P9-BIT-676

Britain

written and researched by
Robert Andrews, Jules Brown,
Rob Humphreys, Phil Lee and Donald Reid

with additional contributions by
Paul Gray and Geoff Wallis

ROUGH
GUIDES

www.roughguides.com

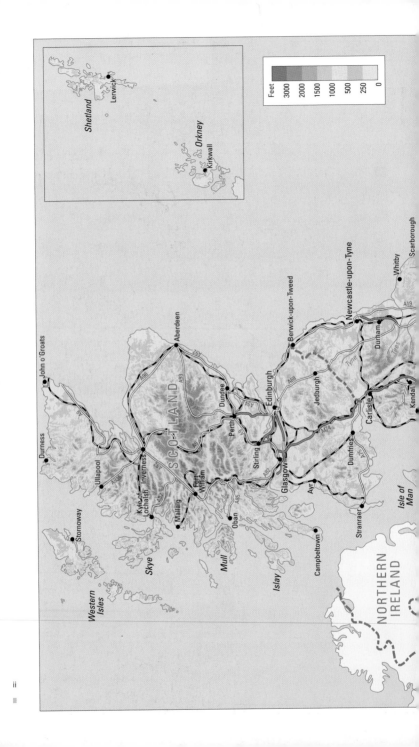

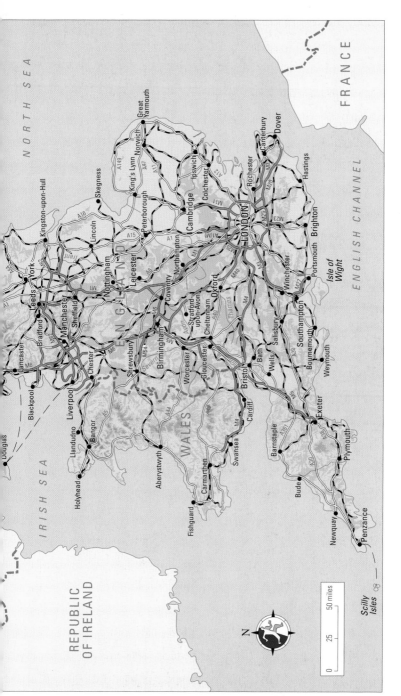

Introduction to

Britain

If ever a nation were both hostage to and beneficiary of its history, it's Britain. The single most important thing to remember when travelling here is that you're visiting not one country, but three: England, Wales and Scotland. For visitors foreign and domestic, that means contending with three capital cities (London, Cardiff and Edinburgh) and three sets of national identity – not to mention the myriad accent shifts as you move between them.

The truth is that were you to plan a country from scratch, you wouldn't even try to corral these three fiercely contradictory nations into a United Kingdom★. They've had centuries to get used to each other, but there's still very little love lost: Wales has long been resentful of English dominance, Scotland is happiest as far away from both as possible, northern England is contemptuous of the south, and Londoners are convinced they're in a league of their own.

That said, most visitors don't let a little social disunity get in the way of seeing the sights. There's enough here for a lifetime's travels – from London, a city of world renown, to remote Scottish fishing villages; from the Welsh valleys to England's post-industrial heartland; from Land's End to John O'Groats; and the North Sea to the Irish Sea.

However, travelling around Britain today is not without its idiosyncrasies. The train system, infamously, is in disarray, with commuters and

---

★ "Britain" (or "Great Britain") is a geographical term, referring to the largest of the British Isles. "United Kingdom" is a political term, referring to a state comprising England, Scotland, Wales and Northern Ireland.

Fact file

• The **population** of Britain – which, at 93,000 square miles, is slightly smaller than the US state of Oregon – is about 58 million: 50 million in England, 5 million in Scotland and 3 million in Wales. Biggest city is London, with some 7.4 million inhabitants. **Ethnic minorities** represent about six percent of the total population, the largest being those of Caribbean or African descent (875,000 people), Indians (840,000) and Pakistanis and Bangladeshis (640,000). The official **language** is English, though Welsh also has official status in Wales. Scottish Gaelic is used in parts of Scotland.

• The **lowest point** is in the Fens of eastern England, at 13ft below sea level; the **highest point** is the summit of Ben Nevis at 4406ft. From the south coast of England to the extreme north of Scotland is about 600 miles; the **longest journey**, from Land's End to John O'Groats, is nearer 850 miles.

• The UK, comprising Britain and Northern Ireland, is a **constitutional monarchy**, whose head of state is Queen Elizabeth II. The bicameral parliament is composed of the directly elected **House of Commons** and the unelected **House of Lords**. There is no written constitution, and real power is concentrated in the hands of the **Prime Minister**, head of the largest party in the House of Commons.

long-distance travellers in a semi-permanent state of delay and revolt. The arterial roads aren't much better, often gridlocked around major cities, while the decrepit condition of many state-run hospitals and schools – starved for decades of coherent investment and direction, and now well below European and North American averages – commonly makes headlines in the daily newspapers. And if you've just arrived clutching your euros from a tour of "The Continent", free of border controls and exchange rates, you'll swiftly be disabused of the notion of Britain being an integral part of Europe.

The country has dithered for decades about its postwar – and, more specifically, post-imperial – role: having ruled the roost for several hundred years, Brits are increasingly uncertain about their place in the new order. Paradoxically, it's the Welsh and the Scots, for so long under the English thumb, who have emerged with their national identities intact and tangible political power embodied in their own parliamentary assemblies. The English, still without a regional voice, are left unsure of how to modernize their institutions, ever-fearful of conflict erupting between town and country, north and south, rich and poor, blacks, Asians and whites, and increasingly lagging behind the social and political change that is being wrought as effectively in Edinburgh as in Brussels. England remains the dominant and most urbanized member of the British partnership, but crossing the border into predominantly rural Wales brings you into an unmistakably Celtic land, while in Scotland (a nation whose absorption into the state was rather more recent) the presence of a profoundly non-English worldview is striking.

The A to Z of fish and chips

Britain's one truly significant contribution to world cuisine emerges from the nation's fish-and-chip shops, or "chippies". A marriage made in nineteenth-century cities as cheap food for the working masses, battered fish and thick-cut potato chips – both deep-fried, salted and soused in vinegar – have conquered the world. These days, the traditional staples of cod and haddock are endangered species, so you're just as likely to see skate, hake, rock salmon (ie dogfish) and other coastal beasties on fish shop menus. In most places, ask for "fish and chips" if you want the works, though in Scotland it's a "fish supper". Mushy peas are the traditional accompaniment, while chips or fish in a bread-roll sandwich (with or, more often, without butter) is a "butty". Other available items range from battered sausages and saveloys to pickled eggs. After ordering all this, if you still feel that your meal hasn't got quite enough calories, you can always ask for a scoop of the leftover batter "bits" or "scraps" on top.

Britain's urban culture is as popular a draw as its countryside and history have ever been.

Across the country, virtually every town bears a mark of former wealth and power, whether it be a Gothic cathedral financed from a monarch's treasury, a parish church funded by the tycoons of medieval trade, or a triumphalist Victorian civic building, raised on the income of the British Empire. Elsewhere, you'll find old dockyards from which the Royal Navy patrolled the oceans, and mills that employed whole town populations. Meanwhile Britain's museums and galleries – several of them ranking among the world's finest, and most of the major ones with free admission – are full of treasures trawled from its imperial conquests.

In London's and Bristol's vibrant music scene, in the fashionable restaurants and bars of Manchester and Glasgow, in the outstanding contemporary architecture on show in Cardiff and Newcastle, there's a buzz, a "feel-good" factor, that is palpable. Indeed, there's always been an innovative flair to British popular culture, which contrasts sharply with the bucolic view of Britain that many tourist boards favour. The countryside may yield all manner of delights, from walkers' trails around the hills and lakes, through prehistoric stone circles, to traditional villages and their pubs; but Britain's characterful and diverse urban culture is fast becoming as popular a draw as its countryside and history have ever been.

Where to go

England

London is the place to start. Nowhere in the country can match the scope and innovation of the metropolis, a colossal, frenetic city, perhaps not as immediately attractive as its European counterparts, but with so much variety that the only obstacle to a great time is the shockingly high cost of everything. It's here that you'll find Britain's best spread of nightlife, cultural events, museums, galleries, pubs and restaurants. The other large cities, such as **Birmingham**, **Newcastle**, **Leeds** or **Liverpool** each have their strengths: Birmingham has a resurgent arts scene, for example, while people travel for miles to sample Newcastle's nightlife. These days **Manchester** can match the capital for glamour in cafés and clubs, and also boasts the inimitable draw of the world's best-known football team.

England's ancient cathedral cities, such as **Lincoln**, **York**, **Salisbury**, **Durham** and **Winchester**, cannot be equalled for sheer physical beauty. Wherever you're based, you're never more than a few miles from a ruined castle, a majestic country house, a secluded chapel or a monastery. In the southwest there are remnants of a Celtic culture that was all but eradicated elsewhere by the Romans, and everywhere you can find traces of prehistoric settlers – most famously the megalithic circles of **Stonehenge** and **Avebury**.

Standing stones

Why the prehistoric peoples of Britain built circles of standing stones may never be fully known. The theories are as diverse as the sites themselves: perhaps they were places of sacrifice and celebration, or erected for an astronomical function. But two things remain obvious, even at a distance of five thousand years. Firstly, each series of standing stones represents a highly organized effort by ancient peoples once thought of as unsophisticated. And secondly, whatever their function, the circles retain a powerful presence even today, recognized by the disparate bands of druids and New Age travellers who still seek solace in the stones. Mass tourism has dragged famous sites like Stonehenge into the embrace of the heritage industry, but there are other sites which retain their sense of mystery and isolation. At Castlerigg in the Lake District, Calanais in western Scotland, or Holy Island in North Wales, you can still wander alone, forming your own theories as the early morning mist rises above the stones.

Most beguiling of all are the long-established villages of England, hundreds of which amount to nothing more than a pub, a shop, a gaggle of cottages and a farmhouse offering bed and breakfast. **Devon, Cornwall**, the **Cotswolds** and the **Yorkshire Dales** harbour some especially picturesque specimens, but every county can boast a decent showing. Then, of course, there's the English countryside, an extraordinarily diverse terrain from which Constable, Turner, Wordsworth, Emily Brontë and a host of other writers and artists took inspiration. **Exmoor, Dartmoor, Bodmin Moor**, the **North York Moors** and the **Lake District** are the most dramatic and best known of the national parks, each offering an array of landscapes crisscrossed with walking routes.

Wales

Although **Cardiff** boasts most of Wales' national institutions, including the National Museum, the appeal of a visit lies outside the towns, where there is ample evidence of the war-mongering which shaped the country's development. Castles are everywhere, from hard little stone keeps of the early Welsh princes and the mighty **Carreg Cennen** to Edward I's doughty fortresses such as **Beaumaris, Caernarfon** and **Harlech**. Passage graves and stone circles (such as on **Holy Island**) offer a link to the pre-Roman era when the priestly order of Druids ruled over early Celtic peoples, and great medieval monastic houses, like ruined **Tintern Abbey**, are easily accessible.

All these attractions are enhanced by the beauty of the wild Welsh countryside. The backbone of the Cambrian Mountains terminates in the soaring peaks of **Snowdonia National Park** and the angular ridges of the **Brecon**

Beacons; both are superb walking country, as is the **Pembrokeshire Coast** in the southwest. Much of the rest of the coast remains unspoilt, though long sweeps of sand are often backed by traditional British seaside resorts, such as **Llandudno** in the north or **Tenby** in the south.

Scotland

The Scottish capital, **Edinburgh**, is a handsome and ancient city, famous
for its magnificent **castle** and **Palace of Holyroodhouse** as well as for a
world-acclaimed international arts festival and some excellent museums –
not least the outstanding **National Museum of Scotland**. A short journey west is **Glasgow**, a sprawling industrial metropolis that has done much
to improve its image in recent years and can now boast a range of fine
museums and galleries to complement the impressive architectural legacy
of its eighteenth- and nineteenth-century heyday.

    Southern Scotland, often underrated, features some gorgeous scenery,
but nothing quite to compare to the shadowy glens and well-walked hills
of the **Trossachs**, or to the **Highlands**, whose multitude of mountains, sea
cliffs, glens and lochs cover the northern two-thirds of the country. **Inverness** is an obvious base, although **Fort William**, at the opposite end of the
Great Glen near **Ben Nevis**, Britain's highest mountain, is an alternative.

    Some of Britain's most thrilling wilderness experiences are to be had on the Scottish islands, the most accessible of which extend in a long rocky chain off the Atlantic coast, from **Arran** through **Skye** (the most visited of the Hebrides) to the **Western Isles**, where the remarkably hostile terrain harbours some of the last bastions of the Gaelic language. At Britain's northern extreme lie the sea- and wind-buffeted **Orkney** and **Shetland** islands, whose rich Norse heritage makes them distinct in dialect and culture from mainland Scotland, while their wild scenery offers some of Britain's finest birdwatching and some stunning archeological remains.

When to go

Considering the temperate nature of the British **climate**, it's amazing how much mileage the locals get out of the subject: a two-day cold snap is discussed as if it were the onset of a new Ice Age, and a week in the upper 70s starts rumours of a heatwave. The fact is that summers rarely get hot and the winters don't get very cold, except in the north of Scotland and on the highest points of the Welsh and Scottish uplands. Rainfall is fairly even, though again mountainous areas get higher quantities throughout the year (the west coast of Scotland is especially damp, and Llanberis, at the foot of Snowdon, gets more than twice as much rainfall as Caernarfon, seven miles away). In general, the south gets more hours of sunshine than the north.

The bottom line is that it's impossible to say with any degree of certainty what the weather will be like. May might be wet and grey one year and gloriously sunny the next; November stands an equal chance of being crisp

and clear or foggy and grim. If you're planning to lie on a beach, or camp in the dry, you'll want to visit between June and September – a period when you shouldn't go anywhere without booking your accommodation in advance. Elsewhere, if you're balancing the clemency of the weather against the density of the crowds, the best months to explore are April, May, September and October.

Average daily maximum temperatures

	Jan	Feb	Mar	Apr	May	June	July	Aug	Sept	Oct	Nov	Dec
Birmingham												
°F	42	43	48	54	60	66	68	68	63	55	48	44
°C	5	6	9	12	16	19	20	20	17	13	9	7
Cardiff												
°F	45	45	50	56	60	68	69	69	64	58	51	46
°C	7	7	10	13	16	20	21	21	18	14	11	8
Edinburgh												
°F	42	43	46	51	56	64	65	64	60	54	48	44
°C	5	6	8	11	13	18	18	18	16	12	9	7
Fort William												
°F	43	44	48	52	58	60	62	63	60	54	49	45
°C	6	7	9	11	14	16	17	17	16	12	9	7
London												
°F	43	44	50	56	62	69	71	71	65	58	50	45
°C	6	7	10	13	17	21	22	22	19	14	10	7
Plymouth												
°F	47	47	50	54	59	64	66	67	64	58	52	49
°C	8	8	10	12	15	18	19	19	18	14	11	9
York												
°F	43	44	49	55	60	67	70	69	64	57	49	45
°C	6	7	10	13	16	19	21	21	18	14	9	7

32

things not to miss

It's not possible to see everything that Britain has to offer in one trip – and we don't suggest you try. What follows is a selective taste of the highlights of England, Wales and Scotland: outstanding buildings, spectacular scenery, great festivals and unforgettable journeys. They're arranged in five colour-coded categories, which you can browse through to find the very best things to see and experience. All entries have a page reference to take you straight into the guide, where you can find out more.

01 **Westonbirt Arboretum, Gloucestershire** Page **318** • Autumn is the best time to appreciate the majestic beauty of this amazing collection of trees and plants set in peaceful countryside.

02 **Dunnottar Castle** Page **1177** ● Memorably dramatic ruined Scottish fortress, surrounded by giddy sea cliffs.

04 **Glasgow School of Art** Page **1013** ● Finest example of the unique style of Glasgow architect and designer Charles Rennie Mackintosh.

03 **Cowes Week, Isle of Wight** Page **241** ● The spirited atmosphere and sense of occasion at this yachting jamboree every August draw thousands, infecting even the staunchest landlubbers.

05 **Hillwalking** Page **46** • The array of challenging but accessible hills makes walking one of the best ways to enjoy Scotland.

07 **West Highland railway** Page **1194** • One of the great railway journeys of the world.

06 **Iona** Page **1097** • The home of Celtic Christian spirituality, an island of pilgrimage today as in antiquity.

08 **Notting Hill carnival** Page **134** • One of Europe's biggest and loudest street festivals takes place over a weekend every August in the streets of this district of west London.

09 Eden Project, Cornwall Page **396** • Spectacular and refreshingly ungimmicky display of the planet's plant-life, mainly housed in vast geodesic "biomes".

10 Punting on the Cam Page **466** • The handsome university town of Cambridge is justifiably popular, and punting on the River Cam is de rigueur.

11 Kinloch Castle, Rùm Page **1132** • Stay in the servants' quarters of this Edwardian Scottish-island hideaway or in one of its few remaining four-poster beds.

12 **Caledonian forest** Page **1203** • The few gnarled survivors of the great ancient Highland forests are majestic characters.

13 **WOMAD** Page **281** • Celebrations of World Music, Arts and Dance are now held all over the world, but the first and best is staged at Reading's Rivermead Leisure Complex each July.

14 **Snowdonia** Page **861** • One of Britain's grandest national parks, a wedge of mountainous Welsh territory focused on the Snowdon massif; you're likely, though, to find more peace and quiet on the paths of Cadair Idris, a little south.

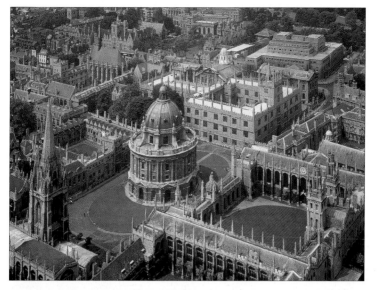

15 **Oxford** Page **284** • The famous old university town boasts many beautiful buildings, including the imposing Italianate rotunda, Radcliffe Camera.

16 **Museum of Scotland, Edinburgh**
Page **928** • The ivory Lewis chessmen are part of this superb collection of arte-facts.

17 **Surfing, Newquay** Page **411** • The beaches strung along the north coast of Devon and Cornwall offer some great breaks, and Newquay is still the top place to see and be seen.

18 Blackpool Tower Page **597** • The British seaside's best-known landmark gives a touch of grace to the Blackpool skyline.

19 Loch Shiel Page **1220** • Among Scotland's myriad lochs, Shiel stands out for its serene beauty and compelling history.

20 Calanais, Lewis Page **1140** • Prehistoric standing stones that occupy a serene lochside setting in the Western Isles.

21 **St Ives Tate, Cornwall** Page **405** • Southwest England's best arts collection occupies a superb site overlooking Porthmeor Beach, and has a wonderful rooftop café.

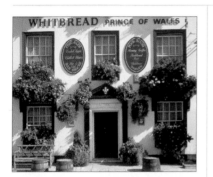

23 **A pint down the pub** Page **36** • From trendy micro-breweries to ancient coaching inns, Britain's pubs are an essential part of any visit.

22 **Machynlleth** Page **844** • Amiable market town in the hills north of Aberystwyth, once proposed as the new capital of Wales.

24 **York Minster** Page **677** • Britain's biggest Gothic church has a thousand-year history and treasures to match, including the world's largest medieval stained-glass window.

25 Castle Arcade, Cardiff Page **777** • Some excellent shopping is to be had in the Victorian and Edwardian arcades occupying the centre of the Welsh capital.

26 Whale-watching, Gairloch Page **1228** • Close encounters with an unusual type of Highland wildlife.

27 Gearrannan, Lewis Page **1140** • Stay in the thatched blackhouse hostel in this beautifully restored former crofting village in the Western Isles.

28 **Maes Howe, Orkney** Page **1258** • Europe's best-preserved Neolithic chambered cairn also contains fine examples of Viking runic inscriptions and drawings.

29 **Tobermory** Page **1095** • Scotland's most picturesque fishing port, bar none.

30 Royal Crescent,

Bath Page **340** •
After visiting the baths, head to England's most elegant Georgian terrace, perfectly sited for views across the town.

31 St David's Cathedral

Page **804** • Serene cathedral set in a small, quiet village that has drawn pilgrims to this westernmost tip of Wales for well over a thousand years.

32 Lizard Point, Cornwall Page **400** • This south-coast headland has none of the razzmatazz of Land's End, but all the views – and some great beaches too.

contents

Using the Rough Guide

We've tried to make this Rough Guide a good read and easy to use. The book is divided into five main sections, and you should be able to find whatever you want in one of them.

colour section

The front colour section offers a quick tour of Britain. The **introduction** aims to give you a feel for the place, with suggestions on where to go. We also tell you what the weather is like and include a basic fact file. Next, our authors round up their favourite aspects of Britain in the **things not to miss** section – whether it's great food, amazing sights or a special hotel. Right after this comes a full **contents** list.

basics

The Basics section covers all the **pre-departure** nitty-gritty to help you plan your trip. This is where to find out which airlines fly to your destination, what paperwork you'll need, what to do about money and insurance, about internet access, food, security, public transport, car rental – in fact just about every piece of **general practical information** you might need.

guide

This is the heart of the Rough Guide, divided into user-friendly chapters, each of which covers a specific region. Every chapter starts with a list of **highlights** and an **introduction** that

helps you to decide where to go, depending on your time and budget. Likewise, introductions to the various towns and smaller regions within each chapter should help you plan your itinerary. We start most town accounts with information on arrival and accommodation, followed by a tour of the sights, and finally reviews of places to eat and drink, and details of nightlife. Longer accounts also have a directory of practical listings. Each chapter concludes with **public transport** details for that region.

contexts

Read Contexts to get a deeper understanding of what makes Britain tick. We include a brief **history** and a detailed further reading section that reviews dozens of **books** and **films** relating to Britain.

index + small print

Apart from a **full index**, which includes maps as well as places, this section covers publishing information, credits and acknowledgements, and also has our contact details in case you want to send in updates and corrections to the book – or suggestions as to how we might improve it.

contents ▶

basics ▶

guide ▶

① London ② Surrey, Kent and Sussex ③ Hampshire, Dorset and Wiltshire
④ Oxford and around ⑤ The Cotswolds and Somerset ⑥ Devon and Cornwall
⑦ East Anglia ⑧ The West Midlands and the Peak District ⑨ The East Midlands
⑩ The Northwest ⑪ The Lake District ⑫ Yorkshire ⑬ The Northeast ⑭ South Wales
⑮ Mid-Wales ⑯ North Wales ⑰ Edinburgh and around ⑱ Southern Scotland
⑲ Glasgow and the Clyde ⑳ Central Scotland ㉑ Argyll ㉒ Skye and the Western Isles
㉓ Northeast Scotland ㉔ The Highland Region ㉕ Orkney and Shetland

contexts ▶

index ▶

chapter map of **Britain**

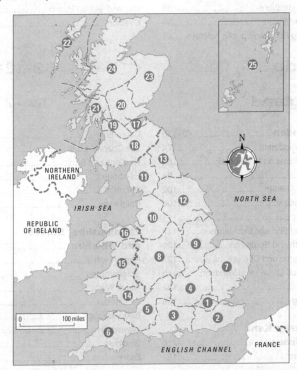

contents

colour section   i–xxiv

Colour map of Britain ....ii–iii
Where to go ix

When to go xii
Things not to miss xiv

basics   9–61

Getting there 11
Red tape and visas 18
Information, maps and websites..........19
Health and insurance 21
Costs, money and banks 23
Getting around 25
Accommodation 30
Food and drink 34
Communications..................................38
The media 39
Opening hours and public holidays 41

Admission to museums
and monuments 42
Festivals 43
Sports and outdoor pursuits...............46
Spectator sports 53
Crime and personal safety 56
Work 57
Travellers with disabilities 58
Gay and lesbian Britain......................59
Directory 60

guide   63–1283

England   64–755

❶ **London** 65–176
Accommodation 74
Westminster and Whitehall 85
Soho 98
Covent Garden 102
Bloomsbury..104
The City..111
The East End and Docklands 117
Lambeth and Southwark....................121
Kensington and Chelsea....................127
Out west: Chiswick to Windsor..........145
Eating 152
Drinking..159

❷ **Surrey, Kent
and Sussex** 177–226
Guildford 182

Canterbury 189
The Channel ports 194
Hastings and Battle 202
Eastbourne 209
Brighton 215
Chichester..223

❸ **Hampshire, Dorset
and Wiltshire** 227–274
Portsmouth 232
Southampton 235
Isle of Wight 237
Winchester 242
Bournemouth 248
Weymouth...257
Salisbury 264
Stonehenge..269

❹ Oxford and around 275–303
Reading...281
Oxford...284
Buckingham 299
St Albans..301

❺ The Cotswolds and Somerset......................305–351
Cirencester 315
Cheltenham 318
Gloucester..323
Bristol 328
Bath..336
Wells 343
Glastonbury 345
Taunton 349

❻ Devon and Cornwall ..353–421
Exeter 359
Torquay 366
Plymouth 372
Dartmoor 375
North Devon 381
Exmoor 386
St Austell 395
The Lizard peninsula..........................400
Penzance 402
St Ives 405
Newquay 411
Bodmin 417

❼ East Anglia......................423–473
Colchester..427
Bury St Edmunds 434
Ipswich 435
Norwich...442
The Norfolk Broads............................450
Ely 460
Cambridge 461

❽ The West Midlands and the Peak District......475–527
Stratford-upon-Avon...........................479
Warwick 485
Worcester 487
Hereford 491
Shrewsbury...498

Birmingham..502
Derby and the Peak District 515

❾ The East Midlands 529–564
Nottingham 533
Leicester 541
Northampton.......................................549
Lincoln 553

❿ The Northwest 565–610
Manchester...569
Chester 582
Liverpool 586
Blackpool 597
Preston 600
Lancaster 601
The Isle of Man 604

⓫ Cumbria and the Lakes 611–640
Kendal 616
Windermere..617
Grasmere 621
Coniston 623
Keswick...627
Ullswater 632
Penrith 633
Carlisle 638

⓬ Yorkshire 641–700
Sheffield 646
Leeds 648
Bradford 653
The Yorkshire Dales 656
Harrogate 667
Ripon...670
York 672
Hull 683
The North York Moors........................686
Whitby...696

⓭ The Northeast................701–755
Durham 706
The Tees Valley 717
Newcastle upon Tyne 720
Hadrian's Wall 734
Northumberland National Park 741

Wales

⑭ South Wales.................759–810
Newport 766
The Valleys 768
Cardiff 773
Swansea 784
Carmarthen 791
Tenby.......................................796
Pembroke 800
St David's 804

⑮ Mid-Wales.......................811–855
The Brecon Beacons 816
Hay-on-Wye 823
Welshpool 831

Llangollen 835
Harlech 840
Machynlleth...............................844
Aberystwyth 846

⑯ North Wales 857–898
Snowdonia 861
Caernarfon 879
Anglesey 882
Bangor 885
Conwy 887
Llandudno 891
Wrexham 896

Scotland

**⑰ Edinburgh and
the Lothians** 901–960
Accommodation 910
The Old Town 913
The New Town 931
Eating 939
Drinking....................................943
Leith 952
Dunbar 955
Linlithgow 958

⑱ Southern Scotland 961–994
Melrose 966
Kelso 970
Jedburgh...................................972
Peebles 974
Dumfries 977
Kirkcudbright 983
Stranraer 987
Ayr...988

**⑲ Glasgow and
the Clyde** 995–1038
Accommodation 1004
The City Centre 1005
The West End 1015
Clydeside 1018
The Southside............................1020

Eating 1024
Drinking....................................1027
Paisley.....................................1031
Dumbarton 1033
Lanark 1035

⑳ Central Scotland 1039–1082
Stirling 1044
Falkirk 1051
Loch Lomond 1053
The Trossachs............................1056
Dunfermline...............................1062
St Andrews 1066
Perth 1073
Pitlochry 1079

㉑ Argyll...........................1083–1116
Cowal 1088
Bute...1090
Oban 1092
Mull 1093
Iona 1097
Kilmartin Glen 1103
Kintyre 1105
Arran 1108
Islay 1110
Jura 1114

㉒ Skye and the Western Isles 1117–1150

Skye 1121
Rùm...1132
Lewis..1136
Harris..1141
North Uist 1144
Benbecula.................................1146
Barra 1148

㉓ Northeast Scotland 1151–1188

Dundee 1156
Arbroath 1162
Montrose...................................1163
Aberdeen...................................1169
Deeside.....................................1178
Speyside 1181
Peterhead 1184
Elgin 1185

㉔ The Highland region.............................1189–1250

Inverness...................................1195
Aviemore...................................1204

Loch Ness..................................1209
Fort William 1212
Glen Coe 1215
Ardnamurchan 1219
Mallaig......................................1223
Kyle of Lochalsh 1224
Gairloch....................................1228
Ullapool.....................................1229
Kylesku.....................................1233
Durness.....................................1235
Thurso......................................1238
The Black Isle 1241
Dornoch 1245
Wick 1248

㉕ Orkney and Shetland 1251–1283

Stromness..................................1256
Kirkwall 1260
Hoy 1263
Westray 1267
Lerwick 1273
Fair Isle 1276
Foula 1278
The North Isles 1280

contexts

1285–1334

A brief history of Britain 1287
Books 1311

Film 1324

index + small print

1333–1358

Full index...................................1334
Twenty years of Rough Guides........1352
Rough Guide credits......................1353
Publishing information 1353

Help us update 1353
Acknowledgements 1354
Readers' letters............................1356
Photo credits..........................1357–1358

map symbols

maps are listed in the full index using coloured text

M4	Motorway	∴	Ruins
	Main road	☻	Cave
	Minor road	⚔	Battle site
	Pedestrianized street	♥	Museum
⊞⊞⊞⊞⊞	Steps	♈	Public gardens
- - - - -	Path	▲	Mountain peak
⊷⊷⊷	Railway	☼	Hill
– – –	Ferry route	⚲	Waterfall
——	Waterway	⚶	Marshland
▪▪▪▪▪▪	National border	⚑	Lighthouse
▪▪ ▪▪	County border	⚐	Ski area
– ▪ – ▪	Chapter division boundary	⊠—⊠	Gate
▪▪▪▪	Wall	⏝	Bridge
♦	General point of interest	⚱	Whisky distillery
✈	Airport	Å	Campsite
⊖	London Underground station	◉	Accommodation
Ⓤ	Glasgow Underground station	■	Café/restaurant
Ⓜ	Metro station	ⓘ	Tourist office
★	Bus stop	⊠	Post office
◘	Parking		Building
⛪	Stately home	+	Church (town maps)
♖	Castle	⁺₊⁺	Cemetery
⌂	Abbey		Park
⚰	Church/chapel (regional maps)		Forest
⊙	Monument		Beach

basics

basics

Getting there 11

Red tape and visas 18

Information, maps and websites 19

Health and insurance 21

Costs, money and banks 23

Getting around 25

Accommodation 30

Food and drink 34

Communications 38

The media 39

Opening hours and public holidays 41

Admission to museums and monuments 42

Festivals 43

Sports and outdoor pursuits 46

Spectator sports 53

Crime and personal safety 56

Work 57

Travellers with disabilities 58

Gay and lesbian Britain 59

Directory 60

Getting there

For most visitors to Britain, the range of options will be greatest – and the fares usually the lowest – flying into London, one of the busiest transport hubs of the world. The city's Heathrow and Gatwick airports take the bulk of transatlantic and long-haul flights, and in terms of convenience, they are about equal. If you're planning to tour the north of England, Scotland or Wales, you might consider one of the growing number of direct flights into Manchester, Birmingham or Glasgow (there are no transatlantic flights into Wales). It's also possible to connect in London to several other regional airports, such as Newcastle and Aberdeen, on one of Britain's domestic carriers. Domestic services to Cardiff are minimal.

Airfares always depend on the season, with the highest being around early June to mid-September, when the weather is best; fares drop during the "shoulder" seasons – mid-September to early November and mid-April to early June – and you'll get the best prices during the low season, November through to April (excluding Christmas and New Year when prices are hiked up and seats are at a premium; it's wise to book at least two or three months ahead for this period). Note also that flying at weekends is generally more expensive; price ranges quoted below assume midweek travel.

You can often cut costs by going through a specialist flight agent – either a **consolidator**, who buys up blocks of tickets from the airlines and sells them at a discount, or a **discount agent**, who in addition to dealing with discounted flights may also offer special student and youth fares and a range of other travel-related services such as travel insurance, rail passes, car rental and tours. Some agents specialize in **charter flights**, which may be cheaper than anything available on a scheduled flight, but departure dates are fixed and withdrawal penalties are high. Don't automatically assume that tickets purchased through a travel specialist will be cheapest, however – once you get a quote, check with the airlines and you may turn up an even better deal. A further possibility is to see if you can arrange a **courier flight**, although you'll need a flexible schedule, and preferably be travelling alone with very little luggage. In return for shepherding a parcel through customs, you can expect to get a deeply discounted ticket. You'll probably also be restricted in the duration of your stay.

If Britain is only one stop on a longer journey, you might want to consider buying a **Round-the-World** (RTW) ticket. Some travel agents can sell you an "off-the-shelf" RTW ticket that will have you touching down in about half a dozen cities (London is usually on the itinerary); others will have to assemble one for you, which can be tailored to your needs but is apt to be more expensive. Prices start from $1850 from Australia, $1295 from the US; for tailor-made itineraries and more flexible options such as Qantas/British Airways "Global Explorer", you'll be paying a lot more.

Booking flights online

Many airlines and discount travel websites offer you the opportunity to book your tickets online, cutting out the costs of agents and middle-men. Good deals can often be found through discount or auction sites, as well as through the airlines' own websites.

Useful websites

ⓦ **www.cheapflights.com** Flight deals, travel agents, plus links to other travel sites.

ⓦ **www.cheaptickets.com** Discount flight specialists.

ⓦ **www.expedia.com** Discount airfares, all-airline search engine and daily deals.

ⓦ **www.gaytravel.com** Gay online travel agent, concentrating mostly on accommodation.

ⓦ **www.hotwire.com** Bookings from the US only. Last-minute savings of up to 40 percent on regular published fares. Travellers must be at least 18 and there are no refunds, transfers or changes allowed. Log-in required.

Ⓦ www.lastminute.com Offers good last-minute holiday package and flight-only deals.

Ⓦ www.priceline.com Name-your-own-price website that has deals at around 40 percent off standard fares. You cannot specify flight times (although you do specify dates) and the tickets are non-refundable, non-transferable and non-changeable.

Ⓦ www.skyauction.com Bookings from the US only. Auctions tickets and travel packages using a "second bid" scheme. The best strategy is to bid the maximum you're willing to pay, since if you win you'll pay just enough to beat the runner-up regardless of your maximum bid.

Ⓦ www.travelocity.com Destination guides, hot web fares and best deals for car rental, accommodation and lodging as well as fares. Provides access to the travel-agent system SABRE, the most comprehensive central reservations system in the US.

Ⓦ www.travelshop.com.au Australian website offering discounted flights, packages, insurance and online bookings.

Ⓦ www.uniquetravel.com.au Australian site with a good range of packages and good-value flights.

Ⓦ travel.yahoo.com Incorporates a lot of Rough Guide material in its coverage of destination countries and cities across the world, with information about places to eat and sleep.

Flights from the US and Canada

Figure on six and a half hours' **flying time** from New York to any of the British airports (it's an hour extra coming the other way, due to headwinds). Most eastbound flights cross the Atlantic overnight, leaving you at your destination the next morning without much sleep, but if you can manage to stay awake until after dinner that night, you should be over the worst of the jet lag the next morning. Some flights from the East Coast depart early in the morning, arriving late the same evening, but this lands you at your destination just as everything is shutting down – a recipe for a disorienting and expensive first night.

Dozens of airlines fly from New York to **London**, and a few fly direct from other East Coast and Midwestern hubs. The best low-season **fares** from New York to London hover around $360 return with a similar price from Boston. In the same period you'll pay in the region of $390 from Washington DC, $430 from Chicago and $440 from Houston.

You can pick up flights from Los Angeles for under $400, but for the west coast in general you're looking at paying $500 or more. For high-season fares, add $150–250 and bear in mind that travelling late on a Saturday can considerably reduce the fare.

In Canada, you'll get the best deal flying to London from the big gateway cities of Toronto and Montréal, where low-season deals start from around CDN$510 return; direct flights from Ottawa and Halifax will probably cost only slightly more. From Edmonton, Calgary and Vancouver, the equivalent fare is CDN$710. If you're travelling in high season, fares are likely to be about $200 higher.

Many of the above airlines also fly nonstop to **Manchester**, with several also running direct flights to **Birmingham** and **Glasgow International**. Manchester and Birmingham are common rated with London, which means that the Apex fare should be the same. For flights to Glasgow, expect to pay around $700 (low season) or $1000 (high season) from New York or Chicago, and $1000/$1150 from Toronto. It will probably work out cheaper to get a flight into London and make an onward connection there; expect to pay about $100 each way for an internal flight.

Airlines in the US and Canada

Aer Lingus ☎1-800/223-6537, Ⓦ www.aerlingus.ie. Boston, Chicago, Los Angeles and New York to Dublin or Shannon with connections to many major British airports.

Air Canada ☎1-888/247-2262, Ⓦ www.aircanada.ca. Calgary, Halifax, Montréal, Ottawa, Toronto and Vancouver to London; Ottawa and Toronto to Manchester; Toronto to Glasgow.

American Airlines ☎1-800/433-7300, Ⓦ www.aa.com. Chicago, Dallas/Fort Worth, Los Angeles, Miami, New York and Raleigh to London; Chicago to Birmingham and Manchester; Dallas/Forth Worth to Manchester; Chicago to Glasgow.

bmi/British Midland ☎1-800/788-0555, Ⓦ www.flybmi.com. Washington and Chicago to Manchester.

British Airways ☎1-800/247-9297, Ⓦ www.british-airways.com. Atlanta, Baltimore, Boston, Charlotte, Chicago, Dallas/Fort Worth, Denver, Detroit, Houston, Los Angeles, Miami, Montréal, New York, Orlando, Philadelphia, Phoenix, Pittsburgh, San Diego, San Francisco, Seattle,

Tampa, Toronto, Vancouver and Washington DC to London (with extensive connections on to other UK destinations); also Chicago, New York and Toronto to Birmingham and Manchester.
Continental Airlines ☎1-800/231-0856, ⓦwww.continental.com. Cleveland, Houston and Newark to London; Newark to Manchester; New York to Glasgow.
Delta Air Lines ☎1-800/241-4141, ⓦwww.delta.com. Atlanta and Cincinnatti to London; Atlanta and New York to Manchester.
Northwest/KLM Airlines ☎1-800/447-4747, ⓦwww.nwa.com. Detroit and Minneapolis to London.
United Airlines ☎1-800/538-2929, ⓦwww.ual.com. Chicago, Los Angeles, Newark, New York, San Francisco and Washington DC to London.
Virgin Atlantic Airways ☎1-800/862-8621, ⓦwww.virgin-atlantic.com. Boston, Chicago, Los Angeles, Miami, Newark, New York, Orlando, San Francisco and Washington DC to London.

Courier flights from the US and Canada

Air Courier Association ☎1-800/282-1202, ⓦwww.aircourier.org.
Now Voyager ☎212/431-1616, ⓦwww.nowvoyagertravel.com.

Discount travel companies from the US and Canada

Air Brokers International ☎1-800/883-3273 or 415/397-1383, ⓦwww.airbrokers.com. Consolidator and specialist in RTW packages.
Airtech ☎212/219-7000, ⓦwww.airtech.com. Standby seat broker. Also deals in consolidator fares and courier flights, mainly from northeastern US cities.
Council Travel ☎1-800/226-8624 or 617/528-2091, ⓦwww.counciltravel.com. Nationwide organization that mostly, but by no means exclusively, specializes in student/budget travel.
Educational Travel Center ☎1-800/747-5551 or 608/256-5551, ⓦwww.edtrav.com. Student/youth discount agent.
New Frontiers/Nouvelles Frontières ☎1-800/677-0720 or 212/986-6006, ⓦwww.NewFrontiers.com. French discount-travel firm. Other branches in LA, San Francisco and Québec City.
STA Travel ☎1-800/777-0112 or 1-800/781-4040, ⓦwww.sta-travel.com. Worldwide specialists in independent travel; also student IDs, travel

insurance, car rental and rail passes.
TFI Tours International ☎1-800/745-8000 or 212/736-1140. Consolidator.
Travac ☎1-800/872-8800, ⓦwww.thetravelsite.com. Consolidator and charter broker.
Travel Avenue ☎1-800/333-3335, ⓦwww.travelavenue.com. Full-service travel agent that offers discounts in the form of rebates.
Travel Cuts Canada ☎1-800/667-2887, US ☎416/979-2406. Canadian student-travel organization.
Worldtek Travel ☎1-800/243-1723, ⓦwww.worldtek.com. Discount travel agency for worldwide travel.

Package holidays and organized tours

Although you'll want to see Britain at your own speed, you shouldn't dismiss the idea of a **package deal** out of hand. Many agents and airlines put together very flexible deals, sometimes amounting to nothing more restrictive than a flight plus accommodation and car or rail pass, and these can actually work out cheaper than the same arrangements made on arrival – especially car rental, which is fairly expensive in Britain. A package can also be great for your peace of mind, if only to ensure a worry-free first week while you're finding your feet for a longer tour. It's worth checking, too, for last-minute deals, especially out of season.

There's no shortage of **tour operators** specializing in travel to the British Isles. Most can do packages of the standard highlights, but of greater interest are the outfits that help you explore the unique points of each country: many organize walking or cycling trips through the countryside, boat trips along canals and any number of theme tours based around history, pubs, gardens, theatre, golf – you name it. A few of the possibilities are listed on p.14, and a travel agent will be able to point out others. For a full listing, contact the British Tourist Authority (see p.19).

Be sure to examine the fine print of any deal, and bear in mind that everything in brochures always sounds great. Choose only an operator that is a member of the United States Tour Operator Association (USTOA) or has been approved by the American Society of Travel Agents (ASTA).

US and Canadian tour operators

All these companies' tours can be booked through a travel agent at no extra cost.

BCT Scenic Walking ☎1-800/473-1210, ⓦwww.bctwalk.com. Guided walking packages in Cornwall, Snowdonia, the Lake District, the Scottish Highlands and Islands and everywhere in between.

British Airways Holidays ☎1-877/428-2228, ⓦwww.british-airways.com. Flight-inclusive vacations and customized itineraries.

British Travel International ☎1-800/327-6097, ⓦwww.britishtravel.com. Agent for all independent arrangements: rail and bus passes, hotels and a comprehensive B&B and vacation-homes reservation service.

Golf International Inc ☎1-800/833-1389, ⓦwww.golfinternational.com. Scottish golf vacation specialist.

International Gay & Lesbian Travel Association ☎1-800/448-8550, ⓦwww.iglta.org. General.

Lynott Tours ☎1-800/221-2474, ⓦwww.lynotttours.com. Escorted tours, hotel and castle stays, self-drives and cottage rental.

Select Travel Service ☎1-800/752-6787, ⓦwww.selecttravel.com. Customized history, literature, theatre and horticulture tours.

Sterling Tours ☎1-800/727-4359, ⓦwww.sterlingtours.com. Variety of independent itineraries, packages, country-house hotels and activity holidays.

Virgin Atlantic Vacations ☎1-800/862-8621, ⓦwww.virgin-atlantic.com. Custom-made packages for independent travellers, including hotel, theatre and airfare deals.

Wilderness Travel ☎1-800/368-2794, ⓦwww.wildernesstravel.com. Inn-to-inn hiking packages in the Cotswolds, through the Lake District and from coast to coast.

Flights from Australia and New Zealand

Travel time from Australia and New Zealand to Britain is over twenty hours and as long-haul flights can be very taxing you might want to consider taking advantage of a stopover and good night's sleep en route. There are plenty of direct flights into London (and a few to Manchester), from where you can make onward connections to other regional British airports. There are no direct flights to Glasgow or Cardiff.

The route to London is a highly competitive one, with flights via Southeast Asia generally being the cheapest option; the lowest

fares start from A$1500/NZ$2000 with such airlines as Britannia Airways and Garuda Air. More expensive, but worth it for the extras, such as fly-drive, accommodation packages and onward travel to other European destinations, are airlines such as Singapore Airlines, Qantas, British Airways and Air New Zealand, whose fares start at around A$1800/NZ$2275.

Fares **from Australia**'s eastern cities are common rated while flights from Perth via Asia and Africa are $200–400 less, and via the Americas about $400 more. The most direct route **from New Zealand** is via North America, with United Airlines offering the best value, stopping in Los Angeles and Chicago for $2150 low season and $3340 in high season, while Air New Zealand have a similar deal for around $2370/$3500. British Airways are a bit more expensive starting at $2410/$3700, but this does include onward connections to other destinations in Britain. Garuda, Korean Air and Thai Airways fly to London via Asia with either a transfer or stopover in their home city for around $2120; for a little more money and comfort Qantas fly via Sydney and Bangkok from $2350.

Airlines in Australia and New Zealand

Air New Zealand ☎0800/737 000 or 09/357 3000, Australia ☎13/2476. Brisbane, Melbourne and Sydney to London via Asia and from New Zealand via Los Angeles.

Britannia Airways Australia ☎02/9251 1299, New Zealand ☎0800/887 997, ⓦwww.britanniaairways.com. Auckland, Brisbane, Cairns and Sydney to London and to Manchester via Bangkok and Abu Dhabi.

British Airways Australia ☎02/8904 8800, New Zealand ☎09/356 8690, ⓦwww.british-airways.com. Brisbane, Melbourne, Perth and Sydney to London. Code-share with Qantas (part owners of the company) from other major cities to London via Los Angeles and Singapore via Harare or Johannesburg; Auckland via Los Angeles. Onward connections to other destinations in Britain.

Canadian Airlines Australia ☎1300/655 767, New Zealand ☎09/309 9159, ⓦwww.cddnair.ca. Auckland, Melbourne and Sydney to London via Toronto or Vancouver.

Cathay Pacific Australia ☎13/1747 or 02/9931 5500, New Zealand ☎09/379 0861, ⓦwww.cathaypacific.com. Auckland, Brisbane, Cairns, Melbourne, Perth and Sydney to London and

Manchester via Hong Kong.

Garuda Australia ☎13/1223 or 02/9334 9900, New Zealand ☎09/366 1862 or 1800/128 510, ⓦwww.garuda-indonesia.com. Adelaide, Auckland, Brisbane, Cairns, Darwin, Melbourne, Perth and Sydney to London via Denpasar or Jakarta.

KLM Australia ☎1300/303 747, New Zealand ☎09/309 1782, ⓦwww.klm.com. Sydney to London via Singapore and Amsterdam.

Malaysia Airlines Australia ☎13/2627, New Zealand ☎09/373 2741 or 0800/657 472, ⓦwww.malaysiaair.com. Auckland, Melbourne, Perth and Sydney to London via Kuala Lumpur. With onward connections.

Qantas Australia ☎13/1313, New Zealand ☎09/357 8900 or 0800/808 767, ⓦwww.qantas.com.au. Adelaide, Auckland, Brisbane, Christchurch, Darwin, Melbourne, Perth, Sydney and Wellington to London via Bangkok or Singapore.

Singapore Airlines Australia ☎13/1011 or 02/9350 0262, New Zealand ☎09/303 2129 or 0800/808 909, ⓦwww.singaporeair.com. Adelaide, Auckland, Brisbane, Cairns, Christchurch, Melbourne, Perth and Sydney to London and Manchester via Singapore.

Thai Airways Australia ☎1300/651 960, New Zealand ☎09/377 3886, ⓦwww.thaiair.com. Auckland, Brisbane, Melbourne, Perth and Sydney to London via Bangkok.

United Airlines Australia ☎13/1777, New Zealand ☎09/379 3800, ⓦwww.ual.com. Auckland to Melbourne, Sydney and London and Manchester via Los Angeles and Chicago, New York or Washington.

Virgin Atlantic Airways Australia ☎02/9244 2747, New Zealand ☎09/308 3377, ⓦwww.virgin-atlantic.com. Sydney and Melbourne to London via Kuala Lumpur. Code-share with Malaysia Airlines for the first leg.

Travel Agents in Australia and New Zealand

Budget Travel New Zealand ☎09/366 0061 or 0800/808 040. Long-established agent with budget airfares and accommodation packages.

Destinations Unlimited New Zealand ☎09/373 4033. Discount fares with a good selection of tours and holiday packages.

Flight Centres Australia ☎02/9235 3522, nearest branch on 13/1600; New Zealand ☎09/358 4310; ⓦwww.flightcentre.com.au. Concentrates on discounted air fares.

STA Travel Australia ☎13/1776 or 1300/360 960, New Zealand ☎09/309 0458 or 09/366 6673, ⓦwww.statravel.com.au. Fare discounts for students and under 25s as well as student cards, rail passes and accommodation.

Student Uni Travel Australia ☎02/9232 8444, ⓦwwww.sut.com.au. Discounted air fares and student/youth travel specialists

Thomas Cook Australia ☎13/1771 or 1800/801 002, New Zealand ☎09/379 3920, ⓦwww.thomascook.com.au. Low-cost flights, tours and accommodation; also issues travellers' cheques.

Trailfinders Australia ☎02/9247 7666. ⓦwww.trailfinders.com.au. Discounted flights, car rental, accommodation and RTW tours.

Usit Beyond New Zealand ☎09/379 4224 or 0800/788 336, ⓦwww.usitbeyond.co.nz. Student/youth travel specialists.

Tour operators in Australia and New Zealand

Adventure World Australia ☎02/8913 0755, ⓦwww.adventureworld.com.au; New Zealand ☎09/524 5118, ⓦwww. adventureworld.co.nz. Offers a wide variety of independent, customized and escorted tours round Britain.

Best of Britain Australia ☎02/9909 1055. Can organize flights, accommodation, car rental, tours, canal boats and B&Bs in the UK.

Explore Holidays Australia ☎02/9857 6200 or 1300/731 000, ⓦwww.exploreholidays.com.au. Accommodation and package tours to Britain and Ireland.

YHA Travel Centre Australia ☎02/9261 1111 or 03/9670 9611, ⓦwww.yha.com.au; New Zealand ☎09/379 4224, ⓦwww.yha.co.nz. Organizes budget accommodation throughout Britain for YHA members.

Flights from Ireland

Stiff competition on routes between Ireland and London has kept the **cost of flights** relatively low, with airlines offering return tickets from Dublin for as little as €60 off-peak, though these will need to be booked well in advance. There are also good connections to Britain's regional airports, with Ryanair generally offering the cheapest deals and most gateways: they currently fly from Cork, Kerry, Knock and Shannon as well as Dublin. Aer Lingus offer deals from Galway and Sligo to London for around €115, while Go has return flights from Belfast International to Edinburgh and Glasgow from around £35. Other options from Belfast include Easyjet, who fly into Luton Airport for £17.50 (excluding tax), and bmi/British Midland who fly into Heathrow for £73; BA are generally more expensive but have special deals from Belfast and Derry to London and Glasgow from around £80.

Airlines in Ireland

Aer Lingus Northern Ireland ☎0845/973 7747, Republic of Ireland ☎01/886 8888, ⓦwww .aerlingus.ie.

bmi/British Midland Northern Ireland ☎0870/607 0555, Republic of Ireland ☎01/407 3036, ⓦwww.flybmi.com.

British Airways Northern Ireland ☎0845/773 3377, Republic of Ireland ☎1800/626747, ⓦwww.britishairways.com.

EasyJet Northern Ireland ☎0870/600 0000, ⓦwww.easyjet.com.

Go Northern Ireland ☎0870/607 6543, ⓦwww.go-fly.com.

Ryanair Northern Ireland ☎0870/156 9569, Republic of Ireland ☎01/609 7800, ⓦwww.ryanair.com.

Flight agents

Joe Walsh Tours Dublin ☎01/872 2555, ⓦwww.joewalshtours.ie. General budget fares agent.

USIT Now Belfast ☎028/9032 7111, Dublin ☎01/602 1777 or 677 8117, ⓦwww.usitnow.ie. Student and youth specialists for flights and trains.

World Travel Centre Dublin ☎01/671 7155, ⓦwww.worldtravel.ie. Consolidators with excellent fares.

By rail

There are frequent through trains for passengers from Paris, Brussels and Lille to London run by **Eurostar**, which travel through the Channel Tunnel to Waterloo International in London via Ashford in Kent. The least expensive return fare (which must be booked fourteen days in advance, include any two nights away or just a Sat night) is £79 from Paris and Brussels and £69 from Lille. Full **fares** with no restrictions are £298 from Paris and Brussels and £230 from Lille. Youth tickets (for under-26s) are fully flexible and cost £75 from Paris and Brussels and £65 from Lille. Eurail and Britrail pass holders qualify for a Passholder return which allows unrestricted journeys for £75 from Paris and Brussels and £65 from Lille.

Drivers from Europe also have the option of using **Eurotunnel**, crossing underneath the Channel on freight trains which carry coaches, cars and motorbikes. The service runs every fifteen minutes at peak periods and takes thirty-five minutes to get between the loading terminals at Folkestone and Calais. You can just turn up, but booking is advised, especially at weekends; you should arrive at least thirty minutes before departure. A five-day fully flexible return for a car and passengers travelling off-peak costs £180, £215 in high season. Travelling between 10pm and 6am brings the price down to £145.

From the Republic of Ireland, you can get **rail/ferry deals**, but if you're starting from the south or west the best ferry crossings are the more expensive Cork–Swansea or Rosslare–Fishguard/Rosslare–Pembroke routes, which can bring the fare to around the same as a flight. If you're willing to travel overnight, the return fare from Dublin to London works out at £43; it rises to £73 during the day. For more information, contact British and European Rail.

Useful rail contacts

British and European Rail ☎01/703 4095.
Eurostar UK ☎0870/160 6600, France ☎08.36.35.33.39, ⓦwww.eurostar.com.
Eurotunnel UK ☎0870/535 3535, France ☎03.21.00.61.00, ⓦwww.eurotunnel.com.

By ferry

Tariffs on **ferries** are bewilderingly complex: prices vary with the month, day or even hour at certain times of the year, not to mention how long you're staying and the size of your car. You should also bear in mind that some kind of sleeping accommodation is often obligatory on the longer crossings if made at night, pushing the price way above the basic rate.

From mainland Europe the quickest crossings are from Calais, Dieppe and Ostend to the English Channel ports by fast ferry and catamaran; expect to pay from £130 (the return fares are usually just twice the price); for a foot passenger the single fare is £24. On the Bergen–Newcastle route – one of the longest crossings, but depositing you less than an hour's drive south of the Scottish border – the one-way fare for four people and a car runs from £150 at off-peak periods to as much as £350 in high season, with foot passengers paying from £38 to £108. For a cabin supplement you can pay between £14 to £114.

Currently, the only ferries direct to Scotland from Europe are run by Smyril Line to Shetland from Norway, the Faroe Islands and Iceland (mid-May to early Sept only) – fine if you're touring the north of Scotland, but not the most convenient gateway to Britain as a whole. From summer 2002, however, a new Superfast Ferries service, will run daily between Zeebrugge (Belgium) and Rosyth, a little northwest of Edinburgh.

From Ireland, there are several services daily to the west coast of Scotland, to both north and south Wales and to England. The quickest and most convenient crossings are to Scotland with P&O Irish Sea, who run several sea crossings daily from Larne to Cairnryan. Stena Line operates conventional ferries and a high-speed service (HSS) daily from Belfast to Stranraer, while SeaCat run daily catamarans from Belfast to Troon, just outside Ayr. Peak period standard return **fares** can cost over £250, though you can save £50 by booking in advance, and another £50 by travelling off-peak. Passenger-only fares work out at around £50 return.

To Wales, there are several services from Dublin and Cork, run by Stena and Swansea–Cork ferries. Expect to pay around €180 for a small vehicle and up to five adults on the Dublin–Holyhead route (€25–35 for a foot passenger), and €140–240 on the Cork–Swansea route (€30–45 foot passenger). Fares from Dublin to Liverpool with the Isle of Man Steam Packet (SeaCat) and Irish Sea are comparable.

Ferry companies

Brittany Ferries UK ⓣ0870/536 0360, France ⓣ0800.38.28.61, Spain ⓣ942.36.06.11, ⓦwww.brittanyferries.com.
Condor UK ⓣ0845/345 2001, France ⓣ02.99.20.03.00, ⓦwww.condorferries.co.uk.
DFDS Seaways UK ⓣ0875/333000, Holland ⓣ0255/534546, Sweden ⓣ031/650650, Germany ⓣ040/389 0371, Denmark ⓣ79.17.79.17, ⓦwww.dfdsseaways.co.uk.
Fjord Line UK ⓣ0191/296 1313, Norway ⓣ55/548800, ⓦwww.fjordline.com.
Hoverspeed UK ⓣ0870/524 0241, France ⓣ0820.00.35.55, Belgium ⓣ059.53.99.55, ⓦwww.hoverspeed.com.
Irish Ferries UK ⓣ0870/517 1717, Ireland ⓣ01/661 0511, ⓦwww.irishferries.com.
Isle of Man Steam Packet UK ⓣ0870/552 3523, ⓦwww.sea-cat.co.uk.
P&O Irish Sea ⓣ0870/242 4777, Ireland ⓣ1/800 409409, ⓦwww.poirishsea.com.
P&O North Sea Ferries UK ⓣ0870/129 6002, Belgium ⓣ050.54.34.30, Holland ⓣ0181/255555, ⓦwww.ponsf.com or mycruiseferries.co.uk.
P&O Portsmouth UK ⓣ0870/242 4999, France ⓣ0803.01.30.13, Spain ⓣ944.23.44.77, ⓦwww.poportsmouth.com.
P&O Scottish Ferries UK ⓣ01224/572615; ⓦwww.posf.co.uk.
P&O Stena Line UK ⓣ0870/600 0600, France ⓣ08.20.01.00.20, ⓦwww.posl.com.
Sea France UK ⓣ0870/571 1711, France ⓣ08.25.04.40.45, ⓦwww.seafrance.com.
Stena Line UK ⓣ0870/570 7070, Ireland ⓣ01/204 7777, Holland ⓣ017/438 9333, ⓦwww.stenaline.co.uk.
Smyril Line UK ⓣ01224/572615; Norway ⓣ5532 0970; ⓦwww.smyril-line.com.
Swansea Cork Ferries UK ⓣ01792/456116, Ireland ⓣ021/427 1166, ⓦwww.swansea-cork.ie.

By bus

You can, of course, catch **buses** from a long list of **European** countries to Britain. Given the low cost of air fares from many cities, however, you'd have to be a masochist to want to travel by bus from, say, Athens – a journey of two nights and three days that actually costs more than the price of a three-and-a-half-hour flight to London. Eurolines (ⓦwww.eurolines.com) is Britain's largest international coach company, with departures to London from 48 European cities, including Amsterdam, Brussels, Dublin, Frankfurt, Hamburg, Madrid, Paris and Rome.

Red tape and visas

Citizens of most European countries can enter the UK with just a passport; EU citizens can stay indefinitely, other Europeans can stay for up to three months. US, Canadian, Australian and New Zealand citizens can stay for up to six months, providing they have a return ticket and adequate funds to cover their stay. Citizens of most other countries require a visa, obtainable from the British consular or mission office in the country of application.

If you want to extend your visa, you should write, before the expiry date given on the endorsement in your passport, to: The Under Secretary of State, Home Office, Immigration and Nationality Dept, Lunar House, Wellesley Rd, Croydon CR9 2BY (☎0870/606 7766, ⊛www.ind.homeoffice.gov.uk), enclosing your passport or National Identity Card and form IS120 (if these were your entry documents).

British embassies and high commissions abroad

Australia British High Commission, Commonwealth Ave, Yarralumla, Canberra, ACT 2600 ☎02/6270 6666, ⊛www.uk.emb.gov.au.
Canada British High Commission, 80 Elgin St, Ottawa, ON K1P 5K7 ☎613/237-1530, ⊛www.britain-in-canada.org.
Ireland 29 Merrion Rd, Dublin 4 ☎01/205 3700, ⊛www.britishembassy.ie.
New Zealand British High Commission, 44 Hill St, Wellington ☎04/924 2888, ⊛www.britain.org.nz.
USA 3100 Massachusetts Ave, NW, Washington, DC 20008 ☎202/588-6500, ⊛www.britainusa.com.

Customs

Since the inauguration of the EU Single Market, travellers coming into Britain directly from another EU country do not have to make a declaration to Customs at their place of entry. In other words, you can bring almost as many cigarettes and as much French wine or German beer into the country as you can carry. The guidance levels are 10 litres of spirits, 90 litres of wine and 110 litres of beer, which should suffice for anyone's requirements – any more than this and you'll have to provide proof that it's for personal use only. The guidelines for tobacco are 800 cigarettes, 400 cigarillos, 200 cigars or 1kg of loose tobacco. If you're travelling to or from a non-EU country, you can still buy duty-free goods, but within the EU, this perk no longer exists. The duty-free allowances are:

• Tobacco: 200 cigarettes; or 100 cigarillos; or 50 cigars; or 250 grammes of loose tobacco.
• Alcohol: 2 litres of still wine plus 1 litre of drink over 22 percent alcohol, or 2 litres of alcoholic drinks not over 22 percent.
• Perfumes: 60ml of perfume plus 250ml of toilet water.
• Plus other goods to the value of £145.

There are **import restrictions** on a variety of articles and substances, from firearms to furs derived from endangered species, none of which should bother the average tourist. However, if you need any clarification on British import regulations, contact the Excise Contact Centre on ☎0845/010 9000, ⊛www.hmce.gov.uk.

Most goods in Britain, with the chief exceptions of books and food, are subject to **Value Added Tax** (VAT), which increases the cost of an item by 17.5 percent (included in the marked price of goods). Visitors from non-EU countries can save a lot of money through the **Retail Export Scheme** (tax-free shopping), which allows a refund of VAT on goods to be taken out of the country. (Savings will usually be minimal for EU nationals because of the rates at which the goods will be taxed upon import to the home country.) Note that not all shops participate in this scheme (those doing so will display a sign to this effect) and that you cannot reclaim VAT charged on hotel bills or other services.

Pets

Since the UK abandoned its strict **quarantine** rules in 2000, it is now possible to bring cats and dogs from most countries in Europe. However, there are still some restrictions: your pet must not have been out of any of the accepted countries in the six months before entering Britain, must be microchipped, at least three months old and be vaccinated against rabies. For a list of participating countries and more detailed information call ☎0870/241 1710 or check at ⓦwww.defra.gov.uk.

Information, maps and websites

If you want to do a bit of research before arriving in Britain, you could contact the British Tourist Authority (BTA) in your country – the addresses are given on p.20. The BTA will send you a wealth of free literature, some of it just rose-tinted advertising copy, but much of it extremely useful; you'll find their website very comprehensive with plenty of good links. If you want more information on a particular area, you should contact the relevant regional tourist offices, which are also listed on pp.19–20.

In Britain, **tourist offices** (usually called Tourist Information Centres, or "TICs" for short) exist in virtually every town – you'll find their phone numbers and opening hours in the relevant sections of the *Guide*. The average opening hours are much the same as standard shop hours – though hours are extended during the summer months and often curtailed in the depths of winter, especially in more remote areas. All centres offer information on accommodation, local public transport, attractions and restaurants as well as town and regional maps. In many cases this is free, but a growing number of offices make a small charge for an accommodation list or a town guide with an accompanying street plan. Areas designated as **national parks** (such as Snowdonia and the Lake District) also have a fair sprinkling of information centres, which are generally more expert in giving guidance on local walks and outdoor pursuits. For information on accommodation-booking services, see p.30.

Regional tourist boards

In England

Britain Visitor Centre No telephone enquiries, ⓦwww.visitbritain.com.
British Tourist Authority ☎020/8846 9000, ⓦwww.visitbritain.com.
Cumbria Tourist Board ☎01539/444444, ⓦwww.golakes.co.uk.
East of England Tourist Board ☎01473/822922, ⓦwww.eastofenglandtouristboard.com.
Heart of England Tourist Board ☎01905/763436 or 0115/959 8383, ⓦwww.visitheartofengland.com.
London Tourist Board ☎020/7932 2000, ⓦwww.londontouristboard.com.
Northumbria Tourist Board ☎0191/375 3000, ⓦwww.visitnorthumbria.com.
North West Tourist Board ☎01942/821222, ⓦwww.visitnorthwest.com.
South East England Tourist Board ☎01892/540766, ⓦwww.southeastengland.uk.com.
Southern Tourist Board ☎023/8062 5400, ⓦwww.gosouth.co.uk.
South West Tourism ☎0870/442 0830, ⓦwww.westcountrynow.com.
Yorkshire Tourist Board ☎01904/707961, ⓦwww.yorkshirevisitor.com.

In Wales

Wales Tourist Board ☎029/2049 9909, ⓦwww.tourism.wales.gov.uk.
North Wales Tourism ☎01492/531731 or 0800/834820, ⓦwww.nwt.co.uk.
Mid and West Coast Wales Tourism ☎01654/703526 or 0800/273747, ⓦwww.mid-wales-tourism.org.uk.

Tourism south and west Wales
☎01792/781212, ⊛ www.tsww.org.uk.

In Scotland

Aberdeen and Grampian ☎01224/288828,
⊛ www.castlesandwhisky.com.
Angus and City of Dundee ☎01382/527527,
⊛ www.angusanddundee.co.uk.
**Argyll, the Isles, Loch Lomond, Stirling and
the Trossachs** ☎01786/470945,
⊛ www.scottish.heartlands.org.
Ayrshire and Arran ☎01292/288688,
⊛ www.ayrshire-arran.com.
Dumfries and Galloway ☎01387/253862,
⊛ www.dumfriesandgalloway.co.uk.
Edinburgh and the Lothians ☎0131/473 3800,
⊛ www.edinburgh.org.
Greater Glasgow and Clyde Valley
☎0141/204 4480, ⊛ www.seeglasgow.com.
Highlands of Scotland ☎01997/421160,
⊛ www.host.co.uk.
Kingdom of Fife ☎01592/750066,
⊛ www.standrews.com/fife.
Orkney ☎01856/872856,
⊛ www.visitorkney.com.
Perthshire ☎01738/627958,
⊛ www.perthshire.co.uk.
Scottish Borders ☎01750/20555, ⊛ www.scot-
borders.co.uk.
Shetland ☎01595/693434,
⊛ www.visitshetland.com.
Western Isles ☎01851/703088,
⊛ www.witb.co.uk.

British tourist offices overseas

Australia Level 16, The Gateway, 1 Macquarie
Place, Circular Quay, Sydney NSW 2000
☎02/9377 4400, ⊛ www.visitbritain.com/au.
Canada 5915 Airport Rd, Suite 120, Mississanga,
ON 1T1 3J8 ☎1-888/ VISIT UK or 905/405-1720,
⊛ www.visitbritain.com/ca.
Ireland BTA, 18–19 College Green, Dublin 2
☎01/670 8000, ⊛ www.visitbritain.com/ie.
New Zealand Floor 17, NZI House, 151 Queen St,
Auckland ☎09/303 1446,
⊛ www.visitbritain.com/nz.
US 551 5th Ave, 7th Floor, New York, NY 10176
☎1-800/ GO-2-BRITAIN or 212-986-2266,
⊛ www.travelbritain.org.

Websites

Weaving your way in and out of the numerous **websites** before leaving for Britain is a
good way to familiarize yourself with your
destination, book up accommodation and
arm yourself with tips and information.
We've indicated relevant websites throughout this chapter, but listed here are some
useful general sites.

⊛ **www.aboutscotland.com** Useful for
accommodation, easy to use and linked to holiday
activities.
⊛ **www.backpackers.co.uk** Gives the low-down
on the independent hostels and budget
accommodation.
⊛ **www.goodguides.com** A combination of
information from the *Good Britain Guide* and the
Good Pub Guide.
⊛ **www.information-britain.co.uk**
Comprehensive site with a county by county guide.
⊛ **www.knowhere.co.uk** A self-styled user's
guide to Britain. Up-to-date info, with readers'
comments, including best-of and worst-of sections.
⊛ **www.multimap.com** Town plans and area
maps with scales up to 1:10,000.
⊛ **www.ngs.org.uk** Details gardens, many of them
private, open throughout the year for charity.
⊛ **www.tiac.net/users/namarie** The site is
named Anglophilia and provides a host of links to
other sites – from shops to bands.
⊛ **www.ordsvy.gov.uk** Information on the full
range of Ordnance Survey maps, including digital
maps.

Maps

The most comprehensive range of maps is
produced by the **Ordnance Survey**, a series
renowned for its accuracy and clarity. The
204 maps in their 1:50,000 (a little over one-
inch-to-one-mile) Landranger series cover
the whole of Britain and show enough detail
to be useful for most walkers. More detailed,
and invaluable for serious hiking, are the
1:25,000 Outdoor Leisure maps, which deal
with national parks and areas of outstanding
beauty, and the Explorer set of maps, which
is gradually replacing the Pathfinder series;
between them they cover the entire country.
The full range of Ordnance Survey maps is
only available at a few big-city stores, but in
any walking district of Britain you'll find the
relevant maps in local shops or information
offices. Check their website (see above) for
information on the full range of maps.

The best **road atlases** are the large-format
ones produced by the AA, RAC, Collins and
Ordnance Survey, which cover all of Britain at
around three-miles-to-one-inch and include

larger-scale plans of major towns. Virtually every motorway service station in the nation stocks one or more of the big road atlases.

Map outlets

In the US and Canada

The Complete Traveler Bookstore 199 Madison Ave, New York, NY 10016 ☎212/685-9007.

Elliot Bay Book Company 101 S Main St, Seattle, WA 98104 ☎206/624-6600 or 1-800/962-5311, ⓦwww.elliotbaybook.com.

Map Link Inc. 30 S La Patera Lane, Unit 5, Santa Barbara, CA 93117 ☎805/692-6777, ⓦwww.maplink.com.

Open Air Books and Maps 25 Toronto St, Toronto M5R 2C1 ☎416/363-0719 or 1-800/748-9171.

Phileas Fogg's Travel Center #87 Stanford Shopping Center, Palo Alto, CA 94304 ☎1-800/533-3644, ⓦwww.foggs.com.

Rand McNally Mail order on ☎1-800/333-0136 ext 2111, ⓦwww.randmcnally.com. Branches at 444 N Michigan Ave, Chicago, IL 60611 ☎312/321-1751; 150 E 52nd St, New York, NY 10022 ☎212/758-7488; and 595 Market St, San Francisco, CA 94105 ☎415/777-3131.

Ulysses Travel Bookshop 4176 St-Denis, Montréal H2W 2M5 ☎514/843-9882, ⓦwww.ulysses.ca.

World Wide Books and Maps 1247 Granville St, Vancouver V6Z 1G3 ☎604/687-3320, ⓦwww.worldofmaps.com.

In Australia and New Zealand

The Map Shop 6 Peel St, Adelaide ☎08/8231 2033, ⓦwww.mapshop.net.au.

Mapland 372 Little Bourke St, Melbourne ☎03/9670 4383, ⓦwww.mapland.com.au.

Mapworld 173 Gloucester St, Christchurch ☎03/374 5399, ⓦwww.mapworld.co.nz.

Perth Map Centre 1/884 Hay St, Perth ☎08/9322 5733, ⓦwww.perthmap.com.au.

Specialty Maps 46 Albert St, Auckland ☎09/307 2217, ⓦwww.ubd-online.co.nz/maps.

Travel Bookshop Shop 3, 175 Liverpool St, Sydney ☎02/9261 8200.

Worldwide Maps and Guides 187 George St, Brisbane ☎07/3221 4330.

In the UK and Ireland

Blackwell's Map and Travel Shop 53 Broad St, Oxford OX1 3BQ ☎01865/792792, ⓦwww.bookshop.blackwell.co.uk.

Heffers Map and Travel 20 Trinity St, Cambridge CB2 1TJ ☎01223/568568, ⓦwww.heffers.co.uk.

Hodges Figgis Bookshop 56–58 Dawson St, Dublin 2 ☎01/677 4754, ⓦwww.hodgesfiggis.com.

James Thin Melven's 29 Union St, Inverness IV1 1QA ☎01463/233500, ⓦwww.jthin.co.uk.

John Smith 26 Colquhoun Ave, Glasgow G52 4PJ ☎0141/552 3377, ⓦwww.johnsmith.co.uk.

Stanfords 12–14 Long Acre, London WC2E 9LP ☎020/7836 1321, ⓦwww.stanfords.co.uk.

Health and insurance

No vaccinations are required for entry into Britain. Citizens of all EU countries and those with a reciprocal health care agreement are entitled to free medical treatment at National Health Service hospitals. If you don't fall into either of these categories, you will be charged for all medical services, in which case health insurance is strongly advised. Indeed, even though EU health care privileges apply in Britain, visitors from elsewhere in the EU would also do well to take out an insurance policy before travelling to cover against theft and loss as well as illness or injury.

Pharmacies and medical emergencies

Pharmacists (known as chemists in Britain) can dispense only a limited range of drugs without a doctor's prescription. Most pharmacies are open standard shop hours, though in large towns some may stay open as late as 10pm – local newspapers carry lists of late-opening pharmacies. **Doctor**'s surgeries tend to be open from about 9am to noon and then for a couple of hours in the

Rough Guide travel insurance

Rough Guides offers its own travel insurance, customized for our readers by a leading UK broker and backed by a Lloyd's underwriter. It's available for anyone, of any nationality, travelling anywhere in the world.

There are two main Rough Guide insurance plans: **Essential**, for basic, no-frills cover; and **Premier** – with more generous and extensive benefits. Alternatively, you can take out annual multi-trip insurance, which covers you for any number of trips throughout the year (with a maximum of 60 days for any one trip). Unlike many policies, the Rough Guides schemes are calculated by the day, so if you're travelling for 27 days rather than a month, that's all you pay for. If you intend to be away for the whole year, the **Adventurer** policy will cover you for 365 days. Each plan can be supplemented with a "Hazardous Activities Premium" if you plan to indulge in sports considered dangerous. Rough Guides also does good deals for older travellers, and will insure you up to any age, at prices comparable to SAGA's.

For a policy quote, call the Rough Guide Insurance Line on UK freefone ℡0800/0150 906; US ℡1-866/220-5588, or, if you're calling from elsewhere ℡+44-1243/621046. Alternatively, get an online quote and buy your cover at ⓦwww.roughguides.com/insurance.

---

evenings; outside surgery hours, you can turn up at the casualty department of the local hospital for complaints that require immediate attention.

For medical advice by phone you can call **NHS Direct** (℡0845/4647, ⓦwww.nhsdirect.nhs.uk), who also run an increasing number of drop-in centres (usually 7.30am–9pm) in the bigger towns and cities. In an **emergency**, call for an ambulance on ℡999.

Insurance policies

Before spending out on a new policy, it's worth checking whether you are already covered: some all-risks home **insurance policies**, for example, may cover your possessions against loss or theft when overseas, and many private medical schemes include cover when abroad, including baggage loss, cancellation or curtailment and cash replacement as well as sickness or accident. **Canadians** will find that they are usually covered by their provincial health plans, while holders of official student/teacher/youth cards in Canada and the US are entitled to be reimbursed for accident coverage and hospital in-patient benefits. **Students** will often find that their student health coverage extends during the vacations and for one term beyond the date of last enrolment. Some bank and credit cards

include certain levels of medical or other insurance and you may automatically get travel insurance if you use a major credit card to pay for your trip.

After exhausting the possibilities above, you might want to contact a specialist **travel insurance company**, or consider the travel insurance deal we offer (see above). A typical travel insurance policy usually provides cover for the loss of baggage, tickets and – up to a certain limit – cash or cheques, as well as cancellation or curtailment of your journey. Most of them exclude so-called dangerous sports unless an extra premium is paid: in Britain this can mean cliff-diving, rock climbing and mountaineering. Many policies can be chopped and changed to exclude coverage you don't need – for example, sickness and accident benefits can often be excluded or included at will. If you do take medical coverage, ascertain whether benefits will be paid as treatment proceeds or only after you return home, and whether there is a 24-hour medical emergency number. When securing baggage cover, make sure that the per-article limit – typically under £500 – will cover your most valuable possession. If you need to make a claim, you should keep receipts for medicines and medical treatment, and in the event you have anything stolen, you must obtain an official statement from the police.

Costs, money and banks

Britain is an expensive place to visit. The minimum expenditure, if you're camping, or hostelling, using public transport, buying picnic food and eating in pubs and cafés, would be in the region of £30–40 a day. Couples staying at budget B&Bs, eating at unpretentious restaurants and visiting a fair number of tourist attractions are looking at around £50–60 each per day, and if you're renting a car, staying in comfortable B&Bs or hotels and eating well, budget on at least £80 each per day. Single travellers should budget on spending around 60 percent of what a couple would spend (single rooms cost more than half a double), and on any visit to London, work on the basis that you'll need an extra £15 per day to get much pleasure out of the place. For more detail on the cost of accommodation, transport and eating, see below.

Currency

Britain has so far declined to adopt the euro, preferring instead its **pound sterling** (£), divided into 100 pence (p). Coins come in denominations of 1p, 2p, 5p, 10p, 20p, 50p and £1 and £2. Notes are in denominations of £5, £10, £20 and £50. All English and Scottish banknotes are legal tender throughout Britain, but you may want to get rid of your Scottish notes once you head south of the border as some less worldly traders in England and Wales may be unwilling to accept them.

Currency exchange

Banks or the larger post offices are the best places to **change money**. Every sizeable town in Britain has at least one of the big high-street banks: Barclays, Lloyds TSB, HSBC, NatWest, Bank of Scotland, Royal Bank of Scotland and Clydesdale. **Opening hours** are generally Mon–Fri 9.30am–4.30pm, though many branches in larger towns open at 9am, close at 5.30pm and also remain open until 3 or 4pm on Saturdays. Outside banking and office hours you're best advised to go to a **bureau de change**; these are to be found in most city centres, often at train stations or airports. Try to avoid changing money or cheques in hotels, where the rates are normally the poorest on offer.

There are no exchange controls in Britain, so you can bring in as much cash as you like and change travellers' cheques up to any amount.

Travellers' cheques

The easiest and safest way to carry your money is in **travellers' cheques**, available for a small commission (normally 1 percent) from any major bank. The most commonly accepted are issued by American Express, followed by Visa and Thomas Cook. Neither American Express nor Thomas Cook will charge commission if you exchange cheques at their own offices, but banks charge around 1.5 percent commision. Keep a record of the cheques as you cash them, and you can get the value of all uncashed cheques refunded immediately if they are lost.

It pays to get a selection of denominations. Make sure to keep the purchase agreement and a record of cheque serial numbers safe and separate from the cheques themselves. In the event that cheques are lost or stolen, the issuing company will expect you to report the loss immediately; most companies claim to replace lost or stolen cheques within 24 hours.

Credit and debit cards

Credit cards can be very handy as a back-up source of funds, and can be used either in ATMs or over the counter. Mastercard, Visa, American Express and Diners Club are accepted in most hotels, shops and restaurants in Britain, although they're less useful in the most rural areas, and smaller establishments everywhere, such as B&Bs, will often accept cash only. You may also be able to make withdrawals using your **debit**

card – your bank's international banking department should be able to advise on this.

Make sure you have a **personal identification number** (**PIN**) that's designed to work overseas. You'll find ATMs at most large supermarkets, train stations, motorway service areas, some petrol stations and even in some pubs and shops.

Wiring money

Having **money wired** from home through a money-wiring company (see below for contacts) is never convenient or cheap and should be considered a last resort. **Fees** depend on the country, method of payment and amount being transferred, but as an example, wiring £500 to Britain from the US will cost £20–35, Moneygram and Travelex (Thomas Cook) being the cheaper options.

It's also possible to have money wired directly from a bank in your home country to a bank in Britain, although this is somewhat less reliable because it involves two separate institutions. If you go down this route, your home bank will need the address of the branch bank where you want to pick up the money and the address and telex number of the head office, which will act as the clearing house; money wired this way normally takes at least two working days to arrive and costs around £25 per transaction.

Money-wiring companies

Moneygram ☎0800/018 0104, ⓦwww.moneygram.com. Money can be wired in twenty minutes from post offices in the UK; a brochure is available at post offices detailing countries where money can be sent and received.
Travelex (Thomas Cook) ☎01733/318922. The cheapest company to approach if you don't need the money on the spot as it takes up to two days to arrive. They can also credit foreign bank

accounts for the same fee (up to three days).
Western Union Money Transfer ☎0800/833 833, ⓦwww.westernunion.com. Money can be transferred in minutes, either by phone or in person from an agency; call for the nearest location.

Youth and student discounts

Various official and quasi-official youth and student ID cards soon pay for themselves in savings. Full-time students are eligible for the **International Student ID Card** (**ISIC**), which entitles the bearer to special air, rail and bus fares and discounts at museums, theatres and other attractions. For Americans there's also a health benefit, providing up to $3000 in emergency medical coverage and $100 a day for 60 days in the hospital, plus a 24-hour hotline to call in the event of a medical, legal or financial emergency. The card costs $22 for Americans; CDN$16 for Canadians; A$16.50 for Australians; NZ$21 for New Zealanders; and £6 for UK residents. A university photo ID might open some doors, but is not as easily recognizable as the ISIC, although the latter is often not accepted as valid proof of age in bars and pubs.

You only have to be 26 or younger to qualify for the **International Youth Travel Card**, which costs around the same as the ISIC and carries the same benefits. Teachers qualify for the **International Teacher Card**, for the same rates and deals. All these cards are available in the US from Council Travel, STA, Travel CUTS and, in Canada, Hostelling International (see p.32 for addresses); in Australia and New Zealand they are available from STA or Campus Travel; and in the UK from Usit Campus and STA.

Several other travel organizations and accommodation groups also sell their own cards, good for various discounts.

Getting around

As you'd expect of such a small and densely populated island, just about every place in Britain is accessible by train or bus. However, costs are among the highest in Europe – London's commuters spend more on getting to work than any of their European counterparts – while cross-country travel can eat up a large part of your budget. It pays to plan ahead and make sure you're aware of all the passes and special deals on offer – note that some are only available outside Britain and must be purchased before you arrive. It's often cheaper to drive yourself around, though fuel and car rental costs again are among the highest in Europe and will seem prohibitive to North Americans. Congestion around the main cities can be bad, and even the motorways are liable to sporadic gridlocks, especially on public holidays when what seems like half the population takes to the roads

Internal flights

Since the distances involved are so small, **internal flights** are not the most obvious choice for getting around Britain. However, with several regional airports – including Birmingham, Bristol, Manchester, Glasgow and Edinburgh – well served by low-cost airlines – flights can be a cost-effective as well as time-saving way of travelling.

You can fly to Scotland's main airports – Edinburgh, Glasgow and Aberdeen – in an hour or so from London, as well as from various provincial airports. There's usually a confusingly wide range of fares. The best deals are **special-offer tickets**, sold at least three days in advance on specific flights; these tend to fly at less social hours and are subject to availability and certain restrictions, but the savings can make the extra effort well worthwhile. The next cheapest seats are **Apex** tickets, available on all flights, at about half the price of a full-price economy-class ticket. The full amount for Apex must be paid at least two weeks before departure, and only half of the price will be returned if the booking is cancelled. Anyone under 26 should also check out a specialist agency such as Campus Travel or STA Travel, as they offer special youth deals, including Domestic Air Passes (aka "Skytrekker Passes") on British Airways flights, which can get you to Inverness and the Hebrides for a fraction of the published fare. Addresses for discount agents are listed below.

As a broad guide to what you're likely to pay, reckon on £30 for a rock-bottom one-way ticket from Luton or Stansted to Edinburgh or Glasgow with Easyjet or Go. Full return fares for British Airways, bmi/British Midland or KLM, the three main carriers, start at around £100, rising to more than double that for the most flexible tickets; Apex rates and reductions for young persons and students apply in most cases. Note, too, that airport tax is levied on all domestic flights to Scotland.

BA also flies from Cardiff to Glasgow, Edinburgh and London for around £100 return, and to Aberdeen for £140 return.

Airlines

KLM ☎0870/507 4074, ⊛www.klmuk.com. London to Edinburgh and Glasgow.
bmi/British Midland ☎0870/607 0555, ⊛www.flybmi.com. London, Manchester and East Midlands to Edinburgh and Glasgow.
British Airways ☎0845/773 3377, ⊛www.britishairways.com. London, Birmingham, Manchester, Bristol, Plymouth and Cardiff to Edinburgh, Glasgow and Aberdeen; London and Birmingham to Inverness.
EasyJet ☎0870/600 0000, ⊛www.easyjet.com. Luton to Aberdeen, Edinburgh, Glasgow and Inverness.
Go ☎0870/607 6543, ⊛www.go-fly.com. London and Bristol to Edinburgh and Glasgow.
Ryanair ☎0870/156 9569, ⊛www.ryanair.com. Stansted to Prestwick.

Flight agents

North South Travel ☏ 01245/608 291,
ⓦ www.northsouthtravel.co.uk. Friendly,
competitive travel agency, whose profits are used to
support projects in the developing world.
STA Travel ☏ 0870/160 6070,
ⓦ www.statravel.co.uk. Specialists in low-cost
flights and tours for students and under-26s, though
other customers welcome.
Usit Campus ☏ 0870/240 1010,
ⓦ www.usitcampus.co.uk. Student/youth travel
specialists, with branches also in YHA shops and on
university campuses all over Britain.

By train

In the recent past Britain's **rail network** has
suffered a foolhardy privatization process
and a chronic under-investment, resulting in
a severe decline in services. With the ownership of the track and stations put into the
hands of Railtrack, but the trains and services run by a tangle of private companies,
there has been no little confusion when it
comes to trying to figure out routes and
prices. Spiralling prices and unreliable services had already caused many passengers
to run for their cars, but it was the train dis-
asters at Paddington in 1999 and Hatfield in
2000 that brought the crisis on the privatized railways to a head; an urgent and long
overdue overhaul of the tracks followed,
but public confidence in the privatized system – and Railtrack in particular – hit an all
time low. At the end of 2001, the government finally pulled the plug on troubled
Railtrack, and a re-evaluation of how the
privatized network shall be run in the future
is currently underway.

Despite this bleak picture, it is fair to say
that most trains run more-or-less to schedule (except on Sundays when maintenance
work takes place) and that there are but a
few major towns that cannot be reached by
rail. Travelling across country – or reaching
remote corners – can be more tricky, however, and at best will involve connections with
several different services.

You can buy **tickets** at the train station on
the day of travel, but it should hardly come
as a surprise to find that booking as far
ahead as possible ensures the cheapest
fares – or that travelling most places on a
Friday, or just turning up at the station to buy
a ticket, are the most expensive ways to go.

In all instances, an essential first call is
National Rail Enquiries (see rail contacts,
below), which can advise on booking, routes
and services throughout the country. Credit-
card **bookings** are made through the privatized rail companies; if you're booking three
or more days in advance, you can do this
through any of the companies, otherwise
you will need to contact the network that
covers the station you depart from. National
Rail Enquiries will supply the necessary contact name and number.

At the time of going to press, there were
four types of **reduced-fare ticket** – Saver,
SuperSaver, SuperAdvanced and Apex – all
with byzantine restrictions which are often
different from route to route and company to
company (for instance, it's often cheaper to
travel return from the north to London, than
it is from London to the north). **Apex** tickets
are issued in limited numbers on certain
intercity journeys of 150 miles or more, and
have to be booked at least 7 days before
travelling; a seat reservation is included with
the ticket. To give you an idea of the differing
fares, using the London–Manchester service
as an example, an open return fare costs
£164, a Saver £49, a SuperSaver £47 and
an Apex £30, with special deals bringing the
fare as low as £15 at certain times of the
year. For all special-offer tickets you should
book as far in advance as you possibly can
– many Apex tickets are sold out weeks
before the travel date.

Children aged 5–15 inclusive pay half the
adult fare on most journeys – but there are
no discounts on Apex tickets. Under-5s
travel free, although they are not entitled to
a seat.

At weekends and on public holidays, many
long-distance services have a special deal
whereby you can convert your second-class
ticket to a first-class one by buying a **first-
class supplement**, which costs between £5
and £15 and is well worth paying if you're
facing a five-hour journey on a popular route
– every Brit has a horror story about having
to stand all the way from London to
Glasgow in a smelly second-class carriage.

If the station's ticket office is closed –
which is likely at rural stations at weekends
– or does not have a vending machine, you
may buy your ticket on the train. Otherwise,
boarding without a ticket will render you
liable to paying the full fare to your destination.

Rail passes

For foreign visitors who anticipate covering a lot of ground around Britain, a rail pass is a wise investment. The most useful is probably the **BritRail Classic Pass**, which must be bought before you enter the country, is available from the companies listed below and many specialist tour operators outside Britain (see pp.13 & 15). It gives unlimited travel in England, Scotland and Wales for eight days ($265), fifteen days ($400), twenty-two days ($505) or one month ($600). The **BritRail Flexipass** is good for travel on four days out of one month ($235), eight days out of two months ($340), or fifteen days out of two months ($515). Note that with both these passes there are discounts for those under 25 (BritRail Youth passes) or over 60 (BritRail Senior passes). The **BritRail Pass 'n' Drive** allows unlimited train travel for three days plus two days' car rental within a two-month period and costs from $257.50 for two adults, depending on the type of car. Up to five additional car days can be added.

Some passes are available only in Britain itself. The **Young Person's Railcard** costs £18 and is available to full-time students and those aged between 16 and 25 and gives a third off all standard, Saver, Supersaver and day-return fares. A **Senior Citizens' Rail Card**, also £18 and offering the same discounts, is available to those aged 60 or over. Families would do well to make use of the **Family Railcard**, which costs £20 and covers up to four adults who are entitled to a 33 percent discount, and up to four children who travel on a 60 percent reduction of the child's full fare. Up to four adults and four children can travel on a **Network Card** which costs £20 and applies to off-peak services throughout London and the south of England (including Oxford, Cambridge and all the Home Counties). Adults travel at a 34 percent discount and children for a flat fare of £1.

If you are planning to travel widely around Europe by train, then it may be worthwhile buying a **Eurail Pass**, though this is unlikely to pay for itself if you stick to Britain alone. The pass, which must be purchased before arrival in Europe, allows unlimited free train travel in the UK and sixteen other countries. The **Eurail Youthpass** (for under-26s) costs $388 for fifteen days, $499 for twenty-one days, or $623 for one month; if you're 26 or over you'll have to buy a first-class pass, available in fifteen-day ($554), twenty-one-day ($718), and one-month ($890) versions. You stand a better chance of getting your money's worth out of a **Eurail Flexipass**, which is valid for a certain number of travel days in a two-month period. This, too, comes in under-26/first-class versions: ten days, costing $458/$654 and $599/$862 for fifteen days.

Rail information and enquiries

In the US and Canada

BritRail Travel International ☎ 1-888/BRITRAIL or 212/490-6688, Ⓦ www.raileurope.com. All rail passes, rail-drive and multi-country passes and tickets for Eurotunnel. Also sells ferry tickets across the Channel.
Europrail International Inc. ☎ 1/888-667-9734, Ⓦ www.europrail.net. Specializes in Eurail and other rail passes.
Online Travel ☎ 1-800/660-5300 or 847/318-8890, Ⓦ www.eurorail.com. Eurail and Britrail passes.
Rail Europe US ☎ 1-800/438-7245, Canada ☎ 1-800/361-7245, Ⓦ www.raileurope.com/us. Official Eurail Pass agent in North America.

In Australia and New Zealand

Rail Plus Australia ☎ 1300/555 003 or 03/9642 8644, Ⓔ info@railplus.com.au; New Zealand ☎ 09/303 2484. Sells Eurail and Britrail passes.
Trailfinders Australia ☎ 02/9247 7666. Sells Eurail passes.

In the UK

National Rail Enquiries ☎ 08457/48 49 50, Ⓦ www.nationalrail.co.uk. For all timetable and fare information in the UK. Calls are charged at local rates and are usually answered very promptly.

By bus and coach

Inter-town bus services (known as **coaches** in Britain) duplicate many rail routes, very often at half the price of the train or less. The frequency of service is often comparable to rail, and in some instances the difference in journey time isn't great enough to be a deciding factor; buses are generally comfortable, and the ones on longer routes often have drinks and sandwiches available on board. There's a plethora of regional companies operating buses and coaches, but by far the biggest national operator is **National**

Express, whose network extends to every corner of the country. With rail prices becoming exorbitant, National Express services are so popular that for busy routes, and on any route at weekends and during holidays, it's advisable to book ahead, rather than just turn up.

Local bus services are run by a bewildering array of companies, most private, a few not. In many cases, timetables and routes are well integrated, but it's increasingly the case that private companies duplicate the busiest routes in an attempt to undercut the commercial opposition, leaving the farther-flung spots neglected. Thus, if you want to get from one end of a big English city to another, you'll probably have a choice of buses all offering cut-price fares, but to get out into the suburbs or to a satellite village, you may have to wait several hours. As a rule, the further away from urban areas you get, the less frequent and more expensive bus services become, but there are very few rural areas which aren't served by at least the occasional privately owned minibus.

National and local bus enquiries

Local bus information and hotline numbers are listed throughout the *Guide*, but for the latest details contact one of the following:

Traveline ☎0870/608 2 608,
⊛www.traveline.org.uk. Phone enquiries daily 7am–9pm. A new, and very useful service, that can give you the latest details on all national and local services throughout the country.
National Express ☎0870/580 8080,
⊛www.gobycoach.com. For inter-town and city connections.

Bus passes

UK residents in full-time education, under 25 or over 50 can buy a National Express Discount Coach Card, which costs £9, is valid for a year and entitles the holder to a 30 percent discount. Foreign travellers of any age can purchase a Tourist Trail Pass, which offers unlimited travel on the National Express network for two days within three (£39 for students and under-23s, otherwise £49), five days within thirty (£69/£85), eight days within thirty (£99/£135) or fifteen days within thirty (£145/£190). In Britain you can obtain both passes from major travel agents,

at the Britain Visitor Centre (see p.19), and at the main National Express office at Victoria Coach Station, London. In North America these passes are available for the dollar equivalent through specialist tour operators (see p.14) or direct from British Travel Associates, PO Box 299, Elkton, VA 22827 ☎1-800/327-6097.

Post Bus Network

Many rural areas not covered by other forms of public transport are served by the Post Bus Network, which operates minibuses carrying mail and about eight fare-paying passengers. They set off in the morning – usually around 8am from the main post office and collect mail from (or deliver it to) the outlying regions. It's a cheap way to travel (£2–4/journey), and can be a convenient way of getting to hidden-away B&Bs, and even round the M25, although it is often excruciatingly slow. You can get a free booklet of routes and timetables from the Royal Mail, Road Transport Consultancy, Room BT 20/3rd Floor, Rowland Hill House, Boythorpe Road, Chesterfield S49 1HQ (☎0845/774 0740 or 01246/546329, ⊛www.royalmail.com/postbus).

"Jump-On-Jump-Off" minibus and guided tours

A popular service pitched at budget travellers and backpackers is the "Jump-On-Jump-Off" minibus run by the Stray company. Starting in London, it travels three days each week in a clockwise direction around England, Wales and Scotland via Windsor, Bath, Snowdonia, Liverpool, The Lakes, Edinburgh, York, Stratford and Oxford before heading back to the capital. Tickets cost £139, and are valid for for up to four months. There is also a shorter trip from London to Liverpool (£99). You can use this bus as a "Jump-On-Jump-Off" option or as a six-day guided tour, either arranging accommodation (average price £10/night) along the way yourself or letting the company do the hard work for you. Contact Stray, 171 Earls Court Rd, Earls Court, London SW5 9RF (☎020/7373 7737, ⊛www.straytravel.com).

Bus tour operators

In addition to the "Jump-On-Jump-Off" buses, several companies offer organized bus tours of Britain.

Gareloch House ☎0870/514 3433,
ⓦwww.insightvacations.com. Tours of the south of
England, taking in Dartmoor, North Devon and the
Cotswolds (April–Oct), and up to Glasgow via Bristol,
the Cotswolds and the Lake District (March–Dec).
Both tours cost from £499.

Haggis ☎0131/557 9393, ⓦwww.
haggisadventures.com. The bright yellow minibuses
head out of Edinburgh daily on whistlestop tours (one
to six days) of various parts of Scotland. The tours
aim to show backpackers a mix of classic highlights
with a few well-chosen spots off the tourist trail, with
an emphasis on keeping the atmosphere
lively. A three-day round-trip from Edinburgh starts
from £69 (food and accommodation not included).

Road Trip ☎0800/056 0505,
ⓦwww.roadtrip.co.uk. Runs weekend and five-day
tours from London between April and mid-November,
with accommodation, meals and entrance fees
thrown in. Weekend trips (£99) cover Cornwall,
Dartmoor, the Lake District, York and Sherwood
Forest; and the five-day tours (£199) explore either
York, Liverpool, Snowdonia and the Cotswolds or the
southwest, from Wiltshire to Cornwall.

Trafalgar ☎020/7574 7444, ⓦwww.trafalgar.com.
Offers round coach trips from London; four-day trips
covering York, Edinburgh and Chester run all year and
cost from £240. From late April to mid-September their
five-day tours (from £295) also pack in Cornwall.

By car

In order to **drive** in Britain you need a current
full **driving licence**. If you're bringing your own
vehicle, you should also carry your **vehicle
registration** or **ownership document** at all
times. Furthermore, you must be **adequately
insured**: check your existing insurance policy.

In Britain, you **drive on the left**, a situation
which can lead to a few tense days of
acclimatization for overseas drivers. Speed
limits are 30–40mph (50–65kph) in built-up
areas, 70mph (110kph) on motorways and
dual carriageways (freeways) and 50mph
(80kph) on most other roads. As a rule,
assume that in any area with street lighting
the speed limit is 30mph (50kph) unless otherwise stated.

Fuel is expensive compared to North
American prices – unleaded petrol (gasoline)
and diesel cost in the region of 77p per litre,
leaded 4-star 80p. The lowest prices of all
are charged at out-of-town supermarkets;
suburban service stations are usually fairly
reasonable; and the highest prices are
charged by motorway stations.

The AA (Automobile Association), RAC
(Royal Automobile Club) and Green Flag all
operate **24-hour emergency breakdown**.
The first two also provide many other motoring services, including a reciprocal arrangement for free assistance through many overseas motoring organizations – check the situation with your own association before setting out. For emergency help the AA and
RAC can be called from roadside booths on
motorways; elsewhere ring ☎0800/887766
for the AA, ☎0800/828282 for the RAC and
☎0800/400600 for Green Flag. You can
make use of these emergency services if you
are not a member of the organizations, but
you will be required to join at the roadside
and you will incur a hefty surcharge as well.

Car **parking** in cities and in popular
tourist spots can be a nightmare and will
also cost you a small fortune. If you're in a
tourist city for a day, look out for the **Park-
and-Ride schemes** where you can park
your car a short way out and take a cheap
or free bus to the centre. Parking in the
long- or short-stay car parks will be cheaper than using meters, which restrict parking
time to two or three hours at the most. As a
rule, the smaller the town, the cheaper the
parking. A yellow line along the edge of the
road indicates **parking restrictions**; check
the nearest sign to see exactly what they
are. A double-yellow line means no parking
at any time, though you can stop briefly to
unload or pick up people or goods (maximum stop two minutes), but if the lines are
red, that means absolutely no stopping at
all.

Compared to rates in North America, **car
rental** in Britain is expensive, and you'll
probably find it cheaper to arrange things in
advance through one of the multinational
chains, or by opting for a fly/drive deal. If you
do rent a car, the least you can expect to
pay is around £110 a week, which is the rate
for a small hatchback from Thrifty; reckon on
paying around £40 per day for something
direct from one of the multinationals, £10 or
so less at a local firm. Rental agencies prefer
you to pay by credit card and you may have
to leave a deposit of £100 or more on top of
the rental charge. There are very few auto-
matics at the lower end of the price scale – if
you want one, you should book well ahead.
To rent a car you need to show your driving
licence; few companies will rent to drivers
with less than one year's experience and

most will only rent to people between 21 and 75 years of age.

Car rental agencies

Avis US ☎1-800/331-1084, Canada ☎1-800/272-5871, Australia ☎13/6333, New Zealand ☎0800/655111, UK ☎0870/606 0100, Ireland ☎01/605 7555; ⓦwww.avis.com.
Budget US & Canada ☎1-800/527-0700, Australia ☎1300/362848, New Zealand ☎0800/652277, UK ☎0800/181181, Ireland ☎01/878 7814; ⓦwww.budget-international.com.
Hertz US ☎1-800/654-3001, Canada ☎1-800/263-0600, Australia ☎1800/550067, New Zealand ☎0800/655955, UK ☎0870/844 8844, Ireland ☎01/676 7476; ⓦwww.hertz.com.
Thrifty US & Canada ☎1-800/367-2277, Australia ☎1300/367227, New Zealand ☎09/309 0111, UK ☎01494/751600; ⓦwww.thrifty.com.

Motoring organizations

In North America

American Automobile Association (AAA).
ⓦwww.aa.com. Each state has its own club – check the web or the phone book for local address and phone number.
Canadian Automobile Association
ⓦwww.caa.com. Each region has its own club –

check the web or the phone book for local address and phone number.

In Australia and New Zealand

Australian Automobile Association ☎02/6247 7311, ⓦwww.aaa.asn.au.
New Zealand Automobile Association
☎09/377 4660, ⓦwww.nzaa.co.nz.

In the UK and Ireland

AA ☎0800/444500, ⓦwww.theaa.com.
AA Travel ☎01/617 9988, ⓦwww.aaireland.ie.
Green Flag ☎ 0800/000111,
ⓦwww.directline.co.uk.
RAC ☎0800/550550, ⓦwww.rac.co.uk.

Taxis

Taxis are a useful option for finding that hostel or sight that's off the beaten track or when time is limited. Also, if you're with a group hiring a taxi can work out as cheap as taking a bus. Reckon on paying around £3 for the first mile and £1 for subsequent miles in cities, and £1.40 a mile in country districts. Black cabs are generally a little more expensive than minicabs, but are usually more reliable. You can hail a black cab on the street, but you must book minicabs by phone – we have given numbers for reliable minicab services throughout the book.

Accommodation

Britain has scores of upmarket hotels, ranging from bland business-oriented places to plush country mansions, as well as budget accommodation in B&Bs, guest houses and youth hostels. Nearly all tourist offices will book rooms for you, although the fee for this service can vary. In some areas you will pay a deposit that's deducted from your first night's bill (usually 10 percent), in others the office will take a percentage or flat-rate commission – on average around £3. Another useful service operated by the majority of tourist offices is the "Book-a-bed-ahead" service, which locates accommodation in your next port of call – again for a charge of about £3, though the service is sometimes free. For a full explanation of the price-coding system used in this book see the box opposite.

Hotels and B&Bs

To help you in your choice of accommodation, a nationwide system for grading **hotel**

and **B&Bs** has been adopted by the British Tourist Authority and the various private organizations which classify accommodation. Hotels are graded by stars, with five

Accommodation price codes

Throughout this guide, hotel and B&B accommodation is priced on a scale of **①** to **⑨**, the number indicating the lowest price you could expect to pay per night in that establishment for a double room in high season. The prices indicated by the codes are as follows:

① under £40	**④** £60–70	**⑦** £110–150
② £40–50	**⑤** £70–90	**⑧** £150–200
③ £50–60	**⑥** £90–110	**⑨** over £200

stars being the top rank, and B&Bs by diamonds with additional gold and silver awards for those that achieve distinction.

Though there's not a hard and fast correlation between standards and price, you'll probably be paying in the region of £50–60 per night for a double room at a one-star **hotel** (breakfast included), rising to around £100 in a three-star and from around £200 for a five-star – in London you pay twice that. In some larger towns and cities you'll find that the larger hotels often offer **cut-price deals** on Saturdays and Sundays to fill the rooms vacated by the week's business trade, but these places tend to be soulless multinational chain operations. If you have money to throw around, stay in a nicely refurbished old building – Britain's historic towns are chock-full of top-quality old coaching inns and similar ancient hostelries, while out in the countryside there are numerous converted mansions and manor houses, often with brilliant restaurants attached.

At the lower end of the scale, it's sometimes difficult to differentiate between a hotel and a **B&B**. At their most basic, these places – often known as **guest houses** in resorts and other tourist towns – are ordinary private houses with a couple of bedrooms set aside for paying guests and a dining room for the consumption of a rudimentary breakfast. At their best, however, B&Bs offer rooms as well furnished as those in hotels costing twice as much, delicious home-prepared breakfasts and an informal hospitality that a larger place couldn't match. As a guideline on costs, you should be able to find a one-diamond place for under £40 per night for a double room and, though the sky is the limit at the top end of the scale, it is possible to stay in some four-diamond places for as little as £70 – farmhouse B&Bs are especially good value. As many B&Bs, even the pricier ones, have a very small

number of rooms, you should certainly book a place as far in advance as possible, especially if you're travelling on your own. Finally, don't assume that a B&B is no good if it's ungraded. There are so many B&Bs in Britain that the grading inspectors can't possibly keep track of them all, and in the rural backwaters some of the most enjoyable accommodation is to be found in welcoming and beautifully set houses whose facilities may technically fall short of official standards.

Hostels, student halls and camping barns

The **Youth Hostels Association (YHA)** network consists of over 230 properties in England and Wales, with the **Scottish Youth Hostels Association (SYHA)** responsible for around 80 properties in Scotland. Both are affiliated to **Hostelling International (HI)** and offer anything from bunk-bed accommodation in single-sex dormitories to B&B in double and family rooms, and in cities the facilities are often every bit as good as some hotels. Indeed, although a few places are spartan establishments of the sort traditionally associated with the wholesome, fresh-air ethic of the first hostels, most have moved well away from the old-fashioned, institutional ambience, and boast cafés, laundry facilities, internet access, entertainment and bike rental.

If you aren't already a member of Hostelling International, you can join through the YHA or SYHA by writing to the head office of either (address below) or in person at any affiliated hostel. **Membership** costs £6.25 per year for under-18s, £12.50 for others.

Prices at most youth hostels are around £7 per night for under-18s and £10 for the over-18s. Students aged 18–25 can get a £1 reduction on production of a valid student card. Length of stay is normally unlimited and the hostel warden will provide a linen sleeping bag for a small charge. The cost of hostel **meals** is low: breakfast is £3.30, a packed lunch £2.90 or £3.80, and evening meals start at £4.90. Nearly all hostels have kitchen facilities for those who prefer self-catering.

At any time of year it's best to **book your place** well in advance, and it's essential at Easter, from May to August and at Christmas. Most hostels accept payment by Mastercard or Visa, with those that don't, you should confirm your booking in writing, with payment, at least seven days before arrival. Bookings made less than seven days in advance will be held only until 6pm on the day of arrival. If you're tempted to turn up on the spur of the moment, bear in mind that very few are open year-round, many are closed at least one day a week, even in high season, and several have periods during which they take bookings from groups only. We have indicated the months during which individual hostels are closed, but to give the full details of **opening times** within this guide would be impossibly unwieldy, so always phone to check – we've given the number for every hostel mentioned. Most hostels are closed from 10am to 5pm, with an 11.30pm curfew, although all seven of the London hostels offer 24-hour access.

At best, **independent hostels**, which are more likely to be found in town centres than in the backwoods, offer facilities commensurate with those of the YHA and SYHA places, and at a lower price. However, many of these hostels make their money by overcramming their rooms with beds, kitchens are often inadequate or non-existent and washing facilities can be similarly poor. That said, a lot of people find the lack of curfews and lockouts ample compensation. A useful publication to have is the annually updated *Independent Hostel Guide* (£4.95), published by The Backpackers Press.

Some cities also have **YMCA** and **YWCA** hostels, though these are only worth considering if you're staying for at least a week, in which case you can get discounts on rates that otherwise are no better than budget B&Bs.

In university towns you should be able to find out-of-term accommodation in the **student halls**, usually one-bedded rooms either with their own or shared bathrooms. In some instances, this may be the only budget accommodation on offer in the centre of town. All the useful university addresses are given in the *Guide*.

In the wilder parts of Britain, such as the north Pennines, Snowdonia, Dartmoor and Exmoor, the YHA and SYHA also administer some basic accommodation for walkers in **camping barns**. Holding up to twenty people, these agricultural outbuildings are often unheated and are very sparsely furnished, with wooden sleeping platforms – or bunks if you're lucky – a couple of tables, a toilet and a cold-water supply, but they are weatherproof, extremely good value (from £4/night) and perfectly situated for walking tours. You do not have to be an HI member to stay in any of these. Similar barns, often called **bunkhouses**, are run by private individuals in these areas – the useful ones are mentioned in the *Guide*.

Youth Hostel Associations

USA

Hostelling International–American Youth Hostels (HI-AYH) 733 15th St NW, Suite 840, Washington, DC 20005 ☎202/783-6161, ⓦwww.hiayh.org.

Canada

Hostelling International–Canadian Hostelling Association Suite 400, 205 Catherine St, Ottawa, ON K2P 1C3 ☎613/237-7884 or 800/663-5777, ⓦwww.hihostels.ca.

Australia

Australian Youth Hostels Association Level 3, 10 Mallet St, Camperdown, NSW 2050 ☎02/9565 1699, ⓦwww.yha.org.au.

New Zealand

Youth Hostels Association of New Zealand PO Box 436, Christchurch 1 ☎03/379 9970, ⓦwww.yha.co.nz.

England and Wales

Youth Hostels Association (YHA) Trevelyan House, 8 St Stephen's Hill, St Albans, Herts AL1 2DY ☎0870/870 8808, ⓦwww.yha.org.uk.

Scotland

Scottish Youth Hostel Association 7 Glebe Crescent, Stirling FK8 2JA ☎0870/155 3255, ⓦwww.syha.org.uk.

Ireland

An Óige 61 Mountjoy St, Dublin 7 ☎01/830 4555, ⓦwww.irelandyha.org.

Ⓑ

Youth Hostel Association of Northern Ireland
22 Donegal Rd, Belfast BT12 5JN
℡01232/324733, ⓦwww.hini.org.uk.

Camping and caravanning

There are hundreds of **campsites** in Britain, charging from £5 per tent per night to around £12 for the plushest sites, with amenities such as laundries, shops and sports facilities. Some hostels have small campsites on their property, charging half the indoor overnight fee. In addition to these official sites, farmers may offer pitches for as little as £3 per night, but don't expect tiled bathrooms and hair dryers for that kind of money. Even farmers without a reserved camping area may let you pitch in a field if you ask first, possibly for free; setting up a tent without asking is an act of trespass, which will not be well received. Free camping is illegal in national parks and nature reserves.

The problem with many campsites in the most popular parts of rural Britain – especially near the coast – is that tents have to share the space with **caravans**. Every summer the country's byways are clogged by migrations of these cumbersome trailers, which are still far more numerous than camper vans in Britain. The great majority of caravans, however, are permanently moored at their sites, where they are rented out to families for self-catering holidays, and the ranks of nose-to-tail trailers in the vicinity of most of Britain's best beaches might make you think that half the population shacks up in a caravan for the midsummer break.

Detailed, annually revised guides to Brtain's camping and caravan sites include the British Tourist Authority's *Caravan and Camping Parks in Britain* (£5.99), which lists graded sites, and Cade's *Camping, Touring and Motor Caravan Site Guide* (£4.99), published by Marwain.

Self-catering accommodation

There are thousands of BTA-approved properties for rent by the week, ranging from city penthouses to secluded cottages. The least you can expect to pay for four-berth self-catering accommodation in low season would be around £120 per week, but in summer for something attractive – such as a small house near the West Country moors – you should budget for around £400 upwards.

Every regional tourist board has details of cottage rentals in its area. Alternative sources of information on all types of self-catering accommodation, from canal boats to lighthouses, are *Dalton's Weekly* (available from most newsagents) and the Sunday newspapers; and of course most travel agents can offer a range of self-catering holiday packages.

Self-catering accommodation firms

Country Cottages in Scotland ℡0870/444 1133, ⓦwww.countrycottagesinscotland.co.uk. Superior cottages with lots of character scattered across the Scottish mainland, plus Skye and Mull.
Country Holidays ℡0870/072 3723, ⓦwww.country-holidays.co.uk. More than three thousand properties.
English Country Cottages ℡0870/585 1100, ⓦwww.english-country-cottages.co.uk. Around two thousand cottages in various parts of rural England.
Hoseasons Country Cottages ℡01502/501515, ⓦwww.hoseasons.co.uk. Wide range of cottages throughout Britain.
Landmark Trust ℡01628/825925, ⓦwww.landmarktrust.co.uk. Their brochure (£9.50) lists around one hundred and sixty converted historic properties, ranging from restored forts and Martello towers to a tiny radio shack used in the last war.
National Trust England and Wales ℡01225/791199, Scotland ℡0131/243 9331. NT-owned cottages and farmhouses, most set in their own gardens or grounds.
Rural Retreats ℡01386/701177, ⓦwww.ruralretreats.co.uk. Upmarket accommodation in restored old buildings, many of them listed.
Vivat Trust ℡020/7930 8030, ⓦwww.vivat.org.uk. Small, select range of historic properties in Shropshire, Dorset, Cumbria and Derbyshire – including North Lees Hall, Charlotte Brontë's inspiration for Mr Rochester's Thornfield Hall in *Jane Eyre*.

Food and drink

Though the British still tend to regard eating as a functional necessity rather than a focal point of the day, great advances towards a more sophisticated appreciation of the culinary arts have been made in recent years. Every major town has its top-range restaurants, many of them boasting awards for excellence, while it's nearly always possible to eat well and inexpensively, thanks chiefly to the influence of Britain's various immigrant communities. However, the pub will long remain the centre of social life in Britain, a drink in a traditional "local" often making the best introduction to the life of a town.

Eating

In many hotels and B&Bs you'll be offered what's termed an "**English breakfast**" – or Welsh or Scottish in the respective countries – which is basically sausage, bacon and eggs plus tea and toast. This used to be the typical working-class start to the day, but these days the British have adopted the healthier cereal alternative, and most places will give you this option as well. Traditionally, a "**Scottish breakfast**" would include porridge – properly made with genuine oatmeal and traditionally eaten with salt rather than sugar, though the latter is always on offer. You may also be served kippers or Arbroath smokies (delicately smoked haddock with butter), or a large piece of haddock with a poached egg on top. Oatcakes (plain savoury biscuits) and a "buttery" – not unlike a French croissant – will often feature.

For most overseas visitors the quintessential British meal is **fish and chips** (known in Scotland as a "fish supper", even at lunchtime), a dish that can vary from the succulently fresh to the indigestibly oily – it's little wonder that lashings of salt, vinegar and

tomato ketchup or the fruitier brown sauce are common additions. The classier places have tables, but more often they serve **takeaway** (takeout) food only, sometimes supplying a disposable fork so that you can guzzle your roadside meal with a modicum of decorum. Fish-and-chip shops ("**chippies**") can be found on most high streets and main suburban thoroughfares throughout Britain, although in larger towns they're beginning to be outnumbered by **pizza**, **kebab** and **burger** outlets.

Other sources of straightforward food throughout the day are "**greasy spoons**" (which tend to close at around 6–7pm), and **pubs** (which usually stop serving food by 9pm), where you'll often find plain "meat-and-two-veg" dishes: steak-and-kidney pie, shepherd's pie (minced lamb or beef covered in mashed potato, and baked), chops and steaks, accompanied by boiled potatoes, carrots or some such vegetable. However, a lot of British pubs now take their food very seriously indeed, having separate dining areas and menus that can compete with some of the better mid-range restaurants. In the smallest villages the pub may be the only place you can eat. Another recent development is the growing number of specialist **vegetarian restaurants**, especially in the larger towns, and the increasing awareness of vegetarian preferences in other eating places. In Wales especially you'll come across dozens of small, inexpensive wholefood cafés, often doubling up as alternative resource centres. Also on the rise in the major towns are vaguely French **brasseries**, informal **bar/restaurants** offering simple meals from around £10–12 per head and often with a set lunchtime menu for around half that.

Britain has its diverse immigrant communities to thank for the range of foods in the mid-range category. Of the innumerable types of **ethnic restaurants** offering good-value high-quality meals you'll find Chinese, Indian and Bangladeshi specialities in every town of any size, with the widest choice in London and the industrial cities of the Midlands and the North. Other Asian restaurants, particularly Thai and Indonesian, are now becoming more widespread in England, but are generally a shade more expensive, while further up the economic scale there's no shortage of French and Italian places – by far the most popular European cuisines, though most cities also have their share of Spanish tapas bars. Japanese food has been one of the success stories of recent years, with sushi bars joining the expense-account restaurants that have been established for some time in the business centres.

The ranks of Britain's **gastronomic restaurants** grow with each passing year, with cordon-bleu chefs producing high-class French-style dishes, California-influenced menus, internationalist hybrid creations, and traditional British meat and fish dishes that are as delicious as the more arty creations of their cross-Channel counterparts. London of course has the highest concentration of top-flight places, but wherever you are in Britain you're never more than half an hour's drive from a really good meal – some of the very best dining rooms are to be found in the countryside hotels. The problem is that fine food costs more in Britain than it does anywhere else in Europe. If a place has any sort of reputation in foodie circles you're unlikely to be spending less than £30 per head, and for the services of the country's glamour chefs you could be paying up to a preposterous £120.

Regional cuisine

England is not particularly celebrated for its variety of regional cuisines, though most areas have a speciality or two, generally rather robust in character. Lincolnshire, for example, is known for its **sausages**, Lancashire and Yorkshire for their **black puddings** (a type of sausage), Cornwall for its **pasty** (a stodgy envelope of pastry filled with meat, potatoes and other root vegetables), and Melton Mowbray for its leaden **pork pies**. England's traditional **cakes** – among them, Bath buns, Bakewell tarts (or puddings) and Eccles cakes – can be found in bakeries on any high street, though they're at their most authentic in their place of origin. A few delicacies are seasonal, such as hot cross buns, available in the few weeks leading up to Easter. More refined dishes are to be had along the coasts – the best **seafood** is found in Cornwall, while oysters are a speciality in Whitstable – and a few English **cheeses**, notably Stilton, enjoy world recognition. England's regional beers are perhaps more distinctive than its food, however, and you'll find a much stronger emphasis on traditional cooking in Scotland and Wales.

The quality of **Scottish food** has improved by leaps and bounds in recent years. Scottish produce – superb meat, fish and game, a wide range of dairy products and a bewildering variety of traditional baked goodies – is of outstanding quality and has to some extent been rediscovered of late. The quintessential Scottish dish is **haggis**, a sheep's stomach stuffed with spiced liver, offal, oatmeal and onion and traditionally eaten with bashed neeps (mashed turnips) and chappit tatties (mashed potatoes). Among other native staples is **stovies**, a tasty mash of onion and fried potato heated up with minced beef. Home-made soup is generally welcome in what can be a cold climate: try **Scots broth**, made with various combinations of lentil, split pea, mutton stock or vegetables and barley.

Welsh cooking is similarly in resurgence, as attested to by the many restaurants, hotels and pubs displaying the "Taste of Wales" (*Blas ar Cymru*) badge. Traditional dishes, such as the delicious native **lamb**, fresh **salmon** and **trout**, can be found on an increasing number of menus, frequently combined with the national vegetable, the **leek**. Particular Welsh specialities include

laver bread (*bara lawr*), a thoroughly tasty seaweed and oatmeal cake often included in a traditional fried breakfast; **bara brith**, a fruit bread found in all teashops, **Glamorgan sausages**, a vegetarian combination of local cheese and spices; **cawl**, a chunky mutton broth; and **cockles**, trawled from the estuary north of the Gower. Dairy products feature highly in such a predominantly rural country, and there's a superb range of Welsh **cheeses**. The best known is Caerphilly, a soft crumbly white cheese that is mixed with beer and toasted on bread to form an authentic **Welsh Rarebit**.

Drinking

The combination of an inclement climate and a British temperamental aversion to casual chat makes the simple **café** a rare phenomenon outside the biggest cities. A growing number of pubs now serve **tea and coffee** during the day, but in most places you'll attract consternation by asking for a cup; in the more genteel tourist towns – such as Stratford, Harrogate and York – you'll find plenty of **teashops**, unlicensed establishments where the normal procedure is to order a slice of cake or some other pastry with your tea or coffee. Increasingly common in the big cities are **brasseries** or equivalent establishments, where the majority of customers are there for a bite to eat, but where you're generally welcome to spend half an hour nursing a cappuccino or glass of wine.

Nothing is likely to dislodge the **pub** from its status as the great British social institution. Originating as wayfarers' hostelries and coaching inns, pubs have outlived the church and marketplace as the focal points of communities, and at their best they can be as welcoming as the full name – "public house" – suggests. Pubs are as varied as the country's townscapes: in larger market towns you'll find huge oak-beamed inns with open fires and polished brass fittings; in the remoter upland villages there are stone-built pubs no larger than a two-bedroomed cottage; and in the more inward-looking parts of industrial Britain you'll come across no-nonsense pubs where something of the old division of the sexes and classes still holds sway – the "spit and sawdust" public bar is where working men can bond over a pint or two, the plusher saloon bar, with a separate entrance, is the preferred haunt of mutually preoccupied couples, the middle classes and unaccompanied women. Whatever the species of pub, its **opening hours** are daily 11am–11pm (in quieter spots, closed between about 3pm and 5.30pm), with "last orders" called by the bar staff about twenty minutes before closing time. The legal drinking age is eighteen and unless there's a special family room or a beer garden, children are not usually welcome.

Most pubs are owned by large breweries who favour their own **beers** and **lagers**, as well as some "guest beers", all dispensed by the pint or half-pint (a pint costs anything from £1.20 to £2.70, depending on the brew and the locale of the pub; see below for more on types of beer). **Cider**, the fermented produce of apples, is a sweet, alcoholic beverage produced in the English West Country, where it's often preferred to beer; the far more potent and less refined **scrumpy** is the type consumed by aficionados of the apple. The cider sold in pubs all over Britain is a fizzy drink that only approximates the real thing. As with beer, the best scrumpy is available within a short radius of the factory, but the drink has nothing like the variety of beer. **Wines** sold in pubs are generally appalling, a strange situation in view of the excellent range of wine available in off-licences and supermarkets. The wine lists in brasseries and **wine bars** are nearly always better, but the mark-ups are often outrageous, and any members of the party who prefer beer will have to be content with bottled drinks. Nonetheless, many people are prepared to pay the extra in return for a less boozy and less male-dominated atmosphere.

Beer

The most widespread type of English beer is **bitter**, an uncarbonated and dark beverage that should be pumped by hand from the cellar and served at room temperature. Though virtually extinct in England, the sweeter, darker "**mild**" beer and the even stronger porter are quite common in Welsh pubs. The indigenous Scottish beer is ale, much like the English **bitter** (in Scotland known as "**heavy**"). In recent years, boosted by aggressive advertising, **lager** has overtaken beer in popularity, and every pub will have at least two brands on offer, but the major breweries are now capitalizing on a backlash against foreign-sounding, pale, chilly and often tasteless drinks, a reaction in large part due to the work of **CAMRA** (Campaign for Real Ale). Some of the beer touted as good traditional ale is nothing of the sort (if the stuff comes out of an electric pump, it probably isn't the real thing), and some of the genuine beers have been adulterated since being taken over by the big companies, but the big breweries do widely distribute some very good beers – for example, Directors, produced by the giant Courage group, is a very classy strong bitter. Guinness, a very dark, creamy Irish stout, is also on sale virtually everywhere, and is an exception to the high-minded objection to electrically pumped beers (though purists will tell you that it does not compare with the stuff sold in Ireland). Smaller operations whose fine ales are available over a wide area include Young's, Fuller's, Wadworth's, Adnams, Greene King, Flowers and Tetley's.

Scottish beers are graded by the shilling: a system used since the 1870s and indicating the level of potency – the higher the shilling mark, the stronger or "heavier" the beer. Scotland's biggest-name breweries are McEwan's and Younger's, part of the mighty Scottish and Newcastle group, and Tennents, owned by the English firm Bass. The beers produced by these companies tend to be heavier, smoother and stronger than their English equivalents, especially McEwan's Export, a mass-produced, highly potent brew, and Tennents' Velvet, a famously smooth ale. Younger's Tartan, though less flavoursome, is Scotland's biggest seller.

However, if you really want to discover how good British beer can be, you should sample the products of the innumerable small local breweries producing **real ales** to traditional recipes. Every region has its distinctive brew, frequently available at free houses – independently run establishments that sell what they please and are generally more characterful than so-called "tied pubs". In **Scotland**, Edinburgh's Caledonian Brewery makes nine good cask beers, operating from Victorian premises that preserve much of their original equipment. Others to look out for are Belhaven, a brewery near Edinburgh whose 80-shilling Export is a typical Scottish ale; Maclays, a hoppy, lightish ale brewed in Alloa; and in the Borders, Traquair Brewery, the only British brewery still to ferment its ale in oak, does a wonderfully smooth House

Ale. The Orkney Brewery's Raven Ale could be a life-saver in the north, where good beer is hard to come by. Among beers worth sampling in **Wales** are the brews produced by the Cardiff-based Brains, whose Dark, Bitter and SA Best Bitter are among the finest pints in the UK. Llanelli-based Felinfoel and Crown Buckley also produce a number of excellent bitters.

For some serious research, CAMRA's annual *Good Beer Guide* (£10.99) is essential; if you see a recent CAMRA sticker on the window of a pub, the beer inside is certainly worth a try. Also useful is the *Good Pub Guide* (£14.99, Ebury Press), a thousand-page yearly handbook that rates each pub's ambience and food as well as its beer.

Whisky

Scotland's national drink is **whisky** – *uisge beatha*, the "water of life" in Gaelic – traditionally drunk in pubs with a half-pint of beer on the side, a combination known as a "nip and a hauf". Whisky has been produced in Scotland since the fifteenth century, and really took off in popularity after the 1780 tax on claret made wine too expensive for most people. The taxman soon caught up with illicit whisky distilling and drove the stills underground, and today many malt distilleries operate on the site of simple cottages that once distilled the stuff illegally. In 1823 Parliament revised its Excise Laws, in the process legalizing whisky production, and today the drink is Scotland's chief export. There are two types of whisky: **single malt**, made from malted barley, and grain, which, relatively cheap to produce, is made from maize and a small amount of malted barley in a continuous still. **Blended whisky**, which accounts for more than 90 percent of all sales, is, as the name suggests, a blend of the two types.

Grain whisky forms about 70 percent of the average bottle of blended whisky, but the distinctive flavour of the different blends comes from the malt whisky which is added to the grain in different quantities. The more expensive the blend, the higher the proportion of skilfully chosen and aged malts that has gone into it. Among many brand names, Johnnie Walker, Bell's, Teacher's and Famous Grouse are some of the most widely available. All have a similar flavour, and are often drunk with mixers such as lemonade or mineral water.

Despite the dominance of the blended whiskies, **single malt whiskies** are infinitely superior, and best drunk neat to appreciate their distinctive flavours. They vary enormously depending on the peat used for drying, the water used, and the type of oak cask in which they are matured, but they fall into four distinct groups – Highland, Lowland, Campbeltown and Islay, with the majority falling into the Highland category and produced largely on Speyside. You can get the best-known makes – among them Glenlivet, Glenmorangie, MacAllan, Talisker, Laphroaig, Highland Park and Glenfiddich, the top seller – in most pubs.

Communications

You should experience no problems with communications either within Britain or calling from abroad; the only difficulty you're likely to encounter is queues at the post office. The mail service is quick and generally efficient, public payphones are numerous, and the outlets offering internet access are ever increasing.

Phones

Most public **payphones** are operated by BT and, at least in the towns, are widespread. Many payphones take all coins from 10p upwards (minimum payment 20p), although an increasing proportion only accept **phonecards**, available from post offices and newsagents displaying BT's green logo. These cards come in denominations of £3, £5, £10 and £20; many phones also accept **credit cards**.

Inland calls are cheapest at weekends and between 6pm and 8am on weekdays. Reduced rate periods for most **international calls** are 6pm–8am from Monday to Friday and all day Saturday and Sunday. A cheaper way to call is from one of the number of **independent telecom centres**, though you're likely to find these only in the major cities.

Throughout the *Guide*, every telephone number is prefixed by the area code, separated from the subscriber number by an oblique slash, which can be omitted if dialling from within the area covered by that prefix. However, some prefixes relate to the cost of calls rather than the location of the subscriber, and should never be omitted: numbers with ☎0800, ☎0808 and ☎0500 prefixes are free of charge to the caller; ☎0845 numbers are charged at local rates and ☎0870 up to the national rate – irrespective of where in the country you are calling from. Beware of premium-rate numbers, which are common for pre-recorded information services – and have the prefix ☎09; these are charged at anything up to £1.50 a minute. Mobile phone numbers are prefixed ☎07.

Mobile phones

More and more people are taking their **mobile phones** with them when they travel, but it is always worth checking with your phone provider to see if your phone will work abroad, and what the call charges will be. Unless you have a tri-band phone, it is unlikely that a mobile bought for use in the US will work outside the States and vice versa, with many only working within the region designated by the area code in the phone number i.e. 212, 415 etc. Most mobiles in Australia and New Zealand use GSM, so should work well in Britain, where most mobile phones use GSM, too – though it's still advisable to check with your provider before travelling.

Operator services

Domestic operator ☎100
International operator ☎155
Domestic directory assistance ☎192 (20p from payphones, otherwise 36–42p)
International directory assistance ☎153 (minimum 20p from payphones, otherwise £1.50; charged according to length of call)

International calls

To call Britain from overseas dial the international access code (☎011 from the US and Canada, ☎0011 from Australia and ☎00 from New Zealand) followed by 44, the area code minus its initial zero, and then the number. To dial out of Britain it's ☎00 followed by the country code, area code (usually without the zero if there is one) and subscriber number. Country codes are as follows:

Australia ☎61
Republic of Ireland ☎353
New Zealand ☎64
US and Canada ☎1

Email

A useful way of keeping in touch while travelling is using one of the **free internet email sites** that can be accessed from anywhere, for example YahooMail and Hotmail – accessible through ⓦwww.yahoo.com and ⓦwww.hotmail.com. Once you've set up an account, you can use these sites to pick up and send mail from anywhere that provides internet access – cafés, hotels, libraries, etc. You'll find **internet cafés** (£3–5/hour) in the major towns and cities; some public libraries now offer free access, but you'll need to book this in advance.

Mail

Virtually all **post offices** are open Mon–Fri 9am–5.30pm, Sat 9am–12.30 or 1pm; in small communities you'll find sub-post offices operating out of general stores; these are open standard post-office hours, even if the shop itself is open for longer. **Stamps** can be bought at supermarkets and newsagents, as well as from post office counters, in books of six or twelve. A first-class stamp for **letters** and **postcards** to anywhere in the British Isles currently costs 27p and should – in theory, at least – arrive the next day; second-class costs 19p and takes from two to four days. **Airmail** weighing less than 20g (0.7oz) to European countries costs 37p and elsewhere overseas from 45p for 10g, and 65p for 20g. Pre-stamped airletters conforming to overseas airmail weight limits of under 10g can be bought for 40p from post offices only. For more information about Royal Mail postal services, call ☎08457/740740.

The media

Britain is well served with newspapers catering to all tastes; each city produces a local journal and newsagents' shelves are stacked floor to ceiling with magazines of every description. Although the proliferation of channels has caused eyebrows to be raised, and accusations of "dumbing–down" to be hurled, British television and radio programmes still remain among the most highly regarded in the world.

Newspapers and magazines

English daily newspapers are predominantly right wing, with the Murdoch-owned *Times* and the staunchly Conservative *Daily Telegraph* occupying the "quality" end of the market, trailed by the *Independent*, which strives worthily to live up to its self-righteous name, and the *Guardian*, which inhabits a niche marginally to the left of centre. At the opposite end of the scale in terms of intellectual weight and volume of sales is the pernicious *Sun*, the sleaziest occupant of the Murdoch stable; its chief rivals in the sex and scandal stakes are the *Daily Star* and self-consciously ridiculous *Daily Sport* but the only tabloid that manages anything approximating to a thought-out response to the *Sun*'s reactionary politics is the *Daily Mirror*. The middle-brow daily tabloids – the *Daily Mail* and the *Daily Express* – show a depressing preoccupation with the royal family and TV celebrities. The scene is a little more varied on a Sunday, when the Guardian-owned Observer, England's oldest **Sunday newspaper**, supplements the Sunday editions of the dailies, whose ranks are also swelled by the amazingly popular News of the World, a smutty rag commonly known as "The News of the Screws".

All the above publications are available in **Wales**, though they don't cover Welsh news in much depth. The only quality Welsh daily is the Western Mail, an uneasy mix of local, Welsh, British and token international news, though its attempts to give a Welsh slant to British stories can sometimes be ludicrous. The national Sunday paper, Wales on Sunday, is far superior.

In **Scotland**, the principal English papers are widely available, often as specific Scottish editions. The Scottish press produces two major daily papers, the liberal-left Scotsman and the slightly less-so Herald, published in Edinburgh and Glasgow respectively. Scotland's best selling daily paper, though, is the downmarket Daily Record, from the same group as the Daily Mirror. Many national Sunday newspapers have a Scottish section north of the border, but Scotland's own Sunday "heavy" is the wholly serious and somewhat dull Scotland on Sunday. Far more fun is the anachronistic Sunday Post, read by over half of the population.

Every town in Britain seems to publish one or more **local papers**, ranging from quality regional news sheets to little more than a collection of adverts. Even these can, however, be a useful source for local events information; we've given details of specific listings magazines in the relevant parts of the Guide.

When it comes to **specialist periodicals**, British newsagents can offer a range covering just about every subject, with motoring, music, sport, computers, gardening and home improvements all well served. One noticeably poor area is current events – the only high-selling weekly commentary magazine is the Economist, which is essential reading in the boardrooms of England. The socialist alternative, the New Statesman, is subsidized by a few socialist millionaires and is complemented by the glossy monthly Red Pepper. The satirical bi-weekly Private Eye is a much-loved institution that prides itself on printing the stories the rest of the press won't touch, and on surviving the consequent stream of libel suits. If you feel you can stomach a descent into the scatological pit of the British male psyche, take a look at Viz, a fortnightly comic which has managed to lodge its grotesque caricatures in the collective consciousness. Scottish monthly magazines include the widely read Scots Magazine, an old-fashioned middle-of-the-road publication that promotes family values. There's a profusion of Welsh monthlies – Planet, an English-language overview of the arts, history and politics, is the best of the bunch.

Australians and New Zealanders in London will be gratified to find the weekly free magazine TNT, which provides news from the home countries as well as adverts for jobs, accommodation and events in the capital. For **North Americans**, USA Today and the International Herald Tribune are widely distributed as are the magazines Time and Newsweek.

Television and radio

In Britain, there are five analogue television stations. These are divided between the state-owned BBC, with two public service channels, and three independent commercial channels, ITV 1, Channel 4 and Channel 5. Though assailed by critics in the Conservative party, who think that it maintains a definite left-wing bias, the **BBC** is just about maintaining its worldwide reputation for in-house quality productions, ranging from expensive costume dramas to intelligent documentaries. BBC 2 is the more offbeat and heavyweight BBC channel; BBC 1 is avowedly mainstream. Various regional companies together form the **ITV 1** network, but they are united by a more tabloid approach to programme making – necessarily so, because if they don't get the advertising they don't survive. **Channel 4**, a partly subsidized institution, is the most progressive of the bunch, with a reputation for broadcasting an eclectic spread of "arty" and minority-pleasing programmes, and for supporting small-budget motion pictures. In Wales, this is replaced with S4C (Sianel Pedwar Cymru), which, like Channel 4, sponsors diverse animation and feature-film projects; it also features Welsh-language programmes, which are broadcast at lunchtime and for most of the evening, with the rest of the schedule reverting to Channel 4's UK-wide output at other times. **Channel 5**, not widely available through analogue receivers, is a self-consciously "young 'n' fun" alternative distinguished by its lurid colour schemes, breathless presenters and mediocre programming.

As the government plans to switch off the analogue system somewhere between 2006 and 2010, **satellite** and **cable** TV companies are increasingly adopting the **digital** system, through which hundreds of channels are on offer, including interactive shopping, games and internet access; Rupert Murdoch's dominant Sky network (now digital) is receiving serious challenge from the latest player in this field, ITV Digital. Although a large proportion of viewers remain content with their core five analogue channels, the ITV network presents ITV 2 and ITV Sport, and the BBC its News 24, BBC 4, Parliament and Choice channels solely through the digital system.

Market forces are eating away rather more quickly at the BBC's **radio** network, which has five stations: Radio 1 is almost exclusively pop music, with a chart-biased view of the rock world; Radio 2 is a combination of easy listening and sassier jazz, rock and arts programmes; Radio 3 is predominantly classical

music; Radio 4 a blend of current affairs, arts and drama; and Radio 5 Live, a sports and news channel. Radio 1 has rivals on all fronts, with Virgin running a youth-oriented nationwide commercial network, and a plethora of local commercial stations – notably London's Capital Radio – also attracting large sections of Radio 1's target audience. Magic FM has whittled away at the Radio 2 easy listening market, as has Jazz FM, while Classic FM has lured people away from Radio 3 by offering a less earnest approach to its subject, though it sometimes degenerates into a "Greatest Hits" view of the greats. The BBC also operates several regional stations, but they are usually rather like listening to a broadcast of the local newspaper interspersed with the "Top 20"; the commercial stations, some of them real fly-by-wire operations, tend to be much livelier.

One BBC institution that has stayed in front despite the arrival of downmarket pretenders is the *Radio Times*, a weekly **listings magazine** that gives full details on all national TV and radio programmes, not just the ones broadcast by the BBC.

Opening hours and public holidays

Most attractions are open daily in summer, with one or two closed days in the winter, though the major state museums are open daily all year. We've given full details of opening hours in the *Guide*.

General **shop hours** are Mon–Sat 9am–5.30 or 6pm, although you'll find Sunday and late-night shopping in the larger towns, with Thursday and Friday the favoured evenings. The big supermarkets also tend to stay open until 8 or 9pm from Monday to Saturday, some staying open through the night. On Sundays, supermarkets and high-street stores can legally open for just six hours – though in the case of the latter, this tends only to happen in larger centres and out-of-town shopping complexes; supermarkets tend to open from 10am to 4pm, while most stores choose to open from 11am or noon to 5pm or 6pm. By contrast, many provincial towns still retain an **early-closing day**, when shops close at 1pm;

Wednesday is the favourite.

Note that not all **service stations** on motorways are open for 24 hours, although you can usually get fuel around the clock in larger towns and cities.

Public holidays

In **England and Wales** most fee-charging sites are open on Bank Holidays (public holidays), when Sunday hours usually apply. The dates of these are in the box below. In **Scotland**, "bank holidays" mean just that – they are literally days when the banks are closed rather than general public holidays, and they vary from year to year; January 1 is the only fixed public holiday in Scotland,

Public Holidays in England and Wales

January 1	**Last Monday in May**
Good Friday (late March or early April)	**Last Monday in August**
Easter Monday (late March or early April)	**December 25**
First Monday in May	**December 26**

Note that if January 1, December 25 or December 26 falls on a Saturday or Sunday, the next week day becomes a public holiday.

but all Scottish towns and cities have a one-day holiday in both spring and autumn – dates vary from place to place but normally fall on a Monday. If you want to know the exact dates, you should get the booklet detailing them from Glasgow Chamber of Commerce, 30 George Square, Glasgow G2 1EQ (☎0141/204 2121, ⓦwww.glasgowchamber.org).

Admission to museums and monuments

Most attractions in England and Wales are open daily in summer and closed one or two days a week in winter, though the major state museums are open daily all year. In Scotland the tourist season runs from Easter to October and only the biggest museums and most popular indoor attractions are open outside this period, although ruins and gardens are normally accessible year-round. We've given full details of opening hours throughout the guide.

Many of Britain's most treasured sites – from castles, abbeys and great houses to tracts of protected landscape – come under the control of the private **National Trust** and **National Trust for Scotland**. Both organizations charge an entry fee for the majority of their sites, and these can be quite high, especially for the more grandiose estates. If you think you'll be visiting more than half a dozen of their properties, denoted "NT" or "NTS" in the guide, it's worth taking out **annual membership** (NT £30; NTS £28), which allows free entry to both sets of properties, although you'll only receive mailings from the one that you join.

A great many of Britain's other sites are controlled by the state-run **English Heritage; Historic Scotland;** and **CADW Welsh Historic Monuments**, which we've denoted as "EH", "HS" and "CADW" respectively. Annual membership of any one of the three (EH £30; HS £28; CADW £26) entitles you to half-price entry to properties run by the other two.

A lot of **stately homes** remain in the hands of the landed gentry, who tend to charge in the region of £5 for admission to edited highlights of their domain – even more if, as at Longleat, they've added some theme-park attractions to the historic pile. Many other old buildings, albeit rarely the most momentous structures, are owned by the local authorities, which are generally more lenient with their admission charges, sometimes allowing free access. You may find that a history museum or a similar collection has been installed in the local castle or half-rebuilt ruin, and in these cases there's usually a modest entry charge. However, **municipal art galleries and museums** are often free, as are many of the great **state museums** – both the British Museum and the National Gallery are free, for example, though Cardiff's National Museum of Wales is not. On the other hand, these cash-starved institutions are nowadays obliged to request voluntary donations, as are several **cathedrals**. Most cathedrals charge a pound or two for admission to the most beautiful parts of the structure – usually the chapter house or cloister. **Churches**, increasingly, are kept locked except for services, but when they are open entry is free.

You will certainly have to pay to visit any of Britain's burgeoning **heritage museums**, which in some instances are large multi-building sites staffed by people in period costume, but more often consist of interactive displays – some of which take the form of hi-tech animatronic tableaux, while others amount to little more than a few mannequins with video monitors for heads. Tickets for these can cost anywhere between £5 and £10, and expense is not necessarily an indication of quality. However, the most expensive attractions in Britain are those aimed squarely at tourists with cash to spend – Madame Tussaud's, the country's number one earner of foreign cash, now charges £14 for admission.

The majority of fee-charging attractions have **reductions** for senior citizens, the unemployed, full-time students and children under 16, with under-5s being admitted free almost everywhere. Proof of eligibility will be required in most cases, though even the flintiest desk clerk will probably take on trust the age of a babe-in-arms. The entry charges given in the guide are the full adult charges; as a rule, adult reductions are in the range of 25–35 percent, while reductions for children are around 50 percent.

Finally, foreign visitors planning on seeing more than a dozen stately homes, monuments or gardens might find it worthwhile to buy a **Great British Heritage Pass**, which gives free admission to some six hundred sites, many of which are not run by the National Trust or English Heritage. Costing under £30 for seven days, £45 for fifteen days and £60 for a month, the pass can be purchased through most travel agents at home, on arrival at any large UK airport, from most major tourist offices and the Britain Visitor Centre, 1 Regent St, London W1 (walk-in service only).

Useful contacts

CADW Welsh Historic Monuments
℡ 029/2050 0200, Ⓦ www.cadw.wales.gov.uk
English Heritage ℡ 0207/973 3000,
Ⓦ www.english-heritage.org.uk.
Historic Scotland ℡ 0131/668 8600,
Ⓦ www.historic-scotland.gov.uk.
National Trust ℡ 020/7973 3000
Ⓦ www.nationaltrust.org.uk.
National Trust for Scotland ℡ 0131/243 9331,
Ⓦ www.nts.org.uk.

Festivals

In terms of the number of tourists they attract, the biggest occasions in the English calendar are the rituals that have associations with the ruling classes – from the courtly pageant of the Trooping of the Colour to the annual rowing race between Oxford and Cambridge universities. In Scotland many visitors home straight in on bagpipes, ceilidhs and Highland Games; such anachronisms certainly reflect the endemic British taste for nostalgia, but to gauge the spirit of the nation you should sample a wider range of events. London's large-scale festivals range from the riotous street party of the Notting Hill Carnival to the Promenade concerts, Europe's most egalitarian high-class music season, while the Edinburgh Festival and Welsh National Eisteddfod are vast cultural jamborees that have attained international status. Every major town in Britain has its own local arts festival, the best of which, along with various other local fairs and commemorative shows, are mentioned in the main part of the *Guide*; the very biggest ones are also listed below.

To see Britain at its most idiosyncratic, take a look at one of the numerous regional celebrations that perpetuate **ancient customs**, the origins and meanings of which have often been lost or conveniently forgotten. The sight of the entire population of a village scrambling around a field after a barrel (that they call a bottle), or chasing a cheese downhill is not easily forgotten. Some of these strange rituals are mentioned in the *Guide* and included in the list below. Bear in mind that at a few of the smaller, more obscure events casual visitors are not always welcome. If in doubt, check with the local tourist office.

Also included in the list are the main **sports events**, which may often be difficult to get tickets for, but are invariably televised. In addition to these, there are of course football matches every Saturday (and some Sundays) from late August till early May, and cricket matches every day throughout the summer – both interesting social phenomena even for those unenthralled by team sports.

Events calendar

Mid- to late Jan Celtic Connections, Glasgow. A major celebration of Celtic and folk music held in venues across the city.

Jan 25 Burns Night: Scots worldwide get stuck into haggis, whisky and vowel-grinding poetry to commemorate Scotland's greatest poet, Robert Burns.

Mid-Feb Chinese New Year. Festivities in London's and Manchester's Chinatown districts.

Feb–March Six Nations Rugby tournament between Scotland, England, Wales, Ireland, France and Italy.

March 1 St David's Day. Hwyrnos and celebrations all over Wales.

March 1 Whuppity Scourie, Lanark. Local children race round the church beating each other with home-made paper weapons in a representation (it's thought) of the chasing away of winter or the warding off of evil spirits.

Mid-March Cheltenham Gold Cup meeting. England's premier national hunt horseracing event.

End of March or early April University Boat Race. Hugely popular rowing contest on the Thames, between the teams of Oxford and Cambridge.

Shrove Tues Purbeck Marblers and Stonecutters Day, Corfe Castle, Dorset. Ritual football game through the streets of the village.

Maundy Thurs The Queen dispenses the Royal Maundy Money (at a different cathedral annually).

Easter Mon Hare Pie Scramble and Bottle-Kicking, Hallaton, Leicestershire.

Late March or early April Grand National meeting, Aintree, Liverpool. Cruelly testing steeplechase that entices most of Britain's population into the betting shops.

April Scottish Grand National, Ayr. Not quite as testing as the English equivalent steeplechase, but an important event on the Scottish racing calendar nonetheless.

April 6 Tartan Day. Over-hyped celebration of ancestry by North Americans of Scottish descent on the anniversary of the Declaration of Arbroath in 1320. Ignored by most Scots in Scotland, other than journalists.

May English FA Cup Final. The deciding contest in the country's premier football tournament is currently without a home of its own. For the time being, the English national game's most important fixture will be held in the Welsh capital, Cardiff.

May Scottish FA Cup Final in Glasgow. Scotland's premier football event.

May 1 Padstow Hobby Horse, Padstow, Cornwall. Processions, music and dancing through the streets.

May 8 Helston Furry Dance, Helston, Cornwall.

Last Mon in May Cheese Rolling, Brockworth, Gloucestershire. Pursuit of a cheese wheel down a murderous incline – one of the weirdest customs in England.

Late May: Hay-on-Wye Festival of Literature. London's literati flock to the Welsh borders for a week.

Last week in May St David's Cathedral Festival. Superb setting for classical concerts and recitals.

Last week in May Chelsea Flower Show, Royal Hospital, Chelsea, London. Essential event for Britain's green-fingered legions.

Late May and early June Bath International Festival. International arts jamboree.

May–July Glyndebourne Opera Festival, East Sussex. The classiest and most snobbish arts festival in Britain.

June Aldeburgh Festival. Jamboree of classical music held on the Suffolk Coast. Established by Benjamin Britten.

June Shinty Camanachd Cup Final. The climax of the season for Scotland's own stick-and-ball game, normally held in one of the main Highland towns. Also marks the beginning of the Highland Games season across the Highlands, northeast and Argyll.

First week in June Eisteddfod Genedlaethol Urdd. The largest youth festival in Europe, alternating between North and South Wales.

First week in June Derby week, Epsom racecourse, Surrey. The world's most expensive horseflesh competing in the Derby, the Coronation Cup and the Oaks.

First Fri in June Cotswold Olimpicks, Chipping Campden, Gloucestershire. Rustic sports festival and torchlight procession.

First or second Sat in June Trooping the Colour, Horse Guards Parade, London. Equestrian pageantry for the Queen's Official Birthday.

Mid-June Cardiff Singer of the World competition. Huge, televised week-long music festival, with a star-studded list of international competitors.

Mid-June Appleby Horse Fair, Appleby-in-Westmorland, Cumbria.

Mid-June Royal Ascot, Berkshire. High-class horseracing attended by high-class people; the best seats go to royalty and their satellites, while the proles mill around in the outfield.

End of June World Worm-Charming Championships, Willaston, Cheshire.

Last week of June Glastonbury Festival, Somerset. Hugely popular festival, with international bands, indie music and loads of hippies.

Last week of June and first week of July Lawn Tennis Championships, Wimbledon, London. Queues are phenomenal even for the early rounds, and you need to know a freemason or ex-champion to get in to the big games.

Late June Royal Highland Agricultural Show, at Ingliston near Edinburgh.

July Scottish Open Golf Championship, held at a different venue each year. Also Highland Games at Caithness, Elgin, Glengarry, North Uist, Inverness, Inveraray, Mull, Lewis, Durness, Lochaber, Dufftown, Halkirk.

Early July Llangollen International Music Eisteddfod. Over 12,000 participants from all over the world, including choirs, dancers, folk singers, groups and instrumentalists.

Early July Glasgow International Jazz Festival, and T in the Park – the latter Scotland's biggest outdoor music event, held in Glasgow's Strathclyde Park with a star-studded line-up of contemporary bands.

First week in July Henley Royal Regatta, Oxfordshire. Rowing event attended by much the same crew as populates the grandstands at Ascot.

First week of July Tynwald Ceremony, St Johns, Isle of Man.

Second weekend in July Gŵyl Werin y Cnapan, Ffostrasol, near Lampeter, Ceredigion. The best folk and Celtic music festival in the world.

Second week in July York Early Music Festival. The premier early music festival lasts for ten days.

Second or Third Sat in July Durham Miner's Gala, Durham.

Mid-July British Open Golf Championship, variable venue. The season's last Grand Slam golf tournament.

Third week in July Swan Upping, River Thames from Sunbury to Pangbourne. Ceremonial registering of the Thames cygnets.

Last week in July Royal Tournament, Earl's Court Exhibition Centre, London. Precision military displays.

Last week in July Cambridge Folk Festival. Biggest event of its kind in England.

Late July WOMAD, Reading. Three-day world music and dance festival.

Last week in July to first week in Aug Cardiff Festival. Incorporates music, art, drama, opera, literature and street entertainment.

July to early Sept The Promenade Concerts ("The Proms"), Royal Albert Hall, London. Classical music concerts ending in the fervently patriotic Last Night of the Proms.

Aug Edinburgh Festival, one of the world's great arts jamborees.

First week in Aug Royal National Eisteddfod. Wales's biggest single annual event: fun, very impressive and worth seeing if only for the overblown pageantry. Bardic competitions, readings, theatre, TV, debates and copious help for the Welsh language learner.

Early Aug The two-day Lammas Fair at St Andrews, the oldest medieval market in the country.

Early Aug Sidmouth Folk Festival. Folk and roots performers from around the world, plus theatre and dance.

Weekend in mid-Aug Bristol Balloon Fiesta. Hundreds of balloons take to the skies early morning and evening.

Aug Bank Hol Notting Hill Carnival, around Notting Hill, West London. Vivacious celebration by London's Caribbean community – plenty of music, food and floats.

Aug Bank Hol Reading Festival, Berkshire. Three-day hard rock jamboree.

Last Sun in Aug Plague Memorial, Eyam, Derbyshire.

Early Sept Ben Nevis Race (for amateurs), held on the first weekend in the month, running to the top of Scotland's highest mountain and back again. Also Highland Games at Braemar.

First Mon after Sept 4 Abbots Bromley Horn Dance, Abbots Bromley, Staffordshire. Vaguely pagan mass dance in mock-medieval costume – one of the most famous ancient customs.

Early Sept to early Nov Blackpool Illuminations, Lancashire. Five miles of extravagant light displays.

Oct Swansea Festival of Music and the Arts. Concerts, jazz, drama, opera, ballet and art events throughout the city.

Late Oct Glenfiddich Piping Championships at Blair Atholl for the world's top ten solo pipers.

Late Oct to early Nov Huddersfield Contemporary Music Festival. One of Europe's premier showcases for up-to-the-minute highbrow music.

First Sun in Nov London to Brighton Veteran Car Rally. Ancient machines lumbering the 57 miles down the A23 to the seafront.

Nov 5 Guy Fawkes Night. Nationwide fireworks and bonfires commemorating the foiling of the Gunpowder Plot in 1605 – especially raucous celebrations at York (Fawkes' birthplace), Ottery St Mary in Devon and at Lewes, East Sussex.

Mid-Nov Lord Mayor's Procession and Show, the City of London. Cavalcade to mark the inauguration of the new mayor.

Nov 30 St Andrew's Day, celebrating Scotland's patron saint.

Dec 31 New Year Walk-In, Llanwrtyd Wells, Powys. A boozy stagger around the town.

Dec 31 Tar Barrels Parade, Allendale Town, Northumberland.

Dec 31 & Jan 1 Hogmanay and Ne'er Day: traditionally more important to the Scots than Christmas, known for the custom of "first-footing", when groups of revellers troop into neighbours' houses at midnight bearing gifts. More popular these days are huge and highly organized street parties, most notably in Edinburgh, but also in Aberdeen, Glasgow and other centres.

Sports and outdoor pursuits

No matter where you are in Britain, you're never far from a stretch of countryside where you can lose the crowds on a brief walk or cycle ride. For tougher specimens, there are numerous long-distance footpaths, as well as opportunities for the more extreme disciplines of rock climbing and potholing (caving). On the coast and many of the inland lakes you can follow the more urbane pursuits of sailing and windsurfing, and there are plenty of fine beaches for less structured fresh-air activities or just slobbing around.

Walking and climbing

Walking routes trace many of Britain's wilder areas, amid landscapes varied enough to suit anyone. More sedate walkers will be happy enough in England, where many of the footpaths traverse moorlands, but if you're after more demanding exercise, or a feeling of isolation, head for Wales or Scotland. Welsh Snowdonia and the Scottish Highlands offer Britain's best **climbing** and have acted as training grounds for some of the world's greatest mountaineers.

Numerous short walks and several major walks are covered in the *Guide* – however, you should use these notes only as general outlines and always in conjunction with a good **map**. Where possible we have given details of the best maps to use – in most cases one of the Ordnance Survey (OS) series (see p.20) – along with advice, leaflets and specialist guidebooks from tourist offices and shops in walking areas. In England and Wales you need to keep to established routes as you'll often be crossing private land, even within the National Parks: all OS maps mark public rights of way. Scotland, in contrast, has a tradition of **free public access** to most of the countryside, restricted only at certain times of the year.

At the time of writing, some footpaths were closed as a precaution against the further spreading of the **Foot and Mouth** epidemic. For the latest on this situation, contact any local tourist office or one of the companies listed below.

Safety in the British hills

British mountains are not high by European standards, but, due to rapid weather changes, they are potentially extremely dangerous and should be treated with respect. Every year, in every season, climbers and hill walkers die on mountains in Scotland, Wales and the English Lake District. If the weather looks as if it's closing in, get down fast. It is essential that you are properly equipped – even for what appears to be an easy expedition in apparently settled weather – with proper warm and waterproof layered clothing, supportive footwear and adequate maps, a compass (which you should know how to use) and food. Always leave word of your route and what time you expect to return; and remember to contact the person again to let them know that you are back.

In England

England's finest **walking areas** are the granite moorlands and spectacular coastlines of **Devon and Cornwall** in the southwest, and the highlands of the north – the low limestone and millstone crags of the **Peak District**, between Sheffield and Manchester; the **Yorkshire Dales**, the stretch of the Pennines to the north of the **Peak District**; the **North York Moors**, a bleak, treeless upland to the east of the Pennines; and the glaciated Cumbrian Mountains, better known as the **Lake District**. On summer weekends the more accessible reaches of these regions can get very crowded with day-trippers, but at any time of the year you'll find yourself in relative isolation if you undertake one of the **Long Distance Footpaths (LDPs)**. Defined as any route over twenty miles long, LDPs exist all over the country and are marked at frequent intervals with an acorn waymarker. **Youth hostels** are littered along most routes, though you may need a tent for some of the more heroic hikes.

In Scotland

The whole of **Scotland** offers good opportunities for gentle hill walking, from the smooth, grassy hills and moors of the **Southern Uplands** to the wild and rugged country of the northwest. Scotland has three **Long Distance Footpaths (LDPs)**, each of which takes days to walk, though you can of course just cover sections of them. The **Southern Upland Way** crosses Scotland from coast to coast in the south, and is the country's longest at 212 miles; the best known is the **West Highland Way**, a 95-mile hike from Glasgow to Fort William via Loch Lomond and Glen Coe; and the gentler **Speyside Way**, in Aberdeenshire, is a mere thirty miles. The green signposts of the Scottish Rights of Way Society point to these and many other cross-country routes; while in the wilder parts the accepted freedom to roam allows extensive mountain walking, rock climbing, orienteering and allied activities.

Scotland's main **climbing areas** are in the Highlands, which boast many challenging peaks as well as great hill walks. There are 279 mountains over 3000ft (914m) in Scotland, known as **Munros** after the man who first classified them: many walkers "collect" them, and it's possible to chalk up several in a day. Serious climbers will probably head for **Glen Coe** or **Torridon** which offer difficult routes in spectacular surroundings. These and some of the other finest Highland areas (Lawers, Kintail, West Affric) are in the ownership of the National Trust for Scotland, while Blaven and Ladhar Bheinn (Knoydart) are John Muir Trust properties; both allow year-round access. Elsewhere there may be restricted access during lambing (dogs are particularly unwelcome during April and May) and deer-stalking seasons (mid-August to the third week in October). The **booklet** *Heading for the Scottish Hills* (published by the Scottish Mountaineering Club or "SMC"; £6.95) provides such information on all areas.

In Wales

Wales's best **walking country** is to be found within its three national parks. Almost the whole of the northwestern corner of Wales is taken up with the **Snowdonia National Park**, a dozen of the country's highest peaks separated by dramatic glaciated valleys and laced with hundreds of miles of ridge and moorland paths. From Snowdonia, the Cambrian Mountains stretch south to the **Brecon Beacons National Park**, with its striking sandstone scarp at the head of the South Wales coalfield, and lush, cave-riddled limestone valleys to the south. One hundred and seventy miles of Wales's southwestern peninsula make up the third park – the **Pembrokeshire Coast National Park**, best explored by the **Pembrokeshire Coast Path** that traverses the cliff tops, frequently dipping down into secluded coves. This is only one of Wales's four frequently walked **Long Distance Paths** – the other three LDPs are the 168-mile-long **Offa's Dyke Path** that traces the England–Wales border; the 274-mile **Cambrian Way**, cutting north–south over the Cambrian Mountains, and **Glyndŵr's Way**, which weaves through mid-Wales for 120 miles.

As well as being superb walking country, Wales offers some of Britain's best **rock climbing** and some challenging scrambles – ascents that fall somewhere between walks and climbs, requiring some use of your hands. There are a couple of noted climbing spots around the Pembrokeshire coast and in the Brecon Beacons but the vast majority are in Snowdonia, with its predominance of low-lying crags and easy access. The best general **guide** for experienced climbers is *Rock Climbing in Snowdonia* by Paul Williams (£12.95, Constable).

Walking-holiday specialists

Adventureline ☎01209/820847, ⓦwww.chyyco.co.uk/adventureline. Small group tours with local guides around the Celtic landscapes of Cornwall.
Explore Britain ☎01740/650900. Guided or independent walking holidays countrywide with luggage transfer.
Footpath Holidays ☎01985/840049, ⓦwww.footpath-holidays.com. Packages to various hill and coastal districts in England, with experienced group leaders.
HF Walking Holidays ☎020/8905 9556 or 905 9388, ⓦwww.hfholidays.co.uk. A wide choice of locations and lodging in comfortable country houses.
Instep Walking Holidays ☎01903/766475, ⓦwww.instephols.co.uk. Self-guided holidays with accommodation in small country hotels and guest houses, mainly in the south of England.
Sherpa Expeditions ☎0181/577 2717, ⓦwww.sherpa-walking-holidays.co.uk. At-your-own-pace, self-guided walks between country pubs.
Walkabout Scotland ☎0131/661 7168, ⓦwww.walkaboutscotland.com. A great way to get a taste of hiking in the Highlands, with guided hillwalking day-trips from Edinburgh for £40 per person, with all transport included.

Cycling

Although there has been a boom in the sale of mountain bikes and a rise in the number of towns and cities that have incorporated designated cycle routes into their traffic schemes, **cyclists** tend to be treated with disrespect by many motorists. British cyclists are estimated to be twelve times more likely to be killed or injured on the road (per miles cycled) than their counterparts in Denmark, where a network of safe cycle paths and traffic-calming schemes has been created, although the organization **SUSTRANS** (see opposite) is attempting to go some way towards addressing this problem.

Surprisingly, cycle **helmets** are not compulsory in Britain – but if you're hellbent on

tackling the congestion, pollution and aggression of city traffic, you're well advised to get one. You do have to have a **rear reflector** and front and back **lights** when riding at night, and are not allowed to carry children without a special child seat. It is also illegal to cycle on pavements (sidewalks), and in most public parks. A secure **lock** (preferably some kind of "D" lock) is also indispensable and it's always a good idea to make a note of your frame number in case you have to report a theft to the police.

Bike rental is available at cycle shops in most large towns, and at villages within national parks and other scenic areas; the addresses and telephone numbers of these appear in the relevant sections of the *Guide*. Expect to pay in the region of £10–20 per day for something sturdy, with discounts for longer periods.

Carrying your bike on public transport

The majority of **airlines** will carry bicycles as part of your luggage allowance on plane journeys, although protruding parts, such as pedals and handlebars, have to be removed, and the tyres deflated; some carriers also require you to stash the machine in a bike bag or cardboard cover. Check with your airline well in advance to find out exactly what their terms and conditions are, and bear in mind that you may have to pay excess baggage. Transporting cycles by **ferry** is also free, but a lot more straightforward; you just wheel them on and off, and reservations are not normally required.

Carrying your bike by **train** is a good way of getting to the interesting parts of England without a lot of stressful or boring pedalling. For some reason, however, rail companies seem hellbent on making life difficult for cyclists by slapping on hefty surcharges. Most suburban trains will carry cycles outside of morning and evening rush hours (7.30–9.30am & 4–7pm), but they are not allowed at all on some express trains (or Eurostar), while those that do accept cycles charge between £1 and £3; this usually has to be paid at least 24 hours in advance, and for each separate leg of the trip, which can work out to be ridiculously expensive if your journey involves a couple of changes. If you reserve 14 days in advance, Eurotunnel will carry you and your bike on the 12.30pm or

6pm train from Calais and the 9.30am or 3.30pm train from Folkestone. A day-trip costs £15, a five-day return £31 and an open return £59. For information and to book, call ☎01303/288933 or 288680.

Cycle routes

Funded by a £43,500,000 grant by the Millennium Commission, in partnership with local authorities and organizations such as the National Trust and Countryside Agency, the charity **SUSTRANS** is dedicated to expanding the National Cycle Network and aims to cover some 10,000 miles by 2005, passing within two miles of some twenty million people. A large proportion of the network is made up of quiet backroads, dubbed "Cycleways", but more than half runs along disused railways and canal towpaths, including the showpiece section connecting the cities of Bath and Bristol.

Aside from these, the backroads of rural Britain (those labelled with the prefix "B") make infinitely more enjoyable routes than trunk routes (or "A" roads), with generally amiable gradients and a sufficient density of pubs and B&Bs to keep the days manageable. Your main problem out in the countryside will be getting hold of any spare parts – only inner tubes and tyres are easy to find.

Off-road cycling is popular in the highland walking areas, but cyclists should remember to keep to rights of way designated on maps as Bridleways, BOATs ("Byways Open To All Traffic") or RUPFs ("Roads Used As Public Footpaths") and to pass walkers at considerate speeds. Footpaths, unless otherwise marked, are for pedestrian use only. Other rules of the road to bear in mind are that cycles are not permitted on motorways (labelled with the prefix "M").

Armed with a detailed OS **map** of any area, you can improvise scenic routes of your own that avoid the main roads – better still, most good bookshops stock a range of **cycling guides**, featuring suggestions for rides of varying length, with coloured maps and detailed route descriptions. Also useful are SUSTRANS' maps of the official cycle network (£5.99) and their *Official Guide to the National Network* (£9.99).

With more time, you may want to take on one of Britain's challenging **long-distance routes**. The Cycle Touring Club or CTC, publishes special maps for some of these, and

supplies members with touring and technical advice as well as insurance. The classic cross-Britain route is Land's End, in the far southwest of England, to John O'Groats, on the northeast tip of Scotland – roughly a thousand miles that can be covered in two to three weeks, depending on which of the three CTC-recommended routes you choose. Another favourite coast-to-coast option is the journey from Lowestoft, in the southeast county of Suffolk, to the Ardnamurchan peninsula in northwest Scotland. The CTC suggests a ten-day itinerary, but you could easily spend twice that long scaling the English watershed. The same applies to the wonderful 130-mile Wye Valley route, which winds from the Severn Estuary through the forests and moorlands of the Welsh borders to the rough mountains of mid-Wales. Other tempting long-distance tours could take you around the Yorkshire Dales, Pennines, and Peak district, around Dartmoor and the Cornish coast, or across the austere North Yorkshire Moors. Visitors from abroad can get copies of their leaflets (costing £2–4) which detail tour routes in these and other regions.

Useful cycling contacts

The Cycle Touring Club (CTC) ☎ 01483/417217, ⓦ www.CTC.org.uk.
SUSTRANS ☎0117/929 0888, ⓦwww.sustrans.org.uk.

Cycling holidays

For those who want a guaranteed hassle-free **cycling holiday**, there are various companies offering easy-going packages. These can take all sorts of forms, but generally include transport of your gear to each night's halt, pre-booked accommodation, detailed route instructions, a packed lunch and back-up support. Most companies offer some budget cycling holidays, with hostels or B&Bs instead of hotels.

Cycling holiday specialists

Activities ☎0870/740 5055, ⓦ www.acornactivities.co.uk. Weekend and one-week tours, with bikes, accommodation, luggage transportation and maps provided.
Bespoke Highland Tours ☎01687/450272, ⓦwww.scotland-inverness.co.uk/bht-main.htm. Organizes cycle touring in the Scottish Highlands and

Islands, using a reliable and long-standing network of B&Bs and hostels, and arranges transport links and baggage transfer.

Bike Breaks ☎0151/722 8050, ⊛www.bywaysbreaks.com. Tours of varying length in the Cheshire and Shropshire countryside.

Compass Holidays ☎01242/250642, ⊛www.compass-holidays.com. Guided or independent tours in the Cotswolds, the Lake District, Cornwall and Warwickshire.

Country Lanes ☎01425/655022, ⊛www.countrylanes.co.uk. Tours in the New Forest, the Cotswolds and the Lake District starting from train stations.

Rough Tracks ☎0700/0560 749, ⊛www.roughtracks.co.uk. Mountain bike and road weekend tours across the country. Also bike maintenance weekends.

Beaches

Britain is ringed by fine beaches and bays, the best of which are readily accessible by public transport – though of course that means they tend to get very busy in high summer. For a combination of decent climate and good sand, southwest **England** is the best area, especially the coast of north Cornwall and Devon. The beaches of England's southern coast become more pebbly as you approach the southeastern corner of the country – resorts round here are more garish than their southwestern counterparts. Moving up the east coast, the East Anglian shore is predominantly pebbly and very exposed, making it ideal for those who want to escape the crowds rather than bask in the sun, while right up in the northeast there are some wonderful sandy strands and old-fashioned seaside resorts, though the North Sea breezes often require a degree of stoicism. Over in the northwest, the inland hills of Cumbria are a greater attraction than anything on the coast, though Blackpool has a certain appeal as the apotheosis of the "kiss-me-quick" holiday town.

Many of **Scotland's** beaches and bays are deserted even in high summer – perhaps hardly surprising given the bracing winds and icy water. Though you're unlikely to come here for a beach holiday, it's worth sampling one or two beaches, even if you never shed as much as a sweater. A rash of slightly melancholy seaside towns lies within easy reach of Glasgow, while on the east coast, the relatively low cliffs and miles of sandy beaches are ideal for walking. Despite the low temperature of the water, the beaches in the northeast are beginning to figure on surfers' itineraries, attracting enthusiasts from all over Europe. Perhaps the most beautiful beaches of all are to be found on Scotland's islands: endless, isolated stretches that on a sunny day can seem the epitome of the Scottish Hebridean dream.

In **Wales** the best areas to head to for sunbathing and swimming are the Gower peninsula, the Pembrokeshire coast, the Llŷn and the southwest coast of Anglesey. The southwest-facing beaches of Wales offer the best conditions for surfing, key spots being Rhossili, at the western tip of the Gower, and Whitesands Bay near St David's. Windsurfers tend to congregate at Barmouth, Borth, around the Pembrokeshire coast and at The Mumbles. Though the north coast has more resorts than any other section of the Welsh coastline, its beaches are certainly not the most attractive and nor is it a good place to swim.

It has to be said that Britain's beaches are not the cleanest in Europe, and many of those that the British authorities declare to be acceptable actually fall below **EU standards**. Although steps are being taken to improve the situation, far too many stretches of the coastline are contaminated by seaborne effluent or other rubbish. For annually updated, detailed information on the condition of Britain's beaches, the *Good Beach Guide* (£3.50), compiled by the Marine Conservation Society (☎01989/566017, ⊛www.goodbeachguide.co.uk), is the definitive source.

Surfing

For most people, surfing in Britain means surfing in Newquay, and while it's true that the southwest of England is the heartland of the British **surf scene**, it would be a mistake to think that there aren't decent waves elsewhere. You don't get the sunshine of Hawaii, and the waves are steely-grey rather than turquoise-blue, but there are world-class waves to be found if you know where to go. The major difference between Britain and the States or Australia, of course, is the water temperature, which even in mid-summer rarely exceeds 15°C, and in winter can drop to as low as 7°C or colder (on the north coast of Scotland you're surfing at the same latitude as Alaska and Iceland). For this reason, if you're planning to surf in the UK – particularly in winter – make sure you have a good wetsuit, and ideally a 5/3mm "steamer", wetsuit boots and, outside summer, gloves and a hood. You'll also need a shedload of enthusiasm to get out into the waves, although when you do eventually paddle out, you may be pleasantly surprised.

In **England**, the northeast coast, from Yorkshire to Northumberland, has a growing population of hardy surfers willing to endure low temperatures to surf clean northerly groundswells. The coastline here is often spectacular, and although the more popular breaks, such as Saltburn, are now crowded, you can find relative isolation off the beaten track. Nevertheless, the southwest, or more specifically Newquay, Cornwall, remains the country's undisputed surf Mecca. Visitors are often amazed to see the hype surrounding this self-styled "surf city". In summer, every other male seems to be a "surfie", sporting regulation bleached hair and designer gear, but the majority only turn up to cruise surf babes. It can still be hectic out in the water though, especially at the main break, Fistral, which regularly hosts international contests. Head out of town, however, and things quieten down noticeably. Try spots such as Perranporth or Polzeath, or travel up to Devon, which also gets decent waves, despite the overcrowding of its main break, Croyde.

Surfing in **Wales** tends to be concentrated on the south coast, around the Gower peninsula, which boasts a good variety of beach and reef breaks, and a lively social scene. One thing to bear in mind if you surf here, though, is the enormous tidal range of the Bristol Channel – it can be up to thirteen metres, and this can have a major effect on the surf. The tidal range drops as you head west towards Pembrokeshire, where the coastline becomes more scenic, and numbers in the water diminish considerably. This area, comprising Britain's only coastal national park, is where you'll find the most consistent surf beach in Wales, Freshwater West, as well as seals, porpoise, dolphins, basking sharks and sunfish in the water. Washed by the Irish Sea, the west coast gets much less surf than the south, with the waves breaking mostly in winter. Aberystwyth is the main centre hereabouts, and its local breaks tend to be pretty busy.

Heading further north, you come to the Llŷn peninsula, in the shadow of Snowdonia, where Hell's Mouth has the best and most consistent waves in North Wales, drawing lots of weekend surfers from northern England throughout the year.

Scotland may not seem the most promising destination for surfers, but it is fast gaining a reputation for the high quality of its breaks. The number one spot is Thurso on the north coast, which has hosted the European Surfing Championships, and has what is widely acknowledged to be one of the finest reef breaks in Europe. Elsewhere along this coastline are waves which compare to those of Hawaii, Australia and Indonesia. Nor do you have to go all the way to Thurso to get tubed. Many of the best breaks lie within easy reach of large cities (eg Pease Bay, near Edinburgh, and Fraserburgh, near Aberdeen), while the spectacular west coast has numerous possibilities: try Sandwood Bay, the most isolated beach in Britain, or the waves of the Outer Hebrides. All are surrounded by stunning scenery, and you'd be unlucky to encounter another surfer for miles, which is an important consideration in itself. The fact that many of the breaks are quite isolated, the water is cold, and the surf often big and powerful means that, in general, Scottish surf is best left to experienced surfers. If you're a beginner, get local advice before you go in and be aware of your limitations; remember, if you get caught in a current off the west coast the next stop might be Iceland.

Top twenty British breaks

An asterisk (*) Indicates that the breaks are for experienced surfers only.

Bamburgh, Northumberland, northeast England. A wonderfully scenic quiet beach, with seals in the water and a spectacular castle as a backdrop.

Constantine, Cornwall, southwest England. Picks up a lot of swell.

Croyde Bay, Devon, southwest England. Good beach breaks, but crowds can be a problem.

Fistral, Newquay, Cornwall, southwest England. Hype, crowds, but still a good wave if you can get one to yourself.

Freshwater West, Pembrokeshire, South Wales. Quality beach and reef breaks. Beware of currents.

Hell's Mouth, Llŷn Peninsula, North Wales. Popular, quality break.

Llangennith, Gower, South Wales. Long beach

with peaks along its length. Busy.

Newgale, Pembrokeshire. South Wales. Two-mile-long beach with peaks along its length.

Pease Bay, near Dunbar, 26 miles east of Edinburgh, Scotland. A popular break suited to all abilities.

*Pete's Reef, Gower, South Wales. Picks up most swells. Popular.

*Porthleven, Cornwall, southwest England. Heavy reef break, heavy locals.

Machrihanish Bay, Mull of Kintyre. Four miles of beach breaks on one of Scotland's loneliest peninsulas.

Sandwood Bay, a day's hike south of Cape Wrath in Sutherland. Beach breaks on one of the most scenic and remote shorelines in Britain, only accessible on foot.

Sennen Cove, Cornwall, southwest England. Picks up any swell going.

Saltburn, Cleveland, northeast England. Another good beach break, with atmosphere to match.

*Skirza Harbour, three miles south of John O'Groats, northeast Scotland. An excellent left-hand reef break on the far northeast tip of Scotland.

*Staithes, Yorkshire, northeast England. Excellent reef breaks, crowded and jealously guarded by locals.

*Thurso East, just below the castle, Thurso, northern Scotland. One of the best right-hand reef breaks in Europe.

*Torrisdale Bay, Bettyhill, on the north coast of the Scottish Highlands. An excellent right-hand rivermouth break.

*Valtos, on the Uig peninsula, Lewis, Outer Hebrides, Scotland. A break on one of the Outer Hebrides' most exquisite shell-sand beaches.

Golf

There are over 400 **golf courses** in **Scotland**, where the game is less elitist, cheaper and more accessible than anywhere else in the world. The game as it's known today took shape in the sixteenth century on the dunes of Scotland's east coast, and today you'll find some of the oldest courses in the world on these early coastal sites, known as "links". If you want a round of golf, it's often possible just to turn up and play, though it's sensible to phone ahead and book, and essential for the championship courses (see below). It's worth asking at the tourist office for the Golf Pass Scotland which will give you a discount on courses for either three or five days. Prices vary according to area.

Public courses are owned by the local council, while **private courses** belong to a club. You can play on both – occasionally the private courses require that you be a member of another club, and the odd one asks for introductions from a member, but these rules are often waived for overseas visitors and all you need to do is pay a one-off fee. The cost of one round will set you back around £10 for small, nine-hole courses, up to more than £40 for eighteen holes. Simply pay as you enter and play. In remote areas the courses are sometimes unmanned – just put the admission fee into the honour box. Most courses have **resident professionals** who give lessons, and some rent equipment at reasonable rates. Renting a caddy car will add an extra few pounds depending on the swankiness of the course you are playing.

Scotland's **championship courses**, which often host the British Open tournament, are renowned for their immaculately kept greens and challenging holes, and though they're favoured by serious players, anybody with a valid handicap certificate can enjoy them. **St Andrews** (℡01334/466666, ⓦwww.standrews.org.uk) is the top destination for golfers: it's the home of the Royal and Ancient Golf Club, the international controlling body that regulates the rules of the game. Of its six courses, the best known is the Old Course, a particularly intriguing ground with eleven enormous greens and the world-famous "Road Hole". If you want to play, there's no introduction needed, but you'll need to book months in advance and for the Old and the New Courses have a handicap certificate – handicap limits are 24 for men and 36 for women. You could also enter your name for the daily lottery – call before 2pm on the day you'd like to play. One of the easier championship courses to get into is **Carnoustie**, in Angus (℡01241/853249; £75), though you should still try and book as far ahead as possible; a handicap certificate is required – 28 for men and 36 for women. Other championship courses include **Gleneagles** in Perthshire (℡01764/662231; £100), **Royal Dornoch** in Sutherland (℡01862/810219; £60) and **Turnberry** in Ayrshire (℡01655/331000; £120). Near Edinburgh, **Muirfield** (℡01620/842123; £85; Tues & Thurs only), considered by professional players to be one of the most testing grounds in the world, is also one of the most reactionary – women can play only if accompanied by a man, and they aren't allowed into the clubhouse.

Spectator sports

As a quick glance at the national press will tell you, sport in Britain is a serious matter. Football, rugby and cricket are the major spectator sports, and horseracing also has a big following, though a fair proportion of its public has little interest beyond the Grand National, the Brits' most popular opportunity for a gamble until the National Lottery came along. The calendar is chock-full of one-off quality sports events, ranging from the massed masochism of the London Marathon to the Wimbledon championship, one of the world's greatest tennis tournaments.

For the top international events it can be almost impossible to track down a ticket without resorting to the services of a grossly overcharging ticket agency, but for many fixtures you can make credit card bookings. Should you be thwarted in your attempts to gain admission, you can often fall back on TV or radio coverage. BBC Radio 5 has live commentaries on major sporting events, while TV carries live transmission of the big international rugby and cricket matches, though very little is available on the basic analogue stations (see p.40), many pubs offer free big-screen viewing of major sporting events to draw in custom.

Football

English football teams may have lost ground to the more cultured continentals in recent years, but it is still the most passionately supported sport in the land, and if you have the slightest interest in the game, then catching a league or FA Cup fixture is a must. The season runs from mid-August to early May, when the **FA Cup Final** (for which tickets are almost impossible to obtain) rounds things off. There are four league divisions: three, two, one and, at the top of the pyramid, the twenty-club **Premier League**. By far the most famous English club is Manchester United, who's supremacy is challenged most regularly by other northern clubs – Liverpool, who signed the phenomenal star Michael Owen, and Leeds and Newcastle. In the Midlands, Coventry and Birmingham's Aston Villa are the strongest clubs, while in London the contest is between Arsenal, Chelsea and Tottenham. **Wales**'s big three teams are Cardiff City and Wrexham, who play in the second division, and Swansea City, which plays in the third; the rest of the Welsh clubs play in the feeble Konica League of Wales. **Scotland** has three divisions, each with fewer teams than the equivalent south of the border, and of considerably lower standard. Glasgow Rangers has dominated the top flight in recent years, and together with Glasgow Celtic are the only Scottish clubs to currently have the clout or the cash to make big-name signings. Top British clubs also take part in European matches played midweek, particularly early in the season.

The team with the biggest following is Manchester United, whose matches are almost always a sell-out, regardless of how the team is playing. Of the other glamorous English clubs, Liverpool and Newcastle United also command so ardent a following that tickets for their matches are often like gold dust. It's easy enough to get tickets, if booked in advance, for most other Premier League games, unless two local sides are playing each other. In Scotland, only the "Old Firm" clash between Rangers and Celtic (representing the Protestant and Irish Catholic communities of Glasgow respectively) is a certain full house.

Most **fixtures** kick off at 3pm on Saturday, though there are generally a few midweek games (usually 7.30pm on Wednesday), and one each on Sunday (kick-off between 2pm and 4pm) and Monday (kick-off at 8pm). **Tickets** cost from about £20 for Premier games, falling to less than £15 in the lower divisions.

Since the introduction of all-seater Premiership stadiums in 1994, top-flight games have lost their reputation for tribal violence, and there's been a striking increase in the numbers of women and children attend-

53

ing. Nonetheless, it's an intense business, with a lot of foul language, and being stuck in the middle of a few thousand West Ham supporters as their team goes 3–0 down is not one of life's more uplifting experiences.

Cricket

In the glory days of the Empire the **English** took cricket to the colonies as a means of instilling the gentlemanly values of fair play while administering a sound thrashing to the natives. These days the former colonies, such as Australia, the West Indies and India, all beat England on a regular basis, so to see the game at its best you should try to get into one of the series of three, five or six **Test matches** played between England and the summer's touring team. These international matches are played in the middle of the cricket season, which runs from April to September. Two of these matches are played in London – at Lord's, the home of English cricket, and The Oval; the other Test grounds are Trent Bridge (Nottingham), Old Trafford (Manchester), Headingley (Leeds) and Edgbaston (Birmingham). In tandem with the full-blown five-day Tests, there's also a series of **one-day internationals**, two of which are again usually held in London.

Getting to see England play one of the big teams may be difficult unless you book months in advance. If you can't wangle your way into a Test, you could watch it live on TV (the Test series is always televised), listen to ball-by-ball commentary on BBC radio, or settle down to an inter-county match, either in the **county championship** (these are four-day games) or in one of the three fast and furious one-day competitions: the Benson and Hedges Cup and the NatWest Trophy (both knockout competitions), or the CGU National league. Of the eighteen county teams (divided into two divisions) in the championship, two are based in London – Middlesex, who play at Lord's, and Surrey, who play at The Oval.

Prices for Test matches cost £15–40 per day; for one-day internationals you can expect to pay £20–50, but tickets for the sparsely attended county games start at as little as £7.

The rules of cricket

The laws of cricket are so complex that the official rule book runs to some twenty pages. The basics, however, are by no means as byzantine as the game's detractors make out.

There are two teams of eleven players. A team wins by scoring more runs than the other team and dismissing all the opposition – in other words, a team could score many runs more than the opposition, but still not win if the last enemy batsman doggedly stays in (hence ensuring a draw). The match is divided into innings, when one team bats and the other fields. The number of innings varies depending on the type of competition; one-day matches have one per team, Test matches and county championship matches have two.

The aim of the fielding side is to limit the runs scored and get the batsmen "out". Two players from the batting side are on the pitch at any one time. The bowling side has a bowler, a wicket keeper and nine fielders. Two umpires, one standing behind the stumps at the bowler's end and one square on to the play, are responsible for adjudicating if a batsman is out. Each innings is divided into overs, consisting of six deliveries, after which the wicket keeper changes ends, the bowler is changed and the fielders move positions.

The batsmen score runs either by running up and down from wicket to wicket (one length is one "run"), or by hitting the ball over the boundary rope, scoring four runs if it crosses the boundary having touched the ground, and six runs if it flies over. The main ways a batsman can be dismissed are: by being "clean bowled", where the bowler dislodges the bails of the wicket (the horizontal pieces of wood resting on top of the stumps); by being "run out", which is when one of the fielding side dislodges the bails with the ball while the batsman is running between the wickets; by being caught, which is when any of the fielding side catches the ball after the batsman has hit it and before it touches the ground; or "LBW" (leg before wicket), where the batsman blocks with his leg a delivery that would otherwise have hit his stumps.

These are the rudiments of a game whose beauty lies in the subtlety of its skills and tactics. The captain, for example, chooses which bowler to play and where to position his fielders to counter the strengths of the batsman, the condition of the pitch, and a dozen other variables. Cricket also has a beauty in its esoteric language, used to describe such things as fielding positions ("silly mid-off", "cover point", etc) and the various types of bowling delivery ("googly", "yorker", etc). For beginners, some enlightenment may be gained by watching the TV coverage, or befriending a spectator – cricket fans tend to be congenial types, eager to introduce newcomers to the mysteries of the true faith.

Rugby

Rugby gets its name from Rugby public school, where the game mutated from football (soccer) in the nineteenth century. A rugby match may at times look like a bunch of weightlifters grappling each other in the mud – as the old joke goes, rugby is a hooligan's game played by gentleman, while football is a gentleman's game played by hooligans – but it is in reality a highly tactical and athletic game. What's more, England's rugby teams have represented the country with rather more success in the last few years than the cricket and football squads.

There are two types of rugby played in Britain, both professional. Fifteen-a-side **Rugby Union** is very strong in working-class Wales, especially in the valleys of the former South Wales coal fields, but has upper-class associations in England, where it is the preferred character-building sport of the great fee-paying schools. The maintenance of the amateur status of Rugby Union in England contributed to its officer-class image until 1995, when the sport finally went professional. The thirteen-a-side **Rugby League** is played almost exclusively in the north of England. Union's move towards professionalism was in part brought about by the tendency of League clubs to poach the top Union players – such as Welsh golden boy Jonathan Davies, who defected to Widnes (half the Welsh national side is these days made up of former League players).

The Union season runs from September until the end of April, finishing off with the **Pilkington Cup**, Union's equivalent of the FA Cup; the League finishes in May, with the **Challenge Cup**. The Pilkington Cup Final, international Rugby Union Test matches and some games in the Six Nations Cup (a round-robin tournament between England, Scotland, Wales, Ireland, France and Italy)

are played at Twickenham stadium in west London. The other international Union grounds are Murrayfield in Edinburgh and the Millennium Stadium in Cardiff. Unless you are affiliated to one of the 2000 clubs of the Rugby Union, or willing to pay well over the odds at a ticket agency, it is tough to get a ticket for one of these big games. For Union and League club games, however, there should be no problem getting tickets at the gate; expect to pay from £5.

Tennis

Tennis in England is synonymous with **Wimbledon**, the only Grand Slam tournament to be played on grass, and for many players the ultimate goal of their careers. The Wimbledon championship lasts a fortnight, in the last week of June and the first week of July. Most of the tickets, especially those with seats for the main show courts (Centre and No. 1), are allocated in advance to Wimbledon's members, other tennis clubs and corporate "sponsors" – as well as by public ballot – and by the time these have taken their slice there's not a lot left for the general public.

It is possible, however, to turn up on the day and buy tickets, and if you're rich enough you could buy through ticket agencies (although these sales are technically illegal). On tournament days, queues start to form around dawn and if you arrive by around 7am you have a reasonable chance of securing the limited number of Centre and No. 1 court tickets held back for sale on the day. If you're there by around 9am, you should get admission to the outside courts (where you'll catch some top players in the first week of the tournament). Either way, you then have a long wait until play commences at noon.

If you want to see big-name players in Britain, an easier opportunity is the **Stella Artois Championship** at Queen's Club in Hammersmith, London, which finishes a week before Wimbledon. Many of the stars use this tournament to acclimatize themselves to British grass-court conditions. As with Wimbledon, you have to apply for tickets in advance, although there is a limited number of returns on sale at 10am each day.

For the unlucky, there's the consolation of **TV coverage**, which is pretty well all-consuming for the two weeks that the Wimbledon tournament lasts.

Horse racing

For most of the British population there is just one important day in the horseracing calendar – the last Saturday in March or the first in April, when the **Grand National**, the "World's Greatest Steeplechase", is run at Liverpool's Aintree course. Millions of people risk a quid or two on the race, and watch the proceedings anxiously on TV, where it's broadcast live and then repeated at least twice before the end of the day. The National is by far the most arduous (some would say cruel) race of the steeplechasing and hurdling season, which runs from August to April, with races taking place on Saturdays and midweek at a vast array of courses, ranging from ovals of grass in the depths of the countryside to prestigious venues like Windsor. Ticket prices range from £5 to £35.

The horses and the clientele are often more upmarket when it comes to racing on the flat, which is a summer sport, observing an April to October season. Whereas the big events in the steeplechasing season draw a broad-based crowd, the showcase races on the flat are largely about upper-crust networking. That said, thousands of Londoners treat themselves to a day out at **Epsom** on Derby Day, the first Saturday in June. The Derby, a mile-and-a-half race for 3-year-old thoroughbreds, is the most prestigious of the five classics of the flat season, and is preceded in the three-day Derby meeting by another classic, the **Oaks**, which is for fillies only – the other Classics are the **1000 Guineas**, **2000 Guineas** (both run at Newmarket) and the **St Leger** (run at Doncaster).

For sheer snobbery nothing can match the **Royal Ascot** week in mid-June, when the Queen and selected members of the royal family are in attendance, along with half the nation's blue bloods. As with the Derby, the best seats are the preserve of the gentry, but the rabble are allowed into the public enclosure for a mere £8–10, and can get considerably closer to the action for from £37–45, providing they dress smartly. Prices are slightly lower at the country's other flat-racing meetings, where the class divisions of British society are generally less glaring. Many of these meetings take place on courses used for steeplechasing in the winter, though some of the better courses – such as Goodwood – are reserved for the flat.

Betting

Most of the money spent by Britain's gamblers is blown on the horses, though only a small minority of punters actually go to the races. At the course itself you can place a bet with one of the independent trackside book-makers (or "tic-tac men" as they are known, from the bizarre sign language with which they signal the odds), or with the state-run Tote, a system by which the total money placed on a race is divided among the winners.

Competing with Tote and the small bookies are the representatives of the big nationwide betting organizations, such as Ladbrokes, Coral and William Hill, who make their money by taking bets on anything from the result of the 4.15 at Epsom to the name of the rider who will finish fourth in the Tour de France or the likelihood of snow at Christmas.

Anyone aged 18 or over can place a bet.

Crime and personal safety

Although the traditional image of the friendly British "bobby" has become increasingly tarnished by stories of corruption, racism and crooked dealings, the British police continue to be approachable and helpful. If you're lost in a major town, asking a police officer is generally the quickest way to pinpoint your destination – alternatively, you could ask a traffic warden, a species of law-enforcer much maligned in car-loving Britain. Most traffic wardens are distinguishable by

their flat caps with a yellow band (though uniforms do vary), and by the fact that they are generally armed with a hand-set for dispensing parking-fine tickets; police officers on street duty wear a distinctive domed hat with a silver tip, and are generally armed with just a truncheon.

As elsewhere, the major towns of Britain have their dangerous spots, but these tend to be inner-city housing estates where no tourist has any reason to be. The chief risk on Britain's streets is **pickpocketing**, and there are some virtuoso villains at work in the big cities, especially on the major shopping streets and public transport. Carry only as much money as you need, and keep all bags and pockets fastened. Should you have anything stolen or be involved in some incident that requires reporting, go to the

Emergencies

For Police, Fire Brigade, Ambulance and, in certain areas, Mountain Rescue or Coastguard, dial ☏999.

local police station – we've given address and contact numbers throughout the *Guide* for those in the bigger towns and cities; the ☏999 number should only be used in real emergencies.

Work

The kind of work you can expect to find in Britain as a visitor is generally unskilled employment in hotels, bars and restaurants, cleaning companies and on farms. As a casual employee you can expect poor pay of around £4–5 per hour and you may be fired at short notice. If you want to come to grips with the country a little more, you could also consider voluntary work, which can range from work camps, archeological digs and placements with service organizations, or even working holidays, whereby you may be required to contribute a small amount for food and lodging.

The British Tourist Authority's **websites** can provide some information on working in Britain (see p.19), as can ⓦ www.hotrecruit .co.uk, an excellent resource for temporary and seasonal work. There are also several useful **publications**. *Working Holidays*, by the Central Bureau for Educational Visits and Exchanges (CBEVE; £9.99), can provide you with scores of ideas; *Summer Jobs in Britain* by David Woodworth (£9.99) gives comprehensive information on paid seasonal work; and *Work Your Way Around the World* by Susan Griffith (£12.95) is also worth a try.

For **conservation work**, BTCV can fix you up with schemes for improving footpaths or building dry-stone walls (around £70) and so on, as can the National Trust.

If you're aged between 17 and 27, you might also consider **working as an au pair**. This enables you to live for a maximum of two years with an English-speaking family. In

return for your accommodation, food and a small amount of pocket money (say £50 per week), you'll be expected to help around the house and to look after the children for a maximum of five hours each day. The easiest way to find au pair work is through a licensed agency. The Recruitment and Employment Confederation (REC) has a list of reputable agents (ie, those which are vetted annually by the government). Alternatively, look in the listings section of *The Lady* magazine.

Work permits

Unless you're a resident of an EU country, you need a **permit** to work legally in the UK, although without the backing of an established employer or company this can be very difficult to obtain. Those aged between 17 and 27 may, however, apply for a **Working**

Holiday-Maker Entry Certificate, which entitles you to a two-year stay in the UK, during which time you are permitted to undertake work of a casual nature – in other words, not in a profession, or as a sportsperson or entertainer. The certificates are only available abroad, from British embassies and consulates, and when you apply you must be able to convince the officer you have a valid return or onward ticket, and the means to support yourself while you're in Britain without having to claim state benefits of any kind. Note, too, that the certificates are valid from the date of entry into Britain – you won't be able to recoup time spent out of the country in the two-year period of validity.

In **North America**, full-time college students can get temporary work or study permits through BUNAC. Permits are valid for up to six months and cost $250; allow two to three weeks for processing of your application.

Other visitors entitled to work in Britain are **Commonwealth citizens**. Those who have a parent who was born in the UK can apply for a Certificate of Entitlement to the Right of Abode; if you have a grandparent who was born in the UK, or Ireland before 1922, you may be entitled to a UK Ancestry Employment Certificate, allowing you to work for up to four years in the UK. For further information contact your nearest British Mission (embassy or consulate) or the Foreign and Commonwealth Office in London (℡020/7270 1500, ⓦwww.fco.gov.uk).

Useful addresses

BTCV 36 St Mary's St, Wallingford, Oxfordshire OX10 0EU ℡01491/839 766, ⓦwww.btcv.org.uk.
BUNAC PO Box 430, Southbury, CT 06488 ℡ 1-800-GO-BUNAC, ⓦwww.bunac.org.
National Trust (Enterprises) The Stable Block, Heywood House, Westbury, Wiltshire BA13 4NA ℡01225/7911199, ⓦwww.nationaltrust.org.uk.
The Recruitment and Employment Confederation (REC) 36–38 Mortimer St, London W1W 7RG ℡020/7462 3260, ⓦwww.rec.uk.com.

Travellers with disabilities

Should you go it alone, you'll find that British attitudes towards travellers with disabilities are often begrudging and guilt-ridden, and are still way behind advances towards independence made in North America and Australia. Having said that, there is movement in the right direction and newer tourist attractions and hotels make full provision for wheelchair users, and access to museums, theatres, cinemas and other public places has greatly improved. Most towns offer free parking for wheelchair orange/blue badge-holders and you'll find reserved parking bays at the majority of tourist attractions.

Britain has numerous specialist **tour operators** catering for travellers with disabilities, and the number of non-specialist operators who welcome clients with disabilities is increasing. For more information on these operators and on facilities for the disabled traveller, you should get in touch with the organizations listed below. RADAR produces a useful annual holiday guide *Holidays in Britain and Ireland* (£8).

As for **accommodation** needs, disabled travellers will find that modified suites are available only at higher-priced establish-

ments and perhaps at the odd B&B, where a ground-floor room has been adapted. **Public transport** companies rarely make any effort to help disabled people, though some rail services now accommodate wheelchair users in comfort and some new buses (including the post buses, see p.28) have accessible doors and steps. Wheelchair-users and blind or partially sighted people are automatically given a third off the price of train fares, and people with other disabilities are eligible for the **Disabled Persons Railcard** (£14/year), which also gives a third off most tickets, but can take up to two weeks to process. Applications for this card must be made in writing to the Disabled Persons Railcard Office, PO Box 1YT, Newcastle-upon-Tyne NE99 1YT. There are no bus discounts for the disabled, while of the major **car rental** firms only Hertz offer models with hand controls at the same rate as conventional vehicles, and even these are in the more expensive categories.

Contacts for travellers with disabilities

In North America

Ⓦwww.access-able.com. An online resource for travellers with disabilities.
Mobility International USA 451 Broadway, Eugene, OR 97401 ☎541/343-1284 (voice and TDD), Ⓦwww.miusa.org. For an annual membership fee of $35, they will provide support and advice; membership includes a quarterly newsletter.
Society for the Advancement of Travelers with Handicaps (SATH) 347 5th Ave, New York NY 10016 ☎212/447-7284, Ⓦwww.sath.org. Non-profit educational organization that has actively represented travellers with disabilities since 1976.
Travel Information Service ☎215/456-9600. Telephone-only information and referral service.
Wheels Up! ☎1-888/389-4335, Ⓦwww.wheelsup.com. Telephone and website information, including discounted airfare, tour and cruise prices for disabled travellers; also publishes a free monthly newsletter.

In Australia and New Zealand

ACROD (Australian Council for Rehabilitation of the Disabled) PO Box 60, Curtin ACT 2605 ☎02/6282 4333, Ⓦwww.acrod.org.au. Regional offices provide lists of travel agencies, tour operators and accommodation.
Disabled Persons Assembly 173–75 Victoria St, Wellington, New Zealand ☎04/801 9100. Resource centre with lists of travel agencies and tour operators for people with disabilities.

In the UK and Ireland

Ⓦwww.everybody.co.uk Provides information on accommodation suitable for disabled travellers throughout the UK.
Holiday Care 2nd floor, Imperial Building, Victoria Rd, Horley, Surrey RH6 7PZ ☎01293/774535, Minicom ☎01293/776943, Ⓦwww.holidaycare. org.uk. Gives out a free list of accessible attractions in the UK. Also has information on financial help for holidays.
RADAR (Royal Association for Disability and Rehabilitation) 12 City Forum, 250 City Rd, London EC1V 8AF ☎020/7250 3222, Minicom ☎020/7250 4119, Ⓦwww.radar.org.uk. Has a wide range of information and advice for travellers.
Tripscope Vassall Centre, Gill Avenue, Bristol BS16 2QQ ☎08457/585 641 Ⓦwww.justmobility. co.uk/tripscope. Provides a national telephone information service offering free advice on travel and access in the UK.

Gay and lesbian Britain

Homosexual acts between consenting males were legalized in Britain in 1967, but it wasn't until as recently as 1994 that the age of consent was finally reduced from 21 to 18 (still two years older than that for heterosexuals). Lesbianism has never specifically been outlawed, apocryphally owing to the fact that Queen Victoria refused to believe that such a thing existed.

As with so many other aspects of British life, attitudes on homosexuality are riven with contradictions. Despite its draconian laws and the sensationalist trash in the tabloid press, England, at least, offers one of the most diverse and accessible lesbian and gay scenes to be found anywhere in Europe. Nearly every town of any size has some kind of organized gay life – pubs, clubs, community groups, campaigning organizations, shops and phone lines – with the **major scenes** being found in London, Manchester

59

and Brighton. The Scottish scene is lively in Edinburgh and in Glasgow, but pretty much non-existent in the more rural areas. In Wales things are a lot more muted, with few venues outside the main centres of Cardiff, Newport and Swansea. We've listed many venues throughout this book, and you'll be able to pick up a free gay listings sheet in almost any one of them.

Of the **nationwide publications**, the weekly *Pink Paper* is informative and contains limited listings; also worth checking are the frothy weekly *Boyz*, and its monthly women's sibling, *Diva*. The best bet for a comprehensive national directory of pubs, clubs, groups, gay accommodation and local lesbian and gay switchboards is the glossy monthly *Gay Times*, available from many newsagents and alternative book-

shops. Gay Men's Press produce guide-books aimed primarily at gay men, although with some lesbian information included too; there's currently *London Scene*, which includes Brighton. Much of the information in such publications applies both to men and women, as the British scene is far more mixed than in most other European nations.

Useful contacts for Gay and Lesbian travellers in the UK

ⓦ www.gaybritain.co.uk Information on events, restaurants and travel, with good links.
ⓦ www.gayguide.co.uk Lists gay venues by location.
ⓦ www.gaytravel.co.uk Online gay and lesbian travel agent, offering good deals on all types of holidays. Also lists gay- and lesbian-friendly hotels.

Directory

Cigarettes The last decade has seen a dramatic change in attitudes towards smoking and a significant reduction in the consumption of cigarettes. Smoking is now outlawed from just about all public buildings and on public transport, and many restaurants and hotels have become non-smoking establishments. Smokers are advised, when booking a table or a room, to check that their vice is tolerated there.

Drugs Likely-looking visitors coming to England from Holland or Spain can expect scrutiny from customs officers on the lookout for hashish (marijuana resin). Being caught in possession of a small amount of hashish or grass may lead to a fine, but possession of larger quantities or of "harder" narcotics could lead to imprisonment or deportation.

Electricity In England the current is 240V AC. North American appliances will need a transformer and adaptor; those from Australia and New Zealand will only need an adaptor.

Laundry Coin-operated laundries (launderettes) are to be found in nearly all British towns and are open about twelve hours a day from Monday to Friday, less on weekends. A wash followed by a spin or tumble dry costs about £3.50, with "service washes" (your laundry done for you in a few hours) about £1 more.

Public toilets These are found at all train and bus stations and are signposted on town high streets. In urban locations a fee of 10p or 20p is usually charged.

Time Greenwich Mean Time (GMT) is used from late October to late March, when the clocks go forward an hour for British Summer Time (BST). GMT is five hours ahead of the US Eastern Standard Time and ten hours behind Australian Eastern Standard Time.

Tipping There are no fixed rules for tipping in England. If you think you've received good service, particularly in restaurants or cafés, you may want to leave a tip of 10 percent of the total bill (unless service has already been included). It is not normal, however, to leave tips in pubs, although bar staff are sometimes offered drinks, which they may accept in the form of money (the assumption is they'll spend this on a drink after closing time). Taxi drivers, on the other hand, will expect tips on longer journeys – expect to add about 10 percent to the fare. The only other occasions when you'll be expected to tip are in hairdressers, and upmarket hotels where, in common with most other countries, porters, bell boys and table waiters rely on being tipped to bump up their often dismal wages.

Videos Visitors from North America should note

that there is a different format for videotapes in Britain than there is in the US and Canada – so even though they look the same, VHS tapes recorded in Britain (in what's called the PAL format) will not work when you get them home and try to play them back on your VCR (which is NTSC format). If you are shooting with your own camera, however, you can use a blank tape purchased in Britain to record your trip's highlights, since your camera will format the tape while it records.

guide

④ Oxford and around 277–300

England

1 London 65–176

2 Surrey, Kent and Sussex 177–226

3 Hampshire, Dorset and Wiltshire 227–274

4 Oxford and around 275–304

5 The Cotswolds and Somerset 305–352

6 Devon and Cornwall 353–422

7 East Anglia 423–474

8 The West Midlands and the Peak District 475–528

9 The East Midlands 529–564

10 The Northwest 565–610

11 Cumbria and the Lakes 611–640

12 Yorkshire 641–700

13 The Northeast 701–755

London

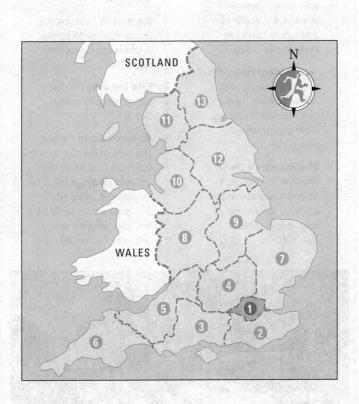

CHAPTER 1 # Highlights

* **British Museum** The BM has reinvented itself with a wonderful new glass-covered courtyard, surrounding the old British Library. See p.105

* **London Eye** The universally loved observation wheel is a graceful new addition to London's skyline. See p.122

* **Tate Modern** Housed in a spectacular disused power station, London's new modern-art gallery is simply awesome. See p.124

* **Shakespeare's Globe Theatre** Try and catch an open-air show in this amazing reconstructed Elizabethan theatre. See p.125

* **Highgate cemetery** Take a guided tour of the steeply sloping terraces of the West Cemetery, whose overgrown graves are the last word in Victorian Gothic gloom. See p.138

* **Greenwich** Probably the single most picturesque riverside spot in London. See p.141

* **Kew Gardens** London's superb botanic gardens. See p.147

* **Hampton Court Palace** The best of the numerous royal palaces in and around London, with exceptional Tudor interiors, architecture by Wren and vast gardens and grounds. See p.149

1

London

What strikes visitors more than anything about **LONDON** is the sheer size of the place. With a population of just under eight million, it's Europe's largest city by far, spreading across an area of more than 620 square miles from its core on the **River Thames**. Londoners tend to cope with this by compartmentalizing the city, identifying with the neighbourhoods in which they work or live, and making the occasional forays into the "centre of town". Ethnically it's also Europe's most diverse metropolis: around two hundred languages are spoken within its confines, and more than thirty percent of the population is made up of first-, second- and third-generation immigrants.

Despite Scottish, Welsh and Northern Irish devolution, London still dominates the national horizon, too: this is where the country's news and money are made, it's where the central government resides and, as far as its inhabitants are concerned, provincial life begins beyond the circuit of the city's orbital motorway. Londoners' sense of superiority causes enormous resentment in the regions, yet it's undeniable that the capital has a unique aura of excitement and success – in most walks of British life, if you want to get on you've got to do it in London.

For the visitor, too, London is a thrilling place. And since the beginning of the new millennium, the city has also been in exceptionally buoyant mood. Thanks to the frenzy of lottery- and millennium-funding of the last few years, virtually every one of London's **world-class museums and galleries** and institutions has been reinvented, from the Royal Opera House to the British Museum. With the Tate Modern, the city can now boast the largest modern art gallery in the world, not to mention the world's largest observation wheel; a new tube extension and the first new bridge to cross the Thames for over a hundred years. And after sixteen years of being the only major city in the world *not* to have its own governing body, London finally has its own elected mayor, and assembly.

In the meantime, London's **traditional sights** – Big Ben, Westminster Abbey, Buckingham Palace, St Paul's Cathedral and the Tower of London – continue to draw in millions of tourists every year. Monuments from the capital's more glorious past are everywhere to be seen, from medieval banqueting halls and the great churches of Sir Christopher Wren to the eclectic Victorian architecture of the triumphalist British Empire. There is also much enjoyment to be had from the city's quiet Georgian squares, the narrow alleyways of the City of London, the riverside walks, and the quirks of what is still identifiably a collection of villages. And even London's traffic pollution – one of its worst problems – is offset by surprisingly large **expanses of greenery**: Hyde Park,

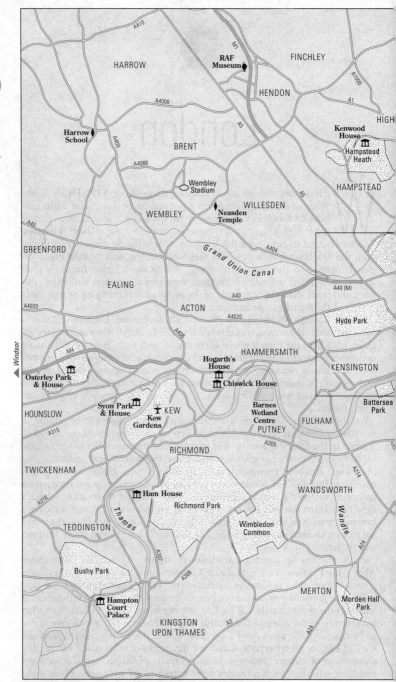

© Crown copyright

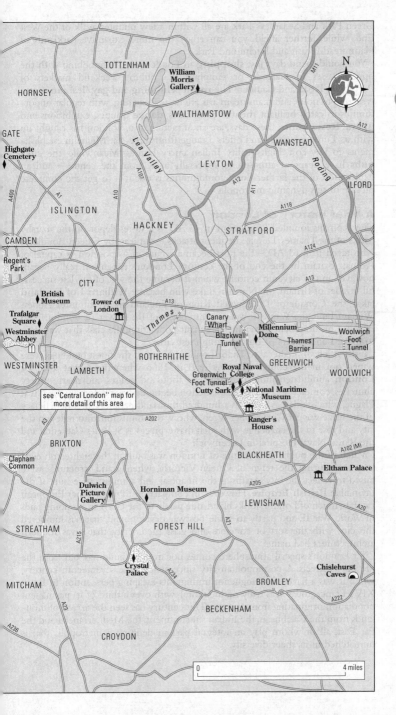

Green Park and St James's Park are all within a few minutes' walk of the West End, while, further afield, you can enjoy the more expansive parklands of Hampstead Heath and Richmond Park.

You could spend days just **shopping** in London, too, hobnobbing with the upper classes in Harrods, or sampling the offbeat weekend markets of Portobello Road and Camden. The **music**, **clubbing** and **gay/lesbian scene** is second to none, and mainstream arts are no less exciting, with regular opportunities to catch brilliant **theatre** companies, **dance** troupes, exhibitions and **opera**. **Restaurants**, these days, are an attraction, too. London has caught up with its European rivals, and offers a range from three-star Michelin establishments to low-cost, high-quality Indian curry houses. Meanwhile, the city's **pubs** have heaps of atmosphere, especially away from the centre – and an exploration of the farther-flung communities is essential to get the complete picture of this dynamic metropolis.

A brief history of London

The Romans founded Londinium in 43 AD as a stores depot on the marshy banks of the Thames. Despite frequent attacks – not least by Queen Boudicca, who razed it in 61 AD – the port became secure in its position as capital of Roman Britain by the end of the century. London's expansion really began, however, in the eleventh century, when it became the seat of the last successful invader of Britain, the Norman duke who became **William I of England** (aka "the Conqueror"). Crowned King of England in Westminster Abbey, William built the White Tower – centrepiece of the Tower of London – to establish his dominance over the merchant population, the class that was soon to make London one of Europe's mightiest cities.

Little is left of medieval or Tudor London. Many of the finest buildings were wiped out in the course of a few days in 1666 when the **Great Fire of London** annihilated more than thirteen thousand houses and nearly ninety churches, completing a cycle of destruction begun the year before by the Great Plague, which killed as many as a hundred thousand people. Chief beneficiary of the blaze was Sir Christopher Wren, who was commissioned to redesign the city and rose to the challenge with such masterpieces as St Paul's Cathedral and the Royal Naval Hospital in Greenwich.

Much of the public architecture of London was built in the eighteenth century and during the reign of Queen Victoria, when grand structures were raised to reflect the city's status as the financial and administrative hub of the invincible **British Empire**. However, in comparison to many other European capitals, much of London looks bland, due partly to the German bombing raids in World War II, and partly to some postwar development that has lumbered the city with the sort of concrete-and-glass mediocrity that gives modern architecture a bad name.

Yet London's special atmosphere comes not from its buildings, but from the life on its streets. A cosmopolitan city since at least the seventeenth century, when it was a haven for Huguenot immigrants escaping persecution in Louis XIV's France, today it is truly multicultural, with over a third of its permanent population originating from overseas. This century has seen the arrival of thousands from the Caribbean, the Indian subcontinent, the Mediterranean and the Far East, all of whom play an integral part in defining a metropolis that is unmatched in its sheer diversity.

Arrival

Flying into London, you'll arrive at one of the capital's five **international airports**: Heathrow, Gatwick, Stansted, Luton or City Airport, all of which are less than an hour from the city centre.

Heathrow (☎0870/000 0123, ⊛www.baa.co.uk), twelve miles west of the city, has four terminals, and two train/tube stations: one for terminals 1, 2 and 3, and a separate one for terminal 4. The high-speed **Heathrow Express** (every 15min; 15–20min; ☎0845/600 1515, ⊛www.heathrowexpress.co.uk) trains travel nonstop to Paddington Station for £12 each way or £22 return (£2 extra if you purchase your ticket on board the train). A much cheaper alternative is to take the slow Piccadilly **Underground** line into central London (every 2–5min; 50min) for £3.60. If you plan to make several sightseeing journeys on your arrival day, buy a multi-zone One-Day Travelcard for £4.90 (see p.73). There is also a **National Express** service from Heathrow, direct to Victoria Coach Station (every 30min; 35min–1hr depending on the traffic; ☎08705/808080, ⊛www.nationalexpress.co.uk), which costs £7 single, £10 return, as well as **Airbus #2** (☎08705/747777, ⊛www.go-by-coach.com), which runs from outside all four Heathrow terminals to several destinations in the city (every 30min; 1hr) and cost £7 single, £10 return. From midnight, you'll have to take **night bus #N97** to Trafalgar Square (every 30min; 1hr 10min) for a bargain £1.50. **Taxis** are plentiful, but cost at least £35 to central London, and take around an hour (longer in the rush hour).

Gatwick (☎01293/535353, ⊛www.baa.co.uk), thirty miles to the south, has two terminals, North and South, connected by a monorail. The nonstop **Gatwick-Express** (every 15–30min; 30min; ☎0990/301530, ⊛www.gatwickexpress.co.uk) train runs day and night between the South Terminal and Victoria Station for £10.50 each way. Other options include the 24-hour **Connex** service to Victoria (every 15min–1hr; 40min) for £8.20 single, or the **Thameslink** to King's Cross (Mon–Sat every 15–30min; 50min) for £9.50 single. **Airbus #5** runs from both terminals to Victoria Coach Station (hourly; 1hr 30min) and costs £7 single, £10 return. A **taxi** ride into central London will set you back £50 or more, and take at least an hour.

Stansted (☎01279/680500, ⊛www.baa.co.uk), London's swankiest international airport, lies 34 miles northeast of the capital and is served by the **Stansted Express** to Liverpool Street (every 15min–30min; 45min), which costs £13 single, £21 return. **Airbus #6 or #7** also run to Victoria Coach Station (every 30min; 1hr 15min) and cost £7 single, £10 return. A **taxi** ride will set you back £50 or more, and take at least an hour.

Luton airport (☎01582/405100, ⊛www.london-luton.com) is roughly thirty miles north of the city centre, and mostly handles charter flights. Luton Airport Parkway station is connected by **rail** to King's Cross (or St Pancras), via **Thameslink** (every 15min; 30–40min); tickets cost £9.50 single. **Bus #757** connects Luton to Victoria Station, taking just over an hour, and costing £6.50 single, £9 return. A **taxi** will cost in the region of £70 and take at least an hour from central London

London's smallest airport, **City Airport** (☎020/7646 0000, ⊛www.londoncityairport.com), is situated in Docklands, nine miles east of central London, and handles European flights only. **Shuttle buses** connect City Airport with Canning Town DLR station (every 10min; 5min; £2), with Canary Wharf DLR and tube (every 10min; 10min; £3), and Liverpool Street station (every 10min; 30min; £6). Another option is to take the North London Line run by Silverlink from Silvertown, which is ten minutes' walk from the airport.

Arriving by **train** from elsewhere in Britain, you'll come into one of London's numerous main-line stations, all of which have adjacent Underground stations linking into the city centre's tube network. **Eurostar** trains arrive at **Waterloo International**, south of the river. Trains from Harwich arrive at Liverpool Street, while trains from Dover arrive at Charing Cross; **coaches** terminate at **Victoria Coach Station**, a couple of hundred yards south of Victoria train station, down Buckingham Palace Road.

Information

The **London Tourist Board** (LTB; ⓦ www.londontown.com) has a desk in the Underground station concourse for Heathrow Terminals 1, 2 and 3 (daily 8am–6pm), but the main central office can be found near Piccadilly Circus in the **British Visitor Centre**, 1 Regent St (Mon 9.30am–6.30pm, Tues–Fri 9am–6.30pm, Sat & Sun 10am–4pm; June–Oct same times except Sat 9am–5pm). There are also offices in the forecourt of Victoria Station (Jan & Feb Mon–Sat 8am–7pm, Sun 8am–6.15pm; March–May & Oct–Dec Mon–Sat closes 8pm; June–Sept Mon–Sat closes 9pm), in the arrivals hall of Waterloo International (daily 8.30am–10.30pm) and in Liverpool Street Underground station (Mon–Fri 8am–6pm, Sat 8am-5.30pm & Sun 9am-5.30pm).

Individual boroughs also run tourist offices at various prime locations. The most useful are in the **City of London** to the south of St Paul's Cathedral (April–Sept daily 9.30am–5pm; Oct–March Mon–Fri 9.30am–5pm, Sat 9.30am–12.30pm; ☎020/7332 1456, ⓦ www.cityoflondon.gov.uk) in **Southwark**, at the south end of London Bridge (April–Sept Mon–Sat 10am–6pm, Sun 11am–6pm; Nov–March closes 4pm; ☎020/7403 8299, ⓦ www .southwark.gov.uk); and in **Greenwich** at 46 Greenwich Church St, SE10 (daily: April–Oct 10am–5pm; Nov–March 11am–4pm; ☎020/8858 6376, ⓦ www.greenwich.gov.uk). These offices will answer enquiries by phone; the best that the LTB can offer is **Visitorcall** (☎0839/123456), a spread of prerecorded phone announcements – you're far better off visiting their website ⓦ www.londontown.com.

Most information offices hand out a useful reference **map** of central London, plus plans of the public transport systems, but to find your way around every cranny of the city you need to invest in either an *A–Z Atlas* or a *Nicholson Streetfinder*, both of which have a street index covering every street in the capital; you can get them at most bookshops and newsagents for around £5. The only comprehensive and critical weekly **listings** magazine is *Time Out*, which costs £2.20 and comes out every Tuesday afternoon. In it you'll find details of all the latest exhibitions, shows, films, music, sport, guided walks and events in and around the capital.

The London Pass

If you're thinking of hitting quite a few of the major sights in a short space of time, it might be worth considering investing in a **London Pass**, which not only gives you entry to a whole range of attractions from the London Aquarium and Buckingham Palace to St Paul's Cathedral and Windsor Castle, but also throws in an all-zone Travelcard, £5 worth of free phone calls and various other perks and incentives. The pass costs from £22 for one day to £79 for six days. The London Pass can be bought over the phone (☎0870/242 9988) or on the internet (ⓦ www.londonpass.com).

City transport

London's transport network is among the most complex and expensive in the world. The **London Transport information office**, at Piccadilly Circus tube station (daily 9am–6pm), will provide free transport maps; there are other desks at Euston Station, Heathrow (terminals 1, 2, & 3), King's Cross, Liverpool Street, Paddington and Victoria stations. There's also a 24-hour phone line for transport information (☎020/7222 1234, ⓦwww.londontransport.co.uk). If you can, avoid travelling during the **rush hour** (Mon–Fri 8–9.30am & 5–7pm) when tubes become unbearably crowded and some buses get so full, you literally won't be allowed on.

The fastest way of moving around the city is by Underground or **Tube** (ⓦwww.thetube.com), as it's known to all Londoners. The eleven different tube lines cross much of the metropolis, although London south of the river is not very well covered. Each line has its own colour and name – all you need to know is which direction you're travelling in: northbound, eastbound, southbound or westbound. Services operate from around 5.30am Monday to Saturday, and from 7.30am on Sundays, and end around midnight every day; you rarely have to wait more than five minutes for a train from central stations. **Tickets** must be bought in advance from the machines or booths in the station entrance hall; ticket inspectors operate throughout the system and if you cannot produce a valid ticket you will be charged an on-the-spot Penalty Fare of £10. A single journey in the central zone costs an unbelievable £1.50; a **Carnet** of ten tickets costs £11.50. If you're intending to travel about a lot, a Travelcard is by far your best bet (see box below).

The network of **buses** is very dense, but much slower going than the Tube. **Tickets** for all bus journeys within, to or from the Central Zone cost a flat fare of £1; journeys outside the central zone cost 70p. Normally you pay the driver on entering, but some routes are covered by older Routemaster buses, staffed by a conductor and with an open rear platform. Note that at request stops (easily recognizable by their red sign) you must stick your arm out to hail the bus you want. In addition to the Travelcards mentioned below, a **One-Day Bus Pass** is also available and can be used before 9.30am; it costs £3 for zones 1 to 4. Regular buses run between about 6am and midnight; **night buses** (prefixed with the letter "N") operate outside this period. Night bus routes radiate out from Trafalgar Square at hourly intervals, more frequently on some routes and on Friday and Saturday nights. Travelcards are valid on night buses; otherwise journeys within, to or from the Central Zone costs a flat fare of £1.50; journeys outside the central zone cost £1.

Travelcards

To get the best value out of the transport system, buy a **Travelcard**. Available from machines and booths at all tube and train stations and at some newsagents as well (look for the sticker), they are valid for the bus, tube, Docklands Light Railway (DLR) and suburban rail networks. **One-Day Travelcards**, valid on weekdays from 9.30am and all day at weekends, cost £4 (central Zones 1 & 2), rising to £4.90 for All Zones (1–6, including Heathrow); the respective **Weekend Travelcards**, for unlimited travel on Saturdays and Sundays, cost £6 and £7.30. If you need to travel before 9.30am on a weekday, but don't need to use suburban trains, you can buy a **One-Day LT Card**, which costs from £5.10 (Zones 1 & 2) to £7.70 (All Zones). **Weekly Travelcards** begin at £15.90 for Zone 1; for these cards you need a **Photocard**, available free of charge from tube and train stations on presentation of a passport photo.

Large areas of London's suburbs are best reached by the **suburban train** network (Travelcards valid). Wherever a sight can only be reached by overground train, we've indicated the nearest train station and the central terminus from which you must depart. If you're planning to use the railway network a lot, you might want to purchase a **Network Card**, which is valid for a year, costs £20, and gives you up to 33 percent discount on fares to destinations in and around the southeast. To find out about a particular service, phone **National Rail Enquiries** on ☎08457/484950 or visit ⓦwww.britrail.co.uk.

If you're in a group of three or more, London's metered **black cabs** can be an economical way of getting around the centre – a ride from Euston to Victoria, for example, should cost around £10. A yellow light over the windscreen tells you if the cab is available – just stick your arm out to hail it. If you want to book one in advance, call ☎020/7272 0272.

Minicabs are less reliable than black cabs, but considerably cheaper, so you might want to take one back from a late-night club. Most minicabs are not metered, so always establish the fare beforehand. If you want to be certain of a woman driver, call Ladycabs (☎020/7254 3501), or a gay/lesbian driver, call Freedom Cars (☎020/7734 1313).

Accommodation

There's no getting away from the fact that **accommodation** in London is expensive. Compared with most European cities, you pay over the odds in every category. The city's hostels are among the most expensive in the world, while venerable institutions such as the *Ritz*, the *Dorchester* and the *Savoy* charge guests the very top international prices – up to £300 and more per luxurious night.

The cheapest places to stay are the dorm beds of the city's numerous independent **hostels**, followed closely by the official YHA hostels. Even the most basic **B&Bs** struggle to bring their tariffs below £40 for a double with shared facilities, and you're more likely to find yourself paying £50 or more.

We've given phone numbers and websites or email addresses where available for all our listed accommodation, but if you fail to find a bed in any of the places we've recommended, you could turn to one of the various **accommodation agencies**. The British Hotel Reservation Centre (BHRC) desks at Heathrow, Gatwick and City airports, at Victoria train and coach stations, and Waterloo International and Paddington train stations, don't charge a fee for booking rooms, and most of their offices are open daily from 6am till midnight. You can also book for free via the 24-hour phone line (☎020/7828 0601) or the internet (ⓦwww.bhrc.co.uk).

In addition, all London tourist offices (listed on p.72) operate a room-booking service, which costs £5; with a credit card you can book over the phone (☎020/7932 2020) or via the internet (ⓦwww.londontown.com). **Thomas Cook** (☎0800/371321) also has accommodation desks at Charing Cross, Euston, Gatwick Airport, King's Cross, Paddington and Victoria train stations, plus Earl's Court and South Kensington tubes, at the British Visitor Centre on Lower Regent Street (see p.72). Most (though not all) of these are open daily from 7am till 11pm, and will book anything from youth hostels (£2 fee) through to five-star hotels (£5 fee).

London postcodes

A brief word on **London postcodes**: the name of each street is followed by a letter giving the geographical location (E for "east", WC for "west central" and so on) and a number that specifies the postal area. However, this is not a reliable indication of the remoteness of the locale – W5, for example, lies beyond the more remote sounding NW10 – so it's always best to check a map before taking a room in what may sound like a fairly central area.

Hotels and B&Bs

With **hotels** you get less for your money in London than elsewhere in the country – generally breakfasts are more meagre and rooms more spartan than in similarly priced places in the provinces. In high season you should phone as far in advance as you can if you want to stay within a couple of tube stops of the West End, and expect to pay around £50 for an unexceptional double room without a private bathroom. If travelling with two or more companions, it's always worth asking the price of the family rooms, which generally sleep four and can save you a few pounds.

When choosing your **area**, bear in mind that the West End – Soho, Covent Garden, St James's, Mayfair and Marylebone – the City or financial district and the western districts of Knightsbridge and Kensington are dominated by expensive, upmarket hotels. For cheaper rooms, the widest choice (and some of the most dubious B&Bs) are close to the main train stations of Victoria and Paddington, and around Earl's Court. Those close to King's Cross tend to cater for people on welfare, or charge by the hour, although neighbouring Bloomsbury is both inexpensive and very central.

St James's, Mayfair and Marylebone

Edward Lear Hotel 28–30 Seymour St, W1 ⓣ020/7402 5401, ⓦwww.edlear.com. A great location close to Oxford Street and Hyde Park, lovely flower boxes and a plush foyer. The rooms themselves need a bit of a makeover, but the low prices reflect this and the fact that most only have shared facilities or shower only. Marble Arch tube. ❺

Durrants Hotel George St, W1 ⓣ020/7935 8131, ⓦwww.durrantshotel.co.uk. Just round the corner from the Wallace Collection and Oxford Street, this Georgian terrace hotel first opened in 1790, and has been run by the same family since 1921. Inside, it's a great exercise in period-piece nostalgia, with lots of wood-panelling, old prints and doormen. Bond Street tube. ❼

The Metropolitan Old Park Lane, W1 ⓣ020/7447 1000, ⓦwww.metropolitan.co.uk. Run by Christina Ong, this terrifyingly trendy hotel adheres to the 1990s fad for pared-down minimalism. The staff are kitted out in designer labels, the Japanese restaurant is outstanding, and the *Met* bar is mem- bers and residents only in the evenings. Double rooms from £300. Green Park or Hyde Park Corner tube. ❾

Wigmore Court Hotel 23 Gloucester Place, W1 ⓣ020/7935 0928, ⓦwww.wigmore-court-hotel.co.uk. The relentlessly pink decor may not be to everyone's taste, but this Georgian town house is a better than average B&B, boasting a high tally of returning clients. Comfortable rooms with en-suite facilities, plus a couple of cheaper rooms for just £80. Unusually, there's also a laundry and basic kitchen for guests' use. Marble Arch or Baker Street tube. ❺

Soho, Covent Garden and The Strand

The Fielding Hotel 4 Broad Court, Bow St, WC2 ⓣ020/7836 8305, ⓦwww.the-fielding-hotel.co.uk. Quietly situated on a traffic-free and gas-lit court, this excellent hotel is one of Covent Garden's hidden gems. A firm favourite with visit-ing performers, since it's just a few yards from the Royal Opera House. Breakfast is extra. Covent Garden tube. ❻

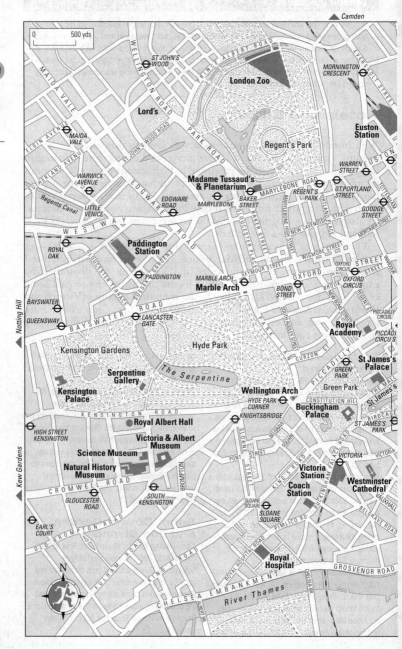

▲ Camden

0   500 yds

ST JOHN'S WOOD

London Zoo

Lord's

Regent's Park

Euston Station

MORNINGTON CRESCENT

WARREN STREET

GT.PORTLAND STREET

Madame Tussaud's & Planetarium

REGENT'S PARK

GOODGE STREET

MARYLEBONE

BAKER STREET

EDGWARE ROAD

Paddington Station

WIGMORE STREET

OXFORD STREET

OXFORD CIRCUS

PADDINGTON

ROYAL OAK

Regents Canal

LITTLE VENICE

MARBLE ARCH

Marble Arch

BOND STREET

PICCADILLY CIRCUS

WARWICK AVENUE

MAIDA VALE

MAIDA VALE

ELGIN AVENUE

SUTHERLAND AVENUE

W E S T W A Y

Royal Academy

PICCADILLY CIRCUS

BAYSWATER

QUEENSWAY

B A Y S W A T E R   R O A D

LANCASTER GATE

Hyde Park

St James's Palace

Kensington Gardens

The Serpentine

GREEN PARK

THE MALL

Serpentine Gallery

Green Park

St James

Kensington Palace

CURZON

Wellington Arch

HYDE PARK CORNER

Buckingham Palace

CONSTITUTION HILL

BIRDCAGE

ST JAMES'S PARK

K E N S I N G T O N   R O A D

KNIGHTSBRIDGE

Royal Albert Hall

HIGH STREET KENSINGTON

Victoria & Victoria Station

VICTORIA

Victoria & Albert Museum

Science Museum

PONT STREET

SLOANE STREET

Coach Station

Westminster Cathedral

Natural History Museum

BROMPTON

VAUXHALL

GLOUCESTER ROAD

SOUTH KENSINGTON

C R O M W E L L   R O A D

SLOANE SQUARE

SLOANE SQUARE

PIMLICO RD

BELGRAVE ROAD

EARL'S COURT

O L D   B R O M P T O N   R O A D

FULHAM ROAD

KING'S ROAD

Royal Hospital

GROSVENOR ROAD

CHELSEA

N

C H E L S E A   E M B A N K M E N T

River Thames

ALBERT BR

▲ Notting Hill

▲ Kew Gardens

MATIDA VALE

WELLINGTON ROAD

PRINCE ALBERT ROAD

EVERSHOLT STREET

ST JOHN'S WOOD ROAD

PARK ROAD

EDGWARE ROAD

GLOUCESTER TERRACE

SUSSEX GARDENS

GLOUCESTER PLACE

BAKER STREET

MARYLEBONE ROAD

MARYLEBONE HIGH STREET

NEW CAVENDISH STREET

PORTLAND PLACE

MORTIMER STREET

TOTTENHAM

EUSTON

WADOUR

SEYMOUR STREET

SOUTH AUDLEY STREET

NEW BOND STREET

REGENT ST

BROOK

PARK LANE

BUCKINGHAM PALACE ROAD

BELGRAVE SQUARE

KING'S ROAD

ROYAL HOSPITAL ROAD

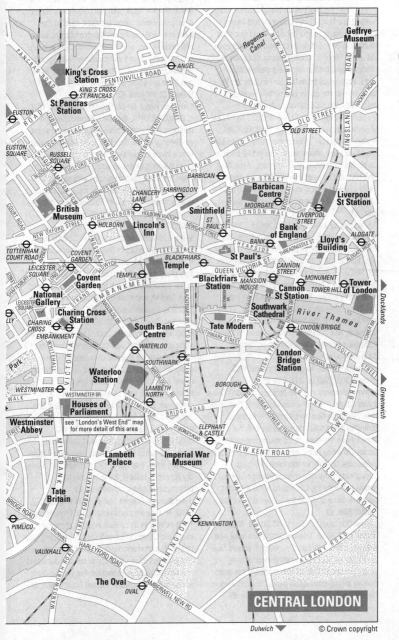

King's Cross
Station
KING'S CROSS
ST PANCRAS
St Pancras
Station
EUSTON
EUSTON
SQUARE
RUSSELL
SQUARE
British
Museum
Lincoln's
Inn
TOTTENHAM
COURT ROAD
COVENT
GARDEN
LEICESTER
SQUARE
Covent
Garden
National
Gallery
LEICESTER
SQUARE
Charing Cross
Station
CHARING
CROSS
EMBANKMENT
Park
WESTMINSTER
WALK
Houses of
Parliament
Westminster
Abbey
Tate
Britain
PIMLICO
VAUXHALL
The Oval
OVAL

ANGEL
PENTONVILLE ROAD
CITY   ROAD
FARRINGDON ROAD
CLERKENWELL ROAD
BARBICAN
Farringdon
Smithfield
ST
PAUL'S
NEWGATE ST
FLEET STREET
BLACKFRIARS
Temple
TEMPLE
EMBANKMENT
WATERLOO BR.
South Bank
Centre
WATERLOO
SOUTHWARK
Waterloo
Station
LAMBETH
NORTH
WESTMINSTER
BRIDGE ROAD
BOROUGH
see ''London's West End'' map
for more detail of this area
LAMBETH
Palace
Imperial War
Museum
ELEPHANT
& CASTLE
KENNINGTON
CAMBERWELL NEW RD

Regents
Canal
OLD STREET
OLD STREET
BEECH STREET
Barbican
Centre
MOORGATE
LONDON WALL
Bank
of England
CHEAPSIDE
BANK
St Paul's
QUEEN VICTORIA ST
Blackfriars
Station
MANSION
HOUSE
Cannon
St Station
Southwark
Cathedral
Tate Modern
SOUTHWARK STREET
London
Bridge
Station
BOROUGH HIGH STREET
GREAT DOVER STREET
NEW KENT ROAD

Geffrye
Museum
NEW NORTH ROAD
KINGSLAND
Liverpool
St Station
LIVERPOOL
STREET
Lloyd's
Building
ALDGATE
Tower
of London
TOWER HILL
MONUMENT
CANNON
STREET
River Thames
LONDON BRIDGE
TOOLEY STREET
LONG LANE
OLD KENT ROAD
ALBANY ROAD

Docklands
Greenwich

CENTRAL LONDON

Dulwich ▼   © Crown copyright

Hazlitt's 6 Frith St, W1 ☏ 020/7434 1771,
ⓦ www.hazlittshotel.com. Located off the south
side of Soho Square, this early-eighteenth-century
building is a hotel of real character and charm,
offering en-suite rooms decorated and furnished
as close to period style as convenience and comfort allow. There is no dining room, but some of
London's best restaurants are a stone's throw
away; continental breakfast isn't included in the
rates, unless you go for one of their weekend
deals. Tottenham Court Road tube. ⓽

Manzi's 1–2 Leicester St, W1 ☏ 020/7734 0224,
ⓦ www.manzis.co.uk. Set over the Italian and
seafood restaurant of the same name, *Manzi's* is
one of very few downtown hotels in this price
range. It's certainly right in the thick of the West
End, just off Leicester Square, although noise
might prove to be a nuisance. Continental breakfast is included in the price. Leicester Square
tube. ⓹

One Aldwych 1 Aldwych, WC2 ☏ 020/7300 1000,
ⓦ www.onealdwych.co.uk. On the outside, this is
one of London's few vaguely Art Nouveau buildings, built in 1907 for the *Morning Post* newspaper. However, little survives from those days, as
the interior of this desperately fashionable luxury
hotel firmly follows the 1990s minimalist trend.
The draws now are the underwater music in the
hotel's vast pool, the oodles of modern art about
the place, and the TVs in the bathrooms of the
£300-plus rooms. Covent Garden or Temple
(Mon–Sat) tube. ⓽

St Martin's Lane 45 St Martin's Lane, WC2
☏ 020/7300 5500 or 0800/634 5500,
ⓦ www.hotelbook.com. So cool you wouldn't know
it was a hotel, this self-consciously chic "boutique
hotel" from the New York-based Ian Schrager
chain has proved an immediate hit with the media
crowd. From the fluorescent yellow-and-white
minimalist lobby to the large Portuguese limestone
bathrooms, the interior has been designed
throughout by the mischievous Philippe Starck.
Rooms currently start at around £300 a double,
but rates come down at the weekend. Leicester
Square tube. ⓽

Strand Continental Hotel 143 Strand, WC2
☏ 020/7836 4880. This tiny Indian-run hotel near
Aldwych offers very basic rooms with shared facilities, plus continental breakfast. Rooms have
recently had a lick of paint, but nothing too drastic,
making this an unbeatable central London bargain.
Covent Garden or Temple (Mon–Sat) tube. ➋

Bloomsbury

Hotel Cavendish 75 Gower St, WC1 ☏ 020/7636
9079, ⓦ www.hotelcavendish.com. Gower Street
is very busy with traffic, but get a room at the
back here and you'll have a peaceful night, and a
real bargain, too, with lovely owners, two beautiful
overrun gardens and some quite well-preserved
original features. All rooms have shared facilities,
and there are some good-value family rooms, too.
Goodge Street tube. ➋

Crescent Hotel 49–50 Cartwright Gardens, WC1
☏ 020/7387 1515, ⓦ www.crescenthoteloflon-
don.com. Very comfortable and tastefully decorated Regency B&B – definitely a cut above the rest,
with a lovely blacked-up range in the breakfast
room. All doubles are en suite and have TVs, but
there are a few bargain singles with shared facilities; guests also have use of tennis courts in the
nearby gardens. Euston or Russell Square tube. ⓹

Jenkins Hotel 45 Cartwright Gardens, WC1
☏ 020/7387 2067,
ⓦ www.jenkinshotel.demon.co.uk. Smartly kept,
family-run place in this fine Regency crescent,
with fourteen fairly small but well-equipped and
very clean rooms, some en suite. The lovely in-
house black labrador is a big hit with visitors, and
a full English breakfast is included in the price.
Euston or Russell Square tube. ⓹

myhotel 11–13 Bayley St, WC1 ☏ 020/7667
6000, ⓦ www.myhotels.co.uk. The aquarium in the
lobby is the tell-tale sign that this is a feng shui
hotel. Despite the positive vibes, and Conran-
designed look, the double-glazed, air-conditioned
rooms are on the small side for the price. Still,
there's a gym, a very pleasant library and a
restaurant, and it's well located for the West End.
Tottenham Court Road tube. ⓽

Ridgemount Hotel 65–67 Gower St, WC1
☏ 020/7636 1141. Old fashioned, family-run
place, with small rooms, mostly with shared facilities, a garden, free hot-drinks machine and a laundry service. A reliable, basic bargain for
Bloomsbury. Goodge Street tube. ➌

Hotel Russell Russell Square, WC1 ☏ 020/7837
6470, ⓦ www.principalhotels.co.uk. From its grand
1898 exterior to its opulent interiors of marble,
wood and crystal, this late-Victorian landmark fully
retains its period atmosphere. The rooms have less
character but all are well appointed and decorated
in a homely manner. Expensive, but various deals
are sometimes available. Russell Square tube. ➐

Clerkenwell and the City

City Hotel 12 Osborn St, E1 ☎020/7247 3313, ⓦwww.cityhotellondon.co.uk. Spacious, clean and modern inside, this hotel stands on the eastern edge of the City, and in the heart of the Bengali East End at the bottom of Brick Lane. The plainly decorated rooms are all en suite, and many have kitchens, too; four-person rooms are a bargain for small groups. Aldgate East tube. ⑥

Great Eastern Hotel Liverpool St, EC2, ☎020/7618 5000, ⓦwww.great-eastern-hotel.co.uk. Without doubt, *the* place to stay if you need or wish to be near the City. This venerable late-nineteenth-century station hotel has had a complete Conran makeover, yet manages to retain much of its clubby flavour. The rooms themselves are impeccably well-appointed and tastefully furnished – to maximize your natural light, get a room facing out. Doubles start from around £250, but rates are cut at the weekend. Liverpool Street tube. ⑨

Jurys Inn 60 Pentonville Rd, N1 ☎020/7282 5500, ⓦwww.jurys.com. This modern Irish chain hotel is not a pretty sight on the busy Pentonville Road, but it's close to the tube, and equally convenient for the City and for Islington and Clerkenwell's trendy bars and restaurants. Service is very friendly, and the fixed room-rate is a bargain for three adults sharing or for those with kids. Breakfast is extra. Angel tube. ⑤

The Rookery Peter's Lane, Cowcross St EC1 ☎020/7336 0931, ⓦwww.rookeryhotel.com. Rambling Georgian town house on the edge of the City in trendy Clerkenwell that makes a fantastically discreet little hideaway. The rooms start at around £225 a double (ask about weekend rates); each one has been individually designed in a sort of modern, camp take on the Baroque period, and all have super bathrooms with lots of character. Farringdon tube. ⑧

The South Bank

Holiday Inn Express 103–109 Southwark St, SE1 ☎020/7401 2525, ⓦwww.hiexpress.com/lonsouthwark. Unbeatable location just a stone's throw from the Tate Modern, and a relative bargain if you can stomach the motorway service station feel of the place. Southwark or Blackfriars tube. ⑤

London Bridge Hotel 8–18 London Bridge St, SE1 ☎020/7855 2200, ⓦwww.london-bridge-hotel.co.uk. Perfectly placed for Southwark and Bankside or the City, this is a tastefully smart new hotel right by the station. As it attracts a mainly business clientele, rates do go down considerably at the weekend. London Bridge tube. ⑧

London County Hall Travel Inn Belvedere Rd, SE1 ☎020/7902 1600, ⓦwww.travelinn.co.uk. Don't expect river views at these prices, but the location in County Hall itself is pretty good if you're up for a bit of sightseeing. Decor and ambience are functional, but for those with kids, the flat-rate rooms are a bargain. Waterloo or Westminster tube. ⑤

London Marriott Hotel, County Hall The County Hall, SE1 ☎020/7928 5200, ⓦwww.marriotthotel.com. If you want river views from County Hall, you'll need to book in here. Over three quarters of the rooms overlook the Thames, and many have little balconies, too, with prices hovering around £300 (weekend rates are lower). It's all suitably pompous inside, and there's a full-size indoor pool. Waterloo or Westminster tube. ⑨

Mad Hatter 3–7 Stamford St, SE1 ☎020/7401 9222, ⓦwww.fullers.co.uk. Situated above a Fuller's pub on the corner of Blackfriars Road, and run by the Fuller's brewery. Breakfast is extra, and is served in the pub, but this is a great location, a short walk from the Tate Modern and the South Bank. Ask about the weekend rates. Southwark or Blackfriars tube. ⑤

Victoria

Dover Hotel 42–44 Belgrave Rd, SW1 ☎020/7821 9085, ⓦwww.dover-hotel.co.uk. One of the best B&Bs in this area. All rooms are tastefully decorated, and have a shower, toilet, phone and TV. Victoria tube. ④

The Goring 15 Beeston Place, SW1 ☎020/7396 9000, ⓦwww.goringhotel.co.uk. This Edwardian hotel, owned and run by the Goring family for three generations, succeeds in creating an atmosphere of elegance and tranquillity. Afternoon tea is served on the delightful private garden-terrace in fine weather; rooms are a pricey £250 and upwards (breakfast not included). Victoria tube. ⑨

Noël Coward Hotel 111 Ebury St SW1 ☎020/7730 2094, ⓦwww.noelcowardhotel.com. Elegant-fronted gay-friendly hotel in the heart of Belgravia, and former home of Coward between 1917 and 1930. Rooms are either en suite or with shared toilet, there's an attractive patio garden, and theatre or club package deals are available. Sloane Square. ⑤

Melbourne House Hotel 79 Belgrave Rd, SW1 ☎020/7828 3516, ⓦwww.melbournehousehotel.co.uk. One of the best B&Bs along Belgrave Road: family-run, well furnished, offering clean and bright rooms, excellent communal areas and friendly service. All doubles have en-suite facilities, but there are a couple of very cheap singles without. Victoria or Pimlico tube. ⑤

Oxford House Hotel 92–94 Cambridge St, SW1 ☎020/7834 6467. Probably the best value rooms you can get in the vicinity of Victoria station. Showers and toilets are shared, but kept pristine. Full English breakfast is included in the price. Victoria tube. ❸

Sanctuary House Hotel 33 Tothill St, SW1 ☎020/7799 4044, ⓦwww.fullers.co.uk. Run by Fuller's Brewery, situated above a Fuller's pub, and decked out like one, too, in smart, pseudo-Victoriana. Breakfast is extra, but the location right by St James's Park is very central. Ask about the weekend deals. St James's Park tube. ❻

Topham's Hotel 26 Ebury St, SW1 ☎020/7730 8147, ⓦwww.tophams.co.uk. Charming family-owned hotel in the English country-house style, just a couple of minutes' walk from the Victoria stations. Sumptuously furnished en-suite twins and doubles, with full English breakfast. Victoria tube. ❼

Windermere Hotel 142–144 Warwick Way, SW1 ☎020/7834 5163, ⓦwww.windermere-hotel.co.uk. Situated at the western end of Warwick Way, this is a tastefully decorated and quietly stylish place, with a few good-value doubles with shared facilities and en-suite doubles for considerably more. There's a good restaurant downstairs, too. Sloane Square, Pimlico or Victoria tube. ❺

Woodville House & Morgan House 107 & 120 Ebury St, SW1 ☎020/7730 1048, ⓦwww.woodvillehouse.co.uk. Two above-average B&Bs, run by the same vivacious couple, with great breakfasts, patio gardens, and an iron and fridge for guests to use. All rooms at *Woodville* are with shared facilities; some at *Morgan* are en suite. Victoria tube. ❹

Paddington, Bayswater and Notting Hill

The Columbia 95–99 Lancaster Gate, W2 ☎020/7402 0021, ⓦwww.columbiahotel.co.uk. The spacious public lounge, well-worn decor and useful late bar make this large white-stucco hotel a rock-band favourite. The en-suite rooms themselves are actually very sober, and retain some original Victorian fittings. Lancaster Gate tube. ❺

Garden Court Hotel 30–31 Kensington Garden Square, W2 ☎020/7229 2553, ⓦwww.garden-courthotel.co.uk. Presentable, family-run B&B on a quiet square close to Portobello market; half the rooms are with shared facilities, half are en suite. Full English breakfast included. Queensway or Bayswater tube. ❸

The Gresham Hotel 116 Sussex Gardens, W2 ☎020/7402 2920, ⓦwww.the-gresham-hotel.co.uk. B&B with a touch more class than many in the area. Rooms are small but tastefully kitted out, and all have TV. Continental breakfast included. Paddington tube. ❺

Inverness Court Hotel 1 Inverness Terrace, W2 ☎020/7229 1444, ⓦwww.cjhotels.com. Late-Victorian facade, reception area, bar and lounges lend a charming ambience, even if most of the en-suite rooms are in an undistinguished modern style. Continental breakfast included. Bayswater or Queensway tube. ❼

Pavilion Hotel 34–36 Sussex Gardens, W2 ☎020/7262 0905, ⓦwww.msi.com.mt/pavilion. The successful rock star's home-from-home, with outrageously over-the-top decor and every room individually themed. Paddington tube. ❻

Pembridge Court Hotel 34 Pembridge Gardens, W11 ☎020/7229 9977, ⓦwww.pemct.co.uk. Attractively converted town house close to Portobello Market, with spacious, fully equipped rooms. Two cats add to the homely feel, as does the lively *Caps Restaurant and Bar*. Notting Hill Gate or Holland Park tube. ❽

Prince William Hotel 42–44 Gloucester Terrace, W2 ☎020/7724 7414, ⓦwww.princewilliamhotel.co.uk. Cheap, gay-friendly place close to the West End. Most rooms are en suite, and the *Pearl of India* restaurant is on site. Paddington or Lancaster Gate. ❺

Knightsbridge, Kensington and Chelsea

Abbey House 11 Vicarage Gate, W8 ☎020/7727 2594, ⓦwww.abbeyhousekensington.com. Inexpensive Victorian B&B in a quiet street just north of Kensington High Street, maintained to a very high standard by its attentive owners. Rooms are large and bright – prices are kept down by sharing facilities rather than fitting the usual cramped bathroom unit. Full English breakfast, with free tea and coffee available all day. Cash only. High Street Kensington tube. ❺

Aster House 3 Sumner Place, SW7 ☎020/7581 5888, ⓦwww.asterhouse.com. Pleasant, non-smoking B&B in a luxurious white-stuccoed South Ken street; there's a lovely garden at the back and a large conservatory, where breakfast is served. Singles with shared facilities start at a bargain £75 a night. South Kensington. ❼

Blakes 33 Roland Gardens, SW7 ☎020/7370 6701, ⓦwww.blakeshotels.com. Blakes' dramatic interior (designed by Anouska Hempel) and glamorous suites have long attracted visiting celebs. A faintly Rafflesesque flavour pervades, with bamboo furniture and old travelling trunks mixing with unusual *objets d'art*, tapestries and prints. Doubles from £250 are smart but small; fully equipped suites are spectacular. The restaurant and bar are excellent, and service is of a very high standard. Gloucester Road tube. ⑨

Five Sumner Place 5 Sumner Place, SW7 ⑦020/7584 7586, ⑩www.sumnerplace.com. Discreetly luxurious B&B in one of South Ken's prettiest white-stucco terraces. All rooms are en suite and breakfast is served in the house's lovely conservatory. South Kensington tube. ⑦ .

The Gore 189 Queen's Gate, SW7 ⑦020/7584 6601, ⑩www.gorehotel.co.uk. Popular, privately owned century-old hotel, only a step away from Hyde Park, and awash with oriental rugs, rich mahogany, walnut panelling and other Victoriana. Ask about weekend rates. South Kensington, Gloucester Road or High Street Kensington tube. ⑧

The Hempel 31–35 Craven Hill Gardens, W2 ⑦020/7298 9000, ⑩www.thehempelhotel.com. Deeply fashionable minimalist hotel, designed by the actress Anouska Hempel, with a huge and very empty atrium entrance. White-on-white rooms start around £300 a double, and there's an excellent postmodern Italian/Thai restaurant called *I-Thai*. Lancaster Gate or Queensway tube. ⑨

Hotel 167 167 Old Brompton Rd, SW5 ⑦020/7373 0672, ⑩www.hotel167.com. Small, stylishly furnished B&B with en-suite facilities, double glazing and a fridge in all rooms. Continental buffet-style breakfast is served in the attractive morning room/reception. Gloucester Road tube. ⑥

Vicarage Hotel 10 Vicarage Gate, W8 ⑦020/7229 4030, ⑩www.londonvicaragehotel. com. Ideally located B&B a step away from Hyde Park. Clean rooms with shared facilities and a full English breakfast. Cash/travellers' cheques only. High Street Kensington or Notting Hill tube. ⑤

Earl's Court

Philbeach Hotel 30–31 Philbeach Gardens, SW5 ⑦020/7373 1244, ⑩www.philbeachhotel. freeserve.co.uk. London's busiest gay hotel, large and friendly, with room-only and en-suite options, internet and pleasant TV lounge area, *Appleby's Bar* and the popular *Wilde About Oscar* conservatory restaurant. Earl's Court tube. ③

Rushmore Hotel 11 Trebovir Rd, SW5 ⑦020/7370 3839, ⑩www.rushmore.activehotels.com. A cut above the average, with its colourful murals and imaginative room decor, in this often dreary area. The attic rooms are especially spacious and comfortable. Full continental breakfast. Earl's Court tube. ⑤

Hampstead

La Gaffe 107–111 Heath St, NW3 ⑦020/7435 4941, ⑩www.lagaffe.co.uk. Small and warren-like but characterful hotel, situated over an Italian restaurant and bar in the heart of Hampstead village. All rooms are en suite and there's a roof terrace for use in fine weather. Hampstead tube. ⑥

Hampstead Village Guest House 2 Kemplay Rd, NW3 ⑦020/7435 8679, ⑥hvguesthouse@dial.pipex.com. Lovely B&B in an old house set in a quiet backstreet between Hampstead village and the Heath. Rooms (some en suite, all non-smoking) have "lived-in" clutter, which makes a pleasant change from anodyne hotels and spartan B&Bs. Hampstead tube. ⑤

Hostels, student halls and camping

London's seven **YHA hostels** are generally the cleanest, most efficiently run hostels in the capital. However, at around £20 a night, they charge around fifty percent more than most private hostels, and tend to get booked up several months in advance. Members of any association affiliated to Hostelling International have automatic membership of the YHA; non-members can join at any of the hostels. Note that you can book a bed in advance with a credit card either by ringing individual hostels or via ⑩www.yha.org.uk. At peak periods, or to get an immediate overview of the availability of beds, and make an immediate booking, contact the **YHA central reservations** (⑦020/7373 3400). In addition to the official hostels, there's a wide range of **independent hostels** which charge less and tend to be more laid-back; unlike YHA hostels, however, there's no quality control, so standards can vary wildly. Some accommodation in **student halls of residence** is available outside term time, but the prices aren't all that attractive and the rooms get booked up quickly. London's **campsites** are all out on the perimeters of the city, offering pitches for around £2–4, plus a fee of around £3–4 per person per night (reductions for children and out of season).

Hostels

YHA hostels

City of London 36 Carter Lane, EC4 ☎020/7236 4965, ⓦwww.yha.org.uk. Two-hundred-bed hostel in a great situation opposite St Paul's Cathedral; some twins, but mostly four- and five-bed dorms or triple-bunks in larger dorms. No groups. St Paul's tube.

Earl's Court 38 Bolton Gardens, SW5 ☎020/7373 7083, ⓦwww.yha.org.uk. Better than a lot of accommodation in Earl's Court, but only offering dorms of mostly ten beds – the triple-bunks take some getting used to. Kitchen, café and patio garden. No groups. Earl's Court tube.

Hampstead Heath 4 Wellgarth Rd, NW11 ☎020/8458 9054, ⓦwww.yha.org.uk. One of London's biggest and best-appointed YHA hostels, with its own garden and the wilds of Hampstead Heath nearby. Rooms with three to six beds and family rooms with two to five beds. Golders Green tube.

Holland House Holland Walk, W8 ☎020/7937 0748, ⓦwww.yha.org.uk. Idyllically situated in the wooded expanse of Holland Park and fairly convenient for the centre of town, this extensive dorm-only hostel offers a decent kitchen and an inexpensive café. Popular with school groups. Holland Park or High Street Kensington tube.

Oxford Street 14 Noel St, W1 ☎020/7734 1618, ⓦwww.yha.org.uk. Its unbeatable West End location and modest size (seventy five beds in rooms of one, two, three and four beds) mean that this hostel tends to be full even out of high season. No children under 6, no groups, no café, but a large kitchen. Oxford Circus or Tottenham Court Road tube.

Rotherhithe Island Yard, Salter Rd, SE16 ☎020/7232 2114, ⓦwww.yha.org.uk. London's largest purpose-built hostel is located in a Docklands area that has little going for it compared to the location of other London YHAs, but it's only a twenty-minute tube ride from the West End and often has space. Rooms have two, four, five or ten beds. Rotherhithe or Canada Water tube.

St Pancras 79–81 Euston Road, NW1 ☎020/7388 9998, ⓦwww.yha.org.uk. Big hostel situated opposite the new British Library, on the busy Euston Road. Rooms are very clean, bright, triple-glazed and air-conditioned – some even

have en-suite facilities. There are a few en-suite doubles and family rooms available with TVs. King's Cross or Euston tube.

Private hostels

Boka Hotel 33 Eardley Crescent SW5 ☎020/7370 1388, ⓦwww.bokahotel.activehotels.com. Famously popular with Aussies and South Africans, this is a laid-back and friendly hotel-cum-hostel with bargain singles and doubles as well as dorm beds. Communal kitchen available. Earl's Court tube.

Generator Compton Place, off Tavistock Place, WC1 ☎020/7388 7666, ⓦwww.thegenerator.co.uk. The neon- and UV-lighting and post-industrial decor may not be to everyone's taste, but the youthful clientele certainly enjoy the cheap bar that's open daily until 2am. You don't share with strangers, so prices get progressively cheaper the more there are in your posse. Russell Square or Euston tube.

Leinster Inn 7–12 Leinster Square, W2 ☎020/7229 9641, ⓦwww.astorhostels.com. The biggest and liveliest of the Astor hostels, with a party atmosphere, and two bars open until the small hours. Singles, doubles and dorm beds available. Under 30s only. Queensway or Notting Hill Gate tube.

Museum Hostel 27 Montague St, WC1 ☎020/7580 5360, ⓦwww.astorhostels.com. In a lovely Georgian house in Bloomsbury, this is the quietest of the Astor hostels. There's no bar, though it's still a sociable, laid-back place, and well situated. Small kitchen, TV lounge and baths as well as showers. Under 30s only. Russell Square tube.

St Christopher's Village 161–165 Borough High St, SE1 ☎020/7407 1856, ⓦwww.st-christophers.co.uk. A new chain of independent hostels, with no fewer than three properties on Borough High Street (and more branches in Camden, Greenwich and Shepherd's Bush). The decor is upbeat and cheerful, the place is efficiently run and there's a party-animal ambience, fuelled by the neighbouring bar and the rooftop sauna and pool. London Bridge tube.

Student halls

Imperial College ☎020/7594 9507, ⓦwww.ad.ic.ac.uk/conferences. Singles and twins

available (with breakfast) in three halls of residence in South Kensington and Notting Hill. You can book online. Open Easter & July to late-Sept.
International Student House 229 Great Portland St, NW1 ☎020/7631 8300, ⓦwww.ish.org.uk. Hundreds of singles, twins, quads and dorm beds in a vast complex at the southern end of Regent's Park. Open year round. Great Portland Street or Regent's Park tube.
John Adams Hall 15–23 Endsleigh St, WC1 ☎020/7387 4086. A hall of residence belonging to the Institute of Education, set in a Georgian terrace in Bloomsbury. Singles and doubles, with breakfast; discounts for students and longer stays. Open Easter & July–Sept. Euston Square tube.
King's College ☎020/7928 3777, ⓦwww.kcl.ac.uk. King's College has a wide range of accommodation available on the South Bank, in Victoria and Hampstead from July to September. You can either contact the Vacation Bureau by phone or book online. All rates including breakfast.
London School of Economics (LSE) ☎020/7955 7370, ⓦwww.lse.ac.uk/vacations.

The LSE offers singles, twins, triples and quads in various halls across London, en suite or with shared facilities, and on either a bed-and-breakfast or self-catering basis. To find out about availability, you can ring the central office, or visit the website and book online.

Campsites

Abbey Wood Federation Rd, Abbey Wood, SE2 ☎020/8311 7708. Enormous, and well equipped Caravan Club site east of Greenwich, ten miles from central London. Train from Charing Cross to Abbey Wood.
Crystal Palace Crystal Palace Parade, SE19 ☎020/8778 7155. Caravan Club site, with maximum stays of two weeks in summer, three weeks in winter. Train from Victoria or London Bridge to Crystal Palace.
Lea Valley Leisure Centre Caravan Park Meridian Way, N9 ☎020/8803 6900. Well-equipped site, situated behind the leisure centre at Pickett's Lock, backing on to a vast reservoir. Ponders End train station from Liverpool Street.

The City

Stretching for more than thirty miles at its broadest point, **London** is by far the largest city in Europe. The majority of its sights are situated to the north of the River Thames, which loops through the city from west to east. However, there is no single predominant focus of interest, for London has grown not through centralized planning but by a process of agglomeration – villages and urban developments that once surrounded the core are now lost within the amorphous mass of Greater London.

One of the few areas which is manageable on foot is **Westminster** and **Whitehall**, the city's royal, political and ecclesiastical power base, where you'll find the **National Gallery** and a host of other London landmarks from **Buckingham Palace** to **Westminster Abbey**. The grand streets and squares of **St James's**, **Mayfair** and **Marylebone**, to the north of Westminster, have been the playground of the rich since the Restoration, and now contain the city's busiest shopping zones.

East of Piccadilly Circus, **Soho** and **Covent Garden** are also easy to walk around and form the heart of the West End entertainment district, containing the largest concentration of theatres, cinemas, clubs, flashy shops, cafés and restaurants. To the north lies the university quarter of **Bloomsbury**, home to the ever-popular British Museum, and the secluded quadrangles of Holborn's Inns of Court, London's legal heartland.

London tours

Standard **sightseeing bus tours** are run by several rival companies, their open-top double-deckers setting off every thirty minutes from Victoria station, Trafalgar Square, Piccadilly, and other conspicuous tourist spots. The Original Tour (☎020/8877 1722, ⊛www.theoriginaltour.com) run several buses on several routes; 24-hour tickets costs around £14, and you can hop on and off as often as you like. Alternatively, you can hop aboard one of the bright yellow World War II amphibious vehicles used by Frog Tours (☎020/7928 3132, ⊛www.frogtours.com) for a combined **bus and boat tour**. After fifty minutes driving round the usual sights, you plunge into the river and go on a half-hour cruise. Tours set off every hour or so from behind County Hall, from 10am to dusk; tickets cost £15. Another money-saving option is to skip the commentary by hopping on a real London bus – the #11 from Victoria will take you past Westminster Abbey, the Houses of Parliament, up Whitehall, round Trafalgar Square, along the Strand and on to St Paul's Cathedral.

Walking tours are infinitely more appealing, mixing solid historical facts with juicy anecdotes in the company of a local specialist. Walks on offer range from a literary pub crawl round Bloomsbury to a tour of places associated with The Beatles. Tours cost around £5 and usually take two hours. To find out what's on offer, check in the "Around Town" section of *Time Out*. The widest range of walks on offer are run by Original London Walks (☎020/7624 3978, ⊛www.walks.com).

The City – the City of London, to give it its full title – is at one and the same time the most ancient and the most modern part of London. Settled since Roman times, it is now one of the world's great financial centres, yet retains its share of historic sights, notably the **Tower of London** and a fine cache of Wren churches that includes **St Paul's Cathedral**. Despite creeping trendification, the **East End**, to the east of the City, is not conventional tourist territory, but to ignore it entirely is to miss out a crucial element of contemporary London. **Docklands** is the converse of the down-at-heel East End, with the Canary Wharf tower, still the country's tallest building, epitomizing the pretensions of the Thatcherite dream.

Lambeth and **Southwark** comprise the small slice of central London that lies south of the Thames. The **South Bank Centre**, London's little-loved concrete culture bunker, is enjoying a new lease of life thanks to its proximity to the new **Tate Modern** in Bankside, which is linked to the City by the famous bouncing **Millennium Bridge**.

The largest segment of greenery in central London is Hyde Park, which separates wealthy **Kensington** and **Chelsea** from the city centre. The **museums** of South Kensington – the Victoria and Albert Museum, the Science Museum and the Natural History Museum – are a must; and if you have shopping on your agenda, you'll want to check out the hive of plush stores in the vicinity of **Harrods**.

The capital's most hectic weekend market takes place around Camden Lock in **North London**. Further out, in the literary suburbs of Hampstead and Highgate, there are unbeatable views across the city from half-wild Hampstead Heath, the favourite parkland of thousands of Londoners. The glory of **South London** is Greenwich, with its nautical associations, royal park and observatory (not to mention its Dome). Finally, there are plenty of rewarding day-trips along the Thames from **Chiswick** to **Windsor**, most notably to Hampton Court Palace and Windsor Castle.

Westminster and Whitehall

Political, religious and regal power has emanated from **Westminster** and **Whitehall** for almost a millennium. It was Edward the Confessor who first established Westminster as London's royal and ecclesiastical power base, some three miles west of the City of London. The embryonic English parliament met in the abbey in the fourteenth century and eventually took over the old royal palace of Westminster. In the nineteenth century, Whitehall became the "heart of the Empire", its ministries ruling over a quarter of the world's population. Even now, though the UK's world status has diminished, the institutions that run the country inhabit roughly the same geographical area: Westminster for the politicians, Whitehall for the civil servants.

The monuments and buildings in and around Whitehall and Westminster also span the millennium, and include some of London's most famous landmarks – **Nelson's Column**, **Big Ben** and the **Houses of Parliament**, **Westminster Abbey** and **Buckingham Palace**, plus two of the city's finest permanent art collections, the **National Gallery** and **Tate Britain**. This is a well-trodden tourist circuit since it's also one of the easiest parts of London to walk round, with all the major sights within a mere half-mile of each other, linked by two of London's most triumphant avenues, **Whitehall** and **The Mall**.

Trafalgar Square

Despite being little more than a glorified, sunken traffic island, infested with scruffy urban pigeons, **Trafalgar Square** is still one of London's grandest architectural set-pieces. John Nash designed the basic layout in the 1820s, but died long before the square took its present form. The Neoclassical National Gallery (see below) filled up the northern side of the square in 1838, followed five years later by the central focal point, **Nelson's Column**; the famous bronze lions didn't arrive until 1868, and the fountains – a rarity in a London square – didn't take their present shape until the eve of World War II.

As one of the few large public squares in London, Trafalgar Square has been both a tourist attraction and a focus for **political demonstrations** since the Chartists assembled here in 1848 before marching to Kennington Common. On a more festive note, the square is graced each December with a giant Christmas tree, donated by Norway in thanks for liberation from the Nazis, and on **New Year's Eve**, thousands of inebriates sing in the New Year.

Stranded on a traffic island to the south of the column, and predating the entire square, is the **equestrian statue of Charles I**, erected shortly after the Restoration on the very spot where eight of those who had signed the king's death warrant were disembowelled. Charles's statue also marks the original site of the thirteenth-century **Charing Cross**, from where all distances from the capital are measured – a Victorian imitation now stands outside Charing Cross train station.

The northeastern corner of the square is occupied by James Gibbs's church of **St Martin-in-the-Fields** (Ⓦ www.stmartin-in-the-fields.org), fronted by a magnificent Corinthian portico and topped by an elaborate and distinctly unclassical tower and steeple. Completed in 1726, the interior is purposefully simple, though the Italian plasterwork on the barrel vaulting is exceptionally rich; it's best appreciated while listening to one of the church's free lunchtime concerts. There's a licensed café in the roomy **crypt**, not to mention a shop, gallery and brass-rubbing centre (Mon–Sat 10am–6pm, Sun noon–6pm).

The National Gallery

Unlike the Louvre or the Hermitage, the **National Gallery**, on the north side of Trafalgar Square (Mon–Sat 10am–6pm, Wed until 8pm, Sun noon–6pm; free; Ⓦwww.nationalgallery.org.uk; Leicester Square or Charing Cross tube), is not based on a royal collection, but was begun as late as 1824 when the government bought 38 paintings belonging to a Russian emigré banker, John Julius Angerstein. The gallery's canny acquisition policy has resulted in a collection of more than 2200 paintings, but the collection's virtue is not so much its size, but the range, depth and sheer quality of its contents.

To view the collection chronologically, begin with the **Sainsbury Wing**, the softly-softly, Postmodern 1980s adjunct which playfully imitates elements of the original gallery's Neoclassicism. However, with more than a thousand paintings on permanent display in the main galleries, you'll need real stamina to see everything in one day, so if time is tight your best bet is to home in on your areas of special interest, having picked up a gallery plan at one of the information desks. A welcome innovation is the **Gallery Guide Soundtrack**, with a brief audio commentary on each of the paintings on display. The Soundtrack is available free of charge, though you're asked for a "voluntary contribution". Another possibility is to join up with one of the gallery's **free guided tours** (daily 11.30am & 2.30pm, plus Wed 6.30pm), which set off from the Sainsbury Wing foyer.

Among the National's **Italian** masterpieces are Leonardo's melancholic *Virgin of the Rocks*, Uccello's *Battle of San Romano*, Botticelli's *Venus and Mars* (inspired by a Dante sonnet) and Piero della Francesca's beautifully composed *Baptism of Christ*, one of his earliest works. The fine collection of Venetian works includes Titian's colourful early masterpiece *Bacchus and Ariadne*, his very late, much gloomier *Death of Acteon*, and Veronese's lustrous *Family of Darius before Alexander*. Elsewhere, Bronzino's erotic *Venus, Cupid, Folly and Time* and Raphael's trenchant *Pope Julius II* keep company with Michelangelo's unfinished *Entombment*. Later Italian works to look out for include a couple by Caravaggio, a few splendid examples of Tiepolo's airy draughtsmanship and glittering vistas of Venice by Canaletto and Guardi.

From **Spain** there are dazzling pieces by El Greco, Goya, Murillo and Velázquez, among them the provocative *Rokeby Venus*. From the **Low Countries**, standouts include van Eyck's *Arnolfini Marriage*, Memlinc's perfectly poised *Donne Triptych*, and a couple of typically serene Vermeers. There are numerous genre paintings, such as Frans Hals' *Family Group in a Landscape*, and some superlative landscapes, most notably Hobbema's *Avenue, Middleharnis*. An array of Rembrandt paintings that features some of his most searching portraits – two of them self-portraits – is followed by abundant examples of Rubens' expansive, fleshy canvases.

Holbein's masterful *Ambassadors* and several of Van Dyck's portraits were painted for the English court, and there's home-grown **British** art, too, represented by important works such as Hogarth's satirical *Marriage à la Mode*, Gainsborough's translucent *Morning Walk*, Constable's ever popular *Hay Wain*, and Turner's *Fighting Téméraire*. Highlights of the **French** contingent include superb works by Poussin, Claude, Fragonard, Boucher and Watteau, and the only two paintings in the country by David.

Finally, there's a particularly strong showing of **Impressionists** and **Post-Impressionists** in rooms 43–46 of the East Wing. Among the most famous works are Manet's unfinished *Execution of Maximilian*, Renoir's *Umbrellas*, Monet's *Thames below Westminster*, Van Gogh's *Sunflowers*, Seurat's pointillist *Bathers at Asnières*, a Rousseau junglescape, Cézanne's proto-Cubist *Bathers* and Picasso's Blue Period *Child with a Dove*.

The National Portrait Gallery

Around the east side of the National Gallery lurks the **National Portrait Gallery** (Mon–Sat 10am–6pm, Sun noon–6pm; free; ⓦ www.npg.org.uk; Leicester Square or Charing Cross tube), founded in 1856 to house uplifting depictions of the good and the great. Though it has some fine works in its collection, many of the studies are of less interest than their subjects, and the overall impression is of an overstuffed shrine to famous Brits rather than a museum offering any insight into the history of portraiture. However, it is fascinating to trace who has been deemed worthy of admiration at any moment: aristocrats and artists in previous centuries, warmongers and imperialists in the early decades of this century, writers and poets in the 1930s and 1940s, and, latterly, retired footballers, and film and pop stars.

The NPG's **new extension** opened in 2000, with a bigger Tudor gallery, and a new contemporary gallery to expand the section that's by far the most popular. There's also a new computer gallery, a lecture theatre and rooftop café/restaurant with a view over the cityscape. The NPG's **Sound Guide**, which gives useful biographical background information to some of the pictures, is provided free of charge, though you're strongly invited to give a "voluntary contribution".

The Mall and St James's Park

The tree-lined sweep of **The Mall** – London's nearest equivalent to a leafy Parisian boulevard – was laid out in the first decade of the twentieth century as a memorial to Queen Victoria, and runs from Trafalgar Square to Buckingham Palace. The bombastic **Admiralty Arch** was erected to mark the entrance at the Trafalgar Square end of The Mall, while at the other end stands the ludicrous Victoria Memorial, Edward VII's overblown tribute to his mother.

The Royal Family

Tourists may still flock to see London's royal palaces, but the British public have become less and less happy about footing the huge tax bill that keeps the **Royal Family** (ⓦ www.royal.gov.uk) in the style to which they are accustomed. This creeping republicanism can be traced back to 1992, which the Queen herself, in one of her few memorable Christmas Day speeches, accurately described as her *annus horribilis*. This was the year that saw the marriage break-ups of Charles and Di, and Andrew and Fergie, and the second marriage of divorcee Princess Anne.

Matters came to a head, though, over who should pay the estimated £50 million costs of repairs after the fire at Windsor Castle (p.150). Misjudging the public mood, the Conservative government offered taxpayers' money to foot the entire bill. After a furore, it was agreed that some of the cost would be raised from astronomical admission charges to Windsor Castle and Buckingham Palace. In addition, under pressure from the media, the Queen also reduced the number of royals paid out of the Civil List, and, for the first time in her life, agreed to pay taxes on her enormous personal fortune.

Given the mounting public resentment against the Royal Family, it was hardly surprising that public opinion tended to side with Princess Diana rather than Prince Charles during their various disputes. Diana's subsequent death, and the huge outpouring of grief that accompanied her funeral, further damaged the reputation of the royals, though her demise has also meant the loss of one of the Royal Family's most vociferous critics. Despite the Royal Family's low poll ratings, none of the political parties currently advocates abolishing the monarchy, and public appetite for stories about the adolescent princes (and their potential girlfriends), or the private life of Charles and Camilla, shows no signs of abating.

Flanking nearly the whole length of the Mall, **St James's Park** is the oldest of the royal parks, having been drained and enclosed for hunting purposes by Henry VIII. It was landscaped by Nash in the 1820s, and today its tree-lined lake is a favourite picnic spot for the civil servants of Whitehall. Pelicans can still be seen at the eastern end of the lake, and there are ducks, swans and geese aplenty. From the bridge across the lake there's also a fine view over to Westminster and the jumble of domes and pinnacles along Whitehall.

Buckingham Palace

The graceless colossus of **Buckingham Palace** (Aug & Sept daily 9.30am–4.15pm; £11; Ⓦ www.royal.gov.uk; Green Park tube), popularly known as "Buck House", has served as the monarch's permanent London residence only since the accession of Victoria. It began its days in 1702 as the Duke of Buckingham's city residence, built on the site of a notorious brothel, and was sold by the duke's son to George III in 1762. The building was overhauled in the late 1820s by Nash and again in 1913, producing a palace that's as bland as it's possible to be.

For two months of the year, the hallowed portals are grudgingly nudged open; timed tickets are sold from the marquee-like box office in Green Park at the western end of The Mall – to avoid queuing, you must book in advance on ☏ 020/7321 2233. The interior, however, is a bit of an anticlimax: of the palace's 660 rooms you're permitted to see around twenty, and there's little sign of life, as the Queen decamps to Scotland every summer. For the other ten months of the year there's little to do here – not that this deters the crowds who mill around the railings, and gather in some force to watch the **Changing of the Guard** (see p.89), in which a detachment of the Queen's Foot Guards marches to appropriate martial music from St James's Palace (unless it rains, that is).

From spring 2002, the public will also be able to view the best of the Royal Collection at the rebuilt, greatly expanded **Queen's Gallery**, on the south side of the palace. Among the highlights will be works by Michelangelo, Reynolds, Gainsborough, Vermeer, van Dyck, Rubens, Rembrandt and Canaletto, as well as the odd Fabergé egg and heaps of Sèvres china.

There's more pageantry on show at the Nash-built **Royal Mews** (Mon–Thurs: Aug & Sept 10.30am–4.30pm; rest of year noon–4pm; £4; Victoria tube), further along Buckingham Palace Road. The royal carriages, lined up under a glass canopy in the courtyard, are the main attraction, in particular the Gold Carriage, made for George III in 1762, smothered in 22-carat gilding and weighing four tons, its axles supporting four life-size figures.

Whitehall

Whitehall, the broad avenue connecting Trafalgar Square to Parliament Square, is synonymous with the faceless, pin-striped bureaucracy charged with the day-to-day running of the country. Since the sixteenth century, nearly all the key governmental ministries and offices have migrated here, rehousing themselves on an ever-increasing scale. The statues dotted about Whitehall recall the days when this street stood at the centre of an empire on which the sun never set. Nowadays, with Scotland, Wales and Northern Ireland each having their own assemblies, Whitehall's remit is ever-decreasing.

During the sixteenth and seventeenth centuries Whitehall was the permanent residence of the kings and queens of England, and was synonymous with royalty. The original **Whitehall Palace** was the London seat of the Archbishop of York, confiscated and greatly extended by Henry VIII after a fire at Westminster

The Changing of the Guard

The Queen is colonel-in-chief of the seven **Household Regiments**: the Life Guards (who dress in red and white) and the Blues and Royals (who dress in blue and red) are the two Household Cavalry regiments; while the Grenadier, Coldstream, Scots, Irish and Welsh Guards make up the Foot Guards.

The Foot Guards can only be told apart by the plumes (or lack of them) in their busbies, and by the arrangement of their tunic buttons. The first three date back to the seventeenth century, and all these regiments still form part of the modern army as well as performing ceremonial functions such as the Changing of the Guard. If you're keen to find out more about the Foot Guards, pay a visit to the **Guards' Museum** (daily 10am–4pm; £2), in the Wellington Barracks on the south side of St James's Park.

The **Changing of the Guard** takes place at two separate locations in London: the two Household Cavalry regiments take it in turns to stand guard at Horse Guards on Whitehall (Mon–Sat 11am, Sun 10am, with inspection daily at 4pm), while the Foot Guards take care of Buckingham Palace (May–Aug daily 11.30am; Sept–April alternate days; no ceremony if it rains). A ceremony also takes place regularly in Windsor Castle (see p.150).

forced him to find alternative accommodation; it was here that Henry celebrated his marriage to Anne Boleyn in 1533, and here that he died fourteen years later.

The chief section of the old palace to survive the fire of 1698 was the **Banqueting House** (Mon–Sat 10am–5pm; £3.90; ⓦ www.hrp.org.uk; Westminster tube), begun by Inigo Jones in 1619 and the first Palladian building to be built in England. The one room now open to the public has no original furnishings, but is well worth seeing for the superlative Rubens ceiling paintings glorifying the Stuart dynasty, commissioned by Charles I in the 1630s. Charles himself walked through the room for the last time in 1649 when he stepped onto the executioner's scaffold from one of its windows.

Across the road, two mounted sentries of the Queen's Household Cavalry and two horseless colleagues, all in ceremonial uniform, are posted daily from 10am to 4pm. Ostensibly they are protecting the **Horse Guards** building, originally built as the old palace guard house, but now guarding nothing in particular. The mounted guards are changed hourly; those standing every two hours. Try to coincide your visit with the Changing of the Guard (see box above), when a squad of twelve mounted troops arrive in full livery. The main action takes place in the parade ground at the rear of the building overlooking Horse Guards' Parade.

Further down this west side of Whitehall is London's most famous address, **Number 10 Downing Street** (ⓦ www.number-10.gov.uk; Westminster tube), the seventeenth-century terraced house that has been the residence of the prime minister since it was presented to Sir Robert Walpole, Britain's first PM, by George II in 1732. Just beyond the Downing Street gates, in the middle of the road, stands Edwin Lutyens' **Cenotaph**, eschewing any kind of Christian imagery, and inscribed simply with the words "The Glorious Dead". The memorial remains the focus of the Remembrance Sunday ceremony in November.

In 1938, in anticipation of Nazi air raids, the basements of the civil service buildings on the south side of King Charles Street were converted into the **Cabinet War Rooms**, now open to the public (daily: April–Sept 9.30am–6pm; Oct–March 10am–6pm; £5; ⓦ www.iwm.org.uk; Westminster tube). It was here that Winston Churchill directed operations and held Cabinet

△ The London Eye

meetings for the duration of World War II. The rooms have been left pretty much as they were when they were finally abandoned on VJ Day 1945, and make for an atmospheric underground trot through wartime London. The museum's free acoustophone commentary helps bring the place to life and includes various eyewitness accounts by folk who worked there.

The Houses of Parliament

Clearly visible at the south end of Whitehall is one of London's best-known monuments, the Palace of Westminster, better known as the **Houses of Parliament**. The city's finest Victorian Gothic Revival building and symbol of a nation once confident of its place at the centre of the world, it is distinguished above all by the ornate, gilded clock tower popularly known as **Big Ben**, after the thirteen-ton main bell that strikes the hour (and is broadcast across the world by the BBC).

The original Westminster Palace was built by **Edward the Confessor** in the first half of the eleventh century, so that he could watch over the building of his abbey. It then served as the seat of all the English monarchs until a fire forced Henry VIII to decamp to Whitehall. The Lords have always convened at the palace, but it was only following Henry's death that the House of Commons moved from the abbey's Chapter House into the palace's St Stephen's Chapel, thus beginning the building's associations with parliament.

In 1834 the old palace burned down. Virtually the only relic of the medieval palace is the bare expanse of **Westminster Hall** (guided tours only, see below), on the north side of the complex. Built by William Rufus in 1099, it's one of the most magnificent secular medieval halls in Europe– you get a glimpse of the hall en route to the public galleries. The **Jewel Tower** (daily: April–Sept 10am–6pm; Oct 10am–5pm; Nov–March 10am–4pm; £1.50; EH; Westminster tube), across the road from parliament, is another remnant of the medieval palace, now housing an excellent exhibition on the history of parliament.

To watch the proceedings in either the House of Commons or the Lords, simply join the queue for the **public galleries** (known as Strangers' Galleries) outside St Stephen's Gate. The public are let in slowly from about 4.30pm onwards from Monday to Thursday and from 10am on Fridays; the security checks are very tight, and the whole procedure can take an hour or more. If you want to avoid the queues, turn up an hour or more later, when the crowds have usually thinned. Recesses (holiday closures) of both Houses occur at Christmas, Easter, and from August to the middle of October; phone ☎020/7219 4272 for more information or visit the parliamentary websites (Ⓦwww.parliament.uk and www.explore.parliament.uk).

To see **Question Time** (Mon–Thurs 2.30–3.30pm) you need to book a ticket several weeks in advance from your local MP (if you're a UK citizen) or your embassy in London (if you're not). To contact your MP, simply phone ☎020/7219 3000 and ask to be put through. In recent years, it's also been possible to join a **guided tour** of the whole of parliament (excluding Big Ben) during the summer recess (Aug & Sept Mon–Sat only; £3.50), lasting an hour and fifteen minutes. Visitors are required to book in advance by phoning ☎020/7344 9966.

Westminster Abbey

The Houses of Parliament dwarf their much older neighbour, **Westminster Abbey** (Mon, Tues, Thurs & Fri 9.30am–4.45pm, Wed 9.30am–4.45pm & 6–8pm, Sat 9.30am–2.45pm; £6; Ⓦwww.westminster-abbey.org; Westminster

Henry Purcell

Henry Purcell (1659–95) is the undisputed father of English classical music and was, until Elgar rose to international prominence in the 1930s, the country's only world-renowned composer. He had a short and fairly remarkable life. His father was a musician in the court of James II, while Henry himself was a chorister at the Chapel Royal. The year after his voice broke in 1673, he became organ tuner at Westminster Abbey and was abbey organist by the tender age of 20. He wrote the music for the coronations of James II and William and Mary. The music he wrote for Queen Mary's funeral was also performed when Purcell, a notorious alcoholic, died just a few months later at the age of 36 and was laid to rest in the abbey. Legend has it that, following a particularly heavy bout of drinking, his wife locked him out and he caught a cold and died.

or St James's Park tube), yet this single building embodies much of the history of England: it has been the venue for all but two coronations since the time of William the Conqueror, and the site of more or less every royal burial for some five hundred years between the reigns of Henry III and George II. Scores of the nation's most famous citizens are honoured here, too (though many of the stones commemorate people buried elsewhere), and the interior is cluttered with hundreds of monuments, reliefs and statues.

Entry is currently via the **north door**, where you can pick up an audioguide for £2, or join a guided tour with one of the vergers for £3 (Mon–Sat only). The north transept is cluttered with monuments to politicians and traditionally known as **Statesmen's Aisle**, shortly after which you come to the abbey's most dazzling architectural set-piece, the **Lady Chapel**, added by Henry VII in 1503 as his future resting place. With its intricately carved vaulting and fan-shaped gilded pendants, the chapel represents the final spectacular gasp of the English Perpendicular style. Unfortunately, the public are no longer admitted to the **Shrine of Edward the Confessor**, the sacred heart of the building, though you do get to inspect Edward I's **Coronation Chair**, a decrepit oak throne dating from around 1300 and still used for coronations.

Nowadays, the abbey's royal tombs are upstaged by **Poets' Corner**, in the south transept, though the first occupant, Geoffrey Chaucer, was in fact buried here not because he was a poet, but because he lived nearby. By the eighteenth century this zone had become an artistic pantheon, and since then, the transept has been filled with tributes to all shades of talent. From the south transept, you can view the central sanctuary, site of the coronations, and the wonderful **Cosmati floor mosaic**, constructed in the thirteenth century by Italian craftsmen, and often covered by a carpet to protect it.

Doors in the south choir aisle lead to the **Great Cloisters** (daily 8am–6pm), rebuilt after a fire in 1298 and now home to a café. At the eastern end of the cloisters lies the octagonal **Chapter House** (daily: April–Oct 10am–5.30pm or dusk; Nov–March 10am–4pm; £2.50 or £1 with an abbey ticket; EH), where the House of Commons met from 1257. The thirteenth-century decorative paving-tiles and wall-paintings have survived intact. Chapter House tickets include entry to some of the few surviving Norman sections of the abbey: the neighbouring **Pyx Chamber** (daily 10.30am–4pm), which displays the abbey's plate, and the **Undercroft Museum** (daily 10.30am–4pm), filled with generations of bald royal death masks and wax effigies.

It's only after exploring the cloisters that you get to see the **nave** itself: narrow, light and, at over a hundred feet in height, by far the tallest in the country. Close by the west door is a doleful fourteenth-century portrait of Richard

II, the oldest-known image of an English monarch painted from life. The most famous monument is the **Tomb of the Unknown Soldier**; it stands right in front of the west door, which now serves as the main exit.

Westminster Cathedral

Halfway down Victoria Street, which runs east from Westminster Abbey, you'll find one of London's most surprising churches, the stripey neo-Byzantine concoction of the Roman Catholic **Westminster Cathedral** (Mon–Fri & Sun 7am–7pm, Sat 8am–7pm; free; Ⓦ www.westminsterdiocese.org.uk; Victoria tube). Begun in 1895, it is one of the last and wildest monuments to the Victorian era: constructed from more than twelve million terracotta-coloured bricks, decorated with hoops of Portland stone, it culminates in a magnificent tapered campanile which rises to 274 feet, served by a lift (daily 9am–5pm; £2). The **interior** is only half finished, so to get an idea of what the place will look like when it's finally completed, explore the series of **side chapels** whose rich, multicoloured decor makes use of over one hundred different marbles from around the world.

Tate Britain

From Parliament Square the unprepossessing Millbank runs south along the river to the **Tate Britain** (daily 10am–5.50pm; free; Ⓦ www.tate.org.uk; Pimlico tube). Founded in 1897 with money from Sir Henry Tate, inventor of the sugar cube, the purpose-built Tate Gallery, half a mile south of parliament, is now devoted exclusively to British art. With the new Tate Modern now established in the disused Bankside Power Station (see p.124), the original building on Millbank has now been rechristened **Tate Britain**. As well as displaying British art from 1500 to 2000, plus a whole wing devoted to Turner, Tate Britain also showcases contemporary British artists, puts on large-scale exhibitions of British art, and continues to sponsor the Turner Prize, the country's most prestigious modern-art prize.

The galleries are rehung more or less annually, but always include a fair selection of **British art** by the likes of Hogarth, Constable, Gainsborough, Reynolds and Blake, plus foreign artists such as van Dyck who spent much of their career over here. The ever-popular **Pre-Raphaelites** are always well represented, as are established twentieth-century greats such as Stanley Spencer and Francis Bacon alongside living artists such as David Hockney and Lucien Freud. Lastly, don't miss the Tate's outstanding **Turner collection**, displayed in the Clore Gallery. The gallery offers audioguides to the collections for £3 each.

St James's, Mayfair and Marylebone

St James's, **Mayfair** and **Marylebone** emerged in the late seventeenth century as London's first real suburbs, characterized by grid-plan streets feeding into grand, formal squares. This expansion set the westward trend for middle-class migration, and as London's wealthier consumers moved west, so too did the city's more upmarket shops and luxury hotels, which are still a feature of the area.

Aristocratic **St James's**, the rectangle of land to the north of St James's Park, was one of the first areas to be developed and remains the preserve of the seriously rich. **Piccadilly**, which forms the border between St James's and Mayfair, is no longer the fashionable promenade it once was, but a whiff of exclusivity still pervades **Bond Street** and its tributaries. **Regent Street** was created as a new "Royal Mile", a tangible borderline to shore up these new fashionable suburbs against the chaotic maze of Soho and the City, where the working population still lived. Now, along with **Oxford Street**, it has become London's busiest shopping district – it's here that Londoners mean when they talk of "going shopping up the West End".

Marylebone, which lies to the north of Oxford Street, is another grid-plan Georgian development, a couple of social and real-estate leagues below Mayfair, but a wealthy area nevertheless. It boasts a very fine art gallery, the **Wallace Collection**, and, in its northern fringes, one of London's biggest tourist attractions, **Madame Tussaud's**, the oldest and largest wax museum in the world.

St James's

St James's, the exclusive little enclave sandwiched between The Mall and Piccadilly, was laid out in the 1670s close to St James's Palace. Royal and aristocratic residences predominate along its southern border, gentlemen's clubs cluster along Pall Mall and St James's Street, while jacket-and-tie restaurants and expense-account gentlemen's outfitters line Jermyn Street. Hardly surprising, then, that most Londoners rarely stray into this area.

St James's does, however, contain some interesting architectural set-pieces, such as **Lower Regent Street**, which was the first stage in John Nash's ambitious plan to link George IV's magnificent Carlton House with Regent's Park. Like so many of Nash's grandiose schemes, it never quite came to fruition, as George IV, soon after ascending the throne, decided that Carlton House – the most expensive palace ever to have been built in London – wasn't quite luxurious enough, and had it pulled down. Instead, Lower Regent Street now opens up into **Waterloo Place**, at the centre of which stands the Guards' Crimean Memorial, fashioned from captured Russian cannon and featuring a statue of Florence Nightingale. Clearly visible, beyond, is the "Grand Old" **Duke of York's Column**, erected in 1833, ten years before Nelson's more famous one in Trafalgar Square.

Cutting across Waterloo Place, **Pall Mall** – named after the croquet-like game of *paglio a maglio* (literally "ball and mallet") that was popular at the time – leads west to **St James's Palace**, whose main red-brick gate-tower is pretty much all that remains of the Tudor palace erected here by Henry VIII. When Whitehall Palace burned down in 1698, St James's became the principal royal residence and, in keeping with tradition, an ambassador to the UK is still known as "Ambassador to the Court of St James", even though the court moved down the road to Buckingham Palace when Queen Victoria ascended the throne. The rambling, crenellated complex now provides a bachelor pad for Prince Charles (Ⓦwww.princeofwales.gov.uk) and is off limits to the public, with the exception of the **Chapel Royal** (Oct to Good Friday Sun 8.30am & 11.15am; Green Park tube), situated within the palace, and the **Queen's Chapel** (Easter–July Sun 8.30am & 11.15am; Green Park tube), on the other side of Marlborough Road; both are open for services only.

One palatial St James's residence you can visit, however, is Princess Diana's ancestral home, **Spencer House** (Feb–July & Sept–Dec Sun 11.30am–4.45pm; £6), a superb Palladian mansion erected in the 1750s. Inside, tour guides take you through nine of the state rooms, the most outrageous of which is Lord Spencer's Room, with its astonishing gilded palm-tree columns. Note that children under 10 are not admitted.

Piccadilly Circus and around

Anonymous and congested it may be, but **Piccadilly Circus** is, for many Londoners, the nearest their city comes to having a centre. A much-altered product of Nash's grand 1812 Regent Street plan and now a major traffic bottleneck, it may not be a picturesque place, but thanks to its celebrated aluminium statue, popularly known as **Eros**, it's prime tourist territory. The fountain's archer is one of the city's top attractions, a status that baffles all who live here. Despite the bow and arrow, it's not the god of love at all but the *Angel of Christian Charity*, erected to commemorate the Earl of Shaftesbury, a bible-thumping social reformer who campaigned against child labour. If Eros's fame remains a mystery, that anyone bothers to wander into the tacky **Trocadero** (daily 10am–1am; ⓦ www.troc.co.uk), is a good deal more perplexing. For all the hype – it's quick to tout its position as Europe's largest indoor virtual-reality theme park – this is really just a glorified amusement arcade with a few virtual-reality rides thrown in.

Regent Street

Drawn up by John Nash in 1812 as both a luxury shopping street and a triumphal way between George IV's Carlton House and Regent's Park, **Regent Street** was the city's first attempt at dealing with traffic congestion, and its first stab at slum clearance and planned social segregation, which would later be perfected by the Victorians.

Despite the subsequent destruction of much of Nash's work in the 1920s, it's still possible to admire the stately intentions of his original Regent Street plan. The increase in the purchasing power of the city's middle classes in the last century brought the tone of the street "down" and heavyweight stores catering for the masses now predominate. Among the best known are **Hamley's**, reputedly the world's largest toy shop, and **Liberty**, the department store that popularized Arts and Crafts designs at the beginning of the last century.

Piccadilly

Piccadilly apparently got its name from the ruffs or "pickadills" worn by the dandies who used to promenade here in the late seventeenth century. Despite its fashionable pedigree, it's no place for promenading in its current state, with traffic careering down it nose to tail most of the day and night. Infinitely more pleasant places to window-shop are the **nineteenth-century arcades**, originally built to protect shoppers from the mud and horse-dung on the streets, but now equally useful for escaping exhaust fumes.

Piccadilly may not be the shopping heaven it once was, but there are still several old firms here that proudly display their royal warrants. One of the oldest institutions is the food emporium of **Fortnum & Mason** (ⓦ www.fortnumandmason.com) at no. 181, established in the 1770s by one of George III's footmen, Charles Fortnum, and his partner, Hugh Mason. In a kitsch addition dating from 1964, the figures of Fortnum and Mason bow to each other on the hour every day as the clock over the main entrance clanks out the Eton school anthem.

Further along Piccadilly, with its best rooms overlooking Green Park, stands the **Ritz Hotel** (ⓦ www.theritzhotel.co.uk), a byword for decadence since it first wowed Edwardian society in 1906; the hotel's design, with its two-storey French-style mansard roof and long arcade, was based on the buildings of Paris's Rue de Rivoli. For a prolonged look inside, you'll need to be in good appetite, dress appropriately, and book in advance, for the famous afternoon tea in the hotel's Palm Court.

Across the road from Fortnum & Mason, the **Royal Academy of Arts** (daily 10am–6pm, Fri until 10pm; £6–8; guided tours of the permanent collection Tues–Fri 1pm; free; ⓦ www.royalacademy.org.uk; Green Park or Piccadilly Circus tube) occupies the enormous Burlington House, one of the few survivors from the ranks of aristocratic mansions that once lined the north side of Piccadilly. The Academy itself was the country's first-ever formal art school, founded in 1768 by a group of English painters including Thomas Gainsborough and Joshua Reynolds. Reynolds went on to become the academy's first president, and his statue now stands in the courtyard, palette in hand.

The Academy has always had a conservative reputation for its teaching and, until recently, most of its shows. The **Summer Exhibition**, which opens in June each year, remains a stop on the social calendar of upper middle-class England. Anyone can enter paintings in any style, and the lucky winners get hung, in rather close proximity, and sold. Supposed gravitas is added by the RA "Academicians", who are allowed to display six of their own works – no matter how awful. The result is a bewildering display, which gets panned annually by highbrow critics.

Along the west side of the Royal Academy runs the **Burlington Arcade**, built in 1819 for Lord Cavendish, then owner of Burlington House, to prevent commoners throwing rubbish into his garden. It's Piccadilly's longest and most expensive nineteenth-century arcade, lined with mahogany-fronted jewellers, gentlemen's outfitters and the like. Upholding Regency decorum, it is still illegal to whistle, sing, hum, hurry or carry large packages or open umbrellas on this small stretch, and the arcade's beadles (known as Burlington Berties), in their Edwardian frock-coats and gold-braided top hats, take the prevention of such criminality very seriously.

Bond Street

While Oxford Street, Regent Street and Piccadilly have all gone downmarket, **Bond Street**, which runs parallel with Regent Street, has carefully maintained its exclusivity. It is, in fact, two streets rolled into one: the southern half, laid out in the 1680s, is known as Old Bond Street; its northern extension, which followed less than fifty years later, is known as New Bond Street. They are both pretty unassuming streets architecturally, being a mixture of modest Victorian and Georgian town houses. However, the shops that line them, and those of neighbouring Conduit Street and South Molton Street, are among the flashiest in London, dominated by perfumeries, **jewellers** and designer clothing stores, including Versace, Gucci, Nicole Farhi and Yves St-Laurent.

In addition to fashion, Bond Street is also renowned for its **auction houses** and for its fine art galleries. Sotheby's, 34–35 New Bond St (ⓦ www.sothebys.com), is the oldest of the auction houses, and its viewing galleries are open free of charge. Bond Street's **art galleries** – exclusive mainstays of the street – are actually outnumbered by those on nearby Cork Street. The main difference between the two locations is that the Bond Street dealers are basically heirloom offloaders, whereas Cork Street galleries sell largely contemporary art. Both have impeccably presented and somewhat intimidating staff, but if you're interested, walk in and look around. They're only shops, after all.

Two famous musicians lived in Brook Street, just off Bond Street. The most recent one was **Jimi Hendrix**, who lived at no. 23 and is commemorated by a blue plaque; some two hundred years earlier, Georg Friedrich Händel lived next door at no. 25. Both houses are now part of the **Handel House Museum**, which should be open by the time you read this. It was here that Handel composed most of his music including the *Messiah* and *Music for the Royal Fireworks*. Highlights of the exhibition include the Byrne Collection which consists of several hundred objects including Mozart's handwritten arrangement of a Handel fugue and early editions of operas and oratorios.

Oxford Street

As wealthy Londoners began to move out of the City in the eighteenth century in favour of the newly developed West End, so **Oxford Street** (ⓦwww.oxfordstreet.co.uk) – the old Roman road to Oxford – gradually became London's main shopping street. Today, despite successive recessions and sky-high rents, this scruffy, two-mile hotchpotch of shops is still one of the world's busiest streets.

East of Oxford Circus, the street forms the border between Soho and Fitzrovia, and features two of the city's main record stores, HMV and Virgin Megastore. West of Oxford Circus, the street is dominated by more upmarket stores, including one great landmark, **Selfridge's** (ⓦwww.selfridges.co.uk), a huge Edwardian pile fronted by giant Ionic columns, with the Queen of Time, riding the ship of commerce and supporting an Art Deco clock, above the main entrance. The store was opened in 1909 by Chicago millionaire Gordon Selfridge, who flaunted its 130 departments under the slogan, "Why not spend a day at Selfridge's?", but was later pensioned off after running into trouble with the Inland Revenue.

The Wallace Collection

Immediately north of Oxford Street, on Manchester Square, stands Hertford House, a miniature eighteenth-century French chateau which holds the splendid **Wallace Collection** (Mon–Sat 10am–5pm, Sun noon–5pm; free; ⓦwww.wallace-collection.org.uk; Bond Street tube), a museum-gallery best known for its eighteenth-century French paintings and decorative art. There's a restaurant in the newly glassed-over courtyard, and a hands-on section downstairs, but at heart, the Wallace Collection remains an old-fashioned place, with exhibits piled high in glass cabinets, and paintings covering every inch of wall space. The fact that these exhibits are set amidst period fittings – and a bloody great armoury – makes the place even more remarkable.

If you're here for the paintings, head for the first floor which has the most famous works, the tone of which is set by **Boucher**'s sumptuous mythological scenes over the staircase. Among the Rococo delights in the West Gallery are **Fragonard**'s coquettes, one of whom flaunts herself to a smitten beau in *The Swing*. In addition to all this French finery there's a good collection of Dutch paintings in the East Galleries: **de Hooch**'s *Women Peeling Apples*, oil sketches by Rubens and landscapes by Ruisdael.

The Great Gallery, the largest room in the house, holds the best paintings, however, including several vast **Van Dyck** portraits, **Titian**'s *Perseus and Andromeda*, **Rembrandt**'s affectionate portrait of his teenage son, Titus, and **Hals'** arrogant *Laughing Cavalier*. Also here are **Velázquez**'s typically searching *Lady with a Fan*, and **Gainsborough**'s deceptively innocent portrait of the actress Mary Robinson, in which she insouciantly holds a miniature of the Prince of Wales, her lover (later George IV).

Baker Street, Madame Tussaud's and the Planetarium

A small percentage of tourists emerging from **Baker Street** tube station are on the trail of English literature's languid super-sleuth, Sherlock Holmes, whose statue now stands outside the main exit. The man himself is celebrated in two museums round the corner in Baker Street itself, though neither place has any real connection with the fictional character (no. 221b doesn't actually exist), nor his creator, Arthur Conan Doyle. The **Sherlock Holmes Museum** (daily 9.30am–6pm; £6; ⓦwww.sherlockholmes.co.uk; Baker Street tube) at no. 239 (in deference to the character, the sign on the door now says 221b) is a competent exercise in period reconstruction, but there's little attempt to impart any insights (or even basic facts) about Holmes or Doyle. Much better value for money is the **Sherlock Holmes Experience** (Mon–Sat 10am–5pm, Sun 11am–4pm; £1.50; ⓣ020/7486 1426; ⓦwww.sh-memorabilia.co.uk; Baker Street tube), situated on the opposite side of the street above a memorabilia shop at no. 230. The curator is a real enthusiast, and has re-created the study from the 1980s British TV series, starring Jeremy Brett, and filled it with artefacts from the show, plus an impressive collection of first editions.

Just round the corner on Marylebone Road, **Madame Tussaud's** (daily: June to mid-Sept 9am–5.30pm; mid-Sept to May Mon–Fri 10am–5.30pm, Sat & Sun 9.30am–5.30pm; £11.50; combined ticket with the Planetarium £13.95; ⓦwww.madame-tussauds.com; Baker Street tube) has been pulling in the crowds ever since the good lady arrived in London from Paris in 1802 bearing the sculpted heads of guillotined aristocrats (she herself only just managed to escape the same fate – her uncle, who started the family business, was less fortunate). The entrance fee might be extortionate, the likenesses occasionally dubious and the automated dummies hardly state-of-the-art, but you can still rely on finding London's biggest queues here – to avoid queuing, book your ticket in advance over the phone or on the internet.

As well as the usual parade of wax figures, the tour of Tussaud's ends with a manic five-minute "ride" through the history of London in a miniaturized taxi cab. The adjoining and equally crowded London **Planetarium** (Mon–Fri 11.30am–5pm, Sat, Sun & school holidays 10am–5pm; £6.50; combined ticket with Madame Tussaud's £13.95) features a thirty-minute high-tech presentation, projected onto a giant dome; a standard romp through the basics of astronomy accompanied by a cosmic astro-babble commentary.

Soho

Soho gives you the best and worst of London. It's here you'll find the city's street fashion on display, its theatres, mega-cinemas and the widest variety of restaurants and cafés – where, whatever hour you wander through, there's always something going on. Uniquely, though, Soho retains an unorthodox and slightly raffish air born of an immigrant history as rich as that of the East End. The porn joints that made the district notorious in the 1970s are still in evidence, especially to the west of Wardour Street, as are the media types who pushed up the rents in the 1980s.

In the 1990s, Soho transformed itself again, this time into one of Europe's leading gay centres, with bars and cafés bursting out from the Old Compton

London bookshops

Charing Cross Road, Soho's eastern border and a thoroughfare from Trafalgar Square to Oxford Street, boasts the highest concentration of **bookshops** anywhere in London. One of the first to open here was the chaotic, antiquated Foyles at no. 119, which now struggles to compete with the nearby heavyweight chain bookshops such as Books Etc, Borders, Blackwell's and Waterstones. The street retains more of its original character south of Cambridge Circus, where you'll find the capital's main feminist bookshop, Silver Moon, along with a cluster of ramshackle second-hand bookshops, such as Quinto.

Street area. Nevertheless, the area continues to boast a lively fruit and vegetable market on **Berwick Street** and a nightlife that has attracted writers and ravers to the place since the eighteenth century. The big movie houses on **Leicester Square** always attract crowds of punters, and the tiny enclave of **Chinatown** continues to double as a focus for the Chinese community and a popular place for inexpensive Chinese restaurants.

Leicester Square and Chinatown

By night, when the big cinemas and discos are doing good business, and the buskers are entertaining the crowds, **Leicester Square** is one of the most crowded places in London, particularly on a Friday or Saturday when huge numbers of tourists and half the youth of the suburbs seem to congregate here. By day, queues form for half-price deals at the Society of West End Theatres booth at the south end of the square, while touts haggle over the price of dodgy tickets for the top shows, and clubbers hand out flyers to likely looking punters.

It wasn't until the mid-nineteenth century that the square actually began to emerge as an entertainment zone, with accommodation houses (for prostitutes and their clients) and music halls such as the grandiose Empire and the Hippodrome (just off the square), edifices which survive today as cinemas and discos. Cinema moved in during the 1930s, a golden age evoked by the sleek black lines of the Odeon on the east side, and maintains its grip on the area. The Empire, at the top end of the square, is the favourite for the big royal premieres and, in a rather half-hearted imitation of the Hollywood (and Cannes) tradition, there are hand prints visible in the pavement by the southwestern corner of the square.

Chinatown, hemmed in between Leicester Square and Shaftesbury Avenue, is a self-contained jumble of shops, cafés and restaurants that make up one of London's most distinct and popular ethnic enclaves. **Gerrard Street**, Chinatown's main drag, has been endowed with ersatz touches – telephone kiosks rigged out as pagodas and fake oriental gates – and few of London's 60,000 Chinese actually live in the three small blocks of Chinatown. Nonetheless, it remains a focus for the community, a place to do business or the weekly shopping, celebrate a wedding, or just meet up for meals, particularly on Sundays, when the restaurants overflow with Chinese families tucking into *dim sum*.

Old Compton Street and around

If Soho has a main drag, it has to be **Old Compton Street**, which runs parallel with Shaftesbury Avenue. The corner shops, peep shows, boutiques and

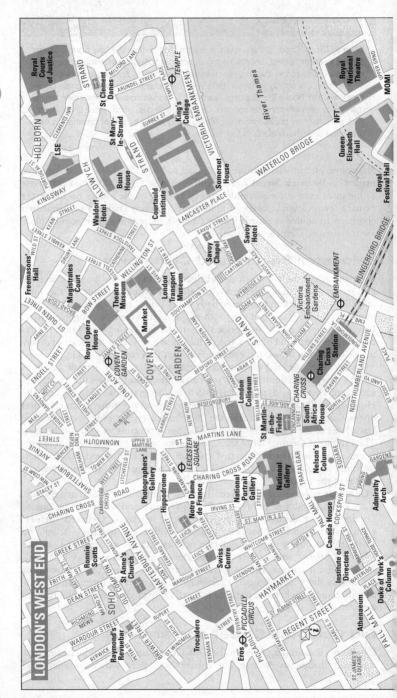

LONDON'S WEST END

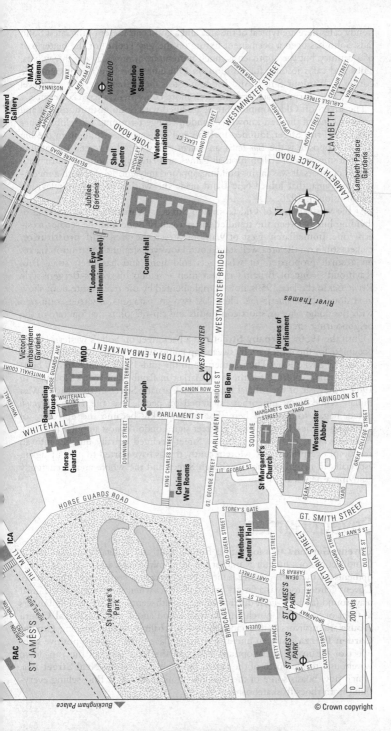

101

© Crown copyright

trendy cafés here are typical of the area and a good barometer of the latest Soho fads. Soho has been a permanent fixture on the **gay scene** for the better part of a century, but the approach is much more upfront nowadays, with gay bars, clubs and cafés jostling for position on Old Compton Street and round the corner in Wardour Street. And it doesn't stop there: there's now a gay travel agency, a gay financial adviser and, even more convenient, a gay taxi service.

The streets off Old Compton Street are lined with Soho institutions past and present. One of the best known is London's longest-running jazz club, *Ronnie Scott's*, on Frith Street, founded in 1958 and still capable of pulling in the big names. Opposite is the *Bar Italia*, an Italian café with a big screen for satellite TV transmissions of Italian football games, and late-night hours popular with Soho's clubbers. It was in this building, appropriately enough for such a media-saturated area, that John Logie Baird made the world's first public television transmission in 1926.

At the western end of Old Compton Street is **Wardour Street**, a kind of dividing line between the trendier, eastern half of Soho and the seedier western zone. Immediately west of Wardour Street, the **vice and prostitution** rackets still have the area well staked out. However, straight prostitution makes up a small proportion of what gets sold here, and has been since Paul Raymond – one of Britain's richest men – set up his Folies-Bergère-style *Revue Bar* in the late 1950s, now complemented by the transvestite floor show next door at *Madame Jo-Jo's*. These last two are paragons of virtue compared with the dodgy videos, short con outfits and rip-off joints that operate in the neighbouring streets.

Until the 1950s, **Carnaby Street** was a backstreet on Soho's western fringe, occupied, for the most part, by sweatshop tailors who used to make up the suits for nearby Savile Row. Then, sometime in the mid-1950s, several trendy boutiques opened catering for the new market in flamboyant men's clothing. In 1964 – the year of the official birth of the Carnaby Street myth – Mods, West Indian Rude Boys and other "switched-on people", as the *Daily Telegraph* noted, began to hangout here. The area quickly became the epicentre of Swinging Sixties' London, and its street sign London's most popular postcard. A victim of its own hype, Carnaby Street declined equally quickly into an avenue of overpriced tack. More recently, things have started to pick up again, especially in neighbouring Newburgh Street, and the whole area is currently enjoying a new lease of life.

Covent Garden

Covent Garden's transformation from a fruit and vegetable market into a fashion-conscious quarter is one of the most miraculous and enduring developments of the 1980s. More sanitized and brazenly commercial than Soho, Covent Garden today is a far cry from its heyday when the piazza was the great playground (and red-light district) of eighteenth-century London. The buskers in front of St Paul's Church, the theatres round about, and the **Royal Opera House** are survivors in this tradition, and on a balmy summer evening, **Covent Garden Piazza** is still an undeniably lively place to be. Another positive side-effect of the market development has been the renovation of the run-down warehouses to the north of the piazza, especially around the **Neal Street** area, which now boasts some of the trendiest shops in the West End, selling everything from shoes to skateboards.

Covent Garden Piazza

London's oldest planned square, laid out in the 1630s by Inigo Jones, **Covent Garden Piazza** was initially a great success, its novelty value alone attracting a rich and aristocratic clientele, but over the next century the tone of the place fell as the fruit and vegetable market expanded, and theatres and coffee houses began to take over the peripheral buildings. When the market closed in 1974, the piazza narrowly survived being turned into an office development. Instead, the elegant Victorian market hall and its environs were restored to house shops, restaurants and arts-and-crafts stalls. Boosted by buskers and street entertainers, the piazza has now become one of London's major tourist attractions, its success prompting a wholesale gentrification of the streets to the north of the market.

Of Jones's original piazza, the only remaining parts are the two rebuilt sections of north-side arcading, and **St Paul's Church**, facing the west side of the market building. The proximity of so many theatres has earned it the nickname of the "Actors' Church", and it's filled with memorials to international thespians from Boris Karloff to Gracie Fields. The space in front of the church's Tuscan portico – where Eliza Doolittle was discovered selling violets by Henry Higgins in George Bernard Shaw's *Pygmalion* – is now a legalized venue for buskers and street performers, who must audition for a slot months in advance.

The piazza's history of entertainment goes back to May 1662, when the first recorded performance of Punch and Judy in England was staged by Italian puppeteer Pietro Gimonde, and witnessed by Samuel Pepys. This historic event is commemorated every second Sunday in May by a **Punch and Judy Festival**, held in the gardens behind the church; for the rest of the year, the churchyard provides a tranquil respite from the activity outside (access is from King, Henrietta and Bedford streets).

The piazza's museums

An original flower-market shed on the piazza's east side is occupied by the **London Transport Museum** (daily 10am–6pm, Fri from 11am; £4.95; Ⓦ www.ltmuseum.co.uk; Covent Garden tube). A herd of old buses, trains and trams make up the bulk of the exhibits, though there's enough interactive fun – touch-screen computers and the odd costumed conductor and vehicles to climb on – to keep most children amused. There's usually a good smattering of London Transport's stylish maps and posters on display, too, and you can buy reproductions, plus countless other LT paraphernalia, at the shop on the way out.

The rest of the old flower market now houses the **Theatre Museum** (Tues–Sun 10am–6pm; £4.50; Ⓦ www.theatremuseum.org), displaying three centuries of memorabilia from every conceivable area of the performing arts in the West (the entrance is on Russell St). The corridors of glass cases cluttered with props, programmes and costumes are not especially exciting, but the various temporary exhibitions are usually much more interactive and fun. There are guides on hand to bring the displays to life, and various workshops and performances to take advantage of. The museum also runs a **booking service** for West End shows and has an unusually good selection of cards and posters.

The Royal Opera House

The Corinthian portico opposite Bow Street magistrates' court belongs to the **Royal Opera House** (backstage tours Mon–Sat 10.30am, 12.30 & 2.30pm; £6; Ⓦ www.royaloperahouse.org; Covent Garden tube), whose main building dates from 1811, but which has recently undergone a £220 million redevelopment. Part and parcel of the rebuilding has been the construction of arcading in the northeast side of the piazza, from which there's now a passageway through to Bow Street. The public can also gain access to the spectacular wrought-iron **Floral Hall** (daily 10am–3pm), on the first floor, which now serves as the opera house's main foyer, and the *Amphitheatre* bar/restaurant, which has a glorious terrace overlooking the piazza.

North of the piazza

The area to the north of Covent Garden Piazza is, on the whole, more interesting in terms of its shops, pubs and eating places than is the piazza itself. Floral Street, Long Acre, Shelton Street and especially Neal Street are all good shopping locales.

Looking east down the gentle curve of Long Acre, it's difficult to miss the austere, Pharaonic mass of the **Freemasons' Hall** (Mon–Fri 10am–5pm; free; Ⓦ www.grand-lodge.org; Covent Garden tube), built as a memorial to all the masons who died in World War I. Whatever you may think of this reactionary, male-only, secretive organization, the interior is worth a peek for the Grand Temple alone, whose pompous, bombastic decor is laden with heavy symbolism. To see the Grand Temple, turn up for one of the free hourly **guided tours** (Mon–Fri 11am–4pm).

North from Long Acre runs **Neal Street**, one of the most sought-after commercial addresses in Covent Garden, which features some fine Victorian warehouses, complete with stair towers for loading and shifting goods between floors. Neal Street is now dominated by trendy fashion stores such as Mango, Diesel and, on nearby Shorts Gardens, About Time. A decade or so ago, the feel of the street was a lot less monied and more alternative, but that ambience only really survives in **Neal's Yard**, a wholefood haven set in a tiny little courtyard off Shorts Gardens, prettily festooned with flower boxes and ivy.

Bloomsbury

Bloomsbury gets its name from its medieval landowners, the Blemunds, though nothing was built here until the 1660s. Through marriage, the Russell family, the earls and later dukes of Bedford, acquired much of the area and established the many formal, bourgeois squares which are the main distinguishing feature of the area. The Russells named the grid-plan streets after their various titles and estates, and kept the pubs and shops to a minimum to maintain the tone of the neighbourhood.

This century, Bloomsbury acquired a reputation as the city's most learned quarter, dominated by the dual institutions of the **British Museum** and **London University** and home to many of London's chief book publishers, but perhaps best known for its literary inhabitants (for more on the Bloomsbury Group, see p.214). Today, the British Museum is clearly the star attraction, but there are other sights, such as the **Dickens' House Museum**, that are high on many people's itineraries. In its northern fringes, the character of the area changes dramatically, becoming steadily more seedy as you near the two big main-line train stations of **Euston** and **King's Cross**, where cheap B&Bs and run-down council estates provide fertile territory for prostitutes and drug dealers, and an unlikely location for the new **British Library**.

The British Museum

One of the great museums of the world, the **British Museum** (daily 10am–5.30pm, Thurs & Fri until 8.30pm; free; ⓦ www.british-museum.ac.uk; Russell Square, Tottenham Court Road or Holborn tube) is Britain's most popular tourist attraction after Blackpool, drawing more than six million visitors a year. With over four million exhibits ranged over two and a half miles of galleries, the BM contains one of the most comprehensive collections of antiquities, prints, drawings and books to be housed under one roof.

The building itself, begun in 1823, is the grandest of London's Greek Revival edifices, dominated by the giant Ionian colonnade and portico that forms the main entrance. The British Library's departure to St Pancras (see p.106) has allowed the museum to open up and re-develop the building's **Great Court** (Mon–Wed 9am–9pm, Thurs–Sat 9am–11pm, Sun 9am–6pm), which now features a remarkable, curving glass-and-steel roof, designed by Norman Foster. At the centre stands the copper-domed former **Round Reading Room**, built in the 1850s to house the British Library. It was here, at desk O7, beneath one of the largest domes in the world, that Karl Marx penned *Das Kapital*. The building continues to function as a public study area, and features a multimedia guide to the museum's collections.

The BM's collection of **Roman and Greek antiquities** is unparalleled, and is perhaps most famous for the Parthenon sculptures, better known as the **Elgin Marbles**, a series of exquisite friezes, metopes and pedimental sculptures, carved between 447 and 432 BC for the **Parthenon**. Removed from Athens in 1801 by Lord Elgin, British ambassador to Constantinople, ostensibly in order to protect them from damage, the sculptures have caused more controversy than any other of the museum's trophies, with the Greek government repeatedly requesting that they be returned. A CD audioguide (£3) is available to rent, but it's by no means essential as the explanatory panels and video are good enough. Amidst the plethora of Greek and Roman statuary and vases, the only other single item with a similarly high profile is the **Portland Vase**, made from cobalt-blue blown glass around the beginning of the first century, and decorated with opaque white cameos.

The museum's **Egyptian collection** is easily the most significant outside Egypt, and ranges from monumental sculptures, such as the colossal granite head of Amenophis III, to the ever-popular **mummies** and their ornate outer caskets. Also on display is the **Rosetta Stone**, which finally unlocked the secret of Egyptian hieroglyphs. Close by the Egyptian Hall, you'll find a splendid series of **Assyrian reliefs** from Nineveh, depicting events such as the royal lion hunts of Ashurbanipal, in which the king slaughters one of the cats with his bare hands. Among the most extraordinary artefacts from **Mesopotamia** are the enigmatic Ram in the Thicket (a lapis lazuli and shell statuette of a goat), an equally mysterious box known as the Standard of Ur, and the remarkable hoard of goldwork known as the Oxus Treasure.

The leathery half-corpse of the 2000-year-old **Lindow Man**, discovered in a Cheshire bog, and the Anglo-Saxon treasure from the **Sutton Hoo** ship burial, are among one of the highlights of the Prehistoric and Romano-British collection. The medieval and modern collections, meanwhile, range from the twelfth-century **Lewis Chessmen**, carved from walrus ivory, to twentieth-century exhibits such as a copper vase by Frank Lloyd Wright. It's also worth seeking out the museum's **Money Gallery**, which begins with the use of grain in Mesopotamia around 2000 BC, ends with a 1990s five hundred thousand million Yugoslav dinar note, and includes coins from all over the world.

The dramatically lit Mexican Gallery, and the North American Gallery, mark the beginning of the return of the museum's **ethnographic collection**, but lack of space means that only a fraction of the BM's enormous collection of prints and drawings can be displayed at any one time. In addition, there are fabulous **Oriental treasures** in the north wing of the museum, closest to the back entrance on Montague Place. The displays include ancient Chinese porcelain, ornate snuffboxes, miniature landscapes, a bewildering array of Buddhist and Hindu gods, and – the showpiece of the collection – dazzling limestone reliefs from the second-century stupa of Amaravati in south India.

Dickens' House

A couple of Bloomsbury's lesser museums, although dwarfed by the British Museum, are worth dipping into. **Dickens' House**, 48 Doughty St (Mon–Sat 10am–5pm; £4; ⓦwww.dickensmuseum.com; Russell Square tube), is the area's only house museum – surprisingly, given the plethora of blue plaques marking the residences of local luminaries. Dickens moved here in 1837 shortly before his marriage to Catherine Hogarth, and they lived here for two years, during which time he wrote *Nicholas Nickleby* and *Oliver Twist*. This is the only one of Dickens' fifteen London addresses to survive intact, but only the drawing room has been restored to its original Regency style. Letters, manuscripts and lots of memorabilia, including first editions, the earliest known portrait and the annotated books he used during extensive lecture tours, are the rewards for those with more than a passing interest in the novelist.

The University

London has more students than any other city in the world (over half a million at the last count), which isn't bad going for a city that only organized its own **University** in 1826 (ⓦwww.lon.ac.uk; Russell Square or Goodge Street tube), more than six hundred years after the likes of Oxford and Cambridge. The university started life in Bloomsbury, but it wasn't until after World War I that the institution really began to take over the area.

However, the university's piecemeal development has left the place with no real focus other than a couple of landmarks in the form of the 1930s **Senate House** skyscraper, behind the British Museum, and the Neoclassical **University College** (UCL; ⓦwww.ucl.ac.uk), near the top of Gower Street. UCL is home to London's most famous art school, the **Slade**, which puts on temporary exhibitions in the **Strang Print Room**, in the south cloister of the main quadrangle (term time: Wed–Fri 1–5pm; free). Also on display in the south cloisters is the fully clothed skeleton of philosopher **Jeremy Bentham** (1748–1832), one of the university's founders, topped by a wax head and wide-brimmed hat.

The university also runs a couple of specialist museums. On the first floor of the Watson building, down Malet Place, the **Petrie Museum of Egyptian Archeology** (Tues–Fri 1–5pm, Sat 10am–1pm; free) has a couple of rooms jam-packed with antiquities, including the world's oldest dress. Tucked away in the southeast corner of Gordon Square, at no. 53, the **Percival David Foundation of Chinese Art** (Mon–Fri 10.30am–5pm; free) houses two floors of top-notch Chinese ceramics.

The British Library

After fifteen years of hassle and £500 million of public money, the new **British Library** (Mon & Wed–Fri 9.30am–6pm, Tues 9.30am–8pm, Sat 9.30am–5pm,

Sun 11am–5pm; free; ⓦwww.bl.uk; King's Cross or Euston tube), located on the busy Euston Road on the northern fringes of Bloomsbury, finally opened to the public in 1998. As the country's most expensive public building, it's hardly surprising that the place has come under fierce criticism from all sides. Architecturally the charge has been led, predictably enough, by Prince Charles, who compared it to an academy for secret policemen. Yet while it's true that the architect, Colin St John Wilson, has a penchant for red-brick brutalism that's horribly out of fashion, and compares unfavourably with its cathedralesque Victorian neighbour, the former Midland Grand Hotel, the interior of the library has met with general approval and the new high-tech exhibition galleries are superb.

With the exception of the reading rooms, the library is open to the general public. The three exhibition galleries are to the left as you enter; straight ahead is the spiritual heart of the BL, a multistorey glass-walled tower housing the vast **King's Library**, collected by George III and donated to the museum by George IV in 1823; to the side of the King's Library is the **philatelic collection**. If you want to explore the parts of the building not normally open to the public, you must sign up for a **guided tour** (Mon, Wed & Fri 3pm, Sat 10.30am & 3pm; Tues 6.30pm & Sun 11.30am & 3pm; to include the reading rooms; £6).

The first of the three exhibition galleries to head for is the dimly lit **John Ritblat Gallery**, where a superlative selection of the BL's ancient manuscripts, maps, documents and precious books, including the richly illustrated Lindisfarne Gospels, are displayed. One of the most appealing innovations is "**Turning the Pages**", a small room off the main gallery, where you can turn the pages of selected texts "virtually" on a computer terminal. The **Workshop of Words, Sounds and Images** is a hands-on exhibition of more universal appeal, where you can design your own literary publication, while the **Pearson Gallery of Living Words** puts on excellent temporary exhibitions, for which there is sometimes an admission charge.

Strand, Holborn and Clerkenwell

This area lies on the periphery of the entertainment zone of the West End and the financial district of the City. The **Strand**, as its name suggests, once lay along the riverbank: it achieved its present-day form when the Victorians shored up the banks of the Thames to create the Embankment. **Holborn** (pronounced "Ho-burn"), to the northeast, has long been associated with the law, and its **Inns of Court** make for an interesting stroll, their archaic, cobbled precincts exuding the rarefied atmosphere of an Oxbridge college, and sheltering one of the city's oldest churches, the twelfth-century **Temple Church**. Close by the Inns, in Lincoln's Inn Fields, is the **Sir John Soane's Museum**, one of the most memorable and enjoyable of London's small museums, packed with architectural illusions and an eclectic array of curios. **Clerkenwell**, further to the northeast, is off the tourist trail, but harbours the vestiges of two pre-Fire-of-London priories, and a whole host of trendy new bars and restaurants.

Strand and Embankment

Once famous for its riverside mansions, and later its music halls, the **Strand** – the main road connecting Westminster to the City – is a shadow of its former self. Nowadays, it's best known for the young homeless who shelter in the shop doorways at night. The **Victoria Embankment**, which runs parallel with the Strand, was built between 1868 and 1874 by the French engineer Joseph Bazalgette, whose project simultaneously relieved congestion along the Strand, provided an extension to the underground railway and sewage systems, and created a new stretch of parkland with a riverside walk – no longer much fun due to the volume of traffic.

London's oldest monument, **Cleopatra's Needle**, languishes little-noticed on the Thames side of the busy Victoria Embankment, guarded by two Victorian sphinxes. The 60-foot-high, 180-ton stick of granite in fact has nothing to do with Cleopatra – it's one of a pair erected in Heliopolis in 1475 BC (the other one is in New York's Central Park) and taken to Alexandria by the Emperor Augustus fifteen years after Cleopatra's suicide. This obelisk was presented to Britain in 1819 by the Turkish viceroy of Egypt, but nearly sixty years passed before it finally made its way to London.

The **Benjamin Franklin House** (☎020/7930 9121, ⓦwww.rsa.org.uk/franklin; Charing Cross or Embankment tube), on the other side of Charing Cross Station at 36 Craven St, will probably attract more visitors than Cleopatra's Needle. Restored with the help of, among others, the nearby Royal Society of Arts, the museum should be open early in 2002. The tenth son of a candlemaker, Franklin (1706–1790) had "genteel lodgings" here more or less continuously from 1757 to 1775. Whilst Franklin was espousing the cause of the British colonies (as the US then was), the house served as the first de facto American Embassy; eventually, he returned to America to help draft the Declaration of Independence, negotiate the peace treaty with Britain and frame the Constitution.

Aldwych

The wide crescent of **Aldwych**, forming a neat "D" with the eastern part of the Strand, was driven through the slums of this zone in the last throes of the Victorian era. A confident ensemble occupies the centre, with the enormous **Australia House** and **India House** sandwiching **Bush House**, home of the BBC's World Service (ⓦwww.bbc.co.uk/worldservice; Holborn tube) since 1940. Despite its thoroughly British associations, Bush House was actually built by the American speculator Irving T. Bush, whose planned trade-centre flopped in the 1930s. The giant figures on the north facade and the inscription, "To the Eternal Friendship of English-speaking Nations", thus refer to the friendship between the US and Britain, and are not, as many people assume, the declaratory manifesto of the current occupants.

Somerset House

South of Aldwych and the Strand stands **Somerset House** (ⓦwww.somerset-house.org.uk; Temple – Mon–Sat only – or Covent Garden tube), sole survivor of the grandiose edifices which once lined this stretch of the riverfront, its four wings enclosing a large courtyard rather like a Parisian *hôtel*. The present building was begun in 1776 by William Chambers as a purpose-built governmental office development. There are now three entrances – off the Strand, via a terrace off Waterloo Bridge, and straight from the Victoria Embankment – all of which will bring you eventually to the main courtyard (daily 7.30am–11pm), which is centred on a startling 55-jet fountain that spouts straight from the cobbles from spring to autumn.

The south wing, overlooking the Thames, now houses the magnificent **Gilbert Collection** (Mon–Sat 10am–6pm, Sun noon–6pm; £4, free Mon 10am–2pm; £7 joint ticket with the Courtauld; ⓦwww.gilbert-collection .org.uk), a new museum of decorative arts displaying European silver and gold, micro-mosaics, clocks, portrait miniatures and snuffboxes. While there's no denying the outstanding craftsmanship of the pieces that attracted the magpie-like attention of the Beverley Hills-based collector Arthur Gilbert, the sheer opulence and gaudiness of many of the exhibits may prove too much for some. Also housed in the south wing are the **Hermitage Rooms** (Mon–Sat 10am–6pm, Sun noon–6pm; £6; ⓦwww.hermitagerooms.com), five galleries featuring changing exhibitions of similarly over-the-top *objets d'art* – drawn from St Petersburg's Hermitage Museum (housed in the Winter Palace).

Part of the north wing has, for some time now, been home to the galleries of the **Courtauld** (Mon–Sat 10am–6pm, Sun noon–6pm; £4, free Mon 10am–2pm; £7 joint ticket with the Gilbert Collection; ⓦwww .courtauld.ac.uk; Temple – Mon–Sat only – or Covent Garden tube), chiefly known for its dazzling collection of Impressionist and Post-Impressionist paintings, whose virtue is quality rather than quantity. Among works by Gauguin, Toulouse-Lautrec, Seurat, Van Gogh and Modigliani, are one or two highly prized paintings: a small-scale version of Manet's *Déjeuner sur l'herbe*, Renoir's *La Loge* and Degas' *Two Dancers*, plus a whole heap of Cézanne's canvases, including one of his series of *Card Players*. The Courtauld also boasts earlier works by the likes of Rubens, van Dyck, Tiepolo and Cranach the Elder. During the course of 2002, the Courtauld plan to move their permanent collection into the south wing, leaving the north wing for large temporary exhibitions.

Temple and the Royal Courts of Justice

Temple is the largest and most complex of the Inns of Court, where every barrister in England must study before being called to the Bar. Temple itself is comprised of two Inns – **Middle Temple** (ⓦwww.middletemple.org.uk) and **Inner Temple** (ⓦwww.innertemple.org.uk) – both of which lie to the south of the Strand, and, strictly speaking, just within the boundaries of the City of London. A few very old buildings survive here, but the overall scene is dominated by the soulless neo-Georgian reconstructions that followed the devastation of the Blitz. Still, the maze of courtyards and passageways is fun to explore – especially after dark, when Temple is gas-lit.

There are several points of access, simplest of which is Devereux Court. Medieval students ate, attended lectures and slept in the **Middle Temple Hall** (Mon–Fri 10am–noon & 3–4pm; Temple tube – Mon–Sat only – or Blackfriars), across the courtyard, still the Inn's main dining room. The present building was constructed in the 1560s and provided the setting for many great Elizabethan masques and plays – probably including Shakespeare's *Twelfth Night*, which is believed to have been premiered here in 1602. The hall is worth a visit for its fine hammer-beam roof, wooden panelling and decorative Elizabethan screen.

The two Temple Inns share use of the complex's oldest building, **Temple Church** (Wed–Sun 11am–4pm; Temple tube – Mon–Sat only – or Blackfriars), built in 1185 by the Knights Templar. An oblong chancel was added in the thirteenth century, and the whole building was damaged in the Blitz, but the original round church – modelled on the Church of the Holy Sepulchre in Jerusalem – still stands, with its striking Purbeck marble piers, recumbent marble effigies of knights and tortured grotesques grimacing in the spandrels of the blind arcading.

Across the Strand from Temple, the **Royal Courts of Justice** (Mon–Fri 8.30am–4.30pm; Temple tube – Mon–Sat only – or Blackfriars), are home to the Court of Appeal and the High Court, where the most important civil cases are tried. Appeals and libel suits are heard here – it was from here that the likes of the Guildford Four and Birmingham Six walked to freedom, and it is where countless pop and soap stars have battled it out with the tabloids. The fifty-odd courtrooms are open to the public, though you have to go through stringent security checks first (strictly no cameras allowed).

Lincoln's Inn Fields

North of the Law Courts lies **Lincoln's Inn Fields**, London's largest square, laid out in the early 1640s with **Lincoln's Inn** (Mon–Fri 9am–6pm; Ⓦwww.lincolnsinn.org.uk; Holborn tube), the first – and in many ways the prettiest – of the Inns of Court on its east side. The Inn's fifteenth-century **Old Hall** is open by appointment only (☎020/7405 1393), but you can view the early seventeenth-century **chapel** (Mon–Fri noon–2pm), with its unusual fan-vaulted open undercroft and, on the first floor, its late Gothic nave, hit by a Zeppelin in World War I and much restored since.

The south side of Lincoln's Inn Fields is occupied by the gigantic **Royal College of Surgeons** (Ⓦwww.rcseng.ac.uk), home to the **Hunterian Museum** (Mon–Fri 9am–5pm; free; Holborn tube), a fascinating collection of pickled bits and bobs. Also on view are the skeletons of the Irish giant, O'Brien (1761–83), who was seven feet ten inches tall, and the Sicilian midget Caroline Crachami (1815–24), who was just one foot ten and a half inches when she died at the age of 9.

A group of buildings on the north side of Lincoln's Inn Fields house **Sir John Soane's Museum** (Tues–Sat 10am–5pm; first Tues of the month also 6–9pm; free; Ⓦwww.soane.org; Holborn tube), one of London's best-kept secrets. The chief architect of the Bank of England, Soane (1753–1837) was an avid collector who designed this house not only as a home and office, but also as a place to stash his large collection of art and antiquities. Arranged much as it was in his lifetime, the ingeniously planned house has an informal, treasure-hunt atmosphere, with surprises in every alcove. At 2.30pm every Saturday, a fascinating, hour-long **free guided tour** takes you round the museum and the enormous research library, next door, containing architectural drawings, books and exquisitely detailed cork and wood models.

Gray's Inn and Staple Inn

North of Lincoln's Inn, **Gray's Inn** (Mon–Fri 10am–4pm; Ⓦwww.graysinn .org.uk; Chancery Lane tube – Mon–Sat only – or Holborn), entered from High Holborn, is named for the de Grey family, who owned the original mansion. The entrance is through an anonymous cream-coloured building next door to the venerable *Cittie of Yorke* pub. Established in the fourteenth century, most of what you see today was rebuilt after the Blitz, with the exception of the **hall** (by appointment only; ☎020/7458 7800), with its fabulous Tudor screen and stained glass, where the premiere of Shakespeare's *Comedy of Errors* is thought to have taken place in 1594.

Heading east along High Holborn, it's worth pausing to admire **Staple Inn** on the right, not one of the Inns of Court, but one of the now defunct Inns of Chancery, which used to provide a sort of foundation course for those aspiring to the Bar. Its overhanging half-timbered facade and gables date from the sixteenth century and are the most extensive in the whole of London; they survived the Great Fire, which stopped just short of Holborn Circus, but had to be extensively rebuilt after the Blitz.

Clerkenwell

Poverty and overcrowding were the main features of nineteenth-century Clerkenwell, and **Clerkenwell Green** became known in the press as "the headquarters of republicanism, revolution and ultra-non-conformity". The Green's connections with **radical politics** have continued into this century, and its oldest building, built as a Welsh Charity School in 1737, is now home to the **Marx Memorial Library** (Mon 1–6pm, Tues–Thurs 1–8pm, Sat 10am–1pm; free; Ⓦ www.marxmemoriallibrary.sageweb.co.uk; Farringdon tube), at no. 37a. One-time headquarters of the Social Democratic Federation press, this is where **Lenin** edited seventeen editions of the Bolshevik paper *Iskra* in 1902–03. Visitors are welcome to visit the poky little back room where he worked, which is maintained as it was then, as a kind of shrine.

Of Clerkenwell's three medieval religious establishments, remnants of two survive, hidden away to the southeast of Clerkenwell Green. The oldest is the priory of the Order of St John of Jerusalem; the sixteenth-century **St John's Gate** (Mon–Fri 10am–5pm, Sat 10am–4pm; free; Ⓦ www.sja.org.uk/history; Farringdon tube), on the south side of Clerkenwell Road, is the most visible survivor of the foundation. Today, the gatehouse forms part of a **museum**, which traces the development of the order before its dissolution in this country by Henry VIII, and its re-establishment in the nineteenth century. In 1877, the St John Ambulance was founded to provide a voluntary first-aid service to the public. It's in this field that the order is now best known in Britain, and a splendid new interactive gallery is now devoted to the history of the service. To get to see the rest of the gatehouse, and to visit the Norman crypt of the Grand Priory Church over the road, you must take a **guided tour** (Tues, Fri & Sat 11am & 2.30pm; £4).

A little to the southeast of St John's, on the edge of Smithfield, lies **Charterhouse** (guided tours only: April–July Wed 2.15pm; £3; Barbican tube), founded in 1371 as a Carthusian monastery. The public school, with which the foundation is now most closely associated, moved out to Surrey in 1872, but forty-odd pensioners – known, in the monastic tradition, as "brothers" – continue to be cared for here. The only way to visit the site is to join one of the exhaustive two-hour **guided tours**, which start at the gatehouse on Charterhouse Square. Very little remains of the original monastic buildings, but there's plenty of Tudor architecture to admire, dating from after the Dissolution when Charterhouse was rebuilt as a private residence.

The City

The City is where London began. Long established as the financial district, it stretches from Temple Bar in the west to the Tower of London in the east – administrative boundaries that are only slightly larger than those marked by the Roman walls and their medieval successors. However, in this Square Mile (as the City is sometimes referred to), you'll find few leftovers of London's early days, since four-fifths of the area burnt down in the Great Fire of 1666. Rebuilt in brick and stone, the City gradually lost its centrality as London swelled west-

The Corporation of London

The one unchanging aspect of the City is its special status, conferred on it by William the Conqueror and extended and reaffirmed by successive monarchs and governments ever since. Nowadays, with its Lord Mayor, its Beadles, Sheriffs and Aldermen, its separate police force and its select electorate of freemen and liverymen, the City is an anachronism of the worst kind. **The Corporation** (ⓦwww.corpoflondon.gov.uk), which runs the City like a one-party mini-state, is an unreconstructed old boys' network whose medievalist pageantry camouflages the very real power and wealth which it holds – the Corporation owns nearly a third of the Square Mile (and several tracts of land elsewhere in and around London). Its anomalous status is all the more baffling when you consider that the City was once the cradle of British democracy: it was the City that traditionally stood up to bullying sovereigns.

wards, though it has maintained its position as Britain's financial heartland. What you see on the ground is mostly the product of three fairly recent building phases: the Victorian construction boom of the late nineteenth century; the overzealous postwar reconstruction following the Blitz and the money-grabbing frenzy of the Thatcherite 1980s, in which nearly fifty percent of the City's office space was rebuilt.

When you consider what has happened here, it's amazing that so much has survived to pay witness to the City's two-thousand-year history. Wren's spires still punctuate the skyline here and there and his masterpiece, **St Paul's Cathedral**, remains one of London's geographical pivots. At the eastern edge of the City, the **Tower of London** still stands protected by some of the best-preserved medieval fortifications in Europe. Other relics, such as the City's few surviving medieval alleyways, Wren's **Monument** to the Great Fire and London's oldest synagogue and church, are less conspicuous, and even locals have problems finding the more modern attractions of the **Museum of London** and the **Barbican** arts complex.

Perhaps the biggest change of all, though, has been in the City's population. Up until the eighteenth century the majority of Londoners lived and worked in or around the City; nowadays 300,000 commuters spend the best part of Monday to Friday here, but only 5000 people remain at night and at weekends. The result of this demographic shift is that the City is fully alive only during office hours. This means that weekdays are by far the best time to visit; many pubs, restaurants and even some tube stations and tourist sights close down at the weekend.

Fleet Street

In 1500 a certain Wynkyn de Worde, a pupil of William Caxton, moved the Caxton presses from Westminster to **Fleet Street**, to be close to the lawyers of the Inns of Court and to the clergy of St Paul's. However, the street really boomed two hundred years later when, in 1702, the now-defunct *Daily Courant*, Britain's first daily newspaper, was published here. By the nineteenth century all the major national and provincial dailies had their offices and printing presses in the Fleet Street district, a situation that prevailed until the 1980s, when the press barons relocated their operations elsewhere.

The best source of information about the old-style Fleet Street is the so-called "journalists' and printers' cathedral", the church of **St Bride's** (Mon–Sat 8am–5pm; Blackfriars tube), which boasts Wren's tallest and most exquisite spire (said to be the inspiration for the tiered wedding cake). The crypt contains a little museum of Fleet Street history, with information on the *Daily Courant* and the *Universal Daily Register*, which later became *The Times*, claiming to be "the faithful recorder of every species of intelligence...circulated for a particular set of readers only."

The western section of Fleet Street was spared the Great Fire, which stopped just short of **Prince Henry's Room** (Mon–Sat 11am–2pm; free), a fine Jacobean house with timber-framed bay windows. The first-floor room now contains material relating to the diarist **Samuel Pepys**, who was born nearby in Salisbury Court in 1633 and baptized in St Bride's. Even if you've no interest in Pepys, the wooden-panelled room is worth a look – it contains one of the finest Jacobean plasterwork ceilings in London, and a lot of original stained glass.

Numerous narrow alleyways lead off the north side of Fleet Street, two of which – Bolt Court and Hind Court – eventually open out into Gough Square, on which stands **Dr Johnson's House** (May–Sept Mon–Sat 11am–5.30pm; Oct–April Mon–Sat 11am–5pm; £3; Ⓦwww.drjh.dircon.co.uk). The great savant, writer and lexicographer lived here from 1747 to 1759, whilst compiling the 41,000 entries for the first dictionary of the English language, two first editions of which can be seen in the grey-panelled rooms of the house. You can also view the open-plan attic, in which Johnson and his six helpers put together the dictionary.

St Paul's Cathedral

St Paul's Cathedral (Mon–Sat 8.30am–4pm; £5; Ⓦstpauls.co.uk; St Paul's tube), topped by an enormous lead-covered dome that's second in size only to St Peter's in Rome, has been a London icon since the Blitz, when it stood defiantly unscathed amid the carnage (or so it appeared on wartime propaganda photos). It remains a dominating presence in the City, despite the encroaching tower blocks – its showpiece west facade is particularly magnificent, and is at its most impressive at night when bathed in sea-green arc lights. Westminster Abbey has the edge, however, when it comes to celebrity corpses, pre-Reformation sculpture, royal connections and sheer atmosphere. St Paul's, by contrast, is a soulless but perfectly calculated architectural set-piece, a burial place for captains rather than kings, though it does contain more artists than Westminster Abbey. The cathedral's services, featuring the renowned St Paul's choir, are held from Monday to Saturday at 5pm and on Sunday at 10.15am, 11.30am and 3.15pm.

The best place from which to appreciate the glory of St Paul's is beneath the **dome**, decorated (against Wren's wishes) by Thornhill's trompe l'oeil frescoes. By far the most richly decorated section of the cathedral, however, is the **chancel**, in particular the spectacular, swirling, gilded mosaics of birds, fish, animals and greenery, dating from the 1890s. The intricately carved oak and limewood **choir stalls**, and the imposing organ case, are the work of Wren's master carver, Grinling Gibbons. Meanwhile, in the south-choir aisle, is the only complete effigy to have survived from Old St Paul's, the upstanding shroud of **John Donne**, poet, preacher and one-time Dean of St Paul's.

A series of stairs, beginning in the south aisle, lead to the dome's three **galleries**, the first of which is the internal **Whispering Gallery**, so called because of its acoustic properties – words whispered to the wall on one side are distinctly audible over one hundred feet away on the other, though the place is usually so busy you can't hear very much above the hubbub except a ghostly murmur. The other two galleries are exterior: the **Stone Gallery**, around the

The City churches

The City of London boasts over forty churches (Ⓦ www.london-city-churches.org), the majority of them built or rebuilt by Wren after the Great Fire. As a general rule, weekday lunchtimes are the best time to visit these churches, many of which put on free lunchtime concerts for the local wage slaves.

On the surface, many of the City churches appear quite similar: plain, light-filled interiors, with white, gold and dark wood furnishings. Below is a list of six of the most varied and interesting churches within the Square Mile:

St Bartholomew-the-Great Cloth Fair; Barbican tube. The oldest surviving church in the City and by far the most atmospheric; a fascinating building. St Paul's aside, if you visit just one church in the City, it should be this one.

St Mary Abchurch Abchurch Lane, Cannon Street; Cannon Street or Bank tube. Uniquely for Wren's City churches, the interior features a huge painted domed ceiling, plus the only authenticated Gibbons reredos.

St Mary Aldermary Queen Victoria Street; Mansion House tube. Wren's most successful stab at Gothic, with fan vaulting in the aisles and a panelled ceiling in the nave.

St Mary Woolnoth Lombard Street; Bank tube. Hawksmoor's only City church, sporting an unusually broad, bulky tower and a Baroque clerestory that floods the church with light from its semicircular windows.

St Olave Hart Street; Tower Hill tube. Built in the fifteenth century, and one of the few pre-Fire Gothic churches in the City.

St Stephen Walbrook Walbrook; Bank tube. Wren's dress rehearsal for St Paul's, with a wonderful central dome and plenty of woodcarving by Gibbons.

balustrade at the base of the dome, and ultimately the **Golden Gallery**, below the golden ball and cross which top the cathedral.

Although the nave is crammed full of overblown monuments to military types, burials in St Paul's are confined to the **crypt**, reputedly the largest in Europe. The whitewashed walls and bright lighting, however, make this one of the least atmospheric mausoleums you could imagine. Immediately to your right you'll find **Artists' Corner**, which boasts as many painters and architects as Westminster Abbey has poets, including Christopher Wren himself, who was commissioned to build the cathedral after its Gothic predecessor was destroyed in the Great Fire. The crypt's two other star tombs are those of **Nelson** and **Wellington**, both occupying centre stage and both with more fanciful monuments upstairs.

Museum of London and the Barbican

Despite London's long pedigree, very few of its ancient structures are now standing. However, numerous Roman, Saxon and Elizabethan remains have been discovered during the City's various rebuildings and many of these finds are now displayed at the **Museum of London** (Mon–Sat 10am–5.50pm, Sun noon–5.50pm; free; St Paul's or Barbican tube), hidden above the western end of London Wall, in the southwestern corner of the Barbican complex. The museum's permanent exhibition is basically an educational trot through London's history from prehistory to the present day. This is interesting enough (and attracts a lot of school groups), but the real strength of the museum lies in the excellent temporary exhibitions, lectures, walks and videos it organizes throughout the year.

The City's only large residential complex is the **Barbican**, a phenomenally ugly and expensive concrete ghetto built on the heavily bombed Cripplegate area. The zone's solitary prewar building is the heavily restored sixteenth-century church of **St Giles Cripplegate** (Mon–Fri 9.30am–5.15pm, Sat 9am–noon); it is situated across from the famously user-repellent **Barbican Arts Centre**, the "City's gift to the nation", which was formally opened in 1982. The complex does, however, serve as home to the London Symphony Orchestra and the London chapter of the Royal Shakespeare Company, and holds various free gigs in the foyer.

Guildhall

Situated at the geographical centre of the City, **Guildhall** (May–Sept daily 10am–5pm; Oct–April Mon–Sat 10am–5pm; free; Ⓦ www.corpoflondon.gov .uk; St Paul's or Bank tube) has been the ancient seat of the City administration for over eight hundred years. It remains the headquarters of the Corporation of London, and is still used for many of the City's formal civic occasions. Architecturally, however, it is not quite the beauty it once was, having been badly damaged in both the Great Fire and the Blitz, and scarred by the addition of a grotesque 1970s concrete cloister and wing.

Nonetheless, the **Great Hall**, basically a postwar reconstruction of the fifteenth-century original, is worth a brief look, as is the **Guildhall Clock Museum** (Mon–Fri 9.30am–4.30pm; free), a collection of over six hundred timepieces, including one of the clocks that won John Harrison the Longitude prize (see p.144). Also worth a visit is the new, purpose-built **Guildhall Art Gallery** (Mon–Sat 10am–5pm, Sun noon–4pm; £2.50, free on Fri and daily after 3.30pm; Ⓦ www.guildhall-art-gallery.org.uk), which contains one or two exceptional works, such as Rossetti's *La Ghirlandata*, and Holman Hunt's *The Eve of St Agnes*, plus a massive painting depicting the 1782 Siege of Gibraltar, commissioned by the Corporation.

The financial centre

Bank is the finest architectural arena in the City. Heart of the finance sector and the busy meeting point of eight streets, it's overlooked by a handsome collection of Neoclassical buildings – among them, the Bank of England, the Royal Exchange and Mansion House (the Lord Mayor's official residence) – each one faced in Portland Stone.

Sadly, only the **Bank of England** (Ⓦ www.bankofengland.co.uk), which stores the nation's vast gold reserves in its vaults, actually encourages visitors. Established in 1694 by William III to raise funds for the war against France, the so-called "Grand Old Lady of Threadneedle Street" wasn't erected on its present site until 1734. All that remains of the building on which Sir John Soane spent the best part of his career from 1788 onwards is the windowless, outer curtain wall, which wraps itself round the three-and-a-half-acre island site. However, you can view a reconstruction of Soane's Bank Stock Office, with its characteristic domed skylight, in the **museum** (Mon–Fri 10am–5pm; free; Bank tube), which has its entrance on Bartholomew Lane.

East of Bank, beyond Bishopsgate, stands Richard Rogers' glitzy **Lloyd's Building**, completed in 1984. A startling array of glass and blue steel pipes – a vertical version of Rogers' own Pompidou Centre – this is easily the most popular of the modern City buildings, at least with the general public. However, it's due to be upstaged by Norman Foster's "upside-down ice-cream cone" building for **Swiss Re** currently being built on the site of the Old Baltic Exchange.

Just south of the Lloyd's building you'll find the picturesque **Leadenhall Market**, whose richly painted, graceful Victorian cast-ironwork dates from 1881. Inside, the traders cater mostly for the lunchtime City crowd, their barrows laden with exotic seafood and game, fine wines, champagne and caviar.

If you walk down Gracechurch Street from Leadenhall Market, you should be able to make out Wren's **Monument** (daily 10am–5.40pm; £1.50; Monument tube), which was designed by Wren to commemorate the Great Fire of 1666. Crowned with spiky gilded flames, this plain Doric column stands 202 feet high, making it the tallest isolated stone column in the world; if it were laid out flat it would touch the bakery where the Fire started, east of Monument. The bas-relief on the base, now in very bad shape, depicts Charles II and the Duke of York in Roman garb conducting the emergency relief operation. The 311 steps to the viewing gallery once guaranteed an incredible view; nowadays it is dwarfed by the buildings around it.

The Tower of London

The **Tower of London** (March–Oct Mon–Sat 9am–5pm, Sun 10am–5pm; Nov–Feb Mon & Sun 10am–4pm, Tues–Sat 9am–4pm; £11.30; Ⓦ www.hrp .org.uk; Tower Hill tube), one of London's main tourist attractions, overlooks the river at the eastern boundary of the old city walls. Despite all the hype and heritage claptrap, it remains one of London's most remarkable buildings, site of some of the goriest events in the nation's history and somewhere all visitors and Londoners should explore at least once. Chiefly famous as a place of imprisonment and death, it has variously been used as a royal residence, armoury, mint, menagerie, observatory and – a function it still serves – a safe-deposit box for the Crown Jewels.

Amidst the crush of tourists and the weight of history surrounding the place, it's easy to forget that the Tower is, above all, the most perfectly preserved (albeit heavily restored) medieval fortress in the country. Begun by William the Conqueror as a simple watchtower, much of what's visible today was already in place by the end of the thirteenth century. Before you set off to explore the Tower complex, it's a good idea to get your bearings by taking one of the free **guided tours**, given every thirty minutes by one of the forty-odd **Beefeaters** (officially known as Yeoman Warders), ex-servicemen in Tudor costume, who can get you into areas otherwise inaccessible.

Visitors today enter the Tower along Water Lane, but in times gone by most prisoners were delivered through **Traitors' Gate**, on the waterfront. The nearby **Bloody Tower**, which forms the main entrance to the Inner Ward, is where the 12-year-old Edward V and his 10-year-old brother were accommodated "for their own safety" in 1483 by their uncle, the future Richard III, and later murdered. It's also where **Sir Walter Raleigh** was imprisoned on three separate occasions, including a thirteen-year stretch.

The **White Tower**, at the centre of the Inner Ward, is the original "Tower", begun in 1076, and now home to displays from the **Royal Armouries**, the majority of which now reside in Leeds (see p.650). Even if you've no interest in military paraphernalia, you should at least pay a visit to the **Chapel of St John**, a beautiful Norman structure on the second floor that was completed in 1080 – making it the oldest intact church building in London. To the west of the White Tower is the execution spot on **Tower Green** where seven highly placed but unlucky individuals were beheaded, among them Anne Boleyn and her cousin Catherine Howard (Henry VIII's second and fifth wives).

The Waterloo Barracks, to the north of the White Tower, hold the **Crown Jewels**, perhaps the major reason so many people flock to the Tower; however, the moving walkways are disappointingly swift, allowing you just 28 seconds' viewing during peak periods. The oldest piece of regalia is the twelfth-century **Anointing Spoon**, but the vast majority of exhibits postdate the Commonwealth (1649–60), when many of the royal riches were melted down for coinage or sold off. Among the jewels are the three largest cut diamonds in the world, including the legendary **Koh-i-Noor**, set into the Queen Mother's Crown in 1937.

The Tower is also home to eight **ravens**, their wings clipped so they can't fly away – legend says that the Tower and the kingdom will fall if they do. The birds are descendants of early scavengers attracted by the waste from palace kitchens, and are the latest in a long line protected by royal decree since the reign of Charles II. They even have their own graveyard, in the moat near the ticket barrier.

Tower Bridge

Tower Bridge (April–Oct 10am–6.30pm; Nov–March 9.30am–6pm; guided tour £6.25; Ⓦ www.towerbridge.org.uk; Tower Hill tube) is less than 110 years old, yet it ranks with Big Ben as the most famous of all London landmarks. Completed in 1894, its neo-Gothic towers are clad in Cornish granite and Portland stone, but conceal a steel frame, which, at the time, represented a considerable engineering achievement, allowing a road crossing that could be raised to give tall ships access to the upper reaches of the Thames. The raising of the bascules (from the French for "see-saw") remains an impressive sight (ring ahead to find out when the next opening is). The elevated walkways linking the summits of the towers (intended for public use) were closed from 1909 to 1982 due to their popularity with prostitutes and the suicidal. You can only visit them now on an overpriced **guided tour**, dubbed the "Tower Bridge Experience", that employs videos and an animatronic chirpy Cockney to describe the history of the bridge.

The East End and Docklands

Few places in London have engendered so many myths as the **East End** (a catch-all title which covers just about everywhere east of the City, but has its heart closest to the latter). Its name is synonymous with slums, sweatshops and crime, as epitomized by antiheroes such as Jack the Ripper and the Kray Twins, but also with the rags-to-riches careers of the likes of Harold Pinter and Vidal Sassoon, and whole generations of Jews who were born in the most notorious of London's cholera-ridden quarters and have now moved to wealthier pastures. Old East Enders will tell you that the area's not what it was – and it's true, as it always has been. The East End is constantly changing as newly arrived immigrants assimilate and move out.

The East End's first immigrants were French Protestant Huguenots, fleeing religious persecution in the late seventeenth century. Within three generations the Huguenots were entirely assimilated, and the Irish became the new immigrant population, but it was the influx of Jews escaping pogroms in eastern Europe and Russia that defined the character of the East End in the second half of the nineteenth century. The area's Jewish population has now dispersed throughout London, though the East End remains at the bottom of the pile; even the millions poured into the **Docklands** development have failed to make much impression on local unemployment and housing problems.

Unfortunately, racism is still rife, and is directed, for the most part, against the extensive Bengali community, who came here from the poor rural area of Sylhet in Bangladesh in the 1960s and 1970s.

Most visitors to the East End come for its famous Sunday **markets** since the area is not an obvious place for sightseeing, and certainly no beauty spot – Victorian slum clearances, Hitler's bombs and postwar tower blocks have all left their mark. However, there's plenty more to get out of a visit, including several **Hawksmoor churches**, and the vast **Canary Wharf** redevelopment, which has to be seen to be believed.

Whitechapel and Spitalfields

The districts of **Whitechapel** and, in particular, **Spitalfields**, within sight of the sleek tower blocks of the financial sector, represent the old heart of the East End, where the French Huguenots settled in the seventeenth century, where the Jewish community was at its strongest in the late nineteenth century, and where today's Bengali community eats, sleeps, works and prays. If you visit just one area in the East End, it should be this zone, which preserves mementoes from each wave of immigration.

The easiest approach is from Liverpool Street Station, a short stroll west of **Spitalfields Market**, the strange-looking red-brick and green-gabled market hall that forms the centrepiece of the area. Originally built in 1893, the market was extended in the 1920s, and it is this extension which is now under threat of demolition to make way for more office blocks. The dominant architectural presence in Spitalfields is **Christ Church** (Mon–Fri 12.30–2.30pm), built between 1714 and 1729 to a characteristically bold design by Nicholas Hawksmoor and now facing the market hall. Best viewed from Brushfield Street, the church's main features are its huge 225-foot-high broach spire and a giant Tuscan portico, raised on steps and shaped like a Venetian window (a central arched opening flanked by two smaller rectangles), a motif repeated in the tower and doors.

Whitechapel Road – as Whitechapel High Street and the Mile End Road are collectively known – is still the East End's main street, shared by all the many races who live in the borough of Tower Hamlets. The East End institution that draws in more outsiders than any other is the **Whitechapel Art**

East End Sunday markets

Most visitors to the East End come here for the **Sunday markets**. Approaching from Liverpool Street, the first one you come to is **Petticoat Lane** (Sun 9am–2pm; Liverpool Street or Aldgate East tube), not one of London's prettiest streets, but one of its longest-running Sunday markets, specializing in cheap (and often pretty tacky) clothing. The authorities renamed the street Middlesex Street in 1830 to avoid the mention of ladies' underwear, but the original name has stuck.

To the north lies **Spitalfields Market** (organic market Fri & Sun 10am–5pm; general market Mon–Fri 11am–3pm & Sun 10am–5pm; Liverpool Street tube), once the capital's premier wholesale fruit and vegetable market, now specializing in organic food, plus clothes, crafts and jewellery. Further east lies **Brick Lane** (Sun 8am–1pm; Aldgate East, Shoreditch or Liverpool Street tube), heart of the Bengali community, famous for its bric-a-brac Sunday market, wonderful curry houses and nonstop bagel bakery, and now also something of a magnet for young designers. From Brick Lane's northernmost end, it's a short walk to **Columbia Road** (Sun 8am–1pm; bus #26 from Aldwych or Liverpool Street tube), the city's best market for flowers and plants.

Gallery (Tues & Thurs–Sun 11am–5pm, Wed 11am–8pm; free; ⓦwww .whitechapel.org), a little further up the High Street in a beautiful crenellated 1899 Arts and Crafts building by Charles Harrison Townsend, architect of the similarly audacious Horniman Museum (see p.141). The gallery stages some of London's most innovative exhibitions of contemporary art, as well as hosting the biennial Whitechapel Open, a chance for local artists to get their work shown to a wider audience.

Just before the point where Whitechapel Road turns into Mile End Road stands the gabled entrance to the former Albion Brewery, where the first bottled brown ale was produced in 1899. Next door lies the **Blind Beggar**, the East End's most famous pub since March 8, 1966, when Ronnie Kray walked into the crowded pub and shot gangland rival George Cornell for calling him a "fat poof". This murder spelled the end of the infamous Kray Twins, Ronnie and Reggie, both of whom were sentenced to life imprisonment, though their well-publicized gifts to local charities created a Robin Hood image that still persists in these parts of town.

East End museums

The East End boasts two fascinating museums, both of them open to the public free of charge. The easiest one to get to is the **Bethnal Green Museum of Childhood** (daily except Fri 10am–5.50pm; free; ⓦwww.vam.ac.uk), situated opposite Bethnal Green tube station. The open-plan, wrought-iron hall, originally part of (and still a branch of) the V&A museum (see p.129), was transported here in the 1860s to bring art to the East End. The variety of exhibits means that there's something here for everyone from 3 to 93, but the museum's most frequent visitors are children – that said, the displays are not very hands-on. The ground floor is best known for its unique collection of antique dolls' houses dating back to 1673. You'll need a pile of 20p pieces with you to work the automata – Wallace the Lion gobbling up Albert is always a favourite. Elsewhere, there are puppets, a jumble of toys, a vast doll collection and excellent temporary exhibitions.

The **Geffrye Museum** (Tues–Sat 10am–5pm, Sun noon–5pm; free; ⓦwww .geffrye-museum.org.uk; bus #67, #149 or #242 from Liverpool Street tube), housed in a peaceful little enclave of eighteenth-century ironmongers' almshouses, set back from Kingsland Road, is essentially a furniture museum. A series of period living rooms, ranging from the oak-panelled seventeenth century through refined Georgian and cluttered Victorian, leads to the state-of-the-art New Gallery Extension, housing the new café and the excellent twentieth-century section, with a room devoted to virtually every decade, and temporary exhibitions in the basement.

Docklands

The architectural embodiment of Thatcherism – a symbol of 1980s smash-and-grab culture according to its critics, a blueprint for inner-city regeneration to its free-market supporters – the **Docklands** redevelopment provokes extreme reactions. Despite its catch-all name, however, Docklands is far from homogeneous. Canary Wharf, with its Manhattan-style skyscraper, is only its most visible landmark; industrial-estate sheds and huge swathes of dereliction are more indicative. Wapping, the westernmost district, has retained much of its old Victorian warehouse architecture, while the Royal Docks, further east, are only just beginning to be transformed from an industrial wasteland.

Docklands transport

Although Canary Wharf is now on the Jubilee line, the best way to view Docklands is either from one of the **boats** that course up and down the Thames (see ⊕www .londontransport.co.uk/river), or from the driverless, overhead **Docklands Light Railway** (DLR; ⊕www.dlr.co.uk), which sets off from Bank and from Tower Gateway, close to Tower Hill tube. Travelcards are valid on the DLR, or you can get a City Flyer South ticket for £2.90, giving you unlimited travel between Tower Gateway or Bank and Lewisham for a whole day. Tour guides give a free running commentary on certain DLR trains that set off from Tower Gateway (Mon–Fri hourly 10am–2pm, Sat & Sun every 30min 11am–4pm; ☏020/7363 9511), but phone ahead to make sure. If you're heading for Greenwich, and fancy taking a boat back into town, it might be worth considering a Sail & Rail ticket (£8.30), which gives you unlimited travel on the DLR, plus a boat trip between Greenwich and Westminster piers.

The docks were originally built from 1802 onwards to relieve congestion on the Thames quays, and eventually became the largest enclosed cargo-dock system in the world. However, competition from the railways, and later, the development of container ships, signalled the closure of the docks in the 1960s. Then, at the height of the recession in the 1980s, regeneration began in earnest. No one thought the old docks could ever be rejuvenated, and twenty years on, more has been achieved than many thought possible (and less than some had hoped). Travelling through on the DLR overhead railway, Docklands comes over as an intriguing open-air design museum, not a place one would choose to live or work – most people stationed here still see it as a bleak business-oriented outpost – but a spectacular sight nevertheless.

Wapping to Limehouse

From the DLR, you get a good view of Hawksmoor's two other landmark East End churches; the first one is **St George-in-the-East**, built in 1726 and visible to the south just before you reach Shadwell station. It's easy to spot thanks to its four domed corner towers and distinctive west-end tower topped by an octagonal lantern. You're missing nothing by staying on the train, though, as the interior was devastated in the Blitz. As the DLR leaves Limehouse station and skirts Limehouse Basin marina, Hawksmoor's **St Anne's Church** is visible to the north. Begun in 1714 and dominated again by a gargantuan west tower, the church is topped by an octagonal lantern and adorned with the highest church clock in London. Again, the interior isn't worth the effort as it was badly damaged by fire in 1850.

An alternative to the DLR is to walk from Wapping to Limehouse, along the Thames Path, which sticks to, or close to, the riverbank. You begin at **St Katharine's Dock**, immediately east of the Tower of London, and the first of the old docks to be renovated way back in the 1970s. St Katharine's redeeming qualities are the old swing bridges and the boats themselves, many of which are beautiful old sailing ships. Continue along desolate **Wapping High Street**, lined with tall brick-built warehouses, most now tastefully converted into yuppie flats, and you will eventually find yourself in Limehouse, beyond which lies the Isle of Dogs. The fairly well-signposted walk is about two miles in length, and will bring you eventually to Westferry DLR station – for details of riverside pubs along the way, see p.161.

The Isle of Dogs

The Thames begins a dramatic horseshoe bend at Limehouse, thus creating the **Isle of Dogs**, currently the geographical and ideological heart of the new Docklands. The area reaches its apotheosis in **Canary Wharf** (Ⓦ www.canary-wharf.com), the strip of land in the middle of the former West India Docks, previously a destination for rum and mahogany, later tomatoes and bananas (from the Canary Islands – hence the name). The only really busy bit of the new Docklands, Canary Wharf is best known as the home of Britain's tallest building. Cesar Pelli's landmark tower is officially known as **One Canada Square**, and at 800ft, it's the highest building in Europe after Frankfurt's Messerturm. The world's first skyscraper to be clad in stainless steel, it's an undeniably impressive sight, both from a distance (its flashing pinnacle is a feature of the horizon at numerous points in London) and close up. Unless you work here, however, there is no access except to the ground-floor marble atrium.

The warehouses to the north of Canary Wharf are currently being converted into flats, bars, restaurants and a **Museum in Docklands** (for more information call Ⓣ 020/7515 1162 or visit the website Ⓦ www.museumindocklands.org; West India Quay DLR), and will include a thirty-storey tower block and a multiplex cinema. Unless you're keen to visit the museum, there's little point in getting off the DLR as it cuts right through the middle of the Canary Wharf office buildings under a parabolic steel and glass canopy.

The rest of the Isle of Dogs remains surreally lifeless, an uneasy mix of drab high-rises, council estates, warehouses converted into expensive apartments, and a lot of new architecture – some of it startling, some of it crass, much of it empty. If you're heading for Greenwich (see p.141), you have a choice: either get off at **Island Gardens**, Christopher Wren's favourite spot from which to contemplate his masterpieces across the river (the Royal Naval College and Royal Observatory), and walk through the 1902 foot-tunnel to Greenwich; alternatively, you can stay on the DLR, which now tunnels underneath the Thames, and alight at Cutty Sark station.

Lambeth and Southwark

Until well into the seventeenth century, the only reason for north-bank residents to cross the Thames, to what is now **Lambeth** and **Southwark**, was to visit the disreputable Bankside entertainment district around the south end of London Bridge, which lay outside the jurisdiction of the City. South London (a catch-all term for everything south of the river) still has a reputation, among north Londoners at least, as a boring, sprawling, residential district devoid of any local culture or life.

As it turns out, this is not too far from the truth: both boroughs are, for the most part, residential. However, along **Lambeth**'s riverbank harbour several important cultural institutions, collectively known as the **South Bank Centre**. Although a mess architecturally, these galleries, theatres and concert halls, plus the nearby **Imperial War Museum**, draw large numbers across the river.

There are even more sights further east along **Southwark**'s riverfront, most notably a reconstruction of Shakespeare's **Globe Theatre**, and the spectacular new **Tate Modern**, housed in a converted power station. Another rash of popular museums can be found along Clink Street and Tooley Street, while further east still, **Butler's Wharf** is a thriving little warehouse development centred on the excellent **Design Museum**.

The South Bank

In 1951, the South Bank Exhibition, held on derelict land south of the Thames, formed the centrepiece of the **Festival of Britain**, an attempt to revive postwar morale by celebrating the centenary of the Great Exhibition (when Britain really did rule over half the world). The most striking features of the site were the Royal Festival Hall (which still stands), the ferris wheel (which returned to the South Bank for the millennium), the saucer-shaped Dome of Discovery (inspiration for the current Millennium Dome), and the cigar-shaped Skylon tower.

The festival's success provided the impetus for the eventual creation of the **South Bank Centre** (Ⓦ www.sbc.org.uk), home to institutions such as the National Theatre, the National Film Theatre, the British Film Institute's new IMAX cinema, and the Museum of the Moving Image or MOMI (due to re-open in 2002). Sadly, the South Bank has become London's much unloved culture bunker, a mess of "weather-stained concrete, rain-swept walkways and urine-soaked stairs", as one critic aptly put it. On the plus side, the South Bank is currently under inspired artistic direction and stands at the heart of the capital's arts scene. Its unprepossessing appearance is softened, too, by its riverside location, its avenue of trees, its fluttering banners, excellent signposting, and its occasional buskers and skateboarders.

London Eye (Millennium Wheel) and County Hall

South of the South Bank Centre proper, beside County Hall, is London's most prominent new landmark, the Millennium Wheel or **London Eye** (daily: April–Sept 10am–8pm or later; Oct–March 10.30am–7pm; £9; Ⓣ0870/500 0600, Ⓦ www.ba-londoneye.com; Waterloo or Westminster tube), British Airways' magnificently graceful observation wheel which spins slowly and silently over the Thames. Standing 450ft high, the wheel is the largest ever built, and it's constantly in slow motion – a full-circle "flight" in one of its 32 pods takes around thirty minutes, and lifts you high above the city. It's one of the few places (apart from a plane window) from which London looks a manageable size, as you can see right out to the very edge of the city where the suburbs slip into the countryside. Queues can be bad at the weekend, and tickets are often completely sold out, so get there early or book in advance over the phone.

The colonnaded crescent of **County Hall** is the only truly monumental building in this part of town. Designed to house the London County Council, it was completed in 1933 and enjoyed its greatest moment of fame as the headquarters of the GLC (Greater London Council), abolished by Margaret Thatcher in 1986, leaving London as the only European city without an elected authority. Since May 2000, London has had its own elected mayor, the former GLC leader Ken Livingstone, as well as a GLA (Greater London Authority), which will eventually be housed in a new building near Tower Bridge. County Hall, meanwhile, is now in the hands of a Japanese property company, and currently houses two hotels, several restaurants, an amusement arcade, the London Aquarium and the Dalí Universe.

So far, the most popular attraction in County Hall is the **London Aquarium** (daily 10am–6pm or later; £8.75; Ⓦ www.londonaquarium.co.uk; Waterloo or Westminster tube), laid out across three floors of the basement. With some super-large tanks, and everything from dog-face puffers to piranhas, this is somewhere that's pretty much guaranteed to please younger kids. The "**Beach**", where children can actually stroke the (non-sting) rays, is particularly popular. Though impressive in scale, the aquarium is fairly conservative in design, however, with no walk-through tanks and only the very briefest of information on any of the fish.

Three giant surrealist sculptures on the riverside walkway in front of County Hall advertise the building's latest attraction, **Dalí Universe** (daily 10am–6pm; £8.50; ⓦ www.daliuniverse.com). There's no denying Salvador Dalí was an accomplished and prolific artist, but you'll be disappointed if you're expecting to see his "greatest hits" – those are scattered across the globe. Most of the works here are little-known bronze and glass sculptures, and various drawings from the many illustrated books which he published, ranging from works by Ovid to the Marquis de Sade. Aside from these, there's one of the numerous Lobster Telephones, which Edward James commissioned for his London home, a copy of his famous Mae West lips sofa, and the oil painting from the dream sequence in Hitchcock's movie *Spellbound*.

South of County Hall

On the south side of Westminster Bridge, in the midst of **St Thomas's Hospital**, on Lambeth Palace Road, is the **Florence Nightingale Museum** (Mon–Fri 10am–5pm, Sat & Sun 11.30am–4.30pm; £4.80; ⓦ www.florence-nightingale.co.uk; Westminster tube), celebrating the woman who revolutionized the nursing profession by establishing the first school of nursing at St Thomas's in 1859. The exhibition hits just the right note, putting the two years she spent in the Crimea in the context of a lifetime of tireless social campaigning. Exhibits include the white lantern that earned her the nickname "The Lady with the Lamp", and a reconstruction of a Crimean military hospital ward.

A short walk south of St Thomas's is the Kentish ragstone church of St Mary-at-Lambeth, which now contains a café and an unpretentious little **Museum of Garden History** (Feb to mid-Dec daily 10.30am–5pm; free). The graveyard has been transformed into a small seventeenth-century garden, where two interesting sarcophagi lurk among the foliage: one belongs to Captain Bligh, the commander of the *Bounty* in 1787; the other is a memorial to John Tradescant, gardener to James I and Charles I.

The domed building at the east end of Lambeth Road, formerly the infamous lunatic asylum of Bethlehem Royal Hospital (better known as Bedlam), is now the **Imperial War Museum** (daily 10am–6pm; free; ⓦ www.iwm.org.uk; Lambeth North or Elephant & Castle tube), by far the best military museum in the capital. The treatment of the subject is impressively wide-ranging and fairly sober, with the main hall's militaristic display of guns, tanks and planes offset by the lower-ground-floor array of documents and images attesting to the human damage of war. The museum also has a harrowing new **Holocaust Exhibition** (not recommended for children under 14), which pulls few punches, and has made a valiant attempt to avoid depicting the victims of the Holocaust as nameless masses by focusing on individual cases, and interspersing the archive footage with eyewitness accounts from contemporary survivors.

Southwark

Southwark – originally the name of the area around the southern end of London Bridge, but now a vast borough reaching as far south as Dulwich – was a lively Roman red-light district whose brothels continued to do a thriving illegal trade until 1161 when they were licensed by royal decree. This measure imposed various restrictions on the prostitutes, who could now be fined three shillings for "grimacing to passers-by", and brought in a lot of revenue for the bishops of Winchester, who owned the area for the four centuries after the Norman Conquest. Under the bishops' rule, bull- and bear-baiting, drinking, cockfighting and gambling were also rife, especially on **Bankside**, to the west. After 1556, Southwark came under the jurisdiction of the City, it was still not subject to its regulations on entertainment, and the area remained the pleasure quarter of Tudor and Stuart London, where brothels and other disreputable institutions banned in the City – notably theatres – continued to flourish until the Puritan purges of the 1640s.

Four hundred years on, and Bankside is once more a magnet for visitors and Londoners alike, thanks to the newly rebuilt **Globe Theatre** (where most of Shakespeare's plays had their first performances), and the **Tate Modern** art gallery housed in the old Bankside power station. In addition, the area will eventually be linked to St Paul's and the City by the notorious Norman Foster-designed **Millennium Bridge**, London's famous bouncing bridge, which wobbled so worryingly when it first opened in 2000 that it was closed indefinitely while the engineers tried to work out how to fix it. By the time you read this, London's first pedestrian-only Thames bridge and the first one to cross the river for over a century should finally be open for business.

Tate Modern

Bankside is dominated by the austere power station of the same name, which has been transformed by the Swiss duo Herzog and de Meuron into the **Tate Modern** (daily 10am–6pm; Fri & Sat till 10pm; free; ⓦwww.tate.org.uk; Southwark or Blackfriars tube). The conversion, completed in May 2000, has been masterfully executed, leaving plenty of the original feel of an industrial giant, while providing wonderfully light and spacious galleries in which to show off the Tate's vast international twentieth-century art collection. The best way to enter is down the ramp from the west, so you get the full effect of the stupendously large turbine hall. It's easy enough to find your way around the galleries, with levels 3 and 5 displaying the permanent collection, level 4 used for fee-paying temporary exhibitions, and level 7 home to a rooftop café with a great view over the Thames – eventually visitors are to be given access to a viewing platform at the top of the central chimney.

Given that Tate Modern is the largest modern art gallery in the world, you really need to spend the best part of a day here to do justice to the place. Pick up a plan (and, for an extra £1, an audioguide), and take the escalator to level 3. As at Tate Britain, the curators have eschewed the usual chronological approach through the "isms", and instead plumped for grouping works together thematically: Landscape/Matter/Environment, Still Life/Object/Real Life, History/Memory/Society and Nude/Action/Body. On the whole this works very well, though the early twentieth-century canvases, in their gilded frames, do struggle when made to compete with contemporary installations.

Although the displays change every six months or so, you're still pretty much guaranteed to see at least some works by **Monet** and Bonnard, Cubist pioneers **Picasso** and Braque, Surrealists such as **Dalí**, abstract artists such as **Mondrian**, Bridget Riley and Pollock, and Pop supremos **Warhol** and Lichtenstein. There are seminal works, including a replica of **Duchamp**'s urinal, entitled *Fountain* and signed "R. Mutt", Yves Klein's totally blue paintings and Carl André's trademark piles of bricks. And such is the space here that several artists get whole rooms to themselves, among them the painter Francis Bacon, Joseph Beuys and his shamanistic wax and furs, and **Mark Rothko**, whose abstract "Seagram Murals", originally destined for a posh restaurant in New York, have their own shrine-like room in the heart of the collection.

From the Globe to the Cathedral

Seriously dwarfed by the Tate Modern is the equally spectacular **Shakespeare's Globe Theatre** (ⓦwww.shakespeares-globe.org; Southwark or Blackfriars tube), a reconstruction of the polygonal playhouse where most of the Bard's later works were first performed, and which was originally erected on nearby Park Street in 1598. To find out more about Shakespeare and the history of Bankside, the Globe's pricey but stylish new **exhibition** (daily 9am–5pm; £7.50) is well worth a visit. It begins by detailing the long campaign by American actor Sam Wanamaker to have the Globe rebuilt, but it's the imaginative hands-on exhibits that really hit the spot. You can have a virtual play on medieval instruments such as the crumhorn or sackbut, prepare your own edition of Shakespeare, and feel the thatch, hazelnut-shell and daub used to build the theatre. Visitors also get taken on an informative **guided tour** round the theatre itself, except in the afternoons during the summer season, when you can only visit the exhibition (for a reduced entrance fee). You can also view the archeological remains of another Elizabethan playhouse, the **Rose Theatre**, nearby at 56 Park St (daily 10am–5pm; £3; ⓦwww.rdg.ac.uk/rose).

East of Bankside, beyond Southwark Bridge, is **Vinopolis** (daily 11am–6pm or later; £11.50; ⓦwww.evinopolis.com), a big-money venture discreetly housed in former wine vaults under the railway arches on Clink Street. The focus of the complex is the **"Wine Odyssey"**, a light-hearted trot through the world's wine regions, equipped with a CD audioguide. There are plenty of visual gags – you get to tour round the Italian vineyards on a Vespa – but the most appealing and educative aspect of the tour is the **wine-tasting**. Visitors get five generous samples – from champagne to vintage port – with the option of buying another five for a mere £2.50 extra.

Further down the suitably gloomy confines of dark and narrow Clink Street is the **Clink Prison Museum** (daily 10am–6pm; £4; ⓦwww.clink.co.uk; London Bridge tube), built on the site of the former Clink Prison, origin of the expression "in the clink". The prison began as a dungeon for disobedient clerics, built under the Bishop of Winchester's Palace – the rose window of the palace's Great Hall survives just east of the museum – and later became a dumping ground for heretics, prostitutes and a motley assortment of Bankside lowlife. Today's exhibition features a handful of prison life tableaux, and dwells on the torture and grim conditions within, but, given the rich history of the place, this is a disappointingly lacklustre museum.

An exact replica of the **Golden Hinde** (daily 10am to dusk; £3; ⓦwww .goldenhinde.co.uk), the galleon in which Sir Francis Drake sailed around the world from 1577 to 1580, nestles in St Mary Overie Dock, at the eastern end of Clink Street. The ship is surprisingly small, and its original crew of eighty-plus must have been cramped to say the least. There's a refreshing lack of interpretive panels, so it's worth paying the little bit extra and getting a guided tour from one of the folk in period garb – ring ahead to check a group hasn't booked the place up (☎0870/011 8700).

Close by the *Golden Hinde* stands **Southwark Cathedral**, built as the medieval Augustinian priory church of St Mary Overie, and given cathedral status only in 1905. Of the original thirteenth-century church, only the choir and retrochoir now remain, separated by a tall and beautiful stone Tudor screen, making them probably the oldest Gothic structures left in London. The nave was entirely rebuilt in the nineteenth century, but the cathedral contains numerous interesting monuments, from a thirteenth-century oak effigy of a knight to an early twentieth-century memorial to Shakespeare, whose brother is buried here.

The London Bridge area

The most educative and strangest of Southwark's museums is the **Old Operating Theatre Museum and Herb Garret** on St Thomas Street (daily 10am–4pm; £3.25; @www.thegarret.co.uk; London Bridge tube). Built in 1821 at the top of a church tower, where the hospital apothecary's herbs were stored, this women's operating theatre dates from the pre-anaesthetic era. Despite being entirely gore-free, the museum is as stomach-churning as the London Dungeon (see below). The surgeons who used this room would have concentrated on speed and accuracy (most amputations took less than a minute), but there was still a thirty percent mortality rate, with many patients simply dying of shock, and many more from bacterial infection, about which very little was known.

A walk under the railway bridges and down Tooley Street brings you to the vaults beneath the railway arches of London Bridge train station, which are now occupied by two museums. Young teenagers and the credulous probably get the most out of the ever-popular **London Dungeon** (daily: April–Sept 10am–5.30pm; Oct–March 10am–5pm; £10.95; @www.thedungeons.com; London Bridge tube) – to avoid the inevitable queue, buy your ticket from the nearby Southwark tourist office at 6 Tooley St. The life-sized waxwork tableaux inside include a man being hung, drawn and quartered and one being boiled alive, the general hysteria being boosted by actors, dressed as top-hatted Victorian vampires, pouncing out of the darkness. Visitors are then herded into a court room, condemned to the "River of Death" boat ride, and forced to endure the "Jack the Ripper Experience", an exploitative trawl through post-mortem photos and wax mock-ups of the victims, followed by the "Great Fire of London", in which visitors get to experience the heat and the smell of the plague-ridden city, before being forced to walk through a revolving tunnel of flames.

A little further east on Tooley Street is **Winston Churchill's Britain at War** (daily: April–Sept 10am–5.30pm; Oct–March 10am–4.30pm; £5.95; @www.britainatwar.co.uk; London Bridge tube), an illuminating insight into the stiff-upper-lip London mentality during the Blitz. The museum contains hundreds of wartime artefacts, including an Anderson shelter, where you can hear the chilling sound of the V1 "doodlebugs" and tune in to contemporary radio broadcasts. The grand finale is a walk through the chaos of a just-bombed street.

There's more World War II history, from a more aggressive angle, at **HMS Belfast** (daily: March–Oct 10am–6pm; Nov–Feb 10am–5pm; £5.40; @www.iwm.org.uk; London Bridge tube), a huge cruiser permanently moored between London Bridge and Tower Bridge. Armed with six torpedoes and six-inch guns with a range of over fourteen miles, the *Belfast* spent over two years of the war in the Royal Naval shipyards, after being hit by a mine in the Firth of Forth at the beginning of hostilities. It later saw action in the Barents Sea and again during the Korean War, before being decommissioned. To find out more about the *Belfast*, head for the exhibition on level 5; otherwise the ship is a bit short on information, but the maze of cabins is fun to explore.

Butler's Wharf

In contrast to the brash offices on Tooley Street, **Butler's Wharf**, east of Tower Bridge, has retained its historical character. **Shad Thames**, the narrow street at the back of Butler's Wharf, has kept the wrought-iron overhead gangways by which the porters used to transport goods from the wharves to the warehouses further back from the river, and is one of the most atmospheric alleyways in the whole of Bermondsey. The eight-storey Butler's Wharf warehouse itself, with its shops and restaurants, forms part of Terence Conran's commercial empire and caters for a moneyed clientele, but the wide promenade on the riverfront is open to the public.

The chief attraction of Butler's Wharf is Conran's superb riverside **Design Museum** (Mon–Fri 11.30am–6pm, Sat & Sun 10.30am–6pm; £5.50; ⓦwww .designmuseum.org; Bermondsey or Tower Hill tube), a stylish, white, Bauhaus-like conversion of a 1950s warehouse at the eastern end of Shad Thames. The museum's excellent temporary **exhibitions** on important designers, movements or single products are staged on the first floor, while the Collection and Review **galleries**, on the top floor, offer a brief overview of mass-produced industrial design from TVs to Tupperware. The small coffee bar in the foyer is a great place to relax, and there's a pricey Conran restaurant on the top floor.

The **Bramah Tea and Coffee Museum** (daily 10am–6pm; £4; ⓦwww .bramahmuseum.co.uk; Tower Hill or Bermondsey tube), housed in an old tea warehouse, Tamarind House, on Maguire Street behind the Design Museum, is not quite in the same league as its neighbour. Still, it's a fun museum, and well worth a visit. Founded in 1992 by Edward Bramah, who began his career on an African tea garden in 1950, the museum's emphasis is firmly on tea. There's an impressive array of teapots from Wedgwood to novelty, and coffee machines spanning the twentieth century, from huge percolator siphons to espresso machines.

Hyde Park, Kensington and Chelsea

Hyde Park, together with its westerly extension, Kensington Gardens, covers a distance of two miles from Speakers' Corner in the northeast to **Kensington Palace** in the southwest. At the end of your journey, you've made it to one of London's most exclusive districts, the Royal Borough of Kensington and Chelsea. Other districts go in and out of fashion, but this area has been in vogue ever since royalty moved into Kensington Palace in the late seventeenth century.

Aside from the shops around Harrods in Knightsbridge, however, the popular tourist attractions lie in **South Kensington**, where three of London's top museums – the **Victoria and Albert**, **Natural History** and **Science museums** – stand on land bought with the proceeds of the Great Exhibition of 1851. **Chelsea**'s character is slightly more bohemian. In the 1960s, the **King's Road** carved out its reputation as London's catwalk, while in the late 1970s it was the epicentre of the punk explosion. Nothing so risqué goes on in Chelsea now, though its residents like to think of themselves as rather more artistic and intellectual than the purely moneyed types of Kensington.

Once slummy, now swanky, Bayswater and **Notting Hill**, to the north of Hyde Park, were the bad boys of the borough for many years, dens of vice and crime comparable to Soho. Despite gentrification over the last twenty-five years, they remain the borough's most cosmopolitan districts, with a strong Arab presence and vestiges of the black community who initiated and still run the city's (and Europe's) largest street **carnival**, which takes place every August Bank Holiday.

Hyde Park and Kensington Gardens

Seized from the Church by Henry VIII to satisfy his desire for yet more hunting grounds, **Hyde Park** (ⓦwww.royalparks.co.uk) was first opened to the public by James I, and soon became a fashionable gathering place for the beau monde, who rode round the circular drive known as the Ring, pausing to gossip and admire each other's *équipage*. Hangings, muggings and duels, the Great Exhibition of 1851 and numerous public events have all taken place in Hyde Park – and it's still a popular gathering point or destination for political demonstrations. For most of the time, however, the park is simply a leisure ground – a wonderful open space which allows you to lose all sight of the city beyond a few persistent tower blocks.

Located at the treeless northeastern corner of the park, **Marble Arch** was originally erected in 1828 as a triumphal entry to Buckingham Palace, but is now stranded on a ferociously busy traffic island at the west end of Oxford Street. This is the most historically charged spot in Hyde Park, as it marks the site of **Tyburn gallows**, the city's main public execution spot until 1783. It's also the location of **Speakers' Corner**, once an entertaining and peculiarly English Sunday tradition, featuring an assembly of characterful speakers and hecklers – now, sadly, a forum for soap-box religious extremists.

A better place to enter the park is at **Hyde Park Corner**, the southeast corner, where **Wellington Arch** (April–Sept daily 10am–6pm; Oct daily 10am–5pm; Nov–March Wed–Sun 10am–4pm; £2.50; EH; Hyde Park Corner tube) stands in the midst of another of London's busiest traffic interchanges. Erected in 1828 to commemorate Wellington's victories in the Napoleonic Wars, the arch originally served as the northern gate into Buckingham Palace grounds. Now it houses a small exhibition on the history of the arch and on the city's numerous outdoor memorials.

Close by stands **Apsley House** (Tues–Sun 11am–5pm; £4.50; Ⓦwww .vam.ac.uk; Hyde Park Corner tube), Wellington's London residence and now a museum to the "Iron Duke". Unless you're a keen fan of the Duke (or Louis XV interiors), the highlight of the museum is the **art collection**, much of which used to belong to the King of Spain. Among the best pieces, displayed in the Waterloo Gallery on the first floor, are works by de Hooch, van Dyck, Velázquez, Goya, Rubens and Murillo. The famous, more than twice life-size nude statue of Napoleon by Antonio Canova stands at the foot of the main staircase.

Hyde Park is divided in two by the **Serpentine Lake**, which has a popular **Lido** (June–Sept daily 10am–6pm; £2.50; Lancaster Gate or Knightsbridge tube) on its south bank. By far the prettiest section of the lake, though, is the upper section known as the **Long Water**, which narrows until it reaches a group of four fountains, laid out symmetrically in front of an Italianate summerhouse designed by Wren.

The western half of the park is officially known as **Kensington Gardens**, and is, strictly speaking, a separate entity, though you hardly notice the change. Its two most popular attractions are the **Serpentine Gallery** (daily 10am–6pm; free; Ⓦwww.serpentinegallery.org; South Kensington tube), which has a reputation for lively, and often controversial, contemporary art exhibitions, and the richly decorated, High Gothic **Albert Memorial** (guided tours Sun 2 & 3pm; £3.50), clearly visible to the west. Erected in 1876, the monument is as much a hymn to the glorious achievements of Britain as to its subject, Queen Victoria's husband (who died of typhoid in 1861). Recently restored to his former gilded glory, Albert occupies the central canopy, clutching a catalogue for the 1851 Great Exhibition that he helped to organize.

The Exhibition's most famous feature, the gargantuan glasshouse of the Crystal Palace, no longer exists, but the profits were used to buy a large tract of land south of the park, now home to South Kensington's remarkable cluster of museums and colleges, plus the vast **Royal Albert Hall**, a splendid iron-and-glass-domed concert hall, with an exterior of red brick, terracotta and marble that became the hallmark of South Ken architecture. The hall is venue for Europe's most democratic music festival, the Henry Wood Promenade Concerts, better known as the **Proms** (ⓦwww.bbc.co.uk/proms), which take place from July to September, with standing-room tickets for as little as £3.

Kensington Palace

On the western edge of Kensington Gardens stands **Kensington Palace** (daily: March–Oct 10am–5pm; Nov–Feb 10am–4pm; £8.80; ⓦwww.hrp.org.uk; High Street Kensington tube), a modestly proportioned Jacobean brick mansion bought by William and Mary in 1689, and the chief royal residence for the next fifty years. KP, as it's fondly known in royal circles, is, of course, best known today as the place where Princess Diana lived up until her death in 1997. It was, in fact, the official London residence of both Charles and Di until the couple formally separated. In the weeks following Diana's death, literally millions of flowers, mementoes, poems and gifts were deposited at the gates to the south of the palace.

Visitors don't get to see Diana's apartments, which were on the west side of the palace, where various minor royals still live. Instead, they are given an audio-guide which takes them round the **Royal Ceremonial Dress Collection**, where they get to view some of the Queen's frocks, and then the sparsely furnished state apartments. The highlights are the trompe l'oeil ceiling paintings by William Kent, in particular the Cupola Room, and the oil paintings in the King's Gallery. En route, you also get to see the tastelessly decorated rooms in which the future Queen Victoria spent her unhappy childhood. To recover from the above, take tea in the exquisite **Orangery** (daily: Easter–Sept 10am–6pm; Oct–Easter 10am–4pm), to the north of the palace.

The Victoria and Albert Museum (V&A)

In terms of sheer variety and scale, the **Victoria and Albert Museum**, on Cromwell Road (daily 10am–5.45pm, Wed also 6.30–9.30pm; free; ⓦwww.vam.ac.uk; South Kensington tube), popularly known as the V&A, is the greatest museum of applied arts in the world. The range of exhibits on display here means that, whatever your taste, there is almost bound to be something to grab your attention.

Beautifully but haphazardly displayed across a seven-mile, four-storey maze of halls and corridors, the V&A's treasures are impossible to survey in a single visit. Floor plans from the information desks can help you decide on which areas to concentrate. If you're flagging, there's *Millburns* restaurant in the basement of the Henry Cole Wing, or a more edifying café in the museum's period-piece **Poynter, Morris and Gamble** refreshment rooms.

The most celebrated of the V&A's numerous exhibits are the **Raphael Cartoons**, seven vast biblical paintings that served as templates for a set of tapestries destined for the Sistine Chapel. Close by, you can view highlights from the country's largest dress collection, and the world's largest collection of **Indian art** outside India. In addition, there are galleries devoted to Chinese, Islamic, Japanese and Korean art, as well as costume jewellery, glassware, metalwork and photography. Wading through the huge collection of European sculpture, you come to the surreal **Plaster Casts** gallery, filled with copies of European art's greatest hits, from Michelangelo's David to Trajan's Column (sawn in half to make it fit). There's even a gallery of **twentieth-century**

objets d'art – everything from Bauhaus furniture to Swatch watches – to rival that of the Design Museum.

Over in the **Henry Cole Wing**, meanwhile, you'll find an entire office interior by Frank Lloyd Wright, a collection of sixteenth-century portrait miniatures, more **Constable** paintings than the Tate, and a goodly collection of sculptures by **Rodin**. As if all this were not enough, the V&A's temporary shows are among the best in Britain, ranging over vast areas of art, craft and technology.

Like all London's major museums, the V&A has big plans for the future, with a £75 million multifaceted extension, known as the "**Spiral**" and designed by controversial Polish-born architect Daniel Libeskind, due to open in 2004.

The Science Museum

Established as a technological counterpart to the V&A, the **Science Museum**, on Exhibition Road (daily 10am–6pm; free; Ⓦ www.nmsi.ac.uk; South Kensington tube), is undeniably impressive, filling seven floors with items drawn from every conceivable area of science, including space travel, telecommunications, time measurement, chemistry, computing, photography and medicine. Keen to dispel the enduring image of museums devoted to its subject as boring and full of dusty glass cabinets, the Science Museum has been busy updating its galleries with more interactive displays, and puts on daily demonstrations to show that not all science teaching has to be deathly dry.

Once you've paid your entrance fee, head for the **information desk** in the Power hall and find out what events and demonstrations are taking place; you can also sign up for a guided tour on a specific subject. Beyond the Power hall and the **Space** exhibition, which follows the history of rockets, lies the old Transport hall, now the **Making of the Modern World**, a display of iconic inventions such as *Puffing Billy*, the world's oldest surviving steam train, and Robert Stephenson's *Rocket* of 1829, as well as a Ford Model T, the world's first mass-produced car.

From here, the darkened, ultra-purple **Wellcome Wing** beckons you on, its ground floor dominated by the floating, sloping underbelly of the museum's state-of-the-art **IMAX cinema** (£6.75). The four floors of the Wellcome Wing are filled with high-tech hands-on computer gadgetry that's great fun to play with: you can morph yourself into the opposite sex or test the gender of your brain, learn about digital technology, and ponder moral questions such as: "should you be able to choose the gender of your child?" There's also plenty of interactive stuff aimed at **younger kids**, from Pattern Pod and the ever-popular Launch Pad, in the Wellcome Wing, to the Garden and Things galleries in the basement.

The rest of the museum – and there's a more than enough to keep you occupied for a whole day – covers such diverse topics as flight and shipping to gas exploration and nuclear physics. Some galleries, such as the one devoted to **Materials**, are admirably stylish; others, such as the sections on **Computing** and **Mathematics**, are rather more old fashioned, though the museum's piecemeal revamping continues apace.

The Natural History Museum

Alfred Waterhouse's purpose-built mock-Romanesque colossus ensures the **Natural History Museum** (Mon–Sat 10am–5.50pm, Sun 11am–5.50pm; free; Ⓦ www.nhm.ac.uk; South Kensington tube) its status as London's most handsome museum. The museum underwent massive redevelopment in the

1990s, and is now, by and large, imaginatively designed, though there are still one or two sections that have changed little since the museum's opening in 1881. To be fair, the museum is caught in a real conundrum, for while its dinosaur collection is a real hit with the kids, its collections are also an important resource for serious zoologists.

The main entrance brings you straight into the Central Hall of the **Life Galleries**, dominated by a plaster-cast skeleton of a Diplodocus. The "side chapels" are filled with wonders of the natural world – the largest egg, a sabretooth tiger – but it's the **Dinosaur gallery** that pulls in the crowds, a show of massive-jawed skeletons and models much enlivened by a grisly life-size animatronic Tyrannosaurus Rex, accompanied by much roaring, slurping and oozing blood. Other popular sections include the Creepy-Crawlies Room and the Ecology Gallery, plus the somewhat ancient displays of stuffed creatures.

If the queues for the museum are long (as they can be at weekends and during school holidays), you're better off heading for the side entrance on Exhibition Road, which leads into the former Geology Museum, now known as the **Earth Galleries**, an expensively revamped and visually exciting romp through the earth's evolution. The most popular sections are the slightly tasteless Kobe earthquake simulator, and the spectacular display of gems and crystals in the Earth's Treasury.

Kensington High Street

Shopper-thronged **Kensington High Street** is dominated architecturally by the twin presences of Sir George Gilbert Scott's neo-Gothic church of St Mary Abbots, whose 250-foot spire makes it London's tallest parish church, and the Art Deco colossus of Barkers department store, remodelled in the 1930s.

Kensington's sights are mostly hidden away in the backstreets, the one exception being the **Commonwealth Institute** (☎020/7603 4535; ⓦwww.commonwealth.org.uk; High Street Kensington tube), housed in a bold 1960s building set back from the High Street. The whole place has recently undergone a massive restoration and refurbishment programme. Gone is the permanent collection with a section on each of the member states; instead, the Institute aims to put on more up-to-date, interactive temporary exhibitions focusing on a particular Commonwealth country.

Two paths along the side of the Commonwealth Institute lead to densely wooded **Holland Park** (daily 7.30am–dusk; High Street Kensington tube), the former grounds of a Jacobean mansion (only the east wing still stands). Theatrical and musical performances are staged here throughout the summer, and several **formal gardens** surround the house, most notably the Japanese-style Kyoto Gardens, while the rest of the park is dotted with a newly installed series of abstract sculptures.

A number of wealthy Victorian artists rather self-consciously founded an artists' colony in the streets that lie between the High Street and Holland Park. It's possible to visit one of the most remarkable of these artist pads, **Leighton House** at 12 Holland Park Rd (daily except Tues 11am–5.30pm; free; ⓦwww.rbkc.cgov.uk). "It will be opulence, it will be sincerity," Lord Leighton opined before starting work on the house in the 1860s – he later became President of the Royal Academy and was ennobled on his deathbed. The big attraction is the domed Arab Hall, decorated with Saracen tiles, gilded mosaics and woodwork drawn from all over the Islamic world. The other rooms are less spectacular but, in compensation, are hung with paintings by Lord Leighton and his Pre-Raphaelite chums.

Knightsbridge and Harrods

Knightsbridge is irredeemably snobbish, revelling in its reputation as the swankiest shopping area in London, a status epitomized by **Harrods** on Brompton Road (Mon, Tues & Sat 10am–6pm, Wed–Fri 10am–7pm; Ⓦ www.harrods.com; Knightsbridge tube). London's most famous department store started out as a family-run grocery store in 1849, with a staff of two. The current 1905 terracotta building is owned by the Egyptian Mohammed Al Fayed and employs in excess of 3000 staff. Tourists flock to Harrods – it's thought to be one of the city's top-ranking tourist attractions – though if you can do without the Harrods' carrier bag, you can buy most of what the shop stocks more cheaply elsewhere.

The store does, however, have a few sections that are architectural sights in their own right: the Food Hall, with its exquisite Arts and Crafts tiling, and the Egyptian Hall, with its pseudo-hieroglyphs and sphinxes, are particularly striking. Now that a fountain dedicated to Di and Dodi is in place, the Egyptian-style escalators are an added attraction, but don't bother taking them to the first floor "washrooms", unless you want to pay £1 for the privilege of relieving yourself. Note, too, that the store has a draconian dress code: no shorts, no ripped jeans, no vest T-shirts and no backpacks.

Chelsea

It wasn't until the latter part of the nineteenth century that **Chelsea** began to earn its reputation as London's very own Left Bank. Its household fame, however, came through **King's Road**'s role as the unofficial catwalk of the "Swinging Sixties". The road remained a fashion parade for hippies, too, and in the Jubilee Year of 1977 it witnessed the birth of punk, masterminded from a shop called Sex, run by Vivienne Westwood and Malcolm McLaren. The posey cafés and boutiques still persist, but these days, the area has a more subdued feel, with high rents and house prices keeping things pretty staid, and chain stores and interior design shops rather than avant-garde fashion the order of the day.

The area's other aspect, oddly enough considering its boho reputation, is a military one. For among the most nattily attired of all those parading down the King's Road are the scarlet or navy-blue clad Chelsea Pensioners, army veterans from the nearby **Royal Hospital** (Mon–Fri 9am–noon & 2–4.30pm, Sat & Sun closes 3pm; free; Sloane Square tube), founded by Charles II in 1681. The hospital's majestic red-brick wings and grassy courtyards became a blueprint for institutional and collegiate architecture all over the English-speaking world. The public are allowed to view the austere hospital chapel, and the equally grand, wood-panelled dining hall, opposite, which has a vast allegorical mural of Charles II.

The concrete bunker next door to the Royal Hospital, on Royal Hospital Road, houses the **National Army Museum** (daily 10am–5.30pm; free; Ⓦ www.national-army-museum.ac.uk; Sloane Square tube). The militarily obsessed are unlikely to be disappointed by the succession of uniforms and medals, but there is very little here for non-enthusiasts. The temporary exhibitions staged on the ground floor are the museum's strong point, but it's rather disappointing overall – you're better off visiting the infinitely superior Imperial War Museum (see p.123).

Cheyne Walk and Cheyne Row

The quiet riverside locale of **Cheyne Walk** (pronounced "chainy") drew artists and writers in great numbers during the nineteenth century. Since the building of the Embankment and the increase in the volume of traffic, however, the character of this peaceful haven has been lost. Novelist Henry James, who lived at no. 21, used to take "beguiling drives" in his wheelchair along the Embankment; today, he'd be hospitalized in the process.

The chief reason to come here nowadays is to visit the **Chelsea Physic Garden** (April–Oct Wed noon–5pm & Sun 2–6pm; £4; ⓦwww.cpgarden. demon.co.uk; Sloane Square tube), which marks the beginning of Cheyne Walk. Founded in 1673, this small walled garden is the second oldest botanical garden in the country. At the entrance (on Swan Walk) you can pick up a map of the garden with a list of the month's most interesting flowers and shrubs, whose labels are slightly more forthcoming than the usual terse Latinate tags. The garden also has an excellent teahouse, where you can get delicious homemade cakes.

It's also worth popping into the nearby **Chelsea Old Church** (daily 9.30am–1pm & 2–4.30pm; Sloane Square tube), halfway down Cheyne Walk, where Thomas More built his own private chapel in the south aisle. The church was badly bombed in the last war, but an impressive number of monuments were retrieved from the rubble and continue to adorn the church's interior.

A short distance inland from Cheyne Walk, at 24 Cheyne Row, is **Carlyle's House** (April–Oct Wed–Sun 11am–5pm; £3.50; NT; Sloane Square tube), where the historian Thomas Carlyle set up home, having moved down from his native Scotland in 1834. The house became a museum just fifteen years after Carlyle's death and is a typically dour Victorian abode, kept much as the Carlyles would have had it: the historian's hat still hanging in the hall, his socks in the chest of drawers. The top floor contains the garret study where Carlyle tried in vain to escape the din of the neighbours' noisy roosters in order to complete his final magnum opus on Frederick the Great.

Notting Hill

Epicentre of the country's first race riots, when bus-loads of whites attacked West Indian homes in the area, **Notting Hill** is now more famous for the eponymous 1998 film, and for its annual Carnival (see box, p.134), which began life in direct response to the riots. The rest of the year, Notting Hill is a lot quieter, though its cafés and restaurants are cool enough places to pull in folk from all over. On Saturdays, big crowds of Londoners and tourists alike descend on the mile-long **Portobello Road Market**, which is lined with stalls selling everything from antiques to cheap second-hand clothes and fruit and vegetables.

Within easy walking distance of Portobello Road, on the other side of the railway tracks, gasworks and canal, is **Kensal Green Cemetery** (daily: April–Sept 8am–6pm; Oct–March 9am–5pm; Kensal Rise tube), opened in 1833 and still a functioning burial ground. Graves of the more famous incumbents – Thackeray, Trollope and Brunel – are less interesting architecturally than those arranged on either side of the Centre Avenue, which leads from the easternmost entrance on Harrow Road.

When it emerged in the 1960s, **Notting Hill Carnival** (@www.nottinghillcarnival.net.uk) was little more than a few church hall events and a Carnival parade, inspired by that of Trinidad – home of many of the area's immigrants. Today the Carnival, held over the August Bank Holiday weekend at the end of the month, still belongs to West Indians (from all parts of the city), but there are participants, too, from London's Latin American and Asian communities, and, of course, Londoners of all description turn out to watch the bands and parades, and just hangout.

The main sights of Carnival are the **costume parades**, which take place on the Sunday (for kids) and Monday (for adults) from around 10am until just before midnight. The parade makes its way around a three-mile route, starting at the top end of Ladbroke Grove, heading south under the Westway, then turning into Westbourne Grove, before looping north again via Chepstow Road, Great Western Road and Kensal Road. The procession consists of "big trucks", which carry the sound systems and **mas** (masquerade) bands, behind which the masqueraders dance in outrageous costumes.

Most of the **mas** bands play a variety of soca music, while others feature steel bands – the "pans" of the steel bands are one of the chief sounds of the Carnival and have their own contest on the Saturday at Horniman's Pleasance. In addition to those playing **mas**, there are three or four **stages for live music** – Portobello Green and Powis Square are regular venues – where you can catch reggae, ragga, drum 'n' bass, jungle, garage, house and much more. A lot of people just mill around the sound systems, dancing as the day progresses, fuelled by cans of Red Stripe, curried goat and Jamaican patties, which are sold by a multitude of weekend entrepreneurs.

Over the last few years, the Carnival has been fairly relaxed, considering the huge numbers of people it attracts. However, this is not an event for those at all bothered by crowds – you can be wedged stationary during the parades – and very loud music. It is worth taking more than usual care about crime, too: leave expensive cameras and jewellery at home, and bring only enough money for the day, as pickpockets turn up from all over. As far as safety goes, don't worry unduly about the media's horror stories as you're in plentiful company. However, the static sound systems are switched off at 7pm every day, and if there's going to be any trouble, it tends to come after that point. If you feel at all uneasy, head home early.

Getting to and from Carnival is quite an event in itself. Ladbroke Grove tube station is closed for the duration, while Notting Hill Gate and Westbourne Park are open only for incoming visitors. The nearest fully operative tube stations are Latimer Road and Royal Oak. Alternatively, there's a whole network of buses running between most points of London and Notting Hill Gate.

North London

Just a handful of the capital's satellite villages in **North London**, now subsumed into the general mass of the city, are worth bothering with. However, all are easily accessible by tube from the centre; in fact, it was the expansion of the Tube which encouraged the forward march of bricks and mortar into many of these suburbs. **Regent's Park**, framed by Nash-designed architecture and home of **London Zoo**, is one of London's finest parks. Within easy walking distance, to the northeast, is **Camden Town**, where the weekend market is now one of the city's big attractions – a warren of stalls selling street fashion, books, records and ethnic goods. The real highlights of north London, though, for visitors and residents alike, are **Hampstead** and **Highgate**, elegant, largely eighteenth-century developments which still reflect their village origins. They have the added advantage of proximity to one of London's wildest patches of greenery, **Hampstead Heath**, where you can enjoy stupendous views, kite-flying and nude bathing, as well as outdoor concerts and high art in the setting of **Kenwood House**.

Regent's Park

As with almost all of London's royal parks, we have Henry VIII to thank for **Regent's Park** (daily 5am–dusk; ⓦ www.royalparks.co.uk; Regent's Park, Baker Street or Great Portland Street tube), which he confiscated from the Church for yet more hunting grounds. However, it wasn't until the reign of the Prince Regent (later George IV) that the park began to take its current form. According to the masterplan, devised by John Nash in 1811, the park was to be girded by a continuous belt of terraces, and sprinkled with a total of 56 villas, including a magnificent pleasure palace for the Prince himself, which would be linked by Regent Street to Carlton House in St James's. The plan was never fully realized, due to lack of funds, but enough was built to create something of the idealized garden city that Nash and the Prince Regent envisaged.

To appreciate the special quality of Regent's Park, take a closer look at the architecture, starting with the Nash terraces, which form a near-unbroken horseshoe of cream-coloured stucco around the Outer Circle. Within the Inner Circle is the **Open Air Theatre**, which puts on summer performances of Shakespeare, opera and ballet, and **Queen Mary's Gardens**, by far the prettiest section of the park. A large slice of the gardens is taken up with a glorious rose garden, featuring some four hundred varieties, surrounded by a ring of ramblers.

Clearly visible on the western edge of the park is the shiny copper dome and minaret of the **London Central Mosque**, an entirely appropriate addition given the Prince Regent's taste for the Orient. Non-Muslim visitors are welcome to look in at the information centre, and glimpse inside the hall of worship, which is packed out with a diversity of communities for the lunchtime Friday prayers.

The northeastern corner of the park is occupied by **London Zoo** (daily: March–Oct 10am–5.30pm; Nov–Feb 10am–4pm; £10; ⓦ www.zsl.org; Camden tube), founded in 1826. It may not be the most uplifting place for animal lovers, but kids will love the place, especially the children's enclosure, where they can actually handle the animals, and the regular "Animals in

---

Regent's Canal by boat

Three companies run **boat services** on the Regent's Canal between Camden (Camden Town tube) and Little Venice (Warwick Avenue tube), stopping off at London Zoo on the way and passing through the Maida Hill tunnel en route. The narrowboat *Jenny Wren* (☎ 020/7485 4433) starts off at Camden, while Jason's narrowboats (☎ 020/7286 3428) start off at Little Venice; the London Waterbus Company (☎ 020/7482 2660) – the only one to run all year round – sets off from both places. Whichever you choose, you can board at either end; **tickets** cost around £5–6 return and journey time is 35–45 minutes one-way.

Those interested in the history of the canal should head off to the **London Canal Museum** (Tues–Sun 10am–4.30pm; £2.50; ⓦ www.canalmuseum.org.uk; King's Cross tube), on the other side of York Way, down New Wharf Road, ten minutes' walk from King's Cross Station.

Action" displays in the Lifewatch House. The zoo boasts some striking architectural features, too, most notably the 1930s modernist, spiral-ramped, concrete penguin pool (where Penguin Books' original colophon was sketched), designed by the Tecton partnership, led by Russian emigré Berthold Lubetkin. Other zoo landmarks include the colossal tetrahedral aluminium-framed tent of the Snowdon Aviary, and the excellent, eco-conscious invertebrate-filled Web of Life.

Camden Town

For all the gentrification of the last twenty years, **Camden Town** retains a seedy air, compounded by the various railway lines that plough through the area, the canal, and Europe's largest dosshouse. The market, however, gives the area a positive lift on the weekends, and is now the district's best-known attribute.

Having started out as a tiny crafts market in the cobbled courtyard by the lock, **Camden Market** has since mushroomed out of all proportion. More than 100,000 shoppers turn up here each weekend, and parts of the market now stay open week-long, alongside a similarly oriented crop of shops, cafés and bistros. The market's overabundance of cheap leather, DM shoes and naff jewellery is compensated for by the sheer variety of what's on offer: from bootleg tapes to furniture, along with a mass of street fashion that may or may not make the transition to mainstream stores. To avoid the crowds, which can be overpowering on a summer weekend afternoon, get here by 10am.

Despite having no significant Jewish associations, Camden is home to London's **Jewish Museum** (Mon–Thurs 10am–4pm, Sun 10am–5pm; £3.50; Ⓦwww.jewmusm.ort.org; Camden Town tube), at 129 Albert St, just off Parkway. The purpose-built premises are smartly designed, but the conventional style and contents of the museum are disappointing: apart from the usual displays of Judaica, there's a video and exhibition explaining Jewish religious practices and the history of the Jewish community in Britain. More challenging temporary exhibitions are held in the museum's Finchley branch on East End Road, N3 (Ⓣ020/8349 1143).

Hampstead

Perched on a hill above Camden Town, **Hampstead** village developed into a fashionable spa in the eighteenth century, after a celebrated physician declared the waters of its spring as being of great medicinal value. Its sloping site, which deterred Victorian property speculators and put off the railway companies, saved much of the Georgian village from destruction, and it's little altered to this day. Later, it became one of the city's most celebrated literary quarters and even now it retains its reputation as a bolt hole of the high-profile intelligentsia. You can get some idea of its tone from the fact that the local Labour MP is currently the actress-turned-politician Glenda Jackson.

The steeply inclined High Street, lined with trendy clothes shops and arty cafés, flaunts the area's ever-increasing wealth without completely losing its picturesqueness. There are several small house museums to explore, but proximity to the Heath is the real joy of Hampstead, for this mixture of woodland, smooth pasture and landscaped garden is quite simply the most exhilarating patch of greenery in London.

Whichever route you take north of Hampstead tube, you'll probably end up at the small triangular green on Holly Bush Hill, on the north side of which stands the late seventeenth-century **Fenton House** (April–Oct Wed–Fri 2–5pm, Sat & Sun 11am–5pm; NT; £4.30; Hampstead tube). As well as housing a collection of European and Oriental ceramics, this National Trust house contains the superb Benton-Fletcher collection of early musical instruments, chiefly displayed on the top floor. Among the many spinets, virginals and clavichords are the earliest extant English grand piano, and an Unverdorben lute from 1580 (one of only three in the world).

The Queen Anne mansion of **Burgh House** (Wed–Sun noon–5pm; free; Hampstead tube), on New End Square, dates from the halcyon spa days of Hampstead Wells – as Hampstead was briefly known – and was at one time occupied by Dr Gibbons, the physician who discovered the spring's medicinal qualities. Surrounded by council housing, it now serves as the **Hampstead Museum**, an exhibition space and a modest local museum, with special emphasis on such notable locals as Constable and Keats; there's also a nice tea room in the basement.

Hampstead's most modern attraction is **2 Willow Road** (guided tours April–Oct Thurs–Sat 12.15–4pm every 45min; £4.30; NT; Hampstead tube), a modernist red-brick terraced house, built in the 1930s by the Hungarian-born architect Ernö Goldfinger. When Goldfinger moved in, this was a state-of-the-art house, but Goldfinger changed little of it in the following sixty years, so what you see is a 1930s avant-garde dwelling preserved in aspic, a house at once both modern and old-fashioned. An added bonus is that the rooms are packed with works of art by the likes of Max Ernst, Duchamp, Henry Moore and Man Ray. There are a limited number of tickets for the **guided tours**, so it's worth booking ahead. Incidentally, James Bond's adversary is indeed named after Ernö, as Ian Fleming lived close by and had a deep personal dislike of both Goldfinger and his modernist abode.

Hampstead's most lustrous figure is celebrated at **Keats' House** (May–Oct Tues–Sun noon–5pm; £3; ⓦwww.keatshouse.org.uk; Hampstead tube), an elegant, whitewashed Regency double villa on Keats Grove, a short walk south of Willow Road. Inspired by the peacefulness of Hampstead and by his passion for girl-next-door Fanny Brawne (whose house is also part of the museum), Keats wrote some of his most famous works here, before leaving for Rome, where he died from consumption in 1821. The neat, rather staid interior contains books and letters, Fanny's engagement ring and the four-poster bed in which the poet first coughed up blood, confiding to his companion, Charles Brown, "that drop of blood is my death warrant".

One of the most poignant of London's house museums is the **Freud Museum**, hidden away in the leafy streets of south Hampstead at 20 Maresfield Gardens (Wed–Sun noon–5pm; £4; ⓦwww.freud.org.uk; Finchley Road tube). Having lived in Vienna for his entire adult life, Freud, by now a semi-invalid with only a year to live, was forced to flee the Nazis, arriving in London in the summer of 1938. The ground-floor study and library look exactly as they did when Freud lived here; the collection of erotic antiquities and the famous couch, sumptuously draped in Persian carpets, were all brought here from Vienna. Upstairs, home movies of family life in Vienna are shown continually and a small room is dedicated to his daughter, Anna, herself an influential child analyst, who lived in the house until her death in 1982.

Hampstead Heath and Kenwood

North London's "green lung", **Hampstead Heath** is the city's most enjoyable public park. It may not have much of its original heathland left, but it packs a wonderful variety of bucolic scenery into its 800 acres. At its southern end are the rolling green pastures of **Parliament Hill**, north London's premier spot for kite-flying. On either side are numerous ponds, three of which – one for men, one for women and one mixed – you can swim in. The thickest woodland is to be found in the **West Heath**, beyond Whitestone Pond, also the site of the most formal section, **Hill Garden**, a secretive and romantic little gem with eccentric balustraded terraces and a ruined pergola. Beyond lies **Golders Hill Park**, where you can gaze at pygmy goats and fallow deer, and inspect the impeccably maintained aviaries, home to flamingos, cranes and other exotic birds.

Finally, don't miss the landscaped grounds of Kenwood, in the north of the Heath, which are focused on the whitewashed, Neoclassical mansion of **Kenwood House** (daily: April–Sept 10am–6pm; Oct 10am–5pm; Nov–March 10am–4pm; free; Hampstead tube or EH bus #210 from Highgate tube). The house is now home to the **Iveagh Bequest**, a collection of seventeenth- and eighteenth-century art, including a handful of real masterpieces by the likes of Vermeer, Rembrandt, Boucher, Gainsborough and Reynolds. Of the house's period interiors, the most spectacular is Robert Adam's sky-blue and gold **library**, its book-filled apses separated from the central entertaining area by paired columns. To the south of the house, a grassy amphitheatre slopes down to a lake where outdoor classical concerts are held on summer evenings.

Highgate

Northeast of the Heath, and fractionally lower than Hampstead (appearances notwithstanding), **Highgate** lacks the literary cachet of its neighbour, but makes up for it with London's most famous cemetery, resting place of Karl Marx. It also retains more of its village origins, especially around **The Grove**, Highgate's finest row of houses, the oldest dating as far back as 1685.

To reach Highgate High Street from the tube, you must walk up Southwood Lane; to reach the cemetery, head south down Highgate High Street and **Highgate Hill**, with its amazing views towards the City. When you get to the copper dome of "Holy Joe", the Roman Catholic Church which stands on Highgate Hill, pop into the pleasantly landscaped **Waterlow Park**, next door, with its fine café and restaurant.

The park provides a through route to **Highgate Cemetery**, which is ranged on both sides of Swain's Lane. Highgate's most famous corpse, that of **Karl Marx**, lies in the **East Cemetery** (daily: April–Sept 10am–5pm; Oct–March 10am–4pm; £2). Marx himself asked for a simple grave topped by a headstone, but by 1954 the Communist movement decided to move his grave to a more prominent position and erect the vulgar bronze bust that now surmounts a granite plinth. Close by lies the much simpler grave of the author George Eliot.

What the East Cemetery lacks in atmosphere is in part compensated for by the fact that you can wander at will through its maze of circuitous paths, whereas to visit the more atmospheric and overgrown **West Cemetery**, with its spooky Egyptian Avenue and terraced catacombs, you must go round with a guided tour (Mon–Fri noon, 2pm & 4pm, Sat & Sun hourly 11am–4pm; £3). Among the prominent graves usually visited are those of artist Dante Gabriel Rossetti and lesbian novelist Radclyffe Hall. No children under 8 admitted.

Hendon: The RAF Museum

A world-class assembly of historic military aircraft can be seen at the **RAF Museum** (daily 10am–6pm; free; ⓦ www.rafmuseum.org.uk; Colindale tube), located in a godforsaken part of north London beside the M1 motorway. Enthusiasts won't be disappointed, but those looking for a balanced account of modern aerial warfare will – the overall tone is unashamedly militaristic, not to say jingoistic. Those with children should head for the hands-on Fun 'n'

Flight gallery; those without might prefer to explore the often overlooked display galleries, ranged around the edge of the Main Aircraft Hall, which contain an art gallery and an exhibition on the history of flight, accompanied by replicas of some of the death-traps of early aviation.

Neasden: the Shri Swaminarayan temple

Perhaps the most remarkable building in the whole of London lies just off the North Circular, in the glum suburb of **Neasden**. Here, rising majestically above the surrounding semi-detached houses like a mirage, is the **Shri Swaminarayan Mandir** (daily 9am–7.30pm; free; Ⓦ www.swaminarayan-baps.org; Stonebridge Park or Neasden tube), a traditional Hindu temple topped with domes and shikharas, erected in 1995 in a style and scale unseen outside of India for more than a millennium. To reach the temple, you must enter through the adjacent Haveli, or cultural complex, with its carved wooden portico and balcony. After taking off your shoes, you can proceed to the **Mandir** (temple) itself, carved entirely out of Carrara marble, with every possible surface transformed into a honeycomb of arabesques, flowers and seated gods. Beneath the Mandir, an **exhibition** (Mon–Fri 9am–6pm, Sat & Sun 7am–7pm; £2) explains the basic tenets of Hinduism and details the life of Lord Swaminarayan, and includes a video about the history of the building.

South London

Now largely built-up into a patchwork of Victorian terraces, one area of **South London** stands head and shoulders above all the others in terms of sightseeing, and that is **Greenwich**. At its heart is the outstanding ensemble of the Royal Naval College and the Queen's House, courtesy of Christopher Wren and Inigo Jones respectively. Most visitors, however, come to see the Cutty Sark, the National Maritime Museum and the Royal Observatory, though Greenwich also pulls in an ever-increasing volume of Londoners in search of bargains at its Sunday **market**.

Greenwich is, of course, also famous as the "home of time", thanks to its status as the **Prime Meridian of the World**, from where time all over the globe is measured. It's partly for this reason that Greenwich was chosen as the centrepiece of the country's millennium celebrations, though the **Dome** is, in fact, situated in the reclaimed industrial wasteland of North Greenwich, a mile or so northeast of Greenwich town centre, and is currently closed to the public.

The only other suburban sights that stand out are the **Dulwich Picture Gallery**, a public art gallery even older than the National Gallery, and the eclectic **Horniman Museum**, in neighbouring Forest Hill.

Dulwich and Forest Hill

Dulwich Village, one of south London's prettier patches, is built on land owned in the seventeenth century by the actor Edward Alleyn, who founded **Dulwich College** in 1619 as almshouses and a school for poor boys on the profits of his whorehouses and bear-baiting pits on Bankside (see p.124). The college has long since outgrown its original buildings, which still stand to the north of the Picture Gallery (see below), and is now housed in a fanciful Italianate complex designed by Charles Barry (son of the architect of the Houses of Parliament), south of Dulwich Common; Alleyn is buried in the college chapel. The college is now a

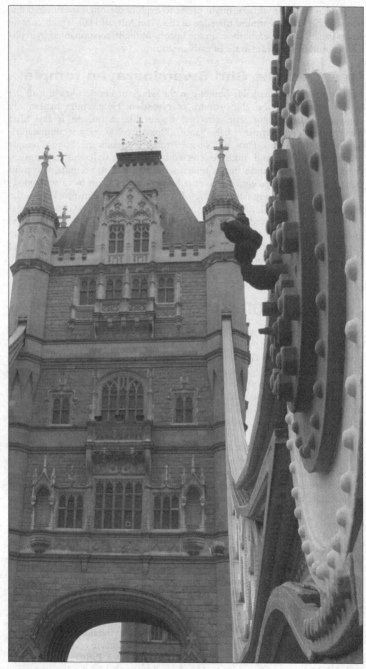

△ Tower Bridge

fee-paying public school, with an impressive roll call of old boys, including Raymond Chandler, P.G. Wodehouse and World War II traitor Lord Haw-Haw, though they tend to keep quiet about the last of the trio.

Recently refurbished, **Dulwich Picture Gallery** (Tues–Fri 10am–5pm, Sat & Sun 11am–5pm; £4, free on Fri; ⓦ www.dulwichpicturegallery.org.uk; West Dulwich train station, from Victoria), on College Road, is the nation's oldest public art gallery, designed by Sir John Soane and opened in 1817. Soane created a beautifully spacious building, awash with natural light and crammed with superb paintings – elegiac landscapes by Cuyp, one of the world's finest Poussin series, and splendid works by Hogarth, Gainsborough, Van Dyck, Canaletto and Rubens. Rembrandt's *Portrait of a Young Man* is probably the most valuable picture in the gallery, and has been stolen no fewer than four times. At the centre of the museum is a tiny mausoleum designed by Soane for the sarcophagi of the gallery's founders.

To the southeast of Dulwich Park, on the busy South Circular road, is the wacky **Horniman Museum** (Mon–Sat 10.30am–5.30pm, Sun 2–5.30pm; free; ⓦ www.horniman.ac.uk; Forest Hill train station, from Victoria or London Bridge), purpose-built in 1901 by Frederick Horniman, a tea trader with a passion for collecting. The museum is principally a monument to its creator's freewheeling eclecticism: in addition to its small aquarium and its large collection of stuffed creatures, there's a wide-ranging anthropology section, and a musical department with more than 1500 instruments from Chinese gongs to electric guitars. However, the museum, including its new "centre for understanding the environment", is undergoing a massive rebuilding programme, which should be completed during the course of 2002.

Greenwich

Greenwich is one of London's most beguiling spots, and the one place in southeast London that draws large numbers of visitors. At its heart stands one of the capital's finest architectural set-pieces, the former Royal Naval College overlooking the Thames. To the west lies Greenwich town centre, while to the south, you'll find Greenwich's two prime tourist sights, the National Maritime Museum and the Royal Observatory.

The Millennium Dome

London's controversial **Millennium Dome** is clearly visible from the riverside at Greenwich and from the upper parts of Greenwich Park. Built at a cost of over £800 million, and designed by Richard Rogers (of Lloyd's Building and Pompidou Centre fame), it is by far the world's largest dome – over half a mile in circumference and 160ft in height – held up by a dozen, 300ft-tall yellow steel masts. In 2000, for one year only, it housed the nation's chief millennium extravaganza: an array of high-tech themed zones set around a stage, on which a circus-style performance took place twice a day.

Like most grand projects, the Dome had a rough ride from the press right from the beginning. The hiccups and headaches continued into the year 2000, with bad reviews and over-optimistic estimates of visitor numbers costing the first Dome chief her job. Nevertheless, millions paid up to £20 each to visit the Dome, and millions went away happy. Nobody quite knows what the future holds for the Dome, which has its very own, very large, very fancy Jubilee line tube station, designed by Norman Foster. Various organizations, including Charlton Athletic football club, have put in bids to take over the site, but as the book went to print, there were still no takers lined up.

If you're heading straight for the National Maritime Museum from central London, the quickest way to get there is to take the **train** from Charing Cross (every 30min) to Maze Hill, on the eastern edge of Greenwich Park. Those wanting to start with the town or the *Cutty Sark* should alight at Greenwich station. A more scenic way of getting to Greenwich is to take a **boat** from one of the piers in central London (see Ⓦwww.londontransport.co.uk/river). A third possible option is to take the **Docklands Light Railway** (DLR) to the Cutty Sark station. For the best view of the Wren buildings, though, get out at Island Gardens, and then take the Greenwich Foot Tunnel under the Thames.

The town centre

Greenwich town centre, laid out in the 1820s with Nash-style terraces, is nowadays plagued with heavy traffic. To escape the busy streets, head for the old covered market, now at the centre of the weekend **Greenwich Market** (Sat & Sun 9am–5pm), a lively place full of antiques, crafts and clothes stalls that have spilled out up the High Road, Stockwell Road and Royal Hill. The best sections are the indoor second-hand book markets, flanking the Central Market on Stockwell Road; the antiques hall, further down on Greenwich High Road; and the flea market on Thames Street.

A short distance in from the old covered market, on the opposite side of Greenwich Church Street, rises the Doric portico and broken pediment of Nicholas Hawksmoor's **St Alfege's Church** (Mon–Sat 10am–4pm, Sun 1–4pm; Ⓦwww.longitude0.co.uk/st-alfege). Built in 1712–18, the church was flattened in the Blitz, but it has been magnificently restored to its former glory.

Wedged in a dry dock by the Greenwich Foot Tunnel is the majestic **Cutty Sark** (daily 10am–5pm; £3.50; Ⓦwww.cuttysark.org.uk), the world's last surviving tea clipper, built in 1869. The *Cutty Sark* lasted just eight years in the China tea trade, and it was as a wool clipper that it actually made its name, making a return journey to Australia in just 72 days. Inside, there's little to see beyond the exhibition in the main hold which tells the ship's story from its inception to its arrival in Greenwich in 1954.

It's entirely appropriate that the one London building that makes the most of its riverbank location should be the **Old Royal Naval College** (Mon–Sat 10am–5pm, Sun 12.30–5pm; £3, free after 3.30pm & all day Sun; Ⓦwww .greenwichfoundation.org.uk), Wren's beautifully symmetrical Baroque ensemble, initially built as a royal palace, but eventually converted into a hospital for disabled seamen. From 1873 until 1998 it was home to the Royal Naval College, but now houses the University of Greenwich and the Trinity College of Music.

The two grandest rooms, situated underneath Wren's twin domes, are open to the public and well worth visiting. The entrance to the college is on King William Walk, and visitors are ushered first into the **RNC Chapel** in the east wing. The exquisite pastel-shaded plasterwork and spectacular, decorative detailing on the ceiling were designed by James "Athenian" Stuart after a fire in 1799 destroyed the original interior. From the chapel, you can take the underground Chalk Walk to gain access to the magnificent **Painted Hall** in the west wing, which is dominated by James Thornhill's gargantuan allegorical ceiling painting and his trompe l'oeil fluted pilasters.

National Maritime Museum

The **National Maritime Museum** (daily 10am–5pm; free; Ⓦwww.nmm .ac.uk), which occupies the old Naval Asylum, has recently undergone a lengthy £20 million redevelopment programme. The main entrance is now on

Greenwich Passport

If you're planning to visit the National Maritime Museum, the Royal Observatory and the *Cutty Sark*, it's worth buying a **Greenwich Passport**, which costs £12 and is valid for two days, and includes a repeat visit to each sight within a year. Alternatively, you can buy a simple combined ticket for the National Maritime Museum and the Royal Observatory for £10.50.

Romney Road, and brings you out into the spectacular glass-roofed central courtyard, which houses the museum's largest artefacts, among them the splendid 63ft-long gilded **Royal Barge**, designed in Rococo style by William Kent for Prince Frederick, the much unloved eldest son of George II.

The various themed galleries are superbly designed to appeal to visitors of all ages. In "Explorers", on Level 1, you get to view some of the museum's most highly prized relics, such as **Captain Cook**'s sextant and K1 marine clock, **Shackleton**'s compass, and **Captain Scott**'s furry sleeping bag and sledging goggles. Sponsors P&O get to display their wares in "Passengers", which traces the history of modern passenger liners, and "Cargoes", which concentrates on containerization. On Level 2, there's a large maritime **art gallery**, an eco-conscious section on the future of the sea and biodiversity, and a gallery devoted to the legacy of the British Empire, warts and all.

Level 3 boasts two **hands-on galleries**: "The Bridge", where you can attempt to navigate a catamaran, a paddle steamer and a rowing boat to shore; and "All Hands", where children can have a go at radio transmission, loading miniature cargo, firing a cannon and so forth. Finally, you reach the **Nelson Gallery**, which contains the museum's vast collection of Nelson-related memorabilia, including Turner's *Battle of Trafalgar, 21st October, 1805*, his largest work and only royal commission.

Inigo Jones's **Queen's House**, originally built amidst a rambling Tudor royal palace, is now the focal point of the Greenwich ensemble, and is an integral part of the Maritime Museum. As royal residences go, it's an unassuming country house, but as the first Neoclassical building in the country, it has enormous architectural significance. An audioguide is available from the desk in the Great Hall; off which lies the beautiful Tulip Staircase, Britain's earliest cantilevered spiral staircase – its name derives from the floral patterning in the wrought-iron balustrade. The ground floor is given over to temporary exhibitions from the Maritime Museum, while the Royal Apartments on the first floor have been decked out with skilful repro furniture, rush matting and damask silk wall hangings.

Royal Observatory

Crowning the hill in Greenwich Park, behind the National Maritime Museum, the **Royal Observatory** (daily 10am–5pm; £5; combined ticket with the National Maritime Museum £10.50; Ⓦ www.rog.nmm.ac.uk) was established in 1675 by Charles II to house the first Astronomer Royal, John Flamsteed. Flamsteed's chief task was to study the night sky in order to discover an astronomical method of finding the longitude of a ship at sea, the lack of which was causing enormous problems for the emerging British Empire. Astrologers continued to work here at Greenwich until the postwar smog forced them to decamp to Herstmonceux Castle and the clearer skies of Sussex (they've since moved to the Pacific); the old observatory, meanwhile, is now a very popular museum.

Greenwich Mean Time

Greenwich's other great claim to fame is of course as the home of **GMT** and the **Prime Meridian** – a meridian being any north–south line used as a basis for astronomical observations, and therefore also for the calculation of longitude and time. In 1852, Britain adopted "London time", which meant, in effect, Greenwich Mean Time (GMT), though, in fact, this wasn't formally acknowledged until 1880. Three years later the USA adopted Greenwich as the Prime Meridian, and in 1884 persuaded an international convention in Washington DC to agree to make Greenwich the Prime Meridian of the World – in other words, zero longitude. As a result, the entire world sets its clocks in relation to GMT.

The red strip in the main courtyard lies along the Greenwich Prime Meridian, which is still used as an absolute today. However, what the Royal Observatory don't tell you is that, as a result of communications problems encountered during the Vietnam War, the Americans starting using satellites to work out longitude in the 1980s. The global standard for air navigation, and used widely by the military, is now the **Global Positioning System** or GPS, which bases its calculations on the centre of the earth not the surface, and places the meridian approximately 336ft to the east of the red strip.

The oldest part of the observatory is the Wren-built **Flamsteed House**, whose northeastern turret sports a bright red time-ball that climbs the mast at 12.58pm and drops at 1pm GMT precisely; it was added in 1833 to allow ships on the Thames to set their clocks. Passing quickly through Flamsteed's restored apartments and the Octagon Room, where the king used to show off to his guests, you reach the Chronometer Gallery, which focuses on the search for the precise measurement of longitude, and displays four of the clocks designed by **John Harrison**, including "H4", which helped win the Longitude Prize in 1763.

Flamsteed's own meridian line is a brass strip in the floor of the Meridian Building. Edmond Halley, Flamsteed's successor, who charted the comings and goings of the famous comet, worked out his own meridian, and the Bradley Meridian Room reveals yet another, standard from 1750 to 1850 and still used for Ordnance Survey maps. Finally, you reach a room that's spliced in two by the present-day Greenwich Meridian, fixed by the cross-hairs in Airy's "Transit Circle", the astrological instrument that dominates the room.

The exhibition ends on a soothing note in the Telescope Dome of the octagonal **Great Equatorial Building**, home to Britain's largest telescope. In addition, there are half-hourly presentations in the **Planetarium** (Mon–Fri 2.30pm; £2), housed in the adjoining South Building.

The Ranger's House and the Fan Museum

Southwest of the observatory, and backing onto Greenwich park's rose garden, is the **Ranger's House** (April–Oct daily 10am–6pm; Oct–March Wed–Sun 10am–4pm; £2.50; EH), a red-brick Georgian villa that has been undergoing a programme of refurbishment which should have finished by spring 2002. If you do visit the house, be sure to check out the Architectural Study Centre across the stable yard, filled with all manner of bits and bobs salvaged from London's buildings.

Croom's Hill boasts some of Greenwich's finest Georgian buildings, one of which houses the **Fan Museum** at no. 12 (Tues–Sat 11am–5pm, Sun noon–5pm; £3.50; ⓦ www.fan-museum.org). It's a fascinating little place (and an extremely beautiful house), revealing the importance of the fan as a social and political document. The permanent exhibition on the ground floor traces the history of the materials employed, from peacock feathers to straw, while temporary exhibitions on the first floor explore such subjects as techniques of production and changing fashion.

Out west: Chiswick to Windsor

Most people experience west London en route to or from Heathrow airport, either from the confines of the train or tube (which runs overground at this point), or the motorway. The city and its satellites seem to continue unabated, with only fleeting glimpses of the countryside. However, in the five-mile stretch from Chiswick to Osterley there are several former country retreats, now surrounded by suburbia, which are definitely worth digging out.

The Palladian villa of **Chiswick House** is perhaps the best known of these attractions. However, it draws nothing like as many visitors as **Syon House**, most of whom come for the gardening centre rather than for the **house** itself, a showcase for the talents of Robert Adam, who also worked at **Osterley House**, another Elizabethan conversion, now owned by the National Trust.

Running through much of the area is the **River Thames**, once known as the "Great Highway of London" and still the most pleasant way to travel in these parts during the summer. Boats plough up the Thames all the way from central London via the **Royal Botanic Gardens** at **Kew** and the picturesque riverside at **Richmond**, as far as **Hampton Court**, home of the country's largest royal residence and the famous maze. To reach the heavily touristed royal outpost of **Windsor Castle**, however, you really need to take the train.

Chiswick

Chiswick House (April to mid-Oct daily 10am–6pm; mid-Oct to March Wed–Sun 10am–4pm; £3.30; EH; Chiswick train station, from Waterloo), is a perfect little Neoclassical villa, designed in the 1720s by Richard Boyle, Earl of Burlington, and set in one of the most beautifully landscaped gardens in London. Like its prototype, Palladio's Villa Rotonda near Vicenza, the house was purpose-built as a "temple to the arts" – here, amid his fine-art collection, Burlington could entertain artistic friends such as Swift, Handel and Pope. Visitors enter via the **lower floor**, where you can pick up an audioguide, before heading up to the **upper floor**, a series of cleverly interconnecting rooms, each enjoying a wonderful view out onto the gardens – all, that is, except the Tribunal, the central octagonal hall, where the earl's finest paintings and sculptures would have been displayed.

To do a quick circuit of the **gardens**, head across the smooth carpet of grass, punctuated by urns and sphinxes that sit under the shadow of two giant cedars of Lebanon. A great place from which to admire the northwest side of the house is from the stone benches of the exedra, the set of yew-hedge niches harbouring lions and copies of Roman statuary, situated beyond the cedars. Elsewhere, there's an Italian garden, a maze of high-hedge alleyways, a lake and a grassy amphitheatre, centred on an obelisk in a pond and overlooked by an Ionic temple.

If you leave Chiswick House gardens by the northernmost exit, beyond the Italian garden, it's just a short walk along the thunderous A4 road to **Hogarth's House** (April–Oct Tues–Fri 1–5pm, Sat & Sun 1–6pm; Nov–March closes 1hr earlier; closed Jan; free), where the artist spent each summer with his wife, sister and mother-in-law from 1749 until his death in 1764. Nowadays it's difficult to believe Hogarth came here for "peace and quiet", but in the eighteenth century the house was almost entirely surrounded by countryside. In addition to scores of Hogarth's engravings, you can see copies of his satirical series *An Election*, *Marriage à la Mode* and *A Harlot's Progress*, and compare the modern view from the parlour with the more idyllic scene in *Mr Ranby's House*.

Barnes: the Wetland Centre

For anyone even remotely interested in wildlife, the new **Wetland Centre** (daily: summer 9.30am–6pm; rest of year 9.30am–5pm; £6.75; @www.wetlandcentre.org.uk; bus #283 from Hammersmith tube, or walk from Barnes train station) in well-to-do Barnes, across the river from Chiswick, is something of an unexpected boon. On the site of four disused reservoirs, the Wildfowl & Wetland Trust (WWT) have created a high-tech 105-acre mosaic of wetland habitats. Heading north from the visitor centre, you enter **World Wetlands**, where a variety of extremely rare wildfowl – from White-faced Whistling Ducks to Blue Ducks – are breeding in captivity in miniature versions of their own endangered wetland habitats. Beyond, in the **Wildside**, are the reedbeds and pools that attract native species, such as lapwing, tufted ducks, grebes and swans. **Waterlife**, east of the visitor centre, includes a chance for younger children to get near some domesticated wildfowl, and, best of all, do some pond-dipping. At the far end is the mother of all hides: a triple-decker octagonal one with a lift, allowing views over the whole of the reserve.

Kew Bridge

Difficult to miss thanks to its stylish Italianate standpipe tower, **Kew Bridge Steam Museum** (daily 11am–5pm; weekdays £3, weekends £4; @www.kbsm.org.uk; Kew Bridge train station, from Waterloo; or bus #237 or #267 from Gunnersbury tube) occupies a former pumping station, on the corner of Kew Bridge Road and Green Dragon Lane, 100m west of the bridge itself. At the heart of the museum is the Steam Hall, which contains a triple expansion steam engine and four gigantic nineteenth-century Cornish beam engines, while two adjoining rooms house the pumping station's original beam engines, one of which is the largest in the world. The steam engines may be things of great beauty, but they are primarily of interest to enthusiasts. Not so the museum's hands-on "Water for Life" gallery in the basement, devoted to the history of the capital's water supply. The best time to visit is at weekends, when each of the museum's industrial dinosaurs is put through its paces, and the small narrow-gauge steam railway runs back and forth round the yard (March–Nov).

Five minutes' walk west of the Steam Museum along Kew Bridge Road and Brentford High Street is the superb **Musical Museum** (April–Oct Sat & Sun 2–5pm; July & Aug also Wed 2–4pm; £3.50), a converted church packed with musical automata and run by wildly enthusiastic and engaging volunteers. During the noisy ninety-minute demonstrations, you get to hear every kind of mechanical music-making machine, from cleverly crafted music boxes to the huge orchestrions that were once a feature of London's swish cafés. The museum also boasts one of the world's finest collections of player-pianos, and an enormous Art Deco Wurlitzer cinema organ.

Syon Park

Across the water from Kew stands **Syon Park** (@www.syonpark.co.uk), seat of the Duke of Northumberland since Elizabethan times, now as much a working commercial concern as a family home, embracing a garden centre, a wholefood shop, an aquatic centre stocked with tropical fish, a mini-zoo and a butterfly house, as well as the old aristocratic mansion and its gardens.

From its rather plain castellated exterior, you'd never guess that **Syon House** (mid-March to Oct Wed, Thurs & Sun 11am–5pm; £6.25, including entry to the gardens; bus #237 or #267, from Gunnersbury tube or Kew Bridge train station) contains the most opulent eighteenth-century interiors in the whole of London. The splendour of Robert Adam's refurbishment is immediately revealed, however, in the pristine **Great Hall**, an apsed double cube with a screen of Doric columns at one end and classical statuary dotted around the edges. There are several more Adam-designed rooms to admire in the house, plus a smattering of works by van Dyck, Lely, Gainsborough and Reynolds.

While Adam beautified Syon House, Capability Brown laid out its **gardens** (daily 10am–5.30pm; £3) around an artificial lake, surrounding it with oaks, beeches, limes and cedars. The gardens' chief focus now, however, is the crescent-shaped **Great Conservatory**, an early nineteenth-century addition which is said to have inspired Joseph Paxton, architect of the Crystal Palace. Those with young children will be compelled to make use of the **miniature steam train**, which runs through the park at weekends from April to October.

Another plus point for kids is Syon's **Butterfly House** (daily: May–Sept 10am–5pm; Oct–April 10am–3pm; £3.50; Ⓦwww.butterflies.org.uk), a small, mesh-covered hothouse, where you can walk amid hundreds of exotic butterflies from all over the world, as they flit about the foliage. An adjoining room houses a collection of iguanas, millipedes, tarantulas and giant hissing Tanzanian cockroaches. If your kids show more enthusiasm for life-threatening reptiles than delicate insects, then you could skip the butterflies and go instead for the adjacent **London Aquatic Experience** (daily 10am–5pm; £3.50; Ⓦwww .aquatic-experience.org), a purpose-built centre with a mixed range of aquatic creatures from the mysterious basilisk, which can walk on water, to the perennially popular piranhas.

Osterley Park and House

Robert Adam redesigned another colossal Elizabethan mansion three miles northwest of Syon at **Osterley Park** (daily 9am–7.30pm or dusk; free), which maintains the impression of being in the middle of the countryside, despite the presence of the M4 to the north of the house. The park itself is well worth exploring, and there's a great café in the Tudor stables, but anyone with a passing interest in Adam's work should pay a visit to **Osterley House** (April–Oct Wed–Sun 1–4.30pm; £4.30; NT; Osterley tube).

From the outside, Osterley bears some similarity to Syon, the big difference being Adam's grand entrance portico, with its tall, Ionic colonnade. From here, you enter a characteristically cool **Entrance Hall**, followed by the so-called State Rooms of the south wing. Highlights include the **Drawing Room**, with Reynolds portraits on the damask walls and a coffered ceiling centred on a giant marigold, and the **Etruscan Dressing Room**, in which every surface is covered in delicate painted trelliswork, sphinxes and urns, a style that Adam (and Wedgwood) dubbed "Etruscan", though it is in fact derived from Greek vases found at Pompeii.

Kew Gardens

Established in 1759, the **Royal Botanic Gardens** (daily 9.30am to 7.30pm or dusk; £6.50; Ⓦwww.kew.org; Kew Gardens tube) have grown from their original eight acres into a three-hundred-acre site in which more than 33,000 species are grown in plantations and glasshouses, a display that attracts over a million visitors every year, most of them with no specialist interest at all. There's always something to see, whatever the season, but to get the most out of the place, come sometime between spring and autumn, bring a picnic and stay for the day. The only drawbacks to Kew are the high entry fee, and the fact that it lies on a frequently used (and very noisy) flight path to Heathrow.

There are four entry points to the gardens, but the majority of people arrive at Kew Gardens tube and train station, a few minutes' walk east of the **Victoria Gate**. Of all the glasshouses, by far the most celebrated is the **Palm House**, a curvaceous mound of glass and wrought-iron, designed by Decimus Burton in the 1840s. Its drippingly humid atmosphere nurtures most of the known palm species, while in the basement there's a small but excellent tropical aquarium. The largest of the glasshouses, however, is the **Temperate House**, to the south, which contains plants from every continent, including one of the largest indoor palms in the world, the sixty-foot Chilean Wine Palm.

Kew's origins as an eighteenth-century royal pleasure garden are evident in the numerous follies dotted about Kew, the most conspicuous of which is the ten-storey 163-foot-high **Pagoda**. The original royal pad, **Kew Palace**, a three-storey red-brick mansion bought by George II as a nursery for his umpteen children, is tentatively scheduled to re-open after a lengthy period of renovation during the course of 2002. Alternatively, you could explore **Queen Charlotte's Cottage** (April–Sept Sat & Sun 10.30am–4pm; free), a tiny thatched summer-house built in the 1770s as a royal picnic spot for George III's wife in the thickly wooded, southwestern section of the park – a sure way to lose the crowds.

Richmond

On emerging from the station at **Richmond**, you'd be forgiven for wondering why you're here, but the procession of chain stores spread out along the one-way system is only half the story. To see Richmond's more interesting side, take one of the narrow pedestrianized alleyways off busy George Street, which bring you to the wide open space of **Richmond Green**, one of the finest village greens in London, and no doubt one of the most peaceful before it found itself on the main flight path into Heathrow. Handsome seventeenth- and eighteenth-century houses line the south side of the green, where the medieval royal palace of **Richmond** once stood, though only its unspectacular **Tudor Gateway** survives.

The other place to head for in Richmond is the **Riverside**, pedestrianized, terraced and redeveloped by Quinlan Terry, Prince Charles's favourite purveyor of ersatz classicism, in the late 1980s. The real joy of the waterfront, however, is **Richmond Bridge**, London's oldest extant bridge, an elegant span of five arches made from Purbeck stone in 1777. The old town hall, set back from the new development, houses the **tourist office** (Mon–Sat 10am–5pm; May–Sept also Sun 10.30am–1.30pm; ☎020/8940 9125, ⓦwww.guidetorichmond.co.uk) and, on the second floor, the **Richmond Museum** (April–Oct Tues–Sat 11am–5pm, Sun 2–5pm; Nov–March Tues–Sat 11am–5pm; £2), but most folk prefer to ensconce themselves in the riverside pubs, or head for the numerous boat- and bike-rental outlets.

Richmond's greatest attraction, though, is the enormous **Richmond Park** (daily: March–Sept 7am–dusk; Oct–Feb 7.30am–dusk; free; ⓦwww.royal-parks.co.uk), at the top of Richmond Hill – 2500 acres of undulating grassland and bracken, dotted with coppiced woodland and as wild as anything in

London. Eight miles across at its widest point, this is Europe's largest city park, famed for its red and fallow deer, which roam freely, and for its ancient oaks. For the most part untamed, the park does have a couple of deliberately land-scaped plantations which feature splendid springtime azaleas and rhododen-drons, in particular the Isabella Plantation.

If you continue along the towpath beyond Richmond Bridge, after a mile or so, you will eventually leave the rest of London far behind and arrive at **Ham House** (April–Oct Mon–Wed, Sat & Sun 1–5pm; £6, including gardens; NT; bus #371 or walk from Richmond tube), home to the Earls of Dysart for near-ly three hundred years. Expensively furnished in the seventeenth century, but little altered since then, the house boasts one of the finest Stuart interiors in the country, from the stupendously ornate Great Staircase to the Long Gallery, featuring six "Court Beauties" by Peter Lely. Elsewhere, there are several fine Verrio ceiling paintings, some exquisite parquet flooring and works by van Dyck and Reynolds. Another bonus are the formal seventeenth-century **gar-dens** (open all year: Mon–Wed, Sat & Sun 11am–6pm; £2), especially the Cherry Garden, laid out with a pungent lavender parterre, surrounded by yew hedges and pleached hornbeam arbours. The Orangery, overlooking the orig-inal kitchen garden, currently serves as a tea room.

Hampton Court

Hampton Court Palace (April–Oct Mon 10.15am–6pm, Tues–Sun 9.30am–6pm; rest of year closes 4.30pm; £10.80; ⓦ www.hrp.org.uk; Hampton Court train station, from Waterloo), a sprawling red-brick ensemble on the banks of the Thames, thirteen miles southwest of London, is the finest of England's royal abodes. Built in 1516 by the upwardly mobile **Cardinal Wolsey**, Henry VIII's Lord Chancellor, it was purloined by Henry himself after Wolsey fell from favour. Charles II laid out the gardens, inspired by what he had seen at Versailles, while William and Mary had large sections of the palace remodelled by Wren.

The **Royal Apartments** are divided into six thematic walking tours. There's not a lot of information in any of the rooms, but guided tours, each lasting 45 minutes, are available at no extra charge for Henry VIII's and the King's apart-ments; all are led by period-costumed historians, who do a fine job of bring-ing the place to life. If your energy is lacking – and Hampton Court is huge – the most rewarding sections are: **Henry VIII's State Apartments**, which fea-ture the glorious double hammer-beamed Great Hall; the **King's Apartments** (remodelled by William III); and the vast **Tudor Kitchens**. The last two are also served by audio tours. The royal art collection is housed in the **Renaissance Picture Gallery** and is chock-full of treasures, among them paintings by Tintoretto, Lotto, Titian, Cranach, Bruegel and Holbein.

Tickets to the Royal Apartments cover entry to the rest of the sites in the grounds. Those who don't wish to visit the apartments are free to wander around the gardens, but will have to pay extra to visit the curious **Royal Tennis Courts** (50p), the palace's famously tricky hedge **Maze** (£2.50), laid out in 1714 north of the palace, and the **South Gardens** (£2.50), where you can view Andrea Mantegna's colourful, heroic canvases, *The Triumphs of Caesar*, housed in the Lower Orangery, and the celebrated **Great Vine**, grown from a cutting in 1768 and now producing about seven hundred pounds of black grapes per year, which are sold at the palace each September. Further afield, across Hampton Court Road, Wren's royal road, Chestnut Avenue, cuts through the semi-wild **Bushy Park**, which sustains a few fallow deer.

Windsor and Eton

Every weekend trains from Waterloo and Paddington are packed with people heading for **WINDSOR**, the royal enclave 21 miles west of London, where they join the human conveyor belt round **Windsor Castle** (April–Sept 9.45am–5.15pm; Oct–March 9.45am–4.15pm; £11; Ⓦwww.royal.gov.uk; Paddington to Windsor & Eton Central via Slough, or Waterloo to Windsor & Eton Riverside). Towering above the town on a steep chalk bluff, the castle is an undeniably awesome sight, its chilly grey walls, punctuated by mighty medieval bastions, continuing as far as the eye can see. The small selection of state rooms open to the public is unexciting, though the magnificent St George's Chapel and the chance to see another small selection of the Queen's private art collection make the trip worthwhile. On a fine day, it pays to put aside some time for exploring Windsor Great Park, which stretches for several miles to the south of the castle.

Windsor has two **train stations**, both very close to the centre. Direct trains from Waterloo (Mon–Sat every 30min, Sun hourly; journey time 50min) arrive at **Windsor & Eton Riverside**, five minutes' walk from the centre; trains from Paddington require a change at Slough (Mon–Fri every 20min, Sat & Sun every 30min; journey time 30–40min), and arrive at **Windsor & Eton Central**, directly opposite the castle. Note that you must arrive and depart from the same station, as tickets are not interchangeable. The **tourist office** is at 24 High St (daily 10am–4pm; longer hours in summer; ☎01753/743900).

Once inside the castle, it's best to head straight for **St George's Chapel** (Mon–Sat 10am–4pm), a glorious Perpendicular structure ranking with Henry VII's chapel in Westminster Abbey, and the second most important resting place for royal corpses after the Abbey. Entry is via the south door and a one-way system operates, which brings you out by the **Albert Memorial Chapel**, built by Henry VII as a burial place for Henry VI, completed by Cardinal Wolsey for his own burial, but eventually converted for Queen Victoria into a High Victorian memorial to her husband, Prince Albert.

Before entering the State Apartments, pay a quick visit to **Queen Mary's Dolls' House**, a palatial micro-residence designed for the wife of George V, and the **Gallery**, where special exhibitions culled from the Royal Art Collection are staged. Most visitors just gape in awe at the monotonous, gilded grandeur of the **State Apartments**, while the real highlights – the paintings from the Royal Collection that line the walls – are rarely given a second glance. The **King's Dressing Room**, for example, despite its small size, contains a feast of art treasures, including a dapper Rubens self-portrait, van Dyck's famous triple portrait of Charles I, and *The Artist's Mother*, a perfectly observed portrait of old age by Rembrandt.

You'd hardly know that Windsor suffered the most devastating **fire** in its history in 1992, so thorough (and uninspired) has the restoration been in rooms such as **St George's Hall**. By contrast, the octagonal **Lantern Lobby**, beyond, is clearly an entirely new room, a safe neo-Gothic design replacing the old chapel. At this point, those visiting during the winter season (Oct–March) are given the privilege of seeing four **Semi-State Rooms**, created in the 1820s by George IV, and still used in the summer months by the Royal Family.

Crossing the bridge at the end of Thames Avenue in Windsor town brings you to **ETON**, a one-street village lined with bookshops and antique dealers, but famous all over the world for **Eton College** (college and chapel: Easter, July & Aug daily 10.30am–4.30pm; after Easter to June & Sept daily 2–4.30pm; £3; guided tours daily 2.15pm & 3.15pm; £4; Ⓦwww.etoncollege.com), a ten-minute walk from the river. When the school was founded in 1440, its aim was to give free education to seventy poor scholars and choristers; how times have changed. The original fifteenth-century **schoolroom**, gnarled with centuries of graffiti, survives, but the real highlight is the **College Chapel**, completed in 1482, a wonderful example of English Perpendicular architecture. The self-congratulatory **Museum of Eton Life**, where you're deposited at the end of the tour, is well worth missing unless you have a fascination with flogging, fagging and bragging about the school's facilities and alumni – Percy Bysshe Shelley is a rare rebellious figure in the roll call of Establishment greats. If you're thinking of going on a guided tour, phone ahead to make sure the school isn't closed for some special reason.

Among younger kids, the attractions of Windsor Castle are overshadowed by the town's **Legoland** (March–Oct daily 10am–5pm or later; adults £18.50, under-15s £15.50, under 3s free; ⓦwww.legoland.co.uk) theme park aimed at pre-teenage children (the perfect age is around 5 to 8). The entrance charges are enough to put off most people, but if you've got the money, and several small kids in tow, it's one way of keeping them happy for a day. Whatever you do, though, try not to go at the weekend or during the school holidays, when the queues for the various rides become grievously long. On arrival, a funicular railway takes visitors down into the park, disgorging them close to Miniland, with its miniature lego depictions of various European landmarks. The rest of the park is really just a series of rides, most of them very gentle. There are numerous places to eat, though it makes sense to take a picnic and save yourself some money

Eating, drinking and nightlife

No matter what your taste in **food**, **drink** or **entertainment**, you'll find what you're looking for in London, a city that in many ways becomes a more appealing place after dark. The capital's rich ethnic mix and concentration of creative talent give it a diversity and energy that no other town in England comes close to matching – Birmingham might have a better concert hall, Manchester might have a couple of top clubs, but nowhere can match the capital's consistent quality and choice. The weekly calendar of gigs, movies, plays and other events is charted most completely in *Time Out*, the main listings magazine, and there are any number of specialist publications for those who want to make sure they are not missing a thing – from solemn books on the foodie shrines of London to esoteric little mags for the dance crowd. However, the listings that follow should be more than enough for any visitor who's planning on spending less than a couple of months in the city.

Eating

London is a great place in which to **eat out**. You can sample more or less any kind of cuisine here, and, wherever you come from, you should find something new and quite possibly unique. Home to some of the best **Cantonese** restaurants in the whole of Europe, London is also a noted centre for **Indian** and **Bangladeshi** food, and has numerous **French**, **Greek**, **Italian**, **Japanese**, **Spanish** and **Thai** restaurants; and within all these cuisines, you can choose anything from simple meals to gourmet spreads. Traditional and **Modern British** food is available all over town, and some of the best venues are reviewed below.

Cheap eats

As well as the places we've listed below, there are several **London-wide chains** that are well worth checking out. **EAT** (Ⓦ www.eatcafe.co.uk) is a promising newcomer, and makes up excellent sandwiches on their own-baked bread; **Prêt à Manger** also does ready-made sandwiches (though it helps if you like mayo), as well as hot stuffed croissants and sushi selections. **Caffè Nero** serves terrific coffee, a range of Italian cakes, and pasta, calzone and pizza. As far as other coffee chains go; there's **Costa Coffee**, the train-station favourite, which serves some of the best coffee in town, as does **Starbucks** (Ⓦ www.starbucks.com), the infamous clean-cut Seattle coffee company – **Coffee Republic** is a slightly less memorable replica.

For more substantial fare, the white and blue, Art Deco-ish **Café Flo** does decent French brasserie fare, as does the red-clad **Café Rouge**; **Crank's**, the original veggie café, is making a bid for world domination, losing its character and flavour en route; **Ed's Easy Diner** (whose main branch is at 12 Moor St in Soho) is a 1950s-theme fast-food joint dishing up some of the city's best burgers and fries; and **Stockpot**, (the main branch is on Soho's Old Compton St), serves big portions of stew and suchlike at rock-bottom prices.

Cafés and fast food

There are plenty of **cafés** and small, basic restaurants all over London that can fill you up for under £10, including tea or coffee. A huge number of them are run by Anglo-Italians, which means you're guaranteed proper coffee and ciabatta sandwiches. Several of the places listed are also open in the evening, but the turnover is fast, so don't expect to linger; they're best seen as fuel stops before – or in a few cases, after – a night out. It's worth bearing in mind that most **pubs** (which are covered in the following section) serve food, and some have restaurants attached.

Mayfair and Marylebone

La Madeleine 5 Vigo St, W1. An authentic French patisserie and café, with mountains of tempting pastries from which to indulge yourself; tables at the back are for punters who want more substantial bistro fare. Green Park or Piccadilly Circus tube.
Mô 25 Heddon St, W1. The ultimate Arabic pastiche, but a successful one at that. The adjacent restaurant is pricey, but the tearoom serves delicious snacks and is a great place to hangout, with tables and hookahs spilling out onto the pavement of this little alleyway off Regent Street. Piccadilly Circus tube.

Patisserie Valerie at Sagne 105 Marylebone High St, W1. Founded as *Maison Sagne* in the 1920s, and preserving its wonderful decor from those days, the café is now run by Soho's fab patisserie makers, and is Marylebone's finest without doubt. Bond Street tube.

Soho

Bar Italia 22 Frith St, W1. A tiny café that's a Soho institution, serving coffee, croissants and sandwiches more or less around the clock – as it has been since 1949. Popular with late-night club-

Internet cafés

If you just need to send a quick email to someone, or go online, head for a branch of *easyEverything* (ⓦwww.easyeverything.com), the no-frills internet café chain – there's a 24-hour branch just up the Strand, off Trafalgar Square: Net access starts at £1. Alternatively, the internet cafés listed below are worth a visit in their own right and offer free or very nearly free internet access.

Cyberia, 39 Whitfield St, W1, ⓦwww.cyberia.co.uk. The city's first internet café, with trip-hop in the background, chilled beers, coffee and cakes for refuelling, and fourteen computers lined up for their netizens. Internet access 50p for 15min, occasionally free. Goodge Street tube.

The Vibe Bar, Truman Brewery, 91 Brick Lane, E1, ⓦwww.vibe-bar.co.uk. Head for "Room Service", a row of terminals in the corner of this trendy bar in a former East End brewery; internet access is free, if you buy a drink. Aldgate East tube.

bers and those here to watch the Italian-league soccer on the giant screen. Leicester Square tube.

Bar du Marché 19 Berwick St, W1. A weird find in the middle of raucous Berwick Street market: a licensed French café serving quick snacks, brasserie staples, fried breakfasts and set meals for under £10. Closed Sun. Tottenham Court Road, Piccadilly Circus or Leicester Square tube.

Centrale 16 Moor St, W1. Tiny, friendly Italian café that serves up huge plates of steaming, garlicky pasta, as well as omelettes, chicken and chops for around £5. You'll almost certainly have to wait for – or share – a formica-topped table. Bring your own booze; there's a 50p–£1 corkage charge. Closed Sun. Leicester Square tube.

Lee Ho Fook 4 Macclesfield St, W1. A genuine Chinese barbecue house – small, spartan and cheap – that is very difficult to find. Macclesfield Street runs from Shaftesbury Avenue to Gerrard Street; on the west side is Dansey Place, and on the corner with a red and gold sign in Chinese and a host of ducks hanging on a rack is this place. Leicester Square tube.

Maison Bertaux 28 Greek St, W1. Long-standing, old-fashioned and downbeat Soho patisserie, with tables on two floors (and one or two outside) and a loyal clientele that keeps things busy. You'll be tempted in by the window full of elaborate cakes, but be warned: the service can be brusque and when it comes to coffee, they only do *café au lait*. Leicester Square tube.

Patisserie Valerie 44 Old Compton St, W1. Popular 1920s coffee, croissant and cake emporium attracting a loud-talking, arty Soho crowd. The same outfit now have a branch at 8 Russell St, WC2, and also run *Patisserie Valerie at Sagne* in Marylebone (see above). Leicester Square or Piccadilly Circus tube.

Tokyo Diner 2 Newport Place, WC2. Providing conclusive proof that you don't need to take out a second mortgage to enjoy Japanese food in London, this friendly eatery on the edge of Chinatown shuns elaboration for fast food, Tokyo style. Minimalist decor lets the sushi and sumo do the talking, which – if the number of Japanese who frequent the place is anything to go by – it does fluently. Leicester Square tube.

Covent Garden and Bloomsbury

Café in the Crypt St Martin-in-the-Fields, Duncannon St, WC2. The self-service buffet food is nothing special, but there are regular veggie dishes, and the handy location – below the church in the crypt – makes this an ideal spot to fill up before hitting the West End. Charing Cross tube.

Coffee Gallery 23 Museum St, WC1. Excellent, if small, café close by the British Museum, serving mouthwatering Italian sandwiches and more substantial dishes at lunchtime. Get there early to grab a seat. Tottenham Court Road tube.

Food for Thought 31 Neal St, WC2. Long-established but minuscule bargain veggie restaurant and takeaway counter – the food is good, with the menu changing twice daily, plus regular vegan and wheat-free options. Expect to queue and don't expect to linger at peak times. Closed Sun. Covent Garden tube.

Frank's Cafe 52 Neal St, WC2. Classic Anglo-Italian café/sandwich bar with easy-going service. All-day breakfasts, plus plates of pasta and omelettes; come either side of lunch to make sure of a table. Closed Sun. Covent Garden tube.

Gaby's 30 Charing Cross Rd, WC2. Busy café and takeaway joint serving a wide range of home-cooked veggie and Middle Eastern specialities. Hard

Liquid refuelling

Over the last few years, lunchtime catering in London has gone liquid, with an explosion of diminutive **soup and juice bars**. The trio below are a mere soupçon:

Crussh 48 Cornhill, EC3. Tiny, unusually funky, City juice bar selling wraps, salads, sushi and, of course, fresh juices. Bank tube. Closed Sat & Sun.

Soup Works 9 D'Arblay St. Noodles served here as well as every type of soup from chicken to chilled borscht. Branches in Monmouth St, WC1, and

Moor St, W1. Mon–Fri 8am–5pm, Sat noon–5pm. Oxford Circus tube.

Squeeze 27 Kensington High St, W8. Fruit smoothies, wraps, salads, sushi and muffins as well as fresh juices at this healthy pitstop. High Street Kensington tube.

to beat for value, choice, location or long hours – it's licensed, too, and the takeaway felafel are a central London bargain. Leicester Square tube.

India Club 143 Strand, WC2. There's a faded period charm to this long established, inexpensive Anglo-Indian eatery, sandwiched between floors of the cheap *Strand Continental Hotel* (see p.78). The "chillie bhajais" are to be taken very seriously. Closed Sun. Covent Garden or Temple (Mon–Sat) tube.

Mode 57 Endell St, WC2. The best things about this stylish Covent Garden café are the Italian sandwiches, the cheeses from nearby Neal's Yard Dairy, and the laid-back, funky atmosphere. Closed Sun. Covent Garden tube.

Monmouth Coffee Company 27 Monmouth St, WC2. The marvellous aroma is the first thing you notice here, while the cramped wooden booths and daily newspapers on hand evoke an eighteenth-century coffee-house atmosphere – pick and mix your coffee from a fine selection (or buy the beans to take home). No smoking. Closed Sun. Covent Garden or Leicester Square tube.

Wagamama 4 Streatham St, WC1. Austere, minimalist canteen-style place where the waiters take your orders on hand-held computers. Diners share long benches and slurp huge bowls of noodle soup or stir-fried plates. You may have to queue, however, and the rapid turnover means it's not a place to consider for a long, romantic dinner. Tottenham Court Road tube.

Clerkenwell, the City and the East End

Arkansas Café Unit 12, Old Spitalfields Market, E1. American barbecue fuel stop, using only the very best ingredients. Try chef Bubb's own smoked beef brisket and ribs, and be sure to taste his home-made barbie sauce (made to a secret formula). Liverpool Street tube.

Brick Lane Beigel Bake 159 Brick Lane, E1. The bagels at this no-frills 24-hour takeaway in the

heart of the East End are freshly made and unbelievably cheap, even when stuffed with smoked salmon and cream cheese. Shoreditch or Aldgate East tube.

Clark & Sons 46 Exmouth Market, EC1. Exmouth Market is currently undergoing something of a transformation, so it's all the more surprising to find this genuine eel and pie shop still going strong. Closed Sun. Angel or Farringdon tube.

Feast 86 St John St, 7 EC1. Delicious tortilla-wrapped sandwiches made to order; takeaway or eat in this small, trendy, designer Clerkenwell café. Closed Sat & Sun. Farringdon or Barbican tube.

The Place Below St Mary-le-Bow, Cheapside, EC2. Something of a find in the midst of the City – a café serving imaginative (albeit slightly pricey) vegetarian dishes. Added to that, the wonderful Norman crypt makes for a very pleasant place in which to dine. Closed Sat & Sun. St Paul's or Bank tube.

The South Bank

Konditor & Cook Young Vic Theatre, 66 The Cut, E1. Cut above your average theatre café, this place gets its cakes and so forth made by the fabulous Konditor & Cook bakery, round the corner in Cornwall Road. You can also get snacks, organic ice creams and sorbets, and, of course, drinks at the bar. Closed Sun. Waterloo tube.

Kensington, Chelsea and Notting Hill

Jenny Lo's Teahouse 14 Ecclestone St, SW1 ☎ 020/7259 0399. Bright, bare and utilitarian yet somehow stylish and fashionable, too, *Jenny Lo's* serves good Chinese food at low prices. Be sure to check out the therapeutic teas. Closed Sun. Victoria tube.

Lisboa Patisserie 57 Golborne Rd, W10. Authentic and friendly Portuguese pastelaria, with coffee and cakes including the best custard tarts this side of Lisbon. The *Oporto*, at 62a Golborne Rd, is a good fallback if this place is full. Ladbroke Grove tube.

Maison Blanc 102 Holland Park Ave, W11. French patisserie (with other branches in St John's Wood, Hampstead, Chelsea and Richmond), where you can guarantee you'll get the real thing when it comes to croissants and the like. Holland Park tube.

New Culture Revolution 305 King's Rd, SW3. Great name, great concept – big bowls of freshly cooked noodles in sauce or soup or dumplings and rice dishes, all offering a one-stop meal at bargain prices in simple, minimalist surroundings. Not a place to linger. Sloane Square tube.

Raison d'Être 18 Bute St, SW7. Smack in the middle of South Kensington's French quarter, this is a top-notch patisserie/boulangerie, serving excellent coffee. Closed Sun. South Kensington tube.

Camden and Hampstead

Brew House Kenwood, Hampstead Lane, NW3. Everything from full English breakfast to lunches, cakes and teas, all served in the old laundry at Kenwood, or enjoyed on the terrace overlooking the lake. Bus #210 from Highgate tube or a walk across the Heath.

Café Mozart 17 Swains Lane, N6. Viennese café that's usefully close to the southeast side of Hampstead Heath, and also serves a few hearty Austrian dishes. Gospel Oak train station, or bus #C2.

Louis Patisserie 32 Heath St, NW3. Popular central-European tea room in Hampstead village serving sticky cakes to a mix of Heath-bound hordes and elderly locals. Hampstead tube.

Marine Ices 8 Haverstock Hill, NW3. Situated halfway between Camden and Hampstead, this is a splendid and justly famous old-fashioned Italian ice-cream parlour; pizza and pasta are served in the adjacent restaurant. Chalk Farm tube.

Greenwich

Pistachio's Café 15 Nelson Rd, SE10. Just about the only decent sandwich café in the centre of Greenwich, serving excellent coffee, and with a small garden out back. Cutty Sark DLR, or Greenwich DLR and train station.

Tai Won Mein 49 Greenwich Church St, SE10. Good quality fast-food noodle bar that gets very busy at weekends. Decor is functional and minimalist; choose between rice, fried or soup noodles and *ho fun* (a flatter, softer, ribbon-like noodle). Cutty Sark DLR or Greenwich DLR and train station.

Restaurants

Many of the restaurants we've listed will be busy on most nights of the week, particularly on Thursday, Friday and Saturday, and you're best advised to **reserve a table** wherever you're headed. As for **prices**, you can pay an awful lot for a meal in London, and if you're used to North American portions, you're not going to be particularly impressed by the volume in most places. For cheaper eats, see the section above.

St James's, Mayfair and Marylebone

Abu Ali 136–138 George St, W1 ☎020/7724 6338. Spartan place that's the Lebanese equivalent to a northern working men's club, serving honest Lebanese fare that's terrific value for money, from the *tabbouleh* to the kebabs – wash it all down with fresh mint tea. Cash or cheque only. Inexpensive. Marble Arch tube.

The Criterion 224 Piccadilly, W1 ☎020/7930 0488. One of the city's most beautiful restaurants, behind Eros on Piccadilly Circus. The high vaulted gold mosaic ceiling sparkles, and the menu is courtesy of scourge of the faint-hearted, Marco Pierre White. The set menu lunch (under £20 a head) is the best value and allows you to keep your table all afternoon. Closed Sun lunch. Expensive. Piccadilly Circus tube.

Mandalay 444 Edgware Rd, W2 ☎020/7258 3696, ⓦwww.bcity.com/mandalay. Small non-smoking restaurant that serves pure, freshly cooked and unexpurgated Burmese cuisine – a *mélange* of Thai, Malaysian, a lot of Indian and a few things that are unique. The portions are huge, flavours hit the mark, the service friendly and the prices low. Closed Sun. Inexpensive. Edgware Road tube.

Quaglino's 16 Bury St, SW1 ☎020/7930 6767, ⓦwww.conran.com. Huge 1930s ballroom revived by Terence Conran as one of the capital's busiest and most glamorous eating spots, so you'll need to book well in advance. There's an unmistakable buzz about the place, the surroundings are splendid, and the fish and seafood dishes are excellent – it's also open late. Closed Sun lunch. Expensive. Green Park tube.

La Spighetta 43 Blandford St, W1 ☎020/7486 7340. Not a spaghetti house – *spighetta* actually means wheat – but a large basement buzzing with activity and serving pizza, pasta and standard Italian main courses. The pizzas and pasta dishes are very good, as are the classic puddings. Closed Sun lunch. Moderate. Bond Street tube.

155

Soho and Chinatown

Aroma II 118 Shaftesbury Ave, W1 ☎020/7437 0370, ⓦwww.aromares.co.uk. Bright, modernist Chinese restaurant with an exhausting and exhaustive menu ranging from traditional hand-pulled noodles to braised sea slug or shark fin. This is one of the more serious but accessible gastronomic Chinatown places, so if you're stuck for what to choose, ask for advice. Inexpensive. Leicester Square tube.

China City White Bear Yard, 25a Lisle St, WC2 ☎020/7734 3388. Large restaurant tucked into a little courtyard off Lisle Street; fresh and bright, with *dim sum* that's up there with the best, service that is "Chinatown brusque", and a menu with eminently reasonable prices. Closed Sun. Inexpensive to Moderate. Leicester Square tube.

Fung Shing 15 Lisle St, WC2 ☎020/7437 1539, ⓦwww.fungshing.com. Bigger and brassier than ever, this is a classy Chinatown restaurant that takes its cooking and its service seriously. Prices are above average, but the portions are large, and the food has an earthy, robust quality redolent of a chef who is absolutely confident of his flavours and textures. Moderate. Leicester Square tube.

Kettner's 29 Romilly St, W1 ☎020/7734 6112. Despite the very handsome *belle époque* Baroque decor and the pianist, this place is by no means exclusive. In fact, it's one of the reliable *Pizza Express* restaurants, serving thin-based pizzas and the like. You can't book and might be forced to hangout a while in the noisy *Champagne Bar* – no great hardship. Closed Sun. Moderate. Leicester Square tube.

Kulu Kulu 76 Brewer St, W1 ☎020/7734 7316. Small, friendly *kaiten* (or conveyor belt) sushi restaurant which pulls off the unlikely trick of serving really good sushi without being impersonal or intimidating. Open your box containing a pair of disposable chopsticks, pickled ginger and soy sauce, grab one or two plates (they're priced/coded by design not colour here) and tuck in. Closed Sun. Inexpensive. Piccadilly Circus tube.

Mezzo 100 Wardour St, W1 ☎020/7314 4000, ⓦwww.conran.com. Mezzo has remained popular ever since Terence Conran opened this six-hundred-seater in 1995. There's a bar, an informal *Mezzonine* restaurant upstairs, and, down the sweeping staircase, the full-on *Mezzo* with a space for performers. The tables are packed close, and there's a fashionable mayhem of noise, but considering the numbers served here, the French/Med food is pretty good. There's a £5 "live music cover charge" after 8pm. Closed Sat lunch. Moderate to Very Expensive. Piccadilly Circus or Tottenham Court Road tube.

Mr Kong 21 Lisle St, WC2 ☎020/7437 7923. One of Chinatown's finest, with a chef/owner who pioneered many of the modern Cantonese dishes now on menus all over town. To sample the restaurant's more unusual dishes – order from the "Today's" and "Chef's Specials" menu, and don't miss the mussels in black-bean sauce or the fresh razor clam with garlic. Moderate. Leicester Square tube.

New World 1 Gerrard Place, W1 ☎020/7734 0396. Very probably the largest single restaurant in London, with four to six hundred seats. The menu is twenty pages long, but luckily you don't need it in order to enjoy the authentic *dim sum*, which is served daily (11am–6pm) from circulating "themed" trolleys. Moderate. Leicester Square tube.

Randall & Aubin 16 Brewer St, W1 ☎020/7287 4447. Converted butcher's, now a champagne-oyster bar, rotisserie, sandwich shop and charcuterie, to boot – in the summer, this is a wonderfully airy place to eat. Closed Sun lunch. Moderate. Piccadilly Circus tube.

Covent Garden

Belgo Centraal 50 Earlham St, WC2 ☎020/7813 2233, ⓦwww.belgo-restaurants.com. Massive metal-minimalist cavern off Neal Street, serving excellent kilo-buckets of moules marinières, with frites and mayonnaise, a bewildering array of Belgian beers to choose from, and waffles for dessert. The £5 lunchtime specials are a bargain for central London. Inexpensive to Moderate. Covent Garden tube.

Café Pacifico 5 Langley St, WC2 ☎020/7379 7728, ⓦwww.cafepacifico-laperla.com. The salsa is hot here – both types – and the menu includes all the favourites, such as fajitas, flautas and tacos. Portions are generous and spicy, and there are nine varieties of Mexican beer and more than sixty types of tequila. The place is very popular and lively in the evening – in fact, you're advised to book. Moderate. Covent Garden tube.

Livebait 21 Wellington St, WC2 ☎020/7836 7161, ⓦwww.sante-gcg.com. Innovative, irrepressible restaurant with a large, bustling, black-and-white-tiled dining room. The emphasis is on fish so fresh you expect to see it flapping on the slab, and superb crustacea. The breads are still a feature and service is friendly. Closed Sun. Expensive. Covent Garden tube.

J. Sheekey 28–32 St Martin's Court, WC2 ☎020/7240 2565. *J. Sheekey's* pedigree goes back to WWI, but the place has recently been totally redesigned and refurbished. The menu is still focused on fish, but in addition to traditional fare such as grilled Dover sole, you're just as likely to find Modernist dishes such as grilled cuttlefish with creamed brandade. The weekend lunches at between £10–15 are great value. Expensive. Leicester Square tube.

Fitzrovia and Bloomsbury

Great Nepalese 48 Eversholt St, NW1 ☎020/7388 6737. Friendly, homely Nepalese restaurant round the back of Euston Station. Delve into the authentic Nepalese dishes, whose names you won't be familiar with, but only try the Coronation rum from Kathmandu if you know what you're doing. Inexpensive. Euston or Euston Square tube.

Ikkyu 67a Tottenham Court Rd, W1 ☎020/7636 9280. Busy, basic basement Japanese restaurant, good enough for a quick lunch or a more elaborate dinner. Either way, prices are infinitely more reasonable than elsewhere in the capital, and the food is tasty and authentic. Be warned, however: it's hard to find, and when you do, shockingly popular. Closed all Sat & Sun lunch. Moderate. Goodge Street tube.

Malabar Junction 107a Great Russell St, WC1 ☎020/7580 5230. Inexpensive yet fully licensed, top quality Keralan restaurant with two entirely (and religiously) separate kitchens: one serving mouthwatering, spicy and nutty veggie dishes, the other dishing out equally tasty meat and fish fare. Inexpensive to Moderate. Tottenham Court Road tube.

Rasa Samudra 5 Charlotte St, W1 ☎020/7637 0222, ⊛www.rasarestaurants.com. Above average prices for exceptional South Indian fish dishes, which are freshly prepared using top quality ingredients, and come complete with accompaniments. The cooking is well-judged and the spices well-balanced, but if you're still nervous of the bill, go for the fixed-price three-course lunch at £10 (vegetarian) or £15 (seafood). Closed Sun. Moderate to Expensive. Goodge Street tube.

Clerkenwell and the City

Cicada 132 St John St, EC1 ☎020/7608 1550. Part bar, part restaurant, *Cicada* is set back from the street and, when the weather's fine, it's a great place for eating alfresco. The unusual Thai-based menu allows you to mix and match from small, large and side dishes ranging from hot, lemony, fishy tom yum soup, to sweet ginger noodles, fresh clams, white miso or kinome leaves. Closed Sat lunch & Sun. Moderate. Farringdon tube.

St John 26 St John St, EC1 ☎020/7272 1587, ⊛www.stjohnrestaurant.co.uk. A genuinely English restaurant, only a stone's throw from Smithfield meat market and specializing in offal. All those strange and unfashionable cuts of meat that were once commonplace in rural England – brains, bone

marrow, meat from a cow's sternum – are on offer at this white-painted former smokehouse. Closed Mon lunch. Expensive. Farringdon tube.

Singapura 1–2 Limeburner Lane, EC4 ☎020/7329 1133, ⊛www.singapura.co.uk. Beautiful, large, modern restaurant off Ludgate Hill that is one of the few places outside Singapore where you can sample *Nonya* cuisine – a fusion of Malayan and Chinese traditions and ingredients. The food is generally (but not always) spicy, and is characterized by a good deal of garlic, galangal, sweetness and lime leaves. Closed Sat & Sun. Moderate. Blackfriars or St Paul's tube.

East End

Café Naz 46–48 Brick Lane, E1 ☎020/7247 0234, ⊛www.cafenaz.com. Self-proclaimed contemporary Bangladeshi restaurant that cuts an imposing modern figure on Brick Lane. The menu has all the standard Indian dishes plus a load of "baltis", the kitchen is open-plan, and the prices keen – as you'd expect in a street replete with rival curry houses. Inexpensive. Aldgate East tube.

Café Spice Namaste 16 Prescott St, E1 ☎020/7488 9242, ⊛www.book2eat.com. Very popular Indian on the fringe of the City that is definitely not your average curry house. Parsee delicacies rub shoulders with dishes from Goa, Hyderabad and Kashmir, and the tandoori specialities are awesome. Be sure to check out the speciality menu, which changes weekly. Closed Sat lunch & Sun. Moderate. Tower Hill tube.

Real Greek 15 Hoxton Market, N1 ☎020/7739 8212, ⊛www.therealgreek.co.uk. Yes, it's run by a real Greek, but this is nothing like your average London Greek-Cypriot joint. Small, modern and comfortable, the menu shows off the authentic dishes of Greece, and the service is excellent. Set lunch and early doors dinner are a bargain. Closed Sun. Moderate. Old Street or Shoreditch tube.

Viet Hoa Café 72 Kingsland Rd, E2 ☎020/7729 8293. Large, light and airy Vietnamese café with a golden parquet floor, situated not far from the Geffrye Museum in Hoxton/Shoreditch, and serving splendid "meals in a bowl" – soups and noodle dishes with everything from spring rolls to tofu. Be sure to try the *Pho* soup, a Vietnamese staple that's eaten at any and every meal. Bus #67, #149 or #242 from Inexpensive to Moderate. Liverpool Street Station.

Lambeth and Southwark

Butlers Wharf Chop House 36e Shad Thames, SE1 ☎020/7403 3403, ⊛www.conran.com. Conran-owned restaurant showcasing British meat, fish and cheeses. Prices are high, but the

Chop House tries to cater for all: you could enjoy a simple dish at the bar, a well-priced set lunch, or an extravagant dinner. You can't reserve the terrace tables but try and book ahead for a window seat. Restaurant closed Sat lunch, bar closed Sun eve. Moderate (bar) to Expensive (restaurant). Tower Hill, London Bridge or Bermondsey tube.

Fina Estampa 150 Tooley St, SE1 ☎ 020/7403 1342. This may be London's only Peruvian restaurant, but it also happens to be the very best, bringing a little of downtown Lima to London Bridge. The menu is traditional Peruvian, with a big emphasis on seafood. Closed Sat lunch & all Sun. Moderate. London Bridge tube.

Fish! Cathedral St, SE1 ☎ 020/7234 3333, ⊛ www.fishdiner.co.uk. Busy, buzzy, tank-like restaurant, with huge windows and a glass ceiling, right in the middle of Borough Market. Choose your fish, decide how you want it cooked, and with what sauce, and then sit back and wait. Portions are huge, and the fish is as good and fresh as you'd expect. Closed Sun eve. Moderate. London Bridge tube.

Little Saigon 139 Westminster Bridge Rd, SE1 ☎ 020/7207 9747. Great Vietnamese spring rolls, grilled squid-cake and crystal pancakes, all served with a wonderful array of sauces, plus great crispy fried noodles. Closed Sat & Sun lunch. Moderate. Waterloo tube.

RSJ 13a Coin St, SE1 ☎ 020/7928 4554, ⊛ www.rsj.uk.com. Regularly high standards of Anglo-French cooking make this a good spot for a meal either before or after an evening at a South Bank theatre or concert hall. The set meals for around £15 are particularly popular. Closed Sat lunch & Sun. Expensive. Waterloo tube.

Kensington and Chelsea

Bibendum Oyster House Michelin House, 81 Fulham Rd, SW3 ☎ 020/7589 1480, ⊛ www.bibendum.co.uk. A glorious tiled affair built in 1911, this former garage is the best place to eat shellfish in London. There are three types of rock oysters, but if you're really hungry, try the *plateau de fruits de mer*, which also has crab, clams, langoustines, prawns, shrimps, whelks and winkles. Moderate. South Kensington tube.

Boisdale 15 Ecclestone St, SW1 ☎ 020/7730 6922, ⊛ www.boisdale.co.uk. Owned by Ranald MacDonald, son of the Chief of Clanranald, this is a very Scottish place, strong on hospitality, and with a befuddlingly large range of rare malt whiskies. Fresh Scottish produce rules wherever possible, including MacSween's haggis (sheep's innards and oatmeal), venison and salmon. Closed Sun. Moderate to Expensive. Victoria tube.

Hunan 51 Pimlico Rd, SW1 ☎ 020/7730 5712. Probably England's only restaurant serving Hunan food, a relative of Sichuan cuisine, with the same spicy kick to most dishes and a fair wallop of pepper in those that aren't actively riddled with chiles. Most people opt for the £25 "Hunan's special leave-it-to-us feast", a multi-course extravaganza which lets the maître d', Mr Peng, show what he can do. Closed Sun. Expensive. Sloane Square tube.

Wódka 12 St Alban's Grove, W8 ☎ 020/7937 6513. The food is cooked with imagination, which makes the smart *Wódka* the place to go if you want to experience the best that Polish cuisine has to offer. It's not an expensive place to eat (especially if you go for the daily set-menu lunch), unless you start working your way through the large selection of flavoured vodkas. Moderate. High Street Kensington or Gloucester Road tube.

Bayswater and Notting Hill

Alounak 44 Westbourne Grove, W2 ☎ 020/7229 0416. Don't be put off by the dated sign outside – this place turns out really good, really cheap Iranian grub. The mixed starter is a fine sampler of all the usual dips, served with freshly baked flat bread; lamb dishes feature heavily, but look out for the daily specials, and wash it all down with a pot of Iranian black tea. Inexpensive. Queensway or Bayswater tube.

The Mandola 139–141 Westbourne Grove, W11 ☎ 020/7229 4734. Small, seriously informal, supremely popular, unlicensed neighbourhood restaurant serving strikingly delicious "urban Sudanese" food at sensible prices. Be sure to check out the Sudanese spiced coffee at the end. Closed Mon lunch. Moderate. Notting Hill Gate tube.

Rodizio Rico 111 Westbourne Grove, W11 ☎ 020/7792 4035. No menu, no prices, but no problem either as this Brazilian eatery specializes in smoky, grilled meat. Carvers come round and lop off chunks of freshly grilled meats, while you help yourself from the salad bar and hot buffet to prime your plate. Closed Mon–Fri lunch. Moderate. Notting Hill Gate or Bayswater tube.

Rôtisserie Jules 133a Notting Hill Gate, W11 ☎ 020/7221 3331, ⊛ www.rotisseriejules.com. One of three consistently sound restaurants – the other two are at 6 Bute St, SW7, and 338 King's Rd, SW3 – which excels in freshly roasted chicken hot off the spit at very reasonable prices. You can have a leg and thigh, a breast and wing, the whole chicken or even an entire leg of lamb, which will feed three or four people. Inexpensive to Moderate. Notting Hill Gate tube.

Camden and Hampstead

Cucina 45a South End Rd, NW3 ⊕020/7435 7814. Brightly painted, wooden-floored, roof-lit first-floor restaurant that's very contemporary, very fashionable and very Hampstead. The Modern British menu changes every two weeks or so and darts about a bit from cuisine to cuisine, but wherever you alight, each dish is well-presented, and the set lunch is a bargain at under £15. Expensive. Belsize Park tube.

Gresslin's 13 Heath St, NW3 ⊕020/7794 8386. Small, Modern European restaurant in the heart of Hampstead, with dishes ranging from Mediterranean French to Thai served up by efficient French waiters. Closed Mon lunch & Sun eve. Moderate. Hampstead tube.

Sauce barorganicdiner 214 Camden High St, NW1 ⊕020/7482 0777. *Sauce* offers food free of chemicals, pesticides and preservatives in a bright, colourful diner, with a juice and cocktail bar attached. Burgers, sandwiches and wraps are on the menu, and it's also fine to go just for a coffee or a beer. Inexpensive. Camden Town tube.

Greenwich

Time 7a College Approach, SE10 ⊕020/8305 9767, ⊛www.timerestaurant.com. *Time* is a small, appealing restaurant, with roomy tables and an elegant clientele. The menu is not long, but it offers plenty of choice, celebrating flavours bor-rowed from around the world. Closed all Mon & Tues–Sat lunch. Expensive. Cutty Sark DLR.

Chiswick to Richmond

Chez Lindsay 11 Hill Rise, Richmond, Surrey ⊕020/8948 7473. Small, bright, authentic Breton creperie, with a loyal local following, and fixed-price lunchtime menus for under £10. Choose between galettes, crepes or more formal French main courses, including lots of fresh fish and shellfish, and wash it all down with Breton cider in traditional earthenware *bolées*. Moderate. Richmond tube.

The Glasshouse 14 Station Parade, Kew, Surrey ⊕020/8940 6777. Clean-cut, modern restaurant on the very doorstep of Kew Gardens tube, with blissfully comfortable chairs. The menu changes on a daily basis, with five or six choices for each course, and set-menu prices hovering around the £20 mark. The cooking is imaginative and straight-forward, and owes much to genuine French food. Closed Sun eve. Expensive. Kew Gardens tube.

Springbok Café 42 Devonshire Rd, W4 ⊕020/8742 3149, ⊛www.springbokcafecuisine.com. Small, informal and ambitious South African restaurant, with an open-plan barbie-oriented kitchen. Many of the ingredients are imported, so there's plenty of bil-tong, game and fish from SA, plus smoked English ostrich to please expats. Closed Mon–Sat lunch & all Sun. Expensive. Turnham Green tube.

Drinking

Older-style inns, with oak beams, open fires and polished-brass fittings survive here and there, but they're not a great feature of the capital. London's great period of **pub** building took place in the Victorian era, to which many pubs still pay homage; genuine Victorian interiors, however, are increasingly difficult to find, as indeed are genuinely individual pubs. Chain pubs can now be found all over the capital: branches of All Bar One, Pitcher & Piano and the Slug & Lettuce are the most obvious, as they all share the chain name, whereas J.D. Wetherspoon and Fuller's pubs do at least vary theirs. The traditional image of London **pub food** is dire but the last couple of decades have seen plenty of improvements. You can get a palatable lunchtime meal at many of the pubs listed below, and at a few of them, you're looking at cooking worthy of high, restaurant-standard praise.

Standard pub **opening hours** are Mon–Sat 11am–11pm, Sun noon–10.30pm (the listings below only specify the exceptions). However, with England's licensing likely to change in the near future, many of the pubs listed will probably stay open later. Until then, in order to drink beyond 11pm, you're probably best off heading for one of the city's bars, which go in and out of fashion with incredible speed. These are very different places to your average pub, catering to a somewhat cliquey, often youngish crowd, with designer interiors and drinks; they also tend to be more expensive (and will charge entry after 11pm). We've listed a fair few – while covering those tied to, or more like, clubs and dance venues on p.164.

Whitehall and Westminster

Albert 52 Victoria St, SW1. Roomy High-Victorian pub, situated halfway between Parliament Square and Victoria, with big bay windows and glass partitions; good bar food, too, and an excellent carvery upstairs. St James's Park or Victoria tube.

ICA Bar 94 The Mall, SW1 ☎020/7930 2402, ⓦwww.ica.org.uk. You have to be a member (or be visiting an exhibition or cinema/theatre/talk event) to drink at the late-opening *ICA Bar* – but anyone can join on the door (Mon–Fri £1.50; Sat & Sun £2.50). It's a cool drinking venue, with a noir dress code observed by the arty crowd and staff. Piccadilly Circus or Charing Cross tube.

Paviour's Arms Page St, SW1. A unique survivor, this large, stylish 1930s Art Deco pub, in the backstreets close to the Tate Gallery, has much of its original decor intact; you can also get decent Thai food with your beer. Be warned, though: the place is heaving with civil servants and locals at lunchtime. Closed Sat & Sun. Pimlico tube.

St James's, Mayfair and Marylebone

Dover Castle 43 Weymouth Mews, W1. A really nice, traditional boozer in a quiet Marylebone mews. Restful, racing-green upholstery, dark wood, a nicotine-stained lincrusta ceiling and cheap Sam Smith's beer on tap. Regent's Park or Oxford Circus tube. Closed Sun.

Mulligans 13–14 Cork St, W1. A fine and very smart Irish pub with an odd mix of clientele – Cork Street gallery staff and Irish lads – and some of the best Guinness in London. Also has a high-class restaurant downstairs, with fine Modern British/Irish cooking. Closed Sun. Green Park or Piccadilly tube.

O'Conor Don 88 Marylebone Lane, W1. A stripped bare, anti-theme Irish pub that's a cut above the average, with excellent Guinness, a pleasantly measured pace and Irish food on offer. Closed Sat & Sun. Bond Street tube.

Red Lion 23 Crown Passage, SW1. Not to be confused with the nearby pub of the same name, this is a small, local, wood-panelled pub hidden away in a passageway off Pall Mall. Green Park tube.

Soho and Fitzrovia

Coach & Horses 29 Greek St, W1. Long-standing – and, for once, little-changed – haunt of the ghosts of old Soho, *Private Eye*, nightclubbers, and art students from nearby St Martin's College. 1950s red plastic stools and black formica tables make up the spartan, unchanging decor. Leicester Square tube.

Dog & Duck 18 Bateman St, W1. Tiny Soho pub that retains much of its old character, beautiful Victorian tiling and mosaics, and a loyal clientele that often includes jazz musicians from nearby *Ronnie Scott's* club. Closed Sat & Sun lunch. Leicester Square or Tottenham Court Road tube.

French House 49 Dean St, W1. The tiny French pub has been a Soho institution since before World War I. Free French and literary associations galore, half pints only at the bar (no real ale) and a fine little restaurant upstairs (book ahead). Leicester Square tube.

The Hope 15 Tottenham St, W1. Chiefly remarkable for its sausage (veggie ones included), beans and mash lunches, and its real ales. Lunchtime only. Goodge Street tube.

Newman Arms 23 Rathbone St, W1. What the *Hope* is to sausages, the *Newman Arms* is to pies, with every sort from gammon to steak-and-kidney. Closed Sat & Sun. Tottenham Court Road tube.

The Toucan 19 Carlisle St ☎020/7437 4123, ⓦwww.thetoucan.co.uk. Small bar serving excellent Guinness and a wide range of Irish whiskey, plus cheap, wholesome and filling food. So popular it can get mobbed. Closed Sun. Tottenham Court Road tube.

Two Floors 3 Kingly St, W1. Relaxed, modernist Soho bar, laid out, unsurprisingly on two floors, attracting a mixed gay/straight crowd, and pumping out drum'n'bass in the evenings – quite a find in an area short of decent drinking holes. Closed Sun. Oxford Circus or Piccadilly Circus tube.

Covent Garden

Freedom Brewing Company 41 Earlham St, WC2, ⓦwww.freedombrew.com. Busy, brick-vaulted basement brewery bar with wrought-iron pillars, lots of brushed steel and pricey, strong brews, made on the premises – in particular, there's a very fine organic honey wheat beer. Covent Garden tube.

Lamb & Flag 33 Rose St, WC2. Busy, tiny and highly atmospheric pub, tucked away down an alley between Garrick Street and Floral Street, where John Dryden was attacked in 1679 for writing scurrilous verses about one of Charles II's mistresses. Leicester Square tube.

Punch & Judy 40 The Market, WC2. Horribly mobbed and loud, but this Covent Garden Market pub does boast an unbeatable location with a very popular balcony overlooking the Piazza – and a stone-flagged cellar. Covent Garden tube.

Salisbury 90 St Martin's Lane, WC2. Easily one of the most beautifully preserved Victorian pubs in the capital – and certainly the most central – with cut, etched and engraved windows, bronze figures, red velvet seating and a fine lincrusta ceiling. Leicester Square tube.

Bloomsbury

Lamb 94 Lamb's Conduit St, WC1. Pleasant pub with a marvellously well-preserved Victorian interior of mirrors, old wood and "snob" screens. Russell Square tube.

Museum Tavern 49 Great Russell St, WC1. Large and characterful old pub, right opposite the main entrance to the British Museum, erstwhile drinking hole of Karl Marx. Tottenham Court Road or Russell Square tube.

Strand, Holborn and Clerkenwell

Café Kick 43 Exmouth Market, EC1. Stylish take on a local French-style café-bar in the heart of newly fashionable Exmouth Market, with table football to complete the retro theme. Farringdon or Angel tube.

Clerkenwell House 23–27 Hatton Wall, EC1. One of a whole host of new bars to open on and off the Clerkenwell Road. The retro 1970s furniture includes some wickedly comfy semi-circular sofas. The Med food is good, and there are four American pool tables in the basement bar. Farringdon tube.

Eagle 159 Farringdon Rd, EC1. The first of London's pubs to go foody, this place is heaving at lunch and dinnertimes, as *Guardian* workers tuck into Med dishes, but you should be able to find a seat at other times. Closed Sun eve. Farringdon tube.

Fox & Anchor 115 Charterhouse St, EC1. Handsome Smithfield market pub famous for its early opening hours (from 7am) and huge breakfasts. Closed Sat & Sun. Farringdon or Barbican tube.

Jerusalem Tavern 55 Britton St, EC1. Cosy little converted Georgian parlour, stripped bare and slightly "distressed", serving tasty food along with an excellent range of draught beers from St Peter's Brewery in Suffolk. Closed Sat & Sun. Farringdon tube.

Na Zdrowie 11 Little Turnstile, WC1. Great Polish bar hidden in an alleyway behind Holborn tube, with a wicked selection of flavoured vodkas, and cheap Polish food. Holborn tube.

Princess Louise 208 High Holborn, WC1. Old-fashioned place, with highly decorated ceilings, lots of glass, brass and mahogany, and a good range of real ales. Closed Sun. Holborn tube.

The City: Fleet Street to St Paul's

Blackfriar 174 Queen Victoria St, EC4. A gorgeous, utterly original pub, with Art Nouveau marble friezes of boozy monks and a wonderful highly decorated alcove – all original, dating from 1905. Closed Sat & Sun. Blackfriars tube.

Old Bank of England 194 Fleet St, EC4. Not the actual Bank of England, but the former Law Courts' branch, this imposing High Victorian banking hall is now a magnificently opulent ale and pie pub. Closed Sat & Sun. Temple (Mon–Sat) or Chancery Lane tube.

Old Cheshire Cheese Wine Office Court, 145 Fleet St, EC4. A famous seventeenth-century watering hole, with several snug, dark panelled bars and real fires. Popular with tourists, but by no means exclusively so. Closed Sun eve. Temple (Mon–Sat) or Blackfriars tube.

The City: Bank to Bishopsgate

The Counting House 50 Cornhill, EC2. Another City bank conversion, with fantastic high ceilings a glass dome, chandeliers and a central oval bar. Naturally enough, given the location, it's wall-to-wall suits. Closed Sat & Sun. Bank tube.

The George Bishopsgate, EC2. *The George* – the pub on the corner of Liverpool Street – is part of Conran's smoothly-run refurbished *Great Eastern Hotel*, and retains its wonderful original mock-Tudor decor. Liverpool Street tube

Hamilton Hall Liverpool Street Station, EC2. Cavernous, gilded, former ballroom of the *Great Eastern* hotel, adorned with nudes and chandeliers. Packed out with City commuters tanking up before the train home, but a great place nonetheless. Liverpool Street tube.

Jamaica Wine House St Michael's Alley, EC3. An old City institution tucked away down a narrow alleyway. Despite the name, this is really just a pub, divided into four large "snugs" by high wooden-panelled partitions. Closed Sat & Sun. Bank tube.

East End and Docklands

Dickens Inn St Katharine's Way, E1. Eighteenth-century timber-framed warehouse transported on wheels from its original site, and then much altered. Still, it's a remarkable building, with a great view, but very firmly on the tourist trail. Tower Hill tube or Tower Gateway DLR.

The Gun 27 Cold Harbour, E14. An old dockers' pub with lots of maritime memorabilia, and – the main attraction – an unrivalled view of the Millennium Dome. South Quay or Blackwall DLR, or Canary Wharf tube.

The Pool 104–108 Curtain Rd, EC2. The three pool tables looking out onto busy, busy Curtain Road give this bar its name; the big bean bags in the basement add a retro touch. Old Street tube.

Prospect of Whitby 57 Wapping Wall, E1. London's most famous riverside pub with a flag-stone floor, a cobbled courtyard and great views over the Thames. Wapping tube.

Town of Ramsgate 62 Wapping High St, E1. Dark, narrow medieval pub located by Wapping Old Stairs, which once led down to Execution Dock. Captain Blood was discovered here with the crown jewels under his cloak, and Admiral Bligh and Fletcher Christian were regular drinking partners in pre-mutiny days.

Via Fossa West India Quay, E14, ☎020/7515 8549. Housed in a nineteenth-century warehouse, and accessible from Canary Wharf via a footbridge. If the weather's warm, the south-facing terrace is great to sit out on. Mon–Sat noon–11pm, Sun noon–7pm. West India Quay DLR.

Lambeth and Southwark

Anchor Bankside 34 Park St, SE1. While the rest of Bankside has changed almost beyond all recognition, this pub still looks much as it did when first built in 1770 (on the inside, at least). Good for alfresco drinking by the river. London Bridge, Southwark or Blackfriars tube.

Fire Station 150 Waterloo Rd, SE1. This gloriously red former fire station is a step away from Waterloo, and therefore a popular place for an after-work pint. The restaurant at the back is good, too. Waterloo tube.

George Inn 77 Borough High St, SE1. London's only surviving coaching inn, dating from the seventeenth century and now owned by the National Trust; it also serves a good range of real ales. Borough or London Bridge tube.

Kensington, Chelsea & Notting Hill

Bunch of Grapes 207 Brompton Rd, SW3. This popular High-Victorian pub, complete with "snob" screens, is the perfect place for a post-V&A (or post-Harrods) pint, pie and chips. South Kensington tube.

The Cow 89 Westbourne Park Rd, W2. Sort of vaguely Irish-themed pub owned by Tom Conran, son of gastro-magnate Terence, which pulls in the beautiful W11 types thanks to its spectacular food, including a daily supply of fresh oysters, and excellent Guinness. Westbourne Park or Royal Oak tube.

Front Page 35 Old Church St, SW3, ⓦwww.front-pagepubs.com. Tucked away in the centre of villagey, boho Chelsea and infinitely preferable to anything on offer on the King's Road, the *Front Page* is small and snug, and serves very good Mediterranean food. Sloane Square tube.

Market Bar 240a Portobello Rd, W11. Self-consciously bohemian pub divided by gilded mirrors and ruched curtains and scattered with weird *objets* – all very Portobello Road. Occasional live music and DJs. Ladbroke Grove tube.

Orange Brewery 37 Pimlico Rd, SW1. The area may be posh, but this is a fairly down-to-earth boozer with its very own micro-brewery. Sloane Square tube.

Prince Bonaparte 80 Chepstow Rd, W2. Pared-down, minimalist pub, with acres of space for sitting and supping or enjoying the excellent Mediterranean food. Closed Tues lunch. Notting Hill Gate or Royal Oak tube.

St John's Wood and Maida Vale

Prince Alfred 9 Formosa St, W9. A fantastic period-piece Victorian pub with all its original 1862 fittings intact, right down to the glazed "snob" screens. The beer and food don't quite live up to the surroundings. Warwick Avenue tube.

Warrington Hotel 93 Warrington Crescent, W9. Yet another architectural gem – this time flamboyant Art Nouveau – in an area replete with them. The interior is rich and satisfying, as are the draught beers and the Thai restaurant upstairs. It is, however, incredibly, spilling-out-onto-the-street, popular. Warwick Avenue or Maida Vale tube.

Camden Town

Bartok 78–79 Chalk Farm Rd, NW1. Mean Fiddler-run bar where punters can sink into one of the sofas and sup beer or wine while listening to classical music and live jazz instead of the usual muzak. Closed Mon–Fri lunch. Chalk Farm or Camden Town tube.

The Engineer 65 Gloucester Ave, NW1. One of a number of gastropubs in the much sought-after residential area of Primrose Hill, the *Engineer* is a smart, grandiose place which serves exceptional Modern Brit/Med food; it's pricey, though, and you're best off booking if you intend to nosh. Chalk Farm tube.

Hampstead and Highgate

The Flask 14 Flask Walk, NW3. Convivial Hampstead local, hidden away along the pedestrianized Flask Walk, which retains its original Victorian snob screen. Serves above-average food and Young's ale. Hampstead tube.

The Flask 77 Highgate West Hill, N6. Ideally situated at the heart of Highgate village green, with a rambling low-ceilinged interior and a summer terrace. The range of beers is good, but the food is nothing special. Highgate tube.

Freemason's Arms 32 Downshire Hill, NW3. Big, smart pub close to the Heath, popular on sunny days primarily for its large beer garden; also does comfort pub food, has a basement skittle alley, and an outdoor pell mell pitch. Hampstead tube.

Holly Bush 22 Holly Mount, NW3. A lovely old wood-panelled, gas-lit pub, tucked away in the steep backstreets of Hampstead village. Mobbed on the weekend. Hampstead tube.

Dulwich and Greenwich

Crown & Greyhound 73 Dulwich Village, SE21. Grand, spacious Victorian pub with an ornate plasterwork ceiling and a nice summer beer garden. Convenient for the Picture Gallery, but be prepared for the Sunday lunchtime crowds. West Dulwich train station from Victoria.

Cutty Sark Ballast Quay, off Lassell St, SE10. The nicest riverside pub in Greenwich, spacious, more of a local and much less touristy than the more famous *Trafalgar Tavern* (it's a couple of minutes walk further east, following the river). The views are great, as is the draught beer, and the bar food is a cut above the norm. Cutty Sark DLR or Maze Hill train station.

Trafalgar Tavern 5 Park Row, SE10. A great riverside position and a mention in Dickens' *Our Mutual Friend* have made this Regency-style inn a firm tourist favourite, which is fair enough really, as it's a convivial period piece, and serves good food. Cutty Sark DLR or Maze Hill train station.

Chiswick to Richmond

Dove 19 Upper Mall, W6. Old, old riverside pub with literary associations, a short walk from Hammersmith Bridge – has the smallest back bar in the UK (4ft by 7ft). Ravenscourt Park tube.

White Cross Hotel Water Lane, Richmond. With a longer pedigree and more character than its clinical chain rival nearby, the *White Cross* is also much closer to the river (its front garden regularly gets flooded), and serves Young's beer and standard pub food. Richmond tube.

White Swan Riverside, Twickenham. Filling pub food, draught beer and a quiet riverside location – with a beer pontoon overlooking Eel Pie Island if you want to get even closer to the water – make this a good halt on any towpath ramble. Twickenham train station.

Nightlife

On any night of the week London offers a bewilderingly range of things to do after dark, ranging from top-flight opera and theatre to clubs with a life span of a couple of nights. The **listings magazine** *Time Out*, which comes out every Tuesday afternoon, is essential if you want to get the most out of this city, giving full details of prices and access, plus previews and reviews.

The **live music** scene remains extremely diverse, encompassing all variations of **rock, blues, roots**, and **world music**; and although London's **jazz** clubs aren't on a par with those in the big American cities, there's a highly individual scene of home-based artists, supplemented by top-name visiting players.

If you're looking for **dance music**, then welcome to Europe's party capital. After dark, London is thriving, with diverse scenes championing everything from hip-hop to house, techno to trance, samba to soca and drum 'n' bass to R&B on virtually any night of the week. Venues once used exclusively by performing bands now pepper the week with club nights, and you often find dance sessions starting as soon as a band has stopped playing. Bear in mind that there's sometimes an overlap between "live music venues" and "clubs" in the listings below; we've indicated which places serve a double function.

As for **theatre**, London has enjoyed a reputation for quality since the time of Shakespeare, and despite the continuing prevalence of fail-safe blockbuster musicals and revenue-spinning star vehicles, the city still provides a platform for innovation. **Cinema** is rather less healthy, for London's repertory film theatres are a dying breed, edged out by the multiscreen complexes, which show mainstream Hollywood fare some months behind America. There are a few excellent independent cinemas, though, including the National Film Theatre, which is the focus of the richly varied **London International Film Festival**, in November.

Live music venues

London is hard to beat for its musical mix: whether you're into **jazz**, **indie rock**, **R&B**, **blues** or **world music** you'll find something worth hearing on almost any night of the week. Entry prices for gigs run from a couple of pounds for an unknown band thrashing it out in a pub to around £30 for the likes of U2, but £10–15 is the average price for a good night out – not counting expenses at the bar. If you have a credit card, it's often cheaper to book tickets in advance via the internet at Ⓦ www.ticketweb.co.uk, Ⓦ www.tickets-online.co.uk or Ⓦ www.gigsandtours.com.

Rock and blues clubs and pubs

12 Bar Club 22–23 Denmark Place, WC2, Ⓦ www.12bar.com. A combination of live blues and contemporary country seven nights a week. Tottenham Court Road tube.

Astoria 157 Charing Cross Rd, WC2, Ⓦ www.meanfiddler.com. One of London's best and most central medium-sized venues, this large, balconied one-time theatre tends to host slightly alternative bands, with club nights on Fri & Sat. More adventurous than most other big venues. Tottenham Court Road tube.

Borderline Orange Yard, off Manette St, W1, Ⓦ www.borderline.co.uk. Intimate basement joint with diverse musical policy; a good place to catch new bands. Also has club nights. Tottenham Court Road tube.

Brixton Academy 211 Stockwell Rd, SW9. This refurbished Victorian hall, complete with Roman decorations, can hold 4000, and usually does, but still manages to seem small and friendly, probably because no one is forced to sit down. Hosts mainly mid-league bands. Brixton tube.

Forum 9–17 Highgate Rd, NW5, Ⓦ www.meanfiddler.com. The *Forum* is perhaps the capital's best medium-sized venue – large enough to attract established bands, and with great views and good bars. Pretty safe music policy. Kentish Town tube.

Mean Fiddler 24–28a Harlesden High St, NW10, Ⓦ www.meanfiddler.com. An excellent, if unfortunately located, small venue with a main hall and smaller acoustic room. The music veers from rock to world to folk to soul (and even, occasionally, gospel). Willesden Junction tube.

Ocean 270 Mare St E8, Ⓦ www.ocean.org.uk. Brand new medium-sized venue (plus two smaller halls) in deepest Hackney, with a very varied music policy, everything from reggae to the latest musak, plus club nights. Hackney Central train station.

Orange 3 North End Crescent, North End Rd W14. Pub-like venue for serious-minded jazz-funkers. There are also club nights (nights vary). West Kensington tube.

Roadhouse Jubilee Hall, 35 The Piazza, WC2, Ⓦ www.roadhouse.co.uk. American food, 1950s US-style decor and a lineup of mainly blues and rock 'n' roll bands performing to a mature, nostalgic crowd. Covent Garden tube.

Rock Garden 35 The Piazza, WC2. Central, loud joint where you can get in free if you dine at the attached burger place first. Live music tends toward conventional rock, but the venue hosts a garage and R&B club night on Saturdays. Covent Garden tube.

Station Tavern 41 Bramley Rd, W10. Arguably London's best blues venue, with free – and occasionally great – blues six nights a week. Latimer Road tube.

Subterania 12 Acklam Rd, W10, Ⓦ www.meanfiddler.com. One of the original live music/club crossover venues in an arch under a bridge. The crowd is as trendy as the music, which is often dance-oriented. Ladbroke Grove tube.

Underworld 174 Camden High St, NW1. This labyrinthine venue is good for new bands and has sporadic club nights. Camden Town tube.

Jazz, world music and roots

100 Club 100 Oxford St, W1. After a brief spell as a stage for punk bands, the *100 Club* is once again an unpretentious and inexpensive jazz venue – in a very central location. Tottenham Court Road tube.

606 Club 90 Lots Rd, SW10. A rare all-jazz venue, located just off the less trendy end of King's Road. You can book a table, and the licensing laws dictate that you must eat if you want to drink, but there's no cover charge. Fulham Broadway tube.

Africa Centre 38 King St, WC2, Ⓦ www.africacentre.org.uk. The packed old hall was the venue that launched Soul II Soul; these days, it hosts African bands and nights like Saturday's P-funk-heavy *Funkin Pussy*, but still draws a vibrantly enthusiastic crowd. Covent Garden tube.

Jazz Café 5 Parkway, NW1, Ⓦ www.jazzcafe.co.uk. Futuristic, white-walled venue with an adventurous booking policy exploring Latin, rap, funk, hip-hop and musical fusions.

Diehard trad-jazz fans won't be happy, despite the fact that there's a rather good restaurant upstairs with a few prime view tables overlooking the stage. Camden Town tube.

Pizza Express 10 Dean St, W1. Enjoy a good pizza, then listen to the resident band or highly skilled guest players in this long-running basement venue. There's also a late-night session on Saturdays which starts at 9pm and finishes in the early hours of Sunday. Oxford Street tube.

Ronnie Scott's 47 Frith St, W1, ⊛ www.ronni-escotts.co.uk. The most famous jazz club in London: small, smoky and still going strong, even though the great man himself has passed away. The place for top-line names, who play two sets – one at around 10pm, the other after midnight. Book a table, or you'll have to stand. Leicester Square tube.

Clubs

More than a decade after the explosion of acid-house, London remains *the* place to come if you want to party after dark. The sheer diversity of dance music has enabled the city to maintain its status as **Europe's dance capital** – and it's still a port of call for DJs from around the globe. The relaxation of late-night licensing has encouraged many venues to keep serving alcohol until 6am or even later, and the resurgence of alcohol in clubland (much to the relief of the breweries) has been echoed by the meteoric rise of the club-bar (see pp.166–167).

Nearly all of London's **dance clubs** open their doors between 10pm and midnight. Some are open six or seven nights a week, some keep irregular days, others just open at the weekend – and very often a venue will host a different club on each night of the week. Many of the best nights take place during the week, especially Wednesdays and Thursdays; for up-to-the-minute details of these, and of all the nights listed below, pop into one of Soho's many record shops (see p.172) to pick up flyers or check magazines such as *7*, *DJ* and *Time Out* for details.

Admission charges vary enormously, with small midweek sessions starting at around £3 and large weekend events charging as much as £25; around £10 is the average for a Friday or Saturday night, but bear in mind that profit margins at the bar are often more outrageous than at live-music venues.

The most notable event in the clubbing world in the past few years has been the rapid growth of **club-bars**: essentially bars with modern decor, a club clientele, and usually a DJ (unknown and otherwise). Perhaps most importantly, though, the club-bar is a more social environment than a club – there's no denying it gets tedious when you have to yell.

Clubs

333 333 Old St, EC1. Three floors of drum 'n' bass, twisted disco and breakbeat madness. Old Street tube.

Aquarium 256 Old St, EC1. The place with the pool – when all the beautiful young things get hot and sweaty they can dive in and cool off. Popular for speed garage nights. Old Street tube.

Bagley's Studios King's Cross Goods Yard, off York Way, N1. Vast warehouse-style venue. The perfect place for enormous raves, with a different DJ in each of the three rooms, and a chill-out bar complete with sofas. King's Cross tube.

Bar Rumba 36 Shaftesbury Ave, W1. Small West End venue with a programme of Latin, jazz-based and funk dance. Many of the punters are regulars. An unpretentious place frequented by happy peo-

ple and well noted in clubbing circles for its amazing diversity. Piccadilly Circus tube.

Café de Paris 3 Coventry St, W1. Elegantly restored ballroom that plays house, garage and disco to a smartly dressed, trendy crowd – no jeans or trainers. Leicester Square tube.

Camden Palace 1 Camden High St, NW1. Most often home to Balearic beats; great lights, great sound, heaving crowds. Camden Town tube.

The Cross Goods Way Depot, off York Way, N1. Hidden underneath the arches the favourite flavours of this renowned club are hard-house, house and garage. It's bigger than you imagine, but always crammed with chic clubby types, and there's a fabulous garden – perfect for those chill-out moments. King's Cross tube.

Cuba 11–13 Kensington High St, W8. Grab a cocktail upstairs in the sociable bar before heading below for club nights that focus around Latin, salsa and Brazilian bossa-nova. Kensington High Street tube.

Electric Ballroom 184 Camden High St, NW1. Attracts a mixed crowd with a wide range of sounds: from rock to hip-hop, jazz to house. Camden Town tube.

The End 18 West Central St, WC1. A club designed for clubbers, by clubbers – large and spacious with chrome minimalist decor. Well known for all music styles, and especially noted for monthly nights hosted by other clubs or record labels. Holborn tube.

Fabric 77a Charterhouse St, EC1, Ⓦ www.fabric-london.com. If you're a serious dance music fan then there really isn't a better weekend venue in London than *Fabric*, a cavernous, underground brewery-like space. Fridays alternate between hard house and hip-hop/drum 'n' bass, while Saturdays concentrate on the most cutting-edge house sounds around, played by the best of the big-name DJs from around the globe. Get there early. Farringdon tube.

Fridge Town Hall Parade, Brixton Hill, SW2. South London's big night out, with a musical policy running from funk to garage. Great gay nights and top techno tunes. Occasional home to *Escape from Samsara*, the night with the psychedelic, trancy vibe and hippie market. Brixton tube.

Gardening Club 4 The Piazza, WC2. Unusually for a central London club, the *Gardening Club* is surprisingly good. A popular choice for house and garage, but be warned, early on you'll be sharing the dance floor with beer-boys and bemused tourists. Covent Garden tube.

Gossips 69 Dean St, W1, Ⓦ www.gossips.co.uk. Cave-like basement club that seems to have been around forever. Located deep in the heart of Soho, it's a popular stop for reggae and hip-hop fans. Tottenham Court Road tube.

Hanover Grand 6 Hanover St, W1, Ⓦ www.hanovergrand.co.uk. A former Masonic hall, that's now a cool and extravagant club, with a great lights-and-sound system, a fine dance floor, lots of alcoves – and air conditioning. Popular with the glammed up, glittery and beautiful crew. Oxford Circus tube.

Home 1 Leicester Square, WC2, Ⓦ www.home-corp.com. Central London rival to *Fabric*, this multi-floored superclub may often feel like a leisure complex, but with some of the best resident DJs in Britain and one of the finest sound systems around, it's hard to feel too depressed. Piccadilly Circus or Leicester Square tube.

HQs West Yard, Camden Lock, NW1. Smallish venue by the canal with a range of nights, although the emphasis is on uplifting house through to salsa. Friendly vibe. Camden Town tube.

The Leisure Lounge 121 Holborn, EC1. This place has had its share of the big-name nights, and is always a good place to check out the latest grooves. Two dance floors – one a full-on dance zone, the other a more relaxed bar area. Chancery Lane or Farringdon tube.

Ministry of Sound 103 Gaunt St, SE1. A vast, state-of-the-art club based on New York's legendary *Paradise Garage*, with an exceptional sound system, but it still draws the top talent. Elephant & Castle tube.

Notting Hill Arts Club 21 Notting Hill Gate, W11. Basement club that's popular for everything from Latin inspired funk, jazz and disco through to soul, house and garage, and famed for its Sunday night deep disco house sessions. Notting Hill Gate tube.

The Office 3–5 Rathbone Place W1. Various music styles, but noted as home to the original mid-week session where you can play silly board games such as Ker-Plunk. Booking a table in advance is advised. Tottenham Court Road tube.

Salsa! 96 Charing Cross Rd, WC2. Funky salsa-based club where you can book a table to eat as you jive. Leicester Square tube.

The Scala 278 Pentonville Rd, N1, Ⓦ www.scala-london.co.uk. Once a cinema, *The Scala* is now one of London's best clubs, holding unusual and multi-faceted nights that take in film, live bands and music ranging from quirky hip-hop to drum 'n' bass and deep house. King's Cross tube.

Turnmills 63 Clerkenwell Rd, EC1, Ⓦ www.turnmills.com. Swanky coffee bar upstairs, fantastic alien-invasion-style bar and funky split-level dance floor in the main room. Saturday night sessions are followed at 4am by the awesomely glorious gay extravaganza, *Trade*. Farringdon tube.

Velvet Room 143 Charing Cross Rd, WC2. Very cool velvet-dripping interior, with house, techno and drum 'n' bass nights. Tottenham Court Road tube.

Club-bars

A.K.A. West Central St, WC1, Ⓦ www.the-end.co.uk. Minimalist, twenty-first century-style bar next door to *The End*. A chrome balcony overlooks the main floor, which includes a well stocked bar and restaurant where you can partake of such delights as chive and butternut squash soup. Tottenham Court Road tube.

Alphabet 61–63 Beak St, W1. Upstairs is light and spacious, with decadent leather sofas, a great choice of European beers and mouthwatering food; downstairs, the dimmed coloured lights and car seats make for an altogether seedier atmosphere. Oxford Circus tube.

Bar Vinyl 6 Inverness St, NW1. Funky glass-bricked place with a record shop downstairs and a break-beat and trip-hop vibe. Camden Town tube.

Bug Bar St Matthew's Church, Brixton Hill, SW2, Ⓦwww.bugbar.co.uk. Set in a church crypt, this place certainly has character. A popular stop-off before the *Fridge*, playing reggae, drum 'n' bass and house. Closed Mon & Tues. Brixton tube.

Detroit 35 Earlham St, WC2. Cavernous underground venue with an open-plan bar area, secluded, Gaudiesque booths and a huge range of spirits. DJs take over at the weekends, with underground house on Saturdays. Closed Sun. Covent Garden tube.

Dog House 187 Wardour St, W1, Ⓦwww.dog-house.co.uk. Colourful basement bar, popular for hip-hop, funk and acid-jazz, that draws a friendly mix of office types, students and film runners. Closed Sun. Leicester Square tube.

Fridge Bar 1 Town Hall Parade, Brixton Hill, SW2, Ⓦwww.fridge.co.uk. The two-floored *Fridge Bar* is a real melting pot, with a multi-tribal clientele grooving to R&B, house and drum 'n' bass in the intimate, pitch-black downstairs club, or slamming shots in the bright upstairs bar. Free entry during

the week, and until 9pm on the weekend (when it gets packed). Brixton tube.

Hoxton Square Bar and Kitchen 2–4 Hoxton Square, N1. Next door to the Lux cinema, this concrete bar attracts the area's artists, writers and wannabees with its mix of modern European food, kitsch-to-club soundtracks, leather sofas and temporary painting and photography exhibitions. Best in the summer, though, when the drinking spills into the square in a carnival-like spirit. Old Street tube.

Jerusalem 33–34 Rathbone Place, W1. Decor is all chandeliers and velvet drapes; especially good music on Thursday nights, though it does attract a large proportion of office workers. Closed Sun. Tottenham Court Road tube.

Lab 12 Old Compton St, W1, Ⓦwww.lab-bar.co.uk. Chic, multi-coloured former strip joint that stirs up some of the best cocktails in town to its style-conscious crowd of beautiful Soho-ites. Tottenham Court Road tube.

The Social 5 Little Portland St, W1, Ⓦwww.social.com. Bacchanalian, industrial club-bar, with great DJs playing everything from rock to rap, a truly hedonistic-cum-alcoholic crowd and the ultimate snacks – beans on toast and cosy soup in a mug – for when you get an attack of the munchies. Fab music on the upstairs jukebox, too. Closed Sun. Oxford Circus tube.

Gay and lesbian bars and clubs

London's **lesbian and gay scene** is so huge, diverse and well-established that it's easy to forget just how much – and how fast – it has grown over the last few years. **Soho** is the obvious place to start exploring, with a mix of traditional gay pubs, trendy café-bars and a range of gay-run services. Details of most events appear in *Time Out* and in *The Pink Paper* and *Axiom News*, which carry news and arts coverage as well as listings. Another excellent source of information is the London **Lesbian and Gay Switchboard** (☎020/7837 7324), which operates around the clock. The biggest annual queer party in the country is **Mardi Gras** (Ⓦwww.londonmardigras.com), a colourful, whistleblowing march through the city streets followed by a huge, ticketed party in Finsbury Park.

Bars

There are loads of lesbian and gay **eating and watering holes** in London, many of them operating as cafés by day and transforming into drinking dens at night. Lots have **cabaret or disco nights** and are open until the early hours, making them a fine alternative to the more expensive clubs. The places listed here are merely a small selection of the most central, although almost every corner of London has its own gay local. Bear in mind that, as ever, "mixed" tends to mean mostly men.

Mixed bars

Bar Aquda 13–14 Maiden Lane, Covent Garden WC2. Bright, modern and fashionable café-bar with good food. Mixed, but mostly boys. Leicester

Square or Covent Garden tube.

The Black Cap 171 Camden High St, NW1. North London institution, offering drag and cabaret of wildly varying quality almost every night. *Mrs*

Shufflewick's Bar upstairs is quieter, and opens onto a lush and lovely roof garden in the summer. Camden Town tube.

The Box 32–34 Monmouth St, WC2. Popular café-bar serving good food for a mixed gay/straight crowd during the day, and becoming queerer as the night draws on. Covent Garden or Leicester Square tube.

The Edge 11 Soho Square, W1. Busy, style-conscious and pricey Soho café-bar spread over several floors, although this doesn't seem to stop everyone ending up on the pavement, especially in summer. Tottenham Court Road tube.

First Out 52 St Giles High St, WC2. The West End's original gay café-bar, and still permanently packed, serving good veggie food at reasonable prices. Upstairs is airy and non-smoking, downstairs dark and foggy. *Girl Friday* is a busy Friday night pre-club session for girls; gay men are welcome as guests. Tottenham Court Road tube.

Freedom 60–66 Wardour St, W1. Hip, busy café-bar, popular with a mixed straight/gay Soho crowd. Great juices and healthy food in the daytime, cocktails and overpriced beer in the evening. Piccadilly Circus tube.

Liquid Lounge 275 Pentonville Rd, N1. Happy-go-lucky weekend dance bar popular with a young, indie-minded crowd. DJs and reliably cheap beer. Thurs–Sat only. King's Cross tube.

Old Compton Café 34 Old Compton St, W1. This enduringly busy Soho institution never closes. Strong coffee and a cosmopolitan range of cakes and snacks make it the obvious solution to sudden mid- or post-party wooziness. Tottenham Court Road or Leicester Square tube.

The Yard 57 Rupert St, W1. Attractive café-bar with courtyard and loft areas. Good food, weekly cabaret and regular fortune tellers. Closed Sun. Piccadilly Circus tube.

Lesbian bars

Candy Bar 23–24 Bateman St, W1. Right in the heart of boys-land, the UK's first seven-day all-girl

bar offers a retro-style cocktail bar-cum-pool room upstairs; a noisy, beery, long and narrow ground level cruising bar, and a range of club nights. Gay men welcome as guests. Tottenham Court Road tube.

The Glass Bar West Lodge, Euston Square Gardens, 190 Euston Rd, NW1, Ⓦwww.glassbar.ndo.co.uk. This friendly and intimate women-only members bar (you become a member once you've found it) is housed in a listed building and features a wrought iron spiral staircase which becomes increasingly perilous as the night goes on. Knock on the door to get in. Closed Sun. Euston tube.

Vespa Lounge Under Centrepoint House, St. Giles High Street, WC1, Ⓦwww.vespalounge.com. London's newest girl bar sets up shop in this prime location at weekends, and it gets busy. Pool table, video screen, cute bar staff and a mostly young crowd. Gay men welcome as guests. Tottenham Court Road tube.

Gay men's pubs

79CXR 79 Charing Cross Rd, WC2. Busy, cruisey men's den on two floors, with industrial decor, late licence and a no-messing atmosphere. Leicester Square tube.

Brief Encounter 41–43 St Martin's Lane, WC2. One of the longest-running men's bars in London. A popular pre-*Heaven* or post-opera hangout (it's next door to the Coliseum); the front bar is light, the back bar dark, and both are busy. Leicester Square tube.

Compton's of Soho 53 Old Compton St, W1. This large, traditional-style pub is a Soho institution, always busy with a youngish crowd, but still a relaxed place to cruise or just hangout. Leicester Square or Piccadilly tube.

Substation Soundshaft Hungerford Lane (behind *Heaven*), WC2. The original late-night cruising pit. Steamy, cruisey and sleazy, offering a diverse seven day menu of sartorial and musical preferences. Charing Cross tube.

Clubs

Clubs move, change and close down fast, so we've listed only the longest-running and most popular nights here – it's always a good idea to check the gay press, listings magazines and websites for up-to-date times and prices before you plan your night out.

Crash 66, Goding St, SE11. Four bars, two dancefloors, chillout areas and plenty of hard bodies make this weekly Saturday-nighter busy, buzzy, sexy and mostly boysy. Vauxhall tube.

DTPM at *Fabric*, 77a Charterhouse St, EC1. This long-running Sunday-nighter can now be found in

Fabric's chic surroundings, with three dancefloors offering soul, jazz, funk, R&B, hip-hop, Latino house and progressive to hard house. Farringdon Road tube.

Duckie at *The Royal Vauxhall Tavern*, 372 Kennington Lane, SE11, Ⓦwww.duckie.co.uk.

Modern rock-based hurdy gurdy for "homosexual-ists", their friends and fans. Regular live art per-formances, occasional bouncy castles, and fabu-lously-titled theme nights. Vauxhall tube.

Exilio Latino 229 Great Portland St, W1. Every other Saturday night, *Exilio* erupts in a fabulous Latin frenzy, spinning salsa, cumbia and merengue, and featuring live acts. Great Portland Street tube.

G.A.Y. at *The Astoria*, 157 Charing Cross Rd, WC2. *The Astoria* hosts huge, unpretentious and fun-lov-ing dance nights for a young crowd on Fridays and Saturdays, which are always packed and often feature big-name PAs. Tottenham Court Road tube.

Heaven under The Arches Villiers St, WC2. Widely regarded as the UK's most popular gay club, this legendary, 2000-capacity club continues to reign supreme. Big nights are Wednesdays (*Fruit Machine*) and Saturdays (just *Heaven*), all with big-name DJs, PAs and shows. More Muscle Mary than Diesel Doris. Charing Cross or Embankment tube.

Love Muscle at *The Fridge*, Town Hall Parade, Brixton Hill, SW2, ⓦwww.fridge.co.uk. A regular Saturday night workout for oiled torsos, disco

dykes and fag-hag friends, this sweaty, eight-year-old all-nighter offers everything from fluffy techno to hard house via Europop. Big stage shows, stun-ning lights, go-go dancers and a chill-out zone top off the party madness. Brixton tube.

Popstarz at the *Scala*, 27 Pentonville Rd, N1. Groundbreaking Friday night indie club, now in its fifth year and its sixth venue, and with a consis-tently winning formula of indie and alternative tunes, 70s and 80s trash, cheap beer and no atti-tude. King's Cross tube.

Queer Nation at *Substation South*, 9 Brighton Terrace, SW9. Long-running and popular New York-style house and garage night for funksters. Brixton tube.

Trade at *Turnmills*, 63b Clerkenwell Rd, EC1, ⓦwww.turnmills.com. This legendary Saturday all-nighter (business kicks off at 4am and will see you well through to Sunday lunchtime) is still going strong. Expect techno and hard house from some of the best DJs in the country, lots of lasers and special effects, and some very sweaty hard bodies – of all genders and flavours, but mostly boys. Farringdon tube.

Theatre, comedy and cinema

London has enjoyed a reputation for quality **theatre** since the time of Shakespeare, and despite the continuing prevalence of fail-safe blockbuster musicals and revenue-spinning star vehicles, the city still provides a platform for innovation. The **comedy** scene in London goes from strength to strength, so much so that the capital now boasts more comedy venues than any other city in the world, while comedians who have made the transition to television also stage shows in major theatres. **Cinema** is rather less healthy, for London's repertory film theatres are a dying breed, edged out by the multiscreen com-plexes which show mainstream Hollywood fare some months behind America. There are a few excellent independent cinemas, though, including the National Film Theatre, which is the focus of the richly varied **London Film Festival** in November.

Theatre

At first glance, it might seem as though London's **theatreland** has become a province of the Andrew Lloyd Webber empire; however, few cities in the world can match the variety of the London scene. The state-funded **Royal Shakespeare Company** and the **National Theatre** often put on extremely original productions of mainstream masterpieces, while some of the most exciting work is performed in what have become known as the **Off West End** theatres, which consistently stage interesting and often challenging produc-tions. Further still down the financial ladder are the **fringe theatres**, more often than not pub venues, where ticket prices are low, and quality variable.

Unfortunately, most theatre-going doesn't come particularly cheap. **Tickets** under £10 are very thin on the ground; the box-office average is closer to £15, with £30 the usual top whack. Tickets for the durable musicals and well-reviewed plays are like gold dust. The Society of London Theatre (SOLT) **half-**

price ticket booth in Leicester Square (Mon–Sat 10am–7pm, Sun noon–3pm) sells tickets for that day's performances of all the West End shows, but they tend to be in the top end of the price range, and carry a service charge of £2.50 per ticket. If the SOLT booth has sold out, you could turn to reputable agencies such as Ticketmaster (☎020/7344 4444; ⓦwww.ticketmaster.co.uk) or First Call (☎020/7497 9977; ⓦwww.firstcalltickets.com), which can get seats for all West End shows, but add a ten percent mark-up on the ticket price.

What follows is a highly selective list. For the most consistent Off West End and fringe venues, check out *Time Out* for what's on at the Almeida, Donmar Warehouse, Royal Court, Young Vic, ICA and Tricycle theatres.

Barbican Centre Silk St, EC2, ☎020/7638 8891, ⓦwww.barbican.org.uk. After a season in the company's HQ at Stratford, Royal Shakespeare Company productions move to one of the Barbican's two venues: the excellently designed Barbican Theatre and the much smaller Pit. A wide range of work is produced, though the writings of the Bard predominate. Barbican or Moorgate tube.

National Theatre South Bank Centre, South Bank, SE1, ☎020/7452 3000, ⓦwww.nt-online.org. The Royal National Theatre, as it's now officially known, consists of three separate theatres: the 1100-seater Olivier, the proscenium-arched Lyttelton and the experimental Cottesloe. Standards set by the late Laurence Olivier, founding artistic director, are maintained by the country's top actors and directors in a programme ranging from *Wind in the Willows* to the work of Arthur Miller. Some productions sell out months in advance, but a few discounted tickets go on sale on the morning of each performance – get there by 8am for the popular shows. Waterloo tube.

Open Air Theatre Regent's Park, Inner Circle, NW1, ☎020/7486 2431. If the weather's good, there's nothing quite like a dose of alfresco drama. This beautiful space in Regent's Park hosts a tourist-friendly summer programme of Shakespeare, musicals, plays and concerts. Regent's Park or Baker Street tube.

Shakespeare's Globe New Globe Walk, SE1, ☎020/7902 1500, ⓦwww.shakespeares-globe.org. This thatch-roofed replica Elizabethan theatre uses only natural light and the minimum of scenery, and currently puts on solid, fun shows from mid-May to mid-September, with "groundling" tickets (standing-room only) for a mere £5. The new indoor Inigo Jones Theatre is set to continue the season throughout the winter months. London Bridge, Blackfriars or Southwark tube.

Comedy and cabaret

London's **comedy scene** continues to live up to its media-coined status as the new rock 'n' roll with the leading comics catapulted to unlikely stardom on both stage and screen. Note that many venues operate only on Friday and Saturday nights, and that August is a lean month, as much of London's talent then heads north for the Edinburgh Festival.

Banana Cabaret *The Bedford*, 77 Bedford Hill, SW12, ☎020/8673 8904. This double-stage pub has become one of London's finest comedy venues – well worth the trip out from the centre of town. Fri & Sat from 9pm. Balham tube.

Comedy Store Haymarket House, 1a Oxendon St, SW1, ☎020/7344 0234, ⓦwww.thecomedystore.co.uk. Widely regarded as the birthplace of alternative comedy, though no longer in its original venue, the Comedy Store has catapulted many a stand-up onto prime-time TV. Improvisation by in-house comics on Wednesdays and Sundays, in addition to a stand-up bill; Thursday night offers try-out spots for those brave enough to handle the hecklers, while Friday and Saturday are the busiest nights, with two shows, at 8pm and midnight – book ahead. Piccadilly Circus tube.

Jongleurs Camden Lock Dingwalls Building, 36 Camden Lock Place, Chalk Farm Rd, NW1, ☎020/7564 2500, ⓦwww.jongleurs.com. Camden link in a top-ranking chain of venues, with a spot of post-revelry disco-dancing included in the ticket price on Fridays, and two shows on a Saturday. Book well in advance. Fri & Sat. Camden Town tube.

Lee Hurst's Backyard Comedy Club 231 Cambridge Heath Rd, E2, ☎020/7739 3122, ⓦwww.leehurst.com. Purpose-built club in Bethnal Green established by comedian Lee Hurst, who has successfully managed to attract a consistently strong line-up. Fri & Sat. Bethnal Green tube.

Cinema

There are an awful lot of **cinemas** in the West End, but only a very few places committed to non-mainstream movies, and even fewer repertory cinemas programming serious films from the back catalogue. November's **London Film Festival**, which occupies half a dozen West End cinemas, is now a huge event, and so popular that most of the films sell out a couple of days after publication of the festival's programme. Below are the city's main arthouse cinemas.

ICA Cinema Nash House, The Mall, SW1, ☎020/7930 3647, ⓦwww.ica.org.uk. Vintage and underground movies shown on one of two tiny screens in the avant-garde HQ of the Institute of Contemporary Arts. Piccadilly Circus or Charing Cross tube.

BFI London Imax Centre South Bank, SE1, ☎020/79021234, ⓦwww.bfi.org.uk. The British Film Institute's remarkable glazed drum sits in the middle of the roundabout at the end of Waterloo Bridge. It's stunning, state-of-the-art stuff alright, showing 2D and 3D films on a massive screen, but like all IMAX cinemas, it suffers from the paucity of good material that's been shot on the format. Waterloo tube.

Lux Cinema 2–4 Hoxton Square, N1, ☎020/7684 0201, ⓦwww.lux.org.uk. Relatively new arts cinema in trendy Hoxton, showing an eclectic mix of films, and with an art gallery on the first floor. Old Street tube.

National Film Theatre South Bank, SE1, ☎020/7928 3232, ⓦwww.bfi.org.uk/nft. Known for its attentive audiences and an exhaustive, eclectic programme that includes directors' seasons and thematic series. Around six films daily are shown in the vast NFT1 and the smaller NFT2. Waterloo tube.

Prince Charles 2–7 Leicester Place, WC2, ☎020/7734 9127. The bargain basement of London's cinemas (entry for most shows is just £3.50/£2.50), with a programme of new movies, classics and cult favourites –Sing-Along-A-Sound-of-Music is a regular. Leicester Square tube.

Classical music, opera and dance

London is spoilt for choice when it comes to **orchestras**. On most days you'll be able to catch a concert by either the London Symphony Orchestra, the London Philharmonic, the Royal Philharmonic, the Philharmonia or the BBC Symphony Orchestra, or a smaller-scale performance from the English Chamber Orchestra, London Sinfonietta or the Academy of St Martin-in-the-Fields. During the week, there are also **free lunchtime concerts** by students or professionals in many of London's churches, particularly in the City; performances in the Royal College of Music and Royal Academy of Music are of an amazingly high standard, and the choice of work a lot riskier than the commercial venues can manage.

The principal **large-scale venue** is the South Bank Centre (☎020/7960 4242, ⓦwww.sbc.org.uk), where the biggest names appear at the Royal Festival Hall, with more specialized programmes staged in the Queen Elizabeth Hall and Purcell. Programming at the Barbican, Silk St, EC2 (☎020/7638 8891, ⓦwww.barbican.org.uk), has become much more adventurous recently, and the free music in the foyer is often very good. For **chamber music**, the intimate and elegant Wigmore Hall, 36 Wigmore St, W1 (☎020/7935 2141, ⓦwww.wigmore-hall.org.uk), is many a Londoner's favourite.

From July to September each year, **the Proms** at the Royal Albert Hall (☎020/7589 8212, ⓦwww.royalalberthall.com) feature at least one concert daily, with hundreds of standing-only tickets sold for just £3 on the night. The acoustics aren't the world's best, but the calibre of the performers is unbeatable and the programme is a fascinating mix of standards and new or obscure works. The hall is so vast that if you turn up half an hour before the show starts there should be little risk of being turned away.

Despite enjoying an increase in popularity, opera remains an elitist genre and has had a bad press in London, largely owing to the travails of Covent Garden's

Royal Opera House (☎020/7304 4000, ⊕www.royaloperahouse.org), which is attempting to make itself more accessible following its multi-million pound refurbishment. The **English National Opera** at the Coliseum, St Martin's Lane (☎020/7632 8300, ⊕www.eno.org), has more radical producers and is a more democratic institution, with all works sung in English.

From the time-honoured showpieces of the **Royal Ballet** (☎020/7304 4000, ⊕www.royaloperahouse.org) to the diverse and exciting range of British and international dance that goes on at the newly rebuilt Sadler's Wells (☎020/7863 8000, ⊕www.sadlers-wells.com), there's always a **dance performance** of some kind afoot in London, and the city also has a good reputation for international dance festivals showcasing the work of a spread of ensembles. The biggest of the annual events is the **Dance Umbrella** (☎020/8741 5881), a six-week season (Oct–Nov) of new work from bright young choreographers and performance artists at venues across the city.

Shopping

Whether it's time or money you've got to burn, London is one big shoppers' playground. And although chains and superstores predominate along the high streets, you're still never too far from the kind of oddball, one-off establishment that makes shopping an adventure rather than a chore. From the *folie de grandeur* that is Harrods to the frantic street markets of the East End, there's nothing you can't find in some corner of the capital.

In the centre of town, **Oxford Street** is the city's most frantic chain store mecca, and together with **Regent Street**, which crosses it halfway, offers pretty much every mainstream clothing label you could wish for. Just off Oxford Street, high-end designer outlets line **St Christopher's Place** and **South Molton Street**, and you'll find even pricier designers and jewellers along the very chic **Bond Street**.

Tottenham Court Road, which heads north from the east end of Oxford Street, is the place to go for electrical goods and furniture and design shops. **Charing Cross Road**, heading south, is the centre of London's book trade, both new and second-hand. At its north end, and particularly on **Denmark Street**, you can find music shops selling everything from instruments to sound equipment and sheet music. **Soho** offers an offbeat mix of sex boutiques, records and silks, while the streets surrounding **Covent Garden** yield art and design shops, mainstream fashion stores and designer wear.

Just off Piccadilly, **St James's** is the natural habitat of the quintessential English gentleman, with **Jermyn Street** in particular harbouring shops dedicated to his grooming. **Knightsbridge**, further west, is home to Harrods, and the big name fashion stores of **Sloane Street** and **Brompton Road** are adjacent.

Books

The biggest bookstore in the capital is Waterstones' Piccadilly branch (Piccadilly Circus), but the largest choice of bookshops is still on **Charing Cross Road**, where you'll not only find all the **chain stores** – Borders at no. 120, and Blackwell's at no. 100 – but also Foyles at no. 113–119, and other smaller **independent shops** such as the feminist outlet Silver Moon at no. 64–68, art specialists Zwemmer at no. 80, crime specialists Murder One at 71–73 and numerous **second-hand stores**, including Any Amount of Books at nos. 56 & 62.

Department stores

Fortnum & Mason, 181 Piccadilly (Green Park or Piccadilly Circus tube), is the place to go for fabulous, gorgeously presented and pricey food, plus upmarket clothes, furniture and stationery. **Harrods**, Knightsbridge (Knightsbridge tube), is famous for its fantastic Art Nouveau tiled food hall, obscenely huge toy department and supremely tasteless memorial to Diana and Dodi; beware the draconian dress code – no backpacks allowed, for example. Nearby, **Harvey Nichols**, 109–125 Knightsbridge (Knightsbridge tube), offers all the latest designer collections and famously frivolous and pricey luxury foods. Over at Oxford Circus, several major stores are close at hand, among them: **John Lewis**, 278–306 Oxford St (Oxford Circus tube), which offers everything from buttons to stockings to furniture and household goods; **Liberty**, 210–220 Regent St (Oxford Circus tube), founded as a retail outlet for the Victorian Arts and Crafts Movement, and still the place to go for regal fabrics and decorative household goods; and **Selfridge's**, 400 Oxford St (Bond Street tube), London's first great department store, which has a wide range of clothing, food and furnishings.

Markets

Camden, running from Camden High Street to Chalk Farm Road (mainly Thurs–Sun 9.30am–5.30pm; Camden Town tube), is top of the list for market shopping on most tourist itineraries; the atmosphere is grungy studenty and the stuff on sale is mainly cheap clothes and jewellery, though the stalls around Camden Lock are generally more interesting; weekends are the best – and busiest – times to visit. **Spitalfields**, Commercial Street (Mon–Fri 11am–3pm, Sun 10am–5pm; Liverpool Street tube), is an arty-crafty market similar to Camden, but on a much smaller scale; it also offers organic fruit and veg on Fridays and Sundays. Nearby, **Brick Lane** (Sun 8am–1pm; Aldgate East, Shoreditch or Liverpool Street tube) has everything from sofas to antique cameo brooches; and **Petticoat Lane**, Middlesex Street and Goulston Street (Sun 9am–2pm; Aldgate East or Liverpool Street tube), offers cheap and cheerful clothes. **Bermondsey** (New Caledonian) Market, Bermondsey Square (Fri 5am–2pm; Borough, London Bridge or Bermondsey tube), is a huge, unglamorous but highly regarded antique market; while **Portobello**, Portobello Rd (Sat 9am–5pm; Notting Hill or Ladbroke Grove tube), is mostly boho-chic clothes and portable antiques. South of the river, **Greenwich**, Market Square (mainly Thurs–Sun, 9.30am–5pm; Greenwich DLR or train station), is a small arty-crafty market, with second-hand clothing and antiques on sale, too.

Music

The **megastores** are: HMV, 150 Oxford St (Oxford Circus tube); Tower Records, 1 Piccadilly Circus (Piccadilly Circus tube); Virgin Megastore, 14–16 Oxford St (Tottenham Court Road tube). For **jazz**, try Ray's Jazz Shop, 180 Shaftesbury Ave (Leicester Square or Tottenham Court Road tube). For **indie music**, there's Sister Ray, 94 Berwick St (Oxford Circus or Piccadilly Circus tube). For **reggae**, **ragga** and **drum 'n' bass**, head to Daddy Kool, 12 Berwick St (Oxford Circus or Tottenham Court Road tube). **Hip-hop** is available at Deal Real Records, Noel St (Oxford Circus tube). For **house**, **techno** and **trance** go to Eukatech, 49 Endell St (Covent Garden tube).

Listings

Airport enquiries Gatwick ☎01293/535353, ⓦwww.baa.co.uk; Heathrow ☎0870/000 0123, ⓦwww.baa.co.uk; London City Airport ☎020/7646 0000, ⓦwww.londoncityairport.com; Luton ☎01582/405100, ⓦwww.london-luton.com; Stansted ☎0870/000 0303, ⓦwww.baa.co.uk.

American Express 30–31 Haymarket, SW1 ☎020/7484 9600, ⓦwww.americanexpress.com. Mon–Fri 9am–7pm, Sat 9am–6pm, Sun 10am–5pm. Piccadilly Circus tube.

Bike rental Bikepark, 14 Stukeley St, WC2 ☎020/7430 0083, ⓦwww.bikepark.co.uk. Mon–Fri 8.30am–7pm, Sat 10am–6pm. Covent Garden tube.

Bus information Long-distance coach services depart from Victoria Coach Station, Buckingham Palace Rd (Victoria tube). National Express have ticket offices here (☎0990/808080) and can tell you about European services operated by Eurolines.

Cricket Two Test matches are played in London each summer: one at Lord's (☎020/7289 1611, ⓦwww.lords.org), the home of English cricket, in St John's Wood, the other at The Oval (☎020/7582 6660, ⓦwww.surreyccc.co.uk), in Kennington. In tandem with the full-blown five-day Tests, there's also a series of one-day internationals, two of which are usually held in London.

Consulates and Embassies Australia, Australia House, Strand, WC2 ☎020/7379 4334, ⓦwww.australia.org.uk; Canada, MacDonald House, 1 Grosvenor Square, W1 ☎020/7258 6600, ⓦwww.canada.org.uk; Ireland, 17 Grosvenor Place, SW1 ☎020/7235 2171, ⓦwww.iolgov.ie/iveagh; New Zealand, New Zealand House, 80 Haymarket, SW1 ☎020/7930 8422, ⓦwww.newzealandhc.org.uk; South Africa, South Africa House, Trafalgar Square, WC2 ☎020/7451 7299, ⓦwww.southafricahouse.com; USA, 24 Grosvenor Square, W1 ☎020/7499 9000, ⓦwww.usembassy.org.uk.

Dentist Emergency treatment: Guy's Hospital, St Thomas St, SE1 ☎020/7955 4317. Mon–Fri 8.45am–3.30pm.

Football London's top club at the moment is Arsenal (☎020/7704 4000, ⓦwww.arsenal.co.uk), who won the double (league and FA Cup) in the 1997–98 season; their closest rivals (geographically) are Tottenham Hotspur (☎020/8365 5000, ⓦwww.spurs.co.uk). Meanwhile, in west London, Chelsea (☎020/7386 7799, ⓦwww.chelseafc.co.uk) waltzed away with the last-ever European Cup Winners' Cup in 1999.

Hospitals For 24-hour accident and emergency: Charing Cross Hospital, Fulham Palace Rd, W6 ☎020/8846 1234; Chelsea & Westminster Hospital, 369 Fulham Rd, SW10 ☎020/8746 8000; Royal Free Hospital, Pond St, NW3 ☎020/7794 0500; Royal London Hospital, Whitechapel Rd, E1 ☎020/7377 7000; St Mary's Hospital, Praed St, W2 ☎020/7886 6666; University College Hospital, Grafton Way, WC1 ☎020/7387 9300; Whittington Hospital, Highgate Hill, N19 ☎020/7272 3070.

Left luggage AIRPORTS Gatwick: North Terminal ☎01293/502013 (daily 6am–10pm); South Terminal ☎01293/502014 (24hr). Heathrow: Terminal 1 ☎020/8745 5301 (daily 6am–11pm); Terminal 2 ☎020/8745 4599 (daily 6am–10.30pm); Terminal 3 ☎020/8759 3344 (daily 5.30am–10.30pm); Terminal 4 ☎020/8745 7460 (daily 5.30am–11pm). London City Airport ☎020/7646 0000 (daily 6.30am–10pm). Stansted Airport ☎01279/680500 (24hr). TRAIN STATIONS Charing Cross ☎020/7839 4282 (daily 7am–11pm); Euston ☎020/7320 0528 (Mon–Sat 6.45am–11.15pm, Sun 7.15am–11pm); Victoria ☎020/7928 5151 ext 27523 (daily 7am–10.15pm, plus lockers); Waterloo International ☎020/7928 5151 (Mon–Fri 4am–11pm, Sat & Sun 6am–11pm).

London Transport enquiries 24-hour information on ☎020/7222 1234, ⓦwww.londontransport.co.uk.

Lost property AIRPORTS Gatwick ☎01293/503162 (daily 7.30am–5.30pm); Heathrow ☎020/8745 7727 (Mon–Fri 8am–5pm, Sat & Sun 8am–4pm); London City Airport ☎020/7646 0000 (Mon–Fri 6am–9.30pm, Sat 6am–1am, Sun 10.30am–9.30pm); Stansted ☎01279/680500 (daily 5.30am–11pm). BUSES ☎020/7222 1234. HEATHROW EXPRESS ☎020/8745 7727. TAXIS (black cabs only) ☎020/7833 0996. TRAIN STATIONS Euston ☎020/7922 6477 (Mon–Sat 6.45am–11pm, Sun 7.15am–11pm); King's Cross ☎020/7922 9081 (daily 8am–7.45pm); Liverpool Street ☎020/7928 9158 (Mon–Fri 7am–7pm, Sat & Sun 7am–2pm); Paddington ☎020/7313 1514 (Mon–Fri 9am–5.30pm); Victoria ☎020/7922 9887 (Mon–Fri 7.30am–10pm); Waterloo ☎020/7401 7861 (Mon–Fri 7.30am–8pm). TUBE TRAINS London Regional Transport ☎020/7486 2496.

Police Central police stations include: Charing Cross, Agar St, WC2 ☎020/7240 1212; Holborn,

70 Theobalds Rd, WC1 ☎020/7404 1212; King's Cross, 76 King's Cross Rd, WC1 ☎020/7704 1212; Tottenham Court Road, 56 Tottenham Court Rd, W1 ☎020/7637 1212; West End Central, 10 Vine St, W1 ☎020/7437 1212. City of London Police, Bishopsgate, EC2 ☎020/7601 2222.

Post offices The only late-opening post office is the Trafalgar Square branch at 24–28 William IV St, WC2 4DL (Mon–Fri 8am–8pm, Sat 9am–8pm; ☎020/7484 9304); it's also the city's poste restante collection point. For general postal enquiries phone ☎08457/740740, or visit the website ⓦwww.royalmail.co.uk.

Tennis Tennis in England is synonymous with Wimbledon (☎020/8946 2244, ⓦwww.wimbledon.org), the only Grand Slam tournament in the world to be played on grass, and for many players the ultimate goal of their careers. To buy tickets on the day, you must arrive by around 7am for tickets on Centre and No. 1 courts, or by around 9am for the outside courts.

Train stations and information As a rough guide, Euston handles services to northwest England and Glasgow; King's Cross northeast England and Edinburgh; Liverpool Street eastern England; Paddington western England; Victoria and Waterloo southeast England. For information, call national rail enquiries on ☎08457/484950.

Travel agents Campus Travel, 52 Grosvenor Gardens, SW1 ☎0870/240 1010, ⓦwww.usit-campus.co.uk; Council Travel, 28a Poland St, W1 ☎020/7437 7767, ⓦwww.destination-group.com; STA Travel, 86 Old Brompton Rd, SW7 ☎020/7361 6161, ⓦwww.statravel.co.uk; Trailfinders, 42–50 Earl's Court Rd, SW5 ☎020/7938 3366, ⓦwww.trailfinders.co.uk.

Travel details

Buses

For information on all local and national bus services, contact Traveline: ☎0870/608 2608, ⓦwww.traveline.org.uk.

Victoria Coach Station to: Bath (11 daily; 3hr 15min); Birmingham (hourly; 2hr); Brighton (hourly; 1hr 45min); Bristol (hourly; 2hr 20min); Cambridge (hourly; 2hr); Canterbury (hourly; 1hr 50min); Carlisle (3–4 daily; 6hr); Chester (5–6 daily; 5hr 30min); Dover (hourly; 2hr 45min); Exeter (8 daily; 4hr); Gloucester (10 daily; 3hr) Liverpool (5–6 daily; 4hr 30min); Manchester (9 daily; 4hr 15min); Oxford (frequently; 1hr 30min); Plymouth (7 daily; 4hr 40min); York (3 daily; 4hr 20min).

Trains

For information on all local and national rail services, contact National Rail Enquiries: ☎08457/48 49 50, ⓦwww.nationalrail.co.uk.

London Charing Cross to: Dover Priory (every 30min; 1hr 45min–2hr).

London Euston to: Birmingham New St (every 30min; 1hr 40min); Carlisle (every 1–2hr; 3hr 50min); Chester (3 daily; 2hr 40min); Crewe (hourly; 2hr); Lancaster (8 daily; 3hr); Liverpool Lime St (hourly; 2hr 45min); Manchester Piccadilly (hourly; 2hr 30min).

London King's Cross to: Brighton (every 10–40min; 1hr 15min); Cambridge (every 30min; 50min); Durham (every 1–2hr; 2hr 50min); Leeds (hourly; 2hr 20min); Newcastle (every 30min; 2hr 40min–3hr); York (every 30min; 1hr 40min–2hr).

London Liverpool Street to: Cambridge (hourly; 1hr 20min); Harwich (every 2hr; 1hr 10min); Norwich (hourly; 2hr); Stansted (every 30min; 45min).

London Paddington to: Bath (every 30min–hourly; 1hr 25min); Bristol Parkway (every 30min–1hr; 1hr 20min); Exeter St Davids (hourly; 2hr 10min); Oxford (every 30min–hourly; 50min–1hr); Penzance (7 daily; 5hr); Plymouth (every 1–2hr; 3hr–3hr 40min); Worcester (11 daily; 2hr–2hr 15min).

London St Pancras to: Leicester (every 30min; 1hr 15min); Nottingham (hourly; 1hr 50min); Sheffield (hourly; 2hr 20min).

London Victoria to: Brighton (every 30min; 1hr–1hr 20min); Canterbury East (every 30min; 1hr 30min); Canterbury West (hourly; 1hr 50min); Dover Priory (hourly; 1hr 50min); Gatwick (frequently; 30min) ; Ramsgate (hourly; 1hr 50min).

London Waterloo to: Portsmouth Harbour (every 30min; 1hr 35min); Southampton Central (every 20min; 1hr 15min); Winchester (every 20min; 55min–1hr 5min).

2

Surrey, Kent and Sussex

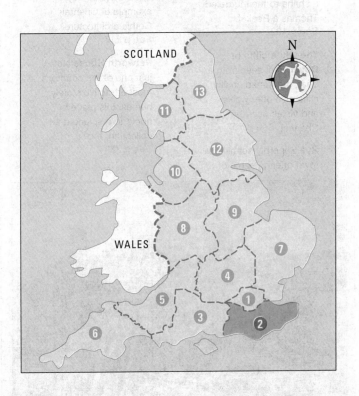

CHAPTER 2

Highlights

* **Canterbury Cathedral**
The mother church of
the Church of England,
this was the destination
of pilgrims in Chaucer's
Canterbury Tales and the
magnificent sixteenth-
century interior includes
a shrine to the murdered
Thomas à Becket.
See p.192

* **The white cliffs of
Dover** Best seen from a
boat, the famed chalky
cliffs also offer walks
and vistas over the
Channel. See p.197

* **Rye** Superbly set hilltop
town offering some of

the best meals, accom-
modation and pubs in
Sussex. See p.201

* **The Royal Pavilion,
Brighton** George IV's
pleasure dome,
designed by Nash, is the
supreme (and only)
example of Oriental-
Gothic architecture.
See p.217

* **Petworth House** Not
just one of the country's
most attractive stately
homes, this place is
home to a splendid art
collection, too.
See p.223

Surrey, Kent and Sussex

The southeast corner of England was traditionally where London went on holiday. In the past, trainloads of Eastenders were shuttled to the hop fields and orchards of **Kent** for a working break from the city; boats ferried people down the Thames to the beach at Margate; and everyone from royalty to cuckolding couples enjoyed the seaside at Brighton, a blot of decadence in the otherwise sedate county of **Sussex**. Of the three, **Surrey** is the least pastoral and historically significant – the home of wealthy metropolitan professionals prepared to commute from what has become known as the "stockbroker belt".

The late twentieth century brought big changes to the southeast region. In purely administrative terms the three counties have become four, since local government reorganization split Sussex into East and West. More significantly, many of the coastal towns have faced an uphill struggle to keep their tourist custom in the face of evermore accessible foreign destinations. To make matters worse, **Brighton**, long known as "London beside the sea", now matches the capital with one of the highest proportions of homeless people in the country.

The proximity of Kent and Sussex to the continent has dictated the history of this region, which has served as a gateway for an array of invaders, both rapacious and benign. **Roman** remains dot the landscape – the most spectacular are at **Bignor**, near Arundel – and many roads, including the London-to-Dover A2, follow the straight lines laid by the legionaries. When post-Roman **Christianity** spread through Europe, it arrived in Britain on the **Isle of Thanet** – the northeast tip of Kent, although older orders already existed among the Celts in the north and west of the country. In 597 AD Augustine moved inland and established a monastery at **Canterbury**, still the home of the Church of England and the county's prime historic attraction. (Surprisingly, Sussex was among the last counties to accept the Cross – due more to the region's then impenetrable forest than to its innate ungodliness.)

The last successful invasion of England took place in 1066, when the **Normans** overran King Harold's army near **Hastings**, on a site now marked by **Battle Abbey**. The Normans left their mark all over this corner of England and Kent remains unmatched in its profusion of medieval castles,

2

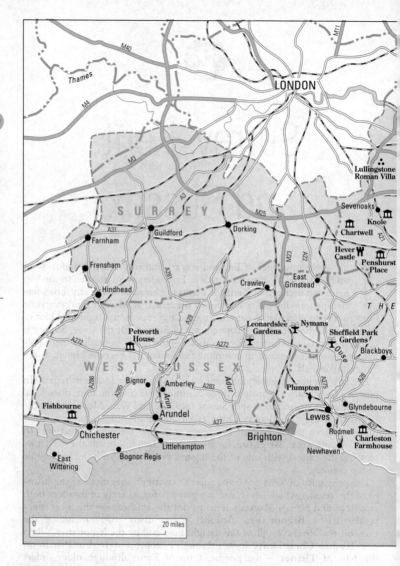

among them **Dover**'s sprawling cliff-top fortress guarding against continental invasion and **Rochester**'s huge, box-like citadel, close to the old dockyards of **Chatham**, power base of the formerly invincible British Navy.

Away from the great historic sites, you can spend unhurried days in elegant old towns such as **Rye**, **Royal Tunbridge Wells** and **Lewes**, or enjoy the less elevated charms of the traditional resorts, of which **Brighton** is far and away the best, combining the buzz of a university town with a good-

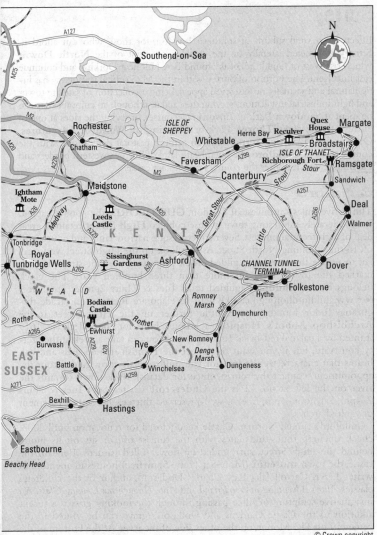

© Crown copyright

time atmosphere and an excellent range of eating options. Dramatic scenery may be in short supply, but in places the **South Downs Way** offers an expanse of rolling chalk uplands that, as much as anywhere in the crowded southeast, gets you away from it all. And of course Surrey, Kent and Sussex harbour some of the country's finest **gardens**, ranging from the lush flowerbeds of **Sissinghurst** to the great landscaped estates of **Petworth** and **Sheffield Park**.

Surrey

Effectively a rural suburb of southern London, for those who can afford it, **Surrey** is bisected laterally by the chalk escarpment of the **North Downs** which rise west of Guildford, peak around Box Hill near Dorking and continue east into Kent. The portion of Surrey within the M25 orbital motorway has little natural and virtually no historical appeal, being a collection of satellite towns and light industrial installations serving the capital, although an enjoyable day can be spent at **Sandown Park** or **Epsom** racecourses, or trying the rides at one of Surrey's theme parks, **Thorpe Park** or **Chessington World of Adventures**. Outside the M25's ring Surrey takes on a more pastoral demeanour, with the county town of **Guildford**, the open heath land of Surrey's western borders and **Farnham**, which houses the county's only intact castle.

Guildford

Thirty-five miles southwest of London, **GUILDFORD**, the county capital, is a moderately interesting town, whose cobbled **High Street** retains a great deal of architectural interest. Several picturesque narrow lanes and courts lead off to the adjoining North Street. As you look up the High Street, you can't fail to notice the wonderful gilded **clock** projecting over the street that has marked the town's time for more than three hundred years. The clock belongs to the **Guildhall** (guided tours Tues & Thurs 2pm & 3pm; free; ⓦ www.guildfordborough.co.uk) with its elaborate Restoration facade disguising Tudor foundations. A little further up the High Street is the **Archbishop Abbot's Hospital**, a hospice built for the elderly in 1619 fronted by a palatial red-brick Tudor gateway. You can take a peek at the pretty courtyard, but if you want to inspect the Flemish stained glass and oak beams that characterize the interior you must sign up for a guided tour (by appointment; contact the tourist office for details). Back down towards the river on the left, at no. 72, is the **Undercroft** (Easter–Sept Tues & Thurs 2–4pm, Sat noon–4pm; free), a well-preserved thirteenth-century basement of vaulted arches.

Guildford's ruined Norman **Castle** keep (closed for renovation until 2003; check opening times and dates with the tourist office) sits on its motte behind the High Street, surrounded by flower-filled gardens. Beneath the castle, the town **museum** (Mon–Sat 11am–5pm; free) houses mementoes of writer Lewis Carroll (aka Rev Charles Dodgson), author of the children's classics *Alice's Adventures in Wonderland* and *Alice Through the Looking Glass*. An imaginative sculpture of Alice passing through the looking glass is a recent addition to the Castle Gardens and Dodgson's grave can be visited in the cemetery off The Mount, on the other side of the river. At the bottom of the High Street runs the **River Wey**, a rather neglected feature of the town, although the once crucial River Wey and Godalming Navigation Canal has been restored into a picturesque waterway. From Easter to October, you can **rent** canoes (swimmers only) and rowing boats (Mon–Sat 9am–5.30pm, Sun 10am–6pm; canoes £4/hour; rowing boats £6/hour; £20 deposit) from Guildford Boat House, based in the Millbrook car park and take the same company's **pleasure cruises** up the river from the town wharf, at the bottom of the High Street (mid-April to mid-July & last 2 weeks Sept Sun & Wed 1.45pm & 3.30pm; mid-July to mid-Sept Tues–Thurs, Sat & Sun noon, 1.45pm & 3.30pm; £4.25; ⓦ www.guildfordboats.co.uk). Half a mile further north up the river is **Dapdune Wharf** (April–Oct Thurs–Sun 11am–5pm; £2.50; NT) whose buildings house an interactive museum recounting the story of what is claimed to be Britain's oldest working waterway, while outside you can visit the restored barge *Reliance*.

Finally, it's difficult to miss Guildford's monumentally unremarkable modern Gothic **Cathedral** (daily 8am–5.30pm; ⓦ www.guildford-cathedral.org), ostentatiously perched on Stag Hill, a mile northwest of the centre. Resembling an outsized crematorium and consecrated in 1961, the cathedral's plain, bright interior has all the spirituality of a concert hall, but without the acoustics. Its most notable claim to fame is having been a location in the film *The Omen*.

Practicalities

Guildford's main **train station** lies just over the river west of the town centre; the **bus station** is between the town centre and the train station, at the foot of North Street. The county's main **tourist office** is at 14 Tunsgate opposite the Guildhall (May–Sept Mon–Sat 9am–5.30pm, Sun 10am–4.30pm; Oct–April Mon–Sat 9.30am–5.30pm; ⓣ 01483/444333, ⓦ www.guildfordborough.co.uk). Guildford's cheaper **accommodation** options are all some distance from the town centre and include the homely *Atkinsons Guest House*, 129 Stoke Rd (ⓣ 01483/538260; ❷), with en-suite rooms, ten minutes' walk up the A320 Woking road. Plusher lodgings can be found at the *Jarvis Guildford Hotel*, 253 High St (ⓣ 01483/564511; ❻) and at the timber-beamed, 500-year-old *Angel Posthouse and Livery*, 91 High St (ⓣ 01483/564555; ❽).

The High Street area offers a fairly routine range of **eating options** – *Café de Paris* at no. 35 (ⓣ 01483/564555; closed Sun), a busy French-style brasserie in a listed building, offers three-course meals from around £14 – while *Olivo*, at 53 Quarry St (ⓣ 01483/564555; closed Sun), is an innovative *focacceria* serving delicious regional Italian dishes, housed in the town's sixteenth-century dispensary. Guildford's better **pubs** include the *King's Head* in Quarry Street, with a courtyard and inexpensive meals, and *Ye Olde Ship Inn*, the town's oldest hostelry, on Portsmouth Road.

Farnham

Tucked into Surrey's southwestern corner, ten miles west of Guildford along the exposed ridgetop of the Hog's Back, lies **FARNHAM**. Smaller and, in parts, more charming than Guildford, Farnham moves at a slower pace. Despite its thousand-year history, the majority of Farnham's architecture dates from the eighteenth century, when the town enjoyed a boom period based on hop farming.

Farnham is home to Surrey's only intact **castle**, built around 1160 by Henry de Blois, Bishop of Winchester, as a convenient residence halfway between his diocese and London. The castle was continuously occupied until 1927, but now houses a conference venue. Its **keep** (April–Sept daily 10am–6pm; Oct daily 10am–5pm; £2.10; EH), from where there are good views over Farnham's red-tile roofs to the Downs beyond, is the only part open to the public and holds a well shaft excavated from an earlier Saxon structure. Farnham's refined Georgian dwellings are at their best along the broad **Castle Street**, which links the town centre with the castle.

The **train station**, with frequent connections to London Waterloo, is over the river on the south edge of town, along South Street and over the bypass. The

tourist office is in the council offices on South Street (Mon–Thurs 9.30am–5.15pm, Fri 9.30am–4.45pm, Sat 9am–noon; ☎01252/715109, ⓦwww.waverley.gov.uk). **B&B** options include *Meads Guest House*, 48 West St (☎01252/715298; ❷) and the excellent *Stafford House Hotel*, 22 Firgrove Hill (☎01252/724336; ❷), close to the station. About a mile south of Farnham Station off the Tilford Road, *High Wray*, 73 Lodge Hill Rd (☎01252/715589; ❷), is located in a peaceful, semi-rural setting, conveniently close to the start of the North Downs Way – it's a little off the beaten track, so be sure to ask for clear directions. Back in town, the oak-beamed *Nelson Arms*, Castle St, offers reasonable bar **food** while, if you prefer to eat Italian, the best bet is the friendly *Caffe Piccolo*, 84 West St (☎01252/723277).

The North Kent coast

It's a commonly held view that the northern part of Kent is a scenic and cultural wasteland, a prejudice that stems partly from the fact that most visitors only glimpse the area as they race to or from the Channel ports. However, the region has its fair share of attractions, all of which are easily accessible from London. The knot of historic sites at **Chatham** and **Rochester** are followed by the seaside towns of **Whitstable**, **Margate**, **Broadstairs** and **Ramsgate**, once-popular resorts that now make an interesting mix of the stuffy and the purely frivolous.

Rochester and around

ROCHESTER was first settled by the Romans, who built a fortress on the site of the present **Castle** (daily: April–Sept 10am–6pm; Oct 10am–5pm; Nov–March 10am–4pm; £3.60; EH) at the northwest end of the High Street; some kind of fortification has remained here ever since. In 1077, William I gave Gundulf, architect of the White Tower at the Tower of London, the see of Rochester and the job of improving the defences on the Medway's northernmost bridge on Watling Street. The castle remains one of the best-preserved examples of a Norman fortress in England. The stark 100-foot-high keep glowers over the town, while its interior is all the better for having lost its floors, allowing clear views up and down the dank interior. It has three square towers and one cylindrical (the southwest), which was rebuilt following its collapse during the siege of 1215, when the bankrupt King John eventually wrested the castle from its archbishop. The outer walls and two of the towers retain their corridors and spiral stairwells, allowing access to the uppermost battlements.

The foundations of the adjacent **Cathedral** (daily 7.30am–6pm; free) were also Gundulf's work, but the building has been much modified over the past nine hundred years. Plenty of Norman touches have endured, particularly in the west front, with its pencil-shaped towers, blind arcading and richly carved portal and tympanum above the doorway. Norman round arches, decorated with zigzags and made from lovely honey-coloured Caen stone, also line the nave. The cathedral once enshrined the remains of one St William of Perth, a pious baker from Scotland, who in 1201 embarked on a pilgrimage to the Holy Land, but got only as far as Rochester, where he was murdered and robbed. The monks of Rochester, envying the popular appeal of St Thomas à Becket's shrine at nearby Canterbury, used William's demise as an opportunity to establish a rival shrine – indeed, substantial additions to the cathedral were financed by donations from pilgrims paying their respects to the canonized baker's tomb, which has long since disappeared. Some fine paintings which survived the Dissolution of the Monasteries decorate the interior, most notably on the walls of the choir where the thirteenth-century depiction of the Wheel of Fortune (only half of which survives) is shown as a treadmill, a trenchant image of medieval life's relentless slog.

Rochester's most famous son is **Charles Dickens**, who spent his youth around here but would seem to have been less than impressed by the place – it appears in two of his novels as "Mudfog" and "Dullborough". Many town buildings, such as the *Royal Victoria and Bull Hotel* at the top of the High Street, also feature in his novels, while most of his last book, the unfinished *Mystery of Edwin Drood*, was set here. A gritty picture of Victorian life is conjured up by the tableaux at the **Charles Dickens Centre** in Eastgate House at the east end of the High Street (daily: April–Sept 10am–6pm; Oct–March 10am–4pm; £3.70; ⓦ www.medway.gov.uk). Key scenes from his well-known books are enacted at the push of a button and the whole place is entertaining and informative whether you're a Dickens enthusiast or not. Further down the High Street stands **Watts' Charity** (March–Oct Tues–Sat 2pm–5pm; free), a sixteenth-century almshouse featuring galleried Elizabethan bedrooms and immortalized in Dickens' short story *The Seven Poor Travellers*.

Not all town museums are worth close scrutiny, but Rochester's excellent **Guildhall Museum**, at the castle end of the High Street (daily 10am–4.30pm; free; ⓦ www.medway.gov.uk), is an exception. Inside, you'll find a vivid model of King John's siege of the castle and a chilling exhibition on the prison ships or **hulks** once moored near the Medway towns. Following American independence from Britain in 1776, England was stuck for a place to transport her growing numbers of convicts – an increase caused as much by desperate poverty and draconian sentencing as any wave of criminality. Until the new penal colony of Botany Bay was established a decade or so later, criminals were housed in appalling and overcrowded conditions inside decommissioned naval vessels moored in the Thames. With the clever use of mirrors the exhibit replicates the grim nightmare inside these floating prisons.

Practicalities

Rochester's **tourist office** stands opposite the cathedral at 95 High St (Mon–Sat 10am–5pm, Sun 10.30am–5pm; ☎01634/843666, ⓦwww.medway.gov.uk); its free guided tours of the town (Easter–Sept Wed, Sat & Sun 2.15pm) set off from the Charles Dickens Centre. The **train station**, served by regular trains from London's Charing Cross and Victoria, is at the southeastern end of the High Street. You could **spend the night** with some Dickensian ghosts at the ancient *Royal Victoria and Bull Hotel*, 16–18 High St (☎01634/846266, ⓦwww.rvandb.co.uk; ❺) or at the plush *Gordon House Hotel* at number 91 (☎01634/83100, ⓦwww.smoothhound.co.uk/hotels/gordon1; ❹). Other options include B&Bs, such as *Grayling House*, 54 St Margaret's St (☎01634/826593; ❷), west of the cathedral. The nearest youth hostel (☎01722/400788) is at Capstone Farm, Gillingham, two miles southeast of Chatham (bus #114). The best **places to eat** include two Italians – choose from *Giannino's* in the *Victoria and Bull* or the modest, family-run *Casa Lina*, at 145 High St – while Southeast Asian food is represented by the *Singapora* at no. 51. Alternatively, try the *Coopers Arms* on St Margaret's Street, just west of the castle and cathedral, which serves good lunches in its small beer garden.

CHATHAM, less than a mile east of Rochester and one stop further on by train, has none of the charms of its neighbour. Its chief attraction is its **Historic Dockyard** (April–Oct daily 10am–5pm; Feb, March & Nov Wed, Sat & Sun 10am–4pm; £8.50; ⓦ www.worldnavalbase.org.uk), originally founded by Henry VIII, and once the major base of the Royal Navy – many of whose vessels were built, stationed and victualled here – it commanded worldwide supremacy from the Tudor era until the end of the Victorian age. Well sheltered, yet close to London and the sea, and lined with tidal mud flats which helped support ships' keels during construction, the port expanded quickly and by the time of Charles II it had become England's largest naval base. This era of ship-building came to an ignominious end when the dockyards were closed in 1984, re-opening soon afterwards as a tourist attraction.

The dockyards occupy a vast eighty-acre site about a mile north of the town centre along the Dock Road; it's a not very pleasant fifteen-minute walk from Chatham town centre, or a short ride on the bus (ask at Rochester's tourist office for the latest timetable). Behind the stern brick wall you'll find an array of historically and architecturally fascinating buildings dating back to the early eighteenth century. In addition to an impressive display of fifteen historic RNLI lifeboats, there's the "**Wooden Walls**" **gallery**, where you can experience life as an apprentice in the eighteenth-century dockyards. Here, too, lies the **Ocelot Submarine**, the last warship built, at Chatham, whose crew endured unbelievably cramped conditions, a major deterrent to visiting claustrophobes. The main part of the exhibition, however, consists of the **Ropery complex**, including the former rope-making room – at a quarter of a mile long, it's the longest room in the country.

Whitstable

Peculiarities of silt and salinity have made **WHITSTABLE** an oyster-friendly environment since classical times, when the Romans feasted on the region's marine delicacies. Before the modern era, oysters were thought of as poor people's food and during the 1950s the town prospered, with offshore **oyster** beds covering five thousand acres and fishing and seaside tourism bringing additional revenue – but then sea pollution, as well as the changing patterns in holiday-making, brought about Whitstable's reversion to humbler status. These days, small-scale boat-building and a mildly Bohemian ambience make Whitstable one of the few pleasant spots along the north Kent coast and it's a popular day-trip destination for Londoners.

Back in 1830, Whitstable became the northern terminus for one of Britain's first steam-powered passenger railway services – the so-called "Crab and Winkle Line" which linked the town via a half-mile tunnel (the world's longest at that time) with Canterbury, ten miles to the south. If you're not satisfied simply eating the local oysters, you can learn more about them at the brand new **Oyster and Fishery Exhibition**, on the harbour, just off Harbour Street. If your fascination with Whitstable's maritime history is still not sated, head for the more staid **Whitstable Museum and Gallery** in Oxford Street (July & Aug Mon–Sat 10am–4pm, Sun 1–4pm; rest of year closed Sun; free), the southern continuation of High Street, with displays on diving and some good photographs of the town's heyday.

Whitstable's **train station** is a five-minute walk along Cromwell Road, east of Oxford Street, while the **tourist office** is beside the museum, at 7 Oxford St (July & Aug Mon–Sat 10am–5pm; rest of year Mon–Sat 10am–4pm;

☎01227/275482, ⓦwww.visitwhitstable.co.uk). For **accommodation** along the seafront, try *Copeland House*, 4 Island Wall (☎01227/266207; ❸), west of the High Street, with a garden which backs on to the beach; the plush *Hotel Continental*, 29 Beach Walk (☎01227/280280, ⓦwww.oysterfishery.co.uk; ❼), off the northern tip of Harbour Street; or homely B&B and a delightful garden at the *Cherry Garden*, 62 Joy Lane (☎01227/266497; ❷), a ten-minute stroll along the Seasalter road. For **campsites**, you're best off heading to *Seaview Caravan Park* (☎01227/792246; closed Nov–March), which backs onto the beach towards Herne Bay.

Whitstable's fishing background is reflected in its **eating** places, from any number of fish-and-chip outlets along the High Street to the very popular *Royal Native Oyster Stores* by the seafront (☎01227/276856; closed Sun eve & Mon), the town's best restaurant, with its own arthouse cinema above. *Pearsons Crab & Oyster House*, opposite (☎01227/272005), is a good alternative. *Tea & Times*, 36 High St, caters for the town's arty fringe and serves a decent English breakfast with real coffee and newspapers. For a **drink** and excellent atmosphere check out the *Old Neptune*, standing alone in its white weatherboards on the shore, while another excellent locals' pub is the *Wall Tavern*, Middle Wall.

The Thanet resorts

The **Isle of Thanet**, a featureless plain fringed by low chalk cliffs and the odd sandy bay, became part of the mainland when the navigable Wantsum Channel began silting up, around the time of the first Roman invasion. This northeastern corner of Kent has witnessed successive waves of incursions. In 43 AD, nearly a century after Julius Caesar's exploratory visit, the Romans got into their stride when they landed near Pegwell Bay and established the port of Richborough in preparation for the march inland. The Saxons followed them four hundred years later (the island is named after the "tenets", which were fire beacons used to warn local residents of the Saxons' raids) and Augustine arrived here in 597 on a divine mission to end English paganism. The evangelist is supposed to have met King Ethelbert of Kent and preached his first sermon at a spot three miles west of Ramsgate – a cross marks the location at Ebbsfleet, next to St Augustine's Golf Club.

Over the next thousand years or so, civilization advanced to the point at which, in 1751, a resident of Margate, one Mr Benjamin Beale, invented the bathing machine, a wheeled cubicle that enabled people to slip into the sea without undue exhibitionism. It heralded the birth of sea bathing as a recreational and recuperative activity, and led to the growth of **seaside resorts**. By the mid-twentieth century the Isle's intermittent expanses of sand had become fully colonized as the "bucket and spade" resorts of the capital's leisure-seeking proletariat. That heyday has passed, but these earliest of resorts still cling to their traditional attractions to varying degrees.

Margate

MARGATE – memorably summarized by Oscar Wilde as "the nom-deplume of Ramsgate" – is a ragged assortment of cafés, shops and amusement arcades wrapped around a broad bay, a rather less elegant place than the one with which it's been twinned, the Black Sea resort of Yalta. Yet two centuries of tourism are embodied by Margate: at its peak thousands of Londoners were ferried down the Thames every summer's day, to be disgorged at the pier – precursor of all such seaside structures.

Other than the agreeable, if small, beach, Margate's main attraction along its unashamedly tacky seafront is **Dreamland** on Marine Terrace (Easter–June & Sept daily 11am–5.30pm; July & Aug 11am–10pm), an amusement park, with a rollercoaster dating back to 1863. If this doesn't appeal you could always visit the **Shell Grotto** (Easter to mid-Oct Mon–Fri 10am–5pm, Sat & Sun 10am–4pm; £1.50), on Grotto Hill, off Northdown Road, which claims to be the world's only underground shell temple and has been open to the public since it was discovered by some children in 1835. Its passages are intricately decorated with shell mosaics and its caverns were once linked to the less interesting **Margate Caves** down Northdown Road (July & Aug daily 10am–5pm; April–June, Sept & Oct daily 10am–4pm; £1.80) – if nothing else, a good place to cool off on a hot day.

Margate's **train station** is on All Saint's Avenue, just a couple of minutes' walk from Dreamland, while the **tourist office** is at 12–13 The Parade (Easter–Sept Mon–Fri 9am–5pm, Sat 9am–4pm, Sun 10am–4pm; Oct–Easter Mon–Sat 9am–4pm; ☎01843/230203, ⓦwww.tourism.thanet.gov.uk). There are plenty of **B&Bs** lining the Regency crescents of the Cliftonville suburb to the east – try the family-run, seafront *Ocean View Hotel*, 8–10 Ethelbert Terrace (☎01843/220641, ⓦwww.oceanviewhotel.co.uk; ❷), or the nearby and welcoming *Hotel Marina*, 8 Dalby Square (☎01843/230120; ❶). Margate's YHA hostel (☎01843/221616, ⓦwww.yha.org.uk), situated in the former Beachcomber Hotel, 3–4 Royal Esplanade, by Westbrook Bay to the west of the train station. Prosaic **seaside food** is on offer at any of the seafront greasy spoons and fish-and-chip shops, but you can get very fine **pastries** and snacks from *Batchelor's Patisserie*, at 246 Northdown Rd, Cliftonville. For **pubs**, try the tiny *Rose & June*, on Trinity Square, or for real ales (and pizzas), there's the *Spread Eagle*, 20 Victoria Rd.

Broadstairs

Said to have been established on the profits of smuggling, **BROADSTAIRS** is the smallest, quietest and most pleasant of Thanet's three resort towns, overlooking the pretty Viking Bay from its cliff-top setting. The town's main claim to fame, though, is as Dickens' holiday retreat: throughout his most productive years he stayed in various hostelries here, and eventually rented an austere dwelling overlooking the bay from Fort Road, since renamed **Bleak House** (July & Aug daily 10am–7.30pm; Sept–Dec & mid-Feb to June daily 10am–6pm; £3) and opened to the public. It was here that he planned the novel of that name as well as finishing *David Copperfield*, and three rooms in the house have been preserved as the author would have known them. There's more of the same at the **Dickens House Museum** in Victoria Parade on the main cliff-top seafront (April to mid-Oct daily 2pm–5pm; £2).

Broadstairs' **train station** is a ten-minute walk from the seafront up the High Street; its **tourist office** is at 6b High St (April–Sept daily 9am–5pm; Oct–March Mon–Sat 9am–4.30pm; ☎01843/862242, ⓦwww.tourism.thanet.gov.uk). The comfortable but pricey **hotel**, the *Royal Albion* on Albion Street (☎01843/868071, ⓦwww.albion-bstairs.demon.co.uk; ❺), cashes in on its association with Dickens – he wrote part of *Nicholas Nickleby* here. There are several ivy-covered establishments in Belvedere Road, behind the High Street: the *Admiral Dundonald Hotel* at no. 43 (☎01843/862236; ❷) and the *Hanson Hotel* next door (☎01843/868936, ⓔhotelhanson@aol.com; ❷) are both good value. There is also a **youth hostel** at 3 Osborne Rd (☎01843/604121, ⓦwww.yha.org.uk), a Victorian villa with a family atmosphere, just two minutes' walk from the train station. For **food**, there are plenty of fish-and-chip outlets and cafés along Albion Street and down Harbour Street. If you're looking for a more congenial setting, *Harpers Wine Bar*, also on Harbour Street (℡01843/602494; eve only), serves moderately priced fish and seafood dishes. For a popular and friendly **pub**, serving the tasty Shepherd Neame beers from Faversham, check out the *Neptune's Hall*, further along at 1–3 Harbour St.

Ramsgate

If Thanet had a capital, it would be **RAMSGATE**, a handsome resort, rich in robust Victorian red brick, but whose centre of boarded-up shops reveal its economic decline. Most of the town is set high on a cliff linked to the seafront and harbour by broad, sweeping ramps, with the villas on the seaward side displaying wrought iron verandas and bricked-in windows – a legacy of the tax on glazed windows. Overall the port has avoided Margate's vulgarity while retaining some of Broadstairs' class.

The most entertaining sight in Ramsgate is the subterranean **Motor Museum** at West Cliff Hall, just by the ferry terminal (April–Oct daily 10.30am–5.30pm; Nov–Easter Sun 10am–5pm; £2.50), which spices up its eclectic collection of cars and motorbikes by placing each vehicle in its historical context. A 1905 Rex pushbike is on show alongside a newspaper proclaiming the increase of third-class steamer fares to the USA to £6, and a 1904 De Dion Bouton is displayed along with details of events from the same year – the founding of Rolls Royce and the arrest of a New York woman for a shocking crime, smoking in public. Ramsgate's other sight, the **Ramsgate Maritime Museum**, in the harbour Clock House (Easter–Sept daily 10am–5pm; Oct–Easter Tues–Fri 10am–4.30pm; £1.50; ⓦwww.ekmt. fsnet.co.uk), is brightened only by an illuminating section on the Goodwin Sands sandbanks – six miles southeast of Ramsgate – the occasional playing field of the eccentric Goodwin Sands Cricket Club.

Ramsgate's **train station** is about a mile northwest of the centre, at the end of Wilfred Road, at the top of the High Street, and the **tourist office** is at 17 Albert Court, York Street (daily 9.30am–4.30pm; ℡01843/583333, ⓦwww .tourism.thanet.gov.uk). For an overnight **stay**, the *Spencer Court Hotel*, 37 Spencer Square (℡01843/594582; ❶), offers comfortable accommodation in a listed Regency building, directly above the ferry terminal; while, in Eastcliff, the Victorian *Eastwood Guest House*, 28 Augusta Rd (℡01843/591505; ❸) has some rooms with balconies. The *Crescent*, 19 Wellington Crescent (℡01843/ 591419; ❶), is an attractive seafront option in a Georgian terrace originally built to house the duke's officers. The nearest **campsite** is *Nethercourt Touring Park*, just two miles southwest of the town centre (℡01843/595485; closed Nov–March).

The *Falstaff* **pub**, on Addington Street by the seafront, does a decent ploughman's lunch, or there's the *Camden Arms*, in nearby La Belle Alliance Square, for good-value fish and chips – for cliff-top views, real ales and occasional live music, head for the *Churchill Tavern* on The Paragon overlooking the harbour.

Canterbury

One of England's most venerable cities, **CANTERBURY** offers a rich slice through two thousand years of history, with Roman and early Christian ruins, a Norman castle, and a famous cathedral that dominates a medieval warren of time-skewed Tudor dwellings. The city began as a Belgic settlement that was

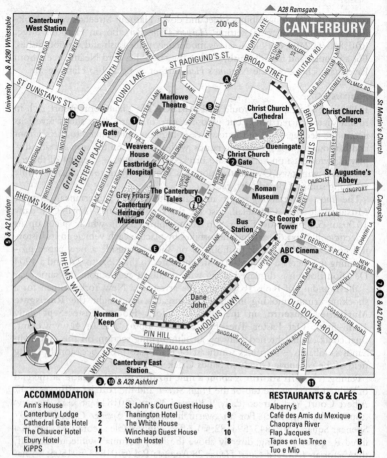

A28 Ramsgate

CANTERBURY

0   200 yds

© Crown copyright

ACCOMMODATION					RESTAURANTS & CAFÉS	
Ann's House	5		St John's Court Guest House	6	Alberry's	D
Canterbury Lodge	3		Thanington Hotel	9	Café des Amis du Mexique	C
Cathedral Gate Hotel	2		The White House	1	Chaopraya River	F
The Chaucer Hotel	4		Wincheap Guest House	10	Flap Jacques	E
Ebury Hotel	7		Youth Hostel	8	Tapas en las Trece	B
KiPPS	11				Tuo e Mio	A

overrun by the Romans and renamed **Durovernum**, from where they proceeded to establish a garrison, supply base and system of roads that was to reach as far as the Scottish borders. With the Roman Empire's collapse came the Saxons, who renamed the town **Cantwarabyrig**; it was a Saxon king, Ethelbert, who in 597 welcomed Augustine, dispatched by the pope to convert the British Isles to Christianity. By the time of his death, Augustine had founded two Benedictine monasteries, one of which – Christ Church, raised on the site of the Roman basilica – was to become the first cathedral in England.

At the turn of the first millennium, Canterbury suffered repeated sackings by the Danes until Canute, a recent Christian convert, restored the ruined Christ Church, only for it to be destroyed by fire a year before the Norman invasion. As the new religion became a tool of control, a struggle for power developed between the archbishops, the abbots from the nearby Benedictine abbey and King Henry II, culminating in the assassination of Archbishop Thomas à Becket in 1170, a martyrdom that effectively established the autonomy of the archbishops and made this one of Christendom's greatest shrines. Geoffrey

Chaucer's *Canterbury Tales*, written towards the end of the fourteenth century, portrays the unexpectedly festive nature of pilgrimages to Becket's tomb, which was plundered and destroyed at the orders of Henry VIII.

In 1830, a pioneering passenger railway service linked Canterbury to the sea and prosperity grew until the city suffered extensive German bombing in the notorious **Baedeker Raids**, when Hitler ordered the destruction of the most treasured historic sites described in the Baedeker travel guide series. The cathedral and compact town centre, however, survived, enclosed on three sides by medieval walls, and today remain the focus for leisure-motivated pilgrims from across the globe.

Arrival, information and accommodation

Canterbury has two **train stations**, Canterbury East for services from London Victoria or Dover Priory, and Canterbury West for services from London Charing Cross and the Isle of Thanet – the stations are northwest and south of the centre respectively, each a ten-minute walk from the cathedral. National Express coaches and local **buses** use the bus station just inside the city walls on St George's Lane. The busy **tourist office** is at 34 St Margaret's St (May–Sept Mon–Sat 9.30am–6pm, Sun 9.30am–5pm; rest of year closed Sun; ℡01227/766567, Ⓦwww.canterbury.co.uk), right in the middle of the city centre, south of the High Street.

Hotels and B&Bs

Ann's House 63 London Rd ℡01227/768767. Traditional Victorian villa offering comfortable rooms, most of which are en suite. ❷

Canterbury Lodge St Margaret's St ℡01227/463271, Ⓔslatters@netcomuk.com. Luxury, lodge-style hotel with an elegant designer bar and restaurant and great central location. ❹

Cathedral Gate Hotel 36 Burgate ℡01227/464381, Ⓔcgate@cgate.demon.co.uk. Built in 1438 and set in the city's medieval heart, this venerable pilgrims' hostelry features crooked floors and exposed timber beams alongside more modern amenities. ❺

The Chaucer Hotel 63 Ivy Lane ℡01227/464427, Ⓦwww.thechaucerhotel.co.uk. Large hotel just beyond the city walls, fully refurbished with modern comforts but retaining some of its early Georgian charm. ❼

Ebury Hotel 65–67 New Dover Rd ℡01227/768433, Ⓦwww.ebury-hotel.co.uk. Very comfortable and spacious family-owned Victorian hotel, fifteen minutes' walk from the centre; indoor pool and well-appointed rooms. ❺

St John's Court Guest House St John's Lane ℡01227/456425, Ⓔnrow5@netscapeonline.co.uk. Good-value guest house, offering B&B in a quiet but central location, just south of the old town. ❶

Thanington Hotel 140 Wincheap ℡01227/453227, Ⓔthanington-hotel.co.uk. Comfortably converted Georgian building, ten minutes' walk from the centre with an indoor pool, games room and friendly, attentive service. ❺

The White House 6 St Peter's Lane ℡01227/761836, Ⓔwhwelcom@aol.com. Small and friendly guest house offering en-suite accommodation in a fine Regency building, midway between the cathedral and Canterbury West station. ❸

Wincheap Guest House 94 Wincheap ℡01227/762309. Good-value Victorian B&B, with shared facilities, close to Canterbury East station. ❶

Hostels and campsites

The Caravan and Camping Club Site Bekesbourne Lane ℡01227/463216. Large year-round caravan park, one and a half miles east of the city off the A257 road to Sandwich.

KiPPS 40 Nunnery Fields ℡01227/786121, Ⓦwww.kipps-hostel.com. Self-catering hostel offering single, double and dormitory accommodation a few minutes' walk from Canterbury East station. £11–16 per person.

Youth Hostel 54 New Dover Rd ℡01227/462 911, Ⓦwww.yha.org.uk. Half a mile out of town, and 15min on foot from Canterbury East station, this friendly hostel is set in a Victorian villa. Closed Jan.

The City

Despite the presence of a university and art college, England's second most visited city is a surprisingly small place with a population of just 35,000. The town centre, ringed by ancient walls, is virtually car-free, but this doesn't stop the High Street seizing up all too frequently with tourists, two million of whom arrive each year. Having said that, the very reason for the city's popularity is its rich tapestry of historical sites, combined with a good selection of places to stay, eat and drink, and no visit to southeast England would be complete without, at the very least, a quick stop here.

The Cathedral

Mother Church of the Church of England, seat of the Primate of All England, **Canterbury Cathedral** (Mon–Sat 9am–7pm, Sun 12.30–2.30pm & 4.30–5.30pm; closes 5pm in winter; also closed on some days in mid-July for university graduation ceremonies; £3.50, free on Sun; Ⓦwww.canterbury-cathedral.org) is ecclesiastically supreme and fills the northeast quadrant of the city with a befitting sense of authority, even if architecturally it's perhaps not among the country's most impressive. A cathedral has stood here since 602, but in 1070 the first Norman archbishop, Lanfranc, levelled that Saxon structure and work began on a replacement. Over successive centuries the masterpiece was heavily modified, and with the puritanical lines of the Perpendicular style gaining ascendancy in late medieval times, the cathedral now derives its distinctiveness from the thrust of the 235-foot-high Bell Harry Tower, completed in 1505. The precincts (daily 7am–9pm) are entered through the superbly ornate early sixteenth-century **Christ Church Gate**, where Burgate and St Margaret's Street meet. This junction, the city's medieval core, is known as the Buttermarket, where religious relics were once sold to pilgrims hoping to prevent an eternity in damnation. Having paid your entrance fee, you pass through the gatehouse and get one of the finest views of the cathedral, foreshortened and crowned with soaring towers and pinnacles.

Once in the magnificent **interior**, look for the tomb of Henry IV and his wife, Joan of Navarre, and for the gilded effigy of Edward III's son, the Black Prince, all of them to be found in the Trinity Chapel, behind the main altar. The **shrine of Thomas à Becket**, in the northwest transept, is marked by the Altar of Sword's Point, where a crude sculpture of the assassins' weapons is suspended above the spot where Becket died and was later enshrined – until Henry VIII's act of ecclesiastical vandalism in 1538. Steps from here descend to the low, Romanesque arches of the **crypt**, one of the few remaining relics of the Norman cathedral and considered the finest such structure in the country, with some amazingly well-preserved carvings on the capitals of the columns.

On the cathedral's north flank are the fan-vaulted colonnades of the **Great Cloister**, from where you enter the **Chapter House**, with its intricate web of fourteenth-century tracery supporting the roof and a wall of stained glass, which illustrates scenes from St Thomas's life and death. In 1935 it was a fitting venue for the inaugural performance of T.S. Eliot's *Murder in the Cathedral*.

The rest of the city

Passing through the cathedral grounds and out through the city walls at the Queningate exit, you come to the vestigial remains of **St Augustine's Abbey** (daily: April–Sept 10am–6pm; Oct 10am–5pm; Nov–March 10am–4pm; £2.60; EH), occupying the site of the church founded by Augustine in 598. It was built outside the city because of a Christian tradition which forbade burials within the walls, and became the final resting place of Augustine, Ethelbert and successive archbishops and kings of Kent, although no trace remains either of them or of the original Saxon church. Shortly after the Normans arrived, the church was demolished in the same construction frenzy which saw the rebuilding of the cathedral. It was replaced by a much larger abbey, most of which was destroyed in the Dissolution so that today only the ruins and foundations remain. To help bring the site to life, pick up an audio tour (free) from the abbey's excellent interpretive centre.

Nearby, on the corner of North Holmes Road and St Martin's Lane is **St Martin's Church** (daily 9am–5pm excluding services), one of England's oldest churches, built on the site of a Roman villa or temple and used by the earliest Christians. Although medieval additions obscure the original Saxon structure, it was here that King Ethelbert was himself baptized, making this perhaps the earliest Christian site in Canterbury.

Back in the city centre, redevelopment of the Longmarket area in the early 1990s exposed Roman foundations and mosaics that are now part of the **Roman Museum** (June–Sept Mon–Sat 10am–5pm, Sun 1.30–5pm; Oct–May closed Sun; £2.50; ⓦwww.canterbury-museum.co.uk). The extant remnants of the larger building are pretty dull and better mosaics can be seen at Lullingstone (see p.208), but the display of recovered artefacts and general design of the museum is tasteful, with re-created Roman domestic scenes as well as a computer-generated view of Durovernum two thousand years ago.

From here a walk down the **High Street** to Mercery Lane and a glance up towards Christ Church Gate presents you with one of the most photographed views in the city: a narrow, medieval street of crooked, overhanging houses behind which loom the turreted gatehouse and the cathedral's towers. Turning in the other direction down St Margaret's Street leads to the former church that's now **The Canterbury Tales** (daily: mid-Feb to June, Sept & Oct 10am–5pm; July & Aug 9.30am–5.30pm; Nov to mid-Feb 10am–4.30pm; £5.90; ⓦwww.canterburytales.org.uk), a quasi-educational show based on Geoffrey Chaucer's book, which was the first ever to be printed in English. Genuinely educational and better value is **Canterbury Heritage Museum**, round the corner in Stour Street (June–Oct Mon–Sat 10.30am–5pm, Sun 1.30–5pm; Nov–May Mon–Sat 10.30am–5pm; £1.90; ⓦwww.canterbury-museums.co.uk), an interactive exhibition spanning local history from the splendour of Durovernum through to the contemporary literary figures of Joseph Conrad (buried in the cemetery in London Road) and local-born Mary Tourtel, creator of the check-trousered philanthropist Rupert Bear. Back on St Margaret's Street, continue to the end to see the simple (but inaccessible) shell of the Norman castle's **keep**.

Where the High Street passes over a branch of the River Stour and turns into St Peter's Street stands **Eastbridge Hospital** (Mon–Sat 10am–4.45pm; £1), founded in the twelfth century to provide poor pilgrims with shelter. Downstairs is an exhibition on Chaucer's life, where storytellers in feudal garb recite parts of his book. Over the road is the wonky, half-timbered **Weavers' House**, built around 1500 and once inhabited by Huguenot textile workers who had been offered religious asylum in post-Reformation England. St Peter's Street terminates at the two massive crenellated towers of the **West Gate**, between which local buses just manage to squeeze. The only one of the town's seven city gates to have survived intact, the West Gate's towers house a small **museum** (Mon–Sat 11am–12.30pm & 1.30–3.30pm; £1; ⓦwww.canterbury-museums.co.uk), which displays contemporary armaments and weaponry used by the medieval city guard, as well as giving access to the battlements.

Eating, drinking and nightlife

The combination of a large student population and the tourist trade means Canterbury has a good selection of places to **eat and drink**, with many establishments in genuinely old settings. Head for *Tapas en las Trece*, 13 Palace St (℡01227/762637), for tasty Spanish snacks, a bargain lunch menu and occasional live music, or the popular and moderately priced *Café des Amis du Mexique*, 95 St Dunstans St (℡01227/464390), for authentic Mexican food. The refined delights of Thai cuisine are available at a reasonable price at *Chaopraya River*, 2 Dover St (℡01227/462876), while *Flap Jacques*, 71 Castle St (℡01227/781000), is a homely little French bistro. For classy Italian dishes at moderate prices, try the long-established *Tuo e Mio*, 16 The Borough (℡01227/761471).

Nightlife in Canterbury keeps a low profile – check what's happening in the free *The Sticks* listings magazine available at the tourist office. **Pubs** to go for include the *Bell & Crown*, a cramped medieval hostelry on Palace Street; the even tinier and very popular *New Inn*, Havelock Street; or the *Miller's Arms*, good for a riverside pint in summer. At *Alberry's* wine bar, opposite the tourist office, and *Simple Simon's*, Radigund's Hall, 3 Church Lane, you can catch the occasional live music act. Also in Northgate, the recently revived Penny Theatre presents local and global live music. The university puts on a good range of arty **films**, and also houses the Gulbenkian Theatre, a venue which shares the city's more edifying cultural events with the Marlowe Theatre in The Friars.

The Channel ports

Dover, just 21 miles from the Continent (Calais' low cliffs are visible on a clear day), is the southeast's principal cross-Channel port, but as a town it is not immensely appealing, even though its key position has left it with a clutch of historic attractions. To its north lie **Sandwich**, once the most important of the Cinque Ports (see box below) but now no longer even on the coast, and the pleasant resort towns of **Deal** and **Walmer**, each with its own set of distinctive fortifications as well as a smattering of traditional seaside B&Bs.

The Cinque Ports

In 1278 Dover, Hythe, Sandwich, New Romney and Hastings – already part of a long-established but unofficial confederation of defensive coastal settlements – were formalized under Edward I's charter as the **Cinque Ports** (pronounced "sink", despite its French origin). In return for providing England with maritime support when necessary, chiefly in the transportation of troops and supplies to the Continent during times of war, the five ports were given trading privileges and other liberties, which enabled them to prosper while neighbouring ports struggled to survive. Some took advantage of this during peacetime, boosting their wealth by various nefarious activities such as piracy and the smuggling of tax-free contraband.

Later, Rye and Winchelsea were added to the confederation along with several other "limb" ports on the southeast coast which joined up at various times. The confederation continued until 1685, when the ports' privileges were revoked. Their maritime services were no longer necessary as Henry VIII had founded a professional navy and, due to a shifting coastline, several of the ports' harbours had silted up anyway. Nowadays, only Dover is still a major working port, though the post of Lord Warden of the Cinque Ports still exists. This honorary title, bestowed by the presiding monarch, is currently held by the Queen Mother.

Sandwich and around

SANDWICH, situated on the River Stour four miles north of Deal, is best known nowadays for giving rise to England's favourite culinary contribution when, in 1762, the fourth Earl of Sandwich, passionately absorbed in a game of cards, demanded some meat between two bits of bread for a quick snack. Aside from this incident, the town's main interest lies in its maritime connections – it was chief among the Cinque Ports (see box opposite) until the Stour silted up. Unlike other former harbour inlets, however, the Stour hasn't silted up completely here and still flows through town, its grassy willow-lined banks adding to the once great medieval port's present charm.

By the bridge over the Stour stands the sixteenth-century **Barbican**, a stone gateway where tolls were once collected. Running parallel to the river is **Strand Street**, whose crooked half-timbered facades front antique shops and private homes. The genteel town is separated from the sandy beaches of Sandwich Bay by the **Royal St George** golf course – frequent venue of the British Open tournament – and a mile of nature reserves. The reserve that most ornithologists make for is the **Gazen Salts Nature Reserve**, three miles north of town, across the Stour.

Overlooking the doleful expanse of Pegwell Bay, two miles northwest of Sandwich, is **Richborough Fort** (April–Sept daily 10am–6pm; Oct daily 10am–5pm; Nov–Feb Sat & Sun 10am–4pm; March Wed–Sun 10am–4pm; £2.70; EH), one of the earliest coastal strongholds built by the Romans along what later became known as the Saxon Shore on account of the frequent raids by the Germanic tribe. Like Reculver, ten miles northwest, it guarded the southern entrance to the Wantsum Channel, which then isolated the Isle of Thanet from the mainland. Rumour has it that Emperor Claudius once rode through a triumphal arch erected inside the fort on an elephant on his way to London, but all that remains now within the well-preserved Roman walls are the relics of an early Saxon church. Richborough's historical significance far outshines its present appearance, especially as Pegwell Bay is now blighted by an ugly chemical works.

Finding **accommodation** in Sandwich shouldn't be much of a problem – the local **tourist office**, housed in the lovely sixteenth-century Guildhall (May–Sept daily 10am–4pm; ☎01304/613565, ⓦwww.whitecliffscountry. org.uk), will provide you with a list of local hotels and guest houses. The golfers' choice, the *Bell Hotel* by the Barbican (☎01304/613388, ⓦwww.hotelworld .com; ❾), is out of most people's range; better value are the en-suite rooms at the old coaching inn, the *Fleur de Lis*, near the Guildhall at 6–8 Delf St (☎01304/611131, ⓦwww.verinitaverns.co.uk/fleurdelis/hotel. htm; ❹), and the modest *Le Trayas* bungalow at 57 St George's St (☎01304/611056, ⓦfree-space.virgin.net/le.trayas; ❶). Alternatively, there's the *St Crispin Inn*, an attractive fifteenth-century pub in the village of Worth, a couple of miles south of Sandwich (☎01304/612081; ❹). Your best choice for top-class food is the pricey *Fisherman's Wharf* on the quayside (☎01304/613636; closed Sun), which serves excellent seafood; for something less expensive try one of the pubs by the Barbican or the *Haven*, 20a King St, for good coffee, light lunches and evening meals. For the definitive Sandwich sandwich, head for the *Little Cottage Tearooms*, on the quay.

Deal and Walmer

One of the most unusual of Henry VIII's forts is the diminutive castle at **DEAL**, six miles southeast of Sandwich and site of Julius Caesar's first successful landfall in Britain in 55 BC. The **Castle** (April–Sept daily 10am–6pm; Oct daily 10am–5pm; Nov–March Wed–Sun 10am–4pm; £3.10; EH) is situated off the Strand at the south end of town. Its unusual shape – viewed from the air it looks like a Tudor rose – is as much an affectation as a defensive design, based on the premise that rounded walls would be better at deflecting missiles. Inside, the comprehensive display on the other similar forts built during Henry VIII's reign is well worth a visit. Much more recently, the town was the focal point of Kent's small-scale coal industry, until the pits were shut down during the bitterly fought retrenchments of the 1980s.

Walmer Castle (April–Sept daily 10am–6pm; Oct daily 10am–5pm; Nov, Dec & March Wed–Sun 10am–4pm; Feb Sat & Sun 10am–4pm; £4.80; EH), a mile south of Deal, is another rotund Tudor-rose-shaped affair, albeit with a more conventional interior, commissioned when the castle became the official residence of the Lord Warden of the Cinque Ports in 1730. Now it resembles a heavily fortified stately home more than a military stronghold. The best-known Lord Warden was the Duke of Wellington, who died here in 1842 – the house is devoted primarily to his life and times; busts and portraits of the Iron Duke crowd the rooms and corridors, where you'll also find the armchair in which he expired and the original Wellington boots in which he triumphed at Waterloo.

Deal's **tourist office** (mid-May to mid-Sept Mon–Fri 9am–5pm, Sat 10am–4pm; rest of year Mon–Fri 9am–12.30pm & 1.30–5pm; ℡01304/ 369576, ⊛www.whitecliffscountry.org.uk) is situated in the Town Hall on the High Street near the sea, about a ten-minute walk from the **train station**. In Deal there's a whole host of places offering **accommodation** on Beach Street: try the winsome *King's Head* pub (℡01304/368194; ❸), or the nearby town house of *Channel View*, at no. 17, run by the same proprietor (same phone number and prices). Another option is *Dunkerley's*, next door at no. 19 (℡01304/375016, ⊛www.dunkerleys.co.uk; ❻), whose **restaurant** is Deal's finest (and priciest). For more reasonably priced seafood try the *Lobster Pot* on Beach Road (℡01304/374713), opposite the pier.

Dover

Badly bombed during the war, **DOVER**'s town centre and seafront just don't have what it takes to induce many travellers to linger before speeding onwards to Europe, or inland to London or Canterbury. That said, the town authorities have put a lot of effort and money into sprucing the place up, particularly the early Victorian New Bridge development along the Esplanade. Despite such

Cross-channel transport services from Dover and Folkestone	
Dover Eastern Docks to Calais: P&O Stena Line (30 daily; journey time 1hr 15min); Seafrance (15 daily; journey time 1hr 30min).	**Dover Western Docks** to Calais: Hoverspeed (10 daily; journey time 40min).
Dover Eastern Docks to Zeebrugge: P&O Stena Line (3–4 daily; journey time 4hr).	**Dover Western Docks** to Ostend: Hoverspeed (July–Sept 3 daily; journey time 2hr).
	Folkestone to Calais: Eurotunnel (up to 4 hourly; journey time 35min).

Reservations: Eurotunnel ℡08705/353535, ⊛www.eurotunnel.co.uk; Hoverspeed ℡08705/240241, ⊛www.hoverspeed.com; P&O Stena Line ℡08706/000600, ⊛www.posl.com; SeaFrance ℡08705/711711, ⊛www.seafrance.com

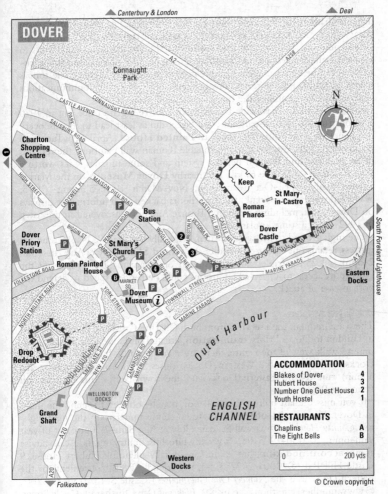

DOVER

Connaught Park

CASTLE AVENUE
CONNAUGHT ROAD
PARK AVENUE
SALISBURY ROAD

Charlton Shopping Centre

HIGH STREET

MAISON DIEU ROAD

LADYWELL PL

Bus Station

Dover Priory Station

BIGGIN ST
KEARSNEY ROAD

St Mary's Church

WOOLCOMBER STREET

CASTLE HILL ROAD
CASTLE HILL
CASTLE ST
LAURESTON PL
VICTORIA PK

Keep

St Mary-in-Castro

Roman Pharos

Dover Castle

Dover Priory Station

Roman Painted House

FOLKESTONE ROAD

CANNON ST

St Mary's Church

CASTLE STREET
RUSSELL ST

MARKET SQ

Dover Museum ℹ

TOWNWALL STREET

MARINE PARADE

MARINE PARADE

Eastern Docks

A2

South Foreland Lighthouse

NORTH MILITARY ROAD

YORK STREET

SNARGATE ST
NEW A20

Drop Redoubt

CAMBRIDGE RD
WATERLOO CRES

Outer Harbour

WELLINGTON DOCKS

Grand Shaft

ESPLANADE

A20

A20

ENGLISH CHANNEL

Western Docks

▼ Folkestone

© Crown copyright

ACCOMMODATION
Blakes of Dover   4
Hubert House   3
Number One Guest House   2
Youth Hostel   1

RESTAURANTS
Chaplins   A
The Eight Bells   B

0   200 yds

valiant attempts, Dover Castle is still by far the most interesting of the numerous attractions which plug the port's defensive history. Entertainment of a saltier nature is offered by Dover's legendary **White Cliffs**, which dominate the town and have long been a source of inspiration for lovers, travellers and soldiers sailing off to war.

The town's chief attraction is **Dover Castle** (daily: April–Sept 10am–6pm; Oct 10am–5pm; Nov–March 10am–4pm; £7; EH), a superbly positioned defensive complex, begun in 1168 and in continuous military use until the 1980s. The **Romans** put Dover on the map when they chose its harbour as the base for their northern fleet and erected a lighthouse here to guide the ships into the river mouth. Beside the lighthouse stands a Saxon-built church, **St Mary in Castro**, dating from the seventh century, with motifs graffitied by irreverent Crusaders still visible near the pulpit. Further up the hill is the impressive, well-preserved **Norman keep**, built by Henry II as a palace. Inside, there's an interactive exhibition on spying; you can also climb its spiral stairs to the lofty battlements for views over the sea to France. The castle's other main attraction is its network of **secret wartime tunnels** dug during the Napoleonic war. Extended during World War II and used as a headquarters to plan the Dunkirk evacuation, "**Hellfire Corner**" – the tunnels' wartime nickname – can be seen on a fifty-minute guided tour (every 20min). The tour is spiced up with a little gore, and reveals the quaintly low-tech communications systems and war rooms of the Navy's command post.

Postwar rebuilding has made Dover **town centre** a grim place, but in 1970 the construction of a car park on New Street did at least lead to the discovery of an ancient guest house. The **Roman Painted House** (April–Sept Tues–Sun 10am–5pm; £2) possesses some reasonable Roman wall paintings, the remains of an underground Roman heating system and some mosaics – it's worth a look if you've some time to kill. The nearby **Dover Museum** on the Market Square (daily: April–Oct 10am–6pm; Nov–March 10am–5.30pm; £1.75; ⓦ www.dovermuseum.co.uk) has three floors packed with informative displays on Dover's past, including a restored Bronze Age boat discovered in the town in 1992 – and a stuffed polar bear.

The high ground to the west of town, originally the site of a Napoleonic-era fortress, retains one interesting oddity, the **Grand Shaft** (July & Aug Tues–Sun 2–5pm; £1.25), a triple staircase, entered on Snargate Street (opposite the Hoverport access road), by which troops could descend at speed to defend the port in case of attack.

Practicalities

There are frequent train services from both Charing Cross and Victoria stations in London to Dover Priory **train station**, situated off Folkestone Road, a ten-minute walk west of the centre; there are regular shuttle buses to the Eastern Docks, but none to the Western Docks. Buses from London (hourly; 2hr 30min) run to the Eastern Docks and the town-centre **bus station** on Pencester Road.

If you miss the last train to London, you may be obliged to spend the night in Dover. The **tourist office**, in the town centre underneath the ugly highrise *County Hotel* on Townwall St (daily: July & Aug 8am–7.30pm; rest of year 9am–6pm; ⓣ01304/205108, ⓦ www.whitecliffscountry.org.uk), can advise about **accommodation**, but rooms are usually plentiful: Hubert House, 9 Castle Hill Rd (ⓣ01304/202253; ❷), is a friendly B&B, convenient for the Eastern Dock, as is the *Number One Guesthouse*, 1 Castle St (ⓣ01304/202007, ⓦ www.number1guesthouse.co.uk; ❷). *Blakes of Dover*, further up Castle Street, at no. 52 (ⓣ01304/202194, ⓔblakes-of-dover@activebooking.com; ❸), is a lovely wood-panelled wine bar, restaurant and hotel with a genial owner. There's a busy **youth hostel**, a mile inland from Dover Priory station, in a listed Georgian town house at 306 London Rd (ⓣ01304/201314, ⓦ www.yha .org.uk), but with an overspill building in Godwyne Road, half a mile north of town. The most convenient **campsite** is *Hawthorn Farm* (ⓣ01304/852658; closed Dec–Feb), close to Martin Mill train station, one stop up the line towards Ramsgate.

Given the town's uninspiring appearance, Dover's **pubs** are surprisingly characterful, although the town gets a rather rough reputation from its shift workers servicing the docks and ferries. Close to Western Docks, the *Cinque Ports Arms* on Clarence Place has guest beers as well as its standard Fremlins ales, while the *Park Inn* on Park Street near the town hall is a big old place with plenty of real ales to choose from. You could do worse than eat pub **food** at the *Eight Bells*, a big Wetherspoon's pub on Cannon Street, as Dover has few other decent places to eat. *Chaplins*, 2 Church St, serves excellent value lunches and probably the town's best coffee

The Romney and Denge marshes

In Roman times, the **Romney and Denge marshes** – now the southernmost part of Kent – were submerged beneath the English Channel. Then the lowering of the sea levels in the Middle Ages and later reclamation created a forty-square-mile area of marshland which, until the last century, was afflicted by malaria and various other malaises. Contrasting strongly with the wooded pastures of Kent's interior, the sheep-speckled marshes have an eerie, forlorn appearance, as if still unassimilated with the mainland and haunted by their maritime origins. The ancient town of **Hythe** is on the eastern edge of the reclaimed marshes and is linked with **Rye** in East Sussex on the marshes' western edge, by the arc of the 23-mile Royal Military Canal. **Folkestone**, Kent's other major port, five miles east of Hythe, and site of the British entrance to the **Channel Tunnel**, is a drab and utterly missable introduction to this swathe of coast.

Hythe

Separated from Folkestone by the massive earthworks of the Channel Tunnel, **HYTHE** is a sedate seaside resort bisected by the disused waterway of the Royal Military Canal, built as a defensive obstacle during the perceived threat of Napoleonic invasion. Hythe's receding shoreline reduced its usefulness as a port and the nearby coast is now just a sweep of beach punctuated by **Martello towers**, part of the chain of 74 citadels built along the southeast coastline for the same reasons as the canal.

There's little to do in Hythe other than enjoy its tranquil antiquity, although a ride on the world's largest toy train – or smallest public railway – the **Romney, Hythe & Dymchurch Railway** (R, H & DR), a fifteen-inch-gauge line which runs the fourteen miles from Hythe to Dungeness, makes a fun day out. Built in the 1920s as a tourist attraction linking the resorts along the shore, its fleet of steam locomotives is now maintained by volunteers (Easter–Sept daily; March & Oct Sat & Sun; plus school holidays throughout the year; £9.20 full return fare; ℡01797/362353, Ⓦwww.rhdr.demon.co.uk). The station is to the west of the town centre, on the south bank of the canal by Station Bridge.

Hythe's **tourist office** is, bizarrely, situated in the old toilets in Red Lion Square (April–June & Sept daily 9am–5.30pm; July & Aug daily 9am–7pm; Oct–March Mon–Sat 9am–5.30pm, Sun 10am–4pm; ℡01303/267799, Ⓦwww.kents-garden-coast.co.uk). For **accommodation** check out the secluded *White House*, 27 Napier Gardens (℡01303/266252; ❸), overlooking the cricket green just a couple of minutes from the sea, or the *Swan Hotel*, a friendly pub on the High Street (℡01303/266311; ❶). The *Capri*, 32–34 High St (℡01303/269898) serves good Italian **food**.

New Romney

NEW ROMNEY, one of the original Cinque Ports and nine miles southwest of Hythe is now really only of interest to connoisseurs of miniature railways, thanks to the R, H & DR's **Toy and Model Train Museum** (same days as the railway; 10am–5pm; £1) at New Romney station, halfway between the town and the seafront. There's a **tourist office** on Church Approach, just off the High Street (April–June & Sept daily 9am–5.30pm; July & Aug daily 9am–7pm; Oct–March Mon–Sat 9am–5.30pm, Sun 10am–4pm; ℡01797/364044,

△ The White Cliffs of Dover

@www.kents-garden-coast.co.uk), where you'll also find the sixteenth-century *Cinque Ports Arms* (@01797/361894; ❸), a nice-looking pub with inexpensive rooms; for something a bit more special, head for *Romney Bay House* (@01797/364747, @www.uk-travelguide.co.uk/rombayho.htm; ❹), a wonderfully secluded place to stay by the beach in neighbouring Littlestone-on-Sea

Dungeness

DUNGENESS, six miles south of New Romney, is the southern terminus for the R, H & DR, set in the sort of wasteland normally used as an army firing-range, but in this case the site of a nuclear power station, though one of the few open to the public (guided tours only: April–Sept daily 10am, 11.30am, 1pm & 2.45pm; Oct–March Mon–Fri same times; free; @www.bnfl.com). The barren environment of the Denge Marsh supports a unique floral ecology and all around you'll see tiny communities of wildflowers struggling against the unrelenting breeze. On the road to the power station, the flotsam sculptures in the late film director **Derek Jarman's garden** (not open to the public) make an eye-catching sight, though the non-indigenous flora he planted around them has attracted the wrath of the local conservation authorities.

Rye and around

Perched on a hill overlooking the Romney Marshes, the town of **RYE** lies over the county border in East Sussex. Added as a "limb" to the original Cinque Ports, the town then became marooned two miles inland with the retreat of the sea and the silting up of the River Rother. It is now one of the most popular places along the Sussex coast – half-timbered, skew-roofed and quintessentially English, but also very commercialized.

From Strand Quay, head up The Deals to Rye's most picturesque street, the sloping cobbled lane of **Mermaid Street**, which will bring you eventually to the peaceful oasis of Church Square. Henry James, who strangely suggested that "Rye would . . . remind you of Granada", spent the last years of his life at **Lamb House** (April–Oct Wed & Sat 2pm–6pm; £2.60; NT) at the east end of Mermaid Street. The house's three rooms and garden are of interest chiefly to fans of James's novels, or to admirers of the novelist E.F. Benson, who lived here after James. A blue plaque in the High Street also testifies that Radclyffe Hall, author of the seminal lesbian novel *The Well of Loneliness*, was also once a resident of the town. At the centre of Church Square stands **St Mary's Church**, boasting the oldest functioning pendulum clock in the country; the ascent of the church tower – whose bells were looted by French raiders in 1377 and then retrieved with similar audacity – offers fine views over the clay-tiled roofs and grid of narrow lanes. In the far corner of the square stands the **Ypres Tower** (April–Oct Mon, Thurs & Fri 10am–1pm & 2pm–5pm, Sat & Sun 10.30am–1pm, 2pm–5pm; Nov–March Sat & Sun 10.30am–3.30pm; £1.90), formerly used to keep watch for cross-Channel invaders, and now a part of the **Rye Castle Museum** on nearby East Street (April–Oct Mon, Thurs & Fri 2pm–5pm, Sat & Sun 10.30am–1pm & 2pm–5pm; £1.90, combined ticket with the tower £2.90). Both sites house a number of relics from Rye's past, including an eighteenth-century fire-engine.

Practicalities

Rye **train station** lies on the Eastbourne–Ashford International rail line and is a short walk north of the centre off Cinque Ports Street; local **buses** use the station forecourt. The town's **tourist office** is on Strand Quay (April–Oct

Mon–Sat 9am–5.30pm, Sun 10am–5pm; Nov–March Mon–Sat 10am–4pm; ℡01797/226696, ⓦwww.rye.org.uk/heritage). Rye's popularity with weekending Londoners gives it an excellent choice of **accommodation**: the most luxurious options are the *Mermaid* (℡01797/223065; ➐), a fifteenth-century inn on Mermaid Street, and *Jeake's House*, also on Mermaid Street (℡01797/222828, ⓔjeakeshouse@btinternet.com; ➌). Alternatively, there's the *Old Vicarage* at 66 Church Square (℡01797/222119, ⓔhomepages.tesco.net/~oldvicaragerye; ➋), a lovely pink Georgian house next to the church, or the best option out of town is *Playden Cottage Guest House*, Military Rd (℡01797/222234; ➌), a listed family house in a semi-rural setting off the A268 and about a mile from the centre. The *Mermaid* is by far the most atmospheric **pub** in town though an excellent alternative is the unspoiled *Ypres Castle* in Gun Gardens (down the steps behind the Ypres Tower). For **food** the pricey *Landgate Bistro* at 5 Landgate (℡01797/222829; eve only; closed Sun & Mon) is also recommended; alternatively, you can sample reasonably priced local seafood at the *Old Forge* on Wish Street (℡01797/223227; closed Sun & Mon, plus Tues & Wed lunch), or the intimate *Gatehouse Restaurant*, 1 Tower St (℡01797/222327; closed Mon lunch).

Winchelsea

WINCHELSEA, two miles southwest of Rye and easily reached by train, bus, foot or bike, shares Rye's indignity of having become detached from the sea, but has a very different character. Rye gets all the visitors, whereas Winchelsea feels positively deserted, an impression augmented as you pass through the Strand Gate and see the ghostly ruined **Church of St Thomas à Becket**. The original settlement was washed away in the great storm of 1287, after which Edward I planned a new port with a chequerboard pattern of streets. Even at the height of Winchelsea's economic activity, however, not all the plots on the grid were used. The town also suffered from incursions by the French in the fourteenth and fifteenth centuries, at which time the church was pillaged; its remains constitute Sussex's finest example of the Decorated style. Head south for a mile and a half and you get to **Winchelsea beach**, a long expanse of pebbly sand.

The fourteenth-century *Strand House* (℡01797/226276, ⓦwww. tuckedup.com/thestrandhouse.html; ➋), at the foot of the cliff below Strand gate, is the best **accommodation** option.

Hastings and Battle

During the twelfth and thirteenth centuries, **Hastings** flourished as an influential Cinque Port. In 1287 its harbour creek was silted up by the same storm which washed away nearby Winchelsea, forcing the settlement to be temporarily abandoned. These days, Hastings is a curious mixture of traditional seaside resort, arty retreat popular with painters (there's even a street and quarter named Bohemia) and unpretentious fishing port. William, Duke of Normandy, landed at Pevensey Bay a few miles west of town and made Hastings his base, but his forces met Harold's army – exhausted after quelling a Nordic invasion near York – at **Battle**, six miles northwest of Hastings. Battle today boasts a magnificent abbey built by William in thanks for his victory, which makes for a good afternoon's excursion from Hastings.

Hastings

HASTINGS' Old Town, east of the pier, holds most of the appeal of this fading seaside resort. With the exception of the oddly neglected Regency architecture of **Pelham Crescent**, directly beneath the castle ruins, **All Saints Street** is the most evocative thoroughfare, punctuated with the odd rickety, timber-framed dwelling from the fifteenth century. The thirteenth-century **St Clement's** church stands in the High Street, on the other side of The Bourne. By a louvred window at the top of the church's tower rests a cannonball that was lodged there by a Dutch galleon in the 1600s – its poignancy rather lost by a companion fitted in the eighteenth century for the sake of symmetry.

Down by the seafront, the area known as The Stade is characterized by its tall, black weatherboard **net shops**, dating from the mid-nineteenth century. To raise Hastings' tone, the town council attempted to shift the fishermen and their malodorously drying nets from the beach by increasing rents per square foot and these sinister-looking towers were their response. There's a trio of nautical attractions on the adjacent Rock-a-Nore Road: the **Fisherman's Museum** (daily: April–Oct 10am–5pm; Nov–March 11am–4pm; free), a converted seaman's chapel, offers an account of the port's commercial activities; the neighbouring **Shipwreck Heritage Centre** (Feb–Easter daily 11am–4pm; Easter–Oct daily 10am–5pm; £1), details the dramas of unfortunate mariners; while the **Underwater World**, opposite (daily: Easter–Sept 10am–5pm; Oct–Easter 10am–4pm; £5.25; ⓦ www.underwaterworld-hastings.co.uk), features walk-through tunnels and magnified tanks housing marine creatures.

Castle Hill, separating the Old Town from the visually less interesting modern quarter, can be ascended by the **West Hill Cliff Railway**, one of two Victorian funicular railways in Hastings (daily: April–Oct 10.30am–5.30pm; Nov–March 11am–4pm; 80p). On top of the hill is where William the Conqueror erected his first **castle** in 1066, one of several wooden prefabricated structures brought over from Normandy in sections. In the thirteenth century, storms caused the cliffs to subside, tipping most of the castle into the sea; the surviving ruins, however, offer an excellent prospect of the town. The castle is home to **The 1066 Story** (daily: April–Sept 10am–5pm; Oct–March 11am–3.30pm; £3.20), in which the events of the last successful invasion of the British mainland are described inside a mock-up of a siege tent. More fun is the **Smugglers' Adventure** (daily: Easter–Sept 10am–5.30pm; Oct–Easter 11am–3.30pm; £5.25, combined ticket with The 1066 Story £7; ⓦ www.smugglersadventure.callnetuk.com), over the hill. Here the labyrinthine St Clement's caves have been converted to house a number of amusing and educational dioramas depicting the town's long history of duty-dodging.

Practicalities

The **train station** is a ten-minute walk from the seafront along Havelock Road; National Express services operate from the **bus station** at the junction of Havelock and Queen's roads. The **tourist office** is located within the Town Hall on Queen's Road (April–Oct Mon–Fri 8.30am–6.15pm, Sat 9am–5pm, Sun 10am–4.30pm; Nov–March Mon & Fri 8.30am–6.15pm, Tues–Thurs 8.30am–5pm, Sat 9am–5pm, Sun 10am–4pm; ⓣ 01424/781111, ⓦ www.hastings.gov.uk); there's also a smaller seafront office (April–Sept Mon–Sat 10am–5pm, Sun 10am–4.30pm; Oct–March Sat & Sun 11am–4pm; ⓣ 01424/781120), near the Boating Lake on East Parade by the old town.

Accommodation available in town includes the *Argyle Guest House*, 32 Cambridge Gardens (ⓣ 01424/421294, ⓔ argyle.1066country@talk21.com;

); timber-framed *Lavender & Lace*, right in the Old Town at 106 All Saints St (☎01424/716290; ❶); and the *Jenny Lind Hotel*, 69 High St (☎01424/421392, Ⓦwww.the-entertainer-online.co.uk/pubs/jenny-lind.html; ❷), in the Old Town. The nearest youth hostel and campsite (☎01424/812373) are in a large manor house at Guestling, three miles along the road to Rye (bus #711).

By far the best prospects for **eating and drinking** are on the High Street and its pedestrianized offshoot, George Street. Above the *Jenny Lind Hotel* is the *Cinnamon Tree* (Wed–Sat 6pm–10pm; ☎01424/437075), serving filling and tasty curries from a mere £5; *Harris* 58 High St (closed Sun), with its wood-panelled walls and potted plants, does decent tapas; *Gannets Bistro*, 45 High St offers everything from breakfast to a wide choice of evening meals, while the waft of garlic from *Bella Napoli*, 9 George St (☎01424/429211), is positively enticing. The best fish and chips in town are at the eat-in *Mermaid*, 2 Rock-a-Nore, right by the beach. There are more than thirty **pubs** to choose from in Hastings: the local fishermen's favourite is the *Lord Nelson* right by the front on the Bourne; others to check out are the ever-popular *First In Last Out*, 15 High St in the Old Town, and the trendy clubby bar, *The Street*, accessible via a tiny entrance on Cambridge Road in the new town centre.

Battle

The town of **BATTLE** – a ten-minute train ride from Hastings – occupies the site of the most famous land battle in British history. Here, on October 14, 1066, the invading Normans overcame the Anglo-Saxon army of King Harold, who was killed not by an arrow through the eye – a myth resulting from the misinterpretation of the Bayeux Tapestry – but from a workaday clubbing about the head. Before the battle took place, William vowed that, should he win the engagement, he would build a religious foundation on the very spot of Harold's slaying to atone for the bloodshed and, true to his word, **Battle Abbey** (daily: April–Sept 10am–6pm; Oct 10am–5pm; Nov–March 10am–4pm; £4.30; EH) was built four years later and subsequently occupied by a fraternity of Benedictines. The magnificent structure, though partially destroyed in the Dissolution and much rebuilt and revised over the centuries, still dominates the town with the huge gatehouse, added in 1338, now containing a good audio-visual exhibition on the battle. You can wander through the ruins of the abbey to the spot where Harold was clubbed – the site of the high altar of William's abbey, now marked by a memorial stone.

Though nothing can match the resonance of the abbey, the rest of the town is worth a stroll. At the far end of the High Street, is the fourteenth-century **Almonry** (Mon–Sat 10am–4.30pm; £1) – the present town hall – which contains a miniature model of Battle and the oldest Guy Fawkes in the country. Every year, on the Saturday nearest to November 5, this 300-year-old effigy is paraded along the High Street at the head of a torch-lit procession culminating in a huge bonfire in front of the abbey gates; similar celebrations occur in Lewes (see p.211).

The **tourist office** is at 88 High St (June–Sept Mon–Sat 9.30am–5.30pm, Sun 9.30am–5.30pm; Oct–May closed Sun; ☎01424/773721, Ⓦwww.battle-town.co.uk). Battle's **accommodation** tends to be agreeable but expensive – a couple of less pricey **B&Bs** are *Abbey View*, Caldbec Hill (☎01424/775513; ❹), only two minutes' walk from town down Mount St, and the en-suite rooms above the *Gateway Café*, 78 High St (☎01424/772856; ❷). Town-centre **pubs** serving decent food include the *Old King's Head* on Mount Street, the *1066* at 12 High St – both of which serve real ales – and the *Chequers Inn* at Lower Lake, on the High Street.

The Kent Weald

The Kent Weald is usually taken to refer to the region around the spa town of **Royal Tunbridge Wells**, but in fact it stretches across a much larger area between the North and South Downs and includes parts of both Kent and Sussex, though the majority of its attractions are in Kent. During Saxon times, much of The Weald was covered in thick forest – the word itself derives from the Germanic word *wald*, meaning forest, and the suffixes -hurst (meaning wood) and -den (meaning clearing) are commonly found in Wealden village names. Now, however, the region is epitomized by gentle hills, sunken country lanes and somnolent villages as well as some of England's most beautiful gardens – **Sissinghurst** being the best known.

Burwash, Bateman's and Bodiam Castle

Thirteen miles northwest of Hastings on the A265, halfway to Tunbridge Wells, **BURWASH**, with its red-brick and weatherboard cottages and Norman church tower, exemplifies the pastoral idyll of inland Sussex. Half a mile south of the village lies the main attraction, **Bateman's** (March Sat & Sun 11am–5pm; April–Oct Mon–Wed, Sat, Sun & public holidays 11am–5pm; £5; NT), home of the Nobel Prize-winning writer and journalist Rudyard Kipling from 1902 until his death in 1936. Built by a local ironmaster in the seventeenth century and set amid attractive gardens, the house features a working watermill converted by Kipling to generate electricity. Inside, the house is laid out as he left it, with letters, early editions of his work and mementoes from his travels on display. Next to the house, a garage houses the last of Kipling's Rolls Royces, one of the many that he owned during his lifetime, although he never actually drove them, preferring the services of a chauffeur.

Bodiam Castle (Feb–Oct daily 10am–6pm or dusk; Nov–Feb Sat & Sun 10am–4pm or dusk; £3.70; NT), eleven miles north of Hastings, is a classic, stout, square castle with rounded corner turrets, battlements and a moat. When it was built in 1385 to guard what were the lower reaches of the River Rother, Bodiam was state-of-the-art military architecture, but during the Civil War a company of Roundheads breached the fortress and removed its roof to reduce its effectiveness as a possible stronghold for the King. Over the next 250 years Bodiam fell into neglect until restoration earlier this century by the philanthropic Lord Curzon. Nowadays, the castle particularly appeals to children who enjoy clambering up the narrow spiral staircases, which lead to crenellated battlements, and watching the absorbing fifteen-minute video portraying medieval life in a castle.

For **accommodation** and **food**, head for the lovely village of **Ewhurst**, two miles southeast of Bodiam, which houses an idyllic country pub, the *White Dog Inn* (☎01580/830264, ⊛www.hey-presto.co.uk/sussex/04bodiam/white-dog/whitedog.htm; ❷).

Royal Tunbridge Wells and around

ROYAL TUNBRIDGE WELLS – not to be confused with the more mundane Tonbridge, a few miles to the north – is the home of the mythical whingeing right-wing letter-writer known as "Disgusted of Tunbridge Wells". Most British people, therefore, view it with derision, but don't be misled – this prosperous spa town, surrounded by gorgeous countryside, is an elegant and diverting place. It was founded in 1606, when Lord North discovered a bubbling spring, and reached its height of popularity during the Regency period, when such restorative cures were in vogue. The well-mannered architecture of that period, surrounded by parklands in which the rejuvenated gentry exercised, gives the southern and western part of town its special character.

The icon of those genteel times, and the best place to start your wanderings, is the **Pantiles**, an elegant colonnaded parade of shops, ten minutes' walk south of the train station, where the fashionable once gathered to promenade and take the waters. The name stems from the chunky Kent tiles made of baked clay, which were put down as paving during Queen Anne's reign. Hub of the Pantiles is the original **Chalybeate Spring** (Easter–Sept daily 10am–5pm) in the Bath House, where a "Dipper" has been employed since the late eighteenth century to serve the ferrous waters. A period-dressed incumbent will fetch you a glass from the cool spring for 25p – or, if you bring your own cup, you can help yourself for free from the adjacent source. The Bath House itself was built in 1804 but failed as an enterprise as the water turns a nasty colour when heated; it closed in 1847 and now houses a pharmacy.

You can view one of the original "pantiles" in the exhibition, **A Day at the Wells** (daily: April–Oct 10am–5pm; Nov–March 10am–4pm; £5.50; ⓦwww.heritageattractions.co.uk), situated in the basement of the nearby Corn Exchange. An audio tour, narrated as if by Richard "Beau" Nash – self-appointed arbiter of good taste – attempts to re-create, with the help of various historical tableaux, eighteenth-century spa life.

Apart from tiles, Tunbridge also produced domestic ceramics, on view with other local relics and historical artefacts in the **Museum and Art Gallery** built in the 1950s at the top of Mount Pleasant Road (Mon–Sat 9.30am–5pm; free; ⓦwww.tunbridgewells.gov.uk/museum), a fifteen-minute walk up the old-fashioned High Street from the Pantiles.

Tunbridge Wells' **train station**, on the line between London Charing Cross and Hastings, is in the centre of town, where the High Street becomes Mount Pleasant Road. The **tourist office** is in the Old Fish Market, The Pantiles (Mon–Sat 9am–6pm, Sun 10am–5pm; ☎01892/515675, ⓦwww.heartofkent.org.uk). For **B&B**, *Ephraim Lodge* (☎01892/523053; ❹), on The Common, and the nearby *Clarken Guest House*, a large Victorian house with gardens at 61 Frant Rd (☎01892/533397, ✉barry.kench@virgin.net; ❸), are good value. The *Swan Hotel* in the Pantiles (☎01892/543319, ⓦwww.the-swan-hotel.com; ❺) is pricey but worth a splurge.

For a small town, Tunbridge Wells has a fair selection of **restaurants** – one of the best (and most expensive) being *Thackeray's House*, one-time home of the writer at 85 London Rd (☎01892/511921; closed Sun eve & Mon). The cheaper end of the market is dominated by the chains, including the reliable *Pizza Express* at 81 High St; *Flippers*, 9 High St (closed Sun), fry superior fish and chips, while veggies can have lunch or pre-theatre grub at the *Trinity Arts Centre Café* in a converted church on Church Road (closed Sun).

Sissinghurst and Leeds Castle

Sissinghurst, twelve miles east of Tunbridge Wells (April to mid-Oct Tues–Fri 1–6.30pm, Sat & Sun 10am–5.30pm; £6.50; NT), was described by Vita Sackville-West as "a garden crying out for rescue" when she and her husband took it over in the 1920s. Gradually, they transformed the five-acre plot into one of England's greatest and most popular modern gardens. Spread over the site of an Elizabethan mansion (of which only one wing remains today), the gardens were designed around the linear pattern of the former building's walls.

Sissinghurst's appeal derives from the way that the flowers are allowed to spill over onto the narrow walkways, defying the classical formality of the great gardens that preceded it. The brick tower Vita restored and used as her study acts as a focal point and offers the best views of the walled gardens. Most impressive are the **White Garden**, composed solely of white flowers and silvery-grey foliage, and the **Cottage Garden**, featuring flora in shades of orange, yellow and red. Sissinghurst gets so busy in summer that timed tickets for half-hourly visits are issued. Food options in the gardens are limited and overpriced – your best bet is to bring a picnic.

   Leeds Castle, fifteen miles north of Sissinghurst, on the edge of the North Downs (daily: March–Oct 10am–5pm; Nov–Feb 10am–3pm; grounds close two hours later than castle; castle, park & gardens £10; park & gardens £7.50; Ⓦwww.leeds-castle.co.uk), is more like a fairy-tale palace than a defensively efficient fortress. The present stone castle dates from Norman times and is set half on an island in the middle of a lake and half on the mainland surrounded by landscaped parkland. Following centuries of regal and noble ownership (and service as a prison) the castle is now run as a commercial concern, hosting conferences as well as sporting and cultural events. Its interior fails to match the castle's stunning external appearance and, in places, twentieth-century renovations have quashed any of its historical charm; possibly the most unusual feature inside is the dog-collar museum. In the grounds, there's a fine aviary with some colourful exotic specimens, as well as manicured gardens and a mildly challenging maze.

Penshurst and Hever Castle

Tudor timber-framed houses and shops line the high street of the attractive village of **PENSHURST**, five miles northwest of Tunbridge Wells. Its village church, St John the Baptist, is capped by an unusual four-spired tower and is entered under a beamed archway which conceals a rustic post office. However, the main reason for coming here is to visit **Penshurst Place** (March Sat & Sun noon–5.30pm; April–Oct daily noon–5.30pm; grounds same days 10.30am–6pm; £6, grounds only £4.50; Ⓦwww.penshurstplace.com), home to the Sidney family since 1552 and birthplace of the Elizabethan soldier and poet, Sir Philip Sidney. The fourteenth-century Barons Hall, built for Sir John de Pulteney, four times Mayor of London, is the chief glory of the interior, with its sixty-foot-high chestnut roof still in place. The ten acres of grounds include a formal Italian garden with clipped box hedges, and double herbaceous borders mixed with an abundance of yew hedges.

   The moated and much-altered **Hever Castle** (March–Nov daily noon–5pm; £7.80; Ⓦwww.hevercastle.co.uk), three miles further west, is where Anne Boleyn, second wife of Henry VIII, grew up, and where Anne of Cleves, Henry's fourth wife, lived after their divorce. In 1903, the castle, having fallen into disrepair, was bought by William Waldorf-Astor, American millionaire owner of *The Times*, who assiduously restored the house, panelling the rooms with reproductions of Tudor woodcarvings. In the Inner Hall hang two fine portraits of Henry VIII and Elizabeth I by Holbein. Upstairs, in Anne of Cleves' room, there's a well-preserved tapestry, depicting the marriage of Henry's sister to King Louis XII, with Anne Boleyn as one of the ladies-in-waiting. Outside in the grounds, next to the gift shop, is the absorbing **Guthrie Miniature Model Houses Collection**, showing the development of aristocratic seats from feudal times onwards. The best feature of the grounds, though, is the beautiful **Italian Garden**, built on reclaimed marshland and decorated with Roman statuary.

Sevenoaks and around

Set among the Greensand ridges of west Kent, 25 miles from London, **SEVENOAKS** lost all but one of the ageing oaks from which it derives its name in the storm that struck southern England in October 1987. With mere saplings having taken their place, the only real reason to come to the town is to visit the immense baronial estate of **Knole** (April–Oct Wed–Sat noon–4pm, Sun 11am–5pm; £5; NT), accessible from the south end of Sevenoaks High Street. Knole House was transformed into a palace in 1456 by Archbishop Thomas Bourchier, for himself and succeeding archbishops of Canterbury. Designed to numerically match the calendar with 7 courtyards, 52 staircases and 365 rooms, it was appropriated by Henry VIII, who lavished further expense on it and hunted in the thousand acres of parkland, still home to several hundred deer. Elizabeth I passed the estate on to her cousin, Thomas Sackville, and it has remained in the family's hands ever since. Vita Sackville-West was born here, and her one-time lover Virginia Woolf derived inspiration for her novel *Orlando* from her frequent visits to the house. Only thirteen rooms are open to the public, featuring an array of fine, if well-worn, furnishings and tapestries. Paintings by Gainsborough and Van Dyck are on display, as are Reynolds' depictions of George III and of Queen Charlotte – between them hangs a painting of their strutting, dandified progeny, George IV, one of the fifteen children she bore the king.

Sevenoaks' **train station** is fifteen minutes' walk north of the town centre on the London Road. The **bus station** is in Buckhurst Lane, off the High Street. The **tourist office** is in the library building, just opposite the bus station (April–Sept Mon–Sat 9.30am–5pm; Oct–March Mon–Fri 9.30am–5pm, Sat 9.30am–4.30pm; ☎01732/450305, ✆www.heartofkent.org.uk). Reasonable **accommodation** options include the spacious family room at *Burley Lodge*, Rockdale Rd (☎01732/455761; ❶), close to the entrance to Knole, or you can have a timber-clad cottage to yourself at *4 Old Timber Top Cottages*, Bethel Rd (☎01732/460506, ✉anthony@ruddassociates.ndo.co.uk; ❸). The nearest **youth hostel** is in Kemsing, four miles northeast of Sevenoaks, and a two-mile hike from Kemsing station (☎01732/761341). Alternatively, take bus #425/6 or #433 from Sevenoaks to Kemsing post office, which is close by – note that no public transport runs to Kemsing on Sundays.

For truly delicious **food**, you need to go to the *Sycamore* restaurant at the *Royal Oak Hotel* on Upper High Street just beyond the entrance to Knole Park, which offers a two-course lunch for over £10 – in the evening, one main dish will cost you more than that. For less expensive evening meals, you should head for the bistro (in other words, the bar).

Lullingstone, Chartwell and Ightham Mote

Lullingstone Roman Villa (daily: April–Sept 10am–6pm; Oct 10am–5pm; Nov–March 10am–4pm; £2.60; EH), seven miles north of Sevenoaks and half a mile along the river west of the village of Eynsford, has some of the best-preserved Roman mosaics in southeast England on show, in a pleasant location alongside the trickle of the River Darent. Believed to have been the first-century residence of a farmer, the site has yielded some fine marble busts (now in the British Museum) and a superb floor depicting the despatching of the chimera, a mythical fire-breathing beast with a lion's head, goat's body and a serpent's tail. Excavation in a nearby chamber has revealed early Christian iconography, suggesting that the villa may have become a Romano-Christian chapel in the third century, pre-empting the official arrival of Christianity by three hundred years and making Lullingstone one of the earliest sites of clandestine Christian worship in England.

The residence of Winston Churchill from 1924 until his death in 1965, **Chartwell**, six miles west of Sevenoaks (April–June, Sept & Oct Wed–Sun 11am–5pm; July & Aug Tues–Sun 11am–5pm; £5.60; NT), is one of the most visited National Trust properties. It's an unremarkable, heavily restored Tudor building, whose main appeal is the wartime premier's memorabilia, including his paintings, which show an unexpectedly contemplative side to the famously gruff statesman. At peak times entry to the house is by timed ticket – expect long queues.

The secluded, moated manor house of **Ightham Mote**, six miles southeast of Sevenoaks just off the A227 (April–Oct Mon, Wed–Fri, Sun & public holidays 11am–5.30pm; £5; NT), originates from the fourteenth century and is one of the southeast's most picturesque National Trust properties, though the original defensive appearance of this half-timbered ragstone building has been muted by Tudor alterations. A tour of the interior reveals a mixture of architectural styles, ranging from the fourteenth-century Old Chapel and crypt, through a barrel-vaulted Tudor chapel with a painted ceiling, to an eighteenth-century Palladian window. This idyllically situated medieval dwelling is being restored by the National Trust, whose efforts are described in a small exhibition on the ground floor.

Eastbourne and around

Like so many of the southeast's seaside resorts, **EASTBOURNE** was kickstarted into life in the 1840s, when the Brighton, Lewes & Hastings railway company built a branch line from Lewes to the sea. Past holiday-makers include George Orwell, the composer Claude Debussy – who finished writing *La Mer* here – as well as Marx and Engels. Nowadays Eastbourne has a solid reputation as a retirement town – albeit one that's a touch livelier than the nearby custom-built Peacehaven. Eastbourne's elegant three-mile seafront consists of houses and hotels and is tainted by barely a shop, but the greatest draw

The South Downs Way

Following the undulating crest of the South Downs, from the village of Buriton on the Sussex–Hampshire border, two miles southwest of Petersfield train station, to their spectacular end at Beachy Head, the **South Downs Way** rises and dips over eighty miles along the chalk uplands, offering the southeast's finest walks. If undertaken in its entirety, the bridle-path is best traversed from west to east, taking advantage of the prevailing wind, Eastbourne's better transport services and accommodation, and the psychological appeal of ending at the sea. **Steyning**, the halfway-point, marks a transition between predominantly wooded sections and more exposed chalk uplands – to the east of here you'll pass the modern **youth hostel** at Truleigh Hill (☎01903/813419). Other hostels along the way are at Telscombe and at Alfriston, where a southern loop can be taken which brings you to Eastbourne along the cliffs of the Seven Sisters, and an old bothy at Gumber Farm (☎01243/814484; closed Nov–Easter), near Bignor Hill.

The OS Landranger **maps** #198 and #199 cover the eastern end of the route; you'll need #185 and #197 as well to cover the lot. Half a dozen guides are available, the best being *South Downs Way* by Miles Jebb (Cicerone Press), or the more detailed *South Downs Way* by Paul Millmore (Aurum Press).

around is the South Downs, which the sea has ground into a series of dramatic chalk cliffs around **Beachy Head**, just west of town.

The Town

Conforming to traditions, Eastbourne's **pier** is the focal point of its seafront: opened in 1872 and among the finest on the south coast. The promenade is framed by two prominent red-brick Martello forts: the northeastern one, the **Redoubt Fortress**, now houses a military museum (April–Nov daily 9.45am–5.30pm; £1.50; ⓦ www.eastbournemuseums.co.uk) and the other, the **Wish Tower** – the name is an old Sussex word meaning "marsh" – has been transformed into a **puppet museum** (mid-July to Sept daily 11am–5pm; April to mid-July, Oct & Nov Sat & Sun 11am–5pm; £1.80; ⓦ www.puppets.co.uk). One bright spark in sedate Eastbourne is the **Towner Gallery and Museum** on the corner of High Street and the Borough in the Old Town (April–Oct Tues–Sat noon–5pm, Sun 2–5pm; Nov–March Tues–Sat noon–4pm, Sun 2–5pm; free; ⓦ www.eastbourne.org/entertainment), a ten-minute walk west of the train station – it shows a refreshingly contemporary and ever-changing range of work.

Eastbourne **train station** is a splendid Italianate terminus ten minutes' walk from the seafront; the **bus station** is on Cavendish Place right by the pier; and the **tourist office** is at 3 Cornfield Rd, on the corner of Hyde Gardens (June–Sept Mon–Sat 9.30am–5.30pm, Sun 10am–1pm; Oct–May closed Sun; ☎01323/411400, ⓦ www.eastbourne.org). Eastbourne has hundreds of places to **stay**: try *Seabreeze Guest House*, 6 Marine Rd (☎01323/725440; ❷), a hundred yards from the sea, or *Sea Beach House Hotel*, 39–40 Marine Parade (☎01323/410458; ⓦ www.seabeachhousehotel.com; ❸). The **youth hostel** is on East Dean Road (☎01323/721081; closed Oct–March), a mile and a half west of town, with spectacular views across Eastbourne; take bus #712. Seaside Road, halfway down Terminus Road, between the train station and the sea, boasts *Tequila Sunset*, at no. 71 (☎01323/732832), offering new Mexican food, including a wide range of fajitas, and the town's best Italian, *Luigi's*, nearby at no. 72 (☎01323/736994; closed Sun); both are moderately priced. The best **pubs** are some distance from the seafront: *Cornfield Garage*, a capacious Wetherspoon's bar at 21–27 Cornfield Rd; the *Hurst Arms* at 76 Willingdon Rd, a ten-minute walk inland from the station up Upperton Road, has Harvey's locally brewed beers on tap.

Beachy Head and the Seven Sisters

A short walk west from Eastbourne takes you out along the most dramatic stretch of Sussex coastline, where the chalk uplands of the Sussex Downs are cut by the sea into a sequence of splendid cliffs. The most spectacular, **Beachy Head**, is 575ft high, with a diminutive-looking lighthouse below, but no beach – the headland's name derives from the French *beau chef* meaning "beautiful head". The beauty certainly went to Friedrich Engels' head – he insisted his ashes be scattered here and depressed individuals regularly try to join him by leaping to their doom from this well-known suicide spot. West of the headland the scenery softens into a diminishing series of cliffs, a landmark known as the **Seven Sisters**. The country park after which they are named provides some of the most impressive walks in the county, taking in the cliff-top walk and the lower valley of the meandering River Cuckmere, into which the Seven Sisters subside.

Lewes and around

East Sussex's county town, **LEWES** straddles the River Ouse as it carves a gap through the South Downs on its final stretch to the sea. The town's core is remarkably good-looking: Georgian and crooked older dwellings still line the High Street and the narrow lanes – or "Twittens" – lead off this main street and its continuations, with views onto the downs. Following the Norman Conquest, William's son-in-law, William de Warenne, built a priory and castle here, the latter still dominating the High Street. In 1264 Henry III's incompetence caused a baronial revolt led by Simon de Montfort, which culminated in the king's surrender at the Battle of Lewes, although de Montfort and his reduced force were annihilated within a year at the Battle of Evesham. De Montfort's name crops up all over the town, as do references to the Lewes Martyrs, the seventeen Protestants burned here in 1556, at the height of Mary Tudor's militant revival of Catholicism – an event commemorated in spectacular fashion every November 5. Intellectual nonconformity is something of a Lewes trademark, its roll call of free-thinkers featuring pioneer paleontologist Gideon Mantell, and the radical humanist Tom Paine, whose works inspired or supported the revolutions in France and America. The conservative spirit triumphed in 1914, however, after a pair of local enthusiasts commissioned a version of Rodin's majestic sculpture *The Kiss*, depicting Paolo and Francesca – lovers from Dante's *Inferno* – clinched in a full-on embrace. Local sentiment was outraged when the piece was unveiled in Lewes Town Hall, leading to its rapid removal amid a flurry of controversy (the sculpture was re-exhibited in the town hall in June 1999, 85 years after the scandal).

The Town

The best way to begin a tour of Lewes from the train station, is to walk up Station Road, then left down the High Street. The town's **Castle** (Mon–Sat 10am–5.30pm, Sun 11am–5.30pm; winter closes at dusk; £4; ⓦwww.sussex-

---

The Bonfire Societies

Each November 5, while the rest of Britain lights small domestic bonfires or attends municipal firework displays to commemorate the foiling of a Catholic plot to blow up the Houses of Parliament (see p.46), Lewes puts on a more dramatic show, whose origins lie in the deaths of the town's Protestant martyrs. By the end of the eighteenth century, Lewes' **Bonfire Boys** had become notorious for the boisterousness of their anti-Catholic demonstrations, in which they set off fireworks indiscriminately and dragged rolling tar barrels through the streets – a tradition still practised today, although with a little more caution. In 1845 events came to a head when the incorrigible pyromaniacs of Lewes had to be read the Riot Act, instigating a night of violence between the police and Bonfire Boys. Lewes' first **bonfire societies** were established soon afterwards, to try to get a bit more discipline into the proceedings, and earlier this century they were persuaded to move their street fires to the town's perimeters.

Today's tightly knit bonfire societies, each with its quasi-militaristic motto ("Death or Glory", "True to Each Other", etc), spend much of the year organizing the Bonfire Night shenanigans, when their members dress up in traditional costumes and parade through the town carrying flaming torches, before marching off onto the downs for their society's big fire. At each of the fires effigies of Guy Fawkes and the Pope are burned alongside contemporary, but equally reviled, figures – Chancellors of the Exchequer and Prime Ministers are popular choices.

past.co.uk) is hidden from view behind the houses on your right. Inside the castle complex – unusual for being built on two mottes, or mounds – the shell of the eleventh-century keep remains, and both the towers can be climbed for excellent views over the town's roofs to the surrounding Downs. Tickets for the castle include admission to the **museum** (same hours as castle), by the castle entrance, which is much better than the usual stuffy town museum. The highlight is a half-hourly audio-visual history of Lewes, aided by the vast Lewes Living History Model on which places of interest within the town are spotlit as the tale unfolds.

A few minutes' walk further west along the High Street past St Michael's Church, with its unusual twin towers – one arcaded and wooden and the other round flint – you come to the steep cobbled and much photographed **Keere Street**, down which the reckless Prince Regent is alleged to have driven his carriage. Keere Street leads eventually to **Southover Grange** (Mon–Sat 8am–dusk, Sun 9am–dusk; free), with its lovely gardens. Built in 1572 from the priory's remains, the Grange was also the childhood home of the diarist John Evelyn. Past the gardens, a right turn down Southover High Street leads to the Tudor-built **Anne of Cleves House** (mid-Feb to Oct Mon–Sat 10am–5pm, Sun noon–5pm; Nov & Dec Tues–Sat 10am–5pm, Sun noon–5pm; Jan to mid-Feb Tues, Thurs & Sat 10am–5pm; £2.60, combined ticket with the castle £5.50; ⓦ www.sussexpast.co.uk), given to her in settlement after her divorce from Henry VIII (although she never actually lived here) and now an absorbing museum. The magnificent oak-beamed Tudor bedroom is impressive, with its cumbersome "bed wagon", a bed-warming brazier which would fail the slackest of fire regulations and which the 400-year-old Flemish four-poster has managed to survive. The house's decor dates from the sixteenth century when the Wealden iron industry was flourishing and Sussex produced most of England's iron, with Lewes being a centre of cannon manufacture.

On the opposite side of the road and closer to the train station, is the church of **St John the Baptist**, with its squat, brick tower capped by a six-foot shark for a weather vane; inside there's some superb stained glass and a tiny chapel with the lead coffins of William de Warenne and his wife Gundrada, William I's daughter. De Warenne was one of the six barons presiding over the new administrative provinces – known as the **Rapes of Sussex** – created by the Normans soon after the Conquest. Behind the church are the ruins of de Warenne's **St Pancras Priory**, once one of Europe's principal Cluniac institutions, with a church the size of Westminster Abbey. Sadly it was dismantled to build town houses following the Dissolution and is now an evocative ruin surrounded by playing fields.

Returning to the town centre, the **Star Brewery Studio** off Fisher Street, north of the High Street, displays the creative talents of a collective of artists, bookbinders, carpenters and other artisans; the attached **Star Gallery** (Mon–Sat 10.30am–5.30pm; free) presents a changing series of exhibitions. At the east end of the High Street, School Hill descends towards Cliffe Bridge, built in 1727 and entrance to the commercial centre of the medieval settlement, although Cliffe High Street's appearance is now predominantly nineteenth century. For the energetic, a path leads up onto the Downs from the end of Cliffe High Street – site of England's worst avalanche disaster in 1836, when a bank of snow slid onto Cliffe village, killing eight people. The path passes close to an obelisk, commemorating the town's seventeen Protestant martyrs.

Practicalities

The **train station**, south of the High Street on Station Road, has regular services from London Victoria and along the coast to Brighton, Eastbourne, Hastings and the ferry port at Newhaven, from where Hoverspeed runs to Dieppe (℡08705/240241). **Buses** to the rest of East Sussex leave from the **bus station** on Eastgate Street, by the river. The **tourist office** (Easter–Sept Mon–Fri 9am–5pm, Sat 10am–5pm, Sun 10am–2pm; Oct–Easter Mon–Fri 9am–5pm, Sat 10am–2pm; ℡01273/483448, ⓦwww.lewes.gov.uk) is at the junction of the High Street and Fisher Street. For **accommodation** try *Castle Banks Cottage*, 4 Castle Banks (℡01273/476291, ⓔa1tourism.com/uk/castle-banks.html; ❷) a beamed period house with great views, tucked away off West Street. The *Crown Inn*, 191 High St, close to the tourist office (℡01273/480670, ⓦwww.crowninn-lewes.co.uk; ❸), is a reasonable fallback. The nearest **youth hostel** is in the village of Telscombe, six miles south of Lewes (see below); there's another – a rustic wooden cabin with basic facilities – eleven miles northeast of Lewes at Blackboys (℡01825/890607; closed mid-Sept to March). Lewes is home to the excellent Harvey's brewery and most of the **pubs** serve its products. The *Brewers' Arms* is central and pleasant enough, as is the *Lewes Arms* tucked behind the *Star Brewery Studios*. **Food** choices include the inexpensive Indian *Dilraj*, 12 Fisher St (℡01273/479279), *La Cucina*, a moderately priced Italian joint at 13 Station St (℡01273/476707), and the inexpensive *Pailin Thai* restaurant, opposite at no. 20 (℡01273/473906).

Around Lewes: Glyndebourne, Rodmell and Charleston

Glyndebourne, Britain's only unsubsidized opera house, is situated near the village of Glynde, three miles east of Lewes. Founded in 1934, the Glyndebourne Festival, which runs from May to August, is an indispensable part of the high-society calendar, with ticket prices and distribution excluding all but the most devoted opera lovers. On one level, Glyndebourne is a repellent spectacle, its lawns thronged with gentry and corporate bigwigs ingesting champagne and smoked salmon – productions have one massive interval to allow for an unhurried repast. On the other hand, the musical values are of the highest standard, mixing young talent with starrier names, and taking the sort of risks Covent Garden wouldn't dream of. The acoustically outstanding new theatre (seating 1200) has broadened the appeal of this exclusive venue to a wider audience. Some tickets are available at reduced prices for dress rehearsals or if you are prepared to stand; call ℡01273/813813 for details or check at ⓦwww.glyndebourne.com.

Three miles south of Lewes lies the village of **RODMELL**, whose main source of interest is the **Monk's House** (April–Oct Wed & Sat 2–5.30pm; £2.60; NT), former home of Virginia Woolf, a leading figure of the Bloomsbury Group (see box on p.214). She and her husband Leonard moved to the weatherboard cottage in 1919 and Leonard stayed there until his death in 1969; both Virginia's and Leonard's remains are interred in the gardens. Nearby lies the River Ouse where Virginia killed herself in 1941 by walking into the water with her pockets full of stones. The house's interior is nothing special and will only really be of interest to Bloomsbury fans, who can look round the study where Virginia wrote several of her novels, and her bedroom, laid out with period editions of her work. Three miles south of Rodmell, in

The Bloomsbury Group

The **Bloomsbury Group** were essentially a bevy of upper middle-class friends, who took their name from the Bloomsbury area of London, where most of them lived before acquiring houses in the Sussex countryside. The Group revolved around Virginia, Vanessa, Thoby and Adrian Stephen, who lived at 46 Gordon Square, the London base of the Bloomsbury Group. Thoby's Thursday evening gatherings and Vanessa's Friday Club for painters attracted a whole host of Cambridge-educated snobs who subscribed to Oscar Wilde's theory that "aesthetics are higher than ethics". Their diet of "human intercourse and the enjoyment of beautiful things" was hardly revolutionary, but their behaviour, particularly that of the two sisters (unmarried, unchaperoned, intellectual and artistic), succeeded in shocking London society, especially through their louche sexual practices (most of the group swung both ways).

All this, though interesting, would be forgotten were it not for their individual work. In 1922 Virginia declared, without too much exaggeration, "Everyone in Gordon Square has become famous": Lytton Strachey had been the first to make his name with *Eminent Victorians*, a series of unprecedentedly frank biographies; Vanessa, now married to the art critic Clive Bell, had become involved in Roger Fry's prolific design firm, Omega Workshop; and the economist John Maynard Keynes had become an adviser to the Treasury (he later went on to become the leading economic theorist of his day). The Group's most celebrated figure, Virginia, married Leonard Woolf and became an established novelist; she and Leonard also founded the Hogarth Press, which published T.S. Eliot's *Waste Land* in 1922.

Eliot was just one of a number of writers, such as Aldous Huxley, Bertrand Russell and E.M. Forster, who were drawn to the interwar Bloomsbury set, but others, notably D.H. Lawrence, were repelled by the clan's narcissism and snobbish narrow-mindedness. Whatever their limitations, the Bloomsbury Group were Britain's most influential intellectual coterie of the interwar years, and their appeal shows little sign of waning – even now scarcely a year goes by without the publication of the biography and or memoirs of some Bloomsbury peripheral.

the village of **TELSCOMBE**, is a quiet **youth hostel** (☎01273/301357; closed mid-Sept to March), whose simple accommodation is in 200-year-old cottages.

Six miles east of Lewes, off the A27, is another Bloomsbury Group shrine, **Charleston Farmhouse** (March–June, Sept & Oct Wed–Sun 2–6pm; July & Aug Wed–Sun 11am–6pm; £5.50; ⓦwww.charleston.org.uk), home to Virginia Woolf's sister Vanessa Bell, Vanessa's husband Clive Bell and her lover Duncan Grant. As conscientious objectors, the trio moved here during World War I so that the men could work on local farms (farm labourers were exempted from military service). The farmhouse became a gathering point for other members of the Bloomsbury Group, including the biographer Lytton Strachey, the economist Maynard Keynes and the novelist E.M. Forster. Duncan Grant continued to live in the house until his death in 1978. Unless it's a Sunday, you have to join a fifty-minute guided tour in order to view the interior of the farmhouse, where almost every surface is painted and the walls are hung with paintings by Picasso, Renoir and Augustus John, alongside the work of the markedly less-talented residents. Many of the fabrics, lampshades and other artefacts bear the unmistakable mark of the Omega Workshop, the Bloomsbury equivalent of William Morris's Arts and Crafts Movement.

Brighton

Recorded as the tiny fishing village of Brithelmeston in the Domesday Book, **BRIGHTON** seems to have slipped unnoticed through history until the mid-eighteenth-century sea-bathing trend established a resort that has never looked back. The fad received royal approval in the 1770s when the decadent Prince Regent, later George IV, began patronizing the town in the company of his mistress, thus setting a precedent for the "dirty weekend", Brighton's major contribution to the English collective consciousness. Trying to shake off this blowsy reputation, Brighton now highlights its Georgian charm, its upmarket shops and classy restaurants and its thriving conference industry. Yet, however much Brighton tries to present itself as a comfortable middle-class town, the essence of its appeal is its faintly bohemian vitality, a buzz that comes from a mix of English holiday-makers, thousands of young foreign students from the town's innumerable language schools, a thriving gay community and an energetic local student population from the art college and two universities.

Arrival, information and accommodation

Brighton **train station** is at the head of Queen's Road, which descends to the Clock Tower and then becomes West Street which eventually collides with the seafront – a distance of about half a mile. **Buses** arrive at Pool Valley bus station, tucked just in from the seafront on the south side of the Old Steine. The **tourist office** is at 10 Bartholomew Square, behind the town hall on the southern side of the Lanes (June–Sept Mon–Fri 9am–6pm, Sat 10am–5pm, Sun 10am–4pm; Oct–May Mon–Sat 9am–5pm; ☏0906/7112255), a maze of narrow alleyways marking Brighton's Old Town. You'll find most budget **accommodation** clustered around the Kemp Town district, to the east of the Palace Pier, with the more elegant and expensive hotels west of the town centre around Regency Square, opposite the West Pier. Brighton's official **campsite** is the year-round *Sheepcote Valley* site (☏01273/626546), just north of Brighton Marina; take bus #1 or #1A to Wilson Avenue, or take the Volks railway and walk up Arundel Road to Wilson Avenue.

Hotels, B&Bs and guest houses

Adelaide Hotel 51 Regency Square ☏01273/205286, ⓦwww.smoothhound.co.uk/hotels/adelaide.html. Top-notch guest house in the fancier part of town. One room has a four-poster bed. ❺

Ainsley House 28 New Steine ☏01273/605310, ⓦwww.ainsleyhotel.com. Friendly, upmarket guest house in an attractive Regency terrace. ❸

Andorra Hotel 15–16 Oriental Place ☏01273/321787. At the west end of town, this hotel has comfortable rooms with good facilities. ❷

Arlanda Hotel 20 New Steine ☏01273/699300, ⓦwww.arlandahotel.co.uk. Plusher than average choice in the New Steine square, with wide price range depending on the room; the cheapest are on the top floor and quite poky. ❷

Ascott House Hotel 21 New Steine ☏01273/688085, ⓦwww.ascotthousehotel.com. Very comfortable guest house near the sea front. ❸

Four Seasons 3 Upper Rock Gardens ☏01273/673574, ⓔjoehalpenny@compuserve.com. Cosy B&B in the Kemp Town area, with good vegetarian breakfast options. ❹

Hudsons 22 Devonshire Place ☏01273/683642. Relaxed and exclusively gay guest house east of the centre off St James St. ❹

Oriental Hotel 9 Oriental Place ☏01273/205050, ⓔinfo@orientalhotel.co.uk. Friendly, laid-back staff and very funky decor throughout; full veggie breakfasts are served in the hotel's mellow café. ❸

Queensbury Hotel 58 Regency Square ☏01273/325558. Comfortable guest house in Brighton's definitive Georgian district. ❸

Sea Spray 25 New Steine ☏01273/680332, ⓔseaspray@brighton.co.uk. Good-value B&B with showers in all rooms. ❷

Westbourne Hotel 46 Upper Rock Gardens ☏01273/686920, ⓔmail@westbournehotel.net. Well-appointed B&B close to the seafront and all amenities. ❸

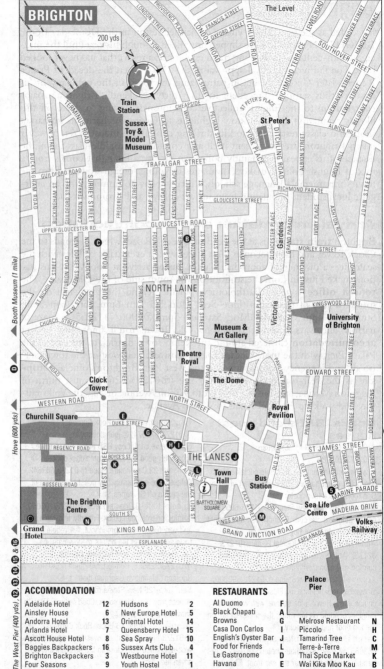

BRIGHTON

0   200 yds

A, Preston Manor, **1** & A23 London   A27 Lewes

The Level

Train Station

Sussex Toy & Model Museum

St Peter's

NORTH LAINE

Museum & Art Gallery

University of Brighton

Theatre Royal

The Dome

Royal Pavilion

Clock Tower

Churchill Square

THE LANES

Town Hall

Bus Station

Sea Life Centre

Volks Railway

The Brighton Centre

Grand Hotel

Palace Pier

Booth Museum (1 mile)

Hove (600 yds)

The West Pier (400 yds)

& Kemp Town (900 yds)

216

ACCOMMODATION

Adelaide Hotel	12
Ainsley House	6
Andorra Hotel	13
Arlanda Hotel	7
Ascott House Hotel	8
Baggies Backpackers	16
Brighton Backpackers	3
Four Seasons	9
Hudsons	2
New Europe Hotel	5
Oriental Hotel	14
Queensberry Hotel	15
Sea Spray	10
Sussex Arts Club	4
Westbourne Hotel	11
Youth Hostel	1

RESTAURANTS

Al Duomo	F
Black Chapati	A
Browns	G
Casa Don Carlos	I
English's Oyster Bar	J
Food for Friends	L
Le Gastronome	D
Havana	E
Melrose Restaurant	N
Piccolo	H
Tamarind Tree	C
Terre-à-Terre	M
Thai Spice Market	K
Wai Kika Moo Kau	B

© Crown copyright

Hostels

Baggies Backpackers 33 Oriental Place
℡01273/733740. Spacious house a little west of the West Pier with large bright dorms, starting at £9 a night, decent showers and plenty of room to spread out.

Brighton Backpackers 75 Middle St
℡01273/777717, Ⓦwww.brightonbackpackers.com. Brighton's established independent hostel with a lively, easy-going atmosphere and vivid murals. A new annexe just round the corner overlooks the seafront and offers a quieter alternative; dorm beds £9, twin rooms £25.

Youth Hostel Patcham Place, London Rd
℡01273/556196, Ⓦwww.yha.org.uk. Brighton's YHA hostel is housed in a splendid Queen Anne mansion, in parkland four miles north of the sea, close to the junction of the roads to Lewes and London. Take bus #5A from the town centre.

The Town

Any visit to Brighton inevitably begins with a visit to its two most famous landmarks – the exuberant **Royal Pavilion** and the wonderfully tacky **Palace Pier**, a few minutes away – followed by a stroll along the seafront promenade or the pebbly beach. Just as interesting, though, is an exploration of Brighton's car-free **Lanes**, where some of the town's diverse restaurants, bars and tiny bric-a-brac, jewellery and antique shops can be found; or an idle meander through the quaint, but more bohemian streets of **North Laine**.

The Royal Pavilion

In any survey to find England's most loved building, there's always a bucketful of votes for Brighton's exotic extravaganza, the **Royal Pavilion** (daily: June–Sept 10am–6pm; Oct–May 10am–5pm; £5.20; Ⓦwww.royalpavilion.brighton.co.uk), which flaunts itself in the middle of the main thoroughfare of Old Steine. The building that originally stood here was a conventional farmhouse. Then in 1787, the fun-loving Prince of Wales commissioned something more regal, and for a couple of decades the prince's south-coast pied-à-terre was a Palladian villa, with mildly oriental embellishments. Shortly after becoming Prince Regent, George commissioned John Nash, architect of London's Regent Street, to build an extraordinary confection of slender minarets, twirling domes, pagodas, balconies and miscellaneous motifs imported from India and China and supported on an innovative cast-iron frame, creating an exterior profile that defines a genre of its own – Oriental-Gothic. Queen Victoria was not amused by George's taste in architecture, and shifted the royal seaside residence to the Isle of Wight, taking the pavilion's valuable fittings back to Buckingham and Kensington palaces and selling the building to the town. The pavilion was then pressed into a series of humdrum roles – tearoom, hospital, concert hall, radar station, ration office – but has now been brilliantly restored.

Inside the pavilion the exuberant compendium of Regency exotica has been enhanced by the return of many of the objects which Victoria had taken away. One of the highlights – approached via the restrained Long Gallery – is the **Banqueting Room**, which erupts with ornate splendour and is dominated by a one-ton chandelier hung from the jaws of a massive dragon cowering in a plantain tree. Next door, the huge, high-ceilinged kitchen, fitted with the most modern appliances of its time, has iron columns disguised as palm trees. Nearby, the stunning **Music Room**, the first sight of which reduced George to tears of joy, has a huge dome lined with more than 26,000 individually gilded scales and hung with exquisite umbrella-like glass lamps. After climbing the famous cast-iron staircase with its bamboo-look bannisters, you can go into Victoria's sober and seldom-used bedroom and the North Gallery where the King's portrait hangs, along with a selection of satirical cartoons. More notable, though, is the **South Gallery**, decorated in sky blue with trompe l'oeil bamboo trellises and a carpet which appears to be strewn with flowers.

The rest of the town

Tucked between the pavilion and the seafront is a warren of narrow, pedestrianized thoroughfares known as **the Lanes** – the core of the old fishing village from which Brighton evolved. Long-established antiques shops, designer outlets and a concentration of bars, pubs and restaurants generate a lively and intimate atmosphere in this part of town. **North Laine**, which spreads north of North Street along Kensington, Sydney, Gardner and Bond streets, is more bohemian with its hub along pedestrianized Kensington Gardens. Here the shops are more eclectic, selling second-hand records, clothes, bric-a-brac and New Age objects, and mingle with earthy coffee shops and downbeat cafés.

Most of the seafront is an ugly mix of shops, entertainment complexes and hotels, ranging from the impressively pompous plasterwork of the *Grand* – scene of the IRA's attempted assassination of the Conservative cabinet in October 1984 – to the green-glass monstrosity on the seaward side of the Lanes. To appreciate fully the tackier side of Brighton, you must take a stroll along the **Palace Pier** whose every inch is devoted to fun and money-making, from the cacophonous Palace of Fun to the Pleasure Dome, and from the state-of-the-art video games to the fairground rides and karaoke sessions at the end of the pier. Brighton's architecturally superior West Pier, built in 1866 half a mile west along the seafront, was damaged in World War II and then fell into disrepair, but looks set to be restored to its former glory by 2002.

Across the road from the Palace Pier, on Marine Parade, is the **Sea Life Centre** (daily 10am–5pm; £5.50; Ⓦ www.sealife.co.uk), one of the best marine life displays of its kind, with a transparent tunnel passing through a huge aquarium – a walk along the bottom of the sea with sharks and rays gliding overhead. Nearby, the antiquated locomotives of **Volks Electric Railway** (April to mid-Sept; £1.60 return) – the first electric train in the country – run eastward towards the Marina and the nudist beach, usually the preserve of just a few thick-skinned souls.

Brighton's museums

Across the gardens from the pavilion stands the **Brighton Museum and Art Gallery** (Mon, Tues & Thurs–Sat 10am–5pm, Sun 2–5pm; free), which is entered just around the corner on Church Street. The paintings here are generally nondescript, but there's an interesting collection of classic Art Deco and Art Nouveau furniture as well as Dalí's famous sofa, based on Mae West's lips. There's also a large selection of pottery, from basic Neolithic earthenware to delicate porcelain figurines popular in the eighteenth century.

Brighton's other big municipal museum is the **Booth Museum of Natural History** (Mon–Wed, Fri & Sat 10am–5pm, Sun 2–5pm; free), a mile up Dukes Road from the centre of town. Purpose-built to house Mr E.T. Booth's prodigious collection of stuffed birds, this is a wonderfully fusty old Victorian museum with beetles, butterflies and animal skeletons galore, but which also puts on very imaginative temporary shows.

Perhaps more immediately gratifying for younger children is the **Sussex Toy and Model Museum** (Mon–Fri 10am–1pm & 2–5pm, Sat 11am–1pm & 2–5pm; £3), housed in an old stables underneath the train station. The collection is impressive, ranging from an entire cabinet full of Smurfs to a set of Pelham puppets, but it's the working model railways that are likely to be the focus of most children's attention.

Eating, drinking and nightlife

Brighton has the greatest concentration of **restaurants** in the southeast after London. Around North Laine are some great, inexpensive **cafés**, but for classier establishments head to the Lanes and out towards Hove. Many of the cheaper places fight hard to attract the large student market with discounted deals of around ten percent, so if you have a student ID, use it. **Nightlife** is hectic and compulsively pursued throughout the year, making Brighton unique in the sedate southeast. There are a couple of outstanding clubs, lots of live music and more cinema screens per head than anywhere else in Britain. Midweek entry into the clubs can cost just a couple of pounds and cinema seats are similarly priced before 6pm. For up-to-date details of **what's on**, pick up a copy of the monthly *Insight* (£1) from newsagents or the free monthly listing magazines *What's On* or *Source* from the tourist office while the similarly free *Gscene*, covering gay events, can be found in gay bars, clubs and shops. If you've access to the internet, you can log on to the highly praised **website**, ⓦwww. brighton.co.uk. Every May the three-week-long **Brighton Festival** (☎01273/700747, ⓦwww.brighton-festival.org.uk) takes place in various venues around town. This arty celebration includes fun fairs, exhibitions, street theatre and concerts from classical to jazz. Brighton is hoping to emulate Berlin by staging its very own version of the latter's Love Parade, a day-and-night-long **Dance Parade**, held in mid-July.

Cafés and bars

Bar Centro 6 Ship St. Brighton's biggest, most spacious pre-club bar with occasional in-house DJs spinning tunes.

Bar Latino 62 Middle St. Tapas bar with regular live screenings of Spanish and Portuguese football matches and a healthy dose of salsa too.

Grinders 10 Kensington Gardens. Upstairs trip-happy café serving tasty cheap snacks and great soups, with a balcony for watching life in North Laine go by, and lots of club fliers to hand.

Mock Turtle 4 Pool Valley. Old-fashioned teashop crammed with bric-a-brac and cheap, home-made cakes. Closed Sun & Mon.

The Sanctuary 51–55 Brunswick St East, Hove ☎01273/770012. Cool and arty vegetarian café with soft furnishings and a cosy, relaxed ambience. Deservedly popular, despite its not-very-central location.

Zanzibar 129 St James's St. Premier pre-club gay bar out towards Kemp Town.

Restaurants

Al Duomo 7 Pavilion Buildings ☎01273/326741. Brilliant pizzeria, with a genuine wood-burning oven. Has a more intimate sister restaurant, *Al Forno* at 36 East St ☎01273/324905. Inexpensive.

Black Chapati 12 Circus Parade ☎01273/699011. Innovative Asian cooking with Japanese and Thai influences as well as more conventional Indian dishes, which are brilliantly executed. Something of a Brighton landmark despite its out-of-the-way location, more than a mile inland, at the point where the London road enters town. Moderate.

Browns 3–4 Duke St ☎01273/323501. A mixture of steak, seafood and pasta dishes as well as traditional favourites such as Guinness-marinated steak-and-mushroom pie, served in a sophisticated continental setting with wooden floors, palms and background jazz. Moderate.

Casa Don Carlos 5 Union St ☎01273/327177. Small, long-established tapas bar in the Lanes with outdoor seating and daily specials. Also serves more substantial Spanish dishes and drinks. Inexpensive.

English's Oyster Bar 29–31 East St ☎01273/327980. Three fishermen's cottages knocked together to house a marble and brass oyster bar and a red velvet dining room. Seafood's the speciality with a mouth-watering menu and better value than you might expect, especially the set menus. Brighton institution famed for its atmosphere as much as its food. Expensive.

Food for Friends 17 Prince Albert St ☎01273/202310. Brighton's ever-popular wholefood veggie eatery is imaginative enough to please die-hard meat-eaters. It's usually busy, but well worth the squeeze and offers discounts for students and music on Sun evenings. Inexpensive.

Le Gastronome 3 Hampton Place ☎01273/777399. Well known for its good-value classic French cuisine, friendly service and outstanding selection of wines; choose the dish of the day for £8 or a five-course blow-out for £22.50. Closed Sun & Mon. Moderate.

Havana 33 Duke St ☏ 01273/773388. Very stylish continental brasserie with just a hint of colonial ambience – palms and rattan chairs – to evoke tropical luxury and a feeling of being pampered. The menu is eclectic, ranging from Med to Thai – the lunchtime menu is particularly good value. Moderate.

Melrose Restaurant 132 King's Rd ☏ 01273/326520. Traditional and decent seafront establishment which has been serving seafood, roasts and custard-covered puddings for over forty years. The *Regency Restaurant* next door is a similar and smaller option. Inexpensive.

Piccolo 56 Ship St ☏ 01273/380380. Informal Italian restaurant with pizza and pasta dishes from around £5 and special deals for students. Inexpensive.

Tamarind Tree 48 Queen's Rd ☏ 01273/298816. Mellow Carribean café decked in turquoise and wickerwork, with a surprisingly large range of veggie dishes. Main dishes around £9, or you could just have a filling starter. Moderate.

Terre-à-Terre 71 East St ☏ 01273/729051. Imaginative, global, veggie cuisine in a modern arty setting. Closed Mon lunch & Sun. Moderate.

Thai Spice Market 13 Boyces St ☏ 01273/325195. Classical Thai interior and cuisine, serving meat, seafood and vegetarian varieties. Inexpensive to moderate.

Yum Yum Noodle Bar 22–23 Sydney St ☏ 01273/606777. Serves anything Southeast Asian – Chinese, Thai, Indonesian and Malaysian noodle dishes at good-value prices – situated above a Chinese supermarket. Lunch only. Inexpensive.

Pubs

The Cricketers 15 Black Lion St. Just west of the Lanes, this is Brighton's oldest pub and it looks it too; very popular with good pub grub served in the pleasant setting of its Courtyard Bar.

Dr Brighton's 16 King's Rd. Popular gay venue.

Druid's Head, 9 Brighton Place. Great, old pub in the heart of the Lanes with a flagstone floor and a raucous jukebox.

Font & Firkin Union St. Spacious converted chapel with a bar in place of the altar and occasional live music.

The Great Eastern 103 Trafalgar St. Relaxing pub with bare boards and bookshelves, lots of real ales, and no fruit machines or TV.

The Hand in Hand 33 Upper St James St. An agreeable pub with its own brewery out the back.

The Prince Albert 48 Trafalgar St. A listed building, right by the train station, popular with students. Live rock upstairs, real ale downstairs; free pool in the afternoon.

The Smugglers 10 Ship St. A young crowd packs out this place, with a good jazz club upstairs, dance club downstairs, and free pool during the day.

Nightlife

The Beach King's Road Arches ☏ 01273/722222. R'n'B, classic grooves and occasional stand-up comedy nights.

Casablanca 3 Middle St ☏ 01273/321817. Basement venue featuring live bands and all types of funk, including latin and jazz.

Concorde 2 Madeira Shelter, Madeira Drive ☏ 01273/207241. Live music venue, with an admirable booking policy featuring everyone from Bert Jansch to Sparklehorse; also has club nights at the weekend and a Tues night comedy club.

Escape 10 Marine Parade ☏ 01273/606906. Brighton's trendiest nightclub packs them in night after night, specializing in funk and techno.

The Jazz Rooms, *Smugglers Inn*, 10 Ship St ☏ 01273/328439. Popular jazz venue in the basement, with the livelier *Enigma* upstairs catering for active ravers and fronting the occasional abstract dance troupe.

Paradox 78 West St ☏ 01273/321628. The best option after the *Zap Club*. Its *Wild Fruits* gay nights on the first Mon of the month are particularly popular.

Revenge 32 Old Steine ☏ 01273/606064. The south's largest gay club with Mon night cabarets plus upfront dance and retro boogie on two floors.

Zap Club 188–193 Kings Rd Arches ☏ 01273/821588. Brighton's most durable club, right on the seafront opposite Ship Street.

Mid-Sussex

The principal attraction of **mid-Sussex** is its wealth of fine gardens, ranging from the majestic **Sheffield Park** to the luscious flowerbeds of **Nymans** and the landscaped lakes of **Leonardslee**. Exploring this region by public transport isn't really feasible unless you take your bike on the train; tourist information is thin on the ground too, so get clued up at Brighton's tourist office before you go.

Sheffield Park and the Bluebell Railway

Around twenty miles northeast of Brighton lies the country estate of **Sheffield Park**, its centrepiece a Gothic mansion built for Lord Sheffield by James Wyatt. The house is closed to the public, but you can roam around the hundred-acre **gardens** (Jan & Feb Sat & Sun 10.30am–4pm; March–Oct Tues–Sun & public holidays 10.30am–6pm; Nov & Dec Tues–Sun 10.30am–4pm; £4.60, combined ticket with Bluebell Railway £10.50; NT), which were laid out by Capability Brown, the Christopher Wren of the grassy knoll. A mile south of the gardens lies the southern terminus of the **Bluebell Railway** (May–Sept daily; Oct–April Sat, Sun & school holidays; day ticket £8; ☎01825/720800, ⓦ www.bluebell-railway.co.uk), whose vintage steam locomotives chuff nine miles north via Horsted Keynes to Kingscote. Although the service gets extremely crowded on weekends – especially in May, when the bluebells blossom in the woods through which the line passes – it's an entertaining and nostalgic way of travelling through the Sussex countryside and your day ticket lets you go to and fro as often as you like.

Nymans and Leonardslee

Nymans (March to early Nov Wed–Sun 11am–6pm; £6; NT), fifteen miles north of Brighton near the village of Handcross (bus #773 from Brighton to Crawley can drop you off on the A23 beside the village), was created by Ludwig Messel, an inspired gardener and plant collector. The **gardens** contain a valuable collection of exotic trees and shrubs as well as more everyday plants, of which the colourful rhododendrons are particularly prolific. Nymans consists of a series of different enclosures and gardens, the highlight of which is the large, romantic walled garden, almost hidden from sight by an abundance of climbing plants and housing a collection of rare Himalayan magnolia trees. The gardens are centred around the picturesque ruins of a mock-Tudor manor house, now covered in wisteria, roses and honeysuckle, and are laced with gently sloping paths linking the huge beds of rhododendrons, azaleas and roses.

The most picturesque of all the mid-Sussex gardens are those at **Leonardslee** (daily: April–Oct 9.30am–6pm; £5, £7 in May; ⓦ www.leonardslee.com), four miles southwest of Nymans, near the village of Crabtree; bus #107 from Brighton to Horsham passes by the garden gates. Set in a wooded valley, the seventy-acre gardens are crisscrossed by steep paths, which link six lakes created – like those at Sheffield Park – in the sixteenth century to power waterwheels for iron foundries. The range of flora is especially impressive here, featuring many hybrid species of rhododendron that were created specifically for this garden and are at their best in May when opening hours are specially extended (and admission charges raised). Wallabies, sika and fallow deer roam freely, adding to the Edenic atmosphere.

Arundel and around

The hilltop town of **ARUNDEL**, eighteen miles west of Brighton, has for seven centuries been the seat of the Dukes of Norfolk, whose fine castle looks over the valley of the River Arun. The medieval town's well-preserved appearance and picturesque setting draws in the crowds on summer weekends, but at any other time a visit reveals one of West Sussex's least spoilt old towns.

Arundel also has a unique place in English cricket: traditionally, the first match of every touring side is played against the Duke of Norfolk's XI on the ground beneath the castle.

Arundel Castle (April–Oct Mon–Fri & Sun noon–5pm; £7.50, grounds & chapel only £2.50; ⓦwww.arundelcastle.org), towering over the High Street, is what first catches the eye and, despite its medieval appearance, most of what you see is only a century old. The structure dated from Norman times, but was ruined during the Civil War, then lavishly reconstructed during the nineteenth century by the eighth, eleventh and fifteenth dukes. From the top of the keep, you can see the current duke's spacious residence and the pristine castle grounds. Inside the castle, the renovated quarters include the impressive Barons Hall and the library, which boasts paintings by Gainsborough, Holbein and Van Dyck. On the edge of the castle grounds, the fourteenth-century **Fitzalan Chapel** houses tombs of past dukes of Norfolk including twin effigies of the seventh duke – one as he looked when he died and, underneath, one of his emaciated corpse. The Catholic chapel belongs to the Norfolk estate, but is actually physically joined to the parish church of St Nicholas, whose entrance is in London Road. It is separated from the altar of the main Anglican church by an iron grille and a glass screen. Although traditionally Catholics, the dukes of Norfolk have shrewdly played down their papal allegiance in sensitive times – such as during the Tudor era when two of the third duke's nieces, Anne Boleyn and Catherine Howard, became Henry VIII's wives.

West of the parish church, further along London Road is Arundel's other major landmark, the towering Gothic bulk of **Arundel Cathedral**. Constructed in the 1870s by the fifteenth Duke of Norfolk over the town's former Catholic church, the cathedral's spire was designed by John Hansom, inventor of the hansom cab, the earliest taxi. Inside are the enshrined remains of St Philip Howard, the fourth duke's son, exhumed from the Fitzalan Chapel after his canonization in 1970. Following a wayward youth, Howard returned to the Catholic fold at a time when the Armada's defeat saw anti-Catholic feelings soar. Caught fleeing overseas and sentenced to death for praying for Spanish victory, he spent the next decade in the Tower of London, where he died. The cathedral's impressive outline is more appealing than the interior, but it fits in well with the townscape of the medieval seaport. The rest of Arundel is pleasant to wander round, with the antique-shop-lined Maltravers and Arun streets the most attractive thoroughfares.

Practicalities

The **train station** is half a mile south of the town centre over the river on the A27, with **buses** arriving either in the High Street or River Road. The **tourist office** is at 61 High St (June–Aug Mon–Fri 9am–5pm, Sat & Sun 10am–5pm; Sept–May Mon–Fri 9am–5pm, Sat & Sun 10am–3pm; ⓣ01903/882268, ⓦwww.sussexbythesea.com). For **accommodation**, try *Portreeves Acre*, The Causeway (ⓣ01903/883277; ❷) a welcoming place with en-suite rooms south of the Queen's Bridge, or the venerable *Swan Hotel* at the bottom of High Street (ⓣ01903/882314, ⓦwww.swan-hotel.co.uk; ❹), a fine old house with a cosy adjoining restaurant. *Castle View* (ⓣ01903/883029; ❷), next door to the tourist office above the tearooms of the same name, is reasonable, and neighbouring *Dukes Restaurant*, 65 High St, with its spectacular gilded ceiling, also has a few rooms available (ⓣ01903/883847, ⓦwww.dukesofarundel.com; ❷). Arundel's **youth hostel** (ⓣ01903/882204; closed Nov to mid-Feb) is in a large Georgian house by the river at Warningcamp, a mile and a half northeast

of town. You can **camp** at the hostel, or try the *Maynards* site
(℡01903/882075) at the top of the hill on the A27 two miles southeast of
town. First choice for reasonably priced, good-quality food is the **restaurant**
attached to the *White Hart* pub over the river at 3 Queen St
(℡01903/882374); alternatively try the *Red Lion*, on the High Street, for solid
pub grub and real ales. *Butlers Wine Bar*, 25 Tarrant St (℡01903/882222), is a
popular choice for steak lovers.

Bignor and Petworth

Six miles north of Arundel, the excavated second-century ruins of the **Bignor
Roman Villa** (March & April Tues–Sun 10am–5pm; May & Oct daily
10am–5pm; June–Sept daily 10am–6pm; £3.50) include some well-preserved
mosaics, of which the Ganymede is the most outstanding. The site, first excavated between 1811 and 1819, is superbly situated at the base of the South Downs
and features the longest extant section of mosaic in England, as well as the
remains of a hypocaust, the underfloor heating system developed by the Romans.

In the pretty little village of **PETWORTH**, eleven miles north of Arundel,
Petworth House (April–June, Sept & Oct Mon–Wed, Sat & Sun 1–5.30pm;
July & Aug Mon–Wed & Fri–Sun 1–5.30pm; park daily 8am–dusk; house £6;
park free; NT), one of the southeast's most impressive stately homes. Built in the
late seventeenth century, the house contains an outstanding art collection,
including paintings by Van Dyck, Titian, Gainsborough, Bosch, Reynolds, Blake
and Turner – the last a frequent guest here. Highlights of the interior decor are
Louis Laguerre's murals around the Grand Staircase and the Carved Room,
where carvings by Grinling Gibbons and Holbein's full-length portrait of
Henry VIII can be seen. The seven-hundred-acre grounds were landscaped by
Capability Brown and are considered one of his finest achievements.

Chichester

The county town of West Sussex and its only city, **CHICHESTER** is an attractive, if stuffy, market town, which began life as a Roman settlement – the Roman
cruciform street plan is still evident in the four-quadrant symmetry of the town
centre, spread around the Market Cross. The city has built itself up as one of
southern England's cultural centres, hosting the **Chichester Festival**
(Ⓦwww.chifest.org.uk) in early July, its focus a fairly safe programme of middle-
brow plays, though the studio theatre is a bit more adventurous. The racecourse
at **Goodwood Park**, north of the city, hosts one of England's most fashionable
racing events at the same time. The Gothic cathedral is the chief permanent
attraction in the city, but two miles west of the town are the restored Roman
ruins of **Fishbourne**, one of the most visited ancient sites in the county.

The City

The main streets lead off to the compass's cardinal points from the Gothic
Market Cross, a bulky octagonal rotunda topped by ornate finials and a large
crown, and built in 1501 to provide shelter for the market traders, although it
appears far too small for its function.

A short stroll down West Street brings you to the neat form of the **Cathedral**
(daily: Easter to mid-Sept 7.30am–7pm; mid-Sept to Easter 7.30am–5pm;
Ⓔvo@chicath.freeserve.co.uk), whose slender spire – a nineteenth-century

addition – is visible from out at sea. Building began in the 1070s, but the church was extensively rebuilt following a fire a century later and has been only minimally modified since about 1300, except for the spire and the unique, free-standing fifteenth-century bell tower, which now houses the cathedral shop. The **interior** is renowned for its contemporary devotional art, which includes a stained-glass window by Marc Chagall and an enormous altar-screen tapestry by John Piper. Other points of interest are the sixteenth-century painting in the north transept of the past bishops of Chichester, and the fourteenth-century Fitzalan tomb which inspired a poem by Philip Larkin. However, the highlight is a pair of **reliefs** in the south aisle, close to the tapestry – created around 1140, they show the raising of Lazarus and Christ at the gate of Bethany. Originally highly coloured, the reliefs once featured semi-precious stones set in the figures' eyes and are among the finest Romanesque stone carvings in England.

Across South Street in the well-preserved Georgian quadrant of the city known as the Pallants, you'll find **Pallant House Gallery**, 9 North Pallant (Tues–Sat 10am–5pm, Sun & public holidays 12.30am–5pm; £4; Ⓦwww.pallanthousegallery.com). Stone dodos stand guard over the gates of this fine mansion, which houses artefacts and furniture from the early eighteenth century. Modern works of art are also included, among them pieces by Henry Moore and Barbara Hepworth and George Sutherland's portrait of Walter Hussey, the former Dean of Chichester, who commissioned much of the cathedral's contemporary art.

Continuing in an anticlockwise direction around the town and crossing East Street to head north up Little London brings you to the **Chichester District Museum** (Tues–Sat 10am–5.30pm; free), housed in an old white weatherboarded corn store. Inside, the modest but entertaining display on local life includes a portable oven carried by Joe Faro, the city pieman, as well as the portable stocks used for the ritual humiliation of petty criminals. The **Guildhall** (June–Aug Sat noon–4pm; free), a branch museum within a thirteenth-century Franciscan church in the middle of Priory Park, at the north end of Little London, has some well-preserved medieval frescoes. It was formerly a town hall and court of law; the poet, painter and visionary William Blake was tried here for sedition.

Practicalities

A regular rail service runs from London Victoria to Chichester's **train station** on Stockbridge Road, the southern continuation of South Street, with the **bus station** across the road. From either station it's a ten-minute walk north to the Market Cross, passing the **tourist office** at 29a South St (April–Sept Mon–Sat 9.15am–5.15pm, Sun 10am–4pm; Oct–March closed Sun; Ⓣ01243/775888, Ⓦwww.chichester.gov.uk).

There should be no problem finding **accommodation**, except during the festival when it's advisable to book ahead. If you want to splash out, try the *Ship Hotel*, North St (Ⓣ01243/778000, Ⓦwww.shiphotel.com; ⑥), a comfortable and characterful inn in the centre of town. Less expensive central B&B options include the brick and flint *Riverside Lodge*, 7 Market Ave, outside the Pallants quarter (Ⓣ01243/783164 Ⓔtregeardavid@aol.com; ❷) or the two hundred-year-old *Friary Close*, Friary Lane (Ⓣ01243/527294, Ⓔfriaryclose@argonet.co.uk; ❹), just inside the city wall. You can **camp** at the *Red House Farm*, Brookers Lane, Earnley (Ⓣ01243/512959; closed Nov–Easter), six miles southwest of town, a mile or so from the beach.

The *Ship* is a good place for a **drink**, or you could try the *Park Tavern*, a convivial pub, serving excellent Gale's ales on Priory Lane, overlooking Priory Park. For something to **eat**, the intimate *Café Coco*, 13 South St (℡01243/786989) specializes in French cuisine and serves splendid set dinners from £11.95; and further down the street there's a branch of *Pizza Express*. Chichester's best Indian is the aptly named *Little London Indian Restaurant*, 38 Little London, off East Street (℡01243/537550).

Fishbourne Roman Palace

Fishbourne, two miles west of Chichester (March–July, Sept & Oct daily 10am–5pm; Aug daily 10am–6pm; Nov to mid-Dec daily 10am–4pm; mid-Dec to Feb Sat & Sun 10am–4pm; £4.50; ℗www.sussexpast.co.uk), is the largest and best-preserved Roman palace in the country. Roman relics have long been turning up here and in 1960 a workman unearthed their source – the site of a depot used by the invading Romans in 43 AD which, it is thought, later became the vast, hundred-room palace of the Romanized Celtic aristocrat Cogidubnus. A pavilion has been built over the north wing of the excavated remains, where floor mosaics depict Fishbourne's famous dolphin-riding cupid as well as the more usual geometric patterns. Like the remains at Bignor (see p.223), only the residential wing of the former quadrangle has been excavated – other parts of the dwelling fulfilled mundane service roles and probably lacked the mosaics which give both sites their singular appeal. The underfloor heating system has also been well restored and an audio-visual programme gives a fuller picture of the palace as it was in Roman times. The extensive gardens attempt to re-create the appearance of the palace grounds as they would have been then.

To get to Fishbourne take the **train** to Fishbourne station, turn right as you leave the station and the palace is a few minutes' walk away. Buses #700 and #56 from Chichester also run to Fishbourne; both services drop you to the bottom of Salt Hill Road, from where it's a clearly signposted five-minute walk to Fishbourne.

Travel details

Buses

For information on all local and national bus services, contact Traveline: ℡0870/608 2 608, ℗www.traveline.org.uk.

Trains

For information on all local and national rail services, contact National Rail Enquiries: ℡08457/48 49 50, ℗www.nationalrail.co.uk.

Arundel to: London Victoria (Mon–Sat 2 hourly, Sun 1 hourly; 1hr 20min).

Battle to: Hastings (hourly; 15min); London Charing Cross (2 hourly; 1hr 15min); Sevenoaks (hourly; 45min); Tunbridge Wells (hourly; 30min).

Brighton to: Chichester (2 hourly; 1hr); Gatwick Airport (every 10–20min; 25–40min); Hastings (2 hourly; 1hr 10min); Lewes (Mon–Sat every 10–20min, Sun 2 hourly; 15min); London Victoria (2 hourly; 1hr–1hr 20min); London King's Cross (Mon–Sat 4 hourly, Sun 2 hourly; 1hr 15min); Oxford (3 hourly; 2hr 50min); Portsmouth Harbour (hourly; 1hr 25min).

Broadstairs to: London Victoria (Mon–Sat 2 hourly, Sun 1 hourly; 2hr); Ramsgate (every 15–20min; 5min).

Canterbury East to: Dover Priory (Mon–Sat 2 hourly, Sun 1 hourly; 30min); London Victoria (Mon–Sat 2 hourly, Sun 1 hourly; 1hr 30min). Canterbury West to: London Charing Cross (hourly; 1hr 40min); Ramsgate (hourly; 20min).

Chatham to: Dover Priory (Mon–Sat 2 hourly, Sun 1 hourly; 1hr 10min); London Victoria (Mon–Sat every 10–30min, Sun 2 hourly; 1hr).

Chichester to: London Victoria (Mon–Sat 2 hourly, Sun 1 hourly; 1hr 45min); Portsmouth Harbour (Mon–Sat 2 hourly, Sun 1 hourly; 40min).

Dover Priory to: Folkestone Central (Mon–Sat 2 hourly, Sun 1 hourly; 15min); London Charing Cross (Mon–Sat 2 hourly, Sun hourly; 1hr 40min); London Victoria (Mon–Sat 2 hourly, Sun 1 hourly; 1hr 50min).

Eastbourne to: Gatwick Airport (2 hourly; 1hr); Hastings (Mon–Sat 3 hourly, Sun hourly; 40min); Lewes (Mon–Sat every 10–30min, Sun hourly; 20–30min); London Victoria (Mon–Sat 2 hourly, Sun hourly; 1hr 40min).

Farnham to: Aldershot (for connections to London Waterloo; Mon–Sat 1–2 hourly, Sun 1 hourly; 10min); Guildford (Mon–Sat 1–2 hourly, Sun hourly; 45min).

Guildford to: Farnham (Mon–Sat 1–2 hourly, Sun 1 hourly; 45min); London Waterloo (Mon–Sat 3–4 hourly, Sun 2 hourly; 40min).

Hastings to: Gatwick Airport (hourly; 1hr 40min); London Victoria (hourly; 2hr); Rye (1 hourly; 20min).

Lewes to: Brighton (Mon–Sat 4 hourly, Sun 2 hourly; 15min); London Victoria (Mon–Sat 2 hourly, Sun hourly; 1hr 15min).

Maidstone East to: London Victoria (Mon–Sat 2 hourly, Sun 1 hourly; 1hr); London Charing Cross (hourly; 1 hr).

Margate to: Canterbury West (hourly; 35–45min); London Victoria (Mon–Sat 2 hourly, Sun 1 hourly; 1hr 40min).

Ramsgate to: London Victoria (Mon–Sat 2 hourly, Sun 1 hourly; 2hr).

Rochester to: Dover Priory (Mon–Sat 2 hourly, Sun 1 hourly; 1hr 10min); Herne Bay (Mon–Sat 2 hourly; Sun hourly; 45min); London Victoria (Mon–Sat 3–4 hourly, Sun 2 hourly; 40min).

Rye to: Hastings (1 hourly; 20min).

Sandwich to: Dover Priory (hourly; 30min); Ramsgate (hourly; 15min).

Sevenoaks to: London Blackfriars (Mon–Sat 2 hourly; 1hr); London Victoria (Mon–Sat 1 hourly, Sun 2 hourly; 1hr).

Tunbridge Wells to: London Charing Cross (Mon–Sat 2 hourly, Sun 1 hourly; 50min).

Whitstable to: London Victoria (hourly; 1hr 20min); Ramsgate (Mon–Sat 2 hourly, Sun 1 hourly; 30min).

Hampshire, Dorset and Wiltshire

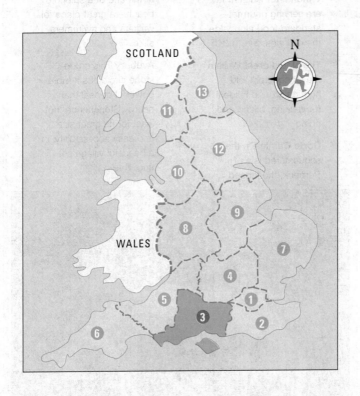

CHAPTER 3 Highlights

* **Cowes Week, Isle of Wight** This yachting jamboree draws thousands, infecting even the staunchest landlubbers. See p.241

* **Wykeham Arms, Winchester** Ancient tavern serving gourmet-standard food alongside the real ales. See p.245

* **The New Forest** William the Conqueror's old hunting ground is ideal for walking, biking and riding. See p.246

* **Corfe Castle** On the sequestered Isle of Purbeck, the jagged keep and shattered remains of this fortress make it one of the country's most dramatic ruins. See p.253

* **Durdle Door** This crumbly natural arch stands at the end of a splendid beach – a great place for walkers and swimmers alike. See p.254

* **Avebury** This crude stone circle has a more powerful appeal than nearby Stonehenge, not least for its great size and easy accessibility, in a peaceful village setting. See p.271

Hampshire, Dorset and Wiltshire

The distant past is perhaps more tangible in **Hampshire**, **Dorset** and **Wiltshire** than in any other part of England. Predominantly rural, these three counties overlap substantially with the ancient kingdom of **Wessex**, whose most famous ruler, Alfred, repulsed the Danes in the ninth century and came close to establishing the first unified state in England. Before Wessex came into being, however, many earlier civilizations had left their stamp on the region. The chalky uplands of Wiltshire boast several of Europe's greatest Neolithic sites, including **Stonehenge** and **Avebury**, while in Dorset you'll find **Maiden Castle**, the most striking Iron Age hill fort in the country, and the **Cerne Abbas Giant**, source of many a legend. The Romans tramped all over these southern counties, leaving the most conspicuous signs of their occupation at the amphitheatre of **Dorchester** – though that town is more closely associated with the novels of Thomas Hardy and his distinctively gloomy vision of Wessex.

None of the landscapes of this region could be described as grand or wild, but the countryside is consistently seductive, its appeal exemplified by the crumbling fossil-bearing cliffs around **Lyme Regis**, the managed woodlands of the **New Forest** and the gentle, open curves of **Salisbury Plain**. Its towns are also generally modest and slow-paced, with the notable exceptions of the two great maritime bases of **Portsmouth** and, to a lesser extent, **Southampton**, a fair proportion of whose visitors are simply passing through on their way to the more genteel pleasures of the **Isle of Wight**. This is something of an injustice, though neither place can compete with the two most interesting cities in this part of England – **Salisbury** and **Winchester**, each of which possesses a stupendous cathedral amid an array of other historic sights. Of the region's great houses, **Wilton**, **Stourhead**, **Longleat** and **Kingston Lacy** are the ones that attract the crowds, but every cranny has its medieval church, manor house or unspoilt country inn – there are few parts of England in which an aimless meander can be so rewarding. But if it's straightforward seaside fun you're after, **Bournemouth** leads the way, with **Weymouth** and **Lyme Regis** heading the ranks of the minor resorts, along with the yachties' havens over on the Isle of Wight.

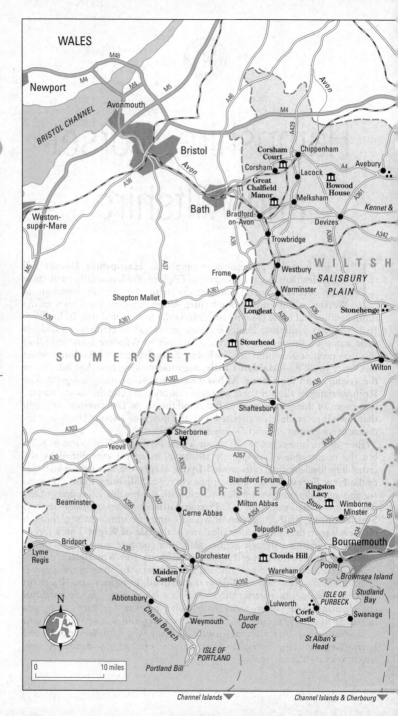

WALES

Newport

M48

M4

M4

M5

Avonmouth

BRISTOL CHANNEL

Weston-
super-Mare

M5

Bristol

Avon

A38

Bath

A46

M4

A429

A4

Corsham
Court

Chippenham

Corsham

Lacock

Avebury

Great
Chalfield
Manor

Bowood
House

Melksham

A361

Kennet &

Bradford-
on-Avon

Devizes

A36

Trowbridge

A360

A342

Frome

Westbury

WILTSH

SALISBURY
PLAIN

Shepton Mallet

A361

Warminster

A36

A39

A361

Longleat

A350

Stonehenge

SOMERSET

Stourhead

A303

A303

Wilton

A30

A303

Shaftesbury

A350

A354

Sherborne

A357

A362

Yeovil

A30

Blandford Forum

Kingston
Lacy

Wimborne
Minster

A35

Beaminster

A37

A356

DORSET

Cerne Abbas

A364

Milton Abbas

Stour

Bridport

A35

Tolpuddle

A31

Bournemouth

Lyme
Regis

Dorchester

Clouds Hill

Poole

A34

Brownsea Island

Maiden
Castle

Wareham

A352

ISLE OF
PURBECK

Studland
Bay

Abbotsbury

Lulworth

Corfe
Castle

Swanage

N

Weymouth

Durdle
Door

St Alban's
Head

Chesil Beach

ISLE OF
PORTLAND

Portland Bill

0   10 miles

Channel Islands ▼

Channel Islands & Cherbourg ▼

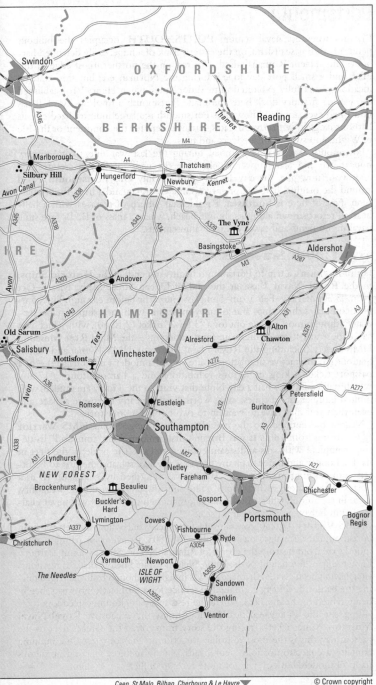

Caen, St Malo, Bilbao, Cherbourg & Le Havre ▼   © Crown copyright

Portsmouth

Britain's foremost naval station, **PORTSMOUTH** occupies the bulbous peninsula of Portsea Island, on the eastern flank of a huge, easily defended harbour. The ancient Romans raised a fortress on the northernmost edge of this inlet, and a small port developed during the Norman era, but this strategic location wasn't fully exploited until Tudor times, when Henry VII established the world's first dry dock here and made Portsmouth a royal dockyard. It has flourished ever since and nowadays Portsmouth is a large industrialized city, its harbour clogged with naval frigates, ferries bound for the continent or the Isle of Wight, and swarms of dredgers and tugs.

Portsmouth was heavily bombed during the last war due to its military importance and bland tower blocks from the nadir of British architectural endeavour now give the city an ugly profile. Only **Old Portsmouth**, based around the original harbour, preserves some Georgian and a little Tudor character. East of here is **Southsea**, a residential suburb of terraces with a half-hearted resort strewn along its shingle beach, where a mass of B&Bs face stoic naval monuments and tawdry seaside amusements.

The Royal Naval Base

For most visitors, a trip to Portsmouth begins and ends at the **Historic Ships**, in the **Royal Naval Base** at the end of Queen Street (daily: March–Oct 10am–5.30pm; Nov–Feb 10am–5pm; last entry 1hr before closing). The complex comprises three ships and as many museums, with each ship visitable separately, though most people opt for a "3 for 2" ticket (£12.50), with which you can choose any three of the main four attractions – the Mary Rose Museum, HMS *Victory* (including the Royal Naval Museum), HMS *Warrior* and Action Stations (an interactive simulation of life aboard a modern naval frigate) – or a passport ticket, taking in various exhibitions and a harbour-tour (£17.50), which will easily take half a day. Note that visits to the *Victory* are guided, with limited numbers at set times, so it's worth booking early to ensure a place, and even then you may have to wait up to two hours for your turn.

Nearest the entrance to the complex is the youngest ship, **HMS Warrior** (£6), dating from 1860. It was Britain's first armoured, or "iron-clad" battleship, complete with sails and steam engines, and was the pride of the fleet in its day. Longer and faster than any previous naval vessel, and the first to be fitted with washing machines, the *Warrior* was described by Napoleon III as a "black snake amongst the rabbits". The ship displays a wealth of weaponry, including cannons, rifles, pistols and sabres, though the *Warrior* was never challenged in her twenty-two years at sea.

HMS Victory (£6.50) was already forty years old when she set sail from Portsmouth for Trafalgar on September 14, 1805, returning in triumph three months later, but bearing the corpse of Admiral Nelson. Shot by a sniper from a French ship at the height of the battle, Nelson expired below decks three hours later, having been assured that victory was in sight. Although badly damaged during the battle, the *Victory* continued in service for a further twenty years, before being retired to the dry dock where she rests today in gleaming splendour.

Opposite the *Victory*, various buildings house the exhaustive **Royal Naval Museum** (same ticket). Tracing the story from Alfred the Great's fleet to the present day, this is the most resistible attraction in the complex. One building contains a collection of jolly figureheads, Nelson memorabilia and numerous nautical models, but coverage of more recent conflicts is very light.

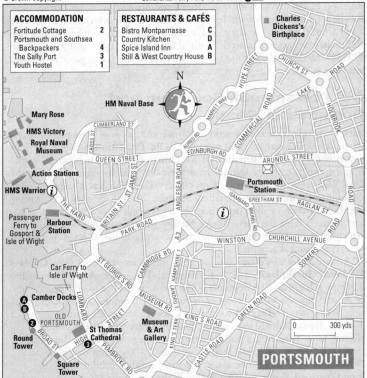

© Crown copyright — Continental Ferry Port, M3 London &

Charles Dickens's Birthplace

HM Naval Base

Mary Rose
HMS Victory
Royal Naval Museum
Action Stations
HMS Warrior (i)
Passenger Ferry to Gosport & Isle of Wight
Harbour Station
Car Ferry to Isle of Wight
Camber Docks
OLD PORTSMOUTH
Round Tower
Square Tower
St Thomas Cathedral
Museum & Art Gallery
Portsmouth Station

0   300 yds

PORTSMOUTH

Southsea, IoW Hovercraft, Southsea Castle, Royal Marine Museum, D-Day Museum, & (i)

In a shed behind the *Victory* are the remains of the **Mary Rose** (£6), Henry VIII's flagship, which capsized before his eyes off Spithead in 1545 while engaging French intruders, sinking swiftly with almost all her seven-hundred-strong crew. In 1982 a massive conservation project successfully raised the remains of the hull, which silt had preserved beneath the seabed. The ship itself is less absorbing than the thousands of objects retrieved near the wreck, which are displayed in an exhibition close to the *Warrior*. Videos of the recovery operation are shown, as well as depictions of life aboard a sixteenth-century warship.

From the harbour

The naval theme is continued at **Submarine World** on Haslar Jetty in Gosport (daily: April–Oct 10am–5.30pm; Nov–March 10am–4.30pm; last tour 1hr before closing; £4), reachable from Harbour train station jetty, just south of the entrance to the Royal Naval Base, on the passenger ferry (daily 5.30am–midnight; £1.60 return) or the water-bus, which gives you a half-hour tour of the harbour before dropping you in Gosport (Easter–Oct 10.30am–5pm; £3.50). The museum elaborates evocatively on the long history of submersible craft, and you'll get a guided tour inside HMS *Alliance*.

From the pontoon beside HMS *Warrior*, regular ferries depart (Wed & Sun 2.45pm; £6.95, including entry to the fort) for the mile-long ride to **Spitbank Fort**, an offshore bastion of granite, iron and brick little altered since its construction in the 1860s. With over fifty rooms linked by passages and steps on two floors, the complex includes a 400-foot deep well, which still draws fresh water from below the seafloor, and an inner courtyard complete with a café and sheltered terrace. The artificial island hosts supper nights and parties – call ☎01329/664286 or ask at the tourist office for details – and you can also stay here (see p.235).

Old Portsmouth, Southsea and Portchester Castle

Back at the Harbour train station in Portsmouth, it's a well-signposted twenty-minute walk south to what remains of **Old Portsmouth**. Along the way, you pass the simple **Cathedral of St Thomas** on the High Street, whose original twelfth-century features have been obscured by rebuilding after the Civil War and again in the twentieth century. The High Street ends at a maze of cobbled Georgian streets huddling behind a fifteenth-century wall protecting the **Camber**, or old port, where Walter Raleigh landed the first potatoes and tobacco from the New World. Nearby, the Round and Square Towers, which punctuate the Tudor fortifications, are popular vantage points for observing nautical activities.

The remainder of Portsmouth has little else of interest apart from **Charles Dickens' Birthplace** at 393 Commercial Rd (daily: April–Sept 10am–5.30pm; £2.50), half a mile north of the town centre, but there are more sites of military interest a mile or so east in the suburb of Southsea. The main attraction here is the **D-Day Museum** on Clarence Esplanade (daily: April–Oct 10am–5.30pm; Nov–March 10am–5pm; last entry 1hr before closing; £5), relating how Portsmouth had a chance to avenge its wartime bombing by being the main assembly point for the D-Day invasion, code-named "Operation Overlord". The museum's most striking exhibit is the 270-feet long **Overlord Embroidery**, which tells the tale of the Normandy landings. Next door to the museum, the squat profile of **Southsea Castle** (April–Oct daily 10am–5.30pm; £2.50), built from the remains of Beaulieu Abbey (see p.247), may have been the spot from where Henry VIII watched the *Mary Rose* sink in 1545. A mile further along the shoreside South Parade, just past South Parade pier, the **Royal Marines Museum** (daily: June–Sept 10am–5pm; Oct–May 10am–4.30pm; last entry 1hr before closing; £4) describes the origins and greatest campaigns of the navy's elite fighting force.

The city's outstanding monument lies six miles north of the centre – just past the burgeoning marina development at Port Solent. **Portchester Castle** (daily: April–Sept 10am–6pm; Oct 10am–5pm; Nov–March 10am–4pm; £3; EH) was built by the Romans in the third century and is the finest surviving example in northern Europe. Its walls are over twenty-feet high and incorporate some twenty bastions, making it so robust that the Normans felt no need to alter it when they moved in. Later, a castle was built within Portchester's precincts by Henry II, which Richard II extended and Henry V used as his garrison when assembling the army that was to fight the Battle of Agincourt. Today its grassy enclosure makes a sheltered spot for a congenial game of cricket or a kickabout with a football.

Practicalities

Portsmouth's main **train station** is in the city centre, but the line continues to **Harbour Station**, the most convenient stop for the main sights and old town.

Passenger **ferries** leave from the jetty at the Harbour station for Ryde, on the Isle of Wight (see p.238) and Gosport, on the other side of Portsmouth Harbour. Wightlink car ferries depart from the ferry port off Gunwharf Road for Fishbourne on the Isle of Wight (see p.237). There are three **tourist offices** (all ☎023/9282 6722, ⊛www.portsmouthharbour.co.uk) in Portsmouth, one on the Hard, by the entrance to the dockyards (daily: Easter–Sept 9.30am–5.45pm; Oct–Easter 9.30am–5.15pm); another in the library at Guildhall Square, near the main train station (Mon–Sat 10am–5pm); and a third on Southsea's seafront, next to the Sea Life Centre (daily 9.30am–5.45pm).

One of the nicest **places to stay** is the *Sally Port*, opposite the cathedral at 57–58 High St (☎023/9282 1860; ❹), an old inn with sloping floors. *Fortitude Cottage*, 51 Broad St (☎023/9282 3748, ✉fortcott@aol.com; ❷) is a beamed harbourside cottage overlooking the boats. Southsea has a better choice of B&Bs, and also has *Portsmouth and Southsea Backpackers,* 4 Florence Rd (☎023/9283 2495 or 9282 2963, ⊛www.portsmouthbackpackers.co.uk), a fifty-bed **hostel** at the east end of Clarence Esplanade (bus #5, #6, #7 from the Harbour station, or any bus to South Parade Pier). *Portsmouth YHA* is at Wymering Manor, Old Wymering Lane, Cosham (☎023/9237 5661, ⊛www.yha.org.uk), an attractive Tudor manor ten minutes west of Cosham train station (bus #5 and #12 from the Harbour station as far as Cosham Health Centre, from where take the first left). You'll find more unusual accommodation at *Spitbank Fort* (☎01329/664286 or 07771/666 6289, ⊛www.spitbankfort.co.uk; ❷), a mile from Portsmouth Harbour and accessible by ferry, where two very basic rooms are available between April and September (weather permitting).

Places to eat are surprisingly scarce in the old town; the best restaurants are all in Southsea. Among these, *Bistro Montparnasse*, 103 Palmerston Rd, Southsea (☎023/9281 6754) is distinguished for its good-quality French and seafood dishes, while *Country Kitchen*, 59 Marmion Rd (☎023/9281 1425) is a more relaxed vegetarian and vegan restaurant with newspapers on hand and free coffee refills. In Old Porstmouth, head for the *Spice Island Inn* and the next-door *Still & West Country House*, in Bath Square, old hostelries with tables outside overlooking the Solent and a great range of hot and cold dishes.

Southampton and around

A glance at the map gives some idea of the strategic maritime importance of **SOUTHAMPTON**, which stands on a triangular peninsula formed at the place where the rivers Itchen and Test flow into Southampton Water, an eight-mile inlet from the Solent. Sure enough, Southampton has figured in numerous stirring events: it witnessed the exodus of Henry V's Agincourt-bound army, the Pilgrim Fathers' departure in the *Mayflower* in 1620 and the maiden voyages of such ships as the *Queen Mary* and the *Titanic*. Unfortunately, since its pummelling by the Luftwaffe and some disastrous postwar planning, the thousand-year-old city is now a sprawling conurbation with little to recommend it for anything more than a fleeting visit.

Core of the modern town is the **Civic Centre**, a short walk east of the train station. Its clock tower is the most distinctive feature of the skyline, and it houses an excellent **art gallery** that's particularly strong on twentieth-century British artists such as Sutherland, Piper and Spencer (Tues–Sat 10am–5pm, Sun 1–4pm; free). The **Western Esplanade**, curving southward from the station, runs alongside the best remaining bits of the old city **walls**. Rebuilt after a French attack in 1338, they feature towers with evocatively chilly names – Windwhistle, Catchcold and **God's House Tower** – the last of these, at the southern end of the old town in Winkle Street, houses a **Museum of Archeology**, though lack of funding has meant that this is currently indefinitely closed except to groups by prior arrangement (☎023/8063 5904). Best preserved of the city's seven gates is **Bargate**, at the opposite end of the old town, at the head of the High Street; an elaborate structure, cluttered with lions, classical figures and machicolations (defensive apertures through which missiles could be dropped), it was formerly the guildhall and court house.

Other ancient buildings survive amid the piecemeal redevelopment of the High Street area. The oldest church is **St Michael's**, to the west of the High Street, with a twelfth-century font of black Tournai marble. The nearby **Tudor House Museum**, in Bugle Street (Tues–Fri 10am–noon & 1–5pm, Sat 10am–noon & 1–4pm, Sun 2–5pm; free), is an impressive fifteenth-century, timber-framed building, its grand banqueting hall and reconstructed Tudor garden outshining the sundry exhibits of Georgian, Victorian and early twentieth-century social history. Down at the southwest corner of the old town, by the seafront, the **Wool House** is a fine fourteenth-century stone warehouse; formerly used as a jail for Napoleonic prisoners, it now houses a **Maritime Museum** (same times as Tudor House Museum; free) with accounts of the heyday of ocean liners, and includes a huge model of the *Queen Mary* and various mementoes from the *Titanic*. The museum also offers the opportunity to listen to the recorded voices of various survivors of the *Titanic* tragedy relating their experiences, while *Titanic* obsessives can follow a *"Titanic* Trail" walking tour around Southampton – ask for the free pamphlet at the tourist office.

Practicalities

The central **train station** is located on Blechynden Terrace, west of the Civic Centre; the **bus** and **coach stations** are immediately south and north of the Civic Centre. For details of **ferry** crossings to the Isle of Wight, see box opposite. The **tourist office** is at 9 Civic Centre Rd (Mon, Tues & Thurs–Sat 8.30am–5.30pm, Wed 10am–5.30pm; ☎023/8083 3333, ⓦwww.southampton.gov.uk).

Southampton isn't a wildly attractive **place to stay**, but there are plenty of business hotels and commercial guest houses in the centre, including *Linden*, just north of the train station on the Polygon (☎023/8022 5653; ❶), which has bright, good-value rooms. For a grander atmosphere, try the four-hundred-year-old *Star* (☎023/8033 9939; ❺) or the slightly younger *Dolphin* (☎023/8033 9955; ❹); both hotels are halfway down the High Street and provide accommodation with all the antique trimmings. The best **eating** choices are clustered on Oxford Street, off Bernard Steet from the High Street, where you'll find the non-smoking *Town House* at no. 59 for vegetarian specialities alongside meat and fish dishes; *Kuti's Brasserie* at no. 39, a moderately priced Bengali restaurant, and the *Oxford Brasserie* at no. 35, a relaxed place for baguettes, salads, pastas and fuller evening meals. As for **pubs**, the ancient *Red Lion*, complete with minstrels' gallery at 55 High St, is a more charismatic alternative to the bars at the *Star* and *Dolphin* hotels.

The Isle of Wight

Having achieved county status after years of being lumped in with Hampshire, the **Isle of Wight** still has difficulty in shaking off its image as a mere adjunct of rural southern England – comfortably off, scrupulously tidy and desperately unadventurous. Yet the island, which measures less than 23 miles at its widest point, packs a surprising variety of landscapes and coastal scenery within its bounds. North of the chalk ridge that runs across its centre, the terrain is low-lying woodland and pasture, deeply cut by meandering rivers, while southwards is open chalky downland fringed by high cliffs. Two **Heritage Coast** paths follow the best of the shoreline, while several historic buildings and a splendid array of well-preserved Victoriana provide added interest. Chief of these is **Osborne House**, near Cowes, originally designed as a summer retreat for Victoria and the royal family, later the queen's permanent home after Albert died. Several other great Victorians also had close associations with the island: Tennyson lived at Freshwater, and Dickens stayed and wrote in Winterbourne House in Bonchurch – the town where Swinburne grew up and is now buried.

If you're dependent upon **public transport**, pick up the Southern Vectis bus route map and timetable (50p) from the tourist office, ferry office or bus station at your point of arrival. The company's hourly Island Explorer buses (routes #7 and #7A) run all round the island in about four hours. A Rover Ticket allows you unlimited travel on the bus network, costing £6.70 for a Day Rover, £10.90 for a Two-Day Rover and £27.50 for a Weekly Rover. The **rail line** is a short east-coast stretch linking Ryde, Sandown and Shanklin. **Cycling** is a very popular way of getting around the Isle of Wight, especially

Sea routes to the Isle of Wight

All the prices quoted are for a ninety-day (Wightlink and Red Funnel) or one-year (Hovertravel) standard return ticket. Wightlink and Red Funnel offer day and half-day returns as well as a range of other short-break deals for cars, with discounts of around 35 percent.

Hovertravel

☎023/9281 1000 or 01983/811000, ⓦwww.hovertravel. co.uk. Year-round hovercraft service from Southsea to Ryde Mon–Fri 7.10am–8.10pm, Sat & Sun 8.15am–8.10pm (early Oct to early April last sailing at 7.35pm); every 30min; 10min; £9.10 for foot passengers only.

Red Funnel

☎023/8033 4010, ⓦwww.redfunnel. co.uk. Year-round ferries on two routes, one of them a high-speed service: **Southampton–East Cowes** daily 6am–1am; hourly; 55min; £9 for foot passengers; £65 for car and driver plus £9 per passenger. **Southampton–West Cowes** high-speed service daily 5.50am–10.35pm (Mon–Wed & Sun) or 11.40pm

(Thurs–Sat); hourly; 22min; £13 for foot passengers only.

Wightlink Ferries

☎0870/582 7744, ⓦwww.wightlink. co.uk. Three year-round ferry routes, including a faster but more expensive catamaran service to Ryde: **Portsmouth–Ryde** catamaran 4.30am–12.40am; 1–2 hourly; 15min; £11.70 for foot passengers only. **Portsmouth–Fishbourne** ferry 3am–1.30am; 1–2 hourly; 35min; £9.50 for foot passengers; £65.50–£81.90 according to season and day for car and driver plus £9.50 per passenger. **Lymington–Yarmouth** ferry (June–Dec) 4am–1am; 1–2 hourly; 30min; £9.50 for foot passengers; £65.50–£81.90 according to season and day for car and driver plus £9.50 per passenger.

as bikes are carried free on all ferry services, but beware that in summer the narrow lanes can get very busy. For **information** about the whole island, call ☎01983/813818, consult ⓦwww.islandbreaks.co.uk, or call the individual tourist offices detailed below.

Ryde and around

As a major ferry terminal, **RYDE** is the first landfall many visitors make on the island, but one where few choose to linger, despite some grand nineteenth-century architecture and decent beach amusements. The **tourist office** (March–Oct Mon–Sat 9am–5.30pm, Sun 9am–5pm; Nov–Feb daily 9am–4.30pm; ☎01983/562905), **bus station**, **Hovercraft terminal** and **Esplanade train station** (the northern terminus of the Island Line train line, which runs south to Shanklin) are all located near the base of the pier. **Boat trips** to the Solent forts leave from Ryde jetty; for details contact Solent & Wight Line Cruises (☎01983/564602).

Accommodation is available at *Yelf's Hotel* on Union Street (☎01983/564062; ❸), right in the town centre; it's one of Ryde's oldest hotels, though mainly geared up for business travellers. Inexpensive **B&Bs** include the *Trentham Guest House*, 38 The Strand (☎01983/563418; ❶), and the similar *Vine Guest House*, 16 Castle St (☎01983/566633; ❶) – both are just south of the Esplanade. Central **eating** options can be found around Union Street, such as *Joe Daflo's Café Bar* at no. 24 and the elegant *Blue Moon* on Castle Street.

As elsewhere on the island, just a couple of miles can remove you from an undistinguished urban setting into one of idyllic rusticity. Just outside the village of Binstead, two miles west of Ryde's centre, lies one of the island's earliest Christian relics, **Quarr Abbey**, founded in 1132. Only stunted ruins survived the Dissolution and ensuing plunder of ready-cut stone, although an ivy-clad archway still hangs picturesquely over a farm track. In 1907 a new abbey was founded just west of the ruins, a striking red-brick building with Byzantine overtones (daily 9am–9pm; Vespers 5pm).

Three miles south of Ryde on the busy A3055 Sandown road, the ancient village of **BRADING** boasts a surprisingly disparate collection of ancient and modern sites. Just south of the village are the remains of **Brading Roman Villa** (April–Oct daily 9.30am–5pm; £2.75), one of two such villas on the island (the other is in Newport; see p.242), both of which were probably sites of bacchanalian worship. The Brading site is renowned for its superbly preserved mosaics, including intact images of Medusa and depictions of Orpheus, associated with the cult of Bacchus.

Signposted off the A3055 less than a mile northwest of Brading, **Nunwell House** (July to early Sept Mon–Wed 1–5pm; £4) was where, in 1647, Charles I spent his last night of freedom before being taken to Carisbrooke Castle (see p.242) and thence to his eventual execution in Whitehall. The house has been in the Oglander family for nearly nine hundred years, with the present building being a mix of Jacobean and Georgian styles with Victorian additions. Guided tours take place at 1.30pm, 2.30pm and 3.30pm, and the entry ticket includes a free guide booklet.

Sandown and Shanklin

The two eastern resorts of Sandown and Shanklin merge into each other across the sandy reach of Sandown Bay, representing the island's holiday-making epicentre. **SANDOWN**, a traditional bucket-and-spade resort, appropriately possesses the island's only surviving pleasure **Pier**, bedecked with amusement arcades, cafeterias, dodgems and a large theatre with nightly entertainment in season. At the northern end of the Esplanade, the **Tiger and Big Cat Sanctuary and Isle of Wight Zoological Gardens** (Easter–Oct daily 10am–5pm; rest of year may also open Sun & school half-term holidays; check on ☎01983/403883; £5.75) is the best of a range of family-oriented entertainments, containing several species of tigers, panthers and other big cats, some of which are heading for extinction in the wild. There are also some frisky lemurs and monkeys, and an exhaustive selection of spiders and snakes.

SHANKLIN, with its auburn cliffs, Old Village and scenic Chine, has a marginally more sophisticated veneer than its northern neighbour. The rose-clad, thatched charm of its **Old Village** is a bit syrupy, but the adjacent **Shanklin Chine** (daily: Easter–May & Oct 10am–5pm; June–Sept 10am–10pm; £2.50), a twisting pathway descending a mossy ravine and decorated on summer nights with fairy lights, is undeniably picturesque, popular since early Victorian times when local resident John Keats drew his Romantic imagery from the environs.

Sandown's **tourist office** is at 8 High St (Easter–Oct Mon–Sat 9am–5.30pm, Sun 9am–5pm; Nov–Easter irregular hours, alternating with Shanklin tourist office; ☎01983/403886); Shanklin's is at 67 High St (same hours; ☎01983/862942). Both towns have Island Line train stations about half a mile inland from their beachfront centres. For **accommodation**, try *St Catherine's Hotel,* 1 Winchester Park Rd, (☎01983/402392; ❸), just five minutes walk from Sandown's beach, or *Mount Brocas*, 15 Beachfield Rd (☎01983/406276; ❷), a good-value B&B at the west end of High Street, Sandown, also very close to the beach. More secluded is *Luccombe Hall*, Luccombe Road, a mile from Shanklin's Old Village (☎01983/862719, Ⓦwww.luccombehall.co.uk; ❺); originally built as the summer palace for the Bishop of Portsmouth, it now sports two pools. *Sandown Youth Hostel*, right in the centre of Sandown on Fitzroy Street (☎01983/402651), lies only a few minutes walk from the beach. For **meals** and refreshment, head for the *King's Bar Café*, a continental-style licensed café with great views over the sea, or *Francine's Restaurant* (☎01983/403289), which serves a good variety of English and seafood dishes, both on Sandown's High Street. In Shanklin, the *Fisherman's Cottage* is an atmospheric seafaring pub with wholesome food, located at the southern end of the Esplanade on Appley Beach.

Ventnor

The attractive seaside resort of **VENTNOR** sits at the foot of St Boniface Down, the island's highest point at 787ft. The Down periodically disintegrates into landslides, creating the jumbled terraces known locally as the **Undercliff**, whose sheltered, south-facing aspect, mild winter temperatures and thick carpet of undergrowth have contributed to the former fishing village becoming a fashionable health spa. Thanks to these unique factors, the town possesses rather more character than the island's other resorts, its Gothic Revival buildings clinging dizzily to zigzagging bends.

The floral terraces of the **Cascade** curve down to the slender Esplanade and narrow beach, where former boat builders' cottages now provide more recreational services. From the Esplanade, it's a pleasant mile-long stroll to Ventnor's famous **Botanical Gardens**, where 22 landscaped acres of subtropical vegetation flourish. Ventnor's **tourist office** is at 34 High St (Easter–Oct Mon–Sat 9.30am–5.30pm, Sun 10am–3pm; ☎01983/853625). For **accommodation**, try the *Spyglass Inn* on the Esplanade (☎01983/855338; ❸), which has a few self-contained rooms with balconies, or, a few doors down, *St Martin's*

(℡01983/852345; ❷), with sea views. East of Ventnor, in the quaintly villagey suburb of Bonchurch, the *Horseshoe Bay House Café* in Horseshoe Bay offers accommodation right on the beach (℡01983/856800; ❷). There's also an excellent **café** here, where you can eat seafood at outdoor tables from which there are 180-degree views. In Ventnor town centre, the *Thistle Café*, 30 Pier St, offers inexpensive seafood and vegetarian snacks and meals.

Appuldurcombe House and St Catherine's Point

Follow the B3327 for a couple of miles inland, over St Boniface Down, through arable farmland and past market gardens, to Wroxall, where a track leads left for half a mile to the ruins of **Appuldurcombe House** (daily: May–Sept 10am–6pm; Oct to mid-Dec & Jan–April 10am–4pm; £2; EH), the island's grandest pre-Victorian house. The present mansion was built in the late eighteenth century in the Palladian style, with gardens landscaped by Capability Brown. Semi-abandoned in the early twentieth century, Appuldurcombe has been preserved in a picturesque state of decay, a partially roofed but intact shell with a stately eastern facade, a spring-fed fountain and an impressive outlook over a fold in the downs.

The western Undercliff begins to recede at the village of Niton, where a foot-path continues to the most southerly tip of the island, **St Catherine's Point**. The prominent landmark on the downs behind it is **St Catherine's Oratory**, known locally as the "Pepper Pot", and originally a lighthouse, reputedly built in 1325 as an act of expiation by Walter de Goditon, who had attempted to pil-fer a cargo of wine owned by a monastic community. A short distance west, **Blackgang Chine** (daily: end March to June & early Sept to Oct 10am–5.30pm; July to early Sept 10am–10pm; £6.50) opened as a landscaped garden in 1843, gradually evolved into a theme park – possibly the world's first – and now offers a half-dozen exhibits from Cowboy Town to Jungleland.

Yarmouth and the western tip

Linked to Lymington in the New Forest by car ferry, the pleasant town of **YARMOUTH**, on the northern coast of the Isle of Wight, makes an appeal-ing arrival or departure point, and is also the best base for exploring the west-ern end of the island. Although razed by the French in 1377 on their way to Newtown and Carisbrooke, the port prospered after **Yarmouth Castle** (April–Sept daily 10am–6pm; Oct 10am–5pm; £2.20; EH), tucked between the quay and the pier, was built on the command of Henry VIII. The top attrac-tions hereabouts, however, lie four miles west of Yarmouth, around the isle's western tip. From the multichrome cliffs at **Alum Bay**, a chair lift (£3 return) runs down to ochre-hued sands, which were used as pigments by local land-scape painters in the Victorian era. From here, it's a twenty-minute walk to the lookout on top of the headland known as **The Needles**, three tall chalk stacks whose grandeur is best appreciated on a boat trip from Alum Bay (℡01983/754477; 25min; £3).

Between the Needles and Freshwater Bay, the breezy four-mile ridge of **Tennyson Down** is one of the island's most satisfying walks, with vistas onto rolling downs and vales. There's a monument here to the poet and local resi-dent from whom it's named – one of the many reminders of some of the ven-erable Victorians who were drawn to the area. On the coastal road at Freshwater Bay, **Dimbola Lodge** (Tues–Sun 10am–5pm; £3; ⓦ www.dimbola.co.uk) was the home of pioneer photographer Julia Margaret Cameron who, after visiting Tennyson in 1860, immediately bought adjacent land on the nearby coast, joining two cottages to make a substantial home for herself and her family. The building now houses a gallery of her work, and also features regular exhibitions.

Yarmouth's **tourist office** is on the Quay (Easter–Oct Mon–Sat 9am–5.30pm, Sun 9am–5pm; Nov–Easter daily 10am–4pm; ℡01983/760015). **Accommodation** in town includes *Jireh House* in St James's Square (℡01983/760513; ❸), a pretty seventeenth-century stone guest house and tea room, and the cosy *Bugle Hotel*, opposite (℡01983/760272; ❸). If you're on the Tennyson trail, book into the swish *Farringford Hotel*, on Bedbury Lane, Freshwater (℡01983/752500, ⓦwww.farringford.co.uk; ❻), Tennyson's former home, where the facilities now include a pool, putting green and tennis courts. There's a **youth hostel** a short walk northeast from the Needles, at Totland Bay (℡01983/752165).

The *Bugle* also holds one of the town's many good **pubs** and has a more sophisticated **restaurant**, *Poacher's*. Alternatively, *Jireh House* serves evening meals in summer, or try *Fender's Bistro* in Bridge Road.

Cowes and around

COWES, at the island's northern tip, is inextricably associated with sailing craft and boat building: Henry VIII built a castle here to defend the Solent's expanding naval dockyards from the French and Spanish, and in the 1950s the world's first hovercraft made its test runs here. In 1820 the Prince Regent's patronage of the yacht club gave the port its cachet with the *Royal Yacht Squadron*, now one of the world's most exclusive sailing clubs, permitted to fly the St George's Ensign guaranteeing free entry to all foreign ports. Only its three hundred members and their guests are permitted within the hallowed precincts of the club house in the remains of Henry VIII's castle, and the club's landing stage is sacrosanct. The first week of August sees the international yachting festival known as **Cowes Week**, which visiting royalty turns into a high-society gala, although most summer weekends see some form of yachting or powerboat racing off Cowes.

The town is bisected by the River Medina, with West Cowes being the older and more interesting half, its High Street meandering up from the waterfront Parade. Along the High Street you'll find shops reflecting the town's gentrified heritage, with boatyards, chandlers and Beken's famous yachting gallery – a photo by Beken of your yacht is considered as prestigious as a family portrait by Snowdon.

Cowes **tourist office** is at the Arcade, Fountain Quay (April–Oct Mon–Sat 9am–5pm, Sun 10am–4pm, with extended hours during Cowes Week; Nov–March Mon–Sat 10am–4pm; ℡01983/291914). **Boat trips** upriver and around the harbour leave from the Parade; for details contact Solent & Wight Line Cruises (℡01983/564602).

The more affordable **accommodation** options include the *Union Inn* in Watch House Lane, off High Street (℡01983/293163; ❷), and *Halcyone Villa*, Grove Road, up Mill Hill Road from the east end of the High Street (℡01983/291334, ⓦwww.halcyonevilla.freeuk.com; ❶), and in East Cowes, there's the *Doghouse* (℡01983/293677; ❸), Crossways Road, opposite Osborne House. The town has a decent selection of places to **eat**: *Baan Thai,* 10 Bath Rd (at the west end of the High Street), offers good-quality oriental food at moderate prices, while the *Octopus's Garden*, 63 High St, is a Beatles-themed café serving baguettes and pies. Along the High Street, you can also pick up a snack or just a pint at the *Fountain*, *Anchor* and *Harbour Lights* **pubs**.

Osborne House and Whippingham

A "floating bridge", or chain ferry (Mon–Sat 5am–midnight, Sun 6.35am–midnight; pedestrians free, cars £1.30) connects West Cowes to the more industrial East Cowes, where the only place of interest is Queen Victoria's family home, **Osborne House** (April–Oct daily 10am–5pm; grounds April–Sept daily 10am–6pm; Oct 10am–5pm; £7.20; EH), signposted one mile southeast of town. The house was built in the late 1840s by Prince Albert and Thomas Cubitt as an Italianate villa, with balconies and large terraces overlooking the landscaped gardens towards the Solent. The state rooms, used for entertaining visiting dignitaries, exude an expected formality, while the private apartments feel more homely, like the affluent family holiday residence that Osborne was – far removed from the pomp and ceremony of state affairs in London. Following Albert's death, the desolate Victoria spent much of her time here, where she eventually died in 1901. Since then, according to her wishes, the house has remained virtually unaltered, allowing an unexpectedly intimate glimpse into Victoria's family life.

At **Whippingham**, a mile south of Osborne, there's another of Albert's architectural extravaganzas, the Gothic Revival **Royal Church of St Mildred** (Easter–Sept Mon–Fri 10am–5pm; Oct closes 4pm). The German Battenberg family, who later adopted the anglicized name Mountbatten, have a chapel here and the parents of the present Queen's late uncle, Earl Mountbatten, the island's last governor, are buried in the churchyard.

Newport and Carisbrooke Castle

NEWPORT, the capital of the Isle of Wight, sits at the centre of the island at a point where the River Medina's commercial navigability ends. Apart from a few pleasant old quays dating from its days as an inland port, the town isn't particularly engaging, content to fulfil its role as the island's municipal and commercial centre. Newport's main attraction is **Carisbrooke Castle** (daily: April–Sept 10am–6pm; Oct 10am–5pm; Nov–March 10am–4pm; £4.50; EH), a hilltop fortress on the southwest outskirts. The austere Norman keep's most famous visitor was Charles I, detained here (and caught one night ignominiously jammed between his room's bars while attempting escape) prior to his execution in London. The **museum** in the centre of the castle features many relics from his incarceration, as well as those of the last royal resident, Princess Beatrice, Queen Victoria's youngest daughter. The castle's other notable curiosity is the sixteenth-century well-house, where donkeys still trudge inside a huge treadmill to raise a barrel 160ft up the well shaft.

Winchester

Nowadays a tranquil, handsome market town, set amid docile hay-meadows and watercress beds, **WINCHESTER** was once one of the mightiest settlements in England. Under the Romans it was Venta Belgarum, the fifth largest town in Britain, but it was **Alfred the Great** who really put Winchester on the map when he made it the capital of his Wessex kingdom in the ninth century. For the next couple of centuries Winchester ranked alongside London, its

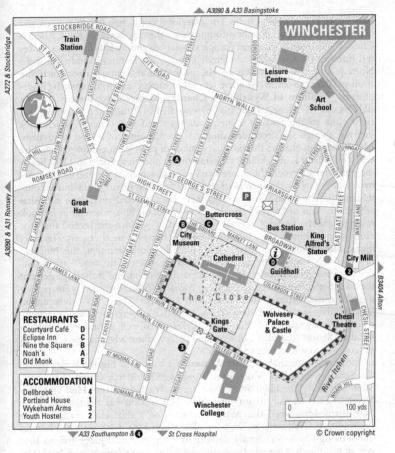

RESTAURANTS

Courtyard Café	D
Eclipse Inn	C
Nine the Square	B
Noah's	A
Old Monk	E

ACCOMMODATION

Dellbrook	4
Portland House	1
Wykeham Arms	3
Youth Hostel	2

© Crown copyright

status affirmed by William the Conqueror's coronation in both cities and by his commissioning of the local monks to prepare the **Domesday Book**. It wasn't until after the Battle of Naseby in 1645, when Cromwell took the city, that Winchester began its decline into provinciality.

Hampshire's county town now has a scholarly and slightly anachronistic air, embodied by the ancient almshouses that still provide shelter for senior citizens of "noble poverty" – the pensioners can be seen wandering round the town in medieval black or mulberry-coloured gowns with silver badges. A trip to this secluded old city is a must – not only for the magnificent **cathedral**, chief relic of Winchester's medieval glory, but for the all-round well-preserved ambience of England's one-time capital.

The City

The first minster to be built in Winchester was raised by Cenwalh, the Saxon king of Wessex in the mid-seventh century and traces of this building have been unearthed near the present **Cathedral** (daily 7.30am–6.30pm; £3.50 donation requested), which was begun in 1079 and completed some three hundred years later, producing a church whose elements range from early

Norman to Perpendicular styles. The exterior is not its best feature – squat and massive, the cathedral crouches stumpily over the tidy lawns of the Cathedral Close. The interior is rich and complex, however, and its 556-foot nave makes this Europe's longest medieval church. Outstanding features include its carved Norman font of black Tournai marble, the fourteenth-century misericords (the choir stalls are the oldest complete set in the country) and some amazing monuments – **William of Wykeham's Chantry**, halfway down the nave on the right, is one of the best. Jane Austen, who died in Winchester, is commemorated close to the font by a memorial brass and slab beneath which she's interred, though she's recorded simply as the daughter of a local clergyman. Above the high altar lie the mortuary chests of pre-Conquest kings, including Canute; William Rufus, killed while hunting in the New Forest in 1100, lies in the presbytery. Beyond the impressive Victorian screen at the end of the presbytery, look out for the memorial shrine to St Swithun: originally buried outside in the churchyard, his remains were later interred inside the cathedral where the "rain of heaven" could no longer fall on him, whereupon he took revenge and the heavens opened for forty days – hence the legend that if it rains on St Swithun's Day (July 15) it will continue for another forty. His exact burial place is unknown. Accessible from the north transept, the Norman **crypt** is only rarely open, since it's flooded for much of the time – the cathedral's original foundations were dug in marshy ground, and at the beginning of the twentieth century a steadfast diver, William Walker, spent five years replacing the rotten timber foundations with concrete (Deep Sea Adventure in Weymouth gives the full story; see p.257). If it's open, you'll see two fourteenth-century statues of William of Wykeham as well as Antony Gormley's standing figure, "Sound II", one of the country's most adventurous ecclesiastical commissions in recent years.

Outside the cathedral, the **City Museum**, a basic local history display, sits on the Square (April–Sept Mon–Sat 10am–5pm; Oct–March closed Mon; free). Walk west along the High Street from here to reach the **Great Hall** on Castle Street (April–Oct daily 10am–5pm; Nov–March Mon–Fri 10am–5pm, Sat & Sun 10am–4pm; free), the vestigial remains of a thirteenth-century castle destroyed by Cromwell. Sir Walter Raleigh heard his death sentence here in 1603, though he wasn't finally dispatched until 1618, and Judge Jeffreys held one of his Bloody Assizes in the castle after Monmouth's rebellion in 1685. The main interest now, however, is a large, brightly painted disc slung on one wall like some curious antique dartboard. This is alleged to be King Arthur's Round Table, but the woodwork is probably fourteenth-century, later repainted as a PR exercise for the Tudor dynasty – the portrait of Arthur at the top of the table bears an uncanny resemblance to Henry VIII.

Heading east along the High Street, you'll pass the Guildhall and the august bronze statue of King Alfred on the Broadway on your way to the River Itchen and the **City Mill** (March Sat & Sun 11am–4.45pm; April–June, Sept & Oct Wed–Sun 11am–4.45pm; July & Aug daily 11am–4.45pm; £2; NT), where you can see restored mill machinery; the building is now part-occupied by a youth hostel. Turning right before the bridge you pass what remains of the Saxon walls, which bracket the ruins of the twelfth-century **Wolvesey Castle** (April–Sept daily 10am–6pm; Oct daily 10am–5pm; £1.90; EH) and the Bishop's Palace, built by Christopher Wren. Immediately to the west up College Street stand the buildings of **Winchester College**, the oldest public school in England – established in 1382 by William of Wykeham for "poor scholars", it now educates few but the wealthy and privileged. The cloisters and chantry are open during term time and the chapel is open all year. Jane Austen moved to the house at 8 College St from Chawton (see p.245) in 1817, when she was already ill with Addison's Disease, dying there later the same year. The thirteenth-century **Kings Gate**, at the top of College Street, is one of the city's original medieval gateways, housing the tiny St Swithun's Church.

About a mile south of College Walk, reached by a pleasant stroll across the watermeadows of the Itchen, lies **St Cross Hospital** (Easter–Sept Mon–Sat 9.30am–5pm; Oct–Easter 10.30am–3.30pm; £2). Founded in 1136 as a hostel for poor brethren, it boasts a fine church, begun in that year and completed a century or so later. Needy wayfarers may still apply for the "dole" at the Porter's Lodge – a tiny portion of bread and beer.

Practicalities

Winchester **train station** is about a mile northwest of the cathedral on Stockbridge Road. If you arrive by **bus**, you'll find yourself on the Broadway, conveniently opposite the **tourist office** in the imposing Guildhall (June–Sept Mon–Sat 10am–6pm, Sun 11am–2pm; Oct–May Mon–Sat 10am–5pm; ☎01962/840500, ⓦwww.winchester.gov.uk). If you're loooking for accommodation with atmosphere, try the *Wykeham Arms*, 75 Kingsgate St (☎01962/853834; ❺), a fine old hostelry where the art of classy inn-keeping has not yet vanished. Nearly as central but not so expensive, *Portland House*, 63 Tower St (☎01962/865195, Ⓔtony@knightworld.com; ❸) is a Georgian house in a quiet mews between the cathedral and train station. *Dellbrook*, Hubert Road (☎01962/865093; ❷) lies a mile south of the city centre, near the watermeadows. Winchester has an exceptionally well-sited **youth hostel** in the eighteenth-century City Mill, 1 Water Lane (☎01962/853723).

The city's best **pub** is the *Wykeham Arms*, 75 Kingsgate St, a maze of characterful, intimate spaces where you can dine on snacks or gourmet-standard food. The picturesque *Eclipse Inn* on the Square, in front of the cathedral, specializes in pies and casseroles, while *Nine The Square*, opposite, is a **restaurant** and wine bar where you can have light meals. The *Old Monk* on Bridge Street has deep comfy sofas and a riverside terrace, while the *Courtyard Café* in the Guildhall, Broadway, has outdoor eating, and more substantial **lunches** in the indoor bistro. *Noah's* on Jewry Street serves inexpensive dishes with Thai, Caribbean and Mediterranean influences.

The Watercress Line and Chawton

ALRESFORD, six miles east of Winchester, is the departure-point for the **Mid-Hants Watercress Line** (March, April & Oct Sat & Sun; May–Sept & school holidays daily; ☎01962/733810, ⓦwww.watercressline.co.uk; £9), a jolly, steam-powered train, so named because it passes through the former watercress beds which once flourished here. The train chuffs ten miles to Alton, with gourmet dinners served on board on Saturday evenings and traditional Sunday lunches.

A mile southwest of Alton, lies the village of **CHAWTON**, where Jane Austen lived from 1809 to 1817, during the last and most prolific years of her life, and where she wrote or revised almost all her six books, including *Sense and Sensibility* and *Pride and Prejudice*. **Jane Austen's House** (Jan & Feb Sat & Sun 11am–4.30pm; rest of year daily 11am–4.30pm; £3), in the centre of the village, is a plain red-brick building, containing first editions of some of her greatest works.

The New Forest

The name of the **NEW FOREST** is misleading, for much of this region's woodland was cleared long before the Normans arrived, and its poor sandy soils support only a meagre covering of heather and gorse in many areas. The forest was requisitioned by William the Conqueror in 1079 as a game reserve, and the rights of its inhabitants soon became subservient to those of his precious deer. Fences to impede their progress were forbidden and terrible punishments were meted out to those who disturbed the animals – hands were lopped off, eyes put out. Later monarchs gradually restored the forest-dwellers' rights, and today the New Forest enjoys a unique patchwork of ancient laws and privileges, enveloped in an arcane vocabulary dating from feudal times. The forest boundary is the "perambulation", and owner-occupiers of forest land have common rights to obscure practices such as "turbary" (peat-cutting), "estover" (firewood collecting) and "mast" (letting pigs forage for acorns and beech mast), as well as the right of pasture, permitting domestic animals to graze freely.

The **trees** of the New Forest are now much more varied than they were in pre-Norman times, with birch, holly, yew, Scots pine and other conifers interspersed with the ancient oaks and beeches. The main wooded areas are around **Lyndhurst**, the "capital" of the New Forest, and one of the most venerable trees is the much-visited **Knightwood Oak**, just a few hundred yards north of the A35 three miles southwest of Lyndhurst, which measures about 22ft in circumference at shoulder height. The most obvious species of New Forest **fauna** are the New Forest **ponies** (reputedly descendants of the Armada's small Spanish horses which survived the battle), now thoroughly domesticated – you'll see them grazing nonchalantly by the roadsides and ambling through some villages. The local deer are less likely to be seen now that some of the faster roads are fenced, although several species still roam the woods, including the tiny **sika deer**, descendants of a pair which escaped from nearby Beaulieu in 1904.

Covering about 144 square miles – a third now in private ownership, the rest administered by the Forestry Commission – the New Forest is one of southern England's main rural playgrounds, and about eight million visitors annually flock here to enjoy a breath of fresh air, often after spending hours in traffic jams. To get the best from the region, you need to **walk** or **ride** through it, avoiding the places cars can reach. There are 150 miles of car-free gravel roads in the forest, making cycling an appealing prospect. The Ordnance Survey Leisure Map 22 of the New Forest is worth getting if you want to explore in any detail, and in Lyndhurst you can pick up numerous walking books and natural history guides. The forest has ten **campsites** run by the Forestry Commission, most closed between October and Easter – to get the full list, write to 231 Corstorphine Rd, Edinburgh EH12 7AT (℡0131/334 0066) – and there's a **youth hostel** in Cottesmore House, Cott Lane, Burley, in the west of the Forest (℡01425/403233).

Lyndhurst and Brockenhurst

LYNDHURST, its town centre skewered by an agonizing one-way system, isn't a particularly interesting place, though the brick **parish church** is worth a glance for its William Morris glass, a fresco by Lord Leighton and the grave of one Mrs Reginald Hargreaves, better known as Alice Liddell, Lewis Carroll's model for Alice. The town is of most interest to visitors for the **New Forest Museum and Visitor Centre** in the central car park off the High Street (daily: mid-July to mid-Sept 10am–6pm; rest of year 10am–5pm; ☎023/8028 2269, ⓦwww.thenewforest.co.uk), where you can buy bus passes and maps for cycling and riding. There's also a small **museum** here focusing on the forest, its history, wildlife and industries (same times as tourist office; £2.75). Nearby in Gosport Lane, AA Bike Hire (☎023/8028 3349) rents **bikes**. For **accommodation** try the clean and airy *Clarendon Villa*, also in Gosport Lane (☎023/8028 2803; ❷), or *Burwood Lodge*, 27 Romsey Rd (☎023/8028 2445; ❸), a large old house a few minutes from the High Street. *Le Café Parisien* at 64 High St, sells **snacks** which you can eat in its small garden in summer; for larger **meals**, head for the nearby *Crown Hotel*.

BROCKENHURST, four miles to the south of Lyndhurst, is a useful centre for visitors without their own transport. There's a train station right in town and **bikes for rent** by the level-crossing at New Forest Cycle Experience (☎01590/624204). The town also has some decent places to **stay**; try the *Cottage Hotel* on Sway Road (☎01590/622296; ❺; closed Dec–Feb) or *Cater's Cottage*, Latchmoor (☎01590/623225; ❸), an above-average B&B on the southern outskirts of Brockenhurst. A short distance farther south in Sway, there's a quiet B&B at *Little Purley Farm* in Chapel Lane (☎01590/682707; ❶), with views over to the Isle of Wight. The *Thatched Cottage* at 16 Brookley Rd can supply everything from three-tier cream teas to light lunches and fine dining.

Beaulieu and Buckler's Hard

The village of **BEAULIEU** (whose name originates from the French meaning "Beautiful Place", but is pronounced "Bewley"), in the southeast corner of the New Forest, was the site of one of England's most influential monasteries, a Cistercian house founded in 1204 by King John – in remorse, it is said, for ordering a group of supplicating Cistercian monks to be trampled to death. Built using stone ferried from Caen and Quarr on the Isle of Wight, the **abbey** managed a self-sufficient estate of ten thousand acres and became a famous sanctuary, offering shelter to Queen Margaret of Anjou among many others. The abbey was dismantled soon after the Dissolution, and its refectory now forms the parish church, which, like everything else in Beaulieu, has been subsumed by the Montagu family who have owned a large chunk of the New Forest since one of Charles II's illegitimate progeny was created duke of the estate.

The estate has been transformed with a prodigious commercial vigour into **Beaulieu** (daily: May–Sept 10am–6pm; Oct–April 10am–5pm; £9.95), a tourist complex comprising **Palace House**, the attractive if unexceptional family home, the abbey and the main attraction, Lord Montagu's **National Motor Museum**. An undersized monorail and an old London bus ease the ten-minute walk between the entry point and Palace House. The house, formerly the abbey's gatehouse, contains masses of Montagu-related memorabilia while the undercroft of the adjacent abbey houses an exhibition depicting medieval monastic life. Inside the celebrated Motor Museum, a collection of 250 cars and motorcycles includes a Formula One McLaren, spindly antiques and recent classics, as well as a couple of svelte land-speed racers, including the record-breaking *Bluebird*. The entertaining "Wheels", a dizzying ride-through display, takes you on a trip through the history of motoring.

If Beaulieu amply deserves its name, **Buckler's Hard**, a couple of miles downstream on the River Beaulieu (daily: Easter–Sept 10am–6pm; Oct–Easter 11am–4pm; £3.50), has an even more wonderful setting. It doesn't look much like a shipyard now, but from Elizabethan times onwards dozens of men o' war were assembled here from giant New Forest oaks. Several of Nelson's ships, including HMS *Agamemnon*, were launched here, to be towed carefully by rowing boats past the sandbanks and across the Solent to Portsmouth. The largest house in this hamlet of shipwrights' cottages, which forms part of the Montagu estate, belonged to Henry Adams, the master builder responsible for most of the Trafalgar fleet; it's now an upmarket hotel and restaurant. At the top of the village, the **Maritime Museum** traces the history of the great ships.

Lymington

The most pleasant point of access for the Isle of Wight (for ferry details, see p.237) is **LYMINGTON**, a sheltered haven which has become one of the busiest leisure harbours on the south coast. Rising from the quay area, the old town is full of cobbled streets and Georgian houses and has one unusual building – the partly thirteenth-century church of **St Thomas the Apostle**, with a cupola-topped tower built in 1670.

Information is available in summer from the local **visitor centre** in New Street, off the High Street (May–Sept Mon–Sat 10am–5pm, Sun 2–5pm; Oct–April Mon–Sat 10am–4pm; ℡01590/689000). Places to **stay** in town include *Dolphins*, 6 Emsworth Rd (℡01590/676108; ❷), which rents out bikes and offers use of a chalet by the beach, and *Wheatsheaf House*, Gosport Lane (℡01590/679208; ❹), a quaint listed building offering two rooms, "Paris" and "Venice", themed accordingly. For **snacks**, try the *Jack in the Basket*, 7 St Thomas St, or head for one of Lymington's excellent **pubs**: the *Chequers* on Ridgeway Lane, on the west side of town; the *Bosun's Chair*, on Station Road, and the harbourfront *Ship Inn*, which has seats looking over the water.

Signposted two miles east of Lymington, the **Sammy Miller Museum**, in New Milton (daily 10am–4.30pm; £3.50) gives classic motorcycles the "Beaulieu" treatment. Many of the once-eminent British marques from Ariel to Vincent are displayed, as well as several acclaimed trials bikes ridden by Sammy Miller himself, one of Britain's most successful trials riders.

Bournemouth and around

Renowned for its clean sandy beaches, the resort of **Bournemouth** is the nucleus of Europe's largest non-industrial conurbation stretching between Lymington and Poole harbour. The resort has a single-minded holiday-making atmosphere, though neighbouring **Poole** and **Christchurch** are more interesting historically. North of this coastal sprawl, the pleasant old market town of **Wimborne** has one of the area's most striking churches, while the stately home of **Kingston Lacy** contains an outstanding collection of old masters and other paintings.

The City

BOURNEMOUTH dates only from 1811, when a local squire, Louis Tregonwell, built a summer house on the wild, unpopulated heathland that once occupied this stretch of coast, and planted the first of the pine trees that now characterize the area. Sadly, the blandly modern town that you see today has little to remind you of Bournemouth's Victorian heyday, though it does boast some exuberant horticultural displays, and exploring Bournemouth's **public gardens** can easily fill a day. Moreover, the pristine sandy beach ranks as one of southern England's cleanest, while the town possesses a first-rate indoor attraction in its **Russell-Cotes Art Gallery and Museum** on East Cliff Promenade (Tues–Sun 10am–5pm; free), which houses a motley assortment of artworks and oriental souvenirs gathered from around the world by the Russell-Cotes family, hoteliers who grew wealthy during Bournemouth's late-Victorian tourist boom. The benefactors' lavishly decorated former home, featuring unusual stained glass and ornate painted ceilings, is jam-packed with their eclectic collections, of which the Japanese artefacts are especially interesting. There are some good examples of Pre-Raphaelite and other British art downstairs, period decor throughout and a cliff-top landscaped garden.

In the centre of town, you might visit the graveyard of **St Peter's** church, just east of the Square, where Mary Shelley, author of the Gothic horror tale *Frankenstein*, is buried, together with the heart belonging to her husband, Percy Bysshe Shelley, former resident of Boscombe. The tombs of Mary's parents – radical thinker William Godwin and early feminist Mary Wollstonecraft – are also here.

Practicalities

The **train station** and **bus station** lie just under a mile east of the centre, to which they're linked by frequent buses. In the centre, the **tourist office** is on Westover Road (mid-July to mid-Sept Mon–Sat 9.30am–7pm, Sun 10.30am–5pm; rest of year Mon–Sat 9.30am–5.30pm; ☏0906/8020234, ⓦwww .bournemouth.co.uk). The town has **accommodation** to suit all budgets: try *Tudor Grange*, 31 Gervis Rd, East Cliff (☏01202/291472; ❹), with attractive interior and gardens, or the friendly *Sea Dene Hotel*, 10 Burnaby Rd, Alum Chine (Thurs–Sun only; ☏01202/761372; ❸), where vegetarians are catered for. The small, friendly **hostel**, *Bournemouth Backpackers*, 3 Frances Rd (☏01202/299491, ⓦwww.bournemouthbackpackers.co.uk), is just three minutes from the train and bus stations.

The *Goat and Tricycle*, 27–29 West Hill Rd, is a quiet and unpretentious **pub**, worth the uphill trek for the real ales and home-made food, while *CH2*, 37 Exeter Rd (☏01202/296296) is an elegant, modern **restaurant** recommended for its steaks and seafood.

Countering its staid image, Bournemouth has thrown up some sizzling **clubs** in recent years. Most are in the centre of town, including the biggest, *Elements*, on Firvale Road, playing mainstream club and house sounds. For something a bit different, try the flamboyant *Opera House*, 570 Christchurch Rd, Boscombe. On a more sedate note, the fortnight at the end of June and the beginning of July sees the **Bournemouth International Festival** draw performers of every musical genre.

Christchurch

CHRISTCHURCH, five miles east of Bournemouth is best known for its colossal parish church, **Christchurch Priory** (Mon–Sat 9.30am–5pm, Sun 2.15–5.30pm; £1 donation requested), bigger than most cathedrals. Built on the site of a Saxon minster dating from 650 AD, but exhibiting chiefly Norman and Perpendicular features, the church is the longest in England, at 311ft, and its fan-vaulted North Porch is the country's biggest. Fine views can be gained from the top of the 120-foot tower (ask at desk; £1).

The area round the old town quay has a carefully preserved charm. The **Red House Museum and Gardens** on Quay Road (Tues–Sat 10am–5pm, Sun 2–5pm; £1.50) contain an affectionate collection of local memorabilia, and **boat**

trips (Easter to mid-Oct daily; ℡01202/429119) can be taken from the grassy banks of the riverside quay east to Mudeford (30min; £4.50 return) or up the river to the *Tuckton Tea Rooms* outside Bournemouth (15 min; £2 return).

The **tourist office** is at 23 High St (June–Sept Mon–Fri 9.30am–5.30pm, Sat 9.30am–5pm; July & Aug also Sun 10am–2pm; Oct–May Mon–Fri 9.30am–5pm, Sat 9.30am–4.30pm; ℡01202/471780, Ⓦwww.resort-guide.co.uk/christchurch). **Accommodation** options in or around town can be fairly pricey, though you'll find a selection of unexciting but reliable guest houses northwest of the centre on Barrack and Stour roads, such as *Grosvenor Lodge*, 53 Stour Rd (℡01202/499008, Ⓦwww.grosvenorlodge.co.uk; ❸); in the centre, try the *King's Arms Toby Hotel*, 18 Castle St (℡01202/484117; ❺). For something to **eat**, try *La Mamma*, 51 Bridge St (℡01202/471608; closed Sun lunch & Mon in winter), where you can enjoy Italian classics (including pizzas), or, at 3 Bridge St, the *Bistro on the Bridge*, which offers coffees and teas, inexpensive lunches and pricier evening meals, and has riverside seating on a veranda. Recommended **pubs** include the *King's Arms Hotel*, right by the priory, and Christchurch's oldest pub, *Ye Olde George Inn*, 2a Castle St – both have gardens and serve food.

Poole

POOLE, west of Bournemouth, is an ancient seaport on a huge, almost land-locked harbour. The town developed in the thirteenth century and was successively colonized by pirates, fishermen and timber traders, more recently replaced by companies prospecting for oil in the shallow waters – the harbour's environmental significance ensures that the extraction process is carefully disguised. The old quarter by the quayside is worth exploring, containing over a hundred historic buildings of which the old Custom House, Scaplen's Court and Guildhall are the most striking.

At the bottom of Old High Street, near the Poole Pottery showroom and crafts centre, the late medieval **Scaplen's Court** once billeted Cromwell's troops (you can see their graffiti around the fireplace). Now restored as an educational centre with very limited opening hours, it holds reconstructions of a Victorian kitchen, pharmacy and school room. Over the road, local history is more accessibly elaborated at the **Waterfront Museum** (April–Oct Mon–Sat 10am–5pm, Sun noon–5pm; Nov–March Mon–Sat 10am–3pm, Sun noon–3pm; £2), which traces Poole's development over the centuries, illustrated by such items as local ceramics and tiles and a rare Iron Age log boat, and there are changing exhibitions.

From Poole's quayside, you can visit **Brownsea Island** (April–June & Sept to early Oct daily 10am–5pm; July & Aug daily 10am–6pm; £3.50; NT) on regular ferries (25min; £5 return). Now a National Trust property, this five-hundred-acre island is famed for its red squirrels, wading birds and other wildlife.

One of the area's most famous gardens lies on the outskirts of Poole, **Compton Acres** (March–Oct daily 10am–6pm; £5.75; Ⓦwww.comptonacres.co.uk), signposted off the A35 Poole Road, towards Bournemouth. Here you'll find seven gardens, each with a different international theme, the best of which is the elegantly understated Japanese Garden.

Poole's **tourist office** is in the Waterfront Museum (April, May & Oct Mon–Sat 10am–5pm, Sun noon–5pm; June, July & Sept Mon–Fri 10am–5.30pm, Sat & Sun 10am–5pm; Aug daily 10am–6pm; Nov–March Mon–Fri 10am–5pm, Sat 10am–3pm, Sun noon–3pm; ℡01202/253253, Ⓦwww.poole.gov.uk/tourism). Best choice for **accommodation** is the

△ Cowes Week, Isle of Wight

Antelope Hotel at the quay end of the High Street (℡01202/672029; ❹), a handsome old hostelry, or try the eighteenth-century *Mansion House*, Thames Street (℡01202/685666, ⓦthemansionhouse.co.uk; ❻). Cheaper rooms can be had at the *Crown Hotel* (℡01202/672137; ❸), an inn on Market Street, and the less central *Harbour Lights Hotel*, 121 North Rd, Parkstone (℡01202/748417; ❷), a mile or so north of the centre. There's a collection of good **restaurants** on and around the High Street: look out for *Storm* at no. 16 (℡01202/674970; closed lunchtime), specializing in seafood, and, at the top end of the street, *Alcatraz*, a trendy Italian brasserie with outdoor tables.

Wimborne Minster and Kingston Lacy

An ancient town on the banks of the Stour, just a few minutes' drive north from the suburbs of Bournemouth, **WIMBORNE MINSTER**, as the name suggests, is mainly of interest for its great church, the **Minster of St Cuthberga** (daily: Jan & Feb 9.30am–4pm; rest of year 9.30am–5.30pm). Built on the site of an eighth-century monastery, its massive twin towers of mottled grey and tawny stone dwarf the rest of the town – and the church was even more imposing before its spire crashed down during morning service in 1602 (amazingly, no-one was injured). What remains today is basically Norman with later features added – such as the Perpendicular west tower, which bears a figure dressed as a grenadier of the Napoleonic era, who strikes every quarter-hour with a hammer. Inside, the church is crowded with memorials and eye-catching details – look out for the orrery clock inside the west tower, with the sun marking the hours and the moon marking the days of the month, and for the organ with trumpets pointing out towards the congregation instead of pipes. The **Chained Library** above the choir vestry (Easter–Oct Mon–Thurs 10.30am–12.30pm & 2–4pm, Fri 10.30am–12.30pm), dating from 1686, is Wimborne's most prized possession and one of the oldest public libraries in the country.

Wimborne's older buildings stand around the main square near the minster, and are mostly from the late eighteenth or early nineteenth century. The **Priest's House** on the High Street started life as lodgings for the clergy, then became a stationer's shop. Now it is an award-winning **museum** (April, May & Oct Mon–Sat 10.30am–5pm; June–Sept Mon–Sat 10.30am–5pm, Sun 2–5pm; £2.40), each room furnished in the style of a different period. A working Victorian kitchen, a Georgian parlour and an ironmonger's shop are among its exhibits, and there's a display of items relating to local archeology and history; a walled garden at the rear provides an excellent place for summer teas.

Kingston Lacy (April–Oct Wed–Sun noon–5.30pm; grounds: Feb–March Sat & Sun 11am–4pm; April–Oct daily 11am–6pm or dusk if earlier; Nov–Dec Fri–Sun 11am–4pm; £6.50; grounds only £3; NT), one of the country's finest seventeenth-century country houses, lies two miles northwest of Wimborne Minster, in 250 acres of parkland grazed by a herd of Red Devon cattle. Designed for the Bankes family, who were exiled from Corfe Castle (see p.254) after the Roundheads reduced it to rubble, the Queen Anne brick building was clad in grey stone during the nineteenth century by Sir Charles Barry, co-architect of the Houses of Parliament. William Bankes, then owner of the house, was a great traveller and collector, and the **Spanish Room** is a superb scrapbook of his Grand Tour souvenirs, lined with gilded leather and surmounted by a Venetian ceiling. Kingston Lacy's **picture collection** is also outstanding, featuring Titian, Rubens, Velázquez and many other old masters. Be warned, though, that this place gets so swamped with visitors that the National Trust has to issue timed tickets on busy weekends.

The Isle of Purbeck

Though not actually an island, the **ISLE OF PURBECK** – a promontory of low hills and heathland jutting out beyond Poole Harbour – does have an insular and distinctive feel. Reached from the east by the **ferry from Sandbanks**, at the narrow mouth of Poole harbour, or by a long and congested landward journey via the bottleneck of **Wareham**, Purbeck can be a difficult destination to reach, but its villages are immensely pretty, none more so than **Corfe Castle**, with its majestic ruins. **Swanage**, a low-key seaside resort, is flanked by more exciting coastlines, all accessible on the Dorset Coast Path. Like Portland, further west, the area is pockmarked with stone quarries – Purbeck marble is the finest grade of the local oolitic limestone.

Wareham and around

The grid pattern of its streets indicates the Saxon origins of **WAREHAM**, and the town is surrounded by even older earth ramparts known as the Walls. A riverside setting adds greatly to its charms, though the major road junction at its heart causes horrible traffic queues in summer, and the scenic stretch along the Quay also gets fairly overrun. Nearby lies an oasis of quaint houses around **Lady St Mary's Church**, which contains the marble coffin of Edward the Martyr, murdered at Corfe Castle in 978 by his stepmother, to make way for her unready son Ethelred. **St Martin's Church**, at the north end of town, dates from Saxon times and the chancel contains a faded twelfth-century mural of St Martin offering his cloak to a beggar, but the church's most striking feature is a romantic effigy of T.E. Lawrence in Arab dress, which was originally destined for Salisbury Cathedral, but was rejected by the dean there who disapproved of Lawrence's sexual proclivities. Lawrence was killed in 1935 in a motorbike accident on the road from Bovington, after returning to Dorset from his Middle Eastern adventures. His simply furnished cottage is at **Clouds Hill**, seven miles northwest of Wareham (April–Oct Wed–Fri & Sun noon–5pm or dusk; £2.60; NT). In Wareham the small **museum** next to the town hall in East Street (Easter–Oct Mon–Sat 11am–1pm & 2–4pm; free) displays some of Lawrence's memorabilia, as does the absorbing **Tank Museum** in Bovington Camp, five miles west of Wareham (daily 10am–5pm; £7; Ⓦ www.tankmuseum.co.uk).

Holy Trinity Church, on South Street, contains Wareham's **tourist office** (June to mid-Sept Mon–Sat 9.30am–5pm, Sun 10am–1pm; mid-Sept to May Mon–Sat 9.30am–1pm & 1.45–5pm; ℡01929/552740). From the nearby Quay, row- and motor-boats are available to rent (£8–12 an hour). The best **accommodation** options are *Anglebury House*, 15 North St (℡01929/552988; ❸), and the *Old Granary* on the Quay (℡01929/552010; ❷), also a **restaurant**, with views over the river.

Corfe Castle

The romantic ruins crowning the hill behind the village of **CORFE CASTLE** (daily: March 10am–5pm; April–Oct 10am–6pm; Nov–Feb 10am–4pm; £4.20; NT) are perhaps the most evocative in England. The family seat of Sir John Bankes, Attorney General to Charles I, this Royalist stronghold withstood a Cromwellian siege for six weeks, gallantly defended by Lady Bankes. One of her own men, Colonel Pitman, eventually betrayed the castle to the Roundheads, after which it was reduced to its present gap-toothed state by gunpowder. Apparently the victorious Roundheads were so impressed by Lady Bankes's courage that they allowed her to take the keys to the castle with her – they can still be seen in the library at the Bankes's subsequent home, Kingston Lacy (see p.252).

The village is well stocked with tearooms and gift shops and has a couple of good **pubs** too: the *Fox* on West Street, and, below the castle ramparts, the *Greyhound*. For moderately priced **accommodation**, head for *The Old Curatage*, 30 East St (℡01929/481441; ❶), or the *Bankes Arms Hotel* (℡01929/480206; ❷), an old inn outside the castle entrance.

Swanage and Shell Bay

Purbeck's largest town is the traditional seaside resort of **SWANAGE**, which sports a pleasant sandy beach and an ornate town hall, the facade of which once adorned the Mercer's Hall in the City of London and was brought back here as ballast on a cargo ship. The town's station is the southern terminus of the **Swanage Steam Railway** (April–Oct daily; Nov, Dec & late Feb to March Sat & Sun; £6 return), which runs as far as Corfe Castle and Norden (on the A351). For timetables, call ℡01929/435800, check at ⓦswanagerailway.co.uk or pick up a leaflet from the tourist office. Swanage is also a good base for exploring **Shell Bay**, to the north, a magnificent beach of icing-sugar sand backed by a remarkable heathland ecosystem that's home to all six British species of reptile – adders are quite common, so be careful. At the top end of the beach, a chain **ferry** (daily 7am–11pm every 20min) crosses the mouth of Poole Harbour, connecting the Isle of Purbeck with Sandbanks in Poole.

Swanage's **tourist office** is by the beach on Shore Road (Easter–Oct daily 10am–5pm; Nov–Easter Mon–Thurs 10am–5pm, Fri 10am–4pm; ℡01929/422885, ⓦwww.swanage.gov.uk), and there's a **youth hostel**, with good views across the bay, on Cluny Crescent (℡01929/422113, ⓦwww.yha.org.uk). The numerous **B&Bs** in Swanage include a handy trio on King's Road near the train station, or try the *Purbeck Hotel*, 19 High St (℡01929/425160; ❷), which also has a decent pub. Swanage has a wide variety of places **to eat**, the best of which is the excellent *Galley*, 9 High St (℡01929/427299; closed Mon except July & Aug), which specializes in well-prepared local fish dishes.

Durlston Head to Durdle Door

Highlights of the coast south and west of Swanage are the cliffs of **Durlston Head**, and the cliff-top path to **St Alban's Head**. West of this headland, **Kimmeridge Bay** may not have a sandy beach but it does have a remarkable marine wildlife reserve much appreciated by divers – there's a Dorset Wildlife Trust **information centre** by the slipway (daily 10am–5pm; ℡01929/481044). The quaint thatch-and-stone villages of East and West Lulworth form a prelude to **Lulworth Cove**, a perfect shell-shaped bite formed when the sea broke through a weakness in the cliffs and then gnawed away at them from behind, forming a circular cave which eventually collapsed to leave a bay enclosed by sandstone cliffs. At the **Lulworth Heritage Centre** the mysteries of the local geology are explained (daily: March–Oct 10am–6pm; Nov–Feb 10am–4pm; free).

Immediately west of the cove you come to **Stair Hole**, a roofless sea cave riddled with arches that will eventually collapse to form another Lulworth, and a couple of miles west is **Durdle Door**, a famous limestone arch that appeals to serious geologist and casual sightseer alike. Most people take the uphill route to the arch which starts from the car park but, if you want to avoid the steep climb, you can drive a mile from the village towards East Chaldon and park at the *Durdle Door Holiday Park* for a small fee.

West Lulworth is the obvious **place to stay** or eat on this section of coast. The *Castle Inn* (℡01929/400311; ❷), *Cromwell House Hotel* (℡01929/400253; ❹), right on the coast path and sporting a heated pool, and *Ivy Cottage* (℡01929/400509; ❶), a seventeenth-century cottage with inglenook fireplace, all make for good stop-offs. You'll find a **youth hostel** at the end of School Lane West (℡01929/400564); a plain chalet with small rooms, it's a stone's throw away from the Dorset Coast Path. In East Lulworth, the *Weld Arms* also has rooms (℡01929/400211; ❷) and the easily overlooked *Sailor's Return* in East Chaldon, four miles northwest of Lulworth Cove, is unsurpassed locally for its mouthwatering pub **food**.

Dorchester and around

The county town of Dorset, **DORCHESTER** still functions as the main agricultural centre for the region, and if you catch it on a Wednesday when the market is in full swing you'll find it livelier than usual. For the local tourist authorities, however, this is essentially **Thomas Hardy**'s town; he was born at Higher Bockhampton, three miles east of here, his heart is buried in Stinsford, a couple of miles northeast (the rest of him is in Westminster Abbey), and he spent much of his life in Dorchester itself, where his statue now stands on High West Street. The town appears in his novels as Casterbridge, and the countryside all around is evocatively depicted, notably the wild heathland to the east (Egdon Heath) and the eerie yew forest of Cranborne Chase. The real Dorchester has an attractive central core of mostly seventeenth-century and Georgian buildings, though the town's origins go back to the Romans, who founded "Durnovaria" in about 70 AD. The Roman walls were replaced in the eighteenth century by tree-lined avenues called "Walks" (Bowling Alley Walk, West Walk and Colliton Walk), but some traces of the Roman period have survived. At the back of County Hall excavations have uncovered a fine Roman villa with a well-preserved mosaic floor, and on the southeast edge of town you'll find **Maumbury Rings**, where the Romans held vast gladiatorial combats in an amphitheatre adapted from a Stone Age site. The gruesome traditions continued into the Middle Ages, when gladiators were replaced by bear-baiting and public executions or "hanging fairs".

Continuing the sanguinary theme, after the ill-fated rebellion of the Duke of Monmouth (another of Charles II's illegitimate offspring) against James II, Judge Jeffreys was appointed to punish the rebels. His "Bloody Assizes" of 1685, held in the Oak Room of the **Antelope Hotel** on Cornhill, sentenced 292 men to death. In the event, 74 were hung, drawn and quartered, and their heads then stuck on pikes throughout Dorset and Somerset; the luckier suspects were merely flogged and transported to the West Indies. Judge Jeffreys lodged just round the corner from the *Antelope* in High West Street, where a half-timbered restaurant now capitalizes on the lurid association.

In 1834 the **Shire Hall**, further down High West Street, witnessed another *cause célèbre*, when six men from the nearby village of Tolpuddle were sentenced to transportation for banding together to form the Friendly Society of Agricultural Labourers, in order to present a request for a small wage increase on the grounds that their families were starving. After a public outcry the men were pardoned, and the **Tolpuddle Martyrs** passed into history as founders of the trades union movement. The room in which they were tried is preserved as a memorial to the martyrs, and you can find out more about them in Tolpuddle itself, eight miles east on the A35, where there's a fine little **museum** (April–Oct Tues–Sat 10am–5.30pm, Sun 11am–5.30pm; Nov–March closes at 4pm; free).

The best place to find out about Dorchester's history is in the engrossing **Dorset County Museum** on High West Street (May–Oct daily 10am–5pm; Nov–April Mon–Sat 10am–5pm; £3.50), where archeological and geological displays trace Celtic and Roman history, including a section on Maiden Castle. Pride of place goes to the re-creation of Thomas Hardy's study, where his pens are inscribed with the names of the books he wrote with them. Other museums in town include the **Keep Military Museum** (July & Aug Mon–Sat 9.30am–5pm, Sun 10am–4pm; rest of year closed Sun; £3; @www.keepmilitarymuseum.org), just west of Hardy's Monument, which traces the fortunes of the Dorset and Devonshire regiments over three hundred years and offers sweeping views over the town; and a small **Dinosaur Museum** off High East Street on Icen Way (daily: April–Sept 9.30am–5.30pm; Oct–March 10am–4.30pm; £4.75; @www.dinosaur-museum.org.uk). Best of all is **Tutankhamun: The Exhibition** on the High Street (daily 9.30am–5.30pm; £4.75; @www.tutankhamun-exhibition.co.uk), a fascinating and thorough exploration of the young pharaoh's life and afterlife through to the eventual discovery of his tomb in 1922. Everything from the mummified remains, complete burial chamber and the celebrated golden mask has been carefully and atmospherically re-created with painstaking detail.

Practicalities

Dorchester has two **train stations**, both of them to the south of the centre: trains from Weymouth and London arrive at Dorchester South, while Bristol trains use the Dorchester West station. Most **buses** stop around the car park on Acland Road, to the east of South Street. The **tourist office** is in Antelope Walk (April–Sept Mon–Sat 9am–5pm, Sun 10am–3pm; Oct Mon–Sat 9am–5pm; Nov–March Mon–Sat 9am–4pm; ☎01305/267992, @www.westdorset.com).

Dorchester has a good selection of **accommodation**, ranging from the superior Georgian *Casterbridge Hotel*, 49 High East St (☎01305/264043, @www.casterbridgehotel.co.uk; ⑤), to such budget options as the *King's Arms*, also on High East St (☎01305/265353; ②), and the small *Maumbury Cottage*, 9 Maumbury Rd (☎01305/266726; ①), near the Rings and the stations. The nearest **youth hostel** is at Litton Cheney (☎01308/482340), halfway between Dorchester and Bridport.

When it comes to **food**, your best bet is a pub meal; try the *King's Arms* (see above), or, on High West Street, the *Royal Oak* or *Old Ship Inn*.

Maiden Castle

One of southern England's finest prehistoric sites, **Maiden Castle** (free access) stands on a hill two miles or so south of Dorchester. Covering about 115 acres, it was first developed around 3000 BC by a Stone Age farming community and then used during the Bronze Age as a funeral mound. Iron Age dwellers expanded it into a populous settlement and fortified it with a daunting series of ramparts and ditches, just in time for the arrival of Vespasian's Second Legion. The ancient Britons' slingstones were no match for the more sophisticated weapons of the Roman invaders, and Maiden Castle was stormed in a bloody massacre in 43 AD.

What you see today is a massive series of grassy concentric ridges about sixty feet high, creasing the surface of the hill. The main finds from the site are displayed in the Dorset County Museum (see above).

Weymouth to Bridport

Whether George III's passion for sea bathing was a symptom of his eventual madness is uncertain, but it was at the bay of **Weymouth** that in 1789 he became the first reigning monarch to follow the craze. Sycophantic gentry rushed into the waves behind him, and soon the town, formerly a workaday harbour, took on the elegant Georgian stamp which it bears today. A likeness of the monarch on horseback is even carved into the chalk downs northwest of the town, like some guardian spirit. Weymouth nowadays plays second fiddle to the vast resort of Bournemouth to the east, but it's still an attractive family holiday destination, which manages to be both sedate and gaudy.

Just south of the town stretch the giant arms of Portland Harbour, and a long causeway links Weymouth to the strange five-mile-long excrescence of the **Isle of Portland**. West of the causeway, the eighteen-mile bank of pebbles known as **Chesil Beach** runs northwest in the direction of **Bridport**.

Weymouth

WEYMOUTH had long been a port before the Georgians popularized it as a resort. It's possible that a ship unloading a cargo here in 1348 first brought the Black Death to English shores, and it was from Weymouth that John Endicott sailed in 1628 to found Salem in Massachusetts. A few buildings survive from these pre-Georgian times: the restored **Tudor House** on Trinity Street (June–Sept Tues–Fri 11am–3.45pm; Oct–May first Sun of month 2–4pm; £1.50) and the ruins of **Sandsfoot Castle** (free access), built by Henry VIII, overlooking Portland Harbour. But Weymouth's most imposing architectural heritage stands along the Esplanade, a dignified range of bow-fronted and porticoed buildings gazing out across the graceful bay, an ensemble rather disrupted by the garish **Clock Tower** commemorating Victoria's jubilee. The more intimate quayside of the Old Harbour is lined with waterfront pubs from where you can view the passing yachts, trawlers and ferries.

Weymouth's slightly faded gentility is now counterbalanced by a number of "all-weather" attractions, the most high-profile of which is the **Sea Life Park** in Lodmoor Country Park east of the Esplanade (daily: 10am–5pm; winter weekdays closes at 4pm; last admission 1hr before closing; £6.50, £4.95 from tourist office; ☎01305/761070), where you can get close to sharks and rays and wander among multichrome birds in the tropical house. Other attractions include the **Deep Sea Adventure** at the Old Harbour (late July to early Sept 9.30am–8pm; rest of year 9.30am–7pm; last entry 1hr 30min before closing; £3.75), which describes the origins of modern diving and the sobering story of the *Titanic* disaster. Over the river on Hope Square, **The Timewalk** housed in Brewer's Quay (Mon–Sat 10am–5.30pm, Sun 11am–4.30pm; public & school holidays open until 9pm; £4.25), contains an entertaining and educational walk-through exhibition of Weymouth's maritime and brewing past. A fifteen-minute walk southwards leads to the Palmerston-era **Nothe Fort** (May to mid-Sept daily 10.30am–5.30pm; rest of year hours are variable; ☎01305/787243; £3), which has a number of displays on military themes, as well as a museum detailing the centuries-old practice of coastal defence, made obsolete in 1956 by advancing technology.

Practicalities

Weymouth's **train** station is a couple of blocks west of the King's Statue, on the Esplanade, which is where you'll find the town's **tourist office** (daily: April–Sept 9.30am–5pm; Oct–March 10.30am–3pm; ☎01305/785747, ⓦwww.weymouth .gov.uk). A cluster of good **accommodation** options lies at the south end of the Esplanade, for instance *Chatsworth*, 14 The Esplanade (☎01305/785012, ⓦwww.thechatsworth.co.uk; ❺), which has a garden terrace, and the Georgian *Cavendish House*, 5 The Esplanade (☎01305/782039; ❷), overlooking the bay with harbour views at the back. At the quieter northern end of the Esplanade, *Bay Lodge*, 27 Greenhill (☎01305/782419, ⓦwww.baylodge.co.uk; ❹), is a better-than-average B&B with great sea views. As for **eating**, you can't do better than *Perry's*, a moderately priced seafood restaurant overlooking the quayside at 4 Trinity Rd (☎01305/785799, ⓦwww.perrysrestaurant.co.uk), while the cheerful *Café 21* at 21 East St is Weymouth's only vegetarian restaurant, with courtyard seating. Amenable **pubs** include the *Old Rooms Inn* on Trinity Road, an inexpensive lunch venue with a strong maritime theme, and the *Nothe Tavern*, buried among Nothe Gardens on Barrack Road, which has bar meals and views from the garden.

Portland

Stark, wind-battered and treeless, the **Isle of Portland** is famed above all for its hard white limestone, which has been quarried here for centuries – Wren used it for St Paul's Cathedral, and it clads the UN headquarters in New York. It was also used for the six-thousand-foot breakwater that protects Portland Harbour – the largest artificial harbour in Britain, which was built by convicts in the mid-nineteenth century. Poorer grades of Portland stone are pulverized for cement – the industrial stone-crushing plant is a prominent and unlovely feature of the island.

The causeway road by which the Isle of Portland is approached stands on the easternmost section of the Chesil shingle. To the east you get a good view of the harbour, a naval base since 1872. The first settlement you come to, **FORTUNESWELL**, overlooks the huge harbour and is itself surveyed by a 450-year-old Tudor fortress, **Portland Castle** (April–Sept daily 10am–6pm; Oct daily 10am–5pm; Nov–March Fri–Sun 10am–4pm; £3; EH), commissioned by Henry VIII. South of **EASTON**, the main village on the island, Wakeham Road holds **Pennsylvania Castle** (now a private house), built in 1800 for John Penn, governor of the island and a grandson of the founder of Pennsylvania. A couple of hundred yards beyond the house, the seventeenth-century **Avice's Cottage**, a gift of Marie Stopes, the pioneer of birth control, is home to a small **museum** (Easter–July, Sept & Oct Mon, Tues & Fri–Sun 10.30am–1pm & 1.30–5pm; Aug & school holidays daily 10.30am–1pm & 1.30–5pm; £2), with exhibitions on local shipwrecks, smuggling and quarrying. The cottage owes its name to Thomas Hardy, who described it in his novel, *The Well-Beloved*. Nearby, in **Church Ope Cove**, you can see the ruins of St Andrew's Church and eleventh-century Rufus Castle.

The craggy limestone of the island rises to 496 feet at **Portland Bill**, where a lighthouse has guarded the promontory since the eighteenth century. You can climb the 153 steps of the present one, dating from 1906, for the views (Easter–Sept Mon–Fri & Sun 11am–5pm; tours £2), and it also houses Portland's tourist office (Easter–Sept Mon, Tues & Thurs–Sun 10am–4pm, Wed 11am–4pm; ☎01305/861233), which can update you on **accommodation** options in the area, for instance *Sturt Corner* (☎01305/822846; ❶) and the *Pulpit Inn* (☎01305/821237; ❷), both nearby on Portland Bill, and there's a **youth hostel** in Portland itself, on Castle Road, Castletown (☎01305/861368).

Chesil Beach to Bridport

Chesil Beach is the strangest feature of the Dorset coast, a two-hundred-yard-wide, fifty-foot-high bank of pebbles that extends for eighteen miles, its component stones gradually decreasing in size from fist-like pebbles at Portland to "pea gravel" at Burton Bradstock in the west. This sorting is an effect of the powerful coastal currents, which make this one of the most dangerous beaches in Europe – churchyards in the local villages display plenty of evidence of wrecks and drownings. Though not a swimming beach, Chesil is popular with sea anglers, and its wild, uncommercialized atmosphere makes an appealing antidote to the south-coast resorts. Chesil Beach encloses a brackish lagoon called The Fleet for much of its length – it was the setting for J. Meade Faulkner's classic smuggling tale, *Moonfleet*.

At the point where the shingle beach attaches itself to the shore is the pretty village of **ABBOTSBURY**, all tawny ironstone and thatch. Its Tithe Barn is a fifteenth-century building, the last remnant of the village's Benedictine abbey, and today, as the **Smuggler's Barn** (daily: Easter–Oct 10am–6pm; Nov–Easter Sat & Sun 11am–dusk; last admissions 1hr before closing; £4.20), illustrates the ins and outs of contrabanding. The village **Swannery** (mid-March to Oct daily 10am–6pm; last admissions 1hr before closing; £5.20), a wetland reserve for mute swans, dates back to medieval times, when presumably it formed part of the abbot's larder. Other attractions include the **Subtropical Gardens** (daily: April–Oct 10am–6pm; Nov–March 10am–dusk; last admission 1hr before closing; £4.70), where delicate species thrive in the microclimate created by Chesil's stones, which act as a giant radiator to keep out all but the worst frosts. Up on the downs a couple of miles inland from Abbotsbury is a monument to Thomas Hardy, not the usual one associated with Dorset, but the flag captain in whose arms Admiral Nelson expired. Abbotsbury offers a couple of good **accommodation** options: *Swan Lodge*, 1 Rodden Row (☎01305/871249; ❷), which has fully-equipped rooms, some en suite, and the *Ilchester Arms* in the village centre, a handsome stone inn with fine food (☎01305/871243; ❷).

BRIDPORT, just beyond the far end of Chesil Beach, is a pleasant old town of brick rather than stone, with unusually wide streets, a hangover from its rope-making days when cords made of locally grown hemp and flax were stretched between the houses. If you want to know about the rope and net industry head for the fishing resort of **West Bay**, Bridport's access to the sea, where the **Harbour Life Exhibition** (April–Oct daily 10am–5pm; £1) will fill you in about "Bridport daggers" (hangmen's nooses) and more besides. West Bay also has the area's best place to **eat**, the *Riverside Restaurant*, a renowned but informal fish place with good views out to sea (☎01308/422011). Across the harbour, the *Bridport Arms Hotel* (☎01308/422994; ❹) offers good **accommodation** near the beach; alternatively, in the centre of town, try *Cranston Cottage*, 27 Church St (☎01308/456240; ❶). Bridport's **tourist office** is at 32 South St (April–Oct Mon–Sat 9am–5pm; Nov–March Mon–Sat 10am–3pm; ☎01308/424901), and there's a seasonal office at West Bay sharing the same premises with the Harbour Life Exhibition (☎01308/422807).

Lyme Regis and around

LYME REGIS, Dorset's most westerly town, shelters snugly between steep hills, just before the grey, fossil-filled cliffs lurch into Devon. Its intimate size and undeniable photogenic qualities mean that in high summer car-borne crowds jostle with pedestrians for the limited space along Lyme's narrow streets. For all that, the town lives up to the classy impression created by its regal name, which it owes to a royal charter granted by Edward I in 1284. It has some upmarket literary associations to further bolster its self-esteem – Jane Austen penned *Persuasion* in a seafront cottage here, while novelist John Fowles is the town's most famous current resident; but it was the film adaptation of his book, *The French Lieutenant's Woman*, shot on location here, that did more than any tourist board production ever could to place the resort firmly on the map.

Colourwashed cottages and elegant Regency and Victorian villas line the seafront and flanking streets, but Lyme's best-known feature is a briskly practical reminder of its commercial origins. **The Cobb**, the curving harbour wall, was first constructed in the thirteenth century but has suffered many alterations since, most notably in the nineteenth century, when its massive boulders were clad in neater blocks of Portland stone.

As you walk along the seafront and out towards The Cobb, look for the outlines of ammonites in the walls and paving stones. The cliffs around Lyme are made up of complex layers of limestone, greensand and unstable clay, a perfect medium for preserving fossils, which are exposed by landslips of the water-logged clays. In 1811, after a fierce storm caused parts of the cliffs to collapse, 12-year-old Mary Anning, a keen fossil-hunter, discovered an almost complete dinosaur skeleton, a 30-foot ichthyosaurus now displayed in London's Natural History Museum (see p.130).

Hammering fossils out of the cliffs is frowned on by today's conservationists, and in any case is rather hazardous. Hands-off inspection of the area's complex geology can be enjoyed on both sides of town: to the west lies the **Undercliff**, a fascinating jumble of overgrown landslips, now a nature reserve. East of Lyme, the Dorset Coast Path is closed as far as jaded **Charmouth** (Jane Austen's favourite resort), but at low tide you can walk for two miles along the beach, then, just past Charmouth, rejoin the coastal path to the headland of **Golden Cap**, whose brilliant outcrop of auburn sandstone is crowned with gorse.

Lyme's excellent **Philpot Museum** on Bridge Street (April–Oct Mon–Sat 10am–5pm, Sun 11am–5pm; Nov–March Sat 10am–5pm, Sun 11am–5pm, also open Christmas & school half-terms at same times; £1.50) provides a crash course in local history and geology, while **Dinosaurland** on Coombe Street (daily: Aug 10am–6pm; rest of year 10am–5pm; £3.50) fills out the story on ammonites and other local fossils. Also worth seeing is the small **marine aquarium** on The Cobb (Easter–Oct 10am–5pm, with later closing in July & Aug; £2), where local fishermen bring unusual catches, and the fifteenth-century **parish church** of St Michael the Archangel, up Church Street, which contains a seventeenth-century pulpit and a massive chained Bible.

Practicalities

Lyme's nearest **train station** is in Axminster, five miles north; the #31 **bus** runs from here to Lyme Regis. The **tourist office** is on Church Street (May–Oct Mon–Sat 10am–5am, Sun 10am–4pm; Nov–April Mon–Sat 10am–2pm; ☏01297/442138, ⊛www.lymeregistourism.co.uk).

Lyme's sole seafront hotel is the pricey *Bay Hotel* on Marine Parade

(☎01297/442059; ❺), but you don't have to walk far for more moderately priced **accommodation** in the centre, such as the *Old Monmouth Hotel*, at 12 Church St (☎01297/442456; ❷), or *Cliff Cottage* on Cobb Road (☎01297/443334; ❶), which has harbour views, a garden chalet and an attached fish **restaurant**. The *Millside Restaurant and Wine Bar*, 1 Mill Lane (☎01297/445999), serving good pasta and fish dishes, is another good place to repair to in the evening; for inexpensive daytime meals, try the *Bell Cliff Restaurant* at 5–6 Broad St. The best **pubs** are the *Royal Standard* on Ozone Parade, and the *Pilot Boat* on Bridge Street, which also does excellent seafood and vegetarian meals.

Inland Dorset and southern Wiltshire

The main pleasures of inland Dorset come from unscheduled meandering through its ancient landscapes and tiny rural settlements, many of which boast preposterously winsome names such as Ryme Intrinseca, Piddletrenthide, Up Sydling and Plush. The rumbustious chalk-carved giant outside the village of **Cerne Abbas** is the county's most photographed site, but the major tourist honeypots are the towns of **Blandford Forum**, **Shaftesbury** and **Sherborne**, the landscaped garden at **Stourhead** across the county boundary in Wiltshire, and the brasher stately home at **Longleat**, an unlikely hybrid of safari park and historic monument.

Blandford Forum

BLANDFORD FORUM, the gateway into mid-Dorset from Bournemouth, owes its latinate name not to the Romans but to medieval pedantry – the original Saxon name Cheping, meaning "market", was translated as Forum by Latin-speaking tax officials in the thirteenth century. The Romans weren't far away, however – their main route from Old Sarum to Dorchester ran through the Iron Age fortification of Badbury Rings, just east of the town, where it made an uncharacteristic bend.

In 1731 Blandford was all but destroyed by fire, the fourth such conflagration since the end of the sixteenth century. The phoenix that rose from these ashes – as the Fire Monument near the church puts it – was designed by the unfortunately named Bastard brothers, John and William, whose "Blandford School" produced buildings characterized by mellow dapplings of brick and stone. Sleepy Blandford still boasts one of the most harmonious and complete Georgian townscapes in England, with its centrepieces being the **Town Hall** and the **Church of St Peter and St Paul**, built in 1739. Outside, the church's distinguishing feature is the cupola perched on its handsome square tower; inside, it has fine box pews and huge Ionic columns. It doesn't quite look as John Bastard intended, though: the church was daringly altered at the end of the nineteenth century, when the chancel was sawn off the nave, stuck on wheels, rolled out of the way so that a new section could be built in the gap, and then stuck back onto the extension. The town **museum** in Bere's Yard, opposite the church (Easter–Sept daily 11am–4pm; £1.50) offers a pithy account of local history, while **Mrs Penny's Cavalcade of Costume** at Lime Tree House, The Plocks (Easter–Sept Mon & Thurs–Sun 11am–5pm; Oct–Easter same days 11am–4pm; £3), presents over five hundred items of costume and accoutrements from 1730 to the 1950s.

Blandford's **tourist office** is in the car park on West Street (Mon–Sat: April–Oct 10am–5pm; Nov–March 10am–1pm; ☎01258/454770, ⓦwww .ruraldorset.com). There are numerous **B&Bs** along Whitecliff Mill Street to choose from, or try *Gone Walkabout*, at 3 Alexandra St (☎01258/455699, ⓔ101454.1674@compuserve.com; no smoking; ❶), a Georgian house close to the town centre where walkers and cyclists are welcome. The local Hall & Woodhouse brewery supplies many local **inns** – the *Greyhound*, in quiet Greyhound Place (off Market Place), is a good-looking pub with outdoor seating and great food.

Cerne Abbas

Sixteen miles west of Blandford, just off the A352 (on the regular #216 bus route between Dorchester and Sherborne), the village of **CERNE ABBAS** has bags of charm in its own right, with gorgeous Tudor cottages and abbey ruins, but its main attraction is carved into the chalk hillside, visible from the main road just to the north. Here, the enormously priapic **giant** stands 180-feet high, and flourishes a club over a disproportionately small head. The age of the monument is disputed: some authorities believe it to be a pre-Roman fertility symbol (accounting for its most prominent feature), others that it might be a Romano-British figure of Hercules; the most interesting theory, however, given that there is no record of the Giant until the end of the seventeenth century, is that it was etched into the hillside around the time of the Civil War as a less-than-subtle piece of propaganda intended to mock Cromwell. Whatever its true origins, folklore has it that lying on the outsize member will induce conception, but the National Trust, who now own the site, do their best to stop people wandering over it and eroding the two-foot trenches that form the outlines.

Shaftesbury

Ten miles north of Blandford, **SHAFTESBURY** perches on a spur of lumpy green-gold hills, with severe gradients on three sides of the town. On a clear day, views from the town are terrific – one of the best vantage points is **Gold Hill**, quaint, cobbled and very steep. The local history **museum** at the top of Gold Hill (Easter–Sept daily 10.30am–4.30pm; also some weekends in winter, call ☎01747/854146 to check; £1) is worth a glance – its contents include a collection of locally made buttons, for which the area was once renowned.

Pilgrims used to flock to Shaftesbury to pay homage to the bones of Edward the Martyr, which were brought to the **Abbey** in 978, though now only the footings of the abbey church survive, just off the main street (April–Oct daily 10am–5pm; £1.50). **St Peter's Church** on the market place is one of the few reminders of Shaftesbury's medieval grandeur, when it boasted a castle, twelve churches and four market crosses.

The **tourist office** is on Bell Street (mid-March to Nov daily 10am–5pm; Dec to mid-March Mon–Wed 10am–1pm, Thurs–Sat 10am–5pm; ☎01747/ 853514, ⓦwww.ruraldorset.com). Local **accommodation** includes *Maple Lodge* on Christy's Lane (☎01747/853945; ❷) and the *Knoll* in Bleke Street (☎01747/855243; ❸), which boasts views over three counties. Three miles south of town in the village of **Compton Abbas**, on the scenic A350 to Blandford, the *Old Forge*, on Chapel Hill (☎01747/811881, ⓔtheoldforge@hotmail.com; ❷), offers B&B in an eighteenth-century cottage with log fires. For a **snack** or main **meal** in Shaftesbury, try the *Salt Cellar* at the top of Gold Hill.

Stourhead

Landscape gardening was a favoured mode of display among the grandest eighteenth-century landowners, and **Stourhead**, ten miles northwest of Shaftesbury, is one of the most accomplished survivors of the genre (April–Oct Mon–Wed, Sat & Sun noon–5.30pm or dusk; garden: daily 9am–7pm or dusk; £8.50; house only £4.80; garden only £4.80, £3.70 in winter; NT). The Stourton estate was bought in 1717 by Henry Hoare, who commissioned Colen Campbell to build a new villa in the Palladian style. Hoare's heir, another Henry, returned from his Grand Tour in 1741 with his head full of the paintings of Claude and Poussin, and determined to translate their images of well-ordered, wistful classicism into real life. He dammed the Stour to create a lake, then planted the terrain with blocks of trees, domed temples, stone bridges, grottoes and statues, all mirrored vividly in the water. In 1772 the folly of **King Alfred's Tower** (April–Oct Tues–Fri 2–5.30pm or dusk, Sat & Sun 11.30am–5.30pm or dusk; £1.60) was added and today affords fine views across the estate and into neighbouring counties. The house, in contrast, is fairly run-of-the-mill, though it has some good Chippendale furniture.

A mile to the southeast, in the showpiece village of **STOURTON**, also now owned by the National Trust, the *Spread Eagle Inn* has five en-suite **rooms** available (℡01747/840587; ⑤) with prices halving in winter – it's also a good place to have **lunch**.

Longleat

If Stourhead is an unexpected outcrop of Italy in Wiltshire, the African savannah intrudes even more bizarrely at **Longleat** (Easter–Sept daily 10am–5.30pm; Oct–Easter guided tours at set times 10am–3pm, call ℡01985/844400; safari park: Easter–Oct Mon–Fri 10am–4pm, Sat, Sun & school holidays 10am–5pm; house £7; safari park £7; combined ticket £14), two and a half miles south of the road from Warminster to Frome. In 1946 the sixth marquess of Bath became the first stately-home owner to open his house to the paying public on a regular basis to help make ends meet, and in 1966 he turned Longleat's Capability Brown landscapes into a drive-through **safari park** – the first in the country. Once committed to such commercial enterprise, the bosses of Longleat knew no limits: other attractions now include the world's largest hedge maze, a Doctor Who exhibition, a hi-tech simulation of the world's most dangerous modes of travel and the seventh marquess's steamy murals encapsulating his interpretation of life and the universe (children may not be admitted). Beyond the brazen razzmatazz, though, there's an exquisitely furnished Elizabethan house, built for Sir John Thynne, Elizabeth's High Treasurer, with the largest private library in Britain and a fine collection of pictures, including Titian's *Holy Family*.

Longleat is about four miles from the train stations of Frome and Warminster and is currently served by a Lion-Link bus (Easter–Oct only) that leaves Warminster train station at 11.10am and returns from the Information Centre at Longleat at 5.15pm – the service is provided free to coach- and rail-ticket holders, and otherwise costs £1.50. Alternatively, there's the #53 bus (Mon–Sat) which shuttles roughly every hour between Warminster and Frome train stations – though be prepared to walk the two and a half miles from the entrance of the grounds to the house.

Sherborne

Tucked away in the northwest corner of Dorset, the pretty town of **SHER-BORNE** was once the capital of Wessex, its church having cathedral status until Old Sarum (see p.267) usurped the bishopric in 1075. This former glory is embodied by the magnificent **Abbey Church** (daily: April–Oct 8.30am–6pm; Nov–March 8.30am–4pm), which was founded in 705, later becoming a Benedictine abbey. Most of its extant parts date from a rebuilding in the fifteenth century, and it is one of the best examples of Perpendicular architecture in Britain, particularly noted for its outstanding **fan vaulting**. The church also has a famously weighty peal of bells, led by "Great Tom", a tenor bell presented to the abbey by Cardinal Wolsey. Among the abbey church's many tombs are those of Alfred the Great's two brothers, Ethelred and Ethelbert, and the Elizabethan poet Thomas Wyatt, all located in the northeast corner. The **almshouse** on the opposite side of the Abbey Close was built in 1437 and is a rare example of a medieval hospital; another wing provides accommodation for Sherborne's well-known public school.

Sherborne also has two "castles", both associated with Sir Walter Raleigh. Queen Elizabeth I first leased, then gave, Raleigh the twelfth-century **Old Castle** (April–Sept daily 10am–6pm; Oct daily 10am–1pm & 2–5pm; Nov–March Wed–Sun 10am–1pm & 2–4pm; £1.80; EH), but it seems that he despaired of feudal accommodation and built himself a more comfortably domesticated house, **Sherborne Castle**, in adjacent parkland (April–Oct Tues, Thurs & Sun 12.30–5pm, Sat 2.30–5pm; gardens: April–Oct daily except Wed 10am–5pm; £5.50; gardens only £2.75). When Sir Walter fell from the queen's favour by seducing her maid of honour, the Digby family acquired the house and have lived there ever since; portraits, furniture and books are displayed in a whimsically Gothic interior, remodelled in the nineteenth century. The Old Castle fared less happily, and was pulverized by Cromwellian cannonfire for the obstinately Royalist leanings of its occupants. The **museum** near the abbey on Church Lane (Easter–Oct Tues–Sat 10.30am–4.30pm, Sun 2.30–4.30pm; £1) includes a model of the Old Castle and photographs of parts of the fifteenth-century Sherborne Missal, a richly illuminated tome weighing nearly fifty pounds, now housed in the British Library.

The **tourist office** is at 3 Tilton Court, Digby Road (Mon–Sat: April–Oct 9am–5pm; Nov–Easter 10am–3pm; ☏01935/815341). For an **overnight stay** try the *Half Moon Hotel*, Half Moon Street (☏01935/812017; ❹), the *Britannia Inn*, on Westbury, just down from the abbey (☏01935/813300; ❷), or the *Cross Keys Hotel*, 88 Cheap St (☏01935/812492; ❷), which has a few tables out front for drinks and meals. *Oliver's* on Cheap Street and the *Church House Gallery* close to the abbey on Half Moon Street are both good for teas and light lunches.

Salisbury and around

SALISBURY, huddled below Wiltshire's chalky plain in the converging valleys of the Avon and Nadder, looks from a distance very much as it did when Constable painted his celebrated view of it from across the water meadows. Prosperous and well-kept, Wiltshire's only city is designed on a pleasantly human scale, with no sprawling suburbs or high-rise buildings to challenge the supremacy of the cathedral's immense spire.

The town sprang into existence in the early thirteenth century, when the

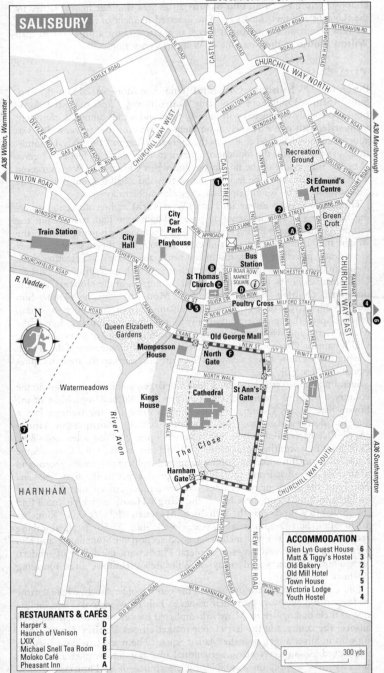

SALISBURY

▲ Old Sarum, Stonehenge (A345) & Campsite

▲ A36 Wilton, Warminster

▲ A30 Marlborough

▲ A36 Southampton

▲ A338 Bournemouth

Train Station

City Hall

Playhouse

City Car Park

Recreation Ground

St Edmund's Art Centre

Green Croft

St Thomas Church

Bus Station

Old George Mall

Mompesson House

North Gate

Queen Elizabeth Gardens

Watermeadows

Kings House

Cathedral

St Ann's Gate

The Close

Harnham Gate

HARNHAM

R. Nadder

River Avon

Poultry Cross

ACCOMMODATION

Glen Lyn Guest House	6
Matt & Tiggy's Hostel	3
Old Bakery	2
Old Mill Hotel	7
Town House	5
Victoria Lodge	1
Youth Hostel	4

RESTAURANTS & CAFÉS

Harper's	D
Haunch of Venison	C
LXIX	F
Michael Snell Tea Room	B
Moloko Café	E
Pheasant Inn	A

0 — 300 yds

© Crown copyright

265

bishopric was moved from **Old Sarum**, an ancient Iron Age hillfort settled by the Romans and their successors. The deserted remnant of Salisbury's precursor now stands on the northern fringe of the town, just a bit closer in than **Wilton House** to the west, one of Wiltshire's great houses.

The City

Begun in 1220, **Salisbury Cathedral** (June–Aug Mon–Sat 7.15am–8.15pm, Sun 7.15am–6.15pm; Sept–May daily 7am–6.15pm; £3.50 suggested donation) was mostly completed within forty years and is thus unusually consistent in its style, with one extremely prominent exception – the **spire**, which was added a century later and at 404ft is the highest in England. Its survival is something of a miracle, for the foundations penetrate only about six feet into a gravel bed in the middle of the floodplain, and when Christopher Wren surveyed it he found the spire to be leaning almost two and a half feet out of true. The tie-rods inserted by Wren helped to arrest the problem for good.

The interior is over-austere after James Wyatt's brisk eighteenth-century tidying, but there's an amazing sense of space and light in its high nave, despite the sombre pillars of grey Purbeck marble, which are visibly bowing beneath the weight they bear. Monuments and carved tombs line the walls, where they were neatly placed by Wyatt, and in the north aisle there's a fascinating clock dating from 1386, one of the oldest functioning clock mechanisms in Europe. Other features not to miss are the vaulted colonnades of the **cloisters**, and the octagonal **chapter house** (June–Aug Mon–Sat 9.30am–7.45pm, Sun noon–5.30pm; rest of year Mon–Sat 9.30am–5.30pm, Sun noon–5.30pm), which displays the best preserved of only four surviving original editions of the Magna Carta, and whose walls are decorated with a frieze of scenes from the Old Testament. On most days, you can join a free 45-minute tour of the church leaving two or more times a day, and there are also tours to the roof and spires (variable times; £3).

Surrounding the cathedral is the **Close**, the largest and most impressive in the country, a peaceful precinct of lawns and mellow old buildings. Most of the houses have seemly Georgian facades, though some, like the Bishop's Palace and the deanery, date from the thirteenth century. **Mompesson House** (April–Oct Mon–Wed, Sat & Sun noon–5.30pm; £3.90; garden only 80p; NT), built by a wealthy merchant in 1701, is a fine example of a Queen Anne house and contains some beautifully furnished eighteenth-century rooms and a superbly carved staircase, as displayed to great effect in the film *Sense and Sensibility*; the entry price includes a thirty-minute guided tour. The other building to head for in the Close is the **King's House**, in which you'll find the **Salisbury and South Wiltshire Museum** (July & Aug Mon–Sat 10am–5pm, Sun 2–5pm; rest of year closed Sun; £3.50) – an absorbing account of local history. It includes a good section on Stonehenge and also focuses on the life and times of General Pitt-Rivers, the father of modern archeology, who excavated many of Wiltshire's prehistoric sites, including Avebury (see p.271).

The Close's **North Gate** opens onto the centre's older streets, where narrow pedestrianized alleyways bear such names as Fish Row and Salt Lane, indicative of their trading origin. Many half-timbered houses and inns have survived all over the centre, and the last of four market crosses, **Poultry Cross**, stands on stilts in Silver Street, near the Market Square. The market, held on Tuesdays and Saturdays, still serves a large agricultural area, as it did in earlier times when the city grew wealthy on wool. Nearby, the church of **St Thomas** – named after Thomas à Becket – is worth a look inside for its carved timber roof and "Doom painting" over the chancel arch, depicting Christ presiding over the Last Judgment. Dating from 1475, it's the largest of its kind in England.

Lastly, to best appreciate the city's inspiring silhouette – the view made famous by Constable – take a twenty-minute walk through the water meadows southwest of the centre to **HARNHAM**; the *Old Mill* here serves drinks and modestly priced meals.

Practicalities

Trains arrive half a mile west of the centre, on South Western Road; the **bus station** is a short way north of the Market Place, on Endless Street.

The **tourist office** is on Fish Row, just off the Market Place (May, June & Sept Mon–Sat 9.30am–6pm, Sun 10.30am–4.30pm; July & Aug Mon–Sat 9.30am–7pm, Sun 10.30am–5pm; Oct–April Mon–Sat 9.30am–5pm; ℡01722/334956) and is the starting point for informative and inexpensive **guided walks** of the city.

Salisbury has a good range of **accommodation** to suit all pockets. One of the best is the *Old Mill Hotel*, Town Path, Harnham (℡01722/327517; ❺), a riverside pub about a mile from the centre, with great views across the meadows to the cathedral. Less expensive options include *Victoria Lodge*, 61 Castle Rd (℡01722/320586, ⓦwww.viclodge.co.uk; ❸), one of several good-value B&Bs along the main road to Stonehenge, and *Glen Lyn*, 6 Bellamy Lane, Milford Hill (℡01722/327880, ⓔglen.lyn@btinternet.com; ❷), an elegant Victorian guest house in a quiet lane ten minutes east of the centre. Among the more central options, try *Town House*, 1 Bridge St (℡01722/415386; ❷), a modern pub with bland but clean rooms upstairs, or the *Old Bakery*, 35 Bedwin St (℡01722/320100; ❶), an oak-beamed, 500-year-old building – there's no breakfast, hence the low rates. There are two **hostels** in town: *Matt and Tiggy's* at 51 Salt Lane (℡01722/327443), which offers eighteen beds in three properties (one a 450-year-old cottage) close to the bus station, and *Salisbury YHA* (℡01722/327572, ⓦwww.yha.org.uk), a 220-year-old building in its own spacious grounds, ten minutes' east of the cathedral at Milford Hill.

For **food and drink**, sample the good-value, traditional English fare at *Harper's*, Market Square (℡01722/333118), or the pub grub at the atmospheric *Haunch of Venison*, Minster Street, where you'll find the mummified hand of a nineteenth-century card player still clutching his cards. For something more upmarket, head for *LXIX*, 69 New St (℡01722/340000), very close to the cathedral, an elegant and expensive modern restaurant with a cheaper bistro next door. The *Michael Snell Tea Room*, 8 St Thomas's Square, is an established and popular patisserie in the city centre, with outdoor tables, and *Moloko Café*, 5 Bridge St, offers coffees and cocktails, as well as croissants, panini and salads.

Old Sarum

The ruins of **Old Sarum** (daily: April–June & Sept 10am–6pm; July & Aug 9am–6pm; Oct 10am–5pm; Nov–March 10am–4pm; £2; EH) occupy a bleak hilltop site two miles north of the city centre – an easy walk, but there are plenty of buses: #5, #6, #8 and #9 running every fifteen minutes or so (less frequent on Sun). Possibly occupied up to five thousand years ago, then developed as an Iron Age fort whose double protective ditches remain, it was settled by Romans and Saxons before the Norman bishopric of Sherborne was moved here in the 1070s. Within a couple of decades a new cathedral had been consecrated at Old Sarum, and a large religious community was living alongside the soldiers in the central castle. Old Sarum was an uncomfortable place, parched and windswept, and in 1220 the dissatisfied clergy – additionally at loggerheads with the castle's occupants – appealed to the pope for permission to decamp to Salisbury (still known officially as New Sarum). When permission was granted, the stone from the cathedral was commandeered for Salisbury's gateways, and once the church had gone the population waned. By the nineteenth century Old Sarum was deserted, but it continued to exist as a political constituency – William Pitt was one of its representatives. The most notorious of the "rotten boroughs", it returned two MPs at a time to Westminster up until the 1832 Reform Act put a stop to it.

Wilton

WILTON, five miles west of Salisbury, is renowned for its carpet industry and the splendid **Wilton House** (mid-April to Oct daily 10.30am–5.30pm; last entry 1hr before closing; £7.25; grounds only £3.75; ⓦ www.wiltonhouse.com), of which Daniel Defoe wrote: "One cannot be said to have seen any thing that a man of curiosity would think worth seeing in this county, and not have been at Wilton House." The Tudor house, built for the First Earl of Pembroke on the site of a dissolved Benedictine abbey, was ruined by fire in 1647 and rebuilt by Inigo Jones, whose classic hallmarks can be seen in the sumptuous Single Cube and Double Cube rooms, so called because of their precise dimensions. Sir Philip Sidney, illustrious Elizabethan courtier and poet, wrote part of his magnum opus *Arcadia* here – the dado round the Single Cube Room illustrates scenes from the book – and the Double Cube room was the setting for the ballroom scene in Ang Lee's film, *Sense and Sensibility*. The easel **paintings** are what makes Wilton really special, however – the collection includes paintings by Van Dyck, Rembrandt, two of the Brueghel family, Poussin, Andrea del Sarto and Tintoretto. In the grounds, the famous **Palladian Bridge** has been joined by ancillary attractions including an adventure playground, garden centre and an audiovisual show on the colourful earls of Pembroke, all designed to subsidize a massive programme of structural renovation.

Salisbury Plain and northwards

The Ministry of Defence is the landlord of much of **Salisbury Plain**, the hundred thousand acres of chalky upland to the north of Salisbury. Flags warn casual trespassers away from MoD firing ranges and tank training grounds, while rather stricter security cordons off such secretive establishments as the research centre at Porton Down, Britain's centre for chemical and biological warfare. As elsewhere, the army's presence has ironically saved much of the plain from modern agricultural chemicals, thereby inadvertently nurturing species that are all but extinct in more trampled landscapes.

Though now largely deserted except by forces families living in ugly, temporary-looking barracks quarters, Salisbury Plain once positively throbbed with communities. Stone Age, Bronze Age and Iron Age settlements left hundreds of burial mounds scattered over the chalklands, as well as major complexes at Danebury, Badbury, Figsbury, Old Sarum and, of course, the great circle of **Stonehenge**. North of Salisbury Plain, beyond the A342 Andover–Devizes road, lies the softer Vale of Pewsey, traversed by the Kennet and Avon Canal. **Marlborough**, to the north of the Vale, makes a good base for another cluster of ancient sites, including the huge stone circle of **Avebury**, the mysterious grassy mound of **Silbury Hill** and the chamber graves of **West Kennet**. Malmesbury, though in Wiltshire, is covered in Chapter 5 (see p.317), as it feels more closely allied to the Cotswolds area than to the rest of its county, from which it's cut off by the M4 and the rail line.

Stonehenge

No ancient structure in England arouses more controversy than **Stonehenge** (daily: mid-March to May & Sept to mid-Oct 9.30am–6pm; June–Aug 9am–7pm; mid-Oct to end Oct 9.30am–5pm; end Oct to mid-March 9.30am–4pm; £4.20; NT & EH; ⓦwww.stonehengematerplan.org), a mysterious ring of monoliths nine miles north of Salisbury. While archeologists argue over whether it was a place of ritual sacrifice and sun-worship, an astronomical calculator or a royal palace, the guardians of the site struggle to accommodate its year-round crowds who are resentful at no longer being able to walk among the stones (though it is now possible to make a supervised tour of the stones by calling ahead on ☎01980/626267). Annual battles between the police and gatherings of druids and New Age travellers trying to celebrate the summer solstice are a thing of the past since the passage of the draconian Criminal Justice Act in 1994 – though low-key solstice celebrations are now permitted.

Conservation of Stonehenge, one of UNESCO's 690 designated World Heritage Sites, is obviously an urgent priority, and the current custodians are trying to address the dissatisfaction that many feel on visiting this landmark. A new visitors' centre is planned two miles east of the stones at the Amesbury roundabout (scheduled to open 2005), and a re-routing of the nearby roads is projected. In the meantime, visitors are issued with handsets programmed to dispense a range of information on the site – some of the soundtrack is interesting, but much is misleading and patronizing.

What exists today is only a small part of the original prehistoric complex, as many of the outlying stones were probably plundered by medieval and later farmers for building materials. The construction of Stonehenge is thought to have taken place in several stages. In about 3000 BC the outer circular bank and ditch were constructed, and the massive Heel Stone placed outside the entrance to the central enclosure; just inside the ditch was dug a ring of 56 pits, which at a later date were filled with a mixture of earth and human ash. Around 2500 BC the first stones were raised within the earthworks, comprising approximately forty great blocks of dolerite (bluestone), whose ultimate source was Preseli in Wales. Some archeologists have suggested that these monoliths were found lying on Salisbury Plain, having been borne down from the Welsh mountains by a glacier in the last Ice Age, but the lack of any other glacial debris on the plain would seem to disprove this theory. It really does seem to be the case that the stones were cut from quarries in Preseli and dragged or floated here on rafts, a prodigious task which has defeated recent attempts to emulate it.

The crucial phase in the creation of the site came during the next six hundred years, when the incomplete bluestone circle was transformed by the construction of a circle of twenty-five **trilithons** (two uprights crossed by a lintel) and an inner horseshoe formation of five trilithons. Hewn from Marlborough Downs sandstone, these colossal stones (called sarsens), ranging from 13ft to 21ft in height and weighing up to thirty tons, were carefully dressed and worked – for example, to compensate for perspectival distortion the uprights have a slight swelling in the middle, the same trick as the builders of the Parthenon were to employ several hundred years later. More bluestones were arranged within the outer circle in various patterns, but the purpose of all this work remains baffling. The symmetry and location of the site (a slight rise in a flat valley with even views of the horizon in all directions) as well as its alignment towards the points of sunrise and sunset on the summer and winter solstices tend to support the supposition that it was some sort of observatory or time-measuring device. The site ceased to be used at around 1600 BC, and by the Middle Ages it had already become a "landmark".

There's a lot less charisma about the reputedly significant Bronze Age site of **Woodhenge** (dawn–dusk; free), two miles northwest of Stonehenge. The site consists of a circular bank about 220ft in diameter enclosing a ditch and six concentric rings of post holes, which would originally have held timber uprights, possibly supporting a roofed building of some kind. The holes are now marked more durably if less romantically by concrete pillars. A child's grave was found at the centre of the rings, suggesting that it may have been a place of ritual sacrifice.

Marlborough

Once a major stop on the old London-to-Bath stagecoach route, **MARLBOROUGH**, at the top end of the Vale of Pewsey, is a relatively tranquil spot now that the M4 deflects traffic to the north. It's a handsome town too: the wide High Street, a dignified assembly of Georgian buildings, has a fine Perpendicular church standing at each end and half-timbered cottages rambling up the alleyways behind. The famous public school is not especially old – it was established in 1843 – but incorporates an ancient coaching inn among its red-brick buildings.

Marlborough **tourist office** is in the car park on George Lane, accessible from the High Street via Hilliers Yard (Easter–Oct Mon–Sat 10am–5pm; Nov–Easter Mon–Sat 10am–4.30pm; ☎01672/513989, Ⓦwww.kennet. gov.uk) and there are several inns and guest houses offering **accommodation** along the High Street. Top of the range are *Ivy House* (☎01672/515333, Ⓦwww.ivyhousemarlborough.co.uk; ❺), a superior guest house at the top of the High Street, and the antique *Castle & Ball* (☎01672/515201; ❺), halfway along. Less expensive central options include the *Lamb Inn* (☎01672/512668; ❷), a coaching inn on the Parade, off the south side of the High Street – sometimes noisy with live music but with good accommodation – and the B&B at 63 George Lane (☎01672/512771; no credit cards; ❶), which overlooks water meadows. **Eating** options in central Marlborough include the reasonable bistro food at *Ivy House*, while *Polly Tea Rooms* serves good snacks and ice cream.

If you fancy a woodland walk or picnic, head out southeast of town into **Savernake Forest**, an ancient royal forest of oak and beech, crossed by eight long avenues that converge at its centre. You can walk there in less than thirty minutes, or else take a bus to Great Bedwyn from Marlborough (roughly hourly), asking the driver to let you off en route.

Silbury Hill, West Kennet and Avebury

The neat green mound of **Silbury Hill**, five miles west of Marlborough, is probably overlooked by the majority of drivers whizzing by on the A4. At 130ft it's no great height, but when you realize it's the largest prehistoric artificial mound in Europe, and was made by a people using nothing more than primitive spades, it commands more respect. It was probably constructed around 2600 BC, but like so many of the sites of Salisbury Plain, no-one knows quite what it was for, though the likelihood is that it was a burial mound. You can't actually walk on the hill – so having admired it briefly from the car park, cross the road to the footpath that leads half a mile to the **West Kennet Long Barrow**. Dating from about 3250 BC, this was definitely a chamber tomb – nearly fifty burials have been discovered at West Kennet.

Immediately to the west, the village of **AVEBURY** stands in the midst of a **stone circle** (free access; NT & EH) that rivals Stonehenge – the individual stones are generally smaller, but the circle itself is much wider and more complex. A massive earthwork 20ft high and 1400ft across encloses the main circle, which is approached by four causeways across the inner ditch, two of them leading into wide avenues stretching over a mile beyond the circle. The best guess is that it was built soon after 2500 BC, and presumably had a similar ritual or religious function to Stonehenge's. The structure of Avebury's diffuse circle is quite difficult to grasp, but there are plans on the site, and you can get an excellent overview at the **Alexander Keiller Museum**, at the western entrance to the site (daily: April–Oct 10am–6pm or dusk if earlier; Nov–March 10am–4pm; £3.50; NT & EH), which displays excavated material and explanatory information. Nearby, the **Barn Gallery** (same times and prices) holds a permanent exhibition of Avebury and the surrounding country, and shows clips from recently discovered home-movies of Keiller excavating the stones aided by a bevy of nubile assistants. Having absorbed the contents of the various collections, you can wander round the peaceful circle, accompanied by sheep and cattle grazing unconcernedly among the stones. To the southeast, an avenue of standing stones leads half a mile beyond West Kennet towards a spot known as the Sanctuary, though there is little left to see here.

Back in the placid **village** of Avebury, you might drop into **Avebury Manor** (April–Oct Tues, Wed & Sun 2–5.30pm; garden: April–Oct Tues, Wed & Fri–Sun 11am–5.30pm; £3.50, garden only £2.50; NT), behind the Alexander Keiller Museum. This sixteenth-century house – incorporating later alterations – has four or five panelled and plastered rooms, for which you are issued with over-shoes to protect the wooden floors from the chalk dust, and a **garden** with topiary and medieval walls. House and garden are distinctly low-key attractions, however, and little to do with the spirit of Avebury; you might find it more satisfying poking around the small village, half inside the circle, and having a **snack** or cream tea at the *Circles* vegetarian restaurant, or a drink in the *Red Lion* **pub** which also serves reasonable **meals** as well as providing a few en-suite rooms should you wish to **stay** over (℡01672/539266; ❸). There's a **tourist office** (daily: summer 10am–5.30pm; rest of year 10am–4.30pm; ℡01672/539425) in the Avebury Chapel Centre on Green Street.

Devizes

DEVIZES, seven miles down the A361 from Avebury at the mouth of the Vale of Pewsey, is a pleasant place, with some attractive eighteenth-century houses, a stately semicircular market place and a couple of fine churches, St Mary's and St John's. It's chiefly worth a stop, however, for the excellent **Museum** at 41 Long St (Mon–Sat 10am–5pm, Sun noon–4pm; £3, free Sun & Mon), housing an exceptional collection of prehistoric finds from barrows and henges throughout the county. Star exhibit is the so-called Marlborough Bucket, decorated with bronze reliefs from the first century BC.

The town offers some appealing nooks to explore: seek out the timbered and jettied row of Elizabethan-era houses on the cobbled St John's Alley, tucked away behind St John's Street. Out of town, you can enjoy a pleasant canalside stroll along the **Kennet and Avon Canal** which boasts 29 locks at Caen Hill, roughly an hour-and-a-half's walk westwards, but easily cyclable too.

Devizes has a very helpful **tourist office** at Cromwell House, Market Place (Mon–Sat 9.30am–5pm; ☎01380/729408). The best place **to stay** is the *Castle Hotel*, on New Park Street, a former coaching inn with a bar and restaurant (☎01380/729300; ❹); less expensive are the *Craven* B&B Station Road (☎01380/723514; ❶) and the *White Bear Inn*, Monday Market Street (☎01380/722583; ❷). For **eating**, try the *Wiltshire Kitchen*, St John's Street, which serves good lunches and snacks, as does the *Cheesecake* in Market Place. Also in Market Place, you'll find *Seafoods Restaurant,* a fish-and-chip takeaway that also provides more substantial sit-down meals at cheap prices.

Lacock and around

LACOCK, ten miles northwest of Devizes, is the perfect English feudal village, albeit one gentrified by the National Trust to within a hair's breadth of natural life, and besieged by tourists all summer. Appropriately for so photogenic a spot, it has a fascinating museum dedicated to the founding father of photography, Henry Fox Talbot, a member of the dynasty which has lived in the local **Abbey** since it passed to Sir William Sharington on the Dissolution of the Monasteries in 1539. Sir William's descendant, William Henry Fox Talbot, was the first to produce a photographic negative, and the **Fox Talbot Museum**, in a sixteenth-century barn by the abbey gates (March–Oct daily 11am–5.30pm; Nov–Feb Sat & Sun 11am–4pm; £3.80; NT), captures something of the excitement he must have experienced as the dim outline of an oriel window in the abbey steadily imprinted itself on a piece of silver nitrate paper. The postage-stamp-sized result is on display in the museum. The **abbey** itself (April–Oct Mon & Wed–Sun 1–5.30pm; £4.80; £6 including museum; NT), preserves a few monastic fragments amid the eighteenth-century Gothic, while the church of **St Cyriac** (free access) contains the opulent tomb of the nefarious Sir William Sharington, buried beneath a splendid barrel-vaulted roof.

The village's delightfully Chaucerian-sounding hostelry, *At the Sign of the Angel*, is a good, if expensive, **hotel** and **restaurant** (☎01249/730230; ❺).

Corsham Court and Bowood House

The main sight within a short drive of Lacock is **Corsham Court** (mid-March to Oct Tues–Sun 2–5.30pm; Oct, Nov & Jan to mid-March Sat & Sun 2–4.30pm; £5; garden only £2), three miles west. It dates from Elizabethan times, though what you see now bears the Georgian stamp of Nash and Capability Brown, and the house, furnished by Robert Adam and Thomas Chippendale among others, contains a fine collection of art, including pieces by Caravaggio, Rubens, Reynolds and Michelangelo. The village of **CORSHAM** is another dignified little cloth-making town of Bath stone, riddled with underground limestone quarries and a long railway tunnel engineered by Brunel.

Ten miles east of Corsham, off the A342 Chippenham–Devizes road and just outside the village of Calne, **Bowood House** (April–Oct daily 11am–6pm; £5.90; ⓦ www.bowood-estate.co.uk) was designed in the eighteenth century by the likes of Henry Keene, Charles Barry and – again – Robert Adam. Adam was primarily responsible for the great south front and the Orangery, and, inside the house, the library – though the present appearance of this owes more to Charles Robert Cockerell, architect of Oxford's Ashmolean Museum, who also built the Neoclassical chapel. But it is the magnificent grounds of Bowood that are the real draw, with rhododendron gardens, a Doric temple on the banks of its placid lake and a waterfall in the woods; there's also an adventure playground for kids, and a restaurant.

Bradford on Avon and around

With its buildings of mellow auburn stone, reminiscent of the townscapes just over the county border in Bath and the Cotswolds, **BRADFORD ON AVON** is the most appealing town in the northwest corner of Wiltshire. Sheltering against a steep wooded slope, it takes its name from its "broad ford" across the Avon, though the original fording place was replaced in the thirteenth century by a **bridge** that was in turn largely rebuilt in the seventeenth century. The domed structure at one end is a quaint old jail converted from a chapel.

The local industry, based on textiles like that of its Yorkshire namesake, was revolutionized with the arrival of Flemish weavers in 1659, and many of the town's handsome buildings reflect the prosperity of this period. Yet Bradford's most significant building is the tiny **St Laurence Church** on Church Street, an outstanding example of Saxon architecture dating from about 700 AD. Wrecked by Viking invaders, and later used as a school and a simple dwelling, it was rehabilitated by a local vicar in 1856. Its distinctive features are the carved angels over the chancel arch.

Bradford's **train station** is on St Margaret's Street close to the town centre. The well-equipped **tourist office** is near the bridge at 34 Silver St (daily: April–Dec 10am–5pm; Jan–March 10am–4pm; ☎01225/865797, ⒲www .bradfordonavontown.com). Bradford has a good range of **accommodation**, none more characterful than *Bradford Old Windmill*, a B&B up the hill at 4 Mason's Lane (☎01225/866842; ❸, ❺), where an imaginative vegetarian menu is served house-party style (evening meals currently on Mon, Thurs & Sat). The lowest rates are given for anyone arriving after 6pm (assuming there's space); winter opening is irregular. *Priory Steps*, closer to the centre on Newtown (☎01225/862230; ❺), is a family home with bags of personality, well-prepared dinners and excellent views over a roofscape of weavers' cottages. For light lunches or cakes, try the *Bridge Tea Rooms* on Bridge Street, or *Scribbling Horse* at 34 Silver St. For alcohol or more substantial food, head for the *Bunch of Grapes* **pub** on Silver Street, also an evening venue for jazz, folk and blues.

Great Chalfield

Great Chalfield Manor (guided tours: April–Oct Tues–Thurs 12.15pm, 2.15pm, 3pm, 3.45pm & 4.30pm; £3.80; NT), two and a half miles northeast of Bradford, is a splendid moated complex of house, church and outbuildings dating from about 1470, sensitively restored at the beginning of the twentieth century as a family home. The exterior looks like a typical Cotswold manor, all gables and mullions; inside, the Great Hall is overlooked by a minstrels' gallery from which three gargoyle-like masks gaze down into the hall, the eyes cut away so that the womenfolk could inspect the proceedings below without jeopardizing their modesty. The interior of the church features some fifteenth-century wall paintings.

Travel details

Buses

For information on all local and national bus services, contact Traveline: ℡0870/608 2 608, ⓦwww.traveline.org.uk.

Trains

For information on all local and national rail services, contact National Rail Enquiries: ℡08457/48 49 50, ⓦwww.nationalrail.co.uk.

Bournemouth to: Brockenhurst (3 hourly; 15–25min); Dorchester (hourly; 45min); London (2 hourly; 1hr 45min–2hr); Poole (1–3 hourly; 10–15min); Southampton (3 hourly; 30–45min); Weymouth (hourly; 1hr); Winchester (1–3 hourly; 1hr).

Dorchester to: Bournemouth (hourly; 45min); Brockenhurst (hourly; 1hr); London (hourly; 2hr 30min); Weymouth (hourly; 12min).

Portsmouth to: London (3 hourly; 1hr 30min–2hr); Salisbury (hourly; 1hr 30min); Southampton (2 hourly; 40–50min); Winchester (hourly; 1hr).

Ryde (Isle of Wight) to: Shanklin (2 hourly; 25min).

Salisbury to: Exeter (every 2hr; 2hr); London (2–3 hourly; 1hr 20min); Portsmouth (hourly; 1hr 30min); Southampton (2 hourly; 30–40min).

Southampton to: Bournemouth (3 hourly; 30–45min); Bristol (hourly; 1hr 50min); Brockenhurst (3 hourly; 15min); London (2 hourly; 1hr 15min–1hr 30min); Portsmouth (2 hourly; 40–50min); Salisbury (2 hourly; 30–40min); Weymouth (hourly; 1hr 30min); Winchester (3–4 hourly; 20min).

Winchester to: Bournemouth (2 hourly; 1hr); London (2 hourly; 1hr); Portsmouth (hourly; 1hr); Southampton (3–4 hourly; 20min).

Ferries and hovercrafts

Lymington to: Yarmouth, Isle of Wight (1–2 hourly; 30min).

Poole to: Cherbourg (1–3 daily; 2hr 15min–7hr); Jersey (April to mid-May & Oct 4–6 weekly; mid-May to Sept 1–2 daily; 3hr–3hr 45min); Guernsey (April to mid-May & Oct 4–6 weekly; mid-May to Sept 1–2 daily; 2hr 30min); St Malo (mid-May to Sept 1 daily; 4hr 35min).

Portsmouth to: Bilbao (1–2 weekly; 35hr); Caen (Jan to mid-Nov 2–3 daily; 6hr–7hr 15min); Cherbourg (6–8 daily; 2hr 45min–7hr 15min); Fishbourne, Isle of Wight (1–2 hourly; 35min); Guernsey (Mon–Sat 1 daily; 6hr 30min); Jersey

(Mon–Sat 1 daily; 10hr); Le Havre (2–3 daily; 5hr 30min–7hr 45min); Ryde, Isle of Wight (1–2 hourly; 15min); St Malo (1 daily Jan to mid-Nov; 8hr 45min).

Southampton to: East Cowes, Isle of Wight (hourly; 55min); West Cowes, Isle of Wight (hourly; 22min).

Southsea to: Ryde, Isle Of Wight (2 hourly;10min).

Weymouth to: Guernsey (April–Oct 1 daily; Nov–March irregular service; 2hr); Jersey (April–Oct 1 daily; Nov–March irregular service; 3hr 15min–3hr 35min).

Oxford and around

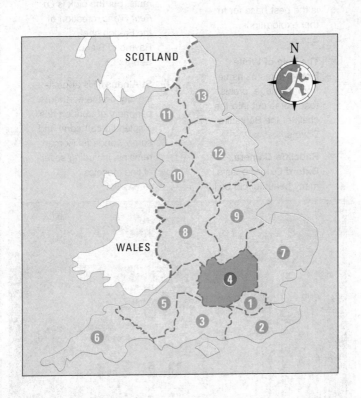

CHAPTER 4

Highlights

✳ **Chiltern Hills** Stretching southwest from Luton to the River Thames near Reading, the Chiltern Hills offer lovely wooded scenery. Henley-on-Thames, site of the famous Henley Regatta, is the best base for further explorations.
See p.279

✳ **The Vale of White Horse** Takes its name from the huge, prehistoric horse cut into the chalk of the Berkshire Downs. See p.282

✳ **Radcliffe Camera, Oxford** Oxford boasts many beautiful old buildings, but the most imposing is the Italianate rotunda, Radcliffe Camera. See p.291

✳ **Le Petit Blanc restaurant, Oxford** Oxford has several excellent restaurants, but the pick is *Le Petit Blanc*, creation of the French chef, Raymond Blanc.
See p.296

✳ **St Albans** This appealing city on the northern periphery of London has a splendid cathedral and some wonderful Roman remains, including several fine mosaics.
See p.301

4

Oxford and around

A rching around the peripheries of London, beyond the orbital M25, the "Home Counties" of England form London's commuter-belt. Beyond the suburban sprawl, however, there is plenty to entice the visitor. The northwestern Home Counties – **Berkshire**, **Buckinghamshire** and **Hertfordshire** – are at their most enticing amidst the **Chiltern Hills**, a picturesque band of chalk uplands whose wooded ridges rise near Luton, beside the M1, and stretch southwest, petering out beside the River Thames near Reading. The hills provide an exclusive setting for many of the capital's wealthiest commuters, but for the casual visitor the obvious target is **Henley-on-Thames**, a good-looking old town famous for its Regatta and with a good supply of accommodation. Henley is also a handy base for further explorations, with the village of **Cookham** – and its Stanley Spencer gallery – leading the way, though **Reading** is also of interest as the host of two of Europe's most prestigious music festivals.

The Chilterns are traversed by the **Ridgeway**, a prehistoric track – and now a national trail – that offers excellent hiking. However, the finest portion of the trail is further to the west, across the Thames, on the downs straddling the Berkshire–Oxfordshire border. Here, the Ridgeway visits a string of prehistoric sites, the most extraordinary being the gigantic chalk horse that gives the **Vale of White Horse** its name. The Vale is dotted with pleasant little villages, and both **Woolstone** and plainer **Uffington** have places to stay; but neither is it far to the university city of **Oxford**, which, with its superb architecture, museums and lively student population, can keep you busy for days. Oxford is this region's star turn and it's also close to **Woodstock**, the handsome little town abutting one of England's most imposing country homes, **Blenheim Palace**.

To the northeast of Oxford, beyond the Chilterns, the plain landscapes of north Buckinghamshire hardly fire the soul, though modest **Buckingham** is pleasant enough and it is also within easy striking distance of **Stowe Gardens**, which hold a remarkable collection of outdoor sculptures, monuments and decorative buildings. Travel east from Buckingham and you soon reach Bedfordshire, mostly flat agricultural land with a hint of industrial Midlands. It is not a county you'd cross England to visit, but **Bedford** is interesting for its John Bunyan connection and possibly useful for its hotels and restaurants.

Hit Bedfordshire and you're on the edge of the East Midlands (see chapter 9), but travel back towards London and you'll cross Hertfordshire. The prime target here is **St Albans**, an ancient and dignified town with Roman remains and a superb cathedral – but marooned amidst a knot of motorways and new towns on the fringes of London.

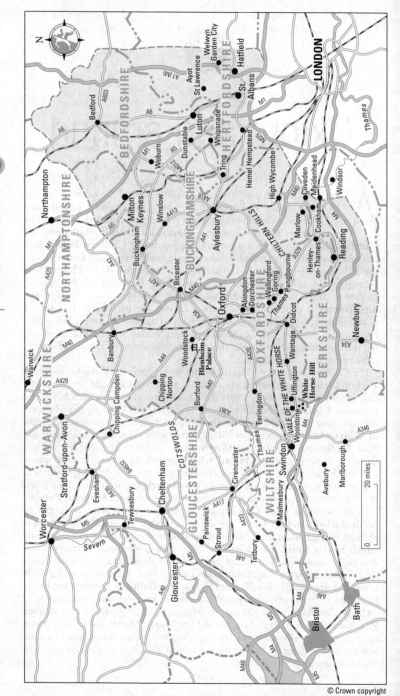

The area covered in this chapter is threaded by five **motorways**, the M25, M4, M40, M1 and A1(M). These give swift access from all directions, though drivers will need a detailed map to successfully explore the rural nooks and crannies. Long-distance **buses** mostly stick to the motorways, too, providing an efficient service to all the larger towns, but local services between the villages are patchy, sometimes non-existent. There are mainline **train** services from London's Paddington station to Oxford, Henley-on-Thames and Reading, and from London's St Pancras to St Albans and Bedford. These main routes are supplemented by a number of branch lines, the most useful of which links Henley-on-Thames with Cookham.

The Chiltern Hills and the Vale of White Horse

The **Chiltern Hills** extend southwest from the workaday town of Luton, beside the M1, bumping across Buckinghamshire and Oxfordshire as far as the River Thames, just to the west of Reading. At their best, the hills offer handsome countryside, comprising a band of forested chalk hills with steep ridges and deep valleys interrupted by easy, rolling farmland. The Chilterns are also one of the country's wealthiest areas, liberally sprinkled with exclusive commuter hideaways-cum-country homes – though there are unappetising suburban blotches too. The obvious base for visitors is **Henley-on-Thames**, a pleasant riverside town within easy striking distance of the area's key attractions and with a reasonable range of accommodation. The particular target to aim for is the village of **Cookham**, home to the fascinating Stanley Spencer gallery. Spare a thought also for **Reading**, beside the Thames at the southern tip of the Chilterns, not so much for itself (it's brusquely modern), but for its two big music festivals, Reading Rock Festival and the World Music extravaganza, WOMAD.

Crossing the Chilterns to the north and west of Henley, the **Ridgeway National Trail** (see box p.282) offers splendid hiking, though the most diverting part of the trail is further to the west, beyond the Chilterns and the Thames, amongst the more open scenery of the Berkshire and Oxfordshire downs. Here, on the edge of the **Vale of White Horse**, the trail sticks to a chalky ridge that provides magnificent views of the surrounding countryside and skirts the giant prehistoric figure after which the Vale is named. Here, you might opt to stay locally in the superb YHA hostel on the ridge above **Wantage**, in the humdrum town itself or in one of the Vale's quaint villages – tiny **Woolstone** is perhaps the most appealing.

Henley-on-Thames and around

Three counties – Oxfordshire, Berkshire and Buckinghamshire – meet at **HENLEY-ON-THAMES**, a long-established stopping place for travellers between London and Oxford. Henley is a good-looking, affluent commuter town that is at its prettiest among the old brick and stone buildings that flank the short main drag, **Hart Street**. At one end of Hart Street is the Market Place and its large and fetching **Town Hall**, at the other stands the easy Georgian curves of **Henley Bridge**. Overlooking the bridge is the parish church of **St Mary**, whose sturdy square tower sports a set of little turrets worked in chequerboard flint and stone, a popular decorative motif in the fifteenth and sixteenth centuries. Several operators run boat trips out along the Thames from near the bridge and there is also an imaginative **River and Rowing Museum** (daily: May–Aug 10am–5.30pm; rest of year closes 5pm; £4.95), a ten-minute walk south along the river bank from the foot of Hart Street via Thames Side. This focuses on three main themes – the history of the town, the development of rowing from the Greeks onwards, and the Thames as both a wildlife habitat and as a trading link.

Henley is, however, best known for its **Royal Regatta**, the world's most important amateur rowing tournament, when the town gets all puffed up and arrogant. Established in 1839, the Regatta is the boating equivalent of the Ascot races, a quintessentially English parade ground for the rich, aristocratic and aspiring, whose champagne-swilling antics are inexplicably found thrilling by larger numbers of the hoi polloi. The Regatta, featuring past and potential Olympic rowers, begins on the Wednesday before the first weekend in July and runs for five days. Further information is available from the Regatta Headquarters on the east side of the Hart Street bridge (℡01491/572153).

Practicalities

Two or three times daily a direct train runs from London's Paddington station to Henley, but mostly you have to change at Twyford. From Henley **train station**, it's a five-minute walk north to Hart Street, along Station Road and its continuation Thames Side. Henley is easy to reach by bus, too, with regular services from Oxford, Reading and London. **Buses** from Reading and points south and west mostly pull in on Hart Street, while those from the north and east – including Marlow and Cookham – stop on Bell Street, immediately to the north of Hart Street. The **tourist office** (April–Sept Mon–Sat 9.30am–6pm, Sun 11am–5pm; Oct–March daily 10am–4pm; ℡01491/578034) is located in a refurbished old barn, in a courtyard across from the Town Hall – it's clearly signed.

Henley has several first-rate **B&Bs**. One especially good option is the smart and tastefully furnished *Alftrudis*, 8 Norman Ave (℡01491/573099, ✉b&b@alftrudis.fsnet.co.uk; no credit cards; ②), which occupies a handsome Victorian town house in a quiet, leafy residential street. There are three guest rooms here, all en suite. Another excellent choice is *Lenwade*, 3 Western Rd (℡01491/573468, ✉lenwadeuk@compuserve.com; no credit cards; ③), an attractive Edwardian house with three en-suite guest rooms, comfortable furnishings and fittings and an unusual stained glass window in the hallway. **Hotels** are thin on the ground here, but pick of the punch is the delightful, wisteria-clad old coaching inn, the *Red Lion*, beside Henley Bridge, with over twenty well-appointed bedrooms, individually decorated in period style (℡01491/572161, ⊛www.redlionhenley.co.uk; ⑦).

The *Red Lion* has the best **restaurant** in town, but there are other more informal and less expensive places on Hart Street, including the *Thai Orchard* at no. 8 (℡01491/412227). **Pubs** line up on Hart Street, but the *Angel*, by the bridge, has the advantage of an outside deck overlooking the river.

Marlow

Heading north and then east out of Henley along the A4155, it's eight leafy miles to bustling **MARLOW**, another pleasant Thames-side town, its centre dotted with comely Georgian buildings. Here, you can while away an hour or two watching boats go through the lock or tracing Marlow's literary connections. In 1817 Shelley and his wife Mary moved to a house on West Street (between Hayes Place and the school) and stayed for a year – just long enough for him to compose the *Revolt of Islam* and for her to write *Frankenstein*. T.S.

Eliot lived down the road at no. 31 for a time in 1918, and Jerome K. Jerome wrote parts of *Three Men in a Boat* in the *Two Brewers* on St Peter's Street, Marlow's best pub.

There are regular **buses** from Henley to Marlow and the two are also linked by **train** – though you have to change twice and it takes about an hour. Buses drop passengers close to Marlow High Street, a couple of minutes walk from the **tourist office**, at no. 31 (Mon–Fri 9am–5pm, Sat 9.30am–5pm; winter closes 4pm; ☎01628/483597). From the train station, it's a short walk west along Station Road to the tourist office.

Cookham

Tiny **COOKHAM**, on the other side of the Thames just three miles southeast of Marlow – and not to be confused with neighbouring Cookham Dean and Cookham Rise – is noteworthy as the former home of **Stanley Spencer** (1891–1959), one of Britain's greatest – and most eccentric – artists. The Bible fired Spencer's imagination and many of his paintings depict biblical tales transposed into his Cookham surroundings – remarkable, visionary works in which the village is turned into a sort of earthly paradise. Spencer made his artistic name in the 1920s, firstly as an official war artist and then for his *Resurrection: Cookham*, which attracted rave reviews when it was exhibited in London in 1927. No one minded much that his brand of Christianity was extremely unorthodox – he called his religious system the "Church of Me" – but in the 1930s his reputation temporarily dipped and he took endless critical flak when his work took an erotic turn. Much of Spencer's most acclaimed work is displayed at the Tate Britain, in London (see p.93), but there's a fine sample here at the **Stanley Spencer Gallery** (Easter–Oct daily 10.30am–5.30pm; Nov–Easter Sat & Sun 11am–5pm; £1), which occupies the old Wesleyan Chapel on the High Street. Three prime exhibits are *Listening from Punts*, *Conversation between Punts* and the wonderful (but unfinished) *Christ Preaching at Cookham Regatta*. The permanent collection is enhanced by regular exhibitions of Spencer paintings and the gallery also contains incidental Spencer letters, documents and memorabilia, including the pram in which he used to wheel his artist's clobber around the village.

There's an hourly **train** service from Marlow to Cookham and from the station it's a pleasant ten-minute walk east across the common to the Spencer Gallery. Cookham's *Bell & Dragon* **pub**, with ancient beams and ample leather chairs, pulls a good pint and serves decent home-made food.

Reading

READING is a modern, prosperous town on the south bank of the River Thames, ten miles south of Henley. Guarding the western approaches to London, it has always been important, long a stopping-off point for kings and queens and once home to one of the country's richest abbeys. Henry VIII took care of the abbey, seizing its lands and hanging the abbot from the main gate, and today almost nothing remains of the old town except the shattered remains of the aforementioned abbey, a short walk to the east of the pedestrianized shopping centre.

There is a flourishing **arts scene** in the town, with both the Reading Film Theatre (☎0118/9868497) and the Hexagon Theatre (☎0118/9606060) offering a good programme of shows, but you wouldn't make a beeline for the place were it not for its two big summertime **music festivals**. The first, the three-day **WOMAD** festival (⊛www.womad.org; tickets ☎0118/9390930), held each

July, is a celebration of World Music, Arts and Dance, originally inspired by Peter Gabriel. Since the first WOMAD in 1982, there have been about a hundred spin-off events in twenty countries, but the Reading festival remains the focus, held at the Rivermead Leisure Complex, Richfield Avenue, just to the north of the town centre. Also held at the Rivermead Leisure Complex, but a little later in the summer, the **Reading Festival** (ⓦ www.readingfestival.com) is a three-day event featuring many of the big names of contemporary music. Details of who is performing are published in the music press at least a couple of months in advance and tickets are available from record shops across the country. The vast majority of festival-goers **camp** on site and special buses run there in their hundreds, or you can walk from Reading train station – it only takes fifteen minutes.

Reading can be reached by train from London Paddington and Waterloo. The **tourist office**, in the town hall, in the town centre on Blagrave Street (Mon–Fri 10am–5pm, Sat 10am–4pm; ☎0118/9566226), runs an accommodation-booking service; be sure to reserve a room months in advance if you're planning on being here for either festival.

The Vale of White Horse

The **Vale of White Horse**, situated between Wantage, a modest market town about thirty miles west of Henley, and Faringdon, seventeen miles southwest of Oxford, is a shallow valley, whose fertile farmland is studded with tiny villages. It takes its name from the prehistoric figure carved into the chalk downs above two of its smaller hamlets – **Uffington** and **Woolstone**. Carved in the first century BC, the horse is the most conspicuous of a string of prehistoric remains that dot the downs and include burial mounds and Iron Age forts. The **Ridgeway National Trail** (see box below), running along – or near – the top of the downs, links several of these sites and offers wonderful, breezy views over the Vale. Originally a prehistoric footpath, the Ridgeway was long used as a drove road, with sheep taken over the downs to market. Nowadays, horses are more common, the well-drained turf providing an ideal training ground for racehorses.

The Ridgeway

The Iron Age inhabitants of Britain developed the **Ridgeway** as a major thoroughfare, a fast route that beetled across the chalky downs of modern-day Berkshire and Oxfordshire, negotiated the Thames and then traversed the Chiltern Hills. The Ridgeway is one of England's fourteen national trails, running from **Overton Hill**, near Avebury in Wiltshire, to **Ivinghoe Beacon**, 85 miles to the northeast near Tring, which is itself just a few miles southwest of Luton. Crossing five counties, the trail avoids densely populated areas, keeping to the hills, except where the Thames slices through the trail at **Goring Gap** and marks the transition from the wooded valleys of the Chilterns to the more open Berkshire–Oxfordshire downs. By and large, the Ridgeway is fairly easy hiking and over half of it is accessible to cyclists and RVs. The prevailing winds mean that it is best walked in a northeasterly direction. The Ridgeway is strewn with prehistoric monuments of one description or another, though easily the finest archeological remains are on the downs edging the **Vale of White Horse** and around **Avebury**. There are several youth hostels within reach of the Ridgeway – most notably the *Ridgeway Centre Youth Hostel* near Wantage – and numerous B&Bs. The *Ridgeway National Trail Companion*, available from the National Trails Office (Cultural Services, Holton, Oxford OX33 1QQ ☎01865/810224), gives the low-down and also includes details of local accommodation. There's also a useful website: ⓦ www.nationaltrails.gov.uk.

Wantage

Workaday **WANTAGE** is an unassuming, somewhat care-worn market town, whose crowded Market Place is overseen by a statue of its most famous son, Alfred the Great (849–99), the most distinguished of England's Saxon kings. Unveiled in 1877, the statue doesn't do Alfred any favours – though he must have been very strong to stand any chance of lifting his over-large axe. From the south side of the Market Place, a couple of alleys lead through to Church Street, where the tourist office shares its premises with the **Vale and Downland Museum** (Mon–Sat 10am–4.30pm, Sun 2.30–5pm; £1.50), which is good on local history.

Wantage is handy for the finest portion of the **Ridgeway** and the museum is also the place to pick up local hiking maps and bus timetables. The quickest way to reach the Ridgeway direct from Wantage is to take bus #38 (Mon–Sat only, hourly; 10min) from the Market Place to **Letcombe Bassett**, less than a mile from the path – and the model for Cresscombe village in Hardy's *Jude the Obscure*. The best walks along the Ridgeway take you westwards from Letcombe Bassett to the White Horse (see below), a distance of about seven miles.

Long distance **buses** drop passengers in Wantage's Market Place, footsteps from the **tourist office**, on Church Street (☎01235/760176). One of the better **B&Bs** is the well-kept *Alfred's Lodge*, 23 Ormond Rd (☎01235/762409; ●), in a detached Victorian house about five minutes' walk southeast of the centre: from the east end of the Market Place, take Newbury Street and watch for Ormond on the left. Alternatively, the **Ridgeway youth hostel** (☎01235/760253; limited opening Oct to mid-March), just off the A338 a couple of miles south of Wantage and a short walk from the Ridgeway, occupies five converted barns. To get there, take bus #38 from Wantage to Letcombe Regis, and walk a mile or so uphill to the hostel from there. Wantage has one excellent **restaurant**, *Foxes* (☎01235/760568), at the foot of Newbury Street near the east end of the Market Place. This serves a changing menu of imaginatively prepared contemporary dishes featuring local ingredients, but it's expensive, with a two-course set meal costing around £20. For a less pricey deal, try either the *Cellar Bar*, a café serving tasty snacks and lunches at the east end of the Market Place on Newbury Street, or the *Lamb* (☎01235/766768), a revamped seventeenth-century building inn at the bottom of Mill Street – head northwest from the Market Place.

White Horse Hill

White Horse Hill, six miles west of Wantage along the B4507, follows close behind Stonehenge (see p.269) and Avebury (see p.271) in the hierarchy of Britain's ancient sites, though it attracts nothing like the same number of visitors. Carved into the north-facing slope of the downs above the villages of Uffington and Woolstone, the 374-foot-long **horse** looks like something created with a few swift strokes of an immense brush, and there's been no lack of weird and wonderful theories as to its origins. Some have suggested it was a glorified signpost, created to show travellers where to join the Ridgeway; others that it represented the horse (or even the dragon) of St George. In fact, burial sites excavated in the surrounding area point to the horse having some kind of sacred function, though frankly no one knows quite what. A detailed 1994 study showed that its creators dug out the soil to a depth of a metre and then filled the hollow with clear white chalk taken from a nearby hilltop. Here also, at the top of the hill, is the Iron Age earthwork of **Uffington Castle**, which provides wonderful views over the Vale.

Getting here by public transport is difficult: the only **bus**, the Ridgeway Explorer, linking Wantage and Swindon via the B4507, runs only on Sundays and Bank Holidays between June and October (timetable details on ☎0870/608 2608).

Woolstone and Uffington

About three quarters of a mile below the White Horse car park, on the north side of the B4057, is the minuscule hamlet of **WOOLSTONE**. Here, the attractive *White Horse Inn* (☎01367/820726; ❸) occupies a rickety, half-timbered, partly thatched old building and offers both good quality pub food and **accommodation**, mostly in a modern annexe. A second option is the *Hickory House* (☎01367/820303; no credit cards; ❷), offering en-suite guest rooms in a spick and span modern house close to the pub. A mile or two to the north of Woolstone, the much larger (and plainer) village of **UFFINGTON** has a couple of **B&Bs**, notably the well-kept and unassuming *Norton House*, next to the post office on the main street (☎01367/820230; no credit cards; ❷).

Oxford

Think of **OXFORD** and inevitably you think of its university, revered as one of the world's great academic institutions, inhabiting honey-coloured stone buildings set around ivy-clad quadrangles. Much of this is accurate enough, but although the university dominates central Oxford both physically and mentally, the wider city has an entirely different character, its economy built on the car plants of Cowley to the south of the centre. It was here that Britain's first mass-produced cars were produced in the 1920s and, despite the fact that there have been more downs than ups in recent years, the plants are still vitally important to the area.

Oxford started late, in Anglo-Saxon times, and blossomed even later, under the Normans, when the cathedral was constructed and Oxford was chosen as a royal residence. The origins of the university are obscure, but it seems that the reputation of **Henry I**, the so-called "Scholar King", helped attract students in the early twelfth century, their numbers increasing with the expulsion of English students from the Sorbonne in 1167. The first colleges, founded mostly by rich bishops, were essentially ecclesiastical institutions and this was reflected in collegiate rules and regulations – until 1877 lecturers were not allowed to marry and women were not granted degrees until 1920. There are common **architectural features**, too, with the private rooms of the students arranged around quadrangles (quads) as are most of the communal rooms – the chapels, halls (dining rooms) and libraries.

Oxford should be high on anyone's itinerary, and can keep you occupied for several days. The university buildings include some of England's finest architecture, and the city can also boast some excellent museums and numerous bars and restaurants.

Arrival, information and guided tours

From Oxford **train station**, it's a five- to ten-minute walk east to the centre along Park End Street and its continuation, Hythe Bridge Street. Long-distance and many county-wide buses terminate at the Gloucester Green **bus station**, in the centre adjoining George Street. Many of these buses make other city stops prior to arriving at the bus station – ask the respective company for

4

details. Most city services – including Park and Ride – are operated by the Oxford Bus Company (℡01865/785400) and many of their buses pull in on the High Street and St Giles. Oxford's (municipally engineered) lack of convenient downtown **parking** makes the city's Park-and-Ride scheme very attractive, except on Sundays when the scheme pretty much closes down and you should be able to park in the centre without much problem. There are Park-and-Ride car parks on all the main access routes into the city.

The Gloucester Green bus station is yards from the **tourist office** (April–Sept Mon–Sat 9.30am–5pm, Sun 10am–3.30pm; Oct–March closed Sun; ℡01865/726871, Ⓦwww.visitoxford.org). They have a wealth of information about the city's sights, though precious little is issued free. There are, however, two free **listings magazines**, the plodding *This Month in Oxford* and the livelier *WOW*.

The tourist office also operates an accommodation-booking service (see below) and offers excellent **guided tours** – a two-hour stroll round the city centre costs £5.85. There are several tours daily, but it's still a good idea to book in advance. More specialized tours are available, too, with one following in the footsteps of Lewis Carroll, others devoted to Tolkien and to British TV's Inspector Morse; these need to be arranged ahead of time – ring the tourist office for details.

Accommodation

With supply struggling to keep pace with demand, Oxford's central **hotels** are almost invariably expensive, though nowhere near as pricey as those in London. There are one or two inexpensive hotels in or near the centre, but by and large they are far from inspiring and, at the cheaper end of the market, you're better off choosing a **guest house** or **B&B**, of which there is a healthy supply. The problem is that the majority (but certainly not all) of these establishments are scattered on the edge of town – and Oxford is much better appreciated if you stay in the centre. That said, **Iffley Road**, southeast of the centre and the location of several reasonably priced B&Bs, gives easy access to the Cowley Road, whose northern extremity holds a gritty student ghetto that is the liveliest part of Oxford outside of the centre. Wherever you stay, book ahead in high season either direct or through the tourist office (see above), which operates an efficient accommodation-booking service and compiles a comprehensive accommodation listings booklet, *Staying in Oxford* (80p).

Hotels

Bath Place Hotel 4 Bath Place ℡01865/791812, Ⓦwww.bathplace.co.uk. This unusual, pink and blue hotel, down an old cobbled courtyard flanked by ancient buildings with higgledy-piggledy roofs, has just thirteen rooms, all of them reasonably attractive. The location is excellent – in the centre, off Holywell Street. ⑤

Old Bank Hotel 92 High St ℡01865/799599, Ⓔinfo@oldbank-hotel.co.uk. Great location for a first-rate hotel, a slick, glistening conversion of an old bank. Over forty immaculate bedrooms decorated in smart, modern style. Some of the rooms have great views over All Souls college. The *Quod* bistro is on the ground floor. ⑧

Parklands Hotel 100 Banbury Rd ℡01865/

554374, Ⓔtheparklands@freenet.co.uk. Pleasant fourteen-room hotel in a Victorian house with a garden, licensed restaurant and bar. North of the centre, but connected to it by a frequent bus service. Standard and en-suite rooms offer good-value for the rate. ⑥

Guest houses and B&Bs

Becket Guest House 5 Becket St ℡01865/724675. Modest but proficient bay-windowed guest house in a plain terrace close to the train station. Most rooms en suite. ②

Brown's Guest House 281 Iffley Rd ℡01865/246822, Ⓦwww.brownsgh.freeserve.co.uk. Well-maintained guest house in a pleasing Victorian property with eight rooms, most of them en suite. ③

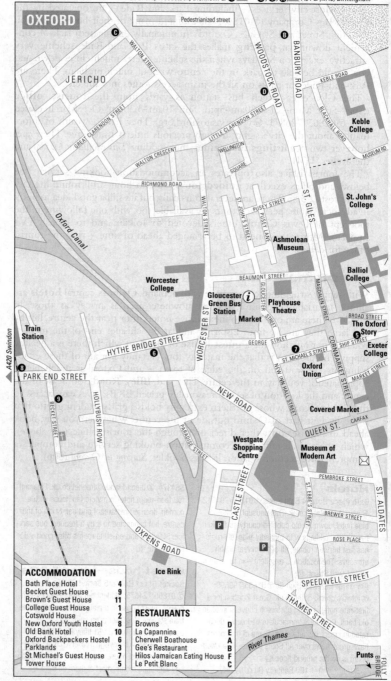

OXFORD

Stratford, Woodstock, Blenheim & ① ▲ ②, ③, Ⓐ ▲ A34 & (M40) Birmingham

Pedestrianized street

JERICHO

WALTON STREET

GREAT CLARENDON STREET

WALTON CRESCENT

RICHMOND ROAD

Oxford Canal

WALTON STREET

LITTLE CLARENDON STREET

WELLINGTON SQUARE

ST. JOHN'S STREET

PUSEY STREET

PUSEY LANE

WOODSTOCK ROAD

BANBURY ROAD

KEBLE ROAD

BLACKHALL ROAD

Keble College

MUSEUM RD.

ST. GILES

St. John's College

Ashmolean Museum

BEAUMONT STREET

Worcester College

Gloucester Green Bus Station ⓘ

Market

Playhouse Theatre

GLOUCESTER STREET

MAGDALEN STREET

Balliol College

BROAD STREET

The Oxford Story ⑤

Exeter College

Train Station

HYTHE BRIDGE STREET

WORCESTER ST.

GEORGE STREET

ST. MICHAEL'S STREET ⑦

Oxford Union

CORNMARKET STREET

SHIP STREET

MARKET STREET

⑥

A420 Swindon

PARK END STREET ⑧

⑨

BECKET STREET

HOLLYBUSH ROW

NEW ROAD

NEW INN HALL STREET

Covered Market

QUEEN ST.

CARFAX

PARADISE STREET

Westgate Shopping Centre

Museum of Modern Art

CASTLE STREET

ST. EBBE'S STREET

PEMBROKE STREET

✉

ST. ALDATES

OXPENS ROAD

Ice Rink

P

P

BREWER STREET

ROSE PLACE

SPEEDWELL STREET

THAMES STREET

River Thames

Punts

FOLLY BRIDGE

Abingdon ▼

ACCOMMODATION
Bath Place Hotel	4
Becket Guest House	9
Brown's Guest House	11
College Guest House	1
Cotswold House	2
New Oxford Youth Hostel	8
Oxford Backpackers Hostel	6
Parklands	3
St Michael's Guest House	7
Tower House	5

RESTAURANTS
Browns	D
La Capannina	E
Cherwell Boathouse	A
Gee's Restaurant	B
Hilos Jamaican Eating House	F
Le Petit Blanc	C

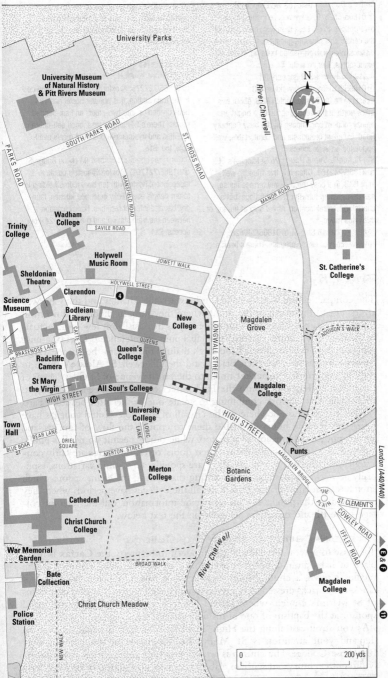

© Crown copyright

College Guest House 103 Woodstock Rd
☎01865/552579, ⌨www.collegeguesthouse.
oxfordpages.co.uk. Less than two miles north of
the centre, this pleasant guest house occupies a
distinctive older, high-gabled building. There are
eight rooms, four en suite. ❸

Cotswold House 363 Banbury Rd
☎01865/310558, ⌨www.house363.
freeserve.co.uk. This top-notch B&B, about two
miles north of the centre, occupies a bright and
breezy modern brick house on the busy Banbury
Road. Excellent breakfasts and comfortable, well-
appointed en-suite rooms. ❹

St Michael's Guest House 26 St Michael's St
☎01865/242101. Often full, this friendly, well-
kept B&B, in a cosy three-storey terrace house,
has unsurprising furnishings and fittings, but a
charming, central location. A real snip at the top of
this price range. ❷

Tower House 15 Ship St ☎01865/246828,
⌨www.scoot.co.uk/towerhouse. There's been a

bit of a hatchet job on an old house here, but the
central location is a plus and the eight rooms –
most en suite – are comfortable enough. ❹, ❻
for en suites.

Hostels

New Oxford Youth Hostel 2A Botley Rd
☎01865/727275, ✉oxford@yha.org.uk. Next door
to the train station, this popular hostel has 184
beds divided up into two-, four- and six-bedded
rooms. There's 24-hour access, good self-catering
facilities and inexpensive prepared meals available, too. £18.

Oxford Backpackers Hostel 9A Hythe Bridge St
☎01865/721761, ✉oxford@hostels.co.uk.
Independent hostel with ten bunkrooms holding up
to ten people each. Fully equipped kitchen, laundry, bar and internet facilities. Handy location
between the train station and the centre; 24-hour
access. £11.

The City

The compact centre of Oxford lies in between the Thames and the Cherwell
rivers, just to the north of the point where they join. In theory, and on most
maps, the Thames is known within the city as the "Isis", but few locals actually use the term. Central Oxford's principal point of reference is **Carfax**, a busy
junction from where three of the city's main thoroughfares begin: the **High
Street** runs east to Magdalen Bridge and the Cherwell; **St Aldate's** south to
the Thames; and **Cornmarket** north to the broad avenue of St Giles. Many of
the oldest **colleges** face onto the High Street or the sidestreets adjoining it,
their mellow stonework combining to create one of the most beautiful parts
of Oxford. Here, as elsewhere in the city, all of the more visited colleges have
restricted opening hours to enable them to control the flow of tourists, and
some impose an admission charge, too, while others permit no regular public
access at all. Of those that do open their doors, **opening times** are fairly consistent throughout the year, but there are sporadic term-time variations, especially at weekends. It's also worth noting that during the exam season, which
stretches from late April to early June, all the colleges have periods when they
are closed to the public. For more specific information, call the relevant college – the **phone numbers** are given in the text below.

From the Carfax to University College

Too busy to be comfortable and too modern to be pretty, the **Carfax** is not a
place to hang around, but it is overlooked by an interesting remnant of the
medieval town, a chunky fourteenth-century **tower**, adorned by a pair of
clock-tower jacks dressed in vaguely Roman gear. The tower is all that remains
of St Martin's church, where legend has it that William Shakespeare stood
sponsor at the baptism of one of his friend's children.

As you stroll east along the High Street from Carfax, the first building to
demand your attention is **St Mary the Virgin** – on the left just after
Brasenose College. The church is a hotchpotch of architectural styles, mostly fifteenth century, but with an elaborate, thirteenth-century pinnacled spire

and a distinctive Baroque porch, flanked by chunky corkscrewed pillars. The church's interior is disappointingly mundane, but the **tower** (daily: July & Aug 9am–7pm; rest of year closes 5pm; £1.60) – entered round the back opposite the Radcliffe Camera (see p.291) – provides exquisite views over the centre.

Further along the High Street is **University College** (no set opening times; ☎01865/276602), where the long curved facade and twin gateway towers date from the seventeenth century. Known as "Univ", the college claims Alfred the Great as its founder, but things really got going with a formal endowment in 1249, making it Oxford's oldest college – though nothing of that period survives. A year Univ may prefer to forget is 1811, when it expelled **Percy Bysshe Shelley** for distributing a paper called *The Necessity of Atheism*. Guilt later induced Univ to accept a memorial to the poet, who drowned in Italy in 1822: the white marble monument, showing the limp body of the poet borne by winged lions and mourned by the Muse of Poetry, occupies a shrine-like domed chamber in the northeast corner of the Front Quad. The college's most famous recent alumnus was Bill Clinton, the non-inhaling Rhodes Scholar; former Australian premier Bob Hawke also studied here.

Merton College

At the east end of the University College, narrow Logic Lane threads through to **Merton College** (Mon–Fri 2–4pm, Sat & Sun 10am–4pm; free; ☎01865/276310), historically the city's most important college. University college may have been founded earlier, but it was Merton – opened in 1264 – which set the model for colleges in both Oxford and Cambridge, being the first to gather its students and tutors together in one place. Furthermore, unlike the other two, Merton retains some of its original medieval buildings with the best of the thirteenth-century architecture clustering around **Mob Quad**, a charming courtyard with mullioned windows and Gothic doorways. The quad's **Library** is of interest too, built in the 1370s and the first library in England to store books upright on shelves as distinct from in piles. Much of the woodwork, including the panelling, screens and bookcases, dates from the Tudor period, but some fittings are original and there's a small display on one of the college's most distinguished alumni, Max Beerbohm. The adjacent **Chapel** is earlier, dating from 1290, and has never had a nave, leaving the transepts as ante-chapels in which a curious monument shows Thomas Bodley (founder of Oxford's most important library) surrounded by masculine-looking women in classical garb.

Other famous Merton alumni include T.S. Eliot, Angus Wilson, Louis MacNeice and Kris Kristofferson.

Magdalen College and around

Doubling back to the High Street, it's a short walk east to **Magdalen College** (pronounced "Maudlin"; Mon–Fri noon–6pm, Sat & Sun 2–6pm; £2; ☎01865/276000), dominated by its chunky medieval bell tower. The college is entered via a grand Victorian gateway, just beyond which is the **Chapel**, which has a handsome reredos – though you have to admire it from a distance, from behind a stone screen. The adjacent **cloisters**, arguably the finest in Oxford, are adorned by standing figures, some of which are biblical and others folkloric – most notably the cacophony of bizarre grotesques. Magdalen also boasts better **grounds** than most other colleges, with a bridge – at the back of the cloisters – spanning the River Cherwell to join **Addison's Walk**, which you can follow along the river and around a water meadow; rare wild fritillaries flower there in spring. Magdalen's alumni include Oscar Wilde, C.S. Lewis, John Betjeman, Julian Barnes, A.J.P. Taylor and Dudley Moore.

Just beyond the college, you can rent punts at **Magdalen Bridge** (see box, p.289); opposite, on the other side of High Street, are the **Botanic Gardens** (daily: April–Sept 9am–5pm; Oct–March 9am–4.30pm; glasshouses: April–Sept 10am–4.30pm; Oct–March 2–4pm; £2), bounded by a graceful curve of the Cherwell. First planted in 1621, the gardens are on the site of a medieval Jewish cemetery and predate all others in the country.

New College

Retracing your steps back along the High Street to Queen's, cut up **Queen's Lane** and you'll dog-leg your way north to **New College** (daily: April–Oct 11am–5pm; Nov–March 2–4pm; £2, free in winter; ☎01865/279555). Founded in 1379, the college has splendid Perpendicular Gothic architecture in its **Front Quad**, even if the addition of an extra storey in 1674 spoiled the overall effect. The **Chapel** has been mucked about, too, yet it can still lay claim to being the finest in Oxford, not so much for its design as its contents. The ante-chapel contains some superb fourteenth-century stained glass and the west window – of 1778 – holds an intriguing (if somewhat unsuccessful) Nativity scene based on a design by Sir Joshua Reynolds. Beneath it, shoved up against the wall, stands the wonderful *Lazarus* by Jacob Epstein – Khrushchev, after a visit to the college, claimed that the memory of this haunting sculpture kept him awake at night. Notable New College alumni include the Labour Party leader Hugh Gaitskell, Tony Benn and the author John Fowles.

An archway on the east side of the Front Quad leads through to the grounds, a pleasant lawn skirted by the best-preserved part of the thirteenth-century **city walls**. You can leave the college either through the north entrance into Holywell Street, or back the way you came and into New College Lane. Both are close to the east end of Broad Street.

The Sheldonian Theatre and the Bodleian Library

The east end of Broad Street abuts some of Oxford's most monumental architecture, beginning with the **Sheldonian Theatre** (Mon–Sat 10am–12.30pm & 2–4.30pm; winter closes 3.30pm; ℡01865/277299; £1.50), ringed by a series of glum-looking, pop-eyed classical heads. The Sheldonian was Christopher Wren's first major work, a reworking of the Theatre of Marcellus in Rome, semi-circular at the back and rectangular at the front. It was conceived in 1663, when the 31-year-old Wren's main job was as professor of astronomy. Designed as a stage for university ceremonies, nowadays it also functions as a concert hall, but the interior, painted in gold and a dull brown, lacks any sense of drama, and even the views from the cupola are disappointing.

Wren's colleague, Nicholas Hawksmoor, designed the **Clarendon Building**, a domineering, solidly symmetrical edifice topped by allegorical figures that is set at right angles to – and lies immediately east of – the Sheldonian. The Clarendon was built to house the University Press, but is now part of the **Bodleian Library** – the UK's largest after the British Library in London – which has an estimated eighty miles of shelves distributed among various buildings. The heart of the Bodleian is located straight across from the Clarendon in the **Old Library**, which inhabits the beautifully proportioned **Old Schools Quadrangle**, built in the early seventeenth-century in the ornate Jacobean-Gothic style that distinguishes many of the city's finest buildings. On the quad's east side is the handsome **Tower of the Five Orders**, which gives a lesson in architectural design, with tiers of columns built according to the five classical styles – Tuscan, Doric, Ionic, Corinthian and Composite. On the west side is the library's main entrance and, although most of the complex is out of bounds to the general public, you can pop into the **Divinity School** (Mon–Fri 9am–5pm, Sat 9am–12.30pm; free). Begun in 1424, and sixty years in the making, the Divinity School boasts an extravagant vaulted ceiling, a riot of pendants and decorative bosses that comprise an exquisite example of late Gothic architecture. However, this elaborate design was never carried right through – funding was a constant problem – and parts of the school were finished off in a much plainer style with the change being especially pronounced on the south wall.

You can also sign up for an hour-long **guided tour** (March–Oct Mon–Fri 10.30am, 11.30am, 2pm & 3pm, Sat 10.30am & 11.30am; £3.50) of **Convocation House**, adjacent to the Divinity School, and **Duke Humfrey's Library**, immediately above. The former is a sombre wood-panelled chamber graced by a fancy fan-vaulted ceiling, completed in 1759 but designed to look much older, while the latter is distinguished by its painted beams and carved corbels, dating from the fifteenth century, but restored and remodelled by Thomas Bodley at the turn of the seventeenth century.

Behind the Old Schools Quadrangle rises Oxford's most imposing – or vainglorious – building, the Bodleian's **Radcliffe Camera** (formerly the Radcliffe Library; no public access), a mighty rotunda, built between 1737 and 1748 by James Gibbs, architect of London's St Martin-in-the-Fields church. Gibbs was one of the few British architects of the period to have been trained in Rome and his rotunda was thoroughly Italian in style, its limestone columns ascending to a delicate balustrade, decorated with pin-prick urns and encircling a lead-sheathed dome. For a less overpowering perspective, climb the tower of the church of **St Mary the Virgin** (daily: July & Aug 9am–7pm; rest of year 9am–5pm; £1.60) to the rear of the rotunda. The views can't be bettered, both across to the rotunda and east over **All Souls College** (Mon–Fri 2–4.30pm;

free; ℡01865/279379), with its twin mock-Gothic towers (the work of Hawksmoor) and a coloured sundial designed by Wren.

Trinity and Exeter colleges

Back on Broad Street, the classical heads that shield the Sheldonian continue along the front of the modest **History of Science Museum** (Tues–Sat noon–4pm; free), where microscopes and early calculators are immaculately displayed alongside Islamic and European astrolabes. Across the street, **Trinity College** (daily 10.30am–noon & 2–4pm; £2; ℡01865/279900) sits back from the road behind trim gardens, its attractive ensemble of old stone buildings begun at the end of the seventeenth century. The expansive **Front Quad** holds the college's architectural pride and joy, its **Chapel**, where Grinling Gibbons did some of his finest carving – a distinctive performance, with cherubs' heads peering out from delicate foliage. Recent alumni include Richard Burton, Terence Rattigan and the Labour Party politician, Anthony Crosland.

From the south side of Broad Street, take Turl Street and you'll soon reach the entrance to **Exeter College** (daily: term-time 2–5pm; otherwise 10am–5pm; free; ℡01865/279600), another medieval foundation whose original buildings were chopped about in the nineteenth century. On this occasion, however, the Victorians did create something of interest in the elaborate, neo-Gothic **Chapel**, whose intricate, almost fussy detail was conceived by Sir Gilbert Scott in the 1850s. The chapel contains a superb Pre-Raphaelite tapestry, the *Adoration of the Magi*, a fine collaboration between William Morris and Edward Burne-Jones. Morris and Burne-Jones were both students here, as were J.R.R. Tolkien, Alan Bennett and Imogen Stubbs.

Near the west end of Broad Street, the **Oxford Story** (daily: April–June, Sept & Oct 9.30am–5pm; July & Aug 9.30am–5.30pm; Nov–March Mon–Fri 10am–4.30pm, Sat & Sun 10am–5pm; £6) is a purpose-built tourist attraction devoted to the history of the city and its university. It begins with an audio-visual display on university life and thereafter you hop on a "time-car", which moves through a series of historical dioramas; the same people designed the Jorvik Viking Centre in York (see p.680).

Broad Street leads into the pedestrianized **Cornmarket**, a busy shopping strip lined by major stores that cuts back to the Carfax.

South from Carfax and Christ Church College

Spreading down St Aldates from the Carfax, Oxford's **Town Hall** is an ostentatious Victorian confection that reflects a municipal determination not to be overwhelmed by the university. A staircase on its south side gives access to the **Museum of Oxford** (Tues–Fri 10am–4pm, Sat 10am–5pm, Sun noon–4pm; £1.50), which makes good use of photographs to tell the history of the city. In the face of tough competition this museum often gets ignored, but you'll discover far more here than at the "Oxford Story" in Broad Street.

Just down from the museum, the Tom Tower, added by Christopher Wren to house the weighty "Great Tom" bell in 1681, marks the main entrance to **Christ Church College** (Mon–Sat 9.30am–5.30pm, Sun 11.30am–5.30pm; £4; ℡01865/276492), Oxford's largest, most prestigious and – some would say – most pretentious college. Albert Einstein, William Gladstone and no fewer than twelve other British prime ministers were educated here, and it claims the distinction of having been founded three times, firstly by Cardinal Wolsey in 1525, then by Henry VIII after the cardinal's fall from favour and finally, after the Reformation – when the second college was suppressed – in 1545, when it assumed its present name. Beyond the main entrance is the striking **Tom**

293

△ Radcliffe Camera, Oxford

Quad, the largest quad in Oxford, so large in fact that the Royalists penned up their mobile larder of cattle here during the Civil War. The Quad's soft, honey-coloured stone makes a harmonious whole, but it was built in two main phases with the southern side dating back to Wolsey, the north finally finished in the 1660s. A staircase in the southeast corner of the quad reaches the **dining hall**, the grandest refectory in Oxford with a fanciful hammer-beam roof and a set of stern portraits of past scholars by a roll-call of well-known artists, including Reynolds, Gainsborough and Millais. A passage at the northeast corner of the Tom Quad leads through to the **Peckwater Quad**, the site of the library, and from here you can pass through to the **Canterbury Quad**, where the **Picture Gallery** provides a pokey home for works by many of Italy's finest artists, from the fifteenth to eighteenth centuries, including Leonardo da Vinci and Michelangelo.

To the rear of the Tom Quad stands the **Cathedral**, which is also – in a most unusual arrangement – the college chapel. The site was originally occupied by the Anglo-Saxon church of St Frideswide Priory, but this disappeared long ago and the present structure is essentially Norman, though it has been hacked at – Wolsey destroyed part of the west end to make space for the Tom Quad and Sir Gilbert Scott made further alterations in 1870. The Norman legacy is most apparent in the choir, where massive Norman columns rise to delicate fifteenth-century stone vaulting. Much fine medieval carving and several impressive tombs have also survived here, most notably the shrine of St Frideswide, by the Lady Chapel. A window in the adjacent Latin Chapel depicts the life of the saint, an early work by Pre-Raphaelite luminary Edward Burne-Jones – and one of several windows he completed in the choir.

Leaving Christ Church by the south entrance, you emerge at the top of **Christ Church Meadow**, which fills in the tapering gap between the rivers Cherwell and Thames. Head east along Broad Walk for the Cherwell or keep straight down tree-lined (and more appealing) New Walk for the Thames. Alternatively, if you stroll west, past the tiny War Memorial Garden, you quickly return to St Aldates, from where it's another short hop to Pembroke Street's **Museum of Modern Art** or MOMA (Tues–Sun 11am–6pm, till 9pm on Thurs; sometimes closed between exhibitions, call ☎01865/722733; £2.50, free till 1pm on Wed & from 6pm on Thurs). The gallery has an excellent programme of temporary exhibitions, featuring international contemporary art in a wide variety of media; the basement café serves good vegetarian food, too.

The Ashmolean

The university's principal museums grew up around the collections of the magpie-like **John Tradescant**, gardener to Charles I and an energetic traveller. During his wanderings, Tradescant built up a huge collection of artefacts and natural specimens, which became known as Tradescant's Ark. He bequeathed his collection to his friend and sponsor, the lawyer Elias Ashmole, who in turn gave it to the university – and they eventually split it up between the Ashmolean and the Pitt-Rivers museums. Tradescant's Ark has been added to ever since.

The **Ashmolean** (June–Aug Tues, Wed, Fri & Sat 10am–5pm, Thurs 10am–7pm, Sun noon–5pm; rest of year Tues–Sat 10am–5pm, Sun 2–5pm; free), the oldest museum in the country, occupies a mammoth Neoclassical building to the north of the centre on the corner of Beaumont Street and St Giles. The building is enormous and so is the collection – far too much to absorb in one visit, so either allow for several or stick to the highlights. Plans are available at reception and the museum shop sells a useful introductory guide for £3.95. Beginning on the ground floor, the **Egyptian** rooms should not be missed: in addition to well-preserved mummies and sarcophagi, there are unusual frescoes, rare textiles from the Roman and Byzantine periods and several fine examples of relief carving, such as on the shrine of Taharqa. Nearby, the **Islamic Art** room includes superb Islamic ceramics, while the five **Chinese Art** rooms contain some remarkable early Chinese pottery with the simple monochrome pots of the Sung dynasty (960–1279) looking surprisingly modern.

On the First Floor, a selection from Tradescant's Ark is gathered together in **Room 27**. Amongst the assorted curiosities, highlights include Guy Fawkes' lantern, Oliver Cromwell's death mask and Powhatan's mantle, a hanging made of deerskin and decorated with shells. Powhatan was the father of Pocahontas, and this mantle dates back to the earliest contacts between English colonists and the Native Americans of modern-day Virginia. Moving on, the archeologist Arthur Evans had close ties with the museum and he gifted it a stunning collection of Minoan finds from his years working at Knossos in Crete (1900–06). These artefacts are displayed in the **Crete & Aegean Room** and pride of place goes to the storage jars, sumptuously decorated with sea creatures and marine plants.

Most of the rest of the first floor is devoted to European painting from the Italian Renaissance to the twentieth century with a series of clearly labelled galleries arranged in roughly chronological order. Amongst the **Italian** works, look out for Piero di Cosimo's *Forest Fire* and Paolo Uccello's *Hunt in the Forest*, though Tintoretto, Veronese and Bellini are all well represented too. There's also a strong showing of **French paintings**, with Pissarro, Monet, Manet and Renoir featuring alongside Cézanne and Bonnard. Part of the Ashmolean's hoard of prints is on display in the **Prints & Drawings Room** with Michelangelo and Raphael taking the lead.

Up on the second floor, one room each is devoted to eighteenth- and nineteenth-century **British art**: Samuel Palmer's visionary paintings run rings around the rest, though there's lashings of Pre-Raphaelite stuff from Rossetti and Holman Hunt to assorted cohorts.

Eating and drinking

With so many students and tourists to cater for, Oxford has developed a wide choice of places to eat and drink. For a midday bite, the numerous **sandwich bars** are ideal – some of the best are listed below and you'll find several others in the Covered Market, between the High and Cornmarket, an Oxford institution as essential to local shoppers as the Bodleian is to academics. There's also a sprinkling of first-rate (and pricey) **restaurants**, but the majority cater for the less expensive end of the market with varying degrees of success – again some of the better options are listed below. Reasonable food is served at most **pubs**, but those listed have been singled out for their ambience or selection of beers rather than for their menus.

Snacks and cafés

Beat Café Little Clarendon St. Hippified café with fancy decor and stained-glass windows. Sells a good line in inexpensive sandwiches, salads and smoothies.

Convocation Coffee House Radcliffe Square. Attached to the church of St Mary the Virgin, this inexpensive café occupies an atmospheric stone-vaulted room and serves up good quality coffee and cake and quiche-and-salad lunches. There's a small outside area, but it's more than a little glum. Daily 10am–5pm. No smoking.

Felson's 32 Little Clarendon St. Another hot contender for Oxford's best sandwich bar, this tiny, friendly place has a huge range of fillings for its baguettes and rolls.

George & Davies Little Clarendon St. An established ice-cream parlour that stays open well after the pubs and cinemas. The cow mural is good fun too.

Nosebag 6 St Michael's St. A civilized but unassuming place, with chintzy decor and classical background music. The hot and cold food attracts queues at lunchtime; not so in the evening, when it is a good place for a quick but wholesome meal. Good selection of veggie food. Open till 9pm.

St Giles' Café 52 St Giles. Oxford's favourite greasy spoon. The huge fry-ups and strong coffee pulls an interesting mix of people, including the poet Elizabeth Jennings, who is said to be a regular here.

Restaurants

Browns 5–11 Woodstock Rd ☎01865/319600. Buzzing and stylish brasserie-restaurant with abundant foliage. Main courses from hamburgers to fresh salmon, in addition to legendary Guinness pies. Open for breakfast. Moderate.

La Capannina 247 Cowley Rd ☎01865/248200. Oxford's most authentic Italian is cosy and unpretentious. A mile or so up the Cowley Road, it's easy to find thanks to the extravagant mock-log-cabin facade. Inexpensive.

Cherwell Boathouse Bardwell Rd, off Banbury Rd ☎01865/552746. A deservedly popular spot for an unhurried meal at a riverside setting, about a mile north of town. Closed Mon & Tues, plus Sun eve. Reservations essential. Moderate.

Gee's Restaurant 61A Banbury Rd ☎01865/553540. Chic conservatory setting, but not as expensive as it looks. The inventive menu includes such items as chargrilled vegetables with polenta, roasted beetroot, a variety of steaks and a wide choice of breads. Strong on fish, too, with seafood main courses for around £14. Open daily for lunch and dinner plus brunch at weekends. Moderate.

Hilos Jamaican Eating House 68 Cowley Rd ☎01865/725984. Legendary West Indian restaurant with oodles of atmosphere and imported Jamaican beer; the menu's meat-oriented (curried goat often features), the lighting low and the background music heavy reggae. Moderate.

Le Petit Blanc 71–72 Walton St ☎01865/510999. Renowned French chef Raymond Blanc's affordable, and much hyped, alternative to his famous *Manoir aux Quat' Saisons* in Great Milton, some seven miles east of Oxford (☎01844/278881). The food is a refreshing mix of French gourmet (corn-fed quail with lime leaf and ginger) and traditional English (pan-fried Gloucester old spot pork). If you want to splash out, this is the place to do it – main courses are a very reasonable £12–15. Expensive.

Pubs and bars

Eagle & Child 49 St Giles. Known variously as the "Bird & Baby", "Bird & Brat" or "Bird & Bastard", this pub was once the haunt of J.R.R. Tolkien and C.S. Lewis, and still attracts a comparatively genteel mix of professionals and academics.

Isis by Iffley Lock ☎01865/242466. Lovely spot amid the flood meadows, just under two miles' walk southeast along the Thames from Folly Bridge; definitely a summer pub. Take any bus running along the Abingdon Road to Donnington Bridge, from where it's a ten-minute walk south along the river.

King's Arms 40 Holywell St. Prone to student overkill on term-time weekends, but otherwise very pleasant, with snug rooms at the back and a good choice of beers.

Lamb & Flag St Giles. Generations of university students have hung out in this old pub, which comes complete with low-beamed ceilings and a series of cramped but cosy rooms. Good range of ales.

The Turf Bath Place, off Holywell St. Small, extraordinarily atmospheric seventeenth-century pub with a fine range of beers, and mulled wine in winter. Abundant seating outside.

White Horse 52 Broad St. A tiny, old pub with snug rooms, pictures of old university sports teams on the walls and Real Ales. It was used as a set for the *Inspector Morse* TV series.

Entertainment and nightlife

Having spawned both Supergrass and Radiohead, you'd think Oxford would be hot on popular music, but the star quality of its local heroes is not reflected in either the **live-music** or **club scene** which, aside from a couple of noteworthy venues, is comparatively lame. Part of the reason for this is that the city's students tend to fall back on college discos, an option closed to the rest. By comparison, devotees of **classical music** are well catered for, with the city's main concert halls and certain college chapels – primarily Christ Church, Merton and New College – offering a wide-ranging programme of concerts and recitals. As regards **theatre**, student productions dominate the city repertoire, but the quality of acting varies, particularly when they tackle

Shakespeare, the favourite for the open-air college productions put on for tourists during the summer.

For **listings** of upcoming gigs and concerts, consult either *This Month in Oxford* or *WOW*, a glossy, listings magazine. Both are available free at the tourist office. The Friday edition of the *Oxford Times* has a listings section too. **Tickets** to most musical events are on sale at the Oxford Playhouse (see below).

Live music and clubs

The Coven Oxpens Rd ☎01865/242770. Formerly a gay disco, but now gone more or less straight. Tacky grottoes for tête-à-têtes, but generally a good atmosphere and decent music with techno/acid/hard house featuring prominently. Open Tues–Sat 9pm–2am.

Freud Walton St ☎01865/311171. Occupying a grand building in the style of a Roman temple, this new and fashionable café-bar-cum-club serves food till 8pm. Frequent live music. About five minutes' walk north of Worcester College – opposite Great Clarendon St. Open Mon & Tues 11am–midnight, Wed–Sat 11am–2am.

Old Fire Station (OFS) 40 George St ☎01865/794494. Multi-purpose venue with musicals and theatre, plus DJ club nights Fri & Sat 9pm–3am.

Park End Club Cantay House, 37 Park End St ☎01865/250181. A slick outfit, currently the most popular mainstream club in Oxford, with heavies on the door and a cattle-market atmosphere at weekends. Open Mon, Wed & Thurs–Sat 9.30pm–2am.

Zodiac 190 Cowley Rd ☎01865/420042. Far and away Oxford's most respected indie and dance venue, with live bands throughout the week. Open Mon–Sat 9pm–2am.

Classical music and theatre

Oxford Playhouse Beaumont St ☎01865/798600, ⊛www.oxfordplayhouse.co.uk. The city's best theatre. Professional touring companies perform a mixture of plays, opera and concerts, with the odd production by Oxford University Dramatic Society (OUDS), the top student group.

Pegasus Theatre Magdalen Rd ☎01865/722851, ⊛www.pegasustheatre.org.uk. Low-budget, avant-garde productions dominate the programme of this east Oxford theatre.

Sheldonian Theatre Broad St ☎01865/277299. Hard seats and less-than-perfect acoustics, but still Oxford's top concert hall.

Listings

Bike rental Bikezone, 6 Lincoln House, Market St, off Cornmarket ☎01865/728877.

Books Blackwells Map & Travel Shop, Broad St ☎01865/792792; Borders, Magdalen St ☎01865/203901; Waterstones, Broad St ☎01865/790212.

Buses Fast and frequent buses to London are operated by Oxford Tube, a subsidiary of Stagecoach (☎01865/772250), who also run most medium-range services across Oxfordshire. Most urban routes – including Park-and-Ride schemes – are operated by the Oxford Bus Company (☎01865/785400), who also offer a frequent service to London. Most other long-distance services are in the hands of National Express (☎08705/808080).

Internet Internet Exchange Café, Costa Coffee, 8–12 George St ☎01865/241601; Wired to, 138 Magdalen St ☎01865/727770.

Post Office 102 St Aldate's ☎0345/223344.

Taxis Ranks are liberally distributed across the city, including at the train station, Broad St, High St and St Giles. Alternatively, call City Taxis ☎01865/201201 or 001 Taxis ☎01865/240000.

Around Oxford

As a base for exploring some of the most delightful parts of central England, Oxford is hard to beat. It's a short drive west to the Cotswolds (see pp.309–322) and near at hand also are the Vale of White Horse (see p.282) and the Chiltern Hills (see p.279). If, on the other hand, you're using public transport, the options are much more limited, the best choice being the short and easy bus ride north to the charming little town of **Woodstock** and its imperious neighbour, **Blenheim Palace**.

Woodstock

WOODSTOCK, eight miles north of Oxford, has royal associations going back to Saxon times, with a string of kings attracted by its excellent hunting. The Royalists used Woodstock as a base during the Civil War, but, after their defeat, Cromwell never got round to destroying either the town or the palace, but the latter was ultimately given to (and flattened by) the Duke of Marlborough, in 1704. Long dependent on royal and then ducal patronage, Woodstock is now both a well-heeled commuter town for Oxford and a provider of food, drink and beds for visitors to Blenheim. It is also an extremely pretty little place, its handsome stone buildings gathered around the main square, at the junction of Market and High streets. It is here that you'll find the town's one specific sight, the **Oxfordshire Museum** (Tues–Sat 10am–5pm, Sun 2–5pm; £1), a well-composed review of the archeology, social history and industry of the county.

The museum shares its premises with the town's **tourist office** (Mon–Sat 9.30am–5.30pm, Sun 1–5pm; ☏01993/813276), which has a useful range of information on the nearby Cotswolds. Woodstock has several good **pubs**, the best being the *Bear*, a delightful old coaching inn with low-beamed ceilings and antique furnishings across from the museum; it offers a varied menu and serves a good range of beers. **Buses** from Oxford run every thirty minutes or so (reduced service on Sun), with some continuing on to Stratford-upon-Avon.

Blenheim Palace

Nowadays, successful British commanders get medals and titles, but in 1704, as a thank-you for his victory over the French at the battle of Blenheim, Queen Anne gave **John Churchill, Duke of Marlborough** (1650–1722) the royal estate of Woodstock, along with the promise of enough cash to build himself a gargantuan palace.

Work started promptly on **Blenheim Palace** (mid-March to Oct daily 10.30am–5.30pm; £9.50) with the principal architect being Sir John Vanbrugh. The end result is the country's grandest example of Baroque civic architecture, an Italianate palace that is more a monument than a house. The **interior** is stuffed with paintings and tapestries, plus all manner of *objets d'art*, including furniture from Versailles, and stone and marble carvings by Grinling Gibbons. The ceiling of the Great Hall sports painted allegories celebrating Marlborough's martial skills and the Dining Saloon holds murals by Louis Laguerre, but frankly it's hard to warm to all this conspicuous consumption. Neither is the guided tour conducive to much idle rumination, with guides whisking visitors through the palace in about an hour. As for the Marlboroughs, John Churchill was one of the few members of the clan to have made anything but a poor impression, the spectacular exception being **Sir Winston Churchill**, born here in 1874. Several rooms are dedicated to the wartime prime minister, who is buried with his wife in the graveyard of **Bladon Church**, visible from the palace.

Formal **gardens** (mid-March to Oct daily 10.30am–5.30pm; entry covered by ticket to palace) flank the house, but the open **parkland** (daily 9am–4.45pm; £2, £6 for cars, including passengers) is more enticing, especially just north of the house, where the ground falls away dramatically to an exquisite artificial lake, Queen Pool. It's said that Capability Brown, who landscaped the grounds, laid out the trees and avenues to represent the battle of Blenheim. Whatever the truth of the tale, fine vistas fan out in every direction, including one from Vanbrugh's Grand Bridge, over the main lake, up to the

Column of Victory, erected by Sarah Jennings and topped by a statue of her husband posing heroically in a toga.

There are two entrances to Blenheim, one just south of Woodstock on the Oxford road and another through the Triumphal Arch at the end of Park Street in Woodstock itself.

North Buckinghamshire and Bedfordshire

The untidy landscapes of **north Buckinghamshire** and **Bedfordshire** herald a transition between the satellite towns of London and the Midlands. Since the war, the character of the region has been transformed by the attempt to solve London's overcrowding. Sprawling suburbs now festoon many of the small country towns of yesteryear and, in the 1960s, Milton Keynes swallowed thirteen existing villages to become the country's largest new town. Nonetheless, there are several interesting targets. North Buckinghamshire has the wonderful **Stowe Gardens**, dotted with a remarkable assortment of outdoor sculptures and follies and, over in Bedfordshire, whose most distinctive feature is the wriggling River Ouse, **Bedford** deserves more than just a sideward glance, if for no other reason than for its links with John Bunyan.

Buckingham and around

Unassuming **BUCKINGHAM** is tucked into a sharp bend in the River Ouse about twenty-five miles northeast of Oxford. It became the county town of Buckinghamshire in the tenth century and flourished during medieval times, but it was bypassed by the Industrial Revolution and remained a forgotten backwater until a recent wave of incomers created the modern suburbs that surround it today. The town centre is at its prettiest along the wide, sloping Market Hill, standing in the middle of which is the **Old Gaol**, a chunky, stone structure that is home to the **tourist office** and a modest, local history **museum** (Mon–Sat 10am–4pm; £1.50). Otherwise, Buckingham is short on sights, though you might take a peek inside the sombre **Church of St Peter and St Paul**, which perches on the hill where the castle once stood – take Castle Street from the west end of Market Hill and you can't miss it.

There's no train service to Buckingham, but there are **bus** links from neighbouring towns, principally Milton Keynes. Buses stop on the High Street a few yards from the **tourist office** in the Old Gaol (July & Aug Mon–Sat 10am–4pm, Sun noon–4pm; rest of year closed Sun; ☎01280/823020). They have a small supply of **B&Bs**, which they will book on your behalf, or you can target Buckingham's best **hotel**, the *Villiers*, which occupies an imaginatively modernized old inn bang in the centre of town at 3 Castle St (☎01280/822444; ❼). Most of the rooms flank the courtyard to the rear of the main building and each is decorated in smart modern style. The best spot for **food** is the *Dipalee Indian Restaurant* (☎01280/813151), just along Castle Street from the hotel and with a good range of dishes; main courses average about £7.

Stowe Gardens

Just three miles northwest of Buckingham off the A422, **Stowe Gardens** (March–Oct Wed–Sun 10am–5.30pm; Dec Wed–Sun 10am–4pm; but call ahead to confirm times, ☎01280/822850; £4.60; NT) contain an extraordinary collection of outdoor sculptures, monuments and decorative buildings by some of the greatest designers and architects of the eighteenth century. They worked at the behest of the prodigiously wealthy Temple and Grenville families and later the dukes of Buckingham and Chandos. This ornamental miscellany has a partly naturalistic setting, representing one of the first breaks with the strictly formal garden tradition that had dominated Europe for decades. On display is work by Sir John Vanbrugh, James Gibbs and William Kent, and the grounds incorporate one of only three Palladian bridges in the country, as well as the "Grecian valley" that was Capability Brown's first large-scale design. The curious obelisk surmounted by a monkey that stands on an island in the middle of the Octagonal Lake is a monument to the dramatist William Congreve, erected in 1736 by William Kent.

At the heart of the gardens, the main **house** (£3) is also open to the public, but much less frequently as it is occupied by Stowe school.

Bedford

BEDFORD, some thirty miles east of Buckingham, has struggled to retain a modicum of character in the face of redevelopment, but the end result is pleasant enough, the town's neat and tidy centre hugging the north bank of the River Ouse. Bedford also makes the most of its connections with **John Bunyan** (1628–88), a blaspheming tinker turned Nonconformist preacher, who lived most of his life in and around the town. Bunyan fought for Parliament in the Civil War and became a well-known public speaker during Cromwell's Protectorate, but the Restoration proved disastrous for him. In 1660, he was arrested for breaking Charles II's new religious legislation, which restricted the activities of Nonconformist preachers, and he spent most of the next seventeen years in Bedford prison. During his incarceration, he wrote *The Pilgrim's Progress*, a seminal text whose simple language and powerful allegories were to have a profound influence on generations of Nonconformists.

Built in 1850 on the spot where Bunyan founded his first Independent Congregation, the **Bunyan Meeting Free Church** (Tues–Sat 10am–4pm), just east of the High Street on Mill Street, is still a Nonconformist church. It bears several memorials to Bunyan, beginning with the splendid bronze doors, decorated with ten finely worked panels depicting scenes from *The Pilgrim's Progress*. Inside, the stained glass windows develop the theme, again depicting scenes from the book, plus one showing Bunyan scribbling away in prison. Next door, the homely **Bunyan Museum** (March–Oct Tues–Sat 11am–4pm; free) features extracts from his book and tracks through the author's life and times.

Bedford's other noteworthy attraction is the **Cecil Higgins Art Gallery**, just to the south of Mill Street on Castle Lane (Tues–Sat 11am–5pm & Sun 2–5pm; £2.10, free on Fri). The gallery holds strong collections of ceramics, glass and local lace as well as a competent range of watercolours and prints, though these are not always on display due to their sensitivity to light. There are also several period rooms, done out in high Victorian style, and it's here you'll find the eccentric Burges Room, a colourful fantasy of ersatz classical and medieval decoration created by William Burges (1827–81), one of the leading figures in the Gothic Revival movement. The gallery's admission charge covers the adjacent **Bedford Museum** (same hours), an extremely dull trawl through the city's history.

Bedford is on the London St Pancras–Sheffield rail line with **trains** arriving at Midland Station, from where it's a ten-minute walk east to the centre – just follow the signs. The **bus station** is on All Hallows and from here it's a couple of minutes' walk east to the short High Street, which runs north–south and spans the River Ouse. The **tourist office** (Mon–Sat 9.30am–5pm; ☏01234/215226) is just off the High Street near the river at 10 St Paul's Square.

The town's best **hotel** is the *Swan* (☏01234/346565, ⓦwww.bedfordswan-hotel.co.uk; ❾), whose Georgian stonework conceals a lavish and tastefully modernized interior; it's down by the river at the foot of the High Street. As a second choice, the *Moat House Hotel* (☏01234/799988; ❼) occupies a blotchy high-rise across the river from the *Swan*, but its upper rooms have great views and there's a good range of fitness facilities. The tourist office has a small cachet of **B&Bs**.

Bedford's large Italian community adds a bit of zip to the local **restaurant** scene. Pick of the bunch, serving the tastiest pizzas and pastas in town, is *Pizzeria Santaniello*, 9 Newnham St, immediately to the east of Mill Street's Bunyan Meeting Free Church. Further down Newnham Street, at no. 36, *Bar Cappuccino* chips in with authentic coffee, ice cream, pizzas and snacks. In between the two, the *Castle*, has bar food and Real Ales, and occupies ancient (but heavily modernized) premises.

St Albans

ST ALBANS is one of the most appealing towns on the peripheries of London, its well-blended medley of medieval and modern features grafted onto the site of **Verulamium**, the town founded by the Romans soon after their successful invasion of 43 AD. Boudicca and her followers burned this settlement to the ground eighteen years later, but reconstruction was swift and the town grew into a major administrative base. It was here, in 209 AD, that a Roman soldier by the name of Alban became the country's first Christian martyr, when he was beheaded for giving shelter to a priest. Pilgrims later flocked to the town that had come to bear his name, with the place of execution marked by a hilltop cathedral that was once one of the largest churches in the Christian world.

Not just a religious centre, St Albans also flourished as a trading town and a staging post on the route to London from the north, its economy further buttressed by two local industries, brewing and straw-hat-making. In the nineteenth century, the coaching trade faded away with the coming of the railways, but when St Albans was connected to London by train in 1868, it rapidly reinvented itself as a prosperous and pleasant commuter town, a description that fits it well today.

St Albans' best-known attraction is its **cathedral**, but the town also possesses the outstanding **Verulamium Museum**, home to several breathtaking Roman mosaics, as well as a likeable riverside park and a number of charming old streets. All the town's main sights are within easy walking distance of each other, making St Albans an ideal day out, but if you do decide to stay the night be sure to try out some of the excellent pubs.

The City

One good way to start a tour of the city is by climbing to the top of the fifteenth-century **Clock Tower**, plumb in the centre of town where the High Street and Market Place meet (Easter–Oct Sat & Sun 10.30am–4.30pm; 35p). The climb is a tight squeeze, but worth it for the view over the **Cathedral** (daily 8.30am–5.45pm; donation requested), a vast brick and flint edifice close by and reached down a narrow passageway across from the foot of the tower. An abbey was constructed here in 1077, on the site of a Saxon abbey founded by King Offa of Mercia, and despite subsequent alterations – including the ugly nineteenth-century west front – the legacy of the Normans remains the most impressive aspect. The sheer scale of their design is breathtaking: the **nave**, almost 300-foot long, is the longest medieval nave in Britain, even if it isn't the most harmonious – the massive Norman **pillars** on the north side stand out from those in the later Early English style opposite. Some of the Norman pillars retain thirteenth- and fourteenth-century paintings, the detail clear though the ochre colours are much faded. Two- and three-tone geometric designs decorate the Norman **arches** in the nave and at the central crossing, where the impact of the original design reaches its peak with the mighty Norman tower.

A few yards to the west of the cathedral's main entrance, the **abbey gateway** is the only other part of the original complex to have survived the Dissolution. From here, Abbey Mill Lane leads down past the *Fighting Cocks* (one of the oldest pubs in the country) and across the trickle of the River Ver to **Verulamium Park**, whose sloping lawns and duck-happy ponds occupy the site of the Roman city. The park holds a scattering of Roman remains – primarily fragments of the old Roman wall and the remains of a town house with its underfloor heating system (hypocaust) – but these are hardly riveting. Instead, follow the signs to the **Verulamium Museum** (Mon–Sat 10am–5.30pm, Sun 2–5.30pm; £3), which occupies an attractive circular building on the northern edge of the park. Inside, a series of well-conceived displays illustrate and explain life in Roman Britain, but these are eclipsed by the **mosaic** room, containing five wonderful floor mosaics unearthed hereabouts in the 1930s and 1950s.

Close by, the **Roman Theatre of Verulamium** (daily: April–Sept 10am–5pm; Oct–March 10am–4pm; £1.50), across a busy road from the museum, and signposted from there, was built around 140 AD, but reduced to the status of municipal rubbish dump by the fifth century. Little more than a small hollow now, the site is still impressive enough and gives a real sense of how these theatres would once have looked. Further excavation is underway nearby, revealing a house and several workshops. From the theatre, you can walk back to the centre along **St Michael's Street**, over one of the prettier stretches of the Ver, past a sixteenth-century **watermill**, now a museum and café (Easter–Oct Mon–Sat 10am–6pm, Sun 11am–6pm; Nov–Easter closes 5pm; £1.10), and up the gently curving **Fishpool Street**, a quiet road lined with medieval inns and handsome Georgian houses.

Practicalities

Trains on the Bedford to London King's Cross line call at St Albans station, from where it's a ten-minute walk west up the hill along Victoria street to the centre – and the Clock Tower. Trains from Watford Junction (for London Euston and the North) serve the small St Albans Abbey Station, a similar distance from the centre, but this time to the south at the bottom of Holywell Hill. Most **buses** terminate at St Albans station, but virtually all services stop along the main commercial drag, St Peter's Street, too. St Peter's Street extends north from the Market Place. The **tourist office** is in the Town Hall, on the Market Place (Easter–Oct Mon–Sat 9.30am–5.30pm; Nov–Easter Mon–Sat 10am–4pm; ☎01727/864511, ⓦwww.stalbans.gov.uk).

St Albans has a good supply of **B&Bs** with several clustered near St Albans station, including the first-rate *Wren Lodge* (☎01727/855540; no credit cards; ❷), a well-maintained Edwardian house with four comfortable and attractively furnished bedrooms – two en suite. Fishpool Street is, however, a much prettier spot to head for and it's here you'll find the pleasant *Black Lion Inn*, at no. 198 (☎01727/851786, ⓔinfo@blacklioninn.abelartis.com; ❹), an ancient pub with sixteen agreeable rooms, fourteen en suite.

When it comes to **food**, St Albans' restaurant scene is a tad humdrum, but the **pubs** serve up some interesting fare. The *Goat*, on Sopwell Lane off Holywell Hill (☎01727/833934), serves some of the best food and beer in town, while the *Blue Anchor*, on Fishpool Street, is a more solidly local pub with an open fire in winter and garden seating in summer. The antique *Fighting Cocks*, on Abbey Mill Lane, has been chopped around a bit and does get mightily crowded on sunny summer days, but still has lots of enjoyable nooks and crannies in which to nurse a pint.

Travel details

Buses

For information on all local and national bus services, contact Traveline: ☎ 0870/608 2 608 (daily 7am–9pm), ⓦ www.traveline.org.uk.

Trains

For information on all local and national rail services, contact National Rail Enquiries: ☎ 08457/48 49 50, ⓦ www.nationalrail.co.uk.

Bedford to: London (1–2 hourly; 30min–1hr); St Albans (1–2 hourly; 40min).

Hatfield to: London (1–2 hourly; 20min).

Henley to: London (3 daily; 1hr).

Oxford to: Birmingham (hourly; 1hr 30min); London (1–2 hourly; 1hr); Worcester (hourly; 1hr 10min).

St Albans to: Bedford (1–2 hourly; 40min); London (14 daily; 20–40min).

The Cotswolds and Somerset

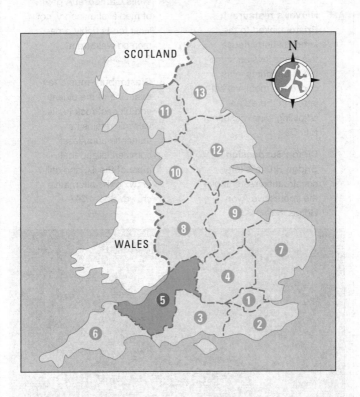

CHAPTER 5 Highlights

* **Westonbirt Arboretum, Gloucestershire** Long boulevards of elegant trees distinguish this tranquil park, an excellent spot for a picnic on a fine autumn day. See p.318

* **Harvey's restaurant, Bristol** Linked to the famous sherry house, this place lays on sumptuous banquets in its converted medieval cellars, and there's an adjoining wine museum, too. See p.335

* **Clifton Suspension Bridge** Brunel's lofty construction rears above the impressive Avon Gorge. See p.334

* **Bath** The beautifully preserved old baths complex at the heart of the town is one of the country's most fascinating Roman remains. See p.336

* **Wells Cathedral** A gem of medieval masonry, not least for its richly ornamented west front. See p.343

* **Glastonbury music festival** One of the oldest and biggest rock festivals still retains its authentic aura, less commercialized than most of the ilk, and still drawing the alternative crowd. See p.347

5

The Cotswolds and Somerset

The rolling green swards of **Gloucestershire** and **Somerset**, a wedge of land linking the Midlands with the West Country, encapsulate a vision of rural England which has very largely survived the inroads of modern urban culture. The relatively remote settlements may not, for the most part, be peopled by shepherds and farmers, but the landscape has preserved its slumberous charm, and wears a mellow tranquillity which has even seeped into the towns which grew rich on its wealth. Occupying the eastern side of Gloucestershire, the **Cotswolds**, in particular, show plenty of evidence of past prosperity, not least in the beautiful old mansions and churches endowed from the fortunes made through the medieval wool trade. Moreover, the remarkable continuity of Cotswold architecture has created villages as picturesque as any in England, though the resulting tourist deluge makes some spots nightmarish in summer. Tourism is less of a nuisance in the south of this region, around the busy market town of **Cirencester**, once an important Roman stronghold and still an important transport hub.

To the west, the land drops sharply from the Cotswold escarpment down to **Cheltenham**, an elegant Regency spa town most famous these days for its horse racing. The town's reputation as a bastion of blue-stockinged conservatism is fairly passé now, and it has developed a more sophisticated veneer in recent years, boasting some of the best restaurants and nightlife in the region. Cheltenham would also make a good base for visits to **Gloucester**, with its superb cathedral and rejuvenated harbour area, and **Stroud**, where the much praised Museum in the Park has recently opened. The Vale of Gloucester follows the route of the **River Severn** northeast towards Worcestershire, the stone cottages of the Cotswolds giving way to the thatched, half-timbered and red-brick houses which are characteristic of **Tewkesbury**, a solidly provincial town with a magnificent abbey.

South down the M5, **Bristol** is the biggest city in these parts, and one of the most go-ahead, cosmopolitan places outside London. Its dynamism and flare has saddled it with dense traffic and some pretty hideous postwar architecture, but all is compensated for by its surviving traces of every phase in its long maritime history. Bristol is within reach of old-fashioned seaside resorts – more alluring for their nostalgic atmosphere than for their swimming possibilities – and only a few miles from Georgian **Bath**, whose symmetrical honey-toned

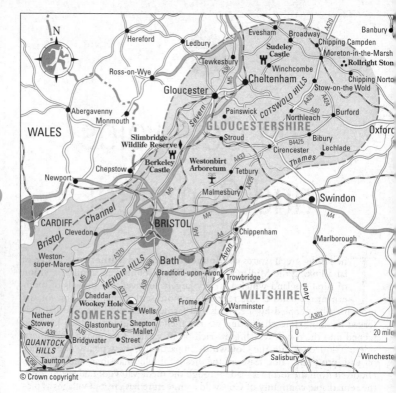

© Crown copyright

terraces contribute to its operatic setting. The proximity of urban grace to panoramic splendour is characteristic of much of **Somerset**, as in the exquisite cathedral city of **Wells**, lying on the edge of the Mendip Hills. The landscape assumes more dramatic lines west of here, where the hills are pocked by cave systems, as at **Wookey Hole**, and sliced through by the **Cheddar Gorge**. The ancient town of **Glastonbury** lies close at hand, a site steeped in Christian lore and Arthurian legend, and popular with New Age mystics. To the west, **Bridgwater** and **Taunton** lie at the southern end of the **Quantock Hills**, where Coleridge and Wordsworth roamed, a time recalled in Coleridge's old house at **Nether Stowey**.

The line between London's Paddington station and Bristol provides the backbone of the **rail network** through this region, though you could also make use of the London–Oxford–Worcester line which runs through Moreton-in-Marsh, in the middle of the Cotswolds. There are also direct lines to Cheltenham and Gloucester, and these towns form the hubs of **bus routes** which connect nearly all the places covered here – though beware that services in the Cotswolds can be extremely sketchy, with little running at all on a Sunday. Your own transport would be ideal for exploring this area, while the M4 and M5 motorways are useful through-routes for longer-distance jaunts.

The Cotswolds

The limestone hills of the **Cotswolds** are preposterously photogenic, strewn with countless picture-book villages built by wealthy cloth merchants. Wool was important here as far back as the Roman era, but the greatest fortunes were made between the fourteenth and sixteenth centuries, during which period many of the region's fine manors and churches were built. Largely bypassed by the Industrial Revolution, which heralded the area's commercial decline, much of the Cotswolds is a relic, its architecture preserved in often immaculate condition. Numerous churches are decorated with beautiful Norman carving, for which the local limestone was ideal: soft and easy to carve when first quarried, but hardening after long exposure to the sunlight. The use of this local stone is a strong unifying characteristic, though its colour modulates as subtly as the shape of the hills, ranging from a deep golden tone in **Chipping Campden** to a silvery grey in **Painswick**.

The consequence of all this is that the Cotswolds have become one of the country's main tourist attractions, with many towns inundated by tea and souvenir and antiques shops. To see the Cotswolds at their best, you should visit in winter or avoid the most popular towns and instead escape into the hills themselves. This might be a tamed landscape, but there is good scope for walks, either in the gentler valleys that are most typical of the Cotswolds or along the dramatic escarpment which marks the boundary with the Severn Valley. A long-distance path called the **Cotswold Way** runs along the top of the ridge, stretching about one hundred miles from Chipping Campden past Cheltenham, Gloucester and Stroud as far as Bath. A number of prehistoric sites provide added interest along the route, with some – such as **Belas Knap** near Winchcombe – being well worth a diversion.

There are a few large settlements in this region, the biggest true Cotswold town being **Cirencester**, a buzzing community dating back to the Romans.

Lechlade and around

Marking the westernmost navigable point of the Thames, **LECHLADE** teems with pleasure boats, but for most people it's handy as a springboard for exploring the southern fringe of the Cotswolds. For **overnight stops** the best place is the modern and stylish *Cambrai Lodge* (℡01367/253173; ❷) in Oak Street, or failing that, the *New Inn* (℡01367/252296, ⓦwww.newinnhotel.com; ❸). The boating and angling fraternities congregate at the *Trout*, a pub lying a mile southeast along the A417 (follow the signs for Faringdon) and reachable by footpath across the meadow near the church. You can **rent boats** from here in summer (£6/hour).

There's lots to see around Lechlade, the nearest sight being the tiny, disused church at **INGLESHAM**, by a farm about a mile south. Its oldest parts are late Saxon, from which period is the carved Madonna and Child on the south wall; the colourful fragments of wall paintings date from the fourteenth century. You can walk to the church along the east bank of the Thames, though you must rejoin the A361 for a short distance at the end. Isolated among fields just three miles east of Lechlade, **KELMSCOTT** has become a place of pilgrimage for devotees of **William Morris** (see box on p.310), who used the Tudor manor as a summer home from 1871 to his death in 1896. The simple beauty of the **house** (April–Sept Wed & first Sat of month 11am–1pm & 2–5pm; July & Aug also third Sat of month 11am–1pm & 2–5pm; £7; ℡01367/252486, ⓦwww.kelmscottmanor.co.uk) is enhanced by the furniture, fabrics, wallpa-

William Morris, the nineteenth-century socialist, writer and craftsman, had a pro-found influence on his contemporaries and on subsequent generations. In some respects he was an ally of Karl Marx, railing against the iniquities of private proper-ty and the squalor of industrialized society. Where he differed from Marx, however, was in his belief that machines necessarily enslave the individual, and in his vision of a world in which each person would be liberated through a sort of communistic, crafts-based economy. His prose/poem story *News from Nowhere* vaguely described his Utopian society, but his main legacy was the **Arts and Crafts Movement**, a direct offshoot of his work and a lasting influence on British crafts.

His career as an artist began at Oxford, where he met Edward Burne-Jones, who shared his admiration for the arts of the Middle Ages. After graduating they both ended up in London, painting under the direction of Dante Gabriel Rossetti, the lead-ing light of the **Pre-Raphaelites** – a loose grouping of artists intent on regaining the spiritual purity characteristic of art before Raphael and the Renaissance tainted the world with humanism. In 1861 Morris founded **Morris & Co** ("The Firm"), whose designs came to embody the ideas of the Arts and Crafts Movement, one of whose basic tenets was formulated by its founder: "Have nothing in your houses that you do not know to be useful or believe to be beautiful." Rossetti and Burne-Jones were among the designers, though the former remains better known for his paintings of Jane Morris, his friend's wife and his own mistress, whom he turned into the arche-typal Pre-Raphaelite woman. Morris's own designs for fabrics, wallpapers and numerous other products were to prove a massive – some would say negative – influence in Britain, as evidenced by the success of the Laura Ashley aesthetic, a lin-eal descendant of Morris's rustic nostalgia.

Morris's energy was not exhausted by his work for The Firm. In 1890 he set up the **Kelmscott Press**, named after but not located at his summer home, whose masterpiece was the so-called *Kelmscott Chaucer*, the collected poems of one of the Pre-Raphaelites' great heroes, with woodcuts by Burne-Jones. Morris also pioneered interest in the architecture of the Cotswolds – it was in response to hideous restoration work in this region that Morris instigated the **Society for the Protection of Ancient Buildings**, still an active force in preserving the country's architectural heritage.

pers and tapestries – some rescued from dog baskets – that were created by Morris and his Pre-Raphaelite friends, including Burne-Jones and Rossetti. Morris and his wife Jane are buried in the southeast corner of the churchyard, in the shadow of the tiny church. Entry is by timed ticket and it's wise to call first to confirm the opening hours, which are erratic. Kelmscott is a pleasant stroll along the north bank of the Thames from Lechlade, and, should you need one, there's a **bed** for the night in the nearby *Plough Inn* (℡01367/253543; ❸) which also serves **meals**.

Burford and the Windrush Valley

Nine miles north of Lechlade you get your first real taste of the Cotswolds at **BURFORD**, where the magnificent High Street, which slopes down to the bridge over the **River Windrush**, holds every variety of golden Cotswold stone. Try to avoid visiting the town in summer, when cars and tourists battle for space, though the huge **parish church**, originally Norman but remodelled in the fifteenth century, is a delight at any time. An unusual monument to Henry VIII's barber, Edmund Harman, shows four Amazonian Indians, said to be the first representation of native Americans in Britain.

Spare a morning to follow the footpath along the Windrush through **WID-BROOK**, a hamlet with an idyllic medieval chapel built in the middle of a field on the site of a Roman villa, and on to **SWINBROOK**, just under three miles east of Burford. The church in this immaculate village contains a monument showing six members of the Fettiplace family reclining comically on their elbows: the Tudor effigies rigid and stony-faced, their Stuart counterparts stylish and rather camp. The best place for lunch or a drink in Swinbrook is the *Swan Inn*.

Burford straddles several main Cotswold routes. **Buses** along the A40 between Oxford and Cheltenham stop several times a day; buses along other routes are mostly once-a-week market-day services. The **tourist office** is situated in Sheep Street (April–Sept Mon–Sat 9.30am–5.30pm, Sun 10am–3pm; Oct–March Mon–Sat 10am–4.30pm; ☎01993/823558, ⊕www.oxfordshire-cotswolds.com). There are several **B&Bs**, including the discreetly signed *Tudor Cottage* at 40 Witney St, off the main High Street, beautifully furnished with antiques (☎01993/823251, ✉bunkered@compuserve.com; ❸), or try the *Highway Hotel* at 117 High St (☎01993/822136, ⊕www.oxlink.co.uk/burford; ❷). For good **food** the *Angel Brasserie* at 14 Witney St, should satisfy; there are three themed bedrooms as well (☎01993/822714; ❸).

Motorists heading to Cirencester, ten miles southwest (see p.315), should take the B4425 via **BIBURY**: this village is completely overrun with visitors, but anyone interested in the early industrial age should make a point of going to the seventeenth-century **Arlington Mill**, for a close-up demonstration of the workings of water power (daily: Easter–Oct 10am–6pm; Nov–Easter 10am–5pm; £2).

Stow-on-the-Wold

Straddling eight roads, including the Roman Fosse Way (now the A429), **STOW-ON-THE-WOLD** sucks in a disproportionate number of visitors for its size and attractions, which essentially comprise an old marketplace surrounded by brassy pubs, antiques shops and souvenir boutiques. The narrow walled alleyways, or "tunes", running into the square were designed for funnelling sheep into the market, which is dominated by an imposing Victorian hall and, just to the south, a medieval cross allegedly raised to instil honesty among the traders.

Stow is the logical springboard for trips deeper into the region with its good bus connections from Moreton-in-Marsh and Cheltenham, and its abundant accommodation options. The **tourist office** is on the Market Square (April–Oct Mon–Sat 9.30am–5.30pm, Sun 10.30am–4pm; Nov–March Mon–Sat 9.30am–4.30pm; ☎01451/831082, ⊕www.cotswold.gov.uk). Among local **B&Bs**, try the central and relaxed *Pear Tree Cottage*, on the High Street (☎01451/831210; ❷), or the secluded and pretty *Honeysuckle Cottage* (☎01451/830973; closed Nov & Jan; ❷), tucked away on Union Street (take the short cut passage through the *King's Arms* pub from the square), while the popular **youth hostel** stands close to the tourist office (☎01451/830497). For **food**, you've a choice of several old coaching inns on the square, including the *Queen's Head*, where main courses are around the £7 mark. The nearby *Royalist*, on the corner of Park and Digbeth streets, is yet another inn billing itself the oldest in Britain, a claim in part substantiated by wooden beams carbon-dated at around one thousand years old; you can eat pub food here or sit down to dinner (£30) in the *947AD* restaurant.

Moreton-in-Marsh and around

MORETON-IN-MARSH, five miles north of Stow and fifteen miles north-west of Burford, has more of a buzz than most Cotswold towns, particularly on Tuesdays, when the High Street disappears beneath a huge market. But the thing not to miss in Moreton is the **Batsford Arboretum** (March to mid-Nov daily 10am–5pm; mid-Nov to Feb Sat & Sun 10am–4pm; £4), a fifteen-minute walk from the High Street. The largest private collection of rare trees in the country, it was planted in the 1880s by Lord Redesdale following his return from a posting in Tokyo. The hilly gardens have a distinctly Japanese flavour, and you can sit here amid magnolias and Chinese pocket-handkerchief trees enjoying wonderful views. Beside the entrance to the arboretum is the **Cotswold Falconry Centre** (March–Nov daily 10.30am–5pm; £4) which, in addition to a collection of beautiful birds of prey, gives flying displays (at 11.30am, 1.30pm, 3pm & 4.30pm; no 4.30pm flight in Nov) against a back-drop of the sweeping Evenlode Valley.

Moreton has better **public transport** services than most other towns in the region, with daily **buses** (except Sun) to Stow-on-the-Wold, Chipping Campden, Evesham, Malvern, Stratford and Cheltenham. In addition, Moreton is on the London–Oxford–Worcester **train** line. There's a useful **tourist office** in the High Street (Mon 8.45am–5pm, Tues–Thurs 8.45am–5.15pm, Fri 8.45am–4.45pm, Sat 9.30am–1pm; ℡01608/650881, ⓦwww.cotswold.gov.uk). Best value of the **hotels** is the lively *Bell Inn* (℡01608/652195, ⓦwww .bellinncotswold.com; ❸), also on the High Street. Inexpensive **B&Bs** include *Acacia*, at 2 New Rd, on the way to the station (℡01608/650130; ❶), and *Townend Coach House* on the High Street (℡01608/650846; ❷). **Places to eat** line the High Street, where blackboards advertise any number of inexpensive pub lunches. For a splash-out gourmet meal, head for the *Marsh Goose* **restaurant** (℡01608/653500; closed Mon & Tues lunch & Sun eve), on the east side of the thoroughfare, which serves superb fresh seafood and game dishes, and you can also snack at the daytime café.

Two miles southwest along the A44, just before you reach Bourton-on-the-Hill, are the blue onion domes and miniature minarets of **Sezincote** (May–July & Sept Thurs & Fri 2.30–5.30pm; garden Jan–Nov Thurs & Fri 2pm–dusk; £5, garden only £3.50), tucked gracefully if incongruously among the Cotswold hills. This extraordinary house, built in the early nineteenth century, was the result of a collaboration between architect Samuel Pepys Cockerell (a distant relative of the diarist), and artist Thomas Daniell, both of whom had spent some time in India and been inspired by Moghul architecture. The end result so impressed the Prince Regent on a visit in 1806 that he ordered the designs for Brighton Pavilion to be changed along these exotic lines. Inside, a curious classical-cum-Chinese style takes precedence; outside, temples, statues and unusual trees and shrubs are scattered about the small but exquisite garden – and in the early months of the year the snowdrops and aconites make a glorious display.

The other stately home in this area worth a visit is **Chastleton House**, three miles southeast of Moreton off the A44 (April–Oct Wed–Sat 1–4pm; £5.20; NT; bookings Tues–Fri 10am–4pm ℡01494/755585); entry is by timed ticket, which it's always wise to pre-book. Built between 1605 and 1612, this ranks among the most splendid Jacobean properties in the country, set amid orna-mental gardens that include England's first-ever croquet lawn (the rules of the game were codified here in 1865). Inside, the air of general shabbiness derives in part from the fact that the resident Jones family lost their fortune after the

Civil War (they supported the losing side), and could not subsequently afford to fill their home with fancy fittings, and in part because the National Trust, who took on the property in 1991, wisely decided the beguiling "lived-in look" should be retained. However, the house and its treasures – which include the huge barrel-vaulted long gallery, elaborate plasterwork and panelling, tapestries and exquisite glassware, geraniums and, in the beer cellar, the longest ladder (dated 1805) you're ever likely to come across – are safely preserved, minus the rope barriers and surface sheen that can sometimes mar NT properties.

Chipping Campden and around

CHIPPING CAMPDEN, six miles northwest of Moreton-in-Marsh, gives a better idea than anywhere else in the Cotswolds as to what a prosperous wool town might have looked like in the Middle Ages. The houses have undulating, weather-beaten roofs and many retain their original mullioned windows, while the fine Perpendicular **church** dates from the fifteenth century, the zenith of the town's wool-trading days. Inside, an ostentatious monument commemorates the family of Sir Baptist Hicks, a local benefactor who built the nearby almshouses and the market hall in the High Street. His own home was burnt down during the Civil War, but you can glimpse the ruins over the wall beside the church.

A fine panoramic view rewards those who make the short but severe hike up the Cotswold Way northwest to **Dover's Hill** (follow Hoo Lane north off the High Street). Since 1610 this natural amphitheatre has been the stage for an Olympics of rural sports, though the event was suspended last century when games such as shin-kicking became little more than licensed thuggery. A more civilized version, the **Cotswold Olimpick Games**, has been staged each June since 1951: no shin-kicking, but still the odd bit of hammer-throwing and tug-of-war pulling.

Such a museum-piece as Chipping Campden must inevitably cope with a bevy of visitors in summer. Try to stay overnight and explore in the evening or at dawn, when the streets are empty and the golden hues of the stone at their richest. **Public transport** to the area is good, with frequent bus services to Moreton, Evesham and Stratford. You can't move for **guest houses** along the High Street, most of which can be booked through the **tourist office** (daily 10am–5.30pm; ☎01386/841206, ⓦwww.chippingcampden.co.uk). Distinguished by its blue door, *Mrs Benfield's* on Lower High Street (☎01386/840163; ❷) has fewer lacy trimmings than most (with correspondingly low prices), as does the *Volunteer Inn* on Park Road, a few doors up on the opposite side of the road (☎01386/840688; ❸). The standard of **pubs** is good, but the *Eight Bells Inn*, around the corner from the church, is particularly cosy, and it serves top food. There's a window in the floor showing the passage once used by Catholic priests escaping from the church.

Winchcombe and around

The journey to **WINCHCOMBE**, twelve miles southwest of Chipping Campden, is stunning, whether you take the dramatic descent over the escarpment or the exhilarating ride down the B4632, which weaves along the lower folds of the cliff. Under the Saxons, Winchcombe became the provincial capital of the kingdom of **Mercia**, and it was the most important town in the Cotswolds until the early Middle Ages. The Saxon abbey didn't survive the Dissolution, and the town's main place of worship is the rather plain fifteenth-century church, most notable for its gargoyles. Apart from that, Winchcombe has an attractive blend of stone and half-timbered buildings and a museum, but the real attractions are **Sudeley Castle**, **Belas Knap** and **Hailes Abbey**, all located just outside the town. These, together with some of the finest scenery in the region and Tewkesbury only a short hop away, make Winchcombe a quieter place to base yourself than Cheltenham, and an appealing alternative to the more touristy towns and villages in the Cotswolds.

Bus #606 runs more or less hourly from Cheltenham to Winchcombe (less frequent on Sun) bound for Broadway. Winchcombe's **tourist office** (April–Oct Mon–Sat 10am–1pm & 2–5pm, Sun 10am–1pm & 1.30–4pm; Nov–March Sat & Sun 10am–1pm & 1.30–4pm; ℡01242/602925, Ⓦwww.winchcombe.co.uk/sites) in the Town Hall is right next to the small **Police and Folk Museum** (April–Oct 10am–5pm; 80p), which has examples of 1829-Peeler, Japanese and Nazi uniforms on display. Of the many **B&Bs** hereabouts, among the best are the Jacobean *Great House* on Castle Street (℡01242/602490; ❷), full of old family furniture; the more modern *Gower House* at 16 North St (℡01242/602616; ❷), and the inexpensive *Clevely*, three miles out of the village on Corndean Lane (℡01242/602059; ❷).

There's little to choose between the town's two main **pubs**, the *White Hart* and the *Plaisterers Arms*, which are both on the main street and serve food, though the latter always has Scandinavian fare on offer.

Sudeley Castle

A short walk west of Winchcombe, **Sudeley Castle** (April–Oct daily 11am–5pm; gardens March–Oct daily 10.30am–5.30pm; £6.20; gardens only £4.70) was once a favourite country retreat of Tudor and Stuart monarchs, though it never belonged to the royal family. It has a particularly strong connection with Catherine Parr, the sixth wife of Henry VIII, who came to live here after her marriage to Thomas Seymour, Lord of Sudeley, following the king's death. During the Civil War the house became a base for the Royalists (Charles I sought refuge here several times), then was later all but destroyed by the Parliamentarians. What remained stood empty until 1830, when the ruins were bought by the Dent family, whose work re-created an extremely handsome exterior but not the atmosphere of a fifteenth-century home. The motley collection inside includes paintings by Turner and Constable, a bed Charles I once slept in and one of Catherine Parr's teeth – her tomb is in the chapel. The real joy of Sudeley lies outside, in the **Queen's Garden**, with its huge yew hedges cut like masonry, and in the creeper-covered ruins of the banqueting hall; and don't miss taking in the majestic setting, with the green slopes of the escarpment behind.

Belas Knap

Up on the ridge overlooking Winchcombe, the Neolithic long barrow of **Belas Knap** occupies one of the most breathtaking spots in the Cotswolds. Dating from around 3000 BC, this is the best-preserved burial chamber in England, stretching out like a strange sleeping beast cloaked in green velvet. The two-mile climb up the Cotswold Way from Winchcombe contributes to the fun, giving good views back over Sudeley Castle. The path strikes off to the right near the entrance to Sudeley; when you reach the road at the top, turn right and then left up into the woods, from where it's a ten-minute hike to Belas Knap.

Hailes Abbey

Hailes Abbey (April–Sept daily 10am–6pm; Oct daily 10am–5pm; Nov–March Sat & Sun 10am–4pm; £2.60), a two-mile stroll northeast of

Winchcombe, was once one of England's great Cistercian monasteries. Pilgrims came here from all over the country to pray before the abbey's phial of Christ's blood, a relic shown to be a fake at the time of the Dissolution, when the thirteenth-century monastery was demolished. Not much of the original complex remains beyond the foundations, but some cloister arches survive, worn by wind and rain. The ruin is undramatic, but Hailes is still worth visiting for the attached museum, where you can get a close-up look at thirteenth-century bosses, for the tranquillity of the spot and for the nearby **church**, which is older than the abbey and contains beautiful wall paintings dating from around 1300. The cartoon-like hunting scene was probably a warning to Sabbath-breakers.

Snowshill Manor

Three miles northeast of Hailes Abbey, the traditional Cotswold manor house of **Snowshill Manor** (April–June & Sept to early Nov Wed–Sun noon–5pm; July & Aug Mon & Wed–Sun noon–5pm; garden same months & days 11am–5.30pm; £6; gardens only £3; NT) invites a detour. Inspired as a boy by his grandmother's "wonderful" Chinese cabinet (now in the Zenith room of the house), the architect, craftsman and poet Charles Paget Wade (1883–1956) spent fifty years of his life in the pursuit of objects which were not "rare or valuable" but "of interest as records of various vanished handicrafts". The results of his forays – model carts, boneshaker bicycles, children's prams, wooden toys, beds, all kinds of musical instruments – were crammed into the house, while he himself lived in a cottage in the garden. It's an endlessly diverting collection, a veritable trove of exotic curiosities. Most dramatic is the arrangement of 26 Samurai warriors dating from the seventeenth to the nineteenth centuries in the Green Room. Note that entry is by timed ticket and there is a ten-minute walk to the house from the entrance to the grounds.

Cirencester and around

On the southern fringes of the Cotswolds, **CIRENCESTER** makes a refreshing change from its more gentrified neighbours, steering clear of the "olde-worlde" image that many Cotswold towns have embraced. Under the Romans, the town was called Corinium and ranked second only to Londinium in size and importance. A provincial capital and a centre of trade, it flourished for three centuries and had one of the largest forums north of the Alps. Few Roman remains are visible in Cirencester itself thanks to the destruction meted out by the Saxons in the sixth century. The new occupiers built an abbey (the longest in England at the time), but the town's prosperity was restored only with the wool boom of the Middle Ages, when the wealth of local merchants financed the construction of one of the finest Perpendicular churches in England. Cirencester has survived as one of the most affluent towns in the area, hence the much-vaunted title "Capital of the Cotswolds".

Cirencester's heart is the **Market Place**, on Mondays and Fridays packed with traders' stalls. An irregular line of eighteenth-century facades along the north side contrasts with the heavier Victorian structures opposite, but the parish church of **St John the Baptist**, built in stages during the fifteenth century, dominates. The extraordinary flying buttresses which support the tower had to be added when it transpired that the church had been constructed upon a filled-in ditch. Its grand three-tiered south porch, the largest in England – big enough to function as the town hall at one stage – leads to the nave, where slender piers and soaring arches create a wonderful sense of space, enhanced by clerestory windows that bathe the nave in a warm light. The church contains much of interest, including a colourful wineglass **pulpit**, carved in stone in around 1450 and one of the few pre-Reformation pulpits to have survived in Britain. North of the chancel, superb fan vaulting hangs overhead in the **chapel of St Catherine**, who appears in a still vivid fragment of a fifteenth-century wall painting. In the adjacent **Lady Chapel**, look out for two good seventeenth-century monuments. Outside, one of the best views of the church is from the **Abbey Grounds**; site of the Saxon abbey, it's now a small park skirted by the modest river Churn and a fragment of the Roman city wall.

Few medieval buildings other than the church have survived in Cirencester. The houses along the town's most handsome streets – Park, Thomas and Coxwell – date mostly from the seventeenth and eighteenth centuries. One of those on Park Street houses the **Corinium Museum** (Mon–Sat 10am–5pm, Sun 2–5pm; £2.50), which devotes itself mainly to the Roman era. Given that the museum has one of the largest Roman collections in Britain, the number of exhibits on display is disappointing, but a lot of space is taken up by **mosaic pavements**, which are among the finest in the country, and the reconstructed triclinium (dining room with couches), kitchen, peristyle and butcher's shop.

Practicalities

Cirencester's **tourist office** (Mon–Sat 9.30am–5pm; ☎01285/654180, ⓦwww.cotswold.gov.uk), in the Corn Hall on the Market Place, covers the whole of the Cotswolds. A string of **B&Bs** lines Victoria Road, a short walk east: facilities and prices barely differ, though the *Ivy House* at no. 2 (☎01285/656626, ⓦwww.ivyhousecotswolds.com; ❷), *Abbeymead*, at no. 39a (☎01285/653740; ❷), and the *Leauses*, at no. 101 (☎01285/653643, ⓔthe.leauses@virgin.net; ❷) – all non-smoking – are cheaper than most. For a little more luxury, stay at the *Crown of Crucis Hotel* in Ampney Crucis (☎01285/851806, ⓦwww.thecrownofcrucis.co.uk; ❺), a sixteenth-century former coaching inn with riverside gardens, a good restaurant and a no-smoking rule; to reach it, head two-and-a-half miles east on the A417. There's a **youth hostel** in Duntisbourne Abbots (☎01285/821682), a lovely rural spot five miles west, reachable on the infrequent bus #52 between Cirencester and Gloucester (weekdays only).

For **snacks** you can't do much better than *Keith's Coffee Shop* on Blackjack Street, which also serves superb coffee. The *Café Bar* **restaurant**, next to the Brewery Centre off Cricklade Street, is inexpensive and has good vegetarian dishes (closed Sun). The best choice for a relaxing evening meal, however, is *Harry Hare's* at 3 Gosditch St (☎01285/652375), just behind the church, which specializes in classy renditions of down-to-earth English dishes for under £20. If you're splashing out and have transport, the *Crown of Crucis* in Ampney Crucis (see accommodation, above) is also worth considering.

Cirencester has plenty of **pubs**, their clientele swollen by students from the nearby Royal Agricultural College. Try the *Kings Head* on the Market Place or, for **bar meals**, the *Waggon & Horses* on London Road, and the *Butcher's Arms* in Ampney Crucis.

Daglingworth, Duntisbourne Rouse and Elkstone

The area northwest of Cirencester has a number of lovely churches well worth seeking out, particularly in the **Dunt Valley**, one of the quietest corners of the Cotswolds yet just a stone's throw from the A417. The hilltop **church** at **DAGLINGWORTH**, just two miles from Cirencester, has an unremarkable exterior, but inside there are four small stone panels – of Christ in Majesty, St Peter and two of the Crucifixion – that are among the best preserved Anglo-Saxon carvings in the country. Less than a mile beyond (you can walk along the Dunt for most of the way), the Saxon **church** at **DUNTISBOURNE ROUSE** perches on a steep bank beneath the road. If you're driving, it's easy to miss; look for the small wooden sign in the hedge. The interior of the church can't quite live up to the setting, but it has a fine Norman chancel arch and a delightful thirteenth-century wall painting of daisies. On the other side of the A417, eight miles north of Cirencester and out of the Dunt Valley, **ELKSTONE** boasts the most beautiful **Norman church** in the Cotswolds. The fifteenth-century tower aside, the church retains its original Norman structure and carving, the latter at its best in the south porch. Inside, the simple harmony of the vaulted chancel outshines even the exquisite stonework around the arches and east window, the whole bathed in golden light from the side windows. A tiny spiral staircase on the left of the altar leads to a rare priest's dovecote above the chancel.

Malmesbury

The striking half-ruin of a Norman abbey presides over the small hilltown of **MALMESBURY**, one of the oldest boroughs in England. Lying eleven miles south of Cirencester, it's not part of the Cotswolds geologically, though the town's early wealth was based on wool. Malmesbury certainly lacks the tweeness of the Cotswold towns to the north, but its new housing estates and modern developments cannot detract from the splendour of the abbey, a majestic structure with some of the finest Romanesque sculpture in the country. The #92 bus service connects Cirencester and Malmesbury every one or two hours (not Sun).

The High Street leads up to the octagonal **Market Cross**, built in around 1490 to provide shelter from the rain. Nearby, the eighteenth-century **Tolsey Gate** leads through to the **Abbey** (daily: April–Oct 10am–5pm; Nov–March 10am–4pm), founded in the seventh century and once a powerful Benedictine foundation, but burnt down in about 1050. The twelfth-century building which replaced it was damaged during the Dissolution, and other parts collapsed at a later date, so that the **nave** is the only substantial Norman part to have survived. Taking pride of place is the south porch, where a multitude of sadly worn figures in three tiers surround the doorway, depicting scenes from the Creation, the Old Testament and the life of Christ, while inside the porch the apostles and Christ are carved in a fine deep relief. The tympanum shows Christ on a rainbow, supported by gracefully gymnastic angels. Within the main body of the church, the pale stone brings a dramatic freshness, particularly to the carving of the nave arches (look out for the Norman beak-heads) and of the clerestory. To the left of the high altar, the pulpit virtually hides the **tomb of King Athelstan**, grandson of Alfred the Great and the first Saxon to be recognized as king of England; the tomb, however, is empty, the location of the king's remains unknown. The abbey's greatest surviving treasures are housed in the parvise (room above the porch), reached via a narrow spiral staircase right of the main doorway, where pride of place is given to four Flemish **medieval Bibles**, written on parchment and sumptuously illuminated with gilt ink and exquisite miniature paintings.

Malmesbury's **tourist office** is in the town hall off Cross Hayes car park (Mon–Thurs 9am–noon & 1–4.50pm, Fri closes 4.20pm, Sat 10am–noon & 1–4pm; ☎01666/823748, ⊛www.wiltshiretourism.co.uk). There are a number of **accommodation** choices right in the centre of town: the *Old Manor House* on Oxford St, above the material shop, has nicely old-fashioned rooms (℡01666/823494; ❶) and on High Street, the pricier *Kings Arms* (℡01666/823383, ⓦwww.malmesburywilts.freeserve.co.uk; ❸) has more standard facilities. For **food** the *Whole Hog*, a stone-walled tearoom-cum-pub overlooking the Market Place, is inexpensive, and *Summer Café* on the High Street, is better for teas and coffees and also does good sandwiches.

Westonbirt Arboretum

Twelve miles southwest of Cirencester, **Westonbirt Arboretum** (daily 10am–8pm or sunset; £4.25; ⓦwww.westonbirtarboretum.com) claims one of the largest collections of temperate trees and shrubs in the world: the maple trees, which set the place ablaze in autumn, and the blankets of bluebells and anemones in spring draw the biggest crowds. Azaleas, rhododendrons and camellias provide other great splashes of colour. Numerous paths crisscross the six-hundred-acre garden: an average circular walk takes about an hour and a half, but you can easily stroll about for much longer than that. The arboretum flanks the A433, just west of Westonbirt village and three miles southwest of Tetbury, a handsome but untouristy Cotswold town. (Keen royalists should keep an eye open for the Prince of Wales and Princess Anne, who live nearby, at Highgrove and Gatcombe Park respectively.)

Cheltenham

Until the eighteenth century **CHELTENHAM** was like any other Cotswold town, but then the discovery of a spring in 1716 transformed it into Britain's most popular **spa**. During Cheltenham's prime, a century or so later, the royal, the rich and the famous descended in hordes to take the waters, which were said to cure anything from constipation to worms. These days, while a fair proportion of Cheltenham's hundred thousand–odd inhabitants are undoubtedly well-heeled, of Conservative persuasion (true of the Cotswolds in general) and above retirement age, the town saves itself from too smug an image by a lively and increasingly cosmopolitan atmosphere. It's by far the best spot around for nightlife and makes a convenient base for touring the area.

Cheltenham races

Cheltenham racecourse, a ten-minute walk north of Pittville Park at the foot of Cleeve Hill, is Britain's main steeplechasing venue. The principal event of the season, the three-day **National Hunt Festival** in March, attracts forty thousand people each day. A fair proportion of them come from Ireland, the birthplace of some of the greatest horses to have raced here, including the supreme steeplechaser, **Arkle**. Other meetings take place in January, April, October, November and December: a list of fixtures is posted up at the tourist office. For the cheapest but arguably the best view, pay £5 (rising to £15 during the Festival) for entry to the Courage Enclosure, as the pen in the middle is known. For schedules and other information, call ℡01242/513014 or access the website at ⓦwww.cheltenham.co.uk. For the National Hunt Festival it's essential to buy tickets in advance.

A popular pre-meet watering hole is the *King's Arms*, a short walk east of the racecourse in **Prestbury**, an old Cotswold village with a reputation for being the most haunted village in England, and which has now been subsumed into the town. **Fred Archer**, considered by many to have been the finest Flat jockey of all time, was brought up here, and he features prominently among the pub's racing memorabilia. The pub has sadly lost much of its character since becoming part of a chain, and you might find the nearby *Royal Oak* more congenial.

The focus of Cheltenham, the broad **Promenade**, sweeps majestically south from the High Street, lined with the town's grandest houses, smartest shops and most genteel public gardens. A short walk north of the High Street, brings you to **Pittville**, which, planned as a spa town to rival Cheltenham, was never completed and is now mostly parkland. Here you can stroll along a few solitary Regency avenues and visit the grandest spa building, the domed **Pump Room** (Mon & Wed–Sun 11am–4pm), whose chief function nowadays is as a concert hall – though you can sample England's only naturally alkaline water for free here. On your return route, the **Holst Birthplace Museum** is worth a glance, at 4 Clarence Rd (Tues–Sat 10am–4pm; £2.50): the former home of the composer of *The Planets*, it holds plenty of Holst memorabilia, including his piano, and also gives a good insight into Victorian family life. Back in the centre, the well-set-out **Art Gallery and Museum** on Clarence Stret (Mon–Sat 10am–5.20pm, Sun 2–4.20pm; free; Ⓦ www.cheltenhammuseum .org.uk) marks the high point of Cheltenham. It's very good on social history, with different eras represented by table displays of personal belongings and a typical dinner of the time. There's also a room dedicated to the Arts and Crafts Movement, containing several pieces by Charles Voysey and Ernest Gimson, two of the period's most graceful designers. Also on display is an array of rare Chinese ceramics and works by Cotswold artists such as Stanley Spencer and Vanessa Bell.

The town is also a thriving arts centre, famous for its festivals of **jazz** (April), **classical music** (July) and **literature** (October) – and then, of course, there are the races (see box opposite). In addition, Coopers' Hill, six miles southwest on the A46, is the venue for the region's most bizarre, and established, competition. On the second bank holiday in May, a steep section of the Cotswold escarpment hosts the annual **Cheese Rolling Festival**, when a large Double Gloucester cheese is rolled down the one-in-two incline and chased by dozens of drunken folk; the first to grab the cheese is the winner.

Practicalities

All long-distance **buses** arrive at the station in Royal Well Road, just west off the Promenade. The **train station** is on Queen's Road, southwest of the centre; buses G and F run into town every fifteen minutes, otherwise it's a twenty-minute walk. The **tourist office**, at 77 Promenade (Mon–Sat 9.30am–5.15pm; ℡ 01242/522878, Ⓦ www.visitcheltenham.gov.uk), sells tickets for walking **tours** of the town (Mon–Fri at 11am; £2.50), and for guided bus tours stopping at several destinations in the Cotswolds that are otherwise difficult to reach on public transport (late June to mid-Sept Tues & Wed; £16); they're popular, so book in advance.

Accommodation is plentiful, though you'll need to book weeks in advance if you're planning to visit during the races and festivals. Some of the best choices are in fine Regency houses, for instance the non-smoking *Crossways*, 57 Bath Rd (℡ 01242/527683, Ⓦ www.cross.ways.btinternet.co.uk; ❷) just two minutes walk from the centre, and *Brennan*, 21 St Luke's Rd (℡ 01242/525904; ❷), on a quiet square. Try also the *Lawn Hotel*, 5 Pittville Lawn (℡ 01242/526638; ❷), near the park, with artistically themed rooms and facilities for vegetarians and vegans, or *Lypiatt House*, Lypiatt Road (℡ 01242/224994, Ⓦ www.travel-uk.net/lypiatthouse; ❹), set in its own grounds and featuring open fires and a conservatory with a small bar.

Cheltenham has experienced a **restaurant** renaissance in the last few years and caters for all tastes and pockets. At *Boogaloos*, 16 Regent St (closed Mon–Sat eve & all Sun), you can munch on salads and sandwiches in the relaxed sofa basement or the brightly coloured upstairs rooms, while vegetarians, vegans and allergy sufferers will appreciate the range of dishes on offer at the moderately priced *Orange Tree*, 317 High St (℡01242/234232; closed Mon eve & all Sun), where there's a pleasant courtyard. For fancier meals, try the *Daffodil*, 18–20 Suffolk Parade, a former cinema with affordable three-course set menus, or *Le Petit Blanc* next to *Queen's Hotel* on The Promenade (℡01242/266800, ⓦwww.petit-blanc.com), an outpost of Raymond Blanc's famed *Manoir Aux Quat' Saisons* where you can eat contemporary French cuisine; the three-course set lunch menu is £15 per head.

Cheltenham also has the area's best bars and **pubs**, for example the *Beehive*, 1–3 Montpellier Villas, an easygoing place with a games shed, a courtyard garden and a bistro upstairs. At *Tailor's Wine Bar*, 4 Cambray Place (just off the High Street), you can relax in old leather armchairs or sit in the courtyard, while at the *Vodka Bar*, 6 Regent St, you can choose from a range of 24 vodkas, served to the accompaniment of DJs playing house and funk. If you're up for it, try the town's **clubs**, which draw in the punters from far and wide: *Subtone*, 115–117 The Promenade, and *Time*, 33–35 Albion St, are the most popular.

Stroud and around

Five heavily populated valleys converge at **STROUD**, ten miles southwest of Cheltenham, creating an exhausting jumble of hills and a sense of high activity atypical of the Cotswolds. The bustle is not a new phenomenon. During the heyday of the wool trade the Frome River powered 150 mills, turning Stroud into the centre of the local cloth industry. Even now, Stroud is very much a working town, and one which doesn't need to peddle its heritage to the tourists in order to survive. While some of the old mills have been converted into flats, others contain factories, but only two continue to make cloth – no longer the so-called Stroudwater Scarlet used for military uniforms, but high-quality felt for tennis balls and snooker tables. In recent years, Stroud has become a thriving alternative centre, its town council Green since 1990. You'll see mountains of organic food and sustainable goods for sale in the centre, while the nearby valleys are home to a growing community of artists and New Agers. Sadly, however, in spite of its scenic setting, the town remains the dowdiest of the region.

For visitors, the main point of interest is the excellent **Museum in the Park**, housed in an eighteenth-century mansion in Stratford Park, half a mile from the centre of town on the Gloucester road (April–Sept Tues–Fri noon–5pm; Sat & Sun 11am–5pm; Oct–March Tues–Fri 1–5pm, Sat & Sun 11am–4pm; £2.50). Beautifully decorated and laid out, the collection demonstrates the history of the town through imaginatively themed rooms such as "Clean, Fit and Tidy" and "Industry and Invention", which are complemented by numerous questions and quotations.

Industrial archeology is strewn the length of the Frome Valley – the so-called Golden Valley. Council offices occupy one of the valley's finest mills, **Ebley Mill**, a twenty-minute walk west of the centre along the old Stroudwater Canal – for the best view you should then walk south across the field to the village of **Selsley**.

Trains on the London–Gloucester rail line stop at Stroud, which is also well served by **buses** from Cirencester. These and other bus services arrive at the station on Merrywalks. The **tourist office** is in the Subscription Rooms on Kendrick Street (Mon–Sat 10am–5pm; ℡01453/760960, ⓦwww.visitthe-cotswolds.org.uk). The most central place to **stay** is the *London Hotel*

(☎01453/759992, ⓦwww.the-london-hotel.co.uk; ❸), otherwise head for the non-smoking *Lay-Bye* at 7 Castlemead Rd (☎01453/751514; ❷), fifteen minutes' walk south of the centre, or the *Downfield Hotel* at 134 Cainscross Rd (☎01453/764496, ⓦwww.downfieldotel.demon.co.uk; ❸), in a Georgian building five minutes from the High Street. You'll find the nearest **youth hostel** at Slimbridge (see below). For **food** in the daytime go straight to *Mills Café* in Withey's Yard off High Street, which sells scrumptious cakes, home-made soups and other wholesome concoctions. In the evenings, the choice narrows down to Indian or Chinese as Stroud's nightlife gives over to laddish pub culture. Its saving grace, however, is the *Retreat* wine bar in Church Street, which is smartish but not overpriced.

Uley

The B4066 cuts a glorious route along the valley ridge southwest of Stroud, passing through **ULEY**, six miles from town. Boasting one of the best settings in the region, the village **church** lords it over the small green and the *Old Crowne* pub, where the local brews include one called Pigor Mortis. **Uley Bury**, among the largest hill forts in Britain, extends along the ridge above the village. The path from the church takes you up the shortest and steepest route, though motorists can opt to drive up to the car park right by the fort. Fences prevent you from clambering on top of the bury, but you can walk around the edge – a distance of about two miles altogether – and take in some staggering views. The atmosphere peaks on a winter's day, when bracing winds blow across the ridge while mist gathers in the valley below.

Slimbridge

Eight miles southwest of Stroud, out of the Cotswolds, **SLIMBRIDGE** sits in a narrow corridor between the M5 and the Severn – a surprising location for the **Slimbridge Wildfowl and Wetlands Centre** (daily: April–Oct 9.30am–6pm; Nov–March 9.30am–5pm; last entry 1hr before closing; £6), covering 120 acres between Sharpness Canal and the river. Since ornithologist Sir Peter Scott created it in 1946, the centre has become Britain's largest **wildfowl sanctuary**, and a breeding ground with an important conservation role. Geese, swans, ducks and a huge gathering of flamingos make up the bulk of the birdlife. While some birds are resident all year round, many are migratory: the greatest numbers congregate in the winter months, when Bewick swans, for example, migrate from Russia. There is an extensive network of trails around the sanctuary, with hides for observation.

Slimbridge has a comfortable, purpose-built **youth hostel** (☎01453/890275), accessible from a lane opposite the *Tudor Arms* pub in the village. The only **buses** to go anywhere near Slimbridge are those between Gloucester and Bristol or Dursley, which stop by the turn-off on the A38, just over a mile east of the village.

Berkeley

Though quite secluded within a swathe of meadows and neat gardens, **Berkeley Castle** (April & May Tues–Sun 2–5pm; June & Sept Tues–Sat 11am–5pm, Sun 2–5pm; July & Aug Mon–Sat 11am–5pm, Sun 2–5pm; Oct Sun 2–5pm; £5.70; grounds only £2) dominates the little village of **BERKELEY**, five miles southwest of Slimbridge on the A38. The fortress has an agreeably turreted medieval look, the robust twelfth-century walls softened by later accretions acquired in its gradual transformation into a family home. The interior is packed with mementoes of its long history, including its grisliest moment in 1327, when Edward II was murdered here – apparently by a red-hot iron thrust into his bowels. You can view the cell where the event took place, along with dungeons, dining room, kitchen, picture gallery and the Great Hall. Outside, the grounds include an Elizabethan terraced garden and a Butterfly Farm (£2), and within easy walking distance, in the village itself, is the **Jenner Museum** (April–Sept Tues–Sat 12.30–5.30pm, Sun 1–5.30pm; Oct Sun 1–5.30pm; £2.80), dedicated to Edward Jenner, discoverer of the principle of vaccination.

Berkeley is fiendishly difficult to reach by public transport, connected only by coaches from Gloucester operated by Beaumont Travel (Mon–Sat 5 daily, none on Sun; ☎01452/309770). For a lunchtime stop near Berkeley, follow the narrow High Street out of the centre of the village for about a mile to reach the *Salutation*, an unpretentious country **pub** with a garden; it serves up bacon sandwiches and suchlike at lunchtimes.

Painswick

The A46 and the B4070 are equally attractive routes linking Stroud and Cheltenham, but the former has the edge because after four miles you reach the old wool town of **PAINSWICK**, where ancient buildings jostle for space on narrow streets running downhill off the busy main street. The fame of Painswick's **church** stems not so much from the building itself as from the surrounding **graveyard**, where 99 yew trees, cut into bizarre bulbous shapes resembling lollipops, surround a collection of eighteenth-century table-tombs unrivalled in the Cotswolds. However, it's the **Rococo Garden** (mid-Jan to April, Oct & Nov Wed–Sun 11am–5pm; May–Sept daily 11am–5pm; £3.30; Ⓦ www.rococogarden.co.uk), about half a mile north up the Gloucester road and attached to Painswick House (not open to the public), that ranks as the town's main attraction. Created in the early eighteenth century and later abandoned, the garden is being restored to its original form with the aid of a painting dated 1748. Although unfinished, it's a beautiful example – and the country's only one – of Rococo garden design, a short-lived fashion typified by a mix of formal geometrical shapes and more naturalistic, curving lines. With a vegetable patch as an unusual centrepiece, the Painswick garden spreads across a sheltered gully – for the best vistas, walk around anticlockwise. In February and March people flock to see the snowdrops that smother the slopes beneath the pond, during which time the garden is open daily (call to check exact dates: ☎01452/813204).

The best **bus** service to Painswick is the #46 between Stroud and Cheltenham, which runs hourly during the week and four times on Sundays. The **tourist office**, housed in an old school at the bottom of the main street (April–Oct Tues–Sun 10am–4pm; ☎01452/813552), can help you find reasonably-priced **accommodation** if the following places are booked: *Thorne Guest House* on Friday Street (☎01452/812476; closed Dec & Jan; ③), one of the oldest houses in the village, or *Cardynham House* on St Mary's Street (☎01452/814006, Ⓦ www.cardynham.co.uk; ④), where all rooms have four-posters or half-testers, and one has a lounge and private pool (£120 a night). In the evenings, there's a set meal on offer in the attached Thai **restaurant** for £21.20 (closed Sun & Mon), which is almost the only place to eat in the village – not counting the nearby *Royal Oak*, reckoned to be the best **pub** hereabouts.

Gloucester

For centuries life was good for **GLOUCESTER**. The Romans chose the spot for a garrison to guard the Severn and spy on Wales, and later for a *colonia* or home for retired soldiers – the highest status a provincial Roman town could dream of. Commercial prestige came with trade up the River Severn, which developed into one of the busiest trade routes in Europe. The city's political importance hit its peak under the Normans, when William the Conqueror met here frequently with his council of nobles. The Middle Ages saw Gloucester's rise as a religious centre, and the construction of what is now the cathedral, but also saw its political and economic decline: navigating the Severn as far up as Gloucester was so difficult that most trade gradually shifted south to Bristol. In a brave attempt to reverse the city's decline, a canal was opened in 1827 to link Gloucester to Sharpness, on a broader stretch of the Severn further south. Trade picked up for a time, but it was only a temporary stay of execution.

Today, the canal is busy once again, though this time with pleasure boats. The Victorian dockyards too have undergone a facelift and are touted as the city's great new tourist attraction, though Gloucester's most prominent sight is the **cathedral**, its tower visible for miles around. Few other buildings in the city have survived the ravages of history and the twentieth century, with the centre a mish-mash of medieval ruins swallowed up by ugly new buildings. A web of roads engulfs Gloucester, and if you're **driving**, the best advice is to head for the docks (well signposted) and park there. National Express runs **buses** from all neighbouring cities and beyond, and there are frequent local services from Cheltenham. **Trains** arrive every one or two hours at the station at Bruton Way, five minutes' walk east of the Cross, from London, Cheltenham, Cardiff, Worcester and Bristol; the **bus** station is right opposite.

The City

Gloucester lies on the east bank of the Severn, its centre spread around a curve in the river. **The Cross**, once the entrance to the Roman forum, marks the heart of the city and the meeting-point of Northgate, Southgate, Eastgate and Westgate streets, all Roman roads. **St Michael's Tower**, the remains of an old church, overlooks it. The main shopping area lies east of the Northgate–Southgate axis, with the **cathedral** and the **docks**, the focus of interest, to the west of it.

Southgate and Westgate streets

The most interesting parish church in Gloucester is **St Mary de Crypt** on Southgate Street, mostly late medieval but with some of its original Norman features. A soft, soothing light filters through the stained-glass windows, and fragments of a sixteenth-century wall painting of the Adoration of the Magi in the chancel shows unusual detail for work of that period. Greyfriars runs alongside St Mary's, past the ruins of a Franciscan church and the Eastgate Market to the **City Museum** on Brunswick Road (July–Sept Mon–Sat 10am–5pm, Sun 10am–4pm; rest of year Mon–Sat 10am–5pm; £2; combined ticket with Folk Museum £3; Ⓦ www.mylife.gloucester.gov.uk), with a good archeological collection including a fragment of the Roman city wall, preserved *in situ* below ground level. Westgate Street, quieter and many times more pleasant than its three Roman counterparts, retains several medieval buildings, one of which, a creaking timber-framed house at the bottom of the street, contains the **Folk Museum** (July–Sept Mon–Sat 10am–5pm, Sun 10am–4pm; rest

△ Royal Crescent, Bath

of year Mon–Sat 10am–5pm; £2; combined ticket with City Museum £3; Ⓦwww.mylife.gloucester.gov.uk). Here, the social history of the Gloucester area is illustrated by an impressive collection of objects, from huge wrought-iron cheese presses to salt-filled rolling pins used to scare off witches. College Court alley leads from Westgate Street to the haven of the cathedral, passing the Beatrix Potter shop and museum – the house sketched by the children's artist and author while she was on holiday here in 1897 and subsequently appearing in every copy of *The Tailor of Gloucester*.

The Cathedral

The superb condition of Gloucester **Cathedral** (daily 7.30am–6pm; Ⓦwww .gloucestercathedral.uk.com) is striking in a city that has lost so much of its past. An abbey was founded on this spot by the Saxons, but four centuries later Benedictine monks came and built their own church, begun in 1069. As a place of worship it shot to importance after the murder at Berkeley Castle of Edward II in 1327: Bristol and Malmesbury wouldn't take his body, but Gloucester did, and the king's shrine became a major place of pilgrimage. The money generated helped to finance the conversion of the church into the country's first and greatest example of the **Perpendicular style**: the magnificent 225-foot tower crowns the achievement. Henry VIII recognized the church's prestige by conferring on it the status of cathedral.

Beneath the reconstructions of the fourteenth and fifteenth centuries, some Norman aspects remain, best seen in the **nave**, flanked by sturdy pillars and arches adorned with immaculate zigzag mouldings. Only when you reach the choir and transepts can you see how skilfully the new church was built inside the old, the Norman masonry hidden beneath the finer lines of the Perpendicular panelling and tracery. The **choir** has extraordinary fourteenth-century misericords, and also provides the best vantage point for admiring the east window, completed in around 1350 and – at almost 80 feet tall – the **largest medieval window** in Britain. Beneath it, to the left (as you're facing the east window) is the **tomb of Edward II**, immortalized in alabaster and marble and in good fettle apart from some graffiti. In the nearby **Lady Chapel**, delicate carved tracery holds a staggering patchwork of windows, virtually creating walls of stained glass. There are well-preserved monuments here, too, but the tomb of Robert II, in the **south ambulatory**, is far more unusual. Robert, eldest son of William the Conqueror, died in 1134, but the painted wooden effigy dates from around 1290. Dressed as a crusader, he lies in a curious pose, with his arms and legs crossed, his right hand gripping his sword ready to do battle with the infidel.

The innovative nature of the cathedral's design can perhaps be best appreciated in the beautiful **cloisters**, completed in 1367 and featuring the first fan vaulting in the country. The fine quality of the work is outdone perhaps only by Henry VII's Chapel in Westminster Abbey, which it inspired. Back inside, an **exhibition** in the upstairs galleries, reached from the north transept (April–Oct Mon–Fri 10.30am–4pm, Sat 10.30am–3pm; £1.50) traces the history of the cathedral, putting it into context with that of the city as a whole. Here, you can try out the **Whispering Gallery**, where you can pick up the tiniest sounds from across the vaulting.

The Docks

The **Docks** complex was developed during the fifty years following the opening of the Sharpness canal in 1827. The import of corn represented the bulk of the port's business at that time, and huge **warehouses** were built for storing the grain. Fourteen of them have survived, mostly now converted into municipal offices, shops and museums. In the southernmost Llanthony Warehouse, the **National Waterways Museum** (daily 10am–5pm, last admission 4pm; £4.95; Ⓦwww.nwm.org.uk) completely immerses you in the canal mania that swept Britain in the eighteenth and nineteenth centuries, touching on everything from the engineering of the locks to the lives of the horses that trod the towpaths. The three floors contain plenty of atmospheric noises off, videos, accessible information and interactive displays. Out from the main building you can practise "walking the wall" in the time honoured manner of boatmen, who propelled their narrowboats through the tunnels by their feet, and explore the boats themselves along the quayside.

Practicalities

Gloucester's **tourist office** is at 28 Southgate St (Mon–Sat 10am–5pm; Ⓣ01452/396572, Ⓦwww.visit-glos.org.uk). Of the few **hotels** within easy walking distance of the train station and centre, the *Albert* at 56–58 Worcester St (Ⓣ01452/502081, Ⓦwww.alberthotel.com; ❷), a listed red-brick building from the 1830s, and the Victorian *Edward* at 88 London Rd (Ⓣ01452/525865; ❸) offer the best value. Central, inexpensive **B&Bs** include *Spalite* (Ⓣ01452/380828; ❷), at the bottom of Southgate Street near the docks (though, right on the main road, it's a bit prone to traffic noise), and the four-storey *Lulworth* at 12 Midland Rd (Ⓣ01452/521881; ❶), in a quiet location behind the park.

The selection of **restaurants** is only slightly more remarkable than the hotels, and many places are open only during the day. You'll find reliable if rather unimaginative fare in the *Orchids at the Undercroft* restaurant in the cathedral, open until 5pm, and at the café-bar in the Guildhall on Eastgate Street – open until 11pm and always lively. *Ye Olde Fish Shoppe* on Hare Lane, even more of a Gloucester institution, occupies a sixteenth-century building and is the fanciest take-away for miles; it serves excellent crispy fish until 6.30pm, though the attached restaurant stays open later (Ⓣ01452/255502; closed all Sun & Mon eve). In the evenings, choice extends to the vaulted *Bearland Restaurant* in Longsmith Street, with a set-price menu at £11.95, and the atmospherically French *Café René*, Greyfriars, Southgate Street, where walls and ceilings are smothered with bottles (closed Mon & Tues). For pizzas go to *Pizza Piazza* at Merchants' Quay – the only reason to venture to the docks in the evening.

There isn't a huge choice of **pubs**, the best are all within spitting distance of the Cross. The rambling fifteenth-century *New Inn* in Northgate Street has a good atmosphere, a splendid galleried courtyard and cheap meals, but for really tasty hot food at rock-bottom prices go to the *Fountain Inn*, down a narrow alley off Westgate Street, this pub pulls a sublime pint of Abbot ale and has tables in an olde-worlde adjacent courtyard – ideal for a sunny day.

Tewkesbury and around

The small market town of **TEWKESBURY**, ten miles north of Gloucester, stands hemmed in by the Avon and Severn rivers, which converge nearby. Pressure of space accounts for the narrow alleys and courts leading off from the main streets, of which thirty of the original ninety still survive. Almost completely bypassed by the Industrial Revolution, Tewkesbury preserves numerous elegant Georgian houses and medieval timber-framed buildings on its main streets – especially Church Street – and the Norman **abbey** has survived as one of the greatest in England.

The site of **Tewkesbury Abbey** (daily 7.30am–6pm, closes 5pm in winter) was first selected for a Benedictine monastery in the eighth century, but virtually nothing of the Saxon complex survived a sacking by the Danes, and a new abbey was founded by a Norman nobleman in 1092. The work took about sixty years to complete, with some additions made in the fourteenth century. Two hundred years later the Dissolution brought about the destruction of most of the monastic buildings, but the abbey itself survived. The sheer scale of its exterior makes a lasting impact: its colossal **tower** is the largest Norman tower in the world, while the west front's soaring recessed arch – 65 feet high – is the only exterior arch in the country to boast such impressive proportions. In the nave, fourteen stout Norman pillars steal the show, topped by a fourteenth-century ribbed and vaulted ceiling, studded with gilded bosses (look for the musical angels). On the blue and scarlet **choir** roof the bosses include a ring of shining suns (emblem of the Yorkist cause), said to have been put there by Edward IV after the defeat of the Lancastrians at Tewkesbury in 1471, the last important battle of the Wars of the Roses. (The battlefield, known as Bloody Meadow, is off Lincoln Green Lane, southwest of the abbey.) The abbey's medieval tombs celebrate Tewkesbury's greatest patrons, the Fitzhamons, De Clares, Beauchamps and Despensers, who turned the building into something of a mausoleum for themselves. The Despensers have the best monuments, particularly Sir Edward, standard-bearer to the Black Prince, who died in 1375 and is shown as a kneeling figure on the roof of the **Trinity Chapel** to the right of the high altar: you can see it best from beside the Warwick Chantry Chapel in the north aisle. Nearby, in the ambulatory, the macabre so-called **Wakeman Cenotaph**, carved in the fifteenth century but of otherwise uncertain origin, represents a decaying corpse being consumed by snakes and other creatures.

Practicalities

The **tourist office** at 64 Barton St (April–Oct Mon–Sat 9am–5pm, Sun 10am–4pm; rest of year closed Sun; ☎01684/295027, ⓦwww.tewkesbury-bc.gov.uk) has inexpensive town and walking maps, plus a small museum (£1) upstairs. You won't have to look far to find a **room**, though noise can be a problem. There are several B&Bs on Barton Road, including *Barton House* at no. 5 (☎01684/292049; ❶), which has an eclectic mix of old furniture. More genteel are the *Two Back of Avon*, a beautiful period building on Riverside Walk, left off Quay Street (☎01684/298935; non-smoking; ❷), and the quiet *Carrant Brook House* on Rope Walk (☎01684/290355; ❸). Tewkesbury's top **hotels** are the *Royal Hop Pole*, Church Street (☎01684/293236, ⓦwww.regal-hotels.co.uk; ❺), whose annexe has a loggia facing the garden, and the *Tudor House*, High Street (☎01684/297755; ❺), where you can take coffee in the panelled Mayor's Parlour.

For daytime **snacks** or **lunches**, choose between the chrome of the *Aubergine* café-bar for good salads and sandwiches or the ancient *Berkeley Arms* **pub** on Church Street, which serves astoundingly cheap but fairly basic food. In the evenings, the blue and oak-furnished *Rendezvous* at 78 Church St (☎01684/290357; closed Sun eve & Mon) concentrates on moderately priced Mediterranean-style fish and meat dishes, but also caters to vegetarians.

Bredon Hill

The most important Iron Age fort in the area once crowned **Bredon Hill**, six miles northeast of Tewkesbury and visible for miles around in the flat Severn Vale. Excavation of the site revealed more than fifty bodies, all hacked to pieces, seemingly the victims of a final assault by unknown attackers in the first century AD. Inside the rampart, a huge expanse covering eleven acres, an eighteenth-century tower called Parson's Folly is an incongruous centrepiece, but the views are supreme, with deer often grazing on the slopes.

Bredon Hill can be approached from various places around the southern foot of the hill. From **Overbury**, one of the prettier villages, the climb takes less than an hour. If you're relying on public transport, buses bound for Evesham from Tewkesbury pass through the village of **Bredon** (except Sun), from where you should allow about three hours to walk to the hill and back.

Bristol

South and west of Gloucester, the distinctive burr that is typical of West Country speech is immediately audible in **BRISTOL**. Alongside it, however, you will also hear the more strident tones of fast money and big business which in recent years have combined to re-energize the city's old commercial traditions. New technology, the arts and a vibrant youth culture have also helped to make this one of Britain's most cutting-edge cities, in the process generating some of the best nightlife in the southwest.

Weaving through its centre, the River Avon forms part of a system of waterways that made Bristol a great inland port, in later years booming on the transatlantic trafficking of such goods as rum, tobacco and slaves. In the nineteenth century the illustrious **Isambard Kingdom Brunel** laid the foundations of a tradition of engineering, creating two of Bristol's greatest monuments – the SS *Great Britain* and the lofty Clifton Suspension Bridge. More recently, spin-offs from the aerospace industry have given the city a high profile in the fields of communications, computing, design and finance. Beneath the prosperous surface, however, Bristol has its negative aspects – one of England's highest homeless populations, some of the most notorious housing estates and the highest proportion of cars to inhabitants. Nonetheless, it remains an attractive city, predominantly hilly, and surrounded by rolling countryside.

Arrival, information and accommodation

Bristol is an easy place to get to. Twice-hourly **trains** from London Paddington arrive at either Bristol Parkway or Bristol Temple Meads. The latter, a twenty-minute walk from the centre, is served by frequent buses #8, #9, #508 and #509, which pass through the centre on their way to Cotham and Clifton. Parkway is too far out of town to walk from: take bus #73 (or #82 or #584 on Sun). The **bus station**, where National Express coaches from London arrive hourly, is in Marlborough Street, right next to Broadmead, the modern shopping centre. For all bus timetables and routes in the Bristol and Bath area, call ℡0870/608 2608 (8am–8pm). The **tourist office** is in the at-Bristol complex, on Wildscreen Walk, Harbourside (March–Oct daily 10am–6pm; Nov–Feb Mon–Sat 10am–5pm, Sun 11am–4pm; ℡0117/926 0767, ⊛www.visitbristol.co.uk).

Most of Bristol's **accommodation** is in the leafy Georgian areas of Cotham and Clifton, which are also the districts where the majority of the city's students live. Price-wise, it's hard to beat *St Michael's Guest House*, 145 St Michael's Hill (℡0117/907 7820; ❶), situated over a popular student café near the university. Lower down, in Cotham, *Arches Hotel*, 132 Cotham Brow (℡0117/924 7398, Ⓦwww.arches-hotel.co.uk; ❷), has small but comfortable non-smoking rooms with or without bath, while Clifton offers a wide range of hotels and B&Bs, from *Downs View*, 38 Upper Belgrave Rd (℡0117/973 7046), which enjoys prospects over Clifton Downs and the city, to *Naseby House Hotel* 105 Pembroke Rd (℡0117/973 7859, Ⓦwww.nasebyhousehotel.co.uk; ❹), a beautifully furnished Victorian building, ten minutes' walk from the centre. With a choice location near Clifton Village, *Glenroy Hotel*, Victoria Square (℡0117/973 9058, Ⓔadmin@glenroyhotel.demon.co.uk; ❺), is pricier, but offers good-value weekend breaks.

Bristol has two **hostels**: the modern and central *Bristol YHA*, in a refurbished warehouse on the quayside, at 14 Narrow Quay (℡0117/922 1659, Ⓦwww.yha.org.uk), and the friendly *Bristol Backpackers*, also very central at 17 St Stephen's St (℡0117/925 7900, Ⓦwww.bristolbackpackers.co.uk) – it's housed in a lovely old building with a late-night bar and cheap internet access, though it can be noisy. The university also has cramped but comfortable B&B during the Easter and summer vacations at The Hawthorns, Woodland Road, Clifton (℡0117/954 5555, Ⓦwww.bris.ac.uk/depts/conferences).

The City

A good place to start exploring, **the Centre** was once an extension of the port but is now the traffic-ridden nucleus of the city, with cars swirling round the statues of Edmund Burke, MP for Bristol from 1774 to 1780, and local benefactor Edward Colston. The Centre is only a few minutes' walk from the cathedral and the oldest quarter of town, and linked by ferry to the sights around the Floating Harbour, the waterway network that runs through the southern part of town and connects with the River Avon. You could cover Bristol's other central attractions on foot without too much sweat, but it's worth using the bus network for more distant sights, especially in the hilly Clifton district.

From the cathedral to the city museum

A short walk west of the Centre lies College Green, dominated by the crescent-shaped Council House and by **Bristol Cathedral** (daily 8am–6pm). Founded around 1140 as an abbey on the supposed spot of St Augustine's convocation with Celtic Christians in 603, it became a cathedral church with the Dissolution of the Monasteries. The two towers on the west front were erected in the nineteenth century in a faithful act of homage to Edmund Knowle, architect and abbot at the start of the fourteenth century. Inside the cathedral, Abbot Knowle's **choir** offers one of the country's most exquisite examples of the early Decorated style of Gothic, while the adjoining **Elder Lady Chapel**, dating from the early thirteenth century, contains some fine tombs and some eccentric carvings of animals, including a monkey playing the bagpipes accompanied by a ram on the violin. The ornate **Eastern Lady Chapel** has some of England's finest examples of heraldic glass. From the south transept, a door leads through to the **Chapter House**, a richly carved piece of late Norman architecture.

Climbing steeply up from College Green, the shop-lined **Park Street** has some elegant Georgian streets leading off it – for instance Great George Street and Berkeley Square, from either of which you can enter **Brandon Hill Park**,

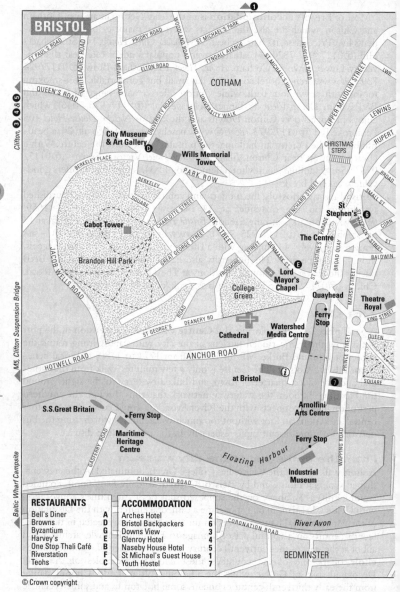

BRISTOL

Clifton, 3, 4 & 5

M5, Clifton Suspension Bridge

Baltic Wharf Campsite

RESTAURANTS	
Bell's Diner	A
Browns	D
Byzantium	G
Harvey's	E
One Stop Thali Café	B
Riverstation	F
Teohs	C

ACCOMMODATION	
Arches Hotel	2
Bristol Backpackers	6
Downs View	3
Glenroy Hotel	4
Naseby House Hotel	5
St Michael's Guest House	1
Youth Hostel	7

© Crown copyright

site of the landmark **Cabot Tower**, built at the end of the last century to commemorate the 400th anniversary of John Cabot's voyage to America. You can climb up the 105-foot tower for the city's best panorama. At the top of Park Street stands central Bristol's other chief landmark, the **Wills Memorial Tower**, erected in the 1920s to lend some stature to the newly opened university. One of the last great neo-Gothic buildings in England, the tower was the gift of the local Wills tobacco dynasty, the university's main benefactors.

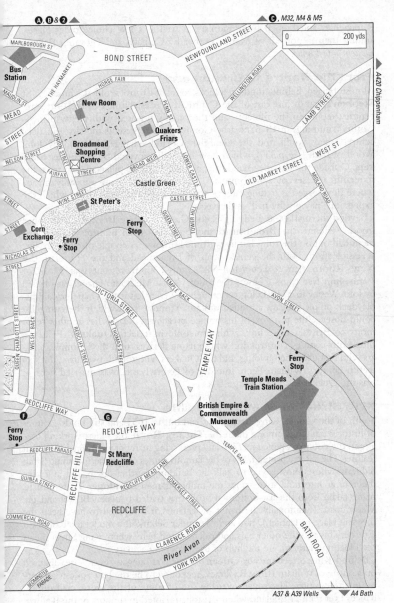

Labels on map:

0   200 yds

MARLBOROUGH ST

BOND STREET

NEWFOUNDLAND STREET

▶ A420 Chippenham

Bus Station

THE HAYMARKET

HORSE FAIR

WELLINGTON ROAD

MAUDLIN ST

MEAD

New Room

PENN ST

LAMB STREET

Quakers' Friars

WEST ST

STREET

UNION STREET

Broadmead Shopping Centre

BROAD WEIR

LOWER CASTLE

OLD MARKET STREET

MIDLAND ROAD

NELSON STREET

FAIRFAX

STREET

Castle Green

CASTLE STREET

STREET

WINE STREET

St Peter's

CASTLE STREET

TOWER HILL

QUEEN STREET

5

Corn Exchange

Ferry Stop

Ferry Stop

NICHOLAS ST

STREET

VICTORIA STREET

TEMPLE BACK

AVON STREET

QUEEN CHARLOTTE STREET

WELSH BACK

REDCLIFFE STREET

ST THOMAS STREET

TEMPLE WAY

Ferry Stop

Temple Meads Train Station

THE COTSWOLDS AND SOMERSET | Bristol

F

G

REDCLIFFE WAY

British Empire & Commonwealth Museum

Ferry Stop

REDCLIFFE PARADE

RECLIFFE HILL

St Mary Redcliffe

REDCLIFFE MEAD LANE

SOMERSET STREET

TEMPLE GATE

GUINEA STREET

COMMERCIAL ROAD

REDCLIFFE

CLARENCE ROAD

River Avon

YORK ROAD

BATH ROAD

BEDMINSTER PARADE

A37 & A39 Wells ▼   ▼ A4 Bath

Next to the tower, on Queen's Road, the **City Museum and Art Gallery** (daily 10am–5pm; free) occupies another building donated by the Wills clan. The sections on local archeology, geology and natural history are pretty well what you'd expect, but the scope of the museum is occasionally surprising – it has the largest collection of Chinese glass on show outside China itself, and some magnificent Assyrian reliefs, carved in the eighth century BC. The second-floor gallery of paintings and sculptures includes work by English Pre-

331

Raphaelites and French Impressionists, as well as a few choice older pieces, among them a portrait of Martin Luther by Cranach and Giovanni Bellini's *Descent into Limbo*.

From the Centre to Broadmead

Almost buried behind modern blocks, one of Bristol's oldest churches, **St Stephen's**, stands just east of the Centre. It was established in the thirteenth century, rebuilt in the fifteenth and thoroughly restored with plenty of neo-Gothic trimmings in 1875. Nearby **Corn Street** represents the city's financial centre, where you'll find the Georgian Corn Exchange, designed by John Wood of Bath (see p.339), which now holds the covered **St Nicholas markets**. Outside the entrance stand four engraved bronze pillars, dating from the sixteenth and seventeenth centuries and transferred from a nearby arcade where they served as trading tables – thought to be the "nails" from which the expression "pay on the nail" is derived.

Beyond the market, and edging Castle Green – where **Bristol Castle** once stood – extends the **Broadmead** shopping centre, an uninspiring development laid out on the ruins left by wartime bombing. A couple of relics survive: accessible from both the central strip of Broadmead and the Horsefair, **the New Room** (Jan & Feb Mon–Sat 11am–2.30pm; rest of year Mon–Sat 10am–4pm; free, tours £2) was the country's first Methodist chapel, established by John Wesley in 1739. Lying very much as Wesley left it, the chapel has a double-deck pulpit beneath a hidden upstairs window, from which the evangelist could observe the progress of his trainee preachers. Nearby lies another testimony to Bristol's close links with nonconformist sects, **Quakers' Friars**, a thirteenth-century construction whose name derives from the Dominican friars who first used the building, and the Quakers who took it over from the sixteenth century. William Penn, founder of Pennsylvania, was married here, as was the Quaker founder George Fox.

King Street to St Mary Redcliffe

South of the Centre, **King Street** was laid out in 1633 and still holds a cluster of historic buildings, among them the **Theatre Royal**, the oldest working theatre in the country, opened in 1766 and preserving many of its original Georgian features. The theatre hosted most of the famous names of its time, including Sarah Siddons, whose ghost is said to stalk the building. Further down, and in a very different architectural style, stands the timber-framed **Llandoger Trow** pub, its name taken from the flat-bottomed boats that traded between Bristol and the Welsh coast. Traditionally the haunt of seafarers, it is reputed to have been the meeting place of Daniel Defoe and Alexander Selkirk, the model for Robinson Crusoe. This and the other bars and cafés around here, where King Street meets the Floating Harbour, are the hub of lively evening activity.

Behind King Street spreads **Queen Square**, an elegant grassy area focused on a statue of William III by Rysbrack, reckoned to be the best equestrian statue in the country. The square was the site of some of the worst civil disturbances ever seen in England when Bristolians rioted in support of the Reform Bill of 1832, burning houses on two sides of the square; among the survivors was no. 37, where the first American consulate was established in 1792.

The southeast corner of the square leads to Redcliffe Bridge and on to the area of Redcliffe, where the spire of **St Mary Redcliffe** (daily 8.30am–5pm) provides one of the distinctive features of the city's skyline. Described by Elizabeth I as "the goodliest, fairest, and most famous parish church in England", the church was largely paid for and used by merchants and mariners who prayed here for a safe voyage. The present building was begun at the end of the thirteenth century, though it was added to in subsequent centuries and the spire was constructed in 1872. Inside, memorials and tombs recall some of the figures associated with the building, including the arms and armour of Sir William Penn, admiral and father of the founder of Pennsylvania, on the north wall of the nave, and the Handel Window in the North Choir aisle, installed in 1859 on the centenary of the death of Handel, who composed on the organ here. The whale bone above the entrance to the Chapel of St John the Baptist is thought to have been brought back from Newfoundland by John Cabot. Above the church's north porch is the muniment room, where **Thomas Chatterton** claimed to have found a trove of medieval manuscripts; the poems, distributed as the work of a fifteenth-century monk named Thomas Rowley, were in fact dazzling fakes. The young poet committed suicide when his forgery was exposed, thereby supplying English literature with one of its most glamorous stories of self-destructive genius. The "Marvellous Boy" is remembered by a memorial stone in the south transept.

A few minutes' walk away, Bristol's **Old Station** stands outside Temple Meads station, the original terminus of the Great Western Railway linking London and Bristol. The terminus, like the line itself, was designed by Brunel in 1840, and was the first great piece of railway architecture. Part of the original building now houses the **British Empire and Commonwealth Museum** (Tues–Sun 9am–5pm; Ⓦwww.empiremuseum.co.uk), which focuses on the history of the empire and Commonwealth.

Around Bristol's waterways

At the southern end of the Centre, the River Frome disappears underground at the **Quayhead**, a spot marked by a statue of Neptune and a memorial plaque to Samuel Plimsoll, inventor of the eponymous line that's painted on the hulls of merchant ships. **St Augustine's Reach**, the central part of the Floating Harbour, is flanked by the **Arnolfini** and **Watershed** arts centres, bastions of Bristol's cultural scene and both housed in refurbished Victorian warehouses. Outside the Arnolfini is a statue of **John Cabot**, the Genoan-born explorer licensed by Henry VII to sail from Bristol in 1497; his landing at Newfoundland formed the basis of England's later claims on the New World (he disappeared on his second expedition the following year).

Beyond the Watershed, Bristol's newly developed Harbourside is the home of Bristol's highest-profile attraction, **at-Bristol** (daily 10am–6pm; £6.50 for one attraction; £11 for two; £15.50 for all, valid for a week; Ⓦwww.at-bristol .org.uk), a large-scale entertainment complex which pivots on three principal sites: Explore-at-Bristol, an interactive science centre; Wildwalk-at-Bristol, a multimedia wildlife complex, including an indoor "tropical forest", and an IMAX cinema (film screenings need to be booked in advance). Although chiefly aimed at families and schoolkids, there's enough here for anyone to occupy a whole day or more. The wildlife displays and scientific wizardry are most impressive, and subsidiary attractions include the Imaginarium (£2), a metal-clad spherical planetarium.

To explore further afield, take advantage of the **ferry service**, which connects the various parts of the Floating Harbour every forty minutes or so (April–Sept Mon–Fri 10.50am–5.45pm, Sat & Sun 10.50am–4.50pm; Oct–March Sat & Sun only; £1 single fare; £3 forty-minute round trip; £3.50 one-hour round trip; Ⓦwww.bristolferryboat.co.uk). Opposite the Arnolfini, the **Industrial Museum**, features a diverse collection of vehicles, mostly with Bristol connections, and a display of maritime models and reconstructions

(April–Oct Mon–Wed, Sat & Sun 10am–5pm; Nov–March Sat & Sun 10am–5pm; free), and about 500 yards west from here, you can visit the **SS Great Britain** (daily: April–Oct 10am–5.30pm; Nov–March 10am–4.30pm; Ⓦ www.ss-great-britain.com; £6.25). Built in 1843 by Brunel, this was the first propeller-driven, ocean-going iron ship, used initially between Liverpool and New York, then between Liverpool and Melbourne, circumnavigating the globe 32 times over a period of 26 years. Her ocean-going days ended in 1886 when she was caught in a storm off Cape Horn, and abandoned in the Falkland Islands; she was recovered from there and in 1968 returned to the same dry dock in Bristol where she was constructed. Alongside is docked a much smaller affair: a replica of the **Matthew** (same times as the *Great Britain*; entry covered by that ticket), the vessel in which John Cabot sailed to America in 1497, rebuilt in time for the voyage to be re-enacted on the 500th anniversary. The adjoining **Maritime Heritage Centre** (same times and ticket) gives the full history of both the *Great Britain* and the *Matthew*, and the few facts which are known about Cabot and his exploits. The museum also illustrates the port's long shipbuilding history from the eighteenth century, when it was second only to London, to its decline in the last century.

Clifton

North and west of the Wills Tower (see p.330) extends **Clifton**, once an aloof spa resort, now Bristol's most elegant quarter. Clifton Village, its select enclave, is centred on the Mall, close to **Royal York Crescent**, the longest Georgian crescent in the country, offering splendid views over the steep drop to the River Avon below.

A few minutes' walk behind the Crescent is Bristol's most famous symbol, **Clifton Suspension Bridge**, 702ft long and poised 245ft above high water. Money was first put forward for a bridge to span the Avon Gorge by a Bristol wine merchant in 1753, though it was not until 1829 that a competition was held for a design, won by Isambard Brunel on a second round, and not until 1864 that the bridge was completed, five years after Brunel's death. Hampered by financial difficulties, the bridge never quite matched the engineer's original ambitious design, which included Egyptian-style towers topped by sphinxes on each end. You can see copies of his plans in the **Visitor Centre** on Sion Place (daily: Easter–Sept 10am–5pm; Oct–Easter Mon–Fri 11am–4pm, Sat & Sun 11am–5pm; £1.90), alongside the other designs proposed by Brunel's rivals, some of them frankly bizarre. The three rooms here give the full background on the various competitions and the vicissitudes which accompanied the bridge's construction.

Just above the bridge in Clifton, a small **Observatory** sits on an arm of Clifton Downs overlooking the gorge, and contains a working camera obscura (daily: summer 11am–5.30pm; rest of year 11am–4pm; £1). You can also buy a ticket (£1) for the 190-foot tunnel leading from here to the "Giant's Cave" set in the cliffs overlooking the gorge; it housed a Roman Catholic chapel in the fifteenth century. Both attractions may be closed in bad weather. Adjoining the Downs is **Bristol Zoo** (daily: June–Aug 9am–5.30pm; Sept–May 9am–4.30pm; Ⓦ www.bristolzoo.org.uk; £8.40), renowned for its animal conservation work, and also featuring a collection of rare trees and shrubs.

Eating, drinking and nightlife

Bristol's numerous **pubs** and **restaurants** are nearly always buzzing – especially those around King Street. Nightlife is equally lively; if you want to check out the **clubs**, look for the music that suits your tastes rather than simply turning up at a venue – and be prepared to queue. You can usually find something happening every night – pick up a copy of *Venue*, the Bristol and Bath fortnightly listings magazine (£1.90) for details of what's on where.

Restaurants

Bell's Diner 1 York Rd ☏0117/924 0357. In the fashionable Montpelier quarter (ten minutes from the bus station up Stokes Croft), this corner bistro offers an inventive menu with good-value, award-winning food. No smoking in dining area. Closed Sat & Mon lunch, plus all day Sun. Moderate.

Browns 38 Queen's Rd ☏0117/930 4777. Spacious and relaxed place for a cocktail, hamburger or delicious fisherman's pie; it's housed in the former university refectory, a Venetian-style structure next to the City Museum. Moderate.

Byzantium 2 Portwall Lane ☏0117/922 1883, ⓦwww.byzantium.co.uk. Opposite St Mary Redcliffe, a warehouse that's been transformed into a highly theatrical dining area, themed along the lines of a Beirut hotel circa 1930. The food is superb, with a good-value set-price menu, and there's an equally exotic bar downstairs that stays open late, with magicians and belly-dancers adding to the ambience. Closed Sun. Expensive.

Harvey's 12 Denmark St ☏0117/927 5034. Owned by a famous name in the world of wines and sherries, this is a showcase restaurant in a medieval cellar complex adjoining a museum of wine that's an attraction in itself, and can be visited while waiting for food. The atmosphere is formal, the food French and the wine list both encyclopedic and outstanding. Closed Sat lunch & all Sun. Very Expensive.

One Stop Thali Café 12 York Rd ☏0117/942 6687. Dhaba-style Asian food in soothing surroundings in the heart of Montpelier. There's no menu, but a combination of dishes are served on a steel plate. Closed Mon. Inexpensive.

Riverstation The Grove ☏0117/914 4424. A former river-police station that has been artfully transformed into two great restaurants: downstairs you can chew on deli-type snacks or just have a drink, while the upstairs restaurant offers a bigger range of international dishes. Inexpensive to Moderate.

Teohs 28–34 Lower Ashley Rd. On the edge of the St Paul's area, this oriental bistro is well worth tracking down for its relaxed atmosphere and extremely low prices, offering thirty-odd dishes from Thailand, Malaysia and Japan. Bottled beers and house wine at £11 a carafe. Closed Mon. Inexpensive.

Pubs, bars and cafés

Arnolfini Narrow Quay. This art centre serves excellent vegetarian and meat dishes, plus drinks at the bar. There are communal wooden benches, and the crowd spills onto the cobbled quayside.

Avon Gorge Hotel Sion Hill. On the edge of the Gorge in Clifton Village, this mediocre bar has a broad terrace with tables from which to contemplate the magnificent views. Snacks available.

Belgo The Old Granary, Queen Charlotte St. Like its London cousins, this branch of the Belgian-food chain – in part of a restored warehouse near King Street – offers a range of Belgian draught and bottled beers. A good deal for early-evening eating is offered, where you pay according to the time you come in, e.g. £6.45 if you come at 6.45pm (until 7.30pm).

Mud Dock Café 40 The Grove. A winning if unlikely combination of bike shop and café-bar/restaurant by the river. There's good food, a barbecue on the balcony in summer, and DJs most nights.

Nova Scotia Cumberland Basin. Traditional dockside pub with seats by the nineteenth-century lock. Inexpensive food available.

Tantric Jazz Café 39–41 St Nicholas St ⓦwww.tantric-jazz.co.uk. Relaxed coffee stop near the Old Markets; there's food too, and live jazz and world music nightly.

Taverna dell'Artista King St. A haunt of theatrical folk as well as a rowdy bunch of regulars, this is a successful Anglo-Italian dive with a late licence. The pizzas, pastas and salads are nothing special, though.

Watershed 1 Canons Rd, St Augustine's Reach ⓦwww.watershed.co.uk. A good bar and café in the arts complex overlooking the boats, with food available until 9pm.

Clubs and venues

Bierkeller All Saints St, off Broadmead ☏0117/926 8514, ⓦwww.bristolbierkeller.co.uk. Steamy venue for live music from thrash metal to 60s and 80s revival bands.

Fleece and Firkin 12 St Thomas St ☏0117/929 9008. Stone-flagged ex-wool warehouse, this loud and sweaty pub puts on live rock and comedy six nights a week.

Lakota 6 Upper York St ☎0117/942 6208. Bristol's most celebrated club, attracting the biggest DJs as well as live bands, and often generating queues to get in. There's also a bistro open day and night.

The Rock Frogmore St ☎0117/927 9227. Near the Centre, this big and popular place is open Thurs, Fri and Sat for mainstream and hard-house parties.

Thekla Phoenix Wharf, off Queen Square ☎0117/929 3301. A youthful riverboat venue staging regular club nights Thurs–Sat, and open until 2am or 4am.

Bath and around

Though only twelve miles from Bristol, **BATH** has a very different feel from its neighbour – more harmonious, compact, leisurely and complacent. The city's elegant crescents and Georgian buildings are studded with plaques naming Bath's eminent inhabitants from its heyday as a spa resort; it was here that Jane Austen wrote *Persuasion* and *Northanger Abbey*, and where Gainsborough established himself as a portraitist and landscape painter. Nowadays Bath ranks as one of Britain's top ten tourist cities, yet the place has never lost the exclusive air those names evoke.

Bath owes its name and fame to its **hot springs** – the only ones in the country – which made it a place of reverence for the local Celtic population, though it had to wait for Roman technology to create a fully fledged bathing establishment. The baths fell into decline with the departure of the Romans, but the town later regained its importance under the Saxons, its abbey seeing the coronation of the **first king of all England**, Edgar, in 973. A new bathing complex was built in the sixteenth century, popularized by the visit of Elizabeth I in 1574, and the city reached its fashionable zenith in the eighteenth century, when **Beau Nash** ruled the town's social scene. It was at this time that Bath acquired its ranks of Palladian mansions and town houses, all built in the local **Bath stone**, which is now enshrined in building regulations as an obligatory element in any new constructions in the city. Three miles southeast of the centre, near the university campus, **Claverton** holds a museum of Americana amid gorgeous rolling countryside.

The swathes of parkland between Bath's Regency developments lend the city a spacious feel, but the sheer weight of traffic pouring through the central streets can be a major turn-off. Drivers are advised to use one of the **Park-and-Ride** car parks around the periphery – and if you're coming from Bristol, note that you can **cycle** all the way along a cycle-path that follows the route of a disused railway line and the course of the Avon.

Arrival, information and accommodation

Bath Spa **train station** and the city's **bus station** are both on Manvers Street, a short walk from the centre. The **tourist office** is right next to the abbey on Abbey Churchyard (May–Sept Mon–Sat 9.30am–6pm, Sun 10am–4pm; Oct–May Mon–Sat 9.30am–5pm, Sun 10am–4pm; ☎01225/477101, ⓦwww.visit-bath.co.uk). Here you can find a detailed list of **accommodation**; most establishments are small, so always phone first.

Hotels and B&Bs

Belmont 7 Belmont, Lansdown Rd ☎01225/423082. Huge rooms – though the single's a bit poky – some with en-suite shower in a house designed by John Wood, very near to the Assembly Rooms, Circus and Royal Crescent. No credit cards. ❷

Cranleigh 159 Newbridge Hill ☎01225/310197, Ⓔcranleigh@btinternet.com. Above the city, with fine views from some of the back rooms. *Objets*

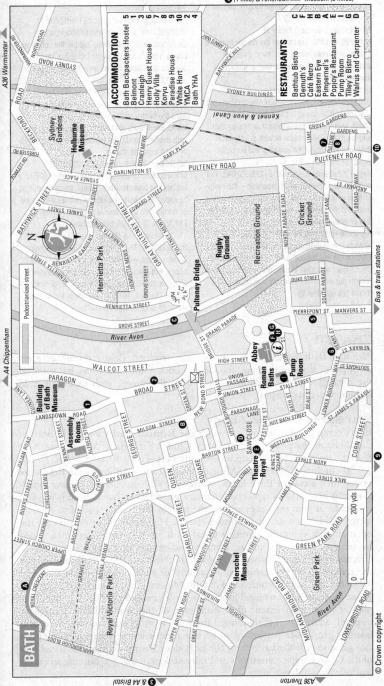

BATH

Pedestrianized street

A36 Warminster ▲

A4 Chippenham ▲

SYDNEY ROAD

NORTH ROAD

BECKFORD ROAD

BATHWICK STREET

FORESTER RD

SYDNEY PLACE

Sydney Gardens

Holburne Museum

SYDNEY MEWS

DARLINGTON ST

SYDNEY PLACE

RABY PLACE

SYDNEY BUILDINGS

Kennet & Avon Canal

ST ANN'S WAY

BATHWICK HILL

SUTTON STREET

HENRIETTA SONS

HENRIETTA MEWS

Henrietta Park

HENRIETTA GARDENS

DANIEL STREET

DANIEL STREET

HENRIETTA STREET

EDWARD STREET

GREEN PULTENEY STREET

GROVE STREET

PULTENEY MEWS

PULTENEY ROAD

Rugby Ground

Recreation Ground

Cricket Ground

NORTH PARADE ROAD

LIME GROVE GARDENS

GROVE GARDENS

PULTENEY ROAD

ARCHWAY ST

BROAD QUAY

FERRY LANE

DUKE STREET

SOUTH PARADE

NEWARK ST

HENRY ST

MANVERS ST

PIERREPONT ST

SOUTHGATE WALLS

LOWER BOROUGH WALLS

ST JAMES'S PARADE

CORN STREET

MILK STREET

AVON STREET

KING'S STREET

JAMES STREET

JAMES STREET WEST

GREEN PARK ROAD

Green Park

MIDLAND BRIDGE ROAD

River Avon

LOWER BRISTOL ROAD

NORFOLK BUILDINGS

GREAT STANHOPE ST

UPPER BRISTOL ROAD

NEW KING STREET

Herschel Museum

MONMOUTH STREET

MONMOUTH PLACE

CHARLES STREET

CHARLES STREET

JAMES STREET

KINGSMEAD SQUARE

Theatre Royal

SAWCLOSE

WESTGATE BUILDINGS

WESTGATE ST

HOT BATH STREET

BEAU ST

BATH ST

STALL ST

Roman Baths

Pump Room

Abbey

YORK ST

Bus & train stations ▶

CHARLOTTE STREET

QUEEN SQUARE

GAY STREET

THE CIRCUS

BROCK STREET

Royal Crescent

Royal Victoria Park

MARLBOROUGH BLDGS

UPPER CHURCH STREET

CATHERINE PL

RIVERS STREET

CIRCUS MEWS

JULIAN ROAD

BENNETT STREET

ALFRED STREET

Assembly Rooms

Building of Bath Museum

LANSDOWN ROAD

PARAGON

BROAD STREET

GEORGE STREET

MILSOM STREET

GREEN ST

NEW BOND STREET

UPPER BOROUGH WALLS

UNION PASSAGE

UNION STREET

PARSONAGE LANE

WALCOT STREET

HIGH STREET

BRIDGE ST

GRAND PARADE

Pulteney Bridge

GROVE STREET

River Avon

HENRIETTA STREET

BRISTOL ROAD

GRAVEL WALK

ROYAL AVENUE

ROYAL CRESCENT

BROCK STREET

QUIET LANE

SION HILL

BARTON STREET

A4 Bristol ▲

A36 & A4 Bristol ▼

A36 Tiverton ▼

5

ACCOMMODATION

Bath Backpackers Hostel	5
Belmont	1
Cranleigh	3
Henry Guest House	6
Holly Villa	7
Koryu	8
Paradise House	9
White Hart	10
YMCA	2
Bath YHA	4

RESTAURANTS

Bathtub Bistro	C
Demuth's	F
Café Retro	H
Eastern Eye	B
Pimpernel's	A
Popjoy's Restaurant	E
Pump Room	I
Tilley's Bistro	G
Walrus and Carpenter	D

200 yds

0 ——— 200

© Crown copyright

d'art abound, and period fittings include original fireplaces. No smoking. ⑤

Henry Guest House 6 Henry St ☎01225/424052. Just round the corner from the abbey, with more rooms than most (none en suite), but its location means that availability is limited. No credit cards. ②

Holly Villa 14 Pulteney Gardens ☎01225/310331, ✉hollyvilla.bb@ukgateway.net. High-class B&B, close to the Kennet and Avon Canal, with friendly management, a nice garden and six rooms (all en suite or with private facilities), one very large. No smoking and no credit cards. Closed Jan & Feb. ②

Koryu 7 Pulteney Gardens ☎01225/337642. The name means "Sunshine" in Japanese – the mother-tongue of the landlady, who has made cleanliness and simplicity the keynotes. No shoes inside and no smoking. No credit cards. ③

Paradise House 88 Holloway ☎01225/317723, ⓦwww.paradise-house.co.uk. The wonderful view justifies the ten-minute uphill trudge from the centre. Croquet or boules in the lush garden and open fires in the winter are other attractions, and all rooms are en suite. ⑤ ②

Hostels

Bath Backpackers Hostel 13 Pierrepoint St ☎01225/446787, ✉stayinbath@backpackers-uk.demon.co.uk. Cheap stop right in the centre of things. There's no curfew, no lockout, a kitchen, bar and pool room, but no breakfast. Dorm beds are £12, doubles with bath £30.

Bath YHA Bathwick Hill ☎01225/465674, ⓦwww.yha.org.uk. An Italianate mansion a mile from the centre, with gardens and panoramic views. Dorm beds (£11 each) and double rooms with evening meals also available. Take buses #18 or #418 from the station.

White Hart Widcombe Hill ☎01225/313985, ⓦwww.whitehartbath.co.uk. The comfiest of Bath's hostels has basic facilities, though these are due to be expanded. There is a kitchen and a café, however, dorms with six to twelve beds with duvets (at £12.50 each), and doubles available (£30).

YMCA International House, Broad St ☎01225/460471, ✉info@ymcabath.u-net.com. Clean, central, with lots of room and convenient prices, this place offers good central accommodation, charging £11 for dorm beds, £16 for singles, £28 for doubles, and with reductions for weekly stays; all prices include breakfast.

The City

Although Bath could easily be seen on a day-trip from Bristol, it really deserves a couple of days on the spot; the city is chock-full of museums, but some of the greatest enjoyment comes simply from the streets, with their pale gold architecture and sweeping vistas.

The Baths and the Abbey

Bath's centrepiece is, naturally enough, the **Roman Baths** located in front of the abbey in the pedestrianized Abbey Church Yard (daily: March–June, Sept & Oct 9am–6pm; July & Aug 9am–10pm; Nov–Feb 9.30am–5.30pm; £7.50, £9.50 combined ticket with Museum of Costume). Although the tickets are pricey, there's two or three hours' worth of well-balanced, informative entertainment here, with a taped commentary provided on handsets allowing you to wander at your own pace around the temple and bathing complex, where a spring still issues water at a constant 46.5°C. Highlights of the remains are the open-air (but originally covered) Great Bath, its vaporous waters surrounded by nineteenth-century pillars, terraces and statues of famous Romans; the Circular Bath, where bathers cooled off; the Norman King's Bath; and part of the temple of Minerva. Among a quantity of coins, jewellery and sculpture exhibited are the gilt bronze head of Sulis Minerva, the local deity, and a grand, Celtic-inspired gorgon's head from the temple's pediment. Models of the complex at its greatest extent give some idea of the awe which it must have inspired, while the graffiti salvaged from the Roman era – mainly curses and boasts – give a nice personal slant on this antique leisure centre. You can get a free glimpse into the baths from the next-door **Pump Room**, the social hub of the Georgian spa community and still redolent of that era, housing an excellent tearoom and restaurant.

Richard "Beau" Nash was an ex-army officer, ex-lawyer, dandy and gambler, who became Bath's Master of Ceremonies in 1704, conducting public balls of an unprecedented splendour. Wielding dictatorial powers over dress and behaviour, Nash orchestrated the social manners of the city and even extended his influence to cover road improvements and the design of buildings. In an early example of health awareness, he banned smoking in Bath's public rooms at a time when pipe-smoking was a general pastime among men, women and children. Less philanthropically, he also encouraged gambling and even took a percentage of the bank's takings. Nonetheless, he was generally held in high esteem and succeeded in establishing rules such as the setting of specific hours and procedure for all social functions. Balls were to begin at six and end at eleven and every ball had to open with a minuet "danced by two persons of the highest distinction present". White aprons were banned, gossipers and scandalmongers were shunned, and, most radical of all, the wearing of swords in public places was forbidden, a ruling referred to in Sheridan's play *The Rivals*, in which Captain Absolute declares, "A sword seen in the streets of Bath would raise as great an alarm as a mad dog." By such measures, Nash presided over the city's greatest period, during the first four decades of the eighteenth century. He lived in Bath until his death at the age of 87, by which time he had been reduced to comparative poverty.

Next to the innovations of Nash and the architectural creations of the two John Woods, the name of **William Oliver** should not be forgotten in the story of Regency Bath. A physician and philanthropist, Oliver did more than anyone to boost the city's profile as a therapeutic centre, thanks to publications such as his *Practical Essay on the Use and Abuse of Warm Bathing in Gouty Cases* (1751), and by founding the Bath General Hospital to enable the poor to make use of the waters. He is remembered today by the Bath Oliver biscuit, which he invented, and by the use of Olivers as the exchange currency in a local community bartering scheme.

Although there has been a church on the site since the seventh century, **Bath Abbey** (daily 9am–5pm; closes 4pm in winter; requested donation £2) did not take its present form until the end of the fifteenth century, when Bishop Oliver King began work on the ruins of the previous Norman building, some of which were incorporated into the new church. The bishop was said to have been inspired by a vision of angels ascending and descending a ladder to heaven, which the present facade recalls on the turrets flanking the central window. The west front also features the founder's signature in the form of carvings of olive trees surmounted by crowns, a play on his name.

The interior is in a restrained Perpendicular style, and boasts splendid fan vaulting on the ceiling, which was not properly completed until the nineteenth century. The floor and walls are crammed with elaborate monuments and memorials, and traces of the grander Norman building are visible in the Norman Chapel.

To the Circus and the Royal Crescent

From Abbey Church Yard, the elegantly colonnaded Bath Street leads onto Hot Bath Street; turn right here to reach Westgate Street and Sawclose, where you can take a glance at the **Theatre Royal**, opened in 1805 and one of the country's finest surviving Georgian theatres. Next door is the house where Beau Nash spent his last years, now a restaurant. Up from the Theatre Royal, off Barton Street, the gracious **Queen Square** was the first Bath venture of the architect **John Wood**, who with his son (also John) was chiefly responsible for the Roman-inspired developments of the areas outside the confines of the

THE COTSWOLDS AND SOMERSET | Bath and around

medieval city. Wood himself lived at no. 24, giving him a vista of the northern terrace's palatial facade.

West of Queen Square, the typical Bath townhouse at 19 New King St was where the musician and astronomer Sir William Herschel, in collaboration with his sister Caroline, discovered the planet Uranus in 1781. You can take a brisk whirl around the small **Herschel Museum** here (March–Oct daily 2–5pm; Nov–Feb Sat & Sun 2–5pm; £3.50), showing contemporary furnishings, musical instruments, a replica of the telescope with which Uranus was identified and various knick-knacks from the Herschels' life.

Up from Queen Square, at the end of Gay Street, is the elder John Wood's masterpiece, **The Circus**, consisting of three crescents arranged in a tight circle of three-storey houses, with a carved frieze running round the entire circle. Wood died soon after laying the foundation stone for this enterprise, and the job was finished by his son. The painter Thomas Gainsborough lived at no. 17 from 1760 to 1774.

The Circus is connected by Brock Street to the **Royal Crescent**, grandest of Bath's crescents, begun by the younger John Wood in 1767. The stately arc of thirty houses is set off by a spacious sloping lawn from which a magnificent vista extends to green hills and distant ribbons of honey-coloured stone. The interior of **No. 1 Royal Crescent**, on the corner with Brock Street, has been restored to reflect as nearly as possible its original Georgian appearance (mid-Feb to Oct Tues–Sun 10.30am–5pm; Nov Tues–Sun 10.30am–4pm; £4; ⓦwww.bath-preservation-trust.org.uk).

At the bottom of the Crescent, Royal Avenue leads onto **Royal Victoria Park**, the city's largest open space, containing an aviary and botanical gardens.

The Assembly Rooms, the Paragon and Milsom Street

The younger John Wood's **Assembly Rooms**, east of the Circus on Bennett Street, were, with the Pump Room, the centre of Bath's social scene. A fire virtually destroyed the building in 1942, but it has now been perfectly restored and houses a **Museum of Costume** (daily 10am–5pm; £4.20, or £9.50 with Baths), an entertaining collection of clothing from the Stuart era to the latest Japanese designs.

From the Assembly Rooms, Alfred Street leads to the area known as the **Paragon**, at the top of Milsom Street. Here, an old Methodist chapel houses the **Building of Bath Museum** (mid-Feb to Nov Tues–Sun 10.30am–5pm; £4), an educational explanation of the construction and architecture of Bath. At the bottom of the Paragon, off George Street, lies **Milsom Street**, a wide shopping strand designed by the elder Wood as the main thoroughfare of Georgian Bath.

The river and Great Pulteney Street

The flow of the River Avon – a crucial ingredient in the city's charm – is interrupted by a graceful V-shaped weir just below the shop-lined **Pulteney Bridge**, an Italianate structure designed by the eighteenth-century Scottish architect Robert Adam. The bridge was intended to link the city centre with **Great Pulteney Street**, a handsome avenue originally planned as the nucleus of a large residential quarter on the eastern bank. The work ran into financial difficulties, however, so the roads running off it now stop short after a few yards, though there is a lengthy vista to the imposing classical facade of the **Holburne Museum** at the end of the street (mid-Feb to mid-Dec Tues–Sat 11am–5pm, Sun 2.30–5.30pm; £3.50; ⓦwww.bath.ac.uk/holburne). The three-storey building contains an impressive range of decorative and fine art, mostly furniture, silverware, porcelain and paintings (including the newly acquired *Byam Family* portrait by Gainsborough) from the eighteenth century, plus a good collection of twentieth-century craftwork.

Behind Holburne House, **Sydney Gardens** make a delightful place to take a breather. When Holburne House was a bustling hotel, the pleasure gardens were the venue for concerts and fireworks, as witnessed by Jane Austen, a frequent visitor here – the family had lodgings across the street at 4 Sydney Place in the autumn of 1801. Today, the bosky slopes are cut through by the railway and the Kennet and Avon Canal. From here, it's a pleasant one-and-a-half mile saunter along the canal to the *George* pub (see below).

If you want to explore the river itself, rent a skiff, punt or canoe in summer from the **Victorian Bath Boating Station** at the end of Forester Road, behind the Holburne Museum (about £6 per person per hour). Organized river trips can be made from Pulteney Bridge and weir, and there are cruises on the Kennet and Avon Canal from Sydney Wharf, near Bathwick Bridge. A two-mile **nature trail** winds along the banks of the restored canal, which itself extends east as far as Reading.

Eating, drinking and nightlife

Bath has a reputation for gourmet cuisine, even if too many of the town's **restaurants** do over-exploit the period trappings. In the less exalted regions of the price scale, there are several decent, inexpensive places to eat, and coffee shops and snack bars are ubiquitous in the centre.

For concerts, gigs and other events, refer to *Venue*, the fortnightly listings magazine (£1.90). **Theatre** and ballet fans should check out what's showing at the Theatre Royal on Sawclose (℡01225/448844), which stages more experimental productions in the Ustinov Studio. Bath also has a great range of festivals throughout the year, offering talks, gigs and other events in often sumptuous surroundings, notably the **Bath International Music Festival** (ⓦwww.bathmusicfest.org.uk), held between mid-May and June and featuring jazz, classical and World Music; the **Bath Fringe Festival** (ⓦwww.bathfringe.co.uk), running from the end of May to mid-June, with the accent on art, theatre and music, and **Bath Literature Festival** (ⓦwww.bathlitfest.org.uk), taking place over ten days in Feb/March. For further information on each, check out the individual websites, or call ℡01225/463362.

The best of the town's **clubs** are *Moles* on George Street, which has live music and DJs; the *Fez Club*, The Paragon, which plays funk, trance and old skool, and *Club Eros*, a gay and lesbian venue situated under the *Bath Tap* pub (see below).

Restaurants

Bathtub Bistro 2 Grove St ℡01225/460593, ⓦwww.bathtubbistro.co.uk. Round the corner from Pulteney Bridge, this place looks tiny from the outside but reveals several eating areas on different levels. The menu includes one hundred percent-beef hamburgers, vegetarian dishes and spiced ice cream. BYOB Mon & Tues. Inexpensive to moderate.

Demuth's 2 North Parade Passage ℡01225/446059. Bath's favourite eating place for veggies and vegans, offering original and delicious dishes, as well as organic beers, wines and coffees. Decor is bright and modern. No smoking. Booking advisable at weekends. Moderate to expensive.

Café Retro 18 York St. A laid-back place near the Abbey offering an inventive international menu, all to mellow sounds. Also a good spot for a cappuccino break during the day. BYOB. Moderate.

Eastern Eye 8 Quiet St ℡01225/422323, ⓦwww.easterneye.co.uk. Just off Milsom Street in the centre of Bath, this designer curry house occupies a Georgian bank, with a spectacular vaulted ceiling. The food's good too, impeccably presented and served. Moderate.

Pimpernel's *Royal Crescent Hotel*, 16 Royal Crescent ☎01225/823333. English-based classics with Mediterranean influences make this the best restaurant in Bath, all in sumptuous surroundings. Non-smoking. Very Expensive.

Popjoy's Restaurant Sawclose ☎01225/460494. Though somewhat twee, this restaurant is worth the splurge for its prime location next to the Theatre Royal, and for the curiosity value of being Beau Nash's house (it's named after his mistress). The food is high-quality Modern British, with great desserts, and there's a good-value pre-theatre menu. Closed Sun. Expensive.

Pump Room Abbey Church Yard ☎01225/444477. If you don't want to splash out on an Eggs Benedict brunch, you might succumb to a Bath bun here in the morning, or a bewildering range of cream teas in the afternoon, or the excellent lunch-time menu, all to the accompaniment of a classical trio. You get a good view of the baths, and a chance to sample the waters, though be prepared to queue. Open daytime only, plus evenings during the Bath Festival. Inexpensive to moderate.

Tilley's Bistro 3 North Parade Passage ☎01225/484200. Informal, rather cramped French restaurant with starter-sized and -priced portions to allow more samplings, good set-price lunchtime menus and a separate vegetarian menu. Closed Sun. Moderate.

Walrus and Carpenter 25 Barton St. Popular spot near the Theatre Royal, serving steaks, burgers, poultry dishes and a full vegetarian menu. Moderate.

Pubs and cafés

The Bath Tap 19–20 St James's Parade. Home of Bath's gay and lesbian scene, though without so much of the "scene". It's lively but relaxed, with a mixed crowd enjoying the regular cabaret.

The Bell 103 Walcot St. Excellent pub with a garden, live music three times a week (Mon & Wed eve, plus Sun lunchtime) and bar billiards.

The George Mill Lane, Bathampton. Popular canalside pub twenty minutes' walk from the centre. Better than average bar food.

Hat & Feather London St. Further up from Walcot Street, this drinking hole continues the quarter's alternative theme, with table football, DJs and live music on some nights.

Pig & Fiddle corner of Saracen and Walcot streets. Real ales and outside terraces, north of Pulteney Bridge. Table football and food helps to pull in the crowds.

The Porter Miles Buildings, George St. Part of *Moles* club (see below), this is the only vegetarian pub in Bath, though it feels more like a café. Live music twice weekly & DJs other nights in the cosy cellar bar.

Claverton

For a quick sample of the lovely countryside around Bath you could make an easy excursion to **CLAVERTON**, on the eastern edge of Bath, where the **American Museum** (late March to July & Sept–Nov Tues–Sun 2–5pm; Aug daily 2–5pm; grounds Tues–Fri 1–6pm, Sat & Sun noon–6pm; £5.50; grounds only £3) merits at least half a day. Occupying the early nineteenth-century Claverton Manor, where Winston Churchill made his maiden political speech in 1897, this consists of a series of reconstructed rooms illustrating life in the New World from the seventeenth to the nineteenth centuries, as well as special sections devoted to textiles, whaling, the opening of the West, Native Americans and Hispano-American culture. The glorious **grounds** contain a replica of George Washington's garden, an arboretum and assorted relics resembling items from a movie set. University buses #18 and #418 run throughout the year to the Avenue (the stop before the campus), from where it's a ten-minute walk to the museum.

Wells, the Mendips and Glastonbury

Wells, twenty miles south of Bristol across the Somerset border and the same distance southwest from Bath, is a miniature cathedral city that has not significantly altered in eight hundred years. You might decide to make it a base for visiting nearby attractions in the **Mendip Hills**, such as the **Wookey Hole** caves and the **Cheddar Gorge**. On the southern edge of the range, and just a jump away from Wells, the town of **Glastonbury** is famed as one of Britain's main Arthurian sites, and has become an enthusiastic centre of New Age cults.

Wells

Technically the smallest city in the country, **WELLS** owes its celebrity entirely to its Gothic Cathedral (daily: May, June & Sept 7am–7pm; July & Aug 7am–8.30pm; Oct–April 7am–6pm; suggested donation £4). Hidden from sight until you pass into its spacious close from the central Market Place, the building presents a majestic spectacle, the broad lawn of the former graveyard providing a perfect foreground. The west front, constructed about fifty years after work on the main building was begun in 1180, teems with some three hundred thirteenth-century figures of saints and kings, once brightly painted and gilded, though their present honey tint has a subtle splendour of its own. Close up, the impact is slightly lessened, as most of the statuary is badly eroded and many figures were damaged by Puritans in the seventeenth century. The **interior** is a supreme example of early English Gothic, the long nave punctuated by a dramatic "scissor arch", one of three that were constructed in 1338 to take the extra weight of the newly built tower. Though some wax enthusiastic about the ingenuity of these so-called "strainer" arches, others argue that they're "grotesque intrusions" from an aesthetic point of view.

Other features worth scrutinizing are the narrative carvings on the **capitals and corbels** in the transepts – including men with toothache and an old man caught pilfering an orchard. In the north transept, don't miss the 24-hour astronomical clock, dating from 1390, whose jousting knights charge each other every quarter-hour, as announced by a figure known as Jack Blandiver, who kicks a couple of bells from his seat high up on the right – on the hour he strikes the bell in front of him. Opposite the clock, a doorway leads to a graceful, much-worn flight of steps rising to the **Chapter House** (closes 4.30pm), an octagonal room elaborately ribbed in the Decorated style. There are some gnarled old tombs to be seen in the aisles of the **choir**, at the end of which is the richly coloured stained glass of the fourteenth-century **Lady Chapel**.

The row of clerical houses on the north side of the cathedral green are mainly seventeenth- and eighteenth-century, though one, the **Old Deanery**, shows traces of its fifteenth-century origins. The chancellor's house is now a **museum** (Easter–July, Sept & Oct daily 10am–5.30pm; Aug daily 10am–8pm; Nov–Easter Mon & Wed–Sun 11am–4pm; £2.50), displaying, among other items, some of the cathedral's original statuary, placed here for conservation reasons (and replaced by replicas), as well as a good geological section with fossils from the surrounding area, including Wookey Hole.

A little further along the street, the cobbled medieval **Vicars' Close** holds more clerical dwellings, linked to the cathedral by the Chain Gate and fronted by small gardens. The cottages were built in the mid-fourteenth century – though only no. 22 has not undergone outward alterations – and have been continuously occupied by members of the cathedral clergy ever since.

On the other side of the cathedral – and accessible through the cathedral shop – are the cloisters, from which you can enter the tranquil grounds of the **Bishop's Palace** (April–July, Sept & Oct Tues–Fri 10.30am–5pm, Sun 2–5pm; Aug daily 10.30am–5pm, though may close on first or second Sat of month for wedding receptions; £3.50), also reachable from Market Place through the Bishop's Eye archway. The residence of the Bishop of Bath and Wells, the palace was walled and moated as a result of a rift with the borough in the fourteenth century, and the imposing gatehouse still displays the grooves of the portcullis and a chute for pouring oil and molten lead on would-be assailants. Its tranquil gardens contain the springs from which the city takes its name and the ruined **Great Hall**, built at the end of the thirteenth century and despoiled during the Reformation.

Practicalities

Wells is not connected to the rail network, but its **bus station**, off Market Street, receives hourly buses from Bristol and Bath (less frequent on Sun). The **tourist office** is on Market Place (daily: April–Oct 9.30am–5.30pm; Nov–March 10am–4pm; ☎01749/672552).

Among the best **B&Bs**, try *Canon Grange*, right on the Cathedral Green, its spacious rooms facing the west front (☎01749/671800, ✉canongrange@email.com; ❷), or *Bekynton House*, a little farther out at 7 St Thomas St (☎01749/672222, ⊛www.bekyntonhouse.freeserve.co.uk; ❷), where en-suite rooms nudge into the next category. The town also has some nice old coaching inns, notably the *Crown Hotel*, Market Place (☎01749/673457; ❻), where William Penn was arrested in 1695 for illegal preaching, and the *Swan*, further down the High Street (☎01749/836300; ❻).

For **food**, head for *Chapel's* in Union Street (off High Street), a modern café-bar with a varied menu, or the Italian-run *Ancient Gate House*, Sadler Street (☎01749/672029); on the same street, *Ritcher's* (☎01749/679085) combines a downstairs bar/patisserie with a restaurant in a plant-filled loft offering set-price menus. Excellent wholefood is served at the *Good Earth* on Priory Road, near the bus station (☎01749/678600; closed Sun), and you can eat inexpensive meals as well as **pub** fare at the *City Arms* on Cuthbert Street, formerly the city jail.

The Mendips

The **Mendip Hills**, rising to the north of Wells, are chiefly famous for **Wookey Hole** – the most impressive of many caves in this narrow limestone chain – and for the **Cheddar Gorge**, where a walk through the narrow cleft might make a starting point for more adventurous trips across the Mendips. From Monday to Saturday there's an hourly bus to Wookey Hole from Wells (#172), from where there's also an hourly bus to the gorge (#126 or #826) – every two hours on Sunday.

Wookey Hole

Hollowed out by the River Axe a couple of miles outside Wells, **Wookey Hole** is an impressive cave complex of deep pools and intricate rock formations, but it's folklore rather than geology that takes precedence on the guided tours (daily: April–Oct 10am–5pm; Nov–March 10.30am–4.30pm; closed Dec 17–25; £7.30). Highlight of the tour is the alleged petrified remains of the Witch of Wookey, a "blear-eyed hag" who was said to have turned her evil eye on crops, young lovers and local farmers until the Abbot of Glastonbury intervened; he despatched a monk who drove the witch into the inner cave, sprinkled her with holy water and turned her into stone. Some substance was lent to the legend when an ancient skeleton – in fact Romano-British – was unearthed here in 1912, together with a dagger, sacrificial knife and a big rounded ball of pure stalagmite, the so-called witch's ball. Beside her were found two skeletons, the remains of goats tied to a stake. At the end of the hour-long tour, you can visit a functioning Victorian paper mill and rooms containing speleological exhibits and a range of gaudy, sometimes ghoulish Edwardian fairground amusements.

Cheddar Gorge

Six miles west of Wookey on the A371, the rather plain village of Cheddar has given its name to Britain's best-known cheese – most of it now mass-produced far from here – and is also renowned for the **Cheddar Gorge**, lying beyond the neighbourhood of Tweentown about a mile to the north. Cutting a jagged gash across the Mendip Hills, the limestone gorge is an impressive geological phenomenon, though its natural beauty is undermined by the minor road running through it and by the Lower Gorge's mile of shops and coach park – and you'll also find here Cheddar's **tourist office** (mid-March to mid-Nov daily 10am–5pm; mid-Nov to mid-March Sun 11am–4pm; ℡01934/744071, ⓦwww .sedgemoor.gov.uk/tourism). Few trippers venture further than the first few curves of the gorge, which admittedly hold its most dramatic scenery, though each turn of the two-mile length presents new, sometimes startling vistas. At its narrowest the path squeezes between cliffs towering almost five hundred feet above, and if you don't want to follow the road as far as **Priddy**, the highest village in the Mendips, you can reach more dramatic destinations by branching off onto marked paths to such secluded spots as **Black Rock**, just two miles from Cheddar, or **Black Down**, at 1067ft the Mendips' highest peak. Cliff-top paths winding along the rim of the gorge provide an alternative to walking on the road. The tourist office can give you details of a two-and-a-half-hour circular walk and of the **West Mendip Way**, a forty-mile route extending from Uphill, near Weston-super-Mare, to Wells and Shepton Mallet.

Beneath the gorge, the **Cheddar Caves** (daily: May to mid-Sept 10am–5pm; mid-Sept to April 10am–4.30pm; £7.90) were scooped out by underground rivers in the wake of the Ice Age, and subsequently occupied by primitive communities. Today, the caves are floodlit to pick out the subtle pinks, greys, greens and whites in the rock, and the array of tortuous rock formations that resemble organ pipes, waterfalls and giant birds. Outside, close to Cox's Caves, the 274 steps of **Jacob's Ladder** (same ticket as caves) lead to a cliff-top viewpoint towards Glastonbury Tor, Exmoor and the sea. It's a muscle-wrenching climb – anyone not in a state of honed fitness can reach the same spot via the narrow lane winding up behind the cliffs. You can also survey the panorama from **Pavey's Lookout Tower** nearby.

Among Cheddar's handful of **B&Bs**, try *Chedwell Cottage*, Redcliffe Street (℡01934/743268; ❷), or *Wossells House*, Upper New Road (℡01934/744317; ❷) – booking ahead is recommended for both of these. There's also a **youth hostel** here, opposite the fire station off the Hayes (℡01934/742494).

Glastonbury

Six miles south of Wells, and reachable from there in twenty minutes on frequent buses, **GLASTONBURY** lies at the centre of the so-called **Isle of Avalon**, a region rich with mystical associations. At the heart of it all is the early Christian legend that the young Christ once visited this site, a story that is not as far-fetched as it sounds. The Romans had a heavy presence in the area, mining lead in the Mendips, and one of these mines was owned by **Joseph of Arimathea**, a well-to-do merchant said to have been related to Mary. It's not inconceivable that the merchant took his kinsman on one of his many visits to his property, in a period of Christ's life of which nothing is recorded. It was this possibility to which William Blake referred in his *Glastonbury Hymn*, better known as *Jerusalem*: – "And did those feet in ancient times/Walk upon England's mountains green?"

Another legend relates how Joseph was imprisoned for twelve years after the Crucifixion, miraculously kept alive by the **Holy Grail**, the chalice of the Last Supper, in which the blood was gathered from the wound in Christ's side. The Grail, along with the spear which had caused the wound, were later taken by Joseph to Glastonbury, where he founded the abbey and commenced the conversion of Britain.

More verifiably, a Celtic monastery was established on this site in the fourth or fifth century – making this the oldest Christian foundation in England. Enlarged by St Dunstan, **Glastonbury Abbey** (daily: Feb 10am–5pm; March 9.30am–5.30pm; April–Sept 9.30am–6pm; Oct 9.30am–5pm; Nov 9.30am–4.30pm; Dec & Jan 10am–4.30pm; £3; ⓦ www.glastonburyabbey.com) became the richest Benedictine abbey in the country. Three Anglo-Saxon kings (Edmund, Edgar and Edmund Ironside) were buried here, the library had a far-reaching fame, and the church had the longest known nave of any monastic church at the time of the Dissolution (580ft – Wells Cathedral's nave reaches 415ft). The original building was destroyed by fire in 1184 and the ruins are the rather scanty remains of what took its place, reduced to their present state at the Dissolution. Hidden behind walls at the centre of town, surrounded by grassy parkland and shaded by trees, the ruins only hint at the extent of the building, which was financed largely by a constant procession of medieval pilgrims. Most prominent and photogenic remains are the transept piers and the shell of the Lady Chapel, with its carved figures of the Annunciation, the Magi and Herod.

The abbey's **choir** introduces another strand to the Glastonbury mythology, for it holds what is alleged to be the tomb of **Arthur and Guinevere**. As told by William of Malmesbury and Thomas Malory, the story relates how, after being mortally wounded in battle, King Arthur sailed to Avalon where he was buried alongside his queen. The discovery of two bodies in an ancient cemetery outside the abbey in 1191 – from which they were transferred here in 1278 – was taken to confirm the popular identification of Glastonbury with Avalon. In the grounds, the fourteenth-century abbot's kitchen is the only monastic building to survive intact, with four huge corner fireplaces and a great central lantern above. Behind the main entrance to the grounds, look out for the thorn-tree that is supposedly from the original **Glastonbury Thorn** said to have sprouted from the staff of Joseph of Arimathea when he landed here to convert the country. The plant grew for centuries on a nearby hill known as Wyrral, or Weary-All, and despite being hacked down by Puritans, lived long enough to provide numerous cuttings whose descendants still bloom twice a year (Easter & Dec). Only at Glastonbury do they flourish, it is claimed – anywhere else they die after a couple of years.

On the edge of the abbey grounds, the medieval abbey barn forms the centrepiece of the engaging **Somerset Rural Life Museum** (April–Oct Tues–Fri 10am–5pm, Sat & Sun 2–6pm; Nov–March Tues–Sat 10am–3pm; £2.50), illustrating a range of local rural occupations, from cheese- and cider-making to peat-digging, thatching and farming.

From the abbey's ruins it's a mile-long hike to **Glastonbury Tor**, at 521ft a landmark for miles around. The conical hill is topped by the dilapidated **St Michael's Tower**, sole remnant of a fourteenth-century church; it commands stupendous views encompassing Wells, the Quantocks, the Mendips, the Somerset Levels – the once-marshy peat moors rolling out to the sea – and sometimes the Welsh mountains. Pilgrims once embarked on the stiff climb here with hard peas in their shoes as penance – nowadays people come to feel the vibrations of crossing ley-lines. If you don't fancy the steep ascent, take the easier path farther up Wellhouse Lane, the road that leads to the Tor Park from the centre of town. You can also save some legwork by taking advantage of the **Glastonbury Tor Bus**, a summer service (July to mid-Sept) which takes people from the High Street to the base of the Tor every thirty minutes; your £1 ticket can be used all day.

At the bottom of Wellhouse Lane, in the middle of a lush garden intended for quiet contemplation, the **Chalice Well** (daily: Feb, March & Nov 11am–5pm; April–Oct 10am–6pm; Dec & Jan noon–4pm; £2.20; ⓦwww .chalicewell.org.uk) is alleged to be the hiding-place of the Holy Grail. The iron-red waters were considered to have curative properties, making the town a spa for a brief period in the eighteenth century, and they are still prized – there's a tap in Wellhouse Lane.

Back in town, you might take a glance at the fifteenth-century church of **St John the Baptist**, halfway along the High Street. The tower is reckoned to be one of Somerset's finest, and the **interior** has a fine oak roof and stained glass illustrating the legend of St Joseph of Arimathea, both from the period of the church's construction. The Glastonbury thorn in the churchyard is the biggest in town.

Further down the street, the fourteenth-century **Tribunal** was where the abbots presided over legal cases; it later became a hotel for pilgrims, and now holds a small museum of finds from the Iron Age lake villages that once fringed the marshland below the Tor (April–Sept Mon–Thurs & Sun 10am–5pm, Fri & Sat 10am–5.30pm; Oct–March closes 1hr earlier; £2).

Glastonbury is of course also famous for its **music festival** which takes place most years over three days at the end of June outside the nearby village of Pilton. Having started in the 1970s, the festival has become one of the biggest and best organized in the country, without shedding too much of its alternative feel. Bands range from huge acts such as REM and Pulp to up-and-coming indie groups and such old hands as Tom Jones. Ticket prices are steep (around £90) and are snapped up early: for general information, contact the promoters on ☎01749/890470, or Glastonbury's tourist office (see below), which is also licensed to sell tickets.

Practicalities

Bus #376 runs once or twice an hour from Wells. Glastonbury's **tourist office** is housed in the Tribunal on the High Street (April–Sept Mon–Thurs & Sun 10am–5pm, Fri & Sat 10am–5.30pm; Oct–March closes 1hr earlier; ☎01458/832954 or 832020 for information on tickets for the festival, ⓦwww.glastonburytic.co.uk).

Good-value **accommodation** in town includes the seventeenth-century *Waterfall Cottage*, 20 Old Wells Rd (☎01458/831707; ❶), which boasts a garden and views, and the *Bolthole*, close to the Chalice Well and Rural Life Museum at 32 Chilkwell St (☎01458/832800; ❶), which caters for vegetarians. Far grander is the *Ramala Centre* on nearby Dod Lane (☎01458/832459; ❸). This old manor house is the headquarters of a meditation group and offers accommodation without strings, including use of a library of esoteric philosophy – smokers and carnivores are not welcome. If you prefer a more medieval mood, head straight for the *George & Pilgrims*, an old oak-panelled inn on the High Street (℡01458/831146; ⑤). Just as central, *Glastonbury Backpackers*, 4 Market Place (℡01458/833353, ✉glastonbury@backpackers-online.com), offers a livelier atmosphere: there's a café, first-floor restaurant and pool room, and occasional live music in the bar. The nearest YHA **hostel**, at the Chalet, Ivythorn Hill (℡01458/442961), lies a couple of miles outside the nearby village of **Street**, an easy bus ride on the #376 between Wells and Glastonbury.

Wedged between the esoteric shops of Glastonbury's High Street are several decent **cafés** serving inexpensive home-made meals, including the *Blue Note Café* at no. 4, a good place to hang out over coffees and cakes with live or recorded music, and *Rainbow's End* at no. 17, which has vegetarian and vegan food and a small garden, and stays open for evening meals on Fridays and Saturdays, for which booking is recommended (℡01458/833896). Halfway up the High Street, the Assembly Rooms has a funky wholefood café, but is better known as the venue for talks and musical and theatrical **performances**, including an international **dance festival** which takes place over a week between July and August. You can also buy tickets for concerts and miracle plays staged within the abbey grounds between mid-June and mid-September – call ℡01458/832267 for details, or view the Abbey's website (see above).

Bridgwater, Taunton and the Quantocks

Travelling west through the Somerset Levels, your route could take you through both **Bridgwater** and **Taunton**, each of which would make a handy starting point for excursions into the gently undulating **Quantock Hills**, a mellow landscape of snug villages set in scenic wooded valleys or "combes". Public transport is fairly minimal round here, but you can see quite a lot on the **West Somerset Railway** between Bishops Lydeard and the coastal resort of Minehead, with stops at some of the thatched, typically English villages along the west flank of the Quantocks. The restored line was built originally to serve the harbour of Watchet, and is now mainly used by tourists, birdwatchers and trekkers.

Bridgwater

Sedate **BRIDGWATER** has seen little excitement since it was embroiled in the Civil War and its aftermath, in particular the events surrounding the **Monmouth Rebellion** of 1685. Having landed from his base in Holland, the Protestant Duke of Monmouth, an illegitimate son of Charles II, was enthusiastically proclaimed king at Taunton, and was only prevented from taking Bristol by the encampment of the Catholic James II's army there. Monmouth turned round and attempted to surprise the king's forces on **Sedgemoor**, three miles outside Bridgwater. The disorganized rebel army was mown down by the royal artillery, Monmouth himself was captured and later beheaded, and a period of repression was unleashed under the infamous Judge Jeffreys, whose Bloody Assizes created a folk-memory in Somerset of gibbets and gutted carcasses displayed around the county.

The town was once one of Somerset's major ports and still has some handsome red-brick buildings around its centre. The thirteenth- to fourteenth-century **St Mary's church** (Mon–Wed & Sat 10.30am–noon, Thurs 10.30am–

noon & 2–3.30pm), immediately identifiable by its polygonal, acutely angled steeple that soars over the town centre, has an oak pulpit and a seventeenth-century Italian altarpiece. By the River Parrett on Blake Street, and just round the corner from the red-brick Christ Church, where Coleridge preached in 1797 and 1798, Bridgwater's **Blake Museum** (Tues–Sat 10am–4pm; free) shows relics, models and a video-documentary relating to the Battle of Sedgemoor. The sixteenth-century building is reputedly the birthplace of local hero Robert Blake, admiral under Oliver Cromwell, whose swashbuckling career against Royalists, Dutch and Spanish is also chronicled and illustrated here.

Bridgwater's **tourist office** is on the High Street (March–Oct Mon–Fri 10am–5pm Sat 10am–4.30pm; Nov–Feb Mon, Wed & Fri 10am–1pm & 1.45–4pm; ℡01278/427652). If you're looking for **accommodation** here-abouts, try *Acorns*, 61 Taunton Rd (℡01278/445577; ❶), on the banks of the Bridgwater–Taunton Canal, or, more centrally, the atmospheric *Old Vicarage*, right opposite St Mary's Church (℡01278/458891, ✉oldvicaragehotel@ aol.com; ❹), which calls itself one of Bridgwater's oldest buildings. For **snacks** head for the *Nutmeg House* in Angel Crescent, behind the shopping centre off the High Street, where good pastas, soups, salads and a breakfast menu are offered (closed Sun).

A good time to be in Bridgwater would be for the **carnival** celebrations, which usually take place on the nearest Thursday or Friday to Guy Fawkes Night (one of the Catholic conspirators of the Gunpowder Plot hailed from nearby Nether Stowey). Grandly festooned floats belonging to the local Carnival Clubs roll through town, before heading off to do the same in vari-ous other Somerset towns and villages, including North Petherton, Glastonbury, Wells and Shepton Mallet.

Taunton

Twelve miles from Bridgwater, Somerset's county town of **TAUNTON** lies in the fertile Vale of Taunton, wedged between the Quantock, Brendon and Blackdown hills. The region is famed for its production of cider and scrumpy (cider's less refined cousin), while Taunton itself is host to one of the country's biggest cattle markets.

Taunton's **Castle**, started in the twelfth century, staged the trial of royal claimant Perkin Warbeck, who in 1490 declared himself to be the Duke of York, the younger of the "Princes in the Tower" – the sons of Edward IV, who had been murdered seven years earlier. Most of the castle was pulled down in 1662, but a part of it now houses the **County Museum** (Tues–Sat: April–Oct 10am–5pm; Nov–March 10am–3pm; £2.50), which includes a portrait of Judge Jeffreys among other memorabilia of local interest. Overlooking the county cricket ground are the pinnacled and battlemented towers of the town's two most important churches: **St James** and **St Mary Magdalene**, both fif-teenth-century though remodelled by the Victorians. St Mary's is worth a look inside for its roof-bosses carved with medieval masks.

Otherwise Taunton should only detain you as a base to visit the Quantock vil-lages or Exmoor. Information is on hand at the **tourist office** in the library building on Paul Street (April–Sept Mon–Thurs 9.30am–5.30pm, Fri 9.30am–7pm, Sat 9.30am–5pm; Oct–March Mon–Fri 9.30am–5.30pm, Sat 9.30am–5pm; ℡01823/336344). Central **B&Bs** include three within a few steps of each other on Wellington Road: *Brookfield* at no. 16 (℡01823/272786; ❷), *Beaufort Lodge* at no. 18 (℡01823/326420; ❷) and *Acorn Lodge* at no. 22 (℡01823/

337613; ❶). A couple of miles outside town, near the village of West Monkton, *Prockters Farm* (☎01823/412269; ❷) is a comfortable old country retreat with brass beds and antiques plus a large garden. For a snack or **meal**, head down East Street from Fore Street to *Brettons*, a congenial wine bar at 49 East Reach (closed Sat & Mon lunch, plus all Sun). Vegetarian dishes are served at the *Brewhouse Theatre and Arts Centre* on Coal Orchard, by the cricket ground, a good place to come in the evening, when there's usually something going on.

The Quantock Hills

Geologically closer to Devon than Somerset, the **Quantock Hills** are a culti-vated outpost of Exmoor, similarly crossed by clear streams and grazed by red deer. Just twelve miles in length and mostly between 800 and 900 feet high, the range is enclosed by a triangle of roads leading up from Bridgwater and Taunton, within which snake a tangle of narrow lanes connecting secluded hamlets, reached by local buses from these two towns.

North of Taunton, the first villages you pass through on the A358 give you an immediate introduction to the flavour of the Quantocks. **BISHOPS LYDEARD**, four miles up, has a splendid church tower in the Perpendicular style; the church's interior is also worth a look for its carved bench-ends. The village is the terminus of the **West Somerset Railway**, linked by buses #28A and, on Sunday, #928 from Taunton's train station (from which you can save money by buying a combined bus-and-rail ticket to Minehead). From mid-March to the first week of November (plus some dates in December) steam and diesel trains depart up to eight times daily, stopping at renovated stations on the way to Minehead, some twenty miles away (see p.388). For a talking timetable call ☎01643/707650, for other enquiries call ☎01643/704996, or log on at ⓦwww.west-somerset-railway.co.uk.

A couple of miles north, **COMBE FLOREY** is almost exclusively built of the pinkish-red sandstone characteristic of Quantock villages. For over fifteen years (1829–45), the local rector was the unconventional cleric Sydney Smith, called "the greatest master of ridicule since Swift" by Macaulay; more recently it's been home to Evelyn Waugh.

Eight miles west of Bridgwater on the A39, on the edge of the hills, the pret-ty village of **NETHER STOWEY** is best known for its association with **Samuel Taylor Coleridge**, who walked here from Bristol at the end of 1796 to join his wife and child at their new home. This "miserable cottage", as Sara Coleridge called it, was visited six months later by William Wordsworth and his sister Dorothy, who soon afterwards moved into Alfoxton House, near Holford, a couple of miles down the road. The year that Coleridge and Wordsworth spent as neighbours was extraordinarily productive – Coleridge composed some of his best poetry at this time, including *The Rime of the Ancient Mariner* and *Kubla Khan*, and the two poets in collaboration produced the *Lyrical Ballads*, the poetic manifesto of early English Romanticism. In **Coleridge Cottage** (April–Sept Tues–Thurs & Sun 2–5pm; £3; NT), you can see the man's parlour and reading room, and, upstairs, his bedroom and an exhibition room containing various letters and first editions.

The village library in nearby Castle Street has a **Quantock Information Centre** (Mon 2.30–5pm, Wed 10am–12.30pm & 2–5pm, Fri 10am–12.30pm, 2–5pm & 5.30–7pm; ☎01278/732845), which can provide walking itineraries and local information. As for **accommodation**, the only choice in the village is the *Rose & Crown Inn*, St Mary Street (☎01278/732265; ❶); this and the tile-fronted *George* next door also provide the only sustenance to be had in the village, including bar meals. The nearby village of **HOLFORD** has *Quantock House* (T01278/741439; ①), a beautiful Elizabethan thatched cottage, and a signposted two-mile walk from the village centre is a **youth hostel** (T01278/741224), where you can also **camp** in the grounds. Holford's *Plough Inn*, where Virginia and Leonard Woolf spent their honeymoon, serves simple **snacks**, and is a stop on the #15 Bridgwater–Minehead bus route.

From Nether Stowey, a minor road winds south off the A39 to the highest point on the Quantocks at **Wills Neck** (1260ft); park at Triscombe Stone, on the edge of Quantock Forest, from where a footpath leads to the summit about a mile distant. Stretching between the Wills Neck and the village of Aisholt, the bracken- and heather-grown moorland plateau of **Aisholt Common** is the heart of the Quantocks – the best place to begin exploring this central tract is near **West Bagborough**, where a five-mile path starts at Birches Corner. Lower down the slopes, outside the village of Aisholt, the banks of **Hawkridge Reservoir** make a lovely picnic stop.

The Quantock seaboard can be seen at its best at **Kilve Beach**, signposted off the A39 below Holford. Not so much a beach as a grand shale-studded foreshore, it's perfect for messing about in the rock pools and roaming the seaweedy shore. Six miles to the west, **WATCHET** is Somerset's only port of any consequence, and the place from which Coleridge's Ancient Mariner set sail. Having made a halt at the harbour, the quiet heart of the village, you can get a good all-round view from **St Decuman's church** above it, built on the site of the saint's martyrdom. Decuman, who floated over the sea from Wales, was decapitated by a Danish invader who was instantly converted when the saint picked up his bleeding head, washed it in a stream, and gently placed it next to him as he lay down to die. Watchet is only a stop away on the West Somerset Railway from **Washford**, from where it's a ten-minute walk to **Cleeve Abbey** (daily: April–Sept 10am–6pm; Oct 10am–5pm; Nov–March 10am–1pm & 2–4pm; £2.60; EH), a Cistercian house founded in 1198. Although the church itself has been mostly destroyed, the convent buildings are in excellent condition, providing the country's most complete collection of domestic buildings belonging to this austere order. An exhibition here illustrates how the monks lived and how the local population unsuccessfully pleaded with Henry VIII for the abbey's survival.

Travel details

Buses

For information on all local and national bus services, contact Traveline: T 0870/608 2 608 (daily 7am–9pm), W www.traveline.org.uk.

Trains

For information on all local and national rail services, contact National Rail Enquiries: T 08457/48 49 50, W www.nationalrail.co.uk.

Bath to: Bristol (every 20min; 20min); Dorchester (Mon–Sat 6–8 daily, Sun 2 daily; 2hr 10min); London (1–2 hourly; 1hr 30min); Salisbury (hourly; 1hr); Southampton (1–2 hourly; 1hr 30min).

Bristol to: Bath (every 20min; 20min); Birmingham (hourly; 1hr 30min); Cheltenham (hourly; 1hr); Exeter (1–2 hourly; 1hr 20min–1hr 40min); Gloucester (hourly; 1hr); London (2 hourly;

1hr 40min); Plymouth (1–2 hourly; 2hr–2hr 50min); Truro (7 daily; 3hr 20min–4hr).

Cheltenham to: Bristol (hourly; 1hr); Gloucester (1–2 hourly; 15min); London (1–2 hourly; 1hr 40min–2hr); Worcester (hourly; 20–30min).

Gloucester to: Bristol (hourly; 1hr); Cheltenham (1–2 hourly; 15min); London (1–2 hourly; 1hr 50min–2hr 10); Stroud (hourly; 15–20min).

6

Devon and Cornwall

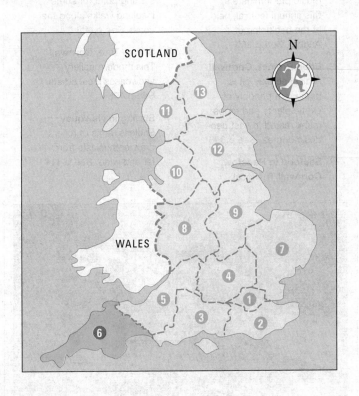

CHAPTER 6

Highlights

* **South West Coast Path**
The ever-changing vistas ensure constant variety on Britain's longest way-marked path. See p.388

* **Sidmouth International Festival** Folk and world music predominate at this annual festival, held at the beginning of August. See p.365

* **Eden Project, Cornwall**
A disused clay pit is home to a panoply of exotic plants and crops, many reared in vast geo-desic domes. See p.396

* **Seafood in Padstow, Cornwall** The local catch goes straight into the excellent restaurants of this bustling port. See p.413

* **Lizard Point, Cornwall**
Battered by waves, this unspoilt headland is the starting point for some inspiring walks along the coast. See p.400

* **St Ives Tate, Cornwall**
This modern gallery showcases local artists. See p.405

* **Surfing in Newquay**
Endless ranks of rollers draw enthusiasts from far and wide. See p.411

6

Devon and Cornwall

At the western extremity of England, the counties of **Devon and Cornwall** encompass everything from genteel, cosy villages to vast Atlantic-facing strands of golden sand and wild expanses of granite moorland. The combination of rural peace and first-class beaches has made the peninsula perennially popular with tourists, so much so that tourism has replaced the traditional occupations of fishing and farming as the main source of employment and income. Enough remains of these beleaguered communities to preserve the region's authentic character, however – even if this can be occasionally obscured during the summer season. Avoid the peak periods and you'll be seduced by the genuine appeal of this region, which beckons ever westwards into rural backwaters where increasingly exotic place-names and idiosyncratic pronunciations recall that this was once England's last bastion of Celtic culture.

Although the human history of the region has left its stamp, it is the natural landscape which exerts the strongest pull, and not just in the beauty of the long, deeply indented seaboard. Straddling the border between Devon and Somerset, **Exmoor** is one of the peninsula's three great moors, its heathery slopes much favoured by hunting parties as well as by hikers. For wilderness, however, nothing can beat the remoter tracts of **Dartmoor**, which takes up much of the southern half of inland Devon. The greatest of the West Country's granite massifs, most of Dartmoor retains its solitude in spite of its proximity to the only major cities at this end of the country, either of which would make a good touring base. Of the two, **Exeter** is by far the more interesting, dominated by the twin towers of its medieval cathedral and offering a rich selection of restaurants and nightlife. Much of the city was destroyed by bombing during World War II, though the largest city of Devon and Cornwall, **Plymouth** suffered far worse, the consequence of its historic role as a great naval port. Bland postwar development inflicted almost as much damage as the Luftwaffe, although enough of Plymouth's Elizabethan core has survived to merit a visit, and the city, by capitalizing on its maritime associations, has succeeded in reviving its port area.

The coastline on either side of Exeter and Plymouth is within easy reach. Warmed by the Gulf Stream, and enjoying more hours of sunshine than virtually anywhere else in England, this part of the country can sometimes come fairly close to the atmosphere of the Mediterranean, and indeed Devon's principal resort, **Torquay**, styles itself the capital of the "English Riviera". St Tropez it ain't, but there's no denying a certain glamour, far removed from the old-fashioned charm of the seaside towns of **East Devon**, or the cliff-backed resorts of the county's northern littoral.

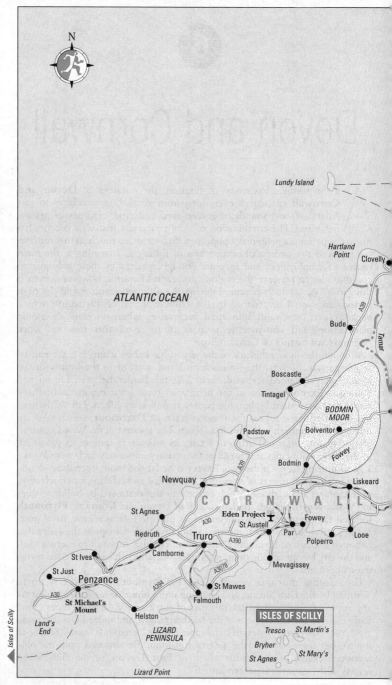

N

ATLANTIC OCEAN

Lundy Island

Hartland
Point

Clovelly

Bude

Boscastle

Tintagel

BODMIN
MOOR

Bolventor

Padstow

Fowey

Bodmin

Liskeard

Newquay

C O R N W A L L

St Agnes

Eden Project

A30

A39

St Austell

Fowey

Redruth

Truro

A390

Par

Looe

St Ives

Camborne

A3078

Polperro

St Just

Mevagissey

Penzance

A394

St Mawes

A30

St Michael's
Mount

Falmouth

Land's
End

Helston

LIZARD
PENINSULA

ISLES OF SCILLY

Tresco   St Martin's

Bryher

St Agnes   St Mary's

Lizard Point

Hartland
Point

Tamar

A39

A39

Bolventor

Fowey

Bodmin

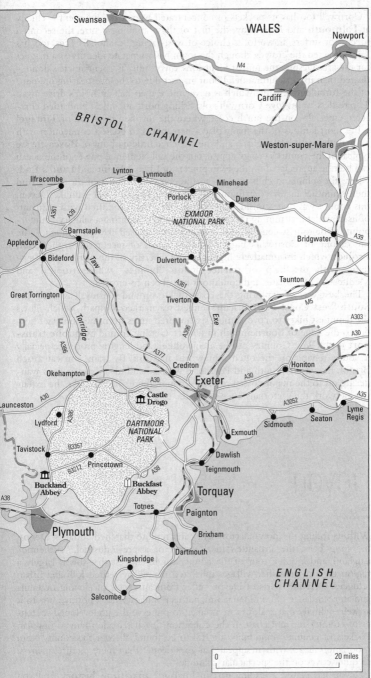

© Crown copyright

Cornwall too has its pockets of concentrated tourist development – chiefly at **Falmouth** and **Newquay**, the first of these a sailing centre, the second a mecca for surfers drawn to its choice of west-facing beaches. **St Ives**, too, has long attracted the crowds, though the town has a separate identity as a magnet for the arts. Despite the tourist incursions, this county is essentially less domesticated than its agricultural neighbour, in part due to the overbearing presence of the turbulent Atlantic, which is never more than half an hour's drive away. The restless waves give Cornwall's old fishing ports an almost embattled character, especially on the north coast, where the fortified headland of **Tintagel** – the most famous of the many places hereabouts to boast a connection with King Arthur and his knights – and the clenched little harbour of **Boscastle** are typical of the county's craggy appeal, but the full elemental power of the ocean can best be appreciated on the twin pincers of **Lizard Point** and **Land's End**, where the splintered cliffs resound to the constant thunder of the waves. And there's another factor contributing to Cornwall's starker feel – unlike Devon, this county was once considerably industrialized, and is dotted with remnants of its now defunct mining industries, their ruins presenting a salutary counterpoint to the tourist-centred seaside towns. One disused clay-pit, though, is the site of one of Cornwall's biggest success stories of recent times, the **Eden Project**, which imaginatively highlights the diversity of the planet's plant-systems, with the help of science-fiction "biomes" where tropical and Mediterranean climates and conditions have been re-created.

The best way of exploring the coast of Devon and Cornwall is along the **South West Coast Path**, Britain's longest waymarked footpath, which allows the dauntless hiker to cover almost six hundred miles from the Somerset border to the edge of Bournemouth in Dorset. Getting around by **public transport** in the West Country can be a convoluted and lengthy process, especially if you're relying on the often skimpy bus network. By train, you can reach Bristol, Exeter, Plymouth and Penzance, with a handful of branch lines wandering off to the major coastal resorts – though there's nothing like the extensive network the Victorians once enjoyed.

Devon

With its rolling meadows, narrow lanes and remote thatched cottages, **Devon** has long been the urbanite's ideal vision of a pre-industrial, "authentic" England, and a quick tour of the county might suggest that this is largely a region of cosy, gentrified villages inhabited mainly by retired folk and urban refugees. Certainly parts of Devon suffer from an excess of cloying nostalgia and an abundance of commercialism, but its popularity has a positive side to it as well – chiefly that zealous care is taken to preserve the undeveloped stretches of countryside and coast in the condition that has made them so popular. Pockets of genuine tranquillity are still to be found all over the county, from moorland villages with an appeal that goes deeper than mere picturesqueness, to quiet coves on the spectacular coastline.

Devon has played a leading part in England's **maritime history**, and you can't go far without meeting some reminder of the great names of Tudor and Stuart seafaring, particularly at the two cities of **Exeter** and **Plymouth**. These days the nautical tradition is perpetuated on a domesticated scale by yachtspeople taking advantage of Devon's numerous creeks and bays, especially on its southern coast, where ports such as Dartmouth and Salcombe are awash with amateur sailors. Land-bound tourists flock to the sandy beaches and seaside resorts, of which **Torquay**, on the south coast, and **Ilfracombe**, on the north, are the busiest – though the most attractive are those which have retained something of their nineteenth-century elegance, such as Sidmouth, in East Devon. Other seaside villages retain a low level of fishing activity but otherwise live on a stilted Old World image, of which **Clovelly** is the supreme example. **Inland**, Devon is characterized by swards of lush pasture and a scattering of sheltered villages, the county's low population density dropping to almost zero on **Dartmoor**, the wildest and bleakest of the West's moors, and **Exmoor**, whose seaboard constitutes one of the West Country's most scenic littorals.

Exeter and Plymouth are on the main **rail** lines from London and the Midlands, with branch lines from Exeter linking the north coast at Barnstaple and the south-coast towns of Exmouth and Torquay. **Buses** from the chief stations fan out along the coasts and into the interior, though the service can be extremely rudimentary for the smaller villages.

Exeter

EXETER's sights are richer than those of any other town in Devon or Cornwall, the legacy of an eventful history since its Celtic foundation and the establishment here of the most westerly Roman outpost. After the Roman withdrawal, Exeter was refounded by Alfred the Great and by the time of the Norman Conquest had become one of the largest towns in England, profiting from its position on the banks of the River Exe. The expansion of the wool trade in the Tudor period sustained the city until the eighteenth century, and Exeter has maintained its status as commercial centre and county town, despite having much of its ancient centre gutted by World War II bombing.

You are likely to pass through this transport hub for Devon at least once on your West Country travels, and Exeter's sturdy cathedral and the remnants of its compact old quarter would repay an overnight stay.

Arrival, information and accommodation

Exeter has two **train stations**, Exeter Central and St David's, the latter a little further out from the centre of town, though connected by frequent city buses. Trains from London Waterloo stop at both, as do trains on the Tarka Line to Barnstaple (see p.381) and those to Exmouth, though Exeter Central is not served by most other long-distance trains. **Buses** stop at the station on Paris Street, right across from the **tourist office** (July & Aug Mon–Sat 9am–5pm, Sun 10am–4pm; rest of year Mon–Fri 9am–5pm, Sat 9am–1pm & 2–5pm; ℡01392/265700, ⓦwww.thisisexeter.co.uk).

Most of Exeter's cheaper **accommodation** lies north of the centre, near the two stations, including two comfortable B&Bs close to each other in a quiet location, *Park View Hotel*, 8 Howell Rd (℡01392/271772, ⓦwww.parkviewhotel.freeserve.co.uk; ❷), a listed Georgian building with peaceful, airy rooms, and *Raffles*, 11 Blackall Rd (℡01392/270200, ⓦwww.rafffles-exeter.co.uk; ❸), an elegant Victorian house with rooms furnished with items

St David's
Train Station

HOWELL ROAD

NEW NORTH ROAD

ELMBRIDGE ROAD

HELE ROAD

ST DAVID'S HILL

NEW NORTH ROAD

Central
Train Station

BONHAY ROAD

River Exe

BISTOCK TERRACE

RICHMOND ROAD

QUEEN'S STREET

Northernhay
Gardens

Rougemont
Gardens

HALDON ROAD

IRON BRIDGE

NORTHERNHAY STREET

Royal Albert
Memorial
Museum

GANDY STREET

Queen
Street

EXE STREET

BARTHOLOMEW ST EAST

PAUL STREET

NORTH STREET

Guildhall

HIGH STREET

MARY ARCHES STREET

BONHAY ROAD

Playing Fields

BARTHOLOMEW ST WEST

St Nicholas
Priory

FORE STREET

MARKET STREET

ST GEORGE'S S

SOUTH STREET

KING STREET

SMITHEN STREET

PRESTON STREET

St Mary's
Steps

STEPCOTE HILL

WEST STREET

TUDOR STREET

NEW BRIDGE STREET

FROG STREET

WESTERN WAY

OKEHAMPTON STREET

QUAY HILL

ALBION STREET

EDMUND STREET

COMMERCIAL ROAD

Custom
House

BULLER ROAD

COWICK ST

ALPHINGTON ST

River Exe

St Thomas
Train Station

HAVEN ROAD

EXETER

© Crown copyright

▼ M5, A30 Okehampton & A38 Plymouth

❶ **❸** **Ⓐ** **Ⓑ** **Ⓒ** **Ⓓ** **Ⓔ** **Ⓕ**

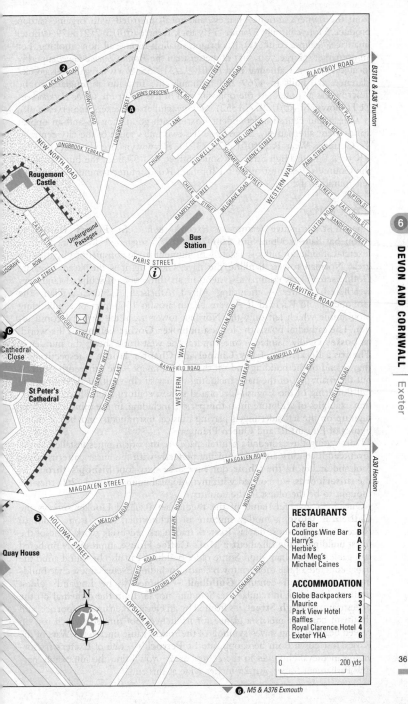

B3181 & A38 Taunton

A30 Honiton

RESTAURANTS

Café Bar	C
Coolings Wine Bar	B
Harry's	A
Herbie's	E
Mad Meg's	F
Michael Caines	D

ACCOMMODATION

Globe Backpackers	5
Maurice	3
Park View Hotel	1
Raffles	2
Royal Clarence Hotel	4
Exeter YHA	6

N

0   200 yds

6, M5 & A376 Exmouth

from the owner's antique business, and meals prepared with organic garden produce. More centrally, *Maurice*, 5 Bystock Terrace (℡01392/213079, ✆hotel .maurice@eclipse.co.uk; ❶), has bright, smallish rooms, all non-smoking. For an upmarket splurge, you can't do better than the *Royal Clarence Hotel*, superbly located right on Cathedral Yard (℡01392/319955, Ⓦwww.regalhotels.co.uk/ clarence; ❻), built in 1769 and reputedly the first inn in England to be described as a "hotel". At the opposite end of the spectrum, *Globe Backpackers*, 71 Holloway St (℡01392/215521, Ⓦwww.globebackpackers.freeserve.co.uk), is a clean and central independent **hostel** with good showers and an upbeat atmosphere; alternatively, *Exeter YHA* lies two miles south of the city centre at 47 Countess Wear Rd (℡01392/873329, Ⓦwww.yha.org.uk); take minibus #K or #T from High Street or South Street, or #57 from the bus station, to the Countess Wear post office on Topsham Road, a fifteen-minute ride, plus a ten-minute walk.

The City

The most distinctive feature of Exeter's skyline, **St Peter's Cathedral** (Mon–Sat 8am–6.30pm, Sun 8am–7.30pm; £3 suggested donation; Ⓦwww .exeter-cathedral.org.uk), is a stately monument made conspicuous by the two great Norman towers flanking the nave. Close up, it is the facade's ornate Gothic screen that commands attention: its three tiers of sculpted (and very weathered) figures – including Alfred, Athelstan, Canute, William the Conqueror and Richard II – were begun around 1360, part of a rebuilding programme which left only the Norman towers from the original construction. The cathedral boasts the longest unbroken **Gothic ceiling** in the world, its **bosses** vividly painted – one, towards the west front, shows the murder of Thomas à Becket. The **Lady Chapel** and **Chapter House** – respectively at the far end of the building and off the right transept – are thirteenth-century, but the main part of the nave, including the lavish rib-vaulting, dates from the full flowering of the English Decorated style, a century later. There are many fine examples of sculpture from this period, including, in the minstrels' gallery high up on the left side, angels playing musical instruments, and, below them, figures of Edward III and Queen Philippa.

Dominating the cathedral's central space are the organ pipes installed in the seventeenth century and harmonizing perfectly with the linear patterns of the roof and arches. In the **Choir** don't miss the sixty-foot **bishop's throne** or the **misericords** – decorated with mythological figures around 1260, they are thought to be the oldest in the country.

Outside, a graceful statue of the theologian Richard Hooker surveys the **Cathedral Close**, a motley mixture of architectural styles from Tudor to Regency, though most display Exeter's trademark red-brick work. One of the finest buildings is the Elizabethan **Mol's Coffee House**, impressively timbered and gabled, now a map shop. Some older buildings can also be found amid the banal concrete of the modern town centre, including Exeter's finest civic building, the fourteenth-century **Guildhall** – claimed to be England's oldest municipal building in regular use. Standing not far from the cathedral on the pedestrianized **High Street**, it's fronted by an elegant Renaissance portico, and the main chamber merits a glance for its arched roof timbers, which rest on carved bears holding staves, symbols of the Yorkist cause during the Wars of the Roses. Just down from here, opposite **St Petrock's** – one of Exeter's six surviving medieval churches in the central area – you'll find the impossibly narrow Parliament Street, just 25 inches wide at this end.

On the west side of Fore Street, the continuation of the High Street, a turn-ing leads to **St Nicholas Priory** (Easter–Oct Mon, Wed & Sat 3–4.30pm; free), part of a small Benedictine foundation that became a merchant's home after the Dissolution; the interior has been restored to what it might have looked like in the Tudor era. On the other side of Fore Street, trailing down towards the river, cobbled **Stepcote Hill** was once the main road into Exeter from the west, though it is difficult to imagine this steep and narrow lane as a main thoroughfare. Another of central Exeter's ancient churches, **St Mary Steps**, stands surrounded by mainly Tudor houses at the bottom, with a fine seventeenth-century clock on its tower and a late Gothic nave inside.

At the north end of the High Street, Romansgate Passage (next to Boots) holds the entrance to a network of **underground passages** first excavated in the thirteenth century to bring water to the cathedral precincts. The passages can be visited as part of a fascinating 35-minute guided **tour** (July–Sept & school holidays Mon–Sat 10am–5.30pm; rest of year Tues–Fri noon–5pm, Sat 10am–5pm; £2.75; July & Aug £3.75) – not recommended to claustrophobes, however. Nearby, Castle Street leads to what remains of **Rougemont Castle**, now little more than a perimeter of red-stone walls that are best appreciated from the surrounding Rougemont and Northernhay Gardens. Following the path through this park, exit at Queen Street to drop in at the excellent **Royal Albert Memorial Museum** (Mon–Sat 10am–5pm; free), the closest thing in Devon to a county museum. Exuding the Victorian spirit of wide-ranging curiosity, this motley assortment includes everything from a menagerie of stuffed animals to mock-ups of the various building styles used at different periods in the city. The collections of silverware, watches and clocks contrast nicely with the colourful ethnography section, and the picture gallery has some good specimens of West Country art.

Exeter's centre is bounded to the southwest by the River Exe, where the port area is now mostly devoted to leisure activities, particularly around the old **Quayside**. Pubs, shops and cafés share the space with handsomely restored nineteenth-century warehouses and the smart **Custom House**, built in 1681, its opulence reflecting the former importance of the cloth trade. Next door, the **Quay House** from the same period has an information desk and, upstairs, a video on Exeter's history (Easter–Oct). The area comes into its own at night, but is worth a wander at any time, and you can **rent bikes** and **canoes** at Saddles & Paddles on the quayside (℡01392/424241, Ⓦwww.saddlepaddle.co.uk) to explore the **Exeter Canal**, which runs five miles to Topsham and beyond.

Eating, drinking and entertainment

Round the corner from the museum, in medieval Gandy Street, *Coolings Wine Bar* is a popular and stylish **snack** stop that's also open until late evening with DJs on Fridays and Saturdays. Opposite the cathedral, the casually modish *Café Bar* serves toasties, salads, burgers and pastas in small or large sizes until 10pm daily. It's part of the next-door *Michael Caine's* (℡01392/310031, Ⓦwww.michaelcaines.com), one of Exeter's classiest **restaurants** where you'll find sophisticated modern European cuisine in sleek surroundings; prices are fairly high, though there are reasonable fixed-price menus at lunchtime. In total con-trast, the "olde worlde" atmosphere is laid on thickly at *Mad Meg's* (closed Mon & Tues lunch) – once a nunnery, now staffed by waitresses in wench costume – but there are some good-value traditional dishes here; it's tucked away near the top of Fore Street, below a bike shop. Nearby *Herbie's*, 15 North St

(℡01392/258473; closed all Sun & Mon eve), is a wholefood restaurant with organic ice cream on the menu, while good-value Mexican and Italian staples are on the menu at *Harry's*, in a converted church at 86 Longbrook St (℡01392/202 234).

Among the **pubs**, the *Ship Inn*, in St Martin's Lane (between the High Street and the cathedral), serves reasonably priced lunches and prides itself on the claim that it was once Francis Drake's local. The pubs and clubs on Exeter's Quay make this a lively spot to while away an evening. You can eat and drink sitting outside at the seventeenth-century *Prospect Inn*.

Behind Exeter's museum, the **Phoenix Arts Centre** (℡01392/667080) is the focus of a medley of cultural pursuits, including films, exhibitions, gigs and various workshops. Of the town's **theatres**, the Northcott, near the university on Stocker Road (℡01392/493493), and the Barnfield, on Barnfield Road (℡01392/271808), have the best productions, with the former also staging ballet and opera performances. The **Exeter Festival** takes place during the first three weeks of July, and features jazz and blues concerts as well as classical performances and cabaret, at various venues around town.

The city's best **dance and live-music venues** are in the centre, including the *Cavern Club*, with entrances in Queen and Gandy streets (also open 10.30am–4pm for snacks), and the *Timepiece*, Little Castle Street, formerly a prison that now also has a good daytime bar with a garden. Exeter's two biggest **club** complexes face each other on the Quay: the *Warehouse*, *Boxes* and *Boogies*, and *Volts* and *Hothouse*, all open in various combinations and playing mainstream dance and retro sounds.

A La Ronde

Five miles south of Exeter off the A376, the Gothic folly of **A La Ronde** (April–Oct Mon–Thurs & Sun 11am–5.30pm; £3.40) was the creation of two cousins, Jane and Mary Parminter, who in the 1790s were inspired by their European Grand Tour to construct a sixteen-sided house, possibly based on the Byzantine basilica of San Vitale in Ravenna. The end product is filled with mementoes of the Parminters' tour as well as some of their more offbeat creations, such as a frieze made of feathers culled from game birds and chickens. In the upper rooms are a gallery and staircase completely covered in shells, too fragile to be visited, though part can be glimpsed on a closed-circuit TV system.

The women intended that the house should be inherited only by female descendants, though the conditions of Mary Parminter's will (she died in 1849) were broken at the end of the nineteenth century when the building was inherited by the Reverend Oswald Reichel, who added dormer windows on the second floor, which afford superb views over the Exe Estuary to Haldon Hill and Dawlish Warren.

Exmouth and Budleigh Salterton

EXMOUTH started as a Roman port and went on to become the first of Devon's resorts to be popularized by holiday-makers in the late eighteenth century. Overlooking lawns, rock pools and a respectable two miles of beach, Exmouth's Georgian terraces once accommodated such folk as the wives of Nelson and Byron – installed at no. 6 and no. 19 The Beacon respectively (on a rise overlooking the seafront, above the public gardens). The resort has a good choice of accommodation options, including, the *Manor Hotel*, The Beacon (℡01395/274477; ③), where you can enjoy wonderful panoramic views from the rooms. From April to October, Exmouth is linked by **ferry** to Starcross, on the other side of the Exe estuary (hourly service; £2.50 single fare), where you can pick up a bus to Torbay (see p.366).

Four miles east of Exmouth, bounded on each side by sandstone cliffs, **BUDLEIGH SALTERTON** continues the genteel theme – its thatched and whitewashed cottages attracted such figures as Noël Coward and P.G. Wodehouse, and John Millais painted his famous *Boyhood of Raleigh* on the shingle beach here. (Sir Walter Raleigh was born in the pretty East Budleigh, a couple of miles inland.) Three miles east, **Ladram Bay** is a popular pebbly beach sheltered by woods and beautiful eroded cliffs. If you want to stay in the area, contact the **tourist office** on Fore Street (Easter–June, Sept & Oct Mon–Sat 10am–5pm; July & Aug Mon–Sat 10am–5pm, Sun 11am–5pm; Nov–Easter Mon–Thurs & Sat 10am–1pm, Fri 10am–3pm; ☏01395/445275).

Sidmouth

East along the East Devon coast, cream-and-white **SIDMOUTH** is the chief resort on this stretch of coast, set amid a shelf of crumbling sandstone. The town boasts nearly five hundred buildings listed as having special historic or architectural interest, among them the stately Georgian homes of **York Terrace** behind the Esplanade. Moreover, the **beaches** are better tended than many along this coast, not only the mile-long main town beach but also Jacob's Ladder, a cliff-backed shingle and sand strip beyond Connaught Gardens to the west of town. To the east, the South Devon Coast Path (part of the South West Coast Path) climbs steep Salcombe Hill to follow cliffs that give sanctuary to a range of birdlife. Farther on, the path descends to meet one of the most isolated and attractive beaches in the area, **Weston Mouth**.

Sidmouth's **tourist office** is on Ham Lane, off the eastern end of the Esplanade (March–July & Sept Mon–Thurs 10am–4pm, Fri & Sat 10am–5pm, Sun 10am–1pm; Aug & Oct Mon–Sat 10am–6pm, Sun 10am–4pm; Nov–Feb Mon–Sat 10am–1.30pm; ☏01395/516441). Of the **B&Bs**, *Cranmere*, close to the Esplanade at 2 Fortfield Place (☏01395/513933; ❶), is one of the cheapest, with a homely atmosphere and most rooms en suite. A little further from the seafront, the *Old Farmhouse*, Hillside Road (☏01395/512284; ❸), offers attractive rooms with plenty of atmosphere and delicious meals on request. There's also a string of guest houses along Salcombe Road; try *Berwick Guest House* at 4 Albert Terrace (☏01395/513621; no smoking; ❸). For **meals** in town, try *Brown's Bistro* on Fore Street (closed Sun); *Osborne's* further down Fore Street serves teas and light **snacks**. On Old Fore Street, two hundred yards from the seafront, the *Old Ship* and *Anchor* **pubs** provide excellent bar meals as well as a good range of ales.

Sidmouth hosts what many consider to be the country's best **folk festival** over eight days at the beginning of August. For details, ask at the tourist office, or call ☏01296/433669 or check out the website at ⓦwww.mrscasey.co.uk/sidmouth. Book early for the main acts.

Beer

Eight miles east along the coast, the fishing village of **BEER** lies huddled within a small sheltered cove between gleaming white headlands. A stream rushes along a deep channel dug into Beer's main street, and if you can ignore the crowds in high summer much of the village looks unchanged since the time when it was a smugglers' eyrie, its inlets used by such characters as Jack Rattenbury, who published his *Memoirs of a Smuggler* in 1837. The village is best known for its quarries, which were worked from Roman times until the last century: **Beer Stone** was used in many of Devon's churches and other buildings. You can visit the complex of **underground quarries** (Easter–Sept 10am–5pm; Oct 11am–4pm; last entry 1hr before closing; £4.25) a mile or so west of the village on a guided tour, along with a small exhibition of pieces carved by medieval masons, among others. Take something warm to wear. *Bay View* (℡01297/20489; ❶), overlooking the sea on Fore Street, is the best of the **B&Bs** and Beer's **youth hostel** is on a hillside half a mile northwest, at Bovey Combe, Townsend (℡01297/20296; closed Nov–March). For **food**, head straight to the *Barrel* pub, on the main street, where the superb menu includes local delicacies such as Devon oysters and home-smoked fish; there are imaginative vegetarian options, too.

The "English Riviera" and the South Hams

The wedge of land between Dartmoor and the sea contains some of Devon's most fertile pastures, backing onto some of the West's most popular coastal resorts. Chief of these is **Torbay**, an amalgam of **Torquay**, **Paignton** and **Brixham** and the nucleus of an area optimistically known as "**The English Riviera**". To the south the port of **Dartmouth** offers a calmer alternative, linked by riverboat to historic and almost unspoilt **Totnes**. West of the River Dart, the rich agricultural district of **South Hams** extends as far as Plymouth, cleft by a web of rivers flowing off Dartmoor. The main town here is **Kingsbridge**, at the head of an estuary down which you can ferry to the sailing resort of **Salcombe**.

Torquay

Sporting a mini-corniche and promenades landscaped with flowerbeds, **TORQUAY**, the main centre of the tourist conglomeration at **Torbay**, comes closest to living up to the self-penned "English Riviera" sobriquet. The much-vaunted palm trees (actually New Zealand cabbage trees) and the coloured lights that festoon the harbour by night contribute to the town's unique flavour, a slightly frayed combination of the exotic and the classically English. Torquay's transformation from a fishing village began with its establishment as a fashionable haven for invalids, among them the consumptive Elizabeth Barrett Browning, who spent three years here. In recent years the most famous figures previously associated with Torquay – crimewriter Agatha Christie and traveller Freya Stark – have given way to the fictional TV hotelier Basil Fawlty, whose jingoism and injured pride perfectly encapsulate the town's adaptation to the demands of mass tourism.

The town is focused on the small **harbour** and marina, separated by limestone cliffs sprouting white high-rise hotels and apartment blocks from Torquay's main beach, **Abbey Sands**. Good for chucking a frisbee about but too busy for serious relaxation, it takes its name from **Torre Abbey**, sited in ornamental gardens behind the beachside road. The Norman church that once stood here was razed by Henry VIII, though a gatehouse, tithe barn, chapter house and tower escaped demolition. The present **Abbey Mansion** (Easter–Oct daily 9.30am–6pm; £3) is a seventeenth- and eighteenth-century construction, now containing the mayor's office, a suite of period rooms with collections of paintings, silver and glass, and one devoted to Agatha Christie. There's more material relating to the Mistress of Murder at the **Torquay Museum**, above the harbour at 529 Babbacombe Rd (Easter–Oct Mon–Sat 10am–5pm, Sun 1.30–5pm; Nov–Easter Mon–Fri 10am–5pm; £3), but most of the space is given over to the local history and natural history collections.

Walking north round the promontory from the harbour, you'll reach some good sand beaches, nearest of which **Meadfoot Beach**, lies at the end of a pretty half-mile coastal walk that takes you through Daddyhole Plain, a large chasm in the cliff caused by a landslide locally attributed to the devil ("Daddy"). If you're searching for something a little more low-key, continue round the point to where a series of beaches extends along the coast as far as the cliff-backed coves of **Watcombe** and **Maidencombe**.

Practicalities

Torquay's main **train station** is off Rathmore Road, just southeast of the Torre Abbey gardens; most **buses** leave from the marina, close to the **tourist office**, Vaughan Parade (late May to Sept Mon–Sat 9.30am–6pm, Sun 10am–6pm; Oct to late May Mon–Sat 9am–5.15pm; ☎0906/680 1268, ⓦwww .TheEnglishRiviera.co.uk). There's plenty of **accommodation** in town, most of the budget choices lying along Belgrave Road and, slightly further out, Avenue Road, for example *Charnwood Guest House*, 8 Bampfylde Rd, off Belgrave Road and a ten-minute walk from the train station (☎01803/293879; ❶). Non-smokers with a yen for antique pine furnishings and crisp bed-linen should head for *Mulberry House*, 1 Scarborough Rd (☎01803/213639; ❸), with a rated restaurant on the premises (see below); for views and statelier surroundings, try the *Allerdale Hotel* on Croft Road (☎01803/292667; ❸), which has a long, lawned garden sloping below it. *Torquay Backpackers*, a ten-minute walk from the station at 119 Abbey Rd (☎01803/299924), offers cheap and friendly **hostel** accommodation, and there's a free pick-up service offered if you give advance notice.

There is a surprisingly high standard of cuisine in Torquay's restaurants, one of the best being the *Mulberry House Restaurant*, 1 Scarborough Rd (☎01803/213639; closed Fri–Sun eve, plus Mon & Tues to non-residents), with the accent on healthy and low-cholesterol eating. Nearby, the inexpensive *Bombay Express* at 98 Belgrave Rd claims to be the southwest's "first and only original Balti House"; you can bring your own bottle and it's also good for takeaways. The cobbled *Hole in the Wall* **pub** on nearby Park Lane serves some vegetarian dishes and has sing-songs round the piano – it was the Irish playwright Sean O'Casey's boozer when he lived in Torquay.

Paignton

Not so much a rival to Torquay as its complement, **PAIGNTON** lacks the gloss of its neighbour, but also its pretensions. Activity is concentrated at the southern end of the wide town beach, around the small harbour that nestles in the lee of the appropriately named Redcliffe headland. Otherwise, diversion-seekers could wander over to **Paignton Zoo** (daily 10am–6pm or dusk if earlier; £7.70; ⓦwww.paigntonzoo.org.uk), a mile out on Totnes Road, or board the **Paignton & Dartmouth Steam Railway** at Paignton's Queen's Park train station near the harbour. Running daily from June to September, with a patchy service in April, May, October and December, the line connects with Paignton's other main beach – **Goodrington Sands** – before trundling alongside the Dart estuary to Kingswear, seven miles south. You could make a day of it by taking the ferry connection from Kingswear to Dartmouth (see p.370), then taking a river boat up the Dart to Totnes, from where you can take any bus back to Paignton – ask about "Round Robin" tickets at the station.

Paignton's **bus and train stations** are next to each other off Sands Road. Five minutes away, the seafront has a **tourist office** (late May to Sept Mon–Sat 9.30am–6pm, Sun 10am–6pm; Oct to late May Mon–Sat 9.30am–5.15pm; ☎0906/680 1268).

Brixham

From Paignton, it's a fifteen-minute bus ride down to **BRIXHAM**, the prettiest of the Torbay towns. Fishing was for centuries Brixham's life-blood, and it still supplies fish to restaurants as far away as London. Among the trawlers on Brixham's quayside is moored a full-size reconstruction of the **Golden Hind**, the surprisingly small vessel in which Francis Drake circumnavigated the world – it has no real connection with the port, however. The harbour is overlooked by an unflattering statue of William III, a reminder of his landing in Brixham to claim the crown of England in 1688. From here, steep lanes and stairways thread up to the older centre around Fore Street, where the bus from Torquay pulls in.

From the harbour, you can reach the promontory of **Berry Head** along a path winding up from the *Berry Head House Hotel*. Fortifications built during the Napoleonic wars are still standing on this southern limit of Torbay, which is now a conservation area, attracting colonies of nesting seabirds and affording fabulous views.

The town's **tourist office** (June to Sept daily 9.30am–6pm, Sun 10am–6pm; Oct Mon–Sat 9.30am–5.15pm; Nov–May Mon–Fri 9.30am–5.15pm; ☎0906/ 680 1268) is on the quayside, next to William's statue. For the views, the best **accommodation** is on King Street, overlooking the harbour, such as the *Harbour View Hotel* at no. 65 (☎01803/853052; ❷) and, two doors down, the classier *Quayside Hotel* (☎01803/855751, ⓦwww.quaysidehotel.co.uk; ❺), which has two bars and a restaurant. Away from the harbour, the reputedly ghost-ridden *Smugglers' Haunt* on Church Hill (☎01803/853050, ⓦwww .smugglershaunt-hotel-devon.co.uk; ❸) is creaky and cramped, but useful if everywhere else is full. The nearest YHA **hostel** is four miles away outside the village of Galmpton, on the banks of the Dart (☎01803/842444), a one-and-a-half-mile walk or bus ride from Churston Bridge – you can also get there on the Paignton & Dartmouth Steam Railway (see above).

When it comes to **eating options**, Brixham offers fish and more fish – from the stalls selling cockles, whelks and mussels on the harbourside to the moderately expensive *Yardarms* (☎01803/858266; closed lunch & all Mon, plus all Tues in winter), on Beach Approach off the quayside. For a relaxed pint, try out the *Blue Anchor* on Fore Street, with coal fires and low beams.

Totnes

Most of the Plymouth buses from Paignton and Torquay make a stop at **TOTNES**, on the west bank of the River Dart. The town has an ancient pedigree, its period of greatest prosperity occurring in the sixteenth century when this inland port exported cloth to France and brought back wine. Some handsome structures from that era remain, and there is still a working port down on the river, but these days Totnes has mellowed into a residential market town, enjoying an esoteric fame as a centre of the New Age crowd.

The town centres on the long main street that starts off as Fore Street, where the local **museum** (April–Oct Mon–Fri 10.30am–5pm; £1.75) occupies a four-storey Elizabethan house at no. 70. Showing how wealthy clothiers lived at the peak of Totnes's success, it is packed with domestic objects and furniture, and also has a room devoted to local mathematician Charles Babbage, whose "analytical engine" was the forerunner of the computer. Fore Street becomes the **High Street** at the East Gate, a much retouched medieval arch. Beneath it, Rampart Walk trails off along the old city walls, curling round the fifteenth-century church of **St Mary**. Inside, an exquisitely carved roodscreen stretches across the full width of the red sandstone building. Behind the church, the eleventh-century **Guildhall** (April–Sept Mon–Fri 10.30am–1pm & 2–4.30pm; £1) was originally the refectory and kitchen of a Benedictine priory. Granted to the city corporation in 1553, the building still houses the town's Council Chamber, which you can see together with the former jail cells and courtroom.

Totnes **Castle** (April–Sept daily 10am–6pm; Oct daily 10am–5pm; Nov–March Wed–Sun 10am–1pm & 2–4pm; £1.60; EH) on Castle Street – leading off the High Street – is a classic Norman structure of the motte and bailey design, its simple crenellated keep atop a grassy mound offering wide views of the town and Dart valley. Totnes assumes a much livelier air at the bottom of Fore Street, at river level. This is the highest navigable point on the **River Dart** for seagoing vessels, and there is constant activity around the craft arriving from and leaving for European destinations. More locally, there are also cruises to Dartmouth between Easter and October, leaving from Steamer Quay, on the other side of the Dart. Riverside walks in either direction pass some congenial pubs, and near the railway bridge you can board a steam train of the **South Devon Railway** on its run along the course of the Dart to Buckfastleigh, adjacent to Buckfast Abbey (see p.378).

Practicalities

Totnes's **tourist office** is in the Town Mill, signposted off the Plains near the Safeway car park (Aug Mon–Sat 9.30am–5pm, Sun 9.30am–1pm; rest of year Mon–Sat 9.30am–5pm; ☎01803/863168). You'll find a good **B&B** a stone's throw from the station: *Number Four*, Queen's Terrace, Station Rd (☎01803/867365, ✉tobsjq@aol.com; ❷), where vegetarian breakfasts include eggs from the hens in the garden, figs and waffles. Opposite the castle car park on North Street, the *Elbow Room* (☎01803/863480; no smoking; ❸) occupies a two-hundred-year-old converted cottage and cider press. For a bit extra, pamper yourself at the atmospheric *Royal Seven Stars Hotel* on The Plains (☎01803/862125; ❹), or, just over the river in Seymour Place, at the *Old Forge* (☎01803/862174; non-smoking; ❸) – a working medieval forge with comfortably modernized rooms and a secluded walled garden. The **youth hostel** (☎01803/862303), in a sixteenth-century cottage, lies next to the River Bidwell two miles from Totnes and half a mile from Shinner's Bridge, a stop on the #X80 Torquay–Plymouth bus route.

You don't need to stray off the Fore Street/High Street axis to find a good place to **eat** in Totnes. *Willow*, 87 High St (☎01803/862605), has inexpensive vegetarian wholefood snacks and evening meals (Wed–Sat) when there is occasional live music (closed Sun). Indonesian food is on offer at *Rickshaws*, 98 High St (☎01803/866171; closed eve, plus all Sun & Mon), while *Rumour*, 30 High St, serves coffees, snacks and good-value full meals including home-made pizzas. There are also several excellent **pubs**: the *Bull Inn* at the top of the High Street and the *Kingsbridge Inn* on Leechwell Street (off Kingsbridge Hill) both have a warm atmosphere, bar snacks and good ale. By the riverside, try the *Steampacket*, on St Peter's Quay.

Dartmouth

South of Torbay, and eight miles downstream from Totnes, **DARTMOUTH** has thrived since the Normans recognized the potential of this deepwater port for trading with their home country, and today its activities embrace fishing, freight and a booming leisure industry – as well as the education of the senior service's officer class at the Royal Naval College, built at the start of this century on a hill overlooking the port. (Coming from Torbay, visitors to Dartmouth can save time and a long detour through Totnes by using the frequent ferries from Kingswear).

Behind the enclosed boat basin at the heart of town stands Dartmouth's most photographed building, the four-storey **Butterwalk**, built in the seventeenth century for a local merchant. Richly decorated with wood carvings, the timber-framed construction looks precarious as it overhangs the street on eleven granite columns. This arcade now holds shops and Dartmouth's small **museum** (Mon–Sat: April–Sept 11am–4.30pm; Oct–March noon–3pm; £1.50), mainly devoted to maritime curios, including old maps, prints and models of ships. Nearby **St Saviour's**, rebuilt in the 1630s from a fourteenth-century church, has long been a landmark for boats sailing upriver. The building stands at the head of Higher Street, the old town's central thoroughfare and the site of another tottering medieval structure, the *Cherub* inn. More impressive is **Agincourt House** on the parallel Lower Street, built by a merchant after the battle for which it is named, then restored in the seventeenth century and again in the twentieth.

Lower Street leads down to **Bayard's Cove**, a short cobbled quay lined with well-restored eighteenth-century houses, where the Pilgrim Fathers touched en route to the New World. A twenty-minute walk from here along the river takes you to **Dartmouth Castle** (April–Sept daily 10am–6pm; Oct daily 10am–5pm; Nov–March Wed–Sun 10am–1pm & 2–4pm; £3.20; EH), one of two fortifications on opposite sides of the estuary. The site includes coastal defence works from the nineteenth century and from World War II, though the main interest is in the fifteenth-century castle, the first in England to be constructed specifically to withstand artillery. The castle was never actually tested in action, and consequently is excellently preserved. If you don't relish the return walk, you can take advantage of a ferry back to town, leaving roughly every fifteen minutes from Easter to October (£1).

Continuing south along the coastal path brings you through the pretty hilltop village of **Stoke Fleming** to **Blackpool Sands** (45min from the castle), the best and most popular beach in the area. The unspoilt cove, flanked by steep, wooded cliffs, was the site of a battle in 1404 in which Devon archers repulsed a Breton invasion force sent to punish the privateers of Dartmouth for their raiding across the Channel.

From Dartmouth there are regular ferries across the river to **Kingswear**, terminus of the **Paignton & Dartmouth Steam Railway** (see p.367). There are also various summer cruises from Dartmouth's quay up the River Dart to Totnes (1hr 15min; £7 return); this is the best way to see the river's deep creeks and the various houses overlooking the river, among them the **Royal Naval College** and **Greenway House**, birthplace of Walter Raleigh's three seafaring half-brothers, the Gilberts, and later rebuilt for Agatha Christie.

Practicalities

Dartmouth's **tourist office** is opposite the car park at Mayor's Avenue (Easter–Oct Mon–Sat 9.30am–5.30pm, Sun 10am–4pm; Nov–Easter Mon–Sat

DEVON AND CORNWALL | Dartmouth

10am–4pm; ☎01803/834224, ⓦwww.dartmouth-tourism.org.uk). The less expensive **accommodation** is either at the top of steep hills or strung along Victoria Road, a continuation of Duke Street. The hilltop choices are preferable for their views, such as the spacious and elegant *Avondale* at 5 Vicarage Hill (☎01803/835831, ⓔavondaleco@aol.com; ❷), though the choices on Victoria Road are also enticing – not least the *Middle House*, offering two large and colourful en-suite rooms at no. 16 (☎01803/833935; ❷), and the nearby *Sunnybanks* at 1 Vicarage Hill (☎01803/832766, ⓦwww.sunnybanks.com; ❷). Alternatively, splurge on the *Royal Castle Hotel* (☎01803/833033, ⓦwww.royalcastle.co.uk; ❺), right on the central quay, converted from two seventeenth-century merchants' houses. For something a little different, book a berth on the *Res Nova Inn* (☎0777/062 8967; may close in winter), a barge moored in mid-river and run by a friendly couple who will ferry guests to and from town.

Dartmouth has a great range of good **restaurants**, from the relaxed *Café Alf Resco* on Lower Street, good for breakfasts and coffees and with outdoor tables (closed Mon & Tues), to posher **restaurants** such as *Bayard's*, 28 Lower St (☎01803/833523), for moderately priced fish and vegetarian dishes, and the expensive *Carved Angel*, at 2 South Embankment (☎01803/832465, ⓦwww.thecarvedangel.com; closed Sun eve, Mon lunch & Jan to mid-Feb), a high-class fish restaurant with views over the riverfront; it also excels in game in winter. If you're put off by the prices and ambience here, drop into its humbler offshoot at 7 Foss St, the *Carved Angel Café* (☎01803/834842; no smoking; closed Sun eve & Mon lunch). The *Res Nova Inn* (see above) also offers fish suppers as well as late-night drinks: call to be picked up.

Salcombe and around

The area between the Dart and Plym estuaries, the **South Hams**, holds some of Devon's comeliest villages and most striking coastline. The "capital" of the region, Kingsbridge, is a useful transport hub but is not particularly inspiring. Far comelier is Devon's southernmost resort of **SALCOMBE**, almost at the mouth of the Kingsbridge estuary and reachable by ferry from Kingsbridge (summer only). Once a nondescript fishing village, Salcombe is now a full-blown sailing and holiday resort, its calm waters strewn with pleasure craft. There is still some fishing activity here, and a few working boatyards, but a certain serenity prevails, with the ruined Fort Charles at the entrance to the harbour injecting a touch of romance amid the villas and hotels. You can bone up on boating and local history at **Salcombe Maritime Museum** on Market Street, off the north end of the central Fore Street (April to late Sept 10.30am–12.30pm & 2.30–4.30pm; £1). From a quay off Fore Street, a regular ferry crosses the narrow channel to **East Portlemouth**, from where you can follow the coastal path past the craggily photogenic Gammon Point to Devon's most southerly tip at **Prawle Point**, where a broken-backed freighter is a reminder of the hazards of this stretch of coast.

Salcombe's museum also houses a **tourist office** (April–June, Sept & Oct Mon–Sat 10am–5pm; July & Aug Mon–Sat 10am–5.30pm, Sun 10am–4pm; Nov–March Mon–Sat 10am–1pm & 2–4pm; ☎01548/844673, ⓦwww.salcombeinformation.co.uk). Most of the **hotels** are above Fore Street, enjoying excellent estuary views, such as *Rocarno* on Grenville Road (☎01548/842732; ❷). Near the car park on Shadycombe Road, *The Old Porch House* (☎01548/842157; ❸) dates back to 1660 but has full modern facilities amid the brass ornaments.

Plymouth

PLYMOUTH's predominantly bland and modern face belies its great historic role as a naval base, a role assured in the sixteenth century by the patronage of such national heroes as John Hawkins and Francis Drake. It was from here that the latter sailed to defeat the Spanish Armada in 1588, and 32 years later the port was the last embarkation point for the Pilgrim Fathers, whose New Plymouth colony became the nucleus for the English settlement of North America. The sustained prominence of the city's Devonport dockyards as a shipbuilding and military base made it a target in World War II, when the Luftwaffe reduced the old centre to rubble, apart from the compact area around the Barbican. Subsequent reconstruction, spurred on by growth that has made Plymouth by far Devon's biggest town, has done nothing to enhance the place. That said, it would be difficult to spoil the glorious vista over **Plymouth Sound**, the basin of calm water at the mouth of the combined Plym, Tavy and Tamar estuaries, which has remained largely unchanged since Drake played his famous game of bowls on the Hoe before joining battle with the Armada.

One of the best local day excursions from Plymouth is to **Mount Edgcumbe**, where woods and meadows provide a welcome antidote to the urban bustle, and are within easy reach of some fabulous sand. East of Plymouth, the aristocratic opulence of **Saltram House** includes some fine art and furniture, while to the north of town you can visit Drake's old residence at **Buckland Abbey**.

The City

A good place to start a tour of the city is **Plymouth Hoe**, an immense esplanade studded with reminders of the great events in the city's history. Resplendent in fair weather, with glorious views over the sea, the Hoe can also attract some pretty ferocious winds, making it well-nigh impossible to explore in wintry conditions. Approaching from the Civic Centre – the hub of the town centre – the most distinctive landmark is a tall white naval war memorial, standing alongside smaller monuments to the defeat of the Spanish Armada and to the airmen who defended the city during the wartime blitz, and a rather portly statue of Sir Francis Drake, gazing grandly out to sea. Appropriately, there's a bowling green back from the brow.

In front of the memorials the red-and-white striped **Smeaton's Tower** (Easter–Sept 10.30am–4.30pm; 90p, free for Plymouth Dome visitors) was erected in 1759 by John Smeaton on the treacherous Eddystone Rocks, fourteen miles out to sea. When replaced by a larger lighthouse in 1882, it was reassembled here, where it gives the loftiest view over Plymouth Sound. Below Smeaton's Tower is **Plymouth Dome** (April–Oct daily 9am–6pm; last entry 1hr before closing; £4.10), which features tricksy audiovisual exhibitions of Plymouth's history and the lives of local heroes such as Drake, the Mayflower Pilgrims and Captain Cook. On the seafront, Plymouth's **Royal Citadel** (May–Sept tours at 2.30pm lasting 1hr 15min; £3; EH) is an uncompromising fortress constructed in 1666 to intimidate the populace of the only town in the southwest to be held by the Parliamentarians in the Civil War. The stronghold is still used by the military, though there are guided tours through some of its older parts, including the seventeenth-century Governor's House and the Royal Chapel of St Katherine; tickets for tours are available from the Plymouth Dome and the tourist office.

Born around 1540 near Tavistock, **Francis Drake** worked in the domestic coastal trade from the age of 13, but was soon taking part in the first English slaving expeditions between Africa and the West Indies, led by his Plymouth kinsman John Hawkins. Later, Drake was active in the secret war against Spain, raiding and looting merchant ships in actions unofficially sanctioned by Elizabeth I. In 1572 he became the first Englishman to sight the Pacific, and soon afterwards, on board the *Golden Hind*, became the first one to **circumnavigate the world**, for which he received a knighthood on his return in 1580. The following year Drake was made mayor of Plymouth, settling in Buckland Abbey (see p.375), but was back in action before long – in 1587 he "singed the king of Spain's beard" by entering Cadiz harbour and destroying 33 vessels that were to have formed part of Philip II's **armada**. When the replacement invasion fleet appeared in the English Channel in 1588, Drake – along with Raleigh, Hawkins and Frobisher – played a leading role in wrecking it. The following year he set off on an unsuccessful expedition to help the Portuguese against Spain, but otherwise most of the next decade was spent in relative inactivity in Plymouth, Exeter and London. Finally, in 1596 Drake left with Hawkins for a raid on Panama, a venture that cost the lives of both captains.

Drake has come to personify the Elizabethan Age's swashbuckling expansionism and patriotism, but England's naval triumphs were as much the result of John Hawkins' humbler work in building and maintaining a new generation of warships as they were of the skill and bravery of their captains. Drake was simply the most flamboyant of a generation of reckless and brilliant mariners who broke the Spanish hegemony on the high seas, laying the foundations for England's later imperialist pursuits.

Round the corner, the old town's quay at **Sutton Harbour** is still used by the trawler fleet and is the scene of a boisterous early-morning fish market. The **Mayflower Steps** here commemorate the sailing of the Pilgrim Fathers and a nearby plaque lists the names and professions of the 102 Puritans on board. All three of Captain Cook's voyages to the South Seas, Australia and the Antarctic also started from here, as did the nineteenth-century transport ships to Australia, carrying thousands of convicts and colonists. Edging the harbour, the **Barbican** district is the heart of old Plymouth. Most of the buildings are now shops and restaurants, but off the quayside, New Street holds most of the oldest buildings, among them the **Elizabethan House** (April–Sept Wed–Sun 10am–5.30pm; £1), a captain's dwelling which retains most of the original architectural features. Cross the bridge over Sutton Harbour to reach Plymouth's newest exhibit, the grand **National Marine Aquarium** (daily: April–Oct 10am–6pm; Nov–March 10am–4pm; £6.50), where a range of marine environments are represented; highlights include Europe's largest collection of seahorse species.

In the centre of town, the mainly seventeenth-century **Merchant's House Museum**, 33 St Andrew St (April–Sept Tues–Fri 10am–1pm & 2–5.30pm, Sat 10am–1pm & 2–5pm; £1) goes into various aspects of Plymouth's history. Behind it, off Royal Parade, stands the city's chief place of worship, **St Andrew's**, a reconstruction of a fifteenth-century building that was almost completely gutted by a bomb in 1941. The entrails of the navigator Martin Frobisher are buried here, as are those of Admiral Blake, the Parliamentarian who died as his ship entered Plymouth after destroying a Spanish treasure fleet off Tenerife. Local boy William Bligh, of *Mutiny on the Bounty* fame, was baptized here.

Practicalities

Plymouth's **train station** is off Saltash Road, from where bus #25 leaves every fifteen minutes for the central Royal Parade. The **bus station** is just over St Andrew's Cross from Royal Parade, at Bretonside. The **tourist office**, off Sutton Harbour at 9 The Barbican (April–Oct Mon–Sat 9am–5pm, Sun 10am–4pm; Nov–March Mon–Fri 9am–5pm, Sat 10am–4pm; ☎01752/304849, ⓦwww .plymouth.gov.uk), has information about guided tours.

Most of the city's central **accommodation** lies a short walk from here: try first the row of B&Bs edging the Hoe on Citadel Road if you want to be near the sights, for example the *Acorns and Lawns*, 171 Citadel Rd (☎01752/ 229474; ❶), or *The Beeches*, at no. 175 (☎01752/266475; ❶). On the west side of the Hoe, the smart *Bowling Green Hotel*, 9–10 Osborne Place, Lockyer St (☎01752/209090, ⓦwww.bowlinggreenhotel.co.uk; ❷) overlooks Francis Drake's fabled haunt, while *Osmond Guest House*, 42 Pier St (☎01752/229705; ❶), is closer to the Great Western Docks, and offers a pick-up service from the bus and train stations. There are two **hostels** in town: *Plymouth Backpackers Hotel*, 172 Citadel Rd (☎01752/225158, ⓦwww.backpackers.co.uk/ply-mouth), and, further out, *Plymouth YHA*, Belmont House, Devonport Rd (☎01752/562189, ⓦwww.yha.org.uk), for which walk a quarter-mile from Devonport train station, or catch a bus from the centre.

You'll find a wildly eclectic range of **restaurants** in and around Plymouth's Barbican area. One of the best places for fish is *Piermaster's*, at 3 Southside St (☎01752/229345; closed Sun), whose kitchen is supplied straight from the nearby harbour. Across the road, the *Barbican Pasta Bar* attracts the crowds, while Notte Street, at the top of Southside, has the inexpensive *Revival*, a Mexican/Italian/American diner with lots of jazzy ambience. *Plymouth Arts Centre*, 38 Looe St, has a self-service vegetarian restaurant open until around 8pm, though the major reason for coming here is to see its films and live per-formances.

The *Dolphin* **pub** on Southside Street is a landmark in the Barbican, and is crowded with fishermen in the morning and locals and boisterous boozers at night; it also serves simple lunchtime snacks.

Mount Edgcumbe

Lying on the Cornish side of Plymouth Sound and visible from the Hoe, **Mount Edgcumbe** features a Tudor house, landscaped gardens and acres of rolling parkland and coastal paths. The **house** (April to Sept Wed–Sun 11am–4.30pm; £4.50) is a reconstruction of the bomb-damaged Tudor origi-nal, though inside the predominant note is eighteenth-century, the rooms ele-gantly restored with authentic Regency furniture. The highlight, though, is the **grounds**, which include impeccable gardens divided into French, Italian and English sections – the first two a blaze of flowerbeds adorned with classical stat-uary, the last an acre of sweeping lawn shaded by exotic trees – while the **park** gives access to the Coastal Path. You can reach the house by the passenger **ferry** to Cremyll, leaving at least hourly from Admiral's Hard, a small mooring in the Stonehouse district (bus #33 or #34 from the Guildhall), and in summer there's also a direct motor launch between the Mayflower Steps and the village of **Cawsand**, an old smugglers' haunt two hours' walk from the house. Cawsand itself is just a mile from the southern tip of the huge **Whitsand Bay**, the best bathing beach for miles around.

Saltram House

The remodelled Tudor mansion **Saltram House** (April–Sept Mon–Thurs & Sun noon–5pm: Oct closes 4pm; garden April–Oct Mon–Thurs & Sun 10.30am–5.30pm; Feb & March Sat & Sun 11am–4pm; £6; garden only £3; NT), two miles east of Plymouth off the A38, is Devon's largest country house, featuring work by the great architect Robert Adam and fourteen portraits by **Joshua Reynolds**, who was born nearby in Plympton. Showpiece is the Saloon, a fussy but exquisitely furnished room dripping with gilt and plaster, and set off by a huge Axminster carpet especially woven for it in 1770. Saltram's landscaped park provides a breather from this riot of interior design, though it is marred by the proximity of the road. You can get here on the hourly #22 bus (#19b on Sun) from Royal Parade to Cot Hill, from where it's a ten-minute signposted walk.

Buckland Abbey

Six miles north of Plymouth, close to the River Tavy and on the edge of Dartmoor, stands **Buckland Abbey** (April–Oct Mon–Wed & Fri–Sun 10.30am–5.30pm; Nov–March Sat & Sun 2–5pm; £4.60, grounds only £2.40; NT), once the most westerly of England's Cistercian abbeys. After its dissolution Buckland was converted to a family home by the privateer Richard Grenville (cousin of Walter Raleigh), from whom the estate was acquired by Sir Francis Drake in 1582, the year he became mayor of Plymouth. It remained his home until his death, but the house reveals few traces of Drake's residence. There are, however, numerous maps, portraits and mementoes of his buccaneering exploits on show, most famous of which is Drake's Drum, which was said to beat a supernatural warning of impending danger to the country. The house stands in majestic grounds which contain a fine fourteenth-century **Great Barn**, buttressed and gabled and larger than the abbey itself. To get here, take bus #83, #84 or #86 from Plymouth to Tavistock, changing at Yelverton to the hourly #55 minibus (not Sun).

Dartmoor

Occupying the main part of Devon between Exeter and Plymouth, **DARTMOOR** is southern England's greatest expanse of wilderness, some 365 square miles of raw granite, barren bogland, sparse grass and heather-grown moor. It was not always so desolate, as testified by the remnants of scattered Stone Age settlements and the ruined relics of the area's nineteenth-century tin-mining industry. Today desultory flocks of sheep and groups of ponies are virtually the only living creatures to be seen wandering over the central fastnesses of the National Park, with solitary birds – buzzards, kestrels, pipits, stonechats and wagtails – wheeling and hovering high above.

The core of Dartmoor, characterized by tumbling streams and high tors chiselled by the elements, is **Dartmoor Forest**, which has belonged to the Duchy of Cornwall since 1307, though there is almost unlimited public access. Camping is permitted out of sight of houses and roads, but fires are strictly forbidden. Though networks of signposts or painted stones do exist to guide **walkers**, map-reading abilities are a prerequisite for any but the shortest walks, and a good deal of experience is essential for longer distances. Information on **guided walks** and **riding** facilities is available from National Park Visitor Centres in Dartmoor's major towns and villages, and from information points in smaller villages.

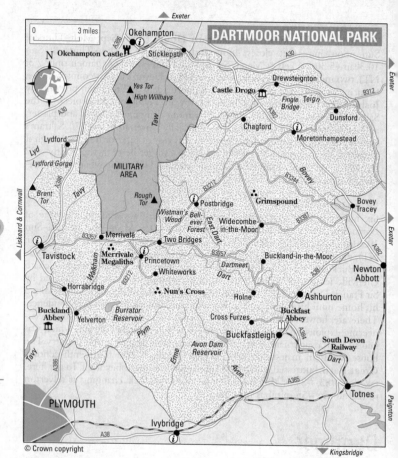

© Crown copyright

Much to the irritation of locals and visitors alike, the **Ministry of Defence** has appropriated a significant portion of northern Dartmoor, an area that contains Dartmoor's highest tors and some of its most famous beauty spots. The MoD firing ranges are marked by red and white posts; when firing is in progress, red flags or red lights signify that entry is prohibited. As a general rule, you can assume that if no warning flags are flying by 9am between April and September, or by 10am from October to March, there is to be no firing on that day.

Princetown and the central moor

PRINCETOWN owes its growth to the presence of Dartmoor Prison, a high-security jail originally constructed for POWs captured in the Napoleonic wars. Its grim spirit seeps into the village, which has a somewhat oppressed air and functional grey stone houses, some of them – like the parish church of St Michael – built by French and American prisoners. What Princetown lacks in beauty is amply compensated for by the surrounding country, the best of which lies immediately to the north.

Information on all of Dartmoor is given by the main **National Park information centre**, on the village's central green (daily: Easter–Oct 10am–5pm; Nov–March 10am–4pm; ℡01822/890414, ⓦwww.dartmoor-npa.gov.uk). The best **places to stay** include the central and friendly *Lamorna* on Two Bridges Road (℡01822/890360; ❶) and the non-smoking *Duchy House* on Tavistock Road (℡01822/890552, Ⓔduchyhouse@aol.com; ❶; closed Nov), which also runs a **café**. Two pubs in Princetown's central square also offer accommodation, the *Railway Inn* (℡01822/890232; ❶) and the *Plume of Feathers* (℡01822/890240; ❶); the latter claims to be the oldest building in town, and also has dormitory accommodation in two bunkhouses as well as a convenient **campsite** – staple bar-food is always available.

Northeast of Princetown, two miles north of the crossroads at Two Bridges, the dwarfed and misshapen oaks of **Wistman's Wood** are an evocative relic of the original Dartmoor Forest, cluttered with lichen-covered boulders and a dense undergrowth of ferns. The gnarled old trees are alleged to have been the site of druidic gatherings, a story unsupported by any evidence but quite plausible in this solitary spot. Two Bridges has a basic example of Dartmoor's **clapper bridges** – simple structures which consist of huge slabs of granite supported by piers of the same material, used by tin-miners and farmers since medieval times – but the largest and best preserved of these crosses the East Dart river three miles northeast of Two Bridges at **POSTBRIDGE**. Walkers from Postbridge can explore up and down the river, or press further south through **Bellever Forest** to the open moor beyond. On the edge of the forest, a couple of miles south of Postbridge on the banks of the East Dart river, lies one of Dartmoor's three **youth hostels** (℡01822/880227) – it's on a minor road from Postbridge, but there's no public transport. There's also a **camping barn** (℡01200/420102) close to Bellever Forest at Runnage Farm with a bunkhouse and outdoor camping facilities alongside – for this and any of Dartmoor's other camping barns, it's wise to book ahead, particularly at weekends. You'll find more luxury in the riverside *Lydgate House Hotel*, signposted off the main road half a mile southwest of Postbridge and offering easy access to Bellever Forest and the moor (℡01822/880209; ❺). Two miles northeast of Postbridge, the solitary *Warren House Inn* offers warm, firelit comfort and **meals** in a bleak tract of moorland.

To the east of the B3212, reachable on a right turn towards Widecombe-in-the-Moor, the Bronze Age village of **Grimspound** lies about a mile off the road. Inhabited some three thousand years ago, this is the most complete example of Dartmoor's prehistoric settlements, consisting of twenty-four circular huts scattered within a four-acre enclosure. The site is thought to have been the model for the Stone Age settlement in which Sherlock Holmes camped in *The Hound of the Baskervilles*, while **Hound Tor**, an outcrop three miles to the southwest, was the inspiration for Conan Doyle's tale – according to local legend, phantom hounds were sighted racing across the moor to hurl themselves on the tomb of a hated squire following his death in 1677.

Buckland, Widecombe and the southeastern moor

Four miles east of the crossroads at Two Bridges, **Dartmeet** marks the place where the East and West Dart rivers merge after tortuous journeys from their remote sources. Crowds home in on this beauty spot, but the valley is memorably lush and you don't need to walk far to leave the car park and ice-cream vans behind. From here the Dart pursues a more leisurely course, joined by the

River Webburn near the pretty moorland village of **BUCKLAND-IN-THE-MOOR**, one of a cluster of moorstone-and-thatched hamlets on this south-eastern side of the moor.

Four miles north, another popular Dartmoor village, **WIDECOMBE-IN-THE-MOOR** is set in a hollow amid high granite-strewn ridges. Its church of **St Pancras** provides a famous local landmark, its pinnacled tower dwarfing the fourteenth-century main building, whose interior boasts a beautiful painted rood screen. Look out here too for the carved one-eared rabbits above the communion rail. The nearby **Church House** was built in the fifteenth century for weary churchgoers from outlying districts, and was later converted into almshouses. Widecombe's other claim to fame is the traditional song, *Widdicombe Fair*: the **fair** is still held annually on the second Tuesday of September, but is now primarily a tourist attraction. You could **stay** in Widecombe in the elegant *Old Rectory* (℡01364/621231, ✉rachel.belgrave@care4free.net; ❶), opposite the post office and set in a lovely garden; or try *Manor Cottage* (℡01364/621218; ❶), next to the post office, which also has a garden where breakfast can be taken.

South of Buckland, the village of **HOLNE** is another rustic idyll surrounded on three sides by wooded valleys. The vicarage here was the birthplace of Charles Kingsley, author of *The Water Babies* and such Devon-based tales as *Westward Ho!*. A couple of miles east, the Dart weaves through a wooded green valley to enter the grounds of **Buckfast Abbey** (daily: May–Oct 9am–5.30pm; Nov–April 10am–4pm; free), a modern monastic complex occupying the site of an abbey founded in the eleventh century by Canute, abandoned two hundred years later, refounded, and finally dissolved by Henry VIII. The present buildings were the work of a handful of French Benedictine monks who consecrated their new abbey in 1932, though work on the other monastic buildings has continued until recently. The church itself is in a traditional Anglo-Norman style, following the design of the Cistercian building razed in 1535.

The northeastern moor

The essentially unspoilt market town of **MORETONHAMPSTEAD**, lying on the northeastern edge of the moor, makes an attractive entry point from Exeter. Local **information** is handled by a Visitor Information Point at 10 The Square (Easter–Oct daily 10am–5pm; Nov–Easter Fri–Sun 10am–1pm & 2–5pm; ℡01647/440043). There is classy **accommodation** on the western edge of the village, the *Old Post House* in Court Street (℡01647/440900, Ⓦwww.theoldposthouse.com; non-smoking; ❶), a friendly B&B which welcomes walkers, and at *Cookshayes*, a little further out at 33 Court St (℡01647/440374; ❷), offering good home cooking. The village also has a first-rate new **hostel**, the *Sparrowhawks Backpackers Hostel* at 45 Ford St (℡01647/440318), and there's another hostel on the outskirts of **Dunsford**, three miles northeast of Moretonhampstead, the *Steps Bridge* youth hostel (℡01647/252435), right on the boundary of the National Park – buses #359 (not Sun) and #82 stop nearby. Its woodland setting overlooking the Teign Gorge makes it a popular overnight stop for hikers.

Moretonhampstead has an historic rivalry with neighbouring **CHAGFORD**, a Stannary town (a chartered centre of the tin trade) that also enjoyed prosperity as a centre of the wool industry. It stands on a hillside overlooking the River Teign, with a fine fifteenth-century church at its centre. The ancient *Globe* (℡01647/433485, Ⓦwww.the-globe.org.uk; ❷), facing the church, is one of a number of decent **pubs** in the village, and offers spacious **rooms**, though subject to noise from the church clock. A quieter alternative is the thatched, seventeenth-century *Lawn House* (℡01647/433329; closed Nov–Feb; no smoking; ❷), on the other side of the main square on Mill Street, and next to a famed local **restaurant**, the non-smoking *22 Mill Street* (℡01647/432244; closed Sun and lunchtime Mon & Tues), which offers pricey, but top quality modern cuisine.

There are numerous **walks** to be made in the immediate vicinity, for instance five miles downstream along the Teign to the twentieth-century extravaganza of **Castle Drogo** (April–Oct Mon–Thurs, Sat & Sun 11am–5.30pm; grounds daily 10.30am–dusk; £5.60; grounds only £2.80; NT), which occupies a stupendous site overlooking the Teign gorge. Having retired at the age of 33, grocery magnate Julius Drewe unearthed a link that suggested his descent from a Norman baron, and set about creating a castle befitting his pedigree. Begun in 1910, to a design by **Sir Edwin Lutyens**, it was not completed until 1930, but the result was an unsurpassed synthesis of medieval and modern elements. Paths lead from Drogo east to **Fingle Bridge**, one of Dartmoor's most noted beauty spots, where shaded green pools hold trout and the occasional salmon; the *Angler's Rest* pub here has an adjoining **restaurant**.

Okehampton and the northwestern moor

The main centre on the northern fringes of Dartmoor, **OKEHAMPTON** grew prosperous as a market town for the medieval wool trade, and some fine old buildings survive between the two branches of the River Okement that meet here, among them the prominent fifteenth-century tower of the **Chapel of St James**. Across the road from the seventeenth-century town hall, a granite archway leads into the **Museum of Dartmoor Life** (Easter–Sept Mon–Sat 10am–5pm, Sun 10am–4.30pm; Oct–Easter Mon–Sat 10am–5pm; £2; ⓦwww.museumofdartmoorlife.eclipse.co.uk), an excellent overview of habitation on the moor since earliest times. Outside town, loftily perched above the West Okement, **Okehampton Castle** (April–Sept daily 10am–6pm; Oct daily 10am–5pm; £2.50; EH) is the shattered hulk of a stronghold laid waste by Henry VIII; its ruins include a gatehouse, Norman keep and the remains of the Great Hall, buttery and kitchens.

Between late May and late September, an old goods line provides Okehampton with a useful Sunday **rail** connection, linking the town with Exeter via Crediton in about forty minutes. The station is a fifteen-minute walk up Station Road from Fore Street in Okehampton's centre, where the **tourist office** (April, May & mid-Sept to Oct Mon–Sat 10am–5pm; June to mid-Sept daily 10am–5pm; Nov–March Mon, Fri & Sat 10am–5pm; ℡01837/53020) sits next to the museum. Alongside them lies the expensive *White Hart* (℡01837/52730; ❹), though cheaper **accommodation** can be found a short walk north of the centre around the station, where traffic noise from the A30 is compensated by views towards Exmoor and the outdoor heated pool at *Heathfield House*, the old station-master's home above the station on Klondyke Road (℡01837/54211, ⓦwww.tgibbins.freeserve.co.uk; no smoking; ❷). Alternatively, opt for the more economical *Meadowlea* lower down at 65 Station Rd (℡01837/53200; ❶). If you prefer rural surroundings, try the comfortable and spacious *Upcott House* on Upcott Hill, half a mile north of the centre (℡01837/53743; ❷). Okehampton's **youth hostel** (℡01837/53916, ⓦwww.yha.org.uk; closed Dec & Jan) provides four- and six-bed bunkrooms in a converted goods shed at the station, and offers a range of outdoor activities. As for **eating**, the *Coffee Pot*, tucked away behind the museum in Fairplace

Terrace, is good for breakfasts, coffees and meals (closed eve Oct–May), while *Le Café Noir* (closed Sun), across West Street in Red Lion Yard, offers inexpensive lunches.

Lydford

Five miles southwest of Okehampton, the village of **LYDFORD** boasts the sturdy but small-scale Lydford Castle, a Saxon outpost, then a Norman keep and later used as a prison. The chief attraction here, though, is **Lydford Gorge** (April–Sept 10am–5.30pm; Oct 10am–4pm; Nov–March 10.30am–3pm; £3.60; NT), whose main entrance is a five-minute walk downhill. Two routes – one above, one along the banks – follow the ravine burrowed through by the River Lyd as far as the hundred-foot White Lady Waterfall, coming back on the opposite bank. Overgrown with thick woods, the one-and-a-half-mile gorge is alive with butterflies, spotted woodpeckers, dippers, herons and clouds of insects. The full course would take you roughly two hours at a leisurely pace, though there is a separate entrance at the south end of the gorge if you only want to visit the waterfall. In winter months, when the river can flood, the waterfall is the only part of the gorge open.

Back in the village, the picturesque *Castle Inn* sits right next to the castle, and provides a fire-lit sixteenth-century bar where you can drink and snack. There's a **restaurant** here too, and en-suite **accommodation** in low-ceilinged oak-beamed rooms (℡01822/820242, ⓔcastleinnlyd@aol.com; ❹), though you'll find lower rates at the family-run *Moorlands* (℡01822/820229; ❶), 300 yards from the A386 on the Lydford turning.

Tavistock

The main town of the western moor, **TAVISTOCK** owes its distinctive Victorian appearance to the building boom that followed the discovery of copper deposits here in 1844. Originally, however, this market and Stannary town on the River Tavy grew around what was once the West Country's most important Benedictine abbey, established in the eleventh century. Some scanty remnants survive in the churchyard of **St Eustace**, a mainly fifteenth-century building with stained glass from William Morris's studio in the south aisle.

Tavistock's **tourist office**, in the town hall on Bedford Square (Easter to late July & early Sept to Oct Mon–Sat 10am–5pm; late July to early Sept daily 9.30am–5pm; Nov–Easter Mon, Tues, Fri & Sat 10am–4pm; ℡01822/612938), can supply you with information on the western moor, for which the town would make an ideal base. There's a good range of **accommodation** choices, including the Georgian *Eko Brae* at 4 Bedford Villas (℡01822/614028, ⓔekobrae@aol.com; ❶), and, about half a mile east of Tavistock off the B3357 Princetown Road, *Mount Tavy Cottage* (℡01822/614253, ⓦwww.mounttavy.freeserve.co.uk; ❷), set in a lush garden and offering organic breakfasts.

North of Tavistock, a four-mile lane wanders up to **Brent Tor**, 1130-foot high and dominating Dartmoor's western fringes. Access to its conical summit is easiest along a path gently ascending through gorse on its southwestern side, leading to the small church of St Michael at the top. Bleak, treeless moorland extends in every direction, wrapped in silence that's occasionally pierced by the shrill cries of stonechats and wheatears. A couple of miles eastwards, **Gibbet Hill** looms over Black Down and the ruined stack of the abandoned Wheal Betsy silver and lead mine.

North Devon

From Exeter the A377 runs alongside the scenic Tarka Line railway to **North Devon**'s major town, **Barnstaple**. Within easy reach of here, the resorts of **Ilfracombe** and **Woolacombe** draw the crowds, though the fine sandy beaches surrounding the latter give ample opportunity to find your own space. The river port of **Bideford** gives its name to a long bay that holds another beach resort, **Westward Ho!**, as well as the precipitous village of **Clovelly**, perhaps Devon's most famous beauty spot. The coastal path follows the bay westwards, particularly inspiring around the stormy **Hartland Point**. Away from the coast, there is plenty of scope for walking and cycling along the **Tarka Trail** long-distance path, passing through some of the region's loveliest countryside, while for a complete break, the tiny island of **Lundy** offers almost complete isolation and a cleansing air.

Barnstaple

BARNSTAPLE, at the head of the Taw estuary, makes an excellent spring-board, being well connected to the resorts of Bideford Bay, Ilfracombe and Woolacombe, as well as to the western fringes of Exmoor. The town's cen-turies-old role as a marketplace is perpetuated in the daily bustle around the huge timber-framed **Pannier Market** off the High Street, alongside which runs **Butchers Row**, most of whose 33 archways are still occupied by butch-ers. Also off the High Street, in the pedestrianized area between that and Boutport Street, lies Barnstaple's **parish church**, itself worth a look, and the fourteenth-century **St Anne's Chapel**, converted into a grammar school in 1549 and later numbering among its pupils John Gay, author of *The Beggar's*

The Tarka Line and the Tarka Trail

Henry Williamson's *Tarka the Otter* (1927), rated by some as one of the finest pieces of nature writing in the English language, has been appropriated as a promotional device by the Devon tourist industry. As parts of the book are set in the Taw valley, it was inevitable that the Exeter to Barnstaple rail route – which follows the Taw for half of its length – should be dubbed the **Tarka Line**. Leaving almost hourly from Exeter St David's station, trains on this branch line cut through the sparsely popu-lated heart of Devon, the biggest town en route being **Crediton**, ancient birthplace of St Boniface (patron saint of Germany and the Netherlands) and site of the bish-opric before its transfer to Exeter in the eleventh century.

Barnstaple forms the centre of the figure-of-eight traced by the **Tarka Trail**, which tracks the otter's wanderings for a distance of over 180 miles. To the north, the trail penetrates Exmoor then follows the coast back, passing through Williamson's home village of **Georgeham** on its return to Barnstaple. South, the path takes in Bideford (see p.383), following a disused rail line to Meeth, and continuing as far as Okehampton (see p.379), before swooping up via Eggesford, the point at which the Tarka Line joins the Taw valley.

Twenty-three miles of the trail follow a former rail line that's ideally suited to **bicy-cles**, and there are rental shops at Barnstaple (near the train station), and Bideford (see p.383). Sculptures have been placed along the route to mark its inclusion in the National Cycle Network. A good ride from Barnstaple is to **Torrington** (fifteen miles south), where you can eat at the *Puffing Billy* pub, formerly the train station.

Tourist offices give out leaflets on individual sections of the trail, but the best over-all book is *The Tarka Trail: A Walker's Guide* (Devon Books; £4.95), available from tourist offices or bookshops.

Opera; it's now closed to the public. At the end of Boutport Street, make time to visit the **Museum of North Devon** (Tues–Sat 10am–4.30pm; £1, free on Sat till noon), a lively miscellany including wildlife displays and a collection of eighteenth-century pottery for which the region was famous. The museum lies alongside the Taw, where footpaths make for a pleasant riverside stroll, with the colonnaded eighteenth-century **Queen Anne's Walk** – built as a merchants' exchange – providing some architectural interest.

Barnstaple's well-equipped **tourist office** lies opposite Butchers Row on Boutport Street (May–Sept Mon–Sat 9.30am–5.30pm; Oct–April Mon–Sat 9.30am–5pm; ☎01271/375000, ⓦwww.northdevon.com). Cyclists on the Tarka Trail can **rent bikes** from Tarka Trail Cycle Hire at the train station (☎01271/324202) or Rolle Quay Cycle Hire on Rolle Street (☎01271/325361), at the top end of the High Street, conveniently placed for the northern section of the Trail towards Braunton. There are plenty of **places to stay** in town, two of them five hundred yards south of Long Bridge, at the bottom of the High Street: the Georgian *Nelson House*, 99 Newport Rd (☎01271/345929; ❶), backing onto Rock Park and the river, and, around the corner on Victoria Road, *Ivy House* (☎01271/371198; ❶). A little further out, on Landkey Road – a continuation of Newport Road – is the excellent *Mount Sandford* (☎01271/342354; ❷), which has a beautiful garden. A mile south of the centre on Bishops Tawton Road, the non-smoking *Lynwood House* (☎01271/343695, ⓦwww.lynwoodhouse.co.uk; ❹) has comfortable accommodation though is better known for its gourmet **restaurant** (closed Sun), where you can pick up moderate set lunches and pricier evening meals. You'll find coffees and **snacks** at the *Old School Coffee House*, a seventeenth-century building on Church Lane, near St Anne's Chapel, and at the coolly modern *PV*, 70 Boutport St (closed Sun), which has an upstairs restaurant and the ground floor becomes a wine bar in the evening.

Ilfracombe and around

The most popular resort on Devon's northern coast, **ILFRACOMBE** is essentially little changed since its evolution into a Victorian and Edwardian tourist centre, large-scale development having been restricted by the surrounding cliffs. Nonetheless, the relentless pressure to have fun and the ubiquitous smell of chips can become oppressive, though in summer you can always escape on a coastal tour, a cruise to Lundy Island (see p.385) or a fishing trip, all available at its small harbour.

For walkers, an attractive stretch of coast runs east out of town, beyond the grassy cliffs of Hillsborough, where a succession of undeveloped coves and inlets is surrounded by jagged slanting rocks and heather-covered hills. There are sandy **beaches** here, though many prefer those past **Morte Point**, five miles west of Ilfracombe, from which the view takes in the island of Lundy, fifteen miles out to sea. Below the promontory stretches a rocky shore whose menacing sunken reef inspired the Normans to give it the name Morte Stone. A break in the rocks makes space for the pocket-sized **Barricane Beach**, famous for the tropical shells washed here from the Caribbean by the Atlantic currents, and a popular swimming spot. There's more space on the two miles of **Woolacombe Sands**, a broad, west-facing expanse much favoured by surfers and families alike. At the quieter southern end, **Putsborough Sands** is a choice swimming spot bracketed by **Baggy Point**, where from September to November the air is a swirl of gannets, shags, cormorants and shearwaters. South of this promontory, **Croyde Bay** is another surfers' delight, more compact than Woolacombe, with stalls on the sand renting surfboards and wet-suits, while **Saunton Sands** is a magnificent long stretch of coast pummelled by endless ranks of classic breakers.

Practicalities

Ilfracombe's **tourist office** is at the Landmark on the Seafront (daily: Easter–Oct 10am–5.30pm; Nov–Easter 10am–5.30pm; ☎01271/863001, ⓦwww .ilfracombe-guide.org.uk). The numerous **accommodation** choices in town include inexpensive **B&Bs** such as *Kinvara*, very central at 6 Avenue Rd (☎01271/863013; ❶; closed Nov–Easter), and the *Cavendish* at 9 Larkstone Terrace (☎01271/863994; ❸), which offers harbour views. There's also an excellent independent **hostel**, *Ocean Backpackers*, near the bus station and harbour at 29 St James Place (☎01271/867835), and the YHA hostel, *Ashmour House* (☎01271/865337), occupies a Georgian building above the harbour on Hillsborough Terrace. There are several **campsites** around Morte Point. The best **place to eat** in Ilfracombe is the *Atlantis*, below *Ocean Backpackers* (see above), with an eclectic range of dishes.

Bideford Bay

BIDEFORD BAY (sometimes called Barnstaple Bay) encapsulates the variety of Devon, encompassing the downmarket beach resort of **Westward Ho!**, the savage windlashed rocks of **Hartland Point** and the photogenic village of **Clovelly**. Picturesquely sited on the River Torridge, **Bideford** itself is mainly a transit centre, with bus connections to all the towns on the bay and regular boats to Lundy, though the old port of **Appledore** makes a more attractive place to spend any time.

Bideford

Like Barnstaple, nine miles to the east, the estuary town of **BIDEFORD** formed an important link in the north Devon trade network, mainly due to its **bridge**, which still straddles the River Torridge. First built in 1300, the bridge was reconstructed in stone in the following century, and subsequently reinforced and widened, hence the irregularity of its twenty-four arches, no two of which have the same span. Bideford's greatest prosperity arose in the seventeenth and eighteenth centuries, when it enjoyed a flourishing trade with the New World, and today the tree-lined quay along the west riverbank is still the focal point for the knot of narrow shop-lined streets.

From the Norman era until the eighteenth century, the port was the property of the Grenville family, whose most celebrated scion was **Richard Grenville**, commander of the ships that carried the first settlers to Virginia, and later a major player in the defeat of the Spanish Armada. Grenville also featured in *Westward Ho!*, the historical romance by **Charles Kingsley** who wrote part of the book in Bideford and is commemorated by a statue at the quay's northern end. Behind, **Victoria Park** extends up the riverbank, containing guns captured from the Spanish in 1588.

Alongside the park, the **tourist office** (Easter–June & Sept Mon–Sat 10am–5pm, Sun 10am–1pm; July & Aug Mon–Sat 10am–5pm, Sun 10am–1pm; Oct–Easter Mon, Tues, Thurs & Fri 10am–4.30pm, Wed & Sat 10am–1pm; ☎01237/477676) can provide information on coastal cruises, the Tarka Trail and ferries to Lundy (see p.385) – buy tickets for the latter from here or from the ticket-booth on the quayside. A useful **B&B** nearby is the *Cornerhouse*, 14 The Strand, two minutes from Victoria Park (☎01237/473722; ❶), or opt for the attractive *Mount* (☎01237/473748, ⓦwww.themount1. cjb.net; ❸), further out on Northdown Road, but linked to the centre by a footpath, and set in its own walled garden; both are non-smoking. For a **meal** or a drink, head up Bridge Street from Bideford's bridge to Market Place, where the porticoed *Old Coach Inn* provides ales and hearty snacks and the more up-to-date *Praxis II* has French sticks and vegan pasties during the day (closed Wed pm & all Sun).

A couple of miles downstream of Bideford, near the confluence of the Taw and Torridge rivers, the old shipbuilding port of **APPLEDORE** is worth a wander and a drink in one of its cosy pubs. The village still has several operating boatyards, but the peaceful pastel-coloured Georgian houses give little hint of the extent of the industry in earlier times.

WESTWARD HO!, three miles northwest of Bideford, is the only English town to be named after a book. After the publication of Kingsley's historical romance in 1855, speculators recognized the tourist potential of what was then an empty expanse of sand and mud pounded by Atlantic rollers, and the first villa was built within a decade. Now densely packed with caravan sites and holiday chalets, the resort has lost much of it's appeal, though the beach still has a mighty impact, backed by **Northam Burrows** – a flat, marshy expanse of dunes and meadows rich in flora and attracting plenty of migratory birds.

Clovelly

The steep cobbled lanes and whitewashed cottages of **CLOVELLY** must have featured on more calendars, biscuit boxes and tourist posters than anywhere else in the West Country. It was put on the map in the second half of the nineteenth century by two books: Charles Dickens' *A Message From the Sea* and, inevitably, *Westward Ho!* – Charles Kingsley's father was rector here for six years. To an extent, the tone of the village has been preserved by limiting hotel accommodation and holiday homes, and restricting coach parties, though there's still a regular stream of visitors and on summer days it's impossible to see past the artifice.

The first hurdle to surmount is the **visitor centre** (daily: April–Oct 9am–5pm; Nov–March 10am–4pm; Ⓦwww.clovelly.co.uk), where you are charged £3.50 for access to shops, snack bars and an audiovisual show, and also for use of the car park (it's well-nigh impossible to leave your motor anywhere else). Walkers, cyclists and users of public transport have right of way to the village (there's a separate entrance to the right of the visitor centre). Below, the traffic-free main street plunges past neat, flower-smothered cottages where sledges are tethered for transporting goods – the only way to carry supplies since the use of donkeys ended.

Clovelly's stony beach and tiny harbour lie snuggled under a cleft in the cliff wall. A lifeboat operates from here, and a handful of fishing boats are the only remnants of a fleet that provided the village's main business before the herring stocks became depleted. If you can't face the return climb, take the Land Rover, which grinds up to the top of the village and leaves about every fifteen minutes from behind the *Red Lion* (Easter–Oct 9am–5.30pm; £1.60). It is here, immediately below the visitor centre, that Hobby Drive begins, a panoramic three-mile **walk** along the cliffs through thick woods.

There are two **hotels** in the village, both pricey: the *New Inn* halfway down the High Street (℡01237/431303; ⑤), and, enjoying a superb position, the *Red Lion* at the harbour (℡01237/431237, Ⓔredlion@clovelly.demon.co.uk; ⑥). Below the *New Inn* is a small **B&B**, *Donkey Hill Cottage* (℡01237/431601; ①), and there's a greater selection of guest houses a twenty-minute walk up from the visitor centre in Higher Clovelly: try the *Old Smithy*, on the main road (℡01237/431202; ①).

Hartland Point and around

You could drive along minor roads to **Hartland Point**, ten miles west of Clovelly, but the best approach is on foot along the coastal path. Shortly before arriving, the path touches at the only sandy beach between Westward Ho! and the Cornish border, **Shipload Bay**. The headland presents one of Devon's most dramatic sights, its jagged black rocks battered by the sea and overlooked by a solitary lighthouse 350ft up. South of Hartland Point, the saw-toothed rocks and near-vertical escarpments defiantly confront the waves, with spectacular waterfalls tumbling over the cliffs. This sheer stretch of coast has seen dozens of shipwrecks over the centuries, though many must have been prevented by the sight of the tower of fourteenth-century **St Nectan's** – a couple of miles south of the point in the village of **STOKE** – which acted as a landmark to sailors before the construction of the lighthouse. At 128ft, it is the tallest church tower in north Devon, and overlooks a weathered old graveyard containing memorials to various members of the Lane family – of the Bodley Head and Penguin publishing empire – who were associated with the area; inside, the church boasts a finely carved rood screen and a Norman font, all covered by a repainted wagon-type roof. Tea and home-made scones are served in summer at *Stoke Barton Farm*, just opposite.

Half a mile east of the church, gardens and lush woodland surround **Hartland Abbey** (May, June & Sept Wed, Thurs & Sun 2–5.30pm; July & Aug also Tues 2–5.30pm; £4.25), an eighteenth-century country house incorporating the ruins of an abbey dissolved in 1539, and displaying fine furniture, old photographs and recently uncovered frescoes. **HARTLAND** itself, further inland, holds little appeal beyond its three pubs and café, but on the coast, **Hartland Quay** deserves a linger: once a busy port, financed in part by the mariners Raleigh, Drake and Hawkins, it was mostly destroyed by storms in the nineteenth century, and now holds a solitary pub and hotel, surrounded by beautiful slate cliffs. About one mile south of here, **Speke's Mill Mouth** is a select surfers' beach.

For **accommodation** in the area, the *Hartland Quay Hotel* (in Hartland Quay) can't be beaten for isolated atmosphere (☎01237/441218; ❷; closed Nov to mid-Feb), but if you want to be nearer Shipload Bay and Hartland Point, try *West Titchberry Farm* (☎01237/441287; ❶), for which you should follow signs for Hartland Lighthouse. In nearby Stoke, *Stoke Barton Farm* (see above) also provides **B&B** (☎01237/441238; ❶) and basic camping facilities, while further south, at Elmscott, at the end of a three-and-a-half-mile signposted footpath from Hartland, and about half a mile inland, there's a **youth hostel** in a converted Victorian schoolhouse (☎01237/441367). The only public transport is bus #319 from Barnstaple, and buses #119 and #128 from Bude; alight at Hartland.

Lundy Island

There are fewer than twenty full-time residents on **Lundy**, a tiny windswept island twelve miles north of Hartland Point. Now a refuge for thousands of marine birds, Lundy has no cars, just one pub and one shop – indeed little has changed since the Marisco family established itself here in the twelfth century, making use of the shingle beaches and coves to terrorize shipping along the Bristol Channel. The family's fortunes only fell in 1242 when one of their number, William de Marisco, was found to be plotting against the king, whereupon he was hanged, drawn and quartered at Tower Hill in London.

After the Mariscos, Lundy's most famous inhabitants were Thomas Benson, MP for Barnstaple in the eighteenth century – who was discovered using slave labour to work the granite quarries, and later found guilty of a massive insurance fraud – and **William Hudson Heaven**, who bought the island in 1834 and established what became known as the "Kingdom of Heaven". His home, **Millcombe House**, an incongruous piece of Georgian architecture in the desolate surroundings, is one of many relics of former habitation scattered around the island, though a recent addition compared with the castle standing on Lundy's southern end, which was erected by Henry III following the downfall of the Mariscos.

Tracks and footpaths interweave all over the island, and **walking** is really the only thing to do here. Inland, the grass, heather and bog is crossed by dry-stone walls and grazed by ponies, goats, deer and the rare soay sheep. The shores – mainly cliffy on the west, softer and undulating on the east – shelter a rich variety of **birdlife**, including kittiwakes, fulmars, shags and Manx shearwaters, which often nest in rabbit burrows. The most famous birds, though, are the **puffins** after which Lundy is named – from the Norse *Lunde* (puffin) and *ey* (island). They can only be sighted in April and May, when they come ashore to mate. Offshore, **grey seals** can be seen all the year round.

Practicalities

The *Oldenburg* crosses to Lundy from Bideford throughout the year apart from a few weeks in January and February, with additional sailings from Ilfracombe and from Clovelly from April to September (1–4 weekly). From Bideford, sailings increase in frequency from twice a week in winter to four times in mid-summer, taking around two hours; day return tickets cost around £25, period returns £40 (to reserve a place, call ☎01237/423233 or 01271/863636). **Accommodation** on the island can be booked up months in advance, and B&B is only available in houses that have not already been taken for weekly rentals. Since B&B bookings can only be made within two weeks of the proposed visit, this limits the options, though outside the holiday season it is still eminently possible to find a double room for under £45 per night. **Bookings** must be made through the Landmark Trust's office in Shottisbrooke (☎01628/825925). Options range from the remote *Admiralty Lookout* (lacking electricity and with only hand-pumped water), through the two-storey granite *Barn*, a hostel sleeping fourteen, to the comfortable *Old House*, where Charles Kingsley stayed in 1849, and the *Old Light*, a lighthouse built in 1820 by the architect of Dartmoor Prison. There's also a **campsite** on the island open throughout the year, though it can get wet and windswept in winter.

Exmoor

A high bare plateau sliced by wooded combes and splashing rivers, **EXMOOR** can be one of the most forbidding landscapes in England, especially when its sea-mists fall. When it's clear, though, the moorland of this National Park reveals rich swathes of colour and an amazing diversity of wildlife, from buzzards to the unique **Exmoor ponies**, a species closely related to prehistoric horses. In the treeless heartland of the moor in particular, it is not difficult to spot these short and stocky animals, though fewer than twelve hundred are registered, and of these only about two hundred are free-living on the moor. Much more elusive are the **red deer**, England's largest native wild animal, of which Exmoor supports England's only wild population; about two and half thousand are thought to inhabit the moor today.

Endless permutations of **walking routes** are possible along a network of some six hundred miles of footpaths and bridleways. **Horseback** is another way of getting the most of Exmoor's desolate beauty, and the most convenient stables are mentioned below. Whether walking or riding, bear in mind that over seventy percent of the National Park is privately owned and that access is theoretically restricted to public rights of way; special permission should certainly be sought before camping, canoeing, fishing or similar.

There are four obvious bases for inland walks: **Dulverton** in the southeast, site of the main information facilities; **Simonsbath** in the centre; **Exford**, near Exmoor's highest point of Dunkery Beacon; and the attractive village of **Winsford**, close to the A396 on the east of the moor. Exmoor's coastline offers an alluring alternative to the open moorland, all of it accessible via the **South West Coast Path**, which embarks on its long coastal journey at **Minehead**, though there is more charm to be found farther west at the sister-villages of **Lynmouth** and **Lynton**, just over the Devon border (over half of the moor lies in Somerset, though for convenience is covered in its entirety here).

Dulverton

The village of **DULVERTON**, on the southern edge of the National Park, is the Park Authority's headquarters and so makes a good introduction to Exmoor. Information on the whole moor is available at the **visitor centre**, 7 Fore St (daily: Easter–Oct 10am–1.15pm & 1.45–5pm; Nov–Easter 10.30am–2.30pm; ☎01398/323841). Dulverton's best **accommodation** choice is *Town Mills* (☎01398/323124; ❶), an old mill house in the centre of the village. If you hanker after beams and four-posters, try the *Lion Hotel* in Bank Square (☎01398/323444; ❸), or the plainer *Crispin's*, in a nook off 26 High St (☎01398/323397; ❶); the latter also serves moderately priced snacks and full evening **meals**. Moorland **horse riding** and tuition is offered at West Anstey Farm (☎01398/341354), a couple of miles west of Dulverton; there's also a **camping barn** here.

Winsford, Exford and Dunkery Beacon

Five miles north of Dulverton, **WINSFORD** – birthplace of the renowned Labour politician Ernest Bevin – lays good claim to being the moor's prettiest village. A scattering of thatched cottages ranged around a sleepy green, it is watered by a confluence of streams and rivers – one of them the Exe – giving it no fewer than seven bridges. *Larcombe Foot* (☎01643/851306; ❷), one mile to the north, offers excellent **B&B** overlooking the Exe, while the *Royal Oak* (☎01643/851455, ⓦwww.royaloak-somerset.co.uk; ❺), a thatched and rambling old inn on the village green, has pricier rooms, and also offers drinks, snacks and full restaurant **meals**.

The hamlet of **EXFORD**, an ancient crossing-point on the River Exe, is popular with hunting folk as well as with walkers here for the four-mile hike to **Dunkery Beacon**, Exmoor's highest point at 1700ft. The village also holds Exmoor's main **youth hostel**, a rambling Victorian house in the centre (☎01643/831288); alternatively, head for *Exmoor Lodge*, a friendly vegetarian and vegan **B&B** (☎01643/831694, ⓦwww.exmoorlodge.co.uk; no smoking; ❶).

Exmoor Forest and Simonsbath

At the centre of the National Park stands **Exmoor Forest**, the barest part of the moor, scarcely populated except by roaming sheep and a few red deer –

the word "forest" denotes simply that it was a hunting reserve. In the middle of it stands the village of **SIMONSBATH**, at a crossroads between Lynton, Barnstaple and Minehead on the River Barle. The village was home to the Knight family, who bought the forest in 1818 and, by introducing tenant farmers, building roads and importing sheep, brought systematic agriculture to an area that had never before produced any income. The Knights also built a wall round their land – parts of which can still be seen – as well as the intriguing Pinkworthy (pronounced "Pinkery") Pond, four miles to the northwest, whose exact function remains unexplained. Simonsbath would make a great base for hikes in the heart of the moor, but there are only two **accommodation** possibilities: the *Exmoor Forest Hotel* (℡01643/831341; ❸), which also has space for free **camping**, and the *Simonsbath House Hotel* (℡01643/831259; ❺), former home of the Knights and now holding a good but expensive **restaurant**. In a converted barn next to the hotel, *Boevey's* offers coffees and **snacks**, while a couple of miles outside the village on the Brayford Road, is the *Poltimore Arms* at **Yarde Down**, a classic country **pub** serving excellent food, including vegetarian dishes.

Minehead and around

A chief port on the Somerset coast, **MINEHEAD** quickly became a favourite Victorian watering-hole with the arrival of the railway, and it has preserved an upbeat holiday-town atmosphere ever since. Steep lanes link the two quarters of **Higher Town**, on North Hill, containing some of the oldest houses, and **Quay Town**, the harbour area. It is in Quay Town that the **Hobby Horse** performs its dance in the town's three-day May Day celebrations, snaring maidens under its prancing skirt and tail in a fertility ritual resembling the more famous festivities at the Cornish port of Padstow (see p.412).

Midway between Higher Town and Quay Town, the **tourist office** at 17 Friday St, off the Parade (April–June, Sept & Oct Mon–Sat 9.30am–5pm; July & Aug Mon–Sat 9.30am–5.30pm, Sun 10am–1pm; Nov–March Mon–Sat 10am–4pm; ℡01643/702624), has information on the moor and coast. If you want to **stay** in Minehead, try the budget *Avill House* on Townsend Road (℡01643/704370; ❶), a short walk from the seafront past the tourist office; or 100 yards further up on the same road, the more comfortable *Kildare Lodge* (℡01643/702009; ❸), a reconstructed Tudor inn designed by a pupil of

---

The South West Coast Path

The South West Coast Path, the longest footpath in Britain, starts at Minehead and tracks the coastline as closely as it possibly can along Devon's northern seaboard, round Cornwall, back into Devon, and on to Dorset, where it finishes close to the entrance to Poole Harbour. The path was conceived in the 1940s, but it is only in the last twenty years that – barring a few significant gaps – the full **six-hundred-mile route** has been open, much of it on land owned by the National Trust, and all of it well signposted.

The relevant Ordnance Survey **maps** can be found at most village shops on the route, while many newsagents, bookshops and tourist offices will stock books or pamphlets containing route plans and details of local flora and fauna. Aurum Press (🌐www.aurumpress.co.uk) produces a series of four books using Ordnance Survey maps and describing different parts of the path, while the **South West Coast Path Association** publishes an annual guide (£7) to the whole path, including accommodation lists, ferry timetables and transport details; contact them at Windlestraw, Penquit, Ermington, Devon PL21 0LU ℡01752/896237, 🌐www.swcp.org.uk.

Lutyens. There's a **youth hostel** a couple of miles southeast, outside the village of Alcombe on the edge of Exmoor (☎01643/702595).

Minehead is the terminus for the **West Somerset Railway**, which curves eastwards into the Quantocks. The line's first stop is about a mile from the old village of **DUNSTER**, three miles inland, and dominated by the towers and turrets of **Dunster Castle** (April–Sept Mon–Wed, Sat & Sun 11am–5pm; Oct Mon–Wed, Sat & Sun 11am–4pm; grounds daily: April–Sept 10am–5pm; Oct–March 11am–4pm; £6; grounds only £3; NT). Most of the castle's fortifications were demolished after the Civil War, following which it became something of an architectural showpiece, and Victorian restoration has made it more like a Rhineland Schloss than a Norman stronghold. A tour of the castle takes in various portraits of the Luttrells, owners of the house for six hundred years before the National Trust took over in the 1970s; a bedroom once occupied by Charles I; a fine seventeenth-century carved staircase; and a richly decorated banqueting hall. The grounds include terraced gardens and riverside walks – and drama productions are periodically staged here in the summer. The nearby hilltop tower is a folly, **Conygar Tower**, dating from 1776.

Dunster village preserves a few picturesque relics of its wool-making heyday, notably the octagonal **Yarn Market**, in the High Street below the castle (1609). At the end of Mill Lane, the three-hundred-year-old **water mill** (April–Oct daily 10.30am–5pm; £2.20; NT) is still used commercially for milling the various grains which go to make the flour and muesli sold in the mill shop and riverside café, making this a good spot for lunch. For somewhere to **stay**, try the *Gables* 33 High St (☎01643/821496; no smoking; ❸), which has rooms under the eaves overlooking the Yarn Market. There's a **visitor centre** at the top of Dunster Steep by the main car park (Easter–Oct daily 10am–5pm; Nov–Easter Sat & Sun 11am–3pm; ☎01643/821835).

Porlock

The real enticement of **PORLOCK**, six miles west of Minehead, is its extraordinary position in a deep hollow, cupped on three sides by Exmoor's hogbacked hills. The thatch-and-cob houses and dripping charm of the village's long main street have led to invasions of tourists, some of whom are also drawn by the place's literary links. According to Coleridge's own less than reliable testimony, it was a "man from Porlock" who broke the opium trance in which he was composing *Kubla Khan*, while the High Street's beamed *Ship Inn* prides itself on featuring prominently in the Exmoor romance *Lorna Doone* and, in real life, having sheltered the poet Robert Southey, who staggered in rain-soaked after an Exmoor ramble.

Porlock's **tourist office** is at West End, High St (Easter–Oct Mon–Sat 10am–5pm, Sun 10am–1pm; Nov–Easter Mon–Fri & Sun 10am–1pm; ☎01643/863150, ⓦwww.porlock.co.uk). The best **accommodation** in town is on the High Street, where you'll find the Victorian *Lorna Doone Hotel* (☎01643/862404; ❷) and the smaller and quainter *Cottage* (☎01643/862687; ❸) – both serve snacks, meals and teas. Porlock has a central **campsite** *Sparkhayes Farm* (☎01643/862470; closed Nov–March), signposted off the main road near the *Lorna Doone*.

If you walk two miles west over the reclaimed marshland, you'll come to the tiny harbour of **PORLOCK WEIR**, a peaceful, sheltered spot with a pub and a hotel. An easy two-mile stroll west from here along the Coast Path brings you to **St Culbone**, a tiny church – claimed to be the country's smallest – buried among woods once inhabited by a leper colony.

Lynton

West from Porlock, the road climbs 1350ft in less than three miles, though cyclists and drivers might prefer the gentler and more scenic toll-road alternative to the direct uphill trawl. Nine miles along the coast, on the Devon side of the county border, the Victorian resort of **LYNTON** perches above a lofty gorge with splendid views over the sea. Almost completely cut off from the rest of the country for most of its history, the village struck lucky during the Napoleonic wars, when frustrated Grand Tourists – unable to visit their usual continental haunts – discovered in Lynton a domestic piece of Swiss landscape. Coleridge and Hazlitt trudged over to Lynton from the Quantocks, but the greatest spur to the village's popularity came with the publication in 1869 of R.D. Blackmore's Exmoor melodrama *Lorna Doone*, a book based on the outlaw clans who inhabited these parts in the seventeenth century. The imposing **town hall** on Lee Road epitomizes the Victorian–Edwardian accent of the village. It was the gift of publisher George Newnes, who also donated the nearby hydraulic **cliff railway** connecting Lynton with Lynmouth (March to mid-July & mid-Sept to Nov daily 9am–7pm; mid-July to mid-Sept daily 9am–10pm; £1).

Lynton's **tourist office** is in the town hall (Easter–Oct Mon–Sat 9.30am–5.30pm, Sun 9.30am–5pm; Nov–Easter Mon–Sat 10am–4pm; ℡01598/752225). There's a good choice of **B&Bs** here, cheapest along Lee Road, including the Victorian *The Turret* at no. 33 (℡01598/753284; ❶), built by the same engineer who built the cliff railway. The more central *St Vincent* (℡01598/752244, ℮keenstvincent@lineone.net; ❶), a whitewashed, Georgian house on Castle Hill, has spacious bedrooms and a garden, and the *Lynhurst*, Lyn Way (℡01598/752241, ℮lynhurst@demon.co.uk; ❸) has striking views over the valley. There is a **youth hostel** (℡01598/753237) in a homely Victorian house about one mile inland from Lynton's centre, and signposted off Lynbridge Road. Pick up wholefoods and quality picnic fare from *Gourmet Organix* at 4 Queen St.

Walks from Lynton and Lynmouth

As well as the draws of the coastal path, there are several popular walks inland in this region. The one-and-a-half-mile tramp to **Watersmeet**, for example, follows the East Lyn River to where it is joined by Hoar Oak Water, a tranquil spot transformed into a roaring torrent after a bout of rain. From the fishing lodge here – now owned by the National Trust and open as a café and shop in summer – you can branch off on a range of less-trodden paths, such as the three-quarters-of-a-mile route south to **Hillsford Bridge**, the confluence of Hoar Oak and Farley Water.

North of Watersmeet, a path climbs up **Countisbury Hill** and the higher **Butter Hill** (nearly 1000ft) giving riveting views of Lynton, Lynmouth and the north Devon coast, and there is also a track leading to the lighthouse at **Foreland Point**, close to the coastal path. East from Lynmouth you can reach the point via a fine sheltered shingle beach at the foot of Countisbury Hill – one of a number of tiny coves that are easily accessible on either side of the estuary.

From Lynton, an undemanding expedition takes you west along the North Walk, a mile-long path leading to the **Valley of the Rocks**, a steeply curved heathland dominated by rugged rock formations. At the far end of the valley, herds of wild goats range free, as they have done here for centuries.

Lynmouth

Five hundred feet below, **LYNMOUTH** the junction and estuary of the East and West Lyn rivers, in a spot des... Gainsborough as "the most delightful place for a landscape painter... try can boast". The pictur-esque scene was shattered in August 1952 ...mouth was almost washed away by floodwaters coming off Exmoor, a[nd] ...of which there are many reminders around the village. Having recovere[d] ...m, Lynmouth is only ruf-fled now by the summer crowds, though noth... compromise the village's unique location. Shelley spent his honeym[oon]... with his 16-year-old bride Harriet Westbrook, making time in his nine... sojourn to write his polemical *Queen Mab* – two different houses claim ...been the Shelleys' love-nest. In summer, the harbour offers boat trips an[d] ...expeditions, and you can explore the **Glen Lyn Gorge** up the wood[y] ...cy with its walks and waterfalls and displays of the uses and dangers ...power (daily 9am–dusk; exhibition Easter–Oct 10am–dusk; £3) – this ...e course taken by the destructive floods of 1952.

Lynmouth has a **National Park Visitor Centre** on the sea, daily 10am–5pm; Nov, Dec & Feb–Easter Sat & Sun 11am–(Easter–Oct 752509). The most inspiring place to stay here is *Harbour Point*, (☎01598/on the harbour at 1 The Esplanade, (☎01598/752321; ❷; closed **&B** right or you might opt for the posh *Shelley's Hotel*, right next to the Glen –April), (☎01598/753219; ❹), where you can sleep in the room supposed to ... Gorge occupied by the poet – he apparently left without paying his bill – or t[he] *Rock House Hotel*, Harbourside (☎01598/753508, ✉dave@ rockh.freeserve..., ❸), which also serves scones in the garden, snacks at the bar and meals i... **restaurant**. The *Village Inn*, Lynmouth Street, does inexpensive lunches a... dinners, including vegetarian options, though you'll find better food at the tra-ditional and fairly expensive *Rising Sun*, on the Harbourside.

Cornwall

When D.H. Lawrence wrote that being in **Cornwall** was "like being at a win-dow and looking out of England", he wasn't just thinking of its geographical extremity. Virtually unaffected by the Roman conquest, Cornwall was for cen-turies the last haven for a **Celtic culture** elsewhere eradicated by the Saxons – a land where princes communed with Breton troubadours, where chroniclers and scribes composed the epic tales of Arthurian heroism, and where itinerant monks from Welsh and Irish monasteries disseminated an elemental and vision-ary Christianity. Primitive granite crosses and a crop of Celtic saints remain as traces of this formative period, and though the Cornish language had ebbed away by the eighteenth century, it is recalled in Celtic place names that in many cases have grown more exotic as they have become corrupted over time.

Another strand of Cornwall's folkloric character comes from the **smugglers** who thrived here right up until the last century, exploiting the sheltered creeks and hidden anchorages of the southern coasts. For many fishing vil-

△ Surfers, Bude Beach

lages, contraband provided an important secondary income, as did the looting of the ships that regularly came to grief on the reefs and rocks. Further distinguishing it from its neighbour, Cornwall has also had a strong **industrial economy**, based mainly on the mining of **copper** and **tin** in the north, and on the deposits of **china clay** in the south, still being mined today in the area around St Austell.

Nowadays, of course, Cornwall's most flourishing industry is tourism. The repercussions of the holiday business on Cornwall have been uneven, for instance shamefully defacing **Land's End** but leaving Cornwall's other great promontory, **Lizard Point**, untainted. All the stops are pulled out in the thronged resorts of **Falmouth** and **Newquay**, though the effects of mass tourism have been more destructive in smaller, quainter places, such as **Mevagissey**, **Polperro** and **Padstow**, whose genuine charms can fade from view in full season. Other villages, such as **Charlestown**, **Port Isaac** and **Boscastle**, are hardly touched, however, and you couldn't wish for anything more remote than **Bodmin Moor**, a tract of wilderness in the heart of Cornwall – and even **Tintagel**, site of what is fondly known as King Arthur's castle, has preserved its sense of desolation. Near **St Austell**, the spectacular and high-profile **Eden Project**, located in an abandoned clay pit, has pointed the way to a less destructive and exploitative form of crowd-pulling, while other places – such **St Ives**, **Fowey** and **Bude** – have reached a happy compromise with the seasonal influx, or else are saved from saturation by sheer distance, as is the case with the **Isles of Scilly**.

From Looe to Veryan Bay

The southeast strip of the Cornish coast from Looe to Veryan Bay holds a string of medieval harbour towns tarnished by various degrees of commercialization, but there are also a few spots where you can experience the best of Cornwall, including some wonderful coastline. The main rail stop is **St Austell**, the capital of Cornwall's china clay industry, though there is a branch line connecting nearby **Par** with the north coast at Newquay. To the east of St Austell Bay, the touristy **Polperro** and **Looe** are easily accessible by bus from Plymouth, and there's a rail link to Looe from Liskeard. The estuary town of **Fowey**, in a niche of Cornwall closely associated with the author Daphne Du Maurier, is most easily reached by bus from St Austell and Par, as is **Mevagissey**, to the west.

Looe

LOOE was drawing crowds as early as 1800, when the first "bathing-machines" were wheeled out, but the arrival of the railway in 1879 was what really packed its beaches. Though Looe now touts itself as something of a shark-fishing centre, most people come here for the sand, the handiest stretch being the beach in front of East Looe – the busier half of the river-divided town. Away from the river mouth, you'll find a cleaner spot to swim a mile eastwards at **Millendreath**. If you're not enticed by Looe's boating and bathing attractions, there's always the **Old Guildhall Museum** (May–Sept Mon–Fri & Sun 11.30am–4.30pm; £1), a diverse collection of maritime models and exhibits, though none so interesting as the building itself, a fifteenth-century construction preserving its prisoners' cells and raised magistrates' benches.

East Looe's **tourist office** is at the Guildhall on Fore Street (Easter & May to mid-Sept daily 10am–5pm; April & mid-Sept to Oct daily 10am–2pm; ☎01503/262072). There's plenty of **accommodation** here: try *Osborne House*, a converted cottage in Lower Chapel Street (☎01503/262970; ❷; closed Nov & Jan), or the chintzier *Sea Breeze*, a three-storey B&B further up the same street (☎01503/263131, ✉johnjenkin@sbgh.freeserve.co.uk; ❶); both are close to the beach and harbour. *Osborne House* also has a moderately priced **restaurant**.

Polperro

Neighbouring **POLPERRO** is smaller and quainter, but has a similar feel. The surrounding cliffs and the tightly packed houses rising on each side of the pretty harbour have an undeniable charm, and the tangle of lanes is little changed since the village's heyday of smuggling and pilchard fishing, but the "discovery" of Polperro has almost ruined it, and its straggling main street – the Coombes – is now an unbroken row of tourist shops and fast-food outlets. The best places to **stay** include the *House on Props*, Talland Street (☎01503/272310; ❷), and the next-door *Talland House* (☎01503/273176; ❶). On the Coombes, the *Plantation Café* provides cream teas and **snacks** and has some outdoor seating (closed Sat), and the non-smoking *Kitchen* **restaurant** (☎01503/272780) is especially popular with vegetarians and seafood fans.

Fowey and around

The ten miles west from Polperro to Polruan are among the best stretches of the coastal path in south Cornwall, giving access to some beautiful secluded sand beaches. Regular ferries cross the River Fowey from Polruan, giving a fine view of the quintessential Cornish port of **FOWEY** (pronounced "Foy"), a cascade of neat, pale terraces at the mouth of one of the peninsula's greatest rivers. The major port on the county's south coast in the fourteenth century, Fowey finally became so ambitious that it provoked Edward IV to strip the town of its military capability, though it continued to thrive commercially, coming into its own as the leading port for china clay shipments in the nineteenth century. In addition to the bulkier freighters sailing from wharves north of the town, the harbour today is crowded with trawlers and yachts, giving the town a brisk, purposeful character lacking in many of Cornwall's south-coast ports.

Fowey's steep layout centres on the church of **St Fimbarrus**, a distinctive fifteenth-century construction replacing a church that was sacked by the French. Next door, the **Literary Centre** on South Street is a small exhibition including a twelve-minute video of Daphne Du Maurier's life and work (daily 10am–5pm; free), while behind the church stands **Place House**, an extravagance belonging to the local Treffry family, with a Victorian Gothic tower grafted onto the fifteenth- and sixteenth-century fortified building. Below the church, the **Ship Inn**, sporting some fine Elizabethan panelling and plaster ceilings, was originally home to the Rashleighs – a recurring name in the annals of this region – and held the local Roundhead HQ during the Civil War. From here, Fore Street, Lostwithiel Street and the Esplanade fan out, the **Esplanade** leading to a footpath that gives access to some splendid walks around the coast. Past the remains of a blockhouse that once supported a defensive chain hung across the river's mouth, is the small beach of **Readymoney Cove**. Close by stand the ruins of **St Catherine's Castle**, built by Thomas Treffry on the orders of Henry VIII, and offering fine views across the estuary.

Practicalities

Separated from eastern routes by its river, Fowey is most accessible by #24 **buses** from St Austell. There's a small **tourist office** in the town's post office on Custom House Hill (May–Sept Mon–Fri 9am–5.30pm, Sat 9am–5pm, Sun 10am–5pm; Oct–April Mon–Sat 9am–5.30pm; ☎01726/833616). All of the central pubs offer **B&B**: try the *Ship* (☎01726/832230; ❷) or the *Safe Harbour* (☎01726/833379; ❷), both on Lostwithiel Street. Alternatively, there's the *Dwelling House*, 6 Fore St (☎01726/833662; ❶), or, up Daglands Road from The Esplanade, *Seahorses* at 14 St Fimbarrus Rd (☎01726/833148, ✉jandh@ globalnet.co.uk; no smoking; ❶; closed Oct–April), which provides stylish rooms, bathrobes and offers Dutch pancakes for breakfast, and has a banjo-playing owner. There is a **youth hostel** outside the nearby riverside hamlet of Golant at *Penquite House*, a Georgian mansion with views over the valley (☎01726/833507, ⊛www.yha.org.uk).

Fowey has some good seafood **restaurants**; among the best is *Ellis's* at 3 The Esplanade (☎01726/832359), specializing in lobster, and *Food For Thought* on the quay, offers a fixed-price menu on weekdays (☎01726/832221) – both are quite formal, expensive places. The area is also well provided with good **pubs**, some of which can be sampled on walkabouts, such as Golant's *Fisherman's Arms*, the *Old Ferry Inn* at Bodinnick, which also has comfortable rooms (☎01726/870237; ❷), and Polruan's excellent *Lugger Inn*.

St Austell and around

It was the discovery of china clay, or kaolin, in the downs to the north of **ST AUSTELL** that spurred the town's growth in the eighteenth century. An essential ingredient in the production of porcelain, kaolin had until then only been produced in northern China, where a high ridge, or *kao-lin*, was the sole known source of the raw material. Still a vital part of Cornwall's economy, the clay is now mostly exported for use in the manufacture of paper, as well as paint and medicines. The conical spoil heaps left by the mines are a feature of the local landscape, especially on Hensbarrow Downs to the north, the great green and white mounds making an eerie sight.

St Austell's nearest link to the sea is at **CHARLESTOWN**, an easy downhill walk from the centre of town. This unassuming and unspoilt port is named after the entrepreneur Charles Rashleigh, who in 1791 began work on the harbour in what was then a small fishing community two miles south of St Austell, widening its streets to accommodate the clay wagons daily passing through. Behind the harbour, the **Shipwreck Museum** (March–Oct daily 10am–6pm; £4.45) is entered through tunnels once used to convey the clay to the docks, and shows a good collection of photos and relics as well as tableaux of historical scenes.

On each side of the dock the coarse sand and stone **beaches** have small rock pools, above which cliff walks lead around St Austell Bay. Eastwards, you soon arrive at overdeveloped **Carlyon Bay**, whose main resort is **Par**. The beaches here get clogged with clay – the best swimming is to be found by pressing on to the sheltered crescent of **Polkerris**. The easternmost limit of St Austell Bay is marked by **Gribbin Head**, near which stands Menabilly House, where Daphne Du Maurier lived for 24 years – it was the model for the "Manderley" of *Rebecca*. The house is not open to the public, but you can walk down to Polridmouth Cove, where Rebecca met her watery end.

Trains on the main London–Penzance line serve St Austell, with most services also stopping at Par. **Bus** service #24 links St Austell, Charlestown, Par and

Polkerris. Charlestown has two really attractive places **to stay**: *T'Gallants* (℡01726/70203; ❷), a smart Georgian B&B at the back of the harbour where cream teas are served in the garden, and *Broad Meadow House*, behind the Shipwreck Centre on Quay Road (℡01726/76636, ✉BestTribe@tiny-world.co.uk; ❶). Behind *T'Gallants*, the *Rashleigh Arms* offers real ale and a range of **food**, though the most highly commended **pub** in the area is the *Rashleigh Inn* at Polkerris.

The Eden Project

A disused clay pit four miles northeast of St Austell holds the newest and high-est-profile of Cornwall's attractions, the **Eden Project** (daily: March–Oct 10am–6pm; Nov–Feb 10am–4.30pm; £9.50; ⓦwww.edenproject.com), reach-able on bus #T9 from St Austell station and #T10 (summer only) from Newquay, and signposted on most roads in the area. Occupying a 160-foot-deep crater, the project showcases the diversity of the planet's plant-life in an imagi-native, sometimes wacky, but refreshingly ungimmicky style. The whole site is stunningly landscaped with an array of various crops and flower beds, but at centre stage are the vast geodesic "biomes", or conservatories made up of eco-friendly Teflon-coated, hexagonal panels. One cluster holds groves of olive and citrus trees, cacti and other plants more usually found in the warm, temperate zones of the Mediterranean, southern Africa and southwestern USA, while the larger group contains plants from the tropics, including teak and mahogany trees, and there's a waterfall and river gushing through. Equally impressive are the external grounds, where plantations of bamboo, tea, hops, hemp and tobac-co are interspersed with brilliant swathes of flowers. The whole "living theatre" presents a constantly changing spectacle, and should ideally be visited in differ-ent seasons. Allow at least half a day for a full exploration, but arrive early to avoid congestion. There are timed "story-telling" sessions, a lawn-carpeted arena where Celtic and other music is played, and good food on hand.

Mevagissey to Veryan Bay

MEVAGISSEY was once known for the construction of fast vessels, used for carrying contraband as well as pilchards. Today the tiny port might display a few stacks of lobster pots, but the real business is tourism, and in summer the maze of back streets is saturated with day-trippers, converging on the inner harbour and overflowing onto the large sand beach at Pentewan a mile to the north. A couple of miles northwest of Mevagissey, the **Lost Gardens of Heligan** (daily: late March to late Oct 10am–6pm, last entry 4.30pm; late Oct to late March 10am–5pm, last entry 3.30pm; £5.50; ⓦwww.heligan.com) are a fascinating resurrection of a Victorian garden which had fallen into neglect and was rescued from a ten-foot covering of brambles by Tim Smit, the vision-ary instigator of the Eden Project (see above). The abundant palm trees, giant Himalayan rhododendrons, immaculate vinery and glasshouses scattered about all look as if they've been transplanted from warmer climes. You can get here on either the #26 or #26a bus, both of which run between St Austell and Mevagissey.

Four miles south of Mevagissey juts the most striking headland on Cornwall's southern coast, **Dodman Point**, cause of many a wreck and topped by a stark granite cross built by a local parson as a seamark in 1896. The promontory holds the substantial remains of an Iron Age fort, with an earthwork bulwark cutting right across the point. Curving away to the west, the elegant parabola of **Veryan Bay** is barely touched by commercialism. Here you'll find a string of exquisite inlets and coves, including **Hemmick Beach**, a fine place for a dip with rocky outcrops affording a measure of privacy, and **Porthluney Cove**, a crescent of sand whose centrepiece is the battlemented **Caerhays Castle** (mid-March to mid-April Mon–Fri 2–4pm; gardens mid-March to mid-May Mon–Fri 10am–4pm; house £3.50; garden £3.50; combined ticket £6), built in 1808 by John Nash and surrounded by beautiful gardens. A little farther on, the minuscule and whitewashed **Portloe** is fronted by jagged black rocks that throw up fountains of seaspray, giving it a good, end-of-the-road kind of atmosphere.

Sequestered inland, **VERYAN** has a pretty village green and pond, but is best known for its curious circular white houses built in the last century by one Reverend Jeremiah Trist. A lane from Veryan leads down to one of the cleanest swimming spots on Cornwall's southern coast, **Pendower Beach**. Two-thirds of a mile long and backed by dunes, Pendower joins with the neighbouring **Carne Beach** at low tide to create a long sandy continuum.

Practicalities

From St Austell's train station, **buses** #26 and #26A leave hourly for Mevagissey, while Veryan and Portloe are reachable on #51 from Truro. Mevagissey's best central **accommodation** option is the fifteenth-century *Fountain Inn*, (℡01726/842320, ✉fountain_meva@hotmail.com; ❷), on Cliff Street, off East Quay; alternatively try *Lawn House*, 1 Church Lane (℡01726/842754; ❷; phone ahead Nov–Easter), with candelabra and brass beds. The nearest **youth hostel** (℡01726/843234) is in **Boswinger**, half a mile from Hemmick Beach and difficult to reach without your own transport, served infrequently by some #26 buses. In **Veryan**, head for the *Elerkey Guest House* (℡01872/501261, ⓦwww.elerkey-guest-house.co.uk; ❷), an ex-farmhouse with a spacious garden and adjoining art gallery and coffee shop; it's the first on the left after the church. The *New Inn* serves pub meals and also provides B&B (℡01872/501362; ❷).

Most of Mevagissey's **restaurants** specialize in fish – try the large harbourfront *Shark's Fin Hotel*. The *Fountain Inn* and the *Ship Inn* on Fore Street both offer pub grub.

Truro, Falmouth and St Mawes

Lush tranquillity collides with frantic tourist activity around **Carrick Roads**, the complex estuary basin to the south of **Truro**, a stop on the main line to Penzance and the region's main centre for transport and accommodation. At the end of a branch line from Truro and at the mouth of the Carrick Roads, **Falmouth** is the major resort hereabouts, and the site of one of Cornwall's mightiest castles, Pendennis. Its sister fort lies across the Carrick Roads in **St Mawes**, the main settlement on the **Roseland** peninsula, a luxuriant backwater of woods and sheltered creeks between the River Fal and the sea.

Truro

TRURO, Cornwall's administrative capital, has a distinctly small-scale provincial feel, even if its Georgian villas do reflect the prosperity that came with the tin-mining boom of the 1800s. Blurring the town's overall identity, its modern shopping centre stands alongside the powerful but chronologically confused **Cathedral**. Completed in 1910, this was the first Anglican cathedral to be built in England since St Paul's in London, but it incorporates part of the fabric of the old parish church that previously occupied the site. The airy interior's best feature is its neo-Gothic baptistry, complete with emphatically pointed arches and elaborate roof vaulting. To the right of the choir, St Mary's aisle is a relic of the original Perpendicular building, other fragments of which adorn the walls, including – in the north transept – a colourful Jacobean memorial to local Parliamentarian John Robartes and his wife.

Truro's other unmissable attraction is the **Royal Cornwall Museum** (Mon–Sat 10am–5pm; £3), housed in an elegant Georgian building on River Street. The exhibits include minerals, Celtic inscriptions and paintings by Cornish artists.

Truro's **tourist office** is on Boscawen Street (Easter–May & Sept Mon–Fri 9am–5.30pm, Sat 9.30am–1pm; June–Aug Mon–Fri 9am–5.30pm, Sat 9.30am–5.30pm; Oct–Easter Mon–Fri 9am–5pm, Sat 9.30am–1pm; ☏01872/274555). **Buses** stop nearby at Lemon Quay, or near the **train station** on Richmond Hill. Among the best **accommodation** choices are the *Gables*, near the train station at 49 Treyew Rd (☏01872/242318; ❶), the *Bay Tree*, 28 Ferris Town (☏01872/240274; ❶), a restored Georgian house halfway between the station and the centre, and *Patmos*, 8 Burley Close, off Barrack Lane, where Lemon Street meets Falmouth Road (☏01872/278018; no smoking; ❶). A good selection of Truro's **restaurants** lie on or around Kenwyn Street, including *Number Ten* at no. 10, where you'll find inexpensive international dishes (☏01872/272363), and the *Feast*, at no. 15, which offers wholefoods and a choice of Belgian beers (daytime only; closed Sun). Elsewhere in town, *Pizza Express* on Boscawen Street is housed in the imposing old Coinage Hall, which sports carpets on the walls alongside portraits of various notables. On the corner of Frances and Castle streets, the *Wig and Pen* is a decent **pub** with bar food, real ale and live jazz.

Falmouth

The construction of Pendennis Castle on the southern point of Carrick Roads in the sixteenth century prepared the ground for the growth of **FALMOUTH**, then no more than a fishing village. The building of its deepwater harbour was proposed a century later by Sir John Killigrew, and Falmouth's prosperity was assured when in 1689 it became chief base of the fast Falmouth Packets, which sped mail to the Americas. However, recent years have seen the port's character submerged beneath waves of tourist traffic attracted to the lush beaches to the south of town, and the long **High Street** and its continuations Market and Church streets are now crammed with humdrum bars and cafés. The southern end of Arwenack Street, though, does have the Tudor remains of the Killigrews' **Arwenack House** (closed to the public); the peculiar granite pyramid standing opposite, built in 1737, is probably intended to commemorate the family, though its exact significance has never been clear.

Falmouth's links with the sea are explored at the **Maritime Museum** at Bell's Court, at the Moor end of the High Street (Easter–Oct daily 10am–5pm; Oct–Easter Mon–Sat 10am–3pm; £2.20), which tracks the evolution of boat design – rather a lacklustre collection at present, but soon to be revitalized when it transfers in 2002 to a purpose-built exhibition space on Arwenack Street. Apart from this, the centre of town only offers a clamber up the precipitous 111 steps of **Jacob's Ladder** from the Moor, the old town's main square, to give a bird's-eye view of the harbour, and the numerous **boat cruises** in summer which leave from the Prince of Wales Pier, below the Moor, for exploring the Carrick Roads.

The highlight of Falmouth is **Pendennis Castle** (daily: April–June & Sept 10am–6pm; July & Aug 9am–6pm; Oct 10am–5pm; Nov–March 10am–4pm; £3.80; EH), standing sentinel at the tip of the promontory separating Carrick Roads from Falmouth Bay. The stronghold shows little evidence of its five-month siege by the Parliamentarians during the Civil War, which ended only when half its defenders had died and the rest had been starved into submission. Though less refined than its sister castle at St Mawes, Pendennis enjoys an unrivalled site, facing right out to sea on its own pointed peninsula, the stout ramparts offering the best all-round views of Carrick Roads and Falmouth Bay. In August, the castle grounds stay open late for concerts and other events. Round Pendennis Point, south of the centre, stretches a long sandy bay with various **beaches** backed by expensive hotels. If you wanted to swim, the best spot is from **Swanpool Beach**, accessible by cliff path from the more popular **Gyllyngvase Beach** – or walk a couple of miles farther on to **Maenporth**, from where there are some fine cliff-top walks.

Falmouth's **tourist office** is off the Moor, on Killigrew Street (Easter–June & Sept Mon–Thurs & Sat 9.30am–5.30pm, Fri 9am–4.45pm; July & Aug also Sun 10am–2pm; Oct–Easter Mon–Thurs 9am–1pm & 2–5pm, Fri 9am–1pm & 2–4.45pm; ☎01326/312300, ⓦwww.falmouth-sw-cornwall.co.uk). Most of the town's **accommodation** is near the train station and beach area; top choices include *Brandywine Lodge*, 3 Bay View Crescent (☎01326/318709; ❶), a cosy cottage just off Castle Drive, and the *Melvill House Hotel*, 52 Melvill Rd (☎01326/316645; ❷), run by a Franco-Scottish couple. Expect to pay more for places nearer the beaches, such as *Gyllyngvase House Hotel*, a staid but comfortable choice on Gyllyngvase Rd (☎01326/312956; ❸), and *Chellowdene* (☎01326/314950; ❸; closed Oct–April) on the parallel Gyllyngvase Hill. You can **eat** in congenial surroundings at *No. 33*, 33 High St (☎01326/211944; closed Sun), an easy-going café/restaurant, while the best fish in town is to be found off the main drag at the *Seafood Bar*, Lower Quay Hill (☎01326/315129; closed lunch, plus all Sun & Mon), where thick crab soup is a speciality. The *Quayside Inn*, further up on Arwenack Street, is the pick of the **pubs**.

St Mawes and the Roseland peninsula

Stuck at the end of a prong of land at the bottom of Carrick Roads, and reached on frequent **ferries** from Falmouth's Prince of Wales Pier, the secluded, unhurried town of **ST MAWES** has an attractive walled seafront overlooked by villas and abundant gardens. Just out of sight at the end of the seafront stands the small and pristine **St Mawes Castle** (April–Sept daily 10am–6pm; Oct daily 10am–5pm; Nov–March Wed–Sun 10am–1pm & 2–4pm; £2.70; EH). Built during the reign of Henry VIII to a cloverleaf design, its round central keep surrounded by robust gun-emplacements, the castle owes its excellent condition to its early surrender during the Civil War when it was placed under siege by Parliamentary forces in 1646. The dungeons and gun installations contain various artillery exhibits as well as some background on local social history.

Outside St Mawes, you could spend a pleasant afternoon poking around the **Roseland peninsula** between the Percuil River and the eastern shore of Carrick Roads. Two and a half miles north, the scattered hamlet of **ST JUST-IN-ROSELAND** holds the strikingly picturesque church of St Just, surrounded by palms and subtropical shrubbery, its gravestones tumbling down to the water's edge. In summer, there's a **ferry** from St Mawes to the southern arm of the Roseland Peninsula, which holds the equally charming twelfth- to thirteenth-century church of **St Anthony-in-Roseland**.

St Mawes makes an attractive – though fairly pricey – **place to stay**. The best budget choices are a ten-minute walk up from the seafront on Newton Road: *Little Newton* (℡01326/270664; ❷) and *Newton Farm*, next door (℡01326/270427; ❷). Otherwise, you'll have to dig deep for the upmarket *St Mawes Hotel*, located right on the seafront with glorious views over the estuary (℡01326/270266; ❽; closed Nov to mid-Feb) – or else cross over to Falmouth, where there's plenty more choice. The *Victory Inn* is a fine old oak-beamed **pub** just off the seafront, which also serves seafood meals.

The Lizard peninsula

The **Lizard peninsula** – from the Celtic *lys ardh*, or "high point" – preserves a thankfully undeveloped appearance in contrast to many other areas of Cornwall. If this flat and treeless expanse can be said to have a centre, it is **Helston**, a junction for buses running from Falmouth and Truro to the spartan villages of the peninsula's interior and the tiny fishing ports on its coast.

The east coast to Lizard Point

To the north of the peninsula, the snug hamlets sprinkled in the valley of the **River Helford** are a complete contrast to the rugged character of most of the Lizard. At the river's mouth stands **MAWNAN**, whose granite church of St Mawnan-in-Meneage is dedicated to the sixth-century Welsh missionary St Maunanus – *Meneage*, means "land of monks". Upstream on the south side, **Frenchman's Creek** is one of a splay of creeks and arcane inlets running off the river, and was the inspiration for Daphne Du Maurier's novel of the same name – her evocation of it holds true: "still and soundless, surrounded by the trees, hidden from the eyes of men".

You can get over to the south bank by the seasonal ferry from Helford Passage to Helford, an agreeable old smugglers' haunt where you can have teas and snacks at *Rose Cottage* or pub lunches in the *Shipwright's Arms*, overlooking the river. South of here, on the B3293, the road splits: left to **ST KEVERNE**, an inland village whose tidy square is flanked by two pubs and a church, right to meet the sea at **COVERACK**, a fishing port at one end of a sheltered bay. The handful of **B&Bs** and restaurants here make this a great place to hole up for a few days: try the pleasant and friendly *Fernleigh* (℡01326/280626; ❶), on Chymbloth Way, a turn-off from Harbour Road, or the diminutive *Bakery Cottage* (℡01326/280474; ❶), just off the seafront. There's a **youth hostel** overlooking the bay just west of Coverack's centre (℡01326/280687). For **eating**, the *Old Lifeboat House Seafood Restaurant* (℡01326/280899; closed Mon & Oct–Easter) is pricey and often fully booked, but the fish is superb, and you can pick up first-class fish and chips from the attached takeaway.

Beyond the safe and clean swimming spot of **Kennack Sands**, the south tip of the promontory, **Lizard Point**, is marked by a plain lighthouse and a couple of low-key cafés and gift shops. Sheltered from the ceaselessly churning sea, a tiny cove holds a disused lifeboat station. Behind the point, a road and foot-path lead a mile inland to the nondescript village called simply **THE LIZARD**, which holds several more **accommodation** options, including the non-smoking *Caerthillian*, behind the *Top House* pub in the centre (℡01326/290019, ⓦwww.connexions.co.uk/caerthillian; ❷) and *Parc Brawse House* (℡01326/290466; ❷) on Penmenner Road. The peninsula's best-known beach, **Kynance Cove**, lies a mile westward. With its sheer hundred-foot cliffs, its stacks and arches of serpentine rock and its offshore islands, the beach has a wild grandeur, and the water quality is excellent – but take care not to be stranded by the tide.

The west coast

Four miles north of Kynance Cove, the inland village of **MULLION** has a fifteenth- to sixteenth-century church dedicated to the Breton **St Mellane** (or Malo), with a dog-door for canine churchgoers. In the centre of the village, behind an enclosed garden at the top of Nansmellyon Road, the *Old Vicarage* (☎01326/240509; ❸) is an elegant **B&B**, and a mile south of Mullion on the coast, next to the car park above **Mullion Cove**, *Criggan Mill* (☎01326/240496; ❷) provides accommodation in timber lodges in a narrow field 200 yards up from the sea. Sheltered behind a lovely harbour and more rock stacks, there's a small beach here, though the neighbouring sands at **Polurrian** and **Poldhu**, to the north, are better and attract surfers. At the cliff-edge, the **Marconi Monument** marks the spot from which the first transatlantic radio transmission was made in 1901. Three miles further north, strong currents make it unsafe to swim at the beautiful beach at **Loe Bar**, a strip of shingle which separates the freshwater **Loe Pool** from the sea. The elongated Pool is one of two places claiming to be where the sword Excalibur was restored to its watery source (the other is on Bodmin Moor), and there's a path running along its western shore as far as Helston, five miles north, making a fine **walk**.

A mile or two up the coast from Loe Bar, **PORTHLEVEN** is a sizeable port that once served to export tin ore from the inland Stannary town of **HELSTON**, the main transport junction and centre for the Lizard peninsula. The town is best known for its **Furry Dance** (or Flora Dance), which dates from the seventeenth century. Held on May 8 (unless this falls on a Sun or Mon, when the procession takes place on the nearest Sat), it's a stately procession of top-hatted men and summer-frocked women performing a solemn dance through the town's streets and gardens. You can learn something about it and absorb plenty of other local history and lore in the eclectic **Helston Folk Museum** (Mon–Sat 10am–5pm; £2), housed in former market buildings behind the Guildhall on Church Street. Helston has the peninsula's only **tourist office** at 79 Meneage St (Aug Mon–Fri 10am–1pm & 2–4.30pm, Sat 10am–4.30pm; rest of year closes 1pm on Sat; ☎01326/565431). For a drink or a **pub** snack, check out the *Blue Anchor*, 50 Coinagehall St, a fifteenth-century monastery rest house, now a cramped pub with flagstone floors and mellow Spingo beer brewed on the premises in three strengths. Next door to the pub, the **B&B** at 52 Coinagehall St (☎01326/569334; ❷) makes a smart night-stop, with solid old furnishings.

The Penwith peninsula

Though more densely populated than the Lizard, the **Penwith peninsula** is a more rugged landscape, with a raw appeal that is still encapsulated by **Land's End**, despite the commercial paraphernalia superimposed on that headland. The seascapes, the quality of the light and the slow tempo of the local fishing communities made this area a hotbed of artistic activity towards the end of the nineteenth century, when the painters of **Newlyn**, near **Penzance**, established a distinctive school of painting. More innovative figures – among them Ben Nicholson, Barbara Hepworth and Naum Gabo – were soon afterwards to make **St Ives** one of England's liveliest cultural communities, and their enduring influence is illustrated in the St Ives branch of the Tate Gallery, showcasing the Modern artists associated with the locality.

Penwith is far more easily toured than the Lizard, with a road circling its coastline and a better network of public transport from the two main towns, St Ives and Penzance, which hold most of the accommodation.

Penzance and around

Occupying a sheltered position at the northwest corner of Mount's Bay, **PENZANCE** has always been a major port, but most traces of the medieval town were obliterated at the end of the sixteenth century by a Spanish raiding party. Today the dominant style of Penzance is Georgian, particularly at the top of **Market Jew Street** (from *Marghas Jew*, meaning "Thursday Market"), which climbs from the harbour and the train and bus stations. At the top of the street is the green-domed Victorian **Market House**, before which stands a statue of **Humphry Davy** (1778–1829), the local woodcarver's son who pioneered the science of electrochemistry and invented the life-saving miners' safety-lamp, which his statue holds.

Turn left here into **Chapel Street**, which has some of the town's finest buildings, including the flamboyant **Egyptian House**, built in 1835 to contain a geological museum but subsequently abandoned until its restoration twenty-odd years ago. Across the street, the **Union Hotel** dates from the seventeenth century, and originally housed the town's assembly rooms. If your interest is roused by the art scene that flourished hereabouts at the turn of the nineteenth century, head for **Penlee House Gallery and Museum** on Morrab Road (Mon–Sat: May–Sept 10am–5pm; Oct–April 10.30am–4.30pm; £2, free on Sat), which holds the biggest collection of the works of the Newlyn School – impressionistic harbour scenes, frequently sentimentalized but often bathed in an evocatively luminous light. There are frequent exhibitions, and also displays on local history. At the bottom of Morrab Road, the Art Deco **Jubilee Pool** (mid-May to mid-Sept daily 10.30am–6pm; £1.70) bulges out of the Promenade into Mount's Bay, a tidal, salt-water (though chlorinated) open-air swimming pool, built to mark the Silver Jubilee of George V in 1935. It's a classic example of the style, and non-swimmers can stroll around (60p) to get a closer view of the pool and bay.

Practicalities

Penzance is the terminus for rail services from London and Birmingham; the **train and bus stations** are right next to each other on the seafront, and adjacent to the **tourist office** (May–Sept Mon–Fri 9am–5pm, Sat 9am–4pm, Sun 10am–1pm; Oct–April Mon–Fri 9am–5pm, Sat 10am–1pm; ℡01736/362207, ⓦ www.west-cornwall-tourism.co.uk). There are a few inexpensive **B&Bs** nearby, though you should venture further afield for a bit more character. On Chapel Street, there's the seventeenth-century *Trevelyan Hotel* (℡01736/ 362494; ❶) – ask for a top-floor room for the view – or you could soak up the atmosphere in the *Union Hotel* (℡01736/362319; ❸) or the seventeenth-century *Abbey Hotel*, just off Chapel Street on Abbey Street (℡01736/366906, ⓦ www.abbey-hotel.co.uk; ❻). Most cheaper B&Bs are a few minutes' walk west of the centre: try *Kimberley House* at 10 Morrab Rd (℡01736/362727; ❶) or *Holbein House* on Alexandra Road (℡01736/332625; ❶). Alexandra Road is also the location of the *Blue Dolphin* **hostel** (℡01736/363836); the YHA hostel is in a Georgian mansion at Castle Horneck, Alverton (℡01736/

326666, ⓦ www.yha.org.uk), a two-mile hike from the station up Market Je Street into Alverton Road, then turn right at the *Pirate Inn* (or take buses from the station as far as the inn).

On Chapel Street, *Co-Co's Tapas Bar* makes a good spot for coffees and cakes as well as beers and tapas, and you can have various snacks at the relaxed *Blue Snappa*, 18 Market Place (at the top of Chapel Street). Quality cuisine can be had at the ultra-modern and expensive *Abbey Restaurant* in Abbey Street (ⓣ01736/330680; closed Sun & Mon). Vegetarians can choose between the tiny *Dandelions*, at the top of the pedestrianized Causeway Head, or the spacious and relaxed *Brown's*, above a health shop in nearby Bread Street. Chapel Street has a couple of characterful **pubs**, the *Admiral Benbow*, crammed with gaudy ships' figureheads and other nautical items, and the *Turk's Head*, the town's oldest inn, reputed to date back to the thirteenth century.

St Michael's Mount

Buses from Penzance bus station leave every thirty minutes for Marazion, five miles east, from where the medieval chimneys and towers of **St Michael's Mount** (April–Oct Mon–Fri 10.30am–5.30pm, plus most weekends; Nov–March call for opening times; ⓣ01736/710507; £4.50; NT) can be seen a couple of hundred yards offshore. A vision of the archangel Michael led to the building of a church on this granite pile around the fifth century, and within three centuries a Celtic monastery had been founded here. The present building derives from a chapel raised in the eleventh century by Edward the Confessor, who handed over the abbey to the Benedictine monks of Brittany's Mont St Michel, whose island abbey was the model for this one. After the Civil War, when it was used to store arms for the Royalist forces, it became the residence of the St Aubyn family, who still inhabit the castle. A good number of the buildings date from the twelfth century, but the later additions are more interesting, such as the battlemented **chapel** and the seventeenth-century decorations of the Chevy Chase Room, the former refectory. At low tide the promontory can be approached via a cobbled causeway; at high tide there are boats from Marazion (£1).

Mousehole to Land's End

Accounts vary as to the derivation of the name of **MOUSEHOLE** (pronounced "Mowzle"), though it may be from a smugglers' cave just south of town. In any case, the name evokes perfectly this minuscule harbour, cradled in the arms of a granite breakwater three miles south of Penzance. The village attracts more visitors than it can handle, so hang around until the crowds have departed before you walk through its tight tangle of lanes to take in its oldest house, the fourteenth-century Keigwin House (a survival of the 1595 attack when the village was burned by the Spaniards), and/or a drink at the *Ship Inn*, which also has **rooms** (ⓣ01736/731234; ❸) – those with a view are slightly more expensive. Half a mile inland, the churchyard wall at Paul holds a monument to Dolly Pentreath, a resident of Mousehole who died in 1777 and was reputed to have been the last person to speak the Cornish language. The inscription includes a Cornish translation of a verse from the Bible.

Eight miles west lies one of Penwith's best beaches, at **PORTHCURNO**, sheltered between granite cliffs. To one side, steep steps lead up to the rock-hewn **Minack Theatre**, created in the 1930s and since enlarged to hold 750 seats, though the basic Greek-inspired design has remained intact. The spectacular backdrop makes this one of the country's most inspiring theatres – providing the weather holds. The summer season lasts from May to September, presenting a gamut of plays, opera and musicals, with inexpensive tickets (℡01736/810181, Ⓦwww.minack.com). Bring a cushion and a rug. You can also visit the **Exhibition Centre** (daily: April–Sept 9.30am–5.30pm; Oct–March 10am–4pm; closed during performances; £2.50), which allows you to see the theatre and follow the story of its creation through photographs and audiovisual displays. On the shore to the east of Porthcurno, a white pyramid marks the spot where the first transatlantic cables were laid in 1880. On the headland beyond lies an Iron Age fort, **Treryn Dinas**, close to the **Logan Rock**, a seventy-ton rocking stone that was knocked off its perch by a nephew of playwright Oliver Goldsmith and a gang of sailors in 1824. Somehow they replaced the stone, but it never rocked again.

The best way to approach **Land's End** is unarguably on foot along the coastal path. Although nothing can completely destroy the potency of this extreme western tip of England, the colossal theme park thrown up behind this majestic headland comes close to violating irreparably the spirit of the place. The trivializing **Land's End Experience** (daily: Easter–Oct 10am–6pm; Oct–Easter 10am–5pm, or earlier at quiet times; ℡0870/4580099) substitutes various laser displays and unconvincing sound effects for the real open-air experience, but the location is still a public right of way, and once past the paraphernalia, nature takes over. Turf-covered cliffs sixty feet high provide a platform to view the Irish Lady, the Armed Knight, Dr Syntax's Head and the rest of the Land's End outcrops, beyond which you can spot the Longships lighthouse, a mile and a half out to sea, and sometimes the Wolf Rock lighthouse, nine miles southwest, or even the Isles of Scilly, twenty-five miles away.

Whitesand Bay to Zennor

To the north of Land's End the rounded granite cliffs fall away at **Whitesand Bay** to reveal a glistening mile-long shelf of beach that offers the best swimming on the Penwith peninsula. The rollers make for good surfing and boards can be rented at **Sennen Cove**, the more popular southern end of the beach. There are a few places to **stay** around the southern end of the strand, including *Myrtle Cottage* (℡01736/871698; ❷) and the nearby *Polwyn Cottage*, tucked away on Old Coastguard Row (℡01736/871349; ❶). If you don't mind being a few minutes' walk inland, *Whitesands Lodge*, a backpackers' **hostel**, would make a good base for the whole area, offering dorms and private rooms (℡01736/871776; ❶).

Cape Cornwall, three miles northward, shelters another superb beach, overlooked by the chimney of the Cape Cornwall Mine, which closed in 1870. Half a mile inland the grimly grey village of **ST JUST-IN-PENWITH** was a centre of the tin and copper industry, and the rows of trim cottages radiating out from Bank Square are redolent of the close-knit community that once existed here. The tone is somewhat lightened by the grassy open-air theatre where the old Cornish miracle plays were staged; it was later used by Methodist preachers as well as Cornish wrestlers. Three out of the four pubs in and off Bank Square have **accommodation** – best is the traditional *Star Inn* (℡01736/788767; ❷) – and there's a **youth hostel** signposted on the outskirts of the village (℡01736/788437). For **lunches** and inexpensive **dinners**, step into *Kegen Teg*, 12 Market Square (closed Sun eve), which offers fish pie, rich chocolate cake and wonderful Kelly's ice creams.

East of St Just, the landscape is all rolling moorland and knobbly granite, the chief building material of **ZENNOR**. D.H. Lawrence and Frieda came to live

6

here in 1916: "It is a most beautiful place," Lawrence wrote, "lovelier even than the Mediterranean". The Lawrences were soon joined by John Middleton Murry and Katherine Mansfield, with the hope of forming a writers' community, but the new arrivals soon left for a more sheltered haven near Falmouth. Lawrence stayed on to write *Women in Love*, spending in all a year and a half in Zennor before being given notice to quit by the local constabulary, who suspected Lawrence and his German wife of unpatriotic sympathies. His Cornish experiences were later described in *Kangaroo*.

At the bottom of the village, the **Wayside Museum** is packed with a fascinating miscellany illustrating Cornish life from prehistoric times (April to late July, Sept & Oct Mon–Fri & Sun 11am–5pm; late July to Aug daily 10.30am–5.30pm; £2.20). Note the "plague stone" on the road outside the building, where a hole containing vinegar was used to disinfect visiting merchants' money during cholera outbreaks. At the top of the lane, the church of **St Sennen** displays a sixteenth-century bench-carving of a mermaid who, according to legend, was so entranced by the singing of a chorister that she lured him down to the sea, from where he never returned – though his singing can still occasionally be heard. Nearby, the *Tinners Arms*, where Lawrence briefly stayed, is a homely place to **drink** and **eat**, while the *Old Chapel Backpackers Hostel*, next to the Wayside Museum, makes a great place **to stay** (☎01736/798307).

Located on a windy hillside a couple of miles inland from Zennor, off the minor road to Penzance, the Iron Age village of **Chysauster** (April–Sept daily 10am–6pm; Oct daily 10am–5pm; £1.70; EH) is the best-preserved ancient settlement in the southwest. Dating from about the first century BC, it contains two rows of four buildings, each consisting of a courtyard with small chambers leading off it, and a garden that was presumably used for growing vegetables.

St Ives

East of Zennor, the road runs four hilly miles on to the steeply built town of **ST IVES**, a place that has smoothly undergone the transition to holiday haunt from its previous role as a centre of the fishing industry. So productive were the offshore waters that a record sixteen and a half million fish were caught in one net on a single day in 1868, and the diarist Francis Kilvert was told by the local vicar that the smell was sometimes so great as to stop the church clock. By the time the pilchard reserves dried up around the early years of the last century, the town was beginning to attract a vibrant **artists' colony**, precursors of the wave later headed by Ben Nicholson, Barbara Hepworth, Naum Gabo and the potter Bernard Leach, who in the 1960s were followed by a third wave including Terry Frost, Peter Lanyon, Patrick Heron and Bryan Wynter.

Sunday painters dominate the dozens of galleries sandwiched between the town's restaurants and bars; the best work created in St Ives can be viewed in the **St Ives Tate Gallery**, overlooking Porthmeor Beach on the north side of town (March to mid-June daily 10am–5.30pm; mid-June to Aug daily 10am–6.30pm; Nov–Feb Tues–Sun 10am–4.30pm; £3.95; combined ticket with Barbara Hepworth Museum £6.50; ⓦwww.tate.org.uk). The sights and sounds of the beach are a constant presence inside the airy, gleaming white building, interacting with the gallery's paintings, sculptures and ceramics, most of which date from the period 1925 to 1975. Apart from these, the Tate has some specially commissioned contemporary works on view. The museum's rooftop **café** is one the best places in town for tea and cake.

A short distance away on Barnoon Hill, the **Barbara Hepworth Museum** (March–Oct daily 10am–5.30pm; Nov–Feb Tues–Sun 10am–4.30pm; £3.75; combined ticket with the Tate £6.50) gives another insight into the local arts scene. One of the foremost non-figurative sculptors of her time, Hepworth lived in the building from 1949 until her death in a studio fire in 1975. The sculptures are arranged in positions chosen by Hepworth in the house and garden, and the museum also has plenty of background, from photos and letters to catalogues and reviews.

The wide expanse of **Porthmeor Beach** dominates the northern side of St Ives; unusually for a town beach, the water quality is excellent, and the rollers make it popular with surfers. South of the station, **Porthminster Beach** is another favourite spot for sunbathing and swimming, but if you hanker for a quieter stretch you need to head east out of town to the string of magnificent golden beaches lining **St Ives Bay** – the strand is especially fine on the far side of the port of Hayle, at the mouth of the eponymous river.

Arrival and information

St Ives **train station** is off Porthminster Beach, just below the **bus station** on Station Hill. The **tourist office** is in the Guildhall, in the narrow Street-an-Pol, two minutes' walk away (July & Aug Mon–Sat 9.30am–6pm, Sun 10am–1pm; Sept–Sat 9.30am–5.30pm; Oct to mid-May Mon–Thurs 9.30am–5.30pm, Fri 9.30am–5pm; mid-May to June Mon–Sat 9.30am–5.30pm, Sun 10am–1pm; ☎01736/796297).You can rent **surfing equipment** on Porthmeor Beach and outlets on and around Fore Street.

There are several good **B&Bs** bordering the seafront near the train and bus stations and a stone's throw from Porthminster Beach for which early booking is recommended: try *Kandahar*, 11 The Warren (☎01736/796183; ❸), or *Kynance*, 24 The Warren (☎01736/796636; ❷); both are closed Nov to Easter and are non-smoking. Opposite the tourist office, *Bowden's*, at 4 Trepolpen, Street-an-Pol (☎01736 796281; ❷), will apeal to anyone tired of the "fisherman's cottage" style of decor; it offers instead bold minimalist designs and modern art on the walls.At the top of the range, go for the *Garrack Hotel*, Burthallan Lane (☎01736/796199, ⓦwww.garrack.com; ❼), outside the town's bustle but within walking distance of Porthmeor Beach; there's an indoor pool and sauna, and an excellent restaurant. There's a **hostel** in a restored Wesleyan chapel school in the centre of town, *St Ives Backpackers*, The Stennack (☎01736/799444, ⓦwww.backpackers.co.uk/st-ives), and the nearest **campsite**, *Ayr*, is at Higher Ayr (☎01736/795855, ⓦwww.ayrholidaypark.demon.co.uk), half a mile west of the centre, above Porthmeor Beach.

St Ives has a good choice of **restaurants**, ranging from the tiny *Café*, Island Square (☎01736/793621), where vegetarian snacks and reasonably priced full evening meals are served, to the *Grapevine*, 7 High St (☎01736/794030), a bistro serving breakfasts and lunches and fresh local fish at night, all in a pleasant woody decor. At the top of Street-an-Pol on Tregenna Place, *Isobar* is a cool place for coffees and chunky ciabattas, with DJs in the evening and a separate club upstairs.

The Isles of Scilly

The **Isles of Scilly** are a compact archipelago of about a hundred islands 28 miles southwest of Land's End, none of them bigger than three miles across, and only five of them inhabited – **St Mary's**, **Tresco**, **Bryher**, **St Martin's** and **St Agnes**. In the annals of folklore, the Scillies are the peaks of the sub-merged land of Lyonesse, in fact they form part of the same granite mass as Land's End, Bodmin Moor and Dartmoor, all swept by an energizing briny air filled with the cries of seabirds. Though rarely rising above a hundred feet, the Isles possess a remarkable variety of landscape, the beaches ranging from small coves to vast untrammelled strands. Other points of interest include Cornwall's greatest concentration of prehistoric remains, some fabulous rock formations, and masses of **flowers**. Along with tourism, the main source of income here is flower-growing, for which the equable climate and the long hours of sunshine – their name means "Sun Isles" – make the islands ideal.

Free of traffic, theme parks and amusement arcades, the Scillies are a welcome respite from the tourist trail, the main drawbacks being the high cost of reaching the islands and the shortage of **accommodation** – making advance booking essential at any time (most places offer a dinner, bed and breakfast package). Apart from Tresco, each of the main islands has a basic campsite. If you're visiting between May and September, try to be here on a Wednesday or Friday evening to witness the **gig races**, performed by six-oared vessels some thirty feet in length.

Getting to the islands

The islands are accessible by sea or air. **Boats from Penzance to St Mary's** are operated by the Isles of Scilly Steamship Company on the South Pier (☎0845/710 5555, ⓦwww.islesofscilly-travel.co.uk). Sailings take place daily and last nearly three hours; day returns cost £32–35, short-break returns (one to three nights) £45–55, and period returns £65–74, with discounts for students, families and children.

The main departure points for **flights** (also operated by the Isles of Scilly Steamship Company) are **Land's End**, near St Just (Mon–Sat; 15min; £50–98 return), **Newquay** (Mon–Sat; 30min; £67–104 return), **Plymouth** (Mon, Wed & Fri; 45min; £110–150 return), **Exeter** (Mon–Sat; 50min; £142–196 return) and **Bristol** (Mon–Sat; 1hr 10min; £148–199 return). In winter, there are departures only from Land's End and Newquay. British International (☎01736/363871, ⓦwww.scillyhelicopter.co.uk) runs **helicopter** flights (not Sun) from the heliport a mile east of Penzance to St Mary's and Tresco taking about twenty minutes; return fares are about £98 – though you can get discounted day returns, advance returns and short-break returns.

Inter-island launches connect the inhabited islands (about £5 return fare), though these are sporadic in winter.

St Mary's

The island of **ST MARY'S** holds the overwhelming majority of the archipelago's population and most of its tourist accommodation. From the airport buses shuttle passengers the mile to **HUGH TOWN**, which straddles a neck of land at the southwestern end of the island. The harbour lies on the north side of town, under a knob of land still known as the Garrison, where the eight-pointed **Star Castle**, built in Elizabeth I's reign, is now a hotel; the rampart walk here affords views over all the islands. On Church Street, the engaging **Isles of Scilly Museum** (April–Oct daily 10am–noon, 1.30–4.30pm & 7.30–9pm; Nov–March Wed 1.30–4.30pm; £1) shows relics salvaged from the many ships foundered on or around the islands. Hugh Town's best bathing **beach** is in the sheltered bay of Porthcressa, where you can also find Buccabu Bike Hire (☎01720/422289), which offers an alternative way for getting around the island to the circular **bus** service leaving from The Parade, at the end of the main street (summer 6 daily, reduced service rest of year) – though walking is best for exploring the coast.

From Porthcressa a path wanders south to skirt the **Peninnis Headland**, passing some impressive sea-sculpted granite rocks. The path follows the coast to **Old Town Bay**, around which the modern houses of **OLD TOWN** give little hint of its former role as the island's chief port. Here, you'll find cafés and a sheltered south-facing beach, and a **diving** school where equipment can be rented (℡01720/422732).

Three-quarters of a mile east, **Porth Hellick** is the next major inlet on the island's southern coast, marked by a rugged quartz monument to the fantastically named Sir Cloudesley Shovell, who in 1707 was washed up here from a shipwreck which claimed four ships and nearly 1700 lives. On one side of the bay is another rock shape, the **Loaded Camel**; near it a gate leads to a 4000-year-old **barrow**, probably used by Bronze Age people from the Iberian peninsula who were the Scillies' first colonists.

Pelistry Bay, on the northeastern side of St Mary's, less than two miles from Hugh Town, is one of the most secluded spots on the island, its sandy beach and crystal-clear waters sheltered by the outlying **Toll's Island**, joined to St Mary's at low tide by a slender strand. The best remnants of early human settlement on the Scillies are to be found at **Halangy Down**, overlooking the sea a mile or so north of Hugh Town. Dating from around 200 BC, it's an extensive complex of stone huts, chief of them a structure built around a courtyard with interconnecting buildings. Most complete is **Bant's Carn**, part of a much earlier site comprising a long rectangular roofed chamber where cremations were carried out.

Hugh Town's **tourist office**, in the Old Wesleyan Chapel on Garrison Lane (Jan–March Mon–Thurs 8.30am–5pm, Fri 8.30am–4.30pm, Sat 10am–1pm; April to mid-June & Oct Mon–Sat 8.30am–5.30pm; mid-June to Sept Mon–Sat 8.30am–5.30pm, Sun 10am–noon; Nov & Dec Mon–Thurs 8.30am–5pm, Fri 8.30am–4.30pm; ℡01720/422536, ⓦwww.simplyscilly .co.uk), has information on all the Scillies. Though accommodation can be scarce in peak season, the town is relatively well supplied with **B&Bs**: The Strand has the friendly, non-smoking *Lyonesse Guest House* (℡01720/422458; ❸; closed Nov–Feb), right on the harbourfront, while the *Boathouse*, on the Thoroughfare, also enjoys a harbour view and has a restaurant (℡01720/ 422688; ❸; closed Nov–Feb). If you can afford it, you might consider the atmospheric *Star Castle Hotel* (℡01720/422317, ⓦwww.starcastlescilly. demon.co.uk; ❼; closed Nov–Feb), on the Garrison. Also here is the more modest *Veronica Lodge* (℡01720/422585; ❷; closed Nov–Feb), with a spacious garden and excellent views. The *Pilot's Gig* is a basement **restaurant** below the Garrison Gate, offering lunchtime snacks and fish dinners. In the middle of the main street, the *Kavorna Bakery* is a handy spot for daytime refreshment, while the *Star Castle Hotel* has two quality restaurants.

Tresco

After St Mary's, **TRESCO** is the most visited island of the Scillies, and, measuring two miles in length, is the second largest in the group. Once the private estate of Devon's Tavistock Abbey, Tresco still retains a cloistered, slightly privileged air, and it has no budget accommodation.

Boats pull in at various quays according to the tide; wherever you land, it is only a few minutes' walk to the entrance to **Abbey Gardens** (daily 10am–

4pm; £6.50), featuring a few ruins from the priory amid subtropical gardens first laid out in 1834. Many of the plants were grown from seeds taken from London's Kew Gardens, others were brought here from Africa, South America and the Antipodes. The entry ticket also admits you to a collection of figure-heads and name plates from shipwrecked vessels. You don't need to walk far to find alluring sandy beaches: one of the best – **Appletree Bay** – is only a few steps from the southern ferry landing at Carn Near. The island's best strands, and good for shell-hunting, stretch south of **Old Grimsby**, on the island's eastern side. Another gorgeous bay lies around the cluster of cottages that make up **New Grimsby**, on the island's eastern shore. North of here, Tresco's tidy fields give way to rough heathland, while a narrow path traces the coast to **Charles' Castle**, built in the 1550s. Strategically positioned on a height to cover the lagoon-like channel separating Tresco from Bryher, the castle was in fact badly designed, its guns unable to depress far enough to be effective, and it was superseded in 1651 by the much better-preserved **Cromwell's Castle**, actually no more than a gun-tower, built at sea level next to a pretty sandy cove. The shore path winds northwest from here, round to **Piper's Hole**, a deep underground cave accessible from the cliff-edge on the northern coast.

Apart from the exclusive *Island Hotel* at the centre of the island (☎01720/422883; ❾; closed Nov to mid-March), the only **accommodation** on the island is the *New Inn* at New Grimsby (☎01720/422844; ❼), which also has pub snacks in its garden and a formal **restaurant**. For gourmet cuisine, head for the restaurant at the *Island Hotel*, where fresh fish is the speciality.

Bryher and Samson

Covered with a thick carpet of bracken, heather and bramble, **BRYHER** is the wildest of the inhabited islands, but the seventy-odd inhabitants have introduced some pockets of order in the form of flower plantations, mostly confined to the small settlement around the quay and climbing up the slopes of **Watch Hill** on Bryher's eastern side. The exposed western seaboard takes the full brunt of the Atlantic, and nowhere more spectacularly than at the aptly named **Hell Bay**, worth catching when the wind's up. In contrast to this sound and fury, peace reigns in the southern cove of **Rushy Bay**, one of the island's best beaches. From the quay, there are frequent tours to seal and bird colonies, and to the small isle of **SAMSON**, deserted since 1855. Most of the famous **gig races** start off from Nut Rock, to the east of Samson, finishing at St Mary's quay.

Among Bryher's tiny choice of **B&Bs** are *Soleil D'Or*, on the eastern side of the island with views over to Tresco (☎01720/422003; ❷), and *Bank Cottage*, on the western side near Gweal Pool (☎01720/422612; ❷) – both of which offer meals, and both are closed November–February. The island's one hotel, the *Hell Bay* (☎01720/422947; ❽; closed Nov–Feb), near the pool below Gweal Hill, has a **bar** and **restaurant**, and you can also eat inexpensively at the *Vine Café*, below Watch Hill, and the *Fraggle Rock Café*, near the post office.

St Martin's

The main landing stage at **ST MARTIN'S** is on the southern promontory, at the head of the majestic sweep of **Par Beach** – a fitting entry to the island that boasts the best of the Scillies' beaches. From the quay, a road leads up to

HIGHER TOWN, the main concentration of houses and location of the only shop as well as St Martin's Diving Centre (℡01720/422848). Beyond the church, follow the road westwards to **LOWER TOWN**, a cluster of cottages on the western extremity, overlooking the uninhabited isles of Teän and **St Helen's**. The latter holds the remains of a tenth-century oratory, monks' dwellings and a chapel, together with a pest house, erected in 1756 to house plague-carriers entering British waters.

Along the gentler southern shore, you'll find the long strand of **Lawrence's Bay** and large areas of flowerbeds; the northern side has the beautiful **Great Bay**, a half-mile recess of sand, utterly secluded and ideal for swimming. From its western end, you can climb across boulders at low tide to the hilly and wild **White Island**, on the northeastern side of which is a vast cave, **Underland Girt**, accessible at low tide. Below **St Martin's Head**, where a red and white Daymark (erected in 1683, not 1637 as inscribed) served as a warning to shipping, another fine beach, **Perpitch**, looks out to the scattered **Eastern Isles** – slivers of rock to which boats take trippers to view puffins and grey seals.

St Martin's has just one **B&B** listed, *Polreath* (℡01720/422046, ✉polreath-scilly@virginnet.co.uk; ❹), in Higher Town, which has all-round views, and there's one select **hotel**, *St Martin's on the Isle* in Lower Town (℡01720/422090; closed Nov–March; ❾), consisting of a cluster of cottages looking onto a sandy beach. Ask around about other possibilities, and consult the notice-board at Higher Town's post office. *Polreath* also has a simple **café** serving light meals, and snacks are available at the *Sevenstones Inn* in Lower Town.

St Agnes

Visitors to the southernmost inhabited island of the Scillies, **ST AGNES**, disembark at **Porth Conger**, from where a road leads to the western side of the island, on the way passing the disused **Old Lighthouse**, one of the oldest in the country – dating from 1680. From here the right-hand fork leads to **Periglis Cove**, a mooring for boats on the western side of the island, and the left-hand fork goes to **St Warna's Cove**, where the patron saint of shipwrecks is reputed to have landed from Ireland, the exact spot being marked by a holy well. Between the two coves the coastal path passes the miniature **Troy Town Maze**, thought to have been created a couple of centuries ago, but possibly much older. Beyond St Warna's Cove, cross Wingletang Down to the southern headland of **Horse Point**, where there are some tortuous wind-eroded rocks. **Beady Pool**, an inlet on the eastern side of the headland, gained its name from the trove of beads washed ashore from the wreck of a seventeenth-century Dutch trader; some of the reddish-brown stones still occasionally turn up. The eastern side of St Agnes has one of the best beaches, the small, sheltered **Covean**, and at low tide you can cross a sand bar to reach the islet of **Gugh**, where there's a scattering of untended Bronze Age remains. St Agnes's western side looks out onto the **Western Rocks**, a horseshoe of bird-populated islets that can be explored on boat tours.

Best of the **B&Bs** on St Agnes is the *Coastguards*, one of a smart row of cottages past the Old Lighthouse and post office on the island's western side (℡01720/422373; ❸; closed Nov–March). Others include *Covean Cottage*, above Porth Conger (℡01720/422620; ❸) and the *Parsonage* (℡01720/422370; ❸), nestled below the lighthouse. Just above the jetty at Porth Conger, the *Turk's Head* serves beer and superb pasties.

The north Cornish coast to Bude

Though generally harsher than the county's southern seaboard, the north Cornish coast is punctuated by some of the finest beaches in England, the most popular of which are to be found around **Newquay**, the surfers' capital. Other major holiday centres are around the Camel estuary, where the port of **Padstow** makes a good base for some remarkable beaches. North of the Camel, the coast is an almost unbroken line of cliffs as far as the Devon border, the gaunt, exposed terrain making a melodramatic setting for **Tintagel**, though the wide strand at **Bude** attracts legions of surfers and family holiday-makers. The more westerly stretches of this coast are littered with the derelict stacks and castle-like ruins of the engine-houses that once powered the region's **copper** and **tin mines**, industries that at one time led the world.

Newquay

It is difficult to imagine a lineage for **NEWQUAY** that extends more than a few decades, but the "new quay" was built in the fifteenth century in what was already a long-established fishing port. Up to then it had been more colour-fully known as Towan Blistra, and was concentrated in the sheltered west end of the bay. The town was given a boost in the nineteenth century when its har-bour was expanded for coal import and a railway was constructed across the peninsula for china clay shipments. With the trains came a swelling stream of seasonal visitors, drawn to the town's superb position on a knuckle of cliffs overlooking fine golden sands and Atlantic rollers, natural advantages which have made Newquay the premier resort of north Cornwall.

The centre of town is a somewhat tacky parade of shops and restaurants, part-ly pedestrianized, from which lanes lead to ornamental gardens and sloping lawns on the clifftops. Below, adjacent to the small harbour in the crook of the massive Towan Head, **Towan Beach** is the most central of the seven miles of firm sandy beaches that follow in an almost unbroken succession. You can reach all of them on foot, though for some of the farther ones, such as **Porth Beach**, with its grassy headland, or the extensive **Watergate Bay**, you might prefer to make use of local buses. The beaches can be unbearably crowded in full season, and all are popular with surfers, particularly Watergate and – west of Towan Head – **Fistral Bay**, the largest of the town beaches. On the other side of East Pentire Head from Fistral, **Crantock Beach** – reachable over the Gannel River by ferry or upstream footbridge – is usually less crowded, and has a love-ly backdrop of dunes and undulating grassland. Try to coincide your visit to Newquay with one of the **surfing competitions** and events that run right through the summer – contact the tourist office for details.

Practicalities

Newquay is accessible by train via a branch line from Par, on the main Penzance line. The **train station** is off Cliff Road, a couple of hundred yards from the **bus station** on East Street, which itself is just across from the **tourist office** at Marcus Hill (May–Sept Mon–Sat 9.30am–5.30pm, Sun 9.30am–3.30pm; Oct–April Mon–Fri 9.30am–4.30pm, Sat 9.30am–12.30pm; ☎01637/854020, ⓦ www.newquay.co.uk). You can rent or buy **surfing** equip-ment from beach stalls or shops on Fore Street; ask at the tourist office for a list of places running courses, or which specialize in kite-surfing, land yacht-ing, surf canoeing and paragliding.

There's no lack of **accommodation** in Newquay, though rooms can still be at a premium in July and August. In the centre of town, the *Bay View House Hotel* on Fore Street offers good value and superb views (℡01637/871214; ❸; closed Nov–Easter), while fans of Fistral Beach will appreciate the proximity of *Links Hotel* on Headland Road (℡01637/873211; ❷). The town has a choice of independent **hostels** offering dorm beds and some double rooms, including *Newquay International Backpackers*, 69 Tower Rd (℡01637/879366, Ⓦwww .backpackers.co.uk/newquay); *Home Surf Lodge*, 18 Tower Rd (℡01637/ 873387, Ⓦwww.newquay-online.com/homesurf), and *Matt's Surf Lodge*, 110 Mount Wise Rd (℡01637/874651, Ⓦwww.matts-surf-lodge.co.uk). The numerous **campsites** in the area include *Porth Beach* (℡01637/876531, Ⓦwww.porthbeach.co.uk; closed Nov to mid-March), behind the beach of the same name to the east of town, and a little further back, on Trevelgue Road, *Trevelgue* (℡01637/851851, Ⓦwww.trevelgue.co.uk).

Most of the town's places to eat are pretty bland. The *Lifebuoy* is one of the best of the casual **cafés** on Tower Road, and at the lattice-windowed *Cottage*, 38 Fore St, you'll find snacks and teas by day and Tex-Mex, steaks and salads in the upstairs **restaurant** in the evenings, with musical accompaniment (closed Sat lunch & all Sun). The *Bay View House Hotel* (see above) has a terrace café open during the day and good-value evening meals. Newquay has become Cornwall's biggest **nightclubbing** centre: current hot spots are *Berties* on East Street, *Sailors* and the *Beach* on Fore Street, and *Tall Trees* on Tolcarne Road, though if you want to explore the livelier surfhead culture, ask around and watch the posters.

Padstow and around

The small fishing port of **PADSTOW** is nearly as popular as Newquay, but has a very different feel. Enclosed within the estuary of the Camel – the only river of any size that empties on Cornwall's north coast – the town long retained its position as the principal fishing port on this coast, and still has something of the atmosphere of a medieval town. Its chief annual festival is also a hangover from times past, the **Obby Oss**, a May Day romp when one of the locals garbs himself as a horse and prances through the town preceded by a masked and club-wielding "teaser" – a spirited if rather institutionalized re-enactment of old fertility rites.

The Saints' Way

Padstow's St Petroc church is the traditional starting point for one of Cornwall's oldest walking routes, the **Saints' Way**. Extending for some thirty miles between Cornwall's north and south coasts, and connecting the principal ports of Padstow and Fowey, the path originates from the Bronze Age when traders preferred the cross-country hike to making the perilous sea journey round Land's End. The route was later travelled by Irish and Welsh missionaries crossing the peninsula between the fifth and eighth centuries, on pilgrimage to the principal shrines of Cornwall's Celtic culture.

Skirting Bodmin Moor, the reconstructed Saints' Way is rarely dramatic, though it passes a variety of scenery and several points of interest along the way, from Neolithic burial chambers to medieval churches and the more austere lines of Wesleyan chapels. The route is well marked and can be walked in stages, the country paths that constitute it stretching for two to six miles each; although it crosses several trunk roads, these do not impinge too much. You can pick up **guides and leaflets** giving detailed directions to local tourist offices.

On the hill overlooking Padstow, the church of **St Petroc** is dedicated to Cornwall's most important saint, a Welsh or Irish monk who landed here in the sixth century, died in the area and gave his name to the town – "Petrock's Stow". The building has a fine fifteenth-century font, an Elizabethan pulpit and unusual carved bench-ends. The walls are lined with monuments to the local Prideaux family, who still occupy nearby **Prideaux Place**, an Elizabethan manor house with grand staircases, richly furnished rooms full of portraits, fantastically ornate ceilings and formal gardens (Easter & June–Sept Mon–Thurs & Sun 1.30–5pm; £5; grounds only £2), all of which have been used as settings for such films as *Twelfth Night* and *Oscar and Lucinda*.

The harbour is jammed with launches and boats offering cruises in Padstow Bay, while a regular **ferry** (daily: Easter–Oct 8am–7.30pm; Nov–Easter Mon–Sat 8am–5pm; £2 return) carries people across the river to **ROCK** – close to the sand-engulfed church of **St Enodoc** (John Betjeman's burial place) and to the good beaches around Polzeath (see below).

The coast on the **south side** of the estuary also offers some good **beaches**, with some terrific coastline. Round **Stepper Point** you can reach the sandy and secluded Harlyn Bay and, turning the corner southwards, **Constantine Bay**, the area's best surfing beach. The dunes backing the beach and the rock pools skirting it make this one of the most appealing bays on this coast; moreover it boasts the best water quality, though the tides can be treacherous and bathing hazardous near the rocks. Three or four miles further south lies one of Cornwall's most dramatic beaches, **Bedruthan Steps**, slate outcrops which were traditionally held to be a giant's stepping-stones. They can be viewed from the cliff-top path – at a point which drivers can reach on the B3276 – and steps lead down to the broad beach below (not advised for swimming).

Practicalities

Padstow's **tourist office** is on the harbour (Mon–Sat 9.30am–5pm, Sun 9.30am–2pm; winter closed Sun; ℡01841/533449, ⓦwww.padstow.uk.com). Central **accommodation** includes the B&B at 4 Riverside (℡01841/532383; ❷), a three-storey building right on the harbour, and nearby *Armside*, 10 Cross St (℡01841/532271; ❸), an elegant eighteenth-century town house. The nearest **youth hostel** has stunning views and is excellently sited almost on the beach at Treyarnon Bay (℡01841/520322); to get there, take a bus to Constantine (#556, also from Newquay) then walk for half a mile. Padstow's quayside is lined with snack bars and pasty shops as well as pubs where you can sit outside, such as the *Shipwright's* on the harbour's north side. But foodies know the town best for its high-class **restaurants**, particularly those associated with star chef Rick Stein, all of which also offer accommodation. The *Seafood Restaurant*, at Riverside (℡01841/532700, ⓦwww.rickstein.com; ❻), is one of England's top fish eateries – and expensive, with a waiting list stretching for months. Alternatively, try Stein's slightly cheaper *St Petroc's Bistro* at 4 New St (℡01841/532700; closed Mon; ❺), or the casual *Rick Stein's Café* nearby at 10 Middle St (closed Sun; ❺). For cheaper eats, the *Old Custom House* on the harbourside serves pub snacks, while *Rojano's* on Mill Square dishes up pizza and pasta (closed Mon & Nov–Feb).

Polzeath to Port Isaac

Facing west into Padstow Bay, the beaches of and around **POLZEATH** are the finest in the vicinity, pelted by rollers which make this one of the best surfing sites in the West Country. Tuition and gear to rent are offered from stalls here. If you want to stay, try *Pentire View*, a pleasant **B&B** a few yards up the hill from Polzeath's beach (☎01208/862484; ●). On the beach itself, the *Galleon* does various snacks and takeaways, and *Finn's* serves full meals as well as cream teas, while the *Oyster Catcher* bar is a lively evening hangout just up the hill.

The next settlement of any size is **PORT ISAAC**, wedged in a gap in the precipitous cliff-wall and dedicated to the crab and lobster trade. Narrow lanes focus on a couple of pubs at the seafront, where a pebble beach and rock pools are exposed by the low tide. The village offers a range of **accommodation**, best of all the *Slipway Hotel* (☎01208/880264, ⊛www.portisaac.com; ●), a sixteenth-century building right opposite the harbour, with a bar and excellent restaurant. Cheaper choices are outside the centre and away from the sea, among them the Victorian *Bay Hotel*, 1 The Terrace (☎01208/880380, ⊜jacki.burns@talk21.com; ●), with light, bright rooms, and *Anchorage Guest House*, 12 The Terrace (☎01208/880629; non-smoking; ●), both with good views. Crab is what Port Isaac does best; try it here or to take away on the harbourfront; other places to sample crab or lobster include the *Slipway Hotel* (see above) and the *Old School*, at the top of the village. The *Golden Lion* is Port Isaac's most cheerful **pub** and has an adjoining bistro and balcony seating overlooking the harbour.

Tintagel

East of Port Isaac, the coast is wild and unspoilt, making for some steep and strenuous walking, and providing an appropriate backdrop for the black, forsaken ruins of **Tintagel Castle** (daily: April to mid-July & late Aug to Sept 10am–6pm; mid-July to late Aug 10am–7pm; Oct 10am–5pm; Nov–March 10am–4pm; £3; EH). It was the twelfth-century chronicler Geoffrey of Monmouth who first popularized the notion that this was the **birthplace of King Arthur**, son of Uther Pendragon and Ygrayne, but by that time local folklore was already saturated with tales of King Mark of Cornwall, Tristan and Iseult, Arthur and the knights of Camelot. Twin influences were at work in Geoffrey's story, which merges the historic figure of Arthur with a separate body of legend centring on the missionary activity of the Celtic monastery that occupied this site in the sixth century. Tintagel is certainly a plausibly resonant candidate for the abode of the Once and Future King, but the **castle** ruins in fact belong to a Norman stronghold occupied by the earls of Cornwall, who after sporadic spurts of rebuilding allowed it to decay, most of it having been washed into the sea by the sixteenth century. The remains of the **Celtic monastery** are still visible on the headland and are an important source of knowledge of how the country's earliest monastic houses were organized.

The easiest access to the site is along a signposted path from the village of **TINTAGEL**. The only item of note in this dreary collection of cafés and B&Bs is the **Old Post Office** (April–Sept daily 11am–5.30pm; Oct daily 11am–5pm; £2.20; NT), a rickety-roofed slate-built construction dating from the fourteenth century, now restored to its appearance in the Victorian era when it was used as a post office.

Buses stop on the main Fore Street close to the octagonal **tourist office** (daily: March–Oct 10am–5pm; Nov–Feb 10.30am–4pm; ☎01840/779084). The village has plenty of **accommodation**, most of it fairly basic, though the *Old Malt House* (☎01840/770461; ●; closed Jan) and the *Tintagel Arms Hotel* (☎01840/770780; ●), both on Fore Street, have more character; alternatively, head a mile or so inland to Trenale, where *Trebrea Lodge* (☎01840/770410; ●;

Did **King Arthur** really exist? If he did, it is likely that he was an amalgam of two people; a sixth-century Celtic warlord who united the local tribes in a series of successful battles against the invading Anglo-Saxons, and a local Cornish saint. Whatever his origins, his role was recounted and inflated by poets and troubadours in later centuries. Though there is no mention of him in the ninth- to twelfth-century *Anglo-Saxon Chronicle*, his exploits were elaborated by the unreliable medieval chroniclers Geoffrey of Monmouth, who made Arthur the conqueror of western Europe, and William of Malmesbury, who narrated the legend that, after being mortally wounded in battle, Arthur sailed to Avalon (Glastonbury), where he was buried alongside Guinevere. The Arthurian legends were crystallized in Thomas Malory's epic, *Morte d'Arthur* (1485), further romanticized in Tennyson's *Idylls of the King* (1859–85) and resurrected in T.H. White's saga, *The Once and Future King* (1937–58).

Although there are places throughout Britain and Europe which claim some association with Arthur, it is England's West Country, and **Cornwall** in particular, that has the greatest concentration of places boasting a link. Relatively untouched by the Saxon invasions, Cornwall has practically appropriated the hero as its own, a far more authentic bond than the efforts of the county's tourist industry might suggest. Here, the legends, fertilized by fellow Celts from Brittany and Wales, have established deep roots, so that, for example, the spirit of Arthur is said to be embodied in the Cornish chough – a bird now almost extinct. Cornwall's most famous Arthurian site is **Tintagel**, which is said to be the birthplace of Arthur. Meanwhile, Merlin is thought to have lived in a cave under the castle – and also on a rock near Mousehole, south of Penzance. Nearby Bodmin Moor is full of places with associated names such as "King Arthur's Bed" and "King Arthur's Downs", while Camlan, the battlefield where Arthur was mortally wounded fighting against his nephew Mordred, is thought to lie on the northern reaches of the moor at Slaughterbridge, near Camelford (which is also sometimes identified as Camelot itself). Nearby, at **Dozmary Pool**, the knight Bedivere was dispatched by the dying Arthur to return the sword Excalibur to the mysterious hand emerging from the water – though Loe Pool in Mount's Bay also claims this honour. According to some, Arthur's body was transported after the battle to **Boscastle**, on Cornwall's northern coast, from where a funeral barge transported the body to Avalon. Cornwall is also the presumed home of King Mark, at the centre of a separate cycle of myths which later became interwoven with the Arthurian one. It was Mark who sent the knight Tristan to Ireland to fetch his betrothed, Iseult; his headquarters is supposed to have been at Castle Dore, north of Fowey. Out beyond Land's End, the fabled, vanished country of Lyonesse is also said to be the original home of Arthur, as well as being (according to Spenser's *Faerie Queene*) the birthplace of Tristan.

Much of the Cornish tourist office's celebration of the Arthurian sagas has the same cynical basis as the more ancient desire to claim Arthur by the various villages and sites throughout England and Wales: the cachet and hence profit to be had from the veneration of a secular saint. Today in Tintagel you will find Arthurian tack galore, including every kind of Merlin-esque hogwash (crystal balls, sugar-coated wands, etc), and even Excaliburgers.

closed Jan) is a manor house in a lush rural location with sea-facing bedrooms. Three-quarters of a mile south of Tintagel at Dunderhole Point, the offices of a former slate quarry now house a **youth hostel** with great views of the coastline (℡01840/770334).

Three miles northeast of Tintagel, the port of **BOSCASTLE** lies compressed within a narrow ravine drilled by the rivers Jordan and Valency, its tidy riverfront bordered by thatched and lime-washed houses giving on to the twisty harbour. Above and behind, a collection of seventeenth- and eighteenth-century cottages can be seen on a circular walk, starting either from Fore Street or the main car park, which traces the valley of the Valency for about a mile to reach Boscastle's graceful **parish church**, tucked away in a peaceful glen. A mile and a half further up the valley lies another church, **St Juliot's**, restored by Thomas Hardy when he was plying his trade as a young architect.

Boscastle's **tourist office** is situated in the car park at the bottom of the main road into the village (daily: March–Oct 10am–5pm; Nov–Feb 10.30am–4pm; ℡01840/250010). One of the most appealing **places to stay** is *St Christopher's Hotel* (℡01840/250412, ⓦwww.stchristophershotel.co.uk; ❷; closed Dec–Feb), a restored Georgian manor house at the top of the High Street, but for a real Hardy experience, head for the non-smoking *Old Rectory*, on the road to St Juliot (℡01840/250225, ⓦwww.stjuliot.com; ❷; closed Dec–Feb), where you can stay in either Hardy's or Emma's bedroom. The harbour has a lovely old **youth hostel** (℡01840/250287) which is right by the sea. Nearby, you can eat at the *Harbour Restaurant* (℡01840/250380; closed mid-Nov to Easter), which serves organic, Asian-influenced food, as well as sandwiches and teas. The village has three good **pubs**: in the upper part of town, the *Napoleon* has the advantage of a good seafood bistro and a spacious lawned garden, while the *Cobweb* down near the harbour rates highly on atmosphere.

Bude and around

There is little distinctively Cornish in Cornwall's northernmost town of **BUDE**, four miles west of the Devon border. Built around an estuary surrounded by a fine expanse of sands, the town has sprouted a crop of holiday homes and hotels, though these have not unduly spoiled the place nor the magnificent cliffy coast surrounding it.

Of the excellent beaches hereabouts, the central **Summerleaze** is clean and wide, though the mile-long **Widemouth Bay**, two and a half miles **south** of Bude, is the main focus of the holiday hordes – it has the cleanest water monitored between Bude and Polzeath, though bathing can be dangerous near the rocks at low tide. Surfers also congregate five miles down the coast at **Crackington Haven**, wonderfully situated between 430-foot crags at the mouth of a lush valley. The cliffs on this stretch are characterized by remarkable zigzagging strata of shale, limestone and sandstone, a mixture which erodes into vividly contorted detached formations.

To the **north** of Bude, acres-wide **Crooklets** is the scene of **surfing** and life-saving demonstrations and competitions. A couple of miles farther on, **Sandy Mouth** holds a pristine expanse of sand with rock pools beneath the encircling cliffs. It is a short walk from here to another surfers' delight, **Duckpool**, a tiny sandy cove flanked by jagged reefs at low tide, and dominated by the three-hundred-foot **Steeple Point**.

Bude's **tourist office** is in the centre of town at the Crescent (April–Sept Mon–Sat 9.30am–5pm, Sun 10am–4pm; Oct–March Mon–Fri 10am–4pm, Sat 10am–2pm; ℡01288/354240, ⓦwww.bude.co.uk). Among the town's **accommodation**, *Tee Side* (℡01288/352351, Ⓔtee_side@hotmail.com; ❶) and *Sea Jade* (℡01288/353404; ❶) at no. 2 and no. 15 Burn View respectively are among a cluster of very similar B&Bs near the golf course. The *Falcon Hotel*, an old coaching inn on Breakwater Road, is a much fancier affair (℡01288/352005; ❻), and also offers bar meals and has a more formal seafood **restaurant**. You can buy or rent **surfing** equipment from numerous places on the beaches or in the town centre.

Bodmin and Bodmin Moor

Bodmin Moor, the smallest, mildest and most accessible of the West Country's great moors, has some beautiful tors, torrents and rock formations, but much of its fascination lies in the strong human imprint, particularly the wealth of relics left behind by its **Bronze Age** population, including such important sites as Trethevy Quoit and the stone circles of the Hurlers. Separated from these by some three millennia, the churches in the villages of **St Neot's**, **Blisland** and **Altarnun** are among the region's finest examples of fifteenth-century art and architecture.

Situated on the main A30 and on the main rail line, the undistinguished town of **Bodmin** stands outside the moor but can provide information on walking routes and has the area's widest choice of accommodation.

Bodmin

BODMIN's position on the western edge of Bodmin Moor, equidistant from the north and south Cornish coasts and the Fowey and Camel rivers, encouraged its growth as a trading town. It was also an important ecclesiastical centre after the establishment of a priory by St Petroc, who moved here from Padstow in the sixth century. Later, the town became increasingly sidelined after refusing access to the Great Western Railway in the 1870s, as a result of which much local business transferred down the road to Truro. **Bodmin Parkway** station lies three miles outside town, with a regular bus connection to the centre.

Bodmin's most prominent landmark is the **Gilbert Memorial**, a 144-foot obelisk honouring a descendant of Walter Raleigh and occupying a commanding location on Bodmin Beacon, a high area of moorland near the centre of town. Below, at the end of Fore Steet, stands **St Petroc's**, built in the fifteenth century and still the largest church in Cornwall; inside, there's an extravagantly carved twelfth-century font and an ivory casket that once held the bones of the saint, while the southwest corner of the churchyard holds a sacred well. Close by, the notorious **Bodmin Jail** (Mon–Fri & Sun 10am–5pm, Sat 11am–6pm; £3.50) glowers darkly on Berrycombe Road, redolent of the public executions that were once guaranteed crowd-pullers. You can visit part of the original eighteenth-century structure, including the condemned cell and some grisly exhibits chronicling the lives of the inmates.

From Parkway it's less than two miles' walk to one of Cornwall's most celebrated country houses, **Lanhydrock** (April–Sept Tues–Sun 11am–5.30pm; Oct Tues–Sun 11am–5pm; £6.80; grounds only £3.70; NT), originally seventeenth-century but totally rebuilt after a fire in 1881. The granite exterior remains true to its original form, but the 42 rooms show a very different style, including a long picture gallery with a plaster ceiling depicting scenes from the Old Testament, and – most illuminating of all – servants' quarters that reveal the daily workings of a Victorian manor house. The grounds have magnificent beds of magnolias, azaleas and rhododendrons, and a huge area of wooded parkland bordering onto the River Fowey.

Practicalities

Bodmin's **tourist office** (May–Sept Mon–Sat 10am–5pm; Oct–April Mon–Fri 10am–5pm, Sat 10am–1pm; ☎01208/76616) is near the main car park at the bottom of St Nicholas Street. Comfortable **B&B** is available at *Higher Windsor Cottage*, 18 Castle St (☎01208/76474, ⓦwww.ji77.dial.pipex.com; ❶), and the beflowered, seventeenth-century *Priory Cottage*, near St

Petroc's church at 34 Rhind St (℡01208/73064, ⊛www.priorycottage1 .co.uk; no smoking; ❶). South of town, the non-smoking *Bokiddick Farm*, two miles east of Lanivet, is convenient for the Lanhydrock estate and boasts magnificent views (℡01208/831481; ❸). Off Fore Street, the *Hole in the Wall* **pub** in Crockwell Street has a courtyard, a pleasant backroom bar in what used to be the debtors' prison, and an upstairs **restaurant**. Wholesome snacks are also served at the *Maple Leaf*, a tiny café just across from St Petroc's at 14 Honey St (closed Sun).

Blisland and the western moor

BLISLAND stands in the Camel valley on the western slopes of Bodmin Moor, three miles northeast of Bodmin. Georgian and Victorian houses cluster around a village green and a church whose well-restored interior has an Italianate altar and a startlingly painted screen. On **Pendrift Common** above the village, the gigantic **Jubilee Rock** is inscribed with various patriotic insignia commemorating the jubilee of George III's coronation in 1809. From this seven-hundred-foot vantage point you look eastward over the De Lank gorge and the boulder-crowned knoll of **Hawk's Tor**, three miles away. On the shoulder of the tor stand the Neolithic **Stripple Stones**, a circular platform once holding 28 standing stones, of which just four are still upright. If you're looking for a **place to stay** in the area, try *Lavethan* (℡01208/850487, ⊛www.cornwall-online.co.uk/lavethan; ❹), a beautiful sixteenth-century manor house set in thirty acres of park-like fields and gardens sloping to a small river; it's ten minutes' walk from the village towards St Mabyn.

Bolventor and Dozmary Pool

The village of **BOLVENTOR**, lying at the centre of the moor midway between Bodmin and Launceston, is an uninspiring place close to one of the moor's chief focuses for walkers and sightseers alike – **Jamaica Inn** (℡01566/86250, ⊛www.jamaicainn.co.uk; ❸). A staging-post even before the precursor of the A30 road was laid here in 1769, the inn was described by Daphne Du Maurier as being "alone in glory, four square to the winds", and the combination of its convenient position and its association with her has led to its growth into a hotel and restaurant complex. One corner exhibits the room where the author stayed in 1930, soaking up inspiration for her smuggler's yarn. At the other end of the building is the entertaining **Museum of Curiosities** (daily: Easter–Oct 10am–6pm, until 8pm during school holidays; Nov–Easter 11am–4pm; £2.50; combined ticket with Smuggler's Museum £4).

The inn's car park is a useful place from which to venture forth on foot. Just over a mile south, **Dozmary Pool** is another link in the West Country's Arthurian mythologies – after Arthur's death Sir Bedivere hurled Excalibur, the king's sword, into the pool, where it was seized by an arm raised from the depths. Despite its proximity to the A30, the diamond-shaped lake usually preserves an ethereal air, though it's been known to run dry in summer, dealing a bit of a blow to the legend that the pool is bottomless. The lake is also the source of another, more obviously Cornish legend, that of John Tregeagle, a steward at Lanhydrock, whose unjust dealings with the local tenant farmers in the seventeenth century brought upon his spirit the curse of endlessly baling out the pool with a perforated limpet shell. As if this were not enough, his ghost is further tormented by a swarm of devils pursuing him as he flies across the moor in search of sanctuary; their infernal howling is sometimes audible on windy nights.

Liskeard and St Neot

LISKEARD, a bus and rail junction just off the southern limits of the moor, makes a decent overnight stop, with good **accommodation** at *Elnor*, 1 Russell St (☎01579/342472; ❶), located on the way to the train station, and the immaculately kept *Hyvue* just north of the centre at Barras Cross (☎01579/348175; non-smoking; ❶). From here, buses go on to **ST NEOT**, one of Bodmin Moor's prettiest villages, approached through a lush wooded valley. Its fifteenth-century **church** contains some of the most impressive stained-glass windows of any parish church in the country, the oldest glass being the fifteenth-century **Creation Window**, at the east end of the south aisle. Next along, **Noah's Window** continues the sequence, but the narration soon dissolves into windows portraying patrons and local bigwigs, while others present cameos of the ordinary men and women of the village. Among the best of St Neot's B&Bs is the seventeenth-century *Dye Cottage* (☎01579/321394, Ⓦwww.cornwall-info.co.uk/dye-cottage; ❶), which has a garden that slopes down to a stream.

This southern edge of the moor is far greener and more thickly wooded than the northern reaches, due to the confluence of a web of rivers. One of the moor's best-known beauty spots is a couple of miles east, below Draynes Bridge, where the Fowey tumbles through the **Golitha Falls**, less a waterfall than a series of rapids. Dippers and wagtails flit through the trees, and there's a pleasant woodland walk you can take to the dam at the Siblyback Lake reservoir just over a mile away.

Camelford and the northern tors

The northern half of Bodmin Moor is dominated by its two highest tors, both of them easily accessible from **CAMELFORD**, a town once associated with King Arthur's Camelot, while Slaughterbridge, which crosses the River Camel north of town, is one of the contenders for his last battleground. Camelford has resisted trading on the Arthurian myths, but does have a couple of diverting museums: the **British Cycling Museum** (daily: Mon–Thurs & Sun 10am–5pm, Fri & Sat call ahead for times; ☎01840/212811; £2.50), housed in the old station one mile north of town on the Boscastle Road and containing some four hundred examples of bikes through the ages, and the **North Cornwall Museum** (April–Sept Mon–Sat 10am–5pm; £1.50) in Camelford's centre, exhibiting domestic items and charting the development of the local slate industry; the same building has a **tourist office** (same hours; ☎01840/212954). Although it lacks excitement, Camelford makes a useful touring base. Among its **accommodation** is the central *Countryman Hotel*, at 7 Victoria Rd (☎01840/212250, Ⓦwww.cornwall-online.co.uk/countryman; ❷); the thirteenth-century *Darlington Inn* on Fore Street (☎01840/213314; ❶), and the *Mason's Arms* on Market Place (☎01840/213309; ❶). The last two places are also useful **refreshment** stops.

Rough Tor, the second highest peak on Bodmin Moor at 1311ft, is four miles' walk southeast from Camelford. The hill presents a different aspect from every angle: from the south an ungainly mass, from the west a nobly proportioned mountain. A short distance to the east stand **Little Rough Tor**, where there are the remains of an Iron Age camp, and **Showery Tor**, capped by a prominent formation of piled rocks. Easily visible to the southeast, **Brown Willy** is, at 1375ft, the highest peak in Cornwall, as its original name signified – Bronewhella, or "highest hill". Like Rough Tor, Brown Willy shows various faces, its sugarloaf appearance from the north sharpening into a long multi-peaked crest as you approach. The tor is accessible by continuing from the summit of Rough Tor across the valley of the De Lank, or, from the south, by foot-path from Bolventor. The easiest ascent is by the worn path which climbs steeply up from the northern end of the hill.

Altarnun and the eastern moor

ALTARNUN is a pleasant, granite-grey village snugly sheltered beneath the eastern heights of the moor. Its prominent **church**, dedicated to St Nonna, mother of David, patron saint of Wales, contains a fine Norman font and 79 bench-ends carved at the beginning of the sixteenth century, depicting saints, musicians and clowns. Accessed by a private gate from St Nonna's (and also from the road), *Penhallow Manor* (☎01566/86206, ⓦwww.penhallow-manor.co.uk; ⑤), originally the vicarage, now offers tasteful **accommodation** and a set three-course dinner at £20 (book ahead if you're not staying); morning coffees and afternoon teas are also available. Cheaper rooms can be found 500 yards towards the A30, where the *King's Head* (☎01566/86241; ①) has beams, saggy ceilings and **meals** for under a fiver.

South of Altarnun, **Withey Brook** tumbles four hundred feet in less than a mile of gushing cascades before meeting up with the River Lynher, which bounds Bodmin Moor to the east. Beyond the brook, on **Twelve Men's Moor**, lie some of Bodmin Moor's grandest landscapes. The quite modest elevations of Hawk's Tor (1079ft) and the lower Trewartha Tor appear enormous from the north, though they are overtopped by **Kilmar**, highest of the hills on the moor's eastern flank at 1280ft.

Withey Brook starts life about six miles from Altarnun on **Stowe's Hill**, site of the moor's most famous stone pile, **The Cheesewring**, a precarious pillar of balancing granite slabs, marvellously eroded by the wind. A mile or so south down Stowe's Hill stands an artificial rock phenomenon, **The Hurlers**, a wide complex of three circles dating from about 1500 BC. The purpose of these stark upright stones is not known, though they owe their name to the legend that they were men turned to stone for playing the Celtic game of hurling on the Sabbath.

The Hurlers are easily accessible just outside **MINIONS**, Cornwall's highest village, three miles south of which stands another Stone Age survival, **Trethevy Quoit**, a chamber tomb nearly nine feet high, surmounted by a massive capstone. Originally enclosed in earth, the stones have been stripped by centuries of weathering to create Cornwall's most impressive megalithic monument. Bus #73 from Liskeard calls at St Cleer and Darite, both of which are close to Trethevy Quoit; alternatively, it's a three-mile walk from Liskeard.

Travel details

Buses

For information on all local and national bus services, contact Traveline: ☎0870/608 2 608 (daily 7am–9pm, ⓦwww.traveline.org.uk).

Trains

For information on all local and national rail services, contact National Rail Enquiries: ☎08457/48 49 50, ⓦwww.rail.co.uk.
Barnstaple to: Exeter (Mon–Sat 9–11 daily, Sun 5 daily; 1hr).

Bodmin to: Exeter (1–2 hourly; 1hr 30min–2hr); London (8–10 daily; 4hr 15min); Penzance (hourly; 1hr 20min); Plymouth (1–2 hourly; 40min).
Exeter to: Barnstaple (Mon–Sat 9–11 daily, Sun 5 daily; 1hr); Birmingham (hourly; 2hr 20min–2hr

40min); Bodmin (1–2 hourly; 1hr 45min); Bristol (1–2 hourly; 1hr 20min); Exmouth (Mon–Sat 2 hourly, Sun hourly; 30min); Liskeard (1–2 hourly; 1hr 30min); London (1–2 hourly; 2hr 30min–3hr 20min); Par (hourly; 2hr); Penzance (hourly; 3hr); Plymouth (2 hourly; 1hr); Salisbury (every 2hr; 2hr); Torquay (hourly; 45min); Totnes (2 hourly; 35min); Truro (1–2 hourly; 2hr 15min).

Falmouth to: Truro (10–12 daily; 25min).

Liskeard to: Exeter (1–2 hourly; 1hr 30min); London (8 daily; 4hr); Looe (8–10 daily, not Sun in winter; 30min); Penzance (hourly; 1hr 30min); Plymouth (1–2 hourly; 30min); Truro (hourly; 50min).

Newquay to: Par (4–7 daily, not Sun in winter; 50min).

Par to: Exeter (hourly; 1hr 50min); Newquay (4–7 daily, not Sun in winter; 50min); Penzance (hourly; 1hr 10min); Plymouth (hourly; 1hr).

Penzance to: Bodmin (hourly; 1hr 20min); Bristol (11 daily; 4hr); Exeter (hourly; 3hr); Liskeard (hourly; 1hr 30min); London (8 daily; 5–6hr); Par (hourly; 1hr 10min); Plymouth (hourly; 2hr); St Ives (3–5 daily; 20min); Truro (1–2 hourly; 40min).

Plymouth to: Bodmin (1–2 hourly; 40min); Bristol (1–2 hourly; 2hr–2hr 50min); Exeter (2 hourly; 1hr); Liskeard (1–2 hourly; 30min); London (8 daily; 3hr–4hr); Par (hourly; 1hr); Penzance (hourly; 2hr); St Erth (hourly; 1hr 50min); Truro (hourly; 1hr 20min).

St Ives to: Penzance (3–5 daily; 20min); St Erth (2 hourly; 15min).

Torquay to: Exeter (hourly; 45min).

Truro to: Bristol (11 daily; 3hr 20min); Exeter (1–2 hourly; 2hr 15min); Falmouth (10–12 daily; 25min); Liskeard (hourly; 50min); London (8 daily; 4hr 40min); Penzance (1–2 hourly; 40min); Plymouth (hourly; 1hr 20min).

East Anglia

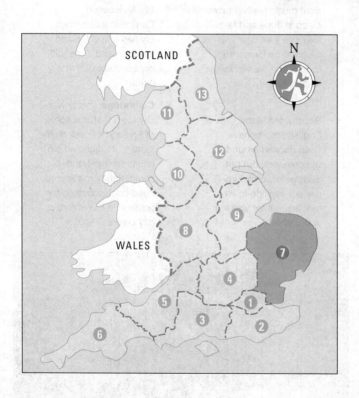

CHAPTER 7 # Highlights

* **Orford** Remote and peaceful, this hamlet is hidden away on the Suffolk coast and makes for a wonderful weekend away. See p.438

* **The Aldeburgh Festival** The region's prime classical music festival takes place in June and lasts for three weeks; it was founded by Benjamin Britten and his works feature heavily. See p.439

* **Southwold** Many English resorts have been hacked around by the planners, but not Southwold, a picture-perfect seaside town that is ideal for walking and bathing. See p.441

* **Norwich Market** Huddled under brightly striped awnings, this open-air market is the region's biggest and best for everything from whelks to wellies. See p.448

* **Ely** An isolated Cambridgeshire town, Ely has a true fenland flavour – and a magnificent cathedral. See p.460

* **Cambridge** This university town features some of England's finest architecture, its dignified old churches and handsome, tightly manicured quadrangles jostling for position in the compact city centre. See p.461

East Anglia

S trictly speaking, **East Anglia** is made up of just three counties – Suffolk, Norfolk and Cambridgeshire – which were settled by Angles from Holstein in the fifth century, though in more recent times it's come to be loosely applied to parts of Essex too. As a region it's renowned for its wide skies and flat landscapes, and of course such generalizations always contain more than a grain of truth – if you're looking for mountains, you've come to the wrong place. That said, East Anglia often fails to conform to its stereotype: parts of Suffolk are positively hilly, and its coastline can induce vertigo; the north Norfolk coast holds steep cliffs as well as wide sandy beaches; and even the pancake-flat fenlands are broken by wide, muddy rivers and hilly mounds, on one of which perches **Ely**'s magnificent cathedral. Indeed, the whole region is sprinkled with fine medieval churches, the legacy of the days when this was England's most progressive and prosperous region.

Of all the region's counties, **Suffolk** is the most varied. Its undulating southern reaches, straddling the River Stour, are home to a string of picturesque, well-preserved little towns – **Lavenham** and **Kersey** are two excellent examples – which enjoyed immense prosperity during the thirteenth to sixteenth centuries, the heyday of the wool trade. Elsewhere, **Bury St Edmunds** can boast not just the ruins of its once-prestigious abbey, but also some fine Georgian architecture on its grid-plan streets. Even the much maligned county town of **Ipswich** has more to offer than it's generally given credit for. Nevertheless, for many visitors it's the north Suffolk coast that steals the local show. In **Southwold**, with its comely Georgian high street, Suffolk possesses a delightful seaside resort, elegant and relaxing in equal measure, while neighbouring **Aldeburgh** hosts one of the best music festivals in the country.

Norfolk, as everyone knows thanks to Noël Coward, is very flat. It's also one of the most sparsely populated and tranquil counties in England, a remarkable turnaround from the days when it was an economic and political powerhouse – until, that is, the Industrial Revolution simply passed it by. Its capital, **Norwich**, is still East Anglia's largest city, renowned for its Norman cathedral and castle, and for its high-tech Sainsbury Centre, a provocative collection of twentieth-century art. The one part of Norfolk which has been well and truly discovered is the **Broads**, a unique landscape of reed-ridden waterways that has been over-exploited by farmers and boat-rental companies for the last twenty years. Too far from London to attract day-trippers, the Norfolk coast – with the exception of touristy **Great Yarmouth** and, to a lesser extent, the Victorian resort of **Cromer** – remains one of the most unspoilt in England, with **Blakeney Point** and the surrounding marshes among the country's top nature

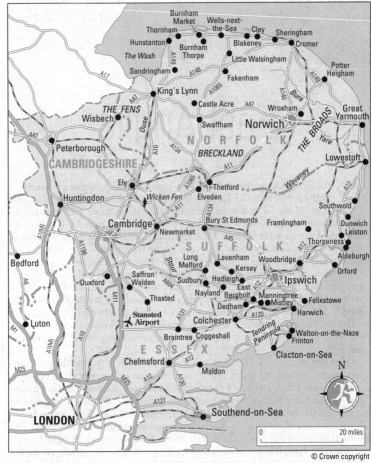

© Crown copyright

reserves. Meanwhile, sheltering inland, is an outstanding stately home – **Blickling Hall** – plus a couple more within easy striking distance of the steady resort of **Hunstanton**.

Cambridge is, however, the one place in East Anglia everyone visits, largely on account of its world-renowned university, whose ancient colleges boast some of the finest medieval and early modern architecture in the country. The rest of Cambridgeshire is dominated by the landscape of the **Fens**, for centuries an inhospitable marshland, which was eventually drained to provide rich alluvial farming land. The one great highlight here is the cathedral town of **Ely**, settled on one of the few areas of raised ground in this region and an easy and popular day-trip from Cambridge.

Heading into the region from the south, almost inevitably takes you through **Essex**, though there's little here to divert you. Not properly part of East Anglia, but generally lumped together with the region, Essex's proximity to London has turned many places into soulless commuter towns with only the historic town of **Colchester** being really worth a detour.

Getting around

The **train** network is at its best to and from London, with quick and frequent services from the capital to all of East Anglia's major towns. One mainline service links Colchester, Ipswich and Norwich, another Cambridge, Ely and Peterborough, which means it is relatively easy to move from one major town to another. However, once you get away from the major towns, you're going to have to rely on local **buses**, whose services, run by a multitude of companies, are very patchy – especially on Sundays and in winter. Indeed, in parts of north Norfolk and inland Suffolk, you may find the only way to get about is by your own transport. The largest regional bus operator is First Eastern Counties, who sell Ranger tickets providing unlimited travel for one day or more on their buses. These are available either in advance or from their drivers. Most tourist offices carry details of local buses and some of the more useful services are detailed in the text.

Colchester and around

If you visit anywhere in Essex, it should be **COLCHESTER**, an agreeable town with a castle, a university and a large army base, fifty miles or so northeast of London. More than anything else, Colchester prides itself on being England's oldest town and there is documentary evidence of a settlement here as early as the fifth century BC. By the first century AD, the town was the region's capital and when the Romans invaded Britain in 43 AD they chose Colchester (Camulodunum) as their new capital, though it was soon eclipsed by London, becoming a retirement colony for legionaries instead. A millennium later, the conquering Normans built one of their mightiest strongholds in Colchester, but the conflict that most marked the town was the Civil War. In 1648, Colchester was subjected to a gruelling siege by the Parliamentarian army led by Lord Fairfax; after three months, during which the population ate every living creature within the walls, the town finally surrendered and the Royalist leaders were promptly executed for their pains.

Today, Colchester makes a good base for further explorations of the surrounding countryside – particularly the Stour valley towns of Constable country (see pp.429–433), within easy reach to the north.

Arrival, information and accommodation

Colchester has two **train stations** with services from London, Ipswich and Harwich arriving at the mainline Colchester North Station, from where it's a fifteen-minute walk south into town – follow North Station Road and its continuation North Hill until you reach the west end of the High Street. The **bus station** is off Queen Street, the northerly continuation of St Botolph's Street, and a couple of minutes' walk from the east end of High Street. You can get bus timetables here from the First Eastern National office (Mon–Fri 8.45am–5pm, Sat 9am–1pm; ☎01206/572478), which also sells Bus Ranger tickets (£6) valid for a day's travel throughout much of East Anglia.

The **tourist office** is at 1 Queen St (April–Oct Mon–Sat 9.30am–6pm, Sun 10am–5pm; Nov–March Mon–Sat 10am–5pm; ☎01206/282920), at the east end of High Street, just behind the castle. As well as helping with accommodation, they sell leaflets detailing local walks and co-ordinate daily **guided walks** around town (June–Sept; £2.50). You can rent a **bike** from Action Bikes, beside the Odeon Cinema on Crouch Street (☎01206/541744; £12/day) – a good way of getting out to see the nearby "Constable Country" (see p.429).

For **accommodation**, Colchester has more than its fair share of old hotels as well as a scattering of pleasant, well-located B&Bs. The *Rose & Crown Hotel*, East Street (℡01206/866677, ⓦwww.rose-and-crown.com; ④), occupies an old, tastefully refurbished Tudor inn – the oldest inn in town, while the *George Hotel*, 116 High St (℡01206/578494; ⑤), is an attractive old coaching inn, whose recently revamped rooms come with all mod cons. The *Red Lion*, 43 High St (℡01206/577986; ⑤), is another old-timer, a fifteenth-century timber building containing 24 modernized en-suite rooms. The *Old Manse*, 15 Roman Rd (℡01206/545154, ⓦwww.doveuk.com/oldmanse; ②), is the best of the many B&B options along Roman Road, with three pleasant guest rooms; Roman Road is on the east side of the Castle.

The Town

Most visitors start off at the town's rugged, honey-coloured **Castle**, the perfect introduction to Colchester's long history, set in attractive parkland, which stretches down to the River Colne. Begun less than ten years after the Battle of Hastings, it boasts a phenomenally large keep – the largest in Europe at the time – built on the site of the defunct Roman temple. The castle's **museum** (Mon–Sat 10am–5pm, Sun 11am–5pm; £3.90) contains the best of the region's Romano-British archeological finds, although, apart from a fine bronze of Mercury, the messenger of the gods, this amounts to little more than a smattering of coins, tombstones, statues and mosaics. The museum also covers the Boudicca revolt and the 1648 siege, and you can sign up for a **guided tour** of the underground tunnels (45min; £1.20), which give access to the foundations of the Roman temple and the Norman chapel and walls – parts not otherwise accessible to regular visitors. Outside, down towards the river in Castle Park is a section of the old **Roman walls**, whose battered remains are still visible around much of the town centre.

The castle stands at the eastern end of the wide, and largely pedestrianized, **High Street**, which lies pretty much along the same route as it did in Roman times. The most arresting building here is the flamboyant **Town Hall**, built in 1902 and topped by a statue of St Helena, mother of Constantine the Great and daughter of "Old King Cole" of nursery-rhyme fame – after whom, some say, the town was named. Immediately north of the High Street is the so-called **Dutch Quarter**, where Flemish refugees settled in the sixteenth century giving a boost to the town's ailing cloth trade. The area's lofty buildings still make this a pleasant place to stroll, particularly along West and East Stockwell streets. South of the High Street, much of the medieval street plan has been subsumed within a vast open-air shopping precinct, complete with three separate indoor shopping centres and an open-air **market** held every Friday and Saturday in Vineyard Street.

With a little time to spare, it's worth strolling down **East Hill**, a continuation of the High Street east of the castle. Splendid Georgian houses line the top end of the hill, one of which – opposite the tourist office – is now the **Hollytrees Museum** (Mon–Sat 10am–5pm, Sun 11am–5pm; free), containing a modest collection of costumes, toys, domestic items, trade implements and decorative arts from the eighteenth to the twentieth century. Over the road at the **Minories** (April–Sept Mon–Sat 10am–5pm, Sun 11am–5pm; rest of year closed Sun; free) another Georgian exterior conceals a contemporary arts centre, with a changing exhibition programme, a garden and a great café. Just along the street, **Priory Galleries** sells the work of local artists, and is well worth a look.

Eating, drinking and nightlife

Colchester's oysters have been highly prized since Roman times and the local vineyards have an equally long heritage, so it's no surprise to find the town has a good choice of first-rate **restaurants**. Pickings are slim on Sundays, however, when most places are closed. Probably the best place in town is the *Red Onion Bistro*, 19 Head St (℡01206/366379; closed Sun eve), which offers tasty dishes at moderate prices from a wide-ranging, contemporary menu. Alternatively, try *Ruan Thai*, 82a East Hill (℡01206/870770), an excellent and moderately priced Thai restaurant near the top of East Hill, or the garden café at the Minories (closed Sun in winter), where the lunches are delicious. The *Lemon Tree*, 48 St John's St (℡01206/767337; closed Sun), is a moderately priced option, popular for its lunch specials and sunny courtyard seating. For pizza, try *Pizza Express*, 1 St Runwald's St, off West Stockwell (℡01206/760680), or *Toto's*, 5–7 Museum St (℡01206/573235).

Colchester's town centre is crowded with **pubs**, with three of the best being the *Red Lion*, 43 High St, the *Foresters Arms*, a nice backstreet local on Castle Road, and the *Goat & Boot*, just one of several lively spots down East Hill. And, as you'd expect in a university town, the town rates reasonably well when it comes to the **arts and nightlife**. The Colchester Arts Centre, on Church Street next to the Balkerne Gate (℡01206/500900), puts on a good programme of rock, folk, jazz, theatre and dance, plus some club nights – all in a converted Victorian church. Nearby is the Mercury Theatre (℡01206/573948), the town's main drama venue.

The Stour Valley and the old wool towns of south Suffolk

Five miles or so north of Colchester, the **Stour River Valley** forms the border between Essex and Suffolk, and signals the beginning of East Anglia proper. Compared with much of the region it is positively hilly, a handsome landscape of farms and woodland latticed by dense, well-kept hedges and thick grassy banks that once kept the Stour in check. The valley is dotted with lovely little villages, where rickety, half-timbered Tudor houses and elegant Georgian dwellings cluster around medieval churches, proud buildings with square, self-confident towers. The Stour's prettiest villages are concentrated along its lower reaches – to the east of the A134 – in Dedham Vale, with **Stoke-by-Nayland** and **Dedham** arguably the most appealing of them all. The vale is also known as "**Constable Country**", as it was the home of John Constable, one of England's greatest artists, and the subject of his most famous works. Inevitably, there's a Constable shrine – the much-visited complex of old buildings down by the river at **Flatford Mill**.

The villages along the River Stour and its tributaries were once busy little places at the heart of East Anglia's weaving trade, which boomed from the thirteenth to the fifteenth century. By the 1490s, the region produced more cloth than any other part of the country, but in Tudor times production shifted to Colchester, Ipswich and Norwich. Bypassed by the Industrial Revolution, south Suffolk had, by the late nineteenth century, become a remote rural backwater, an impoverished area whose decline had one unforeseen consequence. With few exceptions, the towns and villages were never well enough off to modernize, and the architectural legacy of medieval and Tudor times survived. The two best-preserved villages are **Lavenham** and **Kersey**, both of which heave with sightseers on summer weekends, but there are other attractive spots too, notably **Sudbury**. The latter boasts an excellent museum devoted to the work of Thomas Gainsborough, another great English artist and a native of the town who spent much of his time painting the local landscape.

Seeing the region by **public transport** is problematic – distances are small (Dedham Vale is only about ten miles long), but buses between the villages are infrequent and you'll find it difficult to get away from the towns. Several rail lines cross south Suffolk, the most useful being the London– Colchester– Sudbury route. The area is crisscrossed by **footpaths**, some of the most enjoyable of which are in the vicinity of Dedham village.

East Bergholt, Flatford Mill and John Constable

"I associate my careless boyhood to all that lies on the banks of the Stour" wrote **John Constable**, who was born the son of a miller in **EAST BERGHOLT**, nine miles northeast of Colchester in 1776. The house in which he was born has long since disappeared, so it has been left to **Flatford Mill**, a mile or so to the south, to take up the painter's cause. The mill was owned by his father and was where Constable painted his most famous canvas, *The Hay Wain* (now in the National Gallery, London), which created a sensation when it was exhibited in 1824. To the chagrin of many of his contemporaries, Constable turned away from the landscape-painting conventions of the day, rendering his scenery with a realistic directness that harked back to the Dutch landscape painters of the seventeenth century. Typically, he justified this approach in unpretentious terms, observing that, after all "no two days are alike, nor even two hours; neither were there ever two leaves of a tree alike since the creation of the world." The mill itself – not the one he painted, but a Victorian replacement – is not open to the public, but the sixteenth-century thatched **Bridge Cottage** (March & April Wed–Sun 11am–5.30pm; May–Sept daily 10am–5.30pm; Oct daily 11am–5.30pm; Nov & Dec Wed–Sun 11am–3.30pm; Jan & Feb Sat & Sun 11am–3.30pm; free, but parking £1.90; NT), which overlooks the scene, has been painstakingly restored and stuffed full of Constabilia. Unfortunately, none of Constable's paintings are displayed here, though the adjacent granary contains mezzotints of the artist's works and there's a pleasant riverside tearoom to take in the view. Beyond stands **Willy Lott's Cottage** (also closed to the public), which does actually feature in *The Hay Wain*.

In summer, the National Trust organizes **guided walks** around the sites of Constable's paintings (call ☎01206/298260 for details), but there are many other pleasant walks to be had along this deeply rural bend in the Stour. One footpath connects the mill to the **train station** at Manningtree, two miles to the east, and another runs over to the village of Dedham, a mile and a half to the west.

Dedham

Constable went to school in **DEDHAM**, just upriver from Flatford Mill. It's one of the region's most attractive villages, with a scattering of ancient timber-framed houses strung along the wide main street. The only sights as such are **St Mary's Church**, an early sixteenth-century structure which Constable painted on several occasions, and the **Sir Alfred Munnings Art Museum**, in

the highest for miles around, partly to celebrate the Tudor victory at the Battle of Bosworth in 1485, but mainly to show off their wealth.

There are fairly frequent **buses** to Lavenham from Colchester via Sudbury and Long Melford, with the service continuing on to Bury St Edmunds. The **tourist office** is located on Lady Street (April–Oct daily 10am–4.45pm; Nov–March Sat & Sun 11am–3pm; ☎01787/248207, ✉lavenhamtic@babergh .gov.uk), just south off Market Place. They can help with **accommodation** and sell a detailed, street-by-street walking guide. Rooms at the *Swan hotel* (☎01787/247477, ⓦwww.heritage-hotels.com; ⑥), a splendid old inn on High Street, are some of the most comfortable in town. Less expensive options on the Market Place include the ancient *Angel Hotel* (☎01787/247388, ⓦwww.lavenham.co.uk/angel; ⑤), which has eight pleasant rooms above its bar, and the dinky *Angel Gallery* (☎01787/248417, ③), where the three guest rooms are situated above a pocket-sized art shop. For cheaper B&B options, you'll probably end up staying outside Lavenham itself; the tourist office will provide you with details. For **food**, the *Angel Hotel* serves up excellent, moderately priced bar meals, as does the *Swan*. The other choice in Market Place is the *Great House* (☎01787/247431; closed Sun & Mon), whose outstanding restaurant serves moderately priced food on both its à la carte and set menus.

Kersey and Hadleigh

Eight miles southeast off the A1141, **KERSEY** vies with Lavenham as the most photographed village in Suffolk. Another old wool town, Kersey has been bypassed by history and is now little more than one exquisite street of timber-framed houses, which dips in the middle to cross a ford that's inhabited by a family of fearless ducks. Prime real estate today, Kersey's more populous past is recalled by its large and austere parish church, visible for miles around, perched on high ground above the village. There's nowhere to stay, but there are two good **pubs**, the *White Horse* and the *Bell*, both of which serve good, reasonably priced bar food.

Another two miles southeast, the market town of **HADLEIGH** is a positive metropolis compared to Kersey, but everything of interest is within a stone's throw of the **Parish Church of St Mary's**. The church, one block west of the elongated High Street, is mainly fifteenth century, a good-looking replacement for several earlier versions. Legend asserts that Guthrum, the Danish chieftain and arch-rival of **Alfred the Great**, was buried underneath the south aisle in 889, but his remains have never been definitively identified. Opposite the church, across the graveyard, is the half-timbered **Guildhall** (guided tours June–Sept Thurs & Sun 2–5pm; £1.50), every bit as immaculate as Lavenham's, with the earliest sections dating from 1438 – and offering very-English cream teas in the garden from June to September (Mon–Fri & Sun 2.30–5pm). At the back of the church, is the extravagantly ornate **Deanery Tower**, a fifteenth-century gatehouse whose palace was never completed.

Hadleigh is easy to reach by **bus** with regular services from Sudbury, Lavenham, Ipswich and Colchester, though Sundays can be a bit tricky. Several Hadleigh-bound buses pass through Kersey too. Tourist information on Hadleigh is available at the library on the High Street and the town is also home to the **East of England Tourist Board**, just off the High Street at Toppesfield Hall (Mon–Fri 9am–5pm; ☎01473/822922). Both can help with local **accommodation**, though there's no real reason to tarry once you've seen the sights. For a bite **to eat**, Ferguson's Delicatessen, 48 High St (closed Sun), sells delicious sandwiches.

Bury St Edmunds

Appealing **BURY ST EDMUNDS** started out as a Benedictine monastery, founded to house the remains of Edmund, the last Saxon king of East Anglia, who was tortured and beheaded by the marauding Danes in 869. Almost two centuries later, England was briefly ruled by the kings of Denmark and the shrewdest of them, King Canute, made a gesture of reconciliation to his Saxon subjects by conferring on the monastery the status of abbey. It was a popular move and the abbey prospered, so much so that before its dissolution in 1539, it had become the richest religious house in the country. Most of the abbey disappeared long ago, and nowadays Bury is better known for its graceful Georgian streets, its flower gardens and its sugar-beet plant than for its ancient monuments. Nonetheless, it's an amiable, eminently likeable place, one of the prettiest towns in Suffolk, and, with good transport connections on to Cambridge, Colchester, Ipswich and Norwich, it demands at least half a day of anyone's time.

The Town

The town centre has preserved its Norman street plan, a gridiron in which Churchgate was aligned with – and sloped up from – the abbey's high altar. It was the first planned town of Norman Britain and, for that matter, the first example of urban planning in England since the departure of the Romans. Beside the abbey grounds is **Angel Hill**, a broad, spacious square partly framed by Georgian buildings, the most distinguished being the ivy-covered **Angel Hotel**, which features in Dickens' *Pickwick Papers*. Dickens also gave readings of his work in the **Athenaeum**, the Georgian assembly rooms at the far end of the square. A twelfth-century wall runs along the east side of Angel Hill, with the bulky fourteenth-century **Abbey Gate** forming the entrance to the abbey gardens and ruins.

The **abbey ruins** themselves are like nothing so much as petrified porridge, with little to remind you of the grandiose Norman complex that dominated the town. The most significant remnants are behind the more modern cathedral (see below) on the far side of the public **gardens** with the rubbled remains of a small part of the old **abbey church** integrated into a set of unusual Georgian houses. In front, across the green, is the imposing **Norman Tower**, once the main gateway into the abbey and now a solitary monument with dragon gargoyles and fancily decorated capitals.

Incongruously, the tower is next to the front part of Bury's Anglican **Cathedral of St James** (daily: 8.30am–6pm; £2 donation requested), with chancel and transepts added as recently as the 1960s. That its thousand-odd kneelers are often cited as one of its major highlights gives an idea of the paucity of the interior – notwithstanding the hammer-beam roof and a couple of quality stained-glass windows. In fact, it was a toss-up between this place and **St Mary's Church** (Mon–Sat 10am–4pm, 3pm in winter), further down Crown Street, as to which would be given cathedral status in 1914. The presence of the tomb of the resolutely Catholic Mary Tudor in the latter was probably the clinching factor.

Not far away, at the far end of Crown Street, stands Bury's most important industrial concern, the pungent **Greene King Brewery** (June–Aug Mon–Fri 1–4pm, Sat 11am–4pm, Sun 11am–4pm; rest of year closed Sun), whose powerful Abbot Ale is an intense bittersweet beer to be quaffed with caution. The brewery and the National Trust are joint owners of the neighbouring Regency

Theatre Royal, at the junction of Crown and Westgate streets, built in 1819 by William Wilkins and still staging plays.

The town's main commercial area is on the west side of the centre, a five-minute walk up Abbeygate Street from Angel Hill. There's been some intrusive modern planning here, but dignified Victorian buildings flank both **Cornhill** and **Buttermarket**, the two short main streets, as well as the narrower streets in between. Older still is the Cornhill's flint-walled **Moyse's Hall**, one of the few surviving Norman houses in England, while the streets to the south are lined by an attractive medley of architectural styles, from elegant Georgian town houses to Victorian brick terraces. You'll see the best by strolling along Guildhall Street and turning left down Churchgate, which brings you back to Angel Hill.

Practicalities

From Bury St Edmunds' **train station**, it's ten minutes' walk south to Angel Hill, along Northgate Street. The **bus station** is on St Andrew Street North, near Cornhill. The town's **tourist office**, at 6 Angel Hill (Easter–Sept Mon–Sat 9.30am–5.30pm, Sun 10am–3pm; Oct–Easter Mon–Fri 10am–4pm, Sat 10am–1pm; ⓣ01284/764667, ⓔtic@stedsbc.gov.uk), provides free town maps and has a useful range of leaflets.

The pick of the town's **hotels** is the *Angel*, on Angel Hill (ⓣ01284/714000; ❺), an immaculately maintained, county-set hotel with thick carpets, oodles of wood panelling and suitably luxurious rooms. A good alternative is the *Chantry Hotel*, 8 Sparhawk St (ⓣ01284/767427; ❹), which has sixteen comfortable rooms in a converted Georgian building near the Manor House Museum. The town has a good supply of **B&Bs**, including the excellent *South Hill House*, 43 Southgate St (ⓣ01284/755650, ⓦwww.southill.cwc.net; ❷), a handsome old town house with many Georgian features and three large en-suite bedrooms.

For **restaurants**, *Maison Bleue*, 31 Churchgate St (ⓣ01284/760623; closed Sun), serves wonderfully fresh seafood at moderate prices. The *Vaults*, inside the medieval undercroft at the *Angel Hotel*, is also first-rate, with tasty main dishes from £7.50. Otherwise, aim for coffee, cakes and **snacks** in either the Cathedral *Refectory* (closed Sun) or the *Scandinavia Coffee House*, 30 Abbeygate St.

Of the **pubs**, one you shouldn't miss is the *Nutshell* (closed Sun), on The Traverse at the top of Abbeygate, which, at sixteen feet by seven and a half, claims to be Britain's smallest. Greene King's brewery tap is the ancient-looking *Dog & Partridge*, 29 Crown St.

Ipswich and around

Situated at the head of the Orwell estuary, **IPSWICH** was a rich trading port in the Middle Ages, but its appearance today is mainly the result of a revival of fortunes in the Victorian era – give or take some clumsy postwar development. The two surviving reminders of old Ipswich – **Christchurch Mansion** and the splendid **Ancient House** – plus the recently renovated quayside are all reason enough to spend at least an afternoon here. Ipswich also boasts a wealth of medieval flint churches, some now locked and slowly rusting away, but others sympathetically restored. One now houses the tourist office, from where **guided walks** depart a couple of times a week during the season (May–Sept Tues & Thurs 2.15pm; £1.75) – perhaps the best way to see the town on a short visit.

The Town

The ancient Saxon market place, **Cornhill**, is still the town's focal point, a like-able urban space flanked by a bevy of imposing Victorian edifices – the Italianate town hall, the old Neoclassical Post Office and the pseudo-Jacobean Lloyds building. From here, it's just a couple of minutes' walk to the Buttermarket and Ipswich's most famous building, the **Ancient House**, whose exterior was decorated around 1670 in extravagant style, a riot of pargeting and stuccowork that together make one of the finest examples of Restoration artistry in the country. Since the house is now a shop, you're free to take a peek inside to view yet more of the decor, including the hammer-beam roof on the first floor.

From the Ancient House, head up Dial Lane past the fifteenth-century church of **St Lawrence** and you are soon on Tavern Street, where two won-derful mock-Tudor shops, built in the 1930s, face the **Great White Horse Hotel**, the "overgrown tavern" which appears in Dickens' *Pickwick Papers*. Heading north from here up Northgate Street takes you past the much-restored sixteenth-century, half-timbered **Oak House**, once an inn and now housing office space, to busy St Margaret's Plain and the gates of **Christchurch Mansion** (Tues–Sat 10am–5pm, Sun 2.30–4.30pm; free). This handsome, if much-restored Tudor building, sporting seventeenth-century Dutch gables, is set in 65 acres of parkland, an area larger than the town centre itself. The man-sion's labyrinthine interior is well worth exploring, with period furnishings and a good collection of paintings by Constable and Gainsborough, as well as more contemporary art exhibitions.

On the south side of the centre, follow Key Street and you'll soon reach the Neptune Quay marking the northern edge of the **Wet Dock**, the largest in Europe when it opened in 1845 and looking much as it did then, apart from the rash of yachts in the marina. The smell of malt and barley still wafts across the quayside, and several of the granaries continue to function, though other warehouses have been turned into pubs, restaurants and offices. Halfway along the Neptune Quay stands the proud Neoclassical **Customs House**, built for the opening of the dock.

Fifteen minutes' walk south of Neptune Quay via Orwell Quay is the **Tolly Cobbold Brewery** (guided tours £4.50; for latest times & details call ☎01473/261112), which rewards visitors with a sample of its brew after the tour of its Victorian premises. Tours begin in the *Brewery Tap* **pub** (closed Sun) next door.

Practicalities

Ipswich **train station** is on the south bank of the Orwell, ten minutes' walk from Cornhill along Princes Street. The **bus station** is more central, occupy-ing part of the old cattle market, a short walk south of Cornhill and close to the **tourist office** (Mon–Sat 9am–5pm; ☎01473/258070, ✉tourist@ipswich .gov.uk), in the converted St Stephen's Church in St Stephen's Lane. The town is compact enough to walk around, though a special summer **bus** (☎01473/232600) runs a circular route connecting the bus station to all the main sights, including the Wet Dock and the brewery.

There's no real need **to stay**, especially with the Suffolk coast so close, but a full list of B&Bs is available from the tourist office. One of the best is *Burlington Lodge*, 30 Burlington Rd (☎01473/251868, ✉burlingtonlodge@bigfoot.com; ②), an attractive Victorian detached house with five comfortable bedrooms, ten minutes' walk west of the Cornhill. Alternatively, try the ultra-modern *Novotel*

Hotel, in the centre near Wolsey's Gateway, on Grey Friars Road (☎01473/232400; ❹).

There are several good **restaurants** down by the Wet Dock. *Il Punto*, on Neptune Quay (☎01473/289748), which offers good quality cuisine at moderate prices, has the most distinctive premises – on board a Dutch pleasure boat – while the more expensive *Mortimer's On The Quay Restaurant* (☎01473/230225), in one of the old red-brick warehouses down on Wherry Quay, specializes in seafood. Meals here cost £20–30 a head, though it's cheaper at lunch. **Cafés** in town include *Jacey's* at 1 St Stephen's Lane and *Pickwick's*, 1 Dial Lane, with courtyard seating next to St Lawrence's Church.

For a **drink**, try either the *Black Horse* on Black Horse Lane, near the Civic Centre, or the *Glasshouse* on the Buttermarket.

Sutton Hoo and Framlingham

Beyond Ipswich, the obvious destination is the Suffolk coast, but on the way it's worth considering a short stop at **Sutton Hoo**, where a brand new National Trust visitor centre has been built beside an Anglo-Saxon burial site unearthed in 1939. Near here also, a short detour to the north, is the tranquil village of **Framlingham**, a delightful place with a gaunt, ruined castle.

Sutton Hoo

In the summer of 1939, way out in the countryside at **SUTTON HOO**, about ten miles northeast of Ipswich, a local landowner stumbled across the richest single archeological find in Britain, an Anglo-Saxon royal burial site belonging to Raedwald, king of East Anglia, who died around 625 AD. A forty-oar open ship was discovered, containing a wooden tomb stuffed with gold and jewelled ornaments. Further archeological research was conducted on the site in the 1980s, and in November 1991 a second undisturbed grave was uncovered. Most of the artefacts are displayed in London's British Museum (see p.105), but some (along with replicas of others) have been returned to Sutton Hoo, where the National Trust have recently opened an immaculate visitor centre and **exhibition hall** (mid-March to May & Oct Wed–Sun 10am–5pm; June–Sept daily 10am–5pm; Nov–Feb most Sat & Sun 11am–4pm; £3.50). The latter explains the history and significance of the finds and afterwards you can wander out onto the burial site itself. To get to Sutton Hoo, head for **Woodbridge**, a few miles northeast of Ipswich, and from there take the Melton Road – the B1438 – turning right onto the A1152 and right again onto the B1083, the Bawdsey road, at the roundabout.

Framlingham and around

FRAMLINGHAM, ten miles north of Woodbridge, boasts a magnificent **Castle** (daily: April–Oct 10am–6pm; Nov–March 10am–4pm; £3.70; EH), whose severe, turreted walls date from the twelfth century. The original seat of the Dukes of Norfolk, the fortress is little more than a shell inside, but the curtain-wall, with its thirteen towers, has survived almost intact, a splendid example of medieval military architecture topped by ornamental Tudor chimney stacks. Footpaths crisscross the earthen banks encircling the castle and from the internal wall walkways, there are sweeping views across town to the imposing red-brick mass of Framlingham College, but nothing remains of the Great Hall where Mary Tudor was proclaimed Queen of England in 1553.

The sleepy little village next to the castle is a real pleasure to visit, its elongated main street, **Market Hill**, flanked by a harmonious ensemble of sedate old buildings, including the *Crown Hotel* (☎01728/723521; ❺), a traditional seventeenth-century inn with roaring fires, wood panelling and snug bedrooms. The parish **Church of St Michael** is also intriguing, its finely crafted hammer-beam roof sheltering several wonderful, sixteenth-century tombs belonging to the Howard family, who owned the castle at the time.

The district is also a centre of East Anglia's developing wine industry and several local vineyards offer tours and tastings. The well-established **Shawsgate Vineyard** (March–Nov 10.30am–5pm; ☎01728/724060) is situated one mile north of Framlingham along the B1120.

The Suffolk coast

The **Suffolk coast** feels detached from the rest of the county: the road and rail lines from Ipswich to Lowestoft funnel traffic five miles inland for most of the way, and patches of marsh and woodland make the separation still more complete. The coast has long been plagued by erosion and this has contributed to the virtual extinction of the local fishing industry, and, in the case of **Dunwich**, destroyed virtually the entire town. What is left, however, is undoubtedly one of the most unspoilt shorelines in the country – if, that is, you set aside the Sizewell nuclear power station. Highlights include the sleepy isolation of minuscule **Orford** and several genteel resorts, most notably **Southwold**, which has evaded the lurid fate of so many English seaside towns. There are scores of delightful **walks** hereabouts, easy routes along the coast that are best followed with either OS map no.156 or no.169, or the simplified *Footpath Maps* available at most tourist offices. The Suffolk coast is also host to East Anglia's most compelling cultural gathering, the three-week-long **Aldeburgh Festival**, which takes place each June.

Orford

Twelve miles east of Woodbridge, on the far side of the Forest of Rendlesham, the tiny village of **ORFORD** is dominated by two buildings, both of them medieval. The more impressive is the twelfth-century **Castle** (April–Oct daily 10am–6pm; Nov–March Wed–Sun 10am–1pm & 2–4pm; £3.10; EH), built on high ground to the southwest of the village by Henry II, and under siege within months of its completion from Henry's rebellious sons. Most of the castle disappeared centuries ago, but the lofty keep remains, its impressive stature hinting at the scale of the original fortifications. Orford's other medieval edifice, on the far side of the main square, is **St Bartholomew's Church**, where Benjamin Britten premiered his most successful children's work, *Noye's Fludde*, as part of the 1958 Aldeburgh Festival (see box below).

From the top of the castle keep, there's a great view across **Orford Ness**, a six-mile-long shingle spit that has all but blocked off Orford from the sea since Tudor times. Its mud flats and marshes harbour sea lavender beds, which act as feeding and roosting areas for wildfowl and waders. The National Trust offers **boat trips** (July–Sept Tues–Sat outward boats between 10am–2pm, last ferry back 5pm; mid-April to June & Oct Sat only; £5.60; NT members £3.60; ☎01394/450057) across to the Ness from Orford Quay, four hundred yards down the road from the church, and a five-mile hiking trail threads its way along the spit. There are also plenty of walks to be had around Orford itself.

One of the best is the five-mile hike north along the river wall that guards the west bank of the River Alde, returning via Ferry Road, a narrow country lane.

Orford's gentle, unhurried air is best experienced on a night's stay. **Rooms** are available at the *Crown & Castle* (☎01394/450205, ✆www.crownandcastle-hotel.co.uk; ❺), an attractive inn across from the castle with comfortable bedrooms kitted out with all mod cons, and at the marginally less enticing *King's Head* (☎01394/450271; ❸), on Market Hill, the main square. For **meals**, don't miss the *Butley Orford Oysterage* (☎01394/450277; closed Nov–March) also on Market Hill. This has a very reasonably priced café/restaurant, whose menu focuses on fresh oysters and oak-wood smoked fish. Finally, down near the quay, the *Jolly Sailor Inn* serves bar meals, teas and coffee.

Aldeburgh and around

ALDEBURGH is best known for its annual arts festival, the brainchild of composer **Benjamin Britten**, who is buried in the village churchyard alongside the tenor Peter Pears, his lover and musical collaborator. They lived by the seafront in Crag House on Crabbe Street – the street named for the poet who provided Britten with his greatest inspiration (see box below). Outside of June, when the festival takes place, and November, when the three-day international poetry festival fills the town, Aldeburgh is the quietest of places, with just a small fishing fleet selling its daily catch from wooden shacks along the pebbled shore.

The wide **High Street** and its narrow sidestreets run close to the beach, but this was not always the case – hence their garbled appearance. The ocean swallowed most of what was once an extensive medieval town long ago and today

Benjamin Britten and the Aldeburgh Festival

Benjamin Britten was born in Lowestoft in 1913, and was closely associated with Suffolk for most of his life. However, it was during his self-imposed exile in the USA during World War II – he was a conscientious objector – that Britten first read the work of the nineteenth-century Suffolk poet, George Crabbe. Crabbe's *The Borough*, a grisly portrait of the life of the fishermen of Aldeburgh, was the basis of the libretto of Britten's best-known opera, *Peter Grimes* which was premiered in London in 1945 to great acclaim.

In 1947 Britten founded the English Opera Group and the following year launched the **Aldeburgh Festival** as a showpiece for his own works and those of his contemporaries. He lived in the town for the next ten years and it was during this period that he completed much of his best work as a conductor and pianist. For the rest of his life he composed many works specifically for the festival, including his masterpiece for children, *Noye's Fludde* and the last of his fifteen operas, *Death in Venice*.

By the mid-1960s, the festival had outgrown the parish churches in which it began, and moved into a collection of disused malthouses, five miles west of Aldeburgh on the River Alde, just south of the small village of **SNAPE** along the B1069. **Snape Maltings** were subsequently converted into one of the finest concert venues in the country. In addition to the concert hall, there is now a recording studio, a music school, various craft shops and galleries, a tearoom, and a nice pub, the *Plough & Sail*.

For more information on the Aldeburgh Festival, contact the **festival box office**, 152 Aldeburgh High St (☎01728/687110, ✆www.aldeburgh.co.uk). Tickets for the concerts, talks, exhibitions and other special events go on sale to the public towards the end of March, and usually sell out fast for the big-name recitals; prices range from £9 to £50. There are all sorts of concerts and performances at other times of the year too – again details are available from the booking office – with showcase events including the Proms season in August and the three-day Britten Festival in late October.

Aldeburgh's oldest remaining building, the sixteenth-century **Moot Hall** (Easter–May & Oct Sat & Sun 2.30–5pm; June & Sept daily 2.30–5pm; July & Aug daily 10.30am–12.30pm & 2.30–5pm; 50p), which began its days in the centre of town, finds itself on the seashore. It's a handsome building made out of a mixture of red-brick, flint and timber and the interior accommodates a modest museum of local finds and history. One of Aldeburgh's newest buildings, the **RNLI Lifeboat Station**, is situated bang in the middle of the seafront opposite the Jubilee Hall. From the public viewing deck you can look at the town's lifeboat and the tractor used to drag it out to sea.

Several **footpaths** radiate out from Aldeburgh, with the most appealing trail leading southwest to the winding estuary of the River Alde, an area rich in wildfowl.

Practicalities

Aldeburgh's festival box office shares its High Street premises with the local **tourist office** (daily 9am–5.30pm, till 5.15pm in winter; ℡01728/453637), who have a useful range of local leaflets. They will also book **accommodation** on your behalf, though things get very tight during the main festival and leading events when you should book months in advance. The town boasts several splendidly sited **hotels**, including the comfortable *Wentworth* (℡01728/452312, ⓦwww.wentworth-aldeburgh.com; ❻), a family-owned hotel along the seafront from the Moot Hall. Of the **B&Bs**, the *Ocean House*, 25 Crag Path (℡01728/452094; ❹), is probably the best. An immaculately maintained Victorian dwelling right on the seafront in the centre of town, it's decorated in period style, with two of its three guest rooms overlooking the beach; dinner is available by prior arrangement. Also in the town centre is *East Cottage*, 55 King St (℡01728/453010; ❷; closed Sept–May), a brightly painted Victorian cottage a block back from the sea. There's also a **youth hostel** on Heath Walk in the hamlet of Blaxhall (℡01728/688206, ⓦwww.yha.org.uk; closed Nov–March), a couple of miles west of the concert facilities at Snape Maltings. The hostel has forty beds and is housed in a former village school.

There are tearooms and takeaway fish-and-chip shops on the High Street, but Aldeburgh does much better than that with the town's highbrow leanings sustaining a glut of terrific **restaurants**. *Café 152*, 152 High St (℡01728/454152), is the most moderately priced, a simple painted wooden café where stylishly cooked fresh fish is served at lunch and dinner. There are more Mediterranean flavours and adventurous use of local ingredients at both the *Lighthouse*, 77 High St (℡01728/453377), and the *Regatta*, 171–173 High St (℡01728/452011; closed Mon & Tues in winter), each moderately priced and the latter open to the pavement in summer. For **drinks**, head for the *White Lion Hotel*, just along the seafront from the Moot Hall.

Dunwich

Seat of the kings of East Anglia, a bishopric and once the largest port on the Suffolk coast, the ancient city of **DUNWICH**, about twelve miles up the coast from Aldeburgh, reached its peak of prosperity in the twelfth century. Over the last millennium, however, something like a mile of land has been lost to the sea, a process that continues at the rate of about a yard a year. As a result, the whole of the medieval city now lies under the ocean, including all twelve churches, the last of which toppled over the cliffs in 1919. All that survives are fragments of the Greyfriars monastery, which originally lay to the west of the city and now dangles at the sea's edge. For a potted history of the lost city, head for the

museum (April–Sept daily 11.30am–4.30pm; Oct daily noon–4pm; free) in what's left of Dunwich – little more than one small street of terraced houses built by the local landowner in the nineteenth century.

A sprawling, coastline car park gives ready access to this part of the seashore and is also where fishing boats still sell their daily catch off the shingle beach. From the car park, it's a short stroll west to the village and south to Greyfriars. Or you can hike further south, out along the beach to **Dunwich Heath**, where the coastguard cottages have been turned into a National Trust information centre (April–Oct daily; rest of year Wed–Sun) with displays on the heath and local wildlife. The heath is itself next to the **Minsmere RSPB Nature Reserve**, whose star turn is a colony of avocets. You can rent binoculars from the RSPB **visitor centre** (for times, call ℡01728/648281) and strike out on the trails to the birdwatching hides; there's a café on site, too.

The coastline and its heaths have an eerie quality that is best appreciated by **staying** at Dunwich's one and only pub, the *Ship Inn* (℡01728/648219; ❸). With its low wooden beams and open fire, the bar here is a great place for a drink and the **food** is both moderately priced and very tasty with seafood the main event.

Southwold

Perched on robust cliffs just to the north of the River Blyth, **SOUTHWOLD** gained what Dunwich lost, and by the sixteenth century it had overtaken all its local rivals. Its days as a busy fishing port are, however, long gone – though a small fleet still brings in herring, sprats and cod – and today it's a genteel seaside resort, an eminently appealing little town with none of the crassness of many of its competitors. There are fine old buildings, a long sandy beach, open heathland, a dinky harbour and even a little industry – in the shape of the Adnams brewery – but no burger bars and certainly no amusement arcades.

Southwold's breezy **High Street** is framed by attractive, mainly Georgian buildings, which culminate in the pocket-sized Market Place. From here, it's a brief stroll along East Street to the curious **Sailors' Reading Room** (daily 9am–5pm; free), decked out with model ships and nautical texts, and the bluff above the **beach**, where row upon row of candy-coloured huts march across the sands. Queen Street begins at the Market Place too, quickly leading to **South Green**, the prettiest of several greens dotted across town. In 1659, a calamitous fire razed much of Southwold and when the town was rebuilt the greens were left to act as firebreaks. Beyond, both Ferry Road and the Ferry footpath lead down to the **harbour**, at the mouth of the River Blyth, an idyllic spot, where fishing smacks rest against old wooden jetties and nets are spread out along the banks to dry.

Back on the Market Place, it's a couple of hundred yards north along Church Street to East Green, with Adnams Brewery on one side, the stumpy lighthouse on another. Close by is Southwold's architectural pride and joy, the **Church of St Edmund** (daily: June–Aug 9am–6pm; Sept–May 9am–4pm), a handsome fifteenth-century structure whose solid symmetries are balanced by its long and elegantly carved windows. From the church, it's a short walk north to the **pier**, the latest incarnation of a structure that dates from 1899. Built as a landing stage for passenger ferries, the pier has had a troubled history: it has been repeatedly damaged by storms, was hit by a sea-mine and then partly chopped up by the army as a protection against German invasion in World War II. Work started on rebuilding the pier in 1999 and will take several years to complete.

Practicalities

With frequent services from other towns along the coast, Southwold is easy to reach by **bus**. These stop on the Market Place, yards from the **tourist office**, at 69 High St (April–Sept Mon–Fri 10am–5pm, Sat 10am–5.30pm, Sun 11am–4pm; Oct–March Mon–Fri 10.30am–3.30pm, Sat 10am–4.30pm; ☎01502/724729, ◉www.visit-southwold.co.uk), which has details of local attractions and sells walking maps. The town has two well-known **hotels** beside the Market Place, both owned and operated by Adnams. The smarter of the two is the *Swan* (☎01502/722186; ◉), which occupies a splendid Georgian building with lovely period rooms, though the bedrooms – in the main house and in a garden annexe behind – are a little on the small side. The *Crown,* just along the High Street (☎01502/722275; ◉), has just twelve simple bedrooms, all of which are en suite. The best **B&B** in town is the delightful *Acton Lodge*, 18 South Green (☎01502/723217; no credit cards; ◉), which occupies a grand Victorian house complete with its own neo-Gothic tower. The interior is decorated in period style and the three comfortable bedrooms are all en suite. Breakfasts are delicious, too. Alternatively, there's a string of **guest houses** down along the seafront on North Parade: try the *North Parade*, at no. 21 (☎01502/722573; ◉), a well-tended Victorian house with sprucely decorated bedrooms; or the attractive *Dunburgh*, at no. 28 (☎01502/723253; ◉), housed in a rambling building with its own mini-tower.

Southwold has two outstanding **places to eat**. The *Crown*'s front bar provides superb informal meals, encompassing daily fish and meat specials combined with an enlightened wine list where all the choices are available by the glass. Turn up, wait for a table and expect to pay just £12 or so for two courses; you'll have to make a booking if you want to eat in the adjacent restaurant, which is pricier, slightly more adventurous and just as terrific. The *Swan*'s more formal dining room is the place for a gourmet blow-out, offering a choice of set dinners at £20–30 a head. For a **drink**, sample Adnams' brews in the *Crown*'s wood-panelled back-bar or stroll along to the *Red Lion* on South Green.

Norwich

One of the five largest cities in Norman England, **NORWICH** once served a vast hinterland of cloth producers in the eastern counties, whose work was brought here by river and exported to the continent. Its isolated position beyond the Fens meant that it enjoyed closer links with the Low Countries than with the rest of England – it was, after all, quicker to cross the North Sea than to go cross-country to London – and by 1700 Norwich was the second richest city in the country after London.

With the onset of the Industrial Revolution, Norwich lost ground to the northern manufacturing towns – the city's famous mustard company, Colman's is one of its few industrial success stories. This, and its continuing geographical isolation, has helped preserve much of the ancient street plan as well as many of the city's older buildings. Pride of place goes to the beautiful cathedral and the castle, but the city's hallmark is its medieval **churches**, thirty or so squat flintstone structures with sturdy towers and sinuous stone tracery round the windows. Isolation has also meant that the population has never swelled to any great extent and today, with just 170,000 inhabitants, Norwich remains an easy and enjoyable city to negotiate. Yet Norwich is no provincial backwater. In the

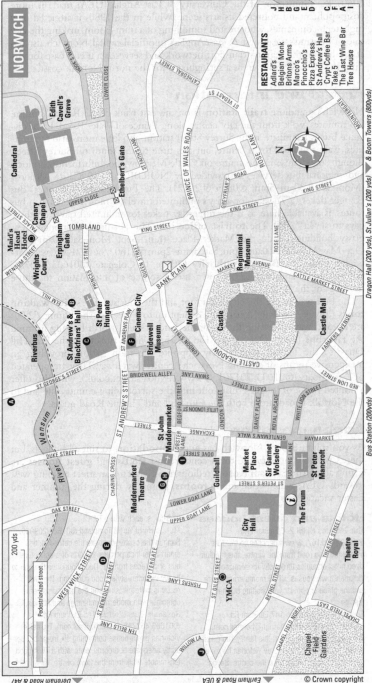

▲ Pulls Ferry & River   Train Station (50 yds) & ▲ A47 Great Yarmouth

RESTAURANTS
Adlard's   J
Belgian Monk   H
Britons Arms   B
Marco's   G
Pinocchio's   E
Pizza Express   D
St Andrew's Hall   C
Crypt Coffee Bar
Take 5   F
The Last Wine Bar   A
Tree House   I

▲ Bishopsgate
▲ Bishopsgate
Edith Cavell's Grave
Cathedral
LOWER CLOSE
CATHEDRAL STREET
ST VEDAST ST
Canary Chapel
PALACE STREET
Ethelbert's Gate
UPPER CLOSE
Maid's Head Hotel
TOMBLAND
MOUNTERGATE
◀ A1151 Wroxham
Erpingham Gate
Wrights Court
WENSUM STREET
ELM HILL
PRINCES STREET
STRAITE'S LANE
PRINCE OF WALES ROAD
KING STREET
GREYFRIARS ROAD
ROSE LANE
KING STREET
N
◀ Broads Authority Office (100 yds)
St Peter Hungate
St Andrew's & Blackfriars' Hall
ST ANDREWS PLAIN
QUEEN STREET
BANK PLAIN
Cinema City
Bridewell Museum
Norbic
MARKET AVENUE
Regimental Museum
ROSE LANE
CATTLE MARKET STREET
KING STREET
Riverbus
A
ST GEORGE'S STREET
BRIDEWELL ALLEY
SWAN LANE
LONDON STREET
CASTLE MEADOW
Castle
Castle Mall
FARMER'S AVENUE
CATTLE MARKET STREET
Wensum
River
ST ANDREW'S STREET
BEDFORD STREET
LITTLE LONDON ST
CASTLE STREET
DAVEY PLACE
Royal Arcade
RED LION STREET
WHITE LION STREET
▶ Bus Station (200yds)
DUKE STREET
ST JOHN STREET
EXCHANGE STREET
LOBSTER LANE
DOVE STREET
St John Maddermarket
GENTLEMAN'S WALK
HAYMARKET
I
CHARING CROSS
Maddermarket Theatre
G   H
Guildhall
LOWER GOAT LANE
Market Place
Sir Garnet Wolseley
PUDDING LANE
St Peter Mancroft
ST PETER'S STREET
OAK STREET
UPPER GOAT LANE
City Hall
The Forum
i
THEATRE STREET
◀ Dereham Road & A47
WESTWICK STREET
D   E
ST BENEDICT'S STREET
POTTERGATE
FISHERS LANE
ST GILES STREET
YMCA
BETHEL STREET
Theatre Royal
TEN BELLS LANE
CHAPEL FIELD NORTH
CHAPEL FIELD EAST
J
WILLOW LA
Chapel Field Gardens
◀ Earlham Road & UEA
© Crown copyright

▶ Dragon Hall (200 yds, St Julian's (200 yds) ▶ & Boom Towers (800yds)

Pedestrianized street
Pedestrian street
200 yds
0

1960s, the foundation of the University of East Anglia (UEA) made it more cosmopolitan and bolstered its arts scene, while in the 1980s it attracted new high-tech companies, who created something of a mini-boom, making the city one of England's wealthiest. As East Anglia's unofficial capital, Norwich also lies at the hub of the region's transport network and serves as a useful base for visiting the Broads, and even as a springboard for the north Norfolk coast.

Arrival and information

Norwich's grandiose **train station** is on the east bank of the River Wensum, ten minutes' walk from the city centre along Prince of Wales Road. Long distance **buses** terminate at the Surrey Street station, also little more than ten minutes' walk from the town centre, but this time to the south off Surrey Street, though some pause in the centre on Castle Meadow too. Information on local and regional bus services is provided by NORBIC, 17–19 Castle Meadow (Mon–Sat 8.30am–5pm; ☎0845/6020121). The First Eastern Counties' Bus Ranger ticket (£7), valid for a day's unlimited travel on most East Anglian bus routes, is available here, as is the three-day ticket for unlimited travel on three days in seven (£16). The **tourist office** is in The Forum, a gleamingly new, glassy building beside the Market Place (June–Sept Mon–Sat 10am–5pm; Oct–May Mon–Fri 10am–4pm, Sat 10am–2pm; ☎01603/666071, Ⓦwww.norwich.gov.uk). The **Broads Authority Office**, 18 Colegate (☎01603/610734, Ⓦwww.broads-authority.gov.uk), is a useful source of information for those heading for the Broads.

The best way to see the city is on foot and the tourist office's **city walking tours** (July & Aug daily; April–June & Sept up to 4 weekly; 1hr 30min; £2.50) are a good way of getting the lie of the land. It's also worth bearing in mind the **riverbus** (April–Oct 5 daily; 15min; 75p), which runs from the Elm Hill Quay to the Thorpe Road Quay, opposite the train station, providing an inexpensive means of cruising Norwich's central waterway. They are operated by City Boats (☎01603/701701, Ⓦwww.cityboats.fsnet.co.uk), who also offer a limited range of longer cruises out into the surrounding countryside and to the Norfolk Broads from both the Elm Hill and Thorpe Road quays.

Accommodation

As you might expect, Norwich has **accommodation** to suit all budgets, but there's precious little in the town centre. Most **B&Bs** and **guest houses** are strung along the Earlham Road, a tedious, mostly Victorian street running west towards UEA, which itself offers **rooms**, primarily during the summer and Easter vacations.

Hotels and guest houses

The Beeches Hotel 2–6 Earlham Rd ☎01603/621167, Ⓦwww.beeches.co.uk. Just across the ring road from the centre, this medium-sized hotel occupies three fully modernized Victorian town houses. All 36 rooms are en suite and the place is popular with visiting business folk. ❺

Earlham Guest House 147 Earlham Rd ☎01603/454169, ℮earlhamgh@hotmail.com. Spick-and-span lodgings at this family-run guest house, located in a two-storey Victorian house a good ten minutes' walk from the centre. Seven

bedrooms, each with a TV. ❷

Maid's Head Hotel Tombland ☎01603/209955. Bang in the centre, opposite the cathedral, this smart hotel incorporates all sorts of architectural bits and pieces from Art Deco flourishes through to heavy Victorian-style wood panelling. The end result is quite pleasing and the bedrooms come complete with modern furnishings and fittings. ❻

Rosedale Guest House 145 Earlham Rd ☎01603/453743, ℮drcbac@aol.com. Typical Victorian guest house containing six frugal but perfectly adequate bedrooms, each with a TV. A good ten-minute walk from the town centre. ❷

Swallow Nelson Hotel Prince of Wales Rd ☎01603/760260. This modern, riverside hotel, directly opposite the train station, caters to a mainly business clientele. It offers spick-and-span rooms, some of which overlook the water, an indoor pool and a health club. ☻

Hostels and student halls

Norwich youth hostel 112 Turner Rd ☎01603/627647, ☻www.yha.org.uk. This straight-forward, sixty-bed hostel is located in the suburbs two miles west of the centre. Closed Nov–March.

University of East Anglia ☎01603/593297. There are sixty en-suite rooms available year-round in Nelson Court (£49 per double), and also single student rooms with shared bathrooms (£23) and en suite (£32) available during Easter and summer vacations. The campus is four miles west of the centre along the Earlham Road; of the many buses running here from the centre – #25, #26 and #27 from Castle Meadow are the most frequent.

The City

Tucked into a sweeping bend of the River Wensum, Norwich's irregular street plan, a Saxon legacy, can make orientation difficult. There are, however, three obvious landmarks to help you find your way – the cathedral with its giant spire, the Norman castle on its commanding mound and the distinctive clock-tower of City Hall. The **cathedral** and the **castle** are the town's premier attractions and the latter also holds one of the region's most satisfying collections of fine art. Finally, note that **Sunday** can be a disastrous day to visit if you want to see anything other than the cathedral: most museums and attractions are closed, not to mention most restaurants.

The Cathedral

Norwich **Cathedral** (daily: May–Sept 7.30am–7pm; Oct–April 7.30am–6pm; free tours May–Oct Mon–Sat; £3 donation requested) is distinguished by its prickly octagonal spire which rises to a height of 315ft, second only to Salisbury. It's best viewed from the Lower Close (see below) to the west, where the thick curves of the flying buttresses, the rounded excrescences of the ambulatory chapels – unusual in an English cathedral – and the straight symmetries of the main body can all be seen to perfection.

The **interior** is pleasantly light thanks to a creamy tint in the stone and the clear glass windows of much of the nave, where the thick pillars are a powerful legacy of the Norman builders who began the cathedral in 1096. Look up to spy the nave's fan vaulting, delicate and geometrically precise carving adorned by several hundred roof **bosses** recounting – from east to west – the story of the Old and New Testaments from the Creation to the Last Judgement. Moving on, wander down the south side of the ambulatory to reach **St Luke's Chapel**, where the cathedral's finest work of art, the *Despenser Reredos*, is a superb painted panel commissioned to celebrate the crushing of the Peasants' Revolt of 1381. Accessible from the south aisle of the nave are the cathedral's unique **cloisters**. Built between 1297 and 1450, and the only two-storey cloisters left standing in England, they contain a remarkable set of sculpted **bosses**, similar to the ones in the main nave, but close enough to be scrutinized without binoculars. The carving is fabulously intricate and the dominant theme is the Apocalypse, but look out also for the bosses depicting green men, pagan fertility symbols. A computer screen by the main entrance gives the low-down on all of the bosses.

Outside, beside the main entrance, stands the medieval **Canary Chapel**. This is the original building of Norwich School, whose blue-blazered pupils are often visible during term time – the rambling school buildings are adjacent. A statue of the school's most famous boy, Horatio Nelson, faces the chapel, stand-

△ Flatford Mill, Suffolk

ing on the green of the **Upper Close**, which is guarded by two ornate and imposing medieval gates, **Erpingham** and, a few yards to the south, **Ethelbert**. Beside the Erpingham gate is a memorial to Edith Cavell, a local woman who was a nurse in occupied Brussels during World War I. Both gates lead onto the old Saxon market place, **Tombland**, a wide and busy thoroughfare whose name derives from the Saxon word for an open space.

Tombland is a convenient place to start an exploration of the rest of the city centre (see below), but instead you might prefer to wander pedestrianized **Cathedral Close**, which extends east to the river from – and including – the Upper Close. Just beyond the Upper Close is the **Lower Close**, where a scattering of silver birches is flanked by attractive Georgian and Victorian houses. Keeping straight, the footpath continues east to **Pull's Ferry**, a landing stage at the city's medieval watergate, named after the last ferryman to work this stretch of the river. It's a picturesque spot and from here you can wander along the riverbank either south to the railway station or north to Bishopgate, by means of which you can regain Tombland.

From Tombland to Elm Hill and Pottergate

At the north end of Tombland, fork left at the *Maid's Head Hotel* and cobbled **Elm Hill** soon appears on the left, its quirky half-timbered houses incorporating **Wright's Court**, down a passageway at no. 43, one of the city's few remaining enclosed courtyards. Elm Hill quickly opens out into a triangular square centred on a plane tree, planted on the spot where the eponymous elm tree from Henry VIII's time once stood. It then veers left up to **St Peter Hungate**, a good-looking, fifteenth-century flint church equipped with a solid square tower and gentle stone tracery round its windows.

Turn right at the church and it's just a few yards to **St Andrew's Hall** and **Blackfriars Hall**, two adjoining buildings that were originally the nave and chancel, respectively, of a Dominican monastery church. Imaginatively recycled, the two halls are now used for a variety of public events, including concerts, weddings and antique fairs; the crypt of the former now serves as a café (Mon–Sat 9am–4.30pm). South of here, off St Andrews Street and along Bridewell Alley, stands the **Bridewell Museum** (April–Sept Mon–Sat 10am–5pm; £2), one of the city's more enjoyable museums. Formerly the city jail, the Bridewell holds a pot-pourri of old machines, adverts, signs, and reconstructed shops celebrating Norwich's old trades and industry. Inevitably, there's much on the all-important mustard industry, which did much to keep the city's economy afloat in its more troubled times.

From the top of Bridewell Alley, Bedford Street and then Lobster Lane lead west to Pottergate's **St John Maddermarket** (June–Sept Tues–Sat 10.30am–5pm; free), one of thirty medieval churches standing within the boundaries of the old city walls. Most are redundant and are rarely open to the public, but this is one of the more accessible, courtesy of dedicated volunteers. Apart from the stone trimmings, the church is almost entirely composed of flint rubble, the traditional building material of east Norfolk, an area chronically short of decent stone. It is a good example of the Perpendicular style, a subdivision of English Gothic which flourished from the middle of the fourteenth to the early sixteenth century and is characterized by straight vertical lines – as you might expect from the name – and large windows framed by flowing, but plain tracery. By comparison, the remodelled interior is something of a disappointment, but it does hold a good selection of **brasses** and the volunteers will kit you out so you can rub away to your heart's content. Back outside, the arch under the church tower leads through to the **Maddermarket Theatre**, built in 1921 in the style of an

Elizabethan playhouse. Incidentally, Maddermarket is named after the yellow flower that the weavers used to make red vegetable dye, or madder.

The Market Place

From Pottergate, several narrow alleys lead through to the city's **Market Place**, site of one of the country's largest open-air markets (closed Sun), with stalls selling everything from bargain-basement clothes to local mussels and whelks. Four very different but equally distinctive buildings oversee the market's stripy awnings, the oldest of them being the fifteenth-century **Guildhall**, an attractive flint and stone structure begun in 1407. Opposite, commanding the heights of the market place, are the austere **City Hall**, a lumbering brick pile with a landmark clock tower built in the 1930s in a Scandinavian style – it bears a striking resemblance to Oslo's city hall – and **The Forum**, a flashy, glassy structure completed in 2001. On the south side of the Market Place is the finest of the four buildings, **St Peter Mancroft** (Mon–Fri 9.30am–4.30pm, Sat 10am–12.30pm; free), whose long and graceful nave leads to a mighty stone tower, an intricately carved affair surmounted by a spiky little spire. The church once delighted John Wesley, who declared "I scarcely ever remember to have seen a more beautiful parish church," a fair description of what remains an exquisite example of the Perpendicular style with the slender columns of the nave reaching up towards the delicate groining of the roof.

Back outside and just below the church is the bubble-gum-orange **Sir Garnet Wolseley** pub, sole survivor of the 44 ale houses that once crowded the Market Place – and stirred the local bourgeoisie into endless discussions about the drunken fecklessness of the working class. Opposite the pub, across **Gentlemen's Walk**, the town's main promenade, which runs along the bottom of the market place, is the **Royal Arcade**, an Art Nouveau extravagance from 1899. The arcade has been beautifully restored to reveal the swirl and blob of the tiling, ironwork and stained glass, though it's actually the eastern entrance, further from Gentlemen's Walk, which is the most appealing section.

The Castle

Perched high on a grassy mound in the centre of town, and imaginatively tailored into a brand new shopping mall down below, the stern walls of **Norwich Castle**, replete with blind arcading and dating from the twelfth century, were built to intimidate the local population. To begin with they were a reminder of Norman power and then, when the castle was turned into a prison, they served as a grim warning to potential law-breakers. Recently refurbished in lavish style, the castle now holds an excellent **Museum and Art Gallery** (July & Aug 10.30am–7pm, Sun 2–5pm; rest of year Mon–Sat 10.30am–5pm; £4.90 all zones), which is divided into three colour-coded zones – yellow for Art and Exhibitions, green for Natural History, and pink for the Castle Keep. The **Natural History** section holds a fairly routine collection of stuffed and mounted wildlife, but **Art and Exhibitions** scores well with its temporary displays and boasts an outstanding selection of work by the **Norwich School**. Founded in 1803, and in existence for just thirty years, this school of landscape painters produced – for the most part at least – richly coloured, formally composed land- and seascapes in oil and watercolour, paintings whose realism harked back to the Dutch landscape painters of the seventeenth century. The leading figures were John Crome – aka "Old Crome" – and more particularly John Sell Cotman, who is generally acknowledged as one of England's finest watercolourists. Both have a gallery to themselves and, helpfully, there's also a gallery given over to those Dutch painters who influenced them.

Moving on, the **Castle Keep** is no more than a shell, its gloomy walls towering above a scattering of local archeological finds and exhibits that illustrate traditional forms of punishment. The gibbet and its instruments of torture attract most attention, but more unusual is a bloated model dragon, known as Snap, which was paraded round town on the annual guilds' day procession – a folkloric hand-me-down from the dragon St George had so much trouble polishing off. To see more of the Keep, join one of the regular **guided tours** (an extra £2.50) that explore the battlements and – at some time in the near future – the dungeons.

Finally, a long and dark (and one-way) tunnel leads down from the Castle Museum to the **Royal Norfolk Regimental Museum** (Mon–Sat 10am–5pm), which tracks through the history of the regiment with remarkable candour – including an even-handed account of the Norfolks' police-keeping role in Northern Ireland. The exit leaves you below the castle on Market Avenue.

The University

The **University of East Anglia** (UEA) occupies a sprawling campus on the western outskirts of the city beside the B1108. Its buildings are resolutely modern concrete-and-glass blocks of varying designs – some quite ordinary, others like the prize-winning "ziggurat" halls of residence, designed by Denys Lasdun, eminently memorable. The main reason to visit is the flashy, high-tech **Sainsbury Centre for Visual Arts** (Tues–Sun 11am–5pm; £2; ⓦwww .uea.ac.uk/scva), built by Norman Foster in the 1970s. The interior houses one of the most varied collections of sculpture and painting in the country – donated by the family which founded the Sainsbury supermarket chain – in which the likes of Degas, Seurat, Picasso, Giacometti, Bacon and Henry Moore rub shoulders with Mayan and Egyptian antiquities. The centre also runs a first-rate programme of temporary exhibitions (call ℡01603/593199 for further details). **Buses** #25, #26 and #27 run frequently to UEA from Castle Meadow.

Eating and drinking

There are plenty of **cafés and restaurants** in the city centre – most of them very good value. Decent **pubs**, though, are harder to find – maybe because previously serviceable places have been turned into ersatz "traditional" drinking dens for students.

Cafés and restaurants

Adlard's 79 Upper Giles St ℡01603/633522. Engaging Modern-British restaurant with accomplished seasonal cooking from a brief but enticing menu. Closed all Sun & Mon lunch. Expensive.

Belgian Monk 7 Pottergate ℡01603/767222. Perhaps too theme-ish for some tastes, this new bar and restaurant specializes in all-things Flemish – from beers through to soup and, of course, mussels and chips. Moderate.

Britons Arms 9 Elm Hill. Home-made quiches, tarts, cakes and scones plus pies and salads in a quaint Elm Hill house with a terraced garden. Closed Sun. Inexpensive.

The Last Wine Bar, 70–76 St George's St ℡01603/626626. Converted factory building holding a smart wine bar, which serves up tasty bistro-style dishes. A couple of minutes' walk north of the river. Closed Sun. Moderate.

Marco's 17 Pottergate ℡01603/624044. The city's oldest and finest Italian restaurant, serving all the classics with panache. Smart and formal. Closed Sun & Mon. Expensive.

Pinocchio's 11 St Benedicts St ℡01603/613318. Relaxed Italian restaurant with inventive food combinations and featuring live music a couple of times a week. Occupies a pleasantly converted old general store. Closed Sun. Moderate.

Pizza Express 15 St Benedicts St. No surprises, of course, on the menu, but you get the city centre's best pizzas. Inexpensive.

St Andrew's Hall Crypt Coffee Bar St Andrews Plain at St Georges St. Bargain spot for budget meals or just a coffee and cake. Closed Sun. Inexpensive.

Take 5 at Cinema City, St Andrews Plain. Imaginative, budget bistro food served in amenable surroundings. A student favourite. Mon–Sat 11am–11pm. Inexpensive.

Tree House 14 Dove St, above the Rainbow wholefood shop. Vegetarian wholefood café/restaurant offering a daily changing menu of soups, salads and main courses, plus organic wines and beers. Closed Sun. Inexpensive.

Pubs, bars and clubs

Adam & Eve Bishopgate. There's been a pub on this site for seven hundred years and it's still the top spot in town for the discerning drinker – with a changing range of real ales and an eclectic wine list supplied by Adnams.

Coach & Horses Bethel St. Pleasant city-centre pub – across the street from City Hall – with lived-in furnishings and fittings. Good for a quiet drink.

Ribs of Beef Wensum St. Boisterous riverside drinking haunt popular with students and townies alike. Well-kept ales and inexpensive bar food.

Waterfront 139–41 King's St ☎01603/632717. Norwich's principal club and alternative music venue, with gigs and DJs most nights. Sponsored by UEA.

Wild Man Bedford St. Long-established, popular city-centre watering hole that has greased many a student wheel.

Entertainment

Predictably, Norwich has its fair share of multi-screen **cinemas** showing Hollywood blockbusters, but it also has the excellent art-house Cinema City, in Suckling House on St Andrew's Plain (☎01603/622047, ⊛www.cinemaci-ty.co.uk). The **arts scene** here is a tad self-conscious, but the city does possess several first-rate **theatres**. The Theatre Royal, on Theatre Street (☎01603/630000, ⊛www.theatreroyalnorwich.co.uk), has a wide-ranging programme of mainstream and more adventurous plays and dance, while the amateur Maddermarket, St John's Alley, off Pottergate (☎01603/620917), offers an interesting range of modern theatre. Predictably enough, **UEA** is a major source of entertainment for students and locals alike, with gigs at the Union and classical concerts at the Music Centre. The annual **Norfolk and Norwich Festival** each October (☎01603/766400) features music, film, theatre, comedy, dance, walks and talks at venues all over the city.

The Norfolk Broads

Three rivers – the Yare, Waveney and Bure – meander across the flatlands to the east of Norwich, converging on Breydon Water before flowing into the sea at Great Yarmouth. In places these rivers swell into wide expanses of water known as "broads", which for years were thought to be natural lakes. In fact they're the result of extensive peat cutting, several centuries of accumulated diggings made in a region where wood was scarce and peat a valuable source of energy. The pits flooded when sea levels rose in the thirteenth and fourteenth centuries to create the **Norfolk Broads**, now one of the most important wetlands in Europe – a haven for many birds, such as kingfishers, grebes and warblers – and the county's major tourist attraction.

The Broads' delicate ecological balance suffered badly during the 1970s and 1980s. The careless use of fertilizers poisoned the water with phosphates and nitrates, encouraging the spread of algae; the decline in reed cutting – previously in great demand for thatching – made the broads partly unnavigable; and the enormous increase in pleasure-boat traffic began to erode the banks. National Park status was, however, accorded to the area in 1988, and efforts are now under way to clear the waters and protect the ecosystem. Co-ordinating the clean up is the **Broads Authority** (℡01603/610734, Ⓦwww.broads-authority.gov.uk), which maintains a series of information centres throughout the region – as well as a **Broads Information Line** (℡01603/782281). At any of these locations, you can pick up a free copy of the *Broadcaster*, a useful newspaper guide to the Broads as a whole.

The region is crossed by several **train** lines, with connections from Norwich to Wroxham, Acle and Reedham, as well as Berney Arms, near Breydon Water, one of the few places in England that can be reached by rail but not road. However, the best – really the only – way to see the Broads themselves is **by boat**, and you could happily spend a week or so exploring the 125 miles of lock-free navigable waterways, visiting the various churches, pubs and windmills en route. Among many **boat rental** companies, two of the more established are Blakes Holiday Boating (℡01603/739400, Ⓦwww.blakes.co.uk) and Broads Tours Ltd (℡01603/782207, Ⓦwww.broads.co.uk), both of whom operate out of Wroxham (see below). Prices for cruisers start at around £700 a week for four people in peak season, but less expensive, short-term rentals are widely available too. Houseboats are much cheaper than cruisers, but they are, of course, static.

Trying to explore the Broads by car is – as you might imagine – pretty much a waste of time, but cyclists and walkers have a much better time, taking advantage of the region's network of footpaths and cycling trails. There are eight Broads Authority **bike rental** points dotted round the Broads (£8/day; ℡01603/782281). **Walkers** might consider the 56-mile Weavers' Way, a long-distance footpath that winds through the best parts of the Broads on its way from Cromer to Great Yarmouth, though there are many shorter options too.

The easiest boating centre to reach from Norwich is **WROXHAM**, seven miles to the northeast and accessible by train, bus and car. Wroxham is itself short on charm, but it has a useful **information centre**, on Station Road (Easter–Oct daily 9am–1pm & 2–5pm; ℡01603/782281), and plenty of places where you can stock up with food before heading out on a cruise.

Some eight miles east of Wroxham, **POTTER HEIGHAM** is the nominal capital of the Broads, taking its name from the pottery which once stood here on the River Thurne and from the Saxon lord of Heacham who founded the first settlement. Again, there's not much to keep your attention, though you can watch boaters struggling with the village's fourteenth-century bridge, regarded as one of the most difficult passages in the Broads. All the major boat rental companies have outlets here and there's also an **information centre** (Easter–Oct daily 9am–1pm & 2–5pm; ℡01692/670779). The only public transport to Potter Heigham is by bus from Great Yarmouth.

Tiny **RANWORTH**, around twelve miles east of Norwich via the B1140, is a quieter spot altogether. There's no point in coming here if you're after a boat, but the village does have its own **information office** (Easter–Oct daily 9am–1pm & 2–5pm; ℡01603/270453), with stacks of stuff on local walking and wildlife. Ranworth also possesses a good-looking **church**, which is graced by a much-admired fifteenth-century rood screen, and from here it's just a couple of miles downstream along the River Bure to the isolated ruins of **St Benet's Abbey** – but note you can't get here by car.

Great Yarmouth

First and foremost, **GREAT YARMOUTH** is a seaside resort, its promenade a parade of amusement arcades and rainy-day attractions, deserted in winter, heaving in summer. But it's also a port with a long history and, despite extensive wartime bomb damage, it retains a handful of sights that give some idea of the place Daniel Defoe thought "far superior to Norwich".

Yarmouth was a major trading port by the fourteenth century, its economy underpinned by its control of the waterways leading inland to Norwich. It also benefited from fishing, especially during the nineteenth century when there was a spectacular boom in the herring industry. The fishing finally fizzled out in the 1960s, but the timely discovery of gas and oil deposits off the Norfolk coast helped mitigate the effects and have since made the town a major base for the offshore gas industry, second only to Aberdeen for North Sea oil.

The Town

Arriving by train or car from Norwich, initial impressions are favourable thanks to the appealing silhouette of the church of **St Nicholas**, which boasts one of the widest naves in the country and, consequently, an impressive west front. The church stands at the northern end of the broad Market Place, which served as the centre of medieval Yarmouth, but is now mostly undistinguished. The one exception, at the square's northeast corner, is the **Hospital for Decayed Fishermen**, almshouses built in 1702 and opening out into a lovely little courtyard flanked by Dutch gables, the central cupola topped by a chilly looking statue of the fishermen's friend himself, St Peter. Just beyond, in Prior Plain and now a teashop, is Sewell House, the childhood home of Anna Sewell, author of *Black Beauty*.

Despite considerable wartime damage, sections of the **medieval walls** remain, with one of the best-preserved portions located along Ferrier Road, just north of St Nicholas. Another interesting feature of the old town is the narrow parallel alleys, known locally as rows, which were built to connect South Quay, running beside the River Yare just to the southwest of the Market Place, with the town. Sixty-nine rows have survived, and English Heritage maintain two seventeenth-century row houses – the **Old Merchant's House** in Row 117 and a **Row 111 House**, each with furnishings and fittings illustrating the life of local folk between the 1870s and the 1940s (April–Oct daily 10am–1pm & 2–5pm; £2.40 combined entry; EH). For more on Yarmouth's past, head for the **Elizabethan House Museum**, at 4 South Quay (April–Oct Mon–Fri 10am–5pm, Sat & Sun 1–5pm; £2; NT), whose period rooms concentrate on domestic life and include a Tudor bedroom and dining room. Here also is the Conspiracy Room where legend has it that Cromwell and his Puritan colleagues plotted the trial and execution of Charles I.

The vast majority of tourists simply head for the Victorian-built seafront, **Marine Parade**, whose wide sandy beach was the unlikely setting for many of the most dramatic events in Dickens' *David Copperfield*. There are the usual promenade gardens and seafront attractions here, bolstered by the presence of the town's **Maritime Museum** (June–Sept Mon–Fri 10am-5pm, Sat & Sun 1.15pm–5pm; £1.10), which traces the history of the herring industry and the inland waterways.

Practicalities

It's a good ten-minute walk east from Great Yarmouth's **train station** to the central Market Place – cross the river by the footbridge and you'll find yourself on North Quay, from where The Conge leads straight there. **Buses** terminate one block from the sea on Wellesley Road and about 600 yards to the northeast of Market Place. There are two **tourist offices**: one in the town hall, on South Quay (Mon–Fri 9am–5pm; ☎01493/846345, ⓦwww.great-yarmouth.co.uk), and a seasonal office on Marine Parade (June–Sept Mon–Sat 9.30am–5.30pm, Sun 10am–5pm; April, May & Oct daily 10am–1pm & 2–5pm; ☎01493/842195). There's also a useful **Broads Information Centre** in the North West Tower, at the foot of North Quay (July–Sept daily 10am–3.45pm; ☎01493/332095).

B&Bs line every street, with price a fair indication of quality, but if you don't have much luck, call in at the tourist office, which operates an accommodation booking service. Among many options, the *Willow Guest House*, 26 Trafalgar Rd (☎01493/332355; ❶), offers sea views from some of its nine bedrooms, while *Senglea Lodge*, 7 Euston Rd (☎01493/859632; ❶), is a cosy, well-maintained terraced house with seven pleasant bedrooms a short walk from Marine Parade. For a **hotel**, try the *Royal*, 4 Marine Parade (☎01493/844215; ❸), arguably Yarmouth's grandest – and where Dickens stayed. Yarmouth's **youth hostel**, with self-catering facilities but no café, is in a large Victorian house near the bus station at 2 Sandown Rd (☎01493/843991, ⓦwww.yha.org.uk).

Far and away the best **restaurant** in town is the reasonably priced *Seafood Restaurant*, 85 North Quay (☎01493/856009; closed Sun), which does a superb fish soup and Mediterranean-influenced seafood dishes.

The north Norfolk coast

Beyond Yarmouth, the first thirty miles of the **north Norfolk coast** is preoccupied by its beach, with barely a village, never mind an estuary or a harbour, in sight. The first place of any note is **Cromer**, a workaday seaside town whose bleak and blustery cliffs have drawn tourists for over a century. A few miles to the west is another well-established resort, **Sheringham**, but thereafter the shoreline becomes a ragged patchwork of salt marshes, dunes and shingle spits which form an almost unbroken series of nature reserves, supporting a fascinating range of flora and fauna. It's a lovely stretch of coast and the villages bordering it, principally **Cley-next-the-Sea**, **Blakeney** and **Wells**, are prime targets for an overnight stay. The other major attractions hereabouts are the string of stately homes that lie a short distance inland – some, such as **Felbrigg** and **Blickling Hall**, are among the finest in the region.

Cromer and Sheringham are the only places reachable by **train**, with an hourly service from Norwich on the Bittern Line. Local **bus** services fill in (most of) the gaps, connecting all of the towns and many of the villages. There's also the **Coasthopper bus** (June–Sept Mon–Sat hourly, Sun 4 daily; ☎0845/3006116), which provides regular services along the whole length of the coast from Cromer to Hunstanton, with some buses continuing to Great Yarmouth and King's Lynn. The Coasthopper Rover ticket (£4) gives a day's unlimited travel on the route.

Cromer and around

Dramatically poised on a high bluff, **CROMER** should be the most memorable of the Norfolk coastal resorts, but its fine aspect is undermined by a dispiriting shabbiness in the streets and shopfronts. The tower of **St Peter and St Paul**, at 160ft the tallest in Norfolk, attests to the port's medieval wealth, but it was the advent of the railway in the 1880s that heralded the most frenetic flurry of building activity. A bevy of grand Edwardian hotels was constructed along the seafront and for a moment Cromer became the most fashionable of resorts, but the gloss soon wore off and only the seen-better-days **Hotel de Paris** has survived. While you're here, be sure to take a stroll out onto the **pier**, which was badly damaged in a storm in November 1993, but has since been repaired and struggles gamely on.

Somewhat miraculously Cromer has managed to retain its rail link with Norwich; the **train station** is a five-minute walk west of the centre. **Buses** terminate on Cadogan Road, next to the **tourist office** (April–June, Sept & Oct Mon–Sat 10am–5pm, Sun 10am–4pm; July & Aug Mon–Sat 9.30am–6pm, Sun 9.30am–5pm; Nov–March 10am–1pm & 1.45–4pm; ☎01263/512497), which is just 200 yards from the cliff-top promenade. An hour or two in Cromer is probably enough, though the beach is first-rate and the cliff-top walk exhilarating. There's no shortage of inexpensive **accommodation** – the tourist office has all the details.

Felbrigg Hall

Just a couple of miles southwest of Cromer off the A148, **Felbrigg Hall** (April–Oct Mon–Wed, Sat & Sun 1–5pm; £5.80; NT) is a charming Jacobean mansion. The main facade is particularly appealing, the soft hues of the ageing limestone and brick intercepted by three bay windows which together sport a large, cleverly carved inscription – *Gloria Deo in Excelsis* – in celebration of the reviving fortunes of the family who then owned the place, the Windhams. The interior is splendid too, with the studied informality of both the dining room and the drawing room enlivened by some magnificent seventeenth-century plasterwork ceilings and sundry *objets d'art*.

The surrounding **parkland** (daily dawn to dusk) divides into two, with woods to the north and open pasture to the south. Footpaths crisscross the park and a popular spot to head for is the medieval church of **St Margaret's** in the southeastern corner, which contains a fine set of brasses and a fancy memorial to William Windham I and his wife by Grinling Gibbons. Nearer the house, there's the extensive **walled garden**, which features flowering borders and an octagonal dove house, and the stables, which have been converted into very pleasant **tearooms**.

Blickling Hall

Blickling Hall (April–Sept Wed–Sun 1–4.30pm; Oct 1–3.30pm; £6.70; gardens only £3.80; NT), set in a sheltered, wooded valley ten miles south of Cromer via the A140 is another grand Jacobean pile. Built for Sir Henry Hobart, a Lord Chief Justice, the hall dates from the 1620s and although it was extensively remodelled over a century later, the modifications respected the integrity of the earlier design. Consequently, the long facade, with its slender chimneys, high gables and towers, is the apotheosis of Jacobean design. Inside, highlights include a superb plasterwork ceiling in the Long Gallery and an extraordinarily grand main staircase. There's also a gargantuan tapestry depicting Peter the Great defeating the Swedes, given to one of the family by Catherine the Great.

The surrounding **parkland** (daily dawn to dusk) incorporates a mile-long lake and a weird pyramidal mausoleum holding the earthly remains of the last of the male Hobarts.

Sheringham

SHERINGHAM, a popular seaside town four miles west of Cromer, has an amiable, easy-going air and makes a reasonable overnight stop, though frankly you're still only marking time until you hit the more appealing places further west. One of the distinctive features of the town is the smooth local beach pebbles that face and decorate the houses, a flinting technique used frequently in this part of Norfolk – the best examples here are off the High Street. The downside is that the power of the waves which makes the pebbles smooth has also forced the local council to spend thousands rebuilding the sea defences. The resultant mass of reinforced concrete makes for a less than pleasing seafront – all the more reason to head, instead, for **Sheringham Park**, the 770-acre woodland park a couple of miles southwest of the town, laid out by Humphrey Repton in the early 1800s. The park boasts a wonderful array of rhododendrons and azaleas, at their best in late May to early June, and a series of lookout posts from which you can admire the view down to the coast. The other out-of-town jaunt is on the **North Norfolk Railway**, whose steam trains operate along the five miles of track southwest from Sheringham to the modest market town of Holt (June–Sept daily; all-day ticket £7.50; ☎01263/820800).

Sheringham's two **train stations** are opposite each other on either side of Station Road. The main station, the terminus of the Bittern Line from Norwich, is just to the east, the North Norfolk Railway station to the west. The **tourist office** (April–Oct Mon–Sat 10am–5pm, Sun 10am–4pm; ☎01263/824329) is in between them on Railway Approach. From the tourist office, it's a five-minute walk north to the seafront, straight down Station Road and its continuation, the High Street. You can rent **bikes** from Bike Riders, 7 St Peter's Rd (☎01263/821906), adjacent to the North Norfolk Railway station.

There are plenty of **B&B** options, with one of the best being *Oak Lodge* at 2 Morris St (☎01263/823158, ⓦwww.oak-lodge.co.uk; ❸), a smart Edwardian house with four attractive bedrooms right in the centre of town. A good alternative is the *Two Lifeboats*, 2 High St (☎01263/822401; ❹), a small hotel on the promenade offering sea views from most of its bedrooms. The **youth hostel** is a short walk south of the main train station at 1 Cremer's Drift (☎01263/823215, ⓦwww.yha.org.uk), set in its own grounds just off Cromer Road. The *Two Lifeboats* serves inexpensive **bar meals** and more formal dinners in its **restaurant**, and prides itself on its fresh fish.

Cley-next-the-Sea and Blakeney Point

Travelling west from Sheringham, the A149 meanders through a pretty rural landscape offering occasional glimpses of the sea and a shoreline protected by a giant shingle barrier erected after the catastrophic flood of 1953, a disaster which claimed over one thousand lives. After seven miles you reach **CLEY-NEXT-THE-SEA**, once a busy wool port but now little more than a row of flint cottages and Georgian mansions set beside a narrow, marshy inlet that (just) gives access to the sea. The original village was destroyed in a fire in 1612, which explains why Cley's fine medieval **Church of St Margaret** is located half a mile inland at the very southern edge of the current village, overlooking the green. The Black Death brought church construction to a sudden halt, hence the contrast between the stunted, unfinished chancel and the splendid nave, which boasts several fine medieval brasses and some folksy fifteenth-century bench ends depicting animals and grotesques. Cley's other great draw – housed in an old forge on the main street – is the excellent **Cley Smoke House**, selling local smoked fish and other delicacies, while nearby Picnic Fayre has long been one of the finest delis in East Anglia.

It's about 400 yards east from the village to the mile-long byroad that leads to the shingle mounds of **Cley beach**. This is the starting point for the four-mile hike west out along the spit to **Blakeney Point**, a nature reserve famed for its colonies of terns and seals. The seal colony is made up of several hundred common and grey seals and the old lifeboat house, at the end of the spit, is now a summer-only National Trust information centre. The shifting shingle can, however, make the going difficult, so keep to the low-water mark – which also means that you won't accidentally trample any nests. The easier alternative is to take one of the boat trips to the point from Blakeney or Morston. The Norfolk Coast Path passes close to the beach too, continuing south along the edge of the **Cley Marshes**, which attract a bewildering variety of waders – and, of course, "twitchers".

Cley has several great places **to stay**, beginning with the *Cley Mill B&B* (☎01263/740209; ❹), housed in a converted windmill complete with sails and a balcony offering wonderful views over the surrounding salt marshes and seashore. Other options in the village include the attractive *Whalebone House*, on the main street (☎01263/740336; ❸), and the *Three Swallows* pub (☎01263/740526; ❷) on the green by the church, which has several pleasant en-suite rooms and serves good **food**.

Blakeney

BLAKENEY is delightful. Once a bustling port exporting fish, corn and salt, it's now a dreamy little place of pebble-covered cottages sloping up from a narrow harbour just a mile west of Cley. Crab sandwiches are sold from stalls at the quayside, the meandering high street is flanked by family-run shops, and footpaths stretch out along the sea wall to east and west, allowing long, lingering looks over the salt marshes. The only sight as such is the **Church of St Nicholas**, beside the A149 at the south end of the village, whose sturdy tower and nave are made of flint rubble with stone trimmings, the traditional building materials of north Norfolk. Inside, the oak and chestnut hammer-beam roof and the delicate rood screen are the most enjoyable features of the nave, which is attached to a late thirteenth-century chancel, the only survivor from the original Carmelite friary church. With its seven stepped lancet windows, the east window is a rare example of Early English design, though the stained glass is much later.

Blakeney **harbour** is linked to the sea by a narrow channel, which wriggles its way through the salt marshes. The channel is, however, only navigable for a few hours at high tide – at low tide the harbour is no more than a muddy creek. Depending on the tides, there are **boat trips** from Blakeney or Morston quay, a mile or two to the west, to Blakeney Point (see above); as well as the two-hour round trips which land passengers at the National Trust information centre on Blakeney Point there are also hour-long seal-watching trips. The main operators advertise departure times on blackboards by the quayside.

For **accommodation**, the quayside *Blakeney Hotel* (☎01263/740797, ⓦwww.blakeney-hotel.co.uk; ❼) is one of the most charming hotels in Norfolk, a rambling building with high-pitched gables and pebble-covered walls. The hotel has a heated indoor swimming pool, a secluded garden, cosy lounges decorated in soft pastel colours, sea views and serves outstanding food. The cheaper rooms can be poky and somewhat airless, but pay a little more and you'll be rewarded with splendid views across the harbour and the marshes. There are discounts for longer stays with full board. A very good alternative is the *Manor Hotel* (℡01263/740376, ⓦwww.blakeneymanor.co.uk; ⑥), which occupies a low-lying courtyard complex a few yards to the east of the harbour; or you might try the excellent *King's Arms*, just back from the quay on Westgate (℡01263/740341; ③), a traditional pub, with low, beamed ceilings and seven en-suite bedrooms. The latter also serves up delicious, reasonably priced **bar food**.

Wells-next-the-Sea and around

Despite its name, **WELLS-NEXT-THE-SEA**, some eight miles west of Blakeney, is situated a good mile or so from open water. In Tudor times, when it enjoyed much easier access to the ocean, it was one of the great ports of eastern England, a major player in the trade with the Netherlands. It's still one of the more attractive towns on the north Norfolk coast, and the only one to remain a commercially viable port. There's nothing specific to see among its narrow lanes, but it does make a very good base for exploring the surrounding coastline.

The town divides into three distinct areas, starting with the broad rectangular green to the south, lined with oak and beech trees and some very fine Georgian houses, and known as **The Buttlands** since the days when it was used for archery practice. North from here, across Station Road, are the narrow lanes of the town centre with **Staithe Street**, the tiny main drag, flanked by quaint old-fashioned shops. At the north end of Staithe Street stands the **quay**, a slightly forlorn affair inhabited by a couple of amusement arcades and fish-and-chip shops. A few yards away is the mile-long road to the **beach**, a handsome sandy tract backed by pine-clad dunes. The road is shadowed by a high flood defence and a tiny narrow-gauge railway, which scoots down to the beach every forty minutes or so during the season.

Buses to Wells stop on the Buttlands, a short stroll from the **tourist office** at the foot of Staithe Street (March to mid-July & Oct Mon–Sat 10am–5pm, Sun 10am–4pm; mid-July to Sept Mon–Sat 9.30am–7pm, Sun 9.30am–6pm; ℡01328/710885). Several of the best **guest houses** are along Standard Road, which runs up from the eastern end of the quayside. First choice should be the elegant *Normans* (℡01328/710657; ③), whose six spacious and tastefully decorated rooms are all en suite; the TV lounge has a log fire and racks of games and the first-floor look-out window provides a wide view over the marshes – binoculars are provided. Other options include *Mill House*, a dignified old millowner's home on Northfield Lane (℡01328/710739; ②), and *Ilex House* on Bases Lane (℡01328/710556; ②); the latter is a good-looking Georgian villa with three guest rooms that sits in its own grounds, just to the west of the centre.

For **pub** food, head straight for the *Crown* on the Buttlands, the best pub in town. *Nelson's*, 21 Staithe St, is a pleasant tea and coffee shop that serves inexpensive meals.

Little Walsingham

For centuries **LITTLE WALSINGHAM**, five miles south of Wells, rivalled Canterbury as the foremost pilgrimage site in England. In 1061 the Lady of the Manor, Richeldis de Faverches, was prompted to build a replica of the **Santa Casa** (Mary's home in Nazareth) here – inspired, it is said, by visions of the

Virgin Mary. Whatever the reason for her actions, it brought instant fame and fortune to this little Norfolk village. By the fourteenth century, both the Augustinians and the Franciscans had established themselves here and every English king since Henry III had visited the place, walking barefoot for the last mile. Henry VIII followed in his predecessors' footsteps in 1511, though he subsequently destroyed the shrine during the Dissolution and brought the village's principal trade to an abrupt halt. Pilgrimages resumed in earnest after 1922, when the local vicar, Alfred Hope Patten, organized an Anglo-Catholic pilgrimage, the prelude to the building of an Anglican shrine in the 1930s. Today the village does good business out of its holy connections and the narrow-gauge **steam railway** from Wells (Easter–Sept daily; ☎01328/710631).

Little Walsingham now has a number of shrines catering to a variety of denominations – there are even two Russian Orthodox shrines – though the main one is the **Anglican shrine** inside the heavily restored parish church, a few yards from the main square beside the road to Holt. It's a strange-looking building – a cross between an English village hall and a Greek Orthodox church – and inside the candle-lit Santa Casa contains the statue of Our Lady of Walsingham.

Shrines apart, Little Walsingham has an attractive **High Street**, overlooked by handsome Georgian and half-timbered houses, several of which are given over to shrine shops and religious bookstores. At its southern end is **Friday Market**, a pretty little square which backs onto the grounds and ruins of the old Franciscan Friary. Along the High Street itself are yet more ecclesiastical ruins, those of **The Abbey** – more accurately the Augustinian Priory – whose landscaped grounds stretch east to the River Stiffkey. The abbey ruins are not much to look at, but the fifteenth-century **gatehouse**, on the High Street, is an impressive affair – look up and you'll spy Christ peering out from a window. At the north end of the High Street is the main square, the **Common Place**, whose half-timbered buildings surround a quaint octagonal structure built to protect the village **pump** in the sixteenth century.

The Coasthopper **bus** – as well as the fairly frequent Fakenham (for Norwich) to Wells bus – stops outside the Anglican shrine. The **train station** (for the steam train from Wells) is a five-minute walk from the north end of the village. To get to the village from the station, turn left along Egmere Road and take the second major right down Bridewell Street. The **tourist office** is on Common Place (April–Oct daily 10am–4.30pm; ☎01328/820510). It's difficult to find accommodation during major **pilgrimages** – the main ones are the national pilgrimage on May 31 and the pilgrimage for the sick and disabled on August 30. That said, the *Black Lion* pub on Friday Market (☎01328/820235; ❸) has comfortable en-suite rooms and a restaurant, as does the *Bull Inn* on Common Place (☎01328/820333; ❸).

Hunstanton and around

The Norfolk coast pretty much ends at **HUNSTANTON**, a Victorian seaside resort that grew up to the southwest of the original fishing village – now Old Hunstanton. Like Yarmouth, it has its fair share of amusement arcades, crazy golf, and entertainment complexes, but it has also hung on to its genteel origins – and its sandy beaches, backed by stripy gateau-like cliffs, are among the cleanest in Norfolk. Incidentally, in "The World of Fun" on Greevegate, Hunstanton possesses the self-proclaimed largest joke shop in Britain with more whoopee cushions and Dracula fangs than even the most unpleasant 10-year-old could want.

The **tourist office** is in the town hall (daily: April–Sept 9.30am–5pm; Oct–March 10.30am–4pm; ☏01485/532610) on the wide sloping green, which serves as the focal point of the town. They can help out with **accommodation**, though it's easy enough to find. The nicest and priciest places are among the cottages of Old Hunstanton. One particular recommendation is *Le Strange Arms*, Golf Course Road (☏01485/534411; ❺), an expansive mansion dating from the nineteenth century and with gardens running down to the beach. At the other end of the market, the **youth hostel** occupies a Victorian town house at 15 Avenue Rd (☏01485/532061, ⓦwww.yha.org.uk; closed Nov–March), south of Hunstanton green.

Sandringham House

Some eight miles south of Hunstanton looms the seven-thousand-acre estate of **Sandringham House** (mid-April to Oct daily 11am–4.45pm; closed for two weeks late-July or early Aug; £6), bought in 1861 by Queen Victoria for her son, the future Edward VII. The house is billed as a private home, but few families have a drawing room crammed with Russian silver and Chinese jade. The **museum**, housed in the old coach and stable block, contains an exhibition of royal memorabilia from dolls to cars, but much more arresting are the beautifully maintained **grounds** (10.30am–5pm), a mass of rhododendrons and azaleas in spring and early summer. The estate's sandy soil is also ideal for game birds, which was the attraction of the place for the terminally bored Edward, whose tradition of posh shooting parties is still followed by the royals.

The Fens – and Wicken Fen

One of the strangest of all English landscapes, the **Fens** cover a vast area from just north of Cambridge right up to Boston in Lincolnshire. For centuries, they were an inhospitable wilderness of quaking bogs and marshland, punctuated by clay islands on which small communities eked out a livelihood cutting peat for fuel, using reeds for thatching and living on a diet of fish and wildfowl. Piecemeal land reclamation took place throughout the Middle Ages, but it wasn't until the seventeenth century that the systematic draining of the fens was undertaken – amid fierce local opposition – by the Dutch engineer **Cornelius Vermuyden**. The transformation of the fens had unforeseen consequences: as it dried out, the peaty soil shrank to below the level of the rivers, causing further flooding, a situation only exacerbated by the numerous windmills, erected to help drain the fens, but which actually resulted in further shrinkage. The problem of shrinkage was only resolved in the 1820s with the introduction of steam-driven pumps, as these leviathans could control water levels with much greater precision, enabling the fens to be turned into the valuable agricultural land of today.

At **Wicken Fen** (daily dawn to dusk; visitor centre Tues–Sun 10am–5pm; ☏01353/720274; £3.70; NT), nine miles south of Ely via the A142, you can visit one of the few remaining areas of undrained fenland. Its survival is thanks to a group of Victorian entomologists who donated the land to the National Trust in 1899, making it the oldest nature reserve in the UK. The seven hundred acres are undrained but not uncultivated – sedge and reed cutting are still carried out to preserve the landscape as it is – and the reserve also features one of the last surviving fenland wind pumps. Traditional "droves" (wide footpaths) enable visitors to explore the fen and a boardwalk nature trail gives access to several hides.

Perched on a mound of clay above the River Ouse, **ELY** – literally "eel island" – was to all intents and purposes a true island until the draining of the fens in the seventeenth century. Up until then, the town was encircled by treacherous marshland, which could only be crossed with the help of the locals, "fen-slodgers" who knew the firm tussock paths. In 1070, **Hereward the Wake** turned this inaccessibility to military advantage, holding out against the Normans and forcing William the Conqueror to undertake a prolonged siege – and finally to build an improvised road floated on bundles of sticks.

Since then, Ely has always been associated with Hereward, which is really rather ridiculous as Ely is, above all else, an ecclesiastical town and a Norman one to boot. The Normans built the **cathedral**, a towering structure visible for miles across the flat landscape and Ely's only significant sight. It's easy to see the town on a day-trip from Cambridge, but Ely does make a pleasant night's stop in its own right. It's also handy for **Wicken Fen** (see box on p.459).

The Town

Ely **Cathedral** (June–Sept daily 7am–7pm; Oct–May Mon–Sat 7.30am–6pm, Sun 7.30am–5pm; £4) is seen to best advantage from the south, the crenellated towers of the west side perfectly balanced by the prickly finials to the east with the distinctive timber lantern rising above them both. To approach from this direction, follow the footpath leading up the hill into the cathedral precincts from **Broad Street** – also the second turning on the right as you walk up Station Road from the train station. At the top of the footpath, pass through the medieval **Porta**, once the principal entrance to the monastery complex, and turn right to reach the main entrance on the lopsided **west front** – one of the transepts collapsed in a storm in 1701.

The first things to strike you as you enter the **nave** are the sheer length of the building and the lively nineteenth-century painted ceiling, largely the work of amateurs. The procession of plain late-Norman arches leads to the architectural feature that makes Ely so special, the **octagon** – the only one of its kind in England – built in 1322 to replace the collapsed central tower. Its construction, employing the largest oaks available in England to support some four hundred tons, is one of the wonders of the medieval world, and the effect, as you look up into this Gothic dome, is simply breathtaking. **Octagon tours** depart several times a day from the desk at the entrance and venture up into the octagon itself.

When the central tower collapsed, it fell eastwards, onto the **choir**, which was subsequently rebuilt in a fussier decorative style. The thirteenth-century presbytery, beyond, houses the relics of **St Ethelreda**, founder of the abbey in 673, who, despite being twice married, is honoured liturgically as a virgin. The other marvel at Ely is the **Lady Chapel**, in actual fact a separate building accessible via the north transept. It lost its sculpture and its stained glass during the Reformation, but its fan vaulting remains, an exquisite example of English Gothic.

The rest of Ely is pretty enough, but hardly compelling after the wonders of the cathedral. To the north, the **High Street**, with its Georgian buildings and old-fashioned shops, makes for an enjoyable browse and, if you push on past the Market Place down Forehill and then Waterside, you'll soon reach the **Babylon Gallery** (Tues–Sat 10am–4pm, Sun 11am–5pm; free), where an imaginative programme of temporary exhibitions featuring contemporary art and craft is displayed in an attractively renovated old brewery warehouse.

Alternatively, head west from the cathedral entrance across the triangular Palace Green, to **Oliver Cromwell's House** at 29 St Mary's St (April–Sept daily 10am–5.30pm; Oct–March Mon–Sat 10am–5pm, Sun 11am–4pm; £3.50), a timber-framed former vicarage, which holds a small exhibition on the Protector's ten-year sojourn in Ely, when he was employed as a tithe collector.

Practicalities

Ely lies on a major rail intersection, with direct **trains** from as far afield as Liverpool, Norwich and London, as well as from Cambridge, just twenty minutes to the south. The **train station** is a ten-minute walk from the cathedral straight up Station Road and its continuation Back Hill. **Buses** (from King's Lynn and Cambridge) stop on Market Street immediately to the north of the cathedral. The **tourist office** is in Oliver Cromwell's House (April–Sept daily 10am–5.30pm; Oct–March Mon–Sat 10am–5pm, Sun 11am–4pm; ☎01353/662062) and they issue free town maps and will help with accommodation.

Ely has several appealing **B&Bs**, the best being the handy *Cathedral House*, 17 St Mary's St (☎01353/662124; ❸), an attractive Georgian town house with three comfortable, en-suite bedrooms. Several other good options are concentrated along Egremont Street, about five minutes' walk north from the cathedral via the Lynn Road. Possibilities here include the spacious *Old Egremont House* at no. 31 (☎01353/663118; ❷), with cathedral views and a walled garden, and the more modern, spick and span *Posthouse* at no. 12a (☎01353/667184; ❶).

Of the numerous **tearooms** in town, *The Almonry* (daily 10am–5pm), in the grounds to the north of the cathedral, is by far the best sited, with garden seats granting great views of the cathedral. Two other good choices are the *Steeplegate Tea* Rooms at 16–18 High St (closed Sun), backing onto the cathedral grounds, and *Dominique's*, 8 St Mary's St (closed Sun). The pick of the town's **restaurants** is the *Old Fire Engine House*, 25 St Mary's St (☎01353/662582; closes 9pm, 5pm on Sun), a gourmet English restaurant of some local repute. Ely's friendliest **pub** is the *Prince Albert*, 62 Silver St.

Cambridge and around

On the whole, **CAMBRIDGE** is a much quieter and more secluded place than Oxford, though for the visitor what really sets it apart from its scholarly rival is "the Backs" – the green swathe of land that straddles the languid River Cam, providing exquisite views over the backs of the old colleges. At the front, the handsome facades of these same colleges dominate the layout of the town centre, lining up along the main streets. Most of the older colleges date back to the late thirteenth and early fourteenth centuries and are designed to a similar plan with the main gate leading through to a series of "courts," typically a carefully manicured slab of lawn surrounded on all four sides by college residences or offices. Many of the buildings are extraordinarily beautiful, but the most famous is **King's College**, whose magnificent **King's College Chapel** is one of the great statements of late Gothic architecture. There are thirty-one university colleges in total, each an independent, self-governing body, proud of its achievements and attracting – for the most part at least – a close loyalty from its students, amongst whom privately educated boys remain hopelessly over-represented despite decades of perfectly adequate state education.

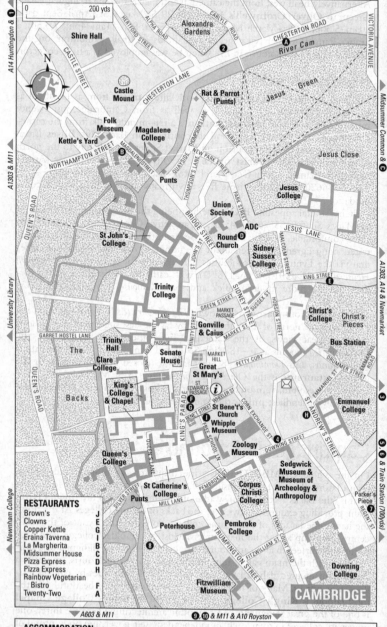

0   200 yds

A14 Huntingdon & 1

A1303 & M11

University Library

Newnham College

Shire Hall

Alexandra
Gardens

CARLYLE ROAD

CHESTERTON ROAD

VICTORIA AVENUE

River Cam

2

A

ALPHA ROAD

HERTFORD STREET

CASTLE STREET

Castle
Mound

CHESTERTON LANE

Rat & Parrot
(Punts)

Jesus   Green

Midsummer Common & C

Folk
Museum

THOMPSON'S LANE

Magdalene
College

QUAYSIDE

NEW PARK STREET

PARK PARADE

Jesus Close

Kettle's Yard

NORTHAMPTON STREET

MAGDALENE STREET

Punts

B

THOMPSON'S LANE

PARK STREET

Jesus
College

QUEEN'S ROAD

BRIDGE STREET

ST JOHN'S ST

Union
Society

ADC

JESUS LANE

A1303, A14 & Newmarket

St John's
College

Round
Church

D

Sidney
Sussex
College

MALCOLM STREET

Trinity
College

GREEN STREET

SIDNEY STREET

ST SUSSEX ST

MARKET
PASSAGE

KING STREET

E

Christ's
College

Christ's
Pieces

Garret Hostel Lane

TRINITY LANE

Gonville
& Caius

TRINITY STREET

MARKET ST

HOBSON STREET

Bus Station

DRUMMER STREET

Trinity
Hall

SENATE HOUSE PASSAGE

Senate
House

MARKET
HILL

PETTY CURY

The

Clare
College

Great
St Mary's

i

EMMANUEL STREET

QUEEN'S ROAD

Backs

King's
College
& Chapel

KING'S PARADE

F

G

ST EDWARD'S
PASSAGE

WHEELER ST

CORN EXCHANGE ST

ST ANDREW'S STREET

Emmanuel
College

H

BENE'T STREET

St Bene't's
Church

FREE SCHOOL LANE

Whipple
Museum

DOWNING STREET

Queen's
College

QUEEN'S LANE

Zoology
Museum

SILVER STREET

St Catherine's
College

Punts

PEMBROKE ST

Corpus
Christi
College

Sedgwick
Museum &
Museum of
Archeology &
Anthropology

Parker's
Piece

5, 6 & Train Station (700yds)

7

REGENT ST

MILL LANE

Peterhouse

TRUMPINGTON STREET

Pembroke
College

TENNIS COURT ROAD

FITZWILLIAM STREET

8

Fitzwilliam
Museum

J

Downing
College

CAMBRIDGE

RESTAURANTS

Brown's	J
Clowns	E
Copper Kettle	G
Eraina Taverna	I
La Margherita	B
Midsummer House	C
Pizza Express	D
Pizza Express	H
Rainbow Vegetarian Bistro	F
Twenty-Two	A

A603 & M11

9, 10 & M11 & A10 Royston

ACCOMMODATION

Arundel House Hotel	2	Cambridge YHA	5	Regent Hotel	7	Sleeperz Hotel	6
Benson House	1	Crown Plaza Cambridge	4	Royal Cambridge		YMCA	3
Cambridge Garden House	8	Lensfield Hotel	9	Hotel	10		

© Crown copyright

Tradition has it that Cambridge was founded in the late 1220s by scholastic refugees from Oxford, who fled the town after one of their number was lynched by hostile townsfolk – though the first proper college wasn't founded until 1271. Rivalry has existed between the two institutions ever since – epitomized by the annual Boat Race on the River Thames – while internal tensions between "**town and gown**" have inevitably plagued a place where the university has long tended to control local life.

During the nineteenth century, the university finally lost its ancient privileges over the town, which was expanding rapidly thanks to the arrival of the railway. The university expanded too, with the number of students increasing dramatically following the broadening of the curriculum to include new subjects such as natural science and history. More recently, change has been much slower in coming to the university, particularly when it comes to **equality of the sexes**. The first two women's colleges were founded in the 1870s, but it was only in 1947 that women were actually awarded degrees and one or two colleges held out against accepting women students until the 1980s. In the meantime, the city and university had been acquiring a reputation as a **high-tech centre** of excellence, what locals refer to half-seriously as "Silicon Fen". Cambridge has always been in the vanguard of scientific research – its alumni have garnered no less than ninety Nobel prizes – and it has now become a major international player in the lucrative electronic communications industry.

Cambridge is an extremely compact place, and you can **walk** round the centre, visiting the most interesting colleges, in an afternoon. A more thorough exploration, covering more of the colleges, a visit to the fine art of the Fitzwilliam Museum and a leisurely afternoon on a **punt**, will however take at least a couple of days – maybe more. If possible you should avoid coming in high summer, when the students are replaced by hordes of sightseers and posses of foreign-language students, though you can still miss the crowds by getting up early – the tourists only start to appear in numbers from around 10.30am. Faced with such crowds, the more popular colleges have restricted their opening times and several have introduced admission charges. Bear in mind, too, that during the exam period (late April to early June), most colleges close their doors to the public at least some of the time.

Arrival, information and getting around

The **train station** is a mile or so southeast of the city centre, off Hills Road. It's an easy but tedious twenty-minute walk into the centre, or take shuttle bus #3, which runs to downtown Emmanuel Road every ten minutes or so (less frequently on Sun). The **bus station** is centrally located on Drummer Street, right by Christ's Pieces – and Emmanuel Road. **Stansted**, London's third airport, with its striking terminal building designed by Norman Foster, is just thirty miles south of Cambridge on the M11; there are hourly trains from the airport to the city, and regular bus services too. Arriving by **car**, you'll find much of the city centre closed to traffic and on-street parking well-nigh impossible – for a day-trip, at least, the best option is a **Park-and-Ride** car park; they are signposted on all major approaches.

The city centre is small enough to walk round comfortably, so apart from getting to and from the train station, you shouldn't have to use the city's buses. On the other hand, cycling is an enjoyable way of getting around and has long been extremely popular with locals and students alike. **Bike rental** outlets are dotted all over town (see p.472), including a couple of places handy for the train station. When and wherever you leave your bike, padlock it to something immovable – bike theft is commonplace.

Cambridge **tourist office** is conveniently situated in the ornate, domed former public library on Wheeler Street, off King's Parade (April–Oct Mon–Fri 10am–6pm, Sat 10am–5pm, Sun 11am–4pm; Nov–March Mon–Fri 10am–5.30pm, Sat 10am–5pm; ☏01223/322640, ⓦwww.tourismcambridge. com). They issue city maps, have lots of leaflets on local attractions and sell an in-depth guide to the city (£4). They can also help with accommodation, which is a useful service especially in the summer when vacant rooms can be hard to find. The best source of **information** on eating out and entertainment is *Adhoc's What's On?*, a free monthly brochure available at the tourist office and larger bookshops.

The tourist office runs very popular **walking tours** of the centre (1–4 daily; 2hr; £7), which are expensive but include entrance to at least one college that normally charges for the privilege. Book well in advance in summer.

Accommodation

Cambridge is short of central accommodation and those few **hotels** that do occupy prime locations are expensive. That said, Chesterton Road, the busy street running east from the top of Magdalene Street, has several reasonably priced hotels and guest houses. There are lots of **B&Bs** on the outskirts of town, with several in the vicinity of the train station and it's here you'll find the **youth hostel** too. In high season, when rooms are often difficult to find, the tourist office's efficient **accommodation booking service** can be very useful (Mon–Fri 9.30am–4pm; ☏01223/457581).

Hotels, guest houses and B&Bs

Arundel House Hotel 53 Chesterton Rd ☏01223/367701, ⓦwww.arundelhousehotels. co.uk. A converted row of late-Victorian houses overlooking Jesus Green makes for one of the better mid-range B&B choices. Neat and tidy rooms with mundanely modern furnishings. Breakfasts are good. ❺

Benson House 24 Huntingdon Rd ☏01223/311594. Pleasant, well-kept guest house in a demure brick house about five minutes' walk north from the Magdalene Bridge near New Hall College. Five rooms, three en suite. ❷

Cambridge Garden House Moat House Granta Place, Mill Lane ☏01223/259988. Disregard the clumsy name, for this is arguably Cambridge's best central hotel, set in its own gardens with a fine riverside location, rooms with balconies, indoor pool and health club. ❻

Crowne Plaza Cambridge Downing St ☏01223/464466. Immaculately tailored behind a dignified facade, this sleek and slick hotel is first-rate. The foyer is adventurously designed and the rooms are resolutely modern in efficient chain-hotel style. Great central location. ❼

Lensfield Hotel 53 Lensfield Rd ☏01223/355017, ⓦwww.lensfieldhotel.co.uk. Small, well-kept family-owned hotel on the ring road, just round the corner from the Fitzwilliam Museum. ❺

Regent Hotel 41 Regent St ☏01223/351470, ⓦwww.regenthotel.co.uk. Small-scale, family-owned hotel in an old brick town house within easy walking distance of the centre, beside Parker's Piece. The thirty-odd rooms are decorated in an efficient modern style. ❻

Royal Cambridge Hotel Trumpington St ☏01223/351631. One of the city's more polished hotels, occupying a rehashed Georgian terrace. The conversion is rather heavy handed, and the furniture and fittings look too chain-like to be at ease, but no quibbles about the location, just down from the Fitzwilliam. ❼

Sleeperz Hotel Station Rd ☏01223/304050, ⓦwww.sleeperz.com. This popular hotel is in an imaginatively converted granary warehouse, right outside the train station. Most of the rooms are bunk-style affairs done out in the manner of a ship's cabin, and there are a few doubles too. All are en suite, with shower and TV. ❷

Hostels and campsites

Cambridge YHA 97 Tenison Rd ☏01223/354601, ⓦwww.yha.org.uk. This well-equipped hostel has laundry and self-catering facilities, a cycle store, a games room and a small courtyard garden. It's close to the train station – Tenison Road is a right turn a couple of hundred yards down Station Road. ❶

YMCA Queen Anne House, Gonville Place ☏01223/356998. Central location on the south side of Parker's Piece. Offers singles (£23) and doubles (£37), with breakfast included in the price, but very busy during summer – book well in advance. ❶

The City

Cambridge's main shopping street is Bridge Street, which becomes Sidney Street, St Andrew's Street and finally Regent Street; the other main thoroughfare is the procession of St John's Street, Trinity Street, King's Parade and Trumpington Street. The university developed on the land west of this latter route along the banks of the Cam, and now forms a continuous half-mile parade of **colleges** from Magdalene to Peterhouse, with sundry others scattered about the periphery. The **Fitzwilliam Museum**, with easily the city's finest art collection, is just along Trumpington Street south of Peterhouse. The account below starts with **King's College**, whose chapel is the university's most celebrated attraction, and covers the rest of the town in a broadly clockwise direction.

King's College

Henry VI founded **King's College** (☎01223/331100) in 1441, but he was disappointed with his initial efforts, so four years later he cleared away half of medieval Cambridge to make room for a much grander foundation. His plans were ambitious, but the Wars of the Roses – and bouts of royal insanity – intervened and by the time of his death in 1471 very little had been finished. Indeed, work on Henry's **Great Court** hadn't even started and the site remained empty for three hundred years. The present complex – facing King's Parade from behind a long stone screen – is largely neo-Gothic, built in the 1820s to a design by William Wilkins. However, Henry's workmen did start on the college's finest building, the much celebrated **King's College Chapel** (term time Mon–Fri 9.30am–3.30pm, Sat 9.30am–3.15pm, Sun 1.15–2.15pm; rest of year Mon–Sat 9.30am–4.30pm, Sun 10am–5pm; £3.50), on the north side of today's Great Court. Committed to canvas by Turner and Canaletto, and eulogized in three sonnets by Wordsworth, it's now best known for its **boys' choir**, whose members process across the college grounds during term time in their antiquated garb to sing evensong (Tues–Sat at 5.30pm) and carols on Christmas Eve. Begun in 1446 and over sixty years in the making, the chapel is an extraordinary building. From the outside, it seems impossibly slender, its streamlined buttresses channelling up to a dainty balustrade and four spiky turrets, but the exterior was, in a sense at least, a happy accident – its design predicated by the carefully composed interior. Here, in the final flowering of the Gothic style, the mystery of the Christian faith was expressed by a long, uninterrupted **nave** flooded with kaleidoscopic patterns of light filtering in through copious stained-glass windows.

Like Oxford's New College, King's enjoyed an exclusive supply of students from one of the country's public schools – in this case, Eton – and until 1851

College admission charges and opening times

All of the more visited colleges now impose an **admission charge**, partly to control the number of tourists and partly to raise cash. It is, however, a creeping trend, so don't be surprised if other, lesser-known colleges follow suit. **Opening times** are fairly consistent throughout the year, though there are sporadic term-time variations especially at the weekend. It's also worth noting that during the exam season, which stretches from late April to early June, all the colleges have periods when they are closed to the public. Where no opening hours are given, you're usually free to tour the grounds at any time during the day. For more specific information, call the relevant college; **phone numbers** are given in the text.

On the river

Punting is the quintessential Cambridge activity, though it's a good deal harder than it looks. First-timers find themselves zigzagging across the water and "punt jams" are very common on the stretch of the Cam beside the Backs in summer. **Punt rental** is available at several points, including the boatyard at Mill Lane (beside the Silver Street bridge), at Magdalene Bridge, and at the *Rat & Parrot* pub on Jesus Green. It costs around £12 an hour (and most places charge a deposit), with up to six people in each punt. If you find it all too daunting you can always hire a **chauffeur punt** from any of the rental places; this works out at about a fiver a head. Cambridge is also famous for its **rowing clubs**, which are clustered along the north bank of the river across from Midsummer Common. For their convenience, this stretch of water is punt-free. The most important inter-college races are the **May Bumps**, which, confusingly, take place in June.

claimed the right to award its students degrees without taking any examinations. The first non-Etonians were only accepted in 1873. Times have changed since those days, and, if anything, King's is now one of the more progressive colleges, having been one of the first to admit women in 1972. Among its most famous alumni are E.M. Forster, who described his experiences in *Maurice*, film director Derek Jarman, poet Rupert Brooke and John Maynard Keynes, whose economic theories did much to improve the college's finances when he became the college bursar.

From King's Parade to Clare College

King's Parade, originally the medieval High Street, is inevitably dominated by King's College and Chapel, but the higgledy-piggledy shops opposite are an attractive foil to William Wilkins's architectural screen. At the northern end of King's Parade is **St Mary's the Great** (daily 8am–6pm; free), the university's pet church, a sturdy Gothic structure dating from the fifteenth century. Its tower (Mon–Sat 9.30am–5.30pm, Sun 12.30–5.30pm; £1.85) offers a good overall view of the colleges and a bird's-eye view of **Market Hill**, east of the church, where food and bric-a-brac stalls are set out daily. Opposite the church stands **Senate House**, an exercise in Palladian classicism by James Gibbs, and the scene of graduation ceremonies on the last Saturday in June, when champagne corks fly around the rabbit-fur collars and black gowns. It's not usually open to the public, though you can wander around the quad if the gate is open.

The northern continuation of King's Parade is Trinity Street, a short way along which, on the left, is the main entrance to **Gonville and Caius College** (℡01223/332400), known simply as Caius (pronounced "keys"), after the co-founder John Keys, who latinized his name, as was then the custom with men of learning. The design of the college owes much to Keys, who placed a gate on three sides of two adjoining courts, each representing a different stage on the path to academic enlightenment: the Gate of Humility, through which the student entered the college, now stands in the Fellows' Garden; the Gate of Virtue, sporting the female figures of Fame and Wealth, marks the entrance to Caius Court; while the Gate of Honour, capped with sundials and decorated with classical motifs, leads to Senate House Passage and on to Senate House.

Senate House Passage continues west beyond the Gate of Honour to Trinity Lane and **Trinity Hall** (℡01223/332500) – not to be confused with Trinity College – where the Elizabethan library retains several of its original chains, designed to prevent students from purloining the texts. A few metres to the south is the much more diverting **Clare College** (daily 10am–5pm; £2;

☎01223/333200). One of seven colleges founded, rather surprisingly, by women, its plain period-piece courtyards, completed in the early eighteenth century, lead to one of the most picturesque of all the bridges over the Cam, **Clare Bridge**. Beyond lies the Fellows' Garden, one of the loveliest college gardens open to the public (times as college). Back at the entrance to Clare, it's a few metres more to the North Gate of King's College, beside the chapel.

Trinity

Trinity College, on Trinity Street (daily 10am–5pm; £1; ☎01223/338400), is the largest of the Cambridge colleges and to ram home the point it also has the largest courtyard. It comes as little surprise then that its list of famous alumni is longer than any other college: literary greats, including Dryden, Byron, Tennyson and Vladimir Nabokov; the Cambridge spies Blunt, Burgess and Philby; two prime ministers, Balfour and Baldwin; William Thackeray, Isaac Newton, Lord Rutherford, Vaughan Williams, Pandit Nehru, Bertrand Russell and Ludwig Wittgenstein, not to mention a trio of (much less talented) royals, Edward VII, George VI and Prince Charles.

A statue of Henry VIII, who founded the college in 1546, sits in majesty over Trinity's **Great Gate**, his sceptre replaced with a chair leg by a student wit. Beyond lies the vast asymmetrical expanse of **Great Court**, which displays a fine range of Tudor buildings, the oldest of which is the fifteenth-century clock tower – the annual race against its midnight chimes is now common currency thanks to the film *Chariots of Fire*. The centrepiece of the court is the delicate fountain, in which, legend has it, Lord Byron used to bathe naked with his pet bear – the college forbade students from keeping dogs.

To get through to **Nevile's Court** – where Newton first calculated the speed of sound – you must pass through "the screens", a passage separating the Hall from the kitchens, a common feature of Oxbridge colleges. The west end of Nevile's Court is enclosed by the university's most famous building after King's College Chapel, the **Wren Library** (term time Mon–Fri noon–2pm, Sat 10.30am–12.30pm; rest of year Mon–Fri noon–2pm; free). Viewed from the outside, it's impossible to appreciate the scale of the interior thanks to Wren's clever device of concealing the internal floor level. In contrast to many modern libraries, natural light pours into the white stuccoed interior, which contrasts wonderfully with the dark lime-wood bookcases, also Wren-designed and housing numerous valuable manuscripts including Milton's *Lycidas*, Wittgenstein's journals and A.A. Milne's *Winnie the Pooh*.

St John's

Next door, **St John's College**, on St John's St (daily 10am–5pm; £2; ☎01223/338600), sports a grandiloquent Tudor gatehouse, distinguished by the coat of arms of the founder, Lady Margaret Beaufort, the mother of Henry VII, held aloft by two spotted, mythical beasts. Beyond, three successive courts lead to the river, but there's an excess of dull reddish brickwork here – enough for Wordsworth, who lived above the kitchens on F staircase, to describe the place as "gloomy". The arcade on the far side of Third Court leads through to the **Bridge of Sighs**, a chunky, covered bridge built in 1831 but in most other respects very unlike its Venetian namesake. The bridge is closed to the public, and in any case is best viewed either from a punt or from the much older, more stylish Wren-designed bridge a few metres to the south. The Bridge of Sighs links the old college with the fanciful nineteenth-century **New Court**, a crenellated neo-Gothic extravaganza topped by a feast of pinnacles and a central cupola – and known as "the wedding cake".

Back on St John's Street, it's a few seconds' walk to Bridge Street and the **Round Church** (daily: June–Sept 10am–5pm; Oct–May 1–4pm; free), built in the twelfth century on the model of the Holy Sepulchre in Jerusalem. It's a curious-looking structure, squat with an ill-considered late medieval extension to the rear, but the Norman pillars of the original church remain, overseen by sturdy arcading and a ring of finely carved faces. The church is also geared up for **brass rubbing**. It holds a varied selection of brasses and sells all the necessary tackle. Staff will help you get started. In addition, the church is the starting point for Christian heritage walks around the city (Feb–Nov Wed 11am, Sun 2.30pm; £3 recommended donation; ℡01223/311602).

Saving nearby Jesus College till later (see below), it only takes a minute or two to stroll up from the Round Church to **Magdalene Bridge**, the site of the old Roman ford. Just beyond is **Magdalene College** (℡01223/332100) – pronounced "maudlin" – which was founded as a hostel by the Benedictines and became a university college in 1542. Magdalene was the last of the colleges to admit women, finally succumbing in 1988. Here, the main focus of attention is the **Pepys Building** (Nov & mid-Jan to mid-March Mon–Sat 2.30–3.30pm; late April to Aug Mon–Sat 11.30am–12.30pm & 2.30–3.30pm; free), in the second of the college's ancient courtyards. Samuel Pepys, a Magdalene student, bequeathed his entire library to the college, where it has been displayed ever since in its original red-oak bookshelves – though his famous diary, which also now resides here, was only discovered in the nineteenth century.

Jesus

Back down Magdalene Street then Bridge Street, take the first left after the Round Church to reach **Jesus College** (℡01223/339339), whose intimate cloisters are reminiscent of a monastic institution. This is not too surprising as the Bishop of Ely founded the college on the grounds of a suppressed Benedictine nunnery in 1496. The main red-brick gateway is approached via a distinctive walled walkway strewn with bicycles and known as "the Chimney". Beyond, much of the ground plan of the nunnery has been preserved, especially around **Cloister Court**, the prettiest of the college's courtyards, dripping with ivy and overflowing hanging baskets. Entered from the court, the college **chapel** occupies the former priory chancel and looks like a medieval parish church; it was imaginatively restored in the nineteenth century, using ceiling designs by William Morris and Pre-Raphaelite stained glass. The poet Samuel Taylor Coleridge was the college's most famously bad student, absconding in his first year to join the Light Dragoons, and returning only to be kicked out for a combination of bad debts and unconventional opinions.

Sidney Sussex and Christ's College

Near Jesus, Malcolm Street cuts off Jesus Lane to reach King Street, from where it's a short stroll through to **Sidney Sussex College** (℡01223/338800), whose sombre, mostly mock-Gothic facade glowers over Sidney Street. Oliver Cromwell studied here and, in 1960, his skull was brought to the college and buried in a secret location in the ante-chapel.

Just to the south of Sidney Sussex, on St Andrew's Street, you hit the hustle and bustle of the town's central shopping area, dominated by the **Lion Yard** shopping centre. This was one of the few town-planning mistakes in the centre of Cambridge, a brutally modern structure that rumbles along **Petty Cury**, formerly a cobbled curve of leaning half-timbered houses. Aesthetic relief is, however, close at hand, just opposite Lion Yard, in the turreted gateway of **Christ's College** (℡01223/334900), which features the coat of arms of the founder, Lady Margaret Beaufort, who also founded St John's. Passing through First Court you come to the Fellows' Building, attributed to Inigo Jones, whose central arch gives access to the **Fellows' Garden** (Mon–Fri 10am–12pm; free). The poet John Milton is said either to have painted or composed beneath the garden's elderly mulberry tree, though there's no definite proof that he did either; Christ's other famous undergraduate was Charles Darwin, who showed little academic promise and spent most of his time hunting and shooting. If you continue walking through the college, you come to its modern adjunct, Denys Lasdun's concrete pyramidal accommodation block, dubbed "the typewriter".

Emmanuel College

A little further along St Andrew's Street is **Emmanuel College** (℡01223/334200), whose stolid Neoclassical facade hides a neat and trim Front Court, where the college **chapel** was designed by Wren in a simple classical style, its wood-panelled nave set beneath a fancy stucco ceiling. The college was founded in 1584 to train a new generation of Protestant clergy following the Reformation. Emmanuel men were numbered among the Pilgrims who settled New England, which not only explains the derivation of the place name Cambridge in Massachusetts but also accounts for Harvard University – **John Harvard**, another alumnus, is remembered by a memorial window in the chapel.

Corpus Christi and Queens'

Opposite Emmanuel, Downing Street leads into **Pembroke Street**, at the west end of which, around the foot of King's Parade, are two more noteworthy town-centre colleges. On the east side of King's Parade is **Corpus Christi College** (℡01223/338000), founded by two of the town's guilds in 1352. Ignore the first court and instead head north into **Old Court**, which dates from the foundation of the college and is where Christopher Marlowe wrote *Tamburlane* before graduating in 1587. The college library, on the south side, contains a priceless collection of Anglo-Saxon manuscripts, while the north side is linked by a gallery to **St Bene't's Church**, which served as the college chapel, but is of much earlier Saxon origin. Inside, Thomas Hobson's Bible is exhibited in a glass case; Hobson was the owner of a Cambridge livery stable, where he would only allow customers to take the horse nearest the door – hence "Hobson's choice".

Nearby **Queens' College** (daily 10am–4.30pm; £1.20; ℡01223/335511), accessed through the gate on Queen's Lane, just off Silver Street, is the most popular college with university applicants, and it's not difficult to see why. In the **Old Court** and the **Cloister Court**, Queens possesses two fairy-tale Tudor courtyards, with the first of the two the perfect illustration of the original collegiate ideal with kitchens, library, chapel, hall and rooms all set around a tiny green. Cloister Court is flanked by the Long Gallery of the President's Lodge, the last remaining half-timbered building in the university, and, in its southeast corner, by the tower where Erasmus is thought to have beavered away during his four years here, probably from 1510 to 1514. Be sure to pay a visit to the college **Hall**, off the screens passage between the two courts, which holds mantel tiles by William Morris, and portraits of Erasmus and one of the college's co-founders, Elizabeth Woodville, wife of Edward IV. Equally eye-catching is the wooden **Mathematical Bridge** over the Cam (visible for free from the Silver

Street Bridge), a copy of the mid-eighteenth-century original which, it was claimed, would stay in place even if the nuts and bolts were removed.

The Fitzwilliam Museum

Of all the museums in Cambridge, the **Fitzwilliam Museum**, on Trumpington Street (Tues–Sat 10am–5pm, Sun 2.15–5pm; £3 donation suggested), stands head and shoulders above the rest. The building itself is a splendidly grandiloquent interpretation of Neoclassicism, built in the mid-nineteenth century to house the vast collection bequeathed by Viscount Fitzwilliam in 1816. Since then, the museum has been bequeathed a string of private collections, most of which are focused on a particular specialism. Consequently, the Fitzwilliam says much about the changing tastes of the British upper class. The **Lower Galleries** contain a wealth of antiquities including Egyptian sarcophagi and mummies, fifth-century BC black- and red-figure Greek vases, plus a bewildering display of European ceramics. Further on, there are sections dedicated to armour, glass and pewterware, medals, portrait miniatures and illuminated manuscripts, and – right at the far end – galleries devoted to Far Eastern applied arts and Korean ceramics.

The **Upper Galleries** concentrate on painting and sculpture with three of the first five rooms containing an eclectic assortment of mostly nineteenth- and early twentieth-century European paintings. Among many, there are works by Picasso, Matisse, Monet, Renoir, Delacroix, Cézanne and Degas. The other two rooms feature on British painting, with works by William Blake, Constable and Turner, Hogarth, Reynolds, Gainsborough and Stubbs. Moving on, the Italian section displays paintings by Fra Filippo Lippi and Simone Martini, Titian and Veronese, while Frans Hals and Ruisdael feature in the Flemish section. The post-1945 gallery is packed with a fascinating selection including pieces by the likes of Lucian Freud, David Hockney, Henry Moore, Ivon Hitchens, Ben Nicholson and Barbara Hepworth.

To the University Botanic Gardens

Past the Fitzwilliam Museum, turn left along busy Lensfield Road for the **Scott Polar Research Institute** (Mon–Fri 2.30–4pm; free), founded in 1920 in memory of the explorer, Captain Scott, with displays from the expeditions of various polar adventurers, plus exhibitions on native cultures of the Arctic. There's more general interest near at hand in the shape of the **University Botanic Gardens** (daily 10am–6pm, 4pm in winter; glasshouses till 3.30pm; £2), whose entrance is on Bateman Street, about 500 yards to the south of Lensfield Road via Panton Street. Founded in 1760 and covering forty acres, the gardens are second only to Kew with glasshouses as well as bountiful outdoor displays. The outdoor beds are mostly arranged by natural order, but there is also a particularly unusual series of chronological beds, showing when different plants were introduced into Britain.

Eating and drinking

Even at Cambridge, students are not the world's greatest customers for restaurateurs, so although the downtown **takeaway** and **café** scene is fine, decent **restaurants** are a little thin on the ground. On any kind of budget, the myriad Italian places – courtesy of Cambridge's large Italian population – will stand you in good stead; otherwise, choose carefully, particularly in the more touristy areas, where quality isn't always all it should be. Happily, Cambridge abounds in excellent **pubs**, and our list rounds up some of the best traditional student and local drinking haunts.

Cafés and restaurants

Brown's 23 Trumpington St. Breezy brasserie with a competent, fairly wide-ranging menu housed in a former hospital outpatients department (the rest of the hospital has become a Management Institute). The grand setting – all plants and fans – sets the meal off a treat. Inordinately popular, but no reservations – wait in line or at the bar. Moderate.

Clowns 54 King St. Italian-style cappuccino and cakes, sandwiches and snacks, plus newspapers to browse. Off the tourist route and not part of a chain – bonuses in anyone's books.

Copper Kettle 4 King's Parade. Generations of students have whiled away time in this resolutely old-fashioned café opposite King's College, sipping coffee, eating pastries and putting the world to rights.

Eraina Taverna 2 Free School Lane ☎01223/368786. Packed Greek taverna which satisfies the hungry hordes with huge platefuls of stews and grills, as well as pizzas, curries and a whole host of other menu madness. Try to avoid getting stuck in the basement, though at weekends (when you'll probably have to queue) you'll be lucky to get a seat anywhere. Inexpensive.

La Margherita 15 Magdalene St ☎01223/315232. Cheapish and cheerful Italian outfit offering pizzas and pastas as well as standard meat and fish dishes. Inexpensive to moderate.

Midsummer House Midsummer Common ☎01223/369299. Lovely riverside restaurant with conservatory, specializing in top-notch French-Mediterranean cuisine. Reservations essential. On the south side of the river, beside the foot bridge just to the east of Victoria Avenue. Expensive.

Nadia's Patisserie 11 St John's St. Good sandwich and cake takeaway in the centre, opposite St John's. One of several outlets – there's another at 20 King's Parade.

Pizza Express 7a Jesus Lane. Superior pizza chain outlet located in the grand, marbled hall of the former Pitt Club. Also, smart premises in an uninspiring modern block at 28 St Andrew's St. Inexpensive.

Rainbow Vegetarian Bistro 9a King's Parade ☎01223/321551. Vegetarian restaurant with main courses – ranging from couscous to lasagne and Indonesian *gado-gado* – all under £7. Good-value breakfasts, and organic wines served with meals. Great location, opposite King's College. Closed Sun. Inexpensive.

Twenty-Two 22 Chesterton Rd ☎01223/351880. Consistently the best restaurant in Cambridge, a candlelit town house in which the good-value, fixed-price menu (at around £25) touches all the modern bases. Closed Sun & Mon. Expensive.

Pubs and bars

Anchor Silver St. Very popular riverside tourist haunt with views of the Backs, adjacent punt rental and an outdoor deck.

Blackwood's Cambridge Arts Theatre, 6 St Edward's Passage. The first-floor bar at the theatre makes a civilized meeting spot. Closed Sun.

Champion of the Thames 68 King St. Gratifyingly old-fashioned central pub with decent beer and a student/academic clientele.

Eagle Bene't St. An ancient inn with a cobbled courtyard where Crick and Watson sought inspiration in the 1950s, at the time of their discovery of DNA. It's been tarted up since and gets horribly crowded, but is still worth a pint of anyone's time.

Elm Tree 42 Orchard St. Cosy local with frequent live music, mainly jazz. Just to the north of Parker's Piece and full of furiously smoking refugees from the nearby *Free Press* (see below). Well worth seeking out: to get there, follow Emmanuel Road north off Drummer Street, near the bus station, and take the third turning on the right – it's on the corner with Eden Street.

Fort St George Midsummer Common. Boisterous pub with a pleasant riverside location, overlooking the boathouses from the south side of the river, beside the foot bridge just to the east of Victoria Avenue.

Free Press 7 Prospect Row. Classic, superbly maintained backstreet local with an admirable no-smoking policy, good beer and fine food. It's located a few yards along the street from the *Elm Tree* – for directions, see above.

Entertainment

The **performing arts** scene is at its best during term time, with numerous student **drama** productions, **classical concerts** and **gigs** culminating in the traditional orgy of excess following the exam season, though the more firmly town-based venues, such as the Corn Exchange, do put on events throughout the year. Apart from the places highlighted below, each college and several churches contribute to the performing arts scene too, with the **King's College choir** being, of course, the most famous attraction (see p.465), though the choral scholars who perform at the chapels of St John's and Trinity are also exceptionally good. For all upcoming events, check the **listings** section of *Adhoc's What's On?* (www.adhoc.co.uk), a free weekly magazine that is widely available in downtown bookshops and newsagents as well as from the tourist office. For advance tickets for most events, pop into the Corn Exchange (see below).

June and July are the busiest times in Cambridge's calendar of **events**. The fortnight of post-exam celebrations, which take place in the first two weeks of June – and are confusingly known as **May Week** – herald the ball and garden-party season, and include boat races, known as the "May Bumps", on the Cam by Midsummer Common. The vaguely hippified **Midsummer Fair**, descendant of the town's famous medieval Stourbridge Fair, discontinued in 1934, takes place in mid-June on Midsummer Common, with bands, theatre and much more besides – all for free. By contrast, you'll have to pay out around £50 for a tent pitch and entry into the three-day **Cambridge Folk Festival**, held annually at the end of July at Cherry Hinton, and attracting a wide variety of loosely folk-based acts.

Arts Picture House 38–39 St Andrew's St ☎01223/504444. Art house cinema with an excellent, wide-ranging programme.

Boat Race 170 East Rd ☎01223/508533. Lively pub venue for all kinds of music, with gigs every night.

Cambridge Arts Theatre 6 St Edward's Passage, off King's Parade ☎01223/503333. The city's main repertory theatre, founded by John Maynard Keynes, and launching pad of a thousand-and-one famous careers, from Derek Jacobi to Stephen Fry, offers a top-notch range of cutting-edge and classic productions.

Cambridge Corn Exchange Wheeler St ☎01223/357851. Revamped nineteenth-century trading hall, now the main city-centre venue for opera, ballet, musicals and comedy as well as regular rock and folk gigs.

Cambridge Modern Jazz Club at Sophbeck Sessions, 14 Tredgold Lane, Napier St ☎01223/722811. Attracts top-ranking artists from around the world. East of the city centre, near the Grafton Centre shopping mall, off Newmarket Road.

Junction Clifton Rd ☎01223/511511. Rock, Indie, jazz, reggae or soul gigs, plus occasional comedy acts and dance groups at this popular arts and entertainments venue.

Listings

Bike rental Geoff's Bike Hire, near the train station at 65 Devonshire Rd ☎01223/365629; Mikes Bikes, 28 Mill Rd ☎01223/312591; and H. Drake, near the train station at 56–60 Hills Rd ☎01223/363468. Rates start at around £7 a day.

Bookshops Heffers has several outlets with its main branch at 20 Trinity St; Cambridge University Press has a shop at 1 Trinity St; Borders are at 12–13 Market St; and Waterstones at 22 Sidney St. For second-hand books try the shops down St Edward's Passage off King's Parade: G. David, at no.3, is an antiquarian's and hard-back hunter's paradise; the Haunted Bookshop, at no. 9, is better for first editions, travel and illustrated books.

Buses Most city buses pull in to – and depart from – the stops along Emmanuel Street. Close by, at the top of Emmanuel Street, the Drummer Street bus station is for long distance services. For information on Cambridgeshire bus services, call the information line (☎0870/608 2608), or drop by

the Premier Travel Agency, beside the Drummer Street station (☎01223/572300). In addition, Airlinks (☎0870/574 7777) operates direct services to the London airports; and National Express (☎0870/5808080) runs services to London and other major cities.

Car rental Avis, 245 Mill Rd ☎01223/212551; Budget, 303–305 Newmarket Rd ☎01223/323838; Europcar, 22 Cambridge Rd ☎01223/233644; National, 264 Newmarket Rd ☎01223/365438.

Pharmacies Boots, 28 Petty Cury ☎01223/350213; Lloyds, 30 Trumpington St ☎01223/359449.

Post office The main office is at 9–11 St Andrew's St (Mon–Sat 9am–5.30pm).

Taxis There are ranks at the train and bus stations. To book, call Diamond ☎01223/523523; or Panther ☎01223/715715.

Around Cambridge – the Imperial War Museum at Duxford

Eight miles south of Cambridge, and visible from the M11 – it's next to junction 10 – are the giant hangars of the **Imperial War Museum** (daily mid-March to mid-Oct 10am–6pm; mid-Oct to mid-March 10am–4pm; £7.70; Ⓦwww.iwm.org.uk/duxford), based at Duxford airfield. Throughout World War II, East Anglia was a centre of operations for the RAF and the USAF, with the flat, unobstructed landscape dotted by dozens of airfields. Duxford itself was a Battle of Britain station, equipped with Spitfires, and there's a reconstructed Operations Room in one of the control towers. In total, Duxford holds over 150 historic aircraft, a wide-ranging collection of civil and military planes from the Sunderland flying boat to Concorde and the Vulcan B2 bombers, which were used for the first and last time in the Falklands; the Spitfires remain the most enduringly popular. Most of the planes are kept in full working order and are taken out for a spin several times a year at **Duxford Air Shows**, which attract thousands of visitors. There are usually three Air Shows a year and tickets cost from £12.50 to £15.50; advance bookings are strongly recommended (Ⓣ01223/499353). For details of the free courtesy bus service linking Duxford with Cambridge, call Ⓣ01223/835000.

Travel details

Buses

For information on all local and national bus services, contact Traveline: Ⓣ 0870/608 2 608 (daily 7am–9pm), Ⓦwww.traveline.org.uk.

Trains

For information on all local and national rail services, contact National Rail Enquiries: Ⓣ 08457/48 49 50, Ⓦwww.nationalrail.co.uk.

Cambridge to: Birmingham (hourly; 2hr 50min); Bury St Edmunds (8 daily; 40min); Ely (hourly; 15min); Ipswich (6 daily; 1hr 20min); Leicester (hourly; 1hr 50min); London (2 hourly; 1hr); Norwich (hourly; 1hr); Stansted (10 daily; 40min).

Colchester to: Ipswich (2 hourly; 25min); London (2 hourly; 30min); Norwich (hourly; 1hr).

Ely to: Liverpool (hourly 4hr 30min); Manchester (hourly; 3hr 30min); Nottingham (hourly 1hr 45min).

Ipswich to: Bury St Edmunds (10 daily; 30min); Ely (7 daily; 1hr); London (2 hourly; 1hr 10min); Norwich (hourly; 45min); Woodbridge (every 1–2hr; 15min).

Norwich to: Ely (hourly; 50min); Cromer (every 1–2hr; 50min); Great Yarmouth (hourly; 30min); Liverpool (hourly; 5hr 30min); London (hourly; 2hr); Lowestoft (hourly; 30–45min); Manchester (hourly; 4hr 30min); Nottingham (hourly; 2hr 30min); Sheringham (every 1–2hr; 1hr).

The West Midlands and the Peak District

SCOTLAND

N

WALES

* **Fischer's Hotel, Baslow**
Fischer's Hotel is one of the Peak District's finest hotels and a great base for some wonderful hiking as well as visits to Chatsworth and Haddon Hall. See p.525

* **Ironbridge Gorge**
Named for the first iron bridge ever to be constructed, the showpiece here is the bridge itself: arching high above the River Severn. See p.495

* **Mappa Mundi, Hereford Cathedral** The complex iconography of this antique map, dating to around 1300, provides a real insight into the medieval mind.
See p.491

* **The theatres, Stratford-upon-Avon** *The* place to see Shakespeare's plays, performed by the world-renowned Royal Shakespeare Company.
See p.483

The West Midlands and the Peak District

The factories of the **West Midlands** were the powerhouses of the Industrial Revolution and **Birmingham**, Britain's second city, was once the world's greatest industrial metropolis. Long saddled with a reputation as a culture-hating, car-loving backwater, Birmingham has redefined its image in recent years, initiating some ambitious architectural and environmental schemes, jazzing up its museums and industrial heritage sites and giving itself a higher profile on the nation's cultural map than it's ever had before. It's not an especially good-looking city, it must be admitted, but it does hold several excellent attractions and it's certainly lively, with nightlife encompassing everything from Royal Ballet productions to all-night raves, and a great spread of restaurants and pubs in between.

The counties to the south and west of Birmingham – Warwickshire, Worcestershire, Herefordshire and Shropshire – comprise a rural stronghold that maintains an emotional and political distance from the conurbation. The left-wing politics of the big city seem remote indeed when you're in Shrewsbury, but in fact it's only seventy miles from the big city. For the most part, the four counties constitute a quiet, unassuming stretch of pastoral England whose beauty is rarely dramatic, but whose charms become more evident the longer you stay. Of the four counties, **Warwickshire** is the least obviously scenic, but draws by far the largest number of visitors, for – as the roadsigns declare at every entry point – this is "Shakespeare Country". The prime target is, of course, **Stratford-upon-Avon**, with its handful of Shakespeare-related sites and world-class theatre, but spare time also for the diverting town of **Warwick**, which has a superb church and a whopping castle.

Neighbouring **Worcestershire**, which stretches southwest from the urban fringes of the West Midlands, holds two principal places of interest, **Worcester**, which is graced by a mighty cathedral, and **Great Malvern**, a mannered inland resort spread along the rolling contours of the **Malvern Hills** – prime walking territory. From here, it's west again for **Herefordshire**, a large and sparsely populated county that's home to several charming market towns, most notably picture-postcard **Ledbury** and **Hay-on-Wye**; the latter has the largest concentration of second-hand bookshops in the world. There's also **Hereford**, where the remarkable medieval Mappa Mundi map is displayed, and pocket-sized **Ross-on-Wye**, which is within easy striking distance of an especially

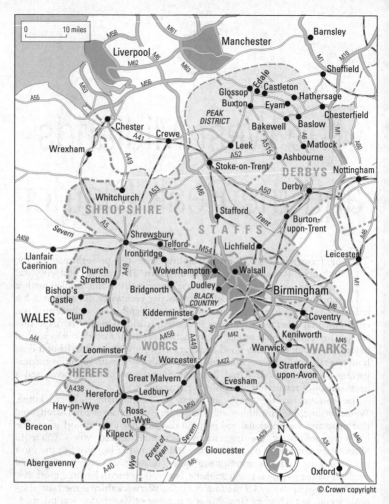

0 10 miles

© Crown copyright

scenic stretch of the **Wye River Valley**. Next door, to the north, rural **Shropshire** weighs in with **Ludlow**, one of the region's prettiest towns, awash with antique half-timbered buildings, and the amiable county town of **Shrewsbury**, which is also close to the hiking trails of the **Long Mynd**. Shropshire has a fascinating industrial history, too, for it was here in the **Ironbridge Gorge** that British industrialists built the world's first iron bridge and pioneered the use of coal as a smelting fuel. These were two key events in the Industrial Revolution and, appropriately, the Gorge's industrial heyday is recalled by a phalanx of first-rate museums.

To the east of Shropshire, sprawling north of the Birmingham conurbation, is **Staffordshire**, where **Lichfield** makes a good hand of its links with **Samuel Johnson**, while **Stoke-on-Trent** remembers the good times, when its potteries dominated the world market, in an excellent museum and several heritage sites – and factory shops. Beyond lies **Derbyshire**, whose northern reaches incorporate the region's finest scenery in the rough landscapes of the **Peak District National Park**. The latter offers great opportunities for moderately strenuous walks, as well as the diversions of the former spa town of **Buxton**, the limestone caverns of **Castleton** and the so-called "Plague Village" of **Eyam**. In addition, there's the grandiose stately pile of **Chatsworth House** and **Haddon Hall**, an exceptionally fascinating old manor house.

Birmingham, the region's public transport hub, is easily accessible by **train** from London Euston, Liverpool, Manchester, Leeds, York and a score of other towns. It is also well served by the National Express **bus** network, with dozens of buses leaving every hour for destinations all over Britain. Local **bus** services are excellent around the West Midlands conurbation and very good in the Peak District, but fade away badly in amongst the villages of Herefordshire and Shropshire.

Stratford-upon-Avon and around

Despite its worldwide fame, **STRATFORD-UPON-AVON** is, at heart, an unassuming market town with an unexceptional pedigree. A charter for Stratford's weekly market was granted in the twelfth century, a tradition continued to this day, and the town later became an important stopping-off point for stagecoaches between London, Oxford and the north. Like all such places, Stratford had its clearly defined class system and within this typical milieu John and Mary **Shakespeare** occupied the middle rank, and would have been forgotten long ago had their first son, **William**, not turned out to be one of the greatest writers ever to use the English language. A consequence of their good fortune is that this ordinary little place is nowadays all but smothered by package-tourist hype and its central streets groan under the weight of thousands of tourists. Don't let that deter you: dodging the multitudes is possible by avoiding the busiest attractions – principally the Birthplace Museum – and the **Royal Shakespeare Company** offers superb theatre. Moreover, Stratford still has the ability to surprise and delight, whether in the excellence of some of its restaurants or by the gentle river views beside the lovely **Holy Trinity Church**.

Arrival and information

Stratford's **train station** is on the northwestern edge of town, ten minutes' walk from the centre. Now the end of the line, it receives hourly services from Birmingham and frequent trains from Warwick, except on Sundays, when there are only a couple of services all day. Local **bus services** arrive and depart from the central Bridge Street; National Express services and most other long-distance and regional buses pull into the Riverside station on the east side of the town centre, off Bridgeway.

The **tourist office** (April–Oct Mon–Sat 9am–6pm, Sun 11am–5pm; Nov–March Mon–Sat 9am–5pm, Sun 11am–4pm; ☎01789/293127, ⓦwww.shakespeare-country.co.uk) is located a couple of minutes' walk from the bus station by the bridge at the junction of Bridgeway and Bridgefoot. They have oodles of information on local attractions and operate an accommodation-booking service (see below), which is very useful during the height of the summer when rooms can be in very short supply. It also issues bus timetables and sells bus tickets. General tourist information is available from the Guide Friday office in the centre at 14 Rother St (☎01789/299866), but they basically exist to flog tickets for their bus tours of the town and environs (£8.50,

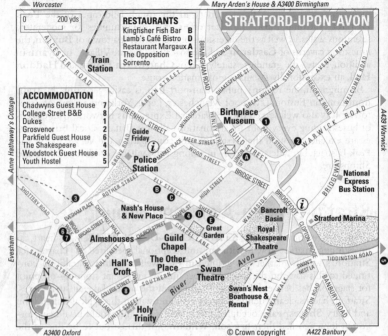

excluding admission to properties). The tourist office will sell you an all-in ticket for all five **Shakespeare Birthplace Trust** properties (£12), or a **Three In-Town Shakespeare Property Ticket** (£8.50) for the three Trust properties in Stratford – both tickets are also available from each of the sites themselves.

Accommodation

As one of the most popular tourist destinations in England, Stratford's **accommodation** is a tad pricey and gets booked up well in advance. In peak months, and during the Shakespeare birthday celebrations around April 23, it's essential to book ahead. The town has a couple of dozen **hotels**, the pick of which occupy old half-timbered buildings right in the centre of town, but most visitors choose to stay in a **B&B**. These have sprung up in every part of Stratford, but there's a particular concentration to the southwest of the centre around Grove Road, Evesham Place and Broad Walk. The tourist office operates an efficient and extremely useful **Accommodation Booking Hotline** (Mon–Fri 9.30am–4.30pm; ☎01789/415061; £3).

Hotels

Dukes Payton St ☎01789/269300, ⓦwww. dukeshotel.co.uk. On the north side of the town centre, a couple of minutes' walk from the Birthplace Museum, this comfortable, privately owned hotel has a pleasant interior dotted with antiques. ④

Grosvenor Warwick Rd ☎01789/269213. Close to the canal, just a couple of minutes' walk from the town centre, the Grosvenor occupies a row of pleasant, two-storey Georgian houses. The interior is crisp and modern and there's ample parking at the back. Discounted short break deals available. ⑤

The Shakespeare Chapel St ☎0870/4008182. Right in the centre of town. Now part of a chain, this old hotel, with its mullion windows and half-timbered facade, is one of Stratford's best known. The interior has low beams and open fires and represents a fairly successful amalgamation of the old and new. **❼**

Guest houses and B&Bs

Chadwyns Guest House 6 Broad Walk ☎01789/269077, ⓦwww.chadwyns. freeserve.co.uk. Just off Evesham Place, this well-maintained, most agreeable guest house occupies pleasant Victorian premises and offers seven en-suite rooms. Great breakfasts with vegetarian options. **❷**

College Street B&B 32 College St ☎01789/266784. Handy location, just west of the centre, for this friendly B&B, which has two bright and cheerful, en-suite guest rooms. No cards. **❷**

Parkfield Guest House 3 Broad Walk ☎01789/293313, ⓔparkfiel@btinternet.com. Very pleasant B&B in a rambling Victorian house in a residential street off Evesham Place. There's a private car park – a useful facility in crowded Stratford – and most rooms are en suite. Under ten minutes' walk from the centre. **❷**

Woodstock Guest House 30 Grove Rd ☎01789/299881, ⓔwoodstockhouse@com-puserve.com. A smart and neatly kept B&B ten minutes' walk from the centre, by the start of the path to Anne Hathaway's Cottage. It has five extremely comfortable bedrooms, all en suite. No credit cards. **❷**

Hostels and camping

Stratford-upon-Avon Youth Hostel
Hemmingford House, Alveston ☎01789/297093, ⓦwww.yha.org.uk. This hostel occupies a rambling Georgian mansion on the edge of the pretty village of Alveston. There are dormitories and family rooms, some of which are en suite. Laundry, internet-access, self-catering facilities and evening meals, too. It's located two miles east of the town centre on the B4086 and served by regular bus from Stratford's Riverside bus station. Open all year. £15.50.

Stratford Racecourse Camp Site Luddington Rd ☎01789/267949. Well-equipped camping and caravan site one mile southwest of the town centre. Regular buses into town (not Sun). Closed Oct–March. Tent pitches from £4, caravans from £6.

The Town

Spreading back from the River Avon, Stratford's **town centre** is fairly flat and compact, its mostly modern buildings filling out a simple gridiron just two blocks deep and four blocks long. Running along the northern edge of the centre is **Bridge Street**, the main thoroughfare lined with shops and chock-a-block with local buses. At its west end, Bridge Street divides into Henley Street, home of the **Birthplace Museum**, and Wood Street, which leads up to the market place. It also intersects with High Street. This, and its continuation Chapel and Church streets, cuts south to pass most of the old buildings that the town still possesses, most notably **Nash's House** and, on neighbouring Old Town Street, **Hall's Croft**. From here, it's a short hop to the charming **Holy Trinity Church**, where Shakespeare lies buried, and then only a few minutes back along the river past the **theatres** to the foot of Bridge Street. In itself, this circular walk only takes about fifteen minutes, but it takes all day if you potter around the attractions. In addition, there are two outlying Shakespearean properties, **Anne Hathaway's Cottage** in Shottery and **Mary Arden's House** in Wilmcote – though you have to be a really serious sightseer to want to see them all.

The Birthplace Museum

Top of everyone's Bardic itinerary is the **Birthplace Museum** (late March to mid-Oct Mon–Sat 9am–5pm, Sun 9.30am–5pm; mid-Oct to late March Mon–Sat 9.30am–4pm, Sun 10am–4pm; £6), comprising an ugly modern visitor centre attached to the heavily restored half-timbered building on Henley Street where the great man was born. The visitor centre pokes into every corner of Shakespeare's life and times, making the most of what little hard evidence there is. His will is interesting in so far as he passed all sorts of goodies to his daughter, but precious little to his wife – the museum commentary tries to gainsay this apparent meanness, but fails to convince. Next door, the half-timbered dwelling is actually two buildings knocked into one. The northern half, now fitted out in the style of a sixteenth-century domestic interior, was the business premises of the poet's father, who is thought to have worked as a glover, though some argue that he was a wool merchant or a butcher. Neither is it certain that Shakespeare was born in this building nor that he was born on April 23, 1564 – it's just known that he was baptized on April 26, and it's an irresistible temptation to place the birth of the national poet three days earlier, on St George's Day. However, both suppositions are now treated as fact at this shrine, where the south half of the building – bought by John Shakespeare in 1556 – displays a modest range of period artefacts designed to illuminate a life which remains distinctly enigmatic.

Nash's House and New Place

Follow the High Street south from the junction of Bridge and Henley streets, and you'll soon come to another Birthplace Trust property, **Nash's House** on Chapel Street (late March to mid-Oct Mon–Sat 9.30am–5pm, Sun 10am–5pm; mid-Oct to late March Mon–Sat 10am–4pm, Sun 10.30am–4pm; £3.50, includes entry to New Place). The house was the property of Thomas Nash, first husband of Shakespeare's granddaughter, Elizabeth Hall. The ground floor is kitted out with a pleasant assortment of period furnishings and upstairs has more of the same, plus a competent potted biography of Shakespeare. The adjacent gardens contain the bare foundations of **New Place** (same hours), Shakespeare's last residence, which was demolished in 1759 by its owner, the Reverend Francis Gastrell, during a bitter dispute with the town council over taxation.

On the other side of Chapel Lane stands the **Guild Chapel**, whose chunky tower and sturdy stonework shelters a plain interior enlivened by some rather crude stained-glass windows and a faded mural above the triumphal arch. The adjoining King Edward VI **Grammar School**, where it's assumed Shakespeare was educated, incorporates a creaky line of fifteenth-century almshouses running along Church Street.

Hall's Croft

Chapel Street continues south as Church Street. At the end, turn left along Old Town Street for Stratford's most impressive medieval house, the Birthplace Trust's **Hall's Croft** (late March to mid-Oct Mon–Sat 9.30am–5pm, Sun 10am–5pm; mid-Oct to late March Mon–Sat 10am–4pm, Sun 10.30am–4pm; £3.50). The former home of Shakespeare's elder daughter, Susanna, and her doctor husband, John Hall, the immaculately maintained Croft, with its creaking wooden floors, beamed ceilings and fine kitchen range, holds a scattering of period furniture and a fascinating display on Elizabethan medicine. Hall established something of a reputation for his medical know-how and after his death some of his case notes were published in a volume entitled *Select Observations on English Bodies*.

Holy Trinity Church

Beyond Hall's Croft, Old Town Street steers right to reach the handsome **Holy Trinity Church** (March–Oct Mon–Sat 8.30am–6pm, Sun 2–5pm; Nov–Feb Mon–Sat 9am–4pm, Sun 2–5pm; free), whose mellow, honey-coloured stonework dates from the thirteenth century. Enhanced by its riverside setting and flanked by the yews and weeping willows of its graveyard, the dignified proportions of this quintessentially English church are the result of several centuries of chopping and changing, culminating in the replacement of the original wooden spire with today's stone version in 1763. Inside, the nave is bathed in light from the **stained-glass windows**, some of which (predominantly along the south aisle) date from the fourteenth century. In the north aisle, beside the transept, is the **Clopton Chapel**, where the tomb of George Carew is a superbly carved Renaissance extravagance decorated with military insignia appropriate to George's job as master in ordnance to James I. But poor old George is long forgotten, unlike William Shakespeare, who lies buried in the **chancel** (£1), his remains overseen by a sedate and studious memorial plaque and effigy added just seven years after his death.

The theatres

Doubling back from the church, turn right along Southern Lane and its continuation, Waterside, home to the town's three Royal Shakespeare Company **theatres** – The Other Place, the Swan Theatre and the Royal Shakespeare Theatre. There was no theatre in Stratford in Shakespeare's day and indeed the first home-town festival in his honour was only held in 1769 at the behest of London-based David Garrick. Thereafter, the idea of building a permanent home in which to perform Shakespeare's works slowly gained momentum, and finally, in 1879, the first Memorial Theatre was opened on land donated by local beer baron Charles Flower. A fire in 1926 necessitated the construction of a new theatre, and the ensuing architectural competition was won by Elisabeth Scott. Her theatre is today's **Royal Shakespeare Theatre**. In the 1980s, the burnt-out original theatre round the back was turned into a replica "in-the-round" Elizabethan stage – the **Swan**; it's used for works by Shakespeare's contemporaries, classics from all eras and one annual piece by the man himself. The third auditorium, **The Other Place**, showcases modern and experimental pieces. The RSC also organizes a number of behind-the-scenes tours – ask at the box office for details.

Anne Hathaway's Cottage and Mary Arden's House

Anne Hathaway's Cottage (late March to mid-Oct Mon–Sat 9am–5pm, Sun 9.30am–5pm; late Oct to mid-March Mon–Sat 9.30am–4pm, Sun 10am–

Tickets for the RSC

As the Royal Shakespeare Company works on a repertory system, you could stay in Stratford for a few days and see four or five different plays. Tickets for the **Royal Shakespeare Theatre** start at around £5 for standing room and a restricted view, rising to £40 for the best seats in the house. However, very popular shows get booked up months in advance. **Swan** tickets are generally between £5 and £36, with tickets for **The Other Place** hovering between £10 and £20.

The RSC's **box office** (Mon–Sat from 9am; ☎01789/403403) serves as the central booking agent for all three houses, although you collect your tickets from the theatre in question. At the Royal Shakespeare Theatre, twenty tickets are kept back for that evening's performance and sold at between £10 and £20 each; for a real blockbuster, arriving to queue at 5am will not be too early. Stand-by tickets (for unsold seats) are also available on the day of performance, but only concessionary groups (OAPs, students, etc) are eligible. If all else fails, turn up about an hour before the performance and try your luck – though last-minute **returns** are quite rare. For more **information**, call ☎01789/403403 or check ⊛www.rsc.org.uk.

4pm; £4.50), also operated by the Birthplace Trust, is located just over a mile west of the town centre in Shottery. The most agreeable way to get there is on the signposted footpath from Evesham Place, at the south end of Rother Street. The cottage, complete with its dinky wooden beams and thatching, was the home of Anne Hathaway before she married Shakespeare in 1582. A few yards away, the **Shakespeare Tree Garden** has a patch that is planted with species mentioned in the plays.

The Birthplace Trust also keeps **Mary Arden's House**, three miles north-west of the town centre in **Wilmcote** (late March to mid-Oct Mon–Sat 9.30am–5pm, Sun 10am–5pm; late Oct to mid-March Mon–Sat 10am–4pm, Sun 10.30am–4pm; £5.50). Mary Arden was Shakespeare's mother, the only unmarried daughter when her father, Robert, died in 1556. Unusually for the time, she inherited the house and land, thus becoming one of the neighbour-hood's most eligible women – John Shakespeare, eager for self-improvement, married her within a year. The house is a well-furnished example of an Elizabethan farmhouse and, though the labelling is rather scant, a platoon of guides fill in the details of family life and traditions.

Eating and drinking

Stratford is used to feeding and watering thousands of visitors, so finding refreshment is never difficult. The problem is that many places are geared to serving the day-tripper as rapidly as possible – not a recipe for much gastro-nomic delight. That said, there is a scattering of very good **restaurants**, sever-al of which have been catering to theatre-goers for many years, and a handful of **pubs** and **cafés** offering good food, too. The best restaurants are concen-trated along Sheep Street, running up from Waterside near the theatres.

Restaurants and cafés

Kingfisher Fish Bar 13 Ely St. The best fish-and-chip shop in town. A five-minute walk from the theatres. Take out only. Closed Sun.

Lamb's Café Bistro 12 Sheep St ☎01789/292554. Smart restaurant serving a mouth-watering range of stylish English and conti-nental dishes. A good option for pasta lovers. Moderate.

Restaurant Margaux 6 Union St ☎01789/269106. Smart and intimate restaurant serving top-quality seafood and meat dishes with a Mediterranean slant. Expensive.

The Opposition 13 Sheep St ☎01789/269980. Top-quality, imaginative international cuisine in a busy but amiable atmosphere. The dishes of the day, chalked up on a board inside, are excellent value. Moderate.

Sorrento 8 Ely St ☎01789/297999. Classy Italian restaurant offering great pizzas, pastas along with meat and seafood. Closed Sun. Moderate.

Pubs

Dirty Duck 53 Waterside. The archetypal actors' pub, stuffed to the gunwales every night with a vocal entourage of RSC employees and hangers-on. Essential viewing.

The Garrick Inn 25 High St. Arguably the town's most photogenic and best-preserved old ale house: exposed beams, real ales and good food.

Windmill Inn Church St. Popular pub of cosy little rooms with low-beamed ceilings. A good range of beers, too.

Listings

Bike rental Pashley Cycles, 3 Guild St ☎01789/205057.

Boat rental and cruises Avon Boating, Swan's Nest Boathouse, Swan's Nest Lane ☎01789/267073, ⊛www.avon-boating.co.uk (Easter–Oct 10am to dusk; cruises £3/person).

Buses Stagecoach Midland Red ☎0870/6082608; Stratford Blue Buses ☎01789/292085; West Midlands Centro Hotline ☎024/76559559.

Laundry Sparklean, 74 Bull St, off Old Town ☎01789/269075.

Pharmacy Boots, 11 Bridge St ☎01789/292173 (Mon–Sat 9am–5.30pm; late opening roster post-ed on the door).

Post office Henley Street (Mon–Fri 9am–5.30pm, Sat 9am–6pm)

Worcestershire

In geographical terms, **Worcestershire** can be compared to a huge saucer, with the low-lying plains of the Severn Valley and the Vale of Evesham, Britain's foremost fruit-growing area, rising to a lip of hills, principally the Malverns in the west and the Cotswolds to the south. In character, the county divides into two broad belts. To the north lie the industrial and overspill towns – Droitwich and Redditch for instance – that have much in common with the Birmingham conurbation, while the south is predominantly rural. Marking the transition between the two is **Worcester** itself, a handy base for further explorations and possessed of a splendid cathedral. The south holds the county's finest scenery in the **Malvern Hills**, excellent walking territory and home to the amiable little spa town of **Great Malvern**.

The proximity of Birmingham ensures Worcestershire has a good network of **trains** and **buses**, though services are spasmodic amongst the villages in the south of the county.

Worcester

Right at the heart of the county, both geographically and politically, **WORCESTER** is something of an architectural hotchpotch, its half-timbered Tudor and stone Georgian buildings standing cheek by jowl with some fairly charmless modern developments. Postwar clumsiness apart, the biggest single influence on the city has always been the River Severn, which flows along Worcester's west flank. It was the river that drew the Romans here and river-trade that made it an important settlement as early as Saxon times. The river's major drawback is its propensity to breach its banks, inundating parts of the city in murky water, though this has at least limited development along the riverside, leaving clear space to view the mighty **cathedral**, Worcester's star turn.

The Cathedral

Worcester's skyline is dominated by the sandstone bulk of its **Cathedral** (daily 7.30am–6.30pm; £2 donation suggested), a rich stew of architectural styles that's best approached from the path that runs along the river's edge and through a gate marked with the city's flood levels. The present structure is the latest of several to stand on the site, but although the interior is mostly medieval, the Victorians remodelled the exterior. Inside, the **nave** is unexceptional except for its two west bays, which are an unusual – and unusually fine – example of the transitional period. They date to the 1160s. Moving on, the **choir**, built between 1220 and 1260, is a beautiful illustration of the Early English style, with a forest of slender pillars soaring over the intricately worked choir stalls. A stairway in the southwest transept leads down to the **crypt**, the oldest part of the cathedral, dating from the 1080s and the largest Norman crypt in the country. In addition, a doorway on the south side of the nave leads to the **Cloisters**, with their delightful roof bosses, and the circular, largely Norman **Chapter House**, which has the distinction of being the first such building constructed with the use of a central supporting pillar.

The rest of the city centre

Tucked behind the cathedral in Severn Street, alongside the canal, the **Royal Worcester Porcelain** complex (Mon–Sat 9am–5.30pm, Sun 11am–5pm; tours Mon–Fri only, reservations advised; factory tour £5; museum only £3; shop free; ℡01905/23221) contains a factory shop, a museum, where a large sample of old Worcester porcelain is displayed in period settings, and the factory itself. Beginning in the mid-eighteenth century, porcelain manufacture was long the city's main industry and Royal Worcester its leading light. Up behind the Royal Worcester complex, on the other side of the busy Sidbury dual carriageway, is the oldest building in the city, the **Commandery**, which dates from the eleventh century and now holds the **Civil War Visitor Centre** (Mon–Sat 10am–5pm, Sun 1.30–5.30pm; £3.90). The Commandery was Charles II's headquarters leading up to the Battle of Worcester in 1651 and has also served as a college for the blind. It now contains a sequence of Tudor and Stuart period rooms plus exhibits on the role of religion in the seventeenth century and the events of the Civil War, focusing on the trial of Charles I and the background to Cromwell's victory.

Pedestrianized **Friar Street**, which forks off Sidbury just west of the Commandery, is blighted by some garish 1960s developments, but these quickly give way to Worcester's most complete ensemble of Elizabethan and Tudor buildings. Sited inside one of these old timber-framed buildings is the **Museum of Local Life** (Mon–Wed, Fri & Sat 10.30am–5pm; free). The museum starts with an examination of Worcester during World War II, interesting chiefly because it paints a picture of ordinary life throughout the war years. The photographs are fascinating, but thereafter the remainder of the museum is given over to anodyne reconstructions of Edwardian and Victorian shops, offices and domestic settings.

Practicalities

Of Worcester's two **train stations**, Foregate Street is the more central and from here it's about half a mile south to the cathedral along Foregate and its continuation The Cross and the High Street. Note, however, that some services only stop at Shrub Hill, the second station, which is located a mile or so northeast of the cathedral. The **bus station** is at the back of the Crowngate shopping mall, on The Butts, about 600 yards northwest of the cathedral. The **tourist office** (Mon–Sat 9.30am–5pm; ☎01905/726311, ⓦ www.cityofworcester.gov.uk) is in the Georgian Guildhall towards the cathedral end of the High Street. **Bike rental** is available from Peddlers, 46 Barbourne Rd (☎01905/24238).

Worcester has a healthy range of accommodation. Amongst several downtown **hotels**, two good choices are the *Fownes' Hotel*, in an old glove factory at the cathedral end of City Walls Road (☎01905/613151; ❺), and the nearby *Loch Ryan*, 119 Sidbury (☎01905/351143; ❹), which is noted for its food and terraced garden. Recommended central **B&Bs** include *Osborne House*, in a traditional Victorian villa at 17 Chestnut Walk (☎01905/22296, ⓦ www.osbornehouse.freeserve.co.uk; ❷), and the excellent *Burgage House*, 4 College Precincts (☎01905/25396; no credit cards; ❷), which occupies a Georgian town house with views over the cathedral.

For **food**, there are several popular café-bars and restaurants dotted along Friar Street and its northerly continuation, New Street. These include the *Lemon Tree*, 12 Friar St (☎01905/27770), a moderately priced café/restaurant serving an imaginative menu featuring several top-notch Mediterranean dishes, and the *King Charles II*, on New Street (☎01905/22449), which has an outstanding traditional English menu – and a rather contrived seventeenth-century ambience. Alternatively, there's *Saffron's*, 15 New St (☎01905/610505), an unpretentious, if expensive, bistro serving mainly chargrilled steaks and chicken.

You'll find a bunch of pleasant old **pubs** in the city centre, with two of the best being the *Ye Olde Talbot*, an ancient coaching inn with a restaurant at the foot of Friar Street, and the *Cardinal's Hat*, a sixteenth-century building complete with a half-timbered interior further along at no. 31. There's also *The Plough*, a lively spot tucked away on the corner of Fish Street and Deansway, and with a patio that gets jam-packed on warm summer evenings. Less touristy is the *Horn & Trumpet*, in Angel Street.

The Malvern Hills and Great Malvern

One of the most exclusive and well-heeled areas of the Midlands, **The Malverns** is the generic name for a string of towns and villages stretched along the eastern lower slopes of the **Malvern Hills**, which rise spectacularly out of the flat plains a few miles to the southwest of Worcester. About nine miles from north to south – between the A44 and the M50 – and never more than five miles wide, the hills straddle the Worcestershire–Herefordshire boundary. Of Pre-Cambrian rock, they are punctuated by over twenty summits, mostly around 1000-feet-high, and in between lie innumerable dips and hollows. Nonetheless, it's easy walking country, with great views, and the hills are criss-crossed by hiking trails.

The centre of the region is **GREAT MALVERN**, a pretty little place – and the most obvious base – served by rail from Worcester, Birmingham and Oxford. The town's medicinal waters became popular towards the end of the eighteenth century, but it was the Victorians who came here in droves, making the steep hike up to **St Ann's Well** on the hill behind town, where you can still try the stuff yourself. The peculiarities of Great Malvern's spa waters are explained in the **Malvern Museum**, housed in the delicately proportioned Abbey Gateway, plum in the centre on Abbey Road (Easter–Oct Mon, Tues & Thurs–Sun 10.30am–5pm, also Wed in school holidays; £1).

The main sight in town is the **Priory Church** (March–Oct daily 9am–6.30pm; Nov–Feb till 4.30pm; donation requested), adjacent to the museum, its patchwork exterior contrasting with the ordered interior, which is notable for its stained glass and hundreds of detailed wall tiles, all added to the building in the mid-fifteenth century. The window of the north transept is especially fine and contains a portrait of Prince Arthur, Henry VII's son – the same Arthur who is commemorated in Worcester cathedral (see p.487). Among the priory's graves is that of Darwin's granddaughter, who died here as a child despite being bathed with Malvern water. From the church, it's a short walk to the **Winter Gardens pavilion**, one of the key venues for the wide range of special events the town puts on each year, including the excellent **Almeida Drama Festival** held in August.

For **walkers**, the Malvern Hills offer splendid day-hikes and a number of historical landmarks, including the remains of an Iron Age fort high on the ridge to the south of town. The panorama from here takes in the contrasts of the surrounding countryside: plains to the east and gentle hills rolling towards the gloomy Black Mountains in the west. The hike along the ridge takes about four and a half hours. Start from the southern end at **Chase End Hill** and work your way north, or head for **British Camp**, midway along the route, and begin there. It's possible to get to both of these starting points by bus, but the service is infrequent; the tourist office (see below) has the timetables.

Great Malvern practicalities

Great Malvern **train station** is on the eastern edge of town, half a mile or so from the centre along Avenue Road and Church Street. A range of inexpensive hiking leaflets are sold at the town's **tourist office**, right in the centre across from the priory church at 21 Church St (April–Nov daily 10am–5pm; Dec–March Mon–Sat 10am–5pm, Sun 10am–4pm; ☎01684/892289, ⓦwww .malvernhills.gov.uk). They also sell the three excellent large-scale **hiking maps**, which are indispensable if you're planning on walking the length of the Malverns. This is also a rewarding, though physically demanding, area to explore by **bike**; at present no one does bike rental, but this may well change – ring the tourist office for details.

Accommodation is plentiful. Amongst the **hotels**, there's the *Great Malvern*, 7 Graham Rd (☎01684/563411, ⓦwww.great-malvern-hotel.co.uk; ❺), a fami-ly-run, medium-sized hotel in a substantial old stone building right in the cen-tre, and, just along the street, at no. 23, is the comparable *Montrose* (☎01684/ 572335; ❷). The smartest hotel in town is the *Foley Arms*, 14 Worcester Rd (☎01684/573397; ❺), which occupies a good-looking Georgian building – with oodles of wrought-iron work – again in the centre. **B&Bs** include the inexpensive *Kylemore*, 30 Avenue Rd (☎01684/563753; no credit cards; ❶), the *Wyche Keep*, an impressive Edwardian house with garden access to the hills at 22 Wyche Rd (☎01684/567018; no credit cards; ❸), and *Elm Bank*, an elegant Regency town house with en-suite rooms at 52 Worcester Rd (☎01684/ 566051; ❷). The homely **youth hostel**, serving simple meals, is a mile south of Great Malvern train station, off the main A449 at 18 Peachfield Rd, Malvern Wells (☎01684/569131, ⓦwww.yha.org.uk; closed Nov to mid-Feb). The nearest **campsite** is at *Odd Fellows Pub*, four miles southwest in Colwall (☎01684/540084).

For **food**, Great Malvern has oodles of cafés and tearooms – one of the more distinctive is the *St Anne's Well Café*, a cosy vegetarian café serving inexpensive wholefood snacks, salads and cakes from its Victorian premises at the Well; just follow the signs up through the park from the centre. They'll also give you a glass to sample the spring water that babbles into a basin outside the door. The town's other café with character lies downhill from the tourist office at the train station. Known as the *Lady Foley's Tea Room* during the day, and *Passionata* in the evening (☎01684/893033; reservations recommended), it's actually on one of the station platforms and makes the most of its Victorian surroundings. Finally, *Cridlans' Restaurant* (☎01684/562676), a French-style brasserie just outside the abbey gates, is a slightly pricier, but still good-value place to eat, serving light lunches and tasty continental dishes on check tablecloths; try their delicious home-made sausage sandwich.

Herefordshire

Over the Malvern Hills from Worcestershire, the rolling agricultural landscapes of **Herefordshire** have an easy-going charm, but the finest scenery hereabouts is along the banks of the **River Wye**, which wriggles and worms its way across the county linking most of the places of interest. Plonked in the middle of the county on the Wye is **Hereford**, a sleepy, rather old-fashioned sort of place whose proudest possession, the cathedral's remarkable Mappa Mundi map, was almost flogged off in a round of ecclesiastical budget cuts, back in the 1980s. Hereford is also close to the delightful little town of **Ledbury**, sitting on the edge of the Malvern Hills and distinguished by its Tudor and Stuart half-tim-bered buildings – sometimes called "Black and Whites". Further afield, in the southeast corner of the county, lies **Ross-on-Wye**, a genial little town with a picturesque river setting and an ideal base for explorations into one of the wilder portions of the **Wye River Valley**. To the west of Hereford, hard by the Welsh border, the key attraction is **Hay-on-Wye**, which has become the world's largest repository of second-hand books, on sale in around thirty bookshops.

Herefordshire possesses one **rail line**, linking Ledbury, Hereford and Leominster and running north to Shrewsbury and east to Great Malvern and Worcester. Otherwise, you'll be restricted to the tender mercies of the county's **buses**, which provide a reasonable service between the villages and towns, except on Sundays when there's almost nothing at all.

Hereford and around

Founded by the Saxons in the seventh century, **HEREFORD** – literally "army ford" – was long a border garrison town against the Welsh, its military importance guaranteed by its strategic position beside the River Wye. It also became a religious centre after the Welsh murdered the Saxon king Ethelbert near here in 794. These were bloody times, so in itself the murder was pretty routine, but legend asserts that Ethelbert's ghost kept on turning up to insist his remains be interred here in Hereford – and eventually it got its way. Ethelbert's posthumous antics made him a military martyr and a Saxon cult soon grew up around his name, prompting the construction of the town's first cathedral. The Welsh were, however, having none of this and, in 1055, they attacked Hereford and burnt the cathedral to the ground.

Today, with the fortifications that once girdled the city all but vanished, it's the second **cathedral**, dating from the eleventh century, which forms the main focus of architectural interest. It lies just to the north of the River Wye at the heart of the city centre, whose compact tangle of narrow streets and squares is clumsily boxed in by the ring road. Taken as a whole, Hereford makes for a pleasant – if not exactly riveting – overnight stay and is also within easy striking distance of pocket-sized **Ledbury**, one of the county's prettiest towns.

The Cathedral and the Mappa Mundi

Hereford **Cathedral** (daily 8.30am–6pm; £2 donation suggested) is a curious building, an uncomfortable amalgamation of architectural styles, with bits and pieces added to the eleventh-century original by a string of bishops and culminating in an extensive – and not especially sympathetic – Victorian refit. From the outside, the sandstone **tower** is the dominant feature, constructed in the early fourteenth century to eclipse the Norman western tower, which subsequently collapsed under its own weight in 1786. The tumbling masonry damaged the **nave** and its replacement lacks the grandeur of most other English cathedrals, though the long rank of surviving Norman arches and piers more than hints at what went before. The **north transept** is, however, a flawless exercise in thirteenth-century taste, its soaring windows a classic example of Early English architecture and a handsome home for the delicately carved shrine of St Thomas Cantilupe.

In the 1980s, financial difficulties prompted the cathedral authorities to plan the sale of one of their most treasured possessions, the **Mappa Mundi**. There was an awful lot of cultural huffing and puffing about this controversial proposal, but the government and John Paul Getty Jnr rode to the rescue, with the oil tycoon stumping up a million pounds to keep the map here and install it in a brand new building. Made of sandstone, this New Library – located next to the cathedral at the west end of the cloisters – blends in seamlessly with the other, older buildings close by. It contains the immaculate **Mappa Mundi and Chained Library Exhibition** (April–Sept Mon–Sat 10am–5pm, Sun 11am–

4pm; Oct–March Mon–Sat 11am–4pm; last admission 45min before closing; £4), which begins with a series of interpretative panels that leads to the Mappa, displayed in a dimly lit room. Dating to about 1300, and 62 by 52 inches in size, the map is quite simply remarkable – and it provides an extraordinary insight into the medieval mind. It is indeed a map (as we know it) in so far as it suggests the general geography of the world – with Asia at the top and Europe and Africa below, to left and right respectively – but it also squeezes in history, mythology and theology. The New Library also holds the **Chained Library**, a remarkably extensive collection of books and manuscripts dating from the eighth to the eighteenth century. A selection is always on display.

The rest of the city

After the Mappa, Hereford's other attractions can't help but seem rather pedestrian. Nonetheless, the **City Museum and Art Gallery**, opposite the cathedral in a flamboyant Victorian building on Broad Street (April–Sept Tues–Sat 10am–5pm, Sun 10am–4pm; rest of year closed Sun; free), holds a mildly diverting collection of wildlife, geological remains, local history and mawkish Victorian art. Broad Street continues up and round into the main square, **High Town**, which is fringed by several Georgian buildings and **The Old House**, sole remnant of the seventeenth-century timber-framed Butchers' Row and now a modest museum with period interiors and bric-a-brac (April–Sept Tues–Sat 10am–5pm, Sun 10am–4pm; Oct–March closed Sun; free).

Set amidst rolling countryside, Hereford's economy is still largely dependent on its agricultural base and the local **cider** industry is one of the city's biggest trades. Cider enthusiasts should make their way to the **Cider Museum and King Offa Distillery**, 21 Ryelands St (April–Oct daily 10am–5.30pm; Nov–March Tues–Sun 11am–3pm; £2.50), which tracks through the history of cider-making, provides views of the distillation process and offers samples of King Offa ciders, including a particularly tasty Cider Brandy. The museum is, however, a dull fifteen-minute walk west of the centre, off the A438. To get there, take Eign Gate west from High Town, cross the ring road onto Eign Street and watch for Ryelands Street on the left.

Practicalities

From Hereford **train station**, it's about half a mile southwest to the High Town along Commercial Road and its continuation Commercial Street; the **bus station** is just off Commercial Road. Most local buses stop in St Peter's Square, at the east end of the High Town. The **tourist office** is directly opposite the cathedral, at 1 King St (May–Sept Mon–Sat 9am–5pm, Sun 10am–4pm; Oct–April closed Sun; ☎01432/268430). **Bicycle rental** is available from Phil Prothero Cycles, Unit 13, Bastion Mews, Union Street (☎01432/359478).

The tourist office has a reasonably long list of **B&Bs**, and the pick of them is *Charades*, 34 Southbank Rd (☎01432/269444; no credit cards; ❷), with six comfortable, en-suite guest rooms in a large Victorian house a short walk from the centre. Further out, in the countryside about two miles south of town off the A49, is *Grafton Villa Farm* (☎01432/268689; no credit cards; ❸), which offers three tastefully decorated bedrooms in the Georgian farmhouse of a working farm. As for **hotels**, the *Green Dragon Hotel*, Broad Street (☎01432/272506; ❼), occupies a grand Georgian building with frilly iron balustrades right in the centre.

For **food**, choices are limited, but one reasonably good option is the inexpensive *Firenze*, a pasta and pizza place just beyond the ring road, five minutes' walk northeast of High Town, at 21 Commercial Rd (☎01432/270183; closed Sun). A second choice is the *Aroon Rai Tai*, 50 Widemarsh St (☎01432/279971), a moderately priced Thai restaurant. When it comes to **drinking**, things get more interesting. **Cider** is a local speciality and there's a local brewery, too – the Wye Valley Brewery, whose trademark **bitter** is the redoubtable Dorothy Goodbody's. You can try both at the best **pub** in town, The *Barrels*, five minutes' walk southeast of High Town, on St Owen's Street.

Ledbury

Heading east from Hereford, it's an easy fifteen miles along the A438 to **LEDBURY**, a good-looking little town perched on the western edge of the Malvern Hills. The focus of the town is the Market Place, home to the dinky **Market House**, a Tudor beamed building raised on oak columns and with herringbone pattern beams. From beside it, narrow **Church Lane** – not to be confused with adjacent Church Street – runs up the slope framed by an especially fine ensemble of half-timbered Tudor and Stuart buildings. Among them is the Butchers' Row House Museum and, pick of the bunch, the so-called **Painted Room** (Easter–Sept Mon–Fri 11am–3pm, Sun 2–5pm; free), featuring a set of bold symmetrical floral frescoes painted on wattle-and-daub walls sometime in the sixteenth century. At the far end of the lane stands **St Michael's parish church**, whose strong and slender spire pokes high into the sky. The nucleus of the church is Norman – note the round pillars and zigzag stonework – but the most interesting features are the funerary monuments inside, including the spectacular seventeenth-century **Skynner Tomb**, where five sons and five daughters kneel in honour of their parents, beneath the canopied slab on which their parents also kneel.

Ledbury **train station** is inconveniently situated on the northern edge of town, about three-quarters of a mile from the Market Place – straight down the A438. **Buses** stop on the Market Place, across from the **tourist office** (daily 10am–5pm; ☎01531/636147, ⓦwww.visitledbury.co.uk). **Accommodation** is thin on the ground, but the *Feathers Hotel* (☎01531/635266; ❻) occupies a smashing "Black and White" on the High Street, footsteps from the Market Place – and has just sixteen very comfortable rooms. As for **food**, the *Malthouse Restaurant*, on Church Lane (☎01531/634443; closed Sun), is exemplary, with a creative menu featuring local ingredients – main courses average around £15. Also on Church Lane, the charming *Prince of Wales* **pub** is a great place to sink a beer amidst its snug, low-beamed rooms.

Ross-on-Wye

ROSS-ON-WYE, perched above a loop of the Wye sixteen miles southeast of Hereford, is a relaxed, easy-going town with an artsy/New Age undertow. It's also the obvious base for exploring one of the more dramatic sections of the Wye River Valley and the Forest of Dean (see below). Ross's jumble of narrow streets zeroes in on the Market Place, which is shadowed by the seventeenth-century **Market House**, a sturdy two-storey sandstone structure that now accommodates a modest **Heritage Centre** (April–Oct Mon–Sat 10am–5pm, Sun 10.30am–4pm; Nov–March Mon–Sat 10am–4pm; free), exploring the town's history. Close by, Ross's other noteworthy building is the mostly thirteenth century **St Mary's church**, whose sturdy stonework culminates in a slender, tapering spire. In front of the church is a large and rare **Plague Cross**, commemorating the three hundred or so townsfolk who were buried here by night without coffins during a savage outbreak of the plague in 1637.

Inside, the church holds several distinctive tombs, one of which – that of a certain William Rudhall (d.1530) – is one of the last great alabaster sculptures from the specialist masons of Nottingham, whose work was prized right across medieval Europe. Opposite the church, **The Prospect** is a neat public garden offering pleasant views over the river.

If you've strolled long enough around town but still have time to spare, strike out along one of the many well-defined **footpaths** that thread their way through the riverine fields and woods bordering the Wye. A collection of leaflets giving detailed descriptions of several circular routes is available at the tourist office (see below).

Practicalities

There are no trains to Ross, but the **bus station** is handily located on Cantilupe Road, from where it's a couple of minutes' walk west to both the Market Place and the **tourist office**, on the corner of High and Edde Cross streets (Easter–Sept Mon–Sat 9am–5.30pm, Sun 10am–4pm; Oct–Easter closed Sun; ☎01989/562768). Ross is strong on **B&Bs** with perhaps the best being the *Linden House*, in a fetching, three-storey Georgian building opposite St Mary's at 14 Church St (☎01989/565373; ❷). The six guest rooms, only one of which is en suite, are cosily decorated in a modern style and the breakfasts are delicious – both traditional and vegetarian. Another convenient choice – if a tad more frugal – is *Vaga House*, another well-maintained Georgian building, this one with oodles of flower boxes, located just below the tourist office on Wye Street (☎01989/563024, ✉vagahouse@hotmail.com; ❶). The nearest **camping** is the *Broadmeadow Caravan Park*, occupying a field on the northeast edge of Ross beside the ring road (☎01989/768076; closed Oct–March). **Bikes** can be rented from Revolutions on Broad Street (☎01989/562639). The main cultural event is the Ross International Festival (☎01989/563330, ⓦwww.festival.org.uk), a mixed bag of music, theatre and dance held over two weeks at the back end of August.

Restaurants range from the *Oat Cuisine*, a straightforward daytime wholefood café at 41 Broad St, to the *Cloisters Wine Bar*, 24 High St (☎01989/567717; eve only), serving a wide range of meat and fish dishes in a candlelit interior. Even better, a few paces further along High Street, is the excellent, reasonably priced *Meader's* (☎01989/562803), which specializes in Hungarian dishes. Of the **pubs**, the ancient, oak-beamed *Eagle Inn,* on Broad Street, is the most appealing, though the *Man of Ross*, at the top of Wye Street, runs it close and serves good pub food.

The Wye River Valley

Heading south from Ross along the B4234, it's just five miles to the sullen sandstone mass of **Goodrich Castle** (daily: April–Oct 10am–6pm; Nov–March 10am–1pm & 2–4pm; £3.60; EH), which commands wide views over the hills and woods of the **Wye River Valley**. Dating from the twelfth century, the castle's strategic location beside a busy river crossing point guaranteed its importance as a border stronghold from the twelfth century onwards. The substantial ruins incorporate a Norman keep, a maze of later rooms and passageways and walkable ramparts, complete with murder holes, slits through which boiling oil or water was poured onto the attackers down below. During the Civil War, a determined Royalist garrison held on until the Parliamentarians built themselves a special cannon, "Roaring Meg", which soon brought victory – a great achievement considering the unreliability of the technology: large cannons had the unfortunate habit of blowing up as soon as anyone fired them.

8

The castle stands next to tiny **GOODRICH VILLAGE**, which is on the Ross to Gloucester bus route – Stagecoach **bus** #34 (not Sun). From the village, it's around a mile and half southeast along narrow country lanes to the solitary **Welsh Bicknor hostel** (℡01594/860300, ⓦwww.yha.org.uk; restricted opening Nov–March), in a Victorian riverside rectory. The hostel, in 25-acre grounds, has 78 beds in anything from two-bed to ten-bed rooms, and provides evening meals on request; you can just show up and hope for a berth, but given the hostel's seclusion booking ahead is strongly recommended.

Symonds Yat Rock and Symonds Yat East

From Goodrich – and beyond all hope of a bus – it's a couple of miles south along narrow roads to the signposted turning that wriggles its way up to the top of **Symonds Yat Rock**, rising high above a wooded, hilly loop in the Wye. This is one of the region's most celebrated views and you'll probably share it with the birdwatchers who come here to spy the raptors gliding the valley below. At the foot of the rock – a two-mile drive away – is **SYMONDS YAT EAST**, a pretty little hamlet that straggles along the east bank of the river. It's a popular spot, with canoe rental and cruises available from Kingfisher (℡01600/891063; closed Nov–Feb), and there are several places to stay. The most appealing **hotel** is the bright and cheerful *Forest View* (℡01600/890210; ❹).

The road to the village is a dead end, so you have to double back to regain the main local road, the B4432.

Shropshire

One of England's largest and least populated counties, **Shropshire** stretches from its long and winding border with Wales to the very edge of the urban Black Country. Its most unique attraction is industrial: it was here that the Industrial Revolution made a huge stride forward with the spanning of the River Severn by the very first **iron bridge**. The assorted industries that subsequently squeezed into the gorge are long gone, but a series of **museums** celebrate their craftsmanship – from tiles and iron through to porcelain and even clay pipes. The River Severn also flows through the county town of **Shrewsbury**, whose antique centre holds dozens of old half-timbered buildings, though **Ludlow**, further to the south, has the edge when it comes to handsome Tudor and Jacobean architecture. One of the most beautiful parts of Shropshire is to the south of Shrewsbury along the ridge of the **Long Mynd**, a prime hiking area that is best explored from the attractive little town of **Church Stretton**.

Yet, for all its attractions, Shropshire remains well off the main tourist routes, one factor protecting the county's isolation being the paucity of its **public transport**. Shrewsbury and Telford are connected to Birmingham, whilst Ludlow, Craven Arms and Church Stretton are connected to Shrewsbury on the Hereford line, but that's about the limit of the **train** services, whilst rural **buses** tend to connect outlying villages on just a few days of the week. Bus timetables are available at tourist offices and from the **Telford Traveline** (℡01952/200005), covering Telford, Ironbridge and Much Wenlock.

Ironbridge Gorge

Both geographically and culturally, **Ironbridge Gorge**, the collective title for a cluster of small villages huddled in the wooded Severn valley to the south of new-town Telford, looks to the cities of the West Midlands conurbation rather than rural Shropshire. Ironbridge Gorge was the crucible of the Industrial Revolution, a process encapsulated by its famous span across the Severn gorge – the world's first **iron bridge**, engineered by Abraham Darby and opened on New Year's Day, 1781. He was the third innovative industrialist of that name – the first Abraham Darby started iron-smelting here back in 1709 and the second invented the forging process that made it possible to produce massive single beams in iron. Under the guidance of such creative figures as the Darbys and Thomas Telford, the area's factories once churned out engines, rails, wheels and other heavy-duty iron pieces in quantities unmatched in England. Manufacturing has now all but vanished, but the surviving monuments make the gorge the most extensive industrial heritage sight in the country – and one that has been granted World Heritage Site status by UNESCO.

Arrival, information and accommodation

There are regular **buses** to Ironbridge village, at the heart of the gorge, from Telford and less frequent services from Shrewsbury and Birmingham. However, travelling round the gorge by bus is well-nigh impossible – the shuttle that used to transport visitors between sights no longer operates and regular buses are few and far between. Even worse, there's currently no **bike** rental in the gorge, though it's possible that this service may be resumed – ring the tourist office (see below) for news.

Ironbridge Gorge contains five museums and an assortment of other industrial attractions spread along a four-mile stretch of the River Severn Valley. A thorough exploration takes at least a day – two for comfort. Each museum charges its own admission fee, but if you're intending to visit several, then buy a **passport ticket** (£10), which allows access to each of them once in any calendar year. Passport tickets are available at all the main sights. **Parking** is free at all the museums, but not in the village of Ironbridge itself. Pick up local maps and information from the **Ironbridge Visitor Information Centre** (Mon–Fri 9am–5pm, Sat & Sun 10am–5pm; ☏01952/432166, ⓦwww.iron-bridge.org.uk), beside the iron bridge in Ironbridge village.

Most visitors to the gorge come for the day, but there are several pleasant **B&Bs** in Ironbridge village, which is where you want to be. Two of the best are the *Library House*, which occupies a charming Georgian villa just yards from the iron bridge at 11 Severn Bank (☏01952/432299, ⓦwww.libraryhouse .com; no credit cards; ❸), and *Eley's Bridge View*, whose spick and span rooms are also a stone's throw from the bridge at 10 Tontine Hill (☏01952/ 432541; ❷). Alternatively, *Coalbrookdale Villa* is an attractive Victorian Gothic ironmaster's house up the hill from the bridge in tiny Paradise (☏01952/ 433450; no credit cards; ❷). The gorge also holds two **youth hostels**: one in the old Workers' Institute opposite the Coalbrookdale Museum of Iron, the other in the former Coalport China factory. They share the same telephone number (☏01952/588755, ⓦwww.yha.org.uk) and are open all year, but only at weekends in the depths of winter.

Ironbridge village

There must have been an awful lot of nervous sweat during the construction of the **iron bridge** over the River Severn in the late 1770s. The first of its kind, no one was quite sure how the new material would wear and although the single-span design looked sound, many feared the bridge would tumble into the river. To compensate, Abraham Darby used more iron than was strictly necessary, but the end result still manages to appear graceful, arching between the steep banks with the river far below. The settlement at the north end of the span was promptly renamed **IRONBRIDGE**, and today its brown-brick houses climb prettily up the river bank. The village is also home to the **Museum of the Gorge** (daily 10am–5pm; £2), in an old riverside warehouse a short walk west of the bridge, which introduces you to the site and its history with a short audiovisual show and small exhibition.

The rest of the Gorge

Just to the west of Ironbridge village, the gorge's big industrial deal was once **COALBROOKDALE**'s iron foundry, which boomed throughout the nineteenth century and employed up to four thousand men and boys. The foundry has been imaginatively converted into the **Museum of Iron** (daily 10am–5pm; £3.90, £4.60 including Darby Houses), with a wide range of displays on iron-making in general and the history of the company in particular. There are superb examples of Victorian and Edwardian ironwork including the art castings – stags, dogs and water fountains for instance – that became the house speciality. Also in the complex is the restored **furnace** where Abraham Darby pioneered the use of coke as a smelting fuel in place of charcoal. From the furnace, it's about 100 yards up to the **Darby Houses** (daily 10am–5pm; £2.65) – Dale House and Rosehill – a pair of attractively restored, old ironmaster's homes with period rooms and items that once belonged to the Darby family.

From Ironbridge village, it's a couple of miles east along the river's edge to the **Tar Tunnel** (April–Oct daily 10am–5pm; £1), where bitumen oozes naturally from the walls. Close by, the **Coalport China Museum** (daily 10am–5pm; £3.90) occupies the restored factory where Coalport porcelain and china was manufactured from 1792 until the works transferred to Stoke-on-Trent in 1926. The complex has several well-preserved examples of the conical bottle-kilns that were long the hallmark of the pottery industry, and inside the museum there's an engrossing assortment of the gaudy crockery for which the company was famous.

It's a mile or so up the hill from the Tar Tunnel to the rambling **Blists Hill Victorian Town** (daily 10am–5pm; £7.50), which encloses various reconstructed Victorian buildings – including a school, a candle-maker's, a doctor's surgery complete with horrific instruments, a gas-lit pub, a wrought-iron works and a slaughterhouse. Jam-packed on most summer days, it's especially popular with school parties, which keep the period-dressed employees very busy.

On the opposite bank of the river, accessible either via the footbridge near the Tar Tunnel or the Jackfield road bridge to the west, is the **Jackfield Tile Museum** (daily 10am–5pm; £3.90). Housed in an old tile factory, the museum features a superb collection of brightly coloured tiles, from the fancy, flowery patterns of washstand splash-backs through to intricate Victorian fireplace tiles and a folksy *Punch and Judy* panel from the 1920s.

Heading west from Jackfield, along the south bank of the River Severn, follow the signs to the enjoyable **Broseley Clay Tobacco Pipe Museum** (April–Oct daily 1–5pm; £2.65). During the late seventeenth and early eighteenth centuries, the satellite settlement of Broseley, formerly a source of raw materials for the foundries across the river, became a boom town in its own right, producing clay pipes for the swelling ranks of tobacco smokers in Britain. Occupying one of three factories that once existed here, the museum charts the history of smoking with a lively exhibition that culminates with some priceless film footage showing how the arm-length "Church Warden" pipes were made.

Eating and drinking

For **food**, there's hardly a plethora of great places to eat in the Gorge, but appealing options kick off with the excellent *Meadow Inn* pub (℡01952/433193), a family-owned Free House with mock-Elizabethan timbers and an excellent line in daily specials – meat, seafood and vegetarian. It's located down by the river on Buildwas Road, about a mile west of the bridge. Also first-rate is the *Horse & Jockey*, 15 Jockey Bank (℡01952/433798), just north of Coalport, whose legendary steak-and-kidney pie draws punters from miles around, whilst the moderately priced *Oliver's Vegetarian Bistro* (℡01952/433086; closed Mon), on the High Street by the bridge, does what it does with flair. **Real-ale** buffs will enjoy the *Coalbrookdale Inn*, past the Museum of Iron, a smashing traditional pub – no pool tables or one-armed bandits – which has the CAMRA stamp of approval for its excellent selection of beers.

Shrewsbury

SHREWSBURY, the county town of Shropshire, sits in a narrow loop of the River Severn, a three-hundred-yard spit of land being all that keeps the town centre from becoming an island. It would be difficult to design a better defensive site, and fortifications were first built on this narrow neck in the fifth century, after the departure of the Roman legions from the nearby garrison town of Viroconium. The Normans were swift to realize the strategic potential of the site, too, building the first stone castle, which was expanded and strengthened by Edward I in the late thirteenth century. The eighteenth century saw the town evolve as a staging post on the busy London to Holyhead route. This traffic withered with the arrival of the railways, but by then the town had become the host of a lively social season, patronized by the sort of people who could afford to send their offspring to the famous Shrewsbury School. The top-notch gatherings are, however, long gone and nowadays Shrewsbury is an easy-going, middling market town, albeit with several especially fine Tudor and Jacobean streetscapes.

Arrival, information and accommodation

Shrewsbury is well connected by **train** to the rest of the country, and its station, at the northeast edge of the centre, is a popular departure point for scenic rail journeys into mid-Wales. **Buses** from London, Birmingham and beyond pull into the National Express stand at the Raven Meadows bus station, off the Smithfield Road, five minutes' walk west of the train station. The **tourist office** is south up the hill from the two stations, on The Square (May–Sept Mon–Sat 10am–6pm, Sun 10am–4pm; Oct–April Mon–Sat 10am–5pm; ℡01743/281200, ⓦwww.shrewsbury.ws). The labyrinthine lanes and alleys of Shrewsbury's centre can be baffling, but fortunately it's too small an area to be lost in for long. As a general guide, Castle Gates/Castle Street runs from the train station up to Pride Hill, a short pedestrianized street that meets St Mary's Street/Dogpole at one end and High Street/Wyle Cop at the other. The Square off the High Street is at the heart of the town centre.

Shrewsbury has one particularly good **hotel**, the *Prince Rupert*, which occupies a tastefully converted old building, right in the centre of town off Pride Hill on Butcher Row (℡01743/499955, ⓦwww.prince-rupert-hotel.co.uk; ⑥). Less expensive options in the centre include the *Lion*, a classic Georgian coaching inn on the Wyle Cop (℡01743/353107; ⑤), and the *College Hill Guest House*, a pleasant **B&B** in an old listed building at 11 College Hill, near The Square (℡01743/365744; no credit cards; ②). Most of the town's B&Bs are beyond the centre, with several dotted along Abbey Foregate, which runs east from the English Bridge at the foot of Wyle Cop: try the unassuming, neat and tidy *Abbey Court Guest House*, at no. 134 (℡01743/364416; no credit cards; ❶). The **youth hostel** is housed in a former Victorian ironmaster's house, about one mile east of the centre, at the far end of Abbey Foregate (℡01743/360179, Ⓦwww.yha.org.uk; closed Nov–Feb). It's near Lord Hill's Column, the monument erected in memory of Wellington's sidekick at the Battle of Waterloo. Take bus #8 or #26 from the bus station.

The Town

The sandstone **Castle**, sitting high above the castellated train station, rests on the site of fortifications that go back a millennium and a half. Today's buildings date mainly from the thirteenth century, although the great architect and engineer Thomas Telford was brought in during the 1780s to shore up the remains and turn the castle into an extravagant private home for local bigwig Sir William Pulteney. It is now home to the dull **Shropshire Regimental Museum** (Easter–Sept Tues–Sat 10am–5pm, Sun 10am–4pm; Oct–Easter Wed–Sat 10am–4pm; £2), a far less interesting attraction than the annual World Music Day (℡01743/231142), which takes place here in July and makes the most of the castle's dramatic setting.

Castle Gates winds up the hill from the station into the heart of the river loop where the medieval town took root. Here, off Pride Hill, several especially appealing half-timbered buildings are dotted along **Butcher Row**, which leads into the quiet precincts of St Alkmund's church, where there's a charming view of the fine old buildings of **Fish Street**. From the church, Bear Steps clambers down to the High Street, on the far side of which, in the narrow Georgian confines of The Square, is the **Old Market Hall**, a heavy-duty stone structure built in 1596.

From The Square, it's a short stroll west to Barker Street and Shrewsbury's most diverting museum, **Rowley's House** (Easter–Sept Mon & Sun 10am–4pm, Tues–Sat 10am–5pm; rest of year Tues–Sat 10am–4pm; free), which occupies an ostentatious 1590s town house with a seventeenth-century brick residence tacked on. The museum contains a wide range of displays relating to local life, with some of the more interesting exhibits coming from the nearby Roman city of Wroxeter, including a unique silver mirror from the third century AD.

Back on The Square, High Street snakes down the hill to become **Wyle Cop**, lined with elegant Georgian buildings and leading to the **English Bridge**, which provides a handsome view of the town as it crosses the Severn. Beyond the bridge is **Shrewsbury Abbey** (daily: April–Oct 9.30am–5.30pm; Nov–March 10.30am–3pm; free), the town's most important ecclesiastical building, but now unceremoniously locked in the middle of a traffic intersection on Abbey Foregate.

Eating and drinking

For daytime **food**, try the *Goodlife Wholefood Restaurant* in the antique surroundings of Barrack's Passage, off Wyle Cop, or snack at *Philpotts' Quality Sandwiches*, which deserves its name and is located at 15 Butcher Row. In the evening, there's the *Sol*, 82 Wyle Cop (℡01743/340560; closed Sun), an outstanding if pricey restaurant featuring local ingredients such as Shropshire lamb cooked in a broadly Mediterranean style, and tasty tandoori at *Shalimar*, by the abbey at 23 Abbey Foregate (℡01743/366658). Some of the best **pub food** in the centre is served at *Loggerheads*, in St Alkmud's Place, with wood-panelled walls and exposed beams; try their filling "Big Head Pie" – steak pieces topped with puff pastry and served with chips, salad and a pint for around £5. Other good **pubs** are the *Severn Stars* on Coleham Head, just over the English Bridge from the town centre; the smoke-free *Three Fishes*, in an ancient building on Fish Street; and the lively *Coach & Horses*, on Swan Hill just south of The Square. The Music Hall **cinema** next door to the tourist office on The Square, screens art-house as well as mainstream releases (℡01743/281281).

The Long Mynd: Church Stretton

Beginning about ten miles south of Shrewsbury, the upland heaths of the **Long Mynd**, some ten miles long and between two and four miles wide, run parallel to and just to the west of the A49. This is prime walking territory and the heath-lands are latticed with footpaths, the best of which offer sweeping views over the border to the Black Mountains of Wales. Nestled at the foot of the Mynd beside the A49 is **CHURCH STRETTON**, a tidy little place and one-time fashionable Victorian resort that makes the best base for hiking the area. The village also possesses the dinky parish **church of St Lawrence**, parts of which – especially the nave – are Norman. Look out also for the fertility symbol over the north doorway – it's a Sheila-na-gig comparable to the one in Kilpeck. In the centre of the village near the church is the **tourist office** (Easter–Sept Mon–Sat 10am–1pm & 2–5pm; ℡01694/723133), which stocks a wide range of leaflets detailing local walks, hikes and off-road cycle routes. Perhaps the most obvious hike is the short, half-mile stroll west up along the National Trust's **Carding Mill Valley** to the **Chalet Pavilion** tearoom and information centre (April–Oct daily 11am–5pm; Nov–March Sat & Sun 11am–4pm).

Church Stretton is accessible from Shrewsbury and Ludlow by **train** and **bus**. Most buses stop in the centre of the village; the train station is a short walk from the tourist office just off the A49. There's no shortage of good-value accommodation in and around Church Stretton, much of it on farms over-looking the Mynd. One particularly good **B&B** is *Acton Scott Farm* (℡01694/781260; no credit cards; ❶; closed Dec & Jan), a seventeenth-century building with log fires and a choice of standard or en-suite rooms, three miles south of Stretton off the A49 in the hamlet of Acton Scott. For a little more luxury, try the *Jinlye Guest House*, on Castle Hill in All Stretton, one mile north, which backs onto the Long Mynd and has great views (℡01694/723243, ⓦwww.jin-lye.co.uk; no credit cards; ❸). **Campers** have a choice of several sites. These include *Small Batch* (℡01694/723358; £8 for caravans or tents; closed Oct–Easter), one mile south at Little Stretton, which enjoys a lovely situation but is small and pretty frugal, and the better equipped *Ley Hill Farm* (℡01694/771366; tents £5; closed Nov–Feb), deep in the countryside near Cardington, with panoramic views of the surrounding hills. **Bike rental** is available from Terry's Cycles, 6 Castle Hill, All Stretton (℡01694/724334).

The **YHA hostel** at **Bridges Long Mynd** (℡01588/650656, ⓦwww.yha.org.uk), five miles' hike west from Church Stretton near **Ratlinghope**, is a splendid base for walks, sitting between the Long Mynd and the **Stiperstones**, a remote range of boggy heather dotted with ancient cairns and earthworks. It's open all year, but bookings are required at least three days in advance from November to March. Marooned amid gentler country east of Church Stretton on the B4371, near Longville-in-the-Dale, **Wilderhope Manor** (℡01694/771363, ⓦwww.yha.org.uk; open Dec 22–26, but otherwise closed Nov–Jan) is the area's other hostel. It occupies a charming Elizabethan mansion, set deep in idyllic countryside. Wilderhope is popular with school groups, so reserva-tions are recommended.

Ludlow

LUDLOW, perched on a hill nearly thirty miles south of Shrewsbury, is one of the most picturesque towns in the Midlands – a cluster of beautifully preserved black-and-white half-timbered buildings packed around a craggy stone castle, with rural Shropshire forming a dreamy backdrop. Close to the Welsh border, the Saxons were the first to recognize the site's defensive qualities, but it was the Normans who got down to business when Roger Montgomery turned up here with his men in 1085. Over the next few decades, Montgomery's fortifications were elaborated into an immense **Castle** (Jan Sat & Sun 10am–4pm; Feb, March & Oct–Dec daily 10am–4pm; April–July & Sept daily 10am–5pm; Aug daily 10am–7pm; £3), strong enough to keep the Welsh at bay and the seat of the Lord President of the Council of the Marches, as the borders were then known. Surviving the attentions of the Parliamentary troops in the Civil War, the rambling and imposing ruins that remain today include towers and turrets, gatehouses and concentric walls as well as the remains of the 110-foot Norman keep and an unusual Round Chapel built in 1120. With its spectacular setting above the rivers Teme and Corve, the castle also makes a fine open-air auditorium during the **Ludlow Festival** (☎01584/872150), two weeks of assorted musical and theatrical fun at the end of June.

The castle entrance opens out onto the **Market Place**, home to the intriguing **Castle Lodge** (daily 10am–5pm; £3), predominantly Elizabethan in style. In the oak-panelled rooms of the ground floor, stained-glass windows depict the coats of arms of Germans summoned by Henry VIII to help sack England's monasteries. In low-beamed chambers upstairs, there's a display on Ludlow's chequered history, which omits the popular rumour that Mary, Queen of Scots hid from Elizabeth's henchmen in the lodge's basement.

At its east end, the Market Place pushes into the Buttercross, off which the magnificently proportioned, fifteenth-century interior of the **church of St Laurence** (daily 10am–5pm; free) boasts vast stained-glass windows and some of the country's finest misericords. In its turn the Buttercross nudges King Street, which intersects with the **Bull Ring**, home of the *Feathers Hotel*, an extraordinary Jacobean building with the fanciest wooden facade imaginable.

Practicalities

From Ludlow **train station**, on the Shrewsbury–Hereford line, it's a five- to ten-minute walk west of the centre – just follow the signs. Most **buses** stop on Mill Street, across the Market Place from the castle entrance. Ludlow's **tourist office**, on the Market Place (summer Mon–Sat 10am–5pm, Sun 10.30am–5pm; rest of year Mon–Sat 10am–5pm; ☎01584/875053, ⒲www.ludlow.org.uk), has a wide range of maps and books for walkers, as well as a selection of inexpensive leaflets detailing day hikes in the area. **Accommodation** is plentiful, though rooms can get scarce during the festival. First choice, if you can afford it, has to be the beautiful *Feathers Hotel* on the Bull Ring (☎01584/875261; ❼), an intricately decorated Jacobean town house with luxury rooms and period furnishings to match. Two other, less expensive options in the town centre are the *Wheatsheaf Inn*, a quaint little pub next to the town gate at the foot of Lower Broad Street (☎01584/872980; ❷), and, just beyond, the excellent *Number Twenty Eight*, in a couple of old properties (☎0800/0815000, ⒲www.no28.co.uk; ❺).

For **food and drink**, the *Feathers* serves up excellent snacks and meals at its café-bar; the popular *Olive Branch*, on the Bull Ring (daily 10am–3pm), specializes in inexpensive light meals and salads; and the *Rose & Crown*, off the marketplace, serves up a good range of beers and delicious bar food and has a sheltered courtyard.

Birmingham

If anywhere can be described as the first purely industrial conurbation, it is **BIRMINGHAM**. Unlike the more specialist industrial towns that grew up across the north and Midlands, "Brum" – and its "Brummies" – turned its hand to every kind of manufacturing, gaining the epithet "the city of 1001 trades". It was here that the pioneers of the Industrial Revolution – James Watt, Matthew Boulton, William Murdock, Josiah Wedgwood, Joseph Priestley and Erasmus Darwin (grandfather of Charles) – formed the **Lunar Society**, a melting-pot of scientific and industrial ideas that spawned the world's first purpose-built factory, the distillation of oxygen, the invention of gas lighting and the mass production of the steam engine. A Midlands market town swiftly mushroomed into the nation's economic dynamo – in the fifty years up to 1830 the population more than trebled to 130,000.

Now the second largest city in Britain, with a population of over one million, Birmingham has long outgrown the squalor and misery of its boom years and today its industrial supremacy is recalled in a crop of excellent heritage museums and an extensive network of canals. It also boasts a thoroughly multiracial population that makes this one of Britain's most cosmopolitan cities. The shift to a post-manufacturing economy is symbolized by the new Convention Centre and by the enormous National Exhibition Centre (NEC) on the outskirts, while Birmingham's cultural initiatives – enticing a division of the Royal Ballet to take up residence here, and building a fabulous new concert hall for the City of Birmingham Symphony Orchestra – are first rate. Nonetheless, there's no pretending that Birmingham is packed with interesting sights – it isn't, though – along with its first-rate restaurant scene and nightlife – it's well worth a day or two – at least.

Arrival, information and city transport

Birmingham's **international airport** is eight miles east of the city centre off the A45 and near the M42 (Junction 6); the main terminal is beside Birmingham International train station, from where there are regular services into the centre. **New Street train station**, to which all InterCity and the vast majority of local services go, is right in the heart of the city. However, trains on the Stratford-upon-Avon, Warwick, Worcester and Malvern lines usually use **Snow Hill** and **Moor Street stations**, both about ten minutes' signposted walk from New Street. National Express **coach** travellers are dumped in the grim surroundings of **Digbeth coach station**, from where it is a ten-minute uphill walk to the centre.

Maps, loads of local leaflets and transport information are provided by all the city's **tourist offices**. The main office is located bang in the centre of town on Victoria Square at 130 Colmore Row (Mon–Sat 9.30am–6pm, Sun 10am–4pm; ☎0121/693 6300, ⓦ www.birmingham.org.uk). Also in the centre is a smaller tourist office – and useful ticket shop – at 2 City Arcade, off New Street (Mon–Sat 9.30am–5.30pm; ☎0121/643 2514). In addition, there are offices at the International Convention Centre (ICC; ☎0121/665 6116), Centenary Square, and in the National Exhibition Centre (NEC; ☎0121/780 4321), next

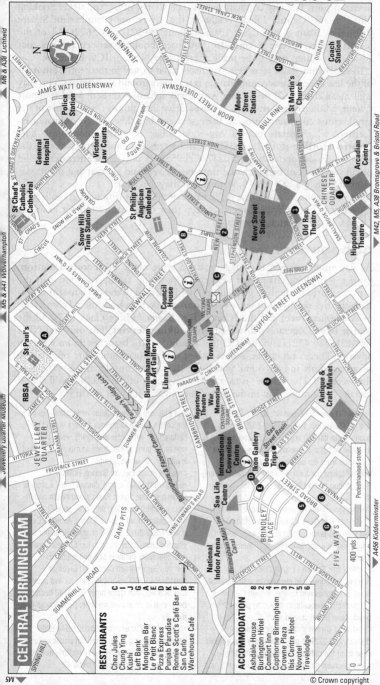

CENTRAL BIRMINGHAM

M42, M6, A45 Coventry, J, K & 8 ▲

M6 & A38 Lichfield ▲

Mb & A41 Wolverhampton ◀

Jewellery Quarter museum ◀

M42, M5, A38 Bromsgrove & Bristol Road ▼

M42, M5, A38 Bromsgrove & Bristol Road ▼

A456 Kidderminster ▼

M5 ▲

JAMES WATT QUEENSWAY

JENNENS ROAD

ASTON STREET

MOOR STREET QUEENSWAY

ST CHAD'S QUEENSWAY

CORPORATION STREET

PRIORY Q'WAY

Police Station

General Hospital

Victoria Law Courts

St Chad's Catholic Cathedral

Snow Hill Train Station

St Philip's Anglican Cathedral

Moor Street Station

St Martin's Church

Coach Station

Rotunda

BULL RING

New Street Station

Old Rep. Theatre

Arcadian Centre

Hippodrome Theatre

CHINESE QUARTER

St Paul's

RBSA

JEWELLERY QUARTER

Council House

Birmingham Museum & Art Gallery

Library

Town Hall

Repertory Theatre

War Memorial

Ikon Gallery

International Convention Centre

Sea Life Centre

National Indoor Arena

Antique & Craft Market

Boat Trips

Gas Street Basin

BRINDLEY PLACE

FIVE WAYS

BROAD STREET

Birmingham & Fazeley Canal

Birmingham Main Line Canal

Farmer's Bridge Locks

SUFFOLK STREET QUEENSWAY

RESTAURANTS

Chez Jules	C
Chung Ying	I
Kushi	J
Left Bank	G
Le Petit Blanc	A
Mongolian Bar	E
Pizza Express	D
Punjab Paradise	K
Ronnie Scott's Café Bar	F
San Carlo	B
Warehouse Café	H

ACCOMMODATION

Ashdale House	8
Burlington Hotel	2
Comfort Inn	4
Copthorne Birmingham	1
Crowne Plaza	3
Ibis Centre Hotel	7
Novotel	5
Travelodge	6

Pedestrianised street

0   400 yds

© Crown copyright

to the airport. The city council runs its own tourist office and ticket booking office in the Central Library, right in the centre on Chamberlain Square (Mon–Fri 10am–5.30pm, Sat 10am–4.30pm; ☎0121/236 5622). All of the tourist offices operate a same-day hotel bed booking service for free, but advance bookings have to be made at either the NEC or ICC branches.

To see Birmingham at its best, you really need to stay in the centre, but most of the less expensive accommodation is scattered around the suburbs. This may well mean that you'll be dealing with Birmingham's excellent local transport system, whose **trains**, **metro** and **buses** delve into almost every corner of the city. Various companies provide these services, but they are co-ordinated by **Centro**, who operate both a city-wide public transport information line, **Centro Hotline** (☎0121/200 2700) and a regional equivalent, covering the West Midlands conurbation (☎0247/655 9559). A one-day **Centrocard**, valid on all services, can be purchased from bus drivers and at train and metro stations; it costs £5 (£4 after 9.30am and at the weekend).

One thing that may confuse is the name of the inner ring road: it's called the Queensway, but individual stretches keep their other names too, for example: Great Charles Street, Queensway.

Accommodation

As you might expect, Birmingham has a wide range of **accommodation**, from tower-block chains out near the airport and family-run hotels in the leafier suburbs through to gritty inner-city B&Bs. All of the city's tourist offices have the full details and there's a selection of hotels in both their *Pocket Guide to Birmingham* (free) and the *Night & Day Essential Visitor Guide* (£2). All the tourist offices operate a **hotel room booking service**, but only the NEC (☎0121/780 4321) and the ICC (☎0121/665 6116) branches do bookings in advance. There's no charge and, even better, the tourist offices are often aware of special deals and discounts, which can slash costs considerably, especially on the weekend. The best bet is to stay in the vicinity of the ICC – you'll almost certainly pay more than in the rest of the city, but it's well worth it.

Ashdale House 39 Broad Rd, Acocks Green ☎0121/706 3598. Well-situated B&B, serving good vegetarian and organic food. Acocks Green is a couple of miles southeast of the centre. There are buses from the centre, but you're probably best off taking the train from Moor Street to Spring Road station and walking the half mile or so from there. ❷

Burlington Hotel 6 Burlington Arcade, 126 New St ☎0121/643 9191. Handsomely refurbished Victorian red-brick hotel with over one hundred bright and well-appointed rooms. Fitness facilities, too. ❻

Comfort Inn Station St ☎0121/643 1134. Routine, medium-sized chain hotel with standard-issue furnishings and fittings, though the rooms are perfectly adequate. In an earthy part of town, beside New Street station. ❸

Copthorne Birmingham Paradise Circus ☎0121/200 2727. It may look rather like a Rubik cube from the outside, but this is a great hotel, partly because its 212 modern bedrooms are neat

and trim, and partly because its location – plum in the centre beside Centenary Square – can't be bettered. It's expensive during the week, but weekends bring prices down to more reasonable levels. ❽ , ❺ at weekends.

Crowne Plaza Central Square, Holliday St ☎0121/631 2000. Large, central hotel, a stone's throw from Gas Street Basin. Good health and fitness facilities, including an indoor pool. ❼

Ibis Centre Hotel Ladywell Walk, Arcadian Centre ☎0121/622 6010. Rather characterless, but well-situated chain hotel, bang in the Chinese Quarter, near the major theatres and nightclubs. ❷

Novotel Birmingham Centre, 70 Broad St ☎0121/643 2000. Great location for this smart, new and well-run chain hotel. Over 140 bedrooms decorated in crisp modern style. Good fitness facilities. ❼

Travelodge 230 Broad St ☎0121/644 5266. Workaday central chain hotel, but prices are very reasonable and it's within easy walking distance of lots of restaurants, bars and clubs. ❸

The City Centre

Many visitors get their first taste of central Birmingham at **New Street station**, whose unreconstructed ugliness – piles of modern concrete – makes a dispiriting start. Fortunately, things soon get better if you stroll west along pedestrianized **New Street**, one of the city's principal shopping streets, to the elegantly revamped **Victoria Square**, with its tumbling water fountain. The adjacent **Chamberlain Square** has been refurbished too, but here pride of place goes to the **Birmingham Museum and Art Gallery**, the city's finest museum, complete with a fabulous collection of Pre-Raphaelite art. Beyond, further west still, is the glossy **International Convention Centre**, from where it's another short hop to the **Gas Street Basin**, the prettiest part of the city's serpentine canal system. Close by is canalside **Brindley Place**, a smart, brick and glass complex with smart cafés and bars and the enterprising **Ikon Gallery** of contemporary art.

From Brindley Place, follow the old tow path along the **Birmingham and Fazeley canal** as far as Newhall Street, which is within easy walking distance of both **St Philip's Cathedral**, back in the centre on Colmore Row, and – in the opposite direction- the **Jewellery Quarter**, which holds an excellent museum and hundreds of workshops and retail outlets.

Victoria and Chamberlain squares

At its west end, New Street opens out into the handsomely refurbished **Victoria Square**, whose centrepiece is a large and particularly engaging water fountain designed by Dhruva Mistry. The waterfall out-does poor old Queen Victoria, whose **statue** is glum and uninspired, though the thrusting self-confidence of her bourgeoisie is very apparent in the flamboyant buildings that frame the adjacent **Chamberlain Square**. Amongst the assorted ornate gables and cupolas, columns and towers, the **Council House** is the most impressive edifice, opened in 1879 and complete with a pair of proud lions.

Very different is Chamberlain Square's **Town Hall** of 1834, whose classical design – by Joseph Hansom, who went on to design Hansom cabs – was based on the Roman temple in Nîmes. The building's simple, flowing lines contrast with much of its surroundings, but it's an appealing structure all the same, erected to house public meetings and musical events in a flush of municipal pride. It's currently undergoing a long-term refurbishment, but you can pop inside for a peek (Mon–Fri 10am–4pm; free), though at present there's nothing much to see. In the middle of the square is a dinky Neo-Gothic memorial in honour of **Joseph Chamberlain** (1836–1914), who made himself immensely popular by taking the city's gas and water supplies into public ownership.

The Birmingham Museum and Art Gallery

The **Birmingham Museum and Art Gallery** occupies a rambling, Edwardian building on Chamberlain Square (Mon–Thurs & Sat 10am–5pm, Fri 10.30am–5pm, Sun 12.30–5pm; free). Its several sections are spread over Floors 2 and 3, but the pick is the **Art** section, which contains one of the world's most comprehensive collections of **Pre-Raphaelite** art, concentrated on Floor 2, in Rooms 14 and 17–19. Founded in 1848, the Pre-Raphaelite Brotherhood consisted of seven young artists, of whom Rossetti, Holman Hunt, Millais and Madox Brown are best known. The name of the group was selected to express their commitment to honest observation, which they thought had been lost with the Renaissance. Many of the Brotherhood's most important paintings are displayed here, including Rossetti's seminal *First Anniversary of the Death of Beatrice* (1849), inspired by Dante, and Brown's powerful image of emigration, *The Last of England* (1855). By 1853, the Brotherhood had effectively disbanded, but a second wave of artists carried on in its footsteps. The most prominent of them was Edward Burne-Jones (1833–98), who has an entire room to himself (Room 14); there, you'll find a remarkable sample of his work, though it's his *Star of Bethlehem* which catches the eye, one of the largest watercolours ever painted, a mysterious, almost magical piece with earnest Magi and a film-star-like Virgin Mary. The rest of the art section, though not quite as memorable, contains a first-rate collection of eighteenth- to twentieth-century British art, including an extensive collection of watercolour landscapes. There's also a significant sample of European paintings from the likes of Jan van Scorel and Lucas Cranach through to the Impressionists.

Sharing Floor 2 is the **Industrial Art** section, which kicks off with the **Industrial Gallery**, set around an expansive atrium whose wrought-iron columns and balconies clamber up towards fancy skylights. This section holds a superb sample of locally produced stained glass, ceramics, metalwork – especially silver – and jewellery that amply illustrates the city's industrial prowess. Here also is the **Edwardian Tea Room**, one of the more pleasant places in Birmingham for a break.

Floor 3 holds the **Science** section, where a rather old-fashioned natural-history collection is linked to a couple of rooms containing incidental archeological artefacts: the Mediterranean finds are in Room 34, the local ones in Room 35. Finally, Floor 1's cavernous **Gas Hall** is an impressive venue for touring art exhibitions.

Gas Street Basin and Brindley Place

From the north side of Chamberlain Square, walk through the hideously kitsch **Paradise Forum** shopping and fast-food complex to get to **Centenary Square**, where there's an unusual World War I war memorial. The square has recently been revamped to complement the showpiece **International Convention Centre** (ICC) and the **Birmingham Repertory Theatre**. Centre-stage on the wide paving is a butter-coloured sculpture called *Forward*, a rousing image of the city's history by Birmingham-born Raymond Mason.

From here, it's a brief stroll along Broad Street to the bridge over – and steps down to – **Gas Street Basin**, the hub of Birmingham's intricate **canal** system. There are eight canals within the city's boundaries, comprising no less than thirty-two miles of canal. The highpoint of canal construction was the late eighteenth century, when almost all heavy goods were transported by water. In the middle of the nineteenth century, the railways made the canals uneconomic, but they struggled on until the 1970s when tourism – and narrow boats – gave them a new lease of life. Much of Birmingham's surviving canal network slices through the city's grimy, industrial bowels, but certain sections have been immaculately restored with Gas Street Basin leading the way. At the junction of the Worcester and Birmingham and Birmingham Main Line canals, the Basin, with its herd of brightly painted narrow boats, is edged by a delightful medley of old brick buildings. There's a good pub here – the *Tap & Spile* – and regular **boat trips** leave to explore the prettier parts of the system. There are several operators, but Second City Canal Cruises are as good as any (℡0121/236 9811; £2/person). In summer, there's also a **water taxi** service between several stops along the central part of the canal system (July & Aug daily 10am–5pm; May, June & Sept Sat & Sun 10am–5pm; 1–2 hourly; one-stop 50p).

From the Basin, it's a short walk north along the canal towpath to the bars, shops and clubs of waterside **Brindley Place**, an extraordinarily successful – and aesthetically pleasing – development and here you'll also find the city's celebrated **Ikon Gallery** (Tues–Sun 11am–6pm; free; ⓦ www.ikon-gallery .co.uk), housed in a lovely old Victorian building and one of the country's most imaginative venues for touring exhibitions of contemporary art.

Along the Birmingham and Fazeley canal to St Philip's Cathedral

Just beyond Brindley Place, in front of the huge dome of the National Indoor Arena (NIA), the **canal forks**: the Birmingham and Fazeley leads northeast (to the right) and the Birmingham Main Line canal cuts west (to the left), though to complicate matters the latter has a spur loop here, going under Sheepcote Street. Also beside the main canal junction is the shell-like **National Sea Life Centre** (daily 10am–6pm, last admission 1hr before closing; £8; ⓦ www.seal-ife.co.uk), which can't help but raise a few eyebrows, given the city's inland location. Nevertheless, it's an enterprising educational venture, giving Birmingham's landlubbers an opportunity to view and even touch many unusual varieties of fish and sea life.

Beyond the main canal fork, the first part of the **Birmingham and Fazeley canal** has been attractively restored, its antique brick buildings cleaned of accumulated grime and leading to the quaint **Farmer's Bridge Locks**. Further on, however, things take a grittier aspect as the canal bores beneath the city centre amidst industrial tangle. Emerging at **Newhall Street** (it's signed), about half a mile from the main canal junction, you're within easy striking distance of **St Paul's Square**, flanked by sturdy Georgian buildings and one of the more agreeable parts of the centre. Here, beside the square in Dakota House, on Brook Street, the **Royal Birmingham Society of Artists** (RBSA; Mon–Wed & Fri 10.30am–5pm, Thurs 10.30am–7pm, Sat 10.30am–5pm; donation), offers an inventive range of fine art exhibitions. Also near at hand is **Colmore Row**, a bustling shopping strip where pride of architectural places goes to **St Philip's Cathedral** (Mon–Fri 7am–7pm, Sat & Sun 9am–5pm), a bijou example of English Baroque. Consecrated in 1715, St Philips was initially a parish church that served as an overspill for St Martin's (see below). It was, however, in a more genteel location than the older church and when, in 1905, the Church of England decided to establish a new diocese here in Birmingham, they made St Philips the cathedral. The church was extended in the 1880s, when four new stained-glass windows were commissioned from local boy **Edward Burne-Jones**, a leading light of the Pre-Raphaelite movement.

The Bull Ring

Colmore Row lies just to the west of the city centre's pedestrianized core with chain stores and shopping precincts lining up along Corporation, New and High streets. At the intersection of New and High streets is the distinctive Modernism of the whopping **Rotunda**, but its neighbour, the notorious Bull Ring indoor shopping centre, which fulfilled every miserable cliché about 1960s town planning, has finally been demolished. At present, the **Bull Ring** is a giant building site rolling down the hill below the Rotunda, but its new incarnation – scheduled to be completed in 2003 – will consist of traditional streets and open spaces radiating out from **St Martin's church**. The church is currently a sooty heap, but underneath the grime it's actually a comely amalgamation of the Gothic and neo-Gothic, with fancifully carved decoration and a Burne-Jones window.

Incidentally, the Bull Ring was where bulls used to be tethered and baited in the belief that if the animal died angry, the meat was better.

The Jewellery Quarter

Birmingham's long-established **Jewellery Quarter** lies just to the northwest of the city centre, about half a mile from Colmore Row via Newhall Street. Buckle-makers and toy-makers first colonized the area in the 1750s, opening the way for hundreds of silversmiths, jewellers and goldsmiths. There are still around five hundred jewellery-related companies in the district with most of the **jewellery shops** concentrated along Vittoria Street and the adjacent Frederick Street and Warstone Lane. The prime attraction hereabouts is the engrossing **Museum of the Jewellery Quarter**, 75–79 Vyse St (Mon–Fri 10am–4pm; Sat 11am–5pm; £2.50), a short walk north of the Frederick Street/Warstone Lane intersection. It is built around a factory that has remained virtually unchanged since the 1950s, though it was in use until 1980. A visitor centre starts proceedings, detailing the growth and decline of the trade in Birmingham, but it's the old factory that steals the show. Here, the atmosphere and conditions of the old works are superbly re-created – the jewellers were wedged into tiny, hot and noisy spaces to churn out hundreds of earrings, brooches and rings. Their modern counterparts use the old machines to show how some of the most common designs were produced.

From the museum, it's a couple of minutes' walk back along Vyse Street to the Jewellery Quarter train station and metro stop, on the Snow Hill line.

The suburbs

Birmingham's suburbs fan out from the centre in every direction, a mammoth industrial – and post-industrial – sprawl intermittently relieved by the municipal parks so much favoured by the Victorians. Inevitably, some districts are much better off than others, and it's in well-heeled **Edgbaston**, a mile or two to the southwest of the centre, you'll find a couple of engaging sights – the leafy, lake-dotted **Cannon Hill Park** and the European paintings of the **Barber Institute** on Birmingham University's campus. Further south still is **Bournville**, the planned workers' village laid out by the Cadburys in Victorian times. The main pull here is **Cadbury World**, where displays about the history and manufacture of chocolate are a prelude to tucking into the stuff.

Edgbaston

Leafy, prosperous and home to one of the most famous cricket grounds in the country, the suburb of **EDGBASTON**, just to the southwest of the city centre, was developed in the 1790s by the Calthorpe family as a genteel residential estate from which industry and commerce were explicitly banned. It's here, about two miles south of central Birmingham, you'll find the most agreeable of Birmingham's many public parks, **Cannon Hill Park** (daily dawn–dusk; free) – take Pershore Road and turn left along Edgbaston Road, which marks the park's northern perimeter. There are boating lakes and bowling greens, tennis courts and woodland, and the greenhouses hold a good collection of tropical plants. Cannon Hill is also home to the excellent **Midland Arts Centre** (mac), which has a popular bar, café, cinema and bookshop and also hosts an imaginative programme of art, craft and photography exhibitions. The centre is opposite the cricket ground on Edgbaston Road. Buses #45 and #47, departing from Corporation Sreet, in the city centre, travel along Pershore Road, from where it's a short hoof to the park along Edgbaston Road.

△ Warwick Castle

For the casual visitor, the campus of **Birmingham University**, on the southern fringe of Edgbaston, has one big draw, the **Barber Institute of Fine Arts**, at the east gate off Edgbaston Park Road (Mon–Sat 10am–5pm, Sun 2–5pm; free). Opened in 1939, the gallery contains a small but eclectic collection of European paintings from the thirteenth century onwards. Notable pieces include an unusual Rubens – *Landscape near Malines* – and Degas' eccentric *Jockeys Before the Race*, a characteristically audacious piece of off-centre composition. Other artists featured include Monet, Magritte, Bellini, Whistler, Gainsborough, Renoir, Gauguin and Turner. The campus has its own train station – University, two stops along the line from New Street.

Bournville

A purpose-built factory-community founded by the Cadbury family in 1879, **BOURNVILLE** is the most distinctive of Birmingham's suburbs, located just beyond the university four miles southwest of the city centre. The first of this Quaker dynasty, **John Cadbury** opened a grocery store in Birmingham in 1824 and from it he sold his home-produced "Cocoa Nibs", part soothing nightcap, part a way of weaning the working class from alcohol by providing a cheap and tempting alternative to beer. The popularity of this sweet concoction exceeded John's wildest dreams and just over fifty years later his sons, George and Richard, were able to move the family business out of their cramped premises in the city centre to Bournville – a so-called "factory in a garden". Much influenced by the utopian ideas of William Morris and the Arts and Crafts movement, the Cadburys' Bournville scheme included gardens for every worker's house, a village green and a half-timbered parade of shops. Despite its unusual history, Bournville village doesn't have much in the way of sights, though the **Village Green**, bounded by Linden Road (the A4040) and Sycamore Road, is pleasant enough and it backs onto Maple Road, where the Cadburys plonked a pair of Tudor buildings that were threatened with demolition. These two timber-framed structures, **Selly Manor** and **Minworth Greaves** (April–Sept Tues–Fri 10am–5pm, Sat & Sun 2–5pm; Oct–March Tues–Fri 10am–5pm; £2) – the first a manor house, the second a hall – are furnished in period style and are flanked by pretty "Tudor" gardens.

However, in terms of popularity, these two buildings are as nothing when compared with the excellent **Cadbury World** (phone for times; £6.50; ☎0121/451 4180, ⓦ www.cadburyworld.co.uk), just to the south off Linden Road, adjoining Cadbury's Bournville Works. Billed as "The Ultimate Chocolate Experience", this attraction tells you all you could ever want to know about the cocoa bean, the manufacture of chocolate and the history of Cadburys' itself – the display on their adverts is especially interesting. But for chocoholics the point of the tour is the opportunity to gorge on free samples from the production line and stock up on the cut-price finished product. Needless to say, it's very popular, so **reservations** are advised; call ☎0121/451 4159.

The easiest way to get to Bournville is by **train** from New Street. Bournville station, the fourth stop along the line, is about three-quarters of a mile from Cadbury World – head west along Bournville Lane and turn right up Linden Road.

Eating and drinking

Birmingham's central **restaurants** long had a reputation as soulless places which emptied quickly, but this state of affairs has changed dramatically, with smart, new venues sprouting up in the slipstream of the growth in the conference- and trade-fair business, particularly along Broad Street, near the ICC.

There's also a concentration of decent, reasonably priced restaurants in the Chinese Quarter, just south of New Street station, on and around Hurst Street. Birmingham's gastronomic speciality is the **balti**, a delicious and astoundingly cheap Kashmiri stew cooked and served in a small wok-like dish called a *karahi*, with nan bread instead of cutlery. Although balti houses have opened up within the city centre, the original and arguably the best balti houses are in the gritty suburbs of **Balsall Heath**, a couple of miles to the south of the centre, and **Sparkhill**, about three miles to the southeast. Some of these are listed here – all are unlicensed, so take your own booze.

City centre **pubs** vary as much as you'd expect. The liveliest, catering for a mixed bag of conference delegates and Brummies-out-on-the-ale, are liberally sprinkled along Broad Street, in the immediate vicinity of the Convention Centre, and in Brindley Place. Most of them are decorated in sharp, modern style, but there are one or two more traditional places here as well – as there are in other parts of the city centre.

Restaurants

Chez Jules 5a Ethel St, off New St ☎0121/633 4664. Best medium-priced French restaurant in the city centre, with especially good lunchtime offers. Moderate.

Chung Ying 16–18 Wrottesley St ☎0121/622 1793. The best Cantonese dishes in the Chinese Quarter, and always busy. Moderate.

Kushi 558 Moseley Rd, Balsall Heath ☎0121/449 7678. Excellent, award-winning balti house that's unlicensed, dirt cheap and deservedly popular. Inexpensive.

Left Bank 79 Broad St ☎0121/643 4464. Swish and classy French and continental restaurant that mops up its fair share of ICC delegates. Moderate.

Mongolian Bar 24 Ludgate Hill ☎0121/236 3842. Lively and enjoyable curry house, where you choose your ingredients and see them flash-fried before you. Just off the inner ring road. Moderate.

Le Petit Blanc 9 Brindley Place ☎0121/633 7333. Directly opposite the Ikon Gallery, this swish restaurant, with its slick modern furnishings and fittings, offers first-rate French cuisine with a touch of Asia thrown in for good measure. Reservations advised. Expensive.

Pizza Express Brindley Place ☎0121/643 2500. Great canalside location for this ultra-reliable chain.

Punjab Paradise 377 Ladypool Rd, Balsall Heath ☎0121/449 4110. One of the city's classic balti houses, specializing in milder dishes. Inexpensive.

Ronnie Scott's Café Bar 258 Broad St ☎0121/643 4525. Serves an imaginative selection of snacks and meals, with jazz sounds and memorabilia as background. Late licence. Inexpensive.

San Carlo 4 Temple St ☎0121/633 0251. Best all-round Italian restaurant in the centre, although somewhat lacking in atmosphere. It's near St Philip's Cathedral, just up from the pizza and pasta chain restaurants on New Street. Moderate.

Warehouse Café 54 Allison St, Digbeth ☎0121/633 0261. Imaginative vegan and vegetarian café; ring for times. Bring your own wine. Just below the Bull Ring, near the start of Digbeth – Allison Street is a turning on the left. Inexpensive.

Pubs and bars

Café des Artistes Custard Factory, Gibb Street, off Digbeth. Popular pre-club haunt in a laid-back arts complex that was once a Custard Factory. The nearest club – the *Medicine Bar* (see below) – is in the same complex. Serves good food too – self-billed as "California-style".

Cube Brindley Place. In the middle of Brindley Place, this chic and lively bar, with its angular furnishings and suspended glass ceiling, heaves on the weekend. Has a canalside restaurant and terrace too.

Fiddle and Bone 4 Sheepcote St ☎0121/200 2223. Canalside pub-cum-restaurant owned by members of the City of Birmingham Symphony Orchestra, hence its musical name and theme. Good old fashioned decor and regular live music, often to a very high standard.

James Brindley next to the Hyatt off Bridge Street ☎0121/644 5971. Frequented by businessfolk in the week, but at weekends the jazz brunches give this place a relaxed air. Great canalside location.

Prince of Wales 84 Cambridge St. Old-fashioned haunt with long-standing custom from the Repertory Theatre, now pulling them in from the neighbouring ICC.

Red Lion 94 Warstone Lane. Appealing, traditional Brummie pub in the Jewellery Quarter.

Tap & Spile 10 Gas St. Charming traditional pub with rickety rooms and low-beamed ceilings beside the canal on Gas Street Basin. Once the hangout of weathered canal men, it now attracts tourists and locals in equal measure.

Nightlife and entertainment

Nightlife in Birmingham is thriving, and the **club scene** is recognized as one of Britain's best, spanning everything from word-of-mouth underground parties to meat-market mainstream clubs. There's a particular emphasis on special/specialist nights with leading DJs turning up at different venues on different nights. **Live music** is strong in the city, too, with big-name concerts at several major venues and other, often local bands appearing at some clubs and pubs (see above). Birmingham's showpiece **Symphony Orchestra** and **Royal Ballet** are the spearheads of the city's resurgent high-cultural scene. The social calendar also gets an added boost from a wide range of up-market **festivals**, including the **Jazz Festival** in the first two weeks in July, and the **Film and TV Festival** in November.

For current **information** on all events, performances and exhibitions, pick up a free copy of the excellent, fortnightly *What's On*, Birmingham's definitive listings guide. It's available at all of the tourist offices and many public venues.

Clubs

Baker's 162 Broad St ☎0121/633 3839. Small, artily designed disco-club with a wide range of speciality evenings. House a favourite.

Bobby Brown's 52 Gas St ☎0121/643 2573. Chart and retro sounds for the over-25s, plus speciality nights. House on Fridays.

House of God various venues. Birmingham's ever-popular techno night is still going strong and loud. This is the sound of the city.

Medicine Bar Custard Factory, Gibb St, off Digbeth ☎0121/604 7777. Adventurous club where every evening is different – from hip-hop to blues and beyond. Part of the arts complex that inhabits an old custard factory.

The Nightingale Essex House, Kent St ☎0121/622 1718, ⊛www.nightingaleclub.co.uk. Arguably Birmingham's best club, consistently popular with gays and straights. Five bars, three levels, two discos, a café-bar and even a garden. About ten minutes' walk south of New Street station, out along Hurst Street.

Que ll Central Hall, Corporation St ☎0121/212 0550. Brum's premier "superclub", a conversion of the old Methodist Central Hall into a full-on, 2000-capacity groove. Frequent all-nighters; speciality nights and big-name DJs.

Ronnie Scott's 258 Broad St ☎0121/643 4525. Second of the late maestro's jazz clubs, good also for big names in blues and World Music.

Waterworks Jazz Club Gough St ☎01562/850765. Up-and-coming specialist jazz joint just off the inner ring road near Holloway Circus.

Classical music, theatre, comedy and dance

Alexandra Theatre Suffolk Street, Queensway ☎0870/607 7533. Mainstream pop concerts, musicals and plays.

Birmingham Repertory Theatre Broad St ☎0121/236 4455. Mixed diet of classics and new work, featuring local and experimental writing.

The Crescent Theatre Sheepcote Street, Brindley Place ☎0121/643 5858. Adventurous theatre group and venue for visiting companies.

Glee Club Arcadian Centre, Hurst St ☎0121/693 2248. Dedicated comedy club, with top national names and up-and-coming stars.

Hippodrome Theatre Hurst St ☎0870/730 1234. Lavishly refurbished – and re-opened at the tail-end of 2001 – the Hippodrome is home to the Birmingham Royal Ballet and regularly hosts the Welsh National Opera. Also features touring plays and big pre- and post-West End productions, plus a splendiferous Christmas pantomime.

National Exhibition Centre (NEC) Bickenhill Parkway ☎0870/789 8841, ⊛www.necgroup.co.uk. The NEC's arena hosts major pop concerts. Ten miles east of the centre beside the M42; train from New Street to Birmingham International station.

Old Rep Theatre Station St ☎0121/236 5622. Britain's oldest repertory theatre, with regular performances by the imaginative Birmingham Stage Company.

Symphony Hall International Convention Centre, Broad St ☎0121/780 3333. Acoustically one of the most advanced concert halls in Europe, home of the acclaimed City of Birmingham Symphony Orchestra (CBSO), as well as a venue for touring music and opera.

Listings

Staffordshire

Spreading north from the Birmingham conurbation, the miscellaneous and low-key landscapes of **Staffordshire** don't enthral too many people. Nonetheless, the county packs in coachloads of visitors owing to the presence of **Alton Towers** (☎0870/5204060, ⓦwww.altontowers.com; closed Nov–March; £23, under-12s £19), the nation's most popular amusement park, with several million visitors annually howling and screaming on rides with names that include *Nemesis* and *Oblivion*. The white-knuckle rides take much more money than do the hoteliers in the cathedral city of **Lichfield**, at the southern end of Staffordshire, both the main historic attraction and the county's most agreeable town. Lichfield is easy to reach by **rail** and **bus** from Birmingham and other major cities.

Lichfield

Some fourteen miles to the north of Birmingham, the pocket-sized town of **LICHFIELD** is a slow-moving but amiable place that demands a visit for one reason – its magnificent sandstone **Cathedral** (daily 8am–6.30pm; £3 donation requested). Begun in 1085, but substantially rebuilt in the thirteenth and fourteenth centuries, the cathedral is unique in possessing three spires – an appropriate distinction for a bishopric that once extended over virtually all of the Midlands. The cathedral's **west front** is adorned by over one hundred statues of biblical figures, English kings and the supposed ancestors of Christ, some of them dating back to the thirteenth century, but mostly Victorian replacements of originals destroyed by Cromwell's troops. Even the central spire was demolished during the skirmishes – Lichfield justly claims to be the cathedral that was most damaged during the Civil War. Extensive and painstaking rebuilding and restoration work, which was begun immediately after the Restoration in 1660, has gone on ever since, although the bulk of the work was only completed at the end of the nineteenth century.

Inside, the **nave** is graced by a long line of slender arches and these, together with the decorated capitals and elaborate roof bosses, more than compensate for its lack of width. Moving on, the first three bays of the **choir** are the oldest part of the church, completed in the Early English style of the twelfth century, but the remainder is middle Gothic. On the south side of the choir a narrow stone stairway leads up to a fine **minstrels' gallery** and the **St Chad's Head Chapel**, where the head of the saint was once displayed to cheer up the faithful. Most impressive of all, however, is the **Lady Chapel**, at the far end of the choir, which boasts a set of magnificent sixteenth-century windows, purchased from the Cistercian abbey at Herkenrode in Belgium in 1802.

The cathedral's greatest treasure, the **Lichfield Gospels**, is displayed (Easter–Christmas) in the **chapter house**, off the north side of the choir. One of the most exquisite and valuable surviving Anglo-Saxon artefacts in the country, this 1250-year-old illuminated manuscript contains the complete gospels of Matthew and Mark, and a fragment of the gospel of Luke, written in Latin and embellished with elaborate decoration. Different pages are exhibited at different times, but a particular favourite is the gorgeous Carpet Page, showing a decorative cross whose blend of Coptic, Celtic and Oriental influences make it the equal of the more famous Irish Book of Kells and Lindisfarne Gospels.

Back outside, the Cathedral is flanked by **The Close**, which, with its good-looking medley of Georgian and Victorian buildings, is the prettiest place in town. From the Close, it's a short walk along Dam Street to the **Market Place**, where there's a statue honouring Lichfield's most famous son, **Samuel Johnson**, eighteenth-century England's most celebrated wit and critic and the compiler of the ground-breaking *Dictionary of the English Language*. The adjacent **Samuel Johnson Birthplace Museum** (April–Sept daily 10.30am–4.30pm; Oct–March Mon–Sat 10.30am–4.30pm; £2) occupies the narrow four-storey house that was both the family home and a bookshop. The museum's ground floor still serves as a bookshop – with copies of many of Johnson's works plus James Boswell's celebrated biography entitled the *Life of Johnson* – whilst up above, on the first floor, a video provides a well-considered potted introduction to the great man. Thereafter, a series of modest displays explore Johnson's life and times. Of particular interest is the biting letter he sent to a certain Lord Chesterfield, after the latter falsely claimed credit for sponsoring Johnson's dictionary. The top floor holds a small collection of personal memorabilia, including Johnson's favourite armchair, his chocolate pot (chocolate was a real Georgian delicacy), bib holder, shoe buckles and ivory writing tablets.

Practicalities

Lichfield has two **train stations**: Lichfield City, with regular connections to and from Birmingham, is about five minutes' walk south of the centre, while Lichfield Trent Valley, served by mainline trains from the northwest and London Euston, is on the eastern fringe of the city, about fifteen minutes' walk from the centre. The **bus station** is in between Lichfield City station and the centre. Clearly signed from all three stations, the city centre is dominated by the sprawling Three Spires Shopping Mall. The **tourist office** is on Bore Street, just off the Market Place (April–Sept Mon–Sat 9am–5pm; Oct–March Mon–Fri 9am–4.45pm & Sat 9am–2pm; ☎01543/308209, ⓦwww.lichfield-tourist.co.uk).

Once you've seen the sights, there's no strong reason to hang around, but Lichfield does have a long list of reasonably priced **B&Bs**. These include the appealing *Mrs Jones's B&B*, in a listed nineteenth-century town house by the Cathedral at 8 The Close (☎01543/418483; ❷), and *Mrs Taylor's B&B*, with just one room, in a pretty, well-kept two-storey old house at 23 The Close (☎01543/306140; ❷).

Generally speaking, Lichfield's **cafés** and **restaurants** hardly inspire the palate, though the *Olive Tree*, 34 Tamworth St (☎01543/263363), serves up tasty Mediterranean-style dishes at moderate prices. Also in the centre is *Don Paco*, a Spanish restaurant at 28 Bird St (☎01543/300789; closed Sun); or you could sample the home-made food of the rather frugal *Cathedral Coffee Shop*, on the south side of the Cathedral (Mon–Sat 9.30am–4.45pm, Sun noon–4.45pm).

Derby and the Peak District

In 1951, the hills and dales of the **Peak District**, at the southern tip of the Pennine range, became Britain's first National Park. Wedged between **Derby**, Manchester and Sheffield, it is effectively the backyard for the fifteen million people who live within an hour's drive of its boundaries, though somehow it accommodates the huge influx with minimum fuss.

Landscapes in the Peak District come in two forms. The brooding high moorland tops of **Dark Peak**, fifteen miles east of central Manchester, take their name from the underlying gritstone, known as millstone grit for its former use – a function commemorated in the millstones demarcating the park boundary. Windswept, mist-shrouded and inhospitable, the flat tops of these peaks are nevertheless a firm favourite with walkers on the **Pennine Way**, which meanders north from the tiny village of **Edale** to the Scottish border (see p.521). Altogether more forgiving, the southern limestone hills of the **White Peak** have been eroded into deep forested dales populated by small stone villages and often threaded by walking trails, some of which follow former rail routes. The limestone is riddled with complex cave systems around **Castleton** and under the region's largest centre, **Buxton**, a former spa town just outside the park's boundaries, at the end of an industrialized corridor that reaches out from Manchester. Two of the country's most distinctive manorial piles, **Chatsworth House** and **Haddon Hall**, stand near **Bakewell**, a town famed locally not just for its cakes but also for its **well-dressing**, a possibly pagan ritual of thanksgiving for fresh water that takes place in about twenty local villages each summer.

There's no obvious **route** around the Peaks, but the one outlined below comes in from the south – from Derby – and then cuts up to Buxton before looping round in a clockwise direction to Castleton, Hathersage, Bakewell and points in between. As for a **base**, you're spoiled for choice, but Castleton and Eyam probably win out.

Access and accommodation

Trains penetrate only as far as Buxton from the north and cut through Edale and Hathersage on the Manchester to Sheffield route. The main **bus access** is via the Trent bus company's TransPeak service from Nottingham to Manchester via Derby, Matlock, Bakewell and Buxton; otherwise bus #272 runs regularly from Sheffield to Castleton, via Hathersage and Hope, and the Peak Express connects Sheffield to Buxton. If you're not planning on walking between towns and villages, you'll need the essential, encyclopedic *Peak District Timetable* (60p), from local tourist and National Park information offices, which lists all the local **public transport** services. Buses are more widespread than you might imagine, though there are limited winter and Sunday services, and often only sporadic links between the major centres. Various one-day **transport passes** allow unlimited travel to and within specified zones. It's a complicated system, but broadly speaking the South Yorkshire Peak Explorer (£5) covers the chunk of the park in Yorkshire, the Peak Wayfarer Manchester (£7), and the Derbyshire Wayfarer (£7.25) covers the rest. For all Peak District bus **timetable information** call ☎0870/608 2608.

There's a full network of dedicated cycle lanes, tracks and old railway lines in the park; the National Park Authority provides a series of **cycle rental** outlets from which to make use of them (£10/day, plus £20 deposit; discounts for YHA members). The centres are located at: Mapleton Lane, Ashbourne (☎01335/343156); Fairholmes, Derwent (☎01433/651261); the Information Centre, Station Road,

Hayfield (☎01663/746222); the Visitor Centre, Middleton- by-Wirksworth, Middleton Top (☎01629/823204); Parsley Hay, Buxton (☎01298/84493); and Old Station Car Park, Waterhouses (☎01538/308609).

There's plenty of **accommodation** in and around the park, mostly in B&Bs, with a dozen youth hostels and numerous campsites scattered among them. A network of YHA-operated **camping barns** is also available. These are located in converted farm buildings and provide simple and inexpensive self-catering accommodation for between six and twenty-four people. For further details contact the YHA Camping Barns Reservation Office (☎01200/420102). The main Peak District National Park Authority office is at Aldern House, Baslow Road, Bakewell DE45 1AE (☎01629/816200, ⓦ www.peakdistrict.org). They also operate a string of **information centres**, which are supplemented by village tourist offices and, in some smaller places, by local stores doubling up as information points. **Maps** and trail **guides** are widely available and guided countryside walks are commonplace – sign-up locally. Finally, be sure to pick up a copy of the free *Peak District* paper, crammed with useful information.

Derby

The proximity of the Peak District might lead you to think that **DERBY**, twenty-five miles northeast of Lichfield, could prove to be an interesting stopping-off point. Sadly, the city – a status conferred as recently as 1977 – is an unexciting place, though its workaday centre is partly redeemed by several long and handsome nineteenth-century stone terraces and its **cathedral**, whose pinnacled tower soars high above its modest surroundings on Queen Street. Of the city's several museums, easily the best is the attractively laid-out **Derby Museum and Art Gallery** on the Strand (Mon 11am–5pm, Tues–Sat 10am–5pm, Sun 2–5pm; free), a five-minute walk from the central market place. The museum exhibits a splendid collection of Derby porcelain, several hundred pieces tracking through the different phases and styles from the late eighteenth century until today. The museum also possesses a first-rate collection of the work of **Joseph Wright** (1734–97), a local artist generally regarded as one of the most talented English painters of his century. Wright's bread and butter came from portraiture, though his attempt to fill the boots of Gainsborough, when the latter moved from Bath to London, came unstuck – his more forceful style did not satisfy his genteel customers and Wright soon hightailed it back to Derby.

With fast and frequent connections to many major cities – including Sheffield and Birmingham – Derby **train station** is a mile to the southeast of the city centre along Midland Road and then London Road; it's a dreary walk, so take a taxi if you can. The **bus station** is about half a mile southeast of the centre. Right in the heart of town, on the market place, is the **tourist office** (Mon–Fri 9.30am–5.30pm, Sat 9.30am–5pm, Sun 10.30am–2.30pm; ☎01332/ 255802).

Ashbourne and Dovedale

Sitting pretty on the edge of the Peaks twelve miles northwest of Derby, **ASHBOURNE** is an amiable little town, whose stubby, cobbled Market Place is flanked by a happy ensemble of old stone buildings. Hikers tramp into town from the neighbouring dales to hang around the square's cafés and pubs, and stroll down the hill to take a peek at the suspended wooden beam spanning Church Street. Once a common feature of English towns, but now a rarity, these **gallows** were not warnings to criminals, but advertising hoardings. Walk west along Church Street and you'll soon spot the soaring spire of **St Oswald's church**, an imposing limestone structure dating from the thirteenth century. The interior is delightful, decorated with all sorts of sculptures, from Green Men through to kings and queens, and graced by handsome stained-glass windows, the best of which are exquisite examples of early twentieth-century Arts and Crafts design.

The **River Dove** wriggles its way across the Peak District, cutting a circuitous course from the high hills of Derbyshire to the flatlands southwest of Derby, where it joins the River Trent. The Dove is at its scenic best near Ashbourne in the stirring two-mile gorge that comprises **Dovedale** – confusingly, other parts of the river are situated in different dales. Dovedale and adjacent Lin Dale are extremely popular with hikers and Ashbourne tourist office (see below) has racks of trail guides to help you through. Generally speaking, this is easy walking country, the only problem being the bogginess of the river valley after rain.

Practicalities

There are no trains to Ashbourne, but the town is easy to reach by bus from Derby, Buxton and Manchester. Dovedale is, however, beyond the reach of public transport. From Ashbourne **bus station**, it's a short walk over the river and up the hill to the Market Place, where the **tourist office** (March–June, Sept & Oct Mon–Sat 9.30am–5pm; July & Aug March–Oct Mon–Sat 9.30am–5pm, Sun 10am–4pm; Nov–Feb Mon–Sat 10am–4pm; ℡01335/343666) has oodles of hiking maps and guides. They can also advise on accommodation, a useful service in the summer when things can get very tight. Amongst many **B&Bs**, the pick is the *Coach House*, an immaculately revamped Victorian house with three en-suite guest rooms in a quiet cul-de-sac a five-minute walk from Market Place on The Firs (℡01335/300145; ❹). Several of the pubs do B&B, too, including *Ye Olde Vaults*, on the Market Place (℡01335/346127; ❷). The nearest **youth hostel** is *Ilam Hall* (℡01335/350212, ⓦwww.yha.org.uk; limited opening Oct to mid-July), in a Victorian Gothic National Trust mansion five miles northwest of town. It's a well-equipped hostel and a perfect base for walking Dovedale. The comfortable *Izaak Walton Hotel* (℡01335/350555; ❼) boasts an even better location, hard by the river.

For **food**, the *White Swan* and *Ye Olde Vaults*, both on the Market Place, serve competent bar meals, whilst the *Patrick & Brooksbank* delicatessen, 22 Market Place, has a superb selection of takeaway food, including local cheeses and hams.

Buxton

BUXTON, twenty miles north of Ashbourne, was founded in 79 AD by the Romans, who happened upon a spring from which 1500 gallons of pure water gushed every hour at a constant 28°C. So famous did the spring become that Mary, Queen of Scots, was allowed by her captors to come here for treatment of her rheumatism. The spa's heyday came at the end of the eighteenth century with the fifth Duke of Devonshire's grand design to create a northern answer to Bath or Cheltenham, a plan thwarted by the climate, but not before some distinguished eighteenth-century buildings had been erected.

Like many former British spas, the town's heritage has been marred by a lack of money to refurbish ageing properties, though a belated attempt has been made to rescue some of the finer buildings. The thermal baths were closed in 1972, but the sweep of the **Crescent**, incorporating the former St Ann's Hotel – its grandest architectural feature, modelled on the Royal Crescent in Bath – has been preserved thanks to a hefty government grant. The little street **fountain** in front of the Crescent, supplied by St Ann's Well, is still used to fill local water bottles and the nearby **Pump Room**, first erected in 1894, provides space for temporary art exhibitions in the summer. At the eastern end of the Crescent, a glass and cast-iron canopy hides the entrance to the Cavendish Arcade shopping centre, which makes a hash of preserving the original eighteenth-century bath houses.

The spa remnants apart, the town is at its best in the nearby landscaped **Pavilion Gardens**, just to the southwest of the Crescent and the home of the grand – and grandly refurbished – thousand-seat **Opera House** (tours usually Sat at 11am; ☎01298/72190), facing Water Street. This is the main venue for the Buxton Festival held over two weeks at the back end of July. The glasshouse gardens next to the Opera House shelter an array of exotic foliage and you can walk through to the double-decker glass-and-iron pavilion itself, where there's a bar, coffee shop and restaurant with nice views.

Fronting the Crescent, an attractive park known as **The Slopes** – laid out in 1818 in the last flush of municipal enthusiasm – leads up to the traffic-choked Market Place. The top of The Slopes offers the best prospect over the Crescent to the *Palace Hotel* (see below) and the **Devonshire Hospital**; the latter, built in 1790 as a riding school, is covered by what for a long time was the world's widest domed roof. Just along Terrace Road from Market Place, the **Buxton Museum and Art Gallery** (Easter–Oct Tues–Fri 9.30am–5.30pm, Sat 9am–5pm, Sun 10.30am–5pm; rest of year closed Sun; £1) houses a collection of ancient fossils, rocks and pots found in the Peak District, among them jawbones from Neolithic lions and bears. The displays on the first floor document the history of the region – and the town – from the Bronze Age through to more recent times.

As rewarding as any of Buxton's architectural attractions is **Poole's Cavern** (Easter–Oct daily 10am–5pm; £4.50; ☎01298/26978), a mile to the south of town: follow the Broadwalk through the Pavilion Gardens and then take Temple Road. The guided-tour patter is irksome, but the orange and blue-grey stalactite formations are amazingly complex and the chambers impressively large; one marks the underground source of the River Wye.

Practicalities

There's an hourly train service from Manchester Piccadilly to Buxton, terminating two minutes' walk from the centre at the **train station** on Station Road. The TransPeak **bus** runs every two hours between Manchester (Lever Street Coach Station) and Nottingham, and stops in Buxton's Market Place, as do the regular buses from Sheffield. Although the town isn't actually in the National Park, its **tourist office**, in the old Natural Mineral Baths on the Crescent (March–Oct daily 9.30am–5pm; Nov–Feb daily 10am–4pm; ☎01298/25106), covers the whole of the Peak District.

Accommodation is plentiful, but at the cheaper end of the market it's none too inspiring, many of the cheaper guest houses being located in dreary backstreets away from the centre, though there are several budget options off Market Place along Grange Road and South Avenue. All told, *Lakenham Guest House*, overlooking Pavilion Gardens at 11 Burlington Rd (☎01298/79209; no credit cards; ❸), is a much better choice, as is the *Grosvenor House Hotel*, 1 Broad Walk (☎01298/72439; no credit cards; ❸), with eight en-suite guest rooms in an immaculate Victorian house – and again with views over the gardens. The historic associations of the *Old Hall Hotel*, a good-looking stone structure in The Square, near the Opera House (℡01298/22841, ⓦwww.oldhallhotelbuxton.co.uk; ⑥), resonate with some – Mary, Queen of Scots stayed here in 1573 – but pride of the old spa was the *Palace Hotel* on Palace Road (℡01298/ 22001; ⑨). This still sits pretty above the town and many of its bedrooms have lovely views. It is a twenty-minute walk to *Sherbrook Lodge* **youth hostel**, a Victorian house set in wooded grounds on Harpur Hill Road, at the end of London Road (℡01298/22287, ⓦwww.yha.org.uk; restricted opening Nov to mid-March). The hostel has self-catering facilities and serves up simple evening meals.

For **food**, Buxton is hardly a gourmet's paradise, but there are one or two more-than-passable cafés, beginning with the *Wild Carrot*, 5 Bridge St (℡01298/22843), an adventurous (mostly vegetarian) café at the end of Spring Gardens. In addition, the restaurant and wine bar of the *Old Hall Hotel* are very good, but otherwise you're left with a motley collection of restaurants and a couple of pubs around Market Place. Amongst them, the *Firenze Pizzeria Ristorante*, 3 Eagle Parade (℡01298/72203; closed Sun) is about the best of the bunch. The annual **Buxton Festival** takes place every July, featuring a full programme of classical music, opera and drama, with supporting fringe events, including a film festival; details are available from the Festival Office (℡01298/70395), in the Opera House, where many events are staged, or from the tourist office.

Castleton

The limestone hills of the White Peaks are riddled with water-worn cave systems, best explored in the four show caves within walking distance of **CASTLETON**, ten miles northeast of Buxton. It's an agreeable small town, overlooked by Mam Tor, ringed by hills and cut through by a babbling river lined with stone cottages. Indeed, as a base for local walks it's hard to beat, and the hikers resting up in the quiet Market Place near the church have the choice of a fine spread of local accommodation and services. Overseeing the whole ensemble is **Peveril Castle** (April–Oct daily 10am–6pm; Nov–March Wed–Sun 10am–4pm; £2.30; EH), from which the village gets its name. Its construction was started by William I's illegitimate son William Peveril to protect the king's rights to the forest that then covered vast areas of the Peak District. After a stiff climb up to the keep, you can trace much of the surviving curtain wall, which commands great views of the Hope Valley.

The closest cavern to town, the **Peak Cavern** (Easter–Oct daily 10am–5pm; Nov–Easter Sat & Sun 10am–4pm; £5; ℡01433/620285) is tucked in a gully at the back of the town, its gaping mouth once providing shelter for a rope factory and a small village, of which a vague floorplan remains. Daniel Defoe, visiting in the eighteenth century, noted the cavern's colourful local name, the "Devil's Arse", after the fiendish fashion in which the interior contours twisted and turned. Twenty minutes' walk out of town along the road west to Winnat's Pass (there's a parallel route, across the fields) lies **Speedwell Cavern** (daily: Easter–Oct 9.30am–6pm; Nov–Easter 10am–5pm; last entry 1hr before closing; £5.50; ℡01433/620512). This is, at 600-feet below ground, the deepest cave accessible to the public in Britain. That said, there's precious little to see, with the main drama coming with the means of access itself – down a hundred dripping steps and then by boat through a quarter-mile-long claustrophobic tunnel that was blasted out in search of lead. At the end lies the

Bottomless Pit, a pool where 40,000 tons of mining rubble were dumped without raising the water level.

The other two caves are the world's only source of the sparkling fluorspar known as **Blue John**. Highly prized for ornaments and jewellery for the past 250 years, this semi-precious stone comes in a multitude of hues from blue through deep red to yellow, depending on its hydrocarbon impurities. Before being cut and polished it must be soaked in pine resin, a process originally carried out in France, where the term *bleu-jaune* (after its primary colours) provided the source of its English name. The **Treak Cliff Cavern** (daily: March–Oct 10am–5pm; Nov–Feb 10am–4pm; last entry 40min before closing; £5.50; ☎01433/620571), a few hundred yards along the hillside from Speedwell, contains the best examples of the stone *in situ* and a good deal more in the shop. This is also the best cave to visit in its own right, dripping – literally – with stalactites (some up to 100,000 years old), flowstone and bizarre rock formations, all visible on an entertaining forty-minute walking tour through the main cave system. Tours of the **Blue John Cavern** (daily: Easter–Oct 9.30am–5.30pm; Nov–Easter 9.30am–dusk; £6; ☎01433/620638) dive deeper into the rock, with narrow steps and sloping paths following an ancient watercourse through whirlpool-hollowed chambers down to the Dining Room Cavern, where a former owner once held a banquet. Blue John Cavern is another fifteen minutes' signposted walk beyond Treak Cliff, and there's direct access off the A625, just west of Castleton.

Practicalities

The A625 slices through the centre of Castleton as the high street. From the east, it's a clear run from Sheffield via Hathersage, but arriving from the west – from the A6 just north of Buxton – the A625 has to negotiate the steep Winnats Pass. There's a marginally shorter and even more dramatic approach from Buxton, too: turn off the A6 along the A623 and, after about a mile, at windblown Sparrowpit, take the B6061 over the hills and you'll join the A625 at Winnats Pass. The main approach by public transport is by **bus** from Sheffield and Hathersage on the #272; there are also reasonably frequent buses from Bakewell and bus #203, a weekend service direct from Buxton in summer. The regular Manchester Piccadilly–Hope Valley–Sheffield trains stop at **Hope train station** two miles east of town, which is linked to Castleton by the #272 bus and other local services. The **Peak District National Park Information Centre** is on Castle Street, near the church (daily: Easter–Oct 10am–1pm & 2–5.30pm; Nov–Easter 10am–1pm & 2–5pm; ☎01433/620679).

Accommodation is plentiful, but should be booked in advance at popular holiday times; the information centre can help if you're stuck. The lively **youth hostel** (☎01433/620235, ⓦwww.yha.org.uk; closed Jan) is housed in eighteenth-century *Castleton Hall* and the adjacent old vicarage on Market Place, just up past the church from the information office. The most welcoming **B&B** is *Bargate Cottage*, also on Market Place (☎01433/620201; no credit cards; ❷), whose frilly rooms are overseen by a friendly proprietor who offers conversation, good breakfasts and welcome extras such as drying baskets for hiking boots. Two or three other B&Bs are sited just over the road from here. *Cryer House*, a little way back down Castle Street (☎01433/620244; no credit cards; ❷), opposite the church, has a lovely conservatory, or try for space at the popular *Kelseys Swiss House* on How Lane (☎01433/621098; no credit cards; ❸), the eastern continuation of the main road through town. All the local pubs have rooms, such as *Ye Olde Cheshire Cheese*, How Lane (☎01433/620330; ❸). The best lodgings are at *Ye Olde Nag's Head* at Cross Street on the main road (☎01433/620248; ❺), a comfortable, if slightly formal, seventeenth-century coaching inn with some good weekend – and dinner, room and breakfast – deals.

The pubs are the mainstay for **eating out**. *Ye Olde Cheshire Cheese* welcomes muddy boots and fills their owners with generous portions, while the *Castle* on Castle Street has an appealing series of rooms warmed by open fires. Best of all are the bar meals at *Ye Olde Nag's Head*, boasting treats such as *bruschetta* and wild mushrooms; you can eat more expensively, and equally well, in their restaurant too.

Edale

There's almost nothing to **EDALE** except for a couple of pubs, a scattering of local B&Bs and a train station, and it's this isolation which is immediately appealing. Walkers arrive in droves throughout the year to set off on the 250-mile **Pennine Way** (see box below) across England's backbone to Kirk Yetholm on the Scottish border; its starting-point is signposted from outside the *Old Nag's Head* at the head of the village.

An excellent **circular walk** (9 miles; 5hr) uses the first part of the Pennine Way, leading up onto the bleak gritstone, table-top of **Kinder Scout** (2088ft), below which the village cowers. The route cuts west from the *Nag's Head* along a packhorse route once used by Cheshire's salt exporters. From the campsite and camping barn at *Upper Booth Farm* (☎01433/670250), you climb the Jacob's Ladder path continuing half a mile west to the carved medieval **Edale Cross**. Backtracking a couple of hundred yards, the Pennine Way branches north along the broken plateau edge to **Kinder Downfall**, Derbyshire's highest cascade. This was the site of the Kinder Scout Trespass of 1932, when dozens of protesters walked onto unused but private land, five subsequently receiving prison

The Pennine Way

The 250-mile-long **Pennine Way** was the country's first long-distance footpath, officially opened in 1965. It stretches north from the boggy plateau of the Peak District's Kinder Scout, through the Yorkshire Dales and Teesdale, crossing Hadrian's Wall and the Northumberland National Park, before entering Scotland to fizzle out at the village of Kirk Yetholm. People had been using a similar route for over thirty years before the official opening, inspired by Tom Stephenson, secretary of the Ramblers' Association, who had first identified the need for such a long-distance path in the 1930s. His idea was to stick to the crest of the Pennines where practicable and link up existing tracks, bridleways and footpaths, only descending to the valleys for overnight accommodation and services. The problem was that much of the route lay on private land, so years of negotiation and re-routing were necessary before the Pennine Way could be officially declared open.

Now it's one of the most popular walks in the country, either taken in sections or completed in two to three weeks, depending on your level of fitness and experience. It's a challenge in the best of weather, since it passes through some of the most remote countryside in England – you must be properly equipped, able to use a map and compass and be prepared to follow local advice about current diversions and re-routing; changes are often made to avoid erosion of the existing path. The National Trail Guides, *Pennine Way: South* and *Pennine Way: North* are essential, though some still prefer to stick to Wainwright's *Pennine Way Companion*. National Park **information** centres along the route – particularly the one at Edale – stock a full selection of guides and associated trail leaflets and can offer advice. Finally, on reaching the end, you can get your certificate stamped at Edale's *Old Nag's Head* in the south or Kirk Yetholm's *Border Hotel* in the north.

sentences. It was the turning-point in the fight for public access to open moorland, leading, three years later, to the formation of the Ramblers' Association. At Kinder Downfall turn east then southeast across the often boggy peat towards the wind-sculpted **Wool Pack** rocks, then across to the eastern rim, where a path to the south along Grindslow Knoll and down into Edale avoids Grindsbrook Clough, the highly eroded route of the original Pennine Way.

Practicalities

Edale is about five miles northwest of Castleton by road, slightly more direct by path. Hourly **trains** from Manchester or Sheffield (stopping in Hathersage) provide surprisingly easy access; the only **bus** is a summer-weekends only hourly service from Castleton. Around 400 yards up the road from the train station is the **National Park Information Centre** (daily: Easter–Oct 9am–1pm & 2–5.30pm; Nov–Easter closes 5pm; ☎01433/670207) at Fieldhead. This sells all manner of trail leaflets and hiking guides and can advise about local **accommodation**. The nearest **youth hostel**, the extremely popular *Edale YHA Activity Centre* (☎01433/670302, ⓦwww.yha.org.uk) lies two miles northeast of Edale station, in an old country house at Rowland Cote, Nether Booth. It's accessible along the road to Nether Booth or across the fields – and the Fieldhead campsite – from behind the information centre. Naturally enough, the hostel is popular with Pennine Way walkers as is the YHA **camping barn** at Cotefield Farm, Ollerbrook (☎01433/620111), which lies on the path to the youth hostel. There are two **campsites**, *Fieldhead* (☎01433/670386), behind the information centre, and *Cooper's* at Newfold Farm (☎01433/670372), in the centre of Edale near the *Old Nag's Head*.

For a bit more luxury, there are several **B&Bs** to chose from, starting with the recently revamped *Old Parsonage*, behind the *Nag's Head* (☎01433/670232; no credit cards; ❶; closed Oct–Easter). *Stonecroft*, a detached Victorian house on the village road near the church (☎01433/670262; no credit cards; ❸) is good, too, while other private home and farmhouse options lie scattered out along the Nether Booth road. Attractive *Edale House* (☎01433/670399; no credit cards; ❶) is typical, a twenty-minute walk from the pub. The *Ramblers' Country House Hotel* (☎01433/670268; ❸), close to the train station at the bottom of the village, has rooms, and is one of only two places to **eat** and drink. Those things, though, are best done at the hiker-friendly *Old Nag's Head* (☎01433/670291), at the top of the village; alternatively, head down to the *Ramblers'*.

Hathersage

The busy little town of **HATHERSAGE** on the A625, five miles east of Castleton and just eleven from Sheffield, has a hard time persuading people not to pass straight through into the heart of the National Park. It's worth at least an hour though, particularly in its quieter reaches on the heights around the much restored village **church of St Michael and All Angels**, where a prominent grave site is said to be the last resting place of the Sherwood outlaw Little John. The footpath up to the church starts by the side of the *Hathersage Inn* on the main road. Hathersage's other claim to fame is as the "Morton" of Charlotte Brontë's **Jane Eyre** – a village name borrowed by the author from the landlord of the *George* in Hathersage, who met Charlotte off the stagecoach from Haworth when she came to stay here in 1845. She was visiting a friend, whose brother was the local vicar and, in the church, Charlotte doubtless was shown the memorial "Eyre brasses". She also used several other local names and buildings for her novel, notably North Lees Hall (Rochester's Thornfield

Hall) and Moorseats (St John Rivers' Moor House) – all of which can be taken in on a four-mile circular walk around the town.

Hathersage also boasts its share of craft and cottage industries, most notably the impressive **Round Building**, just outside town on the B6001 (Mon–Sat 10am–5pm, Sun 11am–5pm; ☎01433/650220), where Sheffield designer David Mellor produces wonderful cutlery, tableware and kitchenware.

Practicalities

Among several services, the frequent #272 Sheffield–Castleton **bus** stops right outside the *George*. The town is also on the Manchester–Sheffield rail line and from the **train station** it's about half a mile north to both Sheffield Road, the main street, and the *George*.

Hathersage has a couple of first-rate **B&Bs** – try *Moorgate*, on Castleton Road (☎01433/650293; no credit cards; ❶) – and there are rooms in several **inns**, most memorably in the venerable *George* on Sheffield Road (☎01433/650436; ❻). Its close rival is the *Scotsman's Pack* (☎01433/650253; ❹), a flagstoned, eighteenth-century inn on School Lane, the way to the church. Brontë fans will be delighted to know that two apartments in the beautifully restored *North Lees Hall* can be rented – contact the Vivat Trust (☎0207/930 8030; ❾); prices run from £420 a week for the two-person apartment. The local **youth hostel** (☎01433/650493), with just forty beds, is on the edge of the village, on Castleton road, a hundred yards past the *George*.

All the pubs serve bar **meals**, but the restaurant at the *George* is probably the best in town. Otherwise, *Longland's Eating House*, on Sheffield Road (☎01433 651978), is a laid-back, licensed, mainly vegetarian, café above a good hiking/outdoors shop.

Eyam

Within a year of September 7, 1665, the lonely lead-mining settlement of **EYAM** (pronounced "Eem"), five miles south of Hathersage and four miles northwest of Baslow, had lost almost half of its population of 750 to the bubonic plague, a calamity that earned it the enduring epithet "The Plague Village". The first victim was one George Vicars, a journeyman tailor who is said to have released some infected fleas into his lodgings from a package of cloth he had brought here from London. Acutely conscious of the danger to neighbouring villages, William Mompesson, the village rector, speedily organized a self-imposed quarantine, arranging for food to be left at places on the parish boundary. One of these was **Mompesson's Well**, half a mile up the hill to the north and still accessible by footpath from the village. Payment was made with coins left in pools of disinfecting vinegar in holes chiselled into the old boundary stones – and these can still be seen. The rector closed the church and held services in the open air at a natural rock arch to the south of the village – and every year since 1906, on the last Sunday in August, a commemorative service has been held here, at Cucklet Delph. Mompesson himself survived the plague, though his wife did not – poor reward for a man whose endeavours prevented the plague from spreading across the Peaks.

Long and thin, Eyam is little more than one main street – Church and then Main Street – which trails west up from **The Square**, where a scrawny green is overlooked by a few old stone houses. First up of interest along Church Street is the comely **church of St Lawrence** (Easter–Sept Mon–Sat 9am–6pm, Sun 1–5.30pm; Oct–Easter Mon–Sat 9am–4pm, Sun 1–5.30pm; free), of medieval foundation but extensively revamped in the nineteenth century. Buried in the church graveyard, in the shadow of a richly carved eighth-century Celtic cross, is Mompesson's wife, whose sterling work nursing sick villagers is recalled every Remembrance Day when red roses are left beside her tomb. Rather more cheerful is the grave of one Harry Bagshawe, a local cricketer whose tomb shows him being bowled with the umpire's finger raised upright, presumably – on this occasion – to heaven. Inside the church, informative panels reveal more of the village's history, highlighting a number of plague sites dotted around the town. The most harrowing of these are the **Riley Graves**, half a mile east of the village beyond The Square in open country, where a Mrs Hancock buried her husband, three sons and three daughters within eight days in August 1666. Adjacent to the church are the so-called **plague cottages**, where plaques explain who died where and when – it was here that Vicars met his maker.

Just along from the cottages, **Eyam Hall** (guided tours June–Aug Tues–Thurs & Sun 11am–4pm; £4.25) was built for Thomas Wright a few years after the plague ended, possibly in an attempt to secure his position as the squire of the depleted village. Wright's heirs have lived in it ever since, building up a mildly diverting collection of furnishings, family portraits, tapestries, costumes and incidental bygones. Some of the adjacent farm buildings have been turned into a **Craft Centre** (Tues–Sun 11am–4pm; free) with a restaurant and gift shop. From the hall, it's a few minutes' walk along Main Street and up Hawkhill Road – follow the signs – to the modest Methodist chapel that now houses the **Eyam Museum** (April–Oct Tues–Sun 10am–4.30pm; £1.50). This tracks through the history of the village and has a good section on the bubonic plague in general – its transmission, symptoms and social aftermath.

Practicalities

Eyam makes a great overnight stop, though you should try and book accommodation in advance, since facilities are limited. **Buses** to the village – from Sheffield, Manchester, Buxton, Hathersage, Bakewell and Baslow – all stop on The Square and a few run along Main/Church Street too.

First choice among the handful of **B&Bs** is the luxurious *Delf View House* (℡01433/631533; no credit cards; ③), a beautifully kept Georgian house set in its own grounds just along from the church; breakfast is served in a superb old dining room with its flagstone floor, imposing fireplace and beamed ceiling. Otherwise, two pubs – the *Miner's Arms*, near The Square on Water Lane (℡01433/630853; ③), and the *Old Rose & Crown*, on The Square (℡01433/630858; ③) – have a few perfectly adequate rooms of a modern disposition. Eyam **youth hostel**, a large Victorian house on Hawkhill Road (℡01433/630335, ⓦwww.yha.org.uk; restriced opening Nov–March), is a steep twenty-minute walk out of the village, past the museum. The best place **to eat** is the *Miner's Arms*, which serves bar meals as well as more formal, but very enjoyable, traditional British dinners in its restaurant in the evenings.

Baslow

On the northern edge of the Chatsworth estate (see below), beside the A619/A623 junction, is **BASLOW**, an inconclusive little hamlet at its prettiest amongst the huddle of old stone houses that flank the River Derwent as it weaves its way south. The village has several **B&Bs**, with one of the most engaging being the *Old School House*, in attractive Victorian premises in the centre on School Lane (℡01246/582488; ③). Even better – and one of the Peak's greatest luxuries – is *Fischer's Baslow Hall* (℡01246/583259; ⑨), a mile or so beyond the village along Calver Road, the A623. In its own grounds, the hall is picture-postcard perfect, a handsome Edwardian building made of local stone with matching gables and a dinky canopy over the front door. The interior is suitably lavish and – as there are only a handful of rooms – the service attentive. The restaurant is superb and has won several awards for its imaginative cuisine; there's a less formal, less expensive café too.

Bakewell

BAKEWELL, flanking the banks of the River Wye some four miles south of Baslow – and twelve miles east of Buxton – is famous for its **Bakewell Pudding**. Known throughout the rest of the country as a Bakewell Tart, this is a wonderful slippery, flaky, almond-flavoured confection – now with a dab of jam – invented here around 1860 when a cook botched a recipe for strawberry tart. Almost a century before this fortuitous mishap, the Duke of Rutland set out to turn what was then a remote village into a prestigious spa, thereby trumping the work of his rival, the Duke of Devonshire, in Buxton. The frigidity of the water made failure inevitable, leaving only the prettiness of **Bath Gardens** beside Rutland Square as a reminder of the venture.

Famous tart apart, Bakewell is an undemanding place today, its main street too crowded by traffic – and tourists – to be much fun, though it is within easy striking distance of several first-rate attractions. In town, there's some interest in the web of narrow shopping streets around **Market Square** as well as in the adjacent **riverside park**, but the most agreeable part of Bakewell trails up the hill at the west end of the centre. Here, strolling up North Church Street, with its line of comely stone cottages, you soon reach **All Saints church**, the result of centuries of tinkering from the Normans onwards. Outside, in the church yard, is a rare **Saxon cross**, carved with saints and decorative circles and scrolls, and inside are the elaborate tombs of the Vernons, local bigwigs who long ruled the Bakewell roost.

Practicalities

The nearest **train** stations are at Matlock and Buxton, leaving **bus** services such as the TransPeak Manchester to Nottingham service, the #X18 from Sheffield, and the #R61 from Derby/Matlock as the main routes into town. All services stop on – or very close to – central Rutland Square. The **tourist office** is just a couple of hundred yards down the road in the restored, seventeenth-century Old Market Hall (daily: Easter–Oct 9.30am–5.30pm; Nov–Easter 10am–5pm; ☎01629/813227). This is very well equipped with public transport timetables as well as local biking and hiking leaflets and guides.

For **B&B**, try the *Avenue House*, whose three attractively furnished rooms occupy part of a spacious Victorian house south of the centre, along Haddon Road (☎01629/812467; no credit cards; ❷; closed Nov–Jan). Alternatively, the homely *Castle Inn*, at the foot of Castle Street (☎01629/812103; ❷) is a sympathetic old inn by the bridge over the Wye with four straightforward, comfortable rooms. The town's **youth hostel**, with just twenty-eight beds, is in a modest, modern building on Fly Hill (☎01629/812313, ⓦwww.yha.org.uk; limited opening Nov–March); it has self-catering facilities and serves evening meals. Fly Hill is near the church – just follow North Church Street round and you'll hit it. There's also pedestrian-only access up a steep lane from the A6. Much more upmarket is a nearby **hotel**, the luxurious *Hassop Hall* (☎01629/640488; ❺), a cannily refurbished old manor house with beautiful bedrooms set in charming parkland two and a half miles north of Bakewell along the A619 and then the B6001.

Bakeries all over town claim to bake Bakewell Pudding to the original recipe, but the best is the *Old Original Bakewell Pudding Shop* beside Rutland Square – open until 9pm in summer and with a full restaurant menu as well as gargantuan, family-sized puddings for a fiver. *Bloomer's*, on Water Lane, is a great place too, an excellent deli and bakery with a special line in home-made sweet and savoury pies. There are also several good **restaurants** in town, beginning with *Aitch's Wine Bar & Bistro* (℡01629/813895; closed Sun in winter), just off Rutland Square along the road to Buxton, which serves tasty Mediterranean-style dishes at very reasonable prices. There's also the first-rate *Renaissance*, in the centre on Bath Street (℡01629/812687), where the emphasis is on French cuisine with a three-course set meal costing £22.

Haddon Hall

The genteel and understated **Haddon Hall** (April–Sept daily 10.30am–5pm; Oct Mon–Thurs 10.30am–4.30pm; £5.90, plus parking 50p), on the banks of the River Wye, two miles south of Bakewell along the A6, is one of the finest medieval manor houses in England. In the mid-twelfth century the property passed from the Avenells, its Norman founders, to the Vernons, who owned it for four hundred years until 1558 when the sole heir, **Dorothy Vernon**, married John Manners, scion of another powerful family, who later became dukes of Rutland. Their union is commemorated on their joint tomb in Bakewell church, but the romantic story of their elopement is probably apocryphal. At the start of the eighteenth century, when the Devonshires outdid the Rutlands by building nearby Chatsworth, the hall fell into two hundred years of neglect, thereby sparing it from Georgian and Victorian meddling.

Restoration at the beginning of this century revealed the **chapel**'s wall paintings of exotic plants and animals, plastered over at the Reformation. Across the courtyard, the fourteenth-century kitchens – originally detached from the house for fear of fire – are now connected by a passage to the banqueting hall, complete with a beautifully restored roof. A couple of less interesting domestic rooms lead to the house's highlight, the **Long Gallery**, built by John Manners for indoor promenades during inclement weather. The **gardens**, too, are gorgeous, and the whole heady ensemble turned up to great effect as Mr Rochester's Thornfield in Zeffirelli's *Jane Eyre*.

Haddon Hall is on the TransPeak **bus** route.

Chatsworth House

Chatsworth House (Easter–Oct daily 11am–5.30pm; last admission 4.30pm; gardens till 6pm; £7, gardens only £3.85), four miles northeast of Bakewell via the A619, was built in the seventeenth century by the first duke of Devonshire, and has been in the family ever since. The monumental Palladian frontage beautifully sets off the hundred acres of formal gardens, redesigned in the 1750s by Capability Brown. In the 1820s, the sixth duke instigated more substantial changes when he added the north wing and set Joseph Paxton (designer of London's Crystal Palace) to work on the gardens, creating the Emperor Fountain. At 296ft, the fountain was the world's highest gravity-fed jet, but it now attains a meagre third of that.

Beginning a visit at the house, a maze of balconies and grand staircases lead, eventually, to the **State Apartments**, their ceilings daubed with overblown cherubic figures. None of the rooms is finer than the **Dining Room** in the north wing, its table set as it was for the visit of George V and Queen Mary in 1933, and its wall hung with seven Van Dycks. Vases of the semi-precious Blue

John stone (see p.520) flank the door through to the **Sculpture Gallery**, where you can admire a Rembrandt and a Frans Hals before exploring the gardens, restaurant, estate shop or children's playground. The gardens are, however, tiny in comparison to the surrounding **park** (daily dawn–dusk; free), whose rolling, partly wooded grasslands are grazed by sheep and latticed with footpaths.

The principal approach to Chatsworth leads through the immaculately maintained estate village of **EDENSOR**, remodelled by the sixth duke for his employees, and well worth a few minutes in its own right. There's an infrequent **bus** service from both Bakewell and Baslow to Edensor, but otherwise the best bet is to catch any Bakewell to Baslow bus and walk from the bus stop through the park to the house – a distance of around a mile. Walking back to Bakewell from Chatsworth is also enjoyable, and Bakewell tourist office has a leaflet outlining a possible route.

Travel details

Buses

For information on all local and national bus services, contact Traveline: ☎ 0870/608 2 608, Ⓦ www.traveline.org.uk.

Trains

For information on all local and national rail services, contact National Rail Enquiries: ☎ 08457/48 49 50, Ⓦ www.nationalrail.co.uk.

Birmingham New Street to: Birmingham International (every 15–30min; 15min); Coventry (every 15–30min; 30min); Derby (hourly; 45min); Great Malvern (every 30min; 1hr); Hereford (10 daily; 1hr 50min); Kidderminster (every 30min; 30min); Leicester (hourly; 50min); Lichfield (every 15min; 45min); London (every 30min; 1hr 40min); Shrewsbury (hourly; 1hr 20min); Stoke-on-Trent (hourly; 1hr); Walsall (every 30min Mon–Sat; 30min); Wolverhampton (every 30min; 20min); Worcester (every 30min; 1hr).

Birmingham Snow Hill to: Stratford-upon-Avon (Mon–Sat hourly; 50min); Warwick (Mon–Sat hourly; 40min).

Derby to: Birmingham (every 20min; 45min); Leicester (hourly; 30min); London (hourly; 1hr 50min); Nottingham (every 20min; 35min).

Hereford to: Birmingham (hourly; 1hr 40min); Great Malvern (hourly; 30min); Leominster (hourly; 15min); London (5 daily; 2hr 45min); Ludlow (hourly; 30min); Shrewsbury (hourly; 1hr); Worcester (every 1hr 30min; 40min).

Shrewsbury to: Birmingham (2–4 hourly; 1hr 10min); Church Stretton (every 30min; 15min); Craven Arms (hourly; 30min); Hereford (2–3 hourly; 1hr); Ludlow (hourly; 30min); Leominster (hourly; 40min); Telford (every 30min; 20min).

Stoke-on-Trent to: Birmingham (hourly; 1hr).

Stratford-upon-Avon to: Birmingham (Mon–Sat hourly; 1hr); Oxford (4 daily; 1hr 10min); Warwick (Mon–Sat 8 daily; 30min).

Worcester to: Birmingham (every 30min; 40min–1hr); Hereford (13 daily; 40min).

9

The East Midlands

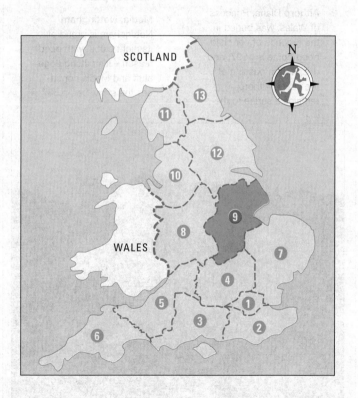

CHAPTER 9

Highlights

✳ Rufford Country Park
Well off the usual tourist track, Rufford offers a wetland and a ceramic gallery, a mill and a sculpture garden with lots of relaxed strolling in between. See p.539

✳ Althorp Diana, Princess of Wales, was buried in the grounds of her childhood home in 1997, and despite the passing of the years, Althorp remains a shrine to the legion of Diana fans. See p.551

✳ Hardwick Hall Elizabeth I was formidable and so was Bess of Hardwick. Her beautiful Elizabethan mansion survives in fine nick. See p.538

✳ Media, Nottingham Nottingham is proud of its night clubs, with good reason – it's cutting edge stuff and Media continues the story. See p.537

9

The East Midlands

Many tourists bypass the four major counties of the **East Midlands** – Nottinghamshire, Leicestershire, Northamptonshire and Lincolnshire – on their way to more obvious destinations, and although there's much to savour it's true they miss little of overriding interest. **Nottingham**, **Leicester** and **Northampton** – three of the four county towns – share a long and eventful history, but have been badly bruised by postwar town planning and industrial development. Embedded in the modernity, however, are a few historical landmarks – an especially fine church in Northampton, the castle in Nottingham, and traces of Roman baths in Leicester – but by and large these are the frills rather than the substance, though Nottingham does have an aesthetic edge. And if few would describe this trio of towns as especially good-looking, the countryside surrounding them can be delightful, with rolling farmland punctuated by wooded ridges and flowing hills, all sprinkled with prestigious country homes, pretty villages and old market towns. In Nottinghamshire, the star turn is **Hardwick Hall**, an especially beautiful Elizabethan country home, but Byron's **Newstead Abbey** runs a close second. Furthermore, the eastern reaches of the county hold two appealing market towns – **Southwell** and **Newark** – whilst west Leicestershire weighs in with the fascinating mansion of **Calke Abbey**. East of Leicestershire, the easy countryside rolls over into **Rutland**, the region's fifth and smallest county, and here you'll find two more pleasant country towns, **Oakham** and **Uppingham**, though tiny **Lyddington** is even more picturesque. Rutland benefits from the use of limestone as the traditional building material and so does **Northamptonshire**. Here, the rural parts of the county are studded with handsome, old stone villages and small towns – most notably **Fotheringhay** and **Oundle** – plus large country estates, the best known of which is **Althorp**, the final resting place of Princess Diana.

Lincolnshire is very different in character from the rest of the region, an agricultural backwater that remains surprisingly remote – locals sometimes call it the "forgotten" county. This was not always the case: throughout medieval times the county flourished as a centre of the wool trade with Flanders, its merchants and landowners becoming some of the wealthiest in the land. Reminders of the high times are legion, beginning with the majestic cathedral that graces **Lincoln**, a dignified old city which, with its cobbled lanes and ancient buildings, well deserves an overnight stay. Equally enticing is the splendidly intact stone town of **Stamford**, but the county's urban attractions pretty much end there. Out in the sticks, the most distinctive feature is **The Fens**, whose pancake-flat fields, filling out much of the south of the county and extending deep into East Anglia, have been regained from the marshes and the

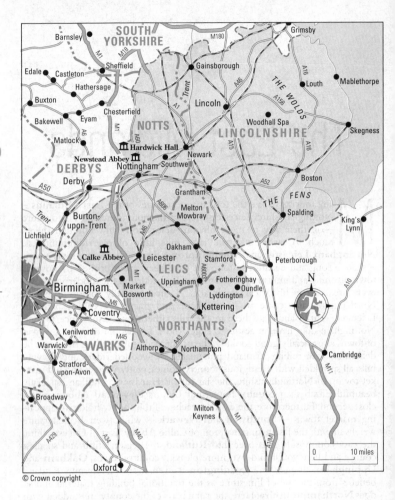

© Crown copyright

sea. Fenland villages are generally short of charm, but the **parish churches**, whose spires regularly interrupt the wide-skied landscape, are simply stunning, the most impressive of the lot being St Botolph's in **Boston**.

In north Lincolnshire, the low-lying chalky hills of the **Lincolnshire Wolds** contain the county's most diverse scenery, including a string of sheltered valleys concentrated in the vicinity of **Louth**, an especially fetching country town. To the east of the Wolds is the **coast**, whose long sandy beach extends, with a few marshy interruptions, from Mablethorpe to **Skegness**, the main resort. The coast has long attracted thousands of holiday-makers from the big cities of the East Midlands and Yorkshire, hence its trail of bungalows, campsites and caravan parks – though, to be fair, chunks of the seashore are now protected as nature reserves.

As for public transport, travelling between the cities of the East Midlands by **train** or **bus** is simple and most of the larger towns have good regional links, too; but things are very different in the country with bus services very patchy.

Nottinghamshire

With a population of over 270,000, **Nottingham** is one of England's big cities, a long-time manufacturing centre for bikes, cigarettes, pharmaceuticals and lace. It is, however, more famous for Nottingham Forest football team (or rather, for its mercurial ex-manager, Brian Clough), for the Trent Bridge cricket ground and for its association with **Robin Hood**, the legendary thirteenth-century outlaw. Unfortunately, the fortress-lair of Hood's bitter enemy, the Sheriff of Nottingham, is long gone, and today the city is at its most diverting in the Lace Market, whose cramped streets are crowded with the mansion-like warehouses of the Victorian lacemakers.

The county town is flanked to the south by the commuter villages of the Nottinghamshire Wolds and to the north by the gritty towns and villages of what was, until Thatcher and her cronies decimated it, the Nottinghamshire coalfield. Both are unremarkable, but encrusted within the old northern Nottinghamshire coalfield are the thin remains of **Sherwood Forest**, the bulk of which is contained within The Dukeries, named after the five dukes who owned most of this area and preserved at least part of the ancient broad-leaved forest. Three of the four remaining estates – Worksop, Welbeck and Thoresby – are still in private hands, though Thoresby Hall has recently been turned into a Warner resort hotel, whilst **Clumber Park** is now owned by the National Trust and offers charming woodland walks. Also within the confines of the former coalfield are two fascinating country houses, **Newstead Abbey**, one-time home of Byron, and, even better, the wonderful Elizabethan extravagance of **Hardwick Hall**. Moving on, eastern Nottinghamshire is agricultural and its most important town is **Newark**, an agreeable, low-key kind of place straddling the River Trent. Newark has a castle, but the main attraction hereabouts is the fine Norman church at nearby **Southwell**.

Fast and frequent **trains** connect Nottingham with, among many destinations, London, Birmingham, Newark, Lincoln and Leicester. County-wide **bus** services radiate out from the city, too, making Nottingham the obvious base for a visit.

Nottingham and around

Controlling a strategic crossing point over the Trent, the Saxon town of **NOTTINGHAM** was built on one of a pair of sandstone hills whose 130-foot cliffs looked out over the river valley. In 1068, William the Conqueror built a castle on the other hill, and the Saxon and Norman communities traded on the low ground in between, the Market Square. The castle was a military stronghold and royal palace, the equal of the great castles of Windsor and Dover, and every medieval king of England paid regular visits. After the Civil War, the Parliamentarians slighted the castle and, in the 1670s, the ruins were cleared by the Duke of Newcastle to make way for a palace, whose continental – and, in English terms, novel – design he chose from a pattern book, probably by Rubens. Beneath the castle lay a market town which, according to contemporaries, was handsome and well kept – "One of the most beautiful towns in England," commented Daniel Defoe. But in the second half of the eighteenth century, the town was transformed by the expansion of the lace and hosiery industries. Within the space of fifty years, Nottingham's population increased from ten thousand to fifty thousand, the resulting slum becoming a hotbed of radicalism. In the 1810s, a recession provoked the hard-pressed workers into action. They struck against the employers and, calling themselves **Luddites**,

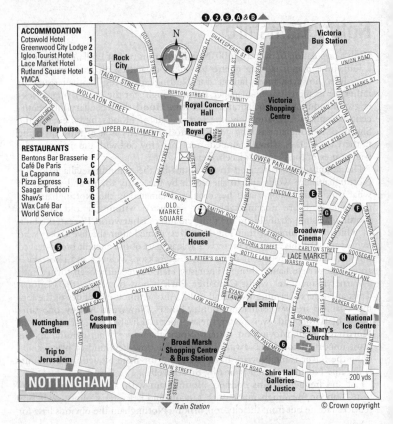

ACCOMMODATION
Cotswold Hotel 1
Greenwood City Lodge 2
Igloo Tourist Hotel 3
Lace Market Hotel 6
Rutland Square Hotel 5
YMCA 4

RESTAURANTS
Bentons Bar Brasserie F
Café De Paris C
La Cappanna A
Pizza Express D & H
Saagar Tandoori B
Shaw's G
Wax Café Bar E
World Service I

NOTTINGHAM

0   200 yds

© Crown copyright

▼ Train Station

after an apprentice-protester by the name of Ned Ludd, raided the factories to
smash the knitting machines. This was but the first of several troubled periods.
During the Reform Bill riots of 1831, the workers set fire to the duke's home
in response to his opposition to parliamentary reform and, in the following
decade, they flocked to the Chartist movement.

The worst of Nottingham's slums were cleared in the late nineteenth century, when the city centre assumed its present structure, with the main commercial area ringed by alternating industrial and residential districts. Crass **postwar
development**, adding tower blocks, shopping centres and a ring road, has
embedded the remnants of the city's past in a townscape that will be disheart-
eningly familiar if you've seen a few other English commercial centres.

Arrival, information and accommodation

Nottingham **train station** is on the south side of the city centre, a five- to ten-
minute walk from the Market Square – just follow the signs. Long-distance
buses arrive at the Broad Marsh **bus station** down the street from the train
station on the way to the centre. The city's **tourist office** is on the Market
Square, on the ground floor of the Council House, at 1 Smithy Row
(Easter–July Mon–Fri 9am–5.30pm, Sat 9am–5pm; Sept & Oct Mon–Fri
9am–5.30pm, Sat 9am–5pm, Sun 10am–3pm; Nov–Easter Mon–Sat 9am–
5.30pm; ☎0115/915 5330, ⓦwww.visitnottingham.com).

As you might expect of a big city, Nottingham has a good range of accommodation, with the more expensive **hotels** concentrated in the centre, the cheaper places and the **B&Bs** mostly located on the outskirts and the main approach roads. Finding a room is rarely difficult, but the tourist office can always help out.

Hotels and guest houses

Cotswold Hotel 330 Mansfield Rd ☏0115/955 1070. Comfortable popular mid-range hotel with cheery half-timbered facade. On a main road about one mile north of the city centre. ❸

Greenwood City Lodge 5 Third Ave, off Sherwood Rise ☏0115/962 1206. Attractive six-bedroomed guest house in a quiet corner of the city, down a narrow lane about a mile north of the city centre. Highly recommended. ❸

Lace Market Hotel 29 High Pavement ☏0115/852 3232. Great location, footsteps from St Mary's church, this smart hotel, in a tastefully modernized Georgian row house, offers thirty individually decorated rooms. ❺

Rutland Square Hotel Rutland Street, off St James' Street ☏0115/941 1114. Attractive and tastefully furnished modern hotel in a great location, just by the castle. ❺

Hostels

Igloo Tourist Hotel 110 Mansfield Rd ☏0115/947 5250. Backpackers' haven in the town centre, opposite the *Golden Fleece* pub, with a convivial atmosphere, good showers and free tea and coffee. Bunk-beds in mixed or single-sex dorms for £12 per person.

YMCA 4 Shakespeare St ☏0115/956 7600. In a handy location, with clean and frugal rooms, but fills up fast. Single rooms are a real bargain at £17.75 a night including breakfast.

The Old Market Square and the Castle

The **Old Market Square** is still the heart of the city, an airy open plaza, whose shops, offices and fountains are watched over by the grand neo-Baroque **Council House**, completed as part of a make-work scheme in 1928. From here, it's a five-minute walk west up Friar Lane to **Nottingham Castle** (daily 10am–5pm; £2 Sat & Sun, free at other times), whose heavily restored gateway stands above a folkloric bronze of Robin Hood. Beyond the gateway, lawns slope up to the squat ducal **palace**, which – after remaining a charred shell for forty years – was opened as the country's first provincial museum in 1878. The mansion occupies the site of the castle's upper bailey and, just outside its main entrance, two sets of steps (guided tours only, call ☏0115/915 3700; £2) lead down into the maze of ancient caves that honeycomb the cliff beneath. One set leads into **Mortimer's Hole**, a three-hundred-foot shaft along which, so the story goes, the young Edward III and his chums crept in October 1330 to capture the queen mother, Isabella, and her lover, Roger Mortimer – his would-be usurpers and the murderers of his father, Edward II. Although the incident certainly took place, it's unlikely that this was the secret tunnel Edward used.

The interior of the ducal mansion holds the **Castle Museum and Art Gallery**, whose lower-level "Story of Nottingham" is a lively, well-presented and entertaining account of the city's development. In particular, look out for a small but exquisite collection of late medieval **alabaster carvings**, an art form for which Nottingham once had an international reputation. It's worth walking up to the top floor, too, for a turn round the main **picture gallery**, which has a curious assortment of mostly English nineteenth-century romantic paintings. The works of Richard Parkes Bonington are perhaps the most evocative, though Laslett John Potts' *Mary Queen of Scots being led to her Execution* comes a close second.

The Lace Market

A ten-minute walk away, on the east side of the Old Market Square up along Victoria Street, is the **Lace Market**, whose narrow lanes and alleys surround the church of **St Mary**, a good-looking, mostly fifteenth-century structure built on top of the hill that was once the Saxon town. The church abuts High Pavement, the administrative centre of Nottingham in Georgian times, and here you'll find the **Shire Hall**, whose Neoclassical columns and dome date from 1770. Now accommodating the **Galleries of Justice** (Tues–Sun 10am–5pm; £7.95), the Shire Hall boasts two superbly preserved Victorian courtrooms as well as an Edwardian police station, some spectacularly unpleasant old cells, a women's prison with bath house and a prisoners' exercise yard. A tour of the whole complex takes around two hours, but note that the interactive nature of a visit (on arrival you are issued with a criminal identity number, and so it continues) is not to everyone's liking. The surrounding Victorian warehouses are at their most striking along **Broadway**, where a line of homogeneous red-brick and sandstone-trimmed buildings perform a neat swerve halfway along the street. Adjacent **Stoney Street** chips in with the imposing Adams Building and, at the corner of Woolpack Lane, a particularly well-composed warehouse that comes equipped with an extravagant stone doorway and slender windows, as well as long attic windows to light the mending and inspection rooms.

Nearby, on Byard Lane, is the first shop of local lad **Paul Smith**, a major success story of recent British fashion, whilst the huge spaceship-like structure on the edge of the Lace Market is the **National Ice Centre**, home of the Panthers ice-skating team and a trainee skaters' paradise. To arrange lessons, call ☏0115/853 3036.

Eating

Nottingham's **restaurant** scene has improved immeasurably in the last five years. French and Mediterranean cuisine are in vogue at present, but the Asian places continue to prosper. In the last couple of years, **cafés** have sprung up all over the city centre. Almost without exception, they've adopted the same formula – angular and ultra-modern furnishings and fittings and a wide range of bottled beers. A few offer tasty, broadly Mediterranean food as well.

Bentons Bar Brasserie corner of Heathcote and Lower Parliament streets. Pleasant café-bar offering tasty dishes from an imaginative menu – salads and pastas through to steaks. Inexpensive.

Petit Paris 2 Kings Walk, off Upper Parliament Street, near the Theatre Royal ☏0115/947 3767. Arguably the best restaurant of its type in town, offering delicious bistro-style French cuisine in neat and informal surroundings. Moderate.

La Cappanna 596 Mansfield Rd ☏0115/985 7411. Outstanding, family-run Italian restaurant with all the usual dishes plus a great line in seafood – the mussels are, so some locals say, the best in England. The regular menu is supplemented by daily specials. The decor is very ordinary, but don't let that put you off. It's located a mile or so north of the city centre. Moderate.

Pizza Express 20 King St ☏0115/952 9095. Fashionable pizza and pasta spot serving the chain's usual delicious pizzas. There's another branch at 24 Goose Gate, Hockley ☏0115/912 7888. Moderate.

Saagar Tandoori Restaurant 473 Mansfield Rd ☏0115/962 2014. Excellent Indian restaurant, a mile or so north of the city centre. The decor is very homely – you feel as if you're in someone's living room – but it's a very popular spot with locals. Moderate.

Shaw's 20 Broad St ☏0115/9500009. Smashing mid-range restaurant in an old, imaginatively converted store with a restaurant in the basement and an agreeable bar upstairs. The menu is lively and creative and the daily specials are first-rate.

Wax Café Bar 27 Broad St. Amongst the city's burgeoning band of café-bars, this is one of the trendiest. The food here is good – all light Mediterranean dishes at very reasonable prices. Inexpensive.

World Service Newdigate House, Castle Gate ☏0115/847 5587. Chic restaurant with bags of flair in charming premises up near the Castle. An international menu done with imagination. Expensive.

Pubs and nightlife

Nottingham's **nightclub** scene is boisterous and fast-moving, with places moving in and out of cool all the time. The **pubs** around Market Square have a tough edge to them, especially on the weekend, but within a few minutes' walk there's a selection of equally lively and more enjoyable drinking-holes. For **live music**, both popular and classical, most big names play at the Royal Centre Concert Hall on Wollaton Street, and nearby **Rock City** pulls in some star turns too. The Broadway, in the Lace Market at 14 Broad St (℡0115/952 6600, ⓦwww.broadway.org.uk), is far and away the best **cinema** in town, featuring the pick of mainstream and avant-garde films.

Pubs and bars

Broadway Cinema Bar Broadway Cinema, 14 Broad St. Informal, fashionable bar serving an eclectic assortment of bottled beers to a cinema-keen clientele. Can get too smoky for comfort, so they have a smaller, smoke-free café-bar upstairs.

The Limelight Wellington Circus. The bar of the Nottingham Playhouse is a popular, easy-going spot with courtyard seating on summer nights. Good supply of real ales.

Lincolnshire Poacher 161 Mansfield Rd. Very popular and relaxed pub, with a wide selection of bottled and real ales. An older clientele than in the (very youthful) city centre – a five- to ten-minute walk away.

Pitcher & Piano High Pavement. Lively, fashionable pub in an imaginatively converted Victorian church on the edge of the Lace Market. Good fun; very youthful.

The Social Pelham St. Just up from the Market Square, this packed, popular bar is very much à la mode. Angular, modern furnishing and fittings plus frequent DJ sounds. It's the sister bar of London's Social.

Ye Olde Trip to Jerusalem Inn below the castle in Brewhouse Yard. Carved into the castle rock, this ancient inn may well have been a meeting point for soldiers gathering for the Third Crusade. Its cave-like bars, with their rough sandstone ceilings, are delightfully secretive.

Clubs

The Bomb 45 Bridlesmith Gate. The frontrunner in the club scene with regular house, techno and jungle nights.

Media Queen St. Grooviest place in town with grand decor and great sounds. Hosted a Renaissance night and features leading DJs.

Rock City Talbot St ℡0115/941 2544. Giant-sized, crowded nightclub/music venue, with different sounds and crowds each night, from Goth to metal to indie. Regularly hosts name bands on UK tours.

Northern Nottinghamshire

Rural **northern Nottinghamshire**, with its easy rolling landscapes and large estates, was transformed in the nineteenth century by coal – deep, wide seams of the stuff that spawned dozens of collieries, and colliery towns, stretching north across the county and on into Yorkshire. Almost without exception, the mines have closed, their passing marked only by the old pit head winding wheels left, bleak and solitary, to commemorate the thousands of men who laboured here. The suddenness of the pit closure programme imposed by the Conservative government in the 1980s knocked the stuffing out of the area and only now is it beginning to revive. One prop has been the tourist industry, for the countryside in between these mining communities holds several enjoyable attractions, the best-known of which is **Sherwood Forest** – or at least the patchy remains of it – one-time haunt (allegedly) of Robin Hood. Byron is a pip-squeak in the celebrity stakes by comparison, but his family home – **Newstead Abbey** – is here too, there are some pleasant woodland walks in the NT's **Clumber Park** and, last but certainly not least, there's **Hardwick Hall**, a beautiful Elizabethan mansion.

To reach this quartet of attractions by **bus** from Nottingham is easy enough with the exception of Hardwick Hall, for which you'll need your own transport.

Hardwick Hall

Born the daughter of a minor Derbyshire squire, Elizabeth, Countess of Shrewsbury (1527–1608) – aka **Bess of Hardwick** – became one of the leading figures of Elizabethan England, renowned for her political and business acumen. She also had a penchant for building and her major achievement, **Hardwick Hall** (April–Oct Wed, Thurs, Sat & Sun 12.30–5pm; gardens same months daily noon–5.30pm; £6.20; gardens only £3.30; NT), begun when she was 62, has survived in amazingly good condition. The house was the epitome of fashionable taste, a balance of symmetry and ingenious detail in which the rectangular lines of the building are offset by line upon line of window – there's actually more glass than stone – whilst up above her giant-sized initials – E.S. – hog every roof line. Inside, the ground floor is relatively routine, but it's here that Hardwick's extensive collection of sixteenth- and seventeenth-century needlework is displayed, including several pieces by Mary, Queen of Scots, who was held in custody by the Earl of Shrewsbury for several years.

On the top floor, the **High Great Chamber**, where Bess received her most distinguished guests, boasts an extraordinary plaster frieze, a brightly painted, finely worked affair celebrating the goddess Diana, the virgin huntress, which was, of course, designed to please the virgin queen herself. Next door, the **Long Gallery** is simply breathtaking, like an indoor cricket pitch only with exquisite furnishings and fittings, from the splendid chimneypieces and tapestries through to a set of portraits, including one each of the queen and Bess. The gallery was where Bess and her chums could exercise – and keep out of the sun at a time when any hint of a suntan was considered peasant-plebeian.

Outside, the **garden** makes for a pleasant wander and, beyond the Ha Ha, rare breeds of cattle and sheep graze the surrounding **parkland**. Finally – and rather confusingly – Hardwick Hall is next to **Hardwick Old Hall** (April–Oct Wed–Sun 11am–6pm; Nov–March Sat & Sun 11am–4pm; £2.75; EH), Bess's previous home, but now little more than a broken-down ruin.

The easiest way to reach Hardwick is along the M1; come off at Junction 29 and follow the signs from the roundabout at the top of the slip road – a three-mile trip. Note, however, that Hardwick is not signed from the motorway itself.

Newstead Abbey

In 1539, Henry VIII granted **Newstead Abbey** (April–Sept daily noon–5pm; grounds daily 9am–dusk; £4; grounds only £2), ten miles north of Nottingham on the A60, to Sir John Byron, who demolished most of the church and converted the monastic buildings into a family home. In 1798, **Lord Byron** inherited Newstead, then little more than a ruin. He restored part of the complex, but most of the present structure dates from later renovations, which maintained much of the shape and feel of the medieval original while creating the warren-like mansion that exists today. Inside, a string of intriguing period rooms includes everything from a neo-Gothic Great Hall to the Henry VII bedroom, fitted with carved panels and painted house screens imported from Japan. Some of the rooms are pretty much as they were when Byron lived here – notably his bedroom and dressing room – and in the library is a small collection of the poet's possessions, from letters and manuscripts through to his pistols and boxing gloves. The surrounding **gardens** are simply delightful, a secretive and subtle combination of walled garden, lake, Gothic waterfalls, yew tunnels and Japanese-style rockeries, complete with eccentric pagodas.

There's a fast and frequent **bus** service from Nottingham's Victoria Centre bus station to the gates of Newstead Abbey, a mile from the house, every twenty minutes or so; the journey takes about twenty-five minutes.

Rufford Country Park

Council-run country parks may be ten-a-penny, but **Rufford Country Park** (daily dawn to dusk; facilities April–Sept 10am–5pm; Oct–March 10am–4pm; free) shows just how things should be done. The remains of the original twelfth-century Cistercian Abbey and the country house built in its stead – but largely demolished in 1956 – are neither very substantial nor especially interesting, but the old buildings are all pleasantly maintained and the former stable block now holds a café and better-than-average craft shop and ceramic gallery. At the back of the stables are the gardens, both informal and formal, and an outstanding **Sculpture Garden**, which manages to be both very accessible and very contemporary. Further afield is a lake and a mill, a bird sanctuary and a wetland area, all accessible by footpath. Country Parks don't come any better and there is a lively programme of special events and temporary art exhibitions too.

Rufford Country Park is right beside the A614 about eighteen miles north of Nottingham and reached on hourly Stagecoach **bus** #33 from Nottingham's Victoria Centre bus station.

Robin Hood – and Sherwood Forest Country Park

Most of **Sherwood Forest**, once a vast royal forest of oak, birch and bracken covering all of northern Nottinghamshire, was cleared in the eighteenth century, and nowadays it's difficult to imagine the protection it provided for generations of outlaws, the most famous of whom was **Robin Hood**. There's no "true story" of Robin's life – the earliest reference to him, in Langland's *Piers Plowman* of 1377, treats him as a fiction – but to the balladeers of fifteenth-century England, who invented most of the folklore, this was hardly the point. For them, Robin was a symbol of yeoman decency, a semi-mythological opponent of corrupt clergymen and evil officers of the law; in the early tales, although Robin shows sympathy for the peasant, he has rather more respect for the decent nobleman, and he's never credited with robbing the rich to give to the poor. This and other parts of the legend, such as Maid Marion and Friar Tuck, were added later.

Robin Hood may lack historical authenticity, but it hasn't discouraged the county council from spending thousands of pounds sustaining the **Major Oak**, the creaky tree where Maid Marion and Robin are supposed to have "plighted their troth". The Major Oak is on a pleasant one-mile trail that begins beside the visitor centre at the main entrance to **Sherwood Forest Country Park** (daily dawn–dusk; free), which comprises 450 acres of oak and silver birch crisscrossed with footpaths. The visitor centre is half a mile north of the village of Edwinstowe, itself just two miles northwest of Rufford Park and twenty-odd miles north of Nottingham via the A614.

There's a regular bus service on Stagecoach bus #33 from Nottingham's Victoria Centre bus station to Edwinstowe via Rufford.

Clumber Park

North of Ollerton, Edwinstowe's immediate neighbour, the A614 trims the edge of Thoresby Park, to reach, after six miles, the eastern entrance to **Clumber Park** (daily dawn–dusk; NT; free, but parking £3), four thousand acres of park and woodland lying to the south of Worksop. The estate was once the country seat of the dukes of Newcastle, and it was here in the 1770s that they constructed a grand mansion overlooking Clumber Lake. The house was dismantled in 1938, when the duke sold the estate, and today all that remains of the lakeside buildings are the Gothic Revival **Chapel** (daily: April–Sept 10.30am–5.30pm; Oct–March 10.30am–4pm; free; NT), built for the seventh duke in the 1880s, and the adjacent **stable block**, which now houses a National Trust office, shop and **café** (same times as chapel). The stables are located about two and a half miles from the A614. The woods around the lake offer some delightful strolls through planted woodland interspersed with the occasional patch of original forest, or you can go for an easy cycle ride by hiring a bike here.

Departing Nottingham's Victoria Centre bus station, Stagecoach East Midlands hourly **bus** #33 runs to Rufford and Edwinstowe, from where it travels on up the west side of Clumber Park en route to Worksop; get off at Carburton for the two-mile walk to the Clumber Park NT office. The excursion is best done as a day-trip from Nottingham, but there is a **campsite** (ⓣ01909/482303; closed Oct–March) in Clumber Park's walled garden, a few minutes' walk north of the chapel.

Eastern Nottinghamshire

Without coal, **eastern Nottinghamshire** escaped the heavy-duty industrialization that fell upon its county neighbours in the late nineteenth century. It remains a largely rural area, its undulating farmland, punctuated by dozens of pint-sized villages, rolling seamlessly over to the River Trent, the boundary with Lincolnshire. By and large, it's a prosperous part of the county and by no means unpleasant, but for the casual visitor the attractions are distinctly low-key, being essentially confined to **Southwell** and **Newark**, both of which are easy to reach by public transport from Nottingham.

Southwell

SOUTHWELL, some twelve miles northeast of Nottingham, is a sedate backwater distinguished by **Southwell Minster** (daily: April–Sept 8am–7pm; Oct–March 8am to dusk; free), whose twin towers are visible for miles around, and the fine Georgian mansions facing it along Church Street. The Normans built the Minster at the beginning of the twelfth century and, although some elements were added later, the Norman design predominates, from the imposing west towers through to the dog-tooth-decorated doorways. Inside, the nave is proud and forceful and in the north transept is the remarkably fine alabaster tomb of a long forgotten churchman, Archbishop Sandys, who died in 1588. The nave's stonework ends abruptly with the clumsy mass of the fourteenth-century rood screen, beyond which lies the Early English **choir** and the extraordinary **chapter house**. The latter is embellished with naturalistic foliage dating from the late thirteenth century, some of the earliest carving of its type in England.

For a bite to **eat**, the daytime *Deli*, a five-minute walk east of the Minster on the main drag through the village at 85a King St, sells a superb range of baguettes and paninis at £2.50 each. There are regular **buses** from the centre of Nottingham to Southwell and Newark. Ask at Nottingham tourist office for the current departure point.

Newark

From Southwell, it's eight miles east to **NEWARK**, an amiable, low-key river port and market town that was once a major staging point on the Great North Road. Fronting the town as you approach from the west are the gaunt riverside ruins of **Newark Castle** (daily dawn to dusk; free), all that's left of the mighty medieval fortress that was pounded to pieces during the Civil War. From here, it's just a couple of minutes' walk east to the expansive **Market**

Place, surrounded by a network of narrow and ancient alleys and overlooked by the mostly thirteenth-century church of **St Mary Magdalene** (Mon–Sat 8.30am–4.30pm), whose massive spire, at 236ft, towers over the town centre. It's a handsome church, its well-proportioned nave cheered by some bright roof paintings and a fine reredos.

There's a regular **bus** service from Nottingham to Newark via Southwell, and Newark is also on the Nottingham–Lincoln **train** line. The Newark Castle **train station** (there is another, so be sure to get off at the right one) is on the west side of the River Trent, a five-minute walk from both the castle and the adjacent **tourist office**, on Castlegate (daily 9am–5/6pm; ☏01636/655765). The **bus station** is on Lombard Street, a couple of minutes' walk south from the tourist office along Castlegate. Newark has a small supply of **hotels** and **B&Bs**, which the tourist office will book on your behalf at no extra charge, but remember that rooms are well-nigh impossible to find during the Newark International Antiques Fair, Europe's biggest such event, held six times a year. For **food**, make for the excellent *Gannets*, 35 Castlegate (Mon–Fri 9am–4pm, Sat 9am–5pm & Sun 9am–4pm), an astoundingly good coffee bar serving daytime snacks and meals, or the simply superb *Café Bleu*, opposite at 14 Castlegate (☏01636/610141), a brilliant French restaurant serving top-class meals from an inventive menu. It's one of the best restaurants in the county, with an outside terrace and live jazz; the decor – all pastel-painted cheerfulness – is delightful too.

Leicestershire and Rutland

The compact county of **Leicestershire** is one of the more anonymous of the English shires, though **Leicester** itself is saved from mediocrity by its role as a focal point for Britain's Asian community. West Leicestershire has rather more to offer, for although its rolling landscape is blemished by a series of industrial settlements, things pick up markedly at **Ashby-de-la-Zouch**, a pleasing little town graced by the substantial remains of its medieval castle, and at **Calke Abbey**, a dishevelled country house set in its own estate. In east Leicestershire, the farmland is studded with long-established market towns. None of them are particularly enthralling, but genial **Market Harborough** does hold several attractive old buildings and an interesting museum.

To the east of Leicestershire lies England's smallest county, **Rutland**, reinstated in 1997 following twenty-three unpopular years of merger with its larger neighbour. Rutland has three places of note, beginning with **Oakham**, the county town, and **Uppingham**, both rural centres with some elegant Georgian architecture. Even prettier is the tiny stone hamlet of **Lyddington**.

Getting around Leicestershire and Rutland can be problematic. **Train** lines radiate out from Leicester, most usefully to Market Harborough and Oakham, and there's a good network of **bus** services between the market towns, but these fade away in the villages where, if there is a bus at all, it only runs once or twice a day.

Leicester

On first impression, **LEICESTER** is a resolutely modern city, but further inspection reveals traces of its medieval and Roman past, situated immediately to the west of the downtown shopping area, near the River Soar. The Romans, choosing this site in the middle of the territory of the rebellious Coritani, developed Leicester's precursor, Ratae Coritanorum, as a fortified town on the

Fosse Way, the military road running from Lincoln to Cirencester, and Emperor Hadrian kitted it out with huge public buildings. Subsequently, in the eighth century, the Danes colonized the town and later still its medieval castle became the base of the earls of Leicester. Since the late seventeenth century, Leicester has been a centre of the hosiery trade and it was this industry that attracted hundreds of Asian immigrants to settle here in the 1950s and 1960s. Today, about one third of Leicester's population is Asian and the city elected the country's first Asian MP, Keith Vaz, in 1987. Leicester's Hindus put on a massive and internationally famous **Diwali**, Festival of Light, in October or November, while the city's sizeable Afro-Caribbean community celebrates its culture in a whirl of colour and music on the first weekend in August. The latter is the country's second biggest street festival after the Notting Hill Carnival (see p.134).

Arrival, information and accommodation

On the line from London's St Pancras station, Leicester **train station** is situated on London Road just to the southeast of the city centre. The **bus station** is on the north side of the centre, just off Gravel Street. The centre is signed from both – the large Haymarket Centre is an easy landmark. The **tourist office** is in between the two stations – and a short walk south of the Haymarket – at 7–9 Every St, on Town Hall Square (Mon–Wed & Fri 9am–5.30pm, Thurs 10am–5.30pm, Sat 9am–5pm; ☎0116/299 8888).

With other more enticing cities near at hand – Nottingham is but one – there's no strong reason to overnight here, but Leicester does have a good crop of business **hotels** close to the centre, within walking distance of the train station. Recommendable options include the *Best Western Belmont House Hotel*, De Montfort Street (☎0116/254 4773; ❻), in an efficiently modernized Georgian property about 500 yards south of the train station, and the nearby and much more personal *Spindle Lodge*, 2 West Walk (☎0116/233 8801; ❹), which occupies an attractively converted Victorian house. There's also the plusher, modern *Holiday Inn*, on the west side of the centre at 129 St Nicholas Circle (☎0116/253 1161; ❺); this has extensive fitness facilities plus a pool. The tourist office has a substantial list of competitively priced **B&Bs**, but most of them are out of the centre. They will help fix you up with somewhere to stay, but things rarely get tight except during Diwali. Leicester also possesses an unofficial **hostel**, *Richard's Students and Backpackers Lodge*, 157 Wanlip Lane, Birstall (☎0116/267 3107; £9). A self-styled backpackers' hostel on the northern edge of town – in a suburban semi, with patio and summerhouse. It has just five beds and is available to those aged between 16 and 26 only.

The city centre

The most conspicuous building in Leicester's crowded centre is undoubtedly the modern Haymarket shopping complex, but the proper landmark is the nearby Victorian **clock tower** of 1868, marking the spot where seven streets meet. From here, Cheapside leads south in a few yards to Leicester's open-air, fresh produce **market** (Mon–Sat), arguably the best in the land. Alternatively, from back at the clock tower, East Gates and then the old High Street run west with Silver Street (subsequently Guildhall Lane), soon branching off to reach **St Martin's Cathedral**, a much modified eleventh-century structure that incorporates a fine medieval wooden entrance porch. Next door is the **Guildhall** (Mon–Sat 10am–5.30pm, Sun 2–5pm; free), a half-timbered building that has served, variously, as the town hall, prison and police station.

From the Guildhall, it's a short walk west to St Nicholas Circle, a large roundabout that is part of the ring road. Go round it to the right – there's a walkway – and on the right is the **Jewry Wall**, a chunk of Roman masonry some 18ft high and 73ft long that was originally part of Hadrian's public baths. The project was a real irritation to the emperor. Hadrian's grand scheme was spoilt by the engineers, who miscalculated the line of the aqueduct that was to pipe in the water, and so bathers had to rely on a hand-filled cistern replenished from the river – which wasn't what he had in mind at all. The adjacent **Jewry Wall and Museum** (April–Sept Mon–Sat 10am–5pm, Sun 1–5pm; Oct–March closes 1hr earlier; free) charts Leicester's history from prehistoric to medieval times in dowdy fashion. The most interesting artefacts are Roman, a hotchpotch of archeological finds from Fosse Way milestones to two splendid mosaics.

From the museum, it's a short stroll south via St Nicholas Circle to **Castle Gardens**, a narrow strip of a park that runs alongside a canalized portion of the Soar. The gardens incorporate the castle motte, the overgrown mound where Leicester's Norman fortifications once stood. At the far end of the gardens, you emerge on The Newarke, the location of the **Newarke Houses Museum** (Mon–Sat 10am–5.30pm, Sun 2–5pm; free), two adjoining Jacobean houses that make a pleasant setting for an exploration of the town's social history. Beside the museum, along Castle View, is the **Turret Gateway**, a rare survivor of the city's medieval castle, and beyond that is the attractive church of **St Mary de Castro** (Easter–Oct Sat 2–5pm), whose mixture of architectural styles incorporates several Norman features, notably a five-seater sedilia in the chancel. Interestingly enough, this was probably where Chaucer got married.

At the east end of The Newarke, ignominiously stranded between the carriageways of the ring road, stands the distinctive and substantial **Magazine Gateway** (no access), once a medieval entrance into the city and arsenal – hence the name. From here, it's a short walk south to the **Jain Centre**, in a totally revamped old Congregational chapel at the beginning of Oxford Street. The rites and beliefs of the Jains, a long-established Indian religious sect, focus on an extreme reverence for all living things – traditional customs include the wearing of gauze masks to prevent the inhalation of passing insects. The temple, the only one of its kind in western Europe, has a splendidly garish white marble facade, and visitors may enter the lobby – or, better, view the interior by prior appointment, call ☏0116/254 3091.

From the Jain Centre, it's about ten minutes' walk east to the **New Walk Museum and Art Gallery** (Mon–Sat 10am–5.30pm, Sun 2–5pm; free), easily the best of the city's museums, located on the New Walk. To get there from the Jain temple, go back to the beginning of Oxford Street, turn right onto Newarke Street and keep going straight until you intersect with – and turn right onto – **New Walk**, a pleasant pedestrianized promenade that runs out from the centre to leafy Victoria Park. On the museum's ground floor is a real surprise – an outstanding collection of German Expressionists, mostly sketches, woodcuts and lithographs by the likes of Otto Dix and George Grosz. The Victorian Gallery is fascinating, too, dominated by extravagant, often mawkish romantic paintings, amongst which is Charles Green's iconic *The Girl I left behind Me* of 1880.

Belgrave

Beginning about a mile to the northeast of the centre, the gritty **Belgrave** neighbourhood is the focus of Leicester's Asian community. Both Belgrave Road and its northerly continuation, Melton Road, are lined with Indian and Pakistani goldsmiths and jewellers, sari shops, Hindi music stores and curry houses. It's never dull down here, but Sunday afternoons are particularly enjoyable, when locals have time to stroll the streets in their finest gear. Belgrave celebrates two major Hindu festivals: **Diwali**, the Festival of Light, held in October or November, when six thousand lamps are strung out along the Belgrave Road and 20,000 come to watch the switch-on alone; and **Navrati**, a nine-day celebration in October held in honour of the goddess Ambaji.

Eating, drinking, nightlife and entertainment

People come from miles around to eat in the **Indian restaurants** on the Belgrave Road – though the opening of lots of Balti places in the Highfields area has provided some intense competition. The most famous of the Belgrave Road restaurants is *Bobby's*, no. 154–156 (☎0116/266 0106). Run by Gujaratis, this moderately priced place is strictly vegetarian and uses no garlic or onions; if you're here on a weekend, try their delicious house speciality, *undhyu*, or the multi-flavoured *Bobby's Special Chaat*. Excellent alternatives include the *Thali*, at no. 49 (☎0116/266 5888), which specializes in set *thali* meals, where several different dishes, breads and pickles are served together on large steel plates, and the *Chaat House* (☎0116/266 0513), south of *Bobby's* on the same side of the road at no. 108. The latter does wonderful *masala dosas* and other south Indian snacks – legendary cricket captain Kapil Dev and his Indian team ate here when they were on tour. In the city centre, and diversifying from the Asian restaurants, there's an outlet of that ultra-reliable chain *Pizza Express* on King Street (☎0116/254 4144), plus the top-notch *Opera House*, 10 Guildhall Lane (☎0116/223 6666), in lovely old premises and with an imaginative, wide-ranging menu.

As for **pubs**, the *Rainbow & Dove*, on Charles Street, attracts real-ale enthusiasts, the *Charlotte*, on Oxford Street, features bands most nights and the *Magazine*, Newarke Street, is a favourite student haunt. Amongst a deluge of new city-centre café-bars, one of the trendier, clubbier spots is *Tabasco Jaz* on Albion Street.

The **performing arts** come up trumps in Leicester at the excellent Phoenix Arts Centre, Newarke Street (☎0116/255 4854, ⊛www.phoenix.org.uk), which features a first-rate mix of comedy, music, theatre and dance, whilst doubling up as an independent cinema. The city's main concert hall is De Montfort Hall, on Granville Road (☎0116/233 3111, ⊛www.demontforthall.co.uk) – adjoining Victoria Park at the end of New Walk.

West Leicestershire

Give or take the odd industrial blip, most of **west Leicestershire** – to the west of the A6 – is rural, its small towns and villages dotted over undulating countryside. The key attractions here are best visited as day-trips, beginning with **Calke Abbey**, technically over the boundary in Derbyshire and not an abbey at all, but an intriguing country house whose faded charms witness the declining fortunes of the landed gentry. There's also a good castle, at **Ashby-de-la-Zouch**, and a fine church, perched on top of one of the few hills hereabouts at **Breedon-on-the-Hill**.

Ashby and Breedon are easy to reach by **bus** from Leicester, but to get to Calke Abbey you'll need your own transport.

Ashby-de-la-Zouch

ASHBY-DE-LA-ZOUCH, fourteen miles northwest of Leicester, takes its fanciful name from two sources – the town's first Norman overlord was Alain

9

△ Lincoln Cathedral

de Parrhoet la Souche and the rest means "place by the ash trees". Nowadays, Ashby is far from rustic, but it's an amiable little place and just off Market Street, the main drag, stands its principal attraction, the **Castle** (April–Oct daily 10am–6pm; Nov–March Wed–Sun 10am–4pm; £2.75; EH), whose rambling ruins mostly date from the fifteenth century. The star turn is the hundred-foot-high **Hastings Tower**, a self-contained four-storey stronghold, which, dating to the 1470s, represented the latest thinking in castle design. It provided a secure inner fastness and it also provided much better accommodation than was previously available. Improved living quarters reflecting the power and pride of the nobility were built all over England at this time and this is a rare survivor – witness the substantial rooms with large windows on the top floors, accessible via the tower's well-worn spiral staircase.

Breedon-on-the-Hill

It's five miles northeast from Ashby to the village of **BREEDON-ON-THE-HILL**, which sits in the shadow of the large but partly quarried hill from which it takes its name. A steep footpath and a winding, half-mile road lead up from the village to the summit, where the fascinating church of **St Mary and St Hardulph** (daily 9.30am–6.30pm or dusk; free) occupies the site of an Iron Age hillfort and an eighth-century Anglo-Saxon monastery. Mostly dating from the thirteenth century, the church is kitted out with Georgian pews and pulpit and also, much rarer, contains a number of Anglo-Saxon carvings, both in the form of wall friezes with folkloric themes and of individual saints and prophets. They are quite extraordinary and the fact that the figures look Byzantine – rather than Anglo-Saxon – has fuelled academic debate. The church has something else too, in the form of several tombs of the Shirley family, who long ruled the local roost. One is a sombre alabaster affair with the kneeling family up above and a skeleton below.

Calke Abbey

The eighteenth-century facade of **Calke Abbey** house (April–Oct Mon–Wed, Sat & Sun 1–5.30pm; garden same days from 11am; £5.20; garden only £2.50; NT) is all self-confidence, its acres of dressed stone and three long lines of windows polished off with an imposing Victorian Greek Revival portico. This all cost oodles of money and the Harpurs and then the Harpur-Crewes, who owned the estate, were doing very well until the economics of the English country estate changed after World War I. Then, at a time when country houses were being demolished by the score, the Harpur-Crewes simply hung on, becoming the epitome of faded gentility and declining to make all but the smallest of changes to the house. The last Harpur-Crewe to live here, Charles, died in 1981 and the estate passed in its entirety to the National Trust. Very much to their credit, the Trust declined to bring in the restorers and have kept the house in its dishevelled state – and this is its real charm. Of particular interest is the caricature room, whose walls are lined (sometimes three to four deep) with satirical cartoons, some of which were executed by the leading cartoonists of their day, including Gillray and Cruikshank. After you've finished in the house, you can wander out into the **gardens** and pop into the Victorian estate **church**.

Calke Abbey is reached via (and signed off from) the B587, which runs north from Ashby to Melbourne.

East Leicestershire and Rutland

For the casual visitor at least, there's nothing compelling about **east Leicestershire**, though the scenery is pleasant enough, with open farmland broken up by hills and ridges, and the middling town of **Market Harborough** is worth a pit-stop. Things improve over in neighbouring **Rutland** with a pair of pleasant country towns – **Oakham** and **Uppingham** – and get even better at the postcard-pretty hamlet of **Lyddington**.

Stamford is on the Leicester–Peterborough branch line, whilst Market Harborough is on the Leicester–London main line. There are reasonably frequent **buses** to and between all the destinations mentioned above, except Lyddington.

Market Harborough

MARKET HARBOROUGH, fifteen miles southeast of Leicester, is an unassuming provincial town that once prospered from its position at the junction of the turnpike roads to Leicester, Nottingham and London. Consequently, the predominantly Georgian High Street's *Three Swans* and *Angel* hotels were originally coaching inns, and the square and solid brick **Town Hall** was designed to help local traders sell their wares – with butchers on the ground floor and cloth merchants up above. Just off the High Street, the triangular Market Place is overlooked by the church of **St Dionysius**, whose striking tower is in stark contrast to the dumpy ironstone nave down below. Here, also, is the **Old Grammar School**, an early seventeenth-century, half-timbered structure mounted on stilts to protect locals from the rain. From 1908 to 1974, the large Victorian building standing directly behind the grammar school on Adam & Eve Street was a factory owned by the Symington family, who designed the world's best-selling corsets. The factory has been redeveloped and now houses both the council offices and the town **museum** (Mon–Sat 10am–4.30pm, Sun 2–5pm; free), which has an intriguing display of Symington corsetry. The **tourist office** (Mon–Fri 9am–5pm & Sat 9.30am–12.30pm; ☏01858/821270) is here, too.

There are frequent services from Nottingham, London and Leicester to Market Harborough's **train station**, fifteen minutes' walk east of the town centre. More conveniently, **buses** stop a couple of minutes' walk from the Market Place, on Northampton Road, a southerly continuation of the High Street. For **food**, *Aldin's Tea Rooms*, on the High Street near the Market Place (closed Sun & Mon), serves home-made food.

Oakham

Some twenty miles east from Leicester, well-heeled **OAKHAM**, Rutland's county town, has a long history as a commercial centre, its prosperity bolstered by Oakham School, a late sixteenth-century foundation that's become one of the country's more exclusive private schools. The town's stone terraces and Georgian villas are too often interrupted by the mundanely modern to assume any grace, but Oakham has its architectural moments – particularly in the L-shaped **Market Place**, where the sturdy awnings of the octagonal Butter Cross shelter the old town stocks. Footsteps from the north side of the Market Place stands **Oakham Castle** (April–Oct Mon–Sat 10am–1pm & 1.30–5pm, Sun 1–5pm; Nov–March Mon–Sat 10am–1pm & 1.30–4pm, Sun 1–4pm; free), comprising part of a fortified house dating from 1191. The banqueting hall is the main survivor, a good example of Norman domestic architecture, and inside the whitewashed walls are covered with horseshoes. This is the result of an ancient custom by which every lord or lady, king or queen, is obliged to present an ornamental horseshoe when they first set foot in the town.

Oakham School is housed in a series of impressive ironstone buildings that frame the west edge of the Market Place. On the right-hand side of the school, a narrow lane allows you to see more of the buildings on the way to **All Saints' church**, whose heavy tower and spire rise high above the town. Dating from the thirteenth century, the church is an architectural hybrid, but the light and airy interior is distinguished by the medieval carvings along the piers beside the chancel, with Christian scenes and symbols set opposite dragons, grotesques, devils and demons.

With regular services from Leicester and Peterborough, Oakham **train station** lies on the west side of town, five minutes' walk from the Market Place. **Buses** connect the town with – amongst many places – Leicester and Nottingham and these pull in on John Street, close to – and also west of – the Market Place. A thorough exploration of Oakham only takes a couple of hours and there are other more interesting places nearby, but, if you do decide to stay, the **tourist office**, at Flore's House, 34 High St (Mon–Sat 9.30am–5pm, Sun 10am–3pm; Nov–March Mon, Wed, Fri & Sat 10am–4pm, Tues & Thurs 10am–1pm; ☎01572/724329, ⓦwww.rutnet.co.uk), can help you find **accommodation**. In addition, the *Whipper-In Hotel*, on the Market Place (☎01572/756971; ❹), is a tempting proposition, its smartly decorated modern rooms set behind an attractive old facade. For **food**, the *Whipper-In* serves excellent bar snacks as does the nearby *Wheatsheaf*, a traditional pub with a good range of brews at 2–4 Northgate. Also near at hand, at 2 Burley Rd, is *Loretta's Bistro* (closed Mon & Tues–Sun eve), which offers a varied range of tasty Greek dishes at very reasonable prices.

Uppingham

The town of **UPPINGHAM**, six miles south of Oakham, has the uniformity of style Oakham lacks, its narrow, meandering High Street flanked by bow-fronted shops and ironstone houses, which mostly date from the eighteenth century. It's the general appearance that pleases, rather than any individual sight, but the town is famous as the home of **Uppingham School**, a bastion of privilege whose imposing fortress-like building stands at the west end of the High Street.

Uppingham has one especially good **hotel**, the *Lake Isle*, in a tastefully modernized eighteenth-century town house at 16 High St East (☎01572/822951; ❹). For en-suite **B&B**, the well-kept *Rutland House*, 61 High St East (☎01572/822497; ❷), occupying a spacious, double-fronted sandstone house, is the place to go. The *Lake Isle* **restaurant** is outstanding, offering a superb and varied menu from guinea fowl to local venison; a three-course meal will set you back about £20. For a **drink**, head for the *Vaults*, on the minuscule Market Place.

Lyddington

Two miles southeast of Uppingham, **LYDDINGTON** is a sleepy village of honey-hued cottages and pubs lining a meandering main street, set against a backdrop of plump hills and broken broadleaf woodland. Early in the twelfth century, the Bishop of Lincoln, whose lands once extended south as far as the Thames, chose this as the site of a small palace – one of thirteen he erected to accommodate himself and his retinue while away on Episcopal business. Confiscated during the Reformation, **Lyddington Bede House**, on Blue Coat Lane (April–Oct daily 10am–6pm; £2.75; EH), was later converted into almshouses by Lord Burghley and has since been beautifully restored by English Heritage. The highlight is the light and airy Great Chamber on the first floor, whose oak cornices are exquisitely carved. Careful lighting in the attic sets off the building's sturdy medieval timber frame to best advantage, the ground floor harbours the tiny rooms that were for centuries occupied by local pensioners and the poor and the gardens are kept in immaculate condition.

Accommodation in Lyddington is limited to the highly recommendable *Marquis of Exeter Hotel* on the main street (☎01572/822477; ④). Gutted by fire and completely restored a few years back, this former coaching inn has sixteen comfortable en-suite rooms and comes complete with a good restaurant serving a classy à la carte menu and less expensive bar meals.

Northamptonshire

Northamptonshire is one of the region's most diverse counties – so diverse in fact that even many Midlanders can't recall what is actually in it and what isn't. With justification, its superabundance of stately homes and historic churches enables it to style itself as the "County of Spires and Squires". It also holds a scattering of charming villages, the most picturesque of which, untouched by all but the vaguest sniff of the twentieth century, are built of local limestone. By contrast, however, three of the county's four big towns – Wellingborough, Corby and Kettering – are primarily industrial and whatever charms they offer to their inhabitants, there's not much to attract the regular tourist. Yet the fourth town, **Northampton**, does something to bridge the gap, its busy centre possessed of several fine old buildings and an excellent museum devoted to shoemaking, the industry that has long made the place tick.

Gentle hills, farmland and patchy woodland stretch right across the county with the A508 forming an easy if arbitrary dividing line – separating west Northamptonshire from the slightly larger east Northamptonshire. The prime target in the former is **Althorp**, family home of the Spencers and the burial place of Diana, Princess of Wales. East Northamptonshire's star turn is the good-looking country town of **Oundle**, which makes the best base for visiting the delightful hamlet of **Fotheringhay**. The county also has a notable **long-distance footpath**, the seventy-mile Nene Way, which follows the looping course of the river right across the county. Nene Way brochures are available at or from Northampton Tourist Office.

Getting to Northampton by **public transport** is no problem, but to reach the villages and stately homes, you'll mostly need your own vehicle – or some careful planning around infrequent bus services.

Northampton

Spreading north from the banks of the River Nene, **NORTHAMPTON** is a workaday modern town whose appearance largely belies its ancient past. Throughout the Middle Ages, this was one of central England's most important towns, a flourishing commercial centre whose now demolished castle was a popular stopping-off point for travelling royalty. A fire in 1675 burnt most of the medieval city to a cinder and the Georgian town that grew up in its stead was itself swamped by the industrial revolution when Northampton swarmed with boot and shoemakers. Their products shod almost everyone in the Empire – from Australia to Canada – as well as the British army.

Northampton's compact **centre** is at its most appealing on and around its main plaza, Market Square, which is where you'll find the town's finest buildings, notably All Saints' Church and the Guildhall. Half a day is enough for a quick gambol round the sights, but if you're tempted to stay the night there's a reasonable supply of hotel accommodation and a scattering of B&Bs.

The Town

Northampton's expansive, cobbled **Market Square** has a busy, self-confident air, its sides flanked by a comparatively harmonious mixture of the old and the new. From here, either of a couple of narrow lanes leads through to the church of **All Saints** (Mon–Sat 9am–2pm; free), whose unusually secular appearance stems from its finely proportioned, pillared portico as well as its towered cupola. A statue of Charles II in Roman attire surmounts the portico, a (flattering) thank you for his donation of a thousand tons of timber after the Great Fire of 1675 had incinerated the earlier church. Inside, the elegant interior looks more like a ballroom than a church, from the sweep of its timber galleries through to its Neoclassical pillars and a ceiling coated in delicately sculpted plasterwork.

Behind the church is St Giles Square, where the **Guildhall** is a flamboyant Victorian edifice constructed in the 1860s to a design by Edward Godwin. Godwin was one of the period's most inventive architects and his Gothic exterior, with its high-pointed windows and dinky turrets and towers, sports kings and queens plus scenes central to the county's history.

The **Central Museum and Art Gallery** (Mon–Sat 10am–5pm, Sun 2–5pm; free), a few yards south on Guildhall Road, celebrates the town's industrial heritage with a surprisingly interesting display of shoes. Along with silk slippers, clogs and high-heeled nineteenth-century court shoes, there's one of the four boots worn by an elephant during the British Expedition of 1959, which retraced Hannibal's putative route over the Alps into Italy. There's celebrity footwear, too – almost inevitably, a pair of Elton John shoes (the giant DMs he wore in *Tommy*) – plus whole cabinets of heavy-duty riding boots, pearl-inlaid raised wooden sandals from Ottoman Turkey and a couple of cabinets showing just how long high heels have been in fashion. Much of the rest of the museum is given over to an excellent display charting the town's history from its Roman days to the present, paying particular attention to the significance of the shoe industry, which employed no less than half the town's population in 1920.

Practicalities

From Northampton **train station**, which has regular services to London Euston and Birmingham, it's a ten-minute walk east to the Market Square – just follow the signs. Buses pull into the **bus station** on Lady's Lane, behind the hideous Grosvenor Shopping Centre, just to the north of the Market Square. The **tourist office** (late May to Aug Mon–Fri 9.30am–5pm, Sat 9.30am–4pm, Sun noon–4pm; rest of year closed Sun; ☎01604/622677) is opposite the Guildhall on St Giles Square, a minute or so to the south of Market Square. They operate an accommodation-booking service, have oodles of information on the county and issue bus timetables.

The smartest **hotel** in the centre is the *Northampton Moat House*, a dependable chain hotel in a large modern block on Silver Street (☎01604/739988; ⑥). More distinctive is the *Lime Trees Hotel*, 8 Langham Place, Barrack Road (☎01604/632188, ⓦwww.limetreeshotel.co.uk; ⑤), in pleasant Georgian premises half a mile north from the centre. The pick of the more central **B&Bs** is the *St Georges Private Hotel*, 128 St Georges Ave (☎01604/792755, ⓦwww .stgeorgeshotel.co.uk; ②). This attractive place has spacious, comfortable guest rooms and occupies a large Edwardian house about a mile and a half from the centre, overlooking Racecourse Park.

A good spot for daytime **snacks** and coffee is *Caffe Nero*, just behind All Saints at 6A Abington St. For more substantial **meals**, try *Joe's Diner*, an American-style joint just along the street at no.104A (closed Sun).

The rest of Northamptonshire

The slice of easy countryside that comprises **west Northamptonshire** falls to the west of the A508 and is dotted with stately homes, amongst which the most diverting are **Althorp**, the last resting place of Diana, Princess of Wales, and **Sulgrave Manor**, which has family links with the USA's own George Washington. **East Northamptonshire** – on the other side of the A508 – is dissected by the River Nene, which wriggles its way through a string of little villages and towns, amongst which **Oundle** and **Fotheringhay** are the most diverting.

Althorp

Some six miles northwest of Northampton off the A428, the ritzy mansion of **Althorp** is the focus of the Spencer estate. The Spencers have lived here for centuries, but this was no big deal until one of the tribe, **Diana**, married Prince Charles in 1981. The disintegration of the marriage and Diana's elevation to sainthood is a story known to millions – and most perceptively analysed by B. Campbell in her book, *Diana, Princess of Wales: How Sexual Politics Shook the Monarchy*. The public outpouring of grief following Diana's death in 1997 was quite astounding and Althorp became the focus of massive media attention as the coffin was brought up the M1 motorway from London to be buried on an island in the grounds of the family estate. Today, visitors troop round the **Diana exhibition**, in the old stable block, as well as the adjacent Althorp house, where there's a large collection of priceless paintings, including works by Gainsborough, Van Dyck and Rubens. From the house, a footpath leads round a lake in the middle of which is the islet (no access) on which Diana is buried. The estate is open in July and August (daily 9am–5pm; £10 in advance, £11 on the gate; ℡0870/167 9000, ⓦwww.visitalthorp.com) and advance reservations are strongly advised.

There are no scheduled **buses** from Northampton to Althorp, but there are sometimes special coaches – contact Northampton tourist office for details.

Sulgrave Manor

Tiny **Sulgrave**, some eighteen miles southwest of Northampton, is home to **Sulgrave Manor**, a neat stone country house built by an ancestor of George Washington – his seven times great-grandfather to be precise (April–Oct Mon, Tues & Thurs–Fri 2–5.30pm, Sat & Sun 10.30am–1pm & 2–5.30pm; March, Nov & Dec Sat & Sun 10.30am–1pm & 2–4.30pm; £3.75). The house remained in the family until 1656, when Colonel John, great-grandfather of the American president, set sail for the New World and settled in Virginia. George Washington never visited Sulgrave, but nevertheless the place has taken on the air of a shrine to American democracy and the interior holds a small museum charting George's remarkable career. The best features of the building are the Great Hall, with its low-beamed ceiling, flagstones and huge fireplace, and the kitchen, set around an ancient hearth hung with copper pots and pans.

Oundle

Arguably Northamptonshire's prettiest town, pocket-sized **OUNDLE** slopes up gently from the River Nene, its congregation of old limestone houses zeroing in on the congenial **Market Place**. Preserving much of its medieval layout, Oundle boasts some of the finest seventeenth- and eighteenth-century streetscapes in the Midlands, and is a suitably exclusive setting for one of England's better-known private schools, **Oundle School**, which has been running since 1556 and owns many of the most prized buildings. Above all it's the general appearance of the place that appeals rather than anything in particular, the exception being the parish church of **St Peter**, whose magnificent two-hundred-foot Decorated spire soars high above the centre, though the interior – give or take the odd stained-glass window – is unremarkable.

Buses from Peterborough and Northampton stop on the Market Place, a short walk from the **tourist office**, at 14 West St (Easter to Aug Mon–Sat 9am–5pm, Sun 1–4pm; rest of year closed Sun; ☎01832/274333). They issue maps and bus timetables, have comprehensive details of local attractions and operate an **accommodation** service. The best place to stay is the *Talbot Hotel*, just along from the Market Place on New Street (☎01832/273621; ❹). This charming hotel dates from 1626 and comes complete with what is thought to be the very oak staircase Mary, Queen of Scots used on her way to her execution at Fotheringhay Castle (see below). Apparently the queen's executioner stayed at the *Talbot* and both his and Mary's ghost are said to wander the upper floor. For somewhere less expensive, head for the very well-kept *Ashworth House*, with two en-suite guest rooms, at 75 West St (☎01832/275312; ❷). The best place to **eat** is at the *Talbot*, unless you want a takeaway or picnic in which case *Trendalls*, on the Market Place, is just dandy for baguettes and sandwiches of all descriptions.

Fotheringhay

Nestling by the River Nene just four miles northeast of Oundle, the tiny hamlet of **FOTHERINGHAY** has long been left to its own devices, but its medieval heyday is recalled by its magnificent church of **St Mary and All Saints**, rising mirage-like above the green riverine meadows. Begun in 1411 and a hundred and fifty years in the making, the church is a paradigm of the Perpendicular, its exterior sporting wonderful arching buttresses, its nave lit by soaring windows and the whole caboodle topped by a splendid octagonal lantern tower. The interior is a tad bleak and bare, though there are two fancily carved medieval pieces to look for – a pulpit and a fine stone font.

Fotheringhay **castle** witnessed two key events – the birth of Richard III in 1452 and the beheading of Mary, Queen of Scots in 1587. On the orders of Elizabeth I, Mary was executed in the castle's Great Hall with no one to stand in her defence – apart, that is, from her dog, who is said to have rushed from beneath her skirts as her head dropped off. Not long afterwards, the castle fell into disrepair and nowadays only a thistle-covered **mound** remains to mark its position; it's signposted – down a narrow lane on the bend of the road as you come into the village from Oundle.

Fotheringhay has an excellent **pub**, the *Falcon*, where the food is delicious and there is a good range of beers.

Lincolnshire

The obvious place to start a visit to **Lincolnshire** is **Lincoln** itself, an old and easy-paced city where the cathedral, the third largest church in England, remains the county's outstanding attraction. Northeast and east of here, the Lincolnshire **Wolds** band the county, their gentle green hills harbouring the pleasant market town of **Louth**, where conscientious objectors were sent to dig potatoes during World War II. The Wolds are flanked by the coast, so different from the rest of Lincolnshire, its brashness encapsulated by the mega resort of **Skegness**, though there are unspoilt stretches, too, most notably at the **Gibraltar Point Nature Reserve**.

Delightful **Stamford**, in the southwest corner of the county, is an alternative base, an attractive town where the narrow streets are flanked by a handsome ensemble of antique stone buildings, and next door stands one of the great monuments of Elizabethan England, **Burghley House**. From Stamford, it's a short hop east into **The Fens**, whose most diverting villages lie along the A17, a road that runs close to the old fenland port of **Boston**, now Lincolnshire's second town. On any tour of the Fens you'll pass some of the county's most imposing medieval **churches**. Several are worth a special visit, especially **St Botolph's** in Boston and **St Andrew's** in Heckington – seen to best advantage, like all the other churches of this area, in the pale, watery sunlight of the fenland evening.

Getting around Lincolnshire by public transport can be difficult. Lincoln is the hub of the county's limited **rail** network with regular services south to Sleaford and Spalding and east via Sleaford to Heckington, Boston and Skegness. There are also links west to Grantham and Newark, in Nottinghamshire, both of which are on the main line from London to the Northeast. In addition, there are reasonable **bus** services between Lincoln and the county's larger market towns, like Louth and Boston, but amongst the villages you'll be struggling without your own transport. This is especially true as many of these villages are long and straggly, built along slight ridges as a precaution against flooding.

Lincoln

Reaching high into the sky from the top of a steep hill, the triple towers of the mighty cathedral of **LINCOLN** are visible for miles across the flatlands. This conspicuous spot was first fortified by the Celts, who called their settlement Lindon, "hillfort by the lake", a reference to the pools formed by the River Witham in the marshy ground below. In 47 AD the Romans occupied Lindon and built a fortified town which subsequently became, as Lindum Colonia, one of the four regional capitals of Roman Britain.

Today, only fragments of the Roman city survive, mostly pieces of the third-century town wall, and these are outdone by reminders of Lincoln's medieval heyday, which began during the reign of William the Conqueror with the building of the **castle** and **cathedral**. Lincoln flourished as a centre of the wool trade with Flanders, until 1369, when the wool market was transferred to neighbouring Boston. It was almost five hundred years before the town revived, the recovery based upon its manufacture of agricultural machinery and drainage equipment for the fenlands. As the nineteenth-century town spread south down the hill and out along the old Roman road – the Fosse Way – so Lincoln became a place of precise class distinctions: the "Up hill" area, spreading north from the cathedral, became synonymous with middle-class respectability, "Down hill" with the proletariat. It's a distinction that remains – locals selling anything from second-hand cars to settees still put "Up hill" in brackets to signify a better quality of merchandise. For the visitor, almost everything of interest is confined to the "Up hill" part of town, and it's here also you'll find the best **pubs** and **restaurants**.

Arrival, information and accommodation

Both Lincoln's **train station**, on St Mary's Street, and its **bus station**, close by off Norman Street, are located "Down hill" in the city centre. From either, it's

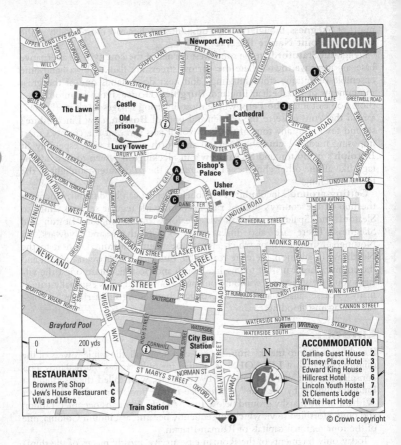

© Crown copyright

a steep, twenty-minute walk to the cathedral, which can also be reached by city bus or (depending on the success of various trials) an electric "people carrier". There are two **tourist offices**. One is in the shopping centre on The Cornhill, close to the train and bus stations (Easter–Sept Mon–Thurs 9.30am–5.30pm, Fri 9.30am–5pm, Sat 10am–5pm; Oct–Easter same days, but closes 4pm; ☎01522/579056, Ⓦwww.lincoln-info.org.uk), the other is at 9 Castle Hill, between the cathedral and the castle (same hours; ☎01522/529828, Ⓦwww.lincoln-info.org.uk). Both have a useful range of literature on Lincoln and its surroundings, take bookings for guided tours of the city, and operate an accommodation-booking service.

Lincoln has a good supply of competitively priced **hotels** and **B&Bs**, though surprisingly few of them are in the vicinity of the Cathedral – "Up hill" – and this is precisely where you want to be. All the places below are "Up hill," unless otherwise indicated. On occasion, demand can exceed supply, in which case head for the tourist office.

Hotels, guest houses and B&Bs

Carline Guest House 1–3 Carline Rd ☎01522/530422. One of the best B&Bs in the city, *Carline* occupies a spick-and-span Edwardian house about ten minutes' walk down from the cathedral – take Drury Lane from in front of the castle and keep going. Breakfasts are first-rate, the rooms smart and tastefully furnished. No credit cards. ❷

D'Isney Place Hotel Eastgate ☎01522/538881, ⓦwww.disneyplacehotel.co.uk. This delightful hotel occupies a lovely eighteenth-century building close to the cathedral. Breakfast is served in the bedrooms, some of which have four-poster beds and spa baths. Highly recommended. ⑤

Edward King House The Old Palace, Minster Yard ☎01522/528778. For something a little different, head for this unusual B&B in a former residence of the bishops of Lincoln. The exterior is a good bit grander than the rooms, but these are perfectly adequate and some have fine views over the city. Next to the cathedral. ①

Hillcrest Hotel 15 Lindum Terrace ☎01522/510182, ⓦwww.hillcrest-hotel.com. Traditional, very English hotel in a large red-brick house that was originally a Victorian rectory. Sixteen comfortable rooms with all mod cons plus a large, sloping garden. The owner, who is often in attendance, has loads of ideas about what to visit. About ten minutes' walk from the cathedral: go down Pottergate, turn right onto Wragby Road and then almost immediately turn left onto Lindum Terrace. ⑤

St Clements Lodge 21 Langworth Gate ☎01522/521532. In a brisk, modern house a short walk from the cathedral, this comfortable B&B offers a handful of pleasant, mostly en-suite guest rooms. To get there, follow Eastgate east from beside the cathedral. ②

White Hart Hotel Bailgate ☎01522/526222. This is one of Lincoln's plushest hotels, a crisply refurbished old coaching inn footsteps from the Castle Hill tourist office. Many of the bedrooms overlook the cathedral. One of the Heritage chain. Weekend deals can half the normal price. ⑦

Hostel

Lincoln youth hostel 77 South Park ☎01522/522076, ⓦwww.yha.org.uk. The town's YHA hostel occupies a Victorian house beside South Common park, one mile south of the train station. There are 46 beds in 2- to 8-bedded rooms. To get there from the train and bus stations, follow Melville Street and its continuation Canwick Road, keep going straight over the island (past South Park Avenue) and it's the first turning on the right opposite the cemetery. Closed Nov–Jan.

The Cathedral

Not a hill at all, **Castle Hill** is a wide, short and level cobbled street that links the castle and the cathedral. It's a charming spot and its east end is marked by the arch of the medieval **Exchequergate**, beyond which soars the glorious west front of **Lincoln Cathedral** (daily: May–Sept 7am–8pm; Oct–April 7am–6pm; except during services when access is restricted; £3.50 with guided tour), a sheer cliff-face of blind arcading mobbed by decorative carving. Most striking of all is the extraordinary band of twelfth-century carved panels which depict biblical themes with passionate intimacy, their inspiration being a similar frieze at Modena cathedral in Italy. The west front's apparent homogeneity is, however, deceptive, and further inspection reveals two phases of construction – the small stones and thick mortar of much of the facade belong to the original church, completed in 1092, whereas the longer stones and finer courses date from the early thirteenth century. These were enforced modifications, for in 1185 an earthquake shattered much of the Norman church, which was then rebuilt under the auspices of **Bishop Hugh of Avalon**, the man responsible for most of the present cathedral, with the notable exception of the (largely) fourteenth-century central tower.

The cavernous **interior** is a fine example of Early English architecture, with the nave's pillars conforming to the same general design yet differing slightly. Looking back up the nave from beneath the central tower, you can also observe a major medieval cock-up: Bishop Hugh's roof is out of alignment with the earlier west front, and the point where they meet has all the wrong angles. It's possible to pick out other irregularities, too – the pillars have bases of different heights, and there are ten windows in the north wall and nine in the south – but these are deliberate features, reflecting a medieval aversion to the vanity of symmetry.

Beyond the rood screen lies **St Hugh's Choir**, its fourteenth-century misericords carrying an eccentric range of carvings, with scenes from the life of Alexander the Great and King Arthur mixed up with biblical characters and folkloric parables. Farther on is the Gothic **Angel Choir**, completed in 1280, its roof embellished by dozens of finely carved statuettes, including the tiny Lincoln Imp (see below). Finally, a corridor off the choir's north aisle leads to the wooden-roofed **cloisters** and the polygonal **chapter house**, where Edward I and Edward II convened gatherings that pre-figured the creation of the English Parliament.

On every day but Sunday, usually a couple of times a day, the cathedral offers two sorts of **guided tour**. The first – the Floor Tour – is a quick gambol round the cathedral's salient features, the second, the Roof Tour, takes in parts of the church otherwise out of bounds. The latter is very popular, so it's a good idea to book in advance – call ☎01522/529241 or see ⓦwww.lincolncathedral.com.

Hidden behind a wall immediately below (and to the south of) the cathedral on Minster Yard are the ruins of what would, in its day, have been among the city's most impressive buildings. This, the medieval **Bishop's Palace** (April–Oct daily 10am–6pm; Nov–March Sat & Sun 10am–4pm; £2.50; EH), once consisted of two grand halls, a lavish chapel, kitchens and ritzy private chambers, but today the only coherent survivor is the battered and bruised Alnwick Tower – where the entrance is. The damage was done during the Civil War when a troupe of Roundheads occupied the palace until they themselves had to evacuate the place after a fierce fire.

The Castle

From the west front of the cathedral, it's a quick stroll across Castle Hill to **Lincoln Castle** (April–Sept Mon–Sat 9.30am–5.30pm, Sun 11am–5.30pm; Oct–March Mon–Sat 9.30am–4pm, Sun 11am–4pm; £2.50). Intact and forbidding, the castle walls incorporate bits and pieces from the twelfth to the nineteenth century and the wall walkway offers great views over town. The earliest remains are those of the **Lucy Tower**, built on the steep grassy mound that was once the site of one of the two original Norman mottes. The castle was turned into a prison in the 1820s and some of the prisoners were unceremoniously buried here at the top of the mound – a sad and lonely spot if ever there was one, especially as the tombs were only allowed to carry the prisoners' initials. The spacious grounds enclosed by the walls hold the old **prison**, a dour red-brick structure that is now home to one of the four surviving copies of the **Magna Carta** as well as a remarkable **prison chapel**. Here, the prisoners – who were kept in solitary confinement – were locked in high-sided cubicles where they could see the preacher and his pulpit but not their fellow internees, an arrangement founded on the pseudo-scientific theory that defined crime as a contagious disease. Unfortunately for the theorists, their so-called Pentonville System of "Separation and Silence", which was introduced here in 1846, drove many prisoners crazy, and it had to be abandoned thirty years later, though nobody bothered to dismantle the chapel.

Leaving the castle via the west gate, you reach **The Lawn**, formerly a lunatic asylum and now a leisure complex incorporating – among several modest attractions – the **Sir Joseph Banks Conservatory** (April–Sept Mon–Fri 9am–5pm, Sat & Sun 10am–4pm; Oct–Easter daily 10am–4pm; free). This is a large tropical glasshouse named after a local botanist who travelled with Cook on his first voyage to Australia.

The rest of the city

As for the rest of **"Up hill" Lincoln**, it's scattered with historic remains, notably several chunks of Roman wall, the most prominent of which is the second-century **Newport Arch** straddling Bailgate and once the main north gate into the city. There's also a bevy of medieval stone houses, at their best on and around the aptly named **Steep Hill** as it cuts down to the city centre. In particular, look out for the tidily restored twelfth-century **Jew's House**, a reminder of the Jewish community that flourished in medieval Lincoln. A rare and superb example of domestic Norman architecture, it now houses the *Jew's House Restaurant* (see below).

The **Usher Gallery**, Lindum Road (Mon–Sat 10am–5.30pm, Sun 2.30–5pm; £2), is on the hillside, too, its well-presented displays featuring some fine paintings of the cathedral and its environs, the best being those of William Logsdail. There's also a *Lincoln* view by Lowry as well as memorabilia celebrating Lincolnshire's own Alfred Tennyson, one of Victorian England's favourite poets. In addition, the gallery holds an eclectic collection of coins, porcelain, and watches and clocks dating from the seventeenth century. The timepieces were given to the gallery by its benefactor, James Ward Usher, a local jeweller and watchmaker who made a fortune by devising the legend of the **Lincoln Imp**, which he turned into the city's emblem in the 1880s. His story has a couple of imps hopping around the cathedral, until one of them is turned to stone for trying to talk to the angels carved into the roof of the Angel Choir. His chum made a hasty exit on the back of a witch, but the wind is still supposed to haunt the cathedral awaiting their return.

Eating and drinking

Lincoln's **café** and **restaurant** scene is a little patchy – with too many places offering mundane food geared to the day-tripping trade – but there are excellent places too, mostly within shouting distance of the Cathedral. First stop must be *Brown's Pie Shop*, 33 Steep Hill – at the top – which has a lively menu where the emphasis is on British ingredients; a main course here will cost you about £10. Next door, and similarly enticing, is the *Wig and Mitre* pub-restaurant, where a wide-ranging, moderately priced menu lists everything from sandwiches through to fillet steak. Another recommendable spot on Steep Hill is the more expensive – and more formal – *Jew's House Restaurant* (☎01522/524851; closed Sun). As for **pubs**, there are a pair of amiable and traditional locals near the cathedral – the *Bull & Chain*, on Langworthgate, and the *Morning Star*, close by on Greetwellgate. The former has a garden.

The Wolds and the coast

The rolling hills and gentle valleys of the **Lincolnshire Wolds**, a narrow band of chalky land running southeast from Caistor to just outside Skegness, stand out amidst the more mundane agricultural landscapes of north Lincolnshire. A string of particularly appealing valleys is concentrated in the vicinity of **Louth**, which, with its striking church and old centre, is easily the most enticing of the region's towns – with the added advantage of being fairly close to the coast. A few miles to the south of Louth, the Wolds dip down to the fens, pancake-flat and making a wide and deep arch around the intrusive stump of The Wash. In the other direction, east of the Wolds, lies the coast, whose bungalows, campsites and caravans are parked beside a sandy beach that extends, with a few marshy interruptions, north from **Skegness**, the main resort, to Mablethorpe and ultimately Cleethorpes. Near Skegness, the **Gibraltar Point Nature Reserve** is a welcome diversion from the bucket-and-spade/amusement-arcade commercialism.

Louth and around

Henry VIII described the county of Lincolnshire as "one of the most brutal and beestlie of the whole realm", his contempt based on the events of 1536, when thousands of northern peasants rebelled against his religious reforms. In Lincolnshire, this insurrection, the **Pilgrimage of Grace**, began in the north-east of the county at **LOUTH**, twenty-three miles from Lincoln, under the leadership of the local vicar, who was subsequently hung, drawn and quartered. There's a commemorative plaque in honour of the rebels beside Louth's church of **St James** (Easter–Christmas Mon–Sat 10.30am–4.30pm), which is the town's one outstanding building, its soaring Perpendicular spire, buttresses, battlements and pinnacles set on a grassy knoll, just to the west of the centre. The interior, clumsily renovated in the 1820s, is a disappointment, but the nave does boast a handsome Georgian wooden roof and the intricate vaulting beneath the tower is an exercise in geometrical precision. Next to the church, the well-tended gardens and Georgian houses of **Westgate** make it one of Louth's prettiest streets and you can grab a drink here at the antique *Wheatsheaf Inn*. Afterwards, it doesn't take long to explore the rest of the town centre, whose cramped lanes and alleys – focusing on the **Cornmarket** – are lined with red-brick buildings dating from the seventeenth century.

With reasonably regular weekday services from Boston and Lincoln, Louth's **bus station** is at the east end of Queen Street, a couple of minutes' walk from the Cornmarket – walk west along Queen Street and turn right onto the Market Place. The **tourist office**, in the Market Hall off Cornmarket (Mon–Sat 9am–5pm; ☎01507/609289), has a competent range of local information including accommodation details. The best **hotel** is the *Priory*, on Eastgate (☎01507/602930, ⓦwww.theprioryhotel.com; ❹), an excellent family-run place in a Georgian villa of 1818 with an idiosyncratic neo-Gothic facade and extensive gardens; it's located at the east end of the centre, about ten minutes' walk from the Cornmarket. There's also a top-notch **B&B**, *Keddington House*, in a pleasant Victorian house with its own heated outdoor pool about three-quarters of a mile to the northeast of the centre at 5 Keddington Rd (☎01507/603973, ⓦwww.keddingtonhouse.co.uk; ❷).

For **food**, it's hard to beat the *Priory*, which serves moderately priced dinners to a very good standard (closed Sun). The miscellaneous snack bars dotted round the Corn Market offer cheaper alternatives. Runner up, and a good bit cheaper, is *Ye Olde Whyte Swanne*, an old pub at 45 Eastgate, that sells tasty bar snacks, including home-made game and pork pies as well as the illustrious (and extremely large) Lincolnshire sausage.

The Saltfleetby-Theddlethorpe dunes

A worthwhile short excursion from Louth takes you east along the **B1200** across about ten miles of fen farmland to the coast. This byroad is built on an old Roman road used to transport salt inland from the seashore salt pans that were once a lucrative source of income for local traders. At the coast, at the end of the B1200, turn right along the main **A1031** and, after about half a mile, take the (poorly signed) track on the left through the dunes to the **Saltfleetby-Theddlethorpe Dunes National Nature Reserve**. Comprising over five miles of sand dune, salt and freshwater marsh, the reserve is at its prettiest in midsummer, when the dunes sprout buckthorn bushes and sea heather flowers, forming a carpet of violet spreading down towards the ocean. A network of trails navigates the dunes and lagoons, with the latter attracting hundreds of migratory wildfowl in spring and autumn.

Skegness and around

SKEGNESS, south along the coast from the Saltfleetby-Theddlethorpe reserve, has been a busy resort ever since the railways reached the Lincolnshire coast in 1875. Its heyday was before the 1960s, when the Brits began to take themselves off to sunnier climes, but it still attracts tens of thousands of city-dwellers each year, who come for the wide, sandy beaches and for a host of attractions ranging from nightclubs to bowling greens. Every inch the traditional English seaside town, Skegness gets the edge over many of its rivals by keeping its beaches clean and its parks spick-and-span, whilst a massive leisure complex in neighbouring Ingoldmells has a whopping indoor "fun pool". Indeed, Skegness has a tradition of keeping ahead of its competitors: in 1908 it came up with the ground-breaking "Skegness is So Bracing" slogan beneath a picture of a "Jolly Fisherman" and it was here in 1936 that ex-showman Billy Butlin opened the first Butlin's Holiday Camp. All that said, the seafront, with its rows of souvenir shops and amusement arcades, can be dismal, especially on rainy days, and you may well decide to sidestep the whole caboodle by heading south three miles along the coastal road to the **Gibraltar Point National Nature Reserve** (daily dawn to dusk). Here, a network of clearly signed footpaths patterns a narrow strip of salt and freshwater marsh, sand dune and beach that attracts an inordinate number of birds, both resident and migratory.

As for practicalities, Skegness **bus** and **train stations** are next door to each other and about ten minutes' walk from the seashore – cut across Lumley Square and go straight up the High Street to the landmark clock tower. The **tourist office** (daily: April–Sept 9.30am–5pm; Oct–March 10am–4pm; ☏01754/764821, ⓦwww.funcoast.co.uk) is yards from the clock tower, behind the beach and opposite the Embassy Centre on Grand Parade. They can provide a colossal list of accommodation, including scores of **B&Bs** and **guest houses**. A series of inexpensive choices is strung out along Drummond Road, near the action but still agreeably residential. Options here include the *Sherwood Lodge*, at no. 100 (☏01754/762548; ●), and the *Singlecote Hotel*, at no. 34 (☏01754/764698; ●). For something a little more original, there's the *Old Mill Guest House*, in an old and imaginatively converted windmill five miles inland at Westend, Burgh Le Marsh (☏01754/810081; ●).

The Lincolnshire Fens

The Lincolnshire section of **The Fens**, the great chunk of eastern England extending from Boston to Cambridge, encompasses some of the most productive farmland in Europe. With the exception of the occasional hillock, this pancake-flat, treeless terrain has been painstakingly reclaimed from the marshes and swamps that once drained into the Wash, a process that has taken almost two thousand years. In earlier times, outsiders were often amazed by the dreadful conditions hereabouts. These dire conditions spawned the distinctive culture of the so-called **fen slodgers**, who embanked small portions of marsh to create pastureland and fields, supplementing their diets by catching fish and fowl, and gathering reed and sedge for thatching and fuel. Their economy was threatened by the large-scale land reclamation schemes of the late fifteenth and sixteenth centuries, and time and again the fenlanders sabotaged progress by breaking down the banks and dams. But the odds were stacked against the saboteurs, and a succession of great landowners eventually drained huge tracts of the fenland; by the end of the eighteenth century the fen slodgers' way of life had all but disappeared. Nonetheless, the Lincolnshire fens remain a distinctive area of introverted little villages, with just one major settlement, the old port of **Boston**.

As it nears The Wash, the muddy River Witham weaves its way through **BOSTON** (a corruption of Botolf's stone, or Botolph's town), which was named after the Anglo-Saxon monk-saint who first established a monastery here, overlooking the main river crossing point in 645 AD. In the thirteenth and fourteenth centuries, the settlement expanded to become England's second largest seaport, its flourishing economy dependent on the wool trade with Flanders. Local merchants, revelling in their success, decided to build a church that demonstrated their wealth, the result being the magnificent medieval church of St Botolph, whose 272-foot tower still presides over the town and surrounding fenland. The church was completed in the early sixteenth century, but by then Boston was in decline as trade drifted west towards the Atlantic and the Witham silted up. The town's fortunes only revived in the late eighteenth century when, after the nearby fens had been drained, it became a minor agricultural centre with a modest port that has, in recent times, been modernized for trade with the EU. A singular mix of fenland town and seaport, Boston is an unusual little place that is at its liveliest on **market days** – Wednesday and Saturday.

Mostly edged by Victorian red-brick buildings, the mazy streets of Boston's cramped and compact centre, on the east side of the Witham, radiate out from the **Market Place**, a dishevelled square of irregular shape. Just to the west looms the massive bulk of **St Botolph** (May–Sept daily 8.30am–4.30pm; Oct–April Mon–Sat 8.30am–4.30pm, Sun 8.30am–12.30pm; free), whose exterior masonry is embellished by the high-pointed windows of the Decorated style. Most of the structure dates from the fourteenth century, but the huge and distinctive **tower**, whose lack of a spire earned the church the nickname the "Boston Stump", is of later construction. The octagonal lantern is later still, added in the sixteenth century and graced by flying buttresses and pointy pinnacles. A tortuous 365-step spiral staircase (closed on Sun) leads to a balcony near the top, from where the panoramic views over Boston and the fens amply repay both the price of the ticket (£2) and the effort of the climb. Down below, St Botolph's light and airy **nave** is an exercise in the Perpendicular, all soaring columns and high windows. The sheer purity of design is stunning, its virtuosity heightened by the narrowness of the annexe-like chancel and the elegance of the Decorated arch that partly screens it from view.

The church's most famous vicar was John Cotton (1584–1652), who helped stir the Puritan stew during his twenty-year tenure, encouraging a stream of Lincolnshire dissidents to head off to the colonies of New England to found their "New Jerusalem". Cotton emigrated himself in 1633 and soon became the leading light among the Puritans of Boston, Massachusetts. The Cotton connection was finally commemorated here in the Stump by the creation of the **Cotton Chapel**, at the west end of the nave, in 1857.

Boston had been alive to religious dissent before Cotton arrived and, in 1607, several of the **Pilgrim Fathers** were incarcerated here after their failed attempt to escape religious persecution by slipping across to Holland. They were imprisoned for thirty days in the old **Guildhall** (Tues–Sat 10am–5pm; £1.25, free on Thurs), on South Street – a brief walk south along the river from St Botolph. A creaky affair, the Guildhall spreads over three levels and incorporates an antique Council Chamber, the court where the Pilgrim Fathers were tried and sentenced, as well as the cells where they were locked up. There's a fascinating hotchpotch of local bygones dotted around – including some spectacularly ferocious anti-poacher traps and a small display on locally born John Fox (1516–87), whose *Book of Martyrs* whipped up an anti-Catholic storm.

It's ten minutes' walk east from Boston **train station** to the town centre – head straight out of the station along Station Street and keep going until you hit the river. The **bus station** is also to the west of the centre, just five minutes' walk away along West Street. The **tourist office** (Mon–Sat 9am–5pm; ☎01205/356656, ⓦwww.boston.gov.uk) is in the Market Place beneath the Assembly Rooms, and here you can pick up details of several **B&Bs**. Among them one good option is the *Bramley House*, in an attractively converted eighteenth-century farmhouse about one mile west of town beyond the train station at 267 Sleaford Rd (☎01205/354538; ❶). Another good choice is *Fairfield Guest House*, in a much enlarged Victorian property about a mile to the south of the centre at 101 London Rd (☎01205/362869; ❶). There are fifteen guest rooms here – seven en suite – and each is decorated in bright and cheerful style. Town centre accommodation is limited and the best you'll do is the *New England Hotel*, Wide Bargate (☎01205/365255, ⓦwww.newenglandboston.co.uk; ❺), an unassuming mid-range place of thirty bedrooms with modern furnishings and fittings.

For **food**, *Goodbarns Yard*, just to the north of the Stump on Wormgate, serves copious pub meals inside or out in a back garden overlooking the river. Vegetarians should make a beeline for *Maud's Tea Rooms*, inside the Maud Foster Windmill, on Willoughby Road (☎01205/352188; open Wed & Sat 11am–5pm, Sun 1–5pm, plus additional days in July & Aug). Built to grind corn in 1819, the windmill, with its five whopping sails, is still in full working order. You can inspect its grinding gears and/or buy the (organic) flour it churns out at the tearoom, which serves a range of vegetarian and vegan meals, as well as a good selection of delicious cakes. The windmill is about ten minutes walk northeast of the Market Place, beside the road to Horncastle.

Heckington

The village of **HECKINGTON**, twelve miles west of Boston, has a tidy little centre that drapes around the church of **St Andrew** (Mon–Sat 9am–5pm or dusk in winter; free), a splendid example of the Decorated style, with a pinnacled spire and elaborate canopied buttresses framing the flowing tracery of the windows. Inside, the original fourteenth-century chancel fittings have survived, including the battered tomb of the founder, Richard de Potesgrave, and an **Easter Sepulchre**, whose folksy and energetic carved figures are set against a dense undergrowth of foliage. The sepulchre, one of the finest in England, was built to accommodate the host between Good Friday and Easter morning. The **sedilia** is intriguing, too, boasting a cartoon strip of domestic scenes on the subject of food – a man eating fruit, a woman feeding the birds and suchlike. Heckington has one other attraction, its unique eight-sailed **windmill**, located a short stroll from the church and worth visiting when it's in operation (Easter to mid-July Thurs–Sun noon–5pm; mid-July to Aug daily noon–5pm; Sept to Easter Sun 2–5pm; £1.50). Afterwards, you could pop over to a good old local, the *Nag's Head*, for a pint.

On the Skegness-Grantham line, Heckington **train station** is in the centre near the windmill.

Stamford

STAMFORD, some thirty miles south of Heckington, is delightful, a handsome little limestone town of yellow-grey seventeenth- and eighteenth-century buildings edging narrow streets that slope up from the River Welland. It was here that the Romans forded this important river, establishing a fortified outpost that the Danes subsequently selected for one of their regional capitals. Later the town became a centre of the medieval wool and cloth trade, its wealthy merchants funding a series of almshouses known as "**callises**" – after Calais, the English-occupied port through which most of them traded. Stamford was also the home of William Cecil, Elizabeth's chief minister, who built his splendid mansion, Burghley House, close by. The town survived the collapse of the wool trade, prospering as an inland port after the Welland was made navigable to the sea in 1570, and, in the eighteenth century, as a staging point on the Great North Road from London. More recently, Stamford escaped the three main threats to old English towns – the Industrial Revolution, wartime bombing and postwar development – and was designated the country's first Conservation Area in 1967. Thanks to this, its unspoilt streets readily lend themselves to period drama- and film-making.

The town centre

Above all, it's the harmony of Stamford's architecture that pleases, rather than any specific sight. There are, nevertheless, a handful of buildings of some special interest amongst the web of narrow streets that make up the town's compact centre, beginning with the church of **St Mary** (no regular opening hours), set beside a pristine close of proud Georgian buildings on St Mary's Street. The church, with its splendid spire, has a small, airy interior, which incorporates the Corpus Christi chapel, whose intricately embossed, painted and panelled roof dates from the 1480s.

From St Mary's, several lanes thread through to the carefully preserved High Street, where Ironmonger Street leads north again to Broad Street, wide and handsome and the site of the **Stamford Museum** (April–Sept Mon–Sat 10am–5pm, Sun 2–5pm; Oct–March Mon–Sat 10am–5pm; free). This features a tasteless exhibit comparing the American midget Tom Thumb with **Daniel Lambert**, the Leicester fat man who died at Stamford in 1809, aged 39 and weighing 52st 11lb (336kg). After Lambert's death his clothes were displayed in a local inn, which Tom Thumb, otherwise Charles Stratton, visited several times to perform a few party tricks, such as standing in Lambert's waistcoat armhole. Nearby, also on Broad Street, is **Browne's Hospital**, the most extensive of the town's almshouses, dating from the late fifteenth century, and from here it's a few paces more to Red Lion Square, which is overseen by **All Saints** (daily dawn to dusk; free). Several centuries in the making, this church is a happy amalgamation of Early English and Perpendicular features that takes full advantage of its position, perched on a grassy mound.

High Street St Martin's and Burghley House

Down the hill from St Mary's, across the Welland on High Street St Martin's, is the **George Hotel**, a splendid old coaching inn whose Georgian facade supports one end of the gallows that span the street – not a warning to criminals, but an advertising hoarding. Just along – and across – the street, the plain and sombre, late fifteenth-century church of **St Martin** (daily 9.30am–4pm; free) shelters the magnificent tombs of the lords Burghley, with a recumbent William Cecil carved beneath twin canopies, holding his rod of office and with a lion at his feet. Just behind, the early eighteenth-century effigies of John Cecil and his wife show the couple as Roman aristocrats, propped up on their elbows, she to gaze at him, John to stare across the nave commandingly.

From St Martin's church, it's a fifteen-minute stroll south along High Street St Martin's to **Burghley House** (April–Oct daily 11am–4.30pm; viewing by guided tours only, except Sat & Sun pm; £6.80), an extravagant Elizabethan mansion standing in parkland landscaped by Capability Brown; you can also drive there along Barnack Road – just follow the signs. Completed in 1587 after twenty-two years' work, the house sports a mellow-yellow ragstone exterior, embellished by dainty cupolas, a pyramidal clock tower and skeletal balustrading, all to a plan by **William Cecil**, the long-serving adviser to Elizabeth I.

With the notable exception of the Tudor kitchen, little remains of Burghley's Elizabethan interior. Instead, the house bears the heavy hand of John, fifth Lord Burghley, who toured France and Italy in the late seventeenth century, commissioning furniture, statuary and tapestries, as well as buying up old Florentine and Venetian paintings, such as Paolo Veronese's *Zebedee's Wife Petitioning our Lord*. To provide a suitable setting for his old masters, John brought in Antonio Verrio and his assistant Louis Laguerre, who between them covered many of Burghley's walls and ceilings with frolicking gods and goddesses. These gaudy and gargantuan murals are at their most engulfing in the Heaven Room, an artfully painted classical temple that adjoins the Hell Staircase, where the entrance to the inferno is through the gaping mouth of a cat.

Practicalities

With frequent services from Peterborough and Oakham, Stamford **train station** is five minutes' walk from the town centre, which lies just to the north across the river. The **bus station** is on the west side of the centre, on Sheepmarket, off All Saints' Street. The **tourist office** is in the centre inside Stamford Arts Centre at 27 St Mary's St (April–Oct Mon–Sat 9.30am–5pm, Sun 11am–4pm; Nov–March closed Sun; ℡01780/755611, ⓦwww.skdc.com).

Stamford has several charming **hotels**, the most celebrated of which is the delightful *George Hotel*, 71 High Street St Martin's (℡01780/750750, ⓦwww.georgehotelofstamford.com; ❼), an old and cleverly remodelled coaching inn with flagstone floors and antique furnishings, where the most appealing rooms overlook the cobbled courtyard. Just along the street is the attractive *Garden House Hotel* (℡01780/763359, ⓦwww.gardenhousehotel.com; ❺), which occupies a tastefully modernized eighteenth-century building with twenty smart bedrooms. Stamford also possesses a clutch of **B&Bs**. As ever, the tourist office has the full list, but one especially good place is *Martin's*, 20 High Street St Martin's (℡01780/752106; no credit cards; ❹), a Georgian house whose three spacious guest rooms are immaculately maintained and tastefully decorated. Breakfasts are delicious; guests have access to the walled garden and dinner is served by prior request.

For **food**, it has to be the *George Hotel* – either in the formal and expensive restaurant, where the emphasis is on British ingredients served in imaginative ways, or in the moderately priced and informal Garden Lounge. There's delicious and inexpensive bar food, too, served in the York Bar at lunchtimes.

Travel details

Buses

For information on all local and national bus services, contact Traveline: ☎ 0870/608 2 608 (daily 7am–9pm), ⊛ www.traveline.org.uk.

Trains

For information on all local and national rail services, contact National Rail Enquiries: ☎ 08457/48 49 50, ⊛ www.nationalrail.co.uk.

Leicester to: Birmingham (every 30min; 1hr); Coventry (hourly; 45min); Derby (hourly; 35min); Lincoln (hourly; 1hr 40min); London (every 30min; 1hr 30min); Market Harborough (every 1–2hr; 15min); Melton Mowbray (hourly; 15min); Nottingham (every 30min; 20min); Oakham (hourly; 30min); Stamford (hourly; 50min).

Lincoln to: Birmingham (hourly; 3hr); Boston (hourly; 1hr); Cambridge (hourly; 1hr); Gainsborough (hourly; 20min); Grantham (every 30min; 45min); London (hourly; 2hr 15min); Leicester (hourly; 1hr 30min); London (hourly; 2hr 15min); Newark (hourly; 25min); Nottingham (hourly; 45min); Peterborough (hourly; 1hr 20min);

Skegness (hourly; 1hr 40min); Spalding (every 1–2hr; 1hr).

Northampton to: Birmingham (every 30min; 1hr); Coventry (hourly; 40min); London Euston (every 30min; 1hr 10min–1hr 40min).

Nottingham to: Leicester (every 30min; 30min); Lincoln (hourly; 1hr 15min); London (hourly; 1hr 40min); Newark (hourly; 30min).

Stamford to: Cambridge (hourly; 1hr 20min); Leicester (hourly; 40min); Oakham (hourly; 10min); Peterborough (hourly; 15min).

The Northwest

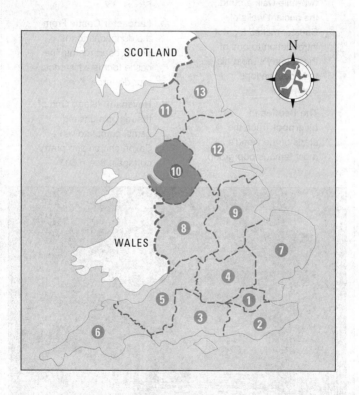

CHAPTER 10 Highlights

* **Café society, Manchester** From breakfast croissant to late-night drinks, Manchester's café-bars set the tone for this happening city. See p.578

* **City walls, Chester** A two-mile walk around the ancient walls of Chester makes a great introduction to one of the country's most historic destinations. See p.584

* **The Beatles in Liverpool** Trace the steps of the world's most famous pop group, who started out in this city's backstreet pubs and clubs. See p.591

* **Blackpool Tower** Blackpool's bold answer to the Eiffel Tower lights up the skyline of the UK's favourite resort. See p.599

* **Lancaster Castle** From the dungeons to the ornate court rooms, the castle tour is a historical tour-de-force. See p.601

* **Heysham Village** One of the region's unsung gems, complete wih Saxon church and pretty cottages. See p.603

10

The Northwest

Within the **northwest** of England lie some of the ugliest and some of the most beautiful parts of the country. The least attractive zones of this region are to be found in the sprawl connecting the country's third and sixth largest conurbations, Manchester and Liverpool, but even here the picture isn't unrelievedly bleak, as the cities themselves have an ingratiating appeal. **Manchester**, in particular, surprises many who don't expect to see beyond its dour, industrial heritage. Where once only a handful of Victorian Gothic buildings lent any grace to the cityscape, Manchester today has been completely transformed by a rebuilding programme that puts it in the vanguard of modern British urban design. **Liverpool**, set on the Mersey estuary, is perhaps less appealing at first glance, though Georgian town houses, grand civic buildings, its twin cathedrals and a burgeoning café scene soon change perceptions. To the south, **Cheshire** boasts the county town, **Chester**, with its complete circuit of town walls and partly Tudor centre. This is as alluring as any of the country's northern towns, capturing the essence of what has always been one of England's wealthiest rural counties.

Lancashire, which historically lay directly to the north of Cheshire, reached industrial prominence in the last century primarily due to the cotton-mill towns around Manchester and to the thriving port of Liverpool. Today, neither of those cities is part of the county, having been excised when England's first substantial county boundary changes since the Domesday Book were enacted in 1974. The urban counties of Merseyside and Greater Manchester chopped off the southern section of Lancashire while Cumbria grabbed a substantial northern chunk leaving Lancashire little more than half its former size. Its oldest town, and major commercial and administrative centre, is **Preston** – home of the national museum of England's national game, football – though tourists are perhaps more inclined to linger in the charming towns and villages of the nearby **Ribble Valley**. Meanwhile, along the coast to the west and north of the major cities stretches a line of **resorts** – from Southport to Morecambe – which once formed the mainstay of the northern British holiday trade before their client base disappeared on cheaper, sunnier holidays to Florida and the Mediterranean. Only **Blackpool** is really worth visiting for its own sake, a rip-roaring resort which has stayed at the top of its game by supplying undemanding entertainment with more panache than its neighbours. For anything more culturally invigorating you'll have to continue north to the historically important city of **Lancaster**, with its Tudor castle. Finally, the semi-autonomous **Isle of Man**, only twenty-five miles off the coast and served by ferries from Liverpool and Heysham (or short flights from Liverpool), provides a terrain almost as rewarding as that of the Lake District but without the seasonal overcrowding.

▲ Isle of Man

NORTH YORKSHIRE

Halifax

Skipton

Rochdale

A65

Oldham

Manchester

PEAK DISTRICT NATIONAL PARK

Hathersage

Edale

Eyam

Castleton

Buxton

Bakewell

A6

Macclesfield

Stockport

LANCASHIRE

Clitheroe

Slaidburn

Newton

FOREST OF BOWLAND

Dunsop Bridge

Bury

Bolton

Knutsford

Warrington

M6

Crewe

M56

Northwich

CHESHIRE

Nantwich

Lancaster

M6

Preston

Chester

M53

Ellesmere Port

Morecambe Bay

Morecambe

Heysham

M55

Fleetwood

Ulverston

Barrow-in-Furness

Blackpool

Southport

Liverpool

M58

M57

M62

Wrexham

WALES

IRISH SEA

Llandudno

A55

A5

Betws-y-coed

Holyhead

A5

ISLE OF MAN

Ramsey

Laxey

Douglas

Peel

Port Erin

Castletown

20 miles

0

N

© Crown copyright

Manchester

Few cities in the world have embraced social change so heartily as **MANCHESTER**. From engine of the Industrial Revolution to test-bed of contemporary urban design, the city has no realistic provincial English rival. Its domestic dominance expresses itself in various ways, most swaggeringly in the success of Manchester United, the richest football club in Britain, but also in a thriving music and cultural scene that has given birth to world-beaters as diverse as the Hallé Orchestra and Oasis. Moreover, the city's concert halls, theatres, clubs and café society are boosted by England's largest student population and a blossoming gay community whose spending-power has created a pioneering Gay Village. For inspiration, Manchester's planners look to Barcelona – another revitalized industrial powerhouse – and, like Barcelona, the promise of a major sports event has powered much of the recent urban regeneration. The city didn't get the Olympics, though it wasn't for the want of trying, but instead landed the 2002 **Commonwealth Games** (see box below).

Manchester's rapid growth was the equal of any flowering of the Industrial Revolution – from little more than a village in 1750 to the world's major cotton-milling centre in only a hundred years. The spectacular rise of **Cottonopolis**, as it became known, came from the production of competitively priced imitations of expensive Indian calicoes, using machines evolved from Arkwright's first steam-powered cotton mill, which opened in 1783. The rapid industrialization of the area brought prosperity for a few but a life of misery for the majority. Exploitation had worsened still further by the time the 23-year-old Friedrich Engels came here in 1842 to work in his father's cotton plant, and the suffering he witnessed – recorded in his *Condition of the Working Class in England* – was a seminal influence on his later collaboration with Karl Marx, the *Communist Manifesto*.

Waterways and railway viaducts form the matrix into which the city's principal buildings have been bedded – as early as 1772 the Duke of Bridgewater had a canal cut to connect the city to the coal mines at Worsley, and the world's

The Commonwealth Games 2002

The seventeenth **Commonwealth Games** take place in Manchester from 25 July to 4 August 2002, with 5000 athletes from 72 nations competing for medals in fourteen individual and three team sports. The new 38,000-seater **City of Manchester Stadium**, in the east of the city, is the centrepiece of the games, staging the opening and closing ceremonies, as well as the athletics events and the Rugby Sevens competition. It's part of a wider **Sportcity** development, incorporating the **Indoor Tennis Centre** and **National Squash Centre**. The **Aquatics Centre**, in the city centre, has been purpose-built for the swimming competitions; other events are at a variety of existing and refurbished venues, including the National Cycling Centre (cycling), G-Mex (gymnastics, judo and wrestling), International Convention Centre (weightlifting), Manchester Evening News Arena (netball and boxing), Belle Vue Leisure Centre (hockey) and Salford Quays (triathlon).

A million tickets will be available for events, with current details contained on the official **website**: ⓦ www.commonwealthgames.com. Although many tickets are expected to be sold well In advance, some will be held back until box-office sales start in early June 2002 while others will be available on the day at certain events. Ticket prices run from £5 to £30, though some events – particularly mountain-biking, the marathon, road-racing and walking – will be free. An accompanying carnival will turn the city centre into a non-stop party for the duration – more details can be obtained from the Manchester Visitor Centre (see p.572).

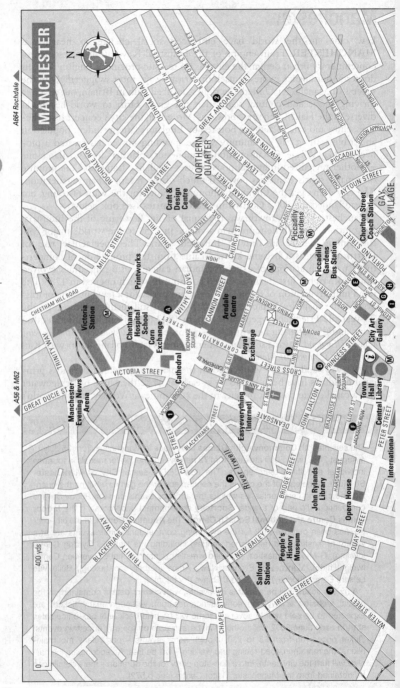

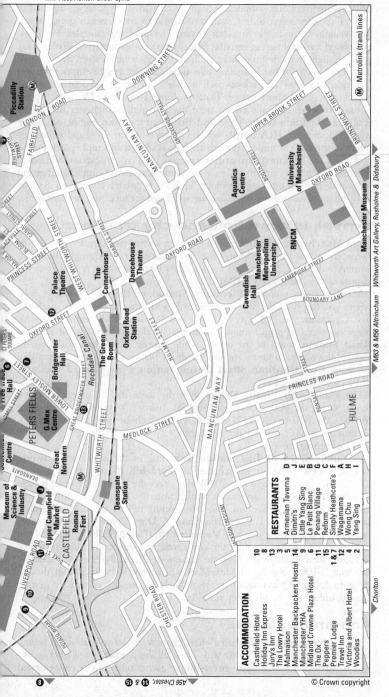

A635 Ashton-under-Lyme

THE NORTHWEST | Manchester

10

ACCOMMODATION

Castlefield Hotel	10
Holiday Inn Express	8
Jury's Inn	13
The Lowry Hotel	3
Malmaison	5
Manchester Backpackers Hostel	14
Manchester YHA	9
Midland Crowne Plaza Hotel	6
The Ox	11
Peppers	15
Premier Lodge	1 & 7
Simply Heathcote's	1 & 7
Travel Inn	12
Victoria and Albert Hotel	4
Woodies	2

RESTAURANTS

Armenian Taverna	D
Dimitri's	J
Little Yang Sing	E
Le Petit Blanc	B
Penang Village	G
Reform	C
Simply Heathcote's	F
Wagamama	A
Wong Chu	H
Yang Sing	I

M Metrolink (tram) lines

M63 & M56 Altrincham   Whitworth Art Gallery, Rusholme & Didsbury

Chorlton

571

© Crown copyright

A56 Chester, 14 & 15

A56 Chester, 8

first passenger rail line, connecting Manchester with Liverpool, was opened in 1830. The Manchester Ship Canal, constructed to entice ocean-going vessels into Manchester and away from burgeoning Liverpool, was completed in 1894, and played a crucial part in reviving Manchester's competitiveness. Within sixty years, though, Manchester's docks, mills and canals were in steep decline. The traditional image of the struggling post-industrial city was of empty mills and factories, and rows of back-to-back houses – an image perpetuated, to an extent, by the popularity of Britain's longest-running TV soap opera, *Coronation Street*. Sporadic efforts were made to pull Manchester out of the economic doldrums of the 1960s and 1970s, but the main engine of change was the devastating **IRA bomb**, which exploded in June 1996 and wiped out much of the city's commercial infrastructure. Rather than simply patch up the buildings, the planning authorities embarked on an ambitious rebuilding scheme, which also came to embrace the Commonwealth Games' facilities and innovative millennium design projects. Entire new districts have taken shape as once-blighted areas along the canals are reclaimed for retail and residential use.

Arrival, information and city transport

From **Manchester Airport**, ten miles south of the city, direct trains run to Piccadilly (every 15min 5.15am–10.15pm, reduced service through the night; 25min) and cost £2.35, £2.80 on weekdays before 9.30am. A taxi from the airport to the centre costs £12–15.

Mainline trains pull into **Piccadilly Station**, on the city's east side, from where you can walk the few hundred yards west into the centre (or catch the free Centreline bus #4 every 10min, not Sunday, to all main locations). Regional trains to points south, east and west call both here and at **Oxford Road Station**, south of the centre, while **Victoria Station**, in the north, services the northern hinterland and Bradford. National Express and long-distance buses use **Chorlton Street Coach Station**, a few hundred yards west of Piccadilly train station.

The **Manchester Visitor Centre** is in the town hall extension on Lloyd Street, facing St Peter's Square (Mon–Sat 10am–5.30pm, Sun 11am–4pm; ☎0161/234 3157 or 0906/8715 533; ⒲www.manchester.gov.uk/visitorcentre). To find out **what's on**, buy the fortnightly *City Life* magazine (⒲www.citylife.co.uk), from any newsstand.

Piccadilly Gardens Bus Station is the hub of the urban bus network, though a new transport interchange at **Shudehill** (north of the Arndale Centre; due for completion by 2003) may affect the location of some routes. **Information** about all services is available from the Travel Shop, in Piccadilly Gardens (Mon–Sat 7am–6pm, Sun 10am–6pm); or call the GMPTE Travel Line (☎0161/228 7811; daily 8am–8pm). A **Day Saver** ticket (£3) gives unlimited travel on any city bus. **Metrolink** (☎0161/205 2000) – the electric tram service – whisks through the city centre and out to the suburbs (every 6–15min 6am–11.30pm). There are stations at Piccadilly Station, Piccadilly Gardens, St Peter's Square, G-Mex, Market Street and Victoria Station, though (trips to Salford Quays aside) you're unlikely to use the system for getting around, unless you simply fancy the ride.

Accommodation

There's a good chance of finding a smart, en-suite, motel-style room in central Manchester for around £50–60, and almost all the plusher hotels offer weekend reductions too. Cheaper **guest-house** accommodation is concentrated some way out of the centre, while **B&B** accommodation in private houses is easy to arrange, though again it won't be particularly central, which makes the city's various **hostels** first choice for most budget travellers. There's no real peak **accommodation season**, though it's also difficult to get a city-centre hotel room when Manchester United play at home.

Hotels, guest houses and B&Bs

Castlefield Hotel Liverpool Rd ☎0161/832 7073, ⒲www.castlefield-hotel.co.uk. Warehouse-style development, with nicely appointed rooms, leisure club and pool. ❺, ❹ at weekends.

Holiday Inn Express Waterfront Quay, Salford Quays ☎0161/868 1000 or ☎0800/897121, ⒲www.hiexpress.com. Reasonably sized rooms in a great Quays location, convenient for The Lowry or Old Trafford – continental breakfast included. ❹

Jury's Inn 56 Great Bridgewater St ☎0161/953 8888, ⒲www.jurys.com. Very handy location – by Bridgewater Hall – for this large, 265-room, no-fuss budget hotel. Rates are room only. ❹, ❷ at weekends.

The Lowry Hotel 50 Dearman's Place, Chapel Wharf, Salford ☎0161/827 4000 or 833 4545, ⒲www.rfhotels.com. Manchester's first five-star hotel sits, exuding class, on the banks of the River Irwell, resplendent in its contemporary finery. ❾

Malmaison Piccadilly ☎0161/278 1000, ⒲www.malmaison.com. An ornate Edwardian facade given sleek interior lines and contemporary design from the Malmaison group. ❼

Midland Crowne Plaza Hotel Peter St ☎0161/236 3333, ⒲www.crowneplaza.com. The apotheosis of Edwardian style, with impressive public rooms and hefty weekend reductions. ❽

The Ox 71 Liverpool Rd ☎0161/839 7740, ⒲www.theox.co.uk. Pleasant rooms above a traditional pub opposite the Science and Industry Museum. Breakfast is extra (£2–6, depending what you have). ❷

Premier Lodge 7–11 Lower Mosley St ☎0870/700 1476; and North Tower, Victoria Bridge St, Salford, ☎0870/700 1488; both ⒲www.premierlodge.com. Good-value, city-cen-

tre, motel-style rooms and comfort from the Premier Lodge chain. ❷

Travel Inn Oxford St ☎0870/242 8000, ⒲www.travelinn.co.uk. Decently equipped motel-style rooms at great rates (breakfast not included). ❸

Victoria and Albert Hotel Water St, Castlefield ☎0161/832 1188, ⒲www.lemeridien-hotels.com. Superb restoration job for a riverside warehouse, with exposed beams, pipes and brickwork part of the interior fabric. ❼, ❻ at weekends.

Hostels and student halls

Manchester Backpackers Hostel 64 Cromwell Rd, Stretford ☎0161/865 9296 or 07711/556157, ⒲www.backpackers.freeserve.co.uk. Attractive Victorian terrace house two miles out of the centre; take Metrolink to Stretford. No credit cards.

Manchester YHA Potato Wharf, Castlefield ☎0161/839 9960, ⒲www.yha.org.uk. Excellent hostel, overlooking the canal, whose en-suite rooms sleep one to four people (you can pay more to have the room to yourself).

Peppers 17 Great Stone Rd, Stretford ☎0161/848 9770. Budget, self-catering accommodation in a terraced house, ten minutes from the centre by Metrolink (to Old Trafford).

University accommodation University of Manchester/UMIST Central Accommodation Office, ☎0161/275 2888. Call for information about vacancies at the various university hostels (available during summer vacations). Office open Mon–Fri 9am–5pm.

Woodies 19 Blossom St, Ancoats ☎0161/228 3456. Independent backpackers' hostel, five minutes' walk from Piccadilly station and handy for the Northern Quarter. Around fifty beds in dorms, singles and doubles.

The City

If Manchester can be said to have a centre, it's **St Peter's Square** and the cluster of buildings focused on it. South of here, the former Central Station now functions as the **G-Mex** exhibition centre, with the Hallé orchestra's home, **Bridgewater Hall**, opposite; **Chinatown** (Britain's largest) and the **Gay Village** are just a short walk to the east; while to the northeast, the revamped **Piccadilly Gardens** provides access to the so-called **Northern Quarter**, the funkiest of the regenerated inner-city areas. To the southwest is the **Castlefield** district, site of the **Museum of Science and Industry**. Eastern spine of the city is **Deansgate**, which runs from Castlefield to the Cathedral and, in its northern environs, displays the most dramatic core of urban regeneration in the country, centred on **Exchange Square**. Other city-centre diversions string out along the main southern artery **Oxford Road**. Southwest of the centre, trams run out to **Salford Quays** where the renovated docks and quays now maintain two high-profile visitor attractions, **The Lowry** arts centre and the **Imperial War Museum North**; and no soccer fan will want to miss the tour of nearby **Old Trafford**, home of Manchester United.

Year-round, two-hour **guided walks** (£4) can be booked at the Visitor Centre in St Peter's Square – there are usually two or three departures a week.

St Peter's Square and around

One of Manchester's boldest Victorian neo-Gothic buildings, Alfred Waterhouse's Town Hall, finished in 1877, divides the plain expanse of **St Peter's Square** from the more harmonious **Albert Square** to the north. You're free to wander inside the **Town Hall** (Mon–Fri 9am–5pm; free) and climb one of the grand staircases to the **Great Hall**, with its iron candelabras, stained-glass windows and paintings by Ford Madox Brown depicting decisive moments from Manchester's past. **Guided tours** of the building set off from the Visitor Centre (Easter–Dec every other Sat & each Wed, usually at 2pm, though times can vary; £4).

On the south side of the Town Hall, the circular **Central Library** (Mon–Thurs 10am–8pm, Fri & Sat 10am–5pm) faces St Peter's Square – built in 1934 as the largest municipal library in the world. Over on Peter Street, the **Midland Hotel** has worn well, and might tempt you in for tea and cakes in its lavish Edwardian interior. The hotel's earlier visitors ventured out for an evening's entertainment at the Italianate **Free Trade Hall** further to the west up Peter Street, original home of the city's own Hallé Orchestra. The Free Trade Hall was erected on the site of St Peter's Fields, where in 1819 eleven demonstrators were killed by the local militia during an event known as the "Peterloo Massacre".

South of St Peter's Square, Lower Mosley Street runs past the **G-Mex Centre**, now an exhibition and events centre but in use as a train station until 1969. On the other side of G-Mex rises the **Bridgewater Hall**, at the junction of Bridgewater Street. One of Britain's finest purpose-built concert halls – venue for concerts by the Hallé – this is balanced on shock-absorbing springs to guarantee clarity of sound. The other way up Mosley Street, north of St Peter's Square, rises Charles Barry's porticoed **City Art Gallery** (Ⓦ www.cityartgalleries.org.uk), where the array of high Victorian art includes the country's finest public collection of works by the Pre-Raphaelite Brotherhood. Following extensive refurbishment, the gallery has doubled in size and has a new extension linked by a glass public area to the original gallery.

Around the corner from here, the grid of streets between Princess and Charlotte streets marks the boundaries of Britain's largest **Chinatown**. To the southeast, the roads off Portland Street lead down to the Rochdale Canal, where Canal Street is the heart of Manchester's thriving **Gay Village**. Here, canalside cafés, clubs, bars and businesses have turned a formerly abandoned warehouse district into something with the verve of San Francisco.

Castlefield

Fifteen minutes' walk southwest of St Peter's Square lies **Castlefield**, Britain's first "urban heritage park". Since the early 1980s, an influx of money allied to a fair amount of speculative vision has resulted in a cobbled canalside, outdoor events arena and some attractive café-bars. Find out about its various festivals, street markets, towpaths and canal cruises at the **Castlefield Visitor Centre** at 101 Liverpool Rd (Mon–Fri 10am–4pm, Sat & Sun noon–4pm; free; ☎0161/ 834 4026, ⓦwww.castlefield.org.uk).

The castle-in-the-field itself is a **Roman fort** whose reconstructed north gate and the foundations of a few houses can be seen on Liverpool Road. This is just a hundred yards from the **Museum of Science and Industry** (daily 10am–5pm; last admission 4pm; free, admission charge for special exhibitions; ⓦwww.msim.org.uk), which mixes technological displays and special block-buster exhibitions with trenchant analysis of the social impact of industrialization. Pride of place goes to a working replica of Robert Stephenson's *Planet* – for which his father George's *Rocket* was the prototype. Built in 1830, the *Planet* reliably attained a scorching 30mph but had no brakes; the museum's version does, and uses them at weekends (usually Easter–Nov Sat & Sun noon–4pm; Dec–Easter Sun only; small charge), dropping passengers a quarter-mile away at the **world's oldest passenger railway station**. A reconstructed Victorian sewer below the station illustrates the problems of sanitation in the 1870s, when poor areas were still using street-end standpipes. There's also a hands-on science centre and interactive gallery, and displays dealing with fibres, fabrics and fashion, while the museum's comprehensive selection of carding machines, bobbin threaders and cotton looms crash into action at weekends in the Textile Gallery. Another glimpse into the past is provided by **Warehouse for the World**, a sound-and-light show (free) which delves into the history of the warehouses whose goods fuelled Manchester's early wealth.

Along Deansgate to the cathedral

Central **Deansgate** cuts through the city from the canal to the cathedral. South of Peter Street, the **Peter's Fields** development has transformed a magnificent sweep of late-nineteenth-century warehousing into the **Great Northern** commercial and leisure complex. North along Deansgate, past Peter Street, keep an eye out for modern **Lincoln Square** (tucked between Queen and Brazenose streets), named after its standing statue of the American President. Across Deansgate, opposite Brazenose Street, is the beautifully detailed **John Rylands Library** (Mon–Fri 10am–5.30pm, Sat 10am–1pm; free; guided tours Wed noon; £1; ⓦwww.rylibweb.man.ac.uk), the city's supreme example of Victorian Gothic. Venture inside to see the superb interior – carved and burnished wood, Art Nouveau metalwork, delicately crafted stone and stained glass. From the library, continue up Deansgate and left into Bridge Street to reach the **People's History Museum** (Tues–Sun 11am–4.30pm; £1, free on Fri; ⓦwww.peopleshistorymuseum.org.uk), an exhibition recording the lives and protests of England's working class over the last two hundred years.

St Ann's Square is tucked away off the eastern side of Deansgate, a couple of blocks up from John Dalton Street. Crowning glory of the square is the **Royal Exchange**, which houses the famous **Royal Exchange Theatre**, the country's largest theatre-in-the-round, whose steel-and-glass cat's cradle sits plonked under the building's immense glass-domed roof. Formerly the Cotton Exchange, this building employed seven thousand people until trading finished on December 31, 1968 – the old trading board still shows the last day's prices for American and Egyptian cotton.

Deansgate ends with the small, Perpendicular **Cathedral** (daily 7.30am–6pm; free organ recitals Thurs at 1pm), the third church on this site since its foundation in the ninth century. A fragment of stone by the choir and a four-teenth-century arch by the tower are all that remain of the earlier structures, and in truth it's been hacked about too much to have any real coherence – the famed widest nave in England (114ft, as opposed to York Minster's 106ft) is entirely a result of rich families adding side chapels to the fifteenth-century church, which were later opened out to provide space for Manchester's burgeoning population of worshippers. The cathedral's choristers are trained in **Chetham's Hospital School**, across the way on Long Millgate (ask at the porter's lodge for entrance), whose oak-panelled **library** (Mon–Fri 9am–12.30pm & 1.30–4.30pm) is a real delight. Someone is usually on hand to show you the restored reading room, with the windowed alcove where, it's claimed, Marx and Engels used to study.

The area around the cathedral is being refashioned as the city's **Millennium Quarter**, with the six-storey **Urbis** at its core. This hi-tech visitor centre (due to open during 2002) explores the experience of the planet's cities – Manchester, naturally, claimed as the world's first industrial city – through a series of interactive exhibits.

Exchange Square and around

Just to the north of St Ann's Square, **Exchange Square** sits at the heart of the ambitious city-centre rebuilding programme launched following the devastating bomb of 1996. A pedestrian boulevard – **New Cathedral Street** – runs from St Ann's Square to the Cathedral, skirting the flanks of the flagship **Marks & Spencer** store whose gigantic glazed facade makes up the south side of Exchange Square. Two historic pubs, the *Old Wellington Inn* and *Sinclair's Oyster Bar*, both moved brick-by-brick to this new site, mop up some of the foot traffic at their outdoor tables.

To the north, the old **Corn Exchange** has been refurbished completely, while retaining its historic facade and glass dome. Relaunched as the **Triangle** (reflecting the unusual shape of its interior), this is a rare wrong foot in the brave new Manchester: gone any sense of the building's tradition, replaced by yet another batch of retail outlets selling expensive shoes and Japanese rice bowls. Across Withy Grove, meanwhile, the former Mirror Building contains the futuristic **Printworks**, an adult "entertainment centre", complete with IMAX screen, cinema megaplex and various themed bars and restaurants.

Piccadilly Gardens and the Northern Quarter

For years, the bleak expanse of **Piccadilly Gardens** divided rather than united the city, though a recent beautification project has dramatically enhanced its character. The gardens are the gateway to the still shabby but improving Oldham Street, which has been adopted by "alternative" entrepreneurs who have dubbed it the **Northern Quarter**. Traditionally, this is Manchester's garment district and you'll still find shops and wholesalers selling high-street fashions, shop fittings, mannequins and hosiery, but there are also new design outlets, lots of music stores, and some funky bars and cafés. The excellent **Manchester Craft and Design Centre**, 17 Oak St (Mon–Sat 10am–5.30pm; free), is a great place to pick up ceramics, fabrics, earthenware, jewellery and decorative art, or just sip a drink in the cosy café.

Oxford Road and points south

From St Peter's Square, **Oxford Road** – initially Oxford Street – stretches to Rusholme (by which time it's become Wilmslow Road) and the leafy suburbs beyond. At its northern end, the **Cornerhouse** is the dynamo of the Manchester arts scene, with its cinema screens and three floors of gallery space (Tues–Sat 11am–6pm, Sun 2–6pm; free). From across the road (outside the

Palace Hotel), an endless stream of buses runs down Oxford Road, passing the buildings and sights detailed below.

Newest addition is the **Manchester Aquatics Centre** (Mon–Fri 6.30am–10pm, Sat 7am–6pm, Sun 7am–10pm; £2.50), at Booth Street, whose two fifty-metre pools under a wave-shaped roof were built with the Commonwealth Games in mind. This is under ten minutes' walk from the Cornerhouse, while another ten minutes along Oxford Road brings you to the Gothic Revival building housing the **Manchester Museum** (Mon–Sat 10am–5pm; free; ⓦwww.museum.man.ac.uk). At the centre of the Egyptology world since the 1890s, the museum has done pioneering work on mummy dissection and captivating displays enlarge upon the burial practices and techniques that their work has revealed. Rocks, minerals, fossils and natural history also get their own exhibition space, while the top-floor Science for Life section concentrates on the human body and biomedical research.

Another half-mile away is the city's modern art collection, housed in the red-brick **Whitworth Gallery** (Mon–Sat 10am–5pm, Sun 2–5pm; free; ⓦwww.whitworth.man.ac.uk). The gallery forms two distinct halves, "historic" and modern, with its pre-1880 historic collection incorporating a strong assembly of watercolours by Turner, Constable, Cox and Blake. The modern collection concentrates on post-1880 British staples, with Moore, Frink and Hepworth setting off contributions from lesser-known artists. With Manchester's cotton connections it is perhaps not surprising that the gallery also displays the country's widest range of textiles outside London's Victoria and Albert Museum. Walk two hundred yards south of the Whitworth Gallery and you'll catch the pungent spicy smell of **Rusholme**'s Wilmslow Road, a "golden mile" of curry houses, sari shops and Asian grocers. In **Platt Fields Park**, at the south end of the curry mile (just past *Hardy's Well* pub), the **Gallery of Costume** (daily 10am–5.30pm; free) fills Georgian Platt Hall. Its collection spans fashion through the ages, giving particular emphasis to Manchester's former role as a textile centre, its large Asian population and the clothes of the working class.

Salford Quays and Trafford

The Metrolink extension to **Salford Quays** provides easy access to one of the city's first urban development projects. For ninety years, from 1894 when the Manchester Ship Canal opened, the Salford docks turned the city into one of Britain's busiest ports. Trade declined in the 1970s and the docks eventually closed in 1982, since which time the Salford Quays development has transformed the run-down quays on the western edge of the city centre into a waterfront residential and leisure complex.

Various Metrolink stations serve the area: for the **Salford Quays tourist information office** (Mon–Fri 8.30am–4.30pm, Sun 10am–4pm; ☎0161/848 8601) get off at Salford Quays station. You can pick up a map here and wander down the Centenary Walkway quayside, which ends at **The Lowry** (daily from 9.30am; free; ⓦwww.thelowry.com), the Quays' shining steel arts centre whose theatres, galleries (Mon–Wed & Sun 11am–5pm, Thurs–Sat 11am–8pm; free) and creative ArtWorks exhibition (Mon–Fri 10am–3pm, Sat & Sun 10am–4pm; £3.75) have quickly become one of Manchester's leading attractions; to travel straight here, stay on the Metrolink until Broadway. The centre, of course, takes its name from L.S. Lowry and no artist is more closely linked with an English city than Lowry is with Manchester – there's always a selection of Lowry works here on show for free.

A footbridge runs from The Lowry across to the Trafford side of the docks where rises the **Imperial War Museum North** (ⓦwww.iwm.org.uk/north), scheduled to open during 2002. This, too, is a dramatic structure, whose three "shards" of fractured steel represent the world's conflicts on land, sea and in the air. It's as resonant in its way as the other great building which looms in the near distance, **Old Trafford**, the self-styled "Theatre of Dreams" and home of Manchester United, arguably the most famous team in the world. **Tours** of Old Trafford and its museum (daily 9.30am–5pm; £8.50; museum only £5.50; advance booking essential, ☎0161/877 8631, ⓦwww.manutd.com) placate out-of-town fans who want to gawp at the silverware, sit in the dug-out and visit the *Red Café*. To get here, take the Metrolink to Old Trafford station and walk up Warwick Road to Sir Matt Busby Way.

Eating, drinking and nightlife

Second only to London in the breadth and scope of its **cafés** and **restaurants**, Manchester has something to suit everyone, from a cheap curry to a night out in a celebrity-chef hotspot. The bulk of Manchester's eating and drinking places are scattered around the city centre – Chinatown, in particular, can always be counted upon for a budget lunch or a late-night meal – while out at Rusholme you'll find the best range of curries this side of the Pennines. Meanwhile, Manchester's **café-bar** scene is its pride and joy. Many of those in the Gay Village, the Northern Quarter and Castlefield are reasonably laidback, though evenings always see the atmosphere ratcheted up a notch; while at the half-dozen places along Deansgate Locks (Whitworth Street West) or in the Printworks (Withy Grove) the emphasis is more on serious partying. Manchester also has a full complement of great **pubs**, including several Victorian classics that have stood the test of time.

For over two decades now, Manchester has been vying with London as Britain's capital of **youth culture**. Banks of fly posters advertise what's going on in the numerous **clubs**; the most enduring are listed below and you can expect to pay £3–15 cover depending on what's on. Manchester has an excellent **live music** scene, with tickets for local bands usually under £5, more like £10–15 for someone you've heard of. Mega-star gigs take place either at **the G-Mex Centre**, Windmill Street (☎0161/834 2700, ⓦwww.g-mex.co.uk), the **Manchester Apollo,** Stockport Road, Ardwick Green (☎0161/242 2560) or the **Manchester Evening News Arena,** Victoria Station, 21 Hunts Bank (☎0161/950 5000). For the broadest coverage of Manchester's musical happenings, check the fortnightly *City Life* magazine or Friday's *Manchester Evening News*.

Cafés and café-bars

Atlas 376 Deansgate. Wood-panel the inside of an old railway arch, add bamboo thickets to a large urban patio and you've got one of the best café-bars in the city.

Barça Arch 8 & 9, Catalan Square. Trendy Castlefield bar/restaurant tucked into the restored railway arches, with a lovely canalside terrace and cosy lounge with fire.

Café Pop 34–36 Oldham St. Retro café full of 70s' kitsch and pop collectables, with the emphasis on veggie fry-ups and hefty sandwiches. Closed Sun.

Cornerhouse 70 Oxford St. Soups, dips, sandwiches and cakes in the first-floor café (daily until 8pm); arty bar downstairs.

Dry Bar 28–30 Oldham St. The earliest of the designer café-bars on the scene, and catalyst for much of what has gone in the Northern Quarter, *Dry* is still as cool as they come.

Eighth Day 107–111 Oxford Rd. Manchester's oldest organic-vegetarian café, with shop, takeaway and juice bar upstairs, café/restaurant downstairs.

KroBar 325 Oxford Rd, opposite Manchester University Students' Union. Half the students in the city crowd into this huge café-bar for value-for-money food, caffeine and a vast range of on-tap beers.

Love Saves the Day Smithfield Building, Tib St. New York style and sass in this Northern Quarter deli-café, where a menu of platters, salads, pasta and sandwiches keep the locals happy. Closed Sun.

Manto 46 Canal St. Gay Village stalwart whose chic crowd laps up the cool sounds and club nights. A canalside Sunday brunch is a treat here.

Metz 3 Brazil St. Classy converted warehouse bar and restaurant. It's great for a pre-club drink or two and its Eastern European food's not bad either.

Mumbo 35a King St. The city's first tea-bar, with sipping and eating on three floors – the coolest perch being the year-round roof-terrace for unique views of St Ann's Church.

Prague V 40 Chorlton St. Gay-friendly hangout on the Canal Street corner, with Czech beer, Mediterranean-inspired meals and snacks, and a late weekend drinks licence.

Velvet 2 Canal St. The redbrick facade hides a stylish, laid-back basement cavern, with good food, outrageous staff, campy clientele and late-night sounds.

Restaurants

Armenian Taverna Albert Square ☎0161/834 9025. Filling meze platters (for vegetarians too) and grilled kebabs are the best deal here. Closed Mon. Moderate.

Dimitri's 1 Campfield Arcade, Deansgate ☎0161/839 3319. Pick and mix from the Greek/Spanish/Italian menu (particularly good for vegetarians), and grab an arcade table. Moderate.

The Lead Station 99 Beech Rd, Chorlton ☎0161/881 5559. Café, bar and restaurant – all three experiences gell in this art-filled spot with a decked rear courtyard. Inexpensive to Moderate.

Lime Tree 8 Lapwing Lane, West Didsbury ☎0161/445 1217. Acclaimed restaurant that char-grills and oven-roasts as if its life depended on it. Closed Mon & Sat lunch, & Sun dinner. Moderate to Expensive.

Little Yang Sing 17 George St, ☎0161/228 7722. Celebrated basement restaurant (forerunner to the larger *Yang Sing*) where the emphasis is on good-value *dim sum*, rice and noodle dishes. Moderate.

The Nose 6 Lapwing Lane, West Didsbury ☎0161/445 3653. Soothing neighbourhood wine bar-café, perfect for a bagel or croissant breakfast, wraps and ciabatta sandwiches, or bistro meals. Inexpensive.

Penang Village 56 Faulkner St ☎0161/236 2650. Friendly Malaysian joint. *Ayam percik* (bar-becued chicken with a curry sauce), beef rendang and veg curry are all recommended. Closed Mon. Moderate.

Le Petit Blanc 55 King St ☎0161/832 1001. Best place in the city for reasonably priced classic and regional French cooking is Raymond Blanc's mid-range brasserie operation. Moderate.

Reform King St, Spring Gardens ☎0161/839 9966. The city's great and good have adopted *Reform* as their pet restaurant, revelling in its spiffy French-inspired food. Closed Sun. Expensive.

Shere Khan IFCO Centre, 52 Wilmslow Rd, Rusholme ☎0161/256 2624. Big Indian brasserie – the grill dispenses marvellous kebabs, or try the *karahi* and *biryani* dishes. Inexpensive to Moderate.

Simply Heathcote's Jackson Row ☎0161/835 3536. Lancastrian chef Paul Heathcote mixes Mediterranean and local flavours, so expect updat-ed working-class dishes alongside the parmesan shavings. Expensive.

Wagamama The Printworks, Corporation St/Withy Grove ☎0161/839 5916. Ace Japanese noodle bar, where you'll quickly learn to tell your *ramen* from your *udon*. Inexpensive.

Wong Chu 63 Faulkner St ☎0161/236 2346. No-frills, paper-tablecloth joint which serves up enor-mous portions of Cantonese staples at bargain prices. Inexpensive.

Yang Sing 34 Princess St ☎0161/236 2200. One of the best Cantonese restaurants in the country, with thoroughly authentic food, from a lunchtime plate of fried noodles to the full works. Moderate to Expensive.

Pubs

The Beer House 6 Angel St. The best place for ale-tasting, with a constant stock of more than thirty brands of beer.

Britons Protection 50 Great Bridgewater St. Elegantly decorated traditional pub opposite Bridgewater Hall, with a couple of cosy, smoky rooms and a brickyard beer garden.

Circus Tavern 86 Portland St. Manchester's smallest pub – a Victorian drinking-hole that's many peoples' favourite city-centre pit-stop.

Dukes '92 Castle St. Former stableblock for goods' horses on the Duke of Bridgewater's canal in Castlefield, now classily revamped. Serves a wide range of pâtés and cheeses.

Marble Arch 73 Rochdale Rd. Real-ale house, whose own Marble Brewery produces some fine brews – the seasonal "Ginger Marble" or the strong "Chocolate Heavy" among them.

The Mark Addy 2 Stanley St. Mainly known for its food, the Mark Addy serves a choice of fifty cheeses and eight pâtés (including vegetarian).

The gay scene

Manchester has one of Britain's most vibrant gay scenes, centred on the Rochdale Canal between Princess and Sackville streets, in the so-called **Gay Village**. Although the annual Mardi Gras carnival bit the dust a while back, it's been replaced by a smaller scale **Gayfest**, held every August bank holiday in and around the village. Other events, including an annual arts festival every May/June, are co-ordinated by **queerupnorth** (information on ☎0161/833 2288, ⓦ www.queerupnorth.com).

Out on the town, early evenings kick off at one of the **café-bars** along Canal Street – *Manto*, *Metz*, *Bar 38*, *Spirit*, or *Velvet* – at the extravagant *Via Fossa* pub or at the more macho *New Union*, 111 Princess St, just off Canal Street. An older crowd drinks in the *Rembrandt Hotel*; *Vanilla* on Richmond Street is a women's café-bar with club nights. **Clubs** include *Essential*, 8 Minshull St (☎0161/237 5445); *Cruz*, 101 Princess St (☎0161/237 1554); the *Hollywood Showbar*, 100 Bloom Street (☎0161/236 6151); and *Follies*, 6 Whitworth St (☎0161/236 8149), a lesbian favourite. And the *Paradise Factory*, 112–116 Princess St (☎0161/273 5422) can always be counted on, too.

For further **information**, call the Lesbian and Gay Foundation (daily 4–10pm; ☎0161/235 8000, ⓦ www.lgfoundation.org.uk).

Mr Thomas' Chop House 52 Cross St. Victorian classic with a Dickensian feel to its nooks and crannies and traditional English "chop-house" food (oysters, bubble and squeak, etc).

The Paramount Oxford Street, at Portland Street. A Wetherspoon's drinking emporium with a sizzling choice of beers, ales and wines, and room to swing a thousand cats.

Peveril of the Peak 127 Great Bridgewater St. The pub that time forgot – one of Manchester's best real-ale houses, with some superb Victorian glazed tilework outside.

Rain Bar 80 Great Bridgewater St. Pub or bar? Experience both, drinking inside the stripped-wood pubby interior, up in the swish bar, or out on the sweeping canalside terraces.

Via Fossa 28–30 Canal St. The elaborate mock-Gothic rooms pack in a high-energy (largely gay) crowd.

Clubs and live music

Band on the Wall 25 Swan St ☎0161/832 6625, ⓦ www.bandonthewall.com. Cosy Northern Quarter joint with a great reputation for its live bands – world and folk to jazz and reggae – and club nights.

The Brickhouse 6 Whitworth St West ☎0161/236 4418. Indie, techno, Seventies, Eighties or glam, depending on the night.

Generation X 11–13 New Wakefield St ☎0161/236 4899, ⓦ www.mantogroup.com. Stylish, studenty café-bar – "eat, drink, slack, loaf" – known for its club nights.

Jilly's Rockworld 65 Oxford St ☎0161/236 9971, ⓦ www.jillys.co.uk. Classic and modern rock, Goth and Indie nights, live bands and club nights.

Manchester Academy 269 Oxford Rd, on the university campus ☎0161/275 2930, ⓦ www.umu.man.ac.uk. Popular student venue for new and established bands.

Manchester Roadhouse 8–10 Newton St ☎0161/237 9789 www.theroadhouse.u-net.com. Regular and varied gigs by local bands seeking glory, and a succession of fine club nights.

Paradise Factory 112–116 Princess St ☎0161/273 5422. One of the hottest clubs on the scene, now fabulously refurbished.

Planet K 46–50 Oldham St ☎0161/839 9941. Indie and student nights, underground sounds, drum and bass, depends on the night.

Sankey's Soap Beehive Mill, Jersey St, Ancoats ☎0161/661 9668, ⓦ www.tribalgathering.co.uk. Many peoples' favourite Friday and Saturday night out, brought to you by the Tribal Gathering crew.

South 4a South King St ☎0161/831 7756. Could be playing anything, depending on the night, from funk, 70s disco and house to punk or Northern Soul. Closed Sun and Mon.

Star & Garter 18–20 Fairfield St ☎0161/273 6726, ⓦ www.starandgarter.co.uk. Thrash/punk pub venue for loud, young bands and Saturday club nights; late bar until 2am.

Arts and culture

Manchester is blessed with the North's most highly regarded **orchestra**, the Hallé, which is resident at the Bridgewater Hall. The Cornerhouse is the local **arts** mainstay, while a full range of mainstream and fringe **theatres** produce a year-round programme of events. The **Printworks**, Manchester's urban entertainment complex, contains the twenty-screen **Filmworks** cinema as well as an IMAX (giant-screen) cinema, while art-house screenings are at the Cornerhouse. The biggest annual fest is the **Manchester Festival**, an arts and TV extravaganza, with events in the city's clubs, theatres and open spaces. The X.Trax/Streets Ahead Festival showcases live theatre, music and entertainment, while other annual **events** include the city's Irish Festival, Jazz Festival, and Food and Drink Festival.

Bridgewater Hall Lower Mosley St ☏0161/907 9000, ⊛www.bridgewater-hall.co.uk. Home of the Hallé (founded 1857); also chamber, classical and jazz concerts.

The Comedy Store Deansgate Locks, Whitworth St West ☏08705/932932, ⊛www.thecomedys-tore.co.uk. Nationwide stand-up comedy talent, with gigs every Wed–Sat.

Contact Theatre 15 Oxford Rd ☏0161/274 3434, ⊛www.contact-theatre.org.uk. One of the most innovative theatre companies, housed in provocatively designed premises.

Cornerhouse 70 Oxford St ☏0161/200 1500, ⊛www.cornerhouse.org. Engaging arts centre, with three cinema screens, art exhibitions, recitals, talks, bookshop, café and bar.

Dancehouse Theatre 10 Oxford Rd ☏0161/237 9753. Home of the Northern Ballet School, and venue for dance, drama and comedy.

The Filmworks Printworks, Exchange Square ☏08700/102030, ⊛www.thefilmworks.co.uk.

State-of-the-art cinema-going – twenty screens, digital projection and comfortable seating.

Green Room 54–56 Whitworth St West ☏0161/950 5900. Rapidly changing fringe programme which includes theatre, dance, mime and cabaret.

Library Theatre St Peter's Square ☏0161/236 7110, ⊛www.libtheatreco.org.net. Classic drama and new writing, in an intimate theatre beneath the Central Library.

The Lowry Pier 8, Salford Quays ☏0161/876 2000, ⊛www.thelowry. com. Full, year-round programme of music events, from opera to country.

Royal Exchange Theatre St Ann's Square ☏0161/833 9833, ⊛www.royalexchange.co.uk. The most famous stage in the city – there's a Studio Theatre (for works by new writers) alongside the main stage.

Royal Northern College of Music (RNCM) 124 Oxford Rd ☏0161/907 5278, ⊛www.rncm.ac.uk. Stages top-quality classical and modern-jazz concerts.

Listings

Airport General enquiries ☏0161/489 3000; flight enquiries ☏0161/489 8000.

Banks and exchange There are ATMs in the city centre shopping streets, as well as in the student areas along Oxford and Wilmslow roads, and in Piccadilly station. Late-night exchanges are at the airport (6am–midnight) and at the Castlefield YHA (daily 7am–11pm); at other times head for: American Express, 10–12 St Mary's Gate (☏0161/833 7303); or Thomas Cook, 22 Cross St (☏0161/839 0832) and 2 Oxford St (☏0161/251 7200).

Bookshops The main chains have outlets on Deansgate and around St Ann's Square. Blackwell's academic bookshop is in the Precinct Centre, Oxford Rd; Sportspages, the sports specialist, is in Barton Square, off St Ann's Square; Gibb's Bookshop, 10 Charlotte St, is great for second-hand books.

Bus information For all city services, call GMPTE on ☏0161/228 7811 or visit ⊛www.gmpte.gov.uk; for intercity services, call National Express on ☏08705/808 080.

Car rental Avis, 1 Ducie St, Piccadilly ☏0161/236 6716 or 436 2020 (airport); Budget, 384 Hyde Rd, Belle Vue ☏0161/231 7100 or 437 0151 (airport); easyRentacar ☏0906/586 0586; Europcar, 41–45 Great Ancoats St ☏0161/236 0311or 436 2200 (airport); Hertz, 31 Aytoun St ☏0161/236 2747 or 437 8208 (airport).

Dentist Dental Hospital of Manchester, Higher Cambridge St ☏0161/275 6666.

Hospital Manchester Royal Infirmary, 13 Oxford Rd ☏0161/276 1234.

Internet easyEverything, 18 Exchange St, St Ann's Square (24hr); Net-Works Centre at the Central Library (Mon, Tues & Thurs 10am–7.30pm, Wed

1–7.30pm, Fri & Sat 10am–4.30pm).

Laundry Several along Wilmslow Road in Rusholme, or you could use the facilities at the YHA hostel.

Left Luggage Chorlton Street coach station (daily 9.30am–5.30pm); or, expensively, at Piccadilly train station, platform 5 (Mon–Fri 8am–10pm, Sat 9am–9pm, Sun 10am–8pm).

Pharmacy Boots, 11–13 Piccadilly Gardens (℡0161/834 8244) and 20 St Ann's St (℡0161/839 1798); Cameolord Ltd, 7 Oxford St (daily 8am–midnight; ℡0161/236 1445).

Police Greater Manchester Police HQ, Chester House, Boyer St ℡0161/872 5050.

Post Office 29 Spring Gardens; 63 Newton St (℡08457/223344). The Spring Gardens office has a *bureau de change* and poste-restante section (Mon–Sat 8.30am-6pm).

Taxis Mantax ℡0161/236 5133; Taxifone ℡0161/236 9974. Airtax (for the airport) ℡0161/499 9000.

Travel Agents STA Travel, 75 Deansgate and 14 Oxford Rd ℡0161/834 0668; Trailfinders, 58 Deansgate ℡0161/839 6969. Also USIT Campus: at YHA shop, Deansgate ℡0161/833 2046; at UMIST, Sackville St ℡0161/200 3278); and at Manchester Academy, Oxford Rd ℡0161/274 3105.

Chester

In 1779 Boswell wrote to Samuel Johnson: "Chester pleases me more than any town I ever saw." **CHESTER**, forty miles southwest of Manchester, has changed since then, but not so much. A glorious two-mile ring of medieval and Roman walls encircle a neat kernel of Tudor and Victorian buildings, including the unique raised arcades called the "Rows". Very much the commercial hub of its county, Chester has enough in the way of sights, restaurants and atmosphere to make it an enjoyable base for a couple of days.

In 79 AD the Romans built Deva Castra here, their largest known fortress in Britain. Later, Ethelfleda, the daughter of King Alfred the Great, extended and refortified the place, only to have it brutally sacked by William the Conqueror's armies. Trade routes to Ireland made Chester the most prosperous port in the northwest, a status it recovered after the English Civil War, which saw a two-year-long siege of the town at the hands of the Parliamentarians. By the middle of the eighteenth century, however, silting of the port had forced the Irish trade to be rerouted first through Parkgate on the Dee estuary, and then to Liverpool. Things improved a little with the Industrial Revolution, as the canal and railway networks made Chester an important regional trading centre, a function it still retains.

Arrival and information

National Express and most regional bus services (including the hourly #X8 from Liverpool) arrive at **Chester bus station**, between Delamere and George streets. Most other local buses use the **bus exchange** just behind the town hall, off Princess Street. Merseyrail **trains** from Liverpool (every 20–30min 6am–11pm; 45min) and all other services call at the **train station**, northeast of the centre, from where it's a ten-minute walk down City Road and along Foregate Street to the central Eastgate Clock. There's a **tourist office** in the Town Hall (May–Oct Mon–Sat 9am–5.30pm, Sun 10am–4pm; Nov–April Mon–Sat 10am–5pm) and also the **Chester Visitor Centre**, on Vicars Lane opposite the amphitheatre (May–Oct Mon–Sat 9am–5.30pm, Sun 10am–4pm; Nov–April Mon–Sat 10am–5pm, Sun 10am–4pm), both with the same telephone enquiries number and website (℡01244/402111, ⓦwww .chestercc.gov.uk).

Accommodation

In high summer **B&B accommodation** can be in short supply, as can space in the more characterful old inns. The places reviewed below are the best of the central choices: if you arrive late, or strike out in the centre, there are lots of budget-rated B&Bs along Brook Street, just a couple of minutes from the train station, and several moderate hotels down City Road, also near the station. Pleasant Victorian B&Bs also line up along Hough Green, a fifteen-minute walk from the centre.

Hotels and B&Bs

Blossom's Hotel St John St ☎01244/346433, ⓦwww.heritage-hotels.com. Seventeenth-century town house with a variety of rooms,. Good full-board rates available. ❻

Castle House 23 Castle St ☎01244/350345. B&B in a sixteenth-century house with good facilities; bang in the centre and excellent value for money. No credit cards. ❷

The Chester Grosvenor Eastgate St ☎01244/324024, ⓦwww.chestergrosvenor.co.uk. Superbly appointed luxury hotel bristling with liveried staff, very comfortable bedrooms and two fine restaurants. Weekdays ❾, weekends ❽.

Chester Town House 23 King St ☎01244/350021, ⓦwww.chestertownhouse.co.uk. A very high-standard B&B in a comfortably furnished seventeenth-century town house. There are five en-suite rooms and private parking. ❸

Commercial Hotel St Peter's Church Yard ☎01244/320749. Friendly Georgian inn with good beer and half-a-dozen pleasant rooms in a brick-walled churchyard. ❷

Grosvenor Place Guest House 2–4 Grosvenor Place ☎01244/324455. Pleasant town house B&B in a good location near the museum. Rooms available with and without shower. ❷

Mill Hotel Milton St ☎01244/350035, ⓦwww.millhotel.com. Sensitive warehouse conversion on the canal, not far from the train station. Rooms with balcony attract a small supplement. ❺

Pied Bull Northgate St ☎01244/325829. Characterful old coaching inn, close to the walls and cathedral. ❷

Youth Hostel

Youth Hostel Hough Green House, 40 Hough Green ☎01244/680056, ⓦwww.yha.org.uk. Twenty-minutes' walk from the centre, this Victorian house has a cafeteria, games room, and coin-op laundry facilities; family rooms available.

The City

Walking tours – assorted Roman, historic and ghost trails – from the Town Hall tourist office and from the Vicar Lane Visitor Centre (May–Oct twice daily; Nov–April once daily; £3) aren't a bad way to orient yourself. The main thoroughfares of Chester's Roman grid plan meet at **the Cross**, where the town crier welcomes visitors to the city (May–Aug Tues–Sat at noon). Both sides of all four streets are lined by **the Rows**, unique galleried arcades running on top of the ground-floor shops. The engaging black-and-white tableau is a blend of genuine Tudor houses and Victorian half-timbered imitations, with the finest Tudor buildings on Watergate Street – though Eastgate Street is perhaps the most picturesque, leading to the filigree **Eastgate Clock**, erected atop a sandstone arch to commemorate Victoria's Diamond Jubilee.

You can get an insight into Chester's Roman heritage at **Deva Roman Experience** tucked away up Pierpoint Lane, off Bridge Street (daily 9am–5pm; £3.95). North of the Cross, the neo-Gothic town hall dominates its square at the end of Northgate Street across from the heavily restored **Cathedral** (daily 7.30am–6pm; free tours Mon–Sat 2.30pm, donation requested; ⓦwww.chestercathedral.co.uk). Taking the role of cathedral in 1541 after the Dissolution of the Monasteries, this Benedictine church is dedicated to St Werburgh, a seventh-century Anglo-Saxon princess who became Chester's patron saint. Parts of the eleventh-century structure can still be seen in the north transept but the highlights are the fourteenth-century choir stalls, with their intricately carved misericords.

East of the cathedral, steps provide access to the top of the two-mile girdle of the medieval and Roman **city walls** – the most complete set in Britain. You can walk past all its towers, turrets and gateways in an hour or two, including the **Water Tower** at the northwest corner, which once stood in the river – evidence of the changes brought about by the gradual silting of the River Dee. South from the Water Tower you'll see the **Roodee**, England's oldest racecourse, laid out on a silted tidal pool where Roman ships once unloaded wine, figs and olive oil from the Mediterranean.

Until nineteenth-century excavation work, much of the wall near the Water Tower was propped up by scores of sculpted tomb panels and engraved headstones, items probably used to rebuild the walls in a hurry in the turbulent fourth century. Many are now on display at the **Grosvenor Museum**, 27 Grosvenor St (Mon–Sat 10.30am–5pm, Sun 2–5pm; free), just inside the city walls near the southern end of the Roodee. This is the best investigation of Roman Chester, with good displays about the legionary system, city buildings, grave sites, defences, daily life and culture. The back of the museum opens into a preserved Georgian house complete with furnished kitchen, parlour, bedrooms, rickety floors and sloping stairs. Across the traffic roundabout on Castle Street, the **Cheshire Military Museum** (daily 10am–5pm; £2.50; @www .chester.ac.uk/militarymuseum) inhabits part of the same complex as the Norman **Chester Castle** (Easter–Sept daily 10am–6pm; Oct–Easter daily 10am–4pm; free; EH). Though the castle was founded by William the Conqueror, most of what you see today is little older than the eighteenth-century Greek Revival Assize Courts and council offices on the same site, the building of which led to the demolition of much of the medieval structure.

South of the castle, the wall is buried under the street, but it rises again alongside the **Roman Gardens** (unrestricted access) on Souters Lane at Little John Street, where Roman foundations and columns dug up during redevelopment are on display. Across the road stands the half-excavated remains of the **Roman Amphitheatre** (Easter–Sept daily 10am–6pm; Oct–Easter daily 10am–1pm & 2–4pm; free; EH); it is estimated to have held seven thousand spectators, making it the largest amphitheatre in Britain, but the stonework is barely head-high now.

The partly ruined pink-stone **Church of St John the Baptist** (daily 9.15am–6pm), a little to the east in Grosvenor Park, was founded by the Saxon king Ethelred in 689 and briefly served as the cathedral of Mercia. Its romantic eastern ruins were left to deteriorate having been cut off from the rest of the church after the Reformation. Steps from the church gardens and from the southern edge of the city walls lead to the tree-shaded **Groves**, on the banks of the Dee, with its bandstand, slender iron footbridge and villas overlooking the willows draped along the opposite bank. Bithells Boats (☎01244/325394, @www.showboatsofchester.co.uk) runs half-hour **cruises** on the river (every 15min; April–Oct 10am–5pm; Nov–March Sat & Sun 11am–4pm; £4) and two-hour trips in the summer (Wed & Sat 11am & 8pm, rest of week 11am only).

Eating, drinking and entertainment

You can't walk more than a few paces in Chester without coming across somewhere good to **eat and drink**, as often as not housed in a medieval crypt or Tudor building. Some of the **pubs** are highly atmospheric and most serve bar meals. A batch of annual **festivals** keeps the town's concert halls and churches busy: the Folk Festival in May, Young Musician's Festival in June and the renowned **Summer Music Festival** every July, which sees outdoor concerts and fireworks in Grosvenor Park, as well as a simultaneous Fringe Festival. There's also a Literature Festival in October.

△ Blackpool

Cafés and restaurants

Alexander's Jazz Theatre and Café Bar 2 Rufus Court ☏01244/340005. Continental-style café-bar with tapas from the counter and live music or comedy nightly. Inexpensive.

Boulevard de la Bastille Bridge St Row. One of the nicest of the arcade cafés, doing a roaring trade in breakfasts, pastries and sandwiches. Inexpensive.

Cathedral Refectory Chester Cathedral, St Werburgh St. Bistro-style dishes served in the thirteenth-century monks' dining room. Closed Sun. Inexpensive.

Chez Jules 69 Northgate St ☏01244/400014. Classic brasserie menu – vegetable cassoulet, Toulouse sausage, or rib-eye steak, all served with dauphinois potatoes. Inexpensive.

The Mediterranean Restaurant 1 Rufus Court, off Northgate St ☏01244/320004. Georgian house with a sunny courtyard garden, serving tapas, pasta, fish, paella and meze. Moderate.

Ristorante Sergio 87 St Werburgh St ☏01244/314663. Popular with a party crowd, this pizzeria-restaurant serves speciality fish and vegetarian dishes. Moderate.

Ruan Orchid 14 Lower Bridge St ☏01244/400661. Their huge menu ranges across all the Thai regions – good for red and green curries, duck dishes and noodles. Moderate.

La Tasca 6–12 Cuppin St ☏01244/400887. Huge tapas selection – Spanish cheeses to grilled prawns – and paella too. Inexpensive to Moderate.

Pubs

Albion Inn corner of Albion and Park streets. Victorian terraced pub in the shadow of the walls with renowned "real British" bar food.

The Boat House The Groves. A riverside pub, decked out with black and white prints of nineteenth-century fishing families, and serving a great selection of ales.

Boot Inn Eastgate Row. A characterful pub in the upper gallery with a back room where fourteen Roundheads were killed, and a highbacked seat once used by soliciting prostitutes.

The Falcon Lower Bridge St. This half-timbered pub was once a town house built by the Grosvenor family by enclosing part of a Row.

Old Harkers Arms 1 Russell St, below the City Road bridge. Canalside real-ale boozer imaginatively sited in a former warehouse.

Chester Zoo

Chester's most popular attraction, **Chester Zoo** (daily: April–Sept 10am–6pm; Oct–March 10am–4pm; last admission 2hr before closing; £10; Ⓦ www .chesterzoo.org), is the second largest in Britain and one of the best in Europe, with new attractions opening all the time. The zoo is well known for its conservation projects and has had notable success with its Asiatic lions, while recent additions include the giant komodo dragons – Chester is the only British zoo to support these creatures – and a new jaguar enclosure. Animals are grouped by region in large paddocks viewed from a maze of pathways or from the creeping monorail, with main attractions being the baby animals (elephants, giraffes and orang-utans), the rainforest habitat, the Twilight Zone bat cave and the Chimpanzee Forest. The zoo entrance is signposted off the A41 to the north of town and reached by buses #4, #14 or #40 (Mon–Sat; every 30min) from Chester's bus exchange, or the #11c and #12c (every 30min, Sun & public holidays) to Liverpool's Albert Dock. Merseyrail stations sell a combined train, bus and zoo-admission ticket (£12), using the #40 bus link from Bache Merseyrail station, one stop north of Chester.

Liverpool

Once the empire's second city, **LIVERPOOL** spent too many of the twentieth-century postwar years struggling against adversity. Things are looking up at last, as economic and social regeneration brightens the centre and old docks. Yet – even as any short-term visitor to the city could tell you – nothing ever broke Liverpool's extraordinary spirit of community, a spirit that emerged strongly in the aftermath of the Hillsborough football stadium disaster of 1989, when the deaths of 95 Liverpool supporters seemed to unite the whole city. Indeed, acerbic wit and loyalty to one of the city's two football teams are the linchpins of Scouse culture – though Liverpool makes great play of its musical heritage, which is reasonable enough from the city that produced The Beatles.

Although it gained its charter from King John in 1207, Liverpool remained a humble fishing village for half a millennium until the silting-up of Chester and the booming slave trade prompted the building of the first dock in 1715. From then until the abolition of slavery in Britain in 1807, Liverpool was the apex of the **slaving triangle** in which firearms, alcohol and textiles were traded for African slaves, who were then shipped to the Caribbean and America. The holds were filled with tobacco, raw cotton and sugar for the return journey. After the abolition of the trade, the port continued to grow into a seven-mile chain of docks, not only for freight but also to cope with wholesale European **emigration**, which saw nine million people from half of Europe leave for the Americas and Australasia between 1830 and 1930. Some never made it further than Liverpool and contributed to a five-fold increase in population in fifty years. An even larger boost came with immigration from the Caribbean and China, and especially Ireland in the wake of the potato famine in 1845.

The docks were busy until the middle of the twentieth century when a number of factors led to the port's **decline**: cheap air fares saw off the lucrative liner business; trade with the dwindling empire declined, while European traffic boosted southeastern ports at Tilbury, Harwich and Southampton; and containerization meant reduced demand for handling and warehousing. The arrival of car manufacturing plants in the 1960s, including Ford at Halewood, stemmed the decline for a while, but during the 1970s and 1980s Liverpool became a byword for British economic malaise as its fundamental businesses withered and died.

There's been a renaissance of sorts since the 1990s as EU development funds and millennium money have kick-started various projects. Financial services, information technology and biotechnology are all major employers while the city is the "call centre" capital of the UK. Compared to the wholesale redevelopment of neighbouring Manchester, the city still has a fair hill to climb but there is at last a welcome new confidence about Liverpool. It's rebranded itself as the "festival city" – on the back of which, it's making a bid to be European Capital of Culture for 2008.

Arrival, information and city transport

Mainline trains pull in to **Lime Street** station, while the suburban **Merseyrail** system (for trains from Chester) calls at four underground stations in the city, including Lime Street. National Express **buses** use the station on Norton Street, northeast of Lime Street. Local buses depart from a variety of terminals: Queen Square (for city centre, Pier Head and Chester services); Paradise Street Bus Station (southbound and a few northbound services); and St Thomas Street (eastbound and cross-river). Liverpool **airport** – now officially named after John Lennon – is eight miles southeast of the city centre. From outside the main entrance, the **Airport Express #500 bus** (every 30min, 6am–1am; £2) runs directly into the city centre, stopping at all major bus terminals and at Lime Street. The slower, cheaper local bus #80A (every 15–30min 6am–11pm) makes the same journey, or a **taxi** to Lime Street costs around £12. **Ferry** arrivals – from the Isle of Man, Dublin and Belfast – dock at the terminals just north of Pier Head, close to Albert Dock and not far from James Street Merseyrail station.

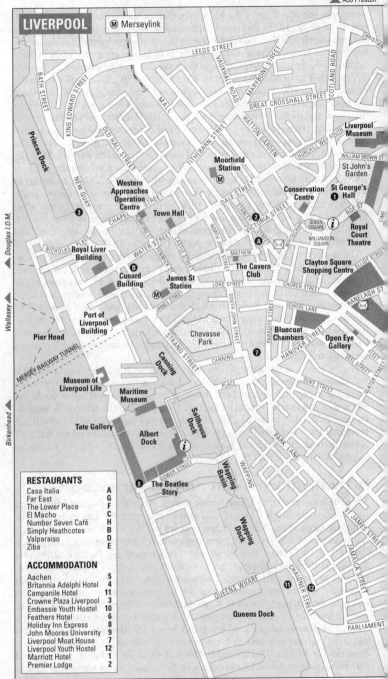

LIVERPOOL

Ⓜ Merseylink

▲ A59 Preston

CHRISTIAN

LEEDS STREET

VAUXHALL ROAD

MARYBONE STREET

GREAT CROSSHALL STREET

SCOTLAND ROAD

BATH STREET

KING EDWARD STREET

OLD HALL STREET

MALL

HATTON GARDEN

CHURCHILL WAY SOUTH

Liverpool Museum

WILLIAM BROWN ST

St John's Garden

Princes Dock

NEW QUAY

CHAPEL STREET

TITHEBARN STREET

Moorfield Station
Ⓜ

DALE STREET

STANLEY

Conservation Centre

St George's Hall ❶

LIME ST

RO ST

Western Approaches Operation Centre

Town Hall

RUMFORD ST

WATER STREET

FENWICK'S ST

CASTLE STREET

NORTH JOHN STREET

VICTORIA STREET

❷

Ⓐ

QUEEN SQUARE

ⓘ

WILLIAMSON SQUARE

WHITECHAPEL

Royal Court Theatre

❸

NICHOLAS PLACE

Royal Liver Building

Ⓑ

Cunard Building

James St Station
Ⓜ

MATHEW

LORD STREET

The Cavern Club

Clayton Square Shopping Centre

CHURCH STREET

ELLIOT STREET

RANELAGH ST

Douglas I.O.M. ◄

Wallasey ◄

Port of Liverpool Building

JAMES STREET

STRAND STREET

SOUTH JOHN STREET

PARADISE STREET

SCHOOL LANE

Bluecoat Chambers

HANOVER STREET

Open Eye Gallery

SEEL STREET

WOOD ST

FLEET ST

SLATER STREET

Pier Head

MERSEY RAILWAY TUNNEL

Birkenhead ◄

Museum of Liverpool Life

Canning Dock

Chavasse Park

CANNING

PLACE

❼

DUKE STREET

Maritime Museum

Tate Gallery

Albert Dock
ⓘ

Salthouse Dock

PARK LANE

WAPPING

Wapping Basin

ST JAMES STREET

GOWER STREET

❽ **The Beatles Story**

Wapping Dock

JAMAICA STREET

CHALONER STREET

❶❶

❶❷

QUEENS WHARF

Queens Dock

PARLIAMENT

RESTAURANTS

Casa Italia	A
Far East	G
The Lower Place	F
El Macho	C
Number Seven Café	H
Simply Heathcotes	B
Valparaiso	D
Ziba	E

ACCOMMODATION

Aachen	5
Britannia Adelphi Hotel	4
Campanile Hotel	11
Crowne Plaza Liverpool	3
Embassie Youth Hostel	10
Feathers Hotel	6
Holiday Inn Express	8
John Moores University	9
Liverpool Moat House	7
Liverpool Youth Hostel	12
Marriott Hotel	1
Premier Lodge	2

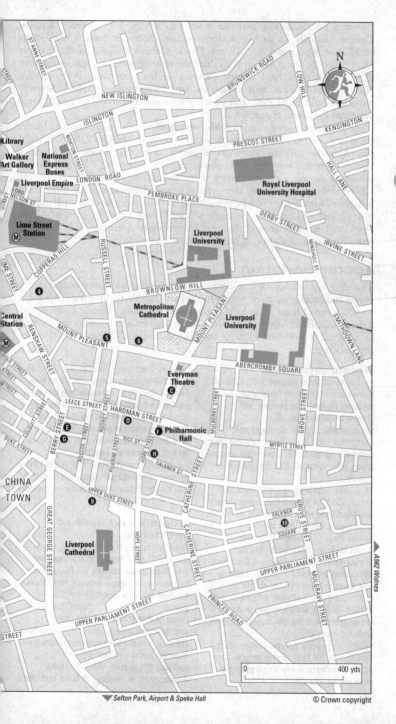

N

Library

Walker
Art Gallery

National
Express
Buses

Liverpool Empire

LORD
NELSON ST

Lime Street
Station
M

Central
Station
M

CHINA
TOWN

ST ANNE STREET

NEW ISLINGTON

ISLINGTON

NORTON STREET

LONDON ROAD

BRUNSWICK ROAD

LOW HILL

KENSINGTON

PRESCOT STREET

HALL LANE

PEMBROKE PLACE

Royal Liverpool
University Hospital

DERBY STREET

IRVINE STREET

MINSHULL ST

Liverpool
University

COPPERAS HILL

RUSSELL STREET

BROWNLOW HILL

SMITHDOWN LANE

Metropolitan
Cathedral

MOUNT PLEASANT

RENSHAW STREET

Liverpool
University

ABERCROMBY SQUARE

MOUNT PLEASANT

GROVE STREET

Everyman
Theatre
C

LEECE STREET

HARDMAN STREET

MULBERRY STREET

COLQUITT STREET

BERRY STREET

RODNEY STREET

Philharmonic
Hall

MYRTLE STREET

DUKE STREET

RICE ST

HOPE STREET

PILGRIM STREET

ROSCOE STREET

FALKNER ST

CATHERINE STREET

UPPER DUKE STREET

FALKNER
SQUARE

GREAT GEORGE STREET

HOPE STREET

Liverpool
Cathedral

CATHERINE STREET

UPPER PARLIAMENT STREET

A562 Widnes

UPPER PARLIAMENT STREET

PRINCES ROAD

MULGRAVE STREET

0   400 yds

4 5 6 E G H 9 10

589

Sefton Park, Airport & Speke Hall

© Crown copyright

Tourist information is available from two offices: the **Queen's Square Centre** centrally located in Queen Square (Mon–Sat 9am–5.30pm, Sun 10.30am–4.30pm) and the **Albert Dock Centre** at the Atlantic Pavilion (daily 10am–5.30pm), which both share the same telephone enquiries number (℡0906/680 6886) and website (Ⓦwww.visitliverpool.com). Both sell the **National Museums and Galleries on Merseyside** (NMGM; Ⓦwww.nmgm.org.uk) Eight Pass (£3) which gives unlimited access into eight local museums for twelve months.

The local transport authority is **Merseytravel**, which co-ordinates all buses, trains and ferries. There's a telephone enquiry line (℡0151/236 7676; daily 8am–8pm) or visit the Merseytravel information office inside the Queen's Square Centre. Daily off-peak, zonal Saveaway tickets (£1.80–£3.20) for unlimited use on most city buses, trains and ferries are available from post offices, newsagents and the Merseytravel offices. The amphibious half-truck-half-boat **Duck Tour** (mid-Feb to Christmas, daily every hour from 10.30am; ℡0151/708 7799; tickets £9) departs from Gower Street, in front of Albert Dock, and trundles around the city centre before splashing down into the water for a spot of aquatic sightseeing.

Accommodation

There's a fair choice of city-centre **accommodation**, from budget hotel chains and small-scale guest houses to business-oriented four-stars. There's also a wide range of hostels and halls of residence, including a terrific youth hostel a short walk from Albert Dock. Both tourist offices will book rooms for you for free; call ℡0845/601 1125 for their details of special-offer weekend breaks and packages.

Hotels and B&Bs

Aachen 89–91 Mount Pleasant ℡0151/709 3477, Ⓦwww.aachenhotel.co.uk. The most popular of the Mount Pleasant budget choices, with a range of value-for-money rooms. ②

Britannia Adelphi Hotel Ranelagh Place ℡0151/709 7200, Ⓦwww.britannia-hotels.co.uk. Liverpool's *Adelphi* catered to passenger-liner customers in its heyday, but it's lost its lustre since then. ⑥

Campanile Hotel Wapping and Chaloner St ℡0151/709 8104. Purpose-built budget property near Albert Dock, where all the rooms are one low price; parking, bistro and bar. ②

Crowne Plaza Liverpool St Nicholas Place, Princes Dock, Pier Head ℡0151/243 8000, Ⓦwww.crowneplaza-liverpool.co.uk. Great dockside location and brimful of facilities, including pool, sauna and gym, brasserie and bar. ⑦

Feathers Hotel 117–125 Mount Pleasant ℡0151/709 9655, Ⓦwww.feathers.uk.com. A converted terrace of Georgian houses, with nicely presented rooms. ⑤

Holiday Inn Express Britannia Pavilion, Albert Dock ℡0151/709 1133, Ⓦwww.hiexpress.com. All 170 of the dockside rooms here go for the same bargain price. ③

Liverpool Moat House Paradise St ℡0151/471 9988. Well-equipped, modern hotel a short walk from the Albert Dock, with comfortable rooms and good sports facilities. ⑦, ⑧ at weekends.

Marriott Hotel 1 Queen Square ℡0151/476 8000, Ⓦwww.marriott.com. Stylish city-centre hotel, featuring a leisure club (with indoor pool and hot tub), restaurant and bar. ⑦

Premier Lodge 45 Victoria St ℡0151/236 1366, Ⓦwww.premierlodge.com. Motel-style comfort near the Cavern Quarter at pretty much unbeatable prices. ②

Hostels and halls of residence

Embassie Youth Hostel 1 Falkner Square ℡0151/707 1089. Twenty minutes' walk from Lime Street station (bus #80), in a Georgian terrace west of the Anglican cathedral. Free showers, tea, toast and coffee included in the price.

John Moores University Cathedral Park, St James Rd ℡0151/709 3197. Self-catering accommodation in the shadow of the metropolitan cathedral. Available with and without continental breakfast. July to early Sept only.

Liverpool YHA Wapping ℡0151/709 8888, Ⓦwww.yha.org.uk. Purpose-built hostel where the accommodation (the price includes breakfast) is in smart two-, three-, four- or six-bed rooms (with private bathroom and heated towel rail). Also a kitchen, licensed café, luggage storage and laundry.

University of Liverpool Halls of Residence Greenbank House, Greenbank Lane ☎0151/794 6440. Set in private parkland, three miles out of the centre (bus #80) and only open June to Aug. Hundreds of single rooms available, with continental breakfast.

The City

Liverpool has a legacy of magnificent municipal and industrial buildings – best seen en masse from across the river or on the Mersey ferry – and these are the chief attractions of the cityscape, along with its two famous **cathedrals**. The city's mercantile past and aspects of its recent history are well covered in a number of fine museums and galleries, especially in the rejuvenated warehouses of **Albert Dock**, which form the largest grouping of Grade I listed buildings in the country. The tourist offices can book you onto a variety of **guided walks and tours** (from £3), or make your own way using the themed trail leaflets on sale in the offices.

Around Lime Street

Emerging from **Lime Street Station** – whose cast-iron train shed was the largest in the world on its completion in 1867 – you can't miss **St George's Hall**, one of Britain's finest Greek Revival buildings. Once Liverpool's concert

The Beatles in Liverpool

No Liverpool band is ever likely to eclipse **The Beatles**. Mathew Street, ten minutes' walk west of Lime Street station, is where *The Cavern* used to be – once the womb of Merseybeat, it's become a little enclave of Beatles nostalgia, most of it bogus and typified by the **Cavern Walks Shopping Centre**, with an awful bronze statue of the boys in the atrium. *The Cavern* itself was where the band was first spotted by Brian Epstein; the club was partly demolished in 1973, though a latterday successor, the **Cavern Club** at 10 Mathew St (ⓦwww.cavern-liverpool.co.uk), complete with souvenir shop, was rebuilt on half of the original site, using, it's claimed, the original bricks. The *Cavern Pub*, immediately across the way, boasts a coiffed Lennon lounging against the wall and an exterior "Wall of Fame", highlighting both the names of all the bands who appeared at the club between 1957 and 1973 (etched into the bricks) and brass discs commemorating every Liverpool No. 1 chart-topper since 1952.

At the Albert Dock, **The Beatles Story** in the Britannia Vaults (daily: April–Sept 10am–6pm; Oct–March 10am–5pm; £7.95) traces The Beatles' rise from the early days at *The Cavern* to their disparate solo careers. Dedicated pilgrims will get more from the two-hour **Magical Mystery Tour** (daily tours; book through Cavern City Tours, ☎0151/236 9091, or Mersey Tourism, ☎0151/709 3285; £10.95; £15 with The Beatles Story), which leaves Albert Dock, visiting Strawberry Fields (a Salvation Army home), Penny Lane (an ordinary suburban street) and the terraced houses where the lads grew up. One of these, **20 Forthlin Rd**, home of the McCartney family from 1955–1964, has been preserved by the National Trust and is open to visitors who duly tramp round the 1950s terraced house where John and Paul wrote songs and where Paul's mother Mary died. The house is only accessible on a pre-booked minibus tour (June–Oct Wed–Sat; £5.50; NT), which leaves six times daily from Speke Hall (see p.594) and the Albert Dock – the price includes the tour, the minibus to Forthlin Road and free access to Speke Hall grounds. Beatlemania is wholeheartedly celebrated on August Bank Holiday Monday (the last Monday of the month) at the culmination of the annual International Beatles Week and **Mathew Street Festival**, filling the town centre with wannabe moptops.

hall and crown courts, its tunnel-vaulted Great Hall is open to the public for monthly craft and antique fairs and for daily **guided tours** in summer (late-July & Aug Mon–Sat 10.30am–4.30pm), when the exquisite floor, tiled with thirty thousand precious Minton tiles, is on show.

Liverpool's **Walker Art Gallery** on William Brown Street (Mon–Sat 10am–5pm, Sun noon–5pm; £3, free with NMGM Eight Pass) houses one of the country's finest provincial art collections, with pieces dating from the fourteenth century to the present day. Major renovations have restored many of the galleries and added new space for temporary exhibitions. There's often a good range of Italian work on show, together with works by Rembrandt, Rubens and other seventeenth-century masters, but here, as in Manchester, British painting occupies centre stage. The gallery also displays exhibits from its large applied-art collection – glassware, ceramics, precious metals, and sculpted furniture, largely retrieved from the homes of the city's early industrial businessmen. Contemporary work floods the building during the John Moores Exhibition, usually held here from October of odd-numbered years to the following January.

Further along William Brown Street the **Liverpool Museum** (Mon–Sat 10am–5pm, Sun noon–5pm; £3, free with NMGM Eight Pass) has also had a major overhaul and certain sections may still be closed during your visit. What is on display is eclectic to say the least, from tarantulas to a space rocket, and it's an appealing diversity which grows on you the longer you stay. The museum had its origins in the natural history collections bequeathed by the Earl of Derby in the mid-nineteenth century, and these have subsequently been augmented by some superior fossil, natural habitat and evolution exhibits. Make time too for the Planetarium (£1); there's also a café.

The cathedrals

On the hill behind Lime Street, off Mount Pleasant, rises the funnel-shaped Catholic **Metropolitan Cathedral of Christ the King** (Mon–Sat 8am–6pm, Sun 8am–5pm; free), denigratingly known as "Paddy's Wigwam" and the "Mersey Funnel". Built in the 1960s in the wake of the revitalizing Second Vatican Council, it was raised on top of the tentative beginnings of Sir Edwin Lutyens's grandiose project to outdo St Peter's in Rome. Bits of Lutyens's cathedral can be seen in the crypt. At the other end of the aptly named Hope Street, the Anglican **Liverpool Cathedral** (daily 8am–6pm; donation requested) looks much more ancient but was actually completed eleven years later, in 1978, after 74 years in construction. The last of the great Neo-Gothic structures, Sir Giles Gilbert Scott's masterwork claims a smattering of superlatives: Britain's largest and the world's fifth largest cathedral, the world's tallest Gothic arches and the highest and heaviest bells. On a clear day, a trip up the 330ft **tower** (11am–4pm; £2) through the cavernous belfry is rewarded by views to the Welsh hills.

The city centre: Bold Street to Pier Head

Having seen the Walker Art Gallery, Liverpool Museum and the cathedrals, you've seen the central showpiece attractions, but you may as well trace a route back through the city centre, stirring after years of neglect. The streets between **Bold Street** and **Duke Street** – Slater, Wood and Fleet streets – feature an increasing number of places in which you can sip a latte, neck a late-night beer or shop for punk records and vintage clothing. **Concert Square**, just off Bold Street, its space once occupied by a factory, was levelled to provide room for warehouse-style bar developments, whose outdoor seats are at a real premium in the summer. On neighbouring Wood Street, the **Open Eye Gallery**, at nos. 28–32 (Tues–Fri 10.30am–5.30pm, Sat 10.30am–5pm; free; ⓦwww.open-eye.org.uk), features temporary exhibitions of photography and the media arts. Bold Street ends at Hanover Street, with the pedestrianized shopping street, Church Street continuing beyond. To the left, School Lane throws up the beautifully proportioned **Bluecoat Chambers**, built in 1717 as an Anglican boarding school for orphans and now a contemporary art gallery (Tues–Sat 10.30am–5pm; free) with a decent café and bookstore (Mon–Sat 9.30am–5pm) and arts centre.

From School Lane turn right on Paradise Street and walk down Whitechapel towards **Queen Square**, through an area which has seen a lot of redevelopment, particularly around **Williamson Square**. One of the neighbourhood's surviving Victorian warehouses, on the corner of Whitechapel and Queen Square, is occupied by the **Conservation Centre** (Mon–Sat 10am–5pm, Sun noon–5pm; £3, free with NMGM Eight Pass). This is where Merseyside's museums and galleries undertake their restoration work and give visitors a hands-on, behind-the-scenes look.

The Pier Head

Though the tumult of shipping which once fought the current here has gone, the **Pier Head** landing stage remains the embarkation point for the **Mersey Ferries** to Woodside (for Birkenhead) and Seacombe (Wallasey). Ride one if only for the magnificent views of the Liverpool skyline and the prominent, 322-feet high **Royal Liver Building** (free tours April–Sept by appointment only; call ⓣ0151/236 2748) – it's topped by the "Liver Birds", a couple of cormorants which have become the symbol of the city.

Straightforward ferry shuttles operate every thirty minutes during morning and evening rush hours (£1.10 each way); at other times the boats run circular "heritage" **cruises** (hourly: Mon–Fri 10am–3pm, Sat & Sun 10am–6pm; £3.75; ⓣ0151/330 1444), complete with sappy commentary and repeated renditions of Gerry Marsden's *Ferry 'cross the Mersey*.

Albert Dock

Albert Dock, five minutes' walk south of the Pier Head, was built in 1846 when Liverpool's port was a world leader. It started to decline at the beginning of the last century, as the new deep-draught ships were unable to berth here, and last saw service in 1972. A decade later the site was given a complete scrub-down and refit. Billed as "Liverpool's Historic Waterfront", it's a type of rescued urban heritage that's been copied throughout the country, but rarely as successfully as here. There's free **parking** – follow the city-centre signs – and **buses** every twenty minutes during the day from Queen Square bus station. All the museums have admission charges: the Maritime Museum, HM Customs Museum and Museum of Liverpool Life are part of the NMGM Eight Pass scheme, while the **Waterfront Pass** (£9.99) saves you money if you want to see the lot.

A trip through the **Merseyside Maritime Museum** (daily 10am–5pm; £3, free with NMGM Eight Pass), filling one wing of the Albert Dock, can easily take two hours. Spread over four floors, it has sections on the history of Liverpool's evolution as a port and shipbuilding centre, and models of seacraft – from Samoan rafts to opulent passenger liners. An illuminating display details Liverpool's role as a springboard for over nine million emigrants – the Irish potato famine and a multiplicity of European wars, combined with the lure of gold and free land, brought people scurrying here to buy their passage to

North America or Australia. On board the ships – there's a walk-through example – people were packed into dark, noisy ranks of bunks where they "puffed, groaned, swore, vomited, prayed, moaned and cried". The museum is at its best in its "Transatlantic Slavery" exhibit, which banishes years of Eurocentric excuses to expose the true horror of the exploitation of African slaves who were kidnapped, abused and sold as property. The conditions they endured on the transatlantic voyage are illustrated by a reconstruction of a slave ship, echoing with haunting voices reading from diaries of slaves and slavers.

The neighbouring **Tate Gallery Liverpool** (Tues–Sun 10am–6pm; free, special exhibitions usually £3–5; Ⓦwww.tate.org.uk) is the country's national collection of modern art in the north. Popular retrospectives and an ever-changing display of individual works are its bread-and-butter, and there's also a full programme of events, talks and tours. The **Museum of Liverpool Life** (daily 10am–5pm; £3, free with NMGM Eight Pass) lies across the dock. Particularly revealing about the hardships that have moulded the resilient Scouse character, it has excellent sections on the city's traditional work, with investigations of the lives of ordinary shipwrights, stevedores, carters and seamen. In the popular-culture sections, Merseyside football gets good coverage, as does Aintree's Grand National, music from the Sixties to the present day, the homegrown soap *Brookside* and local writers, including Alan Bleasdale, Willy Russell, Beryl Bainbridge and Carla Lane.

The outskirts

Located near Liverpool's airport, six miles southeast of the centre, **Speke Hall** (Easter–Oct Tues–Sun 1–5.30pm; Nov to mid-Dec Sat & Sun 1–4.30pm; gardens Easter–Oct same times as house; Nov–Easter Tues–Sun 1–4.30pm; £4.50; gardens only £2.50; NT; Ⓦwww.spekehall.org.uk) is one of the country's finest examples of Elizabethan timbered architecture. Sitting in an oasis of rhododendrons, the house encloses a beautifully proportioned courtyard overlooked by myriad diamond panes. Bus #80/180 to the airport from Paradise Street in the city centre runs within half a mile of the entrance.

For a glimpse of one of the more benign aspects of Merseyside's industrial past, take the Merseyrail under the river to **Port Sunlight**, a garden village created in 1888 by industrialist William Hesketh Lever for the workers at his soap factory. The project is explained at the **Port Sunlight Heritage Centre**, 95 Greendale Rd (April–Oct daily 10am–4pm; Nov–March Sat & Sun 10am–4pm; 60p), set amid the open-planned housing estates. Off Greendale Road, a little further from Port Sunlight station, the **Lady Lever Art Gallery** (Mon–Sat 10am–5pm, Sun noon–5pm; £3, free with NMGM Eight Pass) houses a small collection of English eighteenth-century furniture, Pre-Raphaelite paintings by artists such as Rossetti and Ford Madox Brown, Wedgwood china, porcelain and assorted Greek and Roman artefacts.

Eating, drinking and nightlife

Liverpool's dining scene is slowly shifting up a gear and there's now a good choice of classy **restaurants** alongside a fine selection of cafés and budget places to eat. Fashionable **café–bars** are muscling in on the action too, and you won't want for a decent cup of coffee in most parts of the city. Liverpool's **pubs and bars** stay open later than most, with many serving until 1am or 2am. Fleet Street, Slater Street and Wood Street have seen most development, with ground zero at Concert Square (off Bold Street), where drinkers spill out

Anfield, Goodison Park and Aintree

Liverpool's most popular recreational activity, bar none, is **football**. Liverpool football club plays at **Anfield** (ticket office ☎0151/260 8680, ⓦwww.liverpoolfc.net) in front of some of the nation's most loyal supporters. There's a popular tour around the well-stocked museum, trophy room and dressing rooms (daily 10am–5pm; museum and tour £8.50, museum only £5; booking essential; ☎0151/260 6677). Everton, the city's less glamorous and recently far less successful side, commands equally intense devotion at **Goodison Park** (ticket office ☎0151/330 2300; tours Mon, Wed, Fri & Sun 11am & 2pm; £5.50; booking advised; ⓦwww.evertonfc.com). The first Saturday in April is **Grand National Day** at Aintree – the "World's Greatest Steeplechase". The race is the culmination of a meeting that starts on the previous Thursday, with prices for entry into the grounds ranging from £7 to £65. Catch the Merseyrail to Aintree and buy a ticket on the gate or book on ☎0151/522 2929. A Visitor Centre (☎0151/522 2921, ⓦwww.aintree.co.uk) lets you ride the National on a race simulator as part of a race course tour (£7).

on to the terraces from a variety of cafés, dance bars and theme pubs. Victoria Street in the business district is another fast-developing area.

You'll catch regular gigs at any of the **live music** venues detailed below, and Liverpool has some excellent annual **music festivals and events**, namely the Summer Pops (July) and the Party at the Pier (August) for big-name pop and rock, and Liverpool Now (October) which sees local bands playing in various venues around the city. The evening paper, the *Liverpool Echo*, has **listings** of what's going on, or pick up flyers in the shops, bars and cafés.

Cafés and café-bars

Beluga Bar 40 Wood St. Hip basement space that's great for just a drink, or come to eat – there's a changing, seasonal menu. Opens at 5pm.

Blue Edward Pavilion, Albert Dock. Brick-vaulted café-bar with upstairs grill – a useful stop for a cheap lunch, cappuccino, a pasta or tapas dinner or a late-night drink.

Bluecoat Café Bar Bluecoat Chambers, School Lane. Mainly vegetarian food – salad bar, baked potatoes and dips – served throughout the day. Closed Sun.

Espresso Exchange 6 Victoria St. Locally owned espresso bar with great coffee, snacks and sandwiches.

Everyman Bistro 9–11 Hope St. Long-standing theatre-basement hangout with quiche, pizza and salad-type meals for around a fiver. Closed Sun.

Life Café 1a Bold St. The eighteenth-century

Lyceum Library makes a grand backdrop for this late-opening café-bar, serving pasta, pizza, salads, Thai curries and sandwiches.

The Platinum Lounge Beetham Plaza, 25 The Strand. Feeling smooth? Come right on in to the Liverpool lounge scene where you'll need a bulging wallet and a taste for cocktails.

The Refectory Liverpool Anglican Cathedral, St James' Mount. Appetizing snacks and lunches under the Gothic arches.

Tabac 126 Bold St. A new style for an old favourite sees *Tabac* shed its vaguely hippy leanings and emerge as a contemporary café-bar, serving a wide-ranging menu.

Taste Tate Gallery, Albert Dock. Industrial-lite café-bar at the Tate – bangers and mash, salads and sandwiches during the day, grills and roast vegetables at night.

Restaurants

Casa Italia 40 Stanley St ☎0151/227 5774. Lively trattoria with better than average pasta and pizza dishes. Inexpensive to Moderate.

Far East 27–35 Berry St ☎0151/709 6072. Most reliable of Liverpool's Cantonese eating houses, with authentic *dim sum* (noon–6pm), noodles,

casseroles and rice plates. Moderate.

The Lower Place Philharmonic Hall, Hope St ☎0151/210 1955. Fast winning friends with its chargrilling, oven-roasting, sun-drying ways. Closed Sun. Expensive.

El Macho Hope St ☎ 0151/708 6644.
Longstanding Mexican restaurant that's more
about good times and margarita consumption than
memorable food. Moderate.
Number Seven Café 7 Falkner St ☎ 0151/709
9633. Highly popular, laid-back restaurant with a
daily changing blackboard menu of contemporary
flavours. Moderate.
Simply Heathcotes Beetham Plaza, 25 The
Strand ☎ 0151/236 3536. Lancastrian magic –

roast chump of lamb and Goosnargh duckling fea-
ture among other delights. Expensive.
Valparaiso 4 Hardman St ☎ 0151/708 6036.
Chilean and other Latin-American dishes, with
wines to match. Closed Sun & Mon. Moderate.
Ziba 15–19 Berry St ☎ 0151/708 8870. Stylish
space (formerly a car showroom) now serving cut-
ting-edge Modern British food along with risottos,
Oriental flourishes and vegetarian specialities.
Closed Sun eve. Expensive.

Pubs, bars and clubs

The Baltic Fleet 33a Wapping. Restored pub with
age-old shipping connections. It's got a great period
feel and is known for its fine food and local beer.
Brewery Tap, Stanhope St. Enjoyable Victorian
brewery pub where you can sample Liverpool's
own Cains beers.
The Cavern Club 10 Mathew St ☎ 0151/236
1964. The self-styled "most famous club in the
world" puts on live bands Thursday to Sunday.
Cream Wolstenholme Square, off Hanover St,
☎ 0151/709 1693, ⊛ www.cream.co.uk.
Liverpool's – possibly Britain's – best club, featuring big DJ names. Sponsors the ever-popular
August bank holiday "Creamfields" dance festival.
The Dispensary 87 Renshaw St. Entirely synthetic
but highly sympathetic re-creation of a Victorian pub
using rescued and antique wood, glass and tiles.
The Late Room Life Café, 1a Bold St ☎ 0151/707

2333. Basement lounge featuring stand-up comedy, gigs and club nights, Thurs-Sun.
The Lomax and L2 11–13 Hotham St ☎ 0151/
707 9977. Indie band venue with nightly gigs by
local and touring acts, and weekend club nights.
The Philharmonic 36 Hope St. A superb, traditional
watering-hole where the main attractions – the beer
aside – are the mosaic floors, tiling, gilded wrought-
iron gates and the marble decor in the gents.
Pumphouse Inn Albert Dock. Restored heritage
building at the dock, nice for a waterside pint and
views of the Liver Building.
The Vernon Arms 69 Dale St. Traditional but
smart city-centre boozer with a choice of real ales
and posh pub food.
Ye Cracke 13 Rice St. Crusty backstreet pub off
Hope Street, much loved by the young Lennon, and
with a great jukebox.

Arts, concerts and entertainment

The Royal Liverpool Philharmonic Orchestra, up with Manchester's Hallé as
the northwest's best, dominates the city's **classical music scene** and often plays
at the Philharmonic Hall and the Everyman Theatre. **Theatre** is also well
entrenched in the city, at a variety of venues. Annual **festivals** include the Hope
Street Festival (June); a celebration of African arts and music in Africa Oye
(June); the Summer Pops (July), when the Royal Philharmonic and top pop
names perform beneath a huge marquee on King's Dock; the **Brouhaha Street
Theatre Festival** (August), which involves performances by a host of European
theatre groups; and the **Mathew Street Festival** (August), a free shindig, with
local and national street performers playing the best of The Beatles.

Bluecoat Arts Centre School Lane ☎ 0151/709
5297, ⊛ www.bluecoatartscentre.com. Eclectic
mix of events – drama, dance, poetry, comedy,
music and art exhibitions.
Everyman Theatre and Playhouse Hope St
☎ 0151/709 4776, ⊛ www.everymanplayhouse
.com. Drama, concerts, exhibitions, dance and
musical performances.
Liverpool Empire Lime St ☎ 0151/606 3536,
⊛ www.liverpool-empire.co.uk. The city's largest
theatre, a venue for touring West End shows,
opera, ballet and music.

Philharmonic Hall Hope St ☎ 0151/709 3789,
⊛ www.rlps.co.uk. Home of the Royal Liverpool
Philharmonic Orchestra. Shows classic films once
a month.
Royal Court Theatre Roe St ☎ 0151/709 4321,
⊛ www.royalcourttheatre.net. Art Deco theatre and
concert hall, which sees regular pop and rock concerts among other events.
Unity Theatre Hope Place ☎ 0151/709 4988,
⊛ www.unitytheatreliverpool.co.uk. Puts on the
city's most adventurous range of contemporary
works.

Listings

Airport ☎0151/288 4000, ⓦ www.liverpoolair-port.com. Flights to Belfast, Dublin, the Isle of Man, Madrid, Barcelona, Palma, Nice, Malaga and Amsterdam.

Banks and exchanges American Express, 54 Lord St ☎0151/702 4501; Thomas Cook, 75 Church St ☎0151/552 1300. You can also change money at the two tourist offices, the two main post offices (see below) and at the airport.

Books Most of the bookshops are along Bold Street: Dillons at no. 14, Waterstones at no. 52 and the more radical News from Nowhere at no. 112.

Buses Merseytravel ☎0151/236 7676.

Car rental Alamo, 278 East Prescott Rd, Knotty Ash ☎0151/259 1316; Avis, 113 Mulberry St ☎0151/709 4737; easyRentacar ☎0906/586 0586; Europcar, 8 Brownlow Hill ☎0151/709 7563 and airport ☎0151/448 1652; Hertz, airport ☎0151/486 7444.

Ferries Isle of Man Steam-Packet Company for ferries/Sea Cats ☎08705/523523; Mersey Ferries ☎0151/330 1444; Norse Irish Ferries ☎0151/944 1010.

Hospital Royal Liverpool University Hospital, Prescot Street ☎0151/706 2000.

Internet Planet Electra Internet Café, 36 London Rd ☎0151/708 0303. Daily 10am–6pm.

Laundry Liver Launderette, 170 Aigburth Rd & 104 Prescot Rd.

Left luggage Lime Street Station, daily 7am–10pm.

Pharmacy Boots, Clayton Square ☎0151/709 4711; Moss Pharmacy, 68–70 London Rd ☎0151/709 5271 (daily until 11pm).

Police HQ, Canning Place ☎0151/709 6010.

Post offices City-centre offices at 23–33 Whitechapel; The Lyceum, 1 Bold St. Open Mon–Sat 8.30am–6pm. Taxis Mersey Cabs ☎0151/298 2222; Davy Liver ☎0151/709 4646.

Travel agent Discounted and student tickets from USIT Campus, YHA shop, 25 Bold St ☎0151/709 9200 (plus branches at both universities); STA, 78 Bold St ☎0151/707 1123.

Blackpool

Shamelessly brash **BLACKPOOL** is the archetypal British seaside resort, its "Golden Mile" of piers, fortune-tellers, amusement arcades, tram and donkey rides, fish-and-chip shops, candyfloss stalls, fun pubs and bingo halls making no concessions to anything but low-brow fun-seeking of the finest kind. There are seven miles of wide sandy beach backed by an unbroken chain of hotels and guest houses, and though the sea-water quality is still highly debatable, even after heavy investment in a new sewage system, there's nothing wrong with the beach itself – except for the crowds packing the central stretches on hot summer days. Sixteen million people come here each year, and love every minute.

The coming of the railway in 1846 made Blackpool what it is today: within thirty years, there were piers, promenades and theatres for the thousands who descended. The **Winter Gardens**, with its barrel-vaulted ballroom, the Baroque **Grand Theatre** on Church Street, Blackpool's own "Eiffel Tower" on the seafront and other refined diversions were built to cater to the tastes of the first influx, but it was the Central Pier's "open air dancing for the working classes" that heralded the crucial change of accent. Suddenly Blackpool was favoured destination for the "Wakes Weeks", when whole Lancashire mill towns descended for their annual seven days' holiday.

Where other British holiday resorts have suffered from the rivalry of cheap foreign packages, Blackpool has simply gone from strength to strength by shrewdly providing exactly what its visitors want. Underneath the populist veneer there's a sophisticated marketing approach which balances ever more elaborate rides and attractions with well-grounded traditional entertainment. When other resorts begin to close up for the winter, Blackpool's main season is just beginning, as over half a million light bulbs are used to create **the Illuminations** which decorate the promenade from the beginning of September to early November.

Arrival, information and accommodation

Blackpool's main **train station** is Blackpool North (direct trains from Manchester, Preston and London), half a dozen blocks up Talbot Road from North Pier. A few steps down Talbot Road, towards the sea, stands the combined National Express and local **bus station**. The main **tourist office** at 1 Clifton St (Easter to early Nov Mon–Sat 9am–5pm, Sun 10am–3.45pm; rest of year Mon–Thurs & Sat 8.45am–4.45pm, Fri 8.45am–4.15pm; ☎01253/478222, ⓦwww.blackpooltourism.com) is on the corner of Talbot Road, five minutes' walk from the stations; a seasonal office sits on the prom opposite Blackpool Tower. The main office sells **Travel Cards** (one-day £4.50; three-day £12; five-day £15; seven-day £16) for use on all local buses and trams.

Bed-and-breakfast prices are generally low (from £15 per person, even less on a room-only basis or out of season), but rise at weekends during the Illuminations. In peak season, it's simply a matter of looking for vacancy signs or asking the tourist office for help – anything cheap between North and Central piers is guaranteed to be noisy; for more peace and quiet (an unusual request in Blackpool, it has to be said), look for places along the more restful North Shore, beyond North Pier.

Guest houses and hotels

Boltonia 124–126 Albert Rd ☎01253/620248, ⓦwww.boltoniahotel.co.uk. A qualitative step up from your basic Blackpool boarding house, the Boltonia's 21 rooms are all en suite. ❸

Clifton Hotel Talbot Square ☎01253/621481. On the North Pier prom, this traditional beauty – a Grade 1 listed building – has fine sea views from many rooms; check for special offers. ❺

De Vere East Park Drive ☎01253/838866, ⓦwww.devereonline.co.uk. A reclusive resort-style retreat set in its own grounds, with a fine indoor pool. It's a couple of miles inland. ❼

Dutchman Hotel 269 The Promenade ☎01253/404812. Small, cheery rooms - although those at the front get traffic noise, you do wake up with a view of the sea. No credit cards. ❶

The Garfield 22 Springfield Rd ☎01253/628060. Two blocks west of Talbot Road, this is cheap and convenient for station and town; slightly pricier en-suite rooms are available too. No credit cards. ❶

Grosvenor View 7–9 King Edward Ave ☎01253/352 851. Rooms in this detached property are larger and better equipped than most. ❸

Imperial North Promenade ☎01253/623971, ⓦwww.paramount-hotel.co.uk. The politicians' conference favourite, with excellent sea-facing rooms, pool, a good bar and restaurant. ❼

Ruskin Hotel Albert Rd ☎01253/624063, ⓦwww.ruskinhotel.com. At the prom end of Albert Rd, by Coronation St, the Ruskin exudes repro-Victorian style. ❺

The town and its attractions

With seven miles of beach – the tide ebb is a full half a mile, leaving plenty of sand at low tide – and accompanying promenade, you'll want to jump on and off the electric **trams** if you plan to get up and down much between the piers. South Pier to North Pier – between which lies most of what there is to see and do – costs £1.

The major event in town is Blackpool's **Pleasure Beach** on the South Promenade (March–Easter Sat & Sun 10am–8pm; Easter–June Mon–Fri 2–8pm, Sat & Sun 10am–10pm; July to Nov 5 daily 10am–11pm; hours can vary, call ☎0870/444 5566, ⓦwww.blackpoolpleasurebeach.co.uk), just south of South Pier – visted by over seven million people each year. Entrance to the amusement park is free, but you'll have to fork out for the superb array of "white knuckle" rides including "The Big One", the world's fastest roller coaster (85mph) which involves a terrifying near-vertical drop from 235ft. If you're not leaving until you've been on everything – a sensible course of action – buy an unlimited ride wristband (one-day £25, two-day £40).

Across the road, the **Sandcastle** (June–Oct daily 10am–5.30pm; Nov–May Sat & Sun only; £4.95) is the only place you are likely to want to swim. With every aquatic diversion kept at a constant 29°C it can be a welcome respite from the biting sea air. Jump a tram for the ride up to **Central Pier** with its 108-feet high revolving Big Wheel. The **Sea-Life Centre** (daily 10am–6pm; July & Aug Fri & Sat to 10pm; £7; ⓦwww.sealife.co.uk) here is one of the country's best, with eight-foot sharks looming at you as you march through a glass tunnel. For a taste of what Blackpool attractions used to be like, you could then hit **Louis Tussauds Waxworks**, 87–89 Central Promenade (daily 10am–10pm; £4.50) – these days, more Posh and Becks than Churchill and Margaret Thatcher.

Between Central and North piers stands the 518-feet **Blackpool Tower** – the skyline's only real touch of grace – erected in 1894 when it was thought that the Northwest really ought not to be outdone by Paris. It's now marketed as "Tower World" (Easter to early Nov daily 10am–11pm; rest of year Sat 10am–11pm, Sun 10am–6pm; £10) which offers a ride up to the top (where there's a postbox), an unnerving walk on the see-through glass floor, plus a visit to the Edwardian ballroom and various other attractions. From the very early days, there's been a Moorish-inspired **circus** (shows included in the entry ticket) between the tower's legs, which still functions, though in the spirit of the times it's now animal-free.

Eating, drinking and nightlife

Eating out revolves around the typical British seaside fare of fish and chips, available all over town, but at its supreme best in *Harry Ramsden's*, 60–63 The Promenade, on the corner of Church Street near the Tower. Even more traditional seaside food is available from the wood-panelled, 120-year-old *Robert's Oyster Bar*, 92 The Promenade, near the base of the Tower, where you can buy oysters, cockles and mussels, or fish platters. *Lagoonda*, 37 Queen St (☏01253/293 837), off Talbot Square, is a party-time Afro-Caribbean restaurant, but for a real blowout head for the expensive *September Brasserie*, 15–17 Queen St (☏01253/623282; closed Sun & Mon lunch), or the refined *Palm Court Restaurant* at the *Imperial*.

If you like your **nightlife** late, loud and libidinous, summertime Blackpool has few English peers. *Yates' Wine Lodge* has two branches, in Talbot Square and between Central and South piers, where you can sip an amontillado sherry or champagne on draught. There's a rowdy bar in the *Clifton Hotel*, at North Pier;

Gay Blackpool

Blackpool has become one of the most popular gay resorts in the country, with around forty hotels and guest houses that welcome, or cater specifically for, a gay clientele. Blackpool tourist office can supply a full gay **accommodation** list, but good places to try first include *Raffles Hotel*, set back from Central Pier at 73–75 Hornby Rd (☏01253/294713; ❷), *Mardi Gras*, 41–43 Lord St (☏01253/751087; ❷), the all-male *Trades Hotel*, 51–55 Lord St (☏01253/626041; ❷), and the *Amalfi Guest House*, for women, at 19–21 Eaves St (☏01253/622971; ❷).

There's **nightlife** to match, with *Funny Girls* the most high-profile venue. *Flamingos*, opposite the train station at 174–176 Talbot Rd, is probably the largest and liveliest gay club in Europe, with four storeys of dance floors and eight bars. Other prominent gay **bars** include the *Flying Handbag*, at 170–172 Talbot Rd; *Pepe's*, a basement bar at 94 Talbot Rd; and *Basil's*, 9 The Strand (☏01253/294109).

and a plethora of Irish theme bars, notably *O'Neill's* on the corner of Talbot Road and Abingdon Street, *Finn's* on Talbot Square, and *Scruffy Murphy's*, 32 Corporation St. The *Pump and Truncheon*, 13 Bonny St, behind the Sea Life Centre, is a real-ale pub. For **dancing**, local opinion favours *Blue*, on Corporation Street, near the Grand Theatre, whose club nights bring in star DJs. *Funny Girls*, a transvestite-run bar at 9 The Strand (℡01253/291144), has nightly shows which attract long (gay and straight) queues. Otherwise, **entertainment** is based very heavily on family shows, musicals, crooners and stage spectaculars put on at a variety of end-of-pier and Pleasure Beach theatres or historic venues like the Grand Theatre (℡01253/290190, ⓦwww.blackpool-grand.co.uk), Wintergardens (℡01253/292029, ⓦwww.blackpoollive.co.uk) and Opera House on Church Street (℡01253/292029).

Preston and around

With the siren draws of the Lakes, the Peak District and the Yorkshire Dales so close, the rest of Lancashire often gets bypassed in the rush to the surrounding national parks, and more's the pity. In **Preston**, 25 miles northwest of Manchester, the county has one of England's oldest towns, containing two fine museums and some appealing Georgian and Victorian remnants. North of the town, rural Lancashire is at its most bucolic in the villages of the **Ribble Valley**, particularly in the **Forest of Bowland**, whose gateway is the small market town of **Clitheroe**.

Preston

Strategically placed on the banks of the River Ribble, **PRESTON** was already an important market town in Anglo-Saxon times and received its royal charter in 1179 – origin of the famous Preston Guild celebrations, which since 1542 have taken place every twenty years (the next in 2012). The town was attacked by Robert the Bruce, changed hands in the Civil War and saw action during the Jacobite rebellions, while Charles Dickens gathered material here for *Hard Times*, his coruscating attack on the factory system. Some handsome Victorian public buildings survive, most notably the majestic Greek-Revival-style **Harris Museum and Art Gallery** (Mon–Sat 10am–5pm; free), in the central Market Square. The permanent collection focuses on fine art and decorative art, while temporary exhibitions often explore links with the town's significant Asian population. On either side of the Harris lie the modern shopping streets, converging on Fishergate, the main street through town. For a change in emphasis, cross Fishergate to explore the handsome Georgian development of **Winckley Square**, once home to the town's richest cotton magnates. If you needed any more incentive to stop it would be to make your way to the ground of Preston North End – one of Britain's oldest football clubs – for the marvellous **National Football Museum**, Sir Tom Finney Way, Deepdale Stadium (Tues–Sat 10am–5pm, midweek matchday 10am–7.30pm, Sun 11am–5pm; £6.95; ⓦwww.nationalfootballmusueum.com). On one level, this is simply an unparalleled collection of football memorabilia: those who know about such things will relish the chance to see items like the Geoff Hurst crossbar from the 1966 World Cup Final. But you really don't have to know anything about football to enjoy the museum, since "the true story of the world's greatest game" is backed by fascinating archive material on football's origins, its social importance, the experience of fans through the ages, and other relevant themes.

For the football museum, it's a ten-minute ride on bus #19 from Preston **bus station**, right in the centre of town. The **train station**, on the west coast main line, has regular services to Manchester and Blackpool. The **tourist office** is in the Guild Hall, on Lancaster Road (Mon–Sat 10am–5.30pm; ☎01772/ 253731, ⓦwww.visitpreston.com), just round the corner from the Harris Museum.

The Ribble Valley

When the nineteenth-century Lancashire cotton weavers enjoyed a rare break from their industry they took to the bucolic retreats of the **Ribble Valley**, north of Preston, which cuts through the heart of northern Lancashire to the River Ribble's source in the Yorkshire Dales. In stark contrast to the conurbations to the south, the valley parades a stream of small market towns and isolated villages set among verdant fields and rolling hills.

A tidy little market town on the banks of the River Ribble, **CLITHEROE** (regular trains from Manchester and buses from Preston) is best seen from the terrace of its empty **Norman Keep** which towers above the Ribble Valley floor. From here, the small centre is laid out before you and, if there's little else specific to see – save a **Castle Museum** (May–Sept daily 11am–4.30pm; Oct–Dec & Feb–April closed Thurs & Fri; closed all Jan; £1.50) in the extensive grounds – you can at least spend an hour or two browsing around the shops and old pubs. An obvious target is Pendle Hill, a couple of miles to the east, where the ten **Pendle Witches** allegedly held the diabolic rites that led to their hanging in 1612. The evidence against them came mainly from one small child, but nonetheless a considerable mythology has grown up around the witches, whose memory is perpetuated by a hilltop gathering each Halloween.

Much of the northwestern part of the region is occupied by thinly populated grouse moorland known as the **Forest of Bowland** – the name "forest" is used in its traditional sense of a "royal hunting ground", and much of the land still belongs to the Crown. From Clitheroe, buses run out to Dunsop Bridge, Newton and Slaidburn, the three tiny villages in the heart of the region. Pedal Power on Waddington Road (☎01200/422066) in Clitheroe can sort you out with a **mountain bike** for in-depth exploration. **SLAIDBURN** is the most substantial and attractive of the Forest's settlements. Hoary stone cottages fronted by a strip of aged cobbles set the tone – a truly ancient **inn**, the *Hark to Bounty* (☎01200/446246; ❸), and a popular **youth hostel** (☎01200/446656; closed Oct–March), itself a former inn, complete the picture.

Lancaster and around

LANCASTER, Lancashire's county town, dates back at least as far as the Roman occupation, though only the scant remains of a bath-house and traces of the fort wall survive from that period. It became an important port on the slave triangle, and it's the legacy of predominantly Georgian buildings from that time that gives the town its character, particularly in the leafy areas around the castle. It's no surprise that many people choose to spend a night here on the way to the Lakes or Dales to the north, and it's an easy side-trip a few miles west to the resort of **Morecambe** and to neighbouring **Heysham village** and its ancient churches.

Lancaster Castle (tours: mid-March to mid-Dec daily 10.30am–5pm; last tour at 4pm; £4) has been the city's focal point since Roman times, when there was a fort on this site. Currently, about a quarter of the battlemented building can be visited on an entertaining hour-long tour, though court sittings sometimes affect the schedules. The castle's neighbour, the former Benedictine **Priory Church of St Mary** (Easter–Oct daily 9.30am–5pm; free), has a (possibly) Saxon doorway at the west end and some finely carved fourteenth-century choir stalls. A two-minute walk down the steps between the castle and church brings you to the seventeenth-century **Judges' Lodging** (Easter–June & Oct Mon–Sat 2–5pm; July–Sept Mon–Fri 10am–1pm & 2–5pm, Sat & Sun 2–5pm; £2), once used by visiting magistrates and now home to two museums. Rooms on the ground and first floors house furniture by Gillows of Lancaster, one-time boat builders who, in the early eighteenth century, took to cabinet-making with the tropical timber which came back as ballast in their boats. Their high-quality work eventually earned them contracts to furnish the Houses of Parliament and the great Cunard transatlantic liners, the *Queen Mary* and *Queen Elizabeth*.

Continuing down the hill and left onto Dameside you arrive on the banks of the **River Lune** – which lent Lancaster its name – whose navigable lengths inspired the growth of the port. The river was first bridged in Roman times: the latest span, an eye-catching steel suspension bridge for pedestrians, follows the line of the medieval wooden, later stone, bridge. The top floor of one of the eighteenth-century warehouses here is taken up by part of the **Maritime Museum**, St George's Quay (daily: Easter–Oct 11am–5pm; Nov–Easter 12.30–4pm; £2), entered through the Old Custom House on the riverside. The museum's ample coverage of life on the sea and inland waterways of Lancashire is complemented by the **City Museum** on Market Square back in town (Mon–Sat 10am–5pm; free).

For a panorama of the town, Morecambe Bay and the Cumbrian fells, take a bus from the bus station (or a steep 25-minute walk up Moor Lane) to **Williamson Park** (Easter–Sept daily 10am–5pm; Oct–Easter Mon–Fri 11am–4pm, Sat & Sun 10am–4pm; free), Lancaster's highest point. Funded by local statesman and lino magnate Lord Ashton, the park's centrepiece is the 220-foot-high **Ashton Memorial**, a Baroque folly raised by his son in memory of his second wife.

Practicalities

Lancaster is a regular stop on the West Coast rail line from London to Scotland; there are also hourly trains from Manchester and even more frequently from Preston. From either the **train station** on Meeting House Lane, or the **bus station** on Cable Street in town, it's a five-minute walk to the **tourist office** at 29 Castle Hill (April–June & Oct Mon–Sat 10am–5pm; July–Sept Mon–Sat 10am–6pm, Sun noon–4pm; Nov–March Mon–Sat 10am–4pm; ℡01524/32878, ⑩www.lancaster.gov.uk), in front of the castle. Annual **events and festivals** include an Easter maritime festival, Georgian fair (August bank holiday), and spectacular Bonfire Night celebrations (Saturday nearest Nov 5).

Accommodation

Castle Hill House 27 St Mary's Parade, Castle Hill ℡01524/849137. This attractive renovated Victorian house sits right opposite the castle and has three rooms available (one en suite). ❷

Edenbreck House Sunnyside Lane ℡01524/32464. Large Victorian house, set in its own grounds at the end of Ashfield Avenue, ten minutes'

walk up Meeting House Lane. No credit cards. ❷

Royal King's Arms Market St ℡01524/32451, ⑩www.bookmenzies.com. Lancaster's best-sited hotel, opposite the castle, has fifty-odd prettily furnished rooms. ❺

Shakespeare Hotel 96 St Leonardsgate ℡01524/841041. Hard-working hosts maintain

eight cosy rooms in this town-house hotel on a central street. Advance reservations advised. ❷
Station House 25 Meeting House Lane ☎01524/381060. On a busy road, opposite the train station, but providing budget accommodation just two minutes' from the centre. No credit cards. ❷
Wagon & Horses St George's Quay ☎01524/846094. Pleasant rooms above a riverside pub, just past the Maritime Museum. No credit cards. ❷

Cafés and Restaurants

Il Bistro Morini 26 Sun St ☎01524/846252. The best Italian in town, with regional specialities emphasizing seafood, duck and pork. Closed Sun. Expensive.
Pizza Margherita 2 Moor Lane. Good-natured pizza and pasta restaurant, festooned with plants, where you can fill up for under £10. Inexpensive.
Simply French 27 St George's Quay, ☎01524/843199. Riverside brasserie in a converted warehouse close to the Maritime Museum. Closed Mon, also Tues & Wed lunch. Inexpensive to Moderate.

Som Siam 13–15 Meeting House Lane. Flavourful Thai dishes in a friendly spot – all the old favourites, from noodles to fish cakes. Dinner only. Moderate.
Sun Café 25 Sun St. The food's the draw in this stylish café/restaurant – think gourmet sandwiches and World flavours. Closed Sun evening. Inexpensive to Moderate.
The Whale Tail 78a Penny St. Veggie café serving good breakfasts, tasty dips, salads, burgers, sandwiches and baked potatoes. Closes 5pm, 3pm on Sundays. Inexpensive.

Pubs and nightlife

Dukes Moor Lane ☎01524/66645. The city's main arts centre, with cinema, theatre (including open-air performances in Williamson Park in summer) and other events.
George & Dragon St George's Quay. For a stroll along the river and a quiet drink, either here or the *Wagon & Horses* up the road are the best pubs.

Water Witch Aldcliffe Rd. Canalside pub named after an old canal packet boat. A student crowd munches burgers, shoots pool and hogs the canalside tables.
Ye Olde John O'Gaunt Market St, near the City Museum. City-centre local with home-cooked food, special beers, tea and coffee on request, live music, and a small beer garden.

Morecambe and Heysham

Although the name **MORECAMBE**, meaning "Great Bay", dates from Celtic times, the seaside town five miles west of Lancaster only adopted it in the nineteenth century when it rapidly expanded from a small fishing village into a full-blown resort. The sweep of the bay is still the major attraction, with the local sunsets a renowned phenomenon. The **Stone Jetty**, all that remains of the former harbour, has been remodelled by sculptors and stonemasons and now features bird sculptures, games and motifs. A little way along the prom stands the statue of one of Britain's most treasured comedians – Eric Bartholomew, who took the stage name **Eric Morecambe** when he met his comedy partner, Ernie Wise.

The main historic interest on this side of Morecambe Bay is at **HEYSHAM**, three miles southwest. The nicest approach is on foot, along the promenade from Morecambe. Heysham's hidden gem is the shoreside **Heysham Village**, centred on a group of charming seventeenth-century cottages. Settlement here can be traced back to prehistoric times, though proudest relic is the well-preserved Viking hog's-back tombstone in Saxon **St Peter's** church, set in a romantic churchyard below the headland. Just up the lane, on the headland itself, the earlier ruins of **St Patrick's chapel** occupy a superb vantage-point over the bay and to the lakeland hills beyond.

The Isle of Man

The **Isle of Man**, almost equidistant from Ireland, England, Wales and Scotland, is one of the most beautiful spots in Britain, a mountainous, cliff-fringed island just thirty-one miles by thirteen, into which are shoehorned austere moorlands and wooded glens, sandy beaches, fine castles, beguiling narrow-gauge railways and scores of standing stones and Celtic crosses. It takes some effort to reach, and the weather is hardly reliable, factors which have seen tourist numbers fall since its Victorian heyday. This means, though, that the Isle of Man has been spared the worst excesses of the British tourist trade: there's peace and quiet in abundance, walks around the unspoilt hundred-mile coastline, picket fences and picnic spots, rural villages, steam trains and cream teas – a yesteryear ensemble if ever there was one.

St Patrick is said to have come here in the fifth century bringing Christianity, which struggled for a while when the **Vikings** established garrisons here in the eleventh century, though they converted while they reigned as **Kings of Mann**. The Scots under Alexander wrested power from the Norsemen in 1275, the beginning of an ultimately unsuccessful 130-year struggle with the English for control of the island. The distinct identity of the island remained intact, however, and many true Manx inhabitants, who comprise around half of the island's 72,000 population, insist that the Isle of Man is not part of England, nor even of the UK. Indeed, the island has its own government, **Tynwald**, arguably the world's oldest democratic parliament, which has run continuously since 979 AD. To further complicate matters, the island has its own sterling currency, worth the same as the mainland currency; its own laws, though they generally follow Westminster's; an independent postal service; and a Gaelic-based language which nearly died out but is once again being taught in schools. The island, of course, also produces its own tailless version of the domestic cat, as well as famously good kippers and queenies (scallops). However, much to the locals' chagrin, these thriving marks of identity are still slightly marred by the island's reputation of being a tax haven for greedy Brits and a refuge for the sort of people who think that even Victorian values were a bit on the lax side. It's an image problem which largely stems from the island's archaic human rights legislation. Homosexuality was illegal here until 1992, the death penalty and corporal punishment were only abolished in 1993, and sex discrimination legislation wasn't enforced until 2001.

For most of its history, crofting and fishing, interspersed with a good bit of smuggling, have formed the basis of the economy. The first regular steamship service from England commenced in 1819, and **tourism** began to flourish during the late-Victorian and Edwardian eras with the influx of northwestern factory workers. In recent times the real money-spinner has been the **offshore finance industry**, exploiting the island's low income tax and absence of capital gains tax and death duties. Given its financial expertise, the Isle of Man is also playing a major role in the development of **ebanking and ecommerce**.

Although the landscapes are wonderful, the island's main tourist draw is the **TT (Tourist Trophy) motorcycle races** in the first two weeks in June, a frenzy of speed and burning rubber that's shattered the island's peace annually since 1907. This is only the most famous of a summer-long list of **rallies and races** on the island's roads, from the Manx Rally (May), International Rally and Manx Classic (both Sept) to the Kart Racing Festival (July), when go-carts buzz through the streets of Peel. If you want to stay on the island at these times, book your accommodation well in advance.

Getting to the island

Ferries or the quicker **Sea Cats**, both run by The Isle of Man Steam Packet Company (Mon–Sat 7am–8pm, Sun 9am–8pm; ℡08705/523523, ⓦwww .steam-packet.com), depart from either Heysham (near Lancaster) or Liverpool to Douglas. **Heysham** (Sea Cat 2hr, ferry 3hr 30min) has the most frequent service, with two or three sailings a day in July and August dropping to one or two daily during the rest of the year. **Liverpool** manages two to three Sea Cat services a day (2hr 30min) between April and September, with a reduced ferry service (4hr) at other times (between October and March, down to 1 daily at weekends). One-way **fares** start at £19 for foot passengers and £99 for drivers (covers the car, driver and one passenger), but advance-purchase tickets, special offers and night-time sailings offer substantial savings. The best **flight** deals are with Manx Airlines (℡08457/256256, ⓦwww.manx-airlines.com), which flies several times daily from Liverpool, Manchester and Leeds/Bradford. Meanwhile, British European Airways (℡08705/676676, ⓦwww.british-european.com) flies daily from London City Airport and from Bristol and Belfast. Prices start at £99 return on all routes.

Douglas

A mere market town as late as 1850, the capital **DOUGLAS** was a product of Victorian mass tourism and displays many similarities to Blackpool, just across the water. However, put aside thoughts of Blackpool-style state-of-the-art entertainment and sophisticated nightlife. Although there are pockets of contemporary development, Douglas – despite its financial acumen – has something of an end-of-season feel about it. It's not really the town's fault – where once half a million people a year sported on the sands, package tourism to hotter climates has long since burst the bubble. You can still have a thoroughly enjoyable time here, but it's likely to consist largely of pulling up a candy-striped deckchair and enjoying the extensive sands. When it rains, stroll the covered arcades or attend the afternoon tea dances.

Douglas's seafront vista has changed little since Victorian times, and is still trodden by heavy-footed carthorses pulling **trams** (jump on for a few pence). Up Victoria Street, past the Manx Legislative Building, the **Manx Museum**, on the corner of Kingswood Grove and Crellins Hill (Mon–Sat 10am–5pm; free), makes a good start for anyone wanting to get to grips with Manx culture and heritage. Various rooms provide an absorbing synopsis of the island's history, packed with Neolithic standing stones, Celtic grave markers and other artefacts, notably some excellent displays relating to Viking burials and runic crosses.

Arrival, orientation and information

Ronaldsway airport is at Ballasalla, ten miles southwest of Douglas. Buses (every 30min–1hr 7am–11pm) connect the airport with Castletown/Port St Mary or Douglas. A taxi from the airport costs around £13 to Douglas. **Ferries** and Sea Cats dock by the **Sea Terminal** at the southern end of the Douglas waterfront. Fifty yards beyond the forecourt taxi rank, the Lord Street **bus station** is the hub of the island's bus routes; the **Travel Shop** here (Mon, Wed & Fri 10am–12.30pm & 1.30–5.45pm, Tues, Thurs & Sat 8am–12.30pm & 1.30–5.45pm; ℡01624/662525), at the bottom of Lord Street, has timetable information and sells Island Explorer **travel tickets** for buses and trains – see "The rest of the island" for details.

North Quay runs 300 yards west from the bus station alongside the river and fishing port to Douglas Station, the northern terminus of the **steam railway** to Port Erin. The waterfront (progressively Loch, Central and Queen's promenades) runs a mile and a half north to Derby Castle Station for the **electric railway** to Laxey and Ramsey – take the horse-drawn tram along the promenade or buses #24, #24a, #26 or #26a from Douglas bus station.

The **tourist office** is in the Sea Terminal building (mid-May to Sept daily 9.15am–7pm; April to mid-May & Oct daily 9am–5pm; Nov–March Mon–Thurs 9am–5.30pm, Fri 9am–5pm, Sat 9.30am–12.30pm); ℡01624/686766). The main **websites** for information are ⓦwww.gov.im and ⓦwww.isle-of-man.com.

Accommodation

B&Bs are packed in along Douglas's front and up the roads immediately off Harris Promenade, particularly along Broadway, Castle Mona Avenue, Empress Drive and Empire Terrace. Note that many places demand a two-night minimum stay in the summer. There's also a number of boutique-style **hotels** in renovated seafront buildings, with significantly higher prices.

Guest houses and hotels

Admiral House Hotel Loch Promenade ℡01624/629551, ⓔenquiries@admiralhouse.com. Lovingly restored, club-like retreat with very comfortable rooms, a café-bar and Spanish restaurant. **⑥**

Arrandale Hotel Hutchinson Square ℡01624/674907. Traditional guest house, a few minutes' walk from the promenade, with a wide range of rooms. **②**

Blossoms 4 The Esplanade ℡01624/673360. One of the better choices at the cheaper end of the market – the sea-view rooms tend to go early. No credit cards. **①**

Claremont Hotel 18–19 Loch Promenade ℡01624/698800, ⓦwww.sleepwellhotels.com. Sympathetically renovated promenade hotel. If this is full, try the sister-establishment, the *Chesterhouse Hotel* a few doors up. **⑤**

Cubbon House Loch Promenade ℡01624/670799. Hides its very smart en-suite rooms behind an old-fashioned holiday hotel facade. **③**

Empress Hotel Central Promenade ℡01624/661155, ⓦwww.theempresshotel.net. Victorian hotel that's been remodelled inside to provide a hundred spacious rooms, many with sea views. **⑤**

Sefton Hotel Harris Promenade ℡01624/645500, ⓦwww.seftonhotel.co.im. Sleek rooms offering a sea view or a balcony over the atrium. There's also a pool, internet access and bike rental. **⑥**

Campsites

Glendhoo International Campsite ℡01624/621254. In a sheltered valley, two miles north at the Cronk ny Mona crossroads on the A18; closed Oct–Easter.

Glenlough Farm ℡01624/851326. Three miles west at Union Mills on the Peel road; closed Oct–April.

Grandstand ℡01624/621132. Closest to Douglas, this backs onto Noble's Park Grandstand on Glencrutchery Road, a mile north of the tourist office. Closed Oct–May and during TT and Manx Grand Prix races.

Eating, drinking and entertainment

There's real coffee at the *Spill the Beans Coffee House*, 1 Market Hill (closed Sun), while *Greens*, in the ticket office at the steam railway station, serves vegetarian specials. TV chef and local lad Kevin Woodford has the island's highest culinary profile and runs a couple of **restaurants** in Douglas: the expensive *Waterfront*, at the top of North Quay (℡01624/673222), and the moderate *Blazers* next door (same phone number). Further down the quayside, *Tanroagan* (℡01624/472411; eve only) is the trendy choice for fish. *La Posada*, in the basement of the *Admiral House Hotel* on Loch Promenade (℡01624/629551), is an authentic Spanish restaurant, whose dishes include a rich paella. Locals also like *Paparazzi*, 26 Loch Promenade, a large pizzeria-trattoria.

Manx-brewed beer is on sale at most **pubs** and brews such as "Old Bushy Tail" soon revive flagging spirits. Try it and others at the cosy *Rovers Return*, on

Church Street, around the corner from *Scott's Bistro*. The wine-swilling Euro-crowd frequent the capacious *Bar George*, housed in a converted Sunday School at the end of Hill Street.

Listings

Airport Ronaldsway airport, flight enquiries ☏01624/821600.

Banks ATMs at Barclays, Victoria St; NatWest, Prospect Hill; Lloyds-TSB, Prospect Hill; HSBC, Ridegeway St; Isle of Man Bank, SeaTerminal.

Bicycle rental Eurocycles, 8a Victoria Rd, off Broadway ☏01624/624909.

Buses All bus enquiries ☏01624/662525.

Car rental Most outfits have offices at the airport or can arrange to deliver cars to the Sea Terminal. Contact: Athol, airport and Athol Garage, Peel Road ☏01624/822481, ⓦwww.athol.co.im; Isle of Man Rent-a-Car, airport and deliveries to Sea Terminal ☏01624/825855; Mylchreests, airport and deliveries to Sea Terminal ☏0500/823533; Ocean Ford, Douglas Rd, Castletown ☏01624/820830.

Ferries and Sea Cats Isle of Man Steam Packet Company ☏01624/661661.

Hospital Noble's Hospital, Westmoreland Rd ☏01624/642642.

Internet Feegan's Lounge, Duke St, off Victoria St (Mon–Fri 9am–7pm, Sat 9am–6pm).

Pharmacies Boots, 14 Strand St; John Atkinson, 2 Granville St.

Police Douglas Police Station, Glencrutchery Rd ☏01624/631212.

Post Office Main post office is at 6 Regent St ☏01624/686141.

Trains Steam Railway enquiries ☏01624/673623; Electric Railway and Snaefell Mountain Railway enquiries ☏01624/663366.

The rest of the island

With a car you could see almost everything in a couple of days; even on foot, it only takes around five days to circumnavigate the entire island. But don't miss a trip on one of the two century-old **rail services** which still provide the best public transport to all the major towns and sights except for Peel. The carriages of the **Steam Railway** (Easter–Oct daily 10am–5pm; £7 return to Port Erin) rock their fifteen-mile course from Douglas to Castletown, Port St Mary and Port Erin at a spirited pace. The rolling terrain due north of Douglas was too steep for conventional trains, but by 1893 fledgling technology was available to construct the **Manx Electric Railway** (Easter–May, Sept & Oct daily 10am–5pm; June–Aug 10am–7.30pm; £6 return to Ramsey) which runs for seventeen miles from Douglas's Derby Castle Station to Ramsey via Laxey. The "Island Explorer" ticket gives one (£8), three (£18), five (£26) or seven (£32) days' unlimited travel on all bus services, plus steam and electric train routes, the trip to Snaefell and horse-tram rides in Douglas. Tickets are available from the Travel Shop or the tourist office in Douglas, or main train and tram stations.

Laxey

Filling a narrow valley, the straggling town of **LAXEY**, seven miles north of Douglas, spills down from its train station to a small harbour and long, pebbly beach, squeezed between two bulky headlands. The Manx Electric Railway from Douglas drops you at the station used by the **Snaefell Mountain Railway**. Shops and a couple of cafés here attempt to divert the crowds who disembark and then head inland and uphill to Laxey's pride, the **"Lady Isabella" Great Laxey Wheel** (Easter–Oct daily 10am–5pm; £2.75), the largest working waterwheel in the world. Otherwise Laxey is at its best down in **Old Laxey**, around the harbour, half a mile below the station, where large car parks attest to the popularity of the beach and river. Hourly **buses** #3 and #3A run to Laxey from Douglas; the #3B and #3C run directly to Old Laxey four times a day (not Sun). The *Mines Tavern,* by the station, serves **lunch**, while *Brown's* on the fantastically named Ham and Egg Terrace (by the wheel car park) is the place for fry-ups or some Manx kippers and bread and butter. Down at the harbour, the *Shore Hotel* is a nice **pub** by the bridge which brews its own bitter.

Snaefell

Every few minutes, the tramcars of the **Snaefell Mountain Railway** (Easter–Oct daily 10.30am–3.30pm; £6 return, £7.50 from Douglas) begin their thirty-minute wind from Laxey through increasingly denuded moorland to the island's highest point, the top of **Snaefell** (2036ft) – the Vikings' "Snow Mountain" – from where you can see England, Wales, Scotland and Ireland on a clear day. The four-and-a-half miles of track were built in seven months over the winter of 1895 by two hundred men; one gang worked down from the summit, the other up from Laxey, an unimaginable effort in bitter conditions. At the summit, most people are content to pop into the inelegant café and bar and then soak up the views for the few minutes until the return journey.

St Johns

The trans-island A1 (and hourly bus #5 or #6 from Douglas) follows a deep twelve-mile-long furrow between the northern and southern ranges from Douglas to Peel. A hill at the crossroads settlement of **ST JOHNS**, nine miles along it, is the original site of **Tynwald**, the ancient Manx government, which derives its name from the Norse *Thing Völlr,* meaning "Assembly Field". Nowadays the word refers to the Douglas-based House of Keys and Legislative Council, but acts passed in the capital only become law once they have been proclaimed here on July 5 (ancient Midsummer's Day) in an annual open-air parliament that also hears the grievances of the islanders. Tynwald's four-tiered grass mound – made from soil collected from each of the island's parishes – stands at the other end of a processional path from the stone **St John Chapel**, which traditionally doubled as the courthouse.

Peel

The main settlement on the west coast, **PEEL** immediately captivates, with its fine castle rising across the harbour and a popular sandy beach running the length of its eastern promenade. It's a town of some antiquity and its enduring appeal is as one of the most "Manx" of all the island's towns, a character that is manifested in various ways – from an age-old Tuesday market in the market-place above the harbour to the line of smoke-belching kipper factories along the harbourside. Archeological evidence indicates that **St Patrick's Isle**, which guards the harbour, has had a significant population since Mesolithic times. What probably started out as a flint-working village on a naturally protected spot gained significance with the foundation of a monastery in the seventh or eighth century, parts of which remain inside the ramparts of the red sandstone **Peel Castle** (Easter–Sept daily 10am–5pm; £3). The Vikings built the first fortifications and the site became the residence of the Kings of Mann until 1220, when they moved to Castle Rushen in Castletown.

It's a fifteen-minute walk from the town around the river harbour and over the bridge to the castle. On the way, you'll have passed the excellent harbourside House of Mannannan **heritage centre** (daily 10am–5pm; £5) named after the island's ancient sea-god. You should allow at least two hours to get around the museum, which concentrates strongly on participatory exhibits – whether it's listening to Celtic legends in a replica longhouse, examining the contents and occupants of a life-sized Viking ship, walking through a kipper factory or steering a steamer.

The most regular **bus** service to Peel is the hourly #5 or #6 from Douglas. The much less frequent #8 (not Sun) connects Peel to Port Erin, via St Johns and Castletown. There's central **accommodation** at the Georgian *Merchant's House*, 18 Castle St (℡01624/842541; no credit card; ❷), while for sea views you could try one of the old-fashioned guest houses at the end of Marine Parade, such as *Fernleigh* (℡01624/842435; no credit card; ❶). The *Peel Camping Park*, on Derby Road (℡01624/842341; closed mid-Sept to mid-May), is signposted about half a mile out on the Douglas road. When it comes to **eating**, head for the pub opposite the House of Mannannan: the *Creek Inn* (℡01624/842216) serves a delicious array of specials, from seafood platters to scallops mornay, inside or out, lunch and dinner.

Port Erin to Port St Mary

Plans for the southern branch of the steam railway beyond Castletown included the speculative construction of the new resort of **PORT ERIN**, at the southwestern tip of the island, just over an hour's ride from Douglas. The aspect certainly demanded a resort: a wide, fine sand beach backing a deeply indented bay sits beneath green hills, which climb to the tower-topped headland of **Bradda Head** to the northwest. Families relish the beach here, and the time-warped atmosphere, which appears to have altered little in forty years.

The **train station** is on Station Road, a couple of hundred yards above and back from the beach. **Buses** #1 and #2 from Douglas/Castletown, and #8 from Peel/St Johns, stop on Bridson Street, across Station Road and opposite the *Cherry Orchard* hotel. Most **accommodation** is in holiday apartments or long-stay hotels, booked by the week. Still, you could try one of the large hotels on the cliff-top promenade, such as the *Port Erin Royal* (℡01624/833116; ❺) or *Imperial* (℡01624/832122; ❻), both part of the same group (⚑www.porterin-hotels.com), or check on space at the *Balmoral Hotel* (℡01624/833126; ❸) further down the Promenade. The best rooms, though, are at the *Cherry Orchard Hotel* on Bridson Street (℡01624/833811, ⚑www.cherry-orchard.com; ❺), two hundred yards back from the promenade, with its own pool, sauna, restaurant and bar. Daytime **snacks and meals** are best at *La Patisserie* on Church Road between the *Cherry Orchard* and the promenade, a good deli-bakery which will make up sandwiches to take away. Or call into the *Whistlestop Café* at the train station for a light lunch or afternoon tea.

The harbour at Port Erin marks the start of a six-mile loop around Meayll Hill on the coastal path past **Spanish Head**, the island's southern tip, to Port St Mary. It's one of the best short walks on the island, giving the opportunity of a detour to **Cregneash Village Folk Museum** (Easter–Sept daily 10am–5pm; £2.75), a picturesque cluster of nineteenth-century thatched crofts on the slopes above Spanish Head. It's now peopled at weekends with spinners, weavers, turners and smiths dressed in period costumes.

The fishing harbour still dominates little **PORT ST MARY**, with its houses strung out in a chain above the busy dockside. The best beach is away to the northeast, reached from the harbour along a well-worked Victorian path which clings to the bay's rocky edge.

Castletown

From the twelfth century until 1869, **CASTLETOWN** was the island's capital, but then the influx of tourists and the increase in trade required a bigger harbour, so Douglas took over. So much the better for Castletown, which is a much more pleasant place than it might otherwise have been. Its sleepy harbour and low-roofed cottages are all dominated by **Castle Rushen** (Easter–Sept daily 10am–5pm; £4), one of the most complete and compact medieval castles in Britain. Formerly home to the island's legislature and still the site of the investiture of new lieutenant-governors, the present structure was probably started in the thirteenth century, its limestone walls well under way by the time the last Viking monarch, Magnus, died here in 1256. The heavy defences must have made entry a forbidding objective. Today, a mannequin archer guards access to displays on the castle's history, a prelude to five floors of rooms furnished in medieval and seventeenth-century styles, the most evocative being the tapestry-draped banqueting hall.

The **Old Grammar School** was the former capital's first church, built around 1200, and used as a school from 1570. There's not a lot to see, save a few information boards, but it does house a handy **tourist office** (Easter–Sept daily 10am–5pm). Something of the island's nautical heritage can be gleaned from the little **Nautical Museum** on Douglas Street (daily 10am–5pm; £2.75), just across the harbour footbridge, which displays an armed eighteenth-century yacht ("The Peggy") among other exhibits.

The **steam train station** is five minutes' walk from the centre of Castletown, out along Victoria Road from the harbour; **buses** #8 (from Peel/Port Erin) and #1 (from Douglas) stop in the main square. The only central **accommodation** is the *George Hotel* in the square (℡01624/822533; ❷). There's a clutch of **cafés** around the marketplace, though for a view of the harbour head for the *Chablis Cellar*, 21 Bank St (℡01624/823527; closed Sun eve), which does inexpensive **bistro** lunches and evening meals. The *Castle Arms*, across on the quayside, also serves food.

Travel details

Buses

For information on all local and national bus services, contact Traveline: ℡ 0870/608 2 608 (daily 7am–9pm), ⓦ www.traveline.org.uk.

Trains

For information on all local and national rail services, contact National Rail Enquiries: ℡ 08457/48 49 50, ⓦ www.nationalrail.co.uk.

Blackpool to: Manchester (hourly; 1hr 10min); Preston (hourly; 30min).

Chester to: Liverpool (2 hourly; 45min); Manchester (2 hourly; 1hr–1hr 20min).

Lancaster to: Barrow-in-Furness (17 daily; 1hr); Carlisle (hourly; 1hr); Heysham (1 daily; 30min); Manchester (hourly; 1hr); Morecambe (every 40min; 10min).

Liverpool to: Chester (2 hourly; 45min); Leeds (hourly; 2hr); Manchester (hourly; 50min); Preston (14 daily; 1hr 5min).

Manchester to: Barrow-in-Furness (Mon–Sat 7 daily, Sun 3 daily; 2hr 15min); Blackpool (hourly; 1hr 10min); Carlisle (2 daily; 2hr 30min); Chester (2 hourly; 1hr–1hr 20min); Lancaster (hourly; 1hr); Leeds (hourly; 1hr); Liverpool (every 30min; 50min); Oxenholme (4–6 daily; 40min–1hr 10min); Penrith (2–4 daily; 2hr); Preston (every 20min; 55min).

Cumbria and the Lakes

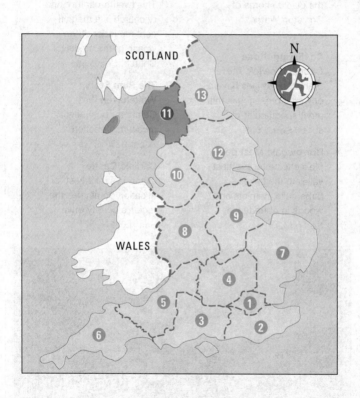

CHAPTER 11

Highlights

* **Hole in't Wall, Bowness-on-Windermere** The very picture of a classic lakeland inn – stone-flagged floors, open fires and real ale. See p.619

* **Brantwood** The home of John Ruskin, sited on the placid shores of Coniston Water. See p.625

* **Castlerigg Stone Circle, Keswick** These prehistoric stones have a powerful presence in this most spectacular of spots. See p.627

* **Borrowdale** Most people's choice for prettiest valley in the Lakes – tarns, falls, hamlets and woods in abundance. See p.629

* **Windermere** England's largest lake never disappoints. Take a cruise – jumping off to hike, to picnic, or even to swim. See p.618

* **Church of St Mary and St Michael, Cartmel** This twelfth-century priory church is a magnificent reminder of the wealth of the medieval Church. See p.635

* **The Rum Story, Whitehaven** West Cumbria's best new museum attraction. See p.637

* **Carlisle Castle** Cumbria's mightiest fortification dominates the region's county town. See p.639

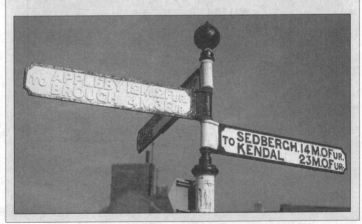

Cumbria and the Lakes

he **Lake District** is England's most hyped scenic area, and for good reasons. Within an area a mere thirty miles across, sixteen major lakes are squeezed between the steeply pitched faces of England's highest mountains, an almost alpine landscape that's augmented by waterfalls and picturesque stone-built villages packed into the valleys. Most of what people refer to as the Lake District – or simply the Lakes – lies within the **Lake District National Park**, England's largest national park, established in 1951. This, in turn, falls entirely within the northwestern county of **Cumbria**, formed in 1974 from the historic counties of Cumberland and Westmorland, and the northern part of Lancashire. Consequently Cumbria contains more than just its lakes, stretching south and west to the **coast**, and north to its county town of **Carlisle**, a place that bears traces of a pedigree that stretches back beyond the construction of Hadrian's Wall. To the east, **Penrith** and the Eden Valley separate the lakes from the near wilderness of the northern Pennines.

Everywhere in the Lakes and Cumbria is connected by local **bus**, with Stagecoach in Cumbria the biggest operator. Their **Explorer Tickets** (one-day £6.50; four-day £15) are valid on the entire network and can be bought on the bus, while other bus-and-boat combination tickets offer a variety of good deals. All routes are all spelled out in detail in the free Lakeland Explorer **timetable**, available on board buses or from local tourist offices. Even more comprehensive is the *Getting Around Cumbria and the Lake District* timetable book produced twice a year by Cumbria County Council and available from tourist offices throughout the region. Or call **Traveline** (daily 7am–8pm; ☏0870/608 2608, ⓦwww.traveline.org.uk), which can advise about all the region's bus, coach, rail and ferry services.

For more **information** about all aspects of the National Park, visit ⓦwww.lake-district.gov.uk; while the official site of the Cumbria Tourist Board is ⓦwww.golakes.co.uk.

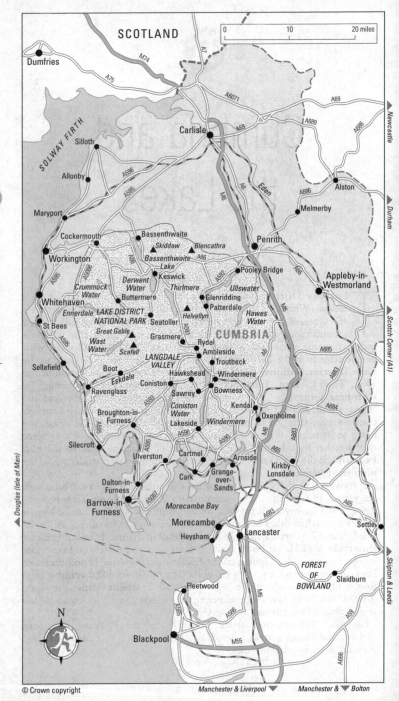

SCOTLAND

0   10   20 miles

Dumfries

Newcastle ▶

SOLWAY FIRTH

Silloth

Allonby

Carlisle

Alston

Durham ▶

Maryport

Melmerby

Cockermouth

Bassenthwaite

Skiddaw   Blencathra

Penrith

Workington

Bassenthwaite
Lake

Appleby-in-
Westmorland

Scotch Corner (A1) ▶

Derwent
Water

Keswick

Pooley Bridge

Crummock
Water

Thirlmere

Ullswater

Whitehaven

Buttermere

Glenridding

Ennerdale

LAKE DISTRICT
NATIONAL PARK

Patterdale

Hawes
Water

St Bees

Seatoller

Helvellyn

CUMBRIA

Great Gable

Grasmere

Wast
Water

Scafell

Rydal

Ambleside

Sellafield

LANGDALE
VALLEY

Troutbeck

Boot

Hawkshead

Windermere

Eskdale

Coniston

Ravenglass

Sawrey

Bowness

Broughton-in-
Furness

Coniston
Water

Kendal

Oxenholme

Silecroft

Lakeside

Windermere

Ulverston

Cartmel

Arnside

Kirkby
Lonsdale

Dalton-in-
Furness

Cark

Grange-
over-Sands

Barrow-in-
Furness

Morecambe Bay

Settle

Morecambe

Skipton & Leeds ▶

Heysham

Lancaster

FOREST
OF
BOWLAND

Slaidburn

Fleetwood

Douglas (Isle of Man) ▶

Blackpool

N

© Crown copyright

Manchester & Liverpool ▼   Manchester & ▼ Bolton

An almost unchartable network of Lake District paths connects the lakes themselves, tracks the broken knife-edge ridges of the fells and mountains or weaves easier courses around the flanks and onto the tops. Wherever you go, you should always be **properly equipped**: wear strong-soled, supportive shoes or boots, carry water, and take a map (and know how to use it). Bad weather can move in quickly, even in the height of summer, so before starting out you should check the weather forecast – many hotels and outdoor shops post a daily forecast – or call ☎017687/75757 (24-hour line).

The best general **map** of the area is the Ordnance Survey inch-to-the-mile (1:63,360) Touring Map and Guide 3, with hill shading and illustrated text on the back. Essential for **walking** are the 1:50,000 OS Landranger maps 89, 90, 96 and 97, or, better, the yellow 1:25,000 OS Outdoor Leisure series, which cover the whole Lake District. Many shops and tourist offices also sell local walk leaflets, and regional trail and hiking guides, of which Alfred Wainwright's hand-drawn masterpieces are the best known.

The Lake District

Although the Lake District might appear too popular for its own good, tourist numbers are concentrated in fairly specific areas and even on the busiest of days it's relatively easy to escape the crowds. Given a week you could see most of the famous settlements and lakes – a circuit taking in the towns of **Ambleside**, **Windermere** and **Bowness**, the Wordsworth houses and sites in pretty villages such as **Hawkshead** and **Grasmere**, and the more dramatic northern scenery near **Keswick** and **Ullswater** would give you a fair sample of the whole. But it's away from the crowds that the Lakes really begin to pay dividends, so aim to steer by central valleys such as **Langdale** and **Eskdale**, and the lesser visited lakes of **Wast Water** and **Buttermere**. Of course, it's only when you start to walk and climb around the Lakes that you can really say you've explored the region. Four peaks top out at over 3000ft – including **Scafell Pike**, the highest in England – but there are literally hundreds of other mountains, crags and fells to roam.

Human interaction has played a significant part in the shaping of the region. As the first settlers, five thousand years ago, learned to shape flints into axes, they began to clear the upland forests, a process accelerated by the road-building Romans. An even greater impact was made by the Norse Vikings in the ninth and tenth centuries, who farmed the land extensively and left their mark on the local dialect: a mountain here is referred to as a "fell", a waterfall is a "force", streams are "becks", a mountain lake is a "tarn", while the suffix "-thwaite" indicates a clearing. Two factors spurred the first waves of **tourism**: the reappraisal of landscape brought about by such painters as Constable and the writings of Wordsworth and his contemporaries, and the outbreak of the French Revolution and its subsequent turmoil, which put paid to the idea of the continental Grand Tour. At the same time, as the war pushed food prices higher, farmers began to reclaim the hillsides, a tendency sanctioned by the General Enclosure Act of 1801. Most of the characteristic dry-stone walls were built at this time, a development that alarmed Wordsworth, who wrote in his *Guide to the Lakes* that he desired "a sort of national property, in which every man has a right and interest who has an eye to perceive and a heart to enjoy." His wish finally came to fruition in 1951 when the government designated 880 square miles of the Lake District as England's largest national park.

Kendal and around

The limestone-grey town of **KENDAL** might be billed as the "Gateway to the Lakes", but it's nearly ten miles from Windermere – the true start of the lakes – and has more in common with the market towns to the east. Nonetheless, it offers rewarding rambles around the "yards" and "ginnels" which make an engaging maze on both sides of Highgate and Stricklandgate, the main streets. The old **Market Place** has long since succumbed to development, with the market hall now converted to the Westmorland Shopping Centre, but traditional stalls still do business outside every Wednesday and Saturday. The town's most visible product is **Kendal Mintcake**, an energy-giving confection of sugar and peppermint oil that has been hoisted to the top of the world's highest mountains.

The town's museums and art gallery have a joint admission policy (each open daily: April–Oct 10.30am–5pm; Nov–March 10.30am–4pm; £3, £1 with a ticket for one of the other museums). The **Kendal Museum**, on Station Road (Ⓦ www.kendalmuseum.org.uk), holds the district's natural history and archeological finds, bolstered by reverential displays on the life of **Alfred Wainwright**. In 1952 this one-time borough treasurer, dissatisfied with the accuracy of existing maps of the paths and ancient tracks across the fells, embarked on what became a series of 47 walking guides, all but two of them painstakingly handwritten with mapped routes and delicately drawn views. The other two museums are in the Georgian **Abbot Hall** (Ⓦ www.abbothall .org.uk) and its stable block, by the river to the south. The main hall, painstakingly restored to its 1760s town-house origins, houses the **Art Gallery**, where cherubic portraits by society painter George Romney line the walls, along with works by Constable, Ruskin, Turner, Edward Lear and lesser local artists. The stables now contain the **Museum of Lakeland Life and Industry**, where reconstructed house interiors stand alongside workshops which make a fairly vivid presentation of rural trades and crafts, from spinning and weaving to tanning.

Just behind Abbot Hall, the wide aisles of the Early English **parish church** (daily: Easter–Oct 9.20am–4.30pm; Nov–Easter 9.20am–noon) house a number of family chapels, including that of the Parr family, who once owned **Kendal Castle**, on a hillock to the east across the river. If you fancy the climb up for the views, follow the footpath from the end of Parr Street, across the footbridge just north of the church and hall.

Practicalities

Kendal's **train station** is the first stop on the Windermere branch line, just five minutes from the **Oxenholme** mainline station. National Express and all regional buses stop at the **bus station** on Blackhall Road (off Stramongate). The **tourist office** (March–Dec Mon–Sat 9am–6pm, Sun 9am–5pm; Jan & Feb closed Sun; ☎01539/725758, Ⓦ www.kendaltown.org) is in the town hall on Highgate. There's **internet** access at Kendal library and at *Dot Café*, inside the Westmorland Shopping Centre.

Most of the local **B&Bs** lie along the road to Windermere, north of the centre, though near the train station there's the Georgian *Bridge House*, 65 Castle St (☎01539/722041, Ⓦ www.bridgehouse-kendal.co.uk; no credit cards; ❷). Best choice is the *Lakeland Natural Vegetarian Guesthouse* at Low Slack, Queen's Road (☎01539/733011, Ⓦ www.landnatural.co.uk; ❸), or look along Milnthorpe Road, a few minutes' south of the centre – walk straight down Highgate and Kirkland – where several places cluster together, including the *Headlands*, 53

Milnthorpe Rd (℡01539/732464, ⓦwww.headlands-hotel.co.uk; ❷). There's a **youth hostel** at 118 Highgate (℡01539/724066, ⓦwww.yha.org.uk), which is attached to The Brewery arts centre.

Kendal certainly doesn't lack decent **cafés**, starting with the *1657 Chocolate House*, on Branthwaite Brow. For inexpensive veggie wholefood lunches and riverside seating, visit the *Waterside Café* on Gulfs Road, at the bottom of Lowther Street. Best **restaurant** is the highly regarded *Moon*, 129 Highgate (℡01539/729254; Wed–Sun dinner only, closed Mon & Tues), an easy-going bistro, or eat Thai at the *Chiang Thai*, 54 Stramongate (closed Mon). For evening entertainment the **Brewery Arts Centre**, on Highgate (℡01539/725133, ⓦwww.breweryarts.co.uk), with its café, bar, cinema, theatre and concert hall, is a good bet.

Sizergh Castle and Levens Hall

Three miles to the south of Kendal stands **Sizergh Castle** (Easter–Oct Mon–Thurs & Sun 1.30–5.30pm; gardens open 12.30pm; £5; gardens only £2.50; NT), tucked away off the A591 amid acres of parkland and reached on bus #555/556. Home of the Strickland family for eight centuries, Sizergh is more of a grand manor house than a castle, but owes its epithet to the fourteenth-century peel tower (which you'll often see spelt "pele" in the North) at its core, one of the best examples of the towers built throughout the region as safe havens during the protracted border raids of the Middle Ages. Like much of the rest of the house, the Great Hall underwent significant changes in Elizabethan times, when extensions were added to the house and most of its rooms were panelled in oak with their ceilings layered in elaborate plasterwork.

Two miles south of Sizergh, just of the A590 (also bus #555/556), **Levens Hall** (April to mid-Oct Mon–Thurs & Sun noon–5pm; gardens open 10am; £6; gardens only £4.50; ⓦwww.levenshall.co.uk), also built around an early peel tower, is more uniform in style than Sizergh, since the bulk of it was built or refurbished in classic Elizabethan style between 1570 and 1640 by James Bellingham. The main entrance opens into the spacious Great Hall, its panelled walls lined with coats of arms; to the left of the hall are the large and small drawing rooms. The other end of the Great Hall leads to the most splendid apartment, the dining room, panelled not with oak but with goat's leather, printed with a deep green floral design – one goat was needed for every forty or so squares.

Windermere, Bowness and around

WINDERMERE town was all but non-existent until 1847 when a railway terminal was built here, making England's longest lake (after which the town is named) an easily accessible resort. Windermere remains the transport hub for the southern lakes, but there's precious little else to keep you in the slate-grey streets. Instead, all the traffic pours a mile down hill to Windermere's older twin town, **BOWNESS** – bus #599 leaves Windermere train station every twenty minutes for the ten-minute run down to its lakeside piers. This is undoubtedly the more attractive of the two settlements, with enough scattered attractions to fill a morning. Most tourists, though, bypass everything in Bowness bar the lake for the chance to visit **The World of Beatrix Potter** in the Old Laundry on Crag Brow (daily: Easter–Sept 10am–5.30pm; Oct–Easter 10am–4.30pm; £3.50; ⓦwww.hop-skip-jump.com). It's unfair to be judgmental – you either like Beatrix Potter or you don't – but it's safe to say that the displays here find more favour with children than the more formal Potter attractions at Hill Top and

Hawkshead. Five hundred yards north of Bowness, on Rayrigg Road, the **Windermere Steamboat Museum** (Easter–Oct daily 10am–5pm; £3.40; steam-launch cruises £5; ⓦ www.steamboat.co.uk) has as its star exhibit the 1850 *Dolly*, claimed to be the world's oldest mechanically driven boat, and extremely well preserved after spending 65 years in the mud at the bottom of Ullswater.

Both, however, come second-best to a trip on **Windermere** itself. Windermere Lake Cruises (ⓣ 015394/31188, ⓦ www.windermere-lakecruises.co.uk) operates stylish steamers and vintage cruisers to Lakeside at the southern tip (£6.20 return) or to Waterhead (for Ambleside) at the northern end (£6 return). A 24-hour **Freedom-of-the-Lake ticket** costs £10.50. Services on both routes are frequent between Easter and October (1–2 hourly at peak times), but much reduced during the winter. The **car-ferry service** across the water to Sawrey (Mon–Sat 7am–10pm, Sun 9am–10pm; departures every 20min; 40p; cars £2), from just south of Bowness, provides access to Beatrix Potter's former home at Hill Top.

A mile and a half south of Bowness, the architect Mackay Hugh Baillie Scott's **Blackwell** (daily 10am–5pm, closes 4pm in winter; £4.50; ⓦ www.blackwell.org.uk) was built in 1900 as a lakeside holiday home for Edward Holt, of the Manchester brewing family. Selected rooms of the restored interior can be viewed, which show off lakeland motifs (particularly trees, flowers, birds and berries) in virtually every nook and cranny. There's a tearoom and gardens too, though no direct bus – the walk from Bowness is about a mile.

Three miles northwest of Windermere, the Lake District National Park has its headquarters at **Brockhole Visitor Centre** (Easter–Oct daily 10am–5pm; grounds & gardens open all year; free; parking £3; ⓦ www.lake-district .gov.uk), a fine mansion set in landscaped grounds on the shores of the lake. Besides the natural history and geological displays, the centre hosts guided walks, children's activities, garden tours, special exhibitions, lectures and film shows. The #555/556 and #559 buses between Windermere and Ambleside run past the visitor centre, or you can get there by Windermere Lake Cruises launch from Waterhead, Ambleside (hourly 10.45am–4.45pm; £4.60 return).

From Bowness piers **cruises** also head south down the lake to **Lakeside**, on Windermere's quieter southern reaches. Lakeside is the terminus of the **Lakeside and Haverthwaite Railway** (Easter–Oct 6–7 daily; £3.90 return; ⓣ 015395/31594, ⓦ www.furnessrailwaytrust.org.uk), whose steam-powered engines chuff along four miles of track through the forests of Backbarrow Gorge. The boat arrivals at Lakeside connect with train departures throughout the day and you can buy a joint boat-and-train ticket (£9.60 return) at Bowness. Also on the quay at Lakeside is the **Aquarium of the Lakes** (daily: April–Sept 9am–6pm; Oct–May 9am–5pm; £5.50; ⓦ www.aquariumofthelakes.co.uk), an entertaining natural history exhibit centred on the fish and animals found in and along a lakeland river, including a pair of captive otters. Again, there's a joint ticket available with the boat ride from Bowness (£10.35 return).

Practicalities

National Express and most local **buses** stop outside Windermere **train station**, a few yards from the **tourist office** on Victoria Street (daily: July & Aug 9am–7.30pm; rest of the year 9am–6pm; ⓣ 015394/46499). There's a second information office down in Bowness, by the piers on Glebe Road (Easter–Oct Mon–Thurs & Sun 9.30am–5.30pm, Fri & Sat 9.30am–6pm; Nov–Easter Fri–Sun 9.30am–5.30pm; ⓣ 015394/42895). For **bike rental**, contact Country Lanes, The Railway Station, Windermere (ⓣ 015394/44544, ⓦ www.country-lanes.co.uk).

The cheapest **rooms in Windermere** are at the *Backpackers Hostel* in the Old Bakery at the top of the High Street (℡015394/46374, Ⓦwww.lakedistrictbackpackers.co.uk no credit cards; ❶), near the tourist office. Otherwise, top **B&B** choices include *Ashleigh Guesthouse* at 11 College Rd (℡015394/42292; no credit cards; ❷), and the *Archway* at no. 13 (℡015394/45613, Ⓦwww.communiken.com/archway; no credit cards; ❸); spick-and-span *Brendan Chase*, 1–3 College Rd (℡015394/45638; no credit cards; ❶); and welcoming, family-run *Broadlands Guest House*, 19 Broad St (℡015394/46532, Ⓦwww.broadlands.clara.co.uk; ❷).

In **Bowness**, *Above The Bay*, 5 Brackenfield (℡015394/88658, Ⓦwww.abovethebay.co.uk; no credit cards; ❸), has lake views, just off the Kendal road a little way south of the centre; or try the seventeenth-century *Laurel Cottage* in St Martin's Square (℡015394/45594, Ⓦwww.laurelcottage-bnb.co.uk; no credit cards; ❷). By far the swankiest central option is the *Old England*, Church Street (℡015394/42444, Ⓦwww.heritage-hotels.com; ❼), a relaxed grande-dame hotel opposite the church, with heated outdoor pool and terraced lakeside gardens.

Eating and drinking is generally better done down in Bowness, but look out in Windermere for the *Miller Howe Café* inside Lakeland Ltd by the train station, which serves up superior snacks, sandwiches and daily specials. In Bowness, budget pizza and pasta is on offer at *Rastelli's,* on Lake Road (closed Wed), while for a **drink**, don't miss the *Hole in't Wall* pub, the town's oldest hostelry, in Falbarrow Road behind Bowness church – cosy in winter when the fires are lit, and pleasant in summer when you can sit outside.

Troutbeck

Troutbeck Bridge, a mile northwest of Windermere along the A591, heralds the start of a gentle valley below Wansfell, where you'll find Windermere's local **youth hostel**, *High Cross* at Bridge Lane (℡015394/43543, Ⓦwww.yha.org.uk), almost a mile uphill from the bridge. A YHA shuttle-bus service operates to the hostel from Windermere train station (meeting arriving trains) and from Ambleside youth hostel, or there's a fine cross-country walking route (3 miles; 1hr 30min) via **Orrest Head** (784ft), whose summit gives a 360° panorama from the Yorkshire fells to the Langdales and Troutbeck Valley – the path branches off the main road a hundred yards south of Windermere train station, by the *Windermere Hotel*.

A little further up the minor valley road from the hostel, **Townend** (Easter–Oct Tues–Fri & Sun 1–5pm; £3; NT) has been preserved as a seventeenth-century yeoman-farmer's house, complete with original furniture and decorative woodwork. Troutbeck's **inn**, the *Mortal Man* (℡015394/33193, Ⓦwww.mortal-man-inns.co.uk; ❻, ❼ with dinner; closed mid-Nov to mid-Feb) has terrific valley views from its rooms and beer-garden, while Troutbeck's other old inn, the *Queen's Head*, down on the main A592 (℡015394/32174, Ⓦwww.queensheadhotel.com; ❹; minimum two-night stay at weekends) serves good food. The *Queen's Head* is a stop on the summer weekend #108A bus route from Bowness and Windermere.

Ambleside

AMBLESIDE, five miles northwest of Windermere, is at the heart of the southern lakes region, making it a first-class base for walkers. The town centre consists of a cluster of grey-green stone houses, shops and B&Bs hugging a circular one-way system, which loops round just south of the narrow gully of stony Stock Ghyll. The rest of town lies a mile south at **Waterhead**, a harbour on the shores of Windermere that's filled with ducks, swans and rowing boats and overlooked by the landscaped gardens of several plush hotels. In Ambleside itself, spare a few minutes for the mural of the rush-bearing ceremony in **St Mary's Church**, whose spire is visible from all over town. A couple of hundred yards north, **Bridge House** (Easter–Oct daily 10am–5pm; free), now a National Trust information centre, straddles Stock Ghyll – scurrilous legend has it that a Scotsman built the two-storey, two-roomed house to evade land taxes. For Ambleside's history, stroll a couple of minutes' along Rydal Road to the **Ambleside Museum** (daily 10am–5pm; £2.50; @www.armitt.com), whose collection catalogues the very distinct contribution to lakeland society made by John Ruskin, Beatrix Potter and longtime Ambleside resident, writer Harriet Martineau. Finally, soccer fans shouldn't miss soccer photographer Stuart Clarke's gallery **The Homes of Football** (daily 10am–5pm; free; @www.homesoffootball.co.uk) at 100 Lake Rd. A permanent archive of over 60,000 images of the country's stadiums and fans, it's quite irresistible.

Practicalities

Buses (including National Express) all stop on Kelsick Road, opposite the library. The **tourist office** is just up the road, in Central Buildings on Market Cross (daily 9am–5.30pm; ☎015394/32582). For **bike rental**, try Biketreks on Compston Road (☎015394/31505, @www.biketreks.co.uk), or Ghyllside Cycles on The Slack (☎015394/33592, @www.ghyllside.co.uk).

Lake Road, running between Waterhead and Ambleside, is lined with **B&Bs**, while there are other options on central Church Street and Compston Road. The cheapest rates are at *Linda's B&B and Bunkhouse* at *Shirland*, Compston Road (☎015394/32999; no credit cards; ❶), while another popular low-cost choice is *3 Cambridge Villas*, Church St (☎015394/32307; no credit cards; ❷). *Mill Cottage* on Rydal Road (☎015394/34830; ❸), near Bridge House, is housed in a sixteenth-century mill building, with a riverside café underneath. Or move up a notch to *Compston House Hotel* on Compston Road (☎015394/ 32305, @www.compstonhouse.co.uk; ❸), a traditional lakeland house with American-style themed rooms. One of the Lake District's best sited **youth hostels** is at Waterhead on the A591 (☎015394/32304, @www.yha.org.uk), a huge lakeside affair; while the nearest **campsite** is the *Low Wray National Trust Campsite* (☎015394/32810; closed Nov–Easter) three miles south of town – hourly bus #505/506 passes within a mile.

Pippins, at 10 Lake Rd, is great for all-day breakfasts, burgers and night-time pizzas, while the *Apple Pie* on Rydal Road is the place for home-made pies. *Zeffirelli's*, Compston Road (☎015394/33845), specializes in inexpensive vegetarian food, either in the daytime *Garden Café* or upstairs in the restaurant for pizzas and pasta. The *Glass House* (☎015394/32137; closed Mon in winter), a renovated mill with waterwheel on Rydal Road, serves accomplished Mediterranean/Modern British cooking – coffee and light lunches are available, too.

Langdale

Three miles west of Ambleside along the A593, **Skelwith Bridge** marks the start of **Great Langdale**, a U-shaped glacial valley overlooked by the prominent rocky summits of the **Langdale Pikes**, the most popular of the central Lakeland fells. The #516 Langdale Rambler **bus** from Ambleside's Kelsick Road runs to Skelwith Bridge, Elterwater and the *Old Dungeon Ghyll Hotel* (see below) at the head of the valley between April and October.

ELTERWATER village lies half a mile northwest of its namesake water, fringed by sheep-filled commonland and centred on a tiny green. It sees its fair share of Langdale-bound hikers, not least because of its two local **youth hostels**: *Elterwater Langdale,* just across the bridge from the village (℡015394/ 37245, Ⓦwww.yha.org.uk); and *Langdale High Close,* a mile from Elterwater (bookings through Ambleside YHA: ℡015394/32304, Ⓦwww.yha.org.uk), with a more spectacular setting, high on the road over Red Bank from Skelwith Bridge to Grasmere. There's traditional hospitality at the *Britannia Inn* (℡015394/37210, Ⓦwww.britinn.co.uk; ❹), a solid old lakeland pub on the green.

The riverside Cumbria Way footpath runs as far as the *New Dungeon Ghyll Hotel,* three miles from Elterwater. A path indicated by the "Stickle Ghyll" sign follows the beck straight up to **Stickle Tarn**, around to the right then left up to **Pavey Ark** (2297ft). It is fairly easy from then on to **Harrison Stickle** (2414ft), down to the stream forming the headwaters of Dungeon Ghyll and slowly up to **Pike of Stickle** (2326ft). Backtracking a short distance, a path leads to the right almost parallel with Dungeon Ghyll, back to the start (4 miles; 2400ft ascent; 4hr).

The traditional **accommodation** in the valley is the peerless *Old Dungeon Ghyll Hotel* (℡015394/37272, Ⓦwww.odg.co.uk; ❺, ❻ with dinner), at the end of the B5343, seven miles northeast of Ambleside; it offers great three-course dinners in its restaurant (book in advance) and has a stone-flagged hikers' bar serving filling food. In the evening, the bar fills up with refugees from the nearby *Great Langdale* **campsite** (℡015394/37668). A mile or so back down the road, rooms at the *New Dungeon Ghyll Hotel* (℡015394/37213, Ⓦwww.dungeon-ghyll.com; ❺, ❼ with dinner) feature dramatic fell views. You can also eat here, or at the adjacent *Sticklebarn Tavern* (℡015394/37356; ❶), which has bunk-barn accommodation.

Grasmere and around

Four miles northwest of Ambleside, the village of **GRASMERE** consists of an intimate cluster of grey-stone houses on the old packhorse road which runs beside the babbling River Rothay. It's an eminently pleasing ensemble, set back from one of the most alluring of the region's small lakes, but it loses some of its charm in summer thanks to the hordes who descend on the trail of the village's most famous former resident, **William Wordsworth** (1770–1850). The poet, his wife Mary, sister Dorothy and other members of his family are buried beneath the yews in **St Oswald's churchyard**, around which the river makes a sinuous curl.

On the southeastern outskirts of the village, on the main A591, stands **Dove Cottage** (daily 9.30am–5.30pm; closed mid-Jan to mid-Feb; £5; Ⓦwww .wordsworth.org.uk), home to William and Dorothy Wordsworth from 1799 to 1808 and where Wordsworth wrote some of his best poetry. Most of the furniture in the cottage belonged to the Wordsworths, while in the upper rooms are various other possessions, including a pair of William's ice skates. In good weather, the **garden** is open for visits as well (same hours as cottage). In the adjacent **museum** are more paintings, manuscripts and personal effects once belonging to the Wordsworths (most poignantly Mary's wedding ring), plus mementoes of Southey, Coleridge and Thomas De Quincey. Exhibits here are likely to be rearranged in the future, now that proposals for a new extension to the museum have been agreed.

William Wordsworth was not the first to praise the Lake District – Thomas Gray wrote appreciatively of his visit in 1769 – but it is Wordsworth that dominates its literary landscape, not solely through his poetry but also through his still useful *Guide to the Lakes* (1810). Born in Cockermouth in 1770, he was sent to school in Hawkshead before a stint at Cambridge, a year in France and two in Somerset. In 1799 he returned to the Lake District, settling in the Grasmere district, where he spent the last two-thirds of his life with his sister Dorothy, who not only transcribed his poems but was an accomplished diarist as well.

Wordsworth and fellow poets **Samuel Taylor Coleridge** and **Robert Southey** formed a clique that became known as the "Lake Poets", a label based more on their fluctuating friendships and their shared passion for the region than on any common subject matter in their writings. A fourth member of the Cumbrian literary elite was the critic and essayist **Thomas De Quincey**, chiefly known today for his *Confessions of an English Opium-Eater*. One of the first to fully appreciate the revolutionary nature of Wordsworth's and Coleridge's collaborative *Lyrical Ballads*, De Quincey became a long-term guest of the Wordsworths in 1807, taking over Dove Cottage from them in 1809. He stayed there until 1820, but it was only in the 1830s that he started writing his *Lake Reminiscences*, offending Wordsworth and Coleridge in the process.

Meanwhile, after short spells at Allan Bank and The Vicarage, both in Grasmere, the Wordsworths made Rydal Mount their home, supported largely by William's position as Distributor of Stamps for Westmorland and his later stipend as Poet Laureate. After his death in 1850, William's body was interred in St Oswald's churchyard in Grasmere, to be joined five years later by Dorothy and by his wife Mary four years after that.

Inspired by Wordsworth's writings and by the terrain itself, the social philosopher and art critic **John Ruskin** also made the Lake District his home, settling at Brantwood outside Coniston in 1872. His letters and watercolours reflect a deep love of the area, also demonstrated by his unsuccessful fight to prevent the damming of Thirlmere. Much of Ruskin's feeling for the countryside permeated through to two other literary immigrants, **Arthur Ransome**, also a Coniston resident and writer of the children's classic *Swallows and Amazons*, and **Beatrix Potter**, whose favourite Lakeland spots feature in her children's stories.

Another mile and a half southeast along the A591 from Grasmere, the hamlet of **RYDAL** consists of an inn, a few houses and **Rydal Mount** (March–Oct daily 9.30am–5pm; Nov–Feb Wed–Mon 10am–4pm; £4, gardens only £1.75), home of William Wordsworth from 1813 until his death in 1850. Parts of the house have been redecorated, but furniture and portraits give a good sense of its former occupants. For many, the highlight is the garden, which has been preserved as Wordsworth designed it, complete with terraces where he used to declaim his poetry. Buses #555/556 and #599 pass the house on the way to Grasmere from Windermere and Ambleside.

Practicalities

Buses stop on the village green. A Stagecoach Round Robin ticket (£5) allows up to five stops on return journeys between Bowness or Ambleside and the Wordsworth houses and Grasmere. The **tourist office** (April–Oct daily 9.30am–5pm; Nov–March Fri, Sat & Sun 10am–3.30pm; ☎015394/35245), five minutes' away from the green down Langdale Road, is tucked in by the main **car park** on Red Bank Road at the southern end of the village.

Accommodation can be hard to come by in summer – book well in advance, especially for popular central places such as the *Harwood*, Red Lion Square (℡015394/35248, ⓦwww.harwoodhotel.co.uk; ❸). *Banerigg Guest House* (℡015394/35204; no smoking; no credit cards; ❸), is a lakeside property fifteen minutes walk out on the Ambleside road (A591); or there's *Titteringdales Guesthouse*, on Pye Lane (℡015394/35439, ⓦwww.grasmere.net; ❷), to the north, just off the A591. The *Red Lion* in central Red Lion Square (℡015394/35456; ❻) is a sympathetically styled eighteenth-century coaching inn. Top of the pile is *White Moss House* (℡015394/35295, ⓦwww.whitemoss.com; ❽, with dinner; closed Dec & Jan), a house once owned by Wordsworth, a mile south on the A591, at the northern end of Rydal Water. Lesser budgets are required for *How Foot Lodge*, at Town End (℡015394/35366; ❸; closed Jan), a Victorian house owned by the National Trust, just yards from Dove Cottage. Grasmere also has three very popular **youth hostels**. The YHA choices are *Butterlip How*, a Victorian house 150 yards north of the green on Easedale Road, and *Thorney How*, a characterful former farmhouse, just under a mile further along the unlit road. Reservations for both are made at *Butterlip How* (℡015394/35316, ⓦwww.yha.org.uk). There's also the excellent *Grasmere Independent Hostel* at Broadrayne Farm (℡015394/35055, ⓦwww.grasmere-accommodation.co.uk; ❶), just north of town on the A591, whose dorm rooms are all en suite.

The *Rowan Tree*, on Church Bridge, Stock Lane, opposite the churchyard, serves vegetarian dishes on a terrace overlooking the river and is open in the evenings, or there's the *Dove Cottage Tea Rooms and Restaurant*, at Town End near Dove Cottage, open during the day for tearoom favourites and at night (℡015394/35268; closed Mon May–Oct, plus Tues & Sun rest of year) for fashionable dinners. The only real **pub** in the village is the *Red Lion* – whose public bar is called the *Lamb Inn*.

Coniston Water

At five miles long and half a mile across at its widest point, **Coniston Water** is not one of the most immediately imposing of the lakes, yet it has a quiet beauty which sets it apart from the more popular destinations. The nineteenth-century art critic and social reformer **John Ruskin** made the lake his home and his isolated house, Brantwood, today provides the most obvious target for a day-trip. Some come here, too, on the *Swallows and Amazons* trail. **Arthur Ransome** was a frequent visitor, his memories and experiences providing much detail later in his famous children's books. In the mid-1960s, the long uninterruptedly glass-like surface of Coniston Water attracted the attention of national hero **Donald Campbell**, who in 1955 had set a world water-speed record of 202mph on Ullswater, bumping it up to 276mph nine years later in Australia. On January 4, 1967, he set out to better his own mark on Coniston Water, but just as his jet-powered *Bluebird* hit an estimated 320mph, a patch of turbulence sent it into a somersault. Campbell was killed immediately and his body and boat lay undisturbed at the bottom of the lake until both were retrieved in 2001, Campbell for reburial at Coniston's cemetery, *Bluebird* into storage while it's decided what to do with the remains of the boat.

Coniston village and Brantwood

A memorial seat and plaque to Campbell decorates the green in the slate-grey village of **CONISTON** (a derivation of "King's Town"), hunkered below the craggy and copper-mine-riddled bulk of **The Old Man of Coniston**. Campbell's grave is nearby, in the new cemetery (behind the *Crown Hotel*).

△ Ullswater

Having studied this and Ruskin's grave, which lies in St Andrew's original churchyard beneath a beautifully worked Celtic cross, you've seen all that Coniston has to offer, save for the excellent **Ruskin Museum** on Yewdale Road (Easter to mid-Nov daily 10am–5.30pm; mid-Nov to Easter Wed–Sun 10am–3.30pm; £3.50; ⓦwww.coniston.org.uk), which combines local history and geology exhibits with a fascinating look at Ruskin's life and work.

Coniston Water itself is hidden out of sight, half a mile southeast of the village. Boat speeds are limited to 10mph, a graceful pace for the sumptuously upholstered **Steam Yacht Gondola** (Easter–Oct 5 daily; £4.80 round trip; ☎015394/63856), built in 1859, which leaves Coniston Pier for hour-long circuits, calling at Park-a-moor landing stage then Ruskin's Brantwood. The wooden **Coniston Launch** (Easter–Oct hourly; Nov–Easter up to 4 daily depending on the weather; ☎015394/36216, ⓦwww.lakefell.co.uk) operates a year-round service to Brantwood on two routes, north (£3.60 return) or south (£5.80) around the lake.

Both steam yacht and motor launches dock beneath the magnificently sited **Brantwood** (mid-March to mid-Nov daily 11am–5.30pm; mid-Nov to mid-March Wed–Sun 11am–4.30pm; £7.50; house only £4.50; gardens only £2; ⓦwww.brantwood.org.uk), two and a half miles by road from Coniston, where art critic and moralist **John Ruskin** lived from 1872 until his death in 1900. Champion of J.M.W. Turner and the Pre-Raphaelites and proponent of the supremacy of Gothic architecture, Ruskin insisted upon the indivisibility of ethics and aesthetics, and was appalled by the conditions in which the captains of industry made their labourers work and live, while expecting him to applaud their patronage of the arts. A twenty-minute video expands on his philosophy and whets the appetite for rooms full of his watercolours. His study and dining room boast superlative lake views, bettered only by those from the Turret Room where he used to sit in later life in his bathchair, itself on display downstairs, along with his mahogany desk and Blue John wine goblet, among other memorabilia. Various other exhibition rooms and galleries display Ruskin-related arts and crafts, while the *Jumping Jenny Tearooms* – named after Ruskin's boat – has outdoor terrace seating for meals and drinks.

Practicalities

Buses stop on the main road through the village, though some of the services also run down to the ferry pier at the lake. A Ruskin Explorer ticket (£9) gets you return bus travel between Bowness and Coniston, plus use of the Coniston Launch and free entry to Ruskin's house – buy the ticket on the bus. The **tourist office** (April–Oct daily 9.30am–5.30pm; Nov–March Fri–Sun 10am–3.30pm; ☎015394/41533) is right in the centre on Ruskin Avenue. You can **rent bikes** from Summitreks on Yewdale Road (☎015394/41212, ⓦwww.summittreks.co.uk).

The most comfortable **B&Bs** are *Shepherds Villa*, Tilberthwaite Avenue (☎015394/ 41337; ❷) – the B5285 into the village – and the vegetarian *Beech Tree Guesthouse*, Yewdale Road (☎015394/41717; no credit cards; ❷) – the Ambleside road. All the pubs have rooms, but the best are those at the *Sun Hotel* (☎015394/41248, ⓦwww.smoothhound.co.uk/hotels/sun; ❹, minimum two-night stay at weekends), a fine old inn 200 yards uphill from the bridge in the centre of Coniston. Of the two **youth hostels**, *Coniston Holly How* (☎015394/41323, ⓦwww.yha.org.uk) is the closer, just a few minutes' walk north of Coniston on the Ambleside road, but *Coniston Coppermines* (☎015394/41261) is more peaceful, in a dramatic mountain setting a steep mile or so from the village. The nearest **campsite** is the *Coniston Hall Campsite*, Haws

Bank (☎015394/41223; booking essential; closed Nov–March), a mile south of town by the lake.

Eating opportunities outside the pubs are limited, but in any case you shouldn't look much further than the *Sun Hotel*, whose cosy bar has filling meals. The *Sun* is also the cheeriest place for a **drink**, though the *Black Bull* in the centre brews its own *Bluebird* beer.

Hawkshead and around

Greystone **HAWKSHEAD**, between Coniston and Ambleside, wears its beauty well, its patchwork of cottages and cobbles backed by woods and fells and barely affected by twentieth-century intrusions. This is partly due to the enlightened policy of banning traffic in the centre – huge car parks at the village edge take the strain and when the crowds of day-trippers leave, Hawkshead regains its natural tranquillity.

The village was an important wool market at the time Wordsworth was studying at **Hawkshead Grammar School** (Easter–Oct Mon–Sat 10am–12.30pm & 1.30–5pm, Sun 1–5pm; £2), founded in 1585, whose entrance lies opposite the tourist office – pride of place is given to the desk on which William carved his signature. While there he attended the fifteenth-century **Church of St Michael** (daily 9am–6pm) above the school, which harks back to Norman designs in its rounded pillars and patterned arches. From its knoll the churchyard gives a good view over the village's twin central squares, and of Main Street, housing the **Beatrix Potter Gallery** (Easter–Oct Mon–Thurs & Sun 10.30am–4.30pm; £3; NT), occupying rooms once used by her solicitor husband. Fans get bustled into rooms full of Potter's original illustrations, though the less devoted might find displays on her life as keen naturalist, conservationist and early supporter of the National Trust more diverting.

The main **bus service** to Hawkshead is the #505/506 between Bowness, Ambleside and Coniston; on reaching Hawkshead it loops down to Hill Top and back for the Beatrix Potter house at Near Sawrey. The **tourist office** is at the main car park (Easter–Oct daily 9.30am–6pm; Nov–Easter Fri, Sat & Sun 10am–3.30pm; ☎015394/36525). Some contend that Wordsworth briefly boarded at what is now *Ann Tyson's Cottage*, on cobbled Wordsworth Street (☎015394/36405, ⊕www.anntysons.co.uk; ❷). The whitewashed *Old School House* (☎015394/36403; ❷) is another historic choice, just behind the Grammar School. The **youth hostel**, *Esthwaite Lodge* (☎015394/36293, ⊕www.yha .org.uk), is a mile to the south down the Newby Bridge road, while **camping** is at Hawkshead's busy *Croft Caravan and Campsite* (☎015394/ 36374, ⊕www.hawkshead-croft.com; closed Nov to mid-March), on North Lonsdale Road, right by the village. **Pubs** provide the main eating options, not bad at either the *Queen's Head* on Main Street (☎015394/36271, ⊕www.queenshead-hotel.co.uk; ❹) or the *King's Arms*, on the main square (☎015394/36372, ⊕www.kingsarmshawkshead.co.uk; ❹), both of which have bar meals as well as a more formal restaurant. Of the **tearooms**, the fifteenth-century *Minstrels' Gallery* on the main square has an espresso machine – ask here, too, about renting cottages in the area.

Hill Top

It's two miles from Hawkshead, down the eastern side of Esthwaite Water on the B5285 to the pretty twin hamlets of Near and Far Sawrey, the first the site of Beatrix Potter's beloved **Hill Top** (Easter–Oct Mon–Wed, Sat & Sun 11am–5pm; £4; NT). A Londoner by birth, Potter bought the farmhouse here with the proceeds from her first book, *The Tale of Peter Rabbit*, and retained it as her study long after she moved out following her marriage in 1913. Its furnishings and contents have been kept as they were during her occupancy – a condition of Potter's will – and the small house is always busy with visitors; so much so that numbers are often limited. In summer, expect to have to wait in line. From April to October, you can travel to Hill Top directly from Bowness (10am–4.30pm every 40min; ☎015394/45161, ⓦwww.mountain-goat.com) on a combined "boat-and-goat" ferry-and-minibus service, which runs on from Hill Top to Hawkshead and back.

Tarn Hows

A minor road off the Hawkshead–Coniston B5285 winds the couple of miles northwest to the highly popular **Tarn Hows**, a body of water surrounded by spruce and pine and circled by paths and picnic spots. The land was donated by Beatrix Potter in 1930, since when the National Trust has carefully maintained it. It takes an hour to walk around the tarn, during which you can ponder on the fact that this miniature idyll is in fact almost entirely artificial – the original owners enlarged two small tarns to make the one you see today, planted and landscaped the surroundings and dug the footpaths. A free National Trust Tarn Hows **bus service** runs between Hawkshead and Coniston on Sundays between Easter and the end of October, linking with the regular #505/506. Otherwise, you'll have to walk the two miles up from Coniston or Hawkshead on country paths and lanes.

Keswick and Derwent Water

Standing on the shores of **Derwent Water** at the junction of the main north–south and east–west routes through the Lake District, **KESWICK** makes a good base for exploring delightful Borrowdale – the start of many walking routes to the central peaks around Scafell Pike – or Skiddaw and Blencathra, which loom over the town. For those not up to a day on the fells, the town remains a popular place throughout the year, with a big enough population (around five thousand) to warrant a bevy of local museums and sights.

Granted its market charter by Edward I in 1276 – **market day** is Saturday – Keswick was an important wool and leather centre until around 1500, when these trades were supplanted by the discovery of local graphite. **The Cumberland Pencil Museum**, west of the centre at Greta Bridge, on Main Street (daily 9.30am–4pm; £2.50; ⓦwww.pencils.co.uk), tells the whole story entertainingly. On the edge of Fitz Park, on Station Road, you'll find the **Keswick Museum and Art Gallery** (Easter–Oct daily 10am–4pm; £1), a quirky Victorian collection of ancient dental tools, fossils and some prized manuscripts and letters written by the Lakeland Poets. Make time, too, for a couple of churches: **St John's**, on St John Street in the centre, where the novelist Sir Hugh Walpole (of Herries novels fame) is buried; and **Crosthwaite Church**, a fifteen-minute walk northwest of town, over Greta Bridge, resting place of the poet Robert Southey.

Keswick's most celebrated landmark, **Castlerigg Stone Circle**, is made especially resonant by its magnificent mountain backdrop. From the end of Station Road, take the Threlkeld rail line path (signposted by the *Keswick Country House Hotel*) and follow the signs. Thirty-eight hunks of Borrowdale volcanic stone, the largest almost eight feet tall, form a circle a hundred feet in diameter; another ten blocks delineating a rectangular enclosure within. Back on the rail path, you can easily continue all the way to **Threlkeld** itself, three miles from town, on a delightful riverside walk with the promise of a drink in one of Threlkeld's old pubs at the end. Keener hikers use Threlkeld as the starting point for the gut-busting climb up **Blencathra**, whose five great ridges loom above the A66: you'll need to be well prepared to tackle this.

On any reasonably decent day, the best move in Keswick is down to the shores of **Derwent Water**, five minutes' walk south of the centre along Lake Road and through the pedestrian underpass. It's among the most attractive of the lakes, ringed by crags and studded with islets, and is most easily seen by hopping on the **Keswick Launch** (Easter–Nov daily 10am–6pm, until 8pm in July & Aug; Dec–Easter Sat & Sun 10am–6pm; £5 round-trip, 80p per stage; ☎017687/72263, ⊛www.keswick-launch.co.uk), which runs right around the lake calling at several points en route. There's also an enjoyable one-hour evening cruise (£5.80) from May Day bank holiday until mid-September.

Practicalities

All **buses**, including National Express services, use the terminal behind Lakes Foodstore, off Main Street. The **tourist office** is in the Moot Hall on Market Square (daily: April–June, Sept & Oct 9.30am–5.30pm; July & Aug 9.30am–7pm; Nov–March 9.30am–4.30pm; ☎017687/72645, ⊛www.keswick.org). George Fisher, at 2 Borrowdale Rd (☎017687/72178), is one of the most celebrated **outdoors stores** on the Lakes, with a full range of equipment and maps, a daily weather information service and café. For **bike rental**, call Keswick Mountain Bikes on Southey Hill (☎017687/75202, ⊛www.keswick-bikes.co.uk). There's **internet access** at *U-Compute*, above the post office at 48 Main St (Mon–Sat 9am–5.30pm, Sun 9.30am–4.30pm; ☎017687/75127).

There's a fair amount of entertainment in Keswick too: a **cinema** on St John's St (often closed Dec–Feb) which hosts an annual film festival, the **jazz festival** each May, **beer festival** in June, and traditional country shows in the locality during the summer. The **Theatre by the Lake** on Lake Road (☎017687/74411, ⊛www.theatrebythelake.com) hosts a full programme of drama, concerts, exhibitions, readings and talks.

B&Bs, guest houses and hotels

Bluestones 7 Southey St ☎017687/74237, ⊛www.members.tripod.com/bluestoneskeswick. Well-kept guest house used to walkers; big breakfasts. No credit cards. ❶

Bridgedale Guesthouse 101 Main St ☎017687/73914. The cheapest central rooms, just around the corner from the bus station. No credit cards. ❶

George Hotel St John St ☎017687/72076, ⊛www.jenningsbrewery.co.uk. Refurbished coaching inn in the centre of town, with bags of character downstairs and fully modernized rooms up. ❸

Greystones Ambleside Rd ☎017687/73108. Non-smoking Victorian terraced house close to the centre at the end of St John's St. Rooms with fell views and TVs. ❸

Highfield Hotel The Heads ☎017687/72508, ⊛www.highfieldkeswick.co.uk. Beautifully restored hotel whose stylish feature rooms include two turret rooms and a converted chapel. ❸, feature rooms ❹.

Howe Keld 5–7 The Heads ☎017687/72417, ⊛www.howekeld.co.uk. Welcoming, non-smoking hotel with a reputation for great breakfasts (vegetarian specialities included). ❸

Keswick Country House Hotel Station Rd ☎017687/72020, ⊛www.principalhotels.co.uk. Grand Victorian hotel, built for the nineteenth-century railway trade. ❼, with dinner.

Campsites and youth hostels

Castlerigg Hall Castlerigg ☎017687/72437, ⊛www.castlerigg.co.uk. Out-of-town campsite, a mile and a half southeast of Keswick. Closed Nov–Easter.

Derwentwater Caravan Club and Camping Site ☎017687/72392. Less than ten minutes' walk from the centre, down by the lake; turn left off Main St beside the supermarket. Closed Dec & Jan.

Derwentwater Youth Hostel Borrowdale ☎017687/77246, ⓦwww.yha.org.uk. An old mansion with fifteen acres of grounds, two miles south of Keswick along the B5289.

Keswick Youth Hostel Station Rd ☎017687/72484, ⓦwww.yha.org.uk. A converted woollen mill by the river in town; free tea and coffee on arrival, plus internet access.

Eating and drinking

Abraham's Tea Rooms in George Fisher's outdoor store, 2 Borrowdale Rd. The top-floor tearoom comes to your aid with warming mugs of *glühwein* and big breakfasts. No credit cards. Inexpensive.

Brysons 42 Main St. Top-notch bakery and tearooms with breakfasts, traditional main dishes and cream teas. No credit cards. Inexpensive.

The Four in Hand Lake Rd, opposite George Fisher's. Popular pub for its food – grilled Cumberland ham and eggs, local trout and other local specialities. Inexpensive to Moderate.

Lakeland Pedlar Henderson's Yard, Bell Close, off Main St. Keswick's best café serves inventive veggie food – from breakfast burritos to veg crumble. Open evenings July & Aug. Inexpensive.

Loose Box Pizzeria King's Arms Courtyard, Main St. Popular pizza-and-pasta joint – the house special is *spaghetti rustica* (tomato, garlic, chilli and prawns). Moderate.

Mayson's 33 Lake Rd. Licensed, self-service café serving bakes, pies and stir-fries (until 8.45pm in summer). No credit cards. Inexpensive.

The Square Orange St John St. The café-bar scene gets a northern lakeland toehold – cappuccino, snacks and meals, day and night. Inexpensive.

Borrowdale and Scafell

It is difficult to overstate the beauty of **Borrowdale**, with its river flats and yew trees, lying at the head of Derwent Water and overshadowed by the peaks of **Scafell** and **Scafell Pike**, the highest in England. Climbs up these, as well as up Great Gable, one of the finest-looking mountains in England, start from the head of the valley, accessible on the #77/77A and #79 **buses** from Keswick.

Just before the *Derwentwater* youth hostel, a narrow road branches left for a steep climb to the photogenic **Ashness Bridge**. The minor road ends two miles further south at **Watendlath**, an idyllic little tarn and tearooms which can be hopelessly overrun at times in summer – the National Trust's free Watendlath Wanderer bus runs here every couple of hours from Keswick on summer Sundays, via Ashness. Back on the B5289, a signposted path heads to the **Lodore Falls**, only really worth the diversion after sustained wet weather. Further south, past the wonderfully sited *Borrowdale Hotel* (☎017687/77224, ⓦwww.theborrowdalehotel.co.uk; ❼, with dinner), there's a slight detour across an old packhorse bridge to **GRANGE**, a peaceful riverside hamlet, peered down upon by Borrowdale's forested crags. At Grange, it's under a mile south to the 1900-ton **Bowder Stone**, a house-sized lump of rock scaled by way of a wooden ladder and worn to a shine on top by thousands of pairs of feet.

Shaded paths through the wood, and the B5289, lead in around a mile to the straggling hamlet of **ROSTHWAITE**, which sustains the most concentrated batch of accommodation in the valley. As well as two or three B&Bs, there are comfortable rooms at the hiker-friendly *Royal Oak Hotel* (☎017687/77214, ⓦwww.royaloakhotel.co.uk; ❻, with dinner) and the smarter, neighbouring *Scafell Hotel* (☎017687/77208, ⓦwww.scafell.co.uk; ❺), whose attached *Riverside Inn* – the only local pub – serves popular bar meals. There's a pleasant **youth hostel**, *Borrowdale Longthwaite* (☎017687/77257, ⓦwww.yha.org.uk), a mile south of Rosthwaite on the riverside footpath to Seatoller; while across the river, on the eastern side of the B5289 is the *Chapel House Farm* **campsite** (☎017687/77602).

Another mile on, **SEATOLLER** and the **Seatoller Barn National Park Information Centre** (Easter–Nov daily 10am–5pm; ☎017687/77294) marks the end of the #79 bus route from Keswick. *Seatoller House* (☎017687/77218;

❸, ❺ with dinner; closed Dec–Feb) here has **rooms**, and there's an informal **campsite** in a small field by the beck along the minor road south to **SEATH-WAITE**, twenty minutes' walk away. This is a popular base for walks up the likes of Great Gable and Scafell Pike (see below): the trout farm at the foot of the valley has a fine **café** (Easter–Sept daily 10am–6.30pm), serving fresh grilled trout or sandwiches.

Scafell, Scafell Pike and Great Gable

In good weather, the minor road to Seathwaite is lined with parked cars by 9am as hikers take to the paths for the rugged climbs up the three major peaks of Scafell, Scafell Pike and Great Gable. The summit of **Scafell Pike** (3205ft), the highest point in England, is close to the second highest point in the Lakes, **Scafell** (3163ft), and an eight-mile, six-hour, loop walk taking in both leaves Seathwaite via Stockley Bridge to the south, branching up Styhead Ghyll to **Styhead Tarn**. This is as far as many get, and on those all-too-rare glorious summer days the tarn is a fine place for a picnic. A direct, but very steep approach to **Great Gable** (2949ft) is also possible from Styhead Tarn, though most people cut west at Seathwaite campsite up Sourmilk Ghyll and approach via **Green Gable** (2628ft), also an eight-mile, six-hour return walk.

Buttermere and Crummock Water

Overlooked by the steep Borrowdale Fells, the B5289 cuts west at Seatoller, up and over the dramatic **Honister Pass**. Bus #77/77A comes this way, making the initial, steep mile-and-a-quarter grind from Borrowdale to the car park at the top of Honister Pass, by the *Honister Hause* **youth hostel** (☎017687/ 77267, ⓦwww.yha.org.uk).

From Honister Pass, the B5289 follows Gatesgarthdale Beck for three miles and makes a dramatic descent into the **Buttermere valley** by *Gatesgarth Farm* **campsite and B&B** (☎017687/70256; no credit cards; ❷), then runs anoth-er mile beside the lake – past more camping and rooms at *Dalegarth* (☎017687/70233; ❷; closed Nov–March) – to the **youth hostel** (☎017687/ 70245, ⓦwww.yha.org.uk) just before **BUTTERMERE** village. The village has two hotels: the *Bridge Hotel* (☎017687/70252, ⓦwww.bridge-hotel.com; ❻, ❼ with dinner) and the smaller *Fish Hotel* (☎017687/70253; ❹). There's simple **camping** at *Syke Farm* right by the lake.

The village itself – set between the two expanses of Buttermere and neigh-bouring **Crummock Water** – makes a good walking base, with a particular-ly easy two-mile hike out along Crummock Water's southwestern edge to the 125ft **Scale Force** falls. The four-mile, **round-lake** stroll circling Buttermere itself shouldn't take more than a couple of hours; you can always detour up Scarth Gap to Haystacks if you want more of a climb and some views.

Wast Water and Eskdale

Great Gable and Scafell stand as a formidable last-gasp boundary between the mountains of the central lakes and the gentler land to the southwest, which smooths out its wrinkles as it descends to the Cumbrian coast. **Wast Water**, which points its slender finger towards the pass between both ranges, remains one of the most isolated of the region's lakes. Public transport is very limited, which makes it one to savour if you fancy getting right off the beaten track. The highest slopes in England frame the northern shores, while on the wild southeastern banks rise the impassable screes which separate the lake from Eskdale to the south. The only road winds from the main coastal A595, through remote settlements, before meeting the lake at its southwestern tip, at the *Wasdale Hall* **youth hostel** (☏019467/26222, ⓦwww.yha.org.uk). The minor road then hugs the shore of the lake, ending four miles away at **Wasdale Head**, a clearing between the mountain ranges, where you'll find the marvellous *Wasdale Head Inn* (☏019467/26229, ⓦwww.wasdale.com; ⑤), one of the most celebrated of all lakeland inns, with legendary breakfasts and hearty four-course dinners. Nearby, there's the National Trust's *Wasdale Head* **campsite** (☏019467/26220; closed Nov–March).

Eskdale is accessed either by the Ravenglass and Eskdale Railway (see p.637), which drops you right in the heart of superb walking country around the hamlet of Boot; or by the east–west minor road route between the coast, via Eskdale Green, and Little Langdale, just west of Skelwith Bridge. The attractive rural ride by road or train through the valley from the west begins to peter out as you approach Dalegarth station (terminus of the Ravenglass and Eskdale Railway), just beyond which nestles the dead-end hamlet of **BOOT**. Three miles beyond Boot and 800-feet up, the remains of granaries, bath houses and the commandant's quarters for **Hardknott Roman Fort** command a strategic and panoramic position.

Boot has a fair smattering of **accommodation and services**. The nearest place to Dalegarth station is *Brook House Inn* (☏019467/23288, ⓦwww.brook-houseinn.co.uk; ③). In Boot itself, the *Burnmoor Inn* (☏019467/23224, ⓦwww.burnmoor.co.uk; ③) is the traditional hikers' choice. Further up the road past the hamlet it's 500 yards to *Hollins Farm* **campsite** (☏019467/23253) and another three-quarters of a mile to the *Woolpack Inn* (☏019467/23230), which as well as rooms (③) has a purpose-built bunkhouse (①). Another 400 yards beyond the pub you'll find *Eskdale* **youth hostel** (☏019467/23219, ⓦwww.yha.org.uk).

Cockermouth

The farming community of **COCKERMOUTH**, midway between the coast and Keswick at the confluence of the Cocker and Derwent rivers, is yet another station on the Wordsworth trail: the **Wordsworth House** on Main Street (Easter–June, Sept & Oct Mon–Fri, 10.30am–4.30pm; July & Aug Mon–Sat, 10.30am–4.30pm; £3; NT) is where William and Dorothy were born and spent their first few years. Some of the original features remain and there are occasional Wordsworthian relics – a chest of drawers here, a pair of candlesticks there – but despite the best endeavours of the enthusiastic staff it's disappointingly lifeless. The rest of Cockermouth tries hard to please, with its tree-lined streets and riverside setting, but after the dramatic fellside approaches from the south and east the town itself falls a little flat. However, there's certainly no shortage of rainy day attractions ranged along Main Street – including museums of printing, toys and models, and motoring – while if you follow your nose, you're likely to stumble upon Jennings Brewery on Brewery Lane near the river. The hour-and-a-half-long **Jenning's Brewery Tour** (July & Aug 4 daily; April–June, Sept & Oct Mon–Sat 2 daily; Nov–Feb Mon–Sat 1 daily; £3.75; booking advisable; ☏01900/821011; ⓦwww.jenningsbrewery.co.uk) culminates with a tasting.

All **buses** stop on Main Street, from where you follow the signs east to the **tourist office** in the Town Hall, off Market Place (April–June & Oct Mon–Sat 9.30am–4.30pm; July–Sept Mon–Sat 9.30am–5pm, Sun 10am–2pm; Nov–March Mon–Sat 9.30am–4pm; ☏01900/822634). The most convenient **B&B** is the biker- and hiker-friendly *Castlegate Guest House*, 6 Castlegate

(☎01900/826749; no credit cards; ❷). The *Trout Hotel* on Crown Street (☎01900/ 823591, ⓦwww.trouthotel.co.uk; ❻), by the river, is the top choice, and there are also rooms available in the *Shepherd's Hotel*, out at the Lakeland Sheep and Wool Centre (☎01900/822673, ⓦwww.shepherdshotel.co.uk; ❷). Ten minutes' walk south along Station Road, then Fern Bank brings you to the *Double Mills* **youth hostel** (☎01900/822561).

All the **pubs** along Main Street compete to sell bar meals at rock-bottom prices, though best choice by far is the *Bitter End* on Kirkgate, a pub housing Cumbria's smallest brewery. Of the **cafés**, the *Norham Coffee House*, 73 Main St (closed Sun), trades on its history – formerly the home of John Christian, grandfather of *Mutiny on the Bounty's* Fletcher Christian. The *Cockatoo*, 16 Market Place (closed Mon, Tues & Sun eve), is a friendly place, with simple lunches and more elaborate dinners. **Market day** in Cockermouth is Monday.

Ullswater

Wordsworth declared **Ullswater** "the happiest combination of beauty and grandeur, which any of the Lakes affords," a judgement that still holds good. At over seven miles long, Ullswater is the second longest lake in Cumbria and much of its appeal derives from its serpentine shape, a result of the complex geology of this area: the glacier that formed the trench in which the lake now lies had to cut across a couple of geological boundaries, from granite in the south, through a band of Skiddaw slate, to softer sandstone and limestone in the north. The only **public transport to Ullswater** is the #108 bus service (May–Oct) from Penrith, which runs via Pooley Bridge, Gowbarrow and Glenridding to Patterdale. On summer weekends, three daily buses continue south over the Kirkstone Pass to Bowness.

The chief lakeside settlements, **PATTERDALE** and **GLENRIDDING**, are less than a mile apart at the southern tip of Ullswater, each with a smattering of cafés and B&Bs. In Glenridding you'll find a few modest places to stay, such as the *Fairlight Guest House* (☎017684/82397; ❷), by Glenridding's main car park; or *Moss Crag Guest House* (☎017684/82500; ❷; closed Dec), across the beck near the shops, which has its own tearooms. *Gillside Caravan & Camping* (☎017684/82346, ⓦwww.gillsidecaravanandcampingsite.co.uk; closed Nov–Feb) is half a mile away up the valley, behind the **tourist office** (Easter–Oct daily 9am–6pm; Nov–Easter Fri–Sun 9.30am–3.30pm; ☎017684/82414) in the main car park. Climbers wanting an early start on Helvellyn stay at the *Helvellyn Youth Hostel* (☎017684/82269, ⓦwww.yha.org.uk), a mile and a half up the valley track from Glenridding. In Patterdale, the cheapest bed is at the rustic **youth hostel** (☎017684/82394, ⓦwww.yha.org.uk), just south of the hamlet on the A592. Patterdale's only **pub**, the *White Lion* (☎017684/82214; ❸), has a few rooms available and serves bar meals. *Side Farm* (☎017684/82337), in the centre (the entrance is across from the church), is open all year for **camping**.

Around the lake

On busy summer days the A592 up the western side of the lake is packed with traffic, all looking for space in one of the few designated car parks. Busiest is usually that below **Gowbarrow Park**, three miles north of Glenridding, where the A5091 meets the A592; the hillside still blazes green and gold in spring, as it was doing when the Wordsworths visited; it's thought that Dorothy's recollections of the visit in her diary inspired William to write his famous "Daffodils" poem. The car park at Gowbarrow is also the start of an easy walk up to **Aira Force**, a

⑪

bush-cloaked seventy-foot fall that's spectacular in spate and can be viewed from bridges spanning the top and bottom of the drop.

The lake itself is traversed by the **Ullswater Steamer** (℡01539/721626, Ⓦwww.ullswater-steamers.co.uk), which – as well as its round-the-lake cruises (one-hour £5.80, two-hour £7) – has services from Glenridding to Howtown, halfway up the lake's eastern side (Easter–Oct daily; £3.60 one way; 35min) and from Howtown to Pooley Bridge, at the northern end of the lake (Easter–Oct daily; £2.60; 20min). **HOWTOWN** is tucked into a little clearing at the foot of beautiful Fusedale, where the *Howtown Hotel* makes a great spot for lunch or a drink in the pocket-sized bar, before hiking back around the lake to Patterdale (6 miles; 3hr). A minor road from Howtown hugs the eastern shore of the lake the four miles to **POOLEY BRIDGE**, passing the incomparable *Sharrow Bay* (℡017684/86301, Ⓦwww.sharrow-bay.com; ❾, with dinner) on the way, one of England's finest hotel-restaurants. Pooley Bridge itself is a cute retreat with a church and three **pubs**, most notably the eighteenth-century *Sun Inn* (℡017684/86205, Ⓦwww.jenningsbrewery.co.uk; ❸).

Climbing Helvellyn

The climb to the summit of **Helvellyn** (3114ft), the most popular of the four 3000ft mountains in Cumbria, is challenging enough for most visitors, who tend to make a day-long circuit from either Glenridding or Patterdale. You are unlikely to be alone or get lost on the yard-wide approaches – on summer weekends and bank holidays the car parks below and paths above are full by 10am – but the variety of routes up and down at least offers a chance of escaping the crowds.

Indeed, if you are hoping to escape the crowds, avoid the most frequently chosen approach via the infamous **Striding Edge**, an undulating rocky ridge offering the most direct access to the summit. With **Red Tarn** – the highest Lake District tarn – a dizzying drop below, purists negotiate the very ridge top of Striding Edge; slightly safer, but no less precipitous tracks follow the line of the ridge, just off the crest. However you get across there's a final, sheer, hands-and-feet scramble to the flat **summit** (2hr 30min from Ullswater). If you're at all nervous of heights you'll find it a challenge to say the least; in poor weather, it's madness even to contemplate it.

The good news is that once you're up the various descents all seem like child's play. The classic return is to the northeast via the less demanding **Swirral Edge**, where a route leads down to Red Tarn, then follows the beck to the disused slate quarry workings and the dramatically sited Helvellyn youth hostel, a mile and a half from Glenridding. Another route, of equal duration, climbs back up to **Catstye Cam** and drops down the northern ridge path into Keppel Cove, where you cross the dam and continue to the hostel. Either of these Helvellyn approaches and descents makes for around a seven-mile (5–6hr) walk.

Penrith

Once a thriving market town on the main north–south trading route, **PEN-RITH** today suffers from undue comparisons with the improbably pretty settlements of the nearby Lakes. The brisk streets, filled with no-nonsense shops and shoppers, have more in common with the towns of the North Pennines than the stone villages of south Cumbria, and even the local building materials emphasize the geographic shift. Its deep-red buildings were erected from the same rust-red sandstone used to construct **Penrith Castle** (daily:

June–Sept 8am–9pm; Oct–May 8am–4.30pm; free) in the fourteenth century, as a bastion against raids from the north; it's now a crumbling ruin, opposite the train station.

Penrith station is five minutes' walk south of the town centre. The **bus station** is on Albert Street, behind Middlegate, and has regular services to Patterdale, Keswick, Cockermouth, Carlisle and Alston. The **tourist office** on Middlegate (Easter–April, Sept & Oct Mon–Sat 9.30am–5pm, Sun 1–4.45pm; May–Aug Mon–Sat 9.30am–6pm, Sun 1–5.45pm; Nov–March Mon–Sat 9.30am–5pm; ☎01768/867466, ⊕www.visiteden.co.uk) can help you find **accommodation**. The bulk of the B&Bs line Victoria Road, the continuation of King Street running south from Market Square: *Victoria Guest House*, at no. 3 (☎01768/863823, ⊕www.vicguesthouse.co.uk; no credit cards; ❷), and *Blue Swallow*, at no. 11 (☎01768/866335, ⊕www.blueswallow.co.uk; no credit cards; ❶), are the two most convenient choices. The *George Hotel*, on Devonshire Street by Market Square (☎01768/862696, ⊕www.georgehotelpenrith.co.uk; ❹), is a central old coaching inn with cosy wood-panelled lounges. For **food**, J. & J. Graham's deli-grocery in Market Square can't be beaten. Otherwise, there's tapas at *Costa's*, 9 Queen St, or elegant dining at *Passepartout*, 51 Castlegate (☎01768/865852; eve only; closed Mon).

Around Penrith

Several attractions lie close to town, the nearest being **Brougham Castle** (April–Sept daily 10am–6pm; Oct daily 10am–5pm; £2.10; EH), a mile and a half south of Penrith by the River Eamont. Slightly further out, three miles southwest of town, reached from either the A66 or A592, is **Dalemain** (Easter–Sept Mon–Thurs & Sun 10.30am–5pm; £5; gardens only £3; ⊕www.dalemain.com), a country house set in ample grounds. This started life in the twelfth century as a fortified tower, but has subsequently been added to by every generation, culminating with a Georgian facade grafted onto a largely Elizabethan house. However, top local attraction is undoubtedly **Rheged** (daily 10am–5.30pm; ⊕www.rheged.com; free) at Redhills on the A66, a couple of minutes' drive from the M6 (junction 40); bus #X4/X5 between Penrith and Keswick stops outside. Billed as Britain's largest earth-covered building, it takes its name from the ancient kingdom of Cumbria and features a spectacular atrium-lit underground visitor centre which fills you in on the region's culture and history by way of exhibitions, local art and craft displays and family activities. There's also a giant-format cinema screen showing *Rheged: The Movie*, documenting a Cumbrian journey through time (£4.95); as well as the separate **National Mountaineering Exhibition** (same times; £4.50, joint ticket with movie £7.80; ⊕www.mountain-exhibition.co.uk), presenting an entertaining history of mountain-climbers and climbing, from the Lake District to Everest.

The Cumbrian coast

South and west of the National Park, the **Cumbrian coast** attracts much less attention than the spectacular scenery inland, but it would be a mistake to write it off. It splits into two distinct sections, the most accessible being the **Furness peninsulas** area, just a few miles from Windermere's Lakeside, where varied attractions include the resort of **Grange-over-Sands**, the monastic priory at **Cartmel**, and market towns such as **Ulverston** and **Broughton-in-Furness**.

Parts of this region share nearby Lancashire's industrial heritage and in the ship-building port of **Barrow-in-Furness** it's possible to see a slow revival that's only just starting to pay dividends in terms of tourism – though the dramatic ruins of nearby **Furness Abbey** have been attracting visitors for almost two hundred years. The **Cumbrian coast** itself is generally judged to begin at Silecroft near Millom and stretches for more than sixty miles to the small resort of Silloth, on the shores of the Solway Firth. In between lie isolated beaches and the headland of **St Bees** as well as the delights of the **Ravenglass and Eskdale Railway** and the attractive Georgian port of **Whitehaven**.

Grange-over-Sands

Before the coming of the railways, the main route to the Lake District was the "road across the sands" from near Lancaster to **GRANGE-OVER-SANDS**, travellers being led by monks from Cartmel Priory, then from the sixteenth century by a royally appointed guide. The tradition continues today with one guide left, who leads the way around the slip sands and hidden channels which claimed so many lives between the fourteenth and nineteenth centuries. The eight-mile walk takes the best part of a day and departures are usually every other week between May and October; ask at the Grange tourist office for further details.

Grange **tourist office** is in Victoria Hall, on Main Street (Easter–Oct daily 10am–5pm; Nov–Easter Mon & Fri–Sun 10am–5pm; ☎015395/34026, ⓦwww.grange-over-sands.com), 400 yards left from the **train station** and National Express stop. Keep walking up Main Street to the top of town to reach Kents Bank Road, which has plenty of **accommodation** lining both sides on the way out of town. *Thornfield House* (☎015395/32512, ⓦwww.thornfield-house.co.uk; no credit cards; ❷) and *Methven Hotel* (☎015395/32031; ❸) are typical. The nearest **youth hostel** is a ten-minute train ride away at the smaller resort of Arnside, on Redhills Road (☎01524/761781, ⓦwww.yha.org.uk).

Cartmel

Sheltered several miles inland from Morecambe Bay, **CARTMEL** grew up around its twelfth-century Augustinian priory and is still dominated by the proud **Church of St Mary and St Michael** (daily: June–Sept 9am–5.30pm; Oct–May 9am–3.30pm; tours Easter–Oct Wed 11am & 2pm; free), the only substantial remnant to survive the Dissolution. A diagonally crowned tower is the most distinctive feature outside, while the light and spacious Norman-transitional interior climaxes at a splendid chancel, illuminated by the 45-foot-high **East Window**. You can spend a good half-hour scanning the immaculate misericords and numerous tombs, chief among them the **Harrington Tomb** in the Town Choir, to the south of the chancel – the weathered figure is that of John Harrington, who rebuilt this section in 1340. Everything else in the village is modest in scale, centred on the attractive **market square**, beyond the church, with its Elizabethan cobbles, water pump and fish slabs.

Trains stop at Cark-in-Cartmel, two miles southwest of the village proper; the #530/#532 **bus** from there or from Grange train station (originating in Kendal) runs to the village. On Market Square, *Market Cross Cottage* (☎015395/ 36143; no credit cards; ❸) is a cosy, seventeenth-century **B&B**. Up a notch, the celebrated *Cavendish Arms* on Cavendish Street (☎015395/36240, ⓦwww.the-cavendisharms.co.uk; ❸, ❹ at weekends), just off the square, is a sixteenth-century inn which retains many of its original features. This is also the best of the **pubs**, offering good (if pricey) food.

Ulverston

The railway line winds westwards from Cartmel to **ULVERSTON**, a close-knit market town, which formerly prospered on the cotton, tanning and iron-ore industries. It's an attractive place, enhanced by its dappled grey limestone cottages and a jumble of cobbled alleys and traditional shops zigzagging off the central **Market Place**. Stalls are still set up here and in the surrounding streets every Thursday and Saturday; on other days (not Wed) the **market hall** on New Market Street is the centre of commercial life.

Ulverston's most famous son is Stan Laurel (born Arthur Stanley Jefferson), the whimpering, head-scratching half of the comic duo who are celebrated in a mind-boggling collection of memorabilia at the **Laurel and Hardy Museum** up an alley at 4c Upper Brook St (Feb–Dec daily 10am–4.30pm; £2), near Market Place. Across King Street, in Lower Brook Street, Ulverston's **Heritage Centre** (Mon, Tues & Thurs–Sat 9.30am–4.30pm; £2) is housed in a former eighteenth-century spice warehouse and gives a good overview of the town's history and its various industrial achievements. It's also worth checking to see what's on at the **Lanternhouse**, on The Ellery (exhibitions, when on, Wed–Sat 11am–4pm; free; Ⓦ www.welfare-state.org), just off the A590, at the bottom of Market Street and across Tank Square (a traffic roundabout). A group of multimedia artists known as Welfare State International occupy this award-winning conversion of an old school.

Ulverston train **station** is only a few minutes' walk from the town centre – head down Prince's Street and turn right at the main road for County Square. **Buses** arrive on nearby Victoria Road from Cartmel, Grange-over-Sands, Barrow, Coniston, Bowness, Windermere and Kendal. The **tourist office** is in Coronation Hall on County Square (Mon–Sat 10am–5pm; ℡01229/587120). **Bike rental** is from Gill Cycles, on The Gill (℡01229/581116). Pick of the **B&Bs** is *Dyker Bank*, 2 Springfield Rd, a Georgian house very near the station (℡01229/582423; no credit cards; ❷). There's also a great *Walker's Hostel* on Oubas Hill (℡01229/585588; no credit cards; ❶), on the A590 near Canal Head, at the foot of the Hoad Monument. **Cafés** include the funky *Hot Mango*, 27 King St, while most of the **pubs** serve food, too, best at the *Farmer's Arms* in Market Place, which has some outdoor tables.

Furness Abbey

Furness Abbey (April–Sept daily 10am–6pm; Oct daily 10am–5pm; Nov–March Wed–Sun 10am–4pm; £2.70; EH), a set of roofless sandstone arcades and pillars hidden in a wooded vale – the so-called "Valley of Deadly Nightshade" – lies a mile and a half out of Barrow-in-Furness on the Ulverston road (local buses to Dalton-in-Furness and Ulverston pass close by). Now one of Cumbria's finest ruins, it was once the most powerful abbey in the northwest, possessing much of southern Cumbria as well as land in Ireland and the Isle of Man. By the fourteenth century it had become such a prize that the Scots raided it twice, though it survived until April 1536, when Henry VIII chose it to be the first of the large abbeys to be dissolved. The transepts stand virtually at their original height, while the massive slabs of stone-ribbed vaulting, richly embellished arcades and intricately carved sedilia in the presbytery are the equal of any of Yorkshire's far busier abbey ruins. The *Abbey Tavern* at the entrance serves drinks at tables scattered about some of the ruined outbuildings.

Ravenglass

On its way between Barrow-in-Furness and Whitehaven, the Cumbrian coast railway stops at **RAVENGLASS**, which preserves a row of characterful nineteenth-century cottages, facing out across the mud flats and dunes. Despite appearances, the village dates back to the arrival of the Romans who established a supply post here in the first century AD for the northern legions manning Hadrian's Wall. Look for the sign to the "Roman Bath House", just past the station: 500 yards up a single-track lane lie the fairly extensive remains of a fort which survived in Ravenglass until the fourth century.

Ravenglass station is the starting point for the **Ravenglass & Eskdale Railway** (Easter week & June–Aug daily; rest of the year Sat & Sun; £7 return; ☏01229/717171, ⓦwww.ravenglass-railway.co.uk), known affectionately as "La'al Ratty". Opened in 1875 to carry ore from the Eskdale mines to the coastal railway, the tiny train, running on a 15-inch gauge track, takes forty minutes to wind its way through seven miles of forests and fields between the fell sides of the Eskdale Valley to Dalegarth station. The stations on the line are popular starting points for walks on and up into the central lakeland peaks, and consequently the railway makes for a fine approach to Eskdale itself (see p.631).

Whitehaven

Some fine Georgian houses mark out the centre of **WHITEHAVEN**, one of the few grid-planned towns in England. The economic expansion that forced this planning was as much due to the booming slave trade as to the more widely recognized coal traffic. Whitehaven spent a brief period during the eighteenth century as Britain's third busiest port (after London and Bristol), making it a prime target for an abortive raid led by Scottish-born American lieutenant **John Paul Jones**. Disgusted with the slave trade he witnessed while ship's mate in America, Jones returned to the port of his apprenticeship to rebel, but, let down by a drunk and potentially mutinous crew, he damaged only one of the two hundred boats in dock and his mini-crusade fell flat. All this and more is explained in **The Beacon** (Easter–Oct Tues–Sun 10am–5.30pm; Nov–Easter 10am–4.30pm; £4), an enterprising heritage centre on the harbour. After seeing this, stroll up Lowther Street to the **Rum Story** (daily: April–Sept 10am–5pm; Oct–March 10am–4pm; £4.50; ⓦwww.rumstory.co.uk), housed in the eighteenth-century shop, courtyard and warehouses of the Jefferson's rum family. This is another place you could easily spend an hour or so, discovering Whitehaven's links with the Caribbean and learning all about rum, the Navy, temperance and the hideousness of the slaves' Middle Passage, amongst other matters. Also on Lowther Street, don't miss Michael Moon's second-hand **book shop** at no. 19 (closed Sun), a bookworm's treasure trove.

Trains follow the coastal route south to Barrow and north to Carlisle. From the station you can walk around the harbour to The Beacon in less than ten minutes; the **bus station** is just across Tesco's car park from the train station. The **tourist office** is in the Market Hall on Market Place (Easter–Oct Mon–Sat 9.30am–5pm, Sun 10am–4pm; Nov–Easter Mon–Sat 10am–4.30pm; ☏01946/852939, ⓦwww.copelandbc.gov.uk), just back from the harbour. For **accommodation**, the best central B&B is the very comfortable *Corcickle Guest House*, 1 Corcickle (☏01946/692073; no credit cards; ❷), five minutes' walk from the centre – keep on up Lowther Street, past Safeway and

McDonald's to find the row of Georgian townhouses. For **meals**, the *Courtyard Café* in the Rum Story, serves wraps, sandwiches, baked potatoes and snacks under a glass roof. In the evening, the bistro at the *Georgian House Hotel* (closed Mon) serves pasta and pizza, while locals like the *Peking Palace* on Duke Street (closed Sun lunch). You can get a decent pint in the *John Paul Jones Tavern*, also on Duke Street.

Carlisle

CARLISLE, the county town of Cumbria and its only city, is also the repository of much of the region's history. Its strategic location has been fought over for more than 2000 years. The original Celtic settlement was superseded by a Roman town, whose first fort was raised here in 72 AD. Carlisle thrived during the construction of Hadrian's Wall and then, long after the Romans had gone, the Saxon settlement was repeatedly fought over by the Danes and the Scots – the latter losing it eventually to the Normans. The struggle with the Scots defined the very nature of Carlisle as a border city: William Wallace was repelled in 1297 and Robert the Bruce eighteen years later, but Bonnie Prince Charlie's troops took Carlisle in 1745 after a six-day siege, holding it for only six weeks before surrendering to the Duke of Cumberland, who bombarded the city with cannon dragged from Whitehaven.

The main thoroughfare of English Street is pedestrianized as far as the expansive **Green Market** square, formerly heart of the medieval city, though a huge fire in 1392 destroyed its buildings and layout. The only historic survivors are the market cross (1682), the Elizabethan former town hall behind it, which now houses the tourist office (see below) and the timber-framed Guildhall beyond that (at the southern end of Fisher Street). The much-restored Guildhall now contains a small **museum** (Easter–Sept Tues–Sun noon–4.30pm; free) of guild and civic artefacts.

It's only a few steps along to **Carlisle Cathedral** (Mon–Sat 7.45am–6.15pm, Sun 7.45am–5pm; £2 donation requested), founded in 1122 but embracing a considerably older heritage. Christianity was established in sixth-century Carlisle by St Kentigern (often known as St Mungo), who became the first bishop and patron saint of Glasgow. The cathedral's sandstone bulk has endured the ravages of time and siege: Parliamentarian troops during the Civil War destroyed all but two powerful arches of the original eight bays of the Norman nave, but there's still much to admire in the ornate fifteenth-century choir stalls and the glorious **East Window**, which features some of the finest pieces of fourteenth-century stained glass in the country. Opposite the main entrance the reconstructed **Fratry**, or monastic building, houses the cathedral library, while its undercroft doubles as the *Prior's Kitchen*, a daytime café (Mon–Sat 10am–4pm) aptly using space that was once the monks' dining hall.

For more on Carlisle's history, head for the **Tullie House Museum and Art Gallery** (Mon–Sat 10am–5pm, Sun noon–5pm; £5), reached up Castle Street or through the cathedral grounds, via Abbey Street. This takes a highly imaginative approach to Carlisle's turbulent past, with special emphasis put on life on the edge of the Roman Empire – climbing a reconstruction of part of Hadrian's Wall you learn about catapults and stone-throwers. There's also plenty on the Jacobite siege of 1745, as well as a dramatic attempt to convey the intensity of the feuds between the "Reivers", border families who lived beyond the jurisdiction of the Scottish and English authorities from the fourteenth to the seventeenth century in the so-called "Debatable Lands".

A subway from outside Tullie House, or the eye-catching Irishgate Bridge – incorporating design elements from the city's former medieval Irish Gate – both cross the fast Castle Way road to **Carlisle Castle** (daily: Easter–Oct 9.30am–6pm; Nov–Easter 10am–4pm; £3.10; EH). This was originally built by William Rufus on the site of a Celtic hillfort, though having now clocked up over nine hundred years of continuous military use, the castle has undergone considerable changes. These are most evident in its outer bailey, which is filled with fairly modern buildings named after battles from the Napoleonic Wars and World War I. Apart from the gatehouse, with its reconstructed warden's quarters, it's the **inner bailey** surrounding the keep that's the real draw. It was here, in 1568, that Elizabeth I kept Mary Queen of Scots as her "guest". There's a **Military Museum** located in the former armoury, but much more interesting are the excellent displays in the **Keep** and the elegant heraldic carvings made by prisoners in a second-floor alcove. **Guided tours** of the castle (Easter–Oct daily; ask at the entrance; an extra £1.50) help bring the history to life. Don't leave without climbing to the battlements for a view of the Carlisle rooftops.

Practicalities

From the **train station**, just off Botchergate, it's a five-minute walk to the **tourist office** in the Old Town Hall on Green Market (July & Aug Mon–Sat 9.30am–6pm, Sun 10.30am–4pm; June & Sept Mon–Sat 9.30am–5pm, Sun 10.30am–4pm; March–May & Oct Mon–Sat 9.30am–5pm; Nov–Feb Mon–Sat 10am–4pm; ☎01228/625600, ⓦwww.historic-carlisle.org.uk). The **bus station** is off Lowther Street, parallel to English Street, and most of the budget **accommodation** is east of here, concentrated on the streets between Victoria Place and Warwick Road. Most B&Bs are less than ten minutes' walk from the centre. Good choices – all of them Victorian town houses in a conservation area, include: *Ashleigh House*, 46 Victoria Place (☎01228/521631; ❸); *Courtfield House*, 169 Warwick Rd (☎01228/522767; no credit cards; ❷); and *Howard House*, 27 Howard Place (☎01228/529159; no credit cards; ❷). Best of the central hotels is the *Lakes Court Hotel*, Court Square (☎01228/531951, ⓦwww.lakescourthotel.co.uk; ❻, ❺ at weekends and winter), right by the train station. A summer-only **youth hostel** occupies the university's Old Brewery Residences, Bridge Lane, Caldewgate (☎01228/597352; July & Aug only), just west of the town centre. The nearest **campsite** is *Orton Grange* caravan park (☎01228/710252) on the Wigton road (A595) four miles southwest of the city – take bus #300.

For daytime **meals** head for *Café Courtyard*, Treasury Court (enter through the gates on Scotch Street or Fisher Street). Near the station *Café Solo*, 1 Botchergate, is a funky little stop for grilled panini, omlettes and coffees. Otherwise, do your dining along Warwick Road, where in the space of 300 yards you can choose from *Casa Romana* (Italian), *David's* (Modern British; eve only, closed Sun & Mon), *Alexandros* (Greek; closed all Sun, plus Mon lunch) and the *Emperor's Palace* (Chinese). The only decent **pub** in the centre is the *Howard Arms*, 107 Lowther St.

Travel details

Buses

For information on all local and national bus services, contact Traveline: ☏ 0870/608 2 608 (daily 7am–9pm), ⓦ www.traveline.org.uk.

Trains

For information on all local and national rail services, contact National Rail Enquiries: ☏ 08457/48 49 50, ⓦ www.nationalrail.co.uk.

Carlisle to: Barrow-in-Furness (5 daily; 2hr 20min); Lancaster (hourly; 1hr); Manchester (2 daily; 2hr 30min); Preston (21 daily; 1hr 20min–1hr 40min); Whitehaven (hourly; 1hr 10min).

Oxenholme (Lake District) to: Carlisle (14 daily; 40–50min); Manchester (1–5 daily; 1hr 40min); Penrith (14 daily; 30min); Preston (hourly; 30–40 min).

Yorkshire

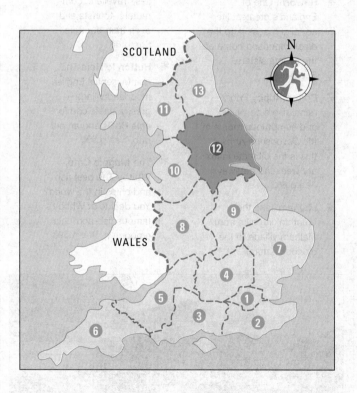

CHAPTER 12

Highlights

* **National Museum of Photography, Film and Television, Bradford** One of the north's most hands-on museums; learn all there is to know about film, photography and TV. See p.653

* **Haworth** One of England's greatest literary pilgrimages is to the bleak moorland home of the Brontë sisters. See p.654

* **Bolton Abbey** Priory ruins, riverside walks and sumptuous rooms at the *Devonshire Arms* – this is the ultimate in luxury weekend getaways. See p.658

* **Malham** Take the breathtaking hike from Malham village to the glorious natural amphitheatre of Malham Cove and the glassy expanse of Malham Tarn. See p.660

* **National Railway Museum, York** York's award-winning railway museum – fun for families, travellers, commuters, tourists and even train-spotters. See p.681

* **Hutton le Hole** The quintessential English moorland village – grassy lanes, comfortable B&Bs and an old pub. See p.690

* **The Magpie Café, Whitby** The best fish and chips in the world? You decide at Whitby's famous fish-and-chip emporium. See p.698

12

Yorkshire

ew visitors pass through **Yorkshire**, England's largest county, without spending time in history-soaked **York**, for centuries England's second city. Famed primarily for its minster, the city is a comprehensive ensemble of medieval alleys, castle ruins, tucked-away churches, riverside gardens and topnotch museums. York's mixture of medieval, Georgian and Victorian architecture is mirrored in miniature in the prosperous north and east of the county by towns such as **Beverley**, centred on another soaring minster; **Richmond**, banked under a crag-bound castle; and **Ripon**, gathered around its honey-stoned cathedral. **Knaresborough** shares similar attributes, but is overshadowed by the faded spa-town gentility of neighbouring **Harrogate**. The Yorkshire coast, too, retains something of the grandeur of the days when its towns were the first to promote themselves as resorts: places such as **Bridlington** and **Scarborough** boomed in the nineteenth century and again in the postwar period, though the best of the Yorkshire coast is found in characterful, historic places such as **Whitby** and **Robin Hood's Bay**.

The engine of growth during the Industrial Revolution was not in the north of the county, but in the south and west. By the nineteenth century, Leeds, Bradford, Sheffield and their satellites were the world's mightiest producers of **textiles** and **steel**. Ruthless economic logic left some of the cities battered by depression in the later years of the twentieth century, though a millennium vigour has infused South and West Yorkshire. The city-centre transformations of **Leeds** and **Sheffield** in particular have been remarkable, both now featuring a series of high-profile attractions, while **Bradford** and its **National Museum of Photography, Film and Television** waylays people on their way to **Haworth** – birthplace of the Brontë sisters.

During even the worst of times, broad swathes of moorland survived above the slum- and factory-choked valleys. The **Yorkshire Dales**, to the northwest, form a lovely patchwork of limestone hills and serene valleys, ranging from the gentle, grassy spans of **Wharfedale** and **Wensleydale** to the majestic heights of Ingleborough, Whernside and Pen-y-ghent, and the wilder valleys of **Swaledale**, **Dentdale**, **Ribblesdale** and **Malhamdale**. Less visited, but still worth as much time as you can spare, is the county's other National Park, the **North York Moors**, divided into bleak upland moors and with a tremendous rugged coastline.

The region is also scattered with a host of historic sites and buildings. The stately home of **Castle Howard** stands out, but there are also imperious relics of the Industrial Revolution, notably the Italianate pastiche of **Saltaire**, a mill-workers' village on the outskirts of Bradford. In an earlier age, before the Reformation, Yorkshire had more monastic houses than any other English

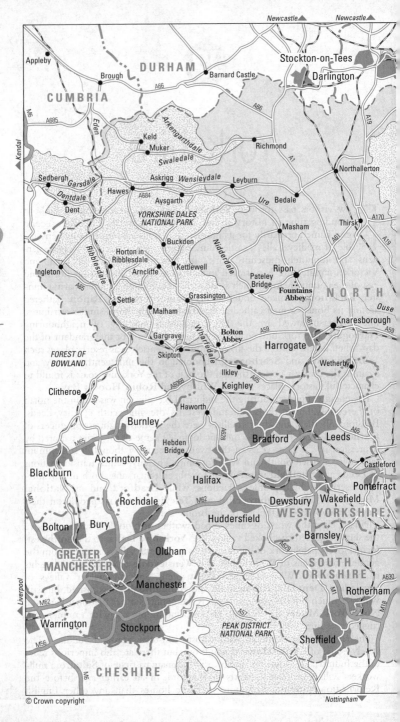

© Crown copyright

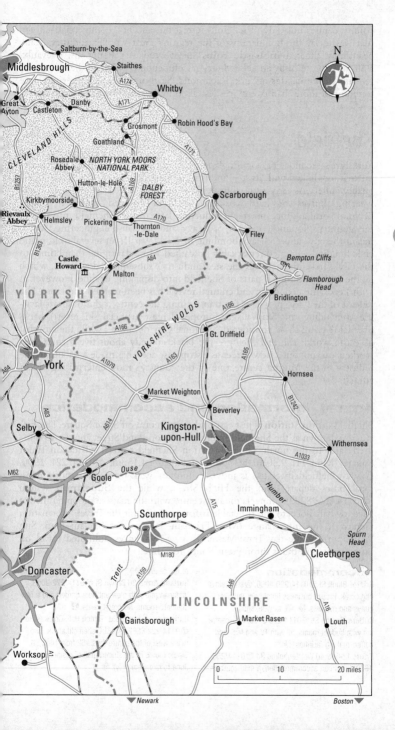

N

Saltburn-by-the-Sea
Middlesbrough
Staithes
A174
Whitby
Great Ayton
Castleton
Danby
A171
Robin Hood's Bay
Grosmont
Goathland
CLEVELAND HILLS
Rosedale Abbey
NORTH YORK MOORS NATIONAL PARK
Hutton-le-Hole
DALBY FOREST
Kirkbymoorside
A169
Scarborough
B1257
Rievaulx Abbey
Helmsley
Pickering
A170
Thornton-le-Dale
Filey
B1363
Bempton Cliffs
Castle Howard
A64
Malton
Flamborough Head
YORKSHIRE
Bridlington
YORKSHIRE WOLDS
A166
A166
Gt. Driffield
A1079
A163
A165
York
A64
Hornsea
A63
Market Weighton
B1242
A614
Beverley
Selby
Kingston-upon-Hull
M62
Withernsea
Goole
Ouse
A1033
Humber
A15
Scunthorpe
Immingham
Spurn Head
M180
Cleethorpes
Doncaster
Trent
A159
LINCOLNSHIRE
A46
A16
Gainsborough
Market Rasen
Louth
Worksop
A1

0   10   20 miles

Newark

Boston

county, centres not only of religious retreat but also of a commercial acumen that was to lay the foundations of the region's great woollen industry. Many beautifully situated **monastic ruins** survive today at Fountains, Rievaulx, Bolton Abbey, Whitby and elsewhere, graceful counterpoints to the more solid remains of the **castles** at York, Richmond, Scarborough and Pickering – the foremost of more than twenty castles raised in Yorkshire by the Normans.

Sheffield

Yorkshire's second city, and England's fourth-largest, **SHEFFIELD** remains inextricably linked with its steel industry, in particular the production of high-quality cutlery. As early as the fourteenth century, the carefully fashioned, hard-wearing knives of hard-working Sheffield enjoyed national repute. Technological advances in steel production later turned Sheffield into one of the country's foremost centres of heavy and specialist engineering, which meant the city suffered heavy bombing in World War II, yet several of its grand civic buildings emerged remarkably unscathed. More damaging than bombs to the city's pre-eminence was the steel industry's subsequent downturn, which by the 1980s had tipped parts of Sheffield into dispiriting decline. However, as with Leeds, the economic and cultural revival has been marked and rapid. The "Heart of the City" project is fast transforming the centre; a glut of sports facil-ities (including the Ski Village, Europe's largest artificial ski resort) backs Sheffield's claim to be considered "National City of Sport"; while the city that gave the world *The Full Monty* – the black comedy about five former steel workers carving out a new career as a striptease act – has made a tribute to the industry in the **Magna** centre, one of the country's most enterprising visitor attractions.

Arrival, information and accommodation

Sheffield's **train station** is just east of the city centre off Sheaf Square. The **bus station**, known as the Sheffield Interchange, is on Pond Street about two hun-dred yards to the north. The Destination Sheffield **tourist office** on Tudor Square (Mon–Fri 9.30am–5.15pm, Sat 9.30am–4.15pm; ☎0114/221 1900, Ⓦwww.sheffieldcity.co.uk) is just five minutes' walk from the stations. Most local buses depart from the High Street, while the **Supertram** system (☎0114/272 8282) connects the city centre with the massive shopping mall at Meadowhall. For fare and timetable **information**, visit the Travel Information Centre at the Interchange (Mon–Fri 8am–5.30pm, Sat 8.30am–5pm, Sun 9am–5pm). A one-day TravelMaster Pass (£4.95) gives unlimited travel on buses, trains and trams throughout South Yorkshire.

Accommodation

Bristol Blonk St ☎0114/220 4000, Ⓔsheffield@ bhg.co.uk. Breezy business hotel near the river, quays and markets. ❺, ❹ at weekends.
Cutlers George St ☎0114/273 9939. City-centre inn with budget rooms, all with TV and tea- and coffee-making facilities. ❹
Priory Lodge 40 Wolstenholme Rd ☎0114/258 4670. Suburban accommodation, a mile southwest

of the centre. ❷
Rutland Arms 86 Brown St ☎0114/272 9003. Victorian pub with pleasant beer garden and a few standard rooms. No credit cards. ❷
University of Sheffield, Tapton Hall, Crookes Rd ☎0114/222 8862, Ⓔb&b@sheffield.ac.uk. Two miles west of the centre (bus #52 from High St) Single rooms in the student hall of residence (mid-June to mid-Sept only). ❶

The City

Millions of pounds have been earmarked to turn Sheffield city centre away from the twin legacies of Victorian solidity and late-twentieth-century sterility. There's been most progress in the revamped post-industrial area near the train station – known as the **Cultural Industries Quarter** – where clubs and galleries exist alongside high-tech arts and media businesses. The interactive museum at the **National Centre for Popular Music** (Ⓦ www.ncpm.co.uk) on Paternoster Row – a Sheffield landmark, consisting of four giant stainless-steel drums – is temporarily closed. But the centre is still a lively night-time venue and the hip ground-floor café-bar shows signs of rivalling the **Showroom** cinema-and-bar complex across the road.

Castlegate and its traditional **markets** are still undergoing ambitious redevelopment, while the main changes so far have been around the impressive Victorian **Town Hall**, at the junction of Pinstone and Surrey streets. The city's new centrepiece is the **Millennium Gallery** (Mon, Tues & Thurs–Sat 10am–5pm, Wed 10am–9pm, Sun 11am–5pm; free). As well as visiting exhibitions (£4) loaned by London's Victoria and Albert Museum, the gallery also holds the Hawley collection of Sheffield hand tools and, of more general interest, the city's Ruskin collection, founded by John Ruskin in 1875 to "improve" the working people of Sheffield. An extension to the gallery in the form of a **Winter Garden** (6am–midnight; free) is due for completion in 2002. North of the town hall, **Fargate** meets Church Street, where the city's **Cathedral of St Peter and St Paul** retains elements of its fifteenth-century origins. Across Cathedral Square sits the **Cutler's Hall** of 1832, an imposing reminder of Sheffield's traditions. The Company of Cutlers was first established in 1624 to regulate the affairs of the cutlery industry, and this is the third hall on the site. South of the town hall, the pedestrianized **Moor Quarter** draws in shoppers, though the nearby **Devonshire Quarter**, centred on Division Street, is the trendiest shopping area.

The **Graves Art Gallery** (Mon–Sat 10am–5pm; free), on the top floor of the City Library (entrance on Surrey Street), leans most heavily towards nineteenth- and twentieth-century British artists. Sheffield's most instructive museums, however, are those devoted to its industrial past, including the **Kelham Island Museum**, Alma Street (Mon–Thurs 10am–4pm, Sun 11am–4.45pm; £3.50), on Kelham Island, one mile north of the city centre (bus #47 or #48 from Flat Street). Exhibits here reveal the breadth of the city's industrial output, ranging from a colossal twelve-thousand horsepower steam engine to a silver-plated penny-farthing made for the tsar of Russia.

This has, however, been eclipsed by **Magna** (daily 10am–5pm; £5.99), the UK's first science adventure centre, set in the building of a former steel works a mile north of the city (bus#69 from the Interchange or the train or supertram to Meadowhall). This offers four gadget-packed, themed pavilions around the four basic elements of earth, air, fire and water. Although most of the centre is aimed at children, the half-hourly *Big Melt* will have everyone gripping onto the railings. An original arc furnace is used in a bone-shaking light and sound show, showing the moment when metal is transformed into white molten steel. For a recovery stop you can chill out in *O2*, an inflatable restaurant designed by Per Lindstrand, Richard Branson's balloon maufacturer.

Eating, drinking and nightlife

Sheffield has plenty of great **café-bars** and good-value **restaurants**. The **pubs** listed below are those with a bit of character and staying power, but for the best insight into what makes Sheffield tick as a party destination take a night-time walk along Division Street and West Street where competing theme and retro bars go in and out of fashion. The Crucible, Lyceum and Studio **theatres** in Tudor Square (℡0114/276 9922) put on a full programme of theatre, dance, comedy and concerts. The Showroom, 7 Paternoster Row (℡0114/275 7727), is the biggest independent **cinema** outside London. Major gigs are held at two edge-of-town **stadium venues**: Don Valley Stadium on Worksop Road (℡0114/278 9199), and Arena, Broughton Lane (℡0114/256 5656). Friday's *Sheffield Telegraph* lists the week's performances, events, concerts and films; look out also for the *Dirty Stop Out's Guide*, a comprehensive listings' booklet, available at the tourist office.

Cafés and café-bars

Casablanca 150–154 Devonshire St. Easygoing bar-bistro with live jazz most nights and a reasonably priced mainstream menu.

The Forum 127–129 Division St. Long the mainstay of the Devonshire Quarter, the Forum has a great menu and laid-back clientele. Closed Sun.

Havana Internet Café 32–34 Division St. All day breakfasts and good cheap food as well as internet access.

Jules and Giovanna Brown St. Lovely little deli-café, serving good coffee, Mediterranean snacks and pastas, and breakfasts until 11.30. Closed Sun.

Showroom 7 Paternoster Row. Café on one side serving Mediterranean-style snacks and sandwiches, and a great bar on the other.

Restaurants

Blue Moon Café 2 St James St. Vegetarian/vegan café, with a few outdoor seats in the summer. Licensed and open until 8pm. Inexpensive.

Encore Crucible Theatre, Tudor Square ℡0114/275 0724. Accomplished Modern British cooking; pre-show dinner and meal-and-ticket deals offer the best value. Moderate to Expensive.

Kashmir Curry Centre 123 Spital Hill ℡0114/272 6253. The curry-lovers' curry house, fifteen-minutes' walk from the city centre, serving the best baltis in town. Inexpensive.

Pizza Volante 255 Glossop Rd ℡0114/273 9056. A rumbustious Italian pasta and pizza place. Inexpensive.

Trippet's Wine Bar 89 Trippets Lane ℡0114/278 0198. Unstuffy wine bar behind West Street. There's live jazz and blues on occasion. Moderate.

Pubs, clubs and live music

Area 51 14–16 Matilda St ℡0114/276 3523. A converted warehouse where the night's clubbing continues well into the wee hours.

Bath Hotel 66 Victoria St. Timeless Victorian pub off Glossop Road – no frills, but well-kept real ale and handsome original features.

The Boardwalk Snig Hill ℡0114/279 9090. Popular venue for indie bands, rock, folk and comedy.

Brown Street 2 Brown St ℡0114/279 6959. Smart bar and chilled club.

Fat Cat 23 Alma St. Cosy, old-fashioned and famed for its umpteen real ales; it's 15mins walk north of the centre. Sister pub *Devonshire Cat* on Devonshire Green offers the same range of beers, but lacks the atmosphere.

Frog & Parrot Division St. A boisterous pub with some dark little nooks and crannies, lots of beers and a good jukebox. Decent mix of locals and students.

The Last Laugh The Lescar Hotel, Sharrowvale Road ℡0114/267 9787. Yorkshire's longest-running comedy club. Thurs & Sun from 8.30pm.

Leadmill 6–7 Leadmill Rd ℡0114/275 4500. Hosts live bands and DJs most nights of the week.

National Centre for Popular Music Paternoster Row ⊛www.ncom.co.uk. Bar, club-nights and gigs. Also home to one of the few gay clubs in Sheffield (every other Sat).

Republic 112 Arundel St ℡0114/276 6777. Club housed in an old steel and engineering works.

The Washington 79 Fitzwilliam St. A good pub with good beer that's a favoured muso's hangout. Just two minutes from Division Street.

Leeds

Yorkshire's commercial capital, and one of the fastest-growing cities in the country, **LEEDS** has undergone a radical transformation in recent years. There's still a true northern grit to its character, and in many of its dilapidated suburbs, but the grime has been removed from the Victorian centre and the city is revelling in its renaissance as a financial, administrative and cultural boomtown. The formerly run-down city quarters have been revitalized and have made Leeds a noted **nightlife** destination. It's long been the region's **cultural** centre, home to Opera North, the noted West Yorkshire Playhouse and a triennial international piano competition that ranks among the world's top musical events. The **Royal Armouries** aside, the **City Art Gallery** has the best collection of British twentieth-century art outside London; **Leeds Industrial Museum** takes care of the city's historical legacy; while further out you might try to see the ruins of **Kirkstall Abbey** and one of the country's great Georgian piles, **Harewood House**.

Arrival, transport and information

Leeds City Station is off City Square on the southern flank of the city centre, and also houses the Gateway Yorkshire **tourist office** in the Arcade (Mon–Sat 9.30am–6pm, Sun 10am–4pm; ☎0113/242 5242, ✉tourinfo@ leeds.gov.uk). The **bus and coach station** occupies a sprawling site to the east, behind Kirkgate Market, on St Peter's Street. The **Metro Travel Centre** at the bus station has up-to-date service details (Mon–Fri 8.30am–5.30pm, Sat 9am–4.30pm; ⊛www.wymetro.com), or call **Metroline** (Mon–Sun 8am–8pm; ☎0113/245 7676). If you're planning to see a slice of West Yorkshire over a day or two, consider buying the bus/train day rover (£4.50), or separate bus or train day rovers (£3.80 each).

Accommodation

There's a good mix of **accommodation** in Leeds, including some budget places near the university campus. Plenty of other cheaper B&Bs lie out to the northwest in Headingley, though these are all a bus ride away. The tourist office can **book you a room**; call ☎0800/808050. Other options include rooms and apartments in halls of residence, rented out during university holidays by the **University of Leeds** (☎0113/233 6100; ❶) – call well in advance and expect a two-night minimum stay. The nearest **youth hostel** is in Haworth and the nearest **campsite** near Roundhay Park on Elmete Lane (☎0113/265 2354), three miles northeast of the city – buses #10 and #12 (#19 or #19a Sun).

42 The Calls 42 The Calls ☎0113/244 0099, ⊛www.42thecalls.co.uk. Leeds' top choice – fashionably converted from an old grain mill on the canal. ❼

Avalon Guest House 132 Woodsley Rd ☎0113/243 2545. Decent budget B&B near the university in a large Victorian house. ❶

Central Hotel 35–47 New Briggate ☎0113/294 1456. Central, simple hotel, handily placed for shopping and café life. ❷

Fairbairn House 71–75 Clarendon Rd ☎0113/233 6633. Victorian house owned by the university. Quiet setting and good value. ❷

Glengarth 162 Woodsley Rd ☎0113/245 7940.

Homely B&B, with good rates and a variety of single and double rooms. No credit cards. ❶

Malmaison Sovereign Quay ☎0113/398 1000. Designer waterside premises (behind Swinegate), with the signature *Malmaison* style. Breakfast isn't included. ❻, ❺ at weekends.

Le Meridien Queen's City Square ☎0113/243 5315. Refurbished Art Deco landmark; weekend rates include breakfast (special deals throw in dinner too). ❽, ❻ at weekends.

Travelodge Blayds Court, off Swinegate ☎0113/244 5793. Reasonable centrally located accommodation. Set price per room, breakfast not included. ❷

The City

City Square opposite the train station hasn't been much of an introduction to Leeds for years, though that's starting to change as the surrounding buildings are renovated and smartened up. From the square it's a short walk up to the main Headrow where you can't miss **Leeds Town Hall**, one of the finest expressions of nineteenth-century civic pride in the country. The masterpiece of local architect Cuthbert Broderick, it's colonnaded on all sides, guarded by white lions and topped by a perky clocktower. Venture further up Calverley Street to see **Millennium Square**. It's not much to look at by day, but hidden beneath the concrete lies state of the art technology to transform the square into a theatre and music venue seating 2,500 people.

The **Leeds City Art Gallery** (Mon–Sat 10am–5pm, Wed 10am–8pm, Sun 1–5pm; free) on the Headrow comprises one of the best arrays outside London of twentieth-century British art. Changing selections from the permanent collection of nineteenth- and twentieth-century art and sculpture are presented, with an understandable bias towards pieces by Henry Moore and Barbara Hepworth, both former students at the Leeds School of Art; Moore's *Reclining Woman* lounges at the top of the steps outside the gallery. From the gallery, a slender bridge connects to the adjacent **Henry Moore Institute** (daily 10am–5.30pm, Wed until 9pm; free), devoted to showcasing temporary exhibitions of sculpture from all periods and nationalities.

Most people make a beeline for the brimming, shop-filled **arcades** further along on either side of **Briggate**. These nineteenth-century palaces of marble, mahogany, stained glass and mosaics have been magnificently restored to house the shops and businesses which are at the heart of Leeds' revival. Perhaps the most splendidly decorated of all is the **Victoria Quarter**, with Harvey Nichols as its designer lodestone. Across Vicar Lane, **Kirkgate Market** (closed Wed afternoon & Sun) is the largest market in the north of England. Housed in a superb Edwardian building, it's a descendant of the medieval woollen markets that were instrumental in making Leeds the early focus of the region's textile industry. On the corner of Vicar Lane and Duncan Street, the elliptical, domed **Corn Exchange** (open daily) was built in 1863, and is now a market for jewellery, retro clothes, furnishings, music and other bits and bobs. Behind here, under the railway arches on Assembley Street and along Call Lane, Leeds' **Exchange Quarter** flexes its fashionable muscles in a series of hip cafés and restaurants.

The biggest transformation in Leeds has been along the **Leeds–Liverpool Canal**, formerly a stagnant relic of industrial decline. At **Granary Wharf**, a couple of minutes' walk from the train station, stores and craftshops fill the extensive cobbled, vaulted arches (the "Dark Arches"), while every weekend (and bank holiday) a market with stalls, bands and entertainers spills out onto the canal basin. Further up on the south side, past Victoria and Leeds bridges, is the gun-metal grey bulk of the **Royal Armouries** (daily: 10am–5pm; free), purpose-built to house the arms and armour collection from the Tower of London. Themed galleries cover concepts such as "War" and "Hunting", while there are enough demonstrations (jousting to falconry), interactive displays, hands-on exhibits and computer simulations to keep everyone interested. Bus #63B runs every fifteen minutes direct to the Armouries from Leeds City Square, a five-minute ride.

Out of the city

The nearest of the surrounding sights is the **Thackray Medical Museum**, on Beckett Street (Tues–Sun 10am–5pm; daily during school holidays; £4.40), next to St James' Hospital ("Jimmy's" from the TV series); catch bus #5a, #13, #17, #41, #42, #43, #50 or #88. Essentially a medical history museum, it's a hugely entertaining place – ghoulish too at times when it delves into topics like surgery before anaesthetics, and the workings of the human intestine. For

Leeds' industrial past, visit the vast **Leeds Industrial Museum**, two miles west of the centre off Canal Road (Tues–Sat 10am–5pm, Sun 1–5pm; £2), which runs between Armley and Kirkstall Road – take bus #5a, #14, #66 or #67. There's been a mill on the site since at least the seventeenth century, and the present building was one of the world's largest woollen mills until its closure in 1969. You can also visit the ruins of **Kirkstall Abbey** (dawn to dusk; free), the city's most important medieval relic. Built between 1152 and 1182 by Cistercian monks from Fountains Abbey, it was the site of 400 years of monastic life before being surrendered to Henry VIII in 1539. The abbey lies about three miles northwest of the city centre on Abbey Road; take bus #732, #733, #734, #735 or #736. The site's still evocatively bucolic, with plenty of signed footpaths around, while the former gatehouse now provides the setting for the **Abbey House Museum** (Tues–Fri & Sun 10am–5pm, Sat 12–5pm; £3), with two floors dedicated to Victorian Leeds. Four miles east of the city, the Jacobean house of **Temple Newsam** (April–Oct Tues–Sat 10am–5pm, Sun 1–5pm; £2) contains many of the paintings and much of the decorative art owned by Leeds City Art Gallery, including one of the largest collections of Chippendale furniture in the country; bus #27 runs here from the centre.

If you were to see just one stately home within the area, however, it should be **Harewood House**, seven miles north of Leeds (Easter–Oct daily 11am–4.30pm; grounds & bird garden 10am–6pm; Nov–Easter Sat & Sun only; £8; grounds & bird garden only £6.25). Conceived in 1759 by York architect John Carr, the building was finished by Robert Adam, the furniture made by Thomas Chippendale and the landscaped gardens laid out by Capability Brown. To cap it all a sweeping terrace designed by Sir Charles Barry (architect of the Houses of Parliament) overlooks the garden, while the ensemble is further enhanced by paintings by artists of such mettle as Turner, Gainsborough, Reynolds, El Greco and a whole host of Italian masters. There are guided tours of the house and galleries throughout the summer every Tuesday and Thursday at 2pm. Buses to Harewood from Leeds include the #36, #781 and #X35.

Eating, drinking and nightlife

Along with its **restaurants**, Leeds rivals Manchester in the number of late-opening, continental-style **café-bars**, while some spruced-up Victorian **pubs** still pull in the punters. The city's **clubs** have a nationwide reputation, too – not least because Leeds lets you dance until 5 or 6am most weekends. For information about **what's on**, the *Yorkshire Evening Post* is your best bet, or look out for the *Absolute Leeds* or *The Leeds Guide* (£1) for listings and features on the city.

Cafés and café-bars

Brodericks Corn Exchange, Call Lane. Relax in the bowels of the Corn Exchange. English and international breakfasts and lunches.

Café Parisa Park Row. Lunches, afternoon tea or just fine wine in this Rustic microbrewery café-bar with a rustic feel.

Café Vitae Granary Wharf ⊛ www.cafévitae.com. "The World's first Recruitment Café" will relax you, refresh you and help you find a job at the same time.

Carpe Diem Basement, Civic Court, Great George St. Wine bar that's tops for good-value food, wine

and decent beer. Resident DJ every Friday until 1am. Closed Sun.

Cuban Heels The Arches, Assembley St. Good food, bottled beers and cool sounds, then pop next door where *Fudge* offers funk and soul until 2am.

Espresso Bar Harvey Nichols, Victoria Quarter Arcade, Briggate. Domain of the high-fashion shopper.

Fibre 168 Lower Briggate. Gay café-bar offering floor-to-ceiling city views and contemporary food served from 11am.

Milo Bar 10–12 Call Lane. Relaxed continental feel in this unpretentious bar. Live DJs most evenings and Saturday afternoons.

Norman Call Lane. Industrial-chic juice-and-booze bar, with noodle-and-satay menu and Saturday-night club sounds.

Pitcher & Piano, Assembley St. Exchange Quarter magnet for city hipsters, drinking or chowing down on food and snacks in the gargantuan interior.

Restaurants

Bibi's Minerva House, 16 Greek St ☎0113/243 0905. Classic old-time Italian, with pizzas and pasta alongside pricier meat and fish concoctions. Moderate.

Brasserie 44 44 The Calls ☎0113/234 3232. Informal, trendy Modern British brasserie, serving everything from Whitby cod to Middle Eastern *meze*. Closed Sat lunch & Sun. Moderate to Expensive.

Fourth Floor Café Harvey Nichols, Briggate ☎0113/204 8000. Souped-up classics (grilled steak, fish and chips, bangers and mash) and exotic flavours. Closed Mon–Wed eve & all Sun. Moderate (lunch) to Expensive (dinner).

Hansa's 72–74 North St ☎0113/244 4408. Gujarati vegetarian restaurant with aromatic Indian food complemented by Indian, vegetarian or organic wines. Inexpensive.

Harry Ramsden's White Cross, Guiseley ☎01943/879531. If you feel like making the pilgrimage to the world's most famous fish-and-chip restaurant (bus #732, #733, #734 or #736 from the bus station), then expect to wait in line. Moderate.

Oporto 31–33 Call Lane ☎0113/245 4444. Funky Exchange Quarter bistro-bar where the flavours mix and match. Moderate.

Pool Court at 42 42–44 The Calls ☎0113/244 4242. Cutting-edge Modern British cuisine, and with a sought-after canalside balcony. Closed Sat lunch & Sun. Expensive to Very Expensive.

Rascasse Canal Wharf, Water Lane ☎0113/244 6611. Pushes all the right Modern-British buttons – if it's not seared, it's roasted or chargrilled. Closed Sat lunch & all Sun. Moderate to Expensive.

Thai Siam 68 New Briggate ☎0113/245 1608. Little local dinner-only Thai place with reliable food and service. Closed Mon. Inexpensive to Moderate.

Pubs, clubs and live music

Club Uropa 54 New Briggate ☎0113/242 2224. Immensely popular club nights, with a good line in guest DJs.

Cockpit Bridge House, Swinegate ☎0113/244 1573. Weekend Mod revival nights; indie sounds and bands, Britpop, and drum'n'bass nights at other times. Gay night "Poptastic" on Thurs.

Creation 55 Cookridge St ☎0113/280 0100. Formerly the Town & Country Club, hosting high-profile live bands as well as regular weekend retro club nights.

Duck & Drake Kirkgate, by the railway bridge. Real-ale pub with a changing selection, and local bands performing for free two or three nights a week.

Heaven & Hell The Grand Arcade ☎0113/243 9963. "Heaven" hosts 70's and 80's disco, soul and chart, while "Hell" serves up house, trance and garage.

Hifi 2 Central Rd ☎0113/242 7353. Smart and stylish Exchange Quarter club, playing everything from funk and soul to drum 'n' bass. Friday gets the local vote.

Po Na Na Unit 2, Waterloo House, Assembley St ☎0113/243 3247. Outrageous club with themed evenings and Leeds' premier salsa night on Tues.

The Ship Ship Inn Yard, off Briggate. The yard tables – crammed into a space about three feet wide – take the city's obsession with continental outdoor ways to extremes.

The Warehouse 19–21 Somers St ☎0113/246 8287. One of the biggest clubs in the city, bringing in clubbers from all over the country.

Whitelocks Turk's Head Yard, off Briggate. Leeds' oldest pub retains its traditional decor, though you'll be hard pushed to see any of it at peak times.

The Whip Duncan St at Briggate. Unchanged Victorian courtyard pub serving great Tetley's beer.

Arts, festivals and entertainment

Opera North, based at the Grand Theatre, gives a free performance each summer at Temple Newsam, as does the **Northern Ballet Theatre** – details from the tourist office. The **Grand Theatre and Opera House**, 46 New Briggate (☎0113/222 6222) is the regular base of Opera North and also puts on a full range of theatrical productions. Classical music can also be heard at the **Leeds Town Hall**, The Headrow (☎0113/247 6962), which supports an annual international concert season. The city's most innovative playhouse is the **West Yorkshire Playhouse**, Quarry Hill Mount (☏0113/213 7700), while for one of the country's last surviving music halls visit the **City Varieties**, Swan Street, off Briggate (☏0113/243 0808), less music-hall fare these days and more tribute bands, middle-of-the-road comedians and cabaret – great building and bar though. Hyde Park Picture House, Brudenell Road, Headingley (☏0113/275 2045; bus #56, #57 or #63) is a classic vintage **cinema** with independent and art-house shows. Finally, August's **West Indian Carnival** is only beaten in size in Britain by Notting Hill.

Bradford and around

In its Victorian heyday, **BRADFORD** was the world's biggest producer of worsted cloth, its skyline etched black with mill chimneys, and its hills clogged with some of the foulest back-to-back houses of any northern city. Today, the city has left this nether world behind and is valiantly laying on tourist attractions to rinse away its associations with urban decrepitude. A few spruced-up buildings and the rejuvenation of the late-Victorian woollen warehouse quarter, Little Germany, signify an attempt to beautify the city centre.

The main interest is provided by the superb **National Museum of Photography, Film and Television** (Tues–Sun & public holidays 10am–6pm; free), one of the most visited national museums outside London. It has recently emerged from a major refit, but still wraps itself around Britain's largest cinema screen (52ft by 64ft), whose daily **IMAX** and 3-D film screenings (£5.80) are billed as "so real you'll think you're there". The museum's ground floor kicks off with the Kodak Gallery, a museum-within-a-museum which houses the contents of Kodak's private collection and traces the story of popular photography. Successive floors are devoted to every nuance of film and television, including some emphasis on state-of-the-art topics like digital imaging and computer animation, and detours into subjects like advertising and news-gathering.

A walk past the restored Venetian-Gothic **Wool Exchange** building on Market Street provides ample evidence of the wealth of nineteenth-century Bradford. Over to the east, north of Leeds Road, the tight grid of streets that is **Little Germany** retains an enclave of warehouse and office buildings in which transplanted German and Jewish merchants once plied their wool trade. The buildings have enticed in new businesses and community ventures, and at the **Design Exchange**, 34 Peckover St (Mon–Fri 9am–5pm; free), the temporary art and design exhibitions are usually worth a peek. The **Peace Museum** (Wed–Fri 11am–3pm, or by arrangement at other times, call ☏01274/754009, ⊛www.peacemuseum.org.uk; free), hidden away on the top floor of 10 Piece Hall Yard, opposite the Wool Exchange, is the only museum of its kind in the country, detailing the history of the peace movement with some panache. The museum will be rehoused in a purpose built International Peace Centre in 2003.

Finally, no one should pass up the chance to drop in on **SALTAIRE**, three miles north of the city, a model industrial village and textile mill built by the industrialist Sir Titus Salt, who built his fortune on the innovative use of alpaca and mohair. **Salt's Mill**, built to emulate an Italian palazzo and larger than St Paul's Cathedral in London, was the biggest factory in the world when it opened in 1853. Its 1200 looms produced over 30,000 yards of cloth a day, and the mill was surrounded by schools, hospitals, a train station, parks, baths and wash-houses, plus 45 almshouses and around 850 houses. Salt's Mill remains the fulcrum of the village, its several floors now housing art, craft and furniture shops, and a craft centre, but its enterprising centrepiece is the **1853 Gallery** (daily 10am–6pm; free; ℡01274/531163), an entire floor of the old spinning shed given over to the world's largest retrospective collection of the works of Bradford-born **David Hockney**. *Salt's Diner* (℡01274/530533) on the same floor has a Hockney-designed logo, menu and crockery. Trains run to Saltaire from Bradford Forster Square, as do buses #662–6 and #679 from the Interchange.

Practicalities

Trains and buses both arrive at **Bradford Interchange** (℡01274/734833) on Croft Street, south of the city-centre grid. The **tourist office** (Mon–Fri 9am–5.30pm, Sat 9am–5pm; ℡01274/753678) is located in Centenary Square's City Hall. The best-value **accommodation** within half a mile of the centre is at the *Ivy*, 3 Melbourne Place (℡01274/727060; no credit cards; ❶), and the *New Beehive Inn*, Westgate (℡01274/721784; no credit cards; ❶). More luxurious digs are available at the Victorian-era *Midland Hotel*, on Forster Square (℡01274/735735; ❺), or the *Quality Victoria Hotel*, on Bridge Street (℡01274/728706; ❺).

Bradford's large Asian population has made the city famous for its **curry houses**. General opinion still favours the Muslim *Mumtaz*, 386–392 Great Horton Rd (℡01274/571861; no alcohol allowed), a twenty-minute walk up towards the university, where the food is sold by weight – a half-pound dish feeds two and the sweet *lassi* is legendary. Closer to town, the *Kashmir*, 27 Morley St (℡01274/726513; open until 2am, 3am at weekends), claims to be Bradford's first-ever curry house. If you don't fancy curry, then head for *Le Café Bleu*, North Parade, which offers a Mediterranean lunch in a small, friendly setting, or *Italia Café*, 344 Great Horton Rd, where home-made Italian bread and pastas are on the menu.

Haworth

Of English literary shrines, probably only Stratford sees more visitors than the quarter of a million who swarm annually into the village of **HAWORTH** to tramp the cobbles once trodden by the Brontë sisters. Quite why the sheltered life of the Brontës should exert such a powerful fascination is a puzzle, though the contrast of their pinched provincial existences with the brooding moors and tumultuous passions of *Wuthering Heights* may well form part of the answer. Whatever the reasons, during the summer the village's steep, cobbled **Main Street** is lost under huge crowds, herded by multilingual signs around the various stations on the Brontë trail.

Of these, the **Brontë Parsonage Museum**, at the top of the main street (April–Sept daily 10am–5.30pm; Oct–March daily 11am–5pm; £4.80), is the obvious focus, a modest Georgian house bought by Patrick Brontë in 1820 to bring up his family. After the tragic early loss of his wife and two eldest daughters, the surviving four children – Anne, Emily, Charlotte and their brother, Branwell – spent most of their short lives in the place, which is furnished as it was in their day, and filled with the sisters' pictures, books, manuscripts and personal treasures. The **parish church** in front of the parsonage – substantially

The Brontës at Haworth

Patrick Prunty or Bronty (it's unclear which) was born in Ireland and became a schoolmaster at the age of sixteen. He later won a place at St John's, Cambridge, where he changed his name to **Brontë**, perhaps influenced by naval hero Lord Nelson, who was made the Duke of Brontë. Later ordained, the Reverend Brontë, and his Cornish wife Maria, took up a living at Thornton, just outside Bradford, where the four youngest of their six children – Maria, Elizabeth, Charlotte, Branwell, Emily and Anne – were born between 1816 and 1820. Later that year, the Brontë family moved into the draughty **parsonage** in nearby Haworth.

Mrs Brontë died within the year and her sister was despatched to help look after the children. The four oldest girls were sent away to school, but withdrawn after first Maria, then Elizabeth, died after falling ill. The surviving daughters, and smothered Branwell, were kept at home, where they amused themselves by making up convoluted stories and writing miniature books. As they successively came of age, the girls took up short-lived jobs as governesses at various local schools; Charlotte and Emily even spent a year in Brussels, learning French. **Branwell**, meanwhile, was already sowing the dissolute seeds of his disappointing future: he had a talent for art, but failed to apply to study at the Royal Academy, got into debt, and then spent two years as a junior stationmaster near Halifax but was later dismissed in disgrace. He then took a tutor's job but was dismissed again and retreated to Haworth, where he made himself overly familiar with the beer in the *Black Bull* and began experimenting with drugs.

Charlotte's, Emily's and Anne's continuing attempts to amuse themselves with their writings led to the private publication, in 1846, of a series of poems, paid for using part of a legacy from their aunt. They used the (male) pseudonyms Currer, Ellis and Acton Bell – corresponding to their own initials – and though few copies of the collection were ever sold, the little volume acted as a catalyst. Keeping the pseudonym, **Charlotte** wrote a novel the same year, which was rejected by various publishers; but her *Jane Eyre*, submitted in 1847, was an instant success. **Emily**'s *Wuthering Heights* and **Anne**'s *Agnes Grey* received similar acclaim the same year; Anne's second novel, the better-known *Tenant of Wildfell Hall*, was published in 1848.

But the next two years destroyed the family, as it was ravaged by consumption. First Branwell, who had sunk ever deeper into addictive misery and ill-health, died in September 1848, followed by Emily in December of that year, and Anne in May of the following year. Charlotte lived on for another six years, writing two more novels – *Shirley* (1849) and *Villette* (1853) – and becoming something of a literary figure once she had revealed her identity. Charlotte finally **married** Reverend Brontë's curate, Arthur Bell Nicholls, who moved into the parsonage, but she died after nine months of marriage in the early stages of pregnancy. The Reverend Brontë lived on until 1861 – the entire family, except Anne (who is buried in Scarborough; see p.694) lies in the **Brontë vault** in the village church, next to the house.

rebuilt since the Brontës lived here – contains the family vault. At the **Sunday School**, between the parsonage and the church, Charlotte, Anne and even Branwell did weekly teaching stints; Branwell, however, was undoubtedly more at home in the **Black Bull**, a pub within staggering distance of the parsonage near the top of Main Street. He got his opium at the pharmacist's over the road (now a gift shop).

The most popular walk runs to **Brontë Falls** and **Bridge**, reached via West Lane and a track from the village, and to **Top Withens**, a mile beyond, a ruin fancifully thought to be the model for Wuthering Heights (3hr round trip). The moorland setting beautifully evokes the flavour of the book, and to enjoy it further you could walk on another two and a half miles to **Ponden Hall**, perhaps the Thrushcross Grange of *Wuthering Heights*.

Practicalities

There are frequent **buses** (#663, #664, #665 and #699) to Haworth from Bradford Interchange, eight miles away, with services every hour during the day; they stop at the bottom of the cobbled Main Street. Haworth **tourist office** is at 2–4 West Lane, at the top of Main Street (daily 9.30am–5.30pm; ☎01535/642329).

You'll need to book ahead for **accommodation** at most times of the year. You can join Branwell's ghost in the *Black Bull Hotel* in Main Street (☎01535/642249; ❷), but the *Old White Lion Hotel*, a little further up (☎01535/642313; ❸), is a more comfortable old inn. The best guest house is the *Apothecary*, 86 Main St (☎01535/643642, ✉apot@sisley86.freeserve.co.uk; ❷), opposite the church. For something a bit more luxurious, try *Weaver's*, 15 West Lane (☎01535/643822; ❺), a converted row of weavers' cottages which also contains one of the best **restaurants** in the county (dinner only, closed Sun & Mon). The **youth hostel**, *Longlands Hall* (☎01535/642234, 🌐www.yha .org.uk), is a mile from the centre at Longlands Drive, Lees Lane, off the Keighley road; the Bradford buses stop on the main road nearby.

The Yorkshire Dales

The **Yorkshire Dales** – "dales" from the Viking word *dalr* (valley) – form a lovely and varied upland area of limestone hills and pastoral valleys at the heart of the Pennines, wedged between the Lake District to the west and the North York Moors to the east. Protected as a **National Park**, the region is crisscrossed by several long-distance footpaths; there's a specially designated circular cycle way, and a host of centres are geared up for caving and other more specialist pursuits.

Most approaches are from the south, via the superbly engineered **Settle to Carlisle Railway**, or along the main A65 road from towns such as **Skipton**, **Settle** and **Ingleton**. This makes southern dales like **Wharfedale** the most visited, while neighbouring **Malhamdale** is also immensely popular, thanks to the fascinating scenery squeezed into its narrow confines around **Malham** village. **Ribblesdale**, approached from Settle, is more sombre, its villages in demand from hikers intent on tackling the Dales' famous **Three Peaks** – the mountains of Pen-y-ghent, Ingleborough and Whernside. To the northwest lies the more remote **Dentdale**, one of the least known but most beautiful of the valleys. Moving north, there are two parallel dales, **Wensleydale** and **Swaledale**, both flowing east, with Swaledale's lower stretches encompassing the appealing historic town of **Richmond**.

Public transport throughout the Dales is surprisingly good. Pick up the free *Dales Explorer* bus timetable (published twice a year), available from tourist offices and from the various **National Park information centres**. There are main centres at Grassington, Aysgarth Falls, Malham, Reeth, Hawes and Clapham, as well as numerous **information points** in shops, post offices and cafés throughout the region. In addition to the Dales' youth hostels there's a series of **bunkhouse barns** – basic self-catering accommodation for around £7 a night per person; **camping barns** are usually more rudimentary versions. Hikers will need the OS *Outdoor Leisure* maps #2, #10 and #30. The **Pennine Way** cuts right through the heart of the Dales, and the region is crossed by the Coast-to-Coast Walk, but the principal local route is the **Dales Way**, an 84-mile footpath from Ilkley to Bowness in the Lake District, which takes around a week to walk.

Skipton

Almost any trip to the southern dales is going to pass through **SKIPTON**, particularly if you want to see Wharfedale, five miles to the east. Apart from practical advantages, however, the town's worth a few hours in its own right, particularly on one of its four weekly **market** days (Mon, Wed, Fri & Sat), when the streets and pubs are filled with what seems like half the Dales population.

Sceptone, or "Sheeptown", was a settlement long before the arrival of the battling Normans, whose **Castle**, located at the top of the High Street (March–Sept Mon–Sat 10am–6pm, Sun noon–6pm; Oct–Feb Mon–Sat 10am–4pm, Sun noon–4pm; £4.40) provided the basis for the present fortress, among England's best preserved, thanks mainly to the efforts of Lady Anne Clifford, who rebuilt much of her family seat between 1650 and 1675 following the pillage of the Civil War. Little survives in the way of furniture or fittings, but starting with the proud battlements – emblazoned with the Clifford cry, *Désormais* ("Henceforth"!) – the castle very much looks the part. Lady Anne also displayed her restorative skills on the **Church of the Holy Trinity**, in front of the castle at the top of the High Street (summer daily 9am–4.30pm; winter daily 9am–dusk; £1 donation requested), which has a fine bossed fifteenth-century roof, beautiful chancel screen (dating from 1533) and a twelfth-century font crowned with a towering wooden Jacobean cover. Down the High Street, on the first floor of the town hall, drop into the entertaining **Craven Museum** (April–Sept Mon & Wed–Sat 10am–5pm, Sun 2–5pm; Oct–March Mon & Wed–Fri 1.30–5pm, Sat 10am–4pm; free), a brief introduction to the geology, flora, fauna, folk history and archeology of the region cradled between Wharfedale and the Lancashire border. The alleys on the western side of the High Street emerge onto the banks of the **Leeds–Liverpool Canal**, which runs right through the centre of Skipton. You can rent boats from the Canal Basin, off Coach Street: Pennine Boat Trips at Waterside Court (℡01756/790829), next to the George Fisher outdoor store, runs daily **canal cruises** (April–Oct; £3.50).

If you're heading for the Settle–Carlisle Railway, note that most **trains** from Skipton are direct – you shouldn't need to change at Settle unless you want to break your journey. The **bus station** is closer in, on Keighley Road, just before Devonshire Place at the bottom of the High Street. You can **rent bikes** for around £12 a day from The Bicycle Shop on Water Street (℡01756/794386), or from Dave Ferguson Cycles at Bowbridge Garage on Skipton Road (℡01756/792526). The **tourist office** is on Coach Street (Mon–Sat 10am–5pm, Sun 11.30am–2pm & 3.30–5pm; ℡01756/792809, ⓦwww.skiptononline.co.uk). **Accommodation** is plentiful, with a host of central pubs offering rooms. Best choice is the *Woolly Sheep Inn*, 38 Sheep Street (℡01756/700966; ❷), a restored seventeenth-century inn. B&Bs tend to lie on the outskirts, ten minutes or so out of the centre, on Gargrave (west) and Keighley (south) roads. *Peace Villas*, 69 Gargrave Rd (℡01756/790672; no credit cards; ❶), and the *Skipton Park Guest 'Otel*, virtually opposite at 2 Salisbury St (℡01756/700640; no credit cards; ❷), are the best places on Gargrave Road; the *Highfield Hotel*, 58 Keighley Rd (℡01756/793182; no credit cards; ❷) is one of a clutch on that road. As for **eating**, *Bizzie Lizzies*, on Swadford Street, is the award-winning fish-and-chip shop of the town, while *Herbs*, 10 High St (closed Tues & Sun), is a veggie place serving homemade soups and home-baked cakes, as well as a daily special for around a fiver. The *Aagrah*, on Devonshire Place, off Keighley Road, has a loyal local following for its fresh, tasty Indian dishes.

Wharfedale

The best of **Wharfedale** starts just east of Skipton at **Bolton Abbey**, and then continues north in a broad, pastoral swathe scattered with villages as picture-perfect as any in northern England. **Grassington** is the main village, a popular walking centre, packed to capacity in summer; lesser hamlets in Upper Wharfedale, like **Kettlewell**, make less frenetic bases. Upland roads lead from the head of the valley up minor dales to cross the watershed into Wensleydale, though the most attractive itinerary would take you up lonely Littondale to **Arncliffe** and then over the tops to either Malham or Ribblesdale. Throughout the year, the #71 **bus** runs roughly hourly (not Sun) to Grassington from Skipton and less frequently on up the B6160 to Kettlewell, Starbotton and Buckden. This is augmented by two seasonal services: the **Dalesbus** (Easter–May & Oct Sun; June–Sept Sat & Sun; Aug Tues, Sat & Sun), from Leeds or Bradford; and the Sunday-only **Wharfedale Wanderer** (late May to Aug), which leaves Ilkley, southeast of Skipton, hourly for Grassington via Bolton Abbey, and then travels on to Kettlewell, Starbotton and Buckden.

Bolton Abbey

BOLTON ABBEY, five miles east of Skipton, is the name of a whole village rather than an abbey, a confusion compounded by the fact that the place's main monastic ruin is known as **Bolton Priory** (Mon–Thurs & Sat 8.30am–7pm, or dusk if earlier, Fri 8.30am–4pm; free), founded here in the 1150s. Turner painted the site, and Ruskin described it as the most beautiful in England, though the priory is now mostly ruined; only the nave, which was incorporated into the village church in 1170, has survived in almost its original state. The priory is the starting point for several highly popular riverside walks, including a footpath that follows the river's west bank to take in Bolton Woods and the **Strid** (from "stride"), an extraordinary piece of white water two miles north of the abbey, where softer rock has allowed the river to funnel into a cleft just a few feet wide. Beyond the Strid, the path emerges at **Barden Bridge**, four miles from the priory, where the fortified **Barden Tower** was another little restoration job for Lady Anne Clifford; there's a tearoom here.

The Wharfedale Wanderer summer bus service calls at Bolton Abbey, or take a taxi from Skipton (around £8 each way). At Bolton Abbey the main **accommodation** is the sumptuous *Devonshire Arms* (℡01756/710441; ❻), just south of the village, owned by the Duke and Duchess of Devonshire. The restaurant is very expensive, though there's an informal, moderately priced brasserie and bar open to the public too. Considerably easier on the pocket is B&B at *Holme House Farm*, a quarter of a mile south of Barden, overlooking the river (℡01756/720661; no credit cards; ❶). *Barden Bunk Barn*, right by the tower (℡01756/720330) is a useful bunkhouse (reserved for groups only at weekends). *Bolton Abbey Tea Cottage*, next to the priory offers traditional afternoon teas.

Grassington and around

GRASSINGTON, the dale's popular main village, is nine miles from Bolton Abbey. The village is at its best by the river and around the cobbled Market Square, home to several inns and shops selling outdoor gear. The **National Park information centre** on Hebden Road (April–Oct daily 9.30am–5pm; Nov–March most weekends 10am–4pm; ℡01756/752774) stands across from the bus stop. Good **B&Bs** include *Kirkfield*, on Hebden Road (℡01756/

752385; no credit cards; ❶), just past the National Park Centre; and *Town Head Guest House*, 1 Low Lane (☎01756/752811; no credit cards; ❷), off Main Street. More expensive, but with a good reputation, is seventeenth-century *Ashfield House* on Summers Fold (☎01756/752584; ❹; closed Dec & Jan), off the square (behind the *Devonshire Hotel*). The local **youth hostel** (☎01756/752400, ⓦwww.yha.org.uk; ❶) is at the village of Linton, a mile to the southwest across the river; you can eat well across the green at the *Fountaine Inn*. Nearest **campsite** is the small *Bell Bank*, Skirethorns Lane, in Threshfield (☎01756/752321), a mile west of Grassington. All the locals **pubs** serve bar meals, the *Black Horse* being the nicest place for a pint. Otherwise, head over to Threshfield where the stone-flagged *Old Hall Inn* (☎01756/752441; closed Sun eve & Mon) wins plaudits for its great food.

A mile beyond the dramatic, glacially carved overhang of Kilnsey Crag (three miles from Grassington), a minor road branches off left into Littondale, a pristine dale with stunning scenery and views. **ARNCLIFFE**, halfway up the dale, is as idyllic a village as you'll find. On foot, the ideal way to see the dale is to follow the valley-floor footpath from Arncliffe to **LITTON** (2–3 miles), where the ancient and unspoilt *Queen's Arms* (☎01756/770208; ❷) could serve as a walking base. There's B&B available at *Litton Hall* (☎01756/770238; no credit cards; ❶).

Upper Wharfedale

KETTLEWELL (Norse for "bubbling spring") is the main centre for the upper dale, with a **National Park information point** in the Over and Under outdoor shop, a **campsite** (☎01756/760886) just to the north at Fold Farm, and the *Whernside House* **youth hostel** (☎01765/760232, ⓦwww.yha.org.uk) in the centre of the village. The *Racehorses Hotel* (☎01756/760233; ❷), on the bridge, is an eighteenth-century hotel with twelve en-suite rooms and beautiful views of the River Wharfe. The village **pubs**, the *Bluebell* and the *King's Head*, are both cosy places for a drink.

It's lovely country north of Kettlewell, accessed either via the dale's single lonely road (B6160) or the Dales Way path. At **STARBOTTON**, two miles away, the *Fox & Hounds* (☎01756/760269; ❸; closed Mon in winter & all Jan) has ancient flagged floors and popular food. Topnotch pub accommodation is also available in **BUCKDEN**, another couple of miles to the north, at the *Buck Inn* (☎01756/760228; ❺, ❻ with dinner). A mile upstream, the river flows through Langstrothdale to **HUBBERHOLME** and the *George* (☎01756/760223; ❷), the favourite pub of archetypal Yorkshireman J.B. Priestley, who's buried in the churchyard of the nearby small chapel of St Michael and All Angels. There's a bunkhouse barn at *Grange Farm* (☎01756/760259), five minutes' walk from the pub on the route back to Buckden.

Malhamdale

A few miles west of Wharfedale lies **Malhamdale**, the uppermost reaches of Airedale and one of the National Park's most heavily visited regions, thanks to its three outstanding natural features: Malham Cove, Malham Tarn and Gordale Scar. Unfortunately for those seeking solitude, all three main attractions are within easy hiking distance of Malham village, so any walking you do locally is likely to be in company, with the Pennine Way further adding to the column of walkers processing through the area. The approach by **public transport** is on the #210 bus or post bus from Skipton (not Sun).

Malham

Unless you're here off-season, some idea of what to expect in **MALHAM** comes at the vast peripheral car park, likely to be packed solid with hikers and day-trippers. The village is home to barely more than a couple of hundred people, who inhabit the huddled stone houses on either side of a bubbling river, but this microscopic gem attracts perhaps half a million visitors a year. Your first stop should be the **National Park information centre** on the southern edge of the village (Easter–Oct daily 10am–5pm; Nov–Easter Sat & Sun 10am–4pm; ℡01729/830363). In summer, you'll need to book ahead to get a bed at the **youth hostel** (℡01729/830321, ⓦwww.yha.org.uk). However, there's also a **bunkhouse barn** at *Hill Top Farm* (℡01729/830320), north of the information centre, and several good village **B&Bs**, including *Beck Hall* (℡01729/830332; ❷), a couple of hundred yards from the fork in the village centre; and *Miresfield Farm* (℡01729/830414; ❷), near the information centre. The comfortable *Riverhouse Hotel* (℡01729/830315; ❸), on the road through the village, serves great evening meals. You can **camp** at *Townhead Farm* (℡01729/830287; reservations advised), near the cove, and under Gordale Scar at *Gordale Scar House Campsite* (℡01729/830333; closed Nov–March). Meals are served in the **pubs**, notably at the *Buck*, but also at the fancier *Lister Arms*, over the bridge.

Malham Cove, Malham Tarn and Gordale Scar

Appearing in spectacular fashion a mile north of Malham, **Malham Cove** is a white-walled limestone amphitheatre rising three hundred feet above its surroundings. Like Gordale Scar's ramparts to the east, it was formed by a shear along the Mid-Craven Fault, a geological tear that runs 22 miles from Wharfedale to Kirkby Lonsdale in Cumbria. A broad **track** leads to the cove, passing some of England's most visible prehistoric field banks en route. Fewer people make the breath-sapping haul to the top, where the rewards are fine views and the famous **limestone pavement**, an expanse of clints (slabs) and grykes (clefts) created by water seeping through weaker lines in the limestone rock. A simple walk over the moors, either via the Pennine Way or the more interesting dry valley to the west, abruptly brings **Malham Tarn** into sight, a lake created by an impervious layer of glacial debris. You can then turn south for **Gordale Scar**, which is also easily approached direct from Malham village. Here the cliffs are if anything more spectacular than at Malham Cove, complemented by a deep ravine to the rear caused by the collapse of a cavern roof. A little to the south of the scar, off the road, lies **Janet's Foss**, a peach of a waterfall set amidst green-damp rocks and overarching trees.

The classic circuit is the clockwise **walk from Malham** (8 miles; 3hr 30min), the only problem being at Gordale Scar, where it may be difficult to scramble down the stream-cut gorge after heavy rain for the last leg back to Malham. From Gordale Scar you could simply follow the Gordale lane back into the village, though the longer path via Janet's Foss, along the beck and across the fields, is more agreeable.

Ribblesdale

Ribblesdale, west of Malhamdale, is more dour and brooding than the bucolic valleys to the east. It's entered from Settle, starting point of the **Settle to Carlisle Railway**, one of the most scenic rail routes in the country (see p.661). The valley's only village of any size is **Horton in Ribblesdale**, a focus not only for the Ribble Way and Pennine Way, but also where most people start the

The Settle to Carlisle railway

With the nineteenth-century railway boom at its height, the Midland Railway company applied to Parliament to build a line which would link the industrial heartlands of West Yorkshire with Carlisle and the Scottish borders beyond. In the six years between 1869 and 1875, when the 72-mile **Settle–Carlisle** line opened, herculean efforts were made by thousands of navvies to blast a route through the unforgiving Dales mountainsides. Living in squalid shanty towns by the sides of the track, and even in the newly opened railway tunnels themselves, six thousand men built twenty viaducts and bored fourteen tunnels in a feat of Victorian engineering that has few equals in Britain. Over two hundred of the workers died, some of smallpox and other diseases, others in horrific accidents.

The attraction in riding the line is the chance to experience what the operators – with no hint of hype – dub "England's most scenic railway". From Settle, the drag up Ribblesdale brings ever more spectacular views – between Horton and Ribblehead the line climbs two hundred feet in five miles, before crossing the famous 24-arched Ribblehead viaduct. Dent is the highest, and bleakest, mainline station in England. Further on, the route heads through Ais Gill, 1100 feet above sea level, before it finally drops into the gentler Eden Valley and on to Carlisle.

The **journey** from Settle to Carlisle takes just under an hour and forty minutes, so it's easy to make a **return trip** (£16.30 for adult day return) along the whole length of the line if you wish. There are connections from Skipton and Leeds (2hr 40min); full **timetable** details are available from National Rail Enquiries, ☏08457/484950, or from the website, ⓦwww.settle-carlisle.co.uk. If you only have time for a short trip, the **best section** is that between Settle and Garsdale (30min), though note that you'll typically have a very short or very long wait for the return train.

Three Peaks Walk, an arduous hike around the Dales' highest peaks. Settle is the **transport** junction for Ribblesdale, with daily **trains** heading north through Horton to Carlisle and south to Skipton and Leeds; a limited service operates on Sundays. The hourly #580 **bus** (not Sun) also connects Skipton with Settle, from where a service runs three or four times daily (not Sun) north to Horton but no further, and northwest via Clapham to Ingleton in the western dales.

Nestled under the wooded knoll of Castleberg, **SETTLE** is well-placed for upper Ribblesdale and a pleasant enough base if you haven't the time to find a more intimate overnight stop within the National Park. The **tourist office** is in the town hall on Cheapside, just off Market Place (daily 10am–5pm; ☏01729/825192). The **train station** is less than five signposted minutes from here. Two comfortable **pubs**, the *Royal Oak* on Market Place (☏01729/822561; ❹), and the *Golden Lion*, just off Market Place along Duke Street (☏01729/822203; ❸), are the best places to stay, while B&B accommodation is available at *Liverpool Guest House* on Chapel Square (☏01729/822247; no credit cards; ❶), and the *Yorkshire Rose* (☏01729/822032; no credit cards; ❷), along Duke Street from the *Golden Lion*. During the day it is hard to see anyone resisting the lure of *Ye Olde Naked Man Café* (closed Wed), serving breakfasts, proper coffee and good home-made food.

The noted walking centre of **HORTON IN RIBBLESDALE** dates from Norman times but the village expanded in the nineteenth century with the arrival of the Settle–Carlisle Railway. The celebrated **Pen-y-ghent Café** (also known as the *Three Peaks Café*) in the village is a **National Park information point** (summer Wed–Fri & Mon 9am–6pm, Sat & Sun 8am–6pm; rest of the year Mon & Wed–Sun 9am–6pm; ☏01729/860333) and an unofficial headquarters for the famous **Three Peaks Walk**, a 25-mile, twelve-hour circuit of Pen-y-ghent (2273ft), Whernside (2414ft) and Ingleborough (2376ft). The village is most convenient for the ascent of sphinx-shaped **Pen-y-ghent** (3–4hr round trip), arguably the most dramatic of the three summits, just to the east on the Pennine Way. Horton straggles along an L-shaped mile of the Settle–Ribblehead road (B6479), with the **train station** at the northern end and the church at the southern end. In between are the café, a post office/store and a campsite. **B&Bs** include the *Willows* (☎01729/860373; no credit cards; ❷) and the more elegant *Rowe House* (☎01729/860212; no credit cards; ❷), both left out of the station and a little way up the Ribblehead road. Of the two **pubs**, the *Crown Hotel* (☎01729/860209; ❷), by the bridge, is the clear winner, a popular walkers' haunt with bar food served until 8.30pm. *Dub Cote* (☎01729/860238) is a **bunkhouse barn** at Brackenbottom, just out of the village on the Settle road, and there's also a tents-only **campsite** at *Holme Farm* (☎01729/860281), near the church.

The Western Dales

The **Western Dales** is a term of convenience for a couple of tiny dales running north from **Ingleton**, a village perfectly poised for walks up Ingleborough and Whernside, and for **Dentdale** one of the loveliest and least-known valleys in the National Park. Ingleton is linked by **bus** to Clapham, Settle (for Skipton) and Horton, and the Settle–Carlisle Railway offers access to upper Dentdale and Garsdale, with fine walks possible virtually off the station platforms.

Clapham

CLAPHAM, four miles north of Settle at the southern foot of Ingleborough, makes a fine introduction to the region. Pop into the **National Park information centre** (April–June & Oct daily 10am–4pm; July–Sept 10am–5pm; Nov–March occasional Sat & Sun 10am–4pm; ☎01524/251419), alongside the car park, for a leaflet on the nature trail through Clapdale Woods to **Ingleborough Cave** (March–Oct daily 10am–5pm; Nov–Feb Sat & Sun 10.30am–dusk; £4.50), the Pennines' oldest show cave. Follow the footpath beyond the caves, and after a little over a mile you reach **Gaping Ghyll**, 365ft deep and 450ft long, probably the most famous of the Dales' many potholes; carry on another two miles northwest from here and the summit of Ingleborough looms – a more interesting approach than the haul up from Ingleton.

Clapham **train station** (on the Leeds/Skipton–Lancaster line) offers another entry to the Dales, but lies over a mile south of the village. There's a post office, general store, and the riverside *New Inn* (☎01524/251203; ❹), with cheaper rooms available at *Arbutus House*, on Riverside (☎01524/251240; no credit cards; ❷). At *Anne's Café*, the invitation at the door is "relax and be happy"(closed Mon & Tues).

Ingleton and around

INGLETON, four miles beyond Clapham, sits at the confluence of two streams, the Twiss and the Doe, whose beautifully wooded valleys are easily the area's best features. The four-and-a-half mile **Falls' Walk** (£1.50; parking – including fee – £5) is the main local attraction, a lovely circular walk up the tree-hung Twiss Valley, past viewing points over the Pecca Falls and Thornton Force. More serious hikers tackle **Ingleborough**, one of the Three Peaks, whose flat plateau is reached by a slightly laborious route to the east (3 miles; 2hr 30min).

Ingleton's **tourist office** is in the community centre car park, just off Main Street (May–Sept daily 10am–4.30pm; Oct Sat & Sun 10am–4.30pm; ☎015242/41049), with the **bus** stop just outside. There's a **youth hostel**, *Greta Tower* (☎015242/41444, ⊛www.yha.org.uk), located centrally in a lane between the market square and the swimming pool. The best **guest houses** include the no-smoking *Seed Hill* on Main Street, near the church and square (☎015242/41799; no credit cards; ❷); *Ingleborough View*, further down Main Street past the tourist office (☎015242/41523; no credit cards; ❷); and the *Bridge End Guest House* on Mill Lane (☎015242/41413; ❶), close to the Falls Walk entrance. You can **camp** at nearby *Moorgarth Farm* (☎015242/41428), while *Stacksteads Farm*, also a mile south but off the minor road to High Bentham (☎015242/41386; ❷), has tent space and a **bunkhouse barn**. The *Inglesport Café* on the first floor of the outdoors store on Main Street (daily 9am–6pm) serves hearty soups and chips with everything.

Northeast of Ingleton, one and a half miles away, is the entrance to the **White Scar Caves** (daily 10am–5pm; £6.25), the longest show cave in England. Don't be put off by the steep price – it's worth every penny for the eighty-minute tour of dank underground chambers, contorted cave formations and glistening stalactites. Three miles farther, the flagstoned **Hill Inn** (☎015242/41256; ❶), near Chapel-le-Dale, is a lively, unpredictable place, with occasional live music and lots of climbers and cavers. Bunkhouse and standard double and twin rooms are available and there's a **campsite** nearby – ask at the bar.

Dentdale

Any rail or road route to **Dentdale** has plenty of scenic rewards, but the most breathtaking is the minor-road route from Ingleton up Kingsdale and down Deepdale, with the vast whalebacks of Gragareth and Whernside rising to each side of the windswept little road. As you might expect, there's next to nothing to do locally except walk or revel in the scenery, but there are few better spots to do either, with **DENT** village an unbeatable base. Here, the main road gives way to grassy cobbles, while the huddled stone cottages sport blooming window-boxes trailing over ancient lintels. You can stay at either of the village's two **pubs**, the *Sun Inn* (☎01539/625208; ❶) and the *George & Dragon* (☎01539/625256; ❷), which are next to each other in the centre and under the same management. The non-smoking *Stone Close Guest House* (☎01539/625231; ❶; closed Jan) has a good café (10.30am–5.30pm) doubling as a **National Park information point**.

Confusion – and not a few sore feet – is caused by Dent's **train station** (on the Settle–Carlisle line) not being in Dent at all, but five miles to the east. Between mid-May and mid-October a **bus** runs between station and village twice a day on Sundays only. **Dentdale youth hostel** at *Dee Side House* (☎01539/625251, ⊛www.yha.org.uk) is a couple of miles south of here down the Dales Way.

Wensleydale

Best known of the Dales, if only for its cheese, **Wensleydale** is the largest, least varied and most serene of the National Park's dales. Known in medieval times as Yoredale, after its river (the Ure), the dale takes its present name from a now-inconsequential village, and while there are towns to detain you – including one of the area's biggest in Hawes – it's Wensleydale's rural attractions that linger longest in the mind. Many will be familiar to devotees of the

James Herriott books and TV series, set and filmed in the dale. The dale is traversed by the National Park's only east–west **main road** (the A684), and linked by high moor roads to virtually all the park's other dales of note. Year-round **public transport** is limited to a post bus from Hawes on varied routes (Mon–Fri 2–3 daily, Sat 1 daily) to Askrigg, Aysgarth and Castle Bolton; and the Arriva services (#156, #157, #159) along the same route between Hawes and Richmond. The **Wensleydale Tourer**, which runs daily in summer (late July to Sept; day-tourer ticket £4.95), meets morning and evening trains at Garsdale and runs on a circular route throughout the day between Aysgarth and Hawes.

Hawes

HAWES – from the Anglo-Saxon *haus*, a mountain pass – is head of Wensleydale in all respects: it is its chief town, main hiking centre, and home to its tourism, cheese and rope-making industries. The cheese trail invariably leads to the **Wensleydale Creamery** on Gayle Lane (Mon–Sat 9.30am–5pm, Sun 10am–4.30pm; £2), a few hundred yards (signposted) south of the centre. The first cheese in Wensleydale was made by medieval Cistercian monks from ewes' milk, and after the Dissolution local farmers made a version from cows' milk which, by the 1840s, was being marketed as "Wensleydale" cheese. The Creamery's "Cheese Experience" tours tell you all this and more, with plenty of opportunity to see the stuff being made, and to sample and purchase in the shop. All three of Wensleydale's industries come together in the **Dales Countryside Museum** (Easter–Oct daily 10am–5pm; Nov–Easter Wed, Fri, Sat & Sun 11am–4pm; £2.50), housed in Station Yard's former train station and warehouses, on the Aysgarth side of town. The comprehensive collection embraces lead-mining, farming, peat-cutting, knitting and all manner of rustic minutiae. Alongside it, in a long shed, the **Hawes Ropemakers Museum** (July–Oct Mon–Fri 9am–5.30pm, Sat 10am–5.30pm; rest of year Mon–Fri 9am–5.30pm; free) presents popular demonstrations of traditional rope-making. A mile and a half out of town to the north, people cough up the 70p toll at the *Green Dragon* pub (℡01969/667392; ❷) to walk to **Hardraw Force**. It's about all the fall is worth for much of the year, for although this is the highest above-ground waterfall in the country there's often barely a trickle dribbling over the edge.

The **National Park information centre** shares the same buildings as the Hawes Ropemakers Museum (July–Oct Mon–Fri 9am–5.30pm, Sat 10am–5.30pm; rest of year Mon–Fri 9am–5.30pm; ℡01969/667450). **Buses** stop in Market Place (except for the post buses which depart from outside the post office), over the road from the information office car park. There's B&B **accommodation** at the *Steppe Haugh Guest House*, Town Head (℡01969/667645; no credit cards; ❷); the *Old Station House*, on Hardraw Road, opposite the museum (℡01969/667785; ❷); and at *Laburnam House*, The Holme (℡01969/667717; no credit cards; ❶), at the turn-off from the main road to the museum. All the **pubs** on and around the market square have rooms, while the fanciest place is *Cocketts Hotel*, on Market Place (℡01969/667312; ❹). There's a **youth hostel** (℡01969/667368, ⓦwww.yha.org.uk) at Lancaster Terrace, at the junction of the main A684 and B6255. **Campers** should head for the *Bainbridge Ings* site (℡01969/667354), half a mile east of the centre, just off the A684 (Aysgarth road). Pub **food** aside, you can pick from snacks and lunches at the first-floor *Wensleydale Pantry* on the main road through town; French-influenced meals at *Herriot's Hotel*, Main Street; and traditional English dinners in the *Cocketts Hotel* restaurant.

Askrigg

The mantle of "Herriot country" lies heavy on **ASKRIGG**, a mile across the valley from Bainbridge, as the TV series *All Creatures Great and Small* was filmed in and around the village. There is, however, little to see or do, though the pubs and Georgian houses have their charms, and you might stroll to a couple of nearby falls, **Whitfield Force** and **Mill Gill Force**, both a mile or so to the west of the village. There's an **information point** in the village shop in the Market Place and plenty of **accommodation**, starting with the *King's Arms*, in Market Place, (℡01969/650817; ❻). B&Bs include the *Apothecary's House* (℡01969/650626; no credit cards; ❷), a fine-looking period house in Market Place. For a rural retreat, you can't beat seventeenth-century *Helm Country House* (℡01969/650443; no credit cards; ❹), a mile west – dinner (£16 a head) is served in the stone-flagged dining room.

Aysgarth and around

The ribbon-village of **AYSGARTH**, straggling along and off the A684, is the vortex that sucks in Wensleydale's largest number of visitors, courtesy of the twin **Aysgarth Falls**, half a mile below the village (there's a path through the fields). A marked nature trail runs through the surrounding woodlands and there's a big car park and **information centre** on the north bank (Easter–Oct daily 10am–5pm; Nov–Easter Fri, Sat & Sun 10am–4pm; ℡01969/663424). The **Upper Falls** and picnic grounds lie just back from here, by the bridge and church; the more spectacular **Lower Falls** are a half-mile stroll to the east through shaded woodland. **B&Bs** along the main road include *Marlbeck* (℡01969/663610; no credit cards; ❶), while the village's only **pub**, the *George & Dragon* (℡01969/663358; ❸), has pleasant en-suite rooms and a bar-meal menu. Other local choices are all down by the falls, where the *Wensleydale Farmhouse* (℡01969/663534; no credit cards; ❷) is on the main road at the turn-off for the falls, with the **youth hostel** (℡01969/663260, ⓦwww.yha.org.uk) just behind. There's a **campsite**, *Westholme Caravan Park* (℡01969/663268; closed Nov–Easter), half a mile east on the A684.

There's a superb **circular walk** northeast from Aysgarth via Castle Bolton (6 miles; 4hr), which starts at the falls themselves and climbs up through Thoresby, with the foursquare battlements of **Castle Bolton** (March–Oct daily 10am–5pm; restricted winter opening, call for details; ℡01969/623981; £4) themselves a magnetic lure from miles away across the fields. Built in 1379 by Richard le Scrope, Lord Chancellor to Richard II, it's a massive defensive structure in which Mary, Queen of Scots was imprisoned for six months in 1568.

Swaledale

The National Park's northernmost dale, **Swaledale** is rivalled only by Dentdale for the lonely grandeur of its landscapes. Narrow and steep-sided in its upper reaches, it emerges rocky and rugged in its central tract, which takes in the remote villages of Keld, Thwaite and Muker, before more typically pastoral scenery cuts in at Reeth. From Richmond, **bus** #30 runs up the valley along the B6270 as far as Keld, but it's a limited service (Mon–Sat 3–4 daily), and the only other access is with the summer-Sunday-only **Swaledale Roamer**, which meets trains at Garsdale and then stops at Hawes, Keld, Muker and Reeth.

KELD, eight miles north of Hawes, is at the crossroads of the Pennine Way and the Coast-to-Coast path, making it an ideal hiking centre. The **youth hostel** is *Keld Lodge*, an old shooting lodge near the telephone kiosk

(☎01748/886259, ⊛www.yha.org.uk), but **B&B** at *Butt House* (☎01748/886374; no credit cards; ❶; closed Sept–Easter), is a more tempting proposition. There's also a **campsite** at *Park Lodge* (☎01748/886274; closed Oct–Easter), but no pub, nor any other facilities, in Keld. North and west of Keld, the upper reaches of Swaledale are wild indeed, with an atmosphere bordering on desolate even in summer. The Kirkby Stephen road (B6270) gives access to short side-valleys such as Stonesdale, Whitsun Dale and Birkdale where you can spend a lonely hour or two, while the Pennine Way shadows the very minor Stonesdale road for the three or four miles across Stonesdale Moor to the splendid **Tan Hill Inn** (☎01833/628246; ❷) – reputedly the highest pub in Britain (1732ft above sea level).

THWAITE is the first hamlet south of Keld, a two-mile walk away and with accommodation and meals at *Kearton Guest House* (☎01748/886277; no credit cards; ❷). Some of the loveliest scenery follows beyond the little village of **MUKER**, which has a **National Park information point** in the village store and a couple of **B&Bs**, including *Hylands* (☎01748/886003; no credit cards; ❷), near the church. There's also a nice Dales pub, the *Farmer's Arms*, serving food, and a **campsite** at *Usha Gap*, half a mile from the village (☎01748/886214). Further east at Low Row, there's a **bunkhouse barn** at the *Punch Bowl Inn* (☎01748/886233; ❶), with inexpensive B&B and basic bar meals also available.

A couple of miles east of Low Row lies **REETH**, the dale's main village and market centre – market day is Friday. Reeth has the biggest range of facilities in the whole dale, including a petrol station, a post office and the only bank, and it also has several local craft workshops making everything from cabinets to guitars. The **National Park information centre** is on the green (daily 10am–5pm; ☎01748/884059), and some cottages around the green post **B&B** signs in their windows. There are also several good **pubs** offering rooms and food, most obviously the *Black Bull* (☎01748/884213; ❷) and the *King's Arms* (☎01748/884259; ❸).

There are numerous paths across the fields on the south side of the river, letting you complete a circular walk from Reeth via Grinton, whose attractive bridge, church and riverside inn, the *Bridge*, are just a mile away by road. The local **youth hostel**, *Grinton Lodge*, is housed in a former shooting lodge spectacularly sited in the hills above (☎01748/884206, ⊛www.yha.org.uk), ten minutes' walk from Grinton. You can rent mountain bikes here.

Richmond

RICHMOND is the Dales' single most tempting historical town, thanks mainly to its magnificent castle, whose extensive walls and colossal keep cling to a precipice above the River Swale. Indeed, the entire town is an absolute gem, centred on a huge cobbled market square backed onto by hidden alleys and gardens housing mainly Georgian buildings of great refinement. The town itself is much older, having been dubbed *Riche-Mont* ("noble hill") by the Normans who first built a castle here in 1071. That heritage is also celebrated in local street names such as Frenchgate and Lombard's Wynd (a "wynd" being a narrow alley).

There's no better place to start than **Richmond Castle** (daily: April–Oct 10am–6pm; Nov–March 10am–1pm & 2–4pm; £2.70; EH), reached by signposted alleys from the market square. Originally built by Alan Rufus, first

Norman Earl of Richmond, it retains many features from its earliest incarnation, principally the gatehouse, curtain wall and Scolland's Hall, the oldest Norman great hall in the country. Most of medieval Richmond – all cobbled streets and narrow wynds – sprouted around the castle, but much of the town now radiates from the vast **Market Place**, with the Market Hall alongside (markets on Thurs, Fri & Sat). The most unusual structure is the defunct **Holy Trinity** church, built in 1135 and now serving as the **Green Howards Museum** (April–Oct Mon–Sat 9.30am–4.30pm; Nov–March Mon–Fri 10am–4pm; £2), honouring North Yorkshire's Green Howards regiment. The **Richmondshire Museum**, reached down Ryder's Wynd, off King Street on the northern side of the square (Easter–Oct daily 11am–5pm; £1.50), is of more general interest. Best of all, though, is the town's **Theatre Royal** (Mon–Sat 2.30–3.45pm; £1.50), dating from 1788, making it one of England's oldest extant theatres. Unassuming from the outside, the theatre's tiny interior is one of England's finest pieces of Georgian architecture. A museum at the rear gives an insight into eighteenth-century the-atrical life, allowing visitors to have a go at scene-shifting, use the thunderbox prop or try on the various masks and costumes.

Practicalities

Buses all stop in the Market Place. The **tourist office**, at Friary Gardens, Victoria Road (summer daily 9.30am–5.30pm; winter Mon–Sat 9.30am–4.30pm; ☎01748/850252), organizes free guided **walking tours** around the town in summer. Recommended **accommodation** includes the *Old Brewery Guest House*, 29 The Green (☎01748/822460; ❷), on a quiet green west of (and below) the castle. The nearby *Restaurant on the Green*, on the corner at 5–7 Bridge St (☎01748/826229; ❷) also has a couple of rooms available. Central Frenchgate features the seventeenth-century *Willance House* at no. 24 (☎01748/824467; no credit cards; ❷) and the *Channel House* at no. 8 (☎01748/823844; no credit cards; ❷). Slightly out of town, the excellent *West End Guest House*, 45 Reeth Rd, along and beyond Victoria Road (☎01748/824783; ❷), gets consistently good reports. The nearest **campsite** is three miles west of town on the Reeth Road at *Swaleview Caravan Park* (☎01748/823106; closed Nov–Easter). For **meals**, the *Bistro* is a pleasant place with an indoor patio on Chantry Wynd (☎01748/850792), off Finkle Street, serving filled croissants, ciabatta sandwiches, and lunches at around the £5 mark; it's also open for dinner from Wednesday to Saturday (6–9.30pm). There are Mediterranean flavours at the *Frenchgate Café*, 29 Frenchgate (☎01748/824949).

Harrogate

HARROGATE – the very picture of genteel Yorkshire respectability – owes its airy, planned appearance and early prosperity to the discovery of Tewit Well in 1571. This was the first of over eighty ferrous and sulphurous springs that, by the nineteenth century, were to turn the town into one of the country's leading spas. Monuments to its past splendours still stand dotted around town, with Harrogate's spa heritage beginning at the **Royal Baths Assembly Rooms** on Crescent Road, built in 1897, where you can still take a **Turkish bath** in the plush, tiled Victorian surroundings (call ☎01423/556746 for hours; from £9.50 a session); the public entrance is on Parliament Street. The contemporaneous **Royal Hall**, built as a concert hall, stands across the way at

△ Tetley Brewery, Leeds

the corner of Ripon Road and King's Road, while just around the corner from the Assembly Rooms stands the **Royal Pump Room**, built 1842, in Crown Place, over the sulphur well that feeds the Royal Baths. The **museum** here (April–Oct Mon–Sat 10am–5pm, Sun 2–5pm; Nov–March Mon–Sat 10am–4pm, Sun 2–4pm; £2) re-creates something of the town's health-fixated past and also lets you sample the water; free **guided walks** leave here several times a week between Easter and October (information from the tourist office). To the southwest, the 120-acre **Valley Gardens** are the venue for the annual Spring Flower Show and Sunday band concerts in summer, while many visitors also make for the **Harlow Carr Botanical Gardens** (daily 9am–6pm or dusk if earlier; £4.50, £3 in winter), the main showpiece of the Northern Horticultural Society. These lie one and a half miles out, on the town's western edge; take the B6162 Otley road, or walk beyond the Valley Gardens, through the Pine Woods.

Practicalities

National Express buses drop you on Victoria Avenue, near the library; local and regional services use the **bus station** on Station Parade. The **train station** is on the same street, just a few minutes from all the central sights. Harrogate's **tourist office** (May–Sept Mon–Sat 9am–6pm, Sun noon–3pm; Oct–April Mon–Fri 9am–5.15pm, Sat 9am–12.30pm; ☎01423/537300) is in the Royal Baths, Crescent Road. Of Harrogate's many **festivals**, the most famous are the **flower shows** (second weeks of April and Sept), the **Great Yorkshire Show** (second week in July) and the **Northern Antiques Fair** (second half of Sept). There are scores of **accommodation** options, starting with the B&Bs on King's Road and Franklin Road, north of the centre. Side streets like Studley Road, off King's Road beyond the conference centre, are quieter.

Accommodation

Alexander Guest House 88 Franklin Rd ☎01423/503348. Victorian-era guest house on a residential street, ten minutes' walk from the centre. No credit cards. ❷

Cavendish Hotel 3 Valley Drive ☎01423/509637. The best rooms here (all en suite) overlook the Valley Gardens. ❸

Fountains Hotel 27 King's Rd ☎01423/530483. Family-run venture just up from the conference centre, with a nice rose garden out front. No credit cards. ❷

The Imperial Prospect Place ☎01423/565071. The doyen of spa-era hotels, the *Imperial* can't be bettered for location. ❺

Old Swan Hotel Swan Rd ☎01423/500055, ⓦwww.oldswanhotel.com. Large ivy-covered inn set in its own grounds, much rebuilt in Victorian times. ❻

Rudding Park Hotel Rudding Park, Follifoot ☎01423/871350, ⓦwww.ruddingpark.com. Stylish country-house hotel with a fine bar and brasserie, three miles southeast of town (down the A661). ❼

Ruskin Hotel 1 Swan Rd ☎01423/502045, ⓦwww.ruskinhotel.co.uk. Appealing Victorian villa with six characterful rooms, terraced bar and charming gardens. ❺

Eating and drinking

Betty's 1 Parliament St ☎01423/502746. Very much a Harrogate institution, *Betty's* has cakes and tarts (of many persuasions) to die for. Full meals served too. Daily 9am–9pm. Inexpensive to Moderate.

Courtyard 1 Montpellier Mews ☎01423/530708. Fashionable food served in a cosy mews cottage. Closed Sun & Mon. Expensive.

Drum and Monkey 5 Montpellier Gardens ☎01423/502650. Long-standing fish and seafood restaurant. Closed Sun. Moderate to Expensive.

Montey's The Ginnel ☎01423/526652. Café-cum-music bar with inexpensive lunches and live music most evenings. Inexpensive.

Rick's Just for Starters 7 Bower Rd ☎01423/502700. Amiable mix-and-match bistro where, a few main courses aside, nothing much costs more than £5. Closed Sun lunch. Inexpensive to Moderate.

Salsa Posada 4 Mayfield Grove ☎01423/565151. Funky Mexican restaurant churning out reasonably authentic *nachos*, *burritos*, *fajitas* and the rest. Closed Sun lunch. Moderate.

Knaresborough

A four-mile hop east from Harrogate, **KNARESBOROUGH** rises spectacularly above the River Nidd's limestone gorge, its old town houses, pubs, shops and gardens clustered together on the wooded northern bank, with the river itself crossed by two bridges ("High" and "Low"). The rocky crag above the town is crowned by the stump of a **Castle** (Easter–Sept daily 10.30am–5pm; £2) dating back to Norman times. Built on the site of Roman and Anglo-Saxon fortifications, it's now little more than a fourteenth-century keep in landscaped grounds, thanks to Cromwell's wrecking tactics during the Civil War. It was here that Henry II's knights fled after the murder of Thomas à Becket in Canterbury Cathedral; here, too, that Richard II was held before being removed to Pontefract, where he was murdered in 1400.

The town's two novelty acts are to be found on the west side of the river. **Mother Shipton's Cave** (daily: Easter–Oct 9.30am–5.45pm; Nov–Easter 10am–4.45pm; £3.95) was home to a sixteenth-century soothsayer who predicted the defeat of the Armada, the Great Fire of London, world wars, cars, planes, iron ships – falling short, however, in the most important oracular chestnut of them all, predicting the End of the World: "The world to an end will come," she prophesied, "in eighteen hundred and eighty one." Close by is an equally tourist-thronged spot, the **Petrifying Well**, where dripping, lime-soaked waters coat everyday objects – gloves, hats, coats, toys – in a brownish veneer that sets rock-hard in a few weeks. Both cave and well are reached along a fine eighteenth-century wooded "Long Walk"; the main entrance is just over the High Bridge, north of the town.

The **bus station** is on the High Street, while **trains** pull up at the station just off the High Street. The **tourist office** is at 9 Castle Courtyard, Market Place (Easter–Oct Mon–Sat 10am–5.30pm, Sun 2–5pm; ✆01423/866886). Free **guided walks** around the town leave from the Castle Yard; for information, call ✆01423/522588. Two good **accommodation** options are *Ebor Mount*, 18 York Place (✆01423/863315; ❷), and the *Yorkshire Lass* on High Bridge (✆01423/862962; ❷), a pub right opposite the entrance to Mother Shipton's Cave. *Pollyanna's Tearooms* up Jockey Lane, off the High Street, is the best **café**, while *Bella Rosa*, 25 Castlegate (✆01423/ 869918; closed Sun), opposite the tourist office, is a good-value pizzeria.

Ripon and around

The unassuming market town of **RIPON**, eleven miles north of Harrogate, only really diverts by virtue of its relatively small but vital **Cathedral** (daily 8am–6.30pm; £2 donation requested), which can trace its ancestry back to its foundation by St Wilfrid in 672; the original crypt is still extant below the central tower. Despite a rather plain exterior, there's plenty that pleases here, from the subtle, twin-towered, thirteenth-century west front to the choir's misericords, full of painted figures of miserable clergymen, executed by the same team that carved the impressive stalls at Beverley. The town's other focus is its **marketplace**, "...the finest and most beautiful square...in England", according to Defoe, linked by Kirkgate to the cathedral; market day is Thursday. At the **Prison and Police Museum**, on St Marygate behind the cathedral (April–Oct daily 11am–3pm; £2), the old cells serve as the backdrop for an exhibition on the evils of previous punishments. It's questionable whether conditions in the nineteenth century were worse here or in the nearby **Ripon Workhouse**, on Allhallowgate (same hours as museum; £1.25), where the "undeserving" poor were incarcerated for such heinous crimes as being unable to pay their bills.

The **bus station** is just off the Market Place, while the town's **tourist office** is on Minster Road opposite the cathedral (April–Oct Mon–Sat 10am–5.30pm, Sun 1–4pm; ☎01765/604625). There's no huge reason to stay the night, though Ripon is the nearest base from which to visit Fountains Abbey (see below). The range of **accommodation** options includes the *Coopers*, 36 College Rd (☎01765/603708; no credit cards; ❶), a quiet spot overlooking countryside; Georgian *Bishopton Grove House*, Bishopton (☎01765/600888; no credit cards; ❶), in a peaceful corner of the town; and the *Unicorn Hotel*, Market Place (☎01765/602202; ❹). There are several small **restaurants** along Kirkgate across from the cathedral.

Fountains Abbey and Studley Royal

It's tantalizing to imagine how the English landscape might have appeared had Henry VIII not dissolved the monasteries, with all the artistic ruin precipitated by that act. **Fountains Abbey**, four miles southwest of Ripon off the B6265, gives a good idea of what might have been, and is the one ruin amongst Yorkshire's many monastic fragments you should make a point of seeing. Linked to it are the elegant water gardens of **Studley Royal**, landscaped in the eighteenth century to form a setting for the abbey. The estate is owned by the National Trust, which organizes an ambitious range of activities and events – from opera and firework displays to **free guided tours** (April–Oct daily; ☎01765/608888). There are regular buses to Ripon from Harrogate and York (amongst other places), but the onward service to the abbey is patchy in summer, paltry in winter. Ring Ripon tourist office or the abbey for the latest.

Beautifully set in a narrow, wooded valley, **Fountains Abbey** (April–Sept daily 10am–7pm; Oct, Feb & March daily 10am–5pm or dusk; Nov–Jan closed Fri; last admission 1hr before closing; £4.50 including Studley Royal and Fountains Hall; NT) was founded in 1133 by thirteen dissident Benedictine monks from the wealthy abbey of St Mary's in York. Within a hundred years, Fountains had become the wealthiest Cistercian foundation in England and it was to this century that the three main phases of the abbey's structural development belong: the church's nave and transepts, the domestic buildings, and the church's east end.

Most immediately eye-catching is the **abbey church**, in particular the **Chapel of the Nine Altars** at its eastern end, whose delicacy is in marked contrast to the austerity of the rest of the nave. A great sixty-foot-high window rises over the chapel, complemented by a similar window at the nave's western doorway, over 370ft away. The **Perpendicular Tower**, almost 180ft high, looms over the whole ensemble, added by the eminent early sixteenth-century Abbot Marmaduke Huby, who presided over perhaps the abbey's greatest period of prosperity. Equally grandiose in scale is the undercroft of the **Lay Brothers' Dormitory** off the cloister, a stunningly vaulted space over three hundred feet long that was used to store the monastery's annual harvest of fleeces. The size of the lay buildings – including a substantial **Lay Brothers' Infirmary** – gives an idea of the number of lay brothers at the abbey. All are considerably larger than the corresponding monks' buildings, of which the most prepossessing are the **Chapter House** and **Refectory** – notice the huge fireplace of the tiny **Warming Room** alongside the refectory, the only heated space in the entire complex. Outside the abbey perimeter, between the gatehouse and the bridge, are the Abbey Mill and **Fountains Hall** (same times; NT), the latter a fine example of early seventeenth-century domestic architecture.

A riverside walk, marked from the visitor centre car park, takes you through the abbey and past Fountains Hall to a series of ponds and ornamental gardens, harbingers of **Studley Royal** (same times as the abbey; NT). This lush medley of lawns, lake, woodland and **Deer Park** (daily dawn to dusk; free) was laid out in 1720. There are some scintillating views of the abbey from the gardens, though it's the cascades and water gardens, fed by canals from the Skell, which command most attention, framed by several small temples positioned for their aesthetic effect. The full circuit, from visitor centre to abbey and gardens and then back, is a good couple of miles' walk.

York

YORK is the north's most compelling city, a place whose history, said George VI, "is the history of England". This is perhaps overstating things a little, but it reflects the significance of a metropolis that until the Industrial Revolution was second only to London in population and importance, not only at the heart of the country's religious life, but also a key player in some of the major events that have shaped the nation. These days a more provincial air hangs over the city, except in summer when York feels like a heritage site for the benefit of tourists. That said, no trip to this part of the country is complete without a visit to the city. York is well placed for any number of **day-trips**, the most essential being that to **Castle Howard**, the gem amongst English stately homes.

Some history

The **Romans** chose York's swampy position, at the confluence of two minor rivers, as the site of a military camp during their campaigns against the Brigantes in 71 AD, and in time this fortress became a city – **Eboracum**, capital of the empire's northern European territories. The base for Hadrian's northern campaigns, it was also ruled for three years by Septimius Severus, one of two emperors to die in the city. The other, Constantine Chlorus, was the father of Constantine the Great, first Christian emperor and founder of Constantinople; at Chlorus' death, his son was proclaimed Roman Emperor here – the only occasion an emperor was enthroned in Britain.

Much fought over after the decline of Rome, the city later became the fulcrum of Christianity in northern England. It was here, on Easter Day in 627, that Bishop Paulinus, on a mission to establish the Roman Church, baptized King Edwin of Northumbria in a small timber chapel built for the purpose. Six years later the church became the first minster and Paulinus the first Archbishop of York. In 867 the city fell to the **Danes**, who renamed it **Jorvik**, and later made it the capital of eastern England (Danelaw). Viking raids culminated in the decisive **Battle of Stamford Bridge** (1066) six miles east of the city, where English King Harold defeated Norse King Harald – a Pyrrhic victory in the event, for his weakened army was defeated by the Normans just a few days later at the Battle of Hastings, with well-known consequences for all concerned. In York, aside from the physical remains left by the Vikings on show in several of the museums, the very street names tell of their profound influence – the suffix "-gate" is derived from an old Norse word for street.

The **Normans** devastated much of York's hinterland in their infamous "Harrying of the North", building two castles astride the Ouse in the city itself. Stone walls were thrown up during the thirteenth century, when the city became a favoured Plantagenet retreat, its importance reflected in the new title of Duke of York, bestowed ever since on the monarch's second son. The 48 **York Mystery Plays**, one of only four surviving such cycles, date from this era, created by the powerful guilds which rose with the city's woollen industry. Although Henry VIII's Dissolution of the Monasteries took its toll on a city crammed with religious houses, York remained strongly wedded to the Catholic cause, and the most famous of the Gunpowder Plot conspirators, **Guy Fawkes**, was born here. During the **Civil War** Charles I established his court in the city, which was strongly pro-Royalist, inviting a Parliamentarian siege that was eventually lifted by Prince Rupert of the Rhine, a nephew of the King. Rupert's troops, however, were routed by Cromwell and Sir Thomas Fairfax at the **Battle of Marston Moor** in 1644, another seminal battle in England's history, which took place just six miles west of York.

Whilst the Industrial Revolution largely passed it by, the arrival of the **railways** brought renewed prosperity, thanks largely to the enterprise of pioneering "Railway King" George Hudson, lord mayor during the 1830s and 1840s. The railway is still a major employer, as is the confectionery industry, together with the proceeds from new service and bioscience industries – not forgetting, of course, the income from four million annual tourists. While a comparatively wealthy place, York is not without its problems, not least its susceptibility to **flooding**. There's river damage most years to low-lying properties near the River Ouse – the floods of 2000 were particularly damaging to the city.

Arrival, information, transport and tours

Trains arrive at **York Station**, just outside the city walls on the west side of the River Ouse, roughly half a mile from the historic core. National Express **buses** and most other regional bus services drop off and pick up on Rougier Street, two hundred yards north of the train station, though National Express services call at the train station, too. There's a **tourist office** at the train station (April–Oct Mon–Sat 9am–8pm, Sun 10am–5pm; Nov–Feb Mon–Sat 9am–5pm, Sun 10am–4pm; March Mon–Sat 9.30am–5.30pm, Sun 10am–5pm; ☎01904/621756), though the main office is in the **De Grey Rooms**, on Exhibition Square (April–June, Sept & Oct Mon–Sat 9am–6pm, Sun 9.30am–6pm; July & Aug daily 9am–7pm; Nov–March Mon–Sat 9am–5pm, Sun 9.30am–3pm; ☎01904/621756). There's **internet access** at Internet Exchange, 13 Stonegate (☎01904/638808) Coffee Express, 60 Goodramgate (☎01904/653463), and at the youth hostels.

Walking is the best way to acquaint yourself with the city, and often the only way to get from A to B, given the confused historic layout of pedestrianized streets, alleys and yards. **Traveline York**, 20 George Hudson St (office Mon–Fri 8.30am–5pm; telephone enquiries Mon–Sat 8am–8pm, Sun 8am–2pm; ☎01904/551400) can advise about all local and regional bus information. Or consider **renting a bike**, as York has over 40 miles of cycle lanes and paths – Bob Trotter, 13–15 Lord Mayor's Walk, at Monkgate (☎01904/622868, ⓦwww.bobtrottercycles.com), Cycle Scene, 2 Ratcliffe St ☎01904/653286), and York Cycleworks, 14–16 Lawrence St (☎01904/626664, ⓦwww.yorkcycleworks.com), can provide bikes from around £10 per day, plus a deposit. The tourist offices all push the various **bus tours** (from £8 per person), but much more interesting are the various **guided walks** on offer, from

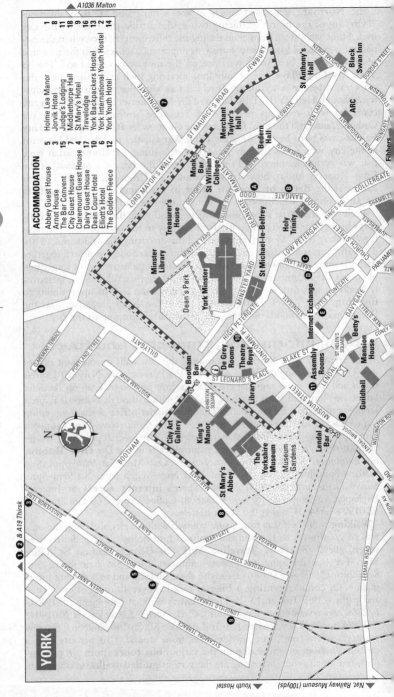

YORK

ACCOMMODATION

Abbey Guest House	5
Arnot House	3
The Bar Convent	15
City Guest House	7
Claremount Guest House	4
Dairy Guest House	17
Dean Court Hotel	10
Elliot's Hotel	6
The Golden Fleece	12
Holme Lea Manor	1
Jorvik Hotel	8
Judge's Lodging	11
Middlethorpe Hall	18
St Mary's Hotel	9
Travelodge	16
York Backpackers Hostel	13
York International Youth Hostel	2
York Youth Hotel	14

Nat. Railway Museum (100yds) ▲   Youth Hostel ▲

1 2 & A19 Thirsk ▲

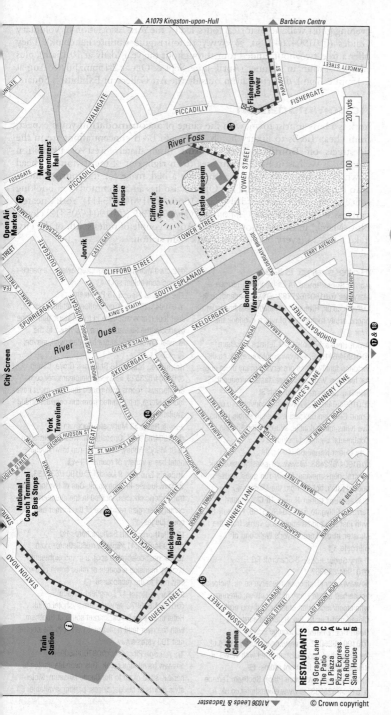

▲ A1079 Kingston-upon-Hull   ▲ Barbican Centre

Fishergate Tower

PICCADILLY

FISHERGATE

FAWCETT STREET

PARAGON ST

River Foss

TOWER STREET

WALMGATE

Merchant Adventurers' Hall

FOSSGATE

Open Air Market

PICCADILLY

Fairfax House

Clifford's Tower

Castle Museum

Jorvik

CASTLEGATE

COPPERGATE

PAVEMENT

HIGH OUSEGATE

TEA MARKET STREET

CLIFFORD STREET

TOWER STREET

SKELDERGATE BRIDGE

TERRY AVENUE

CLEMENTHORPE

SPURRIERGATE

KING STREET

KING'S STAITH

SOUTH ESPLANADE

Bonding Warehouse

SKELDERGATE

BISHOPGATE STREET

City Screen

River   Ouse

QUEEN'S STAITH

OUSE BRIDGE

BRIDGE ST

SKELDERGATE

BUCKINGHAM ST

CROMWELL ROAD

BAILE HILL TERRACE

NORTH STREET

KYME STREET

VICTOR STREET

NEWTON TERRACE

PRICE'S LANE

NUNNERY LANE

ST BENEDICT ROAD

York Traveline

GEORGE HUDSON ST

ROW

MICKLEGATE

TANNER

FETTER LANE

BISHOPHILL SENIOR

ST. MARTIN'S LANE

HAMPDEN STREET

FAIRFAX STREET

LOWER PRIORY STREET

VICTOR ST

BISHOPHILL JUNIOR

SWANN STREET

ST BENEDICT RD

National Coach Terminal & Bus Stops

UGIER STREET

STATION

TRINITY LANE

PRIORY STREET

DEWSBURY TERRACE

NUNNERY LANE

DALE STREET

SCARCROFT LANE

NUNTHORPE ROAD

Micklegate Bar

MICKLEGATE

TOFT GREEN

QUEEN STREET

SEARCROFT ROAD

SOUTH PARADE

STATION ROAD

Train Station

Odeon Cinema

THE MOUNT   BLOSSOM STREET

MOSS STREET

EAST MOUNT ROAD

▲ A1036 Leeds & Tadcaster

© Crown copyright

RESTAURANTS	
19 Grape Lane	D
The Patio	C
La Piazza	A
Pizza Express	F
The Rubicon	E
Siam House	B

0   100   200 yds

675

evening ghost walks to historical tours, led by the York Association of Voluntary Guides (℡01904/640780, ⓦwww.york.touristguides.btinternet.co.uk). They offer a free, two-hour guided tour throughout the year (daily at 10.15am), plus additional tours in summer (April–June, Sept & Oct at 2.15pm; July & Aug at 2.15pm & 7pm), departing from outside the Art Gallery in Exhibition Square.

Accommodation

York is a busy tourist town, with the range of **accommodation** you'd expect, from cheap B&Bs to luxury hotels. The main B&B concentrations are in the sidestreets off **Bootham and Clifton** (immediately west of Exhibition Square), as well as in the **Mount** area (turn right out of the station and head down Blossom Street. If you're stuck for a bed, make for the tourist offices, who'll **book you a room**. First Option also has an accommodation booking office at the train station (daily 8am–10pm; ℡01904/673411). York's nearest **campsite** is the *Riverside Caravan and Camping Park* (℡01904/705812; closed Nov–March) in Bishopsthorpe, off the A64, a couple of miles south of the city. Take bus #23 (every 30min) from York train station.

Hotels and B&Bs

Abbey Guest House 14 Earlsborough Terrace, Marygate ℡01904/627782, ⓦwww.bedandbreakfastyork.co.uk. Riverside terraced guest house with bright, pretty rooms, two of which overlook the river. ❸

Arnot House 17 Grosvenor Terrace, Bootham ℡01904/641966, ⓦwww.arnothouseyork.co.uk. Victorian family house preserving many of its original features. Vegetarian breakfasts on request. ❸

The Bar Convent 17 Blossom St ℡01904/643238, ⓦwww.bar-convent.org.uk. Grand Georgian building with eight single rooms, five twins and a double; self-catering kitchen. Continental breakfast included. ❷

City Guest House 68 Monkgate ℡01904/622483, ⓦwww.cityguesthouse.co.uk. Central, non-smoking, family-run guest house with budget rates, not far from the Minster. ❸

Claremount Guest House 18 Claremount Terrace, Gillygate ℡01904/625158. Friendly B&B with just two rooms about 200 yards from the Minster, at the Lord Mayor's Walk end of Gillygate. ❸

Dairy Guest House 3 Scarcroft Rd ℡01904/639367, ⓦwww.dairyguesthouse.freeserve.co.uk. Victorian house half a mile south of the station, offering wholefood/vegetarian breakfasts if you prefer. Closed mid-Dec to Jan. No credit cards. ❸

Dean Court Hotel Duncombe Place ℡01904/625082, ⓦwww.deancourt-york.co.uk. Perfectly sited neo-Victorian hotel with views of the Minster from the front rooms. ❼

Elliott's Hotel Sycamore Place, Bootham Terrace ℡01904/623333, ⓦwww.elliottshotel.co.uk. A detached Victorian house tucked away in a peaceful and convenient spot. ❹

The Golden Fleece 16 Pavement ℡01904/627151, ⓔgoldenfleece@fibbers.co.uk. Just four rooms available in this historic pub – one overlooks the Shambles, one has views to the Minster towers and all are haunted (well, maybe). ❺–❼

Holme Lea Manor 18 St Peter's Grove, Clifton ℡01904/623529, ⓦwww.holmeleamanor.com. Comfortable rooms with period touches (most have four-posters), ten minutes from the centre. Parking available. ❸

Jorvik Hotel 52 Marygate, Bootham ℡01904/653511. Opposite the western entrance to St Mary's Abbey, this family-run town house hotel has a variety of rooms. ❸–❹

Judge's Lodging 9 Lendal ℡01904/638733, ⓦwww.judges-lodging.co.uk. One of the top central, historic choices, located in the eighteenth-century Georgian residence of the former assize court judges. ❼

Middlethorpe Hall Bishopsthorpe Rd ℡01904/641241, ⓦwww.middlethorpe.com. York's most celebrated spot, a grand eighteenth-century mansion a couple of miles south of the city, next to the racecourse. ❽

St Mary's Hotel 17 Longfield Terrace ℡01904/626972, ⓦwww.stmaryshotel.co.uk. Hotel in a peaceful backstreet south of Bootham, with the river (and a pleasant walk into the centre) just 100 yards away. ❸

Travelodge Piccadilly ℡08700/850950, ⓦwww.travelodge.co.uk. This riverside choice is handily sited close to the Castle Museum. Motel-style rooms at budget prices; parking available. ❸

Hostels

York Backpackers Hostel Micklegate House, 88–90 Micklegate ☎01904/627720, ⓦwww.york-backpackers.mcmail.com. Dorm space, doubles and family rooms. There's a self-catering kitchen, laundry, internet access, TV and games room, and licensed cellar bar.

York International Youth Hostel Water End, Clifton ☎01904/653147, ⓦwww.yha.org.uk. Large Victorian mansion about twenty-minutes'

walk from the centre. Beds mostly in four-bedded dorms, though there are some private rooms (book well in advance). Facilities include a café, internet access, large garden and parking.

York Youth Hotel 11–13 Bishophill Senior ☎01904/625904, ⓦwww.yorkyouthhotel.com. On the west side of the river, off Micklegate – dorm, single and twin rooms available; breakfast extra. Also a kitchen, laundry, games room, TV lounge and internet access.

The City

Take a look at one of the maps dotted around the city centre and you're confronted with a baffling and intimidating prospect. If the tourist office is to be believed, there are around sixty churches, museums and historic buildings crammed within York's walls. In fact the tally of things you really want to see is surprisingly limited, with most sights within easy walking distance of one another. Even so, it's hard to get round everything in less than two days, and equally difficult to stick to any rigid itinerary. The **Minster** is the obvious place to start, followed by the cluster of buildings that circle it; then you might cut south to the **Shambles**, central to the city's old centre and pedestrianized grid, or walk around **the walls** from the Minster to Exhibition Square for the **Yorkshire Museum** and **St Mary's Abbey**, evocative ruins surrounded by the city's loveliest gardens. Thereafter you could walk through the main shopping streets to take in the **Merchant Adventurers' Hall**, most striking of the city's smaller medieval buildings, then deal with **Clifford's Tower** and the nearby **Jorvik Viking Centre** and **Castle Museum**. Lastly, be sure to leave time to take in the **National Railway Museum**, a superb museum whose appeal goes way beyond railway memorabilia. The **York Museums pass** (£9) gives five days' unlimited access to the Castle Museum, Yorkshire Museum and City Art Gallery, offering a fair saving on entry to these attractions.

York Minster

York Minster (daily: June–Sept 7am–8.30pm; Oct–May 7am–6pm; £3 donation requested; ⓦwww.yorkminster.org) ranks as one of the country's most important sights. Seat of the Archbishop of York, it is Britain's largest Gothic building and home to countless treasures, not least of which is the world's largest medieval stained-glass window and an estimated half of all the medieval stained glass in England. In its earliest incarnation the Minster was probably the wooden chapel used to baptize King Edwin of Northumbria in 627. After its stone successors were destroyed by the Danes, the first significant foundations were laid around 1080 and it was from the germ of this Norman church that the present structure emerged. The oldest surviving fabric, in the south transept, dates from 1220 and the reign of Archbishop Walter de Grey. A new chapter house, in the Decorated style, appeared in 1300, and a new nave in the same style was completed in 1338. The Perpendicular choir was realized in 1450 and the western towers in 1472. In 1480, the thirteenth-century central tower, which had collapsed in 1407, was rebuilt, thereby bringing the Minster to more or less its present state.

Nothing else in the Minster can match the magnificence of the stained glass in the nave and transepts. The **West Window** (1338) contains distinctive heart-shaped upper tracery (the "Heart of Yorkshire"), whilst in the nave's north aisle, the second bay window (1155) contains slivers of the oldest stained glass in the country. The north transept's **Five Sisters Window** is named after the five fifty-foot lancets, each glazed with thirteenth-century *grisaille*, a distinctive frosted, silvery-grey glass. Opposite, the south transept contains a sixteenth-century, 17,000-piece **Rose Window**, commemorating the 1486 marriage of Henry VII and Elizabeth of York, an alliance which marked the end of the Wars of the Roses. The greatest of the church's 128 windows, however, is the majestic **East Window** (1405), at 78ft by 31ft the world's largest area of medieval stained glass in a single window. Its themes are the beginning and the end of the world, the upper panels showing scenes from the Old Testament, the lower sections mainly episodes from the book of Revelation.

Before leaving the main body of the interior, give some time to the north transept's 400-year-old wooden clock with its oak knights, and the stone **choir screen**, decorated with life-size figures of English monarchs from William I to Henry VI – all except the latter carved in the last quarter of the fifteenth century. The painted **stone shields** round much of the nave and choir are those of Edward II and the barons who in 1309–10 held a "parliament" in York. Amongst the many **tombs**, those of most interest are the monument in the south transept to Walter de Grey, a beautiful grey-green canopy protecting a recumbent stone figure, and the tomb of the 10-year-old William, second son of Edward III, in the choir aisle.

The foundations, or **undercroft** (£3), have been turned into a museum, fitted into a space excavated during restorations in the 1960s. Amongst precious church relics in the adjoining **treasury** are silver plate found in Walter de Grey's tomb and the eleventh-century Horn of Ulf, presented to the Minster by a relative of the tide-turning King Canute. There's also access from the undercroft to the **crypt**, the spot that transmits the most powerful sense of antiquity, as it contains portions of Archbishop Roger's choir and sections of the 1080 church, including pillars with fine Romanesque capitals. Access to the undercroft, treasury and crypt is from the south transept, also the entrance to the **central tower** (£3), which you can climb for rooftop views over the city. Finally pop into the **Chapter House** (£1), an architectural novelty whose buttressed octagonal walls remove the need for a central pillar, otherwise a common feature of this type of building.

Around the Minster

Past the Minster's west front a gateway leads into **Dean's Park**, a quiet green oasis bordered by a seven-arched fragment of arcade from the Norman archbishop's palace and by **York Minster Library** (Mon–Fri 9am–5pm; free), housed in the thirteenth-century chapel of the same palace. Among its more interesting exhibits is the baptismal entry for Guy Fawkes (April 16, 1570), removed from **St Michael-le-Belfrey** on High Petergate (open for Sunday services only), immediately south of the Minster.

Walk through Dean's Park with the Minster on your right, then through the gate at the top to reach the **Treasurer's House** in Chapter House Street (Easter–Oct Mon–Thurs, Sat & Sun 11am–5pm; £3.70; NT), a glorious seventeenth-century town house that stands on the site of houses used by the Minster's treasurers until the Dissolution. Just around the corner in College Street stands **St William's College**, an eye-catching half-timbered building studded with oriel windows, initially dedicated to the great-grandson of William the Conqueror (first Archbishop of York) and built in its present guise in 1467 for the Minster's chantry priests.

The walls

Although much restored, the city's superb **walls** date mainly from the fourteenth century, though fragments of Norman work survive, particularly in the gates (or "bars"), whilst the northern sections still follow the line of the Roman ramparts. **Monk Bar** at the northern end of Goodramgate is as good a point of access as any, tallest of the city's four main gates and host to a small **Richard III Museum** (daily: March–Oct 9am–5pm; Nov–Feb 9.30am–4pm; £2; Ⓦwww.richardiiimuseum.co.uk), where you're invited to decide on the guilt or innocence of England's most maligned king. For just a taste of the walls' best section, take the ten-minute stroll west from Monk Bar to **Bootham Bar**, the only gate on the site of a Roman gateway and marking the traditional northern entrance to the city. A stroll round the walls' entire two-and-a-half-mile length will take you past the southwestern **Micklegate Bar**, long considered the most important of the gates since it, in turn, marked the start of the road to London. It was built to a Norman design reputedly using ancient stone coffins as building stone, and was later used to exhibit the heads of executed criminals and rebels. The engaging **Micklegate Bar Museum** (daily 9am–5pm; £1.50) occupies a surviving fortified tower.

The Shambles

The Shambles, off King's Square at the southern end of Goodramgate, could be taken as the epitome of medieval York, though the crowds and self-conscious quaintness take the edge off what would otherwise be a perfect medieval thoroughfare. Flagstoned, almost impossibly narrow and lined with perilously leaning timber-framed houses, it was the home of York's butchers, its erstwhile stench and squalor now difficult to imagine, though old meat hooks still adorn the odd house. At no. 35, there's a **shrine** (closed to the public) to Margaret Clitherow, the Catholic wife of a butcher, martyred in 1586 for allegedly sheltering priests; she was pressed to death with rocks piled on top of a board on the city's Ouse Bridge. Newgate **market** (daily 8am–5pm) lies off the Shambles, together with the core of the city's shopping streets.

The Yorkshire Museum and St Mary's Abbey

South of Exhibition Square on Museum Street stands the entrance to the **Yorkshire Museum** (daily 10am–5pm; £4.50), which lies within the beautifully laid-out grounds of St Mary's Abbey, itself now in ruins. It's one of York's better museums, strong on archeological remains which it presents in a series of rooms examining the Roman presence in the city. There are impressive displays of Viking and Anglo-Saxon artefacts, too, though chief exhibit is the fifteenth-century Middleham Jewel, found near Middleham Castle in 1985 – claimed as the finest piece of Gothic jewellery in England.

Part of the museum basement incorporates the fireplace and chapter house of **St Mary's Abbey** (dawn to dusk; free), whose ruins lie around the Museum Gardens, the abbey's former grounds. Founded around 1080, the abbey later became an important Benedictine foundation, additionally significant as it was from here that disenchanted monks fled to found Fountains Abbey.

St Helen's Square and Stonegate

The street called **Lendal** cuts down from Museum Street to **St Helen's Square** – marking the entrance to the Roman city – and the York institution that is **Betty's** tearooms, where you're close to a couple of impressive historic buildings. The Georgian **Mansion House** (1725), in St Helen's Square, is the private home of the city's mayor, and is consequently open only to guided tours by prior arrangement (call ☎01904/551049). However, you can visit the 600-year-old **Guildhall** (May–Oct Mon–Fri 9am–5pm, Sat 10am–5pm, Sun 2–5pm; Nov–April Mon–Fri 9am–5pm; free) behind, which was almost totally destroyed by bombing in 1942, but has since been restored to a near identical replica of its original, timber-roofed state. From St Helen's Square, **Stonegate** leads northeast towards the Minster, a street as ancient as the city itself. Originally the Via Praetoria of Roman York, it's now paved with thick flags of York stone, which were once carried along here to build the Minster, hence the street name. Guy Fawkes' parents lived on Stonegate (there's a plaque opposite the Mulberry Hall shop).

South to Jorvik

At the **Merchant Adventurers' Hall**, off Fossgate (April–Sept Mon–Sat 9am–5pm, Sun noon–4pm; Oct–March Mon–Sat 9am–3.30pm; £2), the overpowering whiff of wood polish prepares you for one of the finest medieval timber-framed halls in Europe. The beautiful building was raised by the city's most powerful guild, dealers in wool from the Wolds, woollens from the Dales and lead from the Pennines, commodities that were traded for exotica from far and wide. **Fairfax House**, on nearby Castlegate (March–Dec Mon–Thurs & Sat 11am–5pm, Sun 1.30–5pm; guided tours Aug & Sept Fri at 11am & 2pm; closed Jan & Feb; £4; ⓦwww.fairfaxhouse.co.uk), celebrates the wealth of a later period. The elegant Georgian town house was restored to house the collection of fine arts left by Noel Terry, scion of one of the city's chocolate dynasties. The bulk of the collection consists of eighteenth-century furniture and clocks, and every December the popular "Keeping of Christmas" exhibition recreates a Georgian Christmas in the house.

Around the corner, in the Coppergate shopping centre, the crowds descend upon the city's blockbuster Viking exhibit – **Jorvik** (daily: April–Oct 9am–5.30pm; Nov–March 10am–4.30pm; £6.95; ⓦwww.vikingjorvik.com). This multi-million-pound affair flies visitors back in "time capsules" to the tenth-century city of York, presenting not just the sights but the sounds and even the smells of a riverside Viking settlement, complete with animatronic figures, street scenes and panoramic views of the re-created city. Not surprisingly, it's a hugely popular exhibit, and great for children, though you can avoid queuing by pre-booking your entrance ticket with a credit card, by calling ☎01904/543043. It's worth noting that the museum organizes York's annual **Viking Festival** every February when themed events take place throughout the city – details from the Festival Office at the centre.

York Castle and the Castle Museum

Despite the rich architectural heritage elsewhere in the city, there's precious little left of **York Castle**, one of two established by William the Conqueror. Only the perilously leaning **Clifford's Tower** (daily: Easter–June & Sept 10am–6pm; July & Aug 10am–7.30pm; Oct 10am–5pm; Nov–Easter 10am–4pm or dusk; £2; EH) remains, as evocative a piece of military engineering as you could wish for: a stark and isolated stone keep built on one of William's mottes between 1245 and 1262.

Immediately east of the tower lies the excellent **Castle Museum** (April–Oct daily 9.30am–5pm; Nov–March Mon–Sat 9.30am–4pm, Sun 10am–4pm; £5.75), a remarkable collection founded by a Dr Kirk of Pickering, who in the 1920s realized that many of the everyday items used in rural areas were in danger of disappearing. He took the unusual step of accepting bric-a-brac from his

12

patients in lieu of fees. A whole range of early craft, folk and agricultural ephemera is complemented by costumes, militaria, workshops, two entire reconstructed streets and special exhibitions on subjects as diverse as chocolate, burials and fire engines. Pride of place is given to a dazzling Viking helmet, discovered during the Coppergate excavations and the only one of its kind ever found.

The National Railway Museum

The **National Railway Museum** on Leeman Road (daily 10am–6pm; free; Ⓦ www.nrm.org.uk), ten minutes' walk from the station, is a must if you have even the slightest interest in railways, history, engineering or Victoriana. The Great Hall alone features some fifty restored locomotives dating from 1829 onwards, among them the *Mallard*, at 126mph the world's fastest steam engine. The Station Hall, a former goods station, complete with tracks and platforms, holds the major permanent exhibitions, where you can see the plush splendour of the royal carriages ("Palaces on Wheels") and the bleak segregation of classes in the Victorian coaches. A separate wing, "The Works", provides access to the engineering workshop where conservation work is undertaken; to a walk-round backstage warehouse area, showcasing the museum's reserve collection; and to a track-and-signal viewing area which has been established over the East Coast main line.

Eating and drinking

In keeping with much else in the city, many establishments are relentlessly and self-consciously old-fashioned, though there are some real highlights – truly historic **pubs**, the remarkable *Betty's*, the ultimate **tea-shop** experience, and a scattering of well-regarded **restaurants**. The **coffee** and **café-bar** scene has flourished too, with the main chain-names all represented, alongside some honourable independents.

Tearooms, cafés and café-bars

Betty's 6–8 St Helen's Square. If there are tea shops in heaven they'll be like *Betty's*, serving a dozen or so fish and meat hot dishes, some extraordinary puddings, and a takeaway counter. Daily 9am–9pm.

Blake Head Vegetarian Café 104 Micklegate. Bookstore-café for freshly baked cakes, pâtés, quiche, brunch, salads and soups. Mon–Sat 9.30am–5pm, Sun 10am–5pm.

Café No. 8 8 Gillygate. Caesar salads, ciabatta sarnies and cool sounds in this funky little café-bar. Mon–Fri 11am–3pm, Thurs & Fri 11am–3pm & 5–11pm, Sat 11am–11pm, Sun 11am–5pm.

City Screen Café-Bar Coney St. York's independent cinema has a splendid riverside café-bar, serving food until 9pm and hosting stand-up comedy, afternoon jazz and poetry evenings. Daily 11am–11pm.

Little Betty's 46 Stonegate. Owned by *Betty's* and in the same league; over 100 years old, it's the picture of a classic teashop. Daily 9am–5.30pm.

National Trust York Tearooms 30 Goodramgate. Choose from the likes of scrambled eggs and smoked ham, BLTs and omlettes, and sample one of Yorkshire's noted "fruit wines". Mon–Sat 10am–5pm.

Spurriergate Centre St Michael's Church, Spurriergate. Quiche, salads and baked potatoes served in the interior of twelfth-century St Michael's. Mon–Fri 10am–4.30pm, Sat 9.30am–5pm.

Restaurants

19 Grape Lane 19 Grape Lane ☏ 01904/636366. Renowned town-house restaurant serving top-quality Modern British dishes, including some great puddings. Closed Sun & Mon. Expensive.

The Patio 13 Swinegate Court East, off Grape Lane ☏ 01904/627879. Plenty of choice in this informal café/restaurant, from overly stuffed baguettes and wraps to a plate of bangers and mash. Closed Sun & Mon eve. Moderate.

La Piazza 45 Goodramgate ☏ 01904/642641. Authentic Italian coffee bar out front, courtyard restaurant out back, tucked into a nice Tudor building. Inexpensive to Moderate.

Pizza Express River House, 17 Museum St. Grand old riverside club rooms with sought-after balcony, the venue for *Pizza Express*'s usual menu of good-quality pizzas. Inexpensive to Moderate.

The Rubicon 5–7 Little Stonegate ℡01904/676076. Contemporary style and vegetarian world flavours, so there's nut roast and veggie lasagne but also *masala dhal* and *burritos* on offer. Inexpensive to Moderate.

Siam House 63a Goodramgate ℡01904/624677. The city's first Thai restaurant rarely disappoints – the menu is huge enough to cater for any tastes. Moderate.

Pubs

Black Swan Peasholme Green. York's oldest (sixteenth-century) pub with some superb stone flagging and wood panelling. Home of the city's folk club.

Golden Fleece 16 Pavement. One of the oldest pubs in the city, squeezed into a narrow town house opposite the Shambles and with a nice beer garden.

Judge's Lodging Cellar Bar 9 Lendal. Cosy drinking hole with good beer, in the eighteenth-century cellars of the *Judge's Lodging*, now a smart hotel.

King's Arms King's Staithe. Close to the Ouse Bridge, this pub has a fine riverside setting with outdoor tables.

The Three-Legged Mare 15 High Petergate. York Brewery's cosy outlet for its own quality beer and definitely a pub for grown-ups – no juke box, no video games and no kids.

Ye Olde Starre Stonegate. Vies with the *Black Swan* for historic precedence; good beer, a beer garden and plenty of atmosphere.

Nightlife, culture and entertainment

There are healthy helpings of **live music**, **culture** and **nightlife**, much of it detailed in the local *Evening Press* (and on their useful website, Ⓦ www.thisisyork .co.uk). Most bigger bands bypass the city in favour of Leeds, though the Barbican Centre pulls in its fair share of major mainstream artists, while the pub **music scene** flourishes. The annual **Early Music Festival**, held in July, is perhaps the best of its kind in Britain, with dozens of events spread over ten days – details are available on ℡01904/658338 or from the tourist offices. The famous **York Mystery Plays** are held every four years – next performances are in 2004.

Clubs and live music

Barbican Centre Barbican Road ℡01904/656688, Ⓦ www.fibbers.co.uk/barbican. Country, rock, folk and MOR stalwarts all appear here sooner or later.

Black Swan Peasholme Green ℡01904/632922. Regular folk nights with a full range of quality bands and singer-songwriters. Sunday lunch jazz too.

Fibbers Stonebow House, Stonebow ℡01904/466148, Ⓦ www.fibbers.co.uk. Indie and guitar-pop bands play most nights of the week at this inventive venue.

Punch Bowl Inn 7 Stonegate ℡01904/615491. Pub venue for jazz and blues, a couple of nights a week.

Cinema, theatre and the arts

City Screen 13–17 Coney St ℡01904/541155, Ⓦ www.picturehouse-cinemas.co.uk. The choice for art-house cinema, with a riverside café-bar.

Grand Opera House Cumberland Street, at Clifford St ℡01904/671818 Ⓦ www.york-opera-house.co.uk. Musicals, ballet and family entertainment in all its guises.

Theatre Royal St Leonard's Place ℡01904/623568 Ⓦ www.theatre-royal-york.co.uk. Musicals, pantos and mainstream theatre, as well as a café-bar.

Castle Howard

Immersed in the deep countryside of the Howardian Hills, fifteen miles northeast of York, off the A64, **Castle Howard** (March–Oct daily 11am–5pm; gardens open at 10am; £7.50; grounds only £4.50; Ⓦ www.castlehoward.co.uk) is the seat of one of England's leading aristocratic families and among the country's grandest stately homes. Since providing the setting for the television version of *Brideshead Revisited*, the house's car parks have been packed every weekend, but fitting it into a public transport itinerary is something of a problem.

In summer there are just two Yorkshire Coastliner buses a day (one on Sun) from York, but various bus tours can bring you out and back, too.

The colossal main house was designed by **Sir John Vanbrugh** in 1699 and was almost forty years in the making – remarkable enough, were it not for the fact that Vanbrugh was, at the start of the commission at least, best known as a playwright and had no formal architectural training. Shrewdly, Vanbrugh recognized his limitations and called upon the assistance of Nicholas Hawksmoor, who had a major part in the house's structural design – the pair later worked successfully together on Blenheim Palace. If Hawksmoor's guiding hand can be seen throughout, Vanbrugh's influence is clear in the very theatricality of the building, notably in the palatial **Great Hall**. This was gutted by fire in the 1940s, but has subsequently been restored from old etchings and photographs to something approaching its original state.

Vanbrugh soon turned his attention to the estate's thousand-acre **grounds** where he could indulge his playful inclinations to excess, and the formal gardens, clipped parkland, towers, obelisks and blunt sandstone follies stretch in all directions, sloping gently to a large artifical lake. He completed the **Temple of the Four Winds** before his death in 1726, leaving Hawskmoor to design the Howard family **Mausoleum**, which is taller than the house itself. Take a look, too, at the fine **stables** which have been converted into the Costume and Regalia Gallery, Britain's largest private collection of period clothes.

Hull

HULL's most famous adopted son, the poet and university librarian Philip Larkin, wrote "I wish I could think of just one nice thing to tell you about Hull, oh yes … *it's very nice and flat for cycling*". Harsh perhaps, but it does capture something of the character of a town that reaches few heights, physical or otherwise. The town – rarely known by its full title of **Kingston-upon-Hull** – undoubtedly suited the poet's curmudgeonly temperament, but he might have mentioned Hull's self-reliant and no-nonsense atmosphere, or that the old docks and restored town centre are surprisingly appealing. Hull's **maritime** pre-eminence dates back to 1299, when it was laid out as a seaport by Edward I. It quickly became England's leading harbour, and was still a vital garrison when the gates were closed against Charles I in 1642, the first serious act of rebellion of what was to become the English Civil War. The central **Princes Dock** sets the tone for Hull's modern refurbishment, the once abandoned waters now lined by landscaped brick promenades and overlooked by **Princes Quay**, a multi-tier, glass-spangled shopping centre, with the revamped **marina** beyond.

The town's maritime legacy is exhaustively detailed in the excellent **Maritime Museum** (Mon–Sat 10am–5pm, Sun 1.30–4.30pm; free), housed in the Neoclassical headquarters of the former Town Docks Offices, flanking the east side of Queen Victoria Square, north of Princes Quay. The main boost to the town's coffers in the eighteenth and nineteenth centuries was whaling, and the museum tells the story well, displaying gruesome whaling equipment, such as a blubber pot cauldron, alongside model ships, old photographs, Inuit relics and a whale skeleton. Leave Queen Victoria Square on its east side by pedestrianized Whitefriargate and, after about 200 yards, turn right down Trinity House Lane for **Holy Trinity** (April–Sept Mon–Fri 11am–3pm, Sat 9.30am–noon; Oct–March Tues–Fri 11am–2pm, Sat 9.30am–noon; free), among the most pleasing parish churches in the country, notable for its brick

12

transepts and chancel. Close by is one of Hull's most revered relics – the **Old Grammar School**, a red-brick edifice built in 1583 and which for 120 years doubled as the town's Merchant Adventurers' Hall. As a school, it numbered amongst its pupils William Wilberforce, instigator of the abolition of slavery in the British Empire, and seventeenth-century poet Andrew Marvell, also MP for Hull. (Hull-born Stevie Smith, incidentally, completes the town's poetic triumvirate.) Two blocks east you hit the **High Street**, whose crop of older buildings and narrow cobbled alleys have seen it designated an "Old Town Conservation Area". At its northern end stands **Wilberforce House** (Mon–Sat 10am–5pm, Sun 1.30–4.30pm; free), the former home of William and containing some fascinating exhibits on slavery and its abolition.

The **train station** is on the west side of town, on the main drag of Ferensway, with the **bus station** just to the north. The main **tourist office** is bang in the centre on Paragon Street at Queen Victoria Square (Mon–Sat 9am–6pm, Sun 11am–3pm; ☏01482/223559, ⓦ www.hullcc.gov.uk). They coordinate richly anecdotal **guided tours** around the old town (April–Oct, Mon, Wed, Thurs, Fri & Sat at 2pm; £2.50). Amongst several **B&Bs**, a good choice is the *Clyde House Hotel*, 13 John St (☏01482/214981; ❷), or try the *Arches*, 38 Saner St (☏01482/211558; ❶). The *Comfort Inn*, just south of the train station at 11 Anlaby Rd (☏01482/323299; ❷), and the *Quality Hotel Royal*, 170 Ferensway (☏01482/325087; ❸), right by the station, have reasonable rooms too. For **food**, *Cerutti's* (☏01482/328501; closed Sat lunch & Sun) leads the way in local seafood; it's down at the end of the east side of the marina at 10 Nelson St. *Studio 10^1/2* (closed Sun), opposite Holy Trinity church on King Street, serves snacks and tasty veggie specials. Next door, *Fiddleheads*, 10 King St (☏01482/224749; open eve, plus Fri & Sat lunch), is a well-thought-of vegetarian and vegan restaurant. Of Hull's many **pubs**, the *Ye Olde White Harte*, 25 Silver St, has a pleasant courtyard and a history going back to the seventeenth century. *Ye Olde Black Boy*, 150 High St, specializes in real ales – and offers cider and fruit wines too.

Beverley

BEVERLEY, nine miles north of Hull, ranks as one of northern England's premier towns, its Minster the superior of many an English cathedral, its tangle of old streets, cobbled lanes and elegant Georgian and Victorian terraces the very picture of a traditional market town. Over 350 buildings are listed as possessing historical or architectural merit, and though you could see its first-rank offerings in a morning, this is one of a handful of places in this part of the world that you might want to stay in for its own sake.

Approaches to the town are dominated by the twin towers of **Beverley Minster** (March, April, Sept & Oct Mon–Sat 9am–5pm; May–Aug Mon–Sat 9am–6pm; Nov–Feb Mon–Sat 9am–4pm; plus Sun year round, depending on services, but usually noon–4pm; £2 donation requested), visible for miles across the wolds and airy flatlands. Initiated as a modest chapel, the minster became a monastery under John of Beverley, who was buried here in 721 and canonized in 1037 – his body lies under the crossing at the top of the nave. Fires and the collapse of the central tower in 1213 paved the way for two centuries of rebuilding, funded by bequests from pilgrims paying homage to the saint, and the result was one of the finest Gothic creations in the country. The **west front**, which crowned the work in 1420, is widely considered without equal, its survival due in large part to Baroque architect Nicholas Hawksmoor, who restored much of the church in the eighteenth century. Similar outstanding work awaits in the interior, most notably the fourteenth-century **Percy Tomb** on the north side of the altar, its sumptuously carved canopy one of the masterpieces of medieval European ecclesiastical art. Other incidental carving throughout the church is magnificent, particularly the 68 misericords of the oak **choir** (1520–24), one of the largest and most accomplished in England. Much of the decorative work here and elsewhere is on a musical theme. Beverley had a renowned guild of itinerant minstrels, which provided funds in the sixteenth century for the carvings on the transept aisle capitals, where you'll be able to pick out players of lutes, bagpipes, horns and tambourines.

Beverley's **train station** is beside Station Square, just a couple of minutes' walk from the Minster; **buses** pull into Station Square. The **tourist office** is at 34 Butcher Row in the main shopping area (June–Aug Mon–Fri 9.30am–5.30pm, Sat 10am–5pm, Sun 10am–2pm; rest of year closed Sun; ☏01482/391672). There's plenty of local **accommodation**, including the *Eastgate*, 7 Eastgate (☏01482/868464; no credit cards; ❷), close to the Minster. Among the hotels, the top town-centre choices are the *Beverley Arms*, North Bar Within (☏01482/869241; ❺), and the *North Bar Hotel*, 28 North Bar Without (☏01482/881375; ❸). Of the pubs, try the *Windmill Inn*, 53 Lairgate (☏01482/862817; ❷), which has a dozen rooms for rent. The **youth hostel** (☏01482/881751, ⓦwww.yha.org.uk; closed Nov–March) occupies one of the town's finer buildings, a restored Dominican friary that was mentioned in the *Canterbury Tales*. It's located in Friar's Lane, off Eastgate. For **food**, *Cerutti's 2*, in Station Square (☏01482/866700; closed Sun), is a sister brasserie to that in Hull. Or you can eat in the **pubs** – the celebrated *White Horse* on Hengate, near St Mary's, is a thoroughly atmospheric traditional drinking den with folk music nights.

The East Yorkshire coast

The **East Yorkshire coast** curves south in a gentle arc from the mighty cliffs of Flamborough Head to Spurn Head, a finger-thin isthmus formed by the constant erosion and shifting currents that scour much of England's eastern shores. Between the two lie a handful of tranquil villages and miles of windswept dunes and mudflats, noted bird sanctuaries, and superbly lonely retreats accessible to anyone prepared to cycle or walk the paths and lanes that fan out amidst the dunes. The two main resorts, Bridlington and Filey, are linked by the regular train service between Hull and Scarborough. There's also an hourly bus service between Bridlington, Filey and Scarborough.

The southernmost major resort on the Yorkshire coast, **BRIDLINGTON** has maintained its harbour for almost a thousand years, though for much of that time it remained a small-scale place of little consequence. Renovations have smartened up the seafront promenade, which looks down upon the town's best asset – its sweeping sandy **beach**. It's an out-and-out family resort, which means plenty of candy-floss, amusement arcades, rides, and other diversions. The **tourist office**, 25 Prince St (Easter–Oct Mon–Sat 9.30am–5.30pm, Sun 9am–5pm; Nov–Easter Mon–Sat 9.30am–5.30pm; ☏01262/673474), has full lists of local accommodation.

Around fourteen miles of precipitous four-hundred-foot cliffs gird **Flamborough Head**, just to the northeast of Bridlington, a chalky knuckle whose 1979 designation as a Heritage Coast has guaranteed a degree of protection not only for a multitude of breeding seabirds, but also for a wealth of geological and archeological features. To see the best of Flamborough Head's coastline, try to walk at least part of the signposted **Heritage Coast path**, a grassy cliff-top track that negotiates most of the headland. One good place to join it is **BEMPTON**, two miles north of Bridlington. From Bempton, you can follow the path all the way round to Flamborough Head or curtail by cutting up paths to Flamborough village. The *Seabirds* (℡01262 674174), at the junction of the roads to the two villages, is a nice **pub** with a good line in fresh-fish bar meals.

FILEY, half a dozen miles further north up the coast has a deal more class as a resort, retaining many of its Edwardian features, including some splendid panoramic gardens. It, too, claims miles of wide sandy **beach**, stretching most of the way south to Flamborough Head and north the mile or so to the jutting rocks of **Filey Brigg**. If you're going to clamber around on the Brigg, check the tide tables first since people do get caught unawares by the incoming waters. **Bus** and **train stations** are just west of the centre on Station Road. Walk down Station Avenue and Murray Street to Filey's **tourist office** in the Borough Council offices on John Street (May–Sept daily 9.30am–5.30pm; Oct–April Sat & Sun 10am–4.30pm; ℡01723/518000). You'll find a clutch of standard **B&Bs** on Rutland Street, off West Avenue, which runs from the church in the centre of town. A couple of pricier hotels sit amongst the holiday flats down on the beachfront. *Downcliffe House* (℡01723/513310; ❸) is the pick of them, with a seaview restaurant serving a decent menu of fresh fish.

The North York Moors

Virtually the whole of the **North York Moors**, from the Hambleton and Cleveland hills in the west to the cliff-edged coastline to the east, is protected by one of the country's finest National Parks. The moors are lonely, heather-covered, flat-topped hills cut by deep, steep-sided valleys, and views here stretch for miles, interrupted only by giant cultivated forests, pale shadows of the woodland that covered the region before it was cleared by Neolithic and later peoples. Barrows and ancient forts provide memorials of these early settlers, mingling on the high moorland with the **Roman remains** of Wades Causeway, the battered stone crosses of the first Christian inhabitants and the ruins of great monastic houses such as Rievaulx.

Helmsley is the best starting point for any exploration of the western and central moors; **Pickering** (actually just outside the National Park) for the eastern moors and northern Esk Valley. The central moors offer the best walking and the most noted landscapes, with **Hutton le Hole** the most picture-perfect village in the region. Any exploration of the district should also include the religious ruins of **Rievaulx Abbey**; the views from **Sutton Bank**; and the gentle landscapes of the **Esk Valley**, blessed with its own small train line.

The main southern artery linking the western, central and eastern divisions is the A170, which runs from Thirsk, through Helmsley and Pickering to Scarborough. Two trans-moor roads, the Helmsley–Stokesley B1257 (west side) and the Pickering–Whitby A169 (east), offer access into the very heart of the moors. The **steam trains** of the North York Moors Railway operate between Pickering and Grosmont (even more renowned since being used as the "Hogwarts Express" in the first *Harry Potter* film). At Grosmont you can connect with the regular trains on the Esk Valley line, running east to Whitby or west through more remote settlements (and ultimately to Middlesbrough). The main **bus** approaches to the moors are from Scarborough and York to Helmsley and Pickering, though beyond these towns local services are limited. You'll need the free *Moors Connections* timetable, available from tourist offices and park information centres.

The western moors

The **western moors** are marked on their western edge by the scarp of the **Hambleton Hills** and the ruler-straight line of the A19 road between York, **Thirsk** (just outside the park) and Middlesbrough. To the east they are closed by Rye Dale, one of the region's more bucolic valleys, and the B1267 from **Helmsley**. Most outings are likely to centre less on the scenery – except for the walks and staggering views from **Sutton Bank** on the A170 – than on a cluster of historic buildings, of which the most prepossessing is **Rievaulx Abbey**, a couple of miles from Helmsley.

Thirsk and Mount Grace Priory

The small market town of **THIRSK**, 23 miles north of York, made the most of its strategic crossroads position on the ancient drove road between Scotland and York and on the historic east–west route from dales to coast. Its medieval prosperity is clear from the large, cobbled **Market Place** (market days are Monday and Saturday), now overrun by traffic, while later well-to-do citizens endowed the town with a bevy of commendable Georgian houses and halls. However, Thirsk's main draw is its attachment to the legacy of local vet Alf Wight, better known as **James Herriott**. Thirsk was the "Darrowby" of the Herriott books, not least because the town was where the vet had his actual surgery. This building at 23 Kirkgate is now the hugely popular **World of James Herriott** (daily: Easter–Oct 10am–6pm; Nov–Easter 10am–5pm, last admission 1hr before closing; £4.50; ⑳www.worldofjamesherriott.org), an entertaining re-creation of the vet's 1940s surgery, dispensary, operating theatre, sitting room and kitchen, each crammed with period pieces and Herriott memorabilia.

Eleven miles north of Thirsk (straight up the A19), the fourteenth-century **Mount Grace Priory** (Easter–Oct daily 10am–6pm; Nov–March Wed–Sun 10am–1pm & 2–4pm; £2.90; NT & EH) is the most important of England's nine Carthusian ruins and the only one in Yorkshire. The Carthusians took a vow of silence and lived, ate and prayed alone in their two-storey cells, each separated from its neighbour by a privy, small garden and high walls. The foundations of the cells are still clearly visible, together with one which has been reconstructed to suggest its original layout and the monks' way of life. Take the

The Moorsbus

The National Park Authority's **Moorsbus** (☏01439/770657, ⑳www.moorsbus.net) runs every Sunday and bank holiday Monday from April to the end of October, and daily in the summer school holidays (late July to late Aug). All local tourist and National Park information offices have timetables, but the **services** connect Helmsley to Sutton Bank, Osmotherley, Rievaulx, Coxwold and Kilburn; Pickering to Hutton le Hole, Castleton and Danby, to Rosedale Abbey and to Dalby Forest; and Helmsley and Pickering to each other. Departures are usually four times daily (hourly on the main routes), and timed so that day-trips are possible to the various sights; all-day **tickets** cost £2.50.

train from Thirsk to Northallerton, six miles southwest of the priory, and then any of the regular Northallerton–Osmotherley buses (hourly, not Sun).

Buses stop in Thirsk's Market Place. The **train station** is a mile west of town on the A61 (Ripon road); minibuses connect the station with the town centre. The **tourist office** is inside the World of James Herriott, 23 Kirkgate (daily: Easter–Oct 10am–5.30pm; Nov–Easter 10am–4.30pm; ☎01845/522755, Ⓦwww.hambleton.gov.uk). For **accommodation**, try *Lavender House*, 27 Kirkgate (☎01845/522224; no credit cards; ❶), and *Kirkgate House*, further along at no. 35 (☎01845/525015; ❹, ❸ for courtyard rooms). The *Golden Fleece* and *Three Tuns* **pubs** both serve meals, while the nicest daytime choice is the *Yorks Tearooms*, next to the clocktower on Market Place. There's a popular **youth hostel** and adjacent campsite at *Cote Ghyll* (☎01609/883575, Ⓦwww.yha .org.uk), half a mile north of the little village of **Osmotherley,** eleven miles north of Thirsk.

Sutton Bank and Coxwold

The main A170 road enters the National Park from Thirsk as it climbs five hundred feet in half a mile to **Sutton Bank** (960ft), a phenomenal viewpoint whose panorama extends across the Vale of York to the Pennines on the far horizon. At the top of the climb stands a North York Moors National Park **Visitor Centre** (Easter–Oct daily 10am–5pm; Nov, Dec & March daily 11am–4pm; Jan & Feb Sat & Sun 11am–4pm; ☎01845/597426, Ⓦwww.nor-thyorkmoors-npa.gov.uk), where you can pick up details about local walks – such as the marked **White Horse Nature Trail** (2–3 miles; 1hr 30min) which skirts the crags of Roulston Scar en route to the **Kilburn White Horse**, northern England's only turf-cut figure, at 314 feet long and 228 feet high.

A diversion off the A170 takes you into **COXWOLD**, as attractive a little village as they come. The majority of its many visitors come to pay homage to the novelist **Laurence Sterne**, who is buried by the south wall (close to the porch) in the churchyard of **St Michael's**, where he was vicar from 1760 until his death in 1768. **Shandy Hall** (150 yards further up the road past the church (May–Sept Wed 2–4pm, Sun 2.30–4.30pm; gardens May–Sept Mon–Fri & Sun 1–4.30pm; £3.50; gardens only £2.50), was Sterne's home, now a museum crammed with literary memorabilia. It was here that he wrote *A Sentimental Journey through France and Italy* and the wonderfully eccentric *The Life and Opinions of Tristram Shandy, Gentleman*. Sterne talked of "A delicious Walk of Romance" from Coxwold to twelfth-century **Byland Abbey** (Easter–Sept daily 10am–6pm; Oct daily 10am–5pm; Nov–Easter Wed–Sun 10am–1pm & 2–4pm; £1.70; EH), a mile and a half northeast of the village. His description captures the appeal of the ruins, which though larger in ground area than the Cistercian houses at Fountains and Rievaulx, are far less well preserved. **Buses** run to Coxwold from Thirsk on Mondays, Fridays and Saturdays (and on to Helmsley), and the Moorsbus runs here from Helmsley in summer. The *Fauconburg Arms* (☎01347/868214; ❹), a superb old **pub** on Main Street, has a cosy bar serving good food and a more formal restaurant.

Helmsley

One of the moors' most appealing towns, **HELMSLEY** makes a perfect base for visiting the western moors and Rievaulx Abbey. Local life revolves around a large cobbled market square (market day is Friday), dominated by a vaunting monument to the second earl of Feversham, whose family were responsible for rebuilding most of the village in the last century. The old **market cross** marks the start of the 110-mile Cleveland Way (see below). Close to the square is **Helmsley Castle** (April–Sept daily 10am–6pm; Nov–March Wed–Sun 10am–1pm & 2–4pm; £2.40; EH), its unique twelfth-century D-shaped keep ringed by massive earthworks.

To the southwest of the town, overlooking a wooded meander of the Rye, stands the Fevershams' country seat, **Duncombe Park** (house & garden: April–Oct Mon–Thurs & Sun 11am–5.30pm; parkland & visitor centre: same days 10.30am–6pm; house, gardens & parkland £6, gardens & parkland £4, parkland only £2; Ⓦwww.duncombepark.com), built for the Fevershams' ancestor Sir Thomas Duncombe in 1713. The **grounds** are perhaps more appealing than the house (which was extensively rebuilt after a fire in 1879), boasting swathes of landscaped gardens and a brace of artfully sited temples.

Helmsley is a hub for the **Moorsbus**, which takes trippers out to Sutton Bank, Rievaulx, Byland Abbey, Coxwold and Kilburn. Make sense of all the connections in the **tourist office** in the town hall on Market Place (Easter–Oct daily 9.30am–5pm; Nov–Easter Sat & Sun 10am–4pm; ☎01439/770173, Ⓦwww.ryedale.gov.uk), which also has full details about the **Cleveland Way,** one of England's premier long-distance National Trails, which starts at Helmsley and follows a route that embraces both the northern rim of the moors and Cleveland Hills and the cliff scenery of the North Yorkshire coast. The **Cleveland Way Project** (The Old Vicarage, Bondgate, Helmsley, YO6 5BP; ☎01439/770657) produces an annual *Accommodation and Information Guide*, an invaluable route-planning aid. There's plenty of **accommodation** in Helmsley itself, starting with *Stilworth House*, 1 Church St, behind the tourist office and square (☎01439/771072; no credit cards; ❸). Other modest B&Bs are scattered along Ashdale Road, a few hundred yards up Bondgate from the Market Place and on the right. Pricier hotels include the classy *Feversham Arms*, 1 High St, behind the church (☎01439/770766; ❻), and the *Black Swan*, on Market Place (☎01439/770466; ❼). The **youth hostel** (☎01439/770433, Ⓦwww.yha.org.uk) is a few hundred yards east of Market Place – follow Bondgate to Carlton Road and turn left. The old **pubs** in the Market Place – the *Royal Oak* and the *Feathers* – are both atmospheric places for a drink and a bite to eat. For a drive out into the country, and a fine meal, you can't do better than the *Star Inn* (☎01439/770397; no food Sun eve & Mon) at **Harome**, a couple of miles south of the A170.

Rievaulx Abbey and Terrace

From Helmsley you can easily hike across country to **Rievaulx Abbey** (daily: April–Sept 10am–6pm; Oct–March 10am–1pm & 2–4pm; £3.60; EH). The signposted path follows the opening two miles of the Cleveland Way, plus a mile's diversion off the Way, and takes around an hour and a half. Founded in 1132, the abbey became the mother church of the Cistercians in England, quickly developing from a series of rough shelters on the deeply wooded banks of the Rye to become a flourishing community with interests in fishing, mining, agriculture and the woollen industry, the latter supported by a chain of associated moorland farms. At its height, 140 monks and up to 500 lay brothers lived and worked at the abbey, though numbers fell dramatically once the Black Death (1348–49) had done its worst. Nemesis came with the Dissolution, when many of the walls were razed and the roof lead stripped – the beautiful ruins, however, still suggest the abbey's former splendour.

Although they form some sort of ensemble with the abbey, there's no access between the ruins and **Rievaulx Terrace and Temples** (Easter–Oct daily

10.30am–5pm; £3.30; NT), a site entered from the B1257, a couple of miles northwest of town. This half-mile stretch of grass-covered terraces and woodland was laid out as part of Duncombe Park in the 1750s, and engineered partly to enhance the views of the abbey. The resulting panorama over the ruins and the valley below is superb, and this makes a great spot for a picnic or simply for strolls along the lawns and woodland trail.

The central moors

The highest and wildest terrain in the North York Moors is in the **central moors**, bounded by Rye Dale in the west and by Rosedale in the east. Purple swathes of summer heather carpet the tops, where ancient crosses and standing stones provide hints of the moorland's distant past.

Lying around eight miles northeast of Helmsley, one of Yorkshire's quaintest villages, **HUTTON LE HOLE**, has become so great a tourist attraction that you'll have to come off-season to get much pleasure from its tidy gardens, its stream-crossed village green and the sight of sheep wandering freely through the lanes. The big draw is the **Ryedale Folk Museum** (Easter–Oct daily 10am–5.30pm; £3.25; ⓦwww.ryedalefolkmuseum.co.uk), an ever-expanding set of displays of local life and work over a two-acre site. The museum also houses a National Park **information centre** (℡01751/417367). For **accommodation**, try the *Barn Hotel* (℡01751/417311; ❸), on the through road just down from the museum, or the Georgian *Hammer and Hand* (℡01751/417300; ❸), a period B&B on the village green. If you stay the night you'll have plenty of time to become acquainted with the *Crown*, the friendly local **pub**.

Farndale is entered from the south by a minor road from **Gillamoor**, a little to the west of Hutton le Hole. Further up the vale the country lanes are packed in spring with tourists come to see the area's wild daffodils, protected by the two-thousand-acre **Farndale nature reserve**. The flowers grow in several parts of the dale, but the best area is north of **Low Mill**, where roads from Gillamoor and Hutton le Hole meet, about four miles north of the latter. The Moorsbus runs a special "Daffodil" service every Sunday in April and over Easter, shuttling visitors from Hutton le Hole.

Rosedale, a couple of miles east of Farndale, is slightly wilder and steeper than the latter, and has a network of wild upland roads ranging over its moors, which are densely studded with prehistoric tumuli and ancient stone crosses, including **Ralph Cross**, which stands sentinel at the isolated crossroads at the top of the dale. The largest of its communities, trim and tidy **ROSEDALE ABBEY**, four miles northeast of Hutton le Hole, preserves only a few fragments of the Cistercian priory (1158) that gave it its name, most of them incorporated into **St Lawrence's** parish church. It's hard to believe now, but in the last century the village had a population of over five thousand, most employed in the ironstone workings whose remnants lie scattered all over the lonely high moors round about. Rosedale village itself gets packed on summer weekends, a fair proportion here to sit outside the *Milburn Arms* (℡01751/417312; ❺; closed Jan), overlooking the small green. There's a popular **campsite** at *Rosedale Caravan Park* (℡01751/417272) down by the river, while north of Rosedale Abbey, you can reach the *Lion Inn* (℡01751/417320, ⓦwww.lionblakey.co.uk; ❸) on windswept **Blakey Ridge**, a couple of miles south of the junction with the Hutton le Hole–Castleton road (along which the Moorsbus travels).

Pickering and the eastern moors

The biggest centre for miles around, **Pickering** takes for itself the title "Gateway to the Moors", which is pushing it a bit, though it's certainly a handy place to stay if you're touring the villages and dales of the **eastern moors**. Its undoubted big pull, and biggest plus if you're using public transport, is the **North Yorkshire Moors Railway**, which provides a beautiful way of travelling up (and walking from) **Newtondale**. Otherwise, Moorsbus services radiate from Pickering and there are regular bus services to and from Helmsley, Scarborough, York and Leeds.

Pickering

A thriving market town at the junction of the A170 and the transmoor A169 (Whitby road), **PICKERING**'s most attractive feature is its **Castle** on the hill north of the market place (Easter–Oct daily 10am–6pm; Nov–March Wed–Sun 10am–4pm; £2.40; EH), reputedly used by every English monarch up to 1400 as a base for hunting in nearby Blandsby Park. Eight monarchs certainly put up here, including Edward II after his trouncing by the Scots at the Battle of Byland Abbey in 1322, and possibly a ninth, Richard II, was kept here as a prisoner shortly before his murder in Pontefract. The **tourist office**, on Eastgate car park (Easter–Oct Mon–Sat 9.30am–5.30pm, Sun 9.30am–4.30pm; Nov–Easter Mon–Sat 10am–4.30pm; ☎01751/473791, ⓦwww.ryedale.gov.uk), just above the Malton/Whitby/Scarborough roundabout, can provide full timetables for the **NYMR** (see box p.692). For **accommodation**, tree-lined Eastgate (the Scarborough road) has *Eden House* at no. 120 (☎01751/472289, ⓦwww.edenhousebandb.co.uk; no credit cards; ❷) and *Heathcote House* at no. 100 (☎01751/476991; ❷). A couple of the pubs also have rooms, top choice the *White Swan*, on the Market Place (☎01751/472288, ⓦwww.white-swan.co.uk; ❻). The nearest **youth hostel** is at the *Old School*, Lockton (☎01751/460376, ⓦwww.yha.org.uk), five miles northeast off the A169 – two miles' cross-country walk from the NYMR station at Levisham, or ask to be dropped at the turn-off by the Whitby bus. The local **campsite** is *Upper Carr* (☎01751/473115, ⓦwww.uppercarr.demon.co.uk; closed Nov–Feb), a mile and half south of town on the Malton Road.

Walks from the North Yorkshire Moors Railway

Most people make a full return journey for the superb scenery of the roadless **Newtondale**, but if you want to combine some walking with the train rides, stop en route at one of the minor stations. The first is **Levisham**, perfect for walks to the village of **LEVISHAM**, a mile and a half to the east, where the *Horseshoe Inn* (☎01751/460240; no credit cards; ❸) is a favourite target. A steep winding road continues another mile beyond Levisham, down across the beck and then up to **LOCKTON**, where there's a youth hostel and a path due north to the **Hole of Horcum**, a natural hollow gouged by the glacial meltwaters that carved out Newtondale – the paths run back to Levisham station from here, and the entire seven-mile circuit is one of the Moors' best short walks. In the other direction, a couple of miles west of the station, the fascinating **Cawthorn Camps** (free access) are the only Roman camps of their kind in the world. The site's jumbled collection of earthworks, spreading over 103 acres, puzzled archeologists for years, as all the previously discovered Roman marching camps in Europe were built on precise geometrical plans. It's now known that this was a military training area, troops from York's Ninth

The North Yorkshire Moors Railway

One of the northeast's big tourist draws, the volunteer-run **North Yorkshire Moors Railway** connects **Pickering** with the Esk Valley (Middlesbrough–Whitby) line at **Grosmont**, 18 miles to the north. The line was completed by George Stephenson in 1835, just nine years after the opening of the Stockton and Darlington Railway, making it one of the earliest lines in the country. Even by the standards of later projects it was a remarkable feat of engineering, navigating 1-in-15 gradients and using thousands of tons of brushwood and heather-stuffed sheepskins to provide bedding for the track through the dale's extensive bogs. For twelve years carriages were pulled by horse, with steam locomotives only arriving in 1847. The line closed in 1965 and was formally reopened in 1973.

Scheduled **services** operate between mid-March and early November (plus Christmas specials), with trains running hourly to three times daily depending on the time of year. For **advance bookings and information**, call ☎01751/472508 (Mon–Fri 9am–5pm, Sat & Sun 10am–2.30pm); for the talking timetables call ☎01751/473535; or check the website at ⊛www.nymr.demon.co.uk. A day-return **fare** along the whole line costs £10. Part of the line's attraction, of course, are the **steam trains**, though be warned that diesels are pulled into service when the fire risk in the forests is high.

Legion garrison being sent here on exercises, many of which obviously involved building camps.

The second stop, **Newtondale Halt**, is only a couple of miles northwest of the Hole of Horcum, or you can head off through the extensive woods of **Cropton Forest** to the west on trails marked by the Forestry Commission. **STAPE** – three miles southwest through the forest – is an archetypal high moors community, just two miles south of the best-preserved stretch of Roman road in Europe, **Wheeldale Roman Road**: the remains show a twenty-foot-wide stretch of sand and gravel studded by sandstone slabs and edged with kerbs and ditches, and the fact that it's plumb in the middle of open moorland only adds to its appeal.

The Esk Valley

The northernmost reaches of the National Park are crossed by the east–west **Esk Valley**, whose pretty river flows into the sea at Whitby. It's a part of the North York Moors overlooked by many visitors – partly, one suspects, because its very attractions, at least in the eastern stretches, are its valley characteristics: there's not much moorland tramping to be done until you reach **Danby**, one of the finest of all moorland villages. **Train** access is easy: the North York Moors Railway connects at **Grosmont**, where you're on the **Esk Valley line** which runs between Middlesbrough and Whitby (4–5 daily).

GROSMONT, little more than a level-crossing, station and a couple of tearooms, sees plenty of summer traffic, as does **EGTON BRIDGE** – similarly tiny but with the bonus of a beautifully sited riverside pub, the *Horseshoe*. Further west, the scenery becomes tinged by the looming moors until at the isolated stone village of **DANBY**, you're once again within striking distance of some excellent walks, all detailed on trail leaflets available from the **Moors Centre** (Easter–Oct daily 10am–5pm; Nov, Dec & March daily 11am–4pm; Jan & Feb Sat & Sun 11am–4pm; ☎01287/660654, ⊛www.northyorkmoors-npa.gov.uk). The *Stonehouse Bakery & Tea Shop* is great for daytime snacks, while a mile out of the village at **Ainthorpe**, the *Fox & Hounds* (☎01287/660218; ❸) looks out over the moors.

South of Grosmont, train, footpath and beck climb out of the Esk Valley towards Goathland. Only on foot will you be able to stop at **BECK HOLE**, after a couple of miles, an idyllic bridgeside hamlet focused on the *Birch Hall Inn*, one of the finest rural pubs in all England. A gentle path from the hamlet runs the mile through the fields up to **GOATHLAND**, another highly attractive village, this time set in open moorland beneath the great expanses of Wheeldale and Goathland moors. If it seems familiar – and if it seems unduly crowded – it's because it's widely known as "Aidensfield", the fictional village at the centre of the *Heartbeat* TV series. Signposts pointing you to the local sight, the **Mallyan Spout**, a seventy-foot-high waterfall. This lies half a mile or so from the imposing, stone *Mallyan Spout Hotel* on the common (☎01947/896486; ❺). Plenty of other local B&Bs offer cheaper rooms, among them *Glendale House*, on the common (☎01947/896281; ❷).

The North Yorkshire coast

A bracing change after the flattened seascapes of East Anglia and much of East Yorkshire, the **North Yorkshire coast** is the southernmost stretch of a cliff-edged shore that stretches almost unbroken to the Scottish border. **Scarborough** is the biggest town and resort, and the terminus for bus and rail links from York and beyond. **Robin Hood's Bay** is the most popular of the many Yorkshire villages, with fishing and smuggling traditions, while bluff **Staithes** – a fishing harbour on the far edge of North Yorkshire – has yet to tip over into full-blown tourist mode. **Whitby**, in between the two, is the best stopover, its fine sands and resort facilities tempered by its abbey ruins, cobbled streets, Georgian buildings and maritime heritage. For those who want to sample the most dizzying clifftops, the **Cleveland Way** provides a marked path along virtually the entire length of the coast.

Hourly **buses** (fewer on Sun) run along the A171 between Scarborough and Whitby, and a similarly frequent service operates to Robin Hood's Bay, and north between Whitby and Staithes. The Yorkshire Coastliner service connects Leeds and York with Scarborough (hourly) or Whitby (2–4 daily). You can also reach Scarborough direct by **train** from York or Hull.

Scarborough

The oldest resort in the country, **SCARBOROUGH** first attracted early seventeenth-century visitors to its newly discovered mineral springs. Fashionable among the Victorians– to whom it was "the Queen of the Watering Places" – Scarborough saw its biggest transformation after World War II, when it became a holiday haven for workers from the industrial heartlands. All the traditional ingredients of a beach resort are here in force, from superb, clean sands, kitsch amusement arcades and Kiss-Me-Quick hats to the more refined pleasures of its tightknit old-town streets and a genteel round of quiet parks and gardens.

There's no better place to acquaint yourself with the local layout than from the walls of **Scarborough Castle** (April–Oct daily 10am–6pm; Nov–March Wed–Sun 10am–1pm & 2–4pm; £2.50; EH), mounted on a jutting headland between two golden-sanded bays east of the town centre. Bronze and Iron Age relics have been found on the wooded castle crag, together with fragments of a fourth-century Roman signalling station, Saxon and Norman chapels and a Viking camp, reputedly built by a Viking with the nickname of *Scardi* (or "harelip"), from which the town's name derives. The present castle consists mainly of a three-storey keep dating from the twelfth century, and a thirteenth-century barbican and raking buttressed walls which trace the cliff edge. As you leave the castle, drop into the church of **St Mary** (1180), immediately below on Castle Road, whose graveyard contains the tomb of Anne Brontë, who died here in 1849.

The town museums are clustered around Valley Road, south of the train station. A "Museum S Pass" (£2; valid for a year) gets you into the Victorian **Wood End** on The Crescent (June–Sept Tues–Sun 10am–5pm; Oct–May Wed, Sat & Sun 11am–4pm), holiday home of the Sitwell family of writers and aesthetes, the adjacent **Art Gallery** (June–Sept Tues–Sun 10am–5pm; Oct–May Thurs, Fri & Sat 11am–4pm) and the nearby **Rotunda Museum** on Vernon Road (June–Sept Tues–Sun 10am–5pm; Oct–April Tues, Sat & Sun 11am–4pm), which holds the local archeological and historic finds.

Most of what passes for family entertainment takes place on the **North Bay** – massive water slides at Atlantis, the kids' amusements at Kinderland, and the miniature North Bay Railway (daily Easter–Sept), which runs up to the most educational of the lot, the **Sea Life Centre**, with its pools of flounders, rock-pool habitats and fishy exhibits. The **South Bay** is more refined, backed by the pleasant Valley Gardens and the Italianate meanderings of the South Cliff Gardens, and topped by an esplanade from which a **hydraulic lift** (daily 10am–4pm, till 10pm July & Aug) putters down to the beach. Here, Scarborough's Regency and Victorian glories are still evident in hotels like the *Crown* and, most impressively of all, the **Grand Hotel** built in 1867.

Practicalities

The **train station** is at the top of town facing Westborough; buses pull up outside or in the surrounding streets, though the National Express services stop in the car park behind the station. Within town, the **seafront buses** run throughout the summer from the *Corner Café* in North Bay to the Spa Complex in South Bay. Scarborough's **tourist office** is in Pavilion House, Valley Bridge Road (daily: May–Sept 9.30am–6pm; Oct–April 10am–4.30pm; ☎01723/ 373333, ⊛www.ycc.org.uk), just over the road from the station.

Scarborough is crammed with inexpensive **hotels and guest houses**. Happy hunting grounds include North Bay's Queen's Parade, where most of the guest houses have sweeping bay views; to be closer to the castle head up its continuation, Blenheim Terrace, where a score more options await. The cheapest places in town are those without the sea views – try along central Aberdeen Walk (off Westborough), or on North Marine Road and Trafalgar Square, behind Queen's Parade. Above South Bay, hotels tend to be pricier, though there's a clutch of B&Bs along and around West Street.

Scarborough is also home to the renowned **Stephen Joseph Theatre**, on the corner of Westborough and Valley Bridge Road, opposite the train station (☎01723/370541, ⊛www.sjt.uk.com). Housed in a former Art Deco cinema, this premieres every new play of local playwright Alan Ayckbourn and promotes strong seasons of theatre and film; a good café/restaurant and bar is open daily except Sunday.

Hotels and guest houses

Hotel Anatolia 21 West St ☎01723/360864. Nice old Victorian red-brick, one block back from the Esplanade. No credit cards. ❷

Crown Hotel Esplanade ☎01723/373491, ⊛www.ScarboroughHotel.com. In a Regency ter-

race above South Bay, the *Crown* makes the most of its period features, views and genteel feel. ❻

Interludes 32 Princess St ☎01723/360513, ⊛www.homepage.ntlworld.com/interludes. Quiet, non-smoking, Georgian town house in the old-town streets behind the harbour. ❸

Red Lea Hotel Prince of Wales Terrace
℡01723/362431, ⓦwww.redleahotel.co.uk. Part of a stylish terrace above South Bay, boasting sea-view rooms and a small indoor pool. B&B ⑤, ⑥ for full board.

Riviera St Nicholas Cliff ℡01723/372277. Restored Victorian hotel opposite the *Grand* (down Bar St, off Westborough) with super bay views and en-suite rooms. ❸

Whiteley Hotel 99 Queen's Parade ℡01723/373514. This is one of the best Queen's Parade options with good-value rooms (a few pounds extra for a sea view). ❷

Youth hostel and camp-sites

Scalby Close Park Burniston Rd ℡01723/ 365908. Tents and caravans. Closed Nov–Easter.

Scalby Manor Caravan Park Burniston Rd ℡01723/366212. There are tent spaces at this huge site, handy for the North Bay. Closed Nov–Easter.

Scarborough YHA Burniston Rd, Scalby Mills ℡01723/361176, ⓦwww.yha.org.uk. Occupies a converted watermill, a mile or so north of the town centre on the A165 and ten minutes' walk from the Sea Life Centre; the Cleveland Way passes close by.

Cafés, restaurants and pubs

Café Italia 36 St Nicholas Cliff. Italian coffee bar next to the *Grand Hotel*, where genuine coffee, focaccia slices and ice cream keep the regulars happy. Inexpensive.

Il Castello 34–36 Castle Rd ℡01723/377312. The town's best pizzas, and some inventive home-made pastas and other Italian dishes. Closed Mon & Tues. Moderate.

Gianni's 13 Victoria Rd ℡01723/507388. The good-natured staff bustle up and down stairs, delivering quality pizzas, pastas and quaffable wine by the carafe. Moderate.

The Golden Grid 4 Sandside ℡01723/360922. The harbourside's choicest fish-and-chip establishment, "catering for the promenader since 1883". Closed Mon–Thurs dinner in winter. Inexpensive–Moderate.

Hole in the Wall Vernon Rd. Cosy, real-ale pub with beer-knowledgeable staff and good food (served noon–2pm). Inexpensive

Lanterna 33 Queen St ℡01723/363616. Long-established, special-night-out destination, featuring traditional, seasonal Italian cooking in quiet, formal surroundings. Closed Sun. Expensive.

Stephen Joseph Theatre Restaurant Westborough ℡01723/368463. Fashionable food in the theatre restaurant. Closed Sun, and other evenings when there's no performance. Moderate.

Robin Hood's Bay

Although known as Robbyn Huddes Bay as early as Tudor times, there's nothing except half-remembered myth to link **ROBIN HOOD'S BAY** with Sherwood's legendary bowman – locals anyway prefer the old name, Bay Town or simply Bay. Perhaps the best-known and most heavily visited spot on the coast, the village fully lives up to its reputation, with narrow streets and pink-tiled cottages toppling down the cliff-edge site, evoking the romance of a time when this was both a hard-bitten fishing community and smugglers' den *par excellence*. From the upper village, lined with Victorian villas, now mostly B&Bs, it's a 1-in-3 walk down the hill to the harbour. Here, Bay is little more than a couple of narrow streets lined with gift shops and cafés, and a steep slipway that leads down to the curving, rocky **shoreline**. When the tide is out, the massive rock beds are exposed, split by a geological fault line and studded with fossil remains. There's an easy walk to **Boggle Hole** and its youth hostel, a mile south, returning inland via South House Farm and the path along the old Scarborough–Whitby railway line.

Buses from Scarborough or Whitby, seven miles north, drop you here too. Whitby has the nearest train station, and the nearest tourist office; **walkers**, along the coastal Cleveland Way, can make Whitby to Robin Hood's Bay in around three hours. **Accommodation** is often in short supply during high season. Two good **pubs** in the lower village have rooms: the tiny *Laurel*, on Main Street (℡01947/880400; ❶; two-night minimum), whose small self-catering flat sleeps two; and the *Bay Hotel*, on the harbour (℡01947/880278; ❸). As well as a score of guest houses in the upper village, there's the late-Victorian *Victoria Hotel*, Station Road (℡01947/880205; ❹), at the top of the hill, with fine views from some of its rooms, and a cliff-top beer garden. The other pub, the eighteenth-century *Dolphin* in King Street, is the oldest in the village, and has folk nights every Friday. Boggle Hole's **youth hostel** is one of Yorkshire's most popular, a former mill located in a wooded ravine a mile south of Robin Hood's Bay (℡01947/880352, ⓦwww.yha.org.uk). Note that a torch is essential after dark, and that you can't access the hostel along the beach once the tide is up. A couple of miles northwest of Robin Hood's Bay at **Hawsker**, on the A171, Trailways (℡01947/820207, ⓦwww.trailways.fsnet.co.uk) is a bike rental outfit based in an old train station, perfectly placed for day-trips along the largely flat railway line in either direction. They'll deliver or pick up from local addresses (including Boggle Hole youth hostel); there's also a small campsite and bunkhouse.

Whitby

If there's one essential stop on the North Yorkshire coast it's **WHITBY**, whose historical associations, atmospheric ruins, fishing harbour and intrinsic charm make it many people's favourite northern resort. The seventh-century abbey here made Whitby one of the key foundations of the early Christian period, and a centre of great learning, though little interfered with the fishing community that scraped together a living on the harbour banks of the River Esk below. For a thousand years, the local herring boats landed their catch until the great whaling boom of the eighteenth century transformed the fortunes of the town. Melville's *Moby Dick* makes much of Whitby whalers such as William Scoresby, while James Cook took his first seafaring steps from the town in 1746, on his way to becoming a national hero. All four of Captain Cook's ships of discovery – the *Endeavour*, *Resolution*, *Adventure* and *Discovery* – were built in Whitby.

Bram Stoker and Dracula

Bram Stoker was born in Dublin in 1847 and wrote his first stories while working in the Irish civil service. A meeting with Sir Henry Irving in 1877 led him to quit his job and move to London, where he became Irving's manager and close friend. Forgettable adventure novels followed, until in 1890, on holiday in Whitby, Stoker began to become interested in writing a story of vampires and the undead, already popularized in "Gothic" novels earlier that century. Using first-hand observation of a town he knew well – he stayed at a house on the West Cliff, now marked by a plaque – Stoker built a story which mixed real locations, legend, myth and historical fact: the grounding of Count Dracula's ship on Tate Hill Sands was based on an actual event reported in the local papers. The novel was published in 1897 and became synonymous with Stoker's name; it's been filmed, with varying degrees of faithfulness, dozens of times since.

With many of the early chapters recognizably set in Whitby, it's hardly surprising that the town has cashed in on its **Dracula Trail** – ask at the tourist office for details. The various sites – Tate Hill Sands, the abbey, church and steps, the graveyard, Stoker's house – can all be visited. Keen interest has also been sparked amongst the **Goth** fraternity, who now come to town en masse a couple of times a year (usually in late spring and around Halloween) for a vampire's ball, concerts and readings; their unofficial headquarters is the otherwise sedate *Elsinore* pub on Flowergate. A kind of truce has been called with the authorities at St Mary's church, who understandably objected to the more lurid goings-on in the churchyard at midnight; these have largely been curtailed and now there's even a special Goths service held at the church.

Hemmed in by steep cliffs and divided by the River Esk, the town splits into two distinct halves joined by a swing bridge: the **old town** to the east, centred on a curving cobbled street of great character, and the newer (though mostly eighteenth- and nineteenth-century) town across the bridge, generally known as **West Cliff**.

Cobbled **Church Street** is the old town's main thoroughfare, barely changed in aspect since the eighteenth century, though now lined with tearooms and gift shops. At the end of Church Street, you climb the famous **199 steps** of the Church Stairs – now paved, but originally a wide wooden staircase built for pallbearers carrying coffins to the church of St Mary above. Having made the climb, you've followed in the fictional footsteps of Bram Stoker's **Dracula**, who in the eponymous novel (see box opposite) takes the form of a large dog that bounds up the steps after the wreck of the ship bearing his coffin. The parish church of **St Mary** at the top of the steps, loftily removed from the town it served, is an architectural dog's dinner dating back to 1110, boasting a Norman chancel arch, a profusion of eighteenth-century panelling, box pews unequalled in England and a triple-decker pulpit – note the built-in ear trumpets, added for the benefit of a nineteenth-century rector's deaf wife.

The cliff-top ruins of **Whitby Abbey** (daily: April–Sept 10am–6pm; Oct–March 10am–4pm; £1.80; EH), beyond St Mary's, are some of the most evocative in England, the nave, soaring north transept and lancets of the east end giving a hint of the building's former delicacy and splendour. Its monastery was founded in 657 by St Hilda of Hartlepool, daughter of King Oswy of Northumberland, and by 664 had become important enough to host the **Synod of Whitby**, an event of seminal importance in the development of English Christianity. It settled once and for all the question of determining the date of Easter, and adopted the rites and authority of the Roman rather than the Celtic Church. **Caedmon**, one of the brothers at the abbey during its earliest years who was reputedly charged with looking after Hilda's pigs, has a twenty-foot cross to his memory which stands in front of St Mary's, at the top of the steps. His nine-line *Song of Creation* is the earliest surviving poem in English, making the abbey not only the cradle of English Christianity, but also the birthplace of English literature.

Whitby likes to make a fuss of Captain Cook who served an apprenticeship here from 1746–49 under John Walker, a Quaker shipowner. The **Captain Cook Memorial Museum** (Easter–Oct daily 9.45am–5pm; March Sat & Sun 11am–3pm; £2.80; ⓦwww.cookmuseumwhitby.co.uk), housed in Walker's rickety old house in Grape Lane (just over the bridge on the east side, on the right), contains an impressive amount of memorabilia, including ships' models, letters and paintings by artists seconded to Cook's voyages.

Final port of call should be the gloriously eccentric **Whitby Museum** in Pannett Park (May–Sept Mon–Sat 9.30am–5.30pm, Sun 2–5pm; Oct–April Mon–Tues 10.30am–1pm, Wed–Sat 10.30am–4pm, Sun 2–4pm; £2), at the back of West Cliff, up from the train station. There's more Cook memorabilia, including various of the ethnic objects and stuffed animals brought back as souvenirs by his crew, as well as casefuls of exhibits devoted to Whitby's seafaring tradition, its whaling industry in particular. Some of the best and largest fossils of Jurassic period reptiles unearthed on the east coast are also preserved here.

Practicalities

The **train station** lies a couple of hundred yards south of the bridge to the old town. Most local **buses** leave from the adjacent bus station, though the Yorkshire Coastliner services (from Leeds, York and Pickering) and National

Express buses (from London and York) stop around the corner on Langborne Road, just down from the tourist office. There's a Travel Centre (☎01947/602146) in the train station, for all local transport enquiries. Whitby's **tourist office** (daily: May–Sept 9.30am–6pm; Oct–April 10am–12.30pm & 1–4.30pm; ☎01947/602674, ⊛www.ycc.org.uk) is a right turn outside the train station to the corner of Langborne Road and New Quay Road.

The main B&B concentrations are on West Cliff, in the streets stretching back from the elegant Royal Crescent. Across the river in the old town, several pubs have rooms, while if you're prepared to travel a couple of miles out of Whitby you can find some pleasant country inns and hotels.

It's also worth nothing that Whitby is at the centre of the local **music scene**, with especially good folk nights in some of its **pubs**. It all comes to a head during the annual **Whitby Folk Week** in August (the week immediately preceding the bank holiday), when the town's streets, pubs and concert halls are filled day and night with singers, bands, traditional dancers, storytellers and music workshops. Other festivals throughout the year include the **Regatta** every August, a weekend of fairground rides, harbourside fireworks and boat races.

Hotels, B&Bs and guest houses

Beehive Newholm, ☎01947/602703. Isolated country pub in a hamlet a couple of miles inland, reached on the Sandsend road. ②

Bramblewick 3 Havelock Place, ☎01947/604504. Victorian house which retains its original fireplaces and wrought-iron balconies. The old attic rooms at the top have the best views. Two-night minimum stay. ②

Duke of York Church St, ☎01947/600324. At the bottom of the 199 steps, this popular pub has en-suite rooms overlooking the harbour. ②

Estbek House Sandsend, ☎01947/893424, ⊛www.fastfix.com/estbek. Georgian house with restaurant and tea garden, at Sandsend, two miles from Whitby and yards from the beach. ②

Number Five 5 Havelock Place, ☎01947/606361. Amiable West Cliff B&B which provides a good breakfast (veggie options available). No credit cards. ②

Shepherd's Purse 95 Church St, ☎01947/820228. Popular wholefood shop and restaurant with its best rooms set around a galleried courtyard. Vegetarian breakfast available. ③

White Horse & Griffin Church St, ☎01947/604857. The most atmospheric place to stay in the old town – an eighteenth-century inn with comfortable rooms. ③

Hostels and campsite

Harbour Grange Spital Bridge, Church St ☎01947/600817. Non-smoking backpackers on the eastern side of the river with five small dorms. Self-catering kitchen and lounge; curfew at 11.30pm.

Sandfield House Caravan Park Sandsend Rd

☎01947/602660. The nearest campsite, a mile west of town on the Sandsend road. Closed Nov–Easter.

Whitby Backpackers 28 Hudson St ☎01947/601794 ⓔmartin@warrener65.freeserve.co.uk. Easygoing West Cliff backpackers, including a couple of private rooms (①) and en-suite family rooms (①). There's a kitchen and lounge, free tea and coffee, and no curfew. Closed Jan & Feb.

Whitby YHA East Cliff ☎01947/602878, ⊛www.yha.org.uk. A converted stable a stone's throw from the abbey, with superb views over the town. Book well in advance. Self-catering kitchen, evening meal available.

Cafés and restaurants

Grapevine 2 Grape Lane, ☎01947/820275. Tiny, funky, dinner-only place dishing up great tapas-style meals. Closed Sun & Mon. Inexpensive.

Green's 13 Bridge St, ☎01947/600284. Whitby's best and most relaxed restaurant, producing stylish meals with contemporary flavours. Moderate.

Java 2 Flowergate ☎01947/821973, ⊛www.java-online.co.uk. From early till late, seven days a week, for cappuccino, latte, all-day breakfasts, grilled sandwiches, the daily papers – even internet surfing. Inexpensive.

Magpie Café 14 Pier Rd, ☎01947/602058. The traditional fish-and-chip choice in town for over forty years, with a wide-ranging menu. In summer you'll have to wait in long queues to get through the doors. Closes 9pm. Moderate.

Trenchers New Quay Rd, ☎01947/603212. Highly rated fish-and-chip restaurant, with snappy service and mountainous portions. Closes 9pm & all Nov–March. Moderate.

Pubs and live music

Black Horse 91 Church St. Idiosyncratic old-town "heritage" pub with a tiny front bar and good Tetley's beer.

Duke of York Church St. Classic Whitby pub, at the bottom of the 199 steps, with harbour views, good-value food and occasional music.

Middle Earth 26 Church St. Regular music nights at this local, down by the marina – outdoor seats provide harbour views.

Tap & Spile New Quay Rd. The town's real-ale haunt, with a changing selection of guest beers and live music nearly every night.

Staithes

Beyond the beach at Sandsend, a fine coastal walk through pretty Runswick Bay leads in around four hours to the fishing village of **STAITHES**; road access is along the A174. At first sight, it's an improbably beautiful grouping of huddled stone houses around a small harbour, backed by the severe outcrop of Cowbar Nab, a sheer cliff face which protects the northern flank of the village. Storms and floods have battered Staithes for centuries: the *Cod & Lobster*, the pub at the harbour, has been rebuilt three times and is shuttered against the wind, while the draper's shop in which James Cook first worked before moving to Whitby collapsed completely in 1745 – its rebuilt successor is now marked by a plaque. Cook is remembered in the **Captain Cook and Staithes Heritage Centre**, on the High Street (daily 10am–5.30pm; £1.75), which re-creates an eighteenth-century street among other interesting exhibits.

You could stay at one of the B&Bs in the houses at the top of the village, but better **accommodation** is available down below, either at the *Endeavour Restaurant* (℡01947/840825; no credit cards; ❸; closed Sun in winter) – itself the best place to eat for miles around, with superb (but pricey) fresh-fish meals – or at the *Black Lion* (℡01947/841132; ❷), a pub with cosy fires and a decent bar menu. There's **camping** back up the road out of the village at *Staithes Caravan Park*, Warp Mill (℡01947/840291; closed Nov–Feb).

Travel details

Buses

Details of minor local bus services are frequently given in the text. It's essential to pick up either the Dales Connections or Moors Connections timetable booklets from a local tourist office if you are visiting those parts of the county. For details of the Moorsbus in the North York Moors National Park see p.687. For information on all other local and national bus services, contact Traveline: ℡0870/608 2608 (daily 7am–9pm), ⓦwww.traveline.org.uk.

Trains

Main routes and services are given below. For more detailed information about specific lines, turn to the following pages: Settle to Carlisle Railway (p.661); North Yorkshire Moors Railway (p.692).

Harrogate to: Knaresborough (every 30min; 15min); Leeds (every 30min; 45min); York (hourly; 30min).

Hull to: Beverley (Mon–Sat hourly, Sun 4 daily; 15min); Leeds (hourly; 1hr); Scarborough (every 2hr; 1hr 30min); York (10 daily; 1hr 15min).

Knaresborough to: Harrogate (every 30min; 15min); Leeds (every 30min; 45min); York (hourly; 30min).

Leeds to: Bradford (every 15min; 20min); Carlisle (3–9 daily; 2hr 40min); Harrogate (every 30min; 45min); Hull (hourly; 1hr); Knaresborough (every 30min; 45min); Settle (3–8 daily; 1hr); Sheffield (every 30min; 45min–1hr 15min); Skipton (hourly; 40min); York (every 30min; 40min).

Pickering to: Grosmont (April–Oct 5–8 daily, plus limited winter service; 1hr).

Scarborough to: Hull (every 2hr; 1hr 30min); York (8–15 daily; 45min).

Sheffield to: Leeds (every 30min; 45min–1hr 15min); York (hourly; 1hr 20min).

Whitby to: Danby (June–Sept 4 daily; Oct–March Mon–Sat 4 daily; 35min); Grosmont (June–Sept 4 daily; Oct–March Mon–Sat 4 daily; 15min).

York to: Bradford (every 45min; 1hr); Harrogate (hourly; 35min); Hull (hourly; 1hr 15min); Leeds (every 30min; 40min); Scarborough (8–15 daily; 45min); Sheffield (hourly; 1hr 20min).

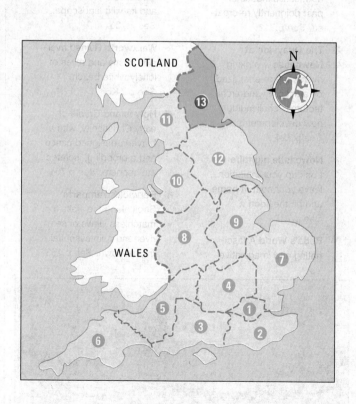

The Northeast

SCOTLAND

N

WALES

13

11

10

12

8

9

4

7

5

1

3

2

6

13

CHAPTER 13 # Highlights

❋ **Durham Cathedral** Awe-inspiring Romanesque church towering above the wooded banks of the River Wear. See p.708

❋ **Beamish Museum** The everyday details of the northeast's industrial past poignantly re-created. See p.712

❋ **The Quayside at Newcastle** A striking riverscape re-energized by artistically and architecturally challenging new developments. See p.724

❋ **Newcastle nightlife** Lock up your inhibitions, leave your coat at home and hit the Toon ... See p.727

❋ **Bede's World** A fascinating and imaginative evocation of the life and times of one of Europe's greatest scholars. See p.732

❋ **Hadrian's Wall** Put your walking boots on to make the most of this extraordinary monument and its wild landscape. See p.735

❋ **Warkworth** Ruined riverside castle and miles of lonely white beach. See p.746

❋ **Holy Island** Cradle of early Christianity, with a Lutyens-designed castle and a brooding, isolated atmosphere. See p.751

❋ **Berwick's ramparts** Stroll along the walls for matchless views of sea, river and quintessential frontier town. See p.753

The Northeast

For England's northeastern region – in particular the counties of **Northumberland** and **Durham** – the centuries between the Roman invasion and the 1603 union of the English and Scottish crowns were a period of almost incessant turbulence. To mark the empire's limit and to contain the troublesome tribes of the far north, **Hadrian's Wall** was built along the seventy-odd miles between the North Sea and the west coast, an extraordinary military structure that is now one of the country's most evocative ruins. When the Romans departed the northeast was plunged into chaos and divided into unstable Saxon principalities until order was restored by the kings of Northumbria, who dominated the region from 600 until the 870s. It was they who nourished the region's early Christian tradition, which achieved its finest flowering with the creation of the **Lindisfarne Gospels** on what is now known as Holy Island. The monks abandoned their island at the end of the ninth century, in advance of the Vikings' destruction of the Northumbrian kingdom, and only after the Norman Conquest did the northeast again become part of a greater England.

The Norman kings and their immediate successors repeatedly attempted to subdue Scotland, passing effective regional control to powerful local lords. Their authority is recalled by a sequence of formidable fortresses, most impressively those at **Bamburgh**, **Alnwick** and **Warkworth**, and also by **Durham Cathedral**, the magnificent twelfth-century church of the prince bishops of Durham, who ruled the whole of County Durham. Long after the northeast had ceased to be a critical military zone, its character and appearance were transformed by the **Industrial Revolution**. Coal had been mined here for hundreds of years, but exploitation only began in earnest towards the end of the eighteenth century, when two main coalfields were established – one dominating County Durham from the Pennines to the sea, the other stretching north along the Northumberland coast from the Tyne. The world's first **railway**, the **Darlington and Stockton** line, was opened in 1825 to move coal to the nearest port for export, while local coal and ore also fuelled the foundries of **Middlesbrough** and Consett, which in turn supplied the ship-building and heavy-engineering companies of Tyneside. The region boomed, creating a score of sizeable towns, amongst which Newcastle was pre-eminent – as it remains today.

Most visitors dodge the industrial areas, bypassing the towns along the **Tees Valley** – Darlington, Stockton, Middlesbrough and Hartlepool – on the way to **Durham**. From Durham it's a short hop to **Newcastle**, an earthy city distinguished by some fine Victorian buildings, the revitalized Quayside and a vibrant cultural scene and nightlife. North, past the old colliery villages, the brighter parts

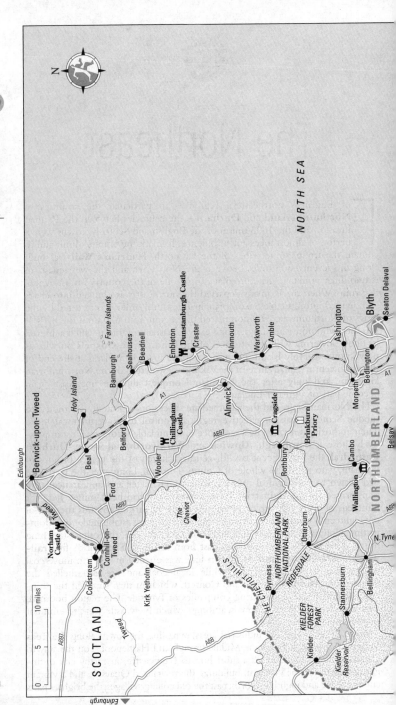

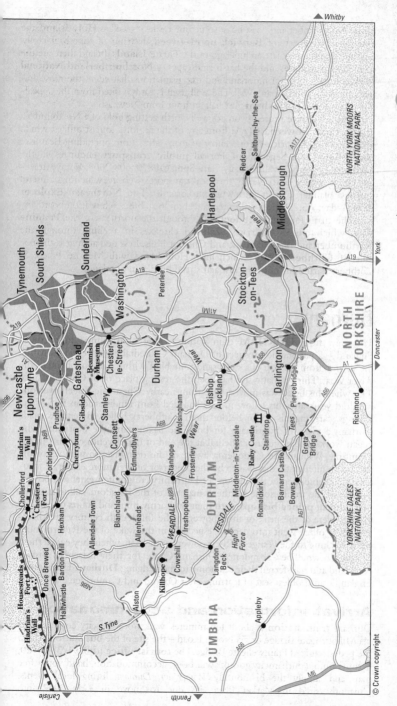

of the Northumberland coast boast some fine castles, as well as **Holy Island**, the extravagant ramparts of **Berwick-upon-Tweed**, a string of superb, if chilly, beaches, and the desolate archipelago of the **Farne Islands**. Inland there are the scenic Durham **dales** and the harsh landscapes of **Northumberland National Park**, a huge chunk of moorland and tree plantations that edges the most dramatic portion of Hadrian's Wall. The wall itself is easily visited from the appealing abbey-town of **Hexham**, just half an hour from Newcastle.

If there are two or more of you, it's well worth getting hold of a Northumbria Tourist Board **Powerpass** (£1) from any of the region's tourist offices, which gives two-for-the-price-of-one entry to many attractions, including Beamish, Bede's World and Segedunum. For all **public transport** enquiries in the northeast, contact Traveline (daily 7am–8pm; ☎0870/608 2608, ⓦwww.traveline.co.uk); or log onto Nexus, the local transport's website, which has a useful journey planner option (ⓦwww.nexus.org.uk). The **Northeast Explorer Pass** (1-day; £5.25) gives unlimited travel on local buses – buy it on board any bus. The main long-distance footpath through the northeast is the **Pennine Way**, which crosses Hadrian's Wall and climaxes in a climb through the Northumberland National Park and Cheviot Hills. Less demanding is the 63-mile **St Cuthbert's Way**, which links Holy Island with Melrose, where St Cuthbert started his ministry, just across the border in Scotland.

Durham

The view from **DURHAM** train station is one of the finest in northern England – a panoramic prospect of Durham Cathedral, its towers dominating the skyline from the top of a steep sandstone bluff within a narrow bend of the River Wear. This dramatic site has been the resting place of St Cuthbert since 995, when his body was moved here from nearby Chester-le-Street, over one hundred years after his fellow monks had fled from Lindisfarne in fear of the Vikings, carrying his coffin before them. Cuthbert's hallowed remains made Durham a place of pilgrimage for both the Saxons and the Normans, who began work on the present cathedral at the end of the eleventh century. In the meantime, William the Conqueror, aware of the defensive possibilities of the site, had built a castle that was to be the precursor of ever more elaborate fortifications. Subsequently, the bishops of Durham were granted extensive powers to control the troublesome northern marches of the kingdom, ruling as semi-independent **prince bishops**, with their own army, mint and courts of law. The bishops were at the peak of their power in the fourteenth century, but thereafter their office went into decline, especially in the wake of the Reformation, yet they clung to the vestiges of their powers until 1836, when they ceded them to the Crown. They abandoned Durham Castle for their palace in Bishop Auckland and transferred their old home to the fledgling **Durham University**, England's third oldest seat of learning after Oxford and Cambridge.

Arrival, information and accommodation

Durham **train station** is about ten minutes' walk from the city centre, either via Millburngate Bridge or via North Road – the site of the **bus station** – then the pedestrianized Framwellgate Bridge. The **tourist office** (☎0191/384 3720, ⓔtouristinfo@durhamcity.gov.uk) will book accommodation, hand you a free map and supply the bi-monthly *What's on: Durham*, listing local events. Currently sited in Market Place, it's due to move in early 2002 into

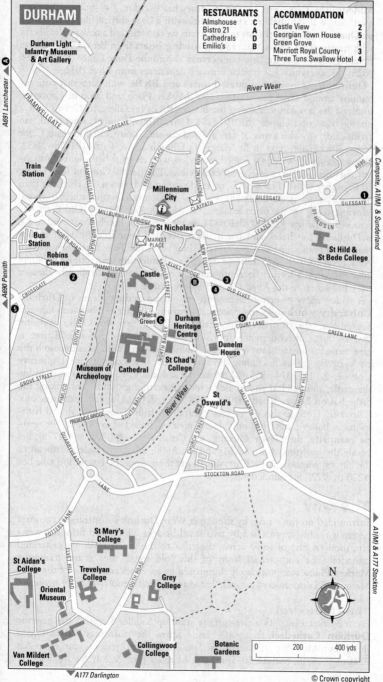

DURHAM

RESTAURANTS
Almshouse C
Bistro 21 A
Cathedrals D
Emilio's B

ACCOMMODATION
Castle View 2
Georgian Town House 5
Green Grove 1
Marriott Royal County 3
Three Tuns Swallow Hotel 4

Durham Light
Infantry Museum
& Art Gallery

River Wear

FRAMWELLGATE

SIDEGATE

A691 Lanchester

Campsite, A1(M) & Sunderland

A690

Train
Station

FREEMANS PLACE

PROVIDENCE ROW

Millennium
City

CLAYPATH

GILESGATE

GILESGATE

ST HILD'S LN

LEAZES ROAD

MILLBURNGATE BRIDGE

FRAMWELLGATE

MILLBURNGATE

NORTH ROAD

Bus
Station

Robins
Cinema

St Nicholas'

MARKET
PLACE

SADDLER STREET

NEW ELVET

ELVET BRIDGE

St Hild &
St Bede College

A690 Penrith

CROSSGATE

FRAMWELLGATE
BRIDGE

Castle

OLD ELVET

COURT LANE

GREEN LANE

Palace
Green

Durham
Heritage
Centre

NEW ELVET

Museum of
Archeology

Cathedral

SOUTH STREET

GROVE STREET

PIMLICO

NORTH BAILEY

SOUTH BAILEY

St Chad's
College

Dunelm
House

St
Oswald's

HALLGARTH STREET

WHINNEY HILL

River Wear

PREBENDS BRIDGE

QUARRYHEADS LANE

CHURCH STREET

STOCKTON ROAD

A1(M) & A177 Stockton

POTTERS BANK

St Mary's
College

St Aidan's
College

Oriental
Museum

Trevelyan
College

ELVET HILL ROAD

Grey
College

SOUTH ROAD

Van Mildert
College

Collingwood
College

Botanic
Gardens

N

0   200   400 yds

A177 Darlington

© Crown copyright

Millennium City on Claypath, a somewhat overdue £40-million development that will also shelter a visitor centre with a large-format film presentation on Durham, a state-of-the-art theatre, crafts workshops, and a new public library with free internet access. You can rent **rowing boats** from Brown's Boathouse, Elvet Bridge, or take the one-hour **cruise** aboard the *Prince Bishop* (☎0191/386 9525; £3.50), which has regular summer departures from Elvet Bridge.

Durham has a long list of **guest houses** and **B&Bs**, with particular concentrations around Gilesgate, northeast of Market Place, and around Crossgate, south of the bus station. Among the budget B&Bs on Gilesgate, *Green Grove* at no. 99 is a good choice (☎0191/384 4361, ✉guesthouse@f.s.net.co.uk; no credit cards; ➊), with a mix of standard and en-suite rooms. On Crossgate, *Castle View Guest House*, next to St Margaret's Church at no. 4 (☎0191/386 8852, ⓦwww.castle-view.net; ➌), is recommended, with en-suite bathrooms throughout, a garden and, of course, great castle views. The nearby *Georgian Town House*, 10 Crossgate (☎0191/386 8070; no credit cards; ➌), boasts more character than most, serves up good breakfasts and has some rooms with cathedral views. Moving swiftly up the price brackets, the *Marriott Royal County*, Old Elvet, just across Elvet Bridge (☎0191/386 6821, ⓦwww.marriotthotels.com/xvudm; ➐), is Durham's top hotel, and has its own riverside leisure centre with indoor swimming pool, sauna and solarium. Its sister hotel, the *Three Tuns Swallow Hotel*, New Elvet (☎0191/375 1504 or 386 1406, ✉threetuns.reservations@btinternet.com; ➐), is a former sixteenth-century coaching inn with slightly cheaper rates and access to the *Royal County's* leisure centre.

A wide variety of private bedrooms are offered at the colleges of **Durham University**, which welcome visitors at Christmas, Easter and between July and September; the tourist office has a full list, or check the website: ⓦwww.dur.ac.uk/conference_tourism. Most university accommodation is now aimed at businessmen as much as holiday-makers, with rates to match the city's B&Bs (➋–➍, including breakfast). The best colleges are University College (☎0191/374 3863, ✉J.A.Marshall@durham.ac.uk), with rooms inside the castle, and St Hild and St Bede, set in beautiful grounds overlooking the cathedral on Leazes Road (☎0191/374 3069, ✉L.C.Hugill@durham.ac.uk). University College also offers very central, no-frills rooms with shared bathrooms at Bailey Court, just off Palace Green (➊, breakfast excluded). The nearest **campsite**, the *Grange Camping and Caravan Site* (☎0191/384 4778), lies beside the junction of the A1(M) and the A690, about two miles northeast of the city on Meadow Lane, Carrville. To get there from the bus station take bus #220 or #222 for Sunderland.

The City

Surrounded on three sides by the River Wear, Durham's surprisingly compact centre is readily approached by two small bridges which lead from the western, modern part of town across the river to the spur containing castle and cathedral. The commercial heart of this "old town" area is the triangular **Market Place**, inappropriately dominated by an equestrian statue of the third Marquis of Londonderry, a much-hated nineteenth-century colliery owner.

The Cathedral

From Market Place, it's a five-minute walk up Saddler Street to the majestic **Durham Cathedral**, facing the castle across the manicured Palace Green (July–Sept Mon–Sat 9.30am–8pm, Sun 12.30–8pm; rest of year Mon–Sat 9.30am–6.15pm, Sun 12.30–5pm; guided tours June & July Sat 10.30am &

2pm; Aug & Sept Mon–Fri 10.30am, 11.30am & 2pm, Sat 10.30am, 11.30am, 2pm & 6.15pm, Sun 5pm; access may be restricted due to services and events, call ℡0191/386 4266 to check; £3 suggested donation; tours £3). Built to house the remains of St Cuthbert, the present cathedral was completed in 1133, and has survived the centuries pretty much intact, a supreme example of the Norman-Romanesque style. Entry is through the northwest porch, where a replica of the lion-head **sanctuary knocker** is a reminder of the medieval distinction between secular and religious law. The church used to be ringed by wooden crosses and, once a fugitive reached them, he or she could claim sanctuary from the lay authorities for up to 35 days.

The awe-inspiring **nave**, completed in 1128, is an inventive structure that used pointed arches for the first time in England, raising the vaulted ceiling to new and dizzying heights. The weight of the stone is borne by massive pillars, their heaviness relieved by striking Moorish-influenced geometric patterns – chevrons, diamonds and vertical fluting. Most of the cathedral's early fixtures and fittings were destroyed by Cromwell's Scottish prisoners, who were deposited inside the church after the Battle of Dunbar in 1650. The Scots did not, however, damage the gaudily painted, sixteenth-century **Prior Castell's clock**, located in the south transept, because it sported their emblem, the thistle. A door here gives access to the **tower** (Mon–Sat: Easter–Sept 9.30am–4pm; Oct–Easter 10am–3pm; £2), from the top of which are gut-wrenching views of the city.

Separated from the nave by a Victorian marble screen is the **choir**, where the dark-stained Restoration stalls are overshadowed by the vainglorious **bishop's throne**, reputedly the highest in medieval Christendom, built on the orders of the fourteenth-century Bishop Hatfield, whose militaristic alabaster tombstone lies just below. Beyond, the **Chapel of the Nine Altars** dates from the thirteenth century, its Early English stonework distinguished by its delicacy of detail. Here, and around the adjoining **Shrine of St Cuthbert**, much of the stonework is Frosterley marble, each dark shaft bearing its own fancy pattern of fossils. Cuthbert himself lies beneath a plain marble slab, his presence and shrine having gained a reputation over the centuries for their curative powers. The legend was given credence in 1104, when the saint's body was exhumed for reburial here, upon the completion of the eastern end of the new Norman cathedral, and was found to be completely uncorrupted, more than four hundred years after his death on Lindisfarne. Almost certainly, this was the result of his fellow monks having (unintentionally) preserved the body by laying it in sand containing salt crystals – though to medieval eyes, here was testament enough to the saint's potency.

Back near the entrance, at the west end of the church, the **Galilee Chapel** was begun in the 1170s, its light and exotic decoration in imitation of the Great Mosque of Cordoba. Subdivided by twelve slender columns, each surrounded by a medley of geometric patterns, the chapel contains the simple tombstone of the **Venerable Bede**, the Northumbrian monk credited with being England's first historian. Bede died at the monastery of Jarrow in 735 (see p.730) and his remains were transferred here in 1020. An ancient wooden doorway opposite the main entrance leads into the spacious **cloisters**, which are flanked by what remains of the monastic buildings. These include the **monks' dormitory** (Easter–Sept Mon–Sat 10am–3.30pm, Sun 12.30–3.15pm; 80p) and the somewhat misleadingly named **Treasures of St Cuthbert** exhibition in the undercroft (Mon–Sat 10am–4.30pm, Sun 2–4.30pm; £2): although the attractive display includes some striking relics of St Cuthbert, including the reassembled fragments of his delicately carved and much-travelled oak coffin, a beautiful gold pectoral cross and a silver-plated portable altar, it's mostly given over to ecclesiastical bric-a-brac, from altar plate, bishops' rings and seals to vestments and illu-minated manuscripts. The original Sanctuary Knocker is here, too, dating from 1140, and a computer terminal giving you a virtual opportunity to see the major illustrated pages of the Lindisfarne Gospels (see p.751). Also in the under-croft is the cathedral café, while next door in the impressively converted monas-tic kitchen is the bookshop.

The rest of the city

Across Palace Green from the cathedral, **Durham Castle** (Easter–Sept Mon–Sat 10am–12.30pm & 2–4pm, Sun 10am–noon & 2–4pm; Oct–Easter Mon, Wed, Sat & Sun 2–4pm; £3; ☎0191/374 3800, ⓦwww.durhamcastle .com) lost its medieval appearance long ago, during refurbishments arranged by a succession of prince bishops, but the university went further by renovat-ing the old keep as a hall of residence. It's only possible to visit the castle on a 45-minute guided tour, highlights of which include rapid visits to the fif-teenth-century kitchen, a climb up the enormous hanging staircase and the jog down to the Norman chapel, notable for its lively Romanesque carved capi-tals. The castle is sometimes closed for functions during its regular opening hours; call ahead to check.

Below the castle and the cathedral are the wooded banks of the **River Wear**, where a pleasant footpath runs right round the peninsula. It takes about thirty minutes to complete the circuit, passing a succession of elegant bridges with fine vantage points over town and cathedral. On the riverbank, south of **Framwellgate Bridge**, the university's **Museum of Archeology** (April–Oct daily 11am–4pm; Nov–March Mon & Fri–Sun 11.30am–3.30pm; £1; ⓦwww .dur.ac.uk/archaeology) occupies an old stone fulling mill. Eighteenth-centu-ry **Prebends Bridge** boasts celebrated views of the cathedral, and the path then continues round to handsome **Elvet Bridge**.

The alternate route from Prebends to Elvet Bridge is along South and North Bailey, a cobbled thoroughfare lined by Georgian houses, many of them occu-pied by university college buildings. The church of St Mary-le-Bow, on North Bailey, immediately below the cathedral, does duty as the **Durham Heritage Centre** (April, May & Oct Sat & Sun 2–4.30pm; June daily 2–4.30pm; July, Aug & Sept daily 11am–4.30pm; £1), a pot-pourri of audiovisual displays, dioramas and exhibitions.

Among Durham's other attractions, the most noteworthy is the university's newly refurbished **Oriental Museum** (Mon–Fri 10am–5pm, Sat & Sun noon–5pm; £1.50; ⓦwww.dur.ac.uk/oriental.museum), set among college buildings a couple of miles south of the city centre on Elvet Hill (off South Road), whose wide-ranging collection contains an outstanding display of Chinese ceramics. Take bus #5 or #6 (to Bishop Auckland) and ask to be put off on South Road. You may as well then continue on foot to the nearby **Botanic Garden** (daily: March–Oct 10am–5pm; Nov–Feb 11am–4pm; £1), whose glasshouses, café and visitor centre are set in eighteen acres of diverse woodland, grassland and gardens near Collingwood College; buses run back to the centre from either Elvet Hill Road or South Road.

North of the centre, a ten-minute walk from the train station takes you to the revamped **Durham Light Infantry Museum and Durham Art Gallery**, at Aykley Heads (daily: April–Oct 10am–5pm; Nov–March 10am–4pm; £2.50; ⓦwww.durham.gov.uk/dli). The museum tells the story of the regiment from World War I to its last parade in 1968, through moving testimonies and wide-ranging artefacts, while the art gallery plays host to an indefinable variety of temporary exhibitions.

Eating, drinking and entertainment

Of the city's **cafés**, *Vennel's*, Saddler's Yard – named after the skinny alley or "vennel" where it stands (next to Waterstone's, off Saddler Street) – serves light lunches in a little hidden courtyard. Further up the hill, on Palace Green, the *Almshouse* conjures up vegetarian and meaty meals for around £5 (open until 8pm in summer). For Italian food, try *Emilio's* at the east end of Elvet Bridge, a smart refurbishment of an eleventh-century chapel with summertime outdoor seating. Excellent Modern British cuisine and service are offered at *Bistro 21*, a converted farmhouse at Aykley Heads, ten minutes' walk on from the DLI museum and art gallery north of the centre (☏0191/384 4354; closed Sun); there's courtyard seating in summer and good-value set menus at lunchtime. If you still can't make your mind up, head for *Cathedrals*, an ambitious and stylish redevelopment of the old police station on Court Lane (☏0191/370 9632), where you can choose among fine dining and great views of the cathedral in the rooftop **restaurant**, Italian-influenced cuisine in the bistro, pub grub amid the impressive copper vats of the bar and microbrewery, and inventive sandwiches and snacks in the coffee house.

Durham's central **pubs** blow hot and cold, depending on whether or not the students are in town. Good bets at most times include the *Court Inn*, which has outdoor seating on Court Lane, and the lively *Hogshead*, 58 Saddler St, with its selection of real ales. The *Victoria*, a quiet, welcoming local at 86 Hallgarth St, is also a favourite.

For more highbrow entertainment, regular **classical concerts** are held at various venues around the city, including the cathedral, while the DLI Museum and Durham Art Gallery (☏0191/384 2214) at Aykley Heads hosts lunchtime recitals as well as summertime brass band concerts, ceilidhs and other events. Durham Student's Union (☏0191/374 2000) puts on **gigs** during term time, with rock, jazz and comedy most regularly performed at Dunelm House, New Elvet. Annual events and **festivals** come thick and fast in the summer. June sees the university's **arts week**, and in the same month the **Durham Regatta** packs the riverbanks and river. Over the first weekend in July, the **Durham Summer Festival** encompasses all manner of musical entertainments, as well as historical re-enactments on Palace Green; on the following Saturday, the **Miners' Gala** – when the traditional lodge banners are paraded through the streets – has been revived as a celebration of the international labour movement.

The rest of County Durham

In the 1910s, **County Durham** produced 41 million tons of coal each year, raised from three hundred pits by 170,000 miners. This was the heyday of an industry that since the 1830s had transformed the county's landscape, spawning scores of pit villages which matted the rolling hills from the Pennines to the North Sea, between Newcastle and Stockton-on-Tees. The miners' union, waging a long struggle against serf-like pay and conditions, achieved a gradual improvement of the miners' lot, but could not prevent the slow decline of the Durham coalfield from the 1920s: just 127 pits were left when the mines were nationalized in 1947, only 34 in 1969, and today not a single pit remains in the county.

For a taste of the old days, most people troop off to the reconstructed colliery village (and much more) at the open-air **Beamish Museum**, north of Durham. The county's other obvious tourist attractions are to the west of the coalfield. There's **Raby Castle**, a stately home to the east of the market town of **Barnard Castle**, itself the setting for the opulent art collection of the **Bowes Museum**. Farther west lie the Pennine valleys of **Teesdale** and **Weardale**, whose upper reaches boast some enjoyable moorland scenery, most dramatically at Teesdale's **High Force** waterfall. If you have your own transport, you can move on north from Weardale via **Blanchland**, a delightful stone village tucked away in the valley of the Derwent River just across the border in Northumberland. For a **public transport** information pack, including the useful *Across the Roof of England* leaflet, which details all bus and train services in this area, contact Durham County Council (☎0191/383 3337, ⓔtransinfo@durham.gov.uk).

Beamish Museum

Established in 1970, the open-air **Beamish Museum** (Easter–Oct daily 10am–5pm; Nov & Jan–Easter Tues–Thurs, Sat & Sun 10am–4pm; last admission 3pm; admission £12, £4 in winter; ⓦwww.beamish.org.uk), spreading out over 300 acres beside the A693 about ten miles north of Durham, is as popular with tourists as it is with local people, who come to chew the fat with the costumed guides, many of whom are recruited for their real-life experience. The collier who takes you down the reopened drift mine may once have been a miner, and some of the blokes driving the steam engine used to work for British Rail, adding a touch of authenticity and sadness to the proceedings, as these industries have deteriorated in tandem with the boom in heritage museums like this one.

To **get there**, drivers should follow signs to the museum off the A1(M) Chester-le-Street exit, then follow the signs along the A693 to Stanley. By **bus**, take the #720 from Durham bus station (hourly) or the #709 from Newcastle's Eldon Square (hourly), which drop you close to the main entrance. In summer, hang on to your bus ticket and you'll get a discount on entrance to the museum, too.

Buildings from all over the region have been reassembled here, and the museum divides into six main sections, linked by restored trams and buses and all painstakingly kitted out with period furnishings and fittings. Four of the sections show life in 1913, before the upheavals brought about by World War I: a pint-sized **colliery village**, complete with cottages, Methodist chapel, school, old stone winding house and drift mine; a **farm** inhabited by breeds of livestock that were popular in the period; a **train station** and goods shed; and a large-scale re-creation of a market **town**, its High Street lined by shops, bank, pub, dentist's surgery, newspaper office, garage, stables, sweet factory and solicitor's office. Two areas date to 1825, at the beginning of the northeast's industrial development: a **manor house**, with horse yard, formal gardens, vegetable plots and orchards; and the **Pockerley Waggonway**, where you can ride behind a replica of George Stephenson's *Locomotion*, the first passenger-carrying steam train in the world, which ran from Darlington to Stockton. There's a great deal to see and what with the summertime Victorian funfair, the *Sun Inn* pub and picnic areas, most people make a day of it – reckon on around four hours to get round the lot in summer, two in winter when only the town and train station are usually open.

Bishop Auckland

Eleven miles southwest of Durham city, **BISHOP AUCKLAND** has been the country home of the bishops of Durham since the twelfth century and their official residence for more than a hundred years. Their palace, the gracious **Auckland Castle** (May to mid-July & Sept Fri & Sun 2–5pm; mid-July to Aug Mon–Fri & Sun 2–5pm; £3.50; ⓦwww.auckland-castle.co.uk), standing in 800-acre grounds, is approached through an imposing gatehouse just off the town's Market Place. The palace has been extensively remodelled since its medieval incarnation, redesigned to satisfy the whims of such occupants as the seventeenth-century Bishop Cosin who refurbished the original banqueting hall to create today's splendid marble and limestone **chapel**. Here, the stained-glass windows relate the stories of early Christian saints familiar throughout the northeast, especially Cuthbert, Bede and Aidan. The other rooms are rather sparse, though – for the moment at least – there's an outstanding exception in the long dining room, with its thirteen paintings of Jacob and his sons by the seventeenth-century Spaniard Zurbarán. However, the Church of England has recently voted to sell the series, its most valuable set of paintings with a price tag of at least £20million; a campaign has started to keep the works at the palace, or possibly at nearby Bowes Museum in Barnard Castle where they would have greater public exposure. In the medieval kitchens there's an exhibition on the life of St Cuthbert and you can stroll into the **Bishop's Deer Park**, too (daily dawn–dusk; free), where an eighteenth-century deer house survives.

The town itself plays second fiddle to the castle, though the Market Place is handsome enough. However, you could follow the mile-long lane that leads north to the remains of **Binchester Roman Fort** (Easter & May–Sept daily 11am–5pm; £1.60) – Roman Vinovia – which boasts the country's best example of a **hypocaust**, built to warm the private bath suite of the garrison's commanding officer.

Bishop Auckland is linked by **train** to Darlington while **buses** drop you just a few minutes' west of the town hall, in Market Place, which houses the **tourist office** (April–Sept Mon–Fri 10am–5pm, Sat 9am–4pm, Sun 1–4pm; rest of year closed Sun; ☎01388/604922). The best **accommodation** option hereabouts is *Five Gables Guest House* in the former colliery manager's house in Binchester (☎01388/608204, ⓦwww.fivegables.co.uk), which offers cosy, en-suite B&B (❷), a self-catering cottage and midweek evening meals for guests if pre-booked. For daytime **food**, the *Laurel Room* in the Town Hall, Market Place, serves up snacks and drinks (closed Sat & Sun), or try the *Castlegate Café* at 8 Market Place for traditional teas and light meals (closed Sun).

Raby Castle

The #8 bus between Bishop Auckland and Barnard Castle runs down the A688 to provide access to the sprawling battlements of **Raby Castle** (May & Sept Wed & Sun 1–5pm; June–Aug Mon–Fri & Sun 1–5pm; gardens same days 11am–5.30pm; £5; gardens only £3; ⓦwww.rabycastle.com), roughly halfway between the two. The castle mostly dates from the fourteenth century, reflecting the power of the Neville family, who ruled the local roost until 1569. It was then that Charles Neville helped plan the "Rising of the North", the abortive attempt to replace Elizabeth I with Mary Queen of Scots. The revolt was a dismal failure, and Neville's estates were confiscated, with Raby subsequently passing to the Vanes, now the Lords Barnard, who still live in the castle. Raby's focal point is the first-floor Baron's Hall, still of cathedral-like dimensions in spite of the floor being raised ten feet in 1787 to let carriages pass through the neo-Gothic entrance below. Outside the castle, in the two-hundred-acre **deer park**, are the walled **gardens**, where peaches, apricots and pineapples once flourished under the careful gaze of forty Victorian gardeners. Heated cavity walls and curtains protected the trees from frost – above the last remaining apricot tree you can still see the hooks for the curtain rail.

Barnard Castle

Fifteen miles southwest of Bishop Auckland, the skeletal remains of **Barnard Castle** (April–Sept daily 10am–6pm; Oct daily 10am–5pm; Nov–March Wed–Sun 10am–4pm; often closed 1–2pm for lunch; £2.40; EH), poking out from a cliff high above the River Tees, overlook the town which grew up in its shadow. First fortified in the eleventh century, the castle was long a stronghold of the Balliols, a Norman family interminably embroiled in the struggle for the Scottish crown. It was one of this clan, Bernard, who built the circular tower which survives to this day, an impressive thirteenth-century fortification just to the right of the later Round Tower, where a beautiful oriel window carries the emblematic boar of Richard III, one of the subsequent owners.

Castle aside, the prime attaction is the grand French-style chateau that constitutes the **Bowes Museum** (daily 11am–5pm; £4, £2 on first Sat of month; free guided tours May–Sept Tues–Sat 11.30am & 2pm, Oct Sat & Sun 11.30am & 2pm; Ⓦ www.bowesmuseum.org.uk), half a mile east of the centre, up Newgate. Begun in 1869, the chateau was commissioned by John and Josephine Bowes, a local businessman and MP and his French actress wife, who spent much of their time in Paris collecting ostentatious treasures and antiques – including furniture, paintings, tapestries, ceramics and incidental curiosities, notably a late eighteenth-century mechanical silver swan in the lobby which still performs daily at 2pm, preening to a brief forty-second melodic burst. Among the paintings, you'll find the most important Spanish collection in the UK, including El Greco's *The Tears of St Peter*; elsewhere, there's varied interest in the French decorative and religious art, English period furniture, and an excellent toy collection – whose nineteenth-century lead soldiers were made possible by the new industry in nearby Stanhope.

Back in the town centre, it's a pleasant mile-and-a-half walk from the castle, southeast along the banks of the Tees, to the shattered ruins of **Egglestone Abbey** (free access), a minor Premonstratensian foundation dating from 1195 (this and other short hikes from the town centre are covered by leaflets available from the tourist office – see below). You can also get here on bus #79 from Barnard Castle, getting off at Abbey Bridge End.

Buses stop on either side of central Galgate – once the road out to the town gallows, hence the name. The **tourist office**, on Flatts Road, is at the end of Galgate by the castle (April–Oct daily 10am–6pm; Nov–March Mon–Sat 11am–4pm; ☎01833/690909, Ⓔ tourism@teesdale.gov.uk). Among several convenient **B&Bs**, the welcoming *Homelands*, 85 Galgate (☎01833/638757, Ⓦ www.barnard-castle.co.uk; no credit cards; ➋), offers pretty bedrooms and good breakfasts, and the similar *Marwood View*, along the same road at no. 98 (☎01833/637493, Ⓦ www.kilgarriff.demon.co.uk; no credit cards; ➋) provides a fitness room and sauna for guests to work off the effects of the home-cooked dinners. Moving upmarket, try the *Old Well Inn*, 21 The Bank (☎01833/690130, Ⓦ www.oldwellinn.co.uk; ➍), an originally Tudor coaching inn with huge en-suite rooms and weekend half-board deals. The town is also ringed by **campsites**, including a Camping and Caravanning Club site with plenty of facilities at Lartington, two miles west of the centre (☎01833/630228; closed Nov–Feb; bus #95 towards Middleton).

For **food**, the *Market Place Teashop*, 29 Market Place, is an excellent traditional tearoom with daily special meals on a blackboard. *Oldfield's*, at 7 The Bank

(☎01833/630700; closed Sun eve), is a smart, modern place with courtyard seating, where you can choose between good-value set menus and à la carte seafood specialities. The town's top restaurant of the moment is *Blagrave's House* at 30–32 The Bank (☎01833/637668; closed Sun), a sixteenth-century former inn sporting low-beamed ceilings and large open fires, with affordable set menus (not Sat).

Teesdale

Extending twenty-odd miles northwest from Barnard Castle, Teesdale begins calmly enough, though the pastoral landscapes of its lower reaches are soon replaced by wilder Pennine scenery. There's a regular **bus service** only as far as Middleton-in-Teesdale, with infrequent (Tues, Wed, Fri & Sat) services on to High Force waterfall and Langdon Beck.

MIDDLETON-IN-TEESDALE, the valley's main settlement, was once the archetypal "company town", owned lock, stock and barrel by the Quaker-run London Lead Company, which began mining here in 1753. There are no specific sights in the village, but it's a quiet and remote spot to spend the night. The **tourist office** in the central Market Place (daily 9.30am–12.30pm & 1.30–5pm, closes 4pm in winter; ☎01833/641001) can give details of **B&Bs**, including the nearby *Bluebell House* (☎01833/640584; no credit cards; ❶). Also in Market Place is the *Teesdale Hotel* (☎01833/640264; ❸), a seventeenth-century coaching inn. It's also well worth knowing about the *Rose & Crown* (☎01833/650213, ⓦwww.rose-and-crown.co.uk; ❺), a couple of miles or so back towards Barnard Castle in **ROMALDKIRK**, which encompasses an impressive church and village green. The ivy-clad eighteenth-century inn has very comfortable rooms and accomplished cooking in the bar or restaurant.

Past Newbiggin, the countryside becomes harsher and the Tees more vigorous as the B6277 travels the three miles on to **Bowlees Country Park and Visitor Centre** (March–Oct daily 10.30am–5pm; Nov–Feb Sat & Sun 10.30am–4pm; 50p), the halt for the short walk to the rapids of **Low Force**. Close by is the altogether more impressive **High Force**, a seventy-foot cascade which rumbles over an outcrop of the Whin Sill, a black dolerite ridge that pokes up in various parts of northern England. The waterfall is on private Raby land, and visitors must pay £1 to view the falls and £1.50 to use the nearby car park, by the B6277. By the car park, the *High Force* **pub** and **hotel** (☎01833/622222; ❸) brews its own beer (a Teesdale Bitter and the stronger, award-winning, Cauldron Snout) to accompany the bar meals.

The Pennine Way – which passes the falls – continues the six miles upstream to **Cauldron Snout**, near the source of the Tees, where the river rolls two hundred feet down a dolerite stairway as it leaves **Cow Green Reservoir**. It's also possible to reach the reservoir by car: turn off the main road at **Langdon Beck** – about a mile north of the stone-built **youth hostel** on the B6277 at Forest-in-Teesdale (☎01833/622228, ⓦwww.yha.org.uk) – and follow the three-mile-long lane to the car park, a mile's walk from the Snout.

Weardale

Seeing **Weardale** by **public transport** can be a frustrating business. Bus #101 runs roughly hourly between Bishop Auckland and Stanhope, with less frequent extensions up the valley to Cowshill; however, to get the bus to take you to the valley's main sight, the lead-mining museum at Killhope, two miles further on, you'll have to ask the driver (or arrange it in advance with the bus company; ☎01388/528235) – and don't forget to request a pick-up for the way back. Otherwise, your only hopes are the #X21 from Newcastle to

Stanhope (Wed & Sat only), and the summer Saturday-only #X85 from Durham to Kendal, which calls at Bishop Auckland, Stanhope and Killhope.

Lead and iron-ore mining flourished in and around Weardale from the 1840s to the 1880s, leaving today's landscape scarred with old workings. One of the bigger mines, situated three miles west of Cowshill, a chilly 1500ft above sea level, has been turned into the **Killhope Lead Mining Museum** (April–July & Sept daily 10.30am–5pm; Aug daily 10.30am–6pm; Oct Sat & Sun 10.30am–5pm; £3.40, £5, including mine visit; Ⓦwww.durham.gov.uk/killhope), whose 34-foot high waterwheel still turns, using six thousand gallons of water per minute from a string of diverted streams. Descending Park Level Mine with hard hat and lamp gives you a taste of the miserable mining life. If you end up walking the two miles back down the Weardale Way to Cowshill to catch the bus, console yourself at the *Cowshill Hotel*, which serves highly recommended bar meals. Two miles east of Cowshill down the main road, tiny **IRESHOPEBURN** is the home of the **Weardale Museum** (Easter, May–July & Sept Wed–Sun 2–5pm; Aug daily 2–5pm; £1), an excellent small folk museum with displays on lead mining, the railways and Methodism, the faith of the majority of Durham's lead miners; entry to the museum also allows you access to the adjacent **High House Chapel**, the oldest Methodist chapel in the world in continuous use, built in 1760 just eight years after John Wesley's first visit to the region.

About nine miles downstream from Ireshopeburn lies **STANHOPE**, the main village of the valley and a useful base for walks across the moors – the **tourist office** (Easter to Oct daily 10am–5pm; Nov to Easter Mon–Fri 10am–4pm, Sat & Sun 11am–4pm; ℡01388/527650, Ⓔdurham.dales.centre@durham.gov.uk), in the Durham Dales Centre, Castle Gardens, opposite Market Place, has all the trail details and a list of B&Bs. Prominent among Stanhope's **accommodation** options is *Stanhope Old Hall* on the main road just west of the town centre (℡01388/528451; ❹), a bargain opportunity to stay in a twelfth-century fortified hunting lodge of the prince bishops of Durham – or make do with a cosy drink in front of a huge open fire.

Blanchland

The trans-moorland B6278, which cuts north from Weardale at Stanhope for ten extraordinarily wild miles, runs to tiny **BLANCHLAND**. Little more than a handful of ancient, lichen-stained cottages huddled round an L-shaped square, the hamlet was once the site of a Premonstratensian abbey, founded in the twelfth century. Blanchland has been preserved and protected since 1721, when Lord Crewe, the childless Bishop of Durham, bequeathed his estate to trustees on condition that they rebuilt the old conventual buildings, for Blanchland had slowly fallen into disrepair after the abbey's dissolution. The original trustees obliged and their successors have allowed but the faintest whiff of the twenty-first century to intrude. Consequently, the village bears many reminders of its monastic past, from the sturdy gatehouse that now accommodates the post office to the parish church where the medieval chancel and tower were all used to good effect during the rebuilding of 1752. But it's the **Lord Crewe Arms Hotel** (℡01434/675251, Ⓦwww.crewearms.freeserve.co.uk; ❼) that steals the show, boasting dark vaulted basements, two big fireplaces left over from the canons' kitchen and a priest's hideaway stuck inside the chimney. The **restaurant** serves expensive *table d'hôte* dinners but there's a fine public bar with cheaper food in the undercroft. By **bus**, you need the #773 from Consett (not Sun), which is itself linked by hourly bus to Newcastle.

The Tees Valley: Darlington to the coast

In a region whose physical face was blighted first by industrial success and then by urban neglect, the towns along the **Tees Valley** take some beating. Whether approaching from Yorkshire to the south or Durham to the north, it seems that a view isn't considered a view hereabouts unless it's blocked by towers and pipes, clouded by smoking chimneys and framed by rusting machinery. This, of course, is a harsh judgement and only half the story – the **River Tees**, along with the Tyne farther north, was one of the great engines of British economic power in the late nineteenth century. Few tourists stop now, but there were once rich pickings here, in places like **Darlington**, twenty miles south of Durham city, where the first public passenger-carrying steam train, George Stephenson's *Locomotion*, made its inaugural run. The line ran first to **Stockton-on-Tees** and was then extended to ports at **Middlesbrough** and **Hartlepool**, to enable ever-increasing amounts of Durham coal to be unloaded and exported. Later in the nineteenth century a branch line was built to the coastal resort of **Saltburn**, which has managed to retain much of its Victorian grandeur.

Darlington

DARLINGTON hit the big time in 1825, when George Stephenson's *Locomotion* hurtled from here to nearby Stockton-on-Tees, with the inventor at the controls and flag-carrying horsemen riding ahead to warn of the onrushing train, which reached a terrifying fifteen miles per hour. This novel form of transport soon proved popular with passengers, an unlooked-for bonus for Edward Pease, the line's instigator: he had simply wanted a fast and economical way to transport coal from the Durham pits to the docks at Stockton. Subsequently, Darlington grew into a rail-engineering centre, and didn't look back till the pruning of the network and the closure of the works in 1966.

It's little surprise, then, that all signs in town point to the **Darlington Railway Centre and Museum** (daily 10am–5pm; £2.10), housed in Darlington's North Road station, a twenty-minute walk up Northgate from the central market place. The museum's pride and joy is the original *Locomotion*, actually built in Newcastle, which continued in service until 1841 – other locally made engines superseded it, and some of these are on show, too. Darlington's origins lie deep in Saxon times, following which it enjoyed a long history as an agricultural centre and staging post on the Great North Road. The monks carrying St Cuthbert's body from Ripon to Durham stopped in Darlington, the saint lending his name to the graceful central, riverside church of **St Cuthbert** (Easter–Sept daily 11am–2pm; Oct–Easter Fri 11am–1pm), where the needle-like spire and decorative turrets herald the delicate Early English stonework inside. One of England's largest market squares spreads beyond the church up to the restored Victorian covered **market** (Mon–Sat 8am–5pm, with a large outdoor market Mon & Sat), next to the clocktower.

The town's helpful **tourist office** is on the south side of Market Place at 13 Horsemarket (Mon–Fri 9am–5pm, Sat 10am–4pm; ☎01325/388666, ✉tic@ darlington.gov.uk). Central **accommodation** options include the *New Grange Hotel*, a smartly refurbished, 200-year-old mansion on Coniscliffe Road, the continuation of Blackwellgate west from the Market Place (☎01325/365858; ⑤), and the more reasonable *Balmoral Guest House*, a grand Victorian town house at 63 Woodland Rd, five minutes' walk northwest of the centre (☎01325/461908; ②). Cheap and basic board is available at the town's Arts Centre (☎01325/483271; ①), about half a mile west of the centre in Vane

Terrace – follow Duke Street from central Skinnergate. Heading west from the Market Place a short way up Blackwellgate, *Joe Rigatoni's* (☎01325/464642) is the town's most reliable Italian **restaurant**, in a grand, airy setting on the corner of Grange Road. Check out the highly enterprising **Arts Centre** and its affiliated **Civic Theatre** (on a separate site on Parkgate, between the Market Place and the train station), which dish up drama, movies, comedy, exhibitions and live music (bookings on ☎01325/486555, ⓦwww.darlington-arts.co.uk).

The Captain Cook trail: Middlesbrough and Stockton

MIDDLESBROUGH, the region's largest town, fifteen miles east of Darlington, is entirely a product of the early industrial age, with nineteenth-century iron and steel barons throwing up factories and housing almost as fast as they could ship their products out of the docks on the River Tees. What was a mere hamlet at the turn of the nineteenth century was a thriving industrial town of 100,000 people by the turn of the twentieth. When iron and steel declined in importance and the local shipbuilding industry collapsed (the last shipyard closed in 1986), Middlesbrough took to the chemical industry. Add to this a contemporary renaissance in light engineering and, compared to many of its neighbours, Middlesbrough can boast relative success in keeping its economic head above water.

Only a pair of bridges recall earlier engineering feats – the **Transporter Bridge** (1911), at Ferry Road just north of the centre, its central section carting cars and pedestrians across the Tees towards Hartlepool (Mon–Sat 5am–11.05pm, Sun 2–11.05pm; cars 80p, pedestrians 30p), is the sole working example left in the country and now sports its own small visitor centre; further southwest, the **Newport Bridge** (1934) was the first vertical lift bridge built in England. Instead the town prefers to trumpet its position as "Gateway to Captain Cook Country", fair enough given that he was born a mile and a half south of the centre in Marton in 1728. Here, at the **Captain Cook Birthplace Museum** in Stewart Park (Tues–Sun: June–Sept 10am–5.30pm; Oct–May 10am–3.30pm; £2.40), are artefacts brought back from the South Seas on Cook's voyages, touch-screen terminals providing contemporary testimony by his botanist Sir Joseph Banks, and background information about a sailor's lot at sea. Buses #28, #29, #30, #66 and #90 from the bus station run every fifteen minutes.

From the **train station** it's just a short walk up Albert Road to the main Corporation Road. Turn right for the **bus station** – five minutes further up on its continuation, Newport Road – and carry straight on for the **tourist office**, 99 Albert Rd (Mon–Thurs 9am–5pm, Fri 9am–4.30pm, Sat 9am–1.30pm; ☎01642/358086, ⓦwww.captaincook.org.uk). To **eat**, the eccentrically decorated *Purple Onion*, 80 Corporation Rd (☎01642/222250; closed Sun eve), is the best place in Middlesbrough, serving bitingly trendy food at middling-to-high prices.

To complete the Captain Cook trail through this part of the country, you'll need to hop on a bus to **STOCKTON-ON-TEES**, three miles west across the river. Tied up at Castlegate Quay in the centre of town is a detailed full-size replica of **HMS Bark Endeavour**, the converted collier in which Cook set sail in 1768 on his first scientific and surveying expedition to Tahiti, New Zealand and Australia. The ship's taken over by youth groups for part of the week, but from Sundays to Wednesdays (April–Oct 10am–5pm; £3) enthusiastic and knowledgeable volunteer guides recount the rigours of life on board during this hazardous voyage.

Hartlepool

If there's one Teesside town trying hard to reinvent itself it's **HARTLEPOOL**, ten miles north of Middlesbrough, England's third largest port in the nineteenth century and a noted shipbuilding centre, but deprived of investment and hope for years following successive economic downturns. These days, though, its image is slowly being transformed by the renaissance of its once decaying dockland area, now spruced up as the popular **Hartlepool Historic Quay** off Marina Way (daily 10am–5pm; last admission 2hr before closing; £5.50). The entrance fee gets you on to the bustling eighteenth-century quayside where active attractions based around pressgangs, the Royal Navy, seaport life and fighting ships stir the senses. There's also a replica eighteenth-century maritime pub, as well as a coffee shop and market, while a separate fee is charged if you want to take a guided tour of **HMS Trincomalee** (daily: April–Oct 10.30am–5pm; Nov–March 10.30am–4pm; £3.50), a navy training ship built in 1817. On the edge of the quay in the entertaining **Museum of Hartlepool** at Jackson Dock (daily 10am–5pm; free), you can climb the port's original lighthouse, board a restored paddle steamer and trace the town's history, including its most notorious episode, which to this day earns Hartlepudlians the nickname "monkey hangers": legend has it that when a French ship sunk off the coast during the Napoleonic Wars, the locals mistook the sole survivor, a monkey, for a Frenchman, and tried and hanged it as a spy. Back in the town centre, ten minutes' walk south, the restored nineteenth-century Christ Church, on Church Square, houses Hartlepool's accomplished **Art Gallery** (Tues–Sat 10am–5.30pm, Sun 2–5pm; free) and the **tourist office** (same hours; ☎01429/869706, ⓦwww.thisishartlepool.com), which can help if you're seduced into staying.

Saltburn

On the coast to the south of the Tees estuary, twelve miles east of Middlesbrough, lies **SALTBURN**, a graceful Victorian resort in a dramatic setting overlooking extensive sands and mottled red sea cliffs. Soon after the railway arrived in 1861 to ferry Teessiders out to the sea on high days and holidays, Saltburn became a rather fashionable spa town boasting all the necessary accoutrements: hydraulic **inclined tramway** (May to mid-Sept daily 10am–1pm & 2–7pm; Easter to end April & mid-Sept to Oct Sat & Sun 10am–1pm & 2–5pm; 55p), complete with stained-glass windows, that connects upper town to pier and promenade; ornate **Italian Gardens** in the more bucolic Valley Gardens that run beneath the eastern side of town, linked to the beach by a **miniature railway** (Easter–Sept Sat & Sun 1–5pm, plus Tues–Fri same times during school holidays; 90p); and prominent hotels, many of which continue to flourish today. Modern attractions include the **Smugglers Heritage Centre** (April–Oct daily 10am–6pm, last tour 5.30pm; £1.85), set in fishermen's cottages to the east of the pier, a vivid audiovisual re-creation of Saltburn's darker past, when "free traders" made themselves popular with locals by sneaking vast quantities of tea, coffee, fine silks, lace and other such illicit cargoes ashore. Afterwards, don't forget to have a **drink** at the *Ship Inn*, the original smugglers' haunt next door. Saltburn's also become something of a **surfing** hub for these parts, with boards available to rent down by the pier (£6/hr including wetsuit; ☎01287/625321; to check on the surf, call ☎09068/545543; ⓦwww.members.tripod.com/eastcoastsurf).

There are regular **train** services to Saltburn's impressive nineteenth-century station from Newcastle, Durham and Bishop Auckland, via Darlington and

⑬

Middlesbrough, while frequent **buses** from Middlesbrough bus station stop in the parade outside the train station. The **tourist office** is handily placed in the railway station buildings (Easter–Sept Mon–Sat 9am–5pm; Oct–Easter Tues–Sat 9am–5pm; ☎01287/622422, ✉saltburn_tic@redcar-cleveland.gov.uk), and has information on a wide selection of good-value **guest houses** and **hotels**. For surroundings in keeping with the town, the *Rushpool Hall Hotel* in Saltburn Valley (☎01287/624111, ⓦwww.rushpoolhall.com; ➐) is a fine choice: a nineteenth-century country house set in extensive grounds about a mile south of the centre off Saltburn Lane, whose turrets, grand staircase and elegant public rooms are straight out of an Agatha Christie whodunnit. If your wallet won't stretch that far, try the *Rose Garden*, just west of the station at 20 Hilda Place (☎01287/622947, ⓦwww.therosegarden.co.uk; ➋), which offers comfortable bedrooms and good breakfasts, including vegetarian options.

Newcastle upon Tyne

At first glance **NEWCASTLE UPON TYNE** – virtual capital of the area between Yorkshire and Scotland – may appear to be just another northern industrial conurbation, but the banks of the Tyne have been settled for nearly two thousand years and the city consequently has a greater breadth of attractions than many of its rivals. The Romans were the first to bridge the river here, and the "new castle" appeared as long ago as 1080. In the seventeenth century a regional monopoly on **coal** export brought wealth and power to Newcastle and – as well as giving a new expression to the English language – engendered its other great industry, shipbuilding. At one time, a quarter of the world's shipping was built here, and the first steam train and steam turbine also emerged from Newcastle factories. In its nineteenth-century heyday, Newcastle's engineers and builders gave the city an elegance which has survived the ravages of recent development. Industrial decline hit Newcastle early, as highlighted by the **Jarrow March** of 1936, but this remains a vibrant place, with a resilience that's symbolized commercially by the hugely successful **MetroCentre** shopping mall across the river at Gateshead, and artistically by Antony Gormley's **Angel of the North**, a magnificent steel sculpture the size of a jumbo jet that welcomes anyone approaching the city from the south by rail or road. There's an impressive energy about Newcastle's handsome city centre, too – encapsulated in the **International Centre for Life**, which combines a cutting-edge biotechnology research centre with noisy and edifying science lessons at the state-of-the-art **LIFE Interactive World** – while its revitalized **Quayside**, scene of much of the city's **nightlife**, goes from strength to strength. Indeed, there's a sharper edge to Newcastle's carousing these days, with new cafés, bars and clubs rivalling the traditional knees-up antics of the notorious Bigg Market. Culturally, too, Newcastle is way ahead of its local rivals – Durham included – boasting the best traditional art gallery in the Northeast, the **Laing**, and a slew of good theatres and all-round arts venues. This pre-eminence will be cemented with the imminent opening of the **BALTIC Centre for Contemporary Art**, a quayside flour mill that's being transformed into the largest visual arts space in the country outside of London, and will be further reinforced in 2003 by the equally adventurous **Music Centre Gateshead** alongside.

Hard times and a sense of remoteness from the capital have given Newcastle's inhabitants, known as **Geordies**, a partisan pride in their city, which finds its most evident expression in fanatical support for the **Newcastle United** foot-

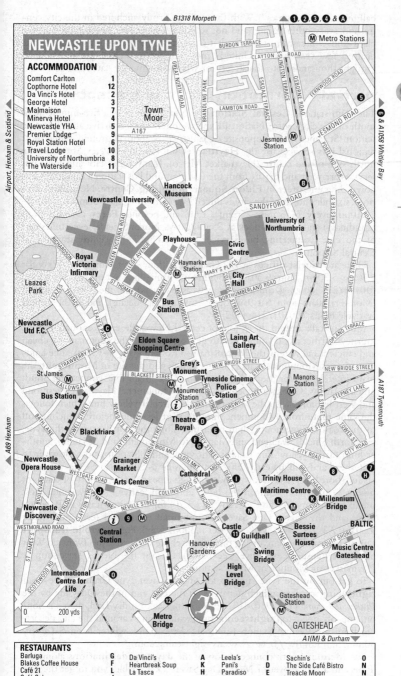

NEWCASTLE UPON TYNE

ACCOMMODATION

Comfort Carlton	1
Copthorne Hotel	12
Da Vinci's Hotel	2
George Hotel	3
Malmaison	7
Minerva Hotel	4
Newcastle YHA	5
Premier Lodge	9
Royal Station Hotel	6
Travel Lodge	10
University of Northumbria	8
The Waterside	11

M Metro Stations

▲ B1318 Morpeth

Airport, Hexham & Scotland

A69 Hexham

6 & A1058 Whitley Bay

A187 Tynemouth

A1(M) & Durham ▼

GATESHEAD

BALTIC

RESTAURANTS

Barluga	G	Da Vinci's	A	Leela's	I	Sachin's	O
Blakes Coffee House	F	Heartbreak Soup	K	Pani's	D	The Side Café Bistro	N
Café 21	L	La Tasca	H	Paradiso	E	Treacle Moon	N
Café Sol	J	La Toscana	C	Sabatini	M	Valley Junction 397	B

© Crown copyright

ball team (the "Magpies"). With the stadium firmly anchored in the city centre, and every other young (and not so young) supporter wearing the familiar black-and-white shirt, it's difficult to overstate the team's importance – the death a few years ago of United's most famous goalscorer, Jackie Milburn, brought thousands onto the streets for what was almost a state funeral.

Arrival, information and city transport

The train station, **Central Station**, on Neville Street, is a five-minute walk south of the city centre. National Express **coach** services arrive at Gallowgate station (St James Metro) opposite St James's Park football ground, while most regional **bus** services use the **Haymarket** bus station on Percy Street on the north side of the centre (Haymarket Metro). Many other city and local bus services arrive at and depart from the underground bus station a hundred yards down the same street in **Eldon Square Shopping Centre**. Newcastle's **airport**, six miles north of the city, is linked by Metro to Central Station (5.50am–11.10pm every 7–15 min; 25min; £1.60) and beyond. **Ferry arrivals** from Scandinavia and Holland dock at Royal Quays, North Shields, seven miles east of the city. Connecting bus services run you into the centre, stopping at Central Station.

There are **tourist offices** at 132 Grainger St (June–Sept Mon–Wed, Fri & Sat 9.30am–5.30pm, Thurs 9.30am–7.30pm Sun 10am–4pm; rest of year closed Sun; ☎0191/277 8000, ✆ tourist.info@newcastle.gov.uk), in the Central Station (Mon–Fri 10am–5pm, Sat 9am–5pm; same contact details), and at the airport (variable hours; ☎0191/214 4422).

You can walk around the whole of central Newcastle easily enough, but for journeys further afield you'll need to get to grips with the conurbation's cheap and efficient rail system, the **Metro** (6am–11.30pm every 4–15min). The landmark Grey's Monument marks the city centre and the site of **Monument**, the main interchange for the Metro's two lines: the green line, connecting South Shields, Jarrow, Gateshead, Central Station, Monument, Haymarket, Jesmond and West Jesmond with the airport; and the circular yellow line which follows the same route from Monument through West Jesmond, before branching off to the coast at Tynemouth, then returning along the north bank of the Tyne, via North Shields, Wallsend and Manors, to Monument (and St James); another limb of the yellow line heads south via Central Station across the river to Gateshead and will, by early 2002, extend as far as Sunderland. One-way tickets for short hops start as low as 60p, though a bewildering variety of discount **passes** – many also valid on the buses and local ferries – are available. Most useful for visitors are the Day Rover (£3.70) for unlimited travel in Tyne and Wear, and the Metro Day Saver for unlimited metro and ferry rides (after 9.30am; £3, £1.50 on Wed and after 6.30pm daily). For all **public transport enquiries**, call Traveline or log onto the website of Nexus, the Tyne and Wear passenger transport executive (see p.706), or visit the Nexus Travelshop at Haymarket or Monument Metro stations.

To get out on the Tyne, sign up for one of River Tyne Cruises' three-hour **sightseeing cruises**, which depart from the east end of the Quayside by the *Pitcher and Piano* (£7.99; ☎0191/296 6740). Back on dry land, there's a hopon, hop-off, open-top **sightseeing bus**, which cruises around the city, departing from the Central Station (summer every 15min; winter Mon–Sat every 30min, Sun hourly; £5; ⓦ www.city-sightseeing.com).

The Metro network connects most of the **day-trip destinations** along the Tyne, and a Day Rover or Metro Day Saver ticket enables you to get the best out of the local transport systems. In addition to the Metro, the Day Rover is valid for most buses in the county of Tyne and Wear and the ferry across the Tyne between North and South Shields (Mon–Sat 6.30am–10.50pm, Sun 10.30am–6pm; every 15–30min; 7min; 85p one-way); there are Metro stations at either end. Note also that Beamish Museum, just across the border in County Durham (see p.712), is within particularly easy reach of Newcastle.

Accommodation

The biggest concentration of **hotels** and **guest houses** is in Jesmond, along and around Osborne Road, a mile north of the city centre: take the Metro to West Jesmond or bus #30B, #31B or #80 from Central Station or Haymarket. Many hotels offer discounts for Friday and Saturday nights, especially at the upper end of the scale where savings can be considerable.

Hotels and guest houses

Comfort Carlton 82–86 Osborne Rd ☎0191/281 3361. Decent value (though breakfast costs extra), with tasteful en-suite rooms, bar and restaurant. ❹

Copthorne Hotel The Close, Quayside ☎0191/222 0333, ✉sales.newcastle@mill-cop.com. Superbly located bang on the riverside, this modern hotel has Tyne views from most of its rooms, a sunny atrium, good restaurants, a gym and swimming pool. Rooms come with modems and voicemail. ❽

Da Vinci's Hotel 73 Osborne Rd ☎0191/281 5284. Light, well-furnished rooms above a classy restaurant complete with piano and Leonardo prints. ❸, ❷ at weekends.

George Hotel 88 Osborne Rd ☎0191/281 4442, ✉georgehotel@dial.pipex.com. Victorian town-house hotel with some of the city's least expensive en-suite rooms, above a popular Chinese restaurant. ❷

Malmaison The Quayside ☎0191/245 5000, ✉newcastle@malmaison.com. Chic lodgings in the former Co-op building, right on the Quayside. Rooms come with great beds, CD players and modems. Jazzy sounds, crushed velvet sofas, brasserie, bar and gym round off the facilities. ❼

Minerva Hotel 105 Osborne Rd ☎0191/281 0190. Family-run place with pleasant rooms (ones with shower in the next price category), a cosy bar, inexpensive dinners, and secure parking. No credit cards. ❶

Premier Lodge The Quayside ☎0870/700 1504, ⓦwww.premierlodge.com. An unbeatable location

for this no-frills chain: in the nineteenth-century Exchange Buildings under the Tyne Bridge. One price for all bedrooms, so singles lose out and families gain – and be sure to ask for a room with a view of the river. ❷

Royal Station Hotel Neville St ☎0191/232 0781, ⓦwww.royalstationhotel.com. The city's original Victorian station hotel in a great central location, opened in 1858 by Victoria herself and now fully modernized. ❺

Travel Lodge Forster St ☎0191/261 5432, ⓦwww.travellodge.co.uk. A purpose-built block in a quiet location off the easterly end of the Quayside; gives *Premier Lodge* a run for its money, with near-identical rates. ❷

The Waterside 48–52 Sandhill ☎0191/230 0111. Small, luxury hotel in a listed building right in the centre of the noisy Quayside night-time action, and with its own decent bar. ❺

Hostel and university accommodation

Newcastle YHA 107 Jesmond Rd ☎0191/281 2570, ⓦwww.yha.org.uk. Popular town-house hostel with sixty beds, including four twin rooms, near Jesmond Metro station – reserve in advance in summer. Breakfast and cheap evening meals served. Closed Mon–Thurs from Christmas to February.

University of Northumbria Coach Lane ☎0191/227 4024. Student hall of residence offering cheap B&B in April and from July to September.

The City

Anyone arriving by train from the north will get a sneak preview of the **Castle** (daily: April–Sept 9.30am–5.30pm; Oct–March Tues–Sun 9.30am–4.30pm; £1.50), as the rail line splits the keep from its gatehouse, the Black Gate, on St Nicholas' Street. A wooden fort was built here on the site of an Anglo-Saxon cemetery – which itself had been dug into the site of the Roman fort of Pons Aelius – by Robert Curthose, illegitimate eldest son of William the Conqueror, but the present keep dates from the twelfth century. Staircases and rooms, including a bare Norman chapel, lie off a draughty Great Hall, where displays relate to the Civil War siege of 1644 by a Scottish army supporting the Parliamentarian cause; a small museum room shows various archeological finds. There's also a great view from the rooftop over the river and city. Little remains of the outer fortifications except the Black Gate, added in 1247–50 and topped by a seventeenth-century house.

Further along St Nicholas' Street stands the **Cathedral** (Mon–Fri 7am–6pm, Sat 8.30am–4pm, Sun 7.30am–noon & 4–7pm; guided tours Easter–Sept Wed 11am; free), remarkable chiefly for its tower – erected in 1470, it is topped with a crown-like structure of turrets and arches supporting a lantern. Inside, behind the high altar, is one of the largest funerary brasses in England, commissioned by Roger Thornton, the Dick Whittington of Newcastle, who arrived penniless and died its richest merchant in 1430. Much of the interior was given a neo-Gothic remodelling in the late nineteenth century under Sir George Gilbert Scott.

The Quayside

From between the castle and the cathedral a road known simply as The Side, formerly the main road out of the city, descends to the **Quayside** where the first bridges across the Tyne stood. There have been fixed river crossings here since Roman times and today the Tyne is spanned by seven bridges in close proximity, the most prominent being the looming **Tyne Bridge** of 1928, symbol of the city, which bears a striking resemblance to the roughly contemporaneous Sydney Harbour Bridge – not surprising really, as both were built by Dorman Long of Middlesbrough. To the west of it, road and rail lines cross the river on the **High Level Bridge**, built by Robert Stephenson in 1849.

Protected by the towering castle, the Quayside became the commercial heart of the city and in the sixteenth and seventeenth centuries its half-timbered houses were the homes of Newcastle's wealthiest merchants. One is **Bessie Surtees' House**, at 41–44 Sandhill (Mon–Fri 10am–4pm; free), the residence of an eighteenth-century woman who scandalously eloped to Scotland with her beau; all ended well and the groom in question went on to become Lord Eldon, Chancellor of England. It's now the regional headquarters of English Heritage, with three rooms, decorated with elaborate panelling and plaster ceilings, open to the public. Directly opposite is the **Guildhall**, rebuilt many times since its foundation in 1316, where court sessions were held; John Wesley preached here in 1742 and had to be rescued from a volatile crowd by a hefty fishwife. On Sundays a busy morning **market** spreads around the nearby hydraulic **Swing Bridge**, which was erected in 1876 by Lord Armstrong, so that larger vessels could reach his shipyards upriver.

East along the quay, up Broad Chare, stands the unspoiled ensemble of **Trinity House** (guided tours Fri 1pm; £3.50), with its enclosed courtyard and own graciously carved chapel, built in 1505 for the Mariners' Guild and still run by the Brethren of Master Mariners. Next door, at no. 29, the **Trinity Maritime Centre** (April–Oct Mon–Fri 11am–4pm; £1.50), housed in an old ship chandler's warehouse, has a few rooms of maritime mementoes and some lovingly detailed model ships.

Beyond Broad Chare, the modern-day regeneration of the Quayside is in full swing. A landscaped promenade, public sculpture and pedestrianized squares have paved the way for a series of fashionable new bars and restaurants, centred around the supremely graceful, £20-million **Millennium Bridge**, the world's first tilting span, which is designed to pivot – at an energy-saving cost of £4 a go – to allow ships to pass. Dubbed the "blinking eye" by locals, it also allows pedestrians and cyclists to cross the Tyne to the Gateshead side, either to complete a mile-long circuit of the riverfronts via the Swing Bridge, or to visit the **BALTIC Centre for Contemporary Art** (due to open March 2002; ⓦwww.balticmill.com). This brick flour mill built in the 1940s is being converted into a huge visual arts space, second only in scale to London's Tate Modern and scheduled to hold some of the most ambitious international art shows of the next few years. As well as galleries, the centre has room to accommodate artists' studios, education workshops, an art performance space and cinema, plus a bar and two restaurants, one at river level with an outdoor terrace, the other on the roof with uninterrupted views of the Newcastle skyline.

The BALTIC will be joined on the Gateshead side by new hotels, restaurants, bars and a multiplex cinema, and in summer 2003 by the similarly ambitious **Music Centre Gateshead**. This billowing steel, aluminium and glass structure designed by Foster and Partners will shelter two concert halls, a rehearsal hall and a wide-ranging music education centre and will be home to the Northern Sinfonia and Folkworks, a charity promoting traditional music.

Grey Street to the city walls

By the mid-nineteenth century, Newcastle's centre of balance had shifted away from the river, uphill to the rapidly expanding Victorian town. In a few short years, businessmen-builders and architects like Richard Grainger, Thomas Oliver and John Dobson fashioned the best-designed Victorian town in England, with classical facades of stone lining splendid new streets, most notably **Grey Street** – "that descending, subtle curve", as John Betjeman described it. The street takes its name from the Northumberland dynasty of political heavyweights whose most illustrious member was the second Earl Grey, prime minister from 1830 to 1834. In the middle of his term of office he carried the Reform Bill through parliament, an act commemorated by **Grey's Monument** at the top of the street. Grey Street still shows off much of its Victorian elegance, best exemplified by the **Theatre Royal**, halfway down, and the nearby **Grainger Market** (Mon–Sat 8am–5pm), Europe's largest undercover market when built in the 1830s, also maintains its style.

West of here, behind Gallowgate, is the most complete stretch of the old **city walls**, leading down to Westgate Road. Once encircling the whole of medieval Newcastle, they remained in place until the sixteenth century, after which time many sections were plundered for building stone. Several towers remained in use by the city guilds as meeting houses and one, the **Morden Tower**, alongside Stowell Street, gained more recent prestige as the haunt of poets such as Allen Ginsberg, Basil Bunting and Tom Pickard. Through the arch, the outer defensive ditch has been restored. Stowell Street, incidentally, is Newcastle's small **Chinatown**. Across Stowell Street from the tower, at Friar's Green, is the tranquil courtyard of **Blackfriars**, a thirteenth-century stone monastery with ruined cloistered grounds, now lovingly restored to house a crafts centre and a café/restaurant.

Museums and galleries

On the south side of Westgate Road, the **Discovery Museum** in Blandford Square (Mon–Sat 10am–5pm, Sun 2–5pm; free), attempts to put into context the city's history – a footnote to which is the museum's own massive £12 million redevelopment, due for completion by early 2002. Expect to find exhibits such as the "Newcastle Story", the interactive "Science Maze" and the *Turbinia*, the world's first steam-turbine-powered ship, built by local engineer, Charles Parsons.

Heading back towards the Central Station along Westmorland Street, you can't miss the sleek modern lines of **LIFE Interactive World** (Mon–Sat 10am–6pm, Sun 11am–6pm; £6.95; ⓦ www.lifeinteractiveworld.co.uk), which aims to convey the scientific secrets of life using the latest entertainment technology, including imaginative and humorous computer games. The emphasis is squarely on learning through having fun rather than the other way round, though you probably don't have to undergo the white-knuckle "Crazy Motion Ride", the world's longest motion simulator, to learn that "life is a rollercoaster" – or that you don't like rollercoasters.

Newcastle's – indeed, the Northeast's – premier art collection is the **Laing Gallery** on New Bridge Street (Mon–Sat 10am–5pm, Sun 2–5pm; free), off John Dobson Street, behind the library. It's a splendidly organized museum, in which local pottery, glassware, costume and sculpture play their part, while on permanent display is a sweep through British art from Reynolds to John Hoyland, with a smattering of Pre-Raphaelites, so admired by English industrial barons. The real treat though is the lashings of **John Martin** (1789–1854), a self-taught Northumberland painter with a penchant for massive biblical and mythical scenes inspired by the dramatic northeastern scenery. The other must-see in the gallery is the **Art on Tyneside** exhibition, which romps through the history of art and applied art in the region since the seventeenth century with considerable gusto, highlighting the contribution of **Thomas Bewick**, England's greatest engraver (1735–1828), whose pastoral works were inspired by the surrounding countryside.

Newcastle University, opposite Haymarket Metro, contains a knot of fine museums and galleries, located off King's Walk: the **Museum of Antiquities** (Mon–Sat 10am–5pm; free) makes a good place to get to grips with the history of Hadrian's Wall, with a fascinating scale model of the whole length of the wall; the small **Shefton Museum of Greek Art and Archeology** (Mon–Fri 10am–4pm; free) contains a valuable collection of armour, sculpture and pottery; while the celebrated **Hatton Gallery** (Mon–Fri 10am–5.30pm, Sat 10am–4.30pm; free), attached to the Fine Art Department, features a collection of African sculpture, the only surviving example of Kurt Schwitters' *Merzbau* (a sort of architectural collage) and a wide variety of temporary exhibitions. Also attached to the university is the **Hancock Museum** on adjacent Claremont Road (Mon–Sat 10am–5pm, Sun 2–5pm; £4.50); based on an eighteenth-century natural history collection, it's grown to immense dimensions – with more than 150,000 insect specimens – and hosts widely touted temporary exhibitions such as the 2001 Star Trek "European Tour". Beyond the university stretches the **Town Moor**, 1200 acres of common land where freemen of the city, including former US president Jimmy Carter, are entitled to graze their cattle. It's the site of the annual "Hoppings" in the last week of June, a huge week-long **fair** of rides, stalls and other attractions which keeps the cows awake until well after dark.

Eating, drinking and nightlife

Newcastle's tastes have moved a long way from the traditional gargantuan bread rolls called "stottie cakes" – you're more likely to find them drizzled with olive oil and stuffed with Parma ham and chargrilled vegetables these days. At the budget end of the market Italian, Indian and Chinese food dominates the scene, while at the top end of the scale the city has attracted some top-class chefs. The Quayside and the streets around it are where the most fashionable hangouts are situated. For **Chinese food**, check out Stowell Street in Chinatown where you'll find cheap all-you-can-eat buffets as well as more refined seafood restaurants. If you're counting the pennies, aim to eat early – many city-centre restaurants offer **early bird/happy hour** deals before 7pm, while others serve **set lunches** at often ludicrously low prices.

Newcastle's boisterous but largely good-natured **nightlife** centres on the pubs and clubs in the older parts of town: between Grainger Street and the cathedral in the area called the Bigg Market – spiritual home of Sid the Sexist and the Fat Slags, from the locally based *Viz* magazine – and around the Quayside, where the bars tend to be slightly more sophisticated. If you want to get away from the mayhem, make a bolt for Westgate Road and Pink Lane, while for those staying in Jesmond, there's a more upmarket but generally unremarkable strip of bars along Osborne Road. The grandiosely named "**Gay Quarter**" of mostly mixed gay and lesbian bars and clubs centres on the International Centre for Life, spreading out to Waterloo Street and Westmorland and Scotswood roads. Top brew is, of course, **Newcastle Brown Ale** – known locally as "Dog" – produced in this city since 1927.

Listings for **theatre** and **cinema** are contained in the local morning paper, the *Journal*, while *The Crack* (monthly; free) is the best way to find out about **gigs**, **clubs** and other entertainments: you can usually get a copy from the tourist office or from pubs such as the *Forth Hotel*. For **classical music**, the City Hall on Northumberland Road is the main concert venue until the completion of Northern Sinfonia's new home at the Music Centre Gateshead, but you'll also find performances in St Nicholas' Cathedral and other atmospheric churches around town.

Cafés

Blakes Coffee House 53 Grey St. Friendly and hugely popular haunt serving sandwiches, salads and daily specials.

Pani's High Bridge St, off Grey St. Just up a side street below the Theatre Royal, this little Italian coffee and sandwich bar – which now also stays open in the evenings to serve cheap meals – has a loyal clientele. Closed Sun.

The Side Café Bistro 1–3 The Side. Snacks and cappuccino downstairs, *bruschetta*, pasta, pizza and more substantial dishes upstairs (open until 9pm Thurs–Sat), in an amiable little place near the Quayside.

Tyneside Coffee Rooms 2nd floor, Tyneside Cinema, 10–12 Pilgrim St. Coffee, light meals and art-house movie talk in the Art Deco cinema café.

Restaurants

Café 21 21 Queen St ☎0191/222 0755. The Michelin star's been handed in and the city's premier restaurant has been scaled down to a Parisian-influenced bistro, but the food, featuring inventive seafood and local meat dishes and a veggie menu as long as your arm, is still excellent. Set lunches are a bargain at £12 for two courses, £14.50 for three. Closed Sun. Moderate to Expensive.

Café Sol Pink Lane ☎0191/221 0122. Off-the-shelf tapas bar (checked tablecloths, bullfight posters, flamenco nights) with food a cut above the average, ranging from open sandwiches to mussels, cured meats and daily specials. Inexpensive.

Da Vinci's 73 Osborne Rd, Jesmond ☎0191/281 5284. Good to know about if you're staying in

Jesmond, this is a pleasing town-house restaurant with great Italian food. Moderate.

Heartbreak Soup Baltic Chambers, 77 Quayside ☎0191/222 1701. Good-value food – originally Tex-Mex but now gone global – with inspiring veggie choices in colour-splashed surroundings down by the river. Eve only, closed Sun. Moderate.

La Tasca Quayside ☎0191/230 400. A veritable tapas barn, near the Millennium Bridge, with Spanish tiling and cast-iron candelabras. The food's not bad, though the place really comes into its own in summer when you can sit out on the terrace, grazing, chatting and drinking. Moderate.

La Toscana 22 Leazes Park Rd ☎0191/232 5871. Probably the city's most reliable and authentic Italian restaurant, close to St James's Park stadium.

Leela's 20 Dean St ☏ 0191/230 1261. A rare treat among the flock-wallpaper curry houses, *Leela's* serves high-quality South Indian cuisine, with plenty of vegetarian options; the wide-ranging lunch set menu is particularly good value. Closed Sun. Moderate to Expensive.

Paradiso 1 Market Lane ☏ 0191/221 1240. Hidden down an alley and up a small flight of stairs off Pilgrim Street, a mellow café/restaurant with great food (try the eclectic and filling meze), amiable staff and welcoming booths. Closed Sun. Moderate.

Sabatini 25 King St ☏ 0191/261 4415. Quayside Italian with Neo-Impressionist daubs on the wall, good pizzas and a full menu besides. Closed Sun. Moderate.

Sachin's Forth Banks ☏ 0191/261 9035. Don't be put off by the grandiose, sickly green exterior – this Punjabi restaurant is a cut above and well worth booking ahead for. Moderate to Expensive.

Treacle Moon 5–7 The Side ☏ 0191/232 5537. Modern British food of distinction, pressing all the right trendy buttons (chargrilling, searing), with a cheaper lunch menu. Closed Mon. Expensive.

Valley Junction 397 Archbold Terrace, Jesmond ☏ 0191/281 6397. Wide-ranging and inventive Indian food in a lavishly refurbished railway carriage and signal box in what used to be Jesmond Station (the theme is continued with train trips to its sister restaurant in Corbridge – see p.737). Moderate to Expensive.

Pubs and bars

Bridge Hotel St Nicholas St. Right opposite the castle, this Victorian pub has a great view of the Tyne from its beer garden and regular live music.

Casa 58 Sandhill, next to the Guildhall. One of the bars of the moment, with comfy sofas, good food and an elegant riverside conservatory.

Crown Posada 31 The Side. Local beers and guest ales in a small but highly attractive wood-and-glass-panelled Victorian pub down by the Quayside.

Forth Hotel Pink Lane. Honest, old-fashioned boozer with a fine juke box, which attracts a lively, varied crowd.

Head of Steam Neville St. In a modern block opposite the *Royal Station Hotel*, a relaxed drinking den, with decent beers, good sounds and big sofas to sink into.

Pitcher & Piano by the Millennium Bridge, Quayside. The riverfront's most spectacular bar – sinuous roof, huge plate-glass walls – is a great place to drink, but there's also fine contemporary cooking in the restaurant. Live jazz Sun eve.

Quayside Bar 35 The Close, Quayside. Newcastle's only surviving medieval warehouse, now a rambling, boisterous pub with a good range of local beers and a few outdoor tables under the High Level Bridge.

Revolution Collingwood St. Full-on DJ-led hedonism in an impressive modern conversion of a landmark bank.

Union Rooms bottom of Westgate Rd. Huge former gentlemen's club, sympathetically restored by Wetherspoon's, and now offering cheap beer and sandwiches to the masses.

Clubs

Baja Beach Club Quayside, Gateshead. Hugely popular mainstream club with a beach-party theme – an excuse for bikini-clad dancers and "tub girls".

Foundation 57–59 Melbourne St ☏ 0191/261 8985. Stylish, well-equipped venue hosting club nights (Mon & Thurs–Sat).

Powerhouse George St. The city's best gay club, open every night of the week, attracts a friendly bunch to its four bars and two dance floors.

Rockshots Waterloo St ☏ 0191/232 9648. Lively, unpretentious place that pulls in a mixed crowd with a wide-ranging menu of club nights.

Scotland Yard Waterloo St ☏ 0191/232 4879. Cavernous venue where current favourite club nights are *Reverb* for techno (Fri) and the eclectic *Traveller* (Sat).

Tuxedo Princess Quayside, Gateshead. Raucous floating nightclub serving up scantily clad dancers and seven different styles of music in seven bars.

Arts, culture and music

The Jazz Café 23 Pink Lane ☏ 0191/232 6505. Intimate jazz club with a late licence, near the station; salsa nights Thurs–Sat. Closed Sun.

Live Theatre 27 Broad Chare ☏ 0191/232 1232, ⓦ www.live.org.uk. Enterprising theatre company

promoting local actors and writers. Also exhibitions and occasional club nights, plus fine live blues, reggae, country, soul and roots at its regular *Jumpin' Hot Club*.

Newcastle Arts Centre 69 Westgate Rd

☎0191/261 5618, ⒲www.newcastle-arts-centre.co.uk. Art gallery, workshops, and concert, drama and club venue.

Newcastle Opera House Westgate Rd ☎0191/232 0899, ⒲www.newcastleoperahouse.com. Beautifully restored Victorian theatre with a wide range of shows, comedy and gigs.

Newcastle Playhouse Barras Bridge ☎0191/232 3366. Modern theatre, home of Newcastle's own Northern Stage company and co-host of the annual RSC season in Nov. The Gulbenkian Studio here hosts small-scale theatre, dance and recitals.

Theatre Royal Grey St ☎0191/232 2061, ⒲www.theatre-royal-newcastle.co.uk. Drama, opera and dance; co-host of the annual RSC season in Nov.

Tyneside Cinema Pilgrim St ☎0191/232 1507, ⒲www.tynecine.org. The city's premier art-house cinema with a wide-ranging international programme.

Listings

Airport and flight enquiries General enquiries ☎0191/286 0966; flight enquiries ☎0191/214 4444; ⒲www.newcastleairport.com.

Banks and exchanges Banks are concentrated around Grey and Northumberland streets. There's a bureau de change at the airport, in the main post office and in Thomas Cook travel agency (see below), and an American Express bureau in Lunn Poly, 124 Northumberland St (☎0191/232 5262).

Car rental All of the following have outlets at the airport as well as in town: Avis, 7 George St ☎0191/232 5283 and at the airport ☎0191/214 0116; Europcar, 90 Westmorland Rd ☎0191/261 0833 and at the airport ☎0191/286 5070; Hertz, 14 Westgate Rd ☎0191/232 5313 and at the airport ☎0191/286 6748.

Ferries North Shields ferry terminal at Royal Quays, seven miles east of the city, has sailings to Scandinavia and Amsterdam. Contact Fjord Line (for Bergen, Haugesund and Stavanger; ☎0191/296 1313, ⒲www.fjordline.com) or DFDS (Gothenberg, Kristiansand and Amsterdam; ☎08705/333000, ⒲www.dfdsseaways.co.uk). Buses leave from Central Station to the terminal before each sailing.

Hospital Royal Victoria Infirmary, Queen Victoria Rd (☎0191/232 5131), behind the university, just 400 yards from Haymarket bus station.

Internet Internet Exchange, 26–30 Market St ☎0191/230 1280.

Left luggage Lockers available at the train station (daily 8am–6pm).

Police Corner of Market and Pilgrim streets ☎0191/214 6555.

Post office St Mary's Place, near the Civic Centre, at Haymarket ☎0191/230 2224.

Taxis There are ranks all over the centre, including those at Haymarket, Bigg Market, and outside Central Station. Weekend nights are the most difficult times to hail a cab; the queues at the Bigg Market ranks can be horrendous. Call Noda (☎0191/222 1888 or 232 7777) at Central Station for advance bookings.

Travel agents STA, 9 St Mary's Place ☎0191/233 2111, ⒲www.statravel.co.uk; Thomas Cook, 110 Grey St ☎0191/230 0773; Usit Campus, Level 5, Student Union Building, King's Walk ☎0191/232 2881, ⒲www.usitcampus.co.uk.

North of Newcastle: the stately homes

One of Vanbrugh's great Baroque houses, **Seaton Delaval Hall** (June–Sept Wed & Sun 2–6pm; £3), lies eleven miles northeast of Newcastle in fine gardens, its gloomy north facade looking over the bleak terrain towards the port of Blyth. Fire badly damaged the hall in 1822, a century after it was built, but subsequent restorations have done ample justice to the sombre grandeur of a building that exemplifies the architect's desire to create country houses with "something of the castle air". Public transport is with the #363 (hourly) or #364 (hourly; not Sun) **bus** from Haymarket, a 35-minute ride to Seaton Delaval Avenue head, from where it's a twenty-minute walk to the hall.

Belsay Hall, Castle and Gardens (daily: April–Sept 10am–6pm; Oct 10am–5pm; Nov–March 10am–4pm; £3.90; EH), fourteen miles northwest of Newcastle, were inherited in 1795 by Sir Charles Monck, who eleven years later decided to build a brand new hall here after his return from a honeymoon-cum-Grand-Tour of Europe. Sir Charles planned a majestic Doric house, an austere one-hundred-foot-square sandstone block raised on a podium of three steps. Built between 1807 and 1817, the **Hall** has now been impressively restored, while to the west a footpath threads through to the magical **Quarry Gardens**. Here, in the shelter of the sandstone quarry used for the building of the Hall, lush exotic vegetation cascades over exposed rock faces, planned by Sir Charles as a Romantic antidote to the severity of the house. The track also leads to the substantial remains of the medieval **castle**, its battlements punctuated by four formidable corner turrets. **Belsay village**, on the main road a mile from the Hall, is readily reached by **bus** from Newcastle; the #808 from Eldon Square (not Sun), or #508 from Haymarket (summer Sun only).

Eight miles northwest of Belsay lies the tiny village of **Cambo**; the summer Sunday #508 service (twice a day) links the two. Just outside the village stands **Wallington House** (April–Sept 1–5.30pm Mon & Wed–Sun; Oct same days 1–4.30pm; £5.50; NT) an ostentatious mansion rebuilt by Sir Walter Blackett, the coal- and lead-mine owner, in the 1740s. The interior's highlight is the Rococo plasterwork, though William Bell Scott's Pre-Raphaelite murals of scenes from Northumbrian history in the central hall are good fun, too. There's a separate charge (£4) if you only want to see the **grounds**, with their lawns, woods and lakes (daily dawn–dusk), and the beautiful **walled gardens**, which shelter conservatories, fountains and a huge variety of plants (daily: April–Sept 10am–7pm; Oct 10am–6pm; Nov–March 10am–4pm).

Along the north bank of the Tyne: Wallsend

On the north bank of the river four miles east of Newcastle, **WALLSEND**, as the name tells you, was the last outpost of Hadrian's great border defence. **Segedunum**, the "strong fort" a couple of minutes' walk from the Metro station here (daily: April–Oct 10am–5pm; Nov–March 10am–3.30pm; £2.95), has been admirably developed as one of the prime attractions along the Wall. Besides extensive excavations, the grounds contain a fully reconstructed bath-house, complete with steaming pools and colourful frescoes, and a rebuilt section of the Wall itself. The cleverly conceived museum combines excavated finds with interactive computer displays to give a strong flavour of life at the fort, as well as bringing the history of the site up to the present day with displays on coalmining and shipbuilding. To complete the picture, climb the 110-foot tower for a spectacular overview of the remains, the adjacent ship-repair yards and the river.

Along the south bank of the Tyne: Jarrow and South Shields

Five miles east of the city on the south side of the river, **JARROW** has been ingrained on the national consciousness since the 1936 **Jarrow Crusade**, a march to London by unemployed protesters which became the most potent image of the hardships of 1930s Britain. However, the town made a mark rather earlier, as the seventh-century St Paul's church and monastery was one of the region's early cradles of Christianity. The first Saxon church was built in 681 by monks from St Peter's at Monkwearmouth, and its monastic buildings soon attracted a reputation for scholastic learning. It was here that the **Venerable Bede** (673–735) came to live as a boy, growing to become one of Europe's greatest scholars and England's first historian – his *History of the English Church and People*, describing the struggles of the island's early Christians, was completed at Jarrow in 731. Access to the tranquil stone church

△ The Tyne Bridges, Newcastle

of **St Paul's** and the adjacent ruins of the monastery buildings (Mon–Sat 10am–4.30pm, Sun 2.30–4.30pm) is free, although they stand within the wider development that is **Bede's World** (April–Oct Mon–Sat 10am–5.30pm, Sun noon–5.30pm; Nov–March Mon–Sat 10am–4.30pm, Sun noon–4.30pm; guided tours Sun 2.30pm; £4.50; Ⓦwww.bedesworld.co.uk), which provides a fascinating exploration of early medieval Northumbria. The elegant multi-media **museum** traces the development of Northumbria and England through the use of extracts from Bede's writings, set alongside archeological finds and vivid re-creations of monastic life. After this you can take a turn through "*Gyrwe*", the eleven-acre demonstration **farm** which features reconstructed timber buildings from the early Christian period, as well as demonstrating contemporary agricultural methods. Bede's World is at Church Bank, a signposted fifteen-minute walk from **Bede Metro station**; alternatively, buses #526 or #527 from Neville Street (Central Station) in Newcastle or Jarrow Metro station stop in front of the church.

Beyond Jarrow lies **SOUTH SHIELDS**, the small but distinctive town which guards the south side of the entrance to the Tyne. The main point of interest here is **Arbeia Roman Fort** (Easter–Sept Mon–Sat 10am–5.30pm, Sun 1–5pm; Oct–Easter Mon–Sat 10am–4pm; free), ten minutes' walk north of the town centre and Metro station off River Drive. Built in 120–160 AD as a supply depot for Hadrian's Wall, the fort encloses substantial granaries where you can usually watch archeologists and stonemasons at work, and a museum that's largely unexceptional apart from the most complete Roman ring-mail shirt found in Britain. Fine views of the site and across towards the sister fort of Segedunum can be had from the stone reconstruction of the huge west gate, and from 2002 you'll be able to poke around the commanding officer's house, with richly decorated living rooms off a central courtyard, and the dark, cramped barracks next door, all rebuilt using authentic Roman materials and construction methods. If you have kids in tow, be sure to take them into Time Quest (Mon–Fri 10am–3pm during school terms, 11am–4pm in the holidays; Easter–Oct also Sat 10am–5pm, Sun 1–5pm; £1.50, children 80p), where they can have a go at being archeologists, digging for finds in a gravel pit, doing Roman weaving and making mosaics.

Southeast of Newcastle: Wearside

There's been a long rivalry between Newcastle and Sunderland, twelve miles to the southeast: both cities outraged about being lumped together in the municipal appellation Tyne *and* Wear; both Geordies (from Newcastle) or Mackems (from Sunderland) indignant at being taken for the other by know-nothing southerners; with supporters of both passionately followed football teams cock-a-hoop at the old enemy's misfortunes. To an outsider it can seem at times to be a bewildering argument over nothing at all, but whisper in **Wearside** at your peril the obviously superior charms of Newcastle as a city. Yet **Sunderland** and the River Wear do have their attractions, and in the adjacent new town of **Washington** stands one of the more intriguing historic sites of the northeast.

Sunderland

SUNDERLAND shares Newcastle's long history, river setting and industrial heritage but cannot match its architectural splendour. Formed from three medieval villages flanking the Wear, it was one of the wealthiest towns in England by 1500, and later supported the Parliamentary cause in the Civil War. The twentieth century made and broke the town: from being the largest shipbuilding town in the world, supporting a dozen shipyards, Sunderland slumped after ferocious bombing during World War II. Depression and recession did the rest.

There's little to turn the head in Sunderland's pedestrianized centre, although the revamped **Sunderland Museum** on Borough Road (Mon 10am–4pm, Tues–Sat 10am–5pm, Sun 2–5pm; free) does a very good, multimedia job of telling the city's history. The attached **Winter Gardens**, housed in an impressive new steel and glass hot-house that belatedly replaces the original Victorian glasshouses bombed by the Germans in 1941, are worth a look, too.

The main interest in Sunderland lies across the River Wear, whose remodelled, landscaped **Riverside** is actually the oldest settled part of the city. Here, in front of the university campus buildings, the early Christian church of **St Peter** (Easter–Oct daily 2–4pm; by arrangement at other times, call ☎0191/567 3726), built in 674 AD, is the elder sibling of St Paul's church at Jarrow. The tower and west wall are original Saxon features and the church displays fragments of the oldest stained glass in the country, the work of seventh-century European craftsmen. The extraordinary building further down on the waterside is the **National Glass Centre** (daily 10am–5pm; £5; ☎0191/515 5555, ⓦwww.nationalglasscentre.com), which tells the story of British glass-making – a traditional industry in Sunderland since the seventh century, when workshops turned out stained glass for the north's monastic houses and churches. There's plenty to get your teeth into, not least glass-making demonstrations in the on-site workshop (call for times).

Further north, out in the beach resort of **Roker** (bus #E1, #E3 or #19) the church of **St Andrew's** on Park Avenue (Mon–Fri 9.30–11.30am) is known as "the cathedral of the Arts and Crafts Movement". The nave echoes the upturned hull of a ship, while the sanctuary has a beautiful painting depicting the heavens, with an electric light fitting at the centre of the sun. The tapestries and carpets are from the William Morris workshop, and like the church they date from the early 1900s.

The main stop for **Metros** from Newcastle is in the central **train station** opposite the Bridges Shopping Centre, but get off at the previous stop, St Peter's, to walk along the north side of the river to the National Glass Centre or St Peter's Church. All buses use the **Park Lane Bus Station**, a five-minute walk south of the train station in the city centre, while the **tourist office** is just to the east on the main shopping drag, Fawcett Street (Mon–Sat 9am–5pm, Sun 10am–4pm; ☎0191/553 2000, ⒺTourist.info@sunderland.gov.uk). For daytime **food** in the city centre, try *21 John Street* (closed Sun), a relaxed, airy Italian café offering everything from made-to-order sandwiches to pasta and more substantial dishes.

Washington

Five miles west of Sunderland, the River Wear keeps to the south of the New Town of **WASHINGTON**, focus of much of the area's contemporary investment and manufacture. Split into planned, numbered districts, and organized on American lines, it's not an obvious stop, although the original **Old Village** has been zealously preserved as a conservation area. Just off the village green, past the leafy churchyard on The Avenue, stands the ancestral home of the family which spawned the first **US president**. The "de Wessyngtons" – later the Washingtons – originally came over with William the Conqueror, and by 1183 were based at the **Old Hall** (April–Oct Mon–Wed & Sun 11am–5pm; £2.80; NT), where they lived until 1613. Carefully preserved as a Jacobean showpiece, the echoing, stone-flagged house has a fine kitchen, Great Hall and garden, and some exemplary wood panelling, and although none of the furniture is original to the Washington family, it is contemporaneous. Every Fourth of July, the raising of the US flag heralds a day of independence celebrations; entry to the Old Hall is free that day.

The other main attraction in the area is the **Washington Wildfowl and Wetlands Centre** (daily: April–Oct 9.30am–5pm; Nov–March 9.30am–4pm; £4.90), east of town and north of the River Wear in District 15, its hundred acres designed by Sir Peter Scott and home to swans, geese, ducks, herons and flamingos. Its trails, hides, play areas, visitor information centre and children's activities make for an enjoyable day out.

For Washington Village and the Old Hall, the best service is on the #185 bus from Sunderland's Park Lane Bus Station (not Sun). The Wildfowl Centre is reached on the #56A from Newcastle's Market Street (not Sun) or the #X4 from Newcastle's Eldon Square or Sunderland's Park Lane (not Sun). If disaster strikes, all these buses (and many others from Newcastle or Sunderland) call or terminate at **Washington Galleries Bus Station**, from where you'll be able to reach either site. Most buses prefixed with a "W" run to Washington Village from the Galleries.

Southwest of Newcastle: Gibside

To the southwest of Newcastle, one of the finest landscaped gardens in the North is a quick, six-mile hop from the city centre (bus #745 from Central Station, then a half-mile signposted walk from the village of Rowlands Gill). The grounds of **Gibside** (Tues–Sun: April–Oct 10am–6pm; Nov–March 10am–4pm; £3; NT) represent a very rare survival of mid-eighteenth-century park design, combining striking formal vistas with naturalistic woodland. Created by coal baron George Bowes between 1729 and 1760, the estate went into decline as early as 1885 after the death of his great-grandson John Bowes (founder of the Bowes Museum at Barnard Castle), and for the last twenty years the National Trust have been slowly attempting to restore the original design. A series of hour-long **trails** will take you past the atmospheric shell of the earlier Jacobean mansion, an orangery and walled garden, the 130-foot Column to Liberty, erected to reaffirm Bowes' loyalty to George II after the Jacobite uprising of 1745, and along the east bank of the River Derwent near its confluence with the Tyne (though not past the neo-Gothic Banqueting House, now administered as self-catering accommodation by the Landmark Trust. Back towards the entrance and tearoom stands the most striking and complete architectural remnant, the **chapel** (April–Oct Tues–Sun 11am–4.30pm). Inspired by Palladio's Villa Rotonda in the Veneto in northeastern Italy, this elegantly symmetrical building features an array of delicate carvings under its portico, but is dominated by one of the grandest pulpits you're ever likely to see – a triple-decker mahogany affair decked out in velvet with a grand inlaid sounding board.

Along Hadrian's Wall

In 55 and 54 BC, Julius Caesar launched two swift invasions of southeast England from his base in Gaul, his success proving that Britain lay within the Roman grasp. The full-scale assault began under Claudius in 43 AD and, within forty years, Roman troops had reached the Firth of Tay. In 83 AD, the Roman governor Agricola ventured farther north, but Rome subsequently

Bellingham ▲   Otterburn ▲

Housesteads   Hadrian's Wall   Chollerford
   B6318
Roman
Army   Cawfields   Steel Rigg   Chesters
Birdoswald   Museum
Walltown   ⓘ Vindolanda
Gilsland   Once   Acomb
Greenhead   Brewed   Hexham   Corbridge
   Haltwhistle   Bardon   Haydon
   Mill   Bridge   0   5 miles

Carlisle   Newcastle

© Crown copyright   Alston ▼   Darlington ▼

transferred part of his army to the Danube, and the remaining legions withdrew to the frontier which was marked by the **Stanegate**, a military roadway linking Carlisle and Corbridge.

Emperor Hadrian, who toured Roman Britain in 122 AD, found this informal arrangement unsatisfactory. His imperial policy was quite straightforward – he wanted the empire to live at peace within stable frontiers, most of which were defined by geographical features. In northern Britain, however, there was no natural barrier and so Hadrian decided to create his own by constructing a 76-mile **wall** from the Tyne to the Solway Firth. It was not intended to be an impenetrable fortification, but rather a base for patrols that could push out into hostile territory. It was to be punctuated by **milecastles**, which were to serve as gates, depots and mini-barracks, and by observation **turrets**, two of which were to stand between each pair of milecastles. Before the Wall was even completed, major modifications were made: the bulk of the garrison had initially been stationed along the Stanegate, but they were now moved into the Wall, occupying a chain of new **forts**, which straddled the Wall at six- to nine-mile intervals. These new arrangements concentrated the Wall's garrison in a handful of key points and brought them nearer the enemy, making it possible to respond quickly to any threat. Simultaneously, a military zone was defined by the digging of a broad ditch, or **vallum**, on the south side of the Wall, crossed by causeways to each of the forts, turning them into the main points of access and rendering the milecastles, in this respect, largely redundant. The revised structure remained in operation until the last Roman soldiers left in 411 AD.

Most of Hadrian's Wall disappeared centuries ago, yet walking its length remains a popular pastime, one which will be made easier by the opening of a waymarked trail, the **Hadrian's Wall Path**, in summer 2002; even if you're not up to tramping the entire course of the Wall, it's well worth walking at least one section to get an idea of the whole enterprise. Approached from Newcastle along the valley of the Tyne, via the Roman museum and site at **Corbridge**, the prosperous-looking market town of **Hexham**, with its fine eleventh-century abbey, makes a good base for transport and accommodation. Most visitors stick to the best-preserved portions of the Wall, which are concentrated between the hamlet of **Chollerford**, three miles north of Hexham, and **Haltwhistle**, sixteen miles to the west, which is also a decent base for accommodation and transport. It's here, especially between **Housesteads** and **Steel Rigg**, that the Wall is at its most beautiful, as it clings to the edge of the Whin Sill, a precipitous line of dolerite crags towering above the austere Northumberland National Park moorland. Walking this part of the Wall couldn't be easier: a footpath runs along the top of the ridge, incorporating a short stretch of the **Pennine Way**, which meets the Wall at Greenhead and leaves at Housesteads, where it cuts off north for Bellingham. Scattered along this section are a variety of key archeological sites and museums, notably **Chesters**

Roman Fort and Museum, near Chollerford, the remains of **Housesteads Fort** and that of **Vindolanda**, and the milecastle remains at **Cawfields**, north of Haltwhistle.

Visiting the Wall

There's a special Hadrian's Wall **bus** service, the cutely tagged **#AD122**, which links Hexham tourist office and bus and train stations with Chesters, Housesteads, Once Brewed Visitor Centre, Vindolanda, Cawfields, Haltwhistle train station, the Roman Army Museum and Greenhead, Birdoswald and Carlisle. This operates between late-May and late-September, four to five times a day in each direction, taking two hours for the whole route (1hr Hexham–Haltwhistle); a typical one-way ticket, from Hexham to Vindolanda, costs £2.10. There's also a year-round service, the #185, which runs between Carlisle and Housesteads, via the Roman Army Museum, Haltwhistle and the Once Brewed Visitor Centre, with two to three departures a day (not Sun). Another year-round service, the #685, runs hourly (Mon–Sat) along the A69 between Carlisle, Greenhead, Haltwhistle, Haydon Bridge, Hexham, Corbridge and Newcastle (Eldon Square); on Sundays, the #685 runs four times from Carlisle to Hexham, connecting with the hourly #85 Hexham–Newcastle service. Finally, the #880 or #882 bus from Hexham (calling at the train station and Acomb youth hostel) runs via Chollerford, from where Chesters is just half a mile's walk along the road to the west; during the period May to mid-September, some of these services divert to Chesters itself.

The nearest **train** stations are on the Newcastle–Carlisle line at Corbridge, Hexham, Haydon Bridge, Bardon Mill and Haltwhistle. Hexham, Bardon Mill and Haltwhistle will leave you a fair walk to Chesters, Vindolanda/Once Brewed and Cawfields/Greenhead respectively, or you can connect at Hexham or Haltwhistle with the bus services described above.

A variety of **passes** are available on these services. Day Rover tickets on the #AD122, which can be bought from the driver or local tourist offices, cost £5.50; holders of Northeast Explorer passes get half-price travel, those with Stagecoach Cumberland Explorer tickets go free. The Hadrian's Wall Rail Rover Ticket (£12.50, available from train stations) is valid for two days in any three-day period (after 9am weekdays), and covers travel on the Newcastle–Carlisle train line, the #AD122 and the Tyne & Wear Metro. Not quite so good-value is the Tyne Valley Ranger (£11), a one-day pass for the Newcastle–Carlisle train and the #AD122 (after 9am weekdays). Details of these services are available from tourist offices, the Once Brewed Visitor Centre, and on the Hadrian's Wall tourism partnership's **website**, Ⓦ www .hadrians-wall.org.

Corbridge

Buses from Newcastle and trains on the Newcastle–Hexham–Carlisle line stop at **CORBRIDGE**, a well-heeled town overlooking the River Tyne from the top of a steep ridge. This spur of land was first settled by the Saxons, and their handiwork survives in parts of the **Church of St Andrew**, on the central Market Place, but it's the adjacent **Vicar's Pele** that catches the eye, a well-preserved fourteenth-century fortified tower-house.

One mile west of the Market Place, accessible by road or along the riverside footpath – take the street opposite the *Watling Coffee House* – lies **Corbridge Roman Site** (April–Sept daily 10am–6pm; Oct daily 10am–5pm; Nov–March Wed–Sun 10am–1pm & 2–4pm; £2.90; EH), the location of the garrison town of Corstopitum. This is the oldest fortified site in the region, first established as a supply base for the Roman advance into Scotland in 80 AD (and thus predating the Wall itself). It remained in regular military use until the end of the second century, after which it became surrounded by a fast-developing town – most of the visible archeological remains date from this period, when Corstopitum served as the nerve centre of Hadrian's Wall. The extensive remains provide an insight into the layout of the civilian town, showing the foundations of temples, public baths, garrison headquarters, workshops and houses as well as the best-preserved Roman granaries in Britain. The site **museum** displays the celebrated *Lion and Stag* fountainhead – the so-called "Corbridge Lion"; to the Romans, the lion and its prey symbolized the triumph of life over death.

Corbridge **train station** is half a mile outside the town, across the river; **buses** stop outside the *Angel Inn* on Main Street or near the post office on Hill Street, around the corner. Corbridge **tourist office** is also on Hill Street, at the library (mid-May to Sept Mon–Sat 10am–1pm & 2–6pm, Sun 1–5pm; Easter to mid-May & Oct Mon–Sat 10am–1pm & 2–5pm, Sun 1–5pm; ☎01434/632815). There's plenty of **accommodation** in and around Corbridge – try the *Riverside Guest House*, a comfortable eighteenth-century house with fine views of the Tyne on Main Street (☎01434/632942, ⓦweb.ukonline.co.uk/riverside; ❷), or spacious, tastefully decorated *Clive House*, in the former schoolhouse just east of here on Appletree Lane (☎01434/632617; ❷). Moving upmarket, there's plenty of space and a fine riverside location at the *Lion of Corbridge Hotel*, Bridge End (☎01434/632504, ⓔlionofcorbridge@talk21.com; ❹), which is right by the bridge on the way in from the train station.

The *Watling Coffee House*, on Watling Street just north of the main square, serves light **meals** throughout the day. Star attraction in the evening is the *Valley* (☎01434/633434; closed Sun), a high-quality Indian restaurant in the old station house on Station Road; for larger parties coming from Newcastle, they'll arrange for a waiter to serve drinks and take orders on the "curry train" from Central Station. Back in the centre of town, at 18 Front St, is *Al Ponte* (☎01434/634214), offering a wide selection of Italian dishes, and good lunch deals. For **bar meals** and beer, visit the *Wheatsheaf*, on Watling Street (visible at the end of the road, beyond the *Watling Coffee House*), an attractive seventeenth-century former farmhouse with a couple of Roman stones in the stableyard.

Hexham and around

In 671, on a bluff above the Tyne, four miles west of Corbridge, St Wilfrid founded a Benedictine monastery whose church was, according to contemporary accounts, the finest to be seen north of the Alps. Unfortunately, its gold and silver proved irresistible to the Vikings, who savaged the place in 876, but the church was rebuilt in the eleventh century as part of an Augustinian priory, and the town of **HEXHAM**, governed by the Archbishop of York, grew up in its shadow.

The stately exterior of **Hexham Abbey** (daily: May–Sept 9am–7pm; Oct–April 9am–5pm; free) still dominates the west side of the Market Place. Entry is through the south transept, where there's an impressive first-century tombstone honouring Flavinus, a standard-bearer in the Roman cavalry, who's shown riding down his bearded enemy. The memorial lies at the foot of the broad, well-worn steps of the canons' **night stair**, one of the few such staircases – providing access from the monastery to the church – to have survived the Dissolution. Beyond, most of the high-arched nave dates from an Edwardian restoration and it's here that you gain access to the **crypt**, a Saxon structure made out of old Roman stones, where pilgrims once viewed the abbey's reliquaries. At the end of the nave is the sixteenth-century **rood screen**, whose complex tracery envelops the portraits of local bishops. Behind the screen, the chancel displays the inconsequential-looking **frith stool**, an eighth-century stone chair that was once believed to have been used by St Wilfrid. Nearby, close to the high altar, there are four panels from a fifteenth-century **Dance of Death**, a grim, darkly varnished painting.

The rest of Hexham's large and irregularly shaped **Market Place** (main market day is Tuesday) is peppered with remains of its medieval past. The massive walls of the fourteenth-century **Moot Hall** were built to serve as the gatehouse to "The Hall", a well-protected enclosure that was garrisoned against the Scots. Nearby, the archbishops also built their own prison, a formidable fortified tower dating from 1330 and constructed using stones plundered from the Roman ruins at Corbridge. Now, as the **Old Gaol**, this accommodates the **Border History Museum** (April–Oct daily 10am–4.30pm; Feb, March & Nov Mon, Tues & Sat 10am–4.30pm; £2), which provides information and displays concerning the border-raiding Reivers (see p.741).

Hexham's **train station** sits on the northeastern edge of the town centre, a ten-minute walk from the abbey; the new **tourist office** is halfway between the two, in the main town car park behind the Safeway superstore (Easter to mid-May & Oct Mon–Sat 9am–5pm, Sun 10am–5pm; mid-May to Sept Mon–Sat 9am–6pm, Sun 10am–5pm; Nov to Easter Mon–Sat 9am–5pm; ☎01434/652220, @hexham.tic@tynedale.gov.uk). The **bus station** can be found off Priestpopple, a few minutes' stroll east of the abbey.

Good **accommodation** options include the welcoming Edwardian retreat that is the *Kitty Frisk House*, a few minutes from the centre on Corbridge Road (☎01434/601533; no credit cards; ❷); the quiet and secluded *West Close House*, on Hextol Terrace off the B6305 Allendale Road (☎01434/603307; no credit cards; ❷), which is very friendly, has a delightful garden and offers wholefood continental breakfasts alongside the usual fry-ups; and the bright and breezy *Topsy Turvy*, 9 Leazes Lane (☎01434/603152; no credit cards; ❶). The *Best Western Beaumont Hotel*, Beaumont Street (☎01434/602331, ❾www.beaumont-hotel .co.uk; ❺, excludes breakfast), has spacious doubles overlooking the abbey and weekend dinner, bed and breakfast deals; alternatively, try the sympathetically renovated *Royal Hotel* on Priestpopple (☎01434/602270, ❾www.hexham-royal-hotel.co.uk; ❹), topped by a gleaming gold dome, which offers a dozen en-suite rooms, a cosy, oak-panelled bar and good discounts for stays of two nights or more. The **youth hostel** (☎01434/602864, ❾www.yha.org.uk) occupies converted stable buildings in the village of **Acomb**, two miles from Hexham – take bus #880, #881 or #882, which all pass the train station. The **campsite** here, at *Fallowfield Dene Caravan Park* (☎01434/603553; closed Nov–March), is a tranquil place with proper laundry facilities.

Mrs Miggins, on St Mary's Wynd, just off Beaumont Street, is a good-value daytime **coffee shop**, and the *Hexham Tans*, off the Market Place at 11 St Mary's Chare, is a homely vegetarian café (closed Sun). Options for **evening meals** in Hexham are limited. Your best bets are *Valley Connection 301* on the Market Place (☎01434/601234; closed Mon), part of a chain of inventive Indian restaurants that stretches to Corbridge and Newcastle, or *Danielle's*, an unpretentious bistro at 12 Eastgate (☎01434/601122; closed Sun). **Out of town** on Dipton Mill Road, two miles south of the centre, *Dipton Mill Inn* is a good all-rounder, with wholesome bar meals (until 8.30pm), own-brewed beer, streamside beer garden and a pleasant setting. It's a 45-minute walk from Hexham on lovely hilly footpaths; the tourist office will point you in the right direction. The main focus of **entertainment** in town is the **Queen's Hall Arts Centre** on Beaumont Street (℡01434/652477), which puts on a year-round programme of theatre, dance, music and art exhibitions.

Chollerford and Chesters Roman Fort

At **CHOLLERFORD**, around four miles north of Hexham, a bridge crosses the North Tyne river, overlooked by the swanky *Swallow George Hotel* (℡01434/681611, ⓦwww.georgehotel-chollerford.com; ❼). Two thousand years ago, the main river crossing was a little way downstream, half a mile west of present-day Chollerford, where **Chesters Roman Fort** (daily: Easter–Sept 10am–6pm; Oct 10am–5pm; Nov–Easter 10am–4pm; £2.90; EH), otherwise known as Cilurnum, was built to guard the erstwhile Roman bridge over the river. Enough remains of the original structure to pick out the design of the fort, and each section has been clearly labelled, but the highlight is down by the river where the vestibule, changing room and steam range of the garrison's **bath-house** are still visible. Back at the entrance, the **museum** has an excellent collection of Roman stonework, including Juno (now headless) in a delicately pleated dress standing on a cow, one of the finest pieces of statuary found along the Wall, and a notable sculpture of Mars from Housesteads.

Housesteads to Vindolanda

Overlooking the bleak Northumbrian moors from the top of the Whin Sill, **Housesteads Roman Fort** (daily: Easter–Sept 10am–6pm; Oct 10am–5pm; Nov–Easter 10am–4pm; £2.90; EH & NT), eight miles west of Chesters, has long been the most popular site on the Wall. The fort was built in the second phase of the Hadrianic construction and is of standard design but for one enforced modification – forts were supposed to straddle the line of the Wall, but here the original stonework tracked along the very edge of the cliff, so Housesteads was built on the steeply sloping ridge to the south. Access is via the tiny **museum**, from where you stroll across to the south gate, beside which lie the remains of the civilian settlement that was dependent on the one thousand infantrymen stationed within. You don't need to pay for entrance to Housesteads if you simply intend to walk west along the Wall from here. The three-mile hike past the lovely wooded **Crag Lough** to **Steel Rigg** offers the most fantastic views, especially when you spy the course of the Wall as it threads over the crags ahead.

Leaving the Wall at Steel Rigg, it's roughly half a mile south to the main road and the **Once Brewed National Park Visitor Centre** (June–Aug daily 9.30am–6pm; mid-March to May, Sept & Oct daily 9.30am–5pm; much reduced hours in winter, usually Sat & Sun only, call for details; ℡01434/344396); the side road beyond the centre continues for half a mile down to Vindolanda. For local **accommodation**, there's the popular *Once Brewed Youth Hostel* (℡01434/344360, ⓦwww.yha.org.uk; closed Dec & Jan), next to the visitor centre, and the *Vallum Lodge* (℡01434/344248; ❸; closed Nov–Feb), a comfortable small hotel with good home cooking, a mile or so west down the main road from the visitor centre. The surrounding countryside also shelters a few scenically located B&Bs, including *Gibbs Hill Farm* (℡01434/344030, ⓦwww.gibbshillfarm.co.uk; ❷; closed Nov–Feb), with attractive, en-suite rooms and great views of the wall, two miles north of Steel Rigg. There's also a very well-equipped backpackers' hostel, the *Hadrian Lodge*, to the southeast on isolated North Road

(☎01434/688688) – from the Wall and the B6318 take the turning for **Haydon Bridge** about a mile east of Housesteads, and you'll reach the hostel two miles before the village. Lying on the main A69 road, Haydon Bridge is home to by far the best local place to **eat**, the *General Havelock Inn* (☎01434/684376), serving fine modern European cuisine either in the bar (closed Mon), in the grand rear restaurant (closed Sun eve & Mon), or even in the garden on the banks of the river.

Vindolanda

The excavated garrison fort of **Vindolanda** actually predates the Wall itself, though most of what you see today dates from the second to third century AD, when the fort was a thriving metropolis of five hundred soldiers with its own civilian settlement attached. The **site** (daily: May & June 10am–6pm; July & Aug 10am–6.30pm; April & Sept 10am–5.30pm; March & Oct 10am–5pm; Nov, Dec & Feb 10am–4pm; £3.90, combined ticket with the Roman Army Museum at Greenhead £5.60) is operated by the private Vindolanda Trust, which has done an excellent job of imaginatively presenting its finds. The ongoing **excavations** at Vindolanda are spread over a wide area, with civilian houses, inn, guest quarters, administrative building, commander's house and main gates all clearly visible. Full-scale re-creations give an idea of what the Wall would have looked like: a stone turret and wall section, alongside a timber milecastle and a bit of turf wall to replicate the original appearance of the western third of the Wall, where limestone was in short supply. The path through the excavations then descends to what's termed the **open-air museum**, where you can walk into reconstructions of a shrine of the water nymphs, a shop and a house, all with lively sound commentaries. Beyond lies the café, shop and **Chesterholm Museum**, the latter housing the largest collection of Roman leather items ever discovered on a single site – dozens of shoes, belts, even a pair of baby boots – which were preserved in the black silt of waterlogged ditches. However, the most intriguing sections are concerned with the excavated hoard of **writing tablets**, now in the British Museum. The writings depict graphically the realities of military life in Northumberland: soldiers' requests for more beer, birthday party invitations, even letters from home containing gifts of underwear for freezing frontline grunts.

Cawfields and Haltwhistle to Birdoswald

Wall-walkers can continue west for around three miles from Steel Rigg/Once Brewed to **Cawfields** (free access), site of a Roman camp and milecastle, perched on one of the most rugged crags on this section. There's not much to the small town of **HALTWHISTLE**, three miles south of the wall here, but there is a **tourist office** (Easter–Oct Mon–Sat 9.30am–1pm & 2–5pm, Sun 1–5pm; Nov–Easter Mon, Tues & Thurs–Sat 10am–noon & 1–3.30pm; ☎01434/322002) in the **train station**, at the western edge of town, and a good selection of **accommodation**. Haltwhistle boasts a fine hotel, the *Centre of Britain* (☎01434/322422, ⓦwww.centre-of-britain.org.uk; ❸), right in the centre of town and – though a few other towns hereabouts lay claim – Britain as well. Built around a fifteenth-century peel tower are a variety of tasteful bedrooms and lounges with wooden beams and stone fireplaces. The town also has plenty of B&Bs, including the attractive, ivy-covered *Hall Meadows*, right at the top of Main Street (☎01434/321021; no credit cards; ❶). Alternatively, there's *Ashcroft* in an elegant former vicarage on Lantys Lonnen, very near the tourist office (☎01434/320213; ❷), which has nice rooms and colourful ter-

13

raced gardens. The *Haltwhistle Camping Site* is in Burnfoot Park (✆01434/320106; closed Nov–Feb), beside the Tyne on the southeast edge of town. There are several tearooms along and around Main Street, while for beer and **bar meals**, the *Spotted Cow Inn*, down on Castle Hill, the eastern extension of Main Street, is an agreeable spot. **Mountain bikes** can be rented for £12 a day from Edens Lawn petrol station on the eastern edge of town (✆01434/320443).

A further four-mile trek west along the wall from Cawfields takes you past the remains of **Great Chesters Fort** before reaching a spectacular section of the Wall, known as the **Walltown Crags**. The views from here are marvellous. Adjacent to the crags, at Carvoran, the Vindolanda Trust's **Roman Army Museum** (daily: May & June 10am–6pm; July & Aug 10am–6.30pm; April & Sept 10am–5.30pm; March & Oct 10am–5pm; early Nov & late Feb 10am–4pm; £3.10; joint admission ticket with Vindolanda £5.60) does its best to inject some interest into its dioramas, reconstructions, films and exhibits, but it's rather tame stuff compared to the archeological sites.

Push on just a mile southwest, and you're soon in minuscule **GREENHEAD**, where the **youth hostel** (✆016977/47401, ⓦwww.yha.org.uk) is located in a converted Methodist chapel. If this doesn't appeal, *Holmhead Guest House* (✆016977/47402, ✉holmhead@hadrianswall.freeserve.co.uk; ❸) probably will, an old stone farmhouse up a track behind the hostel. Sporting exposed beams, and partly built with stones taken from the Wall itself, it also serves an excellent set-menu dinner using local ingredients – book ahead, since there are only four rooms.

Four miles west, and served by the Hadrian's Wall Bus, is **Birdoswald Fort** (March–Nov daily 10am–5.30pm; £2.50; EH). This is the only place along the wall where all tiers of the Roman structure are found intact, the defences comprising an earth ditch, a large section of masonry wall, and the trench and mound foundations behind it. A visitor centre fleshes out the historic background, and you can walk to the nearby Harrow's Scar Milecastle for some spectacular views.

Northumberland National Park

Northwest Northumberland, the great triangular chunk of land between Hadrian's Wall and the coastal plain, is dominated by the wide-skied landscapes of the **Northumberland National Park**, whose four hundred windswept square miles rise to the **Cheviot Hills** on the Scottish border. These uplands are interrupted by great slabs of forest, mostly the conifer plantations of the Forestry Commission, and a string of river valleys, of which Coquetdale, Tynedale and Redesdale are the longest. Remote from lowland law and order, these dales were once the homelands of the **Border Reivers**, turbulent clans who ruled the local roost from the thirteenth to the sixteenth century. The Reivers took advantage of the struggles between England and Scotland to engage in endless cross-border rustling and general brigandage, activities recalled by the ruined **bastles** (fortified farmhouses) and **peels** (defensive tower-houses) that lie dotted across the landscape.

Good walking country can be found right across the National Park. The most popular trail is the **Pennine Way**, which, entering the National Park at Hadrian's Wall, cuts up through Bellingham on its way to The Cheviot, the park's highest peak at 2674ft, finishing at Kirk Yetholm, over the border in

Scotland. This part of the Pennine Way is 64 miles long, but it's easy to break the hike up into manageable portions as the footpath passes through a variety of tiny settlements, several of which have youth hostels, B&B accommodation and campsites. As an introduction, it's hard to beat the lovely moorland scenery of the fifteen-mile stretch from Housesteads at Hadrian's Wall to **Bellingham**, a pleasant town on the banks of the North Tyne. Bellingham is also on the road to **Kielder Water**, a pine-surrounded reservoir which has been vigorously promoted as a water-sports centre and nature reserve since its creation in 1982. Farther north, **Rothbury**, in Coquetdale, is close to both the Simonside Hills and **Cragside**, the nineteenth-century country home of Lord Armstrong, whilst at **Wooler** footpaths lead into the Cheviot Hills. Beyond Wooler, a succession of battle sites and castles attest to the erstwhile military significance of this border region; notable among them is idiosyncratically restored **Chillingham**, which is home to an equally unusual herd of **wild cattle**.

Bellingham

The stone terraces of **BELLINGHAM** (pronounced Bellinjum) slope up from the banks of the Tyne on the eastern edge of the Northumberland National Park. It's a restful spot set in splendid rural surroundings, and it contains the medieval **Church of St Cuthbert**, which has an unusual stone-vaulted roof – designed (successfully) to prevent raiding Border reivers from burning the church to the ground. The **Heritage Centre** just east of the village centre on Woodburn Road (May–Sept Mon & Fri–Sun 10.30am–4.30pm; £1) has more on this turbulent period.

Buses stop in the centre on Market Place, a few hundred yards down from the helpful **tourist office** on Main Street (Mon–Sat 9.30am–1pm & 2–5pm, Sun 1–5pm; ☎01434/220616). Central **lodgings** are available at the modern, en-suite *Lyndale Guest House* (☎01434/220361, ⓦwww.lyndaleguesthouse.co.uk; ❷), just past the *Rose & Crown* pub. *Westfield House*, a large Victorian residence with fine views at the west end of the village (☎01434/220340, Ⓔwestfield .house@virgin.net; ❸), is rather grander, and serves a good dinner to guests. Bellingham's pubs – the *Rose & Crown*, the *Black Bull* and the *Cheviot* – all have a few rooms, too; those at the *Cheviot* (☎01434/220696; ❸) are the nicest. Swankiest choice in Bellingham is *Riverdale Hall Hotel* (☎01434/220254, Ⓔiben@riverdalehall.demon.co.uk; ❺), a nineteenth-century country house on the village's western edge, with an indoor swimming pool and extensive grounds. The **youth hostel** (☎01434/220313, ⓦwww.yha.org.uk) has simple self-catering facilities in a primitive-looking hut some six hundred yards from the centre of the village on Woodburn Road (signposted from Main Street). The local **campsite** is at *Demesne Farm* (☎01434/220258; closed Nov–Feb), right in the centre near the police station.

Kielder Water and Forest

West of Bellingham, the road follows the North Tyne River and skirts the forested edge of **Kielder Water** (ⓦwww.kielder.org), passing the assorted visitor centres, waterside parks, picnic areas and anchorages that fringe its southern shore. First stop is the Visitor Centre at **Tower Knowe** (daily: July & Aug 10am–6pm; June & Sept 10am–5pm; April, May & Oct 10am–4pm; ☎01434/240398), eight miles from Bellingham, with a café and an exhibition (£1) on the history of the valley and lake. Another four miles west, at **Leaplish**, the waterside park (daily: April & Oct 9am–6pm; May–Sept 9am–11pm; Nov–March call to check times on ☎01434/250312), bar and restaurant are the focus of most of Kielder's outdoor activities: water sports and fishing are on offer, and there's a heated indoor pool. The **Bird of Prey Centre** here (March–Oct daily 10.30am–5pm; £3) gives you the chance to handle these vicious predators and lays on flying displays, falconry courses and winter hawk walks. A ten-mile, hour-and-a-half's **cruise** on the Osprey ferry (Easter–Oct 5 daily; ☎01434/250312; £4.20) is always a pleasure; departures are from the piers at either Tower Knowe or Leaplish.

Five miles from Leaplish at the top of the reservoir and just three miles from the Scottish border, Kielder village is dominated by **Kielder Castle** (Easter–July & Oct daily 10am–5pm; Aug daily 10am–6pm; Nov–Easter Sat & Sun 11am–4pm; ☎01434/250209; free, parking £1), built in 1775 as the hunting lodge of the Duke of Northumberland, and now an information centre and exhibition area praising the work of the Forestry Commission. The castle is surrounded by the **Border Forest Park**, several million spruce trees subdivided into a number of approximately defined forest areas: Wark and Kielder are broadly to the south of the reservoir, Falstone and Redesdale to the north. Several easy and clearly marked **footpaths**, dotted with arresting modern sculptures, lead from the castle into the forest – try the "Duke's Trail" through Ravenshill Wood, a slice of ancient and semi-natural woodland. There's **mountain bike rental** available from Kielder Bikes (☎01434/250392) at the castle, too, with thirteen waymarked trails and two off-road routes through the forest to choose from.

If you want to **stay** in the area, options are far-flung but wide-ranging. There's a spacious new **youth hostel** (☎01434/250195, ⓦwww.yha.org.uk; closed Nov–Feb) in Kielder village, with some two-bedded rooms, a self-catering kitchen, and a restaurant offering breakfast and three-course dinners. Leaplish Waterside Park also has **bunk-barn accommodation**, with dorms and two double rooms (❶) available. On the road in from Bellingham, a couple of miles before the water, the early seventeenth-century *Pheasant Inn* (☎01434/240382, ⓔthepheasantinn@kielderwater.demon.co.uk; ❹) at **STANNERSBURN** has eight comfortable rooms in a modern extension and decent meals. The riverside hamlet of **FALSTONE**, a mile to the north, boasts the smaller *Blackcock Inn* (☎01434/240200; ❸). There's also B&B at *Spring Cottage* in Stannersburn (☎01434/240338; ❷), plus several B&Bs in Kielder village and the surrounding area – ask at the information centre. *Kielder* **campsite** (☎01434/250291, ⓔkieldercampsite@aol.com; closed Oct–Easter) is by the banks of the Tyne, about half a mile north of the castle.

Redesdale

From Bellingham, it's a fifteen-mile trek north along the Pennine Way to **BYR-NESS** in **Redesdale**, which can also be reached direct from Kielder Castle via a rough, eleven-mile forestry road. Set beside the main A68 road, Byrness is a tiny village, but walkers can take refuge at the simple **youth hostel** at 7 Otterburn Green (☎01830/520425, ⓦwww.yha.org.uk; closed Oct–Feb).

Redesdale has only one settlement of any size, **OTTERBURN**, ten miles southeast of Byrness down the A68. It's an undistinguished place today, with little except the name of the local pub, the *Percy Arms*, to recall its most notable hour. It was at Otterburn in August 1388 that an English army led by Sir Henry Percy ("Hotspur") was defeated by the Scots under James, Earl of Douglas. Douglas was killed in battle, as were 1800 English troops, while Hotspur was taken prisoner – a chain of events later made the subject of the medieval ballad of *Chevy Chase*. The battle site is about a mile northwest of the village, off the A68, marked by a stone cross set in a little pinewood. (Fittingly, the scenic moorland region immediately north of Otterburn is now a **military training area** – walkers must heed all signs and flags and should take local advice before setting off.)

Otterburn boasts a small **tourist information centre** in the surprisingly thriving **Otterburn Mill** (Mon–Sat 9am–5.30pm, Sun 11am–5pm), which, though it no longer produces textiles, sells them and maintains a small museum. There are several places **to stay**, including the *Butterchurn Guest House*, opposite the church on Main Street (℡01830/520585; ➋), and the comfortable *Percy Arms* (℡01830/520261, ⓦwww.percyarms.co.uk; ➎), further down the road, where you can get coffee, bar meals and full dinners.

Rothbury and around

ROTHBURY, straddling the River Coquet some eighteen miles northeast of Otterburn, prospered as a late Victorian resort because it gave ready access to the forests, burns and ridges of the Simonside Hills. Rothbury remains a popular spot for walkers, and the **Tourist Information and National Park Visitor Centre**, near the Cross on Church Street (April–Oct daily 10am–5pm; Nov–March Sat & Sun 10am–5pm; ℡01669/620887) offers advice on local trails, several of which begin in the Simonside Hills car park, a couple of miles southwest of town.

Buses from Morpeth (with connections from Newcastle) stop on Rothbury's High Street, outside the *Queen's Head*. There are several convenient **B&Bs** – including the well-equipped *Katerina's Guest House* on the High Street (℡01669/620691, ⓦwww.katerinasguesthouse.co.uk; ➋), where all the en-suite rooms boast four-poster beds and TVs; and the comfortable, Georgian *Orchard Guest House*, at the top of the same street (℡01669/620684, ⓦwww.orchardguesthouse.co.uk; ➋), which also serves dinner. Most of the places to **eat and drink** are strung out along the High Street: the *Elmtree Coffee Shop* serves decent light lunches and afternoon teas, and the *Newcastle Hotel* does well-prepared bar meals, high teas and real ales.

Cragside

Victorian Rothbury was dominated by Sir William, later the first **Lord Armstrong**, the nineteenth-century engineer and arms manufacturer, who built his country home at **Cragside** (Easter–Oct Tues–Sun 1–5.30pm; £6.70, gardens only £4.20; NT), a mile to the east of the village. At first, Armstrong was satisfied with his modest house, but in 1869 he decided to build something more substantial, and hired Richard Norman Shaw, one of the period's top architects, to do the job. Work continued until the mid-1880s, the final version being a grandiose Tudor-style mansion, whose black and white timber-framed gables are entirely out of place in the Northumbrian countryside. The interior is stuffed with Armstrong's furnishings and fittings, heavy dark pieces enlivened by the William Morris stained glass in the library and the dining-room inglenook. Armstrong was an avid innovator, fascinated by hydraulic engineering and by hydroelectric power. At Cragside he could indulge himself, damming the Debdon Burn to power several domestic appliances, like the dumb waiter in the massive kitchen, as well as heating his personal Turkish-style plunge bath and steam room. In 1880, he also supplied Cragside with electricity, making this the first house in the world to be lit by hydroelectric power. The remains of the original system – including the powerhouse and pumping station – are still visible in the **grounds**, which, together with the **formal gardens**, have longer opening hours (Easter–Oct Tues–Sun 10.30am–7pm or dusk; Nov to mid-Dec Wed–Sun 11am–4pm).

Brinkburn Priory

From Rothbury the B6344 runs four miles southeast through pretty **Coquetdale**, following the course of the river, to reach **Brinkburn Priory** (April–Sept daily 10am–6pm; Oct daily 10am–5pm; £1.70; EH), nestling in a loop of the Coquet. Founded as an Augustinian priory in 1135, its church – the only surviving building – was built fifty years later and it's this that provides the focus of interest today. Thoroughly but sympathetically restored in the nineteenth century, it's a superb example of northern Transitional architecture, featuring a fine Norman doorway and an echoing nave, empty save for a remarkable series of enormous contemporary wooden religious sculptures by Durham sculptor Fenwick Lawson. English Heritage is also responsible for the rambling manor house adjacent to the church. Built around 1810, but incorporating parts of the earlier monastic buildings, it was rebuilt by the great Newcastle architect John Dobson in the 1830s, and last lived in during the 1950s. It's now a rather forlorn ruin, though essential maintenance work has arrested its decline and the public is free to wander its beautifully proportioned halls.

Wooler and around

There's nothing immediately attractive about stone-terraced **WOOLER**, a grey one-street market town twenty miles north of Rothbury, though its proximity to the **Cheviot Hills** does much to lift the spirits. Local walks provide an introduction to the range, with a particular favourite being the one-mile hike to the top of Humbleton Hill, site of a battle in 1402 in which Hotspur (see p.743) inflicted heavy casualties on forces of the Douglas clan. But to get into the heart of the hills you'll have to tackle the trek to **The Cheviot** itself, seven miles to the southwest and 2674ft above sea level. Starting out from Wooler youth hostel, count on four hours up, a little less back – your reward, an utterly bleak spot with views, on a clear day, to the coast, the castles at Bamburgh and Dunstanburgh, and over to Holy Island. If you're fully prepared for a long day's walking, on the west side of the peak you can join the **Pennine Way** at Scotsman's cairn. Here, you're about seven miles south of the trail end at the Scottish village of **Kirk Yetholm**, where there's a youth hostel (T01573/420631, W www.syha.org.uk; closed Sept to mid-March), down a lane off the village green, and several B&Bs. Wooler is also a staging-post on **St Cuthbert's Way**, which runs west from the town to Kirk Yetholm and Melrose, and northeast to Holy Island.

Wooler's **bus station** is set back off the High Street. Over the road, the **tourist office** at 16 Market Place (Easter–Oct Mon–Sat 10am–1pm & 2–5pm, Sun 10am–2pm; T01668/282123) can help with walking information. There are a couple of good central **B&Bs**: *Tilldale House*, 34 High St (T01668/281450, W www.tilldalehouse.com; no credit cards; ❶), which has spacious en-suite rooms and serves a wide choice of evening meals; and *Winton House*, just off the High Street at 39 Glendale Rd (T01668/281362, W www.wintonhouse.ntb.org.uk; no credit cards; ❷; closed Dec–Feb), a stone-built Edwardian house with garden, owned by a friendly couple who can give information on local walks and provide a packed lunch, too. For a bit more luxury, try the ivy-encrusted *Tankerville Arms* on Cottage Road (T01668/281581, W www.tankervillehotel.co.uk; ❺), a seventeenth-century **coaching inn** just off the A697 below town, which has a good **restaurant** overlooking the attractive garden and a wide range of **bar meals**. Wooler also has a comfortable **youth hostel** at 30 Cheviot St (T01668/281365, W www.yha.org.uk), a five-minute walk up the hill from the bus station, as well as a **campsite**, *Highburn House* on Burnhouse Road (T01668/281344; closed Nov–Feb), just north of town, about half a mile from the bus station.

Chillingham

Six miles southeast of Wooler, and served by bus #470 towards Alnwick, the eccentricities of **Chillingham Castle** (May, June & Sept Mon & Wed–Sun noon–5pm; July & Aug daily noon–5pm; £4.50) provide a refreshing counterpoint to the tidiness of National Trust-restored stately homes. Starting from an eleventh-century tower, the impressive castle was augmented at regular intervals until 1873. For fifty years from 1933, however, Chillingham was largely left to the elements, until the present owner set about restoring it in his own individualistic way: rooms are decorated with all manner of historical flotsam to give an idea of how the place would have looked through the ages, while chatty guides tell tall tales of the castle and its visitors. In the grounds, you can look around a small Elizabethan topiary garden and take a mile-long walk through the woods to the lake. Several apartments within the castle, including the Elizabethan Long Gallery, are available for self-catering (℡01668/215359).

In 1220, the adjoining 365 acres of parkland was enclosed to protect the local wild cattle for hunting and food. And so the **Chillingham Wild Cattle**, a fierce, primeval herd, have remained to this day, cut off from mixing with domesticated breeds. It's possible to visit these unique relics, but only in the company of a warden and from a safe distance – bring binoculars if you can – as the animals are potentially dangerous and need to be protected from outside infection (April–Oct Mon & Wed–Sat 10am–noon & 2–5pm, Sun 2–5pm; £3; ℡01668/215250).

The Northumberland coast

The low-lying **Northumberland coast**, stretching 64 miles north from Newcastle to the Scottish border, boasts many of the region's principal attractions, but first you have to clear the disfigured landscape of the old Northumbrian coalfield. Beyond Amble you emerge into a pastoral landscape that spreads over the thirty-odd miles to Berwick-upon-Tweed. On the way there's a succession of mighty fortresses, beginning with **Warkworth Castle** and **Alnwick Castle**, former and present strongholds of the Percys, the county's biggest landowners. Further along, there's the formidable fastness of **Bamburgh** and then, last of all, the magnificent Elizabethan ramparts surrounding **Berwick-upon-Tweed**. In between you'll find splendid sandy beaches – notably at Warkworth, Bamburgh and the small resort of **Alnmouth** – as well as Lindisfarne monastery on **Holy Island** and the sea-bird and nature reserve of the **Farne Islands**.

Warkworth

WARKWORTH, a coastal hamlet set in a loop of the River Coquet a couple of miles from Amble, is best seen from the north, from where the greystone terraces of the long main street slope up towards the commanding remains of **Warkworth Castle** (daily: April–Sept 10am–6pm; Oct 10am–5pm; Nov–March 10am–1pm & 2–4pm; £2.50; EH). Enough remains of the outer wall to give a clear impression of the layout of the medieval bailey, but – apart from the well-preserved gatehouse through which the site is entered – nothing catches your attention as much as the **keep**. Mostly built in the fourteenth century, this three-storeyed structure, with its polygonal turrets and high central tower, has a honeycomb-like interior, a fine example of the designs developed by the castle-builders of Plantagenet England. It was here that most of the

Percy family, earls of Northumberland, chose to live throughout the fourteenth and fifteenth centuries. The main street sweeps down into the attractive village, flattening out at Dial Place before curving right to cross the River Coquet; just over the bridges – a modern affair flanked by a splendid medieval turreted span – a signposted quarter-mile lane leads to the **beach**, which stretches for five miles from Amble to Alnmouth. Back in Dial Place stands the church of **St Lawrence**, whose many Norman features include the impressive ribbed vaulting of the chancel. From the churchyard (or, further up, from below the castle), a delightful path heads the half-mile inland along the peaceful right bank of the Coquet to the little boat that shuttles visitors across to **Warkworth Hermitage** (April–Sept Wed & Sun 11am–5pm; £1.70; EH), hewn out of the cliff above the river sometime in the fourteenth century.

Warkworth is on the route of the **bus service** linking Alnwick, Alnmouth and Newcastle, and **buses** stop in Dial Place, near the church. For such a small village, Warkworth possesses a surprising number of **accommodation and eating** options. There are several B&Bs just on the other side of the Coquet bridges and handy for the beach, including *Beck'n'Call* (☎01665/711653; ❷). The top spot is the splendid *Sun Hotel*, 6 Castle Terrace (☎01665/711259; ❺), which commands fine views from its perch between the castle and the river, whether from the spacious, pine-furnished bedrooms, the restaurant which specializes in local fare, or the bar and beer garden. Good rooms are also available down the hill at the *Hermitage Inn* (☎01665/711258; ❷), a cosy place with well-kept beers and decent bar meals. At the *Greenhouse*, opposite on the corner of Dial Place (closed Tues & Sun eves), salmon kebabs, cassoulet, and other bistro favourites are served on stripped pine tables.

Alnmouth

It's just three miles north from Warkworth to the seaside resort of **ALN-MOUTH**, whose narrow, mostly nineteenth-century centre is strikingly situated on a steep spur of land between the wide sandy beach and the estuary of the Aln. Alnmouth was a busy and prosperous port up until 1806, when the sea, driven by a freakish gale, broke through to the river and changed its course, moving the estuary from the south to the north side of Church Hill and rendering the original harbour useless. Alnmouth never really recovered, though it has been a low-key holiday spot since Victorian times, as attested by the elegant seaside villas.

There are local bus services from Alnwick and Warkworth, while the regular Newcastle to Alnwick **bus** passes through Alnmouth and calls at its **train station** at Hipsburn, a mile and a half west of the centre. Most of the **accommodation** lies along or just off the main Northumberland Street. Best central B&B is *The Grange* opposite the church (☎01665/830401, ✉the grange .alnmouth@virgin.net; no credit cards; ❷), a reclusive stone house with garden, overlooking the river. A few yards further down Northumberland Street, at no. 56, the friendly *Beaches* (☎01665/830443; no credit cards; ❸) has huge en-suite rooms in a period stone cottage above a good restaurant (see below). A string of **pubs** along Northumberland Street also offers accommodation; the most reasonable is the *Saddle Hotel*, at no. 25 (☎01665/830476; ❸), whose spacious rooms have bath and TV, the top-floor ones enjoying (partial) sea views. The *Tea Cosy Tea Room*, at no. 23 (☎01665/830393), serves bistro **dinners** at weekends in summer, but the best choice is to eat at the oak-beamed *Beaches*, at no. 56 (Tues, Thurs & Fri eve, Sat & Sun lunch & eve), where meals of local cod, Northumbrian game casserole and the like go for around £15 a head; you can take your own wine.

Alnwick

The unassuming town of **ALNWICK** (pronounced "Annick"), thirty miles north of Newcastle and four miles inland from Alnmouth, is renowned for its castle – seat of the dukes of Northumberland – which overlooks the River Aln immediately to the north of the town centre. Alnwick itself is an appealing market town of cobbled streets and Georgian houses, centred on the old cross in Market Place, site of a weekly market (Saturdays) since the thirteenth century.

The Percys – raised to the dukedom of Northumberland in 1750 – have owned the **Castle** (Easter–Oct daily 11am–5pm; £6.75; ⓦ www.alnwickcastle.com) since 1309, when Henry de Percy reinforced the original Norman keep and remodelled its curtain wall. In the eighteenth century, the castle was badly in need of a refit, so the first duke had the interior refurbished by Robert Adam in an extravagant Gothic style – which in turn was supplanted by the gaudy Italianate decoration preferred by the fourth duke in the 1850s. Major building work is again under way, to turn twelve acres of the grounds into an ambitious contemporary water **garden** (ⓦ www.alnwickgarden.com), complete with interactive water displays, sculptures, maze and topiary walks; with some parts of the lengthy project already finished, it's possible to view the state of play by becoming a Friend of the Alnwick Garden (£10), which entitles you to visit as often as you like (daily 10am–5pm).

Entry to the castle is through the carriageway to the right of the fourteenth-century barbican, whose sturdy battlements sport a number of stone soldiers, a piece of eighteenth-century flummery replacing the figurines of medieval times, set up there to ward off the evil eye. The dark and drab entrance hall of the keep leads to the **grand staircase**, a marble pomposity that climbs up to the guard chamber, whose Renaissance-style decor, from the mosaic floor to the stucco ceiling, is typical of the work of the Italian craftsmen hired by the fourth duke. The most lavish decoration is in the **red drawing room**, where the rich polygonal panels of the ceiling bear down on damask-covered walls and some magnificent ebony cabinets rescued from Versailles during the French Revolution. Each room displays part of the duke's extensive collection of paintings, including pieces by Canaletto, Titian, Tintoretto, Van Dyck and Turner. Three of the perimeter towers contain **museum collections** – the Regimental Museum of the Royal Northumberland Fusiliers in the Abbot's Tower, early British and Roman finds in the Postern Tower, and an exhibition dedicated to the Percy Tenantry Volunteers, a private force raised by the second duke during the Napoleonic Wars, in the Constable's Tower – but the bucolic garden walks and Capability Brown-designed **grounds** are a more profitable use of time once you've seen the main rooms.

From outside the castle, it's a few minutes' walk north along Bailiffgate to the gates of **Hulne Park**, a substantial tract of hilly woodland. Deep inside the park, a three-mile hike from the entrance, are the rusticated remains of **Hulne Priory**, a thirteenth-century Carmelite monastery built in a lovely spot above the north bank of the River Aln. There's not much else to see in Alnwick, except for the grandiose **Percy Tenantry Column** just to the southeast of the centre along Bondgate Without. This 75-foot high column, surmounted by the Percy lion with its characteristic horizontal tail, was built by the tenants of the second duke in 1816 after he had reduced their rents by 25 percent. As it turned out, their humble gratitude was somewhat premature. The third duke promptly bumped the rents up again and locals wryly renamed their monument the "Farmers' Folly". A little further on, housed in the listed Victorian train station, **Barter Books** (ⓦ www.barterbooks.co.uk), one of the largest second-hand bookshops in England, is well worth a call; it also offers internet access.

Alnwick **bus station** is on Clayport Street, a couple of minutes' walk west of the Market Place, where you'll find the **tourist office**, in the arcaded Shambles (July & Aug Mon–Sat 9am–6pm, Sun 9am–5pm; April–June & Sept Mon–Sat 9am–5pm, Sun 10am–4pm; Oct–March Mon–Fri 9am–5pm, Sat 10am–4pm; ℡01665/510665). Several **accommodation** options cluster round the gatehouse at the end of Bondgate. Here, the welcoming *Tower Guest Rooms*, above the restaurant of the same name at 10 Bondgate Within (℡01665/603888, ⓦwww.hotspur-tower.com; ❸), stands out for its bright, tasteful, en-suite rooms and hearty breakfasts. Among other cheaper places beyond the gate, you'll find the cosy, ivy-clad *Bondgate House Hotel* at 20 Bondgate Without (℡01665/602025, ⓔkenforbes@lineone.net; ❷). Alnwick's main hotel is the *White Swan*, on Bondgate Within (℡01665/602109; ❺), where you might want to pop in at least for coffee – there's a comfortable lounge, while the hotel's fine panelled dining room was swiped from an old ocean liner, the *Olympic*, the twin of the *Titanic*. You can **camp** at *Alnwick Rugby Club* in Greensfield Park (℡01665/510109; closed Nov–March), a little way south of the centre but walkable.

For evening **meals**, try the *Gate Bistro*, 14 Bondgate Within (closed Mon) – next to the *White Swan Hotel* – which serves some interesting specials, such as Lamb Percy, shoulder cooked with thyme, juniper and red wine. The *Tower Restaurant* next door has a reassuring, pine-furnished feel and serves everything from breakfast to licensed meals, including plenty of vegetarian and chargrilled options. In the other direction, heading towards the castle, *Benvenuti* is a reliable, traditional Italian occupying an atmospheric eighteenth-century town house on Narrowgate (closed Sun). The "Dirty Bottles" in *Ye Olde Cross*'s window on Narrowgate have supposedly not been moved for two centuries, since the person who put them there dropped down dead immediately afterwards. Check to see what's on at the **Alnwick Playhouse**, just through the arch on Bondgate Without (℡01665/510785, ⓦwww.alnwickplayhouse.co.uk), a venue for theatre, music and film throughout the year.

Craster, Dunstanburgh Castle and Beadnell

Heading northeast out of Alnwick along the B1340, it's a six-mile hop to the region's kipper capital, the tiny fishing village of **CRASTER**, perched above its minuscule harbour. There's not a great deal to make you stop long, but you can buy kippers here at Robson's factory and have a pot of tea in the *Bark Pots*. Even better is the *Jolly Fisherman*, the **pub** above the harbour, with sea views from its back window and famously good crab sandwiches. Most spectacularly, however, the village provides access to **Dunstanburgh Castle** (April–Sept daily 10am–6pm; Oct daily 10am–5pm; Nov–March Wed–Sun 10am–4pm; £1.90; NT & EH), whose shattered medieval ruins occupy a magnificent promontory about thirty minutes' windy walk up the coast. Originally built in the fourteenth century, parts of the surrounding walls survive – offering heart-stopping views down to the crashing sea below – though the dominant feature is the massive keep-gatehouse which stands out from miles around on the bare coastal spur.

Half a dozen **buses** a day (the #501/#401) run to Craster from Alnwick, a half-hour journey; the service continues to Beadnell, Seahouses and Bamburgh. There's a small **tourist office** in the village car park (Easter–Oct daily 9.30am–4.30pm; Nov–Easter Sat & Sun 10am–4pm; ℡01665/576007).

The best place to stay hereabouts is **BEADNELL**, nine miles up the coast from Craster, with a couple of fine beaches and the best **windsurfing** on the northeast's coast – boards can be rented from the Outdoor Trust shed (£10/hr, £30/day; ☎01665/721241; closed Nov–Feb), along with kayaks, bodyboards and sailing dinghies. Among several **accommodation** options, the excellent *Beach Court* on Harbour Road (☎01665/720225, ⓦwww.beachcourt.com; ❸) is a distinctive guest house right next to the shore, with sea views and three lovely rooms. There are several local **campsites**, including *Dunstan Hill* (☎01665/576310; closed Nov–Feb), a mile inland from Dunstanburgh castle, close to the B1339.

Seahouses and the Farne Islands

From Beadnell, it's three miles north to **SEAHOUSES**, a desultory fishing-port-cum-resort that's the embarkation point for **boat trips** to the windswept and treeless **Farne Islands**, a rocky archipelago lying a few miles offshore. Owned by the National Trust and maintained as a nature reserve, the Farnes are the summer home of many species of migrating seabirds, especially puffins, guillemots, terns, eider ducks and kittiwakes, and home to the only grey seal colony on the English coastline. To protect the wildlife, only two of the islands are open to visitors: **Inner Farne** (April–Sept daily; landing fee £4.20) and **Staple Island** (same months & prices). The crossing can be rough, but the islands have a wild beauty that makes it all worthwhile, and on Inner Farne you can also visit a tiny, restored fourteenth-century chapel built in honour of St Cuthbert, who spent much of his life here. Weather permitting, several boat owners operate daily **excursions**, usually starting at around 10am: Billy Shiels (Easter–Oct; ☎01665/720308, ⓦwww.farne-islands.com), the best of the bunch, runs a varied programme, from two-and-a-half-hour **cruises** round either island (£8), to all-day trips landing at both (£15); all trips also visit the grey seal colonies off the islands. For more information, call the **tourist office** (daily: April–Oct 10am–5pm; ☎01665/720884), in the Seafield Road car park above the harbour, or the **National Trust Shop**, 16 Main St (☎01665/721099), across from the *Olde Ship*, 9 Main St (☎01665/720200; ❹), easily the most atmospheric place in Seahouses to stay, eat and drink.

Bamburgh

Flanking a triangular green in the lee of its castle, three miles north of Seahouses, the tiny village of **BAMBURGH** is only a five-minute walk from two splendid sandy beaches, backed by rolling, tufted dunes. From the sands **Bamburgh Castle** (April–Oct daily 11am–5pm; £4.50; ⓦwww.bamburgh-castle.com) is a spectacular sight, its elongated battlements crowning a formidable basalt crag high above the beach. This beautiful spot was first fortified by the Celts, but its heyday was as an Anglo-Saxon stronghold, one-time capital of Northumbria and the protector of the preserved head and hand of St Oswald, the seventh-century king who invited St Aidan over from Iona to convert his subjects. Rotted by centuries of seaspray and buffeted by winter storms, Bamburgh Castle struggled on until 1894, when its new owner, Lord Armstrong (see p.744), demolished most of the structure to replace it with a cumbersome castle-mansion. The focal point of the new building was the King's Hall, a soulless teak-ceilinged affair of colossal dimensions, whose main redeeming feature is an exquisite collection of Fabergé stone animal carvings. In the ground floor of the keep, the stone-vaulted ceiling maintains its Norman appearance, making a suitable arena for a display of fetters and man-traps.

Bamburgh is also the home of the **Grace Darling Museum** (Easter to Oct Mon–Sat 10am–5pm, Sun noon–5pm; donation requested), which celebrates the daring sea rescue accomplished by Grace and her lighthouseman father, William, in September, 1838. It began when a gale dashed the steamship *Forfarshire* against the rocks of the Farne Islands. Nine passengers struggled onto a reef, where they were subsequently saved by the Darlings, who left the safety of the lighthouse to row out to them. *The Times* trumpeted Grace's bravery, offers of marriage and requests for locks of her hair streamed into the Darlings' lighthouse home and for the rest of her brief life Grace was plagued by unwanted visitors – she died of tuberculosis aged 26 in 1842. The museum details the rescue and displays the fragile boat the Darlings used; in the churchyard of thirteenth-century **St Aidan's** opposite is the pompous Gothic Revival memorial that covers Grace's body.

A regular **bus** service links Alnwick and Berwick-upon-Tweed with Bamburgh, stopping on Front Street by the green. There are several places **to stay and eat**, including the highly appealing *Lord Crewe Arms Hotel*, Front Street (T01668/214243, Wwww.lordcrewe.com; ❹; closed Dec–Feb), a comfortable old inn with oak beams, open fires and a moderately priced restaurant. Nearby *Green Gates*, 34 Front St (T01668/214535; no credit cards; ❷), offers three rooms with castle views, superior breakfasts and bicycle rental. At the top of the village green, the *Victoria Hotel* (T01668/214431, Wwww.victoriahotel.net; ❺) has been tastefully refurbished, and operates a brasserie with a varied Modern British menu and a pleasant conservatory. Other food options comprise a couple of tearooms – including the very twee and traditional *Copper Kettle* – a small deli for picnics and a bucket-and-spade general store.

Holy Island

There's something rather menacing about the approach to **Holy Island**, past the barnacle-encrusted marker poles that line the causeway. The danger of drowning is real enough if you ignore the safe crossing times posted at the start of the three-mile trip across the tidal flats. (The island is cut off for about five hours every day, so to avoid a tedious delay consult the **tide timetables** at one of the region's tourist offices or in the local newspapers.) Once here, it's easy to picture the furious Viking hordes sweeping across Holy Island, giving no quarter to the monks at this quiet outpost of early Christianity. Today's sole village is plain in the extreme, which doesn't deter summer day-trippers from clogging the car parks as soon as the causeway is open. But Holy Island has a distinctive and isolated atmosphere, especially out of season.

Once known as **Lindisfarne**, Holy Island has an illustrious history. It was here that St Aidan of Iona founded a monastery at the invitation of King Oswald of Northumbria in 634. The monks quickly evangelized the northeast and established a reputation for scholarship and artistry, the latter exemplified by the **Lindisfarne Gospels**, the apotheosis of Celtic religious art, now kept in the British Museum. The monastery had sixteen bishops in all, the most celebrated being **St Cuthbert**, who only accepted the job after Ecgfrith, another Northumbrian king, pleaded with him. But Cuthbert never settled here and, within two years, he was back in his hermit's cell on the Farne Islands, where he died in 687. His colleagues rowed the body back to Lindisfarne, which became a place of pilgrimage until 875, when the monks abandoned the island in fear of marauding Vikings, taking Cuthbert's remains with them – the first part of the saint's long posthumous journey to Durham. In 1082 Lindisfarne, renamed Holy Island, was colonized by Benedictines from Durham, but the monastery was a shadow of its former self, a minor religious house with only a handful of attendant monks, the last of whom was evicted at the Dissolution.

Just off the village green, the pinkish sandstone ruins of **Lindisfarne Priory** (daily: Easter–Sept 10am–6pm; Oct 10am–5pm; Nov–Easter 10am–4pm; £2.90; EH) are from the Benedictine foundation. Enough survives to provide a clear impression of the original structure, notably the tight Romanesque arches of the nave and the gravity-defying stonework of the central tower's last remaining arch. Behind lie the scant remains of the monastic buildings while adjacent is the mostly thirteenth-century church of **St Mary the Virgin**, whose delightful churchyard overlooks the ruins. The **museum** (entrance included in priory fee) features a collection of incised stones that constitute all that remains of the first monastery. The finest of them is a round-headed tombstone showing armed Northumbrians on one side, and kneeling figures before the Cross on the other – presumably a propagandist's view of the beneficial effects of Christianity.

Stuck on a small pyramid of rock half a mile away from the village, past the dock and along the seashore, **Lindisfarne Castle** (April–Oct Mon–Thurs, Sat & Sun, hours according to time of low tide but always including noon–3pm; £4.20; NT; ☎01289/389244) was built in the middle of the sixteenth century to protect the island's harbour from the Scots. It was, however, merely a decaying shell when Edward Hudson, the founder of *Country Life* magazine, stumbled across it in 1901. Hudson bought the castle and turned it into a holiday home to designs by Edwin Lutyens, who used the irregular levels of the building to create the L-shaped living quarters that survive today. The two historic sites are all that most people bother with, but a **walk** around the island's perimeter is a fine way to spend a couple of hours. Most of the northwestern portion of the island is maintained as a **nature reserve**: from a bird hide you can spot terns and plovers, and then plod through the dunes and grasses to your heart's content. Back in the village, the **Lindisfarne Heritage Centre** (daily 10am–5.30pm, though times may vary according to the tides; £2; ☎01289/389004, ⓦwww.lindisfarne-heritage-centre.org), occupying a former coaching inn on the main street, holds computer terminals giving you a virtual opportunity to see the major illustrated pages of the Lindisfarne Gospels, and details the wildlife as well as the former living and working conditions on the island.

Practicalities

The #477 **bus** from Berwick-upon-Tweed to Holy Island is something of a law unto itself given the interfering tides, but basically service is daily in August and twice weekly (Wed & Sat) the rest of the year. Departure times (and sometimes days) vary with the tides, and the journey takes thirty minutes; local tourist offices can provide the latest details. Throughout the year, you can also ask to be dropped off by the Berwick–Newcastle buses at Beal, though from here you face a four-mile walk to the island. Phone Douglas's **taxi** service on the island if you can't face the hike (☎01289/389236).

The island is short on places **to stay** and you should make an advance booking, whenever you visit. Two good places are the *Open Gate*, on Marygate (☎01289/389222; ❸), which offers comfortable rooms in a sixteenth-century listed building; or the cheaper, and very friendly, *Britannia House* (☎01289/389218; ❷; closed Nov–Feb), just by the green. Among the pubs, best is the refurbished *Ship* on Marygate (☎01289/389311; ❷; closed Jan). Camping isn't allowed anywhere on the island. Options for **eating and drinking** are limited to a couple of tearooms and the hostelries, of which the *Ship* is again the pick, with a garden and a cosy panelled bar, good-value meals and well-kept real ales.

Berwick-upon-Tweed and around

Before the union of the English and Scottish crowns in 1603, **BERWICK-UPON-TWEED**, some twelve miles north of Holy Island, was the quintessential frontier town, changing hands no fewer than fourteen times between 1174 and 1482, when the Scots finally ceded the stronghold to the English. Interminable cross-border warfare ruined Berwick's economy, turning the prosperous Scottish port of the thirteenth century into an impoverished garrison town, which the English forcibly cut off from its natural trading hinterland up the River Tweed. By the late sixteenth century, Berwick's fortifications were in a dreadful state of repair and Elizabeth I, apprehensive of the resurgent alliance between France and Scotland, had the place rebuilt in line with the latest principles of military architecture.

The new design recognized the technological development of artillery, which had rendered the traditional high stone wall obsolete. Consequently, Berwick's **ramparts** – one and a half miles long and still in pristine condition – are no more than twenty feet high but incredibly thick: a facing of ashlared stone protects ten to twelve feet of rubble, which, in turn, backs up against a vast quantity of earth. Further protected by ditches on three sides and the Tweed on the fourth, the walls are strengthened by immense bastions, whose arrowhead-shape ensured that every part of the wall could be covered by fire. Begun in 1558, the defences were completed after eleven years at a cost of £128,000, more than Elizabeth paid for all her other fortifications put together. And, as it turned out, it was all a waste of time and money: the French didn't attack and, once England and Scotland were united, Berwick was stuck with a white elephant.

The Town

Today, the easy **stroll** along the top of the ramparts offers a succession of fine views out to sea, across the Tweed and over the orange-tiled rooftops of a town that's distinguished by its elegant Georgian mansions. These, dating from Berwick's resurgence as a seaport between 1750 and 1820, are the town's most attractive feature, with the tapering **Lions' House**, on Windmill Hill, and the daintily decorated facades of **Quay Walls**, beside the river, of particular note. The three bridges spanning the Tweed are worth a second look too – the huge arches of the **Royal Border Railway Bridge**, built in the manner of a Roman aqueduct by Robert Stephenson in the 1840s, contrasting with the desultory concrete of the **Royal Tweed**, completed in 1928 and the modest seventeenth-century **Berwick Bridge**.

Within the ramparts, the Berwick skyline is punctured by the stumpy spire of the eighteenth-century **Town Hall** at the bottom of Marygate, right at the heart of the compact centre. This retains its original jailhouse, now housing the **Cell Block Museum** (Easter–Oct Mon–Fri tours at 10.30am & 2pm; £1.20) with its tales of crime and punishment in Berwick. From here, it's a couple of minutes' walk along Church Street to **Holy Trinity Church**, one of the few churches built during the Commonwealth, the absence of a tower supposedly reflecting the wishes of Cromwell, who found them irreligious. Opposite the church, the elongated **Barracks** (Easter–Sept daily 10am–6pm; Oct daily 10am–5pm; Nov–Easter Wed–Sun 10am–4pm; £2.70; EH) date from the early eighteenth century and were in use until 1964, when the King's Own Scottish Borderers regiment decamped. Inside, there's a predictable regimental museum, as well as the By Beat of Drum exhibition which traces the life of the British infantryman from the sixteenth to the nineteenth century. If all this sounds worthy but dull, it is – rescued only by the temporary summer exhibitions of contemporary art in the **Gymnasium Gallery** and by a superior borough museum and art gallery, sited in the so-called **Clock Block**. Geared up for school parties, the museum features imaginative dioramas, recordings and displays of local traditional life, even a model of a local clergyman haranguing visitors from his pulpit. Upstairs is the kernel of the gallery's fine and applied art collection, the gift of the shipping magnate William Burrell, who lived near Berwick in his retirement.

Practicalities

From Berwick **train station** it's ten minutes' walk down Castlegate to the town centre. Most regional **buses** stop closer in on Golden Square (where Castlegate meets Marygate), on the approach to the Royal Tweed Bridge, though some may also stop in front of the station. The helpful **tourist office** is at 106 Marygate (Easter–Oct Mon–Sat 10am–6pm, Sun 11am–3pm; Nov–Easter Mon–Sat 10am–4pm; ℡01289/330733, ⓦwww.berwickonline.org.uk). For local **bike rental**, call Brilliant Bicycles, 17a Bridge St (℡01289/331476) – you can get details of a scenic route to Holy Island either here or from the tourist office (24 miles return).

In the centre, there's dorm **accommodation** at *Berwick Backpackers* in a well-maintained house at 56–58 Bridge St (℡01289/331481, ⓦwww.berwick-backpackers.co.uk). A highly recommended B&B is *No.1 Sallyport*, 41 Bridge St (℡01289/308827; ❸), a seventeenth-century house next to the city walls (above the Bridge Street Bookshop) with elegant en-suite rooms. Other good options include *Clovelly House*, 58 West St (℡01289/302337, ⓦwww.clovelly53.freeserve.co.uk; ❷), the *Riverview Guest House*, 11 Quay Walls (℡01289/306295; ❷), and *Dervaig Guest House*, 1 North Rd (℡01289/307378, ⒺLdervaig@btinternet.com; ❷). The best central hotel is the *King's Arms*, Hide Hill (℡01289/307454, Ⓔking's_arms.hotel@virgin.net; ❺), one of the myriad English coaching inns in which Charles Dickens is supposed to have slept and lectured. Across Berwick Bridge in Tweedmouth, you can't beat the delightful *Old Vicarage Guest House*, a spacious Victorian villa at 24 Church Rd (℡01289/306909; ❶).

For daytime **snacks**, **coffee** and **lunches**, head for *Popinjays* on Hide Hill or the café on the ground floor of the Town Hall. Berwick's selection of **restaurants** will hardly set the pulse racing – try the *Royal Garden*, a Chinese restaurant in a rather grand converted pub at 35 Marygate, or the *Magna Tandoori*, 39 Bridge St – or head for *Corvi's*, a sparkling chippie with sit-down tables on West Street. The cosy *Barrels Ale House*, 59–61 Bridge St, at the foot of the Berwick Bridge (℡01289/308013, ⓦwww.thebarrelsalehouse.com), has guest beers and an interesting programme of live music. The Maltings on Eastern Lane is Berwick's **arts centre** (℡01289/330999, ⓦwww.maltingsberwick.co.uk), with a year-round programme of music, theatre, comedy, film and dance, and river views from its licensed café.

Norham Castle

It's well worth catching the #23 bus from Berwick for the ten-mile trip west to the atmospheric ruins of **Norham Castle**, set in an inspiring location on the south bank of the Tweed (April–Sept daily 10am–6pm; £1.90; EH). Its surviving pink sandstone walls and foursquare keep, celebrated in paint by J.M.W. Turner and in verse in Sir Walter Scott's *Marmion*, stand out above the flat farming country, the trees lining the green-grassed ramparts stripped bare by the winds in winter and providing a leafy curtain in summer. It was considered one of the strongest of the border castles, but James IV of Scotland nevertheless engineered its capture before meeting his nemesis at Flodden Field.

Travel details

Buses

For information on all local and national bus services, contact Traveline: ☎ 0870/608 2 608 (daily 7am–9pm), ⓦ www.traveline.org.uk. For details of the complicated bus services along Hadrian's Wall, see p.736.

Trains

For information on all local and national rail services, contact National Rail Enquiries: ☎ 08457/48 49 50, ⓦ www.nationalrail.co.uk.

Darlington to: Bishop Auckland (every 1–2hr; 30min).

Durham to: Darlington (every 30min; 20min); London (hourly; 3hr); Newcastle (every 30min; 20min); York (hourly; 50min).

Hexham to: Carlisle (hourly; 1hr); Haltwhistle (hourly; 20min); Newcastle (hourly; 40min).

Middlesbrough to: Durham (hourly; 50min); Grosmont, for North York Moors Railway (see p.692: Mon–Sat 4 daily; 1hr); Newcastle (hourly; 1hr 10min); Saltburn (hourly; 40min); Whitby (Mon–Sat 4 daily; 1hr 30min).

Newcastle to: Alnmouth (Mon–Sat 9–10 daily, Sun 3 daily; 30min); Berwick-upon-Tweed (hourly; 45min); Carlisle (hourly; 1hr 30min); Corbridge (hourly; 40min); Durham (every 30min; 20min); Edinburgh (hourly; 1hr 30min); Haltwhistle (hourly; 1hr); Hexham (hourly; 40min); London (hourly; 2hr 45min–3hr 30min); York (hourly; 1hr).

Wales

Wales

⑭ South Wales 759–810

⑮ Mid-Wales 811–856

⑯ North Wales 857–898

South Wales

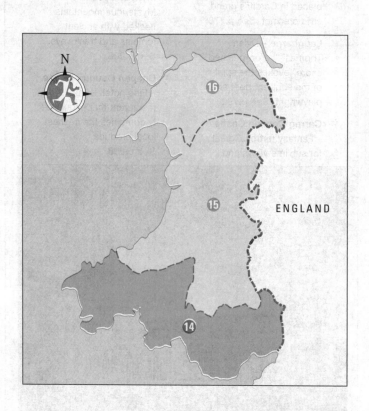

CHAPTER 14

Highlights

* **Blaenafon** – Fascinating ironworking town plus deep mine museum. See p.769

* **National Museum of Wales** – From exquisite art to rugged tales of Welsh history, beautifully placed in Cardiff's grand civic precinct. See p.778

* **Laugharne** – Dylan Thomas' "heron-priested shore" evokes the spirit of the ebullient poet and playwright. See p.792

* **Carreg Cennan Castle** – Fantasy fortress, great for sublime views and exploration. See p.795

* **St David's** – Inspirational village with a splendid cathedral and heart-racing boat trips out to offshore islands. See p.804

* **Mynydd Preseli** – Mysterious mountains flecked with ancient remains and trackways. See p.808

* **Cnapan Country House** – Fine hotel, with a restaurant that exquisitely combines the freshest local produce. See p.808

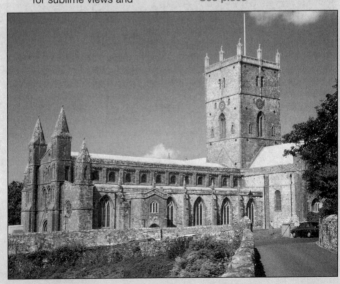

14

South Wales

The most heavily populated, and by far the most anglicized, part of Wales is the **south**. This is a region of distinct character, whether in the resurgent seaport cities of Cardiff and Swansea, the mining-scarred Valleys or the beauty of the Glamorgan, Carmarthenshire and Pembrokeshire coasts. Unlike the rest of Wales, transport connections are fast and frequent, making this region by far the easiest Welsh stop for those on a limited itinerary.

Monmouthshire, the easternmost county in Wales, abuts the English border and contains the full span of south Welsh life, from the bucolic charms of the **River Wye** and **Tintern Abbey**, to **Newport**, Wales's third largest conurbation, near the remains of an extensive Roman settlement at **Caerleon**. West and north are the world-famous **Valleys**. Although all but one of the coal mines have closed, the area is still one of tight-knit towns, with a rich working-class heritage that displays itself in some excellent museums and colliery tours, such as **Big Pit** at Blaenafon and the **Rhondda Heritage Park** in Trehafod. The valleys course down to the great ports of the coast, which once shipped Wales's products all over the world. The greatest of them all was **Cardiff**, now Wales's upbeat capital and an essential stop. Further west is Wales's second city, **Swansea** – rougher, tougher and less anglicized than the capital. It sits on an impressive arc of coast that shelves round to the delightful **Gower Peninsula**, one of the country's favourite playgrounds that juts out into the sea like a mini-Wales of grand beaches, rocky headlands, bracken heaths and ruined castles.

Too many people rush from here straight to the coastal national park of Pembrokeshire, missing out **Carmarthenshire**. Of all the routes that spoke out of the county town of **Carmarthen**, the most glorious is the winding road to **Llandeilo** along the **Tywi Valley**, past ruined hilltop forts and two of the country's finest gardens. Immediately west sits Wales's most impressively sited castle at **Carreg Cennen**, high up on the dizzy rock plug of the Black Mountain.

The wide sands fringing Carmarthen Bay stretch towards the popular seaside resort of **Tenby**, a major stop on the 186-mile **Pembrokeshire Coast Path**. The rutted coastline of **St Bride's Bay** is the most glorious part of the coastal walk, which leads north to brush past the impeccable mini-city of **St David's**, whose exquisite cathedral shelters in its own protective hollow. Nearby are plenty of opportunities for spectacular coast and hill walks, dinghy crossings to local islands and numerous other outdoor activities.

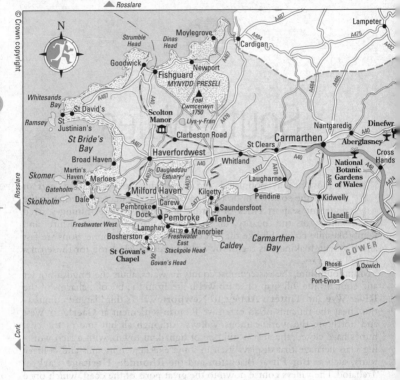
© Crown copyright

The Wye Valley

Perhaps the most anglicized corner of Wales, the **Wye Valley**, along with the rest of Monmouthshire, was only finally recognized as part of Wales in the local government reorganization of 1974. Before then, the county was officially included as part of neither England nor Wales, so that maps were frequently headlined "Wales and Monmouthshire". Most of the rest of Monmouthshire is firmly and redoubtably Welsh, but the woodlands and hills by the meandering River Wye have more in common with the landscape over the border. The two main centres are **Chepstow**, with its massive castle radiating an awesome strength high above the muddy flats and waters of the river estuary; and the spruce, old-fashioned town of **Monmouth**, sixteen miles upstream. Six miles north of Chepstow lie the inspirational ruins of the Cistercian **Tintern Abbey**.

Chepstow and around

Of all the places that call themselves "the gateway to Wales", **CHEPSTOW** (Cas-Gwent) has probably the greatest claim, situated on the western bank of the River Wye just over a mile from where its tidal waters flow out into the muddy Severn estuary. Chepstow is a sturdy place robbed of the immediate charm of many other Welsh market towns by soulless modern developments. Nonetheless, there's an identifiably medieval street plan hemmed in by the thir-

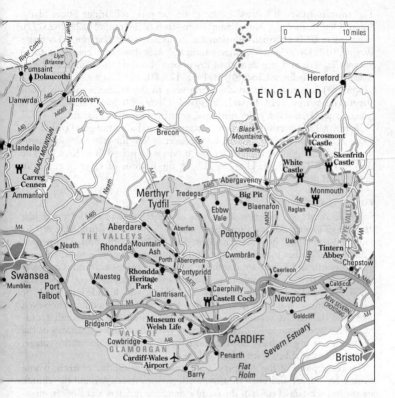

teenth-century **Port Wall**, which encases a tight loop of the River Wye and the strategically sited **Chepstow Castle** (June–Sept daily 9.30am–6pm; April, May & Oct daily 9.30am–5pm; Nov–March Mon–Sat 9.30am–4pm, Sun 11am–4pm; £3). Guarding one of the most important routes into Wales, Chepstow was the first stone castle to be built in Britain, the Great Tower keep being built in 1067 to help subdue the restless Welsh. The Lower Ward is the largest of the three enclosures and dates mainly from the thirteenth century. Here you'll find the **Great Hall**, the home of a wide-ranging exhibition on the history of the castle, with particular emphasis on the English Civil War years, when Royalist Chepstow was twice besieged. Twelfth-century defences separate the Lower Ward from the Middle Ward, which is dominated by the still imposing ruins of the **Great Tower**. Beyond this is the far narrower Upper Ward, which leads up to the Barbican **watchtower** from where there are superb views looking down the cliff to the river estuary.

Opposite is the **Chepstow Museum** (Mon–Sat 11am–1pm & 2–5pm, Sun 2–5pm; £1) containing nostalgic photographs and paintings of the trades supported in the past by the River Wye, and recording Chepstow's brief life in the early part of this century as a shipbuilding centre.

Practicalities

Chepstow's **train station** is five minutes' walk to the south of the High Street; its **bus station** is behind the shops on the other side of the western Town Gate.

The **tourist office** is located in the castle car park, off Bridge Street (daily: Easter–Oct 10am–6pm; Nov–Easter 10am–1pm & 2–4pm; ℡01291/623772). Inexpensive B&B **accommodation** can be found at *Mrs Batchelor*, 7 Lancaster Way (℡01291/626344; ➊), fifteen minutes' walk from the centre of town towards Tintern and, a mile east of town, over the Wye, the wonderful *Upper Sedbury House*, Sedbury Lane (℡01291/627173; ➊). *The George Hotel* (℡01291/625363; ➎) is a grand old coaching inn next to the medieval gate on Moor Street. The nearest YHA **hostel**, *St Briavels Castle* (℡01594/530272, Ⓦwww .yha.org.uk; ➊), is seven miles northeast, over the border in England.

Chepstow has a handful of decent **restaurants** and a host of good **pubs**. *The Grape Escape*, on St Mary's Street, by the river, is best for reasonably inexpensive dining. For gourmet meals, try the moderately priced *Wye Knot*, on The Back (℡01291/622929). The *Five Alls*, at the bottom of High Street, is an earthy local pub.

Tintern Abbey

Six miles north of Chepstow, along one of the River Wye's most spectacular stretches, **Tintern Abbey** (June–Sept daily 9.30am–6pm; April, May & Oct daily 9.30am–5pm; Nov–March Mon–Sat 9.30am–4pm, Sun 11am–4pm; £2.50; CADW) has inspired writers and painters for over two hundred years – Wordsworth and Turner among them. Such is the place's enormous popularity, however, that it's advisable to go out of season or at either end of the day when the hordes have thinned out. The abbey was founded in 1131 by Cistercian monks from Normandy. Most of the remaining buildings, however, date from the massive rebuilding and expansion plan in the fourteenth century, when Tintern was at its mightiest. Its survival after the depredations of the Dissolution is largely thanks to its remoteness, as there were no nearby villages ready to use the abbey stone for rebuilding.

The centrepiece of the complex is the magnificent Gothic **church**, whose remarkable tracery and intricate stonework remains intact. Around the church are the less substantial ruins of the monks' domestic quarters and cloister, mostly reduced to one-storey rubble. The course of the abbey's waste disposal system can be seen in the Great Drain, an irregular channel that links kitchens, toilets and the Infirmary with the nearby Wye. The **Novices' Hall** lies handily close to the Warming House, which together with the kitchen and Infirmary would have been the only heated parts of the abbey, suggesting that novices might have gained a falsely favourable impression of monastic life before taking their final vows.

Monmouth and around

Enclosed on three sides by the rivers Wye and Monnow, **MONMOUTH** (Trefynwy), fifteen miles north of Chepstow, retains some of its quiet charm as an important border post and county town, and makes a good base for a drive – or a long hike – around the **Three Castles** of the pastoral border country to the north.

The centre of the town is **Agincourt Square**, a handsome open space at the top of the wide, shop-lined Monnow Street, which descends gently to the thirteenth-century bridge over the River Monnow. The cobbled square is dominated by the arched, Georgian **Shire Hall**, in which is embedded an eighteenth-century statue of the Monmouth-born King Henry V, victor of the Battle of Agincourt, in 1415. In front is the pompous statue of another local, the Honourable Charles Stewart Rolls, co-founder of Rolls-Royce and, in 1910, the first man to pilot a double-flight over the English Channel. Almost opposite Shire Hall is **Castle Hill**, which you can walk up to glimpse some of the scant ruins of the **castle**, founded in 1068. A small **regimental museum** (April–Oct daily 2–5pm; Nov–March Sat & Sun 2–4pm; free) is the only part that can be visited. More inspiring is the **canoe rental** for trips up the Wye, available at the Monmouth Canoe & Activity Centre (℡01600/713461) in Castle Yard, Old Dixton Road.

Priory Street leads north from Agincourt Square to the market hall, where the **Nelson Museum** (Mon–Sat 10am–1pm & 2–5pm, Sun 2–5pm; £1) attempts to portray the life of one of the most successful sea-going Britons through use of the Admiral's personal artefacts, collected by Charles Rolls' mother, who was an admirer. At the very bottom of Monnow Street, the road narrows to squeeze into the confines of the seven-hundred-year-old **Monnow bridge**, crowned with its hulking stone gate of 1262, that served both as a means of defence for the town and a toll-collection point.

The **bus station** is behind the Kwik Save supermarket, at the bottom of Monnow Street. The **tourist office** is in the Shire Hall, Agincourt Square (daily: April–Oct 10am–6pm; Nov–March 9.30am–5pm; ℡01600/713899). **Accommodation** in town is thin on the ground: try the simple but good *Burton Guesthouse*, on St James Square (℡01600/714958; ❶), the intimate *Riverside Hotel* on Cinderhill Street, over the Monnow Bridge (℡01600/715577; ❸), or the excellent *Church Farm Guesthouse*, two miles south in the village of Mitchel Troy (℡01600/712176; ❷). The nearest tent-friendly **campsites** are both on Drybridge Street (through Monnow Bridge then right): the *Monnow Bridge* (℡01600/714004), behind the *Three Horseshoes* pub, and the slightly pricier *Monmouth Caravan Park* (℡01600/714745), a quarter of a mile beyond.

Inexpensive daytime **eating** can be had at either *Maltsters Coffee Shop*, on St Mary's Street, or at *Cygnet's Kitchen*, White Swan Court, off Church Street, which serves more substantial soups and casseroles, and has outside seating. The *French Horn* (℡01600/772733), handsomely situated at 24 Church St, serves moderately priced French fare for lunch and dinner. You can opt for inexpensive pub grub at the *Punch House*, in Agincourt Square, or the *Green Dragon*, in St Thomas Square, down by the Monnow Bridge.

Raglan

RAGLAN (Rhaglan), seven miles west of Monmouth, is an unassuming village worth visiting for its glorious **Castle** (June–Sept daily 9.30am–6pm; April, May & Oct daily 9am–5pm; Nov–March Mon–Sat 9.30am–4pm, Sun 11am–4pm; £2.50; CADW), whose fussy and comparatively intact style makes it stand out from so many other crumbling Welsh fortresses. The last medieval fortification built in Britain, the design of which combines practical strength with ostentatious style, Raglan was begun on the site of a Norman motte in 1435 by Sir William ap Thomas. The **gatehouse**, still used as the main entrance, houses the best examples of the castle's showy decoration in its heraldic shields, intricate stonework edging and gargoyles. In the mid-fifteenth century, ap Thomas's grandson, William Herbert II, was responsible for the two inner courts, built around his grandfather's original gatehouse, hall and keep. The first is the cobbled **Pitched Stone Court**, designed to house the functional rooms like the kitchen, with its two vast, double-flued chimneys, and the servants' quarters. To the left is **Fountain Court**, a well-proportioned grassy space surrounded by opulent residences that once included grand apartments and state rooms. Separating the two are the original hall, from 1435, the buttery, the remains of the chapel and the dank, cold cellars below.

The Three Castles

The fertile, low-lying land between the Monnow and Usk rivers was important as an easy access route into the agricultural lands of South Wales, and in the eleventh century the Norman invaders built a trio of strongholds here to protect their interests. In 1201, Skenfrith, Grosmont and White castles were presented by King John to Hubert de Burgh, who employed sophisticated new ideas on castle design to replace the earlier, square-keeped castles. In 1260, the advancing army of Llywelyn ap Gruffydd began to threaten the king's supremacy in South Wales, and the three castles were refortified in readiness. Gradually, the castles were adapted as living quarters and royal administration centres, and the only return to military usage came in 1404–05, when Owain Glyndŵr's army pressed down to Grosmont, only to be defeated by the future King Henry V. The castles slipped into disrepair and were finally sold separately in 1902, the first time since 1138 that the three had fallen out of single ownership.

White Castle (Easter–Sept daily 10am–5pm; £2; all other times unrestricted access), eight miles northwest of Monmouth and six miles east of Abergavenny (see p.821), is the most awesome of the three, sited in rolling countryside with some superb views over to the hills surrounding the River Monnow. A few patches of the white rendering that gave the castle its name can be seen on the exterior walls. The grassy Outer Ward is enclosed by a curtain wall with four towers, divided by a moat from the brooding mass of the Inner Ward. A bridge leads to the dual-towered Inner Gatehouse, where you can climb the western tower for its sublime vantage point. At the back of the Inner Ward are the massive foundations of the Norman keep, demolished in about 1260.

Seven miles northeast of White Castle, in the attractive border village of Skenfrith (Ynysgynwraidd), is the thirteenth-century **Skenfrith Castle** (free access), dominated by the circular keep that replaced an earlier Norman structure. Whilst not as impressive as White Castle, Skenfrith has a pretty riverside setting, its castle walls built of a sturdy red sandstone arranged in an irregular rectangle. In the centre of the ward is a low, round keep, raised slightly on an earth mound, containing the vestiges of the private apartments of the castle's lord on the upper floors.

Five miles upstream of Skenfrith, right on the English border, the most dilapidated of the Three Castles, **Grosmont Castle** (free access), sits on a small hill above its village. Entering over the wooden bridge above the dry moat brings you into the small central courtyard, dominated on the right-hand side by the ruins of a large Great Hall dating from the first decade of the thirteenth century.

Newport and Caerleon

Dominating the once industrious valley towns of southern Monmouthshire, **Newport**, Wales's third largest town, is a downbeat, working-class place that grew up around the docks at the mouth of the River Usk. Its rich history has been largely swept away by the twentieth century, but isolated nuggets remain, most notably at Roman **Caerleon** – the "old port" on the River Usk – now a northern suburb of Newport, but predating the town by about a thousand years.

Newport

NEWPORT (Casnewydd), fifteen miles west of Chepstow, is hardly the most prepossessing of towns, with its modern city centre strung along the banks of the foul and muddy River Usk. Overlooking these waters stand both the pathetic remains of **Newport Castle**, and Peter Fink's giant red sculpture *Steel Wave*, a nod to one of Newport's great industries. The place does have a tremendous energy, however, and can be well worth a night's stop.

The central High Street leads to Newport and Westgate squares, and the ornate, Victorian **Westgate Hotel** where, in 1839, soldiers sprayed a crowd of Chartist protesters with gunfire (see box), killing at least twenty – the hotel's original pillars still show bullet marks. A hundred yards along Commercial Street, in John Frost Square, the quirky **Newport clock** shudders, shakes, spits smoke and comes near to apparent collapse every hour, usually drawing an appreciative crowd. In front of the clock is the town's library, tourist office and inspiring civic **museum** (Mon–Thurs 9.30am–5pm, Fri 9.30am–4.30pm, Sat 9.30am–4pm; free). Starting with the origins of the county of Monmouthshire, the displays examine the county's original occupations and early lifestyles, and include a section on mining, with a roll call of those killed in local pit accidents – 3,508 men between 1837 and 1927. Newport's spectacular growth from 1000 townspeople in 1801 to a grimy port town of 70,000 people by a century later is well charted, but the two most interesting sections deal with the Chartist uprising and a fine Roman mosaic.

Dominating the Newport skyline with its comical, spidery legs is the **Transporter Bridge** (May–Sept Mon–Sat 8am–8.50pm, Sun 1–9pm; Oct–April Mon–Sat 8am–5.50pm, Sun 1–5pm; car toll 50p, cyclists and pedestrians free), built in 1906 to enable cars and people to cross the river without disturbing the shipping channel, gliding them across the Usk on a dangling platform. A recently opened visitor centre tells its story.

Newport's **tourist office** is in the museum complex in John Frost Square (daily 9.30am–5pm; ℡01633/842962), a hundred yards from Kingsway **bus station** and five minutes' walk south of the **train station**. Staying in Caerleon is a more amenable option, but there are some decent **B&Bs**, including *Craignair*, 44 Corporation Rd (℡01633/259903; ❶), and the genteel *St Etienne*, 162 Stow Hill (℡01633/262341; ❷). At the western end of Bridge Street, Caerau Road rises up sharply to the south, passing the relaxed, hos-

The Chartists

In an era when wealthy landowners bought votes from the enfranchised few, the struggles of the **Chartists** were perhaps a historical inevitability. Thousands gathered around the 1838 People's Charter that called for universal male suffrage, a secret, annual ballot for Parliament and the abolition of property qualifications for the vote. Demonstrations in support of these principles were held all over the country, with some of the bloodiest and most vociferous taking place in the radical heartlands of industrial South Wales. On November 4, 1839, Chartists from all over Monmouthshire marched on Newport and descended Stow Hill, whereupon they were gunned down by soldiers hiding in the Westgate Hotel; 22 protesters were killed. The leaders of the rebellion were sentenced to death, although the self-righteous and wealthy leaders of the town subsequently commuted their punishment to transportation. Queen Victoria even knighted the mayor who ordered the shooting.

pitable *Kepe Lodge* at no. 46a (℡01633/262351; ❷). There's a **campsite** at *Tredegar House* (℡01633/815600), a couple of miles west – take bus #315 or #30 from the town centre. For **food**, make for the *Oriel* café on the top floor of the museum, the vegetarian *Hunky Dory's* at 17 Charles St, or *Ristorante Vittorio* up by the cathedral at 113 Stow Hill (℡01633/840261). With rock music buoyant in Newport, the best place to catch the vibe is at the legendary *TJ's*, 14 Clarence Place, where Kurt Cobain proposed to Courtney Love.

Caerleon

Compact **CAERLEON** (Caerllion), three miles north of central Newport (bus #2; every 15min), but still within the city limits, is peppered with the remnants of the major Roman town of Isca, named after the River Usk (Wysg). The settlement was built to provide administrative and military services for the smaller, outlying camps in the rest of South Wales and grew to a size and importance on a par with the better-known York and Chester in the north of England. Although the town fell gradually into decay after the Romans had left, there were still some massive remains standing when, in 1188, episcopal envoy Giraldus Cambrensis noted with evident relish the "immense palaces, which, with the gilded gables of their roofs, once rivalled the magnificence of ancient Rome".

Although time has had an inevitably corrosive effect on the remains since Giraldus' time, there's a powerful sense of history running through the Roman **fortress baths** (April–Oct daily 9.30am–5pm; Nov–March Mon–Sat 9.30am–5pm, Sun 1–4pm; £2; CADW). The bathing houses, cold hall and communal pool area are remarkably intact and beautifully presented, with highly imaginative uses of audiovisual equipment, sound commentary and models. On the High Street, a Victorian Neoclassical portico is the sole survivor of the original **Legionary Museum** (April–Oct Mon–Sat 10am–6pm, Sun 2–6pm; Nov–March Mon–Sat 10am–4.30pm, Sun 2–4.30pm; free), now housed in a modern building behind and laden with artefacts unearthed here, including everything from amulets to tweezers.

Opposite the Legionary Museum, Fosse Lane leads down to the hugely atmospheric Roman **amphitheatre** (free access), the only one of its kind preserved in Britain. Hidden under a grassy mound until the 1920s, the amphitheatre was built around 80 AD, at the same time as the Colosseum in Rome. Up to six thousand would take seats to watch animal baiting, military exercises or the gory combat of gladiators.

Caerleon's **tourist office** (daily: April–Oct 10am–1pm & 2–5.30pm; Nov–March 10am–1pm & 2–4pm; ℡01633/422656) lies next to the legionary museum, or there's more informal information in the Ffwrrwm craft centre, down the main street. There's central, shared-bathroom **B&B** at *Pendragon*, 18 Cross St (℡01633/430871; ❷), and *Great House*, Isca Road (℡01633/420216; ❷). The best place to **eat** in Caerleon is *Oriel*, a bistro in the courtyard of the Ffwrrwm centre.

The Valleys

No other part of Wales is as instantly recognizable as the **Valleys**, a generic name for the string of settlements packed into the narrow gashes in the mountainous terrain to the north of Newport and Cardiff. Arriving from England, the change from rolling countryside to sharp contours and a post-industrial landscape is almost instantaneous. Each of the valleys depended almost solely on coal-mining which, although nearly defunct as an industry, has left its mark on the staunchly working-class towns: row upon row of brightly painted terraced housing, tipped along the slopes at some incredible angles, are broken only by austere chapels, the occasional remaining pithead and the dignified memorials to those who died underground.

This is not traditional tourist country, but is doubtless one of the most interesting and distinctive corners of Wales, dripping with sociological and human interest. Some of the former mines have re-opened as gutsy and hard-hitting museums – **Big Pit** at Blaenafon and the **Rhondda Heritage Park** at Trehafod being the best – while other excellent civic museums include those at **Pontypridd** and **Merthyr Tydfil**. A few older sites, such as vast **Caerphilly Castle** and the sixteenth-century manor house of **Llancaiach Fawr**, have been attracting visitors for hundreds of years.

Blaenafon and Big Pit

Fourteen miles north of Newport, the valley of the Llwyd opens out at the airy iron and coal town of **BLAENAFON** (sometimes Blaenavon), whose population has shrunk to five thousand, a quarter of its nineteenth-century size. It's a fascinating and evocative place, a fact recognized by UNESCO, who granted it World Heritage Site status in 2000. The town's boom kicked off at the Blaenafon **ironworks**, just off the Brynmawr road (April–Oct daily 9.30am–4.30pm; call ☎01633/648081 for winter hours; £2; CADW), founded in 1788. Limestone, coal and iron ore – ingredients for successful iron-smelting – were abundant locally, and the Blaenafon works grew to become one of the largest in Britain in the early nineteenth century, until it closed in 1900. The line of Georgian blast furnaces, the water-balance lift and the **museum** in the workers' cottages offer a thorough picture of both the process and the lifestyle that went with it. The ironworks also contains the town's **tourist office** (same hours; ☎01495/792615).

Just as it is now possible to visit the home of Blaenafon's iron industry, the town's defunct coal trade has also been transformed smoothly into the site which most clearly evokes the experience of a miner's work and life. At the **Big Pit National Mining Museum** (mid-Feb to Nov daily 9.30am–5pm; last underground tour 3.30pm; free), a mile west of the town and reached by a half-hourly shuttle bus from Blaenafon, you're kitted out with lamp, helmet and very heavy battery pack and lowered three hundred feet into the labyrinth of shafts and coal faces for a guided tour. The guides – most of whom are ex-miners – lead you through explanations and examples of the different types of coal mining, from the antiquated, risky stack-and-pillar operation to modern, mechanized seam-working. Constant streams of rust-coloured water flow by, adding to the dank and chilly atmosphere that must have terrified the small children who were once paid twopence for a six-day week – of which one penny was taken out for the cost of their candles – pulling the coal wagons along the tracks. Back on the surface, the old pithead baths, smithy, miners' canteen and winding engine house have all been preserved and filled with some fascinating displays about the local mining industry, including a series of characteristically feisty testimonies from the miners made redundant here in 1980.

The Taff and Cynon valleys

The River Taff flows out into the Bristol Channel at Cardiff, after passing through a condensed couple of dozen miles of industry and population. The first town in the Taff vale is **Pontypridd**, one of the most cheerful in the Valleys, and probably the best base. Continuing north, the river splits again at Abercynon, where the River Cynon flows in from Aberdare, site of Wales's only remaining deep mine. Just outside Abercynon is the enjoyable, sixteenth-century **Llancaiach Fawr** manor house. To the north, the Taff is packed into one of the tightest of all the Valleys, passing Aberfan five miles short of the imposing valley head town of **Merthyr Tydfil**.

Pontypridd
PONTYPRIDD, twelve miles north of Cardiff, is built up around its quirky arched **bridge**. Once the largest single-span stone bridge in Europe, it was built in 1775 by local amateur stonemason William Edwards, whose previous attempts had crumbled into the river below. Across the river is **Ynysangharad Park**, where Sir W. Goscombe John's gooey statue honours Pontypridd weaver Evan James, who composed the stirringly nationalistic song *Hen Wlad fy Nhadau (Land of My Fathers)* that has become the Welsh national anthem. By the bridge at the end of Taff Street, a lovingly restored church houses the **Pontypridd Museum** (Mon–Sat 10am–5pm; free), one of the best museums in the Valleys. A treasure trove of photographs, videos, models and exhibits succeeds in painting a warm and human picture of the town and its outlying valleys, as well as paying homage to the town's famous sons, singer Tom Jones and opera star and actor Sir Geraint Evans.

Pontypridd is well connected to bus, train and road networks. The **tourist office** (Mon–Sat 10am–5pm; ☎01443/490748) is in the museum, on Bridge Street. **Accommodation** is rather scarce: in the town centre, try the lively *Millfield Hotel*, Mill Street, near the station (☎01443/480111; ❷), or, right in the thick of the action, the bustling *Market Tavern*, Market Street (☎01443/485331; ❷). Better bets are a few miles out, notably the well-kept and extremely friendly *Fairmead* guesthouse (☎01443/411174; ❸), almost opposite Llancaiach Fawr (see below), and the floral *Llechwen Hall* (☎01443/742050; ❹), signposted off the A470 a couple of miles north of Pontypridd.

Llancaiach Fawr

Five miles north of Pontypridd, the river divides at **Abercynon**, a stark, typical valley town of punishingly steep streets lined with terraced houses that fade out into a coniferous hillside. Two miles east, just north of the village of Nelson, is the sixteenth-century **Llancaiach Fawr** (March–Oct Mon–Fri 10am–5pm, Sat & Sun 10am–6pm, Nov–Feb closed Mon; £4.50), a Tudor house, built around 1530, that has been transformed into a living history museum set in 1645, the time of the Civil War, with all of the guides dressed as house servants, speaking the language of seventeenth-century Britain. Although potentially tacky, it is quite deftly done, with well-researched period authenticity and numerous fascinating anecdotes from the staff; visitors are even encouraged to try on the master of the household's armour. Regular **buses** from Pontypridd and Cardiff pass the entrance.

Merthyr Tydfil

Downtown **MERTHYR TYDFIL** (or Tudful), ten miles north of Pontypridd, is a robust place whose main glory is its location at the top of the Taff Valley, on the cusp of the industrial coal country to the south and the grand, windy heights of the Brecon Beacons to the north. In the eighteenth century it became the largest iron-producing town in the world, as well as by far the most populous town in Wales, with four massive ironworks exploiting the local abundance of the key ingredients: iron ore, coal and limestone. A century earlier, what was then a village became a rallying point for Dissenter and

Aberfan

North of Abercynon, the Taff Valley contains one sight that is hard to forget. Two neat lines of distant arches mark the graves of 144 people killed in October 1966 by an unsecured slag heap collapsing on Pantglas primary school in the village of **Aberfan**. Thousands of people still make the pilgrimage to the village graveyard, to stand silent and bemused by the enormity of the disaster. Among the dead were 116 children, who died huddled in panic at the beginning of their school day. A humbling and beautiful valediction can be seen on one of the gravestones, that of a ten-year-old boy, who, it simply records, "loved light, freedom and animals". Official enquiries all told the sorry tale that this disaster was almost inevitable, given the cavalier approach to safety so often displayed by the coal bosses. Gwynfor Evans, then newly elected as the first Plaid Cymru MP in Westminster, spoke with well-founded bitterness when he said, "Let us suppose that such a monstrous mountain had been built above Hampstead or Eton, where the children of the men of power and wealth are at school...". But that, of course, would never have happened.

Radical movements, which gained adherents as the profits from growing industrialization lined the pockets of the works owners, with little cash finding its way to the workers. Merthyr's radicalism bubbled furiously, breaking out into occasional riots and prompting the election of Britain's first socialist MP, Keir Hardie, in 1900.

Half a mile northwest of the town centre, just off Nant-y-Gwenith Street, the lower end of Neath Road, is **Chapel Row**, a line of skilled ironworkers' cottages built in the 1820s, one of which holds composer **Joseph Parry's Birthplace** (April–Sept Thurs–Sun 2–5pm; Oct–March enquire in advance at the castle, see below; free). Parry wrote the national favourite, *Myfanwy*, which is now piped into the rooms, some of which are given over to a display on his life and music.

Back across the other side of the river, just beyond the Brecon Road, is a home in absolute contrast to Parry's humble and cramped birthplace. **Cyfartha Castle** (April–Sept daily 10am–5.30pm; Oct–March Tues–Fri 10am–4pm, Sat & Sun noon–4pm; free) was built in 1825 as an ostentatious mock-Gothic castle for William Crawshay II, boss of the town's original ironworks. The castle is set within vast, attractive parkland which slopes down to the river and once afforded Crawshay a view over his iron empire. The old wine cellars contain a varied and enjoyable walk through the history of Merthyr, with the political turmoil and massive exploitation of the past couple of centuries picked over in gory detail. Upstairs, the castle's grand main rooms house an **art gallery** with an impressive collection of Welsh pieces, including works by Augustus John, Cedric Morris, Vanessa Bell, Jack Yeats and Kyffin Williams.

The **train station** is a minute's walk from the High Street. North up the High Street from here is Glebeland Street, on which stands the **bus** station and, at no. 14a, the **tourist office** (April–Sept Mon–Sat 9.30am–5.30pm; Oct–March Mon–Sat 10am–5pm; ☎01685/379884). Municipal **bike rental** (April–Oct; ☎01685/376940) is available at the Cyfartha Castle Visitor Centre. **Accommodation** is varied and includes the unpretentious *Tregenna Hotel*, in Park Terrace, next to Penydarren Park (☎01685/723627; ❸), as well as the humbler surroundings of the *Hanover Guest House*, 31 Hanover St (☎01685/ 379303; ❶), and, *Penylan*, 12 Courtland Terrace (☎01685/723179; ❶). There's a **campsite** four miles north of town in the beautiful surroundings of *Grawen Farm*, Cwmtaf, near Cefn-Coed (☎01685/723740).

The Rhondda

Pointing northwest from Pontypridd, the **Rhondda Fawr** – sixteen miles long and never as much as a mile wide – is undoubtedly the most famous of all the Welsh valleys, as well as being the heart of the massive South Wales coal industry. For many it immediately conjures up Richard Llewellyn's 1939 book – and subsequent Oscar-winning weepie – *How Green Was My Valley*, although this was, strictly speaking, based on the author's early life in nearby Gilfach Goch, outside the valley. Between 1860 and 1910 the Rhondda's population grew from 3000 to nearly 160,000, squeezed into ranks of houses grouped around sixty or so pitheads. The Rhondda, more than any other of the valleys, became a self-reliant, hard-living, chapel-going, deeply poor and terrifically spirited breeding ground for radical religion and firebrand politics. For decades, the Communist Party ran the town of Maerdy (nicknamed "Little Moscow" by Fleet Street in the 1930s). The last pit in the Rhondda closed in 1990, but what was left behind was not some dispiriting ragbag of depressing towns, but a range of new attractions, cleaned-up hillsides and some of the friendliest pubs and working men's clubs to be found anywhere in Britain.

Male voice choirs

Fiercely protective of its reputation as a land of song, the voice of Wales is most commonly heard amongst the ranks of **male voice choirs**. Although found all over the country, it is in the southern, industrial heartland that they are loudest and strongest. Their roots lie in the Nonconformist religious traditions of the seventeenth and eighteenth centuries, when Methodism in particular swept the country, and singing was a free and potent way of cherishing the frequently persecuted faith. Classic hymns like *Cwm Rhondda* and the Welsh national anthem, *Hen Wlad Fy Nhadau (Land of My Fathers)*, are synonymous with the choirs, whose full-blooded interpretation of them continues to render all others insipid. Each valleys' town still has its own, often depleted choir, most of whom happily accept visitors to sit in on rehearsals. A leaflet, available from tourist offices, gives contact phone numbers for each choir's secretary. Contact them directly, and take the chance to hear one of the world's most distinctive choral traditions in full, roof-raising splendour.

Specific attractions are few, however. The only one which really stands out is the colliery museum of the **Rhondda Heritage Park** (April–Sept daily 10am–6pm, last admission 4.30pm; Oct–March Tues–Sun same times; £5.60), at **Trehafod**, formed by locals when the Lewis Merthyr pit closed in 1983. You can explore the engine-winding houses, lamp room and fan house, and take a simulated "trip underground", with stunning visuals and sound effects, re-creating 1950s and late nineteenth-century life through the eyes of colliers. The display concludes with a chilling roll call of pit deaths and a moving final narration by Neil Kinnock, the former head of the Labour Party, about the human cost of mining – particularly for the valley women.

A **train** line from Cardiff, punctuated with stops every mile or so, runs the entire length of the Rhondda, stopping at Trehafod, a few minutes walk from the Heritage Park. **Buses** also cover the route, continuing up into the mountains and the Brecon Beacons. **Accommodation** is scarce: near the Heritage Park in Trehafod is the *Bertie*, 1–3 Phillips Terrace (℡01443/688204; ❷), a decent bar-cum-B&B. Also nearby are the *Rickards*, Trebanoy Road, Porth (℡01443/688023; ❶), or *Tegfan*, Celyn Isaf, Tonyrefail (℡01443/670831; ❶), a couple of miles south of Porth.

Cardiff and around

Official capital of Wales since only 1955 (hence the annoyingly ubiquitous "Europe's Youngest Capital" slogan), the buoyant city of **CARDIFF** (Caerdydd) has swiftly grown into its new status. A number of progressive developments, not least the new, sixty-member Welsh National Assembly, are giving the city the feel of an international capital, if not always a very Welsh one: compared with Swansea, Cardiff is very anglicized – you'll rarely hear Welsh on the city's streets.

The second Marquis of Bute built Cardiff's first dock in 1839, opening others in swift succession. The Butes, who owned massive swathes of the rapidly industrializing South Wales valleys, insisted that all coal and iron exports use the family docks in Cardiff, and it became one of the busiest ports in the world. In the hundred years up to the turn of the twentieth century, Cardiff's population had soared from almost nothing to 170,000, and the spacious and ambitious new civic centre in Cathays Park was well under way. The twentieth century saw varying fortunes: the dock trade slumped in the 1930s and the city suffered

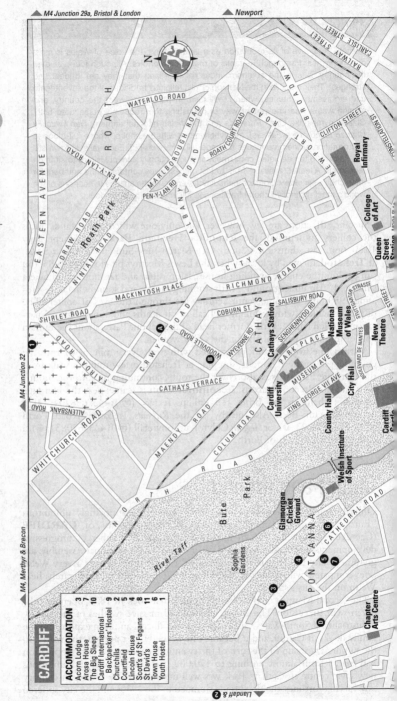

▲ M4 Junction 29a, Bristol & London   ▲ Newport

N

WATERLOO ROAD

ROATH

EASTERN AVENUE

PEN-Y-LAN ROAD

TY-DRAW ROAD

NINIAN ROAD

Roath Park

MARLBOROUGH ROAD

ALBANY ROAD

ROATH COURT ROAD

PEN-Y-LAN RD

CLIFTON STREET

NEWPORT ROAD

BROADWAY

RAILWAY STREET

CARLISLE STREET

CONSTELLATION ST

Royal Infirmary

CITY ROAD

MACKINTOSH PLACE

RICHMOND ROAD

College of Art

SHIRLEY ROAD

COBURN ST

SALISBURY ROAD

Queen Street Station

FAIROAK ROAD

CRWYS ROAD

WOODVILLE ROAD

WYEVERNE RD

Cathays Station

SENGHENNYDD RD

STUTTGARTER STRASSE

National Museum of Wales

New Theatre

❶

Ⓐ

Ⓑ

M4 Junction 32 ▲

ALLENSBANK ROAD

CATHAYS TERRACE

CATHAYS

PARK PLACE

MUSEUM AVE

BOULEVARD DE NANTES

WINDSOR ST

Cardiff University

City Hall

WHITCHURCH ROAD

MAENDY ROAD

COLUM ROAD

KING GEORGE VII AVE

County Hall

Cardiff Castle

M4 Merthyr & Brecon ▲

NORTH ROAD

Bute Park

Welsh Institute of Sport

River Taff

Sophia Gardens

Glamorgan Cricket Ground

CATHEDRAL ROAD

❻

Ⓒ

❸

Ⓓ

❹

❺

❼

PONTCANNA

Chapter Arts Centre

Landaff & 2 ▲

CARDIFF

ACCOMMODATION
Acorn Lodge	3
Arosa House	7
The Big Sleep	10
Cardiff International Backpackers' Hostel	9
Churchills	2
Courtfield	5
Lincoln House	4
Scott's of St Fagans	8
St David's	11
Town House	6
Youth Hostel	1

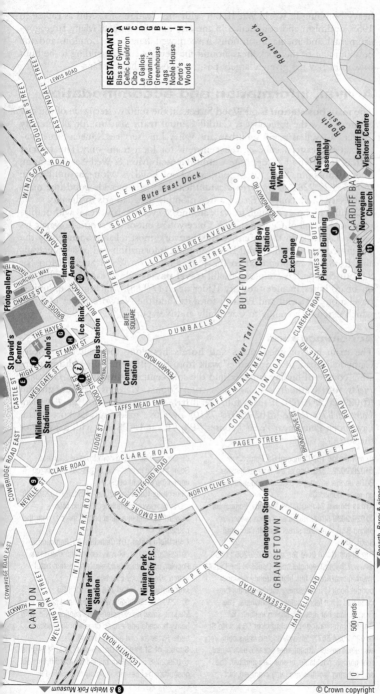

RESTAURANTS

Blas ar Gymru	A
Celtic Cauldron	E
Cibo	C
Le Gallois	D
Giovanni's	G
Greenhouse	B
Jags	F
Noble House	I
Porto's	H
Woods	J

Roath Dock

Roath Basin

National Assembly

Cardiff Bay Visitors' Centre

Atlantic Wharf

CARDIFF BAY

Norwegian Church

CENTRAL LINK

Bute East Dock

SCHOONER WAY

LLOYD GEORGE AVENUE

BUTE STREET

Cardiff Bay Station

Coal Exchange

Pierhead Building

Techniquest

HEMINGWAY RD

BUTE PL

JAMES ST

LEWIS ROAD

EAST TYNDALL STREET

WINDSOR SANDQUAHAR STREET

WINDSOR ROAD

ADAMS ST

International Arena

CHURCHILL WAY

CHARLES ST

Ffotogallery

BRIDGE ST

BUTE TERRACE

HERBERT ST

Ice Rink

BUTE SQUARE

Bus Station

DUMBALLS ROAD

BUTETOWN

STATION TER

The HAYES

St David's Centre

St John's

ST MARY ST

HIGH ST

CASTLE ST

WESTGATE ST

Millennium Stadium

COWBRIDGE ROAD EAST

PARK ST

WOOD STREET

CENTRAL SQUARE

Central Station

PENARTH ROAD

TAFFS MEAD EMB

River Taff

TAFF EMBANKMENT

CORPORATION ROAD

CLARENCE ROAD

AVONDALE RD

FERRY ROAD

TUDOR ST

CLARE ROAD

PAGET STREET

BROMSGROVE ST

CLIVE STREET

NEVILLE ST

COWBRIDGE ROAD EAST

CLARE ROAD

WEDMORE ROAD

STAFFORD ROAD

NORTH CLIVE ST

Grangetown Station

GRANGETOWN

PENARTH ROAD

NINIAN PARK ROAD

Ninian Park Station

Ninian Park (Cardiff City F.C.)

SLOPER ROAD

BESSEMER ROAD

HADFIELD ROAD

CANTON

LECKWITH RD

WELLINGTON STREET

LECKWITH ROAD

▼ & Welsh Folk Museum

▶ Penarth, Barry & airport

0   500 yards

© Crown copyright

heavy bombing in World War II, but with the creation of Cardiff as capital in 1955, optimism and confidence in the city have blossomed. Many large governmental and media institutions have moved here from London, and the development of the dock areas around the new Assembly building to be built in Cardiff Bay has given a largely positive boost to the cityscape.

Arrival, information and accommodation

The main **bus station** is off Wood Street, on the southwestern side of the city centre. Across the forecourt is Cardiff Central **train station**, for all intercity services as well as many suburban and Valley Line services. Queen Street station, at the eastern edge of the centre, is for local trains only. The **tourist office**, at 16 Wood St, opposite Cardiff Central (Mon & Wed–Sat 9am–5pm, Tues 10am–5pm, Sun 10am–2pm; in school holidays Mon–Sat until 6pm; ℡029/2022 7281, Ⓔenquiries@cardifftic.co.uk), will provide good free maps of the city and a copy of *Buzz!*, a free monthly guide to arts in the city.

Cardiff is compact enough to walk around, as even the bay area is within thirty minutes' stroll of Central station. Once you're out of the centre, however, it's best to fall back on the extensive **bus** network, most reliably operated by the garish-orange liveried Cardiff Bus Company. Information and passes are available from the counter next to the tourist office on Wood Street (Mon–Sat 8.30am–5.30pm). A couple of useful **travel passes**, which can also be bought on-board buses, include the City Rider ticket (£2.85), which gives unlimited travel around Cardiff and Penarth for a day and the Network Rider (£4.50), which extends the range to Caerphilly and Newport.

Accommodation

The main belt of guesthouses and **hotels** lies along the genteel and leafy Cathedral Road, fifteen minutes' walk from the city centre. In addition there are a couple of budget **hostels**, and the sole central **campsite**, the *Pontcanna Fields*, off Cathedral Road near the Sophia Gardens cricket ground (℡029/2039 8362). If that's full, you'll have to make do with the *Lavernock Point Holiday Estate* (℡029/2070 7310), over five miles away at Fort Road, Lavernock Point, near Penarth; buses #P4, #P5 and #P8 pass within a mile of the site.

Acorn Lodge 182 Cathedral Rd, Pontcanna ℡029/2022 1373. One of the least expensive B&Bs on this street, yet pleasant and quiet. Some en-suite rooms. ❶

Arosa House 24 Plasturton Gardens, Pontcanna ℡029/2039 5342. Very friendly and reasonably priced B&B in a quiet street just off Cathedral Road. ❶

Big Sleep Hotel Bute Terrace ℡029/2063 6363, Ⓦwww.thebigsleephotel.com. Opposite the Cardiff International Arena, this highly trendy designer budget hotel is a refreshing antidote to the brocade and floral fabric palaces elsewhere. The ground floor bar is worth seeing in itself. ❷

Cardiff International Backpacker 98 Neville St ℡029/2034 5577, Ⓦwww.hostelswales.com. Very well-kept hostel with internet access, bike rental, roof garden, pool table, onsite café and bar. The self-catering facilities are fairly cramped, but

there's easy access to downtown restaurants. Some private rooms, plus single-sex and mixed dorms (up to eight beds). ❶

Churchills Hotel Cardiff Rd, Llandaff ℡029/2056 2372, Ⓦwww.churchillshotel.co.uk. Mock-Edwardian hotel in a quiet part of the city near the cathedral. ❹

Courtfield Hotel 101 Cathedral Rd, Pontcanna ℡029/2022 7701, Ⓦwww.courtfieldhotel.co.uk. Popular, comfortable and nicely furnished hotel with a sizeable gay clientele. ❸

Lincoln House Hotel 118 Cathedral Rd ℡029/2039 5558, Ⓦwww.lincolnhotel.co.uk. Elegant, small hotel restored in Victorian style, with heavy brocade and even a couple of four-poster beds. Rates for bed and breakfast. ❹

Scott's of St Fagans Greenwood Lane, St Fagans ℡029/2056 5400. Four miles from Cardiff, this old post office has been completely remodelled in minimalist style: all white walls, blond ash furniture, chic spotlighting and top quality fittings. Rates include a full breakfast. ④

St David's Hotel and Spa Havannah St, Cardiff Bay ☎029/2045 4045, ⓦwww.rfhotels.com. One of the most luxurious hotels in Cardiff: a tall postmodern structure right on the waterfront that's all clean lines and elegant, understated decor. Rooms come with superb views and access to gorgeous spa facilities. ⑦

Town House 70 Cathedral Rd, Pontcanna

☎029/2023 9399, ⓦwww.thetownhousecardiff .co.uk. Restored Victorian house with en-suite rooms, a comfortable lounge and better-than-average facilities. ③

YHA hostel 2 Wedal Rd, Roath Park ☎029/2046 2303, ⓦwww.yha.org.uk. Large, purpose-built, red-brick building, situated just underneath the A48 Eastern Avenue flyover at the top of Roath Park, almost two miles from the city centre. Buses #78, #80 or #82 go from the central bus station. No curfew. ①

The City

Cardiff's sights are clustered around fairly small, distinct districts. The compact commercial centre is bounded by the **River Taff**, which flows past the tremendous new **Millennium Stadium**, inaugurated for the 1999 Rugby World Cup. In this rugby-mad city, the atmosphere in the pubs and streets when Wales have a home match – particularly against the old enemy, England – is charged with good-natured, beery fervour. Just upstream, the Taff is flanked by the wall of Cardiff's extraordinary **castle**, an amalgam of Roman remains, Norman keep and Victorian fantasy. North of the castle is a series of white Edwardian buildings grouped around **Cathays Park**: the City Hall, Cardiff University and the superb **National Museum**. A mile south of the commercial centre, the area around **Cardiff Bay** is striving to become one of the city's liveliest quarters, home to the new National Assembly of Wales and a welter of new waterfront developments which make it an ideal place for eating, drinking or just ambling about. A couple of miles north of the city centre, **Llandaff Cathedral** warrants a visit for its strange clash of Norman and modern styles.

The city centre

Cardiff **city centre** is surprisingly compact, forming a rough square bounded by the castle, Queen Street and Central stations and the Cardiff International Arena. Dominating the skyline, on the other side of Wood Street from Central Station is the simply magnificent **Millennium Stadium** (tours hourly Mon–Sat 10am–5pm, Sun 10am–4pm, subject to events; ☎029/2082 2228; £5), which has swiftly become an iconic symbol not only of Cardiff but of Wales as a whole. Built to an incredibly tight deadline in order to be ready for the Rugby World Cup of 1999, the stadium has hosted sporting matches of every description (including, bizarrely, the English FA Cup final), as well as an array of huge rock gigs and other musical spectaculars. Its success is due to its amazing adaptability and sensation of intimacy with the action – no mean achievement in a stadium that can seat 72,500 people. The tours include walking the players' tunnel, visiting the dressing rooms, VIP areas and a rugby museum. They start from the **stadium shop** at Entrance Gate 3 on Westgate Street. Don't forget to stroll the walkway along the river that was specially built out on ramps to accommodate the huge swell of the stadium walls.

The districts to the east are Cardiff's main shopping areas. **Queen Street**, running from the castle to Queen Street station, is a pedestrianized thoroughfare containing a predictable clutch of big name chain stores and covered modern malls. Far more interesting are the **Arcades**, a series of Victorian and Edwardian galleries where you'll find all of the city centre's most alluring little independent shops and cafés - great for picking up fliers and information on gigs, club nights and other such events. Particularly impressive are the **High**

Street and **Castle arcades**, either side of the High Street near the castle. A few yards further down towards Central Station is the elegant Edwardian **indoor market** and further still the **Royal** and **Morgan arcades**, linking St Mary's Street with the lower end of The Hayes.

Cardiff Castle

The political, geographical and historical heart of the city is **Cardiff Castle** (daily: March–Oct 9.30am–6pm, tours every 20min; Nov–Feb 9.30am–4.30pm, five tours a day; full tour £5.25, shorter winter tours £3.15, grounds only £2.60), an intriguing hotchpotch of remnants of the city's history. The fortress hides inside a vast walled yard corresponding roughly to the outline of the original fort built by the Romans, Cardiff's first inhabitants. The neat Norman motte, crowned with its eleventh-century **keep**, looks down onto the turrets and towers of the domestic buildings, which date in part from the fourteenth and fifteenth centuries, but were much extended in Tudor times, when residential needs began to overtake military priorities.

In the late nineteenth century, the third Marquis of Bute, one of the richest men on the globe, lavished a fortune on upgrading his pile – although he only lived there for six weeks a year – commissioning architect and decorator William Burges to aid him. With their passion for the religious art and the symbolism of the Middle Ages, they systematically overhauled the buildings, adding a spire to the octagonal tower and erecting a clocktower. But it was inside that their imaginations ran free, and they radically transformed the crumbling interiors into palaces of vivid colour and intricate, high-camp design. These rooms can only be seen as part of the full guided tour, making the extra cost well worthwhile. On the **Animal Wall**, visible from Castle Street, outside, stone creatures are frozen in cheeky poses.

Cathays Park and around

On the north side of the city centre is **Cathays Park**, a large rectangle of lawns and flowerbeds that forms the centrepiece for the impressive buildings of the **civic centre**. Dating from the early twentieth century, the gleaming white buildings are arranged with pompous Edwardian precision, and speak volumes about Cardiff's self-assertion, even half a century before it was officially declared capital of Wales. The dragon-topped, domed **City Hall** is the magnificent centrepiece of the complex, an exercise in every cliché about ostentatious civic self-glory, with a roll call of statues of male Welsh heroes, including Llywelyn ap Gruffudd, St David, Giraldus Cambrensis and Owain Glyndŵr.

National Museum of Wales

To the right stands the **National Museum of Wales** (Tues–Sun 10am–5pm; free), one of Britain's finest, attempting both to tell the story of Wales and to reflect the nation's place in the wider, international sphere. Start off at the back of the entrance lobby with the epic "Evolution of Wales" exhibition, a fabulous mix of natural history, hi-tech gizmos and hugely detailed displays. To the right of the main lobby are various temporary exhibitions and an extensive botany collection, including some stunning silk, paper and wax plant and flower models. In the first-floor archeology gallery, don't miss the Bronze Age remains and the comparatively sophisticated **Caergwrle Bowl**, a delicate, gold-leafed ornament that is 3000 years old. Nearby is the **Tregwynt Treasure Trove**, an impressive cache of gold and silver coins dating back to the Civil War, uncovered near Fishguard in 1996.

The bulk of the East Wing is given over to **fine art**, with ten galleries on the first floor containing the majority of the museum's extraordinary art collection. The oldest part of the collection starts with the fifteenth- and sixteenth-century **Italian schools**, pushing on to seventeenth-century galleries rich in **Flemish** and **Dutch** work, including Rembrandt's coolly aloof portrait of *Catrina Hooghsaet* and Jacob van Ruisdael's mesmerizing *Waterfall*. The most famous, or perhaps infamous, pieces here are the **Cardiff Cartoons**, four monumental tapestries bought at great expense in 1979 and, at the time, presumed to be the work of Rubens. The first of the great Welsh artists is shown to maximum effect in the **eighteenth-century** galleries, where landscapes by Richard Wilson include *Caernarfon Castle* and *Dolbadarn Castle*. The **nineteenth-century** galleries include a round-up of some of the century's greater painters, including J.M.W. Turner, whose *Thames Backwater, with Windsor Castle* is a characteristic wash of diffuse colour and light.

The most exciting art works are contained in galleries eleven to fifteen, kicking off with a fabulous **sculpture collection**, including many by the one-man Welsh Victorian statue industry, Goscombe John, that contrast with the more delicate Rodin pieces nearby. Gallery Thirteen is home to the National Museum's pride, the Davies collection of **Impressionist paintings**. Cézanne, Monet and Degas figure predominantly, alongside Corot's legendary *Distant view of Corbeil, morning*, Pissarro's classic views of Rouen and Paris, and Renoir's chirpy portrait of *La Parisienne*. Gallery Fourteen houses a hearty collection of Post-Impressionists, Futurists and Surrealists, while Gallery Fifteen showcases abstract work with a strong Welsh bent.

Cardiff Bay

The brand new Lloyd George Avenue connects the city centre with **Cardiff Bay**, a thirty-minute walk south (alternatively, use bus #8 or the half-hourly train to Cardiff Bay station from Queen Street station). Like much of the Bay area, the Avenue is a grand example of sweeping recent redevelopment; also like much of the Bay area, it feels soulless and imposed from on high. After all, this area used to be one of Cardiff's spiciest quarters, a multicultural stew of colour and vibrancy, immortalized by local lass Shirley Bassey under its far more pithy epithet of Tiger Bay. Big money has changed it utterly, and the jury is still out as to whether that's for the better.

For those who love these sort of wholesale regeneration projects, Cardiff Bay is nirvana. Gone is the seedy dereliction of the old docks in favour of an area of landscaped walkways, some audacious modern public art, gardens and public attractions. Whatever your opinion, it is hard to disagree that this is a fascinating corner of Cardiff, where ostentatious Victorian shipping company headquarters rub shoulders with spruced-up ex-dockers' housing, and sleek restaurants lurk in the shadow of glittering, postmodern corporate headquarters. Central to the whole project is the **Cardiff Bay Barrage**, across the Ely and Taff estuaries, which has transformed a vast mud flat into a freshwater lake, controversially depriving the wading bird population of a prime habitat.

First stop is the modern, tubular **Cardiff Bay Visitor Centre** (Mon–Fri 9.30am–5pm, Sat & Sun 10.30am–6pm; Oct–April Sat & Sun closes 5pm; free), looking out on to the bay like a giant eye. It's a thinly disguised PR job, but at least it contains a fabulous scale model of the entire docks area, which is well worth seeing.

The adjacent park is graced by the gleaming witch's-hat spire of the **Norwegian church arts centre** (daily 10am–4pm and for evening performances; ☎029/2045 4899), an old seamen's chapel in which the writer Roald Dahl was christened, now converted into a excellent café (see below) and exhibition space. Alongside is the site of the new **National Assembly of Wales** building, unlikely to be open before 2004, as arguments between architects, developers and politicians continue to stall it. If it makes it off the drawing board, the building will be a stunning glass creation that will greatly enhance the Bay's skyline. In the meanwhile, you'll have to content yourself with the undistinguised current Assembly building that lies behind, the red-brick Crickhowell House, and the magnificent **Pierhead Building**, a typically rich, neo-Gothic terracotta pile that now serves as the National Assembly's **Visitor and Education Centre** (Mon–Thurs 9.30am–4.30pm, Fri 10am–4.30pm; free).

On the other side of a newly landscaped basin and the mammoth Exchange Building, built in the 1880s as Britain's central Coal Exchange, is **Techniquest** (Mon–Fri 9.30am–4.30pm, Sat & Sun 10.30am–5pm; £6), a fun, "hands-on" science gallery – perfect for kids. Backing the whole area you'll see the sweeping wavy roofline and vast glass-brick wall of the **Atlantic Wharf**, which makes a striking impression for what is essentially just a big box filled with a twelve-screen cinema, a bowling alley and a few restaurants.

Llandaff Cathedral

Two miles northwest of the city centre along Cathedral Road, the small, quiet suburb of **Llandaff** is home to a church that has now grown up into the city's **cathedral**. It is believed to have been founded in the sixth century by St Teilo, but was rebuilt in Norman style in around 1120, and worked on well into the thirteenth century. From the late fourteenth century onwards, it declined into an advanced state of disrepair, and one of the twin towers and the nave roof eventually collapsed. Restoration only began in earnest in the early 1840s, when **Pre-Raphaelite** artists such as Edward Burne-Jones, Dante Gabriel Rossetti and the firm of William Morris were commissioned to make colourful new windows and decorative panels. Their work is best seen in the south aisle.

The fusion of different styles and ages is evident from outside, especially in the mismatched western towers. Inside, the nave is dominated by Jacob Epstein's overwhelming *Christ in Majesty*, a concrete parabola topped with a soaring Christ figure. At the west end of the north aisle, the **St Illtyd Chapel** features Rossetti's cloying triptych *The Seed of David*. In the south presbytery is a tenth-century Celtic cross, the only survival of the pre-Norman cathedral.

Eating, drinking and nightlife

Cardiff's long-standing internationalism has paid handsome dividends in the range of **restaurants**, with the influence of Italian immigrants particularly evident in the number of cafés, bistros and trattorias. There are numerous places right in the city, most notably in the "café quarter" along Mill Lane. Most other places are within easy walking distance of the city centre, although there are also good hunting grounds in the cheaper quarters of Cathays and Roath, particularly the curry houses along Crwys, Albany and City roads, a stone's throw from the centre, beyond the university. Cardiff's **pub** life has expanded exponentially over recent years, and there are some wonderful Edwardian palaces of etched, smoky glass and deep red wood, where you'll find Cardiff's very own Brains bitter.

Top-flight concert venues such as St David's Hall and the Cardiff International Arena have brought internationally acclaimed orchestras and **musical** performers to the city, although these sterile environments are no match for the sweati-

△ Cyfrwy ridge, Snowdonia

er gigs and traditional rock found in some of Cardiff's earthier pubs and clubs. The burgeoning Welsh rock scene, both English- and Welsh-language, breaks out regularly in the capital. Cardiff also has a modest **gay scene**: the best sources for current information are Friend (Tues–Sat 8–10pm; ☎029/2034 0101) and Lesbian Line (Tues 8–10pm; ☎029/2037 4051).

Cafés and restaurants

Blas ar Gymru 48 Crwys Rd, Cathays ☎029/2038 7185. Meaning "Taste of Wales", this is a comfortable restaurant with a highly imaginative, moderately priced menu made up of delicious traditional recipes from every corner of Wales. Leave room for the selection of Welsh cheeses. Closed Sun. Moderate or expensive.

Celtic Cauldron Castle Arcade. A friendly daytime café, dedicated to bringing a range of simple Welsh food – soups, stews, laver bread, cakes – to an appreciative public. Inexpensive.

Cibo 83 Pontcanna St, off Cathedral Rd ☎029/2223 2226. A slice of Italy in Cardiff: a small, inexpensive and welcoming trattoria serving ciabatta sandwiches and simple, well-cooked food. No credit cards. Moderate.

Giovanni's The Hayes ☎029/2022 0077. One of Cardiff's best Italian restaurants, lively and enormously friendly, with a wide menu of old favourites and some unusual house specialities. Closed Sun. Moderate.

Greenhouse 38 Woodville Rd ☎029/2023 5731. Licensed vegetarian restaurant with a modern take on traditional dishes, often with an inventive twist. Closed Sun & Mon. Moderate.

Jags 4 Church St. Eat-in and take-out sandwich bar serving stuffed baguettes and good coffee. Inexpensive.

Le Gallois Romilly Crescent, Canton ☎029/2034 1264. Fantastic modern French cuisine in a cheerful environment. Moderate.

Noble House 9–10 St David's House, Wood St ☎029/2038 8317. Excellent Chinese restaurant, with a good range of Peking and Szechuan dishes. Moderate.

Norwegian Church Café Harbour Drive. Cosy spot for Norwegian open sandwiches, salads, some scrumptious cakes and filter coffee. Inexpensive.

Porto's St Mary's St ☎029/2022 0060. Authentic restaurant in a dark, wood-beamed room serving massive portions of Portuguese and Madeiran favourites, including endless variations on dried cod. Moderate.

Woods Brasserie Stuart St, Cardiff Bay ☎029/2049 2400. One of Cardiff's most stylish establishments, where you'll definitely need to book in advance to sample the excellent Modern British cuisine. Moderate (lunch); expensive (evening).

Bars, pubs and clubs

Caio Arms Cathedral Road. Great new pub, airy and comfortable. Popular with Welsh speakers.

Chapter Market Rd, Canton ☎029/2030 4400. A smart and popular bar in this arts complex with a good choice of real ales, guest beers and whiskies.

Club Metropolitan Bakers Row ☎029/2037 1549. Slightly scruffy venue for some of the best indie dance nights in town, with plenty of students drawn by the drink specials.

Clwb Ifor Bach Womanby St ☎029/2023 2199. A sweaty and enjoyable live-music and DJ club with

nightly gigs and sessions, many featuring Welsh-language bands.

Exit Bar 48 Charles St. Frantic, noisy disco-bar, popular among the gay community for pre-club drinks before heading to *Club X*, opposite. Open until midnight.

Sam's Bar 63 St Mary St ☎029/2034 5189. Lively club-bar, with everything from live heavy metal through comedy and drag shows to house DJs. A good place to check the pulse of the Mill Lane "cafe quarter".

Theatre, cinema and classical music

Cardiff International Arena Bute Terrace ☎029/2022 4488. For mega concerts, both rock and classical.

Chapter Arts Centre Market Rd, Canton ☎029/2030 4400. Multi-use arts complex that hosts British and touring theatre and dance companies, as well as Cardiff's main art-house cinema.

New Theatre Park Place ☎029/2087 8889. Splendid Edwardian city-centre theatre that plays host to big London shows. Currently the home of the Welsh National Opera.

The Point West Bute St, Cardiff Bay ☎029/2049 9979. Experimental performance space in an old church.

Sherman Theatre Senghenydd Rd, Cathays ☎029/2064 6900. An excellent, two-auditorium repertory theatre hosting a mixed bag of classic Welsh-language pieces (both original and translated), stand-up comedy, children's entertainment, drama classics, music and dance.

St David's Hall The Hayes ☎029/2087 8444. Part of the massive St David's shopping centre, this large and glamorous venue is possibly the most architecturally exciting building in town. Home to visiting orchestras and musicians from jazz to opera, it's frequently used by the excellent BBC Welsh Symphony Orchestra and Chorus.

Listings

Airport Cardiff International Airport (☎01446/711111, ⓦwww.cial.co.uk) is at Rhoose, ten miles southwest of the city centre in the Vale of Glamorgan.
Banks and exchange All major banks have branches along High Street or Queen Street. American Express is at 3 Queen St (Mon–Fri 9am–5.30pm, Sat 10am–1pm; ☎029/2066 5843), Thomas Cook at 16 Queen St (Mon–Fri 9.30am–5pm, Sat 10am–1pm; ☎029/2022 4886).
Bike rental Waterfront Bike Hire (☎029/2048 4110) rent decent machines from their stand in Britannia Park, right by the Cardiff Bay Visitor Centre.
Bus information Traveline (☎0870/608 2608) has details of Cardiff Bus and National Express services.
Car rental Avis, 14–22 Tudor St (☎029/2034 2111); Enterprise, 45 Penarth Rd (☎029/2038

9222); Hertz, 9 Central Sq (☎029/2022 4548).
Laundries Drift Inn, 104 Salisbury Rd, Cathays Park; GP, 244 Cowbridge Rd, Canton; Launderama, 60 Lower Cathedral Rd.
Left luggage At Central Station.
Medical facilities University of Wales Hospital, Heath (☎029/2074 7747). For emergency dental work: Riverside Health Centre, Wellington St, Canton (☎029/2037 1221).
Pharmacy Boots, 5 Wood St (Mon–Sat 8am–8pm, Sun 6–7pm; ☎029/2023 4043).
Police Central Police Station, King Edward VII Ave, Cathays Park (☎029/2022 2111).
Post office The Hayes (Mon–Fri 9am–5.30pm, Sat 9am–12.30pm; ☎029/2022 7363).
Travel agencies Usit, in the YHA shop, 13 Castle St (☎029/2022 0744); John Cory Travel, Park Place (☎029/2037 1878); Welsh Travel Centre, 240 Whitchurch Rd, Cathays (☎029/2062 1479).

Around Cardiff

On the edge of the northern Cardiff suburbs, the thirteenth-century fairy-tale castle of **Castell Coch** stands on a hillside in the woods, while just further north is the massive **Caerphilly Castle**. West of the city, the massively popular **Museum of Welsh Life**, in the grounds of the rambling Elizabethan country house of **St Fagans Castle**, tells the country's history through a collection of buildings salvaged from all over Wales.

Castell Coch

Four miles north of Llandaff, the turreted **Castell Coch** (June–Sept daily 9.30am–6pm; April, May & Oct daily 9.30am–5pm; Nov–March Mon–Sat 9.30am–4pm, Sun 11am–4pm; £2.50; CADW) was once a ruined thirteenth-century fortress. Like Cardiff Castle, it was rebuilt and transformed into a fantasy structure in the late 1870s by William Burges for the third Marquess of Bute. With its working portcullis and drawbridge, Castell Coch is the ultimate wealthy man's medieval fantasy, isolated on its almost alpine hillside, yet only a few hundred yards from the motorway and Cardiff suburbs. There are many similarities with Cardiff Castle, notably the outrageously lavish decor, culled from religious and moral fables, that dazzle in each room. **Bus** #136 from Central Station turns round at the castle gates, while bus #26 drops in Tongwynlais village, ten minutes' walk away.

Caerphilly

Caerphilly (Caerffili), seven miles north of Cardiff, is a flattened and colour-less town, notable mainly for its **castle** (June–Sept daily 9.30am–6pm; April, May & Oct daily 9.30am–5pm; Nov–March Mon–Sat 9.30am–4pm, Sun 11am–4pm; £2.50; CADW), the first in Britain built concentrically, with an inner system of defences overlooking the outer ring. Looming out of its vast surrounding moat, the medieval fortress with its cock-eyed tower occupies over thirty acres, presenting an awesome promise not entirely fulfilled inside. The castle was begun in 1268 by Gilbert de Clare as a defence against Llywelyn the Last. Two years later, Llywelyn largely destroyed the castle. It was swiftly rebuilt, but for the next few hundred years Caerphilly was little more than a decaying toy, given at whim by kings to their favourites. By the turn of the twentieth century, it was in a sorry state, sitting amidst a growing industrial town that saw fit to build in the then-dry moat and castle precincts. Houses and shops were demolished in order to allow the moat to be reflooded in 1958.

You enter the castle through the much restored **gatehouse**, where there's an exhibition on the castle's history. A platform behind the barbican wall exhibits medieval war and siege engines, overlooked on the left by the southeastern tower, out-leaning its rival in Pisa. Of the rest of the castle, the most interesting section is the massive eastern gatehouse, which includes an impressive upper hall and oratory and, to its left, the wholly restored and re-roofed **Great Hall**.

Caerphilly is also known for its crumbly white **cheese**, made in dairies around the town, and available in a ploughman's lunch at the *Courthouse* pub, on Cardiff Road, right by the castle and a five minute stroll from the **bus** and **train** stations.

The Museum of Welsh Life and St Fagans Castle

St Fagans (Sain Ffagan), four miles west of Cardiff city centre, has a rural feel that is only partially disturbed by the bus-loads of tourists that roll in regular-ly to visit the excellent **Museum of Welsh Life** (daily: May–Aug 10am–6pm; Sept–April 10am–5pm; free), built around **St Fagans Castle**, a country house erected in 1580 and furnished in early nineteenth-century style. The most impressive part of the museum is the fifty-acre outdoor collection of buildings from all corners of Wales which have been carefully dismantled and rebuilt on this site since the museum's inception in 1946. There are particular highlights, including the diminutive, whitewashed Pen-Rhiw Chapel, built in Dyfed in 1777; the pristine and evocative St Mary's Board School, built in Lampeter in Victorian times; and the stern mini-fortress of a tollhouse that once guarded the southern approach to Aberystwyth, from 1772. The superb Rhyd-y-car **ironworkers' cottages**, from Merthyr Tydfil, were originally built in around 1800. Each of the six houses, with its accompanying strip of garden, has been furnished in the style of a different period, stretching between 1805 to 1985. Even the frontages and roofs are true to their age, offering a wade through working-class Welsh life over the past century. **Buses** #32 (hourly) and #C1 (variable times) run to the museum from Central Station.

Swansea and Gower

Dylan Thomas called **SWANSEA** (Abertawe) – his birthplace – an "ugly, love-ly town", an epithet which poet Paul Durcan updated to "pretty, shitty city". Both ring true. Large, sprawling and boisterous, it is the second city of Wales, with around 200,000 people, and has great aspirations to be the first; it's certainly far more Welsh than Cardiff. The city centre was massively rebuilt after devastating bomb attacks in World War II, and a jumble of tower blocks now dot the horizon. But closer inspection reveals Swansea's multifarious charms: some intact old corners of the city centre, the spacious and graceful suburb of Uplands, a wide **seafront** overlooking Swansea Bay and a bold marina development around the old docks. Spread throughout are some of the best-funded **museums** in Wales. Situated on the edge of the **Gower peninsula**, which holds some of the country's most popular and inspirational coastal and rural scenery, Swansea makes a logical base: transport out into the surrounding areas is good, and beds tend to be less expensive in the city than in the more picturesque parts of Gower.

The city's Welsh name, Abertawe, means the settlement at the mouth of the River Tawe, a grimy ditch that is slowly being teased back to life after centuries of use as a sewer for Swansea's metal trades. The first reliable mention of Swansea dates from 1099, when a Norman castle was built here as an outpost of William the Conqueror's empire. A small settlement grew near the coalfields and the sea, developing into a mining and shipbuilding centre that, by 1700, was the largest coal port in Wales. Copper smelting became the area's dominant industry in the eighteenth century, soon attracting other metal trades to pack out the lower Tawe Valley, making it one of the world's most prolific metal-bashing centres. Over the years, the valley became a five-mile stretch of rusting, stagnant land and water that has only recently begun to be re-landscaped.

Arrival, information and accommodation

The **train station** is at the top end of the High Street, a ten-minute hike from the **bus station**, which lies adjacent to the Quadrant Shopping Centre. Nearby, on Plymouth Street, is the **tourist office** (Mon–Sat 9.30am–5.30pm, May–Sept also Sun 10am–4pm; ☏01792/468321). Most of the sights are within walking distance of each other; popular suburbs, such as Uplands and Sketty, near the university, are a bracing thirty-minute walk from the centre, although buses cover the suburbs extremely thoroughly. **Ferries** to Cork in Ireland leave roughly once a day from the docks, around a mile east of the town centre (☏01792/456116, ⓦwww.swansea-cork.ie).

Accommodation

There are dozens of dirt-cheap **hotels** and **B&Bs** stretched out along the seafront Oystermouth Road, whose trade is largely pitched at those catching the Swansea–Cork ferry. Better places congregate in leafy Uplands, a ten- to fifteen-minute walk from town. There are no **campsites** or **hostels** in the city itself, although nearby places in Gower are easily reached.

Crescent 132 Eaton Crescent, Uplands ☏01792/466814, ⓦwww.crescentguesthouse .co.uk. Large, pleasant, well-converted Edwardian guesthouse. All rooms have en-suite showers, and half have superb views over the city and the bay. ❷

Harlton 89 King Edward Rd, Brynmill ☏01792/466938. Budget guesthouse that is a little yellow around the edges but perfectly adequate – and very inexpensive. ❶

Oyster 262 Oystermouth Rd ☏01792/654345. Small and friendly hotel with some en-suite rooms. Serves great local cuisine. ❶

St James 76b Walter Rd, Uplands ☏01792/649984. Small, welcoming hotel in an airy Victorian house. ❷

Uplands Court 134 Eaton Crescent, Uplands ☏01792/473046. Appealing guesthouse in a gracious Victorian villa situated in a pleasant area. ❶

White House Hotel 4 Nyanza Terrace, Uplands ☏01792/473856. Excellent-value and extremely well-kept guesthouse: all the well-appointed rooms have satellite TV and some have en-suite facilities. Great breakfasts, and good three-course evening meals for £10. You can even check your

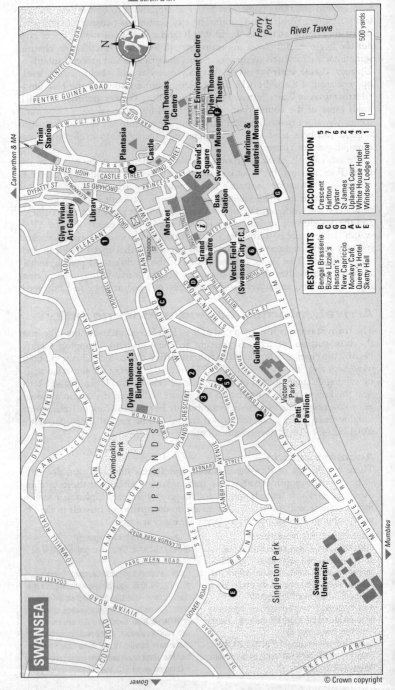

▲ Cardiff & M4

River Tawe

Ferry Port

0 — 500 yards

SWANSEA

© Crown copyright

Gower ▶

Mumbles ▶

ACCOMMODATION

Crescent	5
Harlton	7
Oyster	6
St James	2
Uplands Court	4
White House Hotel	3
Windsor Lodge Hotel	1

RESTAURANTS

Bengal Brasserie	B
Bizzie Lizzie's	C
Hanson's	G
New Capriccio	D
Monkey Café	A
Queen's Hotel	F
Sketty Hall	E

email for the price of the call. ❷
Windsor Lodge Hotel Mount Pleasant
℡ 01792/642158. A two-century-old house like a

country hotel in the city, with nicely decorated en-
suite rooms and elegant but comfortable lounges.
British and French cuisine served in the evenings. ❹

14

SOUTH WALES | Swansea and Gower

The City

Alexandra Road forks right off the High Street immediately south of the train station, leading down to the **Glynn Vivian Art Gallery** (Tues–Sun 10am–5pm; free), a delightful Edwardian showcase of inspiring Welsh art including the huge, frantic canvases of Ceri Richards, Wales' most respected twentieth-century painter, and works by Gwen John and her brother, Augustus, whose mesmerizing portrait of Caitlin Thomas, Dylan's wife, is a real highlight. In the early nineteenth century, Swansea was a noted centre of fine porcelain production, of which the gallery houses a large collection, together with contemporary works from Nantgarw, near Cardiff.

The main shopping streets – considerably tarted-up in recent years – lie to the south, notably underneath the Quadrant Centre where the curving-roofed **market** makes a lively sight, with traditional and long-standing stalls selling local delicacies such as laver bread (a delicious savoury made from sea-weed), as well as cockles trawled from the nearby Loughor estuary, typical Welsh cakes, fish and cheeses. If you're a Dylan Thomas fan, or just keen on books, it's worth popping down Wind Street to Salubrious Passage for the **Dylan Thomas Bookshop**, filled to the rafters with material on the poet. Wind Street has become something of a magnet for bars and restaurants recently, and it's fast become one of the city's more pleasant places to hang out and watch the world drift by.

Hourly buses leave the Quadrant depot for Uplands, a thirty-minute walk from the city centre. North of the main road, leafy avenues rise up the slopes past the sharp terraces of **Cwmdonkin Park**, at the centre of which is a memorial to Dylan Thomas inscribed with lines from *Fern Hill*, one of his best-known poems. On the eastern side of the park is Cwmdonkin Drive, a sharply rising set of solid Victorian semis, notable only for the blue plaque on no. 5, birthplace of the poet in 1914.

The spit of land between Oystermouth Road, the sea and the Tawe estuary has been christened the **Maritime Quarter** – tourist-board-speak for the old docks – built around a vast marina surrounded by legions of modern flats. The city's old South Dock, now cleaned and spruced up, features the enticingly old-fashioned **Swansea Museum** (Tues–Sun 10am–5pm; free). A small grid of nineteenth-century streets around the museum has been thoughtfully cleaned up and now houses some enjoyable cafés, pubs and restaurants.

Behind the museum, in Somerset Place, is the airy **Dylan Thomas Centre**, the national literature centre of Wales (Tues–Sun 10am–4.30pm; free), complete with theatre space, book and craft shops, a great café, and two galleries. One of these is devoted to Dylan Thomas, and includes a mock-up of the shed in which he wrote, in which you can see a fascinating video on his life and work. From here, Burrows Place leads down to the marina and the ever-expanding **Maritime and Industrial Museum** (Tues–Sun 10am–5pm; free). Taking Swansea's maritime tradition as its starting-point, the museum presents a lively history of the city, and includes a working woollen mill, where rows of black machinery, greasy with the wool's lanolin, are operated by staff who gradually turn raw fleece into blankets. A large number of vehicles include an old tram that once rattled along the seafront to Mumbles, and a rare example of Gilbern cars, Wales's principal – and long-dead – contribution to the motor industry.

Eating, drinking and nightlife

Swansea's metamorphosis from a working-class, industrial city into a would-be tourist centre is well demonstrated in the **pubs**, **restaurants** and **entertainment** venues of the city. For nightlife, the city is well placed as a major centre in Wales, with most passing theatre, opera and music of all sorts being obliged to make a stop here. The BBC Welsh Symphony Orchestra appears at the Brangwyn Hall in the Art Deco Civic Centre. Thomas' classics get a regular airing at the Dylan Thomas Theatre, by the marina, while the Taliesin Arts Centre, in the university, is the city's more offbeat venue.

Cafés and restaurants

Bengal Brasserie 47 Walter Rd ☎01792/643747. Best of the many Indian restaurants in Swansea, well worth the ten-minute hike from the city centre. Moderate.

Bizzie Lizzie's 55 Walter Rd ☎01792/473379. Relaxed and informal cellar-bar bistro, with a good range of Welsh, international and vegetarian dishes. Reservations recommended. Inexpensive or moderate.

Hanson's Pilot House Wharf ☎01792/466200. Low-key restaurant on the far side of the marina, at the end of Bathurst Street, serving tasty and well-presented British and Mediterranean dishes. Closed Sun eve. Moderate.

Monkey Café 13 Castle St. Groovy, mosaic-floored café with a relaxed atmosphere, great sandwiches and cakes, and a selection of Mexican and Italian dishes, including many vegetarian options. Inexpensive.

New Capriccio 89 St Helen's Rd ☎01792/648804. Popular Italian restaurant, with a bargain lunch menu. Closed Mon & Sun eve. Inexpensive.

Queen's Hotel Gloucester Place, near the marina. Large old seafaring hotel and pub, with good ales, snack lunches and Sunday roasts. Inexpensive.

Sketty Hall Singleton Park ☎01792/284011. Catering academy in beautiful surroundings, where you can sample the excellent student cuisine for bargain prices. Booking essential. Inexpensive.

Pubs and clubs

Adam and Eve 205 High St. Traditional pub, with a great atmosphere and varied clientele. Well known for the excellence of its beer.

Duke of York Princess Way. Home of *Ellington's* club (small cover charge), Swansea's best venue for jazz and blues music, which hosts nightly gigs.

Escape Club Northampton Lane, off Kingsway ☎01792/652854. Enormous and glitzy mainstream dance club.

Green Dragon Green Dragon Lane, off Wind St ☎01792/641437. Decent pub in the café quarter of town, good for Sunday lunch carvery.

Po Na Na 22 Wind St. New but thriving club with Moroccan "souk" decor, playing mostly garage and hip-hop. Small cover charge on Sat & DJ nights.

Gower

A fifteen-mile-long peninsula of undulating limestone, **Gower** (Gŵyr) points down into the Bristol Channel to the west of Swansea. The area is fringed by sweeping yellow bays and precipitous cliffs, with caves and blowholes to the south, and wide, flat marshes and cockle beds to the north. Bracken heaths dotted with prehistoric remains and tiny villages lie between, and there are numerous castle ruins and curious churches to be found. Out of season, the winding lanes afford wonderful opportunities for exploration, but in the height of the summer – July and August especially – they are congested with caravans shuffling between one overpriced car park and the next.

Gower can be said to start in Swansea's western suburbs, along the coast of Swansea Bay that curves round to a point at the pleasantly old-fashioned resort of **Mumbles**. It finishes with **Rhossili Bay**, a spectacular four-mile yawn of sand backed by the village of Rhossili and occupying the entire western end of the peninsula. The southern coast is punctuated by the village of **PORT EYNON**, home to an excellent YHA **hostel** (☎01792/390706, ⓦwww.yha.org.uk;

April–Oct) and a beautiful beach. West of Port Eynon, the coast becomes a wild, frilly series of inlets and cliffs, topped by a five-mile path that stretches all the way to the peninsula's glorious westernmost point, **Worms Head**. The northern coast merges into the tidal flats of the estuary.

Mumbles and Oystermouth

At the far westernmost end of Swansea Bay, **Mumbles** (Mwmbwls) derives its name from the French *mamelles*, or breasts, a reference to the twin islets off the end of Mumbles Head, and is now used as the name for all of the loose sprawl around **OYSTERMOUTH** (Ystumllwynarth). Here, the seafront is an unbroken curve of budget hotels, breezy pubs and cafés, leading down to the refurbished pier and the rocky plug of Mumbles Head. Around the headland, reached either by the longer, barren coast road or by a short walk over the hill, is the district of **Langland Bay**, whose sandy beach is fairly popular with surfers. The small **tourist office** (daily: June–Aug 9.30am–5.30pm; April, May, Sept & Oct 10am–4pm; ℡01792/361302) is in Oystermouth Square, near the hilltop ruins of **Oystermouth Castle** (April–Sept daily 11am–5.30pm; £1). Founded as a Norman watchtower, the castle was strengthened to withstand attacks by the Welsh before being converted for more amenable residential purposes during the fourteenth century. Today you can see the remains of a late thirteenth-century keep next to a more ornate three-storey ruin incorporating an impressive banqueting hall and state rooms.

The Mumbles is a lively and enjoyable base for the southern Gower coast, with a good clutch of typically tacky seaside entertainment on offer. **Accommodation** is plentiful: try *Henfaes Guesthouse*, 4 Rotherslade Rd (℡01792/366003; ❶); the Victorian shorefront *Tides Reach*, 388 Mumbles Rd (℡01792/404877; ❸); the superb *Alexandra House*, 366 Mumbles Rd (℡01792/406406; ❸); or the sumptuous *Osborne Hotel* (℡01792/366274; ❻), high on a cliff top on Rotherslade Road in Langland Bay. There are several good **places to eat** including the inexpensive *Coffee Denn*, 34 Newton Rd, which is good for light lunches and imaginative ice cream sundaes. *Seafront 604*, 604 Mumbles Rd, does moderately priced light meals, while the expensive, fairly formal *Patricks*, 636 Mumbles Rd (℡01792/360199; closed Sun eve), serves an eclectic range of wonderful modern dishes. *Castell Amare* (℡01792/368486) is a stunning new Italian eatery on the headland overlooking Bracelet Bay. The scores of pubs along the seafront constitute the **Mumbles Mile**, one of Wales's most notorious pub crawls. The ones to linger in are the *Antelope*, the *Oystercatcher* and the *White Rose*.

Rhossili and Worms Head

The village of **RHOSSILI** (Rhosili), at the western end of Gower, is a centre for walkers and beach loungers alike. Dylan Thomas described the terrain to the west of the village as "rubbery, gull-limed grass, the sheep-pilled stones, the pieces of bones and feathers", and you can tread in his footsteps to **Worms Head**, an isolated string of rocks, accessible for only five hours, at low tide. At the head of the road, near the village, is a well-stocked National Trust **information centre** (April–Oct daily 10.30am–5.30pm; ℡01792/390707). They post the tide times outside, for those heading for Worms Head, and hold details of local companies renting surfing and hang-gliding equipment.

Below the village, a great curve of white sand stretches away into the distance, a dazzling coastline vast enough to absorb the crowds, especially if you are prepared to head north towards **Burry Holms**, an islet that is cut off at high tide. The northern end of the beach can also be reached along the small lane which runs from Reynoldston, in the middle of the peninsula, to **LLANGENNITH**, on the other side of the towering, 633-foot **Rhossili Down**. In the village, PJ's Surfshop (℡01792/386669) rents a wide range of **surfboards** (£8/day) and boogie boards (£6/day), and there's a Surf School (℡01792/386426), a mile away at the *Hillend* campsite (see below), which runs half-day (£20) and full-day (£30) **surfing courses**.

In Rhossili village, there are some great **B&Bs**, including *Hampstead* (℡01792/390545; ②), almost half a mile back from the beach but with superb views from the large rooms; and the very friendly *Meadow View*, a mile from the beach (℡01792/390518; ①), with small but nicely furnished rooms. **Campsites** can be found at *Pitton Cross Park* (℡01792/390593), close to Meadow View, at the foot of the northern slopes of Rhossili Down; and at *Hillend* (℡01792/386204), at the end of the southern lane from Llangennith, behind the dunes that bump down to the glorious beach. There's a rather dingy **restaurant** and bar in Rhossili, but you're better off at the *King Arthur*, in nearby Reynoldston, which serves hearty meals and hosts live folk and rock music nights. If you're feeling particularly flush, exquisite food and accommodation can be found at *Fairyhill* (℡01792/390139, Ⓦwww.fairyhill.net; ⑦), just north of Reynoldston.

Southern Carmarthenshire

Frequently overlooked in the stampede towards the resorts of Pembrokeshire, **southern Carmarthenshire** is a quiet part of the world, with few of the problems of mass tourism suffered by more popular parts of Wales. **Kidwelly**, with its dramatically sited castle, is the only reason to stop before **Carmarthen**, the unquestioned capital of its region but one which fails to live up to the promise of its status. There's little of great interest in town, but it does make a good enough base for forays up the **Tywi Valley**. On the western side of the Taf estuary, the village of **Laugharne** has become a place of pilgrimage for Dylan Thomas devotees.

Kidwelly

The sleepy little town of **KIDWELLY** (Cydweli) is dominated by its imposing **castle** (June–Sept daily 9.30am–6pm; April, May & Oct daily 9.30am–5pm; Nov–March Mon–Sat 9.30am–4pm, Sun 11am–4pm; £2.50; CADW). Established around 1106 by the Bishop of Salisbury as a satellite of Sherborne Abbey in Dorset, the castle is situated at a strategic point overlooking the River Gwendraeth and vast tracts of coast. On entering through the massive fourteenth-century gatehouse, you can still see portcullis slats and murder holes, through which noxious substances could be tipped onto unwelcome visitors. The gatehouse forms the centrepiece of the impressively intact semicircular outer ward walls, which can be climbed for some great views over the grassy courtyard and rectangular inner ward to the river. This is the oldest surviving part of the castle, dating from around 1275. The upper stories were added in the fourteenth century by the nephew of warlord Edward I. On the northwest edge of the town is the small-scale **Industrial Museum**, on Priory Street (Easter–Sept Mon–Fri 10am–5pm, Sat & Sun 2–5pm; free), housed in an old tin-plate works. Many of the original features have been preserved, including the rolling mills where long lines of tin were rolled and spun into wafer-thin slices.

There's decent pub **accommodation** at the *Old Malthouse*, by the castle (℡01554/891091; ❸), and superb B&B at *Penlan Isaf Farm* (℡01554/890084, Ⓦwww.visitcarmarthenshire.co.uk/penlanisaf; ❷), on a dairy farm overlooking the town. You can **camp** at *Tanylan Farm* (℡01267/267306), which perches alongside the estuary west of Kidwelly. Good **food** and **drink** are available at the cosy *Boot & Shoe*, 2 Castle St, or at the excellent *King's Arms* in the village of Llansaint, up in the hills a couple of miles west of town.

Carmarthen and around

CARMARTHEN (Caerfyrddin), the ancient capital of the region, is a solid, if hardly thrilling, sort of place. It remains the major town in west Wales where the native language is heard at all times, and was once – in the early eighteenth century – the largest town in Wales. Founded as a Roman fort, it is now best known as the supposed birthplace of the wizard Merlin (Myrddin in Welsh gives the town its name). A good place to catch up on the town's past is the small **Heritage Centre** (Wed–Sat 11am–4pm; free), tucked away down on the Quay Side, by the river.

The most picturesque part of town lies spread out at the base of Edward I's **castle**, around King Street and Nott Square, the main shopping hub. The town's handsome eighteenth-century **Guildhall** sits just off Nott Square, from the bottom of which Darkgate leads to Lammas Street, a wide Georgian thoroughfare flanked by coaching inns. From the top of Nott Square, King Street heads northeast towards the undistinguished **St Peter's Church** and the Victorian School of Art, which has now metamorphosed into **Oriel Myrddin** (Mon–Sat 10.30am–5pm; free), a craft centre and excellent gallery that acts as an imaginative showcase for local artists.

The severe grey Bishop's Palace at **Abergwili**, two miles east of Carmarthen, was the seat of the Bishop of St David's between 1542 and 1974, and now houses the **Carmarthenshire County Museum** (Mon–Sat 10am–4.30pm; free), a spirited amble through the history of the area. This surprisingly interesting exhibition covers the history of Welsh translations of the New Testament and Book of Common Prayer – both first translated here, in 1567. Local pottery, archeological finds, wooden dressers and a lively history of local castles are presented in well-annotated displays. The upstairs section examines a number of topics including geology, the local coracle industry and the origins of one of Wales's first eisteddfodau (Welsh cultural festivals), held in Carmarthen in 1450.

The **train station** lies over Carmarthen Bridge, on the south side of the river. All **buses** terminate at the bus station on Blue Street, just on the north side of the bridge, and many connect with trains. The town's **tourist office** is on Lammas Street, close to the Crimea Monument (daily: Easter–Oct 9.30am–5.30pm; Nov–Easter 10am–4.30pm; ℡01267/231557). For **bike rental**, go to Ar Dy Feic (On Yer Bike), over the river on Llangunnor Road (℡01267/221182).

There's lots of **accommodation** in town, especially on Lammas Street, where you'll find the *Boar's Head* (℡01267/222789, Ⓦwww.boars-head-hotel.demon.co.uk; ❷), one of the town's grandest old coaching inns, and the *Drovers Arms* (℡01267/237646; ❷). The best B&Bs are *Y Dderwen Fach*, 98 Priory St (℡01267/234193; ❶), and the *Old Priory* guesthouse, 20 Priory St (℡01267/237471; ❶), both out along the main road to Lampeter and Llandeilo. If you're looking for something a little more remote, don't pass up *Tŷ Mawr* (℡01267/202332, Ⓦwww.tymawrbrechfa.co.uk; ❺), an oak-beamed country house hotel in the entirely unspoilt village of **BRECHFA**, some twelve miles northeast of Carmarthen. You can find good snack **food** at the old-fashioned *Morris Tea Rooms*, almost opposite the Lyric Theatre in King Street, and at the vegetarian café in the Waverley Stores health-food shop, on 23 Lammas St. The best meals in town can be found at the wonderful *Quayside Brasserie*, on the Tywi quay (☎01267/223000; closed Sun).

Laugharne

The village of **LAUGHARNE** (Talacharn), on the western side of the Taf estuary, is a delightful spot, with its ragged castle looming over the reeds and tidal flats and narrow lanes snuggling in behind. Catch it in high season though and you're immediately aware that Laugharne is increasingly being taken over by the legend of the poet **Dylan Thomas**.

At the end of a narrow lane bumping along the estuary is the **Dylan Thomas Boathouse** (daily: Easter & May–Oct 10am–5.30pm; Nov–Easter 10.30am–3.30pm; £2.75), the simple home of the Thomas family from 1949 until Dylan's death in 1953. It's an enchanting museum, with views of the peaceful, ever-changing water and light of the estuary and its "heron-priested shore". Inside, a period wireless set in the intact living room regales you with the rich tones of the poet reading his own work, while contemporary newspaper reports of his demise show how he was, while alive, a fairly minor literary figure. Back along the narrow lane, you can peer into the blue garage where he wrote: curled photographs of literary heroes, a pen collection and numerous scrunched-up balls of paper on the cheap desk suggest quite effectively that he is about to return at any minute. Thomas is buried in the graveyard of the parish church in the village centre, his grave marked by a simple white cross.

Dylan Thomas

Dylan Thomas was the stereotypical Celt – fiery, verbose, richly talented and habitually drunk. Born in 1914 into a snugly middle-class family in Swansea's Uplands district, Dylan's first glimmers of literary greatness came when he was posted, as a young reporter, to the *South Wales Evening Post* in Swansea. Some of his most popular tales in the *Portrait of the Artist as a Young Dog* were inspired during this period.

Rejecting the coarse provincialism of Swansea and Welsh life, Thomas arrived in London as a broke twenty-year-old in 1934, weeks before the appearance of his first volume of poetry, which was published as the first prize in a *Sunday Referee* competition. Another volume followed shortly afterwards, cementing the engaging young Welshman's reputation in the British literary establishment. He married in 1937, and the newlyweds returned to Wales, settling in the hushed, provincial backwater of Laugharne. Short stories – crackling with rich and melancholy humour – tumbled out as swiftly as poems, further widening his base of admirers, though, like so many other writers, Thomas has only gained star status posthumously. Perhaps better than anyone, he writes in an identifiably Welsh, rhythmic wallow in the language.

Thomas, especially in public, liked to adopt the persona of what he perceived to be an archetypal stage Welshman: sonorous tones, loquacious, romantic and inclined towards a stiff tipple. This role was particularly popular in the United States, where he journeyed on lucrative lecture tours. It was on one of these that he died, in 1953, poisoned by a massive whisky overdose. Just one month earlier, he had put the finishing touches to what many regard as his masterpiece: *Under Milk Wood*, a "play for voices". Describing the dreams, thoughts and lives of a straggling Welsh seaside community called Llareggub – mis-spelt Llaregyb by the po-faced BBC, who couldn't sanction the usage of the expression "bugger all" backwards – it is loosely based on Laugharne, New Quay in Cardiganshire and a vast dose of Thomas's own imagination.

Laugharne has numerous Thomas connections, and plays them with curiously disgruntled aplomb – none more so than the great alcoholic's old boozing hole, **Brown's Hotel** on the main street where, in the nicotine-crusted front bar, Thomas's cast-iron table still sits in a window alcove. At the bottom of the main street, the gloomy hulk of **Laugharne Castle** (Easter–Sept 10am–5pm; £2; CADW) broods over the estuary. Two of the early medieval towers survive, although most of the ruins are those of the Tudor mansion built over the original for Sir John Perrot. The views from the domed roof over the tight, huddled little town are sublime.

Surprisingly, Laugharne has little B&B **accommodation**. *Castle House*, on Market Lane in the village centre (T01994/427616, W www.laugharne.co.uk; ❷), has large en-suite rooms and gorgeous estuary views from some rooms; while *Swan Cottage*, 20 Gosport St (T01994/427409; ❷), is very welcoming. The nearest **campsite** is *Ants Hill Camping Park*, just north of Laugharne (T01994/427293). For **eating**, the choice is a little wider: try the moderately priced *Stable Door* (closed Mon & Tues), near the central town hall, or the *Under Milk Wood Inn*, on the square. If your budget's a little more generous, treat yourself at *The Cors* (T01994/427219; Thurs–Sat) on Newbridge Road, which serves wonderful food in a genteel country house atmosphere.

The Tywi Valley

The **River Tywi** curves and darts its way east from Carmarthen through some of the most magical scenery in south Wales. The thirty-mile trip to Llandovery is punctuated by gentle, impossibly green hills topped with ruined castles, notably the wonderful **Carreg Cennen**. It's not hard to see why the Merlin legend has taken such a hold in these parts – the landscape does seem infused with a kind of eerie splendour. Along the way, a couple of budding gardens have sprung up in the last couple of years: one completely new in the form of the **National Botanic Garden of Wales**, the other a faithful reconstruction of linked walled gardens around the long-abandoned house of **Aberglasney**. Further upstream, the market town of **Llandovery** makes a good base for visiting the Roman gold mine at **Dolaucothi**.

The National Botanic Garden and around

The new **National Botanic Garden of Wales**, nine miles west of Carmarthen (daily: Easter–Aug 10am–6pm, Sept & Oct 10am–5.30pm, Nov–Easter 10am–4.30pm; £6.50, discounts for groups and those who arrive by bike or public transport; W www.gardenofwales.org.uk) is slowly beginning to warrant its considerable hype. Although it will be years before the place is anything like complete, enough of the jigsaw pieces are in place to see its huge potential. Buses #165 and #166 run every two hours from Carmarthen train station to the garden, where, at the entrance, you'll find a fully-functioning **tourist office** (same times; T01558/669084).

From the entrance, you pass up the central broadwalk, past lakes, sculpture and geological outcrops from all over Wales. Walks head down past the lakes towards slate bed plants and different wood and wetland habitats. On the other side of the broadwalk, the double-walled garden is being teased back to life. On the estate's outer edges are recreations of moorland, spring wood, prairie and native Welsh habitats.

At the top of the hill is the garden's most audacious feature: the vast oval **glasshouse** designed by Norman Foster, a truly stunning piece of architecture that justifies a visit on its own. Inside are plants from regions with a Mediterranean climate: the Cape region of South Africa, southwestern Australia, Chile, California and the Mediterranean itself. Near the glasshouse lie the remains of **Middleton Hall**, whose old estate forms the centrepiece of the gardens. A nearby group of buildings house the restaurant, an excellent exhibition about the Welsh herbalists known as the Physicians of Myddfai and the new Theatre Botanica, all focused around **Millennium Square**, the venue for open-air concerts and performances. The entire garden has been designed around principles of sustainability: rainwater is caught and used for irrigation; the glasshouses are heated by burning wood coppiced on the grounds; and human waste is transformed into essentially pure water by means of a series of reed beds. The theme runs through to a large section of the surrounding land which is being turned over to organic farming using Welsh breeds of cattle and sheep – which eventually end up on a plate in the visitors' restaurant.

Aberglasney

A complementary and much older garden has recently opened a few miles to the east, around the dilapidated stately home of **Aberglasney** (April–Oct daily 10am–6pm; Nov–March Mon–Fri 10.30am–3pm; £5; ⓦ www.aberglasney .org), half a mile south of the A40 near Broad Oak. There's little to see in the stabilized shell of the house itself, but archeological work has pretty much peeled back half a century of neglect to reveal a set of interlinking walled gardens mostly constructed between the sixteenth and eighteenth centuries. The basic framework – the walls, ponds and outline of the beds – is largely intact, but detailed digging continues to uncover more about the site, and extensive restoration is underway in the kitchen garden and secular cloister garden – thought to be the only one in Britain. A walkway leads around the top of the cloister, giving access to a set of six Victorian aviaries from where there are great views over the Jacobean pool garden. The highlight of the garden must be the **yew tunnel**, planted around three hundred years ago and trained over to root on the far side.

Llandeilo and around

Fifteen miles east of Carmarthen, the main street – Rhosmaen Street – of the handsome small market town of **LLANDEILO** climbs up from the Tywi bridge. Although there is little in the way of actual sights in the town, Llandeilo is brilliantly situated in a bowl of hills, a quiet, rustic place whose few streets cluster around the main thoroughfare. Behind the main street are the **tourist office** (Easter–Oct Mon–Sat 10am–5pm; ☎01558/824226) in the principal car park and, a couple of blocks to the north, the **train station**. **Accommodation** in town includes the very decent *Glynceirch* B&B (☎01558/823378; ❶), near the station at the northern end of Rhosmaen Street, or, further down the same street into the town centre, the relatively plush *Cawdor Arms* (☎01558/823500; ⓦ www.cawdor-arms.co.uk; ❾), which serves expensive but beautifully cooked evening meals. *Y Capel Bach* bistro, a couple of doors down, serves tasty, moderately priced **meals**, and there is good drinking to be had across the road at the *Castle Hotel*.

A mile west of Llandeilo is the gorgeous parkland of **Plas Dinefwr**, site also of two splendid castles. On a wooded bluff above the Tywi sits the tumbledown shell of **Dinefwr Old Castle** which became ill-suited to the needs of the landowning Rhys family, who aspired to something a little more luxurious. The "new" castle, now named **Newton House** (April–Oct Mon & Thurs–Sun

11am–5pm; house & park £3, park only £2; NT), was built in 1523, and given a new limestone facade in the 1860s.

Carreg Cennen

Isolated in rural hinterland, four miles southeast of Llandeilo, is one of the most magnificently sited castles in the whole of Wales, **Carreg Cennen Castle** (daily: April–Oct 9.30am–7.30pm; Nov–March 9.30am–dusk; £2.50; CADW), just beyond the tiny hamlet of Trap. Sir Urien, one of King Arthur's knights, is said to have built his fortress on the fearsome rocky outcrop, although the first known construction dates from 1248. Carreg Cennen fell to the English in 1277, during Edward I's initial invasion of Wales, and was finally abandoned after being partially destroyed in 1462 by the Earl of Pembroke, who believed it to be the base of a group of lawless rebels. The most astounding aspect of the castle is its commanding position, 300ft above a sheer drop down into the green valley of the small River Cennen. The highlights of a visit are the views down into the river valley and the long descent down into a watery, pitch-black **cave** that is said to have served as a well. Torches are essential (rented from the excellent tearoom near the car park) – it's worth continuing as far as possible and then turning them off to experience absolute darkness.

Llandovery

Twelve miles beyond Llandeilo, the town of **LLANDOVERY** (Llanymddyfri) has architecture and a layout that have changed little for centuries. As with so many mid-Wales settlements to the north, an influx of New Agers since the 1960s has had a discernible effect on the town: there's a thriving independent theatre, and bookshops and wholefood stores abound. Alongside this more alternative flavour, Llandovery is still a major centre for its cattle market, held every other Tuesday.

On the south side of the main Broad Street, a grassy mound holds the scant remains of the town's **castle**. Just in front, an eerie new stainless-steel sculpture commemorates the gruesome death here, in 1401, of Llywelyn ap Gruffydd Fychan at the hands of Henry IV's men in Owain Glyndŵr's war of independence.

Broad Street has been Llandovery's thoroughfare for years, as can be seen from the solid early nineteenth-century town houses and earlier inns that line the road as it widens towards the cobbled, rectangular Market Square. Above the tourist office on Kings Road, the excellent **Llandovery Heritage Centre** (Easter–Sept daily 10am–5.30pm; Oct–Easter Mon–Sat 10am–4pm, Sun 2–4pm; donation appreciated) depicts some powerful local legends and tales. Stone Street heads north from the Market Square to the **Llandovery Theatre**, a shadow of its former self but worth keeping an eye on for an update on events in the area.

Llandovery **train station** sits on the main A40 just before Broad Street; **buses** leave from Broad Street and Market Square. The joint **tourist office** and **Brecon Beacons National Park office** (Easter–Sept daily 10am–5.30pm; Oct-Easter Mon-Sat 10am-4pm, Sun 2-4pm; ☎01550/720693) is on Kings Road, the continuation of Broad Street.

The best central **accommodation** is at *The Drovers*, 9 Market Square (☎01550/721115; ❶), an eighteenth-century town house full of antique furniture. Less central B&Bs include: *Pencerrig*, New Road, on the way out of town towards Llandeilo (☎01550/721259; ❶); the superb Gothic-styled en-suites at *Cwm Rhuddan Mansion* (☎01550/721414; ❷), a mile southwest on the A4069; and, a mile further out on the same road, *Cwmgwyn Farm*, Llangadog Road (☎01550/720410; ❷). The nearest **campsite**, a mile east off the A40, is the

Erwlon (☎01550/720332). Llandovery has precious few good **places to eat**, though there are a number of daytime cafés and tearooms, mainly around the Market Square, and the *Castle Hotel*, on Broad Street, offers delicious, moderately priced lunchtime and evening food. For **drinking**, the eccentric and bizarrely old-fashioned *Red Lion*, a red, colonnaded house nestled in an easy-to-miss corner at 2 Market Square, can't be beaten.

The Dolaucothi Gold Mine

The countryside to the west of Llandovery is blissfully quiet, with just a handful of main roads and lanes that rarely contain traffic of any volume. The principal route off the A40 between Llandeilo and Llandovery, the A482, heads towards the straggling village of **PUMSAINT** (Five Saints). The origin of the name is explained by a stone found near the entrance of the **Dolaucothi Gold Mine** (Easter to mid-Sept daily 10am–5pm; £2.60; NT), half a mile off the main road. Indentations in the rock are said to be the marks left by five sleeping saints, who rested here one night. Pumsaint is the only place in Britain where it is certain that the Romans mined gold, laying complicated and astoundingly advanced systems to extract the precious metal from the rock. The remains of Roman workings – a few water channels and an open cast mine – can still be seen around the site. An underground **tour** (£3.60) goes deep into the mine workings and usually allows visitors to prospect for gold themselves.

Tenby and Caldey Island

On a natural promontory of great strategic importance, the beguilingly old-fashioned resort of **TENBY** (Dinbych-y-Pysgod), wedged between two sweeping beaches fronting an island-studded seascape, is everything a seaside resort should be. Narrow streets wind down from the medieval centre to the harbour past miniature gardens fashioned to catch the afternoon sun. Steps lead down the steeper slopes to dockside arches which still house fishmongers selling the morning's catch.

Tenby has a long pedigree. First mentioned in a ninth-century bardic poem, the town grew under the twelfth-century Normans, who erected a castle on the headland in their attempt to colonize south Pembrokeshire and create a "**Little England beyond Wales**" – an appellation by which the area is still known today. Three times in the twelfth and thirteenth centuries the town was ransacked by the Welsh. In response, the castle was fortified once more and the stout town walls – largely still intact – were built. Tenby prospered as a major port for a wide variety of foodstuffs and fine goods between the fourteenth and sixteenth centuries, and although decline followed, the arrival of the railway brought renewed wealth as the town became a fashionable resort. Lines of neat, prosperous hotels and expensive shops still stand haughtily along the seafront.

Although the town is extremely conservative, with a large population of retired people, there is plenty of entertainment and a huge number of pubs and restaurants. Not for nothing has the town become one of Britain's most fashionable venues for hen and stag parties, something the authorities here are keen to discourage. In the middle of summer, it can seem full to bursting point, with heavy traffic restrictions and a considerable rush on decent accommodation. Tenby is also one of the major stopping-off points along the **Pembrokeshire Coast Path**, a welcome burst of glitter and excitement amidst mile upon mile of undulating cliff scenery. The **National Park** boundary skirts around the edge of the town. A couple of miles offshore, the old monastic ruins of **Caldey Island** make for a pleasant day-trip.

The Town

Tenby is shaped like a triangle, with two sides formed by the coast meeting at Castle Hill. The third side is formed by the remains of the twenty-foot-high town **walls**, first built in the late thirteenth century and massively strengthened by Jasper Tudor, Earl of Pembroke and uncle of Henry VII, in 1457. Further refortification came in the 1580s, when Tenby was considered to be in the frontline against a possible attack by the Spanish Armada. In the middle of the remaining stretch is the only town gate still standing, at **Five Arches**, a semi-circular barbican that combined practical day-to-day usage with hidden look-outs and angles acute enough to surprise invaders.

The centrepiece and most notable landmark of the town centre is the 152-foot spire of the largely fifteenth-century **St Mary's Church**, between St George's Street and Tudor Square. A pleasantly light interior shows the elaborate ceiling bosses in the chancel to good effect, and fifteenth-century tombs of local barons demonstrate Tenby's important mercantile tradition.

Wedged between the town walls and the two bays, the **old town** is a great place to wander, with many of the original medieval lanes still intact in the immediate area around the parish church. **Sun Alley** is a tiny crack between overhanging whitewashed stone houses that connects Crackwell and High streets. Due east, on the other side of the church, **Quay Hill** runs parallel, a narrow set of steps and cobbles tumbling down past some of the town's oldest houses to the top of the harbour. Wedged in a corner of Quay Hill is the **Tudor Merchant's House** (April–Sept Mon, Tues & Thurs–Sat 10am–5pm, Sun 1–5pm; Oct Mon, Tues, Thurs & Fri 10am–3pm, Sun noon–3pm; £2; NT), built in the late fifteenth century for a wealthy local merchant at the time when Tenby was second only to Bristol as an important west-coast port. The rambling house is on three floors, packed with period furniture from the six-teenth century, although more notable are the tapering Flemish-style chimney pieces, a prominent local fashion.

During the day, the **harbour** is the scene of considerable activity as the departure point for numerous excursion boats, the most popular being the short trip over to Caldey Island (see below). Above the harbour is the headland and **Castle Hill**, where paths and flower beds have been planted around the remaining **gatehouse** of the Norman castle. Here, the town **museum** (Easter–Oct daily 10am–6pm; Nov–Easter Mon–Fri 10am–5pm; £2) doubles as a small art gallery and is typical of Tenby: slightly ponderous and municipal-ly minded, but still interesting.

Practicalities

Tenby's **train station** is at the western end of the town centre, at the bottom of Warren Street. Some **buses** stop at South Parade, at the top of Trafalgar Road, although most call at the bus shelter on Upper Park Road. The **tourist office** faces the North Beach, on The Croft (daily: Easter–Sept 10am–6pm; mid-July to Aug closes 8pm; Oct 10am–5.30pm; Nov–Easter Mon–Sat 10am–4pm; ☎01834/842404).

As a major resort, Tenby has dozens of **hotels** and **guest houses**, all pressed from pretty much the same mould, though paying more gets you a wider range of facilities and a sea view. The best budget place is the spotless *Boulston Cottage*, 29 Trafalgar Rd (☎01834/843289; ❶). *Lyndale Guest House*, Warren Street

(☎01834/842836; ❶), is a welcoming B&B near the station, happy to cater for vegetarians; and *Ashby House*, 24 Victoria St (☎01834/842867; ❷), is good too. The *Atlantic*, The Esplanade (☎01834/842881, ⓦwww.atlantic-hotel.uk.com; ❺), is at the top of the range, with a couple of good restaurants and even a small indoor pool. There are a couple of YHA **hostels** nearby: bus #350 runs to *Pentlepoir*, four miles north, near Saundersfoot train station (☎01834/812333, ⓦwww.yha.org.uk; ❶; April–Sept); while four miles west of Tenby, overlooking the cliffs, is the bright and modern *Manorbier*, at Skrinkle Haven (☎01834/871803, ⓦwww.yha.org.uk; ❶; March–Oct). You can **camp** there, and at the small and semi-official *Meadow Farm*, Northcliff, on the northern fringes of town (☎01834/844829; April–Sept).

There are dozens of **cafés** and **restaurants** around town. For ice cream and Italian snacks, try *Fecci and Sons*, Upper Frog Street. *Quay Room*, on Quay Hill, is good for coffee and snacks, while the moderately priced *La Cave*, Upper Frog Street (☎01834/843038), *Paxton's Bistro* at the *Tenby House Hotel*, Tudor Square (☎01834/842000) and the more expensive *Plantagenet*, Quay Hill (☎01834/842350), offer well-cooked local specialities. For **pubs**, head for the *Lifeboat Tavern*, Tudor Square, or the *Coach and Horses*, Upper Frog Street. The *Three Mariners*, on St George's Street, has good beer and live music.

Caldey Island

Looming large over Tenby's seascape is **Caldey Island** (Ynys Pyr), a couple of miles offshore. Celtic monks first settled here in the sixth century, perhaps establishing an offshoot of St Illtud's monastery at Llantwit Major. Little is then known of the island until 1136, when it was given to the Benedictine monks of St Dogmael's at Cardigan, who founded their priory here. Upon the Dissolution of the monasteries in 1536, the Benedictine monks left the island and a fanciful succession of owners bought and sold it on a whim, until it was, once again, sold to a Benedictine monastic order in 1906 and subsequently to an order of Reformed Cistercians. The island has been a monastic home almost constantly ever since.

Boats leave Tenby Harbour (mid-May to mid-Sept Mon–Sat 10am–4pm every 15min; Easter to mid-May & mid-Sept to Oct Mon–Fri 10am–3pm every 30min; weather permitting; ☎01834/842296 or 844453; £7). Tickets for the twenty-minute journey (not tied to any specific sailing) are sold at the kiosk in Castle Square, directly above the harbour. On landing at Caldey's jetty, a short walk leads through the woods to the island's main settlement.

The village itself is the main hub of Caldey life. As well as a tiny post office and popular tearoom, there's a **perfume shop** selling the herbal fragrances distilled by the monks from Caldey's abundant flora. The narrow road going to the left leads down to the heavily restored **chapel of St David**, whose most impressive feature is its round-arched Norman door. Opposite is the gathering point for tours of the garish twentieth-century **monastery** (July & Aug every 2hr; rest of year 1 daily; men only), a white, turreted heap that resembles a Disney castle. A lane leads south from the village to the old **priory**, abandoned at the Dissolution and restored at the turn of the twentieth century. The centrepiece of the complex is the remarkable, twelfth-century **St Illtud's Church**, which houses one of the most significant pre-Norman finds in Wales, the sandstone **Ogham Cross**, found under the stained-glass window on the south side of the nave. It is carved with an inscription from the sixth century which was added to, in Latin, during the ninth. The lane continues south from the site, climbing up to the gleaming white island **lighthouse**, built in 1828, from which there are memorable views.

Southern Pembrokeshire

The southern zigzag of coast that darts west from Tenby is a strange mix of caravan parks, Ministry of Defence shooting ranges, spectacularly beautiful bays and gull-covered cliffs. From Tenby, the A4139 passes through **Penally**, with its wonderful beach, and continues past idyllic coves, the lily ponds at **Bosherston** and the remarkable and ancient **St Govan's Chapel**, squeezed into a rock cleft above the crashing waves. The ancient town of **Pembroke** really only warrants a visit to its impressive castle before pressing on to neighbouring **Lamphey**, with its fine Bishop's Palace. **Buses** to most corners of the peninsula radiate out from Haverfordwest (see p.802).

Penally to Bosherton

Just over a mile down the A4139 from Tenby, the dormitory village of **PENALLY** is unremarkable save for its vast beach. The coastal path hugs the clifftop from the viewpoint at Giltar Point, just below Penally, reaching the glorious privately owned beach at the headland of **Lydstep Haven** after two miles (fee charged for the sands). A mile further west is the cove of **Skrinkle Haven**, and above it the excellent *Manorbier* YHA **hostel** (☎01834/871803, ⓦwww.yha.org.uk), where you can also **camp**.

The next part of the coast path heads inland to avoid the artillery range that occupies the beautiful outcrop of **Old Castle Head**, then leads straight into the quaint village of **MANORBIER** (Maenorbŷr), pronounced "manner-beer", birthplace in 1146 of the Welsh-Norman historian, writer and ecclesiastical reformer Giraldus Cambrensis. Manorbier's **castle** (April–Sept daily 10.30am–5pm; £2.50), founded in the early twelfth century as an impressive baronial residence, sits above the village and its beach on a hill of wild gorse. The Norman walls are in a good state of repair, surrounding an inner grass courtyard in which the extensive remains of the castle's chapel and state rooms jostle for position with the nineteenth-century domestic residence. In the walls

The Pembrokeshire National Park and Coast Path

The **Pembrokeshire Coast** is Britain's only predominantly sea-based national park (ⓦwww.pembrokeshirecoast.org.uk), hugging the rippled coast around the entire western section of Wales. Established in 1952, the park is not one easily identifiable mass, rather a series of occasionally unconnected coastal and inland scenic patches.

Crawling around almost every wriggle of the coastline, the **Pembrokeshire Coast Path** winds 186 miles from St Dogmael's near Cardigan in the north to its southern point at Amroth, near Tenby. For the vast majority of the way, the path clings precariously to cliff-top routes, overlooking seal-basking rocks, craggy offshore islands, unexpected gashes of sand and shrieking clouds of sea birds. The most popular and ruggedly inspiring segments of the coast path are: either side of St Bride's Bay, around St David's Head and the Marloes Peninsula; the stretch along the southern coast from the castle at Manorbier to the tiny cliff chapel at Bosherston; and the generally quieter northern coast either side of Fishguard, past undulating contours, massive cliffs, bays and old ports.

Of all the seasons, spring is perhaps the finest for walking as the crowds are yet to arrive and the cliff-top flora is at its most vivid. There are numerous publications available about the coast path, of which the best is Brian John's *National Trail Guide* (£11), which includes sections of 1:25,000 maps of the route. The National Park publishes a handy *Coast Path Accommodation* guide (£2.25), detailing B&Bs and campsites along its entire length.

and buildings are a warren of dark passageways to explore, occasionally opening out into little cells with lacklustre wax figures purporting to illustrate the castle's history.

The rocky little harbour at **Stackpole Quay**, reached via the small lane from Freshwater East through East Trewent, is a good starting point for walks along the breathtaking cliffs to the north. Another walk leads half a mile south to one of the finest beaches in Pembrokeshire, **Barafundle Bay**, with its soft beach fringed by wooded cliffs at either end. The path continues around the coast, through the dunes of **Stackpole Warren**, to **BROAD HAVEN**, where a pleasant small beach overlooks several rocky islets, now managed by the National Trust. Basing yourself here gives good access to the nearby **Bosherston Lakes** inland, three artificial fingers of water beautifully landscaped in the late eighteenth century. The westernmost lake is the most scenic, especially in late spring and early summer when the lilies that form a carpet across its surface are in full bloom.

Another lane dips south from the village of **BOSHERSTON**, across the MoD training grounds, to a spot overlooking the cliffs where tiny **St Govan's Chapel** is wedged: it's a remarkable building, known to be at least eight hundred years old. Steps descend straight into the sandy-floored chapel, now devoid of any furnishings save for the simple stone altar.

Pembroke and around

The old county town of **PEMBROKE** (Penfro) and its fearsome castle sit on the southern side of the River Pembroke, a continuation of the massive Milford Haven waterway, described by Nelson as the greatest natural harbour in the world. Despite its location, Pembroke is surprisingly dull, with one long main street of attractive Georgian and Victorian houses, some intact stretches of medieval town wall but little else to catch the eye. The town grew up solely to serve the castle, the mightiest link in the chain of Norman strongholds built across southern Wales. The walled town, drawn out along a hilltop ridge, flourished as a port for Pembrokeshire goods, which were sold throughout Britain and exported to Ireland, France and Spain. The castle was destroyed by Cromwell during the Civil War, and though the town developed as a centre of leather-making, weaving, dyeing and tailoring, it never really regained its former importance.

Pembroke's history is inextricably bound up with that of its impregnable **castle** (daily: April–Sept 9.30am–6pm; March & Oct 10am–5pm; Nov–Feb 10am–4pm; £3), founded by the Normans, but rebuilt between 1189 and 1245. During the Civil War, Pembroke was a Parliamentarian stronghold until the town's military governor suddenly switched allegiance to the king, whereupon Cromwell's troops sacked the castle after a 48-day siege. Yet despite Cromwell's battering, and centuries of subsequent neglect, Pembroke still inspires feelings of awe at its sheer, bloody-minded bulk, even if it is largely due to extensive restoration over the last century. The soaring gatehouse leads into the large, grassy courtyard around the vast, round Norman **keep**, 75ft high and with walls 18ft thick, crowned by a dome. In the domestic quarters, there's a dungeon tower, a Norman hall where the period arch has been disappointingly over-restored and reinforced, and the Oriel or Northern hall, a Tudor re-creation of an earlier antechamber. The intact towers and battlements contain many heavily restored communal rooms, now empty of furniture and, to a large extent, atmosphere too, although some of the rooms, mainly in the gatehouse, are used to house some excellent displays on the history of the castle and the Tudor empire.

Opposite the castle walls is the delightfully eccentric **Museum of the Home**, at 7 Westgate Hill, the northward continuation of Main Street (May–Sept Mon–Thurs 11am–5pm; £1.50). Packed into the steep town house is a collection of utterly ordinary items dating from the eighteenth to the twentieth centuries. The objects are loosely gathered into themes, including toiletries, bedroom accessories and children's games – all demonstrated with great enthusiasm.

Practicalities

Pembroke's **train station** is east of the town centre on Station Road. The **tourist office**, on Commons Road, parallel to Main Street (Easter–Oct daily 10am–5.30pm; ☎01646/622388), provides a useful, free town guide and has limited information on the Pembrokeshire National Park. If you decide to **stay**, don't miss *Beech House B&B*, 78 Main St (☎01646/683746; ❶), which easily outdoes places charging twice as much – one room even boasts a four-poster. If it is full, try the slightly pricier *Merton Place House*, a few doors up at 3 East Back (☎01646/684796; ❶), which has a pleasant walled garden at the back. More expensive places in town aren't great shakes, but you could stay in Lamphey (see below), a couple of miles away. Trains continue from Pembroke to Pembroke Dock, two miles northwest, where **Irish Ferries** (☎0870/517 1717, ⓦwww.irishferries.ie) operates two daily services to Rosslare in Ireland.

For **food**, try the *Pantry*, 4 Main St, during the daytime and early evening, or the well-cooked bar food at the *King's Arms Hotel*, 13 Main St. Further along, at no. 63, the expensive *Left Bank* (☎01646/622333) serves well-thought-out French cuisine in stylish surroundings. The best of the dozens of **pubs** is the *Old Cross Saws*, 109 Main St, although it's hard to beat a summer evening on the veranda overlooking the Mill Pond at the *Waterman's Arms*, over the bridge on Northgate Street.

Lamphey

The pleasant village of **LAMPHEY** (Llandyfai), two miles southeast of Pembroke, is best known for the ruined **Bishop's Palace** (daily 10am–5pm; £2; CADW), off a quiet lane to the north of the village. A country retreat for the bishops of St David's, the palace dates from around the thirteenth century, but was abandoned following the Reformation. Stout walls surround the ruins, which are scattered over a large area. Many of the palace buildings have long been lost under grassy banks. Most impressive are the remains of the Great Hall, extending across the entire eastern end of the complex. You can still see Bishop Gower's hallmark arcaded parapets running along the top, similar to those he built in the Bishop's Palace of St David's.

One of the area's swankiest **hotels** is here, in the shape of the Neoclassical *Lamphey Court Hotel* (☎01646/672273, ⓦwww.lampheycourt.co.uk; ❾), opposite the Bishop's Palace. Otherwise, there's the more modest *Lamphey Hall Hotel* (☎01646/672394; ❸) by the church, or great bunkhouse **dorms** at the *Barn at the Back of Beyond* (☎01646/672047; ❶), half a mile east of the village along The Ridgeway.

Carew

A tiny village that can become unbearably packed in high season, **CAREW**, four miles east of Pembroke, by the River Carew, is a pretty place. Just south of the river crossing, by the main road, is the village's **Celtic cross**, the graceful, remarkably intact taper of the shaft covered in fine tracery of ancient Welsh designs. A small hut beyond the cross serves as the ticket office for **Carew**

Castle and Mill (Easter–Oct daily 10am–5pm; castle £1.90; castle & mill £2.80). The castle, a hybrid of Elizabethan fancy and earlier defensive necessity, is reached across a field. A few hundred yards to the west is the **Carew French Mill**, used commercially until 1937 and now the only tide-powered mill in Wales. The impressive eighteenth-century exterior belies the rather pedestrian exhibitions and audiovisual displays inside, which describe the milling process.

Mid and Northern Pembrokeshire

The most western point of Wales – and the very furthest you can get from England – is one of the country's most enchanting areas. The chief town of the region, **Haverfordwest**, remains rather soulless despite some handsome architecture, but it is useful as a jumping-off point for **St Bride's Bay**. The coast here is broken into rocky outcrops, islands and broad, sweeping beaches curving between two headlands that sit like giant crab pincers facing out into the warm Gulf Stream. The southernmost headland winds around every conceivable angle, offering calm, east-facing sands at **Dale** and sunny expanses of south-facing beach at **Marloes**. Near **Martin's Haven**, boats depart for the offshore islands of **Skomer**, **Skokholm** and **Grassholm**. To the north, the spectacularly lacerated coast veers to the left and the **St David's peninsula**, along stunning cliffs interrupted only by occasional strips of sand. Just north of **St Non's Bay**, the tiny cathedral city of **St David's** is definitely a highlight. Rooks and crows circle above the impressive ruins of the huge Bishop's Palace, sitting beneath the delicate bulk of the cathedral, the most impressive in Wales.

The north-facing coast that forms the very southern tip of Cardigan Bay is noticeably less commercialized and far more Welsh than the touristy shores of south and mid-Pembrokeshire. From the crags and cairns above St David's Head, the coast path perches precariously on the cliffs where only the thousands of sea birds have access. There are only the modest charms of small bays and desolate coves to detain you en route to the charming town of **Newport** – unless you're heading for **Fishguard** and the ferries to Ireland.

Haverfordwest

In the seventeenth and eighteenth centuries, the town of **HAVERFORD-WEST** (Hwlffordd), ten miles north of Pembroke, prospered as a port and trading centre, but despite its natural advantages, it is scarcely a place to linger. A cursory look at the dingy shell of the thirteenth-century **castle** and the less-than-exciting **town museum** (Easter–Oct Mon–Sat 10am–4pm; £1) is enough, though as the main transport hub and shopping centre for western Pembrokeshire you are likely to pass through.

The **tourist office** (May–Sept Mon–Sat 10am–5.30pm; Oct–April Mon–Sat 10am–4pm; ☎01437/763110) is next to the bus terminus, at the end of the Old Bridge. There's also a highly informative **National Park office** at 40 High St. Next to the tourist office, the Holiday Information Centre includes an excellent booking agency for self-catering cottages in Pembrokeshire (☎01437/765765, ⓦwww.coastalcottages.co.uk). Low-cost **accommodation** is provided at *College Guest House*, 93 Hill St (☎01437/763710; ❶) and there are slightly pricier rooms at the solidly Georgian *Castle Hotel*, in Castle Square (☎01437/769322; ❸). For **lunch**, duck into *Morillo's*, on the pedestrian Bridge Street, a successful combination of Italian café and chippy. Evening meals are best at *The George's* pub, at the top of town on Market Street (closed Sun).

Four miles northeast of town, along the B4329, **Scolton Manor** (April–Oct Tues–Sun 9am–6pm; £2) is a modest stately home that now forms the nucleus of the diverting **Pembrokeshire County Museum**. Aside from the enchanting period rooms indoors, outhouses showcase all manner of quirky exhibits, and there is a good café and an environmentally aware visitor centre onsite.

Dale and around

DALE, fourteen miles west of Haverfordwest, can be unbearably crowded in peak season, but it is a pleasant enough village, whose east-facing shore makes it excellent for watersports in the lighter seas. All the activity happens around the beachside shack of West Wales Wind, Surf and Sailing (℡01646/636642), who give instruction in power-boating, windsurfing, surfing, sailing and kayaking (£30–£50 per half-day). A few yards away is the village's cheapest **accommodation** in the shape of the *Richmond House* B&B and superior bunkhouse (℡07974/925009; ❶). Alternatively, there's the *Post House Hotel* (℡01646/636201; ❷), in the middle of the village just behind the real-ale *Griffin Inn*, which has en-suite rooms and optional evening meals; and for a touch of luxury, there's *Allenbrook* (℡01646/636254; ❷; closed Dec), a charming country house close to the beach.

The calm waters of Dale are deceptive, and as soon as you head further south towards **St Ann's Head**, one of the most invigoratingly desolate places in the county, the wind speed whips up, with waves and tides to match. The coast path sticks tight to the undulating coastline, passing tiny bays en route to the St Ann's lighthouse.

The most useful **bus** for accessing the central Pembrokeshire coast is the #400 summer service (2 daily) which runs from Milford Haven to Dale (25min), Martin's Haven (40min), Broad Haven (1hr 15min) and St David's (2hr).

Marloes

The coast turns and heads north from St Ann's Head to the unexciting hamlet of **MARLOES**. Only a mile away from the village, the broad, deserted beach is a safe place to swim, and looks out towards the island of Skokholm. From here, the coast path and a narrow road continue for two miles to the National Trust-owned swathe of **Deer Park** – which has no deer but is the name given to the grassy far tip of the southern peninsula of St Bride's Bay – and **Martin's Haven**, from where you can take a **boat** out to the islands of Skomer, Skokholm and Grassholm.

Marloes is tolerably well off for **accommodation**, with the excellent *Foxdale Guesthouse*, Glebe Lane, opposite the church (℡01646/636243; ❷), and the en-suite *Lobster Pot* (℡01646/636233; ❸), nearby in the centre of the village, above the village's only real restaurant. You can pitch a **tent** behind *Foxdale*, up the street at the field-and-toilets *Greenacre* site, and at *Runwayskiln* (℡01646/636257), close to the *Marloes Sands* YHA **hostel** (℡01646/636667, ⓦwww.yha.org.uk; April–Oct), which consists of a series of converted farm buildings overlooking the northern end of the beach. *West Hook Farm*, near Martin's Haven (℡01646/636424), also has **camping**.

Skomer, Skokholm and Grassholm islands

Weather permitting, **boats** run from Martin's Haven to **Skomer Island** (April–Oct Tues–Sun 10am, 11am & noon; £12), a 722-acre flat-topped island rich in sea birds and spectacular carpets of wild flowers, perfect for birdwatching and walking. You can also cross to **Skokholm Island** (June–Aug Mon 10am; £16; booking essential on ☎01646/636234), a couple of miles south of Skomer and far smaller, more rugged and remote, noted for its cliffs of warm red sandstone. Britain's first bird observatory was founded here as far back as the seventeenth century, and there is still a huge number of petrels, gulls, puffins, oystercatchers and rare Manx shearwaters. The trip includes a guided tour by the island's warden. Boat trips also head out even further, to the tiny outpost of **Grassholm Island**, over five miles west of Skomer (boats June–Sept; landing trip Fri noon; guided trip Thurs 5pm; £20; ☎01646/603123). Visiting the island is an unforgettable experience, largely due to the 70,000 or so screaming gannets who call it home. No booking is required for Skomer trips or the guided trips to Grassholm on Thursdays, although these can be arranged via National Park centres.

St David's and its peninsula

ST DAVID'S (Tyddewi) is one of the most enchanting spots in Britain. This miniature city sits back from its purple- and gold-flecked cathedral at the very westernmost point of Wales in bleak, treeless countryside. Spiritually, it is the centre of Welsh ecclesiasticism. Traditionally founded by the Welsh patron saint himself in 550 AD, the see of St David's has drawn pilgrims for a millennium and a half – William the Conqueror included – and by 1120, Pope Calixtus II decreed that two journeys to St David's were the spiritual equivalent of one to Rome. The surrounding city – in reality, never much more than a large village – grew up in the shadow cast by the cathedral, and St David's today still relies on the imported wealth of pilgrims and visitors to the area, attracted by its savage beauty.

The City

The main road from Haverfordwest enters St David's past the tourist office, before descending to the main square, around a **Celtic cross**, and continuing under the thirteenth-century **Tower Gate**, which forms the entrance to the serene **Cathedral Close**, backed by a windswept landscape of treeless heathland. The cathedral lies down to the right, hidden in a hollow by the River Alun. This apparent modesty is explained by reasons of defence, as a towering cathedral, visible from the sea on all sides, would have been vulnerable to attack. On the other side of the babbling Alun lie the ruins of the Bishop's Palace. New Street heads north past the enjoyable **Oceanarium** (daily: April–Sept 10am–6pm; Oct–March 10am–4pm; £3.50), complete with a shark tank overlooked by a viewing gallery.

From beyond the powerfully solid Tower Gate, the Thirty-Nine Articles – steps named after Thomas Cranmer's key tenets of Anglicanism – approach the purple and golden stone **cathedral** (Ⓦwww.stdavidscathedral.org.uk). The 125-foot tower, topped by pert golden pinnacles, has clocks on only three sides – the people of the northern part of the parish couldn't raise enough money for one to be constructed facing them. You enter through the south side of the low, twelfth-century nave in full view of its most striking feature, the intricate latticed oak **roof**. This was added to hide emergency restoration work carried out in the sixteenth century, when the nave was in danger of collapse. The nave floor still has a discernible slope and the support buttresses inserted in the northern aisle look incongruously new and temporary. At the crossing, an elaborate **rood screen** was constructed under the orders of fourteenth-century Bishop Gower, who envisaged it as his own tomb. Behind the screen and the organ, the choir sits directly under the magnificently bold and bright lantern ceiling of the tower, another addition by Gower. At the back of the south choir stalls is a unique **monarch's stall**, complete with royal crest, for, unlike any other British cathedral, the Queen is an automatic member of the St David's Cathedral Chapter.

Separating the choir and the presbytery is a finely traced, rare **parclose screen**. The back wall of the **presbytery** was once the eastern extremity of the cathedral, as can be seen from the two lines of windows. The upper row has been left intact, while the lower three were blocked up and filled with delicate gold mosaics in the nineteenth century. The colourful fifteenth-century roof, a deceptively simple repeating medieval pattern, was extensively restored by Gilbert Scott in the mid-nineteenth century. At the back of the presbytery, around the altar, the **sanctuary** has a few fragmented fifteenth-century tiles still in place. On the south side is a beautifully carved sedilla, a seat for the priest and deacon celebrating mass. To its right are thirteenth-century tombs of two thirteenth-century bishops, Iorwerth and Anselm de la Grace, and on the other side of the sanctuary is the disappointingly plain thirteenth-century tomb of St David, largely destroyed in the Reformation.

From the cathedral, a path leads to the splendid **Bishops' Palace** (June–Sept daily 9.30am–6pm; April, May & Oct daily 9.30am–5pm; Nov–March Mon–Sat 9.30am–4pm, Sun 11am–4pm; £2; CADW), built by bishops Beck and Gower around the turn of the fourteenth century. The huge central quadrangle is fringed by a neat jigsaw of ruined buildings built in extraordinarily richly tinted stone. The **arched parapets** that run along the top of most of the walls were a favourite feature of Gower, who did more than any of his predecessors or successors to transform the palace into an architectural and political powerhouse. Two ruined but still impressive halls – the **Bishops' Hall** and the enormous **Great Hall**, with its glorious rose window – lie off the main quadrangle, above and around a myriad of rooms adorned by some eerily eroded corbels. Underneath the Great Hall are dank vaults containing an interesting exhibition about the palace and the indulgent lifestyles of its occupants. The destruction of the palace is largely due to sixteenth-century Bishop Barlow, who supposedly stripped the buildings of their lead roofs to provide dowries for his five daughters' marriages to bishops.

Practicalities

The main road from Haverfordwest enters St David's past the attractive new **tourist office** (Easter–Oct daily 9.30am–5.30pm; Nov–Easter Mon–Sat 10am–4pm; ☎01437/720392), and continues for two hundred yards down High Street to the **bus station** in New Street. You can **rent bikes** at Ramsey Island Cruises, located behind TYF No Limits, 1 High St (☎01437/721611, ⓦwww.tyf.com), who rent surf gear and kayaks as well as running various **outdoor courses**. The best among these is "coasteering" (full day £60; half-day £35), which involves scrambling over rocks, jumping off cliffs and swimming across the narrow bays of St David's Peninsula.

There are numerous places to **stay**. Good, inexpensive options in town are *Pen Albro*, 18 Goat St (☎01437/721865; ❶), and *Y Glennydd*, 51 Nun St (☎01437/720576; ❶), which has some en-suite rooms. *The Waterings*, on High Street by the tourist office (☎01437/720876; ❸), has luxurious suites in a former marine research establishment, while *Twr-y-Felin*, High Street (☎0800/132588; ❷), offers B&B, camping and a lively bar in a converted windmill. *Ramsey House*, Lower Moor (☎01437/720321; ❺), is an excellent small hotel a quarter of a mile out on the road to Porth Clais, with superb Welsh evening meals included in the price.

Apart from *Twr-y-Felin* (see above), St David's nearest **campsite** is at *Caerfai Farm*, Caerfai Bay (☎01437/720548; May–Sept), a fifteen-minute walk from the city. A delightful thirty-minute walk west of town are the cliff-top camping fields of *Pencarnon Farm* (☎01437/720324), just short of St Justinian's, with amazing views and a virtually private beach below; and there's a YHA **hostel** in a former farmhouse two miles northwest, near Whitesands Bay (☎01437/720345; April–Oct).

For inexpensive **eating**, there are a number of adequate tearooms and the traveller-oriented *Low Pressure Café*, at 1 High St. For more of a treat, *Morgan's Brasserie*, 20 Nun St (☎01437/720508), serves meals made with wonderfully fresh local produce. **Nightlife** boils down to the lively *Farmers Arms*, Goat Street, the city's only real pub, with a terrace overlooking the cathedral.

The St David's peninsula

Surrounded on three sides by inlets, coves and rocky stacks, St David's is an easy base for some excellent walking around the headland of the same name. A mile due south, accessed along the signposted lane from the main Haverfordwest road just near the school, popular **Caerfai Bay** provides a sandy gash in the purple sandstone cliffs, rock which was used in the construction of the cathedral. To the immediate west is the craggy indentation of **St Non's Bay**, reached from Goat Street in St David's down the tiny rhododendron-flooded lane signposted to the *Warpool Court Hotel*. St Non reputedly gave birth to St David at this spot during a tumultuous storm around 500 AD, when a spring opened up between Non's feet, and despite the crashing thunder all around, an eerily calm light filtered down on to the scene. St Non's Bay has received pilgrims for centuries, resulting in the foundation of a tiny, isolated chapel in the pre-Norman age. The ruins of the subsequent thirteenth-century chapel now lie in a field to the right of the car park, beyond the sadly dingy well and coy shrine where the nation's patron saint is said to have been born.

The road from St David's to St Non's branches at the *St Non's Hotel*, where Catherine Street becomes a winding lane that leads a mile down the tiny valley of the River Alun to its mouth at **Porth Clais**. Supposedly the place at which St David was baptized, Porth Clais was the city's main harbour, the spruced-up remains of which can still be seen at the bottom of the turquoise river creek. Today, commercial traffic has long gone, replaced by a boaties' haven.

Running due west out of St David's, Goat Street ducks past the ruins of the Bishop's Palace and over the rocky plateau for two miles to the harbour at **St Justinian's**, little more than a lifeboat station and ticket hut for the boats over to **Ramsey Island**. This dual-humped plateau, less than two miles long, has been under the able stewardship of the RSPB since 1992 and is quite enchanting. Birds of prey circle the skies above the island, but it's better known for the tens of thousands of sea birds that noisily crowd the sheer cliffs on the island's western side. On the beaches, seals laze sloppily below the paths beaten out by a herd of red deer. Two companies run boats – weather permitting – around Ramsey, but the only ones that land are Thousand Islands Expeditions' trips (April–Oct daily; ☎0800/163621; £10); you can stay up to five hours. Worth trying – for the more adventurous – is their two-hour high-speed rigid inflatable tour around Ramsay (£22.50). During the springtime nesting season you actually see more from boats which circle the island but don't land: try Ramsey Island Cruises (year-round daily; ☎01437/721911 or ☎0800/854367; £15), who also operate longer whale-watching trips (£40). Thousand Island Expeditions operate a similar Ramsey circumnavigation from **Whitesands Bay** (Porth Mawr), two miles to the north and reached from St David's, via the B4583 off the Fishguard road.

Fishguard

From St David's, the coast road runs northeast, parallel to numerous small and less-commercialized bays, to **Strumble Head**, which protects the harbour at **FISHGUARD** (Abergwaun), an attractive, hilltop town seldom seen as anything more than a brief stopoff to or from the Stena Line **ferries** (℡0870/570 7070, ⓦwww.stenaline.com), which leave regularly for Rosslare in Ireland from the suburb of Goodwick (Wdig).

Near the town hall is the **Royal Oak Inn**, where a bizarre Franco-Irish attempt to conquer Britain in 1797 at nearby Carregwastad Point is remembered. The hapless forces arrived to negotiate a cease-fire, which was turned by the assembled British into an unconditional surrender. Part of the invaders' low morale – apart from the drunken farce in which they'd become embroiled – is said to have been sparked off by the sight of a hundred local women marching towards them. The troops mistook their stovepipe hats and red flannel dresses for the outfit of a British infantry troop and instantly capitulated. Even if this is not true, it is an undisputed fact that 47-year-old cobbler Jemima Nicholas, the "Welsh Heroine", single-handedly captured fourteen French soldiers. Her grave can be seen next to the uninspiring Victorian parish church, St Mary's, behind the pub. At the time of writing, the fabulous **Fishguard Tapestry**, which tells the story of this ramshackle invasion, is out of public view – a new, more permanent home is being sought.

Buses stop by the town hall in the central Market Square, right outside Fishguard's **tourist office** (June–Aug daily 10am–5.30pm; April, May, Sept & Oct daily 10am–5pm; Nov–March Mon–Sat 11am–4pm; ℡01348/873484). There's a subsidiary tourist office in the foyer of the Ocean Lab in Goodwick (same hours; ℡01348/874737), around half a mile from the Rosslare ferry terminus. Local **boat trips** aboard *The Sea Spirit* (Easter–Oct; ℡01348/874864; £15) go from Goodwick up and down the coast. The **train station** is next to the ferry terminal on Quay Road. Buses usually meet ferries, though seldom the more frequent catamarans; a **taxi** (℡01348/874491) into town costs around £3.

Accommodation is plentiful and cheap, with most places well used to visitors coming and going at odd times. Next to the port is the faded elegance of the *Fishguard Bay Hotel*, on Quay Road (℡01348/873571; ❹); and you'll find comfortable rooms at *Glanmoy Lodge*, on Trefwrgi Road, ten minutes' walk from the port (℡01348/874333; ❷). In Fishguard proper is *Three Main Street* (℡01348/874275; ❺), easy to find and with an expensive and highly praised restaurant; or there are **dorms** at *Hamilton Backpackers Lodge*, 21–23 Hamilton St (℡01348/874797; ❶), just a minute's walk from the tourist office. The nearest **camping** is at *Tregroes Touring Park* (℡01348/872316), a mile southwest of Fishguard just off the A40.

Newport

NEWPORT (Trefdraeth) is an ancient and proud little town set on a gentle slope that courses down to the estuary of the Afon Nyfer. There's little to do except stroll around, but you'd be hard pressed to find a better place to do just that. Just short of the Nevern estuary bridge, on the town side, **Carreg Coetan Arthur**, a well-preserved, capped Neolithic burial chamber, can be seen behind the newish holiday bungalows. The footpath that runs along the river either side of the bridge is marked as the Pilgrims' Way; follow it eastwards for a delightful riverbank stroll to Nevern, a couple of miles away. Another popular local walk is up to the craggy and magical peak of **Carn Ingli**, the Hill of Angels, behind the town. On Lower St Mary Street, the old school has metamorphosed into the excellent **West Wales Eco Centre** (Mon–Fri 9.30am–4.30pm; variable extended hours in summer; free), a venue for exhibitions, advice and resources on various aspects of sustainable living.

Newport's nearest beach, the **Parrog**, is complete with sandy stretches at low tide. On the other side of the estuary is the vast dune-backed **Traethmawr beach**, reached over the town bridge down Feidr Pen-y-Bont. Newport also makes a good jumping-off point for exploring the wooded vales and gnarled hills of **Mynydd Preseli**, just inland, which are scattered with prehistoric remains, notably the four-thousand-year-old capstone at **Pentre Ifan**, a couple of miles south of Newport.

The **tourist office** (April–Sept Mon–Sat 10am–5.30pm; ☎01239/820912) is on Long Street, just off the main road. **Bike rental** is available in town from the *Llysmeddyg* guesthouse, on East Street. There's plenty of **accommodation**: the *Golden Lion* pub, on the main street (☎01239/820321; ❶), does inexpensive B&B, as does *Trewarren*, half a mile to the north (☎01239/820455; ❷), overlooking the estuary and with great views – follow Feidr Pen-y-Bont from town. For more luxury, try the superb *Cnapan Country House*, on East Street (☎01239/820575, ⓦwww.online-holidays.net/cnapan; ❸; closed Jan & Feb). The new YHA **hostel** is tucked in behind the Eco Centre (☎01239/820080; ❶; April–Oct); and a mile south of town, there's a great independent bunkhouse at *Brithdir Mawr*, on Ffordd Cilgwyn, at the bottom of the slopes of Carn Ingli (☎01239/820164; ❶). The nearest **campsite** is the *Morawelon* (☎01239/820565), just west of town, at the Parrog, with nice gardens and its own café. For **food**, the *Cnapan Country House* serves exquisite meals, or there are solid pub classics, including a good veggie menu, at the *Royal Oak*, on Bridge Street. Great snacks can be found at the *Fountain House Foods* deli, and *Fronlas Café*, both on Market Street.

Travel details

Trains

Cardiff to: Abergavenny (hourly; 40min); Birmingham (8 daily; 2hr); Bristol (every 30min; 50min); Caerphilly (every 20min; 20min); Carmarthen (7 daily; 1hr 30min); Chepstow (hourly; 30min); Fishguard Harbour (2 daily; 2hr 20min); Haverfordwest (5 daily; 2hr 40min); London (every 30min; 2hr); Merthyr Tydfil (hourly; 1hr); Newport (every 15–30min; 10min); Pontypool (hourly; 30min); Swansea (hourly; 50min); Tenby (4 daily; 2hr 30min); Ystrad Rhondda (every 30min; 50min).

Carmarthen to: Cardiff (7 daily; 1hr 30min); Fishguard (2 daily; 1hr); Haverfordwest (9 daily; 40min); Pembroke (8 daily; 1hr 10min); Swansea (hourly; 50min); Tenby (8 daily; 40min).

Haverfordwest to: Carmarthen (9 daily; 40min); Swansea (7 daily; 1hr 30min).

Newport (Monmouthshire) to: Abergavenny (hourly; 30min); Cardiff (every 15–30min; 10min); Chepstow (hourly; 20min); London (every 30min; 1hr 50min).

Pembroke to: Lamphey (7 daily; 3min); Manorbier (7 daily; 10min); Pembroke Dock (7 daily; 10min); Tenby (7 daily; 20min).

Swansea to: Cardiff (hourly; 50min); Carmarthen (hourly; 50min); Fishguard (2 daily; 1hr 30min); Haverfordwest (7 daily; 1hr 30min); Llandrindod Wells (5 daily; 2hr 20min); London (hourly; 3hr); Newport (hourly; 1hr 20min); Pembroke (6 daily; 2hr); Tenby (7 daily; 1hr 40min).

Tenby to: Carmarthen (8 daily; 40min); Pembroke (7 daily; 20min); Swansea (7 daily; 1hr 40min).

Buses

Cardiff to: Abergavenny (hourly; 1hr 20min); Aberystwyth (2 daily; 4hr); Blaenafon (hourly; 1hr 40min); Brecon (1 daily; 1hr 20min); Caerphilly (every 30min; 40min); Cardiff–Wales Airport (hourly; 30min); Chepstow (hourly; 1hr 20min); London (8 daily; 3hr 10min); Merthyr Tydfil (every 30min; 45min); Newport, Monmouthshire (every 30min; 30min); Swansea (every 30min; 1hr).

Carmarthen to: Aberystwyth (2 daily; 1hr 45min); Haverfordwest (5 daily; 1hr); Kidwelly (hourly; 25min); Laugharne (hourly; 30min); Llandeilo (15 daily; 40min); National Botanic Garden (4 daily; 20min); Swansea (hourly; 1hr 30min); Tenby (2 daily; 1hr).

Chepstow to: Monmouth (16 daily; 50min); Newport (hourly; 50min); Tintern (8 daily; 20min); Usk (6 daily; 45min).

Fishguard to: Cardigan (hourly; 50min); Haverfordwest (hourly; 40min); Newport, Pembrokeshire (hourly; 20min); St David's (7 daily; 50min).

Haverfordwest to: Carmarthen (5 daily; 1hr); Fishguard (hourly; 40min); Manorbier (hourly; 1hr 10min); Newport, Pembrokeshire (hourly; 1hr 10min); Pembroke (hourly; 50min); St David's (hourly; 40min); Tenby (hourly; 1hr 20min).

Llandovery to: Brecon (Mon–Sat 5 daily, none on Sun; 40min); Llandeilo (9 daily; 45min).

Merthyr Tydfil to: Abergavenny (hourly; 1hr 30min); Brecon (10 daily; 40min); Cardiff (every 30min; 45min).

Monmouth to: Abergavenny (6 daily; 40min); Chepstow (16 daily; 50min); Raglan (8 daily; 20min); Tintern (8 daily; 30min).

Newport (Monmouthshire) to: Abergavenny (hourly; 1hr 10min); Blaenafon (every 30min; 1hr 10min); Cardiff (every 20min; 40min); Chepstow (hourly; 50min).

Newport (Pembrokeshire) to: Fishguard (hourly; 20min); Haverfordwest (hourly; 1hr 10min).

Pembroke to: Bosherston (Mon–Fri 2 daily, none on Sat & Sun; 1hr); Haverfordwest (hourly; 50min); Manorbier (hourly; 20min); Pembroke Dock (every 10min; 10min); Stackpole (Mon–Fri 2 daily, none on Sat & Sun; 50min); Tenby (hourly; 40min).

St David's to: Broad Haven (2 daily; 40min); Fishguard (7 daily; 50min); Haverfordwest (hourly; 40min).

Swansea to: Brecon (3 daily; 1hr 30min); Cardiff (every 30min; 1hr); Dan-yr-ogof (4 daily; 1hr); Merthyr Tydfil (hourly; 1hr); Mumbles (every 10min; 15min); Oxwich (6 daily; 40min); Port Eynon (7 daily; 50min); Rhossili (Mon–Sat 10 daily; 1hr).

Tenby to: Carmarthen (2 daily; 1hr); Haverfordwest (hourly; 1hr 20min); Manorbier (hourly; 20min); Pembroke (hourly ; 40min).

Ferries

Fishguard to: Rosslare, Ireland (4–6 daily; ferry 3hr 30min, catamaran 1hr 40min).

Pembroke Dock to: Rosslare, Ireland (2 daily; 4hr).
Swansea to: Cork, Ireland (1 daily; 10hr).

Mid-Wales

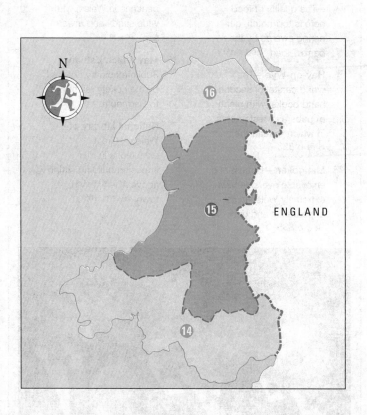

N

ENGLAND

16

15

14

CHAPTER 15 # Highlights

* **Sgwd-yr-Eira waterfall** – A waterfall you can dive through, in the midst of the Brecon Beacons National Park. See p.819

* **Bear Hotel, Crickhowell** – The quality of food here is top-notch, garnering awards by the barrow-load. See p.821

* **Hay-on-Wye** – The world capital of second-hand books, with plenty of pubs and restaurants in which to read them. See p.823

* **Llangollen** – Robust and enjoyable riverside town, extremely Welsh in its appearance and outlook. See p.835

* **Harlech** – A perfect castle and beautiful town wedged between the mountains and the sea. See p.840

* **Ardudwy Beach** – Eight miles of one of the best beaches in Wales, with wide sands and a warm sea. See p.840

* **Mawddach Estuary** – Sublime estuary crossed by the rickety rail bridge to Barmouth. See p.840

* **National Library of Wales** – Great exhibitions in this imposing building sitting above Aberystwyth town. See p.848

15

Mid-Wales

M id-Wales is a huge, beautiful region, crisscrossed by breathtaking mountain passes, dotted with characterful little towns and never far from water – whether sparkling rivers, great lakes or the sea of the Cambrian coast. This is certainly the least-known part of Wales, and that is, perhaps, to its advantage, for it is here that you'll find Welsh culture at its most beguiling and most natural, folded into the contours of the land as it has been for centuries.

A quarter of the area of Wales is occupied by the inland county of **Powys**, whose name harks back to a fifth-century Welsh kingdom. By far the most popular attraction is **Brecon Beacons National Park**, stretching from the dramatic limestone country of Fforest Fawr in the west through to the English border beyond the Black Mountains. The best bases are the tiny city of **Brecon**, the market town of **Abergavenny**, or the characterful border town **Hay-on-Wye** that buzzes all year round with devotees of its abundant secondhand book trade.

North of the Beacons lie the old spa towns of Radnorshire, among them twee **Llandrindod Wells**. The quiet countryside to the north, crossed by spectacular mountain roads such as the **Abergwesyn Pass** from Llanwrtyd, is barely populated, dotted with ancient churches and introspective villages. In the east, the border town of **Knighton** is the home of the flourishing **Offa's Dyke path** industry. **Montgomeryshire** is the northern portion of Powys, similarly underpopulated and remote. Like many country towns in mid-Wales, beautiful **Llanidloes** has a healthy stock of old hippies amongst its population, contributing to a thriving arts and crafts community and a relaxed atmosphere. It's also a great base for the mountains, forests and boggy heathland that surround it.

Continuing north are the mountains that course down into the **Dee Valley**, a fertile landscape much fought over between the English and the Welsh. With the language still thriving hereabouts, there's more of a tangibly Welsh feel to towns like the fabulous **Llangollen**, a great base for a variety of ruins, rides and rambles, as well as the venue each summer for the colourful International Eisteddfod festival. Further west is the old county of **Meirionydd**, which stretches to the enduringly popular Cambrian Coast, peppered with coastal resorts. Between the towns of **Harlech** and **Barmouth** lie some great beaches, backed by burbling rivers and stunning mountains.

The southern tranche of Meirionydd is dominated by mountain scenery, most notably around the massif of **Cadair Idris**. South of the great mountain is **Machynlleth**, a great base for beaches, mountains, shopping and the **Centre for Alternative Technology**, an impressive showpiece for community living and renewable energy resources.

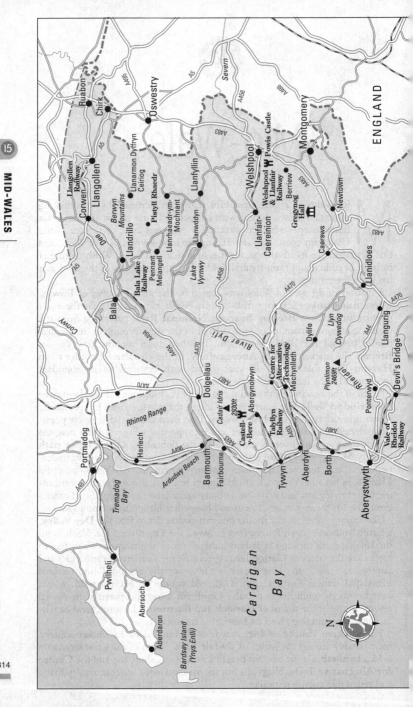

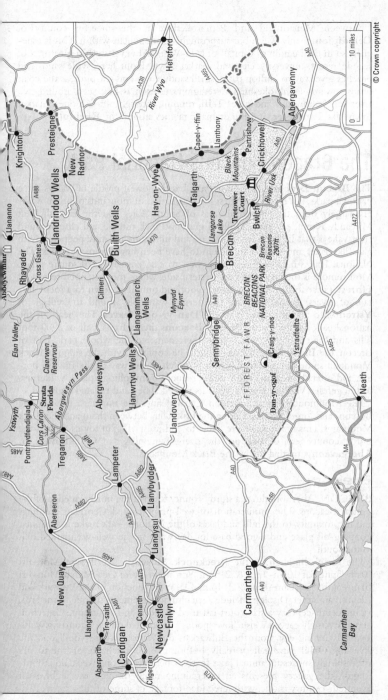

0   10 miles

Between Meirionydd and Pembrokeshire is the cheerful county of **Ceredigion**, firmly Welsh but surprisingly cosmopolitan with it. This is especially so in the beguiling "capital" of Mid-Wales, **Aberystwyth**, a great mix of seaside resort, university city and market town. From here, wide sands and beaches give way to clifftop paths, small sandy coves and sea-birds, as the coast heads towards Pembrokeshire. Ceredigion's interior is best seen around two river valleys: the lush and quiet **Teifi**, running through old-fashioned market towns like **Lampeter**, and the dramatic ravines around the **Rheidol**.

The Brecon Beacons National Park

The **Brecon Beacons National Park** has the lowest profile of Wales's three national parks, but it is nonetheless the destination of thousands of urban walkers, largely from the industrial areas of South Wales and the English West Midlands. Rounded, spongy hills of grass and rock tumble and climb around river valleys that lie between sandstone and limestone uplands, peppered with glass-like lakes and villages that seem to have been hewn from one rock. The National Park straddles Powys from west to east, covering 520 square miles. Most remote is the area at the far western side, where the vast, open terrain of **Fforest Fawr** forms miles of tufted moorland tumbling down to a rocky terrain of rivers, deep caves and spluttering waterfalls around the village of **Ystradfellte** and the chasms of the **Dan-yr-ogof caves**. The heart of the national park comprises the **Brecon Beacons** themselves, a pair of 2900-foot hills and their satellites which lend their name to the whole park. East of Brecon, the **Black Mountains** – not to be confused with the singular Black Mountain some distance to the west – stretch all the way to the English border, and offer the region's most varied scenery, from rolling upland wilderness to the gentler **Vale of Ewyas**, with its ruined abbey and isolated churches.

The Monmouthshire and Brecon Canal defines the northern limit of the Beacons and forges a passage along the Usk Valley between them and the Black Mountains. This is where you're likely to end up staying; in towns such as the sturdy county seat of **Brecon**, the overgrown village of **Crickhowell**, or **Abergavenny**, nestled below the Black Mountains.

Brecon

BRECON (Aberhonddu) is a sturdy county town at the northern edge of the central Beacons. The proliferation of well-proportioned Georgian buildings and its proximity to the hills and lakes of the National Park make it a popular stopping-off place and a good base for day walks in the well-waymarked hills to the south.

The town's highlight is the **Brecknock Museum** (April–Sept Mon–Fri 10am–5pm, Sat 10am–1pm & 2–5pm, Sun noon–5pm; Oct–March Mon–Fri 10am–5pm, Sat 10am–1pm & 2–4pm; £1), at the junction of the Bulwark and Glamorgan Street. Displays include agricultural implements unique to the area, a nineteenth-century assize court last used in 1971, and an antique collection of painstakingly carved Welsh "love spoons" – betrothal gifts for courting Welsh lovers. Running east from the Bulwark is the Watton, where you'll find the diverting **Oriel Jazz** gallery (daily 1–4pm; free). Capitalizing on the town's astonishingly successful annual **jazz festival**, held over a long weekend in mid-August, the gallery presents an entertaining romp through the archives of twentieth-century music, with rare video footage of some of the jazz greats.

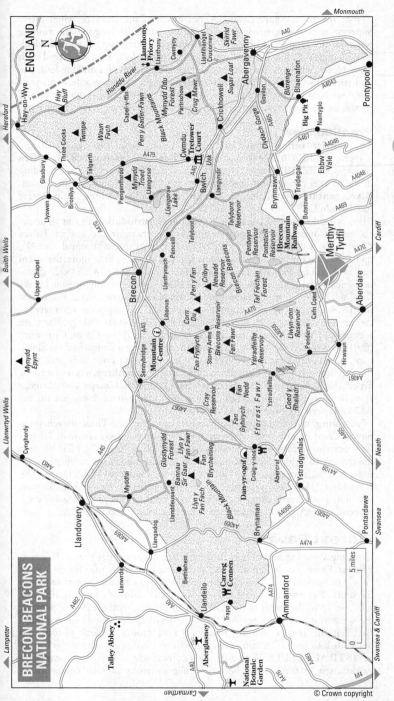

BRECON BEACONS
NATIONAL PARK

ENGLAND

N

Monmouth

Hay-on-Wye

Hereford

Buith Wells

Llanwrtyd Wells

Lampeter

Hay Bluff
Honddu River
Llanthony Priory
Llanthony
Cwmyoy
Llanfihangel Crucorney
Skirrid Fawr
A40
Capel-y-ffin
Twmpa
Waun Fach
Pen y Gader-Fawr
Mynydd Ddu Forest
Black Mountains
Partrishow
Crug Mawr
Sugar Loaf
Abergavenny
Crickhowell
Govilon
Blorenge
Blaenafon
A4043
Pontypool

Three Cocks
Glasbury
Talgarth
A479
Pengenffordd
Mynydd Troed
Llangorse
Llangorse Lake
Cwmdu
Tretower Court
Usk
A40
Bwlch
Llangynidr
Clydach Gorge
A465
Big Pit
Nantyglo
A461
A4046
Ebbw Vale
A469
Cardiff

Llyswen
Bronllys
Talybont Reservoir
Talybont
Pentwyn Reservoir
Pontsticill Reservoir
Brynmawr
Butetown
Tredegar
A4048

Upper Chapel
Brecon
Llanfrynach
Pencelli
Pen y Fan
Cribyn
Neuadd Reservoir
Brecon Beacons
Taf Fechan Forest
Brecon Mountain Railway
Merthyr Tydfil
A470
Aberdare

Libanus
Mountain Centre
Corn Du
Fan Frynych
Storey Arms
Brecons Reservoir
Fan Fawr
A470
Llwyn-on Reservoir
Cefn Coed
A465
Penderyn
Hirwaun
A4061

Sennybridge
A40
A4067
Cray Reservoir
Fan Nedd
Fan Gyhirych
Ystradfellte Reservoir
Ystradfellte
Coed y Rhaladr
A4109
Neath

Mynydd Epynt

Cynghordy

Llandovery
A483
A40
Myddfai
Llanddeusant
Glastynydd Forest
Bannau Sir Gaer
Fan Fawr
Llyn y Fan Fach
Fan Brycheiniog
Black Mountain
Craig-y-nos
Dan-yr-ogof
Brynaman
A4069
A4067
A4068
Abercraf
Ystradgynlais
Pontardawe
Swansea

Llangadog
A40

Bethlehem
Llandeilo
Carreg Cennen
Trapp
Talley Abbey
Llanwrda
Aberglasney
National Botanic Garden
A40
Ammanford
A474
A483
A476
M4
Swansea & Cardiff

5 miles
0

Carmarthen

© Crown copyright

From the town-centre crossroads, northwest of the Bulwark, High Street Superior goes north, becoming The Struet, running alongside the rushing waters of the Honddu. Off to the left, a footpath climbs up to the **cathedral**. The building's dumpy external appearance belies its lofty interior, graced with a few Norman features from the eleventh century, including a hulking font. The mid-sixteenth-century **Games Monument**, in the southern aisle, is made of three oak beds and depicts an unknown woman whose hands, clasped in prayer, remain intact, but whose arms and nose have been unceremoniously hacked off.

Practicalities

The **tourist office** (daily: Easter–Oct 9.30am–5pm; Nov–Easter 10am–4.45pm; ℡01874/622485) and **Brecon Beacons National Park office** (Easter–Oct daily 9.30am–5.30pm; ℡01874/623156) share the same building in the Market car park off Lion Street, next to the new Safeway supermarket. **Bike rental** is available at the Brecon Cycle Centre, Ship Street (℡01874/622557).

Brecon and adjacent Llanfaes bulge with **accommodation** to suit all pockets, except during the August jazz festival. Best bets are the budget *Tirbach Guest House*, 13 Alexandra Rd (℡01874/624551, ✉tirbach@hotmail.com; ❶), up behind Safeway, and a couple of lovely places costing a little more: the warm and welcoming *Pickwick House*, St John's Road (℡01874/624322, ✉isobel@pickwick.prestel.co.uk; ❸), with excellent, predominantly organic breakfasts and evening meals; and the non-smoking *Cantre Selyf*, 5 Lion St (℡01874/622904, ⓦwww.cantreselyf.co.uk; ❸), an imposing seventeenth-century town house, all creaking floors and moulded plaster ceilings. There are a couple of YHA **hostels**, the closest of which is *Ty'n-y-Caeau*, Groesfford (℡01874/665270; ❶), two miles east of the town. It can be reached via Slwch Lane, a path from Cerrigcochion Road in Brecon, or it's a one-mile walk from the bus stops at either Cefn Brynich lock (Brecon–Abergavenny buses) or Troedyrharn Farm (Brecon–Hereford buses). *Brynich Caravan and Camping Park*, Brynich (℡01874/623325), is situated a mile east of town, just off the A470, overlooking the town and the river.

For **eating**, the inexpensive *Waterfront Bistro* in the new Theatr Brycheiniog on the Canal Basin is open in the daytime for tasty café food and until 7.30pm for superb pre-theatre suppers; the *Beacons Guest House* (℡01874/623339), over the river at 16 Bridge St, Llanfaes, is open to non-residents for excellent meals, many of which are inspired by local produce and traditional Welsh recipes. The *Bull's Head*, The Struet, is the pick of the town's **pubs**, or you could make your way four miles north along the B4520 to the *Seland Newydd*, at Pwllgloyw, a peaceful country pub that offers much the best eating around Brecon.

Fforest Fawr

Covering a vast expanse of hilly landscape west of the central Brecon Beacons, **Fforest Fawr** (Great Forest) seems something of a misnomer for an area of largely unforested sandstone hills dropping down to a porous limestone belt in the south. The name, however, refers to its former status as a hunting area. The hills rise up to the south of the A40, west of Brecon, with the A4067 piercing the western side of the range and the A470 defining the Fforest's eastern limit. Between the two, a twisting mountain road crosses a bleak plateau and descends into one of Britain's classic limestone landscapes, around the hamlet of **YSTRADFELLTE**. With a dazzling countryside of lush, deep ravines on its doorstep. Ystradfellte has become a phenomenally popular centre for its walks over great pavements of bone-white rock next to cradling potholes, disappearing rivers and crashing waterfalls.

A mile to the south, the River Mellte tumbles into the dark mouth of the **Porth-yr-ogof** (White Horse Cave), emerging into daylight a few hundred yards further south. A signposted path heads south from the Porth-yr-ogof car park and into the green gorge of the River Mellte. After little more than a mile, the first of three waterfalls is reached at **Sgwd Clun-Gwyn** (White Meadow Fall), where the river crashes fifty feet over two huge, angular steps of rock before hurtling down course for a few hundred yards to the other two falls – the impressive **Sgwd Isaf Clun-Gwyn** (Lower White Meadow Fall) and, around the wooded corner, the **Sgwd y Pannwr** (Fall of the Fuller). The path continues to the confluence of the rivers Mellte and Hepste, half a mile further on. A quarter of a mile along the Hepste is the most popular of the area's falls, the **Sgwd yr Eira** (Fall of Snow), whose rock below the main tumble has eroded back six feet, allowing you to walk directly behind a dramatic twenty-foot curtain of water. A shorter two-mile walk to Sgwd yr Eira leads from **PENDERYN** village, off the A4059, three miles north of Hirwaun: to get there, catch **bus** #9 (hourly) from Merthyr Tydfil to Hirwaun and change to bus #15 to Penderyn (every 30min).

For **accommodation**, there's a cosy YHA hostel (☎01639/720301, ⓦwww.yha.org.uk; April–Oct) at **TAI'R HEOL**, half a mile south of Ystradfellte and just a short walk from Porth-yr-ogof, plus numerous informal **camping** spots in the woods.

Dan-yr-ogof Showcaves

Six miles of upland forest and squelchy moor lie between Ystradfellte and the **Dan-yr-ogof Showcaves** (April–Oct daily 10am–3pm; call ☎01639/730801 for winter hours; £7.50), off the A4067 to the west. Only discovered in 1912, they are claimed to form the largest system of subterranean caverns in northern Europe, and, although relentless marketing has turned them into something of an overdone theme park, the caverns are truly awesome in their size. A concrete path leads into the first of three caverns, the **Dan-yr-ogof** cave, and a bewildering subterranean warren, the crags and walls framed by stalactites and frothy limestone deposits. Emerging back outside, you pass a downbeat recreated Iron Age "village" and a hideous park of fibreglass dinosaurs, and walk through a succession of spookily lit caverns, where water cascades relentlessly down the walls. A swelling classical soundtrack and a dancing light show come together in the final 150-foot-long **Cathedral Cave** – impressive despite its tawdriness. A precarious path leads to the **Bone Cave** where the owners have fenced off an assortment of dressed-up mannequins that make Bronze Age woman look like a reject from Miss Selfridge. **Camping** is available just up the road at the *Tafarn-y-Garreg* pub (☎01639/730236).

The Brecon Beacons

Far more popular for walking and pony trekking than the Fforest Fawr, the central **Brecon Beacons**, grouped around the two highest peaks in the National Park, are easily accessible from Brecon, which lies just six miles to the north. This is classic old red sandstone country, sweeping peaks rising up out of glacial scoops of land. Although the peaks never quite reach 3000ft, the terrain is unmistakably, and dramatically, mountainous. The panorama fans out from the **Brecon Beacons Mountain Centre** (daily: July & Aug 9.30am–6pm; March–June, Sept & Oct 9.30am–5pm; Nov–Feb 10.30am–4.30pm; ☎01874/

623366; small parking fee), on a windy ridge just off the A470 turn-off at Libanus, six miles southwest of Brecon. As well as a fantastic café that specializes in local ingredients, there are interesting displays on the flora, fauna, geology and history of the area, together with a well-stocked shop of maps, books and guides.

Pen y Fan (2907ft) is the highest peak in the Beacons. Together with **Corn Du** (2863ft), half a mile to the west, they form the most popular ascents in the park, particularly along the well-trampled muddy red path that starts from Pont ar Daf, half a mile south of Storey Arms, on the A470, midway between Brecon and Merthyr Tydfil. This is the most direct route from a road, where a comparatively easy five-mile round trip gradually climbs up the southern flank of the two peaks. A longer and generally quieter ascent leads up to the two peaks along the "Gap" route, the ancient road that winds its way north from the Neuadd reservoirs, immediately south of Brecon. This passes through the only natural break in the sandstone ridge of the central Beacons, heading to the bottom of the lane that eventually joins the main street in Llanfaes, Brecon, as Bailihelig Road. Although the old road is no longer accessible for cars, car parks at either end open out onto the track for an eight-mile round-trip ascent up Pen y Fan and Corn Du from the east.

The Black Mountains

The easternmost section of the National Park centres on the **Black Mountains**, far quieter than the central belt of the Brecon Beacons and skirted by the wide valley of the River Usk. The only exception to the Black Mountains' unremitting sandstone is an isolated outcrop of limestone, long divorced from the southern belt, that peaks due north of Crickhowell at Pen Cerrig-calch (2302ft). The Black Mountains have the feel of a landscape only partly tamed by human habitation: tiny villages, isolated churches and delightful lanes are folded into an undulating green landscape which levels out to the south around the pretty villages of **Tretower** and **Crickhowell**.

Tretower

Rising out of the valley floor, dominating the view from both the A40 and A479 mountain road, the solid round tower of the **Castle and Court** (daily: June–Sept 10am–6pm; April, May, Sept & Oct 10am–5pm; March 10am–4pm; £2.50; CADW) at **TRETOWER** (Tre-tûr), ten miles southeast of Brecon, was built to guard the pass. The bleak, thirteenth-century round tower replaced an earlier Norman fortification, and in the late fourteenth century was supplemented by a comparatively luxurious manor house, itself being gradually expanded over the ensuing years. An enjoyable audioguide tour takes you around an open-air gallery and wall walk, and explains late medieval building methods using the exposed plaster and beams where work is still under way. In the summer, contemporary and Shakespeare **plays** are performed in the inspirational surroundings of the fully restored court (box office ☎01874/730279), with its ostentatious, beam-ceilinged Great Hall facing in on the central cobbled courtyard and square sandstone gatehouse.

Crickhowell

Compact **CRICKHOWELL** (Crucywel), four miles southeast of Tretower, on the northern bank of the wide and shallow Usk, makes for a lively base from which to explore the surrounding area. There isn't much to see in town, however, apart from a grand seventeenth-century **bridge**, with thirteen arches visible from the eastern end and only twelve from the west, spawning many a local myth. **Table Mountain** (1481ft) provides a spectacular northern backdrop, topped by the remains of the 2500-year-old hill fort (*crug*) of Hywel, accessed on a path past The Wern, off Llanbedr Road. Many walkers follow a route north from Table Mountain, climbing two miles up to the plateau-topped limestone hump of **Pen Cerrig-calch** (2302ft).

The **tourist office** (April–Sept daily 9am–1pm & 2–5pm; ☎01873/812105) is in Beaufort Chambers, on Beaufort Street, and you can **rent bikes** from Mountain and Water, in the Riverside Centre, on New Road (☎01873/831825). **Accommodation** is abundant, with a grandiose coaching inn, the *Bear Hotel*, on Beaufort Street (☎01873/810408, ⓦwww.bear-hotel.co.uk; ❹), and the *Dragon*, on High Street (☎01873/810362, ⓦwww.dragonhotel.co.uk; ❸); for cheaper B&B, try *Greenhill Villas*, Beaufort Street (☎01873/811177; ❶). The town-centre *Riverside Park* **campsite** lies on New Road (☎01873/810397). Just beyond the turning for the delightful nearby village of Llanbedr, *Perth-y-pia* (☎01873/810050; ❷) is an outdoor centre with decent **hostel** accommodation, B&B and home-cooked evening meals; it's handily close to Llanbedr's *Red Lion* pub. Across the river from Llanbedr, *Gellirhydd Farm* (☎01873/810466; ❶) offers great B&B and woodcraft classes.

For straightforward snacks and **lunches** at low, low prices you can't go past the *Queen Coffee Tavern* on Standard Street, just off High Street, even if you're not immediately drawn to dining to the strains of Cliff Richard overlooked by floor-to-ceiling Cliff photos and memorabilia. If you really can't bear it, visit the *Cheese Press* on the High Street. The *Bear Hotel* wins legions of awards for its delectable, pricier-than-average bar and inexpensive to moderately priced restaurant food. The *Bridge End* pub, by the town bridge, offers inexpensive local delicacies and veggie specialities. A couple of miles out on the Brecon road, by the A40/A479 junction, the lovely *Nantyffin Cider Mill Inn* (☎01873/810775) is great for real ales and ciders, as well as tasty food.

Abergavenny and around

Flanking the Brecon Beacons National Park, the lively market town of **ABERGAVENNY** (Y Fenni), seven miles southeast of Crickhowell, makes one of the best bases for an extended stay. There's not a whole lot to do, but there's a fine range of places to eat, drink and sleep, and the town is a magnet to walkers bound for the local mountains: **Sugar Loaf** and the legend-infused **Holy Mountain** (Skirrid Fawr). Stretching north from town, the **Vale of Ewyas** runs along the foot of the Black Mountains, where the astounding churches at Partrishow and Cwmyoy are lost in rural isolation. Abergavenny also makes a good base for visiting Monmouthshire's "Three Castles" (see p.766), set in the pastoral border country to the east.

Although only a couple of miles and a few hills away from the iron and coal towns of the Valleys (see p.768), Abergavenny grew on the basis of its weaving and tanning trades, giving it an entirely different feel. These industries prospered alongside a flourishing market, which is still the focal point for a wide area, drawing many people up from the Valleys every Tuesday. In World War II, Hitler's deputy, Rudolf Hess, was kept in the town's mental asylum as a prisoner, after his plane crash-landed in Scotland in 1941. He was allowed a weekly walk in the nearby hills, growing, it is said, to love the Welsh countryside.

From the train station, Monmouth Road rises gently, eventually becoming High Street, off which you'll find the fragmented remains of the medieval **castle**, whose ugly Victorian keep houses the **town museum** (March–Oct

15

Mon–Sat 11am–1pm & 2–5pm, Sun 2–5pm; Nov–Feb Mon–Sat 11am–1pm & 2–4pm; £1), which displays ephemera from the town's history and a reconstruction of Basil Jones' grocery shop, once on Main Street. After the death of Jones' son in 1989, the contents of the shop were transported to the museum lock, stock and biscuit barrel. Some goods are of recent origin, but much dates from the 1930s and 1940s – some even from the nineteenth century. Abergavenny's parish church of **St Mary**, on Monk Street, contains some superb tombs that span the entire medieval period. There are effigies of members of the notorious de Braose family, along with the tomb and figure of Sir William ap Thomas, founder of Raglan Castle (see p.765). Look out for the **Jesse Tree**, a recumbent, twice-life-size statue of King David's father which would once have formed part of an altarpiece tracing the family lineage from Jesse to Jesus.

Practicalities

Abergavenny's **train station** lies on the well-used line between Newport and Hereford. Buses depart from Swan Meadow **bus station**, right by the joint **tourist office** (daily: April–Oct 10am–5.30pm; Nov–March 10am–4pm; ☎01873/857588) and **Brecon Beacons National Park office** (Easter–Sept daily 9.30am–5.30pm; ☎01873/853254). You can **rent bikes** from Abergavenny Mountain Bike Hire (☎01873/850910), and from Pedalabikeaway (☎01873/830219), who are based out of town but deliver.

   Accommodation comes in the form of B&Bs, many on the Monmouth Road between the town centre and the train station: *Maes Glas*, Raglan Terrace, Monmouth Road (☎01873/854494; ❶), is the best. Nearby, the Georgian *Park Guest House*, 36 Hereford Rd (☎01873/853715; ❶), is also very good, while the central *King's Arms* pub, on Neville Street (☎01873/855074; ❷), has inexpensive and well-appointed rooms. If you've got transport, *Glangrwney Court* (☎01873/811288; ❷), off the A40 midway to Crickhowell, is an excellent option. The nearest place to pitch a **tent** is *Pyscodlyn Farm Caravan and Camping Site* (☎01873/853271), two miles west of town, off the A40. There are plenty of **places to eat** in Abergavenny, including the moderately priced *Greyhound Vaults*, Market Street, great for a wide range of tasty Welsh and English specialities, including the best vegetarian dishes in town. The very expensive *Walnut Tree Inn* (☎01873/852797), on the B4521 at Llanddewi Sgyrrid, two miles north of town, is a famous foodies' paradise for Mediterranean cuisine. Of Abergavenny's **pubs**, the best is the staunchly traditional *Hen & Chickens*, Flannel Street, just off the High Street, with a separate dining room for inexpensive food.

The Vale of Ewyas

In total contrast to the urban blights in the northern Valleys, just a few miles to the south, the northern finger of Monmouthshire, stretching along the English border, is one of the most enchanting and reclusive parts of Wales. The main A465 Hereford road leads six miles north out of Abergavenny to Llanfihangel Crucorney, where the B4423 diverges off to the north into the beautiful **Vale of Ewyas**, along the banks of the Honddu River.

   After a mile, a lane heads west towards the enchanting valley of Gwyrne Fawr, and the delightful church and well of St Issui in the hamlet of **Partrishow**. First founded in the eleventh century, the tiny church was refashioned in the thirteenth and fourteenth centuries. In the fifteenth century, it acquired a lacy rood screen, carved out of solid Irish oak and adorned with crude symbols of good and evil – most notably in the corner, where an evil dragon consumes a vine, a symbol of hope and well-being. The rest of the whitewashed church breathes simplicity by comparison. Of special note are the wall texts painted over the doom picture of a skeleton and scythe. Before the Reformation, such pictures were widely used to teach an illiterate population about the scriptures, until King James I ordered that such "popish devices" should be whitewashed over and repainted with scripture texts.

Back on the main B4423, the road winds its way up the valley's western side, past the fork at the *Queen's Head* inn (℡01873/890241; ❸), excellent for B&B and **pony trekking**, and a budget place to **camp**. In the adjacent village of **Cwmyoy**, the parish church of St Martin has substantially subsided due to geological twists in the underlying rock. Nothing squares up: the tower leans at a severe angle from the bulging body of the church, and the view inside from the back of the nave towards the sloping altar, askew roof and straining windows is unforgettable.

Llanthony and around

Four miles further up this most remote of valleys is the hamlet of **LLAN-THONY**, little more than a small cluster of houses, an inn and a few outlying farms around the wide open ruins of **Llanthony Priory** – a grander setting, and certainly a quieter one, than Tintern, though the buildings are far more modest in scale. It was founded in around 1100 by the Norman knight William de Lacy, who, it is said, was so captivated by the spiritual beauty of the site that he renounced worldly living and founded a hermitage, attracting like-minded recluses and forming Wales' first Augustinian priory. The roofless church, with its pointed transitional arches and squat tower, was constructed in the latter half of the twelfth century and retains a real sense of spirituality and peace. There are two good places to **stay**: the *Abbey Hotel* (℡01873/890487; ❸; Nov–March weekends only), fashioned out of part of the tumbledown priory, was built in the eighteenth century as a hunting lodge; along the road is the *Half Moon Inn* (℡01873/890611; ❷), serving superb beer and good-value meals.

From Llanthony, the road slowly climbs four miles alongside the narrowing Honddu River to the isolated hamlet of **CAPEL-Y-FFIN**, from where it's a further mile to the YHA **hostel** (℡01873/890650, ⓦwww.yha.org.uk; ❶; Feb–Nov), which also has pony trekking and **camping**. The road then weaves a tortuous route up over **Gospel Pass** and onto the howling, windy moor of **Hay Bluff**, on the glorious roof of the Black Mountains, before descending five miles to Hay-on-Wye.

Hay-on-Wye

Straddling the Anglo-Welsh border at the northern tip of the Brecon Beacons National Park, the sleepy little town of **HAY-ON-WYE** (Y Gelli) is known to most people for one thing – **books** (see box). Hay is a bibliophile's paradise, with just about every spare inch of the town being given over to the trade, including the old cinema and the ramshackle stone castle. Most of Hay's inhabitants are outsiders, which means that it has little indigenous feel, but its setting, against the spectacular backdrop of Hay Bluff and the Black Mountains, together with its creaky little streets, is delightful. In summer, the town fills with life as it plays host to a succession of riverside parties and travelling fairs, the pick of which is the **Hay Festival of Literature** (℡01497/821299, ⓦwww.hayfestival.co.uk) in the last week of May, when London's literary world decamps here.

The tourist office has a free leaflet that gives the low-down on all the **book-shops** in town. As good a place to start as any is Richard Booth's Bookshop,

The King of the Hay

Richard Booth, whose family originates from the area, opened the first of his Hay-on-Wye secondhand bookshops in 1961. Since then, he has built an astonishing empire and attracted other booksellers to the town, turning it into the greatest market of used books in the world. There are now over thirty such shops in this minuscule town, the largest of which – Booth's own – contains around half a million volumes.

Whereas many of the region's country towns have seen their populations ebb in recent decades, Hay has boomed on the strength of its bibliophilic connections. Booth regards this success as a prototype for other endangered communities, placing the emphasis firmly on local initiatives and unusual specializations. He is unequivocal in his condemnation of government regeneration programmes, which, he asserts, have done little to stem the flow of jobs and people out of the region. This healthy distaste for bureaucracy, coupled with Hay's geographical location slap on the Anglo-Welsh border and Booth's own self-promotional skills, led him to declare Hay independent of the UK in 1977, with himself, naturally, as **king**. He appoints his own ministers and offers "official" government scrolls, passports and car-stickers to bewitched visitors. Although such a proclamation of independence carries no official weight, most of the people of Hay seem to have rallied behind King Richard and are delighted with the publicity, and visitors, that the town's high profile attracts.

44 Lion St, a huge, draughty warehouse of almost unlimited browsing potential. It's owned – like so much else in Hay – by Richard Booth (see box), who lives in part of the castle, a careworn Jacobean mansion built into the walls of a thirteenth-century fortress right in the centre. In another part of the mansion is the Hay Castle Booth Books, a sedate collection of fine-art, cinema, antiquarian and photography books. Nearby, Castle Street Books, 23 Castle St, is great for historical guides and maps. Bag of Books, also on Castle Street, sells all its books at £1 each. Neighbouring Broad Street holds Y Gelli Auctions, with regular sales of books, maps and prints, and West House Books, best for Celtic and women's works.

Practicalities

Buses from Brecon and the English town of Hereford (see p.491) stop in the car park in the town centre off Oxford Road. The adjacent **tourist office** (daily: Easter–Oct 10am–1pm & 2–5pm; Nov–Easter 11am–1pm & 2–4pm; ☎01497/820144, ⊛www.hay-on-wye.co.uk) stocks an exhaustive range of hiking books and maps, and can help arrange accommodation in the area. **Bike rental** is available from Paddles & Peddles, 15 Castle St (☎01497/820604).

Accommodation in town is plentiful, though things get booked up long in advance for the Hay Festival of Literature. Arguably the best option is the *Famous Old Black Lion*, Lion Street (☎01497/820841; ❹), a captivating inn dating back to medieval times with beamed ceilings, comfortable rooms and a penchant for candlelight in the evenings. Also in the centre are *Belmont House*, Belmont Road (☎01497/820718; ❶), a classy guest house in an appealing Georgian villa packed with antiques, and *Brookfield House*, Brook Street (☎01497/ 820518, ⊛www.brookfieldguesthouse.btinternet.co.uk; ❶), an immaculate B&B in a tastefully modernized old building with stone walls, beamed ceilings and eight attractive guest rooms. In addition, the *Old Post Office*, Llanigon (☎01497/820008, ⊛www.oldpost-office.co.uk; ❶), is a wonderful seventeenth-century B&B two miles south of Hay, especially well placed for local walks; it serves up delicious vegetarian breakfasts. The nearest **campsite** is *Radnors End* (☎01497/820780), in a beautiful setting five minutes' walk from town across the Wye bridge on the Clyro road; washing and toilet facilities here are rudimentary, but pitches are cheap (£4) and the views over Hay and the Black Mountains are great.

Several of Hay's **pubs** offer top-quality bar food and meals, but you'll be hard pushed to find anywhere better than the *Famous Old Black Lion* on Lion Street. Another favourite is the *Granary* on Broad Street (☎01497/820790), the vegetarian's choice, specializing in wholefood snacks, soups and filling main meals made mostly with organic produce; it also has a roadside terrace that is a great place for hikers to kick off their boots and relax over a pint.

The Wells towns

The **spa towns** of mid-Wales, strung out along the Heart of Wales rail line between Swansea and Shrewsbury, were once all obscure villages, but with the arrival of the great craze for spas in the early eighteenth century, anywhere with a decent supply of apparently healing water joined in on the act. Royalty and nobility spearheaded the fashion, but the arrival of the railways opened them to all. The westernmost, **Llanwrtyd Wells**, was a popular haunt of the Welsh middle classes, some of whom arrived over the bleak moors by the **Abergwesyn Pass**, a narrow road still connecting the area to the Cambrian Coast. Far prettier – although considerably more twee and anglicized – is **Llandrindod Wells** to the north, whose spa is the only one of the four in any state of decent repair. In between, the larger town of Builth Wells was very much the spa of the Welsh working classes and there's no reason to stop other than to change buses. The fourth spa town, Llangammarch Wells, warrants even less attention.

Llanwrtyd Wells and around

Of the four spa towns, **LLANWRTYD WELLS**, twenty miles northwest of Brecon, is the most appealing. It's more Welsh, less spoilt and in more beautiful surroundings than the other three. This was the spa to which the Welsh – farmers of Dyfed alongside the Nonconformist middle classes from Glamorgan – came to the great *eisteddfodau* (festivals of Welsh music, dance and poetry) in the valley of the Irfon.

South of where the Main Street crosses the turbulent Irfon, a lane winds for half a mile along the river to the *Dolecoed Hotel*, built near the original sulphurous spring. Although the distinctive aroma had been noted in the area for centuries, it was truly "discovered" in 1732 by the local priest, Theophilus Evans, who drank from an evil-smelling spring after seeing a rudely healthy frog pop out of it. The spring, named **Ffynon Droellwyd** (Stinking Well), can still be sniffed out in the fields beyond the hotel, now erupting around a dome-shaped extension behind the dilapidated red-and-white spa buildings. The *Neuadd Arms* pub is the base for a wide range of bizarre and entertaining annual events, including a Man-versus-Horse race and a Drovers' Walk (both in June); a town festival (first weekend in Aug); a snorkelling competition in a local bog (end of Aug); a beer festival (Nov); and a torchlight procession through the town (New Year's Eve).

Llanwrtyd's **tourist office** is in *Tŷ Barcud*, on the main square (June–Aug daily 10am–5pm; rest of year Mon–Sat 10am–4pm; ☎01591/610666). **Accommodation** includes the *Neuadd Arms*, on the square (☎01591/610236; ❸), which also rents out **bikes**; the solidly Victorian *Belle Vue Hotel*, a few yards away (☎01591/610237; ❶); and the cheaper *Oakfield House*, Dol-y-coed Road (℡01591/610605; ●). The *Stonecroft Inn*, also on Dol-y-coed Road (℡01591/610332; ●), is a superb pub with great food and regular live music, plus a self-catering **hostel** with bunks. Both the *Neuadd Arms* and the *Belle Vue* provide cheap, hearty **food**. The moderately priced *Drovers* restaurant (℡01591/610264), by the bridge, serves wholesome and highly acclaimed traditional Welsh dishes.

The Abergwesyn Pass

A lane from Llanwrtyd meets up with another road from Beulah at the riverside hamlet of **ABERGWESYN**, five miles north of Llanwrtyd. From here, you can drive the quite magnificent winding thread of an ancient cattle drovers' road – the **Abergwesyn Pass** – up the perilous **Devil's Staircase** and through dense conifer forests to miles of wide, desolate valleys where sheep graze unhurriedly. At the little bridge over the tiny Tywi River, a track heads south past an isolated, gas-lit YHA **hostel** at **DOLGOCH** (℡01974/298680; ●; May–Sept). This is as remote a walking holiday as can be had in Wales. Paths lead from the hostel through the forests and hillsides to the tiny chapel at **Soar-y-Mynydd** and over the mountains to the next, and equally primitive, YHA **hostel** at **TY'N-Y-CORNEL** (℡01550/740225; ●; April–Sept), five miles from Dolgoch. Although the Abergwesyn Pass, which ends in the market square of Tregaron in Ceredigion, is less than twenty miles long, it takes a good hour in a car to negotiate the twisting, narrow road safely. The old drovers, driving their cattle to Shrewsbury or Hereford, would have taken a day or two to cover the same stretch.

Llandrindod Wells

If anything can sum up a town succinctly, it is the plaque at **LLANDRINDOD WELLS** station, commemorating the 1990 "Revictorianisation of Llandrindod railway station". The town, fifteen miles northeast of Llanwrtyd, has not been slow to follow suit, peddling itself furiously as Wales' most upmarket Victorian inland resort, despite its one-time reputation for licentiousness. It was the railway that made Llandrindod, bringing carriages full of well-to-do Victorians to the fledgling spa from 1864 onwards. The town blossomed, new hotels were built, neat parks were laid out and it came to rival many of the more fashionable spas and resorts over the border. Even now, Llandrindod can seem like a breath of fresh air, with its finer buildings swabbed and sandblasted, its ornate cast-iron railings restored, and the spa brought back to some kind of life.

Llandrindod's Victorian opulence is still very much in evidence in the town's grandiose public buildings, especially the lavishly restored **spa pump room** in the pleasant **Rock Park**, with its trickling streams and well-manicured glens. EU regulations sanction the use of only one of Llandrindod's spa taps in the café inside: a tiny – but more than ample – glass costs 10p, or you can step outside for a free gulp from the chalybeate fountain outside. The architecture around the park entrance is Llandrindod at its most confidently Victorian, with elaborately carved terracotta frontages and expansive gabling.

The High Street, running from here to the centre, contains antique, junk and book shops. The tourist office, on Temple Street, behind, houses the small **Radnorshire Museum** (Tues–Thurs 10am–1pm & 2–5pm, Fri 10am–1pm & 2–4.30pm, Sat & Sun 11am–5pm; £1), which is largely dedicated to excavated remains from the Roman fort at Castellcollen, a mile northwest of Llandrindod. Kitsch Victoriana makes up the bulk of the rest of the collection, although there's also one of the better red-kite galleries, including a video with stunning footage. The **National Cycle Collection**, on the corner of Temple Street and Spa Road (March–Oct daily 10am–4pm; call ☎01597/825531 for winter hours; £2.50), is a nostalgic collection of over 250 bikes, from a repro-duction 1818 Hobbyhorse to relatively modern folding bikes and choppers, including styles that look far too uncomfortable to have been a success.

Practicalities

Buses pull in by the **train station** in the heart of town, between High Street and Station Crescent. The **tourist office** is on Temple Street (April–Sept Mon–Fri 9.30am–5.30pm, Sat & Sun 9.30am–5pm; Oct–March Mon–Fri 10am–1pm & 2–5pm; ☎01597/822600). **Bikes** can be rented from the Greenstiles Bike Shed (☎01597/824594), next to the Cycle Exhibition.

As mid-Wales' major tourist centre for the past 130 years, Llandrindod is well served for **accommodation**. For something smart and reasonably close to the station, try *Greylands*, High Street (☎01597/822253; ❶), or nearby *Rhydithon*, Dyffryn Road (☎01597/822624; ❶). The *Kincoed Hotel*, Temple Street (☎01597/822656; ❶), is well appointed but not a patch on the Edwardian ele-gance of the *Metropole Hotel*, on the same street (☎01597/822881, ⓦwww.metropole.co.uk; ❺), an old spa hotel with a pool, the centrepiece of the town. Well worth a visit, for non-residents too, is their superb *Radnor* **restaurant** (☎01597/823700), with some dazzling interpretations of local cuisine. For rea-sonably priced food, head for the *Herb Garden*, Spa Road, a welcoming veggie and wholefood restaurant, or the *Llanerch Inn*, Llanerch Lane, central Llandrindod's only **pub**, and an excellent one at that – a cosy sixteenth-cen-tury inn that predates most of the surrounding town, serving a solid menu of good-value, well-cooked classics. Even nicer is the *Drovers' Arms*, a cosy food-ies' pub, a couple of miles south of town in the village of Howey.

North and East Radnorshire

Radnorshire has long been one of the most sparsely populated counties in England and Wales, its north and east still being especially remote. In the north-west, Rhayader is the only settlement of any size, a gateway to the four inter-locking reservoirs of the **Elan Valley** and the surrounding wild, spartan coun-tryside of waterfalls, bogland and bare peaks. The countryside to the northeast of Rhayader is tamer, and lanes and bridle paths delve in and around the woods and farms, occasionally brushing through minute settlements like the village of **Abbeycwmhir**, whose name is taken from its deserted Cistercian abbey. The hills roll eastwards towards the handsome town of **Knighton**, perched right on the English border, beside some of the most intact parts of **Offa's Dyke**.

Elan Valley and around

The poet Shelley spent his honeymoon in buildings now submerged by the waters of the **Elan Valley** reservoirs, a nine-mile-long string of four lakes built between 1892 and 1903 to supply water to the rapidly growing industrial city of Birmingham, 75 miles east. Although the lakes enhance an already beautiful and idyllic part of the world, the way in which Welsh valleys, villages and farm-steads were seized and flooded to provide water for English cities is something that Welsh nationalists have long protested. The tourist board prefers to adver-tise the profusion of rare plants and birds that resulted, notably the red kites.

From the workaday market town of **RHAYADER**, ten miles west of Llandrindod Wells, the B4518 heads southwest four miles to **ELAN** village, a curious collection of stone houses built in 1909 to replace the reservoir constructors' village that had grown up on the site. Just below the dam of the first reservoir, Caban Coch, the **Elan Valley Visitor Centre** (mid-March to Oct daily 10am–5.30pm; ☎01597/810898) incorporates a tourist office and a permanent exhibition stressing just how awful conditions were in nineteenth-century Birmingham, how rich the wildlife and flora around the lakes is and even how some of the water is now drunk in Wales. Frequent guided **walks** head off from the centre, and a road tucks in along the bank of Caban Coch to the **Garreg Ddu** viaduct, where it winds along for four spectacular miles to the vast, rather chilling 1952 dam on **Claerwen Reservoir**. More remote and less popular than the Elan lakes, Claerwen is a good base for a serious **walk** from the far end of the dam across eight or so harsh but beautiful miles to the monastery of Strata Florida (see p.853). Alternatively, you can follow the path that skirts around the northern shore of Claerwen to the lonely **Teifi Pools**, glacial lakes from which the River Teifi springs.

Back at the Garreg Ddu viaduct, a more popular road continues north along the long, glassy finger of Garreg Ddu reservoir, before doubling back on itself just below the awesome **Pen-y-garreg** dam and reservoir; if the dam is overflowing, the vast wall of foaming water is mesmerizing. At the top of Pen-y-garreg lake, it's possible to drive over the final dam on the system, at **Craig Goch**. Thanks to its gracious curve, elegant Edwardian arches and neat little green cupola, this is the most photographed of all the dams.

ABBEYCWMHIR (Abaty Cwm Hir), seven miles northeast of Rhayader, takes its name from the **abbey** whose sombre ruins (free access) lie behind the village. Cistercian monks founded the site in 1146, planning one of the largest churches in Britain. Destruction by Henry III's troops in 1231 scuppered plans to continue building, but the sparse ruins – a rocky outline of the floor plan – lie in a conifer-carpeted valley alongside a gloomy green lake, lending weight to the site's melancholic associations. Llywelyn ap Gruffydd's body was rumoured to have been buried here, and a new granite slab carved with a Celtic sword lies on the altar to commemorate this last native prince of Wales.

Practicalities

Bus #103 runs to the Elan Valley Visitor Centre from Llandrindod and Rhayader (Mon–Fri 2 daily). The main **accommodation** base in the area is the *Elan Valley Hotel* (☎01597/810448, ⓦwww.elanvalleyhotel.co.uk; ❸), an imposing, neocolonial pile on the Rhayader side of Elan village. It's also very good for eating, drinking and entertainment. Otherwise, you may want to make use of Rhayader, where buses stop opposite the **tourist office** (April–Oct daily 9.30am–12.30pm & 1.30–5.30pm; Nov–March Mon, Tues & Thurs–Sat 10am–4pm; ☎01597/810591), housed in the leisure centre. Eighteenth-century coaching inns, including the *Elan Hotel*, West Street (☎01597/810373; ❷), still line Rhayader's main streets, or there's more modern accommodation at the *Bryncoed* B&B, opposite the tourist office on Dark Lane (☎01597/811082; ❶); the *Horseshoe*, Church Street (☎01597/810982; ❶); or *The Mount*, East Street (☎01597/810585; ❶), a friendly B&B and the base for Clive Powell Mountain Bikes (☎01597/811343), from whom you can **rent bikes** or join one of his organized trips around the tracks of mid-Wales. There's a **campsite** (☎01597/810183) at Wyeside, off the A44 north of Rhayader.

Knighton

A town that straddles King Offa's eighth-century border as well as the modern Wales–England divide, **KNIGHTON** (Tref-y-clawdd, the "Town on the Dyke"), twenty miles northeast of Llandrindod, has come into its own as the most obvious centre for those walking the **Offa's Dyke Path**. Located almost exactly halfway along the route, it's a lively, attractive place that easily warrants a stopoff, although has few specific sights. The town is so close to the border that its **train station** is actually in England. From here, Station Road crosses the River Teme into Wales and climbs a couple of hundred yards to Brookside Square. Further up the hill is the town's alpine-looking Victorian clocktower, at the point where Broad Street becomes West Street and the steep High Street soars off up to the left, past rickety Tudor buildings and up to the mound of the old **castle**.

In West Street, the excellent **Offa's Dyke Centre** also houses the **tourist office** (Easter–Oct daily 9am–5.30pm; Nov–Easter Mon–Fri 9am–5pm; ☎01547/529424). **Accommodation** is plentiful: try *Fleece House*, Market Street (☎01547/520168; ❷), the basic but cheerful *Red Lion*, West Street (☎01547/528231; ❶), or the bargain *Offa's Dyke House*, 4 High Street (☎01547/528634; ❶), which serves evening meals. Limited **camping** is available at *Jenny Stothert's B&B* (☎01547/520075) at 15 Mill Green, down towards the river. For **eating** and drinking, it's hard to beat the comfortable *Horse & Jockey*, at the town end of Station Road. There's folk and jazz **music** in the *Plough* on Market Street.

Offa's Dyke

Offa's Dyke has provided a potent symbol of Welsh–English antipathy ever since it was created in the eighth century as a demarcation line by King Offa of Mercia, ruler of central England. George Borrow, in his classic *Wild Wales*, notes that, once, "it was customary for the English to cut off the ears of every Welshman who was found to the east of the dyke, and for the Welsh to hang every Englishman whom they found to the west of it".

The earthwork – up to 20ft high and 60ft wide – made use of natural boundaries like rivers in its run north to south, and is best seen in the sections near Knighton. Today's England–Wales border crosses the dyke many times, although the basic boundary has changed little since Offa's day. A glorious, 177-mile **long-distance footpath**, opened in 1971, runs the length of the dyke from Prestatyn in the north to Chepstow, and is one of the most rewarding walks in Britain.

Montgomeryshire

The northern part of Powys is made up of the old county of **Montgomeryshire** (Maldwyn), an area of enormously varying landscapes and few inhabitants. The solid little town of **Llanidloes** is a base for ageing hippies on the River Severn (Afon Hafren). To the east, the muted old county town of **Montgomery**, with its fine Georgian architecture, perches amid gentle, green hills above the border and Offa's Dyke. Further north, **Welshpool**, the only major settlement, is packed in above the wide floodplain of the Severn; an excellent local museum, toy rail line, good pubs and reasonable hotels make it a fair stop. On the southern side of Welshpool is Montgomeryshire's one unmissable sight, the sumptuous **Powis Castle** and its exquisite terraced gardens.

Llanidloes and around

Thriving when so many other small market towns seem in danger of atrophying, the secret of success for **LLANIDLOES**, twelve miles north of Rhayader, seems to be in its adaptability. It has developed from a rural village to a weaving town, and has latterly become a centre for artists, craftspeople and assorted alternative lifestylers. One of mid-Wales's prettiest towns, the four main streets meet at the black and white **market hall**, built on timber stilts in 1600 to allow the market – which has long since moved – to take place on the cobbles beneath. Running parallel with the length of the market hall are China Street and Longbridge Street, the latter good for some interesting little shops, including the very browsable Nature Gallery art store. Off Longbridge Street is Church Street, which opens out into a yard surrounding the dumpy parish church of **St Idloes**, the impressive fifteenth-century hammerbeam roof of which is said to have been poached from Abbeycwmhir. The fantastic new **millennium window** in the church was designed and built by two local stained-glass artists.

From the market hall, the broad Great Oak Street heads west to the **Town Hall**, originally built as a temperance hotel to challenge the boozy *Trewythen Arms* opposite. A plaque on the hotel commemorates Llanidloes as an unlikely-seeming place of industrial and political unrest, when, in April 1839, Chartists stormed the hotel, dragging out and beating up special constables who had been despatched to the town in a futile attempt to suppress political activism amongst the town's flannel weavers. In the town hall, you'll also find the wonderfully eclectic and much revamped town **museum** (Easter–Sept daily except Wed 11am–1pm & 2–5pm; Oct–Easter Mon, Tues, Thurs & Fri 11am–1pm & 2–5pm, Sat 10am–1pm; £1), with its inevitable red-kite centre.

China Street curves down to the car park, from where all **bus** services operate. The **tourist office** (April–Sept daily 9.30am–5pm, Oct–March Mon–Sat 10am–5pm; ℡01686/412605) is just north of the market hall, on Longbridge Street. **Accommodation** includes the *Red Lion Hotel*, Longbridge Street (℡01686/412270; ❷) and the genteel *Unicorn*, on the same street (℡01686/413167; ❶).You can **camp** at *Dol-llys Farm* (℡01686/412694), on the northern fringe of town. Among the many options for **food**, the best bet is the wholesome fare in the laid-back *Great Oak Café*, on Great Oak Street.The lively *Red Lion* **pub** also does good food, or you could treat yourself at the *Orchard House*, China Street (℡01686/413700). One event worth investigating is the annual **Fancy Dress Night**, held on the first Friday of July, when the pubs open late, the streets are cordoned off and virtually the whole town gets kitted out.

Montgomery and around

Tiny **MONTGOMERY** (Trefaldwyn), around twenty miles northeast of Llanidloes, is Montgomeryshire at its most anglicized. From the mound of its **castle**, situated just on the Welsh side of Offa's Dyke, there are wonderful views over the lofty church tower and the handsome Georgian streets, notably the impressively symmetrical main street – well-named Broad Street – which swoops up to the perfect little red-brick **Town Hall**, crowned by a pert clock-tower. The rebuilt tower of Montgomery's parish **Church of St Nicholas** dominates the snug proportions of the buildings around it. Largely thirteenth-century, the highlights of its spacious interior include a 1600 monument to local landowner Sir Richard Herbert and his wife.Their eight children – who included prominent Elizabethan poet George – have been carved in beatific kneeling positions behind them. Call in too at the engaging **Old Bell Museum**, just by the town hall (July & Aug Mon–Fri & Sun 1.30–5pm, Sat 10.30am–5pm; April–June & Sept Wed–Fri & Sun 1.30–5pm, Sat 10.30am–5pm; £1), an enjoyable collection of excavated artefacts, scale models of local castles and mementoes from Montgomery civic life.

Montgomery is within striking distance of one of the best-preserved sections of **Offa's Dyke**, traced by the long-distance footpath (see box on p.829), which runs on either side of the B4386. Ditches almost twenty feet high give one of the best indications of the dyke's original appearance. To the south of the main road, the England–Wales border still runs along the line of the dyke, twelve hundred years after it was built. If you want to **stay** here, *Little Brompton Farm*, two miles north on the B4385 (☎01686/668371; ❷), is handily close to the Offa's Dyke Path or, in town, the *Bronwylfa*, Broad Street (☎01686/668630; ❶), is a good B&B in a Georgian town house. For **food** and **drink** there's *The Checkers* pub, on Broad Street.

Berriew

Three miles northwest of Montgomery, the neat village of **BERRIEW** (Aberrhiw) is more redolent of the Tudor settlements over the English border than anywhere in Wales. Its black and white houses are grouped picturesquely around a small church, the shallow waters of the River Rhiw and the slightly twee *Lion Hotel* (☎01686/640452; ❺), excellent nonetheless for food. Just over the river bridge, the **Andrew Logan Museum of Sculpture** (July & Aug Wed–Sun noon–6pm; Easter, May, June, Sept & Oct Sat & Sun noon–6pm, £2.50) makes for an incongruous attraction in such a setting, with a good selection of the notable modern sculptor's work. Logan inaugurated the great 1970s drag-and-grunge ball known as the "Alternative Miss World Contest", astounding costumes and memorabilia from which form a large part of the exhibits at the museum. Logan's oversized horticultural sculpture, including giant lilies encrusted with shattered mirrors and vast metal irises, rises to scrape the roof, while his smaller-scale jewellery and model goddesses only add to the sublime camp of the exhibition.

Welshpool and around

Eastern Montgomeryshire's chief town of **WELSHPOOL** (Y Trallwng), seven miles north of Montgomery, was formerly known as just Pool, its prefix added in 1835 to distinguish it from the English seaside town of Poole in Dorset. Welshpool lies in the valley of the River Severn, just three miles from the English border, and was dependent largely upon the patronage of English landlords and kings. As a result, the town never developed a very Welsh character, but it's an attractive place to visit, with a number of attractive Tudor, Georgian and Victorian buildings in the centre, and the sumptuous Powis Castle nearby.

Along Severn Street from the **train station**, a hump-backed bridge over the much-restored **Montgomery Canal** hides the wharf, from where gaudily painted **boats** will chug you up the navigable section for a few miles and a couple of hours (☎01938/553271; £4.25). Nearby, a carefully restored warehouse contains the **Powysland Museum** (May–Sept Mon, Tues, Thurs & Fri 11am–1pm & 2–5pm, Sat & Sun 10am–1pm & 2–5pm; Oct–April Mon, Tues, Thurs & Fri 11am–1pm & 2–5pm, Sat 2–5pm £1). The impressive local history collection includes archeological nuggets such as those from an old local woodhenge and displays medieval remains from the now obliterated local Cistercian abbey of Strata Marcella.

From the *Royal Oak Hotel*, at the centre of town, follow Broad Street – which changes name five times as it rises up the hill – towards the tiny Raven Square terminus station of the **Welshpool and Llanfair Light Railway** (April–Oct weekends; Easter, Whitsun week and June–Aug daily; generally 2 trains a day; ☎01938/810441; return ticket £8.50). The eight-mile narrow-gauge rail line was open to passengers for less than thirty years prior to its closure in 1931. Now, scaled-down engines once more chuff their way along to the peaceful little village of **Llanfair Caereinion**, a good base for daytime walks, with good pub food at the *Goat Hotel*. The post office, opposite the church, stocks free leaflets of some good local circular walks.

Practicalities

The pompous neo-Gothic turrets of Welshpool's old Victorian **train station** (its modern replacement is directly behind) sit at the top of Severn Street, which leads down into the town centre – the intersection of Severn, Berriew, Broad and Church streets. The **tourist office** (daily 9.30am–5pm; ☎01938/552043) is fifty yards up Church Street in the Vicarage Gardens car park.

There is plenty of **accommodation** in town, including the central *Royal Oak* (☎01938/552217; ❺), a traditional coaching inn at the main crossroads. Dozens of **B&Bs** line Salop Road; *Montgomery House* (☎01938/552693; ❶) is the surest bet. Further from the centre are a couple of options: the beautiful *Lower Trelydan Farm* (☎01938/553105; ❷), out towards the village of Guilsfield (Cegidfa); and *Severn Farm*, on Leighton Road (☎01938/553098; ❶), just beyond the industrial estate to the east of the station, which allows **camping**. The best **eating** in town is at the *Royal Oak* pub (see above), which has managed to retain its olde-worlde grandiosity while including a superb all-day café-bar. Failing that, up the High Street, the *Talbot* pub serves excellent lunchtime and evening meals, and there are numerous stodgy cafés around town.

Powis Castle

In a land of ruined castles, the sheer scale and beauty of **Powis Castle** (April–Oct Wed–Sun castle 1–5pm, gardens 11am–6pm; July & Aug also Tues same times; castle £7.50; gardens only £5; NT), a mile from Welshpool up Park Lane, is reason enough for coming to the town. On the site of an earlier Norman fort, the castle was started in the reign of Edward I by the Gwenwynwyn family; to qualify for the site and the barony of De la Pole, they had to renounce all claims to Welsh princedom. In 1587, Sir Edward Herbert bought the castle and began to transform it into the Elizabethan palace that survives today. Inside, the **Clive Museum** – named after Edward Clive, son of Clive of India, who married into the family in 1784 – forms a lively account of the British in India, through diaries, letters, paintings, tapestries, weapons and jewels. But it is the sumptuous period rooms that impress most, from the vast, kitsch frescoes by Lanscroon above the balustraded staircase, to the mahogany bed, brass and enamel toilets and decorative wall hangings of the state bedroom. The elegant **Long Gallery** has a rich sixteenth-century plasterwork ceiling overlooking winsome busts and marble statuettes of the four elements, placed between the glowering family portraits. The **gardens**, designed by Welsh architect William Winde, are spectacular. Dropping down from the castle in four huge stepped terraces, the design has barely changed since the seventeenth century, with a charmingly precise orangery and topiary that looks as if it is shaved daily. In summer, outdoor **concerts**, frequently with firework finales, take place in the gardens.

△ St David's Cathedral

Llanfyllin and around

The hills and plains of northern Montgomeryshire conceal a maze of deserted lanes and farm outposts along the contours that swell up towards the north and the foothills of the Berwyn Mountains. The only real settlement of any size is **Llanfyllin**, ten miles northwest of Welshpool, a peaceful but friendly hillside town with a Thursday market. There is really nothing to do though, and you'd do better continuing on to the hiking and nature-communing around **Lake Vyrnwy**, or pressing north to **Pistyll Rhaeadr**, Wales' highest waterfall.

Llanrhaeadr-ym-mochnant and Pistyll Rhaeadr

For a place so near the English border, **LLANRHAEADR-YM-MOCHNANT**, six miles north of Llanfyllin, is surprisingly Welsh in its language and appearance. The small, low-roofed village is remembered as the serving parish of Bishop William Morgan, who translated the Bible into Welsh in 1588, but it's mostly visited as a base for **Pistyll Rhaeadr**, Wales' highest waterfall, at 240ft. The village lies at the foot of a lane which runs four miles northwest alongside the River Rhaeadr through an increasingly rocky valley to the falls. The river tumbles down the crags in two stages, flowing furiously under a natural stone arch that has been christened the Fairy Bridge. When it's quiet, tame chaffinches swoop and settle all around this enchanting spot, although the charms are a little hard to appreciate amid the tourists on a warm summer Sunday.

The summer-only *Tan-y-Pistyll* licensed café, by the waterfall car park, is tolerable and they run a decent **B&B** (☎01691/780392; ❷) with a **campsite** in the back field. The village has a bargain B&B, *Powys House*, on the central square (☎01691/780201; ❶), and two great **pubs** – the *Three Tuns* and the *Wynnstay Arms*.

Lake Vyrnwy

A monument to the self-aggrandizement of the Victorian age, **Lake Vyrnwy** (Llyn Efyrnwy) combines its functional role as a water supply for Liverpool with a touch of architectural genius in the shape of the huge nineteenth-century dam at its southern end and the Disneyesque turreted straining tower which edges out into the icy waters. It's a magnificent spot, and a popular centre for walking and birdwatching, with nature trails. The village of **LLAN-WDDYN** was flattened and rebuilt at the eastern end, the inhabitants receiving compensation of just £5 for losing their homes. The story is told, somewhat apologetically, in the RSPB **Vyrnwy Visitor Centre** (April–Dec daily 10am–5.30pm; Jan–March Sat & Sun 10am–4.30pm; free), which includes a whizzy new 3D film presentation on local wildlife. Down the lane are the **tourist office** (Easter–Oct daily 10am–5pm; Nov–Easter Sat & Sun 10am–4pm; ☎01691/870346) and a **birdwatching centre**, in the cluster of buildings on the western side of the dam. **Bikes** can be rented from Mandy's Tea Shop, next door.

Lake Vyrnwy's immediate surroundings have some of the best **accommodation** in the region, notably the grand *Lake Vyrnwy Hotel* (☎01691/870692; ❼), overlooking the waters above the southeastern shore. If you just want a look, the hotel serves a full afternoon tea in a chintzy lounge overlooking the lake. Close by, *Ty Uchaf* (☎01691/870286; ❷) has B&B and a good tearoom. Farmhouse B&B is available not far away at *Tynymaes* (☎01691/870216; ❶), a couple of miles east of Llanwddyn on the B4393; and at the sublime, ivy-draped *Cyfie Farm* (☎01691/648451; ❸), just over a mile south of Llanfihangel-yng-

Ngwynfa. If you're **camping**, there are five tent pitches at *Fronheulog* (℡01691/870662), at the top of the hairpin bends on the road to Llanfyllin, or in Llanwddyn itself, at *Bryn Fedwen* (℡01691/870288).

The Dee Valley

Llangollen, along with the smaller town of Bala, grew up partly as a market centre, but also served the needs of cattle drovers who used the passage carved by the **River Dee** (Afon Dyfrdwy) through the hills – the easiest route from the fattening grounds of northwest Wales to the markets in England. Long before rail and road transport pushed the dwindling numbers of drovers out of business at the end of the nineteenth century, they had already been joined by early tourists. Most made straight for **Llangollen**, where the ruins of both a Welsh castle and a Cistercian abbey lent a gaunt Romantic charm to a dramatic gorge naturally blessed with surging rapids. The arrival of the railway, in the middle of the nineteenth century, made Llangollen a firm favourite with tourists from the mill towns of northwest England. The line closed in the 1960s, but **Bala** has fought neglect to become one of Wales' top **watersports** venues, a mecca for windsurfing and white-water kayaking. Between Llangollen and the English border, the Dee is joined by one of its major tributaries, the Ceiriog, which flows down its peaceful valley to the Marcher fortress of **Chirk Castle**.

Llangollen and around

LLANGOLLEN, thirty miles north of Welshpool, is the embodiment of a Welsh town in both setting and character, clasped tightly in the narrow Dee Valley between the shoulders of the Berwyn and Eglwyseg mountains. Along the valley's floor, the waters of the River Dee run down to the town, licking the angled buttresses of the weighty Gothic bridge, which has spanned the river since the fourteenth century. On its south bank, half a dozen streets, their houses harmoniously straggling up the rugged hillsides, are labelled in both Welsh and English, and form the core of the scattered settlement flung out across the low hills. Every July, the town comes alive for the **International Music Eisteddfod**.

As the only river crossing point for miles, Llangollen was an important town long before the early Romantics arrived at the end of the eighteenth century, when they were cut off from their European Grand Tours by the Napoleonic Wars. Turner came to paint the swollen river and the Cistercian ruin of **Valle Crucis**, a couple of miles up the valley; John Ruskin found the town "entirely lovely in its gentle wildness"; and writer George Borrow made Llangollen his base for the early part of his 1854 tour detailed in *Wild Wales*. The rich and famous came not just for the scenery, but to visit the "Ladies of Llangollen", an eccentric couple who became the toast of society from their house, Plas Newydd. But by this stage some of the town's rural charm had been eaten up by the works of one of the century's finest engineers, Thomas Telford, who squeezed both his London–Holyhead trunk road and the **Llangollen Canal** alongside the river.

The Town

Standing in twelve acres of formal gardens, half a mile up Hill Street from the southern end of Castle Street, the two-storied mock-Tudor **Plas Newydd**

The Llangollen International Music Eisteddfod

Llangollen is heaving in summer, but never more so than during the first week of July, when for six days the town explodes into a frenzy of music, dance, poetry and colour. The **International Music Eisteddfod** comes billed as "the world's greatest folk festival" but unlike the National Eisteddfod, which is a purely Welsh affair, the Llangollen event draws amateur performers from thirty countries, all competing for prizes in their chosen disciplines. Throughout the week, performers present their works at numerous sites around the town, but mainly in the much-derided 6000-seat white plastic structure designed to evoke the shape of the traditional marquee which was formerly erected on the site each year.

The Eisteddfod has been held in its present form since 1947, when it was started more or less on a whim by one Harold Tudor. Forty choirs from fourteen countries performed at the first event. Today, more than 12,000 musicians, singers, dancers and choristers from countries around the world descend on this town of 3000 people, further swamped by up to 150,000 visitors. While the whole set-up can seem oppressive, there is an irresistible *joie-de-vivre* as brightly costumed dancers walk the streets and fill the fish-and-chip shops. Recent years have seen a superbly eclectic **Fringe Festival** grow up alongside the Eisteddfod, with rock gigs, comedy and performance events and some unexpected treats bursting out in every possible venue.

Unless you're arriving specifically for the Eisteddfod, the week after the first Tuesday of July is probably a good time to stay away from Llangollen; otherwise, book early for both accommodation and **tickets** (℡01978/862000, ⓦwww.international-eisteddfod.co.uk).

(Easter–Oct daily 10am–5pm; £2.75) was, for almost fifty years, home to the celebrated **Ladies of Llangollen**. Lady Eleanor Butler and Sarah Ponsonby were a lesbian couple from Anglo-Irish aristocratic backgrounds, and tried to elope together at the end of the eighteenth century. After two botched attempts dressed in men's clothes, they were grudgingly allowed to leave their family seats in 1778 with an annual allowance of £280, enough to settle in Llangollen, where they became celebrated hosts and legendary local characters. Despite their desire for a "life of sweet and delicious retirement", they didn't seem to mind the constant stream of gentry who called on them. Walter Scott was well received, though he found them "a couple of hazy or crazy old sailors" in manner, and like "two respectable superannuated clergymen" in their mode of dress. Visitors' gifts of sculpted **wood panelling** formed the basis of the riotous friezes of gloomy woodwork that weigh on your every step around the modest black and white timbered house. Most of the rooms have been left almost empty, so as not to hide the panelling; only one upper room has been devoted to a few of the ladies' possessions and panels detailing their life story. Llangollen takes its name from the **Church of St Collen**, on Bridge Street (May–Sept daily 1.30–6pm; free), outside which is a triangular railed-off monument to the Ladies and their devoted maid.

The hills around Llangollen echo to the shrill cry of steam engines easing along the **Llangollen Steam Railway** (Easter–Oct daily; plus weekends and holidays throughout the year; ℡01978/860979), shoe-horned into the north side of the valley. From Llangollen's time-warped station it runs along a restored section of the disused Ruabon–Barmouth line, the belching steam engines creeping west along the riverbank, hauling ancient carriages which proudly sport the liveries of their erstwhile owners. The restored line currently runs the eight miles to Carrog, although plans to push through to Corwen are well in hand.

A short riverside walk from the station leads to Lower Dee Exhibition Centre, Mill Street, home to the **Doctor Who Exhibition** (daily 10am–5.30pm; £5.95; joint ticket with Model Railway World £9), an endearing homage to this much-loved British sci-fi drama, and **Model Railway World** (same hours; £4.50), with plenty of layouts and engines to play with. Entry to either gives you the opportunity to watch model-making in progress in the parent Dapol toy factory.

Across the street is the Llangollen Canal, one of the finest feats of British canal building. Its architect, Thomas Telford, succeeded in building a canal without locks through fourteen miles of hilly terrain, most spectacularly by means of the thousand-foot-long **Pontcysyllte Aqueduct**, passing 127ft over the River Dee at Froncysyllte, four miles east. **Canal trips** (Easter–Oct daily; horse-drawn trip £4, aqueduct trip £7; ☎01978/860702) over the aqueduct leave from Llangollen Wharf, just above the steam train station on Wharf Hill.

Walking west from the town bridge, you'll soon come to the site of the International Eisteddfod, crowned by the extraordinary **Royal International Pavilion**, which – especially from the walk up the hill to Dinas Brân – resembles some giant armoured reptile dropped from a great height into the valley. Outside the Eisteddfod season, the auditorium acts as a concert venue and sports hall, with temporary exhibitions in the foyer (Mon–Fri 10am–4pm; free).

Practicalities

Buses stop on Market Street, while the nearest **train station** is five miles away at Ruabon, which is passed by frequent buses on the Llangollen–Wrexham run. The **tourist office**, on Castle Street (daily: Easter–Oct 10am–6pm; Nov–Easter daily except Wed 9.30am–5pm; ☎01978/860828), is fifty yards from the bridge and less than a hundred yards from the bus stop on Market Street. There's **internet** access at The Gallery Computer World, 22 Chapel St (☎01978/869384; £3 per half hour), and **bike rental** from the town's hostel – you don't have to be staying there.

Finding **rooms** in Llangollen can be a chore in summer, especially during the Eisteddfod. Low-cost B&Bs worth checking out include the bright, simply furnished rooms at *Greenbank Guesthouse*, Victoria Square (☎01978/861835, Ⓦ www.greenbank.uk.com; ❶); *Bryant Rose*, 31 Regent St (☎01978/860389; ❶), a central B&B with large, airy rooms; and *Jonkers*, 9 Chapel St (☎01978/ 861158; ❶), which has a couple of compact, low-beamed rooms in an ancient house with uneven floors and narrow stairways. Moving upmarket, go for *Gales*, 18 Bridge St (☎01978/860089; ❸), a comfortable guesthouse above a wine bar; the central *Four Poster Hotel* (☎01978/861062; ❸) at 1 Mill St; *Fron Deg* (☎01978/860126; ❷), a top-class B&B a mile west along Abbey Road; or *Bodidris Hall* (☎01978/790434; ❻), seven miles north of Llangollen on the A5104, which offers secluded luxury in a largely Tudor building with log fires, oak beams and an award-winning restaurant. The excellent YHA **hostel**, on Tyndwr Road (☎01978/860330, Ⓦ www.yha.org.uk; ❶), is a mile and a half from town – go along the A5 towards Shrewsbury, turn right up Birch Hill, then right again. *Eirianfa* (☎01978/860919), a mile west of the town on the A5, is the closest **campsite** – they also rent out bikes.

Though not extensive by city standards, Llangollen boasts a fairly good selection of **restaurants** and no shortage of cafés around town. *The Gallery*, 15 Chapel St (☎01978/860076), is a good start for moderately priced pizza and pasta dishes. *Jonkers*, steps away at 9 Chapel St (☎01978/861158; closed Sun &

Mon), is well worth the extra pound or two for its classy meals, and there's outside seating in summer. *Gales Wine Bar*, 18 Bridge St (☎01978/860089; closed Sun), has great old church pews and an extensive cellar, and serves decent bistro-style food. The *Hand Hotel*, 26 Bridge St, is a straightforward local **pub** where you can listen to a male voice choir in full song (Mon & Fri 7.30pm) or sink a pint in their gorgeous riverside garden. Another good watering hole is *Jenny Jones*, Abbey Road, with live country and western music (Wed) and jazz (Thurs). Top no-nonsense boozing haunt is the youthful *Bull Hotel* on Castle Street.

Around Llangollen

The panoramic view, especially at sunset, justifies the 45-minute slog up to **Castell Dinas Brân** (Crow's Fortress Castle), perched on a hill 800ft above the town, and reached by a path beginning near Llangollen Wharf. The lure certainly isn't the few sad – if powerfully evocative – stumps which stand as a poor testament to what was once the district's largest and most important Welsh fortress. Built in the 1230s by the ruler of northern Powys, Prince Madog ap Gruffydd Maelor, the castle rose on the site of an earlier Iron Age fort. Edward I soon captured it as part of his first campaign against Llywelyn ap Gruffydd, but the castle was left to decay. In 1540, John Leland, Henry VIII's antiquarian, found it "all in ruin".

The gaunt ruin of **Valle Crucis Abbey** (Easter–Sept daily 10am–5pm, £2; all other times free access; CADW), a mile or so west of Llangollen, greets you with its best side, the largely intact west wall of the church pierced by the frame of a rose window. Though one of the last Cistercian foundations in Wales, and the first Gothic abbey in Britain, it is no match for Tintern Abbey (see p.764), but nevertheless stands majestically in a pastoral – and much less visited – setting. Despite a devastating fire in its first century, and a complement of far from pious monks, it survived until the Dissolution, in 1535. The church fell into disrepair, after which the monastic buildings, in particular the monks' dormitory, were employed as farm buildings. Now they hold displays on monastic life, reached by a detour through the mostly ruined cloister and past the weighty vaulting of the chapter house.

Chirk Castle

Seven miles southeast of Llangollen, the busy Dee Valley contrasts with the parallel valley of the River Ceiriog, its entrance guarded by the massive, drum-towered **Chirk Castle** (April–Sept Wed–Sun noon–5pm, garden 11am–6pm; rest of year closes 1hr earlier; castle £5, garden only £2.80; NT), squatting ominously on a rise half a mile to the west of **Chirk** (Y Waun). Construction was begun in the thirteenth century, at the behest of Edward I, who wanted to control the borderlands between England and Wales. The structure is designed to mimic Beaumaris Castle, although it lacks its purity and symmetry. At the end of a long avenue of oaks, the approach is guarded by a magnificent Baroque gate screen, the finest work done by the Davies brothers of Bersham, who wrought it between 1712 and 1719. The ebullient floral designs are capped by the coat of arms of the Myddletons who have lived here for the past four hundred years. The exterior has been extensively remodelled, as have the interiors, leaving a legacy of sumptuous rooms reflecting sixteenth- to nineteenth-century tastes, many now returned to their former states after some Victorian meddling by Pugin in the 1840s.

Meirionydd

Containing stunning scenery and precious few people, the old county of **Meirionydd** (now part of Gwynedd) covers an enormous area from the lushness of the upper Dee Valley, through harsh mountain landscape to the gentle beaches of the west coast. Traditionally, Meirionydd was known as the most remote, and poorest, area in all of Wales, cut off behind the peaks of the Rhinog range. But the landscape tells an even older story: here lie some of Wales's greatest concentrations of Neolithic remains, many from early Irish and Celtic settlers.

Bala was one of Meirionydd's major market towns. Although its agricultural base has waned, the town is a fine place for visitors, especially watersports enthusiasts, who are well catered for on the shores of **Llyn Tegid**, next to the town. Crossing the moors and mountains brings you to the coast, in particular the hilltop fortress of **Harlech**, the bucket-and-spade resort of **Barmouth** and the fabulous stretch of **Ardudwy beach** between them. Barmouth sits at the head of the beautiful **Mawddach estuary**, which snakes its way inland to the old county town of **Dolgellau**, sheltering beneath the northern flank of **Cadair Idris** (2930ft), one of Wales' most inspirational mountains.

Bala

The little town of **BALA** (Y Bala), twenty miles west of Llangollen, is set at the northern end of Wales' largest natural lake, **Llyn Tegid** (Bala Lake). The town was renowned for its piety in the nineteenth century, but these days it has become a major **watersports** centre, and there's little else to do here now. The lake is perfect for windsurfing in particular, due to the winds buffeting up the Talyllyn valley, which slices thirty miles northeast from the coast, along the Bala geological fault.

Slalom kayak fans can make for the **Canolfan Tryweryn** white-water course, four miles west up the A4212. When water is released from the dam, around two hundred days a year, it crashes down a mile and a half through the slalom site, the venue for frequent summer-weekend competitions and commercial **white-water rafting** trips (℡01678/521083). It is a fairly steep £10 for a single heart-stopping run down the roughest part, but for a minimum of £150 a group of up to seven can rent a raft and instructor for two hours, or about four runs. Down on the shores of Llyn Tegid, by the tourist office, the Bala Adventure and Watersports Centre (℡01678/521059) runs courses and rents equipment for **windsurfing**, **kayaking** and **sailing**.

The only public transport access is on **bus** #94, which runs from Llangollen to Dolgellau, stopping on Bala's High Street. The **tourist office** (Easter–Oct daily 10am–6pm; Nov–March Fri–Mon 10am–4pm; ℡01678/521021) is on Pensarn Road on the lakeside, five minutes' walk away. Bala has plenty of **places to stay**, or you can make the most of the surrounding countryside by staying in the Vale of Edeirnion, northeast of the town. Centrally, try the welcoming and good-value *Trem Aran House* B&B, 1 Tegid St (℡01678/520848; ➊). A little further out there's *Abercelyn*, a fine country house half a mile south of Bala on the A494 (℡01678/521109, ⓦwww.abercelyn.co.uk; ➋), and *Fron Feuno Hall* (℡01678/521115, ⓔmair@moneypennyuk.com; ➍), a gracious place with lots of thoughtful touches. One and a half miles north on the A494, there's a great independent **hostel**, the *Coach House*, at Tomen Y Castell (℡01678/520738, ⓦwww.balawales.com/coach-house; ➊). *Pen-y-Bont*, just by the lakeside steam railway station off the B4391 Llandrillo back road (℡01678/520549; April–Oct), is the nearest **campsite**.

Harlech

One of the undoubted highlights of the Cambrian Coast is charming **HARLECH**, 25 miles due west of Bala, with its time-worn castle dramatically clinging to its rocky outcrop, and the town cloaking the ridge behind commanding one of Wales' finest views over Cardigan Bay to the Llŷn. There are good beaches nearby, and the town's twisting, narrow streets harbour places where you can eat and sleep surprisingly well for such a small place.

Harlech's substantially complete **castle** (June–Sept daily 9.30am–6pm, April, May & Oct daily 9.30am–5pm, Nov–March Mon–Sat 9.30am–4pm, Sun 11am–4pm; £3; CADW) sits on its 200-foot-high bluff, a site chosen by Edward I for one more link in his magnificent chain of fortresses. Begun in 1285, it was built of a hard Cambrian rock, known as Harlech grit, hewn from the moat. The sea, which originally protected one side of the fortress, has now receded, leaving the castle dominating a stretch of duned coastline. Harlech withstood a siege in 1295, but was taken by Owain Glyndŵr in 1404. The young Henry VII withstood a seven-year siege at the hands of the Yorkists until 1468, when the castle was again taken. It fell into ruin, but was put back into service for the king during the Civil War; in March 1647, it was the last Royalist castle to fall. The first defensive line comprised the three successive pairs of gates and portcullises built between the two massive half-round towers of the **gatehouse**, where an **exhibition** now outlines the castle's history. Much of the castle's outermost ring has been destroyed, leaving only the twelve-foot-thick curtain walls rising up forty feet to the exposed **battlements**. Only the towering gatehouse prevents you from walking the full circuit.

Harlech's **train station** is below the castle on the main A496. Most **buses** call both here and on High Street, a few yards from the **tourist office** (daily: June–Aug 10am–6pm; April, May, Sept & Oct 10am–1pm & 2–6pm; ℡01766/780658). The pick of the local places to **stay** are the *Morlun* guesthouse (℡01766/780776; ❷) on the Old Llanfair Road and the cosy, informal *Castle Cottage* hotel, on Pen Llech, near the castle (℡01766/780479; ❸), which has the trappings of a place charging twice as much. Other possibilities include the *Plas Newydd* **hostel** (℡01341/241287), three miles south in Llanbedr (buses #38 & #94), where the lane also heads west to the sprawling **camping** resort at *Shell Island* (℡01341/241453, ⓦwww.shellisland.co.uk), great for camp fires in the dunes and walks on the splendid **Ardudwy beach** (part of which, near the village of Dyffryn Ardudwy, is officially nudist). If you want to camp in Harlech itself, head for the *Min y Don* campsite, Beach Road (℡01766/780286; Easter–Sept), three minutes' walk from the beach; take the first right out of the station. There are some wonderful places to **eat** on High Street, including the inexpensive but licensed *Plas Café*, with a good range of food and fabulous views from the garden and conservatory; the bistro-style *Yr Ogof*, where you'll find a good-value range of inventive vegetarian and meat dishes; and the classy, modern *Castle Cottage*.

Barmouth and around

Continuing along the coast, the best approach to **BARMOUTH** (Abermaw) is from the south, where the Cambrian Coast rail line sweeps across the Mawddach River from tiny **Fairbourne**, over 113 rickety-looking wooden spans. It's still the haunt of English holidaymakers from the Midlands, who fashioned Barmouth as a sea-bathing resort in the nineteenth century, but also warrants some attention for breezy rambles on the cliffs of **Dinas Oleu**, above the town, and a great walk around the mouth of the estuary (see box). Central

Walking the Barmouth–Fairbourne Loop

The best lowland walk in the Cambrian Coast region, the **Barmouth–Fairbourne Loop** (5 miles; 300ft ascent; 2–3hr) is a fine way to spend an afternoon with impressive mountain scenery, and estuarine and coastal views all the way. The walking component can be virtually eradicated by using both the mainline and Fairbourne railways. The route first crosses the estuary rail bridge (50p) to Morfa Mawddach mainline station, then follows the lane to the main road, crossing it onto a footpath that loops behind a small wooded hill to Pant Einion Hall, then follows another lane back to the main road near Fairbourne. In Fairbourne, turn north, either walking along the beach to the quay at the end of the spit or catching the **Fairbourne Railway** (Easter–Oct 3–6 daily) to the **passenger ferry** (Easter–Oct; hourly) across the estuary mouth back to Barmouth.

attractions don't extend beyond the **Tŷ Gwyn Museum** (July–Sept Tues–Sun 10.30am–5pm; free), a medieval tower house – now a Tudor museum – where Henry VII's uncle, Jasper Tudor, is thought to have plotted Richard III's downfall; and the **Tŷ Crwn Roundhouse**, on the hill behind (same times) which once acted as a lockup for drunken sailors.

Buses from Harlech and Dolgellau stop in the leisure centre car park by the train station, just a few yards from the **tourist office** in the Old Library on Station Road (Easter–Oct daily 10am–6pm; ☏01341/280787). **Accommodation** is plentiful, and best at *The Gables*, Mynach Road (☏01341/280553; ②), ten minutes' walk north of town and particularly welcoming to walkers, or the seafront *Wavecrest Hotel*, 8 North Parade (☏01341/280330, ⓦwww.lokalink.co.uk/wavecrest; ②). The closest of a long string of **campsites** is *Hendre Mynach*, Llanaber Road (☏01341/280262; March–Oct), a mile north of town and just off the beach. Basic **cafés** are plentiful, though for just a little more money you can get mammoth French sticks and pancakes at the *Anchor Restaurant*, The Quay, and good pizzas next door at the *Isis*. Close to The Quay, in Church Street, *The Last Inn*, in a former cobbler's shop, serves good **pub** meals.

Dolgellau

Its distance from England and its historical position in the heartland of Welsh nationalism should make **DOLGELLAU** (pronounced "dol-geth-lye") the most Welsh of towns, but the town's granite architecture draws more from nineteenth-century England, with a dour series of small neo-Georgian squares all bearing English names. Victorian tourists came to marvel at **Cadair Idris** and the Mawddach Estuary – still the best policy, as the town has little to offer beyond the **Quaker Interpretive Centre**, above the tourist office (Easter–Oct daily 10am–1pm & 2–6pm; Nov–Easter Mon & Thurs–Sun 10am–5pm). This details the lives of Quakers forced by persecution to seek a better life in Pennsylvania, where some towns still bear Welsh names: Bangor, Bryn Mawr and others.

Dolgellau has no train station but is well served by **buses**, all of which pull into the central Eldon Square, close by the **tourist office** (Easter–Oct daily 10am–1pm, 2–6pm; Nov–Easter Mon & Thurs–Sun 10am–5pm; ☏01341/422888). Central **accommodation** is best found at the *Ivy House*, Finsbury Square (☏01341/422535; ②), and the good-value *Royal Ship Hotel*, Queens Square (☏01341/422209; ③). Outside town, the eighteenth-century *Tyddyn*

Dolgellau is a good base for **walks**, whether fairly easy rambles, like the first two described here, or more strenuous mountain hiking. For the **Cadair Idris** ascent, you'll need a map and walking equipment. You're best off with the 1:25,000 OS *Outdoor Leisure* map #23, "Cadair Idris & Bala Lake", though the 1:50,000 map #124, "Dolgellau", will do.

Torrent Walk

Victorians seldom missed the lowland, beechwood **Torrent Walk** (2 miles; 100ft ascent; 1hr) which follows the course of the River Clywedog as it carves its way through bedrock to the *Clywedog Tea Garden*, where home-baked scones are served beside the river. Bus #2 takes you the two miles east along the A470 to the start, by the junction of the B4416 road to Brithdir.

Precipice Walk

Nowadays, more people head for the not-remotely-precipitous **Precipice Walk** (3–4 miles; negligible ascent; 2hr), a circuit around the bracken and heather-covered Foel Cynach, with great views along the Mawddach Estuary and towards the thousand-foot ramparts of Cadair Idris. Best done in the late afternoon, when the sun is low on the estuary, the walk is fairly well signposted from the start, three miles north of Dolgellau along the Llanfachreth road, which turns off the A494 by Big Bridge. Bus #33 (Tues & Fri 3 daily) runs to the start.

Cadair Idris ascents

More ambitious Victorians climbed **Cadair Idris** on the since-eroded Fox's Path, now widely ignored in favour of the straightforward, classic **Pony Path** (6–7 miles; 2500ft ascent; 4–5hr), starting three miles up Cadair Road in the car park at Ty Nant. As you begin by the sign near the telephone box, the view to the craggy flanks of the massif are tremendous, but they disappear as you climb steeply to the col, where a left turn leads to the summit shelter on **Penygadair** (2930ft). The most impressive ascent of Cadair Idris, however, is up the **Minffordd Path** (6 miles; 2900ft ascent; 5hr), which leads up to and then around the glacial lake of Cwm Cau before reaching the summit. The path starts from the car park just west of the *Minffordd Hotel* where the A487 meets the B4405; buses between Dolgellau and Machynlleth pass the spot.

Mawr Farmhouse, Islawrdref (℡01341/422331; ❸), stands on the slopes of Cadair Idris at the foot of the Pony Path, while the superb seventeenth-century *George III Hotel*, Penmaenpool (℡01341/422525; ❻), overlooks the Mawddach Estuary, two miles west of Dolgellau. There's a decent town-centre independent **hostel** in the shape of *Plas Isa* on Lion Street (℡01341/440666 or ℡01766/540569; ❶). The tent-only *Bryn-y-Gwyn* **campsite**, Cader Road (℡01341/422733), is less than a mile southeast of town. There's a fair choice for **eating** in Dolgellau: the best bets are the creative and moderately priced *Bwyty Dylanwad Da*, 2 Smithfield St (℡01341/422870), and the *Tyn-y-Groes Hotel*, Glanllwyd (℡01341/440275), four miles north of town in the Coed y Brenin forest, with good beer, fine bar meals and à la carte dinners. Back in town, the *Tafarn Caetanws*, Smithfield Street, is a great **pub** for food and occasional music and comedy. Dolgellau's Sesiwn Fawr folk and rock **festival** in mid-July (Ⓦwww.sesiwnfawr.demon.co.uk) has rapidly grown into one of Wales' finest.

Tywyn and around

TYWYN is primarily of interest as a base for the Talyllyn and Dysynni valleys, although the town does have miles of sandy beach and the five-foot-high **Ynysmaengwyn**, or St Cadfan's Stone, within the Norman nave of the **Church of St Cadfan** (daily 9am–5pm; hours extended in summer; tours Wed 5pm), which bears the earliest example of written Welsh, dating back to around 650 AD.

Tywyn's three main roads meet at the joint **train station** and main **bus stop**, a short walk from the **tourist office**, opposite the entrance to the leisure centre on High Street (Easter–Oct daily 9.30am–1pm & 2–5.30pm; ☎01654/710070), and, two hundred yards to the south, the Talyllyn narrow-gauge train station (Tywyn Wharf). The Talyllyn Valley is served by **bus** #30, running from Tywyn to Abergynolwyn, continuing to Minffordd (where you can catch bus #2 to Dolgellau) and Machynlleth. Decent **accommodation** can be found at the *Ivy Guest House*, High Street (☎01654/711058; ❷), opposite the tourist office, or the cheaper, non-smoking *Glenydd Guest House*, 2 Maes Newydd (☎01654/711373; ❷), two hundred yards from the beach off Pier Road. The handiest **campsite** is *Ynysmaengwyn Caravan Park*, a mile out on the Dolgellau road (☎01654/710684; April–Sept). The best **eating** in town is upstairs at the moderately priced, non-smoking *The Proper Gander*, High Street.

The Talyllyn and Dysynni valleys

The **Talyllyn narrow-gauge railway** (April–Oct 2–8 daily; also at Christmas; £9.50 return; ☎01654/710472, ⓦwww.talyllyn.co.uk) belches seven miles inland through the delightful wooded Talyllyn Valley to Nant Gwernol. From 1866 to 1946, the rail line was used to haul slate to Tywyn Wharf station. Just four years after its closure, enthusiasts restarted services, making this the world's first volunteer-run railway. At a leisurely 15mph, the round trip takes two hours, longer if you get off to take in some fine broadleaf forest walks. The best of these starts at Dolgoch Falls station, where three well-marked trails (maximum 1hr) lead off to the lower, mid and upper falls. At the end of the line, more woodland walks take you around the site of the old slate quarries.

From Tywyn, the road runs parallel to the Talyllyn Railway, meeting it at Dolgoch Falls, a couple of miles short of the valleys' largest settlement, **Abergynolwyn**, comprising a few dozen quarry workers' houses, a shop and a pub, the excellent *Railway Inn*. The Dysynni Valley branches northwest here, but Talyllyn Valley continues northeast to **Tal-y-llyn Lake** (Llyn Mwyngil) and the fifteenth-century **St Mary's**, a fine example of a small Welsh parish church, unusual because of its chancel arch painted with an alternating grid of red and white roses, separated by grotesque bosses.

The **Dysynni Valley** has more to offer in the way of sights, though the lack of public transport makes it difficult to get to. A mile and a half northwest of Abergynolwyn, a side road cuts northeast to the hamlet of **Llanfihangel-y-Pennant** and the scant, but impressive, ruins of **Castell-y-Bere** (free access; CADW), a fortress built by Llywelyn the Great in 1221 to protect the mountain passes. One of the most massive of the Welsh castles, it was besieged twice before being consigned to seven centuries of obscurity and decay. There's still plenty to poke around, with large slabs of the main towers still standing, but it's primarily a great place just to sit gazing at Cadair Idris, or three miles seaward to **Craig yr Aderyn** (Birds' Rock), a 760-foot-high cliff where thirty breeding pairs of cormorants have remained loyal to the spot as, over the centuries, the sea has receded. Also worth seeing is the fabulous three-dimensional patchwork map of the Dysynni Valley that can be found just up the road in the vestry of Llanfihangel-y-Pennant church.

Good places to **stay** include *Tan-y-Coed-Uchaf* (℡01654/782228; ❷; March–Nov), a superb farmhouse B&B close to Dolgoch Falls; the excellent *Riverside Guesthouse*, Cwrt, in Abergynolwyn (℡01654/782235, ⓦwww.snowdonia-wales.co.uk; ❶); or the *Minffordd Hotel* (℡01654/761665; ❻; March–Dec), an eighteenth-century farmhouse and coaching inn by Tal-y-llyn Lake, open to non-residents for moderately priced traditional British **dinners** (Thurs–Sat). There is a basic **campsite** at *Cedris Farm*, a mile northeast of Abergynolwyn (℡01654/782280), and plenty of others dotted about the two valleys.

Machynlleth

A finger of Montgomeryshire poking out between Meirionydd and Ceredigion, the flat river plain and rolling hills of **Dyfi Valley** lay justifiable claim to being one of the greenest corners of Europe, an area replete with B&Bs and other businesses started up by idealistic New Agers who have flocked to this corner of Wales since the late 1960s. The focal point is the genial town of **MACHYNLLETH** (pronounced "ma-hun-thleth"), eighteen miles northeast of Aberystwyth, a candidate for the Welsh capital in the 1950s and site of Owain Glyndŵr's embryonic fifteenth-century Welsh parliament. In the hills to the north, the renowned, self-contained **Centre for Alternative Technology** runs on co-operative lines and makes for one of the most interesting days out in Wales.

The town that might have been the nation's capital consists essentially of just two streets. The wide main street, **Heol Maengwyn**, is busiest on Wednesdays, when a lively market springs up out of nowhere; **Heol Penrallt** intersects at the fussy clocktower. Glyndŵr's partly fifteenth-century **Parliament House** (Easter–Sept daily 10am–5pm; in winter, call ℡01654/702827 for an appointment; free) sits halfway along Heol Maengwyn, a modest looking black and white fronted building, concealing a large interior. Displays chart the course of Glyndŵr's life, his military campaign, his downfall and the 1404 parliament, when he controlled almost all of what we now know as Wales. The sorriest tales are from 1405 onwards when tactical errors and the sheer brute might of the English forced a swift retreat and an ignominious end to the greatest Welsh uprising.

On the Aberystwyth road, at Y Plas, the **Celtica** exhibition (daily 10am–6pm; last admission 4.40pm; £4.95) combines audiovisual trickery with tales of the Celtic peoples in a thunderous romp through history. The overall effect is certainly impressive, even if the old Welsh addiction to sentimentality is evident on occasion. Upstairs are more detailed exhibitions relating to Celtic history and language. On the other side of the central clocktower, on Heol Penrallt, is **Y Tabernacl** (Mon–Sat 10am–4pm; free), a serene old chapel whose spectacular new sculpted entrance by David Thomas is an audacious addition to the Machynlleth streetscape. The chapel has now been converted into a cultural centre, with a programme of temporary exhibitions augmenting the small collection of the **Wales Museum of Modern Art**. It also hosts films, theatre and the annual **Gŵyl Machynlleth** festival in mid- to late August, with a combination of classical music, debate, theatre and some folk music.

Owain Glyndŵr

No name is so frequently invoked in Wales as that of **Owain Glyndŵr**, a potent fig-urehead of Welsh nationalism since he rose up against the occupying English in the early fifteenth century. Little is known about the real Glyndŵr, although he is described in Shakespeare's *Henry IV, Part I* as "not in the roll of common men". There's little doubt that the charismatic Owain fulfilled many of the mystical medieval prophecies about the rising up of the red dragon. Born in the late fourteenth centu-ry to an aristocratic family, he had a conventional upbringing, part of it studying English in London, where he became a loyal and distinguished soldier of the English king. He returned to Wales to take up his claim as Prince of Wales, being directly descended from the princes of Powys and Cyfeiliog, but became the focus of a rebellion born of discontent simmering since Edward I's stringent policies of subor-dinating Wales.

Goaded by a parochial land dispute in North Wales in which the courts failed to back him, Glyndŵr garnered four thousand supporters and declared anew that he was Prince of Wales. He attacked Ruthin, and then Denbigh, Rhuddlan, Flint, Hawarden and Oswestry, before encountering English resistance at Welshpool, but whole swathes of North Wales were his for the taking. The English king, Henry IV, dispatched troops and rapidly drew up a range of severely punitive laws against the Welsh, even outlawing Welsh-language bards and singers. Battles continued to rage until, by the end of 1403, Glyndŵr controlled most of Wales.

In 1404, Glyndŵr assembled a parliament at Machynlleth, drawing up mutual recognition treaties with France and Spain, and being crowned king of a free Wales. A second parliament in Harlech took place a year later, with Glyndŵr making plans to carve up England and Wales into three as part of an alliance against the English king. The English army, however, attacked the Welsh uprising with increased vigour, and the Tripartite Indenture was never realized. From then on, Glyndŵyr lost battles, ground and castles, and was forced into hiding, dying, it is thought, in Herefordshire. The draconian anti-Welsh laws stayed in place until the accession to the English throne of Henry VII, who had Welsh origins, in 1485. Wales became subsumed into English custom and law, and Glyndŵr's uprising became an increasingly powerful symbol of frustrated Welsh independence. Even in the 1980s, a shadowy organiza-tion that razed several English holiday homes took the name Meibion Glyndŵr – the Sons of Glyndŵr.

Practicalities

The old Victorian **train station** and **bus stop** are both a five-minute walk from the clocktower, up Heol Penrallt and its continuation, Heol Doll. The **tourist office** (daily: Easter–Sept 9.30am–6pm; Oct–Easter 10am–5pm; ☏01654/702401) is next to the Glyndŵr Parliament House on Heol Maengwyn. **Bike rental** is available from Greenstyles Cycles, 4 Heol Maengwyn near the clocktower (☏01654/703543).

B&B **accommodation** includes the *Maenllwyd*, on Newtown Road, the eastern extension of Heol Maengwyn (☏01654/702928, ⓦwww.maenll-wyd.co.uk; ❷), and *Gwelfryn*, in the town centre at 6 Greenfields, Bank Street (☏01654/702532, ⓦwww.gwelfryn.co.uk; ❶). Best of the hotels is the won-derful, if slightly pricy, *Wynnstay Arms,* on Heol Maengwyn (☏01654/702941; ❹). There's a lovely **campsite** three miles north, opposite the Centre for Alternative Technology, at *Llwyngwern Farm* (☏01654/702492), or a very sim-ple tent site at *Plas Forge* (☏01654/703228), a mile or so out on the road to Dylife. There's a great **hostel** (☏01654/761686; ❶; March–Oct daily, Nov–Feb weekends only) six miles north in the slate village of Corris, easily reached by regular bus. There are plenty of **cafés**, **restaurants** and **pubs** in town, includ-ing a great wholefood shop and café at *Siop y Chwarel*, opposite the *Wynnstay*

Arms on Heol Maengwyn. The *Wynnstay Arms* does fantastic lunches and evening meals, and the *Glyndŵr*, on Heol Doll, has live music at the weekend. The bar at *Y Tabernacl* is the most arty hangout in town.

Centre for Alternative Technology

Since its foundation in the middle of the oil crisis of 1974, the **Centre for Alternative Technology**, or Canolfan y Dechnoleg Amgen (daily: April–Oct 10am–7pm, last entry 5pm; £7; Nov–March 10am–5pm; £5; discounts for visitors arriving by bike or public transport) – just over two miles north of Machynlleth off the A487 – has become one of the biggest attractions in Wales. A former derelict slate quarry covering seven acres, over the last 25 years the centre has become an entirely self-sufficient community, generating its own power and water from onsite equipment. It's not a museum, but it is open to the public. It's a fascinating place to visit, combining earnest education about renewable resources and practices with flashes of pizzazz, such as the water-powered cliff rail line (April–Oct) that whisks you 197ft up from the car park. Whole houses have been constructed to showcase energy-saving ideas and the fifty-strong staff – who all live communally and receive identical (very low) wages – are ebullient and helpful in explaining the ideas. There are also organic gardens, beehives, a water wheel, an adventure playground and numerous hands-on exhibits. Two new buildings are the stunning straw-bale theatre and the superb shop, which stocks a vast range of eco-related literature and all sorts of gadgetry. Don't miss the wholefood **restaurant**, which is excellent.

Ceredigion

South of Machynlleth is the county of **Ceredigion**, formerly known as Cardiganshire. Lying as it does between the two national parks of the Pembrokeshire Coast and Snowdonia, Ceredigion is often overlooked by visitors, but it shouldn't be. In many ways, it combines the best of both national parks – the stunning mountain scenery of southern Snowdonia with the little ports and sandy coves of Pembrokeshire, and all soaked in a relaxed, upbeat and firmly Welsh culture. The county's main town is ebullient **Aberystwyth**, a top spot for everything from serious study and exhibitions in the National Library to student-oriented raves and bar culture. It's also a great base for the luscious countryside inland, especially the waterfalls and woods of the **vale of Rheidol** out towards mythical **Devil's Bridge**.

The southern Ceredigion coast is broken by some spirited little ports: most notably Georgian **Aberaeron**, higgledy-piggledy **New Quay** and the old county town of **Cardigan**, where the **River Teifi** flows into the sea. Towns and sights inland along the Teifi are worth exploring, especially the mighty castle at **Cilgerran** and the charming little university town of **Lampeter**. Near the source of the Teifi is the atmospheric **Strata Florida Abbey**.

Aberystwyth and around

The liveliest seaside resort in Wales, **ABERYSTWYTH** is an essential stop along the Ceredigion coast. Being rooted in all aspects of Welsh culture, it is possibly the most enjoyable and relaxed place to gain an insight into the national psyche. As the capital of sparsely populated mid-Wales, and with one of the most prestigious colleges of the University of Wales in the town, there are plenty of cultural and entertainment diversions, as well as an array of

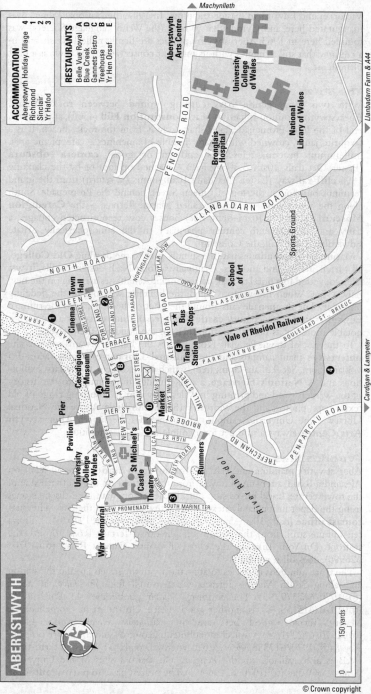

ABERYSTWYTH

N

0   150 yards

▲ Machynlleth

◀ Constitution Hill & Cliff railway

ACCOMMODATION

Aberystwyth Holiday Village 4
Richmond 1
Sinclair 2
Yr Hafod 3

RESTAURANTS

Belle Vue Royal A
Blue Creek D
Gannets Bistro C
Treehouse B
Yr Hen Orsaf E

PENGLAIS ROAD

Aberystwyth
Arts Centre

University College
of Wales

National
Library of Wales

Bronglais
Hospital

▶ Llanbadarn Farm & A44

LLANBADARN ROAD

Sports Ground

NORTH ROAD

Town Hall

QUEEN'S ROAD

Cinema

BATH STREET

PORTLAND ST

i

TERRACE ROAD

PORTLAND ROAD

NORTHGATE ST

POPLAR ROW

NORTH PARADE

School
of Art

STANLEY ROAD

ALEXANDRA ROAD

PLASCRUG AVENUE

★ ★
Bus
Stops

MARINE TERRACE

Pier

Pavilion

Ceredigion
Museum

Library

A

EASTGATE

B

DARKGATE STREET

PIER ST

NEW ST

E
Train
Station

Vale of Rheidol Railway

PARK AVENUE

BOULEVARD ST BRIEUC

QUEENS ST

GRAYS INN RD

QUEENS RD

D

Market

University College
of Wales

War Memorial

NEW PROMENADE

KING STREET

NEW PROMENADE

St Michael's

Castle

Theatre

C

VULCAN ST

BRIDGE ST

HIGH ST

MILL STREET

Rummers

SOUTH MARINE TER.

SOUTH RD

BOVIL RD

SPRING PL

River Rheidol

TREFECHAN RD

PENPARCAU ROAD

4

▶ Cardigan & Lampeter

© Crown copyright

Victorian and Edwardian seaside trappings. In 1907, the National Library was inaugurated here, and Cymdeithas yr Iaith (the Welsh Language Society) was founded here in 1963. Aberystwyth's politics are firmly radical Welsh, and in a country that still struggles with its inherent conservatism, the town is a blast of fresh air.

The Town

With two long, gentle bays curving around between rocky heads, Aberystwyth's position is hard to beat. **Constitution Hill** (430ft), at the north end of the long Promenade, rises sharply away from the rocky beach. It is a favourite jaunt, crowned with a tatty jumble of amenities – café, picnic area, millennium beacon, telescopes and an octagonal **camera obscura** (Easter–Oct daily 10am–5.30pm; free) – reached on foot or by the clanking 1896 **cliff railway** (Easter–Oct daily 10am–6pm; £2 return) from the grand terminus building at the top of Queen Street, behind the Promenade. South along the promenade – officially called Marine Terrace – the **Ceredigion Museum** (Mon–Sat 10am–5pm; free) houses cosy reconstructed cottages, a dairy and a nineteenth-century pharmacy in the atmospherically ornate Edwardian music hall, the Coliseum.

Marine Terrace continues past the spindly **pier** to the dazzling **Old College**, all turrets, friezes and mosaics. Originally a John Nash-designed villa, it was later converted to a hotel to soak up the anticipated masses arriving on the new railway line. When the venture failed, the building was sold to the fledgling university. The Promenade cuts around the front of the building to the ruins of Edward I's thirteenth-century **castle** (free access), a fine place for a picnic, but notable more for its breezy position than for the buildings themselves.

To the east of town, Penglais Road climbs the hill northwards towards the **university**'s main campus and the **National Library of Wales** (Mon–Fri 9.30am–6pm, Sat 9.30am–5pm; free), which has excellent temporary exhibitions and **A Nation's Heritage**, a well-rounded introduction to the history of the written word and printing in Wales, shown in an absorbing range of old texts, maps, photos, and the Morgan's 1588 Welsh Bible. Above the National Library is the University campus, which includes the superb **Aberystwyth Arts Centre**, always a sure bet for a couple of decent exhibitions.

Practicalities

Aberystwyth's mainline and Vale of Rheidol **train stations** are adjacent on Alexandra Road, a ten-minute walk from the seafront on the southern side of the town centre. Local **buses** stop outside the station, with long-distance ones using the depot immediately next door, by the entrance to the park. The busy **tourist office** (daily 10am–5pm; July & Aug until 6pm; ☎01970/612125) is a ten-minute stroll from the station, straight down Terrace Road towards the seafront. On Your Bike, in the Old Police Yard, Queens Road (☎01970/626996), does **bike rental**.

There are hundreds of places to **stay**, mostly in the streets around the station and along South Marine Terrace, where you'll find *Yr Hafod*, at no. 1 (☎01970/617579; ❷). The intimate *Sinclair* guesthouse, 43 Portland St (☎01970/615158; ❷), is another good choice. On the main Promenade, or Marine Terrace, good bets are the *Richmond Hotel* at no. 44–45 (☎01970/612201, ⓦwww.richmondhotel.uk.com; ❹) and the smart *Belle Vue Royal* (☎01970/617558, ⓦwww.bellevueroyal.co.uk; ❺). Outside term-time, B&B is also available on the Penglais and seafront sites of the University College of Wales (☎01970/621960; ❷). The nearest place to pitch a **tent** is the

Aberystwyth Holiday Village (☎01970/624211), off the main Penparcau Road to the south of town, a twenty-minute walk from the station.

Aberystwyth's cultural and gastronomic life is an ebullient, year-round affair, thriving on students in term-time and visitors in the summer. Just behind the market, *Gannets Bistro*, at 7 St James Square (closed Tues), creates imaginative, inexpensive dishes from local farm and sea produce. The *Blue Creek Café*, on the other side the market hall in St James Square, is a fantastic daytime café, as is the organic *Treehouse* (☎01970/615791), a warming veggie café in the daytime and superb evening option (Thurs–Sat) for all tastes. For decent, and very reasonable, **pub food**, you're best off at *Yr Hen Orsaf*, which, as its name implies, is in the old station buildings on Alexandra Road – you can even have a pint or a meal under a stunning glass canopy on the platform. For no-nonsense **drinking**, Aberystwyth has scores of options, and many pubs stay open until 1am in the summer: try the *Castle Hotel* on South Road, a harbourside pub that's built in the style of an ornate Victorian gin palace, and which has regular gigs. *Y Cûps* (Coopers Arms), Llanbadarn Road, is fun and friendly, with regular Welsh folk and jazz nights. For a slice of Edwardian gentility, take afternoon tea in any of the seafront hotels along the Promenade. The Aberystwyth Arts Centre, at the university's Penglais site (☎01970/623232), has art-house **cinema** and touring **theatre**.

The Vale of Rheidol

Inland from Aberystwyth, the River Rheidol winds its way up to a secluded, wooded valley, where occasional old industrial workings have moulded themselves into the contours, rising up past waterfalls and hamlets to Devil's Bridge. It's a glorious route, and by far the best way to see it is on board one of the trains of the **Vale of Rheidol railway** (April–Oct; £11.50 return), a narrow-gauge steam train that wheezes its way along sheer rock faces from the terminus in Aberystwyth to Devil's Bridge. It was built in 1902, ostensibly for the valley's lead mines but with a canny eye on its tourist potential as well, and has run ever since. Partway along, a punishing path on the north side of the river from the Rhiwfron halt scrambles up over the mines for a mile to the sombre little village of Ystumtuen, a former lead-mining community whose school has been converted into a basic **hostel** (☎01970/890693). From here it's a couple of miles' walk to Devil's Bridge.

Devil's Bridge

Folk legend, idyllic beauty and travellers' lore combine at **DEVIL'S BRIDGE** (Pontarfynach), twelve miles east of Aberystwyth, a tiny settlement built solely for the growing visitor trade of the last few hundred years. Be warned, however, that Devil's Bridge is a seriously popular day excursion: in order to escape some of the inevitable congestion, it is wisest to come here at the beginning or end of the day, or out of season.

The main attraction here is the **bridge** itself, which is actually three stacked bridges spanning the chasm of the churning River Mynach, yards upstream from its confluence with the Rheidol. The road bridge in front of the striking *Hafod Arms* **hotel** (☎01970/890232, ⓦwww.hafodarms.co.uk; ❸) is the most modern of the three, dating from 1901. Immediately below it, wedged between the rock faces, are the stone bridge from 1753 and, at the bottom, the original bridge, dating from the eleventh century and reputedly built by the monks of Strata Florida Abbey (see p.853). For a remarkable view of the bridges, you have to enter the turnstile (£1) downstream of the bridge and head down slippery steps to the deep cleft of the **Punch Bowl**, where the water pounds and hurtles through the gap crowned by the bridges. More dramatic still, the gate on the other side (Easter–Oct daily 9.30am–5.30pm; £2.50; at other times access through turnstiles; £2) leads west to a path that tumbles down into the valley below the bridges, descending ultimately to the crashing **Mynach Falls**. The scenery here is magnificent: sharp, wooded slopes rise away from the frothing river and distant mountain peaks surface on the horizon. Platforms overlook the series of falls, from where a set of steep steps takes you further down to a footbridge dramatically spanning the river at the bottom of the falls.

There's a **campsite** – *Woodlands Caravan Park* (☎01970/890233) – by the petrol station, just beyond the bridges.

Aberaeron

ABERAERON, sixteen miles along the coast from Aberystwyth, is a handsome place, even if it is almost unique amongst the Ceredigion resorts for being on an unappealing stretch of coastline. Nonetheless, the town, with its pastel-shaded houses encasing a large harbour inlet, has a rare unity of design, the result of a complete nineteenth-century rebuilding by the Reverend Alban Gwynne. He spent his way through his wife's inheritance by dredging the Aeron Estuary and constructing a formally planned town around it as a new port for mid-Wales.

The A487 runs straight through the heart of town, down Bridge Street and past the large **Alban Square**, named after the rich rector. On the north side of the town bridge, a grid of streets stretches down to a neat line of ordered, colourful houses on the seafront. Right on the harbour, the **Hive on the Quay** (late May to mid-Sept daily 10am–5pm; £1.50) combines an exhibition of bees with chances to sample honey products, including delicious ice cream. Quay Parade runs down the side of the seafront past some of the old fisherman's houses and pubs to the fairly humdrum **Sea Aquarium** (Easter–Oct daily 10am–5pm; £3.95).

A trip to the exquisite kitchen gardens at **Llanerchaeron**, three miles east of Aberaeron (April–Oct Thurs–Sun 11am–5pm; £2; NT), makes an excellent excursion. Once an integrated smallholding typical of this region, the estate is currently undergoing restoration; occasional open days allow access to the Nash-designed main house.

Aberaeron's **tourist office** is on Quay Parade, the seafront road (June–Aug daily 10am–6pm, Sept–May Mon–Sat 10am–5pm; ☎01545/570602). There are two town-centre **B&B**s overlooking the harbour on Cadwgan Place: *Coedmor* (☎01545/571615; ❷) and the lovely *Arosfa* (☎01545/570120, ⓦwww.arosfaguesthouse.co.uk; ❷). A B&B that's better than most small hotels can be found nearby on South Road: the neo-colonial *Hazeldene* (☎01545/570652, ⓦwww.aberaeron.co.uk/hazeldene; ❷). The nearest local **campsite** is the *Aeron Coast*, on the A487 just north of town (☎01545/570349). For **food**, there's the moderate *Arosfa*, 8 Cadwgan Place, for traditional and new Welsh specialities, and an excellent fish restaurant at the *Hive on the Quay* (see above). Good seafood, together with some imaginative French cuisine, can be found at the *Harbourmaster* pub, by the tourist office.

New Quay and around

Along with Laugharne in Carmarthenshire (see p.792), **NEW QUAY** (Cei Newydd), seven miles from Aberaeron, lays claim to being the original Llareggub in Dylan Thomas' *Under Milk Wood*. Certainly, it has the little tumbling streets, prim Victorian terraces, cobbled stone harbour and air of dreamy isolation that Thomas evoked in his play but, in the height of summer, the quiet isolation can be hard to find. Although there is a singular lack of excitement in New Quay, it is a truly pleasant base for good beaches, walking, surfing, eating and drinking.

The pretty **harbour** and small, curving beach are backed by a higgledy-piggledy line of multi-coloured shops and houses. The beachfront streets comprise the **lower town** – the more traditionally "seaside" part of New Quay, full of cafés, pubs and beach shops. Tucked away down the slipway above the beach is the interesting **Marine Wildlife Centre** (April–Sept daily 10am–5pm; donation requested), with some good displays on the dolphins, seals and sea birds of Cardigan Bay. Sharply inclined streets lead to the residential **upper town**, with some delightful views over the sweeping shoreline below. The northern beach soon gives way to a rocky headland, **New Quay Head**, where an invigorating path steers along the top of the the aptly named **Bird Rock**.

Buses stop on Park Street, from where it's a walk down any of the steep streets to the seafront, where you'll find the **tourist office**, centrally located at the junction of Church Street and Wellington Place (daily: July & Aug 10am–6pm; April–June & Sept 10am–5pm; ℡01545/560865). **Accommodation** includes cheap B&Bs at *Elvor*, on George Street, the main road to Llanarth, in the upper town (℡01545/560554; ❷); *The Moorings*, on Glanmor Terrace, near the beach (℡01545/560375; ❷); and the chintzy luxury of *Ffynnon Feddyg*, out towards Cei Bach on the eastern edge of town (℡01545/560222; ❷; March–Oct). The nearest **campsite** is the *Neuadd* (℡01545/560709), fifteen minutes' walk away, behind the *Penrhiwllan Inn*, at the top of the hill on the way to Synod Inn. New Quay contains innumerable cheap, chips-with-everything **cafés**, amongst which the *Mariner's Café*, by the harbour wall, is a sure bet. Most of the **pubs** serve food, the best being the *Seahorse*, Margaret Street, and the *Wellington*, by the tourist office on the seafront.

Tre-Saith and Llangranog

The most popular stopping-off point on the stretch of coast south of New Quay is Aberporth, an elderly resort built around two less than appealing bays, easily shown up by the neighbouring hamlet of **TRE-SAITH**, a mile to the east, which staggers down the tiny valley to a delightful beach. There are **dinghy races** from the beach every Sunday in summer. Around the rocks to the right of the beach, the River Saith plummets over the mossy black rocks in a waterfall. Among the places to **stay** in Tre-Saith, the *Bryn Berwyn* B&B, a ten-minute walk up the hill from Tre-Saith beach (℡01239/811126, ⓦwww.tresaith.fsnet.co.uk; ❷), is a good bet. You could also **camp** right above the beach in one of the quieter outlying fields of the *Llety Caravan Park*, reached by road en route to Aberporth (℡01239/810354).

Three miles north of the A487, **LLANGRANOG** is the most attractive village on the Ceredigion coast, wedged in between bracken and gorse-beaten hills, the main streets winding to the tiny seafront. The beach can become horribly congested in mid-summer, when it's better to follow the cliff path to **Cilborth Beach**, and on to the glorious NT-owned headland, **Ynys Lochtyn**. In Llangranog, you can **stay** on the seafront either at the excellent *Ship Inn* (℡01239/654423; ❸) or the earthier *Pentre Arms* (℡01239/654345; ❷); both do good **food**. Between Penbryn and Llangranog is the *Maesglas* caravan park (℡01239/654268), which takes **tents**.

Cardigan

An ancient borough and fomer port at the lowest bridging point of the Teifi Estuary, **CARDIGAN** (Aberteifi) was founded by the Norman lord Roger de

Montgomery around its castle in 1093. From the castle mound by the bridge, Bridge Street sweeps through High Street to the turreted oddity of the **Guildhall**, with the Welsh flag skewered adamantly to its grey frontage. Through the Guildhall courtyard is the town's **covered market**, a typically eclectic mix of fresh food, local crafts and secondhand stalls. Across the bridge from the town centre, the **Cardigan Heritage Centre** (March–Oct daily 10am–5pm; call ☏01239/614404 for winter hours; £2), housed in an old granary, tells the story of the port's rise and fall.

The helpful **tourist office** (June–Aug daily 10am–6pm; Sept–May Mon–Sat 10am–5pm; ☏01239/613230) is in the foyer of Theatr Mwldan, Bath House Road. There's plenty of **accommodation**, with numerous B&Bs along the Gwbert Road, off North Road: the *Brynhyfryd*, at the town end (☏01239/612861; ❷), and the *Garth*, further up Gwbert Road (☏01239/613085; ❷), are the best. On the High Street, the old-fashioned *Black Lion* pub (☏01239/612532; ❸) does good B&B and evening meals. There's a YHA **hostel** four miles away at Poppit Sands, at the end of the Pembrokeshire Coast Path (☏01239/612936; March–Oct); buses connect in July and August, but for the rest of the year they terminate at St Dogmael's, two miles short. For **food**, try the inexpensive Theatr Mwldan café or *Jackets*, 58 North Rd, which serves pizzas, potatoes, kebabs and pies. The best pub food is at the *Eagle*, at the southern end of the town bridge.

The Teifi Valley

The Teifi is one of Wales' most eulogized rivers, for its rich spawn of fresh fish, its meandering rural charm and the coracles that were a regular feature from pre-Roman times. On the way to its estuary at Cardigan, it flows through some gloriously green and undulating countryside, winding its way over the falls at **Cenarth** and passing the massive ramparts of **Cilgerran Castle**. Further upstream, the river also takes in the proudly Welsh university town of **Lampeter**, and the river's infancy can be seen near the ruins of **Strata Florida Abbey**, beyond which the river emerges from the dark and remote **Teifi Pools**.

Cilgerran Castle

Just a couple of miles up the Teifi River from Cardigan, the attractive village of **CILGERRAN** clusters around its wide main street. Behind is the bulk of the **castle** (April–Oct daily 9.30am–6.30pm; Nov–March daily 9.30am–4pm; £2; CADW), founded in 1100 at a commanding vantage point on a high wooded bluff above the river, then still navigable for sea-going ships. This is the legendary site of the 1109 abduction of Nest (the "Welsh Helen of Troy") by a love-struck Prince Owain of Powys. Her husband, Gerald of Pembroke, escaped by slithering down a toilet waste chute through the castle walls. The two massive drum towers still dominate the castle, and the outer walls, some four feet thicker than those facing the inner courtyard, are traced by vertiginously high walkways. The outer ward, over which a modern path now runs from the entrance, is a good example of the keepless castle that evolved throughout the thirteenth century. The views over the forested valley towards the pink and grey Georgian fantasy castle of **Coedmore**, on the opposite bank, are inspiring.

A footpath runs down from the castle to the river's edge; an exhibition at the quay about local industries – coracles included – also covers the story of America-bound emigrants leaving from Cardigan. Guided two-hour Canadian **canoe trips** leave from the quay in summer.

Cenarth and around

A tourist magnet since it was swooped on by nineteenth-century Romantics and artists, **CENARTH**, five miles east of Cilgerran, is a pleasant spot but hardly merits the mass interest that it receives. The village's main asset, its **waterfalls**, are close to the main road, connected by a path from opposite the *White Hart* pub. This runs past the **National Coracle Centre** (Easter–Oct daily except Sat 10am–5.30pm; other times by arrangement ☎01239/710980; £2.75), a small museum with displays of original coracles from all over the world, before continuing to a restored seventeenth-century flour mill by the falls' edge.

The area's prolific past as a weaving centre is best seen at the **Museum of the Welsh Woollen Industry** (April–Sept Mon–Sat 10am–5pm, Oct–March Mon–Fri 10am–5pm; free), in the village of **Dre-Fach Felindre**, eight miles southeast of Cenarth, which once had over forty working mills.

Lampeter

Twenty miles east of Cenarth, **LAMPETER** (Llanbedr Pont Steffan or, popularly, Lambed) is the home of possibly the most remote university in Britain. St David's University College, now a constituent of the University of Wales, was Wales' first university college, founded in 1822 by the Bishop of St David's to aid Welsh students who couldn't afford the trip to England to receive a full education. With a healthy student population and large numbers of resident hippies, the small town is well geared up for young people and visitors.

There's not a great deal to see, and what you are able to visit is fairly low-key. **Harford Square** forms the hub of the town. Around the corner, at 2 Bridge St, is **Celtic Edge**, a showcase for local artists' work at the back of the Mulberry Bush health-food shop, which has a good bulletin board. The main buildings of the **University College** lie off College Street, and include a quadrangle modelled on an Oxbridge college and the motte of Lampeter's long-vanished castle – a strange sight amidst such order. The High Street is the most architecturally distinguished part of town, its eighteenth-century coaching inn, the *Black Lion*, dominating the streetscape; you can see its old stables and coach house through an archway.

There is a basic **tourist office** in the new civic buildings at the back of Market Street (Mon–Fri 9am–5pm; ☎01570/422718). *Haulfan*, 6 Station Terrace, behind University College (☎01570/422718; ❷), is the best **B&B**, or you could try the recently refurbished *Black Lion*, High Street (☎01570/422172; ❹). Just off the B4343 is one of the area's best farmhouse B&Bs, at *Pentre Farm*, near Llanfair Clydogau, five miles from Lampeter (☎01570/493313; ❸). The nearest **campsite** is five miles northeast, at Moorlands, near Llangybi (☎01570/493543). There are plenty of fine places to **eat** in town. *Lloyds* is an upmarket fish-and-chip restaurant in Bridge Street; the *Cottage Garden* restaurant, opposite the university, on College Street, is cheap and popular with students, as is the *King's Arms*, on Bridge Street, a small stone pub with well-kept beer. Don't miss *Conti's Café*, on Harford Square, a wonderfully timewarped place renowned for its home-made ice-cream. Just south of town, where the A485 joins the A482, the *Cwmann Tavern* is the best bet for catching the extremely lively local **music** scene.

Strata Florida Abbey

Twenty miles northeast of Lampeter, the mighty **Strata Florida Abbey** (Easter–Sept daily 10am–5pm; £2; all other times free access; CADW) dominates the bucolic Ystrad Fflur, the Valley of the Flowers. This Cistercian abbey was founded in 1164, swiftly growing into a centre for milling, farming and weaving, and becoming an important political centre for Wales. In 1238, Llywelyn the Great, whose conquering exploits throughout the rest of Wales had brought him to the peak of the Welsh feudal pyramid, summoned the lesser Welsh princes here. He was near death, and worried that his work of unifying Wales under one ruler would disintegrate, so he commanded the assembled princes to pay homage not just to him but also to his son, Dafydd, so sealing the succession. The church here was vast – larger than the cathedral at St David's – and, although very little survived Henry VIII's dissolution of the monasteries, the huge Norman west doorway gives some idea of its dimensions. Fragments of one-time side chapels include beautifully tiled medieval floors, and there's also a serene cemetery, but it's really the abbey's position that impresses most, in glorious rural solitude amongst wide open skies and fringed with a scoop of sheep-flecked hills. A sinewy yew tree reputedly shades the spot where Dafydd ap Gwilym, fourteenth-century bard and contemporary of Chaucer, is buried.

Travel details

Trains

Abergavenny to: Cardiff (hourly; 40min); Hereford (hourly; 20min); Newport (hourly; 30min).

Aberystwyth to: Birmingham (8 daily; 3hr); Machynlleth (10 daily; 30min); Shrewsbury (8 daily; 2hr); Welshpool (8 daily; 1hr 30min).

Barmouth to: Harlech (6 daily; 30min); Machynlleth (6 daily; 1hr); Porthmadog (6 daily; 45min).

Harlech to: Barmouth (6 daily; 30min); Birmingham (5 daily; 4hr 15min); Machynlleth (6 daily; 1hr 20min); Porthmadog (7 daily; 20min).

Knighton to: Llandrindod Wells (4 daily; 40min);

Llanwrtyd Wells (4 daily; 1hr 10min); Swansea (4 daily; 3hr 10min).

Llandrindod Wells to: Knighton (4 daily; 40min); Llanwrtyd Wells (4 daily; 30min); Shrewsbury (4 daily; 1hr 40min); Swansea (4 daily; 2hr 20min).

Machynlleth to: Aberystwyth (10 daily; 30min); Barmouth (6 daily; 1hr); Birmingham (9 daily; 2hr 30min); Harlech (6 daily; 1hr 20min); Porthmadog (6 daily; 1hr 45min); Shrewsbury (9 daily; 2hr).

Welshpool to: Aberystwyth (8 daily; 1hr 30min); Birmingham (8 daily; 1hr 30min); Machynlleth (8 daily; 1hr).

Buses

Aberaeron to: Aberystwyth (hourly; 40min); Cardigan (6 daily; 1hr 10min); Carmarthen (7 daily; 1hr 40min); Lampeter (7 daily; 35min); New Quay (hourly; 20min).

Abergavenny to: Brecon (Mon–Sat 7 daily, none on Sun; 1hr); Cardiff (hourly; 1hr 20min); Crickhowell (Mon–Sat 7 daily, none on Sun; 20min); Llanfihangel Crucorney (6 daily; 15min); Merthyr Tydfil (hourly; 1hr 30min); Monmouth (6 daily; 40min); Raglan (6 daily; 20min).

Aberystwyth to: Aberaeron (hourly; 40min); Caernarfon (1 daily; 2hr 40min); Cardiff (2 daily; 3hr 50min); Cardigan (9 daily, most change at Synod Inn; 1hr 50min); Carmarthen (2 daily; 1hr 40min); Devil's Bridge (2 daily; 40min); Dolgellau

(6 daily; 1hr 15min); Lampeter (5 daily; 1hr 30min); Machynlleth (8 daily; 45min); New Quay (hourly; 1hr); Swansea (2 daily; 2hr 45min).

Bala to: Dolgellau (9 daily; 40min); Llangollen (8 daily; 1hr).

Barmouth to: Bala (8 daily; 1hr); Blaenau Ffestiniog (4 daily; 1hr); Dolgellau (8 daily; 20min); Harlech (9 daily; 30min); Llangollen (7 daily; 1hr 50min); Wrexham (7 daily; 2hr 20min).

Brecon to: Abergavenny (Mon–Sat 7 daily, none on Sun; 1hr); Cardiff (1 daily; 1hr 20min); Craig-y-nos/Dan-yr-ogof (2 daily; 30min); Crickhowell (Mon–Sat 7 daily, none on Sun; 25min); Hay-on-Wye (6 daily; 50min); Libanus (9 daily; 10min); Llandrindod Wells (Mon–Sat 2 daily, none on Sun;

1hr); Merthyr Tydfil (10 daily; 40min); Swansea (2–3 daily; 1hr 30min).

Cardigan to: Aberaeron (10 daily; 1hr 10min); Aberporth (hourly; 30min); Aberystwyth (9 daily, most change at Synod Inn; 1hr 50min); Carmarthen (hourly; 1hr 30min); Fishguard (hourly; 50min); Newcastle Emlyn (hourly; 30min); Newport, Pembrokeshire (hourly; 30min); New Quay (hourly; 1hr).

Dolgellau to: Aberystwyth (6 daily; 1hr 15min); Bala (9 daily; 40min); Barmouth (8 daily; 20min); Blaenau Ffestiniog (3 daily; 50min); Caernarfon (5 daily; 1hr 40min); Llangollen (8 daily; 1hr 30min); Machynlleth (10 daily; 40min); Porthmadog (6 daily; 50min); Tywyn (6 daily; 50min); Wrexham (8 daily; 2hr).

Harlech to: Barmouth (9 daily; 30min); Blaenau Ffestiniog (4 daily; 40min).

Hay-on-Wye to: Brecon (6 daily; 50min); Hereford (5 daily; 1hr).

Knighton to: Ludlow (3 daily; 1hr 10min); Presteigne (5 daily; 30min).

Lampeter to: Aberaeron (7 daily; 40min); Aberystwyth (5 daily; 1hr 30min); Carmarthen (8 daily; 1hr 10min); Machynlleth (1 daily; 2hr 30min).

Llandrindod Wells to: Abbeycwmhir (Mon–Fri 1 postbus daily; 2hr); Aberystwyth (1 daily; 1hr 40min); Brecon (Mon–Sat 2 daily, none on Sun; 1hr); Elan Village (Mon–Fri 1 postbus daily; 40min); Hay-on-Wye (Wed & Sat 1 daily; 1hr); Rhayader (3 daily; 30min).

Llanfyllin to: Llanwddyn for Lake Vyrnwy (Mon–Sat 3 daily, none on Sun; 30min); Welshpool (Mon–Sat 1 daily; 40min).

Llangollen to: Bala (8 daily; 1hr); Chirk (7 daily; 20min); Wrexham (at least hourly; 30min).

Llanidloes to: Aberystwyth (1 daily; 1hr); Welshpool (5 daily; 1hr 10min).

Llanwrtyd Wells to: Abergwesyn (Mon–Fri 1 postbus daily; 20min); Builth Wells (2 daily; 50min).

Machynlleth to: Aberystwyth (8 daily; 45min); Bala (4 daily; 1hr 20min); Cardiff (1 daily; 5hr 15min); Dolgellau (6 daily; 40min); Lampeter (1 daily; 2hr 30min); Llangollen (6 daily; 3hr); Porthmadog (4 daily; 1hr 45min); Tywyn (4–6 daily; 40min).

New Quay to: Aberaeron (hourly; 20min); Aberporth (hourly; 40min); Aberystwyth (hourly; 1hr); Cardigan (hourly; 1hr).

Welshpool to: Berriew (Mon–Sat 6 daily, none on Sun; 20min); Llanfyllin (Mon–Sat 1 daily, none on Sun; 40min); Llanidloes (5 daily; 1hr 10min); Montgomery (school bus; 25min).

North Wales

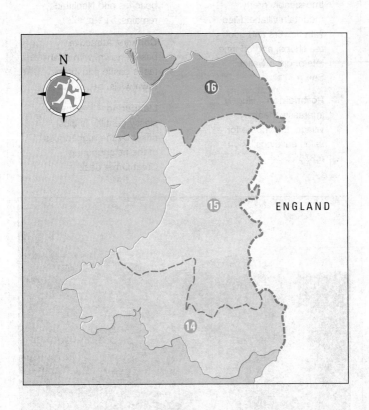

CHAPTER 16 Highlights

✳ **Snowdon** – Wales's highest mountain is a stunning climb, or a gentle ascent by rack-and-pinion railway. See p.869

✳ **Beddgelert** – Impeccably pretty mountain village, filled with flowers and good tea shops, and offering lots of great walks. See p.871

✳ **Portmeirion** – Hugely impressive fantasy village, the "home for fallen buildings". See p.876

✳ **Caernarfon Castle** – The mightiest link in Edward I's chain of Welsh castles. See p.880

✳ **Beaumaris** – A good base for Anglesey's beaches and Neolithic remains. See p.882

✳ **Conwy** – Attractive bastide town, with a fantastic castle and intact town walls. See p.887

✳ **Llandudno** – The town's classy gentility is nicely offset by the ruggedness of the neighbouring Great Orme peak. See p.891

16

North Wales

With the advent of the A55 dual carriageway across the width of **North Wales**, the region has become considerably more accessible in recent times. This, however, has not tamed the wilder aspects of this stunningly beautiful area, especially in the western parts of Snowdonia and the Llŷn peninsula. Wales's north coast and its natural off-shoot, the isle of Anglesey, not only encompass the geographical extremities of the country, but comprise an area exhibiting the extremes of Welsh life. As you walk around most of the brash seaside towns along the eastern section of the coast, only the street signs give any indication that you are in Wales at all; further west, there are places where English is seldom spoken other than to visitors. Scattered along the coast, dramatically sited castles act as a superb anti-dote to low-brow fun-seeking.

Without doubt, **Snowdonia** is the crowning glory of North Wales. This tightly packed bundle of soaring cliff faces, jagged peaks and plunging water-falls measures little more than ten miles by ten, but packs enough mountain paths to keep even the most jaded walking enthusiast happy for weeks. Even if lakeside ambles and rides on antiquated steam trains are more your style, you can't fail to appreciate the natural grandeur of the scenery, occasionally reveal-ing an atmospheric Welsh castle ruin or decaying piece of quarrying equip-ment. The area's small settlements – well geared up for walking and other out-door activities – make for lively bases, whether long-standing tourist towns like **Betws-y-Coed** and **Llanberis**, or old mining and quarry towns such as **Beddgelert** and **Blaenau Ffestiniog**.

Snowdonia is the heart – and undisputed highlight – of the massive **Snowdonia National Park** (Parc Cenedlaethol Eryri), an 840-square-mile area which extends north and south, beyond the bounds of Snowdonia and this chapter, to encompass the Rhinogs, Cadair Idris (see p.841) and 23 miles of superb coastal scenery. To the west, this coast is the highlight, in the gentle rockiness of the **Llŷn peninsula**, where Wales ends in a flourish of small coves and seafaring villages, offering almost unlimited rambling potential around the high-hedged lanes. Roads loop back along the Llŷn to the tip of the north coast, where **Caernarfon** sits overshadowed by its stupendous castle, the mightiest link in Edward I's Iron Ring of thirteenth-century fortresses across north Wales.

Across the Menai Strait lies the island of **Anglesey**, a gentle patchwork of beautiful beaches and sites of ancient heritage, well worth exploration. Edward's final castle, a masterpiece of design, is sited in **Beaumaris**, and cata-marans and ferries from Anglesey's main town, **Holyhead**, provide the fastest route to Dublin.

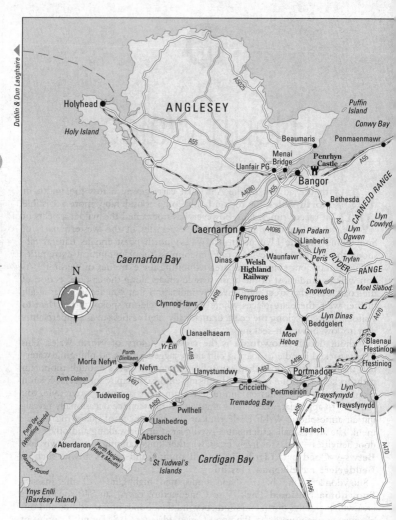

Back on the mainland, the university and cathedral city of **Bangor** is the area's most cosmopolitan haunt, while remaining solidly Welsh in outlook and language. The same could certainly not be said for the string of seaside resorts along the north Wales coast, among which **Conwy** – another walled bastide town built by Edward I – and genteel **Llandudno**, always a cut above the rest, are the highlights. Further east towards England, faded Victorian resorts are the mainstay. However, a few surprises come embedded into this matrix of bingo halls and caravan sites: the allegedly miraculous waters at **Holywell** have attracted the hopeful since the seventh century, while others come for the National Portrait Gallery's collection at **Bodelwyddan**, and Britain's smallest cathedral at **St Asaph**.

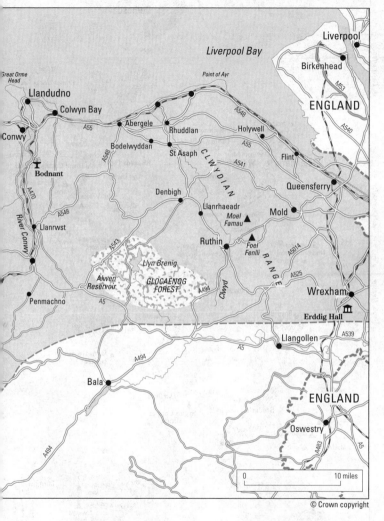

© Crown copyright

Snowdonia

What the coal valleys are to the south of the country, the mountains of **Snowdonia** (Yr Eryri) are to the north – the defining feature, not just in their physical form, but in the way they have shaped the communities within them. To Henry VIII's antiquarian John Leland, the region seemed "horrible with the sight of bare stones"; now it is widely acclaimed as the most dramatic and alluring of all Welsh scenery, a compact, barren land of tortured ridges dividing glacial valleys, whose sheer faces belie the fact that the tallest peaks only just top three thousand feet. It was to this mountain fastness that Llywelyn ap Gruffydd,

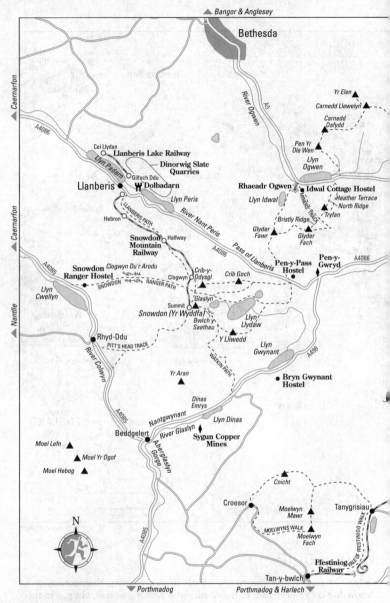

the last true Prince of Wales, retreated in 1277 after his first war with Edward I; it was also here that Owain Glyndŵr held on most tenaciously to his dream of regaining for the Welsh the title of Prince of Wales. Centuries later, the English came to remove the mountains: slate barons built huge fortunes from Welsh toil and reshaped the patterns of Snowdonian life forever, as men looking for steady work in the quarries left the hills and became town dwellers. By the mid-nineteenth century, those with the means began flocking here to mar-

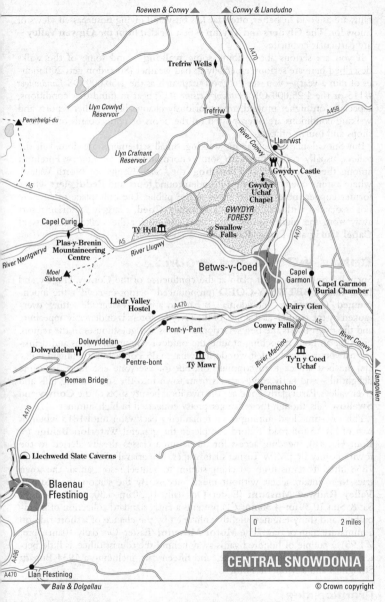

Roewen & Conwy ▲   ▲ Conwy & Llandudno

Trefriw Wells ♦

Llyn Cowlyd
Reservoir

▲ Penyrhelgi-du

Trefriw

A470

A458

River Conwy

Llanrwst

Llyn Crafnant
Reservoir

A5

Gwydyr Castle ♜

Gwydyr
Uchaf
Chapel ♦

GWYDYR
FOREST

Capel Curig

Plas-y-Brenin
Mountaineering
Centre

River Nantgwryd

Tŷ Hyll ⌂

Swallow
Falls

A5

River Llugwy

Betws-y-Coed

Capel
Garmon

Capel Garmon
Burial Chamber ♦

Moel
Siabod ▲

Lledr Valley
Hostel

A470

Fairy Glen

Conwy Falls

A5

River Conwy

Pont-y-Pant

River Machno

Dolwyddelan ♜

Dolwyddelan

Tŷ Mawr ⌂

Tŷ'n y Coed
Uchaf ⌂

Pentre-bont

Roman Bridge

Penmachno

Llangollen ▼

A470

▲ Llechwedd Slate Caverns

Blaenau
Ffestiniog

A496

A470

0   2 miles

CENTRAL SNOWDONIA

Llan Ffestiniog

▼ Bala & Dolgellau

© Crown copyright

vel at the plunging waterfalls and walk the ever-widening paths to the mountaintops. Numbers have increased rapidly since then and thousands of hikers
arrive every weekend for some of the country's best walks over steep, exacting
and constantly varying terrain.

Not surprisingly, the **Snowdon** massif (Eryri) is the focus of the Snowdonia
National Park. Several of the ascent routes are superb, and you can always take
the cog railway up to the summit café from **Llanberis**. But the other moun-

tains are as good or better, often far less busy and giving unsurpassed views of Snowdon. The **Glyders** and **Tryfan** – best tackled from the **Ogwen Valley** – are particular favourites.

If you are serious about doing some **walking** – and some of the walks described here are serious, especially in bad weather (Snowdon gets 200 inches of rain a year) – you need a good map such as the 1:50,000 OS *Landranger* #115 or the 1:25,000 OS *Outdoor Leisure* #17; bear in mind that conditions, especially on higher ground, are notoriously changeable. Weather reports and walking conditions are often posted on the doors or noticeboards of outdoor shops and tourist offices.

But Snowdonia isn't all about walking. Small settlements are dotted in the valleys, usually coinciding with some enormous mine or quarry. Foremost among these are **Blaenau Ffestiniog**, the "Slate Capital of North Wales", where a mine opens its caverns for underground tours, and **Beddgelert** whose former copper mines are also open to the public. The only place of any size not associated with slate mining is **Betws-y-Coed**, a largely Victorian resort away from the higher peaks, and a springboard for the walkers' hamlets of **Capel Curig** and **Pen-y-Pass**.

Betws-y-Coed and around

Sprawled out across a flat plain at the confluence of the Conwy, Llugwy and Lledr valleys, **BETWS-Y-COED** (pronounced "betoos-er-coyd"), the much-vaunted "Gateway to Snowdonia", is hard to avoid. Its riverside setting, over-looked by the conifer-clad slopes of the Gwydyr forest, is undeniably appealing, and the town boasts the best selection of hotels and guesthouses in the region, but after an hour mooching around the outdoor equipment shops and drinking tea you may well be left wondering what to do. For serious mountain walkers, the best advice is to continue on, but for everyone else there are some delightful – and fairly easy – strolls from town into the surrounding hills and river valleys. Particularly good are the two local beauty spots of the **Conwy** and **Swallow** falls, though these can get pretty congested in high summer.

This one-time lead-mining town remained a backwater until 1815 when, as part of his A5 toll road, Telford completed the graceful **Waterloo Bridge** (Y Bont Haearn), speeding access for the leisured classes already alerted to the town's beauty by J.M.W. Turner's landscapes. The arrival of the railway line in 1868 lifted its status from coaching station to genteel resort, an air the town tries to maintain, albeit without much success. By the station, the **Conwy Valley Railway Museum** (Easter–Oct daily 10.30am–5.30pm; Nov–Easter Sat & Sun 10.30am–4.30pm; £1) presents a fairly standard collection of memorabilia and shiny engines, slightly enlivened by the chance of a short ride on a miniature train or tram. The **Motor Museum** (Easter–Oct daily 10am–5pm; £1.95), a couple of hundred yards away behind the tourist office, is little better, with a half-dozen classic bikes and fifteen cars, including a 1934 Bugatti Straight 8 and a Model T Ford.

Practicalities

The **train station**, for services from Llandudno Junction up the Conwy Valley and on to Blaenau Ffestiniog, is just a few paces across the grass from the **tourist office**, at Royal Oak Stables (daily: Easter–Oct 10am–6pm; Nov–Easter 9.30am–12.30pm & 1.30–4.30pm; ☎01690/710426), and the **bus stop**, outside St Mary's church, on the main street. Whether you're a beginner or intermediate climber, you can arrange **scrambling**, **climbing** and **abseil-**

ing courses with Snowdonia Mountain Guides (℡01690/750554; £30–50 a day). **Mountain bikes** can be rented from Beics Betws (℡01690/710766), on Church Hill, at the top of the road beside the post office; permits and information on routes through the Gwydyr Forest are obtainable from the tourist office. The Ultimate Outdoors shop, opposite Pont-y-Pair bridge, is good for all kinds of equipment and information.

The town has plenty of **accommodation**, but has to cope with an ever-larger number of visitors pushing prices up in the summer, when you need to book ahead. The cheapest rooms are above the award-winning *Riverside Restaurant*, Holyhead Road, near the central Pont-y-Pair bridge (℡01690/710650; ❶). *Glan Llugwy*, on the A5, a short way beyond Pont-y-Pair (℡01690/710592; ❶), is another inexpensive option, while *Tŷ Gwyn*, also on the A5 (℡01690/710383; ❸), is a prettified old coaching inn half a mile east of the centre, just over Waterloo Bridge. The luxury option is *Tan-y-Foel*, Capel Garmon (℡01690/710507, ⓌWwww.tyfhotel.co.uk; ❹), with a heated indoor pool and superb cuisine; take the A470 towards Llanrwst then turn right after about a mile. The nearest **hostel** is at Capel Curig (see below); the closest **campsite** is *Riverside* (℡01690/710310; Easter–Oct), right behind the station.

For a town so geared to tourism that you can hardly turn around without knocking someone's cream tea to the floor, there are surprisingly few places to **eat** other than the pubs. The aforementioned *Riverside Restaurant*, with its fresh Mediterranean cuisine, or *Tŷ Gwyn*, on the A5, are the best places to eat in town. The low-cost bar meals at the lively *Royal Oak Hotel*, High Street, are decent value.

The Conwy and Swallow Falls

Nothing in Betws-y-Coed can compete with getting out to the gorges and waterfalls in the vicinity, and **walking** is the ideal way to see them. In the final gorge section of the River Conwy, a couple of miles above Betws-y-Coed, the river plunges fifty feet over the **Conwy Falls** into a deep pool. The *Conwy Falls Café*, reached by bus #49 (4 daily), collects a small fee entitling you to view the falls and a series of rock steps which once formed part of a primitive fish ladder.

After carving out a mile or so of what kayakers regard as some of North Wales' toughest white water, the Conwy negotiates a staircase of drops and enters the **Fairy Glen**, a cleft in a small wood which takes its name from the Welsh fairies, the Tylwyth Teg, who are said to be seen hereabouts. The two sights are linked by a mile-long path following a cool green lane giving glimpses of the river through the woods. The path continues a short distance to Beaver Bridge from where you can walk back along the road to Betws-y-Coed – an excellent round trip.

The **Swallow Falls**, two miles west along the A5 towards Capel Curig, is the region's most visited sight, a straightforward, pretty waterfall with the occasional mad kayaker scraping down the precipitous rock. Pay your 50p and you can walk down to a series of viewing platforms. Better still, leave the car park on the north side of Pont-y-Pair, in town, and follow the **Llugwy Valley Walk** (3 miles; 400ft ascent; 1hr 30min), a forested path following the twisting and plunging river upstream towards Capel Curig. Less than a mile from Pont-y-Pair you reach the steeply sloping **Miners' Bridge**, which linked miners' homes at Pentre Du, on the south side of the river, to the lead mines in Llanrwst. Just beneath the bridge are a series of idyllic plunge pools, perfect for swimming. The path follows the river on your left for another mile to a slightly obscured view of Swallow Falls. Detailed maps are available from the tourist office showing numerous routes back through the Gwydyr Forest, or you can continue half a mile to the road bridge from where you can wait for the bus back to Betws-y-Coed.

Capel Curig

Tantalizing flashes of Wales' highest mountains are glimpsed through the forested banks of the Llugwy as you climb west from Betws-y-Coed on the A5, but Snowdon eludes you until the final bend before **CAPEL CURIG**. The tiny, scattered village, six miles west of Betws-y-Coed, is the site of a major centre for outdoor enthusiasts. A quarter of a mile along the A4086 to Llanberis from the main road junction, **Plas-y-Brenin** (the **National Mountaineering Centre**) was built around a former coaching inn and hotel, and now runs renowned residential courses. Two-hour abseiling, canoeing and dry-slope skiing sessions are held during July and August, there's a dry ski slope (daily 10am–9pm; prices vary), a state-of-the-art climbing wall open throughout the year (daily 10am–11pm; £3), and the opportunity to hear talks or watch slide shows of expeditions (usually Mon–Thurs & Sat 8pm; free).

There are plenty of places to **stay**, though none is especially luxurious. The best is either the *Bron Eryri* (℡01690/720240; ❷), a comfortable and welcoming B&B half a mile outside the village towards Betws-y-Coed, or the wonderful *Bryn Tyrch Hotel* (℡01690/720223; ❷), also on the A5, but closer to the main road junction. The *Llugwy Guesthouse* (℡01690/720218; ❶) is on the A4086 towards the adventure centre of Plas-y-Brenin (℡01690/720214, Ⓦwww.pyb.co.uk; ❶), which has a limited amount of accommodation. The cheapest option in the village is the YHA **hostel** (℡01690/720225, Ⓦwww.yha.org.uk; mid-Feb to mid-Dec), five hundred yards along the A5 towards Betws-y-Coed. Two and a half miles west down the Ogwen Valley you can stay for a good deal less in the *Williams Barn* bunkhouse and **campsite** (see p.868). During the day, walkers patronize the *Pinnacle Café*, grafted onto the post office and general store at the main road junction. In the evening they retire to the warm and lively **bar** of the *Bryn Tyrch Hotel*, which serves great **food**, much of which is vegan and vegetarian, or head for the sociable bar at the Plas-y-Brenin centre.

The Ogwen Valley

Prising apart the Carneddau and Glyder ranges northwest from Capel Curig, the A5 forges through the **Ogwen Valley** to Bethesda, where one of Wales's last surviving slate quarries continues to tear away the end of the Glyders range, only just keeping the tatty town viable. To the north, the frequently mist-shrouded Carneddau range glowers across at the **Glyders** range and its triple-peaked **Tryfan**, perhaps Snowdonia's most demanding mountain, which forms a fractured spur out from the main ridge, blocking the view down the valley. West of Tryfan, the road follows a perfect example of a U-shaped valley, carved and smoothed by rocks frozen into the undersides of the glaciers that creaked down Nant Ffrancon ten thousand years ago.

The time-compacted moraine left by the retreating ice formed Llŷn Ogwen. On its shores, **Idwal Cottage**, a settlement so small it isn't named on maps, provides the valleys with a mountain rescue centre, a snack bar and a YHA hostel (see below), all clustered around the car park. This is the start of some of Wales's most demanding and rewarding hikes (see box), and the easier half-hour walk to the magnificent cirque, **Cwm Idwal**. The cwm's scalloped floor traps the beautifully still **Llŷn Idwal**, which reflects the precipitous grey cliffs

Tourists hike up Snowdon, but mountain connoisseurs invariably prefer the sharply angled peaks of **Tryfan and the Glyders**, with their challenging terrain, cantilevered rocks and views back to Snowdon. The sheer number of good walking paths on the Glyders make it almost impossible to choose one definitive circular route. The individual sections of the walk have therefore been defined separately in order to allow the greatest flexibility. All times given are for the ascents: expect to take approximately half the time to get back down. **Maps** are essential for all these walks: the OS *Outdoor Leisure* 1:25,000 "Snowdonia" #17 is by far the best bet.

If you've got the head for it, the **North Ridge of Tryfan**, at 3002ft (1 mile; 2000ft ascent; 1hr–1hr 30min), is one of the most rewarding scrambles in the country. It's never as precarious as Snowdon's Crib Goch, but you get a genuine mountaineering feel as the valley floor drops rapidly. The route starts in the lay-by at the head of Idwal Lake and goes left across rising ground, until you strike a path heading straight up, following the crest of the ridge to the twin monoliths of **Adam and Eve** on the summit. The courageous, or foolhardy, make the jump between them as a point of honour at the end of every ascent. In fact, the leap is trivial, but the consequences of overshooting would be disastrous.

There are two other main routes up Tryfan. The first follows the so-called **Miners' Track** (2 miles; 1350ft ascent; 2hr) from Idwal Cottage, taking the path to Cwm Idwal, then, as it bears sharply to the right, keeping straight ahead and making for the gap on the horizon. This is **Bwlch Tryfan**, the col between Tryfan and Glyder Fach, from where the **South Ridge** of Tryfan (800yd; 650ft ascent; 30min) climbs from the Far South Peak to the summit. This last section is an easy scramble. The second route, which is more often used in descent, follows **Heather Terrace** (1.5 miles; 2000ft ascent; 2hr), which keeps to a fault in the rock running diagonally across the east face.

The assault on **Glyder Fach** (3260ft) begins at Bwlch Tryfan, reached either by the Miners' Track from Idwal Cottage or by the south ridge from Tryfan's summit. The trickier route follows **Bristly Ridge** (1000yd; 900ft ascent; 40min) which isn't marked on OS maps but runs steeply south from the col up past some daunting-looking towers of rock. It isn't that difficult in dry conditions, and saves a long hike southeast along a second section of the *Miners' Track* (1.5 miles; 900ft ascent; 1hr 30min). The summit lies to the west of the ridge, a chaotic jumble of huge grey slabs that many people don't bother climbing up, preferring to be photographed on a massive cantilevered rock a few yards away.

From Glyder Fach, it's an easy enough stroll to **Glyder Fawr** (3280ft), reached by skirting round the tortured rock formations of **Castell y Gwynt** (the Castle of the Winds) then following a cairn-marked path to the dramatic summit of frost-shattered slabs angled like ancient headstones (1 mile; 200ft ascent; 40min). Glyder Fawr is normally approached from Idwal Cottage, following the **Devil's Kitchen Route** (2.5 miles; 2300ft ascent; 3hr) past Idwal Lake, then to the left of the Devil's Kitchen, zigzagging up to a lake-filled plateau. Follow the path to the right of the lake and turn left for the summit where two paths cross.

behind, split by the jointed cleft of Twll Du, the **Devil's Kitchen**. Down this, a fine watery haze runs off the flanks of **Glyder Fawr**, soaking the crevices where early botanists found rare arctic-alpine plants, the main reason for designating Cwm Idwal as Wales's first **nature reserve** in 1954. An easy, well-groomed path leads up to the reserve from the car park, where the café (daily 8.30am–5pm; later on summer weekends) will sell you a nature trail booklet for 75p. A five-minute walk down from the car park, the road crosses a bridge over the top of **Rhaeadr Ogwen** (Ogwen Falls), which cascade down a step in the valley floor.

A couple of inconveniently timed **buses** run along the valley daily between Betws-y-Coed and Bangor. **Accommodation** in the valley is limited to a self-catering bunkhouse and **campsite** at *Williams Barn*, Gwern Gof Isaf Farm, two and a half miles west of Capel Curig (℡01690/720276; ❶), the smaller *Gwern Gof Uchaf* campsite, a mile further west, and the Idwal Cottage YHA **hostel** (℡01248/600225, ⊛www.yha.org.uk; March–Oct), at the western end of Llŷn Ogwen, five miles from Capel Curig. Residents can get meals at the hostel; the valley is otherwise self-catering.

Llanberis and Snowdon

Mention **LLANBERIS** to any mountain enthusiast and they will think of **Snowdon**. The two seem inseparable, and it's not just the five-mile-long umbilical of the **Snowdon Mountain Railway**, Britain's only rack-and-pinion railway, which bonds the town, located ten miles west of Capel Curig, to the summit, nor the popular path running parallel to it (see box). This is the nearest you'll get to an alpine climbing village in Wales, its single main street thronged with weatherbeaten walkers and climbers decked out in fleeces, high fashion for what is otherwise a dowdy town. At the same time, Llanberis is very much a Welsh rural community, albeit a depleted one now that slate is no longer being torn from the flanks of Elidir Fawr, the mountain across the town's twin lakes. The quarries, which for the best part of two centuries employed up to three thousand men, closed in 1969, making way for the construction of the Dinorwig Pumped Storage Power Station.

Three of the routes up Snowdon start five miles east of Llanberis at the top of the Llanberis Pass, one of the deepest, narrowest and craggiest in Snowdonia. At the summit, a hostel, café and car park comprise the settlement of **PEN-Y-PASS**. Frequent, year-round Sherpa **buses** travel up daily to Pen-y-Pass, and from mid-July to August there is also the #96 Pen-y-Pass shuttle from Llanberis, the recommended approach even if you have a car, since the Pen-y-Pass car park is expensive and almost always full. Use the "Park and Ride" car park at the bottom of the pass, near the *Vaynol Arms*.

The Town

Scattered remains are all that is left of thirteenth-century **Dolbadarn Castle** (free access; CADW), on the road to **Parc Padarn**, where lakeside oak woods are gradually recolonizing the discarded workings of the defunct Dinorwig Slate Quarries. Here, the **Welsh Slate Museum** (Easter–Oct daily 10am–5pm, Nov–Easter Sun–Fri 10am–4pm; free) occupies the former maintenance workshops of what was once one of the largest slate quarries in the world. The line shafts and flapping belts driven by a fifty-foot-diameter waterwheel provide a backdrop to workbenches where former quarry workers demonstrate their skills at turning an inch-thick slab of slate into six, or even eight, perfectly smooth slivers. The craftsmen here operate an ageing foundry, producing pieces for the scattered branches of the National Museum of Wales, as well as repairing the rolling stock belonging to the nearby **Llanberis Lake Railway** (July & Aug daily 4–10pm; March–June & Sept to early Oct Mon–Fri & Sun 3–6pm; £4.75 return), which formerly transported slate and workers between the Dinorwig quarries and Port Dinorwig on the Menai Strait. It's a tame forty-minute round trip with little to do at the end except come back and explore the old slate workings.

In 1974, five years after the quarry closed, work began on hollowing out the vast underground chambers of the **Dinorwig Pumped Storage Hydro**

Station, designed to provide power on demand. If you can bear the thinly disguised electricity industry advertisement which comes before it, you can take an hour-long minibus tour around the enormous pipework in the depths. For this, you need to call at **Electric Mountain** (Easter–Sept daily 9.30am–5.30pm; Oct–Dec daily 10.30am–4.30pm; mid-Jan to Easter Thurs–Sun 10.30am–4.30pm; £5), by the lake beside the A4086, the town-centre bypass. The museum complex has some tolerably interesting displays on local glaciation, flora and fauna, and an exhibition about mammoths.

Practicalities

All **buses** to Llanberis stop near the **tourist office**, 41b High St (Easter–Oct daily 10am–6pm, Nov–Easter Wed–Sun 11am–4pm; ☎01286/870765). Adventurous types should contact Blue Peris (☎01286/870853, ⓦwww.blue-peris.co.uk) for mountaineering, sea kayaking, mine exploration and coasteering, but with a charge of £150 per day for instructors, you'd best be in a group. Alternatively, High Trek Snowdonia, Tal y Waen, Deiniolen (☎01286/871232), offers guided walking and courses. Padarn Watersports at Bryn Du, Tydu Road (☎01286/870556), offers organized climbing, abseiling, canoeing and other mountain activities. The Llanberis Path (see box), Snowdon Ranger Path and Pitt's Head Track to Rhyd-Ddu are open to **cyclists**, although a voluntary agreement exists restricting cycle access to and from the summit between 10am and 5pm (June–Sept).

There is plenty of low-cost **accommodation** in or close to town: *The Heights*, 74 High St (☎01286/871179; ❶), caters to the walking and climbing set, offering B&B and dorms, not to mention a climbing wall, good restaurant and lively bar. Two other options on the High Street are the *Dolafon Hotel* (☎01286/870993; ❷), a comfortable B&B in its own grounds, and the family-run *Padarn Lake Hotel* (☎01286/870260; ❸). The only luxurious place is the *Royal Victoria Hotel*, opposite the Mountain Railway (☎01286/870253, ⓦwww.royal-victoria-hotel.co.uk; ❺). Llanberis YHA **hostel**, *Llwyn Celyn* (☎01286/870280, ⓦwww.yha.org.uk), is half a mile uphill along Capel Goch Road, signposted off High Street. Four miles east of town is the *Pen-y-Pass* YHA hostel (☎01286/870428, ⓦwww.yha.org.uk), with the *Pen-y-Gwryd Hotel* (☎01286/870211; ❷; March–Oct) a mile further east; they're used to muddy boots in the bar. A cheaper option is *Gwastadnant B&B and Bunkhouse*, three miles east of Llanberis in Nant Peris (☎01286/870356; ❶), which also has **camping** facilities.

For **food** of gut-splitting proportions, climbers and walkers flock to *Pete's Eats*, 40 High St, while *Y Bistro*, 43–45 High St (☎01286/871278; Sept–May closed Sun), is the best restaurant for miles around. The *Vaynol Arms*, two miles east of Llanberis and the only pub before Pen-y-Gwryd, serves good beer and very tasty food in a convivial atmosphere; it's usually full of campers from across the road.

Snowdon and the Snowdon Mountain Railway

The highest British mountain outside Scotland, the **Snowdon massif** (3560ft) forms a star of shattered ridges with four major peaks: Crib Goch, Crib-y-ddysgl, Y Lliwedd and the main summit, **Yr Wyddfa**. Snowdon sports some of the finest walking and scrambling in the park and, in winter, the longest season for ice climbers and cramponed walkers. Hardened outdoor enthusiasts dismiss it as overused, and it can certainly be crowded, especially in summer, when a thousand visitors a day can be pressed into the postbox-red carriages of the Snowdon Mountain Railway, while another 1500 pound the well-maintained paths.

The following are justifiably the most popular of the seven accepted **walking** routes up **Snowdon**. Maps are essential for all these walks: the OS *Outdoor Leisure* 1:25,000 map of "Snowdonia" #17 is highly recommended.

Llanberis Path

The easiest, longest and most derided route up Snowdon, the **Llanberis Path** (5 miles to summit; 3200ft ascent; 3hr) follows the rail line past the *Halfway Station* café (March to late Sept daily; rest of year Sat & Sun only); posted on the wall inside are the barely believable times of the annual Snowdon Race, which passes on the fourth Saturday in July. Continuing up, the path gets steeper to the "Finger Stone" at **Bwlch Glas** (Green Pass), marking the arrival of the Snowdon Ranger Path, and three routes coming up from Pen-y-Pass to join the Llanberis Path for the final ascent to **Yr Wyddfa**, the summit.

The Miners' and Pig tracks

The **Miners' Track** (4 miles to summit; 2400ft ascent; 2hr 30min) is the easiest of the three routes up from Pen-y-Pass, a broad track leading south then west to the dilap- idated remains of the former copper mines in Cwm Dyli. Skirting around the right of a lake, the path climbs more steeply to the lake-filled Cwm Glaslyn, then again to Upper Glaslyn, from where the measured steps of those ahead warn of the impend- ing switchback ascent to the junction with the Llanberis Path.

The stonier **Pig Track** (3.5 miles to summit; 2400ft ascent; 2hr 30min) is really just a variation on the Miners' Track, leaving from the western end of the Pen-y-Pass car park and climbing up to **Bwlch y Moch** (the Pass of the Pigs) before meeting the Miners' Track prior to the zigzag up to the Llanberis Path.

Snowdon Horseshoe

Some claim that the **Snowdon Horseshoe** (8 miles round; 3200ft ascent; 5–7hr) is one of the finest ridge walks in Europe. The route makes a full anticlockwise circuit around the three glacier-carved cwms of Upper Glaslyn, Glaslyn and Llydaw. Not to be taken lightly, it includes the knife-edge traverse of **Crib Goch**, which requires a minimum of an ice axe and crampons in winter. The path follows the Pig Track to Bwlch y Moch, then pitches right for the moderate scramble up to Crib Goch. If you balk at any of this, turn back: if not, pick your way along the sensational ridge to **Crib-y-ddysgl** (3494ft) and, on easier ground, to the summit. The return to Llyn Llydaw and the Miners' Track is via **Bwlch-y-Saethau** (Pass of the Arrows) and **Y Lliwedd** (2930ft).

Watkin Path

The most spectacular of the southern routes up Snowdon, the **Watkin Path** (4 miles to summit; 3350ft ascent; 3hr) begins at Bethania Bridge, three miles northeast of Beddgelert in Nantgwynant. The path starts on a broad track, lined with oaks, which narrows before heading past a disused tramway to a series of cataracts. A natural amphitheatre contains the ruins of a slate works and **Gladstone Rock**, at which, in 1892, the 83-year-old prime minister officially opened the route.

Opprobrium is chiefly levelled at the **Snowdon Mountain Railway** (mid- March to Oct 6–25 trains daily; £16.90 return; ☏01286/870223, ⓦwww .snowdonrailway.co.uk), completed in 1896, purely for the fact that it exists. Seventy-year-old carriages pushed by equally old steam locos still climb, in just under an hour, from the eastern end of Llanberis opposite the *Royal Victoria Hotel* to the summit café and bar (open when the trains are running to the top). A "Railway Stamp" (10p) affixed to your letter – along with the usual Royal

Mail one – entitles you to use the highest postbox in the UK and enchant your friends with a "Summit of Snowdon – Copa'r Wyddfa" postmark. Times, type of locomotive and final destination vary with demand and ice conditions at the top: to avoid disappointment, buy your tickets early on clear summer days. If you walk up by one of the routes detailed in the "Walks on Snowdon" box, you can take the train down, if there is space (£8).

Beddgelert

Almost all of the prodigious quantity of rain which falls on Snowdon spills down either the Glaslyn or Colwyn rivers, which meet at the huddle of grey houses, prodigiously brightened with floral displays in summer, that make up **BEDDGELERT**. A sentimental tale fabricated by a wily local publican to lure punters tells how the town got its name. **Gelert's Grave** (*bedd* means burial place), an enclosure just south of town, is supposedly the final resting place of Prince Llywelyn ap Iorwerth's faithful dog, Gelert, who was left in charge of the prince's infant son while he went hunting. On his return, the child was gone and the hound's muzzle was soaked in blood. Jumping to conclusions, the impetuous Llywelyn slew the dog, only to find the child safely asleep beneath its cot and a dead wolf beside him. Llywelyn hurried to his dog, which licked his hand as it died.

Beyond the "grave", the river crashes down the bony and picturesque **Aberglaslyn Gorge** towards Porthmadog. You can walk along the right bank of the river, past Gelert's Grave, crossing over the bridge onto the Fisherman's Path. This then hugs the left bank for a mile, heading gently down to Pont Aberglaslyn, at the bottom of the gorge, affording a closer look at the river's course through chutes and channels in sculpted rocks. You have to return the same way.

A mile in the opposite direction up Nantgwynant, the **Sygun Copper Mine** (Easter–Sept Mon–Fri 10am–5pm, Sat 10am–4pm, Sun 11am–5pm; Oct, Feb & March Mon–Sat 10.30am–4pm, Sun 11am–4pm; Nov–Jan Sat & Sun 11am–3.30pm; £4.95) is the dilapidated remnant of what, until a century ago, had been the valley's prime source of income from Roman times. Restored and made safe, the multiple levels of tunnels and galleries can now be visited on a 45-minute guided tour, accompanied by the disembodied voice of a miner describing his life in the mine.

Buses all stop by the National Trust shop, just by the bridge in Tŷ Llywelyn (daily: June–Aug 11am–6pm; April, May, Sept & Oct 11am–5pm), which houses some interesting exhibits on Snowdonia and the Victorian Romantics. The **tourist office** (Easter–Oct daily 10am–6pm; ☎01766/890615) is in Canolfan Hebog, a restored chapel just up the road by the main village car park. The best places to **stay** are the *Beddgelert Antiques and Tea Rooms*, Waterloo House, directly opposite the bridge (☎01766/890543; ❷), with limited accommodation above the restaurant; *Plas Tan-y-Graig* (☎01766/890310, ⓦwww.plastany-graig.co.uk; ❶), also near the bridge, a decent budget B&B aimed at walkers and cyclists; and *Sygun Fawr Country House*, three quarters of a mile away off the A498 (☎01766/890258; ❸), a partially sixteenth-century house in its own grounds with a sauna and good, moderately priced evening meals. The excellent *Beddgelert Forest Campsite* (☎01766/890288) is a mile out on the Caernarfon road, four miles before the highly rated *Snowdon Ranger* YHA **hostel** (☎01286/650391, ⓦwww.yha.org.uk; mid-Feb to Dec). The *Bryn Gwynant* YHA hostel (☎01766/890251, ⓦwww.yha.org.uk; Jan–Oct), is beautifully sited in Nantgwynant, four miles northeast of Beddgelert on the A498, and has a **campsite** where you can use the hostel's facilities for half the adult rate.

Blaenau Ffestiniog and around

Every approach to **BLAENAU FFESTINIOG** is dramatic, but none more so than the train journey through the Lledr Valley from Betws-y-Coed. Following the twists of the river, the railway passes through broadleaf woods which give way to the smooth, grassy slopes of the Moel Siabod, where the longest rail tunnel in Wales bores through over two miles of slate to suddenly emerge in the town. Blaenau means "head of the valley", in this case the lush Vale of Ffestiniog, a dramatic contrast to the forbidding town, hemmed in by stark slopes strewn with heaps of discarded, splintered slate. When clouds hunker low in this great cwm and rain sheets the grey roofs, grey walls and grey paving slabs, it can be a terrifically gloomy place. Thousands of tons of slate were once hewn from the labyrinth of underground caverns here each year, but these days the town is only kept alive by its extant slate cavern tour, and by tourists who change from the Lledr Valley train line onto the wonderful, narrow-gauge **Ffestiniog Railway** (see p.875), which winds up from Porthmadog.

It is difficult to get a real feeling of what slate means to the town without a visit to the **Llechwedd Slate Caverns** (daily: March–Sept 10am–5.15pm; Oct–Feb 10am–4.15pm; single tour £7.25, both tours £11), on the edge of

The Welsh slate industry

Slate derives its name from the Old French word *esclater*, meaning to split – an apt reflection of its most highly valued quality. The Romans recognized the potential of the substance, roofing the houses of Segontium with it (see p.881), and Edward I used it extensively in his Iron Ring of castles around Snowdonia. It wasn't until around 1780 that Britain's Industrial Revolution kicked in, leading to greater urbanization and boosting the demand for Welsh roofing slates. Cities grew: Hamburg was re-roofed with Welsh slate after its fire of 1842, and it is the same material which still gives that rainy-day sheen to interminable rows of English mill-town houses.

For the 1862 London Exhibition, one skilled craftsman produced a sheet of slate ten feet long, a foot wide and a sixteenth of an inch thick – so thin it could be flexed – firmly establishing Welsh slate as the finest in the world. By 1898, Welsh quarries – largely run, like the coal and steel industries of the south, by the English – were producing half a million tons of dressed slate a year, almost all of it from Snowdonia. At Penrhyn and Dinorwig, mountains were hacked away in terraces, sometimes rising 2000ft above sea level, with the teams of workers negotiating with the foreman for the choicest piece of rock and the selling price for what they produced. They often slept through the week in damp dormitories on the mountain, and tuberculosis was common, exacerbated by the slate dust. At Blaenau Ffestiniog, the seams required mining underground rather than quarrying, but conditions were no better, with miners even having to buy their own candles, the only light they had. In spite of this, thousands left their hillside smallholdings for the burgeoning quarry towns. Few workers were allowed to join Undeb Chwarelwyr Gogledd Cymru (the North Wales Quarrymen's Union), and in 1900 the workers in Lord Penrhyn's quarry at Bethesda went out on strike. They stayed out for three years, but failed to win any concessions. Those who got their jobs back were forced to work for even less money as a recession took hold, and although the two world wars heralded mini-booms as bombed houses were replaced, the industry never recovered its nineteenth-century prosperity, and most quarries and mines closed in the 1950s.

Sadly, what little slate is produced today mostly goes for things besides roofing: floor tiles, road aggregate and an astonishing array of nasty ashtrays and coasters etched with mountainscapes.

town on the road to Betws-y-coed. There are two tours available. On the **Miners' Tramway Tour**, you are plied with facts about slate mining as a small train takes you a third of a mile along one of the oldest levels to the enormous Cathedral Cave and the open-air Chough's Cavern. The awe-inspiring scale of the place justifies the trip, even without the tableaux of Victorian miners at work. On the more dramatic **Deep Mine Tour**, a steeply inclined railway takes you down to a labyrinth of tunnels through which you are guided by an irksome taped spiel of a Victorian miner. The long caverns angling back into the gloom are increasingly impressive, culminating in one filled by a beautiful opalescent pool.

Practicalities

The **train station** on the High Street serves both the Ffestiniog line to Porthmadog and mainline train services from Betws-y-coed, and is a short walk up the main drag from the **tourist office** (April–Oct daily 10am–6pm; ☏01766/830360), opposite the *Queen's Hotel*. **Buses** stop either in the car park around the back or outside *Y Commercial* pub, on High Street. A vast number of Blaenau Ffestiniog's visitors ride the train up from Porthmadog, visit a slate mine and leave, and this is reflected in the limited range of **accommodation**. But try the excellent, welcoming cheapie *Afallon*, Manod Road (☏01766/830468; ❶), almost a mile south of the tourist office, or, in town itself, the *Queen's Hotel*, 1 High St (☏01766/830055; ❸). A mile or so south on the A470 is *Cae Du*, Manod Road (☏01766/830847; ❷), in a seventeenth-century farmhouse.

Good **food** isn't especially abundant. *Caffi Glen*, south of the tourist office at 36 High St, does decent all-day breakfasts and snacks, but for something more substantial you're limited to the moderate, broad-ranging menu at *Myfanwys*, 4 Market Place (☏01766/830059), or a bar meal at the *Queen's Hotel*. Most locals head for the *Grapes* (☏01766/590208) at Maentwrog, four miles south down the A496, where there's the moderately priced and gamey *Flambard's* restaurant, although the place is also lauded for its gargantuan and inexpensive bar meals.

A walk from Blaenau Ffestiniog

One of the most scenic, and easiest, walks around Blaenau Ffestiniog leads down into the **Vale of Ffestiniog** (4–5 miles; descent only; 2–3hr) following the Ffestiniog Railway past its 360° loop, through sessile oak woods and past several cascades all the way to Tan-y-bwlch. From here, you can return to Blaenau Ffestiniog, or continue on to Porthmadog by train; check the times at the station and buy your ticket to ensure a place on the return train.

The walk can be done from Blaenau Ffestiniog, but it involves a fairly dull first mile easily avoided by catching the railway or driving to the reservoir at **Tanygrisiau**. From the station, turn right past the Tanygrisiau information centre then take the second left, not the road beside the reservoir but the next one, following the footpath signs. Cross the train line, then pass a car park on your left before turning left down a track and skirting behind the powerhouse. The path then sticks closely to the train line, occasionally crossing it. Even when there are several paths you can't go far wrong if you keep the train lines in sight. *The Grapes* pub at Maentwrog, half a mile beyond Tan-y-bwlch, is a great place to while away the time until the next train – or the one after that.

△ The Ffestiniog railway

The Llŷn

The Llŷn takes its name from an Irish word for peninsula – aptly so, for this most westerly part of North Wales, which, until the fifth century, had a significant Irish population. The cliff- and cove-lined finger of land juts out south and west, separating Cardigan and Caernarfon bays, its hills tapering away along the ancient route to Aberdaron, where pilgrims sailed for Ynys Enlli (Bardsey Island). Today, it's the beaches that lure people to the south coast family resorts of **Cricieth**, **Pwllheli** and **Abersoch**, and unless you want to rent windsurfers or canoes, it's preferable to press on along the narrow roads that dawdle down towards Aberdaron. Not even Snowdonia can match the remoteness of the tip of the Llŷn, and nowhere in Wales is more staunchly Welsh: road signs are still bilingual but the English is frequently obliterated; Stryd Fawr is used instead of High Street, and in most local shops you'll only hear Welsh spoken.

The Llŷn is reached through one of the two gateway towns, Porthmadog and Caernarfon, linked by the A487, an effective boundary between Snowdonia proper and the peninsula's gentler contours. **Porthmadog**, nestling into the crook of the elbow where the Cambrian coast takes a sharp left turn, is of interest for its proximity to the private "dream village" of **Portmeirion**, reached on Wales's finest narrow-gauge train line, the **Ffestiniog Railway**. The Llŷn's northern coast comes to an abrupt end at the mouth of the Menai Strait, guarded by the magnificent fortress which forms the centrepiece of **Caernarfon**, a good base for both the Llŷn and central Snowdonia.

Porthmadog and around

Located right at the point where the Llŷn peninsula turns sharply south down the Cambrian coast, **PORTHMADOG** was once the busiest slate port in North Wales. Nowadays, it's a pleasant enough town to spend a night or two, although it sadly makes little of its situation on the north bank of the vast, mountain-backed estuary. Two things it does make a fuss about are the Italianate folly of Portmeirion, two miles east of town, and the Ffestiniog Railway that originally carried slate down from Blaenau Ffestiniog through verdant mountain scenery. Porthmadog would never have existed at all without the entrepreneurial ventures of a Lincolnshire MP named William Alexander Madocks, who named the town after both himself and the Welsh prince Madog, who some say sailed from the nearby Ynys Fadog (Madog's Island) to North America in 1170. Between 1808 and 1812, Madocks fought tides and currents to build the mile-long embankment of The Cob, southeast of present-day Porthmadog, enclosing 7000 acres of the estuary. A wharf was built and, with the completion of the Blaenau Ffestiniog Railway in 1836, the town spread along a waterfront thick with orderly heaps of slate and the masts of merchant ships.

Without a doubt, the **Ffestiniog Railway** (Easter–Oct 4–10 trains daily; Nov–Easter mainly weekends; return to Blaenau Ffestiniog £13.80, to Tan-y-Bwlch £8.40; ☎01766/512340, ⓦwww.festrail.co.uk) ranks as Wales' finest narrow-gauge rail line, twisting and looping up 650ft from the wharf at Porthmadog to the slate mines at Blaenau Ffestiniog, thirteen miles away. When the line opened in 1836, it carried slate from the mines down to the port with the help of gravity, horses riding with the goods then hauling the empty carriages back up again. Steam had to be introduced to cope with the 100,000 tons of slate a year that Blaenau Ffestiniog was churning out by the late nineteenth century, but the slate roofing market collapsed between the wars and the line was abandoned in 1946. Most of the tracks and sleepers had disappeared by 1954, when a bunch of dedicated volunteers began reconstruction, only completing the entire route in 1982. Leaving Porthmadog, trains cross The Cob and then stop at **Minffordd**, a mile from Portmeirion and a convenient place to change onto the mainline railway. Two stops later is Tan-y-Bwlch, from where it's a short stroll to *The Grapes* pub at Maentwrog and the start of the Vale of Ffestiniog walk (see box p.873).

Practicalities

Cambrian coast trains pull into Porthmadog mainline **train station** at the north end of the High Street; the **Ffestiniog station** is located down by the harbour, about half a mile to the south. In between the two, National Express **coaches** stop on Avenue Road outside the *Royal Sportsman*; local **bus** servic-es stop outside the *Australia Inn*, on High Street. The helpful **tourist office**, adjoining the community centre on the High Street (Easter–Oct daily 10am–6pm; Nov–Easter Mon & Wed–Sun 10am–5pm; ☎01766/512981), is over the bridge from the Ffestiniog Railway station.

While limited budgets are well catered for, there's not much really decent **accommodation**, unless you're prepared to splash out for a night at the swanky *Portmeirion Hotel* in Portmeirion (see below). The *Royal Sportsman* pub, 131 High St (☎01766/512015, ⓦwww.royalsportsman.co.uk; ❸), is a safe town-centre bet. *Skellerns*, 35 Madog St, near the Ffestiniog Railway station (☎01766/512843; ❶), is a good budget place. *Eric's Bunkhouse*, at Prenteg (☎01766/512199), two miles north of Porthmadog on the A498 to Beddgelert, opposite *Eric Jones' Café*, has acceptable dorms for around £4 a night. At the top of High Street, Bank Place forks left, becoming Borth Road, on the way out to numerous family-oriented **campsites** at Black Rock and Morfa Bychan. Along this way, about fifteen minutes' walk from town, you'll come to the pleasant enough *Tyddyn Llwyn* site (☎01766/512205).

For **food** in Porthmadog, there's *Yr Hen Fecus*, Lombard Street (☎01766/514625), an unpretentious restaurant with some good veggie options, or the seafood specialities of the excellent *Harbour Restaurant*, High Street (☎01766/512471; winter Thurs–Sat only), almost opposite the tourist office. For bar meals, try *The Ship*, a popular pub on Lombard Street, noted for its ori-ental beer and its food – predominantly Thai and Malaysian, with some vege-tarian options. If you've got transport or want to walk up an appetite, there's fantastic pub food to be had in nearby Tremadog, less than a mile north, at either the *Union Inn* or the *Golden Fleece*, both on the main square.

Portmeirion

The area's main lure is the unique, Italianate private village of **PORTMEIRI-ON** (daily 9.30am–5.30pm; £5), set on a small rocky peninsula in Tremadog Bay, three miles east near Minffordd. Both the mainline and Ffestiniog trains, as well as buses #1 and #2, stop in Minffordd, from where it's a 25-minute walk to Portmeirion. Perhaps best known as "The Village" in the 1960s' cult British TV series *The Prisoner*, Portmeirion was the brainchild of eccentric architect Clough Williams-Ellis, and his dream to build an ideal village which enhances rather than blends in with the surroundings, using a "gay, light-opera sort of approach". The result is certainly theatrical: a stage set with a lucky dip of buildings arranged to distort perspectives and reveal tantalizing glimpses of the seascape behind.

In the 1920s, Williams-Ellis bought the site and turned an existing house into a hotel, the income from this providing funds for his "Home for Fallen Buildings". Endangered buildings from all over Britain and abroad were broken down, transported and rebuilt, every conceivable style being plundered: a Neoclassical colonnade from Bristol, Siamese figures, a Jacobean town hall, and the Italianate touches – a campanile and a pantheon. Williams-Ellis designed his village around a Mediterranean piazza, piecing together a scaled-down nest of loggias, grand porticoes and tiny terracotta-roofed houses and painting them in pastels: turquoise, ochre and buff yellows. Continually surprising, with hidden entrances and cherubs popping out of crevices, the ensemble is eclectic yet never quite inappropriate. A recent addition to the family is the Victorian folly of Castell Deudraeth, opened with a canny eye on the conference trade, but worth a look for other visitors too.

Portmeirion is in need of a lick of paint here and there, but even so, more than three thousand visitors a day come to ogle in summer, when it can be a delight; there are fewer in winter, when it seems just bizarre. In the evening, when the village is closed to the public, patrons at the opulent, waterside *Portmeirion Hotel* (T01766/770000, W www.portmeirion-village.com;) get to see the place at its best – peaceful, even ghostly. Other than walking in the delightful grounds, there's little to actually do, except for viewing a film on the town, popping into the shops selling china and *Prisoner* memorabilia, and eating.

Cricieth and around

When sea-bathing became the Victorian fashion, English families descended on the sweeping sand and shingle beach at **CRICIETH** (sometimes Criccieth), five miles west of Porthmadog, a quiet, amiable resort which curiously abounds with good places to stay and great restaurants, making it a good touring base for the peninsula and Porthmadog. There isn't much here, however, other than the battle-worn remains of **Cricieth Castle** (daily: June–Sept 10am–6pm; April & May 10am–5pm; all other times free access; £2.50; CADW), dominating the coastline with its twin-towered gatehouse. Started by Llywelyn ap Iorwerth in 1230, it was strengthened by Edward I around 1283, and razed by Owain Glyndŵr in 1404, leaving little besides a plan of broken walls. It's a great spot to sit and look over Cardigan Bay to Harlech, but leave time for the ticket office, where there's a workaday exhibition on Welsh castles and a wonderful animated cartoon based on the twelfth-century Cambrian travels of Giraldus Cambrensis as he gathered support for the Third Crusade.

Buses and **trains** along the Cambrian coastline stop a couple of hundred yards west of Y Maes, the open square at the centre of Cricieth. **Accommodation** is plentiful, with a good cheap seafront option being *Awel Môr*, 29 Marine Terrace (T01766/522086;). The *Moelwyn*, 27–29 Mona Terrace (T01766/522500;) is a smarter choice but with similarly great sea views. More luxurious places are further afield: *Mynydd Ednyfed*, Caernarfon Road (T01766/523269;), is a classy country hotel a mile north on the B4411, while *Bron Eifion* (T01766/522385, W www.broneifion.co.uk;) is a beautiful Victorian country house hotel set in its own grounds a mile west of town. You'll find the **campsite**, *Mynydd Du*, a mile towards Porthmadog on the A497 (T01766/522533; April–Oct).

For such a small town, good **restaurants** are surprisingly abundant in Cricieth, and offer the best range of eating on the peninsula. The two plusher hotels listed above both serve innovative and moderately priced meals. *Tir-a-Môr*, 1–3 Mona Terrace (T01766/523084; closed Sun), isn't strictly Italian, but offers a large range of expensive Italian-influenced dishes, with definite Welsh overtones, in airy surroundings. *Moelwyn* (see above) has a superb sea-facing restaurant; and the *Prince of Wales*, Stryd Fawr, offers a great **pub** atmosphere and decent bar meals.

Llanystumdwy

A mile west of Cricieth, the village of **LLANYSTUMDWY** celebrates its most famous son, the Welsh patriot, social reformer and British prime minister David Lloyd George. He grew up in Highgate House, now part of the **Lloyd George Museum** (July–Sept daily 10.30am–5pm; June Mon–Sat 10.30am–5pm; Easter–May & Oct Mon–Fri 10.30am–4.30pm; £3.50), comprising a fairly dull collection of gifts, awards and caskets honouring the statesman, displays full of anecdotes and little-known facts, and a couple of short films giving a broad sweep of his life. Lloyd George is buried under a memorial by the River Dwyfor – a boulder and two simple plaques by Portmeirion designer Clough Williams-Ellis. **Bus** #3 from Porthmadog and Cricieth passes through the village on its way to Pwllheli.

Pwllheli

PWLLHELI (pronounced "poolth-heli") is the market town for the peninsula, a role it has maintained since 1355 when it gained its charter, though there's little sign of its history nowadays. The overall tenor is one of low-brow fun-seeking, as holidaymakers flood in from the nearby holiday camp. Pwllheli's one defining feature is its Welshness. Even in the height of summer, you'll hear far more Welsh spoken here than English.

Pwllheli is hard to avoid – it's the terminus for National Express **coaches**, which stop on Y Maes, the main square, and is also the final stop for Cambrian coast **trains** – but you should push on if possible. The **tourist office** is bang opposite the station on Sgwar yr Orsaf (daily: April–Oct 10am–6pm; Nov–March Fri–Wed 10am–4.30pm; ℡01758/613000). During the summer you can rent **mountain bikes** at Llŷn Cycle Hire, 2 Ala Road (£10 per day; ℡01758/612414). If you decide to **stay**, try *Bank Place* on Stryd Fawr (℡01758/612103; ❶) or, four hundred yards away, *Llys Gwyrfai*, 14 West End Parade (℡01758/614877; ❶), a comfortable guesthouse with sea views and home-cooked meals.

Abersoch

After the distinctly Welsh feel of Pwllheli, **ABERSOCH**, seven miles south-west along the coast, comes as a surprise. This former fishing village pitched in the middle of two golden bays has, over the last century, become a thoroughly anglicized resort, with a distinctly haughty opinion of itself. Such high self-esteem isn't really justified, but at high tide the harbour is attractive, and the long swathe of the beach-hut-backed Town Beach is a fine spot, even if it is barely visible under towels at busy times. A short walk along the beach shakes off most of the crowds, but a better bet is to make for three-mile-long **Porth Neigwl** (Hell's Mouth), two miles to the southwest, which ranks as one of the country's best **surf beaches**; you'll need your own gear, and beware of the undertow if you are swimming. You can **rent windsurfers**, surfboards and wetsuits from Abersoch Watersports, Lôn Pont Morgan (℡01758/712483), by the harbour. If you need instruction, check out the West Coast Surf Shop on Lôn Pen Cei.

Buses from Pwllheli make a loop through the middle of Abersoch, stopping by the **tourist office**, Lôn Pen Cei (Easter to mid-Sept daily 10am–5pm; ☎01758/712929). For **accommodation**, try the *Trewen*, Lôn Hawen, just off Lôn Sarn Bach (☎01758/712755; ❶). Two good places on Lôn Sarn Bach itself are *Angorfa Guest House* (☎01758/712967; ❷; Jan–Nov), and the superb *Neigwl Hotel* (☎01758/712363; Ⓦwww.neigwl.com; ❸). There are some decent **places to eat**: *Mañana*, on Lôn Pen Cai, serves Mexican and Italian food; *Champers* bistro in the *Vaynol Arms*, on Lôn Sarn Bach is fun and friendly; and the *Ship*, out of town in Llanbedrog, near Pwllheli, is excellent.

Aberdaron and Bardsey Island

The small, lime-washed fishing village of **ABERDARON** backs a pebble beach two miles short of the tip of the Llŷn. For a thousand years, from the sixth century onwards, it was the last stop for pilgrims to **Bardsey Island**, or Ynys Enlli (the Island of the Currents), just offshore; three visits were proclaimed equivalent to one pilgrimage to Rome. Many pilgrims came to die there, earning the place its epithet "The Isle of Twenty Thousand Saints". Bardsey is heart-stoppingly beautiful and well worth a visit – there are self-catering cottages available on the island, or you could just go for a day-trip. For details of both, contact the Bardsey Island Trust (☎01758/730740, Ⓦwww.bardsey-island.co.uk). In olden days, the final gathering place before the treacherous crossing was the fourteenth-century Y Gegin Fawr (Great Kitchen), a stone building which still operates as a **café** in the middle of Aberdaron. Today, pilgrims are more likely to be attracted by poetry, as until 1978, **R.S. Thomas** (1913–2000) was the minister at Aberdaron's seafront church of St Hywyn.

Without your own transport, the only way to get to Aberdaron is to catch bus #17 from Pwllheli (Mon–Sat). **Accommodation** is fairly limited; the least expensive option is *Brynmor* (☎01758/760344; ❶), overlooking the bay, just up the road to Porth Oer, the "whistling sands". The *Tŷ Newydd* hotel (☎01758/760207; ❸) is a good bet too; make time for a pint or meal on their beach terrace as the sun sets. The best and quietest **campsite** around is *Mur Melyn* (no phone) just over a mile out from Aberdaron, mid-way to Porth Oer; take the B4413 west, fork right, then turn left at Pen-y-Bont house.

Caernarfon

It was in **CAERNARFON**, in 1969, that Charles, the current heir to the throne, was invested as Prince of Wales, a ceremony which re-affirmed English sovereignty over Wales in this, one of the most nationalist of Welsh-speaking regions. Since 1282, when the English defeated Llywelyn ap Gruffydd, the last Welsh Prince of Wales, the title has been bestowed on heirs to the English (and then British) throne, but it wasn't until 1911 that the machinations of David Lloyd George – MP for Caernarfon and future prime minister – brought a theatrical investiture ceremony to the centre of his constituency: an odd move for a proto-nationalist considering the symbolic implications. Caernarfon's vastly imposing **castle** and near-complete rectangle of town walls make it an appealing place, but apart from the castle, there isn't too much to see: you can only walk a small section of the wall and the rest of the town has been ripped through by a main road and boxed in by modern buildings. That said, it's a spirited and lively town, is well situated on the Menai Strait, between the mainland and Anglesey, and has good bus connections to Llanberis and Snowdonia.

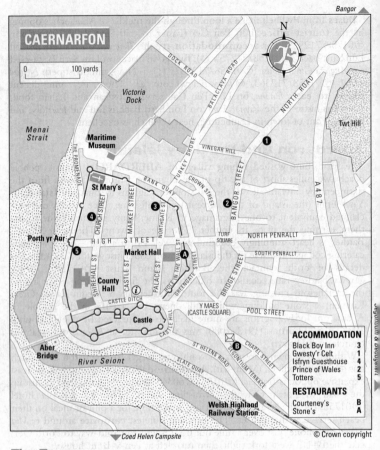

CAERNARFON

0   100 yards

Bangor

N

Victoria
Dock

Menai
Strait

Twt Hill

Maritime
Museum

VINEGAR HILL

BALACLAVA ROAD

NORTH ROAD

DOCK ROAD

TURKEY SHORE

BANGOR STREET

A 487

St Mary's

BANK QUAY

CROWN STREET

❶

CHURCH STREET

MARKET STREET

NORTHGATE ST

❸

❷

TURF
SQUARE

NORTH PENRALLT

SOUTH PENRALLT

❹

Porth yr Aur

HIGH STREET

❺

Market Hall

SHIREHALL ST

CASTLE ST

PALACE ST

GREENGATE STREET

HOLE IN THE WALL ST

Ⓐ

County
Hall

ⓘ

CASTLE DITCH

BRIDGE STREET

Y MAES
(CASTLE SQUARE)

POOL STREET

Castle

CASTLE HILL

Ⓑ

CHAPEL STREET

Aber
Bridge

River Seiont

ST HELENS ROAD

SLATE QUAY

SEGONTIUM TERRACE

Welsh Highland
Railway Station

Coed Helen Campsite

© Crown copyright

Bangor & Beaumaris

ACCOMMODATION	
Black Boy Inn	3
Gwesty'r Celt	1
Isfryn Guesthouse	4
Prince of Wales	2
Totters	5
RESTAURANTS	
Courteney's	B
Stone's	A

The Town

In 1283, Edward I started work on **Caernarfon Castle** (June–Sept daily
9.30am–6pm; April–May & Oct daily 9.30am–5pm; Nov–March Mon–Sat
9.30am–4pm, Sun 11am–4pm; £4.20; CADW), the strongest link in his Iron
Ring (see box on p.888), a decisive hammer-blow to any Welsh aspirations to
autonomy and the ultimate symbol of Anglo-Norman military might. With the
Welsh already smarting from the loss of their prince, Edward is said to have
promised "a prince born in Wales who could speak never a word of English",
a vow he fulfilled to the letter by moving his pregnant wife to Caernarfon. The
story is almost certainly apocryphal. Instead, Edward attempted to appease the
Welsh by paying tribute to aspects of local legend. The Welsh had long associated their town with the eastern capital of the Roman Empire: Caernarfon's
old name, Caer Cystennin, was also the name used for Constantinople, and
Constantine himself was believed to have been born at Segontium (see opposite). Edward's architect, James of St George, exploited this connection in the
distinctive limestone and sandstone banding and the polygonal towers, both
reminiscent of the Theodosian walls in present-day Istanbul.

In military terms, the castle is supreme. It was taken once, before building was
complete, but then withstood two sieges by Owain Glyndŵr with a garrison

of only 28 men-at-arms. Entering through the **King's Gate**, the castle's strength is immediately apparent. Embrasures and murder holes between the octagonal towers face in on no fewer than five gates and six portcullises, and that's once you have crossed the moat, now bridged by an incongruous modern structure. Inside, the huge lawn gives a misleading impression since both the wall dividing the two original wards and all the buildings which filled them crumbled away long ago. The towers are in a much better state, and linked by an exhausting honeycomb of wall-walks and tunnels. The tallest and most striking is the **King's Tower**, at the western end, whose three slender turrets are adorned with eagle sculptures and give the best views of the town. To the south, the Queen's Tower is entirely taken up by the numbingly thorough **Museum of the Royal Welch Fusiliers**, while the Northeast Tower houses the **Prince of Wales Exhibition**, just outside which is the Dinorwig slate dais used for Charles' investiture.

A ten-minute walk along the A4085 Beddgelert road brings you to the western end of the Roman road from Chester, at **Segontium Roman Fort** (Mon–Sat 10am–5pm, Sun 2–5pm; Nov–March closes 4pm; free). The Romans occupied this five-acre site for three centuries from around 78 AD, though most of the remains are from the final rebuilding after 364. The ground plan is seldom more than shin-high and somewhat baffling, making the museum and displays in the ticket office pretty much essential.

Wales's newest narrow-gauge railway also starts in Caernarfon, just near the harbour on St Helen's Road. Ultimately, the **Welsh Highland Railway** (WHR, or Rheilffordd Eryri) will run all the way to Porthmadog via Beddgelert, a route of 25 miles. It currently goes as far as Waunfawr (£7.80 return), but is hoped to reach the village of Rhyd-Ddu, starting point for southerly ascents of Snowdon, by late 2002. That said, timescales are constantly slipping as the project remains mired in much controversy.

Practicalities

With no mainline train station, the hub of Caernarfon's public transport system is Y Maes (Castle Square), right under the walls of the castle, where **buses** stop. The **tourist office** is in Oriel Pendeitsh on Castle Street (Easter–Oct daily 10am–6pm; Nov–Easter daily except Wed 10am–4.30pm; ☎01286/ 672232), just a few steps away.

There are a number of **accommodation** options close to the centre: try *Isfryn Guesthouse*, 11 Church St (☎01286/675628; ❶), or the *Prince of Wales* pub on Bangor Street (☎01286/673367; ❷). The characterful *Black Boy Inn*, Northgate Street (☎01286/673023; ❷), is one of the town's oldest buildings, but for more upmarket accommodation, your best bet is the *Gwesty'r Celt* hotel, Bangor Street (☎01286/674477, Ⓦwww.celtic-royal.co.uk; ❺), which comes complete with an indoor pool and smart restaurant. Away from town are some excellent country houses, including *Pengwern Farm* in Saron, three miles southwest of Caernarfon (☎01286/831500; ❷; Feb–Nov), which has a lovely rural setting, and serves inexpensive, farm-fresh evening meals. Take the A487 south across the river then turn right towards Saron; Pengwern is just over two miles down on the right. *Totters*, at Plas Porth Yr Aur, 2 High St (☎01286/672963; ❶), is a superb and very friendly independent **hostel**. The *Coed Helen* **campsite** (☎01286/676770; March–Oct) sits right on the Seiont River, just across the footbridge from the base of the castle.

Caernarfon boasts a number of low-key and likeable **restaurants**: you can sample the eclectic menu at *Courteney's*, 9 Segontium Terrace (closed Sun, Mon & Tues lunch), or the bistro-style fare at *Stone's*, 4 Hole in the Wall St (closed

Sun). The cheapest option is the excellent **bar meals** at the aforementioned *Black Boy Inn*. For **nightlife**, you might catch a Welsh-language band at *Tafarn Yr Albert*, 11 Segontium Terrace, on Saturday nights, or live music at the *Prince of Wales*, Bangor Street. Thursday's *Caernarfon Chronicle* newspaper has gig information for both Bangor and Caernarfon.

The island of Anglesey

Across the Menai Strait from Caernarfon, **Anglesey** (Ynys Môn) welcomes visitors to "Mam Cymru", the Mother of Wales, attesting to the island's former importance as the national breadbasket. In the twelfth century Giraldus Cambrensis noted that "when crops have failed in other regions, this island, from its soil and its abundant produce, has been able to supply all Wales", and while feeding their less productive kin in Snowdonia is no longer a priority, the land remains predominantly pastoral, with small fields, stone walls and white houses reminiscent of parts of Ireland or England. Linguistically and politically, though, Anglesey is intensely Welsh, with seventy percent of the islanders being first-language Welsh-speakers. The island was the crucible of pre-Roman druidic activity in Britain, and there are still numerous Neolithic remains at which to soak up the atmosphere of a pagan past. Especially since the recent advent of the A55 main road, many people charge straight through to **Holyhead** and the Irish ferries, missing out on the many charms of Anglesey. There's the ancient town of **Beaumaris**, with its fine castle, the Whistler mural at **Plas Newydd** and some superb coastal scenery: a necklace of fine sandy coves and rocky headlands that's a match for anywhere in the country.

Beaumaris

The original inhabitants of **BEAUMARIS** (Biwmares) were evicted by Edward I to make way for the construction of his new castle and bastide town (see p.888), dubbed "beautiful marsh" in an attempt to attract English settlers. Today the place can still seem like the small English outpost Edward intended, with its elegant Georgian terrace along the front (designed by Joseph Hansom, of cab fame) and more plummy English accents than you'll have heard for a while. Many of their owners belong with the flotilla of yachts, an echo of the port's fleet of merchant ships, which disappeared with the completion of bridges to the mainland and subsequent growth of Holyhead. While Beaumaris repays an afternoon mooching around and enjoying the views across the Strait, it also boasts more sights than the rest of the island put together, inevitably drawing the crowds in summer.

Beaumaris Castle (June–Sept daily 9.30am–6pm; April, May & Oct daily 9.30am–5pm; Nov–March Mon–Sat 9.30am–4pm, Sun 11am–4pm; £2.50; CADW) might never have been built had Madog ap Llywelyn not captured Caernarfon in 1294. When asked to build the new castle, James of St George abandoned the Caernarfon design in favour of a concentric plan, developing it into a highly evolved symmetrical octagon. Sited on flat land at the edge of town, the castle is denied the domineering majesty of Caernarfon or Harlech, its low outer walls appearing almost welcoming until you begin to appreciate the concentric layout of the defences protected by massive towers, a moat linked to the sea and the Arab-influenced staggered entries through the two gatehouses. Despite more than thirty years' work, the project was never quite finished, leaving most of the inner ward empty and the corbels and fireplaces built into the walls unused. You can explore the internal passages in the walls but the low-parapet wall-walk, from where you get the best idea of the castle's defensive capability, remains off limits. Impressive as they are, none of these defences was able to prevent siege by Owain Glyndŵr, who held the castle for two years from 1403, although they did withhold a Parliamentarian siege during the Civil War.

Almost opposite the castle stands the Jacobean **Beaumaris Courthouse** (Easter & June–Sept daily 11am–4.30pm, May Sat & Sun same times; £1.50; joint ticket with gaol £3), built in 1614 and the oldest active court in Britain. It is now used only for the twice-monthly Magistrates Court, but until 1971, when they were moved to Caernarfon, the quarterly Assize Courts were held here. These were traditionally held in English, giving the jury little chance to follow the proceedings and Welsh-speaking defendants no defence against prosecutors renowned for slapping heavy penalties on minor offences. On session days you can watch the trials, but won't be able to take the recorded tour or inspect *The Lawsuit*, a plaque in the magistrates' room depicting two farmers pulling the horns and tail of a cow while a lawyer milks it.

Many citizens were transported from the courthouse to the colonies for their misdemeanours; others only made it a couple of blocks to **Beaumaris Gaol**, Steeple Lane (Easter & June–Sept daily 11am–5pm; £2.50; joint ticket with courthouse £3) which, when it opened in 1829, was considered a model prison, with running water and toilets in each cell, an infirmary and, eventually, heating. Women prisoners did the cooking and were allowed to rock their babies' cradles in the nursery above by means of a pulley system. Advanced perhaps, but nonetheless a gloomy place: witness the windowless punishment cell, the yard for stone-breaking and the treadmill water pump operated by the prisoners. The least fortunate inmates were publicly hanged, the fate of a certain Richard Rowlands, whose disembodied voice leads the recorded tour of the building and various displays on prison life.

After all this gloom, a good way to lift the spirits is aboard one of the **pleasure cruises** (℡01248/810251 or 810379) on the *Island Princess* out to (but not landing on) Puffin Island. The booking kiosk is at the foot of the pier.

Practicalities

With no trains, long-distance coaches or tourist office, Beaumaris seems poorly served, but it does have a regular **bus** service to Bangor (#53 & #57; infrequent on Sun). The best of the **hotels** is the ancient and luxurious *Ye Olde Bull's Head Inn*, 18 Castle St (℡01248/810329, ⓦwww.bullsheadinn.co.uk; ❺), used as General Mytton's headquarters during the Civil War. The *Bishopsgate Hotel*, 54 Castle St (℡01248/810302; ❹; mid-Feb to Dec), is only a stone's throw away and almost of the same standard. Cheaper **B&Bs** can be found in the summer, though none are very special – you'd be better off at *Plas Cichle* (℡01248/810488; ❷), an elegant farmhouse a couple of miles north near Llanfaes, or back in the town of Menai Bridge at the superb *Bwthyn*, 5 Brynafon (℡01248/713119; ❶). *Kingsbridge* is the nearest **campsite**, two miles north in Llanfaes (℡01248/490636). There are plenty of daytime cafés serving snacks, and more substantial **restaurants** are also in good supply, the best being *Ye Olde Bull's Head Inn* and the moderately priced *Bishopsgate House Hotel*, both of which also do great bar meals. For a great pint and good food, there's the wonderfully cosy *Sailor's Return* pub on Church Street. *Y Gragen Cocos/The Cockleshell*, 13 Castle St (℡01248/810623), offers good seafood specialities.

Llanfair PG and around

In the 1880s a local tailor invented the longest place name in Britain in a successful attempt to draw tourists. However, it is an utter disappointment to arrive at Llanfairpwllgwyngyllgogerychwyrndrobwllllandysiliogogogoch, which translates as "St Mary's Church in the hollow of white hazel near a rapid whirlpool and the Church of St Tysilio near the red cave" – commonly known as **LLANFAIR PG** – to find only a railway station, a vast car park, a tacky wool shop and a **tourist office** (April–Oct Mon–Sat 9.30am–5.30pm, Sun 10am–5pm; Nov–March Mon–Sat 9.30am–5pm, Sun 10am–5pm; ☎01248/713177), the only one worth its salt on the island.

The marquises of Anglesey still live at **Plas Newydd** (April–Oct Mon–Wed, Sat & Sun: house noon–5pm, garden 11am–5.30pm; house & garden £4.50, garden only £2.50; NT), a mile and a half south of Llanfair PG, a modest three-storey mansion with incongruous Tudor caps on slender octagonal turrets. Inside, architect James Wyatt was given free stylistic rein, producing a Gothic music room followed by a Neoclassical staircase hall with a cantilevered staircase and deceptively solid-looking Doric columns – actually just painted wood. Endure the slog through corridors of oils and period rooms to the highlight, a 58-foot-long wall consumed by a trompe l'oeil painting by **Rex Whistler**, who spent a couple of years here in the 1930s. Walking along his imaginary seascape, your position appears to shift by over a mile as the mountains of Snowdonia and a whimsical composite of elements, culled from Italy as well as Britain, change perspective. Portmeirion (see p.876) is there, as are the Round Tower from Windsor Castle and the steeple from St Martin-in-the-Fields in London. Whistler himself appears as a gondolier, and again as a gardener in one of the two right-angled panels at either end, which appear to extend the room further. The prize exhibit in the **Cavalry Museum**, a few rooms further on, is the world's first articulated leg, all wood, leather and springs, designed for the first marquis, who lost his leg at Waterloo.

Holyhead and around

Holy Island (Ynys Gybi) is blessed with Anglesey's best scenery and cursed with its most unattractive town. The spectacular sea cliffs around South Stack, and the Stone Age and Roman remains on Holyhead Mountain are just a couple of miles from workaday Holyhead (pronounced as "holly-head"), whose ferry routes to Ireland and good transport links mean you'll probably find your way there at some stage.

Ferries and catamarans to Dublin

Ferries and catamarans run regularly from Holyhead to both **Dun Laoghaire** (pronounced "dun-leery"), six miles south of Dublin, and to **Dublin Port** itself. Up-to-date **catamaran** sailing times can be checked with any travel agent, but at the time of writing Stena Line (☎0870/570 7070, ⓦwww.stenaline.co.uk) leave for Dun Laoghaire at 8.55am, 1.45pm and 6.30pm, with additional 4am sailings on most Saturdays. Irish Ferries (☎0870/517 1717, ⓦwww.irishferries.ie) have catamarans sailing for Dublin Port at 2.30am, 8.30am, 3.15pm and 8.45pm. All take under two hours; high-season passenger fares are around £70 return. Catamarans are £10 more expensive than the **ferries** to Dublin Port, which take 3hr 45min, run by Stena Line (3am & 3.15pm) and Irish Ferries (3.45am & 3.45pm, subject to change). Travelling by day is more convenient, shorter and twice as expensive as night-time crossings. Irish Ferries generally offer the cheaper **day-trips** to Dublin, starting from as little as £10, though this does entail getting the 3.45am boat.

The local council's valiant attempts to brighten up **HOLYHEAD** (Caergybi) somehow make this town of dilapidated shopfronts and high unemployment even more depressing. In 1727, Swift found it "scurvy, ill provided and comfortless", and little seems to have changed. Fortunately, train and ferry timings are reasonably well integrated, so you shouldn't need to spend much time here. If you do have an hour to kill, worth seeing is the **Holyhead Maritime Museum** (Easter–Oct Tues–Sun 1–5pm; £2), down on the Newry Beach seashore in the old lifeboat station. From the combined **train station**, **bus station** and **ferry terminal**, a pedestrian bridge over London Road, past the A5, leads into the town centre. The **tourist office** (daily 10am–6pm; ☎01407/762622) is in the ferry terminal.

Shun the bunch of poor **B&Bs** along the A5 into the town in favour of those around Walthew Avenue, most easily reached by turning left just before the tourist office onto the beachfront Prince of Wales Road, then left again into Walthew Avenue. *Glan Ifor*, at no. 8 (☎01407/764238; ❶), and *Orotavia*, no. 66 (☎01407/760259; ❶), are both good, as is *Hendre*, Porth-y-Felin, at the top of Walthew Avenue (☎01407/762929; ❷), a former manse where you can get inexpensive evening meals. Fast **food** is the staple diet in Holyhead, but you can still eat well: the budget *Omar Khayyam Tandoori*, 8 Newry St, serves the tastiest curries around, and great daytime **pub** food can be found at *The Seventy-Nine* on Market Street, a good start as well for a pub crawl through the many bars of the town centre. Good bets for a pint include the old-fashioned *George Hotel* on Stanley Street, or the *Britannia* on Thomas Street, where you might also catch a gig.

Holyhead Mountain and South Stack

The northern half of Holy Island is ranged around the skirts of the 700-foot **Holyhead Mountain** (Mynydd Twr), its summit ringed by the seventeen-acre **Caer y Twr** (free access; CADW), one of the largest Iron Age sites in North Wales. The best approach is by car or bus #44 to the car park at **South Stack** (Ynys Lawd), two miles west of Holyhead, from where a path (30min) leads to the top of Holyhead Mountain. Most visitors only walk the few yards to the cliff-top **Ellin's Tower Seabird Centre** (Easter–Sept daily 11am–5pm; free) where, from April until the end of July, binoculars and closed-circuit TV give an unparalleled opportunity to watch up to three thousand birds – razorbills, guillemots and the odd puffin – nesting on the nearby sea cliffs while ravens and peregrines wheel outside the tower's windows. When the birds have gone, rock climbers picking their way up the same cliff face replace them as the main interest. A twisting path leads down from the tower to a suspension bridge over the surging waves, leading over to the now fully automated pepper-pot **lighthouse** (Easter–Sept daily 10.30am–5.30pm; £2). Tickets are issued at the *South Stack Kitchen*, a café-cum-interpretative centre a hundred yards back down the lane. Nearby, nineteen low stone circles make up the **Cytiau'r Gwyddelod** or the "Huts of the Irish", a common name for any ancient settlement – in this case late Neolithic or early Bronze Age.

Bangor

After spending a few days in the North Wales rural hinterland, **BANGOR**, across the bridges from Anglesey, makes a welcome change. It is not big, but as the largest town in Gwynedd and home to Bangor University, it passes in these parts for cosmopolitan. The students decamp for the summer, leaving only a trickle of visitors to replace them. Bangor is a hotbed of passionate Welsh nationalism, hardly surprising in such a staunchly Welsh-speaking area, and it's a dramatic change from the largely English-speaking north-coast resorts.

The **university** takes up much of upper Bangor, straddling the hill that separates the town centre from the Menai Strait. The shape of the college's main building is almost an exact replica of the thirteenth- to fifteenth-century **cathedral** (daily 11am–5pm), which boasts the longest continuous use of any cathedral in Britain, easily predating the town. Pop in if only to see the sixteenth-century wooden **Mostyn Christ**, depicted bound and seated on a rock.

Just over the road, the **Bangor Museum and Art Gallery**, Ffordd Gwynedd (Tues–Fri 12.30–4.30pm, Sat 10.30am–4.30pm; free), offers snippets of local history enlivened by a traditional costume section and an archeology room, containing the most complete Roman sword found in Wales. The art gallery concentrates on predominantly Welsh contemporary works. For a good look down the Menai Strait to Telford's bridge, walk along Garth Road to Bangor's rejuvenated and pristine **Victorian Pier** (50p), which reaches halfway across to Anglesey.

Penrhyn Castle

There can hardly be a more vulgar testament to the Anglo-Welsh landowning gentry's oppression of the rural Welsh than the oddly compelling **Penrhyn Castle** (Mon & Wed–Sun: July & Aug 11am–5pm; April–June, Sept & Oct noon–5pm; castle & grounds £6; grounds only £4; NT), two miles east of Bangor, which overlooks Port Penrhyn from its acres of isolating parkland. Built on the backs of slate miners for the benefit of their hated bosses, this monstrous nineteenth-century neo-Norman fancy, with over three hundred rooms dripping with luxurious fittings, was funded by the quarry's huge profits. The sugar and slate fortune built by anti-abolitionist Richard Pennant, first Baron Penrhyn, provided the means for his self-aggrandizing great-great-nephew George Dawkins to hire architect Thomas Hopper, who spent thirteen years from 1827 encasing the neo-Gothic hall in a Norman fortress complete with monumental five-storey keep.

Sour grapes aside, the decoration is glorious, and fairly true to the Romanesque style, with its deeply cut chevrons, billets and double-cone ornamentation. Hopper even looked to Norman architecture for the design of the furniture, but abandoned historical authenticity when it came to installing the central heating system, which piped hot air through ornamental brass ducts at the cost of twenty tons of coal a month. Everything is on a massive scale. Three-foot-thick oak doors separate the rooms, ebony is used to dramatic effect and a slate bed was built for, but declined by, Queen Victoria when she visited. The family amassed Wales' largest private painting collection, including numerous family likenesses, a Gainsborough landscape, Canaletto's *The Thames at Westminster* and a Rembrandt portrait. Newly opened to the public are the Victorian kitchen and servants' quarters, something of an antidote to the opulence "above stairs".

Gleaming examples of rolling stock from Richard Pennant's slate railway and the country's other private industrial lines are on display in the **Industrial Railway Museum** (same times as castle; entry with castle or grounds ticket), including Lord Penrhyn's luxurious coach, linked to a quarrymen's car. Buses #5, #6 and #7 run frequently from Bangor to the gates, from where it is a mile-long walk to the house.

Practicalities

All trains on the North Coast line stop at Bangor **train station**, on Station Road, at the bottom of Holyhead Road. The **tourist office** is in the Town Hall on Deiniol Road (Easter–Sept daily 10am–6pm; Oct–March Tues–Sat 10am–5pm; ☏01248/352786). Bangor doesn't have a huge choice of places to **stay**, although the *Garden Hotel* (☏01248/362189, ⓦwww.gardenhotelbangor.co.uk; ❹) is handy for the station and is pretty good. Most of the cheaper accommodation is bundled at the northern end of Garth Road, about twenty minutes' walk from the train station: try *Dilfan* (☏01248/353030; ❷). *Eryl Môr*, 2 Upper Garth Rd (☏01248/353789; ❸), is a quiet and comfortable hotel with views over Bangor's pier and the Menai Strait. The university lets out clean, functional rooms on Ffriddoedd Road (☏01248/372104; ❶) from late June to late September and over the Easter vacation. Bangor's YHA **hostel**, Tan-y-Bryn (☏01248/353516, ⓦwww.yha.org.uk; Jan–Nov), is signposted off the A56, ten minutes' walk east of the centre (bus #6 or #7 along Garth Road). The nearest **campsite** is the very laid-back *Treborth Hall Farm* (☏01248/364104), fifteen minutes' walk (or bus #5) from Upper Bangor, on the road out towards the Menai Bridge.

With the possible exception of Llandudno, Bangor offers the widest selection of **eating** possibilities in North Wales. Packed out with students and locals, the *Fat Cat Café Bar*, 161 High St, has a menu ranging from huge burgers to salmon and broccoli pasta quills; another good bet is the classy *Greek Taverna Politis*, 12 Holyhead Rd. *Herbs Cookshop*, 307 High St (☏01248/351249), is a great veggie daytime cafe that is also open for swankier (and meatier) meals on weekend evenings. The expensive restaurant of the *Menai Court Hotel*, Craig-y-Don Road, earns plaudits from foodies for its traditional British and European dishes. If you've tried to learn any of the language you can put it to good use at *Tafarn Y Glôb*, a traditional **pub** on Albert Street, where ordering in Welsh is pretty much a house rule. For "a pint of beer, please" try *un peint o gwrw, os gwelwch chi'n dda* (pronounced "een paint o gooroo, os gweloch un tha"). *Y Castell*, on Glanrafon, is a greate spot opposite the cathedral, is a very popular and studenty pub, while *O'Shea's*, on High Street, is your best bet for local **live music**.

Conwy and around

CONWY, twenty miles east of Bangor, has been much prettified since completion of a bypass tunnel under the Conwy River (Afon Conwy), making it one of the highlights of the north coast. Backed by a forested fold of Snowdonia, the town boasts a fine castle, a nearly complete belt of town walls and a wonderful setting on the Conwy estuary. Nowhere in the core of medieval and Victorian buildings is more than two hundred yards from the irregular triangle of protective masonry formed by the town walls. This makes it wonderfully easy to potter around and though you'll get to see everything you want to in a day, you may well want to stay longer.

Conwy Castle

Conwy Castle (June–Sept daily 9.30am–6pm; April, May & Oct daily 9.30am–5pm; Nov–March Mon–Sat 9.30am–4pm, Sun 11am–4pm; £3.60; CADW), now entered through a separate ticket office and over a modern

The Iron Ring

Dotting the North Wales coast, Edward I's fearsome **Iron Ring** of colossal fortresses, each within a day's march of the next, represents Europe's most ambitious and concentrated medieval building project, designed to prevent the recurrence of two massively expensive military campaigns. After Edward's first successful campaign in 1277, he was able to pin down his adversary, Llywelyn ap Gruffydd ("the Last") in Snowdonia and on Anglesey. In his first attempt at subjugation, this gave Edward room and time enough to build the now largely ruined castles at **Flint**, **Rhuddlan**, **Builth Wells** and **Aberystwyth**, as well as to commandeer and upgrade Welsh castles. Llywelyn's second uprising, in 1282, was ultimately unsuccessful, and Edward, determined not to have to fight a third time for the same land, set about extending his ring of fortifications in an immensely costly display of English might. Together with the Treaty of Rhuddlan in 1284, this saw the Welsh resistance effectively crushed. The castles at **Harlech**, **Caernarfon** and **Conwy**, though nearly contemporary, display a unique progression towards the later, highly evolved concentric design of **Beaumaris**. All this second batch, including the town walls of Caernarfon and Conwy, were the work of the master military architect of his age, James of St George d'Espéranche, whose work in Conwy is now recognized with **UNESCO World Heritage Site** status.

Each of the castles was integrated with a **bastide town**, an idea borrowed from Gascony in southwest France, where Edward I was duke – the town and castle mutually reliant on each other for protection and trade. The bastides were always populated with English settlers, the Welsh permitted to enter the town during the day but not to trade and certainly not to carry arms. It wasn't until the eighteenth century that the Welsh would have towns they could truly call their own.

bridge, is the toughest-looking link in Edward I's "Iron Ring" of fortresses. After advancing west of the Conwy River in 1283, Edward decided to maintain a bridgehead by establishing another of his bastide towns (see box). He chose a strategic knoll at the mouth of the river and set James of St George to fashion a castle to fit its contours. With the labour of 1500 men it took only five years.

Richard II stayed at the castle on his return from an ill-timed trip to Ireland in 1399, until lured from safety by Bolingbroke's vassal the Earl of Northumberland. Northumberland swore in the castle's chapel to grant the king safe passage, but Richard was taken and Bolingbroke became Henry IV. Just two years later, on Good Friday, when the fifteen-strong castle guard were at church, two cousins of Owain Glyndŵr took the castle and razed the town for Glyndŵr's cause. The castle then fell into disuse, and was bought in 1627 for £100 by Charles I's Secretary of State, Lord Conway of Ragley, who then had the task of refortifying it for the Civil War. At the restoration of the monarchy in 1665, the castle was stripped of all its iron, wood and lead, and was left substantially as it is today.

Being overlooked by a low hill, the castle appears less easily defended than others along the coast, but James constructed eight massive **towers** in a rectangle around the two wards, the inner one separated from the outer by a **drawbridge** and **portcullis**, and further protected by turrets atop the four eastern towers, now the preserve of crows. Strolling along the wall-top gallery, you can look down onto something unique in the Iron Ring fortresses, a roofless but largely intact interior. The outer ward's 130-foot-long **Great Hall** and the **King's Apartments** are both well preserved, but the only part of the castle to have kept its roof is the **Chapel Tower**, named for the small room built

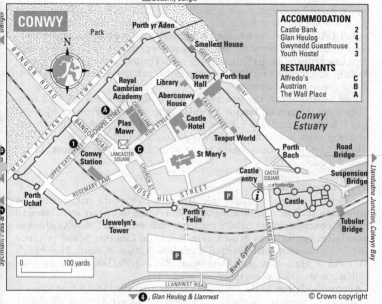

On the map:

CONWY

Butterfly Jungle

Park

Porth yr Aden

Smallest House

Royal Cambrian Academy

Library

Town Hall

Porth Isaf

Aberconwy House

Plas Mawr

Castle Hotel

Conwy Station

Teapot World

St Mary's

Porth Bach

Road Bridge

Castle entry

Suspension Bridge

Porth Uchaf

Llewelyn's Tower

Porth y Felin

Castle

Tubular Bridge

Conwy Estuary

Llandudno Junction, Colwyn Bay

0   100 yards

LLANRWST ROAD

Glan Heulog & Llanrwst

into the wall whose semicircular apse still shows some heavily worn carving. On the floor below, there's a small exhibition on religious life in medieval castles which won't detain you long from exploring the passages.

The rest of the town

Anchored to the castle walls as though a drawbridge, Telford's narrow **suspension bridge** (July & Aug daily 10am–5pm; April–June, Sept & Oct daily except Tues same times; £1; joint ticket with Aberconwy House £2.50; NT) was part of the 1826 road improvement scheme, prompted by the need for better communications to Ireland after the Act of Union, and contemporary with his far greater effort spanning the Menai Strait. Restored to its original state, without tarmac, signs or street lighting, it now operates as a footbridge.

The approach to the modern replacement bridge has created the only breach in the thirty-foot high **town walls**, which branch out from the castle into a three-quarter-mile-long circuit, enclosing Conwy's ancient quarter. Inaccessible from the castle they were designed to protect, the walls are punctuated by 21 evenly spaced horseshoe towers, seven of which can be visited on the **wall walk**, starting from Porth Uchaf on Upper Gate Street and running down to a spur into the estuary. Here, you come down off the walls beside brightly rigged trawlers, mussel boats and the self-proclaimed **smallest house in Britain** (daily: July & Aug 10am–9pm; Easter–June & Sept to mid-Oct 10am–6pm; 50p), only 9ft by 5ft in total. Porth Isaf, the nearby gate in the town walls, leads up Lower High Street to the fourteenth-century timber-and-stone **Aberconwy House**, Castle Street (April–Oct daily except Tues 11am–5pm; £2; joint ticket with suspension bridge £2.50; NT), a former merchant's house, its rooms decked out in styles that recall its past. Continue along the High Street to the Dutch-style **Plas Mawr** at no. 20 (Tues–Sun: June–Aug 9.30am–6pm; April, May & Sept 9.30am–5pm; Oct 9.30am–4pm; £4.10; CADW), a beautifully restored Elizabethan town house, built in 1576 for Robert Wynn, one of the first Welsh people to live in the town. Much of the dressed stonework was replaced during renovations in the 1940s and 1950s, but the interior sports more original features, in particular the friezes and superb moulded plaster ceilings depicting fleurs-de-lis, griffons, owls and rams. The tour concludes with a wonderfully scatological exhibition on sixteenth- and seventeenth-century ideas about disease and cleanliness.

Light relief from all the worthy history is on hand across the road from Aberconwy House, at **Teapot World**, Castle Street (Easter–Oct Mon–Sat 10am–5.30pm, Sun 11am–5.30pm; £1.50), which has a thousand pots, mostly dating from before the 1950s: Wedgwood and majolica to Bauhaus and Clarice Cliff. If you fancy taking to the water, regular **river cruises** operate from the quay.

Practicalities

Llandudno Junction, less than a mile across the river to the east, serves as the main **train station**; only slow, regional services stop in Conwy itself. National Express **coaches** pull up outside the town walls on Town Ditch Road, while local **buses** use the stops in the centre, mostly on Lancaster Square or Castle Street. The **tourist office** (April–Oct daily 9.30am–6.30pm; Nov–March Mon–Sat 9.30am–4pm, Sun 11am–4pm; ☎01492/592248) shares the same building as the castle ticket office.

Accommodation in the centre of town is a bit thin, so booking ahead is advisable in summer. *Gwynedd Guesthouse*, 10 Upper Gate St (☎01492/596537; ❶), is the least expensive central B&B and consequently often full. *Glan Heulog*, Llanrwst Road, on the outskirts of town half a mile towards Llanrwst on the B5106 (☎01492/593845, ⓦwww.walesbandb.com; ❶), is about the best B&B within easy walking distance of Conwy. Further afield, there's *Castle Bank Hotel*, Mount Pleasant (☎01492/593888; ❸), a licensed, non-smoking hotel with country house atmosphere, ten minutes' walk from the town centre: turn first left outside the town walls on the Bangor road. Take bus #19 to the nearest **campsite**, the family-oriented *Conwy Touring Park*, a mile or so south along the B5106 (☎01492/592856; April–Oct). The YHA **hostel** (☎01492/593571, ⓦwww.yha.org.uk) is on Lark Hill, a ten-minute hike from town up the road to Sychnant Pass, where people staying can also hire bikes. There's another YHA hostel a mile up a steep hill above Rowen village, four miles south of Conwy (☎01492/650089, ⓦwww.yha.org.uk; Easter–Sept); bus #19 connects hourly in summer.

Conwy has relatively few **restaurants**. In town, you're best off going veggie at *The Wall Place*, Bishop's Yard, Chapel Street (☎01492/596326), one of Conwy's trendier spots; it even has the occasional night of live folk and Welsh music. Otherwise, you can eat Italian at *Alfredo's*, Lancaster Square (☎01492/592381; closed Sun), or Austrian at the *Austrian Restaurant*, west of town on Old Conwy Road, Capelulo (☎01492/622170; closed Sun eve & Mon). Good **pubs** are easier to find: try *Ye Olde Mail Coach*, 16 High St, for decent beer, food and occasional music, or the scruffy *Malt Loaf*, opposite the station on Rosehill Street, where you'll find regular live folk and other music. The best pub in the vicinity is the fifteenth-century *Groes Inn*, in Tyn-y-Groes, two miles south on the B5106 to Llanrwst, which serves excellent bar meals and good cask ales.

Around Conwy

The best short walk from Conwy is on to **Conwy Mountain** and the 800-foot peaks behind, all giving great views right along the coast. Follow a sign up Cadnant Park off the Bangor road just outside the town walls, then take the road around until Mountain Road heads off on the right towards a hill fort on the summit. This group is separated from the foothills of the Carneddau range by the narrow cleft of **Sychnant Pass**.

Thousands come to Conwy specifically to see **Bodnant Garden** (mid-March to Oct daily 10am–5pm; £5; NT), beside the lower reaches of the Conwy, eight miles to the south. During May and June, the Laburnum Arch flourishes and banks of rhododendrons are in full and glorious bloom all over what ranks as one of the finest formal gardens in Britain. Laid out in 1875 around Bodnant Hall (no public access) by its then owner, English industrialist Henry Pochin, the garden spreads out over eighty acres of the eastern Conwy Valley. Facing southwest, the bulk of the gardens – divided into an upper terraced garden and lower pinetum and wild garden – catch the late afternoon sun as it sets over the Carneddau range. Though it's arranged so that shrubs and plants provide a blaze of colour throughout the opening season, autumn is a perfect time to be here, with hydrangeas still in bloom and fruit trees shedding their leaves. Bus #25 runs here from Llandudno (every 2hr), calling at Llandudno Junction, or it's a two-mile walk from the Tal-y-Cafn train station on the Conwy Valley line.

Llandudno

Set on a low isthmus, across the river and a couple of miles north of Conwy, **LLANDUDNO** has an undeniably dignified air, its older set of promenading devotees often huddled in the glassed frontages of once-grand hotels, content to sit and watch the more rumbustious younger visitors. Almost invariably, the wind funnels between the limestone hummocks of the 680-foot **Great Orme** and its southern cousin the **Little Orme**, which flank the gently curving Victorian frontage; but don't let that put you off visiting this archetype of the genteel British seaside town.

Llandudno's early history revolves around the Great Orme, where St Tudno, who brought Christianity to the region in the sixth century, built the monastic cell that gives the town its name. When the early Victorian copper mines looked about to be worked out, in the mid-nineteenth century, local landowner Edward Mostyn exploited the growing craze for sea bathing and set about a speculative venture to create a seaside resort for the upper middle classes. Work got under way around 1854 and the town rapidly gained popularity over the next fifty years, becoming synonymous with the Victorian ideal of a respectable resort.

The Town

Despite the pavilion being destroyed by fire in early 1994, Llandudno's nineteenth-century **pier** (open all year; free) is one of the few remaining in Wales. It juts out 2220 feet into Llandudno Bay, a leisurely ten-minute stroll along The Promenade from Vaughan Street and the region's premier contemporary art gallery, the **Oriel Mostyn**, 12 Vaughan St (Mon–Sat 10am–1pm & 1.30–5pm; free), which hosts temporary shows featuring works by artists of international renown, with a particular leaning towards the current Welsh arts scene.

Kids are better entertained at the **Alice in Wonderland Visitor Centre**, 3–4 Trinity Square (daily 10am–5pm; Nov–Easter closed Sun; £2.95), where they are guided through the "Rabbit Hole", full of fibre-glass Mad Hatters and March Hares, while a headset treats them to readings of *Jabberwocky* and the like. The Alice books were inspired by Lewis Carroll's meeting with one Alice Liddell, the daughter of friends, here in Llandudno.

The Great Orme

The view from the top of the **Great Orme** (Pen y Gogarth) ranks with those from the far loftier summits in Snowdonia, combining the seascapes east towards Rhyl and west over the sands of the Conwy Estuary with the brooding, quarry-chewed northern limit of the Carneddau range where Snowdonia crashes into the sea.

This huge lump of carboniferous limestone was subject to some of the same stresses that folded Snowdonia, producing fissures filled by molten mineral-bearing rock. A Bronze Age settlement developed when people began to smelt the contents of the malachite-rich veins, supplying copper – if current speculation turns out to be true – throughout Europe. The result of their labour is evident at the **Great Orme Copper Mines** (Feb–Oct daily 10am–5pm; £4.40), accessed via the tramway (see below). What were, until recently, considered to be Roman workings have recently revealed 4000-year-old animal bones which had been used as scrapers. Hard hats and miners' lamps are provided for the **guided tour** through just a small portion of the tunnels, enough to get a feel for the cramped working conditions and the dangers of falling rock.

The base of the Great Orme is traditionally circumnavigated on **Marine Drive**, a five-mile anticlockwise circuit from just near Llandudno's pier. To ascend to the dry-ski slope and toboggan run at the **Summit Complex** (Easter–Oct daily; Nov–Easter Sat & Sun only), you can take the road, which runs past the mines, or the San Francisco-style **Great Orme Tramway** (April–Sept 10am–6pm; Oct–March 10am–4pm; £4 return), which creaks up from the bottom of Old Road, much as it has done since 1902. Alternatively, a **Cabin Lift** (daily: July & Aug 10am–5.30pm; Easter–June, Sept & Oct 10am–1pm & 2–4.20pm; £5) carries you up over the Orme from the **Happy Valley** formal gardens, at the base of the pier.

Practicalities

Llandudno's central **train station** (not to be confused with the mainline Llandudno Junction, three miles south), is at the corner of Augusta and Vaughan streets, five minutes' walk southeast from the **tourist office**, 1–2 Chapel St (Easter–Sept daily 9.30am–6pm; Oct–Easter Mon–Sat 9.30am–5pm; ☎01492/876413). Chapel Street runs parallel to Mostyn Street, where local **buses** stop. Less than ten minutes' walk south, National Express **coaches** pull in to the coach park on Mostyn Broadway. **Bike rental** is available from West End Cycles, 22 Augusta St (☎01492/876891), across the road from the train station. Snowdonia Cycle Hire (☎01492/878771) will deliver and collect bikes within a six-mile radius of Llandudno.

With over seven hundred **hotels**, finding a place to stay is not usually a problem, though in high summer and especially on bank holidays, booking ahead is wise. The greatest concentration of budget places is along St David's Road, just west of the station, where you'll find the *Cliffbury Hotel*, 34 St David's Rd (℡01492/877224, ⓦwww.cliffburyhotel.co.uk; ❶). *Fernbank*, 9 Chapel St (℡01492/877251; ❶), is one of the least expensive and best equipped of a string of low-cost hotels just along from the tourist office, while the *Gwesty Leamore Hotel*, 40 Lloyd St (℡01492/875552; ❶), is one of the few guesthouses in Llandudno actually run by Welsh people. If you've a head for heights, try *The Lighthouse*, Marine Drive (℡01492/876819; ❺), three miles from Llandudno, and 370ft above the Irish Sea. Topnotch accommodation is available at *St Tudno Hotel*, a superb, small, seafront hotel on North Parade, just behind the pier (℡01492/874411, ⓦwww.st-tudno.co.uk; ❺). The closest **camping** is at *Dinarth Hall Farm*, Dinarth Hall Road, Rhos-on-Sea (℡01492/548203), three miles east of Llandudno, accessible on buses #13, #14 and #15.

Llandudno has plenty of excellent **restaurants**. The basement bistro at *Richards*, 7 Church Walks (℡01792/877924), dishes up delicious meals, many based on local seafood, while the *Garden Room* at the *St Tudno Hotel* (see above) is one of Wales' best restaurants, serving French cuisine based on fresh Welsh produce. For substantial, tasty bar food, try the *Cottage Loaf*, Market Street, a flag-floored **pub** built from old ships' timbers on top of an old bakehouse, or the *King's Head*, on Old Road, the oldest pub in town, where Edward Mostyn and his surveyor mapped out the town. For sheer raucous drinking, the bars along Upper Mostyn Street are generally full and extremely lively.

Around the turn of the last century all the best performers clamoured to play Llandudno, but today you're lucky to get anything more than faded stars plying the resorts throughout the summer. However, with the 1500-seat **North Wales Theatre**, The Promenade (Theatr Gogledd Cymru; ℡01492/872000) and various little festivals throughout the year, things are looking a little rosier.

Flintshire and Denbighshire

Making for the coastal resorts or mountains of Snowdonia, you might be tempted to charge headlong through **Flintshire** and **Denbighshire**, two small counties hard up against the English border. No sooner have you cleared the industrial hinterland that spreads over the border from Chester (see p.582) than you hit the North Wales coast, a twenty-mile stretch from the end of the Dee estuary to Colwyn Bay which constitutes the ugliest piece of Welsh coastline: almost the entire length is taken up by caravan parks. Inland, however, there are one or two very interesting diversions, notably **St Asaph**, home to Britain's smallest cathedral. Two miles to the north is the second of Edward I's castles at **Rhuddlan**, and a few miles west, the National Portrait Gallery's Welsh outpost at **Bodelwyddan**; all are easily accessed from the brash resort town of Rhyl.

The country flanking the salt marshes of the Dee estuary was once contested by Marcher lords, but skirmishes were quashed by the construction of Flint Castle, the earliest of Edward I's Iron Ring of fortresses and now an insubstantial ruin overlooking the estuary at Flint. Understated **Holywell** has been an important pilgrimage site for the last thirteen hundred years, but now quietly ticks by almost unvisited.

St Asaph and around

ST ASAPH (Llanelwy), some eighteen miles east of Conwy along the A55, ranks as Britain's second-smallest "city" after St David's in Pembrokeshire, and its **cathedral** (daily 8am–dusk) is the country's smallest, no bigger than many village churches. It was founded around 570 by St Kentigern, the patron saint of Glasgow, and takes its name from the succeeding bishop, St Asaph. Both are commemorated in the easternmost window in the north aisle. From 1601 until his death in 1604, the bishopric was held by **William Morgan**, whose grave under the presbytery has gone unmarked since Giles Gilbert Scott's substantial restoration in the 1870s. Morgan was responsible for the translation of the first Welsh-language bible in 1588, replacing the English ones used up until that time. Over 25 years, he and three other clergymen produced a translation so successful that the Privy Council decreed that a copy of *Y Beibl* should be allocated to every Welsh church, thereby setting a standard for prose and codifying the language. Without his efforts, many claim, Welsh would have died out. A thousand Morgan bibles were printed, of which only nineteen remain, one of them displayed in the north transept along with notable prayer books and psalters.

Buses stop right outside the cathedral. The best central **rooms** are at the *Kentigern Arms*, towards the bottom of the High Street (℡01745/584157; ❸). The nicely furnished, non-smoking *Chalet*, The Roe (℡01745/584025; ❷), is a quarter of a mile away – across the river bridge then right – while the plush *Plas Elwy*, The Roe (℡01745/582263; ❹), is further down the same road. St Asaph's best **food** is served at the moderately priced *Barrow Alms*, High Street (℡01745/582260), followed by the bar meals at the *Kentigern Arms*, which is the most alluring **pub**.

Rhuddlan

RHUDDLAN, two miles north of St Asaph, lies on the banks of a tidal reach of the Clwyd River (Afon Clywedog), which finally meets the sea at Rhyl. The town would be an insignificant suburb of Rhyl but for the diamond-shaped ruin of **Rhuddlan Castle** (Easter–Sept daily 10am–5pm; £2; CADW), built between 1277 and 1282 as a garrison and royal residence for Edward I. The impressive castle commands a canalized section of the river protected by **Gillot's Tower**. Behind, the castle's massive towers were the work of James of St George, who was responsible for the concentric plan that allowed archers on both outer and inner walls to fire simultaneously. Important though the castle was, Rhuddlan earns its position in history as the place where Edward I signed the **Statute of Rhuddlan** on March 19, 1284, consigning Wales to centuries of subjugation by the English. A large – and somewhat ironic – plaque in Rhuddlan's main street details the terms of the statute.

Bodelwyddan

Barrelling west along the A55 towards the coast brings you to the small village of **BODELWYDDAN**. The slender 202-foot limestone spire of **Marble Church** heralds the finest art showcase in North Wales, at **Bodelwyddan Castle** (July & Aug daily 10.30am–5pm; April–June, Sept & Oct Mon–Thurs, Sat & Sun 10.30am–5pm; Nov–March Tues–Thurs, Sat & Sun 10.30am–4pm; castle £4, gardens £1.50), set amidst landscaped gardens on its hill, half a mile south of the village. The opulent Victorian interiors of what is essentially a nineteenth-century mansion were restored in the 1980s to house one of four provincial outposts of the **National Portrait Gallery**, specializing in works contemporary with the castle. As well as the NPG's collection, each summer sees children-oriented temporary exhibitions.

Most of the two hundred-odd paintings are on the ground floor, approached through the "Watts Hall of Fame", a long corridor specially decorated in William Morris-style to accommodate a chair by Morris and 26 portraits of eminent Victorians by G.F. Watts, among them Millais, Rossetti, Browning and Walter Crane. In the Ladies' Drawing Room opposite, a beautiful Biedermeier sofa outshines paintings of little-celebrated nineteenth-century women around the walls. Of the three main rooms, it is the Dining Room that stands out. Two sensitive portraits here highlight the Pre-Raphaelite support for social reform: William Holman Hunt's portrayal of the vociferous opponent of slavery and capital punishment, Stephen Lushington; and Ford Madox-Brown's double portrait of Henry Farell, prime mover in the passing of the 1867 Reform Bill, and suffragette Millicent Garrett. Works by John Singer Sargent and Hubert von Herkamer also adorn the room, which, like the others, is furnished with pieces from London's Victoria and Albert Museum. Upstairs, nineteenth-century portraiture, portrait photography and works by female artists get generous coverage along with animal painters, Landseer in particular.

Holywell and around

A place of pilgrimage for thirteen hundred years, **HOLYWELL** (Treffynnon), just off the A55 ten miles east of St Asaph, comes billed as "The Lourdes of Wales" – but without the tacky souvenir stalls, it doesn't really warrant such a comparison. **St Winefride's Well** (daily: mid-May to Sept 9.30am–5.15pm; rest of year 10am–4pm; donation requested) – half a mile from the bus station at the far end of the High Street, then turn right and follow the signs – is the source of all the fuss, a calm pool capacious enough to accommodate the dozens of the faithful who dutifully wade through the waters three times in the hope of curing their ailments, a relic of the Celtic baptism by triple immersion.

The existence of the spring was first noted by the Romans, who used the waters to relieve rheumatism and gout. The traditional legend, however, states that in around 660, the virtuous Winefride (Gwenfrewi in Welsh) was decapitated here after resisting the amorous advances of Prince Caradoc; the well is said to have sprung up at the spot where her head fell. Richard I and Henry V provided regal patronage, ensuring a steady flow of believers to what became one of the great shrines of Christendom, and James II came here to pray for a son and heir. Pilgrims formerly spent the night praying in the Perpendicular **St Winefride's Chapel** (key from the ticket office; CADW), built in around 1500 to enclose three sides of the well. The site's importance is waning, but pilgrimages do still take place, mainly on St Winefride's Day, the nearest Sunday to June 22, when a couple of thousand pilgrims are led through the streets behind a relic, part of Winefride's thumb-bone.

From St Winefride's Well, a mile-long path runs past the remains of the copper and brass factories which now constitute the **Greenfield Valley Heritage Park** (April–Oct daily 10am–5pm; £2), whose moderately interesting farm and museum preserves agricultural and other buildings from around the area. Over the way are the ruined domestic buildings used by the abbot and twelve monks of the Savignac order at **Basingwerk Abbey** (free access; CADW), and there's a good exhibition about it in the Greenfield Valley visitor centre (April–Oct daily 10am–5pm; free).

Holywell has no train station, but frequent **buses** run to Rhyl and Chester from the bus station at the southern end of High Street.

Wrexham and around

WREXHAM (Wrecsam) is odds-on favourite to be named a city in 2002, as part of the celebrations for the Queen's Golden Jubilee. Don't be fooled into thinking, however, that this gives the place much of a cosmopolitan edge. Its industrial past is all too evident and, as a border town, its Welshness is often hidden. There's little reason to stop except to use it as a base for the nearby attractions, which in any case – if you have your own transport – are better visited from Llangollen (see p.835). You might call in at **St Giles' Church** (Easter–Oct Mon–Fri 10am–4pm), its Gothic tower rising gracefully above the kernel of small lanes at the end of Hope Street. Topped off with a steeple in the 1520s, the tower has five distinct levels, stepping up to four hexagonal pinnacles. The same design was used at Yale University, in homage to the ancestral home of the college's benefactor, Elihu Yale, whose tomb can be seen at the base of St Giles' tower.

Wrexham has two **train stations**, half a mile apart, all services stopping at Wrexham General on Mold Road, ten minutes' walk northwest of the centre. Walking into town from here, Mold Street becomes Regent Street and then Hope Street, from which King Street branches off left to the **bus station**, for National Express coaches (tickets from Key Travel, King Street) and frequent local buses serving Chester and Llangollen. The **tourist office**, Lambpit Street (Mon–Sat 10am–5pm; Oct–Easter closes 4pm; ☎01978/292015), is reached by turning left where Hope Street turns to the right. If you need to **stay**, make for *Lyndhurst Guesthouse*, 3 Gerald St, off Grosvenor Road (☎01978/290802; ❶), a short walk from the centre, or the much-refurbished town-centre *Wynnstay Arms* (☎01978/291010; ❸) on Yorke Street, which is also a good place to grab a snack or full meal.

Clywedog Valley and Erddig

The **Clywedog Valley**, which forms an arc around the western and southern suburbs of Wrexham, was the crucible of industrial success in the northern Welsh borders during the eighteenth century. Iron mining and smelting were the principle industries, but as the Industrial Revolution forged ahead, water power harnessed from the Clywedog became less important, and factories moved closer to their raw materials, leaving the valley barely disturbed. A series of former industrial sites – ironworks, lead mines and the like – are now linked by the seven-mile-long **Clywedog Trail**. It's all a bit heavy on packaged heritage, but if you're interested, pick up a leaflet from the Wrexham tourist office.

Despite the closure of the ironworks and the consequent drop in demand, coal continued to be mined in the valley until 1986. After World War II, coal mines were tunnelled under the nearby stately home of **Erddig** (April–Sept Mon–Wed, Sat & Sun: house noon–5pm, gardens 11am–6pm; Oct both close 1hr earlier; full tour £6, gardens and outbuildings only £2.50; NT), two miles south of Wrexham, adding subsidence to the troubles of an already decaying seventeenth-century building. The house has now been restored to its 1922 appearance, but it isn't particularly distinguished. While the State Rooms upstairs have their share of fine furniture and portraits – including one by Gainsborough – the real interest lies in the quarters of the servants, whose lives were fully documented by their unusually benevolent masters. Eighteenth- and early nineteenth-century portraits of staff are still on display in the Servants' Hall, and each has a verse written by one of the Yorkes. You can also see the blacksmith's shop, lime yard, stables, laundry, kitchen and still-used bakehouse.

Travel details

Trains

Bangor to: Chester (20 daily; 1hr); Colwyn Bay (20 daily; 30min); Conwy (7 daily; 20min); Holyhead (21 daily; 30–40min); Llandudno Junction (20 daily; 20min); Llanfair PG (7 daily; 10min).
Betws-y-Coed to: Blaenau Ffestiniog (6 daily; 30min); Llandudno Junction (6 daily; 30min).
Blaenau Ffestiniog to: Betws-y-Coed (6 daily 30min); Llandudno Junction (6 daily; 1hr); Porthmadog by Ffestiniog Railway (April–Oct 4–10 daily; 1hr).
Criccieth to: Barmouth (6 daily; 55min); Machynlleth (6 daily; 1hr 45min); Porthmadog (6 daily; 10min); Pwllheli (6 daily; 15min).
Conwy to: Bangor (7 daily; 20min); Holyhead (8 daily; 1hr); Llandudno Junction (8 daily; 5min).
Holyhead to: Bangor (20 daily; 30–40min); Chester (15 daily; 1hr 40min); Llandudno Junction (20 daily; 1hr); Llanfair PG (7 daily; 30min).

Llandudno to: Betws-y-Coed (5 daily; 40min); Blaenau Ffestiniog (5 daily; 1hr 10min); Llandudno Junction (at least hourly; 10min).
Llandudno Junction to: Bangor (20 daily; 20min); Betws-y-Coed (6 daily; 30min); Holyhead (20 daily; 1hr).
Llanfair PG to: Bangor (7 daily; 10min); Holyhead (7 daily; 30min).
Porthmadog to: Barmouth (6 daily; 45min); Blaenau Ffestiniog by Ffestiniog Railway (Easter–Oct 4–10 daily; 1hr); Harlech (6 daily; 20min); Machynlleth (6 daily; 1hr 40min); Pwllheli (6 daily; 25min).
Pwllheli to: Criccieth (6 daily; 15min); Machynlleth (6 daily; 2hr); Porthmadog (6 daily; 25min).
Wrexham to: Chester (every 2hr; 20min); Chirk (every 2hr; 10min); Liverpool (change at Bidston; hourly; 1hr 15min).

Buses

Aberdaron to: Pwllheli (9 daily; 40min).
Abersoch to: Pwllheli (9 daily; 20min).
Bangor to: Beaumaris (at least hourly; 30min); Betws-y-Coed (3 daily; 50min); Caernarfon (every 30min; 30min); Capel Curig (2 daily; 40min); Cardiff (1 daily; 7hr 45min); Chester (2 daily; 2hr 40min); Conwy (every 30min; 45min); Holyhead (every 30min; 1hr); Llanberis (every 30min; 30min); Llandudno (every 30min; 1hr); Llanfair PG (every 30min; 15min).
Beaumaris to: Bangor (at least hourly; 30min).
Beddgelert to: Caernarfon (8 daily; 30min); Llanberis (5 daily; 40min); Porthmadog (8 daily; 30min).
Betws-y-Coed to: Bangor (2 daily; 50min); Blaenau Ffestiniog (1 daily; 30min); Capel Curig (8 daily; 15min); Conwy (6 daily; 55min); Llanberis (3 daily; 40min).
Blaenau Ffestiniog to: Caernarfon (roughly hourly; 1hr 20min); Harlech (4 daily; 35min); Porthmadog (hourly; 30min).
Caernarfon to: Bangor (every 30min; 30min); Beddgelert (6 daily; 30min); Blaenau Ffestiniog (roughly hourly; 1hr 20min); Criccieth (4 daily; 40min); Llanberis (every 30min; 25min); Llandudno (hourly; 1hr 40min); Porthmadog (hourly; 45min); Pwllheli (at least hourly; 45min).
Capel Curig to: Bangor (2 daily; 40min); Betws-y-Coed (8 daily; 15min); Llanberis (3 daily; 30min).
Conwy to: Bangor (every 30min; 45min); Betws-y-Coed (5 daily; 1hr); Llanberis (3 daily; 1hr 30min);

Llandudno (every 30min; 20min).
Criccieth to: Caernarfon (4 daily; 40min); Llanystumdwy (hourly; 5min); Porthmadog (hourly; 15min); Pwllheli (hourly; 20min).
Holyhead to: Bangor (every 30min; 1hr); Chester (1 daily; 3hr 30min); Llanfair PG (every 30min; 45min).
Llanberis to: Bangor (7 daily; 40min); Beddgelert (4 daily; 40min); Betws-y-Coed (3 daily; 40min); Caernarfon (every 30min; 25min).
Llandudno to: Bangor (every 30min; 1hr); Betws-y-Coed (5 daily; 1hr 15min); Caernarfon (every 30min; 1hr 40min); Llanberis (4–6 daily in summer only; 2hr).
Llanfair PG to: Bangor (every 30min; 15min); Holyhead (every 30min; 45min).
Porthmadog to: Beddgelert (6 daily; 30min); Blaenau Ffestiniog (hourly; 30min); Caernarfon (hourly; 45min); Cardiff (1 daily; 6hr 40min); Criccieth (hourly; 15min); Dolgellau (6 daily; 50min); Machynlleth (3 daily; 1hr 45min); Pwllheli (hourly; 40min).
Pwllheli to: Aberdaron (7 daily; 40min); Abersoch (9 daily; 15min); Caernarfon (hourly; 45min); Criccieth (hourly; 20min); Porthmadog (hourly; 40min).
Wrexham to: Barmouth (7 daily; 2hr 20min); Chester (every 15min; 40min); Chirk (hourly; 40min); Dolgellau (6 daily; 2hr); Llangollen (at least hourly; 40min).

Ferries

Holyhead to: Dublin (4 ferries daily; 3hr 45min; 3 catamarans daily; 1hr 45min); Dun Laoghaire (4 catamarans daily; 1hr 45min).

Scotland

Scotland

⑰ Edinburgh and the Lothians 901–960

⑱ Southern Scotland 961–994

⑲ Glasgow and the Clyde 995–1038

⑳ Central Scotland 1039–1082

㉑ Argyll 1083–1116

㉒ Skye and the Western Isles 1117–1150

㉓ Northeast Scotland 1151–1188

㉔ The Highland region 1189–1250

㉕ Orkney and Shetland 1251–1283

Edinburgh
and the Lothians

CHAPTER 17

Highlights

* **Edinburgh Castle** –
Perched on an imposing
volcanic crag, the castle
still dominates
Scotland's capital.
See p.913

* **The Old Town** – The
evocative heart of the
historic city, with its tenements, courtyards,
ghosts and catacombs.
See p.913

* **Holyrood Park** – Wild
moors, rocky crags and
the 800-ft Arthur's Seat
all slap in the middle of
the city. See p.925

* **Museum of Scotland** –
The treasures of
Scotland's past in a
dynamic and superbly
conceived new building.
See p.928

* **Café Royal Circle Bar** –
There are few finer pubs
in which to sample a pint
of local "80 shilling"
beer. See p.944

* **Edinburgh Festival** –
The world's biggest arts
festival – bewildering,
inspiring, exhausting and
endlessly entertaining.
See p.947

* **Leith** – Take your pick
from the fine seafood
bistros on the cobbled
waterfront of Edinburgh's
historic port. See p.952

Edinburgh
and the Lothians

Venerable, dramatic **EDINBURGH**, the showcase capital of Scotland, is a historic, cosmopolitan and cultured city. The setting is wonderfully striking; the city is perched on a series of extinct volcanoes and rocky crags which rise from the generally flat landscape of the Lothians, with the sheltered shoreline of the Firth of Forth to the north. "My own Romantic town", Sir Walter Scott called it, although it was another native author, Robert Louis Stevenson, who perhaps best captured the feel of his "precipitous city", declaring that "No situation could be more commanding for the head of a kingdom; none better chosen for noble prospects."

The centre has two distinct parts, divided by **Princes Street Gardens**, which run roughly east–west under the shadow of **Castle Rock**. To the north, the dignified, Grecian-style **New Town** was immaculately laid out during the Age of Reason, after the announcement of a plan to improve conditions in the city. The **Old Town**, on the other hand, with its tortuous alleys and tightly packed closes, is unrelentingly medieval, associated in popular imagination with the underworld lore of schizophrenic Deacon Brodie, inspiration for Stevenson's *Dr Jekyll and Mr Hyde*, and the bodysnatchers Burke and Hare. Edinburgh earned its nickname of "Auld Reekie" for the smog and smell generated by the Old Town, which for centuries swam in sewage tipped out of the windows of cramped tenements.

Set on the crag which sweeps down from the towering fairytale **castle** to the royal **Palace of Holyroodhouse**, the Old Town preserves all the key reminders of its role as a capital, plus a brand new **parliament building** rising up opposite the palace. A few hundred yards away a tantalizing glimpse of the wild beauty of Scotland's scenery can be had immediately beyond the palace in **Holyrood Park**, an extensive area of open countryside dominated by **Arthur's Seat**, the largest and most impressive of the volcanoes.

In August and early September, around a million visitors flock to the city for the **Edinburgh Festival**, in fact a series of separate festivals that make up the largest arts extravaganza in the world. Among the many museums, the exciting new **National Museum of Scotland** houses ten thousand of Scotland's most precious artefacts, while the **National Gallery of Scotland** and its offshoot, the **Scottish National Gallery of Modern Art**, have two of Britain's finest collections of paintings.

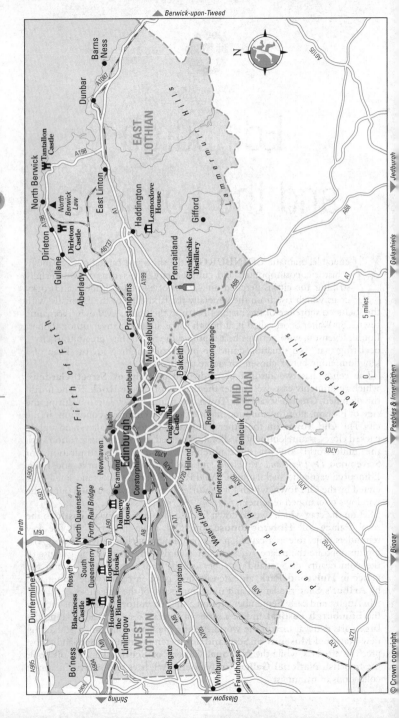

© Crown copyright

On a less elevated theme, the city's distinctive howffs (pubs), allied to its brewing and distilling traditions, make Edinburgh a great **drinking** city. The presence of three **universities**, plus several colleges, means that there is a youthful presence for most of the year – a welcome corrective to the stuffiness which is often regarded as Edinburgh's Achilles heel.

Beyond the city centre, the most lively area is **Leith**, the city's medieval port, whose seedy edge is softened by a series of great bars and upmarket seafood restaurants, along with the presence of the former royal yacht *Britannia*, now open to visitors. The wider rural hinterland of Edinburgh, known as the **Lothians**, mixes rolling countryside and attractive country towns with some dramatic historic ruins. In East Lothian, blustery cliff-top paths lead to the romantic battlements of **Tantallon Castle**, while nearby North Berwick, home of the **Scottish Seabird Centre**, looks out to the gannet-covered Bass Rock. The most famous sight in Midlothian is the mysterious fifteenth-century **Rosslyn Chapel**, while West Lothian boasts the towering, roofless **Linlithgow Palace**, thirty minutes from Edinburgh by train.

Some history

It was during the Dark Ages that the name of Edinburgh – at least in its early forms of **Dunedin** or Din Eidyn ("fort of Eidyn") – first appeared. Castle Rock, a strategic fort atop one of the volcanoes, served as the nation's southernmost border post until 1018, when King Malcolm I established the River Tweed as the permanent frontier. In the reign of Malcolm Canmore, the castle became one of the main seats of the court, and the town, which was given privileged status as a **royal burgh**, began to grow. In 1128 King David established Holyrood Abbey at the foot of the slope, later allowing its monks to found a separate burgh, known as **Canongate**.

Robert the Bruce granted Edinburgh a new charter in 1329, giving it jurisdiction over the nearby port of Leith, and during the following century the prosperity brought by foreign trade enabled the newly fortified city to establish itself as the permanent **capital of Scotland**. Under King James IV, the city enjoyed a short but brilliant Renaissance era, which saw not only the construction of a new palace alongside Holyrood Abbey, but also the granting of a royal charter to the College of Surgeons, the earliest in the city's long line of academic and professional bodies.

This period came to an abrupt end in 1513 with the calamitous defeat by the English at the **Battle of Flodden**, which led to several decades of political instability. In the 1540s, King Henry VIII's attempt to force a royal union with Scotland led to the sack of Edinburgh, prompting the Scots to turn to France: French troops arrived to defend the city, while the young queen Mary was dispatched to Paris as the promised bride of the Dauphin. While the French occupiers succeeded in removing the English threat, they themselves antagonized the locals, who had become increasingly sympathetic to the ideals of the **Reformation**. When the radical preacher John Knox returned from exile in 1555, he quickly won the city over to his Calvinist message.

James VI's rule saw the foundation of the University of Edinburgh in 1582, but following the **Union of the Crowns** in 1603 the city was totally upstaged by London: although James promised to visit every three years, it was not until 1617 that he made his only return trip. In 1633 Charles I visited Edinburgh for his coronation, but soon afterwards precipitated a crisis by introducing episcopacy to the Church of Scotland, in the process making Edinburgh a bishopric for the first time. Fifty years of religious turmoil followed, culminating in the triumph of **Presbyterianism**. Despite these vicissitudes, Edinburgh expanded throughout the seventeenth century and, constrained by its walls, was forced to build both upwards and inwards.

The **Union of the Parliaments** of 1707 dealt a further blow to Edinburgh's political prestige, though the guaranteed preservation of the national church and the legal and educational systems ensured that it was never relegated to a purely provincial role. On the contrary, it was in the second half of the eighteenth century that Edinburgh achieved the height of its intellectual influence, led by an outstanding group including David Hume and Adam Smith. Around the same time, the city began to expand beyond its medieval boundaries, laying out a **New Town**, a masterpiece of the Neoclassical style.

Industrialization affected Edinburgh less than any other major city in the nation, and it never lost its white-collar character. Nevertheless, it underwent an enormous **urban expansion** in the course of the nineteenth century.

In 1947 Edinburgh was chosen to host the great **International Festival** which served as a symbol of the new peaceful European order; despite some hiccups, it has flourished ever since, in the process helping to make tourism a mainstay of the local economy. In 1975 the city carried out another territorial expansion, moving its boundaries westwards as far as the old burgh of South Queensferry and the Forth Bridges. Four years later, an inconclusive referendum on Scottish devolution delayed Edinburgh's revival of its role as a governmental capital, and Glasgow, previously the poor relation but always a tenacious rival, began to challenge the city's status as a cultural centre.

However, while the 1990s saw Glasgow establish a clear lead in driving Scotland's contemporary arts scene, the decade also marked the return of power and influence to Edinburgh. Following a referendum in 1997, in which Scotland voted resoundingly in favour of re-establishing its own **parliament**, elections were held in May 1999. On July 1, 1999 the Queen formally opened the parliament, temporarily housed in the twin-towered Church of Scotland Assembly Halls on the Mound. Inevitably, the early years of the parliament have seen petty squabbling mixed with rather dizzying constitutional manoeuvring, but with debates, decisions and demonstrations about crucial aspects of the government of Scotland now taking place in Edinburgh, there has been a notable upturn in the sense of importance of the city. Added to this, recent acquisitions and mergers involving Scotland's two major banks, the Royal Bank of Scotland and the Bank of Scotland, have affirmed Edinburgh's significant place as a financial centre not just in Britain, but also Europe. Meanwhile, construction teams are at work on the parliament building, which will take its place opposite the ancient Palace of Holyroodhouse at the foot of the Royal Mile.

Arrival, information and transport

Although Edinburgh occupies a large area relative to its population – less than half a million people – most places worth visiting lie within the compact city centre, which is easily explored on foot. This is divided clearly and unequivocally between the maze-like **Old Town**, which lies on and around the crag linking the castle and the Palace, and the **New Town**, laid out in a symmetrical pattern on the undulating ground to the north.

Edinburgh International Airport (☎0131/333 1000) is at Turnhouse, seven miles west of the city centre; regular Airlink shuttle buses (£3.30) connect to Waverley Bridge in the town centre; taxis charge around £15 for the same journey. Conveniently situated at the eastern end of Princes Street in the New Town, **Waverley Station** (timetable and fare enquiries ☎0845/748 4950) is the terminus for all mainline trains. There's a second mainline train stop, **Haymarket Station**, just under two miles west on the lines from Waverley to Glasgow, Fife and the Highlands, although this is only really of use if you're staying nearby. The **bus** terminal for local and intercity services is on St Andrew Square, two minutes' walk from Waverley Station, on the opposite side of Princes Street.

Information

Edinburgh's main **tourist office** is on top of Princes Mall near the northern entrance to the station (July & Aug Mon–Sat 9am–8pm, Sun 10am–8pm; May, June & Sept 9am–7pm, Sun 10am–7pm; April & Oct Mon–Sat 9am–6pm, Sun 10am–6pm; Nov–March Mon–Sat 9am–5pm, Sun 10am–4pm; ☎0131/473 3800, ⓦwww.edinburgh.org). The much smaller airport branch is in the main concourse, directly opposite Gate 5 (daily: April–Oct 6.30am–10.30pm; Nov–March 7.30am–9.30pm). For backpacker-related information head to the **Haggis Office** at 60 High St (daily 9am–6pm; ☎0131/557 9393, ⓦwww.haggisadventures.com). Although their main function is to run minibus tours of Scotland, they're a good source of general information about the backpacker scene around Scotland and you can book hostels and intercity coaches from here, as well as change money. For up-to-date **maps** of the city head for one of the major book stores: Waterstone's, 13–14 Princes St, is the nearest to Waverley Station.

City transport

Edinburgh is well served by **buses**, although even locals are confused by the consequences of deregulation, with several companies offering competing services along similar routes. Most bus stops have a useful diagram indicating which services pass the stop and which routes they take.

Most useful are the maroon buses operated by Lothian Regional Transport (LRT); all buses referred to in the text are run by them unless otherwise stated. Timetables and passes are available from their ticket centres on Waverley Bridge or at 27 Hanover St (enquiry line ☎0131/555 6363), or from the city council-run Traveline, at 2 Cockburn St (☎0800/232323). Of the various passes available, there's an LRT **day pass** for £2.20 (£1.50 if you buy it after 9.30am, or £4.20 including the airport bus), or, of course, you can buy individual tickets from the driver, for which you'll need exact change – the most common fare is 80p.

Edinburgh is well endowed with **taxi** ranks, and you can also hail black cabs on the street. Phone numbers for taxi firms are listed on p.951. It is emphatically not a good idea to take a **car** into central Edinburgh: despite the presence of several expensive multistorey car parks, finding somewhere to park involves long and often fruitless searches. In addition, street parking restrictions are famously draconian. Edinburgh is, however, a reasonably cycle-friendly city – although hilly – with several **cycle paths**. The local cycling action group, Spokes (☎0131/313 2114, ⓦwww.spokes.org.uk), publishes an excellent cycle map of the city. For bike rental, see p.951.

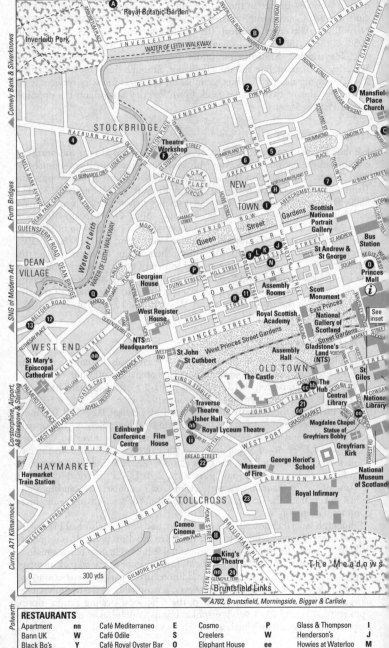

Inverleith
Bonnington & Leith

Royal Botanic Garden

Inverleith Park

INVERLEITH TERRACE

WATER OF LEITH WALKWAY

GLENOGLE ROAD

HENDERSON ROW

STOCKBRIDGE

RAEBURN PLACE

CUMBERLAND STREET

GREAT KING STREET

NEW TOWN

Theatre Workshop

ROYAL CIRCUS PLACE

DEAN VILLAGE

Georgian House

Queen Street

Gardens

Scottish National Portrait Gallery

St Andrew & St George

Bus Station

Princes Mall

West Register House

NTS Headquarters

Assembly Rooms

Scott Monument

St John St Cuthbert

PRINCES STREET

West Princes Street Gardens

Royal Scottish Academy

National Gallery of Scotland

East Princes Street Gardens

Gladstone's Land (NTS)

St Giles

National Library

St Mary's Episcopal Cathedral

WEST END

The Castle

OLD TOWN

The Hub

Central Library

Traverse Theatre

Usher Hall

Royal Lyceum Theatre

Edinburgh Conference Centre

Film House

JOHNSTON TERRACE

GRASSMARKET

Magdalen Chapel

Statue of Greyfriars Bobby

Greyfriars Kirk

WEST PORT

Museum of Fire

George Heriot's School

Royal Infirmary

National Museum of Scotland

HAYMARKET

Haymarket Train Station

MORRISON STREET

BREAD STREET

TOLLCROSS

FOUNTAIN BRIDGE

Cameo Cinema

King's Theatre

Bruntsfield Links

The Meadows

A702, Bruntsfield, Morningside, Biggar & Carlisle

0   300 yds

RESTAURANTS

Apartment	nn	Café Mediterraneo	E	Cosmo	P	Glass & Thompson	I
Bann UK	W	Café Odile	S	Creelers	W	Henderson's	J
Black Bo's	Y	Café Royal Oyster Bar	O	Elephant House	ee	Howies at Waterloo	M
Blue Parrot	F	Café St Honoré	L	Favorit	mm	Igg's	U
Café Hub	bb	Caffè DOC	K	Fishers in the City	N	Jasmine	ii

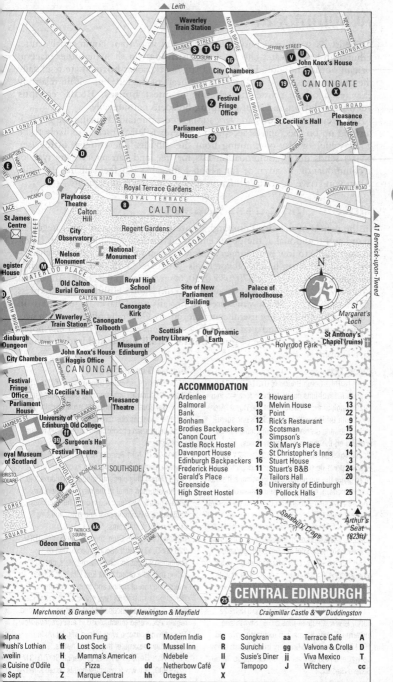

CENTRAL EDINBURGH

ACCOMMODATION

Ardenlee	2	Howard	5
Balmoral	10	Melvin House	13
Bank	18	Point	22
Bonham	12	Rick's Restaurant	9
Brodies Backpackers	17	Scotsman	15
Canon Court	1	Simpson's	23
Castle Rock Hostel	21	Six Mary's Place	4
Davenport House	6	St Christopher's Inns	14
Edinburgh Backpackers	16	Stuart House	3
Frederick House	11	Stuart's B&B	24
Gerald's Place	7	Tailors Hall	20
Greenside	8	University of Edinburgh	
High Street Hostel	19	Pollock Halls	25

alpna	kk	Loon Fung	B	Modern India	G	Songkran	aa	Terrace Café	A
hushi's Lothian	ff	Lost Sock	C	Mussel Inn	R	Suruchi	gg	Valvona & Crolla	D
weilin	H	Mamma's American		Ndebele	ll	Susie's Diner	jj	Viva Mexico	T
a Cuisine d'Odile	Q	Pizza	dd	Netherbow Café	V	Tampopo	J	Witchery	cc
e Sept	Z	Marque Central	hh	Ortegas	X				

Accommodation

As befits its status as a busy tourist city and important commercial centre, Edinburgh has a greater choice of **accommodation** than any other place in Britain outside London. **Hotels** (and large backpacker **hostels**) are essentially the only options you'll find right in the heart of the city, but within relatively easy reach of the centre the selection of **guest houses**, **B&Bs**, **campus accommodation** and even **camping** broadens considerably.

Advance reservations are very strongly recommended during the Festival: turning up on spec entails accepting whatever is left (which is unlikely to be good value) or else commuting from the suburbs. The **tourist office** (see p.907) sends out accommodation lists for free, and can reserve any type of accommodation in advance for a non-refundable £5 fee: call in personally when you arrive or contact them in advance, stating requirements.

Hotels and guest houses

In the centre of the city, Edinburgh's **hotels** tend to fall into two categories: grand and traditional at the upper end of the market, and budget chain hotels in the middle to low price range. While we haven't listed the generally characterless budget chain hotels, Novotel/Ibis (☎020/8283 4530, ⓦwww.accorhotels.com), Travelodge (☎0870/085 0950, ⓦwww.travelodge.co.uk), Travel Inn (☎0870/242 8000, ⓦwww.travelinn.co.uk), and Holiday Inn Express (☎0800/897121, ⓦwww.hiexpress.com), all now have large hotels in Edinburgh, often in very useful central locations. Generally offering much better value for money and a far more cosy experience than the larger city hotels are Edinburgh's vast range of **guest houses**, **small hotels** and **bed & breakfast** establishments.

Old Town

Bank Hotel 1 South Bridge ☎0131/556 9043, ⓦwww.festival-inns.co.uk. Notable location in a 1920s bank at the crossroads of the Royal Mile and South Bridge, with Logie Baird's bar downstairs and nine unusual but comfortable rooms upstairs on the theme of famous Scots. ⑤

Point Hotel 34–59 Bread St ☎0131/221 5555, ⓦwww.point-hotel.co.uk. A former department store given the modern design treatment: it's thoroughly modern, comfortable and glamorous. There's a popular bar and an excellent restaurant at street level. ⑥

The Scotsman Hotel 20 Northbridge ☎0131/556 5565, ⓦwww.thescotsmanhotel.co.uk. The most talked-about new hotel in Edinburgh, a plush, smart but non-stuffy new occupant of the grand old offices of the *Scotsman* newspaper. The marble staircase and walnut panelled lobby have been retained, and you can sleep in the editor's office. ⑧

Tailors Hall Hotel 139 Cowgate ☎0131/622 6800, ⓦwww.festival-inns.co.uk. Stylish and modern en-suite rooms in a recently converted 1621 trades hall and brewery in otherwise dingy Cowgate, linked to the lively mock-Gothic *Three Sisters Bar*. ⑥

New Town

Ardenlee Guest House 9 Eyre Place ☎0131/556 2838. Welcoming, non-smoking guest house near the Royal Botanic Garden, with exceptionally comfortable and spacious rooms. Breakfast includes some vegetarian options, and large family rooms are available. ③

Balmoral Hotel 1 Princes St ☎0131/556 2414, ⓦwww.rfhotels.com. Originally known as the *North British*, this elegant Edinburgh landmark is the finest grand hotel in the city. The *Balmoral* boasts nearly two hundred rooms, full business facilities, a swimming pool and gym, and two highly rated restaurants. ⑧

Bonham Hotel 35 Drumsheugh Gardens ☎0131/226 6050, ⓦwww.thebonham.com. One of Edinburgh's most stylish modern hotels, cheekily hiding behind a grand West End Victorian facade. An interesting mix of period and modern furniture. ⑧

Davenport House 58 Great King St ☎0131/558 8495, ⓔdavenporthouse@btinternet.com. A grand, regally decorated guest house in an attractive New Town town house; a well-priced and intimate alternative to some of the nearby hotels. ④

Frederick House Hotel 42 Frederick St ☎0131/226 1999, ⓦwww.townhousehotels.co.uk. A reasonable if slightly plain hotel in a superb location just off George Street in the New Town. ④

Gerald's Place 21b Abercromby Place ☎0131/558 7017, ⓦwww.scotland2000.com/geraldsplace. A real taste of New Town life at an upmarket but wonderfully hospitable and comfy basement B&B. ⑤

Greenside Hotel 9 Royal Terrace ☎0131/557 0022, ⓦwww.townhousehotels.co.uk. One of a number of small hotels on Calton Hill with great views from the top floors – in this case across to Leith and beyond to the Firth of Forth. Value for money considering the location. ④

Howard Hotel 34 Great King St ☎0131/557 3500, ⓦwww.thehoward.com. Top-of-the-range elegant town-house hotel, with fifteen exclusive rooms lavishly decorated in grand and rather refined style. ⑨

Melvin House Hotel 3 Rothesay Terrace ☎0131/225 5084, ⓦwww.melvinhouse.co.uk. One of Edinburgh's grandest Victorian terrace houses, with exquisite internal wood panelling, a galleried library and decent rooms, some with outstanding views over Dean village and the city skyline. ⑦

Rick's Restaurant with rooms 55a Frederick St ☎0131/622 7800, ⓦwww.ricksedinburgh.co.uk. Four much sought-after rooms at the back of the popular New Town bar and restaurant. Beautifully styled and fitted with walnut headboards and top quality fabrics, they look out onto a cobbled lane behind. ⑥

Six Mary's Place Raeburn Place ☎0131/332 8965, Ⓔsixmarysplace@btinternet.com. Collectively run "alternative" guest house; has a no-smoking policy and offers excellent home-cooked vegetarian meals. ④

Stuart House 12 E Claremont St ☎0131/557 9030, Ⓔstuartho@globalnet.co.uk. Cosy, bright Georgian house in the Broughton area. No smoking. ④

Leith and Inverleith

A-Haven Town House 180 Ferry Rd, Leith ☎0131/554 6559, Ⓔreservations@a-haven.co.uk. A terrifically friendly place – among the best of a number of guest houses on one of Edinburgh's main east–west arteries. ⑤

Ashlyn Guest House 42 Inverleith Row, Inverleith ☎0131/552 2954. Right by the Botanic Garden, a half-hour walk to the centre or an easy bus trip. Non-smoking. ③

Bar Java 48–50 Constitution St, Leith ☎0131/467 7527, ⓦwww.java-bedandbreakfast.com. Simple but brightly designed rooms above one of Leith's funkiest bars. Great breakfasts served, and food and drink available till late in the bar itself. ②

Malmaison 1 Tower Place ☎0131/468 5000, ⓦwww.malmaison.com. Chic modern hotel in a converted harbourside building with bright, bold original designs in each room, as well as CD players and cable TV. Also has gym, room service, Parisian brasserie and café-bar serving lighter meals. ⑦

South of the centre

Ashdene House 23 Fountainhall Rd, Grange ☎0131/667 6026, Ⓔ Ashdene_House_Edinburgh@compuserve.com. Well-run, non-smoking and environmentally friendly guest house in the quiet southern suburbs. ③

Cluaran House 47 Leamington Terrace, Viewforth ☎0131/221 0047, ⓦwww.scotland2000.com/cluaran. Pleasant B&B in a nicely decorated, non-smoking house near Brunstfield serving wholefood breakfasts. ③

The Greenhouse 14 Hartington Gardens, Viewforth ☎0131/622 7634, Ⓔgreenhouse_edin@hotmail.com. A fully vegetarian/vegan guest house, right down to the soaps and duvets, though a relaxed rather than right-on atmosphere prevails. The rooms are neat and tastefully furnished, with fresh fruit and flowers in each. ③

International Guest House 37 Mayfield Gardens, Mayfield ☎0131/667 2511, Ⓔintergh@easynet.co.uk. One of the best of the Mayfield guest houses, with comfortable well equipped rooms. ③

Prestonfield House Hotel Priestfield Road, Bruntsfield ☎0131/668 3346, ⓦwww.prestonfieldhouse.com. A unique Edinburgh hotel: a seventeenth-century mansion set in its own park below Arthur's Seat with upmarket rooms in the main house and a tasteful annexe. Peacocks strut around on the lawns and Highland cattle low in the adjacent fields. ⑦

Simpson's Hotel 79 Lauriston Place ☎0131/622 7979, ⓦwww.simpsons-hotel.com. Well-priced and smart medium-sized hotel located in the former maternity hospital near Tollcross and the Meadows. Named after Sir James Young Simpson, pioneer of modern anaesthetics. ⑤

The Stuarts B&B 17 Glengyle Terrace, Bruntsfield ☎0131/229 9559, Ⓔreservations@the-stuarts.com. A five-star bed and breakfast in central Edinburgh, with three comfortable and well-equipped rooms in a basement beside Bruntsfield Links. ⑤

Teviotdale House Hotel 53 Grange Loan, Grange ☎0131/667 4376, Ⓔteviotdale.house@btinternet.com. Peaceful non-smoking hotel, offering luxurious standards at reasonable prices. Particularly good (and huge) home-cooked Scottish breakfasts. ③

East of the centre

Joppa Turrets Guest House 1 Lower Joppa, Joppa ☎0131/669 5806, ⓦwww.joppaturrets .demon.co.uk. The place to come if you want an Edinburgh holiday by the sea: a quiet establishment right by the beach in Joppa, five miles east of the city centre. ❷

Portobello House 2 Pittville St, Portobello ☎0131/669 6067. Pleasant rooms and good (organic) breakfasts at this family-run guest house, only two minutes from the shore. ❷

Hostel, self-catering and campus accommodation

Edinburgh now has a wealth of **hostels**, including two grand SYHA-run establishments and a cluster of independent outfits on or near the Royal Mile. Competition is fierce, so be prepared for a bit of enthusiastic marketing when you make an enquiry. All hostels are open all year round, unless stated. Custom-built **self-catering apartments** are well worth considering for longer stays, for example during the Festival. **Campus accommodation** is available in the city during the summer months, though it's neither as useful or cheap as might be expected.

Argyle Backpackers Hotel 14 Argyle Place, Marchmont ☎0131/667 9991, ⓦwww.sol.co.uk/a/argyle. Quieter, less intense version of the typical backpackers' hostel, with small dorms with single beds and a dozen double/twin rooms, though prices are a pound or two higher. Pleasantly located near the Meadows in studenty Marchmont.

Brodies Backpackers Hostel 12 High St, Old Town ☎0131/556 6770, ⓦwww.brodieshostels.co.uk. Tucked down a typical Old Town close, with four fairly straightforward dorms and limited communal areas. Smaller than many others, and a little bit more cosy.

Bruntsfield Hostel 7 Bruntsfield Crescent, Bruntsfield ☎0131/447 2994, ⓦwww.syha.org.uk. Large SYHA youth hostel overlooking Bruntsfield Links a mile south of Princes Street; take bus #10, #11 or #16. Note that as well as the similarly sized Eglinton hostel (see p.912), SYHA also take over two central student residences with single rooms during July and August – one on The Pleasance and one on Cowgate; both have over 100 single bedrooms for around £16 per night (☎0131/556 5566).

Canon Court Apartments 20 Canonmills ☎0131/474 7000, ⓦwww.canoncourt.co.uk. All mod cons available in these smart, comfortable self-catering apartments on the northern edge of the New Town, near the Water of Leith. Prices start at £87 a night for a studio apartment.

Castle Rock Hostel 15 Johnston Terrace, Old Town ☎0131/225 9666, ⓦwww.scotlands-top-hostels.com. Busy 200-bed hostel tucked below the castle ramparts. Dorms are large and bright, and the communal areas include a games room with pool and ping-pong tables.

Edinburgh Backpackers Hostel 65 Cockburn St, Old Town ☎0131/539 8695, booking hotline ☎0800/096 6868, ⓦwww.hoppo.com. Big hostel with a great central location in a side street off the Royal Mile. Accommodation is mostly in large but bright dorms, although a few doubles are available.

Eglinton Hostel 18 Eglinton Crescent, Haymarket ☎0131/337 1120, ⓦwww.syha.org.uk. Slightly more expensive but the more central of the two main SYHA hostels, in a characterful town house west of the centre, near Haymarket Station.

High Street Hostel 8 Blackfriars St, Old Town ☎0131/557 3984, ⓦwww.scotlands-top-hostels.com. Large but lively and well-known hostel in a sixteenth-century building just off the Royal Mile.

Napier University 219 Colinton Rd, Merchiston ☎0131/455 4331, ⓔvacation.lets@napier.ac.uk. Three- to five-person self-catering flats in the Tollcross/Bruntsfield area of the city. Minimum stay one week; from £315 per week.

St Christopher's Inns 9–13 Market St, Old Town ☎0131/226 1446, ⓦwww.st-christophers.co.uk. Edinburgh's first sighting of the mega-hostels now common in London; 110 beds (all bunks) with smaller rooms as well as dorms. There's a small communal area and a noisy bar for beer and food on ground level. A little corporate but clean and with good service; slightly more expensive than most other hostels.

University of Edinburgh Pollock Halls of Residence 18 Holyrood Park Rd, Newington ☎0131/651 2007 or ☎0800/028 7118, ⓦwww.edinburghfirst.com. Unquestionably the best setting of any of the campuses, right beside the Royal Commonwealth Pool and Holyrood Park, but relatively expensive (rates are for bed and breakfast). Easter & late June to mid-Sept. ❺

Campsites

Davidson's Mains Caravan Site Marine Drive, Silverknowes ☎ 0131/312 6874. Edinburgh Caravan Club site in a pleasant location close to the shore in the northwestern suburbs, a thirty-minute ride from the centre by bus #14. Open year-round.

Drummohr Caravan Park Levenhall, Musselburgh ☎ 0131/665 6867. A large, pleasant site in this coastal satellite town to the east of Edinburgh, with excellent transport connections to the city, including buses #15, #15A, #26, #44, #66 (SMT) and #85. Open March–Oct.

The Old Town

The **Old Town**, although only about a mile long and 300 yards wide, represents the total extent of the twin burghs of Edinburgh and Canongate for the first 650 years of their existence, and its general appearance and character remain indubitably medieval. Containing as it does the majority of the city's most famous tourist sights, it makes by far the best starting point for your explorations.

In addition to the obvious goals of the **castle**, the **Palace of Holyroodhouse** and **Holyrood Abbey**, you'll find scores of historic buildings along the length of the **Royal Mile**. Inevitably, much of the Old Town is sacrificed to hard-sell tourism, and can be uncomfortably crowded throughout the summer, especially during the Festival. Yet the area remains at the heart of Edinburgh, with daily business of the greatest importance being conducted in **Parliament House**, home of the Scottish Parliament until 1707 and now the location of Scotland's highest Law Courts, and in the **Assembly Hall**, temporary home of the new Scottish Parliament. It's well worthwhile extending your explorations to the area immediately to the south of the Royal Mile, and in particular to the stunning new **National Museum of Scotland**. Close by is the wonderfully varied scenery and breathtaking vantage points of **Holyrood Park**, an extensive tract of open countryside on the eastern edge of the Old Town which includes Arthur's Seat, the peak which rises so distinctively in the midst of the city.

Edinburgh Castle

The history of Edinburgh, and indeed of Scotland, is indissolubly bound up with its **castle** (daily: April–Oct 9.30am–6pm; Nov–March 9.30am–5pm; £7.50), which dominates the city from its lofty seat atop an extinct volcanic rock. It requires no great imaginative feat to comprehend the strategic importance that underpinned the castle's, and hence Edinburgh's, importance in Scotland: from Princes Street, the north side rears high above an almost sheer rockface; the southern side is equally formidable; the western, where the rock rises in terraces, only marginally less so. Would-be attackers, like modern tourists, were forced to approach the castle from the crag to the east on which the Royal Mile runs down to Holyrood.

The castle's disparate styles reflect its many changes in usage, as well as advances in military architecture: the oldest surviving part, **St Margaret's Chapel**, is from the twelfth century, while the most recent additions date back to the 1920s. It last saw action in 1745, when the Young Pretender's forces, fresh from their victory at Prestonpans, made a half-hearted attempt to storm it. Subsequently, advances in weapon technology diminished the castle's importance, but under the influence of the Romantic movement it came to be seen as a great national monument.

Though you can easily take in the views and wander round the castle yourself, you might like to join one of the somewhat overheated **guided tours**, with their talk of war, boiling oil and the roar of the cannon. Alternatively, **audioguides** with personal headphones are available from a booth just inside the gatehouse. Both the guided tours and audioguides are included in the entrance price.

The Esplanade and lower defences

The castle is entered via the **Esplanade**, a parade ground laid out in the eighteenth century and enclosed a hundred years later by ornamental walls. For most of the year it acts as a coach park, though in July and August huge grandstands are erected for the Edinburgh Military Tattoo (see p.950), which takes place every night during August, coinciding with the Edinburgh Festival. A shameless and spectacular pageant of swinging kilts and massed pipe bands, the Tattoo makes full use of its dramatic setting.

The **gatehouse** to the castle is a Romantic-style addition of the 1880s, complete with the last drawbridge ever built in Scotland. It was later adorned with appropriately heroic-looking statues of Sir William Wallace and Robert the Bruce. Standing guard by the drawbridge are real-life soldiers, members of the regiment in residence at the castle; while their presence in full dress uniform is always a hit with camera-toting tourists, it's also a reminder that the castle is still a working military garrison.

Rearing up behind is the most distinctive and impressive feature of the castle's silhouette, the sixteenth-century **Half Moon Battery**, which marks the outer limit of the actual defences. Once through the gatehouse, continue uphill along Lower Ward, passing through the **Portcullis Gate**, a handsome Renaissance gateway of the same period as the battery above, marred by the addition of a nineteenth-century upper storey equipped with anachronistic arrow slits rather than gunholes.

Beyond this the wide main path is known as Middle Ward, with the six-gun **Argyle Battery** to the right. Further west on **Mill's Mount Battery**, a well-known Edinburgh ritual takes place – the daily firing of the one o'clock gun. Originally designed for the benefit of ships in the Firth of Forth, these days it's an enjoyable ceremony for visitors to watch and a useful time-signal for city-centre office workers. Both batteries offer wonderful panoramic views over Princes Street and the New Town to the coastal towns and hills of Fife across the Forth.

National War Museum of Scotland

Located in the old hospital buildings, down a ramp between the café/restaurant immediately behind the one o'clock gun and the Governor's House, the **National War Museum of Scotland** (free), part of the collection of the National Museums of Scotland, is a recently refurbished exhibition covering the last 400 years of Scottish military history. While the various rooms are packed with uniforms, medals, paintings of heroic actions and plenty of interesting memorabilia, the museum manages to convey a reflective, human tone.

Back on Middle Ward, the **Governor's House** is a 1740s mansion whose harled masonry and crow-stepped gables are archetypal features of vernacular Scottish architecture. It now serves as the officers' mess for members of the garrison, while the governor himself lives in the northern side wing. Behind stands the largest single construction in the castle complex, the **New Barracks**, built in the 1790s in an austere Neoclassical style. From here a cobbled road then snakes round towards the enclosed citadel at the uppermost point of Castle Rock, entered via **Foog's Gate**.

St Margaret's Chapel

At the eastern end of the citadel, **St Margaret's Chapel** is the oldest surviving building in the castle, and probably also in Edinburgh itself. Used as a powder magazine for 300 years, this tiny Norman church was rediscovered in 1845 and was eventually rededicated in 1934, after sympathetic restoration. Externally, it is plain and severe, but the interior preserves an elaborate zigzag archway dividing the nave from the sanctuary. Although once believed to have been built by the saint herself, and mooted as the site of her death in 1093, its architectural style suggests that it actually dates from about thirty years later, and was thus probably built by King David I as a memorial to his mother.

The battlements in front of the chapel offer the best of all the castle's panoramic views. Just below the battlements there's a small **cemetery**, the last resting place of the **soldiers' pets**: it is kept in immaculate condition, particularly when contrasted with the dilapidated state of some of the city's public cemeteries. Continuing eastwards, you skirt the top of the Forewall and Half Moon Batteries, passing the 110-foot **Castle Well** en route to **Crown Square**, the highest, most secure and most important section of the entire complex.

Crown Square

The eastern side of Crown Square is occupied by the **Palace**, a surprisingly unassuming edifice built round an octagonal stair turret heightened in the nineteenth century to bear the castle's main flagpole. Begun in the 1430s, the Palace owes its Renaissance appearance to King James IV, though it was remodelled for Mary, Queen of Scots and her consort Henry, Lord Darnley, whose entwined initials (MAH), together with the date 1566, can be seen above one of the doorways. This gives access to a few historic rooms, the most interesting of which is the tiny panelled bedchamber at the extreme south-eastern corner, where Mary gave birth to James VI.

Another section of the Palace has recently been refurbished with a detailed audiovisual presentation on the **Honours of Scotland**, the originals of which are housed in the Crown Room at the very end of the display. Though you

---

The Stone of Destiny

Legend has it that the **Stone of Destiny** (also called the **Stone of Scone**) was "Jacob's Pillow", on which he dreamed of the ladder of angels from earth to heaven. Its real history is obscure, but it is known that it was moved from Ireland to Dunadd by missionaries, and thence to Dunstaffnage, from where Kenneth MacAlpine, king of the Dalriada Scots, brought it to the abbey at Scone in 838. There it remained for almost five hundred years, used as a coronation throne on which all kings of Scotland were crowned.

In 1296, an over-eager Edward I stole what he believed to be the Stone and installed it at Westminster Abbey, where, apart from a brief interlude in 1950 when it was removed by Scottish nationalists and hidden in Arbroath for several months, it remained for seven hundred years. All this changed in December 1996 when, after an elaborate ceremony-laden journey from London, the Stone returned to Scotland. Much to the annoyance of the people of Perth and the curators of Scone Palace (see p.1075), it was placed in Edinburgh Castle.

However, speculation surrounds the authenticity of the Stone, for the original is said to have been intricately carved, while the one seen today is a plain block of sandstone. Many believe that the canny monks at Scone palmed this off onto the English king (some say that it's nothing more sacred than the cover for a medieval septic tank), and that the real Stone of Destiny lies hidden in an underground chamber, its whereabouts a mystery to all but the chosen few.

might be put off by the slow-moving, claustrophobic queues that shuffle past the displays, the interest in them is justified: these magnificent crown jewels – the only pre-Restoration set in the United Kingdom – serve as one of the most potent images of Scotland's nationhood. They were last used for the Scottish-only coronation of Charles II in 1651, an event which provoked the wrath of Oliver Cromwell, who made exhaustive attempts to have the jewels melted down. Having narrowly escaped his clutches by being smuggled out of the castle and hidden in a rural church, the jewels later served as symbols of the absent monarch at sittings of the Scottish Parliament before being locked away in a chest following the Union of 1707. For over a century they were out of sight and eventually presumed lost, before being rediscovered in 1818 as a result of a search initiated by Sir Walter Scott.

Of the three pieces comprising the Honours, the oldest is the **sceptre**, given to James IV in 1494 by Pope Alexander VI. Even finer is the **sword**, a swaggering Italian High Renaissance masterpiece presented to James IV by the great artistic patron Pope Julius II. The jewel-encrusted **crown**, made for James V by the Scottish goldsmith James Mosman, incorporates the gold circlet worn by Robert the Bruce. The glass case containing the Honours has recently been rearranged to create space for its newest addition, the **Stone of Destiny** (see box). This remarkably plain object now lies incongruously next to the opulent crown jewels.

The south side of **Crown Square** is occupied by the **Great Hall**, built under James IV as a venue for banquets and other ceremonial occasions. It later underwent the indignity of conversion and subdivision, firstly into a barracks, then a hospital. During this time, its hammer-beam roof – the earliest of three in the Old Town – was hidden from view. It was restored towards the end of the nineteenth century, when the hall was decked out in the full-blown Romantic manner. In 1755, the castle church of St Mary on the north side of the square was replaced by a barracks, which in turn was skilfully converted into the quietly reverential **Scottish National War Memorial** in honour of the 150,000 Scots who fell in World War I.

The rest of the complex

From Crown Square, you can descend to the **Vaults**, a series of cavernous chambers erected by order of James IV. They were later used as a prison for captured foreign nationals, who have bequeathed a rich legacy of graffiti. One of the rooms houses the famous fifteenth-century siege gun, **Mons Meg**, which could fire a 500-pound stone nearly two miles. Directly opposite the entrance to the Vaults is the **Military Prison**, built in 1842, when the design and function of jails was a major topic of public debate. The cells, though designed for solitary confinement, are less forbidding than might be expected.

The Royal Mile

The **Royal Mile**, the name given to the ridge linking the castle with Holyrood, was described by Daniel Defoe, in 1724, as "the largest, longest and finest street for Buildings and Number of Inhabitants, not in Bretain only, but in the World". Almost exactly a mile in length, it is divided into four separate streets – **Castlehill**, **Lawnmarket**, **High Street** and **Canongate**. From these, branching out in a herringbone pattern, are a series of tightly packed closes and steep lanes entered via archways known as "pends". After the construction of the New Town, much of the housing along the Royal Mile degenerated into a notorious slum, but has since shaken off that reputation, becoming once again a highly desirable place to live. Although marred somewhat by rather too many tacky tourist shops and the odd misjudged new development, it is still among the most evocative parts of the city, and one that particularly rewards detailed exploration.

Castlehill

The narrow uppermost stretch of the Royal Mile is known as **Castlehill**. The first building on the northern side of the street as you leave the Castle Esplanade is the former reservoir for the Old Town, which has been converted into the **Edinburgh Old Town Weaving Centre** (daily 9am–5.30pm). Very much a commercial enterprise, the centre contains various large shops selling kilts, rugs and other tartan adornments while noisy looms rhymically churn the stuff out on the floors below. You can see these up close and try your hand at weaving on a self-guided tour (£4), or for £7 dress up in rather ridiculous-looking ancient tartan dress and have your photo snapped.

On the corner of the wall of the Weaving Centre facing the castle, a pretty Art Nouveau **Witches' Fountain** commemorates the three hundred or more women burnt at the spot on charges of sorcery, the last of whom died in 1722. Rising up behind is **Ramsay Gardens**, surely some of the most picturesque city-centre flats in the world. The oldest part is the octagonal Goose Pie House, home of the eighteenth-century poet Allan Ramsay, while the rest dates from the 1890s.

Opposite the Weaving Centre at the top of the southern side of Castlehill, the so-called **Cannonball House** takes its name from the cannonball embedded in its masonry, which according to legend was the result of a poorly targeted shot fired by the castle garrison at Bonnie Prince Charlie's encampment at Holyrood. The truth is far more prosaic: the ball marks the gravitation height of the city's first piped water supply. Alongside, the **Scotch Whisky Heritage Centre** (daily: June–Sept 9.30am–6.30pm; Oct–May 10am–5.30pm; £6.50; barrel-ride only £4.50) gives the lowdown on all aspects of Scotland's national beverage. The full tour starts off with a free dram (a measure) of whisky and then launches into a detailed explanation of how it's made, with a film, a brief lecture and a visit from an entertaining "ghost" who explains some of the specialized art of blending whisky. The climax is a gimmicky ride in a moving "barrel" through a series of uninspiring historical tableaux; there's little on offer here which you won't find done rather better on a tour of a real distillery.

Across the street, the **Outlook Tower** (April–Oct Mon–Fri 9.30am–6pm, Sat & Sun 10am–6pm; Nov–March daily 10am–5pm; £4.25) has been one of Edinburgh's top tourist attractions since 1853, when the original seventeenth-century tenement was equipped with a *camera obscura*. It makes a good introduction to the city: live images are beamed through a periscope mounted at the highest point of the tower onto a white table in the auditorium, accompanied by a running commentary. For the best views, visit at noon when there are fewer shadows.

A few doors further on is the **Assembly Hall**, normally used as the meeting place of the annual General Assembly of the Church of Scotland but, since May 1999, the home of the **Scottish Parliament** while it awaits more permanent accommodation (see p.925). It is possible to visit the debating chamber of the parliament by going to the public entrance in Milne's Court, one of the closes off the Royal Mile just past the Assembly Hall (Mon–Fri 10am–noon & 2–4pm; free). When the parliament is in session, you can sit and watch the **debates** from the large public gallery – tickets are available on an ad hoc basis either from the desk at the public entrance or from the Scottish Parliament **visitor centre** on the corner of George IV Bridge and High Street

(☎0131/348 5000, 🌐www.scottish.parliament.uk). The best time to see a debate is First Minister's Questions on Thursday afternoon; if the house is not in session, it is still possible to view the empty debating chamber from the public gallery.

The imposing black church building opposite the Assembly Hall at the foot of Castlehill is **The Hub** (daily 8am–late; ☎0131/473 2010, 🌐www.eif.co.uk/thehub), also known as "Edinburgh's Festival Centre". Although the Festival only takes place for three weeks every August and early September, The Hub is open year round, providing performance, rehearsal and exhibition space, a ticket centre and a café. The building was constructed in 1845 to designs by James Gillespie Graham and Augustus Pugin, one of the co-architects of the Houses of Parliament in London. On the ground floor is the *Hub Café* (daily 8am–11pm); also worth checking out is the main hall upstairs, where the original neo-Gothic woodwork and high-vaulted ceiling is enlivened with a fabulous fabric design in Rastafarian colours. Permanent works of art have been incorporated into the centre, including over 200 delightful foot-high sculptures by Scottish sculptor Jill Watson, depicting festival performers and audiences.

Lawnmarket

Below the Tolbooth Kirk, the Royal Mile opens out into the broader expanse of **Lawnmarket**, which, as its name suggests, was once a marketplace. At its northern end is the entry to **Milne's Court**, whose excellently restored tenements now serve as student residences, and immediately beyond, **James Court**, one of Edinburgh's most fashionable addresses prior to the advent of the New Town; David Hume and James Boswell were among those who lived there.

Back on Lawnmarket itself, **Gladstone's Land** (April–Oct Mon–Sat 10am–5pm, Sun 2–5pm; £3.50) takes its name from the merchant Thomas Gledstane [sic], who in 1617 acquired a modest dwelling on the site, transforming it into a magnificent six-storey mansion. The arcaded ground floor, the only authentic example left of what was once a common feature of Royal Mile houses, has been restored to illustrate its early function as a shopping booth. Several other rooms have been kitted out in authentic period style to give an impression of the lifestyle of a well-to-do household of the late seventeenth century; the Painted Chamber, with its decorated wooden ceiling and wall friezes, is particularly impressive.

A few paces further on, steps lead down to Lady Stair's Close, in which stands the **Writers' Museum** (Mon–Sat 10am–5pm; also Sun 2–5pm during the Festival; free), housed in Lady Stair's House, another fine seventeenth-century residence. Dedicated to the three lions of Scottish literature – Robert Burns, Sir Walter Scott and Robert Louis Stevenson – the museum shows off various manuscripts, first editions and portraits, plus personal mementoes (among them locks of hair and walking sticks). Continuing the literary theme, the courtyard outside, called the **Makars' Court** after the Scots word for the "maker" of poetry or prose, has quotations by Scotland's most famous writers and poets inscribed on paving stones.

On the south side of Lawnmarket is **Brodie's Close**, named after the father of one of Edinburgh's most morbid characters, Deacon William Brodie, apparent pillar of society by day, burglar by night. Following his eventual capture, he managed to escape to Holland, but was betrayed, brought back to Edinburgh and hanged in 1788 on gallows of his own design. His ruse of trying to cheat death by secretly wearing an iron collar under his shirt failed. You can visit the popular *Deacon Brodie's Tavern* on the corner of the Lawnmarket and Bank

Though **Robert Louis Stevenson** (1850–94) is sometimes dismissed for his straight-up writing style, he was undoubtedly one of the best-loved writers of his generation, whose travelogues, novels, short stories and essays remain enormously popular more than a century after his death.

Born in Edinburgh into a distinguished family of engineers, Stevenson was a sickly child, with a solitary childhood dominated by his governess, Alison "Cummie" Cunningham, who regaled him with tales drawn from Calvinist folklore. Sent to the university to study engineering, Stevenson rebelled against his upbringing by spending much of his time in the lowlife howffs and brothels of the city, and eventually switching to law. Although called to the bar in 1875, by then he had decided to channel his energies into literature: his early successes were two **travelogues**, *An Inland Voyage* and *Travels with a Donkey in the Cevennes*, kaleidoscopic jottings based on his journeys in France, where he went to escape Scotland's weather, which was damaging his health. It was there that he met Fanny Osbourne, an American ten years his senior, who was estranged from her husband and had two children in tow. His voyage to join her in San Francisco formed the basis for his most important factual work, *The Amateur Emigrant*, a vivid firsthand account of the great nineteenth-century European migration to the United States.

Having married the now-divorced Fanny, Stevenson began an elusive search for an agreeable climate that led to Switzerland, the French Riviera and the Scottish Highlands. He belatedly turned to the novel, achieving immediate acclaim in 1881 for **Treasure Island**. In 1886, his most famous short story, **Dr Jekyll and Mr Hyde**, despite its nominal London setting, offered a vivid evocation of Edinburgh's Old Town – an allegory of its dual personality of prosperity and squalor, and an analysis of its Calvinistic preoccupations with guilt and damnation. The same year saw the publication of the historical romance **Kidnapped**, an adventure novel which exemplified Stevenson's view that literature should seek above all to entertain.

In 1887 Stevenson left Britain for good, travelling first to the United States; a year later, he set sail for the South Seas, and eventually settled in **Samoa**; his last works include a number of stories with a local setting, such as the grimly realistic *The Ebb Tide* and *The Beach of Falesà*. He died suddenly from a brain haemorrhage in 1894 and was buried on the top of Mount Vaea overlooking the Pacific Ocean.

Street and ruminate over a beer on the connections between Brodie, Robert Louis Stevenson's similarly themed tale *Dr Jekyll and Mr Hyde*, and the various split personalities of Edinburgh itself, not least its Old Town and New Town.

The High Kirk of St Giles

Across George IV Bridge is the third section of the Royal Mile, known as the **High Street**, which occupies two blocks either side of the intersection between North Bridge and South Bridge. The dominant building of the southern side of the street is the **High Kirk of St Giles** (April–Sept Mon–Fri 9am–7pm, Sat 9am–5pm, Sun 1–5pm; Oct–March Mon–Sat 9am–5pm, Sun 1–5pm; free) which closes off Parliament Square from High Street. The sole parish church of medieval Edinburgh, where John Knox (see box) launched and directed the Scottish Reformation, the Kirk is almost invariably referred to as a cathedral, although it has been the seat of a bishop on only two brief and unhappy occasions in the seventeenth century. According to one of the city's best-known legends, the attempt in 1637 to introduce the English prayer book, and thus episcopal government, so incensed a humble stallholder named Jenny Geddes that she hurled her stool at the preacher, prompting the rest of the congregation to chase the offending clergy out of the building. A tablet in the north aisle marks the spot from where she let rip.

John Knox

The Protestant reformer **John Knox** has been alternately credited with, or blamed for, the distinctive national culture that emerged from the Calvinist Reformation, which has cast its shadow over Scottish history and the Scottish character right up to the present.

Little is known about Knox's early years: he was born between 1505 and 1514 in East Lothian, and trained for the priesthood at St Andrews University under John Major, author of a *History of Great Britain* that advocated the union of Scotland and England. Ordained in 1540, Knox then served as a private tutor, in league with Scotland's first significant Protestant leader, **George Wishart**. After Wishart was burnt at the stake for heresy in 1546, Knox became involved with the group who had carried out the revenge murder of the Scottish primate, Cardinal David Beaton, subsequently taking over his castle in St Andrews. The following year this was captured by the French, and Knox was carted off to work as a galley slave.

He was freed in 1548, as a result of the intervention of the English, who invited him to play an evangelizing role in the spread of their own Reformation. When the Catholic Mary Tudor acceded to the English throne in 1553, Knox fled to the continent, ending up as minister to the English-speaking community in Geneva, which was then in the grip of the theocratic government of the Frenchman **Jean Calvin**. Knox was quickly won over to his radical version of Protestantism, declaring Geneva to be "the most perfect school of Christ since the days of the Apostles". In exile, Knox wrote his infamous treatise, *The First Blast of the Trumpet Against the Monstrous Regiment of Women*, a specific attack on the three Catholic women then ruling Scotland, England and France, which has made his name synonymous with misogyny ever since.

When Knox was allowed to return to Scotland in 1555, he took over as spiritual leader of the Reformation, becoming minister of St Giles in Edinburgh, where he established a reputation as a charismatic preacher. However, the establishment of Protestantism as the official religion of Scotland in 1560 was dependent on the forging of an alliance with Elizabeth I, which Knox himself rigorously championed. Although the return of Mary, Queen of Scots the following year placed a Catholic monarch on the Scottish throne, reputedly Knox was always able to retain the upper hand in his famous disputes with her.

For all his considerable influence, Knox was not responsible for many of the features which have created the popular image of Scottish Presbyterianism – and of Knox himself – as austere and joyless. A man of refined cultural tastes, he did not encourage the iconoclasm that destroyed so many of Scotland's churches and works of art: indeed, much of this was carried out by English hands. Nor did he promote unbending Sabbatarianism, an obsessive work ethic or even the inflexible view of the doctrine of predestination favoured by his far more fanatical successors. Ironically, though, by fostering an irrevocable rift in the "Auld Alliance" with France, he did do more than anyone else to ensure that Scotland's future was to be linked with that of England.

In the early nineteenth century, St Giles received a much-needed but over-drastic restoration, covering most of the Gothic exterior with a smooth stone coating that gives it a certain Georgian dignity while sacrificing its medieval character almost completely. The only part to survive this treatment is the late fifteenth-century tower, whose resplendent crown spire is formed by eight flying buttresses. The **interior** has survived in much better shape. Especially notable are the four massive piers supporting the tower, which date back, at least in part, to the church's Norman predecessor. Look out for the great **west window**, whose dedication to Robbie Burns in 1985 caused enormous controversy: as a hardened drinker and womanizer, the national bard was far from being an upholder of accepted Presbyterian values.

At the southeastern corner of St Giles, the **Thistle Chapel** was built by Sir Robert Lorimer in 1911 as the private chapel of the sixteen knights of the Most Noble Order of the Thistle, the highest chivalric order in Scotland. Self-consciously derivative of St George's Chapel in Windsor, it's an exquisite piece of craftsmanship, with an elaborate ribbed vault, huge drooping bosses, and extravagantly ornate stalls.

Parliament Square

The rest of **Parliament Square** is dominated by the continuous Neoclassical facades of the **Law Courts**, originally planned by Robert Adam (1728–92), one of four brothers in a family of architects (their father William Adam designed Hopetoun House; see p.958) whose work helped imbue the New Town with much of its grace and elegance. Because of a shortage of funds, the present exteriors were built to designs by Robert Reid (1776–1856), the designer of the northern part of New Town, who faithfully quoted from Adam's architectural vocabulary without matching his flair.

Around the corner, facing the southern side of St Giles, is **Parliament House**, built in the 1630s for the Scottish Parliament, a role it maintained until the Union, when it passed into the hands of the legal fraternity. To enter the impressive main hall go through the entrance lobby (Mon–Fri 9am–5pm); the most notable feature is the extravagant hammer-beam roof and the delicately carved stone corbels from which it springs – in addition to some vicious grotesques with accurate depictions of several castles, including Edinburgh. In the far corner a small exhibition explains the history of the building and courts, but it's more fun simply to watch the everyday business, with solicitors and bewigged advocates in hushed conferrals. Most of the court rooms have public galleries, which you can sit in if you're interested – ask one of the attendants in the lobby to point you in the right direction.

Upper High Street

The first main building on the northern side of the **High Street** after the intersection of George IV Bridge and Bank Street is the High Court of Justiciary, Scotland's highest criminal court, outside which is a statue of David Hume, the philosopher and one of Edinburgh's greatest sons, who looks decidedly wan and chilly dressed in nothing but a Roman toga. A little further on, opposite the Mercat Cross, the U-shaped **City Chambers** were designed by John Adam, brother of Robert, as the Royal Exchange. Local traders never warmed to the exchange, however, so the town council established its headquarters there instead. Beneath the City Chambers lies **Mary King's Close**, one of Edinburgh's most unusual attractions. Built in the early sixteenth century, it was closed off for many years after the devastation of the 1645 plague, before being entirely covered up by the chambers in 1753. Brief tours of this rather spooky "lost city" are run regularly through the day by Mercat Tours (℡0131/557 6464).

Across the road you'll find the **Tron Kirk**, a popular focal point for hardy Hogmanay revellers to count down the seconds to the new year. The church was built in the 1630s and remained in use until 1952. It was then closed for forty years, during which time excavations revealed sections of an old close, Marlin's Wynd, which ran from High Street down to the Cowgate. Today the building houses the **Old Town Information Centre** (June–Sept daily 10am–7pm; Easter–May Mon & Thurs–Sun 10am–1pm & 2–5pm), where you can peruse information boards on the buildings of the Old Town and look down from raised walkways on the Marlin's Wynd excavations.

Lower High Street

Beyond the intersection of North Bridge and South Bridge, **Trinity Apse** is a poignant reminder of the fifteenth-century Holy Trinity Collegiate Church, formerly one of Edinburgh's most outstanding buildings, but demolished in 1848 to make way for an extension to Waverley Station. The stones were carefully numbered and stored on Calton Hill so that it could be reassembled at a later date, but many were pilfered before sufficient funds became available, and only the apse could be reconstructed on this new site. It's now home to a **Brass Rubbing Centre** (Mon–Sat 10am–5pm; Sun noon–5pm during the Festival only; last rubbing sold 1hr before closing; free), where you can rub your own impressions from Pictish crosses and medieval church brasses from £1.20 upwards.

On the other side of High Street, the noisy **Museum of Childhood** (Mon–Sat 10am–5pm; also Sun noon–5pm during the Festival; free) was, oddly enough, founded by an eccentric local councillor who heartily disliked children. Although he claimed that the museum was a serious social archive for adults, and dedicated it to King Herod, it has always attracted swarms of kids, who delight in the dolls' houses, teddy bears, train sets, marionettes and other paraphernalia.

Almost directly opposite is what's thought to be the city's oldest surviving dwelling, the early sixteenth-century **Moubray House** (no public access). The uses of the four-storey house have included tavern, bookshop and even, towards the end of the nineteenth century, temperance hotel. Next door lies the picturesque **John Knox's House** (Mon–Sat 10am–5pm; July & Aug also Sun noon–5pm; £2.25), built some thirty years later. With its outside stairway, biblical motto, and sundial adorned with a statue of Moses, it gives a good impression of how the Royal Mile must have once looked. Whether or not it was ever really the home of Knox is debatable: he may have moved here for safety at the height of the religious troubles. The rather bare interiors, which give a good idea of the labyrinthine layout of Old Town houses, display explanatory material on Knox's life and career. The house is linked to the neighbouring **Netherbow Arts Centre**, a busy venue during the Festival which displays paintings and photography throughout the year and has a popular lunchtime café selling wholesome soups and light meals.

Canongate

For over seven hundred years, the district through which Canongate runs was a burgh in its own right, officially separate from the capital, which was entered through the Netherbow Port. A notorious slum area even into the 1960s, it has been the subject of some of the most ambitious **restoration** programmes in the Old Town, though the lack of harmony between the buildings renovated in different decades can be seen fairly clearly. For such a central district, it's interesting to note that most of the buildings here are residential, and by no means are they all bijou apartments. The development of the Canongate is ongoing, particularly at its lower end around the site of the new parliament building. This section of the Royal Mile features an eclectic range of shops, from a gallery of historic maps and sea charts to genuine bagpipe makers.

Near the top of Canongate, a good example of the restoration work can be seen at **Chessel's Court**, a mid-eighteenth-century development with fanciful Rococo chimneys. Over the road the **Morocco Land** is a reasonably faithful reproduction of an old tenement, incorporating the original bust of a Moor from which its name derives.

Dominated by a turreted steeple and an odd external box clock, the late sixteenth-century **Canongate Tolbooth**, a little further down the north side of the street, has served both as the headquarters of the burgh administration and as a prison, and now houses **The People's Story** (Mon–Sat 10am–5pm, also Sun 2–5pm during the Festival; free), a lively museum devoted to the everyday life and work of Edinburgh people down the centuries. Next door, **Canongate Kirk** was built in the 1680s to a curiously archaic design, still Renaissance in outline, and built to a cruciform plan wholly at odds with the ideals and requirements of Protestant worship. Its churchyard, one of the city's most exclusive cemeteries, commands a superb view across to Calton Hill. Among those buried here are Adam Smith, Mrs Agnes McLehose (better known as Robert Burns'"Clarinda") and Robert Fergusson, regarded by some as Edinburgh's greatest poet, despite his death at the age of 24; his headstone was donated by Burns, a fervent admirer, who also wrote the inscription.

Opposite the church, the **Museum of Edinburgh** in Huntly House (Mon–Sat 10am–5pm, also Sun 2–5pm during the Festival; free) includes a quirky array of old shop signs, some dating back to the eighteenth century, as well as displays on indigenous industries such as glass, silver, pottery and clock-making. Also on view is the original version of the National Covenant of 1638; modern science has failed to resolve whether or not some of the signatories signed with their own blood, as tradition has it.

Among the intriguing series of closes and entries on this stretch of Canongate, **Dunbar's Close**, on the north side of the street, has a beautiful seventeenth-century walled garden tucked in behind the tenements. Opposite this is the entry to Crichton's Close, through which you'll find the **Scottish Poetry Library** (Mon–Fri noon–6pm, Sat noon–4pm; free), a small island of modern architectural eloquence amid a sea of construction work and large-scale developments. At the very foot of the street, the entrance to the residential **Whitehorse Close** was once the site of the inn from where stagecoaches began the journey to London. Stridently quaint, it drips with the characteristic features of Scottish vernacular architecture: crow-stepped gables, dormer windows, overhanging upper storeys and curving outside stairways.

Holyrood

At the foot of Canongate lies **Holyrood**, Edinburgh's royal quarter, the legend of whose foundation in 1128 is described in a fifteenth-century manuscript which is still kept there. The story goes that King David I, son of Malcolm Canmore and St Margaret, went out hunting one day and was suddenly confronted by a stag who threw him from his horse and seemed ready to gore him. In desperation, the king tried to protect himself by grasping its antlers, but instead found himself holding a crucifix, whereupon the animal ran off. In a dream that night, he heard a voice commanding him to "make a house for Canons devoted to the Cross"; he duly obeyed, naming the abbey Holyrood (rood being an alternative name for a cross). A more prosaic explanation is that

Admissions to Holyrood

Guided tours of Holyrood take place from November to March only; at other times of the year, you're free to move around at your own pace. It is worth remembering that Holyrood is still a working palace, so the buildings are closed to the public for long periods during state functions: you won't be able to visit for a fortnight in the middle of May, and during the annual royal visit which usually takes place in the last two weeks of June and the first in July.

David, the most pious of all Scotland's monarchs, simply acquired a relic of the True Cross and decided to build a suitable home for it.

Holyrood soon became a favoured **royal residence**, its situation in a secluded valley making it far more agreeable than the draughty castle. At first, monarchs lodged in the monastic guest house, to which a wing for the exclusive use of the court was added during the reign of James II. This was transformed into a full-blown palace for James IV, which in turn was replaced by a much larger building for Charles II, although he never actually lived there. Indeed, it was something of a white elephant until Queen Victoria started making regular trips to her northern kingdom, a custom that has been maintained by her successors.

The Palace of Holyroodhouse

In its present form, the **Palace of Holyroodhouse** (daily: April–Oct 9.30am–6pm; Nov–March 9.30am–4.30pm; £6.50) is largely a seventeenth-century creation, planned for Charles II. However, the tower house of the old palace was skilfully incorporated to form the northwestern block, with a virtual mirror-image of it erected as a counterbalance at the other end. Inside, the **State Apartments**, as Charles II's palace is known, are decked out with oak panelling, tapestries, portraits and decorative paintings, all overshadowed by the magnificent white stucco **ceilings**, especially in the Morning Drawing Room. The most eye-catching chamber, however, is the **Great Gallery**, which takes up the entire first floor of the northern wing. During the 1745 sojourn of the Young Pretender this was the setting for a banquet, described in detail in Scott's novel *Waverley*, and it is still used for big ceremonial occasions. Along the walls are 89 portraits commissioned from the seventeenth-century Dutch artist Jacob de Wit to illustrate the royal lineage of Scotland from its mythical origins in the fourth century BC; the result is unintentionally hilarious, as it is clear that the artist's imagination was taxed to bursting point by the need to paint so many different facial types without having an inkling as to what the subjects actually looked like.

The oldest parts of the palace, the **Historical Apartments**, are mainly of note for their associations with Mary, Queen of Scots and in particular for the brutal murder, organized by her husband, Lord Darnley, of her private secretary, David Rizzio, who was stabbed 56 times and dragged from the small closet, through the Queen's Bedchamber, and into the Outer Chamber. Until a few years ago, visitors were shown apparently indelible bloodstains on the floor of the latter, but these are now admitted to be fakes and have been covered up. A display cabinet in the same room shows some pieces of **needlework** woven by the deposed queen while in English captivity; another case has an outstanding **miniature portrait** of her by the French court painter, François Clouet.

Holyrood Abbey

In the grounds of the Palace are the wonderfully evocative ruins of **Holyrood Abbey**. The only surviving fragment of King David's original Norman church is a doorway in the far southeastern corner. Most of the remainder dates from a late twelfth- and early thirteenth-century rebuilding in the Early Gothic style.

The surviving parts of the **west front**, including one of the twin towers and the elaborately carved entrance portal, show how resplendent the abbey must once have been. Unfortunately, its sacking by the English in 1547, followed by the demolition of the transept and chancel during the Reformation, all but destroyed the building.

The Scottish Parliament site

Immediately opposite Abbey Strand, the massive construction site between the Royal Mile and Holyrood Road is where the new **Scottish Parliament** is being built. For decades, campaigners for home rule for Scotland envisaged the Old Royal High School building on Calton Hill (see p.936) as the place where the long-awaited Scottish Parliament would sit. In the run-up to the devolution referendum, however, the Scottish Office unexpectedly announced that the Old Royal High School was too small to accommodate the proposed parliament and its offices, and a disused brewery at the foot of the Royal Mile was identified as the ideal location. Originally designed by the late Catalan architect **Enric Miralles**, the structure will cost something in the region of £100 million, and is due to be ready by late 2002.

While the building is being completed, a temporary **visitor centre** (daily 10am–4pm; free) has been established on Holyrood Road, next door to Dynamic Earth, where you can view plans, models and computer images of the proposed structure.

Our Dynamic Earth

On the Holyrood Road, beneath a pin-cushion of white metal struts which make it look like a miniature version of London's Millennium Dome, **Our Dynamic Earth** (April–Oct daily 10am–6pm; Nov–March Wed–Sat 10am–5pm; £7.95), is a hi-tech attraction about the natural world aimed mainly at families. A "time machine" elevator takes you to a room where the creation of the universe, 15 billion years ago, is described using wide-screen video graphics, eerie music and a sonorous commentary. Subsequent galleries describe the formation of the earth and continents with crashing sound-effects and a shaking floor, the calmer grandeur of glaciers and oceans being explored through magnificent large-screen landscape footage. The "Casualties and Survivors" gallery describes the history of life on earth, from primordial swamps to life-size models of some of the odd creatures who once inhabited the earth, with interactive computer screens and special effects at every turn.

Holyrood Park

Holyrood Park, or Queen's Park – a natural wilderness in the very heart of the modern city – is unquestionably one of Edinburgh's main assets, as locals (though relatively few tourists) readily appreciate. Packed into an area no more than five miles in diameter is an amazing variety of landscapes – hills, crags, moorland, marshes, glens, lochs and fields – representing something of a microcosm of Scotland's scenery. The park is a great place for outdoor activities, with toddlers, cyclists and rock-climbers all being catered for. A single tarred road, the **Queen's Drive**, circles the park. In a small stone-built gate lodge at the entrance to the park from Holyrood Road, the **Holyrood Park Ranger Service** has a small information point (Mon–Thurs 10am–4pm, Fri 10am–3.30pm) where you can pick up a map of suggested walks or find out about ranger-led walks which depart from the lodge at 2pm on Wednesdays. Note that some time in 2002 the ranger service will move to a brand-new Park HQ in the area behind the Palace of Holyroodhouse.

Two of the most rewarding walks begin opposite the southern gates of the palace: one, a pathway nicknamed the Radical Road, traverses the ridge immediately below the **Salisbury Crags**, one of the main features of the Edinburgh skyline, while you can also walk along the top of the basalt crags, from where there are excellent views of the Palace of Holyroodhouse and Holyrood Abbey.

From the palace gates, the best way to follow Queen's Drive is in a clockwise direction. Soon you arrive at **St Margaret's Loch**, a nineteenth-century artificial pond, above which stand the scanty ruins of **St Anthony's Chapel**, another fine vantage point. From here, the road's loop is one-way only for vehicular traffic, ascending to **Dunsapie Loch**, again an artificial stretch of water, which makes an excellent foil to the crag behind.

This is the usual starting point for the ascent of **Arthur's Seat**, a majestic extinct volcano rising 823ft above sea level. The Seat is Edinburgh's single most prominent landmark, resembling a huge crouched lion when seen from the west. The views from the top are all you'd expect, covering the entire city and much of the Firth of Forth; on a clear day, you can even see the southernmost mountains of the Highlands.

From Dunsapie Loch, Queen's Drive continues round beneath the summit to meet itself again at a roundabout near the southern point of the Salisbury Crags. At a second roundabout the second exit leads out of the park; the first exit takes you beneath **Samson's Ribs**, a group of basalt pillars strikingly reminiscent of the Hebridean island of Staffa (see p.1097), and onto **Duddingston Loch**, the only natural stretch of water in the park, now a bird sanctuary. Perched above it, just outside the park boundary, **Duddingston Kirk** dates back in part to the twelfth century and is the focus of one of the most unspoilt old villages within modern Edinburgh. In the village, the *Sheep Heid Inn* (see p.944) is a great spot to pull in for a drink or a bar meal, and you can also try your hand at the traditional skittle alley.

Cowgate and the Grassmarket

At the bottom of the valley immediately south of the Royal Mile, and following a roughly parallel course from the Lawnmarket to St Mary's Street, is the **Cowgate**. One of Edinburgh's oldest surviving streets, it was also formerly one of the city's most prestigious addresses. However, the construction of the great **viaducts** of George IV Bridge and South Bridge entombed it below street level. In the last decade or so the Cowgate has experienced something of a revival, with various nightclubs and festival venues establishing themselves, though few tourists venture here and the contrast with the neighbouring Royal Mile remains stark.

At the corner with Niddry Street, which runs down from the High Street near its junction with North Bridge and South Bridge, unprepossessing **St Cecilia's Hall** (Wed & Sat 2–5pm; also Mon–Sat 10.30am–12.30pm during the Festival; £1) was built in the 1760s for the Musical Society of Edinburgh. Inside, Scotland's oldest and most beautiful concert room, oval in shape and set under a shallow dome, makes a perfect venue for concerts of Baroque and early music, held during the Festival and occasionally at other times of the year. The building is primarily worth visiting for the **Russell Collection** of antique keyboard instruments.

The Grassmarket

At its western end, Cowgate opens out into the **Grassmarket**, which has played an important role in the murkier aspects of Edinburgh's turbulent history. The public gallows were located here, and it was the scene of numerous riots and other disturbances down the centuries. It was here, in 1736, that Captain Porteous was lynched after he had ordered shots to be fired at the crowd watching a public execution. The notorious duo William Burke and William Hare had their lair in a now-vanished close just off the western end of the Grassmarket, luring to it victims whom they murdered with the inten-

respectful but imaginative treatment of the nation's treasures, this is undoubtedly Scotland's premier museum. The fresh, open atmosphere of the building is
combined with terrific features: specially commissioned art works; the
Discovery Centre, specifically aimed at 5- to 14-year-olds; the **exhibIT**
computer bank with databases of the museum's collections; and the **Tower
Restaurant**, a sleek, stylish place with fabulous views which is also open in the
evenings (for a review, see p.940).

The main entrance to the museum is at the base of the tower (although it is
also possible to enter through the neighbouring Royal Museum of Scotland;
see p.930). Make your way to the information desk in **Hawthornden Court**,
the central atrium of the museum and a useful orientation point; on this level
you'll also find the museum shop and access to the Royal Museum café. Free
guided tours on different themes take place through the day, and free audioguides give detailed information on artefacts and displays.

Level 0

To get to the first section, "**Beginnings**", take the lift or stairs from
Hawthornden Court down to Level 0. Here, Scotland's story before the
arrival of humans is presented with audiovisual displays, artistic recreations
and a selection of rocks and fossils, including some Lewisian gneiss, the oldest
rock in Europe, and "Lizzie" (*Westlothiana lizziae*), the oldest known fossil reptile in the world.

The second section, "**Early People**", also on Level 0, covers the period from
the arrival of the first people to the end of the first millennium AD. This, in
many ways, is the most engrossing section of the entire museum, an eloquent
testament to the remarkable craftsmanship, artistry and practicality of Scotland's
early people. From the doors of the main lift you're confronted by eight giant
bronze figures in the distinctive post-industrial style of Edinburgh-born sculptor **Sir Eduardo Paolozzi**. His trademark incorporation of geometric shapes
into the human form allows the figures to "wear" different artefacts. The innovative use of contemporary art is continued with installations by the environmental artist **Andy Goldsworthy**, who shapes natural materials into sinuous-
ly beautiful geometrical patterns. Among the artefacts on display, highlights are
the **Trappain treasure** hoard, 20kg of silver plates, cutlery and goblets found
buried in East Lothian, and the **Cramond Lioness**, a sculpture from a Roman
tombstone found recently in the Firth of Forth.

Levels 1 and 3

The "**Kingdom of the Scots**" on Level 1 covers the period between
Scotland's development as a single independent nation and the union with
England in 1707. At the entrance to the section in Hawthornden Court is the
Dupplin Cross, a symbol of the different peoples who united under King
Kenneth MacAlpine to form a single kingdom in 843. Star exhibits include the
Monymusk reliquary, an intricately decorated box said to have carried the
remains of St Columba; the **Lewis chessmen**, exquisitely idiosyncratic
twelfth-century pieces carved from walrus ivory; and the "**Maiden**", an early
form of the guillotine.

Level 3 shows exhibits under the theme "**Scotland Transformed**", covering the century or so following the Union of Parliaments in 1707. This was the
period which saw the last of the Highland uprisings under Bonnie Prince
Charlie (whose silver travelling canteen is on display), yet also witnessed the
expansion of trade links with the Americas and developments in industries
such as weaving and iron and steel production. Dominating the floor is a

reconstructed steam-driven **Newcomen engine**, which was still being used to pump water from a coal mine in Ayrshire in 1901. Alongside it, in contrast, is part of a thatched, cruck-frame house of the 1720s of a type in which many Scots still lived during this time.

Levels 4, 5 and 6

Following the early innovations of steam and mechanical engineering, Scotland went on to pioneer many aspects of heavy engineering, with ship and locomotive production to the fore. Largest of the exhibits in "**Industry and Empire**" on Level 4 is the steam locomotive *Ellesmere*. As well as industrial progress, other fields are covered too, including domestic life, leisure activities and the influence of Scots around the world, both as a result of emigration, and through such luminaries as James Watt, Charles Rennie Mackintosh and Robert Louis Stevenson.

For the **Twentieth Century Gallery** on Level 6, a range of Scots, from schoolchildren to celebrities, were asked to pick a single object to represent the twentieth century. Choices are intriguing, controversial and unexpected, from computers to football strips, cans of Irn Bru to a black Saab convertible. Tony Blair, who went to Fettes School in Edinburgh, chose a guitar, and former Edinburgh milkman Sean Connery a milk bottle. The **roof garden**, accessed by a lift, offers sweeping views out to the Firth of Forth, the Pentland hills, and across to the castle and Royal Mile skyline.

The Royal Museum of Scotland

Interlinked with the National Museum, though also with its own entrance, is the **Royal Museum of Scotland** (same hours; free), a dignified Venetian-style palace with a cast-iron interior which contains an extraordinarily eclectic range of exhibits, from exotic stuffed animals to colonial loot. The **sculpture** in the lofty entrance hall includes a superb Assyrian relief from the royal palace at Nimrud and a totem pole from British Columbia. Also on the ground floor are the **Power Collections**, with a double-action beam engine designed by James Watt in 1786 alongside the control desk from Hunterston "A" nuclear reactor. Upstairs there's a fine array of Egyptian mummies, ceramics from ancient Greece to the present day, costumes, jewellery, natural-history displays and a splendid selection of European decorative art, including some stunning French silverware made during the reign of Louis XIV.

The University of Edinburgh

Immediately alongside the Royal Museum is the earliest surviving part of the **University of Edinburgh**, variously referred to as Old College or Old Quad, although nowadays it houses only a few university departments; the main campus colonizes the streets and squares to the south. Founded in 1582 by James VI (later James I of England), the university is now the largest in Scotland, with over 13,000 students.

The Old College was designed by Robert Adam, but was built after his death in a considerably modified form by William Playfair (1789–1857), one of Edinburgh's greatest architects. The small **Talbot Rice Art Gallery** (Tues–Sat 10am–5pm; free), housed in the southwest corner of the Old College, displays in rather lacklustre fashion some of the university's large art and bronze collection, though touring and temporary avant-garde exhibitions are mounted here on a regular basis. The show held during the Festival is normally of a high standard.

The New Town

The **New Town**, itself well over two hundred years old, stands in total contrast to the Old Town: the layout is symmetrical, the streets are broad and straight, and most of the buildings are Neoclassical. Originally intended to be residential, the entire area, right down to the names of its streets, is something of a celebration of the Union, which was then generally regarded as a proud development in Scotland's history. Today the New Town is the bustling hub of the city's professional, commercial and business life, dominated by shops, banks and offices.

The existence of the New Town is chiefly due to the vision of **George Drummond**, who made schemes for the expansion of the city soon after becoming Lord Provost in 1725. The North Bridge, linking the Old Town with the port of Leith, was built between 1763 and 1772. In 1766, following a public competition, a plan for the New Town by 22-year-old architect **James Craig** was chosen. Its gridiron pattern was perfectly matched to the site: central George Street, flanked by showpiece squares, was laid out along the main ridge, with parallel Princes Street and Queen Street on either side below, and two smaller streets, Thistle Street and Rose Street in between the three major thoroughfares providing coach houses, artisans' dwellings and shops. Princes and Queen streets were built up on one side only, so as not to block the spectacular views of the Old Town and Fife.

In many ways, the layout of the New Town is its own most remarkable sight, an extraordinary grouping of squares, circuses, terraces, crescents and parks with a few set pieces such as **Register House**, the north frontage of **Charlotte Square** and the assemblage of curiosities on and around **Calton Hill**. However, it also contains assorted Victorian additions, notably the **Scott Monument**, as well as two of the city's most important public collections – the **National Gallery of Scotland** and, further afield, the **Scottish National Gallery of Modern Art**.

Princes Street

Although allocated only a subsidiary role in the original plan of the New Town, **Princes Street** had developed into Edinburgh's principal thoroughfare by the middle of the nineteenth century, a role it has retained ever since. Its unobstructed views across to the castle and the Old Town are undeniably magnificent. Indeed, without the views, Princes Street would lose much of its appeal; its northern side, dominated by ugly department stores, is almost always crowded with shoppers, and few of the original eighteenth-century buildings remain.

It was the coming of the railway, which follows a parallel course to the south, that ensured Princes Street's rise to prominence. The tracks are well concealed at the far end of the sunken **gardens** that replaced the Nor' Loch, which provide ample space to relax or picnic during the summer.

The East End

Register House (Mon–Fri 9am–4.45pm; free), Princes Street's most distinguished building, is at its extreme northeastern corner, framing the perspective down North Bridge, and providing a good visual link between the Old and New Towns. It was designed in the 1770s by Robert Adam to hold Scotland's historic records, a function it has maintained ever since. Opposite is one of the few buildings on the south side of Princes Street, the **Balmoral Hotel**, formerly known as the *North British*. Among the most luxurious hotels in the city, it has always been associated with the railway, and the timepiece on its bulky clocktower is always kept two minutes fast in order to encourage passengers to hurry to catch their trains.

The Scott Monument and the Royal Scottish Academy

Facing the Victorian shopping emporium Jenners, and set within East Princes Street Gardens, the 200ft-high **Scott Monument** (June–Sept Mon–Sat 9am–8pm, Sun 10am–6pm; March–May & Oct daily 9am–6pm; Nov–Feb daily 9am–4pm; £2.50) was erected in memory of the writer by public subscription within a few years of his death. The elaborate Gothic spire was created by George Meikle Kemp, a carpenter and joiner whose only building this is; underneath the archway is a **statue** of Scott with his deerhound Maida, carved from a thirty-ton block of Carrara marble. Visitors are able to use a tightly winding internal spiral staircase to climb up to a series of platforms which offer some inspiring – if heady – vistas of the city below and hills and firths beyond.

The Princes Street Gardens are bisected by the **Mound**, which provides one of only two direct road links between the Old and New Towns (the other is the Northbridge). Its name is an accurate description: it was formed in the 1780s by dumping piles of earth and other waste brought from the New Town's building plots. At the foot of the Mound on the Princes Street level are two grand sandstone buildings; nearest to Princes Street, Playfair's **Royal Scottish Academy** (Mon–Sat 10am–5pm, Sun 2–5pm; admission varies) is the more elaborate of the two, a Grecian-style Doric temple topped with a statue of Queen Victoria and four sphinxes. The £26-million Playfair Project, due for completion in 2005, will eventually see it used as an extension of its more important neighbour, the National Gallery.

The National Gallery of Scotland

To the rear of the Royal Scottish Academy, the less elaborate **National Gallery of Scotland** (Mon–Sat 10am–5pm, Sun noon–5pm; permanent collection free; admission charged for some temporary exhibitions) is another of Playfair's Athenian constructions, built in the 1840s and now housing Scotland's premier collection of pre-twentieth-century European art. Though by no means as vast as national collections elsewhere in Europe, the National Gallery of Scotland benefits not just from a clutch of exquisite Old Masters and Impressionist works, but also from the fact that it is a manageable gallery enlivened by imaginative displays and a pleasantly unrushed atmosphere. Elsewhere in the city, the Scottish National Portrait Gallery (see p.936), the Scottish National Gallery of Modern Art (p.938) and its neighbour the Dean Gallery (p.939), display other parts of the National Galleries' collection.

The innovative and often controversial influence of the National Galleries' flamboyant director, Timothy Clifford, is immediately apparent on the ground floor, where the rooms have been restored to their 1840s appearance, with the pictures hung closely together on claret-coloured walls, often on two levels,

A **free bus** (Mon–Sat 11am–5pm, Sun noon–5pm; ☎0131/624 6200) runs on the hour between the National Gallery of Scotland, the Scottish National Portrait Gallery (see p.936), the Scottish National Gallery of Modern Art (p.938) and its neighbour the Dean Gallery (p.939).

and intermingled with sculptures and *objets d'art* to produce a deliberately cluttered effect.

Though individual works are frequently rearranged, the layout is broadly chronological, starting in the upper rooms above the entrance and continuing clockwise around the ground floor. The gallery has a programme of temporary exhibitions, which may mean that some of the paintings described here will not be on display. There are no guided tours; instead, audioguides available in five languages (£2) provide commentaries on the gallery's more important works.

Early Netherlandish and German works

Among the gallery's most valuable treasures are the *Trinity Panels*, the remaining parts of the only surviving pre-Reformation altarpiece made for a Scottish church. Painted by **Hugo van der Goes** in the mid-fifteenth century, they were commissioned for the Holy Trinity Collegiate Church (which was demolished to make way for Edinburgh's Waverley Station) by its provost Edward Bonkil, who appears in the company of organ-playing angels in the finest and best preserved of the four panels. On the reverse sides are portraits of James III, his son (the future James IV) and Queen Margaret of Denmark. Their feebly characterized heads, which stand in jarring contrast to the superlative figures of the patron saints accompanying them, were modelled from life by an unknown local painter after the altar had been shipped to Edinburgh. The panels are turned every half-hour.

Of the later Netherlandish works, **Gerard David** is represented by the touchingly anecdotal *Three Legends of St Nicholas*, while the *Portrait of a Man* by **Quentin Massys** is an excellent early example of northern European assimilation of the forms and techniques of the Italian Renaissance.

Italian Renaissance works

The Italian section includes a wonderful array of **Renaissance** masterpieces, the latest addition to which is a superb painting by Botticelli, *The Virgin Adoring the Sleeping Christ Child*, which was carefully restored and now positively glows with colour and light. Equally graceful are three works by **Raphael**, particularly *The Bridgewater Madonna* and the tondo *The Holy Family with a Palm Tree*, the latter another example of the striking luminosity restoration can reveal.

Of the four mythological scenes by **Titian**, the sensuous *Three Ages of Man*, an allegory of childhood, adulthood and old age, is one of the most accomplished compositions of his early period. The companion pair *Diana and Acteon* and *Diana and Calisto*, painted for Philip II of Spain, show the almost impressionistic freedom of his late style. **Bassano**'s truly regal *Adoration of the Kings*, a dramatic altarpiece *The Deposition of Christ* by **Tintoretto**, and several other works by **Veronese**, complete a fine Venetian collection.

Seventeenth-century works

Among the seventeenth-century works, **El Greco**'s *A Fable*, painted during his early years in Italy, takes a mysterious subject whose exact meaning is unclear. Indigenous Spanish art is represented by **Velázquez**'s *An Old Woman Cooking Eggs*, an astonishingly assured work for a lad of nineteen, and by **Zurbarán**'s *The Immaculate Conception*, part of his ambitious decorative scheme of the Carthusian monastery in Jerez.

The series *The Seven Sacraments* by **Poussin** are displayed in their own room, whose floor and central octagonal seat repeat some of the motifs in the paintings. The series marks the first attempt to portray scenes from the life of Jesus and the early Christians in an authentic manner, rather than one overlaid by artistic conventions. The result is profoundly touching, with a myriad of imaginative and subtle details.

Rubens' *The Feast of Herod* is an archetypal example of his grand manner, in which the gory subject matter is overshadowed by the lively depiction of the delights of the table. The trio of large upright canvases by **Van Dyck** date from his early Genoese period; of these, *The Lomellini Family* shows his mastery in creating a definitive dynastic image. Among the four canvases by **Rembrandt** is the poignant *Self-Portrait Aged 51*, and the ripely suggestive *Woman in Bed*, which probably represents the biblical figure of Sarah on her wedding night, waiting for her husband Tobias to put the devil to flight. *Christ in the House of Martha and Mary* is the largest and probably the earliest of the thirty or so surviving paintings by **Vermeer**; as the only one with a religious subject, it inspired a notorious series of forgeries by Han van Meegeren. There are two portraits by **Hals**, while his *Verdonck* stands in animated contrast to Rembrandt's self-portrait.

Eighteenth- and nineteenth-century works

Of the large-scale eighteenth-century works, **Tiepolo**'s *The Finding of Moses*, a gloriously bravura fantasy (the Pharaoh's daughter and her attendants appear in sixteenth-century garb) stands out. By way of contrast, the gems of the French section are the smaller panels, in particular **Watteau**'s *Fêtes Vénitiennes*, an effervescent Rococo idyll, and **Chardin**'s *Vase of Flowers*, a copybook example of still-life painting. There's also a superb group of early Impressionist works such as Jean Bastien Lepage's beautifully innocent *Pas Meche* and Camille Pissarro's *Kitchen Garden L'Hermitage*. Impressionist masters are also well represented; there's a collection of sketches, painting and bronzes by **Degas**, including the influential *Portrait of Diego Marteli*, as well as Monet's *Haystacks (Snow)* and Renoir's *Woman Nursing Child*. Representing the post-Impressionists are three outstanding examples of **Gauguin**'s work, including *Vision After the Sermon*, set in Brittany; **Van Gogh**'s *Olive Trees*; and **Cézanne**'s *The Big Trees* – a clear forerunner of modern abstraction.

The gallery's relatively few English paintings are impressive. **Hogarth**'s *Sarah Malcolm*, painted in Newgate Prison the day the murderess was executed, once belonged to Horace Walpole. **Gainsborough**'s *The Honourable Mrs Graham* is one of his most memorable society portraits, while **Constable** himself described *Dedham Vale* as being "perhaps my best". The gallery owns a wonderful array of watercolours by **Turner**, faithfully displayed each January when damaging sunlight is at its weakest, though visitors at other times of year can enjoy two of his fine Roman views displayed in one of the darker galleries.

Scottish works

On the face of it, the gallery's Scottish collection is something of an anticlimax. There are, however, some important works displayed within a broad European context: **Gavin Hamilton**'s *Achilles Mourning the Death of Patroclus*, for example, painted in Rome, is an unquestionably arresting image. **Allan Ramsay**, who became court painter to George III, is represented by his *Portrait of a Lady*. The swaggering masculinity of **Sir Henry Raeburn**'s *Sir John Sinclair*, featuring the subject in Highland dress, is a fine example of Raeburn's technical mastery. He was equally sure when working on a small scale, as shown in one of the gallery's most popular pictures, *The Rev Robert Walker Skating on Duddingston Loch*.

Other Scottish painters represented include the versatile **Sir David Wilkie**, whose huge historical painting, *Sir David Baird Discovering the Body of Sultan*

Tippo Saib, is in marked contrast to the genre scenes displayed in the basement, and **Alexander Nasmyth**, whose tendency to gild the lily can be seen in his *View of Tantallon Castle and the Bass Rock*, where the dramatic scenery is further spiced up by the inclusion of a shipwreck.

George Street and around

The street parallel to Princes Street to the north is **George Street**, rapidly changing its role from a thoroughfare of august financial institutions to a high-brow version of Princes Street, where the big deals are these days done in designer-label shops. George Street was designed to be the centrepiece of the First New Town, joining two grand squares. At its eastern end lies **St Andrew Square**, now home to Edinburgh's bus station, which shares space with the city's newest shopping mall. Beside this on the eastern side stands a handsome eighteenth-century town mansion, designed by Sir William Chambers. Headquarters of the Royal Bank of Scotland since 1825, the palatial mid-nineteenth-century banking hall is a symbol of the success of the New Town. Heading west along George Street, on the south side of the street, the oval-shaped church of **St Andrew** (now known as St Andrew and St George) is chiefly famous as the scene of the 1843 Disruption led by Thomas Chalmers, which split the Church of Scotland in two.

Charlotte Square

At the western end of George Street, **Charlotte Square** was designed by Robert Adam in 1791, a year before his death. Once the most exclusive quarter of the city, when the New Town began to change to commercial use, the square maintained its prestige by attracting the offices of the city's most celebrated law firms. The north side of the square is once more the city's premier address, with the official residence of the First Minister of the Scottish Parliament at no. 6 – also the place where the Scottish cabinet meets.

Restored by the National Trust for Scotland (NTS), the lower floors of neighbouring no. 7 are open to the public under the name of the **Georgian House** (March–Oct Mon–Sat 10am–5pm, Sun 2–5pm; £5), whose contents give a good idea of what the house must have looked like during the period of the first owner, the head of the clan Lamont. The rooms are decked out in period furniture, including a working barrel organ which plays a selection of Scottish airs, and hung with fine paintings, including portraits by Ramsay and Raeburn. Meanwhile the love affair of the NTS with the square is continued on the south side, most of which they occupy as their main headquarters in Scotland. It's well worth paying a visit to no. 28 to peer at the sumptuous interior. One floor up, a small **gallery** (Mon–Sat 10am–5pm, Sun noon–5pm; free) shows a collection of twentieth-century Scottish art, including a number of attractive examples of the work of the Scottish Colourists. Downstairs there's a **shop** selling National Trust books and souvenirs, as well as a very pleasant **café**.

Queen Street

Queen Street, the last of the three main streets of the First New Town, is bordered to the north by gardens, and commands sweeping views across to Fife. Occupied mostly by offices, it's the best preserved of the area's three main streets, although it's principally notable for the striking late nineteenth-century home of the National Portrait Gallery.

The Scottish National Portrait Gallery

At the eastern end of Queen Street is the **Scottish National Portrait Gallery** (Mon–Sat 10am–5pm, Sun noon–5pm; free). See p.932 for details of the free bus linking it to other major galleries. The remarkable building is itself a fascinating period piece, its red sandstone exterior, modelled on the Doge's Palace in Venice, encrusted with statues of famous Scots – a theme taken up in the stunning entrance hall, which has a mosaic-like frieze procession by William Hole of great figures from Scotland's past, with heroic murals by the same artist adorning the balcony above.

Temporary exhibitions are mounted in the galleries on the ground floor; elsewhere on this floor are the gallery shop and café. The **permanent collection** is located on the two upper floors. In contrast to the more global outlook of its sister National Galleries, the Portrait Gallery devotes itself to images of famous Scots – a definition stretched to include anyone with the slightest Scottish connection – and is dominated by Scottish artists. Taken as a whole, the gallery offers an engaging procession through Scottish history, with familiar images of famous Scots such as Bonnie Prince Charlie, Mary, Queen of Scots and Robert Burns.

Highlights include portraits of the philosopher-historian David Hume by Allan Ramsay, and the bard Robert Burns by his friend Alexander Nasmyth, plus a varied group by Raeburn: subjects include Sir Walter Scott, the fiddler Niel Gow and the artist himself. Thomas Gainsborough's *John, 4th Duke of Argyll* (1768) depicts the man who "pacified" the Highlands after the Jacobite rebellion; though an enemy to many he was feted by the establishment. The star portrait from the nineteenth century is that of physician Sir Alexander Morison by his patient, the mad painter Richard Dadd. Twentieth-century portraits occupy the first floor and include clever photo-montages of sporting stars Stephen Hendry and Alex Ferguson, a larger-than-life bright red bust of socialist Jimmy Reid by Kenny Hunter, and many other royals, inventors, politicians, tycoons and celebrities.

Calton

Of the various extensions to the New Town, the most engaging is **Calton**, which branches out from the eastern end of Princes Street and encircles a volcanic hill. **Waterloo Place** forms a ceremonial way from Princes Street to Calton Hill. On its southern side is the sombre and overgrown **Old Calton Burial Ground**, in which you can see Robert Adam's plain, cylindrical memorial to David Hume and a monument, complete with a statue of Abraham Lincoln, to the Scots who died in the American Civil War. Next door is the massive **St Andrew's House**, built in the 1930s to house civil servants.

Further on, set majestically in a confined site below Calton Hill, sits one of Edinburgh's greatest buildings, the Grecian **Old Royal High School**, which for many years was assumed to be where Scotland's new parliament would sit. Less than a year before the first elections, however, it was announced that the building was too small for the parliament envisaged. Across the road, Hamilton also built the **Burns Monument**, a circular Corinthian temple modelled on the Monument to Lysicrates in Athens, as a memorial to the national bard.

Robert Louis Stevenson reckoned that **Calton Hill** was the best place to view Edinburgh, "since you can see the castle, which you lose from the castle, and Arthur's Seat, which you cannot see from Arthur's Seat". Though the panoramas from ground level are spectacular enough, those from the top of the **Nelson Monument** (April–Sept Mon 1–6pm, Tues–Sat 10am–6pm;

Oct–March Mon–Sat 10am–3pm; £2; joint ticket with Scott Monument £4), perched near the summit of Calton Hill, are even better. Begun just two years after Nelson's death at Trafalgar, this is one of Edinburgh's oddest buildings, resembling a gigantic spyglass. Each day at 1pm a white ball drops down a mast at the top of the monument; together with the one o'clock gun fired from the castle battlements these were a daily check for the mariners of Leith who needed accurate chronometers to ensure reliable navigation at sea.

Alongside, the **National Monument** was begun in 1822 by Playfair to plans by the English architect Charles Cockerell. Had it been completed, it would have been a reasonably accurate replica of the Parthenon, but funds ran out with only twelve columns built. Various later schemes to finish it similarly foundered, earning it the nickname "Edinburgh's Disgrace". Playfair also built the **City Observatory** for his uncle, the mathematician and astronomer John Playfair. At the opposite end of the complex is the **Old Observatory**, one of the few surviving buildings by James Craig, designer of the New Town.

The Northern New Town

The **Northern New Town** was the earliest extension to the New Town, begun in 1801, and today roughly covers the area north of Queen Street between India Street to the west and Broughton Street to the east, and as far as Fettes Row to the north. This has survived in far better shape than its predecessor: with the exception of one street, almost all of it is intact, and it has managed to preserve a predominantly residential character.

One of the area's most interesting buildings is the neo-Norman **Mansfield Place Church**, home of a cycle of murals by the Dublin-born Phoebe Anna Traquair, a leading light in the Scottish Arts and Crafts movement. She laboured for eight years on this decorative scheme, which has all the freshness and luminosity of a medieval manuscript, yet it was almost lost due to leaks and rot in the fabric of the building in recent decades. The building is currently undergoing major refurbishment.

The Royal Botanic Garden

Just beyond the northern boundaries of the New Town, with entrances on Inverleith Row and Arboretum Place, is the seventy-acre site of the **Royal Botanic Garden** (daily: April–Aug 9.30am–7pm; March & Sept 9.30am–6pm; Feb & Oct 9.30am–5pm; Nov–Jan 9.30am–4pm; free), particularly renowned for the rhododendrons, which blaze out in a glorious patchwork of colours in April and May. In the heart of the grounds a group of hothouses designated the **Glasshouse Experience** (daily: March–Oct 10am–5pm; Nov–Feb 10am–3.30pm; donation requested) displays orchids, giant Amazonian water lilies, and a 200-year-old West Indian palm tree, the latter being in the elegant 1850s glass-topped Palm House. Guided tours (£2) of the garden leave from the West Gate on Arboretum Place at 11am and 2pm (April–Sept).

Dean Village

Work began on the western end of the New Town in 1822, in a small area of land north of Charlotte Square and west of George Street. Instead of the straight lines of the earlier sections, there were now the gracious curves of Randolph Crescent, Ainslie Place and the magnificent twelve-sided Moray Place. Round the corner from Randolph Crescent, the four-arched **Dean**

Bridge, a bravura feat of 1830s engineering by Thomas Telford, carries the main road high above Edinburgh's placid little river, the Water of Leith. Down to the left lies **Dean Village**, an old milling community that is one of central Edinburgh's most picturesque yet oddest corners, its atmosphere of decay arrested by the conversion of some of the mills into designer flats. There's now a riverside path which runs almost the entire length of the river; though a little gloomy in parts, some stretches are charming and colourful.

The West End and around

The western extension to the New Town was the last part to be built, deviating from the area's overriding Neoclassicism with a number of Victorian additions, including the city's principal Episcopal church, **St Mary's Cathedral**. With its proximity to the city centre the West End is now mostly used for offices, with a decent clutch of bars and restaurants, though there is some elegant terraced housing towards its outer edges. Here, enjoying some green space and a dignified setting are two compelling collections of contemporary art, the well-established **Scottish National Gallery of Modern Art** and its newer neighbour, the **Dean Gallery**. Further out, Edinburgh's **Zoo**, a popular family attraction, is located on one of the city's prominent rises, Corstorphine Hill.

The Scottish National Gallery of Modern Art

Set in spacious wooded grounds at the far northwestern fringe of the New Town, about ten minutes' walk from either the cathedral or Dean Village (or accessed by free shuttle bus; see p.932), the **Scottish National Gallery of Modern Art** on Belford Road (Mon–Sat 10am–5pm, Sun noon–5pm; free), was established as the first collection in Britain devoted solely to twentieth-century painting and sculpture. The display space is divided between temporary loan exhibitions and selections from the gallery's own holdings; the latter are arranged thematically, but are almost constantly moved around. What you get to see at any particular time is therefore a matter of chance, though the most important works are nearly always on view.

French painters are particularly well represented, beginning with early twentieth-century work such as **Bonnard**'s *Lane at Vernonnet* and **Vuillard**'s jewel-like *Two Seamstresses*. There are a few examples of the Fauves, notably **Matisse**'s *The Painting Session* and **Derain**'s dazzlingly brilliant *Still Life*, as well as a fine group of late canvases by **Léger**, notably *The Constructors*. Cubism is represented by **Picasso**'s *Soles* and **Braque**'s *Candlestick*.

Of works by Americans, **Roy Lichtenstein**'s *In the Car* is a fine example of his Pop Art style, while **Duane Hanson**'s fibreglass *Tourists* is typically unflinching. English artists on show include Sickert, Nicholson, Spencer, Freud, Hockney and Hirst but, as you'd expect, slightly more space is allocated to Scottish artists. Of particular note are the Colourists, whose works are attracting fancy prices on the art market, as well as ever-growing posthumous critical acclaim. Also worth exploring is the vivid realism of the more recent

Approaches to the Modern Art and Dean galleries

The most scenic way of getting to the neighbouring Modern Art and Dean galleries is along the **Water of Leith walkway**, which can be joined at Stockbridge or Dean Village. A **free bus** runs from outside the National Gallery on the Mound (see p.932). The only regular **public transport** running along Belford Road is bus #13, which leaves from the western end of George Street.

Edinburgh School, whose members include **Anne Redpath**, **Sir Robin Philipson** and **William Gillies**, and the distinctive styles of contemporary Scots such as **John Bellany**, a portraitist of striking originality, and the poet-artist-gardener **Ian Hamilton Finlay**.

The Dean Gallery

Opposite the Modern Art Gallery, on the other side of Belford Road, is the latest addition to the National Galleries of Scotland, the **Dean Gallery** (same hours; free), housed in an equally impressive Neoclassical building completed in 1833 as an orphanage and later used as an education centre. The interior has been dramatically refurbished specifically to make room for the work of Edinburgh-born sculptor **Sir Eduardo Paolozzi**. Visitors are given an awesome introduction to Paolozzi's work by the huge *Vulcan* – half-man, half-machine – which squeezes into the Great Hall immediately opposite the main entrance. No less persuasive of Paolozzi's dynamic creative talents are the rooms to the right of the main entrance, where his London studio has been expertly recreated, right down to the clutter of half-finished casts, toys and empty pots of glue. In the adjoining room a selection of his sculptures and drawings are exhibited in a more traditional manner.

Also on the ground floor is the **Roland Penrose Gallery**, which houses an impressive collection of Dada and Surrealist art. **Marcel Duchamp**, **Max Ernst** and **Man Ray** are all represented, and look out too for **Dali**'s *The Signal of Anguish* and **Magritte**'s *Magic Mirror* along with work by **Miró** and **Giacometti** – all hung on crowded walls with an assortment of artefacts and ethnic souvenirs gathered by Penrose and his artist companions while travelling.

The Zoo

A couple of miles west of the galleries, **Edinburgh Zoo** (daily: April–Sept 9am–6pm; Oct & March 9am–5pm; Nov–Feb 9am–4.30pm; £7) is set on an eighty-acre site on the slopes of Corstorphine Hill (served by buses #2, #26, #31, #36, #69, #85 and #86 from Princes Street). Here you can see over a thousand animals, including a number of endangered species such as white rhinos, red pandas, pygmy hippos and poison-arrow frogs. Making the most of the space offered by the setting, the "African Plains Experience" has a walkway leading you out over the animals to viewing platforms. The zoo's chief claim to fame is its crowd of penguins (the largest number in captivity anywhere in the world), a legacy of Leith's whaling trade in the South Atlantic. The "penguin parade" (April–Sept daily 2.15pm; also on sunny days in March & Oct) has gained something of a cult status.

Cafés and restaurants

The last decade has seen an upsurge in style, sophistication and good taste in Edinburgh's cafés and restaurants. **Café** culture has hit the centre of the city, with tables spilling onto the pavements in the summer, and this has been matched by the rise of a clutch of original, upmarket and stylish **restaurants**, many identifying their cuisine as "contemporary" or "modern Scottish" and championing top-quality meat, game and fish. As with most large British cities, the culinary map of Edinburgh is colourful and global, with long-established Chinese, Indian and Mexican places competing with outlets for Thai, Japanese, North African and Spanish cuisine.

Generally, small **diners** and **bistros** predominate, many adopting a casual French style and offering good-value set menus. Traditional Scottish cooking can still be found at some of the more formal restaurants, and inevitably some tourist-oriented places offer haggis and other classic clichés. Edinburgh excels in **vegetarian** restaurants, including a couple of classic Indian vegetarian places, and **seafood** – it's long been a speciality of the Leith waterfront, and you'll now also find a number of great seafood bistros in the centre of town.

The Royal Mile and around

Bistros, cafés and diners

Café Hub Lawnmarket. Colourful, well-run café in the Edinburgh Festival centre, with light modern meals served right through the day and evening. Teas, coffees, snacks and drinks also served. The large terrace is usefully central on sunny days. Inexpensive.

Café Odile Stills Gallery, 23 Cockburn St. Not the easiest place to find, but worth seeking out. French home-cooking at its best, with tasty, original savoury tarts, flans, salads and sandwiches, as well as delicious cakes and coffee. Inexpensive.

Elephant House 21 George IV Bridge. A popular café with a large selection of coffees, teas, sandwiches, light meals and big cakes. The cavernous back room is great for reading newspapers and having philosophical discussions. Open every day 8am–11pm. Inexpensive.

Lower Aisle In the High Kirk of St Giles, High Street. Popular with bewigged advocates from the High Court, this café in the crypt serves good-value light lunches, with excellent home baking. Closed evenings and all day Sat. Inexpensive.

Netherbow Café Netherbow Arts Centre, 43 High St. Decent wholefood and vegetarian soups and light meals, with a courtyard for sunny days and kids' corner. Lunchtimes only. Closed Sun. Inexpensive.

Restaurants

Bann UK 5 Hunter Square ☎0131/226 1112. Thoroughly modern vegetarian restaurant, with interesting, non-conventional dishes, stylish design and DJs playing ambient music late on. Mon–Thurs & Sun 10am–1am, Fri & Sat 10am–3am. Moderate.

Black Bo's 57 Blackfriars St ☎0131/557 6136. Inventive non-meat diner with an earthy atmosphere and friendly service. Open evenings daily and lunch Fri & Sat. Moderate.

Creelers 3 Hunter Sq ☎0131/220 4447. The only specialist seafood restaurant in the Old Town, with fresh produce brought in from a sister restaurant/fish shop on Arran. Moderate–expensive.

Igg's 15 Jeffrey St ☎0131/557 8184. A Spanish-owned hybrid, offering tapas snacks and Mediterranean dishes alongside traditional Scottish

food. Smart but not intimidating. Closed Sun. Expensive.

Khushi's Lothian Restaurant 16 Drummond St. One of the first Indian places to open in the capital, *Khushi's* is still essentially a basic cafeteria with few frills, but it's a characterful and friendly place and the food is reliable and cheap. Bring your own drink. Closed Sun. Inexpensive.

Le Sept Old Fishmarket Close ☎0131/225 5428. Long-established French brasserie tucked down a cobbled close off the Royal Mile specializing in fish dishes and filling savoury crepes. Moderate.

Mamma's American Pizza Co. 30 Grassmarket. The best pizzas in this part of town, popular with students and larger groups, with outside tables in the summer and reasonably priced wine. Open Sun–Thurs until midnight, Fri & Sat until 1am. Inexpensive–moderate.

Ortegas 38 St Mary's St ☎0131/557 5754. Comfortable local bistro with some refreshingly original dishes, including good vegetarian options. Although the name is Spanish, the food isn't easily pigeonholed. Moderate.

Suruchi 14a Nicolson St ☎0131/556 6583. Popular establishment serving genuine South Indian dishes – the menu is written in bizarre but entertaining broad Scots. Look out for cross-cultural specials such as tandoori trout. Moderate.

The Tower Museum of Scotland, Chambers Street ☎0131/225 3003. Unique setting on Level 5 of the museum; at night you are escorted along the empty corridors to the restaurant, where spectacular views to the floodlit castle are revealed. Excellent Modern Scottish food in a self-consciously chic setting. Expensive.

Viva Mexico 10 Anchor Close, off Cockburn Street ☎0131/226 5145. For many years one of Edinburgh's best Mexicans, doing the staples well in a friendly, easygoing atmosphere. Moderate.

The Witchery by the Castle 352 Castlehill, Royal Mile ☎0131/225 5613. The restaurant that only Edinburgh could create, with Gothic panelling, tapestries and heavy stonework only a broomstick-hop from the castle. The superb fish and game dishes are pricey, but you can steal a sense of it all with a pre- or post-theatre set menu (£10). Expensive.

The New Town and the West End

Bistros, cafés and diners

Glass & Thompson 2 Dundas St. An unusually airy deli with huge bowls of olives and an extensive cheese counter; scattered tables and chairs mean you can linger over a made-to-order sandwich, an irresistible cake and coffee. Closed evenings. Inexpensive.

Hadrian's 2 North Bridge ☎0131/557 5000. Although it's strictly part of the upmarket *Balmoral Hotel*, this brasserie isn't too overpriced, and the elegance of the design and atmosphere, along with good quality Modern British cooking, make it worth seeking out. Moderate.

Howies at Waterloo 29 Waterloo Place ☎0131/556 5766. Flagship of the small local Howies chain, with a pleasant dining area on the fringe of Calton Hill and reliably well priced, comforting modern Scottish food. Moderate.

Restaurants

Café Royal Oyster Bar 17a W Register St ☎0131/556 4124. An Edinburgh classic, with its splendidly ornate Victorian interior (featured in *Chariots of Fire*), stained-glass windows, marble floor and Doulton tiling. Classic seafood dishes, including freshly caught oysters, served in a civilized, chatty atmosphere. Very expensive.

Café St Honoré 34 Thistle St Lane ☎0131/226 2211. A little piece of Paris tucked away in a New Town back lane. Fairly traditional French fare, but top quality. Closed Sun. Expensive.

Caffè DOC 49a Thistle St. Modern Italian style and a genuine dedication to good food are evident here, with a dining room rather hidden behind the sleek street-front coffee bar. Moderate–expensive.

Cosmo 58a N Castle St ☎0131/226 6743. Straightforward but genuine and delicious Italian cuisine in a long-established, fairly exclusive restaurant. Closed Sun. Expensive.

Fishers in the City 58 Thistle Lane ☎0131/225 5109. New Town incarnation of Leith's best-loved seafood bistro. This one has a sleek modern interior, great service and some stunning seafood. Expensive.

Henderson's Salad Table 94 Hanover St. A much-loved Edinburgh institution with a self-service basement restaurant offering freshly prepared hot dishes, plus a great choice of salads, soups, sweets and cheeses. The slightly antiquated cafeteria feel can put people off, but the food is rarely short of outstanding. Light jazz every evening. Open Mon–Sat 8am–10.30pm. Inexpensive–moderate. *Henderson's Bistro*, next door at 25 Thistle St (☎0131/225 2605) offers moderately priced bistro-style vegetarian meals, and is open during the day and Thurs–Sat evenings. Closed Mon.

Kweilin 19–21 Dundas St ☎0131/557 1875. One of the most reliable Chinese restaurants in town, serving Cantonese and Szechuan dishes in a pleasant atmosphere. Slightly more expensive than some. Moderate.

La Cuisine d'Odile 13 Randolph Crescent, West End ☎0131/225 5685. Genuine French home cooking in a West End basement under the French Institute. Lunch only (noon–2pm). Closed Sun, Mon & July. Inexpensive.

Loon Fung 2 Warriston Place, Canonmills ☎0131/556 1781. Something of a trailblazer for Cantonese cuisine in Scotland, near the eastern entrance to the Botanic Garden. Moderate.

Mussel Inn 61–65 Rose St ☎0131/225 5979. After feasting on a kilo of mussels and a basket of chips for under £10 you'll realize why there's a demand to get in here. Owned by two west-coast shellfish farmers, which ensures that the time from sea to stomach is minimal. Closed Sun. Moderate.

Songkran 24a Stafford St, West End ☎0131/225 7889. A simple basement restaurant with some nice authentic decor and good-value tasty Thai food, including "banquet" options. Moderate.

Tampopo 25a Thistle St ☎0131/220 5254. Tiny budget noodle bar offering filling Japanese meals from around £5, but engaging owner Katsuo Honjigawa will guide you through more interesting choices including sushi and bento boxes. Tues–Sat noon–2.30pm & 6–9pm. Inexpensive–moderate.

North and west of the New Town

Bistros, cafés and diners

Café Mediterraneo 73 Broughton St. A great little place with a deli counter and a small dining space serving Italian food in unpretentious style. Not a red-checked tablecloth to be seen. Moderate.

The Gallery Café Scottish National Gallery of Modern Art, Belford Road, Dean. Far more than a standard refreshment stop for gallery visitors, the cultured setting and strong menu attracts reassuring numbers of locals. Serves salads, filled croissants, light meals, coffee and cakes. Open Mon–Sat 10am–4.30pm, Sun noon–4.30pm. Moderate.

Lost Sock Diner 11 East London St, Broughton. Fill up on burgers, wraps and blackboard specials, all at surprising low prices, while your dirty clothes take a spin in the adjacent laundrette. Try the parsnip chips. Open Tues & Wed until 9pm, Thurs–Sat until 10pm. Inexpensive.

Terrace Café Royal Botanic Garden, Inverleith. Superior spot with outside tables offering stunning views of the city skyline, though the food is not that exciting. Their changing menu includes hot dishes, sandwiches and cakes. Inexpensive.

Valvona and Crolla 19 Elm Row, Leith Walk ☎0131/556 6066. The café at the back of this exquisite Italian deli serves authentic and delicious breakfasts, lunches and snacks. The best advert for the café is the walk through the shop – which has food stacked from floor to ceiling, with display cabinets full of sublime olives, meats and cheeses. Open Mon–Sat 8am–5pm. Moderate.

Restaurants

Blue Parrot Cantina 49 St Stephen's St, Stockbridge ☎0131/225 2941. Cosy Stockbridge basement restaurant, with a small, frequently changing menu which deviates from the Mexican clichés. Moderate.

Modern India 20 Union Place ☎0131/556 4547. Edinburgh's best example of the contemporary curry-house, with bright new decor and a menu daring to stray from the conventional. A little bit of Bollywood right across from the Playhouse Theatre. Moderate.

South and west of the Old Town

Bistros, cafés and diners

The Apartment 7–13 Barclay Place, Bruntsfield ☎0131/228 6456. Hugely popular, highly fashionable modern diner, with IKEA furniture, sisal flooring and abstract modern art on the walls. Their "Chunky, Healthy Lines" feature filling kebabs of meat, fish or vegetables. Moderate.

blue 10 Cambridge St ☎0131/221 1222. Long-standing super-stylish café/bistro in the same building as the avant-garde Traverse Theatre. Modern minimalist decor, with tasty modern dishes for under £10 per main course. Open Mon–Sat until 11pm. Moderate.

Favorit 30-32 Leven St, Bruntsfield. Thoroughly modern café-diner dishing up coffees, fruit shakes, cakes and big sandwiches, as well as drinks, right through to 3am.

Ndebele 57 Home St. Colourful African café offering sandwiches with lots of alternative fillings, imaginative salads and biltong for homesick South Africans. Open daily until 10pm. Inexpensive.

Restaurants

The Atrium 10 Cambridge St ☎0131/228 8882. Proving resilient in its position among the most impressive restaurants in the city. Quirky arty design with railway-sleeper tables and innovative nouvelle cuisine focusing on high-quality Scottish produce. Closed Sunday. Very expensive.

Jasmine 32 Grindlay St ☎0131/229 5757. Modern looking, good-value Cantonese restaurant, with a strong line in fresh fish. Across the street from the Lyceum and the Usher Hall. Moderate.

Kalpna 2 St Patrick Square, Newington ☎0131/667 9890. Outstanding vegetarian restaurant serving authentic Gujarati dishes. Four set meals, including a vegan option, stand alongside the main menu. Closed Sun. Moderate.

The Marque 19–21 Causewayside, Newington ☎0131/466 6660. One of the best exponents of classy-but-casual dining in Edinburgh, with Modern Scottish recipes and some top-value pre- and post-theatre deals. Closed Mon. Moderate–expensive.

Marque Central 30b Grindlay St ☎0131/229 9859. Sister restaurant to the original Southside venture, moving into the theatreland patch with its great value pre- and post-theatre deals. At any time a place for imaginative modern Scottish food. Closed Sun. Moderate–expensive.

Point Hotel 34 Bread St ☎0131/221 5555. A classy feel with modern decor, white linen tablecloths and smartly dressed waiters, and well-presented food based on fresh local fish and meat. One of the best-value deals in town: a three-course set menu is just £12.90. Moderate.

Susie's Diner 51 W Nicolson St, Newington. Popular café serving inventive soups, savouries and puddings, and a range of vegan food, to crowds of students. Inexpensive.

Leith and Newhaven

Bistros, cafés and diners

Daniel's, 88 Commercial St ☎0131/553 5933. Top-grade bistro in an attractive setting on the ground floor of a converted warehouse in Leith. Food is from the Alsace region of France; the *tarte flambée*, one of the specialist dishes, is a sort of pizza with a French name and German ingredients. Moderate.

Malmaison Café Bar 1 Tower Place ☎0131/468 5001. Successful attempt to create the feel of a French café, serving excellent steak and chips as well as indulgent breakfasts and brunches. Moderate.

Restaurants

Britannia Spice 150 Commercial St ☎0131/555 2255. The decor's nautical, the food is prepared by specialist chefs from the sub-continent and the awards for this relatively new but ambitious Indian restaurant have been piling up. Moderate

Restaurant Martin Wishart 52 The Shore ☎0131/553 3557. Edinburgh's only Michelin-star holder wows the gourmets with French-influenced Scottish food by the Water of Leith. The food's incredible but the ambience is rather stark. Closed Sun & Mon. Expensive.

Ship on the Shore 24–26 The Shore ☎0131/555 0409. The homeliest and least expensive of the waterfront brasseries, serving good fresh fish and with a changing range of cask ales. Moderate.

Skippers Bistro 1a Dock Place ☎0131/554 1018. More relaxed than it looks from the outside,

with a vaguely nautical atmosphere and a superb fish-oriented menu that changes according to what's fresh. Worth booking ahead. Expensive.

The Shore 3 The Shore ☎0131/553 5080. A bar/restaurant with huge mirrors, wood panelling and aproned waiters who serve up good fish dishes and decent wines. Live jazz, folk and hubbub floats through from the adjoining bar. Moderate.

The Vintner's Rooms 87 Giles St ☎0131/554 6767. Splendid restaurant in a seventeenth-century warehouse; the ornate Rococo dining room is a marvel and the food – ranging from seafood to game – isn't bad either. Very expensive.

Waterfront Wine Bar 1c Dock Place ☎0131/554 7427. Housed in the former lock-keeper's cottage, you can eat in the wonderfully characterful wine bar (smoking) or non-smoking conservatory attached. Fish dishes dominate. Moderate.

Pubs and bars

Many of Edinburgh's **pubs**, especially in the Old Town, have histories that stretch back centuries, while others, particularly in the New Town, are unaltered Victorian or Edwardian period pieces. Add a plentiful supply of trendy modern **bars**, and there's a variety of styles and atmospheres to cater for all tastes.

Edinburgh has a long history of brewing beer, though only two principal **breweries** remain: the giant Scottish & Newcastle (who produce McEwan's and Younger's) and the small independent Caledonian Brewery, which uses old techniques and equipment to produce some of the best beers in Britain. Once upon a time Edinburgh's main drinking strip was the near-legendary **Rose Street**, and the ultimate Edinburgh pub crawl was to drink a half-pint in each of its dozen or so establishments. Things are a bit more sophisticated these days, with **George Street** taking a lead: various former financial institutions have been converted into bars, with a predictable invasion of suits by day and style by night. While many of the **Royal Mile**'s pubs aren't ashamed to make the most of local historical connections to draw in the tourists, you don't have to travel far to find some lively places, notably the student-filled pubs in and around the **Grassmarket**. **Leith** has a range of bars, from rough spit-and-sawdust places to polished pseudo-Victoriana, while we've also listed a number of characterful places further away from the centre.

The Royal Mile and around

Bannermans 212 Cowgate. Once the best pub in the street; now its late-night music can be a bit intrusive. Still atmospheric, however – a former vintner's cellar, it has a labyrinthine interior deep under the Old Town and good beer on tap. Open daily until 1am.

Bow Bar 80 West Bow. Wonderful old wood-panelled bar that won an award as the best drinkers' pub in Britain a few years back. Choose from

among nearly 150 whiskies or a changing selection of first-rate Scottish and English cask beers. Closed Sun afternoons.

City Café 19 Blair St. Long-standing but determinedly trendy bar on the street linking the Royal Mile to the clubbers' hub along the Cowgate. The blue pool tables are always popular and you can buy candies behind the American-style bar.

Doric Tavern 15 Market St. Long-established upstairs wine bar (open until 1am) is a favoured watering hole of journalists and artists. The downstairs *McGuffie's Tavern* is a traditional Edinburgh howff, while the brasserie beside the wine bar serves reliable good quality Scottish food.

Jolly Judge 7a James Court. Atmospheric, low-ceilinged bar in a close just down from the castle. Cosy in winter and pleasant outside in summer.

Last Drop 74–78 Grassmarket. The "drop" refers to the Edinburgh gallows, which were located in front, and whose former presence is symbolized in the red paintwork of the exterior. Cheapish pub food, and, like its competitors in the same block, patronized mainly by students. Open until 1am.

New Town and West End

Café Royal Circle Bar 17 W Register St. As notable as the *Oyster Bar* restaurant next door, the *Café Royal* is worth a visit just for its Victorian decor, notably the huge elliptical "island" counter and the tiled portraits of renowned inventors. Thurs until midnight, Fri & Sat until 1am. Upstairs, the *Café Royal Bistro Bar* is an unlovely rugby-themed affair.

The Dome 14 George St. Opulent conversion of a massive New Town bank, thronging with well dressed locals. Probably the most impressive bar interior in Edinburgh, though the ultra-chic atmosphere can be a bit intense. Sun–Thurs until 11.30pm, Fri & Sat until 1am.

Indigo Yard 7 Charlotte Lane, West End. For many years one of Edinburgh's "it" bars, although the moment has probably passed. Still busy and lively, with decent food as well as designer lager. Daily until 1am.

Milne's Bar 35 Hanover St. Cellar bar once beloved of Edinburgh's literati, earning the nickname "The Poets' Pub" courtesy of Hugh MacDiarmid *et al*. Recent redevelopment hasn't done it many favours. Serves a good range of cask beers.

Oxford Bar 8 Young St. Traditional city bar, unpretentious and somewhat of a shrine for rugby fans, off-duty policemen and readers of the books of Ian Rankin. Open until 1am.

Pivo Caffé 2–6 Calton Rd. The theme is essentially Czech, but the result is a laid-back and popular bar with good DJs. Eastern European food and beer is prominent. Open until 1am.

North and west of the New Town

Baillie Bar 2 St Stephen St. Traditional basement bar at the corner of Edinburgh's most self-consciously bohemian street. English and Scottish ales are available, as well as better-than-average pub grub. Open Mon–Thurs until midnight; Fri & Sat until 1am; Sun until 11pm.

The Barony Bar 81–85 Broughton St. A fine old-fashioned bar, which manages to be big and lively without being spoilt. Real ale and some good food, though it can be a wait to get served. Open until midnight.

Bert's Bar 2–4 Raeburn Place, Stockbridge, & 29 William St, West End. Popular locals' pubs, despite their relatively recent arrival. Both have excellent beer, tasty pies and strive to be authentic, non-theme-oriented venues, though the telly rarely misses any sporting action.

The Basement 10a Broughton St. Packed out, especially at the weekends, with a pre-club crowd, this trendy bar is run by young and enthusiastic staff and serves cheap Mexican food until 10pm every day. Open until 1am.

The Outhouse 12a Broughton Street Lane. Busy pre-club bar tucked away down a cobbled lane off Broughton Street, with a lively beer garden and funky music. Open until 1am.

Hector's 47–49 Deanhaugh St. A magnet for trendy Stockbridgers, full of tall stools, chocolate-coloured leather couches and rough-hewn walls. Good place for weekend brunches; food is served all day in a dining area to the rear.

South and west of the Old Town

Bennets Bar 8 Leven St, Tollcross. Edwardian pub with mahogany-framed mirrors and Art Nouveau stained glass; gets packed in the evening, particularly when there's a show at the King's Theatre next door. Mon–Sat serves lunch; open until midnight.

Blue Blazer 2 Spittal St. Traditional Edinburgh howff with oak-clad bar and church pews; serves a good selection of ales. Open Wed & Thurs until midnight, Fri & Sat until 1am.

Human Be-In 2–8 West Crosscauseway, Newington. Despite the silly name, this is one of the trendiest student bars around, with huge plate glass windows to admire the beautiful people and tables outside for summer posing. Good food too. Open until 1am.

Peartree House 36 W Nicolson St, Newington. Fine bar in an eighteenth-century house with old sofas and a large courtyard, one of central Edinburgh's very few beer gardens; serves budget bar lunches. Open Mon–Wed & Sun until midnight, Thurs–Sat until 1am.

Sheep Heid Inn 43 The Causeway, Duddingston. This eighteenth-century inn with a family atmosphere makes an ideal refreshment stop at the end of a tramp through Holyrood Park. Decent home-cooked meals are available at the bar, while the old-fashioned skittle alley is always popular with students.

Traverse Bar Café Traverse Theatre, 10 Cambridge St. Much more than just a theatre bar, attracting a lively, sophisticated crowd which dispels any notion of a quiet interval drink. Good food available in the bar and also at *blue* upstairs. One of the hot places to be during the Festival.

Leith and around

Bar Java 48–50 Constitution St, Leith. Friendly bar in an area where you'd expect all the pubs to have sawdust on the floor. Serves decent food, has a small courtyard beer garden and even B&B rooms upstairs. Open Sun–Wed until midnight,

Thurs–Sat until 1am.

Carriers' Quarters 42 Bernard St, Leith. Intimate pub that dates back to 1785, with many original features, including a tiny "snug" and blazing log fire. Open Fri & Sat until 1am.

Cramond Inn Cramond Village ☎ 0131/336 2035. An authentic old inn by the riverside at Cramond – the perfect place for a drink or a pub meal after a stroll along the coastal path.

Kings Wark 36 The Shore, Leith. Real ale in an atmospheric restored eighteenth-century pub right in the heart of Leith, with bar meals chalked up on the rafters. Open Fri & Sat until midnight.

Nightlife and entertainment

Inevitably, Edinburgh's **nightlife** is at its best during the Festival (see p.947), which can make the other 49 weeks of the year seem like an anticlimax. However, at any time the city has plenty to offer, especially in the realm of **theatre** and **music**.

The **club** scene is lively, with some excellent venues hosting a changing selection of one-nighters. In the bigger venues, you may find different clubs taking place on each floor. Most of the city-centre clubs stay open until around 3am. You can normally hear **live jazz**, **folk** and **rock** every evening in one or other of the city's pubs. The city has permanent venues large enough to host large touring **orchestras** and **ballet** companies; elsewhere you can also uncover a lively **comedy** club and a couple of excellent art-house **cinemas**.

Edinburgh has a dynamic **gay** culture, for years centred round the top of Leith Walk and Broughton Street, where the first gay and lesbian centre appeared in the 1970s. Since the start of the 1990s, more and more gay enterprises, especially cafés and nightclubs, have moved into this area, now dubbed the "Pink Triangle".

The best way to find out **what's on** is to pick up a copy of *The List*, a fortnightly listings magazine covering both Edinburgh and Glasgow (£1.95). Alternatively, get hold of the *Edinburgh Evening News*, which appears daily except Sunday: its listings column gives details of performances in the city that day, hotels and bars included.

Clubs

The Bongo Club 14 New St ☎ 0131/556 5204. Great venue above a car park near Waverley Station, attracting some of the most interesting DJs around. Look out for the mighty Messenger Sound System monthly on Saturdays and Club Latino monthly on Fridays.

The Cavendish West Tollcross ☎ 0131/228 3252. Slightly dingy but still a packed venue for roots, ragga and reggae night on Friday; the *Mambo Club* on Saturday plays African and Latin rhythms.

Ego 14 Picardy Place ☎ 0131/478 7434. A former casino, this big venue hosts *Joy*, one of the city's longest running nights, which plays house and trance to a gay and mixed crowd monthly on Saturdays. The smaller *Cocteau Lounge* downstairs

is another popular venue.

La Belle Angèle 11 Hasties Close ☎ 0131/225 7536. A rotating selection of Latin, soul, hip-hop and jazz. Look out for the infamous *Radio Babylon* nights on Fridays, while house rules on Saturdays. Occasionally hosts important touring bands.

Gay clubs and bars

Blue Moon Café 1 Barony St ☎ 0131/556 2788. Coffee, drinks and light meals available at this long-standing friendly café-bar which attracts a mixed crowd. Mon–Fri 11am–10pm, Sat & Sun 9.30am–10pm.

CC Bloom's 23 Greenside Place ☎ 0131/556 9331. Big dance floor, stonking rhythms and a young, friendly crowd.

Hogmanay

Hogmanay is the name Scots give to **New Year's Eve**, a celebration they have made all their own with a unique mix of tradition, hedonism, sentimentality and enthusiasm. The roots of the Hogmanay are in ancient pagan festivities based around the winter solstice, which in most places gradually merged with Christmas. When hardline Scottish Protestant clerics in the sixteenth century abolished Christmas for being a Catholic mass, the Scots, not wanting to miss out on a mid-winter knees-up, instead put their energy into greeting the New Year.

Houses were cleaned from top to bottom, debts were paid and quarrels made up, and, after the bells of midnight were rung, great store was laid by welcoming good luck into your house. This still takes the form of the tradition of "first-footing" – visiting your neighbours and bearing gifts. The ideal first-foot is a tall dark-haired male carrying a bottle of whisky; women or redheads, on the other hand, bring bad luck . . . though to be honest no one carrying a bottle of whisky tends to be turned away these days, whatever the colour of their hair. All this neighbourly greeting meant that a fair bit of partying went on, of course, and after a while no one was expected to go to work the next day, or, if the party was that good, the day after that either. Even today, January 1 is a public holiday in the rest of the UK, but only in Scotland does the holiday extend to the next day too. In fact, right up to the 1950s Christmas was a normal working day for many people in Scotland, and Hogmanay was widely regarded as by far the more important celebration.

Over the years, Hogmanay street parties in the middle of towns and cities became popular, often centred around a prominent clockface which would ring out "the bells" at midnight. These days, the largest New Year's Eve street party in Europe takes place in Edinburgh, with around 100,000 people on the streets of the city enjoying the culmination of a week-long series of events. On the night itself, stages are set up in different parts of the city centre, with big name rock groups and local ceilidh bands playing to the increasingly inebriated masses. The high point of the evening is, of course, midnight, when hundreds of tons of fireworks are let off into the night sky above the castle, and Edinburgh joins the rest of the world singing **"Auld Lang Syne"**, an old Scottish tune with lyrics by Robert Burns, Scotland's national poet.

For more details about Hogmanay in Edinburgh, and how to get hold of tickets for the street party, go to ⓦwww.edinburghshogmanay.org.

Nexus Café 60 Broughton St ☎0131/478 7069. Light meals, snacks and drinks in a relaxed atmosphere at the Edinburgh Gay, Lesbian and Bisexual Centre. Open 11am–11pm.

Live music pubs and venues

Henry's Jazz Bar 8 Morrison St, off Lothian Road ☎0131/221 1288. Edinburgh's premier jazz and hip-hop venue, with live music every night and regular top performers.

The Liquid Room 9c Victoria St ☎0131/225 2528. Good-sized venue frequented by visiting indie and local R&B bands.

Sandy Bell's 25 Forrest Rd ☎0131/225 2751. A friendly bar and a good bet for folk music most nights of the week.

Whistlebinkies 4–6 South Bridge ☎0131/557 5114. One of the most reliable places to find live music every night of the week – often it's rock and pop covers, though there are some folk evenings. Daily until 3am.

The Venue 15 Calton Rd ☎0131/557 3073. Small, intimate sweaty club hosting up-and-coming indie bands.

Theatre and comedy

Festival Theatre Nicolson Street ☎0131/529 6000. The largest stage in Britain, principally used for Scottish Opera's appearances in the capital and other major orchestral performances, but also for everything from the children's show *Singing Kettle* to Engelbert Humperdinck.

King's Theatre 2 Leven St ☎0131/228 5955. Stately Edwardian civic theatre that majors in pantomime, touring West End plays and the occasional major drama or opera performance.

Netherbow Arts Centre 43 High St ☎0131/556

9579. Small auditorium used heavily through the Festival but with an adventurous year-round programme concentrating on children's theatre and storytelling events.

Playhouse Theatre 18–22 Greenside Place ☎0131/557 2692. The most capacious theatre in Britain, formerly a cinema. Recently refurbished, and used largely for extended runs of popular musicals and occasional rock concerts.

Royal Lyceum Theatre 30 Grindlay St ☎0131/248 4848. Fine Victorian civic theatre with a compact auditorium. The leading year-round venue for mainstream drama.

The Stand Comedy Club 5 York Place ☎0131/558 7272. The city's top comedy spot, with a different act on every night and some of the UK's top comics headlining at the weekends. The bar is worth a visit in itself.

Theatre Workshop 34 Hamilton Place ☎0131/226 5425. Enticing programmes of international innovative theatre and performance art all year round.

Traverse Theatre, 10 Cambridge St ☎0131/228 1404. Unquestionably one of Britain's premier venues for new plays and avant-garde drama from around the world. Going from strength to strength in its new custom-built home beside the Usher Hall, with a great bar downstairs and the popular *blue* café-bar upstairs.

Concert halls

Queen's Hall 89 Clerk St ☎0131/668 2019.

Converted Georgian church with a capacity of around eight hundred, though many seats have little or no view of the platform. Home base of both the Scottish Chamber Orchestra and Scottish Ensemble, and much favoured by jazz, blues and folk groups. Also hosts established comedians.

Usher Hall Corner of Lothian Road and Grindlay Street ☎0131/228 1155. Edinburgh's main civic concert hall, seating over 2500. Excellent for choral and symphony concerts, but less suitable for solo vocalists. The upper circle seats are cheapest and have the best acoustics; avoid the back of the grand tier and the stalls, where the sound is muffled by the overhanging balconies.

Cinemas

Cameo 38 Home St, Tollcross ☎0131/228 2800; bookings ☎0131/228 4141. A treasure of an art-house cinema; screens more challenging mainstream releases and cult late-nighters. Tarantino's been here and thinks it's great.

Filmhouse 88 Lothian Rd ☎0131/228 2688. Three screens showing an eclectic programme of independent, arthouse and classic films. Their café is a hangout for the city's dedicated film-buffs.

Odeon 7 Clerk St ☎0131/667 0971; information and bookings ☎0870/505 0007. Five-screen cinema showing the latest releases.

UGC Fountainpark, Dundee St, Fountainbridge ☎0870/902 0417. Big, reasonably central multiplex. Buses #1, #28, #34 & #35.

The Edinburgh Festival

The world's largest celebration of the arts, the **Edinburgh Festival** is a massive explosion of cultural and artistic expression, with every available performance space in August – from the grandest concert halls to pub courtyards – helping play host to a packed programme of drama, comedy, performance, music and film. All over the city the streets fill with buskers, craft stalls, tourists,

Edinburgh's other festivals

Quite apart from August's main Edinburgh Festival, the city is now promoting itself as a year-round festival venue, with number of different events well established. The climax of various Christmas events is **Edinburgh's Hogmanay** (see p.946), one of the world's largest New Year street parties, involving torchlight processions, folk and rock concerts and fireworks galore. The **Science Festival** in April incorporates hands-on children's events as well as numerous lectures on a vast array of subjects. There is a **Puppet and Animation Festival** in March, and a **Children's Festival** in late May, with readings, magicians and specialist children's drama. The Caledonian Brewery, 42 Slateford Rd, runs its own German-style **beer festival** in early June. Check out ⓦwww.edinburghfestivals.co.uk for links to the official sites of all Edinburgh's main festivals.

celebrities, performers, media types and festival-goers; posters plaster every vertical space and the centre of town takes on a slightly surreal, vital atmosphere. The Edinburgh Festival is actually an umbrella term which encompasses different festivals taking place at around the same time. The principal events are the **International Festival** and the much larger **Festival Fringe**, but there are also **film**, **book**, and **jazz and blues** festivals, the **Military Tattoo** and the **Edinburgh Mela**.

August is when most things happen. The jazz and blues festival occupies the first week of August; the Fringe and the Tattoo run for the next three weeks, culminating on the last weekend of the month; the International Festival runs over the last two weeks of August and the first week of September; the film and book festivals occupy the last two weeks of August; and the Mela is held on the first weekend in September.

The sheer volume of the Festival's output can be bewildering: it can be a struggle to find accommodation, get hold of the tickets, book a table in a restaurant or simply get from one side of town to another; you can end up seeing something truly dire, or something mind-blowing, and most people inevitably try to do too much. The unpredictable nature of the event is one of its greatest charms, so be prepared for – and enjoy – the unexpected. For year-round up-to-the-minute information, check out ⓦ**www.edinburghfestivals.co.uk**.

In addition to each festival's own programme, various publications give full **information** about what's on day by day. Every day the Fringe Office publishes *The Guide*, giving a chronological listing of virtually every Fringe show scheduled for that day. It's available free from the Office and hundreds of other spots around Edinburgh. Of the local newspapers, the best coverage is in The *Scotsman*, which issues an excellent daily Festival supplement; their reviews and star-rating system carry a lot of weight. *The List*, a locally produced arts and entertainment guide, comes out weekly during the Festival and manages to combine comprehensive coverage with a reliably on-the-pulse sense of what's hot and what's not.

The Edinburgh International Festival

The **Edinburgh International Festival** (sometimes called the "Official Festival") attracts truly international stars, along with some of the world's finest orchestras and opera, theatre and ballet companies. Performances take place at the city's larger venues such as the Usher Hall and the Festival Theatre, and while ticket prices at the top end run to over £35, it is possible to see shows for £10 or less. The most popular events sell out quickly, although for every show fifty tickets are kept back and sold at The Hub (the International Festival's headquarters; see p.918) on the morning of the performance, when queues can begin forming at dawn.

The most popular single event in the Festival is the dramatic **Fireworks Concert**, held late at night on the final Saturday of the International Festival accompanied by a spectacular fireworks display high up above the ramparts of the castle. Unless you want a seat right by the orchestra you don't need a ticket for this event: hundreds of thousands of people view the display from various vantage points throughout the city, the prime spots being Princes Street, Northbridge, Calton Hill or Inverleith Park and the Botanic Gardens by Stockbridge.

The Edinburgh Festival Fringe

Even standing alone from its sister festivals, the **Edinburgh Festival Fringe** is easily the world's largest arts gathering. Each year sees over 15,000 performances from over 600 companies, with more than ten thousand participants from all over the world. There are something in the region of 1500 shows every day, round the clock, in 200 venues around the city.

The first **Fringe Programme** appeared in 1951, the bright idea of a local printer. A single sheet of paper then, it's now a fat magazine crammed with information on most, though not all, participating shows. In 1959, the **Fringe Society** was founded by participants to provide basic marketing and co-ordination between events. Crucially, no artistic control was imposed on those who wanted to produce a show, a defining element of the Fringe which continues to this day: anyone who can afford the registration fee can take part. This means that the shows range from the inspired to the diabolical, and ensures a highly competitive atmosphere, in which one bad review in a prominent publication means box-office disaster. Many unknowns rely on self-publicity, taking to the streets to perform highlights from their show, or pressing leaflets into the hands of every passer-by. Performances go on round the clock: if so inclined, you could sit through twenty shows in a day.

The full Fringe **programme** is usually available in June from the Festival Fringe Office (☎0131/226 5257, ⓦwww.edfringe.com). During the Festival, tickets are sold at the Fringe office (daily 10am–7pm), the venue itself, or at various locations around the city; most Fringe shows start at £5, and average from £8 to £12 at the main venues, with the better known acts going for even more.

The smaller festivals

The **Edinburgh International Film Festival** offers a chance to see some of the year's big cinema hits before they go on general release, along with a varied and exciting bill of reissued movies. For those in the industry, it is also a vital talking shop, with debates, seminars and workshops, spiced up by the attendance of Hollywood stars at the succession of glittering parties which accompany the launches. The main venue is the Filmhouse, 88 Lothian Road.

The **Edinburgh International Book Festival** is the largest celebration of the written word worldwide. It's held in a tented village in the douce setting

---

Fringe venues

In addition to the many tiny and unexpected auditoriums, the three main **Fringe venues** are The Assembly Rooms, The Pleasance and The Gilded Balloon. If you're new to the Fringe, these aren't a bad place to start.

The atmosphere at the **Pleasance** is usually less frenetic than at the other venues, with classy drama and whimsical appearances by media stars sitting easily alongside the wackier acts. The **Assembly Rooms** provide a grand setting for top-of-the-range drama by companies such as the Royal Shakespeare Company and big-name music and comedy acts. The Fringe's premier comedy venue, **The Gilded Balloon**, hosts the "Late and Live" show, crammed with TV performers and wannabes competing to be noticed.

The **Traverse Theatre**, long a champion of new drama, combines the avant-garde with slick presentation. Less glam, but with an excellent line-up of thought-provoking drama, is the **Theatre Workshop**, an intimate venue located in Stockbridge.

of Charlotte Square, and offers talks, readings and signings by a star-studded line-up of visiting authors, as well as panel discussions and workshops.

The **Edinburgh International Jazz and Blues Festival** eases the city into the festival spirit with a full programme of gigs in many different locations. Like all the other festivals, this one has grown over the years from a concentrated international summer camp to a bigger, more modern affair, reflecting the panoply of generations and styles which appear under the banner of jazz and blues. Highlights include "Jazz On A Summer's Day", a musical extravaganza in Princes Street Gardens, and a colourful New Orleans-style street parade.

Staged in the spectacular stadium of Castle Esplanade, the **Military Tattoo** is an unashamed display of pomp and military pride. The programme of choreographed drills, massed pipe bands, historical tableaux, energetic battle re-enactments, national dancing and pyrotechnics has been a feature of the Festival for fifty years, the emotional climax provided by a lone piper on the castle battlements. Tickets need to be booked well in advance, and it's advisable to take a cushion and rainwear.

A festival within a festival, the **Edinburgh Mela** is held at different venues each year, coinciding with the finale of the International Festival. The word "Mela" is a Sanskrit term meaning "gathering", and is used to describe many different community events and festivals on the Asian subcontinent. In Edinburgh, it's about cultural diversity, and the family-oriented programme includes music, dance, foods, carnivals, fashion shows, sports, children's events, crafts and a two-day careers fair for school-leavers. Further details at Ⓦwww.edinburgh-mela.co.uk.

Shopping

Despite the relentless advance of the big chains, it's still possible to track down some characterful and unusual shops in central Edinburgh. **Princes Street**, one of Britain's most famous shopping streets, is all but dominated by standard chain outlets, though no serious shopper should miss out on a visit to Edinburgh's venerable department store, Jenners, at no. 48 opposite the Scott Monument. More fashionable upmarket shops and boutiques are to be found on parallel **George Street**, while for more original outlets, head for **Cockburn Street**, a hub for trendy clothes and record shops. On **Victoria Street** and in and around the **Grassmarket** you'll find an eclectic range of antique and arts and crafts shops plus some antiquarian booksellers.

Books Long-standing Edinburgh bookseller James Thin has large shops at 53–59 South Bridge and 57 George St. Waterstone's is, at present, the only major chain in Edinburgh, with branches at 128 Princes St, 13–14 Princes St and 83 George St. There's a good selection of antiquarian and second-hand bookshops: Peter Bell, 68 West Port; Castle Books, 20 Rankeillor St; West Port Books, 147 West Port; and McNaughtan's Bookshop 3a–4a Haddington Place, Leith Walk.

Haggis Charles MacSween & Son, Dryden Road, Bilston Glen, Loanhead (☎0131/440 2555), has an international reputation, and also makes a tasty vegetarian version; buy it from the factory or various outlets around Edinburgh, such as the Food

Hall in Jenners, 48 Princes St, or Peckhams, 155–159 Bruntsfield Place.

Music Check out Avalanche, 17 West Nicolson St, 28 Lady Lawson St and 63 Cockburn St for indie music; Coda, 12 Bank St, for contemporary Scottish folk and roots music; and Vinyl Villains, 5 Elm Row, for second-hand records, tapes and ephemera.

Tartan Kinloch Anderson, on the corner of Commercial and Dock streets, Leith, has a large showroom; Geoffrey Tailor, 57–59 High St, is one of the largest and most respected retailers on the Royal Mile – they also have a shop in the Edinburgh Old Town Weaving Co by the Castle Esplanade, where "live" weaving takes place.

Whisky Royal Mile Whiskies, 379–381 High St;
William Cadenhead, 172 Canongate.
Woollen goods Bill Baber Knitwear, 66

Grassmarket, has garments designed and made on
the premises; Ragamuffin, 2a St Mary's St, features Skye knitwear.

Listings

Banks Bank of Scotland, The Mound (head office),
38 St Andrew Sq; Barclays, 1 St Andrew Sq;
Clydesdale, 20 Hanover St; HSBC, 76 Hanover St;
Lloyds TSB, 120 George St; NatWest, 80 George
St; Royal Bank of Scotland, 42 St Andrew Sq.
Bike rental Biketrax, 11 Lochrin Place
⊕0131/228 6633; Edinburgh Cycle Hire, 29
Blackfriars St ⊕0131/556 5560.
Car rental Arnold Clark, Lochrin Place
⊕0131/229 8911; Avis, 100 Dalry Rd ⊕0131/337
6363; Budget, 394 Ferry Rd ⊕0800/181181; Easy
Rent-a-Car ⊕0906/586 0586; Europcar, 24 E
London St ⊕0131/557 3456; Hertz, Waverley
Station ⊕0131/557 5272; Mitchells, 32
Torphichen St ⊕0131/229 5384; Thrifty Car
Rental, 42 Haymarket Terrace ⊕0131/337 1319.
Consulates Australia, 69 George St ⊕0131/624
3333; Canada, 30 Lothian Rd ⊕0131/220 4333;
Germany, 16 Eglington Crescent ⊕0131/337
2323; Netherlands, 53 George St ⊕0131/220
3226; USA, 3 Regent Terrace ⊕0131/556 8315.
Dentist The National Health Service Line
(⊕0800/224488) will tell you where the nearest
surgery is. For emergencies go to Edinburgh Dental
Institute, Lauriston Place (⊕0131/536 4920).
Exchange Post offices will exchange currency
commission-free. There are currency exchange
bureaus in the main tourist office (Mon–Wed
9am–5pm, Thurs–Sat 9am–6pm, Sun 10am–5pm)
and beside platform 1 at Waverley Station (July &
Aug Mon–Sat 7am–10pm, Sun 8am–10pm; rest of
year Mon–Sat 7.30am–9pm, Sun 8.30am–9pm).
Hospital Royal Infirmary, 1 Lauriston Place
(⊕0131/536 1000), has a 24hr A&E department,
although note that it is moving in stages to a new

location to the southeast of the centre. Also at the
Western Infirmary, Crewe Road North.
Internet access The Cottage, 136 Nicolson St
(daily 24hr; ⊕0131/531 1881); easyEverything, 58
Rose St (daily 24hr; ⊕0131/220 3580); Web 13,
13 Bread St (Mon–Fri 9am–5.30pm, Thurs until
7pm, Sat 9am–6pm, Sun 11am–5pm; ⊕0131/229
8883).
Laundry Capital Launderette, 208 Dalkeith Rd,
Newington ⊕0131/667 0825; Sundial
Launderette, 7–9 East London St, Broughton
⊕0131/556 2743; Tarvit Launderette, 7–9 Tarvit
St, Tollcross ⊕0131/229 6382.
Left luggage Lockers at Waverley Station and St
Andrew Square bus station.
Libraries Central Library, George IV Bridge. The
National Library of Scotland, George IV Bridge, is
for research purposes only.
Lost property Edinburgh Airport ⊕0131/333
1000; Edinburgh Police HQ ⊕0131/311 3141;
Lothian Regional Transport ⊕0131/554 4494;
Scotrail ⊕0141/335 3276.
Pharmacy Boots, 48 Shandwick Place (Mon–Fri
8am–9pm, Sat 8am–7pm, Sun 10am–5pm;
⊕0131/225 6757).
Police In an emergency call ⊕999. Otherwise
contact Lothian and Borders Police HQ, Fettes
Avenue ⊕0131/311 3131.
Post office 8–10 St James Centre (Mon
9am–5.30pm, Tues–Fri 8.30am–5.30pm, Sat
8.30am–6pm; ⊕0845/722 3344).
Rape crisis centre ⊕0131/556 9437.
Taxis Airport Taxis ⊕0131/344 3344; Central
Radio Taxis ⊕0131/229 2468; City Cabs
⊕0131/228 1211.

Out from the centre

There's a great deal to be discovered by exploring just beyond the compact
centre of Edinburgh, in particular along the Firth of Forth coastline to the
north and the rise of the Pentland Hills to the south. Just over a mile northeast
of the city centre is **Leith**, the historic port of Edinburgh, a fascinating mix of
cobbled streets and new developments. Nearby you can find a flavour of the
city's maritime and fishing heritage at the atmospheric harbour of **Newhaven**.

In the southern suburbs of the city, the imposing fifteenth-century
Craigmillar Castle is incongruously set amid a rather grim housing estate,

but there is also a rural aspect to the area, with various hills, parks and, on the southern edge of the city, the range of the **Pentland Hills** which offer some wild walking country and terrific views.

Attractions further afield in the counties of East Lothian, Midlothian and West Lothian that fringe the city are outlined separately below.

Leith and around

For several hundred years, **LEITH** was separate from Edinburgh. As Scotland's major east coast port, it played a key role in the nation's history, even serving as the seat of government for a time, and in 1833 finally became a burgh in its own right. In 1920, however, it was incorporated into the capital and, in the decades that followed, went into seemingly terminal decline: the population dropped dramatically, and much of its centre was ripped out, to be replaced by grim housing schemes.

The 1980s, however, saw an unexpected turnaround, and today the port boasts arguably the best concentration of good restaurants (particularly seafood) in Edinburgh (see p.942 for reviews). The surviving historic buildings were spruced up and large blocks of yuppie flats appeared among the crumbling tenements and council housing. Meanwhile the dock areas are being transformed by Europe's largest ongoing waterfront development, most notably the vast building housing civil servants from the Scottish Executive and the new Ocean Terminal, a shopping and entertainment complex beside which the former royal yacht **Britannia** is settling into retirement.

Around the port

While you're most likely to come to Leith for the bars and restaurants, the area itself warrants exploration; though the shipbuilding yards have gone, it remains an active port with a rough-edged character. Most of the showpiece Neoclassical buildings lie on or near **The Shore**, the tenement-lined road along the final stretch of the Water of Leith, just before it disgorges into the Firth of Forth. **Leith Links** is an area of predominantly flat parkland just east of the police station. Documentary evidence suggests that The Links was a golf course in the fifteenth century, giving rise to Leith's claim to be regarded as the birthplace of the sport: in 1744 its first written rules were drawn up here, ten years before they were formalized in St Andrews.

Britannia

A little to the west of The Shore, moored alongside **Ocean Terminal** (a huge shopping and entertainment centre designed by Terence Conran), is one of the world's most famous ships, **Britannia** (daily: April–Sept 9.30am–4.30pm; Oct–March 10am–3.30pm; booking advised ☏0131/555 5566; £7.75). Launched in 1953 at John Brown's shipyard on Clydeside, *Britannia* was used by the royal family for 44 years for state visits, diplomatic functions and royal holidays. Leith acquired her following decommission in 1997, against the wishes of many of the royal family, who felt that scuttling would have been a more dignified end.

Visits to *Britannia* begin in the **visitor centre**, within Ocean Terminal. You get a free audioguide and are allowed to roam around the yacht, taking in the **bridge**, the **admiral's quarters**, the **officers' mess** and a large part of the **state apartments**, including the state dining and drawing rooms and the (separate) cabins used by the Queen and the Duke of Edinburgh. The ship has been largely kept as she was when she was in service, with a well-preserved 1950s dowdiness which the audioguide loyally attributes to the Queen's good taste and astute frugality in the lean postwar years. Certainly the atmosphere is a far cry from the opulent splendour which many expect.

To get to Ocean Terminal, jump on one of the tour buses which leave from Waverley Bridge in the city centre; otherwise, buses #10 and #16 from Princes Street, and bus #22 from St Andrew Square, run down Leith Walk to the junction of Commercial Street and North Junction Street, from where it's a five-minute walk down to the visitor centre.

Newhaven

To the west of Leith lies the village of **NEWHAVEN**, built by James IV at the start of the sixteenth century as an alternative shipbuilding centre to Leith: his massive warship, the *Great Michael*, was built here. It has also been a ferry station and an important fishing centre, landing some six million oysters a year at the height of its success in the 1860s. Today, the harbour still has a pleasantly salty feel. Among various modern developments, the old fish market remains, housing *Harry Ramsden's* fish-and-chip café, a couple of fish merchants and the small **Newhaven Heritage Museum** (daily noon–5pm; free), a fascinating collection of costumes and other memorabilia staffed by enthusiastic members of local fishing families.

South of the centre

In a green belt five miles southeast of the centre lies **Craigmillar Castle** (April–Sept daily 9.30am–6.30pm; Oct–March Mon–Wed & Sat 9.30am–4.30pm, Thurs 9.30am–noon, Fri & Sun 2–4.30pm; HS; £2), where the murder of Lord Darnley, second husband of Mary, Queen of Scots was plotted. It's one of the best preserved medieval fortresses in Scotland, and before Queen Victoria set her heart on Balmoral, it was being considered as her royal castle north of the border, a possibility which seems odd now given its proximity to the ugly council housing scheme of Craigmillar, one of Edinburgh's most deprived districts. Take bus #30, #33 or #82, or any bus heading for Hawick or Jedburgh, from the city centre to the district called Little France, from where the castle is a ten-minute walk along Craigmillar Castle Road.

The southern hills

The **hills** of Edinburgh's southern suburbs offer good, not overly demanding, walking opportunities, with plenty of sweeping panoramic views. The **Royal Observatory** (Mon–Sat 10am–5pm, Sun noon–5pm; £3.50) stands at the top of Blackford Hill, just a short walk south of Morningside, or accessible by buses #24 and #41 direct from the centre. The visitor centre here seeks to explain the mysteries of the solar system by means of various hands-on exhibits and CD-ROMs, and you also get to see the observatory's two main telescopes.

Further south are the **Pentland Hills**, a chain some eighteen miles long and five wide. Numerous walks, from gentle strolls along well-marked paths to a ten-mile traverse of the hills and moors, are outlined on a pamphlet available from the Regional Park Information Centre at **FLOTTERSTONE**, ten miles south of the city centre on the A702, an old staging post on the route south.

East Lothian

East Lothian consists of the coastal strip and hinterland immediately east of Edinburgh, bounded by the Firth of Forth to the north and the Lammermuir Hills to the south. All of it is within easy day-trip range from the capital though there are places you can stay overnight if you're keen to explore it properly. Often mocked as the "home counties" of Edinburgh, there's no denying its well-ordered feel, with prosperous farms and large estate houses dominating the scenery. The most immediately attractive part of the area is the coastline, extending from **Musselburgh**, all but joined onto Edinburgh, round to **Dunbar**, including the enjoyable Seabird Centre at **North Berwick** which looks out to the volcanic plug of the Bass Rock, and the dramatic – and romantic – cliff-top ruins at **Tantallon**. The inland region is often ignored in favour of the coast, or by traffic speeding along the main A1 road from Edinburgh which cuts through the region before turning south for Berwick. At the foot of the Lammermuirs is the county town of **Haddington**, a pleasant enough place, though the attractions of Edinburgh's "local" whisky distillery by Pencaitland is always likely to be a stronger draw.

North Berwick and around

NORTH BERWICK, twenty miles east of Edinburgh, has a great deal of charm and a somewhat faded, old-fashioned air, its guest houses and hotels extending along the shore in all their Victorian and Edwardian sobriety. The town's small harbour is set on a headland which cleaves two crescents of sand, providing the town with an attractive coastal setting. The small **museum** on School Road (April–Oct daily 11am–5pm; free), housed in the old school house, displays local curios including the old town stocks.

Located in an attractively designed new building by the harbour, the **Scottish Seabird Centre** (daily: April–Oct 10am–6pm; Nov–March 10am–4pm; £4.50) offers an introduction to all types of seabird found around the Scottish coast, particularly the 100,000-plus gannets and puffins which nest on the Bass Rock every summer. Such is the connection between the rock and its annual visitors that the gannet, once known as the solan goose, takes its Latin name, *Morus bassana*, from the Bass Rock. Thanks to a live link from the centre to cameras mounted on the volcanic island, you're able to view close-up pictures of the birds in their nesting grounds. Elsewhere in the centre, hands-on games and exhibits explain more about different seabirds, and a mock-up of a cliff face has various stuffed birds nesting on it – all of which, the centre insists, were ethically gathered.

Resembling a giant molar, the **Bass Rock** rises 350ft above the sea some three miles east of North Berwick. This massive chunk of basalt has had an interesting history, having held out as a Jacobite stronghold for six years longer than anywhere else in the country, then served as a prison, a fortress and a monastic retreat. The last lighthouse keepers left in 1988, leaving it, quite literally, to the birds: it's Scotland's second-largest gannet colony after St Kilda but also hosts razorbills, terns, puffins, guillemots and fulmars.

Tantallon Castle

The melodramatic ruins of **Tantallon Castle** (April–Sept daily 9.30am–6.30pm; Oct–March Mon–Wed & Sat 9.30am–4.30pm, Thurs 9.30am–noon, Fri & Sun 2–4.30pm; HS; £2.80), three miles east of North Berwick on the A198, stand on the precipitous cliffs facing the Bass Rock.

With a sheer drop down to the sea on three sides and a sequence of moats and ditches on the fourth, the castle's desolate invincibility is daunting, especially when the wind howls over the remaining battlements and the surf crashes on the rocks far below. Built at the end of the fourteenth century, the castle was a stronghold of the Douglases, the Earls of Angus, one of the most powerful noble families in Scotland.

Besieged several times, the castle was finally destroyed by Cromwell in 1651 after a twelve-day bombardment. The ruins, including a seventeenth-century dovecote left untouched by Cromwell's men, enjoy a wonderfully photogenic setting, with the Bass Rock and the Firth of Forth in the background.

The **bus** between North Berwick and Dunbar (Mon–Sat 6 daily, 2 on Sun) passes by the castle, or you can walk there from North Berwick along the cliffs in around an hour.

Practicalities

North Berwick is served by a regular half-hour **train** from Edinburgh Waverley, with special travel and entry deals available for those heading for the Seabird Centre (ask at Waverley ticket office). From the station it's a ten-minute walk east to the town centre along Abbey Road, Westgate and High Street. **Buses** from Edinburgh (every 30min) run along the coast via Aberlady, Gullane and Dirleton and stop on High Street, while the hourly service from Haddington and Dunbar terminates outside the **tourist office**, on Quality Street (July Mon–Sat 9am–7pm, Sun 11am–6pm; Aug Mon–Sat 9am–8pm, Sun 11am–6pm; June & Sept Mon–Sat 9am–6pm, Sun 11am–4pm; April & May Mon–Sat 9am–6pm; Oct–March Mon–Sat 9am–5pm; ☎01620/892197).

As befits a well-to-do holiday resort, there are several excellent **B&Bs**, including *Windrow*, 20 Marmion Rd (☎01620/892066; ❷; April–Sept), a Victorian house within easy walking distance of the sea, and *Tantallon House*, 2 West Bay Rd (☎01620/892873; ❸; April–Oct), next to the golf course. Of the **guest houses**, the seafront *Craigview*, 5 Beach Rd (☎01620/892257; ❹), has four-poster beds and serves good vegetarian breakfasts. The nearest **campsite**, *Tantallon Caravan Park* (☎01620/893348, ⓔTantallonP@aol.com; March–Oct), occupies a prime cliff-top location a couple of miles east of the centre – take the Dunbar bus.

One of the best **cafés** in town is at the Seabird Centre, which has panoramic views over the beach. As well as lunches, coffees and cakes, it's also open as a **bistro** in the evenings (May–Sept Wed–Sat; call for winter hours; ☎01620/893342). In town, the *Grange*, 35 High St (☎01620/893344; closed Mon), is a pleasant restaurant serving good quality, moderately priced meals, while both the *Tantallon Inn* on Marine Parade and the *Marine Hotel* on Cromwell Road do decent bar food.

Dunbar

Twelve miles southeast along the coast from North Berwick lies **DUNBAR**, which bears some resemblance to its near-neighbour with its wide, recently spruced-up High Street graced by several grand old stone buildings. One of these is the three-storey **John Muir House**, 128 High St (call ☎01368/860187 for opening hours; free), birthplace of the explorer and naturalist who created the United States' national park system. Recently refurbished, the house now acts as an interpretative and education centre inspired by the pioneer's life and legacy. A more appropriate tribute, in some respects, is the **country park** in Muir's honour, where an easy three-mile walk west of the harbour takes you along a rugged stretch of coast to the sands of Belhaven Bay.

The **tourist office** is at 143 High St (Aug Mon–Sat 9am–8pm, Sun 11am–6pm; June, July & Sept Mon–Sat 9am–7pm, Sun 11am–4pm; May Mon–Sat 9am–6pm, Sun 11am–4pm; Oct–April Mon–Sat 9am–5pm; ☎01368/863353). For a light **lunch**, the *Food Hamper* and *William Smith's* on the High Street do good sandwiches, while the best evening meal options are the *Creel* (☎01368/863279) by the old harbour, where you can eat steaks and seafood, including a speciality Jamaican seafood dish served with bananas, and *Cuckoo Wrasse* (☎01368/865384), also by the harbour at 1 Shore St, which serves rather pricey seafood dishes in a bistro-style setting.

Haddington and around

The East Lothian gentry keep a careful eye on **HADDINGTON**, their favourite country town. Its compact centre preserves an intriguing ensemble of seventeenth- to nineteenth-century architectural styles where everything of any interest has been labelled and plaqued. Haddington's centre is best approached from the west, where tree-trimmed **Court Street** ends suddenly with the soaring spire, stately stonework and dignified Venetian windows of the **Town House**, designed by William Adam in 1748.

Heading east from the town centre along High Street, it's a brief walk down Church Street – past the hooped arches of Nungate Bridge – to the hulking mass of **St Mary's Church** (April–Sept Mon–Sat 11am–4pm, Sun 1–4.30pm; free), Scotland's largest parish church. Built close to the reedy River Tyne, the church dates from the fourteenth century but it's a real hotch-potch of styles, the squat grey tower uneasy above clumsy buttressing and pinkish-ochre stone walls. Inside, on the **Lauderdale Aisle**, a munificent tomb features the best of Elizabethan alabaster carving, moustached knights and their ruffed ladies lying beneath a finely ornamented canopy. The church also offers brass rubbing, has a good tearoom and in the summer hosts internationally acclaimed concerts.

Fast and frequent **buses** connect Haddington with Edinburgh, fifteen miles to the west, and with North Berwick; all services stop on High Street. There's no tourist office. For **food**, seek out the snacks and lovely deli lunch platters at daytime *Jaques & Lawrence* at 37 Court St, opposite the post office. The best place for an evening meal is the *Waterside Bistro* (☎1620/825674), on the far side of Nungate Bridge, justifiably popular for its delicious seafood and varied vegetarian dishes.

Glenkinchie Distillery

Six miles from Haddington along the A6093, the village of Pencaitland is the closest place to Edinburgh where **malt whisky** is made. Set in a peaceful dip in the rolling countryside about two miles outside Pencaitland, the **Glenkinchie Distillery** (June–Oct Mon–Sat 9.30am–5pm, Sun noon–5pm; March–May Mon–Fri 10am–5pm; Nov–Feb Mon–Fri 11am–4pm; £3.50) is one of only a handful found in the Lowlands of Scotland. Here, of course, they emphasize the qualities which set Glenkinchie, a lighter, drier malt, apart from the peaty, smoky whiskies of the north. Also in the tour there's an impressive scale model of a distillery, allowing you to place all the different processes in context, and a room where the art of blending is explained.

Midlothian

Immediately south of Edinburgh lies the old county of **Midlothian**, once called Edinburghshire. It's one of the hilliest parts of the Central Lowlands, with the Pentland chain running down its western side, and the Moorfoots defining its boundary with the Borders to the south. Though predominantly rural, it contains a belt of former mining communities, which are struggling to come to terms with the recent decline of the industry. Such charms as it has are mostly low-key, with the exception of the riotously ornate chapel at **Roslin**.

Dalkeith and around

Despite its Victorian demeanour, **DALKEITH**, eight miles southeast of central Edinburgh – to which it is linked by very regular buses (#3, #30, #82) – grew up in the Middle Ages as a baronial burgh under the successive control of the Douglases and Buccleuchs. Today it's a bustling shopping centre, with an unusually broad High Street at its heart.

A mile or so south is **NEWTONGRANGE**, whose Lady Victoria Colliery is now open to the public as the **Scottish Mining Museum** (daily: Feb–Oct 10am–5pm, Nov–Jan 11am–4pm; £4), with a 1625-foot shaft and a winding tower powered by Scotland's largest steam engine. A great place for kids, the visitor centre brings the mine and the local community to life with "magic helmets", which enable you to go on shift and experience a virtual-reality tour of life below ground.

Roslin

The tranquil village of **ROSLIN** lies seven miles south of the centre of Edinburgh, from where it can be reached by bus #87a or by regular Eastern Scottish services from St Andrew Square. The village has two unusual claims to fame: it was near here, at the Roslin Institute, that the world's first cloned sheep, Dolly, was created in 1997; and it also boasts the mysterious, richly decorated late-Gothic **Rosslyn Chapel** (Mon–Sat 10am–5pm, Sun noon–4.45pm; £4). Only the choir, Lady Chapel and part of the transepts were built of what was intended to be a huge collegiate church dedicated to St Matthew: construction halted soon after the founder's death in 1484, and the vestry built onto the facade nearly four hundred years later is the sole subsequent addition. After a long period of neglect, a massive restoration project has recently been undertaken: a canopy has been placed over the chapel which will remain in place for several years in order to dry out the saturated ceiling and walls, and other essential repairs are due to be carried out within the chapel.

The exterior bristles with pinnacles, gargoyles, flying buttresses and canopies, while inside the foliage carving is particularly outstanding, with botanically accurate depictions of over a dozen different leaves and plants. Among them are cacti and Indian corn, providing fairly convincing evidence that the founder's grandfather, the daring sea adventurer Prince Henry of Orkney, did indeed, as legend has it, set foot in the New World a century before Columbus. The greatest and most original carving of all is the extraordinary knotted **Prentice Pillar** at the southeastern corner of the Lady Chapel. According to local legend, the pillar was made by an apprentice during the absence of the master mason, who killed him in a fit of jealousy on seeing the finished work.

A number of books have been published in recent years about Rosslyn Chapel, drawing on everything from Freemasons and the Turin Shroud to the True Gospels and the regular sightings of UFOs over Midlothian. Conspiracy theories notwithstanding, the chapel is very definitely worth a visit.

West Lothian

To many, **West Lothian** is a poor relative to the rolling, rich farmland of East and Midlothian, with a landscape dominated by motorways, industrial estates and giant hillocks of ochre-coloured mine waste called "bings". However, anywhere this close to the centres of power through Scottish history would find it hard not to have something to show for itself, and in the ruined royal palace at **Linlithgow** the area boasts one of Scotland's more magnificent ruins. The village of **South Queensferry** (strictly speaking no longer part of West Lothian) lies under the considerable shadow of the Forth rail and road bridges. A mile or two beyond South Queensferry is **Hopetoun House**, an impressive stately home.

South Queensferry and around

Ten miles northwest of Edinburgh city centre is **SOUTH QUEENSFERRY**, a compact little town used by St Margaret as a crossing point for her frequent trips between her palaces in Edinburgh and Dunfermline. The small **museum**, 53 High St (Mon & Thurs–Sat 10am–1pm & 2.15–5pm, Sun noon–5pm; free), contains relics of the town's history and information on the building of the two bridges which loom over the village. A dedicated museum to the bridge can be found in North Queensferry (see p.1063), while the best way to get a good view of the magnificent Rail Bridge is to walk (or cycle) across the adjacent parallel Road Bridge.

Hopetoun House

Immediately beyond the western edge of South Queensferry, **Hopetoun House** (April–Sept daily 10am–5.30pm; £5.30, grounds only £2.90) is one of Scotland's grandest stately homes. The original house was built at the turn of the eighteenth century for the first Earl of Hopetoun by Sir William Bruce, the architect of Holyroodhouse. A couple of decades later, William Adam carried out an enormous extension, engulfing the house in a curvaceous main facade and two projecting wings – superb examples of Roman Baroque pomp and swagger. The scale and lavishness of the Adam interiors, most of the decoration of which was carried out by his sons after the architect's death, make for a stark contrast with the intimacy of those designed by Bruce. Particularly impressive are the Red and Yellow Drawing Rooms, with their splendid ceilings by the young Robert Adam. The **grounds** of the house are also open, with magnificent walks along the banks of the Forth and great opportunities for picnics.

Linlithgow

Roughly equidistant from Falkirk and Edinburgh – fifteen miles from both – is the ancient royal burgh of **LINLITHGOW**. The town itself has largely kept its medieval layout, but development since the 1960s has sadly stripped it of some fine buildings, notably close to the **Town Hall** and **Cross** – the former marketplace – on the long High Street.

Hidden from the main street, **Linlithgow Palace** (April–Sept daily 9.30am–6.30pm; Oct–March Mon–Sat 9.30am–4.30pm, Sun 2–4.30pm; HS; £2.80) is a splendid fifteenth-century ruin romantically set on the edge of Linlithgow Loch and associated with some of Scotland's best-known historical figures – including Mary, Queen of Scots, who was born here on December 8, 1542, and became queen six days later. A royal manor house is believed to have existed on this site since the time of David I. Fire razed the manor in 1424, after which James I began construction of the present palace, a process that continued through two centuries and the reign of no fewer than eight monarchs.

This is a great place to take children: the rooflessness of the castle creates unexpected vistas, the elegant, bare rooms echo with footsteps and the fluttering of birds flying out through the empty windows, and there's a labyrinthine feel to the place with spiral staircases and endless nooks and crannies. The galleried **Great Hall** is magnificent, as is the adjoining kitchen, which has a truly cavernous fireplace. Don't miss the dank downstairs **brewery**, which produced vast quantities of ale; 24 gallons was apparently a good nightly consumption in the sixteenth century.

Practicalities

Frequent **buses** between Stirling and Edinburgh stop at the Cross, and the town is on the main **train** routes from Edinburgh to both Glasgow Queen Street and Stirling; the train station lies at the southern end of town. The **tourist office** is in the Town Hall building at the Cross (April–Sept daily 10am–5pm; ☎01506/844600), between the palace and the High Street.

There are a few decent places to **eat** in Linlithgow: for good pub food try The *Four Marys*, opposite the Cross on High Street, which also has real ales, while *Marynka* (☎01506/840123), also on the High Street at no. 57, is a brighter, more modern bistro-style place. Best of the lot is a place just outside town on the way to Blackness called the *Champany Inn* (☎01506/834532), which serves delicious steaks, chops and seafood.

Travel details

Trains

Edinburgh Waverley to: Aberdeen (hourly; 2hr 40min); Birmingham (6 daily; 5hr 30min); Dunbar (hourly; 30 min); Dundee (hourly; 1hr 45min); Falkirk (every 30min; 25min); Fort William (change at Glasgow; 3 daily; 4hr 55min); Glasgow (2–4 hourly; 50min); Inverness (4 daily; 3hr 50min); London (20 daily; 4hr 30min); Manchester (direct: 4 daily; 4hr; change at Preston: 7 daily; 4hr); Newcastle-upon-Tyne (27 daily; 1hr 30min); North Berwick (hourly; 30 min); Oban (change at Glasgow; 3 daily; 4hr 10min); Perth (6 daily; 1hr 15min); Stirling (every 30min; 45min); York (24 daily; 2hr 30min).

Buses

Edinburgh (St Andrew Square) to: Aberdeen (22 daily; express 3hr, standard 3hr 50min); Birmingham (2 daily; 6hr 50min); Dundee (22 daily; express 1hr 25min–2hr); Fort William (4 daily; 4hr); Glasgow (every 30min; 1hr 10min); Inverness (13 daily; 3–4hr); London (6 daily; 7hr 50min); Newcastle-upon-Tyne (3 daily; 3hr 15min); Oban (3 daily; 5hr); Perth (21 daily; 1hr 20min); York (1 daily; 5hr).

Flights

Edinburgh to: Dublin (Mon–Fri 5 daily, Sat & Sun 4 daily; 1hr); Kirkwall (Mon–Sat 1 daily; 1hr 20min); Lerwick (1 daily; 1hr 30min); London City (Mon–Fri 16 daily, 1 on Sat, 6 on Sun; 1hr 15min); London Gatwick (Mon–Fri 6 daily, Sat & Sun 4 daily; 1hr 15min); London Heathrow (Mon–Fri 20 daily, Sat & Sun 15 daily; 1hr); London Luton (Mon–Fri 6 daily, Sat & Sun 4 daily; 1hr 20min); London Stansted (Mon–Fri 8 daily, Sat & Sun 4–6 daily; 1hr 10min); Stornoway (Mon–Fri 1 daily; 1hr 10min).

Southern Scotland

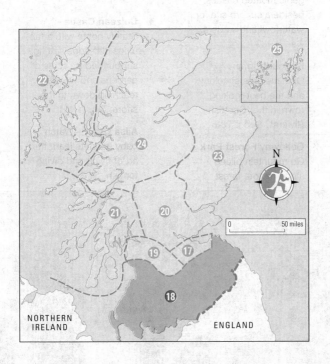

* **Melrose Abbey** – The Border Abbey with the best-preserved sculptural detail, set within the most charming of the Border towns. See p.966

* **Caerlaverock** – One of Scotland's most photogenic moated castles, beside a superb site for waterfowl and waders. See p.980

* **Kirkcudbright** – Onetime artists' colony, and the best-looking town in the "Scottish Riviera". See p.983

* **Galloway Forest Park** – Go mountain biking along remote forest tracks, or hiking on the Southern Upland Way. See p.986

* **Alloway** – The village where poet Robert Burns was born, and the best of many Burns' pilgrimage spots in the region. See p.991

* **Culzean Castle** – Stately home with a fabulous cliff-edge setting, surrounded by acres of gardens and woods reaching down to the shore. See p.991

* **Ailsa Craig** – Watch baby gannets learn the art of flying and diving for fish. See p.991

Southern Scotland

Southern **Scotland** divides neatly into three distinct regions: the Borders, Dumfries and Galloway, and Ayrshire. Although none of the regions has the highest of tourist profiles, those visitors who whizz past on their way to Edinburgh, Glasgow or the Highlands are missing out on a huge swathe of Scotland that is in many ways the very heart of the country. Its inhabitants, particularly in the Borders, bore the brunt of long wars with the English, its farms have fed Scotland's cities since industrialization, and two of the country's literary icons, Sir Walter Scott and Robbie Burns, lived and died here.

Geographically, the region is dominated by the **Southern Uplands**, a chain of bulging round-topped hills and weather-beaten moorland, punctuated by narrow glens, fast-flowing rivers and blue-black lochs. This region is at its most dramatic in the **Galloway Forest Park** to the southwest, with peaks reaching to over 2000ft, crisscrossed by numerous popular walking trails. Meanwhile on the coast, you'll find enormous variety: the east coast is fairly bleak, with dramatic cliffs interspersed with tiny fishing villages; the **Solway coast**, in the southwest, is much gentler, indented by sandy coves and estuaries; while the Ayrshire coast, by contrast, is much more heavily populated, and in parts, an almost continuous stretch of seaside resorts and industrial centres.

Lying north of the inhospitable Cheviot Hills, which separate Scotland from England, the **Borders** region is dominated by the meanderings of the **River Tweed**. None of the towns along the Tweed is of any great size, yet they have provided inspiration for countless folkloric ballads telling of bloody battles with the English and clashes between the notorious warring families, the Border Reivers (see p.966). The small but delightful town of **Melrose**, in the heart of the Borders, is the most obvious base for exploring the region, and has the most impressive of the four **Border abbeys** founded by the medieval Canmore kings, all of which are now reduced to romantic ruins.

Dumfries and Galloway, occupying the southwestern corner of Scotland, gets even more overlooked than the Borders, though the region remains popular with Lowland Scots and folk from the north of England. If you do make the effort to get off the main north–south highway to Glasgow, you'll find several more ruined abbeys, medieval castles, forested hills and dramatic tidal flats and seacliffs ideal for birdwatching. The key resort is the charming town of **Kirkcudbright** halfway along the marshy Solway coast, well placed for exploring the rest of the county.

Ayrshire is rich farming country, and not an obvious destination for first-time visitors to Scotland. It has fewer sights than its neighbours, with almost

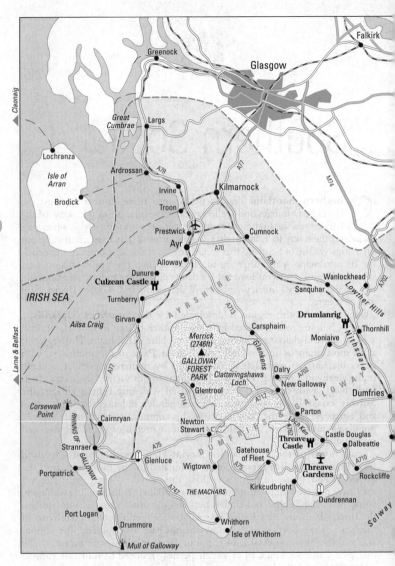

everything of interest confined to the coast. However, the **golf courses** along its gentle coastline are among the finest links courses in the country, and golfers can buy three- and five-day passes from tourist offices allowing free or reduced-fee access to many of the region's golf courses. Fans of Robert Burns could happily spend several days exploring the author's old haunts, especially at **Ayr**, the handsome county town, and the nearby village of Alloway, the poet's birthplace.

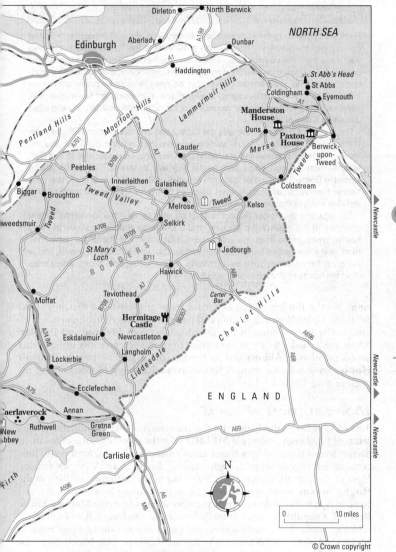

Newcastle

Newcastle

Newcastle

© Crown copyright

The Borders

Sandwiched between the **Cheviot Hills** on the English border and the Pentland and Moorfoot ranges to the south of Edinburgh, is the **Borders** region (Ⓦ www.scot-borders.co.uk). If you've travelled from the south across the bleak moorland of neighbouring Northumberland, you'll be struck by the green lushness of the **Tweed valley**, the pivotal feature of the region's geog-

The Border Reivers

From the thirteenth to the early seventeenth centuries, the wild, inhospitable border country stretching from the Solway Firth in the west to the Tweed Valley in the east, well away from the power bases of both the Scottish and English monarchs, was overrun by outlaws known as the **Border Reivers**, *reive* being a Scots word for plunder. This, was no cross-border dispute, but an open struggle for power among the tribes of the region. Cattle-rustling, blackmail and kidnapping led to an anarchical mindset, where feuding families would wreak havoc and devastation on each other almost as a way of life.

The source of this behaviour was the destruction and devastation wrought upon the region by virtually continual warfare between England and Scotland, and the "slash and burn" policy of the era. With many residents no longer able to find sustenance from the land, crime became the only way to survive. Those who "shook loose the Border" included people from all walks of life – agricultural labourers, gentleman farmers, small-holders, even peers of the realm – for whom theft, raiding, tracking and ambush became second nature.

The legacy of the Border Reivers can still be seen today in the fortified farms and churches of the region's architecture; in the **Common Riding** traditions of many border towns; in the language – the words "blackmail" and "bereaved" have their roots in the destructive behaviour that was so characteristic of this period; and in the great family names such as Armstrong, Graham, Kerr and Nixon, which once filled the hearts of Borderers with dread.

raphy. Yet the Borders also incorporates some of the wildest stretches of the Southern Uplands, with bare, rounded peaks and heathery hills punctuated by valleys. The finest section of the Tweed lies between **Melrose** and **Peebles**, where you'll find a string of attractions, from the eccentricities of Sir Walter Scott's mansion at **Abbotsford** to the intriguing Jacobite past of **Traquair House**, along with the region's famous **ruined abbeys**, founded during the reign of King David I (1124–53).

Melrose and around

Tucked in between the Tweed and the gorse-backed Eildon Hills, thirty miles south of Edinburgh, minuscule **MELROSE** is the most beguiling of towns, its narrow streets trimmed by a harmonious ensemble of styles, from pretty little cottages and tweedy shops to high-standing Georgian and Victorian facades. Most of the year it's a sleepy little place, but as the birthplace in 1883 of the **Rugby Sevens** (seven-a-side games), it swarms during Sevens Week (second week in April), and again in early September when it hosts the **Melrose Music Festival**, a popular weekend of traditional music attracting folkies from afar.

To the north of the town square, the pink- and red-tinted stone ruins of **Melrose Abbey** (April–Sept daily 9.30am–6.30pm; Oct–March Mon–Sat 9.30am–4.30pm, Sun 2–4.30pm; HS; £3.50) soar above their riverside surroundings. Founded in 1136, Melrose was the first Cistercian settlement in Scotland and grew rich selling wool and hides to Flanders, but its prosperity was fragile: the English repeatedly razed Melrose, most viciously under Richard II in 1385 and the Earl of Hertford in 1545. Most of the present remains date from the intervening period, when extensive rebuilding abandoned the original Cistercian austerity for an elaborate Gothic style inspired by the abbeys of northern England, though it seems likely that the abbey was never fully finished before the Reformation. The sculptural detailing at Melrose is of the highest quality, but it's easy to miss if you don't know where to look, so taking advantage of the free audioguide, or buying yourself a guidebook, is a good idea.

The site is dominated by the **Abbey Church**, which has lost its west front, and whose nave is reduced to the elegant window arches and chapels of the south aisle. Amazingly, however, the stone **pulpitum** (screen), separating the choir monks from their lay brothers, is preserved. Beyond, the **presbytery** has its magnificent perpendicular window, lierne vaulting and ceiling bosses intact, with the capitals of the surrounding columns sporting the most intricate of curly kale carving. In the **south transept**, another fine fifteenth-century window sprouts yet more delicate, foliate tracery and the adjacent cornice is enlivened by angels playing musical instruments, though these figures are badly weathered. This kind of finely carved detail is repeated everywhere you look in Melrose: look for the statue of the Virgin and Child, high on the south side of the westernmost surviving buttress, the Coronation of the Virgin on the east end gable, and the numerous mischievous **gargoyles**, from peculiar crouching beasts to the pig playing the bagpipes on the roof on the south side of the nave.

Legend has it that the heart of **Robert the Bruce** is buried here (his body having been buried at Dunfermline Abbey), and this theory received an unexpected boost in 1997, when a heart cask was publicly exhumed. However, the burial location was not in accordance with Bruce's own wishes. In 1329, the dying king told his friend, Sir James Douglas, to carry his heart on a Crusade to the Holy Land in fulfilment of an old vow: "Seeing therefore, that my body cannot go to achieve what my heart desires, I will send my heart instead of my body, to accomplish my vow." Douglas tried his best, but was killed fighting the Moors in Spain – and Bruce's heart ended up in Melrose. A new commemorative stone marks its current resting-place in the chapter house, to the north of the sacristy.

The paltry ruins of the old monastic buildings edge the church to the north and lead over the road to the **Commendator's House** (same hours as the abbey), a lovely red sandstone building now housing a modest collection of ecclesiastical bric-a-brac. Back towards the town, to the south of the abbey, you should pop into the delightful **Priorwood Garden** (April–Sept Mon–Sat 10am–5.30pm, Sun 1.30–5.30pm; Oct–Dec Mon–Sat 10am–4pm, Sun 1.30–4pm; NTS; free), whose compact walled precincts are given over to an orchard and flowers that are suitable for drying. Melrose's other museum, the **Trimontium Exhibition**, just off Market Square (April–Oct Mon–Fri 10.30am–4.30pm, Sat & Sun 10.30am–1pm & 2–4.30pm; ⓦ www.trimontium.freeserve.co.uk; £1.50), is a quirky little centre outlining the three Roman occupations of the region, that merits a browse.

Practicalities

Buses to Melrose stop in Market Square, a brief walk south from the abbey ruins and the **tourist office** opposite (July & Aug Mon–Sat 9.30am–6.30pm, Sun 10am–6pm; June & Sept Mon–Sat 10am–6pm, Sun 10am–2pm; March–May & Oct Mon–Sat 10am–5pm, Sun 10am–1pm; ☎01896/822555). Melrose has a clutch of **hotels**, the best of which is *Burt's*, a smartly converted old inn on Market Square (☎01896/822285, ⓦ www.burtshotel.co.uk; ⑥); rooms are small, but very comfortable. Across the street is the ten-bedroom *Millars* (☎01896/822645; ⑤), recently smartened up and with fewer pretensions than *Burt's*. It's among Melrose's simple **B&Bs**, however, that you'll get the real flavour of the place, most notably at the easygoing and comfortable *Braidwood*, on Buccleuch Street (☎01896/822488; ②), a stone's throw from the abbey, and the equally agreeable *Dunfermline House* (☎01896/822148,

Ⓦwww.dunmel.freeserve.co.uk; ②) opposite. The town also has an SYHA **hostel** (☎01896/822521, Ⓦwww.syha.org.uk; Feb–Oct & New Year) in a sprawling Georgian villa overlooking the abbey from beside the access road into the bypass. The *Gibson Caravan Park* **campsite** (☎01896/822969) is in the town centre, just off the High Street, opposite the Greenyards rugby grounds.

Melrose offers a reasonable choice of **eating** options. *Marmion's Brasserie* (☎01896/822245), housed in a spacious Victorian house on Buccleuch Street, serves well-prepared meals from an imaginative, moderately expensive menu. *Burt's* does excellent bar meals, and if you're feeling energetic, walk past the abbey and across the old suspension bridge to Gattonside, where the *Hoebridge Inn* (☎01896/823082; closed Mon), once a bobbin mill and now one of the Borders' best restaurants, serves home-made Scottish food in relaxed, low-key surroundings. If you want a light lunch or snack, head to *Russell's*, a popular, very traditional tearoom on Market Square; or *Haldane's Fish & Chip Shop* (closed Wed), next door. For **pubs**, try the friendly *King's Arms* on the High Street, or the *Ship Inn*, on East Port at the top of the square, the liveliest in town. Be sure to check out what's on at The Wynd (☎01896/823854, Ⓦwww.the-wynd-theatre.co.uk), Melrose's very own pint-sized **theatre**, tucked away down the alleyway, north off the main square, which shows films and puts on gigs as well as live drama.

Abbotsford

The stately home of **Abbotsford** (June–Sept daily 9.30am–5pm; mid-March to May & Oct Mon–Sat 9.30am–5pm, Sun 2–5pm; £4), three miles up the Tweed from Melrose, was designed to satisfy the Romantic inclinations of **Sir Walter Scott**, who lived here from 1812 until his death twenty years later. Abbotsford (as Scott chose to call it) took twelve years to evolve, with the fanciful turrets and castellations of the Scots Baronial exterior incorporating copies of medieval originals: the entrance porch imitates that of Linlithgow Palace and the screen wall in the garden echoes Melrose Abbey's cloister. Despite all the exterior pomp, the interior is surprisingly small and poky, with just six rooms open for viewing on the upper floor. Visitors start in the wood-panelled study, with its small writing desk made of salvage from the Spanish Armada, at which Scott banged out the Waverley novels at a furious rate. The heavy wood-panelled library boasts Scott's collection of more than nine thousand rare books and an extraordinary assortment of memorabilia, the centrepiece of which is Napoleon's pen case and blotting book, but which also includes Rob Roy's purse and *skene dhu* (knife), and the inlaid pearl crucifix that accompanied Mary, Queen of Scots to the scaffold. You can also see Henry Raeburn's famous portrait of Scott hanging in the drawing room, and all sorts of weapons – notably Rob Roy's sword, dagger and gun – in the armoury.

The fast and frequent Melrose–Galashiels **bus** provides easy access to Abbotsford: ask for the Tweedbank island on the A6091, from where the house is a ten-minute walk up the road.

Dryburgh Abbey

Hidden away in a U-bend in the Tweed, ten miles upstream from Kelso, the remains of **Dryburgh Abbey** (April–Sept daily 9.30am–6.30pm; Oct–March Mon–Sat 9.30am–4.30pm, Sun 2–4.30pm; HS; £2.80) occupy an idyllic position against a hilly backdrop, with ancient cedars, redwoods, beech and lime trees and wide lawns flattering the pinkish-red hues of the stonework. The Premonstratensians founded the abbey in the twelfth century, but they were never as successful as their Cistercian neighbours in Melrose. The romantic set-

Walter Scott (1771–1832) was born in Edinburgh to a solidly bourgeois family whose roots were in Selkirkshire. As a child he was left lame by polio and his anxious parents sent him to recuperate at his grandfather's farm in Smailholm, where the boy's imagination was fired by his relatives' tales of derring-do, the violent history of the Borders retold amidst the rugged landscape that he spent long summer days exploring. Scott returned to Edinburgh to resume his education and take up a career in law, but his real interests remained elsewhere. Throughout the 1790s he transcribed hundreds of old Border ballads, publishing a three-volume collection entitled *Minstrelsy of the Scottish Borders* in 1802. An instant success, *Minstrelsy* was followed by Scott's own *Lay of the Last Minstrel*, a narrative poem whose strong story and rose-tinted regionalism proved very popular.

More poetry was to come, most successfully *Marmion* (1808) and *The Lady of the Lake* (1810), not to mention an eighteen-volume edition of the works of John Dryden and nineteen volumes of Jonathan Swift. However, despite having two paid jobs, one as the Sheriff-Depute of Selkirkshire, the other as clerk to the Court of Session in Edinburgh, his finances remained shaky. He had become a partner in a printing firm, which put him deeply into debt, not helped by the enormous sums he spent on his mansion, Abbotsford. From 1813, Scott was writing to pay the bills and thumped out a veritable flood of historical novels using his extensive knowledge of Scottish history and folklore. He produced his best work within the space of ten years: *Waverley* (1814), *The Antiquary* (1816), *Rob Roy* and *The Heart of Midlothian* (both 1818), as well as two notable novels set in England, *Ivanhoe* (1819) and *Kenilworth* (1821). In 1824 he returned to Scottish tales with *Redgauntlet*, the last of his quality work.

A year later Scott's money problems reached crisis proportions after an economic crash bankrupted his printing business. Attempting to pay his creditors in full, he found the quality of his writing deteriorating with its increased speed and the effort broke his health. His last years were plagued by illness, and in 1832 he died at Abbotsford and was buried within the ruins of Dryburgh Abbey.

Although Scott's interests were diverse, his historical novels mostly focused on the Jacobites, whose loyalty to the Stuarts had riven Scotland since the "Glorious Revolution" of 1688. That the nation was prepared to be entertained by such tales was essentially a matter of timing: by the 1760s it was clear the Jacobite cause was lost for good and Scotland, emerging from its isolated medievalism, had been firmly welded into the United Kingdom. Thus its turbulent history and independent spirit was safely in the past, and ripe for romancing – as shown by the arrival of King George IV in Edinburgh during 1822 decked out in Highland dress. Yet for Sir Walter the romance was tinged with a genuine sense of loss. Loyal to the Hanoverians, he still grieved for Bonnie Prince Charlie; he welcomed a commercial Scotland but lamented the passing of feudal ties, and so his heroes are transitional, fighting men of action superseded by bourgeois figures searching for a clear identity.

---

ting is second to none, but the ruins of the **Abbey Church** are much less substantial than, say, at Melrose or Jedburgh. Virtually nothing survives of the nave, but the transepts have fared better, their chapels now serving as private burial grounds for, among others, Sir Walter Scott and Field Marshal Haig, the World War I commander whose ineptitude cost thousands of soldiers' lives. The night stairs, down which the monks stumbled in the early hours of the morning, survive in the south transept, and lead even today to the monks' dormitory. Leaving the church via the east processional door in the south aisle, with its dog-tooth decoration, you enter the cloisters, the highlight of which is the barrel-vaulted **Chapter House**, complete with low stone benches and blind interlaced arcading.

Next door to the abbey is the *Dryburgh Abbey Hotel* (℡01835/822261, Ⓦwww.dryburgh.co.uk; ⑦), a sprawling red-sandstone **hotel** that's a hunting, shooting, fishing kind of place. You can enjoy the indoor pool, or simply have a cup of tea or a drink in the bar. Dryburgh is not easy to get to by **public transport**, though it's only a mile's walk north from St Boswell's on the A68, and a pleasant three or four miles from Melrose. Drivers and cyclists should approach the abbey via the much-visited **Scott's View**, to the north on the B6356, overlooking the Tweed Valley, where the writer and his friends often picnicked and where Scott's horse stopped out of habit during the writer's own funeral procession. The scene inspired Joseph Turner's *Melrose 1831*, now on display in the National Gallery of Scotland (see p.932).

Kelso and around

KELSO, ten miles or so downstream from Melrose, at the confluence of the Tweed and Teviot, grew up in the shadow of its now-ruined Benedictine **abbey** (April–Sept Mon–Sat 9.30am–6pm, Sun 2–6pm; Oct–March Mon–Sat 9.30am–4pm, Sun 2–4pm; free), once the richest and most powerful of the Border abbeys. Unfortunately, the English savaged Kelso three times in the first half of the sixteenth century: the last (and by far the worst) assault was part of the "Rough Wooing" led by the Earl of Hertford when the Scots refused to ratify a marriage treaty between Henry VIII's son and the infant Mary, Queen of Scots. Such was the extent of the devastation – compounded by the Reformation – that less survives of Kelso than any of the Border abbeys. Nevertheless, at first sight, it looks pretty impressive, with the heavy Norman west end of the abbey church almost entirely intact. Beyond, little remains, though it is possible to make out the two transepts and towers which gave the abbey the shape of a double cross, unique in Scotland.

Kelso town managed to rebuild itself and is now centred on the **Square**, an unusually large cobbled expanse presided over by the honey-hued Ionic columns, pediment and oversized clock belltower of the elegant **Town Hall**. To one side stands the imposing *Cross Keys Hotel*, with its distinctive rooftop balustrade, with a supporting chorus of three-storey eighteenth- and nineteenth-century pastel buildings on every side. Leaving the Square along Roxburgh Street, take the alley down to the **Cobby Riverside Walk**, where a brief stroll leads to Floors Castle (see below). En route, but hidden from view by the islet in the middle of the river, is the spot where the Teviot meets the Tweed. This bit of river, known as The Junction, has long been famous for its **salmon fishing**, with permits – costing thousands – booked years in advance. Permits for fishing other, less expensive reaches of the Tweed and Teviot are available from Tweedside Tackle, 36 Bridge St (℡01573/225306).

Practicalities

Kelso **bus station** on Roxburgh Street is a brief walk from The Square, where you'll find the **tourist office** in the Town Hall (July & Aug Mon–Sat 9am–6pm, Sun 10am–5pm; April–June & Sept Mon–Sat 10am–5pm, Sun 10am–1pm; Oct Mon–Sat 10am–4.30pm, Sun 10am–1pm; ℡01573/223464). **Accommodation** is usually not a problem: one of the best B&Bs in town is *Abbey Bank*, near Kelso Pottery on The Knowes (℡01573/226550, Ⓔdiah@abbeybank.freeserve.co.uk; ②), a Georgian house with large double beds and a lovely south-facing garden. Another good choice is the *Ednam House Hotel* (℡01573/224168, Ⓦwww.ednamhouse.com; ⑤), a splendid Georgian mansion set back off Bridge Street, with antique furnishings and fittings and gardens that abut the Tweed; make sure, though, that you're not put in the modern extension. Lastly, there's the *Roxburghe Hotel* (☎01573/450331, Ⓦ www.roxburghe.net; ❼), a luxury hotel two miles south of Kelso on the A698 at Heiton, owned by the Duke and Duchess of Roxburghe, which also boasts an eighteen-hole championship golf course.

Most **eating** places are just off The Square: the *Cobbles Inn* restaurant is housed in a former pub just up Bowmont Street – check the specials menu for the best dishes – and *The Queen's Head*, on Bridge Street, has an extremely adventurous bar meal menu. The moderately expensive *Ednam House Hotel* (see above) restaurant is more upmarket and often features some unusual dishes, while the restaurant at the *Roxburghe Hotel* is even more formal, its top-quality food and service matched by correspondingly high prices.

Floors Castle

If you stand on Kelso's handsome bridge over the Tweed, you can easily make out the pepperpot turrets and castellations of **Floors Castle** (Easter–Oct daily 10am–4.30pm; Ⓦ www.floorscastle.com; £5.50), a vast, pompous mansion a mile or so northwest of the town. The bulk of the building was designed by William Adam in the 1720s, and, picking through the Victorian modifications, the interior still demonstrates his uncluttered style. However, you won't see much of it, as just ten rooms and a basement are open to the public. Highlights include Hendrick Danckert's splendid panorama of Horse Guards Parade in London in the entrance hall; the Brussels tapestries in the ante- and drawing-rooms; paintings by Augustus John and Henri Matisse in the Needle Room; and all sorts of snuff boxes and cigarette cases in the gallery.

Mellerstain House

Six miles northwest of Kelso off the A6089, **Mellerstain House** (Easter & May–Sept daily except Sat 12.30–5pm; Ⓦ www.scot-borders.co.uk/mellerstain; £5) represents the very best of the Adams' brothers' work: William designed the wings in 1725, and his son Robert the castellated centre fifty years later. Robert's love of columns, roundels and friezes culminates in a stunning sequence of plaster-moulded, pastel-shaded ceilings, from the looping symmetry of the library ceiling, adorned by medallion oil paintings *Learning* and *Reading* on either side of *Minerva*, to the whimsical griffin and vase pattern in the drawing room. The art collection, which includes works by Constable, Van Dyck, Gainsborough, Ramsay and Veronese, is also noteworthy. It takes an hour to tour the house; afterwards you can wander the formal Edwardian **gardens**, which slope down to the lake.

Smailholm Tower

In marked contrast to Mellerstain is the craggy **Smailholm Tower** (April–Sept daily 9.30am–6.30pm; HS; £2), perched on a rocky outcrop a few miles to the south. A remote and evocative fastness recalling Reivers' raids and border skirmishes, the fifteenth-century tower was designed to withstand sudden attack. The rough rubble walls average six feet in thickness and both the entrance – once guarded by a heavy door plus an iron yett (gate) – and the windows are disproportionately small. These were necessary precautions: on both sides of the border, clans were engaged in endless feuds, a violent history that stirred the imagination of Sir Walter Scott, who was but a "wee, sick laddie" when he was brought here to live in 1773. Inside, press on up to the roof, where two narrow **wallwalks**, jammed against the barrel-vaulted roof and the crow-stepped gables, provide panoramic views. On the north side the watchman's seat has also survived, stuck against the chimney stack for warmth and with a recess for a lantern.

Jedburgh

Ten miles south of Melrose, **JEDBURGH** nestles in the lush valley of the Jed Water near its confluence with the Teviot, out on the edge of the wild Cheviot Hills. During the interminable Anglo-Scottish Wars, Jedburgh was the quintessential frontier town, a heavily garrisoned royal burgh incorporating a mighty castle and abbey. Though the castle was destroyed by the Scots in 1409 to keep it out of the hands of the English, its memory has been kept alive by stories: in 1285, for example, King Alexander III was celebrating his wedding feast in the great hall when a ghostly apparition predicted his untimely death and a bloody civil war; sure enough, he died in a hunting accident shortly afterwards and chaos ensued. Today, Jedburgh is the first place of any size that you come to on the A68, having crossed over Carter Bar from England, and as such gets quite a bit of passing tourist trade, most of it heading straight for the town's ruined abbey.

Founded in the twelfth century as an Augustinian priory, **Jedburgh Abbey** (April–Sept daily 9.30am–6.30pm; Oct–March Mon–Sat 9.30am–4.30pm, Sun 2–4.30pm; HS; £3.30) is the best-preserved of all the Border abbeys, its vast abbey church towering over a sloping site right in the centre of town, beside the Jed Water. Built in red, yellow and grey sandstone, the abbey church can appear by turns gloomy, calm or richly warm, depending on the weather and the light. The abbey was burned and badly damaged on a number of occasions, but by far the worst destruction was inflicted by the English in the 1540s. Entry is through the bright **visitor centre** at the bottom of the hill, where you can view Jedburgh's most treasured archeological find, the **Jedburgh Comb**, carved around 1100 from walrus ivory and decorated with a griffin and a dragon. All that remains of the conventual buildings where the canons lived are the foundations and basic ground-plan, but then Jedburgh's chief glory is really its **Abbey Church**, which remains splendidly preserved. Entering via the west door, the three-storey nave's perfectly proportioned parade of columns and arches lies before you, a fine example of the transition from Romanesque to Gothic design, with pointed window arches surmounted by the round-headed arches of the triforium, which, in turn, support the lancet windows of the clerestory. Be sure you climb up the narrow staircase in the west front to the balcony overlooking the nave, where you can contemplate how the place must have looked all decked out for the marriage of Alexander III to Yolande de Dreux in 1285.

It's a couple of minutes' walk from the abbey round to the small square **Market Place**, up the hill from which, at the top of Castlegate, stands **Jedburgh Castle Jail** (April–Oct Mon–Sat 10am–4.30pm, Sun 1–4pm; £1.25), an impressive castellated nineteenth-century pile built on the site of

---

Jedburgh festivals

Jedburgh is at its busiest during the town's two main **festivals**. The **Common Riding**, or Callants' Festival, takes place in late June or early July, when the young people of the town – especially the lads – mount up and ride out to check the burgh boundaries, a reminder of more troubled days when Jedburgh was subject to English raids. In similar spirit, early February sees the day-long **Jedburgh Hand Ba'** game, an all-male affair between the "uppies" (those born above Market Place) and "downies" (those born below). In theory the aim of the game is to get hay-stuffed leather balls – originally representing the heads of English men – from one end of town to the other, but there's more at stake than that: macho reputations are made and lost during the two two-hour games.

the old royal castle, with displays on prison life throughout the ages. Back down near the Market Place, signs will guide you to **Mary, Queen of Scots' House** (June–Aug daily 10am–4.30pm; April–Oct Mon–Sat 10am–4.30pm, Sun noon–4pm; March & Nov Mon–Sat 10.30am–3.30pm, Sun 1–4pm; £2). Despite the name, it seems unlikely that Mary ever actually stayed in this particular sixteenth-century house, though she did visit the town during the eventful year of 1566, staying at a place owned by her protector, Sir Thomas Kerr. The attempt to unravel her complex life is cursory, the redeeming features being a copy of Mary's death mask and one of the few surviving portraits of the Earl of Bothwell. One curious feature of all Kerr houses is that the staircases spiral to the left for ease of sword-drawing, giving rise to the Scottish term for left-handedness, "kerry haunded" or "kerry fisted".

Practicalities

Buses pick up and drop off at Canongate near the town centre. Yards away on Murray's Green is the **tourist office** (July & Aug Mon–Fri 9am–8.30pm, Sat 9am–7pm, Sun 10am–7pm; June & Sept Mon–Sat 9.30am–6pm, Sun noon–4pm; April, May & Oct Mon–Sat 10am–5pm, Sun noon–4pm; Nov–March Mon–Fri 10am–4pm; ℡01835/863435). For **accommodation**, try *Meadhon House*, 48 Castlegate (℡01835/862504; ❷), which has a conservatory round the back overlooking a lovely garden. Another great choice is *Hundalee House* (℡01835/863011, Ⓦwww.accommodation-scotland.org; March–Oct; ❷), a seventeenth-century mansion house in open grounds, a mile south of town on the A68. Of the two **campsites** nearby, the *Jedwater Caravan Park* (℡01835/840219; March–Oct) is cheaper and more secluded, in a pleasant riverside site four miles south of town on the A68.

The best place to **eat** is *Simply Scottish*, 6–8 High St (℡01835/864696), a smart but relaxed bistro-style café-restaurant, serving inexpensive Scottish meals, as well as pasta dishes, baked potatoes and the usual snacks.

Selkirk and around

Just south of the River Tweed, some five miles southwest of Melrose, lies the royal burgh of **SELKIRK**. The old town sits high up above Ettrick Water; down in the valley by the riverside, the town's imposing greystone woollen mills are mostly boarded up now, an eerie reminder of a once prosperous era. There's precious little reason to linger in Selkirk itself, though the town sits on the edge of some lovely countryside, and serves as the gateway to the picturesque, sparsely populated valleys of Yarrow Water and Ettrick Water, to the west.

At the centre of Selkirk, at one end of the High Street, you'll find the tiny **Market Square**, overlooked by a statue of Sir Walter Scott, behind which stands the former Town House, now dubbed **Sir Walter Scott's Courtroom** (April–Sept Mon–Sat 10am–4pm; July & Aug also Sun 2–4pm; Oct–March Mon–Sat 1–4pm; free), where he served as sheriff for 33 years. At the other end of the High Street is a rather more unusual statue of **Mungo Park**, the renowned explorer and anti-slavery advocate, born in the county in 1771. Just off Market Square to the south is **Halliwell's House Museum** (April–Oct Mon–Sat 10am–5pm, Sun 2–4pm; July & Aug Sun until 6pm; free), an old-style hardware shop and an informative exhibit on the industrialization of the Tweed Valley. Down by the river at the junction of the A7 with the B7014, **Selkirk Glass** (Mon–Sat 9am–5pm, Sun 11am–5pm; free) is a thriving craft industry that stands in stark contrast to the neighbouring mills. Visitors arrive by the coachload to sit in the café and watch glass-blowers making intricate paperweights and the like.

The **tourist office** (same hours as Halliwell's House; ☎01750/720054) is in Halliwell's House off Market Square, and can help with **accommodation**. First choice for those with an unlimited budget is the upmarket *Philipburn House Hotel* (☎01750/720747, ⓦwww.philipburnhousehotel.co.uk; ⑥), an unusual eighteenth-century house set in its own grounds a mile west of the town centre; the hotel offers expensive, but excellent Scottish cuisine. More modest in price, but still full of character is the *Heatherlie House Hotel* (☎01750/721200, ⓦwww.heatherlie.freeserve.co.uk; ④), a Victorian mansion a sharp left turn up from the road to Ettrick at Heatherlie Park.

Bowhill House

Three miles west of Selkirk off the A708, **Bowhill House** (July daily 1–4.30pm; £4.50) is the property of the Duke of Buccleuch and Queensberry, a seriously wealthy man. Beyond the grandiose mid-nineteenth-century mansion's facade of dark whinstone is an outstanding collection of French antiques and European **paintings**: in the dining room, for example, there are portraits by Reynolds and Gainsborough and a Canaletto cityscape, while the drawing room boasts Boulle furniture, Meissen tableware, paintings by Ruysdael, Leandro Bassano and Claude Lorrain, as well as two more family portraits by Reynolds. Look out also for the Scott Room, which features another splendid portrait of Sir Walter by Henry Raeburn, and the Monmouth Room, commemorating James, Duke of Monmouth, the illegitimate son of Charles II, who married Anne of the Buccleuchs. After several years in exile, Monmouth returned to England when his father died in 1685, hoping to wrest the crown from James II. He was defeated at the Battle of Sedgemoor in Somerset and subsequently sent to the scaffold; among other items, his execution shirt is on display.

The wooded hills of **Bowhill Country Park** adjoining the house (July daily noon–5pm; Easter–June & Aug daily except Fri noon–5pm; £2) are crisscrossed by scenic footpaths and cycle trails: you can rent **mountain bikes** from the visitor centre.

Getting to Bowhill by **public transport** is difficult. The Peebles bus, leaving Selkirk daily at 2pm, will drop you at General's Bridge (takes 10min), from where it's a mile or so's walk through the grounds to the house.

Peebles and around

Fast, wide, tree-lined and fringed with grassy banks, the Tweed looks at its best at **PEEBLES**, a handsome royal burgh that sits on the north bank, about fifteen miles northwest of Selkirk. The town itself has a genteel, relaxed air, its wide, handsome High Street bordered by houses in a medley of architectural styles, mostly dating from Victorian times, and ending in the soaring crown spire of the **Old Parish Church** at the western end. Halfway down the High Street is the **Tweedale Museum & Gallery** (Mon–Fri 10am–noon & 2–5pm, Sat 10am–1pm, Sun 2–4pm; Nov–March closed Sat & Sun; free), housed in the Chambers Institute, named after a local worthy who presented the building to the town in 1859, complete with an art gallery dedicated to the enlightenment of his neighbours. He stuffed the place with casts of the world's most famous sculptures and, although most were lost long ago, today's "Secret Room", once the Museum Room, boasts two handsome friezes: one a copy of the Elgin marbles taken from the Parthenon; the other of the Triumph of Alexander, originally cast in 1812 to honour Napoleon.

Of the various walks through the hills surrounding Peebles, the five-mile **Sware Trail** is one of the easiest and most scenic, weaving west along the north bank of the river and looping back to the south. On the way, it passes **Neidpath Castle** (Easter, Whitsun, July & Aug daily 11am–6pm; £3), a gaunt medieval tower house perched high above the river on a rocky buff. It's a superb setting, and the interior possesses a pit prison and a great hall bedecked with stunning batik wall hangings depicting the life of Mary, Queen of Scots.

Practicalities

Buses stop outside Peebles' post office, a few doors down from the well-stocked **tourist office** on the High Street (July & Aug Mon–Sat 9am–7pm, Sun 10am–6pm; June Mon–Sat 10am–5.30pm, Sun 10am–4pm; Sept Mon–Sat 9.30am–5.30pm, Sun 10am–4pm; April & May Mon–Sat 10am–5pm, Sun 10am–2pm; Oct Mon–Sat 9.30am–5.30pm, Sun 10am–2pm; Nov–March Mon–Sat 9.30am–4.30pm; ☎01721/720138). Peebles boasts a vast number of **B&Bs**; try *Rowanbrae*, a trim, pint-sized Victorian place on a quiet cul-de-sac on Northgate, off the east end of High Street (☎01721/721630, Ⓔjohn@rowanbrae.freeserve.co.uk; ❶); or *Viewfield*, 1 Rosetta Rd (☎01721/721232, Ⓔmmitchell38@yahoo.com; ❶), an attractive detached Victorian house a ten-minute walk west of the bridge, with rooms overlooking a lovely garden. For upmarket **hotels** you have to head out of town: *Castle Venlaw Hotel* (☎01721/720384, Ⓦwww.venlaw.co.uk; ❻) is a Scots Baronial house set in its own grounds on the edge of town up the Edinburgh Road; the *Cringletie House Hotel* (☎01721/730233, Ⓦwww.cringletie.com; ❽) is a still more splendid Baronial pile a couple of miles further up the Edinburgh Road. Of the two **campsites** on the edge of town, the *Rosetta Caravan Park* (☎01721/720770; April–Oct) is the quieter, set in fields surrounded by mature woods, a fifteen-minute walk north of the High Street.

The best place to **eat** is the *Sunflower* (☎01721/722420), a tiny, brightly coloured restaurant at 4 Bridgegate, just off Northgate, which does inexpensive hot sandwiches and a few main dishes for lunch, and more adventurous (and slightly pricier) evening meals, for which it's advisable to book. *Tatlers*, on the High Street, is a normal café, though it does serve good coffee. As for **pubs**, the *Crown Hotel* on the High Street, is a cosy place to hunker down; the *Tontine Hotel*, opposite, is a grander place with the views south over the Tweed. For really good pub food, try one of the bar meals at the *Castle Venlaw Hotel*.

Traquair House

Six miles east of Peebles, a mile or so south of the A72, **Traquair House** (daily: June–Aug 10.30am–5.30pm; April, May, Sept & Oct 12.30–5.30pm; Ⓦwww.traquair.co.uk; £5.30; grounds only £2) is the oldest continuously inhabited house in Scotland, with the present owners – the Maxwell Stuarts – having lived here since 1491. Persistently Catholic, the family paid for its principles: the fifth earl got two years in the Tower of London for his support of Bonnie Prince Charlie, Protestant mill workers repeatedly attacked their property, and by 1800 little remained of the family's once enormous estates – certainly not enough to fund any major rebuilding.

Inside, the house has kept many of its oldest features. You can see original vaulted cellars, where locals once hid their cattle from raiders; the twisting main staircase as well as the earlier medieval version, later a secret escape route for persecuted Catholics; a carefully camouflaged priest's hole; and even a priest's room where a string of resident chaplains lived in hiding until the Catholic Emancipation Act freed things up in 1829. Of the furniture and fittings, the carved oak door at the foot of the stairs is outstanding, as are the Dutch trompe l'oeil carvings in the still room and the bright-yellow four-

△ Dumfries

poster of the king's room, with a bedspread allegedly embroidered by Mary, Queen of Scots. In the museum room there are several fine examples of Jacobite or Amen glass, inscribed with pictures of the Bonnie Prince or verses in his honour; a handful of personal items thought to have been owned by Mary, Queen of Scots; and the cloak worn by the fourth earl during his dramatic escape from the Tower of London.

It's worth sparing time for the surrounding **gardens** where you'll find a hedge maze, several craft workshops and the **Traquair House Brewery** dating back to 1566, which was revived in 1965 and claims to be the only British brewery that still ferments totally in oak. You can learn about the brewery and taste the ales in the Brewery Shop, as well as buy them from the laid-back tearoom and gift shop. There's also a redundant avenue which leads to the locked **Bear Gates**; Bonnie Prince Charlie departed the house through the gates, and the then owner promised to keep them locked until a Stuart should ascend the throne.

If you're really taken by the place, you can stay in one of its two double guest **rooms** (℡01896/830323; ⑧), decked out with antiques and four-posters, on a bed-and-breakfast basis only.

Dumfries and Galloway

The southwest corner of Scotland, now known as **Dumfries and Galloway** (Ⓦwww.dumfriesandgalloway.co.uk), is a region set apart. Some folk heading north from England might pause to explore the Borders region, but few bother to exit the main Carlisle–Glasgow motorway. Yet Dumfries and Galloway have stately homes, deserted hills and ruined abbeys to compete with the best of the Borders. They also have something the Borders don't have, and that's the **Solway coast**, a long, indented coastline of sheltered sandy coves that's been dubbed the "Scottish Riviera" – an exaggeration perhaps, but it's certainly Scotland's warmest, southernmost stretch of coastline.

Dumfries is the obvious gateway to the region, a pleasant enough town that's only really a must for those on the trail of **Robert Burns**, who spent the last part of his life here. Further west, and even more attractive is **Kirkcudbright**, once a bustling port thronged with sailing ships, later an artists' retreat, and now a tranquil, well-preserved little eighteenth- and early nineteenth-century town. Contrasting with the essentially gentle landscape of the Solway coast, is the brooding presence of the **Galloway Hills** to the north, their beautiful moors, mountains, lakes and rivers centred on the 150,000-acre **Galloway Forest Park**, a seriously underused hill-walking and mountain-biking paradise.

Dumfries and around

Situated on the wide banks of the River Nith a short distance inland from the Solway Firth, **DUMFRIES** is by far the largest town in southwest Scotland, with a population of more than thirty thousand. Long known as the "Queen of the South" (as is its football club), the town flourished as a medieval seaport and trading centre, its success attracting the attention of many English armies. The invaders managed to polish off most of the early settlement in 1448, 1536 and again in 1570, but Dumfries survived to prosper with its light industries and port supplying the agricultural hinterland. The town planners of the 1960s badly damaged the town, but enough remains of the warm red sandstone buildings that distinguish Dumfries from other towns in the southwest, to make it worth at least a brief stop. It also acts as a convenient base for exploring the Solway coast, to the east and west, and is second only to Ayr for its associations with Robbie Burns, who spent the last five years of his life here employed as an exciseman.

Dumfries is characterized by its red sandstone buildings, which survive in sufficient quantity to distinguish it from other towns in the southwest. Orientation is easy, with the railway to the east, and the river to the north and west. The pedestrianized **High Street** runs roughly parallel to the Nith; at its northern end, presiding over a floral roundabout, is the **Burns Statue**, a sentimental piece of Victorian frippery in white Carrara marble, featuring the great man holding a posy in one hand while the other clutches at his heart. His faithful hound, Luath, lies curled around his feet – though it doesn't look much like a Scots collie (as Luath was). Further down the High Street, Burns' body lay in state at the town's most singular building, the **Midsteeple**, an appealingly wonky hotchpotch of a building, built in 1707 to fulfil the multiple functions of town prison, clocktower, courthouse and arsenal.

If you're on Burns' trail, make sure you duck down the alleyway to the whitewashed **Globe Inn**, a little further down the High Street, which was Burns' most famous "howff" (pub). Southeast of the High Street, in Burns Street, stands **Burns' House** (April–Sept Mon–Sat 10am–5pm, Sun 2–5pm; Oct–March Tues–Sat 10am–1pm & 2–5pm; free), a simple sandstone building where the poet died of rheumatic heart disease in 1796, a few days before the birth of his last son, Maxwell. Inside, along with the usual collection of Burns memorabilia, one of the bedroom windows bears his signature, scratched with his diamond ring. As a member of the Dumfries Volunteers, Burns was given a military funeral, before being buried nearby in a simple grave by **St Michael's Church** (Mon–Fri 10am–4pm; free), a large red sandstone church, built in 1745. In 1815, Burns was dug up and moved across the graveyard to a purpose-built **Mausoleum**, a bright white Neoclassical eyesore, which houses a slightly ludicrous statue of Burns being accosted by the Poetic Muse.

From the church, head down to the shallow and fast-running Nith, and cross the pedestrian-only **Devorgilla Bridge**, a little further upstream, built in 1431 and one of the oldest bridges in Scotland. Attached to its southwestern end is the town's oldest house, built in 1660, now housing the tiny **Old Bridge House Museum** (April–Sept Mon–Sat 10am–5pm, Sun 2–5pm; free), stuffed full of Victorian domestic bric-a-brac, including a teeth-chattering range of Victorian dental gear. Downstream from the Old Bridge House, an old water mill has been converted into the **Robert Burns Centre**, or RBC (April–Sept Mon–Sat 10am–8pm, Sun 2–5pm; Oct–March Tues–Sat 10am–1pm & 2–5pm; free), with an optional twenty-minute slide show (£1.50) and a simple exhibition on the poet's years in Dumfries upstairs.

On the hill above the RBC stands the **Dumfries Museum** (April–Sept Mon–Sat 10am–5pm, Sun 2–5pm; Oct–March Tues–Sat 10am–1pm & 2–5pm; free), from which there are great views over the town. The museum is housed partly in an eighteenth-century windmill, which was converted into the town's observatory in the 1830s, and features a **camera obscura** on its top floor (April–Sept; £1.50), well worth a visit on a clear day.

Practicalities

Dumfries **train** station is five minutes' walk east of the town centre, while **buses** drop you off at Whitesands beside the River Nith, where you'll also find the **tourist office** (Mon–Sat 10am–5pm; June–Sept also Sun noon–5pm;

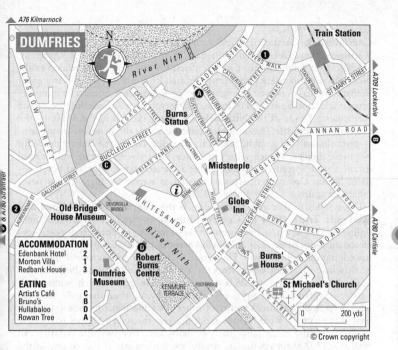

A76 Kilmarnock

DUMFRIES

N

River Nith

Train Station

A709 Lockerbie

ACADEMY STREET

LOVERS WALK

CATHERINE STREET

RAE STREET

NEWALL TERRACE

ST MARY'S STREET

SAVOY ROAD

LOREBURN STREET

QUEENSBERRY STREET

CASTLE STREET

GEORGE STREET

GLASGOW STREET

Burns
Statue

HIGH STREET

ANNAN ROAD

BUCCLEUCH STREET

GALLOWAY STREET

FRIARS VENNEL

IRISH STREET

ENGLISH STREET

Midsteeple

BANK STREET

LEAFIELD ROAD

LAURIEKNOWE ST

Old Bridge
House Museum

DEVORGILLA
BRIDGE

WHITESANDS

River Nith

MILL ROAD

HIGH STREET

Globe
Inn

SHAKESPEARE STREET

QUEEN STREET

A780 Carlisle

18

CHURCH STREET

Robert
Burns
Centre

Dumfries
Museum

NITH STREET

BURNS STREET

Burns'
House

BROOMS ROAD

KENMURE
TERRACE

FOOTBRIDGE

ST MICHAEL STREET

St Michael's Church

0   200 yds

ACCOMMODATION
Edenbank Hotel   2
Morton Villa   1
Redbank House   3

EATING
Artist's Café   C
Bruno's   B
Hullabaloo   D
Rowan Tree   A

© Crown copyright

① & A780 Stranraer

❶
Ⓐ
Ⓑ
Ⓒ
❷
Ⓓ

ℹ️

SOUTHERN SCOTLAND | Dumfries

☎01387/253862). Dumfries abounds in **guest houses** and **B&Bs**. For value and convenience, you can't beat *Morton Villa*, 28 Lovers Walk (☎01387/255825; ❷), a large Victorian house with a pleasant garden near the station. If you're looking for a **hotel**, head for Laurieknowe Street, a five- to ten-minute walk west of Devorgilla Bridge, where you'll find the welcoming, family-run *Edenbank* (☎01387/252759; ❸). *Redbank House* (☎01387/247034, ⓦwww.redbankhouse.co.uk; ❷) is a pristine red-brick mansion set within its own wooded garden at the edge of town on the A710, boasting a sauna, snooker room and gym.

By far the best option for **food** is *Hullabaloo* (☎01387/259679), a stylish restaurant on the top floor of the RBC, with a summer terrace overlooking the river. Another daytime option is the *Artists' Café*, 6 Buccleuch St, which has an eclectic, inexpensive menu featuring wraps, tortillas, toasties and soup. For the evening, there's also the *Rowan Tree Bistro*, 20 Academy St (closed Mon & Tues), which offers a small, but simple selection of inexpensive local fish and meat dishes. *Bruno's* is a family-friendly Italian restaurant on Balmoral Road that's become a Dumfries institution, with the equally popular *Balmoral* chippie round the side which justifiably claims to sell the best chips in the southwest.

Two of Burns' favourite drinking places are still in operation: the *Hole in the Wa'* **pub**, down an alley opposite Woolworth's on High Street, but for somewhere with a bit more atmosphere, make for the smoky, oak-panelled *Globe Inn* on the High Street. The *Robert the Bruce* pub, with its Neoclassical portico at the top of Buccleuch Street, is a typical and very popular church conversion by the J.D. Wetherspoons chain. **Films** are regularly shown at the RBC (☎01387/264808; Tues–Sat). Grierson and Graham, 10 Academy St (☎01387/259483), offer **bike rental**, useful for reaching the nearby Solway coast.

Caerlaverock

Caerlaverock Castle, eight miles southeast of Dumfries (April–Sept daily 9.30am–6.30pm; Oct–March Mon–Sat 9.30am–4.30pm, Sun 2–4.30pm; HS; £2.80), eight miles southeast of Dumfries, is a picture-perfect ruined castle. Not only is it moated, it's built from the rich local red sandstone, is triangular in shape and has preserved its mighty double-towered gatehouse. The most surprising addition, however, lies inside, where you're confronted by the ornate Renaissance facade of the **Nithsdale Lodging**, erected in the 1630s by the first Earl of Nithsdale. The decorated tympana above the windows feature lively mythological and heraldic scenes in what was clearly the latest style. Sadly, Nithsdale didn't get much value for money: just six years later he and his royal garrison were forced to surrender after a thirteen-week siege and bombardment by the Covenanters, who proceeded to wreck the place. It was never inhabited again.

Three miles further east, at Eastpark, is the **Caerlaverock Wildfowl and Wetlands Trust (WWT) Centre** (daily 10am–5pm; Ⓦ www.wwtck.free-online.co.uk; £4, with concessions for those arriving by public transport, bicycle or on foot), more than a thousand acres of protected salt marsh and mud flat edging the Solway Firth. The centre is equipped with screened approaches that link the main observatory to a score of well-situated birdwatchers' hides. It's famous for the 25,000 or so barnacle geese which winter here between September and April. The rest of the year, when the geese are away nesting in Svalbard, there's plenty of other flora and fauna to look out for, as well as the natterjack toad. Throughout the year the wild whooper swans have a daily feeding time and the wardens run free wildlife safaris; call Ⓣ 01387/770200 for up-to-date details. You can **camp** or stay in one of the **rooms** in the centre's converted farmhouse (❸), which has its own observation tower, plus a kitchen and washing machine for guests' use. Both the castle and the centre are reached along the B725; this is the route the bus takes, mostly terminating at the castle but sometimes continuing to the start of the two-mile lane leading off the B725 to the centre.

Ruthwell

From Caerlaverock, it's about seven miles east along the B725 to the village of **RUTHWELL** whose modest country church houses the remarkable eighteen-foot **Ruthwell Cross** (the keys are kept at one of the houses at the foot of the lane; look out for the information notice). An extraordinary early Christian monument from the early or mid-eighth century when Galloway was ruled by the Northumbrians, the cross was considered idolatrous during the Reformation, smashed to pieces and buried. Only in the nineteenth century was the cross finally reassembled and given its own purpose-built semicircular apse. The decoration on the cross reveals a strikingly sophisticated style and iconography, probably derived from the eastern Mediterranean. The main inscriptions are in Latin, but running round the edge is a poem written in the Northumbrian dialect in runic figures. However, it's the biblical carvings on the main face that really catch the eye, notably Mary Magdalene washing the feet of Jesus.

Drumlanrig Castle

Seventeen miles north of Dumfries, **Drumlanrig Castle** (Easter & May–Aug Mon–Fri 11am–4pm, Sat & Sun noon–4pm; Ⓦ www.drumlanrigcastle.org.uk; £6; gardens and country park only £3) is not a castle at all, but the grandiose stately home of the Duke of Buccleuch and Queensberry. Visitors approach via an impressive driveway that sweeps along an avenue of lime trees to the pink sandstone house with its forest of cupolas, turrets and towers. The highlights of the richly furnished interior are really the paintings in the oak-panelled stair-case hall. The most famous trio of works are Rembrandt's *Old Woman Reading*, an extremely sensitive composition dappling the shadow of the subject's hood against her white surplice, Hans Holbein's formal portrait of Sir Nicholas Carew, Master of the Horse to Henry VIII, and the *Madonna with the Yarnwinder* by Leonardo da Vinci. Also be sure to check out the striking 1950s portrait of the present duchess, all débutante coiffure and high-society décolletage, by John Merton in the morning room, and, in the serving room, John Ainslie's *Joseph Florence, Chef*, a sharply observed and dynamic portrait much liked by Walter Scott.

As well as the house, Drumlanrig offers a host of other attractions, including formal **gardens** and a forested **country park** (mid-April to Sept daily 11am–5pm). The old stableyard beside the castle contains a visitor centre, a few shops, the inevitable tearoom, and also a useful **bike rental** outlet, as the park is crisscrossed by footpaths and cycle routes; elsewhere in the grounds, there's an adventure playground. If you're heading here by bus from Dumfries or Ayr, bear in mind it's a one-and-a-half-mile walk from the road to the house.

New Abbey and Sweetheart Abbey

NEW ABBEY is a tidy little one-street village, eight miles south of Dumfries, that originally evolved in order to service its giant neighbour, **Sweetheart Abbey** (April–Sept daily 9.30am–6.30pm; Oct–March Mon–Wed & Sat 9.30am–4.30pm, Thurs 9.30am–12.30pm, Sun 2–4.30pm; HS; £1.50), which now lies romantically ruined to the east. The abbey takes its unusual name from its founder, Devorgilla de Balliol, who carried the embalmed heart of her husband, around with her for the last 22 years of her life – her stone effigy, clutch-ing a heart casket, can be seen in the south transept. The last of the Cistercian abbeys to be founded in Scotland in 1273, Sweetheart is dominated by the red sandstone remains of the abbey church, which remains intact, albeit minus its roof. Standing in the grassy nave, flanked by giant compound piers supporting early Gothic arches, and above them a triforium, it's easy to imagine what the completed church must have looked like. The rest of the conventual buildings are revealed only in the outline of the foundations, with the exception of the precinct wall, to the north and east of the abbey. This massive structure – up to ten feet high and four feet wide in places – is made from rough granite boul-ders, and is the most complete of its kind in the country.

The *Abbey Cottage* **tearoom** is renowned for its good coffee, teas and home-made cakes, and enjoys an unrivalled view over the abbey. At the centre of the village, two **pubs** face one another across a cobbled square: go to the *Abbey Arms* for the best pint, and seats outside, but head for the *Criffel Inn* (☎01387/850244; ❷) if you need a bed for the night.

The Colvend coast and beyond

The **Colvend coast**, twenty miles or so southwest of Dumfries, is probably one of the finest stretches of coastline along the so-called "Scottish Riviera". The best approach is via the A710, which heads south through New Abbey, before cutting across a handsome landscape of rolling farmland to the aptly named Sandyhills, and, beyond, to **ROCKCLIFFE**, a beguiling little place of comfortable villas sheltered beneath wooded hills and nestled around a beau-tiful rocky, sand and shell bay. Excellent B&B **accommodation** is available at

Millbrae House (☎01556/630217; ❷; March–Oct), a whitewashed cottage a short stroll from the bay. For **camping**, the *Castle Point Caravan Site* (☎01556/630248; March–Oct) is in a secluded spot, just south of the village, a stone's throw from the seashore. The *Garden House* tearoom (closed Mon & Tues), at the entrance to the village, can give you simple sustenance and has a garden at the back.

For vehicles, Rockcliffe is a dead end, but it's the start of a pleasant half-hour's walk along the Jubilee Path to neighbouring **KIPPFORD**, a tiny, lively yachting centre strung out along the east bank of the Urr estuary. En route, the path passes the Celtic hill fort of the **Mote of Mark**, a useful craggy viewpoint. At low tide you can walk over the Rough Firth causeway from the shore below across the mud flats to **Rough Island**, a humpy twenty-acre bird sanctuary owned by the National Trust for Scotland – it's out of bounds in May and June when the resident terns and oystercatchers are nesting. The reward for your gentle stroll is a drink and a bite to eat at the ever-popular *Anchor Hotel* (☎01556/620205; ❸), on Kippford's waterfront, which serves excellent **bar meals** – be sure to check the specials board. If you need to stay the night, though, you might find it more peaceful at the *Rosemount* (☎1556/620214; ❷; Feb–Nov), an excellent **guest house** close by on the seafront.

Castle Douglas and around

Most folk come to **CASTLE DOUGLAS** (ⓦwww.castledouglas.net), eighteen miles southwest of Dumfries, simply in order to visit the nearby attractions of Threave Garden and Castle. The man responsible for the town's late eighteenth-century grid-plan streets (and its name) is William Douglas, a local lad who made a fortune trading in the West Indies. Douglas had ambitious plans to turn his town into a prosperous industrial and commercial centre, but, like his scheme to create an extensive Galloway canal system, it didn't quite work. Still, thanks to Douglas, the town now has a distinctive, dead straight main street, **King Street**, that slopes down past the landmark clocktower, built in a mixture of red sandstone and grey granite that's typical of the town.

Threave Garden (daily 9.30am to sunset; NTS; £4.50) is a pleasant mile or so's walk or cycle south of Castle Douglas, along the shores of Loch Carlingwark. The garden features a magnificent spread of flowers and woodland, sixty acres subdivided into more than a dozen areas, from the bright, old-fashioned blooms of the Rose Garden to the brilliant banks of rhododendrons in the Woodland Garden and the ranks of primula, astilbe and gentian in the Peat Garden. In springtime, thousands of visitors turn up for the flowering of more than two hundred types of daffodil and, from late May onwards, the herbaceous beds are the main attraction, with most of them arranged like islets in a sea of lawn (so that they can be viewed from all sides). The exception is the more formal beds of the Walled Garden which adjoin the greenhouses and the nursery.

The nicest way of reaching **Threave Castle** (April–Sept daily 9.30am–6.30pm; HS; £2), a mile or so north of the gardens, is to walk through the estate. However you decide to get there, you should follow the signs to the Open Farm, from where it's a lovely fifteen-minute walk down to the River Dee, where you ring a brass bell for the boat to take you over to the flat and grassy island on which the stern-looking tower house stands. Built for one of the Black Douglases, Archibald the Grim, in around 1370, the fortress was among the first of its kind, a sturdy, rectangular structure completed shortly after the War of Independence when clan feuding spurred a frenzy of castle-building. The rickety curtain wall to the south and east is all that remains of the artillery fortifications, hurriedly constructed in the 1450s in a desperate – and unsuccessful – attempt to defend the castle against James II's new-fangled cannon. The Covenanters wrecked the place in 1640 after a thirteen-week siege, but enough remains of the interior to make it worth exploring.

Practicalities

Castle Douglas **tourist office** (July & Aug Mon–Sat 10am–6pm, Sun 10.30am–5pm; April–June, Sept & Oct Mon–Sat 10am–4.30pm, Sun 11am–4pm; ☎01556/502611) is at the top end of King Street. All the old coaching inns on King Street offer **accommodation**, but you're better off trying one of the well-built Victorian guest houses out on Ernespie Road: try *Albion House* at no. 49 (☎01556/502360; ❶; March–Oct), or head out of town to the *Smithy House* (☎01556/503841, ⓦwww.smithyhouse.co.uk; ❷), a nicely converted smiddy overlooking Loch Carlinwerk, just to the south of Castle Douglas. Campers should make for the *Lochside* **campsite** (☎01556/502949; Easter–Oct), beside Loch Carlingwark, a short walk from the bottom of King Street down Marle Street. **Bike rental** – useful for getting out to Threave – is available from Ace Cycles, 11 Church St (☎01556/504542).

Kirkcudbright and around

KIRKCUDBRIGHT (pronounced "kir-*coo*-bree"), hugging the muddy banks of the River Dee ten miles southwest of Castle Douglas, is the only major town along the Solway coast to have retained a working harbour. In addition, it has a ruined castle and the most attractive of town centres, a charming medley of simple two-storey cottages with medieval pends, Georgian villas and Victorian town houses, all built in a mixture of sandstone, granite and brick, and attractively painted up, with their windows and quoins picked out. It comes as little surprise, then, to find that Kirkcudbright became something of a magnet for Scottish artists from the late nineteenth century onwards. It may no longer live up to the tourist board's "artists' town" label, but it does have a rich artistic heritage that's easy and enjoyable to explore.

The most surprising sight in Kirkcudbright is **MacLellan's Castle** (April–Sept daily 9.30am–12.30pm & 1.30–6pm; HS; £1.80), a pink-flecked sixteenth-century tower house that sits at one end of the High Street by the harbourside. Part fortified keep and part spacious mansion, the castle was built in 1570s for the then-Provost of Kirkcudbright, Sir Thomas MacLellan of Bombie, when a degree of law and order permitted the aristocracy to relax its former defensive preoccupations and satisfy its increasing desire for comfort and domestic convenience. The interior is well preserved from the kitchen (complete with bread oven) to the spyhole known as the "**laird's lug**", behind the fireplace of the Great Hall. Sir Thomas MacLellan is buried in the neighbouring **Greyfriars Kirk** (daily 10am–noon & 2–4pm; key from 7 Castle St), where his tomb is an eccentrically crude attempt at Neoclassicism; it even incorporates parts of someone else's gravestone.

Near the castle, on the L-shaped High Street, is **Broughton House** (daily: Easter, July & Aug 11am–5.30pm; April–June, Sept & Oct 1–5.30pm; Nov garden only Mon–Fri 11am–4pm; NTS; £3.50), a smart Georgian town house, former home of the artist **Edward Hornel** (1863–1933), an important member of the late nineteenth-century Scottish art scene, who spent his childhood a few doors down the street, and returned in 1900 to establish an artists' colony in Kirkcudbright with some of the "Glasgow Boys" (see p.1016). At the back of the house Hornel added a studio and a vast, glass-roofed, mahogany-panelled gallery, now filled with the mannered, vibrantly coloured paintings of girls at play, which he churned out in the latter part of his career. Hornel's trip to Japan in 1893 imbued him with a lifelong affection for the country, and his surprisingly large, densely packed, wonderful, rambling **gardens** have a strong Japanese influence.

Before visiting Broughton House, you should really pay a visit to the imposing, church-like **Tolbooth**, with its stone-built clocktower and spire. Built in the 1620s, the building now houses the **Tolbooth Art Centre** (Mon–Sat 11am–4pm; June–Sept also Sun 2–5pm; £1.50), which has, on the upper floor, a small permanent display of works by some of Kirkcudbright's erstwhile resident artists, including Hornel's striking *Japanese Girl*, and S.J. Peploe's Colourist view of the Tolbooth. The ten-minute video gives you a good, succinct overview of Kirkcudbright's artistic heritage. Don't miss the **Stewartry Museum** on St Mary Street (Mon–Sat 11am–4pm; June–Sept also Sun 2–5pm; £1.50), an extraordinary collection of local exhibits packed into a purpose-built Victorian building on St Mary Street.

Practicalities

Buses to Kirkcudbright stop by the harbour car park, next to the **tourist office** (July & Aug Mon–Sat 9.30am–6pm, Sun 10am–5pm; April–June, Sept & Oct Mon–Sat 10am–5pm, Sun noon–4pm; ☎01557/330494), where you can get help finding **accommodation**. One of the best is *14 High St* (☎01557/330766, ✉14highstreet@kirkcudbright.co.uk; ❸), next door to Broughton House, with a garden overlooking the river, or *Baytree House*, at no. 110 (☎01557/330824; ❹), another Georgian house with comfortable rooms, good cooking, and a beautiful garden with sundeck. Cheaper B&B can be had from 1 Gordon Place (☎01557/330472; ❷), at the castle end of the High Street. The *Silvercraigs* caravan and **campsite** (☎01557/330123; Easter to late Oct) is five or ten minutes' walk from the centre down St Mary's Street and Place, on a bluff overlooking town.

Kirkcudbright is strangely limited when it comes to **restaurants**. Top choice is the *Auld Alliance*, 5 Castle St (☎01557/330569), a superior, if pricey, restaurant offering an imaginative mixture of French and Scottish cuisine. More reasonable is the *Casa Mia*, an Italo-Scottish restaurant within the *Gordon House Hotel*, 116 High St. Otherwise, there's the usual bar food at the Best-Western-run *Selkirk Arms Hotel* on the High Street, which boasts a large garden out the back. A stylish daytime **café**, *Mulberries*, is on St Cuthbert's Street. For a **drink**, the busy *Masonic Arms*, on Castle Street, pulls a reasonable pint.

Gatehouse of Fleet

Like Castle Douglas, **GATEHOUSE OF FLEET**, ten miles west of Kirkcudbright, has a distinctive long, dead straight main street. However, the quiet streets of Gatehouse have none of the life and bustle of Castle Douglas. By contrast, in the late eighteenth and early nineteenth century, the town was a thriving industrial centre with cotton mills, shipbuilding and a brewery. The man who made all this happen (and made himself immeasurably rich in the process) was the local laird James Murray (1727–99). Yorkshire mill owners provided the industrial expertise, imported engineers designed aqueducts to improve the water supply, and dispossessed crofters – and their children – contributed the labour. Between 1760 and 1790, Murray achieved much success, but his custom-built town failed to match its better-placed rivals. By 1850 the boom was over, the town was bypassed by the railway, the mills slipped into disrepair, and nowadays tiny Gatehouse is sustained by tourism and forestry.

It's the country setting that sets Gatehouse apart, rather than any particular sight. As at Castle Douglas, the sloping whitewashed High Street has a landmark clocktower, in this case an incongruous free-standing one, built in grey granite and topped by strange mitre-shaped crenellations. More picturesque is Ann Street, beside the tower, at the end of which you can gain access to the wooded grounds of **Cally House** (now the *Cally Palace Hotel*), and its gardens (Easter–Sept Tues–Fri 2–5pm, Sat & Sun 10am–5.30pm; £1.50). A palatial Neoclassical country mansion, Cally House was built in the 1760s, and is proof positive of the fortune already owned by the Murray family, even before James Murray began his cotton enterprise. Back in town, the **Mill on the Fleet** (March–Oct daily 10.30am–4.30pm; £1.50), opposite the car park by the river at the bottom of the High Street, traces the economic and social history of Gatehouse and Galloway from inside a restored grey granite bobbin mill. Perched on a hill a mile southwest of Gatehouse stands **Cardoness Castle** (April–Sept daily 9.30am–6.30pm; Oct–March Sat 9.30am–4.30pm, Sun 2–4.30pm; HS; £2), a classic late fifteenth-century fortified tower house, which boasts some fashionably decorated fireplaces and plenty of en-suite latrines, plus excellent views out to Fleet Bay in the distance.

Practicalities

The **tourist office** (July & Aug Mon–Sat 10am–5.30pm, Sun 10.30am–4.30pm; May, June & Sept Mon–Sat 10am–5pm, Sun 11am–4pm; March, April & Oct Mon–Sat 10am–4.30pm, Sun noon–4pm; ☎01557/ 814212) is situated by the car park by the river. The place to stay is the sumptuous *Cally Palace* **hotel** (☎01557/814341, Ⓦwww.callypalace.co.uk; ❼; closed Jan), though make sure you're placed in the old house rather than the ugly modern extension. The best **B&B** in Gatehouse itself is the *Bay Horse*, 9 Ann St (☎01557/814073; ❷; March–Oct). The *Masonic Arms*, just up Ann Street, is the most welcoming pub, and serves good **pub food** in the bar or in its conservatory. For the ultimate array of whiskies, head for the *Anwoth Hotel*, at the bottom of the High Street. The *Gatehouse* **tearoom**, inside the original "Gatehouse", the oldest (and once the only) house in town, serves snacks washed down with Sulwath ales from Castle Douglas.

Newton Stewart

NEWTON STEWART, famous for its salmon and trout fishing, is an unassuming market town on the west bank of the River Cree. Originally known as Fordhouse of Cree, it was renamed in the seventeenth century by the local laird, William Stewart. A hundred years later, the estate was bought by William Douglas (of Castle Douglas fame), who preferred Newton Douglas, though neither the name, nor the cotton and carpet industry he established lasted long.

Newton Stewart's most intriguing sight is on the eastern riverbank in what used to be the separate village of Minnigaff, where the **Minnigaff parish church** (mid-June to mid-Sept Mon & Fri 1.30–4pm; free) houses three eleventh-century carved grave-slabs. Otherwise, the town's attractions are pretty much confined to the local **museum** (July & Aug Mon–Fri 10am-12.30pm & 2–5pm, Sat & Sun 2–5pm; Easter–June Mon–Sat 2–5pm; Sept daily 2–5pm; £1), housed in the deconsecrated Church of St Andrew, to the west of the main street. There's also a remarkable collection of over fifty dolls' houses on display at **Sophie's Puppenstube and Dolls' House Museum** (April–Dec

Galloway Forest Park

Newton Stewart is a popular base for hikers and cyclists heading for the nearby **Galloway Forest Park,** Britain's largest forest park, which stretches all the way from the southern part of Ayrshire right down to Gatehouse of Fleet, laid out on land owned by the Forestry Commission. Many hikers aim for the park's **Glen Trool** by following the A714 north for about ten miles to Bargrennan, where a narrow lane twists the five miles over to the glen's Loch Trool. The Forestry Commission *Caldons* **campsite** (☏01671/840218, ⓦwww.forestholidays.co.uk; Easter–Sept) sits in the woods close to the western edge of the loch. From here, there's a choice of mag-nificent **hiking** and **cycling** trails, as well as lesser tracks. Several longer routes curve round the grassy peaks and icy lochs of the Awful Hand and Dungeon ranges, whilst another includes part of the Southern Upland Way, which threads through the Minnigaff Hills to Clatteringshaws Loch.

A twenty-mile stretch of the A712 from Newton Stewart east to New Galloway, known as the **Queen's Way,** cuts through the southern periphery of Galloway Forest Park, a landscape of glassy lochs, wooded hills and bare, rounded peaks. You'll pass all sorts of **hiking trails,** some the gentlest of strolls, others long-distance treks. For a short walk, stop at the **Grey Mare's Tail Bridge,** about seven miles east of Newton Stewart, where the Forestry Commission has laid out various trails, all delving into the pine forests beside the road, crossing gorges, waterfalls and burns. A few miles further on is **Clatteringshaws Loch,** a reservoir surrounded by pine for-est, with a fourteen-mile footpath running right round.

Mon–Sat 10am–5pm; Jan–March Tues–Sat 10am–4pm; £2.75), located at 29 Queen St, on the road heading west from the main square.

On the main square itself, by the bus station, you'll find the local **tourist office** (July & Aug 10am–6pm; May, June & Sept 10am–5pm; April & Oct 10am–4.30pm; ☏01671/402431), which has plenty of helpful literature. The finest **hotel** is the warm and friendly *Creebridge House Hotel* (☏01671/402121, ⓦwww.cree-bridge.co.uk; ❺), in an appealing eighteenth-century granite hunting lodge near the main bridge. A cheaper option is to go for one of the substantial red sandstone Victorian villa **B&Bs**, such as *Rowallan House* (☏01671/402520), on Corsbie Road, west of the main street up Church Lane. There's also an SYHA **hostel** (☏01671/402211, ⓦwww.syha.org.uk; April–Sept) in an old schoolhouse in Minnigaff, up Millcroft Road from the bridge.

Whithorn and around

A one-street town twenty miles south of Newton Stewart, in the low-lying triangular peninsula known as the Machars, **WHITHORN** (ⓦwww .whithorn.com) nevertheless occupies an important place in Scottish history, for it is thought that here in 397 **St Ninian** founded the first Christian church north of Hadrian's Wall. According to the Venerable Bede, Ninian built a church in "a manner to which the Britons were not accustomed", and it became known as *Candida Casa*, "a bright and shining place", translated by the southern Picts he had come to convert as "Hwiterne" (White House) – hence Whithorn. No one can be sure where the *Candida Casa* actually stood, and very little is known about Ninian's life, but his tomb at Whithorn soon became a popular place of pilgrimage and, in the twelfth century, a Premonstratensian priory was established to service the shrine. For generations the rich and the royal made the trek here, the last being Mary, Queen of Scots in 1563, but then came the Reformation and the prohibition of pilgrimages in 1581.

These days, it takes a serious leap of the imagination to envisage Whithorn as a medieval pilgrimage centre. For this reason, it's a good idea to start by watching the audiovisual show at the **Whithorn Dig** (April–Oct daily 10.30am–5pm; £2.70; HS members £1.90) on the main street. Heading outside, the dig site is pretty uninspiring, as are the nearby ruins of the nave of **Whithorn Priory**, though the latter does have a couple of finely carved thirteenth-century south-facing doorways. The most compelling early Christian relics found in the vicinity – a series of standing crosses and headstones – are housed in the onsite **Whithorn Museum**.

The pilgrims who crossed the Solway to visit St Ninian's shrine landed at the **ISLE OF WHITHORN**, four miles south of Whithorn, no longer an island, but an antique and picturesque little seaport. If you continue to the end of the harbour, you'll pick up signs to the minuscule remains of the thirteenth-century **St Ninian's Chapel**, which some believe was the site of the original *Candida Casa*. If you want to **stay**, try the unassuming *Steam Packet Inn* (☎01988/500334; ❸), right on the quay in Isle of Whithorn; it does pub food that's above average in quality and price, and has a moderately expensive **restaurant**.

Stranraer

No one could say that **STRANRAER** was beautiful, and if you're heading to (or coming from) Northern Ireland, there's really no reason to linger longer than you have to. If you find yourself with time to kill, head for the town's one specific attraction, the **Castle of St John** (Easter to mid-Sept Mon–Sat 10am–1pm & 2–5pm; £1.20), a ruined four-storey tower house built around 1500, which stands on the main street, one block inland from the harbour front. If you've yet more time on your hands, pop into the **Stranraer Museum** in the Old Town Hall a short distance west along George Street (Mon–Fri 10am–5pm, Sat 10am–1pm & 2–5pm; free) for a brief foray into local history.

The **train station** is right by the Stena Line **ferry** terminal (☎0870/570 7070, ⓦwww.stenaline.co.uk) on the East Pier, from where boats depart for Belfast. A couple of minutes' walk away, on Port Rodie, is the **bus station**. Stena Line's fast HSS **catamarans** depart for Belfast from the West Pier on the other side of the harbour. P&O Irish Sea ferries (☎0870/242 4777, ⓦwww.poirishsea.com) to and from Larne arrive at the port of **CAIRN-RYAN**, some five miles north; note, though, that bus services to Cairnryan are infrequent and aren't integrated with the ferry times.

Stranraer's **tourist office** is at 28 Harbour St (April–Oct 9.30am–5.30pm, Sun 10am–4.30pm; Nov–March Mon–Sat 10am–4pm; ☎01776/702595) between the two piers. Should you need **accommodation**, head for the *Harbour Guest House* (☎01776/704626, ⓦwww.harbourguesthouse.com; ❷), a decent **B&B** on the seafront on Market Street, just a short stroll from either pier, or the vast, whitewashed crenellated *North West Castle* (☎01776/704413, ⓦwww.mcmillanhotels.com; ❺), next to the police station on Port Rodie. For **campers**, *Aird Donald Caravan Park* (☎01776/702025, ⓦcome-to/airddonald.co.uk) is ten minutes' walk east of the town centre along London Road, though there are much nicer sites elsewhere.

Portpatrick to the Mull of Galloway

Situated roughly halfway along the west shore of the Rhinns of Galloway, the hilly, hammer-shaped peninsula at the end of the Solway coast, **PORT-PATRICK** has an attractive pastel-painted seafront that wraps itself round a small rocky bay, sheltered by equally rocky cliffs. Until the mid-nineteenth century, when sailing ships were replaced by steamboats, Portpatrick was a thriving seaport, serving as the main embarkation point for Northern Ireland, with coal, cotton and British troops heading in one direction, Ulster cattle and linen in the other.

Portpatrick has several good **hotels** and **guest houses**, the best of which is the lilac-painted *Waterfront Hotel* (☎01776/810800, ⓦwww.waterfronthotel.co.uk; ❹), which has gone for the contemporary look inside. Cheaper choices include the neighbouring *Knowe Guest House* (☎01776/810441; ❶), a bright, white B&B which runs a tearoom in its conservatory, and the equally comfortable Victorian *Carlton Guest House*, also on the harbour at 21 South Crescent (☎01776/810253; ❶). It's impossible to miss the *Portpatrick Hotel* (☎01942/824824, ⓦwww.shearingsholidays.com; ❺; Feb–Nov), a grand turreted Edwardian mansion on the hill above the harbour; inside, it's a bit tatty round the edges, but it goes down well with the tour groups, for whom there's live music more or less every night.

There are several caravan and **campsites** in a row on the hill overlooking Portpatrick and Dunskey Castle, quite a distance from town (and the sea), but accessed by a pleasant walk along the disused railway and cliff-top trail; *Sunnymeade* (☎01776/810293) has the better facilities, but *Castle Bay* (☎01776/810462) has the more informal atmosphere. The best place for a **meal** and a **drink** is the *Crown* pub on the seafront. For something more formal and slightly pricier, head to the *Waterfront Bistro* next door.

It's twenty miles south from Portpatrick to the **Mull of Galloway** (ⓦwww.mull-of-galloway.co.uk), a bleak and precipitous headland, where wheeling guillemots, razorbills and kittiwakes and whistling winds circle a bright whitewashed lighthouse. This is the southernmost point in Scotland and on clear days you can see over to Cumbria, Ireland and the Isle of Man. The headland is also an RSPB reserve and there's a new **visitor centre** (Easter to mid-Oct daily 10am–5pm) in a building near the lighthouse.

Ayrshire

The rolling hills and rich soil of **Ayrshire** (ⓦwww.ayrshire-arran.com) make for prime farming country, and as such, are not really top of most visitors' Scottish itinerary. **Ayr**, the county town and birthplace of Robert Burns, is handsome enough, but won't keep you long. Most folk wisely stick to the coastline, attracted by the wide, flat sandy **beaches** and the region's vast number of **golf** courses. South of Ayr, the most obvious points of interest are **Culzean Castle**, with its Robert Adam interior and extensive wooded grounds, and the off-shore islands of **Ailsa Craig**, home to the world's second largest gannetry. North of Ayr, where the towns benefited from the industrialization of Glasgow, there are even fewer places to detain you, with the exception of **Irvine**, home to the ever-expanding Scottish Maritime Museum.

Ayr and around

With a population of around fifty thousand, **AYR** is by far the largest town on the Firth of Clyde coast. It was an important seaport and trading centre for many centuries, and rivalled Glasgow in size and significance right up until the late seventeenth century. Nowadays, the town won't detain you long, though its presti-

Robert Burns

The first of seven children, **Robert Burns**, the national poet of Scotland, was born in Alloway on January 25, 1759. His father, William, was employed as a gardener until 1766 when he became a tenant farmer at Mount Oliphant, near Alloway, moving to Lochlie farm, Tarbolton, eleven years later. A series of bad harvests and the demands of the landlord's estate manager bankrupted the family, and William died almost penniless in 1784. These events had a profound effect on Robert, leaving him with an antipathy towards political authority and a hatred of the land-owning classes.

With the death of his father, Robert became head of the family and they moved again, this time to a farm at Mossgiel, near Mauchline. Burns had already begun writing **poetry** and **prose** at Lochlie, recording incidental thoughts in his *First Commonplace Book*, but it was here at Mossgiel that he began to write in earnest, and his first volume, *Poems Chiefly in the Scottish Dialect*, was published in Kilmarnock in 1786. The book proved immensely popular, celebrated by ordinary Scots and Edinburgh literati alike, with the satirical trilogy *Holy Willie's Prayer*, *The Holy Fair* and *Address to the Devil* attracting particular attention. The object of Burns' poetic scorn was the kirk, whose ministers had obliged him to appear in church to be publicly condemned for fornication – a commonplace punishment in those days.

Burns spent the winter of 1786–87 in the capital, lionized by the literary establishment. Despite his success, however, he felt trapped, unable to make enough money from writing to leave farming. He was also in a political snare, fraternizing with the elite, but with radical views and pseudo-Jacobite nationalism that constantly landed him in trouble. His frequent recourse was to play the part of the unlettered ploughman-poet, the noble savage who might be excused his impetuous outbursts and hectic womanizing.

He had, however, made useful contacts in Edinburgh and as a consequence was recruited to collect, write and rearrange two volumes of songs set to traditional Scottish tunes. These volumes, James Johnson's *Scots Musical Museum* and George Thomson's *Select Scottish Airs*, contain the bulk of his **songwriting**, and it's on them that Burns' international reputation rests, with works like *Auld Lang Syne*, *Scots*, *Wha Hae*, *Coming Through the Rye* and *Green Grow the Rushes, O*. At this time, too, though poetry now took second place, he produced two excellent poems: *Tam o' Shanter* and a republican tract, *A Man's a Man for a' That*.

Burns often boasted of his sexual conquests, and he fathered several illegitimate children, but in 1788, he eventually married **Jean Armour**, a stonemason's daughter from Mauchline, with whom he already had two children, and moved to Ellisland Farm, near Dumfries (see p.977). The following year, he was appointed excise officer and could at last leave farming, moving to Dumfries in 1791. Burns' years of comfort were short-lived, however. His years of labour on the farm, allied to a rheumatic fever, damaged his heart, and he died in Dumfries on July 21, 1796, aged 37. Burns' work, inspired by a romantic nationalism and tinged with a wry wit, has made him a potent symbol of "Scottishness". Ignoring the anglophile preferences of the Edinburgh elite, he wrote in Scots vernacular about the country he loved, an exuberant celebration that filled a need in a nation culturally colonized by England. Today, Burns Clubs all over the world mark every anniversary of the poet's birthday with the Burns' Supper, complete with Scottish totems – haggis, piper and whisky bottle – and a ritual recital of Burns' *Ode to a Haggis*.

gious racecourse, venue for the Scottish Grand National, pulls in huge crowds, and the local tourist industry continues to do steady business out of the fact that Robbie Burns was born in the neighbouring village of **Alloway** (see p.991).

Ayr's busy town centre, wedged between Sandgate and the south bank of the treacly River Ayr, was rebuilt by the Victorians, and is now busy most days with shoppers from all over the county. The most conspicuous landmark is the big, grey, rather ugly castellated **Wallace Tower**, erected in 1828 at the southern end of the High Street. It stands on what is thought to have been the site of the Edward I's barracks, which was set alight by Wallace in 1297. At the junction of the High Street and Sandgate stands the rather more impressive Neoclassical **Town Buildings**, completed in 1832, whose spectacular 226ft spire is guarded by griffins, eagles and a Triton.

Ayr's medieval **Auld Brig**, just east off the High Street, survived the threat of demolition in the early twentieth century, thanks largely to its featuring in a Burns' poem, and is now one of the oldest stone bridges in Scotland, having been built during the reign of James IV (1488–1513). A short stroll upstream from the bridge stands the much restored **Auld Kirk**, the church funded by Cromwell as recompense for the one he incorporated into the town's fortress. The church's dark and gloomy interior retains the original pulpit (call ☎01292/262580 for access).

All you can see of Cromwell's zigzag **Citadel**, built to the west of the town centre in 1650s, is a small section of the old walls – the area is still known locally as "the Fort". To the south of the citadel are the wide, gridiron streets of Ayr's main Georgian and Regency residential development. **Wellington Square** is the area's showpiece, its trim gardens and terraces overlooked by the **County Buildings**, a vast, imposing Palladian pile from 1820. The opening of the Glasgow-to-Ayr train line in 1840 brought the first major influx of holiday-makers to the town, but today, only a few hardy visitors and local dog-walkers take a stroll along Ayr's bleak, long **Esplanade** and beach, which look out to the Isle of Arran.

Practicalities

Ayr is the nearest large town to **Glasgow Prestwick airport** (Ⓦwww.gpia.co.uk), which lies three miles north and has regular transport to Ayr and Glasgow. Ayr **train** station is ten minutes' walk southeast of the town centre; the **bus** station is in the centre at the foot of Sandgate; nearby is the **tourist office**, at 22 Sandgate (July & Aug Mon–Sat 9am–6pm, Sun 10am–5pm; Oct–June Mon–Sat 9am–5pm; ☎01292/290300), which can help with **accommodation**. Of the numerous choices on Queen's Terrace, head for *Craggallan* (☎01292/264998, Ⓦwww.craggallan.com; ➋), a friendly little guest house with a dining table that converts into a billiards table, or opt for the *Horizon Hotel* (☎01292/264384, Ⓦwww.horizonhotel.com; ➍), a purpose-built modern hotel nearby on the seafront. The best-value luxury option is the *Savoy Park Hotel* (☎01292/266112, Ⓦwww.savoypark.com; ➎), a splendid red sandstone Scots Baronial building on 16 Racecourse Rd. Ayr's SYHA **hostel** (☎01292/262322, Ⓦwww.syha.org.uk; March–Oct) also occupies a Scots Baronial mansion, at 5 Craigweil Rd off Racecourse Road. Campers should head for the *Heads of Ayr* caravan and **campsite** (☎01292/442269; March–Nov), three miles south of town along the A719.

Arguably the town's best **restaurant** is *Fouters*, 2a Academy St, a cellar bistro off Sandgate (☎01292/261391, Ⓦwww.fouters.co.uk; closed Sun & Mon). For filling and inexpensive Scottish staples, try the *Stables* coffee house, tucked away in the Queen's Court Centre, on the corner of Sandgate and Newmarket Street. The *Rupee Room*, a popular, eye-catching Indian restaurant, on the eastern side of Wellington Square; the same family also run the snackier and even more designer *Pakora Bar*, 56–58 Sandgate. A mixed crowd packs out the *West Kirk*, a **pub** in a converted church on Sandgate, but the most historic pub in town is the thatched *Tam o' Shanter*, on the High Street, whose ancient walls sport quotes from Robert Burns.

Alloway

ALLOWAY, formerly a small village but now on the outskirts of Ayr, is the birthplace of Robert Burns (1759–96), Scotland's national poet. The first port of call is the **Burns Cottage and Museum** (April–Oct daily 9am–6pm; Nov–March Mon–Sat 10am–4pm, Sun noon–4pm; £2.80), the poet's birthplace, a low, whitewashed, thatched cottage where animals and people lived under the same roof. Much altered over the years, you can nevertheless gain an impression of what the place must have been like when Burns, the first of seven children, was born in the box bed in the only room in the house.

Ten minutes' walk down the road from the cottage are the plain, roofless ruins of **Alloway Kirk**, where Robert's father William is buried, and where Burns set much of *Tam o' Shanter*. Down the road from the church, the **Brig o' Doon**, the picturesque thirteenth-century hump-backed bridge over which Tam is forced to flee for his life, still stands, curving gracefully over the river. High above the river and bridge, towers the **Burns Monument** (May–Sept Mon–Sat 9am–5pm; same ticket as Cottage), a striking Neoclassical temple in a small carefully manicured garden and housing yet another museum. For the populist approach to Burns, head for the **Tam o' Shanter Experience** (daily: April–Sept 9am–6pm; Oct–March 9am–5pm; £2.80 for each video), on the opposite side of the road from Alloway Kirk, housed in a modern, faceless building that belies a marginally more interesting interior.

True Burns junkies might want to eat, drink and stay at the *Brig o' Doon* **hotel** on the banks of the River Doon (☎01292/442466; ❸), reputed to be another of Burns' drinking haunts. To reach Alloway from Ayr town centre, take the A1 bus (Mon–Sat every 15min, Sun hourly; journey time 10min) from Burns Statue Square near the train station.

Culzean Castle

Sitting on the edge of a sheer cliff, looking out over the Firth of Clyde to Arran, **Culzean Castle** (daily: April–Oct 11am–5pm; Nov–April park only 9am to dusk; NTS; ⓦwww.culzeancastle.net; £8; park only £4), ten miles south of Ayr, couldn't want for a more impressive situation. The current castle is actually a grand, late eighteenth-century stately home, designed by highly successful Scottish Neoclassical architect, **Robert Adam**, for the tenth Earl of Cassillis (pronounced "cassles"). Since passing into the hands of the National Trust for Scotland in 1945, Culzean, and in particular its surrounding 560-acre **country park**, has become one of Ayrshire's premier tourist attractions.

Ailsa Craig

If the weather's half decent, it's impossible to miss the views of the island of **Ailsa Craig**, which lies ten miles off the Ayrshire coast in the middle of the Firth of Clyde. The island's name means "Fairy Rock" in Gaelic, though the island looks more like an enormous muffin than a place of enchantment. It would certainly have been less-than-enchanting for the persecuted Catholics who escaped to the island during the Reformation. With its jagged cliffs and 1114ft summit, Ailsa Craig is now a privately owned **bird sanctuary** that's home to thousands of gannets. The best time to make the trip is at the end of May and in June when the fledglings are trying to fly – boats leave from the port of Girvan, accessible by bus and train from Ayr. Several companies **cruise** round the island, but only Mark McCrindle is licensed to land (May to late Sept 1–2 daily; exact timings and prices depend on the length of trip and the tides; ☎01465/713219). It takes about an hour to reach the island, so you've enough time to walk up to the summit of the rock and watch the birds, weather permitting.

The best place to start is at the **visitor centre** in the modernized Home Farm buildings. Here, you can watch an audiovisual show on the house, and pick up **free maps** – as well as wildlife leaflets – that help you get your bearings, the layout of the place being rather confusing; consult staff about taking a guided walk in the grounds. You can **stay** at Culzean (℡01655/884455; April–Oct; ❾), on the top floor, where six double bedrooms have been done out in a comfortably genteel style. Another option is the nearby *Culzean Castle* **campsite** (℡01655/760627; April–Oct), located in the woods by the castle entrance, though not in fact run by the National Trust.

Irvine

IRVINE, twelve miles north of Ayr, was once the principal port for trade between Glasgow and Ireland, and later for coal from Kilmarnock, its halcyon days recalled by the enjoyable **Scottish Maritime Museum** (April–Oct daily 10am–5pm; £2.50), which is spread across several locations down at the town's beautifully restored old harbour. The best place to start is in the late nineteenth-century **Linthouse Engine Shop**, on Harbour Road, a hangar-like building housing everything from old sailing dinghies and canoes to a giant ship's turbines, and a kids' corner for learning Morse code and semaphore. Free guided tours set off regularly for the nearby **Shipbuilder's Flat**, which has been restored to something like its appearance in 1910, when a family of six to eight would have occupied its two rooms and scullery. You're also shown round the rusting hulk of the SV *Carrick*, the world's oldest colonial clipper, currently in a parlous state. Moored at the **pontoons** on Harbour Street is an assortment of craft, which you can board, including a tug, a trawler, a "puffer" boat and the SY *Carola*, the oldest seagoing steam yacht in the country.

Close by, opposite **Magnum** (ⓦwww.themagnum.co.uk), Scotland's largest leisure and swimming complex, a funky retracting footbridge leads visitors to Irvine's newest attraction, the **Big Idea** (daily 10am–6pm; ⓦwww .bigidea.org.uk; £7.95), a half-submerged glass eye of a building with a turf roof. The theme of the place is invention, and it has endless high-tech hands-on exhibits where children can play with robots, check out a toilet flush system, and get to grips with the scientific principles of cams, rods, levers, gears and valves. There's also a "pink-knuckle" ride called **The History of Explosions**, which is little more than a promotional film for the munitions industry, watched from jolting seats. More informative is the nearby static exhibition telling the story of Nobel's Explosives Company (later to become ICI), which once ran the world's largest explosives factory on the Ardeer peninsula behind the museum.

Arriving at Irvine's adjacent **train** or **bus stations**, you'll find yourself exactly halfway between the harbour, to the west, and the Riverfront shopping complex and old town, to the east. The **tourist office** (July & Aug Mon–Sat 10am–4pm; Easter–June, Sept & Oct Tues–Sat 10am–4pm; ℡01294/313886) is situated near the stations beside the shopping mall's giant car park. Kilwinning Road, heading north out of Irvine, has several inexpensive **B&Bs**; should you wish to pamper yourself a bit more, head for *Annfield House*, 6 Castle St (℡01294/278903; ❻), a big Victorian mansion overlooking the river at the end of Sandgate, that has spacious bedrooms and its own bar and **restaurant**.

Travel details

Trains

Ayr to: Dumfries (Mon–Sat 2 daily; 1hr 30min); Girvan (Mon–Sat 12 daily, 2 on Sun; 25min); Glasgow Central (Mon–Sat every 30min, Sun hourly; 55min); Irvine (Mon–Sat every 30min, Sun hourly; 20min); Prestwick Airport (every 30min; 8min); Stranraer (Mon–Sat 6–7 daily, 2 on Sun; 1hr 20min).

Dumfries to: Carlisle (Mon–Sat 13–15 daily, 4 on Sun; 40min); Glasgow Central (Mon–Sat 8 daily, 2 on Sun; 1hr 50min); Stranraer (Mon–Sat 2 daily; 3hr).

Glasgow Central to: Ardrossan Harbour (4–5 daily; 55min); Ayr (Mon–Sat every 30min, Sun hourly; 55min); Dumfries (Mon–Sat 8 daily, 2 on Sun; 1hr 50min); Kilmarnock (hourly; 40min); Prestwick Airport (Mon–Sat every 30min, Sun hourly; 45min); Stranraer (3–5 daily; 2hr).

Stranraer to: Ayr (Mon–Sat 6–7 daily, 2 on Sun; 1hr 20min); Dumfries (Mon–Sat 2 daily; 3hr); Girvan (Mon–Sat 6–7 daily, 3 on Sun; 50min); Glasgow Central (3–5 daily; 2hr).

Buses

Ayr to: Culzean Castle (Mon–Sat hourly, Sun every 2hr; 30min); Dumfries (Mon–Sat every 2hr; 2hr 10min); Girvan (Mon–Sat hourly, Sun every 2hr; 1hr 10min); Glasgow (hourly; 55min); New Galloway (Mon–Sat 2 daily; 1hr 20min).

Castle Douglas to: Dumfries (Mon–Sat hourly, 11 on Sun; 30–45min); Kirkcudbright (Mon–Sat hourly, 6 on Sun; 20min); New Galloway (Mon–Sat 6 daily, 1 on Sun; 30min).

Dumfries to: Ayr (Mon–Sat every 2hr; 2hr 10min); Caerlaverock (Mon–Sat every 2hr, 2 on Sun; 30min); Carlisle (Mon–Sat hourly, Sun every 2hr; 1hr 25min); Castle Douglas (Mon–Sat hourly, 11 on Sun; 30–45min); Gatehouse of Fleet (Mon–Sat 9 daily, 5 on Sun; 1hr–1hr 25min); Kirkcudbright (Mon–Sat hourly, 6 on Sun; 1hr 10min); Moffat (Mon–Sat 8 daily, 4 on Sun; 45min); New Galloway (Mon–Sat 1–2 daily; 55min); Newton Stewart (Mon–Sat 5 daily, 3 on Sun; 1hr 20min); Rockcliffe (5 daily; 1hr); Stranraer (Mon–Sat 5 daily, 3 on Sun; 2hr).

Edinburgh to: Dumfries (Mon–Sat 4 daily, 2 on Sun; 2hr 40min); Jedburgh (2–3 daily; 2hr); Kelso (Mon–Fri 5 daily, Sat & Sun 2–3 daily; 2hr); Melrose (Mon–Sat hourly, 6 on Sun; 2hr 15min); Peebles (Mon–Sat hourly, 9 on Sun; 1hr 10min); Selkirk (Mon–Sat hourly, Sun every 2hr; 1hr 40min).

Gatehouse of Fleet to: Kirkcudbright (Mon–Sat 5–6 daily, 2 on Sun; 20min); Newton Stewart (Mon–Sat 6 daily, 3 on Sun; 25min); Stranraer (Mon–Sat 6 daily, 3 on Sun; 1hr 10min).

Jedburgh to: Kelso (Mon–Sat 14–15 daily, 4 on Sun; 25min); Melrose (Mon–Sat 1–2 hourly, 7 on Sun; 30min).

Kelso to: Melrose (Mon–Sat 8–12 daily, 4 on Sun; 30min).

Melrose to: Jedburgh (Mon–Sat 1–2 hourly, 7 on Sun; 30min); Kelso (Mon–Sat 8–12 daily, 4 on Sun; 30min); Peebles (Mon–Sat hourly, 6 on Sun; 1hr 10min); Selkirk (Mon–Sat hourly, 2 on Sun; 20min).

Newcastleton to: Carlisle (Mon–Sat 2–5 daily; 50min).

Newton Stewart to: Glentrool (Mon–Sat 7 daily, 3 on Sun; 20min); Stranraer (Mon–Sat 5 daily, 3 on Sun; 45min); Whithorn (Mon–Sat hourly, 4 on Sun; 50min); Isle of Whithorn (Mon–Sat hourly, 4 on Sun; 1hr).

Stranraer to: Portpatrick (Mon–Sat 8–10 daily, 3 on Sun; 25min).

Ferries (summer timetable)

Ardrossan to: Brodick, Isle of Arran (4–6 daily; 55min).

Cairnryan to: Larne (8 daily; 1hr–1hr 45min).

Stranraer to: Belfast (8–10 daily; 1hr 45min–3hr 15min).

Troon to: Belfast (3 daily; 2hr 30min).

Glasgow
and the Clyde

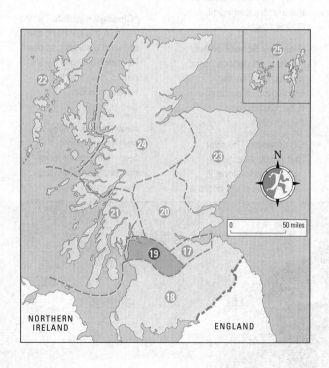

CHAPTER 19   # Highlights

✴ **Gallery of Modern Art** –
Idiosyncratic but populist
collection of contempo-
rary artworks, bang in
the heart of the city.
See p.1007

✴ **Necropolis** – Elegantly
crumbling graveyard on
a city-centre hill, behind
the ancient cathedral.
See p.1012

✴ **Glasgow School of Art**
– Take a student-led tour
of Charles Rennie
Mackintosh's architec-
tural masterpiece.
See p.1013

✴ **Clydeside** – The river
that made Glasgow:
walk or cycle along it,
take a boat on it, cross a
bridge over it, or view it
from the top of the
Glasgow Tower.
See p.1018

✴ **Burrell Collection** – An
inspired and eclectic art
collection displayed in a
purpose-built museum in
Pollok Park. See p.1022

✴ **"Glaesga nightlife"** –
Sample the glitz and the
grit with cocktails at the
Rogano followed by a
pint of heavy at the
Horseshoe Bar.
See p.1026

✴ **New Lanark** – Stay for
next-to-nothing at this
fascinating nineteenth-
century planned village.
See p.1036

19

Glasgow
and the Clyde

R ejuvenated, upbeat **Glasgow**, Scotland's largest city, has not traditionally enjoyed the best of reputations. Once an industrial giant set on the
banks of the mighty River Clyde, it can still initially seem a grey and
depressing place, with the M8 motorway screeching through the centre and dilapidated housing estates on its outskirts. However, Glasgow's image
of itself has changed irrevocably and few visitors will be left in any doubt that
the city is, in its own idiosyncratic way, a cultured and dynamic place well
worth getting to know.

The city has much to offer: here are some of the best-financed and most
imaginative museums and galleries in Britain – among them the showcase
Burrell Collection of art and antiquities – and nearly all of them are free.
Glasgow's **architecture** is some of the most striking in the UK, from the
restored eighteenth-century warehouses of the **Merchant City** to the hulking
Victorian prosperity of George Square. Most distinctive of all is the work of
local luminary Charles Rennie Mackintosh, whose elegantly streamlined Art
Nouveau designs appear all over the city, reaching their apotheosis in the stunning **School of Art**. Recent development of the old shipyards of the Clyde,
notably in the space-age shapes of the new **Glasgow Science Centre**, hint at
yet another string to the city's bow: combining design with innovation. The
city boasts thriving live-music venues, distinctive places to eat and drink, busy
theatres, concert halls and an opera house. Above all, the feature that best
defines the individualism and peculiar attraction of the city is its **people**,
whether rough-edged comedians on the football terraces or bright young
things dressed to the nines in the trendiest of style bars.

Despite all the upbeat hype, Glasgow's gentrification has passed by deprived
inner-city areas such as the **East End**, home of the **Barras market** and some
staunchly change-resistant pubs. This area has historically been the breeding
ground for the city's much-lauded **socialism**, celebrated in the wonderful
People's Palace social history museum. Indeed, even in the more stylish quarters of Glasgow there's a gritty edge that's never far away, reinforcing a peculiar mix of grime and glitz which the city seems to have patented.

Quite apart from its own attractions, Glasgow makes an excellent base from
which to explore the **Clyde Valley and coast**, made easily accessible by a reliable train service. Chief among the draws is the remarkable eighteenth-centu-

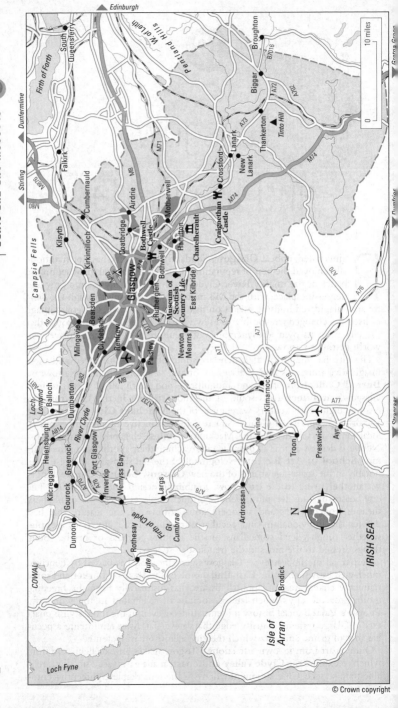

ry **New Lanark** mills and workers' village, a World Heritage Site, while other day trips might take you to the new **National Museum of Scottish Country Life** near East Kilbride or on a boat heading "doon the watter" past the old shipbuilding centres on the Clyde estuary.

Glasgow

GLASGOW's earliest history, like so much else in this surprisingly romantic city, is obscured in a swirl of myth. The city's name is said to derive from the Celtic *Glas-cu*, which loosely translates as "the dear, green place" – a tag that the tourist board are keen to exploit as an antidote to the sooty images of popular imagination. It is generally agreed that the first settlers arrived in the sixth century to join Christian missionary **Kentigern** – later to become St Mungo – in his newly founded monastery on the banks of the tiny Molendinar Burn.

William the Lionheart gave the town an official charter in 1175, after which it continued to grow in importance, peaking in the mid-fifteenth century when the **university** was founded on Kentigern's site – the second in Scotland after St Andrews. This led to the establishment of an archbishopric, and hence city status, in 1492, and, due to its situation on a large, navigable river, Glasgow soon expanded into a major industrial **port**. The first cargo of tobacco from Virginia offloaded in Glasgow in 1674, and led to a boom in trade with the colonies until American independence. Following the **Industrial Revolution** and James Watt's innovations in steam power, coal from the abundant seams of Lanarkshire fuelled the ironworks all around the Clyde, worked by the cheap hands of the Highlanders and, later, those fleeing the Irish potato famine of the 1840s.

The **Victorian** age transformed Glasgow beyond recognition. The population boomed from 77,000 in 1801 to nearly 800,000 at the end of the century, and new tenement blocks swept into the suburbs in an attempt to cope with the choking influxes of people. At this time Glasgow became known as the "Second City of the Empire" – a curious epithet for a place that today rarely acknowledges second place in anything.

By the turn of the twentieth century, Glasgow's industries had been honed into one massive **shipbuilding** culture. Everything from tugboats to transatlantic liners were fashioned out of sheet metal in the yards that straddled the Clyde. In the harsh economic climate of the 1930s, however, unemployment spiralled, and Glasgow could do little to counter its popular image as a city dominated by inebriate violence and – having absorbed vast numbers of Irish emigrants – sectarian tensions.

Shipbuilding, and many associated industries, died away almost completely in the 1960s and 1970s, leaving the city depressed, jobless and directionless. Then, in the 1980s, the self-promotion campaign began, snowballing towards the 1988 Garden Festival and year-long party as European City of Culture in 1990. More recently, Glasgow was **UK City of Architecture and Design** in 1999, an event which strove valiantly to showcase the city's rich architectural heritage.

Arrival, orientation and information

Glasgow International airport (☎0141/887 1111, ◉www.glasgow-airport .com) is at Abbotsinch, eight miles southwest of the city – not to be confused with Glasgow Prestwick airport, which is thirty miles south near Ayr. From the international airport, the Glasgow Airport Link bus (£3.30; information ☎0870/608 2608) runs from bus stops 1 or 2 into the central Buchanan Street bus station every fifteen minutes during the day. White airport taxis charge around £15.

From **Glasgow Prestwick** airport (☎01292/511000, ◉www.gpia.co.uk), buses to Glasgow depart from directly outside the terminal: there's an express bus (hourly; £3.50; 50min), or Airbus #4 (Mon–Sat every 30min, Sun hourly), which costs just 50p if you have an air ticket but takes an hour and a half. The **train** station is a short walk from the terminal (alight at the airport not Prestwick Town), with trains taking 45 minutes to reach Glasgow (Mon–Sat every 30min, Sun hourly; £4.90).

Nearly all **trains** from England come into **Central station**, which sits over Argyle Street, one of the city's main shopping thoroughfares. Bus #398 from the front entrance on Gordon Street shuttles every ten minutes to **Queen Street station**, at the corner of George Square, terminus for trains serving Edinburgh and the north. The walk between the two takes about ten minutes. Bus #398 also stops at **Buchanan Street bus station**, arrival point for regional and inter-city **coaches**.

Orientation

Glasgow is a sprawling place, built on some punishingly steep hills, and with no really obvious focus, although, as most transport services converge on the area around **Argyle Street** and, 200 yards to the north, **George Square**, this pocket is the most obvious candidate for city-centre status. However, with the renovated, upmarket **Merchant City** immediately to the east and the main business and commercial areas to the west, the centre, when the term is used, actually refers to a large swathe from **Charing Cross** and the M8 in the west through to **Glasgow Green** in the rundown **East End**.

The **West End** begins just over a mile west of Central station, and covers most of the area beyond the M8 motorway. Today, this is still very much the student quarter of Glasgow, exuding a decorous air, with graceful avenues and parks, and inexpensive, interesting shops and cafés. Parts of the **Southside** have always been very pleasant: the leafy enclaves of **Queen's Park** are home to the national football stadium, Hampden Park, while **Pollok Park** and the **Burrell Collection** are undisputed highlights of the city.

Information

The city's efficient **tourist office**, at 11 George Square (July & Aug Mon–Sat 9am–8pm, Sun 10am–6pm; June & Sept Mon–Sat 10am–7pm, Sun 10am–6pm; rest of year Mon–Sat 9am–6pm, Sun 10am–6pm; ☎0141/204 4400, ◉www.seeglasgow.com), provides a wide array of maps and leaflets, and has an accommodation-booking service (fee £2). They also sell travel passes, theatre tickets and organize car rental. Pick up their free *Essential Guide to Glasgow*, a chunky brochure with details of every tourist attraction for miles around. If you're heading for the suburbs or want to explore the tiny streets and alleys that are invariably airbrushed off the tourist maps, it's probably worth investing in a *Bartholomew Glasgow Streetfinder* (£2.99), which you can pick up at the tourist office and most bookshops.

There's also a branch of the tourist office in the **airport's** international arrivals hall (daily 7.30am–5pm, except Oct–April Sun 8am–3.30pm; ℡0141/848 4440).

City transport

The best way to get between the city centre and the West End is to use the **Underground** (Mon–Sat 6.30am–11.30pm, Sun 11am–6pm), whose stations are marked with a large orange U. The service is extremely easy to use: there's a flat fare of 90p, or you can buy a **day ticket** for £1.60 (Mon–Fri after 9.30am and all day weekends). The main stations are **Buchanan Street**, near George Square and connected to Queen Street train station by a moving walkway, and **St Enoch**, at the junction of Buchanan Street pedestrian precinct and Argyle Street. **Hillhead** station is bang in the heart of the West End, near the university.

The array of different **bus** companies and the various routes they take is perplexing even to locals, and there's no easy guide to using them other than picking up individual timetables at the Travel Centre on St Enoch's Square (see below). The main operator is First Glasgow (℡0141/423 6600), which runs the "Overground" buses. Arriva (℡0141/885 4040) also operates many services. Information on relevant services is given at some bus stops.

The suburban **train** network is swift and convenient. There are two grim but functional **cross-city lines**: the one running through Central station connects to southeastern districts as far out as Lanark, while the Queen Street line links to the East End and points east. Trains on both lines go through **Partick** station, near the West End, which is also an underground stop; beyond Partick, the trains are an excellent way to link to points west and northwest of Glasgow, including Milngavie (for the start of the West Highland Way), Dumbarton and Helensburgh.

Transport passes and information

Various **public transport passes** are available if you plan to do lots of travelling on one day or are in the city for more than a few days. For train and underground travel the **Roundabout Glasgow** ticket (£3.50; available Mon–Fri after 9am, and all day Sat & Sun) gives unlimited travel for a day. The simplest of a complicated system of **Zonecards** costs £11.20 and gives travel for a week in central Glasgow, including Partick in the west and the Burrell Collection in the south. Neither of these are valid on the buses, which have their own systems of daily and weekly tickets.

To help demystify the system, and get detailed information on local public transport, make for the neo-Gothic hut of the **Travel Centre** (Mon–Sat 9.30am–5.30pm), located a couple of hundred yards southwest of the tourist office above St Enoch underground station, where you can pick up sheaves of maps, leaflets and bus timetables. There are smaller Travel Centres at Buchanan Street bus station and Hillhead underground station. For information on all transport within the city and further afield, call ℡0870/608 2608.

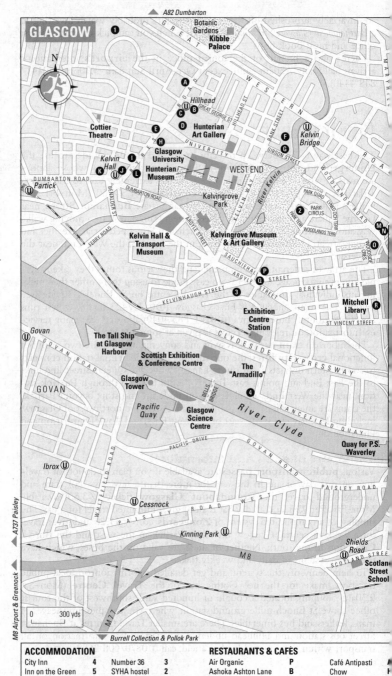

GLASGOW

▲ A82 Dumbarton

Botanic Gardens
Kibble Palace

Cottier Theatre

Hillhead

Hunterian Art Gallery

Kelvin Bridge

Glasgow University

Hunterian Museum

Kelvin Hall

Partick

WEST END

Kelvingrove Park

River Kelvin

PARK CIRCUS

Kelvingrove Museum & Art Gallery

Kelvin Hall & Transport Museum

Mitchell Library

Exhibition Centre Station

Govan

The Tall Ship at Glasgow Harbour

Scottish Exhibition & Conference Centre

The "Armadillo"

Glasgow Tower

GOVAN

Pacific Quay

Glasgow Science Centre

BELL'S BRIDGE

River Clyde

Quay for P.S. Waverley

Ibrox

Cessnock

Kinning Park

M8

Shields Road

Scotland Street School

0   300 yds

▼ Burrell Collection & Pollok Park

ACCOMMODATION				RESTAURANTS & CAFÉS			
City Inn	4	Number 36	3	Air Organic	P	Café Antipasti	
Inn on the Green	5	SYHA hostel	2	Ashoka Ashton Lane	B	Chow	
Kirklee Hotel	1			Brel	D	Fusion	

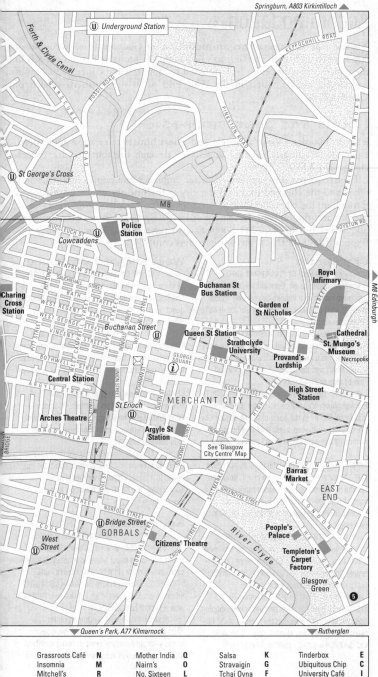

Springburn, A803 Kirkintilloch

KEPPOCHHILL ROAD

Forth & Clyde Canal

GARSCUBE ROAD

FOSSIL ROAD

PINKSTON ROAD

SPRINGBURN ROAD

(U) St George's Cross

M8

ROYSTON RD

M8 Edinburgh

(U) Underground Station

BUCCLEUCH ST
(U) Cowcaddens

Police Station

RENFREW STREET
SAUCHIEHALL STREET
BATH STREET
WEST REGENT STREET
WEST GEORGE STREET
WEST NILE STREET
HOPE STREET
RENFIELD STREET

Charing Cross Station

Buchanan St Bus Station

Royal Infirmary

Garden of St Nicholas

CATHEDRAL STREET

CASTLE STREET

Buchanan Street

(U) Queen St Station

Strathclyde University

Cathedral
St. Mungo's Museum
Necropolis

Provand's Lordship

PITT STREET
BOTHWELL STREET
VINCENT STREET
WEST CAMPBELL STREET

GEORGE SQUARE
(i) GEORGE STREET

Central Station

ARGYLE STREET

UNION STREET

BUCHANAN ST

QUEEN ST

INGRAM STREET

HIGH STREET

High Street Station

DUKE ST

St Enoch (U)

MERCHANT CITY

Arches Theatre

BROOMIELAW

Argyle St Station

STOCKWELL STREET

TRONGATE

See 'Glasgow City Centre' Map

GALLOWGATE

Barras Market

EAST END

NELSON STREET
NORFOLK STREET
COOK STREET

BRIDGE ST

(U) Bridge Street

GORBALS

West Street (U)

GORBALS STREET

Citizens' Theatre

CROWN

SALTMARKET

GREENDYKE STREET

River Clyde

BALLATER STREET

People's Palace

LONDON RD

THE GREEN

Templeton's Carpet Factory

Glasgow Green

5

Queen's Park, A77 Kilmarnock

Rutherglen

Grassroots Café	N	Mother India	Q	Salsa	K	Tinderbox	E
Insomnia	M	Nairn's	O	Stravaigin	G	Ubiquitous Chip	C
Mitchell's	R	No. Sixteen	L	Tchai Ovna	F	University Café	I

1003

Accommodation

There's a good range of **accommodation** in Glasgow, from a couple of large, well-run hostels through to some highly fashionable designer hotels in the centre. The city centre is dominated by hotels, while cosier guest houses and B&Bs can be found in the West End or in the southern suburb of Queen's Park.

Hotels and guest houses

It's worth booking ahead at **hotels and guest houses** to ensure a good room, especially in summer – either directly or through the tourist office (which charges a £2 fee).

If you're prepared to sacrifice character, ambience and home comforts, you'll often find the cheapest rooms in the city at the **budget chain hotels** found throughout the city centre. Big players include Novotel/Ibis ☎020/8283 4530, ⓦ www.accorhotels.com; Travelodge ☎0870/085 0950, ⓦ www.travelodge.co .uk; Travel Inn ☎0870/242 8000, ⓦ www.travelinn.co.uk; and Holiday Inn Express ☎0800/897121, ⓦ www.hiexpress.com.

City centre

Adelaide's 209 Bath St ☎0141/248 4970, ⓦ www.adelaides.co.uk. Eight simple, well-appointed rooms in a beautifully restored church building, with pleasant staff and an attractive café. Breakfast excluded. ❷

Baird Hall 460 Sauchiehall St ☎0141/553 4148. The most distinctive student halls of residence in the country, in a lavish Art Deco building near the School of Art and the upper end of Sauchiehall Street (June to mid-Sept). ❶

Brunswick 106 Brunswick St ☎0141/552 0001, ⓦ www.brunswickhotel.co.uk. Under the banner "Eat Drink Sleep" in the heart of the Merchant City, a fashionable but good-value designer hotel with minimalist furniture and a smart bar and restaurant. ❹

Inn on the Green 25 Greenhead St ☎0141/554 0165, ⓦ www.theinnonthegreen.co.uk. Neat and tasteful small hotel off the beaten track on the edge of Glasgow Green, with live jazz most evenings in the restaurant downstairs. Breakfast excluded. ❺

Malmaison 278 West George St ☎0141/572 1000, ⓦ www.malmaison.com. Glasgow's version of the sleek, chic mini-chain, an austere Grecian-temple frontage masking a superbly comfortable designer hotel. Breakfast excluded. ❼

Rennie Mackintosh 218–220 Renfrew St ☎0141/333 9992, ⓦ www.renniemackintoshhotels .com. An obvious theme, but the "Mockintosh" furniture and designs are elegant rather than tacky, and the hotel is small, smart and intimate. ❸

West End and Clydeside

Ambassador 7 Kelvin Drive ☎0141/946 1018, ⓦ www.glasgowhotelsandapartments.co.uk. Smallish and comfortable, a standard mid-sized guest house in lovely surroundings next to the River Kelvin and Botanic Gardens. ❸

City Inn Finnieston Quay ☎0141/240 1002, ⓦ www.cityinn.com. Chain hotel with stylish rooms and decent rates made interesting by its riverside location right under the Finnieston crane. Breakfast excluded. ❸

Kirklee 11 Kensington Gate ☎0141/334 5555, ⓦ www.scotland2000.com/kirklee. Characterful West End B&B in an Edwardian town house, with antique furniture and walls crammed with paintings and etchings. ❹

Number 36 36 St Vincent Crescent ☎0141/248 2086, ⓦ www.no36.co.uk. Neat, comfortable guest house in a lovely crescent well located for Kelvingrove, the SECC and transport links to the city centre. ❷

Southside

Balmoral Guest House 124 Queens Drive ☎0141/401 8866, ⓦ www.balmoral.kirion.net. Smart five-room guest house in a honey-coloured sandstone terrace right beside Queen's Park. ❸

Boswell 27 Mansionhouse Rd ☎0141/632 9812. Informal, relaxing hotel in an old Queen's Park villa with a superb real-ale bar. ❹

Glasgow Guest House 56 Dumbreck Rd ☎0141/427 0129. Pleasant four-room guest house with old furniture, good disabled facilities and handy transport links into the city centre. ❷

Hostels, campsites and self-catering

Glasgow doesn't have nearly as many **hostels** as Edinburgh, though it isn't short of bed space, thanks to the arrival of the bright-pink liveried, seven-storey *Euro Hostel* smack in the centre of the city at 318 Clyde St (☏0141/222 2828, ⓦwww.euro-hostels.com), which tries to bridge the gap between back-packer hostel and budget hotel. Its 360 beds are all bunks but they're in smart en-suite rooms sleeping two, four, six or more − some of which have great views. Bed and continental breakfast is from £13.75.

The popular SYHA hostel, 7–8 Park Terrace (☏0141/332 3004, ⓦwww.syha.org.uk), is located in a large town house in one of the West End's grandest terraces. It's a ten-minute walk south of Kelvinbridge underground station; bus #11 or #44 from the city centre leaves you with a short stroll west up Woodlands Road. Beds, mainly in en-suite four-bed dorms, are £11.50 per person in July and August and £11 the rest of the year; book in advance.

Campsite

The only **campsite** within a decent distance of Glasgow is *Craigendmuir Park*, Campsie View, Stepps (☏0141/779 4159, ⓦwww.craigendmuir.co.uk), four miles northeast of the centre, about fifteen minutes' walk from Stepps train station. It has adequate facilities with showers, a laundry and a shop, but there are only ten pitches.

Self-catering

Low-priced **self-catering** rooms and flats are available at the University of Glasgow (☏0141/330 5385, ⓦwww.glas.ac.uk) from June to mid-September, mostly located in the West End, with prices starting at £13.50 per night. The University of Strathclyde (☏0141/553 4148, ⓦwww.strath.ac.uk) has various sites available during the same period, most of which are gathered around the cathedral: you can pick up rooms for as little as £10 if you have your own bedding and spurn breakfast.

The City Centre

Glasgow's large **City Centre** is ranged across the north bank of the River Clyde. At its geographical heart is **George Square**, a nineteenth-century municipal showpiece crowned by the enormous **City Chambers** at its eastern end. Behind this lies one of the greatest marketing successes of the 1980s, the **Merchant City**, an area which blends magnificent Victorian architecture with yuppie conversions. The grand buildings and trendy cafés cling to the borders of the run-down **East End**, a strongly working-class district that chooses to ignore its rather showy neighbour. The oldest part of Glasgow, around the **Cathedral**, lies immediately north of the East End.

Called by poet John Betjeman "the greatest Victorian city in the world", Glasgow's commercial core spreads west of George Square, and is mostly built on a large grid system − possibly inspired by Edinburgh's New Town − with ruler-straight roads soon rising up severe hills to grand, sandblasted buildings. The same style was copied by many North American cities, and indeed parts of Glasgow have been pressed into service as nineteenth-century New York in films such as *House of Mirth*. The main shopping areas here are **Argyle Street**,

© Crown copyright

running parallel to the river, and **Buchanan Street**, which links Argyle Street to the pedestrianized shopping thoroughfare, **Sauchiehall Street**. Just to the northwest of here is Charles Rennie Mackintosh's famous **Glasgow School of Art**.

George Square and around

Now hemmed in by the city's grinding traffic, the imposing architecture of **George Square** reflects the confidence of Glasgow's Victorian age. The wide-open plaza almost has a continental airiness about it, although there isn't much subtlety about the eighty-foot column rising up at its centre. It's topped by a statue of Sir Walter Scott, even though his links with Glasgow are, at best, sketchy. The florid splendour of the **City Chambers**, opened by Queen Victoria in 1888, occupies the entire eastern end of the square. Built from wealth gained by colonial trade and heavy industry, it epitomizes the aspirations and optimism of late-Victorian city elders. Its intricately detailed facade includes high-minded friezes typical of the era: the four nations which then comprised the United Kingdom (England, Scotland, Wales and Ireland) at the feet of the throned queen, the British colonies and allegorical figures representing Religion, Virtue and Knowledge. It's worth taking a free **guided tour** of the labyrinthine interior (Mon–Fri 10.30am & 2.30pm; booking recommended on ℡0141/287 4018) to get a look at the acres of intricate gold leaf and Italian marble.

The Gallery of Modern Art

Queen Street leads south from George Square to **Royal Exchange Square**, where the focal point is the graceful mansion built in 1780 for tobacco lord William Cunninghame. This was the most ostentatious of the Glasgow merchants' homes and, having served as the city's Royal Exchange and central library, now houses the **Gallery of Modern Art** (Mon–Thurs & Sat 10am–5pm, Fri & Sun 11am–5pm; free). Surrounded by controversy from the day it opened in 1996, the gallery has tended to please the punters more than the critics, who have damned the place for emphasizing presentation over content.

The mirrored reception area leads you straight into the **Earth Gallery**, a spacious zone that effortlessly absorbs large-scale socially committed works by the "New Glasgow Boys" – Peter Howson, Adrian Wiszniewski, Ken Currie and Steven Campbell. Right in the middle of the gallery the kinetic sculpture *Titanic* by Eduard Bersudsky, made of scrap metal and old junk, whirrs into life every hour on the half-hour. Downstairs is the **Fire Gallery**, containing an imaginative new art library, while upstairs you'll find the **Water Gallery**, a brightly lit room dealing with the flow of life and death through art, ranging from Andy Goldsworthy's cracked and sun-baked red clay floor to intricate aboriginal paintings on canvas and bark. The blinding-white upper-floor **Air Gallery** generally features work with vivid visual impact, though in the summer it is filled by major temporary exhibitions. A small set of stairs at the far end of the gallery leads down to an area filled with pop art such as the wavy lines of Bridget Riley's *Arrest III* and Alan Davie's jazz-inspired *Cornucopia*, along with the gruesome row of guillotined heads in baskets by Scottish conceptual artist Ian Hamilton Finlay. Don't miss the top-floor **café** (see p.1025), where a huge mural by Adrian Wiszniewski competes with the view over the rooftops.

Along Buchanan Street

Buchanan Street runs north–south one block west of George Square, defining Glasgow's main shopping district. At the southern end of the street is **Princes Square**, one of the most stylish and imaginative shopping centres in the country, hollowed out of the innards of a soft sandstone building. The interior, all recherché Art Deco and ornate ironwork, has lots of pricey, highly fashionable shops, the whole place set to a soothing background of classical music.

Glaswegians' voracious appetite for shopping is fed further at the northern end of Buchanan Street, just beyond the underground station, where the **Buchanan Galleries** is a bewilderingly vast shopping mall of some 600,000 square feet which includes the largest Habitat store in Europe. Next door, almost anonymous beside its massive neighbouring auditorium of consumerism, is the £30-million **Royal Concert Hall**, with an excellent auditorium which plays host to world-class musical events from touring orchestras to rock acts.

The Lighthouse

At 11 Mitchell Lane, an otherwise nondescript alleyway between Buchanan Street and Union Street, is **The Lighthouse** (Mon, Wed, Fri & Sat 10.30am–5.30pm, Tues 11am–5.30pm, Thurs 10.30am–7pm, Sun noon–5pm; free; ⓦwww.thelighthouse.co.uk), a spectacularly converted Charles Rennie

Glasgow's architecture

Glasgow, founded on religion, built on trade and now well established as a cultural centre, has become recognized for its architectural riches, from the medieval cathedral to the modern glass-lined galleries of the Burrell Collection. Most dominant is the legacy of the **Victorian age**, when booming trade and industry allowed merchants to commission the finest architects of the day, and the celebrated work of **Charles Rennie Mackintosh** (see p.1013), which took Glasgow architecture to the forefront of early twentieth-century design.

The city's expansion: 1750–1850

Glasgow's great expansion was initiated in the eighteenth century by wealthy tobacco merchants who built the grand edifices of public and municipal importance that still make up much of the **Merchant City**. Further west, **Royal Exchange Square** is one of the best examples of a typical Glasgow square: treeless, bare and centred around a building of importance, the 1829 **Royal Exchange**, now housing the Gallery of Modern Art. As workers piled into the centre of Glasgow in the early nineteenth century, wealthy residents began moving west to the gridded streets that line **Blythswood Hill** (mostly developed after 1820) with two- or three-storey terraces, their porches and heavy cornices providing textural relief to the endless sandstone monotony. Above all, the long streets provide a beautiful selection of open-ended views, one moment leading into the heart of the city, the next filled with distant hills and sky.

Desiring to surround themselves with trees and fields, the well-to-do continued their migration west; **Woodside Crescent**, leading into Woodside Terrace, is a severe line of buildings with splendid Doric porches and neatly organized gardens. **Park Circus**, on the other hand, is a parade of uninterrupted Georgian magnificence, with delicate detail – such as narrow window slots on either side of the doors – enhancing the dignified crescent.

Greek Thomson and the Victorians

Long since overshadowed by Charles Rennie Mackintosh, the design of **Alexander "Greek" Thomson**, in the latter half of the nineteenth century, though well respected in its time, has been sadly neglected. As his nickname suggests, his work took the principles of Greek architecture, but reprocessed them in a highly unique manner. The 1857 **St Vincent Street Church**, his best work, has a massive simplicity

Mackintosh building which has found new life as Scotland's Centre for Architecture, Design and the City. The 1895 building was Mackintosh's first public commission, and housed the offices of the *Glasgow Herald* newspaper; despite glass and sandstone additions by architects Page & Park, it retains many original features, including the distinctive tower from which the building takes its name. The venue played a central role in Glasgow's reign as City of Architecture and Design in 1999, and acts as a permanent legacy of that year, mounting temporary exhibitions on design and architecture alongside the permanent **Mackintosh Interpretation Centre** (£2.50), a great place to learn more about the man and his work. The Lighthouse Tower itself gives fantastic views out over the city skyline to a number of his important buildings, including the School of Art and Scotland Street School.

The Merchant City

The grid of streets that lies immediately east of the City Chambers is known as the **Merchant City** (Ⓦ www.glasgowmerchantcity.net), an area of eigh-

and serenity lightened by the use of exotic Egyptian and Hindu motifs, particularly in the tower with its decorated egg-shaped dome. Most recently, the National Trust has opened his finest domestic dwelling, **Holmwood House**, on the Southside, to the public (see p.1024).

West from Park Circus lies **Glasgow University** (1866–86), its Gothic Revivalism – the work of Sir George Gilbert Scott – representing everything that Greek Thomson despised; he called it "sixteenth-century Scottish architecture clothed in fourteenth-century French details". Scottish features abound, such as crow-stepped gables, round turrets with conical caps and the top-heavy central tower. Inside, cloisters and quadrants sum up a suitably scholastic severity.

Originally conceived as a convenient way to house the influx of workers in the late 1800s, the Glasgow **tenement** design became more refined as the wealthy middle-classes began to realize its potential. Mainly constructed between 1860 and 1910, tenements have three to five storeys with two or three apartments per floor. A fascinating example of the style of these buildings, as well as the typical style of life inside them, can be seen at the **Tenement House** (see p.1014).

From World War I to the present

World War I put an end to the glorious century of Glasgow building, and the Depression years did little to enhance the city. However, since World War II bombing was targeted on the shipbuilding district of Clydebank, west of the centre, most of the city's legacy of fine sandstone buildings survived intact.

Glassy office buildings have sprung up in recent years, their mirrored walls basking in the reflected glory of the surrounding buildings to disguise their banality of design. The 1980s onwards have seen the return of the grand public building as inheritor of architectural innovation. Beginning with the imaginative **Burrell Collection**, the theme has been taken up by the titanium-clad behemoths of Clydeside: the unmistakable Clyde Auditorium, better known as the "**Armadillo**", and the futuristic glass-walled **Science Centre**, flanked by a bubble-like IMAX theatre and the 100-metre-high Glasgow Tower. This is not to ignore the poverty of artistry which went into great works such as the Kingston Bridge and Royal Concert Hall, but few could argue that Glasgow has failed to open itself to innovation and ideas. Above all, the city can be credited with involving its citizens in an awareness that everyone is influenced, as well as represented, by the buildings around them.

teenth-century warehouses and homes once bustling with cotton, tobacco and sugar traders, which in the last two decades has been sandblasted and swabbed clean with greater enthusiasm and municipal money than any other part of Glasgow in an attempt to bring residents back into the city centre. The expected flood of yuppies, however, was more like a trickle, and the latest efforts to woo them centre on New York-style loft conversions. Yet the expensive designer shops, style bars and bijou cafés continue to flock here, giving the area a pervasive air of sophistication and chic.

At the junction of Ingram and John streets, look out for the **Italian Centre**, a revitalized eighteenth-century warehouse now housing lively cafés, outdoor sculpture and some of the city's most fashionable boutiques – Versace established his first shop in Britain here. Immediately opposite, across John Street, is the delicate white spire of the National Trust for Scotland's regional headquarters, **Hutcheson Hall**, at 158 Ingram St (Mon–Sat 10am–5pm; free). The ground floor houses an exhibition of "Glasgow Style", with some attractive work by contemporary designers and craftsmen on sale, while there's a particularly fine ornately decorated hall upstairs. Here you can pick up a Merchant

City Trail leaflet, which guides you around a dozen of the most interesting buildings in the area.

Almost opposite in the other direction, a little way down Glassford Street, the Robert Adam-designed **Trades House** (Mon–Sat 9am–6pm, depending on functions; free) still functions as the headquarters of the Glasgow trade guilds. Its history can be traced back to 1605 when fourteen societies of well-to-do city merchants, who were the forerunners of the trade unions, first incorporated. The former civic pride and status of the guilds is still evident, however, from the rich assortment of carvings and stained-glass windows, with a lively pictorial representation of the different trades in the silk frieze around the walls of the first-floor banqueting hall.

Glasgow Cross

Before 1846, **Glasgow Cross** – the junction of Trongate, Gallowgate and the High Street, at the southeastern corner of the Merchant City – was the city's principal intersection, until the construction of the new train station near George Square shifted the city's emphasis west. The turreted seventeenth-century **Tolbooth Steeple** still stands here, although the rest of the building has long since disappeared, and today the stern tower is little more than a traffic hazard at a busy junction.

The East End

East of Glasgow Cross, down Gallowgate beyond the train lines, lies the **East End**, the district that perhaps most closely corresponds to the old perception of Glasgow. The Depression caused the closure of many factories, leaving communities stranded in an industrial wasteland. Today isolated pubs, tatty shops and cafés sit amidst this dereliction, in sharp contrast to the gloss of the Merchant City only a few blocks to the west. Walking around here you definitely get the sense that you're off the tourist trail, but unless you're here after dark it's not as threatening as it may feel, and there's no doubt that the area advertises a rich flavour of working-class Glasgow.

Three hundred yards down either London Road or Gallowgate is **The Barras**, Glasgow's largest and most popular weekend market (Sat & Sun 9am–5pm). Selling household goods, bric-a-brac, second-hand clothes and records, none of it particularly high quality, the stalls spill out into the surrounding cobbled streets. The fast-talking traders, lively atmosphere and entertaining vignettes of Glasgow life make it an off-beat diversion from shopping-mall banality.

Between London Road and the River Clyde are the wide and tree-lined spaces of **Glasgow Green**. Reputedly the oldest public park in Britain, the Green has been common land since at least 1178, when it was first mentioned in records. On the northeast side of the Green, just beyond the People's Palace, it's worth taking a look at the extraordinary **Templeton's Carpet Factory**, a massive brick edifice of turrets, arched windows, mosaic-style patterns and castellated grandeur designed in the style of the Doge's Palace in Venice and built in 1892. Subsequent to its days as a carpet factory it has been a small business centre and health centre, but is now disused.

The People's Palace

Opposite the Templeton's carpet factory on Glasgow Green you can still see some poles erected to hang out washing, recalling the days when the Green was very much a public space in daily use. Beside these, the **People's Palace**

(Mon–Thurs & Sat 10am–5pm, Fri & Sun 11am–5pm; free) houses a wonderfully haphazard evocation of the city's history. This squat, red-sandstone Victorian building, with a vast semicircular glasshouse tacked on the back, was purpose-built as a museum back in 1898 – almost a century before the rest of the country caught on to the fashion for social history collections. While many of the displays are designed to instil a warm glow in the memories of older locals, the museum is refreshingly unpretentious, and visitors are almost always outnumbered by Glaswegian families.

On the **top floor**, glowing murals by local artist Ken Currie powerfully evoke the spirit of radical Glasgow, from the Carlton Weavers strike in 1787 to the Red Clydesiders of the 1920s. The **west wing** looks at famous Glasgow products through history, with displays of everything from cast-iron railings and biscuit wrappers to a giant portrait of Billy Connolly. In the **East Gallery** is a reconstructed "single-end" or one-roomed house, a typical setting for the daily life of hundreds of thousands of Glasgow people through the years. Downstairs, various themes are explored, including alcohol, the traditional holiday excursion "doon the watter" by steamer to various Clyde coastal resorts, and some guidance to understanding "the Patter", Glaswegians' idiosyncratic version of the Queen's English. The glasshouse at the back of the palace contains the **Winter Gardens**, with a café, water garden, twittering birds and assorted tropical plants and shrubs.

The Cathedral area

Rising north up the hill from the Tolbooth Steeple at Glasgow Cross is Glasgow's **High Street**. In British cities, the name is commonly associated with the busiest central thoroughfare, and it's a surprise to see how forlorn and dilapidated Glasgow's version is, long superseded by the grander thoroughfares further west. The High Street leads up to the **Cathedral**, on the site of Glasgow's original settlement.

Glasgow Cathedral

Built in 1136, destroyed in 1192 and rebuilt soon after, stumpy-spired **Glasgow Cathedral** (April–Sept Mon–Sat 9.30am–6pm, Sun 2–5pm; Oct–March Mon–Sat 9.30am–4pm, Sun 2–4pm; free) was not completed until the late fifteenth century, with the final reconstruction of the chapterhouse and the aisle designed by Robert Blacader, the city's first archbishop. Thanks to the intervention of the city guilds, it is the only Scottish mainland cathedral to have escaped the hands of religious reformers in the sixteenth century. The cathedral is dedicated to the city's patron saint and reputed founder, St Mungo, about whom four popular stories are frequently told – they even make an appearance on the city's coat of arms. These involve a bird that he brought back to life, the bell with which he summoned the faithful to prayer, a tree that he managed to make spontaneously combust and a fish that he caught with a repentant adulterous queen's ring on its tongue.

On entering, you arrive in the impressively lofty nave of the **upper church**, with the lower church entirely hidden from view. Either side of the nave, the narrow **aisles** are illuminated by vivid stained-glass windows, most of which date from the last century. Threadbare Union flags and military pennants hang listlessly beneath them, serving as a reminder that the cathedral is very much a part of the Unionist Protestant tradition. Beyond the nave, the **choir** is hidden from view by the curtained stone pulpit, making the interior feel a great deal smaller than might be expected from the outside.

Two sets of steps from the nave lead down into the **lower church**, where you'll see the dark and musty **chapel** surrounding the tomb of St Mungo. The saint's relics were removed in the late Middle Ages, although the tomb still forms the centrepiece. The chapel itself is one of the most glorious examples of medieval architecture in Scotland, best seen in the delicate fan vaulting rising up from the thicket of cool stone columns.

The Necropolis

Rising up behind the Cathedral, the atmospheric **Necropolis** is a grassy mound covered in a fantastic assortment of crumbling and tumbling gravestones, ornate urns, gloomy catacombs and Neoclassical temples. Inspired by the Père Lachaise cemetery in Paris, developer John Strong created a garden of death in 1833, and it quickly became a fitting spot for the great and the good of wealthy nineteenth-century Glasgow to indulge their vanity. Various paths lead through the rows of eroding, neglected graves, and from the summit, next to the column topped with an indignant John Knox, there are superb **views** which capture the city and its trademark mix of grit and grace – the steaming chimneys of the Tennants brewery, the traffic on the M8 motorway, the crowded city-centre offices, the serene cathedral itself, and a wide cityscape of spires and high-rise blocks to the south and east.

Cathedral Square

Back in Cathedral Square, the **St Mungo Museum of Religious Life and Art** (Mon–Thurs & Sat 10am–5pm, Fri & Sun 11am–5pm; free) focuses on objects, beliefs and art from Christianity, Buddhism, Judaism, Islam, Hinduism and Sikhism. Portrayals of Hindu gods are juxtaposed with the stunning Salvador Dalí painting *St John of the Cross*. In addition to the main exhibition there is a small collection of photographs, papers and archive material looking at religion in Glasgow, the power and zealotry of the nineteenth-century Temperance movement and Christian missionaries.

Across the square, the oldest house in the city, the **Provand's Lordship** (same times; free) dates from 1471, and has been used, among other things, as an ecclesiastical residence and an inn. Inside, the recreations of life in the fifteenth century aren't particularly arresting unless you've an interest in period furniture. Behind the Provand's Lordship lies the small **Garden of St Nicholas**, a herb garden contrasting medieval and Renaissance aesthetics and approaches to medicine, with muddled clusters of herbs amid stone carvings of the heart and other organs.

Sauchiehall Street and around

Glasgow's most famous street, **Sauchiehall Street**, runs in a straight line west from the northern end of Buchanan Street, past some unexciting shopping malls to a few of the city's most interesting sights. Charles Rennie Mackintosh fans should head for the **Willow Tea Rooms**, not all that easy to spot at first, above a jewellery shop at 217 Sauchiehall St. This is a faithful reconstruction on the site of the 1904 original, which was created for Kate Cranston, one of Rennie Mackintosh's few contemporary supporters in the city, opened in 1980 after more than fifty years of closure. Taking inspiration from the word *Sauchiehall*, which means "avenue of willow", he chose the willow leaf as a theme to unify the whole structure from the tables to the mirrors and the ironwork. Tea is served here daily from 9.30am until 5pm (for a review, see p.1025). A few blocks further west at no. 350 is the recently remodelled **CCA** (Centre for Contemporary Arts; ☎0141/332 7521, ⓦwww.cca-glasgow.com), where eclectically internationalist exhibitions and performances consistently make the centre one of the city's cultural hotspots.

The Glasgow School of Art

Rising above Sauchiehall Street to the north is one of the city centre's steepest hills, where Dalhousie and Scott streets veer up to Renfrew Street, where you'll find Charles Rennie Mackintosh's **Glasgow School of Art**, 167

Charles Rennie Mackintosh

The work of the architect **Charles Rennie Mackintosh** (1868–1928), has come to be synonymous with the image of Glasgow. Historians may disagree over whether his work was a forerunner of the Modernist movement or merely a sunset of Victorianism, but he nonetheless undoubtedly created buildings of great beauty, idiosyncratically fusing Scots Baronial with Gothic, Art Nouveau and modern design. Though the bulk of his work was conceived at the turn of the twentieth century, since the postwar years Mackintosh's ideas have become particularly fashionable, giving rise to a certain amount of ersatz **"Mockintosh"** in his home city, with his distinctive lettering and small design features used time and again by shops, pubs and businesses. Fortunately, there are also plenty of examples of the genuine article, making the city something of a pilgrimage centre for art and design students from all over the world.

He joined the Glasgow School of Art in 1884, where the vibrant new director, Francis Newberry, encouraged his pupils to create original and individual work. Here he met Herbert MacNair and the sisters Margaret and Frances MacDonald; nicknamed **"The Spook School"**, the four created a new artistic language, using extended vertical design, stylized abstract organic forms and muted colours, reflecting their interest in Japanese design and the work of Whistler and Beardsley. However, it was architecture that truly challenged Mackintosh, allowing him to use his creative artistic impulse in a three-dimensional and cohesive manner.

His big break came in 1896, when he won the competition to design a new home for the **Glasgow School of Art** (see p.1014). This is his most famous work, but a number of smaller buildings document the development of his style. One of his earliest commissions was for a new building to house the *Glasgow Herald* on Mitchell Lane, off Argyle Street. A massive tower rises up from the corner, giving the building its popular name of **The Lighthouse**; it now houses the Mackintosh Interpretation Centre (see p.1008).

In the 1890s Glasgow went wild for tearooms, and the imposing Miss Cranston, who dominated the Glasgow teashop scene, gave Mackintosh great freedom of design. Over the next twenty years he designed articles from teaspoons to furniture and, finally, as in the case of the **Willow Tea Rooms** (see p.1012), the structure itself. Mackintosh designed few **religious buildings**: the Queens Cross Church of 1896, still at the junction of Garscube and Maryhill roads in the northwest of the city, is the only completed example standing. It is now home to the **Charles Rennie Mackintosh Society** (Mon–Fri 10am–5pm, Sat 10am–2pm, Sun 2–5pm; ☎0141/946 6600, ⊛www.crmsociety.com).

The spectre of limited budgets was to haunt Mackintosh throughout his career, and he never had the chance to design and construct with complete freedom. However, these constraints didn't manage to dull his creativity, as demonstrated by the **Scotland Street School** of 1904, just south of the river (see p.1021). It is his most symmetrical work, with a whimsical nod to history in the Scots Baronial conical tower roofs and sandstone building material. The building which arguably displays Mackintosh at his most flamboyant was one he never saw built, the **House for an Art Lover** (see p.1021), constructed in Bellahouston Park in 1996, 95 years after plans for it were submitted to a German architectural competition.

Renfrew St (guided tours Mon–Fri 11am & 2pm, Sat 10.30 & 11.30am; July & August also Sat 1pm, Sun 10.30 & 11.30am; booking advised; ☏0141/353 4526, ⓦwww.gsa.ac.uk; £5). This is one of the most prestigious art schools in the country, with such notable alumni as artists Robert Colquhoun and Robert Macbryde and, more recently, Steven Campbell, Ken Currie and actor Robbie Coltrane. Widely considered to be the pinnacle of Mackintosh's work, the school is a characteristically angular building of warm sandstone which, due to financial constraints, had to be constructed in two sections (1897–99 and 1907–09). There's a clear change in the architect's style from the earlier severity of the mock-Baronial east wing to the softer lines of the western half.

The only way to see the school is to take one of the student-led **guided tours**, the extent of which are dependent on curricular activities. You can, however, be sure of seeing at least some of the differences between the two halves and a handful of the most impressive rooms. All over the school, from the roof to the stairwells, Mackintosh's unique touches recur – light Oriental reliefs, tall-backed chairs and stylized Celtic illuminations. Even before entering the building up the gently curving stairway, you cannot fail to be struck by the soaring height of the north-facing windows, which light the art studios and were designed, in the architect's inimitable style, to combine aesthetics with practicality.

You can peer down from the **Furniture Gallery** into the school's most spectacular room, the glorious two-storey **Library**. Here, sombre oak panelling is set against angular lights adorned with primary colours, dangling down in seemingly random clusters. The dark bookcases sit precisely in their fitted alcoves, while of the furniture, the most unusual feature is the central periodical desk, whose oval central strut displays perfect and quite beautiful symmetry.

The school also puts on various **exhibitions** through the year, which you can view without going on a tour. For details, contact the school or check up-to-date listings.

The Tenement House

Just a few hundred yards north of the School of Art – on the other side of a sheer hill – is the **Tenement House**, 145 Buccleuch Street (March–Oct daily 2–5pm; Nov–Feb by appointment only; NTS; £3.20). This is a typical tenement block still lived in on most floors, except for the ground and first floor, where you can see the perfectly preserved home of Agnes Toward, who moved here with her mother in 1911, changing nothing and throwing very little out until she was hospitalized in 1965. On the ground floor, the National Trust for Scotland has constructed a fascinating display on the development of the humble tenement block as the bedrock of urban Scottish housing. Upstairs, the flat gives every impression of still being inhabited, with a cluttered hearth and range, kitchen utensils, recess beds, framed religious tracts and sewing machine all untouched.

The Piping Centre

Behind the hulking Royal Scottish Academy for Music and Drama, a short way east of the Tenement House, the immaculate **Piping Centre**, at 30–34 McPhater Street, prides itself on being a national centre for the promotion of the bagpipe. Equipped with rehearsal rooms, performance halls, conference centre, accommodation, museum and an attractive café, it is a meeting place for fans and performers from all over the world. For the casual visitor, the single-room **museum** (daily 10am–4.30pm; £3; ⓦwww.thepipingcentre.co.uk) is of most interest, with a collection of instruments and related artefacts from the fourteenth century to the present day.

The West End

The urbane veneer of the **West End** seems a world away from Glasgow's industrial image and the hustle and bustle of the city centre. In the 1800s, the city's wealthy merchants established huge estates away from the soot and grime of city life, and in 1870 the ancient university was moved from its cramped home near the cathedral to a spacious new site overlooking the River Kelvin. Elegant housing swiftly followed, the Kelvingrove Art Gallery was built to house the 1888 International Exhibition and, in 1896, the Glasgow District Subway – today's Underground – started its circuitous shuffle from here to the city centre.

The hub of life in this part of Glasgow is **Byres Road**, running between Great Western Road and Dumbarton Road past Hillhead underground station. Shops, restaurants, cafés, some enticing pubs and hordes of roving young people, including thousands of students, give the area a sense of style and vitality. The main sights straddle the banks of the cleaned-up River Kelvin, where the slopes, trees and statues of **Kelvingrove Park** are framed by a backdrop of the Gothic towers and turrets of **Glasgow University** and the **Kelvingrove Museum and Art Gallery**, off Argyle Street.

Kelvingrove Museum and Art Gallery

Founded on donations from the city's chief industrialists, the huge, red-brick fantasy castle of **Kelvingrove Museum and Art Gallery** (Mon–Thurs & Sat 10am–5pm, Fri & Sun 11am–5pm; free) is a brash statement of Glasgow's nine-teenth-century self-confidence. On the ground floor, the central hall is an impressive, airy introduction to the style of the place. However, it's the art col-lections, the majority of which are upstairs, that are of most interest. **Room 22** contains some superb Italian paintings, notably Botticelli's delicate *Annunciation*, Giorgione's rich and vibrant *The Adulteress Brought Before Christ*, and some fervent landscapes by Salvator Rosa. Further down the gallery, Rembrandt's symbolic portrayal of a carcass of an ox stands out darkly, along with his quiet portrait, *The Man in Armour*. Continuing from the seventeenth century and leading up to the early nineteenth century, **room 23** contains pre-dominantly British work, dominated by two paintings by Jacob More, a Scottish artist who worked in the elegiacally classical style of Claude.

Room 24 is filled with quality work from Scottish and European artists from the eighteenth century to the early twentieth century, among them Corot, Degas and Millet. As for the Scots, the angelic face of *Mrs William Urquhart* is testimony to Sir Henry Raeburn's skill as an informal portraitist. **Room 25** is dominated by French impressionists and post-impressionists, including work by

At the time of going to press, the Kelvingrove Museum and Art Gallery was on the point of securing a grant for a complete **refurbishment** of the building. This would mean that the museum would be closed to the public from early 2003 for about one year. For the latest information, contact the tourist office or the Kelvingrove project office on ☏0141/287 2757.

Monet and Van Gogh, while **room 26** sets such continental luminaries as Picasso and Derain alongside excellent work by the increasingly popular Scottish Colourists. *The Pink Parasol* by J.D. Fergusson, for example, reveals what he learned from Matisse and Cézanne, while Cadell's *Orange Blind*, with its unexpectedly strident blocks of colour contrasting with the precise, flat brushwork, is one of the gallery's best-loved works.

In the east wing, **The Scottish Gallery** is entirely devoted to native artists. Here Raeburn's magnificent *Mr and Mrs Robert N. Campbell of Kailzie* almost overwhelms the room, the golden, life-size figures emerging from the loosely brushed background. On the far wall hangs the famous portrait of Robert Burns by Alexander Naysmyth, now found on biscuit tins the world over.

The **Glasgow Style** room is dedicated to the era when Charles Rennie Mackintosh was in his prime: this marvellous collection of furniture is crowned by a pair of domino tables and chairs designed by Mackintosh for the tearooms of Miss Cranston. The **Glasgow Boys** are well represented, with the decoratively patterned *In a Japanese Garden* by George Henry alongside his collaborative work with Hornel, *The Druids Bringing in the Mistletoe*.

The Glasgow Boys

The traditional rivalry between Glasgow and Edinburgh was alive and kicking in the late nineteenth century when the Royal Scottish Academy resolutely refused to accept the work of any west-coast artist. That was soon to change, however, when in the 1870s a group of painters formed a loose association, centred in Glasgow, that was to invest Scottish painting with a fresh approach inspired by contemporary European trends (in particular the *plein air* painting of the Impressionists). Derisively nicknamed "The Glasgow Boys", the group was dominated by five men – Guthrie, Lavery, Henry, Hornel and Crawhall – who, despite coming from very different backgrounds, all violently rejected the eighteenth-century conservatism which spawned little other than sentimental, anecdotal renditions of Scottish history peopled by "poor but happy" families, in a detailed, exacting manner. They began to experiment with colour, liberally splashing paint across the canvas. The content and concerns of the paintings, often showing peasant life and work, were as offensive to the effete art establishment as their style: until then most of Glasgow's public art collections had been accrued by wealthy tobacco lords and merchants.

Of the Glasgow Boys, **Sir James Guthrie**'s *A Highland Funeral* (on display in St Mungo's Museum; see p.1012) was hugely influential for the rest of the group, who found inspiration in its restrained emotional content, colour and unaffected realism. Seeing it persuaded **Sir John Lavery**, then studying in France, to return to Glasgow. Lavery was eventually to become an internationally popular society portraitist, but his earlier work, depicting the middle class at play, is filled with fresh colour and figures in motion. Rather than a realistic aesthetic, an interest in colour and decoration united the work of friends **George Henry** and **E.A. Hornel**. The predominance of colour, pattern and design in Henry's *Galloway Landscape*, for example, is remarkable, while their joint work *The Druids* (both on display in the Glasgow Style room at Kelvingrove; see above), in thickly applied impasto, is full of Celtic symbolism. Newcastle-born **Joseph Crawhall** combined superb draughtsmanship and simplicity of line with a photographic memory to create watercolours of an outstanding naturalism and freshness. William Burrell was an important patron, and a good collection of Crawhall's works resides at the Burrell Collection (see p.1022).

The Glasgow Boys school reached its height by 1900, and once its members had achieved the artistic respect – and for some the commercial success – they craved, it began to disintegrate and did not outlast World War I. However, the influence of their work cannot be underestimated, shaking the foundations of the artistic elite and inspiring the next generation of Edinburgh painters, now known as the "Colourists".

The Transport Museum

Twin-towered **Kelvin Hall** opposite the Kelvingrove Museum is home to the excellent **Transport Museum**, an enormous collection of trains, cars, trams, circus caravans and prams, along with an array of old Glaswegian ephemera (Mon–Thurs & Sat 10am–5pm, Fri & Sun 11am–5pm; free). Just inside the Bunhouse Road entrance, "Kelvin Street" is a re-created 1938 cobbled street featuring an old Italian coffee shop, a butcher (complete with plastic meat joints dangling in the window), a bakery (where labels claim that the buns were provided by the university's taxidermy department) and an old-time underground station. The Clyde Room displays intricate models of ships forged in Glasgow's yards, everything from tiny schooners to ostentatious ocean liners such as the *QE2*.

Glasgow University and the Hunterian bequests

Dominating the West End skyline, the gloomy turreted tower of **Glasgow University**, designed by Sir Gilbert Scott in the mid-nineteenth century, overlooks the glades of the River Kelvin. Access to the main buildings and museums is from University Avenue, running east from Byres Road. In the dark neo-Gothic pile under the tower you'll find the **University Visitor Centre** (Mon–Sat 9.30am–5pm; May–Sept also Sun 2–5pm), which, as well as giving information for potential students, distributes leaflets about the various university buildings and the statues around the campus. From May to September **historical tours** of the campus are run from here (check schedules on ☎0141/330 5511; £2). It's possible to join a tour up the sky-piercing university **tower** (May–Sept Fri 2pm; free), climbing 228 narrow spiral-staircase steps to some heady views; places, though, are limited to twenty people, with tickets available only in person that morning from the Visitor Centre.

Beside the Visitor Centre is the **Hunterian Museum** (Mon–Sat 9.30am–5pm; free), Scotland's oldest public museum, dating back to 1807. The collection was donated to the university by ex-student William Hunter, a pathologist and anatomist whose eclectic tastes form the basis of a fairly diverting zoological and archeological jaunt. Exhibitions include Scotland's only dinosaur, a look at the Romans in Scotland – the furthest outpost of their massive empire – and a vast numismatic collection.

The Hunterian Art Gallery

Opposite the university, across University Avenue, is Hunter's more frequently visited bequest, the **Hunterian Art Gallery** (Mon–Sat 9.30am–5pm; free), best known for its wonderful works by James Abbott McNeill Whistler: only Washington DC has a larger collection. Whistler's breathy landscapes are less compelling than his portraits of women, which give his subjects a resolute strength in addition to their fey and occasionally winsome qualities: look out especially for the trio of full-length portraits, *Harmony of Flesh Colour* and *Black, Pink and Gold – the Tulip* and *Red and Black – the Fan*.

A side gallery leads to the **Mackintosh House** (closed 12.30–1.30pm; free), a re-creation of the interior of the now-demolished Glasgow home of Margaret and Charles Rennie Mackintosh. An introductory display contains photographs of the original house sliding irrevocably into terminal decay, from where you are led into an exquisitely cool interior that contains over sixty pieces of Mackintosh furniture on three floors.

The Botanic Gardens

At the northern, top end of Byres Road, where it meets the Great Western Road, is the main entrance to the **Botanic Gardens** (daily 7am–dusk; free). The best-known glasshouse here, the hulking, domed **Kibble Palace** (daily 10am–4.45pm; winter closes 4.15pm; closed for restoration after autumn 2002), was built in 1863 for wealthy landowner John Kibble's estate on the shores of Loch Long, where it stood for ten years before he decided to transport it into Glasgow, drawing it up the Clyde on a vast raft pulled by a steamer. Today the palace houses a damp, musty collection of swaying palms from around the world, along with an unremarkable but well-placed café. Nearby, the **Main Range Glasshouse** (same times) is home to lurid, blooming flowers and plants luxuriating in the humidity, including stunning orchids, cacti, ferns and tropical fruit. Between the two in the old curator's house is a small **visitor centre** (daily 11am–4pm; free) with art exhibitions an interactive computer aimed at younger visitors.

Clydeside

"The **Clyde** made Glasgow and Glasgow made the Clyde" runs an old saw, full of sentimentality for the days when the river was the world's premier shipbuilding centre, and when its industry lent an innovation and confidence which made Glasgow the second city of the British Empire. The last of the great liners to be built on **Clydeside** was the *QE2* in 1967, yet such events are hard to visualize today, with the banks of the river all but devoid of any industry: shipbuilding is now restricted to a couple of barely viable yards, as derelict warehouses, crumbling docks and overgrown wastelands crowd the river's flanks.

Glasgow is often accused of failing to capitalize on its river, and it's only in the last few years, with a number of large, striking Clydeside buildings going up, such as the Scottish Exhibition and Conference Centre, or **SECC**, the **Armadillo** and the **Science Centre**, that the river is once again becoming a focus of attention. The easiest way to reach the cluster of Clydeside attractions is to **walk** the mile or so west along the riverside footpath from the city centre. Otherwise, **trains** from Glasgow Central low-level station and half-hourly **bus** #30 from the centre of town run to the Exhibition Centre. Bell's Bridge runs across the river to the Science Centre on the south bank, also served by bus #24 from Renfield Street.

The Waverley

One of Glasgow's best-loved treasures is the **Waverley**, the last sea-going paddlesteamer in the world, which spends the summer cruising "doon the watter" to various ports on the Firth of Clyde and the Ayrshire coast from its base at Anderson Quay between Finnieston and the Kingston Bridge. Built on Clydeside as recently as 1947, she's an elegant vessel to look at, not least when she's thrashing away at full steam with the hills of Argyll or Arran in the background. Call the booking office on ☎0141/243 2224 or check ⓦwww.waverleyexcursions.co.uk for her sailing times and itinerary.

△ Statue of Mercury, Merchant City, Glasgow

The north bank

On Clydeside immediately south of the West End, just over a mile west of the city centre, is the harshly re-landscaped Scottish Exhibition and Conference Centre, or **SECC**, two vast adjoining red and grey sheds that make a dutifully utilitarian venue for travelling fairs, mega-concerts and anonymous bars and cafés. Although the huge **Finnieston Crane**, retained as an icon of shipbuilding days, stands alongside the SECC, the site was rescued from bland obscurity by the arrival in 1997 of a supplementary concert hall officially entitled the Clyde Auditorium but universally nicknamed "**the Armadillo**" for its rounded exterior of armour-plating. It resembles a poor man's version of the Sydney Opera House but has quickly established itself as one of the city's architectural landmarks.

A few hundred yards downstream on the north bank of the river is an attraction known as the **Tall Ship at Glasgow Harbour** (daily: April–Sept 10am–5pm, Oct–March 11am–4pm; £4.50). A 245-foot-long, three-masted barque, the *Glenlee* was launched on the river in 1896 and is now one of only five large sailing vessels built on Clydeside still afloat. The sheer scale of the *Glenlee* is her most impressive feature, though various parts of the ship are imaginatively set up to offer an insight into life aboard when she was a hard-working merchant vessel carrying cargo round Cape Horn.

The Glasgow Science Centre

On the south bank of the river, linked to the SECC by Bell's Bridge, are the three space-age, titanium-clad constructions which make up the **Glasgow Science Centre**, a massive, hands-on collection opened in 2001 (Tower £5.50, Science Mall £6.50, IMAX £5.50; any two £9.50; all three £14; Ⓦwww.gsc.org.uk). Of the three buildings, the most obvious from afar is the 127-metre **Glasgow Tower** (daily 10am–6pm, Thurs–Sat until 9pm), an aerofoil-like construction which can rotate to face into the prevailing wind and which is the tallest free-standing structure in Scotland. Glass lifts ascend to the viewing cabin at the top, offering suitably panoramic views.

Alongside the tower is the centrepiece of the development, the curvaceous, wedge-shaped **Science Mall** (daily 10am–6pm). Behind the vast glass wall which faces the river are four floors of interactive exhibits ranging from lift-you-own-weight pulleys to high-tech thermograms. The centre covers almost every aspect of science from simple optical illusions to cutting-edge computer technology, including a section on moral and environmental issues – lots of good fun, although weekends and school holidays are busy and noisy.

The smallest of the three buildings on the site is the bubble-like **IMAX theatre**, which shows a range of mostly science- and nature-based documentaries on its giant screen, with programmes changing regularly.

The Southside

On the Clyde's **Southside**, immediately facing the city centre, are the notoriously deprived districts of the Gorbals and Govan – sprinkled with new developments but still obviously derelict and tatty in many parts. There's little reason to venture here unless you're making your way to the Science Centre (see above), the famously innovative Citizen's Theatre (see p.1029), or one of the revived architectural gems of Charles Rennie Mackintosh, the **Scotland Street School** and the **House for an Art Lover**.

Moving further south, inner-city decay fades into altogether gentler and more salubrious suburbs, including Queen's Park, home to Scotland's national football stadium, **Hampden Park**; Pollokshaws and the rural landscape of Pollok Park, which contains two of Glasgow's major museums, the **Burrell Collection** and **Pollok House**; and Cathcart, location of Alexander "Greek" Thomson's **Holmwood House**.

Southside attractions are fairly widely spread. The **underground** will get you to Scotland Street School and the House for an Art Lover, while a **train** from Central station is best for Hampden Park (Mount Florida station) and Holmwood House (Cathcart station). For Pollok Park either take the train to Pollokshaws West station (not to be confused with Pollokshields West), or **bus** #45, #47, #48 or #57 to Pollokshaws Road, or a **taxi** (£12–14 from the centre). From the park gates a **free minibus** runs every half-hour between 10am and 4.30pm to both the Burrell Collection and Pollok House.

Scotland Street School Museum of Education

Opposite Shields Road underground station is the **Scotland Street School Museum of Education** (Mon–Thurs & Sat 10am–5pm, Fri & Sun 11am–5pm; free), another of the city's Charles Rennie Mackintosh treasures. Opened as a school in 1906 to Mackintosh's distinctively angular design, it closed in 1979, since when it has been entertainingly refurbished to house a fascinating collection of memorabilia related to classroom life. There are reconstructed classrooms from the Victorian and Edwardian eras, World War II and the 1960s, as well as changing rooms, a primitive domestic science room and recreations of the school matron's sanatorium and a janitor's lair.

House for an Art Lover

West of Scotland Street School, tucked just inside Bellahouston Park, is Charles Rennie Mackintosh's **House for an Art Lover** (April–Sept daily except Fri 10am–4pm; Oct–March Sat & Sun 10am–4pm but closed occasionally for functions; ☎0141/353 4449; £3.50). Designed in 1901 for a German competition, it was not until 1996, after years of detailed research and painstaking work, that the building was actually constructed and opened as a centre for Glasgow School of Art postgraduate students, with a limited number of rooms open to the public.

It's all quintessential Mackintosh, almost unimaginable as a living space but exquisitely stylish and original at the same time. On the upper floor is the main **hallway**, where massive windows cast a cool light upon an area designed for large parties. In direct contrast, the dazzling, white **Music Room** has bow windows opening out to a large balcony. The **Dining Room** is decorated with darkened stained wood and enhanced by some beautiful gesso tiles. On the ground floor, the **café** (☎0141/353 4779) is particularly popular with locals on Sunday mornings; there's an attractive menu, and it's open through the day and sometimes also in the evenings.

Hampden Park and the Scottish Football Museum

Two and a half miles due south of the city centre, just to the west of the tree-filled Queen's Park, the floodlights and giant stands of Scotland's national football stadium, **Hampden Park**, loom over the surrounding suburban tenements

Football in Glasgow

Football, or *fitba'* as it's pronounced locally, is one of Glasgow's great passions – and one of its great blights. While the city can claim to be one of Europe's premier footballing centres, it's known above all for one of the most bitter rivalries in any sport, that between **Celtic** and **Rangers**. Two of the largest clubs in Britain, with weekly crowds regularly topping 60,000, the Old Firm, as they're collectively known, have dominated Scottish football for a century, most notably in the last fifteen years as they have lavished vast sums of money on foreign talent in an often frantic effort to out-do the other while at the same time stay in touch with the standards of the top English and European teams.

The roots of Celtic, who play at Celtic Park in the eastern district of Parkhead (℡0141/551 8653), lie in the city's immigrant Irish and **Catholic** population, while Rangers, based at Ibrox Park in Govan on the Southside (℡0870/600 1993), have traditionally drawn support from local **Protestants**. As a result, sporting rivalries have been enmeshed in a sectarian divide which many argue would not have remained so long, nor so deep, had it been divorced from the footballing scene: although Catholics do play for Rangers, and Protestants for Celtic, sections of supporters of both clubs seem intent on perpetuating the feud. While large-scale violence on the terraces and streets has not been seen for some time – thanks in large measure to canny policing – Old Firm matches often seethe with bitter passions, and sectarian-related assaults do still occur in parts of the city.

However, there is a less intense side to the game, found not just in the fun-loving "Tartan Army" which follows the (often rollercoaster) fortunes of the Scottish national team, but also in Glasgow's smaller clubs, who actively distance themselves from the distasteful aspects of the Old Firm and plod along with homegrown talent in the lower reaches of the Scottish league. **Queen's Park**, residents of Hampden (℡0141/632 1275), **St Mirren**, the Paisley team (℡0141/889 2558), and the much-maligned **Partick Thistle**, who play at Firhill Stadium in the West End (℡0141/579 1971), offer the best chances of experiencing the more down-to-earth side of Glaswegian football – mixed with all-important reminders that it is, in the end, only a game.

and terraces. Home of Queen's Park Football Club, the fact that it's the venue for Scotland's international fixtures and major cup finals makes it a place of pilgrimage for the country's football fans. Regular **guided tours** (daily 10.30am–3.30pm; £2.50; ⊛www.hampdenpark.co.uk) offer the chance to see inside the stadium itself. Also here is the engaging **Scottish Football Museum** (Mon–Sat 10am–5pm, Sun 11am–5pm; £5), with extensive collections of memorabilia, video clips and displays covering almost every aspect of the game.

The Burrell Collection

Located in Pollok Park some six miles southwest of the city centre, the outstanding **Burrell Collection** (Mon–Thurs & Sat 10am–5pm, Fri & Sun 11am–5pm; free), the lifetime collection of shipping magnate Sir William Burrell (1861–1958), is, for some, the principal reason for visiting Glasgow. Unlike many other art collectors, Sir William's only real criterion for buying a piece was whether he liked it or not, enabling him to buy many "unfashionable" works, which cost comparatively little but subsequently proved their worth. He wanted to leave his collection of art, sculpture and antiquities for public display, but stipulated in 1943 that they should be housed "in a rural setting far removed from the atmospheric pollution of urban conurbations, not less than sixteen miles from the Royal Exchange". For decades, these conditions proved too difficult to meet, with few open spaces available and a pall of industrial smoke ruling out any city site. However, by the late 1960s, after the nationwide Clean Air Act had reduced pollution, and the vast land of **Pollok Park**, previously privately owned, had been donated to the city, plans began for a new, purpose-built gallery, which finally opened in 1983. Today the simplicity and clean lines of the Burrell building are its greatest assets, with large picture windows giving sweeping views over woodland and serving as a tranquil backdrop to the objects inside.

The courtyard

On entering the building, head past the information desk and shop to an airy covered **courtyard** where the most striking piece, by virtue of sheer size, is the **Warwick Vase**, a huge bowl containing fragments of a second-century AD vase from Emperor Hadrian's villa in Tivoli. Next to it are a series of sinewy and naturalistic bronze casts of **Rodin sculptures**, among them *The Age of Bronze*, *A Call to Arms* and the famous *Thinker*. On three sides of the courtyard, a trio of dark and sombre panelled rooms have been re-erected in faithful detail from the Burrells' Hutton Castle home, their heavy tapestries, antique furniture and fireplaces displaying the same eclectic taste as the rest of the museum.

The ground floor

From the courtyard, go through the massive sandstone portal and door from Hornby Castle to the start of the **Ancient Civilizations** collection which includes an exquisite mosaic Roman cockerel from the first century BC and a 4000-year-old Mesopotamian lion's head. Nearby, also illuminated by enormous windows, the **Oriental Art** collection forms nearly one-quarter of the whole display, ranging from Neolithic jades through bronze vessels and Tang funerary horses to cloisonné. The earliest piece, from around the second century BC, is a loveable earthenware watchdog from the Han Dynasty, but most dominant is the serene fifteenth-century *Lohan* (disciple of Buddha), who sits cross-legged and contemplative up against the window and the trees of Pollok Park.

Burrell considered his **Medieval and Post-Medieval European Art**, which encompasses silverware, glass, textiles and sculpture, to be the most valuable part of his collection. Ranged across a maze of small galleries, the most impressive sections are the sympathetically lit stained glass and the numerous tapestries, among them the riotous fifteenth-century *Peasants Hunting Rabbits with Ferrets*. Nearby is a selection from Burrell's vast art collection, the highlight of which is one of Rembrandt's evocative early self-portraits.

The mezzanine

Upstairs, the cramped and comparatively gloomy **mezzanine** is probably the least satisfactory section of the gallery, not the best setting for its sparkling array of paintings. The selection incongruously leaps from a small gathering of fifteenth-century religious works to Géricault's darkly dynamic *Prancing Grey Horse* and Degas's thoughtful and perceptive *Portrait of Émile Duranty*. Pissarro, Manet and Boudin are also represented, along with some exquisite watercolours by Glasgow Boy Joseph Crawhall, revealing his accurate and tender observations of the animal world.

Pollok House

Within Pollok Park, a quarter of a mile down rutted tracks west of the Burrell Collection, lies the lovely eighteenth-century **Pollok House** (daily 10am–5pm; NTS; April–Oct £4, rest of year free; café and gardens free year-round), the manor of the Pollok Park estate and once home of the Maxwell family. Designed by William Adam in the mid-1700s, the house is typical of its age: graciously light and sturdily built, looking out onto the pristine raked and parterre gardens.

The house recently came under the management of the National Trust for Scotland, which has made a deliberate effort to return the house to the layout and style it would have enjoyed in the 1920s and 1930s. As a result, the **paintings** range from the Spanish masterpieces in the Morning Room and some splendid Dutch hunting scenes in the Dining Room to the family's worthy but noticeably amateur efforts which line the upstairs corridors. The servants' quarters downstairs do manage to capture the imagination – a virtually untouched labyrinth of tiled Victorian parlours and corridors that includes a good tearoom in the old kitchen. Free tours of the house are available from the front desk, or you can wander around at your own pace.

Holmwood House

Four miles south of the city centre in the suburb of Cathcart, the finest domestic design by rediscovered Glasgow architect Alexander "Greek" Thomson, **Holmwood House** (April–Oct daily 1.30–5.30pm; NTS; £3.50), has recently been restored and opened to the public. A commission by James Couper, co-owner of a paper mill on the nearby River Carth, the house shows off Thomson's bold Classical concepts, with exterior pillars on two levels and a raised main door, as well as his detailed and highly imaginative interiors. The restoration is ongoing, as you'll see from the patches of exquisite stencilling revealed beneath the wallpaper, and the fact that the rooms are unfurnished. One room upstairs is given over to a series of displays about Thomson and the history of the house. Also on the upper floor is the **drawing room** – look for the white marble fireplace and the night-time star decorations on the ceiling, which contrast with a black marble fireplace and sunburst decorations in the room immediately underneath on the downstairs level, the **parlour**, which also boasts a delightful round bay window.

Eating

The huge growth in restaurants, bars and cafés in Glasgow over recent years shows little sign of abating. **Eating** options are fairly diverse: the city's restaurants offer everything from tapas to sushi, dim sum to every variety of dansak at the city's renowned Indian restaurants. Contemporary Scottish cuisine – fresh local produce prepared under French and other international influences – has seen a boom in recent years.

Worth knowing about if you're watching the pennies is the restaurant-booking website ⓦ www.5pm.co.uk, which every day receives a significant number of good-quality restaurants around Glasgow posting special good-value dining deals (sometimes with restrictions, for example that a table should be clear for a certain time).

Cafés, diners and café-bars

City centre

Café Gandolfi 64 Albion St ☎0141/552 6813. This bona fide landmark (now also with a branch in Buchanan Street's Habitat shop) was one of the first to test the waters in the Merchant City.

Designed with distinctive wooden furniture that creator Tim Stead once called "sculpture in disguise," it serves up healthy and hearty portions of soup, salad, fish dishes, and more. Only drawback is the queue. Moderate.

Gallery of Modern Art rooftop café Queen St. Serving light meals during lunch hours (with cakes and coffee at other times), this café is worth a visit for Adrian Wiszniewski's massive mural and, of course, the views. Open Mon–Sat 10am–4.30pm, Sun 11am–4.30pm. Inexpensive.

Tron Theatre Chisholm St off the Trongate. Another arty hangout (see p.1029), this time for writers and theatrical types in either the modern designed street-side pub/café or a more traditional Victorian bar. One all-day menu serves both spaces with pre-theatre specials most evenings. Mon–Sat noon–10pm, Sun 10.30am–4pm. Moderate.

Grassroots Café 93 St Georges Rd. Although the competition is not particularly stiff, this is the best vegetarian outlet in the city. Fresh, creative cooking and a relaxed atmosphere. Inexpensive.

Where the Monkey Sleeps 182 West Regent St. Staffed by cordial art graduates who acquired their barista skills while still in school, and carrying an unstudied hipness. While food is limited to soups and sandwiches, the espresso is supreme and the space doubles as a gallery. Mon–Sat 8am–11pm, Sun 10am–11pm. Inexpensive.

Willow Tea Rooms 217 Sauchiehall St. Refined elevenses, lunches and afternoon tea amid the splendour of the Mackintosh-designed building and interiors. A similarly themed branch at 97 Buchanan Street is less authentic but less frenetic. Moderate.

West End

Air Organic 36 Kelvingrove St ☎0141/564 5200. This hip bistro (and pre-club bar downstairs) has earned design awards, while the menu is dominated by veg and meaty organic offerings cooked with an Asian touch. Excellent for Sunday brunch, and open late on Fri & Sat until 2am. Moderate.

Brel 39–43 Ashton Lane. Popular with students and post-grads, offering a smattering of Belgian food *(moules et frites)* and beers. The rear conservatory which opens on to a grassy knoll is an attractive spot on fine days. Moderate.

Insomnia 38–42 Woodlands Rd. A classic 24/7 café conveniently located about halfway between the city centre and the middle of the West End. Very crowded once the clubs close, it is renowned for its convenience rather than its cuisine. Daily 24hr. Inexpensive.

Tchai Ovna 42 Otago Lane. With live acoustic gigs and pre-club nights, this largely alcohol-free zone with lovely cakes and an array of sixty teas is a bohemian favourite. Inexpensive.

Tinderbox 189 Byres Rd. A style café which aspires – with an array of espresso-based drinks and its designer looks – to lure people who might ordinarily fancy a pint at the pub. Even in trendy Glasgow, it is amazingly successful. Inexpensive.

University Café 87 Byres Rd. A 70-year-old institution dearly loved by generations of students and West End residents. Formica tables in snug booths, glass counters and other original features, where the favourites are fish'n'chips or mince'n'tatties rounded off with an ice-cream cone. Inexpensive.

Southside

The Granary 10–16 Kilmarnock Rd ☎0141/632 8487. At Shawlands Cross, in the commercial heart of the Southside, this bar with a bistro-style dining room to the rear serves an international selection of food and rich satisfying desserts. Moderate.

1901 1534 Pollokshaws Rd. Formerly the *Stoat & Ferret*, this bistro/pub near Pollok Country Park is a lesser-known gem serving a basic French-Mediterranean menu. There's often live jazz on a Sunday afternoon. Moderate.

Restaurants

City centre restaurants

El Sabor Merchant Sq, Bell St ☎0141/552 3400. Casual split-level Spanish cantina with a frequently changing tapas menu as well as mains such as chicken rellenos. Moderate.

Esca 27 Chisholm St ☎0141/553 0880. Italian place across from the Tron Theatre, a relative newcomer that is casual and brightly designed, with a light touch in the kitchen. Moderate.

Fratelli Sarti 133 Wellington St or 121 Bath St. This Italian café/deli/restaurant all under one roof is both authentic and popular. The more formal dining space is off Bath Street, but the same selection of pizzas, pastas and daily specials is also available in the atmospheric café. Open from 8am Mon–Sat, and noon on Sun. Moderate.

Gamba 225a West George St ☎0141/572 0899. A stylish modern basement restaurant that acknowledges the Mediterranean both in decor and seafood menu, and has been known to impress hard-to-please visitors from London. Closed Sun. Expensive.

Groucho St Judes 190 Bath St ☎0141/352 8800. Part of booming Bath St, the ground floor restaurant is a hip, comfortable place for filling meals of a mostly Scottish nature, whether Aberdeen Angus steaks or mussels. Meanwhile the basement bar is a real scene spot. Moderate or Expensive.

Ichiban Japanese Noodle Café 50 Queen St. Japanese-style setting, with long benches you share with fellow diners. Bowls of noodles and sushi selections are the staples here; service is friendly and efficient. Completely non-smoking. Inexpensive.

Kama Sutra 331 Sauchiehall St ☎0141/332 0055. Deep velvet curtains and wrought-iron decoration highlight the unusual design, while a wide-ranging menu which includes dishes from the Northeast frontier make this a favourite central curry house. Daytime buffet is a popular bargain. Open Sun–Thurs until midnight, Fri & Sat until 1am. Moderate.

Le Bouchon 17 King St ☎0141/552 7411. Fairly traditional French cooking in a basic brasserie setting, with excellent pre-theatre offers. Closed Sun. Moderate.

Le Chardon d'Or 176 West Regent St ☎0141/248 3801. Backed by the Roux brothers and featuring the Scottish-born head chef from their *Le Gavroche* restaurant in London, this recently opened French restaurant has Michelin star potential. Closed Sun. Expensive.

Mao 84 Brunswick St. Bright, fully glazed corner café-bar in the Merchant City offering a range of Asian cuisine, with spicy Korean and Indonesian specialities of particular note, and a pre-club feel at the weekend. Moderate.

Mitchell's 157 North St ☎0141/204 4312. Next to the domed Mitchell's Library, this is a comfortable brasserie without airs. The menu is fairly meaty and moderately priced. Good beer and an excellent refuge. Mon–Thurs noon–2.30pm & 5–10pm, Fri noon–2.30pm & 5–11pm, Sat 5–11pm.

Mussel Inn 157 Hope St ☎0141/572 1405. Like its Edinburgh flagship, this branch concentrates on simply prepared pots of fresh mussels and grilled scallops in casual environs. Mon–Sat noon–10pm, Sun 1.30–6pm. Moderate.

Oko 68 Ingram St ☎0141/572 1500. Locally owned restaurant bringing freshly prepared sushi on colour-coded plates and the conveyor belt thing to the stylish Merchant City. Closed Sun. Moderate.

Pattaya 437 Sauchiehall St. In order to cater to post-clubbing crowds, this basic and satisfying Thai restaurant has decided to stop serving lunches and instead stay open into the wee small hours. Daily 5pm–5am. Moderate.

Rogano 11 Exchange Place ☎0141/248 4055. A shockingly expensive fish restaurant decked out as an art-deco replica of the *Queen Mary* that has long been a Glasgow institution. *Café Rogano*, in the basement, is cheaper. Restaurant: daily noon–2.30pm & 6.30–10.30pm. Café: daily noon–11pm, Fri & Sat until midnight. Expensive.

Wee Curry Shop 7 Buccleuch St. Tiny Indian café near the Glasgow Film Theatre, serving home-made, inexpensive meals to compete with the best in town. BYOB and marvel. Closed Sun. Inexpensive.

West End restaurants

Amaryllis At "Number 1 Devonshire Gardens", corner of Great Western and Hyndland roads ☎0141/337 3434. Gordon Ramsay, the Glaswegian celebrity chef who made it big in London, opened this long-awaited and critically acclaimed French restaurant in spring 2001. It's less pricey than you'd expect, though the main man still spends most of his time down south. Closed Sun evening. Expensive.

Ashoka Ashton Lane 19 Ashton Lane ☎0141/337 1115. Lively curry house in the Harlequin chain, which dominates the Indian restaurant community throughout the west of Scotland; all have consistent quality and this branch is particularly popular with students. There are other Ashoka restaurants at 1284 Argyle St, and on the Southside at 268 Clarkston Rd. Mon–Sat noon–midnight, Sun 5pm–midnight. Moderate.

Café Antipasti 337 Byres Rd ☎0141/337 2737. A busy Italian bistro near the Botanic Gardens serving tasty and well-priced pastas and salads. No bookings are taken, so anticipate a queue on busy nights. Second branch in town on Sauchiehall Street. Inexpensive.

Chow 98 Byres Rd. Proof that Chinese restaurants can be modern and not crammed with Oriental kitsch. This bijou diner with extra tables upstairs offers excellent value-for-money meals. No smoking. Moderate.

Fusion Sushi Bar 41 Byres Rd ☎0141/339 3666. Funky sushi bar with rolls and sashimi at various prices as well as yakitori, teriyaki, katsu and the like. No smoking. Moderate.

Mother India 28 Westminster Terrace, off Sauchiehall St ☎0141/221 1663. By near-unanimous consent, this is the best Indian restaurant in Glasgow. Excellent authentic home-cooking with some original Goanese specials as well as the old favourites at affordable prices in refreshingly laid-back surroundings. BYOB; small corkage fee. Moderate.

Nairn's 13 Woodside Crescent ☎0141/353 0707. Showcase restaurant for Scotland's celebrity chef Nick Nairn, on the garden level of a lovely Georgian town house. Fresh, specially sourced ingredients go into artfully presented dishes. Closed Sun & Mon. Expensive.

No. Sixteen 16 Byres Rd ☎0141/339 2544.
Undoubtedly the best under-£15 meal in Glasgow,
in a tiny, family-run neighbourhood bistro that is a
rising star. Booking essential. Closed Sun. Moderate.
Salsa 184 Dumbarton Rd ☎0141/337 1416. A
smaller version of sister restaurant *Cantina Del
Rey* in the Merchant City, this West End branch
serves similar, basic Mexican-style favourites,
whether burritos or fajitas, in a colourful and laid-
back atmosphere. Moderate.
Stravaigin 28–30 Gibson St ☎0141/334 2665.
Local meats and fish are given an international
make-over using a host of unexpected ingredients.
Adventurous fine-dining selections and an excep-
tional-value bar menu, too. Basement restaurant
open until 10.30pm, bar until 11pm Sun–Thurs,
midnight Fri & Sat. Moderate upstairs, expensive
downstairs.
The Ubiquitous Chip 12 Ashton Lane
☎0141/334 5007. Opened in 1971, *The Chip*, as
it's affectionately known, led the way in Glasgow
in headlining Scotland's quality fresh produce at
the heart of its contemporary, upmarket dining
experience. Some say it's living on its well-

deserved reputation, but it's still up there. Less
expensive options upstairs. Expensive.

Southside restaurants

Arigo 67 Kilmarnock Rd ☎0141/636 6616. Some
claim this is the best Italian restaurant in the city.
Lamb and veal dishes are noteworthy, with everything made fresh to order. Moderate.
Art Lovers' Café In House for an Art Lover,
Bellahouston Park, 10 Dumbreck Rd ☎0141/353
4779. This show-case Rennie Mackintosh house
(see p.1021) offers sublime lunches with views of
the garden. Moderate.
The Cook's Room 205 Fenwick Rd, Giffnock
☎0141/621 1903. Chef/owner Tom Battersby has
earned an admirable reputation, and his restaurant
with its rustic furniture and friendly service merits
a special trip for dinner or a weekend brunch.
Moderate.
Greek Golden Kebab 34 Sinclair Drive
☎0141/649 7581. The longest-running Greek
restaurant in Glasgow hasn't changed its rustic
cooking in probably thirty years. Worth seeking
out. Thurs–Sun 5pm–1am. Moderate.

Drinking

If you tire of the trendier pre-club bars in the **city centre** and its buzzing
Merchant City, set out for the **East End** or the **Saltmarket** district near the
Clyde, where the local spit-and-sawdust establishments offer a welcome
change. The liveliest area is the **West End**, with students mixing with fun-
seeking locals around Byres Road. Decent pubs are more widely scattered in
the **Southside**, but you'll find a handful of pleasant spots, ranging from stylish
hangouts to historic locals.

As for **opening hours**, Glasgow's pubs and bars often keep serving until
midnight; some do close at 11pm during the week, but then again in certain
areas you'll find pubs open at the weekend until 1am. After closing-time, your
only option is to head to a nightclub (see below), some of which don't close
until 5am.

City centre pubs and bars

The Arches 253 Argyle St. This contemporary arts
centre under Central station made its new bar one
of the focal points in a recent interior redesign.
Good happy-hour bargains; arty clientele.
Babbity Bowster 16–18 Blackfriars St, off the
High Street. Lively place with a natural Scottish
feel – and thankfully without any kitsch. Good
place to hear spontaneous folk sessions. Excellent
beer and good basic food all day and night, with
pricier restaurant upstairs.
Bar 91 91 Candleriggs. Merchant City-style bar
that tends to be friendlier and less pretentious

than some others.
Bargo 80 Albion St. Design-award winner with a
spacious wood and stainless-steel interior that
opens onto the pavement. Popular with students
who appreciate the scene and the cheap eats.
Corinthian 191 Ingram St. A remarkable renovation of an old bank, with some over-the-top
Italianate architecture dating to early Victoriana.
Three distinct bars, one restaurant and a private
club: dress smartly.
Horseshoe Bar 17 Drury St. A must for visiting
real-pub aficionados. Traditional 'Gin Palace pub',
with the longest continuous bar in the UK, this is
reputedly Glasgow's busiest drinking hole, with a

mixed clientele, including recent rock darlings Travis; karaoke upstairs for aspiring Fran Healys.

Mitre Bar 12–16 Brunswick St. Tucked away up a lane between Wilson Street and the Trongate, this tiny unpretentious traditional retreat festooned with football banners sells decent beer to a mixed bunch of locals.

Republic Bier Halle 9 Gordon St. Intense modern industrial design using shuttered concrete and caissons of stone with chunky seating. Serves 130 different beers and hearty Eastern European grub from sausages to goulash.

Variety Bar 401 Sauchiehall St. Crowded with faded faux Art Nouveau details and frequented by nearby Glasgow Art School students, here for the eclectic array of different DJs every night.

East End and Saltmarket pubs and bars

Clutha Vaults 167 Stockwell St. Slightly more scrubbed and less atmospheric than the *Scotia* (see below) but host to a similar line-up of free live music.

Saracen Head 209 Gallowgate, opposite the Barras market and near the Barrowland ballroom. The *Sarry Heid* is notorious for its rough-edged atmosphere and its historic relics displayed in glass cabinets. The mildly mental atmosphere is pure Glasgow. Look out for the tax demand from Robbie Burns up on the wall, dating from the days when he was the local tax collector. Often open weekends only.

Scotia Bar 112 Stockwell St. Management says this is the oldest pub in the city – not convincingly proven, but it looks the part, with low, exposed timber ceilings. Still the place for live blues, folk and skiffle sessions; Billy Connolly began his career here, telling jokes in between singing folk songs.

West End pubs and bars

Attic 44–46 Ashton Lane. Proof that New York doesn't have a monopoly on creative loft conversions, this bar above the *Cul-de-Sac* restaurant is the smart place to drink on busy Ashton Lane.

Firebird 1321 Argyle St. Fully glazed, airy drinking spot near the Kelvingrove Art Gallery, with a wood-stoked pizza oven producing some tasty snacks plus DJs to keep the pre-clubbing crowd entertained.

Lismore Lounge 206 Dumbarton Rd. One-time working man's pub, tastefully redecorated with specially commissioned stained-glass panels depicting the Highland Clearances, this friendly bar is a meeting point for the local Gaels, who come here to chat, relax and listen to the impromptu music sessions.

Living Room 5–9 Byres Rd. Hotbed for the young and hip, at the southern end of Byres Road. Wrought iron and candles enhance the pre-club atmosphere.

Tennent's 191 Byres Rd. No-nonsense, beery pub that offers a refreshing antidote to designer-driven bars nearby. Large and popular, with real ale and a no-music policy.

Uisge Beatha 232 Woodlands Rd. Unexceptional white frontage belies the eclectic interior, with lots of sofas and ironic Scots kitsch. Barmen wear kilts and keep the atmosphere lively. The name is Gaelic for "the water of life" – that is, whisky.

Southside pubs and bars

Cul de Sac Southside 1179 Pollokshaws Rd. Relaxing if fashionable spot; the only calculated style bar on the Southside, with the *Attic* upstairs serving food.

Heraghty's Free House 708 Pollokshaws Rd. Authentic Irish pub on the corner of Pollokshaws and Nithsdale roads which prides itself on pouring the perfect pint of Guinness. Still living down its history of not having a women's loo: one's been installed for several years now.

The Taverna 778 Pollokshaws Rd. A favourite for many who stay in this neck of the Southside; fully glazed corner location with potted palms and selection of real ales.

Nightlife and entertainment

Glasgow's **clubbing scene** is highly rated, with the city attracting top DJs from around the world and also breeding a good deal of local talent. Opening hours hover between 11pm to 3am, though some stay open until 5am. Cover charges are variable: expect to pay around £4 during the week and up to £15 at the weekend. Drinks are usually about thirty percent more expensive than in the pubs.

Glasgow is home to Scottish Opera, Scottish Ballet and the Royal Scottish National Orchestra, and the city's cultural programme offers a breadth of **music** (from hip contemporary to heavyweight classical), plus **dance**, **theatre**,

film and performance art. For detailed **listings**, pick up the comprehensive fortnightly magazine *The List* (£1.95), which also covers Edinburgh, or consult Glasgow's *Herald* or *Evening Times* newspapers. To book **tickets** for theatre productions or big concerts, call at the Ticket Centre, City Hall, Candleriggs (Mon–Sat 10.30am–6.30pm, Sun noon–5pm), or call Ticket Link on ☎0141/287 5511.

Clubs

Archaos 25 Queen St ☎0141/204 3189. Massive, multi-level place with designer decor and a mainstream music policy.

The Arches 30 Midland St, off Jamaica St ☎0141/221 4001. In converted railway arches under Central station, the club portion of this arts venue offers an eclectic array of music: hard house, trance, techno and funk.

Fury Murray's 96 Maxwell St, behind the St Enoch Centre ☎0141/221 6511. Student-oriented and lively, with music spanning the 1960s to recent indie and chart favourites.

The Tunnel 84 Mitchell St ☎0141/204 1000. Pre-eminent contemporary and progressive house music club with arty decor (dig the gents' cascading waterfall walls) and fairly strict dress codes.

The Velvet Rooms 520 Sauchiehall St ☎0141/332 0755. Consists of a small bar with postage-stamp dance area for mainstream dance, garage and soul.

Gay clubs and bars

Gay and Lesbian Centre 11 Dixon St ☎0141/221 7203. Licensed café in addition to more institutional support such as information and reading rooms.

Polo Lounge 84 Wilson St, off Glassford Street ☎0141/553 1221. The original decor – marble tiles and open fires – and gentleman's club atmosphere upstairs combine with the dark, pounding nightclubs underneath which attract a gay and gay-friendly crowd.

Revolver 6a John St ☎0141/553 2456. Recently opened gay bar geared more towards the art of conversation than dance, with a popular Sunday chill-out.

Live music venues

Barrowland 244 Gallowgate ☎0141/552 4601. Legendary East End ballroom that hosts some of the liveliest, sweatiest and best gigs you may ever encounter. With room for a couple of thousand, it mostly books bands securely on the rise but still hosts some big-time acts who return to it as their favourite venue in Scotland.

King Tut's Wah Wah Hut 272a St Vincent St ☎0141/221 5279. Famous as the place where

Oasis were discovered, and still presenting one of the city's best live music programmes. Also has a good downstairs bar, with an excellent jukebox should you want to sit out the gig.

Scotia Bar 112 Stockwell St ☎0141/552 8681. The folkies' favourite, a mellow musical pub with regular live gigs and jam sessions. Free.

The 13th Note 50–60 King St ☎0141/553 1638. The basement of this relaxed bar and vegetarian restaurant is the place to sample local and cutting-edge musical talent, including jazz and R&B; the club of the same name at 260 Clyde St is a bit louder and livelier.

Theatres and comedy venues

Arches Theatre 253 Argyle St ☎0901/022 0300. Andy Arnold runs the *Arches* theatre company, reviving old classics and introducing new talent in this recently refurbished, hip venue.

Citizens' Theatre 119 Gorbals St ☎0141/429 0022. The "Citz" has evolved from its 1960s working-class roots into one of the most respected contemporary theatres in Britain. Three stages, concession rates for students and free preview nights.

Cottier Theatre 935 Hyndland St ☎0141/357 3868. This performance space in the old Dowanhill church hosts touring shows, dance and music gigs. An adjoining bar with beer garden is a favourite on dry summer evenings.

The Stand 333 Woodlands Rd ☎0870/600 6055. Recent addition and sister to the first-rate comedy club in Edinburgh, booking national and international acts.

Tron Theatre 63 Trongate ☎0141/552 4267. Varied repertoire of mainstream and more challenging productions from itinerant companies, such as Glasgow's *Vanishing Point*.

Concert halls

Glasgow Royal Concert Hall 2 Sauchiehall St ☎0141/287 5511. Chunky modern monstrosity that is the venue for big-name touring orchestras and the home to the Royal Scottish National Orchestra, as well as booking some big-name rock and soul stars and middle-of-the-road music hall acts.

Scottish Exhibition and Conference Centre, and Clyde Auditorium Finnieston Quay ☎0870/040 4000. The SECC is a gigantic airplane hangar-like space with dreadful acoustics that, unfortunately, is the only indoor venue in Scotland for world-touring megastars from Tom Jones to Eminem. The adjacent Clyde Auditorium – better known as the Armadillo – is smaller but more melodic.

Theatre Royal 282 Hope St ☎0141/332 9000. This late nineteenth-century theatre was revived in the mid-1970s as the opulent home of Scottish Opera, and plays regular host to visiting orchestras, opera and theatre groups, including the Royal Shakespeare Company.

Cinemas

Glasgow Film Theatre 12 Rose St ☎0141/332 8128. Dedicated art, independent and repertory cinema house. Its inhouse *Café Cosmo* is an excellent place for pre-show drinks.

Grosvenor Ashton Lane ☎0141/339 4298. Eclectic mix of mainstream and art-house movies on two screens in this eighty-year-old cinema, which has plans to open a restaurant and bar. Occasional theme nights and frequent late shows for local students.

Odeon City Centre 56 Renfield St ☎0141/332 3413. Multiscreen cinema with the latest releases.

Odeon at the Quay Paisley Road ☎0141/418 0111. Another multiplex, just over the river on the Southside.

Listings

Bike rental Only a few bike shops rent out bikes. Dales, 150 Dobbies Loan ☎0141/332 2705, a block north of the Buchanan Street bus station, has a few bikes available. There's a better selection at West End Cycles, 16 Chancellor St ☎0141/357 1344, conveniently placed close to the start of the Glasgow to Loch Lomond route, one of a number of special cycle routes which radiate out from the city. For further details, check ⓦ www.sustrans.co.uk.

Books Borders, 98 Buchanan St; Waterstone's, 153 Sauchiehall St. For second-hand: Caledonian Bookshop, 483 Great Western Rd, or Voltaire & Rousseau, 12–14 Otago Lane.

Car rental Arnold Clark, Castlebank St ☎0141/339 9886; Avis, 161 North St ☎0141/221 2827; Budget, 101 Waterloo St ☎0141/221 9241; Europcar, 38 Anderston Quay ☎0141/248 8788. Car-rental firms at the airport include Budget ☎0141/889 1479, Europcar ☎0141/887 0414 and Hertz ☎0141/887 2451.

Dentist National Health Service line ☎0800/224488 lists local and emergency dentists. Glasgow Dental Hospital, 378 Sauchiehall St (☎0141/211 9600).

Hospital 24hr casualty department at the Royal Infirmary, 84 Castle St ☎0141/211 4000.

Internet EasyEverything is open 24hr at 57–61 St Vincent St. Internet Exchange is at 136 Sauchiehall St.

Laundry Harvey's, 161 Great Western Rd; Laundromat, 39 Bank St; Majestic Laundrette, 1110 Argyle St.

Police Strathclyde Police HQ, Pitt Street ☎0141/532 2000; Stewart Street station, Cowcaddens ☎0141/532 3000.

Post office General information ☎0845/722 3344. Main office at 47 St Vincent St (Mon–Fri 8.30am–5.45pm, Sat 9am–5.30pm); other city centre offices at 87–91 Bothwell St and 228 Hope St.

Taxis TOA ☎0141/429 7070.

The Clyde

The **River Clyde** is the dominant physical feature of Glasgow and its environs, the largest urban concentration in Scotland, with almost two million people living in the city and satellite towns. Little of this immediate hinterland can be described as beautiful, with crisscrossing motorways and relentlessly grim housing estates dominating much of the landscape. However, there are pockets of interest, many related to the river itself or the industries which grew up from it.

West of the city is **Paisley**, where the distinctive cloth pattern gained its name, and the former shipbuilding towns of **Port Glasgow**, **Greenock** and **Gourock**. On the north bank of the Firth of Clyde the ancient Strathclyde capital of **Dumbarton**, and **Helensburgh**, birthplace of architect Charles Rennie Mackintosh and television pioneer John Logie Baird.

Heading southeast out of Glasgow, the industrial landscape of the **Clyde Valley** eventually gives way to a far more attractive scenery of gorges and towering castles. Here lie the stoic town of **Lanark**, where eighteenth-century philanthropists built their model workers' community around the mills of **New Lanark**, and the spectacular **Falls of Clyde**, a mile upstream. Even further beyond, deep into the rolling countryside of South Lanarkshire where the Clyde is little more than a widening stream, the market town of **Biggar** with its unusual clutch of museums serves as a useful orientation point to the hill farming country of the Scottish Borders beyond.

The Firth of Clyde – south bank

The swift journey from Glasgow along the M8, coupled with the proximity of the international airport, can belie the fact that **Paisley** is not a suburb of Glasgow but a town in its own right, with a long and distinctive history, particularly in the textile trade. Further west, as the estuary widens, the former shipbuilding centres of Port Glasgow and **Greenock** crowd the river bank, followed by the old-fashioned seaside resort of **Gourock**, and eventually **Wemyss Bay**, jumping-off point for the ferry to Rothesay on Bute.

Paisley

Founded in the twelfth century as a monastic settlement around an abbey, **PAISLEY** expanded rapidly after the eighteenth century as a linen manufacturing town, specializing in the production of highly fashionable imitation Kashmiri shawls. Paisley quickly eclipsed other British centres producing the cloth, eventually lending its name to the swirling pine-cone design.

South of the train station, the **Abbey** (Mon–Sat 10am–3.30pm; free) was built on the site of the town's original settlement and was massively overhauled in the Victorian age. The unattractive, fat grey facade of the church does little justice to the renovated interior, which is tall, spacious and elaborately decorated; the elongated choir, rebuilt extensively throughout the last two centuries, is illuminated by jewel-coloured stained glass from a variety of ages and styles. Along Paisley's bland pedestrianised **High Street**, the town's **Museum and Art Gallery** (Tues–Sat 10am–5pm, Sun 2–5pm; free) shelters behind pompous Ionic columns that face the grim buildings of Paisley University. The main reason for coming here is to see the Shawl Gallery, which deals with the growth and development of the Paisley pattern and shawls, showing the familiar pine- cone (or teardrop) pattern from its simplistic beginnings to elaborate later incarnations. Leading on from this is the largest gallery, mixing local social history with blown-up photos of locals (or "buddies", as inhabitants of Paisley like to be known) selecting their favourite exhibits in the museum. The Upper Gallery houses a small art collection including works by Glasgow Boys Hornel, Guthrie and Lavery (see p.1016), as well as one or two paintings by local boy John Byrne, artist and playwright best known for his plays *The Slab Boys* and *Tutti Frutti*.

Regular **trains** from Glasgow Central connect with Paisley's Gilmour Street station in the centre of town, and they're a faster, more convenient option than **buses** #9, #36 or #38 from Glasgow city centre. Buses leave Paisley's Gilmour Street forecourt every ten minutes for Glasgow International Airport, two miles north of the town. The **tourist office** is right in the centre at 9a Gilmour Street (June–Sept Mon–Sat 9.30am–5.30pm, Sun noon–5pm; Oct–May Mon–Fri 9am–1pm & 2–5pm; ☎0141/889 0711). Decent lunchtime and early-evening bar **meals** can be had at the stylish *Bar Bossa*, 40 New St, while nearby the Paisley Arts Centre has a small bar with seating outside. Most of the pubs in the centre, including the *Last Post* pub in the old Post Office building in County Square, serves a range of bar meals. *Aroma Room* is a more modern spot right opposite the Museum and Art Gallery, which serves coffees, snacks and lunches.

Greenock and around

GREENOCK, west of Glasgow, was the site of the first dock on the Clyde, founded in 1711, and the community has grown on the back of shipping ever since. Despite its ranks of anonymous tower blocks and sterile shopping centres, the town still retains a few features of interest. From the Central train station in Greenock (also served by hourly Citylink buses from Glasgow's Buchanan Street station), it's a short walk down the hill to **Cathcart Square**, where an exuberant 245-foot Victorian tower looms high over the elegant Council House. A small council-run local **information** service operates from the building opposite the Council House, which houses the central library (Mon–Fri 8.45am–4.45pm, Fri 8.45am–4pm, Sat 9.30am–12.30pm; ☎01475/ 712555). On the dockside, reached by crossing the dual carriageway behind the square, the Neoclassical **Custom House** has an informative **museum** (Mon–Fri 10am–4pm; free) featuring the work of the Customs and Excise departments, with a display on illicit whisky distilleries and a computer game in which you search a ship for contraband. **Clyde Marine Cruises** (mid-June to Aug; ☎01475/721281, ⓦwww.clydesite.co.uk/cruises) operates from Victoria Harbour, a few minutes from Central station, with daily sailings on a 1938 Clyde-built vessel which take in various Clyde coastal towns, including Dunoon, Rothesay, Tighnabruaich, Tarbert and Lochranza on Arran.

A hundred yards from the well-proportioned George Square, close to Greenock West station, the **McLean Museum and Art Gallery** in Union Street (Mon–Sat 10am–5pm; free) contains pictures and contemporary records of the life and achievements of Greenock-born James Watt, prominent eighteenth-century industrialist and pioneer of steam power. The small art gallery on the ground floor contains work by Glasgow Boys Hornel and Guthrie plus Colourists Fergusson, Cadell and Peploe.

The best place to **eat** is the *Port and Harbour Restaurant* at Custom House Place (☎01475/730370), which serves both a bar menu and finer-dining in a "Dutch brown bar" atmosphere. *Morgan's* brasserie on West Blackhall Street, west of the shopping centre, serves a decent selection of bistro-style food.

Gourock

West of Greenock lies the dowdy old resort of **GOUROCK**, once a holiday destination for generations of Glaswegians, but today only of significance as a **ferry** terminal: both CalMac (enquiries ☎01475/650100, sales ☎0870/565 0000, ⓦwww.calmac.co.uk) and the more frequent Western Ferries (☎01369/704452, ⓦwww.westernferriesclyde.com) ply the 20-minute route across the Firth of Clyde to Dunoon on the Cowal peninsula (see p.1089).

Wemyss Bay

There's not much south of Gourock apart from a gruesome power-station chimney and large yacht marina at **Inverkip**, until you reach **WEMYSS BAY**, the terminus of the southern branch of the train line from Port Glasgow. The most memorable part of the journey is the arrival at the breathtaking Wemyss Bay station, a startling wrought-iron and glass palace which serves as a reminder of the great glory days when thousands of Glaswegians would alight for their steamer trip "doon the watter". Today the only steamer connection is the rather prosaic CalMac **ferry** over to Rothesay, capital of the Isle of Bute (see p.1090).

The Firth of Clyde – north bank

Heading west out of Glasgow, the A82 road and the train tracks both follow the north bank of the river, passing through Clydebank, another ex-shipbuilding centre, and Bowling, the western entry point of the newly re-opened Forth & Clyde canal (see p.1051). At **Dumbarton**, an ancient regional capital, the main road swings north towards Loch Lomond (see p.1055), while the railway and A814 carry on along the shores of the Firth of Clyde to wealthy **Helensburgh**, before themselves turning north along the shores of Gare Loch and Loch Long to Arrochar, which marks the beginning of Argyll (see p.1088).

Dumbarton

Founded in the fifth century, today the town of **DUMBARTON** is a brutal concrete sprawl, fulfilling every last cliché about postwar planning and architecture. Avoid the town itself and head one mile southeast to **Dumbarton Castle** (April–Sept Mon–Sat 9.30am–6.30pm, Sun 2–6.30pm; Oct–March Mon–Wed & Sat 9.30am–4.30pm, Thurs 9.30am–1pm, Sun 2–4.30pm; £2), which sits atop a twin outcrop of volcanic rock overlooking the Clyde. As a natural site, Dumbarton Rock could not be bettered – surrounded by water on three sides and with commanding views. First founded as a Roman fort, the structure was expanded in the fifth century by the Damnonii tribe, and remained Strathclyde's capital until its absorption into the greater kingdom of Scotland in 1034. The castle then became a royal seat, from which Mary, Queen of Scots, sailed for France to marry Henri II's son in 1548, and to which she was attempting to escape when she and her troops were defeated twenty years later at the Battle of Langside. Since the 1600s, the castle has been used as a garrison and artillery fortress to guard the approaches to Glasgow; most of the current buildings date from this period.

Regular **trains** run from Glasgow's Queen Street station to Dumbarton East and Dumbarton Central stations; the former gives best access to the castle and accommodation. The **tourist office** (daily: July & Aug 10am–7pm; June & Sept 10am–6pm; May & Oct 10am–5pm; Nov–April 10am–4pm; ☏01389/742306, ⦿www.visitscottishheartlands.org) is situated a couple of miles east of town on the A82 and mainly caters for the vast number of car-bound tourists on their way to the Highlands.

Helensburgh

HELENSBURGH, twenty miles or so northwest of Glasgow, is a smart, Georgian grid-plan settlement laid out in an imitation of Edinburgh's New

Town and overlooking the Clyde estuary. In the eighteenth century it was a well-to-do commuter town for Glasgow and also a seaside resort, whose bathing-master, **Henry Bell**, invented one of the first steamboats, the *Comet*, to transport Glaswegians "doon the watter". The **tourist office** is on the ground floor of the old Italianate church tower by the Clyde (daily: July & Aug 10am–6pm; June & Sept 10am–5.30pm; April & May 10am–5pm; early Oct 10am–4.30pm; ①01436/672642).

The inventor of TV, John Logie Baird, was born here, as was Charles Rennie Mackintosh, who in 1902 was commissioned by the Glaswegian publisher Walter Blackie to design **Hill House** on Upper Colquhoun Street (April–Oct daily 1.30–5.30pm; NTS; £6). Without doubt the best surviving example of Mackintosh's domestic architecture, the house is stamped with his very personal interpretation of Art Nouveau, right down to the light fittings, characterized by his sparing use of colour and stylized floral patterns. The effect is occasionally overwhelming – it's difficult to imagine actually living in such an environment – yet it is precisely Mackintosh's attention to detail that makes the place so special.

The Clyde valley

The journey southeast of Glasgow into Lanarkshire, while mostly following the course of the Clyde upstream, is dominated by endless suburbs, industrial parks and wide strips of concrete highway. The principal road here is the M74, though you'll have to get off the motorway to find the main points of interest, which tend to lie on or near the banks of the river. Less than ten miles from central Glasgow, **Bothwell Castle** lies about a mile northeast of the **Blantyre** millworkers' tenement in which the explorer David Livingstone was born. Five miles west of Blantyre, on the outskirts of the new town of East Kilbride, the **National Museum of Scottish Country Life**, set on a historic farm, offers a in-depth look at the history of agriculture in Scotland. South of here the Clyde winds through lush market gardens and orchards, before passing beneath the sturdy little town of **Lanark**, probably the best base from which to explore the valley. **New Lanark**, on the riverbank, is a remarkable eighteenth-century planned village. Ten miles further upstream, the country town of **Biggar** is a pleasant spot with a surprising number of rather quirky museums, and marks the transition from the industrial central belt to rolling Border country.

Blantyre and around

BLANTYRE, now a colourless suburb of Hamilton, was a remote hamlet based around a mill on the banks of the Clyde when explorer and missionary David Livingstone was born there in 1813. First Bus's **bus** #263 or #267 from Glasgow (Buchanan Street) to Hamilton runs via Blantyre, or there are frequent **trains** from Glasgow Central's lower-level. From Blantyre station, a right turn brings you through suburban housing to a quiet country park. The separate tenement block near the river, now painted a brilliant white, has been taken over by the **David Livingstone Centre** (April–Oct Mon–Sat 10am–5.30pm, Sun 12.30–5.30pm; Nov–March Mon–Sat 10am–4.30pm, Sun 12.30–4.30pm; NTS; £3), exploring his life, from his boyhood up until his death in 1873 when he was searching for the source of the Nile. In 1813, the block consisted of 24 one-room tenements, each occupied by an entire family of mill workers. Today, the Livingstone family room shows the claustrophobic conditions under which he was brought up; all the others feature slightly defensive exhibitions on the missionary movement, with tableaux of scenes from his life in Africa, including his "discovery" of the Victoria Falls and the famous meeting of November 10, 1871, with Henry Stanley.

A mile or so north of Blantyre, **Bothwell Castle** (April–Sept daily 9.30am– 6.30pm; Oct–March Sat–Wed 9.30am–4.30pm, Thurs 9.30am–12.30pm, Sun 2–4.30pm; HS; £2) is one of Scotland's most dramatic citadels, its great red sandstone bulk looming high above a loop in the river. The oldest section is the solid donjon, or circular tower, at the western end, built by the Moray family in the late thirteenth century to protect themselves against the English king Edward I during the Scottish wars of independence. Despite its jigsaw construction, today the overwhelming impression is of the near-impenetrable strength of the castle, its solid red towers – whose walls stand almost sixteen feet thick in places – holding firm centuries after their construction. First Bus operate **bus** #255 from Glasgow (Buchanan Street) to Hamilton, which will drop you off on the Bothwell Road near the castle entrance. By car, it is best approached from the B7071 Bothwell–Uddingston road.

National Museum of Scottish Country Life

On the edge of **EAST KILBRIDE** new town, five miles west of Blantyre and seven miles southeast of Glasgow centre, the **National Museum of Scottish Country Life** (daily 10am–5pm; NTS; £3) at **Kittochside** incorporates a 170-acre farm and a custom-built, £6-million museum building. The exhibition has three principal sections: the **Land Gallery** is concerned with how Scots have used the land over centuries, and how the landscape has changed as a result; the **People Gallery** looks at the way of life for farmers and their families; and the **Tools Gallery**, occupying the large central hall, displays all kinds of farm equipment from early ploughs to a combine harvester.

What really makes the museum, however, is its contextual setting. A tractor and trailer shuttles visitors the half-mile up to the eighteenth-century **farmhouse** and its steading, still in daily use for hand-milking cows and, in season, threshing grain. You can wander round the farmhouse, furnished much as it would have been in the 1950s, the crucial decade that the farm as a whole is meant to capture, just before traditional methods using horses and hand-tools were replaced by tractors and mechanization. There are **paths** leading from the farmhouse around the surrounding fields, and you're encouraged to wander along these, not just to get a sense of the wider farm, but also to see and experience the farm in use.

Transport isn't straightforward. If you don't have your own vehicle, aim for East Kilbride by **bus** #31 from Glasgow's St Enoch Centre or #205 from Blantyre shopping centre, or **train** from Glasgow Central, and then take a taxi for the final three miles to the museum.

Lanark and New Lanark

The neat little market town of **LANARK** is an old and distinguished burgh, sitting in the purple hills high above the River Clyde, its rooftops and spires visible for miles around. Beyond the **world's oldest bell**, cast in 1130 and visible in the Georgian Church of St Nicholas, there's little to see in town unless you around during the lively **Lanimer** celebrations in early June, one of Scotland's oldest ceremonies of riding the marches or boundaries, which goes back to 1140. Most people head straight on to the village of **NEW LANARK** (Ⓦ www.newlanark.org), a mile below the main town on Braxfield Road, whose importance as a centre of social and industrial innovation has recently been recognized by UNESCO, who included it on their list of World Heritage Sites.

Although New Lanark is served by an hourly **bus** from Lanark train station, it's well worth the steep downhill walk to get there. The first sight of the village, hidden away down in the gorge, is unforgettable: large broken curving walls of honeyed warehouses and tenements, built in Palladian style, are lined up along the turbulent river's edge. The community was founded by David Dale and Richard Arkwright in 1785 to harness the power of the Clyde waterfalls in their cotton-spinning industry, but it was Dale's son-in-law, Robert Owen, who revolutionized the social side of the experiment in 1798, creating a "village of unity". Believing the welfare of the workers to be crucial to industrial success, Owen built adult educational facilities, the world's first day nursery and playground, and schools in which dancing and music were obligatory and there was no punishment or reward.

While you're free to wander around the village, which rather unexpectedly for such a historical site is still partially residential, to get into any of the **exhibitions** (all daily 11am–5pm) you need to buy a passport ticket (£4.75; various discount tickets are available, including an all-in ticket covering admission and the return train and bus trip from Glasgow). Of the three vast old mill buildings open to visitors, one houses the **New Millennium Experience**, where a chair lift whisks visitors through a social history of the village, conveying Robert Owen's vision not just for the idealized life at New Lanark, but also what he predicted for the year 2000. New Lanark village itself is just as fascinating: everything, from the co-operative store to the workers' tenements and workshops, was built in an attempt to prove that industrialism need not be unaesthetic. In the **School for Children** there's a clever cinematic show giving an unsentimental picture of village life through the imaginary perspective of a young mill girl. Situated in the Old Dyeworks, the **Scottish Wildlife Trust Visitor Centre** (April–Sept Mon–Fri 11am–5pm, Sat & Sun 1–5pm; Feb, March & Oct–Dec Sat & Sun 1–5pm; £1) provides information about the history and wildlife of the area. Beyond the visitor centre, a riverside path leads you the mile or so to the major **Falls of the Clyde**, where at the stunning tree-fringed Cora Linn, the river plunges 90ft in three tumultuous stages.

Practicalities

Lanark is the terminus of **trains** from Glasgow Central. The town's **tourist office** (May–Sept Mon–Sat 10am–6pm, Sun noon–5pm; Oct–April Mon–Sat 10am–5pm; ☎01555/661661) is housed in a circular building in the Horsemarket, next to Somerfields supermarket, 100 yards west of the station.

By far the most original **accommodation** options in the area, at both ends of the market, make use of reconstructed mill buildings in New Lanark: the SYHA **hostel** (☎01555/666710, ⓦwww.syha.org.uk) has sixteen four-bed rooms in the cutely named Wee Row on Rosedale Street, while the *New Lanark Mill* (☎01555/6672000, ⓦwww.newlanark.org; ❹) is a four-star **hotel** with good views and lots of character, as well as a brasserie serving some tasty dishes.

Biggar and around

On the journey upstream, you leave industrial Lanarkshire behind and come instead into the gentle undualtions of the Border hills. **BIGGAR**, twelve miles from Lanark, has the sense of being slightly adrift, formally in Lanarkshire but more a Border town, as close to Edinburgh as it is to Glasgow but with no strong connection to either. For a town of its size, Biggar has an inordinate number of museums; none could be described as essential, though each has its own quirky appeal. The most general is the **Moat Park Heritage Centre** (Easter to mid-Oct Mon–Sat 10.30am–5pm, Sun 2–5pm; £2), which occupies a grand neo-Romanesque church near the foot of Kirkstyle (off High Street). Inside, the geological and archeological history of Upper Clydesdale is traced. Tucked in behind the High Street, the **Gladstone Court Museum** (Easter–Oct Mon–Sat 10.30am–5pm, Sun 2–5pm; £2) has a recreated street of Victorian shops, including a telephone exchange, bank and cobbler. Beside Biggar burn lies **Biggar Gasworks Museum** (June–Sept daily 2–5pm; £1), which has the appearance of a Lilliputian power station. Built in 1839, it is the only coal-based gasworks still standing; most were demolished in the 1970s when the North Sea gas grid was developed.

Regular **bus** services to Biggar arrive from a wide range of towns; from Lanark, take bus #191, but there are also services from Edinburgh, Peebles, Moffat, Dumfries and more. They stop on High Street, near the **tourist office** (Easter–Oct daily 10am–5pm; ☎01899/221066). There's a **B&B**, *Daleside*, a few doors down at 165 High St (☎01899/220097; ❶), and **camping** at *Biggar Caravan Park* on Broughton Road (☎01899/220319). For **food**, both the *Elphinstone Hotel* and the *Crown*, on High Street, serve up hearty pub grub.

Around Biggar

Six miles west of Biggar along the A72/73, near the village of Thankerton, the solitary peak of **Tinto Hill**, or "hill of fire" was the site of Druidic festivals in honour of the sun-god Baal, or Bel. It's relatively easy to walk the footpath up to the 2320ft summit, from where the views are splendid – you'll also see a Druidic Circle and a Bronze Age burial cairn on the summit. Regular **buses** between Biggar and Lanark stop at Thankerton. Four miles east of Biggar along the B7016 is the village of **BROUGHTON**, where, inside the old Free Church, the **John Buchan Centre** (May to Sept daily 2–5pm; £1) commemorates the novelist, who spent his childhood holidays in the district.

Travel details

Trains

Glasgow Central to: Ardrossan (every 30min; 45min); Ayr (every 30min; 50min); Birmingham (5 daily; 3hr 50min); Blantyre (every 30min; 20min); Carlisle (hourly; 2hr 25min); Crewe (6 daily; 3hr 35min); East Kilbride (Mon–Sat every 30min; 30min); Gourock (every 30min; 50min); Greenock (every 30min; 40min); Hamilton (every 30min; 25min); Kilmarnock (hourly; 40min); Lanark (Mon–Sat hourly; 50min); Largs (hourly; 1hr); London (10 daily; 5hr 45min); Manchester (1 daily; 3hr 50min); Motherwell (every 20min; 30min); Newcastle-upon-Tyne (8 daily; 2hr 30min); Paisley (every 15min; 10min); Port Glasgow (every 15min; 30min); Queen's Park (every 15min; 6min); Rutherglen (every 20min; 10min); Stranraer (6 daily; 2hr 10min); Wemyss Bay (hourly; 55min); York (7 daily; 3hr 30min). **Glasgow Queen St** to: Aberdeen (hourly; 2hr 35min); Aviemore (3 daily; 2hr 40min); Balloch (Mon–Sat every 30min; 45min); Dumbarton (every 20min; 25min); Dundee (hourly; 1hr 20min); Edinburgh (every 15min; 50min); Fort William (3 daily; 3hr 40min); Helensburgh (every 30min; 45min); Inverness (3 daily; 3hr 25min); Mallaig (3 daily; 5hr 15min); Milngavie (every 30min; 22min); Oban (3 daily; 3hr); Perth (hourly; 1hr); Springburn (every 30min; 13min); Stirling (hourly; 30min).

Buses

Glasgow Buchanan St to: Aberdeen (20 daily; 4hr 15min); Aviemore (hourly; 3hr 30min); Campbeltown (4 daily; 4hr 20min); Dundee (hourly; 2hr 15min); Edinburgh (every 15min; 1hr 10min); Fort William (4 daily; 3hr); Glen Coe (4 daily; 2hr 30min); Inverness (hourly; 4–5hr); Kyle of Lochalsh (3 daily; 5hr); Lochgilphead (3 daily; 2hr 40min); Loch Lomond (hourly; 45min); London (5 daily; 7hr 30min); Newcastle-upon-Tyne (2 daily; 4hr); Oban (4 daily; 3hr); Perth (hourly; 1hr 35min); Pitlochry (hourly; 2hr 20min); Portree (3 daily; 6hr); Stirling (hourly; 45min); York (1 daily; 6hr 30min).

Flights

Glasgow International to: Barra (Mon–Fri 2 daily; 1hr 5min); Dublin (4 daily; 1hr); Islay (Mon–Fri 2 daily; 40min); Kirkwall (Mon–Sat 1 daily; 2hr); Lerwick (Mon–Fri 2 daily, Sat & Sun 1 daily; 2hr 20min); London City (Mon–Fri 6 daily, Sun 1 daily; 1hr 30min); London Gatwick (Mon–Fri 6 daily, Sat & Sun 4 daily; 1hr 30min); London Heathrow (Mon–Fri 20 daily, Sat & Sun 12 daily; 1hr 30min); London Luton (Mon–Fri 7 daily, Sat 3 daily, Sun 4 daily; 1hr 15min); London Stansted (Mon–Fri 4 daily, Sat 3 daily, Sun 4 daily; 1hr 30min); Stornoway (Mon–Sat 2 daily; 1hr).

Glasgow Prestwick to: Dublin (Mon–Fri 3 daily, Sat & Sun 2 daily; 45min); London Stansted (Mon–Fri 8 daily, Sat & Sun 6 daily; 1hr 10min).

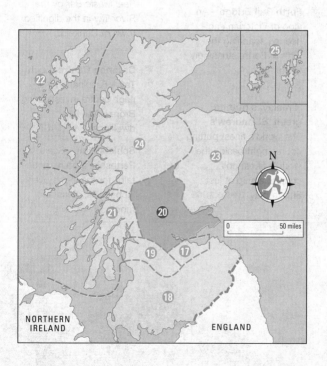

Central Scotland

CHAPTER 20

Highlights

* **Stirling Castle** – Scotland's finest castle – impregnable and highly explorable. See p.1047

* **The Trossachs** – Pocket Highlands with shining lochs, wooded glens and noble peaks. See p.1056

* **Forth Rail Bridge** – An icon of Victorian engineering spanning the Firth of Forth, stunningly floodlit at night. See p.1064

* **Himalayas putting green, St Andrew's** – The world's finest putting course right beside the world's finest golf course; a snip at just 80p to play. See p.1069

* **The East Neuk** – Buy freshly cooked lobster at Crail's historic stone harbour or dine in style at the *Cellar* restaurant in Anstruther. See p.1071

* **Folk music** – Join in a session at *Maclean's Real Music Bar* by the River Tay in the dignified town of Dunkeld. See p.1077

* **Crannog Centre, Loch Tay** – Fascinating heritage centre investigating Bronze Age lake dwellings. See p.1078

* **Schiehallion** – Scale Perthshire's "fairy mountain" for the views over lochs, hills, glens and moors. See p.1080

20

Central Scotland

Central Scotland, the strip of mainland north of the densely populated Glasgow–Edinburgh axis and south of the main swathe of
Highlands, is an accessible, popular and richly varied region. The
Highland Boundary Fault, running southwest-to-northeast across
the region, has rendered central Scotland the main stage for some of the
most important events in Scottish history. Today the landscape is not only
littered with remnants of the past – well-preserved medieval towns and castles, royal residences and battle sites – but also coloured by the many
romantic myths and legends that have grown up around it.

Stirling, its imposing castle perched high above the town, was historically the most important bridging point across the River Forth, and from the
castle battlements you can see the site of two of Scotland's most famous battlefield victories. Beyond Stirling are the fabled mountains, glens, lochs and
forests of the **Trossachs**, often conveniently described as the Highlands-in-
miniature for its taste of archetypal Scottish scenery. Popular for walking
and, in particular, cycling, much of the Trossachs, together with the attractive islands and "bonnie banks" of **Loch Lomond**, form part of Scotland's
first National Park, established in 2001.

In the eastern part of this central region, between the firths of Forth and
Tay, lies the county of **Fife**, a Pictish kingdom which boasts a fascinating
coastline sprinkled with historic fishing villages and sandy beaches, while on
the North Sea fringe lies the historic university town of **St Andrews**,
famous worldwide for its venerable golf courses and as the home of the
game's governing body.

Occupying the same strategic position at the mouth of the River Tay as
Stirling holds on the Forth, the ancient town of **Perth** has as much claim as
anywhere to be the gateway to the Highlands. At nearby **Scone**, Kenneth
Mcalpine established the capital of the kingdom of the Scots and the Picts
in 846. When this settlement was washed away by floods in 1210, William
the Lion founded Perth as a royal burgh and it stood as Scotland's capital
until 1452. North and west of Perth, **Highland Perthshire** begins to weave
its charms: mighty woodlands blend with gorgeously rich scenery, particularly along the banks of the River Tay, leading to **Loch Tay**, overlooked by
Ben Lawers, the area's tallest peak. Further north, the countryside becomes
more sparsely populated and more spectacular, with some wonderful walking country, especially around **Pitlochry, Blair Atholl** and the wild
expanses of **Rannoch Moor** to the west.

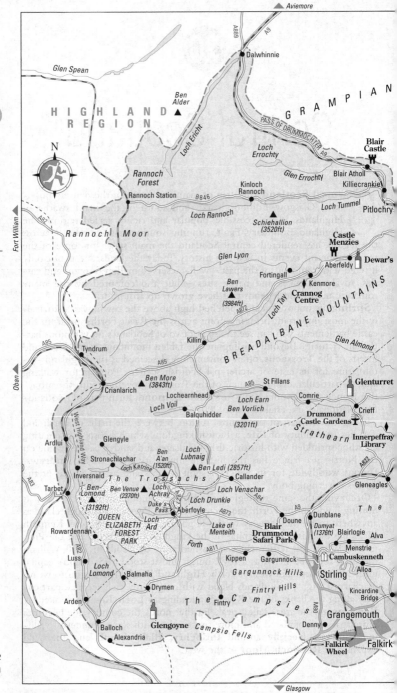

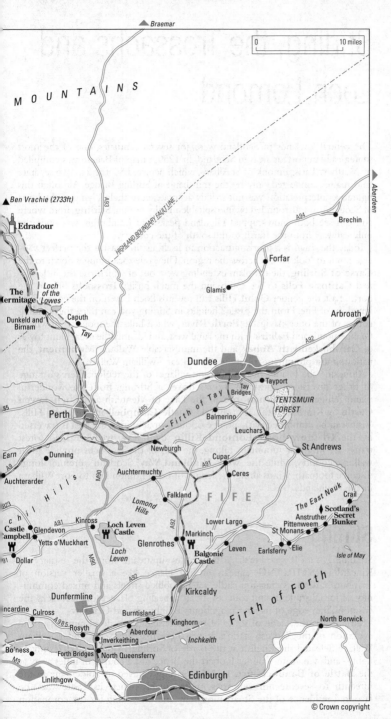

Braemar

0   10 miles

MOUNTAINS

HIGHLAND BOUNDARY FAULT LINE

Aberdeen

Ben Vrachie (2733ft)

Edradour

A93

Brechin

A94

Forfar

Loch of the Lowes

The Hermitage

Glamis

A9

Dunkeld and Birnam

Caputh

Arbroath

Tay

A92

Dundee

Tayport

Firth of Tay

Tay Bridges

TENTSMUIR FOREST

Perth

Balmerino

A85

Leuchars

Earn

Dunning

Newburgh

Cupar

St Andrews

A9

A91

A90

Auchterarder

Auchtermuchty

Ceres

Hills

Falkland

FIFE

Lomond Hills

Crail

The East Neuk

Scotland's Secret Bunker

Kinross

Lower Largo

Anstruther

Castle Campbell

Glendevon

Loch Leven Castle

A92

Pittenweem

St Monans

Yetts o'Muckhart

Markinch

Elie

Dollar

Glenrothes

Leven

Earlsferry

Balgonie Castle

Loch Leven

Isle of May

M90

Kirkcaldy

Firth of Forth

Dunfermline

Culross

Burntisland

North Berwick

A985

incardine

Rosyth

Aberdour

Kinghorn

Inchkeith

Bo'ness

Inverkeithing

M9

Forth Bridges

North Queensferry

Linlithgow

Edinburgh

© Crown copyright

Stirling, the Trossachs and Loch Lomond

The central lowlands of Scotland were, for several centuries, one of the most strategically important areas in Scotland. In 1250, a map of Britain was compiled by Matthew Paris, a monk of St Albans, which depicted Scotland as two separate land masses connected only by the thin band of Stirling Bridge. Although this figurative interpretation was not strictly accurate, nevertheless lying at the heart of Scotland and surrounded with inhospitable marshy terrain, **Stirling**, from where you can see both snow-capped Highland peaks and Edinburgh, was once the only gateway from the north to the south of the country.

Today the town is a tourist attraction in itself, its fine **castle** the perfect vantage point to look far out across the region. The castle rock plunges down to the **Carse of Stirling**, the flat plain extending west, out of which rise the little-visited **Campsie Fells** to the south and the much busier **Trossachs** hills to the north. East, the gentler **Ochil Hills** run towards Loch Leven on the edge of the kingdom of Fife. From the castle's heights in Stirling you can trace the winding course of the once-navigable **Forth River**, which links the industrial towns of Grangemouth and **Falkirk** with the rural west, and identify the great blunt tower of **Cambuskenneth Abbey** and the unmistakable **Wallace Monument**, the nation's most prominent tribute to "Braveheart" William Wallace.

Alongside the beauty of the hills and villages of the region, there's a range of other diversions within an hour's drive of Stirling, from the wonderful island refuges of **Inchmahome** in the Lake of Menteith and **Loch Leven Castle** by Kinross, to the atmospheric **Castle Campbell** in the Ochil Hills. Visits can be combined with a range of outdoor activities; the area is traversed by the **Glasgow–Loch Lomond–Killin cycleway**, well-managed forest tracks are ideal for mountain biking, the hills of the Trossachs provide great walking country, while the **West Highland Way**, Scotland's premier long-distance footpath, winds along the length of Loch Lomond up to Fort William in the Highlands.

Stirling

Straddling the River Forth a few miles upstream from the estuary at Kincardine, **STIRLING** appears at first glance like a smaller version of Edinburgh. With its crag-top castle, steep, cobbled streets and mixed community of locals, students and tourists, it's an appealing place, though it lacks the cosmopolitan edge of its near neighbours Edinburgh and Glasgow.

Stirling was the scene of some of the most significant developments in the evolution of the Scottish nation. It was here that the Scots under William Wallace defeated the English at the Battle of Stirling Bridge in 1297, only to fight – and win again – under Robert the Bruce just a couple of miles away at the **Battle of Bannockburn** in 1314. Stirling enjoyed its golden age in the fifteenth to seventeenth centuries, most notably when its castle was the favoured residence of the Stuart monarchy and the setting for the coronation in 1543 of the young Mary, future Queen of Scots. By the early eighteenth century the town was again besieged, its location being of strategic importance during the Jacobite rebellions of 1715 and 1745.

Today Stirling is known for its **castle** – as atmospheric and explorable as Edinburgh's – and the lofty **Wallace Monument**, a mammoth Victorian monolith high on Abbey Craig to the northeast which has become a place of pilgrimage for admirers both of William Wallace and of Mel Gibson's Oscar-winning film epic *Braveheart*, based on Wallace.

Arrival and information

Stirling's **train station** (☏0845/748 4950) is near the centre of town on Station Road, near the **bus station** (☏01324/613777) on Goosecroft Road. The resourceful **tourist office** is in the heart of the town centre at 41 Dumbarton Rd (July & Aug Mon–Sat 9am–7.30pm, Sun 9.30am–6.30pm;

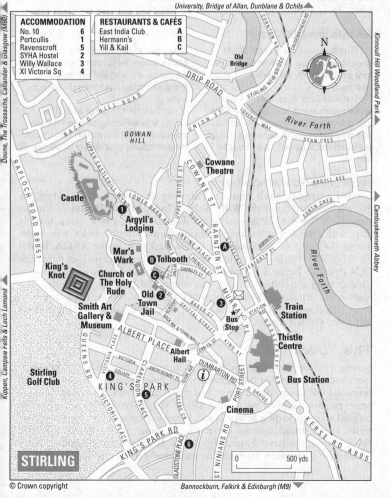

University, Bridge of Allan, Dunblane & Ochils

ACCOMMODATION		RESTAURANTS & CAFÉS	
No. 10	6	East India Club	A
Portcullis	1	Hermann's	B
Ravenscroft	5	Yill & Kail	C
SYHA Hostel	2		
Willy Wallace	3		
XI Victoria Sq	4		

Doune, The Trossachs, Callander & Glasgow (M80)

Kinnoull Hill Woodland Park

Cambuskenneth Abbey

Kippen, Campsie Fells & Loch Lomond

Castle

Argyll's Lodging

Mar's Wark

Tolbooth

Church of The Holy Rude

Old Town Jail

Smith Art Gallery & Museum

King's Knot

Stirling Golf Club

Albert Hall

Bus Stop

Train Station

Thistle Centre

Bus Station

Cinema

River Forth

Cowane Theatre

GOWAN HILL

STIRLING

0   500 yds

© Crown copyright

Bannockburn, Falkirk & Edinburgh (M9)

June & Sept Mon–Sat 9am–6pm, Sun 10am–4pm; rest of year Mon–Sat 10am–5pm; ℡01786/475019, ⓦwww.scottish.heartlands.org). Because of Stirling's compact size – barely five miles from the centre to the outermost fringes – sightseeing is best done **on foot**, though to avoid the steep hills you can take the hop-on hop-off **open-top bus tours** (April–Sept 10am–5pm; £6.50) run by Guide Friday, whose circular route takes in the castle, Wallace Monument, university and the bus and train stations. Actor-led **ghost walks** leave from the Old Town Jail on summer evenings; for details contact the tourist office or the Old Town Jail itself (see below).

Accommodation

Between May and October, you'll need to book **accommodation** as far in advance as possible. A good area to look in is King's Park, an opulent Victorian suburb of tree-lined avenues and splendid villas immediately south of the tourist office. There's a high concentration of B&Bs on Causewayhead Road, which leads north to the university.

Hotels and B&Bs

No. 10 10 Gladstone Place ℡01786/472681, ⓦwww.cameron-10.co.uk. Modernized Victorian home providing friendly and pleasant B&B accommodation. ❷

The Portcullis Castle Wynd ℡01786/472290, ⓦwww.theportcullishotel.com. Small, traditional hotel in an imposing two-hundred-year-old building that's recently been refurbished, in a dramatic location adjacent to the castle at the top of the town. ❺

Ravenscroft 21 Clarendon Place ℡01786/473815, ⓦwww.ravenscroft.stirling.co.uk. A lovely Victorian house offering B&B with antiques throughout, stripped pine floors and views to the castle. ❷

XI Victoria Square 11 Victoria Sq ℡01786/475545, ⓦwww.xivictoriasquare.com. A slightly more upmarket B&B with designer rooms, sumptuous breakfasts and great views of the old town. ❹

Hostels and campsite

Located a hundred yards from the station in an old Victorian building, the liveliest budget option is the **Willy Wallace Independent Hostel**, 77 Murray Place (℡01786/446773; ⓦwww.willywallace.f9.co.uk), a welcoming, friendly place with a big, bright common room, six dorms, a double and a twin. At the top of the town (a strenuous trek with a backpack) is the **SYHA hostel** (℡01786/473442), in a converted church on St John Street with an impressive 1824 Palladian facade. It's modern and a little lacking in character; all rooms have showers and toilets en suite, and continental breakfast is included. The high-season price is £13.75 per person. The pleasant *Witches Craig* **campsite** is at Blairlogie, three miles east off the A91 road to St Andrews (℡01786/474947; April–Oct).

The Town

Stirling evolved from the top down, starting with its **castle** and gradually spreading south and east onto the low-lying flood plain. At the centre of the original **Old Town**, Broad Street was the main thoroughfare, with St John Street running more or less parallel, and St Mary's Wynd forming part of the original route to Stirling Bridge below. In the eighteenth and nineteenth centuries, as the threat of attack decreased, the centre of commercial life crept down towards the River Forth, with the modern town growing on the edge of the plain over which the castle has traditionally stood guard.

Stirling Castle

Stirling Castle (daily 9.30am–6.30pm; Oct–March closes 5pm; HS; £6.50, includes entry to Argyll's Lodging) must have presented would-be invaders with a formidable challenge. Its impregnability is most daunting when you approach the town from the west, from where the sheer 250ft drop down the side of the crag is most obvious. The rock was first fortified during the Iron Age, though what you see now dates largely from the fifteenth and sixteenth centuries. Built on many levels, the main buildings are interspersed with delightful gardens and patches of lawn, while endless battlements, cannon ports, hidden staircases and other nooks and crannies make it thoroughly explorable and inspiring.

The **visitor centre**, in a whitewashed cottage on one side of the esplanade car park, shows an introductory film giving a potted history of the castle, but the best place to get an impression of its gradual expansion is the **Outer Close**, the first main courtyard beyond the imposing inner gatehouse to the castle. Here you can join a **guided tour** (free), which leaves every half-hour.

Looming over the courtyard is the magnificent **Great Hall**, dating from 1501–3 and used as a barracks by the British army until 1964. The building stands out not just in the courtyard but across Stirling for its controversially bright, creamy yellow cladding, added after the discovery during renovations of a stretch of the original sixteenth-century limewash behind a bricked-up doorway. Inside, the hall has been restored to its original state as the finest medieval secular building in Scotland, complete with five gaping fireplaces and an impressive hammer-beam ceiling of rough-hewn wood. To one side of the Great Hall, displays in the restored castle **kitchens** make a lively attempt to re-create the preparations for the spectacular Renaissance banquet given by Mary, Queen of Scots for the baptism of the future James VI.

The exterior of the **Palace**, the largest building in the castle, dates from 1540–42 and is richly decorated with grotesque carved figures and Renaissance sculpture, including, in the left-hand corner, the glaring bearded figure of James V in the dress of a commoner. Inside in the royal apartments are the **Stirling Heads**, 56 elegantly carved oak medallions which once comprised the ceiling of the Presence Chamber, where visitors were presented to royalty. Otherwise the royal apartments are mostly bare, their emptiness emphasizing the fine dimensions and wonderful views.

On the opposite side of the Inner Close, the sloping upper courtyard of the castle, the **Chapel Royal** was built in 1594 by James VI for the baptism of his son, to replace an earlier chapel that was deemed insufficiently impressive. The interior is lovely, with a seventeenth-century fresco of elaborate scrolls and patterns. Alongside, the **King's Old Building**, at the highest point in the castle, now houses the museum of the Argyll and Sutherland Highlanders regiment, with its collection of well-polished silver and memorabilia, including a seemingly endless display of Victoria Crosses. Go through a narrow passageway between the King's Old Building and the Chapel Royal to get to the **Douglas Gardens**, reputedly the place where the eighth Earl of Douglas, suspected of treachery, was thrown to his death by James II in 1452. It's a lovely, quiet corner of the castle, with mature trees and battlements over which there are splendid views of the rising Highlands beyond, as well as a bird's-eye view down to the **King's Knot**, a series of grassed octagonal mounds which in the seventeenth century were planted with box trees and ornamental hedges.

The Old Town

Leaving the castle, head downhill into the old centre of Stirling, fortified behind the massive, whinstone boulders of the **town walls**, built in the mid-sixteenth century and intended to ward off the advances of Henry VIII, who had set his sights on the young Mary, Queen of Scots as a wife for his son, Edward. The walls now constitute some of the best-preserved town defences in Scotland, and can be traced by following the path known as **Back Walk**. This circular walkway was built in the eighteenth century and in the upper reaches encircles the castle, taut along the edge of the crag, offering panoramic views of the surrounding countryside.

Five minutes' walk down the hill from the castle's visitor centre, you'll find **Argyll's Lodging** (daily: April–Sept 9.30am–6pm; Oct–March 9.30am–5pm; HS; £3), a romantic Renaissance mansion built by Sir William Alexander of Menstrie. The oldest part of the building, marked by low ceilings and tiny windows, is the Great Kitchen, whose enormous fireplace comes complete with a special recess for salt, while the Drawing Room, hung with lavishly decorated purple tapestries, contains the ninth earl's imposing chair of state.

Further down Castle Wynd at the top of Broad Street, a richly decorated facade hides the dilapidated **Mar's Wark**, a would-be palace which the first Earl of Mar, Regent of Scotland and hereditary Keeper of Stirling Castle, started in 1570. Behind here is the **Church of the Holy Rude** (May–Sept Mon–Fri 10am–5pm; Sat times vary; Sunday service), a fine medieval structure, the oldest parts of which, including the impressive oak hammer-beam ceiling, date from the early fifteenth century. A short walk down St John Street, a sweeping driveway leads up to the impressive **Old Town Jail** (April–Sept daily 10am–5pm; Oct–March Mon–Sat 10am–5pm, Sat & Sun 11.30am–3pm; £3.95), a formidable building rescued from dereliction in 1992 and superbly refurbished. Tours are brought to life by enthusiastic actors who change costumes and character a number of times, and there's a working example of the dreaded crank, a lever which prisoners had to turn 14,400 times per day for punishment. Take the glass lift up to the prison roof to admire spectacular views across Stirling and the Forth Valley.

The Lower Town

The further downhill you go in Stirling's Lower Town, the more recent the buildings become. By the time the two main streets of the old town merge into King Street, austere Victorian facades block the sun from the cobbled road. Stirling's main **shopping** area is down here, along Port Street and Murray Place. The only other sight of note within the centre is the **Smith Art Gallery and Museum** (Tues–Sat 10am–5pm, Sun 2–5pm; free), a short walk west up Dumbarton Road near the King's Knot. Founded in 1874 with a legacy from local painter and collector Thomas Stuart Smith, it houses "The Stirling Story", a reasonably entertaining whirl through the history of the town, balancing out the stories of kings and queens with more social and domestic history.

Eating, nightlife and entertainment

For **eating**, the upmarket option is *Hermann's* in the historic Mar Place House at the top of Broad Street (℡01786/450632); its downstairs brasserie is open at lunchtime and their Austrian/Scottish evening main courses start around £10. Across the road, the *Yill & Kail*, 39 Broad St, has a relaxed bar downstairs and a restaurant upstairs, seving a broad range of moderately priced Scottish food. At the *East India Company*, 7 Viewfield Place (℡01786/471330), a five-minute walk from the centre, you can enjoy fabulous Indian food, Raj-style decor, and the friendliest service in town; their buffet (Sun–Thurs) costs around £10 for as much as you can eat.

Nightlife in Stirling revolves around **pubs** and **bars** and is dominated by the student population. The lively *Barnton Bar and Bistro*, on Barnton Street, serves a good selection of beers and food in a setting of wrought-iron and marble tables. Try to visit in the morning (from 10.30am) to sample one of their huge breakfasts. Also popular with students is the real ale at the *Settle Inn*, 91 St Mary's Wynd, Stirling's oldest alehouse, built in 1733; nearby at no. 73, *Whistlebinkies* has regular folk music sessions and reasonable bar meals. The main venue for **theatre** and **film** is the excellent MacRobert Arts Centre (☎01786/461081) on the university campus (see below), which shows a good selection of drama plus mainstream and art-house films.

Stirling University and around

North of Stirling, a ten-minute walk from the fine Victorian spa town of **BRIDGE OF ALLAN**, lies **Stirling University**, until 1992 (when all British colleges and polytechnics acquired university status), the youngest university in Scotland and once one of the most radical. Its buildings exemplify successful 1960s architecture, and the landscaped grounds are beautiful – resplendent with daffodils in spring, rhododendrons along the sides of the artificial Airthrey Loch in summer, and the rich colours of the Ochil Hills as a backdrop in autumn. Frequent **buses** run to the university and Wallace Monument from Murray Place in Stirling, including the Guide Friday tour and local buses #62 and #63.

The National Wallace Monument

Overlooking the university one mile to the southwest is the prominent **National Wallace Monument** (daily: July & Aug 9.30am–6.30pm; June 10am–6pm; March–May, Sept & Oct 10am–5pm; Nov–Feb 10.30am–4pm; £3.95), a freestanding, five-storey tower built in the 1860s as a tribute to Sir William Wallace, the freedom fighter who led Scottish resistance to Edward I, the "Hammer of the Scots", in the late thirteenth century. Though a hero to generations of Scots, Wallace shot to international fame on the back of his depiction by Mel Gibson in the epic movie *Braveheart*. Though derided by critics for its historical inaccuracies the film was hugely popular not just in Scotland but around the world, and with the general lack of historic buildings closely associated with Wallace, the monument has become a focus for Wallace (and *Braveheart*) fans. The crag on which it is set was the scene of Wallace's greatest victory, when he sent his troops charging down the hillside onto the plain to defeat the English at the Battle of Stirling Bridge in 1297. Exhibits inside the tower include Wallace's long steel sword and the Hall of (Scottish) Heroes, a row of stern white marble busts featuring John Knox and Adam Smith, as well as a life-size "talking" model of Wallace, who tells visitors about his preparations for the battle. If you can manage the climb – up 246 spiral steps – there are superb views across to Fife and Ben Lomond from the top of the 220ft tower.

Bannockburn

A couple of miles south of Stirling centre, all but surrounded by suburban housing, the **Bannockburn Heritage Centre** (daily: April–Oct 10am–5.30pm; March, Nov & Dec 11am–4pm; NTS; £2.50) commemorates the most famous battle in Scottish history, when King Robert the Bruce won his mighty victory over the English at the **Battle of Bannockburn** on June 24,

1314. It was this battle, the climax of the Wars of Independence, which united the Scots under Bruce and led to independence under the Declaration of Arbroath (1320) and the Treaty of Northampton (1328).

The centre shows an audiovisual presentation on the battle and the background to it, highlighting the brilliantly innovative tactics Bruce employed in mustering his army to defeat a much larger English force. Outside is a stirring equestrian **statue** of Bruce, set against the skyline of Stirling Castle, the English army's approach to which he was intentionally blocking. The actual site of the main battle is, oddly, still a matter of debate. Most agree that it didn't take place near the present visitor centre; the most cogent theory argues that it took place on a boggy carse a mile or so to the west. Buses #51 and #52 leave for Bannockburn from Murray Place every half-hour.

Around Stirling

Stirling's strategic position between the Highlands and Lowlands was not only important in medieval times, but as the industrial revolution grew across Scotland's central belt so the town's proximity to the Forth gave it renewed significance. To the north of Stirling, the historic aspect of the region is reflected in the cathedral at **Dunblane** and the imposing castle at **Doune**, while to the east and south, on either side of the Forth, the **Clackmannanshire** mill towns and the area around **Falkirk** tell of a rich industrial heritage. An undoubted highlight of this hinterland is the massive **Falkirk Wheel**, a spectacular feat of engineering which transfers canal boats up and down a 100-foot drop at the interchange of the newly restored Forth & Clyde and Union canals.

Dunblane and Doune

Frequent trains, bus #58 (and bus #358 in school term-time) make the journey four miles north of Stirling to **DUNBLANE**, a small, attractive place which has been an important ecclesiastical centre since the seventh century, when the Celts founded the Church of St Blane here. Despite the length of its history, however, it is the more recent past which the town prefers to put gently to one side, Dunblane having witnessed a horrific massacre in March 1996, when one Thomas Hamilton entered a local primary school and shot dead fifteen children and their teacher before turning the gun on himself. Scene of an intensely moving memorial service following the killings, **Dunblane Cathedral** (April–Sept Mon–Sat 9.30am–6.30pm, Sun 1–6.30pm; Oct–March Mon–Sat 9.30am–4.30pm, Sun 2–4.30pm; HS; free) dates mainly from the thirteenth century, and restoration work carried out a century ago has returned it to its Gothic splendour. Inside, note the delicate blue-purple stained glass, and the exquisitely carved pews, screen and choir stalls, all crafted in the early twentieth century. The cathedral, praised in the highest terms by John Ruskin ("I know not anything so perfect in its simplicity, and so beautiful, in all the Gothic with which I am acquainted"), stands serenely amid a clutch of old-world buildings, among them the seventeenth-century Dean's House, which houses the tiny cathedral **museum** (May–Oct Mon–Sat 10am–12.30pm & 2–4.30pm; free) with exhibits on local history.

DOUNE, eight miles northwest of Stirling and three miles due west of Dunblane, is a sleepy village with a violent past. The fourteenth-century **castle** (April–Sept Mon–Sat 9.30am–6.30pm, Sun 2–6.30pm; Oct–March Mon–Wed & Sat 9.30am–4.30pm, Thurs 9.30am–1pm, Fri & Sun 2–4.30pm;

HS; £2.50) is a marvellous semi-ruin standing on a small hill in a bend of the River Teith. Built by Robert, Duke of Albany, it eventually ended up in the hands of the earls of Moray (whose descendants still live here), following the execution of the Albany family by James I. Today the most prominent features of the castle are its mighty 95ft gatehouse, with spacious vaulted rooms, and the kitchens, complete with medieval rubbish chute. Close to the castle, **accommodation** is available at the excellent *Glenardoch House*, Castle Road (☎01786/841489; ❷), an eighteenth-century country-house B&B with two comfortable en-suite rooms and a beautiful riverside garden.

Falkirk and around

Southeast of Stirling along the south bank of the widening Forth Estuary, farmland gives way to industry, notably BP's gargantuan petrochemical plant nearby at Grangemouth. The lights and fires of the refineries are spectacular at night, and inspired Bertrand Tavernier to make his dour 1979 sci-fi film *Death Watch* in Scotland. Strangely, given its nondescript industrial surroundings, **FALKIRK** – located about halfway between Stirling and Edinburgh on the M9 motorway – has a good deal of visible history, going right back to the remains of the Roman Antonine wall. It was also the site of two major battles, one in 1298, when William Wallace's army fell victim to the English under Edward I, and the other in 1746, when Bonnie Prince Charlie's disintegrating force, retreating northwards, sent the Hanoverians packing in one of its last victories. Traditionally a livestock centre, Falkirk became an industrial node with the development of the now-redundant Carron Ironworks, founded in 1759, which manufactured "carronades" (small cannons) for Nelson's fleet. The town was further transformed later in the eighteenth century by the construction of first the Forth and Clyde Canal, allowing easy access to Glasgow and the west coast, and then the Union Canal, which continued the route through to Edinburgh. Just twenty years later, the trains arrived, and the canals gradually fell into disuse.

Falkirk is now the focal point for the massive £78 million **Millennium Link** project. This has restored the canals to working order in recent years, bringing to life a valuable part of the country's industrial heritage and also encouraging leisure activities, from walking or cycling along the towpaths to canal boat trips. At the interchange of the two canals in Falkirk, in place of an exhausting flight of eleven locks, the Union Canal from Edinburgh has been diverted to a point a mile west of the town centre where the remarkable **Falkirk Wheel**, due to be completed in 2002, is set to become the most impressive engineering spectacle in Scotland since the building of the Forth Rail Bridge. Over 100ft high, the awe-inspiring steel wheel uses two giant caissons to lower up to four boats at a time from the Union Canal down to a holding basin on the Forth and Clyde Canal. Visitors will be able to take a 40-minute trip on a boat which traverses the newly built section of the Union Canal and the Wheel itself, before being dropped off at a high-tech new **visitor's centre** (@www.millenniumlink.org.uk) by the side of the basin.

Practicalities

Falkirk's centrally located **bus** station is at Callender Riggs. Regular **trains** run from Edinburgh to Stirling via Falkirk **Grahamston Station**, while Falkirk **High Station**, which is further from the centre, is a stop on the Edinburgh–Glasgow line. From Grahamston Station it's a five-minute walk to the **tourist office**, 2–4 Glebe St (June–Oct daily 9.30am–6pm, Aug until 7pm; April & May daily 9.30am–5pm; Nov–March Mon–Sat 9.30am–

12.30pm & 1.30–5pm; ☎01324/620244). The town has a good selection of decent places to **eat** and **drink**. *Comma Bar Cafe*, 14 Lint Riggs, is a brasserie-style café and trendy bar, while *Quenelles* (☎01324/877411) is a **restaurant** serving pleasant Scottish fare in a whitewashed cottage at 4 Weir St, right in the centre.

Around Falkirk

In **BONNYBRIDGE**, five miles west of Falkirk by bus #37, is **Rough Castle**, one of the forts which were set up, at two-mile intervals, to defend the entire length of the Roman **Antonine Wall**. The most northerly frontier of the Roman Empire, it was built in 142 AD of turf rather than stone, stretching for 37 miles right across the country from the Forth to the Clyde. Assailed by skirmishing Picts and the grim Scottish weather, it didn't take long for the Romans to abandon the wall and retreat to Hadrian's Wall between the Solway and the Tyne, just south of Scotland's present border with England. The remains at Rough Castle are the best-preserved part of the Antonine Wall, but if you're interested in tracking down further parts of the wall, pick up the factsheet available at Falkirk tourist office.

The Ochil Hills

The rugged **Ochil Hills** stretch for roughly forty miles northeast of Stirling, forming a steep-faced range which drops down to the flood plain of the Forth Valley and is sliced by a series of deep-cut, richly wooded glens. Tucked up against the southern slopes of the Ochils are a string of settlements known as the **Hillfoot villages**, which have been at the centre of Scotland's wool production for centuries, rivalled only by the Borders. The cottage industry of **Clackmannanshire**, immediately east of Stirling, capitalized on the technological advances of the Industrial Revolution, and by the mid-nineteenth century there were more than thirty mills in a fifteen-mile stretch between the Ochils and the banks of the Forth.

The main highlights here are Castle Campbell at **Dollar**, an atmospheric spot with some great walks nearby, and **Kinross**, on the shores of **Loch Leven**, where you can take a boat out to wander round the ruins of a castle in which Mary, Queen of Scots was once imprisoned.

Dollar and around

Nestling in a fold of the Ochils on the northern bank of the small River Devon, where mountain waters rush off the hills, affluent **DOLLAR** is known for its Academy, founded in 1820 with a substantial bequest from local lad John MacNabb, and now one of Scotland's most respected private schools; its pupils and staff account for around a third of the town's population. Above the town, the dramatic chasm of **Dollar Glen** is commanded by **Castle Campbell** (April–Sept daily 9.30am–6.30pm; Oct–March Mon–Sat 9.30am–4.30pm, Thurs & Fri closes noon, Sun 2–4.30pm; NTS/HS; £2.80), formerly, and still unofficially, known as Castle Gloom – a fine and evocative tag but, prosaically, a derivation of "Gloume", an old Gaelic name. A one-and-a-half-mile road leads up from the main street, but becomes very narrow, very steep, and stops short of the castle, with only limited parking at the top. There is a marked **walk** through the glen to the castle, past mossy crags and rushing streams.

The castle came into the hands of the Campbells in 1481, who changed its name from Castle Gloom in 1489. In 1654 the castle was burnt by Cromwell's troops; however, the oldest part of the castle, the fine fifteenth-century tower built by Sir Colin Campbell, survived the fire. You can walk round the roof of the tower, where there's a wonderful vista of the hills behind the castle, and down the glen to Dollar.

Kinross and Loch Leven

Although by no means a large place, **KINROSS**, ten miles east of Dollar, has been transformed in the last couple of decades by the construction of the near-by M90 Edinburgh–Perth motorway. The old village is still there, at the southern end of the main street, but apart from the views of Loch Leven its charm has been eroded by amorphous splodges of modern housing, which threaten to nudge it into the loch itself.

Without doubt the most attractive part of Kinross is by the shores of trout-filled **Loch Leven**, signposted from the main street. In recent years the loch has become a National Nature Reserve and as well as some interesting birds, including visiting geese and various types of duck, you'll almost always find a number of fishermen casting from small boats. From the shore a small ferry chugs over to an island on which stands the ruined fourteenth-century **Loch Leven Castle** (April–Sept daily 9.30am–6.30pm; Oct Mon, Wed, Thurs & Sat 9.30am–4.30pm; Sun 2–4.30pm; HS; £3.30), where Mary, Queen of Scots was imprisoned for eleven months in 1567–68. This isn't the only island fortress Mary spent time in, and it's easy to imagine the isolation of the tragic queen, who is believed to have miscarried twins while here. She managed to charm the eighteen-year-old son of Lady Douglas into helping her escape: he stole the castle keys, secured a boat in which to row ashore, locked the castle gates behind them and threw the keys into the loch – from where they were retrieved three centuries later.

Loch Lomond

The largest stretch of fresh water in Britain (23 miles long and up to five miles wide), and now at the centre of Scotland's first National Park, **Loch Lomond** is the epitome of Scottish scenic splendour, thanks in large part to the ballad which fondly recalls its "bonnie, bonnie banks". The song was said to be have been written by a Jacobite prisoner captured by the English, who, sure of his fate, wrote that his spirit would return to Scotland on the low road much faster than his living compatriots on the high road. However, all is not so bonnie at the loch nowadays, especially on its overdeveloped western and southern banks, which are mobbed by tour coaches and day-trippers from Glasgow, just twenty or so miles away. The upgraded A82 no longer meanders along the lochside, but speeds traffic past giving only the occasional glimpse across the water. On the loch itself, speedboats tear up and down on summer weekends, destroying the tranquillity which so impressed Queen Victoria, the Wordsworths and Sir Walter Scott. The only place to find any peace and quiet now is on the eastern banks, large sections of which are only accessible on foot.

Balloch and around

The main settlement on Loch Lomond-side is **BALLOCH**, at the southwestern corner of the loch, where the water channels into the River Leven for its short journey south to the sea in the Firth of Clyde. Surrounded by housing estates and overstuffed with undistinguished guest houses, Balloch has few redeeming features, and is little more than a suburb of the much larger factory town of **ALEXANDRIA**, to the south. Balloch has big plans for a new marina and pier development to the north of the town, which will include a visitor centre showing a film entitled "The Legend of the Loch", as well as numerous shopping outlets, due to be completed in 2002 (ⓦwww.lomond-shores.com). For a more edifying view over the loch, walk over the river and then into extensive mature grounds of **Balloch Castle Country Park**, to the northeast. Formerly a Lennox stronghold, the present mock-Gothic castle dates from 1808 and was built by local capitalist and one-time Tory MP John Buchanan. It's now a **visitor centre** (Easter–Oct daily 10am–6pm; free), and really only of use as a wet-weather refuge; the views from its terrace over the loch, however, are lovely.

Balloch has a direct **train** connection with Glasgow Queen Street, and opposite the train station stands the area's main **tourist office** (daily: July & Aug 9.30am–6.30pm; June & Sept 9.30am–6pm; April, May & Oct 10am–5pm; ⓣ01389/753533). There's really little point in basing yourself in Balloch, though it's worth mentioning that Scotland's most beautiful SYHA **hostel**, a turreted building complete with ghost (ⓣ01389/850226, ⓦwww.syha.org.uk; April–Oct), lies two miles northwest of Balloch train station, just off the A82; you can either walk there from Balloch, or if you're travelling by bus, ask the driver to drop you off close by. In Balloch itself there's the year-round *Lomond Woods Holiday Park*, in Tullichewan (ⓣ01389/759475, ⓦwww.holiday-parks.co.uk), an excellent **campsite** which also rents out **bikes**.

Various operators offer **boat cruises** from beside the bridge over the River Leven, taking you around the 33 islands scattered across the loch: Mullens Cruises (ⓣ01389/751481) operates daily trips on the *Lomond Duchess* and the *Lomond Maid* (£5); Sweeney's Cruises (ⓣ01389/752376, ⓦwww.sweeney.uk.com) runs one-hour trips departing hourly (starting at around £5), while their daily Balloch–Luss cruise leaves at 2.30pm (£7.50), and ninety-minute evening cruises operate daily during July and August only, leaving at 7.30pm (£6.50).

The eastern shore of Loch Lomond

The tranquil **eastern shore** is far better for walking and appreciating the loch's natural beauty than the western. The dead-end B837 from Drymen will take you halfway up the east bank, while the West Highland Way sticks close to the shores for the entire length of the loch, beginning at the tiny lochside settlement of **BALMAHA**. Balmaha has a **Loch Lomond Park Centre** (Easter–Oct daily 10am–6pm; ⓣ01360/870470), one of two principal **information** points on the shores of the loch (the other is in Luss). You can **stay** at purpose-built *Oak Tree Inn* (ⓣ01360/870357, ⓦwww.oaktreeinn.co.uk; ③). opposite the big car park, either in one of their double rooms or in their cheaper bunk-bed quads.

Public transport stops at Balamaha, but a couple of miles or so further up the road, at Cashel, is a lovely secluded Forestry Commission **campsite** (ⓣ01360/870234, ⓦwww.forestholidays.co.uk; April–Oct). Another three miles north through the woods brings you to **ROWARDENNAN**, a scattered settlement which sits below the mountain Ben Lomond. Passenger ferries (Easter–Sept 3 daily) cross between Inverbeg and Rowardennan, where **accommodation** is available at the *Rowardennan Hotel* (ⓣ01360/870273; ⑤), whose lawns slope down to the shore, and half a mile beyond, at a wonderfully situated SYHA **hostel** (ⓣ01360/870259, ⓦwww.syha.org.uk; March–Oct), strategically placed on the West Highland Way.

The West Highland Way

Opened in 1980, the spectacular **West Highland Way** was Scotland's first long-distance footpath, stretching some 95 miles from Milngavie (pronounced "mill-guy", six miles north of central Glasgow, to Fort William, where it reaches the foot of Ben Nevis, Britain's highest mountain. Today, it is by far the most popular footpath in Scotland, and while for many the range of scenery, relative ease of walking and nearby facilities make it a classic route, others find it a little too busy in high season, particularly in comparison with the relative isolation which can be found in many other parts of the Highlands.

The route follows ancient **drove roads**, along which Highlanders herded their cattle and sheep to market in the lowlands, as well as military roads built by troops to control the Jacobite insurgence in the eighteenth century, old coaching roads and even disused railway lines. In addition to the stunning scenery, which is increasingly dramatic as the path heads north, walkers may see some of Scotland's rarer **wildlife**, including red deer, feral goats – ancestors of those left behind after the Highland clearances – and, soaring over the highest peaks, golden eagles.

Passing through the lowlands north of Glasgow, the route runs along the eastern shores of Loch Lomond, over the Highland Boundary Fault Line, then round Crianlarich, crossing open heather moorland across the **Rannoch Moor** wilderness area. It passes close to **Glen Coe**, notorious for the massacre of the MacDonald clan, before reaching **Fort William**. Apart from a stretch between Loch Lomond and Bridge of Orchy, when the path is within earshot of the main road, this is wild, remote country: north of Rowardennan on Loch Lomond, the landscape is increasingly exposed, and you should be well prepared for sudden and extreme weather changes.

Though this is emphatically not the most strenuous of Britain's long-distance walks – it passes between lofty mountain peaks, rather than over them – a moderate degree of fitness is required as there are some steep ascents. If you're looking for an added challenge, you could work a climb of Ben Lomond or Ben Nevis into your schedule. You might choose to walk individual sections of the Way (the eight-mile climb from Glen Coe up the Devil's Staircase is particularly spectacular), but to tackle the whole thing you need to set aside at least **seven days**; avoid a Saturday start from Milngavie and you'll be less likely to be walking with hordes of people, and there'll be less pressure on accommodation. Most walkers tackle the route from south to north, and manage between ten and fourteen miles a day, staying at hotels, B&Bs and bunkhouses en route. Camping is permitted at recognized sites.

Although the path is clearly waymarked, you may want to check the **official guide**, published by Mercat Press (£14.99), which includes Ordnance Survey maps as well as descriptions of the route, with detailed cultural, historical, archeological and wildlife information. Further details about the Way, including an accommodation list, can be had from the West Highland Way ranger at Balmaha (℡01389/870470). The very useful **website** ⊛www.west-highland-way.co.uk has comprehensive accommodation listings as well as links to tour companies and transport providers, who can take your luggage from one stopping point to the next.

The western shore of Loch Lomond

Despite the roar of traffic hurtling along the upgraded A82, the **west bank** of Loch Lomond is an undeniably beautiful stretch of water and gives better views of the loch's wooded islands and surrounding peaks than the heavily wooded east side. **LUSS**, setting for the Scottish TV soap *High Road*, is without doubt the prettiest village on the west coast, with its prim, identical sandstone and slate cottages garlanded in rambling roses, and its narrow sandy, pebbly strand. However, its charms are no secret, and its streets and beach can become unbearably crowded in summer. If you want to escape the crowds, pop into the parish **church**, which is a haven of peace and has a lovely ceiling made from Scots pine rafters and some good Victorian stained-glass windows. The **Loch Lomond Park Centre** (Easter–Oct 10am–6pm; ℡01436/860601), adjacent to the massive village car park, can help with any enquiries. The *Coach House*, just off the main street towards the church, is the place to grab tea, coffee, cake or a roll.

Seventeen miles north at **TARBET**, the West Highland **train** – the line from Glasgow to Mallaig, with a branch line to Oban – reaches the shoreline at the point where the A83 heads off west into Argyll; the A82 continues north along the banks of the loch towards Crianlarich. Tarbet has a small **tourist office** (July & Aug 10am–7pm; June & Sept 10am–6pm; April, May & early Oct 10am–5pm; ℡01301/702260), situated opposite the *Tarbet Hotel*, but no other reason for stopping, unless you want to join one of the **loch cruises**, run by *Cruise Loch Lomond* (℡01301/702356) that depart from the pier.

North of Tarbet, the A82 turns back into the narrow, winding road of old, making for slower but much more interesting driving. There's one more **train station** on Loch Lomond at **ARDLUI**, at the mountain-framed head of the loch, and a couple of miles further north at Inverarnan, is the *Drover's Inn* (℡01301/704234; ❷) one of the most idiosyncratic **hotels** in Scotland: typically, the bar has a roaring fire, barmen dressed in kilts, weary hillwalkers sipping pints and bearded musicians banging out old folk songs. Down the creaking corridors, which are filled with moth-eaten stuffed animals, are a number of haunted and resolutely old-fashioned rooms.

Crianlarich

At **CRIANLARICH**, some eight miles north of the head of Loch Lomond, the A82 is joined briefly by the A85 Perth–Oban road. Crianlarich is an important staging-post on various transport routes, including the West Highland railway which divides here, one branch heading due west towards Oban, the other continuing north over Rannoch Moor to Fort William. The West Highland Way long-distance footpath (see box) also trogs past. Otherwise there's little reason to stop here, unless you're keen on tackling some of the steep-sided hills that rise up from the glen.

The Trossachs

Often described as the Highlands in miniature, the **Trossachs** area boasts a magnificent diversity of scenery, with dramatic peaks and mysterious, forest-covered slopes that live up to all the images ever produced of Scotland's wild land. It is country ripe for stirring tales of brave kilted clansmen, a role fulfilled by Rob Roy Macgregor, the seventeenth-century outlaw whose name seems to attach to every second waterfall, cave and barely discernible path. Strictly speaking, the name "Trossachs", normally translated as either "bristly country" or "crossing place", originally referred only to the wooded glen between **Loch Katrine** and Loch Achray, but today it is usually taken as being the whole area from Callander in the east to Queen Elizabeth Forest Park in the west, right up to the eastern banks of Loch Lomond.

The Trossachs' high tourist profile was largely attributable in the early days to Sir Walter Scott, whose novels *Lady of the Lake* and *Rob Roy* were set in and around the area. According to one contemporaneous account, after Scott's *Lady*

Rob Roy

A member of the outlawed Macgregor clan, **Rob Roy** (meaning "Red Robert" in Gaelic) was born in 1671 in Glengyle, just north of Loch Katrine, and lived for some time as a respectable cattle farmer and trader, supported by the powerful Duke of Montrose. In 1712, finding himself in a tight spot when a cattle deal fell through, Rob Roy absconded with £1000, some of it belonging to the duke. He took to the hills to live as a brigand, his feud with Montrose escalating after the duke repossessed Rob Roy's land and drove his wife from their house. He was present at the Battle of Sheriffmuir during the earlier Jacobite uprising of 1715, ostensibly supporting the Jacobites but probably as an opportunist: the chaos would have made cattle-raiding easier. Eventually captured and sentenced to transportation, Rob Roy was pardoned and returned to **Balquhidder**, where he remained until his death in 1734.

Rob Roy's status as a local hero in the mould of Robin Hood should be tempered with the fact that he was without doubt a notorious bandit and blackmailer. His life has been much romanticized, from Sir Walter Scott's 1818 novel *Rob Roy* to the 1995 film starring Liam Neeson, although the tale does serve well to dramatize the clash between the doomed clan culture of the Gaelic-speaking Highlanders and the organized feudal culture of lowland Scots, which effectively ended with the defeat of the Jacobites at Culloden in 1746. His **grave** in Balquhidder, a simple affair behind the ruined church, is one of the principal sights on the unofficial Rob Roy trail, though the peaceful graveyard is mercifully underdeveloped and free of the tourist trappings which has seen the Trossachs dubbed "Rob Roy Country".

of the Lake was published in 1810, the number of carriages passing Loch Katrine rose from 50 the previous year to 270. Since then, neither the popularity nor beauty of the region have waned, and in high season the place is jam-packed with coaches full of tourists as well as walkers and mountain-bikers taking advantage of the easily accessed richness of the scenery. Autumn is a better time to come, when the hills are blanketed in rich, rusty colours and the crowds are thinner. In terms of where to stay, **Aberfoyle** has a rather dowdy air while **Callander** feels rather overrun, and you're often better seeking out one of the guest houses or B&Bs tucked away in secluded corners of the region.

The **Trossachs Trundler** is a minibus which loops usefully round Callander, Loch Katrine and Aberfoyle four times a day from July to mid-Sept (not Wed), stopping at various points en route; contact any tourist office for details. The bus is timed to connect with sailings of the SS *Sir Walter Scott* on Loch Katrine (see p.1059), and costs £4 for a day-pass or £8 including the bus fare from Stirling to Callander.

Aberfoyle and the Lake of Menteith

Each summer the sleepy little town of **ABERFOYLE**, twenty miles west of Stirling, dusts itself down for its annual influx of tourists. Though of little appeal itself, Aberfoyle's position in the heart of the Trossachs is ideal, with **Loch Ard Forest** and **Queen Elizabeth Forest Park** stretching across to Ben Lomond and Loch Lomond to the west, the long curve of Loch Katrine and Ben Venue to the northwest, and Ben Ledi to the northeast. Regular **buses** from Stirling pull into the car park on Aberfoyle's Main Street. The **tourist office** next door (daily: July & Aug 9.30pm–6pm; March–June, Sept & Oct 10am–5pm; ☎01877/382352) has full details of local accommodation, sights and outdoor activities.

Accommodation options in Aberfoyle aren't all that inspiring. Best of the B&Bs is *Creag-Ard House* (☎01877/382297; ❸; March–Oct) in the pretty village

Hiking and biking in the Trossachs

Despite the steady flow of coach tours taking in the scenic highlights of the area, the Trossachs is at its best when you take to it **on foot** or on a **mountain bike**. This is partly because the terrain is slightly more benign that the Highlands proper, but much is due to the excellent management of the **Queen Elizabeth Forest Park**, which covers 75,000 acres of land between Loch Lomond and Loch Lubnaig. The park's visitor centre just outside Aberfoyle is well worth a visit if you want to get some orientation on the region and learn about the local trees, geology and wildlife, which includes roe deer and birds of prey.

For **hillwalkers**, the prize peak is Ben Lomond (3192ft), best accessed from Rowardennan (see p.1054). Other highlights include Ben Venue and Ben A'an on the shores of Loch Katrine, as well as Ben Ledi, just northwest of Callander, which all offer relatively straightforward but very rewarding climbs and, on clear days, stunning views. Walkers can also choose from any number of waymarked routes through the forests and along lochsides; pick up a map of these at the visitor centre.

The area is also a popular spot for **mountain-biking**, with a number of useful rental shops, a network of forest paths and one of the more impressive stretches of the National Cycle Network cutting through the region from Loch Lomond to Killin. If you don't have your own bike, Wheels Cycling Centre, next to *Trossachs Backpackers* a mile and a half southwest of Callander (☎01877/331200), is the best place in the area to **rent**, with front or full suspension models available, as well as baby seats and children's cycles. Also well set up is Trossachs Cycles, at the *Trossachs Holiday Park* on the A81 two miles south of Aberfoyle (☎01877/382614).

of Milton, two miles west of Aberfoyle. It looks out on Ben Lomond and Loch Ard, to which it has fishing and boating rights. The Lake of Menteith is a beautiful place to stay: the *Lake Hotel and Restaurant* (☎01877/385258, ⓦwww.lake-of-menteith-hotel.com; ⓞ) at Port of Menteith has a lovely waterfront setting next to the Victorian Gothic parish church, as well as a classy restaurant. For **camping**, a couple of miles south of Aberfoyle on the edge of Queen Elizabeth Forest Park is *Cobleland* (☎01877/382392; April–Oct), run by the Forestry Commission, which covers five acres of woodland by the River Forth (little more than a stream here). Further south, the excellent family-run *Trossachs Holiday Park* (☎01877/382614; March–Oct), is twice the size and has **bikes** for rent.

For **food** in Aberfoyle, your best bet is to stick with the local hotels: the *Forth Inn* (☎01877/382372) on the main street or the *Covenanters Inn* at the large, turreted *Inchrie Castle Hotel*, five minutes walk from the centre; both serve bar food and smarter restaurant meals.

The Lake of Menteith

About four miles east of Aberfoyle towards Doune, the **Lake of Menteith** is a superb fly-fishing centre and Scotland's only lake (as opposed to loch), so named due to a historic mix-up with the word *laigh*, Scots for "low-lying ground", which applied to the whole area. To rent a **fishing boat**, contact the Lake of Menteith Fisheries (☎01877/385664; April–Oct).

From the northern shore of the lake, you can take a little ferry (April–Sept daily 9.30am–5.15pm; HS; £3.30) out to the **Island of Inchmahome** in order to explore the lovely Augustine abbey. Founded in 1238, the ruined **Inchmahome Priory** is the most beautiful island monastery in Scotland, its remains rising tall and graceful above the trees. Five-year-old Mary, Queen of Scots was hidden at Inchmahome in 1547 before being taken to France, and there's a formal garden in the west of the island, known as Queen Mary's bower, where legend has it she played.

Duke's Pass and around

North of Aberfoyle, the A821 road to Loch Katrine plunges into the Queen Elizabeth forest, winding its way up **Duke's Pass** (so called because it once belonged to the Duke of Montrose). You can walk or drive the short distance to the park's excellent **visitor centre** (daily 10am–6pm; Nov–March closes 4pm; ☎01877/382258; car park fee £1), where you can pick up maps of the walks and cycle routes in the forest, find out background information on the flora and fauna of the area (there's a video relay to a peregrine falcon's nest), or settle into the café with its splendid views out over the tree tops. From the centre, various marked paths wind through the forest, giving glimpses of the lowlands and surrounding hills.

Loch Katrine

Heading down the northern side of the Duke's Pass you come first to **Loch Achray**, tucked under Ben A'an. Look out across the loch for the small **Callander Kirk** in a lovely setting alone on a promontory. At the head of the loch a road branches the short distance through to the southern end of **Loch Katrine** at the foot of Ben Venue (2370ft), from where the elegant Victorian passenger **steamer**, the SS *Sir Walter Scott*, has been plying the waters since 1900, chugging up the loch to the wild country of Glengyle. It does two runs from the pier each day, the first departing at 11am and stopping off at Stronachlachar before returning (April–Oct daily except Wed; £4.40 single, £6.50 return), the afternoon cruise departing at 1.45pm but not making any stops (April–Oct daily; £5.40). A popular combination is to rent a bike from the Katrinewheels hut by the pier, take the steamer up to Stronachlachar, then cycle back by way of the road around the north side of the loch.

Callander

CALLANDER, on the eastern edge of the Trossachs, sits quietly on the banks of the River Teith roughly ten miles north of Doune, at the southern end of the **Pass of Leny**, one of the key routes into the Highlands. Significantly larger than Aberfoyle, it is a popular summer holiday base and suffers in high season for being right on the main tourist trail from Stirling through to the west Highlands. The chief attraction in town is the **Rob Roy and Trossachs Visitor Centre** in a converted church at Ancaster Square on the main street (July & Aug daily 9.30am–8pm; June daily 9.30am–6pm; Sept 10am–6pm; March–May & Oct–Dec daily 10am–5pm; Jan & Feb Sat & Sun 11am–4.30pm; £3.25). Downstairs is the tourist office and bookshop; upstairs a hammed-up audiovisual display offers an entertaining and partisan account of the life and times of Rob Roy and those who have portrayed him in film and fiction.

Callander's **tourist office** is in the Rob Roy and Trossachs Visitor Centre (same times as above; ☎01877/330342), and can book **accommodation**. The best options include the *Priory*, on Bracklinn Road (☎01877/330001, ✉judith@bracklinnroad.fsnet.co.uk; ❹), a highly recommended Victorian house in its own gardens with good views; and *Arden House*, also on Bracklinn Road (☎01877/330235; ❸). Budget travellers are also well served: a couple of miles southwest of town down a turn-off from the A81 to Port of Menteith you'll find *Trossachs Backpackers* (☎01877/331200, ⓦwww.scottish-hostel.co.uk), a friendly and comfortable 32-bed **hostel** and activity centre with self-catering dorms, family rooms and excellent **bike rental** (☎01877/331100).

△ Lake of Menteith

Fife

The ancient Pictish kingdom of **Fife** is barely fifty miles at its widest point, but it has a definite identity, inextricably linked with the waters which surround it on three sides – the Tay to the north, the Forth to the south, and the cold North Sea to the east. Despite its small size, Fife encompasses several different regions, with a marked difference between the semi-industrial south and the rural north. In the south the most notable attractions are the perfectly preserved town of **Culross,** with its cobbled streets and collection of historic buildings, the town of **Dunfermline**, a former capital of Scotland, and the dramatic **Forth Rail Bridge** and Road Bridge. To the north in Central Fife is the absorbing village of **Falkland** with its impressive ruined palace and the country town of **Cupar**, a charming market town set in rolling countryside.

In the **northeast** corner of Fife the landscape varies from the gentle hills in the rural hinterland to windswept cliffs, rocky bays and sandy beaches. Most visitors are drawn to **St Andrews**, Scotland's oldest university town and the home of the world-famous Royal and Ancient golf club. South of St Andrews, the tiny stone harbours of the fishing villages of the **East Neuk** are an undeniably appealing extension to any visit to this part of Fife.

The main **transport route** through the region is the M90 from Edinburgh to Perth, which edges Fife's western boundary. The coastal route is more attractive, however, and also affords relatively easy access into the centre of Fife. The train line follows the coast as far north as Kirkcaldy and then cuts inland towards Dundee, stopping on the way at Cupar and Leuchars (from where buses run to St Andrews). Exploration by public transport of the eastern and western fringes requires some planning as there is no train service and buses are few and far between. However, if you're planning on tackling a large swathe of Fife in one day, ask for a **Fife Rover** ticket from any bus driver; this costs £10 for a day and is valid on all Stagecoach Fife buses (℡01592/416060), including those connecting with Glasgow, Edinburgh, Dundee and Stirling.

Southern Fife

Although the coast of **southern Fife** is predominantly industrial – with everything from cottage industries to the refitting of nuclear submarines – thankfully only a small part has been blighted by insensitive development. Even in the old coal-mining areas, disused pits and left-over slag heaps have either been well camouflaged through landscaping or put to alternative use as recreation areas. **Culross** was once a lively port which enjoyed a thriving trade with Holland, the Dutch influence obvious in its lovely gabled houses. It was from nearby **Dunfermline** that Queen Margaret ousted the Celtic Church from Scotland in the eleventh century; her son, David I, founded an abbey here in the twelfth century. Fife is linked to Edinburgh by the two **Forth bridges**, the red-painted girders of the Rail Bridge representing one of Britain's great engineering spectacles.

Culross

The A985 crosses the Forth Road Bridge, with unattractive views of the shipyard at Inverkeithing and the naval dock at Rosyth (newly commissioned as a port for ferry crossings to Zeebrugge in Belgium), before heading west along the river to **CULROSS** (pronounced "coorus"), one of Scotland's most picturesque settlements. The town's development began in the fifth century with the arrival of St Serf on the northern side of the Forth at Cuileann Ros ("point where holly grows"), and is also said to have been the birthplace of St Mungo, founder of Glasgow cathedral. Culross today is in excellent condition, thanks to the work of the NTS, which has been renovating its whitewashed, red-tiled buildings since 1932.

For an excellent introduction to the burgh's history, make your first stop in Culross the **National Trust Visitor Centre** (Easter week & June–Aug daily 10am–5pm; April, May & Sept daily 12.30–4.30pm; Oct Sat & Sun 12.30–4.30pm; joint ticket for Town House, Palace and Study £5), located in the **Town House** on the main road in the centre. The focal point of the community is the nearby ochre-coloured **Culross Palace** (same hours), built by wealthy coal merchant George Bruce in the late sixteenth century; it's not a palace at all – its name comes from the Latin *palatium*, or "hall" – but a grand and impressive house, with lots of small rooms and connecting passageways. The garden is planted with grasses, herbs and vegetables of the period, carefully grown from seed. The **café** (11am–4.30pm) serves home-made food.

Culross Abbey

Further up the hill from the Study lie the remains of **Culross Abbey**, founded by Cistercian monks on land given to the church in 1217 by the Earl of Fife. The nave of the original building is a ruin, a lawn studded with great stumps of columns. Although it is difficult to get a sense of what the abbey would have looked like, the overall effect is of grace and grandeur. A ladder leads to a vaulted chamber, now exposed to the elements on one side, which feels as if it is suspended in mid-air. This adjoins the fine seventeenth-century **manse**, hung with clematis, and the choir of the abbey, which became the **Parish Church** in 1633. The **graveyard** of the church is fascinating. Many of the graves are eighteenth-century, with symbols depicting the occupation of the person who is buried; the gravestone of a gardener has a crossed spade and rake and an hourglass with the sand run out – the latter a symbol of mortality used on many of the graves. Note the Scottish custom, still continued, of marking women's graves with maiden names, even when they are buried with their husbands.

Dunfermline

Scotland's capital until the Union of the Crowns in 1603, **DUNFERMLINE** lies inland seven miles east of Culross, north of the Forth bridges. This "auld, grey toun" is built on a hill, dominated by the **abbey** and ruined **palace** at the top. In the eleventh century, Malcolm III (Malcolm Canmore) offered refuge here to Edgar Atheling, heir to the English throne, and his family, who were shipwrecked in the Forth while fleeing the Norman Conquest. Malcolm married Edgar's Catholic sister Margaret in 1067, and in so doing started a process of reformation that ultimately supplanted the Celtic Church. Until the late nineteenth century, Dunfermline was one of Scotland's foremost linen producers, as well as a major coal-mining centre, and today the town is a busy place, its ever-increasing sprawl attesting to a growing economy.

The Town

Dunfermline's **centre**, at the top of the hill around the abbey and palace, holds an appeal of its own, with its narrow, cobbled streets, pedestrianized shopping areas and gargoyle-adorned buildings. The oldest part of **Dunfermline Abbey** (April–Sept Mon–Sat 9.30am–6.30pm, Sun 2–4.30pm; Oct–March Mon–Wed & Sat 9.30am–4.30pm, Thurs 9.30am–12.30pm, Fri & Sun 2–4.30pm; HS; £2) is attributable to Queen Margaret, who began building a Benedictine priory in 1072, the remains of which can still be seen beneath the nave of the present church; her son, **David I**, raised the priory to the rank of abbey in the following century. In 1303, during the first of the **Wars of Independence**, the English king Edward I appears to have ordered the destruction of most of the monastery buildings. **Robert the Bruce** helped rebuild the abbey, and when he died of leprosy was buried here 25 years later, although his body went undiscovered until building began on a new parish church in 1821. The enormous stonework graffiti, "King Robert the Bruce", at the top of the tower is attributable to an overexcited architect thrilled by the discovery of Bruce's remains.

The guest house of Margaret's Benedictine monastery, south of the abbey, became the **palace** in the sixteenth century under James VI, who gave both it and the abbey to his consort, Queen Anne of Denmark. Charles I, the last monarch to be born in Scotland, entered the world here in 1600. All that is left of it today is a long, sandstone facade, especially impressive when silhouetted against the evening sky.

Pittencrieff Park, known to locals as "the Glen", covers a huge area in the centre of Dunfermline. Bordering the ruined palace, the 76-acre park used to be owned by the Lairds of Pittencrieff; in 1902, however, the entire plot was purchased by the local rags-to-riches industrialist and philanthropist Andrew Carnegie, who donated it to his home town. Just beyond the southeast corner of the park, the modest little cottage at the bottom of St Margaret Street is **Andrew Carnegie's Birthplace** (April–Oct Mon–Sat 11am–5pm, Sun 2–5pm; £2). The son of a weaver, Carnegie (1835–1919) lived as a child upstairs with his family, while the room below housed his father's loom shop. After the family emigrated to America in 1848, Carnegie worked first on the railroads and then in the iron and steel industries; he began acquiring steel-production firms in the 1870s and was so successful that by the time he retired in 1901 he was a multi-millionaire and one of the richest men in the world. For the next 18 years he devoted himself to giving the money away, endowing educational establishments and free libraries around the world, including some 600 in Britain.

Practicalities

Trains from Edinburgh stop at Dunfermline's **train station**, halfway down the long hill of St Margaret's Drive, southeast of the centre. It's a fifteen-minute walk up the hill from here to the **tourist office** at 1 High St, immediately opposite the City Chambers (April–Sept Mon–Sat 10am–5pm; Aug also Sun 11.30am–3.30pm; phone for winter hours; ☏01383/720999). An hourly bus from Edinburgh and two-hourly services from Glasgow, Perth and Dundee come in at the **bus station**, in the Kingsgate Centre, on the north side of town. There are some good, well-priced **places to eat**, including the stylish modern *Bar Café Brio* on the corner of Canmore and Guildhall streets, *Blossom's*, 6–8 Chalmers St (☏01383 623092), for Chinese food, or you can get bar meals at the *Old Inn*, just down Kirkgate, which has the *Creepy Wee Pub* right next door.

The Forth bridges and the coast

Cowering beneath the Forth bridges is **NORTH QUEENSFERRY**, a small fishing village, which, until the opening of the road bridge, was the northern landing point of the ferry from South Queensferry (see p.958) and a nine-teenth-century bathing resort. The cantilevered **Forth Rail Bridge**, built from 1883 to 1890 by Sir John Fowler and Benjamin Baker, ranks among the supreme achievements of Victorian engineering. Some 50,000 tons of steel were used in the construction of a design that manages to express grace as well as might. Derived from American models, the suspension format chosen for the **Forth Road Bridge** alongside makes an interesting modern complement to the older structure. Erected between 1958 and 1964, it finally killed off the 900-year-old ferry, and now attracts a heavy volume of traffic.

While the geometric girders of the rail bridge are one of the most spectacular sights in Scotland, particularly after dark now that they are **floodlit**, the road bridge which parallels it is grand but comparatively dull. The only way to cross the rail bridge is aboard a train heading to or from Edinburgh, though inevitably this doesn't allow much of a perspective of the spectacle itself. For the best **panorama** of the rail bridge, make use of the pedestrian and cycle lane on the east side of the parallel road bridge. For some background to the construction of the bridges, head to the **Forth Bridges Exhibition** (daily 9am–9pm; free), occupying a couple of rooms tacked onto the modern *Queensferry Lodge Hotel*, which has a series of storyboards, photographs, models and displays.

Tucked underneath the mighty geometry of the rail bridge is **Deep-Sea World** (July & Aug daily 10am–6.30pm; April–June, Sept & Oct daily 10am–6pm; Nov–March Mon–Fri 11am–5pm; £6.50), one of Scotland's most popular family attractions. Full of weird and wonderful creatures from sea horses to piranhas, the highlight is a huge aquarium that boasts the world's largest underwater viewing tunnel, through which you glide on a moving walkway while sharks, conger eels and all manner of fish from the deep swim nonchalantly past.

The coast

Fife's **south coast** curves sharply north at the mouth of the Forth, exposing the towns and villages to an icy east wind that somewhat undermines the sunshine image of their beaches. For a pleasant, but time-consuming alternative route to St Andrews, you can head east along the A921 after crossing the **Forth Road Bridge**, following the train line as it clings to the northern shore of the mouth of the Forth. Here you'll find a straggle of Fife fishing communities which have depended on the sea for centuries, and now make popular, although not especially attractive, holiday spots. The **train** line from Inverkeithing and twice-hourly **buses** #7 and #7a from Dunfermline run along this coast, stopping at all towns. The most interesting route is the **Fife Coastal Path**, a waymarked walking trail which picks its way for over fifty miles along the coast all the way from North Queensferry to Crail.

Kirkcaldy

KIRKCALDY (pronounced "kir-coddy"), at a junction of roads from the Forth bridges, St Andrews, the East Neuk and Falkland, doesn't hold a great deal of interest, its charms largely obliterated by overdevelopment. If you're here in mid-April, you'll see the historic **Links Market**, a week-long funfair that dates back to 1305 and is possibly the largest street fair in Britain. The town's history is chronicled in its **Museum and Art Gallery** (Mon–Sat 10.30am–5pm, Sun 2–5pm; free) in the colourful War Memorial Gardens between the train and bus stations. Since its inception in 1925, the gallery has built up its collection to around three hundred works by some of Scotland's finest painters from the late eighteenth century onwards, including works by the fine portraitist Sir Henry Raeburn, the historical painter Sir David Wilkie, the Scottish "Colourists", the "Glasgow Boys" and William McTaggart. For a town which is known primarily for linoleum production and whose reputation is firmly rooted in the prosaic, the art gallery is an unexpected boon.

The **train** and **bus stations** are in the upper part of town – keep heading downhill to get to the centre. For the **tourist office**, 19 Whytescauseway (Mon–Sat 10am–5pm; ☎01592/267775), follow the road for about ten minutes round to the right from the bus station. The tourist office's accommodation booking service is a life-saver; there are few places **to stay** in the centre, and the layout of the rest of the town is not easy to follow because of the way it falls across the hillside. In the town centre the refined *Dunnikier House Hotel*, Dunnikier Park, Dunnikier Way (☎01592/268393, ⓦwww.dunnikier-house-hotel.co.uk; ❹), serves fine local food and is set in pleasant grounds. Otherwise, the *Bennochy Bank Guest House* (☎01592/200733; ❷) offers decent B&B in a relatively central location.

Central Fife

The main A92 road cuts right through **Central Fife**, ultimately connecting the Forth Road Bridge on the southern coast of Fife with the Tay Road Bridge on the northern coast. The main settlement of this inland region is Glenrothes, a new town created after World War II in old coal mining territory. Generally the scenery in this part of the county is pleasant rather than startling, though it is worth diverting off the road, however, to seek out **Falkland** and its magnificent ruined palace, and **Cupar**, the county town on the road to St Andrews.

Falkland

The **Howe of Fife**, north of Glenrothes, is a low-lying stretch of ground (or "howe") at the foot of the twin peaks of the heather-swathed **Lomond Hills** – West Lomond (1696ft) and East Lomond (1378ft). Nestling in the lower slopes of East Lomond, the narrow streets of **FALKLAND** are lined with fine and well-preserved seventeenth- and eighteenth-century buildings. The village grew up around **Falkland Palace** (June–Aug Mon–Sat 10am–5.30pm, Sun 1.30–5.30pm; April, May, Sept & Oct Mon–Sat 11am–5.30pm, Sun 1.30–5.30pm; NTS; £5, gardens only £2.50), which stands on the site of an earlier castle, home to the Macduffs, the Earls of Fife. James IV began the construction of the present palace in 1500; it was completed and embellished by James V, and became a favoured royal residence. Charles II stayed here in 1650, when he was in Scotland for his coronation, but after the Jacobite rising of 1715 and temporary occupation by Rob Roy the palace was abandoned, remaining so until the late nineteenth century when the keepership was acquired by the third Marquess of Bute. He completely restored the palace, and today it is a stunning example of Early Renaissance architecture, complete with corbelled parapet, mullioned windows, round towers and massive walls. A **guided tour** (40min) takes in a cross-section of public and private rooms in the south and east wings. Outside, the **gardens** are also worth a look, their well-stocked herbaceous borders lining a pristine lawn, and they feature the oldest tennis court in Britain – built in 1539 for James V and still used.

Accommodation includes the *Burgh Lodge*, a newly renovated independent **hostel** on Back Wynd (℡01337/857710) which has facilities for families and people with disabilities. Both the *Hunting Lodge Hotel*, on High Street, directly opposite the palace (℡01337/857226, ⓦwww.huntinglodgehotel.com; ❸), and the *Covenanter Hotel* (℡01337/857224, ⓦwww.covenanterhotel.com; ❸), just up the road, are comfortable traditional inns, with great pubs as well as a couple of rooms upstairs. The *Greenhouse* (℡01337/858400; closed Mon & Tues), also on the High Street, is a small modern restaurant serving organic food.

Cupar

Straddling the small River Eden and surrounded by gentle hills, **CUPAR**, the capital of Fife, has retained much of its medieval character – and its self-confident air – from the days when it was a bustling market centre. The **Mercat Cross**, stranded in the midst of the lorries and cars which speed through the centre, now consists of salvaged sections of the seventeenth-century original, following its destruction by an errant lorry some years ago.

One of the best reasons for stopping off at Cupar is to visit the **Hill of Tarvit** (July & Aug daily 11am–5.30pm; Easter, May, June & Sept daily 1.30–5.30pm; Oct Sat & Sun 1.30–5.30pm; NTS; £5; gardens daily 9.30am–sunset), an Edwardian mansion two miles south of town remodelled by Sir Robert Lorimer from a late seventeenth-century building. The estate includes the five-storey, late sixteenth-century **Scotstarvit Tower**, a fine example of a Scots tower house, providing both fortification and comfort.

St Andrews and the East Neuk

Confident, poised and well groomed, if a little snooty, **ST ANDREWS**, Scotland's oldest **university town** and a pilgrimage centre for **golfers** from all over the world, is situated on a wide bay on the northeastern coast of Fife. Of all Scotland's universities, St Andrews is most often compared to Oxford or Cambridge both for the dominance of gown over town, and for the intimate, collegiate feel of the place. Accentuating the comparison is the fact that the student population has a significant proportion of English undergraduates, among them, famously, Prince William, rather to the chagrin of townsfolk who imagine there to be a tabloid photographer lurking round every street corner.

According to legend, the town was founded, pretty much by accident, in the fourth century. **St Rule** – or Regulus – a custodian of the bones of St Andrew in Patras in southern Greece, had a vision in which an angel ordered him to carry five of the saint's bones to the western edge of the world, where he was to build a city in his honour. The conscientious courier set off, but was shipwrecked on the rocks close to the present harbour. Struggling ashore with his precious burden, he built a shrine to the saint on what subsequently became the site of the **cathedral**; St Andrew became Scotland's patron saint and the town its ecclesiastical capital.

St Andrews isn't a large place, with only three main streets and an open, airy feel encouraged by the long stretches of sand on either side of town and the acreage of golf links all around. Local residents are proud of their town, with its refined old-fashioned ambience. Thanks to a strong and well-informed local conservation lobby, many of the original buildings have survived. Almost the entire centre consists of listed buildings, while the ruined castle and cathedral have all but been rebuilt in the efforts to preserve their remains.

From St Andrews the attractive beaches and little fishing villages of the **East Neuk** (*neuk* is Scots for "corner") are within easy reach, although the area can also be approached from the Kirkcaldy side. Though golf and coastal walks are a shared characteristic, the East Neuk villages have few of the grand buildings and important bustle of St Andrews, with old cottages and merchants' houses huddling round stone-built harbours in scenes fallen upon with joy by artists and photographers.

Arrival and information

St Andrews is not on the train line. The nearest **train station** is on the Edinburgh–Dundee line at Leuchars, five miles northwest across the River Eden, from where regular buses make the fifteen-minute trip into town. (When you buy your rail ticket to Leuchars, ask for a St Andrews Rail-bus ticket which includes the bus fare.) Frequent **buses** from Edinburgh and Dundee terminate at the bus station on City Road at the west end of Market Street. The **tourist office**, 70 Market St (July & Aug Mon–Sat 9.30am–7pm, Sun 10am–5pm; May & June Mon–Sat 9.30am–5.30pm, Sun 11am–4pm; Sept Mon–Sat 9.30am–6pm, Sun 11am–4pm; April Mon–Sat 9.30am–5pm, Sun 11am–4pm; Oct–March Mon–Sat 9.30am–5pm; ☎01334/472021, ⓦwww.standrews.com), holds comprehensive information about St Andrews and northeast Fife. If you're **driving**, the town's fiendish **parking** system requires vouchers (Mon–Sat 9am–5pm; 40p/hr) which you can get from the tourist office and some local shops.

An open-topped bus (July & Aug daily; June & Sept Fri–Mon; £5.50) takes a one-hour **tour** around town. Audio headsets with a historical tour of the main sights are available from the tourist office. In summer, a **witches tour** seeks out the spooky spots around town (get details on ☎01334/655057).

Accommodation

There's no shortage of **accommodation** both in town and around. Upmarket **hotels** are thick on the ground, notably around the golf courses, though what many take to be the finest hotel location, the red sandstone building immediately behind the R&A clubhouse and 18th green of the Old Course, is in fact Hamilton Hall, a student residence. There are plenty of **guest houses** in a central location, notably huddled together around Murray Place and Murray Park, though rooms often get booked up in the summer, when you should definitely book in advance.

In-town accommodation
Hotels

Inn on North Street 127 North St ☎01334/473387, ⓦwww.theinnonnorthstreet.com. Appealing mid-range option with a youthful feel, full of tasteful rooms, wooden floors, modern Gaelic twists and a lively bar and restaurant area. ❺

Old Course Hotel ☎01334/474371, ⓦwww.old-coursehotel.co.uk. The best known hotel in St Andrews, located but a sliced two-iron from the 17th tee. A large, luxurious modern complex with all the facilities including a spa. ❾

B&Bs and hostels

Aslar House 120 North St ☎01334/473460,

ⓦwww.aslar.com. A smarter guest house in a three-storey town house with an unusual round tower at the back. ❸

Craigmore 3 Murray Park ☎01334/472142, ⓦwww.standrewscraigmore.com. A neat, non-smoking guest house with seven rooms in a very central location. ❷

St Andrews Tourist Hostel St Mary's Place ☎01334/479911, ⓦwww.hostelsaccommodation.com. Recently established backpacker hostel in a pleasantly converted town house right above *La Posada* Mexican restaurant with plenty of dorm beds but no doubles.

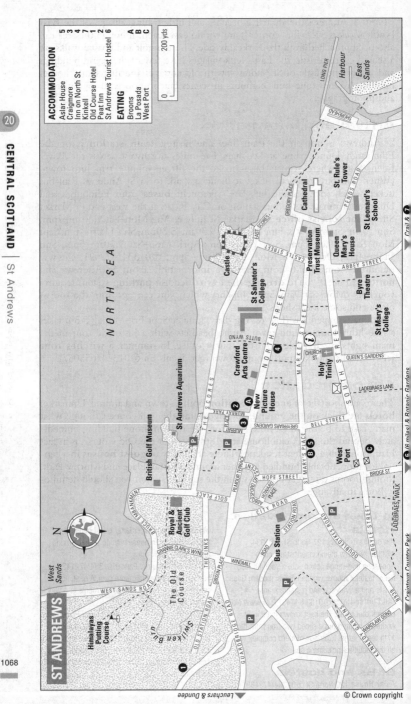

ST ANDREWS

ACCOMMODATION
Aslar House   5
Craigmore   3
Inn on North St   4
Kinkell   7
Old Course Hotel 1
Peat Inn   2
St Andrews Tourist Hostel 6

EATING
Broons   A
La Posada   B
West Port   C

0   200 yds

NORTH SEA

West Sands

Himalayas
Putting
Course

The Old
Course

Swilken Burn

British Golf Museum

Royal & Ancient
Golf Club

St Andrews Aquarium

Castle

St Salvator's
College

Crawford
Arts Centre

New
Picture
House

Cathedral

St. Rule's
Tower

St Leonard's
School

Preservation
Trust Museum

Queen Mary's
House

Byre
Theatre

St Mary's
College

Holy
Trinity

Bus Station

West Port

THE SCORES
THE LINKS
WEST SANDS ROAD
BRUCE EMBANKMENT
GRANNIE CLARK'S WYND
GOLF PLACE
PILMOUR TERRACE
MURRAY PLACE
MURRAY PARK
GREYFRIARS GARDENS
NORTH STREET
BUTTS WYND
MARKET STREET
CASTLE STREET
EAST SCORES
GREGORY PLACE
PENDS ROAD
ABBEY STREET
SHOREHEAD
LONG PIER
Harbour
East Sands

HOPE STREET
CITY ROAD
STATION ROAD
OLD STATION ROAD
GUARDBRIDGE ROAD
BROOM PLACE
WINDMILL ROAD
ABBOTSFORD CRESCENT
HOWARD PLACE
ST MARY'S PLACE
BELL STREET
SOUTH STREET
QUEEN'S GARDENS
CHURCH ST.
LADEBRAES LANE
BRIDGE ST.
DOUBLEDYKES ROAD
ARGYLE STREET
LADEBRAES' WALK
WARDLAW GDNS.
KENNEDY GARDENS
B939

Leuchars & Dundee

Craigtoun Country Park

6 (6 miles) & Botanic Gardens

Crail & 7

© Crown copyright

Out-of-town accommodation

The Peat Inn Peat Inn ☎01334/840206, ⓦwww.thepeatinn.co.uk. Five miles south of town on the A915 and then one mile west on the B940 in a village named after it, this old coaching inn has eight plush suites in a modern building tucked behind, and is renowned for its wonderful restau-

rant (see p.1071). ❼

Kinkell By Brownhills ☎01334/472003, ⓦwww.kinkell.com. Rather more affordable is the B&B at a lovely family farmhouse near the beach about two miles south of town off the A917. ❹

The Town

The centre of St Andrews still follows its medieval layout. On the three main thoroughfares, North Street, South Street and Market Street, which run west to east towards the ruined Gothic cathedral, are several of the original university buildings from the fifteenth century. Narrow alleys connect the cobbled streets, attic windows and gable ends shape the rooftops, and here and there you'll see old wooden doors with heavy knockers and black iron hinges.

The ruin of the great **cathedral** (visitor centre April–Sept daily 9.30am–6.30pm; Oct–March Mon–Sat 9.30am–4.30pm, Sun 2–4.30pm; £2, joint ticket with castle £4: grounds year-round Sun 9am–6.30pm; HS; free), at

---

Golf in St Andrews

St Andrews **Royal and Ancient Golf Club** (or "R&A") is the international governing body for golf, and dates back to a meeting of 22 of the local gentry in 1754, who founded the Society of St Andrews Golfers, being "admirers of the ancient and healthful exercise of golf". The game itself has been played here since the fifteenth century. Those early days were instrumental in establishing Scotland as the home of golf, for the rules were distinguished from those of the French game by the fact that participants had to manoeuvre the ball into a hole, rather than hit an above-ground target. It was not without its opponents, however – particularly James II who, in 1457, banned his subjects from playing since it was distracting them from archery practice.

The approach to St Andrews from the west runs adjacent to the famous **Old Course**, one of seven courses in the immediate vicinity of the town. The Old Course's strictly private **clubhouse**, a stolid, square building dating from 1854, is at the eastern end of the course overlooking both the eighteenth green and the long beach made famous in the film *Chariots of Fire*. Pictures of golfing greats from Tom Morris to Tiger Woods, along with clubs and a variety of memorabilia donated by famous players, are displayed in the admirable **British Golf Museum** on Bruce Embankment, along the waterfront below the clubhouse (April to mid-Oct daily 9.30am–5.30pm; rest of year Thurs–Mon 11am–3pm; £3.75).

Where to play

It is possible to **play** any of the town's courses, ranging from the nine-hole Balgove course (£10 per round) to the venerated Old Course itself – though for the latter you'll need a valid handicap certificate and must enter a daily ballot for tee times; if you're successful the green fees are £85 in summer. All this and more is explained at the clubhouse of the **St Andrews Links Trust** (ⓦwww.standrews.org.uk), the organization which looks after all the courses in town, located alongside the fairway of the first hole of the Old Course.

Arguably the best golfing experience in St Andrews, even if you can't tell a birdie from a bogey, is the **Himalayas**, a fantastically lumpy eighteen-hole putting course in an ideal setting right next to the Old Course and the sea. Officially the Ladies Putting Club, founded in 1867, with its own clubhouse, the grass is as perfectly manicured as the championship course, and you can have all the thrill of sinking a six-footer in the most famous location in golf, all for just 80p per round.

the east end of town, gives only an idea of the former importance of what was once the largest cathedral in Scotland. Though founded in 1160, it was not finished and consecrated until 1318, in the presence of Robert the Bruce. On June 5, 1559, the Reformation took its toll, and supporters of John Knox, fresh from a rousing meeting, plundered the cathedral and left it to ruin. Stone was still being taken from the cathedral for various local building projects as late as the 1820s.

The cathedral site, above the harbour where the land drops to the sea, can be a blustery place, with the wind whistling through the great east window and down the stretch of turf that was once the central aisle. In front of the window a slab is all that remains of the high altar, where the relics of St Andrew were once enshrined. Previously, it is believed that they were kept in **St Rule's Tower**, the austere Romanesque monolith next to the cathedral, which was built as part of an abbey in 1130. From the top of the tower (a climb of 157 steps), there's a good view of the town and surroundings, and of the remains of the monastic buildings which made up the priory.

Down at the **harbour**, gulls screech above the fishing boats, keeping an eye on the lobster nets strewn along the quay. If you come here on a Sunday morning, you'll see students parading down the long pier, red gowns billowing in the wind, in a time-honoured after-church walk.

St Andrews Castle

North of the beach, the rocky coastline curves inland to the ruined **castle** (same hours as cathedral; HS; £2.80, joint ticket with cathedral £4), with a drop to the sea on two sides and a moat on the inland side. Founded around 1200 and extended over the centuries, it was built as part of the Palace of the Bishops and Archbishops of St Andrews and was consequently the scene of some fairly grim incidents at the time of the Reformation. There's not a great deal left of the castle, since it fell into ruin in the seventeenth century, and most of what can be seen dates from the sixteenth century, apart from the fourteenth-century Fore Tower.

Protestant reformer George Wishart was burnt at the stake in front of the castle in 1546, as an incumbent Cardinal Beaton looked on. Wishart had been a friend of John Knox's, and it wasn't long before fellow reformers sought vengeance for his death. Less than three months later, Cardinal Beaton was stabbed to death and his body displayed from the battlements before being dropped into the "bottle dungeon", a 24ft pit hewn out of solid rock which can still be seen in the Sea Tower. The perpetrators then held the castle for over a year, and during that time dug the secret passage which can be entered from the ditch in front. Outside the castle, the initials "GW" are carved in stone.

Around the university

A little way down North Street from the cathedral, housed in a rather cute little sixteenth-century cottage with a low wooden door, the **St Andrews Preservation Trust Museum and Garden** (June–Sept daily 2–5pm; free) presents a cosy picture of the town's history often forgotten in its towering ruins and glamorous golf connections. As you progress towards the centre of town, it's clear that you're in amongst the buildings of St Andrews University, the oldest in Scotland, founded in 1410 by Bishop Henry Wardlaw, although James I, to whom the bishop was tutor, is the nominal founder (and was a great benefactor of the university). A **guided tour** of the university buildings starts from the International Office, Butts Wynd, near St Salvator's Chapel (June–Aug Mon–Fri 11.30am & 2pm; £4), or you can wander freely around the buildings at your own pace.

Eating and drinking

St Andrews has no shortage of **restaurants** and **cafés** and, given the local student population, there's plenty of choice in **pubs**.

Restaurants

La Posada Inchcape House, St Mary's Place. Located opposite the student union, this is a lively Mexican place with a bit more originality in its design and menu than many Tex-Mex efforts. Moderate.

Peat Inn Five miles southwest of town ☎01334/840206, ⊛www.thepeatinn.co.uk (see p.1071). One of Britain's top restaurants, serving a varied menu of local specialities. The dining area is intimate without being cramped, and a three-course meal – perhaps featuring lobster broth, venison or roast monkfish – will set you back at least £40 per head. Very expensive.

West Port 170–172 South St ☎01334/473186. Designer restaurant serving ambitious Modern Scottish fare, though they also have simpler, well-priced set menus. Can attract a few too many rich, loud students in term-time. Moderate–expensive.

Pubs and bars

Broons Bistro and Bar North Street. Right beside the classic New Picture House cinema, quickly established as a young and fun café-bar-bistro with regular live music sessions.

Inn on North Street 127 North St. Tends to attract slightly older students, but houses the happening *Lizard* basement nightclub at weekends.

Ma Belle's 40 The Scores. In the basement of the *St Andrews Golf Hotel*, a lively pub serving cheap food which is often thronged with students.

Rusacks Lounge Bar 16 Pilmour Links. Hotel bar with the best views of the Old Course. Settle into one of their comfy chairs and watch golfers through huge windows as you sip pricey drinks.

The East Neuk

Extending south of St Andrews as far as Largo Bay, the **East Neuk** is famous for its series of quaint fishing villages, all crow-stepped gables and tiled roofs, the Flemish influence in the architecture indicating a history of strong trading links with the Low Countries. Inland, gently rolling hills provide some of the best farmland in Scotland, with quiet country lanes more redolent of parts of southern England than north of the border. Not surprisingly the area is dotted with windy **golf courses**, though if you prefer your walk unspoilt there are plenty of bracing coastal paths, including one out to Fife Ness, the "nose" of Fife sticking out into the North Sea, or along the waymarked **Fife Coastal Path**, which traces the shore from Crail southwest to the Forth Rail Bridge, and is at its most scenic in the East Neuk stretch. **Bus #95** runs from Leven around the coast to Dundee.

Well patronized by holidaymakers and weekenders from the Central Belt, the various **restaurants** of the East Neuk are one of the highlights of the area, with freshly landed seafood a speciality, but often complemented by produce gleaned from the fertile Fife farmland which rolls off pleasantly into the hinterland.

Crail

CRAIL is the archetypal cute East Neuk fishing village, its maze of rough cobbled streets leading down to a tiny stone-built harbour surrounded by piles of lobster creels and fishermen's cottages tucked into every nook and cranny in the cliff. Though often populated by artists at their easels and camera-toting tourists, it is still a working harbour, and if the boats have been out you can often buy fresh lobster cooked to order from a small shack right on the harbour edge. You can trace the history of the town at the fascinating **Crail Museum and Heritage Centre**, 62 Marketgate (Easter–Sept daily 10am–1pm & 2–5pm, Sun 2–5pm; free), which also doubles up as the town's **tourist office**. The **Crail Pottery**, 75 Nethergate (Mon–Fri 9am–5pm, weekends 10am–5pm), is worth a visit for its wide range of locally made pottery, while the **Crail Gallery**, 22 High St, has an attractive selection of lino-cuts, prints and photographs on display and for sale.

Anstruther and around

ANSTRUTHER, the largest settlement and least attractive fishing harbour in the East Neuk, is home to the wonderfully unpretentious **Scottish Fisheries Museum** (April–Oct Mon–Sat 10am–5.30pm, Sun 11am–5pm; Nov–March Mon–Sat 10am–4.30pm, Sun noon–4.30pm; £3.50), quite in keeping with the no-frills integrity of the area in general. Set in an atmospheric complex of six-teenth- to nineteenth-century buildings with timber ceilings and wooden floors, it chronicles the history of the Scottish fishing and whaling industries with ingenious displays, including a whole series of exquisite ships' models built on site by a resident model maker. Anstruther's helpful **tourist office** (Easter–Sept Mon, Fri & Sat 10am–5pm, Tues–Thurs 10am–1pm & 2–5pm, Sun 11am–4pm; ☎01333/311073) is next to the museum. There is a fine fish **restaurant**, the *Cellar*, at 24 East Green (☎01333/310378), in one of the vil-lage's oldest buildings, once a cooperage and smokehouse. For fish and chips that are reputed to be the best in Fife, head for the *Anstruther Fish Bar*, 44 The Shore.

Pittenweem, St Monan's and Elie

Two miles from Anstruther, **PITTENWEEM** has a busy harbour and fish market, as well as a number of small art galleries. Pittenweem almost merges into **ST MONANS**, smallest of the East Neuk fishing villages, though if you take the coastal path between the two you'll encounter a reconstructed stone windmill – a reminder of the area's link with the Low Countries – standing above some old salt pans. St Monans is worth a visit for its splendid *Seafood Restaurant*, at the far end of the harbour (☎01333/730327), where you can **eat** or drink in the dignified old bar or eat in the smarter restaurant with its panoramic views over the coastline. The meals, while expensive, make imagi-native use of the freshest local fish and crustaceans.

Three miles on from St Monans is **ELIE**, gathered round a curve of gold-en brown sand twelve miles south of St Andrews, a popular escape for middle-class Edinburgh families who come for the bracing air and golf courses. The top local **restaurant** is the *Bouquet Garni* (☎01333/330374), which specializes in fresh seafood and game, though a lot more relaxed and convivial is the *Ship Inn*, located behind the beach near the harbour, where you'll find great bar food and, come summer, lots of lively local banter in the beer garden. You can stay beside the pub at *Rockview Guest house* (☎01333/330246; ❸).

Perthshire

Genteel, attractive **Perthshire** is, in many ways, the epitome of well-groomed rural Scotland. An area of gentle glens, mature woodland, rushing rivers and peaceful lochs, it's the long-established domain of Scotland's country-club set. First settled over eight thousand years ago, it was taken by the Romans and then the Picts before Celtic missionaries established themselves, enjoying the amenable climate, fertile soil and ideal defensive and trading location.

Out and about in Perthshire

To many, Perthshire is an extended celebration of the great outdoors, and you'll find here **activities** ranging from gentle strolls through ancient oak forests to river-rafting down the rapids of the River Tay. The variety of landscapes and their relative accessibility from the Central Belt also mean that there are a significant number of operators based in the area. Many of these are linked to the tourist board's **Activity Line** (℡01577/861186, ⌨www.adventureperthshire.co.uk), which can give advice and contacts for around thirty different outdoor activities and sports. For canyoning, cliff-jumping and white-water kayaking, get in touch with adrenalin junkies Nae Limits (℡01250/876310, ⌨www.nae-limits.com); while for rafting on larger craft through the best rapids on the Tay at Grandtully try Splash (℡01887/829706) or Freespirits (℡01887/829280), both based in Aberfeldy. Also near Aberfeldy are Highland Adventure Safaris (℡01887/820071), giving an inspiring introduction to wild Scotland in which you're taken by four-wheel-drive vehicle to search for golden eagle eyries, stags and pine martens.

The hub of the region is the port of **Perth**, which for centuries has benefited from its inland position on the River Tay. Salmon, wool and, by the sixteenth century, whisky – Bell's, Dewar's and the Famous Grouse brands all hail from this area – were exported, while a major import was Bordeaux claret. Today, it remains a prosperous-feeling place and has some excellent restaurants and a fine gallery commemorating the Scottish Colourist J.D. Fergusson.

A place of magnificent natural beauty, where the snow-capped peaks fall away to forested slopes and long, deep lochs, Perthshire is dominated by the gathering mountains of the Highlands, topography which inevitably controls transport routes, influences the weather and tolerates little development. The various mountains, woods and lochs provide walking and water sports, and the area is dotted with fine towns and villages like **Aberfeldy** at the western tip of Loch Tay and **Dunkeld** with its eighteenth-century whitewashed cottages and lovely ruined cathedral.

Transport connections in the region are at their best if you head straight north from Perth, along the train line to Inverness, but buses – albeit often infrequent – also serve the more remote areas. Keep asking at bus stations for details of services, as the further you get from the main villages the less definitive timetables become.

Perth

Surrounded by fertile agricultural land and beautiful scenery, **PERTH** was for several centuries Scotland's capital. During the reign of James I, Parliament met here on several occasions, but its glory was short-lived: the king was murdered in the town's Dominican priory in 1437 by the traitorous Sir Robert Graham. Despite decline in the seventeenth century, the community expanded in the eighteenth and has prospered ever since; today the whisky and insurance trades employ significant numbers, and Perth remains an important and bustling market town.

The Town and around

Perth's compact **centre** occupies a small area on the west bank of the Tay. Two large areas of green parkland, known as the North and South Inch, flank the

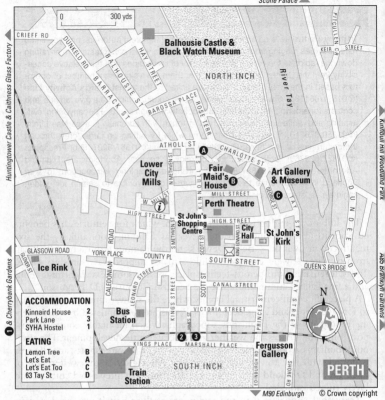

Scone Palace ▲

CRIEFF RD

**Balhousie Castle &
Black Watch Museum**

NORTH INCH

River Tay

PITCULLEN CR

KEIR CR STREET

DUNKELD RD

BALHOUSIE ST

BARRACK ST

HAY STREET

BAROSSA PLACE

ROSE TERR

ATHOLL ST

CHARLOTTE ST

**Lower
City
Mills**

N. METHVEN ST

KINNOULL ST

Ⓐ

**Fair
Maid's
House** **Ⓑ**

MILL STREET

**Art Gallery
& Museum**

GEORGE ST

Ⓒ

W. MILL ST

HIGH STREET

Perth Theatre

HIGH STREET

**St John's
Shopping
Centre**

**City
Hall**

**St John's
Kirk**

SCOTT ST

KING EDWARD ST

GLASGOW ROAD

YORK PLACE

COUNTY PL

Ice Rink

GLOVER ST

CALEDONIAN

LEONARD STREET

SOUTH STREET

CANAL STREET

KINGS STREET

SCOTT ST

PRINCES ST

TAY STREET

QUEEN'S BRIDGE

DUNDEE ROAD

Ⓓ

N

VICTORIA STREET

ACCOMMODATION
Kinnaird House   2
Park Lane   3
SYHA Hostel   1

EATING
Lemon Tree   B
Let's Eat   A
Let's Eat Too C
63 Tay St   D

**Bus
Station**

JAMES ST

Ⓩ Ⓩ

KINGS PLACE   MARSHALL PLACE

EDINBURGH RD

SHORE RD

**Fergusson
Gallery**

SOUTH INCH

**Train
Station**

PERTH

Huntingtower Castle & Caithness Glass Factory

& Cherrybank Gardens

Kinnoull Hill Woodland Park

& Branklyn Gardens

0   300 yds

▼ M90 Edinburgh   © Crown copyright

centre. The **North Inch** was the site of the Battle of the Clans in 1396, in which thirty men from each of the clans Chattan and Quhele (pronounced "kay") clashed, while the **South Inch** was the public meeting-place for witch-burning in the seventeenth century. Both are now used for more civilized public recreation, with sports matches to the north, and boating and putting to the south.

A good variety of shops line **High Street** and **South Street**, as well as filling St John's shopping centre on King Edward Street. Opposite the entrance to the centre, the imposing **City Hall** is used by Scotland's politicians for party conferences. Behind here lies the solid and attractive **St John's Kirk** (Mon–Sat 10am–4pm, Sun 12.30–2pm, except during services; free), surrounded by cobbled lanes and cafés. It was founded by David I in 1126, although the present building dates from the fifteenth century and was restored to house a war memorial chapel designed by Robert Lorimer in 1923–28.

The **Art Gallery and Museum**, 78 George St (Mon–Sat 10am–5pm; free), another of Perth's grand buildings, has exhibits on local history, art, natural history, archeology and whisky, and gives a good overview of local life through the centuries. From here, a five-minute stroll south along the paved path between Tay Street and the river brings you to the corner of Marshall Place and a round Victorian water tower with ornate Neoclassical flourishes. This is the unlikely setting for the excellent **Fergusson Gallery** (Mon–Sat 10am–5pm; free), which holds a collection of the paintings, drawings and sculpture of J.D. Fergusson, the foremost artist of the Scottish Colourist movement.

Perth Ice Rink, in the Dewar's Centre, Glasgow Road, is one of the best places in the country to watch a game of **curling**, a winter sport popular in Scotland, Canada and northern Europe but little-known elsewhere.

Scone Palace

Just a couple of miles north of Perth on the A93 (catch the Guide Friday tour bus, or bus #58 from South Street) is **Scone Palace** (pronounced "skoon"; April–Oct daily 9.30am–5.15pm; £6.20; grounds only £3.10), one of Scotland's finest historical country homes. Owned and occupied by the Earl and Countess of Mansfield, whose family has owned it for almost four centuries, the two-storey building on the eastern side of the Tay is stately but not overpowering, far more a home than an untouchable monument: the rooms, although full of priceless antiques and lavish furnishings, feel lived-in and used.

Restored in the nineteenth century, the palace today consists of a sixteenth-century core surrounded by earlier buildings, most built of red sandstone, complete with battlements and the original gateway. The abbey that stood here in the sixteenth century, where all Scottish kings until James I were crowned, was one of those destroyed following John Knox's sermon in Perth. Long before that, Scone was the capital of Pictavia, and it was here that Kenneth MacAlpine brought the famous Coronation **Stone of Destiny** (see p.915) and ruled as the first king of a united Scotland.

Practicalities

Perth's **tourist office** is on West Mill Street (July & Aug Mon–Sat 9am–7pm, Sun 11am–6pm; April–June, Sept & Oct Mon–Sat 9am–6pm, Sun 11am–4pm; Nov–March Mon–Sat 9am–5pm; ℡01738/450600, Ⓦwww.perthshire.co.uk). While it's easy to walk to all the main attractions in the centre of Perth, an open-topped Guide Friday **tour bus** (June–Aug) loops around town stopping off at the sights on the outskirts, including Scone Palace.

There are **B&Bs** and guest houses all over town, notably on the approach roads from Crieff and Stirling. In the centre, Marshall Place, overlooking the South Inch, is the place to look; of the many possibilities along here *Kinnaird House*, 5 Marshall Place (℡01738/628021, Ⓦwww.kinnaird-guest house.co.uk; ❷), offers a warm welcome in a lovely town house with well-equipped en-suite rooms. In an elegant Georgian terrace nearby is the *Park Lane Guest House*, 17 Marshall Place (℡01738/637218, Ⓦwww.parklaneuk .com; ❷). An SYHA **hostel** is housed in an impressive old 64-room mansion beyond the west end of York Place at 107 Glasgow Rd (℡01738/623658, Ⓦwww.syha.org.uk; reception closed 10.30am–5pm; March–Oct). It's a fair walk from the bus station; if you've got a heavy rucksack you might want to take bus #7. You can **camp** in pleasant surroundings by Scone Palace (℡01738/552323) on the outskirts of town, from where there are regular bus connections to Perth town centre.

Perth has an excellent collection of quality **restaurants**. For truly delicious wholefood lunches and home baking through the day head to the *Lemon Tree*, 29–41 Skinnergate; at the top end of the market are places such as *63, Tay Street* (℡01738/441451), in a designer setting serving classy and expensive Modern Scottish fare; and there are the two award-winning *Let's Eat* restaurants – the original at 77 Kinnoull St (℡01738/643377) has a lighter, livelier atmosphere but both this and *Let's Eat Too* at 33 George St (℡01738/633771) serve innovative, top-notch and reasonably priced food.

Strath Tay to Loch Tay

From Perth both the railway and main A9 trunk road carry much of the traffic heading into the Highlands, often speeding straight through some of Perthshire's most attractive countryside in its eagerness to get to the bleaker country to the north. Perthshire has been dubbed "**Big Tree Country**" by the tourist board in recognition of some magnificent woodland in the area, including a number of individual trees which rank among Europe's oldest, tallest, and certainly most handsome specimens. Many of these are found around the valley – or "strath" – of the River Tay as it heads towards the sea from attractive Loch Tay, set up among the high Breadalbane mountains. Near the eastern end of the loch is the prosperous small town of **Aberfeldy**; from here the Tay drifts southeast between the unspoilt twin villages of **Dunkeld** and **Birnam** before meandering its way past Perth.

Dunkeld and Birnam

DUNKELD, twelve miles north of Perth on the A9, also served by trains between Perth and Inverness and buses #23 and #27 (bus #22 on Sun), was proclaimed Scotland's ecclesiastical capital by Kenneth MacAlpine in 850. The town is one of the area's most pleasant communities, with handsome whitewashed houses, appealing arts and crafts shops and a lovely cathedral. The **tourist office** is at The Cross in the town centre (July & Aug Mon–Sat 9am–6.30pm, Sun 11am–5pm; April–June, Sept & Oct Mon–Sat 9.30am–5pm, Sun 11am–4pm; Nov–March Wed–Sun 9.30am–5pm; ☎01350/727688). Dunkeld's partly ruined **cathedral** is on the northern side of town, in an idyllic setting amid lawns and trees on the east bank of the Tay. The present structure, in Gothic and Norman style, consists of the fourteenth-century choir and the fifteenth-century nave. The choir, restored in 1600 (and several times since), now serves as the parish church, while the nave remains roofless apart from the clocktower.

Dunkeld is linked to its sister community, **BIRNAM**, by Thomas Telford's seven-arched bridge of 1809. This little village has a place in history thanks to Shakespeare, for it was on Dunsinane Hill, to the southeast of the village, that Macbeth declared: "I will not be afraid of death and bane/Till Birnam Forest come to Dunsinane", only to be told later by a messenger:

As I did stand my watch upon the Hill,
I look'd toward Birnam, and anon me thought
The Wood began to move . . .

The **Birnam Oak**, a gnarly old character propped up by crutches just on the edge of the village, is inevitably claimed to be a survivor of the infamous mobile forest. Several centuries after Shakespeare another literary personality, Beatrix Potter, drew inspiration from the area, recalling her childhood holidays here when penning the *Peter Rabbit* stories. An exhibition on Potter, directed both at children and parents, can be found in the impressive barrel-fronted **Birnam Institute** on the main road, an Arts Lottery-funded theatre and community centre. It incorporates the **Beatrix Potter Garden** (Mon–Sat 10am–4pm, Sun 2–4pm; free), where various characters from the books are hidden amongst the bushes.

Practicalities

Of the **hotels** in Dunkeld and Birnam, the *Taybank Hotel* (☎01350/727340, ⓦwww.taybank.com; ❶), owned by popular Scottish folk singer Dougie MacLean, is a real beacon for music fans and at *MacLean's Real Music Bar* in the hotel there are live sessions at least three times each week. The rooms are simple and inexpensive, and the rate includes a continental breakfast. Local **B&Bs** include *Waterbury Guest House* (☎01350/727324, ⓔbrian@waterburyguest house.co.uk; ❷) on Murthly Terrace in Birnam, or the more luxurious *The Pend* (☎01350/727586, ⓦwww.thepend.com; ❹).

Around Dunkeld

Dunkeld and Birnam are surrounded by some lovely countryside, both along the banks of the Tay and into the deep forests which seem to close in on the settlement. A good way to explore the area is by **bike** – you can rent good-quality mountain bikes, as well as tandems, child seats and maps of local routes, from Dunkeld Bike Hire (☎01350/728744), based in the Old Police Station on the Perth Road in Birnam.

On the other side of the busy A9 from Birnam, paths lead the mile and a half to **The Hermitage**, set in a grandly wooded gorge of the plunging River Braan. Here you'll find a pretty eighteenth-century folly, also known as Ossian's Hall, which was once mirrored to reflect the water, but the mirrors were smashed by Victorian vandals and the folly more tamely restored. Two miles east of Dunkeld, the **Loch of the Lowes** is a nature reserve which offers a rare chance to see breeding ospreys and other wildfowl; the visitor centre (April–Sept 10am–5pm; £1) has video relay screens and will point you in the direction of the best vantage points.

Aberfeldy and around

From Dunkeld the A9 runs north alongside the Tay for eight miles before the road leaves the river near Ballinluig, a small settlement which marks the turn-off along the A827 to **ABERFELDY**, a prosperous settlement of large stone houses and 4WD vehicles which acts as a service centre for the wider Loch Tay area. The **tourist office** at The Square in the town centre (July & Aug Mon–Sat 9.30am–6.30pm, Sun 11am–5pm; April–June, Sept & Oct Mon–Sat 9.30am–5.30pm, Sun 11am–4pm; Nov–March Mon–Fri 9.30am–5pm, Sat 10am–2pm; ☎01887/820276) gives details of local trails to take in all the main sights.

Aberfeldy sits at the point where the Urlar Burn flows into the River Tay. The Tay is spanned by the humpbacked, four-arch **Wade's Bridge**, built by General Wade in 1733 during his efforts to control the unrest in the Highlands, and one of the general's more impressive pieces of work. The small town centre is a busy mixture of craft and tourist shops, with its main attraction the superbly restored early nineteenth-century **Aberfeldy Water Mill** (Easter–Oct Mon–Sat 10am–4.30pm, Sun 11am–4.30pm; £2.50), which harnesses the water of the Urlar to turn the wheel that stone-grinds oatmeal in the traditional Scottish way. **Dewar's World of Whisky** at the Aberfeldy Distillery (April–Oct Mon–Sat 10am–6pm; Sun noon–4pm; Nov–March Mon–Fri 10am–4pm; £3.95) puts on an impressive show describing the making of whisky – worthwhile if you haven't been given a similar low-down at distilleries elsewhere.

Accommodation includes *Novar*, 2 Home St (☎01887/820779; ❶), or *Mavisbank*, Taybridge Drive (☎01887/820223; ❶; March–Oct), both attractive stone cottages. Up on the hillside above Weem, about two and a half miles from the centre of Aberfeldy, *Glassie Farm* (☎01887/820265, ⓦwww.the-bunkhouse.co.uk) has a **bunkhouse** which is popular with those taking part in outdoor activities locally.

Decent bar **meals** can be found just over the Wade Bridge in Weem at the *Ailean Chraggan Inn* (☎01887/820346; ❹); in town, you can get tasty home-made food at 7 *The Square Café & Bistro* (☎01887/829120; closed Sun & Mon).

Loch Tay

Aberfeldy grew up around a crossing point on the River Tay, which leaves it slightly oddly six miles adrift of Loch Tay, a fourteen-mile-long stretch of fresh water which all but hooks together the western and eastern Highlands. Guarding over the northern end of the loch is **KENMORE**; the main attraction here is the **Scottish Crannog Centre** (April–Oct daily 10am–4.30pm; £3.50), one of the most effective reconstruction-style heritage museums in the country. Crannogs are houses on stilts built by Bronze Age inhabitants of Scotland a short distance from the shore of a freshwater loch, essentially as a defensive measure – the walkway leading to the house could be demolished at a moment's notice to defy an intruder. Following extensive underwater acheological excavations, the team here have reconstructed a crannog in the traditional fashion, and visitors can now walk out over the loch to the thatched wooden dwelling, complete with sheepskin rugs, wooden bowls and other evidence of the way life was lived 2500 years ago.

Dominating the northern side of Loch Tay is moody **Ben Lawers** (3984ft), Perthshire's highest mountain; from the top there are incredible views towards both the Atlantic and the North Sea. The ascent – which should not be tackled without all the right equipment – takes around three hours from the NTS visitor centre (mid-April to Sept daily 10am–5pm; ☎01567/820397), located at 1300ft and reached by a track off the A827.

Glen Lyon

North of Ben Lawers, the mountains tumble down into **Glen Lyon** – at 34 miles long, the longest enclosed glen in Scotland. The narrow single track road down the glen starts at **Keltneyburn**, near Kenmore at the northern end of the loch, although a road does struggle over the hills past the Ben Lawers Visitor Centre to **Bridge of Balgie**, halfway down the glen, where the post office has an art gallery and does good tea and scones. Either way, it's a long, winding journey, much more the place for flights of imagination than tight deadlines. A few miles on from Keltneyburn, the village of **FORTINGALL** is little more than a handful of pretty thatched cottages, although locals make much of their 5000-year-old yew tree – believed (by them at least) to be the oldest living thing in Europe. The venerable tree can be found in the churchyard, showing its age a little but well looked after, with a timeline built into the pathway leading to it suggesting some of the events the yew has lived through. One of these, bizarrely, is the birth of Pontius Pilate, reputedly the son of a Roman officer stationed near Fortingall in the last years BC.

Highland Perthshire

North of the Tay valley, Perthshire doesn't discard its lush richness immediately, but there are clear indications of the more rugged, barren influences of the Highlands proper. The principal settlements of **Pitlochry** and **Blair Atholl**, both just off the A9, are separated by the narrow gorge of Killiecrankie, a crucial strategic spot in times past for anyone seeking to control movement of cattle or armies from the Highlands to the Lowlands. Though there are reasons to stop in both places, inevitably the greater rewards are to be found further from the main drag, and are often best explored on foot.

Pitlochry

PITLOCHRY has, on the face of it, a lot going for it, not least the backdrop of Ben Vrackie (see box) and the River Tummel slipping by. However, there's little charm to be found on the main street, filled with crawling traffic and seemingly endless shops selling cut-price woollens, knobbly walking sticks and glass baubles. The town has grown comfortable in its utilitarian, mass-market role, and, given its self-appointed role as a "gateway to the Highlands", you'd be perfectly excused if you carried straight on through. The one attraction with some distinction in the immediate vicinity is the **Edradour Distillery** (March–Oct Mon–Sat 9.30am–5pm, Sun noon–5pm; Nov & Dec Mon–Sat 10am–4pm; free), Scotland's smallest, set in an idyllic position tucked into the hills a couple of miles east of Pitlochry on the A924. Although the whistle-stop audiovisual presentation and tour of the distillery itself isn't out of the ordinary, the lack of industrialization and the fact that the whole traditional process is done onsite gives Edradour more personality than many of its rivals.

Pitlochry is on the main **train** line to Inverness, and has regular **buses** running from Perth which stop near the train station on Station Road, at the north

---

Walks around Pitlochry

Ordnance Survey Landranger maps Nos. 43 & 52

Pitlochry is surrounded by good walking country. The biggest lure has to be **Ben Vrackie** (2733ft), which provides a stunning backdrop for the town and deserves better than a straight up-and-down walk; however, the climb should only be attempted in settled weather conditions, with the right equipment and following the necessary safety precautions (see p.46).

The direct route up the hill follows the course of the Moulin burn past the inn of the same name. Alternatively, a longer but much more rewarding circular route heads north out of Pitlochry, along the edge of attractive Loch Faskally, then up the River Garry to go through the **Pass of Killiecrankie**. This is looked after by the NTS, which has a visitor centre detailing the famous battle here as well as the abundant natural history of the gorge. From the NTS centre walk north up the old A9 and branch off on the small tarred road signposted **Old Faskally**, which twists up under the new A9. The route from here is signposted.

Other worthwhile walks in the area include the trip right round **Loch Faskally**, or you could follow the walk above but turn back from Killiecrankie. A lovely short hill walk from the south end of Pitlochry follows a path through oak forests along the banks of the **Black Spout** burn; when you emerge from the woods it's a few hundred yards further uphill to the lovely Edradour Distillery (see above).

end of town, ten minutes' walk from the centre and the **tourist office**, 22 Atholl Rd (mid-May to Sept daily 9am–7pm, Sun closes 6pm; Easter to mid-May & Oct Mon–Sat 9am–6pm, Sun 11am–5pm; Nov–Easter Mon–Fri 9am–5pm, Sat 10am–2pm; ☎01796/472215). The office can sell you a guide to walks in the surrounding area (50p), and also offers an accommodation booking service.

As a well-established holiday town, Pitlochry is packed with grand houses converted into large and medium-sized **hotels**. The *Moulin Hotel* (☎01796/472196, ⓦwww.moulin.u-net.com; ❸), at Moulin on the outskirts of Pitlochry, is a welcoming travellers' inn with a great bar and its own brewery. Of the many guest houses and **B&Bs**, try *Kinnaird House*, Kirkmichael Road (☎01796/472843, ⓦwww.kinnaird-house.co.uk; ❸) or *Ferryman's Cottage*, Port-na-Craig (☎01796/473681; ❷), also in a beautiful position next to the River Tummel. The *Old Bank House Lodge* (☎01796/470022, ⓦwww.scottishlodge.com) is a friendly place with some en-suite rooms as well as bunkrooms and good facilities for walkers and cyclists.

Pitlochry is the domain of the tearoom and is pitifully short of **restaurants** and pubs; the best bet for good **pub grub** is the *Moulin Inn*, handily placed at the foot of Ben Vrackie.

Loch Tummel and Loch Rannoch

West of Pitlochry, the B8019/B846 makes a memorably scenic traverse of the shores of **Loch Tummel** and then **Loch Rannoch**. This is a spectacular stretch of countryside and one which deserves leisurely exploration. **Queen's View** at the eastern end of Loch Tummel is a fabulous vantage point, looking down the loch across the hills to the misty peak of **Schiehallion** (3520ft) or the "Fairy Mountain", one of the few free-standing hills in Scotland. It's a popular and inspiring mountain to climb, with views on a good day to both sides of Scotland; the path up starts at Braes of Foss, just off the B846 which links Aberfeldy with Kinloch Rannoch.

Beyond Loch Tummel, marking the eastern end of Loch Rannoch, the small community of **KINLOCH RANNOCH** doesn't see a lot of passing trade – fishermen and hill-walkers are the most common visitors. Otherwise, the only real destination here is Rannoch Station, a lonely outpost on the Glasgow–Fort William West Highland train (see p.1194), six miles or so beyond the western end of Loch Rannoch. The road goes no further. Here you can contemplate the bleakness of **Rannoch Moor**, a wide expanse of bog, heather and wind-blown pine tree which stretches right across to the imposing entrance to Glen Coe (see p.1216). There is a tearoom and hotel here, but even these struggle to diminish the feeling of isolation.

North of Pitlochry

Four miles north of Pitlochry, the A9 cuts through the **Pass of Killiecrankie**, a breathtaking wooded gorge which falls away to the River Garry below. This dramatic setting was the site of the **Battle of Killiecrankie** in 1689, when the Jacobites quashed the forces of General Mackay. Legend has it that one soldier of the Crown, fleeing for his life, made a miraculous jump across the 18ft **Soldier's Leap**, an impossibly wide chasm halfway up the gorge. Exhibits at the slick NTS **visitor centre** (April–Oct daily 10am–5.30pm; ☎01796/473233; parking £1) recall the battle and examine the gorge in detail. The surroundings here are thick, mature forest, full of interesting plants and creatures – the local ranger often sets off on **guided walks** which are well worth joining if you're around at the right time. Walks leave from the visitor centre and they'll let you know what's scheduled when.

Blair Atholl

Three miles north of Killiecrankie, the village of **BLAIR ATHOLL** makes for a much quieter and more idiosyncratic stop than Pitlochry. At the **Atholl Estates Information Centre** (April–Oct daily 9am–4.45pm; ☎01796/ 481464) you can get details of the extensive network of local walks and bike rides; alongside is Atholl Mountain Bike Hire. **Blair Castle** (April–Oct daily 10am–6pm; £6.25; grounds only £2), a whitewashed, turreted castle, surrounded by parkland and dating from 1269, presents an impressive sight as you approach up the drive. A piper may be playing in front of the castle, one of the Atholl Highlanders, a select group retained by the duke as his private army – a unique privilege afforded to him by Queen Victoria, who stayed here in 1844. Thirty or so rooms are open for inspection, and display a selection of paintings, antique furniture and plasterwork that is sumptuous in the extreme. Highlights are the soaring **entrance hall**, with every spare inch of wood panelling covered in weapons of some description; the **Tapestry Room**, on the top floor of the original Cumming's Tower; and the vast **ballroom**, with its timber roof, antlers and mixture of portraits.

Travel details

Trains

Balloch to: Glasgow (every 30min; 40min).
Crianlarich to: Fort William (3 daily; 2hr); Glasgow (3 daily; 2hr); Oban (3 daily; 1hr 10min).
Dunfermline to: Edinburgh (every 30min; 30min); Kirkcaldy (hourly; 40min).
Falkirk Grahamston to: Edinburgh (every 30min; 35min); Glasgow Queen Street (every 30min; 25min); Stirling (every 30min; 15min).
Glasgow Queen Street to: Ardlui (2–4 daily; 1hr 35min); Arrochar & Tarbet (2–4 daily; 1hr 15min); Balloch (every 30min; 45min); Crianlarich (2–4 daily; 1hr 50min).
Kirkcaldy to: Aberdeen (hourly; 2hr); Dundee (hourly; 40min–1hr); Edinburgh (every 30min; 50min); Perth (7 daily; 40min).
Leuchars (for St Andrews) to: Dundee (5 daily; 20min); Edinburgh (5 daily; 1hr 45min).
Perth to: Aberdeen (hourly; 1hr 40min); Dundee (hourly; 25min); Edinburgh (9 daily; 1hr 25min); Glasgow Queen Street (hourly; 1hr 5min); Inverness (5 daily; 2hr); Stirling (hourly; 30min).
Stirling to: Aberdeen (hourly; 2hr 15min); Dundee (hourly; 1hr); Edinburgh (hourly; 1hr); Falkirk Grahamston (hourly; 30min); Glasgow Queen Street (hourly; 30min); Linlithgow (hourly; 35min); Perth (hourly; 30min); Inverness (3–5 daily; 2hr 30min).

Buses

Balloch to: Balmaha (every 2hr; 30min); Luss (Mon–Sat 9 daily, 7 on Sun; 15min); Stirling (1 daily; 1hr 25min).
Dunfermline to: Dundee (every 30min; 1hr 30min); Edinburgh (every 30min; 40min); Glasgow (hourly; 1hr 20min); Glenrothes (every 30min; 30min); Kirkcaldy (every 30min; 25min); St Andrews (hourly; 2hr); Stirling (hourly; 40min).
Glenrothes to: Dundee (every 30min; 1hr); Dunfermline (every 30min; 30min); Kirkcaldy (hourly; 20min); St Andrews (hourly; 45min).
Kirkcaldy to: Dundee (10 daily; 1hr 30min); Dunfermline (every 30min; 25min); Glenrothes (hourly; 20min); St Andrews (16 daily; 1hr).
Luss to: Tarbet (Mon–Sat 2–3 daily; 10min).
Perth to: Aberfeldy (6 daily; 1hr 45min); Dunblane (every 30min; 35min); Dunfermline (every 30min; 50min); Edinburgh (hourly; 1hr 20min); Glasgow (hourly; 1hr 35min); Gleneagles (hourly; 25min); Inverness (10 daily; 2hr 30min); London (4 daily; 9hr); Stirling (20 daily; 50min).
St Andrews to: Dundee (every 20min; 40min);

Dunfermline (hourly; 1hr 30min); Edinburgh (hourly; 2hr); Glasgow (6 daily; 2hr 50min); Glenrothes (hourly; 45min); Kirkcaldy (16 daily; 1hr); Stirling (6 daily; 2hr).

Stirling to: Aberfoyle (4 daily; 45min); Bo'ness (3 daily; 35min); Callander (11 daily; 45min); Dollar (13 daily; 35min); Doune (14 daily; 30min); Dunblane (20 daily; 1hr 15min); Dundee (12 daily; 1hr 30min); Dunfermline (13 daily; 50min); Edinburgh (hourly; 1hr 35min); Falkirk (every 45min; 30min); Glasgow (hourly; 1hr 10min); Gleneagles (16 daily; 30min); Inverness (12 daily; 3hr 30min); Killin (2 daily; 2hr); Lochearnhead (2 daily; 1hr 40min); Perth (20 daily; 50min); Pitlochry (2 daily; 1hr 30min); St Andrews (6 daily; 2hr).

Argyll

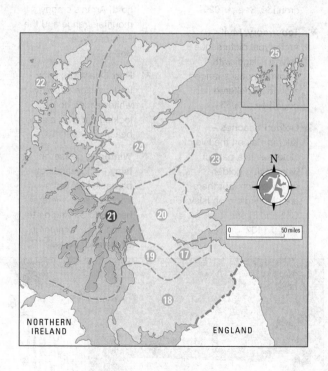

NORTHERN
IRELAND

ENGLAND

N

0   50 miles

22

25

24

23

20

21

19

17

18

CHAPTER 21

Highlights

* **Loch Fyne Oyster Bar, Cairndow** – Scotland's finest smokehouse and seafood outlet. See p.1089

* **Mount Stuart, Bute** – Overblown aristocratic mansion, set in beautiful grounds. See p.1090

* **Tobermory, Mull** – Archetypal picturesque fishing village, with colourful houses ranged around a sheltered harbour. See p.1095

* **Golden beaches** – Kiloran Bay on the Isle of Colonsay is a perfect west-facing golden sandy beach, but there are plenty more on Islay, Coll and Tiree. See p.1102

* **Isle of Gigha** – The perfect island escape: sandy beaches, friendly folk, decent hotel and lovely gardens. See p.1106

* **Goat Fell, Arran** – Spectacular views over north Arran's craggy mountain range and the Firth of Clyde. See p.1110

* **Port Charlotte, Islay** – Idyllic village of pretty whitewashed houses, looking out over a sandy beach. See p.1113

* **Wintering geese on Islay** – Thousands of barnacle and white-fronted geese winter here before flying off to breed each summer in Greenland. See p.1113

21

Argyll

C ut off for centuries from the rest of Scotland by the mountains and sea
lochs that characterize the region, **Argyll** remains remote, its scatter of
offshore islands forming part of the Inner Hebridean archipelago (the
remaining Hebrides are dealt with in the next chapter). Geographically
as well as culturally, this is a transitional area between Highland and Lowland,
boasting a rich variety of scenery, from lush, subtropical gardens warmed by the
Gulf Stream to flat and treeless islands on the edge of the Atlantic. It's in the
folds and twists of the countryside, the interplay of land and water and the
views out to the islands, that the strengths and beauties of mainland Argyll lie.
The one area of man-made sights you shouldn't miss, however, is the cluster of
Celtic and **prehistoric sites** near Kilmartin. Overall, the population is tiny;
even **Oban**, Argyll's chief ferry port, has just seven thousand inhabitants, while
the prettiest, **Inveraray**, boasts a mere four hundred.

The eastern duo of **Bute** and **Arran** are the most popular of Scotland's more
southerly islands, the latter – now, strictly speaking, part of North Ayrshire –
justifiably so, with spectacular scenery ranging from the granite peaks of the
north to the Lowland pasture of the south. Of the Hebridean islands covered
in this chapter, mountainous **Mull** is the most visited, though it is large enough
to absorb the crowds, many of whom are only passing through en route to the
tiny isle of **Iona**, a centre of Christian culture since the sixth century. **Islay**,
best known for its distinctive malt whiskies, is fairly quiet even in the height of
summer, as is neighbouring **Jura**, which offers excellent walking opportunities.
And, for those seeking further solitude, there are the more remote islands of
Tiree and **Coll**, which, although swept with fierce winds, boast more sunny
days than anywhere else in Scotland.

The region's name derives from *Aragaidheal*, which translates as "Boundary of
the Gaels", the Irish Celts who settled here in the fifth century AD, and whose
kingdom of Dalriada embraced much of what is now Argyll. Known to the
Romans as *Scotti* – hence "Scotland" – it was the Irish Celts who promoted
Celtic Christianity, and whose Gaelic language eventually became the national tongue. In the twelfth century, the immensely powerful Somerled became
King of the Hebrides and Lord of Argyll. His successors, the MacDonalds,
established Islay as their headquarters in the 1200s, but were in turn dislodged
by Robert the Bruce, whose allies, the **Campbells**, eventually gained control
of the entire area as the dukes of Argyll; even today, they remain one of the
largest landowners in the region.

In the aftermath of the Jacobite uprisings, Argyll, like the rest of the
Highlands, was devastated by the **Clearances**, with thousands of crofters evicted to make room for profitable sheep farming – "the white plague" – and cat-

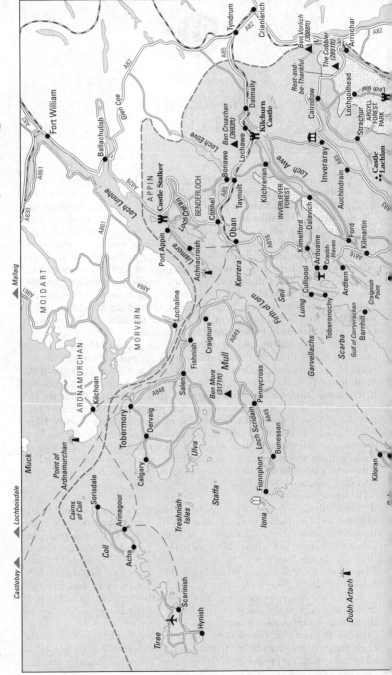

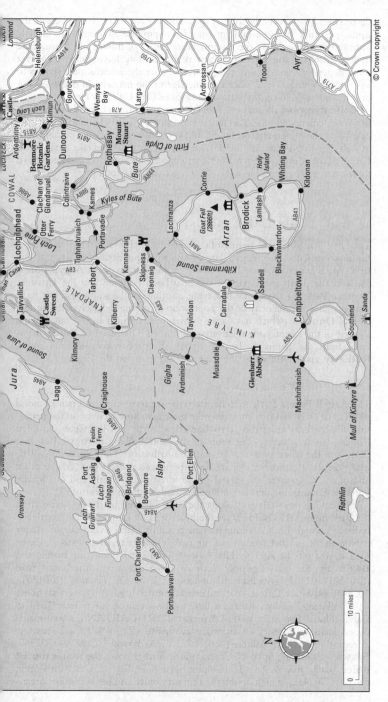

10 miles

0

N

tle-rearing. More recently forestry plantations have dramatically altered the landscape, while purpose-built marinas have sprouted all around the heavily indented coastline. Today the traditional industries of fishing and farming are in deep crisis, as is the modern industry of fish-farming, leaving the region ever more dependent on tourism, EU grants and a steady influx of new settlers to keep things going. Gaelic, once the language of the majority in Argyll, retains only a tenuous hold on the outlying islands of Islay, Coll and Tiree.

Public transport throughout Argyll is minimal, though buses do serve most major settlements, and the train line reaches all the way to Oban. In the remoter parts of the region and on the islands, you'll have to rely on a combination of walking, shared taxis and the postbus. If you're planning to take a **car** across to one of the islands, it's essential that you book both your outward and return journeys as early as possible, as the ferries get very booked up.

Cowal and Bute

The claw-shaped **Cowal peninsula**, formed by Loch Fyne and Loch Long, is the most-visited part of Argyll, largely due to its proximity to Glasgow. The landscape is extremely varied, ranging from the Munros of the **Argyll Forest Park** in the north (now part of the new Loch Lomond and the Trossachs National Park), to the gentle low-lying coastline of the southwest, but most visitors – and the majority of the population – confine themselves to the area around **Dunoon** (which has Cowal's chief tourist office) in the east, leaving the rest of the countryside relatively undisturbed. The island of **Bute** is separated from the peninsula by the merest sliver of water; its chief town, **Rothesay**, rivals Dunoon as the major seaside resort on the Clyde.

Argyll Forest Park

The **Argyll Forest Park** stretches from the western shores of Loch Lomond south as far as Holy Loch, providing the most grandiose scenery on the peninsula. The park includes the **Arrochar Alps**, north of Glen Croe and Glen Kinglas, whose Munros offer some of the best climbing in Argyll: Ben Ime (3318ft) is the tallest of the range, and Ben Arthur or "The Cobbler" (2891ft) easily the most distinctive. All are for experienced walkers only. At the other end of the scale, there are several gentle forest walks clearly laid out by the Forestry Commission and helpful leaflets available from tourist offices.

Approaching from Glasgow along the A82, followed by the A83, you enter the park from **ARROCHAR**, at the head of Loch Long. The village itself is ordinary enough, but the setting is dramatic, and it makes a convenient base for exploring the northern section of the park. There's a **train station** a mile or so east, just off the A83 to Tarbet (see p.1105), and numerous **hotels** and **B&Bs**; try the very friendly *Lochside Guest House* on the main road (℡01301/702467, Ⓔlochsidegh@aol.com; ❷), or the *Fascadail* (℡01301/702344, Ⓦwww.vacations-scotland.co.uk/fascadail.html; ❷), a guest house with a glorious garden, situated a little to the south on the quieter A814 to Garelochhead. Two miles west of Arrochar at **ARDGARTAN** is a well-maintained lochside Forestry Commission **campsite** (℡01301/702293, Ⓦwww.forestholidays.co.uk; March–Oct), an SYHA **hostel** (℡01301/702362, Ⓦwww.syha.org.uk; April–Nov) and, a little further down the road, a **tourist office** (daily: July & Aug 10am–6pm; April–June, Sept & Oct 10am–5pm; ℡01301/702432), which doubles as a forestry office and has occasional organized walks. There are also waymarked **walks** starting from the tourist office, and a bike rental place called South Park (℡01301/702288).

Approaching Cowal from the east, you're forced to climb **Glen Croe**, a strategic hill pass whose saddle is called Rest-and-be-Thankful, for obvious reasons. From here, continue along the A83 down the grand Highland sweep of **Glen Kinglas** to **CAIRNDOW**, at the head of Loch Fyne. A mile or so around the head of the loch on the main road is the **Loch Fyne Oyster Bar** (℡01499/600264, ⓦwww.loch-fyne.com), which sells more oysters than anywhere else in the country, plus lots of other fish and seafood treats. You can easily assemble a gourmet picnic here or stock up on provisions for the week, and the moderately expensive **restaurant** is excellent, though booking is advisable at busy times. Inveraray (see p.1091) is only six miles along the western shores of Loch Fyne on the A83.

To delve further into Cowal, take the A815 southwest to Strachur before heading inland to **Loch Eck**, an exceptionally narrow freshwater loch, squeezed between steeply banked woods, is a favourite spot for trout fishing. At the loch's southern tip are the beautifully laid-out **Benmore Botanic Gardens** (March–Oct daily 9.30am–6pm; £3), an offshoot of Edinburgh's Royal Botanic Gardens, famed for their rhododendrons and especially striking for their avenue of Great Redwoods, planted in 1863 and now over 100ft high. There's an excellent, inexpensive **café** by the entrance, open in season, with an imaginative menu; you can eat there without visiting the gardens if trees aren't your thing.

Dunoon

In the nineteenth century, **DUNOON**, Cowal's capital, grew from a mere village to a major Clyde seaside resort and favourite holiday spot for Glaswegians. Nowadays, tourists tend to arrive by ferry from Gourock and, though their numbers are smaller, Dunoon remains by far the largest town in Argyll, with 13,000 inhabitants. Apart from its practical uses and its fine pier, however, there's little to tempt you to linger.

The **Castle House Museum** (Easter–Oct Mon–Sat 10.30am–4.30pm, Sun 2–4.30pm; ⓦwww.castlehousemuseum.org.uk; £1.50) has some good hands-on nature stuff for kids, an excellent section on the Clyde steamers as well as details of "Highland Mary", betrothed to Robbie Burns (despite the fact that he already had a pregnant wife), who nursed the poet through typhus while they planned to elope to the West Indies only to die from the disease herself. A statue of her is in the grounds. With an hour or so to spare, you could visit the **Cowal Bird Garden** (April–Oct daily 10.30am–6pm; £3.25), one mile northwest along the A885 to Sandbank, and wander through their woodland amid exotic caged birds as well as free-roaming peacocks, macaws and pot-bellied pigs. If the weather's fine, take the **Ardnadam Heritage Trail**, a mile further up the road, to the wonderful Dunan viewpoint looking out to the Firth of Clyde.

It's a good idea to take advantage of Dunoon's **tourist office**, the principal one in Cowal, located on Alexandra Parade (May–Sept Mon–Fri 9am–6pm, Sat & Sun 10am–5pm; April & Oct Mon–Fri 9am–5.30pm, Sat 10am–5pm, Sun 11am–3pm; Nov–March Mon–Thurs 9am–5.30pm, Fri 9am–5pm; ℡01369/703785). There are two **ferry crossings** across the Clyde from Gourock to Dunoon; the shorter, more frequent service is half-hourly on Western Ferries to Hunter's Quay, a mile north of the town centre; CalMac's boats, though, arrive at the main pier, and have better transport connections if you're on foot.

There's an enormous choice of **B&Bs**, none of them outstanding. You're better off heading out of town or persuading the tourist office to help you out, since availability is the biggest problem. For real quality, head for the highly reputable *Ardfillayne House*, West Bay (☎01369/702267, ⓦwww.ardfillayne .activebooking.com; ❹). A **hostel**, run by the Baptist Church, is due to open on Alexandra Parade (for the latest, call the church on ☎01369/706665). *Chatters*, 58 John St (Wed–Sat only; closed Jan & Feb), is Dunoon's best **restaurant**, offering delicious Loch Fyne seafood and Scottish beef. Dunoon boasts a two-screen **cinema** (a rarity in Argyll) on John Street, but the town's most famous entertainment is the **Cowal Highland Gathering** (ⓦwww.cowal-gathering.com), the largest of its kind in the world, held here on the last weekend in August, and culminating in the awesome spectacle of the massed pipes and drums of more than 150 bands marching through the streets.

The Isle of Bute

Thanks to its consistently mild climate and its ferry link with Wemyss Bay (see p.1116), the island of **Bute** has been a popular holiday and convalescence spot for Clydesiders – particularly the elderly – for over a century. Even considering the island's small size (fifteen miles long and five miles wide) you can find peace and quiet; most of its inhabitants are centred on the two wide bays on the east coast of the island.

Bute's only town, **ROTHESAY**, is a handsome Victorian resort set in a wide sweeping bay, backed by green hills, with a classic palm-tree promenade and 1920s pagoda-style Winter Gardens. It creates a much better general impression than Dunoon, with its period architecture and the occasional flourishes of wrought-ironwork. Even if you're just passing through, you should pay a visit to the ornate **Victorian toilets** (daily: Easter–Oct 8am–9pm; Nov–Easter 9am–5pm; 10p) on the pier, which were built by Twyfords in 1899 and have since been declared a national treasure. Men have the best time, since the porcelain urinals steal the show, but women can ask for a guided tour. Rothesay also boasts the militarily useless, but architecturally impressive, moated ruins of **Rothesay Castle** (April–Sept daily 9.30am–6.30pm; Oct–March Mon–Wed 9.30am–4.30pm, Thurs 9.30am–noon, Sat 9.30am–4.30pm, Sun 2–4.30pm; HS; £2), hidden amid the town's backstreets but signposted from the pier. Built around the twelfth century, it was twice captured by the Vikings in the 1200s; such vulnerability was the reasoning behind the unusual, almost circular curtain wall, with its four big drum towers, only one of which remains fully intact.

A very good reason for coming to Bute is to visit **Mount Stuart** (May–Sept Mon, Wed & Fri–Sun 11am–5pm; £6.50, gardens only £3), three miles south of Rothesay. Seat of the fantastically wealthy seventh Marquis of Bute, the mansion was built for the third marquis between 1879 and World War II, as an incredible High Gothic fancy, drawing architectural inspiration from all over Europe. The sumptuous interior was decked out by craftsmen who worked with William Burges on the marquis's earlier medieval concoctions at Cardiff Castle. The gardens, established in the eighteenth century by the third Earl of Bute, who had a hand in London's Kew Gardens, are equally lovely.

For the best overall view of the island, take a walk up **Canada Hill** above the freshwater Loch Fad, which all but divides Bute in two. The northern half of the island is hilly, uninhabited and little visited, while the southern half is made up of Lowland-style farmland. The early monastic history of the island is recalled at **St Blane's Chapel**, a twelfth-century ruin beautifully situated in open countryside on the west coast, close to the very southernmost tip. Bute's finest sandy beach is **Scalpsie Bay**, further up the west coast, beyond which lies **St Ninian's Point**, where the ruins of a sixth-century chapel overlook another fine sandy strand and the deserted island of **Inchmarnock**.

Practicalities

Rothesay's **tourist office** is opposite the pier at 15 Victoria St (July & Aug Mon–Fri 9am–7pm, Sat 10am–7pm, Sun 10am–5pm; May, June & Sept Mon–Fri 9am–5.30pm, Sat & Sun 10am–5pm; April & Oct Mon–Fri 9am–5.30pm, Sat & Sun 9.30am–5pm; Nov–March Mon–Thurs 9am–5.30pm, Fri 9am–5pm; ☎01700/502151). There's no shortage of modest places to **stay** along the seafront, but one of the most attractive is *Cannon House* (☎01700/ 502819; ⑤), a Georgian house close to the pier on Battery Place. Another excellent option, a mile to the north in Ardbeg, is *Ardmory House* (☎01700/ 502346, ⓔardmory.house.hotel@dial.pipex.com; ⑤), which is also one of the area's best places to eat. Further out, one mile north of Mount Stuart, *New Farm* (☎01700/831646; ②) has a few rooms in a lovely converted farmhouse, above a moderately expensive restaurant. The best **food** options in Rothesay itself are *Oliver's*, on Victoria Street, or fish and chips at the *West End Café* on Gallowgate. The *Harbour Café* on the seafront combines coffee, cakes and **internet** surfing. Rothesay's **cinema** is in the Winter Gardens. Bute holds its own **Highland Games** on the second-to-last weekend in August – Prince Charles, the Duke of Rothesay, occasionally attends.

Inveraray

A classic example of an eighteenth-century planned town, **INVERARAY** was built on the site of a ruined fishing village in 1745 by the third Duke of Argyll, head of the powerful Campbell clan, in order to distance his newly rebuilt castle from the hoi polloi in the town and to establish a commercial and legal centre for the region. Today Inveraray, an absolute set piece of Scottish Georgian architecture, has a truly memorable setting, the brilliant white arches of Front Street reflected in the still waters of **Loch Fyne**, which separate it from the Cowal peninsula.

Squeezed onto a promontory some distance from the duke's new castle, there's not much more to Inveraray's "New Town" than its distinctive **Main Street** (set at a right angle to Front Street), flanked by whitewashed terraces, whose window casements are picked out in black. At the top of the street, the road divides to circumnavigate the town's Neoclassical church, originally built in two parts: the southern half served the Gaelic-speaking community, while the northern half served those who spoke English.

East of the church is **Inveraray Jail** (daily: April–Oct 9.30am–6pm; Nov–March 10am–5pm; £4.90), whose attractive Georgian courthouse and grim prison blocks ceased to function in the 1930s. The jail is now an imaginative and thoroughly enjoyable museum, which graphically recounts prison conditions from medieval times up until the nineteenth century – and even brings it up to date by including a picture of life in Barlinnie Prison. You can also sit in the beautiful semicircular courthouse and listen to the trial of a farmer accused of fraud.

A ten-minute walk north of the New Town, the neo-Gothic **Inveraray Castle** (July & Aug Mon–Sat 10am–5.45pm, Sun 1–5.45pm; April–June, Sept & Oct Mon–Thurs & Sat 10am–1pm & 2–5.45pm, Sun 1–5.45pm; £5.50) remains the family home of the Duke of Argyll. Built in 1745 by the third duke, it was given a touch of the Loire in the nineteenth century with the addition of dormer windows and conical roofs. Inside, the most startling feature is the armoury hall, whose displays of weaponry – supplied to the Campbells by the British government to put down the Jacobites – rise through several storeys; look out for Rob Roy's rather sad-looking sporran and dirk handle (a "dirk" being a dagger, traditionally worn in Highland dress).

Practicalities

Inveraray's **tourist office** is on Front Street (July & Aug daily 9am–6pm; May & June Mon–Sat 9am–5pm, Sun 11am–5pm; April, Sept & Oct Mon–Sat 9am–5pm, Sun noon–5pm; Feb, March & Nov Mon–Fri 11am–4pm, Sat & Sun noon–4pm; Jan & Dec Mon–Fri 10am–3pm, Sat & Sun 11am–3pm; ☏01499/302063), as is the town's chief **hotel**, the historic *Argyll* (☏01499/302466; ❹), now part of the Best Western chain. A cheaper, but equally well-appointed alternative is the Georgian *Fernpoint Hotel* (☏01499/302170, ✉fernpoint.hotel@virgin.net; ❶), round by the pier, which has a nice pub garden. The SYHA **hostel** (☏01499/302454, ⓦwww.syha.org.uk; mid-March to Oct) is in a modern building a short distance north on the A819 Dalmally road. The **bar** of the central *George Hotel* is the town's liveliest spot. The best place to sample Loch Fyne's delicious fresh fish and seafood is the superb, moderately priced restaurant of the *Loch Fyne Oyster Bar* (see p.1089), six miles northeast back up the A83 towards Glasgow.

Oban

The solidly Victorian resort of **OBAN** enjoys a superb setting – the island of Kerrera providing its bay with a natural shelter – distinguished by a bizarre granite amphitheatre, dramatically lit at night, on the hilltop above the town. Despite a population of just eight thousand, it's by far the largest port in northwest Scotland, the second-largest town in Argyll, and the main departure point for ferries to the Hebrides. If you arrive late, or are catching an early boat, you may have to spend the night here (there's no real need otherwise); if you're staying elsewhere, it's a useful base for wet-weather activities and shopping, although it does get uncomfortably crowded in the summer.

The only truly remarkable sight in Oban is the town's landmark, **McCaig's Tower**, a stiff ten-minute climb from the quayside. Built in imitation of Rome's Colosseum, it was the brainchild of a local businessman a century ago, who had the twin aims of alleviating off-season unemployment among the local stonemasons and creating a museum, art gallery and chapel. In his will, McCaig gave instructions for the lancet windows to be filled with bronze statues of the family, though no such work was ever undertaken. Instead, the folly has been turned into a sort of walled garden, and simply provides a wonderful seaward panorama, particularly at sunset.

Down in the centre of town, you can pass a few hours admiring the boats in the harbour and looking out for scavenging seals in the bay. If the weather's bad, the best option is to sign up for one of the excellent guided tours around **Oban Distillery** (Mon–Fri 9.30am–5pm; Easter–Oct also Sat; July–Sept Mon–Fri until 8.30pm, Sun noon–5pm; ⓦwww.scotch.com; £3.50), in the centre of town off George Street. The tour ends with a generous dram of Oban's lightly peaty malt (and a refund of the admission fee if you buy a bottle).

Practicalities

The CalMac **ferry terminal** (℡01631/566688, ⓦwww.calmac.co.uk) for the islands is on Railway Pier, a stone's throw from the **train station**, which is itself adjacent to the **bus station** on Station Square. The **tourist office** (July & Aug Mon–Sat 9am–8pm, Sun 9am–7pm; mid- to late June & Sept Mon–Sat 9am–6.30pm, Sun 10am–5pm; May to mid-June Mon–Sat 9am–5.30pm, Sun 10am–5pm; late Sept to Oct Mon–Sat 9am–5.30pm, Sun 10am–4pm; April Mon–Fri 9am–5pm, Sat & Sun 10am–5pm; Nov–March Mon–Fri 9.30am–5pm, Sat & Sun noon–4pm; ℡01631/563122; ⓦwww.oban.org.uk) is housed in a converted church on Argyll Square.

Oban is positively heaving with **hotels** and **B&B**s. Top choices include the *Glenbervie Guest House* (℡01631/564770; ❶), a superior Victorian guest house set slightly above the town on Dalriach Road, the *Glenburnie Hotel* (℡01631/562089; April–Oct; ❸), an efficiently run medium-sized Victorian hotel on the quieter section of the Corran Esplanade, beyond the cathedral, and the *Royal Hotel*, on Argyll Square (℡01631/563021; ❺), the best of Oban's big central hotels. There are also three **hostels**, the friendliest, cheapest and most central of which is the *Oban Backpackers*, on Breadalbane Street (℡01631/562107, ⓔoban@scotlands-top-hostels.com). **Campers** should head for *Oban Caravan & Camping Park,* Gallanachmore Farm, Gallanach Road (℡01631/562425; April to mid-Oct), two miles southwest of Oban along the Gallanach Road.

For sit-down snacks, *F'Eats*, a modern café on John Street, offers delicious toasted panini and good cappuccino. On the corner of George and John Street is Oban's swankiest new designer **restaurant**, *Ee-usk*, which serves up superb fish and seafood dishes. Vegetarians might prefer to head for *Café Na Lusan,* in Craigard Road (closed Mon), an internet café serving inexpensive veggie food. Oban's only half-decent **pub** is the *Oban Inn* opposite the North Pier, with a classic dark-wood-flagstone-and-brass bar downstairs and lounge bar with stained glass upstairs. It's worth noting, however, that Oban is one of the few places in Argyll with a **cinema**, confusingly known as The Highland Theatre (℡01631/562444), at the north end of George Street. The annual **Argyllshire Gathering** takes place on the last Thursday in August, featuring piping competitions and Highland Games.

The Isle of Mull

The second largest of the Inner Hebrides, **Mull** (ⓦwww.holidaymull.org.uk) is by far the most accessible: just forty minutes from Oban by ferry. As so often, first impressions largely depend on the weather – it is the wettest of the Hebrides (and that's saying something) – for without the sun the large tracts of moorland, particularly around the island's highest peak, Ben More (3196ft), can appear bleak and unwelcoming. There are, however, areas of more gentle pastoral scenery around **Dervaig** in the north and the indented west coast varies from the sandy beaches around **Calgary** to the cliffs of Loch na Keal. The most common mistake is to try and "do" the island in a day or two: flogging up the main road to the picturesque capital of **Tobermory**, then covering the fifty-odd miles between there and Fionnphort, in order to visit **Iona**. Mull is a place that will grow on you only if you have the time and patience to explore.

Historically, crofting, whisky distilling and fishing supported the islanders (*Muileachs*), but the population – which peaked at 10,000 – decreased dramat-

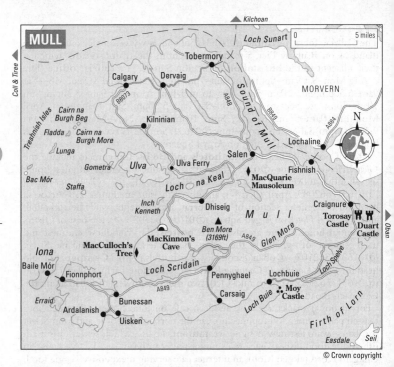

© Crown copyright

ically in the late nineteenth century due to the Clearances and the 1846 pota-to famine. On Mull, it is a trend that has been reversed, mostly due to the large influx of settlers from elsewhere in the country which has brought the current population up to over 2500. One of the main reasons for this resurgence is, of course, tourism – more than half a million visitors come here each year – although, oddly enough, there are very few large hotels or campsites.

Craignure is the main arrival point, with a frequent daily **car ferry** link with Oban (booking advised). Two much smaller car ferries operate on a first-come first-served basis: from Lochaline on the Morvern peninsula to the slipway at Fishnish, six miles northwest of Craignure; and from Kilchoan on the Ardnamurchan peninsula to Tobermory, 24 miles northwest of Craignure. **Public transport** on Mull is not too bad on the main A849, but there's more or less no service along the west coast (for more information, visit ⓦwww.mict.co.uk/travel).

Craignure and around

CRAIGNURE is little more than a scattering of cottages, though there is a small shop, a bar, some toilets and a CalMac and **tourist office** – the only one on the island open all year round – situated opposite the pier (mid-June to mid-Sept Mon–Thurs 8.30am–7pm, Fri 8.30am–5.15pm, Sat 9am–6.30pm, Sun 10am–5.30pm; April to mid-June Mon–Fri 8.30am–5.15pm, Sat 9am–6.30pm, Sun 10.30am–5.30pm; mid-Sept to mid-Oct Mon–Fri 8.30am–5.15pm, Sat 9am–5pm, Sun 10.30am–5.30pm; mid-Oct to mid-April Mon–Sat 10am–5pm, Sun 10.30am–noon & 3.30–5pm; ☎01680/812377). The *Craignure Inn* (☎01680/812305, ⓦwww.craignure-inn.co.uk; ❸), just a minute's stroll up the road towards Fionnphort, is a snug **pub** to hole up in. There's also a well-equipped **campsite** (☏01680/812496, ⓦwww.sheiling-holidays.co.uk; April–Oct) on the south side of Craignure Bay, behind the new village hall.

Two castles lie immediately southeast of Craignure. **Torosay Castle** (Easter to mid-Oct daily 10.30am–5.30pm; £4.50, gardens only £3.50), a full-blown Scottish Baronial creation, is linked to Craignure by the narrow-gauge Mull Rail (Easter to mid-Oct; ☏01680/812494, ⓦwww.holidaymull.org.uk/rail; £3.50 return). The magnificent **gardens** (all year daily 10.30am–5.30pm) with their avenue of eighteenth-century Venetian statues, Japanese section, and views over to neighbouring Duart. The house itself, in the mid-nineteenth-century style, is stuffed with junk relating to the present owners, the little-known Guthries.

Lacking the gardens, but perched on a picturesque spit of rock a couple of miles east of Torosay, **Duart Castle** (May to mid-Oct daily 10.30am–6pm; ⓦwww.duartcastle.com; £3.80) is clearly visible from the Oban–Craignure ferry. Headquarters of the once-powerful MacLean clan from the thirteenth century, it was burnt down by the Campbells and confiscated after the 1745 rebellion. Finally in 1911, the 26th clan chief, Fitzroy MacLean (1835–1936) managed to buy it back and restore it. You can peek at the dungeons, climb up to the ramparts, study the family photos, and learn about the world scout movement – the 27th clan chief became Chief Scout in 1959. After your visit, you can enjoy home-made cakes and tea at the castle's excellent tearoom.

Tobermory

Mull's chief town, **TOBERMORY**, at the northern tip of the islands, is easily the most attractive fishing port on the west coast of Scotland, its clusters of brightly coloured houses and boats sheltering in a bay backed by a steep bluff. Founded in 1788 by the British Society for Encouraging Fisheries, it never really took off as a fishing port and only survived due to the steady influx of crofters evicted from other parts of the island during the Clearances. With a population of more than 800, it is, without doubt, the capital of Mull, and if you're staying any length of time on the island you're bound to end up here, not least because it has a Womble named after it.

Practicalities aside, the harbour's shops are good for browsing, and you could pay a visit to the **Hebridean Whale and Dolphin Trust** (April–Oct daily 10am–5pm; Nov–March Mon–Fri 11am–5pm; ⓦwww.hwdt.org; free), run by a welcoming bunch of enthusiasts. The small office has lots of information on how to identify marine mammals, and on recent sightings. They're very child-friendly, too, and will keep kids amused for an hour or so with computer marine games, word searches and a bit of artwork. Sea Life Surveys (☏01688/302787, ⓦwww.sealifesurveys.co.uk), who offer a variety of whale- and dolphin-watching **tours**, are run from the same office.

Another good wet-weather retreat is the **Mull Museum** (Easter to mid-Oct Mon–Fri 10.30am–4pm, Sat 10am–1pm; £1), further along Main Street, which packs a great deal of information and artefacts – including a few objects salvaged from the sixteenth-century wreck of the *San Juan* – into one tiny room. A stiff climb up Back Brae will bring you to the island's main arts centre, **An Tobar** (Tues–Sat 10am–4pm; free), housed in a converted Victorian schoolhouse. The centre hosts exhibitions, a variety of live events, and contains a café with comfy sofas set before a real fire. The rest of the upper town is laid out on a classic grid-plan, and merits a stroll, if only for the great views over the bay.

The **tourist office** (July & Aug Mon–Sat 9.30am–6pm, Sun 10am–5pm; May & June Mon–Sat 10am–5pm, Sun 11am–5pm; April Mon–Fri 10am–5pm, Sat & Sun noon–5pm; Sept & Oct Mon–Sat 10am–5pm, Sun noon–5pm; ☎01688/302182) is in the same building as the CalMac ticket office at the far end of Main Street. There are several **accommodation** options on Main Street: try the excellent *Fàilte* (☎01688/302495; ❷), the *Harbour Guest House* (☎01688/302209; ❶), or the small, friendly SYHA **hostel** (☎01688/302481, ⓦwww.syha.org.uk; March–Oct). The grand Victorian *Western Isles Hotel* (☎01688/302012, ⓔwihotel@aol.com; ❺) sits high above the bay. The nearest **campsite** is *Newdale* (☎01688/302525; April–Oct), nicely situated one and a half miles outside Tobermory on the B8073 to Dervaig.

Main Street is heaving with places to **eat**. You can get huge bar meals in the lounge bar at the *Mishnish*, but for more imaginative local seafood and meat dishes, you need to go to *Back Brae* (evenings only), which does moderately expensive set menus and à la carte, or to the *Western Isles Hotel*, which serves superior bar food in the conservatory overlooking the Sound of Mull. The *Mishnish* has been the most popular local **pub** for many years, and features live music at the weekend, It's also the focus of Mull's annual **Traditional Music Festival**, a feast of Gaelic folk music held on the last weekend in April. Mull's other major musical event, after the folk festival, is the annual **Mendelssohn on Mull Festival**, held over ten days in early July, which commemorates the composer's visit here in 1829.

Dervaig and Calgary

The gently undulating countryside west of Tobermory, beyond the freshwater Mishnish lochs, provides some of the most beguiling scenery on the island. Added to this, the road out west, the B8073, is exceptionally dramatic, with fiendish switchbacks much appreciated during the annual Mull Rally, which takes place each October. The only village of any size is **DERVAIG**, which nestles beside narrow Loch Chumhainn, just eight miles southwest of Tobermory, distinguished by its unusual pencil-shaped church spire and dinky whitewashed cottages set in twos along its main street. Dervaig is best known as the home of **Mull Theatre**, one of the smallest professional theatres in the world, which puts on an adventurous season of plays adapted for a handful of resident actors (April–Sept; ☎01688/302828, ⓦwww.mulltheatre.org.uk); booking is recommended. The box office is in the main street, while the theatre itself lies within the grounds of the Victorian *Druimard Country House* (☎01688/400345, ⓦwww.druimard.co.uk; ❼; late March–Oct), which has a decent bar, and offers top-class, expensive pre-theatre dinners. Dervaig has a wide choice of **places to stay**: the *Druimnacroish Hotel* (☎01688/400274, ⓦwww.drumnacroish.co.uk; ❺), a lovely country house two miles out on the Salen road, and several good B&Bs ranging from the vegetarian-friendly *Glen Bellart House* (☎01688/400282; ❶; Easter–Oct), on the main street to *Glenview* (☎01688/400239; ❷; April–Oct), a really lovely 1890s house on the edge of the village.

The road continues cross-country to **CALGARY**, once a thriving crofting community, now an idyllic holiday spot boasting Mull's finest sandy bay, backed by low-lying dunes and machair, with wonderful views over to Coll and Tiree. There's just one hotel, the delightful *Calgary Farmhouse* (☎01688/400256, ⓦwww.calgary.co.uk; ❹; April–Oct), whose excellent, moderately priced *Dovecote* restaurant (closed Mon) is (unsurprisingly) housed in a converted dovecote. The south side of the beach is a favourite spot for **camping** rough, though the only facilities are the public toilets.

The Isle of Staffa

Seven miles off the west coast of Mull, **Staffa** is the most romantic and dramatic of Scotland's many uninhabited islands. On its south side, the perpendicular rockface features an imposing series of black basalt columns, known as the Colonnade, which have been cut by the sea into cathedralesque caverns, most notably **Fingal's Cave**. The Vikings knew about the island – the name derives from their word for "Island of Pillars" – but it wasn't until 1772 that it was "discovered" by the world. Turner painted it, Wordsworth explored it, but Mendelssohn's *Die Fingalshöhle*, inspired by the sounds of the sea-wracked caves he heard on a visit here in 1829, did most to popularize the place – after which Queen Victoria gave her blessing, too. The geological explanation for these polygonal basalt organ pipes is that they were created by a massive subterranean explosion some sixty million years ago. A huge mass of molten basalt burst forth onto land and, as it cooled, solidified into what are, essentially, crystals. To **get to Staffa**, you can join one of the many boat trips from Fionnphort, Iona, Ulva Ferry, Dervaig or even Oban. Staffa-only trips run from April to October and cost £12.50 per person on the *Iolaire* (℡01681/700358), which sails out of Fionnphort and Iona twice daily; Turus Mara (℡0800/085 8786, Ⓦwww.turus-mara.com), which operates out of Ulva Ferry, costs a bit more as do Inter-Island Cruises (℡01688/400264, Ⓦwww.jenny.mull.com), which run from Dervaig.

Ben More and the Ross of Mull

From the southern shores of Loch na Keal, which almost splits Mull in two, rise the terraced slopes of **Ben More** (3169ft) – literally "big mountain" – a mighty extinct volcano, and the only Munro in the Hebrides outside of Skye. Stretching for twenty miles west of Ben More as far as Iona is Mull's rocky southernmost peninsula, the **Ross of Mull**, which, like much of Scotland, appears blissfully tranquil in good weather, and desolate and bleak in bad climes.

The road ends at **FIONNPHORT**, facing Iona, probably the least attractive place to stay on the Ross, though it has a nice sandy bay backed by pink granite rocks to the north of the ferry slipway. Partly to ease congestion on Iona, and to give their neighbours a slice of the tourist pound, Fionnphort was chosen as the site for the **St Columba Centre** (Easter–Sept daily 10.30am–1pm & 2–5.30pm; free); inside, a small exhibition outlines Iona's history, tells a little of Columba's life (for more on which, see p.1098), and has a few facsimiles of the illuminated manuscripts produced by the islands's monks.

If you're in need of a **B&B** in Fionnphort, try the granite *Seaview* (℡01681/700235, Ⓦwww.holidaymull.org/seaview; ❶), or the whitewashed *Staffa House* (℡01681/700677; ❷; March–Oct), both of which are close to the ferry, and have views over to Iona. The basic *Fidden Farm* campsite (℡01681/700427; April–Sept), a mile south along the Knockvologan road by Fidden beach, is the nearest to Iona.

The Isle of Iona

Less than a mile off the southwest tip of Mull, **IONA** – just three miles long and not much more than a mile wide – has been a place of pilgrimage for several centuries, and a place of Christian worship for more than 1400 years. For it was to this flat Hebridean island that St Columba fled from Ireland in 563 and established a monastery which was responsible for the conversion of more

A brief history of Iona

Legend has it that **St Columba** (Colum Cille), born in Donegal in northwestern Ireland some time around 521, was a direct descendant of the semi-legendary Irish king, Niall of the Nine Hostages. A scholar and soldier priest, who founded numerous monasteries in Ireland, he is thought to have become involved in a bloody dispute with the king when he refused to hand over a copy of *St Jerome's Psalter* copied illegally from the original owned by St Finian of Moville. This, in turn, provoked the Battle of Cúl Drebene (Cooldrumman) – also known as the **Battle of the Book** – at which Columba's forces won, though with the loss of over 3000 lives. The story goes that, repenting this bloodshed, Columba went into exile with twelve other monks, eventually settling on Iona in 563. The bottom line, however, is that we know very little about Columba, though he undoubtedly became something of a cult figure after his death in 597. He was posthumously credited with miraculous feats such as defeating the Loch Ness monster and banishing snakes (and, some say, frogs) from the island.

Whatever the truth about Columba's life, in the sixth and seventh centuries, Iona enjoyed a great deal of autonomy from Rome, establishing a specifically **Celtic Christian** tradition. Missionaries were sent out to the rest of Scotland and parts of England, and Iona quickly became a respected seat of learning and artistry; the monks compiled a vast library of intricately **illuminated manuscripts** – most famously the *Book of Kells* (now on display in Trinity College, Dublin) – while the masons excelled in carving peculiarly intricate crosses. Two factors were instrumental in the demise of the Celtic tradition: a series of Viking raids, the worst of which was the massacre of 68 monks on the sands of Martyrs' Bay in 806; and relentless pressure from the established Church, beginning with the Synod of Whitby in 664, which chose Rome over the Celtic Church, and culminated in the suppression of the Celtic Church by King David I in 1144.

In 1203, Iona became part of the mainstream church with the establishment of an **Augustinian nunnery** and a **Benedictine monastery** by Reginald, son of Somerled, Lord of the Isles. During the Reformation, the entire complex was ransacked, the contents of the library burnt and all but three of the island's 360 crosses destroyed. Although plans were drawn up at various times to turn the abbey into a Cathedral of the Isles, nothing came of them until in 1899, when the then owner, the eighth duke of Argyll, donated the abbey buildings to the **Church of Scotland**, who restored the abbey church for worship over the course of the next decade. Iona's modern resurgence began in 1938, when **George MacLeod**, a minister from Glasgow, established a group of ministers, students and artisans to begin rebuilding the remainder of the monastic buildings. What began as a mostly male, Gaelic-speaking, strictly Presbyterian community is today a lay, mixed and ecumenical retreat. The entire abbey complex has been successfully restored, and is now looked after by Historic Scotland, while the island, apart from the church land and a few crofts, is in the care of the National Trust for Scotland.

or less all of pagan Scotland as well as much of northern England. This history and the island's splendid isolation have lent it a peculiar religiosity; in the much-quoted words of Dr Johnson, who visited in 1773, "that man is little to be envied . . . whose piety would not grow warmer among the ruins of Iona". Today, however, the island can barely cope with the constant flood of day-trippers, and charges visitors entry to its abbey, so to appreciate the special atmosphere and to have time to see the whole island, including the often overlooked west coast, you should plan on staying at least one night.

The passenger ferry from Fionnphort drops you off at the island's main village, **BAILE MÓR** (literally "large village"), which is in fact little more than a single terrace of cottages facing the sea. Just inland lie the extensive pink granite ruins of the **Augustinian nunnery**, built with pink granite around 1200, but disused since the Reformation – if nothing else, it gives you an idea of the state of the present-day abbey before it was restored. Across the road to the north is the **Iona Heritage Centre** (April–Oct Mon–Sat 10.30am–4.30pm; £1.50), with displays on the social history of the island over the last 200 years, including the Clearances, which nearly halved the island's population of 500 in the mid-nineteenth century. At a bend in the road, just south of the manse and church, stands the fifteenth-century **MacLean's Cross**, a fine late medieval example of the distinctive, flowing, three-leaved foliage of the Iona school.

No buildings remain from Columba's time: the present **abbey** (daily: April–Sept 9.30am–6.30pm; Oct–March 9.30am–4.30pm; HS; £2.80) dates from the arrival of the Benedictines in around 1200, was extensively rebuilt in the fifteenth and sixteenth centuries, and restored virtually wholesale early last century. Adjoining the facade is a small steep-roofed chamber, believed to be St Columba's grave, now a small chapel. The three high crosses in front of the abbey date from the eighth to tenth centuries, and are decorated with the Pictish serpent and boss and Celtic spirals for which Iona's early Christian masons were renowned. For reasons of sanitation, the cloisters were placed, contrary to the norm, on the north side of the church (where running water was available); entirely reconstructed in the late 1950s, they now shelter a useful historical account of the abbey's development.

Iona's oldest building, the plain-looking **St Oran's Chapel**, lies south of the abbey, and boasts an eleventh-century door. Oran's Chapel stands at the centre of Iona's sacred burial ground, **Reilig Odhráin** (Oran's Cemetery), which is said to contain the graves of sixty kings of Norway, Ireland, France and Scotland, including Duncan and Macbeth. The best of the early Christian gravestones and medieval effigies which once lay in the Reilig Odhráin have unfortunately been removed to the Infirmary Museum, behind the abbey.

Practicalities

There's no **tourist office** on Iona, and as demand far exceeds supply you should organize **accommodation** well in advance. Of the island's two **hotels**, the stone-built *Argyll* (☎01681/700334, ⓦwww.argyllhoteliona.co.uk; ❷–❻; April–Oct), in the terrace of cottages overlooking the Sound of Iona, is by far the nicer. As for **B&Bs**, try the secluded *Sithean House* (☎01681/700331; ❶), a mile from the ferry, on the peaceful west side of the island. **Camping** is not permitted on Iona, but there is a **hostel** (☎01681/700642), a mile or so from the ferry, past the abbey. If you want to stay with the **Iona Community**, contact the *MacLeod Centre* (☎01681/700404, ⓦwww.iona.org.uk), popularly known as the "Mac". **Food** options are limited: the eclectic bar menu of the *Argyll* is probably your best option or, for something lighter, head for the tearoom, beside the Heritage Centre, which serves home-made soup and delicious cakes.

Coll, Tiree and Colonsay

Coll and **Tiree** are among the most isolated of the Inner Hebrides, and if anything have more in common with the outlying Western Isles than with their closest neighbour, Mull. Each is roughly twelve miles long and three miles wide, both are low-lying, treeless and exceptionally windy, with white sandy beaches and the highest sunshine records in Scotland. Isolated between Mull

△ Tobermory harbour, Mull

and Islay, **Colonsay** (Ⓦ www.colonsay.org.uk) – eight miles by three at its widest – is nothing like as bleak and windswept as Coll or Tiree. All the islands have strong Gaelic roots, but the percentage of English-speaking newcomers is rising steadily.

The Isle of Coll

The fish-shaped rocky island of **Coll** (population 180) lies less than seven miles off the coast of Mull. The CalMac ferry drops off at Coll's only real village, **ARINAGOUR**, whose whitewashed cottages dot the western shore of Loch Eatharna. Half the island's population lives in the village, and it's here you'll find the hotel and pub, post office, churches and a couple of shops.

On the southwest coast there are two edifices, both confusingly known as **Breachacha Castle**, and both built by the MacLeans. The older, at the head of Loch Breachacha, is a fifteenth-century tower house with an additional curtain wall, recently restored, and is now a training centre for Project Trust overseas aid volunteers. The less attractive "new castle", to the northwest, is made up of a central block built around 1750 and two side pavilions added a century later, and is currently being restored. It was here that Dr Johnson and Boswell stayed in 1773 after a storm forced them to take refuge en route to Mull; they considered the place to be "a mere tradesman's box". Much of the area around the castles is now owned by the RSPB, in the hope of protecting the island's precious corncrake population. A vast area of **giant sand dunes** lies to the west of the castles, with two glorious golden sandy bays stretching for over a mile on either side. At the far western end is *Caolas*, where you can get a cup of tea and home-baked goodies, and where you can book ahead to stay (Ⓣ01879/230438; ❶).

The CalMac **ferry** from Oban calls at Coll (2hr 40min) every day except Thursdays and Sundays. In Arinagour, the small, family-run *Coll Hotel* (Ⓣ01879/230334; ❸) can provide **accommodation**; otherwise, there's the comfortable, modern *Taigh Solas* (Ⓣ01879/230333; ❷), overlooking the bay. *Achamore* (Ⓣ01879/230430, Ⓔjim@achamore.freeserve.co.uk; ❷), a traditional nineteenth-century farmhouse B&B, lies two miles west of Arinagour. The *Coll Hotel* doubles as the island's social centre, does excellent **food** and has a dining-room overflow. Another eating option is the *First Port of Coll* restaurant in Arinagour, which does inexpensive light meals. For **bike rental**, phone Ⓣ01879/230382 or 230873; for whale-watching trips, phone Ⓣ01879/230333 or 230426.

The Isle of Tiree

Tiree, as its Gaelic name *tir-iodh* ("land of corn") suggests, was once known as the breadbasket of the Inner Hebrides, thanks to its acres of rich machair. Nowadays crofting and tourism are the main sources of income for the resident population of around 800. One of the most distinctive features of Tiree is its architecture, in particular the large numbers of "pudding" or "spotty" houses, where only the mortar is painted white. Tiree's sandy beaches also attract large numbers of windsurfers for the Tiree Wave Classic every October.

The CalMac ferry calls at Gott Bay Pier, close to the village of **SCARINISH**, home to a post office, some public toilets, a supermarket, a butcher's and a bank, with a petrol pump back at the pier; to the east is **Gott Bay**, backed by a two-mile stretch of sand. It's just one mile across the island from Gott to Vaul Bay, on the north coast, where the well-preserved remains of a drystone broch, **Dun Mor** – dating from the first century BC – lie hidden in the rocks to the west of the bay. From here it's another two miles west along the coast to the *Clach a'Choire* or **Ringing Stone**, a huge glacial boulder decorated with mysterious prehistoric markings, which when struck with a stone gives out a metallic sound. The story goes that, should the Ringing Stone ever be broken in two, Tiree will sink beneath the waves. A mile further west you come to the lovely **Balephetrish Bay**, where you can watch waders feeding in the breakers, and look over the sea to Skye and the Western Isles.

The most intriguing sights, however, lie in the bulging western half of the island, where Tiree's two landmark hills rise up. The highest of the two, **Ben Hynish** (463ft), is unfortunately occupied by a "golf-ball" radar station, which tracks incoming transatlantic flights; the views from the top, though, are great. Below Ben Hynish, to the east is **HYNISH**, with its recently restored **harbour**, designed by Alan Stevenson in the 1830s to transport building materials for the magnificent 140-foot-tall **Skerryvore Lighthouse**, which lies on a sea-swept reef some twelve miles southwest of Tiree. Up on the hill behind the harbour, a stumpy granite signal tower, whose signals used to be the only contact the lighthouse keepers had with civilization, now houses a **museum** telling the history of the Herculean effort required to erect the lighthouse; weather permitting, you can see the lighthouse from the tower's viewing platform.

The CalMac **ferry** from Oban calls at Tiree (3hr 40min) every day except Thursdays and Sundays. Tiree also has an **airport** with flights (Mon–Sat) to and from Glasgow. Of the island's two **hotels**, the *Skerryvore House* (℡01879/220368; ❷), a mile or so east of Scarinish along Gott Bay, is preferable to the *Scarinish*. Better still are *Kirkapol House* (℡01879/220729; ❸), just beyond *Skerryvore House*, a great B&B in a converted kirk, and the *Glassary* (℡01879/220684; ❸), over on the west coast in Sandaig. There are no official campsites, but **camping** is allowed with the local crofter's permission. As for **eating**, apart from the *Skerryvore House*, the best option is the unpretentious, moderately priced *Glassary* (see above) over in Sandaig.

The Isle of Colonsay

Isolated between Mull and Islay, **Colonsay** is not as bleak and windswept as Coll or Tiree. Its craggy, heather-backed hills even support the occasional patch of woodland, plus a bewildering array of plant and birdlife, wild goats and rabbits, and one of the finest quasi-tropical gardens in Scotland. The population is currently around 200, down from a pre-Clearance peak of just under 1000, and the ferry links with the mainland are infrequent: three a week from Oban (Wed, Fri & Sun; 2hr 15min); one a week from Kennacraig via Islay (Wed; 3hr 35min), when a day-trip is possible, giving you around six hours on the island. There's a large number of self-catering cottages, but, with no camping or caravanning and just one hotel, a couple of B&Bs and a bunkhouse, there's no fear of mass tourism taking over.

The CalMac ferry terminal is at **SCALASAIG**, on the east coast, where there's a post office/shop, a petrol pump, a restaurant and the island's hotel. Right by the pier, the old waiting room now serves as the island's heritage centre and is usually open when the ferry docks. Two miles north of Scalasaig is **Colonsay House**, built in 1722 by Malcolm MacNeil. In 1904, the island and house were bought by Lord Strathcona, who made his fortune building the Canadian Pacific Railway (and whose descendants still own the island).

To the north of Colonsay House, where the road ends, you'll find the island's finest sandy beach, the breathtaking **Kiloran Bay**, where the breakers roll in from the Atlantic. There's another unspoilt sandy beach backed by dunes at Balnahard, two miles northeast along a rough track; en route, you might spot wild goats, choughs, and even a golden eagle. The island's west coast forms a sharp escarpment, quite at odds with the gentle undulating landscape that characterizes the rest of the island.

The **Isle of Oronsay**, half a mile to the south, is only an island when the tide is in, and, as you can't stay overnight, it can only be visited as a day-trip from Colonsay. The two are separated by "The Strand", a mile of tidal mud flats which act as a causeway for two hours either side of low tide; check locally for current timings. Although legends (and etymology) link saints Columba and Oran with both Colonsay and Oronsay, the ruins of the **Oronsay Priory** only date back to the fourteenth century. Abandoned since the Reformation, it still has the original church and cloisters, but the highlight is the Oronsay Cross, a superb example of late medieval artistry from Iona, and the numerous finely carved grave slabs that lie within the Prior's House.

Colonsay's only **hotel**, the *Isle of Colonsay* (℡01951/200316; ❺), is within easy walking distance of the pier in Scalasaig; and serves very decent bar snacks. The best alternative is to stay at the superb *Seaview* **B&B** (℡01951/200315; ❸; April–Oct), and the budget option is to sleep in the *Backpackers' Lodge* **hostel**, in the former keeper's lodge in Kiloran, run by the Colonsay Estate (℡01951/200312). An alternative to **eating out** at the hotel bar is the *Pantry*, above the pier in Scalasaig, which offers simple home-cooking as well as teas and cakes (ring ahead if you want to eat on Thurs or Fri eve; ℡01951/200325).

Mid-Argyll

Mid-Argyll is a vague term which loosely describes the central wedge of land south of Oban and north of Kintyre. The highlights of this gently undulating scenery lie along the sharply indented west coast, in particular the rich Bronze Age and Neolithic remains in the **Kilmartin** valley, one of the most important prehistoric sites in Scotland.

LOCHGILPHEAD, on the shores of Loch Fyne, is the chief town in the area, though it has little to offer beyond its practical use: it has a supermarket, several banks and a **tourist office** at 27 Lochnell St (July & Aug Mon–Sat 9.30am–6pm, Sun 10am–5pm; May & June Mon–Sat 10am–5pm, Sun 11am–5pm; April Mon–Fri 10am–5pm, Sat & Sun noon–5pm; Sept & Oct Mon–Sat 10am–5pm, Sun noon–5pm; ℡01546/602344).

Kilmartin Glen

The **Kilmartin Glen** is the most important prehistoric site on the Scottish mainland. The most remarkable relic is the **linear cemetery**, where several cairns are aligned for more than two miles, to the south of the village Kilmartin. These are thought to represent the successive burials of a ruling family or chieftains, but nobody can be sure. The best view of the cemetery's configuration is from the Bronze Age **Mid-Cairn**, but the Neolithic **South Cairn**, dating from around 3000 BC, is by far the oldest and the most impressive, with its large chambered tomb roofed by giant slabs.

Close to the Mid-Cairn, the two **Temple Wood stone circles** appear to have been the architectural focus of burials in the area from Neolithic times to the Bronze Age. Visible to the south are the impressively cup-marked **Nether Largie standing stones** (no public access), the largest of which looms over 10ft high. **Cup- and ring-marked rocks** are a recurrent feature of prehistoric sites in the Kilmartin Glen and elsewhere in Argyll. There are many theories as to their origin: some see them as Pictish symbols, others as primitive solar calendars. The most extensive markings in the entire country are at **Achnabreck**, off the A816 towards Lochgilphead.

Situated on high ground to the north of the cairns is the tiny village of **KILMARTIN**, where the old manse adjacent to the village church now houses a **Museum of Ancient Culture** (daily 10am–5.30pm; ⓦ www.kilmartin.org; £3.90), which is both enlightening and entertaining. Not only can you learn about the various theories concerning prehistoric crannogs, henges and cairns, but you can practise polishing an axe, examine different types of wood and fur, and listen to a variety of weird and wonderful sounds (check out the Gaelic bird imitations). The nearby church is worth a brief reconnoitre, as it shelters the badly damaged and weathered **Kilmartin crosses**, while a separate enclosure in the graveyard houses a large collection of medieval grave slabs of the Malcolms of Poltalloch.

To the south of Kilmartin, beyond the linear cemetery, lies the raised peat bog of Mòine Mhór (Great Moss), best known as home to the Iron Age fort of **Dunadd**, one of Scotland's most important Celtic sites, occupying a distinctive 176-foot-high rocky knoll once surrounded by the sea but currently stranded beside the winding River Add. It was here that Fergus, the first King of Dalriada, established his royal seat, having arrived from Ireland in around 500 AD. Its strategic position, the craggy defences and the view from the top are all impressive, but it's the **stone carvings** between the twin summits which make Dunadd so remarkable: several lines of inscription in ogam (an ancient alphabet of Irish origin), the faint outline of a boar, a hollowed-out footprint and a small basin. The boar and the inscriptions are probably Pictish, since the fort was clearly occupied long before Fergus got there, but the footprint and basin have been interpreted as being part of the royal coronation rituals of the kings of Dalriada. It is thought that the Stone of Destiny was used at Dunadd before being moved to Scone Palace, then to Westminster Abbey in London, where it languished until it was returned to Edinburgh in 1996.

Great-value **B&B** is available at *Tibertich* (☎01546/810281, ⓦwww.tibertich.com; ❶; March–Oct), a working sheep farm in the hills to the north of Kilmartin, off the A816, and also in the supremely isolated *Ardifuir* (☎01546/510271, Ⓔduntrune@msn.com; ❷), a farmhouse in the grounds of Duntrune Castle, very close to the sea. Alternatively, you could hole up in Crinan or Cairnbaan (see below). The aforementioned café/restaurant at Kilmartin House is a great lunchtime **eating** option; alternatively, the *Cairn* (☎01546/510254; March–Oct), opposite the church in Kilmartin, is open in the evening, and features moderately expensive Scottish and Mediterranean dishes.

Crinan Canal

In 1801 the nine-mile-long **Crinan Canal** opened, linking Loch Fyne, at Ardrishaig south of Lochgilphead, with the Sound of Jura, thus cutting out the long and treacherous journey around the Mull of Kintyre. John Rennie's original design, although an impressive engineering feat, had numerous faults, and by 1816 Thomas Telford was called in to take charge of the renovations. The canal runs parallel to the sea for quite some way before cutting across the bottom of Mòine Mhór and hitting a flight of locks either side of **CAIRNBAAN** (there are fifteen in total); a walk along the towpath is both picturesque and pleasantly unstrenuous. A useful pit stop can be made at the *Cairnbaan Hotel* (☎01546/603668; ❻), an eighteenth-century coaching inn overlooking the canal.

There are usually one or two yachts passing through the locks, but the most relaxing place from which to view the canal in action is **CRINAN**, the pretty little fishing port at the western end of the canal. Crinan's tiny harbour is, for the moment at least, still home to a small fishing fleet. Every room in the *Crinan Hotel* (℡01546/830261, ⓦwww.crinanhotel.com; ⓽) looks across Loch Crinan to the Sound of Jura. If the *Crinan* is beyond your means, try the secluded **B&B** *Tigh-na-Glaic* (℡01546/830261; ⓷), perched above the harbour, also with views out to sea. Bar **meals** at the *Crinan* are expensive, but utterly delicious, as is the hotel's even more expensive seafood restaurant, *Lock 16*, on the top floor, which commands a panoramic view; there's only one sitting, at 8pm, so booking is advisable. Down on the lockside there is a cheaper, cheerful **café** called the *Coffee Shop* (Easter–Oct), serving mouthwatering home-made cakes and wonderful clootie dumplings..

Kintyre

But for the mile-long isthmus between West Loch Tarbert and the much smaller East Loch Tarbert, the little-visited peninsula of **KINTYRE** (ⓦwww.kintyre.org) – from the Gaelic *ceann tire*, "land's end" – would be an island. Indeed, in the eleventh century, when the Scottish king, Malcolm Canmore, allowed Magnus Barefoot, King of Norway, to lay claim to any island he could circumnavigate by boat, Magnus succeeded in dragging his boat across the Tarbert isthmus and added the peninsula to his Hebridean kingdom. During the Wars of the Covenant, the vast majority of the population and property was wiped out by a combination of the 1646 potato blight and the destructive attentions of the Earl of Argyll. Kintyre remained a virtual desert until the earl began his policy of transplanting Gaelic-speaking Lowlanders to the region. They probably felt quite at home here, as the southern half of the peninsula lies on the Lowland side of the Highland Boundary Fault.

Public transport around Kintyre is slow, though services have improved. There are regular daily **buses** from Glasgow to Campbeltown, via Tarbert and the west coast, and even a skeleton service down the east coast. **Ferries** run to Tarbert from Portavadie on the Cowal peninsula, and Campbeltown has an airport, with daily **flights** from Glasgow.

Tarbert

A distinctive rocket-like church steeple heralds the fishing village of **TARBERT** (in Gaelic *An Tairbeart*, meaning "isthmus"), sheltering an attractive little bay backed by rugged hills. Tarbert's herring industry was mentioned in the Annals of Ulster as far back as 836 AD, though right now the local fishing industry is down to its lowest level ever, due to the strict EU quota system. Tourism is now an increasingly important source of income, as is the money that flows through the town during the last week in May, when the yacht races of the famous Scottish Series take place. Tarbert's harbourfront is pretty, and is best appreciated from the rubble of Robert the Bruce's fourteenth-century **castle** above the town to the south.

Tarbert's **tourist office** (July & Aug Mon–Sat 9.30am–6pm, Sun 10am–5pm; May & June Mon–Sat 10am–5pm, Sun 11am–5pm; April Mon–Fri 10am–5pm, Sat & Sun noon–5pm; Sept & Oct Mon–Sat 10am–5pm, Sun noon–5pm; ℡01880/820429) is on the harbour. If you need to **stay**, there's no shortage of B&Bs, though none are outstanding – try *Springside* B&B on Pier Road (℡01880/820413, ✉marshall.springside@virgin.net; ❶), which overlooks the harbour. Highly recommended, however, are the wonderful *Columba Hotel*, a detached Victorian town house further along Tarbert waterfront (℡01880/820808, ⓦwww.columbahotel.com; ❺), and the *Victoria Hotel* (℡01880/820236; ❹), the comfortable bright yellow pub on the opposite side of the harbour. The best bar **food** is to be had at the *Victoria*, where you can sit in the conservatory and look out across the harbour. For some excellent local meat, fish and seafood dishes, head for the moderately expensive *Anchorage* (℡01880/820881; Wed–Sat eves only), on the opposite side of the harbour.

The Isle of Gigha

Gigha (ⓦwww.isle-of-gigha.co.uk) – pronounced "gheeya" – is a low-lying, fertile island three miles off the west coast of Kintyre, reputedly occupied for 5000 years. The island's Ayrshire cattle produce over a quarter of a million gallons of milk a year, though since the closure of Gigha's creamery in the 1980s, the island's distinctive fruit-shaped cheese has been produced on the mainland. Like many of the smaller Hebrides, Gigha has been bought and sold numerous times after its original lairds, the MacNeils, sold up, and was finally bought by the 140 or so inhabitants themselves in 2001.

The ferry from Tayinloan, 23 miles south of Tarbert, deposits you at the island's only village, **ARDMINISH**, where you'll find the post office and shop. The main attraction on the island are the **Achamore Gardens** (daily 9am–dusk; £2), a mile and a half south of Ardminish. Established by the first postwar owner, Sir James Horlick of hot drink fame, their spectacularly colourful display of azaleas are best seen in early summer. The real draw of Gigha, however, apart from the peace and quiet, are the white sandy beaches – including one at Ardminish itself – that dot the coastline.

Gigha is so small – six miles by one mile – that most visitors come here just for the day. It is, however, possible to **stay** at either the *Post Office House* (℡01583/505251; ❷) or the *Gigha Hotel* (℡01583/505254; ❻; March–Oct), the very pleasant social centre of the island. The *Gigha Hotel* is also the place to go for tea and cakes, and for bar meals (with tables outside should the weather be fine).

Campbeltown

CAMPBELTOWN's best feature is its setting, in a deep bay sheltered by Davaar Island and the surrounding hills. With a population of 6500, it is also one of the largest towns in Argyll and, if you're staying in the southern half of Kintyre, its shops are by far the best place to stock up on supplies. As is evident from the architecture, Campbeltown's heyday was the Victorian era, when shipbuilding was going strong, coal was shipped by canal from Drumlemble, the fishing fleet was vast and Campbeltown Loch was said to be made of whisky. The decline of all its old industries has left the town permanently depressed, and unemployment and under-employment remain a persistent problem.

Nineteenth-century visitors to Campbeltown frequently found the place engulfed in a thick fog of pungent peat smoke from the town's 34 **whisky distilleries** – today, only two remain. The deeply traditional, family-owned Springbank, off Longrow, is the only distillery in Scotland that does absolutely everything from malting to bottling, on its own premises. There are regular no-nonsense guided tours but it's best to phone ahead to check (Easter–Sept Mon–Thurs 2pm; ℡01586/552085; £3). At the end, you get a voucher to exchange for a miniature at Eaglesomes, on Longrow South, whose range of whiskies is awesome.

On the town's palm-tree-dotted waterfront you'll find the "**Wee Picture House**", a little Art Deco cinema on Hall Street, built in 1913 and still going strong (daily except Fri). Next door is the equally delightful **Campbeltown Museum and Library** (Tues–Sat 10am–1pm & 2–5pm, Tues & Thurs 5.30–7.30pm; free), built in 1897 in the local sandstone, crowned by a distinctive lantern, and decorated on its harbourside wall with four relief panels depicting each of the town's main industries at the time. Inside, there's a timber-framed ceiling and etched glass partitions to admire, but the museum itself is inferior to the **Campbeltown Heritage Centre** on the Machrihanish Road (April–Oct Mon–Sat noon–5pm, Sun 2–5pm; £2), housed in the church known locally as the "Tartan Kirk", partly due to its Gaelic associations, but mainly for its stripy bell-cote and pinnacles.

Campbeltown's **tourist office** is currently on the Old Quay (July & Aug Mon–Sat 9am–6pm, Sun 11am–5pm; May & June Mon–Sat 9am–5pm, Sun noon–5pm; April Mon–Sat 10am–5pm; Sept & Oct Mon–Fri 10am–5pm, Sat 10am–4pm; Nov–March Mon–Fri 9am–4pm; ☏01586/552056), and will happily hand out a free map of the town. The best centrally located **accommodation** is the delightful family-run *Ardshiel Hotel*, on Kilkerran Road (☏01586/552133; ❸), situated on a lovely leafy square, just a block or so back from the ferry terminal. On the north side of the bay, *Craigard House* (☏01586/554242, ⓦwww.craigard-house.co.uk; ❻), a former whisky distiller's sandstone mansion is even more palatial. For an inexpensive, central B&B, head for *Westbank Guest House*, on Dell Road (☏01586/553660). The best bar **food** is to be found at the *Ardshiel Hotel*.

Southend and the Mull of Kintyre

The bulbous, hilly end of Kintyre, to the south of Campbeltown, features some of the most spectacular scenery on the whole peninsula, mixed with large swaths of Lowland-style farmland. **SOUTHEND** itself, a bleak, blustery spot, comes as something of a disappointment, though it does have a golden sandy beach. Below the cliffs to the west of the beach, a ruined thirteenth-century chapel marks the alleged arrival point of St Columba prior to his trip to Iona, and on a rocky knoll nearby a pair of footprints carved into the rock are known as **Columba's footprints**, though only one is actually of ancient origin.

Most people venture south of Campbeltown to make a pilgrimage to the **Mull of Kintyre** – the nearest Britain gets to Ireland, whose coastline, just twelve miles away, appears remarkably close on fine days. Although the Mull was made famous by the mawkish number-one hit by sometime local resident Paul McCartney, with the help of the Campbeltown Pipe Band, there's nothing specifically to see in this godforsaken storm-racked spot but the view. The roads up to the "**Gap**" (1150ft) – where you must leave your car – and particularly down to the lighthouse, itself 300ft above the ocean waves, are terrifyingly tortuous.

Southend still has a **pub**, the *Argyll Arms*, unremarkable except for the fact that it has a post office inside it. The only hotel has been closed for a long time now and cuts a forlorn figure, set back from the bay, but there are a couple of excellent **B&Bs**: *Ormsary Farm* (☏01586/830665; ❶; April–Sept), a small dairy farm up Glen Breakerie, and the nearby picturesque croft of *Low Cattadale* (☏01586/830205; ❶; March–Nov). **Camping** is possible right in the field right by the beach, run by *Machribeg Farm* (☏01586/830249; Easter–Sept).

The Isle of Arran

Shaped like a kidney bean, **Arran** (Ⓦwww.arran.net) is the most southerly (and therefore the most accessible) of all the Scottish islands. The Highland–Lowland dividing line passes right through its centre – hence the tourist board's aphorism about it being like "Scotland in miniature" – leaving the northern half sparsely populated, mountainous and bleak, while the lush southern half enjoys a much milder climate. Despite its immense popularity, the tourists, like the population of around 4500 – many of whom are incomers – tend to stick to the southeastern quarter of the island, leaving the west and the north relatively undisturbed.

Although tourism is now by far its most important industry, Arran, at twenty miles in length, is large enough to have a life of its own. While the island's post-1745 history and the Clearances (set in motion by the local lairds, the dukes of Hamilton) are as depressing as elsewhere in the Highlands, in recent years Arran has not suffered from the depopulation which has plagued other, more remote islands. Once a county in its own right (along with Bute), Arran has been left out of the new Argyll and Bute district in the latest county boundary shake-up, and is coupled instead with mainland North Ayrshire, with which it enjoys year-round transport links, but little else.

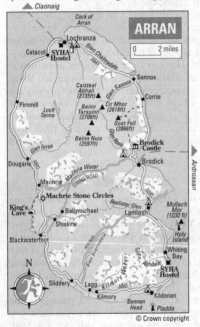

© Crown copyright

Transport on Arran is pretty good: daily **buses** circle the island and link in with the two **ferry services**: a year-round one from Ardrossan in Ayrshire to Brodick, and a smaller ferry from Claonaig on Kintyre to Lochranza (April to mid-Oct).

Brodick

Although the resort of **BRODICK** (from the Norse *breidr vik*, "broad bay") is a place of only moderate charm, it does at least have a grand setting in a wide, sandy bay set against a backdrop of granite mountains. Its development as a tourist resort was held back for a long time by its elitist owners, the dukes of Hamilton, though nowadays, as the island's capital and main communication hub, Brodick is by far the busiest town on Arran.

The dukes lived at **Brodick Castle** (daily: April–June, Sept & Oct 11am–4.30pm; July & Aug 11am–5pm; £6; NTS), on a steep bank on the north side of the bay. The interior is comfortable if undistinguished, but the walled **gardens** (daily 9.30am–dusk; gardens and country park only £2.50) and extensive grounds, contain a treasury of exotic plants and trees and command a superb view across the bay. Buried in the grounds there is a bizarre

Bavarian-style summerhouse lined entirely with pine cones, one of three built by the eleventh duke to make his wife, Princess Marie of Baden, feel at home.

Brodick's **tourist office** (May–Sept Mon–Sat 9am–7.30pm, Sun 10am–5pm; Oct–April Mon–Sat 9am–5pm; ☎01770/302401) is by the CalMac pier, and has reams of information on every activity from pony trekking to paragliding. Unless you've got to catch an early-morning ferry, however, there's little reason to stay in Brodick, though should you need to, the best **rooms** close to the ferry terminal are at the excellent *Dunvegan House Hotel* (☎01770/302811; ❹), the Art Deco *Invercloy Hotel* (☎01770/302225, ⓔinvercloyhotel@sol.co.uk; ❹; March–Oct) or *Carrick Lodge* (☎01770/302550; ❷), a sandstone manse, south of the pier on the Lamlash road. The nearest **campsite** is *Glenrosa* (☎01770/302380), a lovely, but very basic farm site (cold water only and no showers), two miles from town off the B880 to Blackwaterfoot. For **food**, the only place that really stands out is the moderately expensive seafood restaurant *Creelers* (☎01770/302810; mid-March to Oct), on the road to the castle. The *Wineport*, near the castle, does above-average bar meals, offering panini, pizzas.

The south of Arran

The southern half of Arran is less spectacular and less forbidding than the north; it's more heavily forested and the land is more fertile, and for that reason the vast majority of the population lives here. With its distinctive Edwardian architecture and mild climate, **LAMLASH** epitomizes the sedate charm of southeast Arran. Its major drawback is its bay, which is made not of sand but of boulder-strewn mud flats. You can take a boat out to the slug-shaped hump of **Holy Island**, which shelters the bay, and is now owned by a group of Tibetan Buddhists who have set up a meditation centre – providing you don't dawdle, it's possible to scramble up to the top of Mullach Mór (1030ft), the island's highest point, and still catch the last ferry back. To **stay** in style, head for the comfortable *Lilybank* (☎01770/600230, ⓦwww.smoothhound.co.uk/hotels/lilybank; ❸), which does good home-made food. You can **camp** at the fully equipped *Middleton Camping Park* (☎01770/600255; April–Oct), just five minutes' walk south of the centre. Food options are limited to the **bar meals** at the *Pier Head Tavern*, or at the friendly *Drift Inn* by the shore; there's even a Chinese takeaway behind the post office.

An established Clydeside resort for over a century now, **WHITING BAY**, four miles south of Lamlash, is spread out along a very pleasant bay, though it doesn't have quite the distinctive architecture of Lamlash. However, there are some excellent places to **stay**, including the *Royal* (☎01770/700286, ⓦwww.royalarran.co.uk; March–Oct; ❸), the *Argentine House Hotel*, run (confusingly) by a multilingual Swiss couple (☎01770/700662, ⓦwww.argentinearran.co.uk; closed Feb; ❷), both on Shore Road, and the beautiful, whitewashed *Swan's Guest House* (☎01770/700729, ⓦwww.rowallanbb.co.uk; ❷; Feb–Nov), up the hill on School Road. Whiting Bay also boasts an SYHA **hostel** (☎01770/700339, ⓦwww.syha.org.uk; March–Oct), at the southern end of the bay. The **food** is good at the *Burlington Hotel* on Shore Road, and at the *Argentine House Hotel*, though the latter's more expensive.

The north of Arran

The desolate north half of Arran – effectively the Highland part – features bare granite peaks, the occasional golden eagle and miles of unspoilt scenery, within reach only to those prepared to do some serious hiking. Arran's most accessible peak is also the island's highest, **Goat Fell** (2866ft) – take your pick from the Gaelic, *goath*, meaning "windy", or the Norse, *geit-fjall*, "goat mountain" – which can be ascended in just three hours from Brodick or from Corrie (return journey 5hr), though it's a strenuous hike.

Another good base for hiking is the pretty little seaside village of **CORRIE**, six miles north of Brodick, where a procession of pristine cottages lines the road to Lochranza and wraps itself around an exquisite little harbour and pier. The top choice for **accommodation** is *Blackrock* (☎01770/810282, Ⓦ www.arran.net/corrie/blackrock; ❷), a large, traditional seafront guest house on the edge of the village. A good budget option is the *North High Corrie Croft*, a **bunkhouse** (☎01770/302203), ten minutes' steep climb above the village on a raised beach; it has one large room for group bookings, and an annexe with eight beds (advance booking advisable). Corrie Golf Club, confusingly in Sannox, offers good-value **meals** all day in summer.

The ruined castle which occupies the mud flats of the bay, and the brooding north-facing slopes of the mountains which frame it, make for one of the most spectacular settings on the island – yet **LOCHRANZA**, despite being the only place of any size in this sparsely populated area, attracts far fewer visitors than Arran's southern resorts. The castle is worth a brief look inside (get the key from the post office), but Lochranza's main sight now is the island's brand new whisky **distillery** (April–Oct daily 10am–5pm; Nov–March phone ☎01770/830264, Ⓦ www.arranwhisky.com; £3.50), a pristine complex distinguished by its pago-da-style roofs at the south end of the village. The tours are entertaining and slick, and end with a free sample of the island's newly emerging single malt. The finest **accommodation** is to be had at the superb *Apple Lodge* (☎01770/830229, Ⓔ applelodge@easicom.com; ❹), the old village manse where you'll get excel-lent home-cooking, or at *Butt Lodge* (☎01770/830240, Ⓦ www.buttlodge.co.uk; ❹; March–Oct), another hotel with real character (and real log fires). Cheaper, but equally welcoming, is the *Lochranza Hotel* (☎01770/830223, Ⓦ www .lochranza.co.uk; ❷), whose bar is the centre of the local social scene. Lochranza also has an SYHA **hostel** (☎01770/830631, Ⓦ www.syha.org.uk; closed Jan), situated halfway between the distillery and the castle, and a well-equipped **campsite** (☎01770/830273, Ⓦ www.arran.net/lochranza; April-Oct) beauti-fully placed by the golf course on the Brodick Road, where deer come to graze in the early evening. The best place to eat is the inexpensive but excellent *Harold's* **restaurant**, a state-of-the-art place in the distillery (☎01770/830264; closed Mon eve). If you're just passing through, you can also get decent food at the *Pier Tearoom*, situated opposite the CalMac terminal, which doubles as a licensed restaurant, with good views across to Kintyre.

Islay and Jura

The fertile, largely treeless island of **ISLAY** (pronounced "eye-la") is famous for one thing – single malt **whisky**. The smoky, peaty, pungent quality of Islay whisky is unique, recognizable even to the untutored palate, and all seven of the island's distilleries will happily take visitors on a guided tour, ending with the customary complimentary tipple. Yet, despite the fame of its whiskies, Islay remains relatively undiscovered, much as Skye and Mull were some twenty years ago. Part of the reason may be the expense of the two-hour ferry jour-ney from Kennacraig on Kintyre, or perhaps the relative paucity of luxury hotels or fancy restaurants. If you do make the effort, however, you'll be rewarded with a genuinely friendly welcome from islanders proud of their history, landscape and Gaelic culture. The long whale-shaped island of **Jura** is one of the wildest and most mountainous of the Inner Hebrides, its entire west coast uninhabited and inaccessible except to the dedicated walker.

In medieval times, Islay was the political centre of the Hebrides, with **Finlaggan**, near Port Askaig, the seat of the MacDonalds, Lords of the Isles. The picturesque, whitewashed villages you see on Islay today, however, date from the planned settlements founded by the Campbells in the late eighteenth and early nineteenth centuries. Apart from whisky and solitude, the other great draw is the **birdlife** – there's a real possibility of spotting a golden eagle, or the rare crow-like chough, and no possibility at all of missing the scores of white-fronted and barnacle geese who winter here in their thousands. A good time to visit is in late May/early June, when the **Islay Festival** (*Feis Ile*; ⓦ www.ileach.co.uk/festival), takes place, with whisky tasting, piping recitals, folk dancing and other events celebrating the island's Gaelic roots.

Public transport, in the form of buses and postbuses, will get you from one end of the island to the other, but it's as well to know that there is one solitary bus on a Sunday. The **airport**, which lies between Port Ellen and Bowmore, has regular flights to and from Glasgow.

Port Ellen and around

Laid out as a planned village in 1821 by Walter Frederick Campbell, and named after his wife, **PORT ELLEN** is the chief port on Islay, with the island's largest fishing fleet, and main CalMac ferry terminal. The neat whitewashed terraces of Frederick Crescent, which overlook the town's bay of golden sand, are pretty enough, but the strand to the north, up Charlotte Street, is dominated by the modern maltings, on the Bowmore road, whose powerful odours waft across the town. For **accommodation** in Port Ellen itself, the best place is *Tighcargaman* (ⓣ01496/302345; ❶), a pottery set back from the road to Bowmore, half a mile from the ferry, followed by the artistic *Carraig Fhada* B&B by the lighthouse (ⓣ01496/302114; ❶). However, you'd be better off heading up the A846 towards the airport, to the excellent *Glenmachrie Farmhouse* (ⓣ01496/302560, ⓦ www.isle-of-islay.com/group/guest/glenmachrie; ❹), a whitewashed, family-run guest house, which does superb home-cooking. Alternatively, there's an independent **hostel** at the stone-built *Kintra Farm* (ⓣ01496/302051), three miles northwest of Port Ellen, at the southern tip of Laggan Bay; the farm also does B&B (❶; April–Sept), has an adjoining **campsite**, and serves food and drink at the *Granary* (late May to Aug evenings only).

From Port Ellen, a dead-end road heads off east along the coastline, passing three distilleries in as many miles. First comes **Laphroaig**, which, as every bottle tells you, is Gaelic for "the beautiful hollow by the broad bay", and, true enough, the whitewashed distillery is indeed in a gorgeous setting by the sea. A mile down the road lies **Lagavulin** distillery, beyond which stands **Dunyvaig Castle** (*Dún Naomhaig*), a romantic ruin on a promontory looking out to the tiny isle of Texa. Another mile further on is **Ardbeg** distillery, whose *Old Kiln Café* is the best place to grab a bite to eat in the area. In common with all Islay's distilleries, the above three offer guided tours (see box). There are a few **B&Bs** along the rapidly deteriorating road – *Tigh-na-Suil* (ⓣ01496/302483; ❷) has a lovely secluded position. A mile beyond this, slightly off the road, the simple thirteenth-century **Kildalton Chapel** boasts a wonderful eighth-century Celtic ringed cross made from the local "bluestone", which is a rich blue-grey. The quality of the scenes matches any to be found on the crosses carved by the monks in Iona.

Islay has only recently woken up to the fact that its **whisky** distilleries are a major tourist attraction. Nowadays, each distillery offers guided tours, traditionally ending with a generous dram, and a refund for your entrance fee if you buy a bottle in the shop – be warned, however, that a bottle of the stuff is no cheaper at source, so expect to pay over £20 for the privilege. Pick up the tourist board's "Islay and Jura Whisky Trail" leaflet, and phone ahead to make sure there's a tour running, as times do change frequently.

Ardbeg ☎01496/302244, ⊛www.ard-beg.com. The ten-year-old Ardbeg is traditionally considered the saltiest, peatiest malt on Islay (and that's saying something). Bought by Glenmorangie in 1997, the distillery has been thoroughly overhauled and restored, yet it still has bags of character inside. The *Old Kiln Café* is excellent (June–Aug daily 10am–5pm; rest of year Mon–Fri 10am–4pm). Guided tours regularly 10.30am–3.30pm; £2.

Bowmore ☎01496/810441, ⊛www.morrisonbowmore.com. Bowmore is probably the best place to head if this is your first distillery tour, as it is the most central on Islay (also with unrivalled disabled access). Bowmore is also one of the few distilleries still doing its own malting and kilning. The standard twelve-year-old Bowmore you get at the end is smooth, with just a hint of Islay peat. Guided tours: Easter–Sept Mon–Fri 10.30am, 11.30am, 2pm & 3pm, Sat 10.30am; Oct–Easter Mon–Fri 10.30am & 2pm; £2.

Bruichladdich ☎01496/850221. Bruichladdich only came back into production in 2001, and is the only independent distillery left on Islay. Regular guided tours (Mon–Fri 10.30am, 11.30am & 2.30pm, Sat 10.30am & 2.30pm; £3) have only just started again, so it's best to phone ahead.

Bunnahabhainn ☎01496/840646. A visit to Bunnahabhain (pronounced "bunna-have-in") is really only for whisky obsessives. The road from Port Askaig is windy, the whisky is the least characteristically Islay, and the distillery itself is only in production for a few months each year. Guided tours are by appointment (Mon–Fri only; free).

Caol Ila ☎01496/3027600. Caol Ila (pronounced "cul-eela"), just north of Port Askaig, is a modern distillery, the majority of whose lightly peaty malt goes into blended whiskies. No-frills guided tours are by appointment (Mon–Fri only; £3).

Lagavulin ☎01496/302400, ⊛www.scotch.com. Lagavulin probably is the classic, all-round Islay malt, with lots of smoke and peat. The distillery enjoys a fabulous setting and is extremely busy all year round. Phone ahead for details of the guided tours (Mon–Fri only; £3), at the end of which you'll get a taste of the best-selling sixteen-year-old.

Laphroaig ☎01496/302418, ⊛www.laphroaig.com. Another classic smokey, peaty Islay malt, and another great setting. One bonus at Laphroaig is that you get to see the malting and see and smell the peat kilns. There are regular guided tours (Mon–Fri 10.15am & 2.15pm; free), but phone ahead to make sure.

Bowmore

At the northern end of the seven-mile-long Laggan Bay, across the monotonous peat bog of Duich Moss, lies **BOWMORE**, Islay's administrative capital, with a population of around 800. It's a striking place, laid out in a grid-plan rather like Inveraray, with the whitewashed terraces of Main Street climbing up the hill in a straight line from the pier on Loch Indaal to the town's crowning landmark, the **Round Church**, whose central tower looks uncannily like a lighthouse. Built in the round, so that the devil would have no corners in which to hide, it has a plain, wood-panelled interior, with a lovely tiered balcony and a big central mushroom pillar. A little to the west of Main Street is **Bowmore distillery** (see box), the first of the legal Islay distilleries, founded in 1779, and still occupying its original whitewashed buildings by the loch.

Islay's only official **tourist office** is in Bowmore (July & Aug Mon–Sat 9.30am–5.30pm, Sun 2–5pm; May & June Mon–Sat 9.30am–5pm, Sun 2–5pm; April, Sept & Oct Mon–Sat 10am–5pm; Nov–March Mon–Fri noon–4pm; ☎01496/810254); it can help you find **accommodation** anywhere on Islay or Jura. Like Port Ellen, Bowmore itself is, in fact, not necessarily the best place to stay on the island. If you must, however, the *Harbour Inn* (☎01496/810330, ⓔharbour@harbour-inn.co.uk; ❹) on Main Street, Bowmore's cosiest and most central pub, or in one of the town's better B&Bs, such as *Lambeth House* (☎01496/810597; ❶), centrally located on Jamieson Street.

If you're visiting Islay between mid-September and the third week of April, it's impossible to miss the island's staggeringly large wintering population of **barnacle** and **white-fronted geese**. During this period, the geese dominate the landscape, feeding incessantly off the rich pasture, strolling by the shores, and flying in formation across the winter skies. You can see the geese just about anywhere on the island – there are an estimated 15,000 white-fronted and 40,000 barnacles here (and rising) – though in the evening, they tend to congregate in the tidal mud flats and fields around **Loch Gruinart**, which is now an **RSPB nature reserve**.

Port Charlotte

PORT CHARLOTTE, named after the founder's mother, is generally agreed to be Islay's prettiest village, its immaculate whitewashed cottages cluster around a sandy cove overlooking Loch Indaal. On the northern fringe of the village, in a whitewashed former chapel, the imaginative **Museum of Islay Life** (Easter–Oct Mon–Sat 10am–5pm, Sun 2–5pm; £2), has a children's corner, quizzes, a good library of books about the island, and tantalizing snippets about eighteenth-century illegal whisky distillers. The **Wildlife Information Centre** (Easter–Oct Mon, Tues, Thurs & Fri 10am–3pm, Sun 2–5pm; June–Aug Mon, Tues, Thurs & Fri until 5pm; £2), housed in the former distillery warehouse, is also worth a visit for anyone interested in the island's fauna and flora. As well as an extensive library to browse, there's lots of hands-on stuff for kids: microscopes, a touch table full of natural goodies, a seawater aquarium, a bugworld, and owl pellets to examine.

Port Charlotte is the perfect place in which to base yourself on Islay. The welcoming *Port Charlotte Hotel* (☎01496/850360, ⓔcarl@portcharlottehot .demon.co.uk; ❹) has the best **accommodation** – the seafood lunches served in the bar are very popular, and there's a good (moderately expensive) restaurant. For B&B, you're actually better off going for *Octofad Farm* (☎01496/850225; ❶; April–Oct), a dairy farm a few miles down the road beyond Nerabus. Port Charlotte itself is also home to Islay's SYHA **hostel** (☎01496/850385, ⓦwww.syha.org.uk; May–Sept), housed in an old bonded warehouse next door to the Wildlife Information Centre. The *Croft Kitchen* (☎01496/850230; mid-March to mid-Oct), opposite the museum, serves simple **food**, such as sandwiches and cakes, as well as inexpensive seafood, during the day, and more adventurous fare in the evenings (except Wed). The **bar** of the *Port Charlotte* is very easy-going, while the local crack (and occasional live music) goes on at the *Lochindaal Inn*, down the road, where you can also tuck into a very good local-bred steak.

Finlaggan and Port Askaig

Just beyond Ballygrant, on the road to Port Askaig, a narrow road leads off north to **Loch Finlaggan**, site of a number of prehistoric crannogs (artificial islands) and, for four hundred years from the twelfth century, headquarters of the Lords of the Isles, semi-autonomous rulers over the Hebrides and Kintyre. Unless you need shelter from the rain, or are desperate to see the head of the commemorative medieval cross found here, you can happily skip the **visitor centre** (Easter & Oct Tues, Thurs & Sun 2–4pm; May–Sept daily except Sat 2.30–5pm; £2), to the northeast of the loch, and simply head on down to the site itself (access at any time), which is dotted with interpretive panels. Duckboards allow you to walk out across the reed beds of the loch and explore the main crannog, **Eilean Mor**, where several carved gravestones can be seen among the ruins, which seem to support the theory that the Lords of the Isles buried their wives and children, while having themselves interred on Iona.

Islay's other ferry connection with the mainland, and its sole link with Colonsay and Jura, is from **PORT ASKAIG**, a scattering of buildings which tumble down a little cove by the narrowest section of the Sound of Islay (*Caol Ila*). The only real reason to come here is to catch one of the ferries or go to the hotel bar; if you've time to kill, you can wander round the island's **RNLI lifeboat station** or through the nearby woods of Dunlossit House. Easily the most comfortable **place to stay** is the lovely whitewashed *Kilmeny Farmhouse* (T01496/840668, Wwww.kilmeny.com; ⑤), southwest of Ballygrant, a place which richly deserves all the superlatives it regularly receives. The *Ballygrant Inn* is a good **pub** in which to grab a pint, as is the bar of the *Port Askaig Hotel*, which enjoys a wonderful position by the pier at Port Askaig, with views over to the Paps of Jura.

The Isle of Jura

Jura's distinctive Paps – so called because of their smooth breast-like shape, though there are in fact three of them – seem to dominate every view off the west coast of Argyll, their glacial rounded tops covered in a light dusting of quartzite scree. The island's name is commonly thought to derive from the Norse *dyr-oe* (deer island) and, appropriately enough, the current deer population of 6000 outnumbers the 180 humans by 33-to-one. With just one road, which sticks to the more sheltered eastern coast of the island, and only one hotel and a smattering of B&Bs, Jura is an ideal place to go for peace and quiet and some great walking.

If you're just coming over for the day from Islay, and don't fancy climbing the Paps, you could happily spend the day in the lovely wooded grounds of **Jura House** (daily 9am–5pm; £2), five miles up the road from Feolin Ferry, where the car ferry from Port Askaig arrives. Pick up a booklet at the entrance to the grounds, and follow the path which takes you down to the sandy shore, a perfect picnic spot in fine weather. Closer to the house itself, there's an idyllic **walled garden**, divided in two by a natural rushing burn that tumbles down in steps. The garden specializes in Antipodean plants, which flourish in the frost-free climate; in season, you can buy some of the garden's organic produce or take tea in the tea tent.

Anything that happens on Jura happens in the island's only real village, **CRAIGHOUSE**, eight miles up the road from Feolin Ferry. The village enjoys a sheltered setting, overlooking Knapdale on the mainland – so sheltered, in fact, that there are even a few palm trees thriving on the seafront.

There's a shop/post office, the island hotel and a tearoom, plus the tiny **Isle of Jura distillery** (℡01496/820240; tours by appointment), which welcomes visitors. In April 1946, Eric Blair (better known by his pen name of **George Orwell**), suffering badly from TB and intending to give himself "six months' quiet" in which to write his novel *1984*, moved to a remote farmhouse called Barnhill, on the northern tip of Jura. He lived out a spartan existence there for two years but was forced to return to London shortly before his death. The house, 23 miles north of Craighouse up an increasingly poor road, is as remote today as it was in Orwell's day, and sadly there is no access to the interior.

The family-run *Jura Hotel* in Craighouse is the island's one and only **hotel** (℡01496/820243, ⓦmembers.aol.com/jurahotel; ❹), not much to look at from the outside, but warm and friendly within, and centre of the island's social scene. The hotel does moderately expensive bar meals, and has a shower block and laundry facilities round the back for those who wish to camp in the hotel gardens. For **B&B**, look no further than Mrs Boardman at 7 Woodside (℡01496/820379; ❶; April–Sept). There's an infrequent **minibus service** on the island (phone ℡01496/820314 to find out when it's running). The **ferry** from Port Askaig occasionally fails to run if there's a strong northerly or southerly wind, so bring your toothbrush if you're coming for a day-trip.

Travel details

Trains

Glasgow (Queen Street) to: Arrochar & Tarbert (2–4 daily; 1hr 15min); Dalmally (2–4 daily; 2hr 15min); Oban (2–4 daily; 3hr).

Mainland buses (excluding postbuses)

Arrochar to: Carrick Castle (Mon–Sat 3 daily; 1hr); Garelochhead (Mon–Fri 2 daily; 20min); Inveraray (Mon–Sat 5 daily, Sun 2 daily; 35min); Lochgilphead (Mon–Sat 3 daily, Sun 2 daily; 1hr 30min).
Campbeltown to: Campbeltown airport (Mon–Fri 2 daily; 10min); Southend (Mon–Sat 5–6 daily, Sun 2 daily; 23min).
Dunoon to: Inveraray (Mon–Fri 5 daily, Sat 3 daily; 1hr 15min).
Glasgow to: Arrochar (Mon–Sat 6 daily, Sun 3 daily; 1hr 10min); Campbeltown (Mon–Sat 3 daily, Sun 2 daily; 4hr 25min); Dalmally (Mon–Sat 4 daily, Sun 2 daily; 2hr 20min); Inveraray (Mon–Sat 6 daily, Sun 3 daily; 1hr 45min); Kennacraig (Mon–Sat 2 daily, Sun 1 daily; 3hr 30min); Lochgilphead (Mon–Sat 3 daily, Sun 2 daily; 2hr 40min); Oban (Mon–Sat 4 daily, Sun 2 daily; 3hr); Tarbert (Mon–Sat 3 daily, Sun 2 daily; 3hr 15min); Taynuilt (Mon–Sat 4 daily, Sun 2 daily; 2hr 45min).
Inveraray to: Dalmally (Mon–Sat 3 daily, Sun 1 daily; 25min); Dunoon (Mon–Fri 5 daily, Sat 3 daily; 1hr 15min); Lochgilphead (Mon–Sat 3 daily, Sun 2 daily; 40min); Oban (Mon–Sat 3 daily, Sun 1 daily; 1hr 5min); Tarbert (Mon–Sat 3 daily, Sun 2 daily; 1hr 30min); Taynuilt (Mon–Sat 3 daily, Sun 1 daily; 45min).
Kennacraig to: Claonaig (Mon–Sat 3 daily; 15min); Skipness (Mon–Sat 3 daily; 20min).
Lochgilphead to: Campbeltown (Mon–Sat 4 daily, Sun 2 daily; 1hr 25min); Crinan (Mon–Fri 1–3 daily, Sat 2 daily; 20min); Inveraray (Mon–Sat 3 daily, Sun 2 daily; 40min); Kilmartin (Mon–Sat 1–5 daily; 15–40min); Oban (Mon–Sat 1 daily; 1hr 30min); Tarbert (2–4 daily; 30min).
Oban to: Kilmartin (Mon–Sat 1 daily; 1hr 10min); Lochgilphead (Mon–Sat 1 daily; 1hr 30min).
Tarbert to: Campbeltown (Mon–Sat 4 daily, Sun 2 daily; 1hr 10min); Claonaig (Mon–Sat 3 daily; 30min); Kennacraig (Mon–Sat 5 daily, Sun 1 daily; 15min).

Island buses

Arran

Brodick to: Corrie (Mon–Sat 5–6 daily, Sun 4 daily; 20min); Lamlash (Mon–Sat 12–13 daily, Sun 4 daily: 10min); Lochranza (Mon–Sat 5–6 daily, Sun 4 daily; 45min); Whiting Bay (Mon–Sat 12–13 daily, Sun 4 daily: 25min).

Bute

Rothesay to: Kilchattan Bay (Mon–Sat 4 daily, Sun 3 daily; 30min); Mount Stuart (1 daily except Tues & Thurs every 45min; 15min); Rhubodach (Mon–Sat 1–2 daily; 20min).

Colonsay

Scalasaig to: Kilchattan (Mon–Fri 2–4 daily; 30min); Kiloran Bay (Mon–Fri 2–3 daily; 12min); The Strand (Mon–Fri 1 daily).

Islay

Bowmore to: Port Askaig (Mon–Sat 8–10 daily, Sun 1 daily; 30–40min); Port Charlotte (Mon–Sat 5–6 daily; 25min); Port Ellen (Mon–Sat 9–12 daily, Sun 1 daily; 20–30min); Portnahaven (Mon–Sat 5–7 daily; 50min).

Mull

Craignure to: Fionnphort (Mon–Sat 3–4 daily, Sun 1 daily; 1hr 10min); Fishnish (Mon–Sat 4 daily, Sun 3 daily; 10min); Tobermory (Mon–Sat 4–5 daily, Sun 2 daily; 50min).

Tobermory to: Calgary (Mon–Fri 3–6 daily, Sat 2 daily; 45min); Dervaig (Mon–Fri 3–6 daily, Sat 2 daily; 30min); Fishnish (Mon–Sat 4 daily, Sun 3 daily; 40min).

Car ferries (summer timetable)

To Arran: Ardrossan–Brodick (Mon–Sat 5–6 daily, Sun 4 daily; 55min); Claonaig–Lochranza (10 daily; 30min).

To Bute: Colintraive–Rhubodach (frequently; 5min); Wemyss Bay–Rothesay (every 45min; 30min).

To Campbeltown: Ballycastle (Northern Ireland)–Campbeltown (2 daily; 3hr).

To Coll: Oban–Coll (1 daily except Thurs & Sun; 2hr 40min).

To Colonsay: Kennacraig–Colonsay (Wed 1 daily; 3hr 40min); Oban–Colonsay (Wed, Fri & Sun 1 daily; 2hr 10min); Port Askaig–Colonsay (Wed 1 daily; 1hr 20min).

To Dunoon: Gourock–Dunoon (hourly; 20min); McInroy's Point–Hunter's Quay (every 30min; 20min).

To Gigha: Tayinloan–Gigha (hourly; 20min).

To Islay: Colonsay–Port Askaig (Wed 1 daily; 1hr 20min); Kennacraig–Port Askaig (Mon–Sat 1–2 daily; 2hr); Kennacraig–Port Ellen (1–2 daily except Wed; 2hr 10min); Oban–Port Askaig (Wed 1 daily; 4hr).

To Jura: Port Askaig–Feolin Ferry (Mon–Sat 14–16 daily, Sun 6 daily; 10min).

To Kintyre: Portavadie–Tarbert (hourly; 25min).

To Lismore: Oban–Lismore (Mon–Sat 2–4 daily; 50min).

To Luing: Cuan Ferry (Seil)–Luing (every 30min; 5min).

To Mull: Kilchoan–Tobermory (Mon–Sat 7–8 daily; July & Aug also Sun 5 daily; 35min); Lochaline–Fishnish (Mon–Sat every 50min, Sun hourly; 15min); Oban–Craignure (Mon–Sat 6 daily, Sun 4–5 daily; 40min).

To Tiree: Oban–Tiree (1 daily except Thurs & Sun; 3hr 40min).

Passenger-only ferries (summer timetable)

To Helensburgh: Kilcreggan–Helensburgh (Mon–Sat 3 daily, Sun 1 daily; 25min); Gourock–Helensburgh (Mon–Sat 4 daily, Sun 3 daily; 40min).

To Iona: Fionnphort–Iona (Mon–Sat frequently, Sun hourly; 5min).

To Lismore: Port Appin–Lismore (daily every 2hr; 5min).

Flights

Glasgow to: Campbeltown (Mon–Fri 2 daily; 35min); Islay (Mon–Fri 2 daily, Sat 1 daily; 40min); Tiree (Mon–Sat 1 daily; 45min).

22

Skye and the Western Isles

CHAPTER 22 # Highlights

* **Kinloch Castle, Rùm** –
  The most outrageous
  Edwardian pile in the
  Hebrides. See p.1132

* **Loch Coruisk boat trip,
  Skye** – Take the boat
  from Elgol to the beautiful remote glacial Loch
  Coruisk in the midst of
  the Skye Cuillin, and
  walk back. See p.1125

* **Skye Cuillin** – Jagged
  peaks which make Skye
  a great place to visit.
  See p.1125

* **Calanais (Callanish),
  Lewis** – Scotland's finest
  standing stones are set
  in a serene lochside setting. See p.1140

* **Gearrannan (Garenin),
  Lewis** – A painstakingly
  restored crofting village
  of thatched blackhouses.
  See p.1140

* **Roghadal (Rodel)
  Church, Harris** – The
  pre-Reformation St
  Clement's Church boasts
  the most ornate sculp-
  tural decoration in the
  Outer Hebrides.
  See p.1144

* **Golden sandy beaches**
  – South Harris and the
  Uists have some stun-
  ning, mostly deserted,
  golden beaches, backed
  by flower-strewn
  machair. See p.1143

Skye and the Western Isles

A procession of Hebridean islands, islets and reefs off the northwest shore of Scotland, **Skye and the Western Isles** between them boast some of the country's most alluring scenery. It's here that the turbulent seas of the Atlantic smash up against an extravagant shoreline hundreds of miles long, a geologically complex terrain whose rough rocks and mighty sea cliffs are interrupted by a thousand sheltered bays and, in the far west, a long line of sweeping sandy beaches. The islands' interiors are equally dramatic, a series of formidable mountain ranges soaring high above great chunks of boggy peat moor, a barren wilderness enclosing a host of lochans, or tiny lakes.

Each island has its own distinct character, though the grouping splits quite neatly into two. **Skye** and the so-called **Small Isles** – the improbably named **Rùm**, **Eigg**, **Muck** and **Canna** – are part of the Inner Hebrides, which also include the islands of Argyll (see p.1085). Beyond Skye, across the unpredictable waters of the Minch, lie the Outer Hebrides or Outer Isles, nowadays known as the **Western Isles**, a 130-mile-long archipelago stretching from **Lewis** and **Harris** in the north to **Barra** in the south.

Although this area is one of the most popular holiday spots in Scotland, the crowds only become oppressive on Skye, and even there most visitors stick to a well-trodden sequence of roadside sights that leaves the rest of the island unaffected. The main attraction, the spectacular scenery, is best explored on **foot**, following the scores of paths that range from the simplest of cross-country strolls to arduous treks. There are four obvious areas of outstanding natural beauty to aim for: on Skye, the harsh peaks of the **Cuillin** and the bizarre rock formations of the **Trotternish** peninsula; on the Western Isles, the mountains of **North Harris** and the splendid sandy beaches that string along the Atlantic seaboard of **South Harris** and the **Uists**.

Skye and the Western Isles were first settled by Neolithic farming peoples in around 4000 BC. They lived along the coast, where they are remembered by scores of remains, from passage graves through to stone circles, most famously at **Calanais** (Callanish) on Lewis. Viking colonization gathered pace from 700 AD onwards – on Lewis four out of every five place-names is of Norse origin – and it was only in 1266 that the islands were returned to the Scottish crown. James VI (James I of England), a Stuart and a Scot, though no Gaelic-speaker, was the first to put forward the idea of clearing the Hebrides, though it was-

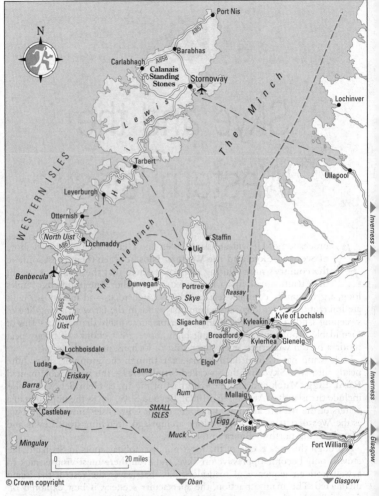

© Crown copyright

n't until after the Jacobite uprisings, in which many Highland clans disastrously backed the wrong side, that the **Clearances** began in earnest.

The isolation of the Hebrides exposed them to the whims and fancies of the various merchants and aristocrats who bought them up. Time and again, from the mid-eighteenth century to the present day, both the land and its people were sold to the highest bidder. Some proprietors were well-meaning but insensitive, like Lord Leverhulme, who wanted to turn Lewis into a centre of the fishing industry in the 1920s – while others were simply autocratic, such as **Colonel Gordon of Cluny**, who bought Benbecula, South Uist, Eriskay and Barra, and forced the inhabitants onto ships bound for North America at gunpoint. Always the islanders were powerless and almost everywhere they were driven from their ancestral homes. However, their language survived, ensuring a degree of cultural continuity, especially in the Western Isles, where even today the first language of the vast majority is **Gaelic** (pronounced "gallic").

Skye

Jutting out from the mainland like a giant wing, the bare and bony promontories of the **Isle of Skye** (An t-Eilean Sgiathanach) fringe a deeply indented coastline that makes the island never more than twenty-five, and sometimes as little as seven, miles wide. Justifiably, Skye was named after the Norse word for "cloud" (*skuy*), earning itself the Gaelic moniker, *Eilean a Cheo* (Island of Mist). Yet, despite the unpredictability of the weather, **tourism** has been an important part of the island's economy for a hundred years, since the train line pushed through to **Kyle of Lochalsh** in the western Highlands in 1897. From Kyle, it was the briefest of boat trips across to Skye, and the Edwardian bourgeoisie was soon swarming over to walk its mountains, whose beauty had been proclaimed by an earlier generation of Victorian climbers.

You might not guess it from the large number of English settlers who run much of the tourist industry – the B&Bs, museums and so forth – but Skye also remains the most important centre for **Gaelic culture** and language outside the Western Isles. Despite the Clearances, which saw an estimated 30,000 emigrate in the mid-nineteenth century, around forty percent of the population is fluent in Gaelic, the Gaelic college on Sleat is the most important in Scotland, and the Free Church (see p.1137) maintains a strong presence. As an English-speaking visitor, it's as well to be aware of the tensions that exist within this idyllic island, even if you never experience them firsthand. For a taste of the resurgence of Gaelic culture, try and get here in time for the Skye and Lochalsh Festival, *Feis an Eilean*, which takes place over two weeks in mid-July.

The most popular destination on Skye is the **Cuillin** ridge, whose jagged peaks dominate the island during clear weather; to explore them at close quarters you'll need to be a fairly experienced and determined walker. Equally dramatic in their own way are the rock formations of the **Trotternish** peninsula in the north, from which there are inspirational views across to the Western Isles. If you want to escape the summer crush, shuffle off to **Glendale** and the cliffs of Neist Point or head for the island of **Raasay**, off Skye's east coast. Of the two main settlements, **Broadford** and **Portree**, only the latter has any charm attached to it, though both have tourist offices, and make useful bases, especially for those without their own transport.

Transport practicalities

Most visitors still reach Skye from **Kyle of Lochalsh**, linked with Inverness by train; frequent buses use the controversially expensive Skye Bridge to reach **Kyleakin**, on the western tip of the island. The more scenic approach is from the **ferry** port of **Mallaig**, further south, crossing to **Armadale** on the gentle southern slopes of the Sleat peninsula. A third option is the privately operated summer-only car ferry which leaves the mainland at Glenelg, south of Kyle of Lochalsh, to arrive at **Kylerhea**, between Armadale and Kyleakin. Most visitors arrive by car, as the **bus** services, while adequate between the villages, peter out in the more remote areas, and virtually close down on Sundays.

Sleat

Ferry services from Mallaig (Mon–Sat 6–7 daily; June to mid-Sept also Sun; 30min) connect with the **Sleat** (pronounced "slate") **peninsula**, Skye's southern tip, an uncharacteristically fertile area that has earned it the sobriquet "The Garden of Skye". The CalMac ferry terminal is at **ARMADALE** (Armadal), an elongated hamlet stretching along the wooded shoreline. If you're leaving

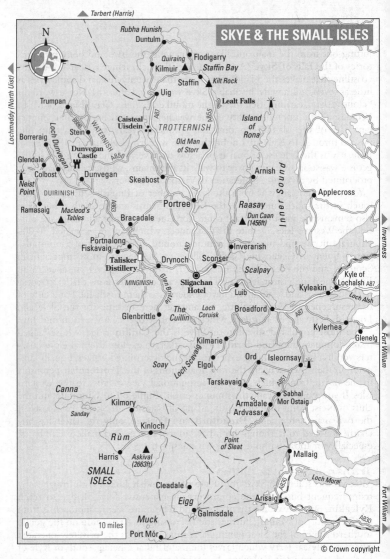

SKYE & THE SMALL ISLES

Tarbert (Harris)

N

Lochmaddy (North Uist)

Rubha Hunish
Duntulm
Flodigarry
Quiraing
Kilmuir
Staffin Bay
Staffin
Kilt Rock
Uig
Lealt Falls
Trumpan
Caisteal
Uisdein
TROTTERNISH
Island
of
Rona
WATERNISH
Borreraig
Loch Dunvegan
Stein
Old Man
of Storr
Dunvegan
Castle
Glendale
A850
Colbost
Dunvegan
Arnish
Skeabost
Applecross
Neist
Point
DUIRINISH
Inner Sound
Ramasaig
Macleod's
Tables
Portree
Raasay
Dun Caan
(1456ft)
Bracadale
A863
Portnalong
Fiskavaig
Inverarish
Talisker
Distillery
Drynoch
Sconser
Scalpay
Glen Brittle
MINGINISH
Sligachan
Hotel
Luib
Kyle of
Lochalsh
A87
Broadford
Kyleakin
Loch Alsh
The
Cuillin
Loch
Coruisk
Glenbrittle
Kylerhea
Kilmarie
Glenelg
Soay
Loch Scavaig
Elgol
Ord
Isleornsay
Tarskavaig
SLEAT
A851
Canna
Sabhal
Mor Ostaig
Kilmory
Armadale
Ardvasar
Sanday
Kinloch
Rùm
Point
of Sleat
Mallaig
Harris
Askival
(2663ft)
SMALL
ISLES
Loch Morar
Cleadale
A830
Eigg
Arisaig
Muck
Galmisdale
A830
Port Mór

0   10 miles

Inverness

Fort William

Fort William

© Crown copyright

Skye on the early-morning ferry and you need **accommodation** near Armadale, head a mile southwest to neighbouring Ardvasar, where the traditional, whitewashed *Ardvasar Hotel* (☎01471/844223, ⓦwww.ardvasarhotel .com; ⑤; March–Dec) has an excellent seafood restaurant, and a lively bar; or for **B&B** try *Holme Leigh* (☎01471/844361, ⓦwww.homeleigh.plus.com; ①). Of the three **hostels** on the peninsula, Armadale SYHA hostel (☎01471/844260, ⓦwww.syha.org.uk; mid-March to Sept) is a convenient ten-minute walk up the A851 towards Broadford and has a good position overlooking the bay; the hostel **rents bikes**, as does the local petrol station (☎01471/844249), close to the pier.

A little further along the A851, past the SYHA hostel, you'll find the **Armadale Castle Gardens & Museum of the Isles** (April–Oct daily 9.30am–5.30pm; ⓦwww.highlandconnection.org/clandonaldcentre.htm; £3.90), housed in the neo-Gothic Armadale Castle, which was built by the MacDonalds as their clan seat in 1815. Part of the castle has been restored to create a touristy museum that traces the history of the Gaels, concentrating on medieval times when the MacDonalds were in their glory as the Lords of the Isles. There's a lot of fairly confusing historical text on the walls, and the romantic sound effects – the cries of seabirds and battle songs – don't really compensate for the lack of original artefacts, but the handsome forty-acre **gardens** (April–Oct daily 9.30am–5.30pm; Nov–March dawn–dusk; free) are the highlight, with guided nature walks in the grounds.

Continuing northeast, it's another eight miles to **ISLEORNSAY** (Eilean Iarmain), a secluded little village of whitewashed cottages that was once Skye's main fishing port. With the mountains of the mainland on the horizon, the views out across the bay are wonderful, overlooking a necklace of seaweed-encrusted rocks and the tidal **Isle of Ornsay**, which sports a trim lighthouse built by Robert Louis Stevenson's father. You can **stay** at the mid-nineteenth-century *Isleornsay Hotel* – also known by its Gaelic name *Hotel Eilean Iarmain* – a pricey place with excellent service, whose **restaurant** serves great seafood (ⓣ01471/833332, ⓦwww.eilean-iarmain.com; ➏). Another couple of miles brings you to the turning for *Kinloch Lodge Hotel* (ⓣ01471/833333, ⓦwww.kinloch-lodge.co.uk; ➐), centred on an old hunting lodge still in the possession of Lord Macdonald of Macdonald with excellent food guaranteed by wife Claire whose cookery books are internationally famous.

Kyleakin and Kylerhea

Sir Iain Noble, an Edinburgh merchant banker and untiring Gaelic enthusiast, is one of the leading advocates of (and investors in) the privately financed **Skye Bridge**, which now links the tidy hamlet of **KYLEAKIN** (pronounced "ka-LA-kin") with the Kyle of Lochalsh, just half a mile away on the mainland. The well-orchestrated campaign by SKAT (Skye and Kyle Against Tolls), 350 of whose members have refused to pay the tolls, provides fierce opposition to the current system and may yet succeed in either reducing or abolishing the fee. Strictly speaking there are, in fact, two bridges which rest on an island in the middle, **Eilean Ban**, once the home of author and naturalist Gavin Maxwell, and now a wildlife sanctuary with the emphasis on otters. Visitors, limited to twelve, arrive by boat and must book through the **Bright Water Visitor Centre** in Kyleakin (ⓣ01599/530040; £8) for a guided tour. The centre itself is well worth a visit as it's full of hands-on things for kids of all ages and it's free.

With its ferry now defunct, Kyleakin has reinvented itself as something of a backpackers' paradise – to the consternation of many villagers – in summer, the population more than doubles. If you're intent on joining the throng, the SYHA **hostel** (ⓣ01599/534585, ⓦwww.syha.org.uk; open all year) is an ugly, modern building a couple of hundred yards from the old pier; nearby *Skye Backpackers* (ⓣ01599/534510, ⓦwww.scotlands-top-hostels.com; open all year) is a more laid-back option, as is *Dun Caan Hostel* (ⓣ01599/534087, ⓔleisureplus@supernet.com; open all year). **Bike rental** is available from *Dun Caan* and Skye Bikes (ⓣ01599/534795) on the pier.

You can still avoid crossing the Skye Bridge by taking the ferry service (mid-March to mid-May & Sept to mid-Oct Mon–Sat 9am–6pm; mid-May to Aug Mon–Sat 9am–8.30pm, Sun 10am–6pm; 15min) from Glenelg to **KYLERHEA** (pronounced "kile-ray"), a peaceful little place some four miles down the coast from Kyleakin. From here you can walk half an hour up the coast to the Forestry Commission **Otter Hide**, where, if you're lucky, you may be able to spot one of these elusive creatures.

Broadford

Heading west out of Kyleakin or Kylerhea brings you eventually to the island's second-largest village, charmless **BROADFORD** (An t-Ath Leathann), whose mile-long main street curves round a wide bay. Despite its rather unlovely appearance, Broadford makes a useful base for exploring the southern half of Skye; its **tourist office** (June–Sept Mon–Sat 9am–6pm, Sun 10am–2pm; April & May Mon–Sat 9.30am–5.30pm; Oct Mon–Sat 9.30am–5pm; ☎01471/ 822361), next to the Esso garage on the main road, contains a laundry, small shop and *bureau de change*, all open 24 hours. At the west end of the village there's a bank, a bakery, a tearoom and a post office. The SYHA **hostel** is on the west shore of Broadford Bay (☎01471/822442, ⓦwww.syha.org.uk; Feb–Dec), or there's the much smaller, more beautiful and primitive *Fossil Bothy* hostel (☎01471/822644 or 822297, ⓔfiona-mandeville@talk21.com; open all year; booking essential), a mile or so east of the bay, in Lower Breakish, off the road to Kyleakin. You can **rent bikes** from the SYHA hostel or from *Fairwinds*, another good place to stay (☎01471/822270; ❷; March–Oct), just past the *Broadford Hotel*.

Isle of Raasay

Travelling west from Broadford, with the Skye Cuillin to your left and the sea to your right, it's thirteen miles to Sconsor, where a CalMac car ferry leaves for the **Isle of Raasay** (Mon–Sat 9–10 daily; 15min), a nature conservancy area, which offers great walks across its bleak and barren hills, and remains well off the tourist trail. Raasay's population stands at around 160, most of them members of the Free Presbyterian Church (see p.1137). Strict observance of the Sabbath – no work or play on Sundays – is the most obvious manifestation for visitors, who should respect the islanders' feelings.

The ferry docks at the southern tip of the island, an easy fifteen-minute walk from **INVERARISH**, a tiny village set within thick woods on the island's southwest coast. **Raasay House,** built by the MacLeods in the late 1740s, is now the *Raasay Outdoor Centre*, offering comfortable **accommodation** in tastefully bohemian rooms (☎01478/660266, ⓔraasay.house@virgin.net; ❶; March to mid-Oct). You can **camp** in the grounds and, for a daily cost of around £25, join in the centre's activity programme: anything from sailing, windsurfing and canoeing, to climbing and hillwalking. Close by is the likeably old-fashioned *Isle of Raasay Hotel* (☎01478/660222; ❸), which serves delicious traditional Scottish food (bunkroom accommodation is also provided at £10 per person); in the village is a pleasant Victorian guest house, *Churchton House* (☎01478/660260; ❶).

A rough track cuts up the steep hillside from the village to Raasay's isolated but beautifully placed SYHA **hostel** (☎01478/660240; ⓦwww.syha.org.uk; mid-May to Sept). Most of the rest of Raasay is starkly barren, a rugged and rocky terrain of sandstone in the south and gneiss in the north, with the most obvious feature being the curiously truncated basalt cap on top of **Dun Caan** (1456ft), where Boswell "danced a Highland dance" on his visit to the island with Dr Johnson in 1773.

The Cuillin and the Red Hills

For many people, the **Cuillin**, whose sharp snowcapped peaks rise mirage-like from the flatness of the surrounding terrain, are Skye's main draw. When the clouds finally disperse, they are the dominating feature of the island, visible from every other peninsula on Skye. There are basically three approaches to the Cuillin: from the south, by foot or by boat from Elgol; from the *Sligachan Hotel* to the north; or from Glen Brittle to the west of the mountains. Glen Sligachan is one of the most popular routes, dividing as it does the granite of the round-topped **Red Hills** (sometimes known as the Red Cuillin) to the east from the dark, coarse-grained jagged-edged gabbro of the real Cuillin (also known as the Black Cuillin), to the west. With some twenty Munros between them, these are mountains to be taken seriously, and many routes through the Cuillin are for experienced climbers only.

Elgol and Loch Coruisk

The road to **ELGOL** (Ealaghol), fourteen miles southwest of Broadford at the tip of the Strathaird peninsula, is one of the most dramatic on the island, leading right into the heart of the Red Hills and then down a precipitous slope, with a stunning view from the top down to Elgol pier. The chief reason for visiting Elgol is, weather permitting, to take a boat across Loch Scavaig (March–Sept 2–4 daily), past a seal colony, to a jetty near the entrance of **Loch Coruisk** (from *coire uish*, "cauldron of water"). An isolated, glacial loch, this needle-like shaft of water, nearly two miles long but only a couple of hundred yards wide, lies in the shadow of the highest peaks of the Black Cuillin, a wonderfully overpowering landscape.

The journey by sea takes 45 minutes and passengers are dropped to spend about one and a half hours ashore; for booking (essential) and details of sailing times, ring the *Bella Jane* (℡0800/731 3089 before 10am and after 7.30pm). Walkers can use the boat on a one-way trip simply to get to Loch Coruisk, from where there are numerous possibilities for hiking amidst the Red Hills, the most popular (and gentle) of which is the eight-mile trek north over the pass into **Glen Sligachan**. Alternatively, you could walk round the coast to the sandy bay of **Camasunary**, over two miles to the east – a difficult walk that involves a tricky river crossing and negotiating "The Bad Step", an overhanging rock with a thirty-foot drop to the sea – and either head north to Glen Sligachan or continue south three miles along the coast to Elgol.

The only public transport is the morning **postbus** from Broadford (Mon–Fri 2 daily, Sat 1 daily; 2hr; check with the Broadford tourist office about connections). Rather than staying in Elgol, head for *Rowan Cottage* (℡01471/866287, Ⓔ Rowan@rowancottage.demon.co.uk; ❷; March–Nov), a lovely **B&B** a mile or so east in Glasnakille, or the larger, more luxurious *Strathaird House* (℡01471/866269, Ⓦ www.strathairdhouse.skye.co.uk; ❸; April–Sept) just beyond Kilmarie, three miles up the road to Broadford. By far the most popular place to stay, though, is the **campsite** (April–Oct) by the *Sligachan Hotel* (℡01478/650204, Ⓦ www.sligachan.co.uk; ❷) on the A87, at the northern end of Glen Sligachan. The hotel's huge *Seamus Bar* serves **food** for weary walkers until 10pm, and quenches their thirst with the full range of real ales produced by Skye's very own microbrewery in Uig; there's also a more formal restaurant with splendid food.

Glen Brittle

Six miles along the A863 to Dunvegan from the *Sligachan Hotel*, a turning signed "Carbost and Portnalong" quickly leads to the entrance to stony **Glen Brittle**, edging the most spectacular peaks of the Cuillin; at the end of the glen, idyllically situated by the sea, is the village of **GLENBRITTLE**. Climbers and serious walkers tend to congregate at the SYHA **hostel** (☎01478/640278, ⓦwww.syha.org.uk; March–Sept) or the fairly basic **campsite** (☎01478/640404; April–Oct), a mile or so further south behind the wide sandy beach at the foot of the glen. During the summer, two buses a day (not Sun) from Portree will drop you at the top of the glen, but you'll have to walk the last seven miles; both the youth hostel and the campsite have grocery stores, the only ones for miles.

From the valley a score of difficult and strenuous trails lead east into the **Black Cuillin**, a rough semicircle of peaks rising to about 3000ft, which surround Loch Coruisk. One of the easiest walks is the five-mile round-trip from the campsite up **Coire Lagan**, to a crystal-cold lochan squeezed in among the sternest of rockfaces. Above the lochan is Skye's highest peak, **Sgurr Alasdair** (3258ft), one of the more difficult Munros, while Sgurr na Banachdich (3166ft) is considered the most easily accessible Munro in the Cuillin.

One wet-weather activity is to visit the **Talisker whisky distillery** (July–Sept Mon–Sat 9am–4.30pm; April–June & Oct Mon–Fri 9am–4.30pm; Nov–March Mon–Fri 2–4.30pm; by appointment ☎01478/640314), which produces a very smoky, peaty single malt. Talisker is the island's only distillery, situated on the shores of Loch Harport at **CARBOST** (and not, confusingly, at the village of Talisker itself).

Dunvegan and Duirinish

After the Glen Brittle turning, the A863 slips across bare rounded hills to skirt the bony sea cliffs and stacks of the west coast twenty miles or so north to **DUNVEGAN** (Dùn Bheagain). It's an unimpressive place, strung out along the east shore of the sea loch of the same name, though it does make quite a good base for exploring the interesting peninsula of Duirinish.

The main tourist trap in the village is **Dunvegan Castle** (daily: April–Oct 10am–5.30pm; Nov–March 11am–4pm; £5.50, gardens only £4) which sprawls on top of a rocky outcrop, sandwiched between the sea and several acres of beautifully maintained gardens. It's been the seat of the Clan MacLeod since the thirteenth century, but the present greying, rectangular fortress, with its uniform battlements and dummy pepper pots, dates from the 1840s. Inside, you don't get a lot of castle for your money and the contents are far from stunning, the most intriguing being the battered remnants of the **Fairy Flag** in the drawing room. This yellow silken flag from the Middle East may have been the battle standard of the Norwegian king, Harald Hardrada, who had been the commander of the imperial guard in Constantinople.

The hammerhead **Duirinish peninsula** lies to the west of Dunvegan, much of it inaccessible to all except walkers prepared to scale or skirt the area's twin flat-topped basalt peaks: Healabhal Bheag (1600ft) and Healabhal Mhor (1538ft). The mountains are better known as **MacLeod's Tables**, for legend has it that the MacLeod chief held an open-air royal feast on the lower of the two for James V. The main areas of habitation lie to the north, along the western shores of Loch Dungeon, and in the broad green sweep of **Glen Dale**, attractively dotted with white farmhouses and dubbed "Little England" by the locals, due to its high percentage of "white settlers", English incomers searching for a better life. Glen Dale's current predicament is doubly ironic given its history, for it was here in 1882 that local crofters staged a rent strike against their landlords, the MacLeods. Five locals – who became known as the "Glen Dale Martyrs" – were given two-month prison sentences, and eventually, in 1904, the crofters became the first owner-occupiers in the Highlands.

All this, and a great deal more about nineteenth-century crofting, is told through fascinating contemporary news cuttings at **Colbost Folk Museum** (Easter–Oct daily 10am–6.30pm; £1), the oldest of Peter MacAskill's three Skye museums, situated in a restored blackhouse, four miles up the road from Dunvegan. A guide is usually on hand to answer questions, the peat fire smokes all day, and there's a restored illegal whisky still round the back. Further up the road, at **BORRERAIG** itself, where there was a famous piping college, is the **MacCrimmon Piping Heritage Centre** (late May to early Oct daily 11am–5.30pm; Easter to late May Tues–Sun same times; £1.50), on the ancestral holdings of the MacCrimmons, hereditary pipers to the MacLeod chiefs for three centuries, until they were sent packing in the 1770s. The plaintive sounds of the *piobaireachd* of the MacCrimmons, the founding family of Scottish piping, fill this illuminating museum.

As a result of such Clearances, the west coast of Duirinish is mostly uninhabited now. For walkers, though, it's a great area to explore, with blustery but easy footpaths leading to the dramatically sited lighthouse on **Neist Point**, Skye's most westerly spot, which features some fearsome sea cliffs and wonderful views across the sea to the Western Isles.

Practicalities

Dunvegan is a useful base, with a **tourist office** (Mon–Sat 9am–5.30pm; ☎01470/521581) and several excellent **hotels** and **B&Bs** dotted along the main road, such as the converted traditional croft *Roskhill House* (☎01470/521317, ✉stay@roskhill.demon.co.uk; ❸). Other possibilities include the beautifully situated *Silverdale* (☎01470/521251; ❶), just before you get to Colbost, or the luxurious *Harlosh House* (☎01470/521367; ❻; April–Oct), four miles south of Dunvegan. There's an excellent lochside **campsite** at Loch Greshornish, eight miles east of Dunvegan on the A850 (☎01470/582230, ✉info@greshcamp.co.uk; April–Sept).

The culinary mecca in the area is the expensive *Three Chimneys* **restaurant** (☎01470/511258, ⓦwww.threechimneys.co.uk; closed Sun), located beside Colbost Folk Museum; if you want to stay for bed and breakfast as well, there are six fabulous **rooms** at the adjacent *House Over-By* (❽). More reasonably priced meals can be had at *An Strupag* in Lephin (☎01470/511204), deeper into Glen Dale. There are welcoming fires and good food at the sixteenth-century *Stein Inn* (☎01470/592362, ⓦwww.steininn.co.uk; ❷), in Stein, and outstanding seafood at the *Lochbay Seafood Restaurant* (☎01470/592235, ⓦwww.lochbay-seafood-restaurant.co.uk; closed Sat & Sun); you can also stay for bed and breakfast (Easter–October; ❸). Eating in Dunvegan is a little problematic; however, there is a snug **café** attached to *Dunvegan Bakery* (closed Sat afternoon & Sun).

Portree

Although referred to by the locals as "the village", **PORTREE** is the only real town on Skye. It's also one of the most attractive fishing ports in northwest Scotland, its deep cliff-edged harbour filled with fishing boats and circled by multicoloured restaurants and guest houses. The harbour is overlooked by **The Lump**, a steep and stumpy peninsula with a flagpole on it that was once the site of public hangings on the island, attracting crowds of up to five thousand; it also sports a folly built by the celebrated Dr Ban, a visionary who wanted to make Portree into a second Oban. Up above the harbour is the spick-and-span town centre, spreading out from **Somerled Square**, built in the late eighteenth century as the island's administrative and commercial centre, and now housing the bus station and car park. The **Royal Hotel** on Bank Street occupies the site of the *McNab's Inn* where Bonnie Prince Charlie took leave of Flora MacDonald (see p.1129), and where, 27 years later, Boswell and Johnson had "a very good dinner, porter, port and punch".

A mile or so out of town on the Sligachan road is one of Skye's most successful tourist attractions, the **Aros Centre** (daily 9am–6pm; open later in summer). Here, you can enjoy the dramatic Aros Experience (£3), an unsentimental presentation of episodes of the island's history, with stunning life-size figures and special effects, ending with an audiovisual show. If it's fine, there are waymarked forest walks and a Gaelic alphabet trail starting just outside. For a view of the contemporary visual art scene, it's well worth seeking out **An Tuireann Arts Centre**, housed in a converted fever hospital on the Struan road (Mon–Sat 10am–5pm; free), which puts on exhibitions, stages concerts, and has an excellent small café where even the counter is a work of art, with an imaginative range of food on offer (Easter–Oct).

Practicalities

Hours vary enormously at Portree's **tourist office**, just off Bridge Street, so the ones we give here are just a guideline (April–Oct Mon–Sat 9am–8pm, Sun 10am–4pm; Nov–March Mon–Sat 9am–5.30pm; ☏01478/612137). Probably the best **hotel** is the comfortable *Cuillin Hills* (☏01478/612003, Ⓦwww.cuillinhills.demon.co.uk; ❺), ten minutes' walk out of town along the northern shore of the bay. *Viewfield House Hotel* (☏01478/612217; ❺), on the southern outskirts of town, is worth investigating for the Victorian atmosphere, stuffed polecats and antiques. In the lower price range, try *Conusg*, a B&B in a quiet spot by the *Cuillin Hills Hotel*, originally built for the coachman in the 1880s (☏01478/612426; ❶; Easter–Sept) or *Balloch* in Viewfield Road (☏01478/612093; ❷; Easter–Oct). Of Portree's year-round **hostels**, the smartest is the *Portree Independent Hostel* (☏01478/613737, Ⓔportreeindhostel@hotmail.co.uk) housed in the Old Post Office on the Green, though the *Portree Backpackers Hostel* (☏01478/613641), ten minutes' walk up the Dunvegan road, enjoys a more secluded location. Torvaig **campsite** (☏01478/612209; April–Oct) lies a mile and a half north of town off the A855 Staffin road.

The best **food** in town is on Bosville Terrace, but it's pricey: within the *Bosville Hotel*, the *Chandlery* restaurant serves excellent meals, with its sister *Bosville* restaurant being much cheaper; *Harbour View* has a seafood **restaurant** with candlelit ambience. The popular *Lower Deck Seafood Restaurant* on the harbour has a wood-panelled warmth to it, and is reasonably priced at lunchtime (less so in the evenings); for good **fish and chips**, pop next door to their excellent chippy. As for **pubs**, the bar of the *Pier Hotel* on the quayside is the fishermen's drinking hole, and the *Tongadale* on Wentworth Street is lively. Currently the most popular evening venue by far is the *Isles Inn* on Somerled Square which also has excellent bar meals.

Trotternish

Protruding twenty miles north from Portree, the **Trotternish peninsula** boasts some of Skye's most bizarre scenery, particularly on the east coast, where volcanic basalt has pressed down on the softer sandstone and limestone underneath, causing massive landslides. These, in turn, have created sheer cliffs, peppered with outcrops of hard, wizened basalt, which run the full length of the peninsula. These pinnacles and pillars are at their most eccentric in the Quiraing, above Staffin Bay, on the east coast. Trotternish is best explored with your own transport, but an occasional bus service (Mon–Sat 2–4 daily) along the road encircling the peninsula gives access to almost all the coast.

The east coast

The first geological eccentricity on the peninsula, six miles north of Portree along the A855, is the **Old Man of Storr**, a distinctive column of rock shaped like a willow leaf, which, along with its neighbours, is part of a massive land-

---

Bonnie Prince Charlie

Prince Charles Edward Stewart – better known as **Bonnie Prince Charlie** or "The Young Pretender" – was born in Rome in 1720, where his father, "The Old Pretender", claimant to the British throne, was living in exile. At the age of 25, having little military experience, no knowledge of Gaelic, an imperfect grasp of English and a strong attachment to the Catholic faith, the prince set out for Scotland on a French ship, disguised as a seminarist from the Scots College in Paris. He arrived on the Outer Hebridean island of Eriskay on July 23, 1745, and was immediately implored to return to France by the clan chiefs, who were singularly unimpressed by his lack of army. Charles was unmoved and went on to raise the royal standard at Glenfinnan, gather together a Highland army, win the Battle of Prestonpans, march on London and reach Derby before finally (and foolishly) agreeing to retreat. Back in Scotland, he won one last victory, at Falkirk, before the final disaster at Culloden in April 1746.

The prince spent the following five months in hiding, with a price of £30,000 on his head, and literally thousands of government troops searching for him. He certainly endured his fair share of cold and hunger whilst on the run, but the real price was paid by the Highlanders themselves, who risked their lives (and often paid for it with them) by aiding and abetting the prince. The most famous of these was, of course, 23-year-old **Flora MacDonald**, whom Charles met on South Uist in June 1746. Flora was persuaded – either by his beauty or her relatives, depending on which account you believe – to convey Charles "over the sea to Skye", disguised as an Irish servant girl by the name of Betty Burke. She was arrested just seven days after parting with the prince in Portree, and held in the Tower of London until July 1747. She went on to marry a local man, had seven children, and in 1774 emigrated to America, where her husband was taken prisoner during the American War of Independence. Flora returned to Scotland and was reunited with her husband on his release; they resettled in Skye and she died at the age of 68.

Charles eventually boarded a ship back to France in September 1746, but, despite his promises – "for all that has happened, Madam, I hope we shall meet in St James's yet" – never returned to Scotland, nor did he ever see Flora again. After mistreating a string of mistresses, he eventually got married at the age of 52 to the 19-year-old Princess of Stolberg, in an effort to produce a Stewart heir. They had no children, and she eventually fled from his violent drunkenness; in 1788, a none-too-"bonnie" Prince Charles died in the arms of his illegitimate daughter in Rome. Bonnie Prince Charlie became a legend in his own lifetime, but it was the Victorians who really milked the myth for all its sentimentality, conveniently overlooking the fact that the real consequence of 1745 was the virtual annihilation of the Highland way of life.

slip. Huge blocks of stone still occasionally break off the cliff face of the Storr (2358ft) above and slide downhill. At 165ft, the Old Man is a real challenge for climbers; less difficult is the half-hour trek up the new footpath to the foot of the column from the woods beside the car park. Eight miles further north, there's another car park for the **Kilt Rock**, whose tube-like, basaltic columns rise precipitously from the sea, set amongst sea cliffs dotted with nests for fulmars and kittiwakes. A mile or two up the minor road which cuts across the peninsula from Staffin Bay, there's a path up to the savage rock formations of the **Quiraing** – a forest of mighty pinnacles including the Needle, the Prison and the Table, where Victorian ramblers used to picnic and play cricket.

The **accommodation** on the east coast is among the best on Skye, with most places enjoying spectacular views out over the sea. Just beyond the Lealt Falls there's the very welcoming and comfortable *Glenview Inn* (☎01470/562248, Ⓔvaltos@lineone.net; ❸; March–Oct), with an excellent adjoining restaurant, and a **campsite** (☎01470/562213; April–Sept) south of Staffin Bay. In fine weather, you can enjoy good bar snacks on the castellated terrace of the stylish, award-winning *Flodigarry Country House Hotel* (☎01470/552203, Ⓦwww.flodigarry.co.uk; ❻), three miles up the coast from Staffin. Behind the hotel (and now part of it) is the cottage where local heroine Flora MacDonald lived, and had six of her seven children, from 1751 to 1759. If the hotel's rooms are beyond your means, try the neat and attractive *Dun Flodigarry Backpackers' Hostel* (☎01470/552212), a couple of minutes' walk away – you can ring the hostel to arrange transport or catch the local bus.

The west coast

Beyond Flodigarry, the A855 veers off to the **west coast**, rounding the tip of the Trotternish ridge before reaching the shattered remains of a headland fortress at **DUNTULM** (Duntuilm), once a major MacDonald power base, abandoned by the clan in 1732 after a clumsy nurse dropped one of their babies from a window onto the rocks below. The imposing *Duntulm Castle Hotel* (☎01470/552213; ❷; March–Nov) is close by, and provides good bar meals as well as wonderful views across the Minch to the Western Isles. Heading down the west shore of the Trotternish, it's two miles to the **Skye Museum of Island Life** (Easter–Oct Mon–Sat 9.30am–5.30pm; £1.75), an impressive cluster of thatched blackhouses on an exposed hill overlooking Harris. The museum, run by locals, gives a fascinating insight into a way of life that was commonplace on Skye a hundred years ago. The blackhouse, now home to the ticket office, is much as it was when it was last inhabited in 1957, while the two houses to the east contain interesting snippets of local history. Behind the museum in the cemetery up the hill are the graves of **Flora MacDonald** and her husband. Thousands turned out for her funeral in 1790, creating a funeral procession a mile long – indeed, so widespread was her fame that the original family mausoleum fell victim to souvenir hunters and had to be replaced. The Celtic cross headstone is inscribed with a simple tribute by Dr Johnson, who visited her in 1773: "Her name will be mentioned in history, if courage and fidelity be virtues, mentioned with honour."

A further four miles south is the ferry port of **UIG** (Uige), which curves its way round a dramatic, horseshoe-shaped bay, and is the arrival point for CalMac ferries from Tarbet (Harris) and Lochmaddy (North Uist). The **tourist office** (April–Oct Mon–Sat 8.45am–6.30pm; mid-July to mid-Sept also Sun 8.45am–2pm; ☎01470/542404) is inside the CalMac office on the pier. Most folk come to Uig to take the ferry to the Western Isles, but if you need to stay near the ferry terminal, try the inexpensive **B&B**, *Orasay*, 14 Idrigill (☎01470/

542316; ❶), or one of the static *Orasay* **caravans** (☎01470/542316). By contrast, the SYHA **hostel** (☎01470/542211, ⓦwww.syha.org.uk; April–Oct) is high up on the south side of the village, with exhilarating views over the bay. The *Pub at the Pier* offers filling meals, and serves the local Skye beers. **Bike rental** is available from Skye Bicycle Hire on the pier (☎01470/542316); **pony trekking**, from the *Uig Hotel* (☎01470/542205).

The Small Isles

The history of the **Small Isles** – Rùm, Eigg, Muck and Canna – which lie south of Skye, is typical of the Hebrides: early Christianization, followed by a period of Norwegian rule that ended in 1266 when the islands fell into Scottish hands. Their support for the Jacobite cause resulted in hard times after the failed rebellion of 1745, but the biggest problems came with the introduction of the **potato** in the mid-eighteenth century. The success of the crop and its nutritional value – when grown in conjunction with traditional cereals – eliminated famine at a stroke, prompting a population explosion. In 1750, there were just a thousand islanders, but by 1800 their numbers had almost doubled.

At first, the problem of overcrowding was camouflaged by the **kelp** boom, in which the islanders were employed and the islands' owners made a fortune, gathering and burning local seaweed to sell for use in the manufacture of gunpowder, soap and glass. But the economic bubble burst with the end of the Napoleonic Wars and, to maintain their profit margins, the owners resorted to drastic action. Alexander Maclean sold Rùm as grazing land for sheep and gave its people a year's notice to quit, and also cleared Muck to graze cattle, as did the MacNeills on Canna. On Eigg, though, the new, more compassionate owner gave some of his tenants extended leases.

Since the Clearances, each of the islands has been bought and sold several times, though only **Muck** is now privately owned by the benevolent laird, Lawrence MacEwen. **Eigg** hit the headlines in 1997, when the islanders finally managed to buy the island themselves and put an end to more than 150 years of property speculation. The other islands were bequeathed to national agencies: **Rùm**, by far the largest and most-visited of the group, with a cluster of formidable volcanic peaks and the architecturally remarkable Kinloch Castle, passed to the Nature Conservancy Council (now Scottish Natural Heritage) in 1957; and **Canna**, in many ways the prettiest of the four with its high basalt cliffs, has been in the hands of the National Trust for Scotland since 1981.

Transport practicalities

CalMac run passenger-only **ferries** to the Small Isles from Mallaig (Mon–Sat; ☎01687/462403, ⓦwww.calmac.co.uk). Day-trips are possible to each of the islands on certain days, and to all four islands on Saturdays, if you catch the 6.30am ferry. The CalMac ferry only docks at Canna; for the other three islands, you (and all the island supplies) have to be transferred to an island tender or "flit boat". However, new piers are currently being constructed, and a new car ferry should be in operation by 2003.

From Easter to September, you can also reach Rùm, Eigg and Muck from Arisaig with **Arisaig Marine**, run by Murdo Grant (daily; ☎01687/450224, ⓦwww.arisaig.co.uk). This is a much more pleasant way to get there, as the boat is licensed, and, if any marine mammals are spotted en route, the boat will pause for a bit of whale-watching. Day-trips are possible to Eigg on most days, allowing four to five hours ashore, and to Rùm and Muck on a few days, allowing two to three hours ashore. With careful studying of both CalMac and Murdo Grant timetables, you should be able to organize a visit to suit you, especially as Arisaig and Mallaig are linked by train.

Rùm

Like Skye, **Rùm** is dominated by its Cuillin, which, though only reaching a height of 2663ft at the summit of Askival, rises up with comparable drama straight up from the sea in the south of the island. Rùm's chief formal attraction is **Kinloch Castle** (guided tours most days at 2pm; £3), a squat red sandstone edifice fronted by colonnades and topped by crenellations and turrets, that dominates the village of Kinloch. Completed at enormous expense in 1900 – the red sandstone was shipped in from Arran and the soil for the gardens from Ayrshire – its interior is a perfectly preserved example of Edwardian decadence, "a living memorial of the stalking, the fishing and the sailing, the tenantry and plenty of the days before 1914". From the galleried hall, with its tiger rugs, stags' heads and giant Japanese incense burners, to the "Extra Low Fast Cushion" of the Soho snooker table in the Billiard Room, the interior is packed with knick-knacks and technical gizmos accumulated by **Sir George Bullough** (1870–1939), the spendthrift son of self-made millionaire Sir John Bullough, who bought the island as a sporting estate in 1888. As such, it was only really used for a few weeks each autumn, during the "season", yet employed an island workforce of one hundred all year round. Bullough's guests were woken at eight each morning by a piper; later on, an orchestrion, an electrically driven barrel organ (originally destined for Balmoral) crammed in under the stairs, would grind out an eccentric mixture of pre-dinner tunes – *The Ride of the Valkyries* and *Ma Blushin' Rosie* among others; a demo is included in the tour. The ballroom has a sprung floor, the library features a gruesome photographic collection from the Bulloughs' world tours, but the *pièce de résistance* has to be Bullough's **Edwardian bathrooms**, whose baths have hooded walnut shower cabinets, fitted with two taps and four dials, which allow the bather to fire high-pressure water at their body from every angle.

For those with limited time or energy, there are two gentle waymarked **heritage trails**, both of which start from Kinloch and take around two hours to complete. For longer walks, you must fill in route cards and pop them into the White House (Mon–Fri 9am–12.30pm), where the reserve manager can give useful advice. The island's best beach is at **KILMORY**, to the north (5hr round-trip), though this part of the island is only open to the public on the weekend as it's given over to the study of red deer; it's also closed completely in June, during calving, and October, during rutting. When the island's human head count peaked at 450 in 1791, the hamlet of **HARRIS** on the southwest coast (6hr round-trip) housed a large crofting community; all that remains now are several ruined blackhouses and the extravagant **Bullough Mausoleum**, built by Sir George to house the remains of his father in the style of a Greek Doric temple, overlooking the sea.

You need to book **accommodation** in advance. There's just one **B&B** on the island, *Ferry Cottage* (☎01687/462767; ❶; Easter–Oct), in Kinloch, with only one twin room with shared facilities. Kinloch Castle was a luxury hotel until the early 1990s, and still lets a few of its four-poster rooms (❻), but it's basically run as an independent **hostel** (☎01687/462037), with dormitories in the old servants' quarters and a farmhouse bothy (March–Oct). SNH also run two simple mountain **bothies** (three nights maximum stay), in Dibidil and

Guirdil, and basic **camping** on the foreshore near the jetty; book ahead by contacting the reserve manager at the *White House* (℡01687/462026). Wherever you're staying, you can either do self-catering – hostellers can use the hostel kitchen – or eat the unpretentious **food** offered in the hostel's licensed bistro. There is also a small shop/off-licence/post office in Kinloch. Bear in mind that Rùm is the wettest of the Small Isles, and is known for having some of the worst **midges** in Scotland – come prepared for both.

Eigg

Eigg (Ⓦwww.isleofeigg.org) is without doubt the most easily distinguishable of the Small Isles from a distance, since the island is mostly made up of a basalt plateau 1000ft above sea level, and a great stump of columnar pitchstone lava, known as An Sgurr, rising out of the plateau another 290ft. It's also by far the most vibrant, populous and welcoming of the Small Isles, with a strong sense of community.

Visitors arrive in the southeast corner of the island – which measures just five miles by three – where **An Laimhrig** (The Anchorage), the island's community centre stands, housing a shop, post office, tearoom and information centre. The island minibus meets incoming ferries, and will take you to wherever you need to go on the island. If time is limited, you could simply head for the nearby **Lodge**, the former laird's house and gardens which the islanders plan to renovate in the future. With the island's great landmark, **An Sgurr** (1292ft), watching over you wherever you go, many folk feel duty bound to climb it, and enjoy the wonderful views over to Muck and Rùm; the return trip takes between three and four hours.

The nicest place to **stay** on Eigg is *Kildonnan House* (℡01687/482446; full board ❹), a beautiful eighteenth-century wood-panelled house where the cooking is superb. The island boasts a comfortable new **bunkhouse** (Ⓦwww.isleofeigg.org) where you must book ahead, and several **bothies**, including one, run by Sue Holland (℡01687/482480), where **camping** is also possible; wild camping is restricted to the beach by the pier. **Bike rental** is available from the craftshop by the pier.

Muck

Smallest and most southerly of the Small Isles, **Muck** is low-lying, mostly treeless and extremely fertile, and as such shares more characteristics with the likes of Coll and Tiree than its nearest neighbours. **PORT MÓR**, the village on the southeast corner of the island, is where visitors arrive. A road, just over a mile in length, connects Port Mór with the island's main farm, **GALLANACH**, which overlooks the rocky seal-strewn skerries on the north side of the island. The nicest sandy beach is Camas na Cairidh, to the east of Gallanach. Despite being only 452ft above sea level, it really is worth climbing **Beinn Airein**, in the southwest corner of the island, for the 360-degree panoramic view of the surrounding islands; the return journey from Port Mór takes around two hours.

You can **stay** with one of the MacEwen family, who have owned the island since 1896, at *Port Mór House* (℡01687/462365; full board ❹); the rooms are pine-clad and enjoy great views, and the food is delicious. Alternatively, you can stay at the island's **bunkhouse** (℡01687/462042), a characterful, wood-panelled bothy. With permission from the landowner you may also **camp rough**, but bring supplies with you as there is no shop. The craftshop in Port Mór springs into life when day-trippers arrive, and doubles as a licensed **restaurant**.

Canna

Measuring a mere five miles by one, and with a population of just twenty, **Canna** is run as a single farm by the National Trust for Scotland. The island enjoys the best harbour in the Small Isles, a horn-shaped haven at its south-eastern corner protected by the tidal island of Sanday, now linked to Canna by a footbridge. For visitors, the chief pastime is walking: from the dock it's about a mile across a grassy basalt plateau to the bony sea cliffs of the north shore, which rise to a peak around **Compass Hill** (458ft) – so called because its high metal content distorts compasses – in the northeastern corner of the island, from where you get great views across to Rùm and Skye. The cliffs of the buffeted western half of the island are a breeding ground for both Manx shear-water and puffin. Some seven miles offshore, stands the **Heiskeir of Canna**, a curious mass of stone columns sticking up thirty feet above the water.

Accommodation is extremely limited. With permission from the NTS you may **camp rough** on Canna; otherwise, the only other option is **B&B** with Wendy MacKinnon (℡01687/462465; full board ⑤). The NTS rep on Canna is Winnie MacKinnon, who can help answer most queries (℡01687/462466). Remember, however, that there are no shops on Canna (bar the post office), so you must bring your own supplies, or order them to be delivered from Mallaig.

The Western Isles

The wild and windy **Western Isles** (ⓦ www.witb.co.uk) – also known as the Outer Hebrides or the Long Isle – vaunt a strikingly hostile mix of landscapes from windswept golden sands to harsh, heather-backed mountains and peat bogs. An elemental beauty pervades each of the more than two hundred islands that make up the archipelago, only a handful of which are actually inhabited by a total of just over 30,000 people. The influence of the Atlantic Gulf Stream ensures a mild but moist climate, though you can expect the strong Atlantic winds to blow in rain on two out of every three days even in summer. Weather fronts, however, come and go at such dramatic speed in these parts that there's little chance of mist or fog settling and few problems with midges.

The most significant difference from Skye is that tourism on the Western Isles is much less important to the fragile economy, which is still mainly concentrated around crofting, fishing and weaving; the percentage of "white settlers" is also a lot lower. The Outer Hebrides remain the heartland of **Gaelic** culture, with the language spoken by the vast majority of islanders, though its every-

---

Gaelic in the Western Isles

Except in Stornoway, and Balivanich on North Uist, **roadsigns** in the Western Isles are now almost exclusively in **Gaelic**, a difficult language to the English-speaker's eye, with complex pronunciation, though as a (very) general rule, the English names can often provide a rough pronunciation guide. Particularly if you're driving, it's essential to buy the bilingual Western Isles **map**, produced by the local tourist board, Bord Turasachd nan Eilean, and available at most tourist offices. To reflect the signposting, we've put the Gaelic first in the text, with the English equivalent in brackets. Thereafter we've stuck to the Gaelic names, to try to familiarize readers with their (albeit variable) spellings. The only exceptions are in the names of islands and ferry terminals, where we've stuck to the English names (with the Gaelic in brackets), partly to reflect CalMac's own policy.

△ Quiraing, Skye

day usage remains under constant threat from the national dominance of English. Its survival is due, in no small part, to the all-pervading influence of the Free Church and its offshoots, whose strict Calvinism is the creed of the vast majority of the population, with the sparsely populated South Uist, Barra and parts of Benbecula adhering to the more relaxed demands of Catholicism.

The interior of the northernmost island, **Lewis**, is mostly peat moor, a barren and marshy tract that gives way abruptly to the bare peaks of **North Harris**. Across a narrow isthmus lies **South Harris**, presenting some of the finest scenery in Scotland, with wide beaches of golden sand trimming the Atlantic in full view of the mountains and a rough boulder-strewn interior lying to the east. Further south still, a string of tiny, flatter islets, mainly **North Uist**, **Benbecula**, **South Uist** and **Barra**, offer breezy beaches, whose fine sands front a narrow band of boggy farmland, which, in turn, is mostly bordered by a lower range of hills to the east.

In direct contrast to their wonderful landscapes, villages in the Western Isles are rarely picturesque in themselves, and are usually made up of scattered, relatively modern croft houses strung out along the elementary road system. **Stornoway**, the only real town in the Outer Hebrides, is eminently unappealing. Many visitors, walkers and nature watchers forgo the settlements altogether and retreat to secluded cottages and B&Bs, though for this you really need your own transport.

Transport practicalities

British Regional Airlines and Loganair operate fast and frequent **flights** (not Sun) from Glasgow and Inverness to Stornoway on Lewis, and Barra and Benbecula on North Uist. But be warned: the weather conditions on the islands are notoriously changeable, making flights prone to both delay and stomach-churning bumpiness. On Barra, the other complication is that you land on the beach, so the timetable is adjusted with the tides. CalMac **car ferries** run from Ullapool to Stornoway (not Sun); from Uig on Skye to Tarbert and Lochmaddy (not Sun); and from Oban and Mallaig to South Uist and Barra (daily). There's also an **inter-island ferry** from Leverburgh on Harris to Otternish on North Uist, and between South Uist and Barra. For more on ferry services, see "Travel details" on p.1149.

Lewis (Leodhas)

Lewis is the largest and most populous of the Western Isles and the northernmost island in the Hebridean archipelago. After Viking rule ended in 1266, the island was fought over by the MacLeods and MacKenzies, until eventually being sold by the latter in 1844. The new owner, Sir James Matheson, invested heavily in new industries, as did **Lord Leverhulme** with the fishing industry when he acquired the island (along with Harris) in 1918. Though undoubtedly a benevolent despot, Leverhulme's unpopularity with crofters on Lewis, and his financial difficulties, forced him to give up his grandiose plans in 1923, when he gave the island to its inhabitants. His departure, however, left a big gap in the economy, and between the wars thousands more emigrated.

Most of the island's 20,000 inhabitants – two-thirds of the Western Isles' total population – now live in the crofting and fishing villages strung out along the northwest coast, between **Calanais** and **Port Nis**, in one of the most densely populated rural areas in the country. On this coast you'll also find the islands' best-preserved **prehistoric remains** – Dùn Charlabhaigh broch and Calanais standing stones – as well as a smattering of ancient crofters' houses in various

It is difficult to overestimate the importance of **religion** in the Western Isles, which are sharply divided – though with little enmity – between the Catholic southern isles of Barra and South Uist, and the Protestant islands of North Uist, Harris and Lewis. Most conflicts arise from the very considerable power the ministers of the Protestant Church, or Kirk, wield in secular life in the north, where the creed of **Sabbatarianism** is very strong. Here, Sunday is the Lord's Day, and virtually the whole community (irrespective of their degree of piety) stops work – all shops close, all pubs close, all garages close and there's no public transport and, perhaps most famously of all, even the swings in the children's playgrounds are padlocked.

The other main area of division is, paradoxically, within the Protestant Church itself. Scotland is unusual in that the national church, the **Church of Scotland**, is presbyterian (ruled by the ministers and elders of the church) rather than episcopal (ruled by bishops). At the time of the main split in the Presbyterian Church – the so-called **1843 Disruption** – a third of its ministers left the Church of Scotland, protesting at the law which allowed landlords to impose ministers against parishioners' wishes, and formed the breakaway **Free Church of Scotland**. Since those days there has been a gradual reconciliation although, in 1893, there was another break, when a minority of the Free Church became the Free Presbyterian Church of Scotland; meanwhile, others slowly made their way back to the Church of Scotland. To confuse matters further, both the Free Church and the Free Presbyterians are referred to as **"Wee Frees"**. In recent years, there have been still more schisms within the Wee Frees: in 1988 the Free Presbyterian Church split over a minister, Lord Mackay of Clashfern, who attended a Requiem Mass during a Catholic funeral of a friend – he and his supporters went on to form the break-away Associated Presbyterian Churches. More recently still, the Free Church split over the "heresies" of Professor Donald MacLeod, one of its more liberal members, who writes a regular column in the West Highland Free Press. A minority within the church have now formed the Free Church of Scotland (Continuing), accompanied by the usual battles over church buildings and congregations.

The various brands and subdivisions of the Presbyterian Church may appear trivial to outsiders, but to the churchgoers of Lewis, Harris and North Uist (as well as much of Skye and Raasay) they are still keenly felt. In part, this is due to social and cultural reasons: Free Church elders helped organize resistance to the Clearances, and the Wee Frees have done the most to help preserve the Gaelic language. A Free Church service is a memorable experience, and in some villages it takes place every evening (and twice on Sundays): there's no set service or prayer book and no hymns; only Biblical readings, psalm singing and a fiery sermon all in Gaelic; the pulpit is the architectural focus of the church, not the altar, and communion is taken only on special occasions. If you want to attend one, the Free Church on Kenneth Street in Stornoway has reputedly the largest Sunday-evening congregation in the UK, of up to 1500 people.

stages of abandonment. The landscape is mostly flat peat bog – hence the island's name, derived from the Gaelic *leogach* ("marshy") – with a gentle shoreline that only fulfils its dramatic potential around Rubha Robhanais (Butt of Lewis), a group of rough rocks on the island's northernmost tip, near Port Nis. To the south, where Lewis is physically joined with Harris, the land rises to just over 1800ft, providing a more exhilarating backdrop for the excellent beaches that pepper the isolated coastline of **Uig**, to the west of Calanais.

Most visitors use **Stornoway**, on the east coast, as a base for exploring the island, though this presents problems if you're travelling by **bus**. There's a regular service to Port Nis and Tarbert, and although the most obvious excursion

– the 45-mile round trip from Stornoway to Calanais, Carlabhagh, Arnol and back – is difficult to complete by public transport, minibus tours make the trip on most days from April to October (see p.1149).

Stornoway (Steornabhagh)

In these parts, **STORNOWAY** is a buzzing metropolis, with some eight thousand inhabitants, a one-way system, pedestrian precinct with CCTV and all the trappings of a large town. It's a centre for employment, a social hub for the island and, perhaps most importantly of all, home to the **Comhairle nan Eilean Siar** (Western Isles Council), set up in 1974, which has done much to promote Gaelic language and culture, and try to stem the tide of anglicization. For the visitor, however, the town is unlikely to win any great praise – aesthetics are not its strong point, and the urban pleasures on offer are limited.

Stornoway's old Town Hall on South Beach houses the **An Lanntair Art Gallery** (Mon–Sat 10am–5.30pm; free) on the first floor, with exhibitions featuring the work of local artists plus a very pleasant café. Anyone remotely interested in Harris tweed should head for the **Lewis Loom Centre** (Mon–Sat 9am–6pm; £1), run by an eccentric and engaging man and located at the far end of Cromwell Street, in the Old Grainstore off Bayhead. Continuing up the pedestrian precinct into Francis Street, you'll eventually reach the **Museum nan Eilean** (April–Sept Mon–Sat 10am–5.30pm; Oct–March Tues–Fri 10am–5pm, Sat 10am–1pm; free), with lots of information about the island's history and its herring and weaving industries.

Practicalities

The best thing about Stornoway is the convenience of its services. The island's **airport** is four miles east of the town centre (£5 by taxi); the swanky new octagonal CalMac **ferry terminal** is on South Beach, close to the **bus station**. You can get bus timetables, a map of the town and other useful information from the **tourist office**, near North Beach at 26 Cromwell St (June–Aug Mon, Tues, Thurs & Sat 9am–6pm & 8–9pm, Wed & Fri 9am–8pm; April, May & Sept to mid-Oct Mon–Fri 9am–6pm, Sat 9am–5pm; rest of year Mon–Fri 9am–5pm; ℡01851/703088).

Of the **hotels**, the *Royal Hotel* on Cromwell Street (℡01851/702109; ❺) is your best bet. Otherwise try the modern and rather pretentious *Caberfeidh* on Macauley Road, north of the town centre, (℡01851/702604, ⓦwww.calahotels.com; ❻); or the more reliable choice of the *Park Guest House* (℡01851/702485; ❷) on James Street where the public areas have bags of lugubrious late Victorian character; the bedrooms significantly less. Of the **B&Bs** along leafy Matheson Road, try *Fernlea*, a listed Victorian house, at no. 9 (℡01851/702125; ❷). The *Stornoway Backpackers'* **hostel** is a basic affair about five minutes' walk from the ferry at 47 Keith St (℡01851/703628, ⓦwww.stornoway-hostel.co.uk). The nearest **campsite**, *Laxdale Holiday Park* (℡01851/703234, ⓦwww.laxdaleholidaypark.force9.co.uk; open all year), lies a mile or so along the road to Barabhas, on Laxdale Lane.

Decent **food** options are disappointingly limited. The best place is the *Thai Café*, 27 Church St (℡01851/701811), which serves inexpensive but authentic **Thai** food – as a consequence it's very popular, so book ahead. There are excellent light lunches to be had from the *An Lanntair* tearoom, and good-value snacks from *An Leabharlann*, the coffee shop in the new library on Cromwell Street. For local food head to the restaurant of the *Park Guest House* on James Street (closed Sun & Mon) – it's expensive unless you go for the "early bird" option. As for **pubs**, *MacNeills* on Cromwell Street is the liveliest central pub, with a mixed clientele of keen drinkers. The *Criterion*, a tiny wee pub on Point Street, is another option, as is the very pleasant bar of the *Royal Hotel*. There's sometimes live music as well as pub grub at the *Whaler's Rest* in Francis Street.

The road to Port Nis (Port of Ness)

Northwest of Stornoway, the A857 crosses the vast, barren **peat bog** of the interior, an empty undulating wilderness riddled with stretchmarks formed by peat cuttings and pockmarked with freshwater lochans. The whole area was once covered by forests, but these disappeared long ago, leaving a smothering deposit of peat that is, on average, six feet thick, and is still being formed in certain places. For the people of Lewis, the peat represents a valuable energy resource, with each crofter being assigned a slice of the bog. The islanders spend several very sociable weeks each spring cutting the peat, turning it over and leaving it neatly laid out in the open air to dry, returning in summer to collect the dried sods and stack them outside their houses. Peat remains the island's main source of domestic fuel, its pungent smoke one of the most characteristic smells of the Western Isles.

Twelve miles across the peat bog the road approaches the west coast of Lewis and divides, heading southwest towards Calanais (see p.1140), or northeast through **BARABHAS** (Barvas), and a whole string of bleak and fervently Free Church crofting and weaving villages. These scattered settlements have none of the photogenic qualities of Skye's whitewashed villages: the churches are plain and unadorned; the crofters' houses relatively modern and smothered in grey, pebble-dash rendering or harling; the stone cottages and enclosures of their forebears often lie half-abandoned in the front garden; while a rusting assortment of discarded cars and vans store peat bags and the like.

The road eventually terminates at the fishing village of **PORT NIS** (Port of Ness), with a tiny harbour and lovely golden beach. Shortly before you reach Port Nis, a minor road heads two miles northwest to the hamlet of **EOROPAIDH** (Europie) – pronounced "yor-erpee". Here, by the road junction that leads to the Butt of Lewis, stands the simple stone structure of **Teampull Mholuaidh** (St Moluag's Church), thought to date from the twelfth century. From Eoropaidh, a narrow road twists to the bleak and blustery northern tip of the island, Rubha Robhanais – well known to devotees of the BBC shipping forecast as the **Butt of Lewis** – where a lighthouse sticks up above a series of sheer cliffs and stacks, alive with seabirds, and a great place for marine mammal-spotting.

There are between four and six **buses** a day from Stornoway to Port Nis (not Sun). The best place to **stay** is *Galson Farm Guest House* (℡01851/850492, Ⓦwww.galsonfarm.freeserve.co.uk; ❺), an eighteenth-century farmhouse in Gabhsann Bho Dheas (South Galson), halfway between Barabhas and Port Nis, with a **bunkhouse** close by. Another, more modest option is the modern croft of *Eisdean* (℡01851/810240; ❶), in Coig Peighinnean (Five Penny Borve), near Port Nis, or *Cross Inn* (℡01851/810378; ❶), remarkable primarily for being the only **pub** in the entire parish.

Arnol and around

Heading southwest from the crossroads near Barabhas brings you to **ARNOL**. The remains of numerous blackhouses lie abandoned in the village, one of which, at the far end, has been restored as a **Black House Museum** (May–Sept Mon–Sat 9.30am–6.30pm; Oct–March 9.30am–4.30pm; £2.80; HS). Dating from the 1870s and inhabited until 1964, its chimneyless roof is overlaid with grassy sods and oat-straw thatch, lashed down with fishnets and ropes. Beneath, a simple system of wooden tie beams supports the roof, which covers both the living quarters and the attached byre and barn. The postwar wallpaper inside has been removed to reveal sooty rafters above the living room, where, in the centre of the stone and clay floor, the peat fire was the focal point of the house. Today, many visitors look back with nostalgia at the old abandoned blackhouses, but it's as well to remember that they were a breeding ground for disease, and that, essentially, life in the blackhouse was pretty grim. There's a great **B&B**, three miles from Arnol, in Siabost Bho Deas (South Shawbost) at *Airigh* (℡01851/710478, ℮eileenmaclean@lineone.net; ❷; March–Nov) and behind the church is the *Eilean Fraoich* **campsite** (℡01851/710504; May–Oct). You can grab a bite to eat at the *Shawbost Inn*.

Five miles on at Carlabhagh (Carloway), a mile-long road leads off north to the beautifully remote coastal settlement of **GEARRANNAN** (Garenin), where nine thatched crofters' houses – the last of which was abandoned in 1973 – have been restored. There's a visitor centre with a **café** serving soup and sandwiches, and also offering guided tours of the village (£1.75). One black-house now serves as a Gatliff Hebridean Hostels Trust (GHHT) **hostel** (℡01851/643416, ⓦwww.gearrannan.com), while another contains public toilets. A night here is unforgettable, and there's a beautiful stony beach from which to view the sunset.

Just beyond Carlabhagh, about 400 yards from the road, **Dùn Charlabhaigh Broch** perches on top of a conspicuous rocky outcrop overlooking the sea. Scotland's Atlantic coast is strewn with the remains of over 500 brochs, or for-tified towers, but this is one of the best-preserved, its dry-stone circular walls reaching a height of more than 30ft on the seaward side. The broch consists of two concentric walls, the inner one perpendicular, the outer one slanting inwards, the two originally fastened together by roughly hewn flagstones, which also served as lookout galleries reached via a narrow stairwell. The only entrance to the roofless inner yard is through a low doorway set beside a crude and cramped guard cell. Dùn Charlabhaigh now has its very own **Doune Broch Centre** (April–Oct Mon–Sat 10am–6pm; free), situated at a discreet distance, stone-built and sporting a turf roof. It's a good wet-weather retreat, and fun for kids, who can walk through the hay-strewn mock-up of the broch as it might have been. A mile or so beyond the broch, beside a lochan, is the *Doune Braes Hotel* (℡01851/643252, ℮hebrides@doune_braes.co.uk; ❹), a friendly, unpretentious place whose bar serves up the same tasty seafood dish-es as its restaurant, only cheaper.

Calanais (Callanish)

Five miles south of Carlabhagh lies the village of **CALANAIS** (Callanish), site of the islands' most dramatic prehistoric ruins, the **Calanais Standing Stones**, whose monoliths – nearly fifty of them – occupy a serene lochside setting. There's been years of heated debate about the origin and function of the stones – slabs of gnarled and finely grained gneiss up to 15ft high – though almost everyone agrees that they were lugged here by Neolithic peoples between 3000 and 1500 BC. It's also obvious that the planning and construction of the site – as well as several other lesser circles nearby – was spread over many gen-erations. Such an endeavour could, it's been argued, only be prompted by the desire to predict the seasonal cycle upon which these early farmers were entirely dependent, and indeed many of the stones are aligned with the posi-tion of the sun and the stars. This rational explanation, based on clear evidence that this part of Lewis was once a fertile farming area, dismisses as coincidence the ground plan of the site, which resembles a colossal Celtic cross, and explains away the central burial chamber as a later addition of no special significance. These two features have, however, fuelled all sorts of theories ranging from alien intervention to human sacrifice.

A blackhouse adjacent to the main stone circle has been refurbished as a **tea-room** and shop, and it's to this you should head for refreshment rather than the superfluous **Calanais Visitor Centre** (Mon–Sat: April–Sept 10am–7pm; Oct–March 10am–4pm; museum £1.75) on the other side of the stones (and thankfully out of view), to which all the signs direct you from the road. The centre runs a decent restaurant and a small museum on the site, but with so much information on the panels beside the stones there's little reason to visit it. You're politely asked not to walk between the stones, only along the path that surrounds them, so if you want to commune with standing stones in solitude, head for the smaller circles in more natural surroundings a mile or two southeast of Calanais, around Gearraidh na h-Aibhne (Garynahine).

There are several inexpensive **B&Bs** in Calanais itself: try Mrs Catherine Morrison, 27 Calanais (☎01851/621392; ➊; March–Sept), or an excellent B&B, which caters well for veggies and is run by Debbie Nash (☎01851/621321; ➊) in neighbouring Tolastadh a Chaolais (Tolsta Chaolais), three miles north. Calanais also has a modern *Eschol Guest House* (☎01851/621357; ➌), no beauty from the outside, but very comfortable within. If it's just **food** you want, *Tigh Mealros* (closed Sun), in Gearraidh na h-Aibhne, serves good, inexpensive lunches and evening meals, featuring local seafood.

Harris (Na Hearadh)

Lewis and **Harris** are, in fact, one island, the division between the two embedded in a historical split in the MacLeod clan, lost in the mists of time. The border between the two was a county boundary until 1975, with Harris lying in Inverness-shire, and Lewis belonging to Ross and Cromarty. Nowadays, the dividing line is rarely marked even on maps; for the record, it comprises Loch Resort in the west, Loch Seaforth in the east, and the six miles in between. Harris itself is more clearly divided by a minuscule isthmus, separating the wild, inhospitable mountains of **North Harris** from the gentler landscape and sandy shores of **South Harris**.

Along with Lewis, Harris was purchased in 1918 by Lord Leverhulme, and after 1923, when he pulled out of Lewis, all his efforts were concentrated here. In contrast to Lewis, though, Leverhulme and his ambitious projects were broadly welcomed by the people of Harris. His most grandiose plans were drawn up for Leverburgh, but he also purchased an old Norwegian whaling station in Bun Abhain Eadara in 1922, built a spinning mill at Geocrab and began the construction of four roads. Financial difficulties, a slump in the tweed industry and the lack of market for whale products meant that none of the schemes was a wholehearted success, and when he died in 1925 the plug was pulled on all of them by his executors. Since then, **unemployment** has been a constant problem in Harris. Crofting continues on a small scale, supplemented by the tweed industry, though the main focus of this has shifted to Lewis. Shellfish fishing continues on Scalpay, while the rest of the population gets by on whatever employment is available: roadworks, crafts and, of course, tourism. There's a regular **bus** connection between Stornoway and **Tarbert**, and an occasional service which circumnavigates South Harris.

Harris tweed

Far from being a picturesque cottage industry, as it's sometimes presented, the production of **Harris tweed** is vital to the local economy, with a well-organized and unionized workforce. Traditionally the tweed was made by women, from the wool of their own sheep, to provide clothing for their families, using a 2500-year-old process. Each woman was responsible for plucking the wool by hand, washing and scouring it, dyeing it with lichen, heather flowers or ragwort, carding (smoothing and straightening the wool, often adding butter to grease it), spinning and weaving. Finally the cloth was dipped in sheep's urine and "waulked" by a group of women, who beat the cloth on a table to soften and shrink it whilst singing Gaelic waulking songs. Harris Tweed was originally made all over the islands, and was known simply as *clò mór* (big cloth).

In the mid-nineteenth century, the Countess of Dunmore, who owned a large part of Harris, started to sell surplus cloth to her aristocratic friends, thus forming the genesis of the modern industry, which serves as a vital source of employment, though demand (and therefore employment levels) can fluctuate wildly as fashions change. To earn the official Harris Tweed Association trademark of the Orb and the Maltese Cross – taken from the Countess of Dunmore's coat of arms – the fabric has to be hand-woven on the Outer Hebrides from 100 percent pure new Scottish wool, while the other parts of the manufacturing process must take place only in the local mills.

The main centre of production is now Lewis, where the wool is dyed, carded and spun; you can see all these processes by visiting the **Lewis Loom Centre** in Stornoway (see p.1138). In recent years there has been a revival of traditional tweed-making techniques, with several small producers, like Anne Campbell at *Clò Mór* in Liceasto (Mon–Fri 9am–5pm; ☎01859/530364), religiously following old methods. One of the more interesting aspects of the process is the use of indigenous plants and bushes to dye the cloth: yellow comes from rocket and broom, green from heather, grey and black from iris and oak, and, most popular of all, reddish brown from crotal, a flat grey lichen scraped off rocks.

Tarbert (Tairbeart)

The largest place on Harris is the ferry port of **TARBERT**, sheltered in a green valley on the narrow isthmus that marks the border between North and South Harris. The mountainous backdrop is impressive, and the town is attractively laid out on steep terraces sloping up from the dock. It also boasts Harris's only **tourist office** (April–Oct Mon–Sat 9am–1pm & 2–5pm; also open to greet the ferry; winter hours variable; ☎01859/502011), close to the ferry terminal. The office can arrange modest, inexpensive B&B **accommodation** and has a full set of bus timetables, but its real value is as a source of information on local walks.

Tarbert has an excellent new **hostel**, the *Rockview Bunkhouse* (☎01859/502626), on Main Street, which also offers **bike rental**. Close to the ferry terminal, there's a very good B&B, *Tigh na Mara* (☎01859/502270, ⓔtighnamara@tarbert-harris.freeserve.co.uk; ❶), or the easygoing, old-fashioned *Harris Hotel* (☎01859/502154, ⓔcameronharris@btinternet.com; ❹), five minutes' walk away. You'll need to book ahead to stay in Tarbert's two most popular **guest houses**: *Allan Cottage* (☎01859/502146; ❸; May–Sept), in the old telephone exchange, or *Leachin House* (☎01859/502157, ⓦwww.leachinhouse.com; ❺), further up the Stornoway road. The purpose-built hotel **bar** acts as the local social centre and serves excellent bar meals; the adjacent *Crofters* **restaurant** serves moderately expensive standard fare. During the day, you're best off heading for the very pleasant *First Fruits* **tearoom** (April–Sept; closed Sun), behind the tourist office.

North Harris (Ceann a Tuath na Hearadh)

The A859 north to Stornoway takes you over a boulder-strewn saddle between mighty **Sgaoth Aird** (1829ft) and An Cliseam or the **Clisham** (2619ft), the highest peak in the Western Isles. This bitter terrain, littered with debris left behind by retreating glaciers, offers but the barest of vegetation, with an occasional cluster of crofters' houses sitting in the shadow of a host of pointed peaks, anywhere between 1000ft and 2500ft high. These bulging, pyramidal mountains reach their climax around the dramatic shores of the fjord-like **Loch Seaforth**. If you're planning on walking in North Harris, and can afford it, consider using the spectacular *Ardvourlie Castle* (☎01859/502307; ●; April–Oct), ten miles north of Tarbert by the shores of Loch Seaforth, as a launch pad. A cheaper, but equally idyllic spot is the GHHT **hostel** (no phone; open all year) in the lonely coastal hamlet of Reinigeadal (Rhenigdale). To reach the hostel without your own transport, walk east five miles from Tarbert along the road to **Caolas Scalpaigh** (Kyles Scalpay). After another mile or so, watch for the sign marking the start of the path which threads its way through the peaks of the craggy promontory that lies trapped between Loch Seaforth and East Loch Tarbert. It's a magnificent hike, with superb views out along the coast and over the mountains, but you'll need to be properly equipped, and should allow three hours for the one-way trip.

South Harris (Ceann a Deas na Hearadh)

The mountains of **South Harris** are less dramatic than those of the north, but the scenery is equally breathtaking. There's a choice of routes from Tarbert to the ferry port of Leverburgh, which connects with North Uist; the east coast, known as Bays (Na Baigh), is rugged and seemingly inhospitable, while the west coast is endowed with some of the finest stretches of golden sand in the whole of the archipelago, buffeted by the Atlantic winds. Paradoxically, most people on South Harris live along the harsh eastern coastline rather than the more fertile west side, though not by choice – they were evicted from their original crofts to make way for sheep-grazing.

The main road from Tarbert into South Harris snakes its way west for ten miles across the boulder-strewn interior to reach the coast. Once there, you get a view of the most stunning **beach**, the vast golden strand of **Tràigh Losgaintir**. The road continues to ride above a chain of sweeping sands, backed by rich machair, that stretches for nine miles along the Atlantic coast. In good weather, the scenery is particularly impressive, foaming breakers rolling along the golden sands set against the rounded peaks of the mountains to the north and the islet-studded turquoise sea to the west – and even on the dullest day the sand manages to glow beneath the waves. A short distance out to sea is the large island of **Taransay** (Tarasaigh), which once held a population of nearly a hundred, but was abandoned as recently as 1974. In 2000 it was the scene of the BBC series *Castaway*, in which thirty-odd contestants were filmed living on the island for the best part of a year; you can now take day-trips to the island (☎07747/842218, ⓦwww.visit-taransay.com). Nobody bothers much if you **camp** or park beside the dune-edged beach, as long as you're careful not to churn up the machair, and there are two very good B&Bs, *Moravia* (☎01859/550262; ●; March–Oct), overlooking the sands at Losgaintir (Luskentyre) and *Beul na Mara* at Seilebost (☎01859/550205, Ⓔmorrison-cl@talk21.com; ●). The most luxurious accommodation, though, is five miles further south in **SGARASTA** (Scarista), where one of the first of the Hebridean Clearances took place in 1828, when thirty families were evicted and their homes burnt. Here, the Georgian former manse of *Scarista House*

(☎01859/550238, 🌐www.scaristahouse.com; ❼; May–Sept) overlooks the nearby golden sands; if you can't afford to stay, it's worth splashing out and booking for dinner, as the meat and seafood served here is among the freshest and finest on the Western Isles.

From Taobh Tuath the road veers to the southeast to trim the island's south shore, eventually reaching the sprawling settlement of **LEVERBURGH** (An t-Ob), named after Lord Leverhulme, who planned to turn the place into the largest fishing port on the west coast of Scotland. From a jetty about a mile south of the main road, a CalMac **car ferry** runs to Otternish on North Uist. There are several **B&Bs** strung out within a two-mile radius of Leverburgh: try *Caberfeidh House* (☎01859/520276; ❶), a lovely stone-built Victorian building by the turn-off to the ferry, or *Sorrel Cottage* (☎01859/520319, ❻sorrel-cottage@talk21.com; ❶), which specializes in vegetarian and seafood cooking. A cheaper alternative is the welcoming purpose-built timber-clad *An Bothan* **bunkhouse** (☎01859/520251), which has great facilities, and is only a few minutes' walk from the ferry.

Three miles southeast of Leverburgh and a mile or so from Renish Point, the southern tip of Harris, is the old port of **ROGHADAL** (Rodel), where a smattering of ancient stone houses lies among the hillocks surrounding the dilapidated harbour where the ferry from Skye used to arrive. On top of one of these grassy humps, with sheep grazing in the graveyard, is **St Clement's Church** (Tur Chliamainn), burial place of the MacLeods of Harris and Dunvegan in Skye. Dating from the 1520s, the church's bare interior is distinguished by its wall tombs, notably that of the founder, Alasdair Crotach (also known as Alexander MacLeod), whose heavily weathered effigy lies beneath an intriguing backdrop and canopy of sculpted reliefs depicting vernacular and religious scenes – elemental representations of, among others, a stag hunt, the Holy Trinity, St Michael, and the devil and an angel weighing the souls of the dead. Look out, too, for the *sheila-na-gig* halfway up the south side of the church tower; unusually, she has a brother displaying his genitalia, below a carving of St Clement on the west face. Beyond the church, tucked away by a quiet harbour, the newly restored *Rodel Hotel* is excellent (☎01859/520210, 🌐www.rodelhotel.co.uk; ❺).

North Uist (Uibhist a Tuath)

Compared to the mountainous scenery of Harris, **North Uist** – seventeen miles long and thirteen miles wide – is much flatter and for some comes as something of an anticlimax. Over half the surface area is covered by water, creating a distinctive peaty-brown lochan-studded "drowned landscape". Most visitors come here for the trout and salmon fishing and the deerstalking, both of which (along with poaching) are critical to the survival of the island's economy. Others come for the smattering of prehistoric sites and sheer peace of this windy isle, and the solitude of North Uist's vast sandy beaches, which extend – almost without interruption – along the north and west coast.

Despite being situated on the east coast, some distance away from any beach, the ferry port of **LOCHMADDY** (Loch nam Madadh, or "Loch of the Dogs") makes a good base for exploring the island. The village itself, occupying a narrow, bumpy promontory, is nothing special, though, one place that's well worth visiting is **Taigh Chearsabhagh** (Mon–Sat 10am–5pm), a converted eighteenth-century merchant's house, now home to an arts centre, airy café, shop and excellent museum (£1) which is a replica Norse house where children can dress up in costume and touch everything. There's a **sculpture trail** starting outside the arts centre on the shore; to see the highlight, **Both nam Faileas** (Hut of the Shadow), an ingenious drystone, turf-roofed camera obscura, take a walk out past the Uist Outdoor Centre and across the footbridge that leads to the derelict Sponish House. The **tourist office** (mid-April to mid-Oct Mon–Fri 9am–5pm, Sat 9.30am–5.30pm; also open to greet the evening ferry; ℡01876/500321), near the quayside, has local bus and ferry timetables, and can help with **accommodation**. There are a couple of nice Victorian B&Bs, north off the main road: try the *Old* ℡ *Courthouse* (℡01876/500358, ✉mjohn-son@oldcourthouse.fsnet.co.uk; ➋). A little further north lies the *Uist Outdoor Centre* (℡01876/500480, ⓦwww.uistoutdoorcentre.co.uk), which has **hostel** accommodation in four-person bunk rooms, and offers a wide range of outdoor activities, from canoeing round the indented coastline to "rubber tubing". The **bar** in the *Lochmaddy Hotel* is lively and serves the usual bar meals, but it's currently not a place to recommend staying in.

Several prehistoric sights lie within easy cycling distance of Lochmaddy (or even walking distance if you use the postbus for the outward journey). The most significant is the **Barpa Langass**, a large, mostly intact, chambered cairn seven barren miles to the southwest along the A867; a mile to the southeast is the small stone circle of **Pobull Fhinn**. Three miles northwest of Lochmaddy along the A865 is **Na Fir Bhreige** (The Three False Men), three standing stones which, depending on your legend, mark the graves of three spies buried alive, or three men who deserted their wives and were turned to stone by a proto-feminist witch.

North Uist's other main draw is the **Balranald RSPB Reserve**, one of the last breeding grounds of the corncrake, among Europe's most endangered birds. Sightings are rare, partly because the birds are very good at hiding in long grass, but the males' loud "craking" is relatively easy to hear from May to July. From the excellent new **visitor centre**, there's a two-hour walk along the headland, marked out by discreet white pegs, giving you ample opportunity for appreciating the wonderful carpet of flowers that covers the machair in summer, and for spotting corn buntings and arctic terns inland and gannets and Manx shearwaters out to sea – guided walks take place throughout the summer (May–Aug Tues & Thurs 2pm; ℡01878/602188). On a clear day you can see the unmistakable shape of St Kilda, seeming miraculously near. Another **hostel** worth noting is *Taigh mo Sheanair* (℡01876/580246), a very welcoming, family-run place, where you can also **camp**; it's a clearly signposted fifteen-minute walk from the main road, south of the crossroads at Clachan.

Bhearnaraigh (Berneray)

For those in search of still more seclusion, there's the low-lying island of **Berneray** – two miles by three, with a population of about 140 – now accessible via a brand-new causeway from **Otternish**, eight miles north of Lochmaddy. The island's main claim to fame is as the birthplace of Giant MacAskill, a nineteenth-century circus character who used to tour with Tom Thumb, and as the favoured holiday hideaway of that other great eccentric, Prince Charles, lover of Gaelic culture and royal potato-picker to local crofter, "Splash" MacKillop. Apart from the sheer peace and isolation, the island's main draw for non-royals is a three-mile-long sandy beach on the west and north coast, backed by rabbit-free dunes and machair. The other great draw is the wonderful GHHT **hostel**, which occupies a pair of thatched blackhouses in a lovely spot by a beach, beyond Loch a Bhàigh and the main village. Alternatively you can follow in the prince's footsteps and stay (and help out) at "Splash" MacKillop's *Burnside Croft* **B&B** (℡01876/540235, ✉splashmackillop@burnsidecroft.fsnet.co.uk; ❷ ; Feb–Nov), and enjoy "storytelling evenings"; bike rental is also available. There are several **tearooms** currently functioning along the main road, including one in the community centre at the end of the road to **Borgh** (Borve), all of which serve simple refreshments, and, with the new causeway in place, there's now a **bus** connection with Lochmaddy.

Benbecula (Beinn na Faoghla)

Blink and you could miss the pancake-flat island of **Benbecula** (pronounced with stress on the second syllable), sandwiched between Protestant North Uist and Catholic South Uist. Most visitors simply trundle along the main road that cuts across the middle of the island in less than five miles – not such a bad idea, since the island is scarred from the postwar presence of the Royal Artillery who until recently used to make up half the local population. Economically, of course, the area benefited enormously from the military presence, though the impact on the environment and Gaelic culture (with so many English-speakers around) has been less positive.

The legacy of Benbecula's military past is only too evident in the depressing, barracks-like housing developments **BALIVANICH** (Baile a Mhanaich), the grim, grey capital of Benbecula in the northwest. The only reason to come here at all is if you happen to be flying into or out of **Benbecula airport** (direct flights to Glasgow, Barra and Stornoway), need to take money out of the Bank of Scotland ATM (the only one on the Uists), or stock up on provisions, best done at the old NAAFI store (now a Spar supermarket; open daily), to the west of the post office. The modern **hostel** *Taigh-na-Cille* (☎01870/602522) is within easy walking distance of the airport, on the road to North Uist. The best thing about Balivanich is *Stepping Stone*, the purpose-built **café–restaurant** situated opposite the post office: the lunchtime café is cheap and cheerful, offering filled rolls and chips with everything, while in the evening, it's home to *Sinteag* restaurant, where the à la carte menu will set you back around £20 a head.

South Uist (Uibhist a Deas)

To the south of Benbecula, the island of **South Uist** is arguably the most appealing of the southern chain of islands. The west coast boasts some of the region's finest machair and beaches – a necklace of gold and grey sand strung twenty miles from one end to the other – while the east coast features a ridge of high mountains rising to 2034ft at the summit of Beinn Mhor. The only blot on South Uist's landscape is the old Royal Artillery missile range, which occupies the northwest corner of the island.

The Reformation never took a strong hold in South Uist (or Barra), and the island remains Roman Catholic, as is evident from the various roadside shrines and the slender modern statue of Our Lady of the Isles that stands by the main road below the small hill of **Rueval**, known to the locals as "Space City" for its forest of aerials and golf balls. To the south of Rueval is the freshwater **Loch Druidibeg**, a breeding ground for greylag geese and a favourite spot for mute swans; there's a waymarked path through the reserve that begins just by the telephone box on the main road in Stadhlaigearraidh (Stilligarry). One of the best places to gain access to the sandy shoreline is at **TOBHA MÒR** (Howmore), a pretty little crofting settlement with a fair number of restored houses, many still thatched, including one distinctively roofed in brown heather. A GHHT **hostel** (no phone) occupies one such house near the village church, from where it's an easy walk across the flower-infested machair to the gorgeous beach. Close by the hostel are the shattered, lichen-encrusted remains of no fewer than four medieval churches and chapels, and a burial ground now harbouring just a few scattered graves.

Five miles south of Tobha Mòr, the **Kildonan Museum** (Mon–Sat 10am–5pm, Sun 2–5pm; £1.80) contains mock-ups of Hebridean kitchens through the ages, two lovely box beds and an impressive selection of old photos are accompanied by a firmly unsentimental yet poetic written text on crofting life in the last two centuries. Among the more unusual exhibits is a pair of ornamental shoes made of deer hooves. The museum also runs a café serving sandwiches and home-made cakes, and has a choice of historical videos for those really wet and windy days.

The best **hotel** on the Uists is the *Orasay Inn* (℡01870/610298, Ⓔorasayinn@btinternet.com; ➌), located in a peaceful spot off the road to Loch a Charnain (Lochcarnan), in the northeastern corner of the island. By contrast, **LOCHBOISDALE**, South Uist's chief settlement and ferry port, five miles southeast of Kildonan, has just the *Lochboisdale Hotel* for somewhere to have a drink and a proper meal. The **tourist office** (Easter to mid-Oct Mon–Sat 9am–5pm; ℡01878/700286) opens to meet the night ferry from Oban. There are several small, ordinary **B&Bs** within comfortable walking distance of the dock, one of the nearest being *Brae Lea House* (℡01878/700497; ➋). Perhaps the best place to hole up in this part of South Uist is the *Polochar Inn* (℡01878/700215; ➍), eight miles from Lochboisdale, right on the south coast overlooking the Sound of Barra, with its own sandy beach close by. If you're heading for Barra you could take the passenger **ferry** (3–4 daily), which also takes bikes, from **Ludag jetty** (℡01851/701702), two miles east of the *Polochar Inn*, and lands at Eoligarry on Barra's north coast. Now that the causeway to Eriskay is complete, there are plans to establish a car ferry service to Barra from there.

Eriskay (Eiriosgaigh)

To the south of South Uist lies the barren, hilly island of **Eriskay**, famous for its patterned jerseys (on sale at the community centre), and a peculiar breed of pony, originally used for carrying peat and seaweed. The island, which measures just over two miles by one, shelters a small fishing community of about 150, and makes a great day-trip from South Uist, as long as the weather's fine. It's now connected by a newly-built and impressive **causeway**, which misleadingly signposts you at the other end to the car ferry to Barra: this, however, does not yet exist since Barra has only just got the funding.

For a small island, Eriskay has had more than its fair share of historical headlines. The island's main beach on the west coast, Coilleag a Phrionnsa (Prince's Cockle Strand), was where **Bonnie Prince Charlie** landed on Scottish soil on July 23, 1745 – the sea bindweed that grows there to this day is said to have sprung from the seeds Charles brought with him from France. Eriskay's other claim to fame came in 1941 when the 8000-ton **SS Politician** or *Polly* as it's fondly known, sank on its way from Liverpool to Jamaica, along with its cargo of bicycle parts, £3 million in Jamaican currency and 264,000 bottles of whisky, inspiring Compton MacKenzie's book – and the Ealing comedy (filmed here in 1948) – *Whisky Galore!* (released in the US as *Tight Little Island*). The ship's stern can still be seen to the northwest of the Isle of Calvey at low tide, and one of the original bottles (and lots of other related memorabilia) is on show in the island's purpose-built pub, *Am Politician*, on the west coast.

Barra (Barraigh)

Just four miles wide and eight miles long, **Barra** has a well-deserved reputation for being the Western Isles in miniature. It has sandy beaches, backed by machair, glacial mountains, prehistoric ruins, Gaelic culture, and a welcoming Catholic population of just over 1300. The only settlement of any size is **CASTLEBAY** (Bagh a Chaisteil), which curves around the barren rocky hills of a wide bay on the south side of the island. It's difficult to imagine it now, but Castlebay was a herring port of some significance back in the nineteenth century, with up to 400 boats in the harbour and curing and packing factories ashore. Barra's religious allegiance is immediately announced by the large Catholic church, Our Lady, Star of the Sea, which overlooks the bay; to underline the point, there's a Madonna and Child on the slopes of **Heaval** (1260ft), the largest peak on Barra, and a fairly easy hike from the bay. Castlebay has a castle in its bay, the medieval islet-fortress of **Kisimul Castle** (April–Sept daily 9.30am–6.30pm; Oct Mon–Wed & Sat 9.30am–4.30pm, Thurs 9.30am–12.30pm, Sun 2–4.30pm; HS; £3), ancestral home of the MacNeil clan. The castle burnt down in the eighteenth century, but when the 45th MacNeil chief – conveniently enough an architect by training – bought the island back in 1937, he set about restoring the castle. You can take a stroll round it by heading down to the slipway at the bottom of Main Street, where you can signal to the HS ferryman to come over and get you (weather permitting; ☎01871/810313).

To learn more about the history of the island, and about the postal system of the Western Isles, it's worth paying a visit to **Barra Heritage Centre** (Mon–Fri 11am–5pm; £1), housed in an unprepossessing block on the road that leads west out of town. One of Barra's most fascinating sights is its **airport**, on the north side of the island, where planes land and take off from the crunchy shell sands of Tràigh Mhór, better known as **Cockle Strand**; the exact timing of the flights depends on the tides, since at high tide the beach (and therefore the runway) is covered in water. As its name suggests, the strand is also famous for its cockles and cockleshells, the latter being used to make harling, the rendering used on most Scottish houses. In 1994, mechanical cockle extraction using tractors was introduced, and quickly began to decimate the cockle stocks and threaten the beach's use as an airport; as a result it has now been banned, in favour of traditional hand-raking.

Barra's **tourist office** (April to mid-Oct Mon–Sat 9am–5pm; also open to greet the ferry; ☎01871/810336) is situated on Main Street in Castlebay just round from the pier. In Castlebay itself, the *Castlebay Hotel* (☎01871/810223; ❹) is the most comfortable **place to stay**, followed by *Tigh-na-Mara* (☎01871/810304; ❷; April–Oct), a guest house a couple of minutes' walk from the pier by the sea; another good choice is *Grianamul* (☎01871/810416, Ⓔronnie.macneil@virgin.net; ❸; April–Oct). There's a GHHT **hostel** (no phone) in Breibhig (Brevig), a couple of miles east of Castlebay, where you can also **camp**. Places to eat include the *Kisimul Galley* **café** which specializes in cheap-and-cheerful Scottish fry-ups. For more fancy fare, head to the *Castlebay Hotel*'s cosy **bar**, which regularly has cockles, crabs and scallops on its menu, and good views out over the bay.

Travel details

Trains

Aberdeen to: Kyle of Lochalsh (Mon–Sat 1 daily; 5hr).
Fort William to: Mallaig (4–5 daily; 1hr 25min).
Glasgow (Queen Street) to: Mallaig (Mon–Sat 3 daily, Sun 1 daily; 5hr 20min); Oban (2–4 daily; 3hr).
Inverness to: Kyle of Lochalsh (Mon–Sat 3 daily, Sun 1 daily; 2hr 30min).

Buses

Mainland

Edinburgh to: Broadford (2 daily; 6hr 30min); Oban (1 daily; 4hr); Portree (2 daily; 7hr 40min).
Glasgow to: Broadford (3 daily; 5hr 25min); Oban (Mon–Sat 4 daily, Sun 2 daily; 3hr); Portree (3 daily; 6hr–6hr 30min); Uig (Mon–Sat 2 daily; 7hr 40min).
Inverness to: Broadford (2 daily; 2hr 50min); Portree (2 daily; 3hr 15min); Ullapool (Mon–Sat 2–3 daily; 1hr 20min).
Kyle of Lochalsh to: Broadford (7 daily; 30min); Portree (7daily; 1hr).

Skye

Armadale to: Broadford (Mon–Sat 4–5 daily; 45min); Portree (Mon–Sat 3–4 daily; 1hr 20min); Sligachan (Mon–Sat 3–4 daily; 1hr 10min).
Broadford to: Portree (Mon–Sat 5–6 daily; 40min).
Dunvegan to: Glendale (Mon–Sat 1–4 daily; 30min).
Kyleakin to: Broadford (Mon–Sat 12–14 daily, Sun 7 daily; 15min); Portree (Mon–Sat 6–7 daily, Sun 5 daily; 1hr); Sligachan (Mon–Sat 7–8 daily, Sun 5 daily; 45min); Uig (Mon–Sat 2 daily; 1hr 20min).
Portree to: Carbost (Mon–Fri 2–3 daily, Sat 1 daily; 35min); Duntulm (Mon–Sat 2–3 daily; 1hr); Dunvegan (Mon–Sat 4 daily; 50min); Staffin (Mon–Sat 3 daily; 40min); Uig (Mon–Sat 4–5 daily; 30min).

Lewis/Harris

ⓦ www.witb.co.uk/services/bus.htm
Stornoway to: Barabhas (Mon–Sat 8–12 daily; 25min); Calanais (Mon–Sat 4–6 daily; 40min); Carlabhagh (Mon–Sat 4–6 daily; 1hr); Leverburgh (Mon–Sat 4–5 daily; 2hr); Port Nis (Mon–Sat 4–6 daily; 1hr); Siabost (Mon–Sat 4–6 daily; 45min); Tarbert (Mon–Sat 4–5 daily; 1hr 10min).
Tarbert to: Leverburgh (Mon–Sat 8 daily; 50min); Leverburgh via the Bays (Mon–Sat 3–4 daily; 1hr 10min).

The Uists and Benbecula

Lochboisdale to: Eriskay (Mon–Sat 5 daily; 30–45min).
Lochmaddy to: Balivanich (Mon–Sat 5–6 daily; 45min–2hr); Balranald (Mon–Sat 3 daily; 50min); Berneray (Mon–Sat 6–7 daily; 30min); Lochboisdale (Mon–Sat 5–6 daily; 2hr).
Otternish to: Balivanich (Mon–Sat 3–4 daily; 1hr–2hr 20min); Lochmaddy (Mon–Sat 6–7 daily; 20–50min).

Barra

Castlebay to: Airport/Eoligarry (Mon–Sat 6–7 daily; 35min/45min).

Ferries (summer timetable)

To Barra: Lochboisdale–Castlebay (Tues, Thurs, Fri & Sun; 1hr 35min); Mallaig–Castlebay (Sun; 3hr 45min); Oban–Castlebay (Mon, Wed, Thurs & Sat; 5hr).
To Canna: Eigg–Canna (Mon & Sat; 2hr 45min–3hr); Mallaig–Canna (Mon, Wed, Fri & Sat; 2hr 30min–4hr 15min); Muck–Canna (Sat; 2hr 15min); Rùm–Canna (Mon, Wed, Fri & Sat; 1hr–1hr 15min).
To Eigg: Canna–Eigg (Mon & Sat; 2hr 15min–3hr); Mallaig–Eigg (Mon, Tues & Thurs–Sat; 1hr 30–1hr 50min); Muck–Eigg (Tues & Thurs–Sat; 45–50min); Rùm–Eigg (Mon & Sat; 1hr 15min–2hr).
To Harris: Lochmaddy–Tarbert via Uig (Mon–Sat 1–2 daily; 4hr); Otternish–Leverburgh (Mon–Sat 4 daily; 1hr 10min); Uig–Tarbert (Mon–Sat 1–2 daily; 1hr 45min).
To Lewis: Ullapool–Stornoway (Mon–Sat 2–3 daily; 2hr 40min).
To Muck: Eigg–Muck (Tues, Thurs & Sat; 1hr); Canna–Muck (Sat; 2hr 15min); Mallaig–Muck (Tues, Thurs, Fri & Sat; 2hr 40min–4hr 45min); Rùm–Muck (Sat; 1hr 15min).
To North Uist: Leverburgh–Otternish (Mon–Sat 4 daily; 1hr 10min); Tarbert–Lochmaddy via Uig (Mon–Sat 1–2 daily; 4hr); Uig–Lochmaddy (1–2 daily; 1hr 50min).

To Raasay: Sconser–Raasay (Mon–Sat 9–11 daily; 15min).

To Rùm: Canna–Rùm (Mon, Wed, Fri & Sat; 1hr–1hr 15min); Eigg–Rùm (Mon & Sat; 1hr 30min–2hr); Mallaig–Rùm (Mon, Wed, Fri & Sat; 1hr 45min–3hr 30min); Muck–Rùm (Sat; 1hr 15min).

To Skye: Glenelg–Kylerhea (daily frequently;

15min); Mallaig–Armadale (Mon–Sat 6–7 daily; June–Aug also Sun; 30min).

To South Uist: Castlebay–Lochboisdale (Mon, Wed, Thurs & Sat; 1hr 40min); Mallaig–Lochboisdale (Tues; 3hr 30min); Oban–Lochboisdale (daily except Tues & Sun; 5hr–6hr 50min).

Flights

Benbecula to: Barra (Mon–Fri 1 daily; 20min); Stornoway (Mon–Fri 1 daily; 35min).
Glasgow to: Barra (Mon–Sat 1 daily; 1hr 5min); Benbecula (Mon–Sat 2 daily; 1hr); Stornoway

(Mon–Sat 2 daily; 1hr).
Inverness to: Stornoway (Mon–Fri 2 daily, Sat 1 daily; 20min).

Northeast Scotland

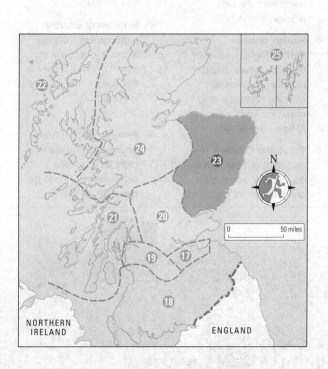

* **DCA** – Arts centre/cinema/cinema/café at the hip new heart of Dundee's up-and-coming cultural scene. See p.1160

* **Arbroath smokie** – A true Scottish delicacy: succulent haddock still warm from the oak smoker. See p.1162

* **Pictish stones** – Fascinating carved relics of a lost culture, standing alone in fields all over the northeast or in museums such as at Meigle. See p.1165

* **Dunnottar Castle** – The moodiest cliff-top ruin in the country, and a great scene-setter for the northeast's trail of castles. See p.1177

* **Speyside Way** – Walking route taking in Glenfiddich, Glenlivet and Glen Grant, with the chance to drop in and taste their whiskies too. See p.1181

* **Museum of Scottish Lighthouses** – Lights, lenses and legends at one of the best small museums in the country, in Fraserburgh. See p.1184

* **Pennan** – A one-street fishing village: there's no room for any more between the cliff and the sea. See p.1184

Northeast Scotland

large triangle of land thrusting into the North Sea, **northeast Scotland** comprises the area east of a line drawn roughly from Perth north to the fringe of the Moray Firth at Forres. The area takes in the county of Angus and the city of Dundee to the south and, beyond the **Grampian Mountains**, the counties of Aberdeenshire and Moray and the city of Aberdeen. Geographically diverse, the landscape in the south of the region is made up predominantly of undulating farmland, but, as you get further north of the Firth of Tay, this gives way to wooded glens, mountains and increasingly harsh land fringed by a dramatic coast of cliffs and long sandy beaches.

The northeast was the southern kingdom of the **Picts**, reminders of whom are scattered throughout the region in the form of numerous symbolic and beautifully carved stones found in fields, churchyards and museums (such as the one at **Meigle**). Remote, self-contained and cut off from the centres of major power in the south, the area never grew particularly prosperous, and a handful of feuding and intermarrying families, such as the Gordons, the Keiths and the Irvines, grew to wield disproportionate influence, building many of the region's **castles** and religious buildings and developing and planning its towns.

Many of the most appealing settlements are along the coast, but while the fishing industry is but a fondly held memory in many parts, a number of the northeast's ports have been transformed by the discovery of **oil** in the North Sea in the 1960s – particularly **Aberdeen**, Scotland's third-largest city. Despite its relative isolation in the Scottish context, Aberdeen remains a sophisticated city which, for the time being, still rides a diminishing wave of oil-based prosperity. At the same time, **Dundee**, the northeast's next-largest metropolis, is fast losing its depressed post-industrial image with an reinvigorated cultural scene and some heavily marketed tourist attractions, including *Discovery*, the ship of Captain Scott ("of the Antarctic"). A little way up the Angus coast lie the historically important towns of **Arbroath** and **Montrose**, while, inland, the picturesque **Angus glens** cut into the Grampian mountains, offering a readily accessible taste of wild Highland scenery to both hikers and skiers.

North of the glens and west of Aberdeen, **Deeside** is a fertile yet ruggedly attractive area made famous by the Royal Family, who have favoured the estate at **Balmoral** as a summer holiday retreat ever since Queen Victoria fell in love with it back in the 1840s. Beyond, the **Don Valley** is similarly endowed although less visited, while tranquil **Speyside**, a little way northwest, is best known as Scotland's premier whisky-producing region, where **malt whisky trails**, both official and unofficial, can be followed. The northeast coast offers yet another aspect of a diverse region, with rugged cliffs, empty beaches and historic fishing villages tucked into coves and bays.

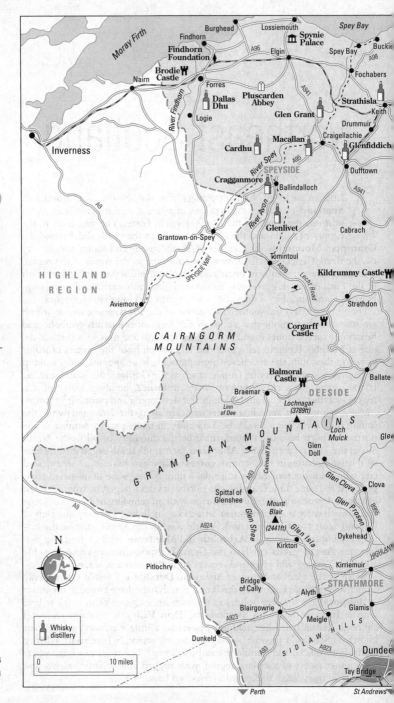

Moray Firth

Burghead
Lossiemouth
Spey Bay
Findhorn
Spynie Palace
Spey Bay
Buckie
A96
Elgin
A98
Findhorn Foundation
Fochabers
Brodie Castle
Nairn
Forres
Strathisla
Dallas Dhu
Pluscarden Abbey
Keith
River Findhorn
Logie
Glen Grant
Drummuir
Macallan
Craigellachie
Cardhu
Glenfiddich
Inverness
River Spey
Dufftown
SPEYSIDE
Cragganmore
Ballindalloch
A941
River Avon
A95
Glenlivet
Cabrach
Grantown-on-Spey
Tomintoul
Kildrummy Castle
HIGHLAND REGION
Lecht Road
SPEYSIDE WAY
Strathdon
Aviemore
Corgarff Castle
CAIRNGORM MOUNTAINS
Balmoral Castle
Ballate
Braemar
DEESIDE
Linn of Dee
Lochnagar (3789ft)
Loch Muick
Gle
GRAMPIAN MOUNTAINS
Glen Doll
A93
Cairnwell Pass
Glen Clova
Clova
Spittal of Glenshee
Glen Prosen
B955
Mount Blair (2441ft)
Glen Isla
Dykehead
A9
Glen Shee
Kirkton
HIGHLAN
A924
Kirriemuir
Pitlochry
Bridge of Cally
STRATHMORE
Alyth
Glamis
Blairgowrie
Meigle
N
SIDLAW HILLS
Dunkeld
A923
A93
Dundee

Whisky distillery

0   10 miles

A923
Tay Bridge

Perth   St Andrews

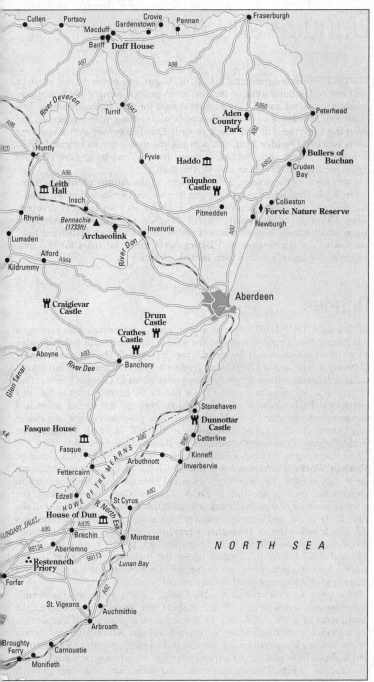

Cullen
Portsoy
Crovie
Gardenstown
Pennan
Fraserburgh
Macduff
Banff **Duff House**

River Deveron

A97
A98

A950
Peterhead

Turriff
A947

Aden Country Park

A96
Huntly

A920

Fyvie
Haddo

Bullers of Buchan

A952
Cruden Bay

A96
Leith Hall

Insch

Tolquhon Castle

Rhynie

Bennachie (1733ft)
Archaeolink

Pitmedden

Forvie Nature Reserve
Collieston

Lumsden

Inverurie

River Don

Newburgh

A92

Alford
A944

Kildrummy

Aberdeen

Craigievar Castle

Drum Castle

Crathes Castle

Aboyne
A93
River Dee
Banchory

Glen Tanar

Stonehaven
Dunnottar Castle

Fasque House

A90
Catterline
B967

Fasque

HOWE OF THE MEARNS

Kinneff
Inverbervie

Arbuthnott
A92

Fettercairn

Edzell

R. North Esk

St Cyrus

House of Dun

BOUNDARY FAULT
A90
A935

Brechin
Montrose

NORTH SEA

B9134
Aberlemno
B9113

Restenneth Priory

Lunan Bay

Forfar

St. Vigeans
A92
Auchmithie

Arbroath

Broughty Ferry
Carnoustie

Monifieth

Dundee and Angus

The predominantly agricultural county of **Angus**, east of the A9 and north of the Firth of Tay, holds some of the northeast's greatest scenery and is relatively free of tourists, who tend to head further west for the Highlands proper. The coast from **Montrose** to **Arbroath** is especially inviting, with scarlet cliffs and sweeping bays, then, further south towards Dundee, gentler dunes and long sandy beaches. **Dundee** itself, although not the most obvious tourist destination, has in recent years become a more dynamic and progressive city, and makes for a less snooty alternative to Aberdeen.

In the north of the county, the long fingers of the **Angus glens** – heather-covered hills tumbling down to rushing rivers – are overlooked by the southern peaks of the Grampian Mountains. Each has its own feel and devotees, **Glen Clova** being, deservedly, one of the most popular, along with **Glen Shee**, which attracts large numbers of people to its ski slopes. Handsome market towns like **Kirriemuir** and **Blairgowrie** are good bases for the area. Angus is also liberally dotted with **Pictish** remains.

Dundee

At first sight, **DUNDEE** can seem a grim place. In the nineteenth century it was Britain's main processor of jute, the world's most important vegetable fibre after cotton, which earned the city the tag "Juteopolis". The decline of manufacturing wasn't kind to Dundee, but regeneration is very much the buzz-word today, with some commentators drawing comparisons to Glasgow's reinvention of itself as a city of culture in the 1980s and 1990s. Less apparent is the city's international reputation as a centre of biotechnology and cancer research, a theme soon to be given a notable monument in the construction of a cancer care centre, the first public commission in the UK of Frank O. Gehry, the world-famous US architect responsible for Bilbao's Guggenheim.

The major sight is Captain Scott's Antarctic explorer ship, RRS *Discovery*. **Verdant Works** is a recreated jute mill which has picked up tourism awards for its take on the city's distinctive industrial heritage. You should also try to spend some time at the upbeat **DCA** (Dundee Contemporary Arts), the totemic building of the developing cultural quarter around which most of the city's lively artistic and social life revolves. Four miles east of the city centre lies the seaside settlement of **Broughty Ferry**, now engulfed as a reluctant suburb. Comprising an eclectic mix of big villas built by jute barons up the hillside and small fishermen's cottages along the shoreline, "The Ferry", as it's known, has experienced a recent resurgence in popularity, and is a pleasant and relaxing spot with some good restaurants and pubs.

Even prior to its Victorian heyday, Dundee was a town of considerable importance. It was here in 1309 that **Robert the Bruce** was proclaimed the lawful King of Scots, and during the Reformation it earned itself a reputation for tolerance, sheltering leading figures such as **John Knox**. After destruction by the Jacobite Viscount Dundee, the city picked itself up in the 1800s, its train and harbour links making it a major centre for shipbuilding, whaling and the manufacture of **jute**. This, along with jam and journalism – the three Js which famously defined the city – has all but disappeared, with only local publishing giant D.C. Thomson, publisher of the timelessly popular *Beano* and *Dandy* comics, as well as a spread of other comics and newspapers, still playing a meaningful role in the city.

Arrival, information and city transport

Dundee's **airport** (☎01382/643242) is five minutes' drive west of the city centre (£2–3 by taxi). By **train**, you'll arrive at Taybridge Station on South Union Street (☎0845/748 4950), about 300 yards south of the city centre near the river. Long-distance **buses** arrive at the Seagate bus station (☎0870/608 2608), a couple of hundred yards east of the centre.

The very helpful **tourist office** is right in the centre of things at 21 Castle St (June–Sept Mon–Sat 9am–6pm, Sun noon–4pm; Oct–May Mon–Sat 9am–5pm; ☎01382/527527, ⓦwww.angusanddundee.co.uk or ⓦwww.dundeecity.gov.uk), and sells bus tickets as well as booking accommodation. You can also pick up the free *Accent* listings magazine here, which details local theatre, music and exhibitions. The city's two daily newspapers are the morning *Courier & Advertiser* and the *Evening Telegraph & Post*.

Dundee's centre is reasonably compact and you can walk to most sights; **local buses** leave from the High Street or from Albert Square, one block to the north; for bus information, call ☎01382/201121 or go to the Travel Dundee Travel Centre, 95 Commercial St. A Daysaver ticket, with unlimited bus travel for a day, costs £2.

Accommodation

Dundee has no recommended hostel or backpacker **accommodation** – the cheaper B&Bs on the fringes of the city centre are the most reasonable alternative. You'll find plenty of rooms out by the suburb of Broughty Ferry, a twenty-minute bus ride (90p) into the city on Travel Dundee buses #7, #8 or #9X, or Strathtay buses #73 and #76 (all leave from either Commercial Street or Seagate in the town centre).

Hotels, guest houses and B&Bs

Discovery Quay Travel Inn Riverside Drive ☎01382/203240, ⓦwww.travelinn.co.uk. Bland, modern chain hotel well positioned right beside Discovery Point and the railway station. ❸

Fisherman's Tavern 12 Fort St, Broughty Ferry ☎01382/775941, ⓦwww.fishermans-tavern-hotel.co.uk. Creaky rooms above a cosy pub with decent food, great real ales and malt whiskies. ❷

Hillside 43 Constitution St ☎01382/223443, ⓔinfo@tildab.co.uk. Homely, central B&B with four comfortable, no-smoking rooms. ❷

Homebank 9 Ellieslea Rd, Broughty Ferry ☎01382/477481. B&B an in elegant mansion house set in walled gardens, a good example of why Broughty Ferry was the suburb of choice for the wealthy. ❸

Nelson Guest House 8 Nelson Terrace ☎01382/225354. Inexpensive B&B with three twin rooms, located up the hill from the downtown area. ❶

Queens Hotel 160 Nethergate ☎01382/322515, ⓦwww.queenshotel-dundee.com. Grand old hotel with refurbished rooms and a friendly welcome. Its location is good too, right in the heart of the action between the city and the university, and it has discount rates at the weekend. ❹

Campsite

Riverview Caravan Park Marine Drive, Monifieth ☎01382/535471. Well-run camping park in a suburb beyond Broughty Ferry, with an easy train link to Dundee. March–Oct.

The City

The best approach to Dundee is across the mile-and-a-half-long **Tay Road Bridge** from Fife. While the Tay bridges aren't nearly as spectacular as the

DUNDEE

▲ Broughty Ferry   ❸ & ❹ ▲ ❶ , Riverside Caravan Park & Broughty Ferry

ALBERT STREET

PEEP O' DAY LANE

EAST DOCK STREET

VICTORIA STREET

PRINCES STREET

BLACKSCROFT

FOUNDRY LANE

City Quay

KING STREET

ALLAN STREET

QUEEN'S ST

NELSON ST

COWGATE

Unicorn

VICTORIA ROAD

Bus Station

TRADER LANE

SEAGATE

VICTORIA DOCK ROAD

Wellgate Shopping Centre

PANMURE ST

MURRAYGATE

St. Paul's Cathedral

COMMERCIAL ST

Tay Road Bridge (Toll)

ALBERT SQUARE

Travel Dundee

CASTLE ST

COCKBURN ST

DOCK ST

❷

DUDHOPE STREET

McManus Galleries

REFORM STREET

ⓖ

ℹ

SHORE TERRACE

BELL STREET

Howff Burial Ground

Overgate Shopping Centre

HIGH STREET

Caird Hall

DISCOVERY QUAY

Olympia Leisure Centre

MARKET GAIT

BARRACK ST

CONSTITUTION ROAD

UNION ST

RRS Discovery

❶

WARD ROAD

NORTH LINDSAY STREET

SOUTH WARD STREET

St Mary's Church

OVERGATE LANE

Discovery Point

Leuchars ▶

Dundee Law ▲

WEST BELL STREET

Train Station

❻

BROWN STREET

MILN STREET

MARKETGATE

NETHERGATE

DOUGLAS STREET

SESSION STREET

SOUTH TAY ST

ⓑ

TAY ST

DCA

❺

Sensation

RIVERSIDE DRIVE

Verdant Works

WEST HENDERSON WYND

HAWKHILL

GUTHRIE STREET

WEST PORT

PARK PLACE

Dundee Repertory Theatre

PERTH ROAD

University of Dundee

N

0   200 yds

▲ ❹

© Crown copyright

ACCOMMODATION	
Discovery Quay	6
Fisherman's Tavern	3
Hillside	1
Homebank	4
Nelson	2
Queens	5

RESTAURANTS	
Agacan	A
Howies	B
Twin City Café	C
Visocchi's	D

bridges over the Forth near Edinburgh, they do offer a magnificent panorama of the city on the northern bank of the firth. The bridge, opened in 1966, has a central walkway for pedestrians. An 80p toll is levied on cars leaving the city, but you can enter from the south for free. Running parallel half a mile upstream is the **Tay Rail Bridge**, opened in 1887 to replace the spindly structure which collapsed in a storm in May 1878 only eighteen months after it was built, killing the crew and 75 passengers on a train passing over the bridge at the time.

Dundee's city centre is focused on **City Square**, a couple of hundred yards north of the Tay. The attractive square, set in front of the city's imposing Caird Hall, has been much spruced up in recent years, with fountains, benches and extensive pedestrianization making for a relaxing environment, though the grand old buildings and churches close to the centre have been rather overwhelmed by large shopping malls filled with a mundane mass of chain stores.

The main street, which is pedestrianized as it passes City Square, starts as Nethergate in the west, becomes High Street in the centre, then divides into Murraygate (which is also pedestrianized) and Seagate. Opposite this junction is the mottled spire of **St Paul's Episcopal Cathedral** (open to the public, though hours vary; free), a rather gaudy Gothic Revival structure by George Gilbert Scott, notable for its vividly sentimental stained glass and floridly gilded high altar.

At the other old church in the centre, St Mary's, now engulfed by the vast Overgate Shopping Centre, is an attraction called **The Old Steeple** (April–Sept Mon–Sat 10am–5pm, Sun noon–4pm; Oct–March Mon–Sat 11am–4pm, Sun noon–4pm; £2; joint ticket with Verdant Works and Discovery Point £12.15). Led by a guide, you'll have to tackle a lot of steps, encountering along the way the belfry and the church's massive, seven-ton bells, followed by the mechanism for the steeple's clock. At the top you step out onto a parapet for great views over the city and the Tay with its bridges.

A hundred yards north of City Square, at the top of Reform Street, is the attractive **Albert Square**, home of the imposing D.C. Thomson building, Dundee High School and, on its eastern side, the **McManus Art Galleries and Museum** (Mon–Sat 10.30am–5pm, Thurs until 7pm, Sun 12.30–4pm; free). Designed by Gilbert Scott, the museum is Dundee's most impressive Victorian structure, with a delightful sweep of outside curved stone staircases and elaborate Gothic touches. Inside, the museum gives an excellent overview of the city's past, with displays ranging from Pictish stones to the Tay Bridge disaster. On the ground floor, the most impressive exhibit is the skeleton of a whale, washed up on a nearby beach in 1883 and eulogized in a poem by William McGonagall, a strong contender for the title of the world's worst poet ("'Twas in the month of December, and in the year 1883,/That a monster whale came to Dundee"). Upstairs, the magnificent **Albert Hall** – crowned by a roof of 480 pitch-pine panels in a Gothic arch – houses antique musical instruments, decorative glass, gold, silver, sculpture and some exquisite furniture. On the same floor, the barrel-roofed **Victoria Gallery**'s red walls are packed with nineteenth- and twentieth-century paintings, including some notable Pre-Raphaelite and Scottish collections, William McTaggart's seascapes being a particular highlight.

Across Ward Road from the museum, the **Howff Burial Ground** on Meadowside (daily 9am to dusk) has some great carved tombstones dating from the sixteenth to nineteenth centuries. Originally gardens belonging to a monastery, the land was given to Dundee for burials in 1564 by Mary, Queen of Scots. Five minutes' walk west of here, on West Henderson Wynd in Blackness, an award-winning museum, **Verdant Works**, tells the story of jute from its harvesting in India to its arrival in Dundee on clipper ships (opening hours under review – check on ☎01382/225282; £5.95; joint ticket with Discovery Point and Old Steeple £12.15). In the nineteenth century, Dundee's jute mills employed fifty thousand people and were responsible for the rapid industrialization and development of the city as a trading port. The museum, set in an old jute mill, makes a lively attempt to recreate the turn-of-the-century factory floor, the highlight being the chance to watch jute being processed on fully operational quarter-size machines originally used for training workers.

The Cultural Quarter

Immediately west of the city centre, High Street becomes Nethergate and passes into what is now being dubbed, with a fair amount of justification, Dundee's "**Cultural Quarter**". As well as the university and the highly respected Rep theatre, the area is also home to the best concentration of pubs and cafés in the city. Principal among the area's many arts venues is the hip and exciting **DCA**, or Dundee Contemporary Arts, at 152 Nethergate (Mon–Sat 10.30am–midnight, Sun 10.30am–11pm; galleries Tues–Sun 11.30am–5.30pm; ☎01382/432000, ⓦwww.dca.org.uk), a stunningly designed centre which incorporates galleries, a print studio and an airy café-bar. The centre, opened in 1999, was designed by Richard Murphy, who converted an old brick building which had been a garage and car showroom into an inspiring new space, given energy and confidence by its bright, sleek interior and distinctive ship-like exterior. It's worth visiting for its stimulating temporary and touring exhibitions of contemporary art and eclectic programme of art-house films and cult classics.

Tucked in behind DCA is another new building, **Sensation** (daily 10am–6pm; Nov–March closes 5pm; ⓦwww.sensation.org.uk; £5), best approached from Greenmarket, off Marketgate. Aimed squarely at families and schoolchildren, it's a fun-packed exploration of science, using sixty different interactive exhibits and participatory experiments.

The waterfront

Just south of the city centre, at the water's edge alongside the Tay Road Bridge, the domed **Discovery Point** is an impressive development centring on the Royal Research Ship *Discovery* (April–Oct Mon–Sat 10am–5pm, Sun 11am–5pm; Nov–March Mon–Sat 10am–4pm, Sun 11am–4pm; £5.95; joint ticket with Verdant Works and Old Steeple £12.15). Something of an icon for Dundee's renaissance, *Discovery* is a three-mast steam-assisted vessel built in Dundee in 1901 to take Captain Robert Falcon Scott on his polar expeditions. A combination of brute strength and elegance, she has been beautifully restored, with polished wood panels and brass trimmings giving scant indication of the privations suffered by the crew. Temperatures on board would plummet to -28°C in the Antarctic, and turns at having a bath came round every 47 days. As a introduction before stepping aboard you're led through a series of displays about the construction of the ship and Scott's journeys, including the chill-inducing "Polarama" about life in Antarctica and a compelling, if overhyped, audiovisual spectacular involving a model ship bursting through the screen and lots of dry ice.

Eating, drinking and nightlife

The West End of Dundee, around the main university campus and Perth Road, is the best area for **eating and drinking**, while the city centre, though good for a few pubs, is a bit of a non-starter for decent food. The suburb of Broughty Ferry is a pleasant spot with a good selection of pubs and restaurants, which get particularly busy on summer evenings.

Cafés and restaurants

Agacan 113 Perth Rd ℡ 01382/644227. Tiny Turkish restaurant with an unmistakeable colourful exterior and rough-hewn walls inside; they serve up decent kebabs and stuffed pittas, and also do take-aways. Moderate. Closed lunchtimes & all day Mon.

Howies 25 Tay St ℡ 01382/322999. Large restaurant serving Modern Scottish dishes, with the *Lounge* café-bar on the lower ground floor for cocktails and light snacks. Moderate.

Jute In DCA (Dundee Contemporary Arts), 152 Nethergate. Trendy spot occupying a large open-plan space on the lower level of the new arts centre, with large windows looking out over the industrial wasteland and railway tracks which line the Tay. Has table service and a decent range of sandwiches and light meals, served until 11pm. Inexpensive.

Twin City Café 4 City Sq ℡ 01382/223662. Almost achieves a continental feel, with tables and chairs spilling out onto City Square. The menu ranges through light dishes and snacks associated with all the different cities twinned with Dundee, from the US to Croatia. Inexpensive. Closes Mon–Thurs 7pm, Fri & Sat 9pm.

Visocchi's 40 Gray St, Broughty Ferry. Authentic Italian fare served in an informal, popular ice-cream café. Inexpensive.

Pubs

Drouthie Neebours 142–146 Perth Rd. A cheerful bar with a Robbie Burns theme, lavish painted murals and a lively student clientele.

Nosey Parkers 160 Nethergate. Recently smartened-up bar and bistro on the ground floor of the *Queen's Hotel*, between the DCA and the university.

Ship Inn 121 Fisher St, Broughty Ferry. A narrow pub with a warm atmosphere right on the waterfront. The bistro upstairs has views over the Tay and serves great food.

Nightlife

Right at the heart of the Cultural Quarter on Tay Square, north of Nethergate, is the prodigious Dundee Repertory Theatre (℡01382/223530, ℡www.dundeereptheatre.co.uk), an excellent place for indigenously produced contemporary **theatre** and the home of the only permanent repertory company in Scotland. The best venue for **classical** music, including visits by the Royal Scottish Orchestra and other bigwigs, is Caird Hall (℡01382/434451), whose bulky frontage dominates City Square. For **movies**, DCA (℡01382/606220, ℡www.dca.org.uk) has two comfy auditoriums showing an appealing range of foreign and art movies alongside the more challenging mainstream releases; otherwise you have to head a fair way out of the centre to the UGC multiplex at Camperdown Leisure park (℡0870/902 0407; bus #4/4a).

Listings

Bike rental Just Bikes, 57 Grey St, Broughty Ferry (℡01382/732100).

Books James Thin, 7 High St; Waterstone's, 34 Commercial St.

Bus information Scottish Citylink (℡0870/550 5050); Strathtay Scottish for regional buses (℡01382/228345); Travel Dundee (℡0870/608 2608).

Car rental Arnold Clark, East Dock St (℡01382/225382); Alamo National, 45–53 Gellatly St (℡01382/224037); Hertz, 18 West Marketgate (℡01382/223711).

Internet Webgate Internet (℡01382/434332) at the Central Library in the Wellgate Shopping Centre, (Mon–Fri 9.30am–8.30pm, Sat 9.30am–4.30pm). The tourist office also has internet access.

Medical facilities Ninewells Hospital in the west of the city has an Accident and Emergency department (℡01382/660111). Boots pharmacy is at 49–53 High St (Mon–Sat 8.30am–5.45pm, Thurs until 7pm, Sun 12.30–5pm).

Police Tayside Police HQ, West Bell St (℡01382/223200).

Post office 4 Meadowside (Mon–Fri 9am–5.30pm, Sat 9am–12.30pm; ℡0845/722 3344).

Taxis There are taxi ranks on Nethergate, or call City Cabs (℡01382/566666), Handy Taxis (℡01382/225825) or, in nearby Broughty Ferry, Discovery Taxis (℡01382/732111).

The Angus coast

Two roads link Dundee to Aberdeen and the northeast coast of Scotland. By far the more pleasant option is the slightly longer A92 coast road which joins the inland A90 at Stonehaven, just south of Aberdeen. Intercity **buses** follow both roads, while the coast-hugging train line from Dundee is one of the most picturesque in Scotland, passing attractive beaches and impressive cliffs, and stopping in the old seaports of **Arbroath** and **Montrose**.

Arbroath

Since it was settled in the twelfth century, local fishermen have been landing their catches at **ARBROATH**, situated on the Angus coast where it starts to curve in from the North Sea towards the Firth of Tay, about fifteen miles northeast of Dundee. The town's most famous product is the **Arbroath smokie** – line-caught haddock, smoke-cured over smouldering oak chips, and still made here in a number of family-run smokehouses tucked in around the harbour. One of the most approachable and atmospheric is M&M Spink's tiny whitewashed premises at 10 Marketgate; chef and cookery writer Rick Stein described the fish here, warm from the smoke, as "a world-class delicacy".

By the late eighteenth century, chiefly due to its harbour, Arbroath had become a trading and manufacturing centre, famed for boot-making and sail-making (the *Cutty Sark*'s sails were made here). The town's real glory days, however, came much earlier in the thirteenth century with the completion in 1233 of **Arbroath Abbey** (April–Sept daily 9.30am–6.30pm; Oct–March Mon–Wed & Sat 9.30am–4.30pm, Thurs 9.30am–12.30pm, Sun 2–4.30pm; HS; £2.50), whose rose-pink sandstone ruins, described by Dr Johnson as "fragments of magnificence", stand on Abbey Street. Founded in 1178 but not granted abbey status until 1285, it was the scene of one of the most significant events in Scotland's history when, on April 6, 1320, a group of Scottish barons drew up the **Declaration of Arbroath**, asking the Pope to reverse his excommunication of Robert the Bruce and recognize him as king of a Scottish nation independent from England. The wonderfully resonant language of the document still makes for a stirring expression of Scottish nationhood: "For so long as one hundred of us remain alive, we will never in any degree be subject to the dominion of the English, since it is not for glory, riches or honour that we do fight, but for freedom alone, which no honest man loses but with his life." It was duly despatched to Pope John XXII in Avignon, who in 1324 agreed to Robert's claim. A new **visitors' centre** at the Abbey Street entrance offers some in-depth background on these events and other aspects of the history of the building.

Practicalities

Arbroath's helpful **tourist office** is at Market Place in the middle of town (June–Aug Mon–Sat 9.30am–5.30pm, Sun 10am–3pm; April, May & Sept Mon–Fri 9am–5pm, Sat 10am–5pm; Oct–March Mon–Fri 9am–5pm, Sat 10am–3pm; ☎01241/872609). Staff can recommend local walks and book accommodation. For somewhere to **stay**, it's hard to beat the isolation of the *Auchmithie Hotel* (☎01241/873010; ❸), perched on a cliff top four miles north in tiny Auchmithie, with a bar and restaurant staring out over the North Sea. Alternatively, try the *Harbour House Guest House*, 4 The Shore (☎01241/878047; ❶), down by Arbroath's harbour, which is also where you'll find the best **restaurants** and **pubs**. The *Old Brewhouse* (☎01241/879945) is a convivial and moderately priced restaurant-cum-pub by the harbour wall at the end of High Street.

Montrose and around

"Here's the Basin, there's Montrose, shut your een and haud your nose." As the old rhyme indicates, **MONTROSE**, a seaport and market town since the thirteenth century, can sometimes smell a little rich, mostly because of its position on the edge of a virtually landlocked two-mile-square lagoon of mud known as the Basin. On the south side of the Basin, a mile out of Montrose along the A92, the **Montrose Basin Wildlife Centre** (redevelopment is planned during 2002; call ☎01674/676336 to confirm opening times and admission charges; previously daily 10.30am–5pm, Nov–March closes 4pm) has binoculars, high-powered telescopes, bird hides and remote-control video cameras. In addition, the centre's resident ranger leads regular guided walks around the reserve.

Montrose locals are known as "Gable Endies", because of the unusual way in which the town's eighteenth- and nineteenth-century merchants, influenced by architectural styles they had seen on the continent, built their houses gable-end to the street. The few remaining original gabled houses line the wide **High Street**, off which are numerous tiny alleyways and quiet courtyards.

Two blocks behind the soaring kirk steeple at the lower end of High Street, the **Montrose Museum and Art Gallery** (Mon–Sat 10am–5pm; free) in Panmure Place on the western side of Mid Links park, is one of Scotland's oldest museums, dating from 1842. For a small-town museum, it has some particularly unusual exhibits, among them the so-called Samson Stone, a Pictish relic dating from 900 AD bearing a carving of Samson slaying the Philistines. In the local history section, look out for the mechanical paper sculpture of the town of Montrose, with a green train running along the top and yachts sailing by.

Outside the museum entrance stands a winsome study of a boy by local sculptor William Lamb (1893–1951). More of his work can be seen in the moving **William Lamb Memorial Studio** on Market Street (July to mid-Sept daily 2–5pm; at other times, ask at the museum; free), including bronze heads of the Queen, Princess Margaret and the Queen Mother. Finally, don't ignore the town's fabulous golden **seashore**. The beach road, Marine Avenue, across from the town museum, heads down through sand dunes and golf links to car parks fringing the fine, wide beach overlooked by a slender white lighthouse.

The House of Dun

Across the Basin, four miles west of Montrose, is the Palladian **House of Dun** (July & Aug daily 11am–5.30pm; Easter weekend, May, June & Sept daily 1.30–5.30pm; Oct Sat & Sun 1.30–5.30pm; NTS; £6, grounds only £1), accessible on the regular Montrose–Brechin bus #30 – ask the driver to let you off outside. Built in 1730 for David Erskine, Laird of Dun, to designs by William Adam, the house was opened to the public in 1989 after extensive restoration, and is crammed full of period furniture and *objets d'art*. Inside, the ornate relief plasterwork is the most impressive feature, extravagantly emblazoned with Jacobite symbolism.

Practicalities

Montrose **tourist office** is squeezed into a former public toilet next to the library, at the point where Bridge Street merges into the lower end of High Street (July & Aug Mon–Sat 9.30am–5.30pm; April–June & Sept Mon–Sat 10am–5pm; ☎01674/672000). Most **buses** stop in the High Street, while the **train** station lies a block back on Western Road. For B&B **accommodation**, try *Oaklands*, over the river bridge at 10 Rossie Island Rd (☎01674/672018, ⓦwww.nebsnow.com/oaklands; ❶), or *Kirkside* (☎01674/830780; ❷), an isolated converted fishing bothy situated on the edge of the sand dunes by St Cyrus Nature Reserve, just over two miles north of Montrose at the mouth of the North Esk River. For **eating**, the liveliest place in town is unquestionably *Roo's Leap*, a sports bar and restaurant by the golf club off the northern end of Traill Drive, with an unlikely, but excellent, mix of Scottish, American and Australian cuisine.

Strathmore and the Angus glens

Immediately north of Dundee, the low-lying Sidlaw Hills divide the city from the rich agricultural region of **Strathmore**, whose string of tidy market towns lies on a fertile strip along the southernmost edge of the heather-covered lower slopes of the Grampian Mountains. These towns act as gateways to the **Angus glens**, a series of tranquil valleys penetrated by single-track roads and offering some of the most rugged and majestic landscapes of northeast Scotland. It's a rain-swept, wind-blown, sparsely populated area, whose roads become impassable with the first snows; in summer, there are ferocious midges to contend with. The most useful road is the A93, which cuts through **Glen Shee** to Braemar (see p.1180) over Britain's highest main-road pass, the **Cairnwell Pass** (2199ft).

Blairgowrie and Glen Shee

The upper reaches of **Glen Shee**, the most dramatic and best known of the Angus glens, are dominated by its ski fields, ranged over four mountains above the Cairnwell mountain pass. To get to Glen Shee from the south you'll pass through the well-heeled town of **BLAIRGOWRIE**, little more than one main road set among raspberry fields on the glen's southernmost tip, but a good place to pick up information and plan your activities. Blairgowrie **tourist office** (July & Aug Mon–Sat 9.30am–6.30pm, Sun 11am–5pm; April–June, Sept & Oct Mon–Sat 9.30am–5.30pm, Sun 11am–4pm; Nov–March Mon–Fri 9.30am–5pm, Sat 10am–2pm; ☎01250/872960, ⓦwww.perthshire.co.uk), on the high side of the Wellmeadow, can help with **accommodation**. Over the bridge spanning the fast-flowing River Ericht, Blairgowrie melts into its twin community of **RATTRAY**, where, on the main street (Boat Brae) is the B&B *Ivy Bank House* (☎01250/873056, ⓦwww.ivybankhouse.com; ❶), in a central location and offering sweeping views of the river and surrounding hills. **Camping** is available at the year-round *Blairgowrie Holiday Park* on Rattray's

---

Skiing at Glenshee

Glenshee is the most accessible of Scotland's **ski** areas, just over two hours from both Glasgow and Edinburgh; for information, contact Ski Glenshee (☎013397/41320, ⓦwww.ski-glenshee.co.uk), who also offer ski rental and lessons. In addition, lessons, skis and boards are available from Cairnwell Mountain Sports (☎01250/885255), at the Spittal of Glenshee. **Ski rental** starts at around £12 a day, while lessons are around £10 for two hours. **Lift passes** cost £18 per day or £72 for a five-day (Mon–Fri) ticket. For the latest snow and **weather conditions**, phone the Ski Hotline (☎0900/165 4656) or check out the Ski Scotland website (ⓦwww.ski.scotland.net). Should you be more interested in **cross-country** skiing, there are some good touring areas in the vicinity; contact Cairnwell Mountain Sports (see above) or Braemar Mountain Sports (☎013397/41242) for information and equipment rental.

Hatton Road (℡01250/876666). Blairgowrie boasts plenty of places to **eat**: *Cargills* by the river on Lower Mill Street (℡01250/876735; closed Mon) is the best bet for a formal meal or civilized coffee and cakes, while, for good **pub** grub try the youthful *Driftwood*, just off the Wellmeadow, which has a terrace overlooking the river, or head six miles north of town on the A93 to the delightfully situated *Bridge of Cally Hotel* (℡01250/886231; ❸). You can rent **bikes** from Crichton's Cycle Hire, 87 Perth Rd (℡01250/876100).

Nearly twenty miles north of Blairgowrie, the **SPITTAL OF GLEN-SHEE**, though ideally situated for skiing, is little more than a tacky service area, only worth stopping at for a quick drink or bite to eat. However, it does boast the excellent *Gulabin Bunkhouse* on the A93, run by Cairnwell Mountain Sports (℡01250/885255), which rents out skis and bikes and offers hang-gliding lessons.

Meigle and Glen Isla

Fifteen miles north of Dundee on the B954 lies the tiny settlement of **MEIGLE**, home to Scotland's most important collection of early Christian and Pictish inscribed stones. Housed in a modest former schoolhouse, the **Meigle Museum** (April–Nov daily 9.30am–6pm; HS; £2) displays some thirty pieces dating from the seventh to the tenth centuries, all found in and around the nearby church-yard. The majority are either gravestones that would have lain flat, or cross slabs inscribed with the sign of the cross, usually standing. Most impressive is the 7ft-tall great cross slab, said to be the gravestone of Guinevere, wife of King Arthur, carved on one side with a portrayal of Daniel surrounded by lions, a beautifully executed equestrian group, and mythological creatures including a dragon and a centaur.

Three miles north of Meigle is **Alyth**, near which, legend has it, Guinevere was held captive by Mordred. The sleepy village lies at the south end of **Glen Isla**, which runs parallel to Glen Shee and is linked to it by the A926. The tiny hamlet of **KIRKTON OF GLENISLA** is ten miles or so up the glen. Here, the cosy *Glenisla Hotel* (℡01575/582223, ⓦwww.glenisla-hotel.co.uk; ❹) is great for classy bar meals and convivial drinking. In the nearby Glenisla forest there are some **hiking** trails, while just before Kirkton, a turn-off on the right-hand side leads northeast up a long bumpy road to the unexpected Glenmarkie Farmhouse Health Spa and Equestrian Centre (℡01575/582295; ❷) which offers pedicures and pony trekking.

Forfar and around

Around fifteen miles north of Dundee on the main A90 lies **FORFAR**, Angus's county town and the ancient capital of the Picts. The wide High Street is framed by some impressive Victorian architecture and small old-fashioned shops. Midway along, at 20 West High St, the **Meffen Institute Museum and Art Gallery** (Mon–Sat 10am–5pm; free) exhibits Neolithic, Pictish and Celtic remains and a thoroughly enjoyable collection of re-created historical street scenes. The most disturbing examines the town's seventeenth-century passion for witch-hunting, with a taped re-creation of locals baying for blood. There is also a comprehensive interactive computer catalogue of all the Pictish stones in Angus, and an excellent art gallery.

Forfar's small **tourist office** (July & Aug Mon–Sat 9.30am–5.30pm; April–June & Sept Mon–Sat 10am–5pm; ℡01307/467876) is at 45 East High St, opposite the soaring steeple of the parish church. Numerous shops and bakers stock the famous "Forfar Bridie", a semi-circular folded pastry-case of mince, onion and seasonings, including Saddlers, a few doors down from the tourist office, and McLarens (the locals' favourite), at 8 West High St.

Glamis Castle

Bus #125 from Forfar runs regularly to Dundee via the pink sandstone **Glamis Castle** (April–Oct daily 10.30am–4.45pm; £6.20, grounds only £3.10), located a mile north of the picturesque village of **GLAMIS** (pronounced "glahms"). A wondrously over-the-top, L-shaped five-storey pile set in an extensive landscaped park complete with deer and pheasants, this is one of the most famous Scottish castles. Shakespeare chose it as a central location in *Macbeth* and its royal connections (as the childhood home of the Queen Mother and birthplace of Princess Margaret) make it one of the essential stops on every coach tour of Scotland, though for many visitors the Queen Mum gloss is laid on rather thick.

The guided tour starts upstairs in the Victorian **Dining Room**, notable for its fine rose-and-thistle ceiling. The atmosphere changes dramatically in the fifteenth-century **Crypt**, more properly the Lower Hall of the original tower house, which you enter through a door in the wood panelling of the Dining Room. The crypt's 12ft-thick walls enclose a haunted "lost" room, reputed to be have been sealed with the red-bearded Lord of Glamis and Crawford (also known as Beardie Crawford) inside, after he dared to play cards with the Devil one Sabbath. From here, the tour passes up a seventeenth-century staircase, whose hollow central pillar provided a primitive system of central heating.

The highlight of the tour is the family **Chapel**, completed in 1688. The chapel is said to be haunted by the spectre of a grey lady, the ghost of the sixth Lady Glamis who was burnt as a witch on the order of James V. The **Billiard Room**, complete with full-sized table and a beautiful polished walnut piano that cost £199 when it was commissioned in 1866, is decorated with various species of stuffed bird and lined with paintings and tapestries, of which the vast and colourful *Fruit Market* by Flemish artist Frans Snyders draws the most attention.

Glamis' **grounds** are worth a few hours in their own right, holding lead statues of James VI and Charles I at the top of the main drive, a seventeenth-century Baroque sundial, a formal Italian Garden and verdant walks out to Earl John's Bridge and through the woodland.

Kirriemuir, Glen Clova and Glen Doll

The sandstone town of **KIRRIEMUIR**, known locally as "Kirrie", is set on a hill six miles northwest of Forfar on the cusp of glens Clova and Prosen. The main cluster of streets have all the appeal of an old film set, with their old-fashioned bars, tiled butcher's shop, tartan outlets and haberdasheries somehow managing to avoid being contrived and quaint – although the recent recobbling of the town centre around a twee statue of Peter Pan undermines this somewhat. Peter Pan's presence is justified, however, since Kirrie was the birthplace of his creator, **J.M. Barrie**. A local handloom-weaver's son, Barrie first came to notice with his series of novels about "Thrums", a village based on his hometown, in particular *A Window in Thrums* and his third novel, *The Little Minister*. **Barrie's birthplace**, a plain little whitewashed cottage at 9 Brechin Rd (April–Sept Mon–Sat 11am–5.30pm, Sun 1.30–5.30pm; Oct Sat 11am–5.30pm, Sun 1.30–5.30pm; NTS; £3), displays his writing desk, photos and newspaper clippings. The washhouse outside – romantically billed as Barrie's first "theatre" – was apparently the model for the house built by the Lost Boys for Wendy in Never-Never Land.

△ Union Street, Aberdeen

More on other notable residents can be found in the **Kirriemuir Museum** (Mon–Wed, Fri & Sat 10am–5pm, Thurs 1–5pm; free), in the old Town House on the main square. The oldest building in Kirrie, it has seen service as a tolbooth, court, jail, post office, police station and chemist; these days you can find two floors of information and exhibits on the town and the Angus Glens, including scale models of the town in 1604, the year the tolbooth was erected, and one of Glen Clova, showing the relief of the hills.

Kirrie's helpful **tourist office** is in Cumberland Close (July & Aug Mon–Sat 9.30am–5.30pm; April–June & Sept Mon–Sat 10am–5pm; ☎01575/574097), in the new development behind *Visocchi's* in the main square. **Accommodation** is available at *Crepto B&B*, Kinnordy Place (☎01575/572746; ❷), or the respectable *Airlie Arms*, St Malcolm's Wynd (☎01575/572487, ⓦwww.airliearms-hotel.co.uk; ❸).

Glen Clova and Glen Doll

Of all the Angus glens, **Glen Clova** – which in the north becomes **Glen Doll** – with its stunning cliffs, heather slopes and valley meadows, is the firm favourite of many. Wildlife is abundant, with deer on the mountains, wild hares and even grouse and the occasional buzzard. The meadow flowers on the valley floor and arctic plants (including great splashes of white and purple saxifrage) on the rocks also make it something of a botanist's paradise.

The B955 from Dykehead and Kirriemuir divides at the Gella bridge over the swift-coursing River South Esk; six miles north of Gella, the two branches of the road join up once more at the hamlet of **CLOVA**, little more than the hearty *Glen Clova Hotel* (☎01575/550350, ⓦwww.clova.com; ❸), which also has a refurbished bunkhouse (£9.50 per night). Meals and real ale are available in the lively *Climbers' Bar* at the side of the hotel.

North from Clova village, the road turns into a rabbit-infested lane coursing along the riverside for four miles to the car park and informal **campsite** in **GLEN DOLL**, a useful starting point for numerous superb **walks**. From the car park, it's only a few hundred yards further to the SYHA **hostel** (☎01575/550236, ⓦwww.syha.org.uk; May–Sept), a restored hunting lodge that boasts a squash court along with the usual facilities and is typically busy with climbers and youth groups.

Aberdeenshire and Moray

Aberdeenshire and Moray cover some 3500 square miles of open and varied country dotted with historic and archeological sights, from neat National Trust for Scotland properties and eerie prehistoric rings of standing stones to quiet kirkyards, serene abbeys and a rash of dramatic castles. Geographically, the counties break down into two distinct areas: the **hinterland**, once barren and now a patchwork of fertile farms, rising towards high mountains, sparkling rivers and gentle valleys; and the **coast**, a classic stretch of rocky cliff, remote fishing villages and long, sandy beaches.

The large city of **Aberdeen** is the obvious focal point of the region, and while it's not a place to keep you engrossed for long, it does boast some intriguing architecture, attractive museums and a lively social scene. From here, it's a short hop west to **Deeside**, visited annually by the Royal Family and an easily accessed gateway to some spectacular mountain scenery. To the north lies the **Don Valley**, a quiet area which leads into the Cairngorms at the Lecht, a remote mountain pass where there's a skiing centre in winter, and **Speyside**, the heart of Scotland's malt whisky industry. Further north, the **coast** offers some dramatic scenery, punctuated by picturesque villages left almost unchanged by the centuries.

Aberdeen

The third-largest city in Scotland, **ABERDEEN**, commonly known as the Granite City, lies 120 miles northeast of Edinburgh, on the banks of the rivers Dee and Don smack in the middle of the northeast coast. Based around a working harbour, it's a place that people either love or hate. Certainly, while some extol the many tones and colours of Aberdeen's **granite** buildings, others see only uniform grey and find the city grim, cold and unwelcoming. The weather doesn't help: Aberdeen lies on a latitude north of Moscow and the cutting wind and driving rain (even if it does transform the buildings into sparkling silver) can be tiresome.

Since the 1970s, **oil** has made Aberdeen a hugely wealthy and self-confident place: only four percent of Scotland's population live in the city, yet it has eight percent of the country's spending power. Despite (or perhaps because of) this, it can seem a soulless city; there's a feeling of corporate sterility and sometimes, despite its long history, Aberdeen seems to exist only as a departure point and service station for the transient population of some ten to fifteen thousand who live on the 130 oil platforms out to sea.

Staying in such a prosperous place has its advantages. There are plenty of good restaurants and hotels, local transport is efficient and certain sights, including Aberdeen's splendid **Art Gallery** and the excellent **Maritime Museum**, are free. Furthermore, the fact that the city is the bright light in a wide hinterland helps it to sustain a lively nightlife with some decent pubs and a colourful arts and cultural scene.

Some history

In the twelfth century, Alexander I noted "Aberdon" as one of his principal towns, and by the thirteenth century it had become a centre for **trade and fishing**, a jumble of timber and wattle houses perched on three small hills, with the castle to the east and St Nicholas's kirk outside the gates to the west.

It was here that **Robert the Bruce** sought refuge during the Scottish Wars of Independence, leading to the garrison of the castle by Edward I and Balliol's supporters. In a night-time raid in 1306, the townspeople attacked the garrison and killed them all, an event commemorated by the city's motto "Bon Accord", the watchword for the night. A century later Bishop Elphinstane founded the Catholic university in the area north of town known today as **Old Aberdeen**, while the rest of the city developed as a mercantile centre and important port.

By the mid-twentieth century, Aberdeen's traditional industries were in decline, but the discovery of **oil** in the North Sea transformed the place from

Oil and Aberdeen

When **oil** was discovered in BP's Forties Field in 1970, Aberdonians rightly viewed it as a massive financial opportunity, and – despite fierce competition from other east coast British ports, Scandinavia and Germany – the city succeeded in persuading the oil companies to base their headquarters here. The city's **population** swelled by sixty thousand, and earnings escalated from fifteen percent below the national average to a figure well above it. At the peak of production in the **mid-1980s**, 2.6 million barrels a day were being turned out, and the price had reached $80 a barrel. The effect of the slump of 1986 – when oil prices dropped to $10 a barrel – was devastating: jobs vanished at the rate of a thousand a month, house prices dropped and Aberdeen soon discovered just how dependent on oil it was. The moment oil prices began to rise, crisis struck again with the loss of 167 lives when the **Piper Alpha oilrig** exploded, precipitating an array of much-needed but very expensive safety measures.

Oil remains the cornerstone of Aberdeen's economy, keeping unemployment down to one of the lowest levels in Britain and driving up house prices not just in the city itself but in an increasingly wide area of its rural hinterland. Predictions of the imminent decline in oil reserves and the end of Aberdeen's economic boom are heard frequently, as they have been since 1970, but reliable indicators suggest that the black gold will be flowing well into the new millennium.

a depressed port into a boom town (see box). The oil-borne prosperity may have served to mask the thinness of the region's other wealth creators, but it has nonetheless allowed Aberdeen to hold its own as a cultural and academic centre and as a focus of the northeast's identity into the new century.

Arrival, information and city transport

Aberdeen's Dyce **airport** is seven miles northwest. The airport bus #27 and Aberdeen–Inverness bus #10 run to the city centre; a taxi costs around £10. The main **train station** is on Guild Street, in the centre (℡0845/748 4950), with the **bus** terminal for intercity and regional services right beside it (regional buses ℡0870/608 2608; intercity buses ℡0870/550 5050). **Ferries** run from Jamieson's Quay in the harbour to Lerwick in Shetland and Stromness in Orkney. Note that from October 2002, Northlink will be taking over this service from P&O Scottish Ferries.

From the train and bus station it's a two-minute walk up the hill to Union Street, Aberdeen's main thoroughfare, and an even shorter stroll to the **tourist office** in Old Provost Ross's House, beside the Maritime Museum on Ship Row (July & Aug Mon–Sat 9.30am–7pm, Sun 10am–4pm; June & Sept Mon–Sat 9.30am–5pm; rest of year Mon–Fri 9.30am–5pm, Sat 10am–2pm; ℡01224/288828, ⓦwww.agtb.org).

Almost all **local buses** (℡01224/650065) pass along Union Street; buy a Farecard (in £2, £5 or £10 denominations) from the main **transport office**, 395 King St, or the busy city-centre kiosk outside Marks & Spencer on Union Street, which also hands out transport **maps**; each time you travel the fare is deducted from the card. A open-topped **bus tour** passing the main sights runs regularly (July–Sept) from the Town House on Union Street (£4; or an "explorer" £6 ticket also buys a day's free travel on local buses).

Accommodation

As befits a high-flying business city, Aberdeen has a large choice of **accommodation** – much of it characterless and expensive. Many **B&Bs** and **guest**

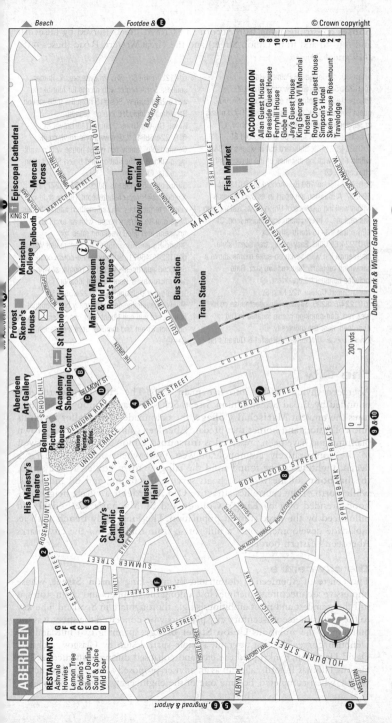

ABERDEEN

RESTAURANTS
Ashvale   G
Howies   F
Lemon Tree   A
Poldino's   C
Silver Darling   E
Soul & Spice   D
Wild Boar   B

ACCOMMODATION
Allan Guest House   9
Braeside Guest House   8
Ferryhill House   10
Globe Inn   3
Jay's Guest House   1
King George VI Memorial Hostel   5
Royal Crown Guest House   7
Simpson's Hotel   6
Skene House Rosemount   2
Travelodge   4

© Crown copyright

Beach

Footdee & E

Episcopal Cathedral

Mercat Cross

KING ST

Marischal College Tolbooth

Provost Skene's House

St Nicholas Kirk

Aberdeen Art Gallery

Belmont Picture House

Academy Shopping Centre

His Majesty's Theatre

Maritime Museum & Old Provost Ross's House

Harbour

Ferry Terminal

Fish Market

Bus Station

Train Station

Music Hall

St Mary's Catholic Cathedral

Duthie Park & Winter Gardens

MARISCHAL STREET

VIRGINIA STREET

REGENT QUAY

BLAIKIES QUAY

JAMESON'S QUAY

FISH MARKET

MARKET STREET

N. ESPLANADE W.

PALMERSTONE RD

GUILD STREET

COLLEGE STREET

BRIDGE STREET

CROWN STREET

DEE STREET

BON ACCORD STREET

SPRINGBANK TERRACE

BON ACCORD CRESCENT

BON ACCORD TERRACE

SQUARE

BON ACCORD

UNION STREET

SUMMER STREET

HUNTLY STREET

CHAPEL STREET

ROSE STREET

THISTLE STREET

ALBYN PL

JUSTICE MILL LANE

ALFORD LANE

HOLBURN STREET

WELLINGTON RD

ROSEMOUNT VIADUCT

SKENE STREET

SCHOOLHILL

BELMONT ST

DENBURN ROAD

UNION TERRACE

Union Terrace Gdns

GOLDEN SQUARE

THE GREEN

THE GREEN

SHIPROW

CASTLE STREET

NETHERKIRKGATE

Ringroad & Airport

N

200 yds

0

Duthie Park & Winter Gardens

houses are strung along Bon Accord and Crown streets (served by buses #6 and #17 to and from Union Street) and the Great Western Road (buses #18, #19 and #24).

Allan Guest House 56 Polmuir Rd
℡01224/584484, Ⓦwww.camtay.co.uk.
Unexpectedly tasteful and enthusiastically run guest house not far from Duthie Park. Good meals or supper available if arranged in advance. ❸
Braeside Guest House 68 Bon Accord St
℡01224/571471. Standard but inexpensive B&B within easy walking distance of the station and city centre. ❶
Ferryhill House 169 Bon Accord St ℡01224/590867. A mansion set apart in its own grounds within walking distance of Union St. Its historic pub has real ale, a beer garden and decent food. ❺
Globe Inn 13–15 North Silver St
℡01224/624258. Easy-going, traditional-style city-centre inn with seven en-suite rooms above a bar which regularly features live jazz. Rate includes continental breakfast. ❷
Jay's Guest House 422 King St
℡01224/638295, Ⓦwww.jaysguesthouse.co.uk.
Well-run, non-smoking house located in Old Aberdeen, near the university. ❸
King George VI Memorial Hostel 8 Queen's Rd

℡01224/646988, Ⓦwww.syha.org.uk. Rather soulless SYHA hostel with rooms for four to six, and a 2am curfew. Bus #15 from the train station. Breakfast is included in high season.
Royal Crown Guest House 111 Crown St
℡01224/586461, Ⓦwww.royalcrown.co.uk.
Comfortable, family-run guest house within walking distance of the station and Union Street. Non-smoking. ❷
Simpson's 59 Queen's Rd ℡01224/327777,
Ⓔaddress@simpsonshotel.com. Highly style-conscious, terracotta-coloured modern interior to this large granite terrace house, with an excellent brasserie and good weekend rates. ❼
Skene House Rosemount 96 Rosemount Viaduct
℡01224/645971, Ⓦwww.skene-house.co.uk.
Serviced apartments with 1–3 rooms, all with TVs and microwaves. Good central location. ❹
Travelodge 9 Bridge St ℡01224/584555,
Ⓦwww.travelodge.co.uk. Typically bland budget hotel – but you can't beat it for convenience, right on Union Street and minutes from the station.
❷–❸

The City

Aberdeen divides neatly into five main areas. The **city centre**, roughly bounded by Broad Street, Union Street, Schoolhill and Union Terrace, features the opulent **Marischal College**, the colonnaded **Art Gallery** with its fine collection, and homes that predate Aberdeen's nineteenth-century town planning and have been preserved as **museums**. Union Street continues west to the comparatively cosmopolitan West End, where much of the city's decent nightlife can be found amid the tall grey town houses. To the south, the **harbour** still heaves with boats serving the fishing and oil industries, while north of the centre lies attractive **Old Aberdeen**, a village neighbourhood presided over by **King's College** and **St Machar's Cathedral** and influenced by the large student population. The long sandy **beach** with its esplanade development, only a mile or so from the heart of the city, marks Aberdeen's eastern border.

The city centre

The centre of Aberdeen is dominated by mile-long **Union Street**, whose impressive architecture, sometimes lost among the shoppers and chain stores, is still the grandest and most ambitious single thoroughfare in Scotland. The key to the early nineteenth-century city planners who conceived the street was the building of the ambitious **Union Street bridge**, spanning two hills and the Denburn gorge. The first attempt, a triple-span design by Glasgow architect David Hamilton, bankrupted the city and collapsed during construction. The famous Thomas Telford, called in as an adviser, proposed a single-arch structure which, when completed, became one of the engineering wonders of its age.

Any exploration of the city centre should begin at the open, cobbled **Castlegate**, where Aberdeen's long-gone castle once stood. At its centre is the late seventeenth-century **Mercat Cross**, carved with a unique gallery of Stewart sovereigns alongside some fierce gargoyles. Castlegate was once the focus of city life but nowadays is rather lifeless, with litter swirling around and pigeons easily outnumbering shoppers. However, the view up gently rising Union Street – a jumble of grey spires, turrets and jostling double-decker buses – is quintessential Aberdeen and well worth taking a moment or two to savour.

As Union Street begins you have to crane your neck to get a good view of the towering, turreted spire of the granite **Town House**, though the steely-grey nineteenth-century exterior is in fact simply a facade behind which lurks the early seventeenth-century **Tolbooth**, one of the city's oldest buildings. Used as a jail for many centuries, the Tolbooth presently houses a mothballed museum on the theme of crime and imprisonment.

Nearby, on King Street, the sandstone **St Andrew's Episcopal Cathedral** (mid-May to mid-Sept Mon–Sat 11am–4pm), where Samuel Seabury, America's first bishop, was ordained in 1784, offers a welcome relief from the uniform granite. Inside, its spartan whiteness is broken by florid gold ceiling bosses representing the (then) 48 states of the USA and 48 local families who remained loyal to the Episcopal Church during the eighteenth-century Penal Laws.

The Marischal College and around

On Broad Street itself stands Aberdeen's most imposing edifice and the world's second-largest granite building after the Escorial in Madrid – the exuberant **Marischal College**, whose tall, steely-grey pinnacled neo-Gothic facade is in absolute contrast to the hideously utilitarian concrete office blocks which face it. This spectacular architecture with all its soaring, surging lines has been painted and sketched more than any other in Aberdeen. The college itself was founded in 1593 by the fourth Earl Marischal, and coexisted as a separate Protestant university from Catholic King's, just up the road, for over two centuries. It was long Aberdeen's boast that their city had as many universities as the whole of England, and it wasn't until 1860 that the two were united as the University of Aberdeen. The **Marischal Museum** (Mon–Fri 10am–5pm, Sun 2–5pm; free), is made up of two large rooms that contain a wealth of weird exhibits, many gathered by Victorian anthropologists and other collectors who roamed the world filling their luggage with objects. The museum, sensitive to the cultural crassness this represents to the modern world, concentrates as much on the phenomenon of these collectors as the objects they brought back.

Aberdeen's oldest-surviving private house, **Provost Skene's House**, dating from 1545, is hemmed in by ghastly modern office blocks at 45 Guestrow (Mon–Sat 10am–5pm, Sun 1–4pm; free). In the sixteenth century all the well-to-do houses in the area looked like this, with mellow stone and rounded turrets – yet it was only the intervention of the Queen Mother in 1938 which saved this house from the fate of its neighbours. The house is now a museum, with a costume gallery, archeological exhibits and a series of period room settings illustrating life in the seventeenth, eighteenth and nineteenth centuries.

Between Upperkirkgate and Union Street stands the long **St Nicholas Kirk** (May–Sept Mon–Fri noon–4pm, Sat 1–3pm, Oct–April Mon–Fri 10am–1pm; free), actually two churches in one, with a solid, central bell tower rising from the middle, from where the 48-bell carillon, the largest in Britain, regularly chimes across the city. The Renaissance-style **West Church**, formerly the nave of St Nicholas, was designed in the mid-eighteenth century by James Gibbs, architect of St-Martin-in-the-Fields in London. The **East Church** was rebuilt over the groin-vaulted crypt of the restored fifteenth-century St Mary's Chapel (entered from Correction Wynd), which back in the 1600s was a place to imprison witches: you can still see the iron rings to which they were chained. Take time to explore the large peaceful churchyard, which with its green marble tombs and Baroque monuments seems a million miles from the bustling main street.

The Aberdeen Art Gallery

A little further west up Schoolhill, Aberdeen's engrossing **Art Gallery** (Mon–Sat 10am–5pm, Sun 2–5pm; free) was purpose-built in 1884 to a Neoclassical design by Mackenzie. You enter via the airy **Centre Court**, dominated by Barbara Hepworth's central fountain and the thick pillars running down from the upper balcony, each hewn from a different local marble. The walls here highlight the gallery's policy of acquiring contemporary art, with British work to the fore. From here, the **Side Court** contains selected work by YBAs (Young British Artists) gifted by the Saatchi Collection in 2000, including Jordan Baseman's extraordinary *I Love You Still*, made from tree limbs and human hair.

The **upstairs** rooms house the main body of the gallery's painting collection. The permanent collection is moved around on an occasional basis, and some of the rooms are given over to temporary and touring exhibitions: you'll find these advertised downstairs as well as in the local press.

Starting at the top of the staircase, the sheer number of landscapes crowding the walls of **Room One** can be disconcerting at first, but closer inspection reveals a superb collection of Victorian narrative art. **Room Two** concentrates on eighteenth-century painters such as Scotland's famous portraitists, Henry Raeburn and Alan Ramsay. **Room Three** includes works by Boudin, Courbet, Sisley, Monet, Pissarro and a deliciously bright Renoir, *La Roche Guyon*. The strong connections between the French schools and the development of modernism in Scottish painting saw the emergence of the "Glasgow Boys" in the 1880s (see p.1016), exemplified here by John Lavery's *The Tennis Party*. Inheritors of the Glasgow Boys' mantle, the now much in-vogue Scottish Colourists, can be found in **Room Four**. Here, Peploe's *Landscape, Cassis* shows off his instinct for colour, with daringly angled foreground tree trunks in rich blue, chocolate and purple shadows. In **Room Six** and on the balcony overlooking the Central Court you'll find some superb works by British Impressionists and Modernists.

The harbour

The old cobbled road of Ship Row winds down from Castlegate at the east end of Union Street to the north side of the **harbour**. Just off this steep road, peering out at the harbour through a striking modern glass facade, is the **Maritime Museum** (Mon–Sat 10am–5pm, Sun noon–3pm; free), which combines a thoroughly modern, airy museum with Aberdeen's oldest-surviving building, **Old Provost Ross's House**, laced with labyrinthine corridors, low doorways and small rooms. Suspended above the foyer and visible from five different levels is a spectacular 27ft-high model of an oil rig, which, along with terrific views over the bustling harbour, serves as a constant reminder that Aberdeen's maritime links are very much alive today. While large sections of the museum are devoted to telling the story of North Sea oil and gas production, the older industries of herring-fishing, whaling, shipbuilding and lighthouses also have their place, with well-designed displays and audiovisual presentations, many of which draw heavily on personal reminiscences. Passages lead from various levels of the museum into Provost Ross's House, where intricate ships' models and a variety of nautical paintings and drawings are on display.

At the bottom of Ship Row, the cobbles meet Market Street, which runs the length of the **harbour**. Here, brightly painted oil-supply ships, sleek cruise ships and peeling fishing boats jostle for position to an ever-constant clatter and the screech of well-fed seagulls. It's not the most attractive part of the city, but you'll encounter plenty of life and colour if you follow your nose down the road to the **fish market**, best visited early (7–8am).

At the east corner of the harbour is Aberdeen's **Footdee** or "fitee"(an easy walk or bus #14 from Union Street), a quaint nineteenth-century fishermen's village of higgledy-piggledy cottages which back onto the sea, their windows and doors facing inwards to protect from storms but also, so they say, to prevent the Devil from sneaking in the back door. Here, in a great setting beside the lighthouse which marks the channel into the harbour, you'll find the *Silver Darling*, one of the finest seafood restaurants in the Northeast.

Old Aberdeen

An independent burgh until 1891, the tranquil district of **Old Aberdeen**, a twenty-minute ride north of the city centre on bus #20, has always maintained a separate village-like identity. Its medieval cobbled streets, tiny wynds and little lanes are beautifully preserved.

The southern half of High Street is overlooked by **King's College Chapel** (Mon–Fri 9am–5pm; free), the first and finest of the college buildings, completed in 1495, with a chunky Renaissance spire. Named in honour of James IV, the chapel's west door is flanked by his coat of arms and those of his queen. The screen, the stalls (each unique) and the ribbed arched wooden ceiling are rare and beautiful examples of medieval Scottish woodcarving. The remains of Bishop Elphinstone's tomb and the carved pulpit from nearby St Machar's are also here.

From the college, the cobbled High Street leads a short way north to **St Machar's Cathedral** on the leafy Chanonry (daily 9am–5pm, except during services; free), overlooking Seaton Park and the River Don. The site was reputedly founded in 580 by Machar, a follower of Columba, when he was sent by the latter to find a grassy platform near the sea, overlooking a river shaped like the crook on a bishop's crozier. This setting fitted the bill perfectly, and the cathedral, a huge fifteenth-century fortified building, became one of the city's first great granite edifices.

The beach

Aberdeen can surely claim to have the best **beach** of all Britain's large cities. Less than a mile east of Union Street is a great two-mile sweep of clean sand, broken by groynes and lined all along with an esplanade, where most of the city's population seems to gather on a sunny day. Towards the southern end of the beach is a burgeoning concrete expanse of cinemas and fast-food outlets, a couple of fairly tatty amusement parks and a vast leisure centre. As you head further north, most of the beach's hinterland is devoted to successive golf links. Bus #14 goes along the southern esplanade.

A few hundred yards inland, the city's old tram depot at 179 Constitution Street, just across from the *Patio Hotel*, houses **Satrosphere** (Mon–Sat 10am–5pm, Sun 1.30–5pm; Ⓦwww.satrosphere.net; £5), Aberdeen's thoroughly entertaining hands-on science exhibition.

Eating, drinking and nightlife

Union Street and the surrounding area has a glut of attractive **cafés** and **restaurants**. Like most ports, Aberdeen caters for a transient population with a lot of disposable income and a desire to get drunk as quickly as possible: although you'll find no shortage of loud, flashy **bars** catering to such needs, there are still a number of more traditional old **pubs** which are well worth a visit.

Cafés and restaurants

Ashvale 46 Great Western Rd. One of Scotland's finest, and biggest, fish-and-chip shops, with seating for 300. Restaurant open daily until 11pm; takeaway until 1am. Inexpensive.

Howies 50 Chapel St ☎01224/639500. Aberdeen outpost of an Edinburgh institution, serving Modern Scottish cooking in a very accessible environment. Good price set meal deals and cheap house wine. Moderate.

Lemon Tree 5 West North St. Easy-going café inside the arts centre; serves good vegetarian and vegan snacks and meals. Inexpensive.

Poldino's 7 Little Belmont St ☎01224/647777. Lively, authentic Italian restaurant in a happening area of the city. Moderate. Closed Sun.

Silver Darling Pocra Quay, North Pier ☎01224/576229. Attractively located right at the mouth of the Dee in Footdee, this pricey restaurant serves the best seafood in town. Expensive. Closed Sat lunch & Sun.

Soul & Spice 15–17 Belmont St ☎01224/645200. Entertaining and colourful café serving up fantastic African and Caribbean dishes. Moderate. Open evenings only Tues-Fri, all day Sat & Sun.

Wild Boar 19 Belmont St ☎01224/625357. Upbeat gallery/coffee shop/brasserie with well-priced vegetarian food, soups, salads and oriental-style noodles, as well as great cake and coffee through the day. Food served until 9pm (Fri & Sat 8pm), after which DJs move in. Moderate.

Pubs and bars

Archibald Simpson 5 Castle St. A J.D. Wetherspoon chain-pub on the corner of Union Street, named after one of the architects of the Granite City, in typically ornate style with tiled floors and an extravagant interior.

Ma Cameron's Inn Little Belmont Street. Aberdeen's oldest pub, though only a section remains of the original. Serves food.

Prince of Wales 7 St Nicholas Lane. The quintessential Aberdeen pub with a long bar and flagstone floor. Serves fine pub grub, is renowned for its real ales and has a Sunday evening folk session; little

wonder that it's often crowded.

RSVP Academy Shopping Centre, Schoolhill ☎01224/625590. Stylish and busy venue with designer furniture and live jazz on a Sunday afternoon.

St Machar Bar 97 High St, Old Aberdeen. The medieval quarter's only pub, a pokey, old-fashioned bar inevitably full of King's College students.

Clubs and live music

The Blue Lamp 121 Gallowgate. A big bar featuring live bands (Fri & Sat) and a folk session (Mon); there's also a much smaller snug for relative peace and quiet.

The Globe Inn 13–15 North Silver St. Pleasant city-centre inn with jazz and blues on Tues, Fri, Sat & Sun.

Franklyn's 44 Justice Mill Lane. Contains three very different rooms: a piano bar; a club bar with live bands (Fri & Sat); and crowd-pleasing chart music pumping out in the main dance area.

Lemon Tree 5 West North St. The fulcrum of the city's arts scene, with a great buzz and regular live music, comedy and folk.

Theatres and cinemas

Belmont Picture House 9 Belmont St ☎01224/343536, ⓦ www.picturehouse-cinema.co.uk/ab. Art-house cinema showing the more cultured new releases and a back-list of classic, cult and foreign-language films. There's a decent café inside and some good places nearby for a bite before or after.

His Majesty's Rosemount Viaduct ☎01224/637788. Aberdeen's main theatre, in a beautifully restored Edwardian building, with a programme that ranges from highbrow drama and opera to pantomime.

Lemon Tree 5 West North St ☎01224/642230, ⓦ www.lemontree.org. Avant-garde events with off-the-wall comedians and plays, many coming hotfoot from the Edinburgh festivals.

UGC Beach Esplanade ☎0870/155 0502. Huge multiplex cinema in a beach-side development showing all the mainstream releases.

Listings

Airport ☏ 01224/722331.

Bike rental Alpine Bikes, 66–70 Holburn St
☏ 01224/211455; Cycling World, 460 George St
☏ 01224/632994.

Bookshops The largest are Waterstone's,
269–271 Union St, and Ottakar's, in Trinity
Shopping Centre, Union Bridge. Bon Accord Books,
69–75 Spittal, is the best for second-hand.

Bus information Grampian Transport Busline
☏ 01224/650065.

Car rental Arnold Clark, Girdleness Rd (☏ 01224/
249159), and at the airport (☏ 01224/663723);
Budget, Wellheads Drive (☏ 01224/793333), and
at the airport (☏ 01224/771777); National, 46
Summer St and at the airport (both ☏ 0870/400
4502).

Exchange Thomas Cook in the Bon Accord Centre
(Mon–Sat 9.30am–5.30pm, Sun noon–5pm;
☏ 01224/807100).

Ferry information P&O Scottish Ferries
☏ 01224/572615, ⊛ www.posf.co.uk.

Internet There's free access in the Reference sec-
tion of the main library on Rosemount Viaduct
(Mon–Thurs 9am–8pm, Fri & Sat 9am–5pm).
Costa Coffee on Loch Street, at the back of the
Bon Accord Centre, also offers access.

Left luggage Small 24hr lockers at the train station cost £2.

Medical facilities The Royal Infirmary, on
Foresterhill, northeast of the town centre, has a
24hr casualty department (☏ 01224/681818).
Boots pharmacy is at 161 Union St (Mon–Sat
8am–6pm; ☏ 01224/211592). Late-night pharmacies are listed each day in the Evening Express.

Police Main station is on Queen Street
☏ 01224/386000.

Post office The central post office is in the St
Nicholas Centre, between Union Street and
Upperkirkgate (Mon–Sat 9am–5.30pm), with a
branch at 489 Union St (Mon–Fri 9am–5.30pm,
Sat 9am–12.30pm).

Taxis Mairs Taxis ☏ 01224/353535.

Stonehaven and the Mearns

South of Aberdeen, the A92 and the main train line follow the coast to the busy
pebbledashed town of **STONEHAVEN**, which attracts hordes of holiday-
makers in the summer due to its sheltered Kincardine coastline, and in mid-
July in particular because of its respected **folk festival**. The old High Street,
lined with some fine town houses and civic buildings, connects the harbour
and its surrounding old town with the late eighteenth-century planned centre
on the other side of the River Carron. On New Year's Eve, High Street is the
location for the ancient ceremony of **Fireballs**, when locals parade its length,
swinging metal cages full of burning debris around their heads to ward off evil
spirits for the year ahead.

The **tourist office** is at 66 Allardice St, the main street past the square (July
& Aug Mon–Sat 10am–7pm, Sun noon–6pm; April–June, Sept & Oct
Mon–Sat 10am–5pm; ☏01569/762806). For **B&B** accommodation, try the
non-smoking *Sirdhana* at 11 Urie Crescent (☏01569/763011; ❷), or, a few
miles south of town on the A92, *Dunnottar Mains Farm* (☏01569/762621; ❷),
a decent farmhouse B&B beautifully situated right beside Dunnottar Castle.
For **food**, the *Tolbooth Seafood Restaurant* (☏01569/762287; closed Mon),
above the museum on the harbour, is the place to go – it's pricey but worth it.
For cheaper **pub** food or just a drink, try the entertaining *Marine Hotel* or the
attractive *Ship Inn*, both on the harbour.

Dunnottar Castle and Arbuthnott

Two miles south of Stonehaven (the tourist office sells a walking guide for the scenic amble), **Dunnottar Castle** (Easter–Oct Mon–Sat 9am–6pm, Sun 2–5pm; rest
of year Mon–Fri 9am–4pm, Dec & Jan closes 3pm; £3.50) is one of the finest of
Scotland's ruined castles, a huge ninth-century fortress set on a three-sided sheer
cliff jutting into the sea – a setting striking enough to be chosen as the backdrop
for Zeffirelli's movie version of *Hamlet*. Once the principal fortress of the north-

23

east, the ruins are worth a good root around, and there are any number of dramatic views out to the crashing sea. Siege and bloodstained drama splatter the castle's past: in 1297 William Wallace burnt alive the whole English Plantagenet garrison here, while one of the more gruesome tales from the castle's history tells of the imprisonment and torture of 122 men and 45 women Covenanters in 1685 – an event, as it says on the Covenanters' Stone in the churchyard, "whose dark shadow is for evermore flung athwart the Castled Rock".

Inland is the **Mearns**, an agricultural district of scattered population and gathering hills. Here, the straggling village of **ARBUTHNOTT** was the home of prolific local author Lewis Grassic Gibbon (1901–35), whose romanticized realism perfectly encapsulates the spirit of the agricultural Mearns area. *Sunset Song*, his most famous work, is an essential read for those travelling in this area. The community-run **Grassic Gibbon Centre** (April–Oct daily 10am–4.30pm; £2), on the B967 through the village, is a great introduction to this fascinating and self-assured man who died so young. He is buried (under his real name of James Leslie Mitchell) in the corner of the little village graveyard, overlooking the forested banks of the Bervie Water off the main road.

Deeside

More commonly known as **Royal Deeside**, the land stretching west from Aberdeen along the River Dee revels in its connections with the Royal Family, who have regularly holidayed here, at **Balmoral**, since Queen Victoria bought the estate. Eighty thousand Scots turned out to welcome her on her first visit in 1848, but some weren't so charmed: one local journalist remarked that the area was about to be "desolated by cockneys and other horrible reptiles". Today, most locals are fiercely protective of the royal connection.

Many of Victoria's guests weren't as enthusiastic about Deeside as she was: Count von Moltke, then aide-de-camp to Prince Frederick William of Prussia, observed, "It is very astonishing that the Royal Power of England should reside amid this lonesome, desolate, cold mountain scenery", while Tsar Nicholas II whined, "The weather is awful, rain and wind every day and on top of it no luck at all – I haven't killed a stag yet." However, Victoria adored the place, and the woods were said to remind Prince Albert of Thuringia, his homeland.

Deeside is undoubtedly handsome in a fierce, craggy, Scottish way, and the royal presence has helped keep a lid on any unattractive mass development. The villages strung along the A93, the main route through the area, are well-heeled and the facilities for visitors first-class, with a number of bunkhouses and hostels, some outstanding hotels and plenty of castles and grounds to snoop around. It's also an excellent area for **outdoor activities**, with hiking routes into both the Grampian and Cairngorm mountains, and good mountain biking, horse-riding and skiing.

Bluebird **bus** #201 from Aberdeen regularly chugs along the A93, serving most of the towns on the way to Braemar.

West of Aberdeen

West of Aberdeen, you'll pass through low-lying land of mixed farming, forestry and suburbs. Easily reached from the main road are the castles of **Drum** and **Crathes**, both interesting fortified houses with pleasant gardens, while the uneventful town of **Banchory** serves as gateway to the heart of Royal Deeside. Further west, **Glen Tanar** is a great example of the area's attractive blend of forest, river and mountain scenery.

Drum Castle and Crathes Castle

Ten miles west of Aberdeen on the A93, **Drum Castle** (June–Aug daily 11am–5.30pm; April, May & Sept daily 1.30–5.30pm; Oct Sat & Sun 1.30–5.30pm; grounds same days 10am–6pm; NTS; £6, grounds only £1) stands in a clearing in the ancient **woods of Drum**, made up of the splendid pines and oaks that once covered this whole area before the shipbuilding industry precipitated mass forest clearance. The castle itself combines a 1619 Jacobean mansion with Victorian extensions and the original, huge thirteenth-century keep which has recently been restored and reopened.

Further along the A93, four miles west of Drum Castle, **Crathes Castle** (daily: April–Sept 10.30am–5.30pm; Oct 10.30am–4.30pm; NTS; £3.50, or £7 including grounds and walled garden) is a splendid sixteenth-century granite tower house adorned with flourishes such as overhanging turrets, gargoyles and conical roofs. Its thick walls, narrow windows and tiny rooms loaded with heavy old furniture make Crathes rather claustrophobic, but it is saved by some wonderfully painted ceilings, either still in their original form or sensitively restored; the earliest dates from 1602. Don't miss the Room of the Nine Nobles, where great heroes of the past, among them Julius Caesar, King David and King Arthur, are skilfully painted on the beams.

Aboyne and Glen Tanar

Twelve miles west of Banchory on the A93, **ABOYNE** is a typically well-mannered Deeside village at the mouth of **Glen Tanar**, which runs southwest from here for ten miles or so deep into the Grampian hills. The glen, with few steep gradients and some glorious stands of mature Caledonian pine, is ideal for walking, mountain biking or horse-riding; the ranger information point two miles into the glen off the B976 has details of suitable routes, while the Glen Tanar Equestrian Centre (☎013398/86448) offers one and two-hour horse trails.

Ballater

Ten miles west of Aboyne is the neat and ordered town of **BALLATER**, attractively hemmed in by the river and fir-covered mountains. It was in Ballater that Queen Victoria first arrived in Deeside by train from Aberdeen back in 1848; she wouldn't allow a station to be built any closer to Balmoral, eight miles further west. Although the line has long been closed, the town's rather self-important royalism is much in evidence at the restored **train station** in the centre of town (same hours as the tourist office), where various video presentations and life-sized models relive the comings and goings of generations of royals. The local shops, having provided Balmoral with groceries and household basics, also flaunt their connections, with oversized 'By Appointment' crests sported above the doorways of most businesses from the butcher to the newsagent.

If you prefer to discover the fresh air and natural beauty that Victoria came to love so much, Ballater is an excellent base for local **walks and outdoor activities**. There are numerous hikes from Loch Muik (pronounced "mick"), nine miles southwest of town, including the Capel Mounth drovers' route over the mountains to Glen Doll, and a well-worn but strenuous all-day trek up and around Lochnagar (3789ft), the mountain much painted and written about by the current Prince of Wales. The starting point for all these walks is the Balmoral Rangers' **visitors' centre**, on the shores of the loch (call ☎013397/55059 for opening hours), which also offers a series of free guided nature walks. Good-quality **bikes** can be rented from Wheels and Reels (℡013397/55864) at 2 Braemar Rd, just over the railway bridge from Station Square.

Practicalities

Ballater's **tourist office** is in the disused, renovated train station (July & Aug Mon–Sat 9.30am–7pm, Sun 1–7pm; June & Sept Mon–Sat 10am–1pm & 2–6pm, Sun 1–6pm; April, May, Oct & Nov Mon–Sat 10am–1pm & 2–5pm, Sun 1–5pm; Dec–March Sat & Sun 10am–5pm; ℡013397/55306). **Bunkhouse** accommodation is available for groups or backpackers at the *Schoolhouse*, Ferndean, Anderson Road (℡013397/56333, Ⓔschoolhousebal-later@btinternet.com; ❶), while there are plenty of reasonable **B&Bs** in town, including the no-smoking *Inverdeen House*, on Bridge Square (℡013397/ 55759, Ⓦwww.inverdeen.com; ❷), which offers a wide choice of breakfasts, most involving local produce and home baking. A few miles north of town on the road to Tomintoul (see p.1181) is *Gairnshiel Lodge* (℡013397/55582; ❶). In a remote but beautiful setting, it's a particularly child-friendly place and a great base for walking or cycling. For **camping**, the *Anderson Road Caravan Park* (℡013397/55727; Easter–Oct) down towards the river, has around sixty tent pitches.

Balmoral Estate

Originally a sixteenth-century tower house built for the powerful Gordon family, **Balmoral Castle** (mid-April to July daily 10am–5pm; £4.50) has been a royal residence since 1852, when it was converted to the Scottish Baronial mansion that stands today. The Royal Family traditionally spend their summer holidays here, but despite its fame it can be something of a disappointment even for a dedicated royalist. For the three months when the doors are nudged open, the general riffraff are permitted to view only the ballroom and the grounds; for the rest of the year it is not even visible to the paparazzi who converge en masse when the royals are in residence here in August.

Braemar

Continuing for another few miles, the road rises to 1100ft above sea level in the upper part of Deeside and the village of **BRAEMAR**, situated where three passes meet and overlooked by an unremarkable **castle** (July & Aug daily 9.30am–5.30pm; Easter–June, Sept & Oct closed Fri; £3). This is an invigorating, outdoor kind of place, well patronized by committed hikers, but probably best known for its Highland Games, the annual **Braemar Gathering**, on the first Saturday of September (Ⓦwww.braemargathering.org). Games were first held here in the eleventh century, when Malcolm Canmore set contests for the local clans in order to pick the bravest and strongest for his army. Since Queen Victoria's day, successive generations of royals have attended, and the world's most famous Highland Games have become rather an overcrowded, overblown event. You're not guaranteed to get in if you just turn up; the website has details of how to book tickets in advance.

Braemar's **tourist office** is in the modern building known as the Mews in the middle of the village on Mar Road (July & Aug daily 9am–7pm; June & Sept daily 10am–6pm; rest of year Mon–Sat 10am–1pm & 2–5pm, Sun noon–5pm; ℡013397/41600). **Accommodation** is scarce in Braemar in the lead-up to the Games, but at other times there's a wide choice. *Clunie Lodge Guest House*, Clunie Bank Road (℡013397/41330, Ⓔclunielodge@msn.com; ❷), on the edge of town, is a good **B&B** with lovely views up Clunie Glen, and there's a large SYHA **hostel** at Corrie Feragie, 21 Glenshee Rd (☎013397/41659, ⓦwww.syha.org.uk; Jan–Oct). The cheery *Rucksacks*, an easy-going bunkhouse well equipped for walkers and backpackers, is just behind the Mews complex (☎013397/41517). The *Invercauld Caravan Club Park* (☎013397/41373), just south of the village off Glenshee Road, has fifteen **camping** pitches.

Speyside

Strictly speaking, **Speyside** is the region surrounding the Spey River, but to most people the name is synonymous with the **whisky triangle**, stretching from just north of Craigellachie down towards Tomintoul in the south, and west to Huntly. Indeed, there are more whisky distilleries and famous brands concentrated in this small area (including Glenfiddich and Glenlivet) than in any other part of the country. Running through the heart of the region is the River Spey, whose clean clear waters play such a vital part in the whisky industry and are home to thousands of salmon. At the centre of Speyside is the quiet market town of **Dufftown**, which along with nearby **Craigellachie** makes the best base for a tour of the distilleries.

Dufftown and Craigellachie

The cheery community of **DUFFTOWN**, founded in 1817 by James Duff, the fourth Earl of Fife, proudly proclaims itself "Malt Whisky Capital of the World", and indeed it exports more of the stuff than anywhere else in Britain. There isn't a great deal to do in the town, but it's a useful starting point for orienting yourself towards the whisky trail, and if you're keen to immerse yourself in some of the local history and lore relating to the precious liquid, the small **museum** at 24 Fife St (Mon–Fri 2–7pm, Sat & Sun 10am–5pm) has a collection of illicit distilling equipment, books and old photographs.

> ### The Speyside Way
>
> The **Speyside Way**, with its beguiling mix of mountain, river, wildlife and whisky, is fast establishing itself as an appealing alternative to the popular West Highland and Southern Upland long-distance footpaths. Starting at **Buckie** on the Moray Firth coast, it follows the fast-flowing River Spey from its mouth at Spey Bay south to **Aviemore**, with branches linking it to **Dufftown**, Scotland's malt whisky capital, and **Tomintoul** on the remote edge of the Cairngorm mountains. Some 65 miles long without taking on the branch routes, the whole thing is a five- to seven-day expedition, but its proximity to main roads and small villages means that it is excellent for shorter walks or even bicycle trips, especially in the heart of **distillery** country between Craigellachie and Glenlivet: Glenfiddich, Glenlivet, Macallan and Cardhu distilleries, as well as the Speyside Cooperage, lie directly on or a short distance off the route. Other highlights include the chance to encounter an array of **wildlife**, from dolphins at Spey Bay to ospreys at Loch Garten, as well as the restored **railway** trips on offer at Dufftown and Aviemore. The path uses disused railway lines for much of its length, and there are simple campsites and good B&Bs at strategic points along the route. For more details contact the Speyside Way Visitor Centre at Craigellachie (☎01340/881266, ⓦwww.moray.org/area/speyway/webpages/index.htm).

The Malt Whisky Trail

Speyside's **Malt Whisky Trail** is a clearly signposted seventy-mile meander around the region via eight distilleries. Unless you're seriously interested in whisky, it's best to just pick out a couple that appeal, perhaps choosing one because you know the whisky and another for its setting. All the distilleries offer a guided **tour** (some are free, others charge but then give you a voucher which is redeemable against a bottle of whisky from the distillery shop) with a tasting to round it off; if you're driving you'll be offered a miniature to take away with you. Most people travel the route by car, though you could cycle parts of it, or even walk using the Speyside Way (see box p.1181). The following are selected highlights.

Cardhu, on the B9102 at Knockando (July–Sept Mon–Fri 10am–6pm, Sat 10am–4.30pm & Sun 11am–4pm; March–June & Oct Mon–Fri 10am–4.30pm; Nov–Feb Mon–Fri 11am–3pm; £3 including voucher). This distillery was established over a century ago when the founder's wife was nice enough to raise a red flag to warn local crofters if the authorities were on the lookout for their illegal stills. Sells rich, full-bodied whisky which has distinctive peaty flavours and comes in an attractive bulbous bottle.

Glen Grant, Rothes (April–Oct Mon–Sat 10am–4pm, Sun 12.30–4pm; £3). A well-known, floral whisky which you can sample in a heather-thatched tasting pavilion. It's well worth taking time to wander through the attractive Victorian gardens.

Glenfiddich, on the A941 just north of Dufftown (April to mid-Oct Mon–Sat 9.30am–4.30pm, Sun noon–4.30pm; rest of year Mon–Fri 9.30am–4.30pm; free). Probably the best known of the malt whiskies, and the biggest and slickest of all the distilleries. It's a light, sweet whisky which comes in triangular shaped bottles. Uniquely, the whisky is bottled on the premises – an interesting process to watch. The tours are informative, though the place is thronged with tourists.

Glenlivet, on the B9008, ten miles north of Tomintoul (April–Oct Mon–Sat 10am–4pm, Sun 12.30–4pm; £3 including voucher). A famous name in a lonely hillside setting. This was the first licensed distillery in the Highlands, following the 1823 Act of Parliament which aimed to reduce illicit distilling and smuggling. The Glenlivet twelve-year-old malt is a floral, fragrant medium-bodied whisky.

Speyside Cooperage, Craigellachie (Mon–Fri 9.30am–4.30pm; £2.95). Not a distillery, but a fascinating adjunct to the industry. After a short exhibition explaining the ancient and skilled art of cooperage, you're shown onto a balcony overlooking the large workshop where the oak casks for whisky are made and repaired by fast-working, highly skilled coopers.

Strathisla, Keith (April–Oct Mon–Sat 10am–4pm, Sun 12.30–4pm; £4, including a voucher worth £2). A small old-fashioned distillery claiming to be Scotland's oldest (1786); it's certainly one of the most attractive, situated in a highly evocative highland location on the strath of the Isla River. The malt itself has a rich almost fruity taste and is pretty rare, but is used as the heart of the better-known Chivas Regal blend.

There are also **other distilleries** not on the official trail that you can visit: the **Macallan** distillery near Craigellachie (Mon–Sat 10am–3.30pm; booking advised ☏01340/871471; free) has in-depth tours limited to a maximum of ten people, and **Cragganmore** at Ballindalloch (tours June–Sept Mon–Fri 10am, 1pm & 3pm; booking essential ☏01479/874700; £5) also offers a personalized, exclusive tour.

Four miles north of Dufftown, the small settlement of **CRAIGELLACHIE** sits above the confluence of the sparkling waters of the Fiddich and the Spey. From the village, you can look down on a beautiful iron bridge over the Spey built by Thomas Telford in 1815. By the River Fiddich on the A95 Huntly road, there's a **visitor centre** for the Speyside Way (Easter–Oct generally daily 9am–5pm; ☎01340/881266), which sells maps of the route and gives advice on what to look for along the way.

Practicalities

Dufftown's four main streets converge on Main Square. The official **tourist office** is located inside the handsome clocktower at the centre of the square (July & Aug Mon–Sat 10am–6pm, Sun 1–6pm; April–June, Sept & Oct Mon–Sat 10am–1pm & 2–5pm; ☎01340/820501), though an informal information and accommodation booking service has developed at The Whisky Shop (☎01340/821097) across the road. You'll certainly need to look no further than this for a vast array of whiskies produced not just on Speyside but all over Scotland; nosings and other special events are organized regularly here.

There's a good range of places to **stay** in Dufftown itself, as well as in the surrounding countryside. The only hostel accommodation is the small self-catering *Swan Bunkhouse* (☎01542/810334) located at Drummuir, three miles northeast of Dufftown, is a pleasant spot and the owners will arrange pick-ups from Dufftown or Keith. In Craigellachie there's the extremely welcoming and tasteful B&B attached to the *Green Hall Gallery* on Victoria Street (☎01340/871010, ⓦwww.greenhall-gallery.co.uk; ❷). For unquestionable style and luxury, head to *Minmore House* (☎01807/590378, Ⓔminmore-house@ukonline.co.uk; limited opening Nov–March; ❺), the former home of Glenlivet owner George Smith, which sits right beside the Glenlivet distillery on a quiet hillside above the Livet Water.

The smartest of Dufftown's **restaurants** are the expensive *La Faisanderie*, on the corner of the square and Balvenie Street (☎01340/821273) and *Taste of Speyside*, 10 Balverie St (☎01340/820860). For more down-to-earth pub grub you're better off heading to the busy *Highlander Inn* (☎01340/881446; ❷) on Victoria Street in Craigellachie, which serves decent meals, has frequent folk **music sessions** in its bar, and five guest rooms.

You can rent **bikes** from Clarke's Cycle Hire (☎01340/881525), beside the *Fiddichside Inn* at Craigellachie.

The coast

The **coast** of northeast Scotland from Aberdeen to Inverness is a rugged, often bleak, landscape. Still, if the weather is good, it's well worth spending a couple of days meandering through the various little fishing villages and along the miles of deserted, unspoilt beaches. Keen walkers have the best run of the area: some of the cliffs are so steep that you have to hike considerable distances to get the best views of the coast.

The largest towns along the coast are **Peterhead** and **Fraserburgh**, both dominated by sizeable fishing fleets, and while neither has much to offer, the latter's Museum of Scottish Lighthouses is one of the most attractive small museums in Scotland. More appealing to most visitors are the quieter spots along the Moray coast, including the idyllic villages of **Pennan**, **Portsoy** and nearby **Cullen**. The other main attractions are **Duff House**, a branch of the National Gallery of Scotland, in Banff; the working abbey at **Pluscarden** by Elgin; and the **Findhorn Foundation**, near Forres.

The main towns and larger villages are fairly well served by **buses**, while **trains** from Aberdeen and Inverness stop at Elgin, Forres and Nairn. Even so, it's preferable to have your own transport for reaching some of the far-flung places.

Peterhead and around

PETERHEAD, the easternmost mainland town in Scotland, stands in sharp contrast to the picturesque fishing villages on this stretch of coast. As notable for its high-security prison and ugly power station as its busy harbour, it's an unashamedly functional place. Although in recent years the oil industry has created a surge in wealth and population, Peterhead's *raison d'être* is **fishing**, and it was for many years the busiest white-fish port in Europe. The oldest building in town is the 400-year-old **Ugie Salmon Fish House** on Golf Road at the mouth of the River Ugie, at the north end of town (Mon–Fri 9am–5pm, Sat 9am–noon; free), where you can watch the traditional methods of oak-smoking salmon and trout in Scotland's oldest smoke-house; the finished product is for sale at reasonable prices. One of the town's newest buildings houses the **Peterhead Maritime Heritage Museum** (April–Oct daily 10.30am–5pm; call ☎01779/473000 for winter opening; £2.60), on the beach just off the main road. It's an airy, pleasant place with a café, and the helpful staff are happy to help with tourist **information**. The museum tells the story of the town's fishing industry from the old herring fleet to the modern day, with a live relay of the harbourmaster's radio channel.

Fraserburgh and the north coast

FRASERBURGH is a large and fairly severe-looking town in the same vein as Peterhead, although its economy still relies on fishing alone. At the northern tip of the town, an eighteenth-century lighthouse protrudes from the top of sixteenth-century **Fraserburgh Castle**, where the highest wind speeds on mainland Britain were recorded in 1989 (they reached 140mph). The lighthouse was one of the first to be built in Scotland and is now part of the excellent **Museum of Scottish Lighthouses** (April–Oct Mon–Sat 10am–6pm, Sun noon–6pm; Nov–March closes 4pm; £3.50), where you can see a collection of huge lenses and prisms gathered from decommissioned lighthouses, and a display on various members of the famous "Lighthouse" Stevenson family, who designed many of them (including the father and grandfather of author Robert Louis Stevenson). Highlight of the museum is the tour of Kinnaird Head light itself, preserved as it was when the last keeper left in 1991, with its century-old equipment still in perfect working order.

West of Fraserburgh

The coast road between Fraserburgh and Pennan, twelve miles west, is particularly attractive: it's lined with pretty churches and cottages, while countless paths lead off it to ruined castles, cliff-top walks and lonely beaches. **PENNAN** itself, a tiny fishing hamlet, lies just off the road, down a steep and hazardous hill. Consisting of little more than a single row of whitewashed stone cottages tucked between a cliff and the sea, the village leapt into the limelight when the British movie *Local Hero* was filmed here in 1982. You can stay at one of the identifiable landmarks from the film, the *Pennan Inn* (☎01346/561201; ❷), a convivial, lively spot with an excellent seafood **restaurant** and a cosy bar, whose customers spill out onto the sea wall on summer evenings. The tiny village of **CROVIE** (pronounced "crivie"), whose residents frequently have their doorsteps washed by the sea, is just as appealing. Tucked against the steep cliffs, it's so narrow that its residents have to park at one end of the village and continue to their houses on foot. **GARDENSTOWN**, another village of the same style on the other side of Troup Head from Pennan, is a little larger and slightly down-at-heel, but has a nice beach.

Heading west from Pennan brings you, after ten miles, to **MACDUFF** and its neighbour **BANFF**, separated by little more than the beautiful seven-arch bridge over the River Deveron. Banff's **tourist office** (July & Aug Mon–Sat 10am–1pm & 2–6pm, Sun 1–6pm; April–June & Sept Mon–Sat closes 5pm; ☎01261/812419) is housed in the old gatehouse of Duff House in St Mary Square.

Banff's undoubted highlight is the extravagant **Duff House** (generally April–Oct daily 11am–5pm, Nov–March Thurs–Sun 11am–4pm, though hours can be irregular; call ☎01261/818181 to check; HS; £4). Built to William Adam's design in 1730, this elegant four-floor Georgian Baroque house was originally intended for one of the northeast's richest men, William Braco, who became Earl of Fife in 1759. The house has been painstakingly restored and reopened as an outpost of the National Gallery of Scotland's extensive collection, although the emphasis is to display period artwork rather than any broader selection of the Gallery's paintings. The downstairs rooms set the tone, principally the Rococo vestibule and the **dining room**, hung with ponderous eighteenth-century portraits, among which Allan Ramsay's *Elizabeth, Mrs Daniel Cunyngham* leaps out for its delightfully cool composition. To the left is the **Private Drawing Room**, containing a bust of William Adam and the sweeping canvases of Welsh landscapist Richard Wilson (1714–82). Ascending the **Great Staircase**, all eyes are drawn to the enormous copy of Raphael's *Transfiguration* by Inverness's Grigor Urquhart (1797–1846). Most of the accompanying portraits are also Scottish. Upstairs, the **North Drawing Room** contains the only piece of furniture original to the house, a 1760s mirror, but more obvious is the bewilderingly bold gold and cherry-red ceiling, a not entirely successful Victorian pastiche of Adam's style. Beyond the house there are extensive grounds with some pleasant parkland walks, notably along the River Deveron to a local beauty spot, the **Bridge of Alvah**, a couple of miles south.

Buckie and around

The dull fishing and service town of **BUCKIE** is home to the **Buckie Drifter** heritage museum (April–Oct Mon–Sat 10am–5pm, Sun noon–5pm; £2.75), a hands-on exhibition telling the history of the area's fishing industry. It's well geared to families, though inevitably given the dominance of fishing a century and more ago, it's only one of half-a-dozen maritime heritage museums found up and down this coast.

Buckie also marks the terminus of the **Speyside Way** long-distance footpath (see p.1181). This follows the coast west for five miles to windy **Spey Bay**, also reached by a small coastal road from Buckie, at the mouth of the river of the same name. It's a remote spot bounded by sea and river and sky; interpretation is offered by a small **wildlife centre** (daily July & Aug 10.30am–7pm; April–June, Sept & Oct closes 5.30pm; ⓦwww.mfwc.co.uk; £1.50), whose main mission is research of the Moray Firth dolphin population (for more on which, see p.1201).

Elgin and around

The lively market town of **ELGIN**, just inland about fifteen miles west of Cullen, grew up in the thirteenth century around the River Lossie. It's an appealing place, still largely sticking to its medieval street plan, with a busy main street opening out onto an old cobbled marketplace and a tangle of wynds and pends.

On North College Street, just round the corner from the tourist office and clearly signposted, is the lovely ruin of **Elgin Cathedral** (April–Sept daily 9.30am–6.30pm; Oct–March Mon–Sat 9.30am–4.30pm, Thurs closes noon, Sun 2–4.30pm; HS; £2.80, joint ticket with Spynie Palace £3.30). Once considered Scotland's most beautiful cathedral, rivalling St Andrews in importance, today it is little more than a shell, though it does retain its original facade. Founded in 1224, the three-towered building was extensively rebuilt after a fire in 1270, and stood as the region's highest religious house until 1390 when the inimical Wolf of Badenoch (Alexander Stewart, Earl of Buchan and illegitimate son of Robert II) burned the place down, along with the rest of the town, in retaliation for having been excommunicated by the Bishop of Moray when he left his wife. Unusual features include the Pictish cross slab in the middle of the ruins and the cracked gravestones with their *memento mori* of skulls and crossbones.

At the very top of High Street is one of Britain's oldest museums, the **Elgin Museum** (April–Oct Mon–Fri 10am–5pm, Sat 11am–4pm, Sun 2–5pm; £2), housed in this building since 1843. Along with the usual local exhibits, there's a weird anthropological collection including reptilian skulls, a shrunken head from Ecuador and a grinning mummy from Peru. In addition, you can see an excellent collection of fossils and well-explained Pictish relics.

Practicalities

Elgin is well served by public transport, with the Aberdeen–Inverness train stopping here several times a day. The **bus station** is on Alexandra Road (☎01343/544222), a block from St Giles Church, while the **train station** is slightly less convenient, on the south side of town on Station Road (turn right out of the station, left at the island and up Moss Street to reach the centre).

The **tourist office**, 17 High St (July & Aug Mon–Sat 10am–6pm, Sun 11am–6pm; April–June & Sept Mon–Sat 10am–5pm, Sun 11am–3pm; Oct–March Mon–Sat 10am–4pm; ☎01343/542666), will book **accommodation**. Central *Belleville B&B*, 14 South College St (☎01343/541515, ✉belleville@talk21.com; ❶) is good value; five miles east of town in Urquhart, the *Old Church of Urquhart* (☎01343/843063; ❷) is an unusual and comfortable B&B in a striking converted church on Meft Road.

For **food**, the *Abbey Court* restaurant (☎01343/552849) on Greyfriars Street offers good food at low prices, while the *Emperor* (☎01343/551133), next to the Elgin Museum on North College Street, serves commendable Thai and Chinese dishes. For great **picnic** foods, head to the old-fashioned high-street store Gordon & McPhail, 58–60 South St, an Aladdin's cave of aromas, colours and delicacies, which sells one of the widest range of malt whiskies in the world.

Pluscarden Abbey

Set in a verdant valley seven miles southwest of Elgin, **Pluscarden Abbey** (daily 4.30am–8.45pm; ⓦwww.geocities.com/athens/thebes/2553; free), looms impressively large in a peaceful clearing off an unmarked road. One of only two abbeys in Scotland with a permanent community of monks, it was founded in 1230 for a French order and, in 1390, became another of the properties burnt by the Wolf of Badenoch (see above); recovering from this, it became a priory of the Benedictine Abbey of Dunfermline in 1454 and continued as such until monastic life was suppressed in Scotland in 1560.

The abbey's revival began in 1897 when the Catholic antiquarian, John, third Marquis of Bute, started to repair the building. In 1948 his son donated it to a small group of Benedictine monks from Gloucester, who established the present community. They are an active bunch, running stained-glass workshops, making honey and even recording Gregorian chants on CDs, all of which is detailed on their website. The abbey itself is airy and tranquil, with the monks' singing often eerily floating through from the connecting chapel. It is possible to **stay** here on retreat for a few days; see the website for details.

Findhorn

A little north of the town of Forres, and a mile beyond the controversial **Findhorn Foundation** (see box), is the tidy village of **FINDHORN**, which has a magnificent beach, a delightful harbour, a small **Heritage Centre** (June–Aug daily except Tues 2–5pm; May & Sept Sat & Sun 2–5pm; free) and a couple of good pubs: on a sunny day, a pint on the terrace at the *Kimberbey Inn* is hard to beat.

The Findhorn Foundation

In 1962, with little money and no employment, Eileen and Peter Caddy, their three children and friend Dorothy Maclean, settled on a caravan site at **Findhorn**. Dorothy believed she had a special relationship with what she called the "devas... the archetypal formative forces of light or energy that underlie all forms in nature – plants, trees, rivers", and from the uncompromising sandy soil they built a remarkable garden filled with plants and vegetables, far larger than had ever been seen in the area. Today, the **Findhorn Foundation** (Mon–Sat 9am–noon & 2–5pm, Sun 2–5pm; free) has blossomed from its early core of three adults and three children into a full-blown community of a couple of hundred people, with classes and facilities for around eight thousand visitors a year. The Original Caravan – as it is marked on the site's map – still stands, surrounded by a whole host of newer timber buildings and other caravans employing solar power, earth roofs and other green initiatives, such as an ecological sewage treatment centre. **Guided tours** (Mon, Wed & Fri–Sun 2pm; £1) allow visitors a more informed look at the different activities of the foundation, as well as some of the site's more interesting buildings, while residential workshops and short-term stays are also available.

As can be expected, the foundation is not without controversy: one community leader declared that "behind the benign and apparently religious front lies a hard core of New Agers experimenting with hallucinatory techniques marketed as spirituality". Findhorn, now a public company, is also accused of being overly well-heeled: a glance into the shop or a tally of the large cars parked outside the houses does give some substance to such ideas. However, most people here, although honest about the downsides of community living, are extremely positive about its benefits. The reputation of the place is such that it attracts visitors both sympathetic and cynical – and both find something to feed their impressions.

Bizarrely enough, despite its enormous growth, the foundation is still situated on Findhorn's caravan and **camping park** (☎01309/690203; April–Oct), located on the B9011 about ten miles west of Elgin and served by bus #310 from Forres – which creates an intriguing combination of people onsite. For details of all activities contact the **visitor centre** (Mon–Fri 9am–5pm, Sat & Sun 2–5pm; ☎01309/690311, ⓦwww.findhorn.org), which is clearly signposted from the entrance. There's a smart **café** and richly stocked **delicatessen** and general **shop** on site.

Travel details

Trains

Aberdeen to: Arbroath (every 30min; 1hr); Dundee (every 30min; 1hr 15min); Edinburgh (1–2 hourly; 2hr 35min); Elgin (hourly; 1hr 30min); Forres (hourly; 1hr 45min); Glasgow (1–2 hourly; 2hr 35min); Huntly (hourly; 50min); Insch (hourly; 35min); Inverurie (hourly; 20min); Keith (hourly; 1hr 5min); Montrose (every 30min; 45min); Nairn (hourly; 2hr); Stonehaven (every 30min; 15min).

Dundee to: Aberdeen (every 30min; 1hr 15min); Arbroath (hourly; 20min); Montrose (hourly; 15min).

Elgin to: Forres (hourly; 15min); Nairn (hourly; 25min).

Buses

Aberdeen to: Arbroath (hourly; 1hr 20min); Ballater (hourly; 1hr 45min); Banchory (hourly; 55min); Banff (hourly; 1hr 55min); Braemar (4–6 daily; 2hr 10min); Crathie (for Balmoral) (4–6 daily; 1hr 55min); Cruden Bay (hourly; 50min); Cullen (hourly; 1hr 50min–2hr 30min); Dufftown (2 weekly; 2hr 10min); Dundee (hourly; 2hr); Elgin (hourly; 2hr 35min–3hr 40min); Forfar (2 daily; 1hr 20min); Forres (hourly; 2hr 35min); Fraserburgh (hourly; 1hr 20min); Fyvie (hourly; 1hr); Huntly (hourly; 1hr 35min); Inverurie (hourly; 45min); Macduff (hourly; 1hr 50min); Mintlaw (for Aden Park) (hourly; 50min); Montrose (hourly; 1hr); Nairn (hourly; 2hr 50min); Peterhead (every 30min; 1hr 15min); Pitmedden (hourly; 50min); Stonehaven (every 30min; 25–45min).

Ballater to: Crathie (June–Sept 1 daily; 15min).

Banchory to: Ballater (June–Sept 1 daily; 45min); Braemar (June–Sept 1 daily; 1hr 20min); Crathie (June–Sept 1 daily; 1hr); Spittal of Glenshee (June–Sept 1 daily; 2hr).

Dufftown to: Elgin (hourly; 1hr).

Dundee to: Aberdeen (hourly; 2hr); Arbroath (every 15min; 40min–1hr); Blairgowrie (every 30min; 50min–1hr); Forfar (every 30min; 30min); Glamis (2 daily; 40min); Kirriemuir (hourly; 1hr 10min); Meigle (hourly; 40min); Montrose (hourly; 1hr 15min).

Elgin to: Aberdeen (hourly; 2hr 35min–3hr 40min); Burghead (Mon–Sat hourly; 30min); Duffus (Mon–Sat hourly; 15min); Forres (hourly; 25min); Huntly (3 daily; 50min); Inverurie (3 daily; 1hr 45min); Lossiemouth (every 30min; 20min); Nairn (hourly; 40min); Pluscarden (1 daily; 20min).

Forres to: Elgin (hourly; 25min); Findhorn (Mon–Sat 8 daily; 20min).

Fraserburgh to: Banff (2 daily; 55min); Macduff (2 daily; 45min).

Montrose to: Brechin (hourly; 20min).

Peterhead to: Cruden Bay (every 30min; 20min).

Ferries

Aberdeen to: Lerwick, Shetland (summer only: 4–5 weekly; 14hr); Stromness, Orkney (summer only: 2 weekly; 8–10hr).

Flights

Aberdeen to: Belfast (Mon–Fri 1 daily; 2hr 45min); Birmingham (Mon–Fri 3 daily; 1hr 30min); Glasgow (1 daily; 45min); London Gatwick (5 daily; 1hr 30min); London Heathrow (7 daily; 1hr 30min); London Luton (2 daily; 1hr 30min); London Stansted (4 daily; 1hr 30min); Manchester (Mon–Fri 9 daily, Sat 3 daily, Sun 4 daily; 1hr 20min); Newcastle (Mon–Fri 5 daily; Sat & Sun 2 daily; 1hr); Sumburgh, Shetland (Mon–Fri 4 daily, Sat & Sun 2 daily; 1hr).

Dundee to: London City (Mon–Fri 2 daily; 1hr 15min).

The Highland region

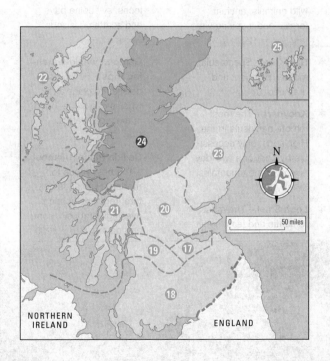

CHAPTER 24 # Highlights

* **West Highland Railway** – From Glasgow to Mallaig via Fort William; the further north it travels, the more spectacular it gets. See p.1194

* **The Cairngorms** – Scotland's unique mountain massif, a place of wild animals, ancient forests and inspiring vistas. See p.1203

* **Glen Coe** – Spectacular, moody, poignant and dramatic. See p.1215

* **Knoydart** – The most remote peninsula in the Highlands, only accessible by boat or a two-day hike over the mountains. See p.1223

* **Loch Shiel** – The most romantic and least spoilt of Scotland's great lochs, the place where Bonnie Prince Charlie first raised an army. See p.1220

* **Wester Ross** – Scotland's finest scenery, a heady mix of dramatic mountains, rugged sea lochs, sweeping bays and scattered islands. See p.1226

* **Gairloch whale-watching trips** – Seals, porpoises, dolphins and whales can all be found in the local waters. See p.1228

* **Ceilidh Place, Ullapool** – The best venue for modern Highlands culture, regularly hosting evenings of music, song and dance. See p.1230

The Highland region

T he **Highland region** of Scotland, covering the northern two-thirds
of the country, holds much of the mainland's most spectacular
scenery: a classic combination of mountains, glens, lochs and rivers
surrounded on three sides by a magnificently pitted and rugged coastline. The inspiring landscape and the tranquillity and space which it offers
are without doubt the main attractions of the region. You may be surprised
at just how remote much of it still is: the vast peat bogs in the north, for
example, are among the most extensive and unspoilt wilderness areas in
Europe, while a handful of the west coast's isolated crofting villages can still
be reached only by boat.

Capital of the Highlands and the only major urban centre in the region,
Inverness is an obvious springboard for more remote areas, with its good
transport links and facilities, and while there are some engaging historic sites
nearby, the city itself is of limited appeal. South of Inverness, the **Strathspey**
region, with a string of villages lying along the River Spey, is dominated by the
dramatic **Cairngorm mountains**, an area brimming with attractive scenery
and opportunities for outdoor activity.

The Monadhliath mountains lie between Strathspey and **Loch Ness**, the
largest and most famous of the necklace of lochs which make up the **Great
Glen**, an ancient geological fault-line which cuts southwest across the region
from Inverness to the town of **Fort William**. From Fort William, located
beneath Scotland's highest peak, Ben Nevis, it's possible to branch out to some
fine scenery – most conveniently the beautiful expanses of **Glen Coe**, but also
in the direction of the appealing **west coast**, notably the remote and tranquil
Ardnamurchan peninsula, the "Road to the Isles" to **Mallaig**, and the lochs
and glens that lead to **Kyle of Lochalsh** on the most direct route to Skye.
Between Kyle of Lochalsh and **Ullapool**, the main settlement in the northwest, lies **Wester Ross**, home to quintessentially west-coast scenes of sparkling
sea lochs, rocky headlands and sandy beaches set against some of Scotland's
most dramatic mountains, with Skye and the Western Isles on the horizon.

The little-visited **north coast** stretching from wind-lashed **Cape Wrath**, at
the very northwest tip of the mainland, east to **John O'Groats** is yet more
rugged, with sheer cliffs and sand-filled bays bearing the brunt of frequently
fierce Atlantic storms. The main settlement on this coast is **Thurso**, jumping-
off point for the main ferry service to Orkney.

On the fertile **east coast**, stretching north from Inverness to the old herring
port of **Wick**, green fields and woodland run down to the sweeping sandy
beaches of the **Black Isle** and the **Cromarty** and **Dornoch firths**. This
region is rich with historical sites, including the **Sutherland Monument** by

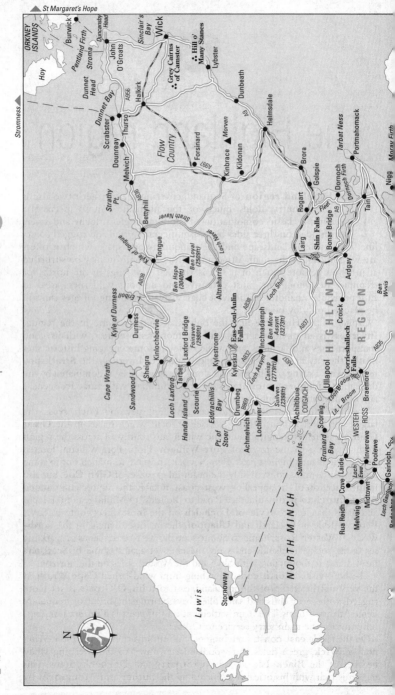

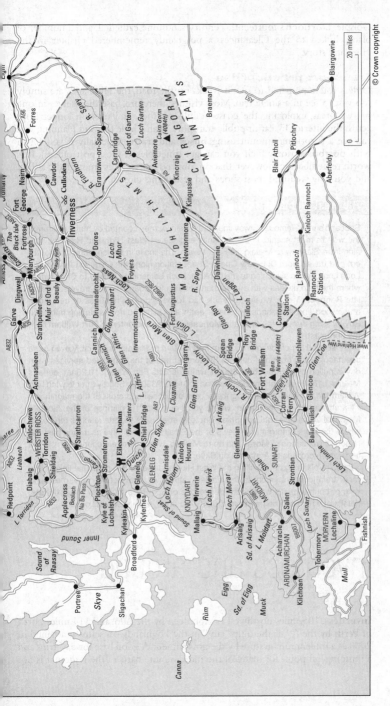

© Crown copyright

0   20 miles

Golspie, **Dornoch**'s fourteenth-century sandstone cathedral, and a number of places linked to the Clearances, a poignantly remembered chapter in the Highland story.

Transport practicalities

Unless you're prepared to spend weeks on the road, the Highlands are simply too vast to see in a single trip. Most visitors, therefore, base themselves in one or two areas, exploring the coast or hills on foot, and making longer hops across the interior by car or public transport. With a little forward planning you can see a surprising amount using **buses** and **trains**, especially if you fill in with **postbuses** (for which you can get timetables at most post offices). It is worth remembering, however, that on Sundays bus services are sporadic at best and you may well find most shops and restaurants closed.

The West Highland Railway

Scotland's most famous railway line, and a train journey counted by many as among the world's most scenic, is the brilliantly engineered **West Highland Railway**, running from Glasgow to Mallaig via Fort William. The line is in two sections: the southern part travels from **Glasgow** Queen Street station along the Clyde estuary and up Loch Long before switching to the banks of Loch Lomond on its way to **Crianlarich**, where the train divides with one section heading for Oban. The line traverses desolate **Rannoch Moor**, where the track had to be laid on a mattress of tree roots, brushwood and thousands of tons of earth and ashes, before swinging into Glen Roy, passing through the dramatic **Monessie Gorge** and entering **Fort William** from the northeast.

The second leg of the journey, from Fort William to Mallaig, is arguably even more spectacular, and from mid-June to September one of the scheduled services each day is pulled by the **Jacobite Steam Train** (departs Fort William 10.20am, departs Mallaig 2.10pm; day return £22; book on ☏01463/239026). Shortly after leaving Fort William the railway travels along the shores of Locheil and crosses the magnificent 21-arch viaduct at **Glenfinnan**, where you'll also catch a glimpse of the Jacobite Memorial at the head of Loch Shiel. Not long afterwards the line reaches the coast, where there are unforgettable views of the Small Isles and Skye as it runs past the famous silver sands of **Morar** and up to **Mallaig**, where there are connections to the ferry which crosses to Armadale on Skye.

If you're planning on travelling the West Highland line, and in particular linking it to other train journeys (such as the similarly attractive route between Inverness and Kyle of Lochalsh), it's worth considering one of ScotRail's multi-day **rover tickets**, details of which can be had from ☏0845/755 0033, ⓦwww.scotrail.co.uk.

Inverness and around

Inverness, 105 miles northwest of Aberdeen by the A96, and 114 miles north of Perth by the A9, is the only "city" in the Highlands – a status it attained in 2000 as a millennium gesture by the government. A good base for day-trips and a jumping-off point for many of the more remote parts of the region, it is not a compelling place to stay for long and inevitably you are drawn to the attractions of sea and mountains beyond. The approach to the city on the A9 over the barren Monadhliath Mountains from Perth and Aviemore provides a spectacular introduction to the district, with the **Great Glen** to the left, stretching southwest towards Fort William and, beyond, the massed peaks of Glen Affric. To the north is the huge, rounded form of Ben Wyvis, whilst to the east lies the **Moray Firth**, boasting a lovely coastline and some of the region's best castles and historic sites. The gentle, undulating green landscape is well tended and tranquil, a fertile contrast to the windswept moorland and mountains that almost surround it.

A string of worthwhile sights punctuates the approaches to Inverness along the main route from Aberdeen. The low-key holiday resort of **Nairn**, with its long white-sand beaches and championship golf course, stands within striking distance of several monuments, including the whimsical **Cawdor Castle**, featured in Shakespeare's *Macbeth*, and **Fort George**, one of several impressive Hanoverian bastions erected in the wake of the Jacobite rebellion. The infamous battle and ensuing massacre that ended Bonnie Prince Charlie's uprising took place on the outskirts of Inverness at **Culloden**, where a small visitor centre and memorial stones beside a heather-clad moor recall the gruesome events of 1746.

Inverness

Straddling a nexus of major road and rail routes, **INVERNESS** is the busy and prosperous hub of the Highlands, and an inevitable port of call if you're exploring the region by public transport. **Buses** and **trains** leave for communities right across the far north of Scotland, and it isn't uncommon for people from as far afield as Thurso, Durness and Kyle of Lochalsh to travel down for a day's shopping here – Britain's most northerly chain-store centre. Though boasting few conventional sights, the city's setting on the banks of the River Ness is appealing.

Arrival, information and accommodation

Inverness **airport** (☎01667/464000) is at Dalcross, seven miles east of the city; from here, bus #11 (Mon–Sat every 1hr–1hr 30min; 20min; £2.50) goes into town, while a **taxi** costs around £10. The **bus station** (☎01463/233371) and **train station** (☎0845/748 4950) both lie just off Academy Street to the east of the centre. The **tourist office** (June–Aug Mon–Fri 9am–6pm, Sat & Sun 9.30am–5pm; mid-July to Aug Mon–Fri until 8pm; rest of year Mon–Fri 9am–5pm, Sat 10am–4pm; ☎01463/234353) is in a 1960s block on Castle Wynd, just five minutes' walk from the station. It stocks a wide range of literature on the area, including free maps, and the friendly staff can book local accommodation for a £3 fee.

Inverness is one of the few places in the Highlands where you're unlikely to have problems finding **accommodation**, although in July and August you'll have to book ahead. Good places to look for B&Bs include both banks of the river south of the Ness Bridge, and Kenneth Street and its offshoots on the west side of the river.

Inverness is the departure point for a range of day **tours** and **cruises**. Guide Friday run an open-topped double-decker tour of **Inverness** itself (May–Sept daily every 45min; 30min; £5.50), which you can hop on and off all day; the bus also goes out to **Culloden** (1hr 20min; £7.50). You can buy tickets on the buses, which leave from Bridge Street near the tourist office, or at Guide Friday's office in the train station (May–Sept daily 9am–6pm). An entertaining if slightly bizarre **Terror Tour** takes groups on foot around Inverness town centre (daily 7pm from the tourist office; £5.50), with grisly tales told along the way of ghosts, torture and witches. There are various **Loch Ness** tours leaving from the tourist office, the most original and personal of which are Tony Harmsworth's Discover Loch Ness (☎01456/450168 or ☎0800/731 5564, ⓦwww.discoverlochness.com). Longer boat trips on Loch Ness are run morning and afternoon by Jacobite Cruises (April–Oct; ☎01463/233999).

To explore the northwest, Dearman Coaches have a daily service to **Ullapool**, **Lochinver**, **Durness**, **Smoo Cave** and back which stops at several hostels en route (June–Sept Mon–Sat; £17.50; or you can buy a £25 rover ticket valid for six days).

Enjoyable trips up to **John O'Groats** and back in a day, with the chance to see puffins and visit prehistoric sites, are run by Puffin Express (☎01463/717181, ⓦwww.puffinexpress.co.uk), who also put together a package which includes an overnight stop on **Orkney**. You can get to the islands and back with a gruelling full-day whistle-stop tour on the Orkney Bus, which leaves Inverness bus station every day during the summer (£44; advance bookings may be made at the tourist office or on ☎01955/611353).

See p.1201 for details of **dolphin**-spotting cruises on the Moray Firth.

Hotels and B&Bs

Brae Ness Ness Bank ☎01463/712266, ⓦwww.braenesshotel.co.uk. A homely Georgian hotel with only ten rooms (all non-smoking) over-looking the river and St Andrews Cathedral. April–Oct. ④

Edenview 26 Ness Bank ☎01463/234397. Very pleasant B&B in a riverside location as good as the more expensive hotels, five minutes' walk from the centre. Non-smoking. ③

Ivybank Guest House 28 Old Edinburgh Rd ☎01463/232796. A grand Georgian home just up the hill from the castle, with open fires and a love-ly wooden interior. ②

Macrae House 24 Ness Bank ☎01463/243658, ⓦwww.macraehouse.co.uk. Right on the river, friendly, and with large, comfortable rooms. Non-smoking. ②

Melrose Villa 35 Kenneth St ☎01463/233745. Very family-friendly, with excellent breakfasts. Three singles as well as doubles and twins, with most rooms en suite. ①

Royal Highland 18 Academy St ☎01463/231926, ⓦwww.royalhighlandhotel.co.uk. The old station hotel, dripping with the grandeur of the golden days of Highland travel. Perfect for those en route to their grouse moor. ⑤

Hostels

Bazpackers Top of Castle Street ☎01463/717663. The most cosy and relaxed of the city's hostels, with thirty beds including two double rooms and a twin; some dorms are mixed. Has good views and a garden, which is used for barbe-cues, as well as the usual cooking facilities. Non-smoking.

Inverness Student Hotel 8 Culduthel Rd ☎01463/236556. A busy fifty-bed hostel with the usual facilities and fine views over the river. Part of the Macbackpackers group, so expect minibus tours to pull in most days.

SYHA hostel Victoria Drive, off Millburn Road, about three-quarters of a mile east of the centre ☎01463/231771, ⓦwww.syha.org.uk. One of SYHA's flagship hostels, fully equipped with large kitchens and communal areas, eco-friendly facili-ties and ten four-bed family rooms among the 188-bed total, but all rather soulless.

The Town

The logical place to begin a tour of Inverness is the central **Town House** on the High Street. Built in 1878, this Gothic pile hosted Prime Minister Lloyd George's emergency meeting to discuss the Irish crisis in September 1921, and now accommodates council offices. Looming above the Town House and

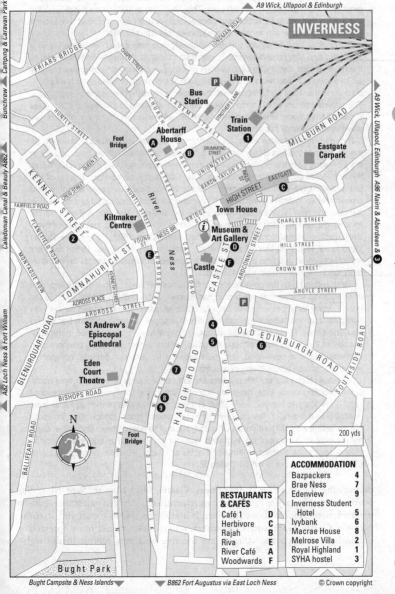

RESTAURANTS
& CAFÉS

Café 1	D
Herbivore	C
Rajah	B
Riva	E
River Café	A
Woodwards	F

ACCOMMODATION

Bazpackers	4
Brae Ness	7
Edenview	9
Inverness Student Hotel	5
Ivybank	6
Macrae House	8
Melrose Villa	2
Royal Highland	1
SYHA hostel	3

0   200 yds

© Crown copyright

To much of the world, **tartan** is synonymous with Scotland. It's the natural choice of packaging for Scottish exports from shortbread to Sean Connery, and when the Scottish football team travels abroad to play a fixture, the high-spirited "Tartan Army" of fans are never far behind. Not surprisingly, tartan is big business for the tourist industry and every year, hundreds of visitors return home from Scotland clutching tartan souvenirs (often manufactured overseas) tied with tartan ribbon, or lengths of cloth inspiringly named Loch This, Ben That or Glen Something-Else. Yet the truth is that romantic fiction and commercial interest have enclosed this ancient Highland art form within an almost insurmountable wall of myth.

The original form of tartan, the kind that long ago was called "**Helande**", was a fine, hard and almost showerproof cloth spun in Highland villages from the wool of the native sheep, dyed with preparations of local plants and with patterns woven by artist-weavers. It was worn as a huge single piece of cloth, or **plaid**, which was belted around the waist and draped over the upper body, rather like a knee-length toga. The natural colours of old tartans were clear but soft, and the broken pattern gave superb camouflage, unlike modern versions, where garish, clashing colours are often used to create impact.

The myth-makers were about four centuries ahead of themselves in dressing up the warriors of the film *Braveheart* in plaid: in fact tartan did not become popular in the Lowlands until the beginning of the eighteenth century, when it was adopted as the anti-Union badge of the **Jacobites**. After Culloden, a ban on the wearing of tartan in the Highlands lasted some 25 years; in that time it became a fondly held emblem for emigrant Highlanders in the colonies and was incorporated into the uniforms of the new Highland regiments in the British Army. Then Sir Walter Scott set to work glamourizing the clans, dressing George IV in a kilt (and, just as controversially, flesh-coloured tights) for his visit to Edinburgh in 1822. By the time Queen Victoria set the royal seal of approval on both the Highlands and tartan with her extended annual holidays at Balmoral, the concept of tartan as formal dress rather than rough Highland wear was assured.

Hand-in-hand with the gentrification of the kilt came "rules" about the correct form of attire, and the idea that every clan had its own distinguishing tartan. To have the right to wear tartan, one had to belong, albeit remotely, to a clan, and so the way was paved for the "what's-my-tartan?" lists that appear in tartan picture books and souvenir shops. Great feats of genealogical gymnastics were performed in the concoction of these lists; where these left gaps, a more recent marketing phenomenon of themed tartans developed, with new patterns for different districts, companies and even football teams being produced.

Scotsmen today will commonly wear the **kilt** for weddings and other formal occasions; properly made kilts, however – comprising some four yards of 100-percent wool – are likely to set you back £300 or more, with the rest of the regalia at least doubling that figure. If the contents of your sporran don't stretch that far, most places selling kilts will rent outfits on a daily basis. The best place to find better quality material is a recognized Highland outfitter rather than a souvenir shop: in Inverness, try the Scottish Kiltmaker Centre at Hector Russell's (see opposite) or Chisholms Kiltmakers at 47–51 Castle St.

dominating the horizon is **Inverness Castle** (mid–May to Sept Mon–Sat 10am–5pm; £3), a predominantly nineteenth-century red sandstone edifice perched picturesquely above the river. It houses the Sheriff Court and, in summer, the **Castle Garrison Encounter**, an entertaining and noisy interactive exhibition in which the visitor plays the role of a new recruit in the eighteenth-century Hanoverian army. Around 7pm during the summer, a lone piper clad in full Highland garb performs for tourists on the castle esplanade.

Below the castle, the **Inverness Museum and Art Gallery** on Castle Wynd (Mon–Sat 9am–5pm; free) gives a good general overview of the development of the Highlands. Informative sections on geology, geography and history cover the ground floor, while upstairs you'll find a muddled selection of silver, taxidermy, weapons and bagpipes, alongside a mediocre art gallery.

Just across Ness Bridge from Bridge Street is the **Kiltmaker Centre** in the Hector Russell shop (mid-May to Sept Mon–Sat 9am–10pm, Sun 10am–5pm; rest of year Mon–Sat 9am–5.30pm; £2). Entered through the factory shop, a small visitor centre sets out everything you ever wanted to know about tartan, and on weekdays you can see various tartan products being made in the workshop. The finished products are, of course, on sale in the showroom downstairs, along with all manner of Highland knitwear, woven woollies and Harris tweed.

Rising from the west bank directly opposite the castle, **St Andrew's Episcopal Cathedral** was intended by its architects to be one of the grandest buildings in Scotland. However, funds ran out before the giant twin spires of the original design could be completed. From here, you can wander a mile or so upriver to the peaceful **Ness Islands**, an attractive, informal public park reached and linked by footbridges.

Eating, drinking and nightlife

Inverness has lots of **eating** places, including some good places for **picnic food**: The Gourmet's Lair, 8 Union St, and Lettuce Eat on Drummond Street.

Restaurants

Café 1 75 Castle St ☎01463/226200. Impressive contemporary Scottish cooking using good local ingredients in a bistro-style setting. Closed Sun. Moderate to expensive.

Herbivore 38 Eastgate ☎01463/231075. Laid-back, modern vegetarian restaurant open right through the day and for decent evening meals. Moderate.

Rajah Post Office Avenue ☎01463/237190. An excellent Indian restaurant, tucked away in a backstreet basement. Moderate.

Riva 4–6 Ness Walk ☎01463/237377. Reasonably authentic modern Italian bistro/café beside the river with antipasta, decent mains and good coffee and cakes. Moderate. Upstairs, inexpensive pasta dishes can be had at *Pazzo's Pasta Bar* (evenings only; closed Sun & Mon).

River Café and Restaurant 10 Bank St ☎01463/714884. Healthy wholefood lunches and evening meals, with a great selection of freshly baked cakes and good coffee. Inexpensive to moderate.

Woodwards 99 Castle St ☎01463/709809. Classy and interesting Modern Scottish cuisine; reasonably formal and upmarket. Expensive.

Nightlife and entertainment

The liveliest **nightlife** in Inverness revolves around the pubs. The far end of Academy Street has a cluster of good **pubs**; the public bar of the *Phoenix* is the most original town-centre place, though *Blackfriars* across the street has a bit more going for it with entertainment seven nights a week, including ceilidhs popular with Australian backpackers searching for their roots. The local **folk music** scene, always lively and authentic, is still recovering from the closure of the widely respected Balnain House. There are normally gigs happening somewhere in Inverness during the week, and particularly at weekends: look out for local adverts or check with the tourist office to find out what's going on.

Listings

Bike rental Barney's, 35 Castle St
☎01463/232249.

Bookshops Leakey's, Greyfriars' Hall on Church
Street, is a great spot to browse for second-hand
books, with a café inside and a warming wood
stove in winter; James Thin, 29 Union St, has an
excellent range of Scottish books and maps; and
Waterstone's is at 50–52 High St.

Car rental Budget is on Railway Terrace, behind
the train station (☎01463/713333); Europcar has
an office on Telfer St (☎01463/235337); Arnold
Clark is at 47–49 Harbour Rd (☎01463/236200);
Thrifty is at 33 Harbour Rd (☎01463/224466); and
Sharps Reliable Wrecks is based at Station Square
(☎01463/236684) as well as the airport.

Cinemas The Eden Court Theatre and the
attached Riverside Screen, on the banks of the

Ness, host touring theatre productions, concerts
and films; La Scala (☎01463/233302) on
Strother's Lane, just off Academy Street, has two
screens; Warner Village (☎01463/711175), on the
A96 Nairn road about two miles from the town
centre, boasts seven screens.

Hospital Raigmore Hospital (☎01463/704000) on
the southeastern outskirts of town close to the A9.

Internet MTC, 2 Grant St (Mon–Thurs 9am–5pm,
Fri 9am–4.30pm). There are also two terminals in
the tourist office.

Post office 14–16 Queensgate (Mon–Thurs
9am–5.30pm, Fri 9.30am–5.30pm, Sat 9am–6pm;
☎0845/722 3344).

Taxis Culloden Taxis (☎01463/790000); Rank
Radio Taxis (☎01463/221111).

East of Inverness

East of Inverness lies the fertile, sheltered coastal strip of the **Moray Firth** and its hinterland. Primary among the sites is **Culloden**, the most poignant battle-field site in Scotland, where Bonnie Prince Charlie's Jacobites were routed in 1746. Further east are **Cawdor Castle** and **Fort George**, two of the best preserved fortified structures in the Highlands. **Nairn**, the main town of the district, has a pretty harbour as well as appealing walks and cycle routes.

The overloaded A96 traverses this stretch and the region is well served by public transport, with all the historic sites and castles accessible on day-trips from Inverness, or en route to Aberdeen. To get to Fort George, Cawdor Castle and Culloden you can juggle the Highland County Tourist Trail buses (#11, #12 and #13; £6 for a day rover ticket) which depart from Queens Gate in Inverness.

Culloden

The windswept moorland of **CULLODEN** (site open all year; free), five miles east of Inverness, witnessed the last-ever battle on British soil when, on April 16, 1746, the Jacobite cause was finally subdued – a turning point in the history of the Scottish nation.

The second Jacobite rebellion had begun on August 19, 1745, with the raising of the Stuarts' standard at **Glenfinnan** on the west coast (see p.1220). Shortly after, Edinburgh fell into Jacobite hands, and Bonnie Prince Charlie began his march on London. The English had appointed the ambitious young Duke of Cumberland to command their forces, and his pursuit, together with bad weather and lack of funds, eventually forced the Jacobites to retreat north. They ended up at Culloden, where, ill-fed and exhausted after a pointless night march, they were hopelessly outnumbered by the English. The open, flat ground of Culloden Moor was totally unsuitable for the Highlanders' style of courageous but undisciplined fighting, which needed steep hills and lots of

The **Moray Firth**, a great wedge-shaped bay forming the eastern coastline of the Highlands, is one of only three areas of UK waters that supports a resident population of **dolphins**. Over a hundred of these beautiful, intelligent marine mammals live in the estuary, the most northerly breeding ground for this particular species – the bottle-nosed dolphin (*Tursiops truncatus*) – in Europe, and you stand a good chance of spotting a few, either from the shore or a boat.

During the summer, herds of thirty to forty have been known to congregate in the Moray Firth; no one is exactly sure why, although experts believe the annual gatherings, which take place between late June and August, may be connected to the breeding cycle. Dolphin-spotting has become something of a craze in the Moray Firth area. One of the best places in Scotland, if not in Europe, to look for them is **Chanonry Point**, on the Black Isle (see p.1241) – a spit of sand protruding into a narrow, deep channel, where converging currents bring fish close to the surface, and thus the dolphins close to shore; the hour or so before high tide is the most likely time to see them. **Kessock Bridge**, one mile north of Inverness, is another prime dolphin-spotting location. You can go all the way down to the beach at the small village of North Kessock, underneath the road bridge, where there's a decent place to have a drink at the pub in the *North Kessock Hotel*, or you can stop above the village in a car park just off the A9 at the visitor centre and listening post (see p.1241).

In addition, several companies run dolphin-spotting **boat trips** around the Moray Firth. Reputable operators approved by the Dolphin Space Programme's Accreditation Scheme include Majestic Cruises, Inverness (☏01463/731661); Benbola Tours, 21 Great Eastern Rd, Portessie, Buckie (☏01542/832289); Macaulay Charters, Inverness (☏01463/751263); Moray Firth Cruises, Shore Street, Inverness (☏01463/717900); and Dolphin Écosse, Bank House, High Street, Cromarty (☏01381/600323). Half-day trips cost around £20.

cover to provide the element of surprise, and they were routed. After the battle, in which 1500 Highlanders were slaughtered (many of them as they lay wounded on the battlefield), Bonnie Prince Charlie fled west to the hills and islands, where loyal Highlanders sheltered and protected him. He eventually escaped to France, leaving his erstwhile supporters to their fate – and, in effect, ushering in the end of the clan system. The clans were disarmed, the wearing of tartan and playing of bagpipes forbidden, and the chiefs became landlords greedy for higher and higher rents. The battle also unleashed an orgy of violent reprisals on Scotland, as unruly English troops raped and pillaged their way across the region; within a century, the Highland way of life had changed out of all recognition.

Today you can walk freely around the battle site; flags show the positions of the two armies, and **clan graves** are marked by simple headstones. The **Field of the English**, for many years unmarked, is a mass grave for the fifty or so English soldiers who died. The **visitor centre** itself (daily: April–Oct 9am–6pm; Nov–March 10am–4pm; closed early to mid-Jan; NTS; £4) provides background information through detailed displays and a film show, as well as a short play set on the day of the battle presented by local actors (June–Sept only; included in admission fee), or you can take the evocative hour-long guided **walking tour** (June–Sept daily; £3).

The site is served by Guide Friday **buses** from Bridge Street in Inverness (May–Sept; 10 daily from 10am; last return bus leaves Culloden at 5.45pm) and Highland Country bus #12 from Inverness post office (Mon–Sat 8 daily).

If you're visiting Culloden with your own transport, a short detour is worthwhile to the **CLAVA CAIRNS**, an impressive collection of prehistoric burial chambers clustered around the south bank of the River Nairn, a mile southeast of the battlefield. Erected some time before 2000 BC, the cairns, which are encircled by standing stones in a spinney of mature beech trees, are of two different kinds: one large and one very small **ring-cairn**, and two **passage graves**, which have a narrow passageway from edge to centre.

Cawdor Castle

The pretty, if slightly self-satisfied village of **CAWDOR**, eight miles east of Culloden, is the site of **Cawdor Castle** (May to mid-Oct daily 10am–5.30pm; £5.90; gardens only £3), a setting intimately linked to Shakespeare's *Macbeth*: the fulfilment of the witches' prediction that Macbeth was to become Thane of Cawdor sets off his tragic desire to be king. Though visitors arrive here in their droves each summer because of the site's literary associations, the castle, which dates from the early fourteenth century, could not possibly have witnessed the grisly historical events on which the Bard's drama was based. However, the immaculately restored monument – a fairy-tale affair of towers, turrets, hidden passageways, dungeons, gargoyles and crenellations whimsically shooting off from the original keep – is still well worth a visit.

As you explore, look out for the **Thorn Tree Room**, a vaulted chamber complete with the remains of an ancient holly tree carbon-dated to 1372 – an ancient pagan fertility symbol believed to ward off fairies and evil spirits. The **grounds** of the castle are impressive, with an attractive walled garden, a topiarian maze, a small golf course, a putting green and nature trails.

Fort George

Eight miles of undulating coastal farmland separate Cawdor Castle from **Fort George** (April–Sept daily 9.30am–6.30pm; Oct–March Mon–Sat 9.30am–4.30pm, Sun 2–4.30pm; HS; £4.50), an old Hanoverian bastion with walls a mile long, considered by military architectural historians to be one of the finest fortifications in Europe. Crowning a sandy spit that juts into the middle of the Moray Firth, it was built between 1747 and 1769 as a base for George II's army, in case the Highlanders should attempt to rekindle the Jacobite flame.

Apart from the sweeping panoramic **views** across the firth from its ramparts, the main incentive to visit Fort George is the **Regimental Museum** of the Queen's Own Highlanders. Displayed in polished glass cases is a predictable array of regimental silver, coins, moth-eaten uniforms and medals, along with some macabre war trophies, ranging from blood-stained nineteenth-century Sudanese battle robes to Iraqi gas masks gleaned in the Gulf War. The heroic deeds performed by various recipients of Victoria Crosses make compelling reading. The **chapel** is also worth a look – squat and solid outside, and all light and grace within.

Nairn and around

One of the driest and sunniest places in the whole of Scotland, **NAIRN**, sixteen miles east of Inverness, began its days as a peaceful community of fishermen and farmers. The former spoke Gaelic, the latter English, allowing James VI to boast that a town in his kingdom was so large that people at one end of the main street could not understand those at the other. It boasts two championship golf courses, and Thomas Telford's **harbour** is filled with leisure craft rather than fishing boats. Nearby, amid the huddled streets of old Fishertown – the town centre is known as new Fishertown – is the tiny **Fishertown Museum** (June–Sept Mon–Sat 10.30am–12.30pm; free).

Nairn's helpful **tourist office** is at 62 King St (June–Aug daily 9am–6pm; Easter–May, Sept & Oct Mon–Sat 10am–5pm; ☎01667/452753). For **accommodation**, try Ben & Iris Murray at 53 King St in Old Fishertown (☎01667/453798; ●), whose small B&B is welcoming and refreshingly kitsch-free. *Greenlawns*, 13 Seafield St (☎01667/452738, ⓦwww.greenlawns.uk.com; ●), is a spacious and friendly B&B with most rooms en suite.

Strathspey and the Cairngorms

Rising high in the heather-clad hills above remote Loch Laggan, forty miles due south of Inverness, the **River Spey**, Scotland's second-longest river, drains northeast towards the Moray Firth through one of the Highlands' most spell-binding valleys. Famous for its ancient forests, salmon fishing and ospreys, Strathspey describes the broad river valley between the rolling Monadhliath mountains and the ice-sculpted **Cairngorm** massif. The Cairngorm range, Britain's most extensive mountainous massif, unique in supporting sub-arctic tundra on its high plateau, is scheduled to become Scotland's second **national park** some time in 2002. Note that Strathspey is distinct from Speyside, located further downstream to the north and famous for its whiskies, which is described on p.1182.

Outdoor enthusiasts flock to Strathspey year-round to take advantage of the superb hiking, water sports and winter snows, aided by the fact that the area is easily accessible from both the Central Belt and Inverness by road and rail. Of Strathspey's scattered settlements, **Aviemore** absorbs the largest number of visitors, particularly in midwinter when it metamorphoses into the UK's busiest ski resort. The village itself isn't up to much, but the 4000ft summit plateau of the Cairngorm is often snowcapped, providing stunning mountain scenery on a grand scale. The planned Georgian town of **Grantown-on-Spey** makes a good alternative base for summer visitors, with similar facilities and more charm than Aviemore. Further upriver, the sedate towns of **Kingussie** and **Newtonmore** are older-established holiday centres, popular more with anglers and grouse hunters than canoeists and climbers. Rather unusually for Scotland, the area boasts a wide choice of good-quality accommodation, particularly in the budget market, with various easy-going hostels run by and for outdoor enthusiasts.

Aviemore and around

The once-sleepy village of **AVIEMORE** was first developed as a ski and tourism resort in the mid-1960s and, over the years, it fell victim to profiteering developers with scant regard for the needs of the local community. Although a large-scale facelift has removed some of the architectural eyesores of that era, the settlement remains dominated by a string of soulless shopping centres and fairly tacky shops surrounding an attractive Victorian railway station. That said, Aviemore is well equipped with services and facilities for visitors to the area and is the most convenient base for the Cairngorms, benefits which for most folk far outweigh its lack of aesthetic appeal.

The main attractions of Aviemore are its outdoor pursuits, though train enthusiasts are drawn to the restored **Strathspey Steam Railway**, which chugs the short distance between Aviemore and Boat of Garten village five times daily through the summer (June–Sept; less regular service at other times; call ☎01479/810725 for details). Another unusual form of transportation is the **Cairngorm funicular railway** (every 10–20min; £7.50), which in 2001 replaced the main chair lift as the principal means of transportation to the top of the ski area. A highly controversial, £15 million scheme, it whisks skiers in

---

Walks around Aviemore

Ordnance Survey Landranger Map No. 36.

Walking of all grades is a highlight of the Aviemore area, though before setting out you should heed the usual safety guidelines. These are particularly important if you want to climb to the high tops, which include a number of Scotland's loftiest peaks. However, as well as the high mountain trails, there are some lovely and well-signposted **low-level walks** in the area. It takes an hour or so to complete the gentle circular walk around pretty **Loch an Eilean** (with its ruined castle) in the Rothiemurchus Estate, beginning at the end of the backroad that turns east off the B970 two miles south of Aviemore. The helpful estate **visitor centres** at the lochside and by the roadside at Inverdruie provide more information on the many woodland trails that crisscross this area. A longer walk through this estate, famous for its atmospheric native woodland of gnarled Caledonian pines and shimmering birch trees, starts at the near end of **Loch Morlich**. Cross the river by the bridge and follow the dirt road, turning off after about twenty minutes to follow the signs to Aviemore. The path goes through beautiful pine woods and past tumbling burns, and you can branch off to Coylumbridge and Loch an Eilean. Unless you're properly prepared for a 25-mile hike, don't take the track to the **Lairig Ghru**, a famous old cattle drovers' route through a dramatic cleft in the mountain range which eventually brings you out near Braemar on the far side of the Cairngorm range.

Another good shortish (half-day) walk leads along a well-surfaced forestry track from *Glenmore Lodge* up towards the **Ryvoan Pass**, taking in An Lochan Uaine, known as the "Green Loch" and living up to its name, with amazing colours that range from turquoise to slate grey depending on the weather. The track narrows once past the loch and leads east towards Deeside, so retrace your steps if you don't want a major trek. The **Glenmore Forest Park Visitor Centre** by the roadside at the turn-off to *Glenmore Lodge* is the starting point for the 3-hour round-trip climb of Meall a' Bhuachaille (2654ft), which offers excellent views and is usually accessible year-round. The centre has information on other trails in this section of the forest.

The **Speyside Way** (see p.1181), the long-distance footpath which begins on the Moray Firth coast at Buckie and follows the course of the Spey through the heart of whisky country, has recently been extended to Aviemore. A pleasant day-trip involves walking from Aviemore to Boat of Garten, on to the RSPB osprey sanctuary at Loch Garten, and returning on the Strathspey Steam Railway.

winter, and tourists in summer, from the Coire Cas car park up to an altitude of 3600 feet. At the top is an exhibition/interpretation area and restaurant from which spectacular views can be had on clear days, though you should note that there is no access beyond the confines of the centre and its open-air viewing terrace unless you're embarking on winter skiing; anyone wanting to walk on the sub-arctic Cairngorm plateau will have to trudge up from the car park at the bottom.

Summer activities

In summer, the main activities around Aviemore are **walking** (see box) and **water sports**, though there are great opportunities to do most things from mountain biking to fly fishing. There are two centres that offer sailing, windsurfing and canoeing: the Loch Morlich Watersports Centre (℡01479/861221, Ⓦwww.aviemore.co.uk/lochmorlich), at the east end of the loch five miles or so east of Aviemore, rents equipment and offers tuition in a lovely setting with a sandy beach, while six miles up-valley near Kincraig, the Loch Insh Watersports Centre (see p.1207) offers the same facilities in equally beautiful surroundings. It also rents mountain bikes, boats for loch fishing, and gives ski instruction on a 164ft dry slope.

Riding and **pony trekking** are on offer up and down the valley: try Ingrid at Alvie Stables near Kincraig (℡01540/651409), or the Carrbridge Trekking Centre, Station Road, Carrbridge, a few miles north of Aviemore (℡01479/841602).

Fishing is very much part of the local scene; you can fish for trout and salmon on the River Spey, and the Rothiemurchus Estate has a stocked trout-fishing loch at **Inverdruie**, where success is virtually guaranteed. Instruction and rod rental is available from the centre beside the loch.

The area is also great for **mountain biking**, with both Rothiemurchus and Glenmore estates more progressive in their attitude to the sport than many. The Rothiemurchus visitor centre at Inverdruie has route maps, and you can also rent bikes here, while Bothy Bikes (℡01479/810111), in the Aviemore Shopping Centre beside the train station on Grampian Road, rents out good-quality mountain bikes with front suspension, as well as offering advice and guided bike tours. For other outdoor equipment, in particular **climbing** and **hill-walking** gear, try Mountain Supplies in Aviemore (℡01479/810903).

Winter activities

Scottish **skiing** on a commercial level first really took off in Aviemore. By continental European and North American standards it's all on a tiny scale, but occasionally snow, sun and lack of crowds coincide and you can have a great day. February and March are usually the best times, but there's a chance of decent snow at any time between mid-November and April. Lots of places – not just in Aviemore itself – sell or rent equipment; for a rundown of ski schools and rental facilities in the area, check out the tourist office's *Ski Scotland* brochure or Ⓦwww.ski.scotland.net.

The **Cairngorm Ski Area**, about eight miles southeast of Aviemore, above Loch Morlich in Glen More Forest Park, is well served during winter by buses from Aviemore. You can rent skis, boards and other equipment from the Day Lodge at the foot of the ski area (℡01479/861261, Ⓦwww.cairngormmountain.com), which also has a shop, a bar and restaurant, and the base station for the **funicular railway**, the principal means of getting to the top of the ski slopes. Various types of ski pass are available from here – in person, by phone or online. If there's lots of snow, the area around **Loch Morlich** and into the

Rothiemurchus Estate provides enjoyable cross-country skiing through lovely woods, beside rushing burns and even over frozen lochs.

For a crash-course in surviving Scottish winters, you could do worse than try a week at the National Outdoor Training Centre at *Glenmore Lodge* (see below) in the heart of the Glenmore Forest Park at the east end of Loch Morlich.

Practicalities

Aviemore's businesslike **tourist office** is just south of the train station on the main drag, Grampian Road (April–Oct Mon–Fri 9am–5.30pm, Sat 10am–5pm, Sun 10am–4pm; Nov–March Mon–Fri 9am–5pm, Sat 10am–5pm; ☎01479/810363). It offers an accommodation booking service and reams of leaflets on local attractions.

There's no shortage of **accommodation** locally. On Grampian Road in Aviemore, *MacKenzies Hotel* (☎01479/810672, ✉mackhotel@aol.com; ➋) is welcoming and family-friendly, while *Ravenscraig* (☎01479/810278, ✉ravenscraig@aol.com; ➋) offers similarly good value. The grandest place in the area is *Corrour House Hotel* at Inverdruie, two miles southeast of Aviemore (☎01479/810220, ⓦwww.corrourhousehotel.com; ➎). Aviemore's large SYHA **hostel** (☎01479/810345, ⓦwww.syha.org.uk; £13.25), is close to the tourist office, while the bunkhouse above Mountain Supplies in the centre of Aviemore (☎01479/810903, ⓦwww.mountainman.co.uk) has good facilities and no curfew. Towards the Cairngorms, there's another SYHA hostel at Loch Morlich (☎01479/861238, ⓦwww.syha.org.uk), as well as excellent accommodation in twin rooms (with shared facilities) at *Glenmore Lodge* (☎01479/861276, ⓦwww.glenmorelodge.org.uk; ➊) – full use of their superb facilities, which include a pool, weights room and indoor climbing wall is included. Two of the best **campsites** are the Campgrounds of Scotland site at Coylumbridge (☎01479/812800) and the Forestry Enterprise site at Glenmore (☎01479/861271).

The *Old Bridge Inn* on the east side of the railway, below the bridge, serves delicious **food** and real ales in a mellow, cosy setting, or you can try *Café Mambo*, in Aviemore Shopping Centre on Grampian Road, with its bright, funky decor and cheerful burger'n'chips-style menu.

Loch Garten and around

The **Abernethy Forest RSPB Reserve** on the shore of **LOCH GARTEN**, seven miles northeast of Aviemore and eight miles south of Grantown-on-Spey, is famous as the nesting site of one of Britain's rarest birds. A little over fifty years ago, the **osprey**, known in North America as the fish hawk, had completely disappeared from the British Isles. Then, in 1954, a single pair of these exquisite white-and-brown raptors mysteriously reappeared and built a nest in a tree half a mile or so from the loch. Although efforts were made to keep the exact location secret, one year's eggs fell victim to a gang of thieves, and thereafter the area became the centre of an effective high-security operation. Now the birds are well established not only here but elsewhere, and there are believed to be up to 150 pairs nesting across the Highlands. The best time to visit is between late April and August, when the ospreys return from West Africa to nest and the RSPB opens an **observation centre** (daily 10am–6pm; £2.50), complete with powerful telescopes and CCTV monitoring of the nest. This is the place to come to get a glimpse of osprey chicks in their nest; you'll be luckier to see the birds perform their trademark swoop over water to pluck a fish out with their talons.

Loch Garten is about a mile and a half west of **BOAT OF GARTEN** village: from the village, if you cross the Spey then take the Grantown road, the reserve is signposted to the right. Boat of Garten has a couple of good **accommodation** options: *Fraoch Lodge*, 15 Deshar Rd (℡01479/831331, ⓦwww .scotmountain.co.uk) is an excellent hostel with bunkhouse and twin rooms (❶), and provides high-quality home-cooked meals along with good facilities. Alternatively, *Craigard House Hotel* (℡01479/831423; ❸) offers stylish accommodation in an old hunting lodge, and includes a restaurant serving local game and fish which is open to non-residents.

Kincraig

At **KINCRAIG**, six miles southwest of Aviemore on the B9152 towards Kingussie, there are a couple of unusual encounters with animals which offer a memorable diversion if you're not setting off on outdoor pursuits. While the style of the **Highland Wildlife Park** (daily: June–Aug 10am–7pm; April, May, Sept & Oct closes 6pm; Nov–March closes 4pm; last entry 2hr before closing; in snowy conditions call in advance; ℡01540/651270; £6.50), with its various captive animals, may not appeal to everyone, it is accredited to the Royal Zoological Society of Scotland and offers a chance to see exotic foreigners such as wolves and bison, as well as many rarely seen natives, including pine martens, capercaillie, wildcat and eagles. Nearby, the engrossing **Working Sheepdogs** show at Leault Farm (open daily; call ℡01540/651310 for the schedule of demonstrations; £3.50) offers the rare opportunity to see a champion shepherd demonstrate how to herd a flock of sheep with up to eight dogs, using whistles and other commands. The fascinating hour-long display also includes geese-herding, a chance to see traditional hand-shearing, and displays on how collie pups are trained.

The Loch Insh Watersports Centre (℡01540/651272, ⓦwww.lochinsh .com), beautifully sited beside the loch, has en-suite **B&B** and self-catering chalets (❶) as well as a handy waterfront café.

Grantown-on-Spey

Buses run from Aviemore and Inverness to the small town of **GRANTOWN-ON-SPEY**, about fifteen miles northeast of Aviemore, which makes a relaxing alternative base for exploring the Strathspey area. Life is concentrated around the central square, with its attractive Georgian architecture, including a small **museum** and resource centre on Burnfield Avenue (Mon–Fri 10am–4pm; £2; ⓦwww.grantown-on-spey.co.uk) which tells the story of the town. The **tourist office** is on the High Street (April–Oct Mon–Fri 9am–5pm, Sat 10am–5pm, Sun 10am–4pm; ℡01479/872773).

As with much of Speyside, there's a decent choice of **accommodation**. For B&B, *Parkburn Guest House* (℡01479/873116; ❷) is welcoming, while, if you're after something more upmarket, head for the large seventeenth-century *Garth Hotel*, at the north end of the square (℡01479/872836; ❸). In the budget range, *Speyside Backpackers* at The Stopover, 16 The Square (℡01479/873514, ⓦwww.scotpackers-hostels.co.uk) has dorms and doubles (❶) with excellent facilities.

Newtonmore and Kingussie

Twelve miles south of Aviemore, close neighbours **NEWTONMORE** and **KINGUSSIE** (pronounced "king-*yoos*-ee") are pleasant towns at the head of the Strathspey Valley separated by a couple of miles of farmland. On the **shinty** field, however, their peaceful co-existence is forgotten and the two become bitter rivals; in recent years Kingussie have been the dominant force in the game, a fierce, homegrown relative of hockey (🌐 www.kingussie.co.uk/shinty).

The chief attraction here is the excellent **Highland Folk Museum** (☎ 01540/661307), split between complementary sites in the two towns. The Kingussie section (April–Sept Mon–Sat 9.30am–5.30pm; winter by appointment; £1 admission covers both sites) contains an absorbing collection of artefacts typical to traditional Highland ways of life, as well as a farming museum, an old smokehouse, a mill, a Hebridean "blackhouse", and a traditional herb and flower garden; most days in summer there's a demonstration of various traditional crafts. The larger outdoor site at Newtonmore (April–Aug daily 10.30am–5.30pm; Sept & Oct Mon–Fri 11am–4.30pm; call for details of weekend opening at other times), tries to create more of a living history museum, with reconstructions of a working croft, a church where recitals on traditional Highland instruments are given through the summer months, and a small village of blackhouses constructed using only authentic tools and materials.

Kingussie is also notable for the ruins of **Ruthven Barracks** (free access), standing east across the river on a hillock. The best-preserved garrison built to pacify the Highlands after the 1715 rebellion, it makes for great exploring by day and is impressively floodlit at night.

Practicalities

Kingussie's friendly **tourist office** is in the same building as the entrance to the Highland Folk Museum, on Duke Street (same hours as museum; ☎ 01540/661297). The Wildcat Centre in Newtonmore (Mon–Fri 9.30am–12.30pm & 2.15–5.15pm, Sat 9.30am–12.30pm) also offers local information and details of walking trails in the area. Bike rental is available at Cairngorm Mountain Tours in Newtonmore. *Dunmhor House* (☎ 01540/661809; ❶) is a good-value **B&B** on the main street in Kingussie, while the best of the local **hostels** are the *Newtonmore Independent Hostel* (☎ 01540/673360, 🌐 www .highlandhostel.co.uk), a welcoming and well-equipped place, and the *Strathspey Mountain Hostel* (☎ 01540/673694), just up the road, which is also of a high standard.

The most ambitious **food** in the area is served at the *Cross* restaurant, in a converted tweed mill on Tweed Mill Brae in Kingussie (☎ 01540/661166, 🌐 www.thecross.co.uk; closed Tues & Dec–Feb). Cheaper food is available at several cafés and pubs in both towns – the *Glen* or the *Brae Riach* in Newtonmore, or the *Royal Hotel* or *Tipsy Laird* in Kingussie.

The Great Glen

The **Great Glen**, cutting diagonally across the Highlands from Inverness to Fort William, follows a major geological fault-line. This huge rift valley was formed when the northwestern and southeastern sides slid against each other along the fault for more than sixty miles, and were later smoothed by glaciers that only retreated around 8000 BC. The glen is impressive more for its sheer scale than its great beauty, but is an obvious and rewarding route between the east and west coast.

Of the Great Glen's four elongated lochs, the most famous is **Loch Ness**, home to the mythical monster; lochs **Oich**, **Lochy** and **Linnhe** (the last of these a sea loch) are less renowned though no less attractive. All four are linked by the **Caledonian Canal**, surveyed by James Watt in 1773 and completed in the early 1800s by Thomas Telford to enable ships to pass between the North Sea and the Atlantic without having to navigate Scotland's treacherous northern coast. Only 22 miles of it are *bona fide* canal – the remaining 38 exploit the glen's natural lochs and west-flowing rivers.

The traditional and most rewarding way to travel through the glen is by **boat**. A flotilla of kayaks, small yachts and pleasure vessels take advantage of the canal and its old wooden locks during the summer, among them Jacobite Cruises (see p.1196 for details). Forest Enterprise (℡01320/366322) has also established an excellent **cycle path** through the glen; a leaflet outlining the route is available at most tourist offices or direct from Forest Enterprise. Following a broadly similar route is a long-distance footpath, the seventy-mile **Great Glen Way**, which takes between five and seven days to walk in full, details of which can be had from tourist offices or Scottish Natural Heritage (℡01463/712221). In addition, the Great Glen is reasonably well served by **buses**, with several daily services between Inverness and Fort William, and a couple of extra buses covering the section between Fort William and Invergarry during school terms.

Loch Ness and around

Twenty-three miles long, unfathomably deep, cold and often moody, **Loch Ness** is bounded by rugged heather-clad mountains rising steeply from a wooded shoreline and attractive valleys opening up on either side. Its fame, however, is based overwhelmingly on its legendary inhabitant Nessie, the "Loch Ness monster", whose fame ensures a steady flow of hopeful visitors to the settlements dotted along the loch, in particular **Drumnadrochit**. Nearby, the impressive ruins of **Castle Urquhart** – a favourite monster-spotting location – perch atop a rock on the lochside and attract a deluge of bus parties during the summer. Almost as busy in high season is the village of **Fort Augustus**, at the more scenic southwest tip of Loch Ness, where you can watch queues of boats tackling one of the Caledonian Canal's longest flight of locks. Away from the lochside, and seeing a fraction of Loch Ness's visitor numbers, the remote **glens** of **Urquhart** and **Affric** make an appealing contrast, with Affric in particular boasting narrow, winding roads, gushing streams and hillsides dotted in ancient Caledonian pine forests.

Although most visitors use the tree-lined A82 road, which runs along the western shore of Loch Ness, the sinuous single-track B862/B852 (originally a military road built to link Fort Augustus and Fort George) that skirts the **eastern shore** is quieter and affords far more spectacular views. However, buses from Inverness along this road only run as far south as Foyers, so you'll need your own transport to complete the whole loop around the loch, a journey which includes a most impressive stretch between Fort Augustus and the high, hidden Loch Mhor.

Drumnadrochit and around

Situated above a verdant, sheltered bay of Loch Ness fifteen miles southwest of Inverness, **DRUMNADROCHIT** is the epicentre of Nessie hype, sporting a rash of tacky souvenir shops and two rival monster exhibitions whose head-to-

The world-famous **Loch Ness monster**, affectionately known as **"Nessie"** (and by serious aficionados as *Nessiteras rhombopteryx*), has been a local celebrity for some time. The first mention of a mystery creature crops up in St Adamnan's seventh-century biography of **St Columba**, who allegedly calmed an aquatic animal which had attacked one of his monks. Present-day interest, however, is probably greater outside Scotland than within the country, and dates from the building of the road along the loch's western shore in the early 1930s. In 1934, the *Daily Mail* published London surgeon R.K. Wilson's sensational photograph of the head and neck of the monster peering up out of the loch, and the hype has hardly diminished since. Recent encounters range from glimpses of ripples by anglers to the famous occasion in 1961 when thirty hotel guests saw a pair of humps break the water's surface and cruise for about half a mile before submerging.

Photographic evidence is showcased in the two "Monster Exhibitions" at Drumnadrochit, but the most impressive of these exhibits – including the renowned black-and-white movie footage of Nessie's humps moving across the water, and Wilson's original head and shoulders shot – have now been exposed as fakes. Indeed, in few other places on earth has watching a rather lifeless and often grey expanse of water seemed so compelling, or have floating logs, otters and boat wakes been photographed so often and with such excitement. Yet while even hi-tech sonar surveys carried out over the past two decades have failed to come up with conclusive evidence, it's hard to dismiss Nessie as pure myth. After all, no-one yet knows where the unknown layers of silt and mud at the bottom of the loch begin and end: best estimates say the loch is over 750 feet deep, deeper than much of the North Sea, while others point to the possibilities of underwater caves and undiscovered channels connected to the sea. What scientists have found in the cold, murky depths, including pure white eels and rare Arctic char, offer fertile grounds for speculation, with different theories declaring Nessie to be a remnant from the dinosaur age, a giant newt or a huge visiting Baltic sturgeon. With the possibility of a definitive answer sending shivers through the local tourist industry, monster-hunters are these days recruited over the web, with the site ⓦwww.lochness.scotland.net offering a list of the latest sightings as well as round-the-clock **webcams** offering views both across the loch and underwater.

head scramble for punters occasionally erupts into acrimonious exchanges, detailed with relish by the local press. Of the pair, the **Loch Ness 2000 Exhibition**, formerly the Official Loch Ness Monster Exhibition (daily: July & Aug 9am–8pm; June & Sept 9am–6pm; Easter–May 9.30am–5pm; Oct–Easter 10am–4pm; £5.95), though more expensive, is the better bet, offering an in-depth rundown of eyewitness accounts through the ages and mock-ups of the various research projects carried out in the loch. A recent upgrade has attempted to offer something to sceptics as well as believers by outlining more of the scientific background to set against the various myths. The **Original Loch Ness Monster Exhibition** (daily: July & Aug 9am–9pm; rest of year 10am–6pm; Dec–March closes 4pm; £3.50) is basically a gift shop with a shoddy audiovisual show tacked on the side.

Cruises on the loch aboard the *Nessie Hunter* (Easter–Oct hourly 9.30am–6pm; 50min; £8) can be booked at the Original Loch Ness Visitor Centre, though a more relaxing alternative is to head out **fishing** with a local gillie – the boat can take 5–8 people and costs around £30 for two hours; contact Bruce on ☎01456/450279 to book.

Most photographs allegedly showing the monster have been taken a couple of miles east of Drumnadrochit, around the fourteenth-century ruined lochside **Castle Urquhart** (daily: July & Aug 9.30am–8.30pm; April–June & Sept 9.30am–6.30pm; Oct–March 9.30am–4.30pm; HS; £3.80). Today it's one of Scotland's classic picture-postcard ruins, crawling with tourists by day but particularly splendid floodlit at night when all the crowds have gone. The castle receives more visitors each year than any other historic site in the Highlands, and to cope with the numbers a new **visitor centre** has been built into the hillside, ostensibly to create sufficient parking above the castle.

Practicalities

Drumnadrochit's **tourist office** (April–Oct daily 9am–5.30pm; Nov–March Mon–Sat 9am–12.30pm; ☎01456/459076) shares space with a Highland Council service point in the middle of the main car park in the village. Two very welcoming **B&Bs** are *Gilliflowers* (☎01456/450641, ✉gillyflowers@cali.co.uk; ❶), a renovated farmhouse tucked away down a country lane in Lewiston, or the modern *Drumbuie* (☎01456/450634, ✉drumbuie@amserve.net; ❶), on the northern approach to Drumnadrochit, which has great views and a resident herd of Highland cattle. For **hostel** beds, head to the immaculate and friendly *Loch Ness Backpackers Lodge* (☎01456/450807, ⓦwww.lochness-backpackers .com), at Coiltie Farmhouse in Lewiston; follow the signs to the left when coming from Drumnadrochit.

Most of the hotels in the area – the *Benleva* in particular – serve good bar **food**; in Drumnadrochit the *Fiddlers' Café Bar*, on the village green, offers local steaks, salmon and appetizing home-baked pizza; it also rents good-quality **mountain bikes** (☎01456/450223), and provides maps and rain capes.

Glen Affric

Due west of Drumnadrochit is a vast area of high peaks, remote glens and few roads. The reason most folk head this way is to explore the native forests and grand mountains of **Glen Affric**, generally held as one of Scotland's most beautiful landscapes. The approach to the glen is through the small settlement of **CANNICH**, 14 miles west of Drumnadrochit on the A831 through **Glen Urquhart**, and also accessible on a direct road from Beauly near Inverness. On weekdays there's a **bus** three times a day from Inverness to Cannich, but to get right into the heart of Glen Affric you'll need a car or a bike.

Glen Affric itself is an inspiring place, with a rushing river and Caledonian pine and birch woods opening out onto an island-studded loch that was considerably enlarged after the building of a **dam**, one of many hydroelectric schemes hereabouts. From the car park at the head of the single-track road along the glen, 10 miles southwest of Cannich, there's a selection of **walks**: the trip round Loch Affric will take you a good five hours but captures the glen and its wildlife and woodlands in all their remote splendour.

Fort Augustus

FORT AUGUSTUS, a tiny village at the scenic southwestern tip of Loch Ness, was named after George II's son, the chubby lad who later became the "Butcher" Duke of Cumberland, of Culloden fame; it was built as a barracks after the 1715 Jacobite rebellion. Today, it's dominated by comings and goings along the Caledonian Canal, which leaves Loch Ness here, and by its large former **Benedictine Abbey**, a campus of grey Victorian buildings founded on the site of the original fort in 1876.

The small **Caledonian Canal Heritage Centre** (July–Sept daily 10am–5pm; Easter–June & Oct Mon–Thurs & Sun 10am–5pm; free) is in

Ardchattan House on the northern bank of the canal, where you can view old photographs and records about the history of the canal and watch a black-and-white film of the days when paddle boats and large barges passed through the locks every day. There's some good **cycling** routes locally, along the Great Glen cycle route and elsewhere; the only place to rent bikes nearby is at South Laggan, eight miles or so southwest at the head of Loch Lochy, where Monster Activities (℡01809/501340) rents bikes, boats and canoes.

Fort Augustus's small **tourist office** (daily: July & Aug 9am–7pm; April–June, Sept & Oct 9am–5pm; ℡01320/366367) hands out free walking maps. The only **hostel** accommodation is at *Morag's Lodge* (℡01320/366289) above the petrol station on the Loch Ness side of town, where the atmosphere livens up with the daily arrival of backpackers' minibus tours. The *Old Pier* (℡01320/366418; ❸) is a particularly appealing B&B right on the loch at the north side of the village; there are log fires in the evenings – often very welcome even in summer – and boats and horse-riding are available to guests. For **food**, your best bet is to head to the lively local pub, the *Lock Inn*, which has regular music and draws a mixed clientele of locals, yachties and backpackers, as does *Poachers* on the main road.

Fort William and around

With its stunning position on Loch Linnhe, tucked in below the snow-streaked bulk of Ben Nevis, **FORT WILLIAM** (known by the many walkers and climbers that come here as "Fort Bill"), should be a gem. Sadly, the same lack of taste that nearly saw the town renamed "Abernevis" in the 1950s is evident in the ribbon bungalow development and ill-advised dual carriageway – complete with grubby pedestrian underpass – which have wrecked the waterfront. The main street and the little squares off it are more appealing, though occupied by some decidedly tacky tourist gift shops.

The countryside around the town is a blend of rugged mountain terrain and tranquil sea loch. Dominating the scene to the south is **Ben Nevis** – Britain's highest peak, best approached from scenic Glen Nevis. Some of the best views

The Nevis Range

Seven miles northeast of Fort William by the A82, on the slopes of **Aonach Mhòr**, one of the high mountains abutting Ben Nevis, the **Nevis Range** (℡01397/705825, ⓦwww.nevis-range.co.uk) is, in winter, Scotland's highest ski area. All year round, however, Highland County bus #41 runs from Fort William four times a day (June–Oct) to the base station of the country's only **gondola** system (July & Aug daily 9.30am–6pm, Thurs & Fri until 8.30pm; Sept to mid-Nov & mid-Dec to June daily 10am–5pm; £6.90 return). The one-and-a-half mile gondola trip (15min), rising 2000ft, gives an easy approach to some high-level walking as well as spectacular views from the terrace of the self-service restaurant at the top station. Active Highs (℡01397/712188, ⓦwww.active-highs.co.uk) offer dual **paragliding** flights off the mountain, while Britain's only championship-grade **downhill mountain-bike course**, a hair-raising 3-km route, starts at the gondola top station. There's also 25 miles of waymarked off-road bike routes on the mountainside and in the Leanachan Forest, ranging from gentle paths to cross-country scrambles. Off Beat Bikes (℡01397/704008, ⓦwww.offbeatbikes.co.uk) rent general mountain bikes as well as full-suspension bikes for the downhill course from their shops in Fort William and at the gondola base station (June–Sept).

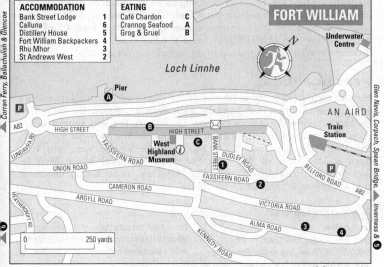

© Crown copyright

of "the Ben", as it's sometimes called, can be found at the Commando Memorial by **Spean Bridge**, a small village which marks the junction of the Great Glen with **Glen Roy**, which stetches east into some remote high country in the centre of Scotland. The most famous glen of all, **Glen Coe**, lies on the main A82 road half an hour's drive south of Fort William, the two separated by the coastal inlet of **Loch Leven**. Nowadays the whole area is unashamedly given over to tourism, and Fort William is swamped by bus tours throughout the summer, but, as ever in the Highlands, within a thirty-minute drive you can be totally alone.

The Town

Fort William's downfall started in the nineteenth century, when the original fort, which gave the town its name, was demolished to make way for the train line. Today, the town is a sprawl of dual carriageways, and there's little to detain you except the splendid and idiosyncratic **West Highland Museum**, on Cameron Square, just off the High Street (June–Sept Mon–Sat 10am–5pm; July & Aug also Sun 2–5pm; Oct–May Mon–Sat 10am–4pm; £2). Its collections cover virtually every aspect of Highland life and the presentation is traditional, but very well done, making a refreshing change from state-of-the-art heritage centres.

   Excursions from town include the popular day-trip to Mallaig (see p.1223) on the **Jacobite Steam Train** (mid-June to Sept Mon–Fri; Aug also Sun; depart Fort William 10.20am, depart Mallaig 2.10pm; day return £22; bookings ☎01463/239026). Heading along the north shore of Loch Eil to the west coast via historic Glenfinnan (see p.1220), the journey takes in some of the region's most spectacular scenery. Several **cruises** also leave from the town pier every day, offering the chance to spot the marine life of Loch Linnhe, which includes seals, otters and seabirds.

   At the suburb of **Banavie**, three miles north of the centre of Fort William along the A830 to Mallaig, the Caledonian Canal climbs 64ft in less than half a mile via a punishing but picturesque series of eight locks known as

Neptune's Staircase. There are stunning views from here of Ben Nevis and its neighbours, and it's a popular point from which to walk or cycle along the canal towpath. Bikes and Canadian canoes can be rented from Caledonian Activity Breaks (℡01397/772373), based at Rhiw Goch, one of the cottages backing onto the canal at the top of the sequence of locks.

Practicalities

Next to each other at the north end of the High Street are the **bus station** (with services from Inverness) and the **train station** (a stop on the scenic West Highland Railway direct from Glasgow; see p.1194). The busy **tourist office** is on Cameron Square, just off High Street (July & Aug Mon–Sat 9am–7pm, Sun 10am–6pm; June, Sept & Oct Mon–Sat 9am–5.30pm, Sun 10am–4pm; April & May Mon–Sat 9am–5pm, Sun 10am–4pm; Nov–March Mon–Fri 9am–5pm, Sat 10am–4pm; ℡01397/703781). They can book accommodation around the Fort William area for a £3 fee.

Accommodation

In town

Bank Street Lodge Bank Street ℡01397/700070. New and slightly characterless lodge with neat doubles, twin and family rooms, all with TVs, and a very central location. Also has a couple of rooms used as four- or eight-bed dorms (£11 per person). ❶

Calluna Heathcroft ℡01397/700451, ⓦwww.guide.u-net.com. Family-run budget self-catering flats with twin and four-person rooms and standard facilities. It can be tricky to find – though a free pick-up from town is available. The owner is one of the area's top mountain guides, so there's plenty of good outdoor advice available.

Distillery House North Road, just north of the town centre near the junction for Glen Nevis ℡01397/700103. Very comfortable and well-equipped upper-range B&B. ❸

Fort William Backpackers Alma Road ℡01397/700711. A big, rambling, archetypal backpacker hostel five minutes' walk up the hill from town, with great views and large communal areas. Part of the Macbackpackers chain, so minibus tours pull in at regular intervals.

Rhu Mhor 42 Alma Rd ℡01397/702213, ⓦwww.rhumhor.co.uk. Congenial B&B ten minutes' walk from the town centre, offering good breakfasts; vegetarians and vegans are catered for by arrangement. ❶

St Andrews West Fassifern Road ℡01397/703038, ⓦwww.standrewsguesthouse.co.uk.

Comfortable and extremely central B&B in an attractive converted granite choir school featuring various inscriptions and stained-glass windows. ❶

Out of town

Ben Nevis Bunkhouse Achintee Farm, Glen Nevis ℡01397/702240, ⓦwww.glennevis.com. A more civilized option than the nearby SYHA place, with hot showers, self-catering kitchen and a small licensed restaurant. Located just over the river from the Ben Nevis Visitor Centre – get to it by following the Ben path across the river or by taking Achintee Road along the north side of the River Nevis from Claggan.

Farr Cottage On the main A830 in Corpach ℡01397/772315, ⓦwww.farrcottage.co.uk. One of the liveliest of the local backpacker hostels, with everything from pizza feasts to whisky tastings going on in the evenings. Accommodation, in medium-sized dorms, is slightly more expensive than others locally.

Glen Nevis SYHA hostel Two and a half miles up the Glen Nevis road ℡01397/702336, ⓦwww.syha.org.uk. Large, but best avoided in mid-summer, when it's chock-full of teenagers. Handy for the Ben Nevis path but a long walk from town.

Rhiw Goch Beside Neptune's Staircase, Banavie ℡01397/772373. Modern, non-smoking villa with three twin rooms in a great situation beside the canal looking over to Ben Nevis. ❷

Eating

Fort William has a reasonable range of places **to eat**. On the High Street, the *Grog and Gruel* serves an eclectic mix of pizzas, pasta and Mexican dishes with real ale, while the pick of the bunch is the *Crannog Seafood Restaurant*, an elegantly converted bait store on the pier, where oysters, langoustines, prawns and salmon are cooked with flair. There are also a number of places out of town well worth seeking out: the *Old Pines* near Spean Bridge (see below) is superb, while *An Crann* at Seangan Bridge, a little north of Banavie (☎01497/772077) is a highly regarded place serving tasty Scottish dishes. A good place for **picnic food** as well as a snack is the *Café Chardon*, up a lane off High Street next to A.T. Mays; they do excellent baguettes, croissants and pastries to eat in or take away.

Glen Nevis and Ben Nevis

A ten-minute drive south of town, **Glen Nevis** is indisputably among the Highlands' most impressive glens: a classic U-shaped glacial valley hemmed in by steep bracken-covered slopes and swaths of blue-grey scree. Herds of shaggy Highland cattle graze the valley floor, where a sparkling river gushes through glades of trees. Highland County **bus** #42 runs from An Aird, beside the Safeway supermarket and the railway station, Fort William (roughly hourly) as far as the SYHA hostel, two and a half miles up the Glen Nevis road; some buses carry on another two and a half miles up the glen to the car park by the Lower Falls (mid-May to Sept only; 10–20min beyond the hostel).

Apart from its natural beauty, Glen Nevis is also the starting point for the ascent of Britain's highest peak, **Ben Nevis** (4406ft). The best map is "Harvey's Ben Nevis Walkers Map and Guide", available from the tourist office and most local bookshops and outdoor stores. Despite the fact that it's quite a slog up to the summit, and that it is by no means the most attractive mountain in Scotland, in high summer the trail is teeming with hikers, whatever the weather. However, this doesn't mean the mountain should be treated casually. It can snow round the summit any day of the year and more people perish here annually than on Everest, so take the necessary precautions; in winter, of course, the mountain should be left to the experts. The most obvious **route** to the summit, a Victorian pony path up the whaleback south side of the mountain, starts from the helpful Glen Nevis visitor centre (daily June–Sept 9am–6pm; Easter–May & Oct 9am–5pm), a mile and a half southeast of Fort William along the Glen Nevis road (bus #42 from An Aird in Fort William). Allow a full day for the climb (8hr).

Spean Bridge

Ten miles northeast of Fort William, the village of **Spean Bridge** marks the junction of the A82 with the A86 from Dalwhinnie and Kingussie. If you're here, its well worth heading a mile out of the village on the A82 towards Inverness to the **Commando Memorial**, a group of bronze soldiers sculpted in 1952 by Scott Sutherland in memory of the men who trained in the area and lost their lives during World War II. The statue stands on a raised promontory overlooking an awesome sweep of moor and mountain that takes in Lochaber and the Ben Nevis massif. A few hundred yards from the memorial, on the minor B8004 which heads towards **Gairlochy**, is one of the Highland's great foodie havens, the *Old Pines* "restaurant with rooms" (☎01397/712324, Ⓦwww.oldpines.co.uk; half-board ❼). The house and rooms are welcoming and comfortable, as well as being well set-up for guests with disabilities and families with children.

Glen Coe

Breathtakingly beautiful **Glen Coe** (literally "Valley of Weeping"), sixteen miles south of Fort William on the A82, is one of the best-known Highland glens: a spectacular mountain valley between velvety-green conical peaks, their

Walks around Glen Coe

Ordnance Survey Landranger Map No. 41.

A good introduction to the splendours of Glen Coe is the half-day hike over the **Devil's Staircase**, which follows part of the old military road that once ran between Fort William and Stirling. The trail, part of the West Highland Way and a good option for families and less experienced hikers, starts at the village of **Kinlochleven**, due north across the mountains from Glen Coe at the far eastern tip of Loch Leven (take the B863). The Devil's Staircase was named by 400 soldiers who endured severe hardship to build it in the seventeenth century, but in fine settled weather the trail is safe and affords stunning views of Loch Eilde and Buachaille Etive Mhor. A more detailed account of this hike features in the leaflet *Great Walks: Kinlochleven* (no. 4), on sale at most tourist offices in the area.

Leaflet no. 5 in the Great Walks series (*Glen Coe*) gives a good description of the **Allt Coire Gabhail** hike, another old favourite. The trailhead for this half-day route is in Glen Coe itself, at the car park opposite the distinctive Three Sisters massif on the main A82. From the road, head straight up the Allt Coire Gabhail to get to the so-called "Lost Valley" which the Clan MacDonald used to flee to and hide their cattle in when attacked. Undoubtedly one of the finest walks in the Glen Coe area not entailing the ascent of a Munro is the **Buachaille Etive Beag** (BEB) circuit, for which you should check out the Ordnance Survey Pathfinder Guide: *Fort William and Glen Coe Walks*. Following the textbook glacial valleys of Lairig Eilde and Lairig Gartain, the route entails a 1968ft climb in only nine miles of rough trail.

tops often wreathed in cloud, and cascades of rock and scree. In 1692 it was the site of a notorious massacre, in which the MacDonalds were victims of a long-standing government desire to suppress the clans. Fed up with what they regarded as unacceptable lawlessness, and a groundswell of Jacobitism and Catholicism, the government offered a general pardon to all those who signed an oath of allegiance to William III by January 1, 1692. When clan chief **Alastair MacDonald** missed the deadline, a plot was hatched to make an example of "that damnable sept", and **Campbell of Glenlyon** was ordered to billet his soldiers in the homes of the MacDonalds, who for ten days entertained them with traditional Highland hospitality. In the early morning of February 13, the soldiers turned on their hosts, slaying between 38 and 45 and causing more than 300 to flee in a blizzard, some to die of exposure.

Beyond the small village of **GLENCOE** at the western end of the glen on the shore of Loch Leven, an inlet of Loch Linnhe, the glen itself, a property of the National Trust for Scotland since the 1930s, is virtually uninhabited, and provides outstanding climbing and walking. The emptiness of the glen, and the poignancy that reflects, has been at the heart of a furious local row in recent years as the NTS struggle to reconcile local opinion with their plans to build a new **visitor centre**, dubbed by some "as similar to building a supermarket in the middle of the glen". The rather dated present construction (April–Oct 9.30am–5.30pm; 50p), near Clachaig, shows a short video about the massacre, and has a gift shop selling the usual books, postcards and Highland kitsch. There is a shortish **walk** from the centre through the forest to **Signal Rock**, which offers good views up and down the glen. More substantial are the informative ranger-led **guided walks** (June–Aug): on different days of the week a high-level hike and a low-level walk set off from the visitor centre.

At the eastern end of Glen Coe beyond the demanding Buachaille Etive Mhor, the landscape opens out onto the vast Rannoch Moor, dotted with small lochs and crossed by the West Highland Way, the A82 and, farther east, the West Highland Railway. From the **Glen Coe Ski Centre**

(☎01855/851226), a chairlift climbs 2400ft to Meall a Bhuiridh, giving spectacular views over Rannoch Moor and to Ben Nevis (lift open in ski season and July & Aug; 15min; £4 return). At the base station, there's a simple but pleasant café.

Practicalities

To get to the heart of Glen Coe from Fort William by **public transport** either hop on the Glasgow-bound Scottish Citylink coach service, or catch the daily postbus from Fort William post office (Mon–Fri 9.30am, Sat 9am). The Highland County bus #44 from Fort William to Kinlochleven also stops at Glencoe village.

There's a good selection of **accommodation** in Glen Coe and the surrounding area. Basic options include an SYHA **hostel** (☎01855/811219, W www.syha.org.uk) on a back road halfway between Glencoe village and the *Clachaig Inn* and the year-round *Red Squirrel* **campsite** (☎01855/811256) nearby. Glencoe village has a few comfortable **B&Bs**, such as the secluded *Scorry Breac* (☎01855/811354, E john@scorrybreac.freeserve.co.uk; ❶), and the *Glen Coe Guest House* (☎01855/811244; ❶), while the best-known **hotel** in the area is the stark *Clachaig Inn* (☎01855/811252, W www.glencoe-scotland.co.uk; ❸), a great place to swap stories with fellow climbers and to reward your exertions with pints of beer and heaped platefuls of food; it's three miles up Glen Coe, on the minor road from Glencoe village. At the other, eastern end of the glen, close to the Glen Coe ski area, is another well-established climber's watering hole, the *Kingshouse Hotel* (☎01855/851259; ❷ excludes breakfast), a classic wayfarers' inn which always proves a welcome sight after the wide emptiness of Rannoch Moor. You can rent **mountain bikes** and **tandems** from the *Clachaig Inn*.

The west coast

For many people, the Highlands' starkly beautiful **west coast** – stretching from the **Morvern peninsula** (opposite Mull) in the south to wind-lashed **Cape Wrath** in the far north – is the finest part of Scotland. Serrated by fjord-like sea lochs, the long coastline is scattered with windswept white-sand beaches, cliff-girt headlands, and rugged mountains sweeping up from the shoreline. The fast-changing weather rolling off the North Atlantic can be harsh, but it can also often create memorable plays of light, mood and landscape. When the sun shines, the sparkle of the sea, the richness of colour and the clarity of the views out to the scattered Hebrides are simply irresistible. This also is the least populated part of Britain, with just two small towns, and yawning tracts of moorland and desolate peat bog between crofting settlements. Beware the dreaded midge, which drives even the hardiest of locals to distraction on warm summer evenings.

The **Vikings**, who ruled the region in the ninth century, called it the "South Land", from which the modern district of Sutherland takes its name. After Culloden, the Clearances emptied most of the inland glens of the far north, however, and left the population clinging to the coastline, where a herring-fishing industry developed. Today, tourism, crofting, fishing and salmon farming are the mainstay of the local economy, supplemented by EU construction grants and subsidies to farm the sheep you'll encounter everywhere. For visitors, **cycling** and **walking** are the obvious ways to make the most of the superb scenery, and countless lochans and crystal-clear rivers offer superlative trout and salmon **fishing**. The shattered cliffs of the far northwest are an ornithologist's dream, harbouring some of Europe's largest and most diverse **seabird colonies**. The area's craggy mountaintops are the haunt of the elusive golden eagle.

The most visited part of the west coast is the stretch between Kyle of Lochalsh and Ullapool. Lying within easy reach of Inverness, this sector boasts the region's more obvious highlights: the awesome mountainscape of **Torridon**, **Gairloch**'s sandy beaches, the famous botanic gardens at **Inverewe**, and **Ullapool** itself, a picturesque and bustling fishing town from where ferries leave for the Outer Hebrides. However, press on further north, or south, and you'll get a truer sense of the isolation that makes the west coast so special. Traversed by few roads, the remote northwest corner of Scotland is wild and bleak, receiving the full force of the north Atlantic's frequently ferocious weather. The scattered settlements of the far southwest, meanwhile, tend to be more sheltered, but they are separated by some of the most extensive wilderness areas in Britain – lonely peninsulas with evocative Gaelic names like **Ardnamurchan**, **Knoydart** and **Glenelg**.

There's a reasonable **train** service from Inverness to Kyle of Lochalsh and from Fort William to Mallaig, and a useful **summer bus** service connects Inverness to Ullapool, Lochinver, Scourie and Durness. However, services peter out as you venture further afield, where you'll have to rely on **postbuses**, which go just about everywhere – albeit slowly and at odd times of day.

The "Rough Bounds"

The remote and sparsely-populated southwest corner of the Highlands, from the empty district of Morvern to the isolated peninsula of **Knoydart**, is a dramatic, lonely region of mountain, moorland and almost deserted glens fringed by a coast of stunning white beaches, with wonderful views to Mull and Skye. Its Gaelic name, *Garbh-chiochan*, translates as the "**Rough Bounds**", implying a region geographically and spiritually apart. Even if you have got a car, you should spend a few days here exploring on foot; there are so few roads that some determined hiking is almost inevitable.

The southwest Highlands' main road is the A830, often described as "the Road to the Isles", which winds in tandem with the rail line through the glens from Fort William to the road- and rail-head at **Mallaig**, a busy fishing port with ferry connections to Skye. Along the way, the road passes **Glenfinnan**, the much-photographed spot at the head of stunning **Loch Shiel** where Bonnie Prince Charlie gathered the clans to start the doomed Jacobite uprising of 1745. There are regular buses and trains along the main road; elsewhere in the region you'll usually have to rely on daily post- or schoolbuses. If you have your own transport, the five-minute ferry crossing at **Corran Ferry** (every 15min; foot passengers and bicycles go free), a nine-mile drive south of Fort William down Loch Linnhe, provides a more direct point of entry for Morvern and the rugged **Ardnamurchan** peninsula.

The Ardnamurchan peninsula

The tortuous single-track B8007 road winds west along the northern shore of Loch Sunart to the wild **Ardnamurchan peninsula**, the most westerly point on the British mainland. The peninsula, which lost most of its inhabitants during the infamous Clearances (see p.1302), has only a handful of tiny crofting settlements clinging to its jagged coastline and is sparsely populated. Ardnamurchan, however, can be an inspiring place for its pristine, empty beaches, wonderful vistas of sea and island, and the sense of nature all around. With its variety of undisturbed habitats the peninsula harbours a huge variety of birds, animals and wildflowers such as thrift and wild iris, making **walking** an obvious attraction. A variety of routes, from hill-climbs to coastal scrambles, are detailed in a comprehensive guide to the peninsula produced annually by the local community (available from tourist offices and most shops on the peninsula, priced around £4), while **guided walks** are also available at most of the nature reserves dotted along the Loch Sunart shoreline; these are run under the auspices of the Highland Council Ranger Service (℡01967/402232).

The Glenmore Natural History Centre

An inspiring introduction to the diverse flora, fauna and geology of Ardnamurchan is the superb **Glenmore Natural History Centre** (April–Oct Mon–Sat 10.30am–5.30pm, Sun noon–5.30pm; £2.50), nestled near the shore just west of the hamlet of **GLENBORRODALE**. Brainchild of local photographer Michael MacGregor (whose stunning work enlivens postcard stands along the west coast), the centre is housed in a sensitively designed timber building called "The Living Building", complete with turf roof and wildlife ponds. CCTV cameras relay live pictures of the comings and goings of the surrounding wildlife, from a pine marten's nest, a heronry and from underwater pools in the nearby river, while an excellent audiovisual show features MacGregor's photographs of the area accompanied by specially composed music. The small **café** serves sandwiches and good home-baked cakes and there's a useful bookshop.

Kilchoan and Ardnamurchan Point

KILCHOAN, nine miles west of the Glenmore Centre, is Ardnamurchan's main village – a straggling but appealing crofting township overlooking the Sound of Mull. In summer, a **car ferry** runs from here to Tobermory (Easter to mid-Oct 7 daily; 35min), while in the winter a passenger ferry plies the route for schoolchildren and shoppers. The new community centre in the village houses a **tourist office** (Easter–Oct daily 10am–6pm; ℡01972/510222, ⓦwww.ardnamurchan.com), who will help with, and book, accommodation, though year-round the community centre will act as an informal source of local advice and assistance. For **boat trips** out of Kilchoan – either wildlife-spotting or fishing – contact Nick Peake (℡01972/510212), who also leads guided walks to look for land-based wildlife such as eagles, pine martens and badgers. The only direct **bus** to Kilchoan leaves from Corran Ferry at 12.40pm (Mon–Sat), arriving two hours later.

The road continues beyond Kilchoan to the rocky, windy **Ardnamurchan Point**, with a **lighthouse** and spectacular views of the Hebrides north and south. The lighthouse buildings house a decent café and an enthusiastically run **visitor centre** (April–Oct 10am–5.30pm; £2.50; ℡01972/510210), with well-assembled displays about lighthouses in general, their construction and the people who lived in them. Best of all is the chance to admire the Egyptian-style lighthouse tower, and find a sheltered spot on the nearby cliff to sit peering out to sea.

Also worth exploring around the peninsula are the myriad coves, beaches and headlands along the long coastline. The finest of the sandy beaches is about three miles north of the lighthouse at **Sanna Bay**, a shell-strewn strand and series of dunes which offers truly unforgettable vistas of the Small Isles to the north, circled by gulls, terns and guillemots.

Practicalities

Accommodation isn't plentiful, and in summer you're well advised to book well ahead. *Water's Edge* (☎01972/510261; ❻ half-board) has one double room in a house in Kilchoan village; *Doirlinn House* (☎01972/510209; ❷; March–Oct), is a simpler B&B. The only budget accommodation on the peninsula is *Bruach na Fearna* (☎01972/500208; ❶), an excellent self-catering wooden chalet above the beach at Laga, just east of Glenborrodale. Both the *Salen Inn* (☎01967/431661; ❸) and the *Kilchoan House Hotel* (☎01972/ 510200; ❸) do decent bar **food**.

Acharacle and Castle Tioram

At the eastern end of Ardnamurchan, the main settlement is **ACHARACLE**, an ancient crofting village lying at the seaward end of freshwater **Loch Shiel**. A mile north of Acharacle, a side road running north off the A861 winds for three miles or so past a secluded estuary lined with rhododendron thickets and fishing platforms to **Loch Moidart**, a calm and sheltered sea loch. Perched atop a rocky promontory in the middle of the loch is **Castle Tioram** (pronounced "cheerum"), one of Scotland's most atmospheric historic monuments. Reached via a sandy causeway, the thirteenth-century fortress, whose Gaelic name means "dry land", was the seat of the MacDonalds of Clanranald until it was destroyed by their chief in 1715 to prevent it from falling into Hanoverian hands while he was away fighting for the Jacobites. Today, a certain amount of controversy surrounds the castle: while the setting and approach to the castle are undoubtedly stunning, large notices and fences keep you from getting too close to the castle due to the danger of falling masonry.

The Road to the Isles

The **"Road to the Isles"** from Fort William to Mallaig, followed by the West Highland Railway and the narrow, winding A830, traverses the mountains and glens of the Rough Bounds before breaking out near **Arisaig** onto a spectacularly scenic coast of sheltered inlets, stunning white beaches and wonderful views to the islands of Rùm, Eigg, Muck and Skye. This is country commonly associated with Bonnie Prince Charlie, whose adventures of 1745–46 began and ended on this stretch of coast, with his first, defiant raising of the standard at **Glenfinnan**.

Glenfinnan

GLENFINNAN, 19 miles west of Fort William at the head of Loch Shiel, was where Bonnie Prince Charlie raised his standard to signal the start of the Jacobite uprising of 1745. Surrounded by no more than 200 loyal clansmen, the young rebel prince waited to see if the Cameron of Loch Shiel would join his army. The drone of this powerful chief's pipers drifting up the glen was eagerly awaited, for without him the Stuarts' attempt to claim the English

1221

△ Castle Urquhart, Loch Ness

throne would have been sheer folly. Despite strong misgivings, Cameron did decide to support the uprising, and arrived at Glenfinnan on a sunny August 19 with 800 men, thereby encouraging other, wavering clan leaders to follow suit. Assured of adequate backing, the prince raised his red-and-white silk colour, proclaimed his father King James III of England, and set off on the long march to London – from which only a handful of the soldiers gathered at Glenfinnan would return. The spot is marked by a column (now a little lop-sided, Pisa-like), crowned with a clansman in full battle dress, erected as a tribute by Alexander Macdonald of Glenaladale in 1815.

Glenfinnan is a poignant place, a beautiful stage for the opening scene in a brutal drama which was to change the Highlands for ever. The **visitor centre** and café (daily: June–Aug 9.30am–6pm; April, May, Sept & Oct 10am–5pm; NTS; £1.50), opposite the monument, gives an account of the '45 uprising through to the rout at **Culloden** eight months later (see p.1200). A **boat trip** on the loch with Loch Shiel Cruises (April–Oct; ☏01397/722235) is highly recommended.

Glenfinnan is one of the most spectacular parts of the **West Highland Railway** line (see p.1194), not only for the glimpse it offers of the monument and graceful Loch Shiel, but also the mighty 21-arched **viaduct** built in 1901 and one of the first-ever large constructions made out of concrete. You can learn more of the history of this section of the railway at the **Glenfinnan Station Museum** (June–Sept daily 9.30am–4.30pm; 50p), set in the old booking office of the station. Right beside the station, two old railway carriages have been pressed into use as a highly original **restaurant** and **bunkhouse**; the *Dining Car* (June–Sept daily 10am–5pm; ☏01397/722300) is open for light lunches, home baking and evening meals (Fri–Sun until 8.30pm), while the *Sleeping Car* (☏01397/722295; year-round), a converted 1958 camping coach, sleeps ten in bunkbeds.

Arisaig and around

West of Glenfinnan, the A830 runs alongside captivating Loch Eilt in the district of **Morar**, through Lochailort – where it meets the road from Acharacle – and onto a coast marked by acres of white sands, turquoise seas and rocky islets draped with orange seaweed. **ARISAIG**, scattered round a sandy bay at the west end of the Morar peninsula, makes a good base for exploring this area. A **boat** also leaves from here daily during the summer for the Small Isles (see p.1131), operated by Arisaig Marine (☏01687/450224). **Accommodation** in the village is plentiful. *Kinloid Farm House* (☏01687/450366; ❸; March–Oct) is one of several pleasant B&Bs with sea views, while the more upmarket *Old Library Lodge* (☏01687/450651, ⓦwww.oldlibrary.co.uk; ❺; April–Oct) has a handful of well-appointed rooms, though only two overlook the seafront.

Stretching for eight miles or so north of Arisaig is a string of stunning white-sand **beaches** backed by flowery machair, with barren granite hills and moorland rising up behind and wonderful seaward views of Eigg and Rùm. The next settlement of any significance is **MORAR**, where the famous beach scenes from *Local Hero* were shot. Since then, however, a bypass has been built around the village, and the white sands, plagued by the rumble of frozen-cod lorries, are no longer an unspoilt idyll. Of the string of **campsites** try *Camusdarach* (☏01687/450221, ⓦwww.road-to-the-isles.org.uk/camusdarach), which isn't quite on the beach but is quieter and less officious than others nearby. **B&B** is also available in the converted billiard room of their attractive main house (❶).

Mallaig

A cluttered, noisy port whose pebble-dashed houses struggle for space with great lumps of granite tumbling down to the sea, **MALLAIG**, 47 miles west of Fort William along the A830 (regular buses and trains run this route), is not pretty. Before the railway reached here in 1901, it consisted of only a few cottages, but now it's a busy, bustling place and, as the main ferry stop for Skye and the Small Isles (see p.1131), is always full of visitors. The continuing source of the village's wealth is its thriving **fishing** industry: on the quayside, piles of nets, tackle and ice crates lie scattered around a bustling modern market. Apart from the daily bustle of Mallaig's harbour, the main attraction in town is **Mallaig Marine World**, north of the train station near the harbour (June–Sept Mon–Sat 9am–6pm, Sun 10am–6pm; July & Aug Mon–Sat until 7pm; Oct–May Mon–Sat 9am–5.30pm, Sun 11am–5pm; £2.75), where tanks of local sea creatures and informative exhibits about the port provide an unpretentious introduction to the local waters.

Mallaig is a compact place, concentrated around the harbour, where you'll find the **tourist office** (April–Oct Mon–Sat 10am–6pm; Nov–March Mon, Wed & Fri 11am–3pm; ☎01687/462170), which will book accommodation, and the **bus** and **train stations**. The CalMac ticket office (☎01687/462403), serving passengers for Skye and the Small Isles, is also nearby, and you can arrange transport to Knoydart by calling Bruce Watt Cruises (☎01687/462320 or 462233), which sails to Inverie every morning and afternoon (June to mid-Sept Mon–Fri; otherwise Mon, Wed & Fri), the later cruise continuing east along Loch Nevis to Tarbet.

For **B&B**, head around the harbour to East Bay, where you'll find the immaculate *Western Isles Guest House* (☎01687/462320, ⓔ westrnisles@aol.com; ❶). *Sheena's Backpackers' Lodge* (☎01687/462764), a refreshingly laid-back independent **hostel** overlooking the harbour, has mixed dorms, self-catering facilities and a sitting room. For **eating**, the *Tea Garden* at *Sheena's Lodge* is a great place to watch the world go by while you tuck into a bowl of cullen skink (soup made from smoked haddock), a pint of prawns, or home-made scones. Also worth seeking out are the freshest of fish and chips, served at the *Cornerstone*, just across the road from the tourist office.

The Knoydart peninsula

Many people regard the **Knoydart peninsula** as Britain's most dramatic and unspoilt wilderness area. Flanked by **Loch Nevis** ("Loch of Heaven") in the south and the fjord-like inlet of **Loch Hourn** ("Loch of Hell") to the north, Knoydart's knobbly green peaks – three of them Munros – sweep straight out of the sea, shrouded for much of the time in a pall of grey mist. To get to the heart of the peninsula, you must catch a **boat** from Mallaig or Glenelg, or else **hike** for a couple of days across rugged moorland and mountains and sleep rough in old stone bothies (most of which are marked on Ordnance Survey maps).

At the end of the eighteenth century, around a thousand people eked out a living from this inhospitable terrain through crofting and fishing. These days the peninsula supports around seventy people, most of whom live in the hamlet of **INVERIE**. Nestled beside a sheltered bay on the south side of the peninsula, it has a pint-sized post office, a shop and mainland Britain's most remote pub, the *Old Forge*. Bruce Watt Cruises' **boat** chugs into Inverie from Mallaig. To arrange for a boat crossing from Arnisdale on the Glenelg peninsula to the north coast of Knoydart or Kinloch Hourn, contact Len Morrison (☎01599/522352; £8–25, depending on passenger numbers).

Torrie Shieling (☎01687/462669, ✉torrreidh@aol.com; £15 per person), an upmarket independent **hostel** located three-quarters of a mile east of Inverie on the side of the mountain, is popular with hikers and families, offering top-notch self-catering facilities, comfortable wooden beds in four-person rooms, and superb views across the bay. In Inverie itself, *Pier House* (☎01687/462347, ⓦwww.thepierhouse.co.uk; ⑤ half-board), is a great place to stay, and has its own licensed **restaurant** serving à la carte evening meals, including some good veggie options. The *Old Forge* has generous bar meals, served indoors beside an open fire, and often live music of an evening. You can rent **mountain bikes** from *Pier House*.

Kyle of Lochalsh and around

As the main gateway to Skye, **Kyle of Lochalsh** is an important transit point for tourists, locals and services. However, despite the through traffic and the fact that it is the terminus for the train route from Inverness, the town itself has little to show off. Of much more interest to most visitors is nearby **Eilean Donan Castle**, one of Scotland's most famous and popular sights, perched at the end of a stone causeway on the shores of **Loch Duich**. It's not hard, however, to step off the tourist trail, with the **Glenelg** peninsula on the south side of Loch Duich testimony to how quickly the west coast can seem remote and undiscovered. A few miles north of Kyle of Lochalsh, the delightful village of **Plockton** is a refreshing alternative to its utilitarian neighbour, with cottages grouped around a yacht-filled bay and Highland cattle wandering the streets.

Kyle of Lochalsh

KYLE OF LOCHALSH is not particularly attractive – concrete buildings, rail junk and myriad signs of the fishing industry abound – and is ideally somewhere to pass through rather than linger in. Since the **Skye road bridge** was opened in 1995, traffic has little reason to stop before rumbling over the channel a mile to the west, leaving Kyle's shopkeepers bereft of the passing trade they used to enjoy. The bridge, built with private-sector money, has also sparked controversy over its high tolls.

Buses run to Kyle of Lochalsh's harbour from Glasgow via Fort William and Invergarry (3 daily; 5hr 30min–6hr 15min), and from Inverness via Invermoriston (2 daily; 2hr); there's also a summer service from Edinburgh (1 daily; 7hr 15min). Book in advance for all of them (☎0870/550 5050). All continue at least as far as Portree on Skye. Buses also shuttle across the bridge to Kyleakin on Skye every thirty minutes or so. **Trains** run to Kyle of Lochalsh from Inverness (Mon–Sat 3–4; summer Sun 1–2; 2hr 30min); curving north through Achnasheen and Glen Carron, the train line is a rail enthusiast's dream, even if scenically it doesn't quite match the West Highland line to Mallaig.

Kyle's **tourist office** (July & Aug Mon–Sat 9am–6pm, Sun 10am–4pm; April–June, Sept & Oct Mon–Sat 9am–5pm; ☎01599/534276), on top of the small hill near the old ferry jetty, can book **accommodation** – a useful service as there are surprisingly few options. One of the most pleasant in the area is the *Old Schoolhouse* at Erbusaig, between Kyle and Plockton (☎01599/534369; ③), a good-quality guest house with three reasonably priced and comfortable rooms. To **eat**, head for the *Seagreen Restaurant and Bookshop* (☎01599/534388), on the Plockton road on the edge of town, which has a pleasant, unfussy atmosphere and serves excellent fresh seafood and vegetarian meals. The *Seafood Restaurant* at the train station is also recommended, if a little pricier.

Eilean Donan castle

Skirted on its northern shore by the A87, **Loch Duich**, the boot-shaped inlet just to the south of Kyle of Lochalsh, features prominently on the tourist trail, with buses from all over Europe thundering down the sixteen miles from **SHIEL BRIDGE** to Kyle of Lochalsh on their way to Skye.

After Edinburgh's hilltop fortress, **Eilean Donan castle** (April–Oct daily 10am–5.30pm; £3.75), ten miles north of Shiel Bridge on the A87, has to be Scotland's most photographed monument. Presiding over the once strategically important confluence of lochs Alsh, Long and Duich, the forbidding crenellated tower rises from the water's edge, joined to the shore by a narrow stone bridge and with sheer mountains as a backdrop. The original castle was established in 1230 by Alexander II to protect the area from the Vikings. It lay in ruins until John Macrae-Gilstrap had it rebuilt between 1912 and 1932. Eilean Donan has also been the setting of several major **films**, including *Highlander* and the James Bond adventure *The World is Not Enough*. Three floors, including the banqueting hall, the bedrooms and the troops' quarters are open to the public, with various Jacobite and clan relics also on display, though like many of the region's most popular castles, the large numbers of people passing through make it hard to appreciate the real charm of the place.

The Glenelg peninsula

South of Loch Duich, the **Glenelg peninsula**, jutting out into the Sound of Sleat, is the isolated and little-known crofting area featured in Gavin Maxwell's otter novel, *Ring of Bright Water*. Maxwell disguised the identity of this pristine stretch of coast by calling it "Camusfearnà", and it has remained a tranquil backwater in spite of the traffic that trickles through during the summer for the Kylerhea ferry to Skye (see p.1123 for details of the wildlife sanctuary at Eilean Ban, once Maxwell's home). The peninsula's main settlement, **GLENELG**, is strewn along a pebbly bay on the Sound of Sleat. A row of little whitewashed houses surrounded by trees, the village is dominated by the rambling, weed-choked ruins of Fort Bernera, an eighteenth-century garrison for English government troops, but now little more than a shell. The *Glenelg Inn* (☎01599/522273, ⓦwww.glenelg-inn.com; ⑤) is a wonderful spot to discover at the end of so remote a road, with food served all day and a good chance of live music from any local musicians who happen to be in the pub.

The frequent six-car **Glenelg–Kylerhea ferry** (5min; information ☎01599/511302; April–Oct) shuttles across the Sound of Sleat from a jetty northwest of the village. In former times, this choppy channel used to be an important drovers' crossing: 8000 cattle each year were herded head to tail across from Skye to the mainland.

Plockton

A fifteen-minute train ride north of Kyle at the seaward end of islet-studded Loch Carron lies the unbelievably picturesque village of **PLOCKTON**: a chocolate-box row of neatly painted cottages ranged around the curve of a tiny harbour and backed by a craggy landscape of heather and pine. Its fifteen minutes of fame came in the mid-1990s, when the BBC chose the village as the setting for the TV drama *Hamish Macbeth*. Though the resulting spin-off has quietened down a little, in high season it's still packed full of tourists, yachties and second-home owners. The unique brilliance of Plockton's light has also made it something of an artists' hangout, and during the summer the waterfront, with its row of shaggy palm trees, even shaggier Highland cattle, flower gardens and pleasure boats, is invariably dotted with painters dabbing at their easels.

The friendly, cosy *Haven Hotel*, on Innes Street (☎01599/544223; ⑤), is renowned for its excellent food, while the *Plockton Inn*, also on Innes Street (☎01599/544222; ③), makes an informal and comfortable alternative. Of the fifteen or so **B&Bs**, the *Shieling* (☎01599/544282; ②) has a great location on a tiny headland at the top of the harbour, and at *An Caladh* (☎01599/544356; ①) on the main street, guests have the free use of a wooden sailing dinghy. There's also the attractive new *Station Bunkhouse* (☎01599/544235, ⓔgill@ecosse.com), built in the shape of a signal box next to the railway station, which has four- and six-person dorms and a cosy open-plan kitchen and living area.

Both the *Haven* and the *Plockton Inn* have excellent seafood **restaurants**, while *Off the Rails*, in the train station, serves good-value, imaginative snacks by day, and evening meals. The *Buttery*, part of Plockton Stores on the seafront, is also open all day for snacks and inexpensive meals. For **fishing** or **seal-spotting** boat trips from Plockton, try Leisure Marine (☎01599/544306) or Plockton Activity Holidays (☎01599/544356).

Wester Ross

Wester Ross, the western seaboard of the old Scottish county of Ross-shire, is widely regarded as the most glamorous stretch of this coast. Here all the classic elements of Scotland's **coastal scenery** – dramatic mountains, sandy beaches, whitewashed crofting cottages and shimmering island views – come together in spectacular fashion. Though popular with generations of adventurous Scottish holidaymakers, only one or two places feel blighted by tourist numbers, with places such as **Applecross** and the peninsulas north and south of **Gairloch** maintaining an endearing simplicity and sense of isolation. There is some tough but wonderful **hiking** to be had in the mountains around **Torridon** and **Coigach**, while **boat trips** out among the islands and the prolific sea- and bird-life of the coast are a common feature. The main settlement is the attractive fishing town of **Ullapool**, port for ferry services to Stornoway in the Western Isles, but a pleasant enough place to use as a base, not least for its active social and cultural scene.

The Applecross peninsula

The most dramatic approach to the **Applecross peninsula** (the English-sounding name is a corruption of the Gaelic *Apor Crosan*, meaning "estuary") is from the south, along the infamous **Bealach na Ba** (literally "Pass of the Cattle"). Crossing the forbidding hills behind Kishorn and rising to 2053ft, with a gradient and switchback bends worthy of the Alps, this route – a popular cycling piste – is hair-raising in places, but the panoramic views across the Minch to Raasay and Skye more than compensate. The sheltered, fertile coast around **APPLECROSS** village, where the Irish missionary monk Maelrhuba founded a monastery in 673 AD, comes as a surprise after the bleakness of the moorland approach. It's an idyllic place: you can wander along lanes banked with wild iris and orchids, and explore beaches and rock pools on the shore.

The old *Applecross Inn* (℡01520/744262, Ⓦwww.applecross.net; ❷), right beside the sea, is the focal point of the community, with rooms upstairs and a lively bar serving snacks and tasty platefuls of local seafood. The inn is the first stop for most folk coming here; if their rooms are full they'll happily recommend any houses locally offering B&B. **Camping** (℡01520/744268) is provided at the *Flowertunnel*, as you come into the village from the pass.

Loch Torridon

Loch Torridon marks the northern boundary of the Applecross peninsula, its awe-inspiring setting backed by the appealingly rugged mountains of **Liathach** and **Beinn Eighe**, tipped by streaks of white quartzite. The greater part of this area is composed of the reddish 750-million-year-old Torridonian sandstone, and some 15,000 acres of the massif are under the protection of the National Trust for Scotland. They run a **Countryside Centre** (May–Sept Mon–Sat 10am–5pm, Sun 2–5pm) at Torridon village at the east end of the loch, where you can call in and learn a bit more about the local geology, flora and fauna. At Torridon itself, near the NTS visitors centre, there's a modern SYHA **hostel** (℡01445/791284, Ⓦwww.syha.org.uk; April–Oct), as well as one of the area's grandest **hotels**, the rambling Victorian *Loch Torridon Hotel* (℡01445/791242; ❽), set amid well-tended lochside grounds. Next door, *Ben Damph Lodge* (℡01445/791242, Ⓦwww.bendamph.lochtorridonhotel.com; ❸) is a modern conversion of an old farmstead, with neat if characterless rooms and a large climber's bar. Along at Diabaig, Miss Ross (℡01445/790240; ❶) has comfortable accommodation overlooking the rocky bay. There's no road to the tiny, spartan *Craig* hostel (no phone; May–Aug), a stone cottage by the shore three miles beyond Diabaig.

Loch Maree

About eight miles north of Loch Torridon, **Loch Maree**, dotted with Caledonian pine-covered islands, is one of the west's scenic highlights, best viewed from the A832 road that drops down to its southeastern tip through Glen Docherty. It's also surrounded by some of Scotland's finest **deerstalking**

Walks around Torridon

Ordnance Survey Outdoor Leisure map No. 8.
There can be difficult conditions on virtually all hiking routes around Torridon, and the weather can change very rapidly. If you're relatively inexperienced but want to do the magnificent ridge walk along the **Liathach** (pronounced "*lee*-ach") massif, or the strenuous traverse of **Beinn Eighe** (pronounced "ben *ay*"), you can join a National Trust Ranger Service guided hike (details from the Torridon Countryside Centre; ℡01445/791221).

For those confident to go it alone, one of many possible routes takes you behind Liathach and down the pass, **Coire Dubh**, to the main road in Glen Torridon. This is a great, straightforward walk if you're properly equipped, covering thirteen miles and taking in superb landscapes. Allow yourself the whole day. A rewarding walk even in rough weather is the seven-mile hike up the coast from **Lower Diabaig**, ten miles northwest of Torridon village, to **Redpoint**. On a clear day, the views across to Raasay and Applecross from this gentle undulating path are superlative, but you'll have to return along the same trail, or else make your way back via Loch Maree on the A832.

country: the remote, privately owned *Letterewe Lodge* on the north shore, accessible only by helicopter or boat, lies at the heart of a famous deer forest. At the southeastern end of the loch, the A896 from Torridon meets the A832 from Achnasheen at the small settlement of **KINLOCHEWE**, another good base if you're heading into the hills. *Cromasaig* B&B (☏01455/760234, ⓔcromasaig@msn.com; ❶) is a great place for hill-walkers set in the forest right at the foot of the track up Beinn Eighe. In Kinlochewe itself, MORU outdoor shop at the old petrol station opposite the hotel will furnish you with maps and guidebooks, as well as equipment and sound local advice. The *Kinlochewe Hotel* serves good meals and bar food.

The A832 skirts the southern shore of Loch Maree, passing the **Beinn Eighe Nature Reserve**, the UK's oldest wildlife sanctuary. Parts of the Beinn Eighe reserve are forested with Caledonian pinewood, which once covered the whole of the country, and it is home to pine marten, wildcat, fox, badger, Scottish crossbill, buzzards and golden eagles. A mile north of Kinlochewe, the **Beinn Eighe Visitor Centre** (Easter & May–Sept daily 10am–5pm) on the A832, gives details of the area's rare species and sells pamphlets describing two excellent **walks** in the reserve.

Gairloch and around

Mostly scattered around the sheltered northeastern shore of **Loch Gairloch**, the crofting township of **GAIRLOCH** thrives during the summer as a low-key holiday resort with several tempting sandy beaches and some excellent coastal walks within easy reach. The **Gairloch Heritage Museum** (April–Sept Mon–Sat 10am–5pm, Oct Mon–Fri 10am–1.30pm; call for winter hours; ☏01445/712287; £2.50) has eclectic, appealing displays covering geology, archeology, fishing and farming that range from a mock-up of a croft house to an early knitting machine. One leisurely way to explore the coast is on a wildlife-spotting **cruise**: Gairloch Marine Life Centre & Cruises (Easter–Oct; ☏01445/712636), at the pier, run informative and enjoyable boat trips across the bay in search of dolphins, porpoises, seals and even the odd whale.

Gairloch has a good choice of **accommodation**, most of it mid-range; the **tourist office**, right by the museum (July to mid-Sept Mon–Sat 9am–6pm, Sun noon–5pm; June Mon–Fri 9.30am–5.30pm, Sat 10am–5pm; April, May & mid-Sept to Oct Mon–Fri 10am–5pm, Sat 11am–4pm; ☏01445/712130) can help you search for possibilities. In the heart of the village, the *Mountain Lodge & Restaurant* (☏01445/712316; ❷) offers a refreshingly alternative experience – run by enthusiastic, young outdoor types the ground floor has a shop crammed with wind chimes and travel books, a café serving hearty, wholesome food and a conservatory and deck with great views over the bay, while upstairs are three comfortable rooms. There are good **B&Bs** scattered throughout the area: try Gaelic-speaking Miss Mackenzie's *Duisary* (☏01445/712252; ❶) or *Harbour View* (☏01445/741316; ❶) at Badachro. There's an SYHA **hostel** in a spectacular setting on the edge of a cliff at **Carn Dearg** two miles up the Melvaig road (☏01445/712219, ⓦwww.syha.org.uk; mid-May to Sept), as well as accommodation at Rua Reidh lighthouse (see below). **Camping** is possible at Big Sand or at Redpoint.

For **food**, the fact that the chef at Gairloch's *Scottish Seafood Restaurant* next to the petrol station near the pier is also the harbourmaster means that the fish and shellfish served up will be the pick of the catch. For **snacks**, the *Mountain Lodge* do a busy trade with their massive (and pricey) muffins and decent cups of coffee.

Around Gairloch

The area's real attraction, however, is its beautiful **coastline**. To get to one of the most impressive stretches, head around the north side of the bay and follow the single-track B8021 beyond Big Sand (a cleaner and quieter beach than the one in Gairloch) to the tiny crofting hamlet of **Melvaig** (reachable by the 8.20am Gairloch postbus), from where a narrow surfaced track winds out to **Rua Reidh Point** (pronounced "roo-a-ray"). The converted **lighthouse** here, which looks straight out to Harris in the Outer Hebrides, serves slap-up afternoon teas and home-baked cakes (Easter–Oct Tues & Thurs 11am–5pm; ☎01445/771263, ⑯www.ruareidh.co.uk). You can also stay in its comfortable and relaxed **bunkhouse** or **double rooms** (❶) – popular in high season – or use it as a base for one of the popular walking or activity holidays organized by the folk who run the bunkhouse.

Three miles south of Gairloch, a narrow single-track lane (built with the Destitution Funds raised during the nineteenth-century potato famine) winds west from the main A832, past wooded coves and inlets on its way south of the loch to **BADACHRO**, a sleepy former fishing village in a very attractive setting with a wonderful pub, the *Badachro Inn*, right by the water's edge, where you can sit in the beer garden watching the boats come and go and tuck into some lovely food. Beyond Badachro, the road winds for five more miles along the shore to **Redpoint**, a straggling hamlet with beautiful beaches of peach-coloured sand and great views to Raasay, Skye and the Western Isles.

Poolewe and around

It's a fifteen-minute hop by bus over the headland from Gairloch to the trim little village of **POOLEWE** on the sheltered south side of Loch Ewe, at the mouth of the River Ewe as it rushes down from Loch Maree. Half a mile across the bay from Poolewe on the A832, **Inverewe Gardens** (daily: mid-March to Oct 9.30am–9pm; Nov to mid-March 9.30am–5pm; NTS; £5), a verdant oasis of foliage and riotously colourful flower collections, forms a vivid contrast to the wild, heathery crags of the adjoining coast. The gardens were the brainchild of **Osgood Mackenzie**, who inherited the surrounding 12,000-acre estate from his stepfather, the laird of Gairloch, in 1862. Taking advantage of the area's famously temperate climate (a consequence of the Gulf Stream, which draws a warm sea current from Mexico to within a stone's throw of these shores), Mackenzie collected plants from all over the world for his walled garden, which still forms the nucleus of the complex. Today the National Trust for Scotland strives to develop the place along the lines envisaged by its founder.

Around 180,000 visitors pour through here annually, but the place rarely feels overcrowded. Mid-May to mid-June is the best time to see the rhododendrons and azaleas, while the herbaceous garden reaches its peak in July and August, as does the wonderful Victorian vegetable and flower garden beside the sea. You'll need at least a couple of hours to do the whole lot justice, and leave time for the **visitor centre** (mid-March to Oct daily 9.30am–5.30pm), which houses an informative display on the history of the garden and is the starting-point for **guided walks** (April–Oct Mon–Fri 1.30pm). The **restaurant** at the top of the car park does good snacks and lunches.

Ullapool

ULLAPOOL, the northwest's principal centre of population, was founded at the height of the herring boom in 1788 by the British Fisheries Society, on a sheltered arm of land jutting into Loch Broom. The grid-plan town is still an

Hikes and cycle rides around Ullapool

Ordnance Survey maps nos. 15, 19 & 20.

Ullapool lies at the start of several excellent **hiking trails**, ranging from sedate shoreside ambles to long and strenuous ascents of Munros. However, the weather here can change very quickly, so take the necessary precautions (see p.46). More detailed descriptions of the routes outlined below are available from the hostel on Shore Street (30p); hostellers can also rent the relevant up-to-date OS maps – essential for the hill walks.

An easy **half-day ramble** begins at the north end of Quay Street: cross the walkway/footbridge here and follow the riverbank on the far side left towards the sea. Walk past the golf course and follow the shore line as best you can for around two miles until you reach a hilltop lighthouse from where you gain fine views across the sea to the Summer Isles. Return the same way or via the main A835 road.

If you're reasonably experienced and can use a map and compass, a day-walk well worth tackling is the rock path to **Achininver**, near Achiltibuie. The route, which winds along one of the region's most beautiful and unspoilt stretches of coastline to a small **hostel** (book ahead on ☎01854/622254, Ⓦ www.syha.org.uk; mid-May to Sept), is easy to follow in good weather, but gets very boggy and slippery when wet. Sound footwear, a light pack and a route guide are essential.

A much easier but no less scenic **cycle** route is the tour of Loch Broom, taking in the hamlets of **Letters** and **Loggie** on the tranquil western shore, which you can get to via a quiet single-track road (off the A832 once you've cycled south and round the loch from Ullapool). At the end of this, a jeep track heads for the vitrified Iron Age fort at **Dun Lagaidh**; you have to return by the same route.

important fishing centre, though the **ferry** link to Stornoway on Lewis (see p.1136) means that in high season its personality is practically swamped by visitors. Even so, it's still a hugely appealing place and a good base for exploring the northwest Highlands. Regular **buses** run from here to Inverness and Durness, while there's an early-morning run through to the remote train station at Lairg. Accommodation is plentiful and Ullapool is an obvious hideaway if the weather is bad, with cosy pubs, a new swimming pool and a lively arts centre, the *Ceilidh Place*.

Most of the action centres on the **harbour**, which has an authentic and salty air, especially when the boats are in. By day, attention focuses on the comings and goings of the ferry, fishing boats and smaller craft, while in the evening, yachts swing on the current, the shops stay open late, and customers from the *Ferry Boat Inn* line the sea wall. During summer, booths advertise trips to the **Summer Isles** – a cluster of uninhabited islets two to three miles offshore – to view seabird colonies, dolphins and porpoises. The only conventional attraction in town is the **museum**, in the old parish church on West Argyle Street (April–Oct Mon–Sat 9.30am–5.30pm; March Mon–Sat 11am–3pm; Nov–Feb Wed, Thurs & Sat 11am–3pm; £2), with displays on crofting, fishing, local religion and emigration. During the Clearances, Ullapool was one of the ports through which evicted crofters left to start new lives in Canada, Australia and New Zealand.

Practicalities

Forming the backbone of its grid plan, Ullapool's two main arteries are the loch-side **Shore Street** and, parallel to it, **Argyle Street**, further inland. **Buses** stop at the pier, in the town centre near the ferry dock, from where it's easy to get your bearings. The well-run **tourist office** (June–Aug Mon–Sat 9am–5.30pm, Sun noon–5pm; April, May, Sept & Oct Mon–Sat

9am–5pm, Sun noon–4pm; Oct Mon–Fri 10am–5pm, Sat noon–4pm; Nov & Dec Mon– Fri 2–5.30pm; ℡01854/612135), on Argyle Street, offers an accommodation booking service. There are two or three daily **ferries** to the Outer Hebrides (Mon–Sat; 2hr 30min) run by CalMac (℡0870/565 0000, ⓦwww.calmac.co.uk).

Accommodation

Brae Guest House Shore Street ℡01854/612421. A great guest house in a beautifully maintained traditional building right on the loch-side. ❷

The Ceilidh Place West Argyle Street ℡01854/612103, ⓦwww.theceilidhplace.com. Tasteful and popular hotel, with the west coast's best bookshop, a relaxing first-floor lounge, a great bar-restaurant, sea views, and a laid-back atmosphere. Also has a good-value bunkhouse (May–Oct), for £12 per person in family rooms. ❻

Ferry Boat Inn Shore Street ℡01854/612366. Traditional inn right on the waterfront with a friendly atmosphere and reasonable food. ❸

The Shieling Garve Road ℡01854/612947.

Outstandingly comfortable guest house overlooking the loch with immaculate, spacious rooms (rooms 4 and 5 have the best views), superb breakfasts (try their home-made venison and leek sausages) and a sauna. ❷

SYHA hostel Shore Street ℡01854/612254, ⓦwww.syha.org.uk. Busy hostel on the front, with internet access and lots of good information about local walks. Closed Jan.

West House West Argyle St ℡01854/613126, ⓦwww.scotpackers-hostels.co.uk. Lively, welcoming hostel with four- to six-bed dorms and more civilized B&B on offer in a nearby house. Minibus day-tours organized and bike rental available.

Eating, drinking and entertainment

The two best **pubs** in Ullapool are the *Arch Inn*, home of the Ullapool football team, and the *Ferry Boat Inn* (known as the "FBI"), where you can enjoy a pint of real ale at the lochside – midges permitting. The slightly less characterful *Seaforth* by the pier is the place to catch middle-of-the-road live **music**, while live folk music is a regular occurrence at the *Ceilidh Place* or on Thursday nights at the *FBI*. The *Ceilidh Place* is one of the happening places in the Highlands, with a decent-quality line-up of touring plays, music festivals, poetry-readings and live entertainment.

The *Ceilidh Place* is also one of the best places in town to find something to **eat**, with a coffee shop, a pleasant bar serving filling snacks and a spacious restaurant offering a selection of imaginative seafood and vegetarian dishes. The other main restaurant in town is in the *Morefield Hotel*, on Morefield Lane off North Road (℡01854/612161), which despite the rather uninspiring motel setting is a long-standing locals' favourite. All three pubs also serve bar meals – the *FBI* is probably the pick of the bunch. If you're looking for **picnic** or **self-catering fare**, try John MacLean's wholefood shop and deli on West Argyle Street, or the Ullapool Catering Company at Unit 3, West Morefield Industrial Estate (℡01854/612969) where you can pick up organic vegetables, fresh seafood and sandwiches.

The Coigach peninsula

Ten miles north of Ullapool, a single-track road winds west off the A835 to squeeze between the northern shore of Loch Lurgainn and the lower slopes of Cul Beag (2523ft) and craggy Stac Pollaidh (2012ft) to reach the **Coigach peninsula**. To the southeast, the awesome bulk of Ben More Coigach (2439ft) presides over the district, which contains some spectacular coastal scenery including a string of sandy beaches and the Summer Isles, scattered just offshore.

Coigach's main settlement is **ACHILTIBUIE**, an old crofting village stretched across the hillside above a series of white-sand coves and rocks tapering into the Atlantic, from where a fleet of small fishing boats carries sheep, and tourists, to the enticing pastures of the **Summer Isles** which lie a little way offshore. The village also attracts gardening enthusiasts, thanks to the unlikely presence of the **Hydroponicum** (late May to Sept daily 10am–5pm; £4.75; tours on the hour), a cross between a giant greenhouse and a futuristic scientific research station. All kinds of flowers, fruits and vegetables are grown without using soil and bumper crops of strawberries, salad leaves, figs and even bananas result – guided tours explain how it's all done and show you round the different "climate zones". You can taste whatever's being harvested in the subtropical setting of the *Lily Pond Café*, which serves meals, desserts and snacks and is open in the evening (Thurs–Sun only). Also worth a visit is the **Achiltibuie Smokehouse** (April–Sept Mon–Sat 9.30am–5pm; free), five miles north of the Hydroponicum at **Altandhu**, where you can see meat, fish and game being cured in the traditional way and can buy some afterwards. Next to this, the *Am Fuaran* bar serves evening meals and, like everywhere else along this stretch, enjoys terrific views over to the Summer Isles. For **boat** trips round these attractive islets, including some time ashore on the largest, Tanera Mor, Ian Macleod's boat *Hectoria* (℡01854/622200) runs twice a day from the pier by Achiltibuie.

For **accommodation**, the wonderfully understated *Summer Isles Hotel* (℡01854/622282, ✉summerisleshotel@aol.com; ❻; April–Oct), just up the road from the Hydroponicum, enjoys a near-perfect setting with views over the islands, and has an excellent **restaurant** (open to non-residents). Of Achiltibuie's several **B&Bs**, *Dornie House* (℡01854/622271; ❶), halfway to Altandhu, is welcoming, and there's also a beautifully situated twenty-bed SYHA **hostel** (℡01854/622254, ⓦwww.syha.org.uk; mid-May to Sept), three miles down the coast at Achininver, which is handy for accessing Coigach's many mountain hikes.

The far northwest coast

The stretch of coast north of Wester Ross is sometimes ignored in favour of the rich pickings around places such as Ullapool and Gairloch, yet for many the stark, elemental beauty of the Highlands is to be found on the **far northwest coast** as nowhere else. Certainly the hills of **Assynt**, the area immediately north of Coigach gathered around the port of **Lochinver**, are among the most distinctive in the country, and the features of the ragged coastline, from the towering rock stack **The Old Man of Stoer** to the beautiful strip of sand at **Sandwood Bay**, retain an essence of wildness. Elsewhere, those inspired to explore can discover hidden **waterfalls** and secret **trout lochs**, while a simple ferry can take you to see the puffins of the island wildlife reserve of **Handa**. Places to stay and eat can be thin on the ground, particularly out of season, but the very lack of infrastructure is testimony to the isolation which this corner of Scotland delivers in such sweeping style.

Lochinver and around

The potholed and narrow road north from Achiltibuie through Inverkirkaig is unremittingly spectacular, threading its way through a tumultuous landscape of secret valleys, moorland and bare rock, past the startling shapes of **Cul Beag** (2523ft), **Cul Mòr** (2785ft) and the distinctive sugar-loaf **Suilven** (2398ft). A scattering of pebble-dashed bungalows around a sheltered bay heralds your arrival at **LOCHINVER**, 16 miles due north of Ullapool (although more than twice that by road). There's a better-than-average **tourist office** (April–Oct Mon–Sat 10am–5pm, July & Aug also Sun 10am–5pm; ☎01571/844330), whose visitor centre gives an interesting rundown on the area's geology, wildlife and history; a countryside ranger is available to advise on walks.

Heading **north** from Lochinver, there are two possible routes: the fast A837, which runs eastwards along the shore of Loch Assynt (see below) to join the northbound A894, or the narrow, more scenic B869 **coast road** that locals dub "The Breakdown Zone", because its ups and downs claim so many victims during summer. Hugging the indented shoreline, this route offers superb views of the Summer Isles, as well as a number of rewarding side-trips to beaches and dramatic cliffs. Post- and schoolbuses from Lochinver cover the route as far as Ardvar or Drumbeg (Mon–Sat).

The first village worthy of a detour is **ACHMELVICH**, a couple of miles along a side road, whose tiny bay cradles a stunning white-sand beach lapped by startlingly turquoise water. There's a noisy **campsite** and a basic forty-bed SYHA **hostel** (☎01571/844480, ⓦwww.syha.org.uk; May–Sept) just behind the largest beach. However, for total peace and quiet, head to other, equally seductive beaches beyond the headlands.

The side road that branches north off the B869 between **Stoer** and **Clashnessie**, both of which have sandy beaches, ends abruptly by the automatic lighthouse at **Raffin**, built in 1870 by the Stevenson brothers (one of whom was the author Robert Louis Stevenson's dad). You can continue for two miles along a well-worn track to the Point of Stoer, named after the colossal rock pillar that stands offshore known as "**The Old Man of Stoer**", surrounded by sheer cliffs and splashed with guano from the seabird colonies that nest on its 200ft sides.

East of Lochinver

The area **east of Lochinver**, traversed by the A837 and bounded by the gnarled peaks of the **Ben More Assynt** massif, is a wilderness of mountains, moorland, mist and scree. Dotted with lochs and lochans, it's also an angler's paradise, home to the only non-migratory fish in northern Scotland, the brown trout, and numerous other sought-after species, including the Atlantic salmon, sea trout, Arctic char and a massive prize strain of cannibal ferox. **Fishing** permits for the rivers in this area are like gold dust during the summer, snapped up months in advance by exclusive hunting-lodge hotels, but you can sometimes obtain last-minute cancellations (try the *Inver Lodge* on ☎01571/844496); permits to fish lochs are easier to get hold of.

The *Inchnadamph Hotel* (☎01571/822202; ❺), ten miles further north on **Loch Assynt**, is a wonderfully traditional Highland retreat; inside, the walls are covered with the stuffed catches of its past guests. Just along the road, the **Assynt Field Centre** at *Inchnadamph Lodge* (☎01571/822218, ⓦwww.highland-hostels.co.uk; ❶) has basic but comfortable bunk rooms, some twins as well as more spacious B&B accommodation. Through the year, the centre offers a variety of outdoor activity breaks and holidays, ranging from hill-walking to dry-stone dyke building and cookery courses focusing on local products.

Kylesku to Sandwood Bay

KYLESKU, 33 miles north of Ullapool on the main A894 road, is the point where a graceful, award-winning road bridge sweeps over the mouth of lochs Glencoul and Glendhu. There's very little to the place, though the congenial *Kylesku Hotel* (☎01971/502231; ❹; March–Oct) by the water's edge above the old ferry slipway has en-suite rooms, a welcoming bar popular with locals, and an excellent **restaurant** serving outstanding fresh seafood, including lobster, crab, mussels and local salmon (you can watch the fish being landed on the pier). Statesman Cruises runs entertaining **boat trips** (March–Oct daily 11am, Sun–Thurs also 3pm; Fri & Sat also 2pm; round trip 2hr; £10; ☎01571/844446) from the jetty below the *Kylesku Hotel* to the 650ft **Eas-Coul-Aulin**, Britain's highest waterfall, located at the head of Loch Glencoul; otters, seals, porpoises and minke whales can occasionally be spotted along the way.

Scourie, Tarbet and Handa Island

Ten miles north of Kylesku, the widely scattered crofting community of **SCOURIE**, on a bluff above the main road, surrounds a beautiful sandy beach whose safe bathing has made it a popular holiday destination for families. Visible just offshore to the north of Scourie is **Handa Island**, a huge chunk of red Torridon sandstone surrounded by sheer cliffs, carpeted with machair and purple-tinged moorland, and teeming with seabirds. It's private property, but is administered as an internationally important **wildlife reserve** by the Scottish Wildlife Trust (SWT) and is a real treat for ornithologists, with vast colonies of razorbills and guillemots breeding on its guano-splashed cliffs during summer. From late May to mid-July, large numbers of puffins waddle comically over the turf-covered cliff tops where they dig their burrows.

Apart from a solitary warden, Handa is deserted. Until midway through the nineteenth century, however, it supported a thriving, if somewhat eccentric, community of crofters. Surviving on a diet of fish, potatoes and seabirds, the islanders, whose ruined cottages still cling to the slopes by the jetty, devised their own system of government, with a "queen" (Handa's oldest widow) and "parliament" (a council of men who met each morning to discuss the day's business). Uprooted by the 1846 potato famine, most of the villagers eventually emigrated to Canada's Cape Breton.

Weather permitting, **boats** (☎01971/502347) leave for Handa throughout the day (April–Sept daily 9.30am–2pm; last return 5pm; £7) from the tiny cove of **TARBET**, three miles northwest of the main road and accessible by post-bus from Scourie (Mon–Sat 1 daily; 1.50pm), where there's a small car park and jetty. You're encouraged to make a **donation** of around £1.50 towards Handa's upkeep. It takes about three hours to follow the **footpath** around the island – an easy and enjoyable walk taking in the north shore's Great Stack rock pillar and some fine views across the Minch: a detailed route guide is featured in the SWT's free leaflet, available from the warden's office when you arrive. The SWT maintains a **bothy** for birdwatchers (reservations essential on ☎0131/ 312 7765 or with the warden). In Tarbet, the *Croft House* (☎01971/ 502098; ❶) is a comfortable little **B&B** overlooking the bay. For **food**, Tarbet's unexpected *Seafood Restaurant* (Mon–Sat noon–7pm) serves delicious, moderately priced fish and vegetarian dishes, and a good selection of home-made cakes and desserts, in its airy conservatory just above the jetty.

Kinlochbervie and around

North of Scourie, the road sweeps inland through the starkest part of the Highlands; rocks piled on rocks, bog and water create an almost alien landscape, and the astonishingly bare, stony coastline looks increasingly inhospitable. At Rhiconich, you can branch off the main road to **KINLOCHBERVIE**, which for all the world seems to be a typical, straggling West Highland crofting community until you turn a corner and encounter an incongrously huge fish-processing plant and modern concrete harbour. Don't miss the fish and chips at the Fisherman's Mission (Mon–Thurs 10am–8pm, Fri 10am–4pm). Further sustenance can be found at the *Old Schoolhouse Restaurant and Guest House* (☎01971/521383; ❸), a couple of miles before Kinlochbervie, which provides comfortable accommodation and home-cooked meals.

A single-track road takes you northwest of Kinlochbervie through isolated Oldshoremore, a working crofters' village scattered above a stunning white-sand beach, to **BLAIRMORE**, where you can park for the four-mile walk across peaty moorland to deserted **Sandwood Bay**. Few visitors make this half-day detour north, but the **beach** at the end of the rough track is one of the most beautiful in Scotland. Flanked by rolling dunes and lashed by fierce gales for much of the year, the shell-white sands and its dramatic leaning rock stack are said to be haunted by a bearded mariner. There's a well-equipped **campsite** at Oldshoremore (☎01971/521281), or you can continue through Blairmore to Sheigra, where the road ends, for informal camping behind the beach.

The north coast

Though a constant stream of sponsored walkers, caravans and tour groups makes it to **John O'Groats**, surprisingly few visitors travel the whole length of the Highlands' wild **north coast**. Those that do, however, rarely return disappointed. Pounded by one of the world's most ferocious seaways, Scotland's rugged northern shore is backed by barren mountains in the west, and in the east by lochs and open rolling grasslands. Between its far ends, mile upon mile of crumbling cliffs and sheer rocky headlands shelter bays whose perfect white beaches are nearly always deserted, even in the height of summer – though, somewhat incongruously, they're also home to Scotland's best **surfing** waves (see p.50). This is a great area for **birdwatching**, with huge seabird colonies clustered in clefts and on remote stacks at regular intervals along the coast; **seals** also bob around in the surf offshore, and in winter **whales** put in the odd appearance in the more sheltered estuaries of the northwest.

Public transport around this stretch of coast can be a slow and frustrating business: **Thurso**, the area's main town and springboard for Orkney, is well connected by bus and train with Inverness, but further west, after the main A836 peters into a single-track road, you have to rely on **postbus** connections or, in peak season, the single Highland Country bus #387.

Durness and around

Scattered around a string of sheltered sandy coves and grassy clifftops, **DURNESS**, the most northwesterly village on the British mainland, straddles the turning point on the main A838 road as it swings east from the inland peat bogs of the interior to the north coast's fertile strip of limestone machair. Even if you're only passing through, it's worth pausing here to see the **Smoo Cave**, a gaping hole in a sheer limestone cliff, and to visit beautiful **Balnakiel beach**, to the west. In addition, Durness is the jumping-off point for rugged **Cape Wrath**, the windswept promontory at the Scotland's northwest tip, which has retained an end-of-the-world mystique lost long ago by John O'Groats.

Public transport is sparse; the key service is the Highland Country bus #387 (June to mid-Sept Mon–Sat) leaving Thurso for Durness at 11.30am, and departing Durness on the return journey at 3pm. Durness is also served by the daily Dearman Coaches link (June–Sept) from Inverness via Ullapool and Lochinver. Postbuses provide a more complicated year-round alternative and meet trains at Lairg; check schedules at the post office or tourist office.

Durness's officious **tourist office** (April–Oct Mon–Sat 10am–5pm; July & Aug also Sun 11am–4pm; Oct–March Mon–Fri 10am–1.30pm; ☎01971/511259) can help with accommodation and arranges ranger-guided walks; its small visitor centre also features excellent interpretive panels detailing the area's history, geology, flora and fauna, with some good insights into the day-to-day life of the community. There is some good **accommodation**. The excellent *Lazy Crofter Bunkhouse* (☎01971/511209, ⓦ www.durnesshostel.co.uk) is open all year and has good facilities including a drying room. The basic SYHA **hostel** (☎01971/511244, ⓦ www.syha.org.uk; April–Sept), beside the Smoo Cave car park half a mile east of the village, also rents out mountain bikes. Durness's most picturesque **hotel** is the *Cape Wrath Hotel* (☎01971/511212; main hotel ❺, annexe ❸), which has a beautiful setting near the ferry jetty at Keoldale. Popular with walkers and fishermen, its rather austere character is offset by friendly service and a stunning view from the dining room. Of the **B&Bs**, *Puffin Cottage* (☎01971/511208; April–Oct; ❶) is small but very pleasant.

The Smoo Cave

Half a mile east of Durness village lies the 200ft-long **Smoo Cave**, formed partly by the action of the sea and partly by the small burn that flows through it. Tucked away at the end of a narrow sheer-sided sea cove, guides will show you the illuminated interior (£2.50), although the much-hyped rock formations are less memorable than the short rubber-dinghy trip you have to make in the second of three caverns, where the whole experience is enlivened after wet weather by a waterfall that crashes through the middle of the cavern. A **boat trip** (May–Sept daily; 1hr 30min; £7; call ☎01971/511365 or 511284 for schedule) leaves from Smoo Cave on a wildlife tour of the coast around Durness.

Balnakiel

A narrow road winds northwest of Durness to tiny **BALNAKIEL**, whose name derives from the Gaelic *Baile ne Cille* (Village of the Church). The white-sand beach on the east side of Balnakiel Bay is a stunning sight in any weather, but most spectacular on sunny days when the water turns to brilliant turquoise. The **Balnakiel Craft Village** back towards Durness, is worth a visit. Housed in an imaginatively converted 1940s military base, the campus consists of a dozen or so workshops where you can watch painters, potters, leather workers, candle makers, woodworkers, stone carvers, knitters and weavers in action – there's also a friendly bookshop with an excellent **café-restaurant** (☎01971/511777; daily 10am–6pm, plus evening meals Fri–Mon).

Cape Wrath

An excellent day-trip from Durness begins three miles southwest of the village at **Keoldale**, where a foot-passenger ferry (June–Aug hourly 9.30am–4.30pm; May & Sept approximately 4 daily; no motorcycles; no service in bad weather; ☎01971/511376) crosses the Kyle of Durness estuary to link up with a minibus (☎01971/511287; May–Sept) that runs the eleven miles out to **Cape Wrath**, the British mainland's most northwesterly point. The headland takes its name not from the stormy seas that crash against it for most of the year, but from the Norse word *hvarf*, meaning "turning place" – a throwback to the days when Viking warships used it as a navigation point during raids on the Scottish coast.

Tongue

It's a long slog around Loch Eriboll and east over the top of A Mhùine moor to the pretty crofting township of **TONGUE**. Dominated by the ruins of **Varick Castle**, the village, an eleventh-century Norse stronghold, is strewn over the east shore of the **Kyle of Tongue**, which you can either cross via a new causeway, or by following the longer and more scenic single-track road around its southern side. When the tide recedes, this shallow estuary becomes a mass of golden sand flats, superb on sunny days, with the sharp profiles of **Ben Hope** (3040ft) and **Ben Loyal** (2509ft) looming large to the south. Tongue's relatively temperate maritime climate even allows it to claim Britain's most northerly palm tree.

Accommodation includes *Rhian Cottage* (☎01847/611257, ✉jenny.anderson@tesco.net; ➋), a pretty whitewashed house with an attractive garden about a mile down the road past the post office. *Cloisters* (☎01847/601286, ⓦwww.cloistertal.demon.co.uk; ➋), two miles out of town at Talmire on the west side of the Kyle, has great views out towards the Orkney Islands and is well worth heading out of town for. There's also a well situated SYHA **hostel** with rather inconvenient opening hours (☎01847/611301, ⓦwww.syha.org.uk; April–Sept; lockout 10.30am–5pm), right beside the causeway a mile north of the village centre on the east shore of the Kyle.

Bettyhill and around

BETTYHILL, a major crofting village set among rocky green hills, straggles along the side of a narrow tidal estuary, and down the coast to two splendid beaches. The delightful and loyally maintained **Strathnaver Museum** (April–Oct Mon–Sat 10am–1pm & 2–5pm; £2), housed in the old church set apart from the village near the sea, is full of locally donated bits and pieces, and includes panels by local schoolchildren telling the story of the Strathnaver Clearances. You can also see some Pictish stones and a 3800-year-old, early Bronze Age beaker found in Strathnaver, the river valley south of the village, whose numerous prehistoric sites are mapped on an excellent pamphlet sold at the entrance desk.

As you move east from Bettyhill, the north coast changes dramatically as the hills on the horizon recede to be replaced by fields fringed with flagstone walls. At the hamlet of **MELVICH**, twelve miles east of Bettyhill, the A897 cuts south through Strath Halladale, the Flow Country (see below) and the Strath of Kildonan to Helmsdale on the east coast (see p.1247). Five miles further east, **Dounreay Nuclear Power Station**, a surreal collection of stark domes and chimney stacks marooned in the middle of nowhere, was the first reactor in the world to provide mains electricity. It's still a major local employer, though the reactors themselves were decommissioned in 1994 and the site is now being gradually detoxified, an operation estimated to take forty years or so. A permanent **exhibition** (May–Oct daily 10am–4pm; free) in the old aircraft control tower details the processes (and, unsurprisingly, the benefits) of nuclear power, and does at least make an attempt to address issues such as the area's "leukaemia cluster", and the high levels of radiation reported over the years on the nearby beaches.

South from Melvich: the Flow Country

From Melvich, you can head forty miles or so south towards Helmsdale on the A897, through the **Flow Country**. This huge expanse of bog land came into the news a few years ago when ecology experts, responding to plans to transform the area into forest, drew attention to the threat to this fragile landscape, described by one contemporary commentator as of "unique and global importance, equivalent to the African Serengeti or Brazil's rainforest". Some forest was planted, but the environmentalists won the day, and the forestry syndicates have had to pull out. There's an excellent RSPB Flow Country **visitor centre** (April–Oct daily 9am–6pm; ☎01641/571225), based in the train station at Forsinard, fifteen miles south of Melvich, which is easily accessible from Thurso, Wick and the south by train. Guided walks through the RSPB **nature reserve** leave from the visitor centre (May–Aug Tues & Thurs) and illuminate the importance of the area and its wildlife.

Thurso

Approached from the isolation of the west, **THURSO** feels like a metropolis. In reality, it's a relatively small service centre visited mostly by people passing through to the adjoining port of **Scrabster** to catch the ferry to Stromness in Orkney. Traill Street is the main drag, turning into the pedestrianized Rotterdam Street and High Street precinct at its northern end. The old part of town near the harbour holds **Old St Peter's Church**, a substantial ruin with origins in the thirteenth century, but which has been much altered over the years. There's a long sandy beach nearby. The most intriguing exhibit in the **Thurso Heritage Museum** on High Street (Mon–Sat 10am–1pm, 2–5pm; £1) is the Pictish Skinnet Stone, intricately carved with enigmatic symbols and a runic cross.

From Thurso **train station**, with services to Inverness and Wick, it's a ten-minute walk down Princes Street and Sir George Street to the **tourist office** on Riverside Road (April–Oct Mon–Sat 10am–5pm; also Sun: June & July 10am–5pm, Aug 10am–6pm Aug, Sept & Oct 11am–4pm; ☎01847/892371). The bus station, close by, runs regular **buses** to John O'Groats, Wick and Inverness and a summer service to Durness. Postbuses run as far as Tongue. **Ferries** operate daily from adjoining Scrabster to Orkney, which has less frequent links to Shetland and Aberdeen; you can book ahead through CalMac (☎0870/565 0000, ⓦwww.calmac.co.uk) or through any local tourist office. Scrabster is a mile west of town; a **taxi** (☎01847/892868) will set you back £3.

Thurso is well stocked with **accommodation**, including the cramped but very welcoming **hostel** *Sandra's*, 24 Princes St (☎01847/894575, ⓔsandras-backpackers@ukf.net). Of the **B&Bs**, *Murray House*, 1 Campbell St (☎01847/895759; ❷), is central, comfortable and friendly; there's also *Tigh Na Abhainn* on the river at 21 Millers Lane (☎01847/893443; ❶), or the long-established *Orcadia*, 27 Olrig St (☎01847/894395; ❶). The nearest **campsite** (☎01847/805503) is out towards Scrabster alongside the main road, though there's a much nicer one at Dunnet Bay, a few miles east (see below).

Food options include *Le Bistro*, 2 Traill St (☎01847/893737; Tues–Sat), with a reasonable-value menu of lunchtime snacks and more ambitious evening meals, and *Upper Deck*, by the harbour at Scrabster, serving large, moderately priced steaks and seafood dishes. You can **rent bikes** at *Sandra's* or at Wheels Cycle Shop on the extension of the High Street, beyond its junction with Couper Street, while Harper's fishing shop, a little further along at 57 High St (☎01847/893179) is the place to rent wetsuits or boards, or get hold of other **surfing** supplies, before you take on the mighty north-coast breaks.

East of Thurso

Despite the publicity that John O'Groats customarily receives, Britain's northernmost mainland point is in fact **Dunnet Head**. The headland is at the far side of Dunnet Bay, a vast sandy beach backed by huge dunes about six miles east of Thurso. The bay is popular with surfers, and even in the winter you can usually spot intrepid figures far out in the Pentland Firth's breakers. There's a **Ranger Centre** (April–Sept Tues–Fri 2–5pm, Sat & Sun 2–6pm) beside the excellent campsite at the east end of the bay, where you can pick up information on good local history and nature walks. Nearby is the small village of **DUNNET**, where it's worth stopping in at **Mary-Ann's Cottage** (June–Sept Tues–Sun 2–4.30pm; £1), a farming croft vacated in 1990 by 93-year-old Mary-Ann Calder and full of reminders of the three generations who lived and worked there over the last 150 years.

For Dunnet Head, turn off at Dunnet onto the B855, which runs for four miles over windy heather and bog to the tip of the headland, crowned with a Victorian lighthouse. The red cliffs below are startling, with weirdly eroded rock stacks and a huge variety of seabirds; on a clear day you can see the whole northern coastline from Cape Wrath to Duncansby Head, and across the Pentland Firth to Orkney. It's worth stopping off at the *Dunnet Head Tearoom* (℡01847/851774, ⓦwww.dunnethead.co.uk; ❶), halfway along the road to the headland. It serves snacks and filling meals, has **internet** access, views, and does good-value **B&B**.

John O'Groats

Romantics expecting to find a magical meeting of land and water at **JOHN O'GROATS** are invariably disappointed – sadly, but all too predictably, it's a seedy little tourist trap. The views north to Orkney are fine enough, but the village is little more than a string of overpriced souvenir shops thronged with coach parties. The village gets its name from the Dutchman, Jan de Groot, who obtained the ferry contract for the hazardous crossing to Orkney in 1496. The eight-sided house he built for his eight quarrelling sons (so that each one could enter by his own door) is echoed in the octagonal tower of the much-photographed *John O'Groats Hotel*, which is fast falling into disrepair but remains a good stop-off for a drink.

Aside from the frequent if irregular links with Land's End (the far southwest tip of England), maintained by a succession of walkers, cyclists, vintage-car drivers and pushers of baths, John O'Groats is connected by regular **buses** to Wick (7 daily Mon–Sat; 50min) and Thurso (Mon–Fri 5 daily, 2 on Sat; 1hr).

Ferries to Orkney

John O'Groats Ferries (℡01955/611353, ⓦwww.jogferry.co.uk) operates a daily passenger **ferry** across to Burwick (with a connecting bus to Kirkwall) in the Orkney Islands (May & Sept 2 daily; June–Aug 4 daily; 40min; £26 return): officially this is a foot-passenger service, but it will take bicycles and motorbikes if it isn't too busy. The company also offers a couple of whistle-stop **day-tours** of Orkney, as well as a more leisurely afternoon **wildlife cruise** round the Stacks of Duncansby and the seabird colonies of nearby Stroma Island (1hr 30min; £12), as do North Coast Marine Adventures (℡0786/766 6273, ⓦwww.northcoast-marine-adventures.co.uk). Mr Simpson (℡01955/611252) periodically takes groups across to **Stroma Island** in his boat.

From **Gills Bay**, five miles west of John O'Groats, Pentland Ferries runs a car and passenger ferry over to St Margaret's Hope (℡01856/831226, ⓦwww.pentlandferries.co.uk; 3 daily; 1hr 45min; £10 one-way, plus £25 for a car).

The east coast

The **east coast** of the Highlands, between Inverness and Wick, is nowhere near as spectacular as the west, with gently undulating moors, grassland and low cliffs where you might otherwise expect to find sea lochs and mountains. Washed by the cold waters of the North Sea, it's markedly cooler, too, although less prone to spells of permadrizzle and midges. Although the Inverness–Thurso train line is twice forced by topography to head inland, the region's main transport artery, the A9 road – slower here than in the south – follows the coast, which veers sharply northeast exactly parallel with the Great Glen and formed by the same geological fault.

While many visitors bypass this region in a headlong rush to the Orkneys, those who choose to dally will find prehistoric and historic sites that are equally impressive. The area around the Black Isle and the Tain Peninsula was a Pictish heartland, and has yielded many important finds. Further north, from around the ninth century AD onwards, the **Norse** influence was more keenly felt than in any other part of mainland Britain, and dozens of Scandinavian-sounding names recall the era when this was a Viking kingdom. The whole area is studded with prehistoric brochs, cairns and standing stones, many in remarkable condition.

Culturally and scenically, much of the east coast is more lowland than highland, and Caithness in particular evolved more or less separately from the Highlands, avoiding the bloody tribal feuds that wrought such havoc further south and west. Later, however, the nineteenth-century **Clearances** hit the region hard, as countless ruined cottages and empty glens show. Hundreds of thousands of crofters were evicted and forced to emigrate to New Zealand, Canada and Australia, or else take up fishing in one of the numerous herring ports established on the coast. The oil boom has brought a transient prosperity to one or two places over the past two decades, but this has been countered by the downturn in the North Sea fishing industry, and the area remains one of the country's poorest, reliant on sheep farming, fishing and tourism.

The one stretch of the east coast that's always been relatively rich is the **Black Isle** just over the Kessock Bridge heading north out of Inverness, whose main village, **Cromarty**, is the region's undisputed highlight, with a crop of elegant mansions and appealing fishermen's cottages clustered near the entrance to the Cromarty Firth. In late medieval times, pilgrims including James IV of Scotland poured through here en route to the red-sandstone town of **Tain** to worship at the shrine of St Duthus, where the former sacred enclave has now been converted into one of the many "heritage centres" that punctuate the route north. Beyond **Dornoch**, a famous golfing resort recently famous as the site of Madonna's wedding, the ersatz-Loire château **Dunrobin Castle** is the main tourist attraction, a monument as much to the iniquities of the Clearances as to the eccentricity of Victorian taste. The award-winning **Timespan Heritage Centre** further north at Helmsdale recounts the human cost of the landlords' greed, while the area around the port of **Lybster** is littered with the remains of more ancient civilizations. **Wick**, the largest town on this section of coast, has an interesting past inevitably entwined with the fishing industry, whose story is told in another good heritage centre, but is otherwise uninspiring. The relatively flat landscapes of this northeast corner – windswept peat bog and farmland dotted with lochans and grey and white crofts – are a surprising contrast to the more rugged country south and west of here.

The Black Isle and around

Sandwiched between the Cromarty Firth to the north and, to the south, the Moray and Beauly firths which separate it from Inverness, the **Black Isle** is not an island at all, but a fertile peninsula whose rolling hills, prosperous farms and stands of deciduous woodland make it more reminiscent of Dorset or Sussex than the Highlands. It probably gained its name because of its mild climate: there's rarely frost, which leaves the fields "black" all winter; another explanation is that the name derives from the Gaelic word for black, *dubh* – a possible corruption of St Duthus (see p.1244).

The Black Isle is littered with dozens of **prehistoric sites**, but the main incentive to make the detour east from the A9 is to visit the picturesque eighteenth-century town of **Cromarty**, huddled at the northeast tip of the peninsula. A string of villages along the south coast is also worth stopping off in en route, and one of them, Rosemarkie, has an outstanding small **museum** devoted to Pictish culture. Nearby Chanonry Point is among the best **dolphin-spotting** sites in Europe.

Fortrose and Rosemarkie

Just across the Kessock Bridge from Inverness is a roadside complex with a **tourist office** (Easter–Oct Mon–Sat 10am–5pm, Sun 11am–4pm; July & Aug Mon–Sat until 6pm; ☎01463/731505), as well as two wildlife centres. The **dolphin and seal centre** (May–Oct daily 10am–5pm; £1) offers the chance to see (and listen to) these popular creatures, while the RSPB have set up an observation post for the **red kite**, a bird-of-prey successfully reintroduced to Scotland in 1992.

FORTROSE is a quietly elegant village dominated by the beautiful ruins of an early thirteenth-century **cathedral** (daily 8am–8pm). Founded by King David I, it now languishes on a lovely green bordered by red-sandstone and colourwashed houses, where a horde of gold coins dating from the time of Robert III was unearthed in 1880. There's also a memorial to the Seaforth family, whose demise the Brahan Seer famously predicted (see box). There's a memorial plaque to the seer at nearby **Chanonry Point**, reached by a backroad from the north end of Fortrose; the thirteenth hole of the golf course here marks the spot where he met his death. Jutting into a narrow channel in the Moray Firth (deepened to allow warships into the estuary during World War

The Brahan Seer

A memorial plaque in Fortrose remembers the seventeenth-century visionary **Cùinneach Odhar** (Kenneth Mackenzie), known as the Brahan Seer. Legend has it that he derived his powers of second sight from a small white divination stone passed on to him, through his mother, from a Viking princess. With the pebble pressed against his eye, Cùinneach foretold everything from outbreaks of measles in the village to the building of the Caledonian Canal, the Clearances and World War II. In 1660, Countess Seaforth, wife of the local laird, summoned the seer after her husband was late home from a trip to France. Reluctantly – when pressurized – he told the Countess that he had seen the earl "on his knees before a fair lady, his arm round her waist and her hand pressed to his lips". At this, she flew into a rage, accused him of sullying the family name and ordered him to be thrown head first into a barrel of boiling tar. However, just before the gruesome execution, Cùinneach made his last prediction: when a deaf and dumb earl inherited the estate, the Seaforth line would end. His prediction finally came true in 1815 when the last earl died.

II), the point, fringed on one side by a beach of golden sand and shingle, is an excellent place to look for **dolphins** (see below). Come here around high tide, and you stand a good chance of spotting a couple leaping through the surf in search of fish brought to the surface by converging currents.

ROSEMARKIE, a lovely one-street village a mile north of Fortrose at the opposite (northwest) end of the beach, is thought to have been evangelized by St Boniface in the early eighth century. The cosy **Groam House Museum** (May–Sept Mon–Sat 10am–5pm, Sun 2–4.30pm; Oct–April Sat & Sun 2–4pm; £1.50), at the bottom of the village, displays a bumper crop of intricately carved Pictish standing stones (among them the famous Rosemarkie Cross Slab), and shows an informative video highlighting Pictish sites in the region. Quality bar food is available at the wonderfully old-fashioned *Plough Inn*, just down the main street from the museum. It's owned by the local Black Isle Brewery and is a good spot to try their range.

Cromarty

An ancient legend recalls that the twin headlands flanking the entrance to the **Cromarty Firth**, known as The Sutors (from the Gaelic word for shoemaker), were once a pair of giant cobblers who used to protect the Black Isle from pirates. Nowadays, however, the only giants in the area are Nigg and Invergordon's colossal oil rigs, marooned in the estuary like metal monsters marching out to sea. Built and serviced here for the Forties oil field in the North Sea, they form a surreal counterpoint to the web of tiny streets and chocolate-box workers' cottages of **CROMARTY**, the Black Isle's main settlement. Although a royal burgh since the fourth century, Cromarty didn't became a prominent port until 1772 when the entrepreneurial local landlord, George Ross, founded a hemp mill here. Imported Baltic hemp was spun into cloth and rope in the mill, fuelling a period of prosperity during which Cromarty acquired some of Scotland's finest Georgian houses; these, together with the terraced fishers' cottages of the nineteenth-century herring boom, have left the town with a wonderfully well-preserved concentration of Scottish domestic architecture.

To get a sense of Cromarty's past, head straight for the award-winning **museum** housed in the old **Courthouse** on Church Street (daily: April–Oct 10am–5pm; Nov–Dec & March noon–4pm; £3), which tells the history of the town using audiovisuals and animated figures. You are also issued with a personal stereo, a tape and a map for a walking tour around the town. **Hugh Miller**, a nineteenth-century stonemason turned author, geologist, folklorist and Free Church campaigner, was born in Cromarty, and his **birthplace** (May–Sept Mon–Sat 11am–1pm & 2–5pm, Sun 2–5pm; NTS; £2.50), a modest thatched cottage on Church Street, has been restored to give an idea of what Cromarty must have been like in his day.

The widely respected Dolphin Écosse (☎01381/600323, ⓦwww.dolphinecosse.co.uk) runs half- or full-day **boat trips** to see seals, porpoises, bottle-nosed dolphins and occasionally minke whales from their Dolphin Centre by the harbour behind the *Royal Hotel*. The tiny two-car Nigg–Cromarty **ferry** (May–Sept daily 9am–6pm), Scotland's smallest, also doubles up as a cruiser on summer evenings; you can catch it from the jetty near the lighthouse.

Nine **buses** a day run to Cromarty from Inverness (55min), returning from the car park at the bottom of Forsyth Place. For **B&B**, try one of the attractive old houses on Church Street, such as Mrs Robertson's at no. 7 (☎01381/600488; ❶), where you can also **rent bikes**. Above the town, *Beechfield House*

(☎01381/600308; ❷) offers modern rooms and good views. The most down-to-earth place **to eat** is the *Cromarty Arms*, which has a beer garden and serves basic, inexpensive bar meals – it also has occasional live music. The *Royal Hotel*'s restaurant features Scottish specialities, while cheaper meals are available in the cosy public bar or, on fine nights, on the terrace outside with great views over the firth.

Dingwall and Strathpeffer

Most traffic nowadays takes the upgraded A9 north from Inverness, bypassing the small market town of **DINGWALL** (from the Norse *thing*, "parliament", and *vollr*, "field"), a royal burgh since 1226 and former port that was left high and dry when the river receded during the nineteenth century. Dingwall's only real claim to fame is that it was the birthplace of Macbeth, whose family occupied the now ruined castle on Castle Street. There's a small **museum** in the centre of town (May–Sept Mon–Sat 10am–5pm; £1.50), and it's worth checking out The Casbah on Tulloch Street for a small but quirky collection of secondhand books, vinyl and curios.

STRATHPEFFER, a mannered and leafy Victorian spa town surrounded by wooded hills four miles west of Dingwall, is pleasant enough but does suffer from a high density of coach parties. During its heyday, this was a renowned European **health resort** reached by the tongue-twisting Strathpeffer Spa Express train from Aviemore. Strathpeffer is within striking distance of the bleak **Ben Wyvis**, and so is also a popular base for walkers. One of the best hikes in the area begins from the SYHA hostel, at the west end of the village, from where a forestry track leads through dense woodland towards the hill of Cnoc Mor. Rather less than a mile farther on, you can turn up onto the ridge on the right and follow it to reach the vitrified Iron Age hill fort of **Knock Farril**, which affords superb panoramic views to the Cromarty Firth and the surrounding mountains.

Buses run regularly between Dingwall and Strathpeffer (11 daily Mon–Sat), dropping passengers in the square, where you'll find a small **tourist office** (July & Aug Mon–Sat 9am–5.30pm, Sun 10am–5.30pm; June to mid-Oct Mon–Sat 10am–5pm, Sun 11am–4pm; April & May Mon–Sat 10am–5pm; ☎01997/421415) with information on points west as well as local areas. The *Inver Lodge*, west of the main square (☎01997/421392; ❶; March–Dec), and *Francisville*, just past the church (☎01997/421345; ❶; April–Oct), both offer good **B&B**. The rambling fifty-bed SYHA **hostel** (☎01997/421532, ⓦwww.syha.org.uk; May–Sept) is a mile southwest of the main square up the hill towards Jameston.

The Dornoch Firth and around

North of the Cromarty Firth, the hammer-shaped **Tain peninsula** can still be approached from the south by the ancient ferry crossing from Cromarty to Nigg, though to the north the link is a more recent causeway over the **Dornoch Firth**, the inlet which marks the northern boundary of the peninsula. On the southern edge of the Dornoch Firth the A9 bypasses the quiet town of **Tain**, probably best known as the home of Glenmorangie whisky. Inland, at the head of the firth, there's not much to the village of **Bonar Bridge**, but fans of unusual hostels travel from far and wide to spend a night with the ghosts at the Duchess of Sutherland's imposing former home, **Carbisdale Castle**. Back on the coast, on the north side of the Dornoch Firth, the neat town of **Dornoch** itself, long known for its impressive cathedral and well-manicured golf courses, found renewed fame in 2000 as the venue for an outbreak of Madonna-mania, when it hosted the pop star's wedding.

Tain

The peninsula's largest settlement is **TAIN**, an attractive and pleasant small town of grand whisky-coloured sandstone buildings that was the birthplace of **St Duthus**, an eleventh-century missionary who inspired great devotion in the Middle Ages. A good place to get to grips with the peninsula's past is the **Tain Through Time** exhibition (April–Oct daily 10am–6pm; call for winter opening hours; ☎01862/894089; £3.50), which makes creative use of three old buildings around the church and graveyard, leading you round using an audioguide. Tain's other main attraction is the **whisky distillery** where the highly rated Glenmorangie malt is produced (☎01862/892477; shop Mon–Fri 9am–5pm, June–Aug also Sat 10am–4pm, Sun noon–4pm; tours Mon–Fri 10am–3.30pm, Sat & Sun 10.30am–2.30pm; £2); it lies just off the A9 on the north side of town. Booking is recommended for the tours.

Bonar Bridge and Carbisdale Castle

Before the causeway was built across the Dornoch Firth, traffic heading along the coast used to skirt west around the estuary, crossing the Kyle of Sutherland at the village of **BONAR BRIDGE**. The place has struggled since it was bypassed: there's little of note here other than the **bridge** itself, which has had three incarnations up to the present steel construction of 1973.

Towering high above the River Shin, three miles northwest of Bonar Bridge, the daunting neo-Gothic profile of **Carbisdale Castle** overlooks the Kyle of Sutherland. The castle was erected between 1906 and 1917 for the dowager Duchess of Sutherland, following a protracted family feud. After the death of her husband, the late Duke of Sutherland, the will leaving her the lion's share of the vast estate was contested by his stepchildren from his first marriage. In the course of the ensuing legal battle, the Duchess was found in contempt of court for destroying important documents pertinent to the case, and locked up in London's Holloway prison for six weeks. However, the Sutherlands eventually recanted (although there was no personal reconciliation) and, by way of compensation, built their stepmother a castle worthy of her rank. Designed in three distinct styles (to give the impression it was added to over a long period of time), Carbisdale was eventually acquired by a Norwegian shipping magnate in 1933, and finally gifted, along with its entire contents and estate, to the Scottish Youth Hostels Association, which has turned it into what must be one of the most opulent **hostels** in the world, full of white Italian marble sculptures, huge gilt-framed portraits, sweeping staircases and magnificent drawing rooms alongside standard facilities such as self-catering kitchens, games rooms, TV rooms and thirty dorms, including some recently upgraded four-bed family rooms (☎01549/421232; March–Oct; £13.50), often booked out by groups. The best way to get here by public transport is to take a **train** to nearby Culrain station, which lies within easy walking distance of the castle. **Buses** from Inverness (3 daily; 1hr 30min) and Tain (4 daily; 25min) only stop at **Ardgay**, three miles south.

Dornoch

DORNOCH, a genteel and appealing town eight miles north of Tain, lies on a flattish headland overlooking the **Dornoch Firth**. Surrounded by sand dunes and blessed with an exceptionally sunny climate by Scottish standards, it's something of a middle-class holiday resort, with solid Edwardian hotels, trees and flowers in profusion, and miles of sandy beaches giving good views across the estuary to the Tain peninsula. The town is also renowned for its championship **golf course**, ranked eleventh in the world and the most northerly first-class course. Dornoch was the scene for 2000's most prestigious rock'n'roll wedding, when Madonna married Guy Ritchie at nearby Skibo Castle and had her son baptized in Dornoch cathedral.

Dating from the twelfth century, Dornoch became a royal burgh in 1628. Among its oldest buildings, which are all grouped round the spacious square, the exquisite **cathedral** was founded in 1224 and built of local sandstone. The original building was horribly damaged by marauding Mackays in 1570, and much of what you see today was restored by the Countess of Sutherland in 1835, though her worst Victorian excesses were removed last century, when the interior stonework was returned to its original state.

Buses from Tain and Inverness stop in the Square, where you'll also find a **tourist office** (May–Oct Mon–Fri 9am–5pm; ℡01862/810400). There's no shortage of **accommodation**: *Tordarroch B&B* (℡01862/810855; March–Oct; ❷), has a great location opposite the cathedral, as does the *Trevose* (℡01862/810269; ❶; March–Sept) which is swathed in roses. Expensive gourmet **meals** are available at the *2 Quail* restaurant (℡01862/811811; Tues–Sat) on Castle Street, which also has tasteful rooms (❹); *Mallin House Hotel* (℡01862/810355) is famous for seafood, and *Luigi's*, on Castle Street, is a good spot for snacks and lunches.

North to Wick

North of Dornoch, the A9 hugs the coastline for most of the sixty or so miles to **Wick**, the principal settlement in the far north of the mainland. Perhaps the most important landmark in the whole stretch is the **Sutherland Monument** near Golspie, erected in memory of the first Duke of Sutherland, known as the landowner who oversaw the eviction of thousands of his tenants in a process known as the Clearances. The bitter memory of those times resonates through most of the small towns and villages on this stretch, including **Brora**, the gold-prospecting village of **Helmsdale**, **Dunbeath** and **Lybster**. With sites dotted around recalling Iron Age settlers and Viking rule, many of these settlements also hark back to the days of a thriving fishing trade, none more so than the main town of Wick, once the busiest herring port in Europe.

Golspie and around

Ten miles north of Dornoch on the A9 lies the straggling red-sandstone town of **GOLSPIE**, whose status as an administrative centre does little to relieve its dullness. The main reason to stop in Golspie is to look around **Dunrobin Castle** (April to mid-Oct Mon–Sat 10.30am–4.30pm, Sun noon–4.30pm; June–Sept daily until 5.30pm; £6), overlooking the sea a mile north of town. Approached via a long tree-lined drive, this fairy-tale confection of turrets and pointed roofs – modelled by the architect Sir Charles Barry (designer of the

Houses of Parliament) on a Loire château – is the seat of the infamous Sutherland family, at one time Europe's biggest landowners, with a staggering 1.3 million acres, and the principal driving force behind the Clearances in this area. Staring up at the pile from the midst of its elaborate **formal gardens**, it's worth remembering that such extravagance was paid for by uprooting literally thousands of crofters from the surrounding glens.

Set aside at least an hour for Dunrobin's amazing **museum**, housed in an eighteenth-century building at the edge of the garden. Inside, hundreds of disembodied animals' heads and horns peer down from the walls, alongside other more macabre appendages, from elephants' toes to rhinos' tails. Bagged mainly by the fifth Duke and Duchess of Sutherland, the trophies vie for space with other fascinating family memorabilia, including one of John O'Groat's bones, Chinese opium pipes, and some finely carved Pictish stones. The admission price to the castle includes a falconry display (3 daily).

The Sutherland Monument

A mile northwest of Golspie, you can't miss the 100ft **monument** to the first Duke of Sutherland, which peers proprietorially down from the summit of the 1293ft **Beinn a'Bhragaidh** (Ben Bhraggie). An inscription cut into its base recalls that the statue was erected in 1834 by "a mourning and grateful tenantry [to] a judicious, kind and liberal landlord [who would] open his hands to the distress of the widow, the sick and the traveller". Unsurprisingly, there's no reference to the fact that the duke, widely regarded as Scotland's own Josef Stalin, forcibly evicted 15,000 crofters from his million-acre estate – a fact which, in the words of one local historian, makes the monument "a grotesque representation of the many forces that destroyed the Highlands". The campaign to have the statue smashed and scattered over the hillside has largely died down; the general attitude now seems to be that the statue now stands as a useful reminder of the duke's infamy as much as his achievements.

It's worth the wet, rocky **climb** to the top of the hill (round-trip 1hr 30min) for the wonderful views south along the coast past Dornoch to the Moray Firth and west towards Lairg and Loch Shin. It's steep and strenuous, however, and there's no view until you're out of the trees, about ten minutes from the top. Take the road opposite Munro's TV Rentals in Golspie's main street, which leads up the hill, past a fountain, under the railway and through a farmyard; from here, follow the Beinn a'Bhragaidh footpath (BBFP) signs along the path into the woods. You can go back the way you came, or follow a clear track which initially goes north from the monument and then winds down through Benvraggie Wood to meet a tarred road; turn left here to link into the path of the Big Burn Glen walk.

Rogart

Just to the south of Golspie on the A839 to Lairg is one of Scotland's most unusual and imaginative **hostels**, *Sleeperzzz.com* (℡01408/641343, ⓦwww.sleeperzzz.com), where you can stay in one of two first-class railway carriages parked in a siding beside the station on the Inverness–Thurso line in the tiny settlement of **ROGART**. Each of the comfortable compartments has a bunk bed on one side and the original seats on the other, while the two end compartments are used as a kitchen and common room. The owners have free **mountain bikes** available to let you explore the local countryside, and the place stands 100 yards from a convivial local **pub**, the *Pittentrail Inn*, that serves warming evening meals. A small reduction is even offered to those arriving by train or bicycle.

Helmsdale and around

Eleven scenic miles north along the A9 from Golspie, **HELMSDALE** is an old herring port, founded in the nineteenth century to house the evicted inhabitants of Strath Kildonan, which lies behind it. Today, the sleepy-looking grey village attracts thousands of tourists, most of them coming to see the attractively designed **Timespan Heritage Centre** beside the river (April to mid-Oct Mon–Sat 9.30am–5pm, Sun 2–5pm; July & Aug until 6pm; £3.50). It's a remarkable venture for a place of this size, telling the local story of Viking raids, witch-burning, Clearances, fishing and gold-prospecting through hi-tech displays, sound effects and an audiovisual programme. The centre also has an art gallery, which often has a decent show of works by Scottish artists.

Eating options abound in Helmsdale. On the main street, local fish wars are taking place between the *Mirage* restaurant and the *Bunillidh* opposite: the proprietor of the *Mirage* has become something of a Scottish celebrity, modelling herself on the romantic novelist Barbara Cartland, whose shooting lodge is nearby. The fittings and furnishings reflect her predilection for all things pink and frilly, with fish tanks, fake-straw parasols and plastic seagulls set off by the country-and-western soundtrack. There's obviously no love lost between her and the kitsch-free *Bunillidh* – though the aggressive marketing conceals the happy fact that both serve excellent meals (especially seafood) at rock-bottom prices.

Baile an Or

From Helmsdale the single-track A897 runs up Strath Kildonan and across the Flow Country (see p.1238) to the north coast, at first following the River Helmsdale, a strictly controlled and exclusive salmon river frequented by the Royal Family. Some eight miles up the Strath at **BAILE AN OR** (Gaelic for "goldfield"), gold was discovered in the bed of the Kildonan Burn in 1869; a **gold rush** ensued, hardly on the scale of the Yukon, but quite bizarre in the Scottish Highlands. A tiny amount of gold is still found by some hardy prospectors every year: should you fancy **gold-panning** yourself, you can rent the relevant equipment for £2.50 from Helmsdale's gift and fishing-tackle shop, Strath Ullie, on the harbour, which also sells a booklet with a few basic tips.

Lybster and around

The final stretch of road before Wick gives great views out to sea to the oil rigs perched on the horizon. The spectacular series of green-topped cliffs and churning bays are gorgeous in the sun and impressively bleak in bad weather. The planned village of **LYBSTER** (pronounced "libe-ster"), established at the height of the nineteenth-century herring boom, once had 200-odd boats working out of its harbour. The new **Water Lines** heritage centre on the harbour (April–Sept daily 11am–5pm; £2) is an attractive modern display about the "silver darlings" and the fishermen that pursued them; there's a snug café downstairs. There's not much else to see here apart from the harbour area; the upper town is a grim collection of grey pebble-dashed bungalows centred on a broad main street.

The **Grey Cairns of Camster**, seven miles due north and one of the most memorable sights on the northeast coast, are a different story. Surrounded by bleak moorland, these two enormous reconstructed prehistoric burial chambers, originally built four or five thousand years ago, were immaculately designed, with corbelled drystone roofs in their hidden chambers, which you can crawl into through narrow passageways. More extraordinary ancient remains lie at **East Clyth**, two miles north of Lybster on the A99, where a path leads to the "**Hill o'Many Stanes**". Some 200 boulders stand in the ground here, forming 22 parallel rows that run north to south; no one has yet worked out what they were used for, although archeological studies have shown there were once 600 stones in place. A fourteen-mile track waymarked as a cycle path leads between the two sites, entering the forest at a car park half a mile south of the Camster Cairns and emerging near the single-track road which passes the Hill o'Many Stanes and connects with the A99.

Wick

Originally a Viking settlement named *Vik* (meaning "bay"), **WICK** has been a royal burgh since 1589. It's actually two towns: Wick proper, and **Pultneytown**, immediately south across the river. Wick's heyday was in the mid-nineteenth century, when it was the busiest herring port in Europe, with a fleet of over 1100 boats, exporting tons of fish to Russia, Scandinavia and the West Indian slave plantations. Although Robert Louis Stevenson described it as "the meanest of man's towns, situated on the baldest of God's bays", it's by no means a bad place, although there's no doubt it has a down-at-heel atmosphere. Pultneytown, lined with rows of fishermen's cottages, is the area most worth a wander, with the acres of largely derelict net-mending sheds, stores and cooperages around the harbour giving some idea of the former scale of the fishing trade. The town's story is told in the excellent **Wick Heritage Centre** in Bank Row, Pultneytown (June–Sept Mon–Sat 10am–5pm; £2), which contains a fascinating array of artefacts from the old fishing days, including fully-rigged boats, original boat models, the old Noss Head lighthouse light and a great photographic collection dating from the 1880s. Interestingly, Wick was a dry town for quarter of a century until 1947, although that didn't stop some of the locals heading off to Lybster or Thurso for a quiet beer or two.

The **train** station and **bus** stops are next to each other behind the hospital. Frequent local buses run to Thurso and up the coast to John O'Groats (7 daily). Wick also has an **airport** (℡01955/602215), a couple of miles north of the town, with direct flights from Edinburgh and Aberdeen, and connections further south. From the train station, head across the river down Bridge Street to the cheerful **tourist office**, just off the High Street (April–Oct Mon–Sat 10am–5pm; July–Oct also Sun 11am–4pm; Nov–March Mon–Fri 11am–2.30pm; ℡01955/602596), which can organize local **accommodation**. On Louisburgh Street, the *Nethercliffe Hotel* (℡01955/602044; ❷) is good value, while the best of the hotels is *Mackay's*, by the river in the town centre (℡01955/602323, ⓦ www.mackayshotel.co.uk; ❺). Five miles towards Thurso is the lovely *Bilbster House* (℡01955/621212; April–Oct; in winter by arrangement; ❶). The north bank of the river, at the east end of High Street, is the best spot for **eating** and **drinking**. On Market Street, the *Bord de l'Eau* (℡01955/604400; Tues–Sun) produces gourmet French cuisine at excellent prices, while round the corner *Cabrelli's* may be trapped in a time warp but it serves piles of fish and chips, along with authentic pizza.

Travel details

Trains

Aviemore to: Edinburgh (Mon–Sat 5 daily, 3 on Sun; 3hr); Inverness (Mon–Sat 5 daily, 4 on Sun; 40min); Newtonmore (Mon–Sat 5 daily, 3 on Sun; 20min).

Dingwall to: Helmsdale (Mon–Sat 3 daily, plus 2 on Sun in summer; 2hr); Inverness (Mon–Sat 6–7 daily, plus 4 on Sun in summer; 25min); Kyle of Lochalsh (Mon–Sat 3–4 daily, plus 2 on Sun in summer; 2hr); Lairg (Mon–Sat 3 daily, plus 2 on Sun in summer; 1hr); Thurso (Mon–Sat 3 daily, plus 2 on Sun in summer; 3hr); Wick (Mon–Sat 3 daily, plus 2 on Sun in summer; 3hr 20min).

Fort William to: Arisaig (Mon–Sat 4 daily, 1–3 on Sun; 1hr 10min); Crianlarich (Mon–Sat 3–4 daily, 1–2 on Sun; 1hr 40min); Glasgow (Mon–Sat 3 daily, 1–2 on Sun; 4hr); Glenfinnan (4 daily; 35min); London (1 nightly; 12hr); Mallaig (Mon–Sat 4 daily, 1–3 on Sun; 1hr 25min).

Inverness to: Aviemore (Mon–Sat 5 daily, 3 on Sun; 40min); Dingwall (Mon–Sat 6–7 daily, plus 4 on Sun in summer; 25min); Edinburgh (Mon–Sat 5 daily, 3 on Sun; 3hr 30min); Helmsdale (Mon–Sat 3 daily, plus 2 on Sun in summer; 2hr 20min); Kyle of Lochalsh (Mon–Sat 3–4 daily, plus 2 on Sun in summer; 2hr 40min); Lairg (Mon–Sat 3 daily, plus 2 on Sun in summer; 1hr 40min); London (Mon–Fri & Sun 1 nightly; 8hr 35min); Plockton (Mon–Sat 3–4 daily, plus 2 on Sun in summer; 2hr 15min); Thurso (Mon–Sat 3 daily, plus 2 on Sun in summer; 3hr 25min); Wick (Mon–Sat 3 daily, plus 2 on Sun in summer; 3hr 45min).

Kyle of Lochalsh to: Dingwall (Mon–Sat 3–4 daily, plus 2 on Sun in summer; 2hr); Inverness (Mon–Sat 3–4 daily, plus 2 on Sun in summer; 2hr 40min); Plockton (Mon–Sat 3–4 daily, plus 2 on Sun in summer; 20min).

Lairg to: Dingwall (Mon–Sat 3 daily, plus 2 on Sun in summer; 1hr 10min); Inverness (Mon–Sat 3 daily, plus 2 on Sun in summer; 1hr 40min); Thurso (Mon–Sat 3 daily, plus 2 on Sun in summer; 1hr 50min); Wick (Mon–Sat 3 daily, plus 2 on Sun in summer; 2hr 20min).

Mallaig to: Arisaig (Mon–Sat 4 daily, plus 3 on Sun in summer; 15min); Fort William (Mon–Sat 4 daily, plus 3 on Sun in summer; 1hr 25min); Glasgow (Mon–Sat 3 daily, 1–2 on Sun; 5hr 20min); Glenfinnan (Mon–Sat 4 daily, plus 3 on Sun in summer; 35min).

Newtonmore to: Aviemore (Mon–Sat 5 daily, 3 on Sun; 20min); Inverness (Mon–Sat 5 daily, 3 on Sun; 55min).

Thurso to: Dingwall (Mon–Sat 3 daily, plus 2 on Sun in summer; 3hr); Inverness (Mon–Sat 3 daily, plus 2 on Sun in summer; 3hr 20min); Lairg (Mon–Sat 3 daily, plus 2 on Sun in summer; 1hr 50min).

Wick to: Dingwall (Mon–Sat 3 daily, plus 2 on Sun in summer; 3hr 20min); Inverness (Mon–Sat 3 daily, plus 2 on Sun in summer; 3hr 45min); Lairg (Mon–Sat 3 daily, plus 2 on Sun in summer; 2hr 5min).

Buses

Aviemore to: Grantown-on-Spey (6–9 daily; 35min); Inverness (15 daily; 40min); Newtonmore (8 daily; 20min).

Dornoch to: Thurso (4 daily; 2hr 20min); Inverness (10 daily; 1hr 10min).

Fort William to: Acharacle (Mon–Sat 2–4 daily; 1hr 30min); Aviemore (2 daily; 1hr 50min); Drumnadrochit (6 daily; 1hr 30min); Fort Augustus (6 daily; 1hr); Inverness (6 daily; 2hr); Mallaig (1–2 daily; 2hr).

Gairloch to: Dingwall (3 weekly; 2hr); Inverness (3 weekly; 2hr 20min); Redpoint (1–3 daily; 1hr 35min).

Inverness to: Aberdeen (hourly; 3hr 40min); Aviemore (12–15 daily; 40min); Cromarty (8 daily; 45min); Drumnadrochit (6 daily; 25min); Durness (June–Sept 1 daily; 5hr); Fort Augustus (6 daily; 1hr); Fort William (6 daily; 2hr); Gairloch (1 daily; 2hr 20min); Glasgow (10 daily; 3hr 35min–4hr 25min); Kyle of Lochalsh (2 daily; 2hr); Lairg (Mon–Sat 2 daily; 2hr); Lochinver (June–Sept 1 daily; 3hr 10min); Nairn (Mon–Sat hourly; 35min); Newtonmore (8 daily; 1hr 10min); Oban (Mon–Sat 2 daily; 4hr); Perth (12–15 daily; 2hr 35min); Portree (2 daily; 3hr 20min); Tain (hourly; 1hr 15min); Thurso (Mon–Sat 5 daily, Sun 4 daily; 3hr 30min); Ullapool (2–4 daily; 1hr 25min); Wick (Mon–Sat 5 daily, Sun 4 daily; 3hr).

Kyle of Lochalsh to: Fort William (3 daily; 1hr 50min); Glasgow (3 daily; 5hr); Inverness (2 daily; 2hr).

Lochinver to: Inverness (June–Sept 1 daily; 3hr 10min).

Mallaig to: Acharacle (1–3 daily; 1hr 45min); Fort William (1–2 daily; 2hr).

Thurso to: Bettyhill (2 daily; 1hr 20min); Inverness (Mon–Sat 5 daily, Sun 4 daily; 3hr 30min); Wick (Mon–Fri hourly, Sat & Sun 6 daily; 35min).

Wick to: Inverness (Mon–Sat 3 daily; 3hr); Thurso (Mon–Fri hourly, Sat & Sun 6 daily; 35min).

Ferries

To Lewis: Ullapool–Stornoway, see p.1136.
To Mull: Kilchoan–Tobermory, see p.1219.
To Orkney: Scrabster–Stromness, John O'Groats–Burwick, Gills Bay–St Margaret's Hope, see p.1239.

To Skye: Mallaig–Armadale and Glenelg–Kylerhea, see p.1121.
To the Small Isles: Mallaig–Eigg, Rùm, Muck and Canna, see p.1131.

Flights

Inverness to: Edinburgh (Mon–Fri 2 daily, Sat & Sun 1 daily; 50min); Glasgow (Mon–Fri 3 daily, Sat 1 daily; 50min); Kirkwall (Mon–Sat 2 daily; 45min); London (Gatwick 3 daily; Luton 1–2 daily; 1hr 45min); Shetland (Mon–Sat 1 daily; 1hr 45min); Stornoway (Mon–Fri 2 daily, 1 on Sat; 40min).

25

Orkney
and Shetland

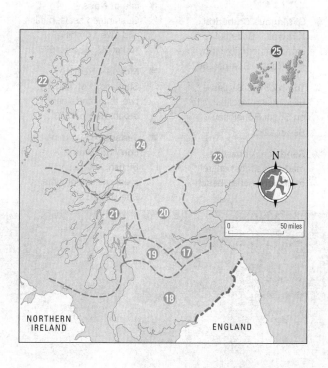

CHAPTER 25

Highlights

＊ **Maes Howe** – Orkney's, and Europe's, finest Neolithic chambered tomb. See p.1258

＊ **Woodwick House** – Beautiful guest house hideaway, producing simple but superb food. See p.1259

＊ **St Magnus Cathedral, Kirkwall** – Beautiful red-stone cathedral built by the Vikings. See p.1260

＊ **Tomb of the Eagles** – Fascinating Neolithic site on South Ronaldsay. See p.1263

＊ **Sanday** – A coastline made up almost entirely of glorious sandy beaches, backed by sand dunes. See p.1269

＊ **Traditional music** – Weekly sessions in Tingwall on Shetland, plus the annual Shetland Folk Festival. See p.1275

＊ **Isle of Noss** – Guaranteed seals, puffins and dive-bombing "bonxies". See p.1275

＊ **Mousa** – Remote Shetland islet with a two-thousand-year-old broch. See p.1276

＊ **Jarlshof** – Site mingling Iron Age, Bronze Age, Pictish, Viking and medieval settlements. See p.1276

Orkney
and Shetland

Reaching up towards the Arctic Circle, and totally exposed to turbulent Atlantic weather systems, the **Orkney** and **Shetland** islands gather neatly into two distinct and very different clusters. Often referring to themselves first as Orcadians or Shetlanders, and with unofficial but widely displayed flags, their inhabitants regard Scotland as a separate entity; the mainland to them is the one in their own archipelago, not the Scottish mainland. This feeling of detachment arises from their distinctive geography, history and culture, in which they differ not only from Scotland but also from each other.

To the south, just a short step from the Scottish mainland, are the seventy or so **Orkney Islands**. With the major exception of **Hoy**, which is high and rugged, these islands are mostly low-lying, gently sloping and richly fertile, and for centuries have provided a reasonably secure living for their inhabitants from farming and, to a much lesser extent, fishing. In spring and summer the days are long, the skies enormous, the sandy beaches dazzling and the meadows thick with wild flowers. There is a peaceful continuity to Orcadian life reflected not only in the well-preserved treasury of Stone Age settlements, such as **Skara Brae**, and standing stones, most notably the **Stones of Stenness**, but also in the rather conservative nature of society here today.

Another sixty miles north, the **Shetland Islands** are in nearly all respects a complete contrast. Dramatic cliffs, teeming with thousands of seabirds, rise straight out of the water to rugged, heather-coated hills, while ice-sculpted sea inlets cut deep into the land, offering memorable coastal walks in Shetland's endless summer evenings. With little fertile ground, Shetlanders have traditionally been crofters rather than farmers, often looking to the sea for an uncertain living in fishing and whaling or the naval and merchant services. Today islanders enthusiastically embrace new opportunities such as fish farming and computing. Nevertheless, the past isn't forgotten; the Norse heritage is clear in every roadsign and there are many well-preserved prehistoric sites, such as **Mousa Broch** and **Jarlshof**.

Since people first began to explore the North Atlantic, Orkney and Shetland have been stepping stones on routes between Britain, Ireland and Scandinavia, and both groups have a long history of settlement, certainly from around 4000–3500 BC. The **Norse settlers**, who began to arrive from about 800 AD, left the islands with a unique cultural character. Orkney was a powerful Norse earldom, and Shetland (at first part of the same earldom) was ruled directly from Norway for nearly three hundred years after 1195. The Norse legacy is clearly evident today in place names and in dialect words; neither group was ever part of the Gaelic-speaking culture of Highland Scotland, and the later Scottish influence is essentially a Lowland one.

It's impossible to underestimate the influence of the **weather**. More often than not, it will be windy and rainy, though you can have all four seasons in one day. The wind-chill factor is not to be taken lightly, and there is often a dampness or drizzle in the air, even when it's not actually raining. Even in late spring and summer, when there can be long dry spells with lots of sunshine, you still need to come prepared for wind, rain and, most frustrating of all, the occasional sea fog. The one good thing is that midges are less of a problem, except on Hoy.

Orkney

Just a short step from John O'Groats, the **Orkney Islands** are a unique and fiercely independent archipelago. In spring and summer, the meadows and cliff tops are a brilliant green, shining with wild flowers, while long days pour light onto the land and sea. In autumn and winter, the islands are often battered by gale-force winds and daylight is scarce, but the temperature stays remarkably mild thanks to the ameliorating effect of the Gulf Stream. For an Orcadian, the "Mainland" invariably means the largest island in Orkney rather than the rest of Scotland, and throughout their history they've been linked to lands much further afield, principally Scandinavia.

Small communities began to settle in the islands around 4000 BC, and the village at **Skara Brae** on the Mainland is one of the best-preserved Stone Age settlements in Europe. This and many of the other older archeological sites, including the **Stones of Stenness** and **Maes Howe**, are concentrated in the central and western parts of the Mainland. Elsewhere the islands are scattered with chambered tombs and stone circles, a tribute to the well-developed religious and ceremonial practices taking place here from around 2000 BC. More sophisticated **Iron Age** inhabitants built fortified villages incorporating stone towers known as brochs, protected by walls and ramparts, many of which are still in place. Later, **Pictish** culture spread to Orkney and the remains of several of their early Christian settlements can still be seen, the best at the **Brough of Birsay** in the West Mainland, where a group of small houses is clustered around the remains of an early church. In the ninth century or thereabouts, **Norse** settlers from Scandinavia arrived and the islands became Norse earldoms, forming an outpost of a powerful, expansive culture which was gradually forcing its way south. The last of the Norse earls was killed in 1231, but they had a lasting impact on the islands, leaving behind not only their language but also the great **St Magnus Cathedral** in Kirkwall, one of Scotland's outstanding examples of medieval architecture.

After the end of Norse rule, the islands became the preserve of **Scottish earls**, who exploited and abused the islanders, although a steady increase in sea trade did offer some chance of escape. French and Spanish ships sheltered here in the sixteenth century, and the ships of the **Hudson Bay Company** recruited hundreds of Orcadians to work in the Canadian fur trade. The islands were also an important staging post in the **whaling industry** and the herring boom, which drew great numbers of small Dutch, French and Scottish boats. More recently,

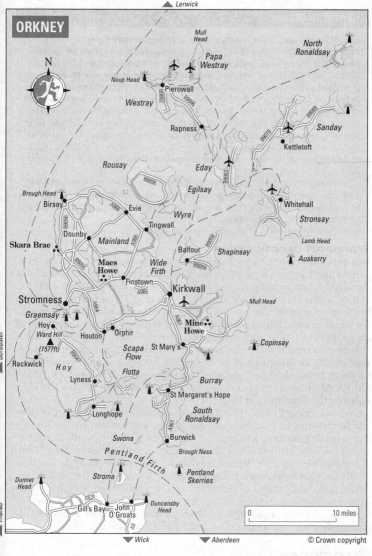

the choice of **Scapa Flow**, Orkney's natural harbour, as the Royal Navy's main base brought plenty of money and activity during both world wars, and left the cliff tops dotted with gun emplacements and the seabed scattered with wrecks – which these days make for wonderful diving opportunities. Since the war, things have quietened down somewhat, although since the mid-1970s the large **oil terminal** on the island of Flotta, combined with EU development grants, have brought surprise windfalls, stemming the exodus of young people. Meanwhile, many disenchanted southerners have become "ferryloupers" (incomers), moving to Orkney in search of peace and the apparent simplicity of island life.

Getting to Orkney

Orkney is connected to the Scottish mainland by several **ferry** routes. Until October 2002, P&O Scottish Ferries (☎01856/850655, ⓦwww.posf.co.uk) runs car ferries to **Stromness** once a week (June–Aug 2 weekly) from **Aberdeen** (takes 8–10hr) and daily on the much shorter and cheaper crossing from **Scrabster** near Thurso (takes 2hr). There's also a weekly (June–Aug 2 weekly) service to Stromness from **Lerwick** in Shetland (takes 2hr). Note that NorthLink take over all the above services as of October 2002, which means timings may change. Pentland Ferries (☎01856/831226, ⓦwww.pentlandferries.co.uk) operates a short car-ferry crossing from **Gills Bay** near John O'Groats to **St Margaret's Hope** on South Ronaldsay (3 daily; takes 1hr). A small passenger ferry run by John O'Groats Ferries (☎0800/731 7872, ⓦwww.jogferry.co.uk) goes from **John O'Groats** to **Burwick** on South Ronaldsay (May–Sept 2–4 daily; 40min).

Direct **flights** serve Kirkwall airport from Sumburgh in Shetland, Wick, Inverness and Aberdeen, and there are good connections from Edinburgh, Glasgow, Manchester, Birmingham and London. All can be booked through British Airways (☎0845/773 3377, ⓦwww.britishairways.com).

Transport practicalities

Bus services on the Orkney Mainland are very poor, and virtually non-existent on Sundays, with some of the most interesting areas not served at all. On the islands, there's usually only a bus service to and from the ferry terminal, making a Day Rover (£6) or Three-Day Rover (£15) of limited value (see ⓦwww.rapsons.co.uk for more). **Cycling** is cheap and relatively easy, though the wind can make it hard going; you can rent bikes in Kirkwall, Stromness and on most of the smaller islands. Bringing a **car** to Orkney is straightforward, if expensive; alternatively, you can **rent** a car in Kirkwall, Stromness or on several of the islands (details are given in the text). You may want to consider one of the informative bus or minibus **tours** on offer: Wildabout (☎01856/851011, ⓦwww.orknet.co.uk/wildabout) have good-value tours of the chief sights on the Mainland and Hoy.

Orkney Ferries (☎01856/872044, ⓦwww.orkneyferries.co.uk) operates several **ferries** daily to Hoy, Shapinsay and Rousay, and between one and three a day, depending on route and season, to all the others except North Ronaldsay, which has a weekly boat. There are also **flights** from Kirkwall to Eday, North Ronaldsay, Westray, Papa Westray, Sanday and Stronsay, operated by Loganair (☎01856/872420, ⓦwww.loganair.co.uk), using a tiny eight-seater plane. Travel between individual islands by sea or air isn't so straightforward, but careful study of timetables can sometimes reduce the need to come all the way back to Kirkwall. It's worth enquiring from Orkney Ferries about their additional sailings on summer Sundays that often make useful inter-island connections.

Stromness

STROMNESS has to be one of the most enchanting ports at which to arrive by boat, its picturesque waterfront a procession of tiny sandstone jetties and slate roofs nestling below the green hill of Brinkies Brae. Its natural sheltered harbour (known as Hamnavoe) must have been used in Viking times, but the town itself only really took off in the eighteenth century. At that time, European conflicts made it safer for ships heading across the Atlantic to travel around the north of Scotland rather than through the English Channel. By 1842, Stromness boasted forty or so pubs; then the herring boom brought large numbers of small boats to the town, along with thousands of young women who gutted, pickled and packed the fish. Things got so rowdy by World War I that the town voted to ban the sale of alcohol, leaving Stromness dry from 1920 until 1947.

The Town

Unlike Kirkwall, the old town of Stromness still hugs the shoreline, its one and only street, a narrow winding affair, built long before the advent of the motor car, still paved with great flagstones and fed by a tight network of alleyways or closes. The central section, which begins at the *Stromness Hotel*, is known as **Victoria Street**, though in fact it takes on several other names – Graham Place, Dundas Street, Alfred Street and South End – as it threads its way southwards. On the east side of the street the houses are gable-end-on to the waterfront, and originally each one would have had its own pier, from which merchants would trade with passing ships.

The first of the old jetties, south of the modern harbour, houses the **Pier Arts Centre** (Tues–Sat 10.30am–12.30pm & 1.30–5pm; free). The art gallery is spread over two buildings, the first often featuring painting and sculpture by local artists, the warehouse housing a remarkable display of twentieth-century British art, including works on marine themes by Cornish artists such as Barbara Hepworth and Ben Nicholson that have a special resonance in this seaport.

At the junction of Alfred Street and South End, is the newly expanded **Stromness Museum** (May–Sept daily 10am–5pm; Oct–April Mon–Sat 10.30am–12.30pm & 1.30–5pm; £2.50), built in 1858, partly to house the collections of the local natural history society. On the ground floor, there's a Halkett cloth boat, an early inflatable like the one used by John Rae, the Stromness-born Arctic explorer, whose fiddle, octant and shotgun are also on display. There are also numerous salty artefacts gathered from shipwrecks, including some barnacle-encrusted crockery from the German High Seas Fleet that sank in Scapa Flow.

Practicalities

Arriving by ferry, you'll disembark at the new ferry terminal, which also houses the **tourist office** (April–Oct Mon–Sat 8am–5pm, Sat 9am–4pm & Sun 10am–3pm; Nov–March Mon–Fri 9am–5pm; ☎01856/850716). As far as **hotels** go, the venerable Victorian *Stromness Hotel* (☎01856/850298, ⓦwww.stromnesshotel.com; ⑤) – the town's first – is probably your best bet. As for **B&Bs**, there's a traditional end-on waterfront house next to the museum at 2 South End (☎01856/850215; ②; April–Oct); if you've got your own transport, you might prefer to head to the modern *Thira* (☎01856/851181; ③), up on the hill above the town, boasting great views overlooking Hoy. Stromness has an SYHA **hostel** on Helliehole Road (☎01856/850589, ⓦwww.syha.org.uk; mid-May to Sept), signposted off the main street; it has a curfew and single-sex dorms. More laid-back is the family-run *Brown's Hostel*, 45–47 Victoria St (☎01856/850661). There's also a **campsite** (☎01856/873535; May to mid-Sept) in a superb, but exposed setting a mile south of the ferry terminal at Point of Ness.

Stromness has a couple of decent **places to eat**, starting with *Julia's Café and Bistro* (lunchtime only except in the height of summer), opposite the ferry terminal. The moderately expensive *Hamnavoe Restaurant,* at 35 Graham Place (☎01856/850606; Thurs–Sun eves only), offers the town's most ambitious cooking in a very pleasant setting. For something less formal, try the specials on offer in the upstairs lounge bar of the *Stromness Hotel*.

The great bulk of the **West Mainland** is fertile, productive farmland, fenced off into a patchwork of fields used either to produce crops or for cattle grazing. It is, however, fringed by some spectacular coastline, particularly in the west, and littered with some of the island's most impressive prehistoric sites, such as the village of **Skara Brae**, the standing **Stones of Stenness** and the chambered tomb of **Maes Howe**.

The Stones of Stenness and Maes Howe

The parish of **STENNESS** lies along the main road from Stromness to Kirkwall, south of the twin lochs of Stenness and Harray, which are separated by a couple of promontories, that once stood at the heart of Orkney's most important Neolithic ceremonial complex. The most visible part of the complex are the **Stones of Stenness**, originally a circle of twelve rock slabs, now just four, the tallest of which is a real monster at over 16ft, though it's more remarkable for its incredible thinness. A broken table-top lies within the circle, which is surrounded by a much-diminished henge (a circular bank of earth and a ditch) with a couple of entrance causeways. Less than a mile to the northwest, you reach another stone circle, the **Ring of Brodgar**, a much wider circle dramatically sited on raised ground. Here there were originally sixty stones, 27 of which now stand; of the henge, only the ditch survives.

There are several quite large burial mounds visible to the south of the Ring of Brodgar, but these are entirely eclipsed by one of the most impressive Neolithic burial chambers in the whole of Europe, **Maes Howe** (April–Sept daily 9.30am–6.30pm; Oct–March Mon–Sat 9.30am–4.30pm, Sun 2–4.30pm; £2.80; HS), which lies less than a mile northeast of the Stones of Stenness. Dating from around 3000 BC, its excellent state of preservation is partly due to the massive slabs of sandstone it was constructed from, the largest of which weighs over thirty tons. Perhaps the most remarkable aspect of Maes Howe is that the tomb is aligned so that the rays of the winter solstice sun reach right down the passage to the ledge of one of the three cells built into the walls of the tomb. When Maes Howe was opened in 1861, it was found to be virtually empty, thanks to the work of generations of grave-robbers, who had left behind only a handful of human bones. The Vikings entered in the twelfth century, probably on their way to the Crusades, leaving large amounts of runic graffiti, some of which are cryptographic twig runes, cut into the walls of the main chamber and still clearly visible today.

Skara Brae

Around seven miles north of Stromness, the beautiful white curve of the Bay of Skaill is home to **Skara Brae** (April–Sept daily 9.30am–6.30pm; Oct–March Mon–Sat 9.30am–4.30pm, Sun 2–4.30pm; £4.50 in summer, £3.50 in winter), where the extensive remains of a small Neolithic fishing and farming village, dating back to 3000 BC, were discovered in 1850 after a fierce storm. The village is very well preserved, its houses huddled together and connected by narrow passages which would originally have been covered over with turf. The houses themselves consist of a single, spacious living room, filled with domestic detail, including dressers, fireplaces, built-in cupboards, beds and boxes, all ingeniously constructed from slabs of stone.

Unfortunately, the sheer numbers now visiting Skara Brae mean that you can no longer explore the site itself properly, but only look down from the outer walls. Before you reach the site you must buy a ticket from the new **visitor**

centre, which houses an excellent **café–restaurant**. After watching a short video, you pass through a small introductory **exhibition**, with a few replica finds, and some hands-on stuff for kids, all of which helps put the site in context. You then proceed to a full-scale replica of House 7 (the best-preserved house); it's all a tad neat and tidy, but it'll give you the general idea.

In the summer months, your ticket to Skara Brae also covers entry to nearby **Skaill House**, an extensive range of buildings 300 yards inland. The original house was built for Bishop George Graham in the 1620s, but it has since been much extended. The house's prize possession is Captain Cook's dinner service from the *Resolution*, which was delivered after Cook's death when the *Resolution* and the *Discovery* sailed into Stromness in 1780.

Birsay and Evie

Occupying the northwest corner of the Mainland, the parish of **BIRSAY** was the centre of Norse power in Orkney for several centuries before the earls moved to Kirkwall, some time after the construction of its cathedral. Today a tiny cluster of homes is gathered around the sandstone ruins of the **Earl's Palace**, which was built in the second half of the sixteenth century by Robert Stewart, Earl of Orkney, using the forced labour of the islanders, who weren't even given food and drink for their work. The palace appears to have lasted barely a century before falling into rack and ruin; the crumbling walls and turrets retain much of their grandeur, although inside there is little remaining domestic detail. However, its vast scale makes the Earl's Palace in Kirkwall seem almost humble in comparison.

Just over half a mile northwest of the palace is the **Brough of Birsay**, a substantial Pictish settlement on a small tidal island that is only accessible during the two hours each side of low tide. The focus of the village was – and still is – the sandstone-built twelfth-century **St Peter's Church**, which is thought to have stood at the centre of a monastic complex of some sort – the foundations of a courtyard and outer buildings can be made out to the west. Close by is a large complex of Viking-era buildings, including several houses, a sauna and some sophisticated stone drains.

Overshadowed by the great wind turbine on Burgar Hill, the village and parish of **EVIE**, on the north coast, looks out across the turbulent waters of Eynhallow Sound towards the island of Rousay. Its chief draw is the **Broch of Gurness** (April–Sept daily 9.30am–6.30pm; £2.80; HS), the best-preserved broch on an archipelago replete with them, and one which is still surrounded by a remarkable complex of later buildings. As at Birsay, the sea has eaten away half the site, but the broch itself, dating from around 100 BC, still stands, its walls reaching a height of 12ft in places, its inner cells still intact. The compact group of homes clustered around the broch have also survived amazingly well, with much of their original and ingenious stone shelving and fireplaces still in place.

Practicalities

The best **B&B** in the West Mainland is the carefully converted *Mill of Eyrland* (℡01856/850136, ⓦ www.orknet.co.uk/mill; ❸), in a delightful setting by a mill stream on the A964 to Orphir. Also worth recommending is the artistically-inclined *Woodwick House* (℡01856/751330, ⓦ www.orknet.co.uk/wood-wick; ❸), situated in a beautiful, secluded position southeast of Evie. At the other end of the scale, you can stay in Evie's modern **bothy and campsite**, run by Dale Farm (℡01856/751270; April–Oct) and situated by the junction of the road to Dounby.

Kirkwall

Initial impressions of **KIRKWALL**, Orkney's capital, are not always favourable. However, it does have one great redeeming feature – its sandstone **cathedral**, without doubt the finest medieval building in the north of Scotland. Part of the reason for Kirkwall's disappointing waterfront is that today's harbour is a largely modern invention; in the mid-nineteenth century, the shoreline ran along Junction Road, and before that it was flush with the west side of Broad Street. Nowadays, the town is very much divided into two main focal points: the busy **harbour**, at the north end of the town, where ferries come and go all year round, and the flagstoned **main street**, which changes its name four times as it twists its way south from the harbour past the cathedral.

The Town

Standing at the very heart of Kirkwall, **St Magnus Cathedral** (Mon–Sat 8.30am–6.30pm, Sun 1.30–6.30pm) is the town's most compelling sight. This beautiful red sandstone building was begun in 1137 by the Orkney Earl Rognvald, who decided to make full use of a growing cult surrounding the figure of his uncle Magnus, killed on the orders of his cousin Haakon in 1117. When Magnus's body was buried in Birsay a heavenly light was said to have shone overhead, and his grave soon became a place of pilgrimage attributed with miraculous powers that drew pilgrims from far afield. When Rognvald finally took over the earldom he built the cathedral in his uncle's honour, moving the centre of religious and secular power from Birsay to Kirkwall.

The first version of the cathedral, built using yellow sandstone from Eday and red sandstone from the Mainland, was somewhat smaller than today's structure, which has been added to over the centuries, with a new east window in the thirteenth century, the extension of the nave in the fifteenth century and a new west window to mark the building's 850th anniversary in 1987. Today much of the detail in the soft sandstone has worn away – the capitals around the main doors are reduced to gnarled stumps – but it's still an immensely impressive building, its shape and style echoing the great cathedrals of Europe. Inside, the atmosphere is surprisingly intimate, the bulky sandstone columns drawing your eye up to the exposed brickwork arches, while around the walls is a series of mostly seventeenth-century tombstones, many carved with a skull and crossbones and other emblems of mortality, alongside chilling inscriptions calling on the reader to "remember death waits us all, the hour none knows".

To the south of the cathedral are the ruined remains of the **Bishop's Palace** (April–Sept daily 9.30am–6.30pm; Oct & Nov Mon–Sat 9.30am–4.30pm, Sun 2–4.30pm; £2; HS), residence of the Bishop of Orkney since the twelfth century. Most of what you see now, however, dates from the time of Bishop Robert Reid, the founder of Edinburgh University, in the mid-sixteenth century. The walls still stand, as does the tall round tower in which the bishop had his private chambers; a narrow spiral staircase takes you to the top for a good view of the cathedral and across Kirkwall's rooftops.

The ticket for the Bishop's Palace also covers entry to the neighbouring **Earl's Palace**, built by the infamous Earl Patrick Stewart around 1600 using forced labour – rather better preserved, and a lot more fun to explore. With its grand entrance, fancy oriel windows, dank dungeons, massive fireplaces and magnificent central hall, it has a confident solidity, and is reckoned to be one of the finest examples of Renaissance architecture in Scotland. The roof may be missing, but many domestic details remain, including a set of toilets and the stone shelves used by the clerk to do his filing. Earl Patrick enjoyed his palace for only a very short time before he was imprisoned.

Opposite the cathedral stands the sixteenth-century Tankerness House, now home to the **Orkney Museum** (Mon–Sat 10.30am–5pm; May–Sept also Sun 2–5pm; free). Among the more unusual artefacts to look out for are a witch's spell box, and a lovely whalebone plaque from a Viking boat grave discovered on Sunday. Further afield, a mile or so south of the town centre on the A961 to South Ronaldsay, is the **Highland Park distillery** (April–Oct Mon–Fri 10am–5pm; July–Sept also Sat noon–5pm, Sun noon–4pm; Nov–March Mon–Fri tours at 2pm; Ⓦwww.highlandpark.co.uk; £3), billed as "the most northerly legal distillery in Scotland".

Practicalities

Buses meet the inter-island car-ferry arrivals at Stromness and passenger-ferry arrivals at Burwick on South Ronaldsay, taking 40–45 minutes to shuttle into Kirkwall. The **bus station** is five minutes' walk west of the town centre. Kirkwall **airport** is three miles southeast of town on the A960 (about £6 by taxi). The helpful **tourist office** is on Broad Street beside the cathedral graveyard (April–Sept daily 8.30am–8pm; Oct–March Mon–Sat 9.30am–5pm; Ⓣ01856/872856). Most events are advertised in *The Orcadian*, which comes out on Thursdays (Ⓦwww.orcadian.co.uk), and there's a *What's on Diary* on BBC Radio Orkney (93.7FM; Mon–Fri 7.30–8am).

The friendly, waterfront *Ayre Hotel* on Ayre Road (Ⓣ01856/873001, Ⓦwww.ayrehotel.co.uk; ❺) offers the smartest **accommodation** in town; equally central is the *Albert* on Mounthoolie Lane (Ⓣ01856/876000, Ⓦwww.alberthotel.co.uk; ❸). The *Lav'rockha* (Ⓣ01856/876103, Ⓦwww.norsecom.co.uk/lavrockha; ❷) is a good, modern guesthouse on Inganess Road, near the Highland Park distillery. The SYHA **hostel** (Ⓣ01856/872243, Ⓦwww.syha.org.uk; April–Sept) is ten minutes' walk out of the centre on the road to Orphir. The small privately-run *Peedie Hostel* (Ⓣ01856/875477) is on the waterfront beside the *Ayre Hotel*. There's also a **campsite** (Ⓣ01856/ 879900; mid-May to mid-Sept) behind the Pickaquoy Leisure Centre, five minutes' walk west of the bus station.

The nicest **café** for lunch is the *Mustard Seed*, 86 Victoria St (closed Wed & Sun), which serves home-made soups and imaginative, inexpensive main courses. In the evening, the *Kirkwall Hotel*, on Harbour Street, is probably the best option, as it offers both **bar meals** and reasonable à la carte, though the bar meals at the *Albert* are OK too. The liveliest **pub** is the *Torvhaug Inn* at the harbour end of Bridge Street. The *Bothy Bar* in the *Albert Hotel* sometimes has live music, while the *Ayre Hotel* hosts regular Orkney Accordion & Fiddle Club nights on Wednesdays. The Pickaquoy Leisure Centre (Ⓦwww.pickaquoy.com) – known locally as the "Picky" – contains the New Phoenix **cinema** (Ⓣ01856/879900).

East Mainland

Southeast from Kirkwall, the narrow spur of the **East Mainland** juts out into the North Sea and is joined, thanks to the remarkable Churchill Barriers, to several smaller islands, the largest of which are Burray and South Ronaldsay. As with the West Mainland, the land here is relatively densely populated and heavily farmed. However, there is one sight you should pay a quick visit to, the recently excavated Iron Age mound of **Mine Howe** (June–Aug daily 11am–5pm; May Wed & Sun 11am–3pm; Sept Wed & Sun 11am–2pm; £2),

Scapa Flow and the Churchill Barriers

The presence of the huge naval base in **Scapa Flow** during both world wars presented an irresistible target to the Germans, and protecting the fleet was always a nagging problem for the Allies. During World War I, blockships were sunk to guard the eastern approaches, but in October 1939, just weeks after the outbreak of World War II, a German U-boat managed to manoeuvre past the blockships and torpedo the battleship HMS *Royal Oak*, which sank with the loss of 833 lives. The U-boat captain claimed to have acquired local knowledge while fishing in the islands before the war. Today the wreck of the *Royal Oak*, marked by a green buoy off the Gaitnip Cliffs, is an official war grave.

The sinking of the *Royal Oak* convinced the First Lord of the Admiralty, Winston Churchill, that Scapa Flow needed better protection, and in 1940 work began on a series of barriers – known as the **Churchill Barriers** – to seal the waters between the Mainland and the string of islands to the south. Special camps were built to accommodate the 1700 men involved in the project; their numbers were boosted by the surrender of Italy in 1942, when Italian prisoners of war were sent to work here.

Besides the barriers, which are an astonishing feat of engineering when you bear in mind the strength of Orkney tides, the Italians also left behind the beautiful **Italian Chapel** (daily: April–Sept 9am–10pm; Oct–March 9am–4.30pm; free) on the first of the islands, Lamb Holm. This, the so-called "miracle of Camp 60", must be one of the greatest adaptations ever, made from two Nissen huts, concrete, barbed wire and parts of a rusting blockship. It has a great false facade, and colourful trompe l'oeil decor, lovingly restored by the chapel's principal architect, Domenico Chiocchetti.

---

just off the A960 beyond the airport. Originally Mine Howe would have been a large mound surrounded by a deep ditch, but only a small section has been excavated. At the top of the mound a series of steps leads steeply down to a half-landing, and then plunges down even deeper to a small chamber some twenty feet below the surface. Visitors don a hard hat and grab a torch, before heading underground. The whole layout is unique and has left archeologists totally baffled, though, naturally, numerous theories as to its purpose abound, from execution by ritual drowning to a temple to the god of the underground.

On the south coast, just before you hit the Churchill Barriers, stands **ST MARY'S**, an old fishing village whose livelihood was destroyed by the building of the causeways. Just east of St Mary's, you'll find the **Norwood Antiques** (June–Sept Tues–Thurs & Sun 2–5pm & 6–8pm; also by arrangement ☎01856/781217; £3), a display of antiques collected by local stonemason Norrie Wood from the age of 13. Only about half of the collection is on display, but it's a fascinating and eccentric selection of bits and pieces from around the world, including pottery, painting, medals, furniture, cutlery, clocks, even a narwhal's tusk, all housed in a grand Orkney home.

South Ronaldsay

At the southern end of the series of four barriers is low-lying **South Ronaldsay**, the largest of the islands linked to the Mainland and, like the latter, rich farming country. The main settlement is **ST MARGARET'S HOPE** – or "The Hope", as it's known locally – a pleasing little gathering of stone-built houses overlooking a sheltered bay. As is obvious from the architecture, and the piers, The Hope was once a thriving port, and locals are backing the new car-ferry link with Caithness, which began in 2001. Until or unless this begins to make serious inroads into Scrabster–Stromness traffic, however, The Hope remains a very peaceful place.

One of the most enjoyable archeological sights on Orkney is the ancient chambered burial cairn at the southeastern corner of South Ronaldsay, known as the **Tomb of the Eagles** (daily: April–Oct 10am–8pm; Nov–March 10am–noon; £3). Discovered, excavated and still owned by local farmer Ronald Simpson, a visit here makes a refreshing change from the usual interpretative centre. First off, you get to look round the family's private museum of prehistoric artefacts; then, you get a brief guided tour of a nearby Bronze Age **burnt mound**, which is basically a Neolithic rubbish dump; and finally you get to walk out to the **chambered cairn**, by the cliff's edge, where human remains were found alongside talons and carcasses of sea eagles. To enter the cairn, you must lie on a trolley and pull yourself in using an overhead rope – something that's guaranteed to put a smile on every visitor's face.

First **accommodation** choice are the comfortable rooms above the *Creel* on the harbourfront (☎01856/831311, ⓦwww.thecreel.co.uk; ❹), one of the best **restaurants** in Scotland; at £25 for two courses, it's expensive, but also friendly and relaxed. More modest bar meals are available from the popular *Galley Inn*, also on the seafront, and the *Murray Arms Hotel* (☎01856/831205, ⓦwww.murrayarmshotel.com; ❷), on Back Road, which has rooms above the pub and a backpackers dorm round the side. The best B&B is *Bellevue Guest House* (☎01856/831294; ❷), a stone-built Victorian house on a hill just west of the village. For a **hostel** with more character, head for *Wheems Bothy* (☎01856/831537; April–Oct), a mile and a half from the war memorial on the main road outside The Hope.

Hoy

Hoy, Orkney's second-largest island, rises sharply out of the sea to the southwest of the Mainland. The least typical of the islands, but certainly the most dramatic, its north and west sides are made up of great glacial valleys and mountainous moorland rising to over 1500ft, dropping into the sea off the red sandstone cliffs of St John's Head.

Much of Hoy's magnificent landscape is embraced by the **North Hoy RSPB Reserve** (which covers most of the northwest end of the island), in which the rough grasses and heather harbour a cluster of arctic plants and a healthy population of mountain hares, as well as numerous great skuas. Walkers arriving by passenger ferry from Stromness at Moaness Pier, near the tiny village of **HOY**, and heading for Rackwick (four miles southwest), can either take the well-marked footpath that passes Sandy Loch or catch the minibus via the single-track road. En route, duckboards head across the heather to the **Dwarfie Stane**, Orkney's most unusual chambered tomb, cut from a solid block of sandstone and dating back to 3000 BC.

RACKWICK is an old crofting and fishing village squeezed between towering sandstone cliffs on the west coast. A small farm building beside the hostel serves as a tiny **museum** (open anytime; free), with a few old photos and a brief rundown of Rackwick's rough history. Take the time, too, to stroll down to the sandy beach, backed by giant sandstone pebbles washed smooth by the sea, which make a thunderous noise when the wind gets up. Despite its isolation, Rackwick has a steady stream of walkers and climbers passing through it en route to the **Old Man of Hoy**, a great sandstone column some 450ft high, perched on an old lava flow which protects it from the erosive power of the sea. The well-trodden footpath from Rackwick is an easy three-mile walk (3hr round-trip) – the great skuas will divebomb you only during the nesting season – and gives the reward of a great view of the stack. Continuing north along the cliff tops, the path peters out before **St John's Head** which, at 1136ft, is one of the highest sea cliffs in the country and mostly too sheer even for nesting seabirds.

Lyness

Along the sheltered eastern shore of Hoy, high moorland gives way to a gentler environment similar to that on the rest of Orkney. Hoy defines the western boundary of Scapa Flow, and **LYNESS** played a major role for the Royal Navy during both world wars. Many of the old wartime buildings have been cleared away over the last few decades, but the harbour and hills around Lyness are still scarred with the scattered remains of concrete structures which once served as hangars and storehouses during World War II, and are now used as barns and cowsheds. The old oil pumphouse, which still stands opposite the new Lyness ferry terminal, has been turned into the **Scapa Flow Visitor Centre & Museum** (Mon–Fri 9am–4.30pm; mid-May to Oct also Sat & Sun 10.30am–3.30pm; free), a fascinating insight into wartime Orkney. The pump house itself retains much of its old equipment – you can even ask for a working demo of one of the oil-fired boilers – used to pump oil off tankers moored at Lyness into sixteen tanks, and from there into underground reservoirs cut into the neighbouring hillside. Every hour (on the half-hour), an audiovisual show on the history of Scapa Flow is screened in the sole surviving tank, which has incredible acoustics.

Practicalities

Two **ferry services** run to Hoy: a passenger ferry from Stromness to the village of Hoy (2–5 daily; takes 25min; ☎01856/850624), which also serves the small island of Graemsay; and the roll-on/roll-off car ferry from Houton on the Mainland to Lyness (Mon–Fri 6 daily, Sat & Sun 2–3 daily; takes 30min–1hr; ☎01856/811397), which sometimes calls in at the oil terminal island of Flotta, and begins and ends its daily schedule at Longhope. There's no bus service on Hoy, but those arriving on the passenger ferry from Stromness should find a **minibus** waiting to take them to Rackwick.

There are two council-run, SYHA-affiliated **hostels** in North Hoy: the *North Hoy Hostel* (May to mid-Sept) in Hoy village and the much smaller *Rackwick Hostel* (mid-March to mid-Sept); to book ahead, you must contact the council (☎01856/873535). You can also **camp** in Rackwick, beside *Burnside Cottage* (☎01856/791316), the heather-thatched **bothy**. Hoy has a handful of very good, friendly **B&Bs**, including *Stonequoy Farm* (☎01856/791234, Ⓦwww.visithoy.com; ➊), a lovely 200-acre stone-built farm south of Lyness, overlooking Longhope; The *Hoy Inn* (closed Mon), near the post office in Hoy village serves good **bar meals**.

Shapinsay

Just a few miles northeast of Kirkwall, **Shapinsay** is the most accessible of Orkney's northern isles. A gently undulating grid-plan patchwork of rich farmland, it's a bit like an island suburb of Kirkwall, which is clearly visible across the bay. Its chief attraction for visitors is **Balfour Castle** (May–Sept Wed & Sun guided tours 3pm; see below for details of the all-inclusive ticket), the imposing Baronial pile designed by David Bryce and completed in 1848 by the Balfour family of Westray, who had made a small fortune in India the previous century. The Balfours died out in 1960 and the castle was bought by a Polish cavalry officer, Captain Tadeusz Zawadski, whose family now run the place as a hotel. The guided tours are great fun, and go down very well with children too, as they finish off with complimentary tea and home-made cakes in the servants' quarters. The old village **Smithy** on the main street (daily noon–4.30pm, Wed & Sun until 5.30pm; free) now serves as a museum of local history, with a tearoom upstairs.

Less than thirty minutes from Kirkwall by **ferry**, Shapinsay is an easy daytrip. If you want to visit the castle, before you set out you must buy an **all-inclusive ticket** from Kirkwall tourist office (£16), which includes a return ferry ticket and castle admission. It's also possible to **stay** in opulent style at *Balfour Castle* (℡01856/711282, ⓦwww.balfourcastle.co.uk; ❺). More modest **B&B** is available at *Girnigoe* (℡01856/711256, ⓔjean@girnigoe.p9.co.uk; ❷), a very comfortable Orcadian croft close to the north shore of Veantro Bay. The only non-hotel **eating** option is the café in the old smithy (May–Sept), which serves teas and sandwiches.

Rousay

Just over half a mile from the Mainland's northern shore, the hilly island of **Rousay** is home to a number of intriguing prehistoric sites. The group of a dozen or so houses above the ferry terminal is the only settlement of any size, but a single road runs around the edge of the island, connecting a string of small farms which make use of the more cultivable coastal fringes. It's easy enough to reach the main points of interest on the south coast by foot or bike from the ferry terminal.

The first trio of archeological sights is spread out over a couple of miles, on and off the road that leads west from the ferry terminal. **Taversoe Tuick**, the nearest chambered cairn, is unusual in that it exploits its sloping site by having two storeys, one entered from the upper side and one from the lower. A little further west is the **Blackhammar Cairn**, which is divided into "stalls" by large flagstones, rather like the more famous cairn at Midhowe (see below). Finally, there's the **Knowe of Yarso**, another stalled cairn dating from the same period that's a stiff climb up the hill from the road, worth it if only for the magnificent view.

The southwestern side of Rousay is home to the most significant of the island's archeological remains. Most lie on the **Westness Walk**, a mile-long heritage trail that begins at Westness Farm, four miles west of the ferry terminal. **Midhowe Cairn**, about a mile on from the farm, comes as something of a surprise, both for its immense size – it's known as "the great ship of death", and measures nearly 100ft in length – and for the fact that it's now entirely surrounded by a stone-walled barn with a corrugated roof. Unfortunately, you can't actually explore the roofless communal burial chamber, dating back to 3500 BC, but only look down from the overhead walkway. A couple of hundred yards beyond Midhowe Cairn is **Midhowe Broch**, built as a sort of fortified family house, surrounded by a complex series of ditches and ramparts. The interior of the broch is divided into two separate rooms, each with their own hearth, water tank and quernstone, all of which date from the final phase of occupation around the second century AD.

Practicalities

Rousay makes a good day-trip from the Mainland, with regular **car ferry** sailings from Tingwall (30min), linked to Kirkwall by buses. Most ferries also call in at Egilsay and Wyre, but some need to be booked the day before at the Tingwall ferry terminal (℡01856/751360). **Bike rental** is available from Arts,

△ Papa Stour, Shetland

Bikes & Crafts, near the pier (☎01856/821398). **Accommodation** on Rousay is limited to a couple of B&Bs: try the Victorian croft *Blackhamar* (☎01856/821333, ⓦwww.orknet.co.uk/blackhamar; ❶). Another option is the hostel at *Trumland Farm* (☎01856/821252), half a mile or so west of the terminal. As well as a couple of dorms, you can also camp, and there's a self-catering cottage, sleeping four. The *Pier Restaurant* (☎01856/821359), right beside the terminal, serves bar meals at lunchtime and functions as a pub in the evenings; if you phone in advance, they will pack you a delicious **picnic** of crab, cheese, fruit and bannock bread.

Westray

Although exposed to the full force of the Atlantic weather in the far northwest of Orkney, **Westray** shelters one of the most tightly knit and prosperous island communities. It has a fairly stable population of 700 or so, producing superb beef, scallops, shellfish and a large catch of white fish, with its own small fish-processing factory and an organic salmon farm. Old Orcadian families still dominate every aspect of life, giving the island a strong individual character.

The main village and harbour is **PIEROWALL** in the north, a good eight miles from the Rapness ferry terminal on the southernmost tip of the island. Pierowall houses the excellent **Westray Heritage Centre** (mid-May to mid-Sept Tues–Sat 9.30am–12.30pm & 2–5pm; £2), a very welcoming wet weather retreat if you've got kids, and somewhere to grab a cup of tea. The island's most impressive ruin is the colossal sandstone hulk of **Noltland Castle** (June–Sept daily 9.30am–6.30pm; £1.50; HS), which stands above the village half a mile west up the road to Noup Head. This Z-plan castle, which is pock-marked with over seventy gun loops, was begun around 1560 by Gilbert Balfour, a shady character from Fife, who was Master of the Household to Mary, Queen of Scots, and was implicated in the murder of her husband Lord Darnley in 1567. To explore the castle, you must first pick up the key from the nearby farm.

The northwestern tip of Westray rises up sharply, culminating in the dramatic sea cliffs of **Noup Head**. The whole area is an RSPB reserve, and during the summer months the guano-covered rock ledges are packed with over 100,000 nesting seabirds, primarily guillemots, razorbills, kittiwakes and fulmars, with puffins as well: a truly awesome sight, sound and smell. The sea cliffs in the southeast of the island around **Stanger Head** are not quite as spectacular as at Noup Head, but it's here that you'll find **Castle o'Burrian**, a sea stack that was once an early Christian hermitage. It's now the best place on Westray at which to see **puffins** nesting.

Practicalities

Westray is served by car **ferry** from Kirkwall (2–3 daily; takes 1hr 25min; ☎01856/872044), or you can **fly** from Kirkwall (Mon–Sat 1–2 daily; 12min). J. & M. Harcus of Pierowall (☎01857/677450) runs a **bus service** which will take you from Rapness to Pierowall, though you should phone ahead to check it's running. For **bike rental**, contact Sand O'Gill (☎01857/677374), Twiness (☎01857/677319), or *Bis Geos* hostel (☎01857/677420).

Westray's finest **accommodation** is at the *Cleaton House Hotel* (☎01857/677508, ⓦwww.orknet.co.uk/cleaton; ❹), a whitewashed Victorian manse about two miles southeast of Pierowall, with great views. This is also the only place on the island where you can sample Westray's organic salmon, either in the expensive hotel **restaurant** or in the congenial **bar**. **B&B** is available at

Sand O'Gill (☎01857/677374; ❶), where you can also **camp**. *Bis Geos* **hostel** (☎01857/677420, ⓦwww.bisgeos.co.uk; May–Sept), on the road to Noup Head, has unbeatable views along the cliffs and out to sea; inside, it's beautifully furnished. The *Barn* (☎01857/677214, ⓦwww.orkneyisles.co.uk/thebarn), is situated in an old farm on the south side of Pierowall Bay, and has a small **campsite** adjacent.

Papa Westray

Across the short Papa Sound from Westray is the island of **Papa Westray**, known locally as "Papay" (ⓦwww.papawestray.co.uk). With a population hovering precariously between sixty and seventy, Papay has had to fight hard to keep itself viable over the last couple of decades, helped by a hefty influx of outsiders. To get an idea how life used to be on Papay, when the Traill family ruled over the island, visit the small **museum** (free access) in an old bothy opposite Holland House, at the centre of the island.

A road leads down from Holland House to the western shore, where the **Knap of Howar** stands. Dating from around 3500 BC, this Neolithic farm building makes a fair claim to being the oldest standing house in Europe. Half a mile north along the coast is **St Boniface Kirk**, a restored pre-Reformation church, with a bare flagstone floor, dry-stone walls, a little wooden gallery and just a couple of surviving box pews. In the surrounding graveyard there's a Viking hogback grave, decorated with carvings in imitation of the wooden shingles on the roof of a Viking longhouse.

Papay is an easy day-trip from Westray, with a regular **passenger ferry** service from Pierowall (3–6 daily; takes 25min). On Tuesdays and Fridays, the **car ferry** from Kirkwall to Westray continues on to Papa Westray. Papay is also connected to Westray by the **world's shortest scheduled flight** (2min; £15 one-way). You can also fly direct from Kirkwall to Papa Westray (Mon–Fri 2 daily, Sat 1 daily). Papay's Community Co-operative (☎01857/644267, ⓔpapaycoop@ orkney .com) has a **minibus** which will take you from the pier to wherever you want on the island; it also runs a shop, a sixteen-bed SYHA-affiliated **hostel** (ⓦwww .syha.org.uk) and the *Beltane House* **hotel** (❷; optional full-board), all housed within the old estate workers' cottages at Beltane, east of Holland House.

Eday

A long, thin island at the centre of Orkney's northern isles, **Eday** shares more characteristics with Rousay and Hoy than with its immediate neighbours, dominated as it is by a great block of heather-covered upland, with farmland confined to a narrow strip of coastal ground. The chief points of interest are all in the northern half of the island, beyond the post office, petrol pump and community shop on the main road. This marks the beginning of the signposted **Eday Heritage Walk**, which covers all the main sights (about 3hr). The walk initially follows the road heading northwest, past the RSPB bird hide overlooking **Mill Loch**, where several pairs of red-throated divers regularly breed. Clearly visible to the north of the road is the fifteen-foot **Stone of Setter**, weathered into three thick, lichen-encrusted fingers. From here, you can climb the hill to reach the **Vinquoy Chambered Cairn**, which has a similar structure to that of Maes Howe. You can crawl into the tomb through the narrow entrance: a skylight inside lets light into the main, beehive chamber, but not into the four side-cells.

Eday's terminal for **ferries** (2–3 daily; takes 1hr 15min–2hr) is at Backaland pier in the south. Car rental and taxis can be organized through Mr A. Stewart by the pier (☎01857/622206); he also runs tailor-made two-hour minibus tours (mid-May to Aug Mon, Wed & Fri). It's also possible to do a day-trip **flight** on Wednesdays from Kirkwall to Eday and back (☎01856/872494 or 873457). **Bike rental** is available from Martin Burkett at Hamarr, in the valley below the post office (☎01857/622331). Friendly **B&B** with full board is available at *Skaill Farm*, a traditional farmhouse just south of the airport (☎01857/622271; ❸; closed April & May). The basic SYHA-affiliated **hostel** (Ⓦwww.syha.org.uk), occupies an exposed spot just north of the airport; it's run by Eday Community Association (☎01857/622206; April–Sept), who will also advise on **camping**.

Stronsay

A beguiling combination of green pastures, white sands and clear turquoise bays, **Stronsay** has seen two economic booms in the last three hundred years. The first was built on collecting vast quantities of seaweed and exporting the **kelp** for use in the chemical industry, particularly in making iodine, soap and glass. Later, **fishing** on a grand scale came to dominate life here, as Whitehall, in the north of the island, became one of the main Scottish centres for the curing of herring. By the 1840s, up to four hundred boats were working out of the port, attracting hundreds of women herring-gutters. By the 1930s, however, the herring stocks had been severely depleted and the industry began a long decline.

WHITEHALL remains the only real village, made up of rows of stone-built fishermen's cottages set between two large piers. Wandering along the tranquil, rather forlorn harbourfront today, you'll find it hard to believe that the village once supported five thousand people in the fishing industry during the summer season, as well as a small army of coopers, coal merchants, butchers, bakers, several Italian ice-cream parlours and a cinema. It was said that, on a Sunday, you could walk across the decks of the boats all the way to **Papa Stronsay**, the tiny island that shelters Whitehall from the north, on which a new monastery is currently being built. The old fish market by the pier used to house a **museum**, with a few photos and artefacts from the herring days; ask at the small café (closed Tues) to see if it's still open.

Stronsay is served by a regular car **ferry** service from Kirkwall to Whitehall (2 daily; takes 1hr 40min–2hr), and weekday **flights**, also from Kirkwall (Mon–Fri 2 daily; takes 25min). There's no bus service, but D.S. Peace (☎01857/616335) operates taxis and **rents cars**. Good **accommodation** choices are the *Stronsay Fish Mart* **hostel** (☎01857/606220) in the old fish market by the pier, or the newly refurbished *Stronsay Hotel* (☎01857/616213; ❹) opposite. A cheaper alternative is the *Stronsay Bird Reserve* (☎01857/616363; ❷), a nicely positioned **B&B** in a lovely old crofthouse, which also tolerates camping on the shores of Mill Bay. The *Stronsay Hotel* does good pub **food**.

Sanday

Sanday, though the largest of the northern isles, is also the most insubstantial, a great low-lying, drifting dune strung out between several rocky points. The island's sweeping aquamarine bays and vast stretches of clean white sand are the finest in Orkney, and in dry, clear weather it's a superb place to spend a day or two. The island has a long history as a shipping hazard, with many wrecks smashed against its shores, although the construction of the **Start Point Lighthouse** in 1802 on the island's exposed eastern tip reduced the risk for seafarers. Today the islanders still survive largely from farming and fishing.

The shoreline supports a healthy seal, otter and wading bird population, and behind the splendid sandy beaches are stretches of beautiful open machair and grassland, thick with wild flowers during the spring and summer. The entire coastline presents the opportunity for superb walks, with particularly spectacular sand dunes to the south of Cata Sand. Sanday is also rich in archeology, with hundreds of mostly unexcavated sites including cairns, brochs and burnt mounds. The most impressive is **Quoyness Chambered Cairn**, on the fertile farmland of Els Ness peninsula, dating from before 2000 BC, and partially reconstructed to a height of around 13ft.

Ferries arrive at the new terminal at the southern tip of the island and are met by the **minibus** (book on ☎01857/600467), which will take you to most points. The airfield is in the centre of the island and there are regular **flights** to Kirkwall (Mon–Fri 2 daily, Sat 1 daily; 10–20min). The fishing port of **KETTLETOFT** is where the ferry used to dock, and where you'll find the island's two **hotels**. Of the two, the *Belsair Hotel* (☎01857/600206, ⓔjoy@ sanday.quista.net; ❷) is probably the one to stay at, and has the slightly more adventurous restaurant menu; the *Kettletoft Hotel* has a lively bar that's popular with the locals. Of the handful of **B&Bs**, try the plain family-run *Quivals* (☎01857/600467; ❶), who can also organize car and bike rental.

North Ronaldsay

North Ronaldsay – or "North Ron" as it's fondly known – has a unique outpost atmosphere, brought about by its extreme isolation. Measuring just three miles by one and rising only 66ft above sea level, the island is almost overwhelmed by the enormity of the sky, the strength of wind and the ferocity of the sea – so much so that its very existence seems an act of tenacious defiance. Despite these adverse conditions, North Ronaldsay has been inhabited for centuries, and continues to be heavily farmed, from old-style crofts whose roofs are made from huge local flagstones.

The island's **sheep** are a unique, tough, goat-like breed, who feed mostly on seaweed, giving their flesh a dark tone and a rich, gamey taste, and making their thick wool highly prized. A high **drystone dyke**, completed in the mid-nineteenth century and running the thirteen miles around the edge of the island, keeps them off the farmland, except during lambing season. The most frequent visitors are ornithologists, who come to catch a glimpse of the rare migrants who land here briefly on their spring and autumn migrations: there's a permanent **Bird Observatory**, established in 1987 by adapting a croft situated in the southwest corner of the island to wind and solar power; they can give advice as to what birds have recently been sighted.

The **ferry** from Kirkwall runs only once a week (usually Fri; takes 2hr 40min–3hr), though day-trips are possible on occasional summer Sundays (phone ☎01856/872044 for details). Your best bet is to catch a **flight** from Kirkwall (Mon–Sat 2 daily): if you stay the night on the island, you're eligible for a bargain £10 return fare. You can **stay** at the *North Ronaldsay Bird Observatory* (☎01857/633200, ⓦwww.nrbo.f2s.com; ❸), which offers full board either in private guest rooms or in dorms. Full-board accommodation is also available at *Garso*, in the northeast (☎01857/633244, ⓔchristine .muir@virgin.net; ❸), which also has a self-catering cottage. The *Burrian Inn*, to the southeast of the war memorial, is the island's small **pub**, and does hot food. **Camping** is possible; for further information, phone Mr Scott on ☎01857/633222.

Shetland

Many maps plonk the **Shetland Islands** in a box somewhere off Aberdeen, but in fact they're a lot closer to Bergen in Norway than Edinburgh. The Shetland **landscape** is a product of the struggle between rock and the forces of water and ice that have, over millennia, tried to break it to pieces. Smoothed by the last glaciation, the surviving land has been exposed to the most violent weather experienced in the British Isles. In winter, gales are routine and Shetlanders take even the occasional hurricane in their stride, marking a calm fine day as "a day atween weathers". There are some good spells of dry, sunny weather from May to September, but it's the "**simmer dim**", the twilight which lingers through the small hours at this latitude, which makes Shetland summers so memorable; in June especially, the northern sky is an unfinished sunset of blue and burnished copper.

People have lived in Shetland since **prehistoric times**, certainly from about 3500 BC, and the islands display spectacular remains. For six centuries they were part of the **Norse empire** which brought together Sweden, Denmark and Norway. In 1469, Shetland followed Orkney in being mortgaged to Scotland, King Christian I of Norway being unable to raise the dowry for the marriage of his daughter, Margaret, to King James III. The Scottish king annexed Shetland in 1472 and the mortgage was never redeemed. Though Shetland retained links with other North Sea communities, religious and administrative practice gradually became Scottish, and **mainland lairds** set about grabbing what land and power they could. Later, especially in rural Shetland, the economy fell increasingly into the hands of **merchant lairds**; they controlled the fish trade and the tenants who supplied it through a system of truck, or forced barter.

During the two world wars, Shetland's role as gatekeeper between the North Sea and North Atlantic meant that the defence of the islands and control of the seas around them were critical. With a rebirth of the local economy in the 1960s, Shetland was able to claim, in the following decade, that the **oil industry** needed the islands more than they needed it. Careful negotiation, backed up by pioneering local legislation, produced a substantial income from oil which has been reinvested in the community. However, it's clear that the oil boom days are over, and the islanders are having to think afresh how to carve out a living in the new millennium.

Getting to Shetland

P&O Scottish Ferries (ⓣ01224/572615 or ⓣ01595/695252, ⓦwww.posf.co.uk) operates a direct overnight **car ferry** from **Aberdeen** to Lerwick four or five times a week (takes 14hr). There's also a once-weekly daytime service from **Stromness** in Orkney (takes 8–10hr), which increases to twice weekly in summer (June–Aug) – one overnight, one daytime. If you're visiting both Orkney and Shetland, be sure to check out the discounted **round-trip fares** advertised by P&O. Note, too, that from October 2002 these services will be run by NorthLink.

There are **flights** on British Airways (ⓣ0845/733 3377) nonstop to Shetland from **Aberdeen**, **Inverness**, **Kirkwall** and **Wick**, with connections into those airports from Edinburgh, Glasgow, Birmingham, Manchester and London. Shetland's main airport is at **Sumburgh**, from where buses make short work of the 25-mile journey north to Lerwick. Standard fares are high, but various cheaper tickets and special offers are sometimes available, often with booking conditions.

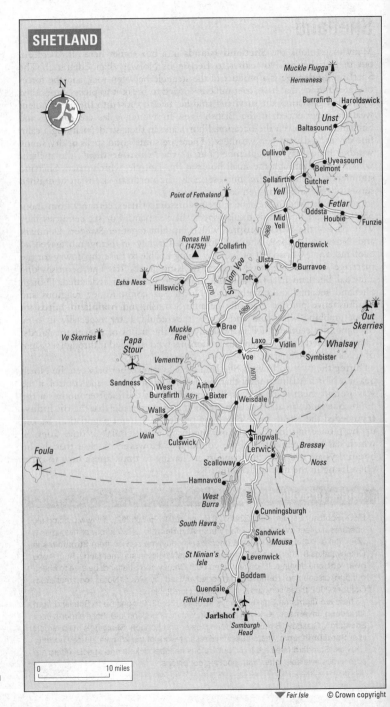

SHETLAND

N

Muckle Flugga
Hermaness
Burrafirth   Haroldswick
Unst
Baltasound
Cullivoe
Uyeasound
Belmont
Sellafirth   Gutcher
Yell
Point of Fethaland
Fetlar
Oddsta   Houbie
Mid
Yell   Funzie
Ronas Hill
(1475ft)   Collafirth
Otterswick
Ulsta
Esha Ness   Sullom Voe   Burravoe
Hillswick   Toft
A970
Out
Skerries
Ve Skerries   Muckle
Roe
Papa
Stour   Brae
Laxo
Vidlin   Whalsay
Vementry   Voe   Symbister
A970
Sandness   Aith
West   Bixter
Burrafirth   A971   Weisdale
Walls
Vaila   Tingwall
Culswick   Bressay
Lerwick   Noss
Scalloway
Foula   Hamnavoe
West
Burra   A970
Cunningsburgh
South Havra
Sandwick
Mousa
St Ninian's
Isle   Levenwick
Boddam
Quendale
Fitful Head
Jarlshof
Sumburgh
Head

0   10 miles

▼ Fair Isle   © Crown copyright

1272

Lerwick

For Shetlanders, there's only one place to stop, meet and do business and that's "da toon", **LERWICK**; it's home to about 7500 people, roughly a third of the islands' population. All year, its sheltered **harbour** at the heart of the town is busy with ferries, fishing boats, oil-rig supply vessels and a variety of more specialized craft including seismic survey and naval vessels from all round the North Sea. In summer, the quaysides come alive with local pleasure craft, visiting yachts, cruise liners, historic vessels such as the restored *Swan*, and the occasional tall sailing ship. Behind the old harbour is the compact town centre, made up of one long main street, Commercial Street; from here, narrow lanes, known as "**closses**", rise westwards to the late-Victorian new town.

Arrival, information and accommodation

The **ferry terminal** is situated in the unprepossessing north harbour, about a mile from the town centre. **Flying** into Sumburgh Airport, you can take one of the regular buses to Lerwick; taxis (around £25) and car rental are also available. Buses stop on the Esplanade, very close to the old harbour and Market Cross, or at the Viking bus station on Commercial Road a little to the north of the town centre. The **tourist office** (May–Sept Mon–Sat 8am–6pm, Sun 10am–1pm; Oct–April Mon–Fri 9am–5pm; ℡01595/693434) is at the Market Cross on Commercial Street.

The *Kvelsdro House Hotel*, Greenfield Place (℡01595/692195, ⓦwww .kgqhotels.co.uk; ⓾), is Lerwick's luxury **accommodation** option, followed by the venerable *Queen's Hotel* right on the waterfront on Commercial Street (℡01595/692826, ⓦwww.kgqhotels.co.uk; ⓹). *Alder Lodge Guest House*, 6 Clairmont Place ℡01595/695705; ⓷), is the best middle-range option, followed by *Carradale Guest House*, 36 King Harald St (℡01595/692251; ⓶), situated in a large, comfortable Victorian family home. The SYHA **hostel** (℡01595/692114, ⓦwww.syha.org.uk; April–Sept) at Islesburgh House on King Harald Street, offers unusually comfortable surroundings, and has useful laundry facilities. The *Clickimin* **campsite** (℡01595/694555; late April to Sept) enjoys the excellent facilities of the neighbouring Clickimin leisure centre.

The Town

Lerwick's attractive, flagstone-clad **Commercial Street** is still very much the core of the town. Its narrow, winding form, set back one block from the Esplanade, provides shelter from the elements even on the worst days, and is where locals meet, shop, exchange news and gossip. The Street's northern end is marked by the towering walls of **Fort Charlotte** (daily: June–Sept 9am–10pm; Oct–May 9am–4pm; free), begun for Charles II in 1665 during the wars with the Dutch, and in the 1780s repaired and named in honour of George III's queen.

Although the closses that connect the Street to Hillhead are now a desirable place to live, it's not so long ago that they were regarded as slum-like dens of iniquity, from which the better-off escaped to the Victorian new town laid out to the west on a grid plan. **Hillhead**, up in the Victorian "new town", is dominated by the splendid **Town Hall** (Mon–Thurs 9am–5pm, Fri 9am–4pm; free), a Scottish Baronial monument to civic pride, built by public subscription. You're free to admire the wonderful stained-glass windows in the main hall, which celebrate Shetland's history, and to climb the castellated central tower which occupies the town's highest point.

Up Helly-Aa

On the last Tuesday in January, whatever the weather, Lerwick's new town is the setting for the most spectacular part of the **Up Helly-Aa**, a huge fire festival, the largest of several held in Shetland from January to March. Around nine hundred torchbearing participants, all male and all in extraordinary costumes, march in procession behind a grand Viking longship. The annually appointed Guizer Jarl and his "squad" appear as Vikings and brandish shields and silver axes; each of the forty or so other squads is dressed for their part in the subsequent entertainment, perhaps as giant insects, space invaders or ballet dancers. Their circuitous route leads to the King George V Playing Field where, after due ceremony, all the torches are thrown into the longship, creating an enormous bonfire. A firework display follows, then the participants, known as "guizers", set off in their squads to do the rounds of more than a dozen "halls" (which usually include at least one hotel and the Town Hall) from around 8.30pm in the evening until 8am the next morning, performing some kind of act – usually a comedy routine – at each.

Up Helly-Aa itself is not that ancient, dating only from Victorian times, when it was introduced to replace the much older Christmas tradition of rolling burning tar barrels through the streets, which was banned in 1874. Seven years later a torchlight procession took place, which eventually developed into a full-blown Viking celebration, known as "Up Helly-Aa". Although this is essentially a community event with entry to halls by invitation only, visitors are welcome at the Town Hall, for which tickets are sold in early January; contact the tourist office well in advance. To catch some of the atmosphere of the event, check out the annual Up Helly-Aa exhibition in the **Galley Shed** on St Sunniva Street (mid-May to mid-Sept Tues 2–4pm & 7–9pm, Fri 7–9pm, Sat 2–4pm; £2.50), where you can see a full-size longship, costumes, shields and photographs.

Opposite the town hall, housed on the first floor of the desperately ugly municipal library, the **Shetland Museum** (Mon, Wed & Fri 10am–7pm, Tues, Thurs & Sat 10am–5pm; Ⓦ www.shetland-museum.org.uk; free) is full to the brim with nauticalia. More unusual exhibits include Shetland's oldest telephone, fitted with a ceramic mouthpiece, and a carved head of Goliath by Adam Christie (1869–1950), a Shetlander who spent much of his life in Montrose Asylum, and who is perhaps best known for his application to patent a submarine built of glass, which would thus be invisible to enemies.

A mile or so southwest of the town centre lies the fortified **Clickimin Broch**, begun around 700 BC and later enclosed by a defensive wall, whose main tower once rose to around 40ft, though the remains are now around 10ft high. Excavation of the site has unearthed an array of domestic goods that suggest international trade, including a Roman glass bowl thought to have been made in Alexandria around 100 AD.

In earlier times the seasonal nature of the Shetland fishing industry led to the establishment of small stores, known as **böds**, often incorporating sleeping accommodation, beside the beaches where fish were landed and dried. Just beyond Lerwick's main ferry terminal, a mile and a half north of the centre, stands the **Böd of Gremista** (June to mid-Sept Wed–Sun 10am–1pm & 2–5pm; Ⓦ www.shetland-museum.org.uk; free), the birthplace of Arthur Anderson (1792–1868), naval seaman, businessman, philanthropist, Shetland's first native MP and founder of the *Shetland Journal*.

Eating, drinking and entertainment

Lerwick's best **restaurant** is *Monty's* on Mounthooly Street (closed Mon & Sun): expect accomplished contemporary cooking at moderate prices. Other places to try include the very good Indian *Raba*, 26 Commercial Rd, and the Chinese/Thai *Great Wall*, located above the Viking Bus Station. *Faerdie-Maet* (closed Sun), near the post office on Commercial Street, is a decent café, as is the relaxed, friendly *Havly Centre* (closed Mon & Sun), a Norwegian lunchtime café on Charlotte Street.

The downstairs bar in the *Thule* on the Esplanade is an archetypal rough-and-ready seaport **pub**, usually heaving. The friendliest place is the upstairs bar in the *Lounge*, up Mounthooly Street, where local musicians often do sessions. The Garrison Theatre, by the Town Hall, shows **films** as well as putting on occasional theatre productions, comedy acts and live gigs. The Islesburgh Community Centre has introduced regular crafts and culture evenings (mid-May to mid-Sept Wed & Fri), where you can buy local knitwear and listen to traditional music.

In late April, musicians from all over the world arrive for the excellent **Shetland Folk Festival**, which embraces a wider range of musical styles than the title might suggest; there are concerts and dances in every corner of the islands. In mid-October, there's an **Accordion and Fiddle Festival**: similar format, same co-ordinating office, but a different musical focus. For details of **what's on**, buy the *Shetland Times* on Fridays, or consult Ⓦ www.shetlandtoday.co.uk. Some events are also advertised on Shetland's independent radio station SIBC, 96.2FM.

Bressay and Noss

Shielding Lerwick from the full force of the North Sea is the island of **Bressay**, dominated at its southern end by the conical Ward Hill (744ft) – "da Wart" – and accessible on an hourly car and passenger ferry from Lerwick (takes 5min). The chief reason most visitors pass through Bressay is in order to visit the tiny but spectacular island of **Noss** – the name means "a point of rock" – just off Bressay's eastern shore. The island was inhabited until World War II but is now given over to sheep farming and is also a National Nature Reserve. Scottish Natural Heritage operates an inflatable as a ferry from the landing stage below the car park at the east side of Bressay (mid-May to Aug daily except Tues & Fri 10am–5pm; takes 2min; £3 return). On the island, the old farmhouse of Gungstie contains a small **visitor centre** where the warden will give you a free map and guide. Behind the house is an old stud farm for **Shetland ponies**, which were sent to work in the mines of county Durham in northeast England. The most memorable feature of Noss is its cliffed coastline rising to a peak at the massive 500-foot **Noup**, home to vast colonies of cliff-nesting gannets, puffins, guillemots, shags, razorbills and fulmars. Be warned: if you stray off the marked path, the great skuas will do their best to intimidate with dive-bombing raids that may hit you hard.

South Mainland

Shetland's **South Mainland** is a long, thin finger of land, only three or four miles wide, but 25 miles long, ending in the cliffs of Sumburgh Head and Fitful Head. It's a beautiful area with wild landscapes but also good farmland, and has yielded some of Shetland's most impressive archeological treasures – in particular, Jarlshof.

From Leebitton, in the district of Sandwick, halfway to Sumburgh Head, you can take the small passenger **ferry** (mid-April to mid-Sept 1–2 daily; takes 15min; £5 return; ☏ 01950/431367, Ⓦ www.mousaboattrips.co.uk) to the small **Isle of Mousa**, on which stands the best-preserved broch in the whole of Scotland. Rising to more than 40ft, and looking rather like a Stone Age cooling tower, **Mousa Broch** has a remarkable presence, and features in both *Egil's Saga* and the *Orkneyinga Saga*, contemporary chronicles of Norse exploration and settlement. The low entrance passage leads through two concentric walls to a central courtyard, divided into separate beehive chambers. Between the walls, a rough (very dark) staircase leads to the top parapet (torch provided). From late May to late July, a large colony of around five thousand **storm petrels** breeds in and around the broch walls, fishing out at sea during the day, and only returning to the nests after dark. The ferry also runs special late-night trips (Wed & Sat weather permitting), setting off in the "simmer dim" twilight around 11pm.

The main road leads eventually to **Sumburgh airport**, beyond which excavations are currently underway at **Old Scatness** (July to early Aug daily except Fri 10am–5.30pm; £2), where a broch, and possibly the best-preserved Iron Age house in Europe, have recently been discovered. A little further along the road lies **Jarlshof** (April–Sept daily 9.30am–6.30pm; £2.50; HS; Oct–March open access to grounds; free), the largest and most impressive of Shetland's archeological sites. There's evidence of more than four thousand years of continuous occupation, with buildings dating from the Stone Age to the early seventeenth century. The best-preserved buildings are the Pictish wheelhouses surrounding a Neolithic broch, and also the Norse longhouses. Sir Walter Scott was responsible for the name: while visiting Shetland in 1814 he decided to use part of the ruins in his novel *The Pirate*. Towering over the whole complex is the laird's house, originally built by Robert Stewart, Earl of Orkney and Lord of Shetland, in the late sixteenth century. Beside Jarlshof is the Scots Baronial *Sumburgh Hotel*, where the bar **food** is surprisingly good.

The Mainland comes to a dramatic end at **Sumburgh Head**, about two miles from Jarlshof. The lighthouse, designed by Robert Stevenson, was built in 1821; although not open to the public its grounds offer great views to Noss in the north and Fair Isle to the south. This is also the easiest place in Shetland to get close to **puffins**. During the nesting season, you simply need to look over the western wall by the lighthouse gate to see them arriving at their burrows with beakfuls of fish or giving flying lessons to their offspring; on no account should you try to climb over the wall.

Fair Isle

Tiny **Fair Isle** is marooned in the sea halfway between Shetland and Orkney and very different from both. The weather reflects its isolated position: you can almost guarantee that it'll be windy, though if you're lucky your visit might coincide with fine weather – what the islanders call "a given day". At one time Fair Isle's population was not far short of four hundred, but by the 1950s, the population had shrunk to just 44, a point at which evacuation and abandonment of the island was seriously considered. George Waterston, who'd bought the island and set up a bird observatory in 1948, passed it into the care of the National Trust for Scotland in 1954 and rejuvenation began.

The croft land and the island's scattered houses are concentrated in the south, but the focus for many visitors is the **Bird Observatory**, built just above the sandy bay of North Haven where the ferry from Shetland Mainland arrives. It's one of the major European centres for ornithology and its work in watching, trapping, recording and ringing birds goes on all year. Fair Isle is a landfall for a huge number and range of migrant birds during the spring and autumn passages. Migration routes converge here and more than 345 species, including many rarities, have been noted. Fair Isle is, of course, even better known for its

knitting patterns, still produced with great skill by the local knitwear cooperative, though not in the quantities which you might imagine from a walk around city department stores. There are a few samples on display at the island's **museum** (Mon 2–5pm, Wed 10am–noon, Fri 2–4.30pm; ☎01595/760244; free), situated next door to the island's Methodist Chapel.

The passenger **ferry** (☎01595/760222) connects Fair Isle with either Lerwick (on alternate Thurs; takes 4hr 30min) or Grutness in Sumburgh (Tues, Sat & alternate Thurs; takes 2hr 40min). **Flights** go from Tingwall (Mon, Wed, Fri & Sat) or Sumburgh (Sat); a one-way ticket costs £38, and day-trips are possible on Mondays, Wednesdays and Fridays. There is full-board **accommodation** at the *Fair Isle Lodge & Bird Observatory* (☎01595/760258, ⓦwww.fairislebirdobs.co.uk; ❹) in rooms or hostel-style dorms. A good **B&B** option is *Upper Leogh* in the south of the island (☎01595/760248, ⒺKathleen.coull@lineone.net; ❷).

Scalloway

Approaching **SCALLOWAY**, six miles west of Lerwick, from the shoulder of the steep hill to the east known as the **Scord**, there's a dramatic view over the town and the islands to the south and west. Once the capital of Shetland, Scalloway's importance waned through the eighteenth century as Lerwick grew in trading success and status. Nowadays, Scalloway is fairly sleepy, though its prosperity, always closely linked to the fluctuations of the fishing industry, has been given a boost with investment in new fish-processing factories.

In spite of modern developments nearby, Scalloway is dominated by the imposing shell of **Scalloway Castle**, a classic fortified tower house built with forced labour in 1600 by the infamous Earl Patrick Stewart, who held court in the castle and gained a reputation for enhancing his own power and wealth through the calculated use of harsh justice. He was eventually arrested and imprisoned in 1609 for his aggressive behaviour towards his fellow landowners; his son, Robert, attempted an insurrection and both were executed in Edinburgh in 1615. On Main Street, the small **Scalloway Museum** (May–Sept Mon 9am–2pm, Tues–Sat 9am–2pm & 4.30–7pm; free), run by volunteers, attempts to tell the story of the Shetland Bus, the link between Shetland and Norway which helped to sustain the Norwegian resistance in World War II.

Scalloway's best **accommodation** is at the very comfortable and welcoming *Hildasay Guest House* (☎01595/880822; ❷), a Hansel-and-Gretel weatherboarded house on the top of the hill above Scalloway, behind the swimming pool. For **food**, head for *Da Haaf* (closed Sat & Sun), the unpretentious licensed restaurant in the North Atlantic Fisheries College, which serves fresh fish, simply prepared.

The Westside

Reached from Lerwick through the attractive coastal landscape of Whiteness and the district of Weisdale, scene of particularly harsh Clearances, the **Westside**'s rolling brown and purple moorland is scattered with dozens of small picturesque lochs gleaming blue or silver and patches of bright green, where cultivation and reseeding have taken place. The coast, cut by several deep voes, is very varied; aside from dramatic cliffs, there are intimate coves and some fine beaches. The crossroads for the area is effectively Bixter, southwest of which lies the finest Neolithic structure in the Westside, dubbed the **Staneydale Temple** by the archeologist who excavated it because it resembled one on Malta.

Whatever its true function, it was twice as large as the surrounding oval-shaped houses (now in ruins) and was certainly of great importance, perhaps as some kind of community centre. The foundations measure more than 40ft by 20ft internally with immensely thick walls, still around 4ft high, whose roof would have been supported by spruce posts (two postholes can still be clearly seen).

At the end of a long winding road across an uninhabited, boulder-strewn landscape, you eventually reach the fertile scattered crofting settlement of **SANDNESS** (pronounced "saaness"). It's an oasis of green meadows in the peat moorland, with a nice beach. The modern **Jamieson's Spinning Mill** (Mon–Fri 8am–5pm; free) is the only one on Shetland producing pure Shetland wool; the factory welcomes visitors, and you can watch how workers take the fleece and then wash, card and spin the exceptionally fine wool into yarn.

The best **accommodation** and **eating** options on the Westside are in and around Walls, halfway between Bixter and Sandness. The best B&B is the wonderfully welcoming *Skeoverick* (℡01595/809349; ❶), a lovely modern croft house which lies a mile or so north of Walls. The only hotel is *Burrastow House* (℡01595/809307, ✉burr.hs.hotel@zetnet.co.uk; ❼), beautifully situated about three miles southwest of Walls; and also one of the best places to **eat** in Shetland.

Papa Stour

A mile offshore from Sandness is the quintessentially peaceful island of **Papa Stour** ("big island of the priests"); apart from early Christian connections, it was home, in the eighteenth century, to people who were mistakenly believed to have been lepers. The sea has eroded its volcanic rocks to produce some of the most impressive coastal scenery in Shetland, with **stacks, caves** and **natural arches**. The east side is the most fecund area, partly because much of the soil from the western side was painstakingly transported here. In the nineteenth century, Papa Stour supported around three hundred inhabitants; today there's only thirty or so. The main settlement, **BIGGINGS**, lies in the west near the pier, and it was here that excavation in the early 1980s revealed the remains of a thirteenth-century Norse house, which is thought to have belonged to Duke Haakon, heir to the Norwegian throne. In summer, the passenger **ferry** runs from West Burrafirth to Papa Stour (Mon, Wed & Fri–Sun). Always book in advance, and reconfirm the day before departure (℡01595/810460); day-trips are only possible on Friday, Saturday and Sunday. There's also a **flight** from Tingwall every Tuesday, and again a day-trip is feasible (£16 one-way). Papa Stour's airstrip is southwest of Biggings, by the school. The only **accommodation** is *North House* B&B (℡01595/873238; ❶), with optional full board, who can arrange boat trips.

Foula

Southwest of Walls, at "the edge of the world", **Foula** is without a doubt the most isolated inhabited island in the British Isles, separated from the nearest point on Mainland Shetland by about fourteen miles of often turbulent ocean. Seen from the Mainland, its distinctive mountainous form changes subtly, depending upon the vantage point, but the outline is unforgettable. Its western **cliffs**, the second highest in Britain after those of St Kilda, rise at **The Kame** to some 1220ft above sea level; a clear day at The Kame offers a magnificent panorama stretching from Unst to Fair Isle. On a bad day, the exposure is complete and the cliffs generate turbulent blasts of wind known in Shetland as "flans", which rip through the hills with tremendous force.

Arriving on Foula, you can't help but be amazed by the sheer size of the island's immense, bare mountain summits. As well as having forty human inhabitants, the island, whose name is derived from the Old Norse for "bird island", also provides a home for a quarter of a million **birds**. Arctic terns wheel overhead at the airstrip, red-throated divers can usually be seen on Mill Loch, while fulmars, guillemots and gannets cling to the rock ledges, but it is the island's colony of **great skuas** or "bonxies" whom you can't fail to notice.

It's essential to book and reconfirm the summer passenger **ferry** from Walls (Tues, Thurs & Sat; 2hr 30min; ☎01595/810460). The boat arrives at Ham, in the middle of Foula's east coast, and has to be winched up onto the pier to protect it. Aside from Tuesdays, day-trips are possible by **flying** from Tingwall (Mon–Wed & Fri; around £22 one-way; ☎01595/753226). Foula's only **B&B** is *Leraback* (☎01595/753226; ❸), near Ham, which does full board only, though they can also rent out a self-catering cottage on a daily basis.

North Mainland

The **North Mainland**, stretching more than thirty miles north from the central belt around Lerwick, is wilder than much of Shetland, with almost relentlessly bleak moorland and some rugged and dramatic coastal scenery. You're bound to pass by **VOE**, as it sits at the main crossroads of the area, but it's easy to miss the picturesque old village, a tight huddle of homes and workshops down below the road around the pier. Set at the head of a deep, sheltered, sea loch, Voe has a Scandinavian appearance, helped by the presence of the **Sail Loft**, painted in a rich, deep red. The building has been converted into a large **hostel** (book through Lerwick tourist office; April–Oct); it has hot showers, a kitchen, and a solid-fuel heater in the smaller of the bedrooms. Across the road is the handy *Pierhead Restaurant & Bar*, a cosy wood-panelled **pub** with a real fire and occasional live music, which offers good food.

From Voe the main road divides; the northern leg leads to Toft, the ferry terminal for the island of Yell (see below), while the other branch cuts northwest to **BRAE**, a sprawling settlement expanded in some haste in the 1970s to accommodate the workforce for the huge **Sullom Voe Oil Terminal** nearby. Brae boasts one of Shetland's finest **hotels**, *Busta House* (☎01806/522506, ⓦwww.bustahouse.com; ❻), a lovely laird's house which sits across the bay of Busta Voe from the modern sprawl of Brae. It's worth coming here for a drink or an excellent meal in the hotel's pub-like bar.

The peninsula of **Northmavine**, to the north of Brae, is connected by the narrow isthmus of Mavis Grind, at which it's said you can throw a stone from the Atlantic to the North Sea. Northmavine is one of the most picturesque areas of Shetland, with its often rugged scenery, magnificent coastline and wide open spaces. **HILLSWICK**, the main settlement, was once served by the steamers of the North of Scotland, Orkney & Shetland Steam Navigation Company and in the early twentieth century the firm also built the **Magnus Bay Hotel**, importing it in the form of a timber kit from Norway; it still stands, albeit somewhat altered. Nearer the shore is the much older Hillswick House and, attached to it, **Da Böd**, once the oldest pub in Shetland, said to have been founded by a German merchant in 1684, now an alternative veggie café and wildlife sanctuary called the *Booth* (☎01806/503348; May–Sept).

Just outside Hillswick, a sideroad leads west to the exposed headland of **Esha Ness** (pronounced "*Ay*sha Ness"), celebrated for its splendid coastline views. Spectacular eroded red granite **cliffs** are spread out before you as the road climbs away from Hillswick: in the foreground are the stacks known as **The**

Drongs off the Ness of Hillswick. A mile or so south off the main road is the **Tangwick Haa Museum** (May–Sept Mon–Fri 1–5pm, Sat & Sun 11am–7pm; free), which tells the often moving story of this remote corner of Shetland and its role in the dangerous trade of deep-sea fishing and whaling. To the north the road ends at the **Esha Ness Lighthouse**, a great place to view the cliffs, stacks and, in rough weather, blowholes of this stretch of coast, and the starting point for an excellent three-hour walk. One of the few places to stay in Esha Ness is *Johnnie Notions* **hostel** (April–Oct; book through Lerwick tourist office; no electricity), up a turning north off the main road, in **Hamnavoe**.

The North Isles

Many visitors never make it out to Shetland's trio of remote **North Isles**, which is a shame, as the ferry links are frequent and inexpensive, and the roads fast. Certainly, there is no dramatic shift in scenery: much of what awaits you is the familiar Shetland landscape of undulating peat moorland, dramatic coastal cliffs and silent glacial voes. However, with Lerwick that much further away, the spirit of independence and self-sufficiency in the North Isles is much more keenly felt. **Yell**, the largest of the three, is best known for its vast otter population. **Fetlar**, the smallest, is home to the rare red-necked phalarope. **Unst**, though, probably has the widest appeal, partly as the most northerly land mass in the British Isles, but also for its nesting seabird population.

Yell

Historically, **Yell** hasn't had good write-ups. The writer Eric Linklater described it as "dull and dark", while the Scottish historian Buchanan claimed it was "so uncouth a place that no creature can live therein, except such as are born there". Certainly, if you keep to the fast main road, which links the island's two ferry terminals of Ulsta and Gutcher, you'll pass a lot of uninspiring peat moorland, but the landscape is relieved by several voes which cut deeply into it, providing superb natural harbours. Yell's coastline, too, is gentler and greener than the interior and provides an ideal habitat for a large population of **otters**.

At **BURRAVOE**, in the southeast corner, there's a lovely whitewashed laird's house that now houses the **Old Haa Museum** (late April to Sept Tues–Thurs & Sat 10am–4pm, Sun 2–5pm; free), which is stuffed with artefacts, and has lots of material on the history of the local herring and whaling industry; there's a very pleasant wood-panelled café on the ground floor. In the north, the area around **CULLIVOE** has relatively gentle, but attractive, coastal scenery. The **Sands of Brekken** are made from crushed shells, and are beautifully sheltered in a cove a mile or two north of Cullivoe. A couple of miles to the west, the road ends at **GLOUP**, with its secretive, narrow voe. This area provides some excellent walking, as does the coast further west, where there's an Iron Age fort and field system at **Burgi Geos**.

Ferries from Toft on the Mainland are frequent and inexpensive, and taking a car over is easy, too (1–2 hourly; takes 20min). One of the best **B&Bs** is *Hillhead* (☎01957/722274; ❶), a comfortable modern house halfway between Ulsta and Burravoe; you can also stay with the very welcoming Tullochs at *Gutcher Post Office* (☎01957/744201; ❶) overlooking the ferry terminal. A cheaper alternative is to stay in the **hostel** at *Windhouse Lodge* (April–Oct; book through Lerwick tourist office), the gatehouse on the main road near Mid Yell. The functional *Hilltop Bar* in Mid Yell offers standard bar **food**, while the *Seaview Café*, opposite the post office at Gutcher provides a welcome shelter, as well as snacks and hot drinks.

Fetlar

Fetlar is the most fertile of the North Isles, much of it grassy moorland and lush green meadows with masses of summer flowers. At the main settlement, **HOUBIE**, you can learn more about the island from the nearby welcoming **Fetlar Interpretive Centre** (May–Sept Tues–Sun noon–5pm; free). Fetlar is also one of very few places in the UK where you'll see graceful **red-necked phalarope** (late May to early Aug): the island boasts ninety percent of the UK's phalarope population, and an RSPB hide has been provided overlooking the marshes (or mires) to the east of the **Loch of Funzie** (pronounced "finny"). **Ferries** (6–8 daily; takes 20min) depart from both Gutcher on Yell and Belmont on Unst, docking at Oddsta, three miles northwest of Houbie. The only public transport is an infrequent postcar (Mon, Wed & Fri). **Accommodation** boils down to *Gord* (☎01957/733227; ❷), a comfortable modern house attached to the island shop in Houbie, and the *Glebe* (☎01957/733242; ❶), a characterful old manse near Papil Water. The *Garths* **campsite** (☎01957/733227; May–Sept) is a simple field just to the west of Houbie.

Unst

Unst has recently been thrown into something of a crisis by the drastic downsizing of the local RAF radar base at Saxa Vord, which used to employ a third of the island's thousand-strong population. Much of the interior is rolling grassland – a blessed relief after the peaty moorland of Yell – but the coast is more dramatic: a fringe of cliffs relieved by some beautiful sandy beaches. As Britain's **most northerly** inhabited island, there is a surfeit of "most northerly" sights: many visitors only come here in order to head straight for Hermaness, to look out over Muckle Flugga and the northernmost tip of Britain.

On the south coast, not far from the ferry terminal, is **UYEASOUND**, east of which lie the ruins of **Muness Castle**, a diminutive defensive structure, built in 1598 with matching bulging bastions and corbelled turrets at opposite corners (keys and torch from the house nearby). Unst's main settlement is **BALTASOUND**, five miles north, whose herring industry used to boost the local population of around five hundred to as much as ten thousand during the fishing season. The excellent **Unst Heritage Centre** (May–Sept daily 2–5pm; free) occupies the old school building by the main crossroads. From Baltasound, the main road crosses a giant boulder field of serpentine, a greyish green, occasionally turquoise rock that weathers to a rusty orange. The **Keen of Hamar**, east of Baltasound, and clearly signposted from the main road, is one of the largest expanses of serpentine debris in Europe, and is home to an extraordinary array of plantlife.

Beyond the Keen of Hamar, the road drops down into **HAROLDSWICK**, where near the shore you'll find the **Unst Boat Haven** (May–Sept daily 2–5pm; otherwise a key is available from the adjacent shop; free), displaying a beautifully presented collection of historic boats with many tools of the trade and information on fishing. The road that heads off northwest leads to the bleak headland of **Hermaness**, now a National Nature Reserve and home to more than 100,000 nesting seabirds. There's an excellent **visitor centre** in the former lighthouse keepers' shore station, where you can pick up a leaflet showing the marked routes across the heather to the view over to **Muckle Flugga** lighthouse and **Out Stack**, the most northerly bit of Britain. The views from here are inevitably marvellous, as is the birdlife; there's a huge gannetry on one of the stacks, and puffins burrow all along the cliff tops.

Book in advance for the regular **ferries** that shuttle from Gutcher on Yell over to **BELMONT** on Unst (every 15–30min; takes 10min; ☎01957/ 722259).

The best and most unusual **accommodation** is *Buness House* (℡01957/711315, Ⓦwww.users.zetnet.co.uk/buness-house; ❹), a seventeenth-century Haa in Baltasound still owned and run by the eccentric Edmondstons (of chickweed fame). Another very good bet is *Prestagaard* (℡01957/755234; ❶), a more modest Victorian B&B in Uyeasound, where there's also the clean and modern *Gardiesfauld Hostel* (℡01957/755259, Ⓔtelecroft2000@ talk21.com; April–Sept) near the pier, which allows **camping** and offers **bike rental**.

Travel details – Orkney

Ferries to Orkney (summer only)

Aberdeen to: Stromness (2 weekly; 8–10hr).
Gill's Bay to: St Margaret's Hope (3 daily; 1hr).
John O'Groats to: Burwick (passengers only; 2–4
daily; 40min).
Lerwick to: Stromness (2 weekly; 8hr).
Scrabster to: Stromness (1–3 daily; 2hr).

Inter-island ferries (summer only)

To Eday : Kirkwall–Eday (2–3 daily; 1hr 15min–2hr).
To Hoy : Houton–Lyness (Mon–Fri 6 daily, Sat & Sun 2–3 daily; 30min–1hr); Stromness–Hoy (passengers only; 2–5 daily; 25min).
To North Ronaldsay : Kirkwall–North Ronaldsay (1 weekly, usually Fri; 2hr 40min–3hr).
To Papa Westray : Kirkwall–Papa Westray (Tues & Fri; 2hr 15min); Pierowall (Westray)–Papa Westray (passengers only; 3–6 daily; 25min).

To Rousay : Tingwall–Rousay (6 daily; 30min).
To Sanday : Kirkwall–Sanday (1–3 daily; 1hr 25min).
To Shapinsay : Kirkwall–Shapinsay (5–6 daily; 45min).
To Stronsay : Kirkwall–Whitehall (2 daily; 1hr 35min–2hr).
To Westray : Kirkwall–Westray (2–3 daily; 1hr 25min).

Inter-island flights (Mon–Sat only)

Kirkwall to: Eday (3 on Wed; 8–36min); North Ronaldsay (2 daily; 15min); Papa Westray (Mon–Fri 2 daily; 12min); Sanday (Mon–Fri 2 daily, 1 on Sat; 10–20min); Stronsay (Mon–Fri 2 daily; 25min); Westray (Mon–Sat 1–2 daily; 12min).

Buses on Orkney Mainland

Kirkwall to: Burwick (4 daily; 45min); Deerness via airport (Mon–Sat 2–4 daily; 25min); Evie (Mon–Sat 2–4 daily; 30min); Houton (Mon–Sat 3–5 daily; 30min); St Margaret's Hope (Mon–Sat 3–4 daily; 40min); Stromness (Mon–Sat 10 daily; 30min); Tingwall (Mon–Sat 5–7 daily; 35min).
Stromness to: Houton (Mon–Sat 2–3 daily; 20min).

Travel details – Shetland

Ferries to Shetland (summer only)

Aberdeen to: Lerwick (4–5 weekly; 14hr).
Stromness (Orkney) to: Lerwick (1–2 weekly; 8–10hr).

Inter-island ferries (summer only)

To Bressay: Lerwick–Bressay (every 30min–1hr; 5min).

To Fair Isle: Lerwick–Fair Isle (1 on alternate Thurs; 4hr 30min); Sumburgh–Fair Isle (1 on Tues, Sat & alternate Thurs; 2hr 40min).

To Fetlar: Belmont (Unst) & Gutcher (Yell)–Oddsta (6–8 daily; 25min).

To Foula: Scalloway–Foula (1 on alternate Thurs; 3hr); Walls–Foula (1 on Tues & alternate Thurs; 2hr 30min).

To Papa Stour: West Burrafirth–Papa Stour (Mon, Wed & Sun 1 daily, Fri & Sat 2 daily; 45min).

To Unst: Gutcher (Yell)–Belmont (every 15–45min; 10min).

To Yell: Toft–Ulsta (every 20–40min; 20min).

Inter-island flights (summer only)

Sumburgh to: Fair Isle (1 on Sat; 15min).

Tingwall to: Fair Isle (Mon, Wed & Fri 2 daily, 1 on Sat; 25min); Foula (Mon, Wed & Fri 2 daily, 1 on Tues; 15min); Papa Stour (2 on Tues; 10min).

Buses

On Shetland Mainland

Lerwick to: Brae (Mon–Fri 4–5 daily, 2 on Sat; 45min); Hamnavoe (Mon–Sat 1–2 daily; 30min); Hillswick (1 daily except Wed & Sun; 1hr 15min); Sandwick (Mon–Sat 5–6 daily, Sun 3 daily; 25min); Scalloway (Mon–Sat hourly; 15min); Sumburgh (2–5 daily; 45min); Toft (Mon–Sat 1 daily; 55min); Voe (Mon–Fri 5–6 daily, Sat & Sun 2–3 daily; 35min); Walls (Mon–Sat 2–4 daily; 45min).

On Unst

Baltasound to: Haroldswick (2–4 daily; 5–10min).

Belmont to: Baltasound (Mon–Fri school term only 1 daily; 1hr); Uyeasound (Mon–Sat 1–3 daily; 5min).

On Yell

Mid Yell to: Gutcher (Mon–Sat 1–3 daily, 1 on Sun in school term; 25min).

Ulsta to: Burravoe (Mon–Sat 1 daily; 10min); Gutcher (Mon–Sat 1–2 daily, 1 on Sun in school term; 30min).

contexts

contexts

A brief history of Britain 1287

Books 1311

Film 1324

A brief history of Britain

Off and on, people have lived in Britain for the best part of half a million years, though the earliest evidence of human life dates from about 250,000 BC. These meagre remains, found near Swanscombe, east of London across the Thames from Tilbury, belong to one of the migrant communities whose comings and goings depended on the fluctuations of the Ice Ages. Renewed glaciation then made the area uninhabitable once more, and the next traces – mainly roughly worked flint implements – were left around 40,000 BC by cave-dwellers at Creswell Crags in Derbyshire, Kent's Cavern near Torquay and Cheddar Cave in Somerset. The last spell of intense cold began about 17,000 years ago, and it was the final thawing of this last Ice Age around 5000 BC that caused the British Isles to separate from the European mainland.

The sea barrier did nothing to stop further migrations of nomadic hunting communities, drawn by the rich forests that covered ancient Britain. In about 3500 BC a new wave of colonists arrived from the continent, probably via Ireland, bringing with them a Neolithic culture based on farming and the rearing of livestock. These tribes were the first to make some impact on their environment, clearing forests, enclosing fields, constructing defensive ditches around their villages and digging mines to obtain flint used for tools and weapons. Fragments of Neolithic pottery have been found near Peterborough and at Windmill Hill, near Avebury in Wiltshire; others – like the well-preserved village of Skara Brae in Orkney – were near the sea, enabling them to supplement their diet by fishing and to develop their skills as boat builders. The most profuse relics of this culture are their graves, usually stone-chambered, turf-covered mounds (called long barrows, cairns or cromlechs), which are scattered throughout the country – the most impressive ones are at Belas Knap in Gloucestershire, Barclodiad y Gawres in Anglesey, and Maes Howe on Orkney.

The transition from the Neolithic to the Bronze Age began around 2000 BC, with the immigration from northern Europe of the so-called Beaker Folk – named from the distinctive cups found at their burial sites. Originating in the Iberian peninsula and bringing with them bronze-workers from the Rhineland, these newcomers had a well-organized social structure with an established aristocracy, and quickly intermixed with the native tribes. Many of Britain's stone circles were completed at this time, including Stonehenge in Wiltshire, and Callanish on the Isle of Lewis, while many others belong entirely to the Bronze Age – for example, the Hurlers and the Nine Maidens on Cornwall's Bodmin Moor. Large numbers of earthwork forts were also built in this period, suggesting a high level of tribal warfare, but none of these were able to withstand the waves of Celtic invaders who, spreading from a homeland in central Europe, began settling in Britain around 600 BC.

The Celts

Highly skilled in battle, the **Celts** soon displaced the local inhabitants all over Britain, establishing a sophisticated farming economy and a social hierarchy that was headed by **Druids**, a ritual priesthood with attendant poets, seers and warriors. Through a deep knowledge of ritual, legend and the mechanics of the heavens, the Druids maintained their position between the people and a pantheon of over four thousand gods. Familiar with Mediterranean artefacts through their far-flung trade routes, they introduced superior methods of metalworking that favoured iron rather than bronze, from which they forged not just weapons but also coins. Gold was used for ornamental works – the first recognizable British art – heavily influenced by the symbolic, patterned **La Tène** style still thought of as quintessentially Celtic.

The principal Celtic contribution to the landscape was a network of hill forts or brochs, and other defensive works stretching over the entire country, the greatest of them at **Maiden Castle** in Dorset, a site first fortified almost 3500 years earlier, and **Mousa** in the Shetland islands. The original Celtic tongue – the basis of modern Welsh and Scottish Gaelic – was spoken over a wide area, gradually dividing into Goidelic (or Q-Celtic) now spoken in Ireland and Scotland, and Brythonic (P-Celtic) spoken in Wales, Cornwall and later exported to Brittany in France. Great though the Celtic technological and artistic achievements were, the people and their pan-European cousins were unable to maintain an organized civic society to match that of their successors, the Romans.

The Romans

Coming at the end of a lengthy but low-level infusion of Roman ideas into the country, the Roman invasion had begun hesitantly, with small cross-Channel incursions by **Julius Caesar** in 55 and 54 BC. Britain's rumoured mineral wealth was a primary motive behind these raids, but the immediate spur to the eventual conquest nearly a century later was the dangerous collaboration between British Celts and the fiercely anti-Roman tribesmen in France, and the need of the emperor **Claudius**, who owed his power to the army, for a great military triumph. The death of the British king Cunobelin, who ruled all southeast England and was the original of Shakespeare's Cymbeline, offered the opportunity Claudius required, and in **August 43 AD**, a substantial force landed in Kent, from where it fanned out, soon establishing a base along the estuary of the Thames. Joined by Claudius and a menagerie of elephants and camels for the major battle of the campaign, the Romans soon reached Camulodunum (Colchester), and within four years were dug in on the frontier of south Wales.

The Catuvellauni chief, Caratacus, continued to conduct a guerrilla campaign from Wales until his eventual betrayal and capture in about 50 AD. About ten years later, a more serious challenge to the Romans arose when the East Anglian Iceni, under their queen **Boudicca** (or Boadicea), sacked Camulodunum and Verulamium (St Albans), and even reached the undefended port of Londinium, precursor of London. The uprising was soon quashed, and turned out to be an isolated act of resistance, with many of the already Romanized southeastern tribes of England probably welcoming absorption into the empire. However, it was not until 79 AD that Wales and the north of England were subdued.

By 80 AD the Roman governor, Agricola, felt secure enough in the south of Britain to begin an invasion of the north, building a string of forts across the Clyde–Forth line and defeating a large force of Scottish tribes at Mons Graupius. The long-term effect of his campaign, however, was slight. In 123

AD the Emperor Hadrian decided to seal the frontier against the northern tribes and built **Hadrian's Wall**, which stretched from the Solway Firth to the Tyne and was the first formal division of the island of Britain. Twenty years later, the Romans again ventured north and built the **Antonine Wall** between the Clyde and the Forth. This was occupied for about forty years, but thereafter the Romans, frustrated by the inhospitable terrain of the Highlands, largely gave up their attempt to subjugate the north, and instead adopted a policy of containment.

The written history of Britain begins with the Romans, whose rule lasted nearly four centuries. For the first time most of England was absorbed into a unified and peaceful political structure, in which commerce flourished and cities prospered, particularly **Londinium**, which immediately assumed a pivotal role in the commercial and administrative life of the province. Although Latin became the language of the Romano-British ruling elite, local traditions were allowed to coexist with imported customs, so that Celtic gods were often worshipped at the same time as the Roman, and sometimes merged with them. Perhaps the most important legacy of the Roman occupation, however, was the introduction of **Christianity** from the third century on, becoming firmly entrenched after its official recognition by the emperor Constantine in 313.

The Anglo-Saxon period

As early as the reign of Constantine, Roman England was being raided by Germanic Saxon pirates. As economic life declined and rural areas became depopulated, individual military leaders began to usurp local authority, so that by the start of the fifth century England had become irrevocably detached from what remained of the Roman Empire. Within fifty years the **Saxons** were settling on the island, the start of a gradual conquest that – despite bitter resistance led by such semi-mythical figures as King Arthur, who is alleged to have held court at Caerleon in Wales – culminated in the defeat of the native Britons in 577 at the **Battle of Dyrham** (near Bath), at which three British kings were killed. Driving the few recalcitrant Celtic tribes deep into Cumbria, Wales and England's West Country, the invaders eliminated the Romano-British culture and by the end of the sixth century the rest of England was divided into the Anglo-Saxon kingdoms of Northumbria, Mercia, East Anglia, Kent and Wessex.

Only in Scotland and Wales did the ancient Celtic traditions survive, untouched by the Teutonic invaders as they had been by the Romans. In the fifth century, Irish-Celtic invaders formed distinct colonies in parts of Wales, and in the northwest of Scotland. Between the fifth and the eighth centuries the **Celtic Saints**, ascetic evangelical missionaries, spread the gospel around Ireland and western Britain, promoting the middle-Eastern eremitical tradition of living a reclusive life. In south Wales, Saint David was the most popular (and subsequently Wales' patron saint), while in northwest Scotland, Saint Columba founded several Christian outposts, the most famous of which was on the island of Iona.

The revival of Christianity in England was driven mainly by the arrival of **St Augustine**, who was dispatched by Pope Gregory I and landed on the Kent coast in 597, accompanied by forty monks. The missionaries were received by **Ethelbert**, who gave Augustine permission to found a monastery at Canterbury, where the king himself was then baptized, followed by ten thousand of his subjects at a grand Christmas ceremony. Despite some reversals in the years that followed, the Christianization of England proceeded quickly, so that by the middle of the seventh century all of the Anglo-Saxon kings had at least nominally adopted the faith. Tensions and clashes between the Augustinian missionaries and the more freebooting Celtic monks inevitably arose, to be resolved by the **Synod of Whitby in 663**, when it was settled that the English church should follow the rule of Rome, thereby ensuring a realignment with the European cultural mainstream.

The central English region of **Mercia** became the dominant Anglo-Saxon kingdom in the eighth century under kings Ethelbald and Offa, the latter being responsible for the greatest public work of the Anglo-Saxon period: **Offa's Dyke**, an earthwork stretching from the River Dee to the Severn, marking the border with Wales. After Offa's death **Wessex** gained the upper hand, and by 825 **Egbert** had conquered or taken allegiance from all the other English kingdoms. The supremacy of Wessex coincided with the first large-scale Norse or **Danish** Viking invasions, which began with coastal pirate raids, such as the one that destroyed the great monastery of Lindisfarne in 793, but gradually grew into a migration, chiefly in the Scottish islands of Orkney, Shetland and the Hebrides.

In 865 a substantial Danish army landed in East Anglia, and within six years they had conquered Northumbria, Mercia and East Anglia, and were attacking Wessex. At about the same time, the leadership of Wessex was assumed by **Alfred the Great**, a warrior whose dogged resistance and acceptance of the need to coexist with the Danes ensured the survival of his kingdom. Having established a border demarcating his domain from the northern **Danelaw**, the part of England in which the rule of the now Christianized Danes was accepted (a border roughly coinciding with the Roman Watling Street), Alfred directed his resources into internal reforms and the strengthening of his defences.

Although Danish attacks had recommenced before the end of Alfred's reign in 899, his successor, **Edward the Elder**, established supremacy over the Danelaw and was thus the de facto overlord of all England, acknowledged even by Scottish and Welsh chieftains. In 973, **Edgar**, king of Mercia and Northumberland, became the first ruler to be crowned king of England, but the aggression from the Danes was unrelenting, and in 1016 Ethelred the Unready – having failed to buy off the enemy – fled to Normandy, establishing links there which were to have a far-reaching effect on ensuing events.

The first and best king of the short-lived Danish dynasty was **Canute**, who was followed by his two unexceptional and disreputable sons, after whom the Saxons were restored under Ethelred's son, **Edward the Confessor**. It was said of Edward that he was better suited to have been a priest than a king, and most of his reign was dominated by Godwin, Earl of Wessex, and by Godwin's son Harold. On Edward's death, the Witan – a sort of council of elders – confirmed **Harold** as king, despite the claim of William, Duke of Normandy, that the exiled and childless Edward had sworn himself to be William's vassal, promising him the succession. Harold's brief reign was overshadowed by the events in the last two of its ten months, when he first marched north to fend off an invasion attempt by his brother Tostig (who had been deprived of his earldom of Northumbria) in league with King Harald of Norway. Having defeated their combined forces at Stamford Bridge in Yorkshire, Harold was immediately forced to return south to meet the invading William, who routed his forces at the **Battle of Hastings** in 1066. Harold was killed, and on Christmas Day of that year William the Conqueror was installed as king in Westminster Abbey.

England: The Normans and the Plantagenets

Making little attempt to reach any understanding with the indigenous Saxon culture, **William I** imposed a new military aristocracy on his subjects, enforcing his rule with a series of strongholds all over England, the grandest of which was the Tower of London. The sporadic rebellions that broke out during the early years of his reign were ruthlessly suppressed by a scorched earth policy, especially in Yorkshire and its surrounding counties, but perhaps the single most effective controlling measure was the compilation of the **Domesday Book** between 1085 and 1086. Recording land ownership, type of cultivation, the number of inhabitants and their social status, it afforded William an unprecedented body of information about his subjects, providing the framework for the administration of taxation, the judicial structure and feudal obligations.

William was succeeded in 1087 by his son William Rufus, an ineffectual ruler but a notable benefactor of the religious foundations that were springing up throughout the realm. Killed by an arrow while hunting in the New Forest, William was in turn followed by William I's youngest son, Henry I, who spent much of his reign in tussles with the country's barons, but at least was the first Norman king to encourage intermarriage, himself marrying a Saxon princess. On his death in 1135, William I's grandson Stephen of Blois contested the accession of Henry's daughter Mathilda (also called Maud), with the consequence that the nineteen years of his reign were spent in civil war. Mathilda's son was eventually recognized as Stephen's heir, and the reign of **Henry II** (1154–89), the first of the **Plantagenet** branch of the Norman line, provided a welcome respite from baronial brawling. Asserting his authority throughout a domain that reached from the Cheviots to the Pyrenees, Henry presided over immense administrative reforms, including the introduction of trial by jury. His attempts to subordinate ecclesiastical authority to the Crown went terribly awry in 1170, when he sanctioned the murder in Canterbury Cathedral of his erstwhile drinking companion **Thomas à Becket**, whose canonization just three years later created an enduring Europe-wide cult.

The last years of Henry's reign were riven by quarrels with his sons, the eldest of whom, **Richard I** (or Lionheart), spent most of his ten-year reign crusading in the Holy Land. Alienated by the king's rift with the Church in Rome, and by his loss of Henry II's huge legacy of French territory, the barons eventually forced Richard's brother **King John** to consent to a charter guaranteeing their rights and privileges, the **Magna Carta**, which was signed in 1215 at Runnymede, on the Thames. The power struggle with the barons continued into the reign of Henry III, who was defeated by their leader Simon de Montfort at Lewes in 1265, when both Henry and Prince Edward were taken prisoner. Edward escaped, defeated the barons' army at the battle of Evesham in 1265 and killed de Montfort, ascending the throne in 1272 as **Edward I**. A great law-maker in the mould of William I and Henry II, Edward presided over the Model Parliament of 1295, a significant step in the evolution of consensual politics, though he was mostly absorbed in extending his kingdom within the island, annexing Wales and imposing English jurisdiction in Scotland.

The conquest of Wales

Though Wales was unable to present a unified opposition to the Norman invaders, William the Conqueror didn't attempt to annex Wales. Instead, he installed a huge retinue of barons, the **Lords Marcher**, along the border to bring as much Welsh territory under their own jurisdiction as possible. Despite generations of squabbling, the barons managed to hold onto their privileges until Henry VIII's Act of Union over four hundred years later.

The status quo between Wales and England changed irrevocably, however, when Edward I succeeded Henry III and began a crusade to unify Britain. The Welsh chief, Llywelyn the Last, had failed to attend Edward's coronation, and refused to pay him homage. With effective use of sea power Edward had little trouble forcing Llywelyn back into Snowdonia. Peace was restored with the **Treaty of Aberconwy** which deprived Llywelyn of almost all his land and stripped him of his financial tributes from the other Welsh princes, but left him with the hollow title of "Prince of Wales". After a relatively cordial four-year period, Llywelyn's brother Dafydd rose against Edward, inevitably dragging Llywelyn along with him. Edward crushed the revolt, captured Llywelyn, and executed him at Cilmeri, after fleeing from the abortive Battle of Builth in 1282. The **Treaty of Rhuddlan** in 1284 set down the terms by which the English monarch was to rule Wales: much of it was given to the Marcher lords who had helped Edward, the rest was divided into administrative and legal districts similar to those in England. Though the treaty is often seen as a symbol of English subjugation, it respected much of Welsh law and provided a basis for civil rights and privileges. Many Welsh were content to accept and exploit Edward's rule for their own benefit, but in 1294 a rebellion led by **Madog ap Llywelyn** gripped Wales and was only halted by Edward's swift and devastating response. Most of the privileges enshrined in the Treaty of Rhuddlan were now rescinded and the Welsh seemed crushed for a century.

Pent-up resentment towards the English sowed seeds of a rebellion led by the tyrannical but charismatic Welsh hero **Owain Glyndŵr**, who declared himself "Prince of Wales" in 1400, and with a crew of local supporters attacked the lands of nearby barons, slaughtering the English. Henry IV misjudged the political climate and imposed restrictions on Welsh land ownership, swelling the general support Glyndŵr needed to take Conwy Castle the following year. In 1404 Glyndŵr summoned a parliament in Machynlleth, and had himself crowned Prince of Wales, with envoys of France, Scotland and Castile in attendance. He then demanded independence for the Welsh Church from Canterbury and set about securing alliances with English noblemen who had grievances with Henry IV. This last ambitious move heralded Glyndŵr's downfall. A succession of defeats saw his allies desert him and by 1408, when the castles at Harlech and Aberystwyth were retaken for the Crown, this last protest against Edward I's English conquest had lost its momentum.

Scotland in the Middle Ages

The victory of the Scottish king, **Malcolm III**, known as Canmore ("big-head"), over Macbeth in 1057 marked the beginning of a period of fundamental change in Scottish society. Having avenged his father Duncan, Malcolm III, who had spent the previous seventeen years at the English court, sought to apply to Scotland a range of ideas he had brought back with him. He and his heirs established a secure dynasty based on succession through the male line and introduced **feudalism** into Scotland, a system that was diametrically opposed to the Gaelic system, which rested on blood ties: the followers of a Gaelic king were his kindred, whereas the followers of a feudal king were vassals bought with land. The Canmores successfully feudalized much of southern and eastern Scotland by making grants to their Norman, Breton and Flemish followers, but beyond that, traditional clan-based forms of social relations persisted.

The Canmores, independent of the local nobility, who remained a military threat, also began to reform the **Church**. This development started with the efforts of Margaret, Malcolm III's English wife, who brought Scottish religious practices into line with those of the rest of Europe and was eventually canonized. **David I** (1124–53) continued the process by importing monks to found a series of monasteries, principally along the border at Kelso, Melrose, Jedburgh and Dryburgh. By 1200 the entire country was covered by a network of eleven bishoprics, although church organization remained weak within the Highlands. Similarly, the dynasty founded a series of **royal burghs**, towns such as Edinburgh, Stirling and Berwick, and bestowed upon them charters recognizing them as centres of trade. The charters usually granted a measure of self-government, vested in the town corporation or guild, and the monarchy hoped this liberality would both encourage loyalty and increase the prosperity of the kingdom. Scotland's Gaelic-speaking clans had little influence within the burghs, and by 1550 Scots – a northern version of Anglo-Saxon – had become the main language throughout the Lowlands.

The policies of the Canmores laid the basis for a cultural rift in Scotland between the Highland and Lowland communities. Before that became an issue, however, the Scots had to face a major threat from the south. In 1286 **Alexander III** died, and a hotly disputed succession gave Edward I, the king of England, an opportunity to subjugate Scotland. In 1291 Edward presided over a conference where the rival claimants to the Scottish throne presented their cases. Edward chose John Balliol, in preference to **Robert the Bruce**, his main rival, and obliged John to pay him homage, thus turning Scotland into a vassal kingdom. Bruce refused to accept the decision, thereby continuing the conflict, and in 1295 Balliol renounced his allegiance to Edward and formed an alliance with France – the beginning of what is known as the "Auld Alliance". In the conflict that followed, the Bruce family sided with the English, Balliol was defeated and imprisoned, and Edward seized control of almost all of Scotland.

Edward had shown little mercy during his conquest of Scotland – he had, for example, had most of the population of Berwick massacred – and his cruelty seems to have provoked a truly national resistance. This focused on **William Wallace**, a man of relatively lowly origins who forged an army of peasants, lesser knights and townsmen that was fundamentally different from the armies raised by the nobility. Figures like Balliol, holding lands in England, France and Scotland, were part of an international aristocracy for whom warfare was merely the means by which they struggled for power. Wallace, by contrast, led proto-nationalist forces determined to expel the English from their country. Probably for that very reason Wallace never received the support of the nobility, and, after a bitter ten-year campaign, he was betrayed and executed in London in 1305.

With Wallace out of the way, feudal intrigue resumed. In 1306 **Robert the Bruce**, the erstwhile ally of the English, defied Edward and had himself crowned king of Scotland. Edward died the following year, but the unrest dragged on until 1314, when Bruce decisively defeated a huge English army under Edward II at the battle of **Bannockburn**. At last Bruce was firmly in control of his kingdom, and in 1320 the Scots asserted their right to independence in a successful petition to the pope, now known as the **Arbroath Declaration**.

From Bannockburn to Bosworth

The defeat at Bannockburn added to the unpopularity of **Edward II**, and the king was eventually overthrown by his wife Isabella and her lover Roger Mortimer, by whom he was horribly put to death in Berkeley Castle, Gloucestershire. Although **Edward III** was initially preoccupied by Scottish wars, his reign is chiefly remembered for his claim to the French throne, a feeble pretence – he had earlier recognized the king of France and done homage to him – but one that launched the **Hundred Years' War** in 1337. Early English victories such as the Battle of Crécy in 1346, and the capture of Calais the following year, were interrupted by the outbreak of the **Black Death** in 1349, a plague which claimed about a third of the English population. The resulting scarcity of labour produced economic turmoil in the land, and attempts to restrict the rise of wages and to levy a poll tax (a tax on each person irrespective of wealth) provoked widespread riots, which peaked with the **Peasants' Revolt** of 1381. After seizing Rochester Castle and sacking Canterbury, the rebels marched on London, where the boy king **Richard II** met Wat Tyler, the leader of the revolt, at Smithfield. The resulting scuffle led to Tyler's murder and the dispersal of the mob, and soon afterwards the Bishop of Norwich routed the Norfolk rebels, the prelude to a wave of repression and terrible retribution.

Parallel with this social unrest were the clerical reforms demanded by the scholar **John Wycliffe**, whose followers made the first translation of the Bible into English in 1380. Another sign of the elevation of the language was the success enjoyed by **Geoffrey Chaucer** (c.1340–1400), a wine merchant's son, whose *Canterbury Tales* was the first major work written in the vernacular and one of the first English books to be printed.

During the later years of Edward III's reign England had in effect been ruled by his son, **John of Gaunt**, Duke of Lancaster, whose influence remained paramount during the minority of Richard II. In 1399 the vacillating Richard II was overthrown by John of Gaunt's son, who took the title **Henry IV** and founded the **Lancastrian** dynasty. Fourteen years later, he in turn was succeeded by his son, **Henry V**, who promptly renewed the war with France, which had been limping along ingloriously since the victory at Poitiers in 1356. After the much-celebrated triumph at **Agincourt**, Henry forced the French king to sign the Treaty of Troyes in 1420, making the English king the heir to the French throne, but on Henry's death just two years later his son was still an infant, which left regents governing the country on behalf of the monarch. Settling their differences, the French rallied under **Joan of Arc** to beat back the English, and by 1454 only Calais was left in English hands.

Meanwhile **Henry VI**, who was temperamentally more inclined to the creation of such architectural coups as King's College Chapel in Cambridge and Eton College Chapel than to warfare, had suffered lapses into insanity. Strongest of the rival contenders for the throne was Richard, Duke of York, by virtue of his direct descent from Edward III. It was no accident that the **Wars of the Roses** – named from the red rose that symbolized the Lancastrian cause and the white Yorkist rose – broke out just a year after the return of the last English garrisons from France, filling the country with footloose knights and archers accustomed to a life of plunder and war. The instability of the time was signalled by **Jack Cade's Rebellion** of 1450, when a disorganized rabble – though with more participation by dissatisfied gentry than had been the case in the 1381 Peasants' Revolt – challenged the king's authority, winning a battle at Sevenoaks before being scattered. Political disputes within the circle surrounding the mad king were to prove more threatening to the regime. The Duke of York's authority over Henry was challenged by the king's accomplished and ambitious wife, Margaret of Anjou, whose forces defeated and slew Richard at Wakefield in 1460. She and Henry were in turn overwhelmed by Richard's son, who was crowned **Edward IV** in 1461 – the first king of the **Yorkist** line.

The civil strife entered a new stage when Edward attempted to shrug off the overbearing influence of Richard Neville, Earl of Warwick and Salisbury, or "Warwick the Kingmaker", as he became known. Warwick then performed a dramatic volte-face by allying himself with his old enemy Margaret of Anjou, forcing Edward into exile and proclaiming Henry king once more. Henry VI's second term was soon interrupted by Edward's unexpected return in 1471, when Warwick was defeated and killed at the Battle of Barnet and the rest of the Lancastrians were crushed at Tewkesbury three months later. Margaret was captured, Henry's heir was killed and Henry himself was soon afterwards dispatched in the Tower.

Edward IV proved to be a precursor of the great Tudor princes – licentious, cruel and despotic, but also a patron of Renaissance learning. In 1483, his twelve-year-old son succeeded as **Edward V**, but his reign was cut short after only two months, when he and his younger brother were murdered in the Tower of London – probably by their uncle, the Duke of Gloucester, who was crowned **Richard III**. Increasingly unpopular as rumours circulated of his part in the fate of the princes in the Tower, Richard was toppled at Bosworth Field in 1485 by **Henry Tudor**, Earl of Richmond, who took the throne as **Henry VII**.

The Tudors

The opening of the **Tudor period** brought radical transformations. A Lancastrian through his mother's descent from John of Gaunt, Henry VII reconciled the Yorkist faction by marrying Edward IV's daughter Elizabeth, putting an end to the internecine squabbling among the discredited gentry. The growth of the wool and cloth trades and the rise of a powerful merchant class brought a general increase of wealth, while England began to assume the status of a major European power partly as a result of Henry's alliances and political marriages – his daughter to James IV of Scotland and his son to Catherine, daughter of Ferdinand and Isabella of Spain.

The relatively easy suppression of the rebellions of Yorkist pretenders Lambert Simnel and Perkin Warbeck ensured a smooth succession for **Henry VIII** in

1509. Although Henry was himself not a Protestant and even received from the pope the title of "Defender of the Faith" for a book he published criticizing Luther's doctrine, this tumultuous king is chiefly noted for the separation of the English Church from Rome. The schism was triggered not by doctrinal issues but by the failure of his wife Catherine of Aragon – widow of his elder brother – to provide Henry with male offspring. Failing to obtain a decree of nullity from Pope Clement VII, he dismissed his long-time chancellor Thomas Wolsey and followed the advice of Thomas Cromwell, forcing the English Church to recognize him as its head. The most far-reaching consequence of this step was the **Dissolution of the Monasteries**, a decision taken mainly to enjoy the profits of the ensuing land sales. The first phase of the Dissolution in 1536, involving the smaller religious houses, was a factor in the only significant rebellion of the reign, the **Pilgrimage of Grace**, a protest largely in the north of the country, which Henry put down with great cruelty, preparing the ground for the closure of the larger foundations in 1539.

In his later years Henry became a corpulent tyrant, six times married but at last furnished with an heir, **Edward VI**, who was only nine years old when he ascended the throne in 1547. His short reign saw Protestantism established on a firm footing, with churches stripped of their images and Catholic services banned, yet on Edward's death most of the country recognized his half-sister **Mary**, daughter of Catherine of Aragon and a fervent Catholic. She restored England to the papacy and married the future Philip II of Spain, forging an alliance whose immediate consequence was war with France and the loss of Calais, last of England's French possessions. Mary's unpopularity increased when she began a savage persecution of Protestants, executing the leading lights of the English Reformation, Hugh Latimer, Nicholas Ridley and Thomas Cranmer, the Archbishop of Canterbury who was largely responsible for the first English Prayer Book, published in 1549.

The accession of the Protestant **Elizabeth I** in 1558 took place in a highly volatile atmosphere, with the country riven between opposing religious loyalties and threatened abroad by Philip II. Heresy and treason were the twin preoccupations of the Elizabethan state, a society in which a sense of English nationhood was evolving on an almost mystical level in the vacuum created by the break with Rome. Aided by a team of exceptionally able ministers, the Virgin Queen provided a focal point for national feeling, enthusiastically supported by a mercantile class which was opposed to foreign entanglements or clerical restrictions, and was represented in a parliament made stronger by the constitutional decisions of the preceding fifty years.

The 45 years of Elizabeth's reign saw the efflorescence of a specifically English Renaissance, especially in the field of literature, which reached its pinnacle in the brilliant career of **William Shakespeare** (1564–1616). It was also the age of the **seafarers** Walter Raleigh, Francis Drake, Martin Frobisher and John Hawkins, whose piratical exploits helped to map out the world for English commerce. English navigational skills – as demonstrated by Drake's voyage round the world (1577–80) – and the country's growing naval strength triumphed with the defeat of the **Spanish Armada** in 1588. The commander of the English fleet, Lord Howard of Effingham, was a practising Catholic, a fact that dashed Philip's hope of a Catholic insurrection in England – a hope in part founded on the widespread sympathy for Elizabeth's cousin Mary Queen of Scots, whose twenty-year imprisonment in England had ended with her beheading in 1587.

Wales under the Tudors

Welsh allegiance during the Wars of the Roses lay broadly with the Lancastrians, who had the support of the ascendant north Welsh Tewdwr (or Tudor) family. Welsh expectations of the first Tudor monarch, Henry VII, were high. Henry lived up to some of them, removing many of the restrictions on land ownership imposed at the start of Glyndŵr's uprising, and promoting many Welshmen to high office, but administration remained piecemeal. Control was still shared between the Crown and largely independent Marcher lords until a uniform administrative structure was achieved under Henry VIII.

Wales had been largely controlled by the English monarch since the Treaty of Rhuddlan in 1284, but the **Acts of Union** in 1536 and 1543 fixed English sovereignty over the country. At the same time the Marches were replaced by shires (the equivalent of modern counties), the Welsh laws codified by Hywel Dda were made void and partible inheritance gave way to primogeniture, the eldest son becoming the sole heir. For the first time the Welsh and English enjoyed legal equality, but the break with native traditions wasn't well received. Most of the people remained poor, the gentry became increasingly anglicized, the use of Welsh was proscribed, and legal proceedings were held in English (a language few peasants understood).

Since Christianity had always been a ritual way of life rather than a philosophical code in Wales, Catholicism was easily replaced by Protestantism during the religious upheavals of Henry VIII's reign. What the Reformation did promote was a more studied approach to religion and learning in general. Under the reign of Elizabeth I, Jesus College was founded in Oxford for Welsh scholars, and the Bible was translated into Welsh for the first time by a team led by Bishop **William Morgan**.

With new land ownership laws enshrined in the Acts of Union, the stimulus provided by the Dissolution hastened the emergence of the Anglo-Welsh gentry, a group eager to claim a Welsh pedigree while promoting the English language and the legal system, helping to perpetuate their grasp. Meanwhile, landless peasants continued in poverty, only gaining slightly from the increase in cattle trade with England and the slow development of mining and ore smelting.

The Stewarts in Scotland

In the years following Bruce's death in 1329, the Scottish monarchy gradually declined in influence. The last of the Bruce dynasty died in 1371, to be succeeded by the "Stewards", hence **Stewarts** (known as Stuarts in England), but thereafter a succession of Scottish rulers, culminating with James VI in 1567, came to the throne when still children. The power vacuum was filled by the nobility, whose key members exercised control as Scotland's regents while carving out territories where they ruled with the power, if not the title, of kings. **James IV** (1488–1513), the most talented of the early Stewarts, might have restored the authority of the Crown, but his invasion of England ended in a terrible defeat for the Scots – and his own death – at the Battle of Flodden Field.

The reign of **Mary Queen of Scots** (1542–87) typified the problems of the Scottish monarchy. Mary came to the throne when just one week old, and immediately caught the attention of the English king, Henry VIII, who sought, first by persuasion and then by military might, to secure her hand in marriage for his five-year-old son, Edward. Beginning in 1544, the English launched a series of devastating attacks on Scotland, an episode Sir Walter Scott later called the "Rough Wooing", until, in the face of another English invasion in 1548, the Scots – or at least those not supporting Henry – turned to the "Auld Alliance". The French king proposed marriage between Mary and the Dauphin Francis, promising in return military assistance against the English. The six-year-old queen sailed for France in 1548, leaving her loyal nobles and their French allies in control, and her husband succeeded to the French throne in 1559. When she returned thirteen years later, following the death of Francis, she had to pick her way through the rival ambitions of her nobility and deal with something entirely new – the religious Reformation.

The **Reformation** in Scotland was a complex social process, whose threads are often hard to unravel. Nevertheless, it is quite clear that, by the end of the sixteenth century, the established Church was held in general contempt. Another spur to the Scottish Reformation was the identification of Protestantism with anti-French feeling. In 1554 Mary of Guise, the French mother of the absent Queen Mary, had become regent, and her habit of appointing Frenchmen to high office caused considerable resentment. In 1557, a group of nobles banded together to form the **Lords of the Congregation**, whose dual purpose was to oppose French influence and promote the reformed religion. With English military backing, the Protestant lords succeeded in deposing the French regent in 1560, and, when the Scottish Parliament assembled shortly afterwards, it asserted the primacy of Protestantism by forbidding Mass and abolishing the authority of the pope. The nobility proceeded to confiscate two thirds of Church lands, a huge prize that did much to bolster their new beliefs.

Even without the economic incentives, Protestantism was a highly charged political doctrine. As the Protestant reformer **John Knox** told Queen Mary at their first meeting in 1561, subjects are not bound to obey an ungodly monarch. Mary ducked and wove, trying to avoid an open breach with her Protestant subjects. Her difficulties were exacerbated by her disastrous second marriage to **Lord Darnley**, a cruel and politically inept character, whose jealousy led to his involvement in the murder of Mary's favourite, David Rizzio, who was dragged from the queen's supper room at Holyrood and stabbed 56 times. The incident caused the Scottish Protestants more than a little unease, but they were entirely scandalized in 1567, when Darnley himself was murdered and Mary promptly married the **Earl of Bothwell**, widely believed to be the murderer. This was too much to bear, and the Scots rose in rebellion, driving Mary into exile in England at the age of just 25. The queen's illegitimate half-brother, the Earl of Moray, became regent and her son, the infant James, was left behind to be raised a Protestant prince. Mary, meanwhile, became perceived as such a threat to the English throne that, after twenty years' imprisonment in England, Queen Elizabeth I had her executed in 1587.

Knox could now concentrate on the organization of the reformed Church, or **Kirk**, which he envisaged as a body empowered to intervene in the daily lives of the people. **Andrew Melville**, another leading reformer, proposed the abolition of all traces of episcopacy – the rule of the bishops in the Church – and that the Kirk should adopt a **presbyterian** structure, administered by a hierarchy of assemblies, part elected and part appointed. At the bottom of the chain, beneath the General Assembly, Synod and Presbytery, would be the Kirk session, responsible for church affairs, the performance of the minister and the morals of the parish. In 1592, the Melvillian party achieved a measure of success when presbyteries and synods were accepted as legal church courts and the office of bishop was suspended.

James VI (1567–1625) disliked Presbyterianism because its quasi-democratic structure – particularly the lack of royally appointed bishops – appeared to threaten his authority. He was, however, unable to resist the reformers until 1610, when, strengthened by his installation as king of England, he restored the Scottish bishops. The argument about the nature of Kirk organization would lead to bloody conflict in the years after James' death.

The Stuarts

On Elizabeth's death in 1603, James VI became **James I** of England, thereby uniting the English and Scottish crowns. James quickly moved to end hostilities with Spain – a move resented by the increasingly powerful English Puritans, an extreme Protestant group – but his intention to exercise tolerance towards the country's Catholics was thwarted by the outcry in the wake of the **Gunpowder Plot** of 1605, when Guy Fawkes and a group of Catholic conspirators were discovered preparing to blow up king and Parliament. Puritan fundamentalism and commercial interests converged in the foundation of Virginia in 1608, the first permanent **colony in North America**, followed in 1620 by the landing in New England of the Pilgrim Fathers, the nucleus of a colony that would absorb about 100,000 mainly Puritan immigrants by the middle of the century.

A split was inevitable between James, who clung to the medieval notion of the divine right of kings, and the landed gentry who dominated the increasingly powerful Parliament, a situation exacerbated by the persecution of the Puritans. Recoiling from the demands of the Parliamentarians, the king relied heavily on court favourites, progressing from the skilful Robert Cecil, Earl of Salisbury, and the philosopher Francis Bacon, to the rash and unpopular George Villiers, Duke of Buckingham, who also had a close influence on the second Stuart king, **Charles I** (1625–49).

Raised in Episcopalian England, Charles had little understanding of Scottish reformism, and like his father, he believed in the divine right of kings. In 1637, Charles attempted to impose a new prayer book on the Scottish Kirk, laying down forms of worship in line with those favoured by the High Anglican Church. The reformers denounced these changes as "popery" and organized the **National Covenant**, a religious pledge that committed the signatories to "Labour by all means lawful to recover the purity and liberty of the Gospel as it was established and professed". Charles declared all the "Covenanters" to be rebels, a proclamation endorsed by his Scottish bishops. Consequently, when the king backed down from military action and called a General Assembly of the Kirk, the assembly promptly abolished the episcopacy. Charles pronounced the proceedings illegal, but lack of finance stopped him from mounting an effective military campaign – whereas the Covenanters, well financed by the Kirk, assembled a proficient army under Alexander Leslie.

In desperation, Charles summoned the English Parliament, the first for eleven years, hoping it would pay for an army. But, like the calling of the General Assembly, the decision was a disaster and Parliament was much keener to criticize his policies than to raise taxes. In 1642, facing the concerted hostility of Parliament, the king withdrew to Nottingham where he raised his standard, the opening military act of the **Civil War**. The Royalist forces were initially successful against the Parliamentarian army, gaining an advantage after the first battle of the war, Edgehill, at which Charles' nephew, the dashing cavalry officer Prince Rupert, displayed the reckless valour which was to distinguish his participation in subsequent engagements. After Edgehill, the Parliamentarian army was completely overhauled by **Oliver Cromwell** as the New Model Army, and won victories at Marston Moor and Naseby. Charles was captured by the Scots at Newark in Nottinghamshire, in 1646 and was finally handed over to the English, by whom, after prolonged negotiations and more fighting, he was executed in January 1649.

The following year, at the invitation of the Earl of Argyll, Charles' son, the future Charles II, came to Scotland. To regain his Scottish kingdom, Charles was obliged to renounce his father and sign the Covenant, two bitter pills taken to impress the population. In the event, the "presbyterian restoration" was short-lived. Cromwell invaded, defeated the Scots at Dunbar and forced Charles into exile. For the next eleven years the whole country was a **Commonwealth** – at first a true republic, then, after 1653, a Protectorate under Cromwell, who was ultimately as impatient of Parliament and as arbitrary as Charles had been. Cromwell's policies were especially savage in Ireland, where his depredations are remembered to this day. At his death in 1658 his son Richard ruled briefly and ineffectually, and in 1660 Parliament voted to restore the monarchy in the person of **Charles II** (1660–85), the exiled son of the previous king.

The Restoration and the Glorious Revolution

The turmoil of the previous twenty years had unleashed a furious debate on every strand of legalistic, theological and political thought, an environment that spawned a host of fringe sects – such as the Levellers, who demanded constitutional reform, and the more radical Ranters, who proposed common ownership of all land. Nonconformist religious groups flourished, prominent among them the pacifist **Quakers**, led by the much-persecuted George Fox (1624–91), and the Dissenters, to whom the most famous writers of the day, John Milton (1608–74) and John Bunyan (1628–88), both belonged. With the **Restoration**, however, these philosophical eddies gave way to a new exuberance in the fields of art, literature and the theatre, a remarkable transition from the sombreness of the Puritan era, when secular drama and other such fripperies were banned outright. In the scientific arena, just six months after his accession Charles founded the **Royal Society**, which numbered Isaac Newton (1642–1727) among its first fellows.

The low points of Charles II's reign came with the **Great Plague** of 1665 and the **Great Fire of London** the following year, though the latter had the positive consequence of allowing Christopher Wren (1632–1723) and other great architects to redesign the capital along more contemporary classical lines. Moreover, the political scene was not entirely tranquil: tensions still existed between king and Parliament, where the traditional divisions of court and country began to coalesce into **Whig** and **Tory** parties, respectively representing the Low-Church gentry and the High-Church aristocracy. A measure of vengeance was also wreaked on the regicides and other leading

Parliamentarians, though its intensity was nothing like that of the anti-Catholic hysteria sparked off by the Popish Plot of 1678, the fabrication of the trickster Titus Oates.

The succession in 1685 of the Catholic **James II** (James VII of Scotland), brother of Charles II, provoked much opposition, though – as one might expect from a country recently racked by civil war – there was an indifferent response when the **Duke of Monmouth**, favourite of Charles II's illegitimate sons, landed at Lyme Regis to mount a challenge to the new king. His undisciplined forces were routed at Sedgemoor, Somerset, in July 1685; nine days later Monmouth was beheaded at Tower Hill, and in the subsequent **Bloody Assizes** of Judge Jeffreys, hundreds of rebels and suspected sympathizers – mainly in Somerset and Devon – were executed or deported.

When seven bishops protested against James' **Declaration of Indulgence** of 1687, removing anti-Catholic restrictions, the king showed something of his father's obstinacy by having them tried for seditious libel, though he was quickly forced to acquit them. When James' son was born, a child destined to be brought up in the Catholic faith, messengers were dispatched to **William of Orange**, the Dutch husband of Mary, the Protestant daughter of James II. William landed in Brixham in Devon, proceeding to London where he was acclaimed king in the so-called **Glorious Revolution** of 1688, the final postscript to the Civil War.

William and Mary were made joint sovereigns, having agreed to a **Bill of Rights** defining the limitations of the monarch's power and the rights of his or her subjects. This, together with the **Act of Settlement of 1701** – among other things, barring Catholics or anyone married to one from succession to the English throne – made Britain the first country to be governed by a **constitutional monarchy**, in which the roles of legislature and executive were separate and interdependent, a model broadly consistent with that outlined by the philosopher and political thinker John Locke (1632–1704), whose essentially Whig doctrines of toleration and social contract were gradually embraced as the new orthodoxy.

Ruling alone after Mary's death in 1694, William regarded England as a prop in his defence of Holland against France, a stance that defined England's political alignment in Europe for the next sixty years. Mary died without leaving an heir and, on William's death in 1702, the Crown passed to her sister **Anne**, who was also childless. In response, the English Parliament secured the Protestant succession through the Act of Settlement, naming the Electress Sophia of Hanover as the next in line to the throne. The Act did not, however, apply in Scotland, and the English feared that the Scots would invite James II's son, James Edward Stuart, back from France to be their king.

Nevertheless, despite the strength of anti-English feeling, the Scottish Parliament passed the **Act of Union** by 110 votes to 69 in 1707. Some historians have explained the vote purely in terms of bribery and corruption, but there were other factors. Scottish politicians were divided between the Cavaliers – Jacobites (supporters of the Stuarts) and Episcopalians – and the Country party, whose presbyterian members dreaded the return of the Stuarts more than they disliked the Hanoverians. There were commercial considerations too. In 1705, the English Parliament had passed the Alien Act, which threatened to impose severe penalties on cross-border trade, whereas the Union gave merchants of both countries free access to each other's markets. The Act of Union also guaranteed the Scottish legal system and the Presbyterian Kirk, though it replaced the two separate parliaments with a new British Parliament based in London.

The Hanoverians

When Anne died in 1714, the succession passed – in accordance with the terms of the Act of Settlement – to a non-English-speaking German, the Elector of Hanover, who became **George I** of England. This prompted the first major **Jacobite uprising** in support of James Edward Stuart, the "Old Pretender" (Pretender in the sense of having pretensions to the throne, Old to distinguish him from his son Charles, the "Young Pretender"). Its timing appeared perfect. Scottish opinion was moving against the Union, which had failed to bring Scotland any tangible economic benefits. Neither were Jacobite sentiments confined to Scotland. There were many in England who toasted the "King across the water" and showed no enthusiasm for the new German ruler. In September 1715, the fiercely Jacobite John Erskine, Earl of Mar, raised the Stuart standard at Braemar Castle. Just eight days later, he captured Perth, where he gathered an army of over 10,000 men, drawn mostly from the Episcopalians of northeast Scotland and from the Highlands. Mar's rebellion took the government by surprise. They had only 4000 soldiers in Scotland, under the command of the Duke of Argyll, but Mar dithered until he lost the military advantage. There was an indecisive battle at Sheriffmuir in November, but by the time the Old Pretender arrived the following month, 6000 veteran Dutch troops had reinforced Argyll. The rebellion disintegrated rapidly and James slunk back to exile in France in February 1716.

As power leaked away from the monarchy into the hands of the Whig oligarchy – many Tories having been discredited for suspected Jacobite sympathies – the king ceased to attend cabinet meetings, his place being taken by his chief minister. Most prominent of these ministers was **Robert Walpole**, regarded as Britain's **first prime minister**, who effectively ruled the country in the period 1721–42. This was a tranquil period politically, with the country standing aloof from foreign affrays, but the financial world was prey to a mania for speculation. Of the numerous fraudulent or ill-conceived financial ventures of this time, the greatest was the fiasco of the **South Sea Company**, which in 1720 sold shares in its monopoly of trade in the Pacific and along the east coast of South America. The "bubble" burst when the shareholders took fright at the extent of their own investments and the value of the shares dropped to nothing, reducing many to penury, and almost wrecking the government, which was saved only by the astute intervention of Walpole.

Peace ended in the reign of **George II**, when in 1739 England declared war on Spain, the prelude to the eight-year War of the Austrian Succession. Then in 1745 the country was invaded by the **Young Pretender**, Charles Edward Stuart (Bonnie Prince Charlie), the Old Pretender's dashing son, in the **Jacobite uprising of 1745**. This second rebellion had little chance of success: the Hanoverians had consolidated their hold on the English throne, Lowland society was uniformly loyalist, and even among the Highlanders Charles only attracted just over half of the 20,000 clansmen who could have marched with him. Nevertheless, after a decisive victory over government forces at Prestonpans, Charles made a spectacular advance into England, getting as far as Derby. London was in a state of panic: its shops were closed and the Bank of England, fearing a run on sterling, slowed withdrawals by paying out in sixpences. But Derby was as far south as Charles got. On December 6, threatened by superior forces, the Jacobites decided to retreat to Scotland.

The Duke of Cumberland was sent in pursuit and the two armies met on

Culloden Moor, near Inverness, in April 1746. Outnumbered and out-gunned, the Jacobites were swept from the field, losing over 1200 men compared to Cumberland's 300 plus. After the battle, many of the wounded Jacobites were slaughtered, an atrocity that earned Cumberland the nickname "Butcher". Jacobite hopes died at Culloden and the prince lived out the rest of his life in drunken exile. In the aftermath of the uprising, the wearing of tartan, the bearing of arms and the playing of bagpipes were all banned. Rebel chiefs lost their land and the Highlands were placed under military occupation. Most significantly, the government prohibited the private armies of the chiefs, thereby effectively destroying the clan system.

Meanwhile, the **Seven Years' War** brought yet more overseas territory, as English armies wrested control of India and Canada from France, then in 1768 **Captain James Cook** departed from Plymouth on his voyage to New Zealand and Australia, further widening the scope of the colonial empire.

In 1760, George II had been succeeded by **George III**, the first native English Hanoverian. The early years of his sixty-year reign saw a revived struggle between king and Parliament, enlivened by the intervention of John Wilkes, first of a long and increasingly vociferous line of parliamentary radicals. The contest was exacerbated by the deteriorating relationship with the thirteen colonies of North America, a situation brought to a head by the American **Declaration of Independence** and Britain's defeat in the Revolutionary War. Chastened by this disaster, Britain chose not to interfere in the momentous events taking place across the Channel, where France, its most consistent foe in the eighteenth century, was convulsed by revolution. Out of the turmoil emerged the country's most daunting enemy yet, Napoleon, whose progress was interrupted by Nelson at Trafalgar in 1805, and finally stopped ten years later by the Duke of Wellington at Waterloo.

The Industrial Revolution

Britain's triumph was largely due to its financial strength, itself largely due to the gradual switch from an agricultural to a manufacturing economy, a process generally referred to as the **Industrial Revolution**. The earliest mechanized production lines were constructed in the Lancashire cotton mills, where cotton-spinning was transformed from a cottage industry into a highly productive factory-based system. Water power became a thing of the past after James Watt patented his **steam engine** in 1781, and the utilization of coal as an engine fuel made it convenient to locate mills and factories near coal mines, a tendency that was accelerated as **ironworkers** took up coal as a smelting fuel, vastly increasing the output from their furnaces. Accordingly there was a shift of population towards the Midlands and north of England, where the great coal reserves were located, resulting in the rapid growth of the industrial towns and the expansion of Liverpool as a commercial port, importing raw materials from India and the Americas and exporting manufactured goods. Commerce and industry were served by steadily improving transport facilities, such as the building of a network of **canals** in the wake of the success of the Bridgewater Canal in 1765, which linked coal mines at Worsley with Manchester and the River Mersey. But the great leap forward occurred with the arrival of the **railway** age, heralded by the opening of the Liverpool–Manchester line in 1830, with power provided by George Stephenson's steam-driven Rocket.

The Highland Clearances

Once the clan chief was forbidden his own army, he had no need of the large tenantry that had previously been a vital military asset. Conversely, the second half of the eighteenth century saw the Highland population double after the introduction of the easy-to-grow and nutritious potato. The clan chiefs adopted different policies to deal with the new situation. Some encouraged emigration, and as many as six thousand Highlanders left for the Americas between 1800 and 1803 alone. Other landowners developed alternative forms of employment for their tenantry, mainly fishing and the gathering of kelp. This brown seaweed was burnt to produce soda ash, which was used in the manufacture of soap, glass and explosives. Other landowners developed sheep runs on the Highland pastures, introducing hardy breeds like the black-faced Linton and the Cheviot. But extensive sheep farming proved incompatible with a high peasant population, and many landowners decided to clear their estates of tenants, some of whom were forcibly moved to tiny plots of marginal land, where they were to farm as crofters.

The pace of the **Highland Clearances** accelerated after the end of the Napoleonic Wars in 1815, when the market price for kelp, fish and cattle declined, leaving sheep as the only profitable Highland product. As the dispossessed Highlanders scratched a living from the acid soils of some tiny croft, they learnt through bitter experience the limitations of the clan. Famine followed, forcing large-scale emigration to America and Canada and leaving the huge uninhabited areas found in the region today. The crofters eked out a precarious existence, but they hung on throughout the nineteenth century, often by taking seasonal employment away from home.

In the 1880s, however, a sharp downturn in agricultural prices made it difficult for many crofters to pay their rent. This time, inspired by the example of the Irish Land League, they resisted eviction, forming the **Highland Land Reform Association** and the **Crofters' Party**. In 1886, in response to the social unrest, Gladstone's Liberal government passed the **Crofters' Holdings Act**, which conceded three of the crofters' demands: security of tenure, fair rents to be decided independently, and the right to pass on crofts by inheritance. But Gladstone did not attempt to increase the amount of land available for crofting and shortage of land remained a major problem until the **Land Settlement Act** of 1919 made provision for the creation of new crofts. Nevertheless, the population of the Highlands continued to decline during the twentieth century, with many of the region's young people finding city life more appealing.

Boosted by influxes of Jewish, Irish, French and Dutch immigrants, many of whom introduced new manufacturing techniques, the country's population rose from about seven and a half million at the beginning of George III's reign to more than fourteen million at its end, an increase whose major cause was a rise in the birthrate as a response to the demand for child labour and the extra income that it would provide for families. But while factories and their attendant towns expanded, the rural settlements of England suffered, inspiring the elegiac pastoral yearnings of Samuel Taylor Coleridge and William Wordsworth, the first great names of the **Romantic** movement in English literature. Later Romantic poets such as Percy Bysshe Shelley and Lord Byron took a more socially engaged stance, inveighing against social injustices that were aggravated by the expenses of the Napoleonic Wars and by its aftermath, when many returning soldiers found their jobs had been taken by machines. Discontent emerged in demands for parliamentary reform, and in 1819 demonstrators in Manchester – centre of the cotton industry and most important of the industrial boom towns still unrepresented in Parliament – were mown down by troops in what became known as the **Peterloo Massacre**.

The following year George III, by now weak, old, blind and insane, died and was succeeded by his son **George IV**. During his reign religious toleration became a reality, as Catholics and Nonconformists were permitted to enter parliament, workers' associations were legalized, and a civilian police force was created, largely the work of **Robert Peel**, a reforming Tory who outlined the basic ideology of modern Conservatism. More far-reaching changes came under **William IV**, with the passing of the **Reform Act** of 1832, whereby the principle of popular representation was acknowledged (though most adult males still had no vote); two years later, the revised **Poor Law** alleviated the condition of the destitute. Significant sections of the middle classes wanted far swifter democratic reform, as was expressed in public indignation over the **Tolpuddle Martyrs** – the Dorset labourers transported to Australia in 1834 for joining an agricultural trade union – and support for **Chartism**, a working-class movement demanding universal male suffrage. Poverty and injustice were the dominant theme of the novels of **Charles Dickens** (1812–70) and the preoccupation of the paternalistic reform movements that were a feature of the nineteenth century. This social concern had been anticipated in the previous century by the Methodism of John Wesley (1703–91) and the anti-slavery campaign promoted by evangelical Christians such as the Quakers and William Wilberforce. As a result of their efforts, slavery was banned in Britain in 1772 and throughout the colonies in 1833 – putting an end to what had been a major factor in the prosperity of ports such as Bristol and Liverpool.

The Victorian Age

In 1837 William IV was succeeded by his niece **Victoria**, who, living through a period in which Britain's international standing reached unprecedented heights, came to be as much a national icon as Elizabeth I had been. Though the intellectual achievements of the Victorian age were immense – as typified by the publication of Charles Darwin's *The Origin of Species* in 1859 – the country saw itself primarily as an imperial power founded on industrial and commercial prowess, its spirit perhaps best embodied by the great engineering feats of Isambard Kingdom Brunel and by the **Great Exhibition** of 1851, a display of manufacturing achievements from all over the world. With trade at the forefront of the agenda, much of the political debate during this period crystallized into a conflict between the **Free Traders** – represented by an alliance of the Peelites and the Whigs, forming the Liberal Party – and the **Protectionists** under Bentinck and **Disraeli**, guiding light of the Tories. During the last third of the century, Parliament was dominated by the duel between Disraeli and the Liberal leader **Gladstone**. Although it was Disraeli who eventually passed the Second Reform Bill in 1867, further extending the electoral franchise, it was Gladstone who had first proposed it, and it was Gladstone's first ministry of 1868–74 that passed some of the century's most far-reaching legislation, including compulsory education, the full legalization of trade unions and an Irish Land Act.

In 1854 troops were sent to protect the Turkish empire against the Russians in the **Crimea**, an inglorious debacle whose horrors were relayed to the public by the first ever press coverage of a military campaign and by the shocking revelations of Florence Nightingale. The fragility of Britain's empire was further exposed by the Indian Mutiny of 1857, though the country's prestige was not sufficiently dented to prevent Victoria from taking the title Empress of

India after 1876. Apart from the Chinese Opium War of 1839–42 and some colonial skirmishes in Asia and Africa, the only other serious conflict to occur in Victoria's reign was the **Boer War** against the Dutch settlers in South Africa (1899–1902), another mishandled affair leading to the establishment of self-government there in 1906 and a military shake-up at home that was to be of significance in the coming European war.

From World War I

Victoria died in the first month of 1901, to be succeeded by her son, **Edward VII**, whose leisurely and dissolute life could be seen as the epitome of the complacent era to which he gave his name. The Edwardian era came to an end on August 4, 1914, when the Liberal government, honouring the Entente Cordiale signed with France in 1904, declared war on Germany. **World War I** was a futile massacre which destroyed millions of lives and eradicated whatever remained of the majority's respect for the ruling classes, whose officers had treated their conscripts as mere cannon fodder.

At the war's end in 1918 the social fabric of the country was changed drastically as the **voting** franchise was extended to all men aged 21 or over and to women of thirty or over, subject to certain residential or business qualifications. This tardy liberalization of women's rights – largely due to the radical **Suffragettes** led by Emmeline Pankhurst and her daughters Sylvia and Christabel – was not completed until 1929, a year after Emmeline's death, when women were at last granted the vote at 21, on equal terms with men.

At around this time the progressive wing of British politics, formerly occupied by the Liberal Party, was taken over by the **Labour Party**, the fruit of an alliance between trade-union interests and middle-class radicals. Labour formed its first government in 1923 under Ramsay MacDonald, but following the publication of the **Zinoviev Letter**, a forged document that seemed to prove Soviet encouragement of British socialist subversion, the Conservatives were returned with a large majority. In 1926, the tensions which had been building up since the end of the war, produced by severe decline in manufacturing and attendant escalating unemployment, erupted with the **General Strike**. Spreading instantly from the coal mines to the railways, the newspapers and the iron and steel industries, the strike lasted nine days and involved half a million workers, provoking the government into draconian action – the army was called in, and the strikers were forced to surrender. The economic situation deteriorated even further after the crash of the New York Stock Exchange in 1929, with unemployment reaching over 2.8 million in 1931, generating a series of mass demonstrations that reached a peak with the **Jarrow March** of 1936. The same year, economist John Maynard Keynes argued in his General Theory of Employment, Interest and Money for a greater degree of state intervention in the management of the economy, though the whole question was soon overshadowed by international events.

Abroad, the structure of the British Empire had undergone profound changes since World War I. The status of Ireland had been partly resolved after the electoral gains of the nationalist Sinn Fein in 1918 led to the establishment of the Irish Free State in 1922, from which the six counties of the mainly Protestant North "contracted out". Four years later, the **Imperial Conference** recognized the autonomy of the British dominions, an agreement formalized in the

1931 Statute of Westminster, whereby each dominion was given an equal footing in a Commonwealth of Nations, though each still recognized the British monarch. The royal family itself was shaken in 1936 by the **abdication of Edward VIII**, following his decision to marry a twice-divorced American, Wallis Simpson. Although the succession passed smoothly to his brother **George VI**, the scandal further reduced the standing of the royals, a process which has gathered pace in recent years.

Non-intervention in the Spanish Civil War and the Sino-Japanese War was paralleled by a policy of appeasement towards **Adolf Hitler**, who had massively rearmed Germany in pursuit of his territorial ambitions. In 1938 Prime Minister Neville Chamberlain returned from meeting Hitler and Mussolini at Munich with an assurance of good intentions from the two fascist leaders, and when **World War II** broke out in September 1939, Britain was still seriously unprepared. In May 1940 the discredited Chamberlain stepped down in favour of a national coalition government headed by the charismatic **Winston Churchill**, whose bulldog persistence and heroic speeches provided the inspiration needed in the backs-against-the-wall mood of the time. Partly through Churchill's manoeuvres, the United States became a supplier of food stuffs and munitions to Britain. Given that the US had broken trade links with Japan in June (in protest at their attacks on China), this factor may have precipitated the Japanese bombing of Pearl Harbor on December 7, 1941 and thus the US's entry into the war as a combatant. This, combined with the heroic resistance of the Russian Red Army, swung the balance.

In terms of the number of casualties it caused, World War II was not as calamitous as the Great War (as World War I is often known), but its impact upon the civilian population was even more terrible. In its first wave of bombing, the Luftwaffe caused massive damage to industrial and supply centres such as London, Coventry, Manchester, Liverpool, Southampton and Plymouth; in later raids, intended to shatter morale rather than factories and docks, the cathedral cities of Canterbury, Exeter, Bath, Norwich and York were targeted. At the end of the fighting, nearly one in three of all the houses in the nation had been destroyed or damaged, nearly a quarter of a million members of the British armed forces had lost their lives and over 58,000 civilians were dead.

Postwar Britain

The end of the war in 1945 was quickly followed by a general election. Hungry for change, the electorate displaced Churchill in favour of the Labour Party under **Clement Attlee**, who, with a large parliamentary majority, set about a radical programme to **nationalize** the coal, gas, electricity, iron and steel industries, as well as the inland transport services. Building on the plans for a social security system presented in Sir William Beveridge's report of 1943, the **National Insurance Act** and the **National Health Service Act** were both passed early in the Labour administration, giving birth to what became known as the **welfare state**. But despite substantial American aid, the huge problems of rebuilding the economy made austerity the keynote, with the rationing of food and fuel remaining in force long after they had ended in most other European countries.

In April 1949 Britain, the United States, Canada, France and the Benelux countries signed the **North Atlantic Treaty** as a counterbalance to Soviet power in eastern Europe, defining the country's postwar international commitments. Yet confusion regarding Britain's post-imperial role was shown up by the Suez Crisis of 1956, when Anglo-French forces invaded Egypt, only to be hastily recalled following international condemnation. Revealing severe limitations on the country's capacity for independent action, the Suez incident resulted in the resignation of Conservative prime minister Anthony Eden and his replacement by the more pragmatic **Harold Macmillan**. Nonetheless, Macmillan maintained a nuclear policy that suggested a continued desire for an international role, and nuclear testing went on against a background of widespread marches under the auspices of the pacifist Campaign for Nuclear Disarmament.

The 1960s, dominated by the Labour premiership of **Harold Wilson**, saw a revival of consumer spending and a corresponding cultural upswing, with London becoming the hippest city on the planet. The good times lasted barely a decade. Though Tory prime minister Edward Heath led Britain into the brave new world of the European Economic Community, the 1970s was a decade of recession and industrial strife. A succession of public-sector strikes and mistimed decisions by James Callaghan's Labour government handed the 1979 general election to **Margaret Thatcher**, who four years earlier had ousted Heath to become the first woman to lead a major political party in Britain.

Thatcher went on to win three general elections, steering the country into a period of ever-greater social polarization. While taxation policies and easy credit fuelled a consumer boom for the professional classes, the erosion of manufacturing industry and the weakening of the welfare state created a calamitous number of people trapped in long-term impoverished unemployment. Social tensions surfaced in sporadic urban rioting and the year-long miners' strike against pit closures (1984–85), while violence in Northern Ireland also intensified and the IRA came close to killing the entire Cabinet when it blew up the Brighton hotel in which the Conservatives were staying for their 1984 annual conference.

The 1990s to the present

The divisive politics of Thatcherism reached their apogee with the introduction of the Poll Tax, a lunatic scheme that led ultimately to Thatcher's overthrow by colleagues who feared annihilation should she lead them into another general election. The uninspiring new Tory leader, **John Major**, won the Conservatives a fourth term of office in 1992, albeit with a much-reduced majority in Parliament. While his government presided over a steady economic growth rate, this was overshadowed by mismanagement, feckless leadership and various "sleaze" scandals involving Conservative MPs. Furthermore, the party was in increasing disarray over Europe with vocal right-wing **Euro-sceptics** calling for Britain to disassociate itself from the planned integration of the economies of the European Union and the introduction of a single European currency, the euro.

Relations with Britain's European partners plummeted further when it was revealed that a brain-wasting disease in cattle (bovine spongiform encephalopathy – **BSE** – or "mad cow disease") was widespread in British beef resulting in an EU ban on its export. The embargo was only lifted after the slaughter of millions of livestock, though concerns still remain regarding the links between BSE and the human degenerative condition, Creutzfeldt-Jacob disease (**CJD**).

Meanwhile, the early 1990s saw the credibility of the **Royal Family** cracked with the break-up of the marriages of Charles and Diana and Andrew and Fergie, along with a growing sense that the monarchy had become an anachronistic institution incapable of relating effectively with its subjects. **Diana**, who formally divorced from Charles in 1996, was championed, in some quarters, as an example of the humanity and glamour lacking in the other royals, and her death in a car accident in Paris in the summer of 1997 had a profound impact on the British population, many of whom joined in spontaneous mourning unprecedented in recent British history. The reaction to her death, as much as her death itself, marked a watershed in the royal family's relationship with both the public and the media.

The Labour Party, itself in disarray through the 1980s, began to regroup under a dynamic young leader, **Tony Blair**, who persuaded the party to distance itself from traditional left-wing socialism and take on a mantle of idealistic, media-friendly populism. The transformation worked to devastating effect, sweeping Blair to power in the general election of May 1997 on a surge of optimism which was immediately reflected in enhanced relations with Europe and progress in the Irish peace talks. Blair's electoral touch was repeated in Labour-sponsored votes in both Scotland and Wales in favour of a devolved regional government, leading to the establishment of a Scottish Parliament and a Welsh Assembly (the difference in title indicating that Scotland's government has stronger powers). While the Parliament has already made an impact through proposals for free nursing care for the elderly and the abolition of the student loan scheme, both it and the Assembly have been bedevilled by leadership issues. The initial Scots First Minister, Donald Dewar, died suddenly and his successor was forced to resign following allegations of financial irregularities. Similarly, the first leader of the Welsh Assembly resigned as a result of losing the confidence of his own Welsh Labour Party.

These changes, along with significant democratizing reform of the **House of Lords**, an institution much derided for its entrenched conservatism and fustiness, undoubtedly set the tone for a period of re-evaluation and modernism in British affairs. However, Blair's popularity was challenged by vociferous complaint from certain countryside factions, who formed the amorphous "**Countryside Alliance**" and in 1998 donned their Wellington boots to march through central London to express dissent about country issues being dictated from Westminster – particularly the proposed ban on fox-hunting, which remains unimplemented – and a feeling that the government wasn't giving sufficient support to beleaguered beef farmers. On the other side of the political spectrum, many found the government's hardline approach to refugees and asylum seekers distasteful, fearing that "New Labour" has abandoned principle - a view ramified by the party's own cases of ministerial "sleaze" - and is swayed too strongly by media opinion.

The government's indisputable drive and energy was substantially threatened in autumn 2000, however: first, by the defeat of Labour's official candidate, Frank Dobson, in the London mayoral election by the former leader of the Greater London Council, **Ken Livingstone**; and secondly, by a widespread protest against taxation on motor fuels, led by a coalition of farmers, truckers and small businesses, which saw blockades of fuel depots and panic-buying of petrol. A further blow came in the form of a huge outbreak of **foot-and-mouth** disease in early 2001, which struck many farms across the country. MAFF, the ministry responsible for agriculture and farming, was ill-prepared for the crisis, and its subsequent dithering over the best means of resolving the matter exacerbated ill-feeling against the government, especially amongst rural communities, and resulted in large areas of the countryside being closed to walkers and tourists. In what was seen as a cynical ploy to salvage his flagging ratings, Blair delayed the calling of a new election until June 2001; while at the same time MAFF guaranteed that the country would be free of foot-and-mouth by that date: of course, it failed to deliver on this promise, although, at the time of writing, most areas of the countryside were free of disease and re-opened to the public. This crisis, along with continued debates about **Northern Ireland**, the dilapidation of the nation's **public transport** system and Labour's failure to reduce **hospital** waiting lists further tarnished New Labour's image, but did not hinder the party's success at the polls. This had much to do with public apathy – voter turnout was lower than any time since World War II – and a lacklustre Conservative Party, led by William Hague, which had unwittingly done its best to help get the Labour party back in by engaging in rigorous political in-fighting in the run-up to the election. The second successive massive defeat for the Tories was followed by Hague's resignation and subsequent replacement by **Iain Duncan Smith**.

However, the events of September 11, 2001, when terrorist-controlled air-planes devastated New York's World Trade Center and the Pentagon in Washington, saw Tony Blair taking a major role alongside US president George Bush in the international coalition formed to wage war against the alleged perpetrators, Al-Qaida, and their protectors, the Taleban rulers of Afghanistan. This diplomatic role took on a new urgency following the overthrow of the Taleban regime and efforts to initiate its replacement by a democratic Afghan government.

Books

Most of the books listed below are in print and in paperback – those that are out of print (o/p) should be easy to track down in second-hand book shops. Publishers are detailed with the British publisher first, separated by an oblique slash from the US publisher, where both exist. Where books are published in only one of these countries, UK or US precedes the publisher's name; where the book is published by the same company in both countries, the name of the company appears just once.

As regards the wealth of Britain's fiction and poetry, the selection below is intended as a very general guide but is, by its nature, partial and partisan.

Finally, while we recommend all those we've listed below, we do have our favourites: we've indicated those that we particularly recommend with a star.

Travel and journals

★ **Bill Bryson**, *Notes from a Small Island* (Black Swan/Avon). Bryson's best-selling and highly amusing account of his farewell journey round Britain.

Giraldus Cambrensis, *The Journey through Wales* and *The Description of Wales* (Penguin). Two witty and frank books in one volume, written in Latin by the quarter-Welsh clergyman after his 1188 tour around Wales recruiting for the third Crusade with Archbishop Baldwin of Canterbury.

James Campbell, *Invisible Country: A Journey Through Scotland* (US New Amsterdam Books) Insightful tour of a country seeking to develop a moden outlook while failing to come to terms with its past.

William Cobbett, *Rural Rides* (UK Penguin). First published in 1830, Cobbett's account of his various fact-finding tours bemoaned the death of the old rural England and its ways while decrying both the growth of cities and the iniquities suffered by the exploited urban poor.

David Craig, *On the Crofter's Trail* (UK Pimlico). Using anecdotes and interviews with descendants, Craig conveys the hardship and tragedy of the Highland Clearances without being mawkish.

★ **Nick Danziger**, *Danziger's Britain* (Flamingo/Trafalgar Square). A well-timed journey through the "other Britain" of council estates and poverty which captures the mood of post-Thatcherite Britain.

Daniel Defoe, *Tour through the Whole Island of Great Britain* (o/p). Defoe, the son of a Stoke Newington butcher, was a novelist, pamphleteer, journalist and sometime spy. This classic travelogue opens a fascinating window onto 1720s Britain.

Charles Jennings, *Up North* (UK Abacus). A provocative, but very readable account of a journey round the north of England, by a self-confessed southerner.

Jan Morris, *The Matter of Wales* (o/p). Prolific half-Welsh travel writer Jan Morris immerses herself in the country that she evidently loves. Highly partisan and fiercely nationalistic, the book combs over the origins of the Welsh character and describes the people and places of Wales with precision and affection. A magnificent introduction to a diverse, and occasionally perverse, nation.

Samuel Pepys, *The Diary of Samuel Pepys* (HarperCollins). Pepys kept a voluminous diary from 1660 until 1669, recording the fall of the Commonwealth, the Restoration, the Great Plague and the Great Fire, as well as describing the daily life of the nation's capital. The unabridged version is published in eleven weighty tomes; Penguin has published an abridged version.

Paul Theroux, *The Kingdom by the Sea* (Penguin). Thoroughly bad-tempered critique of a depressed and drizzly nation.

Dorothy Wordsworth, *Journals* (UK Oxford University Press). The engaging diaries of William's sister, with whom he shared Dove Cottage in the Lake District, provide a vivid account of walks and visits and reflect Dorothy's fascination with the natural world.

History and society

Venerable Bede, *Ecclesiastical History of the English People* (Penguin). First ever English history, written in seventh-century Northumbria.

★ **Asa Briggs**, *Social History of England* (UK Penguin). Immensely accessible overview of English life from Roman times to the 1980s.

Vera Brittain, *Testament of Youth* (Virago/Penguin). Vera Brittain was an exemplar of a golden generation – young, gifted and idealistic – whose lives were shattered by the Great War. She lost her fiancé, brother and two close friends to the trenches, and this book stands testament to the dead, to her own pain, and to the burgeoning pacifism which was to shape her brilliant career as an activist and writer.

★ **David Daiches** (ed.), *The New Companion to Scottish Culture* (UK Polygon). More than 300 articles interpreting Scottish culture in its widest sense, from eating to marriage customs, the Scottish Enlightenment to children's street games.

Friedrich Engels, *The Conditions of the Working Class in England* (Penguin). Portrait of life in England's hellish industrial towns, written in 1844 when Engels was only 24.

Christopher Hill, *The English Revolution* (UK Caliban); *The World Turned Upside-Down* (Penguin). Britain's foremost Marxist historian, Hill is without doubt the most interesting writer on the Civil War and Commonwealth period.

★ **Eric Hobsbawm**, *Industry and Empire* (Penguin/New Press). Ostensibly an economic history of Britain from 1750 to the late 1960s charting Britain's decline and fall as a world power, Hobsbawm's great skill lies in detailed analysis of the effects on ordinary people.

Will Hutton, *The State We're In* (UK Vintage). Widely regarded economic and political survey of Major's Britain by the editor of the *Observer*, spoken of as the textbook for Blair's New Labour.

Philip Jenkins, *A History of Modern Wales 1536–1990* (UK Longman).

Magnificently thorough book, placing Welsh history in its British and European contexts. Unbiased and rational appraisal of events and the struggle to preserve Welsh consciousness, with enough detail to make it of valuable academic interest and sufficient good humour to make it easily readable.

J. Graham Jones, *The History of Wales* (o/p). A concise, easy-paced overview of Welsh life with a welcome bias towards social history.

Michael Lynch (ed.), *The Oxford Companion to Scottish History* (Oxford University Press). A copious collection, covering two thousand years and subjects as varied as climate, archeology, folklore and national identity.

Michael Lynch, *Scotland: A New History* (UK Pimlico). Probably the best available overview of Scottish history, going up to 1992 and the bid for a national parliament.

⭐ **Andrew O'Hagan**, *The Missing* (US New Press) Utterly original, O'Hagan's part-autobiographical journey through Britain's underbelly, focusing on missing persons from bygone Glasgow to the secrets of a Gloucester cellar.

⭐ **George Orwell**, *The Road to Wigan Pier; Down and Out in Paris and London* (both Penguin/Harvest). *Wigan Pier* depicts the effects of the Great Depression on the industrial communities of Lancashire and Yorkshire; *Down and Out* is Orwell's tramp's-eye view of the world, written with first-hand experience – the London section is particularly harrowing.

John Prebble, *Culloden, The Highland Clearances*; and *Glencoe* (all UK Penguin) Ground-breaking trilogy detailing the destruction of the Scottish Highlanders.

Wynford Vaughan-Thomas, *Wales – a History* (o/p). One of the country's most missed broadcasters and writers, Vaughan-Thomas's masterpiece is this warm and spirited history of Wales. Working chronologically through from the pre-Celtic dawn to the aftermath of the 1979 devolution vote, the book offers perhaps the clearest explanation of the evolution of Welsh culture, with the author's patriotic slant evident throughout.

Jennifer Westwood, *Albion: A Guide to Legendary Britain* (o/p). Highly readable volume on the development of myth in literature, with a section on Scottish legends.

Regional guides

⭐ **Joe Fisher**, *The Glasgow Encyclopedia* (o/p). The essential Glasgow reference book, covering nearly every facet of this complex urban society.

Christopher Hibbert (ed.), *Pimlico County History Guides* (o/p). An informative series giving a detailed history of selected English counties. Currently available are guides to Bedfordshire, Cambridgeshire, Dorset, Lincolnshire, Norfolk, Oxfordshire, Somerset (with Bath and Bristol), Suffolk and Sussex.

Daphne Du Maurier, *Vanishing Cornwall* (UK Penguin). Good overall account of Cornwall from an author who lived most of her life there.

Pathfinder Guides, (UK Jarrold-Ordnance Survey). With more than forty titles covering England, Scotland and Wales, these user-friendly walking guides feature Ordnance Survey maps and clear route details.

Richard Sale, *Collins Ramblers Guide: Snowdonia and North Wales* (UK Collins). Describes thirty walks with information on major landmarks and the region's natural history.

★ **A. Wainwright**, *A Coast to Coast Walk* (Michael Joseph). Beautiful palm-sized guide book by acclaimed English hiker and Lake District expert. Printed from his handwritten notes and sketched maps. Also in the series are seven authoritative books covering a variety of walks and climbs in the Lake District. Not all are available in the US.

Ben Weinreb and Christopher Hibbert, *The London Encyclopaedia* (UK Papermac). More than one thousand pages of concisely presented and well-illustrated information on London past and present – the most fascinating single book on the capital.

Art, architecture and archeology

Nicholas Best and Jason Hawkes, *Historic Britain from the Air* (UK Orion). Beautiful aerial photos illustrate this geographical overview of Britain from Roman times to the aftermath of the Blitz.

Alan Crawford, *Charles Rennie Mackintosh* (UK Thames & Hudson). Part of the World of Art series, describing the major contribution of Scotland's premier architect.

Samantha Hardingham, *London: A Guide to Recent Architecture* (UK Ellipsis). A handy pocket-sized book detailing the best of the capital's modern buildings.

Andrew Hayes, *Archaeology of the British Isles* (o/p). Useful introductory history from Stone Age caves to early medieval settlements.

★ **Duncan MacMillan**, *Scottish Art 1460–2000* (Mainstream/ Trafalgar Square); *Scottish Art in the Twentieth Century* (UK Mainstream). The former is a lavish overview of Scottish painting with good sections on landscape, portraiture and the Glasgow Boys while the latter covers the last hundred years in splendid detail.

Nikolaus Pevsner, *The Englishness of English Art* (UK Penguin). Wide-ranging romp through English art concentrating on Hogarth, Reynolds, Blake and Constable, including a section on the Perpendicular style and landscape gardening.

★ **Nikolaus Pevsner and others**, *The Buildings of England & Wales* (UK Penguin). Magisterial series, at least one volume per county, covering just about every inhabitable structure in the country. This project was initially a one-man show, but later authors have revised Pevsner's text, inserting newer buildings but generally respecting the founder's personal tone.

Fiction pre-1900

Jane Austen, *Pride and Prejudice*; *Sense and Sensibility*; *Persuasion* (all Penguin). Austen wrote with wit and vigour on manners, society and the pursuit of happiness, never more enjoyably than in *Pride and Prejudice*. Her amusing sense of irony, especially when delineating acquisitive and socially pretentious characters, is never far from the surface.

R.D. Blackmore, *Lorna Doone* (Oxford University Press). Blackmore's swashbuckling, melodramatic romance, set on Exmoor, has done more for West Country tourism than anything else since.

Charlotte Brontë, *Jane Eyre* (Penguin). A wonderful Victorian "progress" story, following Jane from her pinched, unhappy childhood and schooling to her romance with Mr Rochester. The novel features scenes of quintessential Gothic melodrama – the mad woman in the attic wreaking revenge – and also functions as a deep psychological study of emotional repression.

⭐ **Emily Brontë**, *Wuthering Heights* (Penguin). One of the best, and strangest, novels in the English language. Often falsely claimed as a romance, it is more accurately a work about obsession, and still has the power to disturb. The complex intertwining of the narrative voices in the novel is just one aspect of its genius.

Thomas De Quincey, *Confessions of an English Opium Eater* (Penguin/Oxford University Press). Tripping out with the most famous literary drug-taker since Coleridge. The opium visions only come at the end of the book; the rest is a digressive but entertaining account of the author's childhood and struggles.

⭐ **Charles Dickens**, *Bleak House*; *David Copperfield*; *Little Dorrit*; *Oliver Twist*; *Hard Times* (all Penguin). Many of Dickens' novels are located in London, including *Bleak House*, *Oliver Twist* and *Little Dorrit*, and contain some of his most trenchant passages of social analysis; *Hard Times* is set in a Lancashire mill town; while *David Copperfield* draws on Dickens' own unhappy experiences as a boy, with much of the action taking place in Kent and Norfolk.

George Eliot, *Scenes of Clerical Life* (Penguin/Prometheus); *Middlemarch*; *Mill on the Floss* (both Penguin). Eliot (real name Mary Ann Evans) wrote mostly about the county of her birth, Warwickshire, the setting for the three tales from her fictional debut, *Scenes of Clerical Life*. *Middlemarch* is a gargantuan portrayal of English provincial life prior to the Reform Act of 1832, while *The Mill on the Floss* is based on her own childhood experiences.

Henry Fielding, *Tom Jones* (Penguin). Mock-epic comic novel detailing the exploits of its lusty orphan hero, set in Somerset and London.

Elizabeth Gaskell, *Sylvia's Lovers*; *Mary Barton* (both Penguin/Oxford University Press). *Sylvia's Lovers* is set in a Whitby (Monkshaven in the novel) beset by press gangs, while *Mary Barton* takes place in Manchester and has strong Chartist undertones.

Thomas Hardy, *Far from the Madding Crowd*; *The Mayor of Casterbridge*; *Tess of the D'Urbervilles*; *Jude the Obscure* (all Penguin). Hardy's novels contain some famously evocative descriptions of his native Dorset, but at the time of their publication it was Hardy's defiance of conventional pieties that attracted most attention: *Tess*, in which the heroine has a baby out of wedlock and commits murder, shocked his contemporaries, while his bleakest novel, the Oxford-set *Jude the Obscure*, provoked such a violent response that Hardy gave up novel-writing altogether.

Rudyard Kipling, *Stalky & Co* (Oxford University Press). Nine stories about a mischievous trio of schoolboys, drawn from Kipling's experiences of public school in Devon.

Sir Thomas Malory, *La Morte d'Arthur* (Penguin/Modern Library). Fifteenth-century tales of King Arthur and the Knights of the Round Table, written while the author was in London's Newgate Prison.

Sir Walter Scott, *Waverley* (Penguin). The first of the books that did much to create the romanticized version of Scottish life and history. Others include *Rob Roy* (Wordsworth/NAL), a rich and ripping yarn which transformed the diminutive brigand into a national hero.

Lawrence Sterne, *Tristram Shandy* (Penguin). Anarchic, picaresque eighteenth-century ramblings based on life in a small English village, and full of bizarre textual devices – like an all-black page in mourning for one of the characters.

⭐ **R.L. Stevenson**, *Dr Jekyll and Mr Hyde* (Penguin/Everyman); *Kidnapped* (Penguin/Chain Sales); *The Master of Ballantrae* (Penguin/Everyman); *Treasure Island* (Penguin/Chain Sales); *Weir of Hermiston* (Oxford University Press/Everyman). Superbly imagined and pacily written nineteenth-century tales of intrigue and adventure.

William Makepeace Thackeray, *Vanity Fair* (Penguin). A sceptical but compassionate overview of English capitalist society by one of the leading realists of the mid-nineteenth century.

Anthony Trollope, *The Warden*; *The Small House at Allington* (both Penguin). Trollope was an astonishingly prolific novelist who also, in his capacity as a postal surveyor, found time to invent the letter box. His best-known book, *The Warden*, tells of a collision of family and moral duties in an English cathedral city, while *The Small House at Allington* is a tender story of a failed love affair.

Fiction post-1900

Peter Ackroyd, *English Music* (UK Penguin). A typical Ackroyd novel, constructing parallels between interwar London and distant epochs to conjure a kaleidoscopic vision of English culture. His other novels, such as *Chatterton*, *Hawksmoor* and *The House of Doctor Dee* (all Penguin), are variations on his preoccupation with the English psyche's darker depths.

Martin Amis, *London Fields* (Vintage). A gleefully satirical novel which follows its seedy anti-hero, minor crook Keith Talent, through the mean streets of inner-city London. The rusticity suggested by the title is emphatically ironic.

⭐ **Iain Banks**, An amazingly prolific author, who also writes sci-fi as Iain M. Banks. *The Wasp Factory* (Abacus/Simon and Schuster) was one of the most startling debut novels, chronicling a dysfunctional Scottish childhood. *Complicity* (UK Abacus) was a stunning tale of passion and manipulation while his newest work, *The Business*, explores the political machinations and morality of multi-nationals.

Julian Barnes, *England England* (Picador/Vintage). A satire of the all-pervasive "heritage industry"; a tycoon builds replicas of England's greatest monuments on the Isle of Wight, which gradually come to possess a greater power and importance than the originals.

Arnold Bennett, *Anna of the Five Towns*; *Clayhanger Trilogy* (both UK Penguin). Bennett's first novel, *Anna*, is the story of a miser's daughter and like the later *Clayhanger* trilogy is set in the Potteries.

George Mackay Brown, *Beside the Ocean of Time* (UK Flamingo). A child's journey through the history of an Orkney island, and an adult's effort to make sense of the place's secrets in the late twentieth century.

John Buchan, *The Complete Richard Hannay* (UK Penguin). This one volume includes *The 39 Steps*, *Greenmantle*, *Mr Standfast*, *The Three Hostages* and *The Island of Sheep*. Good gung-ho stories with a great feel for Scottish landscape.

Bruce Chatwin, *On the Black Hill* (Vintage/Penguin). Best known for his travel writing, Bruce Chatwin's talent proved a little too slender for the scope of this subject matter: the sweeping narrative follows the Jones twins' eighty-year tenure of a farm on the Radnorshire border with England. Provides a gentle angle on Welsh–English antipathy.

Joseph Conrad, *The Secret Agent* (Penguin/Oxford University Press). Spy story based on the 1906 Anarchist bombing of Greenwich Observatory, exposing the hypocrisies of both the police and Anarchists.

Daphne Du Maurier, *Frenchman's Creek* (UK Arrow); *Jamaica Inn*; *Rebecca* (both Arrow/Avon). *Frenchman's Creek* and *Jamaica Inn* are nail-biting, swashbuckling romantic novels set in the author's adopted home of Cornwall; but *Rebecca* – in which an unnamed and anonymous bride narrates in terrified thrall the story of her predecessor, the shadowy "first Mrs de Winter" – is perhaps Du Maurier's best-known novel.

E.M. Forster, *Howard's End* (Penguin). Bourgeois angst in Hertfordshire and Shropshire; this is the best book by one of the country's most affectionately regarded modern novelists.

John Fowles, *The Collector*; *The French Lieutenant's Woman* (both Vintage/Back Bay) *Daniel Martin* (UK Vintage). *The Collector*, Fowles's first, is a psychological thriller in which the heroine is kidnapped by a psychotic pools-winner, the story told once by each character. *The French Lieutenant's Woman*, set in Lyme Regis on the Dorset coast, is a tricksy neo-Victorian novel with a famous DIY ending. *Daniel Martin*, a dense, realistic novel, is set in postwar Britain.

Lewis Grassic Gibbon, *A Scots Quair* (UK Penguin). A landmark trilogy, set in northeast Scotland during and after World War I, the events are seen through the eyes of Chris Guthrie, "torn between her love for the land and her desire to escape a peasant culture". Strong, seminal work.

William Golding, *The Spire* (Faber & Faber/Harvest). An atmospheric novel centred on the building of a cathedral spire, taking place in a thinly disguised medieval Salisbury.

Robert Graves, *Goodbye to All That* (UK Penguin). Horrific and humorous memoirs of public school and World War I trenches, followed by postwar trauma and life in Wales, Oxford and Egypt.

Alasdair Gray, *Lanark* (Picador/Harvest). Gray's extraordinary first novel is a postmodern blend of social realism and labyrinthine fantasy featuring his own allegorical illustrations; it takes invention and comprehension to their limits.

★ **Graham Greene**, *Brighton Rock*; *The Human Factor* (both Penguin). Two of the best from the prolific Greene: *Brighton Rock* is an action-packed thriller with heavy Catholic overtones, set in the criminal underworld of a seaside resort; *The Human Factor*, written some forty years later, probes the underworld of London's spies.

★ **Kazuo Ishiguro**, *The Remains of the Day* (Faber & Faber/Vintage). An intelligent novel, beautifully economical in style. It tells of an ageing butler who comes to realize that the master to whom he has devoted himself has Nazi sympathies; it is also a restrained and poignant love story.

Jackie Kay, *The Trumpet* (Picador/Vintage). The poet's debut novel, the powerful tale of a mixed-race jazz trumpeter whose death brings the discovery that 'he' was actually a woman.

James Kelman, *The Busconductor Hines* (UK Phoenix); *How Late It Was, How Late* (Vintage/Delta). *The Busconductor Hines* tells the wildly funny story of a young Glasgow bus conductor with an intensely boring

job and a limitless imagination. *How Late It Was* is Kelman's award-winning and controversial look at life from the perspective of a blind Glaswegian drunk. A disturbing study of personal and political violence, with language to match.

D.H. Lawrence, *Sons and Lovers*; *The Rainbow*; *Women in Love*; *Lady Chatterley's Lover* (all Penguin); *Selected Short Stories* (Penguin/Dover). Lawrence wrote magnificently on the social and emotional aspirations of the working class in Nottinghamshire's pit villages. His early short stories contain some of his finest writing, as does *Sons and Lovers*, a rich semi-autobiographical novel. One of the first writers of the century to write seriously about sex, he brought intensity, integrity and finely tuned feeling to the subject.

Laurie Lee, *Cider with Rosie* (UK Penguin). Reminiscences of adolescent bucolic frolics in the Cotswolds during the 1920s.

Richard Llewellyn, *How Green Was My Valley* (Penguin/Scribner); *Up into the Singing Mountain* (o/p); *Down Where the Moon is Small* (o/p); *Green, Green My Valley Now* (o/p). Vital tetralogy in eloquent and passionate prose, following the life of Huw Morgan from his youth in a South Wales mining valley through emigration to the Welsh community in Patagonia and back to 1970s Wales. A best seller during World War II and still the best introduction to the vast canon of "valleys novels", *How Green was my Valley* captured a longing for a simple if tough life, steering clear of cloying sentimentality.

Compton Mackenzie, *Whisky Galore* (UK Penguin). Comic novel based on a true story of the wartime wreck of a cargo of whisky on a Hebridean island. Full of predictable stereotypes but still funny.

★ **Ian McEwan**, *Atonement* (Cape/Doubleday). McEwan's ninth novel and possibly his most masterful yet, tracing the course of three lives from a swletering country garden in 1935 to seeking absolution in the new century.

Timothy Mo, *Sour Sweet* (UK Paddleless Press). A dense comic novel set in London's Chinatown in the 1960s, which follows the fortunes of the Chen family as they attempt to set up a restaurant, their malevolent rivals posing an increasingly sinister threat.

★ **Ian Rankin**, *The Falls* (Orion/Minotaur). Astonishingly prolific and politically astute Scots writer whose long-running series chronicling the vicissitudes of the dysfunctional Detective Inspector John Rebus whose latest venture concerns the disappearance of the daughter of rich bankers.

Graham Swift, *Waterland* (Picador/Vintage). Postmodern family saga set in East Anglia's fenlands – excellent on the strange history of this superficially drab landscape. *Last Orders* (Picador/Random House) is a bizarre and deceptively simple tale, which follows four men as they take the ashes of their friend, London butcher Jack Dodds, to the sea.

Dylan Thomas, *Under Milk Wood* (UK Penguin); *Collected Stories* (Phoenix/W.W. Norton). *Under Milk Wood* is Thomas' most popular play, telling the story of a microcosmic Welsh seaside town over a 24-hour period. *Collected Stories* contains all of Thomas' classic prose pieces: *Quite Early One Morning*, which metamorphosed into *Under Milk Wood*, the magical *A Child's Christmas in Wales* and the compulsive, crackling autobiography, *Portrait of the Artist as a Young Dog*.

Evelyn Waugh, *Sword of Honour Trilogy* (UK Penguin); *Brideshead Revisited* (Penguin/Little, Brown). The trilogy is a brilliant satire of the World War I officer class laced with some of Waugh's funniest set-pieces. The best-selling *Brideshead Revisited* is possibly his worst book, rank with snobbery, nostalgia and money-worship.

★ **Irvine Welsh**, *Trainspotting* (Minerva/W.W. Norton); *Filth* (Vintage/W.W. Norton); *Glue* (Jonathan Cape/W.W. Norton). *Trainspotting* trawls through the horrors of drug addiction, sexual fantasy, urban decay and hopeless youth, though, thankfully, Welsh's unflinching attention is not without humour. *Filth* focused attention on corrupt policemen, while his most recent offering, *Glue*, reveals a softening of tone in its tale of four boys growing up in slum-clearance flats.

★ **Virginia Woolf**, *Orlando*; *Mrs Dalloway* (both Penguin/Harvest). Woolf's lover, Vita Sackville-West, was the inspiration for *Orlando*, the life of the eponymous protagonist spanning four centuries and both genders. *Mrs Dalloway*, which relates the thoughts of a London society hostess and a shell-shocked war veteran, is a compelling example of her stream of consciousness style.

Poetry anthologies

The New Poetry, ed. Hulse, Kennedy & Morley (UK Bloodaxe). Over fifty poets, all born since World War II.

⭐ **The New Penguin Book of English Verse**, ed. Paul Keegan (Penguin). Seven hundred years of English poetry, listed chronologically rather than by author - a simple innovation, but startlingly effective.

Poetry pre-1900

Beowulf, Séamus Heaney trans. (Faber & Faber/W.W. Norton). A wonderful verse translation of the tenth-century Anglo-Saxon poem, which relates the epic progress of the warrior Beowulf.

William Blake, *The Complete Poems* (Penguin). Blake ranges from the limpid wisdom of *Songs of Innocence and Experience* to the mystical complexities of the prophetic books. He is unique among major poets in illustrating his own work, most of which is set in, or has a significant relationship to, London.

Robert Browning, *Selected Poetry* (Penguin). Browning's poems are marked by intellectual complexity, technical variety and a wide-ranging engagement with the issues of the Victorian age. He also evokes the Italian Renaissance more richly than any other poet in English.

⭐ **Robert Burns**, *Selected Poems* (Penguin). Comprises the best-known work of Scotland's most famous bard, who employed vigorous vernacular language. Immensely popular all over the world, his famous early poems include *Auld Lang Syne* and *My Love Is Like A Red, Red Rose*.

Lord Byron, *Selected Poems* (Penguin/Dover). Byron was a best seller in his day for exotic poems of

adventure such as *The Corsair*, and he is also a master of the Romantic lyric, but the core of his achievement lies in his unfailingly inventive and hilarious satire on all aspects of early nineteenth-century life, *Don Juan*.

Geoffrey Chaucer, *Canterbury Tales* (Penguin). Fourteenth-century collection of bawdy verse tales which follows a pilgrimage to Becket's shrine at Canterbury; translated into modern English blank verse.

Samuel Taylor Coleridge, *The Complete Poetry* (Penguin). Coleridge's output is small, but of the highest quality. *Khubla Khan* and *The Rime Of The Ancient Mariner* are amongst the strangest productions of the Romantic period, but equally noteworthy are the quieter "conversation" poems such as *Frost at Midnight*.

⭐ **John Donne**, *The Complete English Poems* (Everyman). Donne (1572–1631), the greatest of the "metaphysical poets", brought passionate physicality and brilliant intellectual rigour to both his love poetry and religious verse.

Thomas Gray, *Thomas Gray* (UK Everyman). Gray is a minor talent who produced one great poem, *Elegy Written in a Country Churchyard*, a powerful meditation on changes in an apparently changeless English countryside.

George Herbert, *The Complete English Poems* (Penguin). A great seventeenth-century devotional poet, whose passionate dialogues with his Maker ring with energy and deep emotion.

⭐ John Keats, *Selected Poems* (Penguin). Keats was potentially one of the greatest writers who ever lived. Even given his early death – he was only 25 – his achievements in poems such as the *Ode to Autumn* are extraordinary.

Alexander Pope, *Selected Poetry* (Oxford University Press). Pope is the great poetic figure of the eighteenth century and invests the apparent rigidities of the heroic couplet with a flexibility unequalled by any other poet. His *Dunciad* is a steely satire of bad writing in an evil society, while *The Rape of the Lock* is a triumph of charm and delicate eroticism.

Christina Rossetti, *The Complete Poems* (Penguin). Like the American Emily Dickinson, Rossetti is an utterly unpredictable original, capable of producing lyric poems of piercing intensity in addition to the uncanny and gripping long work, *Goblin Market*.

William Shakespeare, *Complete Works* (Oxford University Press). The entire output at a bargain price. For individual plays, you can't beat the Arden Shakespeare series, each volume containing illuminating notes and good introductory essays on the great bard.

Percy Bysshe Shelley, *Selected Poems* (Phoenix Press/Everyman). Shelley's poetry moves from swooning romantic intensity to vigorously expressed hatred of the establishment of his day. He is a seminal figure in the pantheon of English radical dissent.

Alfred Tennyson, *Selected Poems* (Penguin). Tennyson's is perhaps the most purely beautiful and musical poetry in English, filled with sensuous detail and dreamy evocations of natural beauty and the past. *In Memoriam* shows him to be the great poet of Victorian doubt and faith.

⭐ William Wordworth, *Selected Poetry* (Penguin). It is impossible to exaggerate Wordsworth's originality and his influence on the future direction of English culture; his presence is clearly felt in the novels of Dickens and George Eliot as well as in later poets. His understanding of what it means to be human can only be described as profound.

Poetry post-1900

Simon Armitage, *All Points North* (UK Penguin). An engaging and funny poetic travelogue, moving out from Armitage's home town of Marsden in West Yorkshire and taking in Leeds Airport, Huddersfield Town football ground on a Saturday afternoon, amateur dramatics and nights on the town.

⭐ W.H. Auden, *Collected Poems* (Faber & Faber/Vintage).

Auden combines the themes of history, politics and love in poems which seem likely to be definitive expressions of his times. The politically committed work of the 1930s gives way to a later religious commitment, but all his work is marked by stylistic virtuosity.

John Betjeman, *Collected Poems* (UK John Murray). Betjeman (1906–1984) was the English poet laureate; his humorous and often nostalgic work was profoundly concerned with England and the English.

George Mackay Brown, *Selected Poems 1954–1992* (UK John Murray). Brown's work is as haunting, beautiful and gritty as the Orkney islands which inspire it.

Charles Causley, *Collected Poems: 1951-2000* (UK Picador). Contemporary Cornish poet Causley is a champion of the ballad tradition, and writes with precision and beauty about the natural world, and about creativity itself.

Carol Ann Duffy, *Meeting Midnight* (UK Faber and Faber); *Selected Poems* (UK Penguin). *Meeting Midnight* is that rarest of collections – unpretentious poetry for children which actually works. *Selected Poems* shows exactly the reason with its refreshing range of subverted stereotypes.

★ **T.S. Eliot**, *The Wasteland and Other Poems* (UK Faber & Faber); *Collected Poems* (US Harcourt Brace). Published in 1922 and considered one of the cornerstones of Modernist writing, *The Wasteland* offers a revolutionary vision of Western civilization; it is imbued with resonant images of contemporary and ancient London.

★ **Tony Harrison**, *V* (UK Bloodaxe); *Selected Poems* (UK Penguin). One of the most prodigious poets to have emerged over the last thirty years, his longest work *V* explores his feelings at discovering the vandalisation of his parents' grave, while *Selected Poems* sweeps across a broad canvas of sex, politics and the lives of his native Northern English working class.

A.E. Housman, *A Shropshire Lad* (UK Penguin). Housman's poem is a richly detailed evocation of English pastoralism shot through with a strong, if suppressed, vein of homoeroticism.

Ted Hughes, Soon before he died, Hughes published *Birthday Letters* (Faber & Faber/Farrar, Straus & Giroux), a moving account of his relationship with the poet Sylvia Plath, and his response to her suicide. *New Selected Poems 1957–1994* (Faber & Faber/Harper Collins) is the most comprehensive collection of Hughes' work available.

★ **Jackie Kay**, *The Adoption Papers* (UK Bloodaxe); *Other Lovers* (Bloodaxe/Dufour). Kay's poetry explores being black, Scottish and gay and deals with personal relationships in an accessibly intimate way.

Philip Larkin, *Collected Poems* (Faber & Faber/Noonday Press). Larkin used plain language in his work, the subject of which is often the insignificance of human life. Many of the poems achieve an apparently unstudied beauty, though in fact Larkin published very little, preferring to refine his verse to its basic elements.

Norman MacCaig, *Selected Poems* (UK Chatto and Windus). One of the best-known modern Scots poets writes of cityscapes and, in his own words, the "unemphatic marvels" of the natural world.

★ **Hugh MacDiarmid**, *Selected Poems* (UK Penguin). McDiarmid was a poet and nationalist who sought, through his fine lyrical verse, to reinvigorate the use of Scottish literary language.

Sorley Maclean (Somhairle Macgill-Eain), *From Wood to Ridge: Collected Poems* (Birlinn Limited-Carcanet Press/Scholarly Book Services). Written in Gaelic, his poems have been translated into bilingual editions all over the world; they deal with the sorrows of poverty, war and love.

★ **Roger McGough**, *Blazing Fruit: Selected Poems* (UK Penguin). A contemporary Liverpool poet, whose witty rhetorical verse is instantly recognizable. Some of McGough's earlier work, alongside Adrien Henri and Brian Patten, can be found in the influential collection *The Mersey Sound* (UK Penguin).

Edwin Muir, *Collected Poems* (UK Faber & Faber). Muir's childhood on Orkney remained with him as a dream of paradise from which he was banished to Glasgow. His poems are passionately concerned with Scotland.

Wilfred Owen, *The Poems of Wilfred Owen* (Chatto & Windus/W.W. Norton). As with Keats, Owen's early death was a tragedy for English literature. His war poetry is at its best in *Strange Meeting*, with its strikingly original use of half rhymes.

★ **Stevie Smith**, *Selected Poems* (UK Penguin). Smith's best-known poem is *Not Waving But Drowning* (1957), which uses the format of the comic poem but is loaded with economically expressed tragedy.

★ **Dylan Thomas**, *Collected Poems: 1934-1953* (UK Phoenix); *The Poems of Dylan Thomas* (US W.W. Norton). Thomas' beautifully wrought and inventive verse carried a deep, pained concern with mortality and the nature of humanity.

R.S. Thomas, *Collected Poems: 1945-1990* (Bloodaxe/Dufour Editions). Welsh poet R.S. Thomas takes as his theme the enduring nature of Christianity, juxtaposed with the fleeting superficialities of contemporary culture. His finest poems have a strong visionary element, distilled in wonderfully still language.

Benjamin Zephaniah, *Too Black, Too Strong* (UK Bloodaxe). Born in Jamaica but brought up in Britain, Zephaniah is an accomplished dub-poet, and a great performer of his own work.

Film

For much of its history the British film industry has largely been an English affair, with its major studios (Ealing, Pinewood and Shepperton) not far from central London and its stars drawn from the ranks of the capital's stage. However, unlike the Hollywood star system, the English film industry tended and still significantly relies on strong ensemble playing. While Ealing's films were a by-word for social comedy, other significant elements have included the Hammer horror series (usually featuring one or both of Christopher Lee and Peter Cushing), costume dramas typified by the Gainsborough company's productions and the James Bond films, while the Carry On series kept a generation of comedy actors in work long past their sell-by date. In the 1960s, English films developed a justifiable reputation for social realism, which has been maintained in more recent times by directors such as Ken Loach and Mike Leigh.

From its inauguration in the late 1970s the television company Channel 4 began commissioning a wide range of independently-made films and sparked small-scale industries in both Wales and Scotland. Apart from *Gregory's Girl*, success remained relative, however, until the worldwide acclaim received by 1995's *Trainspotting*. Today's British film industry is in a healthier state now than perhaps at any point since the 1930s with a diversity and vitality that reflects the dominance of independent productions. Some film fans might argue that the influence of television means that many such productions are essentially small-screen ventures, but within the last ten years a host of English pictures - *The Full Monty* and *Four Weddings and a Funeral* are just two examples - have enjoyed great success internationally.

The films listed below are all set in England, Scotland or Wales. They are not exclusively greats – though some rank amongst the best movies ever made – but all depict a particular aspect of British life, whether reflecting the experience of immigrant communities, exploring the country's history, or depicting its richly varied landscapes.

Pre-1950

Brief Encounter (David Lean, 1945). Extramarital attraction at a railway station is the theme of this mysteriously popular "classic". Noel Coward is responsible for the clipped dialogue, Rachmaninov for the weepy score, Trevor Howard keeps his upper lip stiff and Celia Johnson wears an improbable hat.

Brighton Rock (John Boulting, 1947). A fine adaptation of Graham Greene's novel, featuring a young, genuinely scary Richard Attenborough as the psychopathic hood Pinkie, who marries a witness to one of his crimes to ensure her silence. Beautiful cinematography and good performances, with a real sense of *film noir* menace.

The Brothers (David MacDonald, 1948). Well worth seeking out as an alternative to cosy Highland mythology. Feisty young Mary moves from Glasgow to the intolerant world of a small Western Isles crofting community, exciting understandable interest from the sons of her savagely patriarchal kinsman. Brilliant interweaving of powerful myth and the hard reality of peasant lives, this has an unusual honesty for its time.

A Canterbury Tale (Michael Powell and Emeric Pressburger, 1944). Set in a wartime Kentish village, where a plucky land girl, a small-town GI and a sardonic English sergeant are billeted. Overseen by a mysterious local magistrate, they make their own pilgrimage to Canterbury, the cathedral glowing high over bomb-damaged streets. A mystical vision of English history is fused with bucolic images of rural life, a restrained exploration of the characters' personal suffering underlying a truly magical masterpiece.

The Edge of the World (Michael Powell, 1937). Michael Powell's first feature, based on the life and evacuation of the tiny isolated island of St Kilda. It is full of embryonic Powell magic, combining an account of the hard life of the islanders and the pull of the modern world with a sense of the power of community and poetry of the island world.

Fires Were Started (Humphrey Jennings, 1943). One of the best films to come out of the prewar documentary tradition in Britain, this is the story of the experiences of a group of firemen through one night of bombing during the Blitz. The use of real firemen as performers rather than professional actors, and the avoidance of formulaic heroics, gives the film great power as an account of the courage of the ordinary people who fought, often uncelebrated, on the home front.

Henry V (Laurence Olivier, 1944). Featuring glowing Technicolor backdrops, this wonderful piece of wartime propaganda is emphatically "theatrical", the action spiralling out from the Globe Theatre itself. Olivier is a brilliantly charismatic king, the

pre-battle scene where he goes disguised amongst his men being delicately muted and atmospheric.

I Know Where I'm Going (Michael Powell and Emeric Pressburger, 1945). Utterly charming fantasy following headstrong Wendy Hiller as she travels to the wilds of west-coast Scotland to wed the ageing tenant of an island castle. Waylaid on the mainland by predictably inclement weather, she begins to fall for Roger Livesey's authentic local laird, and under the spell of the wild landscape and its myths.

Jane Eyre (Robert Stevenson, 1943). Joan Fontaine does a fine job of portraying Jane, and Orson Welles is a suavely sardonic Rochester, the scene where he is thrown from his horse in the mist achieving the perfect melodramatic pitch. With the unlikely tagline, "A Love Story Every Woman Would Die a Thousand Deaths to Live!", it briefly features young Elizabeth Taylor as dying Helen Burns.

Kind Hearts and Coronets (Robert Hamer, 1949). As with the best of the Ealing movies, this is a totally savage comedy on the cruel absurdities of the British class system. With increasing ingenuity, Dennis Price's suave and ruthless anti-hero murders his way through the d'Ascoyne clan (all brilliantly played by Alec Guinness) to claim the family title.

The Life and Death of Colonel Blimp (Michael Powell and Emeric Pressburger, 1943). An epic celebration of the oft-ridiculed romantic spirit of the English, personified by the wonderful Roger Livesey. We follow him through the actual and emotional duels of his youth, against his equally dashing German foe, to crusty old age in World War II. A daring and visually stunning story of love and friendship, it was hated by Churchill for supposedly being unpatriotic, which is surely recommendation enough.

A Matter of Life and Death (Michael Powell and Emeric Pressburger, 1946). From the wartime golden age of British cinema, this remarkable fantasy opens with David Niven's airman miraculously surviving a fall from his stricken bomber. There follows a tussle between the monochrome bureaucracy of Heaven, who seek to reclaim him, and his fast-evolving Earth-bound love affair. Great performances and beautiful Technicolor images in another of Powell and Pressburger's enchanting romances.

Rebecca (Alfred Hitchcock, 1940). Hitchcock does Du Maurier: Laurence Olivier is wonderfully enigmatic as Maxim de Winter, and Joan Fontaine glows in her meek second wife, living in the shadow of her mysterious predecessor. Perfectly paced and beautifully shot, Hitch's first Hollywood picture is a true classic.

The Thirty-Nine Steps (Alfred Hitchcock, 1935). Hitchcock's best-loved British movie, full of wit and bold acts of derring-do. Robert Donat stars as innocent Richard Hannay, inadvertently caught up in a mysterious spy ring and forced to flee both the spies and the agents of Scotland Yard. In a typically perverse Hitchcock touch, he spends a generous amount of time handcuffed to Madeleine Carroll, fleeing across the Scottish countryside, before the action returns to London for the film's great music-hall conclusion.

Whisky Galore! (Alexander Mackendrick, 1949). When a shipwrecked stock of the water of life is washed ashore on a remote Scottish island, the locals contrive all manner of cunning ruses to conceal its presence from the pursuing authorities. A beautiful Ealing comedy, with real sympathy for its eccentric little community as they battle the forces of dull authority in the entirely laudable ambition of having a good time at no expense.

The Wicked Lady (Leslie Arliss, 1945). One of the best of Gainsborough Studio's series of escapist romances, this features a magnificently amoral and headstrong Margaret Lockwood, wooed to a criminal double life by James Mason's quintessentially dashing highwayman. Its opulent recreation of eighteenth-century England is terribly appealing, as are the tempestuous entanglements of its two wayward stars.

1950–1970

Billy Liar! (John Schlesinger, 1963). Tom Courtenay is stuck in a dire job as an undertaker's clerk in a northern town, and spends his time creating extravagant fantasies. His life is lit up by the appearance of Julie Christie, who holds out the glamour and promise of swinging London. Touching and amusing.

Brigadoon (Vincent Minnelli, 1954). Gene Kelly escapes brash New York for the Highland glens, discovering love in the agreeable shape of local lass Cyd Charisse in the eponymous mythical village, which appears from the gloaming only once a century. Despite the slightly awkward studio landscapes, this is a delightful escapist fantasy from the master of serious

Hollywood musicals, with some great Lerner and Loewe tunes.

Culloden (Peter Watkins, 1964). The story of the last battle fought on British soil, made in the style of a BBC documentary, with verité battle footage and interviews with Scottish clansmen and the Duke of Cumberland's opposing modern army. Highly atmospheric, its great strength is the account of the catastrophic aftermath, as Cumberland's men embark on a process of ethnic cleansing.

Far From the Madding Crowd (John Schlesinger, 1967). A largely successful and imaginative adaptation of Hardy's doom-laden tale of the desires and ambitions of wilful Bathsheba Everdene. Julie Christie is a radiant and spirited Bathsheba, Terence Stamp flashes his blade to dynamic effect, Alan Bates is quietly charismatic as dependable Gabriel Oak, and the West Country setting is sparsely beautiful.

If… (Lindsay Anderson, 1968). The stifling world of the English public school as a rather inadequate microcosm of society. Malcolm McDowell plays our iconoclastic hero, leading his little cell in revolution against the arbitrary discipline and cruelty of the school hierarchy. Although beautifully shot and well realized in its own caricatural terms, it seems dated now and rather too narrowly of its time.

I'm Alright Jack (John and Roy Boulting, 1959). The best of The Boulting Brothers' comic explorations of English social mores explores the class system in the context of industrial unrest. Peter Sellers is on top form as the shop steward, while management is represented by a hapless Ian Carmichael (brought in to cause disruption through his own ineptitude) who, naturally, falls in love with Sellers' daughter.

Kes (Kenneth Loach, 1969). Recently re-released to the highest of praise from reviewers, this is the unforgettable story of a neglected Yorkshire schoolboy who finds solace and liberation in training his kestrel. As a still pertinent commentary on poverty and an impoverished school system it is bleak but idealistic, and pale and pinched David Bradley who plays Billy Caspar is hugely affecting.

The Ladykillers (Alexander Mackendrick, 1955). Alec Guinness is fabulously toothy and malevolent as "Professor Marcus", a murderous con man who lodges with a sweet little old lady, Mrs Wilberforce. The professor and his ragbag of criminal accomplices – their sinister intent a hilarious counterpoint to Mrs Wilberforce's genteel tea parties – try to pass themselves off as musicians, while, thanks to her innocent interventions, the body count inexorably mounts. Features some evocative London streetscapes.

A Man For All Seasons (Fred Zinnemann, 1966). Sir Thomas More versus Henry VIII: one of British history's great moral confrontations made skilfully tedious by this film's stage-bound, talky origins in Robert Bolt's play. Despite muted, atmospheric visuals and a heavenly host of theatrical talent (including a cheering appearance by Orson Welles as Cardinal Wolsey), nothing can save this from paralysing dullness.

Night and the City (Jules Dassin, 1950). Great *film noir*, with Richard Widmark as an anxious nightclub hustler on the run. Gripping and convincingly sleazy, the London streetscapes have an expressionist edge of horror.

Only Two Can Play (Sidney Gilliat, 1961). Dryly funny if faintly depressing adaptation of Kinsley Amis's farce

That Uncertain Feeling, with Peter Sellers in convincingly seedy mode as an adulterous Welsh librarian.

Performance (Nicolas Roeg/Donald Cammell, 1970). Credited with precipitating James Fox's breakdown and subsequent retirement from the movies, this shape-shifting tale of gangsters and pop culture is the best account of the hedonistic end to Britain's psychedelic 1960s. Well known for its strange drug-hazed second half, the film is also brilliantly funny in parts and should be cherished for its hilarious destruction of the myth of Kray-style criminals.

This Sporting Life (Lindsay Anderson, 1963). One of the key British films of the 1960s, *This Sporting Life* tells the story of a northern miner turned star player for his local rugby team. The young Richard Harris gives a great performance as the inarticulate antihero, able only to express himself through physical violence, and the film is one of the best examples of the gritty "kitchen sink" genre it helped to usher in.

The 1970s and 1980s

Akenfield (Peter Hall, 1974). A powerfully involving evocation of English rural life whose ingredients include glowing cinematography and Michael Tippett's wonderful music. Past and present are skilfully contrasted, but the heart of the film lies in its sometimes ecstatic, but also harsh, rendering of the past.

Babylon (Franco Rosso, 1980). A moving account of black working-class London life. We follow the experiences of young Blue through a series of encounters which reveal the insidious forces of racism at work in Britain. Good performances and a great reggae soundtrack: an all too rare example of black Britain taking centre stage in British movies.

Chariots of Fire (Hugh Hudson, 1981). This hugely successful movie prompted writer Colin Welland to bombastically – and optimistically – proclaim, "The British are coming". Based around the 1924 Olympics, it tells the true story of Scottish missionary Eric Liddell (Ian Charleson) and repressed Cambridge student Harold Abrahams (Ben Cross). Oscar-winning and overblown, it is distinguished only by Charleson's quiet performance, and some great locations, such as the sweeping beach at St Andrews.

Comrades (Bill Douglas, 1986). In 1830s England, a group of farm workers decide to stand up to the exploitative tactics of the local landowner, and find themselves prosecuted and transported to Australia. Based on the true story of the Tolpuddle Martyrs, this combines political education (the founding of the modern union movement) with a moving and visually stunning celebration of working lives.

Distant Voices, Still Lives (Terence Davies, 1988). Beautifully realized autobiographical tale of growing up in Forties and Fifties Liverpool, juxtaposing contemporary popular songs with isolated scenes from the life of a family ruled by a brutal patriarch. The mesmeric pace is punctuated by astonishing moments of drama, and the whole is a very moving account of how the family survives and triumphs, in small ways, against the odds.

Frenzy (Alfred Hitchcock, 1972). Hitchcock comes back to Blighty in top form, with the story of a man on the run, under suspicion for the vicious "neck tie" murders carried out in Covent Garden. Trademark sly black humour combines with a disturbing exploration of sexual immaturity.

Get Carter (Mike Hodges, 1971). Although not the masterpiece some claim, this is still one of the most vivid and interesting British gangster movies, featuring a monumentally evil outing for Michael Caine as the eponymous villain, returning to his native Newcastle to avenge his brother's death. Great use of its Newcastle locations and a fine turn by playwright John Osborne as the local godfather don't quite, however, compensate for its now faintly ridiculous misogyny.

Gregory's Girl (Bill Forsyth, 1981). John Gordon Sinclair is engaging and gangly as Gregory, whose adolescent dreams are filled with football-playing schoolgirl siren Dorothy. Gregory's gauche attempts to woo her keep the gentle plot tripping along nicely, his teachers making sardonic asides and his little sister proffering grave advice.

Hope and Glory (John Boorman, 1987). A glorious autobiographical feature about the Blitz seen through the eyes of nine-year-old Bill, who revels in the liberating chaos of bomb-site playgrounds, tumbling barrage balloons and shrapnel collections. His older sister's unfettered romps with a Canadian soldier and the adults' privation and occasional despair are an additional source of amusement for Bill and his tiny sister. Sentimental in the best sense, and deliciously nostalgic.

The Last of England (Derek Jarman, 1987). Derek Jarman was a genuine maverick presence in Eighties Britain; this is his most abstract account of a unique vision of the state of the nation. Composed of apparently unrelated shots of decaying London landscapes, rent boys and references to emblematic national events such as the Falklands War, this may not be to all tastes but it is a fitting testament to a unique talent in British film making.

Letter to Brezhnev (Chris Bernard, 1986). Frank Clarke's screenplay about chicken factories, Russian sailors, drink, love and idealism proved a marvellous vehicle for his larger-than-life sister, Margi, and the more considered Alexandra Pigg.

Local Hero (Bill Forsyth, 1983). A genuinely endearing, humane picture which rediscovers some of the subtlety and exuberance of the Ealing comedies. It contrasts the ambitions of a Texan oil baron who wants to buy up a Scottish village with the seductive warmth and vitality of the life of the village. Glorious landscapes, and inspired acting from an imperious Burt Lancaster and a charming Denis Lawson.

The Long Good Friday (John MacKenzie, 1979). Despite a maniacal turn from Bob Hoskins as the East End gang boss threatened by powerful, mysterious new arrivals, this is not all it's cracked up to be. Its vision of East End villains seems self-indulgent and dated, and the plodding TV visual style doesn't help to raise the level.

Made in Britain (Alan Clarke, 1982). One of Alan Clarke's series of savage dissections of Eighties Britain, featuring a seventeen-year-old Tim Roth as skinhead Trevor, on a downbeat odyssey of job centre visits, drug-taking and racist explosions. The energy of the central performance, and the energy of the film making itself, transcend the worthy TV aesthetic and deliver a film of real force, and a very powerful indictment of Thatcher's Britain.

Mona Lisa (Neil Jordan, 1986). This fine London-based thriller has powerful performances from Bob Hoskins, Michael Caine and then-newcomer Cathy Tyson, the latter playing a high-class prostitute who recruits Hoskins to help find her lost friend. This takes him, and us, on a nightmarish exploration of the dark side of Eighties London, lightened only slightly by an utterly convincing, poignant love story, as Bob begins to fall for his beautiful employer.

My Beautiful Laundrette (Stephen Frears, 1985). A slice of Thatcher's Britain, with a young Asian, Omar, on the make, opening a ritzy laundrette. His lover, Johnny, is an ex-National Front glamour boy, angry and inarticulate when forced by the acquisitive Omar into a menial role in the laundrette. The racial, sexual and class dynamics of their relationship are closely observed, and mirror the tensions engendered by the Asian presence in a hostile London. Daring, unexpected and funny, with a wonderful performance from Daniel Day-Lewis as Johnny.

On the Black Hill (Andrew Grieve, 1987). A visually absorbing adaptation of Bruce Chatwin's rather slight novel of Welsh farming folk. Hardyesque characterization and a similar predilection for doom, with a strong performance by Bob Peck as stubborn Amos Jones, trapped in an unhappy marriage to a middle-class woman.

The Wicker Man (Robin Hardy, 1973). A classic more by virtue of its unutterable weirdness than any great achievements of film making. Edward Woodward plays a detective investigating the mysterious disappearance of a local girl on an isolated Scottish island, and finds himself drawn into a strange world of maypole-dancing and inadvertently hilarious pagan rites. Christopher Lee manages to keep a straight face throughout, rather surprisingly.

Withnail and I (Bruce Robinson, 1986). Richard E. Grant is superb as the raddled, drunken Withnail, an out-of-work actor with a penchant for drinking lighter fluid. Paul McGann is the "I" of the title – a bemused and beautiful spectator of Withnail's wild excesses, as they abandon an astonishingly grotty London flat for the wilds of a remote cottage, and the attentions of Withnail's randy uncle Monty. A rare look at the Sixties that avoids nostalgia, and opts instead for emotional truth.

1990 to the present

Bhaji on the Beach (Gurninder Chadha, 1993). An Asian women's group takes a day-trip to Blackpool in this issue-laden but enjoyable picture. A lot of fun is had contrasting the seamier side of British life with the *mores* of the Asian aunties, though the male characters are cartoon villains all.

Billy Elliot (Stephen Daldry, 2000). Set against the backdrop of the turbulent miners' strike of 1984, a young boy (Jamie Bell) is torn between his unexpected love of dance and the disintegration of his family. A way out is offered when the local dancing teacher (Julie Walters) offers him a chance to train and even audition for the Royal Ballet School.

Brassed Off (Mark Herman, 1996). A pacy film about British working-class life that eschews pathos, opting instead for uncompromising anger, underscored by robust black humour. With the imminent demise of the town's coal pit, the future for the Grimley Colliery Brass Band looks hopeless. Danny (Pete Postlethwaite) valiantly attempts to keep the band alive as the emotional lives of the musicians collapse.

Braveheart (Mel Gibson, 1995). Cod-Highland high camp, with a shaggy-haired Mel Gibson wielding his claymore as thirteenth-century Independence hero William Wallace. The English are (naturally enough) thieving effete scum, the Scots all warm-blooded noble savages, and history takes a firm back seat. The Battle of Stirling Bridge, mysteriously, has no bridge, and Wallace's putative fathering of England's royal line is about as historically convincing as Mel's accent. Despite much Scot-nat posturing, the picture was largely filmed in Ireland.

Breaking the Waves (Lars von Trier, 1996). A lyrical, deeply moving drama set in a devout community in the north of Scotland. An innocent young woman, Bess (Emily Watson), falls in love with Danish oil-rig worker Jan (Stellan Skarsgaard). Blaming herself for the injury which cripples him, she embarks on a masochistic sexual odyssey, which rapidly takes her into dark and uncharted waters.

East is East (Damien O'Donnell 1999). Seventies Salford is the setting for this lively comedy, with a Pakistani chip-shop owner struggling to keep control of his seven children as they rail against the strictures of Islam and arranged marriages. Inventively made, and with some pleasing performances.

Elizabeth (Shekahar Kapur, 1998). Charismatic Cate Blanchett is – thankfully – the still heart of this madly over-blown production, where all political and emotional nuance is lost in an orgy of decapitations, swirling cloaks and stagy thunderstorms. Features a host of plodding cameos with, most bizarrely, footballing heart-throb Eric Cantona as the French ambassador.

Enigma (Michael Apted, 2001). This blockbuster, scripted by playwright Tom Stoppard, is a fictional tale using Britain's wartime efforts to crack the GermansÕ' Enigma encrypting machine as its backdrop.

The Full Monty (Peter Cattaneo, 1997). Six Sheffield ex-steel workers throw caution to the wind and become male strippers, their boast being that all will be revealed: the "full monty". Unpromising physical specimens all, they score an unlikely hit with the local lassies. The film was itself an unlikely hit worldwide: the theme of manhood in crisis is sensitively explored, and the long-awaited striptease is a joy to behold.

Hedd Wyn (Paul Turner, 1992). Sentimental and epic Welsh-language feature about World War 1 poet Ellis Evans, who was mortally wounded on the first day of the Battle of Passchendale.

Howards End (James Ivory, 1991). E.M. Forster's tale of the forward-thinking Schlegel sisters, and their relationship with the conventional, domineering Wilcoxes. One of many immaculate British costume dramas, with precise performances from Vanessa Redgrave, Helena Bonham Carter and, most notably, Emma Thompson as Margaret Schlegel.

Little Voice (Mark Herman, 1998). Entertaining screen adaptation of Jim Cartwright's hit play about reclusive

"Little Voice" (Jane Horrocks), who comes miraculously to life only on stage, brilliantly impersonating Fifties stars such as Marilyn Monroe. It features a great performance from Michael Caine as the impossibly seedy agent who seeks to exploit her bizarre talent, and offers a great glimpse of seaside England, with all its eccentric charm.

Lock, Stock and Two Smoking Barrels (Guy Ritchie, 1998). Four lads attempt to pay off gambling debts by making a drug deal in this over-stylized and rather shallow picture, which, though it has a modern setting, pays dubious homage to the London of the Kray twins. However, the suits are sharp, the production is slick and football's hard man turned actor Vinnie Jones turns in a surprisingly solid debut performance.

The Madness of King George (Nicholas Hytner, 1994). Adapted from an Alan Bennett play, this eighteenth-century royal romp has an irritating staginess, with the king's loopy antics played against a cartoon-like court and an England apparently devoid of real people.

Mrs Brown (John Madden, 1997). Demonstrates the Brits' tedious preoccupation with royalty, and concerns the did-she-or-didn't-she relationship between widowed Queen Victoria and her kilted Highland "ghillie" John Brown. Well acted but unchallenging, with Judy Dench as the tight-lipped monarch and Billy Connolly as the plain-speaking Highlander.

Nil by Mouth (Gary Oldman, 1997). Features strong performances by Ray Winstone (Ray) as a boorish south Londoner and Kathy Burke (Valery) as his battered wife. A brave and bleak realist picture, which depicts Ray as a victim of his own violence, as well as the devastatingly vulnerable Valery. Brace yourself.

Notting Hill (Roger Michell, 1999). More smug, middle-class jollity from the writer (Richard Curtis) who brought you *Four Weddings and a Funeral* (1994). Grant reprises his bumbling floppy-haired Englishman role and falls for a glamorous American (Julia Roberts), again. Spans a year in the life of Notting Hill, perversely failing to feature the event for which this part of London is best known: the biggest and best street carnival in Europe.

Orlando (Sally Potter, 1992). Although modest in budget terms, this is a vivid and visually very beautiful adaptation of Virginia Woolf's novel, following its hero/heroine through 400 years of British history. Tilda Swinton is perfectly cast as the androgynous immortal, and choice moments spanning Elizabethan England to the present day (through the Civil War and Victoria's reign, for example) are perfectly and mysteriously realized.

The Ratcatcher (Lynne Ramsay, 1999). Set in 1970s Glasgow during a refuse workers' strike, Ramsay's striking first feature follows twelve-year-old James, who accidentally drowns his friend as the rubbish around the tenement blocks mounts. Weaving rich humour into the gloomy narrative, Ramsay layers poetic images of the city, rejecting realism for a lyrical, symbolic approach.

The Remains of the Day (James Ivory, 1993). Kazuo Ishiguro's masterly study of social and personal repression translates beautifully to the big screen. Anthony Hopkins is the overly decorous butler who gradually becomes aware of his master's fascist connections, Emma Thompson the housekeeper who struggles to bring his real, deeply suppressed feelings to the surface.

Richard III (Richard Loncraine, 1995). A splendid film version of a renowned National Theatre production, which brilliantly transposed the action to a fascist state in the 1930s. The infernal political machinations of a snarling Ian McKellen as Richard are heightened by Nazi associations, and the style of the period imbues the film with the requisite glamour, as does a languorously drugged Kristin Scott-Thomas as Lady Anne. Innovative use of some great London locations, with monumental Battersea Power Station the setting for the Battle of Bosworth.

Rob Roy (Michael Caton-Jones, 1994). Liam Neeson brings a much-needed gravity to the rather sordid goings-on in this moderately successful romanticization of the real-life story of a cattle rustling, blackmailing thug. Some splendid Scottish locations and generally solid performances (including an extravagantly evil Tim Roth) just about redeem the anachronistic script.

Secrets and Lies (Mike Leigh, 1995). Much-loved Mike Leigh slice-of-life drama, with wonderful Timothy Spall at the head of a spectacularly dysfunctional London family. His sister Cynthia (Brenda Blethyn), her heart of gold buried in boozy, cloying unhappiness, is reunited with the black daughter she gave up for adoption at birth. With trademark over-long improvised sequences and a sharp eye for suburban vulgarity which comes uncomfortably close to parody, the film is lifted by stunning ensemble performances and sustained by the simple strength of its central tenet: that secrets and lies in a family will only cause unnecessary pain.

Sense and Sensibility (Ang Lee, 1995). Jane Austen's sprightly essay on the merits of well-modified behaviour is nicely realized by Lee, and neatly scripted by Emma Thompson. Thompson and Kate Winslet are charming as the downtrodden Dashwood sisters: Winslet is a brilliantly overwrought, romantic Marianne, while Thompson turns in another perfect performance as prudent Elinor.

Shakespeare in Love (John Madden, 1998). This irresistible homage to life, love and Shakespeare has an energetic Joseph Fiennes as the quill-chewing bard and Gwyneth Paltrow as his sparky love interest. Sharply scripted by Tom Stoppard, it skips a dainty line between parody and over-reverence, and has fun sending up the British over-fondness for cameos, with Rupert Everett as melancholy Kit Marlowe, off on a one-way trip for a drink in Deptford. No mere piece of frivolity though, the film aspires to, and achieves, real feeling.

Small Faces (Gillies MacKinnon, 1995). A moving little saga about the lives of three brothers growing up in 1960s Glasgow amid feuding gangs of local teenagers. We follow the rough education of young Lex, torn between the excitement and real danger of a life of fighting, and the alternative artistic ambitions of his older brother. A convincing and occasionally very funny re-creation of the period.

Trainspotting (Danny Boyle, 1995). Iconic posters of Ewan McGregor looking wet and wasted in a tight T-shirt fuelled intense *Trainspotting* fever in 1995. An innovative, energetic adaptation of Irvine Welsh's novel, the film features a sensational soundtrack and takes a headlong dive into the drug-fuelled dark side of Edinburgh. Exciting and disturbing in equal measure, with almost insolently superb performances from McGregor, Ewen Bremner and Robert Carlyle.

Twin Town (Kevin Allen, 1997). A Welsh take on *Trainspotting*, with amoral twins Julian and Jeremy wreaking elaborate revenge when their father, Fatty, is hospitalized. The attempt at iconic status largely backfires, but Llyr Evans and Rhys Ifans turn in strong performances as the terrifying Port Talbot twins.

index

and small print

Index

Map entries are in colour

A

À La Ronde.....................364
Abbeycwmhir.................828
Abbotsbury 259
Abbotsford....................968
Aberaeron 850
Aberconwy,
   Treaty of.................1290
Abercynon.....................771
Aberdaron 879
Aberdeen........1169–1177
Aberdeen......................1171
Aberfan 771
Aberfeldy....................1077
Aberfoyle.....................1057
Abergavenny 821
Aberglaslyn Gorge 871
Aberglasney 794
Abergwesyn 826
Abergwili 791
Abergynolwyn 843
Abernethy Garten Forest
   RSPB Reserve 1206
Abersoch.......................878
Aberystwyth 846
Aberystwyth................847
Aboyne........................1179
accommodation..............30
Acharacle 1220
Achiltibuie 1231
Achmelvich 1233
Acomb 738
Act of Union
   (Scotland)...............1299
Acts of Union (Wales) .1295
admission charges..........42
Ailsa Craig.....................991
airlines see flights
Aldeburgh 439
Alexander III 1291
Alexandria 1054
Alfred the Great,
   King..........242, 433, 1288
Alice in Wonderland......892
Alloway 991
Alnmouth......................747
Alnwick 748
Altarnun 421
Althorp 551
Alton Towers 513
Alyth..........................1165
Ambleside 619

America......................1301
Anglesey 882–885
Angus 1162–1168
Anstruther 1072
Antonine Wall....1052, 1287
Aonach Mhòr 1212
Applecross peninsula,
   the 1226
Appledore 384
Appuldurcombe House.240
Arbeia Roman Fort 732
Arbroath 1162
Arbroath Declaration...1292
Arbuthnot 1178
Ardgartan 1088
Ardlui..........................1056
Ardminish 1106
Ardnamurchan
   peninsula.................1219
Argyll 1083–116
Argyll 1086–1087
Argyll Forest Park 1088
Arinagour 1101
Arisaig.........................1222
Arlesford 245
Armadale 1121
Arncliffe.......................659
Arnol 1139
Arran...........................1108
Arran, Isle of 1108–1110
Arrochar 1088
Arthur, King...346, 415, 418
Arundel.........................221
Ashbourne 516
Ashby-de-la-Zouch.......544
Ashmolean, the............294
Askrigg.........................665
Attlee, Clement 1305
Auckland Castle...........713
Austen,
   Jane ...244, 245, 260, 336
Avebury........................271
Aviemore 1204
Ayr...............................988
Ayrshire 988–992
Aysgarth.......................665

B

Badachro 1229
Baile an Or 1247
Baile Mór.....................1098

Baird, John Logie 1034
Bakewell 525
Bala..............................839
Balfour Castle 1264
Ballater.......................1179
Balloch 1053
Balmaha 1054
Balmoral......................1180
BALTIC Centre for
   Contemporary Art 725
Bamburgh 750
Banff 1185
Bangor..........................885
bank holidays.................41
Bank of England   115
banks 23
Bannockburn 1049
Bannockburn,
   Battle of 1292
Barabhas.....................1139
Barafundle Bay 800
Bardsey Island 879
Barmouth 840
Barmouth–Fairbourne
   Loop.........................841
Barnard Castle.............714
Barnstaple....................381
Barnstaple Bay see
   Bideford Bay
Barra, Isle of 1148
Barrie, J.M. 1166
Barvas see Barabhas
Basingwerk Abbey........895
Baslow 524
Batemans.....................205
Bath 336–342
Bath..............................337
Battle...........................204
BBC 40, 108
beaches 50
Beachy Head 210
Beadnell 749
Beamish Museum 712
Beatles, The 591
Beau Nash, Richard.....339
Beaulieu 247
Beaumaris....................882
Beck Hole 693
Becket, Thomas à.......1289
bed and breakfast..........31
Beddgelert 871
Bede, the
   Venerable 709, 730
Bedford 300

Bedfordshire 301–303
beer................................36
Beer 365
Beinn Eighe.................1228
Belas Knap 314
Bellingham 742
Belmont 1281
Belsay 730
Belsay Hall 729
Bempton 686
Ben a'Bhragaidh 1246
Ben Lawes 1078
Ben More 1097
Ben More Assynt 1233
Benbecula, Isle of 1146
Benmore Botanic
   Gardens 1089
Berkeley 321
Berneray, Isle of 1145
Berriew 831
Berwick-upon-Tweed....753
Bess of Hardwick.........538
Bettyhill 1237
Betws-y-Coed...............864
Beverley 684
Bhearnaraigh, Isle of...1145
Bibury...........................311
Bideford 383
Bideford Bay 383
Big Pit National Mining
   Museum 770
Biggar 1036
Biggings 1278
Bignor 223
Binchester Roman
   Fort............................713
Birdoswald Fort 741
BIRMINGHAM 502–513
Birmingham...................503
   accommodation.................504
   arrival 502
   Birmingham Museum and
      Art Gallery.....................505
   Bournville 510
   Brindley Place....................506
   Bull Ring 507
   Cadbury World...................510
   Chamberlain Square 505
   eating and drinking...........510
   Edgbaston 508
   gay and lesbian scene......409
   Ikon Gallery.......................507
   International Convention
      Centre..............................506
   Jewellery Quarter..............508
   listings...............................513
   National Sealife Centre.....507
   nightlife and
      entertainment 512
   Royal Birmingham
      Society of Artists 507
St Philip's Cathedral 507
   tourist offices 502
   transport 504
   Victoria Square 505
Birnam 1076
Birsay 1259
Bishop Auckland...........712
Bishops Lydeard...........350
Black Death, the 1292
Black Isle,
   the 1241–1243
Black Mountains 820
Blackpool 597–600
Blaenafon......................769
Blaenau Ffestiniog 872
Blair Atholl...................1081
Blair Castle 1081
Blair, Tony 1307
Blairgowrie 1164
Blairmore.....................1235
Blakeney 456
Blakeney Point..............456
Blakey Ridge.................690
Blanchland 716
Blandford Forum...........261
Blantyre.......................1034
Blenheim Palace...........298
Blickling Hall 454
Blisland 418
Bloody Assizes 1299
Bloomsbury Group,
   the 214
Bluebell Railway............221
Boat of Garten 1206
Bodelwyddan...............894
Bodiam Castle 205
Bodmin 417
Bodmin Moor........417–420
Bodnant Gardens 891
Boer War, the 1304
Boggle Hole 695
Bolton Abbey 658
Bolventor 418
Bonar Bridge...............1244
Bonfire Societies...........211
Bonnie Prince Charlie
   ...1129, 1147, 1200, 1300
Bonnybridge 1052
books................1309–1321
Boot 631
Booth, Richard..............824
Border Forest Park 743
Border Reivers   966
Borders, the
   Scottish 965–977
Borreraig 1127
Borrowdale 629
Boscastle 415
Bosherton 800
Boston 560
Bothwell Castle...........1035
Bothwell, Earl of.........1296
Boudicca (Boadicea)...1286
Bournemouth 248
Bowes Museum............714
Bowhill House...............974
Bowlees Country
   Park............................715
Bowmore 1112
Bowness 617
Bowood House.............272
Bradford.......................653
Bradford on Avon 273
Brading 238
Brae 1279
Braemar 1180
Brahan Seer, the 1241
Brantwood 625
Breachacha Castle 1101
Brechfa 791
Brecon 816
Brecon Beacons, the.....817
Brecon Beacons
   Mountain Centre 819
Brecon Beacons National
   Park 816–825
Brecon Beacons National
   Park Office 822
Bredon Hill 328
Breedon-on-the-hill.......546
Brent Tor 380
Bressay 1275
Bridge of Allan 1049
Bridgwater 348
Bridlington 685
Bridport.........................259
Brighton 215–220
Brighton.........................216
Brinkburn Priory...........745
Bristol 328–336
Bristol.....................330–331
British Museum.............105
Britten, Benjamin 439
Brixham........................368
Broad Haven.................800
Broadford....................1124
Broadstairs...................188
Broch of Gurness 1259
Brockenhurst 206
Brodick 1108
Brontës, the 655
Brougham Castle..........634
Brown, Capability 526
Brownsea Island 250
Brunel, Isambard
   Kingdom 328, 334
Bryher (Isles of Scilly) ...409
BSE ("mad cow
   disease") 1306

Buckden.............................659
Buckfast Abbey 378
Buckie...........................1185
Buckingham...................299
Buckinghamshire
...........................299–301
Buckland Abbey 375
Buckland-in-the-Moor ..378
Buckler's Hard 247
Bude 416
Budleigh Salterton 365
Bunessan 1097
Bunyan, John................300
Burford.........................310
Burns, Robert
................978, 989, 991
Burry Holms.................789
Burwash........................205
Bury St Edmunds 434
buses
    in Britain............................27
    from Europe.......................17
Bute, Isle of...............1090
Buttermere 630
Buxton 517
Byland Abbey 688
Byrness.........................743
Byron, Lord...................538

C

CADW 42
Caerfai Bay 806
Caerlaverock Castle......980
Caerlaverock Wildfowl and
    Wetlands Centre 980
Caerleon........................768
Caernarfon...........879–882
Caernarfon 880
Caerphilly 784
Caesar, Julius..............1286
Cairndow.....................1089
Cairngorm funicular
    railway.....................1204
Cairngorms, the 1203
Calanais 1140
Calanish see Calanais
Caldey Island 798
Calgary.........................1096
Calke Abbey 546
Callander......................1059
Cally House...................985
Cambo 730
CAMBRIDGE........461–472
Cambridge 462
    accommodation...............464
    airport..............................463
    bike rental 463

Bridge of Sighs 467
Christ's College.................469
Clare College 466
Corpus Christi College 469
eating and drinking...........470
Emmanuel College............469
entertainment...................471
festivals 472
Gonville and Caius
    College 466
information........................464
Jesus College 468
King's College..................465
King's Parade...................466
listings.............................472
Magdalene College...........468
parking.............................463
punting.............................466
Queens' College 469
Round Church...................468
Scott Polar Research
    Institute........................470
Senate House 466
Sidney Sussex College.....468
St John's College..............467
tours................................464
train station 463
Trinity College 467
Trinity Hall 466
University Botanic
    Gardens........................470
Wren Library 467
Camelford......................419
Campbell, Donald 623
Campbeltown 1106
camping 33
Canna, Isle of..............1134
Cannich........................1211
Canolfan Tryweryn 839
Canterbury...........189–194
Canterbury 190
Cape Cornwall 404
Cape Wrath.................1236
Capel Curig...................866
Capel-y-Ffin 823
car rental 29
caravanning 33
Carbisdale Castle 1244
Carbost 1126
CARDIFF 773–783
Cardiff 774–775
    accommodation................773
    Arcades, the.....................777
    arrival 776
    Cardiff Bay 779
    Castle..............................778
    Cathays Park 778
    city centre 777
    City Hall 778
    eating and drinking...........780
    information........................773
    Llandaff............................780
    Millennium Stadium 777
    National Assembly of
        Wales..........................780

    National Museum of
        Wales..........................778
    nightlife and
        entertainment 780
    Norwegian church arts
        centre 779
    Pierhead Building..............780
    Queen Street.....................777
    transport 773
Cardiff Bay 779
Cardigan 851
Cardiganshire see
    Ceredigion
Carew...........................801
Carisbrooke Castle 242
Carlisle 638
Carlyle, Thomas...........133
Carmarthen 791
Carmarthenshire County
    Museum 791
Carn Deag...................1228
Carnegie, Andrew 1065
Carrbridge....................970
Carreg Cennan
    Castle.......................795
Carroll, Lewis 892
Cartmel 635
Castell Coch 783
Castell Dinas Brân 838
Castell-y-Bere 843
Castle Bolton 665
Castle Campbell 1052
Castle Douglas 982
Castle Drogo................379
Castle Howard 682
Castle Tioram..............1220
Castle Urquhart...........1211
Castlebay....................1148
Castlerigg Stone
    Circle.........................627
Castleton......................519
Castletown
    (Isle of Man) 609
Cauldron Snout............715
Cawdor Castle 1202
Cawfields 740
Cawthorn Camps.........691
Celts, the....................1285
Cenarth 853
Centre for Alternative
    Technology.................846
Centre for Contemporary
    Arts (CCA) 1012
Ceredigion 846–854
Cerne Abbas................262
Chagford.......................378
Chanonry Point...........1241
Charles I, King 1297
Charles II, King 1298

Charleston
  Farmhouse 214
Charlestown..................395
Charmouth 260
Chartists, the 767, 1303
Chartwell 209
Chastleton House 312
Chatham 186
Chatsworth House........526
Chatterton, Thomas......333
Chaucer, Geoffrey 1292
Chawton 245
Cheddar Gorge 345
Cheesewring, the..........420
Cheltenham...................318
chemists see pharmacies
Chepstow......................762
Chesil Beach.................259
Chessington World of
  Adventures..................182
Chester..................582–586
Chester Zoo 586
Chester's Roman Fort...739
Cheviot, the 745
Chichester.....................223
Chillingham 746
**Chiltern Hills,
  the**.....................279–282
Chipping Camden.........313
Chirk 838
Chollerford 739
Christchurch 249
Church Stretton 500
Churchill Barriers 1262
Churchill,
  Winston............209, 1305
Chysauster....................405
cigarettes......................60
Cilborth Beach..............851
Cilgerran Castle 852
Cinque Ports.................194
Cirencester....................315
Civil War, the...............1297
Clackmannanshire.......1052
Claerwen Reservoir.......828
Clapham (Yorkshire)......662
Claudius.....................1286
Clava Cairns 1202
Claverton 342
Cleeve Abbey................351
Cleveland Way, the 689
Cley-next-the-Sea 455
Clifton 334
Clifton Suspension
  Bridge 334
Clitheroe.......................601
Clova..........................1168
Clovelly 384
Clumber Park...............539

Clyde, the 1030–1037
Clywedog Valley 896
coaches in Britain 27
Coalbrookdale 497
Cockermouth 631
Coedmore.....................852
Coigach peninsula 1231
Colchester 427–429
Coleridge, Samuel
  Taylor.........................622
Coll, Isle of 1101
Colonsay, Isle of 1102
Colvend coast, the 981
Combe Florey 350
Commonwealth
  Games.........................569
Compton Abbas 262
Compton Acres.............250
Coniston 623
Coniston Water.............623
consolidators see flights
Constable, John............430
Conwy 887–891
Conwy 889
Conwy Falls 865
Conwy Mountain...........891
Cook, ...143, 697,
  Captain 699, 718, 1301
Cookham 281
Corbridge......................736
Corfe Castle.................253
Corn Du 820
Cornwall 391–406
Corrie 1110
Corrieshalloch..............982
Corsham Court 272
costs 23
Cotswolds, the 309–322
Cotswolds, the 308
County Durham ...706–716
Cove.............................981
Coverack.......................400
Cowal Bird Garden 1089
Cowal peninsula 1088
Cowes 241
Coxwold........................688
Cragside 744
Craig Goch....................828
Craig yr Aderyn............843
Craighouse..................1114
Craigmillar Castle 953
Craignure 1094
Craigwellachie............1182
Crail............................1071
Crainlarich..................1056
Craster 749
Crathes Castle 1179
credit cards....................23
Cricieth.........................877

cricket 54
Crickhowell 820
crime 56
Crimean War, the 1303
Crinan 1105
Crinan Canal 1104
Cromarty 1242
Cromer 454
Cromwell,
  Oliver................461, 1298
Crooklets......................416
Cropton Forest.............692
Crovie.........................1184
Crown Jewels 116
Crummock Water..........630
Cuillins, the 1125
cuisine............................34
Cul Beag 1232
Cul Mor 1232
Cullivoe 1280
Culloden.....................1200
Culloden, Battle of......1301
Culross........................1062
Culzean Castle.............991
Cumbria and the
  Lakes.........................614
Cupar 1066
currency 23
customs regulations 18
Cwmyoy........................823
cycling 48, 827, 1205
Cyfartha Castle.............772
Cyon Valley, the 770
Cytiau'r Gwyddelod 885

D

D-Day...........................234
Daglingworth.................316
Dale.............................803
Dalemain 634
Dalkeith 957
Dan-yr-ogof
  Showcaves.................819
Danby...........................692
Danelaw 1288
Darlington 717
Dartmoor............375–381
Dartmoor......................376
Dartmouth 370
Darwin, Charles 1303
De Quincey, Thomas 622
Deal 195
Dedham 430
Dee Valley, the 835–838
Deeside 1178–1181
Denbighshire.................893

Dent 663
Dentdale......................663
Derby 516
Dervaig......................1096
Derwent Water 628
Devil's Bridge..............849
Devizes 271
Devon 358–391
Devon and
   Cornwall 356–357
Diana, Princess of
   Wales 551, 1306
Dickens, Charles.234, 1303
Dinas Oleu 840
Dingwall 1243
disabled travellers...........58
discount agents *see* flights
discounts 24
Disraeli, Benjamin 1303
Dissolution of the
   Monasteries 1294
distilleries *see* whisky
Doctor Who
   (TV series) 837
Dodman Point...............396
Dolaucothi Gold
   Mine 796
Dolbadarn Castle..........868
Dolgellau 841
Dolgoch 826
Dollar..........................1052
dolphins 1201
Domesday Book 1289
Dorchester 255
Dornoch 1245
Dorset..........248–262, 264
Douglas.......................605
Doune 1050
Dounreay....................1237
Dovedale......................517
Dover 196
Dover...........................197
Dover's Hill...................313
Dozmary Pool 418
Dracula........................696
Drake, Sir
   Francis 125, 373
drinking 36
driving in Britain.............29
drugs............................60
Druids, the 1285
Drum Castle 1179
Drumlanrig Castle 980
Drumnadrochit 1209
Dryburgh Abbey............968
Du Maurier,
   Daphne 395, 418
Duff House.................1185
Dufftown 1181

Duirinish peninsula......1126
Duke's Pass 1059
Dulverton 387
Dumbarton.................1033
Dumfries......................977
Dumfries......................979
**Dumfries and
   Galloway**...........977–988
Dunadd 1104
Dunbar 955
Dunblane...................1050
Duncombe Park............689
Dundee...........1156–1161
Dundee 1158
Dundonnell..................982
Dunfermline...............1062
Dungeness...................201
Dunkeld.....................1076
Dunkery Beacon 387
Dunnet 1239
Dunnet Head..............1239
Dunnottar Castle........1177
Dunoon 1089
Dunrobin Castle 1245
Dunstanburgh Castle 749
Dunster 389
Duntisbourne Rouse.....317
Duntulm 1130
Dunvegan...................1126
Dunwich......................440
Durdle Door 254
Durham.............706–711
Durham........................707
Durham County.....706–716
Durlston Head..............254
Durness......................1235
Duxford 473
Dyrham, Battle of.......1287
Dysynni Valley, the........843

E

East Anglia...........425–473
East Anglia 426
East Bergholt 430
East Clyth 1247
East Kilbride...............1035
East Lothian........954–956
East Neuk 1071
Eastbourne 209
Easton.........................258
Edale..........................521
Eday, Isle of 1268
Eden Project, the..........396
Edensor.......................527

EDINBURGH 903–951
Edinburgh
   and the Lotians...........904
Edinburgh,
   Central...............908–909
   accommodation 910–913
   arrival 906
   Arthur's Seat 926
   Calton 936
   Canongate 922
   Castle 913–916
   Castlehill 917
   Charlotte Square...............935
   Cowgate...........................926
   Craigmillar Castle 953
   Dean Gallery, the 939
   Dean Village.....................937
   drinking 943–945
   eating 939–943
   entertainment...................945
   festivals 947–950
   Flotterstone.....................953
   Fringe Festival..................948
   gay scene 945
   George Street 935
   Grassmarket 926
   Greyfriars 928
   High Kirk of St Giles 919
   High Street................921, 922
   history 905
   Holyrood Abbey................924
   Holyrood, Palace of 924
   Holyrood Park...................925
   information 907
   International Festival.........948
   Lawnmarket 918
   Leith...............................952
   lesbian scene...................945
   listings............................951
   National Gallery of
      Scotland 932
   National Museum of
      Scotland 928
   New Town, the 931–939
   Newhaven........................953
   nightlife 945
   Northern New
      Town, the.....................937
   Old Town, the............913–931
   Our Dynamic Earth 925
   Parliament Square 921
   Pentland Hills...................953
   Princes Street 931–935
   Queen Street....................935
   Royal Botanic Garden.......937
   Royal Mile, the 916–923
   Royal Museum of
      Scotland 930
   Royal Observatory 953
   Royal Scottish
      Academy 932
   Scott Monument...............932
   Scottish National Gallery
      of Modern Art 938
   Scottish National Portrait
      Gallery 936

Scottish
  Parliament 917, 925
  shopping 950
  transport 907
  University of Edinburgh 930
  West End, the 938
  Zoo................................939
Edinburgh Festival 947
Edward the
  Confessor 91, 1288
Egglestone Abbey........714
Egton Bridge................692
Eigg, Isle of 1133
Eilean Donan Castle ...1225
Eisteddfod, International
  Music 835, 836
Elan 828
Elan Valley..................827
electricity.....................60
Elgin 1185
Elgin Marbles 105
Elgol 1125
Elie 1072
Elkstone 317
Elterwater 621
Ely 460
email 39
embassies, British 18
emergencies 22, 57
England
Northeast 704–705
England, Northwest.......568
English Heritage.............42
English Riviera.....366–369
Erddig 896
Eriskay, Isle of............1147
Esk Valley, the..............692
Eskdale 631
Ethelbert 1287
Eton...........................150
Europaidh..................1139
Europie see Europaidh
events 43
Evie 1259
Ewhurst......................205
Ewyas, Vale of 822
Exeter 359–364
Exeter...................360–361
Exford 387
Exmoor.................386–391
Exmoor Forest 387
Exmouth......................364
Eyam..........................523

Fairy Glen....................865
Falkirk 1051
Falkland 1065
Falls of Measach..........982
Falmouth 398
Falstone 743
Far Sawrey..................626
Farndale 690
Farne Islands 750
Farnham.....................183
Felbrigg Hall................454
Fens, the
  (Cambridgeshire).......459
Fens, the
  (Lincolnshire).............559
ferries
  in Britain...................237, 274,
    ....407, 884, 1149, 1188,
    .....1239, 1249, 1271, 1282
  from Europe 16
  from Ireland 17, 884
Festival of Britain 122
festivals 43–46, 281,
  ....282, 319, 341, 388,
  ....401, 439, 544, 698,
  ....711, 823, 835, 836,
  ....844, 946, 947–949,
  .....972, 1177, 1180, 1275
Fetlar, Isle of 1281
Ffestiniog Railway.872, 875
Fforest Fawr.................818
fiction 1313–1317
Fife....................1061–1072
Filey............................686
film 1322–1332
Findhorn Foundation ..1186
Fingal's Cave..............1097
Fingle Bridge................379
Fionnphort 1097
Firth of Clyde ...1031–1034
Fishbourne Roman
  Palace 225
Fishguard 807
fishing 1205
Flamborough Head......685
Flatford Mill.................430
flights
  from Australia....................14
  in Britain......................25, 407
  from Canada.....................12
  from Ireland 15
  from New Zealand 14
  from the US 12
  online booking 11
Flintshire 893
Floors Castle................971
Flotterstone 953
Flow Country, the 1238
Folkestone 199
food.............................34

Foot and Mouth
  disease..............46, 1307
football..........53, 576, 620,
 1022
Forest of Bowland 601
Fort Augustus 1211
Fort George................1202
Fort William...............1212
Fort William 1213
Forth Rail Bridge.........1064
Forth Road Bridge 1064
Fortingall....................1078
Fortrose.....................1241
Forтuneswell................258
Fotheringay 552
Foula, Isle of 1278
Fountains Abbey...........671
Fowey 394
Fowles, John................260
Framlingham 437
Fraserburgh................1184
Freud, Sigmund 137
Furness Abbey..............636

G

gaelic 1134
Gairloch 1228
Gairlochy....................1215
Gallanach 1133
Galloway Forest Park....986
Gardenstown 1184
Gatehouse of Fleet 984
gay scene 59
Gearrannan 1140
Gibside........................734
Gigha, Isle of..............1106
Gillamoor 690
Gladstone, William......1303
Glamis 1166
GLASGOW..........999–1030
Glasgow..........1002–1003
Glasgow and
  the Clyde 998
Glasgow City
  Centre....................1006
  airports.............................1000
  architecture....................1008
  Barras, the 1010
  Botanic Gardens............1018
  Buchan Street.................1007
  Burrell Collection,
    the 822, 1022
  Byres Road 1015
  Cathedral 1011
  Centre for Contemporary Arts
    (CCA)..........................1012
  City Chambers................1006
  Clydeside 1018–1020

Fair Isle 1276
Fairbourne..................840

cycle rental........................821
drinking 1027–1028
East End 1010
eating 1024–1027
entertainment........1028–1030
Finnieston Crane.............1020
football 1022
Gallery of Modern Art 1007
gay and lesbian
  scene 1029
George Square.................1006
Glasgow Cross 1010
Glasgow School of Art....1013
Glasgow Science
  Centre...........................1020
Hampden Park.................1021
Holmwood House...........1024
House for an Art
  Lover 823, 1021
Hunterian Museum and
  Art Gallery....................1017
information 1000
Kelvin Hall 1017
Kelvingrove Museum and
  Art Gallery....................1015
Lighthouse, the 1007
listings.............................1030
Mackintosh House..........1017
Merchant City 1008
Necropolis.......................1012
nightlife..................1028–1030
orientation 1000
People's Palace 1010
Piping Centre 1014
Pollok House 822, 1023
Sauciehall Street.............1012
Science Mall 1020
Scotland Street
  School Museum of
  Education 1021
Scottish Exhibition and
  Conference
  Centre (SECC) 1020
Scottish Football
  Museum........................1022
Southside, the.......1020–1024
St Mungo Museum
  of Religious Life
  and Art.........................1012
Tall Ship at Glasgow
  Harbour 1020
Tenement House.............1014
transport 1001
Transport Museum..........1017
University 1017
Waverly, the 1018
West End, the........1015–1018
Willow Tea Rooms 1012
Glasgow Boys, the 1016
Glastonbury 345
Glen Affric 1211
Glen Brittle 1126
Glen Clova 1168
Glen Coe 1215
Glen Dale 1126
Glen Doll 1168

Glen Lyon 1078
Glen Nevis 1215
Glen Shee 1165
Glen Sligachan............1125
Glen Urquhart 1211
Glenborrodale 1219
Glencoe......................1216
Glenelg
  peninsula, the 1225
Glenfinnan...................1220
Glenkinchie Distillery 956
Glenmore Natural History
  Centre........................1219
Glenridding 632
Glorious Revolution 1299
Gloucester 323–326
Gloucestershire ...309–328
Glyders, the 866
Glyndebourne 213
Glyndŵr, Owain............845
Goathland 693
Gobarrow Park.............632
Golden Cap 260
Goldfinger, Ernö...........137
golf..............52, 1069, 1245
Golspie.......................1245
Goodrich Castle...........494
Goodrich Village 495
Gordale Scar 660
Gourock 1032
Gower 788
Grange.......................629
Grange-over-Sands 635
Grantown-on-Spey 1207
Grasmere 621
Grassholm Island..........804
Grassington 658
Great Chalfield
  Manor.......................273
Great Chesters Fort 741
Great Fire of
  London....................1298
Great Gable 630
Great Glen,
  the.................1208–1217
Great Langdale 620
Great Malvern 489
Great Orme 892
Great Plague, the........1298
Great Yarmouth............452
Greenhead 741
Greenock 1032
Grenville, Richard.........383
Grey Cairns of
  Camster 1247
Grimsay, Isle of............913
Grimspound 377
Grosmont 692
Grosmont Castle...........766

Gruinard Bay.................982
Gruinard Island 982
guest houses 31
Guildford 182
Gunpowder Plot, the ..1297
Gŵyl Machynlleth 844

H

Haddington 956
Haddon Hall...................526
Hadleigh.........................433
Hadrian's
  Wall...........734–741, 1287
Hadrian's Wall.................735
Hailes Abbey.................314
Haltwhistle 740
Hampshire, Dorset and
  Wiltshire 230–231
Hampshire............232–248
Handa Island...............1234
Handel............................97
Hanoverians, the.........1300
Hardknott Roman
  Fort.............................631
Hardwick Hall................538
Hardy, Captain
  Thomas 259
Hardy, Thomas 255, 258
Harewood House...........651
Harlech.........................840
Harnham 267
Haroldswick 1281
Harome 689
Harris 1132
Harris, Isle of ...1141–1144
Harris Tweed 1142
Harrison, John 144
Harrogate......................667
Hartland 385
Hartland Point...............386
Hartland Quay...............385
Hartlepool 719
Hastings........................203
Hastings, Battle of 1288
Hathaway, Ann..............483
Hathersage 522
Hatton Gallery, the........726
Haverfordwest...............802
Hawes............................664
Hawkser........................696
Hawkshead 626
Haworth.........................654
Hay-on-Wye..................823
Haydon Bridge..............740
health 21
Heckington....................561

Helensburgh.................1033
Heligan, Lost
  Gardens of 396
Helmsdale 1247
Helmsley 688
Helston.........................401
Helvellyn 633
Hendrix, Jimi 96
Henley-on-Thames 279
Henry Tudor 1293
Hepworth, Barbara 406
Hereford 491
Herefordshire.......490–495
Hermitage, the 1077
Herriot, James 664, 687
Hever Castle 207
Hexham........................737
Heysham......................603
Highland Clearances,
  the.................1240, 1302
Highland Games 1180
**Highland Region,
the**.................1189–1250
Highland Region,
the 1192–1193
Highland Wildlife
  Park..........................1207
hiking 46, 615,
  ....661, 662, 745
Hill of Tarvit 1066
Hill Top 626
Hillfoot villages.............1052
Hillswick 1279
Historic Scotland 42
history 1285–1308
Hitler, Adolf 1305
HMS Victory..................232
Hockney, David.............654
Hogmonay 946
Hole of Horcum 691
Holford 351
holidays, public..............41
Holmes, Sherlock ...98, 377
Holne...........................378
Holy Island
  (England) 751
Holy Island
  (Scotland).................1109
Holy Island (Wales) 884
Holy Mountain..............821
Holyhead......................884
Holyhead Mountain.......885
Holywell 895
Honours of Scotland.....915
Hood, Robin.................539
Hopetoun House...........958
horse racing............56, 318
Horton in Ribblesdale ...660
hostels 31

hotels 31
House of Dun..............1163
Housesteads Roman
  Fort..........................739
Howtown......................633
Hoy, Isle of 1263
Hubberholme 659
Hull..............................683
Hundred Years' War....1292
Hunstanton 458
Hurlers, the 420
Hutton-le-Hole 690
Hynsih 1102
Hythe 199

I

Idwal Cottage 866
Ightham Mote 209
Ilfracombe....................382
Imperial War Musuem
  (London) 123
Imperial War Museum
  North 577
Imperial War Museum
  (Oxfordshire)..............473
Inchmahome,
  Island of 1058
Industrial Revolution,
  the...........................1301
information see tourist
  information
Ingleborough................662
Inglesham 309
Ingleton 662
insurance 22
Inveraray 1091
Inverarish 1124
Inverewe Gardens.......1229
Inverie 1223
Inverkip 1033
Inverness 1195–1200
Inverness....................1197
Iona, Isle of 1097
Ipswich 435–437
Ireshopeburn...............716
Iron Ring, the 888
Ironbridge....................497
**Ironbridge
Gorge**.................495–498
Irvine 992
Islay, Isle of 1110–1114
Isle of Arran 1108–1110
Isle of Barra 1148
Isle of Benbecula........1146
Isle of Canna..............1134
Isle of Coll 1101

Isle of Colonsay 1102
Isle of Eigg 1133
Isle of Eriskay..............1147
Isle of Gigha...............1106
Isle of Iona 1097
Isle of Islay.......1110–1114
Isle of Lewis.......1136–1141
Isle of Man 604–610
Isle of Muck 1133
Isle of Mull 1093
Isle of North Uist.........1144
Isle of Oronsay...........1103
Isle of Portland.............258
Isle of Purbeck 253–255
Isle of Raasay.............1124
Isle of Rùm.................1132
Isle of Skye 1121–1131
Isle of South Uist 1146
Isle of Staffa...............1097
Isle of Thanet 187
Isle of Tiree 1101
Isle of Whithorn...........987
Isle of Wight 237–242
Isleornsay...................1123
**Isles of Scilly,
the**......................406–410

J

Jack Cade's
  Rebellion 1293
Jacobites, the 1300
Jarlshof 1276
Jarrow 730
Jarrow March, the.......1304
Jedburgh.....................972
John O'Groats 1239
John of Gaunt..............1292
Johnson, Samuel..........514
Jones, Inigo 268
Jones, John Paul 637
Jura, Isle of 1114

K

Kame cliffs 1278
Keld............................665
Kelmscott....................309
Kelso..........................970
Kendal.........................616
Kenmore 1078
Kent 184–201
Keoldale 1236
Kersey.........................433
Keswick 627

Kettletoft 1270
Kettlewell 659
Kidwelly........................790
Kielder Castle 742
Kielder Water 742
Kilchoan 1219
Killhope Lead Mining
  Museum....................716
Killiecrankie................1080
Kilmartin 1104
Kilmartin Glen 1103
Kilmory 1132
Kimmeridge Bay 254
Kincraig......................1207
King Arthur....346, 415, 418
King Charles I 1297
King Charles II 1298
King David I 1291
King Edward I 1289
King Edward II 1292
King Edward III 1292
King Edward IV 1293
King Edward V 1293
King Edward VI 1294
King Edward VII 1304
King Edward VIII 1304
King George II.............1300
King George III............1301
King George IV............1303
King George VI............1305
King Harold.................1288
King Henry II 1289
King Henry IV..............1292
King Henry V...............1292
King Henry VI..............1292
King Henry VII............1293
King Henry VIII....149, 1293
King James I...............1297
King James II..............1299
King James VI.............1297
King John....................1289
King Malcolm III..........1290
King Richard I 1289
King Richard II 1292
King Richard III 1293
King William I 1289
King William IV............1303
Kingsley, Charles 383
Kingston Lacy 252
Kingussie 1207
Kingussie 970
Kinloch Rannoch 1080
Kinlochbervie 1234
Kinlochewe 1228
Kinross.......................1053
Kintyre 1105–1107
Kipling, Rudyard 205
Kippford 982
Kirk Yetholm................745

Kirkcaldy 1064
Kirkcudbright 983
Kirkstall Abbey.............651
Kirkwall 1260
Kirriemuir....................1166
Kisimul Castle 1148
Knaresborough 670
Knighton 829
Knock Farril................1243
Knole...........................208
Knox, John 919, 920,
  ....923, 1296
Knoydart Peninsula,
  the..........................1223
Kyle of Lochalsh 1224
Kylerhea 1123
Kylesku 1233

L

Labour party, the 1304
Lacock 272
Ladram Bay 365
Laing Gallery, the.........726
Lake District 615–634
Lake District and
  Cumbria.................614
Lake of Menteith.........1058
Lake Vyrnwy 834
Lamlash 1109
Lampeter.....................853
Lamphey 801
Lanark 1035
Lancaster 601–603
Lancastrians, the 1292
Land's End...................404
Langdale 620
Langdon Beck 715
Lanhydrock 417
Laugharne...................792
Lavenham 432
Lawrence, D.H. 404
Lawrence, T.E. 253
Laxey 607
Leaplish......................742
Lechdale 309
Ledbury.......................493
Leeds..................648–653
Leeds Castle................207
Leicester 541–544
Leicestershire.....541–547
Leith 952
Lenin 111
Leonardslee 221
Lerwick...........1273–1275
lesbian scene................59

Letcombe Bassett 283
Levens Hall 617
Leverburgh..................1144
Levisham 691
Lewes..........................211
Lewis, Isle of....1136–1141
Lichfield 513
Lincoln.................553–557
Lincoln.......................554
Lincolnshire 552–563
Lincolnshire Wolds,
  the....................557–559
Lindisfarne see Holy Island
Linlithgow 958
Liskeard 419
Little Walsingham 457
Litton.........................659
LIVERPOOL...........586–597
Liverpool.............588–589
  accommodation................590
  Albert Dock..................593
  arrival 587
  arts.........................596
  Beatles, The................591
  Bluecoat Chambers.........593
  boat trips..................593
  Bold Street.................592
  city transport..............590
  Concert Square.............592
  Conservation Centre........593
  cruises 593
  eating and drinking 479,
   594–596
  entertainment...............596
  horse racing................595
  information.................590
  Lady Lever Art Gallery 594
  Lime Street Station 591
  Liverpool Cathedral 592
  Liverpool Museum 592
  Merseyside Maritime
    Museum....................478
  Metropolitan Cathedral 592
  Museum of Liverpool
    Life.......................594
  nightlife...................596
  Open Eye Gallery............593
  Pier Head 593
  Port Sunlight...............594
  Royal Liver Building........593
  Speke Hall..................594
  St George's Hall............591
  Tate Gallery Liverpool 594
  tours.................590, 593
  Walker Art Gallery 591
  Williamson Square 593
Livingstone, David 1034
Livingstone, Ken 1307
Lizard Peninsula,
  the....................400–401
Lizard Point..................400
Lizard, the village of......400
Llanberis 868

Llancaiach Fawr............771
Llandaff 780
Llandeilo 794
Llandovery 795
Llandrindod Wells 826
Llandudno 891–893
Llanerchaeron 850
Llanfair Caereinion 832
Llanfair PG 884
Llanfihangel-y-
  Pennant......................843
Llanfyllin 834
Llangennith 790
Llangollen 835–838
Llangollen Steam
  Railway.......................838
Llangranog 851
Llanidloes.....................830
Llanrhaedr-ym-
  Mochnant....................834
Llanthony 823
Llanwrtyd Wells............825
Llanystumdwy...............878
Llewelyn the Great........854
Llugy Valley 865
Llŷn, the 875–882
Llyn Tegid....................839
Loch Achray...............1059
Loch Ard Forest 1057
Loch Assynt................1233
Loch Broom 982
Loch Coruisk...............1125
Loch Duich..................1225
Loch Eck.....................1089
Loch Finlaggan 1114
Loch Fyne 1089, 1091
Loch Gairloch 1228
Loch Garten................1206
Loch Hourn 1223
Loch Katrine 1059
Loch Leven 1053
Loch
  Lomond 1053–1056
Loch Maree.................1227
Loch Moidart 1220
Loch Ness.......1209–1212
Loch Ness Monster 1210
Loch Nevis 1223
Loch of the Lowes......1077
Loch Rannoch 1080
Loch Tay 1078
Loch Torridon.............1227
Loch Tummel 1080
Lochaline 972
Lochgilphead 1103
Lochinver 1232
Lochmaddy 1144
Lochranza 1110
Lockton 691

LONDON 65–176
London.......................68–69
London Central 76–77
London's West
  End.....................100–101
accommodation 74–83
Admiralty Arch 87
airports............................71
Albert Memorial 128
Aldwych 108
Apsley House....................128
Baker Street......................98
ballet 172
Bank.............................115
Bank of England 115
Bankside 124
Banqueting House 89
Barbican.........................115
Benjamin Franklin House..108
Bethnal Green Museum
  of Childhood.................119
Big Ben..........................91
Bloomsbury......................104
Bond Street.......................96
Bramah Tea and
  Coffee Museum 127
Brick Lane......................118
British Library.................106
British Museum...............105
Buckingham Palace...........88
Burlington Arcade............96
cabaret and opera
  venues 170
Cabinet War Rooms 89
Camden Town.................136
Canary Wharf.................121
Carlyle's House.................133
Carnaby Street................102
Cenotaph.........................89
Changing of the Guard 89
Charing Cross 85
Charing Cross Road 99
Charterhouse 111
Chelsea Old Church 133
Chelsea Physic Garden 133
Cheyne Walk...................133
Chinatown..........................99
Chiswick House 145
cinemas 171
classical venues...............171
Cleopatra's Needle 108
Clerkenwell 111
Clink Prison Museum.......125
clubs 165–167
Columbia Road................118
comedy clubs 170
Commonwealth Institute...131
Corporation of London 112
County Hall 122
Covent Garden................102
Crown Jewels 116
Cutty Sark......................142
Dalí Universe..................123
Design Museum...............127
Dickens' House................106
Docklands 119

Downing Street 89
Dr Johnson's House 113
drinking 159–163
Dulwich 139
Dulwich Picture Gallery.....141
East End 117
eating 152–159
Elgin Marbles 105
embassies......................174
Eton.............................150
Fan Museum 144
Flamsteed House............144
Fleet Street 112
Florence Nightingale
  Museum........................123
football..........................174
Freemason's Hall 104
Freud Museum................137
gay scene 167
Geffrye Museum 119
Gerrard Street 99
Globe Theatre 125
Golden Hinde..................125
Gray's Inn 110
Greenwich......................141
Guildhall........................115
Ham House.....................149
Hampstead 136
Hampstead Heath............137
Hampton Court................149
Harrods 132
Hendon RAF Museum 138
Highgate Cemetery..........138
history 70
HMS Belfast...................126
Hogarth's House 145
Holborn.........................107
Holland Park 131
Holocaust Exhibition.........123
Horniman Museum 141
Houses of Parliament 91
Hyde Park 127
Imperial War Museum.......123
information......................72
internet cafés 153
Isle of Dogs.....................121
Keats' House 137
Kensington High Street 131
Kensington Palace............129
Kenwood House...............138
Kew.............................146
King's Road 132
Knightsbridge 132
Leadenhall Market 116
left luggage 174
Legoland 150
Leicester Square...............99
Leighton House 131
lesbian scene 167
Lincoln's Inn Fields 110
live music......................164
Lloyd's..........................115
London Aquarium 122
London Aquatic
  Experience....................147
London Central Mosque...135
London Dungeon 126

London Eye........................122
London Transport
   Museum........................103
London Zoo 135
lost property.....................174
Madame Tussaud's.............98
Mall, the 87
Marble Arch 128
Marx Memorial Library.....111
Millennium Dome.............141
Millennium Wheel.............122
MOMI................................122
Monument........................116
Museum of Garden
   History 123
Museum of London 114
Museum of the Moving
   Image............................122
National Army Museum 132
National Gallery 86
National Maritime
   Museum........................142
National Portrait Gallery......87
Natural History
   Museum........................130
Neal Street 104
Neasdon 139
Nelson's Column.................85
nightlife.................163–173
Notting Hill 133
Notting Hill Carnival........134
Old Compton Street 99
Old Operating Theatre
   Museum........................126
Old Royal Naval
   College 142
Osterley Park and
   House 147
Oxford Street 97
Pall Mall 94
Parliament Hill..................137
Percival David
   Foundation 106
Petticoat Lane...................118
Piccadilly...........................95
Piccadilly Circus 95
Planetarium........................98
Portobello Road................133
Queen's House 143
Ranger's House 144
Regent Street.....................95
Regent's Park 135
Richmond 148
Royal Academy of Arts.......96
Royal Albert Hall..............129
Royal Botanic Gardens.....147
Royal Courts of Justice 110
Royal Hospital, Chelsea ...132
Royal Observatory 143
Royal Opera House 103
St Bride's 112
St James's 94
St James's Park..................88
St John's Gate 111
St Katherine's Dock 120
St Martin-in-the-Fields........85
St Paul's Cathedral 113

Science Museum 130
Serpentine Gallery 128
shopping 172–173
Shri Swaminarayan
   Mandir 139
Sir John Soane's
   Museum........................110
Soho..................................98
Somerset House 108
South Bank 122
South Bank Centre 122
Southwark.........................123
Southwark Cathedral 125
Speaker's Corner 128
Spitalfields 118
Strand, the........................107
Syon Park 146
Tate Britain.........................93
Tate Modern......................124
taxis 74
Temple 109
Theatre Museum...............103
theatres 169
tourist offices 72
tours..................................84
Tower Bridge....................117
Tower of London...............116
Trafalgar Square.................85
train stations 175
transport 73
travel details.....................175
tube, the.............................73
underground trains 73
University..........................106
Victoria and Albert
   Museum........................129
Victoria Embankment.........108
Wallace Collection 97
Wardour Street..................102
Wellington Arch................128
Westminster........................85
Westminster Abbey.............91
Westminster Cathedral 93
Wetland Centre 146
Whitechapel 118
Whitechapel Art Gallery 118
Whitechapel Road 118
Whitehall............................88
Willow Road, no. 2 137
Windsor Castle 150
Winston Churchill's
   Britain at War...............126
Long Mynd....................500
Longleat 263
Looe...............................393
Lords Marcher, the......1290
Lorna Doone 389
Louth.............................558
Luddites, the.................533
Ludlow...........................501
Lullingstone Roman
   Villa..............................208
Lulworth Cove...............254
Lundy Island 385
Luss...............................1055

Lybster 1247
Lyddington 548
Lydford..........................380
Lydstep Haven...............799
Lyme Regis 260
Lymington 248
Lyndhurst 246
Lyness 1264
Lynmouth 391
Lynton 390

M

MacDonald,
   Flora...............1129, 1130
Macduff.......................1185
Machynlleth 844
Mackintosh, Charles
   Rennie...........1013, 1017,
  1034
Macmillan, Harold.......1306
Maes Howe.................1258
magazines......................40
Magna...........................647
Magna Carta 1289
Maiden Castle.....256, 1286
mail.................................39
Major, John 1306
Malham 659
Malham Cove...............660
Malham Tarn 660
Malhamdale 659
Mallaig 1223
Mallyan Spout...............693
Malmesbury 317
Malvern Hills, the 489
Man, Isle of 604–610
MANCHESTER....569–582
Manchester 570–571
   accommodation................572
   arrival............................572
   Bridgewater Hall 574
   Castlefield 574
   Cathedral 575
   Central Library 574
   Chetham's Hospital
      School 576
   Chinatown.......................574
   City Art Gallery.................574
   Corn Exchange 576
   Cornerhouse, the.............576
   Deansgate.......................575
   eating and
      drinking...............578–580
   entertainment..................580
   Exchange Square 576
   Free Trade Hall................574
   G-Mex............................574
   Gallery of Costume...........577
   gay scene 580

Gay Village.........................574
Imperial War Museum
  North..............................577
information.......................572
John Ryland's Library......575
listings............................581
Lowry, the.......................577
Manchester Aquatics
  Museum.........................577
Manchester Craft and
  Design Centre...............576
Manchester Museum.......577
Millennium Quarter..........576
Museum of Science and
  Industry.........................575
nightlife...........................580
Northern Quarter, the.......576
Old Trafford.....................576
Oxford Road....................576
People's History
  Museum.........................575
Piccadilly Gardens...........576
Royal Exchange...............575
Rusholme........................577
Salford Quays.................577
St Peter's Square.............574
transport.........................572
Town Hall.........................574
Whitworth Gallery............577
Manorbier.......................799
Mappa Mundi, the..........491
maps...............................20
Margate............................87
Market Harborough........547
Marlborough...................270
Marloes..........................803
Marlow............................280
Marlowe, Christopher....469
Martins Haven................803
Marx, Karl......................111
Mary Queen of
  Scots...........................1295
Mary Rose......................233
Maumbury Rings............255
Mawnan.........................400
media, the........................39
medical treatment............21
Meigle...........................1165
Mellerstain House..........971
Melrose..........................966
Melvich.........................1237
Melville, Andrew...........1296
Mendips, the..................334
Merthyr Tydfil................771
Mevagissey....................396
Middlesborough..............718
Middleton Hall................794
Middleton-in-
  Teesdale.......................715
Midlands, the......531–564,
 475–528

Midlands, the East.........532
Midlands, the West........478
Midlothian......................957
Millennium Dome...........141
Millennium Stadium........777
Millennium Wheel...........122
Minack Theatre..............230
Mine Howe....................1261
Minehead.......................388
Minffordd.......................876
mining industry.....769, 770
Minions..........................420
MOMI.............................122
money..............................23
Monmouth......................764
Monmouth, Duke of....1299
Monmouth Rebellion....348
Montgomery...................830
Montgomeryshire
 829–835
Montrose.......................1163
Moorsbus, the......687, 689
Morar............................1222
Morecombe....................603
Moreton-in-Marsh.........312
Moretonhampstead......378
Morgan, William..894, 1295
Moriss, William.....309, 310
Morte Point....................382
Morvern peninsula........972
Mote of Mark.................982
Mount Edgecumbe.......374
Mount Grace Priory......687
Mount Stuart................1090
Mousa...........................1286
Mousa, Island of.........1275
Mousehole....................403
Muck, Isle of...............1133
Muir, John.....................955
Muker............................666
Mull...............................1094
Mull of Galloway...........988
Mull of Kintyre.............1107
Mull, Isle of.................1093
Mullion..........................401
Mullion Cove.................401
Mumbles, the...............789
Museum of the Moving
  Image..........................122
Museum of Welsh Life,
  the...............................784
museums.........................42
Mynydd Perseli.............808

Nairn............................1202
Nash, Richard Beau......339
National Botanic Garden
  of Wales.......................793
National Centre for Popular
  Music...........................647
National Coracle
  Centre..........................853
National Cycle
  Museum.........................827
National Gallery..............86
National Gallery of
  Scotland.......................932
National Glass Centre...733
National Mountaineering
  Centre..........................866
National Museum of
  Photography, Film and
  Television.....................653
National Museum of
  Scotland.......................928
National Museum of
  Scottish Country
  Life.............................1035
National Museum of
  Wales...........................778
National Portrait Gallery
  (Bodelwyddan)............894
National Portrait Gallery
  (London).........................87
National Railway
  Museum.........................681
National Trust..................42
National War Museum of
  Scotland.......................914
NATO............................1305
Nayland.........................431
Neidpath Castle.............975
Neist Point...................1127
Nelson, Admiral............765
Nether Stowey..............350
Nevis range, the..........1212
New Abbey....................981
New Forest, the...246–248
New Lanark...................1035
New Quay.....................850
Newark...........................540
Newcastle upon
  Tyne....................720–729
Newcastle upon Tyne....721
Newhaven......................953
Newport (Gwent)...........767
Newport (Isle of Wight).242
Newport
  (Pembrokeshire).........807
Newquay........................411

N

newspapers 39
Newstead Abbey 538
Newton House 794
Newton Stewart 985
Newtondale...................691
Newtondale Halt 692
Newtongrange 57
Newtownmore 1207
Nightingale, Florence 123
Noltand Castle 1267
Norfolk Broads..............450
Norham Castle..............754
North Berwick 954
North Norfolk Railway...455
North Queensferrry 1063
North Ronaldsay,
  Isle of 1270
North Uist, Isle of........1144
**North York
  Moors** 686–693
North York Moors
  Railway.....................692
Northampton...................549
Northamptonshire
 549–552
**Northumberland National
  Park** 741–746
Norwich 442–450
Norwich 443
Noss, Island of............1275
Nottingham 533–537
Nottingham 534
Nottinghamshire
 533–541

O

Oakham 547
Oban 1092
Ochil Hills, the.............1052
Offa's Dyke 829, 831,
 1288
Ogwen Valley 866
Okehampton 379
Old Castle Head 799
Old Man of Coniston 623
Old Man of Hoy 1263
Old Man of Storr 1129
Old Sarum....................267
Once Brewed................739
opening hours...............41
Orford..........................438
Orford Ness 438
Orkney.............1254–1270
Orkney 1255
Oronsay, Isle of 1103
Orrest Head 619

Orwell, George.............1115
Osbourne House...........242
Otterburn 742
Oundle 551
OXFORD 284–297
Oxford 286–287
Oxford and around 278
  accommodation...........285
  Ashmolean, the...........294
  Bodleian Library..........291
  Botanic Gardens..........290
  bus station 284
  Carfax 288
  Cathedral 294
  Christ Church College 292
  Christ Church Meadow.....294
  Cornmarket................292
  drinking 296
  eating 295
  entertainment.............296
  Exeter College 292
  High Street................288
  History of Science
    Museum....................292
  information................285
  Magdalen College.........290
  Merton College 289
  Museum of Modern Art ...294
  Museum of Oxford........292
  New College 290
  nightlife 296
  Oxford Story, the 292
  parking......................285
  punting.....................289
  Radcliffe Camera 291
  St Mary the Virgin 288, 240
  Sheldonian Theatre...........291
  tours.........................285
  Town Hall 292
  train station................284
  Trinity College 292
  University College...........289
Oystermouth 789

P

packages see tours
Padstow........................412
Paignton.......................367
Painswick......................322
Paisley..........................1031
Papa Stour, Isle of 1278
Papa Westray, Isle of ..1268
Parry, Joseph 772
Partrishow.....................822
Pas-y-Brenin 866
Patterdale.....................632
**Peak District,
  the** 515–527

Peasant's Revolt,
  the 1292
Peebles 974
Peel 608
Peel, Robert 1303
Pembroke 800
Pembrokeshire 799–808
Pembrokeshire County
  Museum 803
Pen y Fan.....................820
Pen-y-garreg 828
Pen-y-ghent 662
Pen-y-Pass 868
Penally 799
Penderyn......................819
Pennan 1184
Pennine Way,
  the..............521, 741, 745
Penrhyn Castle 886
Penrith..........................633
Penshurst.....................207
Pentland Hills.................953
Pentre Ifan..................808
**Penwith Peninsula,
  the**.....................401–406
Penzance 402
Pepys, Samuel......113, 468
Perth 1073–1075
Perth 1074
Perthshire 1072–1081
Peter Rabbit.................1076
Peterhead 1184
Peterloo Massacre,
  the 1302
Petworth 223
Peveril Castle...............519
pharmacies 21
phones 38
Pickering......................691
Pierowall 1267
Pilgrim Fathers, the.......560
Pilgrimage of Grace....1294
Piper Alpha disaster ...1170
Pistyll Rhaeadr.............834
Pitcrieff Park................1063
Pitlochry......................1079
Pittenweem 1072
Plantaganets, the.........1289
Plas Dinefwr.................794
Plas Newydd 884
Plockton.......................1225
Pluscarden Abbey.......1186
Plymouth 372–374
poetry 1318–1321
Polperro 394
Polzeath 413
Pontcysyllte
  Aqueduct 837
Pontypridd 770

Poole.............................250
Poolewe 1229
Pooley Bridge 633
Porlock...........................389
Port Askaig 1114
Port Charlotte 1113
Port Ellen 1111
Port Erin 609
Port Isaac......................414
Port Mór......................1133
Port Nis
  (Port of Ness)...........1139
Port St Mary 609
Port Sunlight.................594
Porth Clais 806
Porth Neigwl 878
Porthcurno.....................403
Porthleven......................401
Porthmadog...................875
Portland 258
Portland Bill 258
Portmeirion 876
Portpatrick 987
Portree 1127
Portsmouth 232–235
Portsmouth.....................233
post offices 39
Postbridge 377
Potter Heigham..............451
Potter, Beatrix 617, 622,
.... 626, 627, 1076
Powis Castle..................832
Powys 816–825
Prawle Point...................371
Preston...........................600
Priddy............................345
Princess Diana *see* Diana,
  Princess of Wales
Princetown.....................376
Proms, the 171
public holidays...............41
pubs...............................36
Pumsaint 796
Punch and Judy............103
Purcell, Henry 92
Pwllheli..........................878

Q

Quakers, the 1298
Quantock Hills 350
quarantine regulations 19
Queen Anne 1299
Queen Elizabeth I........1294
Queen Elizabeth Forest
  Park.........................1057

Queen
  Victoria.....242, 459, 1179

R

Raasay, Isle of.............1124
Raby Castle 713
Rackwick 1263
radio................................41
Radnorshire 827–829
Raglan............................765
Railway Museum,
  National......................681
Raleigh, Sir
  Walter.................116, 264
Ramsgate......................189
Rannoch
  Moor.........................1080
Ransome,
  Arthur 622, 623
Ranworth 451
Rattray 1164
Ravenglass 637
Reading.........................281
Reading Festival 282
Redesdale 743
Reeth.............................666
Reformation, the 1296
restaurants 34
Restoration, the 1298
Rheged 634
Rheidol, Vale of.............849
Rhondda Fawr 772
Rhossili 789
Rhuddlan 894
Rhuddlan, Treaty of 1290
Rhyader 828
Ribble Valley, the 601
Ribblesdale 660
Richards, Ceri 787
Richmond (Greater
  London).......................148
Richmond (Yorkshire)....666
Ridgeway, the 282
Rievaulx Abbey.............689
Ripon 670
Rob Roy............1057, 1059
Robert the
  Bruce 1063, 1169,
  ....1291, 1292
Robin Hood....................539
Robin Hood's Bay..........695
Rochester 184
Rock...............................413
Rockliffe 981
Rodmell.........................213
Rogart 1246

Roghadal.....................1146
Romaldkirk.....................715
Romantics, the...........1302
Rosedale........................690
Rosemarkie.................1242
Rosetta Stone...............105
Roslin............................957
Ross of Mull................1097
Ross-on-Wye.................493
Rosthwaite 629
Rothbury 744
Rothesay 1090
**Rough Bounds,
  the** 1218–1224
Rough Castle 1052
Rough Island.................982
Rough Tor 419
Rousay, Isle of 1265
Rowardennan 1054
Royal Academy
  of Arts 96
Royal Family 87
Royal Museum of
  Scotland......................930
Royal Pavilion,
  Brighton 217
Royal Shakespeare
  Company 483
Royal Tunbridge
  Wells............................205
RSC *see* Royal
  Shakespeare Company
Rufford Country Park....539
Rufus, William 244
rugby...............................55
Rùm, Isle of.................1132
Ruskin, John........622, 623,
 624
Ruthwell........................980
Rutland 547–549
Rydal.............................622
Ryde..............................238
Rye................................201
Ryedale Folk
  Museum 690

S

SS Great Britain............334
St Agnes (Isles of
  Scilly)..........................410
St Albans 301
St Andrews 1066–1071
St Andrews 1068
St Ann's Head...............803
St Asaph 893
St Augustine 1287

St Austell.....................395
St Catherine's Point......240
St Colomba.............1097,
..................1098, 1107
St David's....................804
St Fagans Castle 784
St Ives........................405
St Ives Bay...................406
St Johns (Isle of Man)...608
St Just-in-Penwith........404
St Just-in-Roseland......399
St Justinain's................806
St Keverne..................400
St Margaret's Hope.....1262
St Martin's...................409
St Mary's (Isles of
Scilly)......................407
St Mary's (Orkney) 1262
St Mawes....................399
St Michael's Mount.......403
St Monans 1072
St Neot.......................419
St Non's Bay...............806
St Ramsey Island........806
Saints' Way, the...........412
Salcombe....................371
Salisbury.....................265
Salisbury 265–267
Salisbury Plain 268
Saltaire.......................653
Saltburn 719
Saltfleetby-Theddlethorpe
dunes......................558
Saltram House 375
Samson (Isles of
Scilly).......................409
Sanday, Isle of 1269
Sandness 1278
Sandown.....................238
Sandringham
House.......................459
Sandwich 195
Sandwood Bay 1235
Savernake Forest...........270
Saxons, the...............1287
Scafell Pike 630
Scalasaig 1102
Scalloway..................1277
Scapa Flow.......1262, 1264
Scarborough 693
Scarinish 1101
Scolton Manor 803
Scone Palace..............1075
Scoraig.......................982
Scoraig peninsula 982
Scotland,
Central...........1039–1082
Scotland,
Central.............1042–1043
Scotland,
Northeast.........1154–1155
Scotland,
Southern..............964–965
Scott, Captain...............143
Scott, Sir Walter...932, 968,
.........................969, 973
Scottish Exhibition and
Conference Centre
(SECC) 1020
Scottish Maritime
Museum 992
Scottish National Portrait
Gallery 936
Scottish
Parliament..........917, 925
Scourie.......................1234
Scrabster 1238
Seahouses 750
Seathwaite 630
Seatoller.....................629
Seaton Delaval Hall 729
Sedgemoor 348
Segedunnum 730
Segontium Roman
Fort...........................881
self-catering..................33
Selkirk   973
Settle..........................661
Settle to Carlisle
Railway......................661
Seven Sisters...............210
Seven Years' War........1301
Sevenoaks 208
Sezincote 312
Sgarasta......................1143
Shackleton, Ernest........143
Shaftesbury..................262
Shakespeare,
William 125, 479,
..........................481, 1294
Shanklin 239
Shapinsay, Isle of........1264
Sheffield 646–648
Sheffield Park...............221
Shell Bay......................254
Shelley, Percy
Bysshe 289
Sherborne 264
Sheringham..................454
Sherwood Forest 539
Shetland 1271–1282
Shetland 1272
Shiel Bridge 1225
Shipload Bay 385
Shrewsbury...................498
Shropshire............495–502
Sidmouth 365
Silbury Hill....................270
Simonsbath...................388
Simpson, Wallace 1305
singing 773
Sissinghurst 206
Sizergh Castle...............617
Skara Brae 1258
Skegness 559
Skelwith Bridge............620
Skenfrith Castle 766
skiing 1164, 1205, 1216
Skipton.........................657
Skokholm Island 804
Skomer Island..............803
Skrinkle Haven.............799
Skye and the
Small Isles 1122
Skye and the
Western Isles............1120
Skye, Isle of 1121–1131
Slaidburn......................601
Slate industry,
Wales 868, 872
Sleat..........................1121
Slimbridge....................321
Smailholm Tower 971
Small Isles,
the.................1131–1134
Smoo Cave 1236
Snaefell.......................608
Snowdon......................869
Snowdon Mountain
Railway.......................870
Snowdonia 861–875
Snowdonia 862–863
Snowshill Manor 315
soccer 53
Somerset..............336–351
South Downs Way 209
South Hams, the...........371
South Queensferry........958
South Ronaldsay,
Isle of 1262
South Sea Company ..1300
South Shields...............732
South Stack 885
South Uist, Isle of 1146
South West Coast
Path 388
Southampton 235
Southend (Argyll) 1107
Southey, Robert............622
Southsea......................234
Southwell 540
Southwold.....................441
Spanish Armada 1294
Spean Bridge..............1215
Spencer, Stanley...........281
Speyside...........1181–1183

Speyside Way ....1181, ...1185
Spittal of Glenshee 1165
sports events 42
Stackpole Quay 800
Stackpole Warren 600
Staffa, Isle of...............1097
Staithes 699
Stamford 561–563
Staneydale temple 1277
Stanhope 716
Stannersburn 743
Stape 692
Starbotton.....................659
Stathspey....................1203
Sterne, Lawrence..........688
Stevenson, Robert
  Louis 919
Stewarts, the ...1295–1298
Stirling 1044–1050
Stirling 1045
Stirling University........1049
Stockton-on-Tees 718
Stoke (Devon) 385
Stoke-by-Nayland..........431
Stoker, Bram 696
Stone of
  Destiny 915, 1075
Stonehaven.................1177
Stonehenge...................269
Stones of Stenness 1258
Stornoway...................1136
Stour Valley 429–433
Stourhead 263
Stourton 263
Stow-on-the-Wold 311
Stowe Gardens 299
Stowe's Hill 420
Stranraer 987
Strata Florida Abbey.....853
Stratford-upon-Avon 480
**Stratford-upon-
  Avon** 479–484
Strathmore 1164
Strathpeffer 1243
Strathspey....................967
Strathspey Steam
  Railway.....................1204
Stromness...................1256
Stronsay, Isle of 1269
Strontian 972
Stroud 320
Strumble Head..............807
Stuarts, the 1295–1298
student discounts 24
Studley Royal........671, 672
Sudbury 431
Sudeley Castle..............314
Suffragettes, the 1304

Sugar Loaf Mountain 821
Suilven 1232
Sulgrave 551
Sumburgh Head..........1276
Summer Isles, the.......1230
Sunderland 732
surfing 50
Surrey.................182–184
Surrey, Kent and
  Sussex.................180–181
Sussex..................201–224
Sutherland
  Monument...............1246
Sutton Bank 688
Sutton Hoo (British
  Museum) 105
Sutton Hoo (Suffolk) 437
Swaledale 665
Swallow Falls 865
Swanage 254
Swansea................784–788
Swansea 786
Sweetheart Abbey 981
Swinbrook 311
Symonds Yat East 495

T

Table Mountain 821
Taff Valley, the 770
Tai'r Heol 819
Tain.............................1244
Tain peninsula, the.......1243
Tal-y-llyn Lake...............843
Talyllen Valley, the 843
Tantallon Castle 954
Tarbert (Harris) 1142
Tarbert (Kintyre)...........1105
Tarbet (Central
  Scotland).................1056
Tarbet (Highlands).......1234
Tarka Line.....................381
Tarka the Otter..............381
Tarn Hows....................627
tartan..........................1198
Tate Britain 93
Tate Modern   124
Taunton 349
Tavistock 380
tax 18
taxis 30
Tees Valley, the 717
Teesdale.......................715
Teifi Valley, the 852
telephones 38
television 40
Telscombe....................214

Temple Newsam 651
Tenby 796
tennis 55
Tewkesbury 326
Thatcher, Margaret......1306
Thirsk 687
Thomas, Dylan......787, 792
Thorpe Park 182
Threave Castle 982
Threave Garden 982
Three Castles, the.........766
Three Peaks
  Walk 661, 662
Thurso 1238
Thwaite 666
time differences 60
Tintagel 414
Tintern Abbey 764
tipping...........................60
Tiree, Isle of 1101
Tobermory...................1095
toilets 60
Tolpuddle Martyrs,
  the...................255, 1303
Tongue 1237
Torquay 366
Torrington.....................381
Totnes 368
tourist information
  abroad............................20
  in England 19
  in Scotland.....................20
  in Wales 19
  online 20
tourist offices *see* tourist
  information
tours from North
  America......................13
Tower Knowe 742
Traethmawr 808
trains
  in Britain.........................26
  from Europe 16
Traquair House..............975
travel insurance 22
travellers' cheques.........23
Tre-Saith.......................851
Tresco (Isles of Scilly) ...408
Trethevy Quoit...............420
Tretower 820
Trossachs, the ...1056–161
Trotternish
  peninsula.................1129
Troutbeck 619
Truro.............................397
TT racing.......................604
Tudor, Mary 1294
Tudors, the 1293–1293
Tunbridge Wells 205
Twelve Men's Moor.......420

Ty'n-y-Cornel 826
Tywi Valley, the 793–796
Tywyn 843

U

Uffington 284
Uig 1130
Uley 321
Ullapool 1229
Ullswater 632
Ulverston 636
Unst, Isle of.................1281
Uppingham 548
Uyeasound.....................1281

V

Vale of Rheidol...............849
**Vale of White
  Horse** 282–284
Valle Crucis Abbey........838
Varick Castle................1237
VAT 18
Venerable Bede,
  the......................709, 730
Ventnor...........................39
Verulanium 301, 302
Veryan 397
Veryan Bay.....................396
**Victorians,
  the**.................1303–1304
videos 60
Vindolanda 740
visas..............................18
Voe 1279

W

Wales, Mid- 814–815
Wales, North..........860–861
Wales, South 762–763
walking..........46, 745, 1205
Wallace Monument 1049
Wallace, William..........1291
Wallington House..........730
Wallsend 730
Walmer..........................196
Walpole, Robert 1300
Wantage........................283
Wareham......................253
Warkworth....................746

Wars of the Roses 1293
Warwick 485
Warwick..........................485
Washford.......................351
Washington 733
Washington, George 733
Wast Water 630
Watchet.........................351
Watercress Line, the 245
water sports...............1205
Weald, the Kent 205
Weardale 715
Wearside 732–734
Wells 343
Wells-next-the-Sea 457
Welsh choirs 773
Welsh Highland
  Railway.....................881
Welshpool 831
Welshpool and Llanfair
  Light Railway 832
Wemyss Bay 1033
Wensleydale.................663
West Bay (Dorset).........259
West Highland
  Railway....................1222
West Highland Way 1055
West Kennet Long
  Barrow......................271
Wester Ross 1226–1323
**Western Isles,
  the**.................1134–1148
Westonbirt Arboretum...318
Westray, Isle of............1267
Westward Ho! 383
Westward Ho!
  (novel) 383, 384
Weymouth.....................257
Wharfedale....................658
Wheeldale Roman
  Road 692
Whigs, the...................1298
Whippingham.................242
whisky 37, 917, 1077
  Ardbeg Distillery ...1111, 1112
  Bowmore Distillery..........1112
  Bruichladdich Distillery ...1112
  Bunnahabhainn
    Distillery 1112
  Cardhu Distillery 1182
  Edradour Distillery 1079
  Glen Grant Distillery........1182
  Glenfiddich Distillery 1182
  Glenkinchie Distillery 956
  Glenlivet Distillery 1182
  Islay whisky...........1110, 1111
  Isle of Jura Distillery 1115
  Lagavulin Distillery
    ....1111, 1112
  Laphroaig Distillery
    ....1111, 1112

  Oban Distillery 1092
  Speyside Cooperage 1182
  Springbank Distillery.......1106
  Strathisla Distillery 1182
  Tain Distillery...................1244
Whisky Galore! (film) ...1147
Whitby 696–699
White Castle 766
White Horse Hill............283
White Scar Caves 663
Whitehall
  (Isle of Stronsay) 1269
Whitehaven 637
Whitesand Bay
  (Cornwall)............374, 404
Whitesands Bay
  (South Wales).............806
Whithorn 986
Whiting Bay...................1109
Whitstable 186
Wick 1247
Wicken Fen 459
Widbrook 311
Widecombe-in-
  the-Moor 378
Widemouth Bay 416
William of Orange 1299
Wilson, Harold 1306
Wilton House 268
Wiltshire 263, 264–273
Wimborne Minster 252
Winchcombe.................313
Winchelsea 202
Winchester..........242–245
Winchester 243
Windermere 617
Windrush Valley 310
Windsor.........................150
Windsor Castle   150
Winsford........................387
Wistman's Wood...........377
Wolsey, Cardinal 148
WOMAD.........................281
Woodhenge....................270
Woodstock.....................299
Wookey Hole.................344
Wooler...........................745
Woolstone......................284
Worcester......................487
Worcestershire 487–490
Wordsworth,
  William 621, 622,
    ....626, 631
work 57
World War I 1304
World War II 1305
Worms Head 789
Wrexham........................896
Wright, Joseph..............516
Wroxham........................451

INDEX

I

Wycliffe, John 1292
**Wye Valley,
the**.............494, 762–768

Y

Yarmouth.....................240
Yell, Isle of.................1280

Ynys Lochtyn...............851
Ynysangharad Park 770
York......................672–682
York......................674–675
Yorkists, the 1293
Yorkshire 643–699
Yorkshire 644–645
**Yorkshire Dales,
the**.....................656–666
**Yorkshire
Moors** 686–693

youth hostel
associations.................32
youth hostels 31
Ystradfellte...................818

Z

Zennor...........................404

Twenty Years of Rough Guides

In the summer of 1981, Mark Ellingham, Rough Guides' founder, knocked out the first guide on a typewriter, with a group of friends. Mark had been travelling in Greece after university, and couldn't find a guidebook that really answered his needs. There were heavyweight cultural guides on the one hand – good on museums and classical sites but not on beaches and tavernas – and on the other hand student manuals that were so caught up with how to save money that they lost sight of the country's significance beyond its role as a place for a cool vacation. None of the guides began to address Greece as a country, with its natural and human environment, its politics and its contemporary life.

Having no urgent reason to return home, Mark decided to write his own guide. It was a guide to Greece that tried to combine some erudition and insight with a thoroughly practical approach to travellers' needs. Scrupulously researched listings of places to stay, eat and drink were matched by careful attention to detail on everything from Homer to Greek music, from classical sites to national parks and from nude beaches to monasteries. Back in London, Mark and his friends got their Rough Guide accepted by a farsighted commissioning editor at the publisher Routledge and it came out in 1982.

The Rough Guide to Greece was a student scheme that became a publishing phenomenon. The immediate success of the book – shortlisted for the Thomas Cook award – spawned a series that rapidly covered dozens of countries. The Rough Guides found a ready market among backpackers and budget travellers, but soon acquired a much broader readership that included older and less impecunious visitors. Readers relished the guides' wit and inquisitiveness as much as the enthusiastic, critical approach that acknowledges everyone wants value for money – but not at any price.

Rough Guides soon began supplementing the "rougher" information – the hostel and low-budget listings – with the kind of detail that independent-minded travellers on any budget might expect. These days, the guides – distributed worldwide by the Penguin group – include recommendations spanning the range from shoestring to luxury, and cover more than 200 destinations around the globe. Our growing team of authors, many of whom come to Rough Guides initially as outstandingly good letter-writers telling us about their travels, are spread all over the world, particularly in Europe, the USA and Australia. As well as the travel guides, Rough Guides publishes a series of dictionary phrasebooks covering two dozen major languages, an acclaimed series of music guides running the gamut from Classical to World Music, a series of music CDs in association with World Music Network, and a range of reference books on topics as diverse as the Internet, Pregnancy and Unexplained Phenomena. Visit **www.roughguides.com** to see what's cooking.

Rough Guide Credits

Text editors: Judith Bamber & Matthew Teller
Series editor: Mark Ellingham
Editorial: Martin Dunford, Jonathan Buckley, Jo Mead, Kate Berens, Ann-Marie Shaw, Helena Smith, Orla Duane, Olivia Eccleshall, Ruth Blackmore, Geoff Howard, Claire Saunders, Gavin Thomas, Alexander Mark Rogers, Polly Thomas, Joe Staines, Richard Lim, Duncan Clark, Peter Buckley, Lucy Ratcliffe, Clifton Wilkinson, Alison Murchie, Andrew Dickson, Fran Sandham (UK); Andrew Rosenberg, Stephen Timblin, Yuki Takagaki, Richard Koss, Hunter Slaton, Julie Feiner (US)
Production: Susanne Hillen, Andy Hilliard, Link Hall, Helen Prior, Julia Bovis, Michelle Draycott, Katie Pringle, Zoë Nobes, Rachel Holmes, Andy Turner, Michelle Bhatia
Cartography: Melissa Baker, Maxine Repath, Ed Wright, Katie Lloyd-Jones
Cover art direction: Louise Boulton
Picture research: Sharon Martins, Mark Thomas
Online: Kelly Cross, Anja Mutic-Blessing, Jennifer Gold, Audra Epstein, Suzanne Welles, Cree Lawson (US)
Finance: John Fisher, Gary Singh, Edward Downey, Mark Hall, Tim Bill
Marketing & Publicity: Richard Trillo, Niki Smith, David Wearn, Chloë Roberts, Demelza Dallow, Claire Southern (UK); Simon Carloss, David Wechsler, Kathleen Rushforth (US)
Administration: Tania Hummel, Julie Sanderson, Jo Polley

Publishing Information

This fourth edition published May 2002 by
Rough Guides Ltd,
62–70 Shorts Gardens, London WC2H 9AH.
Penguin Putnam, Inc. 375 Hudson Street,
NY 10014, USA.
Distributed by the Penguin Group
Penguin Books Ltd,
80 Strand, London WC2R ORL
Penguin Putnam, Inc.
375 Hudson Street, NY 10014, USA
Penguin Books Australia Ltd,
487 Maroondah Highway, PO Box 257,
Ringwood, Victoria 3134, Australia
Penguin Books Canada Ltd,
10 Alcorn Avenue, Toronto, Ontario,
Canada M4V 1E4
Penguin Books (NZ) Ltd,
182–190 Wairau Road, Auckland 10,
New Zealand
Typeset in Bembo and Helvetica to an
original design by Henry Iles.

Printed in Italy by LegoPrint S.p.A

1360pp includes index
A catalogue record for this book is available from the British Library

ISBN 1-85828-881-9

SMALL PRINT

Help us update

We've gone to a lot of effort to ensure that the fourth edition of **The Rough Guide to Britian** is accurate and up to date. However, things change – places get "discovered", opening hours are notoriously fickle, restaurants and rooms raise prices or lower standards. If you feel we've got it wrong or left something out, we'd like to know, and if you can remember the address, the price, the time, the phone number, so much the better.

We'll credit all contributions, and send a copy of the next edition (or any other Rough Guide if you prefer) for the best letters. Everyone who writes to us and isn't already a subscriber will receive a copy of our full-colour thrice-yearly newsletter. Please mark letters: "**Rough Guide Britain Update**" and send to: Rough Guides, 62–70 Shorts Gardens, London WC2H 9AH, or Rough Guides, 4th Floor, 345 Hudson St, New York, NY 10014. Or send an email to:
mail@roughguides.co.uk or
mail@roughguides.com

Acknowledgements

The authors and researchers would like to thank, in England, the National Trust, English Heritage and all the regional tourist boards for their advice and assistance; and in Scotland, the National Trust for Scotland and Historic Scotland, and Caledonian MacBrayne, P&O Scottish Ferries and Orkney Ferries for help in getting round the islands. Particular thanks go also from:

Robert Andrews to Kate Hughes for incisive tips and discriminating advice, Nina Joquin for sharing holiday enthusiasms, and his mum.

Jules Brown to Mark Mulrooney for his browsing and sluicing skills, and Ian and Linda for their kindness in Manchester. And thanks to Katie, Sam, Greg, Gail and Robert for being pals on holiday.

Rob Humphreys to Alasdair Enticknap for more notes on the west coast; Dick and Sue Courchée for more B&B tips; Sara & Adrian for sussing out the Small Isles; Val & Gordon for researching Skye and Outer Hebrides and for enduring the foot-and-mouth madness in Mull; Gordon (again) for border skirmishing; Val (again) for Orkney & Shetland assistance;

and Kate, Stan & Josh for coming out to Islay, Orkney & Shetland.

Phil Lee to Jan Hull of Oxford Tourism; Dominic Harbour of Hereford Cathedral; Elaine Simpson of the East of England Tourist Board; and Sam Warnock of the Birmingham Marketing Partnership. Thanks also to Suzy Sumner for her contribution to the Yorkshire chapter and Emma Rees for her help with the section on Essex.

Donald Reid to all those who have been generous with beds, meals, ideas, advice and good leads along the way; various tourist offices, in particular those at HOST; Andy Symington for boldly setting off to the far north and producing some redoubtable work; Barry Shelby for the Glasgow listings and loyal support; Ellie Buchanan for her contribution to the Festival material; and especially Mo for sailing the ship around with me.

The editors to Katie Lloyd-Jones and Maxine Repath for cartography; Mark Thomas for picture research; Katie Hughes for Basics research; Geoff Howard for index; Karen Parker for proofreading; and Helen, Zoë, Michelle and Julia for coordinating it all.

SMALL PRINT

Readers' letters

Many thanks to all those readers who took the time to write or email with comments, suggestions and helpful advice (and apologies to anyone whose name we've misspelled or omitted):

Chloe Anderton-Brown, William Preston Fitzhugh, A. & J. Hewitt, Sebastian Rinken, Graeme Alexander, John Rower, Jess Day, Eric J. Sandeen, Steve Cam, T.E. Klimczyk, R.A.D. Norris, Mary Victoria, Andy Winter, Olvia Maehler, Susan Jeacle, P.L. Goldsmith, Katherine Glawe, R. Lancaster, Kelly Cross, Alex Ross, Catherine E. Herriott, Paddy & Toni Cafferky, Norman W. Leslie, R.A. Hempstock, Angus Gordon, Mrs J.M. Foggitt, Pat Corbridge, K.M. Sutherland, Karin MacKinnon, Ben Dipper, Jenny Kohn, Rick Kitson, Sandra Robertson, Philip Hatfield, Rich Rowe, John Deas, Dave Fell & Richard Garvie, John Walton, JPM, Brian Harvey & Viviane van den Boogaard, Donna Ritenour, David & Gwen Bevington, Dr A. Young, Sherry Sparrow, Robert Flemington, James S. McCormick, David Watkins & Emma Dijkstra, Mr J. Shaw, Isabel Raes, Joeri & Christophe, Barbara Phipps, Marie Bridge, Michael Patison, Stephanie Turcotte, Alan Turnball, Ann P. Howard, Geoff Muggeridge, Jodie Ivers, Nick Jones, Anna Rawlinson, Robert L. Holmes, Clare E.

Livingstone, Ros Westcott, Ken Sinnock, Jenny & Ron Farmer, Steve Cann, Peter Goldsmith, Sheila Didcock, Mr A.J. Barclay, Michael Marten, Beatriz Campos, Martin Bodman, Jane Cox, Nigel Renouf, R. Adcock, Kevin Akhurst, John Batt, Theo Berry, Ken Bilski, David Boon, Keith M. Briggs, Myra Campolo, Kath Carrick, Marjorie Clarke, Martine Crepy, Carol Davis, Ian Dickinson, Richard Dillon, Carole Dodds, Peter Dolan, Jon Fletcher, Karl Florczak, Gavin Garth, Cindy Geyer, Eddie Gibbon, Louise Grace, Gerard & Maggi Heelan, Conrad Heine, Craig Holt, Stephen Joyce, Christopher Landau, Ian Leith, Anja Lieder, Teemu Liukkonen, Lilian Lloyd, Antony Macer, Mark & Irina Maze, Andrew McFadyen, Janet Macinnes, Mathew Mead, Kate Minson, Phil Mueller, Andrew K. Mullett, Stuart Nicol, Christa Nuys, Jill Prime, Alistair Oldham, Max Patrick, Chris Pike, Gavin Reeve, E.M. Robb, Joyce Selby, Stan & Joan von Sternberg, Taryn Stanton, L. Stevens, Evan Thornton, Joe Sam Vassar, Dave Watson, Peter Woods.

Photo credits

SMALL PRINT

Cyfrwy ridge, Snowdonia © Dean James/
The Photolibrary Wales
Welsh choir stage © David Williams/
The Photolibrary Wales
St David's Cathedral © Ian Homer/
The Photolibrary Wales
Snowdonia © Ray Wood/
The Photolibrary Wales
Ffestiniog railway © Dave Newbould/
The Photolibrary Wales

Scotland
Calton Hill, Edinburgh © Greg Balfour Evans
Canongate Tollbooth © Greg Balfour Evans
Melrose Abbey © D. Houghton/Trip

Dumfries © Rob Humphreys
"The Armadillo", Glasgow © Edmund Nägele
Mercury, Merchant City © Helena Smith
Stirling Castle © Edmund Nägele
Lake of Menteith © Helena Smith
Islay © Michael Jenner
Tobermory, Mull © Rob Humphreys
Calanais stones, Lewis © B. Woods/Trip
Skye © Sasha Gusov/AXIOM
Dunnottar Castle © Greg Balfour Evans
Union St, Aberdeen © Doug Houghton
Wester Ross © Paul Harris
Urquhart Castle © H. Rogers/Trip
Gannets © K. Robeson/Scotland in Focus
Papa Stour, Shetland © Rob Humphreys

sit us online

roughguides.com

Information on over 25,000 destinations around the world

- **Read** Rough Guides' trusted travel info
- **Share** journals, photos and travel advice with other readers
- Get exclusive Rough Guide **discounts** and travel **deals**
- Earn membership points every time you contribute to the Rough Guide **community** and get **free** books, flights and trips
- Browse thousands of CD reviews and artists in our **music** area